NORTH CAROLINA
STATE BOARD OF COMMUNITY COLLEGES
LIBRARIES
SAMPSON COMMUNITY COLLEGE

For Reference

Not to be taken

from this room

MEDAL OF HONOR RECIPIENTS 1863–1994

Volume I
Civil War to 2nd Nicaraguan Campaign

MEDAL OF HONOR RECIPIENTS 1863–1994

Volume I
Civil War to 2nd Nicaraguan Campaign

Compiled by George Lang, M.H.,
Raymond L. Collins and
Gerard F. White

Facts On File, Inc.
AN INFOBASE HOLDINGS COMPANY

Medal of Honor Recipients 1863–1994

Copyright © 1995 by George Lang, Raymond L. Collins and Gerard F. White

All rights reserved. No part of this book may be reproduced or utilized in any form or by any means, electronic or mechanical, including photocopying, recording, or by any information storage or retrieval systems, without permission in writing from the publisher. For information contact:

Facts On File, Inc.
460 Park Avenue South
New York, NY 10016

Library of Congress Cataloging-in-Publication Data

Lang, George.
   Medal of Honor recipients, 1863–1994 / compiled by George Lang,
Raymond L. Collins, and Gerard F. White
     p. cm.
   Includes bibliographical references and index.
   ISBN 0-8160-3259-9 (set)
   ISBN 0-8160-3260-2 (vol. 1)
   ISBN 0-8160-3261-0 (vol. 2)
   1. Medal of Honor. 2. United States—Armed Forces—Biography.
I. Collins, Raymond L. (Raymond Luther) II. White, Gerard F.
III. Title.
UB433.L36 1995
355.1'342—dc20   95-12529

Facts On File books are available at special discounts when purchased in bulk quantities for businesses, associations, institutions or sales promotions. Please call our Special Sales Department in New York at 212/683-2244 or 800/322-8755.

This book is printed on acid-free paper.

Printed in the United States of America

VB CC 10 9 8 7 6 5 4 3 2 1

TABLE OF CONTENTS

Acknowledgments	vii
Introduction	ix
Methodology	xi
The History of the Medal of Honor	xiii
VOLUME I	
Civil War	1
Interim 1865–1870	251
Indian Campaigns	254
Korean Campaign 1871	315
Interim 1871–1898	318
Spanish-American War	333
Samoa Campaign	352
Philippine Insurrection	353
China Relief Expedition	367
Interim 1899–1910	377
Action Against Outlaws, Philippines 1911	385
Mexican Campaign	387
Haitian Campaign 1915	398
Interim 1915–1916	400
Dominican Campaign	403
World War I	404
Haitian Campaign 1919–1924	434
Second Nicaraguan Campaign	435
Interim 1920–1940	436
VOLUME II	
World War II	441
Korean War	605
Vietnam War	656
Somalia	761
Medals of Honor Awarded to Unknowns	763
Appendixes	765
Abbreviations	766
Recipients by State of Enlistment & Birth	767
Foreign-born Recipients	842
Table of Medal Recipients	851
A Select Medal of Honor Bibliography	852
Index	865

BATTLE IS THE SENSATION OF LIFE.

"A human being is never so alive as he is in combat. He may feel terror or he may not, but the prospect of losing his life makes it surge and flare within him. At no other time do his senses more acutely perceive the world. At no other time does his nerve fire with such spark. Never again will he weld as tight an emotional bond to others around him . . . ."

                 Philip Edwards, in *Soldier of Fortune* magazine

ACKNOWLEDGMENTS

Assistance has been received from the following individuals or organizations:

Jerry Lucino, Director, Institute of Heraldry, Washington, D.C.; Andrew Woods, First Infantry Division Museum, Wheaton, IL; Chuck Lafferty, Irish Brigade, Ft. Schyler, NY; Ron Gough, USAF (Ret), Dover, DE; Joseph L. Murphy, 1st Marine Raiders, Ashland, MA; Albert Lerner, Jewish War Veterans National Museum, Washington, D.C.; Marine Corps Historical Center, Washington Naval Yard; Scott Armstrong, Spring City, PA; Joseph Kralich, Sante Fe, NM; Naval Historical Society, Washington, D.C.; Terrence L. Adkins, USA (Ret), Portland, OR; Wilson Smith, Wilmington, DE; Transportation Museum, Ft. Eustis, VA; Quartermaster Museum, Ft. Lee, VA; U.S. News & World Report, New York City and Washington, D.C.; Rudi Williams, Armed Forces Information Service, Alexandria, VA; Mr. Ednor, United States Navy Still Photo Branch, Washington, D.C.; U.S. Naval Academy Alumni Association, Annapolis, MD; Bernard F. Cavalcante, Naval Historical Center, Washington, D.C.; Johnny Concannon, National Historian, Ancient Order of Hibernians, Flushing, NY; Jerry Anderson, Department of Defense, Indian Affairs, Arlington, VA; Fred Anthony, United States Marine Corps Decorations and Awards Branch & Staff, Washington, D.C.; Robert Aquilina, United States Marine Corps History Department, Washington, D.C.; Rick Arndt, Department of Veterans Affairs, Public Affairs Office, Washington, D.C.; Fred Bauer, Queens, NY; Stan Bozich, Michigan's Own, Inc., Frankenmuth, MI; James Cappadanno, Staten Island, NY; Jack Conway, Woodside, NY; Dave Erbstoesser, Bismarck, ND; John Neilson, Ft. Concho Museum, San Angelo, TX; Judy Van Ben Thuysen, Chief, Public Liaison Branch, Navy Dept., Washington, D.C.; Tom Hennesey, Latham, NY; Frank Lynch, Oneonta, NY; Kenneth Smith-Christmas, USMC History Museum, Quantico, VA; Dr. Robert Morris, National Archives & Records Section, New York, NY; Bill Pierce, 6th Marine Div., Mt. Pleasant, SC; Herb Rosenbleeth, Jewish War Veterans, Washington, D.C.; Military History Institute, Carlisle Barracks, PA; William Linn, National Archives and Records Administration, Washington, D.C.; Charles E. Chambers, Houston, TX; Leonard Close, Saco, ME; Raymond R. Davis, USMC (Ret), CMH, Stockbridge, GA; Francis S. Currey, CMH, Bonneau, SC; Thomas F. Durning, North Haven, CT; John Barry Kelly, Philadelphia, PA; James W. Kenney, San Antonio, TX; Gary F. Lettow, Cedar Falls, IA; Glade H. Lyon, Ashton, ID; Charles A. MacGillivary, CMH, Past President, Congressional Medal of Honor Society, Braintree, MA; Benedict R. Mayrniak, Buffalo, NY; Hank Morris, USA (Ret), Portsmouth, VA; Edward F. Murphy, President, Medal of Honor Historical Society, Mesa, AZ; Michael Robert Patterson, Wantagh, NY; Charles E. Sharrock, Denver, CO; Wes Slusher, McKeesport, PA; Richard Straight, Rensselaer, NY; Timothy M. Touchette, Niagara Falls, NY; all Veteran Service Officers, State of North Carolina; Dan Cole Younger, N., Richland Hills, TX; D. E. Tex Powell, Fullerton, CA; Charles Worman, Curator, Wright-Patterson Air Force Base Museum, Dayton, OH; Stan Smith, Potomac, MD; John and Joyce Davidson, Middletown, RI; Jack McMullen, Seaford, NY; and Sharon Vance Kiernan, Poway, CA.

The generous donation by the Atari Corporation of the Mega4 ST computer on which the original database was created is deeply appreciated as is the technical assistance from Paul Heckel, Producer/Director, of Zoomracks, the database originally used to input the information.

The legal assistance given by Cravath, Swaine & Moore (CS&M), New York, NY is gratefully acknowledged. Our thanks to David O. Brownwood, Philip J. Boeckman, Peter N. Flocos and Douglas J. Kepple (formerly with CS&M).

A special note of thanks to Jean Kirk, Chief, Navy Department, Decorations and Awards Branch, Washington, D.C.; Roger D. Hunt, Bethesda, MD, author of *Brevet Brigadier Generals in Blue;* and many thanks to Harold "Sonny" Wells, Liberty, MO.

We gratefully acknowledge the words of encouragement from Rep. Wendell H. Ford and Sen. Guy V. S. "Sonny" Montgomery.

The Congressional Medal of Honor Society members and the many families of deceased members rendered their encouragement and assistance in our research.

We cannot forget the encouragement and assistance from our families, especially our wives, Grace, Jackie and Pat. The assistance in proofreading this book by Charles and Cathy White and Jackie Lang is deeply appreciated.

Needless to say, we hope that we did not forget anyone that assisted in making this project possible. For those that we may have omitted we apologize for the oversight and wish to thank them here and now.

The authors would like to also acknowledge and thank the "expeditors" for their assistance in getting the copy back and forth from the publisher: Kevin Egan, Seaford, NY and Joseph Williams, Farmingdale, NY.

INTRODUCTION

This history of the Medal of Honor is an attempt to write a systematic account of the decoration's creation and to bring together the stories of the award and its recipients. In the process, it is our hope to uncover, collect and record past events and bring to light new facts. Since the beginning of this massive project we have known that the information previously recorded was incomplete and only partly correct. It required hours of cross checking on our part to uncover the historically correct versions of events.

Since we became a nation, American fighting men have demonstrated a great bravery without regard for personal safety. The history of the United States abounds with stories of the valor of our servicemen. Yet prior to the American Civil war, very little recognition was given to members of the armed forces.

The Medal of Honor was not the idea of any one American. Like most ideas that consolidate into institutions, it was the result of a coordinated effort evolved during the Civil War, in response to the needs of the times. During the first 56 years of the history of the Medal of Honor many changes were made in both the design and the regulations governing its award; and in 1918 additional medals were authorized for acts of bravery that did not merit the Medal of Honor.

The keeping of a Medal of Honor Roll was approved by an act of Congress in 1916. When a recipient reached the age of 65 he was eligible for a pension of $10.00 a month for life. In 1917, to protect the integrity of the Medal, a military board was convened to review all the awards to date, and those who did not meet certain criteria were removed from the Medal of Honor Roll.

These measures may appear to be extremely restrictive, but in reality they are the only means of maintaining the high standards as prescribed by the regulations that govern the award of the Medal. For the same reasons it is imperative that the history of the Medal recipients be preserved. These recipients represent the highest traditions of the armed forces. The many unknown heroes who also give their lives for this nation, and their deeds, just as great, must be preserved as an integral part of our history.

It has been said: "Poor is the Nation that has no heroes, but beggared is that Nation that has and forgets them."

The legacy of the Medal of Honor and the story of its recipients is very much a part of the history of this nation. A handful of 3,401 have been chosen to represent all who have worn the uniform of the armed forces of the United States. Today, we have only 185 recipients living, but they are still to be seen at parades and on patriotic occasions. They will forever keep that flag waving. They have been, and still are, defending our nation, but now it is with words, not guns. They have never let us down and we cannot let their history, which is in essence our history, fade away.

METHODOLOGY

Citation number: To facilitate searching, the entries are indexed to a citation number rather than a page.

Name: The name following the citation number is that under which the recipient served in the armed forces and received the Medal of Honor. Those who received the Medal posthumously are indicated by an asterisk before the name. A double awardee is indicated by a ✢ following his name.

True Name: Many members of the armed forces elected not to use their "given name" in the military. They served under an alias or, as in the case of the foreign born, their names were Americanized or misspelled. Frequently they revealed their true names at the time that they applied for the Medal of Honor pension. In some cases the true name was not known until the recipient died and his family revealed the name.

Rank: Rank is that at time of action for which the individual received the award. If the rank and receipt of award differ from that at time of action, rank at time of action is given in parentheses. The individual's highest rank in the military is also given in parentheses.

Service: Lists the branch of the armed forces in which the individual served.

Birthday: Lists the day, month and year of birth, where known.

Place of Birth: Lists the city, county, and state, territory or country of birth, where known.

Date of Death: Lists the day, month and year of death, where known.

Place of Death: Lists the city, county, and state, territory or country of death, where known.

Cemetery: Lists the name of the cemetery and the city and state in which the cemetery is located. Location of the burial plot is also given where known. If the recipient was cremated or buried at sea, the fact is indicated in this field.

Entered Service at: Lists the city, county and state in which the recipient entered the armed forces.

Unit: Lists the unit to which the recipient was assigned at the time of the action for which he was awarded the Medal of Honor.

Served as: Indicates the job the recipient had at the time of the action for which he received the Medal of Honor.

Battle or Place of Action: Lists the name of the battle for which the recipient received the Medal of Honor. If the action had no commonly known name, the city and state or country of action is given.

Date of Action: Lists the day, month and year of the action for which the recipient won the Medal of Honor

G.O. Number, Date: Lists the general order number and the date of the order under which the recipient received the Medal of Honor.

Date of Issue or Presentation: Lists the day, month and year the Medal of Honor was issued. If the Medal was presented to the recipient, the field gives the date of presentation rather than issue.

Place of Issue or Presentation: Lists the place of issue or presentation. If the Medal was not presented to the individual, the field indicates to whom the Medal was given, if known.

Citation: This field contains the exact wording of the congressional citation. In several cases, the wording contains phrases that contemporary Americans will consider offensive. However, the compilers have chosen to keep the original wording so that readers will have a better understanding of the social and political milieu in which the Medal was awarded.

Notes: Indicates whether the recipient was a prisoner of war or a double awardee.

THE HISTORY OF THE MEDAL OF HONOR

Military leaders have long recognized that awards for valor and extraordinary conduct were a way to recognize good soldiers and inspire others to deeds of greatness. The Greeks and Romans gave laurel wreaths to their best and bravest citizens. Medieval barons gave titles and land. Napoleon created the Legion d'Honneur for soldiers and citizens. This award further inspired loyalty and bravery among the ranks, and Napoleon once remarked that he could conquer Europe with a bolt of ribbon.

It was George Washington who established the first American military award for the enlisted soldier. With the creation of the Badge of Military Merit on August 7, 1782, he had found a way to reward soldiers for "singularly meritorious action." Although it was only awarded to three men, it was a step in recognizing the enlisted man for his military accomplishments. In 1932, the badge was resurrected as the Purple Heart, which is still in existence.

In the days of the American Revolution, Congress awarded specially struck medals for various accomplishments, General Washington being awarded a medal for driving the British from Boston in 1776. General Horatio Gates received a specially struck medal for his victory in the battle of Saratoga, as did General Anthony Wayne for the capture of Stony Point, New York; General Daniel Morgan for the victory at Cowpens, South Carolina; General Nathaniel Greer for victory at Eutaw Springs, South Carolina; General Henry Lee for his attack on Paulus Hook, New Jersey; and Captain John Paul Jones for defeating the British warship HMS *Serapis*. In 1780, Congress created the "Andre" medal to give to the three men who had captured British Major John Andre, who was later hanged as a spy. Andre had been plotting with Benedict Arnold for the overthrow of the American base of West Point. This was the first medal awarded to enlisted men in the American Army. What distinguished Washington's Badge of Military Merit from the Andre medal was the fact that the Badge of Military Merit could be earned by any soldier. The "Andre" medal was a special medal created by Congress to reward three specific men for a very specific act. It was not intended to be an ongoing award.

In the War of 1812 and the Mexican War special medals continued to be voted for generals, but not for enlisted men. But in 1847, during the Mexican War, Congress created the Certificate of Merit. This certificate was originally for privates in the Army who distinguished themselves in action or by acts of heroism in peacetime. A soldier would receive the certificate and an extra $2.00 per month. In 1854, noncommissioned officers were made eligible. The drawback of a certificate, as opposed to a medal, lay in a person being deprived of having something to wear so that others could see and understand that he had performed a heroic deed. It was not until 1905 that a medal was given with the certificate. Different states and military commanders had their own medals created in order to reward soldiers, and this practice continued on into the Civil War, but there still was not a military-wide medal that could be earned by deserving soldiers and sailors.

Prior to the Civil War there was disagreement among the military leadership as to the necessity of having a medal of honor that soldiers could wear on their uniforms. One group of officers thought that the medals awarded to European military were a logical thing to copy, while others felt that since we were a democracy, we should not emulate things that were reminiscent of the old monarchies. In spite of these disagreements, a bill to "promote the efficiency of the Navy" was introduced in the Senate by Senator James W. Grimes of Iowa, chairman of the Senate Naval Committee. Navy Secretary Gideon Welles had been looking for a way to inspire reluctant sailors to improve their work. President Abraham Lincoln approved it on December 21, 1861, and this new act provided for the preparation of 200 Medals of Honor to be awarded "upon such petty officers, seamen, landsmen, and marines as shall most distinguish themselves by their gallantry in action and other seaman like qualities during the present war." Thus the Medal of Honor was created.

Secretary of the Navy Gideon Welles soon opened correspondence with the director of the Philadelphia Mint, James Pollock, in order to create a design for the new Medal. After numerous letters and proposed designs, the Navy Department approved a design and notified the Mint of their decision. The design was for a five-pointed-star-shaped emblem with a single point facing down. Each point of the star held a cluster of laurel leaves and a cluster of oak, the laurel representing victory while the oak stood for strength. In the center of the star were two figures. On the right was Minerva, Roman goddess of wisdom and war. On her helmet perched the owl of wisdom. Her left hand held a fasces, a bundle of rods with an ax blade projecting, which was a classical Roman symbol of authority. Her right hand held the shield of the Union, to dispel Discord, a small male figure on the left clutching snakes in both hands. Encircling both figures were 34 stars, one for each state in the Union at that time. The entire star-shaped emblem was suspended from a ribbon of red, white, and blue by an anchor tangled in rope. The reverse of the Medal was blank except for the inscription "Personal Valor," leaving room for engraving information about the man who had earned it. When one considers that the Medal was created during the Civil War, it is easy to see how the symbolism of the Goddess of Wisdom, using the shield of the Union to dispel Discord, would be favored.

Senator Henry Wilson of Massachusetts introduced a bill for an Army Medal of Honor on February 17, 1862, and on July 12, 1862, President Lincoln signed it into law. This provided for the president to present the medal "in the name of Congress to such noncommissioned officers and privates as shall most distinguish themselves by their gallantry in action, and other soldier-like qualities, during the present insurrection."

The Philadelphia firm of William Wilson & Sons, who had submitted the winning design for the Navy Medal through the Philadelphia Mint, approached Secretary of War Edwin M. Stanton and suggested that the design adopted by the Navy would serve just as well for the Army, and the upshot was that the Army adopted the same emblem for its Medal. The one visible difference between the two Medals was the suspension device between the star-shaped medal itself and the ribbon. Where the Navy had an anchor, the Army had an eagle perched on crossed cannon barrels, holding a saber in its talons. The wording on the reverse of the Army Medal was also different, reading "the Congress to." Underneath this inscription was room for engraving information about the Medal recipient. William Wilson & Sons were awarded contracts to assemble both the Army and Navy Medals using the star-shaped emblem that had been struck by the Philadelphia Mint.

Just four days after the approval of the Army Medal of Honor, the Navy further refined the legislation which had created its Medal. With the passage of the act on July 16, 1862, awards of the Navy Medal were extended beyond "the present war." The act also established a system for recommending sailors for the Medal and offered seamen who distinguished "themselves in battle or by extraordinary heroism in the line of their profession" a chance to be promoted, together with a gratuity of $100.00. By establishing a system for making recommendations for the Medal, the Navy avoided the problem that the Army would face many years later when soldiers began applying for the Medal on their own behalf.

At this time, the Navy and Army Medal legislation had two similarities of note. The first was that only enlisted men were eligible for the award and the second was that it was not a requirement that an act of heroism be performed in action against the enemy. On March 3, 1863, a law was passed for the Army that authorized the president to present Medals of Honor to "such officers, noncommissioned officers, and privates as have most distinguished, or who may thereafter most distinguish, themselves in action." Army officers were now eligible to receive the Medal, and with the use of the word "thereafter," the Medal could be awarded later than the end of the "present insurrection." The act also allowed for awards for action prior to the Civil War. Many years later controversy would arise over whether or not this law negated the original Medal authorization of July 12, 1862. The July 12th act permitted the award of Medals for "soldier-like qualities," which meant that the act of heroism need not be performed in combat; however, the March 3rd law made no mention of "soldier-like qualities." At any rate, most Army awards of the Medal were made for gallantry in action, while the Navy awarded a great number of medals for "seaman-like qualities." Seamen confronted various hazards not commonly faced by soldiers, such as exploding boilers and the danger of drowning, which gave them occasion to distinguish themselves for bravery without having to be under enemy fire.

The Medal of Honor became a success from its very beginning. For Civil War action, 1,520 Medals of Honor were awarded. This number contrasts with the 238 Medals awarded for action in Vietnam, a war which lasted more than twice as long as the four-year Civil War. However, it is necessary to keep in mind that the Medal of Honor was the only military award for valor in the Civil War, and if a man did not receive this medal, there was no other which might be given in its place. Warfare was also very different then, and flags, which played a major part in battle, served as rallying points and as symbols of regimental pride. To have a regimental flag captured or fall to the ground in battle was considered a terrible disgrace. For this reason, 467 Medals of Honor were awarded for either the capture of an enemy flag or the protection of one's own. Capturing an enemy flag could almost guarantee the soldier a 30-day furlough and the Medal of Honor. There were no clear guidelines for earning and awarding the Medal of Honor until the 1890s. Veterans then began to apply for the Medals themselves, based on deeds that had taken place over 30 years before, and because the Army legislation had failed to include the recommendation of a commanding officer as a requirement, as the Navy's legislation had done, the Army continued to award the Medal when the application was initiated by the soldier himself.

The earliest action for which a Medal was awarded took place before the Civil War had even begun, February 13–14, 1861, in what is now Arizona. Bernard J. D. Irwin was an assistant surgeon in the Army who voluntarily led a command of troops to relieve a surrounded detachment of the 7th Infantry. Irwin's Medal was not awarded until January 24, 1894, over 30 years after his act of valor.

The first Medal of Honor in the Civil War was awarded to Francis Brownell of the 11th New York Infantry, on May 24, 1861, at the beginning of the conflict. Brownell's regiment was marching through Alexandria, Virginia when the regimental commander, Colonel Ellsworth, spotted a Confederate flag flying from the Marshall House Inn. Ellsworth went inside and upstairs, removed the flag, and started back down. The angry innkeeper met him on the stairs and shot him; Brownell returned the fire, shot the innkeeper, thereby earning himself the Medal of Honor. Although Francis Brownell performed the first act of the Civil War to be awarded the Medal of Honor, the Medal was not issued until 1877.

The first winner to be formally presented with a Medal of Honor was Private Jacob Parrott, and Secretary of War E. M. Stanton made the presentation. Parrott had been a member of Andrew's Raiders, a group of volunteers who set out to cut telegraph wires and to disrupt railroad lines between Atlanta, Georgia, and Chattanooga, Tennessee. The raiders had infiltrated into Confederate territory, where they stole a train and attempted to return north with it, stopping to cut telegraph wires and to burn bridges along the way. Although the mission was a failure and all of the men were captured, 19 members of the party were awarded the Medal of Honor. Parrott was one of six members of Andrew's Raiders who had been exchanged after their capture. On March 25, 1863, the six met with Stanton at the War Department, where he presented the Medal first to Parrott and then the other five. The group was then received at the White House where they enjoyed "a very interesting interview of half an hour's duration" with President Lincoln.

It was during the Civil War that one of the most amazing and controversial presentations of the Medal of Honor was made. In the summer of 1863 Robert E. Lee's Confederate Army was making its way into Pennsylvania. The War Department feared that the city of Washington would be in danger of attack when Lee turned south again and was looking for all available soldiers to defend the city. The 25th and 27th Maine regiments were two units that had been raised the previous October for a term of nine months and their enlistments were about to expire. They had spent their entire service in training or in garrison around Washington and were untried in combat. The 25th Maine refused to stay past their term to defend the city while the commander of the 27th Maine agreed to ask his men to stay. On June 30th, approximately 300 of the 864 men of the 27th Maine agreed to remain and the rest departed for home. The regimental commander then met with Secretary of War Stanton to offer the service of his volunteers. Surprisingly, Stanton then asked for the names of those who had agreed to stay so that they could each be awarded the Medal of Honor!

A few days later the battle of Gettysburg was resolved in favor of the North, and the volunteers from the 27th Maine left for home on the 4th of July. A record-keeping error eventually led to the submission of the entire roster of the 27th Maine, all 864, for the Medal of Honor authorized by Stanton. An accurate list of the approximately 300 who actually remained could not be produced and the Medals were eventually forwarded to the regimental commander who refused to give them all out, thinking that such an award was improper. All these men, however, were entered onto the list of Medal of Honor recipients, remaining there for over 50 years, until a board was convened to review all Medals of Honor awarded up to that time; as a result, all 864 men of the 27th Maine had their Medals taken away.

After the Civil War, the Indian Wars produced a steady stream of new heroes to earn the Medal. During this period abuses of the Medal began to appear. Because of the loose procedure for awarding the Medal, and poor record keeping, it became very difficult to tell who had actually earned it. In 1869, M. H. Beaumont, publisher of the magazine *The Soldier's Friend*, asked the War Department to give him a list of Medal of Honor recipients to publish. He wrote, "There are some who are using medals for the purpose of soliciting charity who obtained them surreptitiously." His request was granted, partly so that some of the Medals could finally be delivered to those who might read their names on the list. In those days, the Medal of Honor presentation was not the prestigious ceremony that one might imagine. The Medal was often forwarded to the unit commander who might present it at a formation or in private, while for those who had left the service, the Medal was sent by registered mail. If the recipient had moved, the Medal would be returned to Washington, and hence the recipient might never know of the award to which he was entitled.

It was during the Indian Wars, after the disastrous battle at the Little Bighorn River in Montana, that some procedures began to be developed which would enhance the prestige of the Medal of Honor by closely examining the acts that would earn the Medal. While all of the men with General George Custer died at the Battle of the Little Bighorn on June 25, 1876, a detachment that he had sent to attack the Indian camp from the opposite direction managed to survive the fight. The surviving commanders recommended large numbers of their men for Medals of Honor, but Brigadier General Alfred A. Terry rejected them all saying "company commanders have recommended every man in the respective companies that behaved ordinarily well during the action. . . Medals of Honor are not intended for ordinarily good conduct, but for conspicuous acts of gallantry." In response, Colonel S. F. Sturgis assembled a board of officers to review the list of recommended men. One of the criteria the board used was "the conduct which deserves such recognition should not be the simple discharge of duty, but such acts beyond this that if omitted or refused to be done, should not justly subject the person to censure as a shortcoming or failure." As a result of the report of this review board, 24 men eventually received the Medal of Honor. Although the review process was not made standard after the battle of the Little Bighorn, it established a valuable precedent by which future recommendations for Medal awards could be evaluated.

In 1892, the War Department published a circular outlining the differences between the Medal of Honor and the Certificate of Merit. The circular stated that "Medals of Honor should be awarded to officers or enlisted men for distinguished bravery in action, while Certificates of Merit should . . . be awarded for distinguished service, whether in action or otherwise . . . by which the Government is saved losing men or material. Simple heroism in battle, on the contrary, is fitly rewarded by a Medal of Honor." Although the word "simple" does not fit very well when describing the Medal of Honor, this distinction between the Medal and the Certificate of Merit made the matter clear. The circular, however, did not preclude a man from receiving both the Medal and the certificate.

On April 23, 1890, in Washington, D.C., the Medal of Honor Legion was formed by Medal of Honor recipients to perpetuate the ideals and protect the integrity of the Medal of Honor. The Legion was to play a part in lobbying for changes.

Another problem was beginning to develop. Veterans' organizations were adopting medals that looked very similar to the Medal of Honor, and only close examination of these medals could distinguish them. In 1896, Adjutant General George D. Ruggles advised the secretary of war to change the pattern of the ribbon of the Medal of Honor to distinguish it from similar medals. On May 2, 1895, Congress had approved the creation of "a rosette or knot to be worn in lieu of the medal, and a ribbon to be worn with the medal . . . " The secretary of war was also authorized to issue replacement ribbons to those whose ribbons had worn out, and on November 10, 1896, the War Department issued a description of the new ribbon. Instead of having alternating red and white vertical stripes with a strip of blue across the top, it would feature a center stripe of white, flanked on either side by a stripe of blue, bordered by stripes of red. The secretary of war issued regulations for the distribution of the rosettes or knots on February 18, 1897. The regulations required that in order to be sold a rosette or bow, the man had to prove that he had earned the Medal of Honor by showing the Medal or proof of membership in the Medal of Honor Legion, or a statement of entitlement from the War Department. Tiffany & Company was given the contract for the ribbons, and with the proper proof, recipients were permitted to purchase the rosettes or knots directly. On May 4, 1898, a similar resolution passed, authorizing a rosette or knot for the Navy. In this way, the services had distinguished the real Medal from the imitations, and recipients were now also authorized to wear a rosette or knot.

The creation of the Medal of Honor Legion had sparked an increase in the number of applications made to the War Department for the Medal of Honor for deeds performed during the Civil War. This increase seems to have alarmed the members of the Legion for they began to push for legislation to make the Medal of Honor harder to receive and to prevent the Medal being awarded in cases like that of the 27th Maine during the Civil War. They even pushed to have the Medals taken away from those men. Legislation was not quick to come on this matter.

There were, however, stricter guidelines put in place for applying for the Medal, but because there were no regulations in place to deal with these new applications it became necessary to formulate a policy. President William McKinley directed that such a policy be incorporated into the Army Regulations. On June 26, 1897, paragraph 177 of the Regulations was amended to require that Medals only be awarded for service " . . . . performed in action of such a conspicuous character as to clearly distinguish the man for gallantry and intrepidity above his comrades . . . incontestable proof of performance of the service will be exacted." The new regulation also required that the claim for a Medal of Honor be made by someone other than the person in question whenever possible, and official records should also be used to support the claim. Failing this, " . . . testimony must embrace that of one or more eyewitnesses, who, under oath, describe specifically the act or acts they saw wherein the person recommended or applying clearly distinguished himself above his fellows for a most distinguished gallantry in action." Additionally, claims made for action which took place after January 1, 1890, could only be made by the commanding officer or a soldier " . . . having personal cognizance of the act for which the honor is claimed." For the first time, a time limit was set. All claims for a Medal of Honor for action that would take place after June 26, 1897, would have to be submitted within one year of the act.

The amended regulation defined the type of deed for which the Army would award the Medal, set up rules for applications, and set a time limit for award recommendations. All of these things can be found in present-day Medal of Honor regulations.

If one looks back to the review board of 1876, set up to screen the Little Bighorn recommendations, the origins of the June 26, 1897, regulation can be seen.

Elihu Root, when he became secretary of war, did much to push for legislation to tighten up procedures for awarding the Medal. Root wanted to clear up inconsistencies between Army regulations and legislation passed by Congress, and he was interested in setting a time limit in which Medal of Honor acts could be considered. He wrote, "Under existing law there is no limit to the time within which application for the award of Medals of Honor may be filed and considered . . . applications have been filed in recent years for the award of the Medals for gallantry alleged to have been performed more than 40 years ago . . . . It is needless to say that it is impossible at this late date to determine the facts in such cases with any degree of accuracy."

Because Congress was slow to implement his suggestions, on September 21, 1901, Root used his power as secretary of war to set up a review board, whose purpose was to examine claims for the Medal arising from the War with Spain and the Philippine Insurrection. The chairman of this review board was Major General Arthur MacArthur, himself a Civil War Medal of Honor recipient and the father of General Douglas MacArthur. The review board was in session for nine weeks and did such excellent work establishing procedures that it was recommended the board be continued, and this was done. On April 19, 1902, Root issued Special Order Number 95 to establish a board of officers to examine " . . . such applications and recommendations as may be referred to it."

Elihu Root also was in favor of changing the design of the Army Medal of Honor itself. There was a general consensus among military leaders including Medal of Honor winners General George L. Gillespie, chief of engineers, and Horace Porter, ambassador to France. Porter had the company of Messrs. Arthur, Bertrand, and Berenger of Paris draw up designs that he first showed to Root and then sent to the Medal of Honor Legion whose officers agreed to the new design. On April 23, 1904, Congress approved it and authorized the secretary of war to replace those Medals already issued.

The new Medal kept the star shape. The center of the star, however, now featured only the head of the goddess Minerva. A laurel wreath ringed the points of the star, while the oak leaves remained in the points of the star. The head of Minerva was encircled by the words "United States of America" instead of the old ring of 34 stars. The new emblem was suspended from a bar on which the word "valor" was inscribed and which had an eagle holding the olive branch of peace in one talon and the arrows of war in the other. The eagle's head was turned to the arrows of war because valor in time of war is what earns the Medal of Honor. This whole arrangement was suspended from a ribbon of light blue upon which were 13 white stars.

In order to receive the new Medal, Medal winners had to turn in their old decorations. This caused the recipients to complain because they had become attached to their original Medals. On February 27, 1907, Congress removed the requirement that the old Medals be turned in and directed the War Department to send back those Medals that had already been turned in. In order to protect the Medal from duplication, General George Gillespie took out a patent on it. The patent was issued on November 22, 1904, and on December 19, 1904, it was transferred to Secretary of War William Taft "and his successor or successors as Secretary of War of the United States of America." After the patent expired in 1918, Congress protected the Medal of Honor from duplication by passing a law on February 24, 1923, prohibiting the unauthorized manufacture of medals and badges awarded by the War Department.

The Navy changed its ribbon in 1913 to the same light blue with 13 stars that the Army had adopted. The anchor was now a clear one, not fouled by rope. In addition, regulations of 1917 stipulated that the Medal be worn around the neck, rather than pinned to the uniform.

In 1904, it was suggested that the presentation of the Medal be made a special and solemn occasion. As a result, on September 20, 1905, President Theodore Roosevelt issued an Executive Order which stated the presentation " . . . will always be made with formal and impressive . . . " ceremony. When possible, the ". . . presentation will be made by the President as Commander-in-Chief." This procedure has usually been followed, except in wartime, when the order authorized that "on campaign, the presentation will be made by the division or higher commander." This added greatly to the prestige of the Medal. A similar order was issued by the president for the Navy on October 19, 1906. The first person to be so presented the Medal of Honor by the president was Spanish-American War soldier James R. Church, to whom President Roosevelt presented the Medal on January 10, 1906, in a White House ceremony.

On March 3, 1915, Congress approved awarding the Medal of Honor to officers of the Navy. This legislation came exactly 42 years after the act permitting the Army to award the Medal to officers. The Navy bill authorized the president to award the Medal to " . . . any officer of the Navy, Marine Corps, or Coast Guard who shall have distinguished himself in battle or displayed extraordinary heroism in the line of his profession." Note that the act still allowed for the Medal to be awarded for heroism in the line of the naval profession.

The Medal of Honor Legion continued to press for legislation that would " . . . give the Medal of Honor the same position among the military orders of the world which similar medals occupy." Toward this end Representative Isaac R. Sherwood of Ohio introduced the bill to provide a pension for Medal recipients. The bill seemed innocent enough, but it stirred enormous controversy and it is still being argued about today. This bill, passed on April 27, 1916, authorized the establishment of the "Army and Navy Medal of Honor Roll." Those who were listed on the roll were to receive a special $10.00 per month pension for life. This roll was a list of " . . . holders of the Medal of Honor who had reached the age of 65 and who had been awarded the medal for action involving actual conflict with the enemy, distinguished by conspicuous gallantry or intrepidity, at the risk of life, above and beyond the call of duty." The wording of the bill excluded the members of the 27th Maine who had been awarded their Medals without ever seeing combat. In order to determine just who was eligible to be added to the roll, section 122 of the National Defense Act was added. Passed on June 3, 1916, it provided for a board of five retired Army generals who would review each case submitted to them. For those who did not meet the requirements, the bill stated: " . . . in any case in which said board shall find and report that said medal was issued for a cause other than that hereinbefore specified the name of the recipient of the medal so issued shall be stricken permanently from the official Medal of Honor list."

This was a drastic step. The act of July 12, 1862, allowed for soldiers to receive the Medal of Honor for "soldier-like qualities." The March 3, 1865, act did not mention "soldier-like qualities," however, that act had not formally canceled the act of July 12, 1862. It could then be argued that the July 12th act was still in effect, and thus awards such as those made to the 27th Maine should be allowed to stand. The legislation required that the review board, presided over by Lieutenant General Nelson A. Miles, himself a Medal recipient, make a strict interpretation of the previous legislation in order to make its decisions. Nelson was also a past commander of the Medal of Honor Legion, an organization that had announced its disapproval of the awards made to the 27th Maine. As past commander, it is almost certain that he agreed with the Legion's stance. Miles also knew that a strict ruling would require the board to remove from the list some people who had displayed great courage in action, yet because they were not in the Army they could not legally receive the Medal. One of these men was a civilian scout named William F. Cody, better known as Buffalo Bill.

The board met from October 16, 1916, until January 17, 1917. All 2,625 Medals of Honor awarded by the Army up to that time were reviewed. In order to avoid bias, the case of each recipient was given a number so that the review board would not know the person's identity. The findings of the board were announced on February 5, 1917, and the names of 910 men and one woman had been removed from the list. Included in the total were Buffalo Bill and four other civilian scouts; Mary Walker, who had been awarded the Medal for service as a contract surgeon; 29 members of President Lincoln's funeral guard; and all 864 men of the 27th Maine. The board hoped that the Medals of the civilian scouts could be preserved through special legislation. They felt that these men had merited the Medal and they hoped that Congress did not intend to take the Medal away from deserving men on a technicality. The timing was not good, however. With America just about to enter the Great War in Europe, Congress did not have time to worry about such details. Of the 911 names removed from the list, only one, Mary Walker, was restored. This occurred in 1977 after her descendants lobbied for the restoration. Mary Walker remains the only woman to have been awarded the Medal of Honor.

Congress finally moved, in 1918, to establish a clear set of guidelines for awarding the Army Medal of Honor. On July 9 an act was passed that stated that " . . . the President is authorized to present, in the name of the Congress, a Medal of Honor only to each person who, while an officer or enlisted man of the Army, shall hereafter, in action involving actual conflict with an enemy, distinguish himself conspicuously by gallantry and intrepidity at risk of his life above and beyond the call of duty." The use of the word "hereafter" removed for good the problem of claims for Civil War action. The last three Medals for Civil War deeds had been awarded the previous year, in 1917. A time limit was also set. A recommendation had to be made within two years of the deed, and the Medal had to be awarded within three years. The July 9th act also abolished the Certificate of Merit, and the Distinguished Service Medal was created in its place. Two more awards, the Distinguished Service Cross and Silver Star were also created. With the award of any of these new medals or the Medal of Honor, a soldier was entitled to an extra $2.00 per month for the length of his service. The July 9th act also allowed the president to confer medals " . . . upon officers and enlisted men of the military forces of the countries concurrently engaged with the United States in the present war."

Up until this time, the only medal for valor in the military was the Medal of Honor. With the addition of the other medals came the beginning of a "Pyramid of Honor." It was then possible to recognize degrees of bravery and it was felt that this would help to protect the Medal of Honor at the top of the pyramid.

Only four Medals of Honor were awarded while World War I was still in progress. After the war ended, General John Pershing, commander of the American Expeditionary Force, made it a point to see that all worthy acts of bravery were properly reviewed to ensure that the appropriate medal was awarded. A total of 118 men received the Medal of Honor for valor in World War I. In addition, the Unknown Soldiers of Belgium, Great Britain, France, Italy, and Rumania were awarded the Medal of Honor. The Unknown Soldier of the United States was also awarded the Medal as would be the Unknown American Soldiers of World War II, Korea, and Vietnam. While the Army no longer allowed the award of the Medal of Honor for noncombat deeds, the Navy still did. On February 4, 1919, Congress allowed the awarding of two different Medals of Honor for the Navy. A new style of Medal would be designated for gallantry in action, while the old style would be awarded for bravery in the line of the naval profession. Tiffany & Company of New York came up with the new design, which is known by the nickname "Tiffany Cross." This cross featured an eagle in the center encircled by the words "United States Navy" and "1917–1918." In each of the four arms of the cross was an anchor, and on the back, the inscription "Awarded to." The Medal hung from a light blue ribbon with 13 stars, and was made to be either pinned to the uniform or worn with a neck ribbon.

Although it is not known how many "Tiffany Cross" Medals were awarded, it appears that there were at least 18 issued. The reason for the uncertainty is that there was no strict observation of the rules governing which Medal should be awarded in each case. Richard E. Byrd and Floyd Bennett were awarded the combat-style Medal for their flight over the North Pole. It is quite clear that these two should have received the old-style version for bravery in the line of the naval profession rather than the "Tiffany Cross."

The new-style Medal did not prove to be particularly popular, possibly because its shape resembled that of the German Iron Cross. On August 7, 1942, Congress restored the old-style Medal as the only Medal of Honor for the Navy. A sailor could still earn it for duty in the line of his profession, although this was not common during World War II. The last Medal of Honor to be awarded for noncombat bravery was to Owen Hammerberg who died while saving two fellow divers who had become trapped while clearing wreckage in Pearl Harbor on February 17, 1945.

While very few Medals of Honor were awarded posthumously for Civil War action, things began to change after the turn of the century. In World War II, posthumous awards outnumbered living awards and the same held true for Korea and Vietnam. It has become very difficult to earn the Medal of Honor and survive the deed.

Following World War II, the Air Force became its own branch of the military. Prior to that time, and up to the Vietnam War, Army Air Corps or Air Force pilots who earned the Medal of Honor were awarded the Army-style Medal. In 1965 the Air Force adopted its own design. The Air Force Medal is almost twice as large as the Army and Navy Medals. While it retains the basic star shape, the center of the medal contains the head of the Statue of Liberty. A laurel wreath rings the Medal and the points of the star retain the oak leaves representing strength. The star is attached to the ribbon by a bar with the word "valor" on it; between the bar and star is the Air Force coat of arms with thunderbolts shooting out from all sides. The Medal is worn around the neck on a ribbon of blue. The Medal is attached to the ribbon by a pad of the same color as the ribbon, with 13 white stars upon it.

The neck ribbon for the Army Medal of Honor was first authorized on February 1, 1898, although it was usually worn pinned to the uniform until after World War II. The Navy adopted the neck ribbon in 1917 as did the Air Force when it created its own Medal in 1965. Today, the Medal of Honor is the only United States Military medal worn around the neck.

On July 25, 1963, Congress established the guidelines by which the Medal of Honor could be awarded:

1) while engaged in an action against an enemy of the United States;

2) while engaged in military operations involving conflict with an opposing foreign force; or,

3) while serving with friendly forces engaged in an armed conflict against an opposing armed force in which the United States is not a belligerent party.

For each of the three Medals of Honor, Army, Navy, and Air Force, the requirements are now the same. "The President may award, and present in the name of Congress, a Medal of Honor of appropriate design, with ribbons and appurtenances, to a person who, while a member of the Army (Navy, Air Force), distinguished himself conspicuously by gallantry and intrepidity at the risk of his life above and beyond the call of duty."

Currently, the regulations provide that an Army or Air Force Medal of Honor can only be awarded if the recommendation for the award is made within two years of the deed of valor and the award is made within three years. For the Navy, the requirements are that the recommendation be made within three years and the award made within five years of the deed of valor.

Gradually, the special pension awarded to Medal of Honor recipients was increased, and its current level now stands at $400.00 per month without any age requirement. Medal of Honor recipients are also permitted free travel on military aircraft on a space-available basis. A Medal of Honor recipient may be buried in Arlington Cemetery, and the children of Medal recipients may attend the military academies without a congressional appointment.

A reversal of the actions taken by the review board of February 15, 1917, by which 911 recipients had been removed from the Medal of Honor Roll, took place on June 12, 1989, and William F. Cody and the four other civilian scouts had their Medals restored. They were Amos Chapman, William Dixon, James B. Dosher (Dozier), and William H. Woodall. Their medals were presented to the next of kin at a ceremony held at the White House by President George Bush.

On April 24, 1991, President George Bush presented the family of Corporal Freddie Stowers his posthumous award. This soldier was killed in action in World War I.

President Bill Clinton presented Medals of Honor to the widows of two Army sergeants who were killed during "Operation Restore Hope" in Somalia. The two recipients were Master Sergeant Gary Ivan Gordon and Sergeant First Class Randall David Shughart. The presentation was made at the White House on May 23, 1994.

The Medal of Honor was first awarded during the Civil War (1861–1865) and has been awarded for all of the wars that we were engaged in since that date. However, we have also had members of the Armed Forces in many campaigns, actions, and operations over the years in which no Medals of Honor were awarded.

The history of the Medal of Honor is a long and interesting one, which adds to the prestige of the award that is our highest honor. The holders are true American heroes, whose sacrifices and accomplishments should be remembered and honored as an important part of our American heritage.

MEDAL OF HONOR RECIPIENTS 1863–1994

Volume I
Civil War to 2nd Nicaraguan Campaign

CIVIL WAR

1 ◆ ADAMS, JAMES F.

Rank: Private (highest rank: Corporal)
Service: U.S. Army
Birthday: 26 August 1844
Place of Birth: Cabell County, West Virginia
Date of Death: 8 December 1922
Place of Death: Barboursville, West Virginia
Cemetery: Oaklawn Cemetery (MH)—Huntington, West Virginia
Entered Service at: Ceredo, Wayne County, West Virginia
Unit: Company D, 1st West Virginia Cavalry
Battle or Place of Action: Ninevah, Virginia
Date of Action: 12 November 1864
Date of Issue: 26 November 1864
Citation: Capture of state flag of 14th Virginia Cavalry (C.S.A.).
Notes: POW

2 ◆ ADAMS, JOHN GREGORY BISHOP

Rank: Second Lieutenant (highest rank: Captain)
Service: U.S. Army
Birthday: 6 October 1841
Place of Birth: Groveland, Essex County, Massachusetts
Date of Death: 19 October 1900
Place of Death: Lynn, Massachusetts
Cemetery: Pine Grove Cemetery (MH)—Lynn, Massachusetts
Entered Service at: West Newbury, Essex County, Massachusetts
Unit: Company I, 19th Massachusetts Infantry
Served as: Color Bearer
Battle or Place of Action: Fredericksburg, Virginia
Date of Action: 13 December 1862
Date of Issue: 16 December 1896
Citation: Seized the two colors from the hands of a corporal and a lieutenant as they fell mortally wounded, and with a color in each hand advanced across the field to a point where the regiment was reformed on those colors.

3 ◆ AHEAM, MICHAEL

Rank: Paymaster's Steward
Service: U.S. Navy
Entered Service at: France
Unit: U.S.S. *Kearsarge*
Battle or Place of Action: off Cherbourg, France
Date of Action: 19 June 1864
G.O. Number, Date: 45, 31 December 1864
Citation: Serving on board the U.S.S. *Kearsarge* when she destroyed the *Alabama* off Cherbourg, France, 19 June 1864. Carrying out his duties courageously, PmS. Aheam exhibited marked coolness and good conduct and was highly recommended by his divisional officer for gallantry under enemy fire.

4 ◆ ALBER, FREDERICK

Rank: Private
Service: U.S. Army
Birthday: 28 June 1838
Place of Birth: Germany
Date of Death: 12 September 1913
Place of Death: Elba, Michigan
Cemetery: Oregon Township Cemetery—Oregon Township, Michigan
Entered Service at: Manchester, Washtenaw County, Michigan
Unit: Company A, 17th Michigan Infantry
Battle or Place of Action: Spotsylvania, Virginia
Date of Action: 12 May 1864
Date of Issue: 30 July 1896
Citation: Bravely rescued Lt. Charles H. Todd of his regiment who had been captured by a party of Confederates by shooting down one, knocking over another with the butt of his musket, and taking them both prisoners.

5 ◆ ALBERT, CHRISTIAN

Rank: Private
Service: U.S. Army
Birthday: 1 May 1833
Place of Birth: Cincinnati, Hamilton County, Ohio
Date of Death: 6 March 1898
Cemetery: Reading Cemetery—Reading, Ohio
Entered Service at: Cincinnati, Hamilton County, Ohio
Unit: Company G, 47th Ohio Infantry
Battle or Place of Action: Vicksburg, Mississippi
Date of Action: 22 May 1863
Date of Issue: 10 August 1895
Citation: Gallantry in the charge of the "volunteer storming party."

6 ◆ ALLEN, ABNER PEELER

Rank: Corporal
Service: U.S. Army

Birthday: 9 October 1839
Place of Birth: Woodford County, Illinois
Date of Death: 22 August 1905
Cemetery: Centerburg Cemetery (MH)—Centerburg, Ohio
Entered Service at: Bloomington, McLean County, Illinois
Unit: Company K, 39th Illinois Infantry
Battle or Place of Action: Petersburg, Virginia
Date of Action: 2 April 1865
Date of Issue: 12 May 1865
Citation: Gallantry as color bearer in the assault on Fort Gregg.

7 ◆ ALLEN, JAMES

Rank: Private (highest rank: Corporal)
Service: U.S. Army
Birthday: 5 May 1843
Place of Birth: Ireland
Date of Death: 31 August 1913
Place of Death: St. Paul, Minnesota
Cemetery: Oakland Cemetery—St. Paul, Minnesota
Entered Service at: Potsdam, St. Lawrence County, New York
Unit: Company F, 16th New York Infantry
Battle or Place of Action: South Mountain, Maryland
Date of Action: 14 September 1862
Date of Issue: 11 September 1890
Citation: Singlehandedly and slightly wounded he accosted a squad of 14 Confederate soldiers bearing the colors of the 16th Georgia Infantry (C.S.A.). By an imaginary ruse he secured their surrender and kept them at bay when the regimental commander discovered him and rode away for assistance.

8 ◆ ALLEN, NATHANIEL M.

Rank: Corporal
Service: U.S. Army
Birthday: 29 April 1840
Place of Birth: Boston, Suffolk County, Massachusetts
Date of Death: 30 July 1900
Place of Death: South Acton, Massachusetts
Cemetery: Woodlawn Cemetery (MH)—Acton, Massachusetts
Entered Service at: Boston, Suffolk County, Massachusetts
Unit: Company B, 1st Massachusetts Infantry
Battle or Place of Action: Gettysburg, Pennsylvania
Date of Action: 2 July 1863
Date of Issue: 2 July 1899
Citation: When his regiment was falling back, this soldier, bearing the national color, returned in the face of the enemy's fire, pulled the regimental flag from under the body of its bearer, who had fallen, saved the flag from capture, and brought both colors off the field.

9 ◆ AMES, ADELBERT

Rank: First Lieutenant (highest rank: Brevet Major General)
Service: U.S. Army
Birthday: 31 October 1835
Place of Birth: Rockland, Knox County, Maine
Date of Death: 13 April 1933
Place of Death: Ormond, Florida
Cemetery: Hildreth Family Cemetery (MH)—Lowell, Massachusetts
Entered Service at: Rockland, Knox County, Maine
Unit: 5th U.S. Artillery
Battle or Place of Action: Bull Run, Virginia
Date of Action: 21 July 1861
Date of Issue: 22 June 1894
Citation: Remained upon the field in command of a section of Griffin's Battery, directing its fire after being severely wounded and refusing to leave the field until too weak to sit upon the caisson where he had been placed by men of his command.

10 ◆ AMMERMAN, ROBERT WESLEY

Rank: Private
Service: U.S. Army
Birthday: 1841
Place of Birth: Centre County, Pennsylvania
Date of Death: 30 September 1907
Place of Death: McAlisterville, Pennsylvania
Cemetery: Presbyterian Cemetery—McAlisterville, Pennsylvania
Entered Service at: Milesburg, Centre County, Pennsylvania
Unit: Company B, 148th Pennsylvania Infantry
Battle or Place of Action: Spotsylvania, Virginia
Date of Action: 12 May 1864
Date of Issue: 31 January 1865
Citation: Capture of battle flag of the 8th North Carolina (C.S.A.), being one of the foremost in the assault.

11 ◆ ANDERSON, BRUCE

Rank: Private
Service: U.S. Army
Birthday: 19 June 1845
Place of Birth: Mexico City, Mexico
Date of Death: 22 August 1922
Place of Death: Albany, New York
Cemetery: Green Hill Cemetery (MH)—Amsterdam, New York
Entered Service at: Albany, Albany County, New York
Unit: Company K, 142d New York Infantry
Battle or Place of Action: Fort Fisher, North Carolina
Date of Action: 15 January 1865
Date of Issue: 28 December 1914
Citation: Voluntarily advanced with the head of the column and cut down the palisading.

12 ◆ ANDERSON, CHARLES W.

Rank: Private
Service: U.S. Army
Birthday: 15 March 1844
Place of Birth: Baltimore, Baltimore County, Maryland

Date of Death: 25 February 1916
Place of Death: Stanton, Virginia
Cemetery: Thornrose Cemetery—Stanton, Virginia
Entered Service at: near Winchester, Frederick County, Virginia
Unit: 1st New York (Lincoln) Cavalry
Battle or Place of Action: Waynesboro, Virginia
Date of Action: 2 March 1865
Date of Issue: 26 March 1865
Citation: Capture of unknown Confederate flag.

13 ◆ ANDERSON, EVERETT W.

Rank: Sergeant (highest rank: Second Lieutenant)
Service: U.S. Army
Birthday: 12 July 1839
Place of Birth: near Phoenixville, Chester County, Pennsylvania
Date of Death: 4 February 1917
Cemetery: Morris Cemetery (MH)—Phoenixville, Pennsylvania
Entered Service at: Philadelphia, Philadelphia County, Pennsylvania
Unit: Company M, 15th Pennsylvania Cavalry
Battle or Place of Action: Crosby's Creek, Tennessee
Date of Action: 14 January 1864
Date of Issue: 3 December 1894
Citation: Captured, singlehandedly, Confederate Brig. Gen. Robert B. Vance during a charge upon the enemy.

14 ◆ ANDERSON, FREDERICK CHARLES

Rank: Private
Service: U.S. Army
Birthday: 24 March 1842
Place of Birth: Boston, Suffolk County, Massachusetts
Date of Death: 6 October 1882
Place of Death: Providence, Rhode Island
Cemetery: unknown cemetery (family plot)—Somerset, Massachusetts
Entered Service at: Dedham, Norfolk County, Massachusetts
Unit: Company A, 18th Massachusetts Infantry
Battle or Place of Action: Weldon Railroad, Virginia
Date of Action: 21 August 1864
Date of Issue: 3 December 1894
Citation: Capture of battle flag of 27th South Carolina (C.S.A.) and the color bearer.

15 ◆ ANDERSON, MARION T.

Rank: Captain
Service: U.S. Army
Birthday: 13 November 1839
Place of Birth: Decatur County, Indiana
Date of Death: 7 February 1904
Cemetery: Arlington National Cemetery (1-512)—Arlington, Virginia
Entered Service at: Kokomo, Howard County, Indiana
Unit: Company D, 51st Indiana Infantry
Battle or Place of Action: Nashville, Tennessee
Date of Action: 16 December 1864
Date of Issue: 1 September 1893
Citation: Lead his regiment over five lines of the enemy's works, where he fell, severely wounded.

16 ◆ ANDERSON, PETER T.

Rank: Private (highest rank: Brevet Captain)
Service: U.S. Army
Birthday: 4 September 1847
Place of Birth: Darlington, Lafayette County, Wisconsin
Date of Death: 26 July 1907
Place of Death: Storm Lake, Iowa
Cemetery: Newell Cemetery (MH)—Newell, Iowa
Entered Service at: Wiota, Wisconsin
Unit: Company B, 31st Wisconsin Infantry
Battle or Place of Action: Bentonville, North Carolina
Date of Action: 19 March 1865
Date of Issue: 16 June 1865
Citation: Entirely unassisted, brought from the field an abandoned piece of artillery and saved the gun from falling into the hands of the enemy.

17 ◆ ANDERSON, ROBERT N.

Rank: Quartermaster (highest rank: Acting Master's Mate)
Service: U.S. Navy
Birthday: 15 December 1843
Place of Birth: Ireland
Date of Death: 20 June 1900
Place of Death: Portsmouth, New Hampshire
Cemetery: Calvary Cemetery (MH)—Portsmouth, New Hampshire
Entered Service at: New Hampshire
Unit: U.S.S. *Crusader* and the U.S.S. *Keokuk*
Battle or Place of Action: Charleston, South Carolina
Date of Action: 10 July 1863
G.O. Number, Date: 17, 10 July 1863
Citation: Served on board the U.S.S. *Crusader* and the *Keokuk* during various actions of those vessels. Carrying out his duties skillfully while on board the U.S.S. *Crusader*, Q.M. Anderson, on all occasions, set forth the greatest intrepidity and devotion. During the attack on Charleston, while serving on board the U.S.S. *Keokuk*, Q.M. Anderson was stationed at the wheel when shot penetrated the house and, with the scattering of the iron, used his own body as a shield for his commanding officer.

18 ◆ ANDERSON, THOMAS

Rank: Corporal
Service: U.S. Army
Birthday: 12 July 1841
Place of Birth: Scenery Hill, Washington County, Pennsylvania
Date of Death: 8 September 1912
Place of Death: Washington County, Pennsylvania

Cemetery: Dunkard Cemetery—Washington, Pennsylvania
Entered Service at: Wheeling, Ohio County, West Virginia
Unit: Company I, 1st West Virginia Cavalry
Battle or Place of Action: Appomattox Station, Virginia
Date of Action: 8 April 1865
Date of Issue: 3 May 1865
Citation: Capture of Confederate flag.

19 ◆ ANGLING, JOHN

True Name: Anglin, John
Rank: Cabin Boy (highest rank: Cabin Boy First Class)
Service: U.S. Navy
Birthday: 6 October 1850
Place of Birth: Portland, Cumberland County, Maine
Date of Death: 6 September 1905
Cemetery: Calvary Cemetery (MH)—Portland, Maine
Entered Service at: Portland, Cumberland County, Maine
Unit: U.S.S. *Pontoosuc*
Battle or Place of Action: Fort Fisher & Wilmington, North Carolina
Date of Action: 24 December 1864—22 January 1865
G.O. Number, Date: 59, 22 June 1865
Citation: Served on board the U.S.S. *Pontoosuc* during the capture of Fort Fisher and Wilmington, 24 December 1864 to 22 January 1865. Carrying out his duties faithfully during this period, C.B. Angling was recommended for gallantry and skill and for his cool courage while under the fire of the enemy throughout these various actions.

20 ◆ APPLE, ANDREW O.

Rank: Corporal
Service: U.S. Army
Birthday: 1845
Place of Birth: Northampton, Northampton County, Pennsylvania
Date of Death: 7 June 1890
Cemetery: Bluff City Cemetery—Elgin, Illinois
Entered Service at: New Manchester, Hancock County, West Virginia
Unit: Company I, 12th West Virginia Infantry
Battle or Place of Action: Petersburg, Virginia
Date of Action: 2 April 1865
Date of Issue: 12 May 1865
Citation: Conspicuous gallantry as color bearer in the assault on Fort Gregg.

21 ◆ APPLETON, WILLIAM H.

Rank: First Lieutenant (highest rank: Brevet Major)
Service: U.S. Army
Birthday: 24 March 1843
Place of Birth: Chichester, New Hampshire
Date of Death: 9 September 1912
Cemetery: Evergreen Cemetery—Pembroke, New Hampshire
Entered Service at: Portsmouth, Rockingham County, New Hampshire
Unit: Company H, 4th U.S. Colored Infantry
Battle or Place of Action: Petersburg, Virginia
Date of Action: 15 June 1864
Date of Issue: 18 February 1891
Citation: The first man of the Eighteenth Corps to enter the enemy's works at Petersberg, Va., 15 June 1864. Valiant service in a desperate assault at New Market Heights, Va., inspiring the Union troops by his example of steady courage.

22 ◆ ARCHER, JAMES W.

Rank: First Lieutenant & Adjutant
Service: U.S. Army
Birthday: 6 September 1828
Place of Birth: Edgar County, Illinois
Date of Death: 28 January 1908
Cemetery: Riverside Cemetery—Spencer, Indiana
Entered Service at: Spencer, Owen County, Indiana
Unit: 59th Indiana Infantry
Battle or Place of Action: Corinth, Mississippi
Date of Action: 4 October 1862
Date of Issue: 2 August 1897
Citation: Voluntarily took command of another regiment, with the consent of one or more of his seniors, who were present, rallied the command and led it in the assault.

23 ◆ *ARCHER, LESTER

Rank: Sergeant
Service: U.S. Army
Birthday: 1838
Place of Birth: Fort Ann, Washington County, New York
Date of Death: 27 October 1864
Place of Death: Wilderness, Virginia (KIA)
Cemetery: NON-RECOVERABLE
Entered Service at: Plattsburgh, Clinton County, New York
Unit: Company E, 96th New York Infantry
Battle or Place of Action: Fort Harrison, Virginia
Date of Action: 29 September 1864
Date of Issue: 6 April 1865
Citation: Gallantry in placing the colors of his regiment on the fort.

24 ◆ ARCHINAL, WILLIAM J.

Rank: Corporal
Service: U.S. Army
Birthday: 3 June 1840
Place of Birth: Felsburg, Hesse, Germany
Date of Death: 10 May 1919
Cemetery: Riverview Cemetery—Trenton, New Jersey
Entered Service at: Canaldover, Ohio
Unit: Company I, 30th Ohio Infantry
Battle or Place of Action: Vicksburg, Mississippi
Date of Action: 22 May 1863
Date of Issue: 10 July 1894
Citation: Gallantry in the charge of the "volunteer storming party."
Notes: POW

25 ◆ ARMSTRONG, CLINTON LYCURGUS

Rank: Private
Service: U.S. Army
Birthday: 3 March 1844
Place of Birth: Franklin, Johnson County, Indiana
Date of Death: 5 January 1899
Place of Death: Cincinnati, Ohio
Cemetery: Mt. Fountain Park Cemetery—Winchester, Indiana
Entered Service at: Indianapolis, Marion County, Indiana
Unit: Company D, 83d Indiana Infantry
Battle or Place of Action: Vicksburg, Mississippi
Date of Action: 22 May 1863
Date of Issue: 15 August 1894
Citation: Gallantry in the charge of the "volunteer storming party."

26 ◆ ARNOLD, ABRAHAM KERNS

Rank: Captain (highest rank: Brigadier General)
Service: U.S. Army
Birthday: 24 March 1837
Place of Birth: Bedford, Bedford County, Pennsylvania
Date of Death: 23 November 1901
Place of Death: Cold Springs, New York
Cemetery: St. Philips-in-the-Highlands Cemetery—Garrison, New York
Entered Service at: Bedford, Bedford County, Pennsylvania
Unit: 5th U.S. Cavalry
Battle or Place of Action: Davenport Bridge, Virginia
Date of Action: 10 April 1864
Date of Issue: 1 September 1893
Citation: By a gallant charge against a superior force of the enemy, extricated his command from a perilous position in which it had been ordered.

27 ◆ ARTHER, MATTHEW

Rank: Signal Quartermaster
Service: U.S. Navy
Birthday: 1835
Place of Birth: Scotland
Entered Service at: Boston, Suffolk County, Massachusetts
Unit: U.S.S. *Carondelet*
Battle or Place of Action: Forts Henry & Donelson, Tennessee
Date of Action: 6, 14 February 1862
G.O. Number, Date: 17, 10 July 1863
Citation: Served on board the U.S.S. *Carondelet* at the reduction of Forts Henry and Donelson, 6 and 14 February 1862 and other actions. Carrying out his duties as signal quartermaster and captain of the rifled bow gun, S/Q.M. Arther was conspicuous for valor and devotion, serving most faithfully, effectively and valiantly.

28 ◆ ASTEN, CHARLES

True Name: Asten, Michael
Rank: Quarter Gunner
Service: U.S. Navy
Birthday: 1834
Place of Birth: Halifax, Nova Scotia, Canada
Date of Death: 14 September 1885
Place of Death: Providence, Rhode Island
Cemetery: St. Francis Cemetery—Pawtucket, Rhode Island
Entered Service at: Chicago, Cook County, Illinois
Unit: U.S.S. *Signal*
Battle or Place of Action: Red River, Louisiana
Date of Action: 5 May 1864
G.O. Number, Date: 45, 31 December 1864
Citation: Served on board the U.S.S. *Signal*, Red River, 5 May 1864. Proceeding up the Red River, the U.S.S. *Signal* engaged a large force of enemy field batteries and sharpshooters, returning their fire until the Federal ship was totally disabled, at which time the white flag was raised. Although on the sick list, Q.G. Asten courageously carried out his duties during the entire engagement.
Notes: POW

29 ◆ ATKINSON, THOMAS E.

Rank: Yeoman
Service: U.S. Navy
Birthday: 1824
Place of Birth: Salem, Essex County, Massachusetts
Entered Service at: Massachusetts
Unit: U.S.S. *Richmond*
Battle or Place of Action: Mobile Bay, Alabama
Date of Action: 5 August 1864
G.O. Number, Date: 45, 31 December 1864
Citation: On board the U.S.S. *Richmond*, Mobile Bay, 5 August 1864; commended for coolness and energy in supplying the rifle ammunition which was under his sole charge, in the action in Mobile Bay on the morning of 5 August 1864. He was a petty officer on board the U.S. Frigate *Congress* in 1842–46; was present and assisted in the capture the whole of the Buenos Ayrean fleet by that vessel off Montevideo; joined the *Richmond* in September 1860; was in the action with Fort McRea, the Head of the Passes of the Mississippi, Fort Jackson and St. Philip, the Chalmettes, the rebel ironclads and gunboats below New Orleans, Vicksburg, Port Hudson, and the surrender of New Orleans.

30 ◆ AVERY, JAMES

Rank: Seaman
Service: U.S. Navy
Birthday: 1825
Place of Birth: Scotland
Date of Death: 11 October 1898
Cemetery: U.S. Naval Hospital Cemetery (MH)—Norfolk, Virginia
Entered Service at: New York
Unit: U.S.S. *Metacomet*
Battle or Place of Action: Mobile Bay, Alabama
Date of Action: 5 August 1864
G.O. Number, Date: 71, 15 January 1866
Citation: Served on board the U.S.S. *Metacomet*. As a mem-

ber of the boat's crew which went to the rescue of the U.S. Monitor *Tecumseh* when that vessel was struck by a torpedo in passing the enemy forts in Mobile Bay, 5 August 1864, S/man Avery braved the enemy fire which was said by the admiral to be "one of the most galling" he had ever seen, and aided in rescuing from death 10 of the crew of the *Tecumseh*, eliciting the admiration of both friend and foe.

31 ◆ AVERY, WILLIAM B.

Rank: Second Lieutenant (highest rank: Captain)
Service: U.S. Army
Birthday: 10 September 1840
Place of Birth: Providence, Providence County, Rhode Island
Date of Death: 19 July 1894
Place of Death: Bayside, Kent County, Rhode Island
Cemetery: North Burial Grounds—Bayside, Rhode Island
Entered Service at: Providence, Providence County, Rhode Island
Unit: 1st New York Marine Artillery
Battle or Place of Action: Tranter's Creek, North Carolina
Date of Action: 5 June 1862
Date of Issue: 2 September 1893
Citation: Handled his battery with greatest coolness amidst the hottest fire.

32 ◆ AYERS, DAVID

True Name: Ayres, David
Rank: Sergeant (highest rank: Captain)
Service: U.S. Army
Birthday: 29 April 1841
Place of Birth: Kalida, Putnam County, Ohio
Date of Death: 11 December 1916
Place of Death: Chicago, Illinois
Cemetery: Oakwoods Cemetery—Chicago, Illinois
Entered Service at: Upper Sandusky, Wyandot County, Ohio
Unit: Company A, 57th Ohio Infantry
Battle or Place of Action: Vicksburg, Mississippi
Date of Action: 22 May 1863
Date of Issue: 13 April 1894
Citation: Gallantry in the charge of the "volunteer storming party."

33 ◆ AYERS, JOHN G. K.

Rank: Private
Service: U.S. Army
Birthday: 30 October 1837
Place of Birth: Washtenaw County, Michigan
Date of Death: 30 July 1913
Cemetery: Riverside Cemetery—Three Rivers, Michigan
Entered Service at: Pekin, Tazwell County, Illinois
Unit: Company H, 8th Missouri Infantry
Battle or Place of Action: Vicksburg, Mississippi
Date of Action: 22 May 1863
Date of Issue: 31 August 1895
Citation: Gallantry in the charge of the "volunteer storming party."

34 ◆ BABOCK, WILLIAM J.

Rank: Sergeant
Service: U.S. Army
Birthday: 8 April 1841
Place of Birth: Griswold, Connecticut
Date of Death: 29 October 1897
Cemetery: Riverside Cemetery (MH)—Wakefield, Rhode Island
Entered Service at: South Kingston, Washington County, Rhode Island
Unit: 2d Rhode Island Infantry
Battle or Place of Action: Petersburg, Virginia
Date of Action: 2 April 1865
Date of Issue: 2 March 1895
Citation: Planted the flag upon the parapet while the enemy still occupied the line; was the first of his regiment to enter the works.

35 ◆ *BACON, ELIJAH WILLIAM

Rank: Private
Service: U.S. Army
Birthday: 1836
Place of Birth: Burlington, Hartford County, Connecticut
Date of Death: 6 May 1864
Place of Death: Wilderness, Virginia
Cemetery: Maple Cemetery (MH)—Berlin, Connecticut
Entered Service at: New Britain, Hartford County, Connecticut
Unit: Company F, 14th Connecticut Infantry
Battle or Place of Action: Gettysburg, Pennsylvania
Date of Action: 3 July 1863
Date of Issue: 1 December 1864
Citation: Capture of flag of the 16th North Carolina regiment (C.S.A.).

36 ◆ BAIRD, ABSALOM

Rank: Brigadier General (highest rank: Brevet Major General)
Service: U.S. Army
Birthday: 20 August 1824
Place of Birth: Washington, Washington County, Pennsylvania
Date of Death: 14 June 1905
Place of Death: near Relay, Maryland
Cemetery: Arlington National Cemetery (1-55) (MH)—Arlington, Virginia
Entered Service at: Washington, Washington County, Pennsylvania
Unit: U.S. Volunteers
Battle or Place of Action: Jonesboro, Georgia
Date of Action: 1 September 1864
Date of Issue: 22 April 1896

Citation: Voluntarily led a detached brigade in an assault upon the enemy's works.

37 ◆ BAKER, CHARLES

Rank: Quarter Gunner
Service: U.S. Navy
Birthday: 1809
Place of Birth: Georgetown, D.C.
Date of Death: 3 August 1891
Place of Death: Philadelphia, Pennsylvania
Cemetery: Mount Moriah (VA plot 2-22-22) (MH)—Philadelphia, Pennsylvania
Entered Service at: New York, New York
Unit: U.S.S. *Metacomet*
Battle or Place of Action: Mobile Bay, Alabama
Date of Action: 5 August 1864
G.O. Number, Date: 71, 15 January 1866
Citation: Served on board the U.S.S. *Metacomet*. As a member of the boat's crew which went to the rescue of the U.S. Monitor *Tecumseh* when the vessel was struck by a torpedo in passing the enemy forts in Mobile Bay, 5 August 1864, Q.G. Baker braved the enemy fire which was said by the admiral to be "one of the most galling" he has ever seen, and aided in rescuing from death 10 of the crew of the *Tecumseh*, eliciting the admiration of both friend and foe.

38 ◆ BALDWIN, CHARLES H.

Rank: Coal Heaver (highest rank: Acting Master's Mate)
Service: U.S. Navy
Birthday: 30 June 1839
Place of Birth: Wilmington, New Castle County, Delaware
Date of Death: 22 November 1911
Cemetery: Christ Church Cemetery—Accokeek, Maryland
Entered Service at: Philadelphia, Philadelphia County, Pennsylvania
Unit: U.S.S. *Wyalusing*
Battle or Place of Action: Roanoke River, North Carolina
Date of Action: 25 May 1864
G.O. Number, Date: 45, 31 December 1864
Citation: Served on board the U.S.S. *Wyalusing* and participating in a plan to destroy the rebel ram *Albemarle* in Roanoke River, 25 May 1864. Volunteering for the hazardous mission, C.H. Baldwin participated in the transfer of two torpedoes across an island swamp. Weighted by a line which was used to transfer the torpedoes, he swam the river and, when challenged by a sentry, was forced to abandon the plan after erasing its detection and before it could be carried to completion. Escaping the fire of the muskets, C.H. Baldwin spent two days and nights of hazardous travel without food, and finally arrived, fatigued, at the mother ship.
Notes: POW

39 ◆ BALDWIN, FRANK DWIGHT✛

Rank: Captain (highest rank: Major General)
Service: U.S. Army
Birthday: 26 June 1842
Place of Birth: Manchester, Washtenaw County, Michigan
Date of Death: 22 April 1923
Cemetery: Arlington National Cemetery (3-1894)—Arlington Virginia,
Entered Service at: Constantine, St. Joseph County, Michigan
Unit: Company D, 19th Michigan Infantry
Battle or Place of Action: Peach Tree Creek, Georgia
Date of Action: 12 July 1864
Date of Issue: 3 December 1891
Citation: **First Award** Led his company in a countercharge at Peach Tree Creek, Ga., 12 July 1864, under a galling fire ahead of his own men, and singly entered the enemy's line, capturing and bringing back two commissioned officers, fully armed, besides a guidon of a Georgia regiment.
Notes: POW ✛Double Awardee: *see also* Indian Wars

40 ◆ BALLEN, FREDERICK A.

Rank: Private
Service: U.S. Army
Birthday: 11 August 1843
Place of Birth: Germany
Date of Death: 27 April 1916
Place of Death: Exeter Township, Michigan
Cemetery: Carleton Cemetery—Carleton, Michigan
Entered Service at: Adrian, Lenawee County, Michigan
Unit: Company B, 47th Ohio Infantry
Battle or Place of Action: Vicksburg, Mississippi
Date of Action: 3 May 1863
Date of Issue: 6 November 1908
Citation: Was one of a party that volunteered and attempted to run the enemy's batteries with a steam tug and two barges loaded with subsistence stores.

41 ◆ BANKS, GEORGE LOVELL

Rank: Sergeant
Service: U.S. Army
Birthday: 13 October 1839
Place of Birth: Lake County, Ohio
Date of Death: 20 August 1924
Place of Death: Independence, Kansas
Cemetery: Mount Hope Cemetery—Independence, Kansas
Entered Service at: Lafayette, Tippecanoe County, Indiana
Unit: Company C, 15th Indiana Infantry
Battle or Place of Action: Missionary Ridge, Tennessee
Date of Action: 25 November 1863
Date of Issue: 28 September 1897
Citation: As color bearer, led his regiment in the assault, and, though wounded, carried the flag forward to the enemy's works, where he was again wounded. In a brigade of eight regiments this flag was the first planted on the parapet.

42 ◆ BARBER, JAMES ALBERT

Rank: Corporal
Service: U.S. Army

Birthday: 11 July 1841
Place of Birth: Westerly, Washington County, Rhode Island
Date of Death: 26 June 1925
Cemetery: River Bend Cemetery (MH)—Westerly, Rhode Island
Entered Service at: Westerly, Washington County, Rhode Island
Unit: 1st Rhode Island Light Artillery
Battle or Place of Action: Petersburg, Virginia
Date of Action: 2 April 1865
Date of Issue: 20 June 1866
Citation: Was one of a detachment of 20 picked artillerymen who voluntarily accompanied an infantry assaulting party, and who turned upon the enemy the guns captured in the assault.

43 ◆ BARKER, NATHANIEL C.

Rank: Sergeant
Service: U.S. Army
Birthday: 28 September 1836
Place of Birth: Piermont, Grafton County, New Hampshire
Date of Death: 7 March 1904
Place of Death: Somerville, Massachusetts
Cemetery: Last Rest Cemetery (MH)—Merrimack, New Hampshire
Entered Service at: Manchester, Hillsborough County, New Hampshire
Unit: Company E, 11th New Hampshire Infantry
Battle or Place of Action: Spotsylvania, Virginia
Date of Action: 12 May 1864
Date of Presentation: 23 September 1897
Place of Presentation: at the Mass. Assoc. of N.H. Vets 27 Pemberton Square, Boston, Mass
Citation: Six color bearers of the regiment having been killed, he voluntarily took both flags of the regiment and carried them through the remainder of the battle.

44 ◆ BARNES, WILLIAM HENRY

Rank: Private (highest rank: Sergeant)
Service: U.S. Army
Birthday: 1845
Place of Birth: St. Marys County, Maryland
Date of Death: 24 December 1866
Place of Death: Indianola U.S. Army Hospital, Texas
Cemetery: San Antonio National Cemetery as an unknown (MH) ('In Memory' marker)—San Antonio, Texas
Entered Service at: Norfolk, Norfolk County, Virginia
Unit: Company C, 38th U.S. Colored Infantry
Battle or Place of Action: Chapin's Farm, Virginia
Date of Action: 29 September 1864
Date of Issue: 6 April 1865
Citation: Among the first to enter the enemy's works, although wounded.

45 ◆ BARNUM, HENRY ALANSON

Rank: Colonel (highest rank: Brevet Major General)
Service: U.S. Army
Birthday: 24 September 1833
Place of Birth: Jamesville, Onondaga County, New York
Date of Death: 29 January 1892
Place of Death: New York, New York
Cemetery: Oakwood Cemetery (MH)—Syracuse, New York
Entered Service at: Syracuse, Onondaga County, New York
Unit: 149th New York Infantry
Battle or Place of Action: Chattanooga, Tennessee
Date of Action: 23 November 1863
Date of Issue: 16 July 1889
Citation: Although suffering severely from wounds, he led his regiment, inciting his men to greater action by word and example until again severely wounded.
Notes: POW

46 ◆ BARNUM, JAMES

Rank: Boatswain's Mate
Service: U.S. Navy
Birthday: 1816
Place of Birth: Massachusetts
Entered Service at: Massachusetts
Unit: U.S.S. *New Ironsides*
Battle or Place of Action: Fort Fisher, North Carolina
Date of Action: 24-25 December 1864 & 13-15 January 1865
G.O. Number, Date: 59, 22 June 1865
Citation: Barnum served on board the U.S.S. *New Ironsides* during action in several attacks on Fort Fisher, 24 and 25 December 1864; and on 13, 14, and 15 January 1865. The ship steamed in and took the lead in the ironclad division close inshore and immediately opened its starboard battery in a barrage of well-directed fire to cause several fires and explosions and dismount several guns during the first two days of fighting. Taken under fire as she steamed into position on 13 January, the *New Ironsides* fought all day and took on ammunition at night despite severe weather conditions. When the enemy came out of his bombproofs to defend the fort against the storming party, the ship's battery disabled nearly every gun on the fort facing the shore before the cease-fire orders were given by the flagship. Barnum was commended for highly meritorious conduct during this period.

47 ◆ BARRELL, CHARLES L.

Rank: First Lieutenant (highest rank: Captain)
Service: U.S. Army
Birthday: 1 August 1842
Place of Birth: Conquest, New York
Date of Death: 18 April 1914
Place of Death: Ann Arbor, Michigan
Cemetery: Leighton Cemetery—Leighton, Michigan
Entered Service at: Leighton, Allegan County, Michigan
Unit: Company C, 102d U.S. Colored Infantry
Battle or Place of Action: near Camden, South Carolina
Date of Action: April 1865
Date of Issue: 14 May 1891
Citation: Hazardous service in marching through the enemy's country to bring relief to his command.

48 ◆ BARRICK, JESSE T.

Rank: Corporal (highest rank: Second Lieutenant)
Service: U.S. Army
Birthday: 18 January 1841
Place of Birth: Columbiana County, Ohio
Place of Death: Pasco, Washington
Date of Death: 3 November 1923
Cemetery: Pasco Cemetery—Pasco, Washington
Entered Service at: Fort Snelling, St. Paul County, Minnesota
Unit: Company H, 3d Minnesota Infantry
Battle or Place of Action: Duck River, Tennessee
Date of Action: 26 May-2 June 1863
Date of Issue: 3 March 1917
Citation: While on a scout singlehandedly captured two desperate Confederate guerrilla officers who were together and well-armed at the time.

49 ◆ BARRINGER, WILLIAM H.

Rank: Private
Service: U.S. Army
Birthday: 27 May 1841
Place of Birth: Long Bottom, Meigs County, Ohio
Date of Death: 7 April 1917
Place of Death: Oliver Township, Ohio
Cemetery: Mount Olive Cemetery—Racine, Ohio
Entered Service at: Mason City, Mason County, West Virginia
Unit: Company F, 4th West Virginia Infantry
Battle or Place of Action: Vicksburg, Mississippi
Date of Action: 22 May 1863
Date of Issue: 12 July 1894
Citation: Gallantry in the charge of the "volunteer storming party."

50 ◆ BARRY, AUGUSTUS

Rank: Sergeant Major
Service: U.S. Army
Birthday: 1840
Place of Birth: Ireland
Date of Death: 3 August 1871
Cemetery: Cold Harbor National Cemetery (MH) (A-309)—Mechanicsville, Virginia
Entered Service at: New York, New York
Unit: 16th U.S. Infantry
Battle or Place of Action: Tennessee & Georgia
Date of Action: 1863—1865
Date of Issue: 28 February 1870
Citation: Gallantry in various actions during the rebellion.

51 ◆ BARTER, GURDON H.

Rank: Landsman
Service: U.S. Navy
Birthday: 1843
Place of Birth: Williamsburg, Kings County, New York
Date of Death: 22 April 1900
Place of Death: Viola, Idaho
Cemetery: Viola Cemetery—Viola, Idaho
Entered Service at: New York, New York
Unit: U.S.S. *Minnesota*
Battle or Place of Action: Fort Fisher, North Carolina
Date of Action: 15 January 1865
G.O. Number, Date: 59, 22 June 1865
Citation: On board the U.S.S. *Minnesota* in action during the assault on Fort Fisher, 15 January 1865. Landing on the beach with the assaulting party from his ship, Landsman Barter advanced to the top of the sandhill and partly through the breach in the palisades despite enemy fire which killed and wounded many officers and men. When more than two-thirds of the men became seized with panic and retreated on the run, he remained with the party until dark, when it came safely away, bringing its wounded, its arms, and its colors.

52 ◆ BARTON, THOMAS

Rank: Seaman
Service: U.S. Navy
Birthday: 1831
Place of Birth: Cleveland, Cuyahoga County, Ohio
Entered Service at: Ohio
Unit: U.S.S. *Hunchback*
Battle or Place of Action: Franklin, Virginia
Date of Action: 3 October 1862
G.O. Number, Date: 11, 3 April 1863
Citation: On board the U.S.S. *Hunchback* in the attack on Franklin, Va., 3 October 1862. When an ignited shell, with cartridge attached, fell out of the howitzer upon the deck, S/man Barton promptly seized a pail of water and threw it upon the missle, thereby preventing it from exploding.

53 ◆ BASS, DAVID L.

Rank: Seaman
Service: U.S. Navy
Birthday: 3 February 1842
Place of Birth: Ireland
Date of Death: 14 October 1886
Place of Death: Little Falls, New York
Cemetery: Wilcox Cemetery (MH)—Little Falls, New York
Entered Service at: New York, New York
Unit: U.S.S. *Minnesota*
Battle or Place of Action: Fort Fisher, North Carolina
Date of Action: 15 January 1865
G.O. Number, Date: 59, 22 June 1865
Citation: On board the U.S.S. *Minnesota* in action during the assault on Fort Fisher, 15 January 1865. Landing on the beach with the assaulting party from his ship, S/man Bass advanced to the top of the sand hill and partly through the breach in the palisades despite enemy fire which killed and wounded many officers and men. When more than two-thirds of the men became seized with panic and retreated on the run, he remained with the party until dark, when it came safely away, bringing its wounded, its arms, and its colors.

54 ◆ BATCHELDER, RICHARD NAPOLEON

Rank: Lieutenant Colonel and Chief Quartermaster (highest rank: Brigadier General)
Service: U.S. Army
Birthday: 27 July 1832
Place of Birth: Lake Village (Now Lakeport), Belknap County, New Hampshire
Date of Death: 4 January 1901
Place of Death: Washington, D.C.
Cemetery: Arlington National Cemetery (2-998)—Arlington, Virginia
Entered Service at: Manchester, Hillsborough County, New Hampshire
Unit: 2d Corps
Battle or Place of Action: Catlett and Fairfax Stations, Virginia
Date of Action: 13-15 October 1863
Date of Issue: 20 May 1895
Citation: Being ordered to move his trains by a continuous day-and-night march, and without the usual military escort, armed his teamsters and personally commanded them, successfully fighting against heavy odds and bringing his trains through without the loss of a wagon.

55 ◆ BATES, DELAVAN

Rank: Colonel (highest rank: Brevet Brigadier General)
Service: U.S. Army
Birthday: 17 March 1840
Place of Birth: Schoharie County, New York
Date of Death: 19 December 1918
Cemetery: Aurora Cemetery (MH)—Aurora, Nebraska
Entered Service at: Mohawk, Herkimer County, New York
Unit: 30th U.S. Colored Troops
Battle or Place of Action: Cemetery Hill, Petersburg, Virginia
Date of Action: 30 July 1864
Date of Issue: 22 June 1891
Citation: Gallantry in action where he fell, shot through the face, at the head of his regiment.
Notes: POW

56 ◆ BATES, NORMAN FRANCIS

Rank: Sergeant
Service: U.S. Army
Birthday: 6 November 1839
Place of Birth: Derry, Vermont
Date of Death: 16 October 1915
Place of Death: Los Angeles, California
Cemetery: Forest Lawn Memorial Park—Glendale, California
Entered Service at: Grinnell, Poweshiek County, Iowa
Unit: 4th Iowa Cavalry
Battle or Place of Action: Columbus, Georgia
Date of Action: 16 April 1865
Date of Issue: 17 June 1865
Citation: Capture of flag and bearer.

57 ◆ BAYBUTT, PHILIP

Rank: Private
Service: U.S. Army
Birthday: 1844
Place of Birth: Manchester, Greater Manchester County, England
Date of Death: 17 April 1907
Place of Death: Manchester, England
Cemetery: unknown cemetery—Manchester, England
Entered Service at: Fall River, Bristol County, Massachusetts
Unit: Company A, 2d Massachusetts Cavalry
Battle or Place of Action: Luray, Virginia
Date of Action: 24 September 1864
Date of Issue: 14 October 1864
Citation: Capture of flag.

58 ◆ BAZAAR, PHILIP

Rank: Ordinary Seaman
Service: U.S. Navy
Place of Birth: Chile
Entered Service at: New Bedford, Bristol County, Massachusetts
Unit: U.S.S. *Santiago de Cuba*
Battle or Place of Action: Fort Fisher, North Carolina
Date of Action: 15 January 1865
G.O. Number, Date: 59, 22 June 1865
Citation: On board the U.S.S. *Santiago de Cuba* during the assault on Fort Fisher on 15 January 1865. As one of a boat crew detailed to one of the generals onshore, O.S. Bazaar bravely entered the fort in the assault and accompanied his party in carrying dispatches at the height of the battle. He was one of six men who entered the fort in the assault from the fleet.

59 ◆ BEATTY, ALEXANDER MITCHELL

True Name: Beattie, Alexander Mitchell
Rank: Captain
Service: U.S. Army
Birthday: 29 July 1828
Place of Birth: Ryegate, Caledonia County, Vermont
Date of Death: 7 March 1907
Cemetery: Summer Street Cemetery—Lancaster, New Hampshire
Entered Service at: Guildhall, Essex County, Vermont
Unit: Company F, 3d Vermont Infantry
Battle or Place of Action: Cold Harbor, Virginia
Date of Action: 5 June 1864
Date of Issue: 25 April 1894
Citation: Removed, under a hot fire, a wounded member of his command to a place of safety.

60 ◆ BEATY, POWHATAN

Rank: First Sergeant
Service: U.S. Army
Birthday: 8 October 1837

Place of Birth: Richmond, Richmond County, Virginia
Date of Death: 6 December 1916
Cemetery: Union Baptist Cemetery (MH)—Cincinnati, Ohio
Entered Service at: Cincinnati, Hamilton County, Ohio
Unit: Company G, 5th U.S. Colored Infantry
Battle or Place of Action: Chapin's Farm, Virginia
Date of Action: 29 September 1864
Date of Issue: 6 April 1865
Citation: Took command of his company, all the officers having been killed or wounded, and gallantly led it.

61 ◆ BEAUFORT, JEAN J.

True Name: Beaufort, John Joseph
Rank: Corporal
Service: U.S. Army
Birthday: 1832
Place of Birth: France
Date of Death: 15 September 1897
Cemetery: Arlington National Cemetery (13-13784) (MH)—Arlington, Virginia
Entered Service at: New Orleans, Orleans County, Louisiana
Unit: Company A, 2d Louisiana Infantry
Battle or Place of Action: Port Hudson, Louisiana
Date of Action: 20 May 1863
Date of Issue: 20 July 1897
Citation: Volunteered to go within the enemy's lines and at the head of a party of eight destroyed a signal station, thereby greatly aiding in the operations against Port Hudson that immediately followed.

62 ◆ BEAUMONT, EUGENE BEAUHARNAIS

Rank: Major and Assistant Adjutant General (highest rank: Colonel)
Service: U.S. Army
Birthday: 2 August 1837
Place of Birth: Wilks-Barre, Luzerne County, Pennsylvania
Date of Death: 17 August 1916
Place of Death: Harvey's Lake, Pennsylvania
Cemetery: Hollenbeck Cemetery—Wilkes-Barre, Pennsylvania
Entered Service at: Wilks-Barre, Luzerne County, Pennsylvania
Unit: Cavalry Corps, Army of the Mississippi
Battle or Place of Action: Harpeth River, Tennessee; Selma, Alabama
Date of Action: 17 December 1864 & 2 April 1865
Date of Issue: 30 March 1898
Citation: Obtained permission from the corps commander to advance upon enemy's position with the 4th U.S. Cavalry, of which he was a lieutenant; led an attack upon a battery, dispersed the enemy and captured the guns. At Selma, Ala., charged, at the head of his regiment, into the second and last line of the enemy's works.

63 ◆ BEBB, EDWARD JAMES

Rank: Private
Service: U.S. Army
Birthday: 28 April 1839
Place of Birth: Butler County, Ohio
Date of Death: 12 July 1916
Place of Death: Marshalltown, Iowa
Cemetery: New Salem Cemetery—Lynnville, Iowa
Entered Service at: Mount Pleasant, Henry County, Iowa
Unit: Company D, 4th Iowa Cavalry
Battle or Place of Action: Columbus, Georgia
Date of Action: 16 April 1865
Date of Issue: 17 June 1865
Citation: Capture of flag.

64 ◆ BECKWITH, WALLACE A.

Rank: Private
Service: U.S. Army
Birthday: 28 February 1843
Place of Birth: New London, New London County, Connecticut
Date of Death: 22 November 1929
Cemetery: Jordan Cemetery (MH)—Waterford, Connecticut
Entered Service at: New London, New London County, Connecticut
Unit: Company F, 21st Connecticut Infantry
Battle or Place of Action: Fredericksburg, Virginia
Date of Action: 13 December 1862
Date of Issue: 15 February 1897
Citation: Gallantly responded to a call for volunteers to man a battery, served with great heroism until the termination of the engagement.

65 ◆ BEDDOWS, RICHARD

Rank: Private
Service: U.S. Army
Birthday: 27 June 1843
Place of Birth: Liverpool, Merseyside County, England
Date of Death: 15 February 1922
Place of Death: Mt. Vernon, New York
Cemetery: Holy Sepulchre Cemetery—New Rochelle, New York
Entered Service at: Flushing, Queens County, New York
Unit: 34th New York Battery
Battle or Place of Action: Spotsylvania, Virginia
Date of Action: 18 May 1864
Date of Issue: 10 July 1896
Citation: Brought his guidon off in safety under a heavy fire of musketry after he had lost it by his horse becoming furious from the bursting of a shell.

66 ◆ BEEBE, WILLIAM SULLY

Rank: First lieutenant (highest rank: Major)
Service: U.S. Army
Birthday: 14 February 1841
Place of Birth: Ithaca, Tompkins County, New York
Date of Death: 12 October 1898
Cemetery: U.S. Military Academy Cemetery (N-15)—West Point, New York

Entered Service at: Philadelphia, Philadelphia County, Pennsylvania
Unit: Ordnance Department, U.S. Army
Battle or Place of Action: Cane River Crossing, Louisiana
Date of Action: 23 April 1864
Date of Issue: 30 June 1897
Citation: Voluntarily led a successful assault on a fortified position.

67 ◆ BEECH, JOHN P.
Rank: Sergeant
Service: U.S. Army
Birthday: 1 May 1844
Place of Birth: Stratfordshire County, England
Date of Death: 27 November 1926
Cemetery: Mercer Cemetery—Trenton, New Jersey
Entered Service at: Trenton, Mercer County, New Jersey
Unit: Company B, 4th New Jersey Infantry
Battle or Place of Action: Spotsylvania Courthouse, Virginia
Date of Action: 12 May 1864
Date of Issue: 1 June 1894
Citation: Voluntarily assisted in working the guns of a battery, all the members of which had been killed or wounded.

68 ◆ *BEGLEY, TERRENCE
Rank: Sergeant
Service: U.S. Army
Place of Birth: Ireland
Date of Death: 25 August 1864
Place of Death: Weldon RR, Reams Station
Entered Service at: Albany, Albany County, New York
Unit: Company D, 7th New York Heavy Artillery
Battle or Place of Action: Cold Harbor, Virginia
Date of Action: 3 June 1864
Date of Issue: 1 December 1864
Citation: Shot a Confederate color bearer, 26th Virginia Infantry, rushed forward and seized his colors, and although exposed to heavy fire, regained the lines in safety.

69 ◆ BELCHER, THOMAS
Rank: Private
Service: U.S. Army
Birthday: 1834
Place of Birth: Bangor, Penobscot County, Maine
Date of Death: 22 May 1898
Place of Death: Augusta, Maine
Cemetery: Togus, Maine (Per death certificate, no cemetery)
Entered Service at: Bangor, Penobscot County, Maine
Unit: Company I, 9th Maine Infantry
Battle or Place of Action: Chapin's Farm, Virginia
Date of Action: 29 September 1864
Date of Issue: 6 April 1865
Citation: Took a guidon from the hands of the bearer, mortally wounded, and advanced with it nearer to the battery than any other man.

70 ◆ BELL, GEORGE H.
Rank: Captain of the Afterguard
Service: U.S. Navy
Birthday: 12 March 1839
Place of Birth: Sunderland, England
Date of Death: 26 September 1917
Place of Death: Newcastle, England
Cemetery: Elswick Cemetery—Newcastle, England
Entered Service at: New York, New York
Unit: U.S.S. *Santee*
Battle or Place of Action: Galveston Bay, Texas
Date of Action: 7 November 1861
G.O. Number, Date: 17, 10 July 1863
Date of Presentation: 21 November 1864
Place of Presentation: Virginia, Hampton Roads, Virginia, on board the U.S.S. *Brooklyn*, presented by Capt. James Alden
Citation: Served as pilot of the U.S.S. *Santee* when that vessel was engaged in cutting out the rebel armed schooner *Royal Yacht* from Galveston Bay, 7 November 1861, and evinced more coolness, in passing the four forts and the rebel steamer *General Rusk*, than was ever before witnessed by his commanding officer. "Although severely wounded, in the encounter, he displayed extraordinary courage under the most painful and trying circumstances."

71 ◆ BELL, JAMES BENNETT
Rank: Sergeant
Service: U.S. Army
Birthday: 9 August 1835
Place of Birth: Branot, Ohio
Date of Death: 30 June 1910
Place of Death: Elkhart, Indiana
Cemetery: Gettysburg Cemetery (MH)—Gettysburg, Ohio
Entered Service at: Troy, Miami County, Ohio
Unit: Company H, 11th Ohio Infantry
Battle or Place of Action: Missionary Ridge, Tennessee
Date of Action: 25 November 1863
Date of Issue: 9 October 1907
Citation: Though severely wounded, was first of his regiment on the summit of the ridge, planted his colors inside the enemy's works, and did not leave the field until after he had been wounded five times.

72 ◆ BENEDICT, GEORGE GREENVILLE
Rank: Second Lieutenant
Service: U.S. Army
Birthday: 10 December 1826
Place of Birth: Burlington, Chittenden County, Vermont
Date of Death: 8 April 1907
Place of Death: Camden, North Carolina
Cemetery: Green Mount Cemetery—Burlington, Vermont
Entered Service at: Burlington, Chittenden County, Vermont
Unit: Company C (Howard Guards), 12th Vermont Infantry

Battle or Place of Action: Gettysburg, Pennsylvania
Date of Action: 3 July 1863
Date of Issue: 27 June 1892
Citation: Passed through a murderous fire of grape and canister in delivering order and re-formed the crowded lines.

73 ◆ BENJAMIN, JOHN FRANCIS

Rank: Corporal
Service: U.S. Army
Place of Birth: Orange County, New York
Entered Service at: Newburgh, Orange County, New York
Unit: Company M, 2d New York Cavalry
Battle or Place of Action: Deatonsville (Sailor's Creek), Virginia
Date of Action: 6 April 1865
Date of Issue: 3 May 1865
Citation: Capture of battle flag of 9th Virginia Infantry (C.S.A.)

74 ◆ BENJAMIN, SAMUEL NICHOLL

Rank: First Lieutenant (highest rank: Brevet Lieutenant Colonel)
Service: U.S. Army
Birthday: 3 January 1839
Place of Birth: New York, New York
Date of Death: 15 May 1886
Place of Death: Governor's Island, New York
Cemetery: St. Philips In The Highlands Church Cemetery—Garrison, New York
Entered Service at: New York, New York
Unit: 2d U.S. Artillery
Battle or Place of Action: Bull Run to Spotsylvania, Virginia
Date of Action: July 1861—May 1864
Date of Issue: 11 June 1877
Citation: Particularly distinguished services as an artillery officer.

75 ◆ BENNETT, ORRIN

Rank: Private
Service: U.S. Army
Place of Birth: Bradford County, Pennsylvania
Entered Service at: Towanda, Bradford County, Pennsylvania
Unit: Company D, 141st Pennsylvania Infantry
Battle or Place of Action: Deatonsville (Sailor's Creek), Virginia
Date of Action: 6 April 1865
Date of Issue: 10 May 1865
Citation: Capture of flag.

76 ◆ BENNETT, ORSON W.

Rank: First Lieutenant (highest rank: Major)
Service: U.S. Army
Birthday: 17 November 1841
Place of Birth: Union City, Branch County, Michigan
Date of Death: 8 January 1904
Cemetery: Westminster Cemetery—Philadelphia, Pennsylvania
Entered Service at: Dubuque, Dubuque County, Iowa
Unit: Company A, 102d U.S. Colored Infantry
Battle or Place of Action: Honey Hill, South Carolina
Date of Action: 30 November 1864
Date of Issue: 9 March 1887
Citation: After several unsuccessful efforts to recover three pieces of abandoned artillery, this officer gallantly led a small force fully 100 yards in advance of the Union lines and brought in the guns, preventing their capture.

77 ◆ BENSINGER, WILLIAM

Rank: Private (highest rank: Captain)
Service: U.S. Army
Birthday: 14 January 1840
Place of Birth: Waynesburg, Stark County, Ohio
Date of Death: 19 December 1918
Place of Death: McComb, Ohio
Cemetery: Union Cemetery—McComb, Ohio
Entered Service at: McComb, Hancock County, Ohio
Unit: Company G, 21st Ohio Infantry
Battle or Place of Action: Georgia
Date of Action: April 1862
Date of Presentation: 25 March 1863
Place of Presentation: Washington, D.C., presented by Sec. of War Edward M. Stanton
Citation: One of 19 of 24 men (including two civilians) who, by direction of Gen. Ormsby M. Mitchell, penetrated nearly 200 miles south into enemy territory and captured a railroad train at Big Shanty, Ga., in an attempt to destroy the bridges and track between Chattanaooga and Atlanta.

78 ◆ BENYAURD, WILLIAM HENRY HARRISON

Rank: First Lieutenant, Engineers (highest rank: Lieutenant Colonel)
Service: U.S. Army
Birthday: 17 May 1841
Place of Birth: Philadelphia, Philadelphia County, Pennsylvania
Date of Death: 7 February 1900
Cemetery: U.S. Military Academy Cemetery (T-1) (MH)—West Point, New York
Entered Service at: Philadelphia, Philadelphia County, Pennsylvania
Unit: Engineers
Battle or Place of Action: Five Forks, Virginia
Date of Action: 1 April 1865
Date of Issue: 7 September 1897
Citation: With one companion, voluntarily advanced in a reconnaissance beyond the skirmishers, where he was exposed to imminent peril; also, in the same battle, rode to the front with the commanding general to encourage wavering troops to resume the advance, which they did successfully.

79 ◆ BETHAM, ASA

Rank: Coxswain
Service: U.S. Navy
Birthday: 1838
Place of Birth: New York, New York
Entered Service at: New York, New York
Unit: U.S.S. *Pontoosuc*
Battle or Place of Action: Fort Fisher and Wilmington, North Carolina
Date of Action: 24 December 1864—22 June 1865
G.O. Number, Date: 59, 22 June 1865
Citation: Served on board the U.S.S. *Pontoosuc* during the capture of Fort Fisher and Wilmington, 24 December 1864, to 22 January 1865. Carrying out his duties faithfully during this period, Betham was recommended for gallantry and skill and for his cool courage while under the fire of the enemy throughout these various actions.

80 ◆ BETTS, CHARLES MALONE

Rank: Lieutenant Colonel
Service: U.S. Army
Birthday: 9 August 1838
Place of Birth: Bucks County, Pennsylvania
Date of Death: 10 November 1905
Place of Death: Germantown, Pennsylvania
Cemetery: West Laurel Hill Cemetery—Bala-Cynwyd, Pennsylvania
Entered Service at: Philadelphia, Philadelphia County, Pennsylvania
Unit: 15th Pennsylvania Cavalry
Battle or Place of Action: Greensboro, North Carolina
Date of Action: 19 April 1865
Date of Issue: 10 October 1892
Citation: With a force of but 75 men, while on a scouting expedition, by a judicious disposition of his men, surprised and captured an entire battalion of the enemy's cavalry.

81 ◆ BEYER, HILLARY

Rank: Second Lieutenant (highest rank: First Lieutenant)
Service: U.S. Army
Birthday: 28 September 1837
Place of Birth: Montgomery County, Pennsylvania
Date of Death: 24 September 1907
Cemetery: Presbyterian Church Yard Cemetery (MH)—Lower Providence, Pennsylvania
Entered Service at: Philadelphia, Philadelphia County, Pennsylvania
Unit: Company H, 90th Pennsylvania Infantry
Battle or Place of Action: Antietam, Maryland
Date of Action: 17 September 1862
Date of Issue: 30 October 1896
Citation: After his command had been forced to fall back, remained alone on the line of battle, caring for his wounded comrades and carrying one of them to a place of safety.

82 ◆ BIBBER, CHARLES JAMES

Rank: Gunner's Mate
Service: U.S. Navy
Birthday: 22 March 1837
Place of Birth: Portland, Cumberland County, Maine
Date of Death: 8 October 1883
Place of Death: Revere, Massachusetts
Cemetery: Woodlawn Cemetery (MH)—Everett, Massachusetts
Entered Service at: Portland, Cumberland County, Maine
Unit: U.S.S. *Agawam*
Battle or Place of Action: Fort Fisher, North Carolina
Date of Action: 23 December 1864
G.O. Number, Date: 45, 31 December 1864
Date of Presentation: 12 May 1865
Place of Presentation: On board the U.S.S. *Agawam* off New Bern, North Carolina
Citation: Bibber served on board the U.S.S. *Agawam*, as one of a volunteer crew of a powder boat which was exploded near Fort Fisher, 23 December 1864. The powder boat, towed in by the *Wilderness* to prevent detection by the enemy, cast off and slowly steamed to within 300 yards of the beach. After fuses and fires had been lit and a second anchor with short scope let go to assure the boat's tailing inshore, the crew again boarded the *Wilderness* and proceeded a distance of 12 miles from shore. Less than two hours later the explosion took place, and the following day fires were observed still burning at the forts.

83 ◆ BICKFORD, HENRY H.

Rank: Corporal (highest rank: Quartermaster Sergeant)
Service: U.S. Army
Birthday: 13 March 1838
Place of Birth: Ypsilanti, Washtenaw County, Michigan
Date of Death: 20 May 1917
Place of Death: Middleport, New York
Cemetery: Hartland Central Cemetery (MH)—Hartland, New York
Entered Service at: Middleport, Niagara County, New York
Unit: Company E, 8th New York Cavalry
Battle or Place of Action: Waynesboro, Virginia
Date of Action: 2 March 1865
Date of Issue: 26 March 1865
Citation: Recapture of flag.

84 ◆ BICKFORD, JOHN F.

Rank: Captain of the Top (highest rank: Master's Mate)
Service: U.S. Navy
Birthday: 12 March 1843
Place of Birth: Tremont, Maine
Date of Death: 28 April 1927
Place of Death: Glouchester, Massachusetts
Cemetery: Mount Pleasant Cemetery (MH)—East Glouchester, Massachusetts
Entered Service at: Boston, Suffolk County, Massachusetts
Unit: U.S.S. *Kearsarge*

Battle or Place of Action: off Cherbourg, France
Date of Action: 19 June 1864
G.O. Number, Date: 45, 31 December 1864
Citation: Served on board the U.S.S. *Kearsarge* when she destroyed the *Alabama* off Cherbourg, France, 19 June 1864. Acting as the first loader of the pivot gun during this bitter engagement, Bickford exhibited marked coolness and good conduct and was highly recommended for his gallantry under fire by his divisional officer.

85 ◆ BICKFORD, MATTHEW

Rank: Corporal
Service: U.S. Army
Birthday: 10 April 1839
Place of Birth: Peoria County, Illinois
Date of Death: 18 April 1918
Cemetery: Bayview Cemetery (MH)—Bellingham, Washington
Entered Service at: Trivolia, Peoria County, Illinois
Unit: Company G, 8th Missouri Infantry
Battle or Place of Action: Vicksburg, Mississippi
Date of Action: 22 May 1863
Date of Issue: 31 August 1894
Citation: Gallantry in the charge of the "volunteer storming party."

86 ◆ BIEGER, CHARLES

Rank: Private
Service: U.S. Army
Birthday: 25 March 1844
Place of Birth: Wiesbaden, Germany
Date of Death: 10 August 1930
Cemetery: Mount Hope Cemetery—St. Louis, Missouri
Entered Service at: St. Louis, St. Louis County, Missouri
Unit: Company D, 4th Missouri Cavalry
Battle or Place of Action: Ivy Farm, Mississippi
Date of Action: 22 February 1864
Date of Issue: 8 July 1897
Citation: Voluntarily risked his life by taking a horse, under heavy fire beyond the line of battle for the rescue of his captain, whose horse had been killed in a charge and who was surrounded by the enemy's skirmishers.

87 ◆ BINDER, RICHARD

True Name: Bigle, Richard
Rank: Sergeant
Service: U.S. Marine Corps
Birthday: 26 July 1839
Place of Birth: Germany
Date of Death: 26 February 1912
Place of Death: Philadelphia, Pennsylvania
Cemetery: West Laurel Hill Cemetery—Bala-Cynwyd, Pennsylvania
Entered Service at: Pennsylvania
Unit: U.S.S. *Ticonderoga*
Battle or Place of Action: Fort Fisher, North Carolina
Date of Action: 24-25 December 1864 & 13-15 January 1865
Citation: On board the U.S.S. *Ticonderoga* during the attacks on Fort Fisher, 24 and 25 December 1864 and 13 to 15 January 1865. Despite heavy return fire by the enemy and the explosion of the 100-pounder Parrott rifle which killed eight men and wounded 12 more, Sgt. Binder, as captain of a gun, performed his duties with skill and courage during the first two days of battle. As his ship again took position on the 13th, he remained steadfast on the *Ticonderoga*, maintained a well-placed fire upon the batteries onshore, and thereafter, as she materially lessened the power of guns on the mound which had been turned upon our assaulting columns. During this action the flag was planted on one of the strongest fortifications possessed by the rebels.

88 ◆ BINGHAM, HENRY HARRISON

Rank: Captain (highest rank: Brevet Brigadier General)
Service: U.S. Army
Birthday: 4 December 1841
Place of Birth: Philadelphia, Philadelphia County, Pennsylvania
Date of Death: 22 March 1912
Place of Death: Philadelphia, Pennsylvania
Cemetery: Laurel Hill Cemetery (MH)—Philadelphia, Pennsylvania
Entered Service at: Canonsburg, Washington County, Pensylvania
Unit: Company G, 140th Pennsylvania Infantry
Battle or Place of Action: Wilderness Campaign, Virginia
Date of Action: 6 May 1864
Date of Issue: 31 August 1893
Citation: Rallied and led into action a portion of the troops who had given way under the fierce assaults of the enemy.

89 ◆ BIRDSALL, HORATIO L.

Rank: Sergeant
Service: U.S. Army
Birthday: 1833
Place of Birth: Monroe County, New York
Date of Death: 29 November 1891
Cemetery: Arlington National Cemetery (13-6935) (MH)—Arlington, Virginia
Entered Service at: Keokuk, Lee County, Iowa
Unit: Company B, 3d Iowa Cavalry
Battle or Place of Action: Columbus, Georgia
Date of Action: 16 April 1865
Date of Issue: 17 June 1865
Citation: Capture of flag and bearer.

90 ◆ BISHOP, FRANCIS A.

Rank: Private (highest rank: Corporal)
Service: U.S. Army
Birthday: 3 December 1840
Place of Birth: Bradford County, Pennsylvania
Date of Death: 11 October 1937
Place of Death: State Veterans Home, Retsil, Washington

Cemetery: Blanchard Cemetery (MH)—Blanchard, Michigan
Entered Service at: Harrisburg, Dauphin County, Pennsylvania
Unit: Company C, 57th Pennsylvania Infantry
Battle or Place of Action: Spotsylvania, Virginia
Date of Action: 12 May 1864
Date of Issue: 1 December 1864
Citation: Capture of flag.

91 ◆ BLACK, JOHN CHARLES

Rank: Lieutenant Colonel (highest rank: Brevet Brigadier General)
Service: U.S. Army
Birthday: 27 January 1839
Place of Birth: Lexington, Holmes County, Mississippi
Date of Death: 17 August 1915
Place of Death: Chicago, Illinois
Cemetery: Spring Hill Cemetery—Danville, Illinois
Entered Service at: Danville, Vermillion County, Illinois
Unit: 37th Illinois Infantry
Battle or Place of Action: Prairie Grove, Arkansas
Date of Action: 7 December 1862
Date of Issue: 31 October 1893
Citation: Gallantly charged the position of the enemy at the head of his regiment, after two other regiments had been repulsed and driven down the hill, and captured a battery; was severely wounded.

92 ◆ BLACK, WILLIAM PERKINS

Rank: Captain
Service: U.S. Army
Birthday: 11 November 1842
Place of Birth: Woodford, Kentucky
Date of Death: 3 January 1916
Place of Death: Chicago, Illinois
Cemetery: Graceland Cemetery—Chicago, Illinois
Entered Service at: Danville, Vermillion County, Illinois
Unit: Company K, 37th Illinois Infantry
Battle or Place of Action: Pea Ridge, Arkansas
Date of Action: 7 March 1862
Date of Issue: 2 October 1893
Citation: Singlehandedly confronted the enemy, firing a rifle at them, and thus checked their advance within 100 yards of the lines.

93 ◆ BLACKMAR, WILMON WHILLDIN

Rank: Lieutenant (highest rank: Captain)
Service: U.S. Army
Birthday: 25 July 1841
Place of Birth: Bristol, Bucks County, Pennsylvania
Date of Death: 16 July 1905
Place of Death: Boise, Idaho
Cemetery: Cedar Grove Cemetery (MH)—Dorchester, Massachusetts
Entered Service at: Philadelphia, Philadelphia County, Pennsylvania
Unit: Company H, 1st West Virginia Cavalry
Battle or Place of Action: Five Forks, Virginia
Date of Action: 1 April 1865
Date of Issue: 23 October 1897
Citation: At a critical stage of the battle, without orders, led a successful advance upon the enemy.

94 ◆ BLACKWOOD, WILLIAM ROBERT DOUGLAS

Rank: Surgeon (highest rank: Brevet Lieutenant Colonel)
Service: U.S. Army
Birthday: 12 May 1838
Place of Birth: Hollywood, County Wicklow, Ireland
Date of Death: 26 April 1922
Place of Death: Philadelphia, Pennsylvania
Cemetery: Cheltin Hills Crematory (Cremated 29 April 1922. Disposition of remains unknown.)
Entered Service at: Philadelphia, Philadelphia County, Pennsylvania
Unit: 48th Pennsylvania Infantry
Served as: Surgeon
Battle or Place of Action: Petersburg, Virginia
Date of Action: 2 April 1865
Date of Issue: 21 July 1897
Citation: Removed severely wounded officers and soldiers from the field while under a heavy fire from the enemy, exposing himself beyond the call of duty, thus furnishing an example of most distinguished gallantry.

95 ◆ BLAGHEEN, WILLIAM

True Name: Blagden, William
Rank: Ship's Cook
Service: U.S. Navy
Birthday: 1832
Place of Birth: Devonshire County, England
Entered Service at: New York, New York
Unit: U.S.S. *Brooklyn*
Battle or Place of Action: Fort Morgan, Mobile Bay, Alabama
Date of Action: 5 August 1864
G.O. Number, Date: 45, 31 December 1864
Citation: On board the U.S.S. *Brooklyn* during successful attacks against Fort Morgan, rebel gunboats and the ram *Tennessee* in Mobile Bay, on 5 August 1864. Stationed in the immediate vicinity of the shell whips which were twice cleared of men by bursting shells, Blagheen remained steadfast at his post and performed his duties in the powder division throughout the furious action which resulted in the surrender of the prize rebel ram *Tennessee* and in the damaging and destruction of batteries at Fort Morgan.

96 ◆ BLAIR, ROBERT M.

Rank: Boatswain's Mate
Service: U.S. Navy

Birthday: 1836
Place of Birth: Peacham, Caledonia County, Vermont
Date of Death: 2 April 1899
Place of Death: Enid, Oklahoma
Cemetery: Enid Cemetery (MH)—Enid, Oklahoma
Entered Service at: Portland, Cumberland County, Maine
Unit: U.S.S. *Pontoosuc*
Battle or Place of Action: Fort Fisher and Wilmington, North Carolina
Date of Action: 23 December 1864—22 January 1865
G.O. Number, Date: 59, 22 June 1865
Citation: Served on board the U.S.S. *Pontoosuc* during the capture of Fort Fisher and Wilmington, 24 December 1864 to 22 January 1865. Carrying out his duties faithfully throughout this period, Blair was recommended for gallantry and skill and for his cool courage while under the fire of the enemy throughout these actions.

97 ◆ BLAKE, ROBERT

Rank: Contraband
Service: U.S. Navy
Place of Birth: Virginia
Entered Service at: Port Royal, Caroline County, Virginia
Unit: U.S. Steam Gunboat *Marblehead*
Battle or Place of Action: off Legareville, Stono River, John's Island, South Carolina
Date of Action: 25 December 1863
G.O. Number, Date: 32, 16 April 1864
Citation: On board the U.S. Steam Gunboat *Marblehead* off Legareville, Stono River, 25 December 1863, in an engagement with the enemy on John's Island. Serving the rifle gun, Blake, an escaped slave, carried out his duties bravely throughout the engagement, which resulted in the enemy's abandonment of positions, leaving a caisson and one gun behind.

98 ◆ BLASDEL, THOMAS A.

Rank: Private (highest rank: Corporal)
Service: U.S. Army
Birthday: 2 January 1843
Place of Birth: Dearborn County, Indiana
Date of Death: 12 October 1932
Place of Death: Sylvia, Kansas
Cemetery: Fairlawn Cemetery—Hutchinson, Kansas
Entered Service at: Guilford, Dearborn County, Indiana
Unit: Company H, 83d Indiana Infantry
Battle or Place of Action: Vicksburg, Mississippi
Date of Action: 22 May 1863
Date of Issue: 11 August 1894
Citation: Gallantry in the charge of the "volunteer storming party."

99 ◆ BLICKENSDERGER, MILTON

Rank: Corporal (highest rank: Sergeant)
Service: U.S. Army
Birthday: 20 May 1835
Place of Birth: Lancaster, Lancaster County, Pennsylvania
Date of Death: 17 March 1916
Cemetery: Shanesville Cemetery—Shanesville, Ohio
Entered Service at: Shanesville, Ohio
Unit: Company E, 126th Ohio Infantry
Battle or Place of Action: Petersburg, Virginia
Date of Action: 3 April 1865
Date of Issue: 10 May 1865
Citation: Capture of flag.

100 ◆ BLISS, GEORGE NEWMAN

Rank: Captain
Service: U.S. Army
Birthday: 22 July 1837
Place of Birth: Tiverton, Newport County, Rhode Island
Date of Death: 29 August 1928
Cemetery: Lakeside Cemetery (MH)—Rumford, Rhode Island
Entered Service at: Pawtucket, Providence County, Rhode Island
Unit: Company C, 1st Rhode Island Cavalry
Battle or Place of Action: Waynesboro, Virginia
Date of Action: 28 September 1864
Date of Issue: 3 August 1897
Citation: While in command of the provost guard in the village, he saw the Union lines returning before the attack of a greatly superior force of the enemy, mustered his guard, and, without orders, joined in the defense and charged the enemy without support. He received three saber wounds, his horse was shot, and he was taken prisoner.
Notes: POW

101 ◆ BLISS, ZENAS RANDALL

Rank: Colonel (highest rank: Major General)
Service: U.S. Army
Birthday: 17 April 1835
Place of Birth: Johnston, Providence County, Rhode Island
Date of Death: 2 January 1900
Place of Death: Washington, D.C.
Cemetery: Arlington National Cemetery (1-8-B)—Arlington, Virginia
Entered Service at: Johnston, Providence County, Rhode Island
Unit: 7th Rhode Island Infantry
Battle or Place of Action: Fredericksburg, Virginia
Date of Action: 13 December 1862
Date of Issue: 30 December 1898
Citation: This officer, to encourage his regiment which had never before been in action and which had been ordered to lie down to protect itself from the enemy's fire, rose to his feet, advanced in front of the line, and himself fired several shots at the enemy at short range, being fully exposed to their fire at the time.

102 ◆ BLODGETT, WELLS H.

Rank: First Lieutenant (highest rank: Colonel)
Service: U.S. Army

Birthday: 29 January 1839
Place of Birth: Downer's Grove, Du Page County, Illinois
Date of Death: 8 May 1929
Place of Death: St. Louis, Missouri
Cemetery: Bellefontaine Cemetery—St. Louis, Missouri
Entered Service at: Chicago, Cook County, Illinois
Unit: Company D, 37th Illinois Infantry
Battle or Place of Action: Newtonia, Missouri
Date of Action: 30 September 1862
Date of Issue: 15 February 1894
Citation: With a single orderly, captured an armed picket of eight men and marched them in as prisoners.

103 ◆ BLUCHER, CHARLES

Rank: Corporal (highest rank: Sergeant)
Service: U.S. Army
Place of Birth: Germany
Entered Service at: Philadelphia, Philadelphia County, Pennsylvania
Unit: Company H, 188th Pennsylvania Infantry
Battle or Place of Action: Fort Harrison, Virginia
Date of Action: 29 September 1864
Date of Issue: 6 April 1865
Citation: Planted first national colors on the fortifications.

104 ◆ BLUNT, JOHN W.

Rank: First Lieutenant (highest rank: Brevet Major)
Service: U.S. Army
Birthday: 18 May 1840
Place of Birth: Columbia County, New York
Date of Death: 21 January 1910
Cemetery: Chatham Rural Cemetery (MH)—Chatham, New York
Entered Service at: Four Corners, Chatham, Columbia County, New York
Unit: Company K, 6th New York Cavalry
Battle or Place of Action: Cedar Creek, Virginia
Date of Action: 19 October 1864
Date of Issue: 1 June 1908
Citation: Voluntarily led a charge across a narrow bridge over the creek, against the lines of the enemy.

105 ◆ BOEHM, PETER MARTIN

Rank: Second Lieutenant (highest rank: Major)
Service: U.S. Army
Birthday: 10 February 1845
Place of Birth: Albany, Albany County, New York
Date of Death: 14 June 1914
Place of Death: Chicago, Illinois
Cemetery: Arlington National Cemetery (2-3674)—Arlington, Virginia
Entered Service at: Brooklyn, Kings County, New York
Unit: Company K, 15th New York Cavalry
Battle or Place of Action: Dinwiddie Courthouse, Virginia
Date of Action: 31 March 1865
Date of Issue: 15 December 1898
Citation: While acting as aide to Gen. Custer, took a gun from the hands of color bearer, rode in front of a line that was being driven back and, under a heavy fire, rallied the men, re-formed the line, and repulsed the charge.

106 ◆ BOIS, FRANK

Rank: Quartermaster
Service: U.S. Navy
Birthday: 13 September 1841
Place of Birth: Quebec, Canada
Date of Death: 25 January 1920
Place of Death: Seattle, Washington
Cemetery: Grand Army of the Republic Cemetery—Seattle, Washington
Entered Service at: Northampton, Hampshire County, Massachusetts
Unit: U.S.S. *Cincinnati*
Served as: Quartermaster
Battle or Place of Action: Vicksburg, Mississippi
Date of Action: 27 May 1863
G.O. Number, Date: 17, 10 July 1863
Citation: Served as quartermaster on board the U.S.S. *Cincinnati* during the attack on the Vicksburg batteries and at the time of her sinking, 27 May 1863. Engaging the enemy in a fierce battle, the *Cincinnati*, amidst an incessant fire of shot and shell, continued to fire her guns to the last, though so penetrated by enemy shellfire that her fate was sealed. Conspicuously cool in making signals throughout the battle, Bois, after all the *Cincinnati*'s staffs had been shot away, succeeded in nailing the flag to the stump of the forestaff to enable this proud ship to go down, "with her colors nailed to the mast."

107 ◆ BOND, WILLIAM S.

Rank: Boatswain's Mate (highest rank: Boatswain (WO))
Service: U.S. Navy
Birthday: 1839
Place of Birth: Boston, Suffolk County, Massachusetts
Date of Death: 17 March 1892
Cemetery: Sunrise Memorial Cemetery—Vallejo, California
Entered Service at: Boston, Suffolk County, Massachusetts
Unit: U.S.S. *Kearsarge*
Served as: Boatswain's Mate
Battle or Place of Action: off Cherbourg, France
Date of Action: 19 June 1864
G.O. Number, Date: 45, 31 December 1864
Citation: Served on board the U.S.S. *Kearsarge* when she destroyed the *Alabama* off Cherbourg, France, 19 June 1864. Carrying out his duties courageously, Bond exhibited marked coolness and good conduct and was highly recommended for his gallantry under fire by his divisional officer.

108 ◆ BONEBRAKE, HENRY G.

Rank: First Lieutenant
Service: U.S. Army
Birthday: 21 June 1838
Place of Birth: Waynesboro, Franklin County, Pennsylvania
Date of Death: 26 October 1912

Place of Death: Waynesboro, Pennsylvania
Cemetery: Green Hill Cemetery—Waynesboro, Pennsylvania
Entered Service at: Franklin County, Pennsylvania
Unit: Company G, 17th Pennsylvania Cavalry
Battle or Place of Action: Five Forks, Virginia
Date of Action: 1 April 1865
Date of Issue: 3 May 1865
Citation: As one of the first of Devin's Division to enter the works, he fought in a hand-to-hand struggle with a Confederate to capture his flag by superior physical strength.

109 ◆ BONNAFFON JR., SYLVESTER

Rank: First Lieutenant (highest rank: Brevet Lieutenant Colonel)
Service: U.S. Army
Birthday: 14 September 1844
Place of Birth: Philadelphia, Philadelphia County, Pennsylvania
Date of Death: 12 May 1922
Place of Death: Philadelphia, Pennsylvania
Cemetery: Woodlands Cemetery (MH)—Philadelphia, Pennsylvania
Entered Service at: Philadelphia, Philadelphia County, Pennsylvania
Unit: Company G, 99th Pennsylvania Infantry
Battle or Place of Action: Boydton Plank Road, Virginia
Date of Action: 27 October 1864
Date of Issue: 29 September 1893
Citation: Checked the rout and rallied the troops of his command in the face of a terrible fire of musketry; was severely wounded.

110 ◆ BOODY, ROBERT M.

Rank: Sergeant (highest rank: Second Lieutenant)
Service: U.S. Army
Birthday: 6 March 1836
Place of Birth: Lemington, Maine
Date of Death: 22 October 1913
Cemetery: Greenwood Cemetery (MH)—Haverhill, Massachusetts
Entered Service at: Amesbury, Essex County, Massachusetts
Unit: Company B, 40th New York Infantry
Battle or Place of Action: Williamsburg & Chancellorsville, Virginia
Date of Action: 5 May 1862 & 2 May 1863
Date of Issue: 8 July 1896
Citation: This soldier at Williamsburg, Va., then a corporal, at great personal risk, voluntarily saved the lives of and brought from the battlefield two wounded comrades. A year later, at Chancellorsville, voluntarily, and at great personal risk, brought from the field of battle and saved the life of Capt. George B. Carse, Company C, 40th New York Volunteer Infantry.

111 ◆ BOON, HUGH PATTERSON

Rank: Captain
Service: U.S. Army
Birthday: 24 July 1834
Place of Birth: Washington, Washington County, Pennsylvania
Date of Death: 14 January 1908
Cemetery: Washington Cemetery—Washington, Pennsylvania
Entered Service at: Washington, Washington County, Pennsylvania
Unit: Company B, 1st West Virginia Cavalry
Battle or Place of Action: Deatonsville (Sailor's Creek), Virginia
Date of Action: 6 April 1865
Date of Issue: 3 May 1865
Citation: Capture of flag.

112 ◆ BOSS, ORLANDO PHIDELIO

Rank: Corporal
Service: U.S. Army
Birthday: 30 July 1844
Place of Birth: Fitchburg, Worcester County, Massachusetts
Date of Death: 28 December 1931
Cemetery: Laurel Hill Cemetery—Fitchburg, Massachusetts
Entered Service at: Fitchburg, Worcester County, Massachusetts
Unit: Company F, 25th Massachusetts Infantry
Battle or Place of Action: Cold Harbor, Virginia
Date of Action: 3 June 1864
Date of Issue: 10 May 1888
Citation: Rescued his lieutenant, who was lying between the lines mortally wounded; this under a heavy fire from the enemy.

113 ◆ BOUQUET, NICHOLAS S.

Rank: Private (highest rank: Sergeant)
Service: U.S. Army
Birthday: 14 November 1842
Place of Birth: Landau, Bavaria, Germany
Date of Death: 27 December 1912
Place of Death: Burlington, Iowa
Cemetery: Aspen Grove Cemetery (MH)—Burlington, Iowa
Entered Service at: Burlington, Des Moines County, Iowa
Unit: Company D, 1st Iowa Infantry
Battle or Place of Action: Wilson's Creek, Missouri
Date of Action: 10 August 1861
Date of Issue: 16 February 1897
Citation: Voluntarily left the line of battle, and, exposing himself to imminent danger from a heavy fire from the enemy, Bouquet assisted in capturing a riderless horse at large between the lines and hitching him to a disabled gun, saved the gun from capture.

114 ◆ BOURKE, JOHN GREGORY

Rank: Private (highest rank: Brevet Major)
Service: U.S. Army
Birthday: 23 June 1846
Place of Birth: Philadelphia, Philadelphia County,

Pennsylvania
Date of Death: 8 June 1896
Cemetery: Arlington National Cemetery (1-32-A)—Arlington, Virginia
Entered Service at: Chicago, Cook County, Illinois
Unit: Company E, 15th Pennsylvania Cavalry
Battle or Place of Action: Stone River, Tennessee
Date of Action: 31 December 1862—1 January 1863
Date of Issue: 16 November 1887
Citation: Gallantry in action.

115 ◆ BOURNE, THOMAS

Rank: Seaman and Gun Captain (highest rank: Chief Quartermaster)
Service: U.S. Navy
Birthday: 1834
Place of Birth: England
Date of Death: 22 March 1888
Place of Death: Newburg, Michigan
Entered Service at: New York, New York
Unit: U.S.S. *Varuna*
Battle or Place of Action: Forts Jackson & St. Philip, Louisiana
Date of Action: 24 April 1862
G.O. Number, Date: 11, 3 April 1863
Citation: Served as a captain of a gun on board the U.S.S. *Varuna* during an attack on Forts Jackson and St. Philip and while under fire and ramming by the rebel ship *Morgan*, 24 April 1862. During this action at extremely close range, while his ship was under furious fire and was twice rammed by the rebel ship *Morgan*, Bourne remained steadfast at his gun and was instrumental in inflicting damage on the enemy until the *Varuna*, badly damaged and forced to beach, was finally sunk.

116 ◆ BOURY, RICHARD

True Name: Bowry, Richard
Rank: Sergeant
Service: U.S. Army
Birthday: 1836
Place of Birth: Monroe County, Ohio
Date of Death: 5 July 1914
Place of Death: Parkerburg, West Virginia
Cemetery: Odd Fellow Cemetery—Parkerburg, West Virginia
Entered Service at: Wirt Courthouse, West Virginia
Unit: Company G, 1st West Virginia Cavalry
Battle or Place of Action: Charlottesville, Virginia
Date of Action: 5 March 1865
Date of Issue: 25 March 1865
Citation: Capture of flag.

117 ◆ BOUTWELL, JOHN W.

Rank: Private
Service: U.S. Army
Birthday: 3 August 1845
Place of Birth: Hanover, Grafton County, New Hampshire
Date of Death: 11 December 1920
Cemetery: Arlington National Cemetery (33-2937) (MH)—Arlington, Virginia
Entered Service at: West Lebanon, Grafton County, New Hampshire
Unit: Company B, 18th New Hampshire Infantry
Battle or Place of Action: Petersburg, Virginia
Date of Action: 2 April 1865
Citation: Brought off from the picket line, under heavy fire, a comrade who had been shot through both legs.

118 ◆ BOWEN, CHESTER BENNETT

Rank: Corporal (highest rank: Sergeant)
Service: U.S. Army
Birthday: 1 April 1842
Place of Birth: Nunda, Livingston County, New York
Date of Death: 16 March 1905
Cemetery: City Greenwood Cemetery (MH)—Weatherford, Texas
Entered Service at: Nunda, Livingston County, New York
Unit: Company I, 19th New York Cavalry (1st New York Dragoons)
Battle or Place of Action: Winchester, Virginia
Date of Action: 19 September 1864
Date of Issue: 27 September 1864
Citation: Capture of flag.

119 ◆ BOWEN, EMMER

Rank: Private
Service: U.S. Army
Birthday: 25 October 1830
Place of Birth: Erie County, New York
Date of Death: 26 December 1912
Cemetery: Rosedale Cemetery—Los Angeles, California
Entered Service at: Hampshire, Kane County, Illinois
Unit: Company C, 127th Illinois Infantry
Battle or Place of Action: Vicksburg, Mississippi
Date of Action: 22 May 1863
Date of Issue: 21 July 1894
Citation: Gallantry in the charge of the "volunteer storming party."

120 ◆ BOWMAN, EDWARD R.

Rank: Quartermaster
Service: U.S. Navy
Birthday: 1826
Place of Birth: Eastport, Washington County, Maine
Date of Death: 20 October 1898
Cemetery: Hillside Cemetery (MH)—Eastport, Maine
Entered Service at: Maine
Unit: U.S.S. *Ticonderoga*
Battle or Place of Action: Fort Fisher, North Carolina
Date of Action: 13-15 January 1865
G.O. Number, Date: 59, 22 June 1865
Citation: On board the U.S.S. *Ticonderoga* during attacks

on Fort Fisher, 13 to 15 January 1865. Despite severe wounds sustained during the action, Bowman displayed outstanding courage in the performance of duty as his ship maintained its well-placed fire upon the batteries onshore, and thereafter, as she materially lessened the power of guns on the mound which had been turned upon our assaulting columns. During this battle the flag was planted on one of the strongest fortifications possessed by the rebels.

121 ◆ BOX, THOMAS J.

Rank: Captain
Service: U.S. Army
Birthday: 7 November 1833
Place of Birth: Indiana
Date of Death: 18 December 1914
Place of Death: Indianapolis, Marion County, Indiana
Cemetery: Greenhill Cemetery (MH)—Bedford, Indiana
Entered Service at: Bedford, Lawrence County, Indiana
Unit: Company D, 27th Indiana Infantry
Battle or Place of Action: Resaca, Georgia
Date of Action: 14 May 1864
Date of Issue: 7 April 1865
Citation: Capture of flag of the 38th Alabama Infantry (C.S.A.).

122 ◆ BOYNTON, HENRY VAN NESS

Rank: Lieutenant Colonel (highest rank: Brevet Brigadier General)
Service: U.S. Army
Birthday: 22 July 1835
Place of Birth: West Stockbridge, Berkshire County, Massachusetts
Date of Death: 3 June 1905
Place of Death: Atlantic City, New Jersey
Cemetery: Arlington National Cemetery (2-1096)—Arlington, Virginia
Entered Service at: Hamilton, Butler County, Ohio
Unit: 35th Ohio Infantry
Served as: Commanding Officer
Battle or Place of Action: Missionary Ridge, Tennessee
Date of Action: 25 November 1863
Date of Issue: 15 November 1893
Citation: Led his regiment in the face of a severe fire of the enemy; was severely wounded.

123 ◆ BRADLEY, AMOS

Rank: Landsman
Service: U.S. Navy
Birthday: 1837
Place of Birth: Dansville, Livingston County, New York
Entered Service at: New York
Unit: U.S.S. *Varuna*
Battle or Place of Action: Fort Jackson & St. Philip, Louisiana
Date of Action: 24 April 1862
G.O. Number, Date: 11, 3 April 1863
Citation: Served on board the U.S.S. *Varuna* in one of the most responsible positions, during the attacks on Forts Jackson and St. Philip, and while in action against the rebel ship *Morgan* 24 April 1862. Although guns were raking the decks from behind him, Bradley remained steadfast at the wheel throughout the thickest of the fight, continuing at his station and rendering service with the greatest courage until his ship, repeatedly holed and twice rammed by the rebel ship *Morgan*, was beached and sunk.

124 ◆ BRADLEY, CHARLES

Rank: Boatswain's Mate
Service: U.S. Navy
Birthday: 1838
Place of Birth: Ireland
Entered Service at: New York, New York
Unit: U.S.S. *Louisville*
Battle or Place of Action: Fort Hindman, Arkansas
Date of Action: 10-11 January 1863
G.O. Number, Date: 11, 3 April 1863
Citation: Served on board the U.S.S. *Louisville*. Carrying out his duties through the thick of the battle and acting as captain of a 9-inch gun, Bradley consistently showed "attention to duty, bravery, and coolness in action against the enemy."

125 ◆ BRADLEY, THOMAS WILSON

Rank: Sergeant (highest rank: Brevet Lieutenant Colonel)
Service: U.S. Army
Birthday: 6 April 1844
Place of Birth: Sheffield, Yorkshire County, England
Date of Death: 30 May 1920
Cemetery: Wallkill Valley Cemetery—Walden, New York
Entered Service at: Walden, Orange County, New York
Unit: Company H, 124th New York Infantry (American Guard)
Battle or Place of Action: Chancellorsville, Virginia
Date of Action: 3 May 1863
Date of Issue: 10 June 1896
Citation: Volunteered in response to a call and alone, in the face of a heavy fire of musketry and canister, went and procured ammunition for the use of his comrades.

126 ◆ BRADY, JAMES

Rank: Private
Service: U.S. Army
Birthday: 1842
Place of Birth: Boston, Suffolk County, Massachusetts
Date of Death: 7 October 1904
Cemetery: Old Pine Grove Cemetery (MH)—Raymond, New Hampshire
Entered Service at: Kingston, Rockingham County, New Hampshire
Unit: Company F, 10th New Hampshire Infantry (Irish Regiment)
Battle or Place of Action: Chapin's Farm, Virginia

Date of Action: 29 September 1864
Date of Issue: 6 April 1865
Citation: Capture of flag.

127 ◆ BRANDLE, JOSEPH E.

Rank: Private (highest rank: Color Sergeant)
Service: U.S. Army
Birthday: 8 October 1835
Place of Birth: Seneca County, Ohio
Date of Death: 13 May 1909
Place of Death: Coldwater, Michigan
Cemetery: Oak Grove Cemetery (MH)—Coldwater, Michigan
Entered Service at: Colon, St. Joseph County, Michigan
Unit: Company C, 17th Michigan Infantry
Battle or Place of Action: Lenoire, Tennessee
Date of Action: 16 November 1863
Date of Issue: 20 July 1897
Citation: While color bearer of his regiment, having been twice wounded and had the sight of one eye destroyed, Brandle still held to the colors until ordered to the rear by his regimental commander.

128 ◆ BRANNIGAN, FELIX

Rank: Private (highest rank: First Lieutenant)
Service: U.S. Army
Birthday: 1844
Place of Birth: Ireland
Date of Death: 10 June 1907
Cemetery: Arlington National Cemetery (3-1642)—Arlington, Virginia
Entered Service at: Pittsburgh, Allegheny County, Pennsylvania
Unit: Company A, 74th New York Infantry
Battle or Place of Action: Chancellorsville, Virginia
Date of Action: 2 May 1863
Date of Issue: 29 June 1866
Citation: Volunteered on a dangerous service and brought in valuable information.

129 ◆ BRANT JR., WILLIAM

Rank: Lieutenant (highest rank: Brevet Captain)
Service: U.S. Army
Birthday: 1840
Place of Birth: Elizabeth, Union County, New Jersey
Date of Death: 2 March 1898
Place of Death: Elizabeth, New Jersey
Cemetery: The Evergreen Cemetery (MH)—Hillside, New Jersey
Entered Service at: Trenton, Mercer County, New Jersey
Unit: Company B, 1st New Jersey Veteran Battalion
Battle or Place of Action: Petersburg, Virginia
Date of Action: 3 April 1865
Date of Issue: 10 May 1865
Citation: Capture of battle flag of 46th North Carolina (C.S.A.).

130 ◆ BRAS, EDGAR A.

Rank: Sergeant
Service: U.S. Army
Birthday: 6 October 1841
Place of Birth: Jefferson County, Iowa
Date of Death: 24 June 1923
Place of Death: Fort Lauderdale, Florida
Cemetery: Evergreen Cemetery—Fort Lauderdale, Florida
Entered Service at: Wapello, Louisa County, Iowa
Unit: Company K, 8th Iowa Infantry
Battle or Place of Action: Spanish Fort, Alabama
Date of Action: 8 April 1865
Date of Issue: 8 June 1865

131 ◆ BRAZELL, JOHN

Rank: Quartermaster (highest rank: Chief Quartermaster)
Service: U.S. Navy
Birthday: 1837
Place of Birth: Philadelphia, Philadelphia County, Pennsylvania
Date of Death: 12 August 1866
Place of Death: Philadelphia, Pennsylvania
Entered Service at: Pennsylvania
Unit: U.S.S. *Richmond*
Battle or Place of Action: Mobile Bay, Alabama
Date of Action: 5 August 1864
G.O. Number, Date: 45, 31 December 1864
Citation: Served on board the U.S.S. *Richmond* in the action at Mobile Bay, 5 August 1864, where he was recommended for coolness and good conduct as a gun captain during that engagement, which resulted in the capture of the rebel ram *Tennessee* and in the destruction of Fort Morgan. Brazell served gallantly throughout the actions with Forts Jackson and St. Philip, the Chalmettes, batteries below Vicksburg, and was present at the surrender of New Orleans while on board the U.S.S. *Brooklyn*.

132 ◆ BREEN, JOHN

Rank: Boatswain's Mate
Service: U.S. Navy
Birthday: 1827
Place of Birth: New York, New York
Date of Death: 13 December 1875
Place of Death: Milwaukee, Wisconsin
Cemetery: Calvary Cemetery—Milwaukee, Wisconsin
Entered Service at: New York, New York
Unit: U.S.S. *Commodore Perry*
Battle or Place of Action: Franklin, Virginia
Date of Action: 3 October 1862
G.O. Number, Date: 11, 3 April 1863
Citation: On board the U.S.S. *Commodore Perry* in the attack upon Franklin, Va., 3 October 1862. With enemy fire raking the deck of his ship and blockades thwarting her progress, Breen remained at his post and performed his duties with skill and courage as the *Commodore Perry* fought a gal-

lant battle to silence many rebel batteries as she steamed down the Blackwater River.

133 ◆ BRENNAN, CHRISTOPHER

Rank: Seaman
Service: U.S. Navy
Birthday: 1832
Place of Birth: Ireland
Entered Service at: Boston, Suffolk County, Massachusetts
Unit: U.S.S. *Mississippi* (temporarily assigned U.S.S. *Colorado*)
Battle or Place of Action: Forts Jackson & St. Philip and New Orleans, Louisiana
Date of Action: 24-25 April 1862
G.O. Number, Date: 17, 10 July 1863
Citation: On board the U.S.S. *Mississippi* during attacks on Forts Jackson and St. Philip and during the taking of New Orleans, 24–25 April 1862. Taking part in the actions which resulted in the damaging of the *Mississippi* and several casualties on it, Brennan showed skill and courage throughout the entire engagements which resulted in the taking of St. Philip and Jackson and in the surrender of New Orleans.

134 ◆ BREST, LEWIS FRANCIS

Rank: Private
Service: U.S. Army
Birthday: 15 May 1842
Place of Birth: Mercer, Mercer County, Pennsylvania
Date of Death: 2 December 1915
Place of Death: Mercer, Pennsylvania
Cemetery: Citizens Cemetery—Mercer, Pennsylvania
Entered Service at: Pittsburgh, Allegheny County, Pennsylvania
Unit: Company D, 57th Pennsylvania Infantry
Battle or Place of Action: Deatonsville (Sailor's Creek), Virginia
Date of Action: 6 April 1865
Date of Issue: 10 May 1865
Citation: Capture of flag.

135 ◆ BREWER, WILLIAM JOHN

Rank: Private (highest rank: Corporal)
Service: U.S. Army
Birthday: 1843
Place of Birth: Putnam County, New York
Date of Death: 19 June 1878
Place of Death: Cornwall, New York
Cemetery: Quaker Cemetery—Cornwall-on-the-Hudson, New York
Entered Service at: Newburgh, Orange County, New York
Unit: Company C, 2d New York Cavalry
Battle or Place of Action: Appomattox Campaign, Virginia
Date of Action: 4 April 1865
Date of Issue: 3 May 1865
Citation: Capture of engineer flag, Army of Northern Virginia.

136 ◆ BREYER, CHARLES

Rank: Sergeant
Service: U.S. Army
Birthday: 19 June 1844
Place of Birth: England
Date of Death: 9 September 1914
Place of Death: Pottstown, Pennsylvania
Cemetery: St. James Church Cemetery—Limerick, Pennsylvania
Entered Service at: Philadelphia, Philadelphia County, Pennsylvania
Unit: Company I, 90th Pennsylvania Infantry
Battle or Place of Action: Rappahannock Station, Virginia
Date of Action: 23 August 1862
Date of Issue: 8 July 1896
Citation: Voluntarily and at great personal risk, Breyer picked up an unexploded shell and threw it away, thus doubtless saving the life of a comrade whose arm had been taken off by the same shell.

137 ◆ BRIGGS, ELIJAH A.

Rank: Corporal (highest rank: Sergeant)
Service: U.S. Army
Birthday: 26 October 1843
Place of Birth: Salisbury, Litchfield County, Connecticut
Date of Death: 10 March 1922
Place of Death: Beacon, New York
Cemetery: Fishkill Rural Cemetery (MH)—Fishkill, New York
Entered Service at: Salisbury, Litchfield County, Connecticut
Unit: Company B, 2d Connecticut Heavy Artillery
Battle or Place of Action: Petersburg, Virginia
Date of Action: 3 April 1865
Date of Issue: 10 May 1865
Citation: Capture of battle flag.

138 ◆ BRINGLE, ANDREW

Rank: Corporal
Service: U.S. Army
Place of Birth: Buffalo, Erie County, New York
Entered Service at: Buffalo, Erie County, New York
Unit: Company F, 10th New York Cavalry (Porter Guard)
Battle or Place of Action: Deatonsville (Sailor's Creek), Virginia
Date of Action: 6 April 1865
Date of Issue: 3 July 1865
Citation: Charged the enemy and assisted Sgt. Llewllyn P. Norton in capturing a fieldpiece and two prisoners.

139 ◆ BRINN, ANDREW

Rank Seaman
Service: U.S. Navy
Birthday: 1829
Place of Birth: Scotland

Entered Service at: New York, New York
Unit: U.S.S. *Mississippi*
Battle or Place of Action: Port Hudson, Louisiana
Date of Action: 14 March 1864
G.O. Number, Date: 17, 10 July 1863
Citation: Served on board the U.S.S. *Mississippi* during her abandonment and firing in the engagement at Port Hudson, 14 March 1863. Remaining under enemy fire for 2 1/2 hours, Brinn remained on board the grounded vessel until all the abandoning crew had landed. After asking to be assigned some duty, he was finally ordered to save himself and to leave the *Mississippi*, which had been deliberately fired to prevent her falling into rebel hands.

140 ◆ BRONNER, AUGUST FREDERICK

Rank: Private
Service: U.S. Army
Birthday: 1835
Place of Birth: Germany
Date of Death: 31 October 1893
Place of Death: Newark, New Jersey
Cemetery: Fairmount Cemetery (MH)—Newark, New Jersey
Entered Service at: New York, New York
Unit: Company C, 1st New York Artillery
Battle or Place of Action: White Oak Swamp, Virginia
Date of Action: 30 June 1862
Date of Issue: 19 April 1892
Citation: Continued to fight after being severely wounded.

141 ◆ BRONSON, JAMES H.

Rank: First Sergeant
Service: U.S. Army
Birthday: 1838
Place of Birth: Indiana County, Pennsylvania
Date of Death: 16 March 1884
Cemetery: Chartiers Cemetery (MH)—Carnegie, Pennsylvania
Entered Service at: Trumbell County, Ohio
Unit: Company D, 5th U.S. Colored Infantry
Battle or Place of Action: Chapin's Farm, Virginia
Date of Action: 29 September 1864
Date of Issue: 6 April 1865
Citation: Took command of his company, all the officers having been killed or wounded, and gallantly led it.

142 ◆ BROSNAN, JOHN

Rank: Sergeant
Service: U.S. Army
Birthday: 1 July 1846
Place of Birth: Ireland
Date of Death: 7 August 1921
Place of Death: Brooklyn, New York
Cemetery: Holy Cross Cemetery—Brooklyn, New York
Entered Service at: New York, New York
Unit: Company E, 164th New York Infantry
Battle or Place of Action: Petersburg, Virginia
Date of Action: 17 June 1864
Date of Issue: 18 January 1894
Citation: Rescued a wounded comrade who lay exposed to the enemy's fire, receiving a severe wound in the effort.

143 ◆ BROUSE, CHARLES W.

Rank: Captain
Service: U.S. Army
Birthday: 30 November 1839
Date of Death: 26 October 1904
Cemetery: Crown Hill Cemetery (MH)—Indianapolis, Indiana
Entered Service at: Indianapolis, Marion County, Indiana
Unit: Company K, 100th Indiana Infantry
Battle or Place of Action: Missionary Ridge, Tennessee
Date of Action: 25 November 1863
Date of Issue: 16 May 1899
Citation: To encourage his men whom he had ordered to lie down while under severe fire and who were partially protected by slight earthworks, Brouse himself refused to lie down, but walked along the top of the works until he fell severely wounded.

144 ◆ BROWN, CHARLES E.

Rank: Sergeant (highest rank: Captain)
Service: U.S. Army
Birthday: 11 December 1841
Place of Birth: Schuylkill County, Pennsylvania
Date of Death: 20 February 1919
Place of Death: Schuylkill Haven, Pennsylvania
Cemetery: Union Cemetery (MH)—Schuylkill Haven, Pennsylvania
Entered Service at: Schuylkill Haven, Schuylkill County, Pennsylvania
Unit: Company C, 50th Pennsylvania Infantry
Battle or Place of Action: Weldon Railroad, Virginia
Date of Action: 19 August 1864
Date of Issue: 1 December 1864
Citation: Capture of flag of 47th Virginia Infantry (C.S.A.).

145 ◆ BROWN JR., EDWARD

True Name: Browne Jr., Edward
Rank: Corporal (highest rank: Sergeant)
Service: U.S. Army
Birthday: 6 July 1841
Place of Birth: Ireland
Date of Death: 5 November 1911
Place of Death: New York, New York
Cemetery: 1st Calvary Cemetery—Woodside, New York
Entered Service at: New York, New York
Unit: Company G, 62d New York Infantry
Battle or Place of Action: Fredericksburg & Salem Heights, Virginia
Date of Action: 3-4 May 1863
Date of Issue: 24 November 1880

Citation: Severely wounded while carrying the colors, he continued at his post, under fire, until ordered to the rear.

146 ◆ BROWN, HENRI LE FEVRE

Rank: Sergeant
Service: U.S. Army
Birthday: 30 May 1842
Place of Birth: Jamestown, Chautauqua County, New York
Date of Death: 29 April 1910
Place of Death: Jamestown, New York
Cemetery: Lakeview Cemetery—Jamestown, New York
Entered Service at: Ellicott, Erie County, New York
Unit: Company B, 72d New York Infantry
Battle or Place of Action: Wilderness Campaign, Virginia
Date of Action: 6 May 1864
Date of Issue: 23 June 1896
Citation: Voluntarily and under a heavy fire from the enemy, Brown three times crossed the field of battle with a load of ammunition in a blanket on his back, thus supplying the Federal forces, whose ammunition had nearly all been expended, and enabling them to hold their position until reinforcement arrived, when the enemy were driven from their position.

147 ◆ BROWN, JAMES

Rank: Quartermaster
Service: U.S. Navy
Birthday: 1826
Place of Birth: Rochester, Monroe County, New York
Entered Service at: New York
Unit: U.S.S. *Albatross*
Battle or Place of Action: Fort De Russy, Red River, Louisiana
Date of Action: 4 May 1863
G.O. Number, Date: 32, 16 April 1864
Citation: Served on board the U.S.S. *Albatross* during action against Fort De Russy in the Red River area on 4 May 1863. After the steering wheel and wheel ropes had been shot away by rebel fire, Brown stood on the gun platform of the quarterdeck, exposing himself to a close fire of musketry from the shore, and rendered invaluable assistance by his expert management of the relieving tackles in extricating the vessel from a perilous position, and thereby aided in the capture of Fort De Russy's heavyworks.

148 ◆ BROWN, JEREMIAH Z.

Rank: Captain (highest rank: Brevet Major)
Service: U.S. Army
Birthday: 7 November 1839
Place of Birth: near Rural Valley, Armstrong County, Pennsylvania
Date of Death: 19 February 1916
Place of Death: Porter Township, Pennsylvania
Cemetery: Squirriel Hill Cemetery—New Bethlehem, Pennsylvania
Entered Service at: Curllsville, Clarion County, Pennsylvania
Unit: Company K, 148th Pennsylvania Infantry
Battle or Place of Action: Petersburg, Virginia
Date of Action: 27 October 1864
Date of Issue: 22 June 1896
Citation: With 100 selected volunteers, Brown assaulted and captured the works of the enemy, together with a number of officers and men.

149 ◆ BROWN, JOHN

True Name: Hayes, Thomas
Rank: Captain of the Forecastle
Service: U.S. Navy
Birthday: 1826
Place of Birth: Glasgow, Scotland
Date of Death: 1 November 1883
Place of Death: Sonoma, California
Entered Service at: New York, New York
Unit: U.S.S. *Brooklyn*
Battle or Place of Action: Mobile Bay, Alabama
Date of Action: 5 August 1864
G.O. Number, Date: 45, 31 December 1864
Citation: On board the U.S.S. *Brooklyn* during action against rebel forts and gunboats and with the ram *Tennessee* in Mobile Bay, 5 August 1864. Despite severe damage to his ship and the loss of several men on board as enemy fire raked her decks from stem to stern, Brown fought his gun with skill and courage throughout the furious battle which resulted in the surrender of the prize rebel ram *Tennessee* and in the damaging and destruction of batteries at Fort Morgan.

150 ◆ BROWN, JOHN

Rank: First Sergeant (highest rank: Captain)
Service: U.S. Army
Birthday: 1842
Place of Birth: Boston, Suffolk County, Massachusetts
Date of Death: 7 August 1898
Cemetery: Spring Grove Cemetery—Cincinnati, Ohio
Entered Service at: Cincinnati, Hamilton County, Ohio
Unit: Company A, 47th Ohio Infantry
Battle or Place of Action: Vicksburg, Mississippi
Date of Action: 19 May 1863
Date of Issue: 24 August 1896
Citation: Voluntarily carried a verbal message from Col. A.C. Parry to Gen. Hugh Ewing through a terrific fire and in plain view of the enemy.

151 ◆ BROWN, JOHN HARTIES

Rank: Captain
Service: U.S. Army
Birthday: 1834
Place of Birth: New Brunswick, Canada
Date of Death: 30 January 1905
Place of Death: Washington, D.C.
Cemetery: Arlington National Cemetery (3-1486 1/2) (MH)—Arlington, Virginia
Entered Service at: Charlestown, Suffolk County, Massachusetts

Unit: Company D, 12th Kentucky Infantry
Battle or Place of Action: Franklin, Tennessee
Date of Action: 30 November 1864
Date of Issue: 13 February 1865
Citation: Capture of flag.

152 ◆ *BROWN JR., MORRIS

Rank: Captain
Service: U.S. Army
Birthday: August 1842
Place of Birth: Hammondsport, Steuben County, New York
Date of Death: 22 June 1864
Place of Death: Petersburg, Virginia
Cemetery: Lake View Cemetery—Penn Yan, New York
Entered Service at: Geneva, Ontario County, New York
Unit: Company A, 126th New York Infantry
Battle or Place of Action: Gettysburg, Pennsylvania
Date of Action: 3 July 1863
Date of Issue: 6 March 1869
Citation: Capture of flag.

153 ◆ BROWN, ROBERT

Rank: Captain of the Top
Service: U.S. Navy
Birthday: 1830
Place of Birth: Norway
Entered Service at: New York
Unit: U.S.S. *Richmond*
Battle or Place of Action: Fort Morgan, Mobile Bay, Alabama
Date of Action: 5 August 1864
G.O. Number, Date: 45, 31 December 1864
Citation: On board the U.S.S. *Richmond* in action at Mobile Bay, 5 August 1864. Cool and courageous at his station throughout the prolonged action, Brown rendered gallant service as his vessel trained her guns on Fort Morgan and on ships of the Confederacy despite extremely heavy return fire. He participated in the actions at Forts Jackson and St. Philip, with the Chalmette batteries, at the surrender of New Orleans and in the attacks on batteries below Vicksburg.

154 ◆ BROWN, ROBERT BURNS

Rank: Private
Service: U.S. Army
Birthday: 2 October 1844
Place of Birth: New Concord, Muskingum County, Ohio
Date of Death: 30 July 1916
Cemetery: Greenwood Cemetery (MH)—Zanesville, Ohio
Entered Service at: Zanesville, Muskingum County, Ohio
Unit: Company A, 15th Ohio Infantry
Battle or Place of Action: Missionary Ridge, Tennessee
Date of Action: 25 November 1863
Date of Issue: 27 March 1890
Citation: Upon reaching the ridge through concentrated fire, he approached the color bearer of the 9th Mississippi Infantry (C.S.A.), demanded his surrender with threatening gesture, and took him prisoner with his regimental flag.

155 ◆ BROWN, URIAH H.

Rank: Private (highest rank: Corporal)
Service: U.S. Army
Birthday: 4 July 1841
Place of Birth: Covington, Miami County, Ohio
Date of Death: 24 January 1927
Place of Death: Holiday Cove, West Virginia
Cemetery: Paris Cemetery—Paris, Pennsylvania
Entered Service at: Steubenville, Jefferson County, Ohio
Unit: Company G, 30th Ohio Infantry
Battle or Place of Action: Vicksburg, Mississippi
Date of Action: 22 May 1863
Date of Issue: 15 August 1894
Citation: Despite the death of his captain at his side during the assault, he continued carrying his log to the defense ditch. While he was laying his log in place he was shot down and thrown into the water. Unmindful of his own wound he, despite the intense fire, dragged five of his comrades from the ditch, wherein they lay wounded, to a place of safety.

156 ◆ BROWN, WILLIAM H.

Rank: Landsman
Service: U.S. Navy
Birthday: 1836
Place of Birth: Baltimore, Baltimore County, Maryland
Date of Death: 5 November 1896
Cemetery: Arlington National Cemetery (27-565-A) (MH)—Arlington, Virginia
Entered Service at: Maryland
Unit: U.S.S. *Brooklyn*
Battle or Place of Action: Fort Morgan, Mobile Bay, Alabama
Date of Action: 5 August 1864
G.O. Number, Date: 45, 31 December 1864
Citation: On board the U.S.S. *Brooklyn* during successful attacks against Fort Morgan rebel gunboats and the ram *Tennessee* in Mobile Bay, on 5 August 1864. Stationed in the immediate vicinity of the shell whips which were twice cleared of men by bursting shells, Brown remained steadfast at his post and performed his duties in the powder division throughout the furious action, which resulted in the surrender of the prize rebel ram *Tennessee* and in the damaging and destruction of batteries at Fort Morgan.

157 ◆ BROWN, WILSON

Rank: Landsman
Service: U.S. Navy
Birthday: 1841
Place of Birth: Natchez, Adams County, Mississippi
Date of Death: 24 January 1900
Cemetery: National Cemetery (G-3152) (MH)—Natchez, Mississippi
Entered Service at: Mississippi River, Mississippi
Unit: U.S.S. *Hartford*
Battle or Place of Action: Fort Morgan, Mobile Bay, Alabama

Date of Action: 5 August 1864
G.O. Number, Date: 45, 31 December 1864
Citation: On board the flagship U.S.S. *Hartford* during successful attacks against Fort Morgan, rebel gunboats, and the ram *Tennessee* in Mobile Bay, on 5 August 1864. Knocked unconscious into the hold of the ship when an enemy shellburst fatally wounded a man on the ladder above him, Brown, upon regaining consciousness, promptly returned to the shell whip on the berth deck and zealously continued to perform his duties, although four of the six men at this station had been either killed or wounded by the enemy's terrific fire.

158 ◆ BROWN, WILSON W.

Rank: Private (highest rank: Second Lieutenant)
Service: U.S. Army
Birthday: 25 December 1837
Place of Birth: Logan County, Ohio
Date of Death: 25 February 1916
Place of Death: Toledo, Ohio
Cemetery: New Bellville Ridge Cemetery—Dowling, Ohio
Entered Service at: Findlay, Hancock County, Ohio
Unit: Company F, 21st Ohio Infantry
Battle or Place of Action: Georgia
Date of Action: April 1862
Date of Issue: September 1863
Citation: One of the 19 of 24 men (including two civilians) who, by direction of Gen. Ormsby M. Mitchell, penetrated nearly 200 miles south into enemy territory and captured a railroad train at Big Shanty, Ga., in an attempt to destroy the bridges and track between Chattanaooga and Atlanta.
Notes: POW 1862, 1863

159 ◆ BROWNELL, FRANCIS EDWIN

Rank: Private (highest rank: First Lieutenant)
Service: U.S. Army
Birthday: 1840
Place of Birth: Troy, Rensselaer County, New York
Date of Death: 15 March 1894
Place of Death: Washington, D.C.
Cemetery: Bellefontaine Cemetery—St. Louis, Missouri
Entered Service at: Troy, Rensselaer County, New York
Unit: Company A, 11th New York Infantry (Ellsworth's Zouaves)
Battle or Place of Action: Alexandria, Virginia
Date of Action: 24 May 1861
Date of Issue: 26 January 1877
Citation: Killed the murderer of Col. Ellsworth at the Marshall House, Alexandria, Va. First Civil War deed to merit Medal of Honor.

160 ◆ BROWNELL, WILLIAM P.

Rank: Coxswain (highest rank: Acting Master's Mate)
Service: U.S. Navy
Birthday: 12 July 1839
Place of Birth: New York
Date of Death: 26 April 1915
Place of Death: New York, New York
Cemetery: Oak Grove Cemetery (MH)—New Bedford, Massachusetts
Entered Service at: New York
Unit: U.S.S. *Benton*
Battle or Place of Action: Great Gulf Bay and Vicksburg, Mississippi
Date of Action: 2, 22 May 1863
G.O. Number, Date: 32, 16 April 1864
Citation: Served as coxswain on board the U.S.S. *Benton* during the attack on Great Gulf Bay, 2 May 1863, and Vicksburg, 22 May 1863. Carrying out his duties with coolness and courage, Brownell served gallantly against the enemy as captain of a 9-inch gun in the attacks on Great Gulf and Vicksburg and as a member of the Battery Benton before Vicksburg.

161 ◆ BRUNER, LOUIS J.

Rank: Private (highest rank: Quartermaster Sergeant)
Service: U.S. Army
Birthday: 6 October 1843
Place of Birth: Monroe County, Indiana
Date of Death: 28 January 1912
Cemetery: Green Park Cemetery—Portland, Indiana
Entered Service at: Clifty Brumer, Indiana
Unit: Company H, 5th Indiana Cavalry
Battle or Place of Action: Walker's Ford, Tennessee
Date of Action: 2 December 1863
Date of Issue: 9 March 1896
Citation: Voluntarily passed through the enemy's lines under fire and conveyed to a battalion, then in a perilous position and liable to capture, information which enabled it to reach a point of safety.

162 ◆ BRUSH, GEORGE WASHINGTON

Rank: Second Lieutenant (highest rank: Captain)
Service: U.S. Army
Birthday: 4 October 1842
Place of Birth: West Hills, Suffolk County, New York
Date of Death: 18 November 1927
Place of Death: Brooklyn, New York
Cemetery: Huntington Rural Cemetery—Huntington, New York
Entered Service at: Huntington, Suffolk County, New York
Unit: Company B, 34th U.S. Colored Infantry
Battle or Place of Action: Ashepoo River, South Carolina
Date of Action: 24 May 1864
Date of Issue: 21 January 1897
Citation: Voluntarily commanded a boat crew, which went to the rescue of a large number of Union soldiers on board the stranded steamer *Boston*, and with great gallantry succeeded in conveying them to shore, being exposed during the entire time to heavy fire from a Confederate battery.

163 ◆ BRUTON, CHRISTOPHER C.

True Name: Braton, Christopher
Rank: Captain (highest rank: Brevet Major)

164 ◆ BRUTSCHE, HENRY

Service: U.S. Army
Birthday: 1840
Place of Birth: Ireland
Entered Service at: Riga, Monroe County, New York
Unit: Company C, 22d New York Cavalry
Battle or Place of Action: Waynesboro, Virginia
Date of Action: 2 March 1865
Date of Issue: 26 March 1865
Citation: Capture of Gen. Early's headquarters flag. Confederate national standard.

164 ◆ BRUTSCHE, HENRY

Rank: Landsman
Service: U.S. Navy
Birthday: 1846
Place of Birth: Philadelphia, Philadelphia County, Pennsylvania
Entered Service at: Pennsylvania
Unit: U.S.S. *Tacony*
Battle or Place of Action: Plymouth, North Carolina
Date of Action: 23 May 1863
G.O. Number, Date: 45, 31 December 1864
Citation: Served on board the U.S.S. *Tacony* during the taking of Plymouth, N.C., 31 October 1864. Carrying out his duties faithfully during the capture of Plymouth, Brutsche distinguished himself by a display of coolness when he participated in landing and spiking a 9-inch gun while under a devastating fire from enemy musketry.

165 ◆ BRYANT, ANDREW SYMMES

Rank: Sergeant (highest rank: Sergeant Major)
Service: U.S. Army
Birthday: 3 March 1841
Place of Birth: Springfield, Hampden County, Massachusetts
Date of Death: 6 October 1931
Cemetery: Springfield Cemetery (MH)—Springfield, Massachusetts
Entered Service at: Springfield, Hampden County, Massachusetts
Unit: Company A, 46th Massachusetts Infantry
Battle or Place of Action: New Bern, North Carolina
Date of Action: 23 May 1863
Date of Issue: 13 August 1873
Citation: By his courage and judicious disposition of his guard of 16 men, stationed in a small earthwork at the head of the bridge, Bryant held in check and repulsed for a half hour a fierce attack of a strong force of the enemy, thus probably saving the city of New Bern from capture.

166 ◆ *BUCHANAN, GEORGE A.

Rank: Private
Service: U.S. Army
Birthday: 1842
Place of Birth: Victor, Ontario County, New York
Date of Death: 2 October 1864
Place of Death: Chapin's Farm, Virginia
Cemetery: Fort Harrison National Cemetery (A-224) (MH)—Richmond, Virginia
Entered Service at: Canaoaigua, Ontario County, New York
Unit: Company G, 148th New York Infantry
Battle or Place of Action: Chapin's Farm, Virginia
Date of Action: 29 September 1864
Date of Issue: 6 April 1865
Citation: Took position in advance of the skirmish line and drove the enemy's cannoneers from their guns; was mortally wounded.

167 ◆ BUCK, FREDERICK CLARENCE

Rank: Corporal (highest rank: First Lieutenant)
Service: U.S. Army
Birthday: 1843
Place of Birth: Hartford, Hartford County, Connecticut
Entered Service at: Windsor, Hartford County, Connecticut
Unit: Company A, 21st Connecticut Infantry
Battle or Place of Action: Chapin's Farm, Virginia
Date of Action: 29 September 1864
Date of Issue: 6 April 1865
Citation: Although wounded, refused to leave the field until the fight closed.

168 ◆ BUCK, JAMES

Rank: Quartermaster (highest rank: Acting Master's Mate)
Service: U.S. Navy
Birthday: 1808
Place of Birth: Baltimore, Baltimore County, Maryland
Unit: U.S.S. *Brooklyn*
Battle or Place of Action: Forts Jackson and St. Philip, Louisiana
Date of Action: 24-25 April 1862
G.O. Number, Date: 11, 3 April 1863
Citation: Served on board the U.S.S. *Brooklyn* in the attack upon Forts Jackson and St. Philip and at the taking of New Orleans, 24 and 25 April 1862. Although severely wounded by a heavy splinter, Buck continued to perform his duty until positively ordered below. Later stealing back to his post, he steered the ship for eight hours despite his critical condition. His bravery was typical of the type which resulted in the taking of the Forts Jackson and St. Philip and in the capture of New Orleans.

169 ◆ BUCKINGHAM, DAVID EASTBURN

Rank: First Lieutenant (highest rank: Captain)
Service: U.S. Army
Birthday: 3 February 1840
Place of Birth: Pleasant Hill (Stanton), Delaware
Date of Death: 23 November 1915
Cemetery: Arlington National Cemetery (2-3677)—Arlington, Virginia
Entered Service at: Wilmington, New Castle County, Delaware

Unit: Company E, 4th Delaware Infantry
Battle or Place of Action: Rowanty Creek, Virginia
Date of Action: 5 February 1865
Date of Issue: 13 February 1895
Citation: Swam the partly frozen creek under fire, in the attempt to capture a crossing.

170 ◆ BUCKLES, ABRAM J.

True Name: Buckles, Abraham Jay
Rank: Sergeant (highest rank: Second Lieutenant)
Service: U.S. Army
Birthday: 2 August 1846
Place of Birth: Delaware County, Indiana
Date of Death: 19 January 1915
Cemetery: Fairfield Cemetery—Fairfield, California
Entered Service at: Muncie, Delaware County, Indiana
Unit: Company E, 19th Indiana Infantry
Battle or Place of Action: Wilderness Campaign, Virginia
Date of Action: 5 May 1864
Date of Issue: 4 December 1893
Citation: Though suffering from an open wound, Buckles carried the regimental colors until again wounded.

171 ◆ *BUCKLEY, DENIS

True Name: Buckley, Dennis
Rank: Private
Service: U.S. Army
Birthday: 1844
Place of Birth: Canada
Date of Death: 20 July 1864
Place of Death: Peach Tree Creek, Georgia
Entered Service at: Avon, Livingston County, New York
Unit: Company G, 136th New York Infantry
Battle or Place of Action: Peach Tree Creek, Georgia
Date of Action: 20 July 1864
Date of Issue: 7 April 1865
Citation: Capture of flag of 31st Mississippi (C.S.A.).
Notes: POW

172 ◆ BUCKLEY, JOHN C.

Rank: Sergeant
Service: U.S. Army
Birthday: 1 April 1842
Place of Birth: Fayette County, West Virginia
Date of Death: 29 March 1913
Place of Death: Fitzgerald, Georgia
Cemetery: Evergreen Cemetery (MH)—Fitzgerald, Georgia
Entered Service at: Mount Pleasant, West Virginia
Unit: Company G, 4th West Virginia Infantry
Battle or Place of Action: Vicksburg, Mississippi
Date of Action: 22 May 1863
Date of Issue: 9 July 1894
Citation: Gallantry in the charge of the "volunteer storming party."

173 ◆ BUCKLYN, JOHN KNIGHT

Rank: First Lieutenant (highest rank: Brevet Captain)
Service: U.S. Army
Birthday: 15 March 1834
Place of Birth: Foster Creek, Providence County, Rhode Island
Date of Death: 15 May 1906
Cemetery: Lower Mystic Cemetery (MH)—Mystic, Connecticut
Entered Service at: Providence, Providence County, Rhode Island
Unit: Battery E, 1st Rhode Island Light Artillery
Battle or Place of Action: Chancellorsville, Virginia
Date of Action: 3 May 1863
Date of Issue: 13 July 1899
Citation: Though himself wounded, Bucklyn gallantly fought his section of the battery under a fierce fire from the enemy until his ammunition was all expended, many of the cannoneers and most of the horses killed or wounded, and the enemy within 25 yards of the gun, when, disabling one piece, he brought off the other in safety.

174 ◆ BUFFINGTON, JOHN C.

Rank: Sergeant (highest rank: First Lieutenant)
Service: U.S. Army
Birthday: 3 July 1841
Place of Birth: Carroll County, Maryland
Date of Death: 22 November 1924
Place of Death: Washington, D.C.
Cemetery: Trinity Lutheran Cemetery—Tanneytown, Maryland
Entered Service at: Westminster, Carroll County, Maryland
Unit: Company C, 6th Maryland Infantry
Battle or Place of Action: Petersburg, Virginia
Date of Action: 2 April 1865
Date of Issue: 6 March 1908
Citation: Was the first enlisted man of the 3d Division to mount the parapet of the enemy's line.

175 ◆ BUFFUM, ROBERT

Rank: Private (highest rank: Second Lieutenant)
Service: U.S. Army
Birthday: 1828
Place of Birth: Salem, Essex County, Massachusetts
Date of Death: 20 July 1871
Place of Death: Auburn, New York
Cemetery: Auburn Correctional Facility Cemetary ('In Memory' marker only)—Auburn, New York
Entered Service at: Gilead, Wood County, Ohio
Unit: Company H, 21st Ohio Infantry
Battle or Place of Action: Georgia
Date of Action: April 1862
Date of Presentation: 25 March 1863
Place of Presentation: Washington, D.C.; presented by Sec. of War Edward M. Stanton
Citation: One of the 19 of 24 men (including two civilians)

who, by direction of Gen. Mitchell (or Buell), penetrated nearly 200 miles south into enemy territory and captured a railroad train at Big Shanty, Ga., in an attempt to destroy the bridges and track between Chattanooga and Atlanta.

176 ◆ BUHRMAN, HENRY G.

Rank: Private
Service: U.S. Army
Place of Birth: Cincinnati, Hamilton County, Ohio
Date of Death: 1 June 1906
Place of Death: Soldiers Home, Mountain Home, Tennessee
Entered Service at: Cincinnati, Hamilton County, Ohio
Unit: Company H, 54th Ohio Infantry
Battle or Place of Action: Vicksburg, Mississippi
Date of Action: 22 May 1863
Date of Issue: 12 July 1894
Citation: Gallantry in the charge of the "volunteer storming party."

177 ◆ BUMGARNER, WILLIAM

Rank: Sergeant
Service: U.S. Army
Birthday: 12 July 1837
Place of Birth: Mason County, West Virginia
Date of Death: 24 December 1911
Place of Death: Liberty Center, Indiana
Cemetery: Mossburg Cemetery—Wells County, Indiana
Entered Service at: Mason City, Mason County, West Virginia
Unit: Company A, 4th West Virginia Infantry
Battle or Place of Action: Petersburg, Virginia
Date of Action: 2 April 1862
Date of Issue: 10 July 1894
Citation: Gallantry in the charge of the "volunteer storming party."

178 ◆ BURBANK, JAMES H.

Rank: Sergeant
Service: U.S. Army
Birthday: 5 January 1838
Place of Birth: Stavorey, Holland
Date of Death: 15 February 1911
Cemetery: Miltonvale Cemetery (MH)—Miltonvale, Kansas
Entered Service at: Providence, Providence County, Rhode Island
Unit: Company K, 4th Rhode Island Infantry
Battle or Place of Action: Blackwater River, near Franklin, Virginia
Date of Action: 3 October 1862
Date of Issue: 27 July 1896
Citation: Gallantry in action while on detached service on board the gunboat *Barney*.

179 ◆ BURGER, JOSEPH

Rank: Private (highest rank: Captain)
Service: U.S. Army
Birthday: 16 April 1848
Place of Birth: Austria or Swiss Tyrol
Date of Death: 3 January 1921
Place of Death: St. Paul, Minnesota
Cemetery: Oakland Cemetery—St. Paul, Minnesota
Entered Service at: Crystal Lake, Hennepin County, Minnesota
Unit: Company H, 2d Minnesota Infantry
Battle or Place of Action: Nolensville, Tennessee
Date of Action: 15 February 1863
Date of Issue: 11 September 1897
Citation: Was one of a detachment of 16 men who heroically defended a wagon train against the attack of 125 cavalry, repulsed the attack, and saved the train.

180 ◆ BURK, E. MICHAEL

True Name: Burke, Michael
Rank: Private
Service: U.S. Army
Birthday: 1847
Place of Birth: Ireland
Date of Death: 3 February 1878
Cemetery: St. Mary's Cemetery (MH)—Troy, New York
Entered Service at: Troy, Rensselaer County, New York
Unit: Company D, 125th New York Infantry
Battle or Place of Action: Spotsylvania, Virginia
Date of Action: 12 May 1864
Date of Issue: 1 December 1864
Citation: Capture of flag, seizing it as his regiment advanced over the enemy's works. He received a bullet wound in the chest while capturing the flag.

181 ◆ BURK, THOMAS

Rank: Sergeant (highest rank: First Lieutenant)
Service: U.S. Army
Birthday: 7 August 1840
Place of Birth: Lewis County, New York
Date of Death: 15 February 1926
Place of Death: Lowville, New York
Cemetery: Lowville Rural Cemetery—Lowville, New York
Entered Service at: Harrisburgh, Lewis County, New York
Unit: Company H, 97th New York Infantry
Battle or Place of Action: Wilderness Campaign, Virginia
Date of Action: 6 May 1864
Date of Issue: 24 August 1896
Citation: At the risk of his own life, Burk went back while the rebels were still firing and, finding Col. Wheelock unable to move, alone and unaided, carried him off the field of battle.

182 ◆ BURKE, DANIEL WEBSTER

Rank: First Sergeant (highest rank: Brigadier General)
Service: U.S. Army
Birthday: 22 April 1841

Place of Birth: New Haven, New Haven County, Connecticut
Date of Death: 29 May 1911
Cemetery: Arlington National Cemetery (2-3739)—Arlington, Virginia
Entered Service at: New Haven, New Haven County, Connecticut
Unit: Company B, 2d U.S. Infantry
Battle or Place of Action: Shepherdstown Ford, West Virginia
Date of Action: 20 September 1862
Date of Issue: 21 April 1892
Citation: Voluntarily attempted to spike a gun in the face of the enemy.

183 ◆ BURKE, THOMAS

Rank: Private
Service: U.S. Army
Birthday: 1842
Place of Birth: Ireland
Date of Death: 15 March 1902
Cemetery: Calvary Cemetery—Woodside, New York
Entered Service at: New York, New York
Unit: Company A, 5th New York Cavalry
Battle or Place of Action: Hanover Courthouse, Virginia
Date of Action: 30 June 1863
Date of Issue: 11 February 1878
Citation: Capture of battle flag.

184 ◆ BURNS, JAMES MADISON

Rank: Sergeant (highest rank: Lieutenant Colonel)
Service: U.S. Army
Birthday: 9 August 1845
Place of Birth: Wells Township, Jefferson County, Ohio
Date of Death: 30 October 1910
Place of Death: Lebanon, Ohio
Cemetery: Lebanon Cemetery (MH)—Lebanon, Ohio
Entered Service at: Wellsburg, Brooke County, West Virginia
Unit: Company B, 1st West Virginia Infantry
Battle or Place of Action: New Market, Virginia
Date of Action: 15 May 1864
Date of Issue: 20 November 1896
Citation: Under a heavy fire of musketry, rallied a few men to the support of the colors, in danger of capture, and bore them to a place of safety. One of his comrades having been severely wounded in the effort, Sgt. Burns went back a hundred yards in the face of the enemy's fire and carried the wounded man from the field.

185 ◆ BURNS, JOHN M.

Rank: Seaman
Service: U.S. Navy
Birthday: 1835
Place of Birth: Hudson, Columbia County, New York
Entered Service at: New York
Unit: U.S.S. *Lackawanna*
Battle or Place of Action: Fort Morgan, Mobile Bay, Alabama
Date of Action: 5 August 1864
G.O. Number, Date: 45, 31 December 1864
Citation: On board the U.S.S. *Lackawanna* during the successful attacks against Fort Morgan, rebel gunboats and the ram *Tennessee* in Mobile Bay, on 5 August 1864. Although severely wounded and sent below under the surgeon's charge, Burns promptly returned to his station and assisted the powder division throughout the prolonged action which resulted in the capture of the rebel ram *Tennessee* and in the damaging and destruction of Fort Morgan.

186 ◆ BURRITT, WILLIAM WALLACE

Rank: Private
Service: U.S. Army
Birthday: 1831
Place of Birth: Campbell, Steuben County, New York
Date of Death: 18 October 1901
Place of Death: Wadsworth, Kansas
Cemetery: Leavenworth National Cemetery (16-5-7) (MH)—Leavenworth, Kansas
Entered Service at: Chicago, Cook County, Illinois
Unit: Company G, 113th Illinois Infantry
Battle or Place of Action: Vicksburg, Mississippi
Date of Action: 27 April 1863
Date of Issue: 8 July 1896
Citation: Voluntarily acted as a fireman on a steam tug which ran the blockade and passed the batteries under a heavy fire.

187 ◆ BURTON, ALBERT

Rank: Seaman
Service: U.S. Navy
Birthday: 1838
Place of Birth: England
Entered Service at: New York
Unit: U.S.S. *Wabash*
Battle or Place of Action: Fort Fisher, North Carolina
Date of Action: 15 January 1865
G.O. Number, Date: 59, 22 June 1865
Citation: Served on board the U.S.S. *Wabash* in the assault on Fort Fisher, 15 January 1865. Advancing gallantly through the severe enemy fire while armed only with a revolver and cutlass which made it impossible to return the fire at that range, Burton succeeded in reaching the angle of the fort and going on, to be one of the few who entered the fort. When the rest of the body of men to his rear were forced to retreat under a devastating fire, he was forced to withdraw through the lack of support, and to seek the shelter of one of the mounds near the stockade from which point he succeeded in regaining the safety of the ship.

188 ◆ BUTTERFIELD, DANIEL ADAMS

Rank: Brigadier General (highest rank: Major General)
Service: U.S. Army

Birthday: 31 October 1831
Place of Birth: Utica, Oneida County, New York
Date of Death: 17 July 1901
Place of Death: Cold Spring, New York
Cemetery: U.S. Military Academy Cemetery (R-15)—West Point, New York
Entered Service at: Washington, D.C.
Unit: U.S. Volunteers
Battle or Place of Action: Gaines' Mill, Virginia
Date of Action: 27 June 1862
Date of Issue: 26 September 1892
Citation: Seized the colors of the 83d Pennsylvania Volunteers at a critical moment and, under a galling fire of the enemy, encouraged the depleted ranks to renewed exertion.

189 ◆ BUTTERFIELD, FRANKLIN GEORGE

Rank: First Lieutenant (highest rank: Lieutenant Colonel)
Service: U.S. Army
Birthday: 11 March 1842
Place of Birth: Rockingham, Windham County, Vermont
Date of Death: 6 January 1916
Cemetery: Saxtons River Cemetery—Saxtons River, Vermont
Entered Service at: Rockingham, Windham County, Vermont
Unit: Company C, 6th Vermont Infantry
Battle or Place of Action: Salem Heights, Virginia
Date of Action: 4 May 1863
Date of Issue: 4 May 1891
Citation: Took command of the skirmish line and covered the movement of his regiment out of a precarious position.

190 ◆ BUTTS, GEORGE

Rank: Gunner's Mate
Service: U.S. Navy
Birthday: 1838
Place of Birth: Rome, Oneida County, New York
Date of Death: 17 February 1902
Cemetery: Ridgelawn Cemetery—Elyria, Ohio
Entered Service at: Cleveland, Cuyahoga County, Ohio
Unit: U.S.S. *Signal*
Battle or Place of Action: Red River, Louisiana
Date of Action: 5 May 1864
G.O. Number, Date: 45, 31 December 1864
Citation: Served on board the U.S.S. *Signal*, Red River, 5 May 1864. Proceeding up the Red River, the U.S.S. *Signal* engaged a large force of enemy field batteries and sharpshooters, returning their fire until the ship was totally disabled, at which time the white flag was raised. Although entered on the sick list, Butts courageously carried out his duties during the entire engagement.
Notes: POW

191 ◆ BYRNES, JAMES

Rank: Boatswain's Mate (highest rank: Master's Mate)
Service: U.S. Navy
Birthday: 1838
Place of Birth: Ireland
Entered Service at: New York
Unit: U.S.S. *Louisville*
Battle or Place of Action: Fort Hindman, Arkansas
Date of Action: 10-11 January 1863
G.O. Number, Date: 11, 3 April 1863
Citation: Served on board the U.S.S. *Louisville*. Carrying out his duties through the thick of battle and acting as captain of a 9-inch gun, Byrnes consistently showed "Attention to duty, bravery, and coolness in action against the enemy."

192 ◆ CADWALLADER, ABEL G.

Rank: Corporal (highest rank: Sergeant)
Service: U.S. Army
Birthday: 1841
Place of Birth: Baltimore, Baltimore County, Maryland
Date of Death: 6 July 1907
Place of Death: Baltimore, Maryland
Cemetery: Loudon Park Cemetery—Baltimore, Maryland
Entered Service at: Frederick, Frederick County, Maryland
Unit: Company H, 1st Maryland Infantry
Battle or Place of Action: Hatcher's Run & Dabney's Mills, Virginia
Date of Action: 6 February 1865
Date of Issue: 5 January 1897
Citation: Gallantly planted the colors on the enemy's works in advance of the arrival of his regiment.

193 ◆ CADWELL, LUMAN LEWIS

Rank: Sergeant (highest rank: First Lieutenant)
Service: U.S. Army
Birthday: 22 May 1836
Place of Birth: Nanticoke Springs, Broome County, New York
Date of Death: 9 July 1925
Place of Death: Decorah, Iowa
Cemetery: Phelps Cemetery—Decorah, Iowa
Entered Service at: Troy, Rensselaer County, New York
Unit: Company B, 2d New York Veteran Cavalry
Battle or Place of Action: Alabama Bayou, Louisiana
Date of Action: 20 September 1864
Date of Issue: 17 August 1894
Citation: Swam the bayou under fire of the enemy and captured and brought off a boat by means of which the command crossed and routed the enemy.

194 ◆ CALDWELL, DANIEL G.

Rank: Sergeant (highest rank: Captain)
Service: U.S. Army
Birthday: 1 June 1842
Place of Birth: Marble Hill, Montgomery County, Pennsylvania
Date of Death: 15 April 1917
Place of Death: Philadelphia, Pennsylvania
Cemetery: Mount Peace Cemetery—Rockledge, Pennsylvania

Entered Service at: Philadelphia, Philadelphia County, Pennsylvania
Unit: Company H, 13th Pennsylvania Cavalry (Volunteers 117th Regiment)
Battle or Place of Action: Hatcher's Run, Virginia
Date of Action: 6 February 1865
Date of Issue: 25 February 1865
Citation: In a mounted charge, Caldwell dashed into the center of the enemy's line and captured the colors of the 33d North Carolina Infantry.
Notes: POW

195 ◆ CALKIN, IVERS S.

Rank: First Sergeant
Service: U.S. Army
Birthday: 29 May 1836
Place of Birth: Elizabethtown, Essex County, New York
Date of Death: 16 February 1902
Place of Death: Montague, Michigan
Cemetery: Oak Grove Cemetery—Montague, Michigan
Entered Service at: Willsboro, Essex County, New York
Unit: Company M, 2d New York Cavalry
Battle or Place of Action: Deatonsville (Sailor's Creek), Virginia
Date of Action: 6 April 1865
Date of Issue: 3 May 1865
Citation: Capture of flag of 18th Virginia Infantry (C.S.A.).

196 ◆ CALLAHAN, JOHN H.

Rank: Private
Service: U.S. Army
Birthday: 25 January 1845
Place of Birth: Shelby County, Kentucky
Date of Death: 13 March 1914
Cemetery: Sunset Cemetery—Manhattan, Kansas
Entered Service at: Scottville, Macoupin County, Illinois
Unit: Company B, 122d Illinois Infantry
Battle or Place of Action: Fort Blakely, Alabama
Date of Action: 9 April 1865
Date of Issue: 8 June 1865
Citation: Capture of flag.

197 ◆ CAMP, CARLTON N.

Rank: Private
Service: U.S. Army
Birthday: 5 January 1845
Place of Birth: Hanover, Grafton County, New Hampshire
Date of Death: 1 September 1926
Cemetery: Etna Cemetery—Hanover, New Hampshire
Entered Service at: Hanover, Grafton County, New Hampshire
Unit: Company B, 18th New Hampshire Infantry
Battle or Place of Action: Petersburg, Virginia
Date of Action: 2 April 1865
Date of Issue: 21 December 1909
Citation: Brought off from the picket line, under heavy fire, a comrade who had been shot through both legs.

198 ◆ CAMPBELL, JAMES A.

Rank: Private
Service: U.S. Army
Birthday: 20 December 1844
Place of Birth: Brooklyn, Kings County, New York
Date of Death: 6 May 1904
Place of Death: Fort Snelling, Minnesota
Cemetery: Arlington National Cemetery (3-1468-55) (MH)—Arlington, Virginia
Entered Service at: New York, New York
Unit: Company A, 2d New York Cavalry
Battle or Place of Action: Woodstock & Amelia Courthouse, Virginia
Date of Action: 22 January & 5 April 1865
Date of Issue: 30 October 1897
Citation: While his command was retreating before superior numbers at Woodstock, Va., he voluntarily rushed back with one companion and rescued his commanding officer, who had been unhorsed and left behind. At Amelia Courthouse captured two battle flags.

199 ◆ CAMPBELL, WILLIAM

Rank: Private (highest rank: Corporal)
Service: U.S. Army
Birthday: 28 April 1840
Place of Birth: County Down, Ireland
Date of Death: 19 April 1919
Cemetery: Glendale Cemetery—Des Moines, Iowa
Entered Service at: New Philadelphia, Tuscarawas County, Ohio
Unit: Company I, 30th Ohio Infantry
Battle or Place of Action: Vicksburg, Mississippi
Date of Action: 22 May 1863
Date of Issue: 14 August 1894
Citation: Gallantry in the charge of the "volunteer storming party."

200 ◆ CAMPBELL, WILLIAM

Rank: Boatswain's Mate
Service: U.S. Navy
Birthday: 1838
Place of Birth: Indiana
Entered Service at: Indiana
Unit: U.S.S. *Ticonderoga*
Battle or Place of Action: Fort Fisher, North Carolina
Date of Action: 24-25 December 1864 & 13-15 January 1865
G.O. Number, Date: 59, 22 June 1865
Citation: On board the U.S.S. *Ticonderoga* during the attacks on Fort Fisher, 24 and 25 December 1864; and 13 to 15 January 1865. Despite heavy return fire by the enemy and the explosion of the 100-pounder Parrott rifle which killed eight men and wounded 12 more, Campbell, as captain of a

gun, performed his duties with skill and courage during the first two days of battle. As the ship again took position on the line of the 13th, he remained steadfast as the *Ticonderoga* maintained a well-placed fire upon the batteries onshore, and thereafter, as she materially lessened the power of guns on the mound which had been turned upon our assaulting columns. During this action the flag was planted on one of the strongest fortifications possessed by the rebels.

201 ◆ CAPEHART, CHARLES E.

Rank: Major (highest rank: Lieutenant Colonel)
Service: U.S. Army
Birthday: 1833
Place of Birth: Conemaugh Township, Pennsylvania
Date of Death: 11 July 1911
Place of Death: Washington, D.C.
Cemetery: Arlington National Cemetery (3-2033) (MH)—Arlington, Virginia
Entered Service at: Washington, D.C.
Unit: 1st West Virginia Cavalry
Battle or Place of Action: Monterey Mountain, Pennsylvania
Date of Action: 4 July 1863
Date of Issue: 7 April 1898
Citation: While commanding the regiment, Capehart charged down the mountain side at midnight, in a heavy rain, upon the enemy's fleeing wagon train. Many wagons were captured and destroyed and many prisoners taken.

202 ◆ CAPEHART, HENRY

Rank: Colonel (highest rank: Major General)
Service: U.S. Army
Birthday: 18 March 1825
Place of Birth: Johnstown, Cambria County, Pennsylvania
Date of Death: 15 April 1895
Place of Death: Fargo, North Dakota
Cemetery: Arlington National Cemetery (1-140-A&B) (MH)—Arlington, Virginia
Entered Service at: Bridgeport, Belmont County, Ohio
Unit: 1st West Virginia Cavalry
Battle or Place of Action: Greenbrier River, West Virginia
Date of Action: 22 May 1864
Date of Issue: 12 February 1895
Citation: Saved, under fire, the life of a drowning soldier.

203 ◆ *CAPRON JR., HORACE

Rank: Sergeant (highest rank: First Lieutenant)
Service: U.S. Army
Birthday: 1840
Place of Birth: Laurel, Prince George's County, Maryland
Date of Death: 6 February 1864
Place of Death: Blunt County, Tennessee
Cemetery: Springdale Cemetery—Peoria, Illinois
Entered Service at: Peoria, Peoria County, Illinois
Unit: Company G, 8th Illinois Cavalry
Battle or Place of Action: Chickahominy & Ashland, Virginia
Date of Action: June 1862
Date of Issue: 27 September 1865
Citation: Gallantry in action.

204 ◆ *CAREY, HUGH

Rank: Sergeant
Service: U.S. Army
Birthday: 1840
Place of Birth: Ireland
Date of Death: 26 March 1886
Place of Death: Brooklyn, New York
Cemetery: Holy Cross Cemetery—Brooklyn, New York
Entered Service at: New York, New York
Unit: Company E, 82d New York Infantry
Battle or Place of Action: Gettysburg, Pennsylvania
Date of Action: 2 July 1863
Date of Issue: 6 February 1888
Citation: Captured the flag of the 7th Virginia Infantry (C.S.A.), being twice wounded in the effort.

205 ◆ CAREY, JAMES LEMUEL

Rank: Sergeant
Service: U.S. Army
Birthday: 24 December 1839
Place of Birth: Jamesville, Onondaga County, New York
Date of Death: 15 May 1919
Place of Death: Grafton, Pennsylvania
Cemetery: Chartiers Cemetery, Soldier's Plot—Carnegie, Pennsylvania
Entered Service at: Syracuse, Onondaga County, New York
Unit: Company G, 10th New York Cavalry (Porter Guard)
Battle or Place of Action: Appomattox Courthouse, Virginia
Date of Action: 9 April 1865
Citation: Daring bravery and urging the men forward in a charge.

206 ◆ CARLISLE, CASPER R.

Rank: Private
Service: U.S. Army
Birthday: 1841
Place of Birth: Allegheny County, Pennsylvania
Date of Death: 29 April 1908
Cemetery: Mount Lebanon Cemetery (MH)—Pittsburgh, Pennsylvania
Entered Service at: Pittsburgh, Allegheny County, Pennsylvania
Unit: Company F, Independent Pennsylvania Light Artillery
Battle or Place of Action: Gettysburg, Pennsylvania
Date of Action: 2 July 1863
Date of Issue: 21 December 1892
Citation: Saved a gun of his battery under heavy musketry fire, most of the horses being killed and the drivers wounded.

207 ◆ CARMAN, WARREN

Rank: Private (highest rank: Corporal)
Service: U.S. Army

Birthday: 16 March 1845
Place of Birth: England
Date of Death: 17 October 1894
Place of Death: Rochester, New York
Cemetery: Mount Hope Cemetery (MH)—Rochester, New York
Entered Service at: Victor, Ontario County, New York
Unit: Company H, 1st New York (Lincoln) Cavalry
Battle or Place of Action: Waynesboro, Virginia
Date of Action: 2 March 1865
Date of Issue: 26 March 1865
Citation: Capture of flag and several prisoners.

208 ◆ CARMIN, ISAAC HARRISON

True Name: Carman, Isaac Harrison
Rank: Corporal
Service: U.S. Army
Birthday: 17 November 1841
Place of Birth: Monmouth County, New Jersey
Date of Death: 3 June 1919
Place of Death: Fayette County, Ohio
Cemetery: Washington Cemetery (MH)—Washington Courthouse, Ohio
Entered Service at: New Lexington, Perry County, Ohio
Unit: Company A, 48th Ohio Infantry
Battle or Place of Action: Vicksburg, Mississippi
Date of Action: 22 May 1863
Date of Issue: 25 February 1895
Citation: Saved his regimental flag; also seized and threw a shell, with burning fuse, from among his comrades.
Notes: POW

209 ◆ CARNEY, WILLIAM HARVEY

Rank: Sergeant
Service: U.S. Army
Birthday: 29 February 1840
Place of Birth: Norfolk, Norfolk County, Virginia
Date of Death: 9 December 1908
Place of Death: New Bedford, Massachusetts
Cemetery: Oak Grove Cemetery (MH)—New Bedford, Massachusetts
Entered Service at: New Bedford, Bristol County, Massachusetts
Unit: Company C, 54th Massachusetts Colored Infantry
Battle or Place of Action: Fort Wagner, South Carolina
Date of Action: 18 July 1863
Date of Issue: 23 May 1900
Citation: When the color sergeant was shot down, this soldier grasped the flag, led the way to the parapet, and planted the colors thereon. When the troops fell back he brought off the flag, under a fierce fire in which he was twice severely wounded.

210 ◆ CARR, EUGENE ASA

Rank: Colonel (highest rank: Brevet Major General)
Service: U.S. Army
Birthday: 20 March 1830
Place of Birth: Boston Corner, Erie County, New York
Date of Death: 2 December 1910
Cemetery: U.S. Military Academy Cemetery (K-14)—West Point, New York
Entered Service at: Hamburg, Erie County, New York
Unit: 3d Illinois Cavalry
Battle or Place of Action: Pea Ridge, Arkansas
Date of Action: 7 March 1862
Date of Issue: 16 January 1894
Citation: Directed the deployment of his command and held his ground, under a brisk fire of shot and shell in which he was several times wounded.

211 ◆ CARR, FRANKLIN

Rank: Corporal (highest rank: Sergeant)
Service: U.S. Army
Birthday: 1844
Place of Birth: Stark County, Ohio
Date of Death: 16 October 1904
Place of Death: McAlester, Oklahoma
Entered Service at: Toledo, Lucas County, Ohio
Unit: Company D, 124th Ohio Infantry
Battle or Place of Action: Nashville, Tennessee
Date of Action: 16 December 1864
Date of Issue: 24 February 1865
Citation: Recapture of U.S. guidon from a rebel battery.

212 ◆ CARR, WILLIAM M.

Rank: Master-at-Arms
Service: U.S. Navy
Birthday: 25 November 1829
Place of Birth: Baltimore, Baltimore County, Maryland
Date of Death: 2 May 1884
Place of Death: Newtown, Virginia
Cemetery: Norfolk City Cemetery (MH)—Norfolk, Virginia
Entered Service at: Baltimore, Baltimore County, Maryland
Unit: U.S.S. *Richmond*
Battle or Place of Action: Mobile Bay, Alabama
Date of Action: 5 August 1864
G.O. Number, Date: 45, 31 December 1864
Citation: On board the U.S.S. *Richmond* during action against rebel forts and gunboats and against the ram *Tennessee* in Mobile Bay, 5 August 1864. Despite damage to his ship and the loss of several men on board as enemy fire raked her decks, Carr performed his duties with skill and courage throughout the prolonged battle which resulted in the surrender of the rebel ram *Tennessee* and in the successful attacks carried out on Fort Morgan.

213 ◆ CARSON, WILLIAM J.

Rank: Musician
Service: U.S. Army
Birthday: 30 August 1840
Place of Birth: Washington County, Pennsylvania
Date of Death: 13 December 1913
Place of Death: Indianapolis, Indiana
Cemetery: Beech Grove Cemetery (MH)—Muncie, Indiana

Entered Service at: North Greenfield, Highland County, Ohio
Unit: Company E, 1st Battalion, 15th U.S. Infantry
Battle or Place of Action: Chickamauga, Georgia
Date of Action: 19 September 1863
Date of Issue: 27 January 1894
Citation: At a critical stage in the battle when the 14th Corps lines were wavering and in disorder, he on his own initiative bugled "to the colors" amid the 18th U.S. Infantry who formed by him, and held the enemy. Within a few minutes he repeated his action amid the wavering 2d Ohio Infantry. This bugling deceived the enemy who believed reinforcements had arrived. Thus, they delayed their attack.

214 ◆ CART, JACOB

Rank: Private (highest rank: Sergeant)
Service: U.S. Army
Birthday: 1843
Place of Birth: Carlisle, Cumberland County, Pennsylvania
Date of Death: 24 April 1882
Place of Death: Carlisle, Pennsylvania
Cemetery: Ashland Cemetery—Carlisle, Pennsylvania
Entered Service at: Carlisle, Cumberland County, Pennsylvania
Unit: Company A, 7th Pennsylvania Reserve Corps
Battle or Place of Action: Fredericksburg, Virginia
Date of Action: 13 December 1862
Date of Issue: 25 November 1864
Citation: Capture of flag of 19th Georgia Infantry (C.S.A.), wresting it from the hands of the color bearer.

215 ◆ CARTER, JOHN JOICE

Rank: Second Lieutenant (highest rank: Colonel)
Service: U.S. Army
Birthday: 16 June 1842
Place of Birth: Troy, Rensselaer County, New York
Date of Death: 3 January 1917
Cemetery: Woodlawn Cemetery (MH)—Titusville, Pennsylvania
Entered Service at: Nunda, Livingston County, New York
Unit: Company B, 33d New York Infantry
Served as: Commanding Officer
Battle or Place of Action: Antietam, Maryland
Date of Action: 17 September 1862
Date of Issue: 10 September 1897
Citation: While in command of a detached company, seeing his regiment thrown into confusion by a charge of the enemy, without orders made a countercharge upon the attacking column and checked the assault. Penetrated within the enemy's lines at night and obtained valuable information.

216 ◆ CARTER, JOSEPH FRANKLIN

Rank: Captain (highest rank: Major)
Service: U.S. Army
Birthday: 11 September 1842
Place of Birth: Baltimore, Baltimore County, Maryland
Date of Death: 10 April 1922

Cemetery: Arlington National Cemetery (3-1550)—Arlington, Virginia
Entered Service at: Baltimore, Baltimore County, Maryland
Unit: Company D, 3d Maryland Infantry
Battle or Place of Action: Fort Stedman, Virginia
Date of Action: 25 March 1865
Date of Issue: 9 July 1891
Citation: Captured the colors of the 51st Virginia Infantry (C.S.A.). During the battle he was captured and escaped, bringing a number of prisoners with him.

217 ◆ CARUANA, ORLANDO EMANUEL

Rank: Private (Highest rank Sergeant)
Service: U.S. Army
Birthday: 23 June 1844
Place of Birth: Ca Valletta, Malta
Date of Death: 14 September 1917
Cemetery: Mount Olivet Cemetery—Washington, D.C.
Entered Service at: New York, New York
Unit: Company K, 51st New York Infantry
Battle or Place of Action: New Bern, North Carolina & South Mountain, Maryland
Date of Action: 14 March & 14 September 1862
Date of Issue: 14 November 1890
Citation: At New Bern, N.C., brought off the wounded color sergeant and the colors under a heavy fire of the enemy. Was one of four soldiers who volunteered to determine the position of the enemy at South Mountain, Md. While so engaged was fired upon and his three companions killed, but he escaped and rejoined his command in safety.

218 ◆ CASEY, DAVID P.

Rank: Private (highest rank: Corporal)
Service: U.S. Army
Birthday: 1842
Place of Birth: Ireland
Date of Death: 4 January 1893
Cemetery: St. Patrick's Cemetery (MH)—Northbridge, Massachusetts
Entered Service at: Northbridge, Worcester County, Massachusetts
Unit: Company C, 25th Massachusetts Infantry
Battle or Place of Action: Cold Harbor, Virginia
Date of Action: 3 June 1864
Date of Issue: 14 September 1888
Citation: Two color bearers having been shot dead one after the other, the last one far in advance of his regiment and close to the enemy's lines, this soldier rushed forward, and, under a galling fire, after removing the dead body of the bearer therefrom, secured the flag and returned with it to the Union lines.
Notes: POW

219 ◆ CASEY, HENRY

Rank: Private (highest rank: Corporal)
Service: U.S. Army

Birthday: 28 October 1837
Place of Birth: New Geneva, Fayette County, Pennsylvania
Date of Death: 9 May 1919
Place of Death: Bloomingburg, Ohio
Cemetery: Bloomingburg Cemetery (MH)—Bloomingburg, Ohio
Entered Service at: Bloomingburg, Fayette County, Ohio
Unit: Company C, 20th Ohio Infantry
Battle or Place of Action: Vicksburg, Mississippi
Date of Action: 22 April 1863
Date of Issue: 17 September 1897
Citation: Voluntarily served as one of the crew of a transport that passed the forts under a heavy fire.

220 ◆ CASSIDY, MICHAEL

Rank: Landsman (highest rank: Ordinary Seaman)
Service: U.S. Navy
Birthday: 1837
Place of Birth: Ireland
Date of Death: 18 March 1908
Place of Death: Soldier's Home, Hampton, Virginia
Cemetery: Hampton National Cemetery (B-9503) (MH)—Hampton, Virginia
Entered Service at: New York, New York
Unit: U.S.S. *Lackawanna*
Battle or Place of Action: Mobile Bay, Alabama
Date of Action: 5 August 1864
G.O. Number, Date: 45, 31 December 1864
Citation: Served on board the U.S.S. *Lackawanna* during the successful attacks against Fort Morgan, rebel gunboats and the ram *Tennessee* in Mobile Bay, on 5 August 1864. Displaying great coolness and exemplary behavior as first sponger of a gun, Cassidy, by his coolness under fire, received the applause of his officers and the gun crew throughout the action which resulted in the capture of the prize ram *Tennessee* and in the destruction of batteries at Fort Morgan.

221 ◆ CATLIN, ISAAC SWARTWOOD

Rank: Colonel (highest rank: Brevet Major General)
Service: U.S. Army
Birthday: 8 July 1835
Place of Birth: Near Owego, Tioga County, New York
Date of Death: 19 January 1916
Place of Death: Brooklyn, New York
Cemetery: Arlington National Cemetery (2-3397) (MH)—Arlington, Virginia
Entered Service at: Owego, Tioga County, New York
Unit: 109th New York Infantry (Railway Brigade)
Battle or Place of Action: Petersburg, Virginia
Date of Action: 30 July 1864
Date of Issue: 13 January 1899
Citation: In a heroic effort to rally the disorganized troops was disabled by a severe wound. While being carried from the field he recovered somewhat and bravely started to return to his command, when he received a second wound, which necessitated amputation of his right leg.

222 ◆ CAYER, OVILA

Rank: Sergeant
Service: U.S. Army
Birthday: 9 February 1844
Place of Birth: St. Remi, Canada
Date of Death: 7 February 1909
Place of Death: Salinas, California
Cemetery: Garden of Memory Park Cemetery—Salinas, California
Entered Service at: Malone, Franklin County, New York
Unit: Company A, 14th U.S. Volunteer Infantry
Battle or Place of Action: Weldon Railroad, Virginia
Date of Action: 19 August 1864
Date of Issue: 15 February 1867
Citation: Commanded the regiment, all the officers being disabled.

223 ◆ CHAMBERLAIN, JOSHUA LAWRENCE

Rank: Colonel (highest rank: Brevet Major General)
Service: U.S. Army
Birthday: 8 September 1828
Place of Birth: Brewer, Penobscot County, Maine
Date of Death: 24 February 1914
Place of Death: Portland, Maine
Cemetery: Pine Grove Cemetery (MH)—Brunswick, Maine
Entered Service at: Brunswick, Cumberland County, Maine
Unit: 20th Maine Infantry
Battle or Place of Action: Gettysburg, Pennsylvania
Date of Action: 2 July 1863
Date of Issue: 11 August 1893
Citation: Daring heroism and great tenacity in holding his position on the Little Round Top against repeated assaults, and carrying the advance position on the Great Round Top.

224 ◆ CHAMBERLAIN, ORVILLE TYRON

Rank: Second Lieutenant (highest rank: Captain)
Service: U.S. Army
Birthday: 1 September 1841
Place of Birth: Leesburgh, Kosciusko County, Indiana
Date of Death: 27 May 1929
Place of Death: Prescott, Arizona
Cemetery: Gracelawn Cemetery—Elkhart, Indiana
Entered Service at: Elkhart, Elkhart County, Indiana
Unit: Company G, 74th Indiana Infantry
Battle or Place of Action: Chickamauga, Georgia
Date of Action: 20 September 1863
Date of Issue: 11 March 1896
Citation: While exposed to a galling fire, Chamberlain went in search of another regiment, found its location, procured ammunition from the men thereof, and returned with the ammunition to his own company.

225 ◆ CHAMBERS, JOSEPH B.

Rank: Private
Service: U.S. Army

Birthday: 4 May 1833
Place of Birth: Beaver County, Pennsylvania
Date of Death: 8 October 1909
Place of Death: East Brook, Pennsylvania
Cemetery: Oak Park Cemetery—New Castle, Pennsylvania
Entered Service at: East Brook, Pennsylvania
Unit: Company F, 100th Pennsylvania Infantry (Roundheads)
Battle or Place of Action: Petersburg, Virginia
Date of Action: 25 March 1865
Date of Issue: 27 July 1871
Citation: Capture of colors of 1st Virginia Infantry (C.S.A.).

226 ◆ CHANDLER, HENRY FLINT

Rank: Sergeant
Service: U.S. Army
Birthday: 26 September 1835
Place of Birth: Andover, Essex County, Massachusetts
Date of Death: 16 November 1906
Place of Death: Haver Hill, Massachusetts
Cemetery: West Parrish Cemetery (MH)—Andover, Massachusetts
Entered Service at: Andover, Essex County, Massachusetts
Unit: Company E, 59th Massachusetts Infantry
Battle or Place of Action: Petersburg, Virginia
Date of Action: 17 June 1864
Date of Issue: 30 March 1898
Citation: Though seriously wounded in a bayonet charge and directed to go to the rear, he declined to do so, but remained with his regiment and helped to carry the breastworks.

227 ◆ CHANDLER, JAMES B.

True Name: Chandler, John B.
Rank: Coxswain
Service: U.S. Navy
Birthday: 6 October 1837
Place of Birth: Plymouth, Plymouth County, Massachusetts
Date of Death: 12 July 1899
Place of Death: Taunton, Massachusetts
Cemetery: Vine Hill Cemetery (MH)—Plymouth, Massachusetts
Entered Service at: Boston, Suffolk County, Massachusetts
Unit: U.S.S. *Richmond*
Battle or Place of Action: Mobile Bay, Alabama
Date of Action: 5 August 1864
G.O. Number, Date: 45, 31 December 1864
Citation: On board the U.S.S. *Richmond* during action against rebel forts and gunboats and against the ram *Tennessee* in Mobile Bay, 5 August 1864. Cool and courageous although he had just come off the sick list, Chandler rendered gallant service throughout the prolonged action as his ship maintained accurate fire against Fort Morgan and ships of the Confederacy despite extremely heavy return fire. He participated in the actions at Forts Jackson and St. Philip, with the Chalmette batteries, at the surrender of New Orleans and in the attacks on batteries below Vicksburg.

228 ◆ CHANDLER, STEPHEN EDWIN

Rank: Quartermaster Sergeant
Service: U.S. Army
Birthday: 20 November 1841
Place of Birth: Convis, Michigan
Date of Death: 1 February 1919
Place of Death: Minneapolis, Minnesota
Cemetery: Lakewood Cemetery—Minneapolis, Minnesota
Entered Service at: Grandby, Oswego County, New York
Unit: Company A, 24th New York Cavalry
Battle or Place of Action: Amelia Springs, Virginia
Date of Action: 5 April 1865
Date of Issue: 4 April 1898
Citation: Under severe fire of the enemy and of the troops in retreat, Chandler went between the lines to the assistance of a wounded and helpless comrade, and rescued him from death or capture.

229 ◆ CHAPIN, ALARIC B.

Rank: Private
Service: U.S. Army
Birthday: 1847
Place of Birth: Ogdensburg, St. Lawrence County, New York
Date of Death: 27 November 1924
Place of Death: Portland, Oregon
Cemetery: Roselawn Cemetery—Portland, Oregon
Entered Service at: Pamelia, Jefferson County, New York
Unit: Company G, 142d New York Infantry
Battle or Place of Action: Fort Fisher, North Carolina
Date of Action: 15 January 1865
Date of Issue: 28 December 1914
Citation: Voluntarily advanced with the head of the column and cut down the palisading.

230 ◆ CHAPMAN, JOHN

True Name: Kaufman, Charles F.
Rank: Private
Service: U.S. Army
Birthday: 10 February 1844
Place of Birth: Strasburg, France
Date of Death: 30 September 1905
Place of Death: San Francisco, California
Cemetery: Holy Cross Cemetery—Colma, California
Entered Service at: Limerick, York County, Maine
Unit: Company B, 1st Maine Heavy Artillery
Battle or Place of Action: Deatonsville (Sailor's Creek), Virginia
Date of Action: 6 April 1865
Date of Issue: 10 May 1865
Citation: Capture of flag.

231 ◆ CHAPUT, LOUIS G.

Rank: Landsman
Service: U.S. Navy

Birthday: 1845
Place of Birth: Canada
Date of Death: 17 April 1916
Place of Death: Montreal, Canada
Entered Service at: New York, New York
Unit: U.S.S. *Lackawanna*
Battle or Place of Action: Mobile Bay, Alabama
Date of Action: 5 August 1864
G.O. Number, Date: 45, 31 December 1864
Citation: On board the U.S.S. *Lackawanna* during the successful attacks against Fort Morgan, rebel gunboats, and the ram *Tennessee* in Mobile Bay, on 5 August 1864. Severely wounded, Chaput remained at his gun until relieved, reported to the surgeon, and returned to his gun until the action was over. He was then carried below following the action, which resulted in the capture of the prize ram *Tennessee* and in the destruction of batteries at Fort Morgan.

232 ◆ CHASE, JOHN F.

Rank: Private (highest rank: Captain)
Service: U.S. Army
Birthday: 23 April 1843
Place of Birth: Chelsea, Maine
Date of Death: 28 November 1914
Place of Death: St. Petersburg, Florida
Cemetery: St. Bartholomew Cemetery (MH)—St. Petersburg, Florida
Entered Service at: Augusta, Kennebec County, Maine
Unit: 5th Battery, Maine Light Artillery
Battle or Place of Action: Chancellorsville, Virginia
Date of Action: 3 May 1863
Date of Issue: 7 February 1888
Citation: Nearly all the officers and men of the battery having been killed or wounded, this soldier with a comrade continued to fire his gun after the guns had ceased. The piece was then dragged off by the two, the horses having been shot, and its capture by the enemy was prevented.

233 ◆ CHILD, BENJAMIN HAM

Rank: Corporal (highest rank: Second Lieutenant)
Service: U.S. Army
Birthday: 8 May 1843
Place of Birth: Providence, Providence County, Rhode Island
Date of Death: 16 May 1902
Cemetery: Swan Point Cemetery (MH)—Providence, Rhode Island
Entered Service at: Providence, Providence County, Rhode Island
Unit: Battery A, 1st Rhode Island Light Artillery
Battle or Place of Action: Antietam, Maryland
Date of Action: 17 September 1862
Date of Issue: 20 July 1897
Citation: Was wounded and taken to the rear, insensible, but when partialy recovered, Child insisted on returning to the battery and resumed command of his piece, so remaining until the close of the battle.

234 ◆ CHISMAN, WILLIAM W.

Rank: Private (highest rank: Sergeant)
Service: U.S. Army
Birthday: 24 September 1843
Place of Birth: Dearborn County, Indiana
Date of Death: 25 April 1925
Cemetery: Elmwood Cemetery (MH)—Augusta, Kansas
Entered Service at: Wilmington, Indiana
Unit: Company I, 83d Indiana Infantry
Battle or Place of Action: Vicksburg, Mississippi
Date of Action: 22 May 1863
Date of Issue: 15 August 1894
Citation: Gallantry in the charge of the "volunteer storming party."

235 ◆ CHRISTIANCY, JAMES ISAAC

Rank: First Lieutenant
Service: U.S. Army
Birthday: 1844
Place of Birth: Monroe County, Michigan
Date of Death: 18 December 1899
Place of Death: Washington, D.C.
Cemetery: Arlington National Cemetery (1-580) (MH)—Arlington, Virginia
Entered Service at: Monroe County, Michigan
Unit: Company D, 9th Michigan Cavalry
Battle or Place of Action: Hawes Shops, Virginia
Date of Action: 28 May 1864
Date of Issue: 10 October 1892
Citation: While acting as aide, voluntarily led a part of the line into the fight, and was twice wounded.

236 ◆ CHURCHILL, SAMUEL JOSEPH

Rank: Corporal (highest rank: Quartermaster Sergeant)
Service: U.S. Army
Birthday: 1 November 1842
Place of Birth: Rutland, Rutland County, Vermont
Date of Death: 3 June 1932
Cemetery: Oak Hill Cemetery (MH)—Lawrence, Kansas
Entered Service at: DeKalb, DeKalb County, Illinois
Unit: Company G, 2d Illinois Light Artillery
Battle or Place of Action: Nashville, Tennessee
Date of Action: 15 December 1864
Date of Issue: 20 January 1897
Citation: When the fire of the enemy's batteries compelled the men of his detachment for a short time to seek shelter, he stood manfully at his post and for some minutes worked his gun alone.

237 ◆ CILLEY, CLINTON ALBERT

Rank: Captain (highest rank: Brevet Colonel)
Service: U.S. Army
Birthday: 16 February 1837
Place of Birth: Rockingham County, New Hampshire
Date of Death: 9 May 1900

Place of Death: Morgantown, North Carolina
Cemetery: Oakwood Cemetery (MH)—Hickory, North Carolina
Entered Service at: Sasioja, Minnesota
Unit: Company C, 2d Minnesota Infantry
Battle or Place of Action: Chickamauga, Georgia
Date of Action: 20 September 1863
Date of Issue: 12 June 1895
Citation: Seized the colors of a retreating regiment and led it into the thick of the attack.

238 ◆ CLANCY, JAMES T.

Rank: Sergeant (highest rank: Captain)
Service: U.S. Army
Birthday: 1833
Place of Birth: Albany, Albany County, New York
Entered Service at: Camden, Camden County, New Jersey
Unit: Company C, 1st New Jersey Cavalry
Battle or Place of Action: Vaughn Road, Virginia
Date of Action: 1 October 1864
Date of Issue: 3 July 1865
Citation: Shot the Confederate Brig. Gen. John Dunovant dead during a charge, thus confusing the enemy and greatly aiding in his repulse.

239 ◆ CLAPP, ALBERT ADAMS

Rank: First Sergeant (highest rank: Second Lieutenant)
Service: U.S. Army
Birthday: 1 May 1841
Place of Birth: Pompey, Onondaga County, New York
Date of Death: 8 May 1911
Place of Death: Alhambrah, California
Cemetery: Mountain View Cemetery—Altadena, California
Entered Service at: Painesville, Lake County, Ohio
Unit: Company G, 2d Ohio Cavalry
Battle or Place of Action: Deatonsville (Sailor's Creek), Virginia
Date of Action: 6 April 1865
Date of Issue: 24 April 1865
Citation: Capture of battle flag of the 8th Florida Infantry (C.S.A.).

240 ◆ CLARK, CHARLES AMORY

Rank: Lieutenant & Adjutant (highest rank: Brevet Lieutenant Colonel)
Service: U.S. Army
Birthday: 26 January 1841
Place of Birth: Sangerville, Piscataquis County, Maine
Date of Death: 22 December 1913
Cemetery: Oak Hill Cemetery (MH)—Cedar Rapids, Iowa
Entered Service at: Forcroft, Maine
Unit: 6th Maine Infantry
Battle or Place of Action: Brooks Ford, Virginia
Date of Action: 4 May 1863
Date of Issue: 13 May 1896
Citation: Having voluntarily taken command of his regiment in the absence of its commander, at great personal risk and with remarkable presence of mind and fertility of resource, Clark led the command down an exceedingly precipitous embankment to the Rappahannock River and by his gallantry, coolness, and good judgment in the face of the enemy saved the command from capture or destruction.

241 ◆ CLARK, HARRISON

Rank: Corporal (highest rank: Second Lieutenant)
Service: U.S. Army
Birthday: 10 April 1842
Place of Birth: Chatham, Columbia County, New York
Date of Death: 18 April 1913
Cemetery: Albany Rural Cemetery (MH)—Albany, New York
Entered Service at: Chatham, Columbia County, New York
Unit: Company E, 125th New York Infantry
Battle or Place of Action: Gettysburg, Pennsylvania
Date of Action: 2 July 1863
Date of Issue: 11 June 1895
Citation: Seized the colors and advanced with them after the color bearer had been shot.

242 ◆ CLARK, JAMES G.

Rank: Private (highest rank: Drummer)
Service: U.S. Army
Birthday: 31 October 1843
Place of Birth: Germantown, Philadelphia County, Pennsylvania
Date of Death: 16 December 1911
Cemetery: Fernwood Cemetery (MH)—Fernwood, Pennsylvania
Entered Service at: Philadelphia, Philadelphia County, Pennsylvania
Unit: Company F, 88th Pennsylvania Infantry
Battle or Place of Action: Petersburg, Virginia
Date of Action: 18 June 1864
Date of Issue: 30 April 1892
Citation: Distinguished bravery in action; was severely wounded.

243 ◆ CLARK, JOHN WESLEY

Rank: First Lieutenant & Regimental Quartermaster (highest rank: Captain)
Service: U.S. Army
Birthday: 25 October 1830
Place of Birth: Montpelier, Washington County, Vermont
Date of Death: 4 August 1898
Place of Death: Montpelier, Vermont
Cemetery: Green Mount Cemetery—Montpelier, Vermont
Entered Service at: Vermont
Unit: 6th Vermont Infantry
Battle or Place of Action: near Warrenton, Virginia
Date of Action: 28 July 1863
Date of Issue: 17 August 1891
Citation: Defended the division train against a vastly superi-

or force of the enemy, he was severely wounded, but remained in the saddle for 20 hours afterward, until he had brought his train through in safety.

244 ◆ CLARK, WILLIAM A.

Rank: Corporal (highest rank: Sergeant)
Service: U.S. Army
Birthday: 24 July 1828
Place of Birth: Pennsylvania
Date of Death: 9 January 1916
Place of Death: Mankato, Minnesota
Cemetery: Hebron Cemetery (MH)—Nicollet County, Minnesota
Entered Service at: Shelbyville, Minnesota
Unit: Company H, 2d Minnesota Infantry
Battle or Place of Action: Nolensville, Tennessee
Date of Action: 15 February 1863
Date of Issue: 11 September 1897
Citation: Was one of a detachment of 16 men who heroically defended a wagon train against the attack of 125 cavalry, repulsed the attack and saved the train.

245 ◆ CLARKE, DAYTON P.

True Name: Clark, Dayton P.
Rank: Captain
Service: U.S. Army
Birthday: 15 December 1840
Place of Birth: DeKalb, St. Lawrence County, New York
Date of Death: 10 November 1915
Place of Death: Montpelier, Vermont
Cemetery: Green Mount Cemetery—Montpelier, Vermont
Entered Service at: Hermon, St. Lawrence County, New York
Unit: Company F, 2d Vermont Infantry
Battle or Place of Action: Spotsylvania, Virginia
Date of Action: 12 May 1864
Date of Issue: 30 June 1892
Citation: Distinguished conduct in a desperate hand-to-hand fight while commanding the regiment.

246 ◆ CLAUSEN, CHARLES H.

Rank: First Lieutenant
Service: U.S. Army
Birthday: 22 September 1842
Place of Birth: Philadelphia, Philadelphia County, Pennsylvania
Date of Death: 15 August 1922
Place of Death: Glenside, Pennsylvania
Cemetery: Mount Peace Cemetery—Philadelphia, Pennsylvania
Entered Service at: Philadelphia, Philadelphia County, Pennsylvania
Unit: Company H, 61st Pennsylvania Infantry
Battle or Place of Action: Spotsylvania, Virginia
Date of Action: 12 May 1864
Date of Issue: 25 June 1892
Citation: Although severely wounded, he led the regiment against the enemy, under a terrific fire, and saved a battery from capture.

247 ◆ CLAY, CECIL

Rank: Captain (highest rank: Brevet Brigadier General)
Service: U.S. Army
Birthday: 13 February 1842
Place of Birth: Philadelphia, Philadelphia County, Pennsylvania
Date of Death: 23 September 1907
Place of Death: Washington, D.C.
Cemetery: Arlington National Cemetery (2-1012)—Arlington, Virginia
Entered Service at: Philadelphia, Philadelphia County, Pennsylvania
Unit: Company K, 58th Pennsylvania Infantry
Battle or Place of Action: Fort Harrison, Virginia
Date of Action: 29 September 1864
Date of Issue: 19 April 1892
Citation: Led his regiment in the charge, carrying the colors of another regiment, and when severely wounded in the right arm, incurring loss of same, he shifted the colors to the left hand, which also became disabled by a gunshot wound.

248 ◆ CLEVELAND, CHARLES FRANKLIN

Rank: Private
Service: U.S. Army
Birthday: 14 August 1845
Place of Birth: Hartford, Washington County, New York
Date of Death: 29 September 1908
Cemetery: Forest Hill Cemetery—Utica, New York
Entered Service at: Elmira, Chemung County, New York
Unit: Company C, 26th New York Infantry
Battle or Place of Action: Antietam, Maryland
Date of Action: 17 September 1862
Date of Issue: 12 June 1895
Citation: Voluntarily took and carried the colors into action after the color bearer had been shot.

249 ◆ CLIFFORD, ROBERT TELEFORD

True Name: Kelley, Robert Teleford
Rank: Master-at-Arms (highest rank: Master's Mate)
Service: U.S. Navy
Birthday: 1835
Place of Birth: Pennsylvania
Date of Death: 24 July 1873
Place of Death: Philadelphia, Pennsylvania
Cemetery: Laurel Hill Cemetery (MH)—Philadelphia, Pennsylvania
Entered Service at: Pennsylvania
Unit: U.S.S. *Shokokon*
Battle or Place of Action: New Topsail Inlet, off Wilmington, North Carolina
Date of Action: 22 August 1863
G.O. Number, Date: 45, 31 December 1864

Citation: Served on board the U.S.S. *Shokokon* at New Topsail Inlet off Wilmington, N.C., 22 August 1863. Participating in a strategic plan to destroy an enemy schooner, Clifford aided in the portage of a dinghy across the narrow neck of land separating the sea from the sound. Launching the boat in the sound, the crew approached the enemy from the rear and Clifford gallantly crept into the rebel camp and counted the men who outnumbered his party three to one. Returning to his men, he ordered a charge in which the enemy was routed, leaving behind a schooner and a quantity of supplies.

250 ◆ CLOPP, JOHN E.

Rank: Private
Service: U.S. Army
Place of Birth: Philadelphia, Philadelphia County, Pennsylvania
Entered Service at: Philadelphia, Philadelphia County, Pennsylvania
Unit: Company F, 71st Pennsylvania Infantry
Battle or Place of Action: Gettysburg, Pennsylvania
Date of Action: 3 July 1863
Date of Issue: 2 February 1865
Citation: Capture of flag of 9th Virginia Infantry (C.S.A.), wresting it from the color bearer.

251 ◆ CLUTE, GEORGE WASHINGTON

Rank: Corporal
Service: U.S. Army
Birthday: 11 June 1842
Place of Birth: Marathon, Michigan
Date of Death: 13 February 1919
Place of Death: Flint, Michigan
Cemetery: Morris Cemetery (MH)—Mount Morris, Michigan
Entered Service at: Marathon, Michigan
Unit: Company I, 14th Michigan Infantry
Battle or Place of Action: Bentonville, North Carolina
Date of Action: 19 March 1865
Date of Issue: 26 August 1898
Citation: In a charge, captured the flag of the 40th North Carolina (C.S.A.), the flag being taken in a personal encounter with an officer who carried and defended it.

252 ◆ COATES, JEFFERSON

True Name: Coates, Francis Jefferson
Rank: Sergeant
Service: U.S. Army
Birthday: 24 August 1843
Place of Birth: Grant County, Wisconsin
Date of Death: 27 January 1880
Place of Death: Dorchester, Nebraska
Cemetery: Dorchester City Cemetery—Dorchester, Nebraska
Entered Service at: Boscobel, Grant County, Wisconsin
Unit: Company H, 7th Wisconsin Infantry
Battle or Place of Action: Gettysburg, Pennsylvania
Date of Action: 1 July 1863
Date of Issue: 29 June 1866
Citation: Unsurpassed courage in battle, where he had both eyes shot out.

253 ◆ COCKLEY, DAVID L.

Rank: First Lieutenant (highest rank: Captain)
Service: U.S. Army
Birthday: 8 June 1843
Place of Birth: Lexington, Richland County, Ohio
Date of Death: 26 December 1901
Cemetery: Oakland Cemetery (MH)—Shelby, Ohio
Entered Service at: Columbus, Franklin County, Ohio
Unit: Company L, 10th Ohio Cavalry
Battle or Place of Action: Waynesboro, Georgia
Date of Action: 4 December 1864
Date of Issue: 2 August 1897
Citation: While acting as aide-de-camp to a general officer, he three times asked permission to join his regiment in a proposed charge upon the enemy, and in response to the last request, having obtained such permission, joined his regiment and fought bravely at its head throughout the action.

254 ◆ COEY, JAMES

Rank: Major (highest rank: Brevet Colonel U.S. Volunteers)
Service: U.S. Army
Birthday: 12 February 1841
Place of Birth: New York, New York
Date of Death: 14 July 1918
Place of Death: Berkeley, California
Cemetery: San Francisco National Cemetery (OS-89-1) (MH)—San Francisco, California
Entered Service at: Oswego, Oswego County, New York
Unit: 147th New York Infantry
Battle or Place of Action: Hatcher's Run, Virginia
Date of Action: 6 February 1865
Date of Issue: 12 May 1892
Citation: Seized the regimental colors at a critical moment and by a prompt advance on the enemy caused the entire brigade to follow him; and, after himself being severely wounded, he caused himself to be lifted into the saddle and a second time rallied the line in an attempt to check the enemy.

255 ◆ COFFEY, ROBERT JOHN

Rank: Sergeant (highest rank: Major)
Service: U.S. Army
Birthday: 15 December 1842
Place of Birth: St. John, New Brunswick, Canada
Date of Death: 9 July 1901
Cemetery: Green Mount Cemetery—Montpelier, Vermont
Entered Service at: Montpelier, Washington County, Vermont
Unit: Company K, 4th Vermont Infantry

Battle or Place of Action: Bank's Ford, Virginia
Date of Action: 4 May 1863
Date of Issue: 13 May 1892
Citation: Singlehandedly captured two officers and five privates of the 8th Louisiana Regiment (C.S.A.).

256 ◆ COHN, ABRAHAM

Rank: Sergeant Major (highest rank: Captain)
Service: U.S. Army
Birthday: 1832
Place of Birth: Guttentag, Silesia, Prussia
Date of Death: 2 June 1897
Place of Death: New York, New York
Cemetery: Cypress Hills Cemetery (Private)—Brooklyn, New York
Entered Service at: Campton, Grafton County, New Hampshire
Unit: 6th New Hampshire Infantry
Battle or Place of Action: Wilderness Campaign & at the mine, Petersburg, Virginia
Date of Action: 6 May & 30 July 1864
Date of Issue: 24 August 1865
Citation: During Battle of the Wilderness rallied and formed, under heavy fire, disorganized and fleeing troops of different regiments. At Petersburg, Va., 30 July 1864, bravely and coolly carried orders to the advanced line under severe fire.

257 ◆ COLBERT, PATRICK

Rank: Coxswain
Service: U.S. Navy
Birthday: 1842
Place of Birth: Ireland
Date of Death: 19 January 1877
Place of Death: Detroit, Michigan
Cemetery: Mount Elliott Cemetery (MH)—Detroit, Michigan
Entered Service at: New York
Unit: U.S.S. *Commodore Hull*
Battle or Place of Action: Plymouth, North Carolina
Date of Action: 31 October 1864
G.O. Number, Date: 45, 31 December 1864
Citation: Served on board the U.S.S. *Commodore Hull* at the capture of Plymouth, 31 October 1864. Painfully wounded by a shell which killed the man at his side, Colbert, as captain of the forward pivot gun, remained at his post until the end of the action, braving the heavy enemy fire and appearing as cool as if mere target practice.

258 ◆ COLBY, CARLOS W.

Rank: Sergeant (highest rank: First Sergeant)
Service: U.S. Army
Birthday: 15 May 1837
Place of Birth: Merrimack, Hillsborough County, New Hampshire
Date of Death: 19 May 1922
Cemetery: Crest Hill Cemetery—Hillsboro, Illinois
Entered Service at: Madison County, Illinois
Unit: Company G, 97th Illinois Infantry
Battle or Place of Action: Vicksburg, Mississippi
Date of Action: 22 May 1863
Date of Issue: 31 January 1896
Citation: Gallantry in the charge of the "volunteer storming party."

259 ◆ COLE, GABRIEL

Rank: Corporal
Service: U.S. Army
Birthday: 22 March 1831
Place of Birth: Chenango County, New York
Date of Death: 7 January 1907
Cemetery: Sherman Township Cemetery (MH)—Tustin, Michigan
Entered Service at: New Salem, Washtenaw County, Michigan
Unit: Company I, 5th Michigan Cavalry
Battle or Place of Action: Winchester, Virginia
Date of Action: 19 September 1864
Date of Issue: 27 September 1864
Citation: Capture of flag, during which he was wounded in the leg.

260 ◆ COLLINS, HARRISON

Rank: Corporal
Service: U.S. Army
Birthday: 10 March 1836
Place of Birth: Hawkins County, Tennessee
Date of Death: 25 December 1890
Place of Death: Isabella, Missouri
Cemetery: Springfield National Cemetery (26-1357-B)—Springfield, Missouri
Entered Service at: Cumberland Gap, Claiborne County, Tennessee
Unit: Company A, 1st Tennessee Cavalry
Battle or Place of Action: Richland Creek, Tennessee
Date of Action: 24 December 1864
Date of Issue: 24 February 1865
Citation: Capture of flag of Chalmer's Division (C.S.A.).

261 ◆ COLLINS SR., THOMAS D.

Rank: Sergeant
Service: U.S. Army
Birthday: 14 August 1847
Place of Birth: Neversink Flats, Sullivan County, New York
Date of Death: 26 May 1935
Place of Death: Middletown, New York
Cemetery: Hillside Cemetery (MH)—Middletown, New York
Entered Service at: Liberty, Sullivan County, New York
Unit: Company H, 143d New York Infantry (Sullivan County Regiment)

Battle or Place of Action: Resaca, Georgia
Date of Action: 15 May 1864
Date of Issue: 14 August 1896
Citation: Captured a regimental flag of the enemy.

262 ◆ COLLIS, CHARLES HENRY TUCKY

Rank: Colonel (highest rank: Brevet Major General)
Service: U.S. Army
Birthday: 4 February 1838
Place of Birth: Cork, County Cork, Ireland
Date of Death: 11 May 1902
Place of Death: Bryn Mawr, Pennsylvania
Cemetery: Gettysburg National Cemetery (H-1 PA plot)—Gettysburg, Pennsylvania
Entered Service at: Philadelphia, Philadelphia County, Pennsylvania
Unit: 114th Pennsylvania Infantry (Collis' Regiment, Zouaves d'Afrique)
Battle or Place of Action: Fredericksburg, Virginia
Date of Action: 13 December 1862
Date of Issue: 10 March 1893
Citation: Gallantly led his regiment in battle at a critical moment.

263 ◆ COLWELL, OLIVER

Rank: First Lieutenant (highest rank: Captain)
Service: U.S. Army
Birthday: 1834
Place of Birth: Champaign County, Ohio
Date of Death: 12 October 1872
Place of Death: Rush Township, Ohio
Cemetery: Woodstock Cemetery—Rush Township, Ohio
Entered Service at: Columbus, Franklin County, Ohio
Unit: Company G, 95th Ohio Infantry
Battle or Place of Action: Nashville, Tennessee
Date of Action: 16 December 1864
Date of Issue: 24 February 1865
Citation: Capture of flag.
Notes: POW

264 ◆ COMPSON, HARTWELL B.

Rank: Major (highest rank: Brevet Lieutenant Colonel New York Volunteers)
Service: U.S. Army
Birthday: 1840
Place of Birth: Seneca Falls, Seneca County, New York
Date of Death: 31 August 1905
Cemetery: Grand Army of the Republic Cemetery—Portland, Oregon
Entered Service at: Seneca Falls, Seneca County, New York
Unit: 8th New York Cavalry
Battle or Place of Action: Waynesboro, Virginia
Date of Action: 2 March 1865
Date of Issue: 26 March 1865
Citation: Capture of flag belonging to Lt. Gen. Jubal Anderson Early's headquarters.

265 ◆ CONAWAY, JOHN WESLEY

Rank: Private (highest rank: Corporal)
Service: U.S. Army
Birthday: 19 September 1843
Place of Birth: Dearborn County, Indiana
Date of Death: 21 November 1913
Place of Death: Post Falls, Idaho
Cemetery: Evergreen Cemetery (MH)—Post Falls, Idaho
Entered Service at: Hartford, Blackford County, Indiana
Unit: Company C, 83d Indiana Infantry
Battle or Place of Action: Vicksburg, Mississippi
Date of Action: 22 May 1863
Date of Issue: 11 August 1894
Citation: Gallantry in the charge of the "volunteer storming party."

266 ◆ CONBOY, MARTIN

Rank: First Sergeant (highest rank: Second Lieutenant)
Service: U.S. Army
Birthday: 1833
Place of Birth: Roscommon, Ballagh County, Ireland
Date of Death: 21 December 1909
Place of Death: East Orange, New Jersey
Cemetery: Holy Sepulchre Cemetery—East Orange, New Jersey
Entered Service at: New York, New York
Unit: Company B, 37th New York Infantry
Battle or Place of Action: Williamsburg, Virginia
Date of Action: 5 May 1862
Date of Issue: 11 October 1892
Citation: Took command of the company in action, the captain having been wounded, the other commissioned officers being absent, and handled it with skill and bravery.

267 ◆ CONLAN, DENNIS

Rank: Seaman (highest rank: Gunner's Mate)
Service: U.S. Navy
Birthday: 1838
Place of Birth: New York, New York
Date of Death: 2 December 1870
Place of Death: New York, New York
Cemetery: Calvary Cemetery—Woodside, New York
Entered Service at: New York, New York
Unit: U.S.S. *Agawam*
Battle or Place of Action: Fort Fisher, North Carolina
Date of Action: 23 December 1864
G.O. Number, Date: 45, 31 December 1864
Date of Presentation: 12 May 1865
Place of Presentation: On board the U.S.S. *Agawam*, off New Bern, North Carolina
Citation: Conlan served on board the U.S.S. *Agawam*, as one of a volunteer crew of a powder boat which was exploded near Fort Fisher, 23 December 1864. The powder boat, towed in by the *Wilderness* to prevent detection by the enemy, cast off and slowly steamed to within 300 yards of the beach. After fuses and fires had been lit and a second anchor

with short scope let go to assure the boat's tailing inshore, the crew again boarded the *Wilderness* and proceeded a distance of 12 miles from shore. Less than two hours later the explosion took place, and the following day fires were observed still burning at the forts.

268 ◆ CONNELL, TRUSTRIM

Rank: Corporal
Service: U.S. Army
Birthday: 12 May 1844
Place of Birth: Lancaster, Lancaster County, Pennsylvania
Date of Death: 17 February 1937
Place of Death: Phoenix, Arizona
Cemetery: Rosedale Cemetery—Los Angeles, California
Entered Service at: Port Kennedy, Pennsylvania
Unit: Company I, 138th Pennsylvania Infantry
Battle or Place of Action: Deatonsville (Sailor's Creek), Virginia
Date of Action: 6 April 1865
Date of Issue: 10 May 1865
Citation: Capture of flag.

269 ◆ CONNER, RICHARD

Rank: Private (highest rank: Sergeant)
Service: U.S. Army
Birthday: 23 December 1840
Place of Birth: Philadelphia, Philadelphia County, Pennsylvania
Date of Death: 4 November 1923
Place of Death: Philadelphia, Pennsylvania
Cemetery: North Cedar Hills Cemetery—Philadelphia, Pennsylvania
Entered Service at: Burlington, Burlington County, New Jersey
Unit: Company F, 6th New Jersey Infantry
Battle or Place of Action: Bull Run, Virginia
Date of Action: 30 August 1862
Date of Issue: 17 September 1897
Citation: The flag of his regiment having been abandoned during retreat, he voluntarily returned with a single companion under a heavy fire and secured and brought off the flag, his companion being killed.

270 ◆ CONNOR, THOMAS

Rank: Ordinary Seaman
Service: U.S. Navy
Birthday: 1842
Place of Birth: Ireland
Entered Service at: Baltimore, Baltimore County, Maryland
Unit: U.S.S. *Minnesota*
Battle or Place of Action: Fort Fisher, North Carolina
Date of Action: 15 January 1865
G.O. Number, Date: 59, 22 June 1865
Citation: On board the U.S.S. *Minnesota*, in action during the assault on Fort Fisher, 15 January 1865. Landing on the beach with the assaulting party from his ship, Connor charged up to the palisades and, when more than two-thirds of the men became seized with panic and retreated on the run, risked his life to remain with a wounded officer. With the enemy concentrating his fire on the group, he waited until after dark before assisting in carrying the wounded man from the field.

271 ◆ CONNOR, WILLIAM C.

Rank: Boatswain's Mate
Service: U.S. Navy
Birthday: 1832
Place of Birth: Cork, County Cork, Ireland
Entered Service at: Pennsylvania
Unit: U.S.S. *Howquah*
Battle or Place of Action: off Wilmington, Delaware
Date of Action: 25 September 1864
G.O. Number, Date: 45, 31 December 1864
Citation: Served on board the U.S.S. *Howquah* on the occasion of the destruction of the blockade runner *Lynx*, off Wilmington, 25 September 1864. Performing his duty faithfully under the most trying circumstances, Connor stood firmly at his post in the midst of a cross-fire from the rebel shore batteries and our own vessels.

272 ◆ CONNORS, JAMES

Rank: Private
Service: U.S. Army
Birthday: 1838
Place of Birth: Kildare, Ireland
Entered Service at: Canajoharie, Montgomery County, New York
Unit: Company E, 43rd New York Infantry
Battle or Place of Action: Fisher's Hill, Virginia
Date of Action: 22 September 1864
Date of Issue: 6 October 1864
Citation: Capture of flag.

273 ◆ COOK, JOHN

Rank: Bugler
Service: U.S. Army
Birthday: 16 August 1847
Place of Birth: Cincinnati, Hamilton County, Ohio
Date of Death: 3 August 1915
Cemetery: Arlington National Cemetery (17-18613)—Arlington, Virginia
Entered Service at: Cincinnati, Hamilton County, Ohio
Unit: Battery B, 4th U.S. Artillery
Battle or Place of Action: Antietam, Maryland
Date of Action: 17 September 1862
Date of Issue: 30 June 1894
Citation: Volunteered at the age of 15 years to act as a cannoneer, and as such volunteer served a gun under a terrific fire of the enemy.

274 ◆ COOK, JOHN HENRY

Rank: Sergeant
Service: U.S. Army
Birthday: 19 July 1840

Place of Birth: London, England
Date of Death: 22 July 1916
Place of Death: New York, New York
Cemetery: Woodlawn Cemetery—Bronx, New York
Entered Service at: Quincy, Adams County, Illinois
Unit: Company A, 119th Illinois Infantry
Battle or Place of Action: Pleasant Hill, Louisiana
Date of Action: 9 April 1864
Date of Issue: 19 September 1890
Citation: During an attack by the enemy, voluntarily left the brigade quartermaster, with whom he had been detailed as a clerk, rejoined his command, and, acting as first lieutenant, led the line farther toward the charging enemy.

275 ◆ COOKE, WALTER HOWARD

Rank: Captain (highest rank: Major)
Service: U.S. Army
Birthday: 21 July 1838
Place of Birth: Norristown, Montgomery County, Pennsylvania
Date of Death: 28 January 1909
Place of Death: Norristown, Pennsylvania
Cemetery: St. Thomas Church Cemetery (MH)—Whitemarsh, Pennsylvania
Entered Service at: Norristown, Montgomery County, Pennsylvania
Unit: Company K, 4th Pennsylvania Infantry Militia
Battle or Place of Action: Bull Run, Virginia
Date of Action: 21 July 1861
Date of Issue: 19 May 1887
Citation: Voluntarily served as an aide on the staff of Col. David Hunter and participated in the battle, his term of service having expired on the previous day.

276 ◆ COOPER, JOHN✚

True Name: Mather, John Laver
Rank: Coxswain
Service: U.S. Navy
Birthday: 24 July 1828
Place of Birth: Dublin, County Dublin, Ireland
Date of Death: 22 August 1891
Cemetery: Cypress Hills National Cemetery (2-5022) (MH)—Brooklyn, New York
Entered Service at: New York, New York
Unit: U.S.S. *Brooklyn*
Battle or Place of Action: Mobile Bay, Alabama
Date of Action: 5 August 1864
G.O. Number, Date: 45, 31 December 1864
Citation: On board the U.S.S. *Brooklyn* during action against rebel forts and gunboats and with the ram *Tennessee*, in Mobile Bay, on 5 August 1864. Despite severe damage to his ship and the loss of several men on board as enemy fire raked her decks from stem to stern, Cooper fought his gun with skill and courage throughout the furious battle which resulted in the surrender of the prize rebel ram *Tennessee* and in the damaging and destruction of batteries at Fort Morgan.
Notes: ✚Double Awardee: see also Interim 1865–1870

277 ◆ COPP, CHARLES DEARBORN

Rank: Second Lieutenant (highest rank: Captain)
Service: U.S. Army
Birthday: 11 April 1836
Place of Birth: Warren County, New Hampshire
Date of Death: 2 November 1912
Place of Death: Clinton, Massachusetts
Cemetery: Middle Yard Cemetery (MH)—Lancaster, Massachusetts
Entered Service at: Nashua, Hillsborough County, New Hampshire
Unit: Company C, 9th New Hampshire Infantry
Battle or Place of Action: Fredericksburg, Virginia
Date of Action: 13 December 1862
Date of Issue: 28 June 1890
Citation: Seized the regimental colors, the color bearer having been shot down, and, waving them, rallied the regiment under a heavy fire.

278 ◆ CORCORAN, JOHN

Rank: Private
Service: U.S. Army
Birthday: 24 June 1842
Place of Birth: Pawtucket, Providence County, Rhode Island
Date of Death: 19 June 1919
Cemetery: Oak Grove Cemetery (MH)—Pawtucket, Rhode Island
Entered Service at: Pawtucket, Providence County, Rhode Island
Unit: Company G, 1st Rhode Island Light Artillery
Battle or Place of Action: Petersburg, Virginia
Date of Action: 2 April 1865
Date of Issue: 2 November 1887
Citation: Was one of a detachment of 20 picked artillerymen who voluntarily accompanied an infantry assaulting party, and who turned upon the enemy the guns captured in the assault.

279 ◆ CORCORAN, THOMAS E.

Rank: Landsman
Service: U.S. Navy
Birthday: 1838
Place of Birth: Dublin, County Dublin, Ireland
Date of Death: 12 March 1904
Cemetery: 1st Calvary Cemetery—Woodside, New York
Entered Service at: New York, New York
Unit: U.S.S. *Cincinnati*
Battle or Place of Action: Vicksburg, Mississippi
Date of Action: 27 May 1863
G.O. Number, Date: 17, 10 July 1863
Citation: Served on board the U.S.S. *Cincinnati* during the attack on the Vicksburg batteries and at the time of her sinking, 27 May 1863. Engaging the enemy in a fierce battle, the *Cincinnati*, amidst an incessant fire of shot and shell, continued to fire her guns to the last, though so penetrated by shellfire that her fate was sealed. Serving bravely during this

action, Corcoran was conspicuously cool under the fire of the enemy, never ceasing to fight until this proud ship went down, "her colors nailed to the mast."

280 ◆ CORLISS, GEORGE W.

Rank: Captain (highest rank: Brevet Major)
Service: U.S. Army
Birthday: 1834
Place of Birth: Connecticut
Date of Death: 15 May 1903
Place of Death: New York, New York
Cemetery: Maple Grove Cemetery (MH)—Kew Gardens, New York
Entered Service at: Hartford, Hartford County, Connecticut
Unit: Company C, 5th Connecticut Infantry
Battle or Place of Action: Cedar Mountain, Virginia
Date of Action: 9 August 1862
Date of Issue: 10 September 1897
Citation: Seized a fallen flag of the regiment, the color bearer having been killed, carried it forward in the face of a severe fire, and though himself shot down and permanently disabled, planted the staff in the earth and kept the flag flying.

281 ◆ CORLISS, STEPHEN POTTER

Rank: First Lieutenant (highest rank: Brevet Colonel)
Service: U.S. Army
Birthday: 26 July 1842
Place of Birth: Albany, Albany County, New York
Date of Death: 9 May 1904
Place of Death: Pittsfield, Massachusetts
Cemetery: Albany Rural Cemetery (MH)—Albany, New York
Entered Service at: Albany, Albany County, New York
Unit: Company F, 4th New York Heavy Artillery
Battle or Place of Action: South Side Railroad, Virginia
Date of Action: 2 April 1865
Date of Issue: 17 January 1895
Citation: Raised the fallen colors and, rushing forward in advance of the troops, placed them on the enemy's works.

282 ◆ CORSON, JOSEPH KIRBY

Rank: Assistant Surgeon (highest rank: Major USA Ret.)
Service: U.S. Army
Birthday: 26 November 1836
Place of Birth: Plymouth Meeting, Montgomery County, Pennsylvania
Date of Death: 24 July 1913
Place of Death: Plymouth Meeting, Pennsylvania
Cemetery: West Laurel Hill Cemetery—Bala-Cynwyd, Pennsylvania
Entered Service at: Philadelphia, Philadelphia County, Pennsylvania
Unit: 6th Pennsylvania Reserves (35th Pennsylvania Volunteers)
Battle or Place of Action: near Bristoe Station, Virginia
Date of Action: 14 October 1863
Date of Issue: 13 May 1899
Citation: With one companion returned in the face of the enemy's heavy artillery fire and removed to a place of safety a severely wounded soldier who had been left behind as the regiment fell back.

283 ◆ COSGRIFF, RICHARD H.

Rank: Private
Service: U.S. Army
Birthday: 15 December 1844
Place of Birth: Dunkirk County, New York
Date of Death: 2 November 1910
Cemetery: Our Lady of Hope Cemetery—Chippewa Falls, Wisconsin
Entered Service at: Wapello, Louisa County, Iowa
Unit: Company L, 4th Iowa Cavalry
Battle or Place of Action: Columbus, Georgia
Date of Action: 16 April 1865
Date of Issue: 17 June 1865
Citation: Capture of flag in a personal encounter with its bearer.

284 ◆ COSGROVE, THOMAS

Rank: Private
Service: U.S. Army
Birthday: 12 June 1829
Place of Birth: County Galway, Ireland
Date of Death: 27 March 1912
Place of Death: East Lexington, Massachusetts
Cemetery: Munroe Cemetery (MH)—Lexington, Massachusetts
Entered Service at: East Stoughton, Norfolk County, Massachusetts
Unit: Company F, 40th Massachusetts Infantry
Battle or Place of Action: Drewry's Bluff, Virginia
Date of Action: 15 May 1864
Date of Issue: 7 November 1896
Citation: Individually demanded and received the surrender of seven armed Confederates concealed in a cellar, disarming and marching them in as prisoners of war.

285 ◆ COTTON, PETER

Rank: Ordinary Seaman (highest rank: Coxswain)
Service: U.S. Navy
Birthday: 1839
Place of Birth: New York, New York
Entered Service at: New York
Unit: U.S.S. *Baron De Kalb*
Battle or Place of Action: Yazoo River, Mississippi
Date of Action: 23-27 December 1862
G.O. Number, Date: 11, 3 April 1863
Citation: Cotton served on board the U.S.S. *Baron De Kalb* in the Yazoo River expedition, 23 to 27 December 1862. Proceeding under orders up the Yazoo River, the *Baron De Kalb*, with the object of capturing or destroying the enemy's

transports, came upon the steamers *John Walsh*, *R.J. Locklan*, *Golden Age*, and the *Scotland*, sunk on a bar where they were ordered to be burned. Continuing up the river, the *Baron De Kalb* was fired upon but, upon returning the fire, caused the enemy's retreat. Returning down the Yazoo, she destroyed and captured large quantities of enemy equipment and several prisoners. Serving bravely throughout this action, Cotton, as Coxswain, "distinguished himself in the various actions."

286 ◆ COUGHLIN, JOHN

Rank: Lieutenant Colonel (highest rank: Brevet Brigadier General)
Service: U.S. Army
Birthday: 1837
Place of Birth: Vermont
Date of Death: 27 May 1912
Cemetery: Arlington National Cemetery (2-936-WS) (MH)—Arlington, Virginia
Entered Service at: Manchester, Hillsborough County, New Hampshire
Unit: 10th New Hampshire Infantry (Irish Regiment)
Battle or Place of Action: Swift Creek, Virginia
Date of Action: 9 May 1864
Date of Issue: 31 August 1893
Citation: During a sudden night attack upon Burnham's Brigade, resulting in much confusion, this officer, without waiting for orders, led his regiment forward and interposed a line of battle between the advancing enemy and Hunt's Battery, repulsing the attack and saving the guns.

287 ◆ COX, ROBERT MITCHELL

Rank: Corporal
Service: U.S. Army
Birthday: 19 March 1845
Place of Birth: Guernsey County, Ohio
Date of Death: 26 October 1932
Place of Death: Prairie City, Illinois
Cemetery: Prairie City Cemetery (MH)—Prairie City, Illinois
Entered Service at: Prairie City, McDonough County, Illinois
Unit: Company K, 55th Illinois Infantry
Battle or Place of Action: Vicksburg, Mississippi
Date of Action: 22 May 1863
Date of Issue: 31 December 1892
Citation: Bravely defended the colors planted on the outward parapet of Fort Hill.

288 ◆ COYNE, JOHN NICHOLAS

Rank: Sergeant (highest rank: Lieutenant Colonel)
Service: U.S. Army
Birthday: 14 November 1839
Place of Birth: New York, New York
Date of Death: 4 March 1907
Place of Death: East Orange, New Jersey
Cemetery: The Green Wood Cemetery—Brooklyn, New York
Entered Service at: New York, New York
Unit: Company B, 70th New York Infantry
Battle or Place of Action: Williamsburg, Virginia
Date of Action: 5 May 1862
Date of Issue: 18 April 1888
Citation: Capture of a flag after a severe hand-to-hand contest; was mentioned in orders for his gallantry.

289 ◆ CRANSTON, WILLIAM WALLACE

Rank: Private (highest rank: Captain)
Service: U.S. Army
Birthday: 20 November 1838
Place of Birth: near Woodstock, Champaign County, Ohio
Date of Death: 7 December 1907
Place of Death: Parsons, Kansas
Cemetery: Oakwood Cemetery (MH)—Parsons, Kansas
Entered Service at: Urbana, Champaign County, Ohio
Unit: Company A, 66th Ohio Infantry
Battle or Place of Action: Chancellorsville, Virginia
Date of Action: 2 May 1863
Date of Issue: 15 December 1892
Citation: One of a party of four who voluntarily brought in a wounded Confederate officer from within the enemy's line in the face of a constant fire.

290 ◆ CRAWFORD, ALEXANDER

Rank: Fireman
Service: U.S. Navy
Birthday: 1842
Place of Birth: Philadelphia, Philadelphia County, Pennsylvania
Date of Death: 17 March 1886
Cemetery: Cedar Hill Cemetery—Philadelphia, Pennsylvania
Entered Service at: Philadelphia, Philadelphia County, Pennsylvania
Unit: U.S.S. *Wyalusing*
Battle or Place of Action: Roanoke River, North Carolina
Date of Action: 25 May 1864
G.O. Number, Date: 45, 31 December 1864
Citation: On board the U.S.S. *Wyalusing*, Crawford volunteered 25 May 1864, in a night attempt to destroy the rebel ram *Albemarle* in the Roanoke River. Taking part in a plan to explode the rebel ram *Albemarle*, Crawford executed his part in the plan with perfection, but upon being discovered, was forced to abandon the plan and retire, leaving no trace of the evidence. After spending two hazardous days and nights without food, he gained the safety of a friendly ship and was then transferred back to the *Wyalusing*. Though the plan failed, his skill and courage in preventing detection were an example of unfailing devotion to duty.

291 ◆ CREED, JOHN

Rank: Private (highest rank: Corporal)
Service: U.S. Army
Birthday: 1819
Place of Birth: Tipperary, County Tipperary, Ireland

Date of Death: 28 November 1872
Cemetery: Calvary Cemetery—Evanston, Illinois
Entered Service at: Chicago, Cook County, Illinois
Unit: Company D, 23d Illinois Infantry
Battle or Place of Action: Fisher's Hill, Virginia
Date of Action: 22 September 1864
Date of Issue: 6 October 1864
Citation: Capture of flag.

292 ◆ CRIPPS, THOMAS H.

Rank: Quartermaster
Service: U.S. Navy
Birthday: 29 November 1840
Place of Birth: Philadelphia, Philadelphia County, Pennsylvania
Date of Death: 8 December 1906
Place of Death: Philadelphia, Pennsylvania
Cemetery: Woodlands Cemetery (MH)—Philadelphia, Pennsylvania
Entered Service at: Pennsylvania
Unit: U.S.S. *Richmond*
Battle or Place of Action: Mobile Bay, Alabama
Date of Action: 5 August 1864
G.O. Number, Date: 45, 31 December 1864
Citation: As captain of a gun on board the U.S.S. *Richmond* during action against rebel forts and gunboats and with the ram *Tennessee* in Mobile Bay, 5 August 1864. Despite damage to his ship and the loss of several men on board as enemy fire raked her decks, Cripps fought his gun with skill and courage throughout a furious two-hour battle which resulted in the surrender of the rebel ram *Tennessee* and in the damaging and destruction of batteries at Fort Morgan.

293 ◆ CROCKER, HENRY H.

Rank: Captain
Service: U.S. Army
Birthday: 20 January 1839
Place of Birth: Colchester, New London County, Connecticut
Date of Death: 1913
Cemetery: Washington Cemetery (MH)—Washington, New Jersey
Entered Service at: San Francisco, San Francisco County, California
Unit: Company F, 2d Massachusetts Cavalry
Battle or Place of Action: Cedar Creek, Virginia
Date of Action: 19 October 1864
Date of Issue: 10 January 1896
Citation: Voluntarily led a charge, which resulted in the capture of 14 prisoners and in which he himself was wounded.

294 ◆ CROCKER, ULRIC LYONA

Rank: Private
Service: U.S. Army
Birthday: 5 September 1843
Place of Birth: Ohio
Date of Death: 2 February 1913
Place of Death: Manchester, Kansas
Cemetery: Medora Cemetery—Ruyle Township, Illinois
Entered Service at: Vergennes, Ohio
Unit: Company M, 6th Michigan Cavalry
Battle or Place of Action: Cedar Creek, Virginia
Date of Action: 19 October 1864
Date of Issue: 26 October 1864
Citation: Capture of flag of 18th Georgia (C.S.A.).

295 ◆ CROFT, JAMES E.

Rank: Private (highest rank: Second Lieutenant)
Service: U.S. Army
Birthday: 13 November 1833
Place of Birth: Yorkshire, England
Date of Death: 26 May 1914
Place of Death: Janesville, Wisconsin
Cemetery: Oak Hill Cemetery—Janesville, Wisconsin
Entered Service at: Janesville, Rock County, Wisconsin
Unit: 12th Battery, Wisconsin Light Artillery
Battle or Place of Action: Allatoona, Georgia
Date of Action: 5 October 1864
Date of Issue: 20 March 1897
Citation: Took the place of a gunner who had been shot down and inspired his comrades by his bravery and effective gunnery, which contributed largely to the defeat of the enemy.

296 ◆ CRONIN, CORNELIUS

Rank: Chief Quartermaster (highest rank: Chief Gunner)
Service: U.S. Navy
Birthday: 10 March 1838
Place of Birth: Ireland
Date of Death: 18 August 1912
Place of Death: Brooklyn, New York
Cemetery: 1st Calvary Cemetery—Woodside, New York
Entered Service at: Michigan
Unit: U.S.S. *Richmond*
Battle or Place of Action: Mobile Bay, Alabama; Forts Jackson & St. Philip; New Orleans, Louisiana; below Vicksburg, Mississippi
Date of Action: 5 August 1864
G.O. Number, Date: 45, 31 December 1864
Citation: On board the U.S.S. *Richmond* in action at Mobile Bay, 5 August 1864. Cool and vigilant at his station throughout the prolonged action, Cronin watched for signals and skillfully steered the ship as she trained her guns on Fort Morgan and on other ships of the Confederacy despite extremely heavy return fire. He participated in the actions at Forts Jackson and St. Philip, with the Chalmette batteries, at the surrender of New Orleans, and in the attacks on batteries below Vicksburg.

297 ◆ CROSIER, WILLIAM HENRY HARRISON

Rank: Sergeant (highest rank: Color Sergeant)
Service: U.S. Army

Birthday: 5 May 1844
Place of Birth: Skaneateles, Onondaga County, New York
Date of Death: 14 March 1903
Place of Death: Ogdensburg, New York
Cemetery: Oakwood Morningside Cemetery (MH)—Syracuse, New York
Entered Service at: Skaneateles, Onondaga County, New York
Unit: Company G, 149th New York Infantry
Battle or Place of Action: Peach Tree Creek, Georgia
Date of Action: 20 July 1864
Date of Issue: 12 January 1892
Citation: Severely wounded and ambushed by the enemy, he stripped the colors from the staff and brought them back into the line.

298 ◆ CROSS, JAMES EDWIN

Rank: Corporal (highest rank: Sergeant Major)
Service: U.S. Army
Birthday: 27 March 1840
Place of Birth: Darien, Genesee County, New York
Date of Death: 6 January 1917
Place of Death: Albany, New York
Cemetery: Albany Rural Cemetery (MH)—Albany, New York
Entered Service at: Batavia, Genesee County, New York
Unit: Company K, 12th New York Infantry (Independence Guard)
Battle or Place of Action: Blackburn's Ford, Virginia
Date of Action: 18 July 1861
Date of Issue: 5 April 1898
Citation: With a companion, refused to retreat when the part of the regiment to which he was attached was driven back in disorder, but remained upon the skirmish line for some time thereafter, firing upon the enemy.

299 ◆ CROWLEY, MICHAEL

Rank: Private
Service: U.S. Army
Birthday: 1829
Place of Birth: Rochester, Monroe County, New York
Date of Death: 12 May 1888
Place of Death: Worcester, Massachusetts
Cemetery: unknown cemetery—Boston, Massachusetts
Entered Service at: Rochester, Monroe County, New York
Unit: Company A, 22d New York Cavalry
Battle or Place of Action: Waynesboro, Virginia
Date of Action: 2 March 1865
Date of Issue: 26 March 1865
Citation: Capture of flag.

300 ◆ CULLEN, THOMAS

Rank: Corporal
Service: U.S. Army
Birthday: 26 February 1839
Place of Birth: Ireland
Date of Death: 17 August 1913
Cemetery: St. Mary's Cemetery (MH)—Kinny, Pennsylvania
Entered Service at: New York, New York
Unit: Company I, 82d New York Infantry
Battle or Place of Action: Bristoe Station, Virginia
Date of Action: 14 October 1863
Date of Issue: 1 December 1864
Citation: Capture of flag of 22d or 28th North Carolina (C.S.A.).

301 ◆ CUMMINGS, AMOS JAY

Rank: Sergeant Major
Service: U.S. Army
Birthday: 15 May 1838
Place of Birth: Conklin, Broome County, New York
Date of Death: 2 May 1902
Cemetery: Clinton Cemetery (MH)—Irvington, New Jersey
Entered Service at: Irvington, Essex County, New Jersey
Unit: 26th New Jersey Infantry
Battle or Place of Action: Salem Heights, Virginia
Date of Action: 4 May 1863
Date of Issue: 28 March 1894
Citation: Rendered great assistance in the heat of the action in rescuing a part of the field batteries from an extremely dangerous and exposed position.

302 ◆ CUMPSTON, JAMES M.

True Name: Compston, James M.
Rank: Private
Service: U.S. Army
Birthday: 1837
Place of Birth: Gallia County, Ohio
Date of Death: 24 May 1888
Place of Death: Coalton, Ohio
Cemetery: unknown cemetery—Coalton, Ohio
Entered Service at: Portsmouth, Scioto County, Ohio
Unit: Company D, 91st Ohio Infantry
Battle or Place of Action: Shenandoah Valley Campaign, Virginia
Date of Action: August-November 1864
Citation: Capture of flag.

303 ◆ CUNNINGHAM, FRANCIS MARION

Rank: First Sergeant (highest rank: First Lieutenant)
Service: U.S. Army
Birthday: 31 December 1837
Place of Birth: Somerset, Somerset County, Pennsylvania
Date of Death: 11 May 1919
Cemetery: Sugar Grove Cemetery—Ohiopyle, Pennsylvania
Entered Service at: Springfield, Delaware County, Pennsylvania
Unit: Company H, 1st West Virginia Cavalry
Battle or Place of Action: Deatonsville (Sailor's Creek), Virginia
Date of Action: 6 April 1865
Date of Issue: 3 May 1865

Citation: Capture of battle flag of 12th Virginia Infantry (C.S.A.) in hand-to-hand battle while wounded.

304 ◆ CUNNINGHAM, JAMES SMITH

Rank: Private
Service: U.S. Army
Birthday: 31 December 1840
Place of Birth: Washington County, Pennsylvania
Date of Death: 1 April 1921
Cemetery: Big Creek Cemetery—Burlington, Kansas
Entered Service at: Bloomington, McLean County, Illinois
Unit: Company D, 8th Missouri Infantry
Battle or Place of Action: Vicksburg, Mississippi
Date of Action: 22 May 1863
Date of Issue: 30 July 1894
Citation: Gallantry in the charge of the "volunteer storming party."

305 ◆ CURRAN, RICHARD J.

Rank: Assistant Surgeon (highest rank: Surgeon)
Service: U.S. Army
Birthday: 4 January 1834
Place of Birth: Ennis, County Clare, Ireland
Date of Death: 1 June 1915
Cemetery: Holy Sepulchre Cemetery (MH)—Rochester, New York
Entered Service at: Seneca Falls, Seneca County, New York
Unit: 33d New York Infantry
Battle or Place of Action: Antietam, Maryland
Date of Action: 17 September 1862
Date of Issue: 30 March 1898
Citation: Voluntarily exposed himself to great danger by going to the fighting line, there succoring the wounded and helpless, and conducting them to the field hospital.

306 ◆ CURTIS, JOHN CALVIN

Rank: Sergeant Major (highest rank: First Lieutenant)
Service: U.S. Army
Birthday: 19 April 1845
Place of Birth: Bridgeport, Fairfield County, Connecticut
Date of Death: 17 January 1917
Cemetery: Mountain Grove Cemetery (MH)—Bridgeport, Connecticut
Entered Service at: Bridgeport, Fairfield County, Connecticut
Unit: 9th Connecticut Infantry
Battle or Place of Action: Baton Rouge, Louisiana
Date of Action: 5 August 1862
Date of Issue: 16 December 1896
Citation: Voluntarily sought the line of battle and alone and unaided captured two prisoners, driving them before him to regimental headquarters at the point of the bayonet.

307 ◆ CURTIS, JOSIAH M.

Rank: Second Lieutenant (highest rank: First Lieutenant)
Service: U.S. Army
Birthday: 16 November 1844
Place of Birth: Ohio County, West Virginia
Date of Death: 17 June 1875
Place of Death: West Liberty, West Virginia
Cemetery: West Liberty Cemetery—West Liberty, West Virginia
Entered Service at: West Liberty, Ohio County, West Virginia
Unit: Company I, 12th West Virginia Infantry
Battle or Place of Action: Petersburg, Virginia
Date of Action: 2 April 1865
Date of Issue: 12 May 1865
Citation: Seized the colors of his regiment after two color bearers had fallen, bore them gallantly, and was among the first to gain a foothold, with his flag, inside the enemy's works.

308 ◆ CURTIS, NEWTON MARTIN

Rank: Brigadier General (highest rank: Major General)
Service: U.S. Army
Birthday: 21 May 1835
Place of Birth: De Peyster, St. Lawrence County, New York
Date of Death: 8 January 1910
Place of Death: New York, New York
Cemetery: Ogdensburg Cemetery—Ogdensburg, New York
Entered Service at: De Peyster, St. Lawrence County, New York
Unit: U.S. Volunteers
Battle or Place of Action: Fort Fisher, North Carolina
Date of Action: 15 January 1865
Date of Issue: 28 November 1891
Citation: The first man to pass through the stockade, he personally led each assault on the traverses and was four times wounded.

309 ◆ CUSTER, THOMAS WARD✛

Rank: Second Lieutenant (highest rank: Lieutenant Colonel)
Service: U.S. Army
Birthday: 15 March 1845
Place of Birth: New Rumley, Harrison County, Ohio
Date of Death: 25 June 1876
Place of Death: Little Big Horn, Montana
Cemetery: Fort Leavenworth Cemetery (H-1488)—Fort Leavenworth, Kansas
Entered Service at: Monroe, Monroe County, Michigan
Unit: Company B, 6th Michigan Cavalry
Battle or Place of Action: Willicomack (Namozine Church) & Deatonsville (Sailor's Creek), Virginia
Date of Action: 3 April 1865 & 6 April 1865
Date of Issue: 3 May 1865 & 26 May 1865
Citation: **First Award** Capture of flag on 3 April 1865.
Second Award Second Lt. Custer leaped his horse over the enemy's works and captured two stands of colors, having his horse shot from under him and receiving a severe wound.
Notes: ✛Double Awardee

310 ◆ CUTCHEON, BYRON M.

Rank: Major (highest rank: Brevet Brigadier General)
Service: U.S. Army
Birthday: 11 May 1836
Place of Birth: Pembroke, Suncook County, New Hampshire
Date of Death: 12 April 1908
Cemetery: Highland Cemetery—Ypsilanti, Michigan
Entered Service at: Ypsilanti, Washtenaw County, Michigan
Unit: 20th Michigan Infantry
Battle or Place of Action: Horseshoe Bend, Kentucky
Date of Action: 10 May 1863
Date of Issue: 29 June 1891
Citation: Distinguished gallantry in leading his regiment in a charge on a house occupied by the enemy.

311 ◆ CUTTS, JAMES MADISON

Rank: Captain (highest rank: Brevet Lieutenant Colonel)
Service: U.S. Army
Birthday: 1838
Place of Birth: Washington, D.C.
Date of Death: 24 February 1903
Cemetery: Arlington National Cemetery (3-1371-SS) (MH)—Arlington, Virginia
Entered Service at: Providence, Providence County, Rhode Island
Unit: 11th U.S. Infantry
Battle or Place of Action: Wilderness Campaign, Spotsylvania & Petersburg, Virginia
Date of Action: 1864
Date of Issue: 2 May 1891
Citation: Gallantry in actions.

312 ◆ DARROUGH, JOHN S.

Rank: Sergeant
Service: U.S. Army
Birthday: 6 April 1841
Place of Birth: Maysville, Mason County, Kentucky
Date of Death: 14 October 1920
Cemetery: Grand Army of the Republic Cemetery (MH)—Watseka, Illinois
Entered Service at: Concord, Morgan County, Illinois
Unit: Company F, 113th Illinois Infantry
Battle or Place of Action: Eastport, Mississippi
Date of Action: 10 October 1864
Date of Issue: 5 February 1895
Citation: Saved the life of a captain.

313 ◆ DAVIDSIZER, JOHN A.

Rank: Sergeant
Service: U.S. Army
Birthday: 26 April 1834
Place of Birth: Milford, Pike County, Pennsylvania
Date of Death: 19 October 1913
Place of Death: Lewistown, Pennsylvania
Cemetery: First Methodist Cemetery—Lewistown, Pennsylvania
Entered Service at: Lewistown, Mifflin County, Pennsylvania
Unit: Company A, 1st Pennsylvania Cavalry
Battle or Place of Action: Paine's Crossroads, Virginia
Date of Action: 5 April 1865
Date of Issue: 3 May 1865
Citation: Capture of flag.

314 ◆ DAVIDSON, ANDREW

Rank: Assistant Surgeon
Service: U.S. Army
Birthday: 1819
Place of Birth: Middlebury, Addison County, Vermont
Date of Death: 30 June 1901
Cemetery: Forest Rose Cemetery—Lancaster, Ohio
Entered Service at: Cincinnati, Hamilton County, Ohio
Unit: 47th Ohio Infantry
Battle or Place of Action: Vicksburg, Mississippi
Date of Action: 3 May 1863
Date of Issue: 17 October 1892
Citation: Voluntarily attempted to run the enemy's batteries.

315 ◆ DAVIDSON, ANDREW

Rank: First Lieutenant (highest rank: Colonel)
Service: U.S. Army
Birthday: 12 February 1840
Place of Birth: Morebattle, Roxburghshire, Scotland
Date of Death: 10 November 1902
Place of Death: Bath, New York
Cemetery: Lakewood Cemetery (MH)—Cooperstown, New York
Entered Service at: Middlefield, Otsego County, New York
Unit: Company H, 30th U.S. Colored Troops
Battle or Place of Action: Petersburg at the mine, Virginia
Date of Action: 30 July 1864
Date of Issue: 17 October 1892
Citation: One of the first to enter the enemy's works, where, after his colonel, major, and one-third of the company's officers had fallen, he gallantly assisted in rallying and saving the remnant of the command.

316 ◆ DAVIS, CHARLES C.

Rank: Major
Service: U.S. Army
Birthday: 15 August 1830
Place of Birth: Harrisburg, Dauphin County, Pennsylvania
Date of Death: 20 January 1909
Place of Death: Harrisburg, Pennsylvania
Cemetery: Harrisburg Cemetery—Harrisburg, Pennsylvania
Entered Service at: Harrisburg, Dauphin County, Pennsylvania
Unit: 7th Pennsylvania Cavalry
Battle or Place of Action: Shelbyville, Tennessee

Date of Action: 27 June 1863
Date of Issue: 14 June 1894
Citation: Led one of the most desperate and successful charges of the war.

317 ◆ DAVIS, FREEMAN

Rank: Sergeant (highest rank: Captain)
Service: U.S. Army
Birthday: 28 February 1842
Place of Birth: Newcomerstown, Tuscarawas County, Ohio
Date of Death: 23 February 1899
Place of Death: Butler, Missouri
Cemetery: Oak Hill Cemetery (MH)—Butler, Missouri
Entered Service at: Newcomerstown, Tuscarawas County, Ohio
Unit: Company B, 80th Ohio Infantry
Battle or Place of Action: Missionary Ridge, Tennessee
Date of Action: 25 November 1863
Date of Issue: 30 March 1898
Citation: This soldier, while his regiment was falling back, seeing the two color bearers shot down, under a severe fire and at imminent peril recovered both the flags and saved them from capture.

318 ◆ DAVIS, GEORGE EVANS

Rank: First Lieutenant (highest rank: Captain)
Service: U.S. Army
Birthday: 26 December 1839
Place of Birth: Dunstable, Middlesex County, Massachusetts
Date of Death: 28 June 1926
Place of Death: Soldier's Home, Burlington, Vermont
Cemetery: Lake View Cemetery (MH)—Burlington, Vermont
Entered Service at: Burlington, Chittenden County, Vermont
Unit: Company D, 10th Vermont Infantry
Battle or Place of Action: Monocacy, Maryland
Date of Action: 9 July 1864
Date of Issue: 27 May 1892
Citation: While in command of a small force, held the approaches to the two bridges against repeated assaults of superior numbers, thereby materially delaying Early's advance on Washington.

319 ◆ DAVIS, HARRY CLAY

Rank: Private (highest rank: Corporal)
Service: U.S. Army
Birthday: 5 February 1841
Place of Birth: Franklin County, Ohio
Date of Death: 9 July 1929
Place of Death: Pomona, California
Cemetery: Pomona Cemetery—Pomona, California
Entered Service at: Columbus, Franklin County, Ohio
Unit: Company G, 46th Ohio Infantry
Battle or Place of Action: Atlanta, Georgia
Date of Action: 28 July 1864
Date of Issue: 2 December 1864
Citation: Capture of flag of 30th Louisiana Infantry (C.S.A.).

320 ◆ DAVIS, JOHN

Rank: Quarter Gunner
Service: U.S. Navy
Place of Birth: Cedarville, Cumberland County, New Jersey
Entered Service at: New Jersey
Unit: U.S.S. *Valley City*
Battle or Place of Action: off Elizabeth City, North Carolina
Date of Action: 10 February 1862
G.O. Number, Date: 11, 3 April 1863
Citation: Served on board the U.S.S. *Valley City* during action against rebel fort batteries and ships off Elizabeth City, N.C., 10 February 1862. When a shell from the shore penetrated the side and passed through the magazine, exploding outside the screen on the berth deck, several powder divisions protecting bulkheads were torn to pieces and the forward part of the berth deck set on fire. Showing great presence of mind, Davis courageously covered a barrel of powder with his own body and prevented an explosion, while at the same time passing powder to provide the division on the upper deck while under fierce enemy fire.

321 ◆ DAVIS, JOHN

Rank: Private
Service: U.S. Army
Birthday: 1838
Place of Birth: Carroll, Kentucky
Date of Death: 30 December 1901
Place of Death: Cotopaxi, Colorado
Cemetery: unknown cemetery—Cotopaxi, Colorado (Now an abandoned town.)
Entered Service at: Indianapolis, Marion County, Indiana
Unit: Company F, 17th Indiana Mounted Infantry
Battle or Place of Action: Culloden, Georgia
Date of Action: April 1865
Date of Issue: 17 June 1865
Citation: Capture of flag of Worrill Grays (C.S.A.).
Notes: POW

322 ◆ DAVIS, JOSEPH

Rank: Corporal
Service: U.S. Army
Birthday: 22 May 1838
Place of Birth: Monmouth County, Wales
Entered Service at: East Palestine, Columbiana County, Ohio
Unit: Company C, 104th Ohio Infantry
Battle or Place of Action: Franklin, Tennessee
Date of Action: 30 October 1864
Date of Issue: 4 February 1865
Citation: Capture of flag.

323 ◆ DAVIS, MARTIN K.

Rank: Sergeant
Service: U.S. Army
Birthday: 12 March 1843
Place of Birth: Marion, Williamson County, Illinois
Date of Death: 14 December 1936
Cemetery: Demorest Cemetery (MH)—Demorest, Georgia
Entered Service at: Stonington, Christian County, Illinois
Unit: Company H, 116th Illinois Infantry
Battle or Place of Action: Vicksburg, Mississippi
Date of Action: 22 May 1863
Date of Issue: 26 July 1894
Citation: Gallantry in the charge of the "volunteer storming party."

324 ◆ DAVIS, SAMUEL W.

Rank: Ordinary Seaman
Service: U.S. Navy
Birthday: 1845
Place of Birth: Brewer, Penobscot County, Maine
Entered Service at: Maine
Unit: U.S.S. *Brooklyn*
Battle or Place of Action: Mobile Bay, Alabama
Date of Action: 5 August 1864
G.O. Number, Date: 45, 31 December 1864
Citation: On board the U.S.S. *Brooklyn* during successful attacks against Fort Morgan, rebel gunboats and the ram *Tennessee* in Mobile Bay, 5 August 1864. Despite severe damage to his ship and the loss of several men on board as enemy fire raked the decks from stem to stern, Davis exercised extreme courage and vigilance while acting as a lookout for torpedoes and other obstructions throughout the furious battle which resulted in the surrender of the prize rebel ram *Tennessee* and in the damaging and destruction of batteries at Fort Morgan.

325 ◆ DAVIS, THOMAS

Rank: Private
Service: U.S. Army
Birthday: 11 December 1837
Place of Birth: Haverford, West Wales
Date of Death: 24 March 1919
Place of Death: Brooklyn, New York
Cemetery: Mount Olivet Cemetery—Brooklyn, New York
Entered Service at: New York, New York
Unit: Company C, 2d New York Heavy Artillery
Battle or Place of Action: Deatonsville (Sailor's Creek), Virginia
Date of Action: 6 April 1865
Date of Issue: 3 May 1865
Citation: Capture of flag.

326 ◆ DAY, CHARLES

Rank: Private
Service: U.S. Army
Birthday: 28 May 1844
Place of Birth: West Laurens, Otsego County, New York
Date of Death: 29 July 1901
Place of Death: Lambs Creek, Pennsylvania
Cemetery: Prospect Cemetery (MH)—Mansfield, Pennsylvania
Entered Service at: Richmond, Philadelphia County, Pennsylvania
Unit: Company K, 210th Pennsylvania Infantry
Battle or Place of Action: Hatcher's Run, Virginia
Date of Action: 6 February 1865
Date of Issue: 20 July 1897
Citation: Seized the colors of another regiment of the brigade, the regiment having been thrown into confusion and the color bearer killed, and bore said colors throughout the remainder of the engagement.

327 ◆ DAY, DAVID FRAKES

Rank: Private
Service: U.S. Army
Birthday: 7 March 1847
Place of Birth: Dallasburg, Ohio
Date of Death: 22 June 1914
Place of Death: Durango, Colorado
Cemetery: Riverside Cemetery (MH)—Denver, Colorado
Entered Service at: Cincinnati, Hamilton County, Ohio
Unit: Company D, 57th Ohio Infantry
Battle or Place of Action: Vicksburg, Mississippi
Date of Action: 22 May 1863
Date of Issue: 2 January 1895
Citation: Gallantry in the charge of the "volunteer storming party."

328 ◆ DEAKIN, CHARLES

Rank: Boatswain's Mate
Service: U.S. Navy
Birthday: 1837
Place of Birth: New York, New York
Entered Service at: Philadelphia, Philadelphia County, Pennsylvania
Unit: U.S.S. *Richmond*
Battle or Place of Action: Mobile Bay, Alabama
Date of Action: 5 August 1864
G.O. Number, Date: 45, 31 December 1864
Citation: As captain of a gun on board the U.S.S. *Richmond* during action against rebel forts and gunboats and with the ram *Tennessee* in Mobile Bay, 5 August 1864. Despite damage to his ship and the loss of several men on board as enemy fire raked her decks, Deakin fought his gun with skill and courage throughout a furious two-hour battle which resulted in the surrender of the rebel ram *Tennessee* and in the damaging and destruction of batteries at Fort Morgan. He also participated in the actions at Forts Jackson and St. Philip.

329 ◆ DEANE, JOHN MILTON

Rank: Major
Service: U.S. Army

Birthday: 8 January 1840
Place of Birth: Assonet Village, Bristol County, Massachusetts
Date of Death: 2 September 1914
Cemetery: Assonet Burial Grounds (MH)—Freetown, Massachusetts
Entered Service at: Freetown, Bristol County, Massachusetts
Unit: 29th Massachusetts Infantry
Battle or Place of Action: Fort Stedman, Virginia
Date of Action: 25 March 1865
Date of Issue: 8 March 1895
Citation: This officer, observing an abandoned gun within Fort Haskell, called for volunteers, and under a heavy fire, worked the gun until the enemy's advancing line was routed.

330 ◆ DECASTRO, JOSEPH H.

Rank: Corporal (highest rank: Sergeant)
Service: U.S. Army
Birthday: 14 November 1844
Place of Birth: Boston, Suffolk County, Massachusetts
Date of Death: 8 May 1892
Place of Death: New York, New York
Cemetery: Fairmount Cemetery (MH)—Newark, New Jersey
Entered Service at: Boston, Suffolk County, Massachusetts
Unit: Company I, 19th Massachusetts Infantry
Battle or Place of Action: Gettysburg, Pennsylvania
Date of Action: 3 July 1863
Date of Issue: 1 December 1864
Citation: Capture of flag of 19th Virginia regiment (C.S.A.).

331 ◆ DELACEY, PATRICK

Rank: First Sergeant (highest rank: Second Lieutenant)
Service: U.S. Army
Birthday: 25 November 1835
Place of Birth: Carbondale, Lackawanna County, Pennsylvania
Date of Death: 27 April 1915
Place of Death: Scranton, Pennsylvania
Cemetery: St. Catherine's Cemetery (MH)—Moscow, Pennsylvania
Entered Service at: Scranton, Lackawanna County, Pennsylvania
Unit: Company A, 143d Pennsylvania Infantry
Battle or Place of Action: Wilderness Campaign, Virginia
Date of Action: 6 May 1864
Date of Issue: 24 April 1894
Citation: Running ahead of the line, under a concentrated fire, he shot the color bearer of a Confederate regiment on the works, thus contributing to the success of the attack.

332 ◆ DELAND, FREDERICK NELSON

Rank: Private
Service: U.S. Army
Birthday: 25 December 1843
Place of Birth: Sheffield, Berkshire County, Massachusetts
Date of Death: 23 August 1922
Place of Death: Pittsfield, Massachusetts
Cemetery: Mahaiwe Cemetery (MH)—Great Barrington, Massachusetts
Entered Service at: Great Barrington, Berkshire County, Massachusetts
Unit: Company B, 49th Massachusetts Infantry
Battle or Place of Action: Port Hudson, Louisiana
Date of Action: 27 May 1863
Date of Issue: 22 June 1896
Citation: Volunteered in response to a call and, under a heavy fire from the enemy, advanced and assisted in filling with fascines a ditch which presented a serious obstacle to the troops attempting to take the works of the enemy by assault.

333 ◆ DELANEY, JOHN CARROLL

Rank: Sergeant (highest rank: Brevet Captain)
Service: U.S. Army
Birthday: 22 April 1848
Place of Birth: Ireland
Date of Death: 4 April 1915
Cemetery: Arlington National Cemetery (3-2170-WS)—Arlington, Virginia
Entered Service at: Honesdale, Wayne County, Pennsylvania
Unit: Company I, 107th Pennsylvania Infantry
Battle or Place of Action: Danby's Mills, Virginia
Date of Action: 6 February 1865
Date of Issue: 29 August 1894
Citation: Sprang between the lines and brought out a wounded comrade about to be burned in the brush.

334 ◆ DELAVIE, HIRAM H.

True Name: Delavie, Hiram A.
Rank: Sergeant (highest rank: First Sergeant)
Service: U.S. Army
Place of Birth: Stark County, Ohio
Entered Service at: Allegheny County, Pennsylvania
Unit: Company I, 11th Pennsylvania Infantry (Washington Blues)
Battle or Place of Action: Five Forks, Virginia
Date of Action: 1 April 1865
Date of Issue: 10 May 1865
Citation: Capture of flag.

335 ◆ DEMPSTER, JOHN

Rank: Coxswain
Service: U.S. Navy
Birthday: 1839
Place of Birth: Scotland
Entered Service at: Philadelphia, Philadelphia County, Pennsylvania
Unit: U.S.S. *New Ironsides*
Battle or Place of Action: Fort Fisher, North Carolina
Date of Action: 24-25 December 1864 & 13-15 January 1865

G.O. Number, Date: 59, 22 June 1865
Citation: Dempster served on board the U.S.S. *New Ironsides* during action in several attacks on Fort Fisher, 24 and 25 December 1864; and 13, 14, and 15 January 1865. The ship steamed in and took the lead in the ironclad division close inshore and immediately opened its starboard battery in a barrage of well-directed fire to cause several fires and explosions and dismount several guns during the first two days of fighting. Taken under fire as she steamed into position on 13 January, the *New Ironsides* fought all day and took on ammunition at night despite severe weather conditions. When the enemy came out of his bomb-proofs to defend the fort against the storming party, the ship's battery disabled nearly every gun on the fort facing the shore before the cease-fire orders were given by the flagship.

336 ◆ DENIG, J. HENRY

Rank: Sergeant
Service: U.S. Marine Corps
Birthday: 1839
Place of Birth: York, York County, Pennsylvania
Entered Service at: Pennsylvania
Unit: U.S.S. *Brooklyn*
Battle or Place of Action: Mobile Bay, Alabama
Date of Action: 5 August 1864
G.O. Number, Date: 45, 31 December 1864
Citation: On board the U.S.S. *Brooklyn* during action against rebel forts and gunboats and with the ram *Tennessee*, in Mobile Bay, 5 August 1864. Despite severe damage to his ship and the loss of several men on board as enemy fire raked the decks, Sgt. Denig fought his gun with skill and courage throughout the furious two-hour battle which resulted in the surrender of the rebel ram *Tennessee* and in the damaging and destruction of batteries at Fort Morgan.

337 ◆ *DENNING, LORENZO

True Name: Deming, Lorenzo
Rank: Landsman
Service: U.S. Navy
Birthday: 6 September 1843
Place of Birth: Granby, Hartford County, Connecticut
Date of Death: 8 February 1865
Place of Death: Salisbury Prison, North Carolina
Cemetery: Salisbury National Cemetery—Salisbury, North Carolina (One of 11,700 unknowns buried in a long trench.)
Entered Service at: New Britain, Hartford County, Connecticut
Unit: U.S. Picket Boat No. 1
Battle or Place of Action: Plymouth, North Carolina
Date of Action: 27 October 1864
G.O. Number, Date: 45, 31 December 1864
Citation: Denning served on board the U.S. Picket Boat No. 1 in action, 27 October 1864, against the Confederate ram *Albemarle* which had resisted repeated attacks by our steamers and had kept a large force of vessels employed in watching her. The picket boat, equipped with a spar torpedo, succeeded in passing the enemy pickets within 20 yards without being discovered and then made for the *Albemarle* under a full head of steam. Immediately taken under fire by the ram, the small boat plunged on, jumped the log boom which encircled the target and exploded its torpedo under the port bow of the ram. The picket boat was destroyed by enemy fire and almost the entire crew was taken prisoner or lost.
Notes: POW

338 ◆ DENNIS, RICHARD

Rank: Boatswain's Mate
Service: U.S. Navy
Birthday: 1826
Place of Birth: Charlestown, Suffolk County, Massachusetts
Entered Service at: Boston, Suffolk County, Massachusetts
Unit: U.S.S. *Brooklyn*
Battle or Place of Action: Mobile Bay, Alabama
Date of Action: 5 August 1864
G.O. Number, Date: 45, 31 December 1864
Citation: On board the U.S.S. *Brooklyn* during successful attacks against Fort Morgan, rebel gunboats and the ram *Tennessee* in Mobile Bay, 5 August 1864. Despite severe damage to his ship and the loss of several men on board as enemy fire raked her decks from stem to stern, Dennis displayed outstanding skill and courage in operating the torpedo catcher and in assisting in working the bow chasers throughout the furious battle which resulted in the surrender of the prize rebel ram *Tennessee* and in the damaging and destruction of batteries at Fort Morgan.

339 ◆ DENSMORE, WILLIAM

Rank: Chief Boatswain's Mate
Service: U.S. Navy
Birthday: 1843
Place of Birth: New York
Date of Death: 17 June 1865
Place of Death: Philadelphia (Naval Hospital), Pennsylvania
Cemetery: unknown cemetery—Philadelphia, Pennsylvania
Entered Service at: New York
Unit: U.S.S. *Richmond*
Battle or Place of Action: Mobile Bay, Alabama
Date of Action: 5 August 1864
G.O. Number, Date: 45, 31 December 1864
Citation: As captain of a gun on board the U.S.S. *Richmond* during action against rebel forts and gunboats and with the ram *Tennessee* in Mobile Bay, 5 August 1864. Despite damage to his ship and the loss of several men on board as enemy fire raked her decks, Densmore fought his gun with skill and courage throughout a furious two-hour battle, which resulted in the surrender of the rebel ram *Tennessee* and in the damaging and destruction of batteries at Fort Morgan.

340 ◆ DEPUY, CHARLES H.

Rank: First Sergeant
Service: U.S. Army
Birthday: 8 September 1842
Place of Birth: Sherman, Michigan

Date of Death: 6 January 1935
Cemetery: Evergreen Cemetery—Kalkaska, Michigan
Entered Service at: St. Louis, St. Louis County, Missouri
Unit: Company H, 1st Michigan Sharpshooters
Battle or Place of Action: Petersburg, Virginia
Date of Action: 30 July 1864
Date of Issue: 30 July 1896
Citation: Being an old artillerist, De Puy aided Gen. Bartlett in working the guns of the dismantled fort.
Notes: POW

341 ◆ DEWITT, RICHARD WILLIS

Rank: Corporal (highest rank: Sergeant)
Service: U.S. Army
Birthday: 25 June 1838
Place of Birth: Butler County, Ohio
Date of Death: 16 September 1909
Place of Death: Terre Haute, Indiana
Cemetery: Oxford Cemetery—Oxford, Ohio
Entered Service at: Oxford, Butler County, Ohio
Unit: Company D, 47th Ohio Infantry
Battle or Place of Action: Vicksburg, Mississippi
Date of Action: 22 May 1863
Date of Issue: 10 August 1894
Citation: Gallantry in the charge of the "volunteer storming party."

342 ◆ DI CESNOLA, LOUIS PALMA

Rank: Colonel (highest rank: Brevet Brigadier General)
Service: U.S. Army
Birthday: 29 June 1832
Place of Birth: Rivarola, Piedmont, Italy
Date of Death: 20 November 1904
Cemetery: Kensico Cemetery—Valhalla, New York
Entered Service at: New York, New York
Unit: 4th New York Cavalry
Battle or Place of Action: Aldie, Virginia
Date of Action: 17 June 1863
Date of Issue: 6 December 1897
Citation: Was present, in arrest, when, seeing his regiment fall back, he rallied his men, accompanied them, without arms, in a second charge, and in recognition of his gallantry was released from arrest. He continued in the action at the head of his regiment until he was desperately wounded and taken prisoner.
Notes: POW

343 ◆ DICKEY, WILLIAM DONALDSON

Rank: Captain (highest rank: Colonel)
Service: U.S. Army
Birthday: 11 January 1845
Place of Birth: Newburgh, Orange County, New York
Date of Death: 14 May 1924
Place of Death: Brooklyn, New York
Cemetery: The Green Wood Cemetery—Brooklyn, New York
Entered Service at: Newburgh, Orange County, New York
Unit: Battery M, 15th New York Heavy Artillery
Battle or Place of Action: Petersburg, Virginia
Date of Action: 17 June 1864
Date of Issue: 10 June 1896
Citation: Refused to leave the field, remaining in command after being wounded by a piece of shell, and led his command in the assault on the enemy's works on the following day.

344 ◆ DICKIE, DAVID

Rank: Sergeant
Service: U.S. Army
Birthday: 13 July 1841
Place of Birth: Scotland
Date of Death: 26 August 1904
Cemetery: Gillespie Cemetery (MH)—Gillespie, Illinois
Entered Service at: Gillespie, Macoupin County, Illinois
Unit: Company A, 97th Illinois Infantry
Battle or Place of Action: Vicksburg, Mississippi
Date of Action: 22 May 1863
Date of Issue: 29 January 1896
Citation: Gallantry in the charge of the "volunteer storming party."

345 ◆ DIGGINS, BARTHOLOMEW

Rank: Ordinary Seaman
Service: U.S. Navy
Birthday: 9 October 1844
Place of Birth: Baltimore, Baltimore County, Maryland
Date of Death: 23 February 1917
Place of Death: Washington, D.C.
Cemetery: Arlington National Cemetery (13-5400-15)—Arlington, Virginia
Entered Service at: Maryland
Unit: U.S.S. *Hartford*
Battle or Place of Action: Mobile Bay, Alabama
Date of Action: 5 August 1864
G.O. Number, Date: 391, 12 November 1891
Citation: On board the flagship U.S.S. *Hartford*, during action against rebel forts and gunboats and with the ram *Tennessee* in Mobile Bay, 5 August 1864. Despite damage to his ship and the loss of several men on board as enemy fire raked her decks, Diggins as loader of a gun remained steadfast at his post throughout the furious two-hour battle which resulted in the surrender of the rebel ram *Tennessee* and in the damaging and destruction of batteries at Fort Morgan.

346 ◆ DILGER, HUBERT

Rank: Captain
Service: U.S. Army
Birthday: 5 March 1836
Place of Birth: Germany
Date of Death: 14 May 1911
Place of Death: near Front Royal, Virginia
Cemetery: Rock Creek Cemetery—Washington, D.C.

Entered Service at: New York, New York
Unit: Battery I, 1st Ohio Light Artillery
Battle or Place of Action: Chancellorsville, Virginia
Date of Action: 2 May 1863
Date of Issue: 17 August 1893
Citation: Fought his guns until the enemy were upon him, then with one gun hauled in the road by hand he formed the rear guard and kept the enemy at bay by the rapidity of his fire and was the last man in the retreat.

347 ◆ DILLON, MICHAEL A.

Rank: Private
Service: U.S. Army
Birthday: 29 September 1839
Place of Birth: Chelmsford, Middlesex County, Massachusetts
Date of Death: 6 October 1904
Cemetery: Arlington National Cemetery (13-14660)—Arlington, Virginia
Entered Service at: Wilton, Hillsborough County, New Hampshire
Unit: Company G, 2d New Hampshire Infantry
Battle or Place of Action: Williamsburg & Oak Grove, Virginia
Date of Action: 5 May & 25 June 1862
Date of Issue: 10 October 1889
Citation: Bravery in repulsing the enemy's charge on a battery, at Williamsburg, Va. At Oak Grove, Va., crawled outside the lines and brought in important information.

348 ◆ DITZENBACK, JOHN

Rank: Quartermaster
Service: U.S. Navy
Birthday: 1828
Place of Birth: New York, New York
Entered Service at: Indiana
Unit: U.S. Monitor *Neosho*
Battle or Place of Action: near Nashville, Tennessee
Date of Action: 6 December 1864
G.O. Number, Date: 59, 22 June 1865
Citation: Served on board the U.S. Monitor *Neosho* during the engagement with enemy batteries at Bells Mills, Cumberland River, near Nashville, Tenn., 6 December 1864. Carrying out his duties courageously during the engagement, Ditzenback gallantly left the pilot house after the flag and signal staffs of that vessel had been shot away and, taking the flag which was drooping over the wheelhouse, made it fast to the stump of the highest mast remaining, although the ship was still under a heavy fire from the enemy.

349 ◆ DOCKUM, WARREN C.

Rank: Private
Service: U.S. Army
Birthday: 1 January 1844
Place of Birth: Clintonville, Clinton County, New York
Date of Death: 2 October 1921
Place of Death: Colorado Springs, Colorado
Cemetery: Rosemont Cemetery (MH)—Pueblo, Colorado
Entered Service at: Plattsburgh, Clinton County, New York
Unit: Company H, 121st New York Infantry
Battle or Place of Action: Deatonsville (Sailor's Creek), Virginia
Date of Action: 6 April 1865
Date of Issue: 10 May 1865
Citation: Capture of flag of Savannah Guards (C.S.A.), after two other men had been killed in the effort.

350 ◆ DODD, ROBERT FULTON

Rank: Private (highest rank: Corporal)
Service: U.S. Army
Birthday: 1845
Place of Birth: Canada
Date of Death: 4 September 1903
Place of Death: Winnipeg, Canada
Entered Service at: Detroit, Wayne County, Michigan
Unit: Company E, 27th Michigan Infantry
Battle or Place of Action: Petersburg, Virginia
Date of Action: 30 July 1864
Date of Issue: 27 July 1896
Citation: While acting as orderly, voluntarily assisted to carry off the wounded from the ground in front of the crater while exposed to a heavy fire.

351 ◆ DODDS, EDWARD EDWIN

Rank: Sergeant
Service: U.S. Army
Birthday: 1845
Place of Birth: Canada
Date of Death: 12 January 1901
Place of Death: Port Hope, Canada
Cemetery: Canton Cemetery (MH)—Porthope, Ontario, Canada
Entered Service at: Rochester, Monroe County, New York
Unit: Company C, 21st New York Cavalry
Battle or Place of Action: Ashbys Gap, Virginia
Date of Action: 19 July 1864
Date of Issue: 11 June 1896
Citation: At great personal risk rescued his wounded captain and carried him from the field to a place of safety.

352 ◆ DOLLOFF, CHARLES W.

Rank: Corporal (highest rank: Sergeant)
Service: U.S. Army
Birthday: 10 May 1844
Place of Birth: Parishville, St. Lawrence County, New York
Date of Death: 2 August 1884
Place of Death: near Canton, Wisconsin
Cemetery: Forest Cemetery—Stevens Point, Wisconsin
Entered Service at: St. Johnsbury, Caledonia County, Vermont

Unit: Company K, 1st Vermont Heavy Artillery
Battle or Place of Action: Petersburg, Virginia
Date of Action: 2 April 1865
Date of Issue: 10 May 1865
Citation: Capture of flag.

353 ◆ DONALDSON, JOHN P.

Rank: Sergeant (highest rank: Commissary Sergeant)
Service: U.S. Army
Birthday: 14 August 1842
Place of Birth: Butler County, Pennsylvania
Date of Death: 7 January 1920
Place of Death: Dubuque, Iowa
Cemetery: Mars Hill Cemetery—Floris, Iowa
Entered Service at: Butler, Butler County, Pennsylvania
Unit: Company L, 4th Pennsylvania Cavalry
Battle or Place of Action: Appomattox Courthouse, Virginia
Date of Action: 9 April 1865
Date of Issue: 3 May 1865
Citation: Capture of flag of 14th Virginia Cavalry (C.S.A.).

354 ◆ DONNELLY, JOHN C.

Rank: Ordinary Seaman
Service: U.S. Navy
Birthday: 1839
Place of Birth: England
Date of Death: 1895
Entered Service at: New York, New York
Unit: U.S.S. *Metacomet*
Battle or Place of Action: Mobile Bay, Alabama
Date of Action: 5 August 1864
G.O. Number, Date: 71, 15 January 1866
Citation: Served on board the U.S.S. *Metacomet*. As a member of the boat's crew which went to the rescue of the U.S. Monitor *Tecumseh* when that vessel was struck by a torpedo in passing the enemy forts in Mobile Bay, 5 August 1864, Donnelly braved the enemy fire, which was said by the admiral to be "one of the most galling" he had ever seen, and aided in rescuing from death 10 of the crew of the *Tecumseh*, eliciting the admiration of both friend and foe.

355 ◆ DONOGHUE, TIMOTHY

True Name: Donahue, Timothy
Rank: Private
Service: U.S. Army
Birthday: 17 March 1825
Place of Birth: Ireland
Date of Death: 19 March 1908
Cemetery: Holy Cross Cemetery—Brooklyn, New York
Entered Service at: New York, New York
Unit: Company B, 69th New York Infantry
Battle or Place of Action: Fredericksburg, Virginia
Date of Action: 13 December 1862
Date of Issue: 17 January 1894
Citation: Voluntarily carried a wounded officer off the field from between the lines; while doing this he was himself wounded.

356 ◆ DOODY, PATRICK H.

Rank: Corporal (highest rank: First Lieutenant)
Service: U.S. Army
Birthday: 7 July 1840
Place of Birth: Ireland
Date of Death: 5 March 1924
Place of Death: Brooklyn, New York
Cemetery: 1st Calvary Cemetery—Woodside, New York
Entered Service at: New York, New York
Unit: Company E, 164th New York Infantry
Battle or Place of Action: Cold Harbor, Virginia
Date of Action: 7 June 1864
Date of Issue: 13 December 1893
Citation: After making a successful personal reconnaissance, he gallantly led the skirmishers in a night attack, charging the enemy, and thus enabling the pioneers to put up works.

357 ◆ DOOLEN, WILLIAM

Rank: Coal Heaver
Service: U.S. Navy
Birthday: 1841
Place of Birth: Ireland
Date of Death: 14 September 1895
Cemetery: unknown cemetery—Egbert, Wyoming
Entered Service at: Philadelphia, Philadelphia County, Pennsylvania
Unit: U.S.S. *Richmond*
Battle or Place of Action: Mobile Bay, Alabama
Date of Action: 5 August 1864
G.O. Number, Date: 45, 31 December 1864
Citation: On board the U.S.S. *Richmond* during action against rebel forts and gunboats and with the ram *Tennessee* in Mobile Bay, 5 August 1864. Although knocked down and seriously wounded in the head, Doolen refused to leave his station as shot and shell passed. Calm and courageous, he rendered gallant service throughout the prolonged battle, which resulted in the surrender of the rebel ram *Tennessee* and in the successful attacks carried out on Fort Morgan despite the enemy's heavy return fire.

358 ◆ DORE, GEORGE H.

Rank: Sergeant
Service: U.S. Army
Birthday: 24 June 1845
Place of Birth: England
Date of Death: 8 February 1927
Place of Death: Hornell, New York
Cemetery: Hope Cemetery—Hornell, New York
Entered Service at: West Bloomfield, Ontario County, New York
Unit: Company D, 126th New York Infantry
Battle or Place of Action: Gettysburg, Pennsylvania

Date of Action: 3 July 1863
Date of Issue: 1 Decembeer 1864
Citation: The colors being struck down by a shell as the enemy were charging, this soldier rushed out and seized it, exposing himself to the fire of both sides.

359 ◆ DORLEY, AUGUST

True Name: Doerle, August
Rank: Private
Service: U.S. Army
Birthday: 1842
Place of Birth: Germany
Date of Death: 17 October 1867
Cemetery: Natchez City Cemetery (MH)—Natchez, Mississippi
Entered Service at: Natchez, Adams County, Mississippi
Unit: Company B, 1st Louisiana Cavalry
Battle or Place of Action: Mount Pleasant, Alabama
Date of Action: 11 April 1865
Citation: Capture of flag.

360 ◆ DORMAN, JOHN HENRY

Rank: Seaman
Service: U.S. Navy
Birthday: 18 September 1843
Place of Birth: Cincinnati, Hamilton County, Ohio
Date of Death: 29 May 1921
Place of Death: Dayton, Ohio
Cemetery: Spring Grove Cemetery—Cincinnati, Ohio
Entered Service at: Cincinnati, Hamilton County, Ohio
Unit: U.S.S. *Carondelet*
Battle or Place of Action: Fort Henry, Tennessee & Vicksburg, Mississippi
Date of Action: 6 February 1862 & 22 May 1863
G.O. Number, Date: 32, 18 April 1864
Citation: Served on board the U.S.S. *Carondelet* in various actions of that vessel. Carrying out his duties courageously throughout the actions of the *Carondelet*, Dorman, although wounded several times, invariably returned to duty and constantly presented an example of devotion to the flag.

361 ◆ DORSEY, DANIEL ALLEN

Rank: Corporal (highest rank: First Lieutenant)
Service: U.S. Army
Birthday: 31 December 1838
Place of Birth: Lancaster, Fairfield County, Ohio
Date of Death: 10 May 1918
Place of Death: Leavenworth, Kansas
Cemetery: Leavenworth National Cemetery (11-19-8) (MH)—Leavenworth, Kansas
Entered Service at: Chillicothe, Ross County, Ohio
Unit: Company H, 33d Ohio Infantry
Battle or Place of Action: Georgia
Date of Action: April 1862
Date of Issue: 17 September 1863
Citation: One of 19 of 24 men (including two civilians) who, by direction of Gen. Ormsby M. Mitchell, penetrated nearly 200 miles south into enemy territory and captured a railroad train at Big Shanty, Ga., in an attempt to destroy the bridges and track between Chattanaooga and Atlanta.

362 ◆ DORSEY, DECATUR

Rank: Sergeant (highest rank: First Sergeant)
Service: U.S. Army
Birthday: 1836
Place of Birth: Howard County, Maryland
Date of Death: 11 July 1891
Place of Death: Hoboken, New Jersey
Cemetery: Flower Hill Cemetery (MH)—North Bergen, New Jersey
Entered Service at: Baltimore, Baltimore County, Maryland
Unit: Company B, 39th U.S. Colored Infantry
Battle or Place of Action: Petersburg, Virginia
Date of Action: 30 July 1864
Date of Issue: 8 November 1865
Citation: Planted his colors on the Confederate works in advance of his regiment, and when the regiment was driven back to the Union works he carried the colors there and bravely rallied the men.

363 ◆ DOUGALL, ALLAN HOUSTON

Rank: First Lieutenant & Adjutant
Service: U.S. Army
Birthday: 17 July 1836
Place of Birth: Scotland
Date of Death: 22 May 1912
Place of Death: Fort Wayne, Indiana
Cemetery: I.O.O.F. Cemetery—New Haven, Indiana
Entered Service at: New Haven, Allen County, Indiana
Unit: 88th Indiana Infantry
Battle or Place of Action: Bentonville, North Carolina
Date of Action: 19 March 1865
Date of Issue: 16 February 1897
Citation: In the face of a galling fire from the enemy he voluntarily returned to where the color bearer had fallen wounded and saved the flag of his regiment from capture.

364 ◆ DOUGHERTY, MICHAEL

Rank: Private
Service: U.S. Army
Birthday: 10 May 1844
Place of Birth: Falcarragh, County Donegal, Ireland
Date of Death: 19 February 1930
Place of Death: Bristol, Pennsylvania
Cemetery: St. Mark's Cemetery (MH)—Bristol, Pennsylvania
Entered Service at: Philadelphia, Philadelphia County, Pennsylvania
Unit: Company B, 13th Pennsylvania Cavalry (Volunteers 117th Regiment)
Battle or Place of Action: Jefferson, Virginia

Date of Action: 12 October 1863
Date of Issue: 23 January 1897
Citation: At the head of a detachment of his company, he dashed across an open field, exposed to a deadly fire from the enemy, and succeeded in dislodging them from an unoccupied house, which he and his comrades defended for several hours against repeated attacks, thus preventing the enemy from flanking the position of the Union forces.
Notes: POW

365 ◆ DOUGHERTY, PATRICK

Rank: Landsman
Service: U.S. Navy
Birthday: 1844
Place of Birth: Ireland
Entered Service at: New York, New York
Unit: U.S.S. *Lackawanna*
Battle or Place of Action: Fort Morgan, Mobile Bay, Alabama
Date of Action: 5 August 1864
G.O. Number, Date: 45, 31 December 1864
Citation: As a landsman on board the U.S.S. *Lackawanna*, Dougherty acted gallantly without orders when the powder boy at his gun was disabled under the heavy enemy fire, and maintained a supply of powder throughout the prolonged action. Dougherty also aided in the attacks on Fort Morgan and in the capture of the prize ram *Tennessee*.

366 ◆ DOW, GEORGE P.

Rank: Sergeant (highest rank: First Sergeant)
Service: U.S. Army
Birthday: 7 August 1840
Place of Birth: Atkinson, Rockingham County, New Hampshire
Date of Death: 28 September 1910
Cemetery: Old Cemetery—Atkinson, New Hampshire
Entered Service at: Manchester, Hillsborough County, New hampshire
Unit: Company C, 7th New Hampshire Infantry
Battle or Place of Action: near Richmond, Virginia
Date of Action: October 1864
Date of Issue: 10 May 1884
Citation: Gallantry while in command of his company during a reconnaissance toward Richmond.

367 ◆ DOW, HENRY

Rank: Boatswain's Mate
Service: U.S. Navy
Birthday: 1840
Place of Birth: Scotland
Entered Service at: Illinois
Unit: U.S.S. *Cincinnati*
Battle or Place of Action: Vicksburg, Mississippi
Date of Action: 27 May 1863
G.O. Number, Date: 17, 10 July 1863
Citation: Served on board the U.S.S. *Cincinnati* during the attack on the Vicksburg batteries and at the time of her sinking, 27 May 1863. Engaging the enemy in a fierce battle, the *Cincinnati*, amidst an incessant fire of shot and shell, continued to fire her guns to the last, though so penetrated by enemy shellfire that her fate was sealed. Serving courageously throughout this action, Dow carried out his duties to the end on this proud ship that went down with "her colors nailed to the mast."

368 ◆ DOWNEY, WILLIAM

Rank: Private
Service: U.S. Army
Birthday: 1832
Place of Birth: Ireland
Date of Death: 30 June 1909
Place of Death: New Bedford, Massachusetts
Cemetery: St. Mary's Cemetery (MH)—New Bedford, Massachusetts
Entered Service at: Fall River, Bristol County, Massachusetts
Unit: Company B, 4th Massachusetts Cavalry
Battle or Place of Action: Ashepoo River, South Carolina
Date of Action: 24 May 1864
Date of Issue: 21 January 1897
Citation: Volunteered as a member of a boatcrew which went to the rescue of a large number of Union soldiers on board the stranded steamer Boston, and with great gallantry assisted in conveying them to shore, being exposed the entire time to a heavy fire from a Confederate battery.

369 ◆ DOWNS, HENRY W.

Rank: Sergeant (highest rank: Second Lieutenant)
Service: U.S. Army
Birthday: 29 August 1844
Place of Birth: Jamaica, Windham County, Vermont
Date of Death: 2 July 1911
Place of Death: Dayton, Ohio
Cemetery: Dayton National Cemetery (0-7-24) (MH)—Dayton, Ohio
Entered Service at: Newfane, Windham County, Vermont
Unit: Company I, 8th Vermont Infantry
Battle or Place of Action: Winchester, Virginia
Date of Action: 19 September 1864
Date of Issue: 13 December 1893
Citation: With one comrade, voluntarily crossed an open field, exposed to a raking fire, and returned with a supply of ammunition, successfully repeating the attempt a short time thereafter.

370 ◆ DRAKE, JAMES MADISON

Rank: Second Lieutenant (highest rank: First Lieutenant)
Service: U.S. Army
Birthday: 25 March 1837
Place of Birth: Washington Valley, Somerset County, New Jersey

Date of Death: 28 November 1913
Place of Death: Elizabeth, New Jersey
Cemetery: Evergreen Cemetery (MH)—Hillside, New Jersey
Entered Service at: Elizabeth, Union County, New Jersey
Unit: Company D, 9th New Jersey Infantry
Battle or Place of Action: Bermuda Hundred, Virginia
Date of Action: 6 May 1864
Date of Presentation: 3 March 1873
Place of Presentation: The White House, presented by Pres. Ulysses S. Grant
Citation: Commanded the skirmish line in the advance and held his position all day and during the night.
Notes: POW

371 ◆ DRURY, JAMES

Rank: Sergeant
Service: U.S. Army
Birthday: 15 August 1837
Place of Birth: Limerick, County Limerick, Ireland
Date of Death: 25 December 1919
Place of Death: Lovilia, Iowa
Cemetery: St. Peter's Cemetery—Lovilia, Iowa
Entered Service at: Chester, Windsor County, Vermont
Unit: Company C, 4th Vermont Infantry
Battle or Place of Action: Weldon Railroad, Virginia
Date of Action: 23 June 1864
Date of Issue: 18 January 1893
Citation: Saved the colors of his regiment when it was surrounded by a much larger force of the enemy and after the greater part of the regiment had been killed or captured.

372 ◆ DUFFEY, JOHN

True Name: Duffy, John
Rank: Private (highest rank: Farrier)
Service: U.S. Army
Birthday: 17 March 1836
Place of Birth: New Bedford, Bristol County, Massachusetts
Date of Death: 21 August 1923
Cemetery: Oak Grove Cemetery (MH)—New Bedford, Massachusetts
Entered Service at: New Bedford, Bristol County, Massachusetts
Unit: Company B, 4th Massachusetts Cavalry
Battle or Place of Action: Ashepoo River, South Carolina
Date of Action: 24 May 1864
Date of Issue: 21 January 1897
Citation: Volunteered as a member of a boatcrew which went to the rescue of a large number of Union soldiers on board the stranded steamer Boston, and with great gallantry assisted in conveying them to shore, being exposed the entire time to a heavy fire from a Confederate battery.

373 ◆ DUNCAN, ADAM

Rank: Boatswain's Mate
Service: U.S. Navy
Birthday: 1833
Place of Birth: Maine
Entered Service at: Boston, Suffolk County, Massachusetts
Unit: U.S.S. *Richmond*
Battle or Place of Action: Mobile Bay, Alabama
Date of Action: 5 August 1864
G.O. Number, Date: 45, 31 December 1864
Citation: As captain of a gun on board the U.S.S. *Richmond* during action against rebel forts and gunboats and with the ram *Tennessee* in Mobile Bay, 5 August 1864. Despite damage to his ship and the loss of several men on board as enemy fire raked her decks, Duncan fought his gun with skill and courage throughout the prolonged battle, which resulted in the surrender of the rebel ram *Tennessee* and in the successful attacks carried out on Fort Morgan.

374 ◆ DUNCAN, JAMES K. L.

Rank: Ordinary Seaman
Service: U.S. Navy
Birthday: 6 July 1845
Place of Birth: Frankfort Mineral Springs, Washington County, Pennsylvania
Date of Death: 27 March 1913
Place of Death: Wood, Wisconsin
Cemetery: Wood National Cemetery (19-41) (MH)—Wood, Wisconsin
Entered Service at: Pennsylvania
Unit: U.S.S. *Fort Hindman*
Battle or Place of Action: near Harrisonburg, Louisiana
Date of Action: 2 March 1864
G.O. Number, Date: 32, 16 April 1864
Citation: Served on board the U.S.S. *Fort Hindman* during the engagement near Harrisonburg, La., 2 March 1864. Following a shellburst at one of the guns which started a fire at the cartridge tie, Duncan immediately seized the burning cartridge, took it from the gun, and threw it overboard, despite the immediate danger to himself. Carrying out his duties through the entire engagement, Duncan served courageously during this action in which the *Fort Hindman* was raked severely with shot and shell from the enemy guns.

375 ◆ DUNLAVY, JAMES

Rank: Private
Service: U.S. Army
Birthday: 4 February 1844
Place of Birth: Decatur County, Indiana
Date of Death: 6 March 1923
Place of Death: Enid, Oklahoma
Cemetery: Maramec Cemetery—Maramec, Oklahoma
Entered Service at: Bloomfield, Davis County, Iowa
Unit: Company D, 3d Iowa Cavalry
Battle or Place of Action: Osage, Kansas
Date of Action: 25 October 1864
Date of Issue: 4 April 1865
Citation: Gallantry in capturing Maj. Gen. John S. Marmaduke, C.S.A.

376 ◆ DUNN, WILLIAM

Rank: Quartermaster
Service: U.S. Navy
Birthday: 28 April 1834
Place of Birth: Lisbon, Androscoggin County, Maine
Date of Death: 18 March 1902
Place of Death: Lisbon, Maine
Cemetery: West Bowdoin Cemetery (MH)—West Bowdoin, Maine
Entered Service at: Maine
Unit: U.S.S. *Monadnock*
Battle or Place of Action: Fort Fisher, North Carolina
Date of Action: 24-25 December 1864 & 13-15 January 1865
G.O. Number, Date: 59, 22 June 1865
Citation: On board the U.S.S. *Monadnock* in action during several attacks on Fort Fisher, 24 and 25 December 1864; and 13, 14, and 15 January 1865. With his ship anchored well inshore to insure perfect range against the severe fire of rebel guns, Dunn continued his duties when the vessel was at anchor, as her propellers were kept in motion to make her turrets bear, and the shooting away of her chain might have caused her to ground. Disdainful of shelter despite severe weather conditions, he inspired his shipmates and contributed to the success of his vessel in reducing the enemy guns to silence.

377 ◆ DUNNE, JAMES

Rank: Corporal
Service: U.S. Army
Birthday: 26 December 1840
Place of Birth: Detroit, Wayne County, Michigan
Date of Death: 13 February 1915
Place of Death: Chicago, Illinois
Cemetery: Calvary Cemetery (MH)—Evanston, Illinois
Entered Service at: Chicago, Cook County, Illinois
Unit: Chicago Mercantile Battery, Illinois Light Artillery
Battle or Place of Action: Vicksburg, Mississippi
Date of Action: 22 May 1863
Date of Issue: 15 January 1895
Citation: Carried with others by hand a cannon up to and fired it through an embrasure of the enemy's works.

378 ◆ DUNPHY, RICHARD D.

Rank: Coal Heaver
Service: U.S. Navy
Birthday: 12 December 1841
Place of Birth: Ireland
Date of Death: 23 November 1904
Place of Death: San Francisco, California
Cemetery: St. Vincent's Cemetery—Vallejo, California
Entered Service at: New York, New York
Unit: U.S.S. *Hartford*
Battle or Place of Action: Mobile Bay, Alabama
Date of Action: 5 August 1864
G.O. Number, Date: 45, 31 December 1864
Citation: On board the flagship U.S.S. *Hartford*, during successful attacks against Fort Morgan, rebel gunboats, and the rebel ram *Tennessee* in Mobile Bay, 5 August 1864. With his ship under a terrific enemy shellfire, Dunphy performed his duties with skill and courage throughout this fierce engagement which resulted in the capture of the rebel ram *Tennessee*

379 ◆ DU PONT, HENRY ALGERNON

Rank: Captain (highest rank: Brevet Lieutenant Colonel)
Service: U.S. Army
Birthday: 30 July 1838
Place of Birth: Eleutherean Mills, New Castle County, Delaware
Date of Death: 31 December 1926
Place of Death: Winterthur, Delaware
Cemetery: Du Pont Family Cemetery—Christians Hundred, Delaware
Entered Service at: Wilmington, New Castle County, Delaware
Unit: 5th U.S. Artillery
Battle or Place of Action: Cedar Creek, Virginia
Date of Action: 19 October 1864
Date of Issue: 2 April 1898
Citation: By his distinguished gallantry and voluntary exposure to the enemy's fire at a critical moment, when the Union line had been broken, encouraged his men to stand to their guns, checked the advance of the enemy and brought off most of his pieces.

380 ◆ DURHAM, JAMES R.

Rank: Second Lieutenant
Service: U.S. Army
Birthday: 7 February 1833
Place of Birth: Richmond, Richmond County, Virginia
Date of Death: 6 August 1904
Cemetery: Arlington National Cemetery (3-1435)—Arlington, Virginia
Entered Service at: Clarksburg, Harrison County, West Virginia
Unit: Company E, 12th West Virginia Infantry
Battle or Place of Action: Winchester, Virginia
Date of Action: 14 June 1863
Date of Issue: 6 March 1890
Citation: Led his command over the stone wall, where he was wounded.

381 ◆ DURHAM, JOHN S.

Rank: Sergeant
Service: U.S. Army
Birthday: 8 June 1843
Place of Birth: New York, New York
Date of Death: 2 January 1918
Place of Death: Leavenworth, Kansas
Cemetery: Leavenworth National Cemetery (33-10-18) (MH)—Leavenworth, Kansas

Entered Service at: Malone, Fond Du Lac County, Wisconsin
Unit: Company F, 1st Wisconsin Infantry
Battle or Place of Action: Perryville, Kentucky
Date of Action: 8 October 1862
Date of Issue: 20 November 1896
Citation: Seized the flag of his regiment when the color sergeant was shot and advanced with the flag midway between the lines, amid a shower of shot, shell, and bullets, until stopped by his commanding officer.

382 ◆ ECKES, JOHN N.

Rank: Private
Service: U.S. Army
Place of Birth: Lewis County, West Virginia
Date of Death: 20 April 1912
Place of Death: Cushing, Oklahoma
Entered Service at: Weston, Lewis County, West Virginia
Unit: Company E, 47th Ohio Infantry
Battle or Place of Action: Vicksburg, Mississippi
Date of Action: 22 May 1863
Citation: Gallantry in the charge of the "volunteer storming party."

383 ◆ EDDY, SAMUEL E.

Rank: Private
Service: U.S. Army
Birthday: 2 June 1822
Place of Birth: Whitingham, Windham County, Vermont
Date of Death: 7 March 1909
Cemetery: Mount Cemetery (MH)—West Chesterfield, Massachusetts
Entered Service at: Chesterfield, Hampshire County, Massachusetts
Unit: Company D, 37th Massachusetts Infantry
Battle or Place of Action: Deatonville—Sailor's Creek, Virginia
Date of Action: 6 April 1885
Citation: Saved the life of the adjutant of his regiment by voluntarily going beyond the line and there killing one of the enemy then in the act of firing upon the wounded officer. Was assailed by several of the enemy, run through the body with a bayonet, and pinned to the ground, but while so situated he shot and killed his assailant.

384 ◆ EDGERTON, NATHAN HUNTLEY

Rank: First Lieutenant & Adjutant (highest rank: Captain)
Service: U.s. Army
Birthday: 25 August 1838
Place of Birth: Barnesville, Belmont County, Ohio
Date of Death: 27 October 1932
Place of Death: Agnes, Oregon
Cemetery: At his mountain homestead—Agnes, Oregon
Entered Service at: Philadelphia, Philadelphia County, Pennsylvania
Unit: 6th U.S. Colored Infantry
Battle or Place of Action: Chapin's Farm, Virginia
Date of Action: 29 September 1884
Citation: Took up the flag after three color bearers had been shot down and bore it forward, though himself wounded

385 ◆ EDWARDS, DAVID

Rank: Private (highest rank: Corporal)
Service: U.S. Army
Birthday: 1841
Place of Birth: Wales
Date of Death: 14 April 1897
Cemetery: Waterville Cemetery (MH)—Waterville, New York
Entered Service at: Sangerfield, Oneida County, New York
Unit: Company H, 146th New York Infantry
Battle or Place of Action: Five Forks, Virginia
Date of Action: 1 April 1865
Date of Issue: 10 May 1865
Citation: Capture of flag.

386 ◆ EDWARDS, JOHN

Rank: Captain of the Top
Service: U.S. Navy
Birthday: 1831
Place of Birth: Providence, Providence County, Rhode Island
Date of Death: 27 December 1902
Cemetery: Pocasset Cemetery (MH)—Cranston, Rhode Island
Entered Service at: Rhode Island
Unit: U.S.S. *Lackawanna*
Battle or Place of Action: Mobile Bay, Alabama
Date of Action: 5 August 1864
G.O. Number, Date: 45, 31 December 1864
Citation: As second captain of a gun on board the U.S.S. *Lackawanna* during successful attacks against Fort Morgan, rebel gunboats and the ram *Tennessee* in Mobile Bay, 5 August 1864. Wounded when an enemy shell struck, Edwards refused to go below for aid and, as heavy return fire continued to strike his vessel, took the place of the first captain and carried out his duties during the prolonged action which resulted in the capture of the prize ram *Tennessee* and in the damaging and destruction of batteries at Fort Morgan.

387 ◆ ELLIOTT, ALEXANDER

Rank: Sergeant
Service: U.S. Army
Birthday: 1831
Place of Birth: Beaver County, Pennsylvania
Date of Death: 9 February 1905
Place of Death: Emsworth, Pennsylvania
Cemetery: Highwood Cemetery (MH)—Pittsburgh, Pennsylvania
Entered Service at: North Sewickley, Allegheny County, Pennsylvania
Unit: Company A, 1st Pennsylvania Cavalry

Battle or Place of Action: Paine's Crossroads, Virginia
Date of Action: 5 April 1865
Date of Issue: 3 May 1865
Citation: Capture of flag.

388 ◆ ELLIOTT, RUSSELL C.

Rank: Sergeant (highest rank: Second Lieutenant)
Service: U.S. Army
Birthday: 1842
Place of Birth: Concord, Merrimack County, New Hampshire
Date of Death: 23 October 1898
Place of Death: East Somerville, Massachusetts
Cemetery: Woodlawn Cemetery (MH)—Everett, Massachusetts
Entered Service at: Boston, Suffolk County, Massachusetts
Unit: Company B, 3d Massachusetts Cavalry
Battle or Place of Action: Natchitoches, Louisiana
Date of Action: 19 April 1864
Date of Issue: 20 November 1896
Citation: Seeing a Confederate officer in advance of his command, charged on him alone and unaided and captured him.

389 ◆ ELLIS, HORACE

Rank: Private
Service: U.S. Army
Birthday: 23 May 1843
Place of Birth: Mercer County, Pennsylvania
Date of Death: 27 June 1867
Cemetery: O'Neil Creek Cemetery—Eagle Point, Wisconsin
Entered Service at: Chippewa Falls, Chippewa County, Wisconsin
Unit: Company A, 7th Wisconsin Infantry
Battle or Place of Action: Weldon Railroad, Virginia
Date of Action: 21 August 1864
Date of Issue: 1 December 1864
Citation: Capture of flag of 16th Mississippi (C.S.A.).

390 ◆ ELLIS, WILLIAM

Rank: First Sergeant (highest rank: Second Lieutenant)
Service: U.S. Army
Birthday: 1834
Place of Birth: England
Date of Death: 1 February 1875
Place of Death: Cahon Pap, California
Cemetery: County PAP Cemetery—San Bernardino, California
Entered Service at: Watertown, Jefferson County, Wisconsin
Unit: Company K, 3d Wisconsin Cavalry
Battle or Place of Action: Dardanelles, Arkansas
Date of Action: 14 January 1865
Citation: Remained at his post after receiving three wounds, and only retired, by his commanding officer's orders, after being wounded a fourth time.

391 ◆ ELLSWORTH, THOMAS FOULDS

Rank: Captain
Service: U.S. Army
Birthday: 12 November 1840
Place of Birth: Ipswich, Essex County, Massachusetts
Date of Death: 29 August 1911
Place of Death: Pasadena, California
Cemetery: Mountain View Cemetery—Pasadena, California
Entered Service at: Boston, Suffolk County, Massachusetts
Unit: Company B, 55th Massachusetts Colored Infantry
Battle or Place of Action: Honey Hill, South Carolina
Date of Action: 30 November 1864
Date of Issue: 18 November 1895
Citation: Under a heavy fire carried his wounded commanding officer from the field.

392 ◆ ELSON, JAMES M.

Rank: Sergeant (highest rank: First Lieutenant)
Service: U.S. Army
Birthday: 6 November 1838
Place of Birth: Coshocton, Coshocton County, Ohio
Date of Death: 26 March 1894
Place of Death: Vinton, Iowa
Cemetery: Oakwood Cemetery (MH)—Shellsburg, Iowa
Entered Service at: Shellsburg, Benton County, Iowa
Unit: Company C, 9th Iowa Infantry
Battle or Place of Action: Vicksburg, Mississippi
Date of Action: 22 May 1863
Date of Issue: 12 September 1891
Citation: Carried the colors in advance of his regiment and was shot down while attempting to plant them on the enemy's works.

393 ◆ EMBLER, ANDREW HENRY

Rank: Captain (highest rank: Brevet Colonel U.S. Vols.)
Service: U.S. Army
Birthday: 29 June 1834
Place of Birth: New York, New York
Cemetery: Evergreen Cemetery (MH)—New Haven, Connecticut
Entered Service at: New York
Unit: Company D, 59th New York Infantry
Battle or Place of Action: Boydton Plank Road, Virginia
Date of Action: 27 October 1864
Date of Issue: 19 October 1893
Citation: Charged at the head of two regiments, which drove the enemy's main body, gained the crest of the hill near the Burgess house, and forced a barricade on the Boydton road.

394 ◆ ENDERLIN, RICHARD

Rank: Musician (highest rank: Sergeant)
Service: U.S. Army
Birthday: 11 January 1843
Place of Birth: Germany

Date of Death: 11 February 1930
Place of Death: Chillicothe, Ohio
Cemetery: Grandview Cemetery—Chillicothe, Ohio
Entered Service at: Chillicothe, Ross County, Ohio
Unit: Company B, 73d Ohio Infantry
Battle or Place of Action: Gettysburg, Pennsylvania
Date of Action: 1-3 July 1863
Date of Issue: 11 September 1897
Citation: Voluntarily took a rifle and served as a soldier in the ranks during the first and second days of the battle. Voluntarily and at his own imminent peril went into the enemy's lines at night and, under a sharp fire, rescued a wounded comrade.

395 ◆ ENGLE, JAMES EDGAR

Rank: Sergeant (highest rank: Brevet Captain)
Service: U.S. Army
Birthday: 1844
Place of Birth: Chester, Delaware County, Pennsylvania
Date of Death: 19 November 1897
Cemetery: Arlington National Cemetery (1-569)—Arlington, Virginia
Entered Service at: Chester, Delaware County, Pennsylvania
Unit: Company I, 97th Pennsylvania Infantry
Battle or Place of Action: Bermuda Hundred, Virginia
Date of Action: 18 May 1864
Date of Issue: 17 December 1896
Citation: Responded to a call for volunteers to carry ammunition to the regiment on the picket line and under a heavy fire from the enemy, assisted in carrying a box of ammunition to the front, and remained to distribute the same.

396 ◆ ENGLISH, EDMUND

Rank: First Sergeant (highest rank: Captain)
Service: U.S. Army
Birthday: 16 November 1844
Place of Birth: New York, New York
Date of Death: 27 May 1912
Place of Death: Philadelphia, Pennsylvania
Cemetery: Old Cathedral Cemetery—Philadelphia, Pennsylvania
Entered Service at: Newark, Essex County, New Jersey
Unit: Company C, 2d New Jersey Infantry
Battle or Place of Action: Wilderness Campaign, Virginia
Date of Action: 6 May 1864
Date of Issue: 13 February 1891
Citation: During a rout and while under orders to retreat, seized the colors, rallied the men, and drove the enemy back.
Notes: POW

397 ◆ ENGLISH, THOMAS

Rank: Signal Quartermaster
Service: U.S. Navy
Birthday: 1819
Place of Birth: New York, New York
Entered Service at: New York, New York
Unit: U.S.S. *New Ironsides*
Battle or Place of Action: Fort Fisher, North Carolina
Date of Action: 24-25 December 1864—13-15 January 1865
G.O. Number, Date: 59, 22 June 1865
Date of Issue: 22 June 1865
Citation: English served on board the U.S.S. *New Ironsides* during action in several attacks on Fort Fisher, 24 and 25 December 1864; and 13, 14 and 15 January 1865. The ship steamed in and took the lead in the ironclad division close inshore and immediately opened its starboard battery in a barrage of well-directed fire to cause several fires and explosions and dismount several guns during the first two days of fighting. Taken under fire as she steamed into position on 13 January, the *New Ironsides* fought and took on ammunition at night despite severe weather conditions. When the enemy came out of his bombproofs to defend the fort against the storming party, the ship's battery disabled nearly every gun on the fort facing the shore before the cease-fire orders were given by the flagship.

398 ◆ ENNIS, CHARLES D.

Rank: Private
Service: U.S. Army
Birthday: 8 August 1843
Place of Birth: Stonington, New London County, Connecticut
Date of Death: 29 December 1930
Place of Death: Potter Hill, Rhode Island
Cemetery: White Brook Cemetery (MH)—Richmond, Rhode Island
Entered Service at: Charleston, Washington County, Rhode Island
Unit: Company G, 1st Rhode Island Light Artillery
Battle or Place of Action: Petersburg, Virginia
Date of Action: 2 April 1865
Date of Issue: 28 June 1892
Citation: Was one of a detachment of 20 picked artillerymen who voluntarily accompanied an infantry assaulting party and who turned upon the enemy the guns captured in the assault.

399 ◆ ERICKSON, JOHN P.

Rank: Captain of the Forecastle
Service: U.S. Navy
Birthday: 1826
Place of Birth: London, England
Date of Death: 2 August 1907
Place of Death: Brooklyn, New York
Cemetery: The Green Wood Cemetery—Brooklyn, New York
Entered Service at: Brooklyn, Kings County, New York
Unit: U.S.S. *Pontoosuc*
Battle or Place of Action: Forts Fisher & Wilmington, North Carolina
Date of Action: 24 December 1864—22 February 1865
G.O. Number, Date: 59, 22 June 1865

Citation: Served on board the U.S.S. *Pontoosuc* during the capture of Fort Fisher and Wilmington, 24 December 1864 to 22 February 1865. Carrying out his duties faithfully throughout this period, Erickson was so severely wounded in the assault upon Fort Fisher that he was sent to the hospital at Portsmouth, Va. Erickson was recommended for his gallantry, skill, and coolness in action while under the fire of the enemy.

400 ◆ ESTES, LEWELLYN GARRISH

Rank: Captain & Assistant Adjutant General (highest rank: Brevet Brigadier General)
Service: U.S. Army
Birthday: 27 December 1843
Place of Birth: Oldtown, Penobscot County, Maine
Date of Death: 21 February 1905
Place of Death: Washington, D.C.
Cemetery: Arlington National Cemetery (3-1437)—Arlington, Virginia
Entered Service at: Oldtown, Penobscot County, Maine
Unit: U.S. Volunteers
Battle or Place of Action: Flint River, Georgia
Date of Action: 30 August 1864
Date of Issue: 29 August 1894
Citation: Voluntarily led troops in a charge over a burning bridge.

401 ◆ EVANS, CORON D.

Rank: Private
Service: U.S. Army
Birthday: 1844
Place of Birth: Jefferson County, Indiana
Entered Service at: Madison, Jefferson County, Indiana
Unit: Company A, 3d Indiana Cavalry
Battle or Place of Action: Deatonsville (Sailor's Creek), Virginia
Date of Action: 6 April 1865
Date of Issue: 3 May 1865
Citation: Capture of flag of 26th Virginia Infantry (C.S.A.).

402 ◆ EVANS, IRA HOBART

Rank: Captain (highest rank: Brevet Major)
Service: U.S. Army
Birthday: 11 April 1844
Place of Birth: Piermont, Grafton County, New Hampshire
Date of Death: 19 April 1922
Place of Death: San Diego, California
Cemetery: Corners Cemetery—Berlin, Vermont
Entered Service at: Barre, Washington County, Vermont
Unit: Company B, 116th U.S. Colored Infantry
Battle or Place of Action: Hatcher's Run, Virginia
Date of Action: 2 April 1865
Date of Issue: 24 March 1892
Citation: Voluntarily passed between the lines, under a heavy fire from the enemy, and obtained important information.

403 ◆ EVANS, JAMES ROBERT

Rank: Private (highest rank: Captain)
Service: U.S. Army
Birthday: 12 September 1843
Place of Birth: New York, New York
Date of Death: 27 December 1918
Place of Death: Caldwell, New Jersey
Cemetery: First Reformed Church Cemetery—Pompton Plains, New Jersey
Entered Service at: New York, New York
Unit: Company H, 62d New York Infantry
Battle or Place of Action: Wilderness Campaign, Virginia
Date of Action: 5 May 1864
Date of Issue: 25 February 1895
Citation: Went out in front of the line under a fierce fire and, in the face of the rapidly advancing enemy, rescued the regimental flag with which the color bearer had fallen.

404 ◆ EVANS, THOMAS

Rank: Private
Service: U.S. Army
Birthday: 1824
Place of Birth: Wales
Entered Service at: Johnstown, Cambria County, Pennsylvania
Unit: Company D, 54th Pennsylvania Infantry
Battle or Place of Action: Piedmont, Virginia
Date of Action: 5 June 1864
Date of Issue: 26 November 1864
Citation: Capture of flag of 45th Virginia (C.S.A.).

405 ◆ EVERSON, ADELBERT

Rank: Private
Service: U.S. Army
Birthday: 12 April 1841
Place of Birth: Cicero, Onondaga County, New York
Date of Death: 23 July 1913
Place of Death: Brewerton, New York
Cemetery: Riverside Cemetery—Brewerton, New York
Entered Service at: Salina, Onondaga County, New York
Unit: Company D, 185th New York Infantry
Battle or Place of Action: Five Forks, Virginia
Date of Action: 1 April 1865
Date of Issue: 10 May 1865
Citation: Capture of flag.

406 ◆ EWING, JOHN C.

Rank: Private
Service: U.S. Army
Birthday: 4 March 1843
Place of Birth: Ligonier Valley, Westmoreland County, Pennsylvania
Date of Death: 23 May 1918
Place of Death: Johnstown, Pennsylvania
Cemetery: Ligonier Valley Cemetery—Ligonier, Pennsylvania

Entered Service at: Greensburg, Westmoreland County, Pennsylvania
Unit: Company E, 211th Pennsylvania Infantry
Battle or Place of Action: Petersburg, Virginia
Date of Action: 2 April 1865
Date of Issue: 20 May 1865
Citation: Capture of flag.

407 ◆ FALCONER, JOHN A.

Rank: Corporal
Service: U.S. Army
Birthday: 1844
Place of Birth: Washtenaw, Michigan
Date of Death: 1 April 1900
Cemetery: Sunset Hill Cemetery—Warrensburg, Missouri
Entered Service at: Manchester, Washtenaw County, Michigan
Unit: Company A, 17th Michigan Infantry
Battle or Place of Action: Fort Sanders, Knoxville, Tennessee
Date of Action: 20 November 1863
Date of Issue: 27 July 1896
Citation: Conducted the "burning party" of his regiment at the time a charge was made on the enemy's picket line, and burned the house which had sheltered the enemy's sharpshooters, thus insuring success to a hazardous enterprise.

408 ◆ FALL, CHARLES S.

Rank: Sergeant
Service: U.S. Army
Birthday: 1842
Place of Birth: Noble County, Indiana
Date of Death: 4 June 1918
Place of Death: Pasadena, California
Cemetery: I.O.O.F. Cemetery—Alhambra, California
Entered Service at: Hamburg, Livingston County, Michigan
Unit: Company E, 26th Michigan Infantry
Battle or Place of Action: Spotsylvania Courthouse, Virginia
Date of Action: 12 May 1864
Date of Issue: 13 May 1899
Citation: Was one of the first to mount the Confederate works, where he bayoneted two of the enemy and captured a Confederate flag, but threw it away to continue the pursuit of the enemy.

409 ◆ FALLON, THOMAS TIMOTHY

Rank: Private (highest rank: Sergeant)
Service: U.S. Army
Birthday: 12 August 1837
Place of Birth: County Galway, Ireland
Date of Death: 26 August 1916
Cemetery: St. Rose of Lima Cemetery (MH)—Freehold, New Jersey
Entered Service at: Freehold, Monmouth County, New Jersey
Unit: Company K, 37th New York Infantry
Battle or Place of Action: Williamsburg & Fair Oaks, Virginia & Big Shanty, Georgia
Date of Action: 5,30-31 May 1862 & 14-15 June 1864
Date of Issue: 13 February 1891
Citation: At Williamsburg, Va., assisted in driving rebel skirmishers to their main line. Participated in action, at Fair Oaks, Va., though excused from duty because of disability. In a charge with his company at Big Shanty, Ga., was the first man on the enemy's works.

410 ◆ *FALLS, BENJAMIN FRANK

Rank: Color Sergeant
Service: U.S. Army
Place of Birth: Portsmouth, Rockingham County, New Hampshire
Date of Death: 12 May 1864
Place of Death: Wilderness, Virginia
Cemetery: Pine Grove Cemetery (MH)—Lynn, Massachusetts
Entered Service at: Lynn, Essex County, Massachusetts
Unit: Company A, 19th Massachusetts Infantry
Battle or Place of Action: Gettysburg, Pennsylvania
Date of Action: 3 July 1863
Date of Issue: 1 December 1864
Citation: Capture of flag.

411 ◆ FANNING, NICHOLAS

Rank: Private
Service: U.S. Army
Place of Birth: Carroll County, Indiana
Entered Service at: Independence, Buchanan County, Iowa
Unit: Company B, 4th Iowa Cavalry
Battle or Place of Action: Selma, Alabama
Date of Action: 2 April 1865
Date of Issue: 17 June 1865
Citation: Capture of silk Confederate States flag and two staff officers.

412 ◆ FARLEY, WILLIAM

Rank: Boatswain's Mate
Service: U.S. Navy
Birthday: 1835
Place of Birth: Whitefield, Lincoln County, Maine
Entered Service at: Maine
Unit: U.S.S. *Marblehead*
Battle or Place of Action: off Legareville, John's Island, Stono River, South Carolina
Date of Action: 25 December 1863
G.O. Number, Date: 32, 16 April 1864
Citation: Served on board the U.S.S. *Marblehead* off Legareville, Stono River, 25 December 1863, during an engagement with the enemy on John's Island. Behaving in a gallant manner, Farley animated his men and kept up a rapid and effective fire on the enemy throughout the engagement, which resulted in the enemy's abandonment of his positions, leaving a caisson and one gun behind.

413 ◆ FARNSWORTH, HERBERT E.

Rank: Sergeant Major (highest rank: Captain)
Service: U.S. Army
Birthday: 23 August 1834
Place of Birth: Perrysburg, Cattaraugus County, New York
Date of Death: 4 July 1908
Place of Death: Clarkston, Washington
Cemetery: Pomeroy City Cemetery—Pomeroy, Washington
Entered Service at: Gowanda, Cattaraugus County, New York
Unit: 10th New York Cavalry (Porter Guard)
Battle or Place of Action: Trevilian Station, Virginia
Date of Action: 11 June 1864
Date of Issue: 1 April 1898
Citation: Voluntarily carried a message which stopped the firing of a Union battery into his regiment, in which service he crossed a ridge in plain view and swept by the fire of both armies.

414 ◆ FARQUHAR, JOHN MCGREATH

Rank: Sergeant Major
Service: U.S. Army
Birthday: 17 April 1832
Place of Birth: near Ayr, Scotland
Date of Death: 24 April 1918
Place of Death: Buffalo, New York
Cemetery: Forest Lawn Cemetery (MH)—Buffalo, New York
Entered Service at: Chicago, Cook County, Illinois
Unit: 89th Illinois Infantry
Battle or Place of Action: Stone River, Tennessee
Date of Action: 31 December 1862
Date of Issue: 6 August 1902
Citation: When a break occurred on the extreme right wing of the Army of the Cumberland, this soldier rallied fugitives from other commands, and deployed his own regiment, thereby checking the Confederate advance until a new line was established.

415 ◆ FARRELL, EDWARD

Rank: Quartermaster
Service: U.S. Navy
Birthday: 1833
Place of Birth: Saratoga, Saratoga County, New York
Entered Service at: New York, New York
Unit: U.S.S. *Owasco*
Battle or Place of Action: Forts Jackson and St. Philip, Louisiana
Date of Action: 24 April 1862
G.O. Number, Date: 11, 3 April 1863
Citation: Served on board the U.S.S. *Owasco* during the attack upon Forts Jackson and St. Philip, 24 April 1862. Stationed at the masthead during these operations, Farrell observed and reported the effect of the fire of our guns in such a manner as to make his intelligence, coolness, and capacity conspicuous.

416 ◆ FASNACHT, CHARLES H.

Rank: Sergeant (highest rank: First Lieutenant)
Service: U.S. Army
Birthday: 27 March 1842
Place of Birth: Lancaster County, Pennsylvania
Date of Death: 21 July 1902
Cemetery: Greenwood Cemetery (MH)—Lancaster, Pennsylvania
Entered Service at: Philadelphia, Philadelphia County, Pennsylvania
Unit: Company A, 99th Pennsylvania Infantry
Battle or Place of Action: Spotsylvania, Virginia
Date of Action: 12 May 1864
Date of Issue: 2 April 1878
Citation: Capture of flag of 2d Louisiana Tigers (C.S.A.), in a hand-to-hand contest.
Notes: POW

417 ◆ FASSETT, JOHN BARCLAY

Rank: Captain (highest rank: Major)
Service: U.S. Army
Birthday: 1843
Place of Birth: Philadelphia, Philadelphia County, Pennsylvania
Date of Death: 18 January 1905
Place of Death: Pasadena, California
Cemetery: Woodlawn Cemetery—Bronx, New York
Entered Service at: Philadelphia, Philadelphia County, Pennsylvania
Unit: Company F, 23d Pennsylvania Infantry
Battle or Place of Action: Gettysburg, Pennsylvania
Date of Action: 2 July 1863
Date of Issue: 29 December 1894
Citation: While acting as an aide, voluntarily led a regiment to the relief of a battery and recaptured its gun from the enemy.

418 ◆ FERNALD, ALBERT E.

Rank: First Lieutenant
Service: U.S. Army
Birthday: 13 May 1838
Place of Birth: Winterport, Waldo County, Maine
Date of Death: 3 December 1908
Cemetery: Oak Hill Cemetery (MH)—Winterport, Maine
Entered Service at: Winterport, Waldo County, Maine
Unit: Company F, 20th Maine Infantry
Battle or Place of Action: Five Forks, Virginia
Date of Action: 1 April 1865
Date of Issue: 10 May 1865
Citation: During a rush at the enemy, Lt. Fernald seized, during a scuffle, the flag of the 9th Virginia Infantry (C.S.A.).

419 ◆ FERRELL, JOHN H.

Rank: Pilot (Civilian)
Service: U.S. Navy

Birthday: 15 April 1829
Place of Birth: Bedford County, Tennessee
Place of Death: Elizabethtown, Illinois
Cemetery: Price Cemetery—Elizabethtown, Illinois
Entered Service at: Illinois
Unit: U.S. Monitor *Neosho*
Battle or Place of Action: Bells Mills, Cumberland River, near Nashville, Tennessee
Date of Action: 6 December 1864
G.O. Number, Date: 59, 22 June 1865
Citation: Served on board the U.S. Monitor *Neosho* during the engagement with enemy batteries at Bells Mills, Cumberland River, near Nashville, Tenn., 6 December 1864. Carrying out his duties courageously during the engagement, Ferrell gallantly left the pilothouse after the flag and signal staffs of that vessel had been shot away and, taking the flag which was drooping over the wheelhouse, made it fast to the stump of the highest mast remaining, although the ship was still under a heavy fire from the enemy.

420 ◆ FERRIER, DANIEL TWEED

Rank: Sergeant (highest rank: Quartermaster Sergeant)
Service: U.S. Army
Birthday: 26 November 1841
Place of Birth: Indiana
Date of Death: 18 March 1914
Cemetery: Nebo Cemetery (MH)—Camden, Indiana
Entered Service at: Delphi, Carroll County, Indiana
Unit: Company K, 2d Indiana Cavalry
Battle or Place of Action: Varnells Station, Georgia
Date of Action: 9 May 1864
Date of Issue: 30 March 1898
Citation: While his regiment was retreating, voluntarily gave up his horse to his brigade commander who had been unhorsed and was in danger of capture, thereby enabling him to rejoin and rally the disorganized troops. Sgt. Ferrier himself was captured and confined in Confederate prisons, from which he escaped and, after great hardship, rejoined the Union lines.
Notes: POW

421 ◆ FERRIS, EUGENE W.

Rank: First Lieutenant & Adjutant (highest rank: Captain)
Service: U.S. Army
Birthday: 18 November 1841
Place of Birth: Springfield, Windsor County, Vermont
Date of Death: 26 February 1907
Place of Death: Rockville, Indiana
Cemetery: Rockville Cemetery—Rockville, Indiana
Entered Service at: Lowell, Middlesex County, Massachusetts
Unit: 30th Massachusetts Infantry
Battle or Place of Action: Berryville, Virginia
Date of Action: 1 April 1865
Date of Issue: 16 October 1897
Citation: Accompanied only by an orderly, outside the lines of the Army, he gallantly resisted an attack of five of Mosby's cavalry, mortally wounded the leader of the party, seized his horse and pistols, wounded three more, and, though wounded himself, escaped.

422 ◆ FESQ, FRANK E.

Rank: Private
Service: U.S. Army
Birthday: 4 April 1840
Place of Birth: Germany
Date of Death: 6 May 1920
Cemetery: Rosedale Cemetery (MH)—Orange, New Jersey
Entered Service at: Newark, Essex County, New Jersey
Unit: Company A, 40th New Jersey Infantry
Battle or Place of Action: Petersburg, Virginia
Date of Action: 2 April 1865
Date of Issue: 10 May 1865
Citation: Capture of flag of 18th North Carolina (C.S.A.), within the enemy's works.

423 ◆ FINKENBINER, HENRY S.

Rank: Private (highest rank: Corporal)
Service: U.S. Army
Birthday: 29 July 1842
Place of Birth: North Industry, Stark County, Ohio
Date of Death: 3 June 1922
Place of Death: Danville, Illinois
Cemetery: Hopewell Cemetery (MH)—Largo, Indiana
Entered Service at: Pike Township, Ohio
Unit: Company D, 107th Ohio Infantry
Battle or Place of Action: Dingles Mill, South Carolina
Date of Action: 9 April 1865
Date of Issue: 30 March 1898
Citation: While on the advance skirmish line and within direct and close fire of the enemy's artillery, crossed the mill race on a burning bridge and ascertained the enemy's position.

424 ◆ FISHER, JOHN H.

Rank: First Lieutenant
Service: U.S. Army
Birthday: 1837
Place of Birth: Monmouth, Pennsylvania
Date of Death: 16 September 1895
Place of Death: Spencer, Iowa
Cemetery: Mountain View Cemetery (MH)—Longmount, Colorado
Entered Service at: Chicago, Cook County, Illinois
Unit: Company B, 55th Illinois Infantry
Battle or Place of Action: Vicksburg, Mississippi
Date of Action: 22 May 1863
Date of Issue: 2 September 1893
Citation: Gallantry in the charge of the "volunteer storming party."

425 ◆ FISHER, JOSEPH

Rank: Corporal
Service: U.S. Army

Birthday: 24 August 1843
Place of Birth: Philadelphia, Philadelphia County, Pennsylvania
Date of Death: 8 October 1903
Cemetery: Fernwood Cemetery (MH)—Fernwood, Pennsylvania
Entered Service at: Philadelphia, Philadelphia County, Pennsylvania
Unit: Company C, 61st Pennsylvania Infantry
Battle or Place of Action: Petersburg, Virginia
Date of Action: 2 April 1865
Date of Issue: 16 January 1894
Citation: Carried the colors 50 yards in advance of his regiment, and after being painfully wounded attempted to crawl into the enemy's works in an endeavor to plant his flag thereon.

426 ◆ FITZPATRICK, THOMAS

Rank: Coxswain
Service: U.S. Navy
Birthday: 1837
Place of Birth: Canada
Entered Service at: Taunton, Bristol County, Massachusetts
Unit: U.S.S. *Hartford*
Battle or Place of Action: Mobile Bay, Alabama
Date of Action: 5 August 1864
G.O. Number, Date: 45, 31 December 1864
Citation: As captain of the No. 1 gun on board the flagship U.S.S. *Hartford*, during action against rebel gunboats, the ram *Tennessee* and Fort Morgan in Mobile Bay, 5 August 1864. Although struck several times in the face by splinters, and with his gun disabled when a shell burst between the two forward 9-inch guns, killing and wounding 15 men, Fitzpatrick, within a few minutes, had the gun in working order again with new track, breeching, and side tackle, had sent the wounded below, cleared the area of other casualties, and was fighting his gun as before. He served as an inspiration to the members of his crew and contributed to the success of the action in which the *Tennessee* was captured.

427 ◆ FLANAGAN, AUGUSTIN D.

Rank: Sergeant
Service: U.S. Army
Birthday: 10 August 1844
Place of Birth: Loretto, Cambria County, Pennsylvania
Date of Death: 22 January 1924
Place of Death: Tecumseh, Nebraska
Cemetery: Tecumseh Cemetery (MH)—Tecumseh, Nebraska
Entered Service at: Chester Springs, Chester County, Pennsylvania
Unit: Company A, 55th Pennsylvania Infantry
Battle or Place of Action: Chapin's Farm, Virginia
Date of Action: 29 September 1864
Date of Issue: 6 April 1865
Citation: Gallantry in the charge on the enemy's works; rushing forward with the colors and calling upon the men to follow him; was severely wounded.

428 ◆ FLANNIGAN, JAMES

Rank: Private (highest rank: Sergeant)
Service: U.S. Army
Birthday: 1833
Place of Birth: Canada
Date of Death: 4 October 1905
Place of Death: Louisville, New York
Cemetery: St. Lawrence Cemetery (MH)—Louisville, New York
Entered Service at: Fort Snelling, St. Paul County, Minnesota
Unit: Company H, 2d Minnesota Infantry
Battle or Place of Action: Nolensville, Tennessee
Date of Action: 15 February 1863
Date of Issue: 11 September 1897
Citation: Was one of a detachment of 16 men who heroically defended a wagon train against the attack of 125 cavalry, repulsed the attack, and saved the train.

429 ◆ FLEETWOOD, CHRISTIAN A.

Rank: Sergeant Major
Service: U.S. Army
Birthday: 21 July 1840
Place of Birth: Baltimore, Baltimore County, Maryland
Date of Death: 28 September 1914
Place of Death: Washington, D.C.
Cemetery: Harmony Memorial Park (MH)—Landover, Maryland
Entered Service at: Baltimore, Baltimore County, Maryland
Unit: 4th U.S. Colored Infantry
Battle or Place of Action: Chapin's Farm, Virginia
Date of Action: 29 September 1864
Date of Issue: 6 April 1865
Citation: Seized the colors, after two color bearers had been shot down, and bore them nobly through the fight.

430 ◆ FLOOD, THOMAS S.

Rank: Boy
Service: U.S. Navy
Birthday: 1840
Place of Birth: Ireland
Entered Service at: New York
Unit: U.S.S. *Pensacola*
Battle or Place of Action: Forts Jackson and St. Philip, Louisiana
Date of Action: 24-25 April 1862
G.O. Number, Date: 11, 3 April 1863
Citation: Served on board the U.S.S. *Pensacola* in the attack on Forts Jackson and St. Philip and the taking of New Orleans, 24 and 25 April 1862. Swept from the bridge by a shell which wounded the signal quartermaster, Flood returned to the bridge after assisting the wounded man below and taking over his duties, "Performed them with coolness, exactitude and the fidelity of a veteran seaman. His intelligence and character cannot be spoken of too warmly."

431 ◆ FLYNN, CHRISTOPHER

Rank: Corporal (highest rank: Sergeant)
Service: U.S. Army
Birthday: December 1828
Place of Birth: Ireland
Date of Death: 15 October 1889
Place of Death: Sprague, Connecticut
Cemetery: St. Mary's Cemetery (MH)—Sprague, Connecticut
Entered Service at: Hartford, Hartford County, Connecticut
Unit: Company K, 14th Connecticut Infantry
Battle or Place of Action: Gettysburg, Pennsylvania
Date of Action: 3 July 1863
Date of Issue: 1 December 1864
Citation: Capture of flag of 52d North Carolina Infantry (C.S.A.).

432 ◆ FLYNN, JAMES EDWARD

Rank: Sergeant
Service: U.S. Army
Birthday: 17 July 1843
Place of Birth: Pittsfield, Pike County, Illinois
Date of Death: 1 January 1913
Cemetery: Calvary Cemetery—St. Louis, Missouri
Entered Service at: St. Louis, St. Louis County, Missouri
Unit: Company G, 6th Missouri Infantry
Battle or Place of Action: Vicksburg, Mississippi
Date of Action: 22 May 1863
Date of Issue: 19 June 1894
Citation: Gallantry in the charge of the "volunteer storming party."

433 ◆ FOLLETT, JOSEPH LEONARD

Rank: Sergeant (highest rank: Second Lieutenant)
Service: U.S. Army
Birthday: 16 February 1843
Place of Birth: Newark, Essex County, New Jersey
Date of Death: 1 April 1907
Place of Death: New York, New York
Cemetery: Albany Rural Cemetery (MH)—Albany, New York
Entered Service at: St. Louis, St. Louis County, Missouri
Unit: Company G, 1st Missouri Light Artillery
Battle or Place of Action: New Madrid, Missouri & Stone River, Tennessee
Date of Action: 3 March & 31 December 1862
Date of Issue: 19 September 1890
Citation: At New Madrid, Mo., remained on duty though severely wounded. While procuring ammunition from the supply train at Stone River, Tenn., Follett was captured, but made his escape, secured the ammunition, and in less than an hour from the time of his capture had the batteries supplied.

434 ◆ FORCE, MANNING FERGUSON

Rank: Brigadier General (highest rank: Brevet Major General)
Service: U.S. Army
Birthday: 17 December 1824
Place of Birth: Washington, D.C.
Date of Death: 8 May 1899
Cemetery: Spring Grove Cemetery—Cincinnati, Ohio
Entered Service at: Cincinnati, Hamilton County, Ohio
Unit: U.S. Volunteers
Battle or Place of Action: Atlanta, Georgia
Date of Action: 22 July 1864
Date of Issue: 31 March 1892
Citation: Charged upon the enemy's works, and after their capture defended his position against assaults of the enemy until he was severely wounded.

435 ◆ FORD, GEORGE W.

Rank: First Lieutenant (highest rank: Captain)
Service: U.S. Army
Birthday: 1844
Place of Birth: Ireland
Date of Death: 29 November 1883
Cemetery: 1st Calvary Cemetery—Woodside, New York
Entered Service at: New York, New York
Unit: Company E, 88th New York Infantry
Battle or Place of Action: Deatonsville (Sailor's Creek), Virginia
Date of Action: 6 April 1865
Date of Issue: 10 May 1865
Citation: Capture of flag.

436 ◆ FORMAN, ALEXANDER A.

Rank: Corporal
Service: U.S. Army
Birthday: 14 January 1843
Place of Birth: Scipio Township, Hillsdale County, Michigan
Date of Death: 3 March 1922
Cemetery: Cypress Hills Cemetery (Private)—Brooklyn, New York
Entered Service at: Jonesville, Hillsdale County, Michigan
Unit: Company C, 7th Michigan Infantry
Battle or Place of Action: Fair Oaks, Virginia
Date of Action: 31 May 1862
Date of Issue: 17 August 1895
Citation: Although wounded, he continued fighting until, fainting from loss of blood, he was carried off the field.

437 ◆ FOUT, FREDERICK W.

Rank: Second Lieutenant
Service: U.S. Army
Place of Birth: Germany
Date of Death: 6 June 1905
Place of Death: St. Louis, Missouri
Cemetery: Bellefontaine Cemetery—St. Louis, Missouri
Entered Service at: Indanapolis, Marion County, Indiana
Unit: 15th Battery, Indiana Light Artillery
Battle or Place of Action: near Harpers Ferry, West Virginia

Date of Action: 15 September 1862
Date of Issue: 2 November 1896
Citation: Voluntarily gathered the men of the battery together, remanned the guns, which had been ordered abandoned by an officer, opened fire, and kept up the same on the enemy until after the surrender.

438 ◆ FOX, HENRY

Rank: Sergeant (highest rank: Captain)
Service: U.S. Army
Birthday: 3 October 1833
Place of Birth: Reuthingen, Wurtemberg, Germany
Date of Death: 3 September 1906
Cemetery: Oaklawn Cemetery—Dwight, Illinois
Entered Service at: Lincoln, Logan County, Illinois
Unit: Company H, 106th Illinois Infantry
Battle or Place of Action: near Jackson, Tennessee
Date of Action: 23 December 1862
Date of Issue: 16 May 1899
Citation: When his command was surrounded by a greatly superior force, voluntarily left the shelter of the breastworks, crossed an open railway trestle under a concentrated fire from the enemy, made his way out, and secured reinforcements for the relief of his command.

439 ◆ FOX, HENRY M.

Rank: Sergeant (highest rank: Second Lieutenant)
Service: U.S. Army
Birthday: 15 November 1844
Place of Birth: Trumbull, Ohio
Date of Death: 2 March 1923
Place of Death: Middlebury, Indiana
Cemetery: Mottville Cemetery (MH)—Mottville, Michigan
Entered Service at: Coldwater, Branch County, Michigan
Unit: Company M, 5th Michigan Cavalry
Battle or Place of Action: Winchester, Virginia
Date of Action: 19 September 1864
Date of Issue: 27 September 1864
Citation: Capture of flag.

440 ◆ FOX, NICHOLAS

Rank: Private
Service: U.S. Army
Birthday: 1844
Date of Death: 2 October 1929
Place of Death: Port Chester, New York
Cemetery: St. Mary's Cemetery (MH)—Rye Brook, New York
Entered Service at: Greenwich, Fairfield County, Connecticut
Unit: Company H, 28th Connecticut Infantry
Battle or Place of Action: Port Hudson, Louisiana
Date of Action: 14 June 1863
Date of Issue: 1 April 1898
Citation: Made two trips across an open space, in the face of the enemy's concentrated fire, and secured water for the sick and wounded.

441 ◆ FOX, WILLIAM R.

Rank: Private (highest rank: Corporal)
Service: U.S. Army
Birthday: 1837
Place of Birth: Philadelphia, Philadelphia County, Pennsylvania
Entered Service at: Philadelphia, Philadelphia County, Pennsylvania
Unit: Company A, 95th Pennsylvania Infantry
Battle or Place of Action: Petersburg, Virginia
Date of Action: 2 April 1865
Date of Issue: 28 March 1879
Citation: Bravely assisted in the capture of one of the enemy's guns; with the first troops to enter the city, captured the flag of the Confederate customhouse.

442 ◆ FOY, CHARLES H.

Rank: Signal Quartermaster
Service: U.S. Navy
Birthday: 1809
Place of Birth: Portsmouth, Rockingham County, New Hampshire
Entered Service at: Springfield, Hampden County, Massachusetts
Unit: U.S.S. *Rhode Island*
Battle or Place of Action: Fort Fisher and the Federal Point batteries, North Carolina
Date of Action: 13-15 January 1865
G.O. Number, Date: 59, 22 June 1865
Citation: Served on board the U.S.S. *Rhode Island* during the actions with Fort Fisher and the Federal Point batteries, 13 to 15 January 1865. Carrying out his duties courageously during the battle, Foy continued to be outstanding by his good conduct and faithful services throughout the engagement, which resulted in a heavy casualty list when an attempt was made to storm Fort Fisher.

443 ◆ FRANKS, WILLIAM J.

Rank: Seaman (highest rank: Acting Master's Mate)
Service: U.S. Navy
Birthday: 1830
Place of Birth: Chatham County, North Carolina
Entered Service at: De Valls Bluff, Prairie County, Arkansas
Unit: U.S.S. *Marmora*
Battle or Place of Action: off Yazoo City, Mississippi
Date of Action: 5 March 1864
G.O. Number, Date: 32, 16 April 1864
Citation: Served on board the U.S.S. *Marmora* off Yazoo City, Miss., 5 March 1864. Embarking from the *Marmora* with a 12-pound howitzer mounted on a field carriage, Franks landed with the gun and crew in the midst of heated battle and, bravely standing by his gun despite enemy rifle fire

which cut the gun carriage and rammer, contributed to the turning back of the enemy during the fierce engagement.

444 ◆ FRANTZ, JOSEPH
Rank: Private
Service: U.S. Army
Birthday: 9 March 1837
Place of Birth: Eurapae, France
Date of Death: 14 October 1913
Cemetery: Calvary Catholic Cemetery—Northfield, Minnesota
Entered Service at: Osgood, Ripley County, Indiana
Unit: Company E, 83d Indiana Infantry
Battle or Place of Action: Vicksburg, Mississippi
Date of Action: 22 May 1863
Date of Issue: 13 August 1894
Citation: Gallantry in the charge of the "volunteer storming party."

445 ◆ FRASER, WILLIAM W.
Rank: Private (highest rank: Corporal)
Service: U.S. Army
Birthday: 7 March 1844
Place of Birth: Burn Brac, Scotland
Date of Death: 9 February 1915
Place of Death: Los Angeles, California
Cemetery: Odd Fellow Cemetery—Los Angeles, California
Entered Service at: Alton, Madison County, Illinois
Unit: Company I, 97th Illinois Infantry
Battle or Place of Action: Vicksburg, Mississippi
Date of Action: 22 May 1863
Date of Issue: 24 October 1895
Citation: Gallantry in the charge of the "volunteer storming party."

446 ◆ FREEMAN, ARCHIBALD
Rank: Private (highest rank: Sergeant)
Service: U.S. Army
Birthday: 13 August 1847
Place of Birth: Newburgh, Orange County, New York
Date of Death: 26 January 1918
Cemetery: Bethel Cemetery (MH)—Groesbeck, Texas
Entered Service at: Newburgh, Orange County, New York
Unit: Company E, 124th New York Infantry
Battle or Place of Action: Spotsylvania, Virginia
Date of Action: 12 May 1864
Date of Issue: 1 December 1864
Citation: Capture of flag.

447 ◆ FREEMAN, HENRY BLANCHARD
Rank: First Lieutenant (highest rank: Brigadier General)
Service: U.S. Army
Birthday: 17 January 1837
Place of Birth: Mount Vernon, Knox County, Ohio
Date of Death: 16 October 1915
Cemetery: Arlington National Cemetery (2-937)—Arlington, Virginia
Entered Service at: Mount Vernon, Knox County, Ohio
Unit: 18th U.S. Infantry
Battle or Place of Action: Stone River, Tennessee
Date of Action: 31 December 1862
Date of Issue: 17 February 1894
Citation: Voluntarily went to the front and picked up and carried to a place of safety, under a heavy fire from the enemy, an acting field officer who had been wounded, and was about to fall into enemy hands.
Notes: POW

448 ◆ FREEMAN, MARTIN
Rank: 1st Class Pilot (Civilian) (highest rank: Acting Volunteer Lieutenant)
Service: U.S. Navy
Birthday: 18 May 1814
Place of Birth: Germany
Date of Death: 11 September 1894
Place of Death: Pascagoula, Mississippi
Cemetery: Greenwood Cemetery—Pascagoula, Mississippi
Entered Service at: Ship's Island, Jackson County, Mississippi
Unit: U.S.S. *Hartford*
Battle or Place of Action: Mobile Bay, Alabama
Date of Action: 5 August 1864
G.O. Number, Date: 45, 31 December 1864
Citation: As pilot of the flagship U.S.S. *Hartford*, during action against Fort Morgan, rebel gunboats, the ram *Tennessee* in Mobile Bay, 5 August 1864. With his ship under a terrific enemy shellfire, Freeman calmly remained at his station in the maintop and skillfully piloted the ships into the bay. He rendered gallant service throughout the prolonged battle in which the rebel gunboats were captured or driven off, the prize ram *Tennessee* forced to surrender, and the fort successfully attacked.

449 ◆ FREEMAN, WILLIAM HENRY
Rank: Private
Service: U.S. Army
Birthday: 10 May 1844
Place of Birth: Troy, Rensselaer County, New York
Date of Death: 26 August 1911
Place of Death: Troy, New York
Cemetery: Oakwood Cemetery (MH)—Troy, New York
Entered Service at: Troy, Rensselaer County, New York
Unit: Company B, 169th New York Infantry
Battle or Place of Action: Fort Fisher, North Carolina
Date of Action: 15 January 1865
Date of Issue: 27 May 1905
Citation: Volunteered to carry the brigade flag after the bearer was wounded.

450 ◆ FRENCH, SAMUEL S.
Rank: Private
Service: U.S. Army
Birthday: 23 April 1841

Place of Birth: Erie County, New York
Date of Death: 17 February 1913
Place of Death: Gilford, Michigan
Cemetery: Gilford Township Cemetery—Gilford, Michigan
Entered Service at: Gifford, Tuscola County, Michigan
Unit: Company E, 7th Michigan Infantry
Battle or Place of Action: Fair Oaks, Virginia
Date of Action: 31 May 1862
Date of Issue: 24 October 1895
Citation: Continued fighting, although wounded, until he fainted from loss of blood.

451 ◆ FREY, FRANZ

Rank: Corporal
Service: U.S. Army
Birthday: 8 December 1837
Place of Birth: Switzerland
Date of Death: 13 March 1900
Cemetery: Lakeview Cemetery—Cleveland, Ohio
Entered Service at: Cleveland, Cuyahoga County, Ohio
Unit: Company H, 37th Ohio Infantry
Battle or Place of Action: Vicksburg, Mississippi
Date of Action: 22 May 1863
Date of Issue: 14 August 1894
Citation: Gallantry in the charge of the "volunteer storming party."

452 ◆ FRICK, JACOB G.

Rank: Colonel
Service: U.S. Army
Birthday: 23 January 1825
Place of Birth: Northumberland, Northumberland County, Pennsylvania
Date of Death: 5 March 1902
Cemetery: Presbyterian Church Cemetery (MH)—Pottsville, Pennsylvania
Entered Service at: Pottsville, Schuylkill County, Pennsylvania
Unit: 129th Pennsylvania Infantry
Battle or Place of Action: Fredericksburg & Chancellorsville, Virginia
Date of Action: 13 December 1862 & 3 May 1863
Date of Issue: 7 June 1892
Citation: At Fredericksburg seized the colors and led the command through a terrible fire of cannon and musketry. In a hand-to-hand fight at Chancellorsville, recaptured the colors of his regiment.

453 ◆ FRISBEE, JOHN B.

Rank: Gunner's Mate
Service: U.S. Navy
Birthday: 7 January 1825
Place of Birth: Phippsburg, Sagadahoc County, Maine
Date of Death: 9 September 1903
Place of Death: Bath, Maine
Cemetery: Fairview Cemetery (MH)—Winnegance, Maine
Entered Service at: Brookline, Norfolk County, Massachusetts
Unit: U.S. Steam Gunboat *Pinola*
Battle or Place of Action: Forts Jackson & St. Philip and New Orleans, Louisiana
Date of Action: 24 April 1862
G.O. Number, Date: 11, 3 April 1863
Citation: Served on board the U.S. steam gunboat *Pinola* during action against Forts Jackson and St. Philip, and during the taking of New Orleans, 24 April 1862. While engaged in the bombardment of Fort St. Philip, Frisbee, acting courageously and without personal regard, closed the powder magazine which had been set afire by enemy shelling and shut off his avenue of escape, thereby setting a high example of bravery. He served courageously throughout these engagements which resulted in the taking of the Forts Jackson and St Philip and in the surrender of New Orleans.

454 ◆ FRIZZELL, HENRY F.

Rank: Private (highest rank: Corporal)
Service: U.S. Army
Place of Birth: Madison County, Missouri
Date of Death: 25 May 1904
Place of Death: St. Louis, Missouri
Cemetery: Mount Lebanon Cemetery (MH)—St. Louis, Missouri
Entered Service at: Pilot Knob, Iron County, Missouri
Unit: Company B, 6th Missouri Infantry
Battle or Place of Action: Vicksburg, Mississippi
Date of Action: 22 May 1863
Date of Issue: 30 July 1894
Citation: Gallantry in the charge of the "volunteer storming party."

455 ◆ FRY, ISAAC N.

Rank: Orderly Sergeant
Service: U.S. Marine Corps
Place of Birth: Lancaster, Lancaster County, Pennsylvania
Entered Service at: Philadelphia, Philadelphia County, Pennsylvania
Unit: U.S.S. *Ticonderoga*
Battle or Place of Action: Fort Fisher, North Carolina
Date of Action: 13-15 January 1865
G.O. Number, Date: 59, 22 June 1865
Citation: On board the U.S.S. *Ticonderoga* during attacks on Fort Fisher, 13 to 15 January 1865. As orderly sergeant of marine guard and captain of a gun, Orderly Sgt. Fry performed his duties with skill and courage as the *Ticonderoga* maintained a well-placed fire upon the batteries to the left of the palisades during the initial phases of the three-day battle, and thereafter, as she considerably lessened the firing power of guns on the mount which had been turned upon our assaulting columns. During this action the flag was planted on one of the strongest fortifications possessed by the rebels.

456 ◆ FUGER, FREDERICK W.

Rank: Sergeant (highest rank: Lieutenant Colonel USA Ret.)
Service: U.S. Army

Birthday: 18 June 1836
Place of Birth: Wurttemberg, Germany
Date of Death: 13 October 1913
Place of Death: Washington, D.C.
Cemetery: Arlington National Cemetery (1-511)—Arlington, Virginia
Entered Service at: New York, New York
Unit: Battery A, 4th U.S. Artillery
Battle or Place of Action: Gettysburg, Pennsylvania
Date of Action: 3 July 1863
Date of Issue: 24 August 1897
Citation: All the officers of his battery having been killed or wounded and five of its guns disabled in Pickett's assault, he succeeded to the command and fought the remaining gun with most distinguished gallantry until the battery was ordered withdrawn.

457 ◆ FUNK, WEST

Rank: Major
Service: U.S. Army
Place of Birth: Boston, Suffolk County, Massachusetts
Date of Death: 30 July 1897
Place of Death: Philadelphia, Pennsylvania
Entered Service at: Philadelphia, Philadelphia County, Pennsylvania
Unit: 121st Pennsylvania Infantry
Battle or Place of Action: Appomattox Courthouse, Virginia
Date of Action: 9 April 1865
Date of Issue: 15 October 1872
Citation: Capture of flag of 46th Virginia Infantry (C.S.A.).

458 ◆ FURMAN, CHESTER S.

Rank: Corporal
Service: U.S. Army
Birthday: 14 February 1842
Place of Birth: Columbia, Lancaster County, Pennsylvania
Date of Death: 22 July 1910
Cemetery: Old Rosemont Cemetery—Bloomsburg, Pennsylvania
Entered Service at: Bloomsburg, Columbia County, Pennsylvania
Unit: Company A, 6th Pennsylvania Reserves
Battle or Place of Action: Gettysburg, Pennsylvania
Date of Action: 2 July 1863
Date of Issue: 3 August 1897
Citation: Was one of six volunteers who charged upon a log house near Devil's Den, where a squad of the enemy's sharpshooters were sheltered, and compelled their surrender.

459 ◆ FURNESS, FRANK

Rank: Captain
Service: U.S. Army
Birthday: 12 November 1839
Place of Birth: Philadelphia, Philadelphia County, Pennsylvania
Date of Death: 27 June 1912
Place of Death: Media, Pennsylvania
Cemetery: Laurel Hill Cemetery (MH)—Philadelphia, Pennsylvania
Entered Service at: Philadelphia, Philadelphia County, Pennsylvania
Unit: Company F, 6th Pennsylvania Cavalry
Battle or Place of Action: Trevilian Station, Virginia
Date of Action: 12 June 1864
Date of Issue: 20 October 1899
Citation: Voluntarily carried a box of ammunition across an open space swept by the enemy's fire to the relief of an outpost whose ammunition had become almost exhausted, but which was thus enabled to hold its important position.

460 ◆ GAGE, RICHARD J.

Rank: Private
Service: U.S. Army
Birthday: 1842
Place of Birth: Grafton County, New Hampshire
Date of Death: 28 April 1903
Cemetery: Maxton Cemetery (MH)—Seneca, Illinois
Entered Service at: Ottawa, La Salle County, Illinois
Unit: Company D, 104th Illinois Infantry
Battle or Place of Action: Elk River, Tennessee
Date of Action: 2 July 1863
Date of Issue: 30 October 1897
Citation: Voluntarily joined a small party that, under a heavy fire, captured a stockade and saved the bridge.

461 ◆ GALLOWAY, GEORGE NORTON

Rank: Private
Service: U.S. Army
Birthday: 1841/42
Place of Birth: Philadelphia, Philadelphia County, Pennsylvania
Date of Death: 9 February 1904
Place of Death: Philadelphia, Pennsylvania
Cemetery: Mount Moriah Cemetery—Philadelphia, Pennsylvania
Entered Service at: Philadelphia, Philadelphia County, Pennsylvania
Unit: Company G, 95th Pennsylvania Infantry
Battle or Place of Action: Alsops Farm, Virginia
Date of Action: 8 May 1864
Date of Issue: 24 October 1895
Citation: Voluntarily held an important position under heavy fire.

462 ◆ GALLOWAY, JOHN

Rank: Commissary Sergeant (highest rank: First Lieutenant)
Service: U.S. Army
Place of Birth: Philadelphia, Philadelphia County, Pennsylvania
Date of Death: 23 May 1904
Place of Death: Philadelphia, Pennsylvania

Cemetery: Mount Moriah Cemetery—Philadelphia, Pennsylvania
Entered Service at: Philadelphia, Philadelphia County, Pennsylvania
Unit: 8th Pennsylvania Cavalry
Battle or Place of Action: Farmville, Virginia
Date of Action: 7 April 1865
Date of Issue: 30 October 1897
Citation: His regiment being surprised and nearly overwhelmed, he dashed forward under a heavy fire, reached the right of the regiment, where the danger was greatest, rallied the men, and prevented a disaster that was imminent.

463 ◆ GARDINER, JAMES

True Name: Gardner, James Daniel
Rank: Private
Service: U.S. Army
Birthday: 16 September 1839
Place of Birth: Gloucester, Gloucester County, Virginia
Date of Death: 29 September 1905
Place of Death: Clark's Summit, Pennsylvania
Cemetery: Calvary Crest Cemetery (MH)—Ottumwa, Iowa
Entered Service at: Yorktown, York County, Virginia
Unit: Company I, 36th U.S. Colored Infantry
Battle or Place of Action: Chapin's Farm, Virginia
Date of Action: 29 September 1864
Date of Issue: 6 April 1865
Citation: Rushed in advance of his brigade, shot a rebel officer who was on the parapet rallying his men, and then ran him through with his bayonet.

464 ◆ GARDNER, CHARLES N.

Rank: Private (highest rank: Second Lieutenant)
Service: U.S. Army
Birthday: 29 March 1845
Place of Birth: South Scituate, Plymouth County, Massachusetts
Date of Death: 22 February 1919
Place of Death: Accord, Massachusetts
Cemetery: Washington Street Cemetery (MH)—Norwell, Massachusetts
Entered Service at: Scituate, Plymouth County, Massachusetts
Unit: Company E, 32d Massachusetts Infantry
Battle or Place of Action: Five Forks, Virginia
Date of Action: 1 April 1865
Date of Issue: 10 May 1865
Citation: Capture of flag.

465 ◆ GARDNER, ROBERT J.

Rank: Sergeant (highest rank: First Sergeant)
Service: U.S. Army
Birthday: 28 September 1837
Place of Birth: Livingston, Columbia County, New York
Date of Death: 23 September 1902
Place of Death: Iosco, Michigan
Cemetery: Munsell Cemetery—Iosco Township, Michigan
Entered Service at: Egremont, Berkshire County, Massachusetts
Unit: Company K, 34th Massachusetts Infantry
Battle or Place of Action: Petersburg, Virginia
Date of Action: 2 April 1865
Date of Issue: 12 May 1865
Citation: Was among the first to enter Fort Gregg, clearing his way by using his musket on the heads of the enemy.

466 ◆ GARDNER, WILLIAM

Rank: Seaman (highest rank: Ship's Cook)
Service: U.S. Navy
Birthday: 1832
Place of Birth: Ireland
Entered Service at: New York, New York
Unit: U.S.S. *Galena*
Battle or Place of Action: Mobile Bay, Alabama
Date of Action: 5 August 1864
G.O. Number, Date: 45, 31 December 1864
Citation: As seaman on board the U.S.S. *Galena* in the engagement at Mobile Bay, 5 August 1864. Serving gallantly during this fierce battle which resulted in the capture of the rebel ram *Tennessee* and the damaging of Fort Morgan, Gardner behaved with conspicuous coolness under the fire of the enemy.

467 ◆ GARRETT, WILLIAM

Rank: Sergeant
Service: U.S. Army
Birthday: 6 February 1842
Place of Birth: Isle of Man, England
Date of Death: 30 December 1916
Place of Death: Leavenworth, Kansas
Cemetery: Leavenworth National Cemetery (32-3-26) (MH)—Leavenworth, Kansas
Entered Service at: Chardon, Geauga County, Ohio
Unit: Company G, 41st Ohio Infantry
Battle or Place of Action: Nashville, Tennessee
Date of Action: 16 December 1864
Date of Issue: 24 February 1865
Citation: With several companions dashed forward, the first to enter the enemy's works, taking possession of four pieces of artillery and captured the flag of the 13th Mississippi Infantry (C.S.A.).

468 ◆ GARRISON, JAMES R.

Rank: Coal Heaver
Service: U.S. Navy
Birthday: 22 June 1838
Place of Birth: Poughkeepsie, Dutchess County, New York
Date of Death: 19 April 1908
Place of Death: Hampton, Virginia
Cemetery: Hampton National Cemetery (B-9523) (MH)—Hampton, Virginia
Entered Service at: New York, New York

Unit: U.S.S. *Hartford*
Battle or Place of Action: Mobile Bay, Alabama
Date of Action: 5 August 1864
G.O. Number, Date: 45, 31 December 1864
Citation: On board the flagship, U.S.S. *Hartford*, during successful engagements against Fort Morgan, rebel gunboats, the ram *Tennessee* in Mobile Bay, 5 August 1864. When a shell struck his foot and severed one of his toes, Garrison remained at his station at the shell whip and, after crudely bandaging the wound, continued to perform his duties until severely wounded by another shell burst.

469 ◆ GARVIN, WILLIAM

Rank: Captain of the Forecastle (highest rank: Boatswain's Mate)
Service: U.S. Navy
Birthday: 1835
Place of Birth: west Canada
Entered Service at: Plymouth, Litchfield County, Connecticut
Unit: U.S.S. *Agawam*
Battle or Place of Action: Fort Fisher, North Carolina
Date of Action: 23 December 1864
G.O. Number, Date: 45, 31 December 1864
Citation: Garvin served on board the U.S.S. *Agawam*, as one of a volunteer crew of a powder boat which was exploded near Fort Fisher, 23 December 1864. The powder boat, towed in by the *Wilderness* to prevent detection by the enemy, cast off and slowly steamed to within 300 yards of the beach. After fuses and fires had been lit and a second anchor with short scope let go to assure the boat's tailing inshore, the crew again boarded the *Wilderness* and proceeded a distance of 12 miles from shore. Less than two hours later the explosion took place, and the following day fires were observed still burning at the fort.

470 ◆ *GASSON, RICHARD

Rank: Sergeant
Service: U.S. Army
Birthday: 1842
Place of Birth: Ireland
Date of Death: 29 September 1864
Place of Death: Chapins Farm, Virginia
Entered Service at: New York, New York
Unit: Company K, 47th New York Infantry
Battle or Place of Action: Chapin's Farm, Virginia
Date of Action: 29 September 1864
Date of Issue: 6 April 1865
Citation: Fell dead while planting the colors of his regiment on the enemy's works.

471 ◆ GAUNT, JOHN C.

Rank: Private
Service: U.S. Army
Place of Birth: Columbiana County, Ohio
Date of Death: 13 January 1886
Cemetery: unknown cemetery—Garfield, Ohio
Entered Service at: Damascoville, Ohio
Unit: Company G, 104th Ohio Infantry
Battle or Place of Action: Franklin, Tennessee
Date of Action: 30 November 1864
Date of Issue: 13 February 1865
Citation: Capture of flag.

472 ◆ GAUSE, ISAAC

Rank: Corporal (highest rank: Sergeant)
Service: U.S. Army
Birthday: 9 December 1843
Place of Birth: Trumbull County, Ohio
Date of Death: 23 April 1920
Place of Death: Johnson City, Tennessee
Cemetery: Arlington National Cemetery (17-19595) (MH)—Arlington, Virginia
Entered Service at: Canfield, Mahoning County, Ohio
Unit: Company E, 2d Ohio Cavalry
Battle or Place of Action: near Berryville, Virginia
Date of Action: 13 September 1864
Date of Issue: 19 September 1864
Citation: Capture of the colors of the 8th South Carolina Infantry while engaged in a reconnaissance along the Berryville and Winchester Pike.

473 ◆ GAYLORD, LEVI B.

Rank: Sergeant
Service: U.S. Army
Birthday: 23 September 1840
Place of Birth: Boston, Suffolk County, Massachusetts
Date of Death: 6 December 1900
Place of Death: Dorchester, Massachusetts
Cemetery: Cohasset Central Cemetery (MH)—Cohasset, Massachusetts
Entered Service at: Boston, Suffolk County, Massachusetts
Unit: Company A, 29th Massachusetts Infantry
Battle or Place of Action: Fort Stedman, Virginia
Date of Action: 25 March 1865
Date of Issue: 22 June 1896
Citation: Voluntarily assisted in working an abandoned gun, while exposed to heavy fire, until the enemy's advancing line was routed by a charge on its left flank.

474 ◆ GEORGE, DANIEL GRIFFIN

Rank: Ordinary Seaman
Service: U.S. Navy
Birthday: 7 July 1840
Place of Birth: Plaistow, Rockingham County, New Hampshire
Date of Death: 26 February 1916
Place of Death: Amesbury, Massachusetts
Cemetery: Locust Grove Cemetery (MH)—Merrimac, Massachusetts
Entered Service at: New Hampshire
Unit: U.S. Picket Boat No. 1

Battle or Place of Action: Plymouth, North Carolina
Date of Action: 27 October 1864
G.O. Number, Date: 45, 31 December 1864
Citation: George served on board the U.S. Picket Boat No. 1 in action, 27 October 1864, against the Confederate ram *Albemarle*, which had resisted repeated attacks by our steamers and had kept a large force of vessels employed in watching her. The picket boat, equipped with a spar torpedo, succeeded in passing the enemy pickets within 20 yards without being discovered and then made for the *Albemarle* under a full head of steam. Immediately taken under fire by the ram, the small boat plunged on, jumped the log boom which encircled the target, and exploded its torpedo under the port bow of the ram. The picket boat was destroyed by enemy fire and almost the entire crew was taken prisoner or lost.
Notes: POW

475 ◆ GERE, THOMAS PARKE

Rank: First Lieutenant & Adjutant
Service: U.S. Army
Birthday: 10 December 1842
Place of Birth: Wellsburg, Chemung County, New York
Date of Death: 8 January 1912
Cemetery: Arlington National Cemetery (1-361) (MH)—Arlington, Virginia
Entered Service at: Fort Snelling, St. Paul County, Minnesota
Unit: 5th Minnesota Infantry
Battle or Place of Action: Nashville, Tennessee
Date of Action: 16 December 1864
Date of Issue: 24 February 1865
Citation: Capture of flag of 4th Mississippi (C.S.A.).

476 ◆ GESCHWIND, NICHOLAS

Rank: Captain
Service: U.S. Army
Place of Birth: France
Date of Death: 2 January 1897
Cemetery: Springdale Cemetery—Peoria, Illinois
Entered Service at: Pleasant Hill, Pike County, Illinois
Unit: Company F, 116th Illinois Infantry
Battle or Place of Action: Vicksburg, Mississippi
Date of Action: 22 May 1863
Date of Issue: 24 August 1894
Citation: Gallantry in the charge of the "volunteer storming party."

477 ◆ GIBBS, WESLEY

Rank: Sergeant
Service: U.S. Army
Birthday: 24 July 1842
Place of Birth: Sharon, Litchfield County, Connecticut
Date of Death: 29 May 1917
Cemetery: Forest View Cemetery (MH)—Winchester, Connecticut
Entered Service at: Salisbury, Litchfield County, Connecticut
Unit: Company B, 2d Connecticut Heavy Artillery
Battle or Place of Action: Petersburg, Virginia
Date of Action: 2 April 1865
Date of Issue: 10 May 1865
Citation: Capture of flag.

478 ◆ GIFFORD, BENJAMIN

Rank: Private
Service: U.S. Army
Birthday: 13 September 1833
Place of Birth: German Flats, Herkimer County, New York
Date of Death: 14 July 1901
Cemetery: Hinsdale Cemetery (MH)—Hinsdale, New York
Entered Service at: German Flats, Herkimer County, New York
Unit: Company H, 121st New York Infantry
Battle or Place of Action: Deatonsville (Sailor's Creek), Virginia
Date of Action: 6 April 1865
Date of Issue: 10 May 1865
Citation: Capture of flag.

479 ◆ GIFFORD, DAVID L.

Rank: Private
Service: U.S. Army
Birthday: 18 September 1844
Place of Birth: Dartmouth, Bristol County, Massachusetts
Date of Death: 13 January 1904
Place of Death: Dartmouth, Massachusetts
Cemetery: South Dartmouth Cemetery—South Dartmouth, Massachusetts
Entered Service at: New Bedford, Bristol County, Massachusetts
Unit: Company B, 4th Massachusetts Cavalry
Battle or Place of Action: Ashepoo River, South Carolina
Date of Action: 24 May 1864
Date of Issue: 21 January 1897
Citation: Volunteered as a member of a boat crew which went to the rescue of a large number of Union soldiers on board the stranded steamer Boston and with great gallantry assisted in conveying them to shore, being exposed during the entire time to a heavy fire from a Confederate battery.

480 ◆ GILE, FRANK S.

Rank: Landsman
Service: U.S. Navy
Birthday: 15 September 1847
Place of Birth: Massachusetts
Date of Death: 19 March 1898
Place of Death: South Andover, Massachusetts
Cemetery: Ridgewood Cemetery (MH)—North Andover, Massachusetts
Entered Service at: Massachusetts
Unit: U.S.S. *Lehigh*

Battle or Place of Action: Charleston Harbor, South Carolina
Date of Action: 16 November 1863
G.O. Number, Date: 32, 16 April 1864
Citation: On board the U.S.S. *Lehigh*, Charleston Harbor, 16 November 1863, during the hazardous task of freeing the *Lehigh*, which had been grounded and was under heavy enemy fire from Fort Moultrie. After several previous attempts had been made, Gile succeeded in passing in a small boat from the *Lehigh* to the *Nahant* with a line bent on a hawser. This courageous action while under severe enemy fire enabled the *Lehigh* to be freed from her helpless position.

481 ◆ GILLESPIE JR., GEORGE LEWIS

Rank: First Lieutenant (highest rank: Major General)
Service: U.S. Army
Birthday: 7 October 1841
Place of Birth: Kingston, Roane County, Tennessee
Date of Death: 27 September 1913
Place of Death: Saratoga, New York
Cemetery: U.S. Military Academy Cemetery (S-37)—West Point, New York
Entered Service at: Chattanooga, Hamilton County, Tennessee
Unit: Corps of Engineers
Battle or Place of Action: near Bethesda Church, Virginia
Date of Action: 31 May 1864
Date of Issue: 27 October 1897
Citation: Exposed himself to great danger by voluntarily making his way through the enemy's lines to communicate with Gen. Sheridan. While rendering this service he was captured, but escaped; again came in contact with the enemy, was again ordered to surrender, but escaped by dashing away under fire.

482 ◆ GILLIGAN, EDWARD LYONS

Rank: First Sergeant (highest rank: Captain)
Service: U.S. Army
Birthday: 18 April 1843
Place of Birth: Philadelphia, Philadelphia County, Pennsylvania
Date of Death: 2 April 1922
Place of Death: Oxford, Pennsylvania
Cemetery: Oxford Cemetery (MH)—Oxford, Pennsylvania
Entered Service at: Philadelphia, Philadelphia County, Pennsylvania
Unit: Company E, 88th Pennsylvania Infantry
Battle or Place of Action: Gettysburg, Pennsylvania
Date of Action: 1 July 1863
Date of Issue: 30 April 1892
Citation: Assisted in the capture of a Confederate flag by knocking down the color sergeant.

483 ◆ GILMORE, JOHN CURTIS

Rank: Major (highest rank: Brigadier General USA)
Service: U.S. Army
Birthday: 18 April 1837
Place of Birth: Canada
Date of Death: 22 December 1922
Cemetery: Arlington National Cemetery (1-270)—Arlington, Virginia
Entered Service at: Potsdam, St. Lawrence County, New York
Unit: 16th New York Infantry
Battle or Place of Action: Salem Heights, Virginia
Date of Action: 3 May 1863
Date of Issue: 10 October 1892
Citation: Seized the colors of his regiment and gallantly rallied his men under a very severe fire.

484 ◆ GINLEY, PATRICK

Rank: Private
Service: U.S. Army
Birthday: 11 December 1822
Place of Birth: Ireland
Date of Death: 5 April 1917
Place of Death: New York, New York
Cemetery: 1st Calvary Cemetery—Woodside, New York
Entered Service at: New York, New York
Unit: Company G, 1st New York Light Artillery
Battle or Place of Action: Reams' Station, Virginia
Date of Action: 25 August 1864
Date of Issue: 31 October 1890
Citation: The command having been driven from the works, he, having been left alone between the opposing lines, crept back into the works, put three charges of canister in one of the guns and fired the piece directly into a body of the enemy about to seize the works; he then rejoined his command, took the colors, and ran toward the enemy, followed by the command, which recaptured the works and guns.

485 ◆ GION, JOSEPH

Rank: Private
Service: U.S. Army
Birthday: 1826
Place of Birth: Alsace-Lorraine area, Germany
Date of Death: 16 January 1889
Place of Death: Chartiers Township, Pennsylvania
Cemetery: St. Martin's Cemetery (MH)—Pittsburgh, Pennsylvania
Entered Service at: Allegheny County, Pennsylvania
Unit: Company A, 74th New York Infantry
Battle or Place of Action: Chancellorsville, Virginia
Date of Action: 2 May 1863
Date of Issue: 26 November 1884
Citation: Voluntarily and under heavy fire advanced toward the enemy's lines and secured valuable information.

486 ◆ GODLEY, LEONIDAS MAHLON

Rank: First Sergeant
Service: U.S. Army
Birthday: 13 June 1836

Place of Birth: Mason County, West Virginia
Date of Death: 23 May 1904
Place of Death: Ottumwa, Iowa
Cemetery: Ottumwa Cemetery—Ottumwa, Iowa
Entered Service at: Ashland, Iowa
Unit: Company E, 22d Iowa Infantry
Battle or Place of Action: Vicksburg, Mississippi
Date of Action: 22 May 1863
Date of Issue: 3 August 1897
Citation: Led his company in the assault on the enemy's works and gained the parapet, there receiving three very severe wounds. He lay all day in the sun, was taken prisoner, and had his leg amputated without anesthetics.
Notes: POW

487 ◆ GOETTEL, PHILIP

Rank: Private (highest rank: Corporal)
Service: U.S. Army
Birthday: 2 September 1840
Place of Birth: Salina, Onondaga County, New York
Date of Death: 30 January 1920
Place of Death: Syracuse, New York
Cemetery: Woodlawn Cemetery (MH)—Syracuse, New York
Entered Service at: Syracuse, Onondaga County, New York
Unit: Company B, 149th New York Infantry
Battle or Place of Action: Ringgold, Georgia
Date of Action: 27 November 1863
Date of Issue: 28 June 1865
Citation: Capture of flag and a battery guidon.

488 ◆ GOHEEN, CHARLES ARTHUR

Rank: First Sergeant (highest rank: First Lieutenant)
Service: U.S. Army
Birthday: 5 August 1843
Place of Birth: Groveland, Livingston County, New York
Date of Death: 8 May 1889
Place of Death: Mendon, New York
Cemetery: Honeoye Falls Cemetery (MH)—Honeoye Falls, New York
Entered Service at: Rochester, Monroe County, New York
Unit: Company G, 8th New York Cavalry
Battle or Place of Action: Waynesboro, Virginia
Date of Action: 2 March 1865
Date of Issue: 26 March 1865
Citation: Capture of flag.

489 ◆ GOLDSBERY, ANDREW E.

True Name: Goldsberry, Andrew E.
Rank: Private
Service: U.S. Army
Birthday: 25 September 1840
Place of Birth: St. Charles, Kane County, Illinois
Date of Death: 27 October 1910
Place of Death: Fairbank, Iowa
Cemetery: Long Grove Cemetery—Maynard, Iowa
Entered Service at: St. Charles, Kane County, Illinois
Unit: Company E, 127th Illinois Infantry
Battle or Place of Action: Vicksburg, Mississippi
Date of Action: 22 May 1863
Date of Issue: 9 August 1894
Citation: Gallantry in the charge of the "volunteer storming party."

490 ◆ GOODALL, FRANCIS HENRY

Rank: First Sergeant
Service: U.S. Army
Birthday: 10 January 1838
Place of Birth: Bath, Grafton County, New Hampshire
Date of Death: 12 April 1925
Place of Death: Takoma Park, Maryland
Cemetery: Rock Creek Cemetery—Washington, D.C.
Entered Service at: Bath, Grafton County, New Hampshire
Unit: Company G, 11th New Hampshire Infantry
Battle or Place of Action: Fredericksburg, Virginia
Date of Action: 13 December 1862
Date of Issue: 14 December 1894
Citation: With the assistance of another soldier brought a wounded comrade into the lines, under heavy fire.

491 ◆ GOODMAN, WILLAIM ERNEST

Rank: First Lieutenant (highest rank: Major)
Service: U.S. Army
Birthday: 10 December 1838
Place of Birth: Philadelphia, Philadelphia County, Pennsylvania
Date of Death: 22 March 1912
Place of Death: Philadelphia, Pennsylvania
Cemetery: St. Thomas Church Cemetery (MH)—Whitemarsh, Pennsylvania
Entered Service at: Philadelphia, Philadelphia County, Pennsylvania
Unit: Company D, 147th Pennsylvania Infantry
Battle or Place of Action: Chancellorsville, Virginia
Date of Action: 3 May 1863
Date of Issue: 11 January 1894
Citation: Rescued the colors of the 107th Ohio Volunteers from the enemy.

492 ◆ GOODRICH, EDWIN

Rank: First Lieutenant (highest rank: Major)
Service: U.S. Army
Birthday: 22 March 1843
Place of Birth: New York, New York
Date of Death: 26 November 1910
Cemetery: Graceland Cemetery—Chicago, Illinois
Entered Service at: Westfield, Chautauqua County, New York
Unit: Company D, 9th New York Cavalry
Battle or Place of Action: near Cedar Creek, Virginia
Date of Action: November 1864
Date of Issue: 14 May 1894

Citation: While the command was falling back, he returned and in the face of the enemy rescued a sergeant from under his fallen horse.

493 ◆ GOULD, CHARLES GILBERT

Rank: Captain (highest rank: Brevet Major)
Service: U.S. Army
Birthday: 5 May 1845
Place of Birth: Windham County, Vermont
Date of Death: 5 December 1916
Cemetery: Windham Central Cemetery—Windham, Vermont
Entered Service at: Windham County, Vermont
Unit: Company H, 5th Vermont Infantry
Battle or Place of Action: Petersburg, Virginia
Date of Action: 2 April 1865
Date of Issue: 30 July 1890
Citation: Among the first to mount the enemy's works in the assault, he received a serious bayonet wound in the face, was struck several times with clubbed muskets, but bravely stood his ground, and with his sword killed the man who had bayoneted him.

494 ◆ GOULD, NEWTON THOMAS

Rank: Private (highest rank: Sergeant)
Service: U.S. Army
Birthday: 14 May 1843
Place of Birth: Elk Grove, Cook County, Illinois
Date of Death: 2 April 1925
Cemetery: Sacramento City Cemetery (MH)—Sacramento, California
Entered Service at: Elk Grove, Cook County, Illinois
Unit: Company G, 113th Illinois Infantry
Battle or Place of Action: Vicksburg, Mississippi
Date of Action: 22 May 1863
Date of Issue: 6 September 1894
Citation: Gallantry in the charge of the "volunteer storming party."
Notes: POW

495 ◆ GOURAUD, GEORGE EDWARD

Rank: Captain & Aide-de-Camp (highest rank: Brevet Lieutenant Colonel U.S. Vols.)
Service: U.S. Army
Birthday: 1840
Place of Birth: New York, New York
Date of Death: 17 February 1912
Place of Death: England
Entered Service at: New York, New York
Unit: U.S. Volunteers
Battle or Place of Action: Honey Hill, South Carolina
Date of Action: 30 November 1864
Date of Issue: 21 August 1893
Citation: While under severe fire of the enemy, which drove back the command, rendered valuable assistance in rallying the men.

496 ◆ GRACE, PETER

Rank: Sergeant (highest rank: Captain)
Service: U.S. Army
Birthday: 18 March 1845
Place of Birth: Berkshire, Berkshire County, Massachusetts
Date of Death: 27 March 1914
Cemetery: Arlington National Cemetery (3-2556)—Arlington, Virginia
Entered Service at: Berkshire, Berkshire County, Massachusetts
Unit: Company G, 83d Pennsylvania Infantry
Battle or Place of Action: Wilderness Campaign, Virginia
Date of Action: 5 May 1864
Date of Issue: 27 December 1894
Citation: Singlehandedly rescued a comrade from two Confederate guards, knocking down one and compelling the surrender of the other.

497 ◆ GRAHAM, ROBERT

True Name: Hall, Frederick, reenlisted U.S. Marine Corps 1881
Rank: Landsman
Service: U.S. Navy
Birthday: 1841
Place of Birth: England
Entered Service at: New York
Unit: U.S.S. *Tacony*
Battle or Place of Action: Plymouth, North Carolina
Date of Action: 31 October 1864
G.O. Number, Date: 45, 31 December 1864
Citation: Served on board the U.S.S. *Tacony* during the taking of Plymouth, N.C., 31 October 1864. Carrying out his duties faithfully during the capture of Plymouth, Graham distinguished himself by a display of coolness when he participated in landing and spiking a 9-inch gun while under a devastating fire from enemy musketry.

498 ◆ GRAHAM, THOMAS N.

Rank: Second Lieutenant
Service: U.S. Army
Birthday: 16 September 1837
Date of Death: 4 February 1911
Cemetery: Oak Hill Cemetery (MH)—Lawrence, Kansas
Entered Service at: Westville, La Porte County, Indiana
Unit: Company G, 15th Indiana Infantry
Battle or Place of Action: Missionary Ridge, Tennessee
Date of Action: 25 November 1863
Date of Issue: 15 February 1897
Citation: Seized the colors from the color bearer, who had been wounded, and, exposed to a terrible fire, carried them forward, planting them on the enemy's breastworks.

499 ◆ GRANT, GABRIEL

Rank: Surgeon (highest rank: Major)
Service: U.S. Army

Place of Birth: Newark, Essex County, New Jersey
Date of Death: 8 November 1909
Cemetery: Sleepy Hollow Cemetery (MH)—Tarrytown, New York
Entered Service at: Trenton, Mercer County, New Jersey
Unit: U.S. Volunteers
Battle or Place of Action: Fair Oaks, Virginia
Date of Action: 1 June 1862
Date of Issue: 21 July 1897
Citation: Removed severely wounded officers and soldiers from the field while under a heavy fire from the enemy, exposing himself beyond the call of duty, thus furnishing an example of most distinguished gallantry.

500 ◆ GRANT, LEWIS ADDISON

Rank: Colonel (highest rank: Brevet Major General U.S. Vols.)
Service: U.S. Army
Birthday: 17 January 1829
Place of Birth: Winhall, Vermont
Date of Death: 20 March 1918
Cemetery: Lakewood Cemetery—Minneapolis, Minnesota
Entered Service at: Bellows Falls, Windham County, Vermont
Unit: 5th Vermont Infantry
Battle or Place of Action: Salem Heights, Virginia
Date of Action: 3 May 1864
Date of Issue: 11 May 1893
Citation: Personal gallantry and intrepidity displayed in the management of his brigade and in leading it in the assault in which he was wounded.

501 ◆ GRAUL, WILLIAM L.

Rank: Corporal
Service: U.S. Army
Birthday: 27 July 1846
Place of Birth: Reading, Berks County, Pennsylvania
Date of Death: 2 September 1909
Place of Death: Reading, Berks County, Pennsylvania
Cemetery: Charles Evans Cemetery (MH)—Reading, Pennsylvania
Entered Service at: Reading, Berks County, Pennsylvania
Unit: Company I, 188th Pennsylvania Infantry
Battle or Place of Action: Fort Harrison, Virginia
Date of Action: 29 September 1864
Date of Issue: 6 April 1865
Citation: First to plant the colors of his State on the fortifications.

502 ◆ GRAY, JOHN

Rank: Private (highest rank: Musician)
Service: U.S. Army
Birthday: 1836
Place of Birth: Dundee, Scotland
Date of Death: 1 June 1887
Place of Death: Leavenworth, Kansas
Cemetery: Leavenworth National Cemetery (9-1-23) (MH)—Leavenworth, Kansas
Entered Service at: Cincinnati, Hamilton County, Ohio
Unit: Company B, 5th Ohio Infantry
Battle or Place of Action: Port Republic, Virginia
Date of Action: 9 June 1862
Date of Issue: 14 March 1864
Citation: Mounted an artillery horse of the enemy and captured a brass six-pound piece in the face of the enemy's fire and brought it to the rear.

503 ◆ GRAY, ROBERT A.

Rank: Sergeant
Service: U.S. Army
Birthday: 21 September 1834
Place of Birth: Philadelphia, Philadelphia County, Pennsylvania
Date of Death: 22 November 1906
Place of Death: Groton, Connecticut
Cemetery: Colonel Ledyard Cemetery (MH)—Groton, Connecticut
Entered Service at: Groton, New London County, Connecticut
Unit: Company C, 21st Connecticut Infantry
Battle or Place of Action: Drewry's Bluff, Virginia
Date of Action: 16 May 1864
Date of Issue: 13 July 1897
Citation: While retreating with his regiment, which had been repulsed, he voluntarily returned, in the face of the enemy's fire, to a former position and rescued a wounded officer of his company who was unable to walk.

504 ◆ GREBE, M. R. WILLIAM

Rank: Captain (highest rank: Major)
Service: U.S. Army
Birthday: 4 August 1838
Place of Birth: Hildesheim, Germany
Date of Death: 24 December 1916
Place of Death: Bonner Springs, Kansas
Cemetery: Mount St. Mary's Cemetery—Kansas City, Missouri
Entered Service at: St. Louis, St. Louis County, Missouri
Unit: Company F, 4th Missouri Cavalry
Battle or Place of Action: Jonesboro, Georgia
Date of Action: 31 August 1864
Date of Issue: 24 February 1899
Citation: While acting as aide and carrying orders across a most dangerous part of the battlefield, being hindered by a Confederate advance, seized a rifle, took a place in the ranks and was conspicuous in repulsing the enemy.

505 ◆ GREEN, GEORGE

Rank: Corporal
Service: U.S. Army
Birthday: 16 July 1840
Place of Birth: Elsham, Lincolnshire County, England

Date of Death: 10 February 1898
Cemetery: Riverside Cemetery—Troy, Ohio
Entered Service at: Columbus, Franklin County, Ohio
Unit: Company H, 11th Ohio Infantry
Battle or Place of Action: Missionary Ridge, Tennessee
Date of Action: 25 November 1863
Date of Issue: 12 January 1892
Citation: Scaled the enemy's works and in a hand-to-hand fight helped capture the flag of the 18th Alabama Infantry (C.S.A.).

506 ◆ GREENAWALT, ABRAHAM

Rank: Private
Service: U.S. Army
Birthday: 1834
Place of Birth: Montgomery County, Pennsylvania
Date of Death: 27 October 1922
Cemetery: City Cemetery—Alliance, Ohio
Entered Service at: Salem, Columbiana County, Ohio
Unit: Company G, 104th Ohio Infantry
Battle or Place of Action: Franklin, Tennessee
Date of Action: 30 November 1864
Date of Issue: 13 February 1865
Citation: Capture of corps headquarters flag (C.S.A.).

507 ◆ GREENE, JOHN

Rank: Captain of the Forecastle
Service: U.S. Navy
Entered Service at: New York
Unit: U.S.S. *Varuna*
Battle or Place of Action: Forts Jackson and St. Philip, Louisiana
Date of Action: 24 April 1862
G.O. Number, Date: 11, 3 April 1863
Citation: Captain of a gun on board the U.S.S. *Varuna* during the attacks on Forts Jackson and St. Philip, and while under fire and ramming by the rebel ship *Morgan*, 24 April 1862. During this action at extremely close-range while his ship was under furious fire and twice rammed by the rebel ship *Morgan*, Greene remained steadfast at his gun throughout the thickest of the fight and was instrumental in inflicting damage on the enemy until the *Varuna*, badly damaged and forced to beach, was finally sunk.

508 ◆ GREENE, OLIVER DUFF

Rank: Major & Assistant Adjutant General (highest rank: Brevet Brigadier General)
Service: U.S. Army
Birthday: 25 January 1833
Place of Birth: Scott, Cortland County, New York
Date of Death: 19 March 1904
Cemetery: San Francisco National Cemetery OS-49-8—San Francisco, California
Entered Service at: Scott, Cortland County, New York
Unit: U.S. Army
Battle or Place of Action: Antietam, Maryland
Date of Action: 17 September 1862
Date of Issue: 13 December 1893
Citation: Formed the columns under heavy fire and put them into position.

509 ◆ GREGG, JOSEPH OLDS

Rank: Private (highest rank: Captain)
Service: U.S. Army
Birthday: 5 January 1841
Place of Birth: Lithopolis, Fairfield County, Ohio
Date of Death: 25 February 1930
Place of Death: Columbus, Ohio
Cemetery: Lithopolis Cemetery—Lithopolis, Ohio
Entered Service at: Columbus, Franklin County, Ohio
Unit: Company F, 133d Ohio National Guard Infantry
Battle or Place of Action: near the Richmond & Petersburg Railway, Virginia
Date of Action: 16 June 1864
Date of Issue: 13 May 1899
Citation: Voluntarily returned to the breastworks, which his regiment had been forced to abandon, to notify three missing companies that the regiment was falling back; found the enemy already in the works, refused a demand to surrender, returning to his command under a concentrated fire, several bullets passing through his hat and clothing.

510 ◆ GREIG, THEODORE W.

Rank: Second Lieutenant (highest rank: Major)
Service: U.S. Army
Birthday: 13 March 1843
Place of Birth: New York
Date of Death: 17 November 1893
Place of Death: New York, New York
Cemetery: Woodlawn Cemetery—Bronx, New York
Entered Service at: Staten Island, Richmond County, New York
Unit: Company C, 61st New York Infantry
Battle or Place of Action: Antietam, Maryland
Date of Action: 17 September 1862
Date of Issue: 10 February 1887
Citation: A Confederate regiment, the 4th Alabama Infantry (C.S.A.), having planted its battle flag slightly in advance of the regiment, this officer rushed forward and seized it, and, although shot through the neck, retained the flag and brought it within the Union lines.

511 ◆ GRESSER, IGNATZ

Rank: Corporal
Service: U.S. Army
Birthday: 15 August 1835
Place of Birth: Malach, Germany
Date of Death: 1 August 1929
Place of Death: Allentown, Pennsylvania
Cemetery: West Cemetery—Allentown, Pennsylvania

Entered Service at: Allentown, Lehigh County, Pennsylvania
Unit: Company D, 128th Pennsylvania Infantry
Battle or Place of Action: Antietam, Maryland
Date of Action: 17 September 1862
Date of Issue: 12 December 1895
Citation: While exposed to the fire of the enemy, carried from the field a wounded comrade.

512 ◆ GRIBBEN, JAMES H.

Rank: First Lieutenant
Service: U.S. Army
Birthday: April 1839
Place of Birth: Ireland
Date of Death: 6 August 1878
Place of Death: New York, New York
Cemetery: The Green Wood Cemetery—Brooklyn, New York
Entered Service at: New York, New York
Unit: Company C., 2d New York Cavalry
Battle or Place of Action: Deatonsville (Sailor's Creek), Virginia
Date of Action: 6 April 1865
Date of Issue: 3 May 1865
Citation: Capture of flag of 12th Virginia Infantry (C.S.A.).

513 ◆ GRIFFITHS, JOHN

Rank: Captain of the Forecastle
Service: U.S. Navy
Birthday: 1835
Place of Birth: Wales
Entered Service at: Massachusetts
Unit: U.S.S. *Santiago de Cuba*
Battle or Place of Action: Fort Fisher, North Carolina
Date of Action: 15 January 1865
G.O. Number, Date: 59, 22 June 1865
Citation: On board the U.S.S. *Santiago de Cuba* during the assault on Fort Fisher, 15 January 1865. As one of a boatcrew detailed to one of the generals onshore, Griffiths bravely entered the fort in the assault and accompanied his party in carrying dispatches at the height of the battle. He was one of the six men who entered the fort in the assault from the fleet.

514 ◆ GRIMSHAW, SAMUEL

Rank: Private (highest rank: Corporal)
Service: U.S. Army
Birthday: 2 March 1840
Place of Birth: Jefferson County, Ohio
Date of Death: 9 November 1918
Place of Death: Holton, Kansas
Cemetery: Holton Cemetery—Holton, Kansas
Entered Service at: Smithfield, Jefferson County, Ohio
Unit: Company B, 52d Ohio Infantry
Battle or Place of Action: Atlanta, Georgia
Date of Action: 6 August 1864
Date of Issue: 5 April 1894
Citation: Saved the lives of some of his comrades, and greatly imperiled his own by picking up and throwing away a lighted shell which had fallen in the midst of the company.

515 ◆ GRINDLAY, JAMES G.

Rank: Colonel (highest rank: Brevet Brigadier General)
Service: U.S. Army
Birthday: 14 February 1840
Place of Birth: Odinburgh, Scotland
Date of Death: 19 October 1907
Place of Death: Troy, New York
Cemetery: Forest Hill Cemetery—Utica, New York
Entered Service at: Utica, Oneida County, New York
Unit: 146th New York Infantry
Battle or Place of Action: Five Forks, Virginia
Date of Action: 1 April 1865
Date of Issue: 14 August 1891
Citation: The first to enter the enemy's works, where he captured two flags.

516 ◆ GRISWOLD, LUKE M.

Rank: Ordinary Seaman
Service: U.S. Navy
Birthday: 1837
Place of Birth: Massachusetts
Entered Service at: Springfield, Hampden County, Massachusetts
Unit: U.S.S. *Rhode Island*
Battle or Place of Action: off Cape Hatteras, North Carolina
Date of Action: 30 December 1862
G.O. Number, Date: 59, 22 June 1865
Citation: Served on board the U.S.S. *Rhode Island* which was engaged in saving the lives of the officers and crew of the *Monitor*, 30 December 1862. Participating in the hazardous rescue of the officers and crew of the sinking *Monitor*, Griswold, after rescuing several of the men, became separated in a heavy gale with other members of the cutter that had set out from the *Rhode Island*, and spent many hours in the small boat at the mercy of the weather and high seas until finally picked up by a schooner 50 miles east of Cape Hatteras

517 ◆ GRUEB, GEORGE M.

Rank: Private (highest rank: Corporal)
Service: U.S. Army
Birthday: 1835
Place of Birth: Wurttemberg, Germany
Date of Death: 26 September 1893
Cemetery: Bath National Cemetery (A-2-3) (MH)—Bath, New York
Entered Service at: Brooklyn, Kings County, New York
Unit: Company E, 158th New York Infantry
Battle or Place of Action: Chapin's Farm, Virginia
Date of Action: 29 September 1864
Date of Issue: 6 April 1865

Citation: Gallantry in advancing to the ditch of the enemy's works.

518 ◆ GUERIN, FITZ W.

Rank: Private
Service: U.S. Army
Birthday: 17 March 1846
Place of Birth: New York, New York
Date of Death: 11 July 1903
Place of Death: San Francisco, California
Cemetery: Bellefontaine Cemetery—St. Louis, Missouri
Entered Service at: St. Louis, St. Louis County, Missouri
Unit: Battery A, 1st Missouri Light Artillery
Battle or Place of Action: Grand Gulf, Mississippi
Date of Action: 28-29 April 1863
Date of Issue: 10 March 1896
Citation: With two comrades voluntarily took position on board the steamer *Cheeseman*, in charge of all the guns and ammunition of the battery, and remained in charge of the same for a considerable time while the steamer was unmanageable and subjected to a heavy fire from the enemy.

519 ◆ GUINN, THOMAS

Rank: Private
Service: U.S. Army
Birthday: 5 March 1836
Place of Birth: Clinton County, Ohio
Date of Death: 12 September 1908
Place of Death: New Westville, Ohio
Cemetery: Springlawn Cemetery (MH)—New Paris, Ohio
Entered Service at: Oxford, Butler County, Ohio
Unit: Company D, 47th Ohio Infantry
Battle or Place of Action: Vicksburg, Mississippi
Date of Action: 22 May 1863
Date of Issue: 21 August 1894
Citation: Gallantry in the charge of the "volunteer storming party."

520 ◆ GWYNNE, NATHANIEL MCCLEAN

Rank: Private (highest rank: Second Lieutenant)
Service: U.S. Army
Birthday: 5 July 1849
Place of Birth: Urbana, Champaign County, Ohio
Date of Death: 6 January 1883
Place of Death: Kansas City, Missouri
Cemetery: Union Cemetery (MH)—Kansas City, Missouri
Entered Service at: Fairmount, Missouri
Unit: Company H, 13th Ohio Cavalry
Battle or Place of Action: Petersburg, Virginia
Date of Action: 30 July 1864
Date of Issue: 27 January 1865
Citation: When about entering upon the charge, this soldier, then but 15 years old, was cautioned not to go in, as he had not been mustered. He indignantly protested and participated in the charge, his left arm being crushed by a shell and amputated soon afterward.

521 ◆ HACK, JOHN

Rank: Private
Service: U.S. Army
Birthday: 26 November 1842
Place of Birth: Germany
Date of Death: 29 March 1933
Cemetery: Maple Grove Cemetery (MH)—Trenton, Missouri
Entered Service at: Adrian, Lenawee County, Michigan
Unit: Company B, 47th Ohio Infantry
Battle or Place of Action: Vicksburg, Mississippi
Date of Action: 3 May 1863
Date of Issue: 3 January 1907
Citation: Was one of a party which volunteered and attempted to run the enemy's batteries with a steam tug and two barges loaded with subsistence stores.

522 ◆ HACK, LESTER GOODEL

Rank: Sergeant
Service: U.S. Army
Birthday: 18 January 1844
Place of Birth: Cadwell, Warren County, New York
Date of Death: 24 April 1928
Place of Death: Copenhagen, New York
Cemetery: Mount Hope Cemetery (MH)—Ticonderoga, New York
Entered Service at: Salisbury, Addison County, Vermont
Unit: Company F, 5th Vermont Infantry
Battle or Place of Action: Petersburg, Virginia
Date of Action: 2 April 1865
Date of Issue: 10 May 1865
Citation: Capture of flag of 23d Tennessee Infantry (C.S.A.) and several of the enemy.

523 ◆ HADLEY, CORNELIUS MINOR

Rank: Sergeant (highest rank: First Lieutenant)
Service: U.S. Army
Birthday: 27 April 1838
Place of Birth: Sandy Creek, Oswego County, New York
Date of Death: 22 March 1902
Cemetery: Mount Hope Cemetery—Litchfield, Michigan
Entered Service at: Adrian, Lenawee County, Michigan
Unit: Company F, 9th Michigan Cavalry
Battle or Place of Action: Knoxville, Tennessee
Date of Action: 20 November 1863
Date of Issue: 5 April 1898
Citation: With one companion, voluntarily carried through the enemy's lines important dispatches from Gen. Grant to Gen. Burnside, then besieged within Knoxville, and brought back replies, his comrade's horse being killed and the man taken prisoner.

524 ◆ HADLEY, OSGOOD TOWNS

Rank: Corporal (highest rank: Sergeant)
Service: U.S. Army

Birthday: 19 January 1838
Place of Birth: Nashua, Hillsborough County, New Hampshire
Date of Death: 5 October 1914
Place of Death: Southboro, Massachusetts
Cemetery: Rural Cemetery (MH)—Southboro, Massachusetts
Entered Service at: Peterborough, Hillsborough County, New Hampshire
Unit: Company E, 6th New Hampshire Veteran Infantry
Battle or Place of Action: near Pegram House, Virginia
Date of Action: 30 September 1864
Date of Issue: 27 July 1896
Citation: As color bearer of his regiment he defended his colors with great personal gallantry and brought them safely out of the action.

525 ◆ HAFFEE, EDMUND

Rank: Quarter Gunner
Service: U.S. Navy
Birthday: 1832
Place of Birth: Philadelphia, Philadelphia County, Pennsylvania
Entered Service at: Philadelphia, Philadelphia County, Pennsylvania
Unit: U.S.S. *New Ironsides*
Battle or Place of Action: Fort Fisher, North Carolina
Date of Action: 24-25 December 1864 & 13-15 January 1865
G.O. Number, Date: 59, 22 June 1865
Citation: Haffee served on board the U.S.S. *New Ironsides* during action in several attacks on Fort Fisher, 24 and 25 December 1864; and 13, 14, and 15 January 1865. The ship steamed in and took the lead in the ironclad division close inshore, and immediately opened its starboard battery in a barrage of well-directed fire to cause several fires and explosions and dismount several guns during the first two days of fighting. Taken under fire, as she steamed into position on 13 January, the *New Ironsides* fought all day and took on ammunition at night despite severe weather conditions. When the enemy came out of his bombproof to defend the fort against the storming party, the ship's battery disabled nearly every gun on the fort facing the shore before the cease-fire orders were given by the flagship.

526 ◆ HAGERTY, ASEL

True Name: Hagert, Asa
Rank: Private
Service: U.S. Army
Birthday: 30 June 1837
Place of Birth: Canada
Date of Death: 30 March 1919
Cemetery: Riverside Cemetery—Defiance, Ohio
Entered Service at: New York, New York
Unit: Company A, 61st New York Infantry
Battle or Place of Action: Deatonsville (Sailor's Creek), Virginia

Date of Action: 6 April 1865
Date of Issue: 10 May 1865
Citation: Capture of flag.

527 ◆ HAIGHT, JOHN H.

Rank: Sergeant
Service: U.S. Army
Birthday: 1 July 1841
Place of Birth: Westfield, Chautauqua County, New York
Date of Death: 8 April 1917
Place of Death: Westfield, New York
Cemetery: East Ripley Cemetery (MH)—Ripley, New York
Entered Service at: Westfield, Chautauqua County, New York
Unit: Company G, 72d New York Infantry
Battle or Place of Action: Williamsburg & Bristol Station & Manassas, Virginia
Date of Action: 5 May & 27,29,30 August 1862
Date of Issue: 8 June 1888
Citation: At Williamsburg, Va., voluntarily carried a severely wounded comrade off the field in the face of a large force of the enemy; in doing so was himself severely wounded and taken prisoner. Went into the fight at Bristol Station, Va., although severely disabled. At Manassas, volunteered to search the woods for the wounded.
Notes: POW

528 ◆ HAIGHT, SIDNEY

Rank: Corporal
Service: U.S. Army
Birthday: 21 August 1847
Place of Birth: Reading, Hillsdale County, Michigan
Date of Death: 17 September 1918
Cemetery: West Reading Cemetery—Hillsdale, Michigan
Entered Service at: Goodland, Michigan
Unit: Company E, 1st Michigan Sharpshooters
Battle or Place of Action: Petersburg, Virginia
Date of Action: 30 July 1864
Date of Issue: 31 July 1896
Citation: Instead of retreating, remained in the captured works, regardless of his personal safety and exposed to the firing, which he boldly and deliberately returned until the enemy was close upon him.
Notes: POW

529 ◆ HALEY, JAMES

Rank: Captain of the Forecastle
Service: U.S. Navy
Birthday: 1824
Place of Birth: Ireland
Entered Service at: Ohio
Unit: U.S.S. *Kearsarge*
Battle or Place of Action: off Cherbourg, France
Date of Action: 19 June 1864
G.O. Number, Date: 45, 31 December 1864
Citation: Served as captain of the forecastle on board the U.S.S. *Kearsarge* when she destroyed the *Alabama* off

Cherbourg, France, 19 June 1864. Acting as captain of a gun during the bitter engagement, Haley exhibited marked coolness and good conduct and was highly commended by his division officer for his gallantry and meritorious achievement under enemy fire.

530 ◆ HALL, FRANCIS BLOODGOOD

Rank: Chaplain
Service: U.S. Army
Birthday: 16 November 1827
Place of Birth: New York, New York
Date of Death: 4 October 1903
Cemetery: Riverside Cemetery—Plattsburgh, New York
Entered Service at: Plattsburgh, Clinton County, New York
Unit: 16th New York Infantry
Served as: Chaplain
Battle or Place of Action: Salem Heights, Virginia
Date of Action: 3 May 1863
Date of Issue: 16 February 1897
Citation: Voluntarily exposed himself to a heavy fire during the thickest of the fight and carried wounded men to the rear for treatment and attendance.

531 ◆ HALL, HENRY SEYMOUR

True Name: Hall, Hiram Seymour
Rank: Second Lieutenant & Captain (highest rank: Brevet Brigadier General U.S. Vols.)
Service: U.S. Army
Birthday: 26 September 1835
Place of Birth: Barkersville, Saratoga County, New York
Date of Death: 1 July 1908
Place of Death: Kansas City, Kansas
Cemetery: Oak Hill Cemetery (MH)—Lawrence, Kansas
Entered Service at: Elmira, Chemung County, New York
Unit: Company G, 27th New York Infantry; Company F, 121st New York Infantry
Battle or Place of Action: Gaines' Mill & Rappahannock Station, Virginia
Date of Action: 27 June 1862 & 7 November 1863
Date of Issue: 17 August 1891
Citation: Although wounded at Gaines' Mill, Va., he remained on duty and participated in the battle with his company. At Rappahannock Station, Va., while acting as aide, rendered gallant and prompt assistance in reforming the regiments inside the enemy's works.

532 ◆ HALL, NEWTON H.

Rank: Corporal
Service: U.S. Army
Birthday: 4 August 1842
Place of Birth: Brimfield, Portage County, Ohio
Date of Death: 19 October 1911
Cemetery: Standing Rock Cemetery—Kent, Ohio
Entered Service at: Brimfield, Portage County, Ohio
Unit: Company I, 104th Ohio Infantry
Battle or Place of Action: Franklin, Tennessee
Date of Action: 30 November 1864
Date of Issue: 13 February 1865
Citation: Capture of flag, believed to have belonged to Stewart's Corps (C.S.A.).

533 ◆ HALLOCK, NATHAN MULLOCK

Rank: Private (highest rank: Corporal)
Service: U.S. Army
Birthday: 23 August 1844
Place of Birth: Mount Hope, Orange County, New York
Date of Death: 21 March 1903
Place of Death: Los Angeles, California
Cemetery: Hillside Cemetery (MH)—Middletown, New York
Entered Service at: Middletown, Orange County, New York
Unit: Company K, 124th New York Infantry
Battle or Place of Action: Bristoe Station, Virginia
Date of Action: 15 June 1863
Date of Issue: 10 September 1897
Citation: At imminent peril saved from death or capture a disabled officer of his company by carrying him under a hot musketry fire to a place of safety.

534 ◆ HALSTEAD, WILLIAM W.

Rank: Coxswain
Service: U.S. Navy
Birthday: 9 January 1837
Place of Birth: Alplaus, Schenectady County, New York
Date of Death: 23 July 1916
Place of Death: Wyandotte, Michigan
Cemetery: Forest Cemetery—Toledo, Ohio
Entered Service at: New York
Unit: U.S.S. *Brooklyn*
Battle or Place of Action: Mobile Bay, Alabama
Date of Action: 5 August 1864
G.O. Number, Date: 45, 31 December 1864
Citation: On board the U.S.S. *Brooklyn* during action against rebel forts and gunboats and with the ram *Tennessee*, in Mobile Bay, 5 August 1864. Despite severe damage to his ship and the loss of several men on board as enemy fire raked her decks from stem to stern, Halstead fought his gun with skill and courage throughout the furious battle which resulted in the surrender of the prize rebel ram *Tennessee* and in the damaging and destruction of batteries at Fort Morgan.

535 ◆ HAM, MARK G.

Rank: Carpenter's Mate
Service: U.S. Navy
Birthday: 1820
Place of Birth: Portsmouth, Rockingham County, New Hampshire
Date of Death: 11 March 1869
Place of Death: Portsmouth, New Hampshire
Cemetery: Harmony Grove Cemetery (MH)—Portsmouth, New Hampshire
Entered Service at: Portsmouth, Rockingham County, New Hampshire

Unit: U.S.S. *Kearsarge*
Battle or Place of Action: off Cherbourg, France
Date of Action: 19 June 1864
G.O. Number, Date: 45, 31 December 1864
Citation: Served on board the U.S.S. *Kearsarge* when she destroyed the *Alabama* off Cherbourg, France, 19 June 1864. Performing his duties intelligently and faithfully, Ham distinguished himself in the face of the bitter enemy fire and was highly commended by his divisional officer.

536 ◆ HAMILTON, HUGH

Rank: Coxswain
Service: U.S. Navy
Birthday: 1830
Place of Birth: New York, New York
Entered Service at: New York, New York
Unit: U.S.S. *Richmond*
Battle or Place of Action: Mobile Bay, Alabama
Date of Action: 5 August 1864
G.O. Number, Date: 45, 31 December 1864
Citation: On board the U.S.S. *Richmond* during the action against rebel forts and gunboats and with the ram *Tennessee* in Mobile Bay, 5 August 1864. Despite damage to his ship and the loss of several men on board as enemy fire raked her decks, Hamilton performed his duties with skill and courage throughout the prolonged battle, which resulted in the surrender of the rebel ram *Tennessee* and in the successful attacks carried out on Fort Morgan.

537 ◆ HAMILTON, RICHARD

Rank: Coal Heaver
Service: U.S. Navy
Birthday: 1836
Place of Birth: Philadelphia, Philadelphia County, Pennsylvania
Date of Death: 6 July 1881
Place of Death: Camden, New Jersey
Cemetery: Evergreen Cemetery—Camden, New Jersey
Entered Service at: Pennsylvania
Unit: U.S. Picket Boat No. 1
Battle or Place of Action: Plymouth, North Carolina
Date of Action: 27 October 1864
G.O. Number, Date: 45, 31 December 1864
Citation: Hamilton served on board the U.S. Picket Boat No. 1, in action, 27 October 1864, against the Confederate ram, *Albemarle*, which had resisted repeated attacks by our steamers and had kept a large force of vessels employed in watching her. The picket boat, equipped with a spar torpedo, succeeded in passing the enemy pickets within 20 yards without being discovered and then made for the *Albemarle* under a full head of steam. Immediately taken under fire by the ram, the small boat plunged on, jumped the log boom which encircled the target and exploded its torpedo under the port bow of the ram. The picket boat was destroyed by enemy fire and almost the entire crew was taken prisoner or lost.
Notes: POW

538 ◆ HAMILTON, THOMAS W.

Rank: Quartermaster
Service: U.S. Navy
Birthday: 1833
Place of Birth: Scotland
Entered Service at: Weymouth, Norfolk County, Massachusetts
Unit: U.S.S. *Cincinnati*
Battle or Place of Action: Vicksburg, Mississippi
Date of Action: 27 May 1863
G.O. Number, Date: 17, 10 July 1863
Citation: Served as quartermaster on board the U.S.S. *Cincinnati* during the attack on the Vicksburg batteries and at the time of her sinking, 27 May 1863. Engaging the enemy in a fierce battle, the *Cincinnati*, amidst an incessant fire of shot and shell, continued to fire her guns to the last although so penetrated by enemy shell fire that her fate was sealed. Conspicuously gallant during this action, Hamilton, severely wounded at the wheel, returned to his post and had to be sent down below, to hear the incessant roar of guns as the gallant ship went down, "her colors nailed to the mast."

539 ◆ HAMMEL, HENRY A.

Rank: Sergeant (highest rank: First Sergeant)
Service: U.S. Army
Birthday: 20 September 1840
Place of Birth: Germany
Date of Death: 29 November 1902
Cemetery: Bellefontaine Cemetery (MH)—St. Louis, Missouri
Entered Service at: St. Louis, St. Louis County, Missouri
Unit: Battery A, 1st Missouri Light Artillery
Battle or Place of Action: Grand Gulf, Mississippi
Date of Action: 28-29 April 1863
Date of Issue: 10 March 1896
Citation: With two comrades, voluntarily took position on board the steamer *Cheeseman*, in charge of all the guns and ammunition of the battery, and remained in charge of the same for considerable time while the steamer was unmanageable and subjected to a heavy fire from the enemy.

540 ◆ HAND, ALLEXANDER

Rank: Quartermaster
Service: U.S. Navy
Birthday: 1836
Place of Birth: Delaware
Entered Service at: Delaware
Unit: U.S.S. *Ceres*
Battle or Place of Action: near Hamilton, Roanoke River, North Carolina
Date of Action: 9 July 1862
G.O. Number, Date: 11, 3 April 1863
Citation: Served on board the U.S.S. *Ceres* in the fight near Hamilton, Roanoke River, 9 July 1862. Fired on by the enemy with small arms, Hand courageously returned the raking enemy fire and was spoken of for "good conduct and cool bravery under enemy fire" by the commanding officer.

541 ◆ HANEY, MILTON LORENZI

Rank: Regimental Chaplain
Service: U.S. Army
Birthday: 23 January 1825
Place of Birth: Savannah, Ashland County, Ohio
Date of Death: 20 January 1922
Place of Death: Pasadena, California
Cemetery: Mountain View Cemetery—Altadena, California
Entered Service at: Bushnell, McDonough County, Illinois
Unit: 55th Illinois Infantry
Battle or Place of Action: Atlanta, Georgia
Date of Action: 22 July 1864
Date of Issue: 3 November 1896
Citation: Voluntarily carried a musket in the ranks of his regiment and rendered heroic service in retaking the Federal works which had been captured by the enemy.

542 ◆ HANFORD, EDWARD R.

Rank: Private
Service: U.S. Army
Birthday: 1841
Place of Birth: Allegany County, New York
Date of Death: 30 January 1890
Place of Death: Chili Gulch, California
Cemetery: Mokelumne Hill Protestant Cemetery (MH)—Mokelumne Hill, California
Entered Service at: Cortland, Cortland County, New York
Unit: Company H, 2d U.S. Cavalry
Battle or Place of Action: Woodstock, Virginia
Date of Action: 9 October 1864
Date of Issue: 14 October 1864
Citation: Capture of flag of 32d Battalion Virginia Cavalry (C.S.A.).

543 ◆ HANKS, JOSEPH

Rank: Private
Service: U.S. Army
Birthday: 22 March 1843
Place of Birth: Chillicothe, Ross County, Ohio
Date of Death: 28 December 1922
Place of Death: North Bend, Nebraska
Cemetery: Woodland Cemetery (MH)—North Bend, Nebraska
Entered Service at: Chillicothe, Ross County, Ohio
Unit: Company E, 37th Ohio Infantry
Battle or Place of Action: Vicksburg, Mississippi
Date of Action: 22 May 1863
Date of Issue: 19 November 1897
Citation: Voluntarily and under fire went to the rescue of a wounded comrade lying between the lines, gave him water, and brought him off the field.

544 ◆ HANNA, MARCUS A.

Rank: Sergeant
Service: U.S. Army
Birthday: 3 November 1842
Place of Birth: Bristol, Lincoln County, Maine
Date of Death: 12 December 1921
Place of Death: South Portland, Maine
Cemetery: Mount Pleasant Cemetery (MH)—Portland, Maine
Entered Service at: Rockport, Essex County, Massachusetts
Unit: Company B, 50th Massachusetts Infantry
Battle or Place of Action: Port Hudson, Louisiana
Date of Action: 4 July 1863
Date of Issue: 2 November 1895
Citation: Voluntarily exposed himself to a heavy fire to get water for comrades in rifle pits.

545 ◆ HANNA, MILTON

Rank: Corporal (highest rank: Sergeant)
Service: U.S. Army
Birthday: 12 January 1842
Place of Birth: Licking County, Ohio
Date of Death: 21 January 1913
Place of Death: Minnetiaha, Minnesota
Cemetery: Glenwood Cemetery—Mankato, Minnesota
Entered Service at: Henderson, Sibley County, Minnesota
Unit: Company H, 2d Minnesota Infantry
Battle or Place of Action: Nolensville, Tennessee
Date of Action: 15 February 1863
Date of Issue: 11 September 1897
Citation: Was one of a detachment of 16 men who heroically defended a wagon train against the attack of 125 cavalry, repulsed the attack, and saved the train.

546 ◆ HANSCOM, MOSES C.

Rank: Corporal
Service: U.S. Army
Birthday: 1842
Place of Birth: Danville, Androscoggin County, Maine
Date of Death: 26 July 1873
Place of Death: Auburn, Maine
Cemetery: Oak Hill Cemetery (MH)—Auburn, Maine
Entered Service at: Bowdoinham, Sagadahoc County, Maine
Unit: Company F, 19th Maine Infantry
Battle or Place of Action: Bristoe Station, Virginia
Date of Action: 14 October 1863
Date of Issue: 1 December 1864
Citation: Capture of the flag of 26th North Carolina (C.S.A.).

547 ◆ HAPEMAN, DOUGLAS

Rank: Lieutenant Colonel (highest rank: Colonel)
Service: U.S. Army
Birthday: 15 January 1839
Place of Birth: Ephrata, Fulton County, New York
Date of Death: 3 June 1905
Cemetery: Ottawa Avenue Cemetery—Ottawa, Illinois
Entered Service at: Ottawa, La Salle County, Illinois

Unit: 104th Illinois Infantry
Battle or Place of Action: Peach Tree Creek, Georgia
Date of Action: 20 July 1864
Date of Issue: 5 April 1898
Citation: With conspicuous coolness and bravery rallied his men under a severe attack, reformed the broken ranks, and repulsed the attack.
Notes: POW

548 ◆ HARBOURNE, JOHN H.

Rank: Private
Service: U.S. Army
Birthday: 9 September 1840
Place of Birth: England
Date of Death: 29 November 1928
Place of Death: Philadelphia, Pennsylvania
Cemetery: Fernwood Cemetery (no marker at all)—Fernwood, Pennsylvania
Entered Service at: Readville, Suffolk County, Massachusetts
Unit: Company K, 29th Massachusetts Infantry
Battle or Place of Action: Petersburg, Virginia
Date of Action: 17 June 1864
Date of Issue: 24 February 1897
Citation: Capture of flag along with three enemy men.

549 ◆ HARCOURT, THOMAS

Rank: Ordinary Seaman
Service: U.S. Navy
Birthday: 1841
Place of Birth: Boston, Suffolk County, Massachusetts
Entered Service at: Massachusetts
Unit: U.S.S. *Minnesota*
Battle or Place of Action: Fort Fisher, North Carolina
Date of Action: 15 January 1865
G.O. Number, Date: 59, 22 June 1865
Citation: On board the U.S.S. *Minnesota* in action during the assault on Fort Fisher, 15 January 1865. Landing on the beach with the assaulting party from his ship, Harcourt advanced to the top of the sandhill and partly through the breach in the palisades despite enemy fire, which killed and wounded many officers and men. When more than two-thirds of the men became seized with panic and retreated on the run, he remained with the party until dark when it came safely away, bringing its wounded, its arms, and its colors.

550 ◆ *HARDENBERGH, HENRY M.

Rank: Private
Service: U.S. Army
Place of Birth: Noble County, Indiana
Date of Death: 28 August 1864
Place of Death: Petersburg, Virginia
Cemetery: Poplar Grove National Cemetery (D-1283) (MH)—Petersburg, Virginia
Entered Service at: Bremen, Illinois
Unit: Company G, 39th Illinois Infantry

Battle or Place of Action: Deep Run, Virginia
Date of Action: 16 August 1864
Date of Issue: 6 April 1865
Citation: Capture of flag. He was wounded in the shoulder during this action. He was killed in action at Petersburg on 28 August 1864.

551 ◆ HARDING, THOMAS

Rank: Captain of the Forecastle (highest rank: Acting Master's Mate)
Service: U.S. Navy
Birthday: 1837
Place of Birth: Middletown, Middlesex County, Connecticut
Entered Service at: Connecticut
Unit: U.S.S. *Dacotah*
Battle or Place of Action: Beaufort, North Carolina
Date of Action: 9 June 1864
G.O. Number, Date: 45, 31 December 1864
Date of Issue: 31 December 1864
Citation: Served as captain of the forecastle on board the U.S.S. *Dacotah* on the occasion of the destruction of the blockade runner *Pevensey*, near Beaufort, N.C., 9 June 1864. "Learning that one of the officers in the boat, which was in danger of being, and subsequently was, swamped, could not swim, Harding remarked to him: 'If we are swamped, sir, I shall carry you to the beach or I will never go there myself.' He did not succeed in carrying out his promise, but made desperate efforts to do so, while others thought only of themselves. Such conduct is worthy of appreciation and admiration—a sailor risking his own life to save that of an officer."

552 ◆ HARING, ABRAM PYE

Rank: First Lieutenant
Service: U.S. Army
Birthday: 15 November 1840
Place of Birth: New York, New York
Date of Death: 22 February 1915
Place of Death: Montclair, New Jersey
Cemetery: Canterbury Presbyterian Cemetery—Cornwall-on-the-Hudson, New York
Entered Service at: New York, New York
Unit: Company G, 132d New York Infantry
Battle or Place of Action: Bachelor's Creek, North Carolina
Date of Action: 1 February 1864
Date of Issue: 28 June 1890
Citation: With a command of 11 men, on picket, resisted the attack of an overwhelming force of the enemy.

553 ◆ HARLEY, BERNARD

Rank: Ordinary Seaman
Service: U.S. Navy
Birthday: 1842
Place of Birth: Brooklyn, Kings County, New York
Date of Death: 15 January 1886
Cemetery: Holy Cross Cemetery—Brooklyn, New York

Entered Service at: New York, New York
Unit: U.S. Picket Boat No. 1
Battle or Place of Action: Plymouth, North Carolina
Date of Action: 27 October 1864
G.O. Number, Date: 45, 31 December 1864
Citation: Harley served on board the U.S. Picket Boat No. 1, in action, 27 October 1864, against the Confederate ram *Albemarle*, which had resisted repeated attacks by our steamers and had kept a large force of vessels employed in watching her. The picket boat, equipped with a spar torpedo, succeeded in passing the enemy pickets within 20 yards without being discovered and then made for the *Albemarle* under a full head of steam. Immediately taken under fire by the ram, the small boat plunged on, jumped the log boom which encircled the target and exploded its torpedo under the port bow of the ram. The picket boat was destroyed by enemy fire and almost the entire crew taken prisoner or lost.
Notes: POW

554 ◆ HARMON, AMZI DAVIS

True Name: Harman, Amzi Davis
Rank: Corporal
Service: U.S. Army
Birthday: 18 April 1845
Place of Birth: Wilkinsburg, Allegheny County, Pennsylvania
Date of Death: 9 October 1927
Place of Death: St. Cloud, Florida
Cemetery: Mount Peace Cemetery (MH)—St. Cloud, Florida
Entered Service at: Greensburg, Westmoreland County, Pennsylvania
Unit: Company K, 211th Pennsylvania Infantry
Battle or Place of Action: Petersburg, Virginia
Date of Action: 2 April 1865
Date of Issue: 20 May 1865
Citation: Capture of flag.

555 ◆ HARRINGTON, DANIEL C.

Rank: Landsman (highest rank: Acting Masters Mate)
Service: U.S. Navy
Birthday: 1849
Place of Birth: Ireland
Entered Service at: Massachusetts
Unit: U.S.S. *Pocahontas*
Battle or Place of Action: near Brunswick, Georgia
Date of Action: 11 March 1862
G.O. Number, Date: 11, 3 April 1863
Date of Presentation: 1 June 1863
Place of Presentation: Off Wilmington, North Carolina, aboard the U.S.S. Steamer *Sacramento*, presented by Capt. Charles S. Boggs
Citation: Harrington, a landsman from the U.S.S. *Pocahontas*, participated in a shore mission to procure meat for the ship's crew. While returning to the beach, the party was fired on from ambush and several men killed or wounded. Cool and courageous throughout this action, Harrington rendered gallant service against the enemy and in administering to the casualties.

556 ◆ HARRINGTON, EPHRAIM W.

Rank: Sergeant (highest rank: Major)
Service: U.S. Army
Birthday: 16 January 1833
Place of Birth: Waterford, Oxford County, Maine
Date of Death: 19 October 1914
Place of Death: St. Johnsbury, Vermont
Cemetery: Grove Cemetery (MH)—St. Johnsbury, Vermont
Entered Service at: Kirby, Vermont
Unit: Company G, 2d Vermont Infantry
Battle or Place of Action: Fredericksburg, Virginia
Date of Action: 3 May 1863
Date of Issue: 13 December 1893
Citation: Carried the colors to the top of the heights and almost to the muzzle of the enemy's guns.

557 ◆ HARRIS, GEORGE W.

Rank: Private
Service: U.S. Army
Birthday: 6 March 1835
Place of Birth: Schuylkill, Philadelphia County, Pennsylvania
Date of Death: 30 January 1921
Place of Death: Bellefonte, Pennsylvania
Cemetery: Union Cemetery (MH)—Bellefonte, Pennsylvania
Entered Service at: Bellefonte, Centre County, Pennsylvania
Unit: Company B, 148th Pennsylvania Infantry
Battle or Place of Action: Spotsylvania, Virginia
Date of Action: 12 May 1864
Date of Issue: 1 December 1864
Citation: Capture of flag, wresting it from the color bearer and shooting an officer who attempted to regain it.

558 ◆ HARRIS, JAMES H.

Rank: Sergeant
Service: U.S. Army
Birthday: 1828
Place of Birth: St. Mary's County, Maryland
Date of Death: 28 January 1898
Cemetery: Arlington National Cemetery (27-985-H) (MH)—Arlington, Virginia
Entered Service at: Great Mills, St. Mary's County, Maryland
Unit: Company B, 38th U.S. Colored Infantry
Battle or Place of Action: New Market Heights, Virginia
Date of Action: 29 September 1864
Date of Issue: 18 February 1874
Citation: Gallantry in the assault.

559 ◆ HARRIS, JOHN

Rank: Captain of the Forecastle
Service: U.S. Navy

Birthday: 1839
Place of Birth: Norway
Entered Service at: New York, New York
Unit: U.S.S. *Metacomet*
Battle or Place of Action: Mobile Bay, Alabama
Date of Action: 5 August 1864
G.O. Number, Date: 17, 15 January 1866
Citation: As captain of the forecastle on board the U.S.S. *Metacomet*, Harris was a member of the boat's crew which went to the rescue of the officers and crew of the U.S. Monitor *Tecumseh*, when the vessel was struck by a torpedo in passing the enemy forts in Mobile Bay, 5 August 1864. Harris braved the enemy fire which was said by the admiral to be "one of the most galling" he had ever seen, and aided in rescuing from death 10 of the crew of the *Tecumseh*, thereby eliciting the admiration of both friend and foe.

560 ◆ HARRIS, MOSES

Rank: First Lieutenant (highest rank: Major)
Service: U.S. Army
Birthday: 1839
Place of Birth: Andover, Merrimack County, New Hampshire
Date of Death: 27 June 1927
Cemetery: U.S. Military Academy Cemetery (4-C-60)—West Point, New York
Entered Service at: Boston, Suffolk County, Massachusetts
Unit: 1st U.S. Cavalry
Battle or Place of Action: Smithfield, Virginia
Date of Action: 28 August 1864
Date of Issue: 23 November 1896
Citation: In an attack upon a largely superior force, his personal gallantry was so conspicuous as to inspire the men to extraordinary efforts, resulting in complete rout of the enemy.

561 ◆ HARRIS, SAMPSON

Rank: Private
Service: U.S. Army
Place of Birth: Noble County, Ohio
Date of Death: 29 October 1905
Cemetery: Olive Cemetery—Caldwell, Ohio
Entered Service at: Olive, Ohio
Unit: Company K, 30th Ohio Infantry
Battle or Place of Action: Vicksburg, Mississippi
Date of Action: 22 May 1863
Date of Issue: 10 July 1894
Citation: Gallantry in the charge of the "volunteer storming party."

562 ◆ HARRISON, GEORGE H.

Rank: Seaman
Service: U.S. Navy
Birthday: 9 April 1841
Place of Birth: Middleton, Essex County, Massachusetts
Date of Death: 18 January 1919
Place of Death: Chelsea, Massachusetts
Cemetery: Fort Dale Cemetery (MH)—Malden, Massachusetts
Entered Service at: Somerset, Bristol County, Massachusetts
Unit: U.S.S. *Kearsarge*
Battle or Place of Action: off Cherbourg, France
Date of Action: 19 June 1864
G.O. Number, Date: 45, 31 December 1864
Citation: Served on board the U.S.S. *Kearsarge* when she destroyed the *Alabama* off Cherbourg, France, 19 June 1864. Acting as sponger and loader of the 11-inch pivot gun during the bitter engagement, Harrison exhibited marked coolness and good conduct and was highly recommended for his gallantry under fire by the divisional officer.

563 ◆ HART, JOHN WILLIAM

Rank: Sergeant
Service: U.S. Army
Birthday: 30 July 1833
Place of Birth: Germany
Date of Death: 2 June 1908
Place of Death: Cumberland, Maryland
Cemetery: German Lutheran Cemetery—Cumberland, Maryland
Entered Service at: Cumberland, Allegany County, Maryland
Unit: Company D, 6th Pennsylvania Reserves
Battle or Place of Action: Gettysburg, Pennsylvania
Date of Action: 2 July 1863
Date of Issue: 3 August 1897
Citation: Was one of six volunteers who charged upon a log house near the Devil's Den, where a squad of the enemy's sharpshooters were sheltered, and compelled their surrender.

564 ◆ HART, WILLIAM E.

Rank: Private (highest rank: Corporal)
Service: U.S. Army
Birthday: 1843
Place of Birth: Rushville, Yates County, New York
Date of Death: 21 October 1874
Place of Death: Champlain Canal, New York
Cemetery: unknown cemetery—Halfmoon, New York
Entered Service at: Rushville, Yates County, New York
Unit: Company B, 8th New York Cavalry
Battle or Place of Action: Shenandoah Valley, Virginia
Date of Action: 1864 & 1865
Date of Issue: 3 July 1872
Citation: Gallant conduct and services as scout in connection with capture of the guerrilla Harry Gilmore, and other daring acts.

565 ◆ HARTRANFT, JOHN FREDERIC

Rank: Colonel (highest rank: Brevet Major General)
Service: U.S. Army
Birthday: 16 December 1830
Place of Birth: New Hanover Township, Montgomery County, Pennsylvania

Date of Death: 17 October 1889
Cemetery: Montgomery Cemetery (MH)—Norristown, Pennsylvania
Entered Service at: Norristown, Montgomery County, Pennsylvania
Unit: 4th Pennsylvania Militia
Battle or Place of Action: Bull Run, Virginia
Date of Action: 21 July 1861
Date of Issue: 26 August 1886
Citation: Voluntarily served as an aide and participated in the battle after expiration of his term of service, distinguishing himself in rallying several regiments which had been thrown into confusion.

566 ◆ HARVEY, HARRY

True Name: Huckman, Harry
Rank: Corporal
Service: U.S. Army
Birthday: 14 December 1846
Place of Birth: England
Date of Death: 2 April 1896
Place of Death: Elmwood, New York
Cemetery: Myrtle Hill Cemetery (MH)—Syracuse, New York
Entered Service at: Rochester, Monroe County, New York
Unit: Company A, 22d New York Cavalry
Battle or Place of Action: Waynesboro, Virginia
Date of Action: 2 March 1865
Date of Issue: 26 March 1865
Citation: Capture of flag and bearer, with two other prisoners.

567 ◆ HASKELL, FRANK W.

Rank: Sergeant Major
Service: U.S. Army
Birthday: 1843
Place of Birth: Benton, Maine
Date of Death: 9 October 1903
Cemetery: Pine Grove Cemetery—Waterville, Maine
Entered Service at: Waterville, Kennebec County, Maine
Unit: 3d Maine Infantry
Battle or Place of Action: Fair Oaks, Virginia
Date of Action: 1 June 1862
Date of Issue: 8 December 1898
Citation: Assumed command of a portion of the left wing of his regiment, all the company officers present having been killed or disabled, led it gallantly across a stream and contributed most effectively to the success of the action.

568 ◆ HASKELL, MARCUS M.

Rank: Sergeant
Service: U.S. Army
Birthday: 12 February 1843
Place of Birth: Chelsea, Suffolk County, Massachusetts
Date of Death: 29 October 1925
Place of Death: Centerville, Massachusetts
Cemetery: Beechwood Cemetery (MH)—Centerville, Massachusetts
Entered Service at: Chelsea, Suffolk County, Massachusetts
Unit: Company C, 35th Massachusetts Infantry
Battle or Place of Action: Antietam, Maryland
Date of Action: 17 September 1862
Date of Issue: 18 November 1896
Citation: Although wounded and exposed to a heavy fire from the enemy, at the risk of his own life he rescued a badly wounded comrade and succeeded in conveying him to a place of safety.

569 ◆ HASTINGS, SMITH H.

Rank: Captain (highest rank: Colonel)
Service: U.S. Army
Birthday: 27 December 1843
Place of Birth: Quincy, Branch County, Michigan
Date of Death: 13 October 1905
Place of Death: Denver, Colorado
Cemetery: Riverside Cemetery (MH)—Denver, Colorado
Entered Service at: Coldwater, Branch County, Michigan
Unit: Troop M, 5th Michigan Cavalry
Battle or Place of Action: Newbys Crossroads, Virginia
Date of Action: 24 July 1863
Date of Issue: 2 August 1897
Citation: While in command of a squadron in rear guard of a cavalry division, then retiring before the advance of a corps of infantry, was attacked by the enemy and, orders having been given to abandon the guns of a section of field artillery with the rear guard that were in imminent danger of capture, he disregarded the orders received and aided in repelling the attack and saving the guns.

570 ◆ HATCH, JOHN PORTER

Rank: Brigadier General (highest rank: Brevet Major General)
Service: U.S. Army
Birthday: 9 January 1822
Place of Birth: Oswego, Oswego County, New York
Date of Death: 12 April 1901
Place of Death: New York, New York
Cemetery: Arlington National Cemetery (1-333-C)—Arlington, Virginia
Entered Service at: Oswego, Oswego County, New York
Unit: 1st Division, U.S. Volunteers
Battle or Place of Action: South Mountain, Maryland
Date of Action: 14 September 1862
Date of Issue: 28 October 1893
Citation: Was severely wounded while leading one of his brigades in the attack under a heavy fire from the enemy.

571 ◆ HATHAWAY, EDWARD W.

Rank: Seaman
Service: U.S. Navy
Birthday: 9 July 1839
Place of Birth: Plymouth, Plymouth County, Massachusetts
Date of Death: 6 April 1916
Place of Death: Salem, Massachusetts

Cemetery: Woodlawn Cemetery (MH)—Everett, Massachusetts
Entered Service at: Plymouth, Plymouth County, Massachusetts
Unit: U.S.S. *Sciota*
Battle or Place of Action: near Vicksburg, Mississippi
Date of Action: 28 June 1862
G.O. Number, Date: 84, 3 October 1867
Citation: On board the U.S.S. *Sciota* prior to the battle of Vicksburg, 28 June 1862. Struck by a bullet which severed his left arm above the elbow, Hathaway displayed exceptional courage as his ship sustained numerous damaging hits from stem to stern while proceeding down the river to fight the battle of Vicksburg.

572 ◆ HAVRON, JOHN H.

Rank: Sergeant
Service: U.S. Army
Birthday: 23 December 1843
Place of Birth: Ireland
Date of Death: 28 October 1910
Place of Death: New Orleans, Louisiana
Entered Service at: Providence, Providence County, Rhode Island
Unit: Company G, 1st Rhode Island Light Artillery
Battle or Place of Action: Petersburg, Virginia
Date of Action: 2 April 1865
Date of Issue: 16 June 1866
Citation: Was one of a detachment of 20 picked artillerymen who voluntarily accompanied an infantry assaulting party and who turned upon the enemy the guns captured in the assault.

573 ◆ HAWKINS, CHARLES

Rank: Seaman (highest rank: Boatswain's Mate)
Service: U.S. Navy
Birthday: 1834
Place of Birth: Scotland
Date of Death: 29 February 1908
Place of Death: Cranston, Rhode Island
Cemetery: St. Mary's Cemetery—Cranston, Rhode Island
Entered Service at: Portsmouth, Rockingham County, New Hampshire
Unit: U.S.S. *Agawam*
Battle or Place of Action: Fort Fisher, North Carolina
Date of Action: 23 December 1864
G.O. Number, Date: 45, 31 December 1864
Date of Presentation: 12 May 1865
Place of Presentation: On board the U.S.S. *Agawam* off New Bern, North Carolina
Citation: Hawkins served on board the U.S.S. *Agawam* as one of a volunteer crew of a powder boat which was exploded near Fort Fisher, 23 December 1864. The powder boat, towed in by the *Wilderness*, to prevent detection by the enemy, cast off and slowly steamed to within 300 yards of the beach. After fuses and fires had been lit and a second anchor with short scope let go to assure the boat's tailing inshore, the crew again boarded the *Wilderness* and and proceeded a distance of 12 miles from shore. Less than two hours later the explosion took place, and the following day fires were observed still burning at the forts.

574 ◆ HAWKINS, GARDNER C.

Rank: First Lieutenant (highest rank: Colonel)
Service: U.S. Army
Birthday: 11 February 1846
Place of Birth: Pomfret, Vermont
Date of Death: 15 December 1913
Place of Death: Winthrop, Massachusetts
Cemetery: Lindenwood Cemetery—Stoneham, Massachusetts
Entered Service at: Woodstock, Windsor County, Vermont
Unit: Company E, 3d Vermont Infantry
Battle or Place of Action: Petersburg, Virginia
Date of Action: 2 April 1865
Date of Issue: 30 September 1893
Citation: When the lines were wavering from the well-directed fire of the enemy, this officer, acting adjutant of the regiment, sprang forward, and with encouraging words cheered the soldiers on and, although dangerously wounded, refused to leave the field until the enemy's works were taken.

575 ◆ HAWKINS, MARTIN JONES

Rank: Corporal (highest rank: First Lieutenant)
Service: U.S. Army
Place of Birth: Mercer County, Pennsylvania
Date of Death: 7 February 1886
Cemetery: Woodlawn Cemetery (MH)—Quincy, Illinois
Entered Service at: Portsmouth, Scioto County, Ohio
Unit: Company A, 33d Ohio Infantry
Battle or Place of Action: Georgia
Date of Action: April 1862
Date of Issue: September 1863
Citation: One of 19 of 24 men (including two civilians) who, by direction of Gen. Ormsby M. Mitchell, penetrated nearly 200 miles south into enemy territory and captured a railroad train at Big Shanty, Ga., in an attempt to destroy the bridges and track between Chattanaooga and Atlanta.
Notes: POW

576 ◆ HAWKINS, THOMAS R.

Rank: Sergeant Major
Service: U.S. Army
Birthday: 1840
Place of Birth: Cincinnati, Hamilton County, Ohio
Date of Death: 28 February 1870
Place of Death: Washington, D.C.
Cemetery: Harmony Cemetery—Landover, Maryland
Entered Service at: Philadelphia, Philadelphia County, Pennsylvania
Unit: 6th U.S. Colored Infantry
Battle or Place of Action: Chapin's Farm, Virginia
Date of Action: 29 September 1864
Date of Issue: 8 February 1870
Citation: Rescue of regimental colors.

577 ◆ HAWTHORNE, HARRIS SMITH

Rank: Corporal (highest rank: Sergeant)
Service: U.S. Army
Birthday: 29 February 1832
Place of Birth: Salem, Washington County, New York
Date of Death: 23 March 1911
Place of Death: Hoosick Falls, New York
Cemetery: Maple Grove Cemetery—Hoosick Falls, New York
Entered Service at: Otsego County, New York
Unit: Company F, 121st New York Infantry
Battle or Place of Action: Deatonsville (Sailor's Creek), Virginia
Date of Action: 6 April 1865
Date of Issue: 29 December 1894
Citation: Capture of Confederate Maj. Gen. George Washington Custis Lee.

578 ◆ HAYDEN, JOSEPH B.

Rank: Quartermaster
Service: U.S. Navy
Birthday: 1834
Place of Birth: St. Mary's City, St. Mary's County, Maryland
Entered Service at: Maryland
Unit: U.S.S. Ticonderoga
Battle or Place of Action: Fort Fisher, North Carolina
Date of Action: 13-15 January 1865
G.O. Number, Date: 59, 22 June 1865
Citation: On board the U.S.S. Ticonderoga, as quartermaster in charge of steering the ship into action, during attacks on Fort Fisher, 13 to 15 January 1865. Hayden steered the ship into position in the line of battle where she maintained a well-directed fire upon the batteries to the left of the palisades during the initial phases of the engagement. Although several of the enemy's shots fell over and around the vessel, the Ticonderoga fought her guns gallantly throughout three consecutive days of battle until the flag was planted on one of the strongest fortifications possessed by the rebels.

579 ◆ HAYES, JOHN

Rank: Coxswain
Service: U.S. Navy
Birthday: 20 July 1832
Place of Birth: Brogus, Newfoundland, Canada
Date of Death: 28 January 1911
Place of Death: Blairstown, Iowa
Cemetery: Pleasant Hill Cemetery (MH)—Blairstown, Iowa
Entered Service at: New Bedford, Bristol County, Massachusetts
Unit: U.S.S. Kearsarge
Battle or Place of Action: off Cherbourg, France
Date of Action: 19 June 1864
G.O. Number, Date: 45, 31 December 1864
Citation: Served on board the U.S.S. Kearsarge when she destroyed the Alabama off Cherbourg, France, 19 June 1864. Acting as second captain of the No. 2 gun during the bitter engagement, Hayes exhibited marked coolness and good conduct and was highly recommended for his gallantry under fire by the divisional officer.

580 ◆ HAYES, THOMAS

Rank: Coxswain
Service: U.S. Navy
Birthday: 1840
Place of Birth: Rhode Island
Date of Death: 24 May 1914
Entered Service at: Rhode Island
Unit: U.S.S. Richmond
Battle or Place of Action: Mobile Bay, Alabama
Date of Action: 5 August 1864
G.O. Number, Date: 45, 31 December 1864
Citation: As captain of No. 1 gun on board the U.S.S. Richmond during action against rebel forts and gunboats and with the ram Tennessee in Mobile Bay, 5 August 1864. Cool and courageous at his station throughout the prolonged action, Hayes maintained fire from his gun on Fort Morgan and on ships of the Confederacy despite extremely heavy return fire.

581 ◆ HAYNES, ASBURY F.

Rank: Corporal (highest rank: First Sergeant)
Service: U.S. Army
Birthday: 4 September 1842
Place of Birth: Edinburgh, Maine
Date of Death: 8 July 1931
Place of Death: Retsil, Washington
Cemetery: Lakeview Cemetery—Seattle, Washington
Entered Service at: Passadumkeag, Penobscot County, Maine
Unit: Company F, 17th Maine Infantry
Battle or Place of Action: Deatonsville (Sailor's Creek), Virginia
Date of Action: 6 April 1865
Date of Issue: 10 May 1865
Citation: Capture of flag.

582 ◆ HAYS, JOHN H.

Rank: Private
Service: U.S. Army
Birthday: 4 August 1844
Place of Birth: Jefferson County, Ohio
Date of Death: 27 January 1904
Cemetery: Moscow Cemetery—Moscow, Idaho
Entered Service at: Oskaloosa, Mahaska County, Iowa
Unit: Company F, 4th Iowa Cavalry
Battle or Place of Action: Columbus, Georgia
Date of Action: 16 April 1865
Date of Issue: 17 June 1865
Citation: Capture of flag and bearer, Austin's Battery (C.S.A.).

583 ◆ HEALEY, GEORGE WASHINGTON

Rank: Private (highest rank: Corporal)
Service: U.S. Army
Birthday: 22 February 1842
Place of Birth: Dubuque, Dubuque County, Iowa
Date of Death: 9 May 1913
Cemetery: Lindwood Cemetery (MH)—Dubuque, Iowa
Entered Service at: Dubuque, Dubuque County, Iowa
Unit: Company E, 5th Iowa Cavalry
Battle or Place of Action: Newman, Georgia
Date of Action: 29 July 1864
Date of Issue: 13 January 1899
Citation: When nearly surrounded by the enemy, captured a Confederate soldier, and with the aid of a comrade who joined him later, captured four other Confederate soldiers, disarmed the five prisoners, and brought them all into the Union lines.
Notes: POW

584 ◆ HEDGES, JOSEPH S.

Rank: First Lieutenant (highest rank: Captain)
Service: U.S. Army
Birthday: 12 June 1836
Place of Birth: Mansfield, Richland County, Ohio
Date of Death: 12 August 1910
Cemetery: Mansfield Memorial Park—Mansfield, Ohio
Entered Service at: Mansfield, Richland County, Ohio
Unit: 4th U.S. Cavalry
Battle or Place of Action: near Harpeth River, Tennessee
Date of Action: 17 December 1864
Date of Issue: 5 April 1898
Citation: At the head of his regiment charged a field battery with strong infantry supports, broke the enemy's line, and, with other mounted troops, captured three guns and many prisoners.

585 ◆ HEERMANCE, WILLIAM LAING

Rank: Captain
Service: U.S. Army
Birthday: 28 February 1837
Place of Birth: Kinderhook, Columbia County, New York
Date of Death: 25 February 1903
Place of Death: Yonkers, New York
Cemetery: Oakland Cemetery (MH)—Yonkers, New York
Entered Service at: Kinderhook, Columbia County, New York
Unit: Company C, 6th New York Cavalry
Battle or Place of Action: Chancellorsville, Virginia
Date of Action: 30 April 1863
Date of Issue: 30 March 1898
Citation: Took command of the regiment as its senior officer when surrounded by Stuart's Cavalry. The regiment cut its way through the enemy's line and escaped, but Capt. Heermance was desperately wounded, left for dead on the field and was taken prisoner.
Notes: POW

586 ◆ HELLER, HENRY

Rank: Sergeant
Service: U.S. Army
Birthday: 1841
Date of Death: 14 December 1895
Cemetery: Kings Creek Baptist Church Cemetery—Kings Creek, Ohio
Entered Service at: Urbana, Champaign County, Ohio
Unit: Company A, 66th Ohio Infantry
Battle or Place of Action: Chancellorsville, Virginia
Date of Action: 2 May 1863
Date of Issue: 29 July 1892
Citation: One of a party of four who, under heavy fire, voluntarily brought into the Union lines a wounded Confederate officer from whom was obtained valuable information concerning the positions of the enemy.

587 ◆ HELMS, DAVID H.

Rank: Private (highest rank: First Sergeant)
Service: U.S. Army
Birthday: 21 September 1838
Place of Birth: Dearborn County, Indiana
Date of Death: 7 July 1921
Cemetery: Silverlake Cemetery (MH)—Silverlake, Kansas
Entered Service at: Farmers Retreat, Indiana
Unit: Company B, 83d Indiana Infantry
Battle or Place of Action: Vicksburg, Mississippi
Date of Action: 22 May 1863
Date of Issue: 26 July 1894
Citation: Gallantry in the charge of the "volunteer storming party."

588 ◆ HENRY, GUY VERNOR

Rank: Colonel (highest rank: Major General)
Service: U.S. Army
Birthday: 9 March 1839
Place of Birth: Fort Smith, Indian Territory
Date of Death: 27 October 1899
Cemetery: Arlington National Cemetery (2-990)—Arlington, Virginia
Entered Service at: Reading, Berks County, Pennsylvania
Unit: 40th Massachusetts Infantry
Battle or Place of Action: Cold Harbor, Virginia
Date of Action: 1 June 1864
Date of Issue: 5 December 1893
Citation: Led the assaults of his brigade upon the enemy's works, where he had two horses shot under him.

589 ◆ HENRY, JAMES

Rank: Sergeant (highest rank: First Sergeant)
Service: U.S. Army
Birthday: 7 April 1833
Place of Birth: Sunfish, Ohio
Date of Death: 7 June 1911
Place of Death: Geneva, Illinois

Cemetery: Oak Hill Cemetery (MH)—Geneva, Illinois
Entered Service at: Kankakee, Kankakee County, Illinois
Unit: Company B, 113th Illinois Infantry
Battle or Place of Action: Vicksburg, Mississippi
Date of Action: 22 May 1863
Date of Issue: 9 July 1894
Citation: Gallantry in the charge of the "volunteer storming party."

590 ◆ HENRY, WILLIAM WIRT

Rank: Colonel (highest rank: Brevet Brigadier General)
Service: U.S. Army
Birthday: 21 November 1831
Place of Birth: Waterbury, Washington County, Vermont
Date of Death: 31 August 1915
Cemetery: Lake View Cemetery—Burlington, Vermont
Entered Service at: Waterbury, Washington County, Vermont
Unit: 10th Vermont Infantry
Battle or Place of Action: Cedar Creek, Virginia
Date of Action: 19 October 1864
Date of Issue: 21 December 1892
Citation: Though suffering from severe wounds, rejoined his regiment and led it in a brilliant charge, recapturing the guns of an abandoned battery.

591 ◆ HERINGTON, PITT B.

Rank: Private
Service: U.S. Army
Birthday: 5 February 1841
Place of Birth: Michigan
Date of Death: 15 January 1919
Place of Death: Wapalla, Illinois
Cemetery: Park Cemetery—Clinton, Illinois
Entered Service at: Tipton, Cedar County, Iowa
Unit: Company E, 11th Iowa Infantry
Battle or Place of Action: near Kenesaw Mountain, Georgia
Date of Action: 15 June 1864
Date of Issue: 27 November 1899
Citation: With one companion and under a fierce fire of the enemy at close-range, went to the rescue of a wounded comrade who had fallen between the lines and carried him to a place of safety.

592 ◆ HERRON, FRANCIS JAY

Rank: Lieutenant Colonel (highest rank: Major General)
Service: U.S. Army
Birthday: 17 February 1837
Place of Birth: Pittsburgh, Allegheny County, Pennsylvania
Date of Death: 8 January 1902
Cemetery: First Calvary Cemetery—Woodside, New York
Entered Service at: Pittsburgh, Allegheny County, Pennsylvania
Unit: 9th Iowa Infantry
Battle or Place of Action: Pea Ridge, Arkansas
Date of Action: 7 March 1862
Date of Issue: 26 September 1893
Citation: Was foremost in leading his men, rallying them to repeated acts of daring, until himself disabled and taken prisoner.
Notes: POW

593 ◆ HESSELTINE, FRANCIS SNOW

Rank: Lieutenant Colonel
Service: U.S. Army
Birthday: 10 December 1833
Place of Birth: Bangor, Penobscot County, Maine
Date of Death: 17 February 1916
Place of Death: Texas
Cemetery: Wyoming Cemetery (MH)—Melrose, Massachusetts
Entered Service at: Waterville, Kennebec County, Maine
Unit: 13th Maine Infantry
Battle or Place of Action: Matagorda Bay, Texas
Date of Action: 30 December 1863
Date of Issue: 2 March 1895
Citation: In command of a detachment of 100 men, conducted a reconnaissance for two days, baffling and beating back an attacking force of more than 1000 Confederate cavalry, and regained his transport without loss.

594 ◆ HIBSON, JOSEPH C.

Rank: Private (highest rank: Bugler)
Service: U.S. Army
Birthday: 3 August 1843
Place of Birth: London, England
Date of Death: 14 April 1911
Place of Death: Flushing, New York
Cemetery: Cypress Hills Cemetery (Private)—Brooklyn, New York
Entered Service at: New York, New York
Unit: Company C, 48th New York Infantry
Battle or Place of Action: near Fort Wagner, South Carolina
Date of Action: 13-14, 18 July 1863
Date of Issue: 23 October 1897
Citation: While voluntarily performing picket duty under fire, 13 July 1863, was attacked and his surrender demanded, but he killed his assailant. The day following Hibson responded to a call for a volunteer to reconnoiter the enemy's position, and went within the enemy's lines under fire and was exposed to great danger. On 18 July voluntarily exposed himself with great gallantry during an assault, and received three wounds that permanently disabled him for active service.

595 ◆ HICKEY, DENNIS WILLIAM

Rank: Sergeant
Service: U.S. Army
Birthday: 20 September 1844
Place of Birth: Troy, Rensselaer County, New York
Date of Death: 26 October 1908
Place of Death: Newburgh, New York
Cemetery: St. George's Cemetery—Newburgh, New York
Entered Service at: Plattsburgh, Clinton County, New York
Unit: Company E, 2d New York Cavalry

Battle or Place of Action: Stony Creek Bridge, Virginia
Date of Action: 29 June 1864
Date of Issue: 18 April 1891
Citation: With a detachment of three men, tore up the bridge at Stony Creek, being the last man on the bridge and covering the retreat until he was shot down.

596 ◆ HICKMAN, JOHN S.

Rank: Second Class Fireman
Service: U.S. Navy
Birthday: 2 March 1837
Place of Birth: Blair County, Pennsylvania
Date of Death: 24 December 1904
Cemetery: Calvary Cemetery (MH)—Altoona, Pennsylvania
Entered Service at: Pennsylvania
Unit: U.S.S. *Richmond*
Battle or Place of Action: Port Hudson, Louisiana
Date of Action: 14 March 1863
G.O. Number, Date: 17, 10 July 1863
Citation: Served on board the U.S.S. *Richmond* in the attack on Port Hudson, 14 March 1863. Damaged by a 6-inch solid rifle shot which shattered the starboard safety-valve chamber and also damaged the port safety valve, the fireroom of the U.S.S. *Richmond* immediately became filled with steam to place it in an extremely critical condition. Acting courageously in this crisis, Hickman persisted in penetrating the steam-filled room in order to haul the hot fires of the furnaces and continued this action until the gravity of the situation had been lessened.

597 ◆ HICKOK, NATHAN E.

Rank: Corporal
Service: U.S. Army
Birthday: 1839
Place of Birth: Danbury, Fairfield County, Connecticut
Cemetery: Wooster Cemetery—Danbury, Connecticut (Name inscribed on monument honoring local men in unknown graves.)
Entered Service at: Danbury, Fairfield County, Connecticut
Unit: Company A, 8th Connecticut Infantry
Battle or Place of Action: Chapin's Farm, Virginia
Date of Action: 29 September 1864
Date of Issue: 6 April 1865
Citation: Capture of flag.

598 ◆ HIGBY, CHARLES

Rank: Private
Service: U.S. Army
Birthday: 1841
Place of Birth: Pittsburgh, Allegheny County, Pennsylvania
Date of Death: 19 February 1903
Place of Death: McLoud, Oklahoma
Cemetery: unknown cemetery—McLoud, Oklahoma
Entered Service at: New Brighton, Beaver County, Pennsylvania
Unit: Company F, 1st Pennsylvania Cavalry
Battle or Place of Action: Appomattox Campaign, Virginia
Date of Action: 29 March-9 April 1865
Date of Issue: 3 May 1865
Citation: Capture of flag.

599 ◆ HIGGINS, THOMAS J.

Rank: Sergeant
Service: U.S. Army
Birthday: 8 June 1831
Place of Birth: Riverlequerre, Quebec, Canada
Date of Death: 15 August 1917
Place of Death: Hannibal, Missouri
Cemetery: Holy Family Cemetery—Hannibal, Missouri
Entered Service at: Barry, Pike County, Illinois
Unit: Company D, 99th Illinois Infantry
Battle or Place of Action: Vicksburg, Mississippi
Date of Action: 22 May 1863
Date of Issue: 1 April 1898
Citation: When his regiment fell back in the assault, repulsed, this soldier continued to advance and planted the flag on the parapet, where he was captured by the enemy.
Notes: POW

600 ◆ HIGHLAND, PATRICK

Rank: Corporal (highest rank: Sergeant)
Service: U.S. Army
Place of Birth: Tipperary, Ireland
Entered Service at: Chicago, Cook County, Illinois
Unit: Company D, 23rd Illinois Infantry
Battle or Place of Action: Petersburg, Virginia
Date of Action: 2 April 1865
Date of Issue: 12 May 1865
Citation: Conspicuous gallantry as color bearer in the assault on Fort Gregg.

601 ◆ HILL, EDWARD

Rank: Captain (highest rank: Lieutenant Colonel)
Service: U.S. Army
Birthday: 13 April 1835
Place of Birth: Liberty, Sullivan County, New York
Date of Death: 23 October 1900
Place of Death: Green Bay, Wisconsin
Cemetery: Fredericksburg National Military Park Cemetery (OS-2) (MH)—Fredericksburg, Virginia
Entered Service at: Detroit, Wayne County, Michigan
Unit: Company K, 16th Michigan Infantry
Battle or Place of Action: Cold Harbor, Virginia
Date of Action: 1 June 1864
Date of Issue: 4 December 1893
Citation: Led the brigade skirmish line in a desperate charge on the enemy's masked batteries to the muzzles of the guns, where he was severely wounded.

602 ◆ HILL, HENRY

Rank: Corporal (highest rank: Sergeant)
Service: U.S. Army
Birthday: 1843

Place of Birth: Schuylkill County, Pennsylvania
Date of Death: 2 August 1909
Place of Death: Schuylkill Haven, Pennsylvania
Cemetery: Union Cemetery (MH)—Schuylkill Haven, Pennsylvania
Entered Service at: Harrisburg, Dauphin County, Pennsylvania
Unit: Company C, 50th Pennsylvania Infantry
Battle or Place of Action: Wilderness Campaign, Virginia
Date of Action: 6 May 1864
Date of Issue: 23 September 1897
Citation: This soldier, with one companion, would not retire when his regiment fell back in confusion after an unsuccessful charge, but instead advanced and continued firing upon the enemy until the regiment re-formed and regained its position.

603 ◆ HILL, JAMES

Rank: First Lieutenant
Service: U.S. Army
Birthday: 6 December 1822
Place of Birth: Bristol, Avon County, England
Date of Death: 22 September 1899
Cemetery: Cascade Community Cemetery (MH)—Cascade, Iowa
Entered Service at: Cascade, Dubuque County, Iowa
Unit: Company I, 21st Iowa Infantry
Battle or Place of Action: Champion Hill, Mississippi
Date of Action: 16 May 1863
Date of Issue: 15 March 1893
Citation: By skillful and brave management captured three of the enemy's pickets.

604 ◆ HILL, JAMES SAMUEL

Rank: Sergeant
Service: U.S. Army
Birthday: 1845
Place of Birth: Lyons, Wayne County, New York
Date of Death: 10 April 1865
Place of Death: Danville, Virginia
Entered Service at: Lyons, Wayne County, New York
Unit: Company C, 14th New York Heavy Artillery
Battle or Place of Action: Petersburg, Virginia
Date of Action: 30 July 1864
Date of Issue: 1 December 1864
Citation: Capture of flag, shooting a Confederate officer who was rallying his men with the colors in his hand.
Notes: POW

605 ◆ HILLIKER, BENJAMIN F.

Rank: Musician
Service: U.S. Army
Birthday: 23 May 1843
Place of Birth: Golden, Erie County, New York
Date of Death: 18 October 1916
Place of Death: Los Angeles, California
Cemetery: Hollywood Cemetery—Hollywood, California
Entered Service at: Waupaca Township, Waupaca County, Wisconsin
Unit: Company A, 8th Wisconsin Infantry
Battle or Place of Action: Mechanicsburg, Mississippi
Date of Action: 4 June 1863
Date of Issue: 17 December 1897
Citation: When men were needed to oppose a superior Confederate force he laid down his drum for a rifle and proceeded to the front of the skirmish line which was about 120 feet from the enemy. While on this volunteer mission and firing at the enemy he was hit in the head with a minie ball which passed through him. An order was given to "lay him in the shade; he won't last long." He recovered from this wound being left with an ugly scar.

606 ◆ HILLS, WILLIAM GILES

Rank: Private
Service: U.S. Army
Birthday: 26 June 1841
Place of Birth: Conewango, Cattaraugus County, New York
Date of Death: 18 April 1912
Place of Death: St. Louis, Missouri
Cemetery: unknown cemetery—St. Louis, Missouri
Entered Service at: East Randolph, Cattaraugus County, New York
Unit: Company E, 9th New York Cavalry
Battle or Place of Action: North Fork, Virginia
Date of Action: 26 September 1864
Date of Issue: 26 September 1893
Citation: Voluntarily carried a severely wounded comrade out of a heavy fire from the enemy.

607 ◆ *HILTON, ALFRED B.

Rank: Sergeant
Service: U.S. Army
Birthday: 1842
Place of Birth: Harford County, Maryland
Date of Death: 21 October 1864
Place of Death: Fortress Monroe, Virginia
Cemetery: Hampton National Cemetery (E-1231) (MH)—Hampton, Virginia
Entered Service at: Baltimore, Baltimore County, Maryland
Unit: Company H, 4th U.S. Colored Infantry
Battle or Place of Action: Chapin's Farm, Virginia
Date of Action: 29 September 1864
Date of Issue: 6 April 1865
Citation: When the regimental color bearer fell, this soldier seized the colors and carried it forward, together with the national standard, until disabled at the enemy's inner line.

608 ◆ HINCKS, WILLIAM B.

Rank: Sergeant Major (highest rank: Major)
Service: U.S. Army
Birthday: 1841
Place of Birth: Bucksport, Hancock County, Maine

Date of Death: 7 November 1903
Cemetery: Mountain Grove Cemetery (MH)—Bridgeport, Connecticut
Entered Service at: Bridgeport, Fairfield County, Connecticut
Unit: 14th Connecticut Infantry
Battle or Place of Action: Gettysburg, Pennsylvania
Date of Action: 3 July 1863
Date of Issue: 1 December 1864
Citation: During the highwater mark of Pickett's charge on 3 July 1863 the colors of the 14th Tennessee Infantry C.S.A. were planted 50 yards in front of the center of Sgt. Maj. Hincks' regiment. There were no Confederates standing near it but several were lying down around it. Upon a call for volunteers by Maj. Ellis, commanding, to capture this flag, this soldier and two others leaped the wall. One companion was instantly shot. Sgt. Maj. Hincks outran his remaining companion, running straight and swift for the colors amid a storm of shot. Swinging his saber over the prostrate Confederates and uttering a terrific yell, he seized the flag and hastily returned to his lines. The 14th Tenn. carried 12 battle honors on its flag. The devotion to duty shown by Sgt. Maj. Hincks gave encouragement to many of his comrades at a crucial moment of the battle.

609 ◆ HINNEGAN, WILLIAM

Rank: Second Class Fireman
Service: U.S. Navy
Birthday: 1841
Place of Birth: Ireland
Entered Service at: New York
Unit: U.S.S. *Agawam*
Battle or Place of Action: Fort Fisher, North Carolina
Date of Action: 23 December 1864
G.O. Number, Date: 45, 31 December 1864
Date of Presentation: 12 May 1865
Citation: Hinnegan served on board the U.S.S. *Agawam*, as one of a volunteer crew of powder boat which was exploded near Fort Fisher, 23 December 1864. The powder boat, towed in by the *Wilderness* to prevent detection by the enemy, cast off and slowly steamed to within 300 yards of the beach. After fuses and fires had been lit and a second anchor with short scope let go to assure the boat's tailing inshore, the crew again boarded the *Wilderness* and proceeded a distance of 12 miles from shore. Less than two hours later the explosion took place, and the following day fires were observed still burning at the forts.

610 ◆ HODGES, ADDISON J.

Rank: Private (highest rank: Corporal)
Service: U.S. Army
Birthday: 24 October 1841
Place of Birth: Hillsdale, Hillsdale County, Michigan
Date of Death: 28 July 1923
Place of Death: Adrian, Michigan
Cemetery: Zion Cemetery (MH)—Ogden Township, Michigan
Entered Service at: Adrian, Lenawee County, Michigan
Unit: Company B, 47th Ohio Infantry
Battle or Place of Action: Vicksburg, Mississippi
Date of Action: 3 May 1863
Date of Issue: 31 December 1907
Citation: Was one of a party that volunteered and attempted to run the enemy's batteries with a steam tug and two barges loaded with subsistence stores.
Notes: POW

611 ◆ HOFFMAN, HENRY

Rank: Corporal
Service: U.S. Army
Birthday: 23 December 1836
Place of Birth: Wurttemberg, Germany
Date of Death: 8 January 1894
Cemetery: Old Joseph's Cemetery—Cincinnati, Ohio
Entered Service at: Cincinnati, Hamilton County, Ohio
Unit: Company M, 2d Ohio Cavalry
Battle or Place of Action: Deatonsville (Sailor's Creek), Virginia
Date of Action: 6 April 1865
Date of Issue: 3 May 1865
Citation: Capture of flag.

612 ◆ HOFFMAN, THOMAS W.

Rank: Captain (highest rank: Brevet Lieutenant Colonel)
Service: U.S. Army
Birthday: 21 July 1839
Place of Birth: Perrysburg, Allegheny County, Pennsylvania
Date of Death: 18 April 1905
Place of Death: Scranton, Pennsylvania
Cemetery: Pomfret Manor Cemetery—Sunbury, Pennsylvania
Entered Service at: Harrisburg, Dauphin County, Pennsylvania
Unit: Company A, 208th Pennsylvania Infantry
Battle or Place of Action: Petersburg, Virginia
Date of Action: 2 April 1865
Date of Issue: 19 July 1895
Citation: Prevented a retreat of his regiment during the battle.

613 ◆ HOGAN, FRANKLIN

Rank: Corporal
Service: U.S. Army
Birthday: 7 January 1843
Place of Birth: Centre County, Pennsylvania
Date of Death: 5 April 1932
Place of Death: Hutchinson, Kansas
Cemetery: Eastside Cemetery—Hutchinson, Kansas
Entered Service at: Howard, Centre County, Pennsylvania
Unit: Company A, 45th Pennsylvania Infantry
Battle or Place of Action: Petersburg, Virginia
Date of Action: 30 July 1864
Date of Issue: 1 October 1864
Citation: Capture of flag of 6th Virginia Infantry (C.S.A.).

614 ◆ HOGARTY, WILLIAM P.

Rank: Private (highest rank: Lieutenant U.S.A.—Captain U.S. Vols.)
Service: U.S. Army
Birthday: 16 February 1840
Place of Birth: New York, New York
Date of Death: 23 October 1914
Place of Death: Stillwater, Oklahoma
Cemetery: Mount Hope Cemetery—Kansas City, Kansas
Entered Service at: Elmira, Chemung County, New York
Unit: Company D, 23d New York Infantry
Battle or Place of Action: Antietam, Maryland & Fredericksburg, Virginia
Date of Action: 17 September, 13 December 1862
Date of Issue: 22 June 1891
Citation: Distinguished gallantry in actions while attached to Battery B, 4th U.S. Artillery; lost his left arm at Fredericksburg.

615 ◆ HOLCOMB, DANIEL IRVING

Rank: Private (highest rank: Corporal)
Service: U.S. Army
Birthday: 13 November 1845
Place of Birth: Hartford, Trumbull County, Ohio
Date of Death: 14 December 1900
Place of Death: Sedalia, Missouri
Cemetery: Crown Hill Cemetery—Sedalia, Missouri
Entered Service at: Hartford, Trumbull County, Ohio
Unit: Company A, 41st Ohio Infantry
Battle or Place of Action: Brentwood Hills, Tennessee
Date of Action: 16 December 1864
Date of Issue: 22 February 1865
Citation: Capture of Confederate guidon.

616 ◆ HOLEHOUSE, JAMES

Rank: Private
Service: U.S. Army
Birthday: 25 December 1839
Place of Birth: Stockport, Greater Manchester County, England
Date of Death: 20 May 1915
Place of Death: Chelsea, Massachusetts
Cemetery: Oak Grove Cemetery (MH)—Fall River, Massachusetts
Entered Service at: Fall River, Bristol County, Massachusetts
Unit: Company B, 7th Massachusetts Infantry
Battle or Place of Action: Marye's Heights, Virginia
Date of Action: 3 May 1863
Date of Issue: 10 September 1897
Citation: With one companion voluntarily and with conspicuous daring advanced beyond his regiment, which had been broken in the assault, and halted beneath the crest. Following the example of these two men, the colors were brought to the summit, the regiment was advanced, and the position held.

617 ◆ HOLLAND, LEMUEL F.

Rank: Corporal (highest rank: Sergeant)
Service: U.S. Army
Birthday: 28 July 1840
Place of Birth: Burlington, Ohio
Date of Death: 13 January 1914
Cemetery: Greenwood Cemetery—Decatur, Illinois
Entered Service at: Tiskilwa, Bureau County, Illinois
Unit: Company D, 104th Illinois Infantry
Battle or Place of Action: Elk River, Tennessee
Date of Action: 2 July 1863
Date of Issue: 30 October 1897
Citation: Voluntarily joined a small party that, under a heavy fire, captured a stockade and saved the bridge.

618 ◆ HOLLAND, MILTON MURRAY

Rank: Sergeant Major
Service: U.S. Army
Birthday: 1 August 1844
Place of Birth: Austin, Travis County, Texas
Date of Death: 15 May 1910
Place of Death: Silver Springs, Maryland
Cemetery: Arlington National Cemetery (23-21713)—Arlington, Virginia
Entered Service at: Albany, Athens County, Ohio
Unit: 5th U.S. Colored Infantry
Battle or Place of Action: Chapin's Farm, Virginia
Date of Action: 29 September 1864
Date of Issue: 6 April 1865
Citation: Took command of Company C, after all the officers had been killed or wounded, and gallantly led it.

619 ◆ HOLLAT, GEORGE

Rank: Third Class Boy
Service: U.S. Navy
Birthday: 1846
Entered Service at: New York
Unit: U.S.S. *Varuna*
Battle or Place of Action: Forts Jackson and St. Philip, Louisiana
Date of Action: 24 April 1862
G.O. Number, Date: 11, 3 April 1863
Citation: Hollat served as third class boy on board the U.S.S. *Varuna* during an attack on Forts Jackson and St. Philip, 24 April 1862. He rendered gallant service through the perilous action and remained steadfast and courageous at his battle station despite extremely heavy fire and the ramming of the *Varuna* by the rebel ship *Morgan*, continuing his efforts until his ship, repeatedly holed and fatally damaged, was beached and sunk.

620 ◆ HOLMES, LOVILO N.

Rank: First Sergeant (highest rank: Captain)
Service: U.S. Army
Birthday: 10 October 1830

Place of Birth: Farmersville, Cattaraugus County, New York
Date of Death: 7 May 1914
Place of Death: Mankato, Minnesota
Cemetery: Glenwood Cemetery—Mankato, Minnesota
Entered Service at: Mankato, Blue Earth County, Minnesota
Unit: Company H, 2d Minnesota Infantry
Battle or Place of Action: Nolensville, Tennessee
Date of Action: 15 February 1863
Date of Issue: 11 September 1897
Citation: Was one of a detachment of 16 men who heroically defended a wagon train against the attack of 125 cavalry, repulsed the attack, and saved the train.

621 ◆ HOLMES, WILLIAM T.

Rank: Private
Service: U.S. Army
Birthday: 7 June 1846
Place of Birth: Vermilion County, Illinois
Date of Death: 31 August 1916
Place of Death: Osage Township, Missouri
Cemetery: Bean Cemetery—St. Clair County, Missouri
Entered Service at: Indianapolis, Marion County, Indiana
Unit: Company A, 3d Indiana Cavalry
Battle or Place of Action: Deatonsville (Sailor's Creek), Virginia
Date of Action: 6 April 1865
Date of Issue: 3 May 1865
Citation: Capture of flag of 27th Virginia Infantry (C.S.A.).

622 ◆ HOLTON, CHARLES MAYNARD

Rank: First Sergeant (highest rank: Second Lieutenant)
Service: U.S. Army
Birthday: 25 May 1838
Place of Birth: Potter, Yates County, New York
Date of Death: 25 August 1899
Place of Death: Yakima, Washington
Cemetery: Oak Hill Cemetery (MH)—Battle Creek, Michigan
Entered Service at: Battle Creek, Calhoun County, Michigan
Unit: Company A, 7th Michigan Cavalry
Battle or Place of Action: Falling Waters, Virginia
Date of Action: 14 July 1863
Date of Issue: 21 March 1889
Citation: Capture of flag of 55th Virginia Infantry (C.S.A.). In the midst of the battle with foot soldiers he dismounted to capture the flag.

623 ◆ HOLTON, EDWARD A.

Rank: First Sergeant (highest rank: Captain)
Service: U.S. Army
Birthday: 28 August 1835
Place of Birth: Westminster, Windham County, Vermont
Date of Death: 29 January 1906
Place of Death: Bernardston, Massachusetts
Cemetery: Westminster Old Cemetery—Westminster, Vermont
Entered Service at: Williston, Chittenden County, Vermont
Unit: Company I, 6th Vermont Infantry
Battle or Place of Action: Lee's Mills, Virginia
Date of Action: 16 April 1862
Date of Issue: 9 July 1892
Citation: Rescued the colors of his regiment under heavy fire, the color bearer having been shot down while the troops were in retreat.

624 ◆ HOMAN, CONRAD

Rank: Color Sergeant (highest rank: First Lieutenant)
Service: U.S. Army
Birthday: 27 February 1840
Place of Birth: Roxbury, Suffolk County, Massachusetts
Date of Death: 30 January 1922
Cemetery: Edwards Cemetery (MH)—Framingham, Massachusetts
Entered Service at: Boston, Suffolk County, Massachusetts
Unit: Company A, 29th Massachusetts Infantry
Battle or Place of Action: near Petersburg, Virginia
Date of Action: 30 July 1864
Date of Issue: 3 June 1869
Citation: Fought his way through the enemy's lines with the regimental colors, the rest of the color guard being killed or captured.

625 ◆ HOOKER, GEORGE WHITE

Rank: First Lieutenant (highest rank: Brevet Lieutenant Colonel U.S. Vols.)
Service: U.S. Army
Birthday: 6 February 1838
Place of Birth: Salem, Washington County, New York
Date of Death: 6 August 1902
Place of Death: Brattleboro, Vermont
Cemetery: Prospect Hill Cemetery—Brattleboro, Vermont
Entered Service at: Boston, Suffolk County, Massachusetts
Unit: Company E, 4th Vermont Infantry
Battle or Place of Action: South Mountain, Maryland
Date of Action: 14 September 1862
Date of Issue: 17 September 1891
Citation: Rode alone, in advance of his regiment, into the enemy's lines, and before his own men came up, received the surrender of the major of a Confederate regiment, together with the colors and 116 men.

626 ◆ HOOPER, WILLIAM B.

Rank: Corporal (highest rank: Quartermaster Sergeant)
Service: U.S. Army
Birthday: 1841
Place of Birth: Willimantic, Windham County, Connecticut
Date of Death: 16 January 1870
Place of Death: Caldera, Chile
Cemetery: Old Willimatic Cemetery (MH)—Windham, Connecticut
Entered Service at: Jersey City, Hudson County, New Jersey

Unit: Company L, 1st New Jersey Cavalry
Battle or Place of Action: Chamberlains Creek, Virginia
Date of Action: 31 March 1865
Date of Issue: 3 July 1865
Citation: With the assistance of a comrade, headed off the advance of the enemy, shooting two of his color bearers; also posted himself between the enemy and the lead horses of his own command, thus saving the herd from capture.

627 ◆ HOPKINS, CHARLES F.

Rank: Corporal
Service: U.S. Army
Birthday: 16 May 1842
Place of Birth: Hope, Warren County, New Jersey
Date of Death: 14 February 1934
Place of Death: Boonton, New Jersey
Cemetery: Greenwood Cemetery—Boonton, New Jersey
Entered Service at: Trenton, Mercer County, New Jersey
Unit: Company I, 1st New Jersey Infantry
Battle or Place of Action: Gaines' Mill, Virginia
Date of Action: 27 June 1862
Date of Issue: 9 July 1892
Citation: Voluntarily carried a wounded comrade, under heavy fire, to a place of safety; though twice wounded in the act, he continued in action until again severely wounded.
Notes: POW

628 ◆ HORAN, THOMAS

Rank: Sergeant
Service: U.S. Army
Birthday: 1839
Date of Death: 1902
Place of Death: Madison, Illinois
Cemetery: St. Mary's Cemetery—Dunkirk, New York
Entered Service at: Dunkirk, Chautauqua County, New York
Unit: Company E, 72d New York Infantry
Battle or Place of Action: Gettysburg, Pennsylvania
Date of Action: 2 July 1863
Date of Issue: 5 April 1898
Citation: In a charge of his regiment this soldier captured the regimental flag of the 8th Florida Infantry (C.S.A.).

629 ◆ HORNE, SAMUEL BELTON

Rank: Captain
Service: U.S. Army
Birthday: 3 March 1843
Place of Birth: Belleek, County Fermanagh, Ireland
Date of Death: 18 September 1928
Place of Death: Winchester, Connecticut
Cemetery: Forest View Cemetery (MH)—Winsted, Connecticut
Entered Service at: Winsted, Litchfield County, Connecticut
Unit: Company H, 11th Connecticut Infantry
Battle or Place of Action: Fort Harrison, Virginia
Date of Action: 29 September 1864
Date of Issue: 19 November 1897
Citation: While acting as an aide and carrying an important message, Horne was severely wounded and his horse killed, but delivered the order and rejoined his general.

630 ◆ HORSFALL, WILLIAM H.

Rank: Drummer
Service: U.S. Army
Birthday: 3 March 1847
Place of Birth: Campbell County, Kentucky
Date of Death: 22 October 1922
Place of Death: Newport, Kentucky
Cemetery: Evergreen Cemetery (MH)—Southgate, Kentucky
Entered Service at: Fort Cox, Charleston, West Virginia
Unit: Company G, 1st Kentucky Infantry
Battle or Place of Action: Corinth, Mississippi
Date of Action: 21 May 1862
Date of Issue: 17 August 1895
Citation: Saved the life of a wounded officer lying between the lines.

631 ◆ HORTON, JAMES

True Name: Horton, Joseph
Rank: Gunner's Mate (highest rank: Paymaster's Steward)
Service: U.S. Navy
Birthday: 1 July 1840
Place of Birth: England
Date of Death: 15 April 1894
Cemetery: Cypress Hills (Private Sec. 5 Lot 175 East Half—Brooklyn, New York
Entered Service at: Massachusetts
Unit: U.S.S. *Montauk*
Battle or Place of Action: off Port Royal, South Carolina
G.O. Number, Date: 59, 22 June 1865
Citation: Served as gunner's mate on board the U.S.S. *Montauk*, 21 September 1864. During the night of 21 September 1864, when fire was discovered in the magazine lightroom of the vessel, causing a panic and demoralizing the crew, Horton rushed into the cabin, obtained the magazine keys, sprang into the lightroom and began passing out combustibles, including the box of signals in which the fire originated.

632 ◆ HORTON, LEWIS AUGUSTINE

Rank: Seaman
Service: U.S. Navy
Birthday: 26 May 1842
Place of Birth: Bristol County, Massachusetts
Date of Death: 8 June 1916
Place of Death: Boston, Massachusetts
Cemetery: Forest Hill Cemetery—Boston, Massachusetts
Entered Service at: Taunton, Bristol County, Massachusetts
Unit: U.S.S. *Rhode Island*
Battle or Place of Action: off Cape Hatteras, North Carolina
Date of Action: 30 December 1862
G.O. Number, Date: 59, 22 June 1865

Citation: Served on board the U.S.S. *Rhode Island* which was engaged in saving the lives of the officers and crew of the *Monitor*, 30 December 1862. Participating in the hazardous rescue of the officers and crew of the sinking *Monitor*, Horton, after rescuing several of the men, became separated in a heavy gale with other members of the cutter that had set out from the *Rhode Island*, and spent many hours in the small boat at the mercy of the weather and the high seas until finally picked up by a schooner 50 miles east of Cape Hatteras.

633 ◆ HOTTENSTINE, SOLOMON J.

True Name: Hottenstein, Solomon J.
Rank: Private (highest rank: Sergeant)
Service: U.S. Army
Birthday: 5 May 1844
Place of Birth: Lehigh County, Pennsylvania
Date of Death: 24 May 1896
Place of Death: Manassas, Virginia
Cemetery: Manassas Cemetery (MH)—Manassas, Virginia
Entered Service at: Philadelphia, Philadelphia County, Pennsylvania
Unit: Company C, 107th Pennsylvania Infantry
Battle or Place of Action: Petersburg & Norfolk Railroad, Virginia
Date of Action: 19 August 1864
Date of Issue: 2 February 1865
Citation: Captured flag belonging to a North Carolina regiment, and through a ruse led them into the arms of Federal troops.

634 ◆ HOUGH, IRA

Rank: Private
Service: U.S. Army
Birthday: 2 July 1843
Place of Birth: Henry County, Indiana
Date of Death: 18 October 1916
Place of Death: Chipley, Florida
Cemetery: Slocum Church Cemetery—Jackson County, Florida
Entered Service at: Middletown, Henry County, Indiana
Unit: Company E, 8th Indiana Infantry
Battle or Place of Action: Cedar Creek, Virginia
Date of Action: 19 October 1864
Date of Issue: 26 October 1864
Citation: Capture of flag.

635 ◆ HOUGHTON, CHARLES H.

Rank: Captain (highest rank: Colonel)
Service: U.S. Army
Birthday: 30 April 1842
Place of Birth: Macomb, St. Lawrence County, New York
Date of Death: 6 April 1914
Cemetery: Arlington National Cemetery (3-2411-WS)—Arlington, Virginia
Entered Service at: Ogdensburg, St. Lawrence County, New York
Unit: Company L, 14th New York Artillery
Battle or Place of Action: Petersburg, Virginia
Date of Action: 30 July 1864 & 25 March 1865
Date of Issue: 5 April 1898
Citation: In the Union assault at the Crater (30 July 1864), and in the Confederate assault repelled at Fort Haskell, Houghton displayed most conspicuous gallantry and repeatedly exposed himself voluntarily to great danger, was three times wounded, and the suffered loss of a leg.

636 ◆ HOUGHTON, EDWARD J.

Rank: Ordinary Seaman
Service: U.S. Navy
Birthday: 1843
Place of Birth: Mobile, Mobile County, Alabama
Date of Death: 16 July 1865
Place of Death: Norfolk, Virginia
Cemetery: Hollywood Cemetery (MH)—Brookline, Massachusetts
Entered Service at: Alabama
Unit: U.S. Picket Boat No. 1
Battle or Place of Action: Plymouth, North Carolina
Date of Action: 27 October 1864
G.O. Number, Date: 45, 31 December 1864
Citation: Houghton served on board the U.S. Picket Boat No. 1, in action, 27 October 1864, against the Confederate ram, *Albemarle*, which had resisted repeated attacks by our steamers and had kept a large force of vessels employed in watching her. The picket boat, equipped with a spar torpedo, succeeded in passing the enemy pickets within 20 yards without being discovered and then made for the *Albemarle* under a full head of steam. Immediately taken under fire by the ram, the small boat plunged on, jumped the log boom which encircled the target, and exploded its torpedo under the port bow of the ram. The picket boat was destroyed by enemy fire and almost the entire crew taken prisoner or lost.

637 ◆ HOUGHTON, GEORGE L.

Rank: Private
Service: U.S. Army
Birthday: 28 August 1841
Place of Birth: Yarmouth, West Canada
Date of Death: 25 February 1917
Cemetery: Soldier's Home Cemetery—Orting, Washington
Entered Service at: Brookfield, Cook County, Illinois
Unit: Company D, 104th Illinois Infantry
Battle or Place of Action: Elk River, Tennessee
Date of Action: 2 July 1863
Date of Issue: 27 March 1900
Citation: Voluntarily joined a small party that, under a heavy fire, captured a stockade and saved the bridge.

638 ◆ HOULTON, WILLIAM M.

Rank: Commissary Sergeant
Service: U.S. Army
Birthday: 1 September 1835

Place of Birth: Clymer, Chautauqua County, New York
Date of Death: 13 February 1918
Place of Death: Abilene, Kansas
Cemetery: Abilene Cemetery—Abilene, Kansas
Entered Service at: Athens, Athens County, Ohio
Unit: 1st West Virginia Cavalry
Battle or Place of Action: Deatonsville (Sailor's Creek), Virginia
Date of Action: 6 April 1865
Date of Issue: 3 May 1865
Citation: Capture of flag.

639 ◆ HOWARD, HENDERSON CALVIN

Rank: Corporal (highest rank: First Sergeant)
Service: U.S. Army
Birthday: 16 September 1839
Place of Birth: Indiana County, Pennsylvania
Date of Death: 13 December 1919
Place of Death: Fort Collins, Colorado
Cemetery: Grand View Cemetery (MH)—Fort Collins, Colorado
Entered Service at: Indiana, Indiana County, Pennsylvania
Unit: Company B, 11th Pennsylvania Reserves
Battle or Place of Action: Glendale, Virginia
Date of Action: 30 June 1862
Date of Issue: 30 March 1898
Citation: While pursuing one of the enemy's sharpshooters, encountered two others, whom he bayoneted in hand-to-hand encounters; was three times wounded in action.

640 ◆ HOWARD, HIRAM REESE

Rank: Private
Service: U.S. Army
Birthday: 17 February 1843
Place of Birth: Urbana, Champaign County, Ohio
Date of Death: 9 May 1912
Place of Death: Point Pleasant, West Virginia
Cemetery: Lone Oak Cemetery (MH)—Point Pleasant, West Virginia
Entered Service at: Cincinnati, Hamilton County, Ohio
Unit: Company H, 11th Ohio Infantry
Battle or Place of Action: Missionary Ridge, Tennessee
Date of Action: 25 November 1863
Date of Issue: 29 July 1892
Citation: Scaled the enemy's works and in a hand-to-hand fight helped capture the flag of the 18th Alabama Infantry (C.S.A.).

641 ◆ HOWARD, JAMES

True Name: Brown, James
Rank: Sergeant
Service: U.S. Army
Place of Birth: Newton, Sussex County, New Jersey
Place of Death: Brooklyn, New York
Entered Service at: Brooklyn, Kings County, New York
Unit: Company K, 158th New York Infantry
Battle or Place of Action: near Petersburg (Battery Gregg), Virginia
Date of Action: 2 April 1865
Date of Issue: 12 May 1865
Citation: Carried the colors in advance of the line of battle, the flagstaff being shot off while he was planting it on the parapet of the fort.

642 ◆ HOWARD, MARTIN

True Name: Horgan, Michael C.
Rank: Landsman
Service: U.S. Navy
Birthday: 1843
Place of Birth: Ireland
Date of Death: 27 November 1910
Place of Death: Boston, Massachusetts
Cemetery: Holy Cross Cemetery (MH)—Malden, Massachusetts
Entered Service at: New York, New York
Unit: U.S.S. *Tacony*
Battle or Place of Action: Plymouth, North Carolina
Date of Action: 31 October 1864
G.O. Number, Date: 45, 31 December 1864
Citation: Served on board the U.S.S. *Tacony* during the taking of Plymouth, N.C., 31 October 1864. Carrying out his duties faithfully during the capture of Plymouth, Howard distinguished himself by a display of coolness when he participated in landing and spiking a 9-inch gun while under a devastating fire from enemy musketry.

643 ◆ HOWARD, OLIVER OTIS

Rank: Brigadier General (highest rank: Major General)
Service: U.S. Army
Birthday: 8 November 1830
Place of Birth: Leeds, Androscoggin County, Maine
Date of Death: 26 October 1909
Place of Death: Burlington, Vermont
Cemetery: Lake View Cemetery—Burlington, Vermont
Entered Service at: Leeds, Androscoggin County, Maine
Unit: U.S. Volunteers
Battle or Place of Action: Fair Oaks, Virginia
Date of Action: 1 June 1862
Date of Issue: 29 March 1893
Citation: Led the 61st New York Infantry in a charge in which he was twice severely wounded in the right arm, necessitating amputation.

644 ◆ HOWARD, PETER

Rank: Boatswain's Mate (highest rank: Acting Ensign)
Service: U.S. Navy
Birthday: 1829
Place of Birth: France
Date of Death: 25 March 1875
Place of Death: Brooklyn, New York

Entered Service at: Boston, Suffolk County, Massachusetts
Unit: U.S.S. *Mississippi*
Battle or Place of Action: Port Hudson, Louisiana
Date of Action: 14 March 1863
G.O. Number, Date: 17, 10 July 1863
Citation: Served on board the U.S.S. *Mississippi* during the action against Port Hudson, 14 March 1863. Running aground during the darkness and in the midst of battle while exposed to a devastating fire from enemy shore batteries, the *Mississippi* was ordered abandoned after a long and desperate attempt to free her. Serving courageously throughout this period in which a steady fire was kept up against the enemy until the ship was enveloped in flames and abandoned, Howard acted gallantly in his duties as boatswain's mate. Soon after the firing of the *Mississippi* and its abandonment, it was seen to slide off the shoal, drift downstream, and explode, leaving no possibility of its falling into enemy hands.

645 ◆ HOWARD, SQUIRE EDWARD

Rank: First Sergeant (highest rank: Captain)
Service: U.S. Army
Birthday: 15 May 1840
Place of Birth: Jamaica, Windham County, Vermont
Date of Death: 26 November 1912
Place of Death: West Newton, Massachusetts
Cemetery: Newton Cemetery—Newton Center, Massachusetts
Entered Service at: Townshend, Windham County, Vermont
Unit: Company H, 8th Vermont Infantry
Battle or Place of Action: Bayou Teche, Louisiana
Date of Action: 14 January 1863
Date of Issue: 29 January 1894
Citation: Voluntarily carried an important message through the heavy fire of the enemy to bring aid and save the gunboat *Calhoun*.

646 ◆ HOWE, ORION P.

Rank: Musician (highest rank: Corporal)
Service: U.S. Army
Birthday: 29 December 1849
Place of Birth: Hiram, Portage County, Ohio
Date of Death: 27 January 1930
Place of Death: Springfield, Missouri
Cemetery: Springfield National Cemetery (4-207A) (MH)—Springfield, Missouri
Entered Service at: Waukegan, Lake County, Illinois
Unit: Company C, 55th Illinois Infantry
Battle or Place of Action: Vicksburg, Mississippi
Date of Action: 19 May 1863
Date of Issue: 23 April 1896
Citation: A drummer boy, 14 years of age, and severely wounded and exposed to a heavy fire from the enemy, he persistently remained upon the field of battle until he had reported to Gen. W.T. Sherman the necessity of supplying cartridges for the use of troops under command of Col. Malmborg.

647 ◆ HOWE, WILLIAM H.

Rank: Sergeant (highest rank: First Lieutenant)
Service: U.S. Army
Birthday: 11 April 1837
Place of Birth: Haverhill, Essex County, Massachusetts
Date of Death: 23 April 1907
Place of Death: Everett, Massachusetts
Cemetery: Woodlawn Cemetery (MH)—Everett, Massachusetts
Entered Service at: Boston, Suffolk County, Massachusetts
Unit: Company K, 29th Massachusetts Infantry
Battle or Place of Action: Fort Stedman, Virginia
Date of Action: 25 March 1865
Date of Issue: 8 March 1895
Citation: Saved an abandoned gun under heavy fire.

648 ◆ HUBBELL, WILLIAM STONE

Rank: Captain (highest rank: Brevet Major)
Service: U.S. Army
Birthday: 19 April 1837
Place of Birth: Wolcottville, New Haven County, Connecticut
Date of Death: 28 August 1930
Place of Death: Plymouth, Massachusetts
Cemetery: Indian Hill Cemetery (MH)—Middletown, Connecticut
Entered Service at: North Stonington, New London County, Connecticut
Unit: Company A, 21st Connecticut Infantry
Battle or Place of Action: Fort Harrison, Virginia
Date of Action: 30 September 1864
Date of Issue: 13 June 1894
Citation: Led out a small flanking party and by a clash and at great risk captured a large number of prisoners.

649 ◆ HUDSON, AARON R.

Rank: Private
Service: U.S. Army
Place of Birth: Madison County, Kentucky
Date of Death: 7 May 1907
Cemetery: Regan Cemetery (MH)—Neosho, Missouri
Entered Service at: Indianapolis, Marion County, Indiana
Unit: Company C, 17th Indiana Mounted Infantry
Battle or Place of Action: Culloden, Georgia
Date of Action: April 1865
Date of Issue: 17 June 1865
Citation: Capture of flag of Worrill Grays (C.S.A.).

650 ◆ HUDSON, MICHAEL

Rank: Sergeant
Service: U.S. Marine Corps

Birthday: 1834
Place of Birth: County Sligo, Ireland
Date of Death: 28 December 1891
Cemetery: Maple Hill Cemetery (MH)—Charlotte, Michigan
Entered Service at: New York
Unit: U.S.S. *Brooklyn*
Battle or Place of Action: Mobile Bay, Alabama
Date of Action: 5 August 1864
G.O. Number, Date: 45, 31 December 1864
Citation: On board the U.S.S. *Brooklyn* during action against rebel forts and gunboats and with the ram *Tennessee*, in Mobile Bay, 5 August 1864. Despite severe damage to his ship and the loss of several men on board as enemy fire raked the decks, Sgt. Hudson fought his gun with skill and courage throughout the furious two-hour battle, which resulted in the surrender of the rebel ram *Tennessee*.

651 ◆ HUGHES, OLIVER

Rank: Corporal
Service: U.S. Army
Birthday: 21 January 1844
Place of Birth: Fentress County, Tennessee
Date of Death: 5 January 1911
Place of Death: Macon, Missouri
Cemetery: Old Callao Cemetery—Callao, Missouri
Entered Service at: Albany, Clinton County, Kentucky
Unit: Company C, 12th Kentucky Infantry
Battle or Place of Action: Town Creek, North Carolina
Date of Action: 20 February 1865
Date of Issue: 1 August 1865
Citation: Capture of flag of 11th South Carolina (C.S.A.).

652 ◆ HUGHEY, JOHN P.

Rank: Corporal
Service: U.S. Army
Birthday: 1836
Place of Birth: Louisville, Jefferson County, Kentucky
Date of Death: 29 January 1900
Place of Death: Near Hickman, Kentucky
Cemetery: unknown cemetery—Fulton County, Kentucky
Entered Service at: Anna, Union County, Illinois
Unit: Company L, 2d Ohio Cavalry
Battle or Place of Action: Deatonsville (Sailor's Creek), Virginia
Date of Action: 6 April 1865
Date of Issue: 3 May 1865
Citation: Capture of flag of 38th Virginia Infantry (C.S.A.).

653 ◆ HUIDEKOPER, HENRY SHIPPEN

Rank: Lieutenant Colonel (highest rank: Major General) PA National Guard
Service: U.S. Army
Birthday: 7 July 1839
Place of Birth: Meadville, Crawford County, Pennsylvania
Date of Death: 9 November 1918
Place of Death: Philadelphia, Pennsylvania
Cemetery: Greendale Cemetery (MH)—Meadville, Pennsylvania
Entered Service at: Philadelphia, Philadelphia County, Pennsylvania
Unit: 150th Pennsylvania Infantry
Battle or Place of Action: Gettysburg, Pennsylvania
Date of Action: 1 July 1863
Date of Issue: 27 May 1905
Citation: While engaged in repelling an attack of the enemy, received a severe wound of the right arm, but instead of retiring remained at the front in command of his regiment.

654 ◆ HUNT, LOUIS T.

Rank: Private
Service: U.S. Army
Place of Birth: Montgomery County, Indiana
Date of Death: 14 March 1901
Cemetery: Evangelical Lutheran Cemetery—St. Louis, Missouri
Entered Service at: Jefferson County, Missouri
Unit: Company H, 6th Missouri Infantry
Battle or Place of Action: Vicksburg, Mississippi
Date of Action: 22 May 1863
Date of Issue: 12 July 1894
Citation: Gallantry in the charge of the "volunteer storming party."

655 ◆ HUNTER, CHARLES ADAMS

Rank: Sergeant
Service: U.S. Army
Birthday: 26 August 1843
Place of Birth: Spencer, Worcester County, Massachusetts
Date of Death: 31 December 1912
Place of Death: Ashland, Massachusetts
Cemetery: Pine Grove Cemetery (MH)—Spencer, Massachusetts
Entered Service at: Spencer, Worcester County, Massachusetts
Unit: Company E, 34th Massachusetts Infantry
Battle or Place of Action: Petersburg, Virginia
Date of Action: 2 April 1865
Date of Issue: 12 May 1865
Citation: In the assault on Fort Gregg, bore the regimental flag bravely and was among the foremost to enter the work.

656 ◆ HUNTERSON, JOHN C.

Rank: Private
Service: U.S. Army
Birthday: 4 August 1841
Place of Birth: Philadelphia, Philadelphia County, Pennsylvania
Date of Death: 6 November 1927
Place of Death: New Haven, Connecticut
Cemetery: Old Swedes Burial Grounds (MH)—Philadelphia, Pennsylvania

Entered Service at: Philadelphia, Philadelphia County, Pennsylvania
Unit: Company B, 3d Pennsylvania Cavalry
Battle or Place of Action: On the Peninsula, Virginia
Date of Action: 5 June 1862
Date of Issue: 2 August 1897
Citation: While under fire, between the lines of the two armies, voluntarily gave up his own horse to an engineer officer whom he was accompanying on a reconnaissance and whose horse had been killed, thus enabling the officer to escape with valuable papers in his possession.

657 ◆ HUSKEY, MICHAEL

Rank: Fireman (highest rank: Fireman First Class)
Service: U.S. Navy
Birthday: 1841
Place of Birth: Niagara County, New York
Entered Service at: New York
Unit: U.S.S. *Carondelet*
Battle or Place of Action: Deer Creek Expedition, Mississippi
Date of Action: March 1863
G.O. Number, Date: 32, 16 April 1864
Citation: Fireman on board the U.S.S. *Carondelet*, Deer Creek Expedition, March 1863. Carrying out his duties gallantly, Huskey volunteered to aid in the rescue of the tug *Ivy* under the fire of the enemy, and set forth general meritorious conduct during this hazardous mission.

658 ◆ HYATT, THEODORE

Rank: First Sergeant
Service: U.S. Army
Birthday: 3 July 1830
Place of Birth: Pennsylvania
Date of Death: 7 May 1900
Place of Death: Woliet, Illinois
Cemetery: Lockport Cemetery (MH)—Lockport, Illinois
Entered Service at: Gardner, Grundy County, Illinois
Unit: Company D, 127th Illinois Infantry
Battle or Place of Action: Vicksburg, Mississippi
Date of Action: 22 May 1863
Date of Issue: 9 July 1894
Citation: Gallantry in the charge of the "volunteer storming party."

659 ◆ HYDE, THOMAS WORCESTER

Rank: Major (highest rank: Brevet Brigadier General)
Service: U.S. Army
Birthday: 16 January 1841
Place of Birth: Florence, Italy
Date of Death: 14 November 1899
Place of Death: Fortress Monroe, Virginia
Cemetery: Oak Grove Cemetery (Hyde Mausoleum) (MH)—Bath, Maine
Entered Service at: Bath, Sagadahoc County, Maine
Unit: 7th Maine Infantry

Battle or Place of Action: Antietam, Maryland
Date of Action: 17 September 1862
Date of Issue: 8 April 1891
Citation: Led his regiment in an assault on a strong body of the enemy's infantry and kept up the fight until the greater part of his men had been killed or wounded, bringing the remainder safely out of the fight.

660 ◆ HYLAND, JOHN

Rank: Seaman (highest rank: Assistant Gunner)
Service: U.S. Navy
Birthday: 1819
Place of Birth: Ireland
Date of Death: 10 August 1867
Place of Death: Manistee, Michigan
Entered Service at: Illinois
Unit: U.S.S. *Signal*
Battle or Place of Action: Red River, Louisiana
Date of Action: 5 May 1864
G.O. Number, Date: 45, 31 December 1864
Citation: Served as seaman on board the U.S.S. *Signal* which was attacked by field batteries and sharpshooters and destroyed in Red River, 5 May 1864. Proceeding up the Red River, the U.S.S. *Signal* engaged a large force of enemy field batteries and sharpshooters, returning their fire until the ship was totally disabled, at which time the white flag was raised. Although wounded, Hyland courageously went in full view of several hundred sharpshooters and let go the anchor, and again to slip the cable, when he was again wounded by the raking enemy fire.

661 ◆ HYMER, SAMUEL

Rank: Captain
Service: U.S. Army
Birthday: 17 May 1829
Place of Birth: Harrison County, Indiana
Date of Death: 9 May 1906
Cemetery: Rushville Cemetery—Rushville, Illinois
Entered Service at: Rushville, Schuyler County, Illinois
Unit: Company D, 115th Illinois Infantry
Battle or Place of Action: Buzzard's Roost Gap, Georgia
Date of Action: 13 October 1864
Date of Issue: 28 March 1896
Citation: With only 41 men under his command, defended and held a blockhouse against the attack of Hood's Division for nearly 10 hours, thus checking the advance of the enemy and insuring the safety of the balance of the regiment, as well as that of the 8th Kentucky Infantry, then stationed at Ringgold, Ga.

662 ◆ ILGENFRITZ, CHARLES HENRY

Rank: Sergeant (highest rank: First Sergeant)
Service: U.S. Army
Birthday: 4 March 1837
Place of Birth: York County, Pennsylvania
Date of Death: 31 March 1920

Place of Death: York, Pennsylvania
Cemetery: Prospect Hill Cemetery—York, Pennsylvania
Entered Service at: Harrisburg, Dauphin County, Pennsylvania
Unit: Company E, 207th Pennsylvania Infantry
Battle or Place of Action: Fort Sedgwick, Virginia
Date of Action: 2 April 1865
Date of Issue: 20 March 1917
Citation: The color bearer falling, pierced by seven balls, he immediately sprang forward and grasped the colors, planting them upon the enemy's forts amid a murderous fire of grape, canister, and musketry from the enemy.

663 ◆ IMMELL, LORENZO DOW

Rank: Corporal (highest rank: First Lieutenant)
Service: U.S. Army
Birthday: 18 June 1837
Place of Birth: Ross, Butler County, Ohio
Date of Death: 31 October 1912
Cemetery: Jefferson Barracks National Cemetery (4-12342) (MH)—St. Louis, Missouri
Entered Service at: Fort Leavenworth, Leavenworth County, Kansas
Unit: Company F, 2d U.S. Artillery
Battle or Place of Action: Wilson's Creek, Missouri
Date of Action: 10 August 1861
Date of Issue: 19 July 1890
Citation: Bravery in action.

664 ◆ INGALLS, LEWIS J.

Rank: Private
Service: U.S. Army
Birthday: 11 October 1837
Place of Birth: Boston, Suffolk County, Massachusetts
Date of Death: 31 December 1913
Place of Death: Irasburg, Vermont
Cemetery: Irasburg Cemetery—Irasburg, Vermont
Entered Service at: Belvidere, Lamoille County, Vermont
Unit: Company K, 8th Vermont Infantry
Battle or Place of Action: Boutte Station, Louisiana
Date of Action: 4 September 1862
Date of Issue: 20 October 1899
Citation: A railroad train guarded by about 60 men on flat cars having been sidetracked by a misplaced switch into an ambuscade of guerrillas who were rapidly shooting down the unprotected guards, this soldier, under a severe fire in which he was wounded, ran to another switch and, opening it, enabled the train and the surviving guards to escape.

665 ◆ INSCHO, LEONIDAS H.

Rank: Corporal (highest rank: First Lieutenant)
Service: U.S. Army
Birthday: 20 February 1840
Place of Birth: Chatham, Licking County, Ohio
Date of Death: 12 November 1907
Cemetery: Cedar Hill Cemetery (MH)—Newark, Ohio
Entered Service at: Newark, Licking County, Ohio
Unit: Company E, 12th Ohio Infantry
Battle or Place of Action: South Mountain, Maryland
Date of Action: 14 September 1862
Date of Issue: 31 January 1894
Citation: Alone and unaided and with his left hand disabled, captured a Confederate captain and four men.

666 ◆ IRLAM, JOSEPH

Rank: Seaman
Service: U.S. Navy
Birthday: 1840
Place of Birth: Liverpool, Merseyside County, England
Entered Service at: New York, New York
Unit: U.S.S. *Brooklyn*
Battle or Place of Action: Mobile Bay, Alabama
Date of Action: 5 August 1864
G.O. Number, Date: 45, 31 December 1864
Citation: Stationed at the wheel on board the U.S.S. *Brooklyn* during action against rebel forts and gunboats and with the ram *Tennessee* in Mobile Bay, 5 August 1864. When heavy enemy fire struck down several men at their guns and replacements were not available, Irlam voluntarily released two men who were stationed with him and carried on at the wheel with the assistance of only one of the crew throughout the furious battle.

667 ◆ IRSCH, FRANCIS

Rank: Captain
Service: U.S. Army
Birthday: 4 December 1840
Place of Birth: Saarburg, Germany
Date of Death: 19 August 1906
Place of Death: Tampa, Florida
Cemetery: Woodlawn Cemetery (MH)—Tampa, Florida
Entered Service at: New York, New York
Unit: Company D, 45th New York Infantry
Battle or Place of Action: Gettysburg, Pennsylvania
Date of Action: 1 July 1863
Date of Issue: 27 May 1892
Citation: Gallantry in flanking the enemy and capturing a number of prisoners and in holding a part of the town against heavy odds while the Army was rallying on Cemetery Hill.

668 ◆ IRVING, JOHN

Rank: Coxswain
Service: U.S. Navy
Birthday: 1839
Place of Birth: East Brooklyn, Kings County, New York
Entered Service at: New York, New York
Unit: U.S.S. *Brooklyn*
Battle or Place of Action: Mobile Bay, Alabama
Date of Action: 5 August 1864
G.O. Number, Date: 45, 31 December 1864
Citation: On board the U.S.S. *Brooklyn* during action against rebel forts and gunboats and with the ram *Tennessee*,

in Mobile Bay, 5 August 1864. Despite severe damage to his ship and loss of several men on board as enemy fire raked her decks from stem to stern, Irving fought his gun with skill and courage throughout the furious battle which resulted in the surrender of the prize rebel ram *Tennessee* and in the damaging and destruction of batteries at Fort Morgan.

669 ◆ IRVING, THOMAS

Rank: Coxswain (highest rank: Acting Master's Mate)
Service: U.S. Navy
Birthday: 1842
Place of Birth: England
Entered Service at: New York, New York
Unit: U.S.S. *Lehigh*
Battle or Place of Action: Charleston Harbor, South Carolina
Date of Action: 16 November 1863
G.O. Number, Date: 32, 16 April 1864
Citation: Served on board the U.S.S. *Lehigh*, Charleston Harbor, 16 November 1863, during the hazardous task of freeing the *Lehigh*, which had grounded, and was under heavy enemy fire from Fort Moultrie. Rowing the small boat which was used in the hazardous task of transferring hawsers from the *Lehigh* to the *Nahant*, Irving twice succeeded in making the trip, while under severe fire from the enemy, only to find that each had been in vain when the hawsers were cut by hostile fire and chaffing.

670 ◆ IRWIN, NICHOLAS

Rank: Seaman
Service: U.S. Navy
Birthday: 1833
Place of Birth: Denmark
Date of Death: 19 April 1896
Place of Death: Marion, Indiana
Cemetery: Marion National Cemetery (I-382) (MH)—Marion, Indiana
Entered Service at: New York, New York
Unit: U.S.S. *Brooklyn*
Battle or Place of Action: Mobile Bay, Alabama
Date of Action: 5 August 1864
G.O. Number, Date: 45, 31 December 1864
Citation: On board the U.S.S. *Brooklyn* during action against rebel forts and gunboats and with the ram *Tennessee*, in Mobile Bay, 5 August 1864. Despite severe damage to his ship and loss of several men on board as enemy fire raked her decks from stem to stern, Irwin fought his gun with skill and courage throughout the furious battle which resulted in the surrender of the prize rebel ram *Tennessee* and in the damaging and destruction of batteries at Fort Morgan.

671 ◆ IRWIN, PATRICK

Rank: First Sergeant (highest rank: First Lieutenant)
Service: U.S. Army
Birthday: 1839
Place of Birth: Ireland
Date of Death: 6 February 1910
Cemetery: St. Thomas' Cemetery—Ann Arbor, Michigan
Entered Service at: Ann Arbor, Washtenaw County, Michigan
Unit: Company H, 14th Michigan Infantry
Battle or Place of Action: Jonesboro, Georgia
Date of Action: 1 September 1864
Date of Issue: 28 April 1896
Citation: In a charge by the 14th Michigan Infantry against the entrenched enemy, Irwin was the first man over the line of works of the enemy, and demanded and received the surrender of Confederate Gen. Daviel Govan and his command.

672 ◆ JACKSON, FREDERICK RANDOLPH

Rank: First Sergeant (highest rank: Sergeant Major)
Service: U.S. Army
Birthday: 18 February 1844
Place of Birth: New Haven, New Haven County, Connecticut
Date of Death: 14 February 1925
Place of Death: Smithville, New York
Cemetery: Smithfield Cemetery (MH)—Smithville, New York
Entered Service at: New Haven, New Haven County, Connecticut
Unit: Company F, 7th Connecticut Infantry
Battle or Place of Action: James Island, South Carolina
Date of Action: 16 June 1862
Date of Issue: 1863
Citation: Having his left arm shot away in a charge on the enemy, he continued on duty, taking part in a second and a third charge until he fell exhausted from the loss of blood.

673 ◆ JACOBSON, EUGENE PHILIP

Rank: Sergeant Major (highest rank: Brevet Captain U.S. Vols.)
Service: U.S. Army
Birthday: 3 May 1841
Place of Birth: Prussia
Date of Death: 12 April 1881
Place of Death: Denver, Colorado
Cemetery: Green Mount Cemetery—Baltimore, Maryland
Entered Service at: New York, New York
Unit: 74th New York Infantry
Battle or Place of Action: Chancellorsville, Virginia
Date of Action: 2 May 1863
Date of Issue: 29 March 1865
Citation: Bravery in conducting a scouting party in front of the enemy.

674 ◆ JAMES, ISAAC

Rank: Private
Service: U.S. Army
Birthday: 8 March 1838
Place of Birth: Jefferson Township, Ashtabula County, Ohio

Date of Death: 26 September 1914
Place of Death: Union City, Indiana
Entered Service at: Mississinawa Township, Ohio
Unit: Company H, 110th Ohio Infantry
Battle or Place of Action: Petersburg, Virginia
Date of Action: 2 April 1865
Date of Issue: 10 May 1865
Citation: Capture of flag.

675 ◆ JAMES, JOHN H.

Rank: Captain of the Top
Service: U.S. Navy
Birthday: 1835
Place of Birth: Boston, Suffolk County, Massachusetts
Date of Death: 3 August 1914
Cemetery: Dayton National Cemetery (I-19-58) (MH)—Dayton, Ohio
Entered Service at: Massachusetts
Unit: U.S.S. *Richmond*
Battle or Place of Action: Mobile Bay, Alabama
Date of Action: 5 August 1864
G.O. Number, Date: 45, 31 December 1864
Citation: As captain of a gun on board the U.S.S. *Richmond* during action against rebel forts and gunboats and with the ram *Tennessee* in Mobile Bay, 5 August 1864. Despite damage to his ship and the loss of several men on board as enemy fire raked her decks, James fought his gun with skill and courage throughout the furious two-hour battle which resulted in the surrender of the rebel ram *Tennessee* and in the damaging and destruction of batteries at Fort Morgan.

676 ◆ JAMES, MILES

Rank: Corporal (highest rank: First Sergeant)
Service: U.S. Army
Birthday: 1829
Place of Birth: Princess Anne County, Virginia
Date of Death: 28 August 1871
Place of Death: Norfolk, Virginia
Cemetery: unknown cemetery—Norfolk, Virginia
Entered Service at: Portsmouth, Portsmouth County, Virginia
Unit: Company B, 36th U.S. Colored Infantry
Battle or Place of Action: Chapin's Farm, Virginia
Date of Action: 30 September 1864
Date of Issue: 6 April 1865
Citation: Having had his arm mutilated, making immediate amputation necessary, he loaded and discharged his piece with one hand and urged his men forward; this within 30 yards of the enemy's works.

677 ◆ JAMIESON, WALTER

Rank: First Sergeant (highest rank: Captain)
Service: U.S. Army
Birthday: 1842
Place of Birth: Boulogne, France
Date of Death: 6 December 1904

Place of Death: Brooklyn, New York
Cemetery: Cypress Hills Cemetery (Private)—Brooklyn, New York
Entered Service at: New York, New York
Unit: Company B, 139th New York Infantry
Battle or Place of Action: Petersburg & Fort Harrison, Virginia
Date of Action: 30 July, 29 September 1864
Date of Issue: 5 April 1898
Citation: Voluntarily went between the lines under a heavy fire at Petersburg, Va., to the assistance of a wounded and helpless officer, whom he carried within the Union lines. At Fort Harrison, Va., seized the regimental color, the color bearer and guard having been shot down, and, rushing forward, planted it upon the fort in full view of the entire brigade.

678 ◆ JARDINE, JAMES

Rank: Sergeant (highest rank: First Lieutenant)
Service: U.S. Army
Birthday: 16 April 1837
Place of Birth: Helensburgh, Dunbartonshire, Scotland
Date of Death: 9 December 1922
Cemetery: Ohio Veterans' Home Cemetery (MH)—Sandusky, Ohio
Entered Service at: Hamilton County, Ohio
Unit: Company F, 54th Ohio Infantry
Battle or Place of Action: Vicksburg, Mississippi
Date of Action: 22 May 1863
Date of Issue: 5 April 1894
Citation: Gallantry in the charge of the "volunteer storming party."

679 ◆ JELLISON, BENJAMIN H.

Rank: Sergeant (highest rank: Captain)
Service: U.S. Army
Birthday: 29 December 1845
Place of Birth: Newburyport, Essex County, Massachusetts
Date of Death: 5 April 1924
Place of Death: Reading, Massachusetts
Cemetery: Elmwood Cemetery (MH)—Haverhill, Massachusetts
Entered Service at: Newburyport, Essex County, Massachusetts
Unit: Company C, 19th Massachusetts Infantry
Battle or Place of Action: Gettysburg, Pennsylvania
Date of Action: 3 July 1863
Date of Issue: 1 December 1864
Citation: Capture of flag of 57th Virginia Infantry (C.S.A.). He also assisted in taking prisoners.

680 ◆ JENKINS, THOMAS

Rank: Seaman
Service: U.S. Navy
Unit: U.S.S. *Cincinnati*
Battle or Place of Action: Vicksburg, Mississippi

Date of Action: 27 May 1863
G.O. Number, Date: 17, 10 July 1863
Citation: Served on board the U.S.S. *Cincinnati* during the attack on the Vicksburg batteries and at the time of her sinking, 27 May 1863. Engaging the enemy in a fierce battle, the *Cincinnati*, amidst an incessant fire of shot and shell, continued to fire her guns to the last, though so penetrated by shell fire that her fate was sealed. Serving bravely during this action, Jenkins was conspicuously cool under the fire of the enemy, never ceasing to fight until this proud ship went down, "her colors nailed to the mast."

681 ◆ JENNINGS, JAMES T.

Rank: Private (highest rank: Corporal)
Service: U.S. Army
Birthday: April 1818
Place of Birth: Devonshire, England
Date of Death: 22 March 1865
Place of Death: Baltimore, Maryland
Cemetery: Louden Park National Cemetery (A-1410) (MH)—Baltimore, Maryland
Entered Service at: Luzerne, Luzerne County, Pennsylvania
Unit: Company K, 56th Pennsylvania Infantry
Battle or Place of Action: Weldon Railroad, Virginia
Date of Action: 20 August 1864
Date of Issue: 1 December 1864
Citation: Capture of flag of 55th North Carolina Infantry (C.S.A.).

682 ◆ JEWETT, ERASTUS W.

Rank: First Lieutenant
Service: U.S. Army
Birthday: 1 April 1839
Place of Birth: St. Albans, Franklin County, Vermont
Date of Death: 20 February 1906
Cemetery: Church Street Cemetery—Swanton, Vermont
Entered Service at: St. Albans, Franklin County, Vermont
Unit: Company A, 9th Vermont Infantry
Battle or Place of Action: Newport Barracks, North Carolina
Date of Action: 2 February 1864
Date of Issue: 8 September 1891
Citation: By long and persistent resistance and burning the bridges, Jewett kept a superior force of the enemy at a distance and thus covered the retreat of the garrison.
Notes: POW

683 ◆ JOHN, WILLIAM F.

Rank: Private
Service: U.S. Army
Birthday: 23 October 1844
Place of Birth: Germany
Date of Death: 29 August 1927
Place of Death: Hutchings, Kansas
Cemetery: Prattsburg Cemetery (MH)—Macksville, Kansas
Entered Service at: Chillicothe, Ross County, Ohio
Unit: Company E, 37th Ohio Infantry
Battle or Place of Action: Vicksburg, Mississippi
Date of Action: 22 May 1863
Date of Issue: 14 July 1894
Citation: Gallantry in the charge of the "volunteer storming party."

684 ◆ JOHNDRO, FRANKLIN

Rank: Private
Service: U.S. Army
Birthday: 1835
Place of Birth: Highgate Falls, Franklin County, Vermont
Date of Death: 5 April 1901
Place of Death: North Bay City, Michigan
Cemetery: Glens Falls Cemetery—Glens Falls, New York
Entered Service at: Queensbury, Warren County, New York
Unit: Company A, 118th New York Infantry
Battle or Place of Action: Chapin's Farm, Virginia
Date of Action: 30 September 1864
Date of Issue: 6 April 1865
Citation: Capture of 40 prisoners.

685 ◆ JOHNS, ELISHA

Rank: Corporal (highest rank: Sergeant)
Service: U.S. Army
Birthday: 25 August 1837
Place of Birth: Clinton, Summit County, Ohio
Date of Death: 14 June 1920
Place of Death: Elkhart, Indiana
Cemetery: Plum Grove Cemetery—Union, Michigan
Entered Service at: Martinton, Iroquois County, Illinois
Unit: Company B, 113th Illinois Infantry
Battle or Place of Action: Vicksburg, Mississippi
Date of Action: 22 May 1863
Date of Issue: 9 August 1894
Citation: Gallantry in the charge of the "volunteer storming party."

686 ◆ JOHNS, HENRY T.

Rank: Private (highest rank: First Lieutenant)
Service: U.S. Army
Birthday: 8 April 1828
Place of Birth: Philadelphia, Philadelphia County, Pennsylvania
Date of Death: 13 May 1906
Place of Death: Glendale, California
Cemetery: Mountain View Cemetery—Oakland, California
Entered Service at: Hinsdale, Berkshire County, Massachusetts
Unit: Company C, 49th Massachusetts Infantry
Battle or Place of Action: Port Hudson, Louisiana
Date of Action: 27 May 1863
Date of Issue: 25 November 1893
Citation: Volunteered in response to a call and took part in the movement that was made upon the enemy's works under a heavy fire therefrom in advance of the general assault.

687 ◆ JOHNSON, ANDREW

Rank: Private
Service: U.S. Army
Birthday: 1833
Place of Birth: Delaware County, Ohio
Date of Death: 7 February 1912
Place of Death: Tower Hill Township, Illinois
Cemetery: Tower Hill Cemetery (MH)—Tower Hill Township, Illinois
Entered Service at: Assumption, Christian County, Illinois
Unit: Company G, 116th Illinois Infantry
Battle or Place of Action: Vicksburg, Mississippi
Date of Action: 22 May 1863
Date of Issue: 9 August 1894
Citation: Gallantry in the charge of the "volunteer storming party."

688 ◆ JOHNSON, FOLLETT

Rank: Corporal
Service: U.S. Army
Birthday: 20 April 1843
Place of Birth: Brasher, St. Lawrence County, New York
Date of Death: 9 March 1909
Place of Death: Massena, New York
Cemetery: Pine Grove Cemetery No.1 (MH)—Massena, New York
Entered Service at: Ogdensburg, St. Lawrence County, New York
Unit: Company H, 60th New York Infantry
Battle or Place of Action: New Hope Church, Georgia
Date of Action: 27 May 1864
Date of Issue: 6 April 1892
Citation: Voluntarily exposed himself to the fire of a Confederate sharpshooter, thus drawing fire upon himself and enabling his comrade to shoot the sharpshooter.
Notes: POW

689 ◆ JOHNSON, HENRY

Rank: Seaman
Service: U.S. Navy
Birthday: 1824
Place of Birth: Norway
Entered Service at: New York, New York
Unit: U.S.S. *Metacomet*
Battle or Place of Action: Mobile Bay, Alabama
Date of Action: 5 August 1864
G.O. Number, Date: 82, 23 February 1867
Citation: As seaman on board the U.S.S. *Metacomet*, Johnson served as a member of the boat's crew which went to the rescue of the U.S. Monitor *Tecumseh* when that vessel was struck by a torpedo in passing the enemy forts in Mobile Bay, 5 August 1864. He braved the enemy fire, which was said by the admiral to be "one of the most galling" he had ever seen, and aided in rescuing from death 10 of the crew of the *Tecumseh*, thereby eliciting the admiration of both friend and foe.

690 ◆ JOHNSON, JOHN

Rank: Private
Service: U.S. Army
Birthday: 25 March 1842
Place of Birth: Toten Christiana (now Olso), Norway
Date of Death: 3 April 1907
Place of Death: Detroit, Michigan
Cemetery: Rock Creek Cemetery—Washington, D.C.
Entered Service at: Janesville, Rock County, Wisconsin
Unit: Company D, 2d Wisconsin Infantry
Battle or Place of Action: Fredericksburg, Virginia
Date of Action: 13 December 1862
Date of Issue: 28 August 1893
Citation: Conspicuous gallantry in battle in which he was severely wounded. While serving as cannoneer he manned the positions of fallen gunners.

691 ◆ JOHNSON, JOSEPH ESREY

Rank: First Lieutenant (highest rank: Brevet Major)
Service: U.S. Army
Birthday: 5 February 1843
Place of Birth: Lower Merion, Montgomery County, Pennsylvania
Date of Death: 30 April 1911
Cemetery: Arlington National Cemetery (3-2278)—Arlington, Virginia
Entered Service at: Philadelphia, Philadelphia County, Pennsylvania
Unit: Company A, 58th Pennsylvania Infantry
Battle or Place of Action: Fort Harrison, Virginia
Date of Action: 29 September 1864
Date of Issue: 1 April 1898
Citation: Though twice severely wounded while advancing in the assault, he disregarded his injuries and was among the first to enter the fort, where he was wounded for the third time.

692 ◆ JOHNSON, RUEL M.

Rank: Major (highest rank: Colonel)
Service: U.S. Army
Birthday: 5 June 1843
Place of Birth: Harbor Creek Township, Erie County, Pennsylvania
Date of Death: 12 November 1901
Place of Death: Goshen, Indiana
Cemetery: Oak Ridge Cemetery (MH)—Goshen, Indiana
Entered Service at: Goshen, Elkhart County, Indiana
Unit: 100th Indiana Infantry
Battle or Place of Action: Chattanooga, Tennessee
Date of Action: 25 November 1863
Date of Issue: 24 August 1896
Citation: While in command of the regiment bravely exposed himself to the fire of the enemy, encouraging and cheering his men.

693 ◆ JOHNSON, SAMUEL

Rank: Private (highest rank: Second Lieutenant)
Service: U.S. Army
Birthday: 28 January 1845
Place of Birth: Springfield Township, Delaware County, Pennsylvania
Date of Death: 24 November 1915
Place of Death: West Fork, Arkansas
Entered Service at: Connellsville, Fayette County, Pennsylvania
Unit: Company G, 9th Pennsylvania Reserves
Battle or Place of Action: Antietam, Maryland
Date of Action: 17 September 1862
G.O. Number, Date: 160, 30 May 1863
Citation: Individual bravery and daring in capturing from the enemy two colors of the 1st Texas Rangers (C.S.A.), receiving in the act a severe wound.

694 ◆ JOHNSON, WALLACE W.

Rank: Sergeant
Service: U.S. Army
Birthday: 30 December 1842
Place of Birth: Newfield, Thompkins County, New York
Date of Death: 30 December 1911
Place of Death: Walter's Park, Pennsylvania
Cemetery: West Laurel Hill Cemetery—Bala Cynwyd, Pennsylvania
Entered Service at: Waverly, Tioga County, New York
Unit: Company G, 6th Pennsylvania Reserves
Battle or Place of Action: Gettysburg, Pennsylvania
Date of Action: 2 July 1863
Date of Issue: 8 August 1900
Citation: With five other volunteers gallantly charged on a number of the enemy's sharpshooters concealed in a log house, captured them, and brought them into the Union lines.

695 ◆ JOHNSTON, DAVID H.

Rank: Private
Service: U.S. Army
Birthday: 19 August 1838
Place of Birth: Indiana County, Pennsylvania
Date of Death: 1931
Place of Death: Stanfield, Missouri
Cemetery: Pierce Chapel Cemetery (MH)—Clark, Nebraska
Entered Service at: Warsaw, Hancock County, Illinois
Unit: Company K, 8th Missouri Infantry
Battle or Place of Action: Vicksburg, Mississippi
Date of Action: 22 May 1863
Date of Issue: 16 August 1884
Citation: Gallantry in the charge of the "volunteer storming party."

696 ◆ JOHNSTON, WILLIAM P.

Rank: Landsman
Service: U.S. Navy
Birthday: 1849
Place of Birth: Chicago, Cook County, Illinois
Entered Service at: Chicago, Cook County, Illinois
Unit: U.S.S. *Fort Hindman*
Battle or Place of Action: Harrisonburg, Louisiana
Date of Action: 2 March 1864
G.O. Number, Date: 32, 16 April 1864
Citation: Served on board the U.S.S. *Fort Hindman* during the engagement near Harrisonburg, La., 2 March 1864. Badly wounded in the hand during the action, Johnston, despite his wound, took the place of another man to sponge and lead one of the guns throughout the entire action in which the Fort Hindman was raked severely with shot and shell from the enemy guns.

697 ◆ JOHNSTON, WILLIAM (WILLIE)

Rank: Musician
Service: U.S. Army
Birthday: July 1850
Place of Birth: Morristown, Morristown County, New York
Entered Service at: St. Johnsbury, Caledonia County, Vermont
Unit: Company D, 3d Vermont Infantry
Served as: Drummer
Battle or Place of Action: Seven Day Battle & on the Peninsula Campaign, Virginia
Date of Action: 26 June-1 July 1862
Date of Issue: 16 September 1863
Citation: Gallantry in Seven Day Battle and Peninsula campaign.

698 ◆ JONES, ANDREW

Rank: Chief Boatswain's Mate
Service: U.S. Navy
Birthday: 1835
Place of Birth: Limerick, County Limerick, Ireland
Entered Service at: New York, New York
Unit: U.S. Ironclad *Chickasaw*
Battle or Place of Action: Mobile Bay, Alabama
Date of Action: 4 August 1864
G.O. Number, Date: 45, 31 December 1864
Citation: Served as chief boatswain's mate on board the U.S. Ironclad *Chickasaw*, Mobile Bay, 5 August 1864. Although his enlistment was up, Jones volunteered for the battle of Mobile Bay, going on board the *Chickasaw* from the *Vincennes* where he then carried out his duties gallantly throughout the engagement with the enemy, which resulted in the capture of the rebel ram *Tennessee*.

699 ◆ JONES, DAVID

Rank: Private (highest rank: First Lieutenant)
Service: U.S. Army
Birthday: 13 April 1841
Place of Birth: Fayette County, Ohio
Date of Death: 18 June 1911

Cemetery: Good Hope Cemetery—Good Hope, Ohio
Entered Service at: Washington Courthouse, Fayette County, Ohio
Unit: Company I, 54th Ohio Infantry
Battle or Place of Action: Vicksburg, Mississippi
Date of Action: 22 May 1863
Date of Issue: 13 June 1894
Citation: Gallantry in the charge of the "volunteer storming party."

700 ◆ JONES, JOHN

Rank: Landsman
Service: U.S. Navy
Birthday: 25 August 1841
Place of Birth: Bridgeport, Fairfield County, Connecticut
Date of Death: 15 August 1907
Place of Death: Portsmouth, New Hampshire
Cemetery: St. Mary's Cemetery—Portsmouth, New Hampshire
Entered Service at: Acton, Middlesex County, Massachusetts
Unit: U.S.S. *Rhode Island*
Battle or Place of Action: off Cape Hatteras, North Carolina
Date of Action: 30 December 1862
G.O. Number, Date: 59, 22 June 1865
Citation: Served on board the U.S.S. *Rhode Island* which was engaged in saving the lives of the officers and crew of the *Monitor*, 30 December 1862. Participating in the hazardous rescue of the officers and crew of the sinking *Monitor*, Jones, after rescuing several of the men, became separated in a heavy gale with other members of the cutter that had set out from the *Rhode Island*, and spent many hours in the small boat at the mercy of the weather and the high seas until finally picked up by a schooner 50 miles east of Cape Hatteras.

701 ◆ JONES, JOHN E.

Rank: Quartermaster
Service: U.S. Navy
Place of Birth: New York, New York
Entered Service at: New York
Unit: U.S.S. *Oneida*
Battle or Place of Action: Mobile Bay, Alabama
Date of Action: 5 August 1864
G.O. Number, Date: 45, 31 December 1864
Citation: Served as quartermaster on board the U.S.S. *Oneida* in the engagement at Mobile Bay, 5 August 1864. Stationed at the wheel during the fierce action, Jones, though wounded, carried out his duties gallantly by going to the poop to assist at the signals after the wheel ropes were shot away and remained there until ordered to reeve new wheel ropes.

702 ◆ JONES, THOMAS

Rank: Coxswain
Service: U.S. Navy
Birthday: 1820
Place of Birth: Baltimore, Baltimore County, Maryland
Place of Death: Annapolis, Maryland
Entered Service at: Baltimore, Baltimore County, Maryland
Unit: U.S.S. *Ticonderoga*
Battle or Place of Action: Fort Fisher, North Carolina
Date of Action: 24-25 December 1864 & 13-15 January 1865
G.O. Number, Date: 59, 22 June 1865
Citation: On board the U.S.S. *Ticonderoga* during attacks on Fort Fisher, 24 and 25 December 1864; and 13 to 15 January 1865. Despite heavy return fire by the enemy and the explosion of the 100-pounder Parrott rifle which killed eight men and wounded 12 more, Jones, as captain of a gun, performed his duties with skill and courage during the first two days of battle. As his ship again took position on the line on the 13th, he remained steadfast as the *Ticonderoga* maintained a well-placed fire upon the batteries onshore, and thereafter, as she materially lessened the power of the guns on the mound which had been turned upon our assaulting columns. During this action the flag was planted on one side of the strongest fortifications possessed by the rebels.

703 ◆ JONES, WILLIAM

Rank: Captain of the Top
Service: U.S. Navy
Birthday: 1831
Place of Birth: Philadelphia, Philadelphia County, Pennsylvania
Entered Service at: Pennsylvania
Unit: U.S.S. *Richmond*
Battle or Place of Action: Mobile Bay, Alabama
Date of Action: 5 August 1864
G.O. Number, Date: 45, 31 December 1864
Citation: As captain of a gun on board the U.S.S. *Richmond* during action against rebel forts and gunboats and with the ram *Tennessee* in Mobile Bay, 5 August 1864. Despite damage to his ship and the loss of several men on board as enemy fire raked her decks, Jones fought his gun with skill and courage throughout the prolonged battle, which resulted in the surrender of the rebel ram *Tennessee* and in the damaging and destruction of batteries at Fort Morgan.

704 ◆ *JONES, WILLIAM

Rank: First Sergeant
Service: U.S. Army
Birthday: 1836
Place of Birth: Wicklow, County Wicklow, Ireland
Date of Death: 12 May 1864
Place of Death: Spotsylvania, Virginia
Cemetery: Fredericksburg National Military Park (2448) (MH)—Fredericksburg, Virginia
Entered Service at: New York, New York
Unit: Company A, 73d New York Infantry
Battle or Place of Action: Spotsylvania, Virginia
Date of Action: 12 May 1864
Date of Issue: 1 December 1864
Citation: Capture of flag of 65th Virginia Infantry (C.S.A.).

705 ◆ JORDAN, ABSALOM

Rank: Corporal
Service: U.S. Army
Place of Birth: Brown County, Ohio
Date of Death: 3 May 1888
Cemetery: Centerville Cemetery—Lovett, Indiana
Entered Service at: North Madison, Jefferson County, Indiana
Unit: Company A, 3d Indiana Cavalry
Battle or Place of Action: Deatonsville (Sailor's Creek), Virginia
Date of Action: 6 April 1865
Date of Issue: 3 May 1865
Citation: Capture of flag.

706 ◆ JORDAN, ROBERT

Rank: Coxswain
Service: U.S. Navy
Birthday: 1826
Place of Birth: New York, New York
Entered Service at: New York
Unit: U.S.S. *Minnesota* (temporarily on U.S.S. *Mount Washington*)
Battle or Place of Action: Nansemond River, Virginia
Date of Action: 14 April 1863
G.O. Number, Date: 17, 10 July 1863
Date of Issue: 10 July 1863
Citation: Attached to the U.S.S. *Minnesota* and temporarily serving on the U.S.S. *Mount Washington*, during action against the enemy in the Nansemond River, 14 April 1863. When the *Mount Washington* drifted against the bank following several successive hits which struck her boilers and stopped her engines, Jordan boarded the stricken vessel and, for six hours as fierce artillery and musketry continued to rake her decks, calmly assisted in manning a 12-pound howitzer which had been mounted on the open hurricane deck.

707 ◆ JORDAN, THOMAS H.

Rank: Quartermaster
Service: U.S. Navy
Birthday: 12 April 1840
Place of Birth: Portsmouth, Portsmouth County, Virginia
Date of Death: 17 July 1930
Place of Death: Baltimore, Maryland
Cemetery: Mount Olivet Cemetery—Chicago, Illinois
Entered Service at: Baltimore, Baltimore County, Maryland
Unit: U.S.S. *Galena*
Battle or Place of Action: Mobile Bay, Alabama
Date of Action: 5 August 1864
G.O. Number, Date: 59, 22 June 1865
Citation: On board the U.S.S. *Galena* during the attack on enemy forts at Mobile Bay, 5 August 1864. Securely lashed to the side of the *Oneida*, which had suffered the loss of her steering apparatus and an explosion of her boiler from enemy fire, the *Galena* aided the stricken vessel past the enemy forts to safety. Despite heavy damage to his ship from raking enemy fire, Jordan performed his duties with skill and courage throughout the action.

708 ◆ JOSSELYN, SIMEON T.

Rank: First Lieutenant
Service: U.S. Army
Birthday: 14 January 1842
Place of Birth: Buffalo, Erie County, New York
Date of Death: 4 April 1905
Place of Death: Skagway, Alaska
Cemetery: Forest Lawn Cemetery—Omaha, Nebraska
Entered Service at: Amboy, Lee County, Illinois
Unit: Company C, 13th Illinois Infantry
Battle or Place of Action: Missionary Ridge, Tennessee
Date of Action: 25 November 1863
Date of Issue: 4 April 1898
Citation: While commanding his company, deployed as skirmishers, Josselyn came upon a large body of the enemy, taking a number of them prisoner. Lt. Josselyn himself shot their color bearer, seized the colors, and brought them back to his regiment.

709 ◆ JUDGE, FRANCIS W.

Rank: First Sergeant (highest rank: Brevet Major U.S. Vols.)
Service: U.S. Army
Birthday: 10 February 1838
Place of Birth: England
Date of Death: 3 December 1904
Place of Death: New York, New York
Cemetery: Greenwood Cemetery—Brooklyn, New York
Entered Service at: New York, New York
Unit: Company K, 79th New York Infantry
Battle or Place of Action: Fort Sanders, Knoxville, Tennessee
Date of Action: 29 November 1863
Date of Issue: 2 November 1870
Citation: The color bearer of the 51st Georgia Infantry (C.S.A.), having planted his flag upon the side of the work, Sgt. Judge leaped from his position of safety, sprang upon the parapet, and in the face of a concentrated fire seized the flag and returned with it in safety to the fort.

710 ◆ KAISER, JOHN

Rank: First Sergeant (highest rank: Ordnance Sergeant)
Service: U.S. Army
Birthday: 1825
Place of Birth: Nerzogenaurach, Germany
Date of Death: 9 January 1894
Place of Death: Buffalo, New York
Cemetery: Forest Lawn Cemetery (MH)—Buffalo, New York
Entered Service at: New York, New York
Unit: Company E, 2d U.S. Artillery
Battle or Place of Action: Richmond, Virginia
Date of Action: 27 June 1862
Date of Issue: 2 April 1878

Citation: Gallant and meritorious service during the Seven Days' Battles before Richmond, Va.

711 ◆ KALTENBACH, LUTHER
Rank: Corporal (highest rank: Sergeant)
Service: U.S. Army
Birthday: 16 August 1843
Place of Birth: Germany
Date of Death: 1 September 1922
Place of Death: Los Angeles, California
Cemetery: Los Angeles National Cemetery (43-A-15)(MH)—Los Angeles, California
Entered Service at: Honey Creek, Pottawattamie County, Iowa
Unit: Company F, 12th Iowa Infantry
Battle or Place of Action: Nashville, Tennessee
Date of Action: 16 December 1864
Date of Issue: 24 February 1865
Citation: Capture of flag of 44th Mississippi Infantry (C.S.A.).

712 ◆ KANE, JOHN
Rank: Corporal (highest rank: Sergeant)
Service: U.S. Army
Place of Birth: Ireland
Entered Service at: Marilla, Erie County, New York
Unit: Company K, 100th New York Infantry
Served as: Color Bearer
Battle or Place of Action: Petersburg, Virginia
Date of Action: 2 April 1865
Date of Issue: 12 May 1865
Citation: Gallantry as color bearer in the assault on Fort Gregg.

713 ◆ KANE, THOMAS
Rank: Captain of the Hold
Service: U.S. Navy
Birthday: 1841
Place of Birth: Jersey City, Hudson County, New Jersey
Entered Service at: New Jersey
Unit: U.S.S. *Nereus*
Served as: Captain of the Hold
Battle or Place of Action: Fort Fisher, North Carolina
Date of Action: 15 January 1865
G.O. Number, Date: 84, 3 October 1867
Citation: On board the U.S.S. *Nereus* during the attack on Fort Fisher, 15 January 1865. Kane, as captain of the hold, displayed outstanding skill and courage as his ship maintained its well-directed fire against fortifications onshore despite the enemy's return fire. When a rebel steamer was discovered in the river back of the fort, the *Nereus*, with forward rifle guns trained, drove the ship off at the third fire. The gallant ship's participation contributed to the planting of the flag on one of the strongest fortifications possessed by the rebels.

714 ◆ KAPPESSER, PETER
Rank: Private
Service: U.S. Army
Birthday: 8 January 1839
Place of Birth: Germany
Date of Death: 31 May 1930
Place of Death: Syracuse, New York
Cemetery: Woodlawn Cemetery (Soldiers' Plot)(MH)—Syracuse, New York
Entered Service at: Syracuse, Onondaga County, New York
Unit: Company B, 149th New York Infantry
Battle or Place of Action: Lookout Mountain, Tennessee
Date of Action: 24 November 1863
Date of Issue: 28 June 1865
Citation: Capture of Confederate flag (Bragg's army).

715 ◆ KARPELES, LEOPOLD
Rank: Sergeant (highest rank: Color Sergeant)
Service: U.S. Army
Birthday: 9 September 1838
Place of Birth: Prague, Austria-Hungary
Date of Death: 2 February 1909
Place of Death: Washington, D.C.
Cemetery: Hebrew Congregation Cemetery—Washington, D.C.
Entered Service at: Springfield, Hampden County, Massachusetts
Unit: Company E, 57th Massachusetts Infantry
Battle or Place of Action: Wilderness Campaign, Virginia
Date of Action: 6 May 1864
Date of Issue: 30 April 1870
Citation: While color bearer, rallied the retreating troops and induced them to check the enemy's advance.

716 ◆ KAUSS, AUGUST
Rank: Corporal
Service: U.S. Army
Birthday: 6 November 1843
Place of Birth: Germany
Date of Death: 27 April 1913
Place of Death: Hurley, New York
Cemetery: Hurley Cemetery (MH)—Hurley, New York
Entered Service at: New York, New York
Unit: Company H, 15th New York Heavy Artillery
Battle or Place of Action: Five Forks, Virginia
Date of Action: 1 April 1865
Date of Issue: 10 May 1865
Citation: Capture of battle flag.

717 ◆ KEELE, JOSEPH
Rank: Sergeant Major (highest rank: Captain)
Service: U.S. Army
Birthday: 1 August 1840
Place of Birth: Ireland
Date of Death: 16 October 1906
Place of Death: Jersey City, New Jersey
Cemetery: Bayview Cemetery (MH)—Jersey City, New Jersey
Entered Service at: Staten Island, Richmond County, New York

Unit: 182d New York Infantry
Battle or Place of Action: North Anna River, Virginia
Date of Action: 23 May 1864
Date of Issue: 25 October 1867
Citation: Voluntarily and at the risk of his life carried orders to the brigade commander, which resulted in saving the works his regiment was defending.

718 ◆ KEEN, JOSEPH S.

Rank: Sergeant
Service: U.S. Army
Birthday: 24 July 1843
Place of Birth: Vale, Guernsey, England
Date of Death: 3 December 1926
Place of Death: Detroit, Michigan
Cemetery: Elmwood Cemetery (MH)—Detroit, Michigan
Entered Service at: Detroit, Wayne County, Michigan
Unit: Company D, 13th Michigan Infantry
Battle or Place of Action: near the Chattahoochee River, Georgia
Date of Action: 1 October 1864
Date of Issue: 4 August 1899
Citation: While an escaped prisoner of war within the enemy's lines, Keen witnessed an important movement of the enemy, and at great personal risk made his way through the enemy's lines and brought news of the movement to Sherman's army.
Notes: POW

719 ◆ KEENE, JOSEPH

Rank: Private (highest rank: Corporal)
Service: U.S. Army
Birthday: 3 April 1839
Place of Birth: England
Date of Death: 1 December 1921
Place of Death: Willowvale, New York
Cemetery: Grand View Cemetery—Whitesboro, New York
Entered Service at: Utica, Oneida County, New York
Unit: Company B, 26th New York Infantry
Battle or Place of Action: Fredericksburg, Virginia
Date of Action: 13 December 1862
Date of Issue: 2 December 1892
Citation: Voluntarily seized the colors after several color bearers had been shot down and led the regiment in the charge.

720 ◆ KELLEY, ANDREW JOHN

Rank: Private (highest rank: Sergeant)
Service: U.S. Army
Birthday: 2 September 1845
Place of Birth: La Grange County, Indiana
Date of Death: 4 June 1918
Place of Death: Crookston, Minnesota
Cemetery: Oakdale Cemetery (MH)—Crookston, Minnesota
Entered Service at: Ypsilanti, Washtenaw County, Michigan
Unit: Company E, 17th Michigan Infantry
Battle or Place of Action: Knoxville, Tennessee
Date of Action: 20 November 1863
Date of Issue: 17 April 1900
Citation: Having voluntarily accompanied a small party to destroy buildings within the enemy's lines whence sharpshooters had been firing, Kelley disregarded an order to retire, remained, and completed the firing of the buildings, thus insuring their total destruction; this at the imminent risk of his life from the fire of the advancing enemy.

721 ◆ KELLEY, GEORGE V.

Rank: Captain
Service: U.S. Army
Birthday: 23 March 1843
Place of Birth: Massillon, Stark County, Ohio
Date of Death: 4 November 1905
Cemetery: Riverside Cemetery (MH)—Denver, Colorado
Entered Service at: Massillon, Stark County, Ohio
Unit: Company A, 104th Ohio Infantry
Battle or Place of Action: Franklin, Tennessee
Date of Action: 30 November 1864
Date of Issue: 13 February 1865
Citation: Capture of flag supposed to be of Cheatham's Corps (C.S.A.).

722 ◆ KELLEY, JOHN

Rank: Second Class Fireman
Service: U.S. Navy
Place of Birth: Ireland
Unit: U.S.S. *Ceres*
Battle or Place of Action: Roanoke River, near Hamilton, North Carolina
Date of Action: 9 July 1862
G.O. Number, Date: 11, 3 April 1863
Citation: Served as second-class fireman on board the U.S.S. *Ceres* in the fight near Hamilton, Roanoke River, 9 July 1862. When his ship was fired upon by the enemy with small arms, Kelley returned the raking fire, courageously carrying out his duties throughout the engagement, and was spoken of for "good conduct and cool bravery under enemy fire" by the commanding officer.

723 ◆ KELLEY, LEVERETT MANSFIELD

Rank: Sergeant (highest rank: Captain)
Service: U.S. Army
Birthday: 28 September 1841
Place of Birth: Schenectady, Schenectady County, New York
Date of Death: 9 April 1924
Place of Death: Washington, D.C.
Cemetery: Arlington National Cemetery (2-3756)—Arlington, Virginia
Entered Service at: Rutland, La Salle County, Illinois
Unit: Company A, 36th Illinois Infantry
Battle or Place of Action: Missionary Ridge, Tennessee
Date of Action: 25 November 1863
Date of Issue: 4 April 1900

Citation: Sprang over the works just captured from the enemy and calling upon his comrades to follow, rushed forward in the face of a deadly fire and was among the first over the works on the summit, where he compelled the surrender of a Confederate officer and received his sword.

724 ◆ KELLY, ALEXANDER

Rank: First Sergeant
Service: U.S. Army
Birthday: 7 April 1840
Place of Birth: Saltsburg, Indiana County, Pennsylvania
Date of Death: 19 June 1907
Cemetery: St. Peter's Cemetery (MH)—Pittsburgh, Pennsylvania
Entered Service at: Allegheny, Allegheny County, Pennsylvania
Unit: Company F, 6th U.S. Colored Infantry
Battle or Place of Action: Chapin's Farm, Virginia
Date of Action: 29 September 1864
Date of Issue: 6 April 1865
Citation: Gallantly seized the colors, which had fallen near the enemy's lines of abatis, raised them, and rallied the men at a time of confusion and in a place of the greatest danger.

725 ◆ KELLY, DANIEL ARMER

Rank: Sergeant (highest rank: Quartermaster Sergeant)
Service: U.S. Army
Birthday: 19 March 1841
Place of Birth: Groveland, Livingston County, New York
Date of Death: 18 January 1912
Cemetery: Maple Wood Cemetery (MH)—Reading, Michigan
Entered Service at: Groveland, Livingston County, New York
Unit: Company G, 8th New York Cavalry
Battle or Place of Action: Waynesboro, Virginia
Date of Action: 26 March 1865
Date of Issue: 26 March 1865
Citation: Capture of flag.

726 ◆ KELLY, THOMAS

Rank: Private
Service: U.S. Army
Place of Birth: Ireland
Entered Service at: New York, New York
Unit: Company A, 6th New York Cavalry
Battle or Place of Action: Front Royal, Virginia
Date of Action: 16 August 1864
Date of Issue: 26 August 1864
Citation: Capture of flag.

727 ◆ KEMP, JOSEPH BELL

Rank: First Sergeant (highest rank: Captain)
Service: U.S. Army
Birthday: 1 July 1844
Place of Birth: Lima, Allen County, Ohio
Date of Death: 13 July 1917
Place of Death: Ann Arbor, Michigan
Cemetery: Forest Hill Cemetery—Ann Arbor, Michigan
Entered Service at: Sault Ste. Marie, Chippewa County, Michigan
Unit: Company D, 5th Michigan Infantry
Battle or Place of Action: Wilderness Campaign, Virginia
Date of Action: 6 May 1864
Date of Issue: 1 December 1864
Citation: Capture of flag of 31st North Carolina (C.S.A.) in a personal encounter.

728 ◆ KENDALL, WILLIAM WESLEY

Rank: First Sergeant (highest rank: First Lieutenant)
Service: U.S. Army
Birthday: 31 August 1839
Place of Birth: Hall Township, Dubois County, Indiana
Date of Death: 14 August 1920
Place of Death: West Baden, Indiana
Cemetery: Ames Chapel Cemetery—Abydel, Indiana
Entered Service at: Jeffersonville, Clark County, Indiana
Unit: Company A, 49th Indiana Infantry
Battle or Place of Action: Black River Bridge, Mississippi
Date of Action: 17 May 1863
Date of Issue: 12 February 1894
Citation: Voluntarily led the company in a charge and was the first to enter the enemy's works, taking a number of prisoners.

729 ◆ KENDRICK, THOMAS

Rank: Coxswain
Service: U.S. Navy
Birthday: 1839
Place of Birth: Bath, Sagadahoc County, Maine
Entered Service at: Maine
Unit: U.S.S. *Oneida*
Battle or Place of Action: Mobile Bay, Alabama
Date of Action: 5 August 1864
G.O. Number, Date: 45, 31 December 1864
Citation: Served as coxswain on board the U.S.S. *Oneida* in the engagement at Mobile Bay, 5 August 1864. Volunteering for the Mobile Bay action from Bienville, Kendrick displayed courageous devotion to duty, and his excellent conduct throughout the battle which resulted in the capture of the rebel ram *Tennessee* and in the damaging of Fort Morgan, attracted the attention of the commanding officer and those serving around him.

730 ◆ KENNA, BARNETT

Rank: Quartermaster
Service: U.S. Navy
Birthday: 1827
Place of Birth: Canterbury, Kent County, England
Date of Death: 28 May 1890
Place of Death: Glouchester, Massachusetts

Cemetery: Cherry Hill Cemetery (MH)—Glouchester, Massachusetts
Entered Service at: Newburyport, Essex County, Massachusetts
Unit: U.S.S. *Brooklyn*
Battle or Place of Action: Mobile Bay, Alabama
Date of Action: 5 August 1864
G.O. Number, Date: 45, 31 December 1864
Citation: On board the U.S.S. *Brooklyn* during action against rebel forts and gunboats and with the ram *Tennessee*, in Mobile Bay, 5 August 1864. Despite severe damage to his ship and the loss of several men on board as enemy fire raked her decks from stem to stern, Kenna fought his gun with skill and courage throughout the furious action which resulted in the surrender of the rebel ram *Tennessee* and in the damaging and destruction of batteries at Fort Morgan.

731 ◆ KENNEDY, JOHN

Rank: Private (highest rank: Ordance Sergeant Ret.)
Service: U.S. Army
Birthday: 14 May 1834
Place of Birth: Cavan, County Cavan, Ireland
Date of Death: 28 September 1910
Cemetery: Oakland Cemetery (MH)—Little Rock, Arkansas
Entered Service at: New York, New York
Unit: Company M, 2d U.S. Artillery
Battle or Place of Action: Trevilian Station, Virginia
Date of Action: 11 June 1864
Date of Issue: 19 August 1892
Citation: Remained at his gun, resisting with its implements the advancing cavalry, and thus secured the retreat of his detachment.

732 ◆ KENYON, CHARLES W.

Rank: Fireman (highest rank: Acting Third Assistant Engineer)
Service: U.S. Navy
Birthday: 1840
Place of Birth: Oneida, Madison County, New York
Entered Service at: New York, New York
Unit: U.S.S. *Galena*
Battle or Place of Action: Drewry's Bluff, James River, Virginia
Date of Action: 15 May 1862
G.O. Number, Date: 11, 3 April 1863
Citation: On board the U.S.S. *Galena* in the attack upon Drewry's Bluff, 15 May 1862. Severely burned while extricating a priming wire which had become bent and fixed in the bow gun while the ship underwent terrific shelling from the enemy, Kenyon hastily dressed his hands with cotton waste and oil and courageously returned to his gun while enemy sharpshooters in rifle pits along the banks continued to direct their fire at the men at the guns.

733 ◆ KENYON, JOHN SNYDERS

Rank: Sergeant
Service: U.S. Army
Birthday: 5 May 1843
Place of Birth: Grosvenors Corners, Schoharie County, New York
Date of Death: 16 February 1902
Cemetery: Oakwood Cemetery (MH)—Syracuse, New York
Entered Service at: Schenevus, Otsego County, New York
Unit: Company D, 3d New York Cavalry
Battle or Place of Action: Trenton, North Carolina
Date of Action: 15 May 1862
Date of Issue: 28 September 1897
Citation: Voluntarily left a retiring column, returned in the face of the enemy's fire, helped a wounded man upon a horse, and so enabled him to escape capture or death.

734 ◆ KENYON, SAMUEL P.

Rank: Private (highest rank: Quartermaster Sergeant)
Service: U.S. Army
Birthday: 1846
Place of Birth: Ira, Cayuga County, New York
Date of Death: 14 June 1884
Place of Death: Cullen, New York
Entered Service at: Augusta, New York
Unit: Company B, 24th New York Cavalry
Battle or Place of Action: Deatonsville (Sailor's Creek), Virginia
Date of Action: 6 April 1865
Date of Issue: 3 May 1865
Citation: Capture of battle flag.

735 ◆ KEOUGH, JOHN

Rank: Corporal
Service: U.S. Army
Birthday: 1835
Place of Birth: County Tipperary, Ireland
Entered Service at: Annapolis, Anne Arundel County, Maryland
Unit: Company E, 67th Pennsylvania Infantry
Battle or Place of Action: Deatonsville (Sailor's Creek), Virginia
Date of Action: 6 April 1865
Date of Issue: 10 May 1865
Citation: Capture of battle flag of 50th Georgia Infantry (C.S.A.).
Notes: POW

736 ◆ KEPHART, JAMES

Rank: Private
Service: U.S. Army
Birthday: 22 April 1842
Place of Birth: Venango County, Pennsylvania
Date of Death: 17 April 1932
Place of Death: Gooding, Idaho
Cemetery: Elmwood Cemetery (MH)—Gooding, Idaho
Entered Service at: Dubuque, Dubuque County, Iowa
Unit: Company C, 13th U.S. Infantry
Battle or Place of Action: Vicksburg, Mississippi

Date of Action: 19 May 1863
Date of Issue: 13 May 1899
Citation: Voluntarily and at the risk of his life, under a severe fire of the enemy, aided and assisted to the rear an officer who had been severely wounded and left on the field.

737 ◆ KERR, THOMAS R.

Rank: Captain
Service: U.S. Army
Birthday: 24 April 1843
Place of Birth: near Colleraine, County Derry, Ireland
Date of Death: 14 November 1926
Place of Death: Pittsburgh, Pennsylvania
Cemetery: Arlington National Cemetery (3-1623)—Arlington, Virginia
Entered Service at: Pittsburgh, Allegheny County, Pennsylvania
Unit: Company C, 14th Pennsylvania Cavalry
Battle or Place of Action: Moorfield, West Virginia
Date of Action: 7 August 1864
Date of Issue: 13 June 1894
Citation: After being most desperately wounded, he captured the colors of the 8th Virginia Cavalry (C.S.A.).

738 ◆ KIGGINS, JOHN

Rank: Sergeant
Service: U.S. Army
Birthday: 2 February 1837
Place of Birth: Syracuse, Onondaga County, New York
Date of Death: 29 September 1914
Place of Death: Bath, New York
Cemetery: Bath National Cemetery (H-32-9) (MH)—Bath, New York
Entered Service at: Syracuse, Onondaga County, New York
Unit: Company D, 149th New York Infantry
Battle or Place of Action: Lookout Mountain, Tennessee
Date of Action: 24 November 1863
Date of Issue: 12 January 1892
Citation: Waved the colors to save the lives of the men who were being fired upon by their own batteries, and thereby drew upon himself a concentrated fire from the enemy.

739 ◆ KIMBALL, JOSEPH

Rank: Private (highest rank: Corporal)
Service: U.S. Army
Birthday: 2 February 1836
Place of Birth: Littleton, Grafton County, New Hampshire
Date of Death: 20 July 1909
Place of Death: Alma, West Virginia
Cemetery: Beechwood Cemetery (MH)—Middle Bourne, West Virginia
Entered Service at: Ironton, Lawrence County, Ohio
Unit: Company B, 2d West Virginia Cavalry
Battle or Place of Action: Deatonsville (Sailor's Creek), Virginia
Date of Action: 6 April 1865
Date of Issue: 3 May 1865
Citation: Capture of flag of 6th North Carolina Infantry (C.S.A.).

740 ◆ KINDIG, JOHN M.

Rank: Corporal (highest rank: Sergeant)
Service: U.S. Army
Place of Birth: East Liberty, Allegheny County, Pennsylvania
Entered Service at: Wilkins, Allegheny County, Pennsylvania
Unit: Company A, 63d Pennsylvania Infantry
Battle or Place of Action: Spotsylvania, Virginia
Date of Action: 12 May 1864
Date of Issue: 1 December 1864
Citation: Capture of flag of 28th North Carolina Infantry (C.S.A.).
Notes: POW

741 ◆ KING, HORATIO COLLINS

Rank: Major & Quartermaster (highest rank: Brevet Colonel)
Service: U.S. Army
Birthday: 22 December 1837
Place of Birth: Portland, Cumberland County, Maine
Date of Death: 15 November 1918
Place of Death: Brooklyn, New York
Cemetery: The Green Wood Cemetery—Brooklyn, New York
Entered Service at: Brooklyn, Kings County, New York
Unit: U.S. Volunteers
Battle or Place of Action: near Dinwiddie Courthouse, Virginia
Date of Action: 31 March 1865
Date of Issue: 23 September 1897
Citation: While serving as a volunteer aide, carried orders to the reserve brigade and participated with it in the charge which repulsed the enemy.

742 ◆ KING, ROBERT HENRY

Rank: Landsman
Service: U.S. Navy
Birthday: 1845
Place of Birth: New York
Date of Death: 10 April 1865
Cemetery: Albany Rural Cemetery (MH)—Albany, New York
Entered Service at: New York
Unit: U.S. Picket Boat No. 1
Battle or Place of Action: Plymouth, North Carolina
Date of Action: 27 October 1864
G.O. Number, Date: 45, 31 December 1864
Citation: King served on board the U.S. Picket Boat No. 1, in action, 27 October 1864, against the Confederate ram, *Albemarle*, which had resisted repeated attacks by our steamers and had kept a large force of vessels employed in watching

her. The picket boat, equipped with a spar torpedo, succeeded in passing the enemy pickets within 20 yards without being discovered and then made for the *Albemarle* under a full head of steam. Immediately taken under fire by the ram, the small boat plunged on, jumped the log boom which encircled the target, and exploded its torpedo under the port bow of the ram. The picket boat was destroyed by enemy fire and almost the entire crew taken prisoner or lost.
Notes: POW

743 ◆ KING JR., RUFUS

Rank: First Lieutenant (highest rank: Brevet Major)
Service: U.S. Army
Birthday: 21 March 1838
Place of Birth: New York
Date of Death: 18 March 1900
Place of Death: New York, New York
Cemetery: Evergreen Cemetery (MH)—Hillside, New Jersey
Entered Service at: New York
Unit: 4th U.S. Artillery
Battle or Place of Action: White Oak Swamp Bridge, Virginia
Date of Action: 30 June 1862
Date of Issue: 2 April 1898
Citation: This officer, when his captain was wounded, succeeded to the command of two batteries while engaged against a superior force of the enemy and fought his guns most gallantly until compelled to retire.

744 ◆ KINNAIRD, SAMUEL W.

Rank: Landsman (highest rank: Ordinary Seaman)
Service: U.S. Navy
Birthday: 2 May 1840
Place of Birth: New York, New York
Date of Death: 20 April 1923
Place of Death: South Berne, New York
Cemetery: 1st Calvary Cemetery—Woodside, New York
Entered Service at: New York, New York
Unit: U.S.S. *Lackawanna*
Battle or Place of Action: Mobile Bay, Alabama
Date of Action: 5 August 1864
G.O. Number, Date: 45, 31 December 1864
Citation: Served as a landsman on board the U.S.S. *Lackawanna* during successful attacks against Fort Morgan, rebel gunboats, and the ram *Tennessee* in Mobile Bay, 5 August 1864. Showing a presence of mind and cheerfulness that had much to do with maintaining the crew's morale, Kinnaird served gallantly through the action which resulted in the capture of the prize rebel ram *Tennessee* and in the destruction of batteries at Fort Morgan.

745 ◆ KINSEY, JOHN

Rank: Corporal
Service: U.S. Army
Birthday: 1844

Place of Birth: Lancaster County, Pennsylvania
Date of Death: 19 December 1904
Cemetery: Crown Hill Cemetery—Indianapolis, Indiana
Entered Service at: Maytown, Lancaster County, Pennsylvania
Unit: Company B, 45th Pennsylvania Infantry
Battle or Place of Action: Spotsylvania, Virginia
Date of Action: 18 May 1864
Date of Issue: 2 March 1897
Citation: Seized the colors, the color bearer having been shot, and with great gallantry succeeded in saving them from capture.

746 ◆ KIRBY, DENNIS THOMAS

Rank: Major (highest rank: Brevet Brigadier General)
Service: U.S. Army
Birthday: 15 September 1835
Place of Birth: Niagara Falls, Niagara County, New York
Date of Death: 18 April 1922
Place of Death: Washington, D.C.
Cemetery: Arlington National Cemetery (1-334)—Arlington, Virginia
Entered Service at: St. Louis, St. Louis County, Missouri
Unit: 8th Missouri Infantry
Battle or Place of Action: Vicksburg, Mississippi
Date of Action: 22 May 1863
Date of Issue: 31 January 1894
Citation: Seized the colors when the color bearer was killed and bore them himself in the assault.

747 ◆ KIRK, JONATHAN C.

Rank: Captain
Service: U.S. Army
Place of Birth: Clinton County, Ohio
Date of Death: 30 July 1907
Cemetery: Maple Grove Cemetery (MH)—Wichita, Kansas
Entered Service at: Wilmington, Clinton County, Ohio
Unit: Company F, 20th Indiana Infantry
Battle or Place of Action: North Anna River, Virginia
Date of Action: 23 May 1864
Date of Issue: 13 June 1894
Citation: Volunteered for dangerous service and singlehandedly captured 13 armed Confederate soldiers and marched them to the rear.

748 ◆ KLINE, HARRY

True Name: Klien, Henry
Rank: Private (highest rank: Corporal)
Service: U.S. Army
Birthday: 4 October 1841
Place of Birth: Germany
Date of Death: 5 December 1901
Place of Death: Syracuse, New York
Cemetery: Woodlawn Cemetery (MH)—Syracuse, New York

Entered Service at: Syracuse, Onondaga County, New York
Unit: Company E, 40th New York Infantry
Battle or Place of Action: Deatonsville (Sailor's Creek), Virginia
Date of Action: 6 April 1865
Date of Issue: 10 May 1865
Citation: Capture of battle flag.

749 ◆ KLOTH, CHARLES H.

Rank: Private
Service: U.S. Army
Place of Birth: Europe
Entered Service at: Chicago, Cook County, Illinois
Unit: Chicago Mercantile Battery, Illinois Light Artillery
Battle or Place of Action: Vicksburg, Mississippi
Date of Action: 22 May 1863
Date of Issue: 15 January 1895
Citation: Carried with others by hand a cannon up to and fired it through an embrasure of the enemy's works.

750 ◆ KNIGHT, CHARLES H.

Rank: Corporal
Service: U.S. Army
Birthday: 1839
Place of Birth: Keene, Cheshire County, New Hampshire
Date of Death: 9 August 1904
Place of Death: West Springfield, Massachusetts
Cemetery: Oak Grove Cemetery (MH)—Springfield, Massachusetts
Entered Service at: Keene, Cheshire County, New Hampshire
Unit: Company I, 9th New Hampshire Infantry
Battle or Place of Action: Petersburg, Virginia
Date of Action: 30 July 1864
Date of Issue: 27 July 1896
Citation: In company with a sergeant, was the first to enter the exploded mine; was wounded but took several prisoners to the Federal lines.

751 ◆ KNIGHT, WILLIAM J.

Rank: Private
Service: U.S. Army
Birthday: 24 January 1837
Place of Birth: Apple Creek, Wayne County, Ohio
Date of Death: 26 September 1916
Cemetery: Oakwood Cemetery—Stryker, Ohio
Entered Service at: Farmers Center, Defiance County, Ohio
Unit: Company E, 21st Ohio Infantry
Battle or Place of Action: Georgia
Date of Action: April 1862
Date of Issue: September 1863
Citation: One of 19 of 24 men (including two civilians) who, by direction of Gen. Ormsby M. Mitchell, penetrated nearly 200 miles south into enemy territory and captured a railroad train at Big Shanty, Ga., in an attempt to destroy the bridges and track between Chattanaooga and Atlanta.

752 ◆ KNOWLES, ABIATHER J.

Rank: Private (highest rank: Captain)
Service: U.S. Army
Birthday: 15 March 1830
Place of Birth: La Grange, Penobscot County, Maine
Date of Death: 11 February 1905
Place of Death: North Bradfort, Maine
Cemetery: Hill Crest Cemetery (MH)—La Grange, Maine
Entered Service at: Willets Point, Queens County, New York
Unit: Company D, 2d Maine Infantry
Battle or Place of Action: Bull Run, Virginia
Date of Action: 21 July 1861
Date of Issue: 27 December 1894
Citation: Removed the dead and wounded under heavy fire.

753 ◆ KNOX, EDWARD M.

Rank: Second Lieutenant
Service: U.S. Army
Birthday: 12 February 1842
Place of Birth: New York, New York
Date of Death: 28 March 1916
Place of Death: New York, New York
Cemetery: Woodlawn Cemetery—Bronx, New York
Entered Service at: New York, New York
Unit: 15th New York Battery Light Artillery
Battle or Place of Action: Gettysburg, Pennsylvania
Date of Action: 2 July 1863
Date of Issue: 18 October 1892
Citation: Held his ground with the battery after the other batteries had fallen back until compelled to draw his piece off by hand; he was severely wounded.

754 ◆ KOOGLE, JACOB

Rank: First Lieutenant
Service: U.S. Army
Birthday: 5 December 1841
Place of Birth: Frederick, Frederick County, Maryland
Date of Death: 16 March 1915
Place of Death: Hagerstown, Maryland
Cemetery: St. Paul's Lutheran Cemetery (MH)—Myersville, Maryland
Entered Service at: Middletown, Frederick County, Maryland
Unit: Company G, 7th Maryland Infantry
Battle or Place of Action: Five Forks, Virginia
Date of Action: 1 April 1865
Date of Issue: 10 May 1865
Citation: Capture of battle flag.

755 ◆ KOUNTZ, JOHN S.

Rank: Musician
Service: U.S. Army
Birthday: 25 March 1845
Place of Birth: Maumee, Lucas County, Ohio

Date of Death: 14 June 1909
Cemetery: Calvary Cemetery—Toledo, Ohio
Entered Service at: Maumee, Lucas County, Ohio
Unit: Company G, 37th Ohio Infantry
Battle or Place of Action: Missionary Ridge, Tennessee
Date of Action: 25 November 1863
Date of Issue: 13 August 1895
Citation: Seized a musket and joined in the charge in which he was severely wounded.

756 ◆ KRAMER, THEODORE L.

Rank: Private
Service: U.S. Army
Birthday: 1847
Place of Birth: Luzerne County, Pennsylvania
Date of Death: 2 March 1910
Place of Death: Chicago, Illinois
Cemetery: Arlington Cemetery (MH)—Elmhurst, Illinois
Entered Service at: Danville, Montour County, Pennsylvania
Unit: Company G, 188th Pennsylvania Infantry
Battle or Place of Action: Chapin's Farm, Virginia
Date of Action: 29 September 1864
Date of Issue: 6 April 1865
Citation: Took one of the first prisoners, a captain.

757 ◆ KRETSINGER, GEORGE

Rank: Private
Service: U.S. Army
Birthday: 20 June 1844
Place of Birth: Fairfield, Herkimer County, New York
Date of Death: 20 April 1906
Place of Death: Chicago, Illinois
Cemetery: Rose Hill Cemetery—Chicago, Illinois
Entered Service at: Chicago, Cook County, Illinois
Unit: Chicago Mercantile Battery, Illinois Light Artillery
Battle or Place of Action: Vicksburg, Mississippi
Date of Action: 22 May 1863
Date of Issue: 20 July 1897
Citation: Carried with others by hand a cannon up to and fired it through an embrasure of the enemy's works.

758 ◆ KUDER, ANDREW

Rank: Second Lieutenant (highest rank: Captain)
Service: U.S. Army
Birthday: 1838
Place of Birth: Groveland, Livingston County, New York
Date of Death: 30 April 1899
Place of Death: South Livonia, New York
Cemetery: Arnold Cemetery (MH)—Conesus, New York
Entered Service at: Rochester, Monroe County, New York
Unit: Company G, 8th New York Cavalry
Battle or Place of Action: Waynesboro, Virginia
Date of Action: 2 March 1865
Date of Issue: 26 March 1865
Citation: Capture of flag.

759 ◆ KUDER, JEREMIAH

Rank: Lieutenant (highest rank: Captain)
Service: U.S. Army
Birthday: 12 July 1835
Place of Birth: Tiffin, Seneca County, Ohio
Date of Death: 25 May 1916
Place of Death: Marion, Indiana
Cemetery: Marion National Cemetery (4-2464) (MH)—Marion, Indiana
Entered Service at: Warsaw, Kosciusko County, Indiana
Unit: Company A, 74th Indiana Infantry
Battle or Place of Action: Jonesboro, Georgia
Date of Action: 1 September 1864
Date of Issue: 7 April 1865
Citation: Capture of flag of 8th and 19th Arkansas (C.S.A.).

760 ◆ LABILL, JOSEPH S.

True Name: Labille, Joseph S.
Rank: Private
Service: U.S. Army
Birthday: 1837
Place of Birth: Belgium
Date of Death: 1911
Cemetery: South Hill Cemetery (MH)—Vandalia, Illinois
Entered Service at: Vandalia, Fayette County, Illinois
Unit: Company C, 6th Missouri Infantry
Battle or Place of Action: Vicksburg, Mississippi
Date of Action: 22 May 1863
Date of Issue: 14 August 1894
Citation: Gallantry in the charge of the "volunteer storming party."

761 ◆ LADD, GEORGE

Rank: Private
Service: U.S. Army
Place of Birth: Camillus, Onondaga County, New York
Date of Death: 13 August 1869
Place of Death: Bath, New York
Cemetery: Bath National Cemetery (C6-6) (MH)—Bath, New York
Entered Service at: Camillus, Onondaga County, New York
Unit: Company H, 22d New York Cavalry
Battle or Place of Action: Waynesboro, Virginia
Date of Action: 2 March 1865
Date of Issue: 26 March 1865
Citation: Captured a standard bearer, his flag, horse, and equipment.

762 ◆ LAFFERTY, JOHN✢

True Name: Laverty, John
Rank: Fireman
Service: U.S. Navy
Birthday: 1842
Place of Birth: New York, New York
Date of Death: 13 November 1903

Place of Death: Philadelphia, Pennsylvania
Cemetery: Mount Moriah (VA plot 3-3-17) (MH)—Philadelphia, Pennsylvania
Entered Service at: Pennsylvania
Unit: U.S.S. *Wyalusing*
Battle or Place of Action: Roanoke River, North Carolina
Date of Action: 25 May 1864
G.O. Number, Date: 45, 31 December 1864
Date of Issue: 14 March 1865
Citation: **First Award** Served on board the U.S.S. *Wyalusing* and participated in a plan to destroy the rebel ram *Abemarle* in Roanoke River, 25 May 1864. Volunteering for the hazardous mission, Lafferty participated in the transfer of two torpedoes across an island swamp and then served as sentry to keep guard of clothes and arms left by other members of the party. After being rejoined by others of the party who had been discovered before the plan could be completed, Lafferty succeeded in returning to the mother ship after spending 24 hours of discomfort in the rain and swamp.
Notes: ✢Double Awardee: *see also* Interim 1871-1898 during which he served under the name John Laverty

763 ◆ LAFFEY, BARTLETT

Rank: Seaman (highest rank: Acting Master's Mate)
Service: U.S. Navy
Birthday: 1841
Place of Birth: Galway, County Galway, Ireland
Date of Death: 22 March 1901
Place of Death: Chelsea, Massachusetts
Cemetery: Old Calvary Cemetery (MH)—Roslindale, Massachusetts
Entered Service at: Boston, Suffolk County, Massachusetts
Unit: U.S.S. *Marmora*
Battle or Place of Action: off Yazoo City, Mississippi
Date of Action: 5 March 1864
G.O. Number, Date: 32, 16 April 1864
Citation: Off Yazoo City, Miss., 5 March 1864, embarking from the *Marmora* with a 12-pound howitzer mounted on a field carriage, Laffey landed with the gun and crew in the midst of heated battle and, bravely standing by his gun despite enemy rifle fire which cut the gun carriage and rammer, contributed to the turning back of the enemy during the fierce engagement.

764 ◆ *LAING, WILLIAM

Rank: Sergeant
Service: U.S. Army
Birthday: 1831
Place of Birth: Hempstead, Nassau County, New York
Date of Death: 29 September 1864
Place of Death: Chapin's Bluff, Virginia
Entered Service at: Brooklyn, Kings County, New York
Unit: Company F, 158th New York Infantry
Battle or Place of Action: Chapin's Farm, Virginia
Date of Action: 29 September 1864
Date of Issue: 6 April 1865
Citation: Was among the first to scale the parapet.

765 ◆ LAKIN, DANIEL

Rank: Seaman
Service: U.S. Navy
Birthday: 1834
Place of Birth: Baltimore, Baltimore County, Maryland
Entered Service at: Maryland
Unit: U.S.S. *Commodore Perry*
Battle or Place of Action: Franklin, Virginia
Date of Action: 3 October 1862
G.O. Number, Date: 11, 3 April 1863
Citation: On board the U.S.S. *Commodore Perry* in the attack upon Franklin, Va., 3 October 1862. With enemy fire raking the deck of his ship and blockades thwarting her progress, Lakin remained at his post and performed his duties with skill and courage as the *Commodore Perry* fought a gallant battle to silence many rebel batteries as she steamed down the Blackwater River.

766 ◆ LANDIS, JAMES PARKER

Rank: Chief Bugler
Service: U.S. Army
Birthday: 20 July 1843
Place of Birth: Mifflin County, Pennsylvania
Date of Death: 1 December 1924
Place of Death: Yeagertown, Pennsylvania
Cemetery: Holy Communion Lutheran Cemetery—Yeagertown, Pennsylvania
Entered Service at: Reedsville, Mifflin County, Pennsylvania
Unit: 1st Pennsylvania Cavalry
Battle or Place of Action: Paines Crossroads, Virginia
Date of Action: 5 April 1865
Date of Issue: 3 May 1865
Citation: Capture of flag.

767 ◆ LANE, MORGAN D.

Rank: Private
Service: U.S. Army
Birthday: 1844
Place of Birth: Monroe, Orange County, New York
Date of Death: 19 July 1892
Cemetery: Mount Vernon Cemetery (MH)—Atchison, Kansas
Entered Service at: Allegan, Allegan County, Michigan
Unit: Signal Corps
Battle or Place of Action: Jetersville, Virginia
Date of Action: 6 April 1865
Date of Issue: 16 March 1866
Citation: Capture of flag of gunboat *Nansemond*.

768 ◆ LANFARE, AARON STEVEN

Rank: First Lieutenant (highest rank: Captain)
Service: U.S. Army
Birthday: 9 September 1824
Place of Birth: Branford, New Haven County, Connecticut
Date of Death: 19 September 1875
Place of Death: At Sea & buried at Sea

Cemetery: Branford Center Cemetery (MH) (Marker Only)—Branford, Connecticut
Entered Service at: Branford, New Haven County, Connecticut
Unit: Company B, 1st Connecticut Cavalry
Battle or Place of Action: Deatonsville (Sailor's Creek), Virginia
Date of Action: 6 April 1865
Date of Issue: 3 May 1865
Citation: Capture of flag of 11th Florida Infantry (C.S.A.).

769 ◆ LANGBEIN, JOHANN CHRISTOPH JULIUS

Rank: Musician (highest rank: Drummer)
Service: U.S. Army
Birthday: 22 September 1845
Place of Birth: Germany
Date of Death: 28 January 1910
Place of Death: New York, New York
Cemetery: Woodlawn Cemetery (Mausoleum) (125-92)—Bronx, New York
Entered Service at: New York, New York
Unit: Company B, 9th New York Infantry
Battle or Place of Action: Camden, North Carolina
Date of Action: 19 April 1862
Date of Issue: 7 January 1895
Citation: A drummer boy, 15 years of age, he voluntarily and under a heavy fire went to the aid of a wounded officer, procured medical assistance for him, and aided in carrying him to a place of safety.

770 ◆ LANN, JOHN S.

True Name: Lanning, John S.
Rank: Landsman
Service: U.S. Navy
Birthday: 29 August 1843
Place of Birth: Rochester, Monroe County, New York
Date of Death: 13 April 1907
Cemetery: Yankton Municipal Cemetery (MH)—Yankton, South Dakota
Entered Service at: New York, New York
Unit: U.S.S. *Magnolia*
Battle or Place of Action: St. Marks, Florida
Date of Action: 5-6 March 1865
G.O. Number, Date: 59, 22 June 1865
Citation: As landsman on board the U.S.S. *Magnolia*, St. Marks, Fla., 5 and 6 March, Lann served with the Army in charge of the Navy howitzers during the attack on St. Marks and throughout this fierce engagement made remarkable efforts in assisting transport of the gun. His coolness and determination in standing by his gun while under fire of the enemy were a credit to the service to which he belonged.

771 ◆ LARIMER, SMITH

Rank: Corporal
Service: U.S. Army
Birthday: 17 March 1829

Place of Birth: Richland County, Ohio
Date of Death: 20 February 1881
Cemetery: Marlow Cemetery—Ontario, Ohio
Entered Service at: Columbus, Franklin County, Ohio
Unit: Company G, 2d Ohio Cavalry
Battle or Place of Action: Deatonsville (Sailor's Creek), Virginia
Date of Action: 6 April 1865
Date of Issue: 3 May 1865
Citation: Capture of flag of Maj. Gen. Joseph Brezard Kershaw's headquarters.

772 ◆ LARRABEE, JAMES W.

Rank: Corporal (highest rank: First Sergeant)
Service: U.S. Army
Birthday: 1839
Place of Birth: Rensselaer County, New York
Date of Death: 30 December 1907
Place of Death: Lee County, Illinois
Cemetery: Four Mile Grove Cemetery—Meriden, Illinois
Entered Service at: Mendota, La Salle County, Illinois
Unit: Company I, 55th Illinois Infantry
Battle or Place of Action: Vicksburg, Mississippi
Date of Action: 22 May 1863
Date of Issue: 2 September 1893
Citation: Gallantry in the charge of the "volunteer storming party."

773 ◆ LAWSON, GAINES

Rank: First Sergeant (highest rank: Brevet Lieutenant Colonel)
Service: U.S. Army
Birthday: 4 September 1840
Place of Birth: Hawkins County, Tennessee
Date of Death: 12 September 1906
Cemetery: Arlington National Cemetery (1-37-A)—Arlington, Virginia
Entered Service at: Rogersville, Hawkins County, Tennessee
Unit: Company D, 4th East Tennessee Infantry
Battle or Place of Action: Minville, Tennessee
Date of Action: 3 October 1863
Date of Issue: 11 June 1895
Citation: Went to the aid of a wounded comrade between the lines and carried him to a place of safety.

774 ◆ LAWSON, JOHN

Rank: Landsman
Service: U.S. Navy
Birthday: 16 June 1837
Place of Birth: Philadelphia, Philadelphia County, Pennsylvania
Date of Death: 3 May 1919
Place of Death: Philadelphia, Pennsylvania
Cemetery: Mount Peace Cemetery—Camden, New Jersey
Entered Service at: Pennsylvania
Unit: U.S.S. *Hartford*

Battle or Place of Action: Mobile Bay, Alabama
Date of Action: 5 August 1864
G.O. Number, Date: 45, 31 December 1864
Citation: On board the flagship U.S.S. *Hartford* during successful attacks against Fort Morgan, rebel gunboats, and the ram *Tennessee* in Mobile Bay on 5 August 1864. Wounded in the leg and thrown violently against the side of the ship when an enemy shell killed or wounded the six-man crew as the shell whipped on the berth deck, Lawson, upon regaining his composure, promptly returned to his station and, although urged to go below for treatment, steadfastly continued his duties throughout the remainder of the action.

775 ◆ LAWTON, HENRY WARE

Rank: Captain (highest rank: Major General)
Service: U.S. Army
Birthday: 17 March 1843
Place of Birth: Manhattan, Lucas County, Ohio
Date of Death: 19 December 1899
Place of Death: Philippine Islands
Cemetery: Arlington National Cemetery (2-841-842)—Arlington, Virginia
Entered Service at: Fort Wayne, Allen County, Indiana
Unit: Company A, 30th Indiana Infantry
Battle or Place of Action: Atlanta, Georgia
Date of Action: 3 August 1864
Date of Issue: 22 May 1893
Citation: Led a charge of skirmishers against the enemy rifle pits and stubbornly and successfully resisted two determined attacks of the enemy to retake the works.

776 ◆ LEAR, NICHOLAS

Rank: Quartermaster
Service: U.S. Navy
Birthday: 1826
Place of Birth: Rhode Island
Date of Death: 4 July 1902
Place of Death: Philadelphia, Pennsylvania
Cemetery: Mount Moriah Cemetery (VA plot 3-3-3) (MH)—Philadelphia, Pennsylvania
Entered Service at: Philadelphia, Philadelphia County, Pennsylvania
Unit: U.S.S. *New Ironsides*
Battle or Place of Action: Fort Fisher, North Carolina
Date of Action: 24-25 December 1864 & 13-15 January 1865
G.O. Number, Date: 59, 22 June 1865
Citation: Lear served on board the U.S.S. *New Ironsides* during action in several attacks on Fort Fisher, 24 and 25 December 1864; and 13, 14 and 15 January 1865. The ship steamed in and took the lead in the ironclad division close inshore and immediately opened its starboard battery in a barrage of well-directed fire to cause several fires and explosions and dismount several guns during the first two days of fighting. Taken under fire as she steamed into position on 13 January, the *New Ironsides* fought all day and took on ammunition at night, despite severe weather conditions. When the enemy came out of their bombproofs to defend the fort against the storming party, the ship's battery disabled nearly every gun on the fort facing the shore before the cease-fire order was given by the flagship.

777 ◆ LEE, JAMES H.

Rank: Seaman (highest rank: Captain of the Top)
Service: U.S. Navy
Birthday: 1840
Place of Birth: New York
Date of Death: 9 August 1877
Place of Death: Oswego, New York
Cemetery: The Rural Cemetery—Oswego, New York
Entered Service at: New York, New York
Unit: U.S.S. *Kearsarge*
Battle or Place of Action: off Cherbourg, France
Date of Action: 19 June 1864
G.O. Number, Date: 45, 31 December 1864
Citation: Served as seaman on board the U.S.S. *Kearsarge* when she destroyed the *Alabama* off Cherbourg, France, 19 June 1864. Acting as sponger of the No. 1 gun, during this bitter engagement, Lee exhibited marked coolness and good conduct and was highly recommended for his gallantry under fire by the divisional officer.

778 ◆ LELAND, GEORGE W.

Rank: Gunner's Mate (highest rank: Acting Master's Mate)
Service: U.S. Navy
Birthday: 1834
Place of Birth: Savannah, Chatham County, Georgia
Date of Death: 18 March 1880
Cemetery: Riverside Cemetery (MH)—Lewiston, Maine
Entered Service at: Georgia
Unit: U.S.S. *Lehigh*
Battle or Place of Action: Charleston Harbor, South Carolina
Date of Action: 16 November 1863
G.O. Number, Date: 32, 16 April 1864
Citation: Served on board the U.S.S. *Lehigh*, Charleston Harbor, 16 November 1863, during the hazardous task of freeing the *Lehigh*, which had grounded and was under heavy enemy fire from Fort Moultrie. Rowing the small boat which was used in the hazardous task of transferring hawsers from the *Lehigh* to the *Nahant*, Leland twice succeeded in making the trip, only to find that each had been in vain when the hawsers were cut by enemy fire and chaffing.

779 ◆ LEON, PIERRE

Rank: Captain of the Forecastle
Service: U.S. Navy
Birthday: 23 August 1838
Place of Birth: France
Date of Death: 7 December 1915
Place of Death: Riverside, New Jersey
Cemetery: St. Peter's Cemetery (MH)—Riverside, New Jersey

Entered Service at: Philadelphia, Philadelphia County, Pennsylvania
Unit: U.S.S. *Baron De Kalb*
Battle or Place of Action: Yazoo River, Mississippi
Date of Action: 23-27 December 1862
G.O. Number, Date: 11, 3 April 1863
Citation: Served on board the U.S.S. *Baron De Kalb*, Yazoo River Expedition, 23 to 27 December 1862. Proceeding under orders up the Yazoo River, the U.S.S. *Baron De Kalb*, with the object of capturing or destroying the enemy's transports, came upon the steamers *John Walsh*, *R.J. Locklan*, *Golden Age*, and the *Scotland* sunk on a bar where they were ordered fired. Continuing up the river, she was fired on, but upon returning the fire, caused the enemy's retreat. Returning down the Yazoo, she destroyed and captured larger quantities of enemy equipment and several prisoners. Serving bravely throughout this action, Leon, as captain of the forecastle, "distinguished himself in the various actions."

780 ◆ LEONARD, EDWIN

Rank: Sergeant
Service: U.S. Army
Birthday: 17 November 1823
Place of Birth: Agawam, Hampden County, Massachusetts
Date of Death: 5 April 1900
Cemetery: The White Church Cemetery (MH)—West Springfield, Massachusetts
red Service at: Agawam, Hampden County, Massachusetts
Unit: Company I, 37th Massachusetts Infantry
Battle or Place of Action: near Petersburg, Virginia
Date of Action: 18 June 1864
Date of Issue: 16 August 1894
Citation: Voluntarily exposed himself to the fire of a Union brigade to stop their firing on the Union skirmish line.

781 ◆ LEONARD, WILLIAM EDMAN

Rank: Private (highest rank: Second Lieutenant)
Service: U.S. Army
Birthday: 1836
Place of Birth: Greene County, Pennsylvania
Date of Death: 8 February 1891
Place of Death: Harvey's, Pennsylvania
Cemetery: unknown cemetery—Greene County, Pennsylvania
Entered Service at: Jacksonville, Pennsylvania
Unit: Company F, 85th Pennsylvania Infantry
Battle or Place of Action: Deep Bottom, Virginia
Date of Action: 16 August 1864
Date of Issue: 6 April 1865
Citation: Capture of battle flag.

782 ◆ LESLIE, FRANK

Rank: Private (highest rank: Corporal)
Service: U.S. Army
Birthday: 1841
Place of Birth: London, England
Date of Death: 1 August 1882
Place of Death: Minneapolis, Kansas
Entered Service at: New York, New York
Unit: Company B, 4th New York Cavalry
Battle or Place of Action: Front Royal, Virginia
Date of Action: 15 August 1864
Date of Issue: 26 August 1864
Citation: Capture of colors of 3d Virginia Infantry (C.S.A.).
Notes: POW

783 ◆ LEVY, BENJAMIN BENNETT

Rank: Private (highest rank: Color Sergeant)
Service: U.S. Army
Birthday: 22 February 1845
Place of Birth: New York, New York
Date of Death: 20 July 1921
Place of Death: New York, New York
Cemetery: Cypress Hills Cemetery (Private) (Sec.9 Lot 538, Grave 170)—Brooklyn, New York
Entered Service at: Newport News, Newport News County, Virginia
Unit: Company G, 1st New York Infantry
Served as: Orderly
Battle or Place of Action: Glendale, Virginia
Date of Action: 30 June 1862
Date of Issue: 1 March 1865
Citation: This soldier, a drummer boy, took the gun of a sick comrade, went into the fight, and when the color bearers were shot down, carried the colors and saved them from capture.

784 ◆ LEWIS, DEWITT CLINTON

Rank: Captain (highest rank: Brevet Lieutenant Colonel)
Service: U.S. Army
Birthday: 30 July 1822
Place of Birth: West Chester, Chester County, Pennsylvania
Date of Death: 28 June 1899
Place of Death: Morton, Pennsylvania
Cemetery: Oakland Cemetery—West Chester, Pennsylvania
Entered Service at: West Chester, Chester County, Pennsylvania
Unit: Company F, 97th Pennsylvania Infantry
Battle or Place of Action: Secessionville, South Carolina
Date of Action: 16 June 1862
Date of Issue: 23 April 1896
Citation: While retiring with his men before a heavy fire of canister shot at short-range, returned in the face of the enemy's fire and rescued an exhausted private of his company who but for this timely action would have lost his life by drowning in the morass through which the troops were retiring.

785 ◆ LEWIS, HENRY

Rank: Corporal (highest rank: First Sergeant)
Service: U.S. Army
Birthday: 14 December 1844
Place of Birth: Belleville, Wayne County, Michigan

Date of Death: 29 March 1930
Place of Death: Belleville, Michigan
Cemetery: Shoop Cemetery—Belleville, Van Buren Township, Michigan
Entered Service at: Adrian, Lenawee County, Michigan
Unit: Company B, 47th Ohio Infantry
Battle or Place of Action: Vicksburg, Mississippi
Date of Action: 3 May 1863
Date of Issue: 17 April 1917
Citation: Was one of a party that volunteered and attempted to run the enemy's batteries with a steam tug and two barges loaded with subsistence stores.
Notes: POW

786 ◆ LEWIS, SAMUEL E.

Rank: Corporal
Service: U.S. Army
Place of Birth: Coventry, Kent County, Rhode Island
Date of Death: 22 March 1907
Cemetery: North Burial Grounds Cemetery (MH)—Providence, Rhode Island
Entered Service at: Coventry, Kent County, Rhode Island
Unit: Company G, 1st Rhode Island Light Artillery
Battle or Place of Action: Petersburg, Virginia
Date of Action: 2 April 1865
Date of Issue: 16 June 1866
Citation: Was one of a detachment of 20 picked artillerymen who voluntarily accompanied an infantry assaulting party and who turned upon the enemy the guns captured in the assault.

787 ◆ LIBAIRE, ADOLPH

True Name: Libaire, Adolphe
Rank: Captain
Service: U.S. Army
Birthday: 2 May 1840
Place of Birth: Baccarat, France
Date of Death: 5 September 1920
Place of Death: Deal, New Jersey
Cemetery: The Green Wood Cemetery—Brooklyn, New York
Entered Service at: New York, New York
Unit: Company E, 9th New York Infantry
Battle or Place of Action: Antietam, Maryland
Date of Action: 17 September 1862
Date of Issue: 2 April 1898
Citation: In the advance on the enemy and after his color bearer and the entire color guard of eight men had been shot down, this officer seized the regimental flag and with conspicuous gallantry carried it to the extreme front, urging the line forward.

788 ◆ LILLEY, JOHN

Rank: Private
Service: U.S. Army
Birthday: February 1826
Place of Birth: Mifflin County, Pennsylvania
Date of Death: 12 May 1902
Place of Death: Lewistown, Pennsylvania
Cemetery: First Methodist Cemetery—Lewistown, Pennsylvania
Entered Service at: Lewistown, Mifflin County, Pennsylvania
Unit: Company F, 205th Pennsylvania Infantry
Battle or Place of Action: Petersburg, Virginia
Date of Action: 2 April 1865
Date of Issue: 20 May 1865
Citation: After his regiment had began to waiver, he rushed on alone to capture the enemy flag. He reached the works and the Confederate color bearer who, at bayonet point, he caused to surrender with several enemy soldiers. He kept his prisoners in tow when they realized he was alone as his regiment in the meantime withdrawn further to the rear.

789 ◆ LITTLE, HENRY F. W.

Rank: Sergeant (highest rank: First Lieutenant)
Service: U.S. Army
Birthday: 27 June 1842
Place of Birth: Manchester, Hillsborough County, New Hampshire
Date of Death: 7 February 1907
Cemetery: Valley Cemetery (MH)—Manchester, New Hampshire
Entered Service at: Manchester, Hillsborough County, New Hampshire
Unit: Company D, 7th New Hampshire Infantry
Battle or Place of Action: near Richmond, Virginia
Date of Action: September 1864
Date of Issue: 14 January 1870
Citation: Gallantry on the skirmish line.

790 ◆ LITTLEFIELD, GEORGE H.

Rank: Corporal
Service: U.S. Army
Birthday: 2 May 1842
Place of Birth: Skowhegan, Somerset County, Maine
Date of Death: 25 December 1919
Place of Death: Richmond, Maine
Cemetery: The Cotton Cemetery (MH)—Richmond, Maine
Entered Service at: Skowhegan, Somerset County, Maine
Unit: Company G, 1st Maine Veteran Infantry
Battle or Place of Action: Fort Fisher, North Carolina
Date of Action: 25 March 1865
Date of Issue: 22 June 1885
Citation: The color sergeant having been wounded, this soldier picked up the flag and bore it to the front, to the great encouragement of the charging column.

791 ◆ LIVINGSTON, JOSIAH O.

Rank: First Lieutenant & Adjutant (highest rank: Captain)
Service: U.S. Army
Birthday: 3 February 1837
Place of Birth: Walden, Vermont
Date of Death: 23 July 1917
Cemetery: Robinson Cemetery—Calais, Vermont

Entered Service at: Marshfield, Washington County, Vermont
Unit: 9th Vermont Infantry
Battle or Place of Action: Newport Barracks, North Carolina
Date of Action: 2 February 1864
Date of Issue: 8 September 1891
Citation: When, after desperate resistance, the small garrison had been driven back to the river by a vastly superior force, this officer, while a small force held back the enemy, personally fired the railroad bridge, and, although wounded himself, assisted a wounded officer over the burning structure.

792 ◆ LLOYD, BENJAMIN

Rank: Coal Heaver (highest rank: Fireman Second Class)
Service: U.S. Navy
Birthday: 1839
Place of Birth: Liverpool, Merseyside County, England
Entered Service at: Philadelphia, Philadelphia County, Pennsylvania
Unit: U.S.S. *Wyalusing*
Battle or Place of Action: Roanoke River, North Carolina
Date of Action: 25 May 1864
G.O. Number, Date: 45, 31 December 1864
Citation: Serving on board the U.S.S. *Wyalusing* and paticipating in a plan to destroy the rebel ram *Albemarle* in Roanoke River, 25 May 1864. Volunteering for the hazardous mission, Lloyd participated in the transfer of two torpedoes across an island swamp. Serving as boatkeeper, he aided in rescuing others of the party who had been detected before the plan could be completed, but who escaped, leaving detection of the plan impossible. By his skill and courage, Lloyd succeeded in returning to the mother ship after spending 24 hours of discomfort in the rain and swamp.

793 ◆ LLOYD, JOHN W.

Rank: Coxswain
Service: U.S. Navy
Birthday: 1831
Place of Birth: New York, New York
Entered Service at: New York
Unit: U.S.S. *Wyalusing*
Battle or Place of Action: Roanoke River, North Carolina
Date of Action: 25 May 1864
G.O. Number, Date: 45, 31 December 1864
Citation: Serving on board the U.S.S. *Wyalusing* during an attempt to destroy the rebel ram *Albemarle* in Roanoke River, 25 May 1864. Lloyd participated in this daring plan by swimming the Roanoke River heavily weighted with a line which was used for hauling torpedoes across. Thwarted by discovery just before the completion of the plan, Lloyd cut the torpedo guiding line to prevent detection of the plan by the enemy and again swam the river, narrowly escaping enemy musket fire and regaining the ship in safety.

794 ◆ LOCKE, LEWIS

Rank: Private
Service: U.S. Army
Place of Birth: Clintonville, Essex County, New York
Date of Death: 1892
Place of Death: Ashuelot, New Hampshire
Entered Service at: Jersey City, Hudson County, New Jersey
Unit: Company A, 1st New Jersey Cavalry
Battle or Place of Action: Paines Crossroads, Virginia
Date of Action: 5 April 1865
Date of Issue: 3 May 1865
Citation: Capture of a Confederate flag.

795 ◆ LOGAN, HUGH

Rank: Captain of the Afterguard
Service: U.S. Navy
Birthday: 1834
Place of Birth: Ireland
Date of Death: 22 November 1903
Place of Death: Glasgow, Scotland
Entered Service at: Boston, Suffolk County, Massachusetts
Unit: U.S.S. *Rhode Island*
Battle or Place of Action: off Cape Hatteras, North Carolina
Date of Action: 30 December 1862
G.O. Number, Date: 59, 22 June 1865
Citation: On board the U.S.S. *Rhode Island* which was engaged in saving the lives of the officers and crew of the *Monitor*, 30 December 1862. Participating in the hazardous rescue of the officers and crew of the sinking *Monitor*, Logan, after rescuing several of the men, became separated in a heavy gale with other members of the cutter that had set out from the *Rhode Island*, and spent many hours in the small boat at the mercy of the weather and high seas until finally picked up by a schooner 50 miles east of Cape Hatteras.

796 ◆ LONERGAN, JOHN

Rank: Captain
Service: U.S. Army
Birthday: 7 April 1839
Place of Birth: Carrick, County Donegal, Ireland
Date of Death: 6 August 1902
Place of Death: Montreal, Canada
Cemetery: St. Joseph's Cemetery—Burlington, Vermont
Entered Service at: Burlington, Chittenden County, Vermont
Unit: Company A, 13th Vermont Infantry
Battle or Place of Action: Gettysburg, Pennsylvania
Date of Action: 2 July 1863
Date of Issue: 28 October 1893
Citation: Gallantry in the recapture of four guns and the capture of two additional guns from the enemy; also the capture of a number of prisoners.

797 ◆ LONGSHORE, WILLIAM HENRY

Rank: Private
Service: U.S. Army
Birthday: 18 February 1841
Place of Birth: Zanesville, Muskingum County, Ohio

Date of Death: 20 December 1909
Place of Death: Fort Scott, Kansas
Cemetery: Evergreen Cemetery (MH)—Fort Scott, Kansas
Entered Service at: Columbus, Franklin County, Ohio
Unit: Company D, 30th Ohio Infantry
Battle or Place of Action: Vicksburg, Mississippi
Date of Action: 22 May 1863
Date of Issue: 10 August 1894
Citation: Gallantry in the charge of the "volunteer storming party."

798 ◆ LONSWAY, JOSEPH

Rank: Private
Service: U.S. Army
Birthday: 17 March 1844
Place of Birth: Clayton, Jefferson County, New York
Date of Death: 22 January 1925
Place of Death: Clayton, New York
Cemetery: St. Mary's Cemetery (MH)—Clayton, New York
Entered Service at: Sackets Harbor, Jefferson County, New York
Unit: Company D, 20th New York Cavalry
Battle or Place of Action: Murfrees Station, Virginia
Date of Action: 16 October 1864
Date of Issue: 7 March 1917
Citation: Volunteered to swim Blackwater River to get a large flat used as a ferry on the other side; succeeded in getting the boat safely across, making it possible for a detachment to cross the river and take possession of the enemy's breastworks.

799 ◆ LORD, WILLIAM

Rank: Musician
Service: U.S. Army
Birthday: 13 February 1841
Place of Birth: Bradford, England
Date of Death: 4 August 1915
Place of Death: New York, New York
Cemetery: The Lutheran Cemetery—Middle Village, New York
Entered Service at: Lawrence, Essex County, Massachusetts
Unit: Company C, 40th Massachusetts Infantry
Battle or Place of Action: Drewry's Bluff, Virginia
Date of Action: 16 May 1864
Date of Issue: 4 April 1898
Citation: Went to the assistance of a wounded officer lying helpless between the lines, and under fire from both sides removed him to a place of safety.

800 ◆ LORISH, ANDREW J.

Rank: Commissary Sergeant (highest rank: Brevet First Lieutenant)
Service: U.S. Army
Birthday: 8 November 1832
Place of Birth: Dansville, Livingston County, New York
Date of Death: 11 August 1897
Place of Death: Warsaw, New York
Cemetery: Forest Hill Cemetery (MH)—Attica, New York
Entered Service at: Attica, Wyoming County, New York
Unit: 19th New York Cavalry (1st New York Dragoons)
Battle or Place of Action: Winchester, Virginia
Date of Action: 19 September 1864
Date of Issue: 27 September 1864
Citation: Amid the enemy he grabbed the flag from a color bearer who then called for help. When the bearer's comrades were readying their rifles, he dashed directly at them securing their disarming. As he rode away, the Confederates picked up their guns firing at the captor of their flag.

801 ◆ LOVE, GEORGE MALTBY

Rank: Colonel (highest rank: Brevet Brigadier General U.S. Volunteers)
Service: U.S. Army
Birthday: 1 January 1831
Place of Birth: Buffalo, Erie County, New York
Date of Death: 15 March 1887
Place of Death: Buffalo, New York
Cemetery: Forest Lawn Cemetery (MH)—Buffalo, New York
Entered Service at: Elmira, Chemung County, New York
Unit: 116th New York Infantry
Battle or Place of Action: Cedar Creek, Virginia
Date of Action: 19 October 1864
Date of Issue: 6 March 1865
Citation: Capture of battle flag of 2d South Carolina (C.S.A.).

802 ◆ LOVERING, GEORGE MASON

Rank: First Sergeant (highest rank: First Lieutenant)
Service: U.S. Army
Birthday: 10 January 1832
Place of Birth: Springfield, New Hampshire
Date of Death: 2 April 1919
Cemetery: Union Cemetery (MH)—Holbrook, Massachusetts
Entered Service at: East Randolph, Norfolk County, Massachusetts
Unit: Company I, 4th Massachusetts Infantry
Battle or Place of Action: Port Hudson, Louisiana
Date of Action: 14 June 1863
Date of Issue: 19 November 1891
Citation: During a momentary confusion in the ranks caused by other troops rushing upon the regiment, this soldier, with coolness and determination, rendered efficient aid in preventing a panic among the troops.

803 ◆ LOWER, CYRUS B.

Rank: Private
Service: U.S. Army
Birthday: 28 February 1843
Place of Birth: Lawrence, Pennsylvania
Date of Death: 21 May 1924

Place of Death: Washington, D.C.
Cemetery: Arlington National Cemetery (17-19971) (MH)—Arlington, Virginia
Entered Service at: New Castle, Lawrence County, Pennsylvania
Unit: Company K, 13th Pennsylvania Reserves
Battle or Place of Action: Wilderness Campaign, Virginia
Date of Action: 7 May 1864
Date of Issue: 20 July 1887
Citation: Gallant services and soldierly qualities in voluntarily rejoining his command after having been wounded.

804 ◆ LOWER, ROBERT A.

Rank: Private
Service: U.S. Army
Birthday: 1844
Place of Birth: Illinois
Cemetery: Yates City Cemetery—Yates City, Illinois
Entered Service at: Elmwood, Peoria County, Illinois
Unit: Company K, 55th Illinois Infantry
Battle or Place of Action: Vicksburg, Mississippi
Date of Action: 22 May 1863
Date of Issue: 2 September 1893
Citation: Gallantry in the charge of the "volunteer storming party."

805 ◆ LOYD, GEORGE A.

Rank: Private
Service: U.S. Army
Birthday: 9 May 1844
Place of Birth: Muskingum County, Ohio
Date of Death: 13 May 1917
Cemetery: Spring Grove Cemetery—Cincinnati, Ohio
Entered Service at: Zanesville, Muskingum County, Ohio
Unit: Company A, 122d Ohio Infantry
Battle or Place of Action: Petersburg, Virginia
Date of Action: 2 April 1865
Date of Issue: 16 April 1891
Citation: Capture of division flag of Maj. Gen. Henry Heth, (C.S.A.).

806 ◆ LUCAS, GEORGE WASHINGTON

Rank: Private
Service: U.S. Army
Birthday: 1845
Place of Birth: Adams County, Illinois
Date of Death: 17 May 1921
Place of Death: Quincy, Illinois
Cemetery: Mounds Cemetery (MH)—Timewell, Illinois
Entered Service at: Mount Sterling, Brown County, Illinois
Unit: Company C, 3d Missouri Cavalry
Battle or Place of Action: Benton, Arkansas
Date of Action: 25 July 1864
Date of Issue: December 1864
Citation: Pursued and killed Confederate Brig. Gen. George M. Holt, Arkansas Militia, capturing his arms and horse.

807 ◆ LUCE, MOSES AUGUSTINE

Rank: Sergeant
Service: U.S. Army
Birthday: 14 May 1842
Place of Birth: Payson, Adams County, Illinois
Date of Death: 13 April 1933
Place of Death: San Diego, California
Cemetery: Greenwood Memorial Park—San Diego, California
Entered Service at: Adrian, Lenawee County, Michigan
Unit: Company E, 4th Michigan Infantry
Battle or Place of Action: Laurel Hill, Virginia
Date of Action: 10 May 1864
Date of Issue: 7 February 1895
Citation: Voluntarily returned in the face of the advancing enemy to the assistance of a wounded and helpless comrade, and carried him, at imminent peril, to a place of safety.

808 ◆ LUDGATE, WILLIAM

Rank: Captain (highest rank: Brevet Major)
Service: U.S. Army
Birthday: 11 March 1836
Place of Birth: London, England
Date of Death: 14 June 1912
Cemetery: Arlington National Cemetery (3-1488)—Arlington, Virginia
Entered Service at: New York, New York
Unit: Company G, 59th New York Veteran Infantry
Battle or Place of Action: Farmville, Virginia
Date of Action: 7 April 1865
Date of Issue: 10 August 1889
Citation: Gallantry and promptness in rallying his men and advancing with a small detachment to save a bridge about to be fired by the enemy.

809 ◆ LUDWIG, CARL

Rank: Private (highest rank: Corporal)
Service: U.S. Army
Birthday: 10 May 1841
Place of Birth: France
Date of Death: 16 May 1913
Place of Death: College Point, New York
Cemetery: Flushing Cemetery—Flushing, New York
Entered Service at: Flushing, Queens County, New York
Unit: 34th New York Battery
Battle or Place of Action: Petersburg, Virginia
Date of Action: 18 June 1864
Date of Issue: 30 July 1896
Citation: As gunner of his piece, inflicted singly a great loss upon the enemy and distinguished himself in the removal of the piece while under a heavy fire.

810 ◆ LUNT, ALPHONSO M.

Rank: Sergeant
Service: U.S. Army

Birthday: 6 September 1837
Place of Birth: Berwick, York County, Maine
Date of Death: 18 December 1917
Place of Death: Mountain Home, Tennessee
Cemetery: Cambridge Cemetery (MH)—Cambridge, Massachusetts
Entered Service at: Cambridge, Middlesex County, Massachusetts
Unit: Company F, 38th Massachusetts Infantry
Battle or Place of Action: Opequan Creek, Virginia
Date of Action: 19 September 1864
Date of Issue: 10 May 1894
Citation: Carried his flag to the most advanced position where, left almost alone close to the enemy's lines, he refused their demand to surrender, withdrew at great personal peril, and saved his flag.

811 ◆ LUTES, FRANKLIN W.

Rank: Corporal
Service: U.S. Army
Birthday: 1840
Place of Birth: Dundee, Yates County, New York
Date of Death: 6 April 1915
Cemetery: Glenside Cemetery—Wolcott, New York
Entered Service at: Geddes, New York
Unit: Company D, 111th New York Infantry
Battle or Place of Action: Petersburg, Virginia
Date of Action: 31 March 1865
Date of Issue: 3 April 1865
Citation: Capture of flag of 41st Alabama Infantry (C.S.A.), together with the color bearer and one of the color guard.
Notes: POW

812 ◆ LUTHER, JAMES HEZIKIAH

Rank: Private (highest rank: Corporal)
Service: U.S. Army
Birthday: 24 January 1841
Place of Birth: Dighton, Bristol County, Massachusetts
Date of Death: 3 March 1916
Place of Death: North Dighton, Massachusetts
Cemetery: Westville Cemetery (MH)—Taunton, Massachusetts
Entered Service at: Taunton, Bristol County, Massachusetts
Unit: Company D, 7th Massachusetts Infantry
Battle or Place of Action: Fredericksburg, Virginia
Date of Action: 3 May 1863
Date of Issue: 28 June 1890
Citation: Among the first to jump into the enemy's rifle pits, he himself captured and brought out three prisoners.

813 ◆ LUTY, GOTLIEB

Rank: Corporal
Service: U.S. Army
Birthday: 1842
Place of Birth: Allegheny County, Pennsylvania

Date of Death: 12 July 1904
Place of Death: Allegheny, Pennsylvania
Cemetery: Uniondale Cemetery (MH)—Pittsburgh, Pennsylvania
Entered Service at: West Manchester, York County, Pennsylvania
Unit: Company A, 74th New York Infantry
Battle or Place of Action: Chancellorsville, Virginia
Date of Action: 3 May 1863
Date of Issue: 5 October 1876
Citation: Bravely advanced to the enemy's line under heavy fire and brought back valuable information.

814 ◆ LYMAN, JOEL H.

Rank: Quartermaster Sergeant (highest rank: First Lieutenant)
Service: U.S. Army
Birthday: 11 May 1845
Place of Birth: East Randolph, Cattaraugus County, New York
Date of Death: 4 May 1922
Place of Death: Randolph, New York
Cemetery: Randolph Cemetery—Randolph, New York
Entered Service at: East Randolph, Cattaraugus County, New York
Unit: Company B, 9th New York Cavalry
Battle or Place of Action: Winchester, Virginia
Date of Action: 19 September 1864
Date of Issue: 20 August 1894
Citation: In an attempt to capture a Confederate flag, he captured one of the enemy's officers and brought him within the lines.

815 ◆ LYON, FREDERICK A.

Rank: Corporal (highest rank: Sergeant)
Service: U.S. Army
Birthday: 25 June 1843
Place of Birth: Williamsburg, Hampshire County, Massachusetts
Date of Death: 23 September 1911
Place of Death: Jackson, Michigan
Cemetery: Mount Evergreen Cemetery—Jackson, Michigan
Entered Service at: Burlington, Chittenden County, Vermont
Unit: Company A, 1st Vermont Cavalry
Battle or Place of Action: Cedar Creek, Virginia
Date of Action: 19 October 1864
Date of Issue: 26 November 1864
Citation: With one companion, captured the flag of a Confederate regiment, three officers, and an ambulance with its mules and driver.

816 ◆ LYONS, THOMAS G.

Rank: Seaman
Service: U.S. Navy
Birthday: 1838

Place of Birth: Salem, Essex County, Massachusetts
Date of Death: 29 August 1904
Place of Death: Philadelphia, Pennsylvania
Cemetery: Mount Moriah Cemetery (VA plot 3-4-3) (MH)—Philadelphia, Pennsylvania
Entered Service at: Massachusetts
Unit: U.S.S. *Pensacola*
Battle or Place of Action: Forts Jackson & St. Philip, Louisiana
Date of Action: 24 April 1862
G.O. Number, Date: 169, 8 February 1872
Citation: Served as seaman on board the U.S.S. *Pensacola* in the attack on Forts Jackson and St. Philip, 24 April 1862. Carrying out his duties throughout the din and roar of the battle, Lyons never once erred in his brave performance. Lashed outside of that vessel, on the port-sheet chain, with the lead in hand to lead the ship past the forts, Lyons never flinched, although under a heavy fire from the forts and rebel gunboats.

817 ♦ MacARTHUR JR., ARTHUR

Rank: First Lieutenant & Adjutant (highest rank: Lieutenant General)
Service: U.S. Army
Birthday: 2 June 1845
Place of Birth: Springfield, Hampden County, Massachusetts
Date of Death: 5 September 1912
Cemetery: Arlington National Cemetery (2-845-A)—Arlington, Virginia
Entered Service at: Milwaukee, Milwaukee County, Wisconsin
Unit: 24th Wisconsin Infantry
Battle or Place of Action: Missionary Ridge, Tennessee
Date of Action: 25 November 1863
Date of Issue: 30 June 1890
Citation: Seized the colors of his regiment at a critical moment and planted them on the captured works on the crest of Missionary Ridge.

818 ♦ MACHON, JAMES

Rank: Boy (highest rank: Boy First Class)
Service: U.S. Navy
Birthday: 1848
Place of Birth: Derby, Derbyshire, England
Entered Service at: New York, New York
Unit: U.S.S. *Brooklyn*
Battle or Place of Action: Mobile Bay, Alabama
Date of Action: 5 August 1864
G.O. Number, Date: 45, 31 December 1864
Citation: On board the U.S.S. *Brooklyn* during successful attacks against Fort Morgan, rebel gunboats, and the ram *Tennessee* in Mobile Bay, on 5 August 1864. Stationed in the immediate vicinity of the shell whips which were twice cleared of men by bursting shells, Machon remained steadfast at his post and performed his duties in the powder division throughout the furious action which resulted in the surrender of the prize rebel ram *Tennessee* and in the damaging and destruction of batteries at Fort Morgan.

819 ♦ MACK, ALEXANDER

Rank: Captain of the Top (highest rank: Chief Boatswain's Mate Ret.)
Service: U.S. Navy
Birthday: 17 May 1834
Place of Birth: Rotterdam, Holland
Date of Death: 25 September 1907
Place of Death: New London, Connecticut
Cemetery: Oak Grove Cemetery (MH)—Fall River, Massachusetts
Entered Service at: New York, New York
Unit: U.S.S. *Brooklyn*
Battle or Place of Action: Mobile Bay, Alabama
Date of Action: 5 August 1864
G.O. Number, Date: 45, 31 December 1864
Citation: On board the U.S.S. *Brooklyn* during successful attacks against Fort Morgan, rebel gunboats, and the ram *Tennessee* in Mobile Bay, on 5 August 1864. Although wounded and sent below for treatment, Mack immediately returned to his post, took charge of his gun, and, as heavy enemy return fire continued to fall, performed his duties with skill and courage until he was again wounded and totally disabled.

820 ♦ MACK, JOHN

True Name: Connely, Michael
Rank: Seaman
Service: U.S. Navy
Birthday: 1843
Place of Birth: Brooksville, Hancock County, Maine
Date of Death: 10 November 1881
Place of Death: Lynn, Massachusetts
Cemetery: St. Mary's Cemetery (MH)—Lynn, Massachusetts
Entered Service at: Maine
Unit: U.S.S. *Hendrick Hudson*
Battle or Place of Action: St. Marks, Florida
Date of Action: 5-6 March 1865
G.O. Number, Date: 59, 22 June 1865
Citation: As seaman on board the U.S.S. *Hendrick Hudson*, St. Marks, Fla., 5 and 6 March 1865, Mack served with the Army in charge of Navy howitzers during the attack on St. Marks and, throughout this fierce engagement, made remarkable efforts in assisting transport of the gun. His coolness and determination in courageously standing by his gun while under the fire of the enemy were a credit to the service to which he belonged.

821 ♦ MACKIE, JOHN FREEMAN

Rank: Corporal (highest rank: Orderly Sergeant)
Service: U.S. Marine Corps
Birthday: 1 October 1835
Place of Birth: New York, New York

Date of Death: 18 June 1910
Cemetery: Arlington Cemetery—Drexel Hill, Pennsylvania
Entered Service at: New York, New York
Unit: U.S.S. *Galena*
Battle or Place of Action: Fort Darling at Drewry's Bluff, Virginia
Date of Action: 15 May 1862
G.O. Number, Date: 17, 10 July 1863
Place of Presentation: Texas, off Sabine pass, on board the U.S.S. *Seminole*
Citation: On board the U.S.S. *Galena* in the attack on Fort Darling, at Drewry's Bluff, James River, on 15 May 1862. As enemy shellfire raked the deck of his ship, Cpl. Mackie fearlessly maintained his musket fire against the rifle pits along the shore and, when ordered to fill vacancies at guns caused by men wounded and killed in action, manned the weapon with skill and courage.

822 ◆ MADDEN, MICHAEL

Rank: Private
Service: U.S. Army
Birthday: 28 September 1841
Place of Birth: County Limerick, Ireland
Date of Death: 7 August 1920
Place of Death: Harrisburg, Pennsylvania
Cemetery: Mount Calvary Cemetery—Harrisburg, Pennsylvania
Entered Service at: New York, New York
Unit: Company K, 42d New York Infantry
Battle or Place of Action: Mason's Island, Maryland
Date of Action: 3 September 1861
Date of Issue: 22 March 1898
Citation: Assisted a wounded comrade to the riverbank and, under heavy fire of the enemy, swam with him across a branch of the Potomac to the Union lines.

823 ◆ MADDEN, WILLIAM

Rank: Coal Heaver
Service: U.S. Navy
Birthday: 1843
Place of Birth: Devonshire, England
Entered Service at: New York, New York
Unit: U.S.S. *Brooklyn*
Battle or Place of Action: Mobile Bay, Alabama
Date of Action: 5 August 1864
G.O. Number, Date: 45, 31 December 1864
Citation: On board the U.S.S. *Brooklyn* during the successful attacks against Fort Morgan, rebel gunboats, and the ram *Tennessee* in Mobile Bay, 5 August 1864. Stationed in the immediate vicinity of the shell whips, which were twice cleared of men by bursting shells, Madden remained steadfast at his post and performed his duties in the powder division throughout the furious action, which resulted in the surrender of the prize rebel ram *Tennessee* and in the damaging and destruction of batteries at Fort Morgan.

824 ◆ MADISON, JAMES

True Name: Congdon, James
Rank: Sergeant
Service: U.S. Army
Birthday: 1842
Place of Birth: Niagara, Niagara County, New York
Date of Death: 7 August 1926
Cemetery: San Francisco National Cemetery OS-A-7-(MH)—San Francisco, California
Entered Service at: Fairport, Monroe County, New York
Unit: Company E, 8th New York Cavalry
Battle or Place of Action: Waynesboro, Virginia
Date of Action: 2 March 1865
Date of Issue: 26 March 1865
Citation: Recapture of Gen. Crook's headquarters flag.

825 ◆ MAGEE, WILLIAM

Rank: Drummer
Service: U.S. Army
Place of Birth: Newark, Essex County, New Jersey
Entered Service at: Newark, Essex County, New Jersey
Unit: Company C, 33d New Jersey Infantry
Battle or Place of Action: Murfreesboro, Tennessee
Date of Action: 5 December 1864
Date of Issue: 7 February 1866
Citation: In a charge, Magee was among the first to reach a battery of the enemy and, with one or two others, mounted the artillery horses and took two guns into the Union lines.

826 ◆ MAHONEY, JEREMIAH

Rank: First Sergeant
Service: U.S. Army
Birthday: 1840
Date of Death: 24 November 1902
Place of Death: Boston, Massachusetts
Cemetery: Holy Cross Cemetery (MH)—Malden, Massachusetts
Entered Service at: Fall River, Bristol County, Massachusetts
Unit: Company A, 29th Massachusetts Infantry
Battle or Place of Action: Fort Sanders, Knoxville, Tennessee
Date of Action: 29 November 1863
Date of Issue: 1 December 1864
Citation: Capture of flag of 17th Mississippi Infantry (C.S.A.).

827 ◆ MANDY, HARRY J.

Rank: First Sergeant (highest rank: First Lieutenant)
Service: U.S. Army
Birthday: 2 June 1840
Place of Birth: England
Date of Death: 14 August 1904
Place of Death: Hampton, Virginia

Cemetery: Hampton National Cemetery (B-8709) (MH)—Hampton, Virginia
Entered Service at: New York, New York
Unit: Company B, 4th New York Cavalry
Battle or Place of Action: Front Royal, Virginia
Date of Action: 15 August 1864
Date of Issue: 26 August 1864
Citation: Capture of flag of 3d Virginia Infantry (C.S.A.).

828 ◆ MANGAM, RICHARD CHRISTOPHER

Rank: Private
Service: U.S. Army
Place of Birth: Ireland
Date of Death: 17 November 1893
Place of Death: Decatur, New York
Entered Service at: Auburn, Cayuga County, New York
Unit: Company H, 148th New York Infantry
Battle or Place of Action: Hatcher's Run, Virginia
Date of Action: 2 April 1865
Date of Issue: 21 September 1888
Citation: Capture of flag of 8th Mississippi Infantry (C.S.A.).

829 ◆ MANNING, JOSEPH S.

Rank: Private
Service: U.S. Army
Birthday: 13 April 1845
Place of Birth: Ipswich, Essex County, Massachusetts
Date of Death: 27 December 1905
Place of Death: Somerville, Massachusetts
Cemetery: Old North Cemetery (MH)—Ipswich, Massachusetts
Entered Service at: Boston, Suffolk County, Massachusetts
Unit: Company K, 29th Massachusetts Infantry
Battle or Place of Action: Fort Sanders, Knoxville, Tennessee
Date of Action: 29 November 1863
Date of Issue: 1 December 1864
Citation: Capture of flag of 16th Georgia Infantry (C.S.A.).

830 ◆ MARLAND, WILLIAM

Rank: First Lieutenant (highest rank: Brevet Major)
Service: U.S. Army
Birthday: 11 March 1839
Place of Birth: Andover, Essex County, Massachusetts
Date of Death: 17 April 1905
Place of Death: Griffin, Georgia
Cemetery: Oak Hill Cemetery (MH)—Griffin, Georgia
Entered Service at: Andover, Essex County, Massachusetts
Unit: 2d Independent Battery, Massachusetts Light Artillery
Battle or Place of Action: Grand Coteau, Louisiana
Date of Action: 3 November 1863
Date of Issue: 16 February 1897
Citation: After having been surrounded by the enemy's cavalry, his support having surrendered, he ordered a charge and saved the section of the battery that was under his command.

831 ◆ MARQUETTE, CHARLES D.

Rank: Sergeant
Service: U.S. Army
Birthday: 9 February 1845
Place of Birth: Lebanon County, Pennsylvania
Date of Death: 25 November 1907
Place of Death: Carlisle, Pennsylvania
Cemetery: Fairview Cemetery—Wrightsville, Pennsylvania
Entered Service at: Campbelltown, Lebanon County, Pennsylvania
Unit: Company F, 93d Pennsylvania Infantry
Battle or Place of Action: Petersburg, Virginia
Date of Action: 2 April 1865
Date of Issue: 10 May 1865
Citation: Sgt. Marquette, although wounded, was one of the first to plant colors on the enemy's breastworks.

832 ◆ MARSH, ALBERT

Rank: Sergeant
Service: U.S. Army
Birthday: 15 February 1831
Place of Birth: Randolph, Cattaraugus County, New York
Date of Death: 17 February 1895
Place of Death: Randolph, New York
Cemetery: Randolph Cemetery—Randolph, New York
Entered Service at: Randolph, Cattaraugus County, New York
Unit: Company B, 64th New York Infantry
Battle or Place of Action: Spotsylvania, Virginia
Date of Action: 12 May 1864
Date of Issue: 1 December 1864
Citation: Capture of flag.

833 ◆ MARSH, CHARLES H.

Rank: Private
Service: U.S. Army
Birthday: 1840
Place of Birth: Milford, New Haven County, Connecticut
Date of Death: 25 January 1867
Cemetery: Quaker Burying Grounds (MH)—New Milford, Connecticut
Entered Service at: New Milford, Litchfield County, Connecticut
Unit: Company D, 1st Connecticut Cavalry
Battle or Place of Action: Back Creek Valley, near North Mountain, West Virginia
Date of Action: 31 July 1864
Date of Issue: 23 January 1865
Citation: For gallantry in capturing a Black Flag and its bearer from Lt. Gen. Jubal A. Early's (C.S.A.) command, at Back Creek Valley, near North Mountain, W. Va., 31 July 1864.

834 ◆ MARSH, GEORGE

Rank: Sergeant
Service: U.S. Army
Place of Birth: Brookfield, Cook County, Illinois
Date of Death: 18 June 1915
Cemetery: Ottawa Avenue Cemetery—Ottawa, Illinois
Entered Service at: Brookfield, Cook County, Illinois
Unit: Company D, 104th Illinois Infantry
Battle or Place of Action: Elk River, Tennessee
Date of Action: 2 July 1863
Date of Issue: 17 September 1897
Citation: Voluntarily led a small party and, under a heavy fire, captured a stockade and saved the bridge.

835 ◆ MARTIN, EDWARD S.

Rank: Quartermaster
Service: U.S. Navy
Birthday: 1840
Place of Birth: Ireland
Date of Death: 23 December 1901
Place of Death: Brooklyn, New York
Cemetery: Cypress Hills National Cemetery (5766) (MH)—Brooklyn, New York
Entered Service at: Philadelphia, Philadelphia County, Pennsylvania
Unit: U.S.S. *Galena*
Battle or Place of Action: Mobile Bay, Alabama
Date of Action: 5 August 1864
G.O. Number, Date: 59, 22 June 1865
Citation: On board the U.S.S. *Galena* during the attack on enemy forts at Mobile Bay, 5 August 1864. Securely lashed to the side of the *Oneida*, which had suffered the loss of her steering apparatus and an explosion of her boiler from enemy fire, the *Galena* aided the stricken vessel past the enemy forts to safety. Despite heavy damage to his ship from raking enemy fire, Martin performed his duties with skill and courage throughout the action.

836 ◆ MARTIN, JAMES

Rank: Sergeant
Service: U.S. Marine Corps
Birthday: 1826
Place of Birth: Derry, Ireland
Date of Death: 29 October 1895
Cemetery: Mount Moriah Cemetery (VA plot 2-24-5) (MH)—Philadelphia, Pennsylvania
Entered Service at: Pennsylvania
Unit: U.S.S. *Richmond*
Battle or Place of Action: Mobile Bay, Alabama
Date of Action: 5 August 1864
G.O. Number, Date: 45, 31 December 1864
Citation: As captain of a gun on board the U.S.S. *Richmond* during action against rebel forts and gunboats and with the ram *Tennessee* in Mobile Bay, 5 August 1864. Despite damage to his ship and the loss of several men on board as enemy fire raked her decks, Sgt. Martin fought his gun with skill and courage throughout a furious two-hour battle which resulted in the surrender of the rebel ram *Tennessee* and in the damaging and destruction of batteries at Fort Morgan.

837 ◆ MARTIN, SYLVESTER HOPKINS

Rank: Lieutenant (highest rank: Captain)
Service: U.S. Army
Birthday: 9 August 1841
Place of Birth: Chester County, Pennsylvania
Date of Death: 25 September 1927
Place of Death: Erie, Pennsylvania
Cemetery: unknown cemetery—Philadelphia, Pennsylvania
Entered Service at: Philadelphia, Philadelphia County, Pennsylvania
Unit: Company K, 88th Pennsylvania Infantry
Battle or Place of Action: Weldon Railroad, Virginia
Date of Action: 19 August 1864
Date of Issue: 5 April 1894
Citation: Gallantly made a most dangerous reconnaissance, discovering the position of the enemy and enabling the division to repulse an attack made in strong force.

838 ◆ MARTIN, WILLIAM

Rank: Seaman
Service: U.S. Navy
Birthday: 1839
Place of Birth: Ireland
Entered Service at: New York
Unit: U.S.S. *Varuna*
Battle or Place of Action: Forts Jackson and St. Philip, Louisiana
Date of Action: 24 April 1862
G.O. Number, Date: 11, 3 April 1863
Citation: Captain of a gun on board the U.S.S. *Varuna* during an attack on Forts Jackson and St. Philip, 24 April 1862. His ship was taken under furious fire by the rebel *Morgan* and severely damaged by ramming. Steadfast at his station through the thickest of the fight, Martin inflicted damage on the enemy, remaining cool and courageous although the *Varuna*, so badly damaged that she was forced to beach, was finally sunk.

839 ◆ MARTIN, WILLIAM

Rank: Boatswain's Mate (highest rank: Master's Mate)
Service: U.S. Navy
Birthday: 22 September 1835
Place of Birth: New York, New York
Date of Death: 3 April 1914
Place of Death: Alto Pass, Illinois
Cemetery: Alto Pass Cemetery, Block 14, Lot 3—Alto Pass, Illinois
Entered Service at: Cairo, Alexander County, Illinois
Unit: U.S.S. *Benton*
Battle or Place of Action: Haines Bluff, Yazoo River, Mississippi
Date of Action: 27 December 1862

G.O. Number, Date: 11, 3 April 1863
Citation: Served as boatswain's mate on board U.S.S. *Benton* during the attack on Haines Bluff, Yazoo River, 27 December 1862. Taking part in the hour-and-a-half engagement with the enemy, who had the dead-range of the vessel and was punishing her with heavy fire, Martin served courageously throughout the battle until the *Benton* was ordered to withdraw.

840 ◆ MASON, ELIHU H.

Rank: Sergeant (highest rank: Second Lieutenant)
Service: U.S. Army
Birthday: 23 March 1831
Place of Birth: Wayne County, Indiana
Date of Death: 24 September 1896
Cemetery: Pemberville Cemetery—Pemberville, Ohio
Entered Service at: Pemberville, Wood County, Ohio
Unit: Company K, 21st Ohio Infantry
Battle or Place of Action: Georgia
Date of Action: April 1862
Date of Presentation: 25 March 1863
Place of Presentation: Washington, D.C., presented by Sec. of War Edward M. Stanton
Citation: One of 19 of 24 men (including two civilians) who, by direction of Gen. Ormsby M. Mitchell, penetrated nearly 200 miles south into enemy territory and captured a railroad train at Big Shanty, Ga., in an attempt to destroy the bridges and track between Chattanooga and Atlanta.

841 ◆ MATHEWS, WILLIAM HENRY

Rank: First Sergeant (highest rank: Captain)
Service: U.S. Army
Birthday: 3 March 1844
Place of Birth: Devizes, Wiltshire, England
Date of Death: 7 February 1928
Place of Death: Brooklyn, New York
Cemetery: The Green Wood Cemetery—Brooklyn, New York
Entered Service at: Baltimore, Baltimore County, Maryland
Unit: Company E, 2d Maryland Veteran Infantry
Battle or Place of Action: Petersburg, Virginia
Date of Action: 30 July 1864
Date of Issue: 10 July 1892
Citation: Finding himself among a squad of Confederates, he fired into them, killing one, and was himself wounded, but succeeded in bringing in a sergeant and two men of the 17th South Carolina Regiment (C.S.A.) as prisoners.

842 ◆ MATTHEWS, JOHN C.

Rank: Corporal (highest rank: Sergeant)
Service: U.S. Army
Birthday: 1843
Place of Birth: Westmoreland County, Pennsylvania
Date of Death: 20 February 1924
Place of Death: Dayton, Ohio
Cemetery: Dayton National Cemetery (3-7-50) (MH)—Dayton, Ohio
Entered Service at: Greensburg, Westmoreland County, Pennsylvania
Unit: Company A, 61st Pennsylvania Infantry
Battle or Place of Action: Petersburg, Virginia
Date of Action: 2 April 1865
Date of Issue: 13 February 1891
Citation: Voluntarily took the colors, whose bearer had been disabled, and, although himself severely wounded, carried the same until the enemy's works were taken.

843 ◆ MATTHEWS, MILTON

Rank: Private
Service: U.S. Army
Place of Birth: Pittsburgh, Allegheny County, Pennsylvania
Date of Death: 11 April 1896
Place of Death: Milwaukee, Wisconsin
Cemetery: Wood National Cemetery (11-61) (MH)—Wood, Wisconsin
Entered Service at: Pittsburgh, Allegheny County, Pennsylvania
Unit: Company C, 61st Pennsylvania Infantry
Battle or Place of Action: Petersburg, Virginia
Date of Action: 2 April 1865
Date of Issue: 10 May 1865
Citation: Capture of flag of 7th Tennessee Infantry (C.S.A.).

844 ◆ MATTINGLY, HENRY B.

Rank: Private
Service: U.S. Army
Place of Birth: Marion County, Kentucky
Date of Death: 30 November 1893
Place of Death: Shepherdsville, Kentucky
Cemetery: Lebanon Junction Cemetery—Lebanon, Kentucky
Entered Service at: Lebanon, Marion County, Kentucky
Unit: Company C, 10th Kentucky Infantry
Battle or Place of Action: Jonesboro, Georgia
Date of Action: 1 September 1864
Date of Issue: 7 April 1865
Citation: Capture of flags of 6th and 7th Arkansas Infantry (C.S.A.).

845 ◆ MATTOCKS, CHARLES PORTER

Rank: Major
Service: U.S. Army
Birthday: 11 October 1840
Place of Birth: Danville, Caledonia County, Vermont
Date of Death: 16 May 1910
Cemetery: Evergreen Cemetery—Portland, Maine
Entered Service at: Portland, Cumberland County, Maine
Unit: 17th Maine Infantry
Battle or Place of Action: Deatonsville (Sailor's Creek), Virginia
Date of Action: 6 April 1865
Date of Issue: 29 March 1899

Citation: Displayed extraordinary gallantry in leading a charge of his regiment which resulted in the capture of a large number of prisoners and a stand of colors.

846 ◆ MAXHAM, LOWELL MASON

Rank: Corporal
Service: U.S. Army
Birthday: 6 December 1841
Place of Birth: Carver, Plymouth County, Massachusetts
Date of Death: 13 February 1931
Cemetery: Mayflower Hill Cemetery (MH)—Taunton, Massachusetts
Entered Service at: Taunton, Bristol County, Massachusetts
Unit: Company F, 7th Massachusetts Infantry
Battle or Place of Action: Fredericksburg, Virginia
Date of Action: 3 May 1863
Date of Issue: 24 August 1896
Citation: Though severely wounded and in the face of a deadly fire from the enemy at short-range, he rushed bravely forward and was among the first to enter the enemy's works on the crest of Marye's Heights and helped to plant his regimental colors there.

847 ◆ MAY, WILLIAM C.

Rank: Private
Service: U.S. Army
Birthday: 16 January 1826
Place of Birth: Pennsylvania
Date of Death: 21 October 1894
Place of Death: Howard Lake, Minnesota
Cemetery: Winsted Public Cemetery (MH)—Winsted, Minnesota
Entered Service at: Maysville, Franklin County, Iowa
Unit: Company H, 32d Iowa Infantry
Battle or Place of Action: Nashville, Tennessee
Date of Action: 16 December 1864
Date of Issue: 24 February 1865
Citation: Ran ahead of his regiment over the enemy's works and captured from its bearer the flag of Bonanchad's Confederate battery (C.S.A.).

848 ◆ MAYBERRY, JOHN B.

True Name: Maberry, John B.
Rank: Private (highest rank: Sergeant)
Service: U.S. Army
Birthday: 17 December 1841
Place of Birth: Smyrna, Kent County, Delaware
Date of Death: 17 December 1922
Cemetery: Glenwood Cemetery (MH)—Smyrna, Delaware
Entered Service at: Dover, Kent County, Delaware
Unit: Company F, 1st Delaware Infantry
Battle or Place of Action: Gettysburg, Pennsylvania
Date of Action: 3 July 1863
Date of Issue: 1 December 1864
Citation: Capture of flag.

849 ◆ MAYES, WILLIAM B.

Rank: Private
Service: U.S. Army
Birthday: 1838
Place of Birth: Marion County, Ohio
Date of Death: 16 August 1900
Place of Death: Los Angeles, California
Cemetery: Rosedale Cemetery—Los Angeles, California
Entered Service at: DeWitt, Clinton County, Iowa
Unit: Company K, 11th Iowa Infantry
Battle or Place of Action: near Kenesaw Mountain, Georgia
Date of Action: 15 June 1864
Date of Issue: 27 November 1899
Citation: With one companion and under a fierce fire from the enemy at short-range went to the rescue of a wounded comrade who had fallen between the lines and carried him to a place of safety.

850 ◆ MAYNARD, GEORGE HENRY

Rank: Private (highest rank: Brevet Major)
Service: U.S. Army
Birthday: 2 February 1836
Place of Birth: Waltham, Middlesex County, Massachusetts
Date of Death: 26 December 1927
Cemetery: Mount Feake Cemetery—Walthan, Massachusetts
Entered Service at: Boston, Suffolk County, Massachusetts
Unit: Company D, 13th Massachusetts Infantry
Battle or Place of Action: Fredericksburg, Virginia
Date of Action: 13 December 1862
Date of Issue: 1898
Citation: A wounded and helpless comrade, having been left on the skirmish line, this soldier voluntarily returned to the front under a severe fire and carried the wounded man to a place of safety.

851 ◆ McADAMS, PETER

Rank: Corporal (highest rank: Second Lieutenant)
Service: U.S. Army
Birthday: 21 April 1834
Place of Birth: Armagh, County Armagh, Ireland
Date of Death: 29 September 1926
Place of Death: Roxborough, Pennsylvania
Cemetery: St. John the Baptist Cemetery—Philadelphia, Pennsylvania
Entered Service at: Philadelphia, Philadelphia County, Pennsylvania
Unit: Company A, 98th Pennsylvania Infantry
Battle or Place of Action: Salem Heights, Virginia
Date of Action: 3 May 1863
Date of Issue: 1 April 1898
Citation: Went 250 yards in front of his regiment toward the position of the enemy and, under fire, brought within the lines a wounded and unconscious comrade.

852 ◆ McALWEE, BENJAMIN FRANKLIN

Rank: Sergeant (highest rank: Sergeant Major)
Service: U.S. Army
Birthday: 7 January 1838
Place of Birth: Washington, D.C.
Date of Death: 28 June 1918
Place of Death: Washington, D.C.
Cemetery: Congressional Cemetery—Washington, D.C.
Entered Service at: Baltimore, Baltimore County, Maryland
Unit: Company D, 3d Maryland Infantry
Battle or Place of Action: Petersburg, Virginia
Date of Action: 30 July 1864
Date of Issue: 4 April 1898
Citation: Picked up a shell with burning fuse and threw it over the parapet into the ditch, where it exploded; by this act he probably saved the lives of comrades at the great peril of his own.

853 ◆ McANALLY, CHARLES

Rank: Second Lieutenant (highest rank: Captain)
Service: U.S. Army
Birthday: 12 May 1836
Place of Birth: Ireland
Date of Death: 1905
Place of Death: Austin, Texas
Entered Service at: Philadelphia, Philadelphia County, Pennsylvania
Unit: Company D, 69th Pennsylvania Infantry
Battle or Place of Action: Spotsylvania, Virginia
Date of Action: 12 May 1864
Date of Issue: 2 August 1897
Citation: In a hand-to-hand encounter with the enemy captured flag, was wounded in the act, but continued on duty until he received a second wound.

854 ◆ McCAMMON, WILLIAM WALLACE

Rank: First Lieutenant (highest rank: Major Ret.)
Service: U.S. Army
Birthday: 28 May 1838
Place of Birth: Shippensburg, Cumberland County, Pennsylvania
Date of Death: 27 March 1903
Cemetery: Vancouver Barracks Post Cemetery (4-W-412) (MH)—Vancouver, Washington
Entered Service at: Montgomery City, Montgomery County, Missouri
Unit: Company E, 24th Missouri Infantry
Battle or Place of Action: Corinth, Mississippi
Date of Action: 3 October 1862
Date of Issue: 9 July 1896
Citation: While on duty as provost marshal, voluntarily assumed command of his company, then under fire, and so continued in command until the repulse and retreat of the enemy on the following day, the loss to his company during the battle being very great.

855 ◆ McCARREN, BERNARD

Rank: Private (highest rank: Corporal)
Service: U.S. Army
Birthday: 1830
Place of Birth: Ireland
Date of Death: 20 June 1870
Place of Death: Wilmington, Delaware
Cemetery: Old Cathedral Cemetery—Wilmington, Delaware
Entered Service at: Wilmimgton, New Castle County, Delaware
Unit: Company C, 1st Delaware Infantry
Battle or Place of Action: Gettysburg, Pennsylvania
Date of Action: 3 July 1863
Date of Issue: 1 December 1864
Citation: Capture of flag.

856 ◆ McCAUSLIN, JOSEPH

Rank: Private
Service: U.S. Army
Birthday: 1840
Place of Birth: Ohio County, West Virginia
Date of Death: 6 July 1906
Place of Death: West Liberty, West Virginia
Cemetery: West Alexander Cemetery—West Alexander, Pennsylvania
Entered Service at: West Liberty, Ohio County, West Virginia
Unit: Company D, 12th West Virginia Infantry
Battle or Place of Action: Petersburg, Virginia
Date of Action: 2 April 1865
Date of Issue: 12 May 1865
Citation: Conspicuous gallantry as color bearer in the assault on Fort Gregg.

857 ◆ McCLEARY, CHARLES H.

Rank: First Lieutenant (highest rank: Captain)
Service: U.S. Army
Birthday: 1842
Place of Birth: Sandusky County, Ohio
Date of Death: 23 June 1906
Cemetery: McPherson Cemetery (MH)—Clyde, Ohio
Entered Service at: Clyde, Sandusky County, Ohio
Unit: Company C, 72d Ohio Infantry
Battle or Place of Action: Nashville, Tennessee
Date of Action: 16 December 1864
Date of Issue: 24 February 1865
Citation: Capture of flag of 4th Florida Infantry (C.S.A.), while in advance of his lines.

858 ◆ McCLELLAND, JAMES M.

Rank: Private
Service: U.S. Army
Birthday: 12 August 1830

Place of Birth: Harrison County, Ohio
Date of Death: 10 April 1915
Cemetery: Riverside Cemetery (MH)—Cleveland, Ohio
Entered Service at: Ohio
Unit: Company B, 30th Ohio Infantry
Battle or Place of Action: Vicksburg, Mississippi
Date of Action: 22 May 1863
Date of Issue: 13 August 1894
Citation: Gallantry in the charge of the "volunteer storming party."

859 ◆ McCLELLAND, MATTHEW

Rank: First Class Fireman
Service: U.S. Navy
Birthday: 1833
Place of Birth: Brooklyn, Kings County, New York
Date of Death: 30 January 1883
Entered Service at: Brooklyn, Kings County, New York
Unit: U.S.S. *Richmond*
Battle or Place of Action: Port Hudson, Louisiana
Date of Action: 14 March 1863
G.O. Number, Date: 17, 10 July 1863
Citation: Served on board the U.S.S. *Richmond* in the attack on Port Hudson, 14 March 1863. Damaged by a 6-inch solid rifle shot which shattered the starboard safety-valve chamber and also damaged the port safety valve, the fireroom of the *Richmond* immediately became filled with steam to place it in an extremely critical condition. Acting courageously in this crisis, McClelland persisted in penetrating the steam-filled room in order to haul the hot fires of the furnaces and continued this gallant action until the gravity of the situation had lessened.

860 ◆ McCONNELL, SAMUEL

Rank: Captain
Service: U.S. Army
Birthday: 1 June 1830
Place of Birth: Belmont County, Ohio
Date of Death: 26 March 1915
Place of Death: Havelock, Nebraska
Cemetery: Arborville Rural Cemetery (MH)—Bradshaw, Nebraska
Entered Service at: Bushnell, McDonough County, Illinois
Unit: Company H, 119th Illinois Infantry
Battle or Place of Action: Fort Blakely, Alabama
Date of Action: 9 April 1865
Date of Issue: 8 June 1865
Citation: While leading his company in an assault, Capt. McConnell braved an intense fire that mowed down his unit. Upon reaching the breastworks, he found that he had only one member of his company with him, Pvt. Wagner. He was so close to an enemy gun that the blast knocked him down a ditch. Getting up, he entered the gun pit, the gun crew fleeing before him. About 30 paces away he saw a Confederate flag bearer and guard which he captured with the last shot in his pistol.

861 ◆ McCORMICK, MICHAEL

Rank: Boatswain's Mate
Service: U.S. Navy
Birthday: 1833
Place of Birth: Ireland
Date of Death: 19 May 1865
Place of Death: Milwaukee, Wisconsin
Entered Service at: Chicago, Cook County, Illinois
Unit: U.S.S. *Signal*
Battle or Place of Action: Red River, Louisiana
Date of Action: 5 May 1864
G.O. Number, Date: 45, 31 December 1864
Citation: Served as boatswain's mate on board the U.S.S. *Signal*, Red River, 5 May 1864. Proceeding up the Red River, the U.S.S. *Signal* engaged a large force of enemy field batteries and sharpshooters, returning the fire until the ship was totally disabled, at which time the white flag was raised. Serving as gun captain and wounded early in the battle, McCormick bravely stood by his gun in the face of the enemy fire until ordered to withdraw.

862 ◆ McCORNACK, ANDREW

Rank: Private
Service: U.S. Army
Birthday: 2 April 1844
Place of Birth: Kane, Greene County, Illinois
Date of Death: 4 May 1920
Cemetery: Hillside Cemetery (MH)—Monticello, Minnesota
Entered Service at: Rutland, La Salle County, Illinois
Unit: Company I, 127th Illinois Infantry
Battle or Place of Action: Vicksburg, Mississippi
Date of Action: 22 May 1863
Date of Issue: 10 January 1895
Citation: Gallantry in the charge of the "volunteer storming party."

863 ◆ McCULLOCK, ADAM

Rank: Seaman
Service: U.S. Navy
Birthday: 1834
Place of Birth: Maine
Entered Service at: Augusta, Kennebec County, Maine
Unit: U.S.S. *Lackawanna*
Battle or Place of Action: Mobile Bay, Alabama
Date of Action: 5 August 1864
G.O. Number, Date: 45, 31 December 1864
Citation: On board the U.S.S. *Lackawanna* during successful attacks against Fort Morgan, rebel gunboats, and the ram *Tennessee* in Mobile Bay, on 5 August 1864. Wounded when an enemy shell struck and ordered to go below, McCullock refused to leave his station and continued to perform his duties throughout the prolonged action which resulted in the capture of the prize ram *Tennessee* and in the damaging and destruction of Fort Morgan.

864 ◆ McDONALD, GEORGE E.

Rank: Private
Service: U.S. Army
Place of Birth: Warwick, Kent County, Rhode Island
Date of Death: 8 September 1897
Cemetery: Oak Grove Cemetery (MH)—Pawtucket, Rhode Island
Entered Service at: Warwick, Kent County, Rhode Island
Unit: Company L, 1st Connecticut Heavy Artillery
Battle or Place of Action: Fort Stedman, Virginia
Date of Action: 25 March 1865
Date of Issue: 21 July 1865
Citation: Capture of flag of the 26th North Carolina Infantry (C.S.A.).

865 ◆ McDONALD, JOHN

Rank: Boatswain's Mate
Service: U.S. Navy
Birthday: 1817
Place of Birth: Perth, Scotland
Entered Service at: Boston, Suffolk County, Massachusetts
Unit: U.S.S. *Baron De Kalb*
Battle or Place of Action: Yazoo River Expedition, Mississippi
Date of Action: 23-27 December 1862
G.O. Number, Date: 11, 3 April 1863
Citation: Served on board the U.S.S. *Baron De Kalb*, Yazoo River Expedition, 23 to 27 December 1862. Proceeding under orders up the Yazoo River, the U.S.S. *Baron de Kalb*, with the object of capturing or destroying the enemy's transports, came upon the steamers *John Walsh*, *R.J. Locklan*, *Golden Age*, and the *Scotland*, sunk on a bar where they were ordered burned. Continuing up the river, she was fired on but, upon returning the fire, caused the enemy's retreat. Returning down the Yazoo, she destroyed and captured large quantities of enemy equipment and several prisoners. Serving bravely throughout this action, McDonald, as boatswain's mate, "distinguished himself in the various actions."

866 ◆ McDONALD, JOHN WADE

Rank: Private
Service: U.S. Army
Birthday: 10 September 1843
Place of Birth: Lancaster, Fairfield County, Ohio
Date of Death: 27 July 1910
Place of Death: San Diego, California
Cemetery: Greenwood Memorial Park—San Diego, California
Entered Service at: Waynesville, DeWitt County, Illinois
Unit: Company E, 20th Illinois Infantry
Battle or Place of Action: Pittsburg Landing, Tennessee
Date of Action: 6 April 1862
Date of Issue: 27 August 1900
Citation: Was severely wounded while endeavoring, at the risk of his life, to carry to a place of safety a wounded and helpless comrade.

867 ◆ McELHINNY, SAMUEL O.

Rank: Private
Service: U.S. Army
Birthday: 1845
Place of Birth: Meigs County, Ohio
Date of Death: 15 May 1923
Cemetery: Pine Street Cemetery (MH)—Gallipolis, Ohio
Entered Service at: Point Pleasant, Mason County, West Virginia
Unit: Company A, 2d West Virginia Cavalry
Battle or Place of Action: Deatonsville (Sailor's Creek), Virginia
Date of Action: 6 April 1865
Date of Issue: 3 May 1865
Citation: Capture of flag.

868 ◆ McENROE, PATRICK H.

Rank: Sergeant
Service: U.S. Army
Place of Birth: Ireland
Entered Service at: Schodack, Rensselaer County, New York
Unit: Company D, 6th New York Cavalry
Battle or Place of Action: Winchester, Virginia
Date of Action: 19 September 1864
Date of Issue: 19 September 1864
Citation: Capture of colors of 36th Virginia Infantry (C.S.A.).

869 ◆ McFALL, DANIEL ROBERT

Rank: Sergeant
Service: U.S. Army
Birthday: 1836
Place of Birth: Niagara County, New York
Date of Death: 5 November 1919
Place of Death: Milan, Missouri
Cemetery: Rice Cemetery—Dundee, Illinois
Entered Service at: Ypsilanti, Washtenaw County, Michigan
Unit: Company E, 17th Michigan Infantry
Battle or Place of Action: Spotsylvania, Virginia
Date of Action: 12 May 1864
Date of Issue: 27 July 1896
Citation: Captured Col. Barker, commanding the Confederate brigade that charged the Union batteries; on the same day rescued Lt. George W. Harmon of his regiment from the enemy.

870 ◆ McFARLAND, JOHN C.

Rank: Captain of the Forecastle
Service: U.S. Navy
Birthday: 1840
Place of Birth: Boston, Suffolk County, Massachusetts
Date of Death: 3 October 1881

Place of Death: Lowell, Massachusetts
Cemetery: St. Patrick's Cemetery (MH)—Lowell, Massachusetts
Entered Service at: Boston, Suffolk County, Massachusetts
Unit: U.S.S. *Hartford*
Battle or Place of Action: Mobile Bay, Alabama
Date of Action: 5 August 1864
G.O. Number, Date: 45, 31 December 1864
Citation: Stationed at the wheel on board the flagship U.S.S. *Hartford* during successful actions against Fort Morgan, rebel gunboats, and the ram *Tennessee* in Mobile Bay, 5 August 1864. With his ship under terrific enemy shellfire, McFarland performed his duties with skill and courage and, when the *Lackawanna* ran into his ship and every man at the wheel was in danger of being crushed, remained steadfast at his station and continued to steer his ship.

871 ◆ McGINN, EDWARD

Rank: Private (highest rank: First Lieutenant)
Service: U.S. Army
Birthday: 20 November 1843
Place of Birth: New York, New York
Date of Death: 28 September 1908
Place of Death: Milwaukee, Wisconsin
Cemetery: Calvary Cemetery (MH)—Milwaukee, Wisconsin
Entered Service at: Cincinnati, Hamilton County, Ohio
Unit: Company F, 54th Ohio Infantry
Battle or Place of Action: Vicksburg, Mississippi
Date of Action: 22 May 1863
Date of Issue: 28 June 1894
Citation: Gallantry in the charge of the "volunteer storming party."

872 ◆ McGONAGLE, WILSON

Rank: Private
Service: U.S. Army
Birthday: 9 August 1838
Place of Birth: Jefferson County, Ohio
Date of Death: 15 September 1912
Place of Death: Dayton (Soldier's Home), Ohio
Cemetery: unknown cemetery—Saxonburg, Pennsylvania
Entered Service at: Cadiz, Harrison County, Ohio
Unit: Company B, 30th Ohio Infantry
Battle or Place of Action: Vicksburg, Mississippi
Date of Action: 22 May 1863
Date of Issue: 15 August 1894
Citation: Gallantry in the charge of the "volunteer storming party."

873 ◆ McGONNIGLE, ANDREW JACKSON

Rank: Captain & Assistant Quartermaster (highest rank: Colonel)
Service: U.S. Army
Birthday: 4 March 1829
Place of Birth: New York, New York
Date of Death: 25 January 1901
Place of Death: Ashville, North Carolina
Cemetery: Riverside Cemetery (MH)—Ashville, North Carolina
Entered Service at: Cumberland, Allegany County, Maryland
Unit: U.S. Volunteers
Battle or Place of Action: Cedar Creek, Virginia
Date of Action: 19 October 1864
Date of Issue: 21 July 1897
Citation: While acting as chief quartermaster of Gen. Sheridan's forces operating in the Shenandoah Valley, McGonnigle was severely wounded while voluntarily leading a brigade of infantry and was commended for the greatest gallantry by Gen. Sheridan.

874 ◆ McGOUGH, OWEN

Rank: Corporal
Service: U.S. Army
Birthday: 29 June 1829
Place of Birth: Monaghan, Ireland
Date of Death: 5 January 1908
Place of Death: Troy, New York
Cemetery: St. Peter's Cemetery—Troy, New York
Entered Service at: Cornwall, Orange County, New York
Unit: Battery D, 5th U.S. Artillery
Battle or Place of Action: Bull Run, Virginia
Date of Action: 21 July 1861
Date of Issue: 28 August 1897
Citation: Through his personal exertions under a heavy fire, one of the guns of his battery was brought off the field; all the other guns were lost.

875 ◆ McGOWAN, JOHN

Rank: Quartermaster
Service: U.S. Navy
Birthday: 1831
Place of Birth: Ireland
Entered Service at: New York, New York
Unit: U.S.S. *Varuna*
Battle or Place of Action: Forts Jackson and St. Philip, Louisiana
Date of Action: 24 April 1864
G.O. Number, Date: 11, 3 April 1863
Citation: McGowan occupied one of the most responsible positions in the U.S.S. *Varuna*, during the attacks on Forts Jackson and St. Philip and in action against the rebel ship *Morgan*, 24 April 1862. Although guns were raking the decks from behind him, McGowan remained steadfast at the wheel throughout the thickest of the fight, continuing at his station and rendering service with the greatest courage and skill until his ship, repeatedly holed and twice rammed by the enemy, was beached and sunk.

876 ◆ McGRAW, THOMAS

Rank: Sergeant
Service: U.S. Army

Birthday: 1834
Place of Birth: Ireland
Date of Death: 1899
Cemetery: LaCrosse City Cemetery (MH)—LaCrosse, Kansas
Entered Service at: Chicago, Cook County, Illinois
Unit: Company B, 23d Illinois Infantry
Battle or Place of Action: Petersburg, Virginia
Date of Action: 2 April 1865
Date of Issue: 12 May 1865
Citation: One of the three soldiers most conspicuous for gallantry in the final assault.

877 ◆ McGUIRE, PATRICK

Rank: Private
Service: U.S. Army
Birthday: 1840
Place of Birth: Ireland
Date of Death: 8 September 1898
Place of Death: Chicago, Illinois
Cemetery: Calvary Cemetery—Evanston, Illinois
Entered Service at: Chicago, Cook County, Illinois
Unit: Chicago Mercantile Battery, Illinois Light Artillery
Battle or Place of Action: Vicksburg, Mississippi
Date of Action: 22 May 1863
Date of Issue: 15 January 1895
Citation: Carried with others by hand a cannon up to and fired it through the embrasure of the enemy's works.

878 ◆ McHALE, ALEXANDER U.

Rank: Corporal (highest rank: Sergeant)
Service: U.S. Army
Birthday: 16 March 1837
Place of Birth: Ireland
Date of Death: 13 March 1911
Cemetery: Lake View Cemetery—Seattle, Washington
Entered Service at: Muskegon, Muskegon County, Michigan
Unit: Company H, 26th Michigan Infantry
Battle or Place of Action: Spotsylvania Courthouse, Virginia
Date of Action: 12 May 1864
Date of Issue: 11 January 1900
Citation: Captured a Confederate color in a charge, threw the flag over in front of the works, and continued in the charge upon the enemy.

879 ◆ McHUGH, MARTIN

Rank: Seaman
Service: U.S. Navy
Birthday: 1837
Place of Birth: Cincinnati, Hamilton County, Ohio
Entered Service at: Ohio
Unit: U.S.S. *Cincinnati*
Battle or Place of Action: Vicksburg, Mississippi
Date of Action: 27 May 1863
G.O. Number, Date: 17, 10 July 1863
Citation: Served on board the U.S.S. *Cincinnati* during the attack on the Vicksburg batteries and at the time of her sinking, 27 May 1863. Engaging the enemy in a fierce battle, the *Cincinnati*, amidst an incessant fire of shot and shell, continued to fire her guns to the last, though so penetrated by shellfire that her fate was sealed. Serving bravely during this action, McHugh was conspicuously cool under the fire of the enemy, never ceasing to fire until this proud ship went down, "her colors nailed to the mast."

880 ◆ McINTOSH, JAMES

Rank: Captain of the Top
Service: U.S. Navy
Birthday: 17 November 1829
Place of Birth: Canada
Date of Death: 28 May 1908
Place of Death: Kearney, New Jersey
Cemetery: Arlington Cemetery—Kearney, New Jersey
Entered Service at: New York, New York
Unit: U.S.S. *Richmond*
Battle or Place of Action: Mobile Bay, Alabama
Date of Action: 5 August 1864
G.O. Number, Date: 45, 31 December 1864
Citation: On board the U.S.S. *Richmond* during action against rebel forts and gunboats and with the ram *Tennessee* in Mobile Bay, 5 August 1864. Despite damage to his ship and the loss of several men on board as enemy fire raked her decks, McIntosh performed his duties with skill and courage throughout the prolonged battle, which resulted in the surrender of the rebel ram *Tennessee* and in the successful attacks carried out on Fort Morgan.

881 ◆ McKAY, CHARLES W.

Rank: Sergeant (highest rank: Captain)
Service: U.S. Army
Birthday: 25 January 1847
Place of Birth: Mansfield, Cattaraugus County, New York
Date of Death: 25 August 1912
Place of Death: Staples, Minnesota
Cemetery: Oak Grove Cemetery—Fergus Falls, Minnesota
Entered Service at: Allegany, Cattaraugus County, New York
Unit: Company C, 154th New York Infantry
Battle or Place of Action: Dug Gap, Georgia
Date of Action: 8 May 1864
Date of Issue: 13 April 1894
Citation: Voluntarily risked his life in rescuing under the fire of the enemy a wounded comrade who was lying between the lines.

882 ◆ McKEE, GEORGE

Rank: Color Sergeant
Service: U.S. Army
Birthday: 1845
Place of Birth: County Tyrone, Ireland
Date of Death: 8 July 1892

Place of Death: Sawtella, California
Cemetery: Los Angeles National Cemetery (1-6-2) (MH)—Los Angeles, California
Entered Service at: Rochester, Monroe County, New York
Unit: Company D, 89th New York Infantry
Battle or Place of Action: Petersburg, Virginia
Date of Action: 2 April 1865
Date of Issue: 12 May 1865
Citation: Gallantry as color bearer in the assault on Fort Gregg.
Notes: POW

883 ◆ McKEEN, NINEVEH S.

Rank: First Lieutenant (highest rank: Brevet Major)
Service: U.S. Army
Place of Birth: Marshall, Clark County, Illinois
Date of Death: 22 December 1890
Place of Death: Collinsville, Illinois
Cemetery: Greenwood Cemetery (MH)—Collinsville, Illinois
Entered Service at: Marshall, Clark County, Illinois
Unit: Company H, 21st Illinois Infantry
Battle or Place of Action: Stone River & Liberty Gap, Tennessee
Date of Action: 30 December 1862 & 25 June 1863
Date of Issue: 23 June 1890
Citation: Conspicuous in the charge at Stone River, Tenn., where he was three times wounded. At Liberty Gap, Tenn., captured colors of 8th Arkansas Infantry (C.S.A.).

884 ◆ McKEEVER, MICHAEL

Rank: Private (highest rank: First Sergeant)
Service: U.S. Army
Birthday: 25 March 1842
Place of Birth: Ireland
Date of Death: 24 December 1916
Place of Death: Philadelphia, Pennsylvania
Cemetery: Holy Sepulchre Cemetery—Philadelphia, Pennsylvania
Entered Service at: Philadelphia, Philadelphia County, Pennsylvania
Unit: Company K, 5th Pennsylvania Cavalry
Battle or Place of Action: Burnt Ordinary, Virginia
Date of Action: 19 January 1863
Date of Issue: 2 August 1897
Citation: Was one of a small scouting party that charged and routed a mounted force of the enemy six times their number. He led the charge in a most gallant and distinguished manner, going far beyond the call of duty.

885 ◆ McKNIGHT, WILLIAM

Rank: Coxswain (highest rank: Master's Mate)
Service: U.S. Navy
Birthday: 3 May 1842
Place of Birth: Ulster County, New York
Date of Death: 4 November 1914
Place of Death: Woodhaven, New York
Cemetery: The Green Wood Cemetery—Brooklyn, New York
Entered Service at: New York, New York
Unit: U.S.S. *Varuna*
Battle or Place of Action: Forts Jackson & St. Philip, Louisiana
Date of Action: 24 April 1862
G.O. Number, Date: 11, 3 April 1863
Citation: Captain of a gun on board the U.S.S. *Varuna* during the attacks on Forts Jackson and St. Philip and in action against the rebel ship *Morgan*, 24 April 1862. During this action at extremely close-range, while the ship was under furious fire and was twice rammed by the rebel ship *Morgan*, McKnight remained steadfast at his gun throughout the thickest of the fight and was instrumental in inflicting damage on the enemy until the *Varuna*, so badly damaged that she was forced to beach, was finally sunk.

886 ◆ McKOWN, NATHANIEL A.

Rank: Sergeant (highest rank: First Lieutenant)
Service: U.S. Army
Birthday: 11 March 1838
Place of Birth: Susquehanna County, Pennsylvania
Date of Death: 11 August 1902
Cemetery: Sunnyside Cemetery—Tunkhannock, Pennsylvania
Entered Service at: Philadelphia, Philadelphia County, Pennsylvania
Unit: Company B, 58th Pennsylvania Infantry
Battle or Place of Action: Chapin's Farm, Virginia
Date of Action: 29 September 1864
Date of Issue: 6 April 1865
Citation: Capture of flag.

887 ◆ McLEOD, JAMES

Rank: Captain of the Foretop
Service: U.S. Navy
Place of Birth: Scotland
Entered Service at: Maine
Unit: U.S.S. *Pensacola*
Battle or Place of Action: Forts Jackson & St. Philip and New Orleans, Louisiana
Date of Action: 24-25 April 1862
G.O. Number, Date: 11, 3 April 1863
Citation: Captain of the foretop, and a volunteer from the *Colorado*, McLeod served on board the U.S.S. *Pensacola* during the attack on Forts Jackson and St. Philip and the taking of New Orleans, 24 and 25 April 1862. Acting as gun captain of the rifled howitzer aft, which was much exposed, he served this piece with great ability and activity, although no officer superintended it.

888 ◆ McMAHON, MARTIN THOMAS

Rank: Captain & Aide-de-Camp (highest rank: Brevet Major General)

Service: U.S. Army
Birthday: 21 March 1838
Place of Birth: LaPrairie, Quebec, Canada
Date of Death: 21 April 1906
Place of Death: New York, New York
Cemetery: Arlington National Cemetery (2-1101)—Arlington, Virginia
Entered Service at: California
Unit: U.S. Volunteers
Battle or Place of Action: White Oak Swamp, Virginia
Date of Action: 30 June 1862
Date of Issue: 10 March 1891
Citation: Under fire of the enemy, successfully destroyed a valuable train that had been abandoned and prevented it from falling into the hands of the enemy.

889 ◆ McMILLEN, FRANCIS M.

Rank: Sergeant (highest rank: Sergeant Major)
Service: U.S. Army
Birthday: 25 March 1832
Place of Birth: Bracken County, Kentucky
Date of Death: 8 March 1913
Place of Death: Dayton, Ohio
Cemetery: Washington Cemetery (MH)—Washington Courthouse, Ohio
Entered Service at: Piqua, Miami County, Ohio
Unit: Company C, 110th Ohio Infantry
Battle or Place of Action: Petersburg, Virginia
Date of Action: 2 April 1865
Date of Issue: 10 May 1865
Citation: Capture of flag.

890 ◆ *McVEANE, JOHN P.

True Name: McVean, John P.
Rank: Corporal
Service: U.S. Army
Birthday: 1842
Place of Birth: Toronto, Canada
Date of Death: 10 May 1864
Place of Death: Wilderness, Virginia
Cemetery: Forest Lawn Cemetery (MH)—Buffalo, New York
Entered Service at: Buffalo, Erie County, New York
Unit: Company D, 49th New York Infantry
Battle or Place of Action: Fredericksburg Heights, Virginia
Date of Action: 4 May 1863
Date of Issue: 21 September 1870
Citation: Shot a Confederate color bearer and seized the flag; also approached, alone, a barn between the lines and demanded and received the surrender of a number of the enemy therein.

891 ◆ McWHORTER, WALTER F.

Rank: Commissary Sergeant
Service: U.S. Army
Birthday: 14 July 1836
Place of Birth: Lewis County, West Virginia
Date of Death: 17 May 1877
Place of Death: New Milton, West Virginia
Cemetery: Greenbrier (S.B.O.) Cemetery—Nina, West Virginia
Entered Service at: Clarksburg, Harrison County, West Virginia
Unit: Company E, 3d West Virginia Cavalry
Battle or Place of Action: Deatonsville (Sailor's Creek), Virginia
Date of Action: 6 April 1865
Date of Issue: 3 May 1865
Citation: Capture of flag of 6th Tennessee Infantry (C.S.A.).

892 ◆ McWILLIAMS, GEORGE WASHINGTON

Rank: Landsman
Service: U.S. Navy
Birthday: 1844
Place of Birth: Waterford, Erie County, Pennsylvania
Date of Death: 11 August 1900
Place of Death: Ida Grove, Iowa
Cemetery: Ida Grove Cemetery—Ida Grove, Iowa
Entered Service at: Pennsylvania
Unit: U.S.S. *Pontoosuc*
Battle or Place of Action: Fort Fisher & Wilmington, North Carolina
Date of Action: 24 December 1864—22 February 1865
G.O. Number, Date: 59, 22 June 1865
Citation: Served on board the U.S.S. *Pontoosuc* during the capture of Fort Fisher and Wilmington, 24 December 1864 to 22 February 1865. Carrying out his duties faithfully throughout this period, McWilliams was so severely wounded in the assault upon Fort Fisher that he was sent to the hospital at Portsmouth, Va. McWilliams was recommended for his gallantry, skill, and coolness in action while under the fire of the enemy.

893 ◆ MEACH, GEORGE E.

Rank: Farrier (highest rank: Sergeant)
Service: U.S. Army
Birthday: 1844
Place of Birth: New York
Date of Death: 21 March 1873
Cemetery: Pine Grove Cemetery (MH)—Fillmore, New York
Entered Service at: New York, New York
Unit: Company I, 6th New York Cavalry
Battle or Place of Action: Winchester, Virginia
Date of Action: 19 September 1864
Date of Issue: 27 September 1864
Citation: Capture of flag.

894 ◆ MEAGHER, THOMAS

True Name: Marr, Thomas W.
Rank: First Sergeant (highest rank: Brevet First Lieutenant NY Volunteers)

Service: U.S. Army
Birthday: 1842
Place of Birth: Scotland
Date of Death: 16 January 1890
Place of Death: Brooklyn, New York
Cemetery: Holy Cross Cemetery—Brooklyn, New York
Entered Service at: Brooklyn, Kings County, New York
Unit: Company G, 158th New York Infantry
Battle or Place of Action: Chapin's Farm, Virginia
Date of Action: 29 September 1864
Date of Issue: 6 April 1865
Citation: Led a section of his men on the enemy's works, receiving a wound while scaling a parapet.

895 ◆ MEARS, GEORGE W.

Rank: Sergeant
Service: U.S. Army
Birthday: 3 January 1843
Place of Birth: Bloomsburg, Columbia County, Pennsylvania
Date of Death: 24 November 1921
Place of Death: Bloomsburg, Pennsylvania
Cemetery: Old Rosemont Cemetery—Bloomsburg, Pennsylvania
Entered Service at: Bloomsburg, Columbia County, Pennsylvania
Unit: Company A, 6th Pennsylvania Reserves
Battle or Place of Action: Gettysburg, Pennsylvania
Date of Action: 2 July 1863
Date of Issue: 16 February 1897
Citation: With five volunteers he gallantly charged on a number of the enemy's sharpshooters concealed in a log house, captured them, and brought them into the Union lines.

896 ◆ MELVILLE, CHARLES

True Name: Ramsbottom, James
Rank: Ordinary Seaman
Service: U.S. Navy
Birthday: 1828
Place of Birth: Dover, Strafford County, New Hampshire
Date of Death: 5 January 1867
Cemetery: Family Cemetery, Old Dover Road (SR-16B) (MH)—Rochester, New Hampshire
Entered Service at: New Hampshire
Unit: U.S.S. *Hartford*
Battle or Place of Action: Mobile Bay, Alabama
Date of Action: 5 August 1864
G.O. Number, Date: 45, 31 December 1864
Citation: On board the flagship U.S.S. *Hartford* during action against rebel gunboats, the ram *Tennessee*, and Fort Morgan in Mobile Bay, 5 August 1864. Wounded and taken below to the surgeon when a shell burst between the two forward 9-inch guns, killing and wounding 15 men, Melville promptly returned to his gun on the deck and, although scarcely able to stand, refused to go below and continued to man his post throughout the remainder of the action resulting in the capture of the rebel ram *Tennessee*.

897 ◆ MENTER, JOHN WILLIAM

Rank: Sergeant
Service: U.S. Army
Birthday: 7 September 1840
Place of Birth: Palmer, New York
Date of Death: 18 April 1925
Place of Death: Ovid, Michigan
Entered Service at: Detroit, Wayne County, Michigan
Unit: Company D, 5th Michigan Infantry
Battle or Place of Action: Deatonsville (Sailor's Creek), Virginia
Date of Action: 6 April 1865
Date of Issue: 10 May 1865
Citation: Capture of flag.

898 ◆ MERRIAM, HENRY CLAY

Rank: Lieutenant Colonel (highest rank: Major General)
Service: U.S. Army
Birthday: 13 November 1837
Place of Birth: Houlton, Aroostook County, Maine
Date of Death: 18 November 1912
Cemetery: Arlington National Cemetery (1-114-13) (MH)—Arlington, Virginia
Entered Service at: Houlton, Aroostook County, Maine
Unit: 73d U.S. Colored Infantry
Battle or Place of Action: Fort Blakely, Alabama
Date of Action: 9 April 1865
Date of Issue: 28 June 1894
Citation: Volunteered to attack the enemy's works in advance of orders and, upon permission being given, made a most gallant assault.

899 ◆ MERRIFIELD, JAMES K.

Rank: Corporal
Service: U.S. Army
Birthday: 20 August 1844
Place of Birth: Hyde Park, Westmoreland County, Pennsylvania
Date of Death: 7 September 1918
Place of Death: St. Louis, Missouri
Cemetery: Valhalla Cemetery—St. Louis, Missouri
Entered Service at: Manlius, Bureau County, Illinois
Unit: Company C, 88th Illinois Infantry
Battle or Place of Action: Franklin, Tennessee
Date of Action: 30 November 1864
Date of Issue: 28 March 1896
Citation: Captured two battle flags from the enemy and returned with them to his own lines.

900 ◆ MERRILL, AUGUSTUS

Rank: Captain
Service: U.S. Army
Birthday: 4 October 1843
Place of Birth: Byron, Maine
Date of Death: 14 November 1895

Place of Death: Eagle Rock, California
Cemetery: Graceland Cemetery—Chicago, Illinois
Entered Service at: Lyndon, Maine
Unit: Company B, 1st Maine Veteran Infantry
Battle or Place of Action: Petersburg, Virginia
Date of Action: 2 April 1865
Date of Issue: 23 October 1891
Citation: With six men, captured 69 Confederate prisoners and recaptured several soldiers who had fallen into the enemy's hands.

901 ◆ MERRILL, GEORGE

Rank: Private
Service: U.S. Army
Birthday: 11 February 1847
Place of Birth: Queensberry, Warren County, New York
Date of Death: 29 August 1925
Place of Death: Glens Falls, New York
Cemetery: Glens Falls Cemetery—Glens Falls, New York
Entered Service at: Moreau, New York
Unit: Company I, 142d New York Infantry
Battle or Place of Action: Fort Fisher, North Carolina
Date of Action: 15 January 1865
Date of Issue: 28 December 1914
Citation: Voluntarily advanced with the head of the column and cut down the palisading.

902 ◆ MERRITT, JOHN G.

Rank: Sergeant
Service: U.S. Army
Birthday: 31 October 1837
Place of Birth: New York, New York
Date of Death: 17 December 1892
Place of Death: Washington, D.C.
Cemetery: Congressional Cemetery—Washington, D.C.
Entered Service at: Fort Snelling, St. Paul County, Minnesota
Unit: Company K, 1st Minnesota Infantry
Battle or Place of Action: Bull Run, Virginia
Date of Action: 21 July 1861
Date of Issue: 1 April 1880
Citation: Gallantry in action; was wounded while capturing flag in advance of his regiment.

903 ◆ MEYER, HENRY CODDINGTON

Rank: Captain (highest rank: Brevet Major NY Volunteers)
Service: U.S. Army
Birthday: 14 April 1844
Place of Birth: Hamburg, Erie County, New York
Date of Death: 27 March 1935
Place of Death: Montclair, New Jersey
Cemetery: Rosedale Cemetery (MH)—Orange, New Jersey
Entered Service at: Dobbs Ferry, Westchester County, New York
Unit: Company D, 24th New York Cavalry
Battle or Place of Action: Petersburg, Virginia
Date of Action: 17 June 1864
Date of Issue: 29 March 1899
Citation: During an assault and in the face of a heavy fire rendered heroic assistance to a wounded and helpless officer, thereby saving his life and in the performance of this gallant act sustained a severe wound.

904 ◆ MIFFLIN, JAMES

Rank: Engineer's Cook
Service: U.S. Navy
Birthday: 1839
Place of Birth: Richmond, Richmond County, Virginia
Entered Service at: Virginia
Unit: U.S.S. *Brooklyn*
Battle or Place of Action: Mobile Bay, Alabama
Date of Action: 5 August 1864
G.O. Number, Date: 45, 31 December 1864
Citation: On board the U.S.S. *Brooklyn* during successful attacks against Fort Morgan, rebel gunboats, and the ram *Tennessee* in Mobile Bay, 5 August 1864. Stationed in the immediate vicinity of the shell whips, which were twice cleared of men by bursting shells, Mifflin remained steadfast at his post and performed his duties in the powder division throughout the furious action which resulted in the surrender of the prize ram *Tennessee* and in the damaging and destruction of batteries at Fort Morgan.

905 ◆ MILES, NELSON APPLETON

Rank: Colonel (highest rank: Lieutenant General Ret.)
Service: U.S. Army
Birthday: 8 August 1839
Place of Birth: Westminster, Worcester County, Massachusetts
Date of Death: 15 May 1925
Place of Death: Washington, D.C.
Cemetery: Arlington National Cemetery (3-1873) (MH)—Arlington, Virginia
Entered Service at: Roxbury, Suffolk County, Massachusetts
Unit: 61st New York Infantry
Battle or Place of Action: Chancellorsville, Virginia
Date of Action: 2-3 May 1863
Date of Issue: 23 July 1892
Citation: Distinguished gallantry while holding with his command an advanced position against repeated assaults by a strong force of the enemy; was severely wounded.

906 ◆ MILLER, ANDREW

Rank: Sergeant
Service: U.S. Marine Corps
Birthday: 1836
Place of Birth: Germany
Entered Service at: Washington, D.C.
Unit: U.S.S. *Richmond*
Battle or Place of Action: Mobile Bay, Alabama
Date of Action: 5 August 1864
G.O. Number, Date: 45, 31 December 1864

Citation: As a captain of a gun on board the U.S.S. *Richmond* during action against rebel forts and gunboats and with the ram *Tennessee* in Mobile Bay, 5 August 1864. Despite damage to his ship and the loss of several men on board as enemy fire raked her desks, Sgt. Miller fought his gun with skill and courage throughout the furious two-hour battle which resulted in the surrender of the rebel ram *Tennessee* and in the damaging and destruction of batteries at Fort Morgan.

907 ◆ MILLER, FRANK

Rank: Private
Service: U.S. Army
Birthday: 1848
Place of Birth: New York
Date of Death: 12 September 1903
Place of Death: San Francisco, California
Cemetery: unknown cemetery—San Francisco, California
Entered Service at: Jamaica, Queens County, New York
Unit: Company M, 2d New York Cavalry
Battle or Place of Action: Deatonsville (Sailor's Creek), Virginia
Date of Action: 6 April 1865
Date of Issue: 24 April 1865
Citation: Capture of flag of 25th Battalion Virginia Infantry (C.S.A.); was taken prisoner, but successfully retained his trophy until recaptured.

908 ◆ MILLER, HENRY AUGUST

Rank: Captain
Service: U.S. Army
Birthday: 22 March 1839
Place of Birth: Germany
te of Death: 12 June 1919
Place of Death: Urbana, Illinois
Cemetery: Mount Hope Cemetery—Champaign, Illinois
Entered Service at: Decatur, Macon County, Illinois
Unit: Company B, 8th Illinois Infantry
Battle or Place of Action: Fort Blakely, Alabama
Date of Action: 9 April 1865
Date of Issue: 8 June 1865
Citation: Capture of flag.

909 ◆ MILLER, JACOB C.

Rank: Private (highest rank: Sergeant)
Service: U.S. Army
Birthday: 4 August 1840
Place of Birth: Bellevue, Huron County, Ohio
Date of Death: 13 January 1917
Place of Death: Omaha, Nebraska
Cemetery: Cedar Dale Cemetery (MH)—Papillon, Nebraska
Entered Service at: Elgin, Kane County, Illinois
Unit: Company G, 113th Illinois Infantry
Battle or Place of Action: Vicksburg, Mississippi
Date of Action: 22 May 1863
Date of Issue: 20 August 1894
Citation: Gallantry in the charge of the "volunteer storming party."

910 ◆ MILLER, JAMES

Rank: Quartermaster (highest rank: Acting Master's Mate)
Service: U.S. Navy
Birthday: 21 September 1836
Place of Birth: Denmark
Date of Death: 4 March 1914
Place of Death: Philadelphia, Pennsylvania
Cemetery: unknown cemetery—Philadelphia, Pennsylvania
Entered Service at: Boston, Suffolk County, Massachusetts
Unit: U.S. Steam Gunboat *Marblehead*
Battle or Place of Action: off Legareville, John's Island, Stono River, South Carolina
Date of Action: 25 December 1863
G.O. Number, Date: 32, 16 April 1864
Date of Presentation: July 1864
Place of Presentation: Presented by Rear Adm. John A. Dahlgren on his flagship
Citation: Served as quartermaster on board the U.S. steam gunboat *Marblehead* off Legareville, Stono River, 25 December 1863, during an engagement with the enemy on John's Island. Acting courageously under the fierce hostile fire, Miller behaved gallantly throughout the engagement, which resulted in the enemy's withdrawal and abandonment of his arms.

911 ◆ MILLER, JAMES P.

Rank: Private
Service: U.S. Army
Birthday: 29 April 1834
Place of Birth: Franklin, Warren County, Ohio
Date of Death: 2 July 1918
Cemetery: Greenwood Cemetery (MH)—York, Nebraska
Entered Service at: Henry County, Iowa
Unit: Company D, 4th Iowa Cavalry
Battle or Place of Action: Selma, Alabama
Date of Action: 2 April 1865
Date of Issue: 17 June 1865
Citation: Capture of standard of 12th Mississippi Cavalry (C.S.A.).

912 ◆ MILLER, JOHN

True Name: Fey, Henry
Rank: Private
Service: U.S. Army
Birthday: 1839
Place of Birth: Kurhessen, Germany
Date of Death: 8 March 1882
Place of Death: Philadelphia, Pennsylvania
Cemetery: Glenwood Memorial Gardens Cemetery—Broomall, Pennsylvania
Entered Service at: Rochester, Monroe County, New York
Unit: Company H, 8th New York Cavalry

Battle or Place of Action: Waynesboro, Virginia
Date of Action: 2 March 1865
Date of Issue: 26 March 1865
Citation: Capture of flag.

913 ◆ MILLER, JOHN G.

Rank: Corporal (highest rank: Sergeant)
Service: U.S. Army
Birthday: 1841
Place of Birth: Germany
Date of Death: 11 June 1909
Place of Death: Freemont, Ohio
Cemetery: St. Mary's Cemetery—Champaign, Illinois
Entered Service at: Camp Dennison, Hamilton County, Ohio
Unit: Company G, 8th Ohio Infantry
Battle or Place of Action: Gettysburg, Pennsylvania
Date of Action: 3 July 1863
Date of Issue: 1 December 1864
Citation: Capture of two flags.

914 ◆ MILLER, WILLIAM EDWARD

Rank: Captain
Service: U.S. Army
Birthday: 5 February 1836
Place of Birth: West Hill, Cumberland County, Pennsylvania
Date of Death: 10 December 1919
Cemetery: Gettysburg National Military Park (OFF-8) (MH) —Gettysburg, Pennsylvania
Entered Service at: Newville, Cumberland County, Pennsylvania
Unit: Company H, 3d Pennsylvania Cavalry
Battle or Place of Action: Gettysburg, Pennsylvania
Date of Action: 3 July 1863
Date of Issue: 21 July 1897
Citation: Without orders, led a charge of his squadron upon the flank of the enemy, checked his attack, and cut off and dispersed the rear of his column.

915 ◆ MILLIKEN, DANIEL

Rank: Quarter Gunner
Service: U.S. Navy
Birthday: 1838
Place of Birth: Saco, York County, Maine
Entered Service at: New York, New York
Unit: U.S.S. *New Ironsides*
Battle or Place of Action: Fort Fisher, North Carolina
Date of Action: 24-25 December 1864 & 13-15 January 1865
G.O. Number, Date: 59, 22 June 1865
Citation: Milliken served on board the U.S.S. *New Ironsides* during the action in several attacks on Fort Fisher, 24 and 25 December 1864; and 13, 14 and 15 January 1865. The ship steamed in and took the lead in the ironclad division close inshore and immediately opened its starboard battery in a barrage of well-directed fire to cause several fires and explosions and dismount several guns during the first two days of fighting. Taken under fire as she steamed into position on 13 January, the *New Ironsides* fought all day and took on ammunition at night despite severe weather conditions. When the enemy came out of his bombproofs to defend the fort against the storming party, the ship's battery disabled nearly every gun on the fort facing the shore before the cease-fire orders were given by the flagship.

916 ◆ MILLS, CHARLES

Rank: Seaman
Service: U.S. Navy
Birthday: September 1840
Place of Birth: Ulster, Ulster County, New York
Entered Service at: Brooklyn, Kings County, New York
Unit: U.S.S. *Minnesota*
Battle or Place of Action: Fort Fisher, North Carolina
Date of Action: 15 January 1865
G.O. Number, Date: 59, 22 June 1865
Citation: On board the U.S.S. *Minnesota*, in action during the assault on Fort Fisher, 15 January 1865. Landing on the beach with the assaulting party from his ship, Mills charged up the palisades and, when more than two-thirds of the men became seized with panic and retreated on the run, risked his life to remain with a wounded officer. With the enemy concentrating his fire on the group, he waited until after dark before assisting the wounded officer from the field.

917 ◆ MILLS, FRANK W.

Rank: Sergeant (highest rank: First Sergeant)
Service: U.S. Army
Birthday: 5 August 1845
Place of Birth: Middletown, Orange County, New York
Date of Death: 25 November 1923
Place of Death: Pittsburgh, Pennsylvania
Cemetery: St. John's Reformed Church Cemetery (MH)—Chicore, Pennsylvania
Entered Service at: Middletown, Orange County, New York
Unit: Company C, 1st New York Mounted Rifles
Battle or Place of Action: Sandy Cross Roads, North Carolina
Date of Action: 4 September 1862
Date of Issue: 2 April 1898
Citation: While scouting, this soldier, in command of an advance of but three or four men, came upon the enemy, and charged them without orders, the rest of the troops following, the whole force of the enemy, 120 men, being captured.

918 ◆ MINDIL, GEORGE WASHINGTON

Rank: Captain (highest rank: Brevet Major General)
Service: U.S. Army
Birthday: 9 August 1843
Place of Birth: near Frankfort, Germany
Date of Death: 20 July 1907

Cemetery: Arlington National Cemetery (3-1568)—Arlington, Virginia
Entered Service at: Philadelphia, Philadelphia County, Pennsylvania
Unit: Company I, 61st Pennsylvania Infantry
Battle or Place of Action: Williamsburg, Virginia
Date of Action: 5 May 1862
Date of Issue: 25 October 1893
Citation: As aide-de-camp led the charge with a part of a regiment, pierced the enemy's center, silenced some of his artillery, and, getting in his rear, caused him to abandon his position.

919 ◆ MITCHELL, ALEXANDER H.

Rank: First Lieutenant (highest rank: Captain)
Service: U.S. Army
Birthday: 13 November 1840
Place of Birth: Perrysville, Allegheny County, Pennsylvania
Date of Death: 17 March 1913
Cemetery: Arlington National Cemetery (3-2515)—Arlington, Virginia
Entered Service at: Hamilton, Jefferson County, Pennsylvania
Unit: Company A, 105th Pennsylvania Infantry
Battle or Place of Action: Spotsylvania, Virginia
Date of Action: 12 May 1864
Date of Issue: 27 March 1890
Citation: Capture of flag of 18th North Carolina Infantry (C.S.A.), in a personal encounter with the color bearer.

920 ◆ MITCHELL, THEODORE

Rank: Private
Service: U.S. Army
Birthday: 5 May 1835
Place of Birth: Tarentum, Allegheny County, Pennsylvania
Date of Death: 2 March 1910
Place of Death: Cleveland, Ohio
Cemetery: Woodland Cemetery (MH)—Cleveland, Ohio
Entered Service at: Pittsburgh, Allegheny County, Pennsylvania
Unit: Company C, 61st Pennsylvania Infantry
Battle or Place of Action: Petersburg, Virginia
Date of Action: 2 April 1865
Date of Issue: 10 May 1865
Citation: Capture of flag of the Tennessee Brigade (C.S.A.).

921 ◆ MOFFITT, JOHN HENRY

Rank: Corporal (highest rank: Sergeant)
Service: U.S. Army
Birthday: 8 January 1843
Place of Birth: Chazy, Clinton County, New York
Date of Death: 14 August 1926
Place of Death: Plattsburg, New York
Cemetery: Mount Carmel Cemetery—Plattsburg, New York
Entered Service at: Plattsburgh, Clinton County, New York
Unit: Company C, 16th New York Infantry
Battle or Place of Action: Gaines' Mill, Virginia
Date of Action: 27 June 1862
Date of Issue: 3 March 1891
Citation: Voluntarily took up the regimental colors after several color bearers had been shot down and carried them until himself wounded.

922 ◆ MOLBONE, ARCHIBALD

True Name: Malbourne, Archibald
Rank: Sergeant
Service: U.S. Army
Birthday: 3 May 1840
Place of Birth: West Greenwich, Rhode Island
Date of Death: 28 February 1912
Cemetery: Bennett Gardner Cemetery (MH)—Scituate, Massachusetts
Entered Service at: Johnston, Providence County, Rhode Island
Unit: Company G, 1st Rhode Island Light Artillery
Battle or Place of Action: Petersburg, Virginia
Date of Action: 2 April 1865
Date of Issue: 20 June 1866
Citation: Was one of a detachment of 20 picked artillerymen who voluntarily accompanied an infantry assaulting party and who turned upon the enemy the guns captured in the assault.

923 ◆ MOLLOY, HUGH

Rank: Ordinary Seaman
Service: U.S. Navy
Birthday: 25 September 1841
Place of Birth: County Wexford, Ireland
Date of Death: 8 March 1922
Place of Death: Chicago, Illinois
Cemetery: Calvary Cemetery—Evanston, Illinois
Entered Service at: Joliet, Will County, Illinois
Unit: U.S.S. *Fort Hindman*
Battle or Place of Action: near Harrisonburg, Louisiana
Date of Action: 2 March 1864
G.O. Number, Date: 32, 16 April 1864
Citation: Served on board the U.S.S. *Fort Hindman* during the engagement near Harrisonburg, La., 2 March 1864. Following a shellburst which mortally wounded the first sponger, who dropped the sponge out of the forecastle port, Molloy jumped out of the port to the forecastle, recovered the sponge and sponged and loaded the gun for the remainder of the action from his exposed position, despite the extreme danger to his person from the raking fire of enemy musketry.

924 ◆ MONAGHAN, PATRICK H.

Rank: Corporal (highest rank: Lieutenant Colonel)
Service: U.S. Army
Birthday: 19 November 1843
Place of Birth: Ireland
Date of Death: 22 October 1916

Cemetery: St. Joseph's Cemetery—Girardville, Pennsylvania
Entered Service at: Minersville, Schuylkill County, Pennsylvania
Unit: Company F, 48th Pennsylvania Infantry
Battle or Place of Action: Petersburg, Virginia
Date of Action: 17 June 1864
Date of Issue: 1 December 1864
Citation: Recapture of colors of 7th New York Heavy Artillery.

925 ◆ MONTGOMERY, ROBERT WILLIAM

Rank: Captain of the Afterguard
Service: U.S. Navy
Birthday: 1838
Place of Birth: Ireland
Date of Death: 1898
Place of Death: Liverpool, England
Entered Service at: Norwich, New London County, Connecticut
Unit: U.S.S. *Agawam*
Battle or Place of Action: Fort Fisher, North Carolina
Date of Action: 23 December 1864
G.O. Number, Date: 45, 31 December 1864
Date of Presentation: 12 May 1865
Place of Presentation: off New Bern, NC, on board the U.S.S. *Agawam*
Citation: Montgomery on board the U.S.S. *Agawam* as one of a volunteer crew of a powder boat which was exploded near Fort Fisher, 23 December 1864. The powder boat, towed in by the *Wilderness* to prevent detection by the enemy, cast off and slowly steamed to within 300 yards of the beach. After fuses and fires had been lit and a second anchor with short scope let go to assure the boat's tailing inshore, the crew boarded the *Wilderness* and proceeded a distance of 12 miles from shore. Less than two hours later the explosion took place, and the following day fires were observed still burning at the forts.

926 ◆ MOORE, CHARLES

Rank: Seaman
Service: U.S. Navy
Birthday: 1835
Place of Birth: Holland
Date of Death: 30 March 1891
Place of Death: Long Island City, New York
Cemetery: St. Michael's Cemetery—East Elmhurst, New York
Entered Service at: Gibraltar
Unit: U.S.S. *Kearsarge*
Battle or Place of Action: off Cherbourg, France
Date of Action: 19 June 1864
G.O. Number, Date: 45, 31 December 1864
Citation: Served as seaman on board the U.S.S. *Kearsarge* when she destroyed the *Alabama* off Cherbourg, France, 19 June 1864. Acting as sponger and loader on the 11-inch pivot gun of the second division during this bitter engagement, Moore exhibited marked coolness and good conduct and was highly recommended for gallantry under fire by the divisional officer.

927 ◆ MOORE, CHARLES

Rank: Landsman
Service: U.S. Navy
Birthday: 1839
Place of Birth: Ireland
Entered Service at: New York, New York
Unit: U.S. Steam Gunboat *Marblehead*
Battle or Place of Action: off Legareville, John's Island, Stono River, South Carolina
Date of Action: 25 December 1863
G.O. Number, Date: 32, 16 April 1864
Citation: Served on board the U.S. steam gunboat *Marblehead* off Legareville, Stono River, 25 December 1863, during an engagement with the enemy on John's Island. Wounded in the fierce battle, Moore returned to his quarters until so exhausted by loss of blood that he had to be taken below. This engagement resulted in the enemy's abandonment of his positions, leaving a caisson and one gun behind.

928 ◆ MOORE, DANIEL B.

Rank: Corporal (highest rank: Brevet Captain)
Service: U.S. Army
Birthday: 12 June 1838
Place of Birth: Mifflin, Iowa County, Wisconsin
Date of Death: 2 July 1914
Place of Death: Mifflin, Wisconsin
Cemetery: Graceland Cemetery—Mineral Point, Wisconsin
Entered Service at: Mifflin, Iowa County, Wisconsin
Unit: Company E, 11th Wisconsin Infantry
Battle or Place of Action: Fort Blakely, Alabama
Date of Action: 9 April 1865
Date of Issue: 8 August 1900
Citation: At the risk of his own life saved the life of an officer who had been shot down and overpowered by superior umbers.

929 ◆ MOORE, GEORGE

Rank: Seaman
Service: U.S. Navy
Birthday: 1838
Place of Birth: Philadelphia, Philadelphia County, Pennsylvania
Entered Service at: Boston, Suffolk County, Massachusetts
Unit: U.S.S. *Rhode Island*
Battle or Place of Action: off Cape Hatteras, North Carolina
Date of Action: 30 December 1862
G.O. Number, Date: 59, 22 June 1865
Citation: Served on board the U.S.S. *Rhode Island* which was engaged in saving lives of the officers and crew of the *Monitor*, 30 December 1862. Participating in the hazardous task of rescuing the officers and crew of the sinking *Monitor*,

Moore, after rescuing several of the men, became separated in a heavy gale with other members of the cutter that had set out from the *Rhode Island*, and spent many hours in the small boat at the mercy of the weather and high seas until finally picked up by a schooner 50 miles east of Cape Hatteras.

930 ◆ MOORE, GEORGE G.

Rank: Private
Service: U.S. Army
Birthday: 2 July 1844
Place of Birth: Tyler County, West Virginia
Date of Death: 26 November 1925
Place of Death: Greeley, Colorado
Cemetery: Eaton Cemetery (MH)—Eaton, Colorado
Entered Service at: Parkersburg, Wood County, West Virginia
Unit: Company D, 11th West Virginia Infantry
Battle or Place of Action: Fisher's Hill, Virginia
Date of Action: 22 September 1864
Date of Issue: 6 October 1864
Citation: Capture of flag.

931 ◆ MOORE, WILBUR F.

Rank: Private
Service: U.S. Army
Birthday: 1840
Place of Birth: Lebanon, St. Clair County, Illinois
Date of Death: 9 December 1924
Cemetery: Forest Hills Cemetery (MH)—Kansas City, Missouri
Entered Service at: Lebanon, St. Clair County, Illinois
Unit: Company C, 117th Illinois Infantry
Battle or Place of Action: Nashville, Tennessee
Date of Action: 16 December 1864
Date of Issue: 22 February 1865
Citation: Captured the flag of a Confederate battery while far in advance of the Union lines.

932 ◆ MOORE, WILLIAM

Rank: Boatswain's Mate
Service: U.S. Navy
Birthday: 18 May 1837
Place of Birth: Boston, Suffolk County, Massachusetts
Date of Death: 16 February 1918
Place of Death: Austin, Texas
Cemetery: Oakwood Cemetery (MH)—Austin, Texas
Entered Service at: Massachusetts
Unit: U.S.S. *Benton*
Battle or Place of Action: Haines Bluff, Yazoo River, Mississippi
Date of Action: 27 December 1862
G.O. Number, Date: 32, 16 April 1864
Citation: Served as boatswain's mate on board the U.S.S. *Benton* during the attack on Haines Bluff, Yazoo River, 27 December 1862. Wounded during the hour-and-a-half engagement in which the enemy had the dead-range of the vessel and was punishing her with heavy fire, Moore served courageously in carrying lines to the shore until the Benton was ordered to withdraw.

933 ◆ MOREY, DELANO

Rank: Private
Service: U.S. Army
Birthday: 14 July 1845
Place of Birth: Licking County, Ohio
Date of Death: 24 April 1911
Cemetery: Grove Cemetery (MH)—Canton, Ohio
Entered Service at: Kenton, Hardin County, Ohio
Unit: Company B, 82d Ohio Infantry
Battle or Place of Action: McDowell, Virginia
Date of Action: 8 May 1862
Date of Issue: 14 August 1893
Citation: After the charge of the command had been repulsed, he rushed forward alone with an empty gun and captured two of the enemy's sharpshooters.
Notes: POW

934 ◆ MORFORD, JEROME

Rank: Private
Service: U.S. Army
Birthday: 13 June 1841
Place of Birth: Mercer County, Pennsylvania
Date of Death: 11 June 1910
Place of Death: Seattle, Washington
Cemetery: Riverton Crest Cemetery—Seattle, Washington
Entered Service at: Bridgers County, Illinois
Unit: Company K, 55th Illinois Infantry
Battle or Place of Action: Vicksburg, Mississippi
Date of Action: 22 May 1863
Date of Issue: 2 September 1893
Citation: Gallantry in the charge of the "volunteer storming party."

935 ◆ MORGAN, JAMES H.

True Name: Creevey, James H.
Rank: Captain of the Top
Service: U.S. Navy
Birthday: 1840
Place of Birth: New York
Date of Death: 6 April 1877
Cemetery: 1st Calvary Cemetery—Woodside, New York
Entered Service at: New York, New York
Unit: U.S.S. *Richmond*
Battle or Place of Action: Mobile Bay, Alabama
Date of Action: 5 August 1864
G.O. Number, Date: 45, 31 December 1864
Citation: As a captain of a gun on board the U.S.S. *Richmond* during action against rebel forts and gunboats and with the ram *Tennessee* in Mobile Bay, 5 August 1864. Despite damage to his ship and the loss of several men on board as enemy fire raked her decks, Morgan fought his gun with skill and courage throughout the furious two-hour battle

which resulted in the surrender of the rebel ram *Tennessee* and in the damaging and destruction of batteries at Fort Morgan.

936 ◆ *MORGAN, LEWIS

Rank: Private (highest rank: Sergeant)
Service: U.S. Army
Birthday: 1836
Place of Birth: Delaware County, Ohio
Date of Death: 27 October 1864
Place of Death: Hatchers Run, Virginia
Entered Service at: Delaware County, Ohio
Unit: Company I, 4th Ohio Infantry
Battle or Place of Action: Spotsylvania, Virginia
Date of Action: 12 May 1864
Date of Issue: 1 December 1864
Citation: Capture of flag from the enemy's works.

937 ◆ MORGAN, RICHARD H.

Rank: Corporal
Service: U.S. Army
Birthday: 2 April 1840
Place of Birth: Dubois County, Indiana
Date of Death: 17 December 1916
Cemetery: Memory Cemetery (MH)—New Market, Iowa
Entered Service at: Taylor, Freemont County, Iowa
Unit: Company A, 4th Iowa Cavalry
Battle or Place of Action: Columbus, Georgia
Date of Action: 16 April 1865
Date of Issue: 17 June 1865
Citation: Capture of flag inside the enemy's works, contesting for its possession with its bearer.

938 ◆ MORRILL, WALTER GOODALE

Rank: Captain (highest rank: Colonel)
Service: U.S. Army
Birthday: 30 November 1840
Place of Birth: Williamsburg, Maine
Date of Death: 3 March 1935
Cemetery: Village Cemetery (MH)—Pittsfield, Maine
Entered Service at: Brownville, Piscataquis County, Maine
Unit: Company B, 20th Maine Infantry
Battle or Place of Action: Rappahannock Station, Virginia
Date of Action: 7 November 1863
Date of Issue: 5 April 1898
Citation: Learning that an assault was to be made upon the enemy's works by other troops, this officer voluntarily joined the storming party with about 50 men of his regiment, and by his dash and gallantry rendered effective service in the assault.

939 ◆ MORRIS, WILLIAM POWERS

Rank: Sergeant
Service: U.S. Army
Birthday: 18 December 1844
Place of Birth: Philadelphia, Philadelphia County, Pennsylvania
Date of Death: 8 December 1916
Place of Death: Banning, California
Cemetery: Banning Cabazon Cemetery—Banning, California
Entered Service at: Philadelphia, Philadelphia County, Pennsylvania
Unit: Company C, 1st New York (Lincoln) Cavalry
Battle or Place of Action: Deatonsville (Sailor's Creek), Virginia
Date of Action: 6 April 1865
Date of Issue: 3 May 1865
Citation: Capture of flag of 40th Virginia Infantry (C.S.A.).

940 ◆ MORRISON, FRANCIS

Rank: Private
Service: U.S. Army
Birthday: 15 January 1845
Place of Birth: Ohiopyle, Fayette County, Pennsylvania
Date of Death: 30 April 1913
Place of Death: Hopwood, Pennsylvania
Cemetery: Sugar Grove Cemetery (MH)—Ohiopyle, Pennsylvania
Entered Service at: Drakestown, Pennsylvania
Unit: Company H, 85th Pennsylvania infantry
Battle or Place of Action: Bermuda Hundred, Virginia
Date of Action: 17 June 1864
Date of Issue: 2 August 1897
Citation: Voluntarily exposed himself to a heavy fire to bring off a wounded comrade.

941 ◆ MORRISON, JOHN G.

Rank: Coxswain
Service: U.S. Navy
Birthday: 3 November 1842
Place of Birth: Ireland
Date of Death: 9 June 1897
Cemetery: Cypress Hills Cemetery (Private) (MH)—Brooklyn, New York
Entered Service at: Lansingburg, Tompkins County, New York
Unit: U.S.S. *Carondelet*
Battle or Place of Action: Yazoo River, Mississippi
Date of Action: 15 July 1862
G.O. Number, Date: 59, 22 June 1865
Citation: Served as coxswain on board the U.S.S. *Carondelet*, Morrison was commended for meritorious conduct in general and especially for his heroic conduct and his inspiring example to the crew in the engagement with the rebel ram *Arkansas*, Yazoo River, 15 July 1862. When the *Carondelet* was badly cut up, several of her crew killed, many wounded, and others almost suffocated from the effects of escaped steam, Morrison was the leader when boarders were called on deck and the first to return to the guns and give the ram a broadside as she passed. His presence of mind in time of battle or trial is reported as always conspicuous and encouraging.

942 ◆ MORSE, BENJAMIN

Rank: Private (highest rank: Corporal)
Service: U.S. Army
Birthday: 20 September 1844
Place of Birth: Livingston, Columbia County, New York
Date of Death: 24 November 1908
Cemetery: Oakwood Cemetery—Lowell, Michigan
Entered Service at: Grand Rapids, Kent County, Michigan
Unit: Company C, 3d Michigan Infantry
Battle or Place of Action: Spotsylvania, Virginia
Date of Action: 12 May 1864
Date of Issue: 24 February 1891
Citation: Capture of colors of 4th Georgia Battery (C.S.A.).
Notes: POW

943 ◆ MORSE, CHARLES E.

Rank: Sergeant
Service: U.S. Army
Birthday: 5 May 1841
Place of Birth: France
Date of Death: 31 August 1920
Place of Death: Bath, New York
Cemetery: Bath National Cemetery (J-4-24) (MH)—Bath, New York
Entered Service at: New York
Unit: Company I, 62d New York Infantry
Battle or Place of Action: Wilderness Campaign, Virginia
Date of Action: 5 May 1864
Date of Issue: 14 January 1890
Citation: Voluntarily rushed back into the enemy's lines, took the colors from the color sergeant, who was mortally wounded, and, although himself wounded, carried them through the fight.

944 ◆ MORTON, CHARLES W.

Rank: Boatswain's Mate
Service: U.S. Navy
Birthday: 1836
Place of Birth: Ireland
Date of Death: 4 August 1899
Place of Death: Portsmouth, Virginia
Cemetery: U.S. Naval Hospital Cemetery (MH)—Portsmouth, Virginia
Entered Service at: Maryland
Unit: U.S.S. *Benton*
Battle or Place of Action: Yazoo River Expedition, Mississippi
Date of Action: 23-27 December 1863
G.O. Number, Date: 11, 3 April 1863
Citation: Served as boatswain's mate on board the U.S.S. *Benton* during the Yazoo River Expedition, 23 to 27 December 1863. Taking part in the hour-and-a-half engagement with the enemy at Drumgould's Bluff, 27 December, Morton served courageously throughout the battle against the hostile forces, who had the dead-range of the vessel and were punishing her with heavy fire, until the *Benton* was ordered to withdraw.

945 ◆ MOSTOLLER, JOHN WILLIAM

Rank: Private
Service: U.S. Army
Birthday: 14 January 1843
Place of Birth: Stoystown, Somerset County, Pennsylvania
Date of Death: 5 December 1925
Place of Death: Somerset County, Pennsylvania
Cemetery: I.O.O.F. Cemetery—Stoystown, Pennsylvania
Entered Service at: Stoystown, Somerset County, Pennsylvania
Unit: Company B, 54th Pennsylvania Infantry
Battle or Place of Action: Lynchburg, Virginia
Date of Action: 18 June 1864
Date of Issue: 27 December 1894
Citation: Voluntarily led a charge on a Confederate battery (the officers of the company being disabled) and compelled its hasty removal.

946 ◆ MULHOLLAND, ST. CLAIR AGUSTIN

Rank: Major (highest rank: Brevet Major General)
Service: U.S. Army
Birthday: 1 April 1839
Place of Birth: Lisburn, County Antrim, Ireland
Date of Death: 17 February 1910
Place of Death: Philadelphia, Pennsylvania
Cemetery: Old Cathedral Cemetery—Philadelphia, Pennsylvania
Entered Service at: Philadelphia, Philadelphia County, Pennsylvania
Unit: 116th Pennsylvania Infantry
Battle or Place of Action: Chancellorsville, Virginia
Date of Action: 4-5 May 1863
Date of Presentation: 26 March 1895
Place of Presentation: Presented by Ass. Sec. of War Doe
Citation: In command of the picket line, held the enemy in check all night to cover the retreat of the Army.

947 ◆ MULLEN, PATRICK✚

Rank: Boatswain's Mate
Service: U.S. Navy
Birthday: 6 May 1844
Place of Birth: Ireland
Date of Death: 14 February 1897
Cemetery: New Cathedral Cemetery—Baltimore, Maryland
Entered Service at: Baltimore, Baltimore County, Maryland
Unit: U.S.S. *Wyandank*
Battle or Place of Action: Mattox Creek, Virginia
Date of Action: 17 March 1865
G.O. Number, Date: 59, 22 June 1865
Citation: **First Award** Served as boatswain's mate on board the U.S.S. *Wyandank* during a boat expedition up Mattox Creek, 17 March 1865. Rendering gallant assistance to his commanding officer, Mullen, lying on his back, loaded the

howitzer and then fired so carefully as to kill and wound many rebels, causing their retreat.
Notes: ✢Double Awardee: *see also* Interim 1865-1870

948 ◆ MUNDELL, WALTER L.
Rank: Corporal
Service: U.S. Army
Birthday: 4 August 1838
Place of Birth: Michigan
Date of Death: 20 April 1900
Place of Death: Fowler, Michigan
Cemetery: Oak Ridge Cemetery—Bengal Township, Michigan
Entered Service at: Dallas, Michigan
Unit: Company E, 5th Michigan Infantry
Battle or Place of Action: Deatonsville (Sailor's Creek), Virginia
Date of Action: 6 April 1865
Date of Issue: 10 May 1865
Citation: Capture of flag.

949 ◆ MUNSELL, HARVEY MAY
Rank: Sergeant (highest rank: Captain)
Service: U.S. Army
Birthday: 5 January 1843
Place of Birth: Painted Post, Steuben County, New York
Date of Death: 9 February 1913
Place of Death: Mount Vernon, New York
Cemetery: Mount Auburn Cemetery (MH)—Cambridge, Massachusetts
Entered Service at: Philadelphia, Philadelphia County, Pennsylvania
Unit: Company A, 99th Pennsylvania Infantry
Battle or Place of Action: Gettysburg, Pennsylvania
Date of Action: 1-3 July 1863
Date of Issue: 5 February 1866
Citation: Gallant and courageous conduct as color bearer. (This noncommissioned officer carried the colors of his regiment through 13 engagements.)
Notes: POW

950 ◆ MURPHY, CHARLES JOSEPH
Rank: First Lieutenant & Quartermaster (highest rank: Colonel)
Service: U.S. Army
Birthday: 3 June 1832
Place of Birth: Stockport, Greater Manchester County, England
Date of Death: 29 May 1921
Place of Death: New York, New York
Cemetery: Calvary Cemetery—Woodside, New York
Entered Service at: New York, New York
Unit: 38th New York Infantry
Battle or Place of Action: Bull Run, Virginia
Date of Action: 21 July 1861
Date of Issue: 5 April 1898
Citation: Took a rifle and voluntarily fought with his regiment in the ranks; when the regiment was forced back, voluntarily remained on the field caring for the wounded and was there taken prisoner.
Notes: POW

951 ◆ MURPHY, DANIEL J.
Rank: Sergeant (highest rank: Second Lieutenant)
Service: U.S. Army
Birthday: 1843
Place of Birth: Philadelphia, Philadelphia County, Pennsylvania
Date of Death: 19 September 1870
Cemetery: Oakwood Cemetery (MH)—Jefferson, Texas
Entered Service at: Lowell, Middlesex County, Massachusetts
Unit: Company F, 19th Massachusetts Infantry
Battle or Place of Action: Hatcher's Run, Virginia
Date of Action: 27 October 1864
Date of Issue: 1 December 1864
Citation: Capture of flag of 47th North Carolina Infantry (C.S.A.).

952 ◆ MURPHY, DENNIS J. F.
Rank: Sergeant
Service: U.S. Army
Birthday: 28 July 1830
Place of Birth: County Cork, Ireland
Date of Death: 19 June 1901
Place of Death: Green Bay, Wisconsin
Cemetery: Allouez Catholic Cemetery (MH)—Green Bay, Wisconsin
Entered Service at: Lowell, Middlesex County, Massachusetts
Unit: Company F, 14th Wisconsin Infantry
Battle or Place of Action: Corinth, Mississippi
Date of Action: 3 October 1862
Date of Issue: 22 January 1892
Citation: Although wounded three times, carried the colors throughout the conflict.

953 ◆ MURPHY, JAMES T.
Rank: Private (highest rank: Sergeant)
Service: U.S. Army
Birthday: 1839
Place of Birth: Canada
Date of Death: 11 January 1904
Place of Death: New Haven, Connecticut
Cemetery: St. Bernard's Cemetery (MH)—New Haven, Connecticut
Entered Service at: New Haven, New Haven County, Connecticut
Unit: Company L, 1st Connecticut Artillery
Battle or Place of Action: Petersburg, Virginia
Date of Action: 25 March 1865
Date of Issue: 29 October 1886

Citation: A piece of artillery having been silenced by the enemy, this soldier voluntarily assisted in working the piece, conducting himself throughout the engagement in a gallant and fearless manner.

954 ◆ MURPHY, JOHN P.

Rank: Private (highest rank: First Sergeant)
Service: U.S. Army
Birthday: 24 June 1844
Place of Birth: Killarney, County Kerry, Ireland
Date of Death: 1 January 1911
Place of Death: Cincinnati, Ohio
Cemetery: Spring Grove Cemetery—Cincinnati, Ohio
Entered Service at: Cincinnati, Hamilton County, Ohio
Unit: Company K, 5th Ohio Infantry
Battle or Place of Action: Antietam, Maryland
Date of Action: 17 September 1862
Date of Issue: 11 September 1866
Citation: Capture of flag of 13th Alabama Infantry (C.S.A.).

955 ◆ MURPHY, MICHAEL C.

Rank: Lieutenant Colonel (highest rank: Colonel)
Service: U.S. Army
Birthday: 1836
Place of Birth: Limerick, County Limerick, Ireland
Date of Death: 4 March 1903
Cemetery: Kensico Cemetery—Valhalla, New York
Entered Service at: New York, New York
Unit: 170th New York Infantry
Battle or Place of Action: North Anna River, Virginia
Date of Action: 24 May 1864
Date of Issue: 15 January 1897
Citation: This officer, commanding the regiment, kept it on the field exposed to the fire of the enemy for three hours without being able to fire one shot in return because of the ammunition being exhausted.

956 ◆ MURPHY, PATRICK

Rank: Boatswain's Mate (highest rank: Chief Boatswain's Mate)
Service: U.S. Navy
Birthday: 1823
Place of Birth: Ireland
Date of Death: 1 December 1896
Entered Service at: New York, New York
Unit: U.S.S. *Metacomet*
Battle or Place of Action: Mobile Bay, Alabama
Date of Action: 5 August 1864
G.O. Number, Date: 84, 3 October 1867
Citation: Served as boatswain's mate on board the U.S.S. *Metacomet* during action against rebel forts and gunboats and with the ram *Tennessee* in Mobile Bay, 5 August 1864. Despite damage to his ship and the loss of several men on board as enemy fire raked her decks, Murphy performed his duties with skill and courage throughout a furious two-hour battle, which resulted in the surrender of the rebel ram *Tennessee* and in the damaging and destruction of batteries at Fort Morgan.

957 ◆ MURPHY, ROBINSON BARR

Rank: Musician
Service: U.S. Army
Birthday: 11 May 1849
Place of Birth: Oswego, Kendall County, Illinois
Date of Death: 2 October 1934
Place of Death: Washington, D.C.
Cemetery: Arlington National Cemetery (6-9749)—Arlington, Virginia
Entered Service at: Oswego, Kendall County, Illinois
Unit: Company A, 127th Illinois Infantry
Battle or Place of Action: Atlanta, Georgia
Date of Action: 28 July 1864
Date of Issue: 22 July 1890
Citation: Being orderly to the brigade commander, he voluntarily led two regiments as reinforcements into line of battle, where he had his horse shot under him.

958 ◆ MURPHY, THOMAS

Rank: Corporal
Service: U.S. Army
Place of Birth: New York, New York
Entered Service at: Brooklyn, Kings County, New York
Unit: Company K, 158th New York Infantry
Battle or Place of Action: Chapin's Farm, Virginia
Date of Action: 30 September 1864
Date of Issue: 15 October 1864
Citation: Capture of flag.

959 ◆ MURPHY, THOMAS C.

Rank: Corporal
Service: U.S. Army
Birthday: 1842
Place of Birth: Ireland
Date of Death: 31 December 1920
Cemetery: Glendale Cemetery—Washington, Illinois
Entered Service at: Pekin, Tazewell County, Illinois
Unit: Company I, 31st Illinois Infantry
Battle or Place of Action: Vicksburg, Mississippi
Date of Action: 22 May 1863
Date of Issue: 14 August 1893
Citation: Voluntarily crossed the line of heavy fire of Union and Confederate forces, carrying a message to stop the firing of one Union regiment on another.

960 ◆ MURPHY, THOMAS J.

Rank: First Sergeant
Service: U.S. Army
Birthday: 1833
Place of Birth: Ireland
Date of Death: 2 December 1901
Place of Death: High Ridge, Connecticut

Cemetery: Pound Ridge Cemetery (MH)—Pound Ridge, New York
Entered Service at: New York, New York
Unit: Company F, 146th New York Infantry
Battle or Place of Action: Five Forks, Virginia
Date of Action: 1 April 1865
Date of Issue: 10 May 1865
Citation: Capture of flag.

961 ◆ MYERS, GEORGE S.

Rank: Private
Service: U.S. Army
Birthday: 26 January 1843
Place of Birth: Fairfield, Butler County, Ohio
Date of Death: 21 August 1917
Place of Death: Hermosa Beach, California
Cemetery: Inglewood Park Cemetery—Inglewood, California
Entered Service at: Tiffin, Seneca County, Ohio
Unit: Company F, 101st Ohio Infantry
Battle or Place of Action: Chickamauga, Georgia
Date of Action: 19 September 1863
Date of Issue: 9 April 1894
Citation: Saved the regimental colors by greatest personal devotion and bravery.

962 ◆ MYERS, WILLIAM H.

True Name: Meyers, William H.
Rank: Private
Service: U.S. Army
Place of Birth: Philadelphia, Philadelphia County, Pennsylvania
Entered Service at: Baltimore, Baltimore County, Maryland
Unit: Company A, 1st Maryland Cavalry
Battle or Place of Action: Appomattox Courthouse, Virginia
Date of Action: 9 April 1865
Date of Issue: 14 June 1871
Citation: Gallantry in action; was five times wounded.

963 ◆ NASH, HENRY H.

Rank: Corporal
Service: U.S. Army
Birthday: 4 March 1842
Place of Birth: Lenawee County, Michigan
Date of Death: 30 March 1917
Place of Death: Palmyra, Michigan
Cemetery: Palmyra Cemetery (MH)—Palmyra, Michigan
Entered Service at: Adrian, Lenawee County, Michigan
Unit: Company B, 47th Ohio Infantry
Battle or Place of Action: Vicksburg, Mississippi
Date of Action: 3 May 1863
Date of Issue: 15 February 1909
Citation: Was one of a party that volunteered and attempted to run the enemy's batteries with a steam tug and two barges loaded with subsistence stores.
Notes: POW

964 ◆ NAYLOR, DAVID JOHNSON

Rank: Landsman
Service: U.S. Navy
Birthday: 14 November 1843
Place of Birth: Thompsonville, Sullivan County, New York
Date of Death: 7 February 1926
Place of Death: Potter Hill, Rhode Island
Cemetery: River Bend Cemetery (MH)—Westerly, Rhode Island
Entered Service at: New York, New York
Unit: U.S.S. *Oneida*
Battle or Place of Action: Mobile Bay, Alabama
Date of Action: 5 August 1864
G.O. Number, Date: 45, 31 December 1864
Citation: Served on board the U.S.S. *Oneida* in the engagement at Mobile Bay, 5 August 1864. Acting as powder boy at the 30-pounder Parrott rifle, Naylor had his passing box shot from his hands and knocked overboard where it fell into one of the *Galena*'s boats which was under the bow. Jumping overboard, Naylor recovered his box, returned to his station, and continued to carry out his courageous actions throughout the engagement, which resulted in the capture of the rebel ram *Tennessee* and the damaging of Fort Morgan.

965 ◆ NEAHR, ZACHARIAH C.

Rank: Private
Service: U.S. Army
Birthday: 9 December 1830
Place of Birth: Palatine, Montgomery County, New York
Date of Death: 21 July 1903
Place of Death: Canajoharie, New York
Cemetery: Canajoharie Falls Cemetery (MH)—Canajoharie, New York
Entered Service at: Canajoharie, Montgomery County, New York
Unit: Company K, 142d New York Infantry
Battle or Place of Action: Fort Fisher, North Carolina
Date of Action: 16 January 1865
Date of Issue: 11 September 1890
Citation: Voluntarily advanced with the head of the column and cut down the palisading.

966 ◆ NEIL, JOHN

Rank: Quarter Gunner (highest rank: Master-at-Arms)
Service: U.S. Navy
Birthday: 1840
Place of Birth: Newfoundland, Canada
Entered Service at: Norwich, New London County, Connecticut
Unit: U.S.S. *Agawam*
Battle or Place of Action: Fort Fisher, North Carolina
Date of Action: 23 December 1864
G.O. Number, Date: 45, 31 December 1864
Date of Presentation: 12 May 1865
Place of Presentation: off New Bern, NC, on board the U.S.S. *Agawam*

Citation: Neil served on board the U.S.S. *Agawam*, as one of a volunteer crew of a powder boat which was exploded near Fort Fisher, 23 December 1864. The powder boat, towed in by the *Wilderness* to prevent detection by the enemy, cast off and slowly steamed to within 300 yards of the beach. After fuses and fires had been lit and a second anchor with short scope let go to assure the boat's tailing inshore, the crew again boarded the *Wilderness* and proceeded a distance of 12 miles from shore. Less then two hours later the explosion took place, and the following day fires were observed still burning at the forts.

967 ◆ NEVILLE, EDWIN MICHAEL

Rank: Captain
Service: U.S. Army
Birthday: 27 January 1843
Place of Birth: Waterbury, New Haven County, Connecticut
Date of Death: 4 October 1886
Cemetery: Old St. Joseph's Cemetery (MH)—Waterbury, Connecticut
Entered Service at: Waterbury, New Haven County, Connecticut
Unit: Company C, 1st Connecticut Cavalry
Battle or Place of Action: Deatonsville (Sailor's Creek), Virginia
Date of Action: 6 April 1865
Date of Issue: 3 May 1865
Citation: Capture of flag.

968 ◆ NEWLAND, WILLIAM D.

Rank: Ordinary Seaman
Service: U.S. Navy
Birthday: 5 January 1841
Place of Birth: Medway, Norfolk County, Massachusetts
Date of Death: 1914
Cemetery: Prospect Hill Cemetery (MH)—Millis, Massachusetts
Entered Service at: Massachusetts
Unit: U.S.S. *Oneida*
Battle or Place of Action: Mobile Bay, Alabama
Date of Action: 5 August 1864
G.O. Number, Date: 45, 31 December 1864
Citation: Served on board the U.S.S. *Oneida* in the engagement at Mobile Bay, 5 August 1864. Carrying out his duties as loader of the after 11-inch gun, Newland distinguished himself on board for his good conduct and faithful discharge of his station, behaving spendidly under the fire of the enemy and throughout the battle, which resulted in the capture of the rebel ram *Tennessee* and the damaging of Fort Morgan.

969 ◆ NEWMAN, MARCELLUS J.

Rank: Private
Service: U.S. Army
Birthday: 1836
Place of Birth: Richview, Washington County, Illinois
Date of Death: 15 November 1905
Place of Death: Meeker, Oklahoma
Cemetery: Elmwood Cemetery—Centralia, Illinois
Entered Service at: Richview, Washington County, Illinois
Unit: Company B, 111th Illinois Infantry
Battle or Place of Action: Resaca, Georgia
Date of Action: 14 May 1864
Date of Issue: 13 May 1899
Citation: Voluntarily returned, in the face of a severe fire from the enemy, and rescued a wounded comrade who had been left behind as the regiment fell back.

970 ◆ NEWMAN, WILLIAM HENRY

Rank: Lieutenant (highest rank: Captain)
Service: U.S. Army
Birthday: 12 December 1838
Place of Birth: Highland Mills, Orange County, New York
Date of Death: 7 April 1917
Place of Death: Freemont Center, New York
Cemetery: Heavenly Rest Cemetery (MH)—North Branch, New York
Entered Service at: Port Jervis, Orange County, New York
Unit: Company B, 86th New York Infantry
Battle or Place of Action: Amelia Springs, Virginia
Date of Action: 6 April 1865
Date of Issue: 10 May 1865
Citation: Capture of flag.

971 ◆ NIBBE, JOHN H.

Rank: Quartermaster
Service: U.S. Navy
Birthday: 25 November 1847
Place of Birth: Germany
Date of Death: 15 June 1902
Cemetery: Ivy Green Cemetery (MH)—Bremerton, Washington
Entered Service at: New York
Unit: U.S.S. *Petrel*
Battle or Place of Action: Yazoo River, Mississippi
Date of Action: 22 April 1864
G.O. Number, Date: 59, 22 June 1865
Citation: Served as quartermaster on board the U.S.S. *Petrel* during its capture in Yazoo River, 22 April 1864. Standing his ground when a shot came through the stern, raking the gundeck and entering and exploding the boilers, when all the others had deserted the flag, Nibbe assisted in getting the wounded off the guard and proceeded to get ready to fire the ship despite the escaping steam from the boilers, at which time he was surrounded on all sides by the rebels and forced to surrender.
Notes: POW

972 ◆ NICHOLS, HENRY CLAY

Rank: Captain
Service: U.S. Army
Birthday: 30 March 1832

Place of Birth: Brandon, Rutland County, Vermont
Date of Death: 10 February 1904
Place of Death: Coventry, Vermont
Cemetery: Coventry Cemetery—Coventry, Vermont
Entered Service at: St. Albans, Franklin County, Vermont
Unit: Company E, 73d U.S. Colored Infantry
Battle or Place of Action: Fort Blakely, Alabama
Date of Action: 9 April 1865
Date of Issue: 3 August 1897
Citation: Voluntarily made a reconnaissance in advance of the line held by his regiment and, under a heavy fire, obtained information of great value.

973 ◆ NICHOLS, WILLIAM

Rank: Quartermaster
Service: U.S. Navy
Birthday: 1837
Place of Birth: New York, New York
Entered Service at: New York
Unit: U.S.S. *Brooklyn*
Battle or Place of Action: Mobile Bay, Alabama
Date of Action: 5 August 1864
G.O. Number, Date: 45, 31 December 1864
Citation: On board the U.S.S. *Brooklyn* during the successful attacks against Fort Morgan, rebel gunboats, and the ram *Tennessee*, in Mobile Bay, 5 August 1864. Despite severe damage to his ship and the loss of several men on board as enemy fire raked her decks from stem to stern, Nichols fought his gun with skill and courage throughout the furious battle which resulted in the surrender of the prize rebel ram *Tennessee* and in the damaging and destruction of batteries at Fort Morgan.

974 ◆ NIVEN, ROBERT

Rank: Second Lieutenant (highest rank: Captain)
Service: U.S. Army
Birthday: 18 December 1833
Place of Birth: Harlem, New York
Date of Death: 21 December 1921
Place of Death: Providence, Rhode Island
Cemetery: Highland Cemetery—Lakewood, Rhode Island
Entered Service at: Rochester, Monroe County, New York
Unit: Company H, 8th New York Cavalry
Battle or Place of Action: Waynesboro, Virginia
Date of Action: 2 March 1865
Date of Issue: 26 March 1865
Citation: Capture of two flags.

975 ◆ NOBLE, DANIEL

Rank: Landsman
Service: U.S. Navy
Birthday: 1840
Place of Birth: Bath County, Kentucky
Entered Service at: Chicago, Cook County, Illinois
Unit: U.S.S. *Metacomet*
Battle or Place of Action: Mobile Bay, Alabama
Date of Action: 5 August 1864
G.O. Number, Date: 71, 15 January 1866
Citation: As landsman on board the U.S.S. *Metacomet*, Noble served among the boat's crew which went to the rescue of the U.S. Monitor *Tecumseh* when that vessel was struck by a torpedo in passing enemy forts in Mobile Bay, 5 August 1864. Noble braved the enemy fire, which was said by the admiral to be "one of the most galling" he had ever seen, and aided in rescuing from death 10 of the crew of the *Tecumseh*, thereby eliciting the admiration of both friend and foe.

976 ◆ NOLAN, JOHN J.

Rank: Sergeant (highest rank: Second Lieutenant)
Service: U.S. Army
Birthday: 24 June 1842
Place of Birth: Thurles, County Tipperary, Ireland
Date of Death: 13 June 1912
Place of Death: Bronx, New York
Cemetery: St. Raymond's Cemetery—Bronx, New York
Entered Service at: Nashua, Hillsborough County, New Hampshire
Unit: Company K, 8th New Hampshire Infantry
Served as: Color Bearer
Battle or Place of Action: Georgia Landing, Louisiana
Date of Action: 27 October 1862
Date of Issue: 3 August 1897
Citation: Although prostrated by a cannon shot, refused to give up the flag which he was carrying as color bearer of his regiment and continued to carry it at the head of the regiment throughout the engagement.

977 ◆ NOLL, CONRAD

Rank: Sergeant
Service: U.S. Army
Birthday: 20 February 1836
Place of Birth: Germany
Date of Death: 26 May 1925
Place of Death: Ann Arbor, Michigan
Cemetery: Forest Hill Cemetery—Ann Arbor, Michigan
Entered Service at: Ann Arbor, Washtenaw County, Michigan
Unit: Company D, 20th Michigan Infantry
Battle or Place of Action: Spotsylvania, Virginia
Date of Action: 12 May 1864
Date of Issue: 28 July 1896
Citation: Seized the colors, the color bearer having been shot down, and gallantly fought his way out with them, though the enemy were on the left flank and rear.

978 ◆ NORTH, JASPER N.

Rank: Private
Service: U.S. Army
Birthday: 15 September 1842
Place of Birth: Ohio
Date of Death: 10 February 1918
Place of Death: Federal, Ohio

Cemetery: Rightstown Cemetery—Amesville, Ohio
Entered Service at: Amesville, Athens County, Ohio
Unit: Company D, 4th West Virginia Infantry
Battle or Place of Action: Vicksburg, Mississippi
Date of Action: 22 May 1863
Date of Issue: 27 July 1894
Citation: Gallantry in the charge of the "volunteer storming party."

979 ◆ NORTON, ELLIOTT MALLOY

Rank: Second Lieutenant (highest rank: First Lieutenant)
Service: U.S. Army
Birthday: 15 June 1834
Place of Birth: Connecticut
Date of Death: 5 January 1899
Place of Death: Carson City, Michigan
Cemetery: Liberty Street Cemetery—Alamo Township, Michigan
Entered Service at: Cooper, Michigan
Unit: Company H, 6th Michigan Cavalry
Battle or Place of Action: Deatonsville (Sailor's Creek), Virginia
Date of Action: 6 April 1865
Date of Issue: 3 May 1865
Citation: Rushed ahead of his column and captured the flag of the 44th Tennessee Infantry (C.S.A.).

980 ◆ NORTON, JOHN R.

Rank: Second Lieutenant
Service: U.S. Army
Birthday: 20 June 1830
Place of Birth: St. John's Parish, Roscommon, County Ballaugh, Ireland
Date of Death: 19 December 1905
Cemetery: St. Parick's Cemetery—Ada, Michigan
Entered Service at: Grand Rapids, Kent County, Michigan
Unit: Company M, 1st New York (Lincoln) Cavalry
Battle or Place of Action: Deatonsville (Sailor's Creek), Virginia
Date of Action: 6 April 1865
Date of Issue: 3 May 1865
Citation: Capture of flag.

981 ◆ NORTON, LLEWELLYN POWELL

Rank: Sergeant (highest rank: Sergeant Major)
Service: U.S. Army
Birthday: 11 May 1837
Place of Birth: Scott, Cortland County, New York
Date of Death: 16 February 1914
Place of Death: Homer, New York
Cemetery: Elmwood Cemetery—Preble, New York
Entered Service at: Scott, Cortland County, New York
Unit: Company L, 10th New York Cavalry
Battle or Place of Action: Deatonsville (Sailor's Creek), Virginia
Date of Action: 6 April 1865
Date of Issue: 3 July 1865
Citation: Charged the enemy and, with the assistance of Cpl. Andrew Bringle, captured a fieldpiece with two prisoners.

982 ◆ NOYES, WILLIAM W.

Rank: Private
Service: U.S. Army
Birthday: 23 April 1846
Place of Birth: Montpelier, Washington County, Vermont
Date of Death: 1 July 1910
Cemetery: Cutler Cemetery—East Montpelier, Vermont
Entered Service at: Montpelier, Washington County, Vermont
Unit: Company F, 2d Vermont Infantry
Battle or Place of Action: Spotsylvania, Virginia
Date of Action: 12 May 1864
Date of Issue: 22 March 1892
Citation: Standing upon the top of the breastworks, deliberately took aim and fired no less than 15 shots into the enemy's lines, but a few yards away.

983 ◆ NUGENT, CHRISTOPHER

Rank: Orderly Sergeant
Service: U.S. Marine Corps
Birthday: 1838
Place of Birth: County Cavan, Ireland
Date of Death: 6 May 1898
Cemetery: St. Raymond's Cemetery (MH)—Bronx, New York
Entered Service at: Massachusetts
Unit: U.S.S. *Fort Henry*
Battle or Place of Action: Crystal River, Florida
Date of Action: 15 June 1863
G.O. Number, Date: 32, 16 April 1864
Citation: Served on board the U.S.S. *Fort Henry*, Crystal River, Fla., 15 June 1863. Reconnoitering on the Crystal River on this date and in charge of a boat from the *Fort Henry*, Orderly Sgt. Nugent ordered an assault upon a rebel breastwork fortification. In this assault, the orderly sergeant and his comrades drove a guard of 11 rebels into the swamp, capturing their arms and destroying their camp equipage while gallantly withholding fire to prevent harm to a woman among the fugitives. On 30 July 1863, he further proved his courage by capturing a boat off Depot Key, Fla., containing two men and a woman with their baggage.

984 ◆ NUTTING, LEE

Rank: Captain
Service: U.S. Army
Birthday: 14 October 1837
Place of Birth: New York, New York
Date of Death: 11 July 1908
Cemetery: Brookside Cemetery (MH)—Brightwater, Nova Scotia, Canada
Entered Service at: New York, New York
Unit: Company C, 61st New York Infantry

Battle or Place of Action: Todds Tavern, Virginia
Date of Action: 8 May 1864
Date of Issue: 21 August 1893
Citation: Led the regiment in charge at a critical moment under a murderous fire until he fell desperately wounded.

985 ◆ O'BEIRNE, JAMES ROWAN

Rank: Captain (highest rank: Brigadier General)
Service: U.S. Army
Birthday: 25 September 1844
Place of Birth: Roscommon, County Ballagh, Ireland
Date of Death: 17 February 1917
Cemetery: Calvary Cemetery—Woodside, New York
Entered Service at: New York, New York
Unit: Company C, 37th New York Infantry
Battle or Place of Action: Fair Oaks, Virginia
Date of Action: 31 May & 1 June 1862
Date of Issue: 20 January 1891
Citation: Gallantly maintained the line of battle until ordered to fall back.

986 ◆ O'BRIEN, HENRY D.

Rank: Corporal (highest rank: Major)
Service: U.S. Army
Birthday: 21 January 1842
Place of Birth: Colois, Maine
Date of Death: 2 November 1902
Place of Death: St. Louis, Missouri
Cemetery: Bellefontaine Cemetery—St. Louis, Missouri
Entered Service at: St. Anthony Falls, Minnesota
Unit: Company E, 1st Minnesota Infantry
Battle or Place of Action: Gettysburg, Pennsylvania
Date of Action: 3 July 1863
Date of Issue: 9 April 1890
Citation: Taking up the colors where they had fallen, he rushed ahead of his regiment, close to the muzzles of the enemy's guns, and engaged in the desperate struggle in which the enemy was defeated, and though severely wounded, he held the colors until wounded a second time.

987 ◆ O'BRIEN, OLIVER ALBERT

Rank: Coxswain (highest rank: Acting Master's Mate)
Service: U.S. Navy
Birthday: 1839
Place of Birth: Boston, Suffolk County, Massachusetts
Date of Death: 1 October 1894
Place of Death: Glouchester, Massachusetts
Cemetery: St. Ann's Oak Hill Cemetery (MH)—Glouchester, Massachusetts
Entered Service at: Boston, Suffolk County, Massachusetts
Unit: U.S. Sloop *John Adams*
Battle or Place of Action: Sullivan's Island Channel, South Carolina
Date of Action: 28 November 1864
G.O. Number, Date: 45, 31 December 1864
Citation: Served as coxswain on board the U.S. sloop *John Adams*, Sullivan's Island Channel, 28 November 1864. Taking part in the boarding of the blockade runner *Beatrice* while under heavy enemy fire from Fort Moultrie, O'Brien, who was in charge of one of the boarding launches, carried out his duties with prompt and energetic conduct. This action resulted in the firing of the *Beatrice* and the capture of a quantity of supplies from her.

988 ◆ O'BRIEN, PETER

Rank: Private (highest rank: Corporal)
Service: U.S. Army
Birthday: 1842
Place of Birth: Dublin, County Dublin, Ireland
Date of Death: 30 September 1898
Place of Death: Chicago, Illinois
Cemetery: Rose Hill Cemetery—Chicago, Illinois
Entered Service at: New York, New York
Unit: Company A, 1st New York (Lincoln) Cavalry
Battle or Place of Action: Waynesboro, Virginia
Date of Action: 2 March 1865
Date of Issue: 26 March 1865
Citation: Capture of flag and of a Confederate officer with his horse and equipment.

989 ◆ O'CONNELL, THOMAS

Rank: Coal Heaver
Service: U.S. Navy
Birthday: 1842
Place of Birth: Ireland
Date of Death: 1899
Place of Death: New York, New York
Entered Service at: New York, New York
Unit: U.S.S. *Hartford*
Battle or Place of Action: Mobile Bay, Alabama
Date of Action: 5 August 1864
G.O. Number, Date: 45, 31 December 1864
Citation: On board the flagship U.S.S. *Hartford*, during successful attacks against Fort Morgan, rebel gunboats, and the ram *Tennessee* in Mobile Bay, 5 August 1864. Although a patient in the sick bay, O'Connell voluntarily reported at his station at the shell whip and continued to perform his duties with zeal and courage until his right hand was severed by an enemy shellburst.

990 ◆ O'CONNOR, ALBERT

Rank: Sergeant (highest rank: First Sergeant)
Service: U.S. Army
Birthday: 15 July 1843
Place of Birth: Herford, Canada
Date of Death: 3 April 1928
Cemetery: Soldier's Home Cemetery (MH)—Orting, Washington
Entered Service at: Lodi, Columbia County, Wisconsin
Unit: Company A, 7th Wisconsin Infantry
Battle or Place of Action: Gravelly Run, Virginia
Date of Action: 31 March & 1 April 1865

Date of Issue: 27 February 1917
Citation: On 31 March 1865, with a comrade, recaptured a Union officer from a detachment of nine Confederates, capturing three of the detachment and dispersing the remainder, and on 1 April 1865, seized a stand of Confederate colors, killing a Confederate officer in a hand-to-hand contest over the colors and retaining the colors until surrounded by Confederates and compelled to relinquish them.
Notes: POW

991 ◆ O'CONNOR, TIMOTHY

Rank: Private (highest rank: Sergeant)
Service: U.S. Army
Place of Birth: Ireland
Entered Service at: New Creek, Virginia
Unit: Company E, 1st U.S. Cavalry
Battle or Place of Action: near Malvern, Virginia
Date of Action: 28 July 1864
Date of Issue: 5 January 1865
Citation: Capture of flag of the 18th North Carolina Infantry (C.S.A.).

992 ◆ O'DEA, JOHN

Rank: Private
Service: U.S. Army
Birthday: 1839
Place of Birth: Limerick, County Limerick, Ireland
Place of Death: Quincy, Illinois
Cemetery: Sunset Cemetery, Illinois Veterans Home (MH)—Quincy, Illinois
Entered Service at: Bloomington, McLean County, Illinois
Unit: Company D, 8th Missouri Infantry
Battle or Place of Action: Vicksburg, Mississippi
Date of Action: 22 May 1863
Date of Issue: 12 July 1894
Citation: Gallantry in the charge of the "volunteer storming party."

993 ◆ O'DONNELL, MENOMEN

Rank: First Lieutenant (highest rank: Captain)
Service: U.S. Army
Birthday: 20 April 1830
Place of Birth: Drumbarty, Ireland
Date of Death: 3 September 1911
Cemetery: Mount Calvary Cemetery (MH)—Vincennes, Indiana
Entered Service at: Sumner, Lawrence County, Illinois
Unit: Company A, 11th Missouri Infantry
Battle or Place of Action: Vicksburg, Mississippi & Fort DeRussey, Louisiana
Date of Action: 22 May 1863 & 14 March 1864
Date of Issue: 11 September 1897
Citation: Voluntarily joined the color guard in the assault on the enemy's works when he saw indications of wavering and caused the colors of his regiment to be planted on the parapet. Voluntarily placed himself in the ranks of an assaulting column (being then on staff duty) and rode with it into the enemy's works, being the only mounted officer present; was twice wounded in battle.

994 ◆ O'DONOGHUE, TIMOTHY

Rank: Seaman
Service: U.S. Navy
Birthday: 1841
Place of Birth: Rochester, Monroe County, New York
Entered Service at: New York
Unit: U.S.S. *Signal*
Battle or Place of Action: Red River, Louisiana
Date of Action: 5 May 1864
G.O. Number, Date: 45, 31 December 1864
Citation: Served as boatswain's mate on board the U.S.S. *Signal*, Red River, 5 May 1864. Proceeding up the Red River, the U.S.S. *Signal* engaged a large force of enemy field batteries and sharpshooters, returning the fire until the ship was totally disabled, at which time the white flag was raised. Serving as gun captain, wounded early in the battle, O'Donoghue bravely stood by his gun in the face of enemy fire until ordered to withdraw.
Notes: POW

995 ◆ OLIVER, CHARLES

Rank: Sergeant (highest rank: Brevet Captain)
Service: U.S. Army
Birthday: 1840
Place of Birth: Allegheny County, Pennsylvania
Date of Death: 30 August 1920
Cemetery: Richland Cemetery (MH)—Dravosburg, Pennsylvania
Entered Service at: Webster, Westmoreland County, Pennsylvania
Unit: Company M, 100th Pennsylvania Infantry
Battle or Place of Action: Petersburg, Virginia
Date of Action: 25 March 1865
Date of Issue: 3 July 1865
Citation: Capture of flag of 31st Georgia Infantry (C.S.A.).

996 ◆ OLIVER, PAUL AMBROSE

Rank: Captain (highest rank: Brevet Brigadier General)
Service: U.S. Army
Birthday: 18 July 1831
Place of Birth: At sea in the English Channel aboard American flagship Louisiana.
Date of Death: 18 May 1928
Place of Death: Laurel Run, Pennsylvania
Cemetery: The Green Wood Cemetery—Brooklyn, New York
Entered Service at: New York, New York
Unit: Company D, 12th New York Infantry
Battle or Place of Action: Resaca, Georgia
Date of Action: 15 May 1864
Date of Issue: 12 October 1892
Citation: While acting as aide assisted in preventing a disaster caused by Union troops firing into each other.

997 ◆ O'NEILL, STEPHEN

Rank: Corporal (highest rank: Ordance Sergeant Ret.)
Service: U.S. Army
Birthday: 23 December 1837
Place of Birth: St. Johns, New Brunswick, Canada
Date of Death: 20 October 1909
Place of Death: Sault Ste. Marie, Michigan
Cemetery: Riverside Cemetery—Sault Ste. Marie, Michigan
Entered Service at: New York, New York
Unit: Company E, 7th U.S. Infantry
Battle or Place of Action: Chancellorsville, Virginia
Date of Action: 1 May 1863
Date of Issue: 28 September 1891
Citation: Took up the colors from the hands of the color bearer who had been shot down and bore them through the remainder of the battle.

998 ◆ OPEL, JOHN N.

Rank: Private
Service: U.S. Army
Birthday: 30 July 1843
Place of Birth: Hoflas, Bavaria, Germany
Date of Death: 21 February 1925
Place of Death: Cora, Missouri
Cemetery: Mount Zion Cemetery—Pleasant Hill Township, Missouri
Entered Service at: Rossburg, Decatur County, Indiana
Unit: Company G, 7th Indiana Infantry
Battle or Place of Action: Wilderness Campaign, Virginia
Date of Action: 5 May 1864
Date of Issue: 1 December 1864
Citation: Capture of flag of 50th Virginia Infantry (C.S.A.).

999 ◆ ORBANSKY, DAVID

Rank: Private (highest rank: Corporal)
Service: U.S. Army
Birthday: 1843
Place of Birth: Lautenburg, Prussia
Date of Death: 22 January 1897
Cemetery: Cedar Hill Cemetery—Piqua, Ohio
Entered Service at: Columbus, Franklin County, Ohio
Unit: Company B, 58th Ohio Infantry
Battle or Place of Action: Shiloh, Tennessee & Vicksburg, Mississippi, etc.
Date of Action: 1862 & 1863
Date of Issue: 2 August 1879
Citation: Gallantry in actions.

1000 ◆ ORR, CHARLES ALVIN

Rank: Private
Service: U.S. Army
Birthday: 28 June 1848
Place of Birth: Holland, Erie County, New York
Date of Death: 28 October 1923
Place of Death: Buffalo, New York
Cemetery: Forest Lawn Cemetery—Buffalo, New York
Entered Service at: Bennington, Wyoming County, New York
Unit: Company G, 187th New York Infantry
Battle or Place of Action: Hatcher's Run, Virginia
Date of Action: 27 October 1864
Date of Issue: 1 April 1898
Citation: This soldier and two others, voluntarily and under fire, rescued several wounded and helpless soldiers.

1001 ◆ ORR, ROBERT LEVAN

Rank: Major (highest rank: Colonel)
Service: U.S. Army
Birthday: 28 March 1836
Place of Birth: Philadelphia, Philadelphia County, Pennsylvania
Date of Death: 14 November 1894
Cemetery: Lawnview Cemetery—Philadelphia, Pennsylvania
Entered Service at: Philadelphia, Philadelphia County, Pennsylvania
Unit: 61st Pennsylvania Infantry
Battle or Place of Action: Petersburg, Virginia
Date of Action: 2 April 1865
Date of Issue: 28 November 1892
Citation: Carried the colors at the head of the column in the assault after two color bearers had been shot down.

1002 ◆ ORTEGA, JOHN

Rank: Seaman (highest rank: Acting Master's Mate)
Service: U.S. Navy
Birthday: 1840
Place of Birth: Spain
Entered Service at: Pennsylvania
Unit: U.S.S. *Saratoga*
Battle or Place of Action: off the Coast, Georgia
Date of Action: Unknown
G.O. Number, Date: 45, 31 December 1864
Citation: Served as seaman on board the U.S.S. *Saratoga* during actions of that vessel on two occasions. Carrying out his duties courageously during these actions, Ortega conducted himself gallantly through both periods. Promoted to acting master's mate.

1003 ◆ ORTH, JACOB GEORGE

Rank: Corporal (highest rank: Sergeant)
Service: U.S. Army
Birthday: 25 November 1837
Place of Birth: Philadelphia, Philadelphia County, Pennsylvania
Date of Death: 11 September 1907
Place of Death: Philadelphia, Pennsylvania
Cemetery: West Laurel Cemetery (MH)—Bala-Cynwyd, Pennsylvania
Entered Service at: Philadelphia, Philadelphia County, Pennsylvania
Unit: Company D, 28th Pennsylvania Infantry

Battle or Place of Action: Antietam, Maryland
Date of Action: 17 September 1862
Date of Issue: 15 January 1867
Citation: Capture of flag of 7th South Carolina Infantry (C.S.A.), in hand-to-hand encounter, although he was wounded in the shoulder.

1004 ◆ OSBORNE, WILLIAM HENRY

Rank: Private
Service: U.S. Army
Birthday: 16 September 1839
Place of Birth: Scituate, Plymouth County, Massachusetts
Date of Death: 5 June 1910
Cemetery: Village Cemetery of Elmwood (MH)—East Bridgewater, Massachusetts
Entered Service at: East Bridgewater, Plymouth County, Massachusetts
Unit: Company C, 29th Massachusetts Infantry
Battle or Place of Action: Malvern Hill, Virginia
Date of Action: 1 July 1862
Date of Issue: 1 April 1898
Citation: Although wounded and carried to the rear, he secured a rifle and voluntarily returned to the front, where, failing to find his own regiment, he joined another and fought with it until again severely wounded and taken prisoner.
Notes: POW

1005 ◆ OSS, ALBERT

Rank: Private
Service: U.S. Army
Birthday: 1818
Place of Birth: Belgium
Date of Death: 18 December 1898
Place of Death: Kearney, New Jersey
Cemetery: The Holy Sepulchre Cemetery—East Orange, New Jersey
Entered Service at: Newark, Essex County, New Jersey
Unit: Company B, 11th New Jersey Infantry
Battle or Place of Action: Chancellorsville, Virginia
Date of Action: 3 May 1863
Date of Issue: 6 May 1892
Citation: Remained in the rifle pits after the others had retreated, firing constantly, and contesting the ground step by step.

1006 ◆ OVERTURF, JACOB H.

Rank: Private (highest rank: Sergeant)
Service: U.S. Army
Birthday: 7 January 1842
Place of Birth: Jefferson County, Indiana
Date of Death: 10 September 1900
Cemetery: Holton Cemetery (MH)—Holton, Indiana
Entered Service at: Holton, Ripley County, Indiana
Unit: Company K, 83d Indiana Infantry
Battle or Place of Action: Vicksburg, Mississippi
Date of Action: 22 May 1863
Date of Issue: 13 August 1894
Citation: Gallantry in the charge of the "volunteer storming party."

1007 ◆ OVIATT, MILES M.

Rank: Corporal
Service: U.S. Marine Corps
Birthday: 1 December 1840
Place of Birth: Cattaraugus County, New York
Date of Death: 1 November 1880
Cemetery: Pleasant Valley Cemetery (MH)—Olean, New York
Entered Service at: New York
Unit: U.S.S. *Brooklyn*
Battle or Place of Action: Mobile Bay, Alabama
Date of Action: 5 August 1864
G.O. Number, Date: 45, 31 December 1864
Citation: On board the U.S.S. *Brooklyn* during action against rebel forts and gunboat and with the ram *Tennessee* in Mobile Bay, 5 August 1864. Despite severe damage to his ship and the loss of several men on board as enemy fire raked the deck, Cpl. Oviatt fought his gun with skill and courage throughout the furious two-hour battle which resulted in the surrender of the rebel ram *Tennessee*.

1008 ◆ PACKARD, LORON F.

Rank: Private
Service: U.S. Army
Place of Birth: Cattaraugus County, New York
Date of Death: 16 July 1903
Cemetery: Cuba Cemetery (MH)—Cuba, New York
Entered Service at: Cuba, Allegany County, New York
Unit: Company E, 5th New York Cavalry
Battle or Place of Action: Raccoon Ford, Virginia
Date of Action: 27 November 1863
Date of Issue: 20 August 1894
Citation: After his command had retreated, this soldier, voluntarily and alone, returned to the assistance of a comrade and rescued him from the hands of three armed Confederates,

1009 ◆ PALMER, GEORGE HENRY

Rank: Musician (highest rank: Major)
Service: U.S. Army
Birthday: 1842
Place of Birth: New York
Date of Death: 7 April 1901
Cemetery: Arlington National Cemetery (3-2104)—Arlington, Virginia
Entered Service at: Monmouth, Warren County, Illinois
Unit: 1st Illinois Cavalry
Battle or Place of Action: Lexington, Missouri
Date of Action: 20 September 1861
Date of Issue: 10 March 1896
Citation: Volunteered to fight in the trenches and also led a charge which resulted in the recapture of a Union hospital,

together with Confederate sharpshooters then occupying the same.

1010 ◆ PALMER, JOHN GIDEON

Rank: Corporal
Service: U.S. Army
Birthday: 14 October 1845
Place of Birth: Montville, New London County, Connecticut
Date of Death: 17 November 1901
Place of Death: New Haven, Connecticut
Cemetery: Indian Hill Cemetery (MH)—Middletown, Connecticut
Entered Service at: Montville, New London County, Connecticut
Unit: Company F, 21st Connecticut Infantry
Battle or Place of Action: Fredericksburg, Virginia
Date of Action: 13 December 1862
Date of Issue: 30 October 1896
Citation: First of six men who volunteered to assist gunner of a battery upon which the enemy was concentrating its fire, and fought with the battery until the close of the engagement. His commanding officer felt he would never see this man alive again.

1011 ◆ PALMER, WILLIAM JACKSON

Rank: Colonel (highest rank: Brevet Brigadier General)
Service: U.S. Army
Birthday: 17 September 1836
Place of Birth: Leipsic, Kent County, Delaware
Date of Death: 13 March 1909
Place of Death: Colorado Springs, Colorado
Cemetery: Evergreen Cemetery (MH)—Colorado Springs, Colorado
Entered Service at: Philadelphia, Philadelphia County, Pennsylvania
Unit: 15th Pennsylvania Cavalry
Battle or Place of Action: Red Hill, Alabama
Date of Action: 14 January 1865
Date of Issue: 24 February 1894
Citation: With less than 200 men attacked and defeated a superior force of the enemy, capturing their fieldpiece and about 100 prisoners without losing a man.

1012 ◆ PARKER, THOMAS

Rank: Corporal
Service: U.S. Army
Birthday: 1822
Place of Birth: England
Date of Death: 27 April 1872
Cemetery: Mechanics Cemetery—Philadelphia, Pennsylvania
Entered Service at: Providence, Providence County, Rhode Island
Unit: Company B, 2d Rhode Island Infantry
Battle or Place of Action: Petersburg & Deatonsville (Sailors Creek) Virginia
Date of Action: 2 April & 6 April 1865
Date of Issue: 29 May 1867
Citation: Planted the first color on the enemy's works. Carried the regimental colors over the creek after the regiment had broken and been repulsed.

1013 ◆ PARKER, WILLIAM

Rank: Captain of the Afterguard
Service: U.S. Navy
Place of Birth: Boston, Suffolk County, Massachusetts
Entered Service at: Massachusetts
Unit: U.S.S. *Cayuga*
Battle or Place of Action: Forts Jackson & St. Philip and New Orleans, Louisiana
Date of Action: 24-25 April 1862
G.O. Number, Date: 11, 3 April 1863
Citation: At the wheel on board the U.S.S. *Cayuga* during the capture of Forts St. Philip and Jackson, and of New Orleans, 24 and 25 April 1862. As his ship led the advance column toward the barrier and both forts opened fire simultaneously, striking the vessel from stem to stern, Parker conscientiously performed his duties throughout the action in which attempts by three rebel steamers to butt and board were thwarted, and the ships driven off. Eleven gunboats were successfully engaged and the enemy garrisons forced to surrender during this battle in which the *Cayuga* sustained 46 hits.

1014 ◆ PARKS, GEORGE

Rank: Captain of the Forecastle
Service: U.S. Navy
Birthday: 1823
Place of Birth: Schenectady, Schenectady County, New York
Entered Service at: New York, New York
Unit: U.S.S. *Richmond*
Battle or Place of Action: Fort Morgan, Mobile Bay, Alabama
Date of Action: 5 August 1864
G.O. Number, Date: 45, 31 December 1864
Citation: On board the U.S.S. *Richmond* during action against rebel forts and gunboats and with the ram *Tennessee* in Mobile Bay, 5 August 1864. Despite damage to his ship the and loss of several men on board as enemy fire raked her decks, Parks performed his duties with skill and courage throughout a furious two-hour battle which resulted in the surrender of the rebel ram *Tennessee* and in the damaging and destruction of batteries at Fort Morgan.

1015 ◆ PARKS, HENRY JEREMIAH

Rank: Private (highest rank: Captain)
Service: U.S. Army
Birthday: 24 February 1848
Place of Birth: Orangeville, Wyoming County, New York
Date of Death: 19 October 1927
Place of Death: San Diego, California

Cemetery: Arlington National Cemetery (2-1200-SS)—Arlington, Virginia
Entered Service at: Orangeville, Wyoming County, New York
Unit: Company A, 9th New York Cavalry
Battle or Place of Action: Cedar Creek, Virginia
Date of Action: 19 October 1864
Date of Presentation: 26 October 1864
Place of Presentation: Presented by Pres. Abraham Lincoln
Citation: While alone and in advance of his unit and attempting to cut off the retreat of a supply wagon, he fought and sent to flight a Confederate color bearer. After capturing the color bearer and leaving him in the rear, he returned to the front and captured three more wagons and drivers.

1016 ◆ PARKS, JAMES W.

Rank: Corporal
Service: U.S. Army
Birthday: 1840
Place of Birth: Lawrence County, Ohio
Date of Death: 14 January 1906
Place of Death: Massac County, Illinois
Entered Service at: Xenia, Clay County, Illinois
Unit: Company F, 11th Missouri Infantry
Battle or Place of Action: Nashville, Tennessee
Date of Action: 16 December 1864
Date of Issue: 24 February 1865
Citation: Capture of flag.

1017 ◆ PARROTT, JACOB

Rank: Private (highest rank: First Lieutenant)
Service: U.S. Army
Birthday: 17 July 1843
Place of Birth: Fairfield County, Ohio
Date of Death: 22 December 1908
Cemetery: Grove Cemetery (MH)—Kenton, Ohio
Entered Service at: Kenton, Hardin County, Ohio
Unit: Company K, 33d Ohio Infantry
Battle or Place of Action: Georgia
Date of Action: April 1862
Date of Presentation: 25 March 1863
Place of Presentation: Washington, D.C., presented by Sec. of War Edward M. Stanton
Citation: One of 19 of 24 men (including two civilians) who, by direction of Gen. Ormsby M. Mitchell, penetrated nearly 200 miles south into enemy territory and captured a railroad train at Big Shanty, Ga., in an attempt to destroy the bridges and track between Chattanooga and Atlanta.
Notes: POW

1018 ◆ PARSONS, JOEL

Rank: Private
Service: U.S. Army
Birthday: 23 August 1840
Place of Birth: Jackson County, West Virginia
Date of Death: 10 November 1919
Place of Death: Columbus, Ohio
Cemetery: Union Cemetery—Columbus, Ohio
Entered Service at: Mason City, Mason County, West Virginia
Unit: Company B, 4th West Virginia Infantry
Battle or Place of Action: Vicksburg, Mississippi
Date of Action: 22 May 1863
Date of Issue: 16 August 1894
Citation: Gallantry in the charge of the "volunteer storming party."

1019 ◆ PATTERSON, JOHN HENRY

Rank: First Lieutenant (highest rank: Brigadier General Ret.)
Service: U.S. Army
Birthday: 10 February 1843
Place of Birth: New York
Date of Death: 5 October 1920
Place of Death: Selkirk, New York
Cemetery: Albany Rural Cemetery (MH)—Albany, New York
Entered Service at: New York
Unit: 11th U.S. Infantry
Battle or Place of Action: Wilderness Campaign, Virginia
Date of Action: 5 May 1864
Date of Issue: 23 July 1897
Citation: Under the heavy fire of the advancing enemy, picked up and carried several hundred yards to a place of safety a wounded officer of his regiment who was helpless and would otherwise have been burned in the forest.

1020 ◆ PATTERSON, JOHN T.

Rank: Principal Musician
Service: U.S. Army
Birthday: 3 February 1838
Place of Birth: Morgan County, Ohio
Date of Death: 3 March 1922
Place of Death: Mauston, Wisconsin
Cemetery: Oakwood Cemetery—Mauston, Wisconsin
Entered Service at: McConnelsville, Morgan County, Ohio
Unit: 122d Ohio Infantry
Battle or Place of Action: Winchester, Virginia
Date of Action: 14 June 1863
Date of Issue: 13 May 1899
Citation: With one companion, voluntarily went in front of the Union lines, under a heavy fire from the enemy, and carried back a helpless, wounded comrade, thus saving him from death or capture.

1021 ◆ PAUL, WILLIAM H.

Rank: Private (highest rank: First Sergeant)
Service: U.S. Army
Birthday: 3 October 1844
Place of Birth: Philadelphia, Philadelphia County, Pennsylvania
Date of Death: 23 February 1911

Cemetery: Wesleyan Chapel Cemetery—Havre De Grace, Maryland
Entered Service at: Philadelphia, Philadelphia County, Pennsylvania
Unit: Company E, 90th Pennsylvania Infantry
Battle or Place of Action: Antietam, Maryland
Date of Action: 17 September 1862
Date of Issue: 3 November 1896
Citation: Under a most withering and concentrated fire, voluntarily picked up the colors of his regiment, when the bearer and two of the color guard had been killed, and bore them aloft throughout the entire battle.

1022 ◆ PAY, BYRON E.

Rank: Private
Service: U.S. Army
Birthday: 21 October 1844
Place of Birth: LeRoy Township, Jefferson County, New York
Date of Death: 19 February 1906
Place of Death: Volga, South Dakota
Entered Service at: Mankato, Blue Earth County, Minnesota
Unit: Company H, 2d Minnesota Infantry
Battle or Place of Action: Nolensville, Tennessee
Date of Action: 15 February 1863
Date of Issue: 11 September 1897
Citation: Was one of a detachment of 16 men who heroically defended a wagon train against the attack of 125 cavalry, repulsed the attack, and saved the train.

1023 ◆ PAYNE, IRVIN C.

Rank: Corporal (highest rank: Sergeant)
Service: U.S. Army
Birthday: 1830
Place of Birth: Wayne County, Pennsylvania
Date of Death: 3 April 1887
Place of Death: Dunmore, Pennsylvania
Cemetery: Dunmore Cemetery—Dunmore, Pennsylvania
Entered Service at: New York, New York
Unit: Company M, 2d New York Cavalry
Battle or Place of Action: Deatonsville (Sailor's Creek), Virginia
Date of Action: 6 April 1865
Date of Issue: 3 May 1865
Citation: Capture of Virginia state colors.

1024 ◆ PAYNE, THOMAS H. L.

Rank: First Lieutenant (highest rank: Captain)
Service: U.S. Army
Birthday: 5 October 1840
Place of Birth: Boston Suffolk County, Massachusetts
Date of Death: 13 September 1909
Place of Death: Philadelphia, Pennsylvania
Cemetery: Fernwood Cemetery—Fernwood, Pennsylvania
Entered Service at: Mendota, La Salle County, Illinois
Unit: Company E, 37th Illinois Infantry
Battle or Place of Action: Fort Blakely, Alabama
Date of Action: 9 April 1865
Date of Issue: 1 April 1898
Citation: While acting regimental quartermaster, learning of an expected assault, Payne requested assignment to a company that had no commissioned officers present; was so assigned, and was one of the first to lead his men into the enemy's works.

1025 ◆ PEARSALL, PLATT

Rank: Corporal
Service: U.S. Army
Birthday: 27 December 1841
Place of Birth: Meigs County, Ohio
Date of Death: 18 June 1931
Place of Death: Farmington, Missouri
Cemetery: Pendleton Cemetery (MH)—Farmington, Missouri
Entered Service at: Downington, Ohio
Unit: Company C, 30th Ohio Infantry
Battle or Place of Action: Vicksburg, Mississippi
Date of Action: 22 May 1863
Date of Issue: 14 August 1894
Citation: Gallantry in the charge of the "volunteer storming party."

1026 ◆ PEARSON, ALFRED L.

Rank: Colonel (highest rank: Brevet Major General)
Service: U.S. Army
Birthday: 28 December 1838
Place of Birth: Pittsburgh, Allegheny County, Pennsylvania
Date of Death: 6 January 1903
Place of Death: Sewickley, Pennsylvania
Cemetery: Allegheny Cemetery (MH)—Pittsburgh, Pennsylvania
Entered Service at: Pittsburgh, Allegheny County, Pennsylvania
Unit: 155th Pennsylvania Infantry
Battle or Place of Action: Lewis' Farm, Virginia
Date of Action: 29 March 1865
Date of Issue: 17 September 1897
Citation: Seeing a brigade forced back by the enemy, he seized his regimental color, called on his men to follow him, and advanced upon the enemy under a severe fire. The whole brigade took up the advance, the lost ground was regained, and the enemy was repulsed.

1027 ◆ PEASE, JOACHIM

Rank: Seaman
Service: U.S. Navy
Birthday: 1842
Place of Birth: Long Island, New York
Entered Service at: New York, New York
Unit: U.S.S. *Kearsarge*
Battle or Place of Action: off Cherbourg, France

Date of Action: 19 June 1864
G.O. Number, Date: 45, 31 December 1864
Citation: Served as seaman on board the U.S.S. *Kearsarge* when she destroyed the *Alabama* off Cherbourg, France, 19 June 1864. Acting as loader on the No. 2 gun during this bitter engagement, Pease exhibited marked coolness and good conduct and was highly recommended by the divisional officer for gallantry under fire.

1028 ◆ PECK, CASSIUS

Rank: Private (highest rank: Sergeant)
Service: U.S. Army
Birthday: 3 March 1842
Place of Birth: Brookfield, Orange County, Vermont
Date of Death: 12 July 1913
Place of Death: Burlington, Vermont
Cemetery: Brookfield New Cemetery—Brookfield, Vermont
Entered Service at: West Randolph, Orange County, Vermont
Unit: Company F, 1st U.S. Sharpshooters
Battle or Place of Action: near Blackburn's Ford, West Virginia
Date of Action: 19 September 1862
Date of Issue: 12 October 1892
Citation: Took command of such soldiers as he could get and attacked and captured a Confederate battery of four guns. Also, while on a reconnaissance, overtook and captured a Confederate soldier.

1029 ◆ PECK, OSCAR E.

Rank: Second Class Boy
Service: U.S. Navy
Birthday: 1848
Place of Birth: Bridgeport, Fairfield County, Connecticut
Date of Death: 23 October 1906
Place of Death: Norton Heights, Connecticut
Cemetery: Fitch's Home Cemetery (MH)—Darien, Connecticut
Entered Service at: Connecticut
Unit: U.S.S. *Varuna*
Battle or Place of Action: Forts Jackson & St. Philip, Louisiana
Date of Action: 24 April 1862
G.O. Number, Date: 11, 3 April 1863
Citation: Peck served as second class boy on board the *Varuna* during attacks on Forts Jackson and St. Philip, 24 April 1862. Acting as powder boy of the after rifle, Peck served gallantly while the *Varuna* was repeatedly attacked and rammed and finally sunk. This was an extremely close-range action and, although badly damaged, the *Varuna* delivered shells abaft the *Morgan*'s armor.

1030 ◆ PECK, THEODORE SAFFORD

Rank: First Lieutenant (highest rank: Major General)
Service: U.S. Army
Birthday: 22 March 1843
Place of Birth: Burlington, Chittenden County, Vermont
Date of Death: 15 March 1918
Cemetery: Lake View Cemetery—Burlington, Vermont
Entered Service at: Burlington, Chittenden County, Vermont
Unit: Company H, 9th Vermont Infantry
Battle or Place of Action: Newport Barracks, North Carolina
Date of Action: 2 February 1864
Date of Issue: 8 September 1891
Citation: By long and persistent resistance and burning the bridges, kept a superior force of the enemy at bay and covered the retreat of the garrison.

1031 ◆ PEIRSOL, JAMES KASTOR

Rank: Sergeant (highest rank: First Lieutenant)
Service: U.S. Army
Birthday: 21 September 1843
Place of Birth: Beaver County, Pennsylvania
Date of Death: 1 March 1927
Place of Death: Claremont, California
Cemetery: Grove Cemetery—New Brighton, Pennsylvania
Entered Service at: Waynesboro, Ohio
Unit: Company F, 13th Ohio Cavalry
Battle or Place of Action: Paines Crossroads, Virginia
Date of Action: 5 April 1865
Date of Issue: 3 May 1865
Citation: Capture of flag.

1032 ◆ PELHAM, WILLIAM

Rank: Landsman
Service: U.S. Navy
Birthday: 8 December 1847
Place of Birth: Halifax, Nova Scotia, Canada
Date of Death: 30 March 1933
Place of Death: Brooklyn, New York
Cemetery: Holy Cross Cemetery—Brooklyn, New York
Entered Service at: New York, New York
Unit: U.S.S. *Hartford*
Battle or Place of Action: Mobile Bay, Alabama
Date of Action: 5 August 1864
G.O. Number, Date: 45, 31 December 1864
Citation: On board the flagship U.S.S. *Hartford*, during successful actions against Fort Morgan, rebel gunboats and the ram *Tennessee* in Mobile Bay, 5 August 1864. When other members of his crewgun were killed or wounded under the enemy's terrific shellfire, Pelham calmly assisted the casualties below and voluntarily returned and took his place at an adjoining gun where another man had been struck down. He continued to fight his gun throughout the remainder of the battle which resulted in the capture of the *Tennessee*.

1033 ◆ PENNYPACKER, GALUSHA

Rank: Colonel (highest rank: Major General U.S.A.)
Service: U.S. Army
Birthday: 1 June 1844

Place of Birth: Near Valley Forge, Chester County, Pennsylvania
Date of Death: 1 October 1916
Place of Death: Philadelphia, Pennsylvania
Cemetery: Philadelphia National Cemetery (0-175)—Philadelphia, Pennsylvania
Entered Service at: West Chester, Chester County, Pennsylvania
Unit: 97th Pennsylvania Infantry
Battle or Place of Action: Fort Fisher, North Carolina
Date of Action: 15 January 1865
Date of Issue: 17 August 1891
Citation: Gallantly led the charge over a traverse and planted the colors of one of his regiments thereon; was severely wounded.

1034 ◆ PENTZER, PATRICK HENRY

Rank: Captain
Service: U.S. Army
Birthday: 1839
Place of Birth: Marion County, Missouri
Date of Death: 16 October 1901
Place of Death: Nevada, Missouri
Cemetery: Springfield National Cemetery (24-1696) (MH)—Springfield, Missouri
Entered Service at: Gillespie, Macoupin County, Illinois
Unit: Company C, 97th Illinois Infantry
Battle or Place of Action: Fort Blakely, Alabama
Date of Action: 9 April 1865
Date of Issue: 9 October 1879
Citation: Among the first to enter the enemy's entrenchments, he received the surrender of a Confederate general officer and his headquarters flag.

1035 ◆ PERRY, THOMAS

Rank: Boatswain's Mate
Service: U.S. Navy
Birthday: 1836
Place of Birth: New York
Entered Service at: New York
Unit: U.S.S. *Kearsarge*
Battle or Place of Action: off Cherbourg, France
Date of Action: 19 June 1864
G.O. Number, Date: 45, 31 December 1864
Citation: Served as boatswain's mate on board the U.S.S. *Kearsarge* when she destroyed the *Alabama* off Cherbourg, France, 19 June 1864. Acting as captain of the No. 2 gun during this bitter engagement, Perry exhibited marked coolness and good conduct under the enemy fire and was recommended for gallantry by his divisional officer.

1036 ◆ PESCH, JOSEPH M.

Rank: Private
Service: U.S. Army
Birthday: 18 July 1835
Place of Birth: Grossleiton, Prussia

Date of Death: 11 October 1903
Cemetery: Bellefontaine Cemetery—St. Louis, Missouri
Entered Service at: St. Louis, St. Louis County, Missouri
Unit: Battery A, 1st Missouri Light Artillery
Battle or Place of Action: Grand Gulf, Mississippi
Date of Action: 28-29 April 1863
Date of Issue: 10 March 1896
Citation: With two comrades voluntarily took position on board the steamer *Cheeseman*, in charge of all the guns and ammunition of the battery, and remained in charge of the same, although the steamer became unmanageable and was exposed for some time to a heavy fire from the enemy.

1037 ◆ PETERS, HENRY CARLTON

Rank: Private (highest rank: Sergeant)
Service: U.S. Army
Birthday: 29 February 1840
Place of Birth: Monroe County, Michigan
Date of Death: 19 March 1923
Place of Death: Manning, Iowa
Cemetery: Riverside Cemetery (MH)—South Rockwood, Michigan
Entered Service at: Adrian, Lenawee County, Michigan
Unit: Company B, 47th Ohio Infantry
Battle or Place of Action: Vicksburg, Mississippi
Date of Action: 3 May 1863
Date of Issue: 17 April 1917
Citation: Was one of a party that volunteered and attempted to run the enemy's batteries with a steam tug and two barges loaded with subsistence stores.
Notes: POW

1038 ◆ PETERSON, ALFRED

Rank: Seaman
Service: U.S. Navy
Birthday: 1838
Place of Birth: Sweden
Entered Service at: New York, New York
Unit: U.S.S. *Commodore Perry*
Battle or Place of Action: Franklin, Virginia
Date of Action: 3 October 1862
G.O. Number, Date: 11, 3 April 1863
Citation: On board the U.S.S. *Commodore Perry* in the attack upon Franklin, Va., 3 October 1862. With enemy fire raking the deck of his ship and blockades thwarting her progress, Peterson remained at his post and performed his duties with skill and courage as the *Commodore Perry* fought a gallant battle to silence many rebel batteries as she steamed down the Blackwater River.

1039 ◆ PETTY, PHILIP

Rank: Sergeant (highest rank: Color Sergeant)
Service: U.S. Army
Birthday: 17 May 1840
Place of Birth: Tingswich, Buckinghamshire, England
Date of Death: 22 December 1917

Place of Death: Daggett, Pennsylvania
Cemetery: Daggett Cemetery (MH)—Daggett, Pennsylvania
Entered Service at: Troy, Bradford County, Pennsylvania
Unit: Company A, 136th Pennsylvania Infantry
Battle or Place of Action: Fredericksburg, Virginia
Date of Action: 13 December 1862
Date of Issue: 21 August 1893
Citation: Took up the colors as they fell out of the hands of the wounded color bearer and carried them forward in the charge.

1040 ◆ PHELPS, CHARLES EDWARDS

Rank: Colonel (highest rank: Brevet Brigadier General)
Service: U.S. Army
Birthday: 1 May 1833
Place of Birth: Guilford, Vermont
Date of Death: 27 December 1908
Cemetery: Woodlawn Cemetery—Baltimore, Maryland
Entered Service at: Baltimore, Baltimore County, Maryland
Unit: 7th Maryland Infantry
Battle or Place of Action: Laurel Hill, Virginia
Date of Action: 8 May 1864
Date of Issue: 30 March 1898
Citation: Rode to the head of the assaulting column, then much broken by severe losses and faltering under the close fire of artillery, placed himself conspicuously in front of the troops, and gallantly rallied and led them to within a few feet of the enemy's works, where he was severely wounded and captured.

1041 ◆ PHILLIPS, JOSIAH

Rank: Private
Service: U.S. Army
Birthday: 1830
Place of Birth: Wyoming County, New York
Date of Death: 11 December 1894
Place of Death: Lawrence, Wisconsin
Cemetery: Lawrence Cemetery—Lawrence, Wisconsin
Entered Service at: Ulysses, Potter County, Pennsylvania
Unit: Company E, 148th Pennsylvania Infantry
Battle or Place of Action: Sutherland Station, Virginia
Date of Action: 2 April 1865
Date of Issue: 10 May 1865
Citation: Capture of flag.

1042 ◆ PHINNEY, WILLIAM

Rank: Boatswain's Mate
Service: U.S. Navy
Birthday: 1824
Place of Birth: Norway
Entered Service at: New York, New York
Unit: U.S.S. *Lackawanna*
Battle or Place of Action: Fort Morgan, Mobile Bay, Alabama
Date of Action: 5 August 1864
G.O. Number, Date: 45, 31 December 1864
Citation: On board the U.S.S. *Lackawanna* during successful attacks against Fort Morgan, rebel gunboats, and the rebel ram *Tennessee* in Mobile Bay, 5 August 1864. Serving as gun captain, Phinney showed much presence of mind in managing the gun and gave much needed encouragement to the crew during the engagement, which resulted in the capture of the prize rebel ram *Tennessee* and in the damaging and destruction of Fort Morgan.

1043 ◆ PHISTERER, FREDERICK

Rank: First Lieutenant (highest rank: Brevet Major General)
Service: U.S. Army
Birthday: 11 October 1836
Place of Birth: Germany
Date of Death: 13 July 1909
Cemetery: Greenlawn Cemetery—Columbus, Ohio
Entered Service at: Medina County, Ohio
Unit: 18th U.S. Infantry
Battle or Place of Action: Stone River, Tennessee
Date of Action: 31 December 1862
Date of Issue: 12 December 1894
Citation: Voluntarily conveyed, under a heavy fire, information to the commander of a battalion of regular troops by which the battalion was saved from capture or annihilation.

1044 ◆ PICKLE, ALONZO H.

Rank: Sergeant
Service: U.S. Army
Birthday: 2 July 1843
Place of Birth: Canada
Date of Death: 24 May 1925
Cemetery: Home Cemetery (MH)—Sleepy Eye, Minnesota
Entered Service at: Dover, Olmsted County, Minnesota
Unit: Company B, 1st Battalion, Minnesota Infantry
Battle or Place of Action: Deep Bottom, Virginia
Date of Action: 14 August 1864
Date of Issue: 12 June 1895
Citation: At the risk of his life, voluntarily went to the assistance of a wounded officer lying close to the enemy's lines and, under fire, carried him to a place of safety.

1045 ◆ PIKE, EDWARD M.

Rank: First Sergeant
Service: U.S. Army
Birthday: 1 July 1838
Place of Birth: Casco, Cumberland County, Maine
Date of Death: 10 August 1924
Cemetery: Payne Cemetery—Chenoa, Illinois
Entered Service at: Bloomington, McLean County, Illinois
Unit: Company A, 33d Illinois Infantry
Battle or Place of Action: Cache River, Arkansas
Date of Action: 7 July 1862
Date of Issue: 29 March 1899

Citation: While the troops were falling back before a superior force, this soldier, assisted by one companion, and while under severe fire at close-range, saved a cannon from capture by the enemy.

1046 ◆ PINGREE, SAMUEL E.

Rank: Captain (highest rank: Colonel)
Service: U.S. Army
Birthday: 2 August 1832
Place of Birth: Salisbury, Merrimack County, New Hampshire
Date of Death: 1 June 1922
Cemetery: Hartford Cemetery—White River Junction, Vermont
Entered Service at: Hartford, Windsor County, Vermont
Unit: Company F, 3d Vermont Infantry
Battle or Place of Action: Lee's Mills, Virginia
Date of Action: 16 April 1862
Date of Issue: 17 August 1891
Citation: Gallantly led his company across a wide, deep creek, drove the enemy from the rifle pits, which were within two yards of the farther bank, and remained at the head of his men until a second time severely wounded.

1047 ◆ PINKHAM, CHARLES H.

Rank: Sergeant Major (highest rank: Brevet Captain)
Service: U.S. Army
Birthday: 18 August 1844
Place of Birth: Grafton, Worcester County, Massachusetts
Date of Death: 6 November 1920
Cemetery: Hope Cemetery (MH)—Worcester, Massachusetts
Entered Service at: Worcester, Worcester County, Massachusetts
Unit: 57th Massachusetts Infantry
Battle or Place of Action: Fort Stedman, Virginia
Date of Action: 25 March 1865
Date of Issue: 15 April 1895
Citation: Captured the flag of the 57th North Carolina Infantry (C.S.A.), and saved his own colors by tearing them from the staff while the enemy was in the camp.

1048 ◆ PINN, ROBERT A.

Rank: First Sergeant
Service: U.S. Army
Birthday: 1 March 1843
Place of Birth: Stark County, Ohio
Date of Death: 1 January 1911
Cemetery: City Cemetery (MH)—Massillon, Ohio
Entered Service at: Massillon, Stark County, Ohio
Unit: Company I, 5th U.S. Colored Infantry
Battle or Place of Action: Chapin's Farm, Virginia
Date of Action: 29 September 1864
Date of Issue: 6 April 1865
Citation: Took command of his company after all the officers had been killed or wounded and gallantly led it in battle.

1049 ◆ PIPES, JAMES MILTON

Rank: Captain
Service: U.S. Army
Birthday: 10 November 1840
Place of Birth: Morrisville, Bucks County, Pennsylvania
Date of Death: 1 December 1928
Place of Death: Washington, D.C.
Cemetery: Arlington National Cemetery (3-1332-A)—Arlington, Virginia
Entered Service at: Waynesburg, Greene County, Pennsylvania
Unit: Company A, 140th Pennsylvania Infantry
Battle or Place of Action: Gettysburg, Pennsylvania & Reams Station, Virginia
Date of Action: 2 July 1863 & 25 August 1864
Date of Issue: 5 April 1898
Citation: While a sergeant and retiring with his company before the rapid advance of the enemy at Gettysburg, he and a companion stopped and carried to a place of safety a wounded and helpless comrade; in this act both he and his companion were severely wounded. A year later, at Reams Station, Va., while commanding a skirmish line, voluntarily assisted in checking a flank movement of the enemy, and while so doing was severely wounded, suffering the loss of an arm.

1050 ◆ PITMAN, GEORGE J.

Rank: Sergeant
Service: U.S. Army
Birthday: 1839
Place of Birth: Recklestown, New Jersey
Date of Death: 30 April 1884
Place of Death: Philadelphia, Pennsylvania
Cemetery: South Section Laruel Hill Cemetery (MH)—Philadelphia, Pennsylvania
Entered Service at: Philadelphia, Philadelphia County, Pennsylvania
Unit: Company C, 1st New York (Lincoln) Cavalry
Battle or Place of Action: Deatonsville (Sailor's Creek), Virginia
Date of Action: 6 April 1865
Date of Issue: 3 May 1865
Citation: Capture of flag of the Sumter Heavy Artillery (C.S.A.).

1051 ◆ PITTINGER, WILLIAM

True Name: Pittenger, William
Rank: Sergeant
Service: U.S. Army
Birthday: 31 January 1840
Place of Birth: Knoxville, Jefferson County, Ohio
Date of Death: 24 April 1904
Place of Death: Fallbrook, California
Cemetery: Odd Fellow Cemetery (MH)—Fallbrook, California

Entered Service at: Steubenville, Jefferson County, Ohio
Unit: Company G, 2d Ohio Infantry
Battle or Place of Action: Georgia
Date of Action: April 1862
Date of Presentation: 25 March 1863
Place of Presentation: Washington, D.C., presented by Sec. of War Edward M. Stanton
Citation: One of 19 of 24 men (including two civilians) who, by direction of Gen. Ormsby M. Mitchell, penetrated nearly 200 miles south into enemy territory and captured a railroad train at Big Shanty, Ga., in an attempt to destroy the bridges and track between Chattanooga and Atlanta.

1052 ♦ PLANT, HENRY E.

Rank: Corporal (highest rank: Color Sergeant)
Service: U.S. Army
Birthday: 11 October 1841
Place of Birth: Oswego County, New York
Date of Death: 16 April 1925
Cemetery: Nunica Cemetery (MH)—Nunica, Michigan
Entered Service at: Cockery, Michigan
Unit: Company F, 14th Michigan Infantry
Battle or Place of Action: Bentonville, North Carolina
Date of Action: 19 March 1865
Date of Issue: 27 April 1896
Citation: Rushed into the midst of the enemy and rescued the colors, the color bearer having fallen mortally wounded.

1053 ♦ PLATT, GEORGE CRAWFORD

Rank: Private (highest rank: Sergeant)
Service: U.S. Army
Birthday: 17 February 1842
Place of Birth: Ireland
Date of Death: 20 June 1912
Cemetery: Holy Cross Cemetery (MH)—Yeadon, Pennsylvania
Entered Service at: Philadelphia, Philadelphia County, Pennsylvania
Unit: Troop H, 6th U.S. Cavalry
Battle or Place of Action: Fairfield, Pennsylvania
Date of Action: 3 July 1863
Date of Issue: 12 July 1895
Citation: Seized the regimental flag upon the death of the standard bearer in a hand-to-hand fight and prevented it from falling into the hands of the enemy.

1054 ♦ PLIMLEY, WILLIAM

Rank: First Lieutenant (highest rank: Major)
Service: U.S. Army
Birthday: 12 August 1839
Place of Birth: Catskill, Greene County, New York
Date of Death: 2 October 1913
Place of Death: New York, New York
Cemetery: Catskill Rural Cemetery (MH)—Catskill, New York

Entered Service at: Catskill, Greene County, New York
Unit: Company F, 120th New York Infantry
Battle or Place of Action: Hatcher's Run, Virginia
Date of Action: 2 April 1865
Date of Issue: 4 April 1898
Citation: While acting as aide to a general officer, voluntarily accompanied a regiment in an assault on the enemy's works and acted as leader of the movement which resulted in the rout of the enemy and the capture of large numbers of prisoners.

1055 ♦ PLOWMAN, GEORGE H.

Rank: Sergeant Major (highest rank: Captain)
Service: U.S. Army
Birthday: 10 March 1840
Place of Birth: Oxford, Oxfordshire, England
Date of Death: 27 February 1921
Place of Death: Woodward, Oklahoma
Cemetery: Arlington National Cemetery (3-4417-EH) (MH)—Arlington, Virginia
Entered Service at: Washington, D.C.
Unit: 3d Maryland Infantry
Battle or Place of Action: Petersburg, Virginia
Date of Action: 17 June 1864
Date of Issue: 1 December 1864
Citation: Recaptured the colors of the 2d Pennsylvania Provisional Artillery.

1056 ♦ PLUNKETT, THOMAS

Rank: Sergeant
Service: U.S. Army
Birthday: 1841
Place of Birth: Ireland
Date of Death: 10 March 1885
Cemetery: Hope Cemetery—Worcester, Massachusetts
Entered Service at: West Boylston, Worcester County, Massachusetts
Unit: Company E, 21st Massachusetts Infantry
Battle or Place of Action: Fredericksburg, Virginia
Date of Action: 11 December 1862
Date of Issue: 30 March 1866
Citation: Seized the colors of his regiment, the color bearer having been shot down, and bore them to the front where both his arms were carried off by a shell.

1057 ♦ POND, GEORGE F.

Rank: Private
Service: U.S. Army
Birthday: 5 October 1844
Place of Birth: Libertyville, Lake County, Illinois
Date of Death: 21 June 1911
Place of Death: Fort Scott, Kansas
Cemetery: Evergreen Cemetery (MH)—Fort Scott, Kansas
Entered Service at: Fairwater, Fond du Lac County, Wisconsin

Unit: Company C, 3d Wisconsin Cavalry
Battle or Place of Action: Drywood, Kansas
Date of Action: 15 May 1864
Date of Issue: 16 May 1899
Citation: With two companions, attacked a greatly superior force of guerrillas, routed them, and rescued several prisoners.

1058 ◆ POND, JAMES BURTON

Rank: First Lieutenant (highest rank: Major)
Service: U.S. Army
Birthday: 11 June 1838
Place of Birth: Allegany, Cattaraugus County, New York
Date of Death: 21 June 1903
Place of Death: Jersey City, New Jersey
Cemetery: Woodlawn Cemetery—Bronx, New York
Entered Service at: Janesville, Rock County, Wisconsin
Unit: Company C, 3d Wisconsin Cavalry
Battle or Place of Action: Baxter Springs, Kansas
Date of Action: 6 October 1863
Date of Issue: 30 March 1898
Citation: While in command of two companies of cavalry, was surprised and attacked by several times his own number of guerrillas, but gallantly rallied his men, and after a severe struggle drove the enemy outside the fortifications. First Lt. Pond then went outside the works and, alone and unaided, fired a howitzer three times, throwing the enemy into confusion and causing him to retire.

1059 ◆ POOLE, WILLIAM B.

Rank: Quartermaster
Service: U.S. Navy
Birthday: 1833
Place of Birth: Cape Elizabeth Cumberland County, Maine
Date of Death: 15 August 1904
Place of Death: Lynn, Massachusetts
Cemetery: Pine Grove Cemetery (MH)—Lynn, Massachusetts
Entered Service at: Maine
Unit: U.S.S. *Kearsarge*
Battle or Place of Action: off Cherbourg, France
Date of Action: 19 June 1864
G.O. Number, Date: 45, 31 December 1864
Citation: Served as quartermaster on board the U.S.S. *Kearsarge* when she destroyed the *Alabama* off Cherbourg, France, 19 June 1864. Stationed at the helm, Poole steered the ship during the engagement in a cool and most creditable manner and was highly commended by his divisional officer for his gallantry under fire.

1060 ◆ PORTER, AMBROSE

Rank: Commissary Sergeant (highest rank: First Lieutenant)
Service: U.S. Army
Birthday: 2 February 1839
Place of Birth: Allegany County, Maryland
Date of Death: 21 January 1916
Place of Death: Phelps City, Missouri
Cemetery: Elmwood Cemetery (MH)—Rockport, Missouri
Entered Service at: Rockport, Atchison County, Missouri
Unit: Company D, 12th Missouri Cavalry
Battle or Place of Action: Tallahatchie River, Mississippi
Date of Action: 7 August 1864
Date of Issue: 24 August 1905
Citation: Was one of four volunteers who swam the river under a brisk fire of the enemy's sharpshooters and brought over a ferry boat, by means of which the troops crossed and dislodged the enemy from a strong position.

1061 ◆ PORTER, HORACE

Rank: Captain (highest rank: Brevet Brigadier General)
Service: U.S. Army
Birthday: 15 April 1837
Place of Birth: Huntingdon, Huntingdon County, Pennsylvania
Date of Death: 29 May 1921
Place of Death: New York, New York
Cemetery: Old First United Methodist Church—West Long Branch, New Jersey
Entered Service at: Harrisburg, Dauphin County, Pennsylvania
Unit: Ordnance Department
Battle or Place of Action: Chickamauga, Georgia
Date of Action: 20 September 1863
Date of Issue: 8 July 1902
Citation: While acting as a volunteer aide, at a critical moment when the lines were broken, rallied enough fugitives to hold the ground under heavy fire long enough to effect the escape of wagon trains and batteries.

1062 ◆ PORTER, JOHN REED

Rank: Private (highest rank: First Lieutenant)
Service: U.S. Army
Birthday: 14 November 1838
Place of Birth: Delaware County, Ohio
Date of Death: 17 October 1923
Cemetery: Union Cemetery—Macomb, Ohio
Entered Service at: McComb, Hancock County, Ohio
Unit: Company G, 21st Ohio Infantry
Battle or Place of Action: Georgia
Date of Action: April 1862
Date of Issue: September 1863
Citation: One of 19 of 24 men (including two civilians) who, by direction of Gen. Ormsby M. Mitchell, penetrated nearly 200 miles south into enemy territory and captured a railroad train at Big Shanty, Ga., in an attempt to destroy the bridges and track between Chattanooga and Atlanta.
Notes: POW

1063 ◆ PORTER, WILLIAM

Rank: Sergeant
Service: U.S. Army

Place of Birth: New York, New York
Entered Service at: Trenton, Mercer County, New Jersey
Unit: Company H, 1st New Jersey Cavalry
Battle or Place of Action: Deatonsville (Sailor's Creek), Virginia
Date of Action: 6 April 1865
Date of Issue: 3 July 1865
Citation: Among the first to check the enemy's countercharge.

1064 ◆ POST, PHILIP SIDNEY

Rank: Colonel (highest rank: Brevet Brigadier General)
Service: U.S. Army
Birthday: 19 March 1833
Place of Birth: Florida, Orange County, New York
Date of Death: 5 January 1895
Cemetery: Hope Cemetery—Galesburg, Illinois
Entered Service at: Galesburg, Knox County, Illinois
Unit: 59th Illinois Infantry
Battle or Place of Action: Nashville, Tennessee
Date of Action: 15-16 December 1864
Date of Issue: 18 March 1893
Citation: Led his brigade in an attack upon a strong position under a terrific fire of grape, canister, and musketry; was struck down by a grapeshot after he had reached the enemy's works.

1065 ◆ POSTLES, JAMES PARKE

Rank: Captain
Service: U.S. Army
Birthday: 28 September 1840
Place of Birth: Camden, Kent County, Delaware
Date of Death: 27 May 1908
Cemetery: Wilmington Cemetery—Wilmington, Delaware
Entered Service at: Wilmimgton, New Castle County, Delaware
Unit: Company A, 1st Delaware Infantry
Battle or Place of Action: Gettysburg, Pennsylvania
Date of Action: 2 July 1863
Date of Issue: 22 July 1892
Citation: Voluntarily delivered an order in the face of heavy fire from the enemy.

1066 ◆ POTTER, GEORGE W.

Rank: Private
Service: U.S. Army
Birthday: 11 December 1843
Place of Birth: Coventry, Kent County, Rhode Island
Date of Death: 30 November 1918
Cemetery: Swan Point Cemetery (MH)—Providence, Rhode Island
Entered Service at: Coventry, Kent County, Rhode Island
Unit: Company G, 1st Rhode Island Light Artillery
Battle or Place of Action: Petersburg, Virginia
Date of Action: 2 April 1865
Date of Issue: 4 March 1886
Citation: Was one of a detachment of 20 picked artillerymen who voluntarily accompanied an infantry assaulting party, and who turned upon the enemy the guns captured in the assault.

1067 ◆ POTTER, NORMAN F.

Rank: First Sergeant
Service: U.S. Army
Birthday: 10 June 1826
Place of Birth: Pompey, Onondaga County, New York
Date of Death: 25 April 1900
Cemetery: Delphi Falls Baptist Church Cemetery (MH)—Delphi Falls, New York
Entered Service at: Pompey, Onondaga County, New York
Unit: Company E, 149th New York Infantry
Battle or Place of Action: Lookout Mountain, Tennessee
Date of Action: 24 November 1863
Date of Issue: 24 June 1865
Citation: Capture of flag (Bragg's army).

1068 ◆ POWELL, WILLIAM HENRY

Rank: Major (highest rank: Brevet Major General)
Service: U.S. Army
Birthday: 25 May 1825
Place of Birth: Pontypool, Monmouthshire, South Wales
Date of Death: 26 December 1904
Place of Death: Sacket Harbor, New York
Cemetery: Graceland Cemetery—Chicago, Illinois
Entered Service at: Ironton, Lawrence County, Ohio
Unit: 2d West Virginia Cavalry
Battle or Place of Action: Sinking Creek, Virginia
Date of Action: 26 November 1862
Date of Issue: 22 July 1890
Citation: Distinguished services in raid, where with 20 men, he charged and captured the enemy's camp, 500 strong, without the loss of a man or gun.

1069 ◆ POWER, ALBERT

Rank: Private (highest rank: First Sergeant)
Service: U.S. Army
Birthday: 18 June 1842
Place of Birth: Liberty, Guernsey County, Ohio
Date of Death: 26 April 1923
Cemetery: I.O.O.F. Cemetery—Bloomfield, Iowa
Entered Service at: Bloomfield, Davis County, Iowa
Unit: Company A, 3d Iowa Cavalry
Battle or Place of Action: Pea Ridge, Arkansas
Date of Action: 7 March 1862
Date of Issue: 6 March 1899
Citation: Under a heavy fire and at great personal risk went to the aid of a dismounted comrade who was surrounded by the enemy, took him up on his own horse, and carried him to a place of safety.

1070 ◆ POWERS, WESLEY JAMES

Rank: Corporal
Service: U.S. Army
Birthday: 26 October 1845

Place of Birth: Orono, Ontario, Canada
Date of Death: 14 December 1902
Place of Death: St. Charles, Illinois
Cemetery: North Cemetery—St. Charles, Illinois
Entered Service at: Virgil, Kane County, Illinois
Unit: Company F, 147th Illinois Infantry
Battle or Place of Action: Oostanaula River, Georgia
Date of Action: 3 April 1865
Date of Issue: 24 October 1895
Citation: Voluntarily swam the river under heavy fire and secured a ferryboat, by means of which the command crossed.

1071 ◆ PRANCE, GEORGE

Rank: Captain of the Main Top
Service: U.S. Navy
Birthday: 1827
Place of Birth: France
Entered Service at: Boston, Suffolk County, Massachusetts
Unit: U.S.S. *Ticonderoga*
Battle or Place of Action: Fort Fisher, North Carolina
Date of Action: December 1864 & January 1865
G.O. Number, Date: 59, 22 June 1865
Citation: On board the U.S.S. *Ticonderoga* during attacks on Fort Fisher, 24 and 25 December 1864; and 13 to 15 January 1865. Despite heavy return fire by the enemy and the explosion of the 100-pounder Parrott rifle which killed eight men and wounded 12 more, Prance, as captain of a gun, performed his duties with skill and courage during the first two days of battle. As his ship again took position on the line on the 13th, he remained steadfast as the *Ticonderoga* maintained a well-placed fire upon the batteries onshore, and thereafter as she materially lessened the power of guns on the mound which had been turned upon our assaulting columns. During this action the flag was planted on one of the strongest fortifications possessed by the rebels.

1072 ◆ PRENTICE, JOSEPH ROLLIN

Rank: Private
Service: U.S. Army
Birthday: 6 December 1838
Place of Birth: Lancaster, Fairfield County, Ohio
Date of Death: 7 August 1908
Place of Death: Colorado Springs, Colorado
Cemetery: Sacred Heart Cemetery—Hebron, Nebraska
Entered Service at: Fort Wayne, Allen County, Indiana
Unit: Company E, 19th U.S. Infantry
Battle or Place of Action: Stone River, Tennessee
Date of Action: 31 December 1862
Date of Issue: 3 February 1894
Citation: Voluntarily rescued the body of his commanding officer, who had fallen mortally wounded. He brought off the field his mortally wounded leader under direct and constant rifle fire.

1073 ◆ PRESTON, JOHN

Rank: Landsman
Service: U.S. Navy
Birthday: 1841
Place of Birth: Ireland
Entered Service at: Boston, Suffolk County, Massachusetts
Unit: U.S.S. *Oneida*
Battle or Place of Action: Fort Morgan, Mobile Bay, Alabama
Date of Action: 5 August 1864
G.O. Number, Date: 45, 31 December 1864
Citation: Served on board the U.S.S. *Oneida* in the engagement at Mobile Bay, 5 August 1864. Severely wounded, Preston remained at his gun throughout the engagement which resulted in the capture of the rebel ram *Tennessee* and the damaging of Fort Morgan, carrying on until obliged to go to the surgeon to whom he reported himself as "only slightly injured." He then assisted in taking care of the wounded below and wanted to be allowed to return to his battle station on deck. Upon close examination it was found that he was wounded quite severely in both eyes.

1074 ◆ PRESTON, NOBLE DELANCE

Rank: First Lieutenant & Commissary (highest rank: Lieutenant Colonel)
Service: U.S. Army
Birthday: 2 February 1842
Place of Birth: Madison, Madison County, New York
Date of Death: 27 December 1919
Place of Death: Philadelphia, Pennsylvania
Entered Service at: Fulton, Oswego County, New York
Unit: 10th New York Cavalry
Battle or Place of Action: Trevilian Station, Virginia
Date of Action: 11 June 1864
Date of Issue: 22 November 1889
Citation: Voluntarily led a charge in which he was severely wounded.

1075 ◆ PRICE, EDWARD

Rank: Coxswain
Service: U.S. Navy
Birthday: 1840
Place of Birth: New York, New York
Entered Service at: New York, New York
Unit: U.S.S. *Brooklyn*
Battle or Place of Action: Fort Morgan, Mobile Bay, Alabama
Date of Action: 5 August 1864
G.O. Number, Date: 45, 31 December 1864
Citation: On board the U.S.S. *Brooklyn* during successful attacks against Fort Morgan, rebel gunboats and the ram *Tennessee* in Mobile Bay, 5 August 1864. When the sponge broke, leaving the head in the gun and completely disabling the weapon, Price immediately cleared it by pouring powder into the vent and blowing the sponge head out, thereafter continuing to man the weapon until the close of the furious action which resulted in the capture of the prize rebel ram *Tennessee* and in the infliction of damage and destruction of Fort Morgan.

1076 ◆ PROVINCE, GEORGE

Rank: Ordinary Seaman
Service: U.S. Navy
Birthday: 1842
Place of Birth: Newport, Newport County, Rhode Island
Entered Service at: Boston, Suffolk County, Massachusetts
Unit: U.S.S. *Santiago de Cuba*
Battle or Place of Action: Fort Fisher, North Carolina
Date of Action: 15 January 1865
G.O. Number, Date: 59, 22 June 1865
Citation: On board the U.S.S. *Santiago de Cuba* during the assault on Fort Fisher, 15 January 1865. As one of a boat crew detailed to one of the generals onshore, Province bravely entered the fort in the assault and accompanied his party in carrying dispatches at the height of the battle. He was one of six men who entered the fort in the assault from the fleet.

1077 ◆ PURCELL, HIRAM W.

Rank: Sergeant
Service: U.S. Army
Birthday: 1 August 1837
Place of Birth: Upper Black Eddy, Bucks County, Pennsylvania
Date of Death: 13 May 1918
Place of Death: White Haven, Pennsylvania
Cemetery: Laurel Hill Cemetery—White Haven, Pennsylvania
Entered Service at: Doylestown, Bucks County, Pennsylvania
Unit: Company G, 104th Pennsylvania Infantry
Battle or Place of Action: Fair Oaks, Virginia
Date of Action: 31 May 1862
Date of Issue: 12 May 1894
Citation: While carrying the regimental colors on the retreat he returned to face the advancing enemy, flag in hand, and saved the other color, which would otherwise have been captured.

1078 ◆ PURMAN, JAMES JACKSON

Rank: Lieutenant (highest rank: First Lieutenant)
Service: U.S. Army
Birthday: 1841
Place of Birth: Greene County, Pennsylvania
Date of Death: 10 May 1915
Place of Death: Washington, D.C.
Cemetery: Arlington National Cemetery (1-615)—Arlington, Virginia
Entered Service at: Waynesburg, Greene County, Pennsylvania
Unit: Company A, 140th Pennsylvania Infantry
Battle or Place of Action: Gettysburg, Pennsylvania
Date of Action: 2 July 1863
Date of Issue: 30 October 1896
Citation: Voluntarily assisted a wounded comrade to a place of apparent safety while the enemy were in close proximity; he received the fire of the enemy and a wound which resulted in the amputation of his left leg.

1079 ◆ PUTNAM, EDGAR PIERPONT

Rank: Sergeant (highest rank: Brevet Major New York Volunteers)
Service: U.S. Army
Birthday: 4 May 1844
Place of Birth: Stockton, Chautauqua County, New York
Date of Death: 20 May 1921
Cemetery: Lake View Cemetery—Jamestown, New York
Entered Service at: Stockton, Chautauqua County, New York
Unit: Company D, 9th New York Cavalry
Battle or Place of Action: Crumps Creek, Virginia
Date of Action: 27 May 1864
Date of Issue: 13 May 1892
Citation: With a small force on a reconnaissance, drove off a strong body of the enemy, charged into another force of the enemy's cavalry and stampeded them, taking 27 prisoners.

1080 ◆ PUTNAM, WINTHROP D.

Rank: Corporal
Service: U.S. Army
Birthday: 18 September 1837
Place of Birth: Southbridge, Worcester County, Massachusetts
Date of Death: 15 January 1907
Place of Death: Wood, Wisconsin
Cemetery: Wood National Cemetery (16-09) (MH)—Wood, Wisconsin
Entered Service at: Peoria, Peoria County, Illinois
Unit: Company A, 77th Illinois Infantry
Battle or Place of Action: Vicksburg, Mississippi
Date of Action: 22 May 1863
Date of Issue: 4 April 1898
Citation: Carried, with others, by hand, a cannon up to and fired it through an embrasure of the enemy's works.

1081 ◆ PYNE, GEORGE

Rank: Seaman
Service: U.S. Navy
Birthday: 1841
Place of Birth: England
Entered Service at: New York, New York
Unit: U.S.S. *Magnolia*
Battle or Place of Action: St. Marks, Florida
Date of Action: 5, 6 March 1865
G.O. Number, Date: 59, 22 June 1865
Citation: As seaman on board the U.S.S. *Magnolia*, St. Marks, Fla., 5 and 6 March 1865. Serving with the Army in charge of Navy howitzers during the attack on St. Marks and throughout this fierce engagement, Pyne, although wounded, made remarkable efforts in assisting transport of the gun, and his coolness and determination in courageously standing by

his gun while under the fire of the enemy were a credit to the service to which he belonged.

1082 ◆ QUAY, MATTHEW STANLEY

Rank: Colonel
Service: U.S. Army
Birthday: 30 September 1833
Place of Birth: Dillsburg, York County, Pennsylvania
Date of Death: 28 May 1904
Cemetery: Beaver Cemetery—Beaver, Pennsylvania
Entered Service at: Harrisburg, Dauphin County, Pennsylvania
Unit: 134th Pennsylvania Infantry
Battle or Place of Action: Fredericksburg, Virginia
Date of Action: 13 December 1862
Date of Issue: 9 July 1888
Citation: Although out of service, he voluntarily resumed duty on the eve of the battle and took a conspicuous part in the charge on the heights.

1083 ◆ QUINLAN, JAMES

Rank: Major (highest rank: Lieutenant Colonel)
Service: U.S. Army
Birthday: 13 September 1833
Place of Birth: Clomwell, County Tipperary, Ireland
Date of Death: 29 August 1906
Place of Death: New York, New York
Cemetery: Calvary Cemetery—Woodside, New York
Entered Service at: New York, New York
Unit: 88th New York Infantry
Battle or Place of Action: Savage Station, Virginia
Date of Action: 29 June 1862
Date of Issue: 18 February 1891
Citation: Led his regiment on the enemy's battery, silenced the guns, held the position against overwhelming numbers, and covered the retreat of the 2d Army Corps.

1084 ◆ RAFFERTY, PETER F.

Rank: Private (highest rank: Captain)
Service: U.S. Army
Birthday: 12 June 1845
Place of Birth: County Tyrone, Ireland
Date of Death: 30 April 1910
Cemetery: Calvary Cemetery (First)—Woodside, New York
Entered Service at: New York, New York
Unit: Company B, 69th New York Infantry
Battle or Place of Action: Malvern Hill, Virginia
Date of Action: 1 July 1862
Date of Issue: 2 August 1897
Citation: Having been wounded and directed to the rear, declined to go, but continued in action, receiving several additional wounds, which resulted in his capture by the enemy and his total disability for military service.
Notes: POW

1085 ◆ RAND, CHARLES FRANKLIN

Rank: Private (highest rank: Captain)
Service: U.S. Army
Birthday: 1839
Place of Birth: Batavia, Genesee County, New York
Date of Death: 13 October 1908
Cemetery: Arlington National Cemetery (1-125-B)—Arlington, Virginia
Entered Service at: Batavia, Genesee County, New York
Unit: Company K, 12th New York Infantry
Battle or Place of Action: Blackburn's Ford, Virginia
Date of Action: 18 July 1861
Date of Issue: 23 October 1897
Citation: Remained in action when a part of his regiment broke in disorder, joined another company, and fought with it through the remainder of the engagement.

1086 ◆ RANNAHAN, JOHN

Rank: Corporal
Service: U.S. Marine Corps
Birthday: 1836
Place of Birth: County Monaghan, Ireland
Entered Service at: Pennsylvania
Unit: U.S.S. *Minnesota*
Battle or Place of Action: Fort Fisher, North Carolina
Date of Action: 15 January 1865
G.O. Number, Date: 59, 22 June 1865
Citation: On board the U.S.S. *Minnesota*, in the assault on Fort Fisher, 15 January 1865. Landing on the beach with the assaulting party from his ship, Cpl. Rannahan advanced to the top of the sandhill and partly through the breach in the palisades, despite enemy fire which killed or wounded many officers and men. When more than two-thirds of the men became seized with panic and retreated on the run, he remained with the party until dark when it came safely away, bringing its wounded, its arms, and its colors.

1087 ◆ RANNEY, GEORGE E.

Rank: Assistant Surgeon (highest rank: Surgeon)
Service: U.S. Army
Birthday: 13 June 1839
Place of Birth: Batavia, Genesee County, New York
Date of Death: 10 November 1915
Place of Death: Lansing, Michigan
Cemetery: Mount Hope Cemetery—Lansing, Michigan
Entered Service at: Grand Rapids, Kent County, Michigan
Unit: 2d Michigan Cavalry
Battle or Place of Action: Resaca, Georgia
Date of Action: 14 May 1864
Date of Issue: 24 April 1901
Citation: At great personal risk, went to the aid of a wounded soldier, Pvt. Charles W. Baker, lying under heavy fire between the lines and with the aid of an orderly, carried him to a place of safety.
Notes: POW

1088 ◆ RANNEY, MYRON H.

Rank: Private (highest rank: Corporal)
Service: U.S. Army
Birthday: 1846
Place of Birth: Franklinville, Cattaraugus County, New York
Date of Death: 26 September 1910
Cemetery: I.O.O.F. Cemetery—Olympia, Washington
Entered Service at: Dansville, Livingston County, New York
Unit: Company G, 13th New York Infantry
Battle or Place of Action: Bull Run, Virginia
Date of Action: 30 August 1862
Date of Issue: 23 March 1895
Citation: Picked up the colors and carried them off the field after the color bearer had been shot down; was himself wounded.

1089 ◆ RANSBOTTOM, ALFRED

Rank: First Sergeant
Service: U.S. Army
Birthday: 1831
Place of Birth: South Zanesville, Delaware County, Ohio
Date of Death: 14 April 1893
Place of Death: Springfield Township, Ohio
Cemetery: Roseville Cemetery (MH)—Roseville, Ohio
Entered Service at: Nashport, Muskingum County, Ohio
Unit: Company K, 97th Ohio Infantry
Battle or Place of Action: Franklin, Tennessee
Date of Action: 30 November 1864
Date of Issue: 24 February 1865
Citation: Captured the flag of the 2d Mississippi Infantry (C.S.A.), in a hand-to-hand fight with the color bearer.

1090 ◆ RATCLIFF, EDWARD

Rank: First Sergeant (highest rank: Sergeant Major)
Service: U.S. Army
Birthday: 8 February 1835
Place of Birth: James County, Virginia
Date of Death: 10 March 1915
Place of Death: Nelson, Virginia
Cemetery: Chescake Cemetery Naval Station—Lackey, Virginia
Entered Service at: Yorktown, York County, Virginia
Unit: Company C, 38th U.S. Colored Troops
Battle or Place of Action: Chapin's Farm, Virginia
Date of Action: 29 September 1864
Date of Issue: 6 April 1865
Citation: Commanded and gallantly led his company after the commanding officer had been killed; was the first enlisted man to enter the enemy's works.

1091 ◆ RAUB, JACOB F.

Rank: Assistant Surgeon
Service: U.S. Army
Birthday: 13 May 1840
Place of Birth: Raubsville, Northampton County, Pennsylvania
Date of Death: 21 May 1906
Cemetery: Arlington National Cemetery (3-1469)—Arlington, Virginia
Entered Service at: Weaversville, Pennsylvania
Unit: 210th Pennsylvania Infantry
Battle or Place of Action: Hatcher's Run, Virginia
Date of Action: 5 February 1865
Date of Issue: 20 April 1896
Citation: Discovering a flank movement by the enemy, appraised the commanding general at great peril, and though a noncombatant voluntarily participated with the troops in repelling this attack.

1092 ◆ RAYMOND, WILLIAM H.

Rank: Corporal (highest rank: Second Lieutenant)
Service: U.S. Army
Birthday: 30 May 1844
Place of Birth: Penfield, Monroe County, New York
Date of Death: 7 December 1916
Place of Death: Washington, D.C.
Cemetery: Arlington National Cemetery (2-4853) (MH)—Arlington, Virginia
Entered Service at: Penfield, Monroe County, New York
Unit: Company A, 108th New York Infantry
Battle or Place of Action: Gettysburg, Pennsylvania
Date of Action: 3 July 1863
Date of Issue: 10 March 1896
Citation: Voluntarily and under a severe fire brought a box of ammunition to his comrades on the skirmish line.

1093 ◆ READ, CHARLES

Rank: Ordinary Seaman (highest rank: Ship's Cook)
Service: U.S. Navy
Birthday: 1840
Place of Birth: Cambridge, Washington County, New York
Entered Service at: New York, New York
Unit: U.S.S. *Magnolia*
Battle or Place of Action: St. Marks, Florida
Date of Action: 5, 6 March 1865
G.O. Number, Date: 59, 22 June 1865
Citation: As seaman on board the U.S.S. *Magnolia*, St. Marks, Fla., 5 and 6 March 1865. Serving with the Army in charge of Navy howitzers during the attack on St. Marks and throughout this fierce engagement, Read made remarkable efforts in assisting transport of the gun, and his coolness and determination in courageously standing by his gun while under the fire of the enemy were a credit to the service to which he belonged.

1094 ◆ READ, CHARLES A.

Rank: Coxswain
Service: U.S. Navy
Birthday: 1837
Place of Birth: Sweden

Entered Service at: Ohio
Unit: U.S.S. *Kearsarge*
Battle or Place of Action: off Cherbourg, France
Date of Action: 19 June 1864
G.O. Number, Date: 45, 31 December 1864
Citation: Served as coxswain on board the U.S.S. *Kearsarge* when she destroyed the *Alabama* off Cherbourg, France, 19 June 1864. Acting as the first sponger of the pivot gun during this bitter engagement, Read exhibited marked coolness and good conduct and was highly recommended for his gallantry under fire by his divisional officer.

1095 ◆ READ, GEORGE E.

Rank: Seaman
Service: U.S. Navy
Birthday: 1838
Place of Birth: Rhode Island
Date of Death: 1910
Cemetery: Little Neck Cemetery (MH)—Riverside, Rhode Island
Entered Service at: Rhode Island
Unit: U.S.S. *Kearsarge*
Battle or Place of Action: off Cherbourg, France
Date of Action: 19 June 1864
G.O. Number, Date: 45, 31 December 1864
Citation: Served as seaman on board the U.S.S. *Kearsarge* when she destroyed the *Alabama* off Cherbourg, France, 19 June 1864. Acting as the first loader of the No. 2 gun during this bitter engagement, Read exhibited marked coolness and good conduct and was highly recommended for his gallantry under fire by his divisional officer.

1096 ◆ READ, MORTON A.

Rank: First Lieutenant
Service: U.S. Army
Birthday: 1843
Place of Birth: Brockport, Monroe County, New York
Date of Death: 10 July 1921
Place of Death: Danville, Illinois
Cemetery: Danville National Cemetery (10-3033-R-8) (MH)—Danville, Illinois
Entered Service at: Brockport, Monroe County, New York
Unit: Company D, 8th New York Cavalry
Battle or Place of Action: Appomattox Station, Virginia
Date of Action: 8 April 1865
Date of Issue: 3 May 1865
Citation: Capture of flag of 1st Texas Infantry (C.S.A.).

1097 ◆ REBMANN, GEORGE F.

Rank: Sergeant
Service: U.S. Army
Birthday: 10 April 1840
Place of Birth: Schuyler County, Illinois
Date of Death: 20 August 1918
Cemetery: Messerer Cemetery—Rushville, Illinois
Entered Service at: Rushville, Schuyler County, Illinois
Unit: Company B, 119th Illinois Infantry
Battle or Place of Action: Fort Blakely, Alabama
Date of Action: 9 April 1865
Date of Issue: 8 June 1865
Citation: Capture of flag.

1098 ◆ REDDICK, WILLIAM HENRY HARRISON

Rank: Corporal (highest rank: Second Lieutenant)
Service: U.S. Army
Birthday: 18 September 1840
Place of Birth: Locust Grove, Adams County, Ohio
Date of Death: 8 November 1903
Cemetery: Letts Cemetery (MH)—Letts, Iowa
Entered Service at: Portsmouth, Scioto County, Ohio
Unit: Company B, 33d Ohio Infantry
Battle or Place of Action: Georgia
Date of Action: April 1862
Date of Presentation: 25 March 1863
Place of Presentation: Washington, D.C., presented by Sec. of War Stanton
Citation: One of 19 of 24 men (including two civilians) who, by direction of Gen. Ormsby M. Mitchell, penetrated nearly 200 miles south into enemy territory and captured a railroad train at Big Shanty, Ga., in an attempt to destroy the bridges and track between Chattanooga and Atlanta.

1099 ◆ REED, AXEL HAYFORD

Rank: Sergeant (highest rank: Captain)
Service: U.S. Army
Birthday: 13 March 1835
Place of Birth: Hartford, Oxford County, Maine
Date of Death: 21 January 1917
Place of Death: Glencoe, Minnesota
Cemetery: Mount Auburn Cemetery (MH)—Glencoe, Minnesota
Entered Service at: Glencoe, McLeod County, Minnesota
Unit: Company K, 2d Minnesota Infantry
Battle or Place of Action: Chickamauga, Georgia and Missionary Ridge, Tennessee
Date of Action: 19 September 1863 & 15 November 1863
Date of Issue: 2 April 1898
Citation: While in arrest at Chickamagua, Ga., left his place in the rear and voluntarily went to the line of battle, secured a rifle, and fought gallantly during the two-day battle; was released from arrest in recognition of his bravery. At Missionary Ridge Reed commanded his company and gallantly led it, being among the first to enter the enemy's works; was severely wounded, losing an arm, but declined a discharge and remained in active service to the end of the war.

1100 ◆ REED, CHARLES WELLINGTON

Rank: Bugler (highest rank: Chief Bugler)
Service: U.S. Army
Birthday: 1 April 1842
Place of Birth: Charlestown, Suffolk County, Massachusetts

Date of Death: 29 April 1926
Place of Death: Norwell, Massachusetts
Cemetery: Mount Auburn Cemetery (MH)—Cambridge, Massachusetts
Entered Service at: Malden, Middlesex County, Massachusetts
Unit: 9th Independent Battery, Massachusetts Light Artillery
Served as: Bugler
Battle or Place of Action: Gettysburg, Pennsylvania
Date of Action: 2 July 1863
Date of Issue: 16 August 1895
Citation: Rescued his wounded captain from between the lines.

1101 ◆ REED, GEORGE W.

Rank: Private
Service: U.S. Army
Birthday: 1831
Place of Birth: Cambria County, Pennsylvania
Date of Death: 21 December 1906
Place of Death: Chicago, Illinois
Cemetery: Grand View Cemetery—Johnstown, Pennsylvania
Entered Service at: Johnstown, Cambria County, Pennsylvania
Unit: Company E, 11th Pennsylvania Infantry
Battle or Place of Action: Weldon Railroad, Virginia
Date of Action: 21 August 1864
Date of Issue: 6 September 1864
Citation: Capture of flag of 24th North Carolina Volunteers (C.S.A.).

1102 ◆ REED, WILLIAM

Rank: Private
Service: U.S. Army
Birthday: 21 February 1839
Place of Birth: Union County, Pennsylvania
Date of Death: 30 May 1918
Cemetery: Riverview Cemetery (MH)—Huntingdon, Pennsylvania
Entered Service at: Pekin, Tazewell County, Illinois
Unit: Company H, 8th Missouri Infantry
Battle or Place of Action: Vicksburg, Mississippi
Date of Action: 22 May 1863
Date of Issue: 12 December 1895
Citation: Gallantry in the charge of the "volunteer storming party."

1103 ◆ REEDER, CHARLES A.

Rank: Private (highest rank: Corporal)
Service: U.S. Army
Birthday: 20 November 1843
Place of Birth: Harrison, Clay County, West Virginia
Date of Death: 28 September 1902
Place of Death: Morgantown, West Virginia
Cemetery: Masonic Cemetery—Shinnston, West Virginia
Entered Service at: Shinnston, Harrison County, West Virginia
Unit: Company G, 12th West Virginia Infantry
Battle or Place of Action: Battery Gregg, near Petersburg, Virginia
Date of Action: 2 April 1865
Date of Issue: 3 April 1867
Citation: Capture of flag.

1104 ◆ REGAN, JEREMIAH

Rank: Quartermaster
Service: U.S. Navy
Birthday: 1832
Place of Birth: Boston, Suffolk County, Massachusetts
Entered Service at: Boston, Suffolk County, Massachusetts
Unit: U.S.S. *Galena*
Battle or Place of Action: Drewry's Bluff, Virginia
Date of Action: 15 May 1862
G.O. Number, Date: 11, 3 April 1863
Citation: As captain of No. 2 gun on board the U.S.S. *Galena* in the attack upon Drewry's Bluff, 15 May 1862. With his ship severely damaged by the enemy's shellfire and several men killed and wounded, Regan continued to man his gun throughout the engagement despite the concentration of fire directed against men at their guns by enemy sharpshooters in rifle pits along the banks.

1105 ◆ REID, ROBERT ALEXANDER

Rank: Private (highest rank: Ordnance Sergeant)
Service: U.S. Army
Birthday: 22 January 1842
Place of Birth: Raploch, Scotland
Date of Death: 25 April 1929
Place of Death: Pottsville, Pennsylvania
Cemetery: I.O.O.F. Cemetery (MH)—Pottsville, Pennsylvania
Entered Service at: Pottsville, Schuylkill County, Pennsylvania
Unit: Company G, 48th Pennsylvania Infantry
Battle or Place of Action: Petersburg, Virginia
Date of Action: 17 June 1864
Date of Issue: 1 December 1864
Citation: Capture of flag of 44th Tennessee Infantry (C.S.A.).

1106 ◆ REIGLE, DANIEL P.

Rank: Corporal (highest rank: Sergeant)
Service: U.S. Army
Birthday: 19 February 1841
Place of Birth: Adams County, Pennsylvania
Date of Death: 19 March 1917
Place of Death: Gettysburg, Pennsylvania
Cemetery: Mount Carmel Cemetery—Littlestown, Pennsylvania
Entered Service at: Gettysburg, Adams County, Pennsylvania
Unit: Company F, 87th Pennsylvania Infantry
Battle or Place of Action: Cedar Creek, Virginia

Date of Action: 19 October 1864
Date of Issue: 26 October 1864
Citation: For gallantry while rushing forward to capture a Confederate flag at the stone fence where the enemy's last stand was made.

1107 ◆ REISINGER, JAMES MONROE

Rank: Corporal (highest rank: First Lieutenant)
Service: U.S. Army
Birthday: 28 October 1842
Place of Birth: Beaver County, Pennsylvania
Date of Death: 25 May 1925
Place of Death: Franklin, Pennsylvania
Cemetery: Greenville Cemetery (MH)—Meadville, Pennsylvania
Entered Service at: Meadville, Crawford County, Pennsylvania
Unit: Company H, 150th Pennsylvania Infantry
Battle or Place of Action: Gettysburg, Pennsylvania
Date of Action: 1 July 1863
Citation: Specially brave and meritorious conduct in the face of the enemy. Awarded under Act of Congress, January 25, 1907.

1108 ◆ RENNINGER, LOUIS

Rank: Corporal
Service: U.S. Army
Birthday: 25 August 1841
Place of Birth: Liverpool, Ohio
Date of Death: 17 November 1908
Place of Death: Eugene, Oregon
Cemetery: Eugene Pioneer Cemetery—Eugene, Oregon
Entered Service at: Liverpool, Ohio
Unit: Company H, 37th Ohio Infantry
Battle or Place of Action: Vicksburg, Mississippi
Date of Action: 22 May 1863
Date of Issue: 15 August 1894
Citation: Gallantry in the charge of the "volunteer storming party."

1109 ◆ REYNOLDS, GEORGE

Rank: Private
Service: U.S. Army
Place of Birth: Ireland
Entered Service at: New York, New York
Unit: Company M, 9th New York Cavalry
Battle or Place of Action: Winchester, Virginia
Date of Action: 19 September 1864
Date of Issue: 27 September 1864
Citation: Capture of Virginia state flag.

1110 ◆ RHODES, JULIUS DEXTER

Rank: Private (highest rank: Sergeant Major)
Service: U.S. Army
Birthday: 1 October 1841
Place of Birth: Monroe County, Michigan
Date of Death: 19 February 1906
Place of Death: Washington, D.C.
Entered Service at: Springville, Erie County, New York
Unit: Company F, 5th New York Cavalry
Battle or Place of Action: Thoroughfare Gap & Bull Run, Virginia
Date of Action: 28,30 August 1862
Date of Issue: 9 March 1887
Citation: After having had his horse shot under him in the fight at Thoroughfare Gap, Va., he voluntarily joined the 105th New York Volunteers and was conspicuous in the advance on the enemy's lines. Displayed gallantry in the advance on the skirmish line at Bull Run, Va., where he was wounded.

1111 ◆ RHODES, SYLVESTER D.

Rank: Sergeant (highest rank: Captain)
Service: U.S. Army
Birthday: December 1842
Place of Birth: Plains, Pennsylvania
Date of Death: 29 August 1904
Place of Death: Parsons, Pennsylvania
Cemetery: Hollenbeck Cemetery—Wilkes-Barre, Pennsylvania
Entered Service at: Wilkes-Barre, Luzerne County, Pennsylvania
Unit: Company D, 61st Pennsylvania Infantry
Battle or Place of Action: Fisher's Hill, Virginia
Date of Action: 22 September 1864
Date of Issue: 16 February 1897
Citation: Was on the skirmish line which drove the enemy from the first entrenchment and was the first man to enter the breastworks, capturing one of the guns and turning it upon the enemy.

1112 ◆ RICE, CHARLES

Rank: Coal Heaver (highest rank: Fireman Second Class)
Service: U.S. Navy
Birthday: 1840
Place of Birth: Russia
Entered Service at: Portland, Cumberland County, Maine
Unit: U.S.S. *Agawam*
Battle or Place of Action: Fort Fisher, North Carolina
Date of Action: 23 December 1864
G.O. Number, Date: 45, 31 December 1864
Date of Presentation: 12 May 1865
Place of Presentation: On board the U.S.S. *Agawam* off New Bern, North Carolina
Citation: On board the U.S.S. *Agawam* as one of a volunteer crew of a powder boat which was exploded near Fort Fisher, 23 December 1864. The powder boat, towed in by the *Wilderness* to prevent detection by the enemy, cast off and slowly steamed to within 300 yards of the beach. After fuses and fires had been lit and a second anchor with short scope let go to assure the boat's tailing inshore, the crew boarded the *Wilderness* and proceeded a distance of 12 miles from shore. Less than two hours later the explosion took place, and the following day, fires were observed still burning at the fort.

1113 ◆ RICE, EDMUND

Rank: Major (highest rank: Brigadier General)
Service: U.S. Army
Birthday: 2 December 1842
Place of Birth: Brighton, Suffolk County, Massachusetts
Date of Death: 20 July 1906
Place of Death: Boston, Massachusetts
Cemetery: Arlington National Cemetery (3-1875)—Arlington, Virginia
Entered Service at: Cambridge, Middlesex Ccounty, Massachusetts
Unit: 19th Massachusetts Infantry
Battle or Place of Action: Gettysburg, Pennsylvania
Date of Action: 3 July 1863
Date of Issue: 6 October 1891
Citation: Conspicuous bravery on the third day of the battle on the counterchage against Pickett's division where he fell severely wounded within the enemy's lines.

1114 ◆ RICH, CARLOS H.

Rank: First Sergeant
Service: U.S. Army
Birthday: 11 February 1841
Place of Birth: Canada
Date of Death: 29 May 1918
Place of Death: Bennington, Vermont
Cemetery: Roxbury Cemetery—Roxbury, Vermont
Entered Service at: Northfield, Franklin County, Massachusetts
Unit: Company K, 4th Vermont Infantry
Battle or Place of Action: Wilderness Campaign, Virginia
Date of Action: 5 May 1864
Date of Issue: 4 January 1895
Citation: Saved the life of an officer.

1115 ◆ RICHARDS, LOUIS

Rank: Quartermaster (highest rank: Acting Master's Mate)
Service: U.S. Navy
Birthday: 1835
Place of Birth: New York, New York
Date of Death: 7 January 1894
Place of Death: Brooklyn, New York
Cemetery: Evergreen Cemetery—Brooklyn, New York
Entered Service at: New York, New York
Unit: U.S.S. *Pensacola*
Battle or Place of Action: Forts Jackson & St. Philip and New Orleans, Louisiana
Date of Action: 24-25 April 1862
G.O. Number, Date: 11, 3 April 1863
Citation: Richards served as quartermaster on board the U.S.S. *Pensacola* in the attacks upon Forts Jackson and St. Philip, and at the taking of New Orleans, 24 and 25 April 1862. Through all the din and roar of battle, he steered the ship through the narrow opening of the barricade, and his attention to orders contributed to the successful passage of the ship without once fouling the shore or the obstacles of the barricade.

1116 ◆ RICHARDSON, WILLIAM R.

Rank: Private
Service: U.S. Army
Birthday: 1842
Place of Birth: Cleveland, Cuyahoga County, Ohio
Date of Death: 24 October 1873
Cemetery: City Cemetery—Massillon, Ohio
Entered Service at: Washington, Ohio
Unit: Company A, 2d Ohio Cavalry
Battle or Place of Action: Deatonsville (Sailor's Creek), Virginia
Date of Action: 6 April 1865
Date of Issue: 7 April 1866
Citation: Having been captured and taken to the rear, Richardson made his escape, rejoined the Union lines, and furnished information of great importance as to the enemy's position and the approaches thereto.

1117 ◆ RICHEY, WILLIAM E.

Rank: Corporal (highest rank: Sergeant)
Service: U.S. Army
Birthday: 1841
Place of Birth: Athens County, Ohio
Date of Death: 21 June 1909
Cemetery: Harveyville Cemetery—Harveyville, Kansas
Entered Service at: New Concord, Muskingum County, Ohio
Unit: Company A, 15th Ohio Infantry
Battle or Place of Action: Chickamauga, Georgia
Date of Action: 19 September 1863
Date of Issue: 9 November 1893
Citation: While on the extreme front, between the lines of the combatants single-handedly he captured a Confederate major who was armed and mounted.

1118 ◆ *RICHMOND, JAMES

Rank: Private
Service: U.S. Army
Birthday: 1843
Place of Birth: Maine
Date of Death: 3 June 1864
Place of Death: Washington, D.C.
Cemetery: Arlington National Cemetery (27-886) (MH)—Arlington, Virginia
Entered Service at: Fremont, Sandusky County, Ohio
Unit: Company F, 8th Ohio Infantry
Battle or Place of Action: Gettysburg, Pennsylvania
Date of Action: 3 July 1863
Date of Issue: 1 December 1864
Citation: Capture of flag.

1119 ◆ RICKSECKER, JOHN HENRY

Rank: Private
Service: U.S. Army
Birthday: 14 November 1843

Place of Birth: Mansfield, Richland County, Ohio
Date of Death: 2 August 1929
Place of Death: Kansas City, Missouri
Cemetery: Forest Hills Cemetery (MH)—Kansas City, Missouri
Entered Service at: Aurora, Portage County, Ohio
Unit: Company D, 104th Ohio Infantry
Battle or Place of Action: Franklin, Tennessee
Date of Action: 30 November 1864
Date of Issue: 3 February 1865
Citation: Capture of flag of 16th Alabama Artillery (C.S.A.).

1120 ◆ RIDDELL, RUDOLPH R.

Rank: Lieutenant (highest rank: Brevet Lieutenant Colonel)
Service: U.S. Army
Birthday: 11 February 1847
Place of Birth: Hamilton, Madison County, New York
Date of Death: 8 September 1913
Place of Death: Albany, New York
Cemetery: Madison Street Cemetery (MH)—Hamilton, New York
Entered Service at: Hamilton, Madison County, New York
Unit: Company I, 61st New York Infantry
Battle or Place of Action: Deatonsville (Sailor's Creek), Virginia
Date of Action: 6 April 1865
Date of Issue: 10 May 1865
Citation: Captured the flag of the 6th Alabama Cavalry (C.S.A.).

1121 ◆ RILEY, THOMAS

Rank: Private (highest rank: Corporal)
Service: U.S. Army
Place of Birth: Ireland
Entered Service at: New Orleans, Orleans County, Louisiana
Unit: Company D, 1st Louisiana Cavalry
Battle or Place of Action: Fort Blakely, Alabama
Date of Action: 4 April 1865
Date of Issue: 8 June 1865
Citation: Captured the flag of the 6th Alabama Cavalry (C.S.A.).

1122 ◆ RINGOLD, EDWARD

Rank: Coxswain
Service: U.S. Navy
Birthday: 1827
Place of Birth: Baltimore, Baltimore County, Maryland
Entered Service at: Maryland
Unit: U.S.S. *Wabash*
Battle or Place of Action: Pocataligo, South Carolina
Date of Action: 22 October 1862
G.O. Number, Date: 17, 10 July 1863
Citation: Served as coxswain on board the U.S.S. *Wabash* in the engagement at Pocataligo, 22 October 1862. Soliciting permission to accompany the howitzer corps and performing his duty with such gallantry and presence of mind as to attract the attention of all around him, Ringold, knowing there was a scarcity of ammunition, went through the whole line of fire with his shirt slung over his shoulder filled with fixed ammunition which he had brought from two miles to the rear of the lines.

1123 ◆ RIPLEY, WILLIAM YOUNG WARREN

Rank: Lieutenant Colonel (highest rank: Major General)
Service: U.S. Army
Birthday: 31 December 1832
Place of Birth: Middlebury, Addison County, Vermont
Date of Death: 16 December 1905
Cemetery: Evergreen Cemetery (MH)—Rutland, Vermont
Entered Service at: Rutland, Rutland County, Vermont
Unit: 1st U.S. Sharpshooters
Battle or Place of Action: Malvern Hill, Virginia
Date of Action: 1 July 1862
Date of Issue: 11 March 1893
Citation: At a critical moment brought up two regiments, which he led against the enemy himself, being severely wounded.

1124 ◆ ROANTREE, JAMES S.

Rank: Sergeant (highest rank: First Sergeant)
Service: U.S. Marine Corps
Birthday: 1835
Place of Birth: Dublin, County Dublin, Ireland
Date of Death: 24 February 1873
Place of Death: Boston, Massachusetts
Cemetery: Calvary Cemetery—Roslindale, Massachusetts
Entered Service at: New York
Unit: U.S.S. *Oneida*
Battle or Place of Action: Mobile Bay, Alabama
Date of Action: 5 August 1864
G.O. Number, Date: 45, 31 December 1864
Citation: On board the U.S.S. *Oneida* during action against rebel forts and gunboats and with the ram *Tennessee* in Mobile Bay, 5 August 1864. Despite damage to his ship and the loss of several men onboard as the enemy fire raked her decks and penetrated her boilers, Sgt. Roantree performed his duties with skill and courage throughout the furious battle which resulted in the surrender of the rebel ram *Tennessee* and in the damaging and destruction of batteries at Fort Morgan.

1125 ◆ ROBBINS, AUGUSTUS J.

Rank: Second Lieutenant
Service: U.S. Army
Birthday: 17 November 1839
Place of Birth: Grafton, Windham County, Vermont
Date of Death: 6 September 1909
Place of Death: Lakewood, New Jersey
Cemetery: Woodlawn Cemetery (MH)—Lakewood, New Jersey
Entered Service at: Grafton, Windham County, Vermont
Unit: Company B, 2d Vermont Infantry
Battle or Place of Action: Spotsylvania, Virginia

Date of Action: 12 May 1864
Date of Issue: 24 March 1892
Citation: While voluntarily serving as a staff officer, successfully withdrew a regiment across and around a severely exposed position to the rest of the command; was severely wounded.

1126 ◆ ROBERTS, JAMES

Rank: Seaman
Service: U.S. Navy
Birthday: 14 February 1837
Place of Birth: England
Date of Death: 19 October 1908
Place of Death: Bath, New York
Cemetery: Bath National Cemetery (1-26-2) (MH)—Bath, New York
Entered Service at: Hartford, Hartford County, Connecticut
Unit: U.S.S. *Agawan*
Battle or Place of Action: Fort Fisher, North Carolina
Date of Action: 23 December 1864
G.O. Number, Date: 45, 31 December 1864
Date of Presentation: 12 May 1865
Place of Presentation: off New Bern, NC, on board the U.S.S. *Agawam*
Citation: Roberts served on board the U.S.S. *Agawam*, as one of a volunteer crew of a powder boat which was exploded near Fort Fisher, 23 December 1864. The powder boat, towed in by the *Wilderness* to prevent detection by the enemy, cast off and slowly steamed to within 300 yards of the beach. After fuses and fires had been lit and a second anchor with short scope let go to insure the boat's tailing inshore, the crew again boarded the *Wilderness* and proceeded a distance of 12 miles from shore. Less than two hours later the explosion took place, and the following day fires were observed still burning at the fort.

1127 ◆ ROBERTS, OTIS O.

Rank: Sergeant
Service: U.S. Army
Birthday: 20 March 1842
Place of Birth: Sangerville, Piscataquis County, Maine
Date of Death: 8 February 1930
Place of Death: Dexter, Maine
Cemetery: Mount Pleasant Cemetery (MH)—Dexter, Maine
Entered Service at: Dexter, Penobscot County, Maine
Unit: Company H, 6th Maine Infantry
Battle or Place of Action: Rappahannock Station, Virginia
Date of Action: 7 November 1863
Date of Issue: 28 December 1863
Citation: Capture of flag of 8th Louisiana (C.S.A.) in a hand-to-hand struggle with the color bearer.

1128 ◆ ROBERTSON, ROBERT STODDART

Rank: First Lieutenant (highest rank: Brevet Colonel NY Volunteers)
Service: U.S. Army
Birthday: 16 April 1839
Place of Birth: Argyle, Washington County, New York
Date of Death: 25 August 1906
Cemetery: Lindenwood Cemetery—Fort Wayne, Indiana
Entered Service at: Argyle, Washington County, New York
Unit: Company K, 93d New York Infantry
Battle or Place of Action: Corbins Bridge, Virginia
Date of Action: 8 May 1864
Date of Issue: 2 August 1897
Citation: While acting as aide-de-camp to a general officer, seeing a regiment break to the rear, he seized its colors, rode with them to the front in the face of the advancing enemy, and rallied the retreating regiment.

1129 ◆ *ROBERTSON, SAMUEL

Rank: Private
Service: U.S. Army
Birthday: 1843
Place of Birth: Muskingum County, Ohio
Date of Death: 18 June 1862
Cemetery: Chattanooga National Cemetery (H-11177) (MH)—Chattanooga, Tennessee
Entered Service at: Boarneville, Ross County, Ohio
Unit: Company G, 33d Ohio Infantry
Battle or Place of Action: Georgia
Date of Action: April 1862
Date of Issue: September 1863
Citation: One of 19 of 24 men (including two civilians) who, by direction of Gen. Ormsby M. Mitchell, penetrated nearly 200 miles south into enemy territory and captured a railroad train at Big Shanty, Ga., in an attempt to destroy the bridges and track between Chattanooga and Atlanta.

1130 ◆ ROBIE, GEORGE FRANK

Rank: Sergeant (highest rank: First Lieutenant)
Service: U.S. Army
Birthday: 17 June 1844
Place of Birth: Candia, Rockingham County, New Hampshire
Date of Death: 10 June 1891
Place of Death: Galveston, Texas
Entered Service at: Manchester, Hillsborough County, New Hampshire
Unit: Company D, 7th New Hampshire Infantry
Battle or Place of Action: before Richmond, Virginia
Date of Action: September 1864
Date of Issue: 12 June 1883
Citation: Gallantry on the skirmish line.

1131 ◆ ROBINSON, ALEXANDER

Rank: Boatswain's Mate
Service: U.S. Navy
Birthday: 1831
Place of Birth: England
Entered Service at: New York, New York
Unit: U.S.S. *Howquah*
Battle or Place of Action: off Wilmington, North Carolina
Date of Action: 25 September 1864

G.O. Number, Date: 45, 31 December 1864
Date of Issue: 25 August 1868
Citation: Served as boatswain's mate on board the U.S.S. *Howquah* on the occasion of the destruction of the blockade runner, *Lynx*, off Wilmington, 25 September 1864. Performing his duty faithfully under the most trying circumstances, Robinson stood firmly at his post in the midst of a crossfire from the rebel shore batteries and our own vessels.

1132 ◆ ROBINSON, CHARLES

Rank: Boatswain's Mate
Service: U.S. Navy
Birthday: 1840
Place of Birth: Dundee, Scotland
Date of Death: 21 April 1896
Place of Death: Halifax, Nova Scotia, Canada
Cemetery: Holy Cross Cemetery (MH)—Halifax, Nova Scotia, Canada
Entered Service at: New York, New York
Unit: U.S.S. *Baron de Kalb*
Battle or Place of Action: Yazoo River, Mississippi
Date of Action: 23-27 December 1862
G.O. Number, Date: 11, 3 April 1863
Citation: Served on board the U.S.S. *Baron de Kalb* Yazoo River Expedition, 23 to 27 December 1862. Proceeding under orders up the Yazoo River, the U.S.S. *Baron de Kalb*, with the object of capturing or destroying the enemy's transports, came upon the steamers *John Walsh*, *R.J. Locklan*, *Golden Age*, and the *Scotland* sunk on a bar where they were ordered fired. Continuing up the river, she was fired on by the enemy, but upon returning the fire, caused the rebels to retreat. Returning down the Yazoo, she destroyed and captured large quantities of enemy equipment and several prisoners. Serving bravely throughout this action, Robinson, as boatswain's mate, "distinguished himself in the various actions."

1133 ◆ ROBINSON, ELBRIDGE

Rank: Private
Service: U.S. Army
Birthday: 7 January 1844
Place of Birth: Morgan County, Ohio
Date of Death: 19 January 1918
Place of Death: Vernon, Illinois
Cemetery: Patoka Cemetery—Patoka, Illinois
Entered Service at: McConnelsville, Morgan County, Ohio
Unit: Company C, 122d Ohio Infantry
Battle or Place of Action: Winchester, Virginia
Date of Action: 14 June 1863
Date of Issue: 5 April 1898
Citation: With one companion voluntarily went in front of the Union line, under a heavy fire from the enemy, and carried back a helpless wounded comrade, thus saving him from death or capture.

1134 ◆ *ROBINSON, JAMES H.

Rank: Private
Service: U.S. Army
Place of Birth: Oakland County, Michigan
Place of Death: Memphis, Tennessee
Cemetery: Memphis National Cemetery (H-4131) (MH)—Memphis, Tennessee
Entered Service at: Victor, Michigan
Unit: Company B, 3d Michigan Cavalry
Battle or Place of Action: Brownsville Station, Arkansas
Date of Action: 27 January 1865
Date of Issue: 4 April 1865
Citation: Successfully defended himself, singlehandedly, against seven guerrillas, killing the leader (Capt. W.C. Stephenson) and driving off the remainder of the party.

1135 ◆ ROBINSON, JOHN CLEVELAND

Rank: Brigadier General (highest rank: Major General)
Service: U.S. Army
Birthday: 10 April 1817
Place of Birth: Binghamton, Broome County, New York
Date of Death: 18 February 1897
Cemetery: Spring Forest Cemetery (MH)—Binghamton, New York
Entered Service at: Binghamton, Broome County, New York
Unit: U.S. Volunteers
Battle or Place of Action: Laurel Hill, Virginia
Date of Action: 8 May 1864
Date of Issue: 28 March 1894
Citation: Placed himself at the head of the leading brigade in a charge upon the enemy's breastworks; was severely wounded.

1136 ◆ ROBINSON, JOHN H.

Rank: Private
Service: U.S. Army
Birthday: 1846
Place of Birth: Ireland
Date of Death: 30 November 1883
Place of Death: Boston, Massachusetts
Cemetery: St. Benedict Cemetery (MH)—West Roxbury, Massachusetts
Entered Service at: Roxbury, Suffolk County, Massachusetts
Unit: Company I, 19th Massachusetts Infantry
Battle or Place of Action: Gettysburg, Pennsylvania
Date of Action: 3 July 1863
Date of Issue: 1 December 1864
Citation: Capture of flag of 57th Virginia Infantry (C.S.A.).
Notes: POW

1137 ◆ ROBINSON, THOMAS

Rank: Private
Service: U.S. Army
Place of Birth: Ireland
Entered Service at: Tamaqua, Schuylkill County, Pennsylvania
Unit: Company H, 81st Pennsylvania Infantry
Battle or Place of Action: Spotsylvania, Virginia
Date of Action: 12 May 1864

Date of Issue: 1 December 1864
Citation: Capture of flag in a hand-to-hand conflict.

1138 ◆ ROCK, FREDERICK

Rank: Private
Service: U.S. Army
Birthday: 1840
Place of Birth: Darmstadt, Germany
Date of Death: 7 November 1924
Cemetery: Woodlawn Cemetery (MH)—Tampa, Florida
Entered Service at: Cleveland, Cuyahoga County, Ohio
Unit: Company A, 37th Ohio Infantry
Battle or Place of Action: Vicksburg, Mississippi
Date of Action: 22 May 1863
Date of Issue: 10 August 1894
Citation: Gallantry in the charge of the "volunteer storming party."

1139 ◆ ROCKEFELLER, CHARLES MORTIMER

Rank: Lieutenant (highest rank: Major)
Service: U.S. Army
Birthday: 18 September 1844
Place of Birth: Gallatin Columbia County, New York
Date of Death: 28 April 1899
Place of Death: M.I.A. Declared dead near Manila
Entered Service at: New York, New York
Unit: Company A, 178th New York Infantry
Battle or Place of Action: Fort Blakely, Alabama
Date of Action: 9 April 1865
Date of Issue: 2 August 1897
Citation: Voluntarily and alone, under a heavy fire, obtained valuable information which a reconnoitering party of 25 men had previously attempted and failed to obtain, suffering severe loss in the attempt. The information obtained by him was made the basis of the orders for the assault that followed. He also advanced with a few followers, under the fire of both sides, and captured 300 of the enemy who would otherwise have escaped.
Notes: POW

1140 ◆ RODENBOUGH, THEOPHILUS FRANCIS

Rank: Captain (highest rank: Brigadier General)
Service: U.S. Army
Birthday: 5 November 1838
Place of Birth: Easton, Northampton County, Pennsylvania
Date of Death: 19 December 1912
Place of Death: New York, New York
Cemetery: Easton Heights Cemetery (MH)—Easton, Pennsylvania
Entered Service at: Pennsylvania
Unit: 2d U.S. Cavalry
Battle or Place of Action: Trevilian Station, Virginia
Date of Action: 11 June 1864
Date of Issue: 21 September 1893
Citation: Handled the regiment with great skill and valor; was severely wounded.

1141 ◆ ROHM, FERDINAND FREDERICK

Rank: Chief Bugler
Service: U.S. Army
Birthday: 30 August 1843
Place of Birth: Patterson, Juniata County, Pennsylvania
Date of Death: 24 November 1917
Place of Death: Harrisburg, Pennsylvania
Cemetery: Westminster Presbyterian Cemetery—Mifflintown, Pennsylvania
Entered Service at: Juniata County, Pennsylvania
Unit: 16th Pennsylvania Cavalry
Battle or Place of Action: Reams' Station, Virginia
Date of Action: 25 August 1864
Date of Issue: 16 October 1897
Citation: While his regiment was retiring under fire, voluntarily remained behind to succor a wounded officer who was in great danger, secured assistance, and removed the officer to a place of safety.

1142 ◆ ROOD, OLIVER P.

Rank: Private
Service: U.S. Army
Birthday: 1844
Place of Birth: Frankfort County, Kentucky
Date of Death: 11 June 1885
Place of Death: Nashville, Tennessee
Cemetery: Mount Olivet Cemetery (MH)—Nashville, Tennessee
Entered Service at: Terre Haute, Vigo County, Indiana
Unit: Company B, 20th Indiana Infantry
Battle or Place of Action: Gettysburg, Pennsylvania
Date of Action: 3 July 1863
Date of Issue: 1 December 1864
Citation: Capture of flag of 21st North Carolina Infantry (C.S.A.).

1143 ◆ ROOSEVELT, GEORGE WASHINGTON

Rank: First Sergeant (highest rank: Brevet Captain)
Service: U.S. Army
Birthday: 14 February 1844
Place of Birth: Chester County, Pennsylvania
Date of Death: 15 April 1907
Place of Death: Brussels, Belgium
Cemetery: Oak Hill Cemetery—Washington, D.C.
Entered Service at: Chester County, Pennsylvania
Unit: Company K, 26th Pennsylvania Infantry
Battle or Place of Action: Bull Run, Virginia & Gettysburg, Pennsylvania
Date of Action: 30 August 1862 & 2 July 1863
Date of Issue: 2 July 1887
Citation: At Bull Run, Va., recaptured the colors, which had been seized by the enemy. At Gettysburg captured a

Confederate color bearer and colors, in which effort he was severely wounded.

1144 ♦ *ROSS, MARION A.

Rank: Sergeant Major
Service: U.S. Army
Birthday: 1833
Place of Birth: Christianburg, Champaign County, Ohio
Date of Death: 18 June 1862
Cemetery: Chattanooga National Cemetery (H-11179) (MH)—Chattanooga, Tennessee
Entered Service at: Christianburg, Champaign County, Ohio
Unit: 2d Ohio Infantry
Battle or Place of Action: Georgia
Date of Action: April 1862
Date of Issue: September 1863
Citation: One of 19 of 24 men (including two civilians) who, by direction of Gen. Ormsby M. Mitchell, penetrated nearly 200 miles south into enemy territory and captured a railroad train at Big Shanty, Ga., in an attempt to destroy the bridges and track between Chattanooga and Atlanta.

1145 ♦ ROSSBACH, VALENTINE

Rank: Sergeant
Service: U.S. Army
Birthday: 1842
Place of Birth: Germany
Date of Death: 20 February 1897
Cemetery: Cypress Hills National Cemetery (2-5427) (MH)—Brooklyn, New York
Entered Service at: Flushing, Queens County, New York
Unit: 34th New York Battery
Battle or Place of Action: Spotsylvania, Virginia
Date of Action: 12 May 1864
Date of Issue: 10 July 1896
Citation: Encouraged his cannoneers to hold a very dangerous position, and when all depended on several good shots it was from his piece that the most effective were delivered, causing the enemy's fire to cease and thereby relieving the critical position of the Federal troops.

1146 ♦ ROUGHT, STEPHEN

Rank: Sergeant
Service: U.S. Army
Birthday: 3 April 1840
Place of Birth: Bradford County, Pennsylvania
Date of Death: 16 March 1919
Place of Death: Wyalusing, Pennsylvania
Cemetery: Lacy Street Cemetery—Lacyville, Pennsylvania
Entered Service at: Crampton, Pennsylvania
Unit: Company A, 141st Pennsylvania Infantry
Battle or Place of Action: Wilderness Campaign, Virginia
Date of Action: 6 May 1864
Date of Issue: 1 December 1864
Citation: Capture of flag of the 13th North Carolina Infantry (C.S.A.).

1147 ♦ ROUNDS, LEWIS A.

Rank: Private (highest rank: Brevet Major)
Service: U.S. Army
Birthday: 7 June 1843
Place of Birth: Cattaraugus County, New York
Date of Death: 1 May 1916
Place of Death: Wood Soldier's Home, Wisconsin
Cemetery: Wood National Cemetery (MH)—Wood, Wisconsin
Entered Service at: Norwalk, Huron County, Ohio
Unit: Company D, 8th Ohio Infantry
Battle or Place of Action: Spotsylvania, Virginia
Date of Action: 12 May 1864
Date of Issue: 1 December 1864
Citation: Capture of flag.

1148 ♦ ROUNTRY, JOHN

Rank: First Class Fireman
Service: U.S. Navy
Birthday: 1843
Place of Birth: Massachusetts
Date of Death: 3 October 1901
Place of Death: New York, New York
Cemetery: Holy Cross Cemetery—Brooklyn, New York
Entered Service at: Boston, Suffolk County, Massachusetts
Unit: U.S.S. *Montauk*
Battle or Place of Action: off Port Royal, South Carolina
Date of Action: 21 September 1864
G.O. Number, Date: 59, 22 June 1865
Citation: Served as first class fireman on board the U.S.S. *Montauk*, 21 September 1864. During the night of 21 September, when fire was discovered in the magazine lightroom of that vessel, causing a panic and demoralizing the crew, Rountry, notwithstanding the cry of "fire in the magazine," forced his way with hose in hand, through the frightened crowd to the lightroom, and put out the flames.

1149 ♦ ROUSH, JAMES LEVI

Rank: Corporal
Service: U.S. Army
Birthday: 11 February 1838
Place of Birth: Bedford County, Pennsylvania
Date of Death: 12 February 1906
Place of Death: McKee's Gap, Pennsylvania
Cemetery: St. Patrick's Cemetery (MH)—Newry, Pennsylvania
Entered Service at: Chambersburg, Franklin County, Pennsylvania
Unit: Company D, 6th Pennsylvania Reserves
Battle or Place of Action: Gettysburg, Pennsylvania
Date of Action: 2 July 1863
Date of Issue: 3 August 1897
Citation: Was one of six volunteers who charged upon a log house near the Devil's Den, where a squad of the enemy's sharpshooters were sheltered, and compelled their surrender.

1150 ◆ ROWAND JR., ARCHIBALD HAMILTON

Rank: Private
Service: U.S. Army
Birthday: 6 March 1845
Place of Birth: Philadelphia, Philadelphia County, Pennsylvania
Date of Death: 14 December 1913
Cemetery: Allegheny Cemetery (MH)—Pittsburgh, Pennsylvania
Entered Service at: Pittsburgh, Allegheny County, Pennsylvania
Unit: Company K, 1st West Virginia Cavalry
Served as: Scout
Battle or Place of Action: from Columbia Virginia to City Point on the James River, west of Richmond
Date of Action: winter 1864-65
Date of Issue: 3 March 1873
Citation: Was one of two men who succeeded in getting through the enemy's lines with dispatches to Gen. Grant.

1151 ◆ ROWE, HENRY WALKER

Rank: Private
Service: U.S. Army
Birthday: 1 April 1840
Place of Birth: Candia, Rockingham County, New Hampshire
Date of Death: 9 October 1913
Place of Death: Roxbury, Massachusetts
Cemetery: Hill Cemetery—Candia, New Hampshire
Entered Service at: Candia, Rockingham County, New Hampshire
Unit: Company I, 11th New Hampshire Infantry
Battle or Place of Action: Petersburg, Virginia
Date of Action: 17 June 1864
Date of Issue: 1 December 1864
Citation: With two companions, he rushed and disarmed 27 enemy pickets, capturing a stand of flags.

1152 ◆ RUNDLE, CHARLES WESLEY

Rank: Private
Service: U.S. Army
Birthday: 14 December 1842
Place of Birth: Covington, Campbell County, Kentucky
Date of Death: 11 July 1924
Place of Death: Los Angeles, California
Cemetery: Los Angeles National Cemetery (34-I-11) (MH)—Los Angeles, California
Entered Service at: Oakley, Macon County, Illinois
Unit: Company A, 116th Illinois Infantry
Battle or Place of Action: Vicksburg, Mississippi
Date of Action: 22 May 1863
Date of Issue: 26 July 1894
Citation: Gallantry in the charge of the "volunteer storming party."

1153 ◆ RUSH, JOHN

True Name: Little, Israel W.
Rank: First Class Fireman
Service: U.S. Navy
Birthday: 21 February 1837
Place of Birth: Washington, D.C.
Date of Death: 29 April 1916
Place of Death: Washington, D.C.
Cemetery: Arlington National Cemetery (17-18768)—Arlington, Virginia
Entered Service at: Washington, D.C.
Unit: U.S.S. *Richmond*
Battle or Place of Action: Port Hudson, Louisiana
Date of Action: 14 March 1863
G.O. Number, Date: 17, 10 July 1863
Citation: Served on board the U.S.S. *Richmond* in the attack on Port Hudson, 14 March 1863. Damaged by a 6-inch solid rifle shot which shattered the starboard safety-valve chamber and also damaged the port safety valve, the fireroom of the Richmond immediately became filled with steam to place it in an extremely critical condition. Acting courageously in this crisis, Rush persisted in penetrating the steam-filled room in order to haul the hot fires of the furnaces, and continued this action until the gravity of the situation had been lessened.

1154 ◆ RUSSELL, CHARLES L.

Rank: Corporal (highest rank: Second Lieutenant)
Service: U.S. Army
Place of Birth: Malone, Franklin County, New York
Date of Death: 7 June 1910
Cemetery: Hot Springs National Cemetery (3-12-R1)—Hot Springs, South Dakota
Entered Service at: Malone, Franklin County, New York
Unit: Company H, 93d New York Infantry
Battle or Place of Action: Spotsylvania, Virginia
Date of Action: 12 May 1864
Date of Issue: 1 December 1864
Citation: Capture of flag of 42d Virginia Infantry (C.S.A.).

1155 ◆ RUSSELL, MILTON F.

Rank: Captain
Service: U.S. Army
Birthday: 25 September 1836
Place of Birth: Hendricks County, Indiana
Date of Death: 2 July 1908
Place of Death: Oakland, California
Cemetery: Odd Fellow Columbarium Cemetery—San Francisco, California
Entered Service at: North Salem, Hendricks County, Indiana
Unit: Company A, 51st Indiana Infantry
Battle or Place of Action: Stone River, Tennessee
Date of Action: 29 December 1862
Date of Issue: 28 September 1897

Citation: Was the first man to cross Stone River and, in the face of a galling fire from the concealed skirmishers of the enemy, led his men up the hillside, driving the opposing skirmishers before them.

1156 ◆ RUTHERFORD, JOHN T.

Rank: First Lieutenant (highest rank: Brevet Major)
Service: U.S. Army
Birthday: 23 August 1823
Place of Birth: Russell, St. Lawrence County, New York
Date of Death: 27 August 1898
Place of Death: Chicago, Illinois
Cemetery: Brookside Cemetery—Waddington, New York
Entered Service at: Canton, St. Lawrence County, New York
Unit: Company L, 9th New York Cavalry
Battle or Place of Action: Yellow Tavern & Hanovertown, Virginia
Date of Action: 11, 27 May 1864
Date of Issue: 22 March 1892
Citation: Made a successful charge at Yellow Tavern, Va., 11 May 1864, by which 90 prisoners were captured. On 27 May 1864, in a gallant dash on a superior force of the enemy and a personal encounter, captured his opponent.

1157 ◆ RUTTER, JAMES MAY

Rank: Sergeant
Service: U.S. Army
Birthday: 13 May 1841
Place of Birth: Wilkes-Barre, Luzerne County, Pennsylvania
Date of Death: 23 November 1907
Place of Death: Wilkes-Barre, Pennsylvania
Cemetery: Hollenbeck Cemetery—Wilkes-Barre, Pennsylvania
Entered Service at: Wilkes-Barre, Luzerne County, Pennsylvania
Unit: Company C, 143d Pennsylvania Infantry
Battle or Place of Action: Gettysburg, Pennsylvania
Date of Action: 1 July 1863
Date of Issue: 30 October 1896
Citation: At great risk of his life went to the assistance of a wounded comrade and while under fire removed him to a place of safety.

1158 ◆ RYAN, PETER J.

Rank: Private
Service: U.S. Army
Birthday: 1841
Place of Birth: Tipperary, County Tipperary, Ireland
Date of Death: 8 January 1908
Cemetery: Calvary Cemetery—Terre Haute, Indiana
Entered Service at: Terre Haute, Vigo County, Indiana
Unit: Company D, 11th Indiana Infantry
Battle or Place of Action: Winchester, Virginia
Date of Action: 19 September 1864

Date of Issue: 4 April 1865
Citation: With one companion, captured 14 Confederates in the severest part of the battle.

1159 ◆ SACRISTE, LOUIS JEANOTTELLE

Rank: First Lieutenant (highest rank: Brevet Major)
Service: U.S. Army
Birthday: 15 June 1843
Place of Birth: New Castle County, Delaware
Date of Death: 18 August 1904
Place of Death: La Grange, Illinois
Cemetery: Mount Carmel Cemetery—Hillside, Illinois
Entered Service at: Philadelphia, Philadelphia County, Pennsylvania
Unit: Company D, 116th Pennsylvania Infantry
Battle or Place of Action: Chancellorsville & Auburn, Virginia
Date of Action: 3 May & 14 October 1863
Date of Issue: 31 January 1889
Citation: Saved from capture a gun of the 5th Maine Battery. Voluntarily carried orders which resulted in saving from destruction or capture the picket line of the 1st Division, 2d Army Corps.

1160 ◆ SAGELHURST, JOHN CHRISTOPHER

True Name: Segelhurst
Rank: Sergeant (highest rank: First Sergeant)
Service: U.S. Army
Birthday: 1 June 1841
Place of Birth: Buffalo, Erie County, New York
Date of Death: 10 May 1907
Place of Death: Buffalo, New York
Cemetery: Forest Lawn Cemetery (MH)—Buffalo, New York
Entered Service at: Jersey City, Hudson County, New Jersey
Unit: Company B, 1st New Jersey Cavalry
Battle or Place of Action: Hatcher's Run, Virginia
Date of Action: 6 February 1865
Date of Issue: 3 January 1906
Citation: Under a heavy fire from the enemy carried off the field a commissioned officer who was severely wounded and also led a charge on the enemy's rifle pits.

1161 ◆ SANCRAINTE, CHARLES FRANCIS

True Name: Sanscrainte
Rank: Private
Service: U.S. Army
Birthday: 28 February 1838
Place of Birth: Monroe, Monroe County, Michigan
Date of Death: 5 May 1910
Place of Death: Buffalo, New York
Cemetery: Pine Hill Roman Catholic Cemetery (MH)—Buffalo, New York
Entered Service at: Monroe, Monroe County, Michigan

Unit: Company B, 15th Michigan Infantry
Battle or Place of Action: Atlanta, Georgia
Date of Action: 22 July 1864
Date of Issue: 25 July 1892
Citation: Voluntarily scaled the enemy's breastworks and signaled to his commanding officer in charge; also in single combat captured the colors of the 5th Texas Regiment (C.S.A.).

1162 ◆ SANDERSON, AARON

True Name: Anderson
Rank: Landsman
Service: U.S. Navy
Birthday: 1811
Place of Birth: North Carolina
Entered Service at: Philadelphia, Philadelphia County, Pennsylvania
Unit: U.S.S. *Wyandank*
Battle or Place of Action: Mattox Creek, Virginia
Date of Action: 17 March 1865
G.O. Number, Date: 59, 22 June 1865
Citation: Served on board the U.S.S. *Wyandank* during a boat expedition up Mattox Creek, 17 March 1865. Participating with a boat crew in the clearing of Mattox Creek, Landsman Sanderson carried out his duties courageously in the face of a devastating fire which cut away half the oars, pierced the launch in many places, and cut the barrel off a musket being fired at the enemy.

1163 ◆ SANDS, WILLIAM

Rank: First Sergeant
Service: U.S. Army
Birthday: 14 October 1835
Place of Birth: Reading, Berks County, Pennsylvania
Date of Death: 31 October 1918
Place of Death: Norristown, Pennsylvania
Cemetery: Charles Evans Cemetery (MH)—Reading, Pennsylvania
Entered Service at: Reading, Berks County, Pennsylvania
Unit: Company G, 88th Pennsylvania Infantry
Battle or Place of Action: Dabney's Mills, Virginia
Date of Action: 6-7 February 1865
Date of Issue: 9 November 1893
Citation: Grasped the enemy's colors in the face of a deadly fire and brought them inside the lines.

1164 ◆ SANFORD, JACOB

Rank: Private (highest rank: Commissary Sergeant)
Service: U.S. Army
Birthday: 1840
Place of Birth: Fulton County, Illinois
Date of Death: 3 September 1901
Cemetery: Prairie City Cemetery (MH)—Prairie City, Illinois
Entered Service at: Prairie City, McDonough County, Illinois

Unit: 55th Illinois Infantry
Battle or Place of Action: Vicksburg, Mississippi
Date of Action: 22 May 1863
Date of Issue: 2 September 1893
Citation: Gallantry in the charge of the "volunteer storming party."

1165 ◆ SARGENT, JACKSON G.

Rank: Sergeant
Service: U.S. Army
Birthday: 29 December 1841
Place of Birth: Stowe, Lamoille County, Vermont
Date of Death: 2 October 1921
Cemetery: River View Cemetery (MH)—Stowe, Vermont
Entered Service at: Stowe, Lamoille County, Vermont
Unit: Company D, 5th Vermont Infantry
Battle or Place of Action: Petersburg, Virginia
Date of Action: 2 April 1865
Date of Issue: 28 October 1891
Citation: First to scale the enemy's works and plant the colors thereon.

1166 ◆ SARTWELL, HENRY

Rank: Sergeant
Service: U.S. Army
Birthday: 7 March 1837
Place of Birth: Ticonderoga, Essex County, New York
Date of Death: 26 February 1910
Place of Death: Fort Ann, New York
Cemetery: Fish Hill Cemetery (MH)—Fort Ann, New York
Entered Service at: Fort Ann, Washington County, New York
Unit: Company D, 123d New York Infantry
Battle or Place of Action: Chancellorsville, Virginia
Date of Action: 3 May 1863
Date of Issue: 17 November 1896
Citation: Was severely wounded by a gunshot to his left arm, went half a mile to the rear but insisted on returning to his company and continued to fight bravely until he became exhausted from the loss of blood and was compelled to retire from the field.

1167 ◆ SAUNDERS, JAMES

Rank: Quartermaster (highest rank: Chief Quartermaster)
Service: U.S. Navy
Birthday: 1809
Place of Birth: Massachusetts
Entered Service at: Boston, Suffolk County, Massachusetts
Unit: U.S.S. *Kearsarge*
Battle or Place of Action: off Cherbourg, France
Date of Action: 19 June 1864
G.O. Number, Date: 59, 22 June 1865
Citation: Served as quartermaster on board the U.S.S. *Kearsarge* when she destroyed the *Alabama* off Cherbourg, France, 19 June 1864. Carrying out his duties courageously throughout the bitter engagement, Saunders was prompt in

reporting damages done to both ships, and it is testified to by Commodore Winslow that he is deserving of all commendation, both for gallantry and for encouragement of others in his division.

1168 ◆ SAVACOOL, EDWIN F.

Rank: Captain
Service: U.S. Army
Birthday: 1842
Place of Birth: Jackson, Jackson County, Michigan
Date of Death: 5 June 1865
Place of Death: Washington, D.C.
Cemetery: Elmwood Cemetery (MH)—Detroit, Michigan
Entered Service at: Marshall, Calhoun County, Michigan
Unit: Company K, 1st New York (Lincoln) Cavalry
Battle or Place of Action: Deatonsville (Sailor's Creek), Virginia
Date of Action: 6 April 1865
Date of Issue: 24 April 1865
Citation: Capture of flag, during which he was wounded and died several days later in Washington, D.C.

1169 ◆ SAVAGE, AUZELLA

Rank: Ordinary Seaman
Service: U.S. Navy
Birthday: 1846
Place of Birth: Anson, Somerset County, Maine
Date of Death: February 1882
Place of Death: Lost at sea, Atlantic Ocean
Entered Service at: Boston, Suffolk County, Massachusetts
Unit: U.S.S. *Santiago de Cuba*
Battle or Place of Action: Fort Fisher, North Carolina
Date of Action: 15 January 1865
G.O. Number, Date: 59, 22 May 1865
Citation: On board the U.S.S. *Santiago de Cuba* during the assault on Fort Fisher, 15 January 1865. When the landing party to which he was attached charged on the fort with a cheer and the determination to plant the colors on the ramparts, Savage remained steadfast when more than two-thirds of the marines and sailors fell back in panic during the fight. When enemy fire shot away the flagstaff above his hand, he bravery seized the remainder of the staff and brought his colors safely off.

1170 ◆ SAXTON JR., RUFUS

Rank: Brigadier General (highest rank: Brevet Major General)
Service: U.S. Army
Birthday: 19 October 1824
Place of Birth: Greenfield, Franklin County, Massachusetts
Date of Death: 23 February 1908
Place of Death: Washington, D.C.
Cemetery: Arlington National Cemetery (1-20-A) (MH)—Arlington, Virginia
Entered Service at: Deerfield, Franklin County, Massachusetts
Unit: U.S. Volunteers
Battle or Place of Action: Harpers Ferry, West Virginia
Date of Action: 26-30 May 1862
Date of Issue: 25 April 1893
Citation: Distinguished gallantry and good conduct in the defense.

1171 ◆ SCANLAN, PATRICK

True Name: Scanlon, Patrick
Rank: Private (highest rank: Sergeant)
Service: U.S. Army
Birthday: 1838
Place of Birth: Ireland
Date of Death: 5 September 1903
Place of Death: Farmington, Connecticut
Cemetery: St. Mary's Cemetery (MH)—Farmington, Connecticut
Entered Service at: Spencer, Worcester County, Massachusetts
Unit: Company A, 4th Massachusetts Cavalry
Battle or Place of Action: Ashepoo River, South Carolina
Date of Action: 24 May 1864
Date of Issue: 21 January 1897
Citation: Volunteered as a member of a boat crew which went to the rescue of a large number of Union soldiers on board the stranded steamer *Boston*, and with great gallantry assisted in conveying them to shore, being exposed the entire time to a heavy fire from a Confederate battery.

1172 ◆ SCHEIBNER, MARTIN E.

Rank: Private (highest rank: Corporal)
Service: U.S. Army
Birthday: 13 October 1842
Place of Birth: Valdai, Russia
Date of Death: 29 November 1908
Place of Death: Camden, New Jersey
Cemetery: Charles Evans Cemetery (MH)—Reading, Pennsylvania
Entered Service at: Philadelphia, Philadelphia County, Pennsylvania
Unit: Company G, 90th Pennsylvania Infantry
Battle or Place of Action: Mine Run, Virginia
Date of Action: 27 November 1863
Date of Issue: 23 June 1896
Citation: Voluntarily extinguished the burning fuse of a shell which had been thrown into the lines of the regiment by the enemy.

1173 ◆ SCHENCK, BENJAMIN W.

Rank: Private (highest rank: Corporal)
Service: U.S. Army
Birthday: 12 August 1837
Place of Birth: Butler County, Ohio
Date of Death: 28 February 1916
Place of Death: Danville, Illinois
Cemetery: Greenwood Cemetery—Decatur, Illinois
Entered Service at: Maroa, Macon County, Illinois
Unit: Company D, 116th Illinois Infantry

Battle or Place of Action: Vicksburg, Mississippi
Date of Action: 22 May 1863
Date of Issue: 14 August 1894
Citation: Gallantry in the charge of the "volunteer storming party."

1174 ◆ SCHILLER, JOHN

True Name: Schilling, John
Rank: Private
Service: U.S. Army
Birthday: 16 August 1847
Place of Birth: Hessen, Germany
Date of Death: 3 June 1926
Cemetery: Cypress Hills National Cemetery (5-3)—Brooklyn, New York
Entered Service at: New York, New York
Unit: Company E, 158th New York Infantry
Battle or Place of Action: Chapin's Farm, Virginia
Date of Action: 29 September 1864
Date of Issue: 6 April 1865
Citation: Advanced to the ditch of the enemy's works.

1175 ◆ SCHLACHTER, PHILIPP

Rank: Private
Service: U.S. Army
Birthday: 17 June 1841
Place of Birth: Germany
Date of Death: 9 September 1923
Place of Death: Sturgis, Michigan
Cemetery: Oakland Cemetery—Sturgis, Michigan
Entered Service at: New York, New York
Unit: Company F, 73d New York Infantry
Battle or Place of Action: Spotsylvania, Virginia
Date of Action: 12 May 1864
Date of Issue: 1 December 1864
Citation: Capture of flag of 15th Louisiana Infantry (C.S.A.).

1176 ◆ SCHMAL, GEORGE WILLIAM

Rank: Blacksmith
Service: U.S. Army
Birthday: 1849
Place of Birth: Germany
Date of Death: 4 August 1923
Cemetery: Forest Lawn Cemetery (MH)—Buffalo, New York
Entered Service at: Buffalo, Erie County, New York
Unit: Company M, 24th New York Cavalry
Battle or Place of Action: Paines Crossroads, Virginia
Date of Action: 5 April 1865
Date of Issue: 3 May 1865
Citation: Capture of flag.

1177 ◆ SCHMAUCH, ANDREW

Rank: Private (highest rank: First Sergeant)
Service: U.S. Army
Birthday: 1841
Place of Birth: Germany
Entered Service at: Portsmouth, Scioto County, Ohio
Unit: Company A, 30th Ohio Infantry
Battle or Place of Action: Vicksburg, Mississippi
Date of Action: 22 May 1863
Date of Issue: 9 July 1894
Citation: Gallantry in the charge of the "volunteer storming party."

1178 ◆ SCHMIDT, CONRAD

Rank: First Sergeant (highest rank: Quartermaster Sergeant)
Service: U.S. Army
Birthday: 27 February 1830
Place of Birth: Wurttemberg, Germany
Date of Death: 26 December 1908
Cemetery: Catholic Cemetery—Ogden, Kansas
Entered Service at: Fort Leavenworth, Leavenworth County, Kansas
Unit: Company K, 2d U.S. Cavalry
Battle or Place of Action: Winchester, Virginia
Date of Action: 19 September 1864
Date of Issue: 16 March 1896
Citation: Went to the assistance of his regimental commander, whose horse had been killed under him in a charge, mounted the officer behind him, under a heavy fire from the enemy, and returned him to his command.

1179 ◆ SCHMIDT, WILLIAM

Rank: Private
Service: U.S. Army
Birthday: 10 July 1846
Place of Birth: Tiffin, Seneca County, Ohio
Date of Death: 12 January 1888
Cemetery: St. Mary's Cemetery—Cincinnati, Ohio
Entered Service at: Maumee, Lucas County, Ohio
Unit: Company G, 37th Ohio Infantry
Battle or Place of Action: Missionary Ridge, Tennessee
Date of Action: 25 November 1863
Date of Issue: 9 November 1895
Citation: Rescued a wounded comrade under terrific fire.

1180 ◆ SCHNEIDER, GEORGE

Rank: Sergeant
Service: U.S. Army
Birthday: 8 November 1844
Place of Birth: Baltimore, Baltimore County, Maryland
Date of Death: 2 January 1929
Place of Death: Baltimore, Maryland
Cemetery: The Baltimore Cemetery—Baltimore, Maryland
Entered Service at: Baltimore, Baltimore County, Maryland
Unit: Company A, 3d Maryland Veteran Infantry
Battle or Place of Action: Petersburg, Virginia
Date of Action: 30 July 1864
Date of Issue: 27 July 1896
Citation: After the color sergeant had been shot down, seized the colors and planted them on the enemy's works during the charge.

1181 ◆ SCHNELL, CHRISTIAN

Rank: Corporal
Service: U.S. Army
Birthday: 19 February 1838
Place of Birth: Virginia
Date of Death: 14 December 1908
Cemetery: Greenlawn Cemetery—Wapakoneta, Ohio
Entered Service at: Wapakoneta, Auglaize County, Ohio
Unit: Company C, 37th Ohio Infantry
Battle or Place of Action: Vicksburg, Mississippi
Date of Action: 22 May 1863
Date of Issue: 10 July 1894
Citation: Gallantry in the charge of the "volunteer storming party."

1182 ◆ SCHOFIELD, JOHN MCALLISTER

Rank: Major (highest rank: Lieutenant General)
Service: U.S. Army
Birthday: 29 September 1831
Place of Birth: Gerry, Chautauga County, New York
Date of Death: 4 March 1906
Place of Death: St. Augustine, Florida
Cemetery: Arlington National Cemetery (2-1108)—Arlington, Virginia
Entered Service at: Freeport, Stephenson County, Illinois
Unit: 1st Missouri Infantry
Battle or Place of Action: Wilson's Creek, Missouri
Date of Action: 10 August 1861
Date of Issue: 2 July 1892
Citation: Was conspicuously gallant in leading a regiment in a successful charge against the enemy.

1183 ◆ SCHOONMAKER, JAMES MARTINUS

Rank: Colonel
Service: U.S. Army
Birthday: 30 June 1842
Place of Birth: Pittsburgh, Allegheny County, Pennsylvania
Date of Death: 11 October 1927
Place of Death: Pittsburgh, Pennsylvania
Cemetery: Mary S. Brown Memorial Cemetery—Pittsburgh, Pennsylvania
Entered Service at: Pittsburgh, Allegheny County, Pennsylvania
Unit: 14th Pennsylvania Cavalry
Battle or Place of Action: Winchester, Virginia
Date of Action: 19 September 1864
Date of Issue: 19 May 1899
Citation: At a critical period, gallantly led a cavalry charge against the left of the enemy's line of battle, drove the enemy out of his works, and captured many prisoners.

1184 ◆ SCHORN, CHARLES

Rank: Chief Bugler
Service: U.S. Army
Birthday: 1 May 1842
Place of Birth: Germany
Date of Death: 25 March 1915
Place of Death: Pomeroy, Ohio
Cemetery: Catholic Cemetery—Pomeroy, Ohio
Entered Service at: Mason City, Mason County, West Virginia
Unit: Company M, 1st West Virginia Cavalry
Battle or Place of Action: Appomattox, Virginia
Date of Action: 8 April 1865
Date of Issue: 3 May 1865
Citation: Capture of flag of the Sumter Flying Artillery (C.S.A.).

1185 ◆ SCHUBERT, MARTIN

Rank: Private (highest rank: First Lieutenant)
Service: U.S. Army
Birthday: 29 June 1838
Place of Birth: Germany
Date of Death: 25 April 1912
Place of Death: St. Louis, Missouri
Cemetery: Jefferson Barracks National Cemetery 4-12310 (MH)—St. Louis, Missouri
Entered Service at: Elmira, Chemung County, New York
Unit: Company E, 26th New York Infantry
Battle or Place of Action: Fredericksburg, Virginia
Date of Action: 13 December 1862
Date of Issue: 1 September 1893
Citation: Relinquished a furlough granted for wounds, entered the battle, where he picked up the colors after several bearers had been killed or wounded, and carried them until himself again wounded.

1186 ◆ SCHUTT, GEORGE

Rank: Coxswain
Service: U.S. Navy
Birthday: 1833
Place of Birth: Ireland
Entered Service at: New York, New York
Unit: U.S.S. *Hendrick Hudson*
Battle or Place of Action: St. Marks, Florida
Date of Action: 5-6 March 1865
G.O. Number, Date: 59, 22 June 1865
Citation: As coxswain on board the U.S.S. *Hendrick Hudson*, St. Marks, Fla., 5 and 6 March 1865. Serving with the Army in charge of Navy howitzers during the attack on St. Marks and throughout this fierce engagement, Schutt made remarkable efforts in assisting transport of the gun, and his coolness and determination in courageously remaining by his gun while under the heavy fire of the enemy were a credit to the service to which he belonged.

1187 ◆ SCHWAN, THEODORE

Rank: First Lieutenant (highest rank: Major General)
Service: U.S. Army
Birthday: 9 July 1841
Place of Birth: Hanover, Germany
Date of Death: 27 May 1926
Place of Death: Washington, D.C.
Cemetery: Arlington National Cemetery (2-860-)—Arlington, Virginia

Entered Service at: New York
Unit: 10th U.S. Infantry
Battle or Place of Action: Peebles Farm, Virginia
Date of Action: 1 October 1864
Date of Issue: 12 December 1898
Citation: At the imminent risk of his own life, while his regiment was falling back before a superior force of the enemy, he dragged a wounded and helpless officer to the rear, thus saving him from death or capture.

1188 ◆ SCHWENK, MARTIN

Rank: Sergeant
Service: U.S. Army
Birthday: 28 April 1839
Place of Birth: Baden, Germany
Date of Death: 20 June 1924
Cemetery: Arlington National Cemetery (17-20472) (MH)—Arlington, Virginia
Entered Service at: Boston, Suffolk County, Massachusetts
Unit: Company B, 6th U.S. Cavalry
Battle or Place of Action: Millerstown, Pennsylvania
Date of Action: July 1863
Date of Issue: 23 April 1889
Citation: Bravery in an attempt to carry a communication through the enemy's lines; also rescued an officer from the hands of the enemy.

1189 ◆ SCOFIELD, DAVID H.

Rank: Quartermaster Sergeant (highest rank: Regimental Quartermaster Sergeant)
Service: U.S. Army
Birthday: 10 December 1840
Place of Birth: Mamaroneck, Westchester County, New York
Date of Death: 30 September 1905
Place of Death: Bath, New York
Cemetery: Slasson Cemetery (MH)—Darien, Connecticut
Entered Service at: Stamford, Fairfield County, Connecticut
Unit: Company K, 5th New York Cavalry
Battle or Place of Action: Cedar Creek, Virginia
Date of Action: 19 October 1864
Date of Issue: 26 October 1864
Citation: Capture of flag of 13th Virginia Infantry (C.S.A.).

1190 ◆ SCOTT, ALEXANDER

Rank: Corporal
Service: U.S. Army
Birthday: 19 August 1844
Place of Birth: Montreal, Canada
Date of Death: 26 May 1923
Place of Death: Washington, D.C.
Cemetery: Arlington National Cemetery (17-18563) (MH)—Arlington, Virginia
Entered Service at: Winooski, Chittenden County, Vermont
Unit: Company D, 10th Vermont Infantry
Battle or Place of Action: Monocacy, Maryland
Date of Action: 9 July 1864
Date of Issue: 28 September 1897
Citation: Under a very heavy fire from the enemy saved the national flag of his regiment from capture.

1191 ◆ *SCOTT, JOHN MOREHEAD

Rank: Sergeant
Service: U.S. Army
Birthday: 1839
Place of Birth: Stark County, Ohio
Date of Death: 18 June 1862
Cemetery: Chattanooga National Cemetery (H-11182)—Chattanooga, Tennessee
Entered Service at: Findley, Hancock County, Ohio
Unit: Company F, 21st Ohio Infantry
Battle or Place of Action: Georgia
Date of Action: April 1862
Date of Issue: 4 August 1866
Citation: One of 19 of 24 men (including two civilians) who, by direction of Gen. Ormsby M. Mitchell, penetrated nearly 200 miles south into enemy territory and captured a railroad train at Big Shanty, Ga., in an attempt to destroy the bridges and track between Chattanooga and Atlanta.
Notes: POW

1192 ◆ SCOTT, JOHN WALLACE

Rank: Captain (highest rank: Brevet Major)
Service: U.S. Army
Birthday: 31 August 1832
Place of Birth: Chester County, Pennsylvania
Date of Death: 12 May 1903
Place of Death: Philadelphia, Pennsylvania
Cemetery: Presbyterian Church Cemetery—Parkesburg, Pennsylvania
Entered Service at: Philadelphia, Philadelphia County, Pennsylvania
Unit: Company D, 157th Pennsylvania Infantry
Battle or Place of Action: Five Forks, Virginia
Date of Action: 1 April 1865
Date of Issue: 27 April 1865
Citation: Capture of the flag of the 16th South Carolina Infantry, in hand-to-hand combat.

1193 ◆ SCOTT, JULIAN A.

Rank: Drummer
Service: U.S. Army
Birthday: 15 February 1846
Place of Birth: Johnson, Lamoille County, Vermont
Date of Death: 4 July 1901
Cemetery: Hillside Cemetery (MH)—Plainfield, New Jersey
Entered Service at: Johnson, Lamoille County, Vermont
Unit: Company E, 3d Vermont Infantry
Battle or Place of Action: Lee's Mill, Virginia
Date of Action: 16 April 1862
Date of Issue: February 1865
Citation: Crossed the creek under a terrific fire of musketry several times to assist in bringing off the wounded.

1194 ◆ SEAMAN, ELISHA B.

Rank: Private
Service: U.S. Army
Birthday: 1838
Place of Birth: Logan County, Ohio
Date of Death: 12 June 1919
Cemetery: Mount Tabor Cemetery—Salem Township, Ohio
Entered Service at: Logan County, Ohio
Unit: Company A, 66th Ohio Infantry
Battle or Place of Action: Chancellorsville, Virginia
Date of Action: 2 May 1863
Date of Issue: 24 June 1892
Citation: Was one of a party of four who voluntarily brought into the Union lines, under fire, a wounded Confederate officer from whom was obtained valuable information concerning the enemy.

1195 ◆ SEANOR, JAMES

Rank: Master-at-Arms
Service: U.S. Navy
Birthday: 1833
Place of Birth: Boston, Suffolk County, Massachusetts
Entered Service at: New York, New York
Unit: U.S. Ironclad *Chickasaw*
Battle or Place of Action: Fort Morgan, Mobile Bay, Alabama
Date of Action: 5 August 1864
G.O. Number, Date: 45, 31 December 1864
Citation: Served as master-at-arms on board the U.S. Ironclad *Chickasaw*, Mobile Bay, 5 August 1864. Although his enlistment was up, Seanor volunteered for the battle of Mobile Bay, going on board the *Chickasaw* from the *Vincennes* where he carried out his duties gallantly throughout the engagement which resulted in the capture of the rebel ram *Tennessee*.

1196 ◆ SEARS, CYRUS

Rank: First Lieutenant (highest rank: Colonel)
Service: U.S. Army
Birthday: 10 March 1832
Place of Birth: Meredith Township, Delaware County, New York
Date of Death: 30 November 1909
Cemetery: Oak Hill Cemetery (MH)—Upper Sandusky, Ohio
Entered Service at: Bucyrus, Crawford County, Ohio
Unit: Ohio Light Artillery, 11th Battery
Battle or Place of Action: Iuka, Mississippi
Date of Action: 19 September 1862
Date of Issue: 31 December 1892
Citation: Although severely wounded, fought his battery until the cannoneers and horses were nearly all killed or wounded.

1197 ◆ SEAVER, THOMAS ORVILLE

Rank: Colonel
Service: U.S. Army
Birthday: 23 December 1833
Place of Birth: Cavendish, Windsor County, Vermont
Date of Death: 11 July 1912
Place of Death: Woodstock, Vermont
Cemetery: River Street Cemetery—Woodstock, Vermont
Entered Service at: Pomfret, Vermont
Unit: 3d Vermont Infantry
Battle or Place of Action: Spotsylvania Courthouse, Virginia
Date of Action: 10 May 1864
Date of Issue: 8 April 1892
Citation: At the head of three regiments and under a most galling fire, attacked and occupied the enemy's works.

1198 ◆ SEITZINGER, JAMES M.

Rank: Private (highest rank: Sergeant)
Service: U.S. Army
Birthday: 24 November 1846
Place of Birth: Germany
Date of Death: 14 January 1924
Place of Death: Gordon, Pennsylvania
Cemetery: Christ Church Cemetery—Fountain Springs, Pennsylvania
Entered Service at: Worcester, Montgomery County, Pennsylvania
Unit: Company G, 116th Pennsylvania Infantry
Battle or Place of Action: Cold Harbor, Virginia
Date of Action: 3 June 1864
Date of Issue: 1 March 1906
Citation: When the color bearer was shot down, this soldier seized the colors and bore them gallantly in a charge against the enemy.

1199 ◆ SELLERS, ALFRED JACOB

Rank: Major (highest rank: Brevet Colonel)
Service: U.S. Army
Birthday: 2 March 1836
Place of Birth: Plumsteadville, Bucks County, Pennsylvania
Date of Death: 20 September 1908
Place of Death: Philadelphia, Pennsylvania
Cemetery: Mount Vernon Cemetery (MH)—Philadelphia, Pennsylvania
Entered Service at: Philadelphia, Philadelphia County, Pennsylvania
Unit: 90th Pennsylvania Infantry
Battle or Place of Action: Gettysburg, Pennsylvania
Date of Action: 1 July 1863
Date of Issue: 21 July 1894
Citation: Voluntarily led the regiment under a withering fire to a position from which the enemy was repulsed.

1200 ◆ *SESTON, CHARLES H.

Rank: Sergeant
Service: U.S. Army
Birthday: 1840
Place of Birth: New Albany, Floyd County, Indiana
Date of Death: 19 September 1864
Place of Death: Winchester, Virginia

Cemetery: New Albany Cemetery—Floyd County, Indiana
Entered Service at: New Albany, Floyd County, Indiana
Unit: Company I, 11th Indiana Infantry
Battle or Place of Action: Winchester, Virginia
Date of Action: 19 September 1864
Date of Issue: 6 April 1865
Citation: Gallant and meritorious service in carrying the regimental colors.

1201 ◆ SEWARD, RICHARD HENRY

True Name: Seaward, Richard Henry
Rank: Paymaster's Steward (highest rank: Master's Mate)
Service: U.S. Navy
Birthday: 10 October 1840
Place of Birth: Kittery, York County, Maine
Date of Death: 30 May 1899
Cemetery: First Christian Church Cemetery (MH)—Kittery Point, Maine
Entered Service at: Kittery, York County, Maine
Unit: U.S.S. *Commodore*
Battle or Place of Action: Ship Island Sound, Louisiana
Date of Action: 23 November 1863
G.O. Number, Date: 32, 16 April 1864
Citation: Served as paymaster's steward on board the U.S.S. *Commodore*, November 1863. Carrying out his duties courageously, Seward "volunteered to go on the field amidst a heavy fire to recover the bodies of two soldiers which he brought off with the aid of others; a second instance of personal valor within a fortnight." Promoted to acting master's mate.

1202 ◆ SEWELL, WILLIAM JOYCE

Rank: Colonel (highest rank: Brevet Major General)
Service: U.S. Army
Birthday: 6 December 1835
Place of Birth: Castlebar, County Mayo, Ireland
Date of Death: 27 December 1901
Place of Death: Camden, New Jersey
Cemetery: Harleigh Cemetery—Camden, New Jersey
Entered Service at: Camden, Camden County, New Jersey
Unit: 5th New Jersey Infantry
Battle or Place of Action: Chancellorsville, Virginia
Date of Action: 3 May 1863
Date of Issue: 25 March 1896
Citation: Assuming command of a brigade, he rallied around his colors a mass of men from other regiments and fought these troops with great brilliancy through several hours of desperate conflict, remaining in command though wounded and inspired them by his presence and the gallantry of his personal example.

1203 ◆ SHAFTER, WILLIAM RUFUS

Rank: First Lieutenant (highest rank: Major General U.S. Army)
Service: U.S. Army
Birthday: 16 October 1835
Place of Birth: Kalamazoo, Kalamazoo County, Michigan
Date of Death: 12 November 1906
Place of Death: Bakersfield, California
Cemetery: San Francisco National Cemetery OS-30-46 (MH)—San Francisco, California
Entered Service at: Galesburg, Kalamazoo County, Michigan
Unit: Company I, 7th Michigan Infantry
Battle or Place of Action: Fair Oaks, Virginia
Date of Action: 31 May 1862
Date of Issue: 12 June 1895
Citation: Lt. Shafter was engaged in bridge construction and not being needed there returned with his men to engage the enemy participating in a charge across an open field that resulted in casualties to 18 of the 22 men. At the close of the battle his horse was shot from under him and he was severely flesh wounded. He remained on the field that day and stayed to fight the next day only by concealing his wounds. In order not to be sent home with the wounded he kept his wounds concealed for another three days until other wounded had left the area.

1204 ◆ SHAHAN, EMISIRE

Rank: Corporal (highest rank: Sergeant)
Service: U.S. Army
Birthday: 14 August 1843
Place of Birth: Preston County, West Virginia
Date of Death: 17 November 1919
Cemetery: Masonic Cemetery (MH)—Elma, Washington
Entered Service at: Clarksburg, Harrison County, West Virginia
Unit: Company A, 1st West Virginia Cavalry
Battle or Place of Action: Deatonsville (Sailor's Creek), Virginia
Date of Action: 6 April 1865
Date of Issue: 3 May 1865
Citation: Capture of flag of 76th Georgia Infantry (C.S.A.).

1205 ◆ SHALER, ALEXANDER

Rank: Colonel (highest rank: Brevet Major General)
Service: U.S. Army
Birthday: 19 March 1827
Place of Birth: Haddam, Middlesex County, Connecticut
Date of Death: 28 December 1911
Place of Death: New York, New York
Cemetery: English Neighborhood Reform Church Cemetery—Ridgefield, New Jersey
Entered Service at: New York, New York
Unit: 65th New York Infantry
Battle or Place of Action: Marye's Heights, Virginia
Date of Action: 3 May 1863
Date of Issue: 25 November 1893
Citation: At a most critical moment, the head of the charging column being about to be crushed by the severe fire of the enemy's artillery and infantry, he pushed forward with a supporting column, pierced the enemy's works, and turned their flank.
Notes: POW

1206 ◆ SHAMBAUGH, CHARLES

Rank: Corporal
Service: U.S. Army
Birthday: 25 August 1839
Place of Birth: Prussia, Germany
Date of Death: 12 October 1913
Place of Death: Hyattsville, Maryland
Cemetery: Prospect Hill Cemetery—Washington, D.C.
Entered Service at: Indian Town, Lebanon County, Pennsylvania
Unit: Company B, 11th Pennsylvania Reserves
Battle or Place of Action: Charles City Crossroads, Virginia
Date of Action: 30 June 1862
Date of Issue: 17 July 1866
Citation: Capture of flag.
Notes: POW

1207 ◆ SHANES, JOHN

Rank: Private
Service: U.S. Army
Birthday: 23 July 1844
Place of Birth: Monongalia County, West Virginia
Date of Death: 26 January 1904
Place of Death: Brave, Pennsylvania
Cemetery: Lantz Cemetery—Brave, Pennsylvania
Entered Service at: Warren, West Virginia
Unit: Company K, 14th West Virginia Infantry
Battle or Place of Action: Carter's Farm, Virginia
Date of Action: 20 July 1864
Date of Issue: 31 January 1896
Citation: Charged upon a Confederate fieldpiece in advance of his comrades and by his individual exertions silenced the piece.

1208 ◆ SHAPLAND, JOHN

Rank: Private
Service: U.S. Army
Birthday: 4 March 1832
Place of Birth: Barnstable, Devonshire, England
Date of Death: 5 February 1923
Cemetery: Greenwood Cemetery (MH)—York, Nebraska
Entered Service at: Ottawa, La Salle County, Illinois
Unit: Company D, 104th Illinois Infantry
Battle or Place of Action: Elk River, Tennessee
Date of Action: 2 July 1863
Date of Issue: 30 October 1897
Citation: Voluntarily joined a small party that, under heavy fire, captured a stockade and saved the bridge.

1209 ◆ SHARP, HENDRICK

Rank: Seaman
Service: U.S. Navy
Birthday: 1815
Place of Birth: Spain
Entered Service at: New York, New York
Unit: U.S.S. *Richmond*
Battle or Place of Action: Fort Mogan, Mobile Bay, Alabama
Date of Action: 5 August 1864
G.O. Number, Date: 45, 31 December 1864
Citation: As captain of a 100-pounder rifle gun on topgallant forecastle on board the U.S.S. *Richmond* during action against rebel forts and gunboats and against the ram *Tennessee* in Mobile Bay, 5 August 1864. Despite damage to his ship and the loss of several men on board as enemy fire raked her decks, Sharp fought his gun with skill and courage throughout a furious two-hour battle which resulted in the surrender of the rebel ram *Tennessee* and in the damaging and destruction of batteries at Fort Morgan.

1210 ◆ SHEA, JOSEPH HENRY

Rank: Private
Service: U.S. Army
Place of Birth: Baltimore, Baltimore County, Maryland
Entered Service at: New Bern, Craven County, North Carolina
Unit: Company K, 92d New York Infantry
Battle or Place of Action: Chapin's Farm, Virginia
Date of Action: 29 September 1864
Date of Issue: March 1866
Citation: Gallantry in bringing wounded from the field under heavy fire.

1211 ◆ SHELLENBERGER, JOHN

Rank: Corporal
Service: U.S. Army
Birthday: 30 August 1839
Place of Birth: Fayette County, Pennsylvania
Date of Death: 16 January 1911
Cemetery: Welsh Hill Cemetery (MH)—Grandville Township, Ohio
Entered Service at: Perryopolis, Fayette County, Pennsylvania
Unit: Company B, 85th Pennsylvania Infantry
Battle or Place of Action: Deep Run, Virginia
Date of Action: 16 August 1864
Date of Issue: 6 April 1865
Citation: Capture of flag.

1212 ◆ SHEPARD, IRWIN

Rank: Corporal (highest rank: First Sergeant)
Service: U.S. Army
Birthday: 5 July 1843
Place of Birth: Skaneateles, Onondaga County, New York
Date of Death: 17 April 1916
Cemetery: Woodlawn Cemetery—Winona, Minnesota
Entered Service at: Chelsea, Washtenaw County, Michigan
Unit: Company E, 17th Michigan Infantry
Battle or Place of Action: Knoxville, Tennessee
Date of Action: 20 November 1863
Date of Issue: 3 August 1897

Citation: Having voluntarily accompanied a small party to destroy buildings within the enemy's lines, whence sharpshooters had been firing, disregarded an order to retire, remained, and completed the firing of the buildings, thus insuring their total destruction; this at the imminent risk of his life from the fire of the advancing enemy.

1213 ◆ SHEPARD, LOUIS CAPET

Rank: Ordinary Seaman
Service: U.S. Navy
Birthday: 2 September 1841
Place of Birth: Ashtabula, Ashtabula County, Ohio
Date of Death: 27 April 1919
Place of Death: Danbury, Ohio
Cemetery: Lakeview Cemetery—Port Clinton, Ohio
Entered Service at: Ohio
Unit: U.S.S. *Wabash*
Battle or Place of Action: Fort Fisher, North Carolina
Date of Action: 15 January 1865
G.O. Number, Date: 59, 22 June 1865
Citation: Served as seaman on board the U.S.S. *Wabash* in the assault on Fort Fisher, 15 January 1865. Advancing gallantly through severe enemy fire while armed only with a revolver and cutlass which made it impossible to return the fire at that range, Shepard succeeded in reaching the angle of the fort and in going on to be one of the few who entered the fort. When the rest of the body of men to his rear were forced to retreat under a devastating fire, he was forced to withdraw through lack of support and to seek the shelter of one of the mounds near the stockade from which point he succeeded in regaining the safety of his ship.

1214 ◆ SHEPHERD, WILLIAM

Rank: Private (highest rank: Sergeant)
Service: U.S. Army
Birthday: 1837
Place of Birth: Dillsboro, Ohio County, Indiana
Date of Death: 19 March 1899
Cemetery: Conaway Family Cemetery (MH)—Dillsboro, Indiana
Entered Service at: Washington, D.C.
Unit: Company A, 3d Indiana Cavalry
Battle or Place of Action: Deatonsville (Sailor's Creek), Virginia
Date of Action: 6 April 1865
Date of Issue: 3 May 1865
Citation: Capture of flag.
Notes: POW

1215 ◆ SHERIDAN, JAMES

Rank: Quartermaster
Service: U.S. Navy
Birthday: 1831
Place of Birth: Newark, Essex County, New Jersey
Entered Service at: New York, New York
Unit: U.S.S. *Oneida*
Battle or Place of Action: Mobile Bay, Alabama
Date of Action: 5 August 1864
G.O. Number, Date: 45, 31 December 1864
Citation: Served as quartermaster on board the U.S.S. *Oneida* in the engagement at Mobile Bay, 5 August 1864. Acting as captain of the after 11-inch gun, and wounded in several places, Sheridan remained at his gun until the firing had ceased and then took the place of the signal quartermaster who had been injured by a fall. Recommended for his gallantry and intelligence, Sheridan served courageously throughout this battle which resulted in the capture of the rebel ram *Tennessee* and the damaging of Fort Morgan.

1216 ◆ SHERMAN, MARSHALL

Rank: Private
Service: U.S. Army
Birthday: 1823
Place of Birth: Burlington, Chittenden County, Vermont
Date of Death: 19 April 1896
Cemetery: Oakland Cemetery (MH)—St. Paul, Minnesota
Entered Service at: St. Paul, Ramsey County, Minnesota
Unit: Company C, 1st Minnesota Infantry
Battle or Place of Action: Gettysburg, Pennsylvania
Date of Action: 3 July 1863
Date of Issue: 1 December 1864
Citation: Capture of flag of 28th Virginia Infantry (C.S.A.).

1217 ◆ SHIELDS, BERNARD

Rank: Private
Service: U.S. Army
Birthday: 1833
Place of Birth: Ireland
Date of Death: 20 April 1887
Cemetery: Mount Calvary Cemetery—Columbus, Ohio
Entered Service at: Ironton, Lawrence County, Ohio
Unit: Company E, 2d West Virginia Cavalry
Battle or Place of Action: Appomattox, Virginia
Date of Action: 8 April 1865
Date of Issue: 3 May 1865
Citation: Capture of flag of the Washington Artillery (C.S.A.).

1218 ◆ SHIEL, JOHN

True Name: Shields, John
Rank: Corporal (highest rank: Sergeant)
Service: U.S. Army
Birthday: May 1828
Place of Birth: Scotland
Date of Death: 11 June 1908
Place of Death: Philadelphia, Pennsylvania
Cemetery: Greenmount Cemetery—Philadelphia, Pennsylvania
Entered Service at: Philadelphia, Philadelphia County, Pennsylvania
Unit: Company E, 90th Pennsylvania Infantry

Battle or Place of Action: Fredericksburg, Virginia
Date of Action: 13 December 1862
Date of Issue: 21 January 1897
Citation: Carried a dangerously wounded comrade into the Union lines, thereby preventing his capture by the enemy.

1219 ◆ SHILLING, JOHN

Rank: First Sergeant
Service: U.S. Army
Birthday: 15 February 1832
Place of Birth: England
Date of Death: 22 July 1884
Cemetery: Riverside Cemetery—Wilmington, Delaware
Entered Service at: Felton, Kent County, Delaware
Unit: Company H, 3d Delaware Infantry
Battle or Place of Action: Weldon Railroad, Virginia
Date of Action: 21 August 1864
Date of Issue: 6 September 1864
Citation: Capture of flag.

1220 ◆ SHIPLEY, ROBERT F.

Rank: First Sergeant
Service: U.S. Army
Birthday: 8 May 1838
Place of Birth: Wayne, Schuyler County, New York
Date of Death: 29 April 1903
Cemetery: Restland Cemetery—Mendota, Illinois
Entered Service at: Penn Yan, Yates County, New York
Unit: Company A, 140th New York Infantry
Battle or Place of Action: Five Forks, Virginia
Date of Action: 1 April 1865
Date of Issue: 10 May 1865
Citation: Captured the flag of the 9th Virginia Infantry (C.S.A.) in hand-to-hand combat.

1221 ◆ SHIPMAN, WILLIAM

Rank: Coxswain
Service: U.S. Navy
Birthday: 1831
Place of Birth: New York, New York
Date of Death: 17 April 1894
Cemetery: Holy Cross Cemetery—Philadelphia, Pennsylvania
Entered Service at: New York, New York
Unit: U.S.S. *Ticonderoga*
Battle or Place of Action: Fort Fisher, North Carolina
Date of Action: 15 January 1865
G.O. Number, Date: 59, 22 June 1865
Citation: On board the U.S.S. *Ticonderoga* in the attack upon Fort Fisher, 15 January 1865. As captain of No. 2 gun, stationed near the 100-pound Parrott rifle when it burst into fragments, killing eight men and wounding 12 more, Shipman promptly recognized the effect produced by the explosion and, despite the carnage surrounding them and the enemy's fire, encouraged the men at their guns by exclaiming, "Go ahead, boys! This is only the fortunes of war!"

1222 ◆ SHIVERS, JOHN

Rank: Private
Service: U.S. Marine Corps
Birthday: 1830
Place of Birth: Canada
Entered Service at: New Jersey
Battle or Place of Action: Fort Fisher, North Carolina
Date of Action: 15 January 1865
G.O. Number, Date: 59, 22 June 1865
Citation: On board the U.S.S. *Minnesota*, in the assault on Fort Fisher, 15 January 1865. Landing on the beach with the assaulting party from his ship, Pvt. Shivers advanced to the top of the sandhill and partly through the breach in the palisades despite enemy fire which killed or wounded many officers and men. When more than two-thirds of the men became seized with panic and retreated on the run, he remained with the party until dark when it came safely away, bringing its wounded, its arms, and its colors.

1223 ◆ SHOEMAKER, LEVI

Rank: Sergeant
Service: U.S. Army
Birthday: 25 June 1840
Place of Birth: Monongalia County, West Virginia
Date of Death: 3 April 1917
Place of Death: Morgantown, West Virginia
Cemetery: East Oak Grove Cemetery (MH)—Morgantown, West Virginia
Entered Service at: Clarksburg, Harrison County, West Virginia
Unit: Company A, 1st West Virginia Cavalry
Battle or Place of Action: Nineveh, Virginia
Date of Action: 12 November 1864
Date of Issue: 26 November 1864
Citation: Capture of flag of 22d Virginia Cavalry (C.S.A.).

1224 ◆ SHOPP, GEORGE J.

Rank: Private
Service: U.S. Army
Birthday: 8 September 1834
Place of Birth: Equinunk, Wayne County, Pennsylvania
Date of Death: 24 March 1924
Place of Death: Denver, Colorado
Cemetery: Yuma Cemetery (MH)—Yuma, Colorado
Entered Service at: Reading, Berks County, Pennsylvania
Unit: Company E, 191st Pennsylvania Infantry
Battle or Place of Action: Five Forks, Virginia
Date of Action: 1 April 1865
Date of Issue: 27 April 1865
Citation: Capture of flag.

1225 ◆ SHUBERT, FRANK

Rank: Sergeant (highest rank: Second Lieutenant)
Service: U.S. Army
Birthday: 12 January 1841

Place of Birth: Hesse, Germany
Date of Death: 24 December 1920
Cemetery: Prospect Hill Cemetery (MH)—Canojaharie, New York
Entered Service at: Canojaharie, Montgomery County, New York
Unit: Company E, 43d New York Infantry
Battle or Place of Action: Petersburg, Virginia
Date of Action: 2 April 1865
Date of Issue: 10 May 1865
Citation: Capture of two markers.

1226 ◆ SHUTES, HENRY

Rank: Captain of the Forecastle
Service: U.S. Navy
Birthday: 1804
Place of Birth: Baltimore Baltimore County, Maryland
Date of Death: 10 September 1889
Place of Death: Philadelphia, Pennsylvania
Cemetery: Mount Moriah Cemetery VA plot 2-22-01 (MH)—Philadelphia, Pennsylvania
Entered Service at: Maryland
Unit: U.S.S. *Wissahickon*
Battle or Place of Action: New Orleans, Louisiana & Fort McAllister, Georgia
Date of Action: 24-25 April 1862 & 27 February 1863
G.O. Number, Date: 71, 15 January 1866
Citation: Served as captain of the forecastle on board the U.S.S. *Wissahickon* during the battle of New Orleans, 24 and 25 April 1862; and in the engagement at Fort McAllister, 27 February 1863. Going on board the U.S.S. *Wissahickon* from the U.S.S. *Don*, where his seamanlike qualities as gunner's mate were outstanding, Shutes performed his duties with skill and courage. Showing a presence of mind and prompt action when a shot from Fort McAllister penetrated the *Wissahickon* below the water line and entered the powder magazine, Shutes contributed materially to the preservation of the powder and safety of the ship.

1227 ◆ SICKLES, DANIEL EDGAR

Rank: Major General
Service: U.S. Army
Birthday: 20 October 1819
Place of Birth: New York, New York
Date of Death: 3 May 1914
Place of Death: New York, New York
Cemetery: Arlington National Cemetery (3-1906) (MH)—Arlington, Virginia
Entered Service at: New York, New York
Unit: U.S. Volunteers
Battle or Place of Action: Gettysburg, Pennsylvania
Date of Action: 2 July 1863
Date of Issue: 30 October 1897
Citation: Displayed most conspicuous gallantry on the field vigorously contesting the advance of the enemy and continuing to encourage his troops after being himself severely wounded.

1228 ◆ SICKLES, WILLIAM H.

Rank: Sergeant
Service: U.S. Army
Birthday: 27 October 1844
Place of Birth: Danube, Herkimer County, New York
Date of Death: 26 September 1938
Place of Death: Orting, Washington
Cemetery: Soldier's Home Cemetery (MH)—Orting, Washington
Entered Service at: Fall River, Columbia County, Wisconsin
Unit: Company B, 7th Wisconsin Infantry
Battle or Place of Action: Gravelly Run, Virginia
Date of Action: 31 March 1865
Date of Issue: 28 February 1917
Citation: With a comrade, attempted capture of a stand of Confederate colors and detachment of nine Confederates, actually taking prisoner three members of the detachment, dispersing the remainder, and recapturing a Union officer who was a prisoner in hands of the detachment.

1229 ◆ SIDMAN, GEORGE DALLAS

Rank: Private (highest rank: Corporal)
Service: U.S. Army
Birthday: 25 November 1844
Place of Birth: Rochester, Monroe County, New York
Date of Death: 3 February 1920
Place of Death: Lakeland, Florida
Cemetery: Arlington National Cemetery (3-2492) (MH)—Arlington, Virginia
Entered Service at: Owosso, Shiawassee County, Michigan
Unit: Company C, 16th Michigan Infantry
Battle or Place of Action: Gaines' Mill, Virginia
Date of Action: 27 June 1862
Date of Issue: 6 April 1892
Citation: Distinguished bravery in battle. Rallied his comrades to charge vastly superior force until wounded in the hip. He was a 16-year old drummer.
Notes: POW

1230 ◆ SIMKINS, LEBBEUS

True Name: Simpkins, Lebbeus
Rank: Coxswain
Service: U.S. Navy
Birthday: 1836
Place of Birth: Utica, Oneida County, New York
Date of Death: 10 September 1884
Place of Death: Sacramento, California
Cemetery: I.O.O.F. Tier, City Cemetery (MH)—Sacramento, California
Entered Service at: New York
Unit: U.S.S. *Richmond*
Battle or Place of Action: Mobile Bay, Alabama
Date of Action: 5 August 1864
G.O. Number, Date: 45, 31 December 1864
Citation: On board the U.S.S. *Richmond* during action against rebel forts and gunboats and against the ram *Tennessee*

in Mobile Bay, 5 August 1864. Despite damage to his ship and the loss of several men on board as enemy fire raked her decks, Simkins performed his duties with skill and courage throughout the furious two-hour battle, which resulted in the surrender of the rebel ram *Tennessee* and in the damaging and destruction of batteries at Fort Morgan.

1231 ◆ SIMMONS, JOHN

Rank: Private
Service: U.S. Army
Place of Birth: Bethel, Sullivan County, New York
Date of Death: 9 January 1891
Cemetery: Andes Cemetery (MH)—Andes, New York
Entered Service at: Liberty, Sullivan County, New York
Unit: Company D, 2d New York Heavy Artillery
Battle or Place of Action: Deatonsville (Sailor's Creek), Virginia
Date of Action: 6 April 1865
Date of Issue: 24 April 1865
Citation: Capture of flag.

1232 ◆ SIMMONS, WILLIAM THOMAS

Rank: First Lieutenant
Service: U.S. Army
Birthday: 29 January 1843
Place of Birth: Greene County, Illinois
Date of Death: 27 December 1908
Place of Death: Caliatoga, California
Cemetery: St. Helena Public Cemetery (MH)—St. Helena, California
Entered Service at: Springfield, Sangamon County, Illinois
Unit: Company C, 11th Missouri Infantry
Battle or Place of Action: Nashville, Tennessee
Date of Action: 16 December 1864
Date of Issue: 25 February 1865
Citation: Capture of flag of 34th Alabama Infantry (C.S.A.). Being the first to enter the works, he shot and wounded the enemy color bearer.

1233 ◆ SIMONDS, WILLIAM EDGAR

Rank: Sergeant Major (highest rank: Second Lieutenant)
Service: U.S. Army
Birthday: 24 November 1842
Place of Birth: Collinsville, Hartford County, Connecticut
Date of Death: 14 March 1903
Place of Death: Hartford, Connecticut
Cemetery: Collinsville Cemetery (MH)—Collinsville, Connecticut
Entered Service at: Canton, Hartford County, Connecticut
Unit: 25th Connecticut Infantry
Battle or Place of Action: Irish Bend, Louisiana
Date of Action: 14 April 1863
Date of Issue: 25 February 1899
Citation: Displayed great gallantry, under a heavy fire from the enemy, in calling in the skirmishers and assisting in forming the line of battle.

1234 ◆ SIMONS, CHARLES JENKS

Rank: Sergeant (highest rank: First Lieutenant)
Service: U.S. Army
Birthday: 29 March 1843
Place of Birth: Bombay, India
Date of Death: 18 June 1914
Place of Death: Chicago, Illinois
Cemetery: Oakwood Cemetery—Chicago, Illinois
Entered Service at: Exeter, Rockingham County, New Hampshire
Unit: Company A, 9th New Hampshire Infantry
Battle or Place of Action: Petersburg, Virginia
Date of Action: 30 July 1864
Date of Issue: 27 July 1896
Citation: Was one of the first in the exploded mine, captured a number of prisoners, and was himself captured, but escaped.

1235 ◆ SKELLIE, EBENEZER

Rank: Corporal (highest rank: Brevet Second Lieutenant NY Volunteers)
Service: U.S. Army
Birthday: August 1844
Place of Birth: Mina, Chautauqua County, New York
Date of Death: 2 July 1898
Place of Death: Findley Lake, New York
Cemetery: Mina Cemetery (MH)—Mina, New York
Entered Service at: Mina, Chautauqua County, New York
Unit: Company D, 112th New York Infantry
Battle or Place of Action: Chapin's Farm, Virginia
Date of Action: 29 September 1864
Date of Issue: 6 April 1865
Citation: Took the colors of his regiment, the color bearer having fallen, and carried them through the first charge; also, in the second charge, after all the color guards had been killed or wounded he carried the colors up to the enemy's works, where he fell wounded.

1236 ◆ SLADEN, JOSEPH ALTON

Rank: Private (highest rank: Major U.S.A. Retired)
Service: U.S. Army
Birthday: 9 April 1841
Place of Birth: Rockdale, England
Date of Death: 25 January 1911
Place of Death: Portland, Oregon
Cemetery: U.S. Military Academy Cemetery (4-22)—West Point, New York
Entered Service at: Lowell, Middlesex County, Massachusetts
Unit: Company A, 33d Massachusetts Infantry
Battle or Place of Action: Resaca, Georgia
Date of Action: 14 May 1864
Date of Issue: 19 July 1895
Citation: While detailed as clerk at headquarters, voluntarily engaged in action at a critical moment and personal example inspired the troops to repel the enemy.

1237 ◆ SLAGLE, OSCAR

Rank: Private
Service: U.S. Army
Birthday: 2 April 1844
Place of Birth: Fulton County, Ohio
Date of Death: 12 April 1913
Place of Death: Cullom, Illinois
Cemetery: Broughton Township Cemetery—Kempton, Illinois
Entered Service at: Manlius, Bureau County, Illinois
Unit: Company D, 104th Illinois Infantry
Battle or Place of Action: Elk River, Tennessee
Date of Action: 2 July 1863
Date of Issue: 30 October 1897
Citation: Voluntarily joined a small party that, under a heavy fire, captured a stockade and saved the bridge.

1238 ◆ *SLAVENS, SAMUEL

Rank: Private
Service: U.S. Army
Birthday: 1830
Place of Birth: Pike County, Ohio
Date of Death: 18 June 1862
Place of Death: Atlanta, Georgia
Cemetery: Chattanooga National Cemetery (H-11176) (MH)—Chattanooga, Tennessee
Entered Service at: Wakefield, Pike County, Ohio
Unit: Company E, 33d Ohio Infantry
Battle or Place of Action: Georgia
Date of Action: April 1862
Date of Issue: 28 July 1883
Citation: One of 19 of 24 men (including two civilians) who, by direction of Gen. Ormsby M. Mitchell, penetrated nearly 200 miles south into enemy territory and captured a railroad train at Big Shanty, Ga., in an attempt to destroy the bridges and track between Chattanooga and Atlanta.

1239 ◆ SLOAN, ANDREW JACKSON

Rank: Private
Service: U.S. Army
Birthday: 1835
Place of Birth: Bedford County, Pennsylvania
Date of Death: 1875
Cemetery: Platt Cemetery (MH)—Colesburg, Iowa
Entered Service at: Colesburg, Delaware County, Iowa
Unit: Company H, 12th Iowa Infantry
Battle or Place of Action: Nashville, Tennessee
Date of Action: 16 December 1864
Date of Issue: 24 February 1865
Citation: Captured flag of 1st Louisiana Battery (C.S.A.).

1240 ◆ SLUSHER, HENRY C.

Rank: Private
Service: U.S. Army
Birthday: 10 May 1846
Place of Birth: Washington County, Pennsylvania
Date of Death: 12 March 1923
Place of Death: Washington, Pennsylvania
Cemetery: Lone Pine Cemetery—Amwell Township, Pennsylvania
Entered Service at: Washington, Washington County, Pennsylvania
Unit: Troop F, 22d Pennsylvania Volunteer Cavalry
Battle or Place of Action: near Moorefield, West Virginia
Date of Action: 11 September 1863
Date of Issue: 4 April 1898
Citation: Voluntarily crossed a branch of the Potomac River under fire to rescue a wounded comrade held prisoner by the enemy. Was wounded and taken prisoner in the attempt.
Notes: POW

1241 ◆ SMALLEY, REUBEN

Rank: Private
Service: U.S. Army
Birthday: 29 April 1839
Place of Birth: Reading, Schuyler County, New York
Date of Death: 9 July 1926
Place of Death: Greensburg, Indiana
Cemetery: South Park Cemetery (MH)—Greensburg, Indiana
Entered Service at: Holton, Ripley County, Indiana
Unit: Company F, 83d Indiana Infantry
Battle or Place of Action: Vicksburg, Mississippi
Date of Action: 22 May 1863
Date of Issue: 9 July 1894
Citation: Gallantry in the charge of the "volunteer storming party."

1242 ◆ SMALLEY, REUBEN S.

Rank: Private
Service: U.S. Army
Birthday: 8 April 1837
Place of Birth: Washington County, Pennsylvania
Date of Death: 17 February 1916
Place of Death: Quincy, Illinois
Cemetery: Allen Cemetery—Allen, Illinois
Entered Service at: Brookfield, Cook County, Illinois
Unit: Company D, 104th Illinois Infantry
Battle or Place of Action: Elk River, Tennessee
Date of Action: 2 July 1863
Date of Issue: 30 October 1897
Citation: Voluntarily joined a small party that, under a heavy fire, captured a stockade and saved the bridge.

1243 ◆ SMITH, ALONZO

Rank: Sergeant (highest rank: First Lieutenant)
Service: U.S. Army
Birthday: 9 August 1842
Place of Birth: Niagara County, New York
Date of Death: 17 January 1927
Place of Death: Buffalo, New York

Cemetery: St. Stephen's RC Cemetery (MH)—Middleport, New York
Entered Service at: Jonesville, Hillsdale County, Michigan
Unit: Company C, 7th Michigan Infantry
Battle or Place of Action: Hatcher's Run, Virginia
Date of Action: 27 October 1864
Date of Issue: 1 December 1864
Citation: Capture of flag of 26th North Carolina Infantry (C.S.A.), while outside his lines far from his comrades.

1244 ◆ SMITH, CHARLES H.

Rank: Coxswain (highest rank: Master's Mate)
Service: U.S. Navy
Birthday: 1826
Place of Birth: Standish, Cumberland County, Maine
Date of Death: 4 February 1898
Place of Death: West Concord, Vermont
Entered Service at: Maine
Unit: U.S.S. *Rhode Island*
Battle or Place of Action: off Cape Hatteras, North Carolina
Date of Action: 30 December 1862
G.O. Number, Date: 59, 22 June 1865
Citation: Served on board the U.S.S. *Rhode Island* which was engaged in saving the lives of the officers and crew of the *Monitor*, 30 December 1862. Participating in the hazardous rescue of the officers and crew of the sinking *Monitor*, Smith, after rescuing several of the men, became separated in a heavy gale with other members of the cutter that had set out from the *Rhode Island*, and spent many hours in the small boat at the mercy of the weather and high seas until finally picked up by a schooner 50 miles east of Cape Hatteras.

1245 ◆ SMITH, CHARLES HENRY

Rank: Colonel (highest rank: Brevet Major General)
Service: U.S. Army
Birthday: 1 November 1827
Place of Birth: Hollis, York County, Maine
Date of Death: 17 July 1902
Cemetery: Arlington National Cemetery (1-128-A)—Arlington, Virginia
Entered Service at: Eastport, Washington County, Maine
Unit: 1st Maine Cavalry
Battle or Place of Action: St. Mary's Church, Virginia
Date of Action: 24 June 1864
Date of Issue: 11 April 1895
Citation: Remained in the fight to the close, although severely wounded.

1246 ◆ SMITH, DAVID LAFAYETTE

Rank: Sergeant (highest rank: First Lieutenant)
Service: U.S. Army
Birthday: 1 May 1835
Place of Birth: Cameron, Steuben County, New York
Date of Death: 8 June 1916
Place of Death: Orlean, New York
Cemetery: Pleasant Valley Cemetery—Orlean, New York
Entered Service at: Bath, Steuben County, New York
Unit: Battery E, 1st New York Light Artillery
Battle or Place of Action: Warwick Courthouse, Virginia
Date of Action: 6 April 1862
Date of Issue: 6 August 1906
Citation: This soldier, when a shell struck an ammunition chest, exploding a number of cartridges and setting fire to the packing tow, procured water and extinguished the fire, thus preventing the explosion of the remaining ammunition.

1247 ◆ SMITH, EDWIN

Rank: Ordinary Seaman
Service: U.S. Navy
Place of Birth: New York, New York
Entered Service at: New York
Unit: U.S.S. *Whitehead*
Battle or Place of Action: Franklin, Virginia
Date of Action: 3 October 1862
Citation: On board the U.S.S. *Whitehead* in the attack upon Franklin, Va., 3 October 1862. When his ship became grounded in a narrow passage as she rounded a bend in the Blackwater River, Smith, realizing the hazards of lowering a boat, voluntarily swam to shore with a line under the enemy's heavy fire. His fearless action enabled his ship to maintain steady fire and keep the enemy in check during the battle.

1248 ◆ SMITH, FRANCIS M.

Rank: First Lieutenant & Adjutant (highest rank: Captain)
Service: U.S. Army
Birthday: 29 November 1842
Place of Birth: Baltimore, Baltimore County, Maryland
Date of Death: 22 September 1917
Place of Death: Baltimore, Maryland
Cemetery: Loudon Park Cemetery (Private)—Baltimore, Maryland
Entered Service at: Frederick, Frederick County, Maryland
Unit: 1st Maryland Infantry
Battle or Place of Action: Dabney's Mills, Virginia
Date of Action: 6 February 1865
Date of Issue: 13 August 1895
Citation: Voluntarily remained with the body of his regimental commander under a heavy fire after the brigade had retired, and brought the body off the field.

1249 ◆ SMITH, HENRY I.

Rank: First Lieutenant (highest rank: Major)
Service: U.S. Army
Birthday: 4 May 1840
Place of Birth: Nottingham, Nottinghamshire, England
Date of Death: 15 November 1910
Place of Death: Mason City, Iowa
Cemetery: Elmwood Cemetery (MH)—Mason City, Iowa
Entered Service at: Shell Rock Fall, Butler County, Iowa
Unit: Company B, 7th Iowa Infantry
Battle or Place of Action: Black River, North Carolina

Date of Action: 15 March 1865
Date of Issue: 7 September 1894
Citation: Voluntarily and under fire rescued a comrade from death by drowning.

1250 ◆ SMITH, JAMES

Rank: Captain of the Forecastle
Service: U.S. Navy
Birthday: 1826
Place of Birth: Belfast, County Antrim, Ireland
Date of Death: 31 October 1881
Place of Death: New York, New York
Cemetery: Arlington National Cemetery (45-1485) (MH)—Arlington, Virginia
Entered Service at: New York, New York
Unit: U.S.S. *Richmond*
Battle or Place of Action: Mobile Bay, Alabama
Date of Action: 5 August 1864
G.O. Number, Date: 45, 31 December 1864
Citation: As captain of a gun on board the U.S.S. *Richmond* during action against rebel forts and gunboats and against the ram *Tennessee* in Mobile Bay, 5 August 1864. Despite damage to his ship and the loss of several men on board as enemy fire raked her decks, Smith fought his gun with skill and courage throughout the prolonged battle which resulted in the surrender of the rebel ram *Tennessee* and in the successful attacks carried out on Fort Morgan.

1251 ◆ SMITH, JAMES (OVID)

True Name: Smith, Ovid Wellford
Rank: Private (highest rank: Corporal)
Service: U.S. Army
Birthday: 9 November 1844
Place of Birth: Fredericksburg, Fredericksburg County, Virginia
Date of Death: 28 January 1868
Cemetery: Greenlawn Cemetery (MH)—Columbus, Ohio
Entered Service at: Circleville, Pickaway County, Ohio
Unit: Company I, 2d Ohio Infantry
Battle or Place of Action: Georgia
Date of Action: April 1862
Date of Issue: 6 July 1864
Citation: One of the 24 men (including two civilians) who, by direction of Gen. Ormsby M. Mitchell, penetrated nearly 200 miles south into enemy territory. Smith was captured near Huntsville, Ala., and did not participate in the remainder of the raid.

1252 ◆ SMITH, JOHN

Rank: Captain of the Forecastle
Service: U.S. Navy
Birthday: 1831
Place of Birth: Boston, Suffolk County, Massachusetts
Entered Service at: Massachusetts
Unit: U.S.S. *Lackawanna*
Battle or Place of Action: Fort Morgan, Mobile Bay, Alabama
Date of Action: 5 August 1864
G.O. Number, Date: 45, 31 December 1864
Citation: On board the U.S.S. *Lackawanna* during successful attacks against Fort Morgan, rebel gunboats, and the rebel ram *Tennessee* in Mobile Bay, 5 August 1864. Serving as gun captain and finding he could not depress his gun when alongside the rebel ironclad *Tennessee*, Smith threw a hand holystone into one of the ports at a rebel using abusive language against the crew of the ship. He continued his daring action throughout the engagement which resulted in the capture of the prize ram *Tennessee* and in the damaging and destruction of Fort Morgan.

1253 ◆ SMITH, JOHN

Rank: Second Captain of the Top
Service: U.S. Navy
Birthday: 1826
Place of Birth: Albany, Albany County, New York
Entered Service at: New York, New York
Unit: U.S.S. *Richmond*
Battle or Place of Action: Fort Morgan, Mobile Bay, Alabama
Date of Action: 5 August 1864
G.O. Number, Date: 45, 31 December 1864
Citation: As captain of a gun on board the U.S.S. *Richmond* during action against rebel forts and gunboats and against the ram *Tennessee* in Mobile Bay, 5 August 1864. Despite damage to his ship and the loss of several men on board as enemy fire raked her decks, Smith fought his gun with skill and courage throughout a furious two-hour battle, which resulted in the surrender of the rebel ram *Tennessee* and in the damaging and destruction of batteries at Fort Morgan.

1254 ◆ SMITH, JOSEPH SEWALL

Rank: Lieutenant Colonel (highest rank: Brevet Brigadier General)
Service: U.S. Army
Birthday: 27 November 1836
Place of Birth: Wiscasset, Lincoln County, Maine
Date of Death: 25 January 1919
Place of Death: Fort Monroe, Virginia
Cemetery: Arlington National Cemetery (2-996)—Arlington, Virginia
Entered Service at: Wiscasset, Lincoln County, Maine
Unit: 2d Army Corps
Battle or Place of Action: Hatcher's Run, Virginia
Date of Action: 27 October 1864
Date of Issue: 25 May 1892
Citation: Led a part of a brigade, saved two pieces of artillery, captured a flag, and secured a number of prisoners.

1255 ◆ SMITH, OLOFF

Rank: Coxswain
Service: U.S. Navy

Birthday: 1833
Place of Birth: Sweden
Entered Service at: New York, New York
Unit: U.S.S. *Richmond*
Battle or Place of Action: Fort Morgan, Mobile Bay, Alabama
Date of Action: 5 August 1864
G.O. Number, Date: 45, 31 December 1864
Citation: On board the U.S.S. *Richmond* during action against rebel forts and gunboats and against the ram *Tennessee* in Mobile Bay, 5 August 1864. Despite damage to his ship and the loss of several men on board as enemy fire raked her decks, Smith performed his duties with skill and courage throughout the furious two-hour battle, which resulted in the surrender of the rebel ram *Tennessee* and in the damaging and destruction of batteries at Fort Morgan.

1256 ◆ SMITH, OTIS W.

Rank: Private (highest rank: Corporal)
Service: U.S. Army
Birthday: 4 October 1844
Place of Birth: Logan County, Ohio
Date of Death: 10 March 1923
Place of Death: Yountville, California
Cemetery: Arroyo Grande Cemetery—Arroyo Grande, California
Entered Service at: Champaign, Ohio
Unit: Company G, 95th Ohio Infantry
Battle or Place of Action: Nashville, Tennessee
Date of Action: 16 December 1864
Date of Issue: 24 February 1865
Citation: Capture of flag of 6th Florida Infantry (C.S.A.).

1257 ◆ SMITH, RICHARD

Rank: Private
Service: U.S. Army
Birthday: 9 January 1840
Place of Birth: Haverstraw, Rockland County, New York
Date of Death: 13 June 1918
Cemetery: Mount Repose Cemetery—Hayerstraw, New York
Entered Service at: Haverstraw, Rockland County, New York
Unit: Company B, 95th New York Infantry
Battle or Place of Action: Weldon Railroad, Virginia
Date of Action: 21 August 1864
Date of Issue: 13 March 1865
Citation: Captured two officers and 20 men of Hagood's brigade while they were endeavoring to make their way back through the woods.

1258 ◆ SMITH, SAMUEL RODMOND

Rank: Captain (highest rank: Brevet Major)
Service: U.S. Army
Birthday: 20 April 1841
Place of Birth: Wilmington, New Castle County, Delaware
Date of Death: 30 September 1912
Place of Death: Miami, Florida
Cemetery: Wilmington Cemetery—Wilmington, Delaware
Entered Service at: Wilmington, New Castle County, Delaware
Unit: Company C, 4th Delaware Infantry
Battle or Place of Action: Rowanty Creek, Virginia
Date of Action: 5 February 1865
Date of Issue: 8 April 1895
Citation: Swam the partly frozen creek under fire to establish a crossing.

1259 ◆ SMITH, THADDEUS S.

Rank: Corporal
Service: U.S. Army
Birthday: 13 May 1847
Place of Birth: Cumberland, Franklin County, Pennsylvania
Date of Death: 14 March 1933
Place of Death: Port Townsend, Washington
Cemetery: Laurel Grove Cemetery (GAR plot) (MH)—Port Townsend, Washington
Entered Service at: Harrisburg, Dauphin County, Pennsylvania
Unit: Company E, 6th Pennsylvania Reserve Infantry
Battle or Place of Action: Gettysburg, Pennsylvania
Date of Action: 2 July 1863
Date of Issue: 5 May 1900
Citation: Was one of six volunteers who charged upon a log house near the Devil's Den, where a squad of the enemy's sharpshooters were sheltered, and compelled their surrender.

1260 ◆ SMITH, THOMAS

Rank: Seaman
Service: U.S. Navy
Birthday: 1838
Place of Birth: England
Entered Service at: New York, New York
Unit: U.S.S. *Magnolia*
Battle or Place of Action: St. Marks, Florida
Date of Action: 5-6 March 1865
G.O. Number, Date: 59, 22 June 1865
Citation: As seaman on board the U.S.S. *Magnolia*, St. Marks, Fla., 5 and 6 March 1865. Serving with the Army in charge of Navy howitzers during the attack on St. Marks and throughout this fierce engagement, Smith made remarkable efforts in assisting transport of the gun, and his coolness and determination in courageously standing by his gun while under the fire of the enemy were a credit to the service to which he belonged.

1261 ◆ SMITH, WALTER B.

Rank: Ordinary Seaman
Service: U.S. Navy
Birthday: 1827
Place of Birth: New York
Entered Service at: New York, New York

Unit: U.S.S. *Richmond*
Battle or Place of Action: Fort Morgan, Mobile Bay, Alabama
Date of Action: 5 August 1864
G.O. Number, Date: 45, 31 December 1864
Citation: On board the U.S.S. *Richmond* during action against rebel forts and gunboats and with the ram *Tennessee* in Mobile Bay, 5 August 1864. Cool and courageous at his station throughout the prolonged action, Smith rendered outstanding service at the 100-pounder rifle on the topgallant forecastle and while firing his musket into the gun ports of the rebel *Tennessee*.

1262 ◆ SMITH, WILLARD M.

Rank: Corporal
Service: U.S. Marine Corps
Birthday: 1840
Place of Birth: Allegany, Cattaraugus County, New York
Date of Death: 26 March 1918
Place of Death: Brooklyn, New York
Cemetery: Elm Lawn Cemetery—Buffalo, New York
Entered Service at: New York
Unit: U.S.S. *Brooklyn*
Battle or Place of Action: Mobile Bay, Alabama
Date of Action: 5 August 1864
G.O. Number, Date: 45, 31 December 1864
Citation: On board the U.S.S. *Brooklyn* during action against rebel forts and gunboats, and with the ram *Tennessee* in Mobile Bay, on 5 August 1864. Despite severe damage to his ship and the loss of several men on board as enemy fire continued to fall, Cpl. Smith fought his gun with skill and courage throughout the furious two-hour battle which resulted in the surrender of the rebel ram *Tennessee*.

1263 ◆ SMITH, WILLIAM

Rank: Quartermaster (highest rank: Master's Mate)
Service: U.S. Navy
Birthday: 1838
Place of Birth: Ireland
Date of Death: 12 January 1902
Place of Death: Concord, New Hampshire
Cemetery: Blossom Hill Cemetery—Concord, New Hampshire
Entered Service at: Concord, Merrimack County, New Hampshire
Unit: U.S.S. *Kearsarge*
Battle or Place of Action: off Cherbourg, France
Date of Action: 19 June 1864
G.O. Number, Date: 45, 31 December 1864
Citation: Served as second quartermaster on board the U.S.S. *Kearsarge* when she destroyed the *Alabama* off Cherbourg, France, 19 June 1864. Acting as captain of the 11-inch pivot gun of the second division, Smith carried out his duties courageously and deserved special notice for the deliberate and cool manner in which he acted throughout the bitter engagement. It is stated by rebel officers that this gun was more destructive and did more damage than any other gun of the *Kearsarge*.

1264 ◆ SMITH, WILSON

Rank: Corporal (highest rank: Sergeant)
Service: U.S. Army
Birthday: 6 September 1841
Place of Birth: Madison, Madison County, New York
Date of Death: 22 February 1901
Place of Death: Rome, New York
Cemetery: Rome Cemetery (MH)—Rome, New York
Entered Service at: Madison, Madison County, New York
Unit: Battery H, 3d New York Light Artillery
Battle or Place of Action: Washington, North Carolina
Date of Action: 6 September 1862
Date of Issue: 24 April 1896
Citation: Took command of a gun (the lieutenant in charge having disappeared) and fired the same so rapidly and effectively that the enemy was repulsed, although for a time a hand-to-hand conflict was had over the gun.

1265 ◆ SNEDDEN, JAMES

Rank: Musician (highest rank: Bugler)
Service: U.S. Army
Birthday: 19 September 1849
Place of Birth: Edinburgh, Scotland
Date of Death: 14 June 1919
Cemetery: Odd Fellow Cemetery—Lexington, Mississippi
Entered Service at: Johnstown, Cambria County, Pennsylvania
Unit: Company E, 54th Pennsylvania Infantry
Battle or Place of Action: Piedmont, Virginia
Date of Action: 5 June 1864
Date of Issue: 11 September 1897
Citation: Left his place in the rear, took the rifle of a disabled soldier, and fought through the remainder of the action.

1266 ◆ SOUTHARD, DAVID

Rank: Sergeant
Service: U.S. Army
Birthday: 1845
Place of Birth: Ocean County, New Jersey
Date of Death: 6 May 1894
Cemetery: Zion Methodist Cemetery (MH)—Zion, New Jersey
Entered Service at: Florence, Burlington County, New Jersey
Unit: Company C, 1st New Jersey Cavalry
Battle or Place of Action: Deatonsville (Sailor's Creek), Virginia
Date of Action: 6 April 1865
Date of Issue: 3 July 1865
Citation: Capture of flag; and was the first man over the works in the charge.

1267 ◆ SOVA, JOSEPH E.

Rank: Saddler
Service: U.S. Army
Birthday: 1840
Place of Birth: Chili, Monroe County, New York
Date of Death: 23 October 1866
Place of Death: Walworth, New York
Entered Service at: Rochester, Monroe County, New York
Unit: Company H, 8th New York Cavalry
Battle or Place of Action: Appomattox Campaign, Virginia
Date of Action: 29 March-9 April 1865
Date of Issue: 3 May 1865
Citation: Capture of flag.

1268 ◆ SOWERS, MICHAEL

Rank: Private
Service: U.S. Army
Birthday: 14 September 1844
Place of Birth: Pittsburgh, Allegheny County, Pennsylvania
Date of Death: 7 January 1920
Place of Death: Findley, Pennsylvania
Cemetery: Catholic Cemetery—Findley, Pennsylvania
Entered Service at: Pittsburgh, Allegheny County, Pennsylvania
Unit: Company L, 4th Pennsylvania Cavalry
Battle or Place of Action: Stony Creek Station, Virginia
Date of Action: 1 December 1864
Date of Issue: 16 February 1897
Citation: His horse having been shot from under him, he voluntarily and on foot participated in the cavalry charge made upon one of the forts, conducting himself throughout with great personal bravery.

1269 ◆ SPALDING, EDWARD BURSON

Rank: Sergeant (highest rank: First Lieutenant)
Service: U.S. Army
Birthday: 2 February 1840
Place of Birth: Byron, Ogle County, Illinois
Date of Death: 4 March 1920
Cemetery: Floyd Cemetery (MH)—Sioux City, Iowa
Entered Service at: Rockford, Winnebago County, Illinois
Unit: Company E, 52d Illinois Infantry
Battle or Place of Action: Pittsburg Landing, Tennessee
Date of Action: 6 April 1862
Date of Issue: 15 January 1894
Citation: Although twice wounded, and thereby crippled for life, he remained fighting in open ground to the close of the battle.

1270 ◆ SPERRY, WILLIAM JOSEPH

Rank: Major (highest rank: Lieutenant Colonel)
Service: U.S. Army
Birthday: 28 December 1840
Place of Birth: Cavendish, Windsor County, Vermont
Date of Death: 3 March 1914
Cemetery: Mount Union Cemetery—Cavendish Village, Vermont
Entered Service at: Cavendish, Windsor County, Vermont
Unit: 6th Vermont Infantry
Battle or Place of Action: Petersburg, Virginia
Date of Action: 2 April 1865
Date of Issue: 12 August 1892
Citation: With the assistance of a few men, captured two pieces of artillery and turned them upon the enemy.

1271 ◆ SPILLANE, TIMOTHY

Rank: Private (highest rank: Ordnance Sergeant) (highest rank: U.S.A. Ret.)
Service: U.S. Army
Birthday: 1842
Place of Birth: County Kerry, Ireland
Date of Death: 3 December 1901
Place of Death: Knoxville, Tennessee
Cemetery: Knoxville National Cemetery (A-3319) (MH)—Knoxville, Tennessee
Entered Service at: Waterford, Saratoga County, New York
Unit: Company C, 16th Pennsylvania Cavalry
Battle or Place of Action: Hatcher's Run, Virginia
Date of Action: 5-7 February 1865
Date of Issue: 16 September 1880
Citation: Gallantry and good conduct in action; bravery in a charge and reluctance to leave the field after being twice wounded.

1272 ◆ SPRAGUE, BENONA

Rank: Corporal (highest rank: Sergeant)
Service: U.S. Army
Birthday: 15 February 1833
Place of Birth: Satina Onondaga County, New York
Date of Death: 19 June 1908
Place of Death: Cheney Grove, Illinois
Cemetery: Riverside Cemetery—Saybrook, Illinois
Entered Service at: Cheney Grove, Illinois
Unit: Company F, 116th Illinois Infantry
Battle or Place of Action: Vicksburg, Mississippi
Date of Action: 22 May 1863
Date of Issue: 10 July 1894
Citation: Gallantry in the charge of the "volunteer storming party."

1273 ◆ *SPRAGUE, JOHN WILSON

Rank: Colonel (highest rank: Brevet Major General)
Service: U.S. Army
Birthday: 4 April 1817
Place of Birth: White Creek, Washington County, New York
Date of Death: 24 December 1893
Cemetery: Old Tacoma Cemetery—Tacoma, Washington
Entered Service at: Sandusky, Erie County, Ohio

Unit: 63d Ohio Infantry
Battle or Place of Action: Decatur, Georgia
Date of Action: 22 July 1862
Date of Issue: 18 January 1894
Citation: With a small command defeated an overwhelming force of the enemy and saved the trains of the corps.

1274 ◆ SPROWLE, DAVID

True Name: Sprowls, David
Rank: Orderly Sergeant
Service: U.S. Marine Corps
Birthday: 1811
Place of Birth: Lisbon, St. Lawrence County, New York
Cemetery: Red Mills Cemetery—Lisbon, New York
Entered Service at: New York
Unit: U.S.S. *Richmond*
Battle or Place of Action: Mobile Bay, Alabama
Date of Action: 5 August 1864
G.O. Number, Date: 45, 31 December 1864
Citation: On board the U.S.S. *Richmond* during action against rebel forts and gunboats and with the ram *Tennessee* in Moblie Bay, 5 August 1864. Despite damage to his ship and the loss of several men on board as enemy fire raked her decks, Orderly Sgt. Sprowle inspired the men of the marine guard and directed a division of great guns throughout the furious battle which resulted in the surrender of the rebel ram *Tennessee* and in the damaging and destruction of batteries at Fort Morgan.

1275 ◆ SPURLING, ANDREW BARCLAY

Rank: Lieutenant Colonel (highest rank: Brevet Brigadier General)
Service: U.S. Army
Birthday: 20 March 1833
Place of Birth: Cranberry Isles, Hancock County, Maine
Date of Death: 13 August 1906
Place of Death: Chicago, Illinois
Cemetery: Rose Hill Cemetery—Chicago, Illinois
Entered Service at: Augusta, Kennebec County, Maine
Unit: 2d Maine Cavalry
Battle or Place of Action: Evergreen, Alabama
Date of Action: 23 March 1865
Date of Issue: 10 September 1897
Citation: Advanced alone in the darkness beyond the picket line, came upon three of the enemy, fired upon them (his fire being returned), wounded two, and captured the whole party.

1276 ◆ STACEY, CHARLES

Rank: Private
Service: U.S. Army
Birthday: 22 January 1842
Place of Birth: England
Date of Death: 17 October 1924
Cemetery: Woodlawn Cemetery (Mausoleum) (MH)—Norwalk, Ohio
Entered Service at: Norwalk, Huron County, Ohio
Unit: Company D, 55th Ohio Infantry
Battle or Place of Action: Gettysburg, Pennsylvania
Date of Action: 2 July 1863
Date of Issue: 23 June 1896
Citation: Voluntarily took an advanced position on the skirmish line for the purpose of ascertaining the location of Confederate sharpshooters and under heavy fire held the position thus taken until the company of which he was a member went back to the main line.
Notes: POW from 2 July 1863—19 May 1864

1277 ◆ STAHEL, JULIUS H.

Rank: Major General
Service: U.S. Army
Birthday: 5 November 1825
Place of Birth: Szegedin, Hungary
Date of Death: 4 December 1912
Place of Death: New York, New York
Cemetery: Arlington National Cemetery (2-998)—Arlington, Virginia
Entered Service at: New York, New York
Unit: U.S. Volunteers
Battle or Place of Action: Piedmont, Virginia
Date of Action: 5 June 1864
Date of Issue: 4 November 1893
Citation: Led his division into action until he was severely wounded.

1278 ◆ STANLEY, DAVID SLOANE

Rank: Major General
Service: U.S. Army
Birthday: 1 June 1828
Place of Birth: Cedar Valley, Ohio
Date of Death: 13 March 1902
Place of Death: Washington, D.C.
Cemetery: Soldier's Home National Cemetery (O-20)—Washington, D.C.
Entered Service at: Congress, Wayne County, Ohio
Unit: U.S. Volunteers
Battle or Place of Action: Franklin, Tennessee
Date of Action: 30 November 1864
Date of Issue: 29 March 1893
Citation: At a critical moment rode to the front of one of his brigades, reestablished its lines, and gallantly led it in a successful assault.

1279 ◆ STANLEY, WILLIAM A.

Rank: Shell Man
Service: U.S. Navy
Birthday: 1831
Place of Birth: Massachusetts
Entered Service at: Massachusetts
Unit: U.S.S. *Hartford*

Battle or Place of Action: Fort Morgan, Mobile Bay, Alabama
Date of Action: 5 August 1864
G.O. Number, Date: 45, 31 December 1864
Citation: Shell man on No. 8 on board the U.S.S. *Hartford* during successful actions against Fort Morgan, rebel gunboats, and the ram *Tennessee* in Mobile Bay, 5 August 1864. Although severely wounded when his ship sustained numerous hits under the enemy's terrific shellfire, Stanley continued to pass shell until forced by the loss of blood to go below.

1280 ◆ STARKINS, JOHN H.

Rank: Sergeant (highest rank: First Sergeant)
Service: U.S. Army
Birthday: 1841
Place of Birth: Great Neck, Nassau County, New York
Date of Death: 4 April 1897
Place of Death: Flushing, New York
Cemetery: Zion Church Cemetery—Little Neck, New York
Entered Service at: Flushing, Queens County, New York
Unit: 34th New York Battery
Battle or Place of Action: Campbell Station, Tennessee
Date of Action: 16 November 1863
Date of Issue: 30 July 1896
Citation: Brought off his piece without losing a man.

1281 ◆ STEELE, JOHN WHEDON

Rank: Major & Aide-de-Camp (highest rank: Lieutenant Colonel)
Service: U.S. Army
Birthday: 21 December 1835
Place of Birth: Middleburg, Logan County, Ohio
Date of Death: 26 April 1905
Place of Death: Oberlin, Ohio
Cemetery: Westwood Cemetery—Oberlin, Ohio
Entered Service at: Oberlin, Lorain County, Ohio
Unit: U.S. Volunteers
Battle or Place of Action: Spring Hill, Tennessee
Date of Action: 29 November 1864
Date of Issue: 28 September 1897
Citation: During a night attack of the enemy upon the wagon and ammunition train of this officer's corps, he gathered up a force of stragglers and others, assumed command of it, though himself a staff officer, and attacked and dispersed the enemy's forces, thus saving the train.

1282 ◆ STEINMETZ, WILLIAM

Rank: Private (highest rank: Corporal)
Service: U.S. Army
Birthday: 2 September 1847
Place of Birth: Newport, Campbell County, Kentucky
Date of Death: 10 June 1903
Cemetery: Wesleyan Cemetery—Cincinnati, Ohio
Entered Service at: Sunman, Ripley County, Indiana
Unit: Company G, 83d Indiana Infantry
Battle or Place of Action: Vicksburg, Mississippi
Date of Action: 22 May 1863
Date of Issue: 12 July 1894
Citation: Gallantry in the charge of the "volunteer storming party."

1283 ◆ STEPHENS, WILLIAM G.

Rank: Private
Service: U.S. Army
Birthday: 26 December 1843
Place of Birth: New York, New York
Date of Death: 21 March 1904
Place of Death: Chicago, Illinois
Cemetery: Rose Hill Cemetery—Chicago, Illinois
Entered Service at: Chicago, Cook County, Illinois
Unit: Chicago Mercantile Battery, Illinois Light Artillery
Battle or Place of Action: Vicksburg, Mississippi
Date of Action: 22 May 1863
Date of Issue: 21 December 1894
Citation: Carried with others by hand a cannon up to and fired it through an embrasure of the enemy's works.

1284 ◆ STERLING, JAMES E.

Rank: Coal Heaver
Service: U.S. Navy
Birthday: 1838
Place of Birth: Baltimore, Baltimore County, Maryland
Entered Service at: Maryland
Unit: U.S.S. *Brooklyn*
Battle or Place of Action: Fort Morgan, Mobile Bay, Alabama
Date of Action: 5 August 1864
G.O. Number, Date: 45, 31 December 1864
Citation: On board the U.S.S. *Brooklyn* during successful attacks against Fort Morgan, rebel gunboats and the ram *Tennessee* in Mobile Bay, 5 August 1864. Although wounded when heavy enemy return-fire raked the decks of his ship, Sterling courageously remained at his post and continued passing shell until struck down a second time and completely disabled.

1285 ◆ STERLING, JOHN T.

Rank: Private (highest rank: Corporal)
Service: U.S. Army
Birthday: 1841
Place of Birth: Edgar County, Illinois
Date of Death: 2 February 1920
Cemetery: Bethesda Cemetery—West Terre Haute, Indiana
Entered Service at: Indianapolis, Marion County, Indiana
Unit: Company D, 11th Indiana Infantry
Battle or Place of Action: Winchester, Virginia
Date of Action: 19 September 1864
Date of Issue: 4 April 1865
Citation: With one companion captured 14 of the enemy in the severest part of the battle.

1286 ◆ STEVENS, DANIEL DICKERSON

True Name: Stephens, Daniel Dickerson
Rank: Quartermaster (highest rank: Chief Quartermaster)
Service: U.S. Navy
Birthday: 19 December 1839
Place of Birth: La Grange, Fayette County, Tennessee
Date of Death: 7 November 1916
Place of Death: Peabody, Massachusetts
Cemetery: Walnut Grove Cemetery (MH)—Danvers, Massachusetts
Entered Service at: Massachusetts
Unit: U.S.S. *Canonicus*
Battle or Place of Action: Fort Fisher, North Carolina
Date of Action: 13 January 1865
Citation: On board the U.S.S. *Canonicus* during attacks on Fort Fisher, 13 January 1865. As the *Canonicus* moved into position at 700 yards from shore, the enemy troops soon obtained her range and opened with heavy artillery fire, subjecting her to several hits and near misses until late in the afternoon when the heavy ships coming into line drove them into their bombproofs. Twice during the battle, in which his ship sustained 36 hits, the flag was shot away and gallantly replaced by Stevens.

1287 ◆ STEVENS, HAZARD

Rank: Captain & Assistant Adjutant General (highest rank: Brevet Brigadier General)
Service: U.S. Army
Birthday: 9 June 1842
Place of Birth: Newport, Newport County, Rhode Island
Date of Death: 11 October 1918
Place of Death: Olympia, Washington
Cemetery: Island Cemetery—Newport, Rhode Island
Entered Service at: Olympia, Thurston County, Washington Territory
Unit: U.S. Volunteers
Battle or Place of Action: Fort Huger, Virginia
Date of Action: 19 April 1863
Date of Issue: 13 June 1894
Citation: Gallantly led a party that assaulted and captured the fort.

1288 ◆ STEWART, GEORGE W.

Rank: First Sergeant
Service: U.S. Army
Birthday: 25 March 1839
Place of Birth: Salem, Salem County, New Jersey
Date of Death: 17 November 1911
Cemetery: New Camden Cemetery (MH)—New Camden, New Jersey
Entered Service at: Salem, Salem County, New Jersey
Unit: Company E, 1st New Jersey Cavalry
Battle or Place of Action: Paines Crossroads, Virginia
Date of Action: 5 April 1865
Date of Issue: 3 May 1865
Citation: Capture of flag.

1289 ◆ STEWART, JOSEPH

Rank: Private
Service: U.S. Army
Place of Birth: Ireland
Entered Service at: Baltimore, Baltimore County, Maryland
Unit: Company G, 1st Maryland Infantry
Battle or Place of Action: Five Forks, Virginia
Date of Action: 1 April 1865
Date of Issue: 27 April 1865
Citation: Capture of flag.

1290 ◆ STICKELS, JOSEPH

True Name: Stickles, Joseph
Rank: Sergeant
Service: U.S. Army
Birthday: 1843
Place of Birth: Butler County, Ohio
Date of Death: 6 December 1876
Place of Death: Quincy, Illinois
Cemetery: Monroe Cemetery—Monroe, Iowa
Entered Service at: Bethany, Ohio
Unit: Company A, 83d Ohio Infantry
Battle or Place of Action: Fort Blakely, Alabama
Date of Action: 9 April 1865
Date of Issue: 8 June 1865
Citation: Capture of flag.
Notes: POW

1291 ◆ STOCKMAN, GEORGE HENRY

Rank: First Lieutenant
Service: U.S. Army
Birthday: 3 July 1833
Place of Birth: Muenden, Germany
Date of Death: 30 June 1912
Cemetery: West Laurel Hill Cemetery (MH)—Bala-Cynwyd, Pennsylvania
Entered Service at: Chicago, Cook County, Illinois
Unit: Company C, 6th Missouri Infantry
Battle or Place of Action: Vicksburg, Mississippi
Date of Action: 22 May 1863
Date of Issue: 9 July 1894
Citation: Gallantry in the charge of the "volunteer storming party."

1292 ◆ STODDARD, JAMES

Rank: Seaman (highest rank: Acting Master's Mate)
Service: U.S. Navy
Birthday: 1838
Place of Birth: Port Robinson, Canada (West)
Entered Service at: Detroit, Wayne County, Michigan
Unit: U.S.S. *Marmora*
Battle or Place of Action: off Yazoo City, Mississippi
Date of Action: 5 March 1864
G.O. Number, Date: 32, 16 April 1864
Citation: Off Yazoo City, Miss., 5 March 1864. Embarking

from the *Marmora* with a 12-pound howitzer mounted on a field carriage, Stoddard landed with the gun and crew in the midst of heated battle and, bravely standing by his gun despite enemy rifle fire which cut the gun carriage and rammer, contributed to the turning back of the enemy during the fierce engagement.

1293 ◆ STOKES, GEORGE

Rank: Private (highest rank: Corporal)
Service: U.S. Army
Birthday: 24 December 1838
Place of Birth: England
Date of Death: 25 March 1919
Cemetery: Oakland Cemetery—Dolton, Illinois
Entered Service at: Jerseyville, Jersey County, Illinois
Unit: Company C, 122d Illinois Infantry
Battle or Place of Action: Nashville, Tennessee
Date of Action: 16 December 1864
Date of Issue: 24 February 1865
on: Capture of flag.

1294 ◆ STOLZ, FRANK

Rank: Private
Service: U.S. Army
Birthday: 20 July 1844
Place of Birth: Dearborn County, Indiana
Date of Death: 19 November 1926
Place of Death: Indianapolis, Indiana
Cemetery: St. Joseph's Cemetery—Indianapolis, Indiana
Entered Service at: Sunman, Ripley County, Indiana
Unit: Company G, 83d Indiana Infantry
Battle or Place of Action: Vicksburg, Mississippi
Date of Action: 22 May 1863
Date of Issue: 9 July 1894
Citation: Gallantry in the charge of the "volunteer storming party."

1295 ◆ STOREY, JOHN HAMILTON REID

Rank: Sergeant
Service: U.S. Army
Birthday: 14 April 1836
Place of Birth: Philadelphia, Philadelphia County, Pennsylvania
Date of Death: 10 April 1916
Place of Death: Philadelphia, Pennsylvania
Cemetery: Laurel Hill Cemetery (MH)—Philadelphia, Pennsylvania
Entered Service at: Philadelphia, Philadelphia County, Pennsylvania
Unit: Company F, 109th Pennsylvania Infantry
Battle or Place of Action: Dallas, Georgia
Date of Action: 28 May 1864
Date of Issue: 29 August 1896
Citation: While bringing in a wounded comrade, under a destructive fire, he was himself wounded in the right leg, which was amputated on the same day.

1296 ◆ STOUT, RICHARD

Rank: Landsman
Service: U.S. Navy
Birthday: 1836
Place of Birth: Owego, Tioga County, New York
Date of Death: 6 August 1896
Place of Death: Owego, New York
Cemetery: Evergreen Cemetery—Owego, New York
Entered Service at: New York
Unit: U.S.S. *Isaac Smith*
Battle or Place of Action: Stono River, South Carolina
Date of Action: 30 January 1863
G.O. Number, Date: 32, 16 April 1864
Citation: Serving on board the U.S.S. *Isaac Smith*, Stono River, 30 January 1863. While reconnoitering on the Stono River on this date, the U.S.S. *Isaac Smith* became trapped in a rebel ambush. Fired on from two sides, she fought her guns until disabled. Suffering heavy casualties and at the mercy of the enemy who was delivering a raking fire from every side, she struck her colors out of regard for the wounded aboard, and all aboard were taken prisoners. Carrying out his duties bravely through this action, Stout was severely wounded and lost his right arm while returning the rebel fire.
Notes: POW

1297 ◆ STRAHAN, ROBERT

Rank: Captain of the Top
Service: U.S. Navy
Birthday: 1836
Place of Birth: New Jersey
Entered Service at: New Jersey
Unit: U.S.S. *Kearsarge*
Battle or Place of Action: off Cherbourg, France
Date of Action: 19 June 1864
G.O. Number, Date: 45, 31 December 1864
Citation: Served as captain of the top on board the U.S.S. *Kearsarge* when she destroyed the *Alabama* off Cherbourg, France, 19 June 1864. Acting as captain of the No. 1 gun, Strahan carried out his duties in the face of heavy enemy fire and exhibited marked coolness and good conduct throughout the engagement. Strahan was highly recommended by his division officer for his gallantry and meritorious achievements.

1298 ◆ *STRAUSBURGH, BERNARD A.

Rank: First Sergeant
Service: U.S. Army
Birthday: 1831
Place of Birth: Adams County, Pennsylvania
Date of Death: 5 November 1864
Place of Death: Beverly, New Jersey
Cemetery: General Hospital Cemetery Grave 133—Beverly, New Jersey
Entered Service at: Warfordsburg, Fulton County, Pennsylvania
Unit: Company A, 3d Maryland Infantry
Battle or Place of Action: Petersburg, Virginia

Date of Action: 17 June 1864
Date of Issue: 1 December 1864
Citation: Recaptured the colors of 2nd Pennsylvania Provisional Artillery.

1299 ◆ STREILE, CHRISTIAN

Rank: Private
Service: U.S. Army
Birthday: 1839
Place of Birth: Germany
Date of Death: 4 December 1886
Place of Death: New York, New York
Cemetery: The Lutheran Cemetery—Middle Village, New York
Entered Service at: Jersey City, Hudson County, New Jersey
Unit: Company I, 1st New Jersey Cavalry
Battle or Place of Action: Paines Crossroads, Virginia
Date of Action: 5 April 1865
Date of Issue: 3 May 1865
Citation: Capture of flag.

1300 ◆ STRONG, JAMES N.

Rank: Sergeant (highest rank: Second Lieutenant)
Service: U.S. Army
Birthday: 28 February 1818
Place of Birth: Pittsfield, Berkshire County, Massachusetts
Date of Death: 17 December 1900
Place of Death: Fairfield, Iowa
Cemetery: City Cemetery (MH)—Fairfield, Iowa
Entered Service at: Pittsfield, Berkshire County, Massachusetts
Unit: Company C, 49th Massachusetts Infantry
Battle or Place of Action: Port Hudson, Louisiana
Date of Action: 27 May 1863
Date of Issue: 25 November 1893
Citation: Volunteered in response to a call and took part in the movement that was made upon the enemy's works under a heavy fire therefrom in advance of the general assault.

1301 ◆ STURGEON, JAMES K.

Rank: Private
Service: U.S. Army
Birthday: 5 November 1846
Place of Birth: Perry County, Ohio
Date of Death: 19 August 1898
Place of Death: Los Angeles, California
Cemetery: Evergreen Cemetery—Los Angeles, California
Entered Service at: Lancaster, Fairfield County, Ohio
Unit: Company F, 46th Ohio Infantry
Battle or Place of Action: Kenesaw Mountain, Georgia
Date of Action: 15 June 1864
Date of Issue: 2 January 1895
Citation: Advanced beyond the lines and in an encounter with three Confederates shot two and took the other prisoner.

1302 ◆ SULLIVAN, JAMES

Rank: Ordinary Seaman
Service: U.S. Navy
Birthday: 1833
Place of Birth: New York, New York
Entered Service at: Danbury, Fairfield County, Connecticut
Unit: U.S.S. *Agawam*
Battle or Place of Action: Fort Fisher, North Carolina
Date of Action: 2 December 1864
G.O. Number, Date: 45, 31 December 1864
Date of Presentation: 12 May 1865
Place of Presentation: off New Bern, NC, on board the U.S.S. *Agawam*
Citation: On board the U.S.S. *Agawam* as one of a volunteer crew of a powder boat which was exploded near Fort Fisher, 2 December 1864. The powder boat, towed in by the *Wilderness* to prevent detection by the enemy, cast off and slowly steamed to within 300 yards of the beach. After fuses and fires had been lit and a second anchor with short scope let go to assure the boat's tailing inshore, the crew boarded the *Wilderness* and proceeded a distance of 12 miles from shore. Less than two hours later the explosion took place, and the following day fires were observed still burning at the forts.

1303 ◆ SULLIVAN, JOHN

Rank: Seaman
Service: U.S. Navy
Birthday: 17 March 1840
Place of Birth: New York, New York
Date of Death: 23 June 1913
Cemetery: Harmony Grove Cemetery—Portsmouth, New Hampshire
Entered Service at: New York
Unit: U.S.S. *Monticello*
Battle or Place of Action: Wilmington, North Carolina
Date of Action: 23-25 June 1864
G.O. Number, Date: 45, 31 December 1864
Citation: Served as seaman on board the U.S.S. *Monticello* during the reconnaissance of the harbor and water defenses of Wilmington, N.C., 23 to 25 June 1864. Taking part in a reconnaissance of the enemy defenses which covered a period of 2 days and nights, Sullivan courageously carried out his duties during this action, which resulted in the capture of a mail carrier and mail, the cutting of a telegraph wire, and the capture of a large group of prisoners. Although in immediate danger from the enemy at all times, Sullivan showed gallantry and coolness throughout this action, which resulted in the gaining of much vital information of the rebel defenses.

1304 ◆ SULLIVAN, TIMOTHY

Rank: Coxswain
Service: U.S. Navy
Birthday: 1835
Place of Birth: Ireland
Date of Death: 6 October 1910

Place of Death: Sawtella, California
Cemetery: Los Angeles National Cemetery (18-H-2)—Los Angeles, California
Entered Service at: New York, New York
Unit: U.S.S. *Louisville*
Battle or Place of Action: Arkansas, Tennessee & Mississippi
Date of Action: Unknown
G.O. Number, Date: 11, 3 April 1863
Citation: Served on board the U.S.S. *Louisville* during various actions of that vessel. During the engagements of the *Louisville*, Sullivan served as first captain of a 9-inch gun and throughout this period of service was "especially commended for his attention to duty, bravery, and coolness in action."

1305 ◆ SUMMERS, JAMES CALVIN

Rank: Private
Service: U.S. Army
Birthday: 14 February 1838
Place of Birth: on Elk River six miles above Charleston, Kanawha County, West Virginia
Date of Death: 9 May 1927
Place of Death: Frame, West Virginia
Cemetery: Reynolds Cemetery—Elkview, West Virginia
Entered Service at: Point Pleasant, Mason County, West Virginia
Unit: Company H, 4th West Virginia Infantry
Battle or Place of Action: Vicksburg, Mississippi
Date of Action: 22 May 1863
Date of Issue: 25 February 1895
Citation: Gallantry in charge of the "volunteer storming party."

1306 ◆ SUMMERS, ROBERT

True Name: Sommers, Robert
Rank: Chief Quartermaster (highest rank: Chief Gunner)
Service: U.S. Navy
Birthday: 17 December 1837
Place of Birth: Prussia
Date of Death: 1 December 1919
Cemetery: U.S. Naval Academy Cemetery (Lot 235) (MH)—Annapolis, Maryland
Entered Service at: New York, New York
Unit: U.S.S. *Ticonderoga*
Battle or Place of Action: Fort Fisher, North Carolina
Date of Action: 13-15 January 1865
G.O. Number, Date: 59, 22 June 1865
Citation: Summers served on board the U.S.S. *Ticonderoga* in the attacks on Fort Fisher, 13 to 15 January 1865. The ship took position in the line of battle and maintained a well-directed fire upon the batteries to the left of the palisades during the initial phase of the engagement. Although several of the enemy's shots fell over and around the vessel, the *Ticonderoga* fought her guns gallantly throughout three consecutive days of battle until the flag was planted on one of the strongest fortifications possessed by the rebels.

1307 ◆ SURLES, WILLIAM H.

Rank: Private
Service: U.S. Army
Birthday: 24 February 1845
Place of Birth: Steubenville, Jefferson County, Ohio
Date of Death: 19 March 1919
Cemetery: Riverview Cemetery (MH)—East Liverpool, Ohio
Entered Service at: Steubenville, Jefferson County, Ohio
Unit: Company G, 2d Ohio Infantry
Battle or Place of Action: Perryville, Kentucky
Date of Action: 8 October 1862
Date of Issue: 19 August 1891
Citation: In the hottest part of the fire he stepped in front on his colonel to shield him from the enemy's fire.

1308 ◆ SWAN, CHARLES ALEXANDER

Rank: Private
Service: U.S. Army
Birthday: 29 May 1838
Place of Birth: Greene County, Pennsylvania
Date of Death: 8 January 1914
Place of Death: Mount Pleasant, Iowa
Cemetery: Forest Home Cemetery—Mount Pleasant, Iowa
Entered Service at: Mount Pleasant, Henry County, Iowa
Unit: Company K, 4th Iowa Cavalry
Battle or Place of Action: Selma, Alabama
Date of Action: 2 April 1865
Date of Issue: 17 June 1865
Citation: Capture of flag (supposed to be 11th Mississippi, C.S.A.) and bearer.

1309 ◆ SWANSON, JOHN

Rank: Seaman
Service: U.S. Navy
Birthday: 1842
Place of Birth: Gothenburg, Sweden
Entered Service at: Massachusetts
Unit: U.S.S. *Santiago de Cuba*
Battle or Place of Action: Fort Fisher, North Carolina
Date of Action: 15 January 1865
G.O. Number, Date: 59, 22 June 1865
Citation: On board the U.S.S. *Santiago de Cuba* during the assault on Fort Fisher, 15 January 1865. As one of a boat crew detailed to one of the generals onshore, Swanson bravely entered the fort in the assault and accompanied his party in carrying dispatches at the height of the battle. He was one of six men who entered the fort in the assault from the fleet.

1310 ◆ SWAP, JACOB E.

Rank: Private
Service: U.S. Army
Birthday: 12 August 1846
Place of Birth: Coeymans, Albany County, New York

Date of Death: 22 January 1925
Place of Death: Lakeport, California
Cemetery: Oakland Cemetery—Lakeport, California
Entered Service at: Springs, Somerset County, Pennsylvania
Unit: Company H, 83d Pennsylvania Infantry
Battle or Place of Action: Wilderness Campaign, Virginia
Date of Action: 5 May 1864
Date of Issue: 19 November 1897
Citation: Although assigned to other duty, he voluntarily joined his regiment in a charge and fought with it until severely wounded.

1311 ◆ SWATTON, EDWARD

Rank: Seaman
Service: U.S. Navy
Birthday: 1836
Place of Birth: New York, New York
Entered Service at: Boston, Suffolk County, Massachusetts
Unit: U.S.S. *Santiago de Cuba*
Battle or Place of Action: Fort Fisher, North Carolina
Date of Action: 15 January 1865
G.O. Number, Date: 59, 22 June 1865
Citation: On board the U.S.S. *Santiago de Cuba* during the assault on Fort Fisher on 15 January 1865. As one of a boat crew detailed to one of the generals onshore, Swatton bravely entered the fort in the assault and accompanied his party in carrying dispatches at the height of the battle. He was one of six men who entered the fort in the assault from the fleet.

1312 ◆ SWAYNE, WAGER

Rank: Lieutenant Colonel (highest rank: Major General)
Service: U.S. Army
Birthday: 10 November 1834
Place of Birth: Columbus, Franklin County, Ohio
Date of Death: 18 December 1902
Place of Death: New York, New York
Cemetery: Arlington National Cemetery (3-1406)—Arlington, Virginia
Entered Service at: Columbus, Franklin County, Ohio
Unit: 43d Ohio Infantry
Battle or Place of Action: Corinth, Mississippi
Date of Action: 4 October 1862
Date of Issue: 19 August 1893
Citation: Conspicuous gallantry in restoring order at a critical moment and leading his regiment in a charge.

1313 ◆ SWEARER, BENJAMIN

Rank: Seaman (highest rank: Captain of the Foretop)
Service: U.S. Navy
Birthday: 18 May 1825
Place of Birth: Baltimore, Baltimore County, Maryland
Entered Service at: Maryland
Unit: U.S.S. *Pawnee*
Battle or Place of Action: Fort Clark, off Baltimore Inlet, Maryland
Date of Action: 29 August 1861
G.O. Number, Date: 11, 3 April 1863
Date of Issue: 14 April 1864
Citation: Embarked in a surfboat from the U.S.S. *Pawnee* during action against Fort Clark, off Baltimore Inlet, 29 August 1861. Taking part in a mission to land troops and to remain inshore and provide protection, Swearer rendered gallant service throughout the action and had the honor of being the first man to raise the flag on the captured fort.

1314 ◆ SWEATT, JOSEPH SEWELL GERRISH

Rank: Private
Service: U.S. Army
Birthday: 23 October 1843
Place of Birth: Boscawen, Merrimack County, New Hampshire
Date of Death: 14 February 1914
Place of Death: East Billerica, Massachusetts
Cemetery: Oak Grove Cemetery (MH)—Medford, Massachusetts
Entered Service at: Lowell, Middlesex County, Massachusetts
Unit: Company C, 6th Massachusetts Infantry
Battle or Place of Action: Carrsville, Virginia
Date of Action: 15 May 1863
Date of Issue: 22 March 1892
Citation: When ordered to retreat, this soldier turned and rushed back to the front, in the face of heavy fire from the enemy, in an endeavor to rescue his wounded comrades, remaining by them until overpowered and taken prisoner.
Notes: POW

1315 ◆ SWEENEY, JAMES

Rank: Private (highest rank: Corporal)
Service: U.S. Army
Birthday: 24 September 1845
Place of Birth: Manchester, Greater Manchester County, England
Date of Death: 26 June 1931
Place of Death: Sawtella, California
Cemetery: Los Angeles National Cemetery (MH)—Los Angeles, California
Entered Service at: Essex, Chittenden County, Vermont
Unit: Company A, 1st Vermont Cavalry
Battle or Place of Action: Cedar Creek, Virginia
Date of Action: 19 October 1864
Date of Issue: 26 October 1864
Citation: With one companion captured the state flag of a North Carolina regiment, together with three officers and an ambulance with its mules and driver.

1316 ◆ SWEGHEIMER, JACOB

True Name: Swegheimer, John
Rank: Private
Service: U.S. Army
Birthday: 25 February 1843
Place of Birth: Oldtown, Baden, Germany
Date of Death: 15 March 1917

Place of Death: Delaware, Ohio
Cemetery: Oak Grove Cemetery—Delaware, Ohio
Entered Service at: Paducah, McCracken County, Kentucky
Unit: Company I, 54th Ohio Infantry
Battle or Place of Action: Vicksburg, Mississippi
Date of Action: 22 May 1863
Date of Issue: 14 July 1894
Citation: Gallantry in the charge of the "volunteer storming party."

1317 ◆ SWIFT, FREDERIC WILLIAM

Rank: Lieutenant Colonel (highest rank: Brevet Brigadier General)
Service: U.S. Army
Birthday: 30 January 1831
Place of Birth: Mansfield Center, Tolland County, Connecticut
Date of Death: 30 January 1916
Place of Death: Detroit, Michigan
Cemetery: Elmwood Cemetery (MH)—Detroit, Michigan
Entered Service at: Detroit, Wayne County, Michigan
Unit: 17th Michigan Infantry
Battle or Place of Action: Lenoire Station, Tennessee
Date of Action: 16 November 1863
Date of Issue: 15 February 1897
Citation: Gallantly seized the colors and rallied the regiment after three color bearers had been shot and the regiment, having become demoralized, was in imminent danger of capture.

1318 ◆ SWIFT, HARLAN J.

Rank: Second Lieutenant (highest rank: Captain)
Service: U.S. Army
Birthday: 2 October 1843
Place of Birth: New Hudson, Columbia County, New York
Date of Death: 6 October 1910
Cemetery: Cuba Cemetery (MH)—Cuba, New York
Entered Service at: Buffalo, Erie County, New York
Unit: Company H, 2d New York Mounted Rifles
Battle or Place of Action: Petersburg, Virginia
Date of Action: 30 July 1864
Date of Issue: 20 July 1897
Citation: Having advanced with his regiment and captured the enemy's line, saw four of the enemy retiring toward their second line of works. He advanced upon them alone, compelled their surrender and regained his regiment with the four prisoners.

1319 ◆ SYPE, PETER

Rank: Private
Service: U.S. Army
Birthday: 11 October 1841
Place of Birth: Monroe County, Michigan
Date of Death: 20 April 1923
Place of Death: Newport, Michigan
Cemetery: Trinity Lutheran Cemetery (MH)—Monroe, Michigan
Entered Service at: Adrian, Lenawee County, Michigan
Unit: Company B, 47th Ohio Infantry
Battle or Place of Action: Vicksburg, Mississippi
Date of Action: 3 May 1863
Date of Issue: 12 September 1911
Citation: Was one of a party that volunteered and attempted to run the enemy's batteries with a steam tug and two barges loaded with subsistence stores.

1320 ◆ TABOR, WILLIAM L. S.

Rank: Private
Service: U.S. Army
Birthday: 2 June 1843
Place of Birth: Metheun, Essex County, Massachusetts
Date of Death: 15 December 1921
Place of Death: Derry, New Hampshire
Cemetery: Forest Hill Cemetery (MH)—East Derry, New Hampshire
Entered Service at: Concord, Merrimack County, New Hampshire
Unit: Company K, 15th New Hampshire Infantry
Battle or Place of Action: Port Hudson, Louisiana
Date of Action: July 1863
Date of Issue: 10 March 1896
Citation: Voluntarily exposed himself to the enemy only a few feet away to render valuable services for the protection of his comrades.

1321 ◆ TAGGART, CHARLES A.

Rank: Private
Service: U.S. Army
Birthday: 17 January 1843
Place of Birth: Blandford, Hampden County, Massachusetts
Date of Death: 10 April 1938
Place of Death: Dayton, Ohio
Cemetery: Dayton National Cemetery (R-9-14) (MH)—Dayton, Ohio
Entered Service at: Otis, Berkshire County, Massachusetts
Unit: Company B, 37th Massachusetts Infantry
Battle or Place of Action: Deatonsville (Sailor's Creek), Virginia
Date of Action: 6 April 1865
Date of Issue: 10 May 1865
Citation: Capture of flag.

1322 ◆ TALBOTT, WILLIAM

True Name: Talbot, William
Rank: Captain of the Forecastle
Service: U.S. Navy
Birthday: 1812
Place of Birth: England
Date of Death: 5 September 1899
Place of Death: Bath, Maine
Cemetery: Maple Grove Cemetery—Bath, Maine
Entered Service at: Boston, Suffolk County, Massachusetts
Unit: U.S.S. *Louisville*

Battle or Place of Action: Arkansas post (Fort Hindman), Arkansas
Date of Action: 10-11 January 1863
G.O. Number, Date: 32, 16 April 1865
Citation: Served as captain of the forecastle on board the U.S.S. *Louisville* at the capture of the Arkansas post, 10 and 11 January 1863. Carrying out his duties as captain of a 9-inch gun, Talbott was conspicuous for ability and bravery throughout this engagement with the enemy.

1323 ◆ *TALLENTINE, JAMES

Rank: Quarter Gunner
Service: U.S. Navy
Birthday: 1840
Place of Birth: England
Date of Death: 15 January 1865
Place of Death: Fort Fisher, North Carolina
Entered Service at: Baltimore, Baltimore County, Maryland
Unit: U.S.S. *Tacony*
Battle or Place of Action: Plymouth, North Carolina
Date of Action: 31 October 1864
G.O. Number, Date: 45, 31 December 1864
Citation: Served as quarter gunner on board the U.S.S. *Tacony* during the taking of Plymouth, N.C., 31 October 1864. Carrying out his duties faithfully during the capture of Plymouth, Tallentine distinguished himself by a display of coolness when he participated in landing and spiking a 9-inch gun while under devastating fire from enemy musketry. Tallentine later gave his life while courageously engaged in storming Fort Fisher, 15 January 1865.

1324 ◆ TANNER, CHARLES B.

Rank: Second Lieutenant (highest rank: First Lieutenant)
Service: U.S. Army
Birthday: 25 November 1842
Place of Birth: Philadelphia, Philadelphia County, Pennsylvania
Date of Death: 16 December 1911
Place of Death: Floral Park, New York
Cemetery: Greenfield Cemetery—Hempstead, New York
Entered Service at: Wilmimgton, New Castle County, Delaware
Unit: Company H, 1st Delaware Infantry
Battle or Place of Action: Antietam, Maryland
Date of Action: 17 September 1862
Date of Issue: 13 December 1889
Citation: Carried off the regimental colors, which had fallen within 20 yards of the enemy's lines, the color guard of nine men having all been wounded or killed; was himself three times wounded.

1325 ◆ TAYLOR, ANTHONY

Rank: First Lieutenant
Service: U.S. Army
Birthday: 11 October 1837
Place of Birth: Burlington, Burlington County, New Jersey
Date of Death: 21 May 1894
Place of Death: Philadelphia, Pennsylvania
Cemetery: St. James The Less Cemetery—Philadelphia, Pennsylvania
Entered Service at: Philadelphia, Philadelphia County, Pennsylvania
Unit: Company A, 15th Pennsylvania Cavalry
Battle or Place of Action: Chickamauga, Georgia
Date of Action: 20 September 1863
Date of Issue: 4 December 1893
Citation: Held out to the last with a small force against the advance of superior numbers of the enemy.

1326 ◆ TAYLOR, FORRESTER L.

Rank: Captain (highest rank: Brevet Major)
Service: U.S. Army
Birthday: 30 October 1833
Place of Birth: Philadelphia, Philadelphia County, Pennsylvania
Date of Death: 21 April 1907
Place of Death: Lawers, Virginia
Cemetery: Family Cemetery, Wards Road, U.S. 29 South—Lynchburg, Virginia
Entered Service at: Beverly, Burlington County, New Jersey
Unit: Company H, 23d New Jersey Infantry
Battle or Place of Action: Chancellorsville, Virginia
Date of Action: 3 May 1863
Date of Issue: 2 November 1896
Citation: At great risk voluntarily saved the lives of and brought from the battlefield two wounded comrades.

1327 ◆ TAYLOR, GEORGE

True Name: Johnson, George Taylor F.
Rank: Armorer
Service: U.S. Navy
Birthday: 15 November 1830
Place of Birth: Reddich, Hereford & Worcester County, England
Date of Death: 7 October 1893
Place of Death: Paragould, Arkansas
Cemetery: Linwood Cemetery—Paragould, Arkansas
Entered Service at: New York, New York
Unit: U.S.S. *Lackawanna*
Battle or Place of Action: Mobile Bay, Alabama
Date of Action: 5 August 1864
G.O. Number, Date: 45, 31 December 1864
Citation: On board the U.S.S. *Lackawanna* during successful attacks against Fort Morgan, rebel gunboats, and the ram *Tennessee* in Mobile Bay, 5 August 1864. When an enemy shell exploded in the shellroom, Taylor, although wounded, went into the room and, with his hand, extinguished the fire from the explosion. He then carried out his duties during the remainder of the prolonged action which resulted in the capture of the prize rebel ram *Tennessee* and the damaging and destruction of Fort Morgan.

1328 ◆ TAYLOR, HENRY H.

Rank: Sergeant
Service: U.S. Army
Birthday: 4 July 1841
Place of Birth: Near Galena, Jo Daviess County, Illinois
Date of Death: 3 May 1909
Place of Death: Leavenworth, Kansas
Cemetery: Greenwood Cemetery (MH)—Clay Center, Kansas
Entered Service at: Galena, Jo Daviess County, Illinois
Unit: Company C, 45th Illinois Infantry
Served as: Color Sergeant
Battle or Place of Action: Vicksburg, Mississippi
Date of Action: 25 June 1863
Date of Issue: 1 September 1863
Citation: Was the first to plant the Union colors upon the enemy's works.

1329 ◆ TAYLOR, JOSEPH

Rank: Private
Service: U.S. Army
Place of Birth: England
Date of Death: 16 February 1912
Cemetery: Greenwood Cemetery (MH)—Coventry, Rhode Island
Entered Service at: Burrillville, Rhode Island
Unit: Company E, 7th Rhode Island Infantry
Battle or Place of Action: Weldon Railroad, Virginia
Date of Action: 18 August 1864
Date of Issue: 20 July 1897
Citation: While acting as an orderly to a general officer on the field and alone, encountered a picket of three of the enemy and compelled their surrender.

1330 ◆ TAYLOR, RICHARD

Rank: Private
Service: U.S. Army
Birthday: 1834
Place of Birth: Madison County, Alabama
Date of Death: 23 February 1890
Cemetery: St. John's Cemetery (MH)—Washington, Indiana
Entered Service at: Indianapolis, Marion County, Indiana
Unit: Company E, 18th Indiana Infantry
Battle or Place of Action: Cedar Creek, Virginia
Date of Action: 19 October 1864
Date of Issue: 21 November 1864
Citation: Capture of Flag.

1331 ◆ TAYLOR, THOMAS

Rank: Coxswain
Service: U.S. Navy
Birthday: 1834
Place of Birth: Bangor, Penobscot County, Maine
Entered Service at: Maine
Unit: U.S.S. *Metacomet*
Battle or Place of Action: Mobile Bay, Alabama
Date of Action: 5 August 1864
G.O. Number, Date: 59, 22 June 1865
Citation: Served on board the U.S.S. *Metacomet* during the action against rebel forts and gunboats and with the rebel ram *Tennessee* in Mobile Bay, 5 August 1864. Despite damage to his ship and the loss of several men on board as enemy fire raked her decks, Taylor encouraged the men of the forward pivot gun when the officer in command displayed cowardice, doing honor to the occasion.

1332 ◆ TAYLOR, WILLIAM

Rank: Sergeant & Second Lieutenant (highest rank: Captain)
Service: U.S. Army
Birthday: 1836
Place of Birth: Washington, D.C.
Date of Death: 6 April 1902
Place of Death: Baltimore, Maryland
Cemetery: Louden Park National Cemetery (Off-16)—Baltimore, Maryland
Entered Service at: Frederick, Frederick County, Maryland
Unit: Company H & Company M, 1st Maryland Infantry
Battle or Place of Action: Front Royal & Weldon Railroad, Virginia
Date of Action: 23 May 1862 & 19 August 1864
Date of Issue: 2 August 1897
Citation: When a sergeant at Front Royal, Va., he was painfully wounded while obeying an order to burn a bridge, but, persevering in the attempt, he burned the bridge and prevented its use by the enemy. Later, at Weldon Railroad, Va., then a lieutenant, he voluntarily took the place of a disabled officer and undertook a hazardous reconnaissance beyond the lines of the army; was taken prisoner in the attempt.
Notes: POW

1333 ◆ TAYLOR, WILLIAM G.

Rank: Captain of the Forecastle
Service: U.S. Navy
Birthday: 9 August 1829
Place of Birth: Philadelphia, Philadelphia County, Pennsylvania
Date of Death: 28 March 1910
Cemetery: Sunset Cemetery—Quincy, Illinois
Entered Service at: Philadelphia, Philadelphia County, Pennsylvania
Unit: U.S.S. *Ticonderoga*
Battle or Place of Action: Fort Fisher, North Carolina
Date of Action: 24-25 December 1864
G.O. Number, Date: 59, 22 June 1865
Citation: On board the U.S.S. *Ticonderoga* during attacks on Fort Fisher, 24 and 25 December 1864. As captain of a gun, Taylor performed his duties with coolness and skill as his

ship took position in the line of battle and delivered its fire on the batteries onshore. Despite the depressing effect caused when an explosion of the 100-pounder Parrott rifle killed eight men and wounded 12 more, and the enemy's heavy return fire, he calmly remained at his station during the two days' operations.

1334 ◆ TERRY, JOHN DARLING

Rank: Sergeant (highest rank: Major)
Service: U.S. Army
Birthday: 3 September 1845
Place of Birth: Montville, Maine
Date of Death: 4 March 1919
Cemetery: Woodlawn Cemetery—Bronx, New York
Entered Service at: Boston, Suffolk County, Massachusetts
Unit: Company E, 23d Massachusetts Infantry
Battle or Place of Action: New Bern, North Carolina
Date of Action: 14 March 1862
Date of Issue: 12 October 1867
Citation: In the thickest of the fight, where he lost his leg by a shot, still encouraged the men until carried off the field.

1335 ◆ THACKRAH, BENJAMIN

Rank: Private
Service: U.S. Army
Birthday: 13 August 1845
Place of Birth: Scotland
Date of Death: 20 May 1912
Place of Death: Amsterdam, New York
Cemetery: St. Mary's Cemetery (MH)—Fort Johnston, New York
Entered Service at: Johnsonville, Rensselaer County, New York
Unit: Company H, 115th New York Infantry
Battle or Place of Action: near Fort Gates, Florida
Date of Action: 1 April 1864
Date of Issue: 2 May 1890
Citation: Was a volunteer in the surprise and capture of the enemy's picket.

1336 ◆ THATCHER, CHARLES M.

Rank: Private
Service: U.S. Army
Birthday: 1844
Place of Birth: Coldwater, Branch County, Michigan
Date of Death: 13 December 1900
Cemetery: Evergreen Cemetery—Kalkaska, Michigan
Entered Service at: Grand Haven, Ottawa County, Michigan
Unit: Company B, 1st Michigan Sharpshooters
Battle or Place of Action: Petersburg, Virginia
Date of Action: 30 July 1864
Date of Issue: 31 July 1896
Citation: Instead of retreating or surrendering when the works were captured, regardless of his personal safety, continued to return the enemy's fire until he was captured.
Notes: POW

1337 ◆ THAXTER, SIDNEY WARREN

Rank: Major
Service: U.S. Army
Birthday: 8 September 1839
Place of Birth: Bangor, Penobscot County, Maine
Date of Death: 10 November 1908
Place of Death: Portland, Maine
Cemetery: Evergreen Cemetery (MH)—Portland, Maine
Entered Service at: Bangor, Penobscot County, Maine
Unit: 1st Maine Cavalry
Battle or Place of Action: Hatcher's Run, Virginia
Date of Action: 27 October 1864
Date of Issue: 10 September 1897
Citation: Voluntarily remained and participated in the battle with conspicuous gallantry, although his term of service had expired and he had been ordered home to be mustered out.

1338 ◆ THIELBERG, HENRY

Rank: Seaman
Service: U.S. Navy
Birthday: 1833
Place of Birth: Germany
Entered Service at: Dudley, Webster County, Massachusetts
Unit: U.S.S. *Mount Washington* (temporarily assigned) U.S.S. *Minnesota*
Battle or Place of Action: Nansemond River, Virginia
Date of Action: 14 April 1863
G.O. Number, Date: 17, 10 July 1863
Citation: Served temporarily on board the U.S.S. *Mount Washington* during the Nansemond River action, 14 April 1863. After assisting in hauling up and raising the flagstaff, Thielberg volunteered to go up on the pilothouse and observe the movements of the enemy and although three shells struck within a few inches of his head, remained at his post until ordered to descend.

1339 ◆ THOMAS, HAMPTON SIDNEY

Rank: Major (highest rank: Brevet Colonel)
Service: U.S. Army
Birthday: 3 November 1837
Place of Birth: Quakertown, Bucks County, Pennsylvania
Date of Death: 21 May 1899
Place of Death: Philadelphia, Pennsylvania
Cemetery: Lawnview Cemetery—Philadelphia, Pennsylvania
Entered Service at: Harrisburg, Dauphin County, Pennsylvania
Unit: 1st Pennsylvania Veteran Cavalry
Battle or Place of Action: Amelia Springs, Virginia
Date of Action: 5 April 1865
Date of Issue: 15 January 1894
Citation: Conspicuous gallantry in the capture of a field battery and a number of battle flags and in the destruction of the enemy's wagon train. Maj. Thomas lost a leg in this action.

1340 ◆ THOMAS, STEPHEN

Rank: Colonel (highest rank: Brigadier General)
Service: U.S. Army
Birthday: 6 December 1809
Place of Birth: Bethel, Windsor County, Vermont
Date of Death: 18 December 1903
Place of Death: Montpelier, Vermont
Cemetery: Green Mount Cemetery—Montpelier, Vermont
Entered Service at: West Fairlee, Orange County, Vermont
Unit: 8th Vermont Infantry
Battle or Place of Action: Cedar Creek, Virginia
Date of Action: 19 October 1864
Date of Issue: 25 July 1892
Citation: Distinguished conduct in a desperate hand-to-hand encounter, in which the advance of the enemy was checked.

1341 ◆ THOMPKINS, GEORGE W.

True Name: Tompkins, George W.
Rank: Corporal
Service: U.S. Army
Birthday: 9 April 1841
Place of Birth: Orange County, New York
Date of Death: 22 February 1934
Place of Death: Schenectady, New York
Cemetery: Vale Cemetery—Schenectady, New York
Entered Service at: Port Jervis, Orange County, New York
Unit: Company F, 124th New York Infantry
Battle or Place of Action: Petersburg, Virginia
Date of Action: 25 March 1865
Date of Issue: 6 April 1865
Citation: Capture of flag of 49th Alabama Infantry (C.S.A.) from an officer who, with colors in hand, was rallying his men.

1342 ◆ THOMPSON, ALLEN

Rank: Private
Service: U.S. Army
Birthday: 1 October 1847
Place of Birth: New York, New York
Date of Death: 27 February 1906
Cemetery: Lake View Cemetery (MH)—Cheyenne, Wyoming
Entered Service at: Sandy Creek, Oswego County, New York
Unit: Company K, 4th New York Heavy Artillery
Battle or Place of Action: White Oak Road, Virginia
Date of Action: 1 April 1865
Date of Issue: 22 April 1896
Citation: Made a hazardous reconnaissance through timber and slashings, preceding the Union line of battle, signaling the troops, and leading them through the obstructions.

1343 ◆ THOMPSON, CHARLES AUGUSTUS

Rank: Sergeant (highest rank: Second Lieutenant)
Service: U.S. Army
Birthday: 16 February 1843
Place of Birth: Perrysburg, Wood County, Ohio
Date of Death: 24 August 1900
Place of Death: Rutland, Vermont
Cemetery: Evergreen Cemetery—Rutland, Vermont
Entered Service at: Kalamazoo, Kalamazoo County, Michigan
Unit: Company D, 17th Michigan Infantry
Battle or Place of Action: Spotsylvania, Virginia
Date of Action: 12 May 1864
Date of Issue: 27 July 1896
Citation: After the regiment was surrounded and all resistance seemed useless, fought singlehanded for the colors and refused to give them up until he had appealed to his superior officers.

1344 ◆ THOMPSON, FREEMAN C.

Rank: Corporal
Service: U.S. Army
Birthday: 25 February 1845
Place of Birth: Monroe County, Ohio
Date of Death: 10 August 1887
Cemetery: Olive Cemetery—Caldwell, Ohio
Entered Service at: Marietta, Washington County, Ohio
Unit: Company F, 116th Ohio Infantry
Battle or Place of Action: Petersburg, Virginia
Date of Action: 2 April 1865
Date of Issue: 12 May 1865
Citation: Was twice knocked from the parapet of Fort Gregg by blows from the enemy's muskets, but at the third attempt fought his way into the works.

1345 ◆ THOMPSON, HENRY A.

True Name: Connelly, Roderick P.
Rank: Private
Service: U.S. Marine Corps
Birthday: 1841
Place of Birth: England
Date of Death: 16 February 1889
Cemetery: Calvary Cemetery—Woodside, New York
Entered Service at: Pennsylvania
Unit: U.S.S. *Minnesota*
Battle or Place of Action: Fort Fisher, North Carolina
Date of Action: 15 January 1865
G.O. Number, Date: 59, 22 June 1865
Date of Issue: On board the U.S.S. *Minnesota* in the assault on Ft. Fisher, 15 January 1865
Citation: On board the U.S.S. *Minnesota* in the assault on Ft. Fisher, 15 January 1865. Landing on the beach with the assaulting party from his ship, Pvt. Thompson advanced partly through a breach in the palisades and nearer to the fort than any man from his ship despite enemy fire which killed or wounded many officers and men. When more than two-thirds of the men became seized with panic and retreated on the run, he remained with the party until dark, when it came safely away, bringing its wounded, its arms and its colors.

1346 ◆ THOMPSON, JAMES B.

Rank: Sergeant (highest rank: First Sergeant)
Service: U.S. Army
Birthday: 1843
Place of Birth: Juniata County, Pennsylvania
Date of Death: 31 August 1875
Place of Death: Port Royal, Pennsylvania
Cemetery: Old Churchill Cemetery—Port Royal, Pennsylvania
Entered Service at: Perrysville, Allegheny County, Pennsylvania
Unit: Company G, 1st Pennsylvania Rifles
Battle or Place of Action: Gettysburg, Pennsylvania
Date of Action: 3 July 1863
Date of Issue: 1 December 1864
Citation: Capture of flag of 15th Georgia Infantry (C.S.A.).
Notes: POW

1347 ◆ THOMPSON, JAMES GRANVILLE

Rank: Private
Service: U.S. Army
Birthday: 25 December 1849
Place of Birth: Sandy Creek, Oswego County, New York
Date of Death: 23 May 1921
Cemetery: Mount Hope Cemetery (MH)—San Diego, California
Entered Service at: Sandy Creek, Oswego County, New York
Unit: Company K, 4th New York Heavy Artillery
Battle or Place of Action: White Oak Road, Virginia
Date of Action: 1 April 1865
Date of Issue: 22 April 1896
Citation: Made a hazardous reconnaissance through timber and slashings, preceding the Union line of battle, signaling the troops, and leading them through the obstructions.

1348 ◆ THOMPSON, JAMES HARRY

Rank: Surgeon (highest rank: Major)
Service: U.S. Army
Birthday: 1824
Place of Birth: England
Date of Death: 4 November 1896
Place of Death: Great Yarmouth, England
Entered Service at: New York, New York
Unit: U.S. Volunteers
Battle or Place of Action: New Bern, North Carolina
Date of Action: 14 March 1862
Date of Issue: 11 November 1870
Citation: Voluntarily reconnoitered the enemy's position and carried orders under the hottest fire.

1349 ◆ THOMPSON, JOHN J.

Rank: Corporal
Service: U.S. Army
Birthday: 14 August 1838
Place of Birth: Holstein, Germany
Date of Death: 2 July 1915
Place of Death: Baltimore, Maryland
Cemetery: Immanuel Cemetery—Baltimore, Maryland
Entered Service at: Baltimore, Baltimore County, Maryland
Unit: Company C, 1st Maryland Infantry
Battle or Place of Action: Hatcher's Run, Virginia
Date of Action: 6 February 1865
Date of Issue: 10 September 1897
Citation: As color bearer with most conspicuous gallantry preceded his regiment in the assault and planted his flag upon the enemy's works.

1350 ◆ THOMPSON, THOMAS W.

Rank: Sergeant
Service: U.S. Army
Birthday: 27 May 1839
Place of Birth: Champaign County, Ohio
Date of Death: 25 March 1927
Place of Death: Mechanicsburg, Ohio
Cemetery: Maple Grove Cemetery—Mechanicsburg, Ohio
Entered Service at: Urbana, Champaign County, Ohio
Unit: Company A, 66th Ohio Infantry
Battle or Place of Action: Chancellorsville, Virginia
Date of Action: 2 May 1863
Date of Issue: 16 July 1892
Citation: One of a party of four who voluntarily brought into the Union lines, under fire, a wounded Confederate officer from whom was obtained valuable information concerning the enemy.

1351 ◆ THOMPSON, WILLIAM

Rank: Signal Quartermaster
Service: U.S. Navy
Birthday: 1812
Place of Birth: Cape May County, New Jersey
Date of Death: 12 September 1872
Place of Death: Philadelphia, Pennsylvania
Cemetery: Mount Moriah Cemetery VA plot 14-12—Philadelphia, Pennsylvania
Entered Service at: Boston, Suffolk County, Massachusetts
Unit: U.S.S. *Mohican*
Battle or Place of Action: Hilton Head, South Carolina
Date of Action: 7 November 1861
G.O. Number, Date: 17, 10 July 1863
Citation: During action of the main squadron of ships against heavily defended Forts Beauregard and Walker on Hilton Head, 7 November 1861. Serving as a signal quartermaster on board the U.S.S. *Mohican*, Thompson steadfastly steered the ship with a steady and bold heart under the batteries; was wounded by a piece of shell but remained at his station until he fell from loss of blood. Leg since amputated.

1352 ◆ *THOMPSON, WILLIAM P.

Rank: Sergeant (highest rank: First Lieutenant)
Service: U.S. Army

Birthday: 11 January 1844
Place of Birth: Brooklyn, Kings County, New York
Date of Death: 7 October 1864
Place of Death: Wilderness, Virginia
Cemetery: Greenbush Cemetery (MH)—Lafayette, Indiana
Entered Service at: Lafayette, Tippecanoe County, Indiana
Unit: Company G, 20th Indiana Infantry
Battle or Place of Action: Wilderness Campaign, Virginia
Date of Action: 6 May 1864
Date of Issue: 1 December 1864
Citation: Capture of flag of 55th Virginia Infantry (C.S.A.).

1353 ◆ THOMSON, CLIFFORD

Rank: First Lieutenant (highest rank: Brevet Major)
Service: U.S. Army
Birthday: 15 April 1834
Place of Birth: Fulton, Oswego County, New York
Date of Death: 29 September 1912
Cemetery: Holy Sepulchre Cemetery—East Orange, New Jersey
Entered Service at: New York, New York
Unit: Company A, 1st New York Cavalry
Battle or Place of Action: Chancellorsville, Virginia
Date of Action: 2 May 1863
Date of Issue: 27 November 1896
Citation: Volunteered to ascertain the character of approaching troops; rode up so close as to distinguish the features of the enemy, and as he wheeled to return they opened fire with musketry, the Union troops returning same. Under a terrific fire from both sides, Lt. Thompson rode back unhurt to the Federal lines, averting a disaster to the Army by his heroic act.

1354 ◆ THORN, WALTER

Rank: Second Lieutenant (highest rank: Brevet Captain)
Service: U.S. Army
Birthday: 18 November 1844
Place of Birth: Brooklyn, Kings County, New York
Date of Death: 29 July 1920
Place of Death: Hampton, Virginia
Cemetery: Arlington National Cemetery (2-3689-WH) (MH)—Arlington, Virginia
Entered Service at: Camp Nelson, Kentucky
Unit: Company G, 116th U.S. Colored Infantry
Battle or Place of Action: Dutch Gap Canal, Virginia
Date of Action: 1 January 1865
Date of Issue: 8 December 1898
Citation: After the fuse to the mined bulkhead had been lit, this officer, learning that the picket guard had not been withdrawn, mounted the bulkhead and at great personal peril warned the guard of its danger.

1355 ◆ TIBBETS, ANDREW W.

Rank: Private
Service: U.S. Army
Birthday: 1830

Place of Birth: Clark County, Indiana
Date of Death: 18 May 1898
Cemetery: Alberton Cemetery (MH)—Alberton, Iowa
Entered Service at: Centerville, Appanoose County, Iowa
Unit: Company I, 3d Iowa Cavalry
Battle or Place of Action: Columbus, Georgia
Date of Action: 16 April 1865
Date of Issue: 17 June 1865
Citation: Capture of flag and bearer, Austin's Battery (C.S.A.).

1356 ◆ TILTON, WILLIAM

Rank: Sergeant
Service: U.S. Army
Birthday: 27 October 1834
Place of Birth: St. Albans, Franklin County, Vermont
Date of Death: 8 March 1910
Place of Death: Enfield, New Hampshire
Cemetery: Oak Grove Cemetery—Enfield, New Hampshire
Entered Service at: Hanover, Grafton County, New Hampshire
Unit: Company C, 7th New Hampshire Infantry
Battle or Place of Action: Richmond Campaign, Virginia
Date of Action: 1864
Date of Issue: 20 February 1884
Citation: Gallant conduct in the field.

1357 ◆ TINKHAM, EUGENE M.

Rank: Corporal (highest rank: Sergeant)
Service: U.S. Army
Birthday: 19 April 1842
Place of Birth: Sprague, Connecticut
Date of Death: 21 October 1909
Place of Death: Springfield, Massachusetts
Cemetery: New Hanover Cemetery (MH)—Hanover, Connecticut
Entered Service at: Waterloo, Seneca County, New York
Unit: Company H, 148th New York Infantry
Battle or Place of Action: Cold Harbor, Virginia
Date of Action: 3 June 1864
Date of Issue: 5 April 1898
Citation: Though himself wounded, voluntarily left the rifle pits, crept out between the lines and, exposed to the severe fire of the enemy's guns at close-range, brought within the lines two wounded and helpless comrades.

1358 ◆ TITUS, CHARLES

Rank: Sergeant (highest rank: Quartermaster Sergeant)
Service: U.S. Army
Birthday: 1 January 1838
Place of Birth: Millstone, New Jersey
Date of Death: 26 March 1921
Place of Death: Belmar, New Jersey
Cemetery: Gledola Cemetery—Wall Township, New Jersey
Entered Service at: New Brunswick, Middlesex County, New Jersey

Unit: Company H, 1st New Jersey Cavalry
Battle or Place of Action: Deatonsville (Sailor's Creek), Virginia
Date of Action: 6 April 1865
Date of Issue: 3 July 1865
Citation: Was among the first to check the enemy's countercharge.

1359 ◆ TOBAN, JAMES W.

True Name: Toban, Jacobus W.
Rank: Sergeant
Service: U.S. Army
Birthday: 23 November 1845
Place of Birth: Northfield, Michigan
Date of Death: 2 November 1903
Place of Death: Lansing, Michigan
Cemetery: Catholic Cemetery—Northfield, Michigan
Entered Service at: Northfield, Michigan
Unit: Company C, 9th Michigan Cavalry
Battle or Place of Action: Aiken, South Carolina
Date of Action: 11 February 1865
Date of Issue: 9 July 1896
Citation: Voluntarily and at great personal risk returned, in the face of the advance of the enemy, and rescued from impending death or capture, Maj. William C. Stevens, 9th Michigan Cavalry, who had been thrown from his horse.

1360 ◆ TOBIE JR., EDWARD PARSONS

Rank: Sergeant Major (highest rank: Second Lieutenant)
Service: U.S. Army
Birthday: 19 March 1838
Place of Birth: Lewiston, Androscoggin County, Maine
Date of Death: 21 January 1900
Cemetery: Swain Point Cemetery (MH)—Providence, Rhode Island
Entered Service at: Lewiston, Androscoggin County, Maine
Unit: 1st Maine Cavalry
Battle or Place of Action: Appomattox Campaign, Virginia
Date of Action: 29 March-9 April 1865
Date of Issue: 1 April 1898
Citation: Though severely wounded at Sailors Creek, 6 April, and at Farmville, 7 April, refused to go to the hospital, but remained with his regiment, performed the full duties of adjutant upon the wounding of that officer, and was present for duty at Appomattox.
Notes: POW

1361 ◆ TOBIN, JOHN MICHAEL

Rank: First Lieutenant & Adjutant (highest rank: Captain)
Service: U.S. Army
Place of Birth: Waterford, Ireland
Date of Death: 27 December 1898
Cemetery: Mount Auburn Cemetery (MH)—Cambridge, Massachusetts
Entered Service at: Boston, Suffolk County, Massachusetts

Unit: Company I, 9th Massachusetts Infantry
Battle or Place of Action: Malvern Hill, Virginia
Date of Action: 1 July 1862
Date of Issue: 11 March 1896
Citation: Voluntarily took command of the 9th Massachusetts while adjutant, bravely fighting from 3:00 P.M. until dusk, rallying and reforming the regiment under fire; twice picked up the regimental flag, the color bearer having been shot down, and placed it in worthy hands.

1362 ◆ TODD, SAMUEL

Rank: Quartermaster
Service: U.S. Navy
Birthday: 1815
Place of Birth: Portsmouth, Rockingham County, New Hampshire
Entered Service at: New Hampshire
Unit: U.S.S. *Brooklyn*
Battle or Place of Action: Fort Morgan, Mobile Bay, Alabama
Date of Action: 5 August 1864
G.O. Number, Date: 45, 31 December 1864
Citation: Stationed at the conn on board the U.S.S. *Brooklyn* during action against rebel forts and gunboats and with the ram *Tennessee* in Mobile Bay, 5 August 1864. Despite severe damage to his ship and the loss of several men on board as enemy fire raked her decks from stem to stern, Todd performed his duties with outstanding skill and courage throughout the furious battle which resulted in the surrender of the prize rebel ram *Tennessee* and in the damaging and destruction of batteries at Fort Morgan.

1363 ◆ TOFFEY, JOHN JAMES

Rank: First Lieutenant
Service: U.S. Army
Birthday: 1 June 1844
Place of Birth: Quaker Hill, Dutchess County, New York
Date of Death: 13 March 1911
Cemetery: Fishkill Cemetery—Pauling, New York
Entered Service at: Hudson, Hudson County, New Jersey
Unit: Company G, 33d New Jersey Infantry
Battle or Place of Action: Chattanooga, Tennessee
Date of Action: 23 November 1863
Date of Issue: 10 September 1897
Citation: Although excused from duty on account of sickness, went to the front in command of a storming party and with conspicuous gallantry participated in the assault of Missionary Ridge; was here wounded and permanently disabled.

1364 ◆ TOMLIN, ANDREW J.

Rank: Corporal (highest rank: Sergeant)
Service: U.S. Marine Corps
Birthday: 15 March 1845
Place of Birth: Goshen, Cape May County, New Jersey
Date of Death: 1 November 1905

Cemetery: Goshen Methodist Cemetery (MH)—Goshen, New Jersey
Entered Service at: New Jersey
Unit: U.S.S. *Wabash*
Battle or Place of Action: Fort Fisher, North Carolina
Date of Action: 15 January 1865
G.O. Number, Date: 59, 22 June 1865
Citation: As corporal of the guard on board the U.S.S. *Wabash* during the assault on Fort Fisher, 15 January 1865. As one of 200 marines assembled to hold a line of entrenchments in the rear of the fort which the enemy threatened to attack in force following a retreat in panic by more than two-thirds of the assaulting ground forces, Cpl. Tomlin took position in line and remained until morning when relief troops arrived from the fort. When one of his comrades was struck down by enemy fire, he unhesitatingly advanced under a withering fire of musketry into an open plain close to the fort and assisted the wounded man to a place of safety.

1365 ◆ TOMPKINS, AARON B.

Rank: Sergeant (highest rank: First Sergeant)
Service: U.S. Army
Birthday: 15 February 1844
Place of Birth: Orange, Essex County, New Jersey
Date of Death: 25 November 1931
Cemetery: Rosedale Cemetery (MH)—Orange, New Jersey
Entered Service at: Jersey City, Hudson County, New Jersey
Unit: Company G, 1st New Jersey Cavalry
Battle or Place of Action: Deatonsville (Sailor's Creek), Virginia
Date of Action: 5 April 1865
Date of Issue: 3 July 1865
Citation: Charged into the enemy's ranks and captured a battle flag, having a horse shot under him and his cheeks and shoulders cut with a saber.

1366 ◆ TOMPKINS, CHARLES HENRY

Rank: First Lieutenant (highest rank: Brevet Brigadier General)
Service: U.S. Army
Birthday: 12 September 1830
Place of Birth: Fort Monroe, Hampton County, Virginia
Date of Death: 18 January 1915
Place of Death: Washington, D.C.
Cemetery: Oak Hill Cemetery—Washington D.C.
Entered Service at: Brooklyn, Kings County, New York
Unit: 2d U.S. Cavalry
Battle or Place of Action: Fairfax, Virginia
Date of Action: 1 June 1861
Date of Issue: 13 November 1893
Citation: Twice charged through the enemy's lines and, taking a carbine from an enlisted man, shot the enemy's captain.

1367 ◆ TOOHEY, THOMAS

Rank: Sergeant (highest rank: First Sergeant)
Service: U.S. Army
Birthday: 1 January 1835
Place of Birth: New York, New York
Date of Death: 19 November 1918
Cemetery: Mount Washington Cemetery (MH)—Independence, Missouri
Entered Service at: Milwaukee, Milwaukee County, Wisconsin
Unit: Company F, 24th Wisconsin Infantry
Battle or Place of Action: Franklin, Tennessee
Date of Action: 30 November 1864
Date of Issue: 12 March 1917
Citation: Gallantry in action; voluntarily assisting in working guns of battery near right of regiment after nearly every man had left them, the fire of the enemy being hotter at this than at any other point on the line.

1368 ◆ TOOMER, WILLIAM

Rank: Sergeant
Service: U.S. Army
Birthday: 12 January 1830
Place of Birth: Dublin, Ireland
Date of Death: 27 December 1901
Cemetery: Graceland Cemetery—Chicago, Illinois
Entered Service at: Chicago, Cook County, Illinois
Unit: Company G, 127th Illinois Infantry
Battle or Place of Action: Vicksburg, Mississippi
Date of Action: 22 May 1863
Date of Issue: 9 July 1894
Citation: Gallantry in the charge of the "volunteer storming party."

1369 ◆ TORGLER, ERNEST R.

Rank: Sergeant
Service: U.S. Army
Birthday: 29 March 1840
Place of Birth: Mecklenburg, Germany
Date of Death: 3 August 1923
Cemetery: Woodlawn Cemetery (MH)—Toledo, Ohio
Entered Service at: Toledo, Lucas County, Ohio
Unit: Company G, 37th Ohio Infantry
Battle or Place of Action: Ezra Chapel, Georgia
Date of Action: 28 July 1864
Date of Issue: 10 May 1894
Citation: At great hazard of his life he saved his commanding officer, then badly wounded, from capture.

1370 ◆ TOZIER, ANDREW JACKSON

Rank: Sergeant (highest rank: First Sergeant)
Service: U.S. Army
Birthday: 11 February 1838
Place of Birth: Monmouth, Kennebec County, Maine
Date of Death: 28 March 1910
Cemetery: Litchfield Plains Cemetery (MH)—Litchfield, Maine
Entered Service at: Bangor, Penobscot County, Maine
Unit: Company I, 20th Maine Infantry

Battle or Place of Action: Gettysburg, Pennsylvania
Date of Action: 2 July 1863
Date of Issue: 13 August 1898
Citation: At the crisis of the engagement this soldier, a color bearer, stood alone in an advanced position, the regiment having been borne back, and defended his colors with musket and ammunition picked up at his feet.

1371 ◆ TRACY, AMASA SAWYER

Rank: Lieutenant Colonel (highest rank: Brevet Colonel)
Service: U.S. Army
Birthday: 16 March 1829
Place of Birth: Dover, Piscataquis County, Maine
Date of Death: 26 February 1908
Place of Death: Orleans, Vermont
Cemetery: West Cemetery—Middlebury, Vermont
Entered Service at: Middlebury, Addison County, Vermont
Unit: 2d Vermont Infantry
Battle or Place of Action: Cedar Creek, Virginia
Date of Action: 19 October 1864
Date of Issue: 24 June 1892
Citation: Took command and led the brigade in the assault on the enemy's works.

1372 ◆ TRACY, BENJAMIN FRANKLIN

Rank: Colonel (highest rank: Brevet Brigadier General)
Service: U.S. Army
Birthday: 26 April 1830
Place of Birth: Owego, Tioga County, New York
Date of Death: 6 August 1915
Place of Death: New York, New York
Cemetery: The Green Wood Cemetery—Brooklyn, New York
Entered Service at: Owego, Tioga County, New York
Unit: 109th New York Infantry
Served as: Commanding Officer
Battle or Place of Action: Wilderness Campaign, Virginia
Date of Action: 6 May 1864
Date of Issue: 21 June 1895
Citation: Seized the colors and led the regiment when other regiments had retired and then reformed his line and held it.

1373 ◆ TRACY, CHARLES H.

Rank: Sergeant
Service: U.S. Army
Birthday: 1833
Place of Birth: Jewett City, New London County, Connecticut
Date of Death: 13 September 1911
Cemetery: Fairview Cemetery (MH)—Chicopee, Massachusetts
Entered Service at: Springfield, Hampden County, Massachusetts
Unit: Company A, 37th Massachusetts Infantry
Battle or Place of Action: Spotsylvania & Petersburg, Virginia
Date of Action: 12 May 1864 & 2 April 1865
Date of Issue: 19 November 1897
Citation: At the risk of his own life, at Spotsylvania, 12 May 1864, assisted in carrying to a place of safety a wounded and helpless officer. On 2 April 1865, advanced with the pioneers, and, under heavy fire, assisted in removing two lines of chevaux-de-frise; was twice wounded but advanced to the third line, where he was again severely wounded, losing a leg.

1374 ◆ TRACY, WILLIAM GARDNER

Rank: Second Lieutenant (highest rank: Major)
Service: U.S. Army
Birthday: 7 April 1842
Place of Birth: Syracuse, Onondaga County, New York
Date of Death: 8 December 1924
Cemetery: Oakwood Morningside Cemetery (MH)—Syracuse, New York
Entered Service at: Albany, Albany County, New York
Unit: Company I, 122d New York Infantry
Battle or Place of Action: Chancellorsville, Virginia
Date of Action: 2 May 1863
Date of Issue: 2 May 1895
Citation: Having been sent outside the lines to obtain certain information of great importance and having succeeded in his mission, was surprised upon his return by a large force of the enemy, regaining the Union lines only after greatly imperiling his life.

1375 ◆ TRAYNOR, ANDREW

Rank: Corporal
Service: U.S. Army
Birthday: 9 February 1843
Place of Birth: Newark, Essex County, New Jersey
Date of Death: 6 July 1920
Place of Death: Omaha, Nebraska
Cemetery: Forest Lawn Cemetery—Omaha, Nebraska
Entered Service at: Rome, Oneida County, New York
Unit: Company D, 1st Michigan Cavalry
Battle or Place of Action: Mason's Hill, Virginia
Date of Action: 16 March 1864
Date of Issue: 28 September 1897
Citation: Having been surprised and captured by a detachment of guerrillas, this soldier, with other prisoners, seized the arms of the guard over them, killed two of the guerrillas, and enabled all the prisoners to escape.

1376 ◆ TREAT, HOWELL B.

Rank: Sergeant
Service: U.S. Army
Birthday: 31 March 1833
Place of Birth: Painesville, Lake County, Ohio
Date of Death: 21 July 1912
Cemetery: Evergreen Cemetery—Painesville, Ohio
Entered Service at: Painesville, Lake County, Ohio
Unit: Company I, 52d Ohio Infantry
Battle or Place of Action: Buzzard's Roost, Georgia

Date of Action: 11 May 1864
Date of Issue: 14 August 1894
Citation: Risked his life in saving a wounded comrade.

1377 ◆ TREMAIN, HENRY EDWIN

Rank: Major & Aide-de-Camp (highest rank: Brevet Brigadier General)
Service: U.S. Army
Birthday: 14 November 1840
Place of Birth: New York, New York
Date of Death: 9 December 1910
Place of Death: New York, New York
Cemetery: Woodlawn Cemetery—Bronx, New York
Entered Service at: New York, New York
Unit: U.S. Volunteers
Battle or Place of Action: Resaca, Georgia
Date of Action: 15 May 1864
Date of Issue: 30 June 1892
Citation: Voluntarily rode between the lines while two brigades of Union troops were firing into each other and stopped the firing.

1378 ◆ TRIBE, JOHN

Rank: Private (highest rank: Quartermaster Sergeant)
Service: U.S. Army
Birthday: 4 December 1841
Place of Birth: Tioga County, New York
Date of Death: 4 December 1917
Place of Death: Barton, New York
Cemetery: Halsey Valley Cemetery (MH)—Halsey Valley, New York
Entered Service at: Oswego, Oswego County, New York
Unit: Company G, 5th New York Cavalry
Battle or Place of Action: Waterloo Bridge, Virginia
Date of Action: 25 August 1862
Date of Issue: 11 June 1895
Citation: Voluntarily assisted in the burning and destruction of the bridge under heavy fire from the enemy.

1379 ◆ TRIPP, OTHNIEL

Rank: Chief Boatswain's Mate
Service: U.S. Navy
Birthday: 1826
Place of Birth: Maine
Entered Service at: Maine
Unit: U.S.S. *Seneca*
Battle or Place of Action: Fort Fisher, North Carolina
Date of Action: 15 January 1865
G.O. Number, Date: 59, 22 June 1865
Citation: On board the U.S.S. *Seneca* in the assault on Fort Fisher, 15 January 1865. Despite severe enemy fire which halted an attempt by his assaulting party to enter the stockade, Tripp boldly charged through the gap in the stockade although the center of the line, being totally unprotected, fell back along the open beach and left too few in the ranks to attempt an offensive operation.

1380 ◆ TROGDEN, HOWELL G.

Rank: Private
Service: U.S. Army
Birthday: 24 October 1840
Place of Birth: Cedar Falls, Randolph County, North Carolina
Date of Death: 2 December 1910
Cemetery: Calvary Cemetery (MH)—Los Angeles, California
Entered Service at: St. Louis, St. Louis County, Missouri
Unit: Company B, 8th Missouri Infantry
Battle or Place of Action: Vicksburg, Mississippi
Date of Action: 22 May 1863
Date of Issue: 3 August 1894
Citation: Gallantry in the charge of the "volunteer storming party." He carried his regiment's flag and tried to borrow a gun to defend it.

1381 ◆ TRUELL, EDWIN M.

Rank: Private (highest rank: First Lieutenant)
Service: U.S. Army
Birthday: 19 August 1841
Place of Birth: Lowell, Middlesex County, Massachusetts
Date of Death: 12 October 1907
Place of Death: Washington, D.C.
Cemetery: Arlington National Cemetery (13-5274-C)—Arlington, Virginia
Entered Service at: Mantson, Wisconsin
Unit: Company E, 12th Wisconsin Infantry
Battle or Place of Action: near Atlanta, Georgia
Date of Action: 21 July 1864
Date of Issue: 11 March 1870
Citation: Although severely wounded in a charge, he remained with the regiment until again severely wounded, losing his leg.

1382 ◆ TRUETT, ALEXANDER H.

Rank: Coxswain
Service: U.S. Navy
Birthday: 4 July 1833
Place of Birth: Baltimore, Baltimore County, Maryland
Entered Service at: Maryland
Unit: U.S.S. *Richmond*
Battle or Place of Action: Fort Morgan, Mobile Bay, Alabama
Date of Action: 5 August 1864
G.O. Number, Date: 45, 31 December 1864
Date of Issue: 24 October 1865
Citation: On board the U.S.S. *Richmond* during action against rebel forts and gunboats and with the ram *Tennessee* in Mobile Bay, 5 August 1864. Despite damage to his ship the loss of several men on board as enemy fire raked her decks, Truett performed his duties with skill and courage throughout a furious two-hour battle which resulted in the surrender of the rebel ram *Tennessee* and in the damaging and destruction of batteries at Fort Morgan.

1383 ◆ TUCKER, ALLEN

Rank: Sergeant
Service: U.S. Army
Birthday: 1838
Place of Birth: Lyme, Connecticut
Date of Death: 22 February 1903
Place of Death: New Haven, Connecticut
Cemetery: Evergreen Cemetery (MH)—New Haven, Connecticut
Entered Service at: Sprague, Connecticut
Unit: Company F, 10th Connecticut Infantry
Battle or Place of Action: Petersburg, Virginia
Date of Action: 2 April 1865
Date of Issue: 12 May 1865
Citation: Gallantry as color bearer in the assault on Fort Gregg.

1384 ◆ TUCKER, JACOB R.

Rank: Corporal
Service: U.S. Army
Birthday: 1 April 1845
Place of Birth: Chester County, Pennsylvania
Date of Death: 16 February 1926
Cemetery: The Baltimore Cemetery—Baltimore, Maryland
Entered Service at: Baltimore, Baltimore County, Maryland
Unit: Company G, 4th Maryland Infantry
Battle or Place of Action: Petersburg, Virginia
Date of Action: 1 April 1865
Date of Issue: 22 April 1871
Citation: Was one of three soldiers most conspicuous in the final assault.

1385 ◆ TWEEDALE, JOHN

Rank: Private (highest rank: Colonel)
Service: U.S. Army
Birthday: 10 June 1841
Place of Birth: Frankford, Philadelphia County, Pennsylvania
Date of Death: 21 December 1920
Cemetery: Arlington National Cemetery (1-470-WS)—Arlington, Virginia
Entered Service at: Philadelphia, Philadelphia County, Pennsylvania
Unit: Company B, 15th Pennsylvania Cavalry
Battle or Place of Action: Stone River, Tennessee
Date of Action: 31 December 1862—1 January 1863
Date of Issue: 18 November 1887
Citation: Gallantry in action.

1386 ◆ TWOMBLY, VOLTARE PAINE

Rank: Corporal (highest rank: Captain)
Service: U.S. Army
Birthday: 21 February 1842
Place of Birth: Farmington, Van Buren County, Iowa
Date of Death: 24 February 1918
Place of Death: Des Moines, Iowa
Cemetery: Pitsburg Rural Cemetery (MH)—Keosauqua, Iowa
Entered Service at: Keosauqua, Van Buren County, Iowa
Unit: Company F, 2d Iowa Infantry
Battle or Place of Action: Fort Donelson, Tennessee
Date of Action: 15 February 1862
Date of Issue: 12 March 1897
Citation: Took the colors after three of the color guard had fallen, and although most instantly knocked down by a spent ball, immediately arose and bore the colors to the end of the engagement.

1387 ◆ TYRRELL, GEORGE WILLIAM

Rank: Corporal (highest rank: First Sergeant)
Service: U.S. Army
Place of Birth: Ireland
Entered Service at: Cincinnati, Hamilton County, Ohio
Unit: Company H, 5th Ohio Infantry
Battle or Place of Action: Resaca, Georgia
Date of Action: 14 May 1864
Date of Issue: 7 April 1865
Citation: Capture of flag.

1388 ◆ UHRL, GEORGE

True Name: Uhri, George
Rank: Sergeant
Service: U.S. Army
Birthday: 21 October 1838
Place of Birth: Baden, Germany
Date of Death: 28 September 1911
Place of Death: New York, New York
Cemetery: The Lutheran Cemetery—Middle Village, New York
Entered Service at: New York, New York
Unit: Light Battery F, 5th U.S. Artillery
Battle or Place of Action: White Oak Swamp Bridge, Virginia
Date of Action: 30 June 1862
Date of Issue: 4 April 1898
Citation: Was one of a party of three who, under heavy fire of advancing enemy, voluntarily secured and saved from capture a field gun belonging to another battery and which had been deserted by its officers and men.

1389 ◆ URELL, MICHAEL EMMET

Rank: Private (highest rank: Brevet Major)
Service: U.S. Army
Birthday: 8 November 1844
Place of Birth: County Cork, Ireland
Date of Death: 6 September 1910
Place of Death: County Cork, Ireland
Cemetery: Arlington National Cemetery (1-51-D-WS)—Arlington, Virginia
Entered Service at: New York, New York
Unit: Company E, 82d New York Infantry

Served as: Color Bearer
Battle or Place of Action: Bristoe Station, Virginia
Date of Action: 14 October 1863
Date of Issue: 6 June 1870
Citation: Gallantry in action while detailed as color bearer; was severely wounded.
Notes: POW

1390 ◆ VALE, JOHN

Rank: Private (highest rank: Sergeant)
Service: U.S. Army
Birthday: 9 August 1836
Place of Birth: London, England
Date of Death: 4 February 1909
Place of Death: Davenport, Iowa
Cemetery: Oakdale Cemetery—Davenport, Iowa
Entered Service at: Rochester, Olmsted County, Minnesota
Unit: Company H, 2d Minnesota Infantry
Battle or Place of Action: Nolensville, Tennessee
Date of Action: 15 February 1863
Date of Issue: 11 September 1897
Citation: Was one of a detachment of 16 men who heroically defended a wagon train against the attack of 125 cavalry, repulsed the attack and saved the train.

1391 ◆ VANCE, WILSON J.

Rank: Private (highest rank: Brevet Captain)
Service: U.S. Army
Birthday: 20 December 1845
Place of Birth: Findlay, Hancock County, Ohio
Date of Death: 10 November 1911
Place of Death: Chattanooga, Tennessee
Cemetery: Arlington National Cemetery (3-2360-WS) (MH)—Arlington, Virginia
Entered Service at: Findlay, Hancock County, Ohio
Unit: Company B, 21st Ohio Infantry
Battle or Place of Action: Stone River, Tennessee
Date of Action: 31 December 1862
Date of Issue: 17 September 1897
Citation: Voluntarily and under a heavy fire, while his command was falling back, rescued a wounded and helpless comrade from death or capture.

1392 ◆ VANDERSLICE, JOHN MITCHELL

Rank: Private
Service: U.S. Army
Birthday: 31 August 1846
Place of Birth: near Valley Forge, Chester County, Pennsylvania
Date of Death: 12 March 1915
Place of Death: Collegeville, Pennsylvania
Cemetery: St. James Perkiomen Cemetery (MH)—Evansburg, Pennsylvania
Entered Service at: Philadelphia, Philadelphia County, Pennsylvania
Unit: Company D, 8th Pennsylvania Cavalry

Battle or Place of Action: Hatcher's Run, Virginia
Date of Action: 6 February 1865
Date of Issue: 1 September 1893
Citation: Was the first man to reach the enemy's rifle pits, which were taken in the charge.
Notes: POW

1393 ◆ VAN MATRE, JOSEPH

Rank: Private
Service: U.S. Army
Birthday: 9 October 1828
Place of Birth: Mason County, West Virginia
Date of Death: 14 January 1892
Cemetery: Hill Cemetery—Middleport, Ohio
Entered Service at: Middleport, Meigs County, Ohio
Unit: Company G, 116th Ohio Infantry
Battle or Place of Action: Petersburg, Virginia
Date of Action: 2 April 1865
Date of Issue: 12 May 1865
Citation: In the assault on Fort Gregg, this soldier climbed upon the parapet and fired down into the fort as fast as the loaded guns could be passed up to him by comrades.

1394 ◆ VANTINE, JOSEPH E.

Rank: First Class Fireman
Service: U.S. Navy
Birthday: March 1835
Place of Birth: Philadelphia, Philadelphia County, Pennsylvania
Date of Death: 5 May 1904
Cemetery: Globe Cemetery—New Castle, Delaware
Entered Service at: Pennslyvania
Unit: U.S.S. *Richmond*
Battle or Place of Action: Port Hudson, Louisiana
Date of Action: 14 March 1863
G.O. Number, Date: 17, 10 July 1863
Citation: Served on board the U.S.S. *Richmond* in the attack on Port Hudson, 14 March 1863. Damaged by a 6-inch solid rifle shot which shattered the starboard safety-valve chamber and also damaged the port safety valve, the fireroom of the *Richmond* immediately filled with steam, to place it in an extremely critical condition. Acting courageously in this crisis, Vantine persisted in penetrating the steam-filled room in order to haul the hot fires of the furnaces and continued this action until the gravity of the situation had been lessened.

1395 ◆ VAN WINKLE, EDWARD (EDWIN)

Rank: Corporal (highest rank: Sergeant)
Service: U.S. Army
Birthday: 1839
Place of Birth: Phelps, Ontario County, New York
Date of Death: 30 July 1891
Cemetery: Oak Hill Cemetery (MH)—Battle Creek, Michigan
Entered Service at: Phelps, Ontario County, New York
Unit: Company C, 148th New York Infantry

Battle or Place of Action: Chapin's Farm, Virginia
Date of Action: 29 September 1864
Date of Issue: 6 April 1865
Citation: Took position in advance of the skirmish line and drove the enemy's cannoneers from their guns.

1396 ◆ VAUGHN, PINKERTON ROSS

Rank: Sergeant
Service: U.S. Marine Corps
Birthday: 1839
Place of Birth: Downingtown, Chester County, Pennsylvania
Date of Death: 22 August 1866
Cemetery: Laurel Hill Cemetery (MH)—Philadelphia, Pennsylvania
Entered Service at: Pennsylvania
Unit: U.S.S. *Mississippi*
Battle or Place of Action: Port Hudson, Louisiana
Date of Action: 14 March 1863
G.O. Number, Date: 17, 10 July 1863
Citation: Serving on board the U.S.S. *Mississippi* during her abandonment and firing in the action with the Port Hudson batteries, 14 March 1863. During the abandonment of the *Mississippi* which had to be grounded, Sgt. Vaughn rendered invaluable assistance to his commanding officer, remaining with the ship until all of the crew had landed and the ship had been fired to prevent its falling into enemy hands. Persistent until the last, and conspicuously cool under the heavy shellfire, Sgt. Vaughn was finally ordered to save himself as he saw fit.

1397 ◆ VEAL, CHARLES

True Name: Veale, Charles
Rank: Private
Service: U.S. Army
Birthday: 1838
Place of Birth: Portsmouth, Portsmouth County, Virginia
Date of Death: 27 July 1872
Place of Death: Hampton, Virginia
Cemetery: Hampton National Cemetery (F-5097) (MH)—Hampton, Virginia
Entered Service at: Baltimore, Baltimore County, Maryland
Unit: Company D, 4th U.S. Colored Infantry
Battle or Place of Action: Chapin's Farm, Virginia
Date of Action: 29 September 1864
Date of Issue: 6 April 1865
Citation: Seized the national colors, after two color bearers had been shot down close to the enemy's works, and bore them through the remainder of the battle.

1398 ◆ VEALE, MOSES

Rank: Captain (highest rank: Major)
Service: U.S. Army
Birthday: 9 November 1832
Place of Birth: Bridgeton, Cumberland County, New Jersey
Date of Death: 27 July 1917
Place of Death: Philadelphia, Pennsylvania
Cemetery: West Laurel Hill Cemetery—Bala-Cynwyd, Pennsylvania
Entered Service at: Philadelphia, Philadelphia County, Pennsylvania
Unit: Company F, 109th Pennsylvania Infantry
Battle or Place of Action: Wauhatchie, Tennessee
Date of Action: 28 October 1863
Date of Issue: 17 January 1894
Citation: Gallantry in action; manifesting throughout the engagement coolness, zeal, judgment, and courage. His horse was shot from under him and he was hit by four enemy bullets.

1399 ◆ VEAZEY, WHEELOCK GRAVES

Rank: Colonel
Service: U.S. Army
Birthday: 5 December 1835
Place of Birth: Brentwood, Coos County, New Hampshire
Date of Death: 22 March 1898
Cemetery: Arlington National Cemetery (2-1026))—Arlington, Virginia
Entered Service at: Springfield, Windsor County, Vermont
Unit: 16th Vermont Infantry
Battle or Place of Action: Gettysburg, Pennsylvania
Date of Action: 3 July 1863
Date of Issue: 8 September 1891
Citation: Rapidly assembled his regiment and charged the enemy's flank; charged front under heavy fire, and charged and destroyed a Confederate brigade, all this with new troops in their first battle.

1400 ◆ VERNAY, JAMES DAVID

Rank: Second Lieutenant (highest rank: Brevet Major)
Service: U.S. Army
Birthday: 24 December 1834
Place of Birth: Lacon, Marshall County, Illinois
Date of Death: 19 July 1918
Place of Death: Washington, D.C.
Cemetery: Arlington National Cemetery (3-4052) (MH)—Arlington, Virginia
Entered Service at: Lacon, Marshall County, Illinois
Unit: Company B, 11th Illinois Infantry
Battle or Place of Action: Vicksburg, Mississippi
Date of Action: 22 April 1863
Date of Issue: 1 April 1898
Citation: Served gallantly as a volunteer with the crew of the steamer *Horizon* that, under a heavy fire, passed the Confederate batteries.

1401 ◆ VERNEY, JAMES W.

Rank: Chief Quartermaster
Service: U.S. Navy
Birthday: 17 January 1834
Place of Birth: Bath, Sagadahoc County, Maine
Date of Death: 29 November 1902
Place of Death: Boston, Massachusetts

Cemetery: Cedar Grove Cemetery (MH)—Dorchester, Massachusetts
Entered Service at: Portland, Cumberland County, Maine
Unit: U.S.S. *Pontoosuc*
Battle or Place of Action: Fort Fisher & Wilmington, North Carolina
Date of Action: 24 December 1864—22 February 1865
G.O. Number, Date: 59, 22 June 1865
Citation: Seved as chief quartermaster on board the U.S.S. *Pontoosuc* during the capture of Fort Fisher and Wilmington, 24 December 1864 to 22 February 1865. Carrying out his duties faithfully throughout this period, Verney was recommended for gallantry and skill and for his cool courage while under fire of the enemy throughout these various actions.

1402 ◆ VIFQUAIN, VICTOR

Rank: Lieutenant Colonel (highest rank: Brevet Brigadier General)
Service: U.S. Army
Birthday: 20 May 1836
Place of Birth: Brussels, Belgium
Date of Death: 7 January 1904
Place of Death: Lincoln, Nebraska
Cemetery: Calvary Cemetery (MH)—Lincoln, Nebraska
Entered Service at: Salene County, Nebraska
Unit: 97th Illinois Infantry
Battle or Place of Action: Fort Blakely, Alabama
Date of Action: 9 April 1865
Date of Issue: 8 June 1865
Citation: Capture of flag.

1403 ◆ VON VEGESACK, ERNEST

Rank: Major & Aide-de-Camp (highest rank: Brevet Brigadier General)
Service: U.S. Army
Birthday: 18 June 1820
Place of Birth: Gotland, Sweden
Date of Death: 12 January 1903
Place of Death: Stockholm, Sweden
Cemetery: Churchyard Cemetery—Stockholm, Sweden
Entered Service at: New York, New York
Unit: U.S. Volunteers
Battle or Place of Action: Gaines' Mill, Virginia
Date of Action: 27 June 1862
Date of Issue: 23 August 1893
Citation: While voluntarily serving as aide-de-camp, successfully and advantageously charged the position of troops under fire.

1404 ◆ WAGEMAN, JOHN H.

Rank: Private (highest rank: Corporal)
Service: U.S. Army
Birthday: 22 March 1841
Place of Birth: Amelia, Clermont County, Ohio
Date of Death: 9 January 1916
Place of Death: Williamsburg, Ohio

Cemetery: Clover Cemetery—Clover, Ohio
Entered Service at: Amelia, Clermont County, Ohio
Unit: Company I, 60th Ohio Infantry
Battle or Place of Action: Petersburg, Virginia
Date of Action: 17 June 1864
Date of Issue: 27 July 1896
Citation: Remained with the command after being severely wounded until he had fired all the cartridges in his possession, when he had to be carried from the field.

1405 ◆ WAGG, MAURICE

Rank: Coxswain (highest rank: Master's Mate)
Service: U.S. Navy
Birthday: 23 July 1840
Place of Birth: Hampshire, England
Date of Death: 22 June 1926
Place of Death: London, England
Entered Service at: New York, New York
Unit: U.S.S. *Rhode Island*
Battle or Place of Action: off Cape Hatteras, North Carolina
Date of Action: 31 December 1862
G.O. Number, Date: 45, 31 December 1864
Citation: Served on board the U.S.S. *Rhode Island*, which was engaged in saving the lives of the officers and crew of the *Monitor* off Hatteras, 31 December 1862. Participating in the hazardous task of rescuing the officers and crew of the sinking *Monitor*, Wagg distinguished himself by meritorious conduct during this operation.

1406 ◆ WAGNER, JOHN W.

Rank: Corporal
Service: U.S. Army
Birthday: 1837
Place of Birth: Clear Spring, Washington County, Maryland
Date of Death: 24 August 1896
Place of Death: Boston, Massachusetts
Cemetery: Forest Hills Cemetery (PM)—Jamaica Plain, Massachusetts
Entered Service at: St. Louis, St. Louis County, Missouri
Unit: Company F, 8th Missouri Infantry
Battle or Place of Action: Vicksburg, Mississippi
Date of Action: 22 May 1863
Date of Issue: 14 December 1894
Citation: Gallantry in the charge of the "volunteer storming party."

1407 ◆ WAINWRIGHT, JOHN

Rank: First Lieutenant (highest rank: Colonel)
Service: U.S. Army
Birthday: 13 July 1839
Place of Birth: Syracuse, Onondaga County, New York
Date of Death: 15 April 1915
Place of Death: Wilmington, Delaware
Cemetery: Arlington National Cemetery (2-1061)—Arlington, Virginia

Entered Service at: West Chester, Chester County, Pennsylvania
Unit: Company F, 97th Pennsylvania Infantry
Battle or Place of Action: Fort Fisher, North Carolina
Date of Action: 15 January 1865
Date of Issue: 24 June 1890
Citation: Gallant and meritorious conduct, where, as first lieutenant, he commanded the regiment.

1408 ◆ WALKER, JAMES C.

Rank: Private (highest rank: Color Sergeant)
Service: U.S. Army
Birthday: 30 November 1843
Place of Birth: Harmony, Clark County, Ohio
Date of Death: 8 April 1923
Cemetery: Ferncliff Cemetery (MH)—Springfield, Ohio
Entered Service at: Springfield, Clark County, Ohio
Unit: Company K, 31st Ohio Infantry
Battle or Place of Action: Missionary Ridge, Tennessee
Date of Action: 25 November 1863
Date of Issue: 25 November 1895
Citation: After two color bearers had fallen, seized the flag and carried it forward, assisting in the capture of the battery. Shortly thereafter he captured the flag of the 41st Alabama and the color bearer.

1409 ◆ WALKER, MARY EDWARDS

Service: U.S. Army
Birthday: 26 November 1832
Place of Birth: Oswego County, New York
Date of Death: 21 February 1919
Cemetery: The Rural Cemetery (MH)—Oswego, New York
Entered Service at: Louisville, Jefferson County, Kentucky
Served as: Contract Acting Assistant Surgeon (Civilian)
Battle or Place of Action: Battle of Bull Run; Patent Office Hospital, Washington, D.C.; Chattanooga, Tenn.; following Battle of Chickamauga; Battle of Atlanta
Date of Action: 21 July 1861; October 1861; September 1863; September 1864
Date of Issue: 11 November 1865
Citation: *Whereas* it appears from official reports that Dr. Mary E. Walker, a graduate of medicine, "has rendered valuable service to the Government, and her efforts have been earnest and untiring in a variety of ways," and that she was assigned to duty and served as an assistant surgeon in charge of female prisoners at Louisville, Ky., upon the recommendation of Maj. Gens. Sherman and Thomas, and faithfully served as contract surgeon in the service of the United States, and has devoted herself with much patriotic zeal to the sick and wounded soldiers, both in the field and hospitals, to the detriment of her own health, and has also endured hardships as a prisoner of war four months in a Southern prison while acting as contract surgeon; and *Whereas,* by reason of her not being a commissioned officer in the military service, a brevet or honorary rank cannot, under existing laws, be conferred upon her; and *Whereas,* in the opinion of the President an honorable recognition of her services and sufferings should be made; *It is ordered,* That a testimonial thereof shall be hereby made and given to the said Dr. Mary E. Walker, and that the usual medal of honor for meritorious services be given her. Given under my hand in the city of Washington, D.C., this 11th day of November, A.D. 1865. Andrew Johnson
Notes: POW from 10 April 1864—12 August 1864, Richmond, Virginia

1410 ◆ WALL, JERRY C.

Rank: Private
Service: U.S. Army
Birthday: 1 July 1841
Place of Birth: Geneva Ontario County, New York
Date of Death: 8 April 1923
Place of Death: Dansville, New York
Cemetery: Greenmount Cemetery (MH)—Dansville, New York
Entered Service at: Milo, New York
Unit: Company B, 126th New York Infantry
Battle or Place of Action: Gettysburg, Pennsylvania
Date of Action: 3 July 1863
Date of Issue: 1 December 1864
Citation: Capture of flag.

1411 ◆ WALLER, FRANCIS A.

Rank: Corporal (highest rank: First Lieutenant)
Service: U.S. Army
Birthday: 15 August 1840
Place of Birth: Gurney, Ohio
Date of Death: 30 April 1911
Place of Death: Bentford, South Dakota
Cemetery: Walnut Mound Cemetery—DeSoto, Wisconsin
Entered Service at: DeSoto, Vernon County, Wisconsin
Unit: Company I, 6th Wisconsin Infantry
Battle or Place of Action: Gettysburg, Pennsylvania
Date of Action: 1 July 1863
Date of Issue: 1 December 1864
Citation: Capture of flag of 2d Mississippi Infantry (C.S.A.).

1412 ◆ WALLING, WILLIAM HENRY

Rank: Captain (highest rank: Brevet Lieutenant Colonel)
Service: U.S. Army
Birthday: 3 September 1830
Place of Birth: Hartford, Washington County, New York
Date of Death: 16 June 1912
Place of Death: Potsdam, New York
Cemetery: Bayside Cemetery—Potsdam, New York
Entered Service at: Folly Island, Charleston County, South Carolina
Unit: Company C, 142d New York Infantry
Battle or Place of Action: Fort Fisher, North Carolina
Date of Action: 25 December 1864
Date of Issue: 28 March 1892
Citation: During the bombardment of the fort by the fleet, captured and brought the flag of the fort, the flagstaff having been shot down.

1413 ◆ WALSH, JOHN

Rank: Corporal
Service: U.S. Army
Birthday: 4 December 1841
Place of Birth: Tipperary, Ireland
Date of Death: 25 May 1924
Place of Death: Springfield, Massachusetts
Cemetery: St. Benedict's Cemetery—Springfield, Massachusetts
Entered Service at: Springfield, Hampden County, Massachusetts
Unit: Company D, 5th New York Cavalry
Battle or Place of Action: Cedar Creek, Virginia
Date of Action: 19 October 1864
Date of Issue: 26 October 1864
Citation: Recapture of the flag of the 15th New Jersey Infantry.
Notes: POW

1414 ◆ WALTON, GEORGE WASHINGTON

Rank: Private (highest rank: Sergeant)
Service: U.S. Army
Birthday: 27 March 1844
Place of Birth: Upper Oxford Township, Chester County, Pennsylvania
Date of Death: 8 February 1920
Place of Death: Oxford, Pennsylvania
Cemetery: Oxford Cemetery (MH)—Oxford, Pennsylvania
Entered Service at: Upper Oxford Township, Chester County, Pennsylvania
Unit: Company C, 97th Pennsylvania Infantry
Battle or Place of Action: Fort Hell, Petersberg, Virginia
Date of Action: 29 August 1864
Date of Issue: 6 August 1902
Citation: Went outside the trenches, under heavy fire at short-range, and rescued a comrade who had been wounded and thrown out of the trench by an exploding shell.

1415 ◆ WAMBSGAN, MARTIN

Rank: Private (highest rank: Sergeant)
Service: U.S. Army
Birthday: 19 August 1839
Place of Birth: Nusdorof, Bavaria, Germany
Date of Death: 3 May 1911
Place of Death: Baldwinsville, New York
Cemetery: Woodlawn Cemetery (MH)—Syracuse, New York
Entered Service at: Clyde, Wayne County, New York
Unit: Company D, 90th New York Infantry
Battle or Place of Action: Cedar Creek, Virginia
Date of Action: 19 October 1864
Date of Issue: 3 November 1896
Citation: While the enemy were in close proximity, this soldier sprang forward and bore off in safety the regimental colors, the color bearer having fallen on the field of battle.

1416 ◆ WARD, JAMES

Rank: Quarter Gunner (highest rank: Captain of the Forecastle)
Service: U.S. Navy
Birthday: 1833
Place of Birth: New York, New York
Entered Service at: New York, New York
Unit: U.S.S. *Lackawanna*
Battle or Place of Action: Fort Morgan, Mobile Bay, Alabama
Date of Action: 5 August 1864
G.O. Number, Date: 45, 31 December 1864
Citation: Served as gunner on board the U.S.S. *Lackawanna* during successful attacks against Fort Morgan, rebel gunboats, and the rebel ram *Tennessee* in Mobile Bay, 5 August 1864. Although wounded and ordered below, Ward refused to go, but rendered aid at one of the guns when the crew was disabled. He subsequently remained in the chains, heaving the lead, until nearly caught in the collision with the ram *Tennessee*. He continued to serve bravely throughout the action which resulted in the capture of the prize ram *Tennessee* and in the damaging and destruction of Fort Morgan.

1417 ◆ WARD, NELSON W.

Rank: Private (highest rank: Quartermaster Sergeant)
Service: U.S. Army
Birthday: 20 November 1837
Place of Birth: Madison Township, Columbiana County, Ohio
Date of Death: 5 February 1929
Place of Death: Long Beach, California
Cemetery: Sunnyside Cemetery—Long Beach, California
Entered Service at: Rutland, Meigs County, Ohio
Unit: Company M, 11th Pennsylvania Cavalry
Battle or Place of Action: Staunton River Bridge, Virginia
Date of Action: 25 June 1864
Date of Issue: 10 September 1897
Citation: Voluntarily took part in the charge; went alone in the front of his regiment under a heavy fire to secure the body of his captain, who had been killed in the action.

1418 ◆ WARD, THOMAS J.

Rank: Private (highest rank: Sergeant Major)
Service: U.S. Army
Birthday: 18 August 1837
Place of Birth: Romney, Hampshire County, West Virginia
Date of Death: 30 March 1924
Place of Death: Anaconda, Montana
Cemetery: Upper Hill Cemetery (MH)—Anaconda, Montana
Entered Service at: Decatur, Macon County, Illinois
Unit: Company C, 116th Illinois Infantry
Battle or Place of Action: Vicksburg, Mississippi
Date of Action: 22 May 1863
Date of Issue: 27 July 1894

1419 ◆ WARD, WILLIAM HENRY

Rank: Captain
Service: U.S. Army
Birthday: 9 December 1840
Place of Birth: Adrian, Lenawee County, Michigan
Date of Death: 11 April 1927
Place of Death: Kansas City, Kansas
Cemetery: Highland Park Cemetery (MH)—Kansas City, Kansas
Entered Service at: Adrian, Lenawee County, Michigan
Unit: Company B, 47th Ohio Infantry
Battle or Place of Action: Vicksburg, Mississippi
Date of Action: 3 May 1863
Date of Issue: 2 January 1895
Citation: Voluntarily commanded the expedition which, under cover of darkness, attempted to run the enemy's batteries.

1420 ◆ WARDEN, JOHN

Rank: Corporal (highest rank: First Lieutenant)
Service: U.S. Army
Birthday: 11 June 1841
Place of Birth: Cook County, Illinois
Date of Death: 2 July 1906
Place of Death: Sumner, Washington
Cemetery: Orting Cemetery—Orting, Washington
Entered Service at: Lemont, Du Page County, Illinois
Unit: Company E, 55th Illinois Infantry
tle or Place of Action: Vicksburg, Mississippi
Date of Action: 22 May 1863
Date of Issue: 2 September 1893
Citation: Gallantry in the charge of the "volunteer storming party."

1421 ◆ WARFEL, HENRY CLAY

Rank: Private
Service: U.S. Army
Birthday: 14 September 1844
Place of Birth: Mill Creek, Huntingdon County, Pennsylvania
Date of Death: 17 June 1923
Place of Death: Philipsburg, Pennsylvania
Cemetery: Philipsburg Cemetery (MH)—Philipsburg, Pennsylvania
Entered Service at: Monocacy Junction, Maryland
Unit: Company A, 1st Pennsylvania Cavalry
Battle or Place of Action: Paine's Crossroads, Virginia
Date of Action: 5 April 1865
Date of Issue: 3 May 1865
Citation: Capture of Virginia state colors.

1422 ◆ WARREN, DAVID

Rank: Coxswain
Service: U.S. Navy
Birthday: 1836
Place of Birth: Glasgow, Scotland
Date of Death: 2 August 1900
Place of Death: Hampton, Virginia
Cemetery: Hampton National Cemetery (C-7972) (MH)—Hampton, Virginia
Entered Service at: New York, New York
Unit: U.S.S. *Monticello*
Battle or Place of Action: Wilmington, North Carolina
Date of Action: 23-25 June 1864
G.O. Number, Date: 45, 31 December 1864
Citation: Served as coxswain on board the U.S.S. *Monticello* during the reconnaissance of the harbor and water defenses of Wilmington, N.C., 23 to 25 June 1864. Taking part in a reconnaissance of the enemy defenses which lasted two days and nights, Warren courageously carried out his duties during this action which resulted in the capture of a mail carrier and mail, the cutting of the telegraph wire, and the capture of a large group of prisoners. Although in immediate danger from the enemy, Warren showed gallantry and coolness throughout this action which resulted in the gaining of much vital information of the rebel defenses.

1423 ◆ WARREN, FRANCIS EMROY

Rank: Corporal
Service: U.S. Army
Birthday: 20 June 1844
Place of Birth: Hinsdale, Berkshire County, Massachusetts
Date of Death: 24 November 1929
Place of Death: Washington, D.C.
Cemetery: Lake View Cemetery (MH)—Cheyenne, Wyoming
Entered Service at: Hinsdale, Berkshire County, Massachusetts
Unit: Company C, 49th Massachusetts Infantry
Battle or Place of Action: Port Hudson, Louisiana
Date of Action: 27 May 1863
Date of Issue: 30 September 1893
Citation: Volunteered in response to a call, and took part in the movement that was made upon the enemy's works under a heavy fire therefrom in advance of the general assault.

1424 ◆ WEBB, ALEXANDER STEWART

Rank: Brigadier General (highest rank: Major General U.S.A.)
Service: U.S. Army
Birthday: 15 February 1835
Place of Birth: New York, New York
Date of Death: 12 February 1911
Place of Death: Riverdale, New York
Cemetery: U.S. Military Academy Cemetery (M-18)—West Point, New York
Entered Service at: New York, New York
Unit: U.S. Volunteers
Battle or Place of Action: Gettysburg, Pennsylvania
Date of Action: 3 July 1863
Date of Issue: 28 September 1891

Citation: Distinguished personal gallantry in leading his men forward at a critical period in the contest.

1425 ◆ WEBB, JAMES W.

Rank: Private (highest rank: Brevet Captain)
Service: U.S. Army
Birthday: 2 September 1841
Place of Birth: Brooklyn, Kings County, New York
Date of Death: 7 June 1915
Place of Death: Brooklyn, New York
Cemetery: Cypress Hills Cemetery (2-7410) (MH)—Brooklyn, New York
Entered Service at: New York, New York
Unit: Company F, 5th New York Infantry
Battle or Place of Action: Bull Run, Virginia
Date of Action: 30 August 1862
Date of Issue: 17 September 1897
Citation: Under heavy fire voluntarily carried information to a battery commander that enabled him to save his guns from capture. Was severely wounded, but refused to go to the hospital and participated in the remainder of the campaign.

1426 ◆ WEBBER, ALASON P.

True Name: Webber, Alanson P.
Rank: Musician (highest rank: Principal Musician)
Service: U.S. Army
Birthday: 16 March 1828
Place of Birth: Greene County, New York
Date of Death: 27 July 1902
Cemetery: Saratoga Cemetery—Henry, Illinois
Entered Service at: Chillicothe, Ross County, Ohio
Unit: 86th Illinois Infantry
Battle or Place of Action: Kenesaw Mountain, Georgia
Date of Action: 27 June 1864
Date of Issue: 22 June 1896
Citation: Voluntarily joined in a charge against the enemy, which was repulsed, and by his rapid firing in the face of the enemy enabled many of the wounded to return to the Federal lines; with others, held the advance of the enemy while temporary works were being constructed.

1427 ◆ WEBSTER, HENRY S.

Rank: Landsman
Service: U.S. Navy
Birthday: 7 January 1845
Place of Birth: Stockholm, New York
Date of Death: 2 July 1910
Place of Death: Brattleboro, Vermont
Cemetery: Cedar Grove Cemetery—Fairhaven, Vermont
Entered Service at: Brooklyn, Kings County, New York
Unit: U.S.S. *Susquehanna*
Battle or Place of Action: Fort Fisher, North Carolina
Date of Action: 15 January 1865
G.O. Number, Date: 59, 22 June 1865
Citation: On board the U.S.S. *Susquehanna* during the assault on Fort Fisher, 15 January 1865. When enemy fire halted the attempt by his landing party to enter the fort and more than two-thirds of the men fell back along the open beach, Webster voluntarily remained with one of his wounded officers, under fire, until aid could be obtained to bring him to the rear.

1428 ◆ WEEKS, CHARLES H.

Rank: Captain of the Foretop
Service: U.S. Navy
Birthday: 1837
Place of Birth: New Jersey
Entered Service at: New Jersey
Unit: U.S.S. *Montauk*
Battle or Place of Action: off Port Royal, South Carolina
Date of Action: 21 September 1864
G.O. Number, Date: 84, 3 October 1867
Citation: Served as captain of the foretop on board the U.S.S. *Montauk*, 21 September 1864. During the night of 21 September, when fire was discovered in the magazine lightroom of that vessel, causing a panic and demoralizing the crew, Weeks, notwithstanding the cry of "fire in the magazine," displayed great presence of mind and rendered valuable service in extinguishing the flames which were imperiling the ship and the men on board.

1429 ◆ WEEKS, JOHN HENRY

Rank: Private
Service: U.S. Army
Birthday: 15 March 1845
Place of Birth: Hampton, Windham County, Connecticut
Date of Death: 10 March 1911
Cemetery: Hartwick Seminary Cemetery (MH)—Hartwick Seminary, New York
Entered Service at: Hartwick Seminary, Oswego County, New York
Unit: Company H, 152d New York Infantry
Battle or Place of Action: Spotsylvania, Virginia
Date of Action: 12 May 1864
Date of Issue: 1 December 1864
Citation: Capture of flag and color bearer using an empty cocked rifle while outnumbered by five or six.

1430 ◆ WEIR, HENRY CARY

Rank: Captain & Assistant Adjutant General (highest rank: Brevet Lieutenant Colonel)
Service: U.S. Army
Birthday: 22 August 1840
Place of Birth: West Point, Orange County, New York
Date of Death: 22 April 1927
Place of Death: Warwick, New York
Cemetery: The Green Wood Cemetery—Brooklyn, New York
Entered Service at: Bolivar, West Virginia
Unit: U.S. Volunteers
Battle or Place of Action: St. Mary's Church, Virginia
Date of Action: 24 June 1864
Date of Issue: 18 May 1899
Citation: The division being hard-pressed and falling back,

this officer dismounted, gave his horse to a wounded officer, and thus enabled him to escape. Afterwards, on foot, Capt. Weir rallied and took command of some stragglers and helped to repel the last charge of the enemy.

1431 ◆ WELCH, GEORGE W.

Rank: Private
Service: U.S. Army
Place of Birth: Brown County, Iowa
Entered Service at: Keokuk, Lee County, Iowa
Unit: Company A, 11th Missouri Infantry
Battle or Place of Action: Nashville, Tennessee
Date of Action: 16 December 1864
Date of Issue: 24 February 1865
Citation: Captured the flag of the 13th Alabama Infantry (C.S.A.).

1432 ◆ WELCH, RICHARD

Rank: Corporal (highest rank: Sergeant)
Service: U.S. Army
Birthday: 1828
Place of Birth: Ireland
Date of Death: 13 March 1894
Place of Death: Williamstown, Massachusetts
Cemetery: Eastlawn Cemetery (MH)—Williamstown, Massachusetts
Entered Service at: Williamstown, Berkshire County, Massachusetts
Unit: Company E, 37th Massachusetts Infantry
Battle or Place of Action: Petersburg, Virginia
Date of Action: 2 April 1865
Date of Issue: 10 May 1865
Citation: Capture of flag.

1433 ◆ WELCH, STEPHEN

Rank: Sergeant (highest rank: Captain)
Service: U.S. Army
Birthday: 14 June 1824
Place of Birth: Groton, Tompkins County, New York
Date of Death: 30 March 1906
Cemetery: Allegany Cemetery—Allegany, New York
Entered Service at: Allegany, Cattaraugus County, New York
Unit: Company C, 154th New York Infantry
Battle or Place of Action: Dug Gap, Georgia
Date of Action: 8 May 1864
Date of Issue: 13 April 1894
Citation: Risked his life in rescuing a wounded comrade under fire of the enemy.

1434 ◆ *WELLS, HENRY S.

Rank: Private
Service: U.S. Army
Birthday: 1842
Date of Death: 27 October 1864
Place of Death: Fair Oaks, Virginia

Entered Service at: Phelps, Ontario County, New York
Unit: Company C, 148th New York Infantry
Battle or Place of Action: Chapin's Farm, Virginia
Date of Action: 29 September 1864
Date of Issue: 6 April 1865
Citation: With two comrades, took position in advance of the skirmish line, within short distance of the enemy's gunners, and drove them from their guns.
Notes: POW

1435 ◆ WELLS, THOMAS MCCOY

Rank: Chief Bugler (highest rank: First Lieutenant)
Service: U.S. Army
Birthday: 1841
Place of Birth: Ather, Ireland
Date of Death: 5 February 1901
Place of Death: Canton, New York
Cemetery: East Dekalb Cemetery—Dekalb, New York
Entered Service at: DeKalb, St. Lawrence County, New York
Unit: 6th New York Cavalry
Battle or Place of Action: Cedar Creek, Virginia
Date of Action: 19 October 1864
Date of Issue: 26 October 1864
Citation: Capture of colors of 44th Georgia Infantry (C.S.A.).

1436 ◆ WELLS, WILLIAM

Rank: Quartermaster
Service: U.S. Navy
Birthday: 1832
Place of Birth: Germany
Entered Service at: New York, New York
Unit: U.S.S. *Richmond*
Battle or Place of Action: Fort Morgan, Mobile Bay, Alabama
Date of Action: 5 August 1864
G.O. Number, Date: 45, 31 December 1864
Place of Presentation: Lisbon, on board the U.S.S. *Colorado*
Citation: As landsman and lookout on board the U.S.S. *Richmond* during action against rebel forts and gunboats and with the ram *Tennessee* in Mobile Bay, 5 August 1864. Despite damage to his ship and the loss of several men on board as enemy fire raked her decks, Wells performed his duties with skill and courage throughout a furious two-hour battle which resulted in the surrender of the rebel ram *Tennessee* and in the damaging and destruction of batteries at Fort Morgan.

1437 ◆ WELLS, WILLIAM

Rank: Major (highest rank: Brevet Major General)
Service: U.S. Army
Birthday: 14 December 1837
Place of Birth: Waterbury, Washington County, Vermont
Date of Death: 29 April 1892

Place of Death: New York, New York
Cemetery: Lakeview Cemetery—Burlington, Vermont
Entered Service at: Waterbury, Washington County, Vermont
Unit: 2d Battalion, 1st Vermont Cavalry
Battle or Place of Action: Gettysburg, Pennsylvania
Date of Action: 3 July 1863
Date of Issue: 8 September 1891
Citation: Led the second battalion of his regiment in a daring charge.
Notes: POW

1438 ◆ WELSH, EDWARD

Rank: Private (highest rank: Sergeant)
Service: U.S. Army
Birthday: 3 January 1843
Place of Birth: Ireland
Date of Death: 1 February 1929
Place of Death: Soldier's Home, Washington, D.C.
Cemetery: Mount Olivet Cemetery—Washington, D.C.
Entered Service at: Cincinnati, Hamilton County, Ohio
Unit: Company D, 54th Ohio Infantry
Battle or Place of Action: Vicksburg, Mississippi
Date of Action: 22 May 1863
Date of Issue: 11 May 1894
Citation: Gallantry in the charge of the "volunteer storming party."

1439 ◆ WELSH, JAMES

Rank: Private
Service: U.S. Army
Birthday: 11 May 1846
Place of Birth: Ireland
Date of Death: 17 December 1916
Place of Death: Elizabeth City, Virginia
Entered Service at: Slatersville, Providence County, Rhode Island
Unit: Company E, 4th Rhode Island Infantry
Battle or Place of Action: Petersburg, Virginia
Date of Action: 30 July 1864
Date of Issue: 3 June 1905
Citation: Bore off the regimental colors after the color sergeant had been wounded and the color corporal bearing the colors killed, thereby saving the colors from capture.

1440 ◆ WESTERHOLD, WILLIAM

Rank: Sergeant (highest rank: First Lieutenant)
Service: U.S. Army
Birthday: 21 January 1836
Place of Birth: Binde, Prussia
Date of Death: 12 May 1910
Place of Death: New York, New York
Entered Service at: New York, New York
Unit: Company G, 52d New York Infantry
Battle or Place of Action: Spotsylvania, Virginia
Date of Action: 12 May 1864
Date of Issue: 1 December 1864
Citation: Capture of flag of 23d Virginia Infantry (C.S.A.) and its bearer.

1441 ◆ WESTON, JOHN FRANCIS

Rank: Major (highest rank: Major General)
Service: U.S. Army
Birthday: 13 November 1845
Place of Birth: Louisville, Jefferson County, Kentucky
Date of Death: 3 August 1917
Place of Death: Briarcliff Manor, New York
Cemetery: Arlington National Cemetery (2-856)—Arlington, Virginia
Entered Service at: Camp Anderson, Kentucky
Unit: 4th Kentucky Cavalry
Battle or Place of Action: Wetumpka, Alabama
Date of Action: 13 April 1865
Date of Issue: 9 April 1898
Citation: This officer, with a small detachment, while en route to destroy steamboats loaded with supplies for the enemy, was stopped by an unfordable river, but with five of his men swam the river, captured two leaky canoes, and ferried his men across. He then encountered and defeated the enemy, and on reaching Wetumpka found the steamers anchored in midstream. By a ruse obtained possession of a boat, with which he reached the steamers and demanded and received their surrender.

1442 ◆ WHEATON, LOYD

Rank: Lieutenant Colonel (highest rank: Major General)
Service: U.S. Army
Birthday: 15 July 1838
Place of Birth: Penfield, Michigan
Date of Death: 17 September 1918
Cemetery: Greenwood Cemetery—Rockford, Illinois
Entered Service at: Peoria, Peoria County, Illinois
Unit: 8th Illinois Infantry
Battle or Place of Action: Fort Blakely, Alabama
Date of Action: 9 April 1865
Date of Issue: 16 January 1894
Citation: Led the right wing of his regiment, and, springing through an embrasure, was the first to enter the enemy's works, against a strong fire of artillery and infantry.

1443 ◆ WHEELER, DANIEL DAVIS

Rank: First Lieutenant (highest rank: Brigadier General Ret.)
Service: U.S. Army
Birthday: 12 July 1841
Place of Birth: Cavendish, Windsor County, Vermont
Date of Death: 27 July 1916
Place of Death: Fredericksburg, Virginia
Cemetery: Fredericksburg City Cemetery—Fredericksburg, Virginia
Entered Service at: Cavendish, Windsor County, Vermont
Unit: Company G, 4th Vermont Infantry
Battle or Place of Action: Salem Heights, Virginia

1444 ◆ WHEELER, HENRY W.

Date of Action: 3 May 1863
Date of Issue: 28 March 1892
Citation: Distinguished bravery in action where he was wounded and had a horse shot from under him.

1444 ◆ WHEELER, HENRY W.

Rank: Private (highest rank: Brevet Captain, U.S. Volunteers)
Service: U.S. Army
Birthday: 23 September 1841
Place of Birth: Fort Smith, Sebastian County, Arkansas
Date of Death: 18 April 1904
Cemetery: Arlington National Cemetery (3-1496)—Arlington, Virginia
Entered Service at: Bangor, Penobscot County, Maine
Unit: Company A, 2d Maine Infantry
Battle or Place of Action: Bull Run, Virginia
Date of Action: 21 July 1861
Date of Issue: 5 April 1898
Citation: Voluntarily accompanied his commanding officer and assisted in removing the dead and wounded from the field under a heavy fire of artillery and musketry.

1445 ◆ WHERRY, WILLIAM MACKY

Rank: First Lieutenant (highest rank: Brigadier General USA)
Service: U.S. Army
Birthday: 13 September 1836
Place of Birth: St. Louis, St. Louis County, Missouri
Date of Death: 3 November 1918
Place of Death: Cincinnati, Ohio
Cemetery: Bellefontaine Cemetery—St. Louis, Missouri
Entered Service at: St. Louis, St. Louis County, Missouri
Unit: Company D, 3d U.S. Reserve Missouri Infantry
Battle or Place of Action: Wilson's Creek, Missouri
Date of Action: 10 August 1861
Date of Issue: 30 October 1895
Citation: Displayed conspicuous coolness and heroism in rallying troops that were recoiling under heavy fire.

1446 ◆ WHITAKER, EDWARD WASHBURN

Rank: Captain (highest rank: Brigadier General, U.S. Volunteers)
Service: U.S. Army
Birthday: 15 June 1841
Place of Birth: Killingly, Connecticut
Date of Death: 30 July 1922
Place of Death: Washington, D.C.
Cemetery: Arlington National Cemetery (3-1324)—Arlington, Virginia
Entered Service at: Hartford, Hartford County, Connecticut
Unit: Company E, 1st Connecticut Cavalry
Battle or Place of Action: Reams' Station, Virginia
Date of Action: 29 June 1864
Date of Issue: 2 April 1898
Citation: While acting as an aide, voluntarily carried dispatches from the commanding general to Gen. Meade, forcing his way with a single troop of cavalry, through an infantry division of the enemy in the most distinguished manner, though he lost half his escort.

1447 ◆ WHITE, ADAM

Rank: Corporal
Service: U.S. Army
Birthday: 21 December 1823
Place of Birth: Switzerland
Date of Death: 19 May 1895
Place of Death: Tyner, West Virginia
Cemetery: Wadesville Cemetery—Wadesville, West Virginia
Entered Service at: Parkersburg, Wood County, West Virginia
Unit: Company G, 11th West Virginia Infantry
Battle or Place of Action: Hatcher's Run, Virginia
Date of Action: 2 April 1865
Date of Issue: 13 June 1865
Citation: Capture of flag.

1448 ◆ WHITE, JOHN HENRY

Rank: Private
Service: U.S. Army
Birthday: 1 March 1835
Place of Birth: Philadelphia, Philadelphia County, Pennsylvania
Date of Death: 27 April 1912
Place of Death: Darby, Pennsylvania
Entered Service at: Philadelphia, Philadelphia County, Pennsylvania
Unit: Company A, 90th Pennsylvania Infantry
Battle or Place of Action: Rappahannock Station, Virginia
Date of Action: 23 August 1862
Date of Issue: 5 May 1900
Citation: At the imminent risk of his life, crawled to a nearby spring within the enemy's range and, exposed to constant fire, filled a large number of canteens, and returned in safety to the relief of his comrades who were suffering from want of water.
Notes: POW

1449 ◆ WHITE, JOSEPH

Rank: Coxswain
Service: U.S. Navy
Birthday: 1840
Place of Birth: Washington, D.C.
Entered Service at: Philadelphia, Philadelphia County, Pennsylvania
Unit: U.S.S. *New Ironsides*
Battle or Place of Action: Fort Fisher, North Carolina
Date of Action: December 1864 & January 1865
G.O. Number, Date: 59, 22 June 1865
Citation: White served on board the U.S.S. *New Ironsides* during action in several attacks on Fort Fisher, 24 and 25 December 1864; and 13, 14 and 15 January 1865. The ship steamed in and took the lead in the ironclad division close inshore and immediately opened its starboard battery in a barrage of well-directed fire to cause several fires and explosions and dismount several guns during the first two days of fight-

ing. Taken under fire as she steamed into position on 13 January, the *New Ironsides* fought all day and took on ammunition at night, despite severe weather conditions. When the enemy came out of their bombproofs to defend the fort against the storming party, the ship's battery disabled nearly every gun on the fort facing the shore before the cease-fire order was given by the flagship.

1450 ◆ WHITE, PATRICK H.

Rank: Captain
Service: U.S. Army
Birthday: 1 June 1832
Place of Birth: County Sligo, Ireland
Date of Death: 25 November 1915
Place of Death: Albany, New York
Cemetery: St. Agnes Cemetery—Menands, New York
Entered Service at: Chicago, Cook County, Illinois
Unit: Chicago Mercantile Battery, Illinois Light Artillery
Battle or Place of Action: Vicksburg, Mississippi
Date of Action: 22 May 1863
Date of Issue: 15 January 1895
Citation: Carried with others by hand a cannon up to and fired it through an embrasure of the enemy's works.
Notes: POW

1451 ◆ WHITEHEAD, JOHN MILTON

Rank: Chaplain
Service: U.S. Army
Birthday: 6 March 1823
Place of Birth: Wayne County, Indiana
Date of Death: 8 March 1909
Place of Death: Topeka, Kansas
Cemetery: Topeka Cemetery (MH)—Topeka, Kansas
Entered Service at: Westville, La Porte County, Indiana
Unit: 15th Indiana Infantry
Battle or Place of Action: Stone River, Tennessee
Date of Action: 31 December 1862
Date of Issue: 4 April 1898
Citation: Went to the front during a desperate contest and unaided carried to the rear several wounded and helpless soldiers.

1452 ◆ WHITFIELD, DANIEL

Rank: Quartermaster
Service: U.S. Navy
Birthday: 1821
Place of Birth: Newark, Essex County, New Jersey
Entered Service at: New Jersey
Unit: U.S.S. *Lackawanna*
Battle or Place of Action: Fort Morgan, Mobile Bay, Alabama
Date of Action: 5 August 1864
G.O. Number, Date: 45, 31 December 1864
Citation: Serving as quartermaster on board the U.S.S. *Lackawanna* during successful attacks against Fort Morgan, rebel gunboats, and the rebel ram *Tennessee* in Mobile Bay, 5 August 1864. Acting as captain of a gun, Whitfield coolly stood by his gun, holding on to the lock string, and waited alongside the rebel ram *Tennessee* until able to fire the shot that entered her port. Whitfield courageously carried out his duties during the prolonged action which resulted in the capture of the prize ram *Tennessee* and in the damaging and destruction of Fort Morgan.

1453 ◆ WHITMAN, FRANK M.

Rank: Private (highest rank: Sergeant)
Service: U.S. Army
Birthday: 30 September 1838
Place of Birth: Woodstock, Maine
Date of Death: 9 July 1918
Place of Death: Boston, Massachusetts
Cemetery: Riverview Cemetery—Groveland, Massachusetts
Entered Service at: Ayersville, Massachusetts
Unit: Company G, 35th Massachusetts Infantry
Battle or Place of Action: Antietam, Maryland
Date of Action: 17 September 1862
Date of Issue: 21 February 1874
Citation: Was among the last to leave the field at Antietam and was instrumental in saving the lives of several of his comrades at the imminent risk of his own. At Spotsylvania was foremost in line in the assault, where he lost a leg.

1454 ◆ WHITMORE, JOHN W.

Rank: Private
Service: U.S. Army
Birthday: 3 July 1844
Place of Birth: Brown County, Illinois
Date of Death: 26 February 1913
Place of Death: New London, Iowa
Cemetery: Shiner Cemetery—New London, Iowa
Entered Service at: Camden, Schuyler County, Illinois
Unit: Company F, 119th Illinois Infantry
Battle or Place of Action: Fort Blakely, Alabama
Date of Action: 9 April 1865
Date of Issue: 8 June 1865
Citation: Capture of flag.

1455 ◆ WHITNEY, WILLIAM G.

Rank: Sergeant (highest rank: Captain)
Service: U.S. Army
Birthday: 13 December 1840
Place of Birth: Allen, Hillsdale County, Michigan
Date of Death: 7 May 1915
Place of Death: Allen, Michigan
Cemetery: Allen Cemetery—Allen, Michigan
Entered Service at: Quincy, Branch County, Michigan
Unit: Company B, 11th Michigan Infantry
Battle or Place of Action: Chickamauga, Georgia
Date of Action: 20 September 1863
Date of Issue: 21 October 1895
Citation: As the enemy were about to charge, this officer went outside the temporary Union works among the dead and wounded enemy and at great exposure to himself cut off and removed their cartridge boxes, bringing the same within the Union lines, the ammunition being used with good effect in again repulsing the attack.

1456 ◆ WHITTIER, EDWARD NEWTON

Rank: First Lieutenant (highest rank: Captain)
Service: U.S. Army
Birthday: 1 July 1840
Place of Birth: Portland, Cumberland County, Maine
Date of Death: 14 June 1902
Place of Death: Boston, Massachusetts
Cemetery: Pierce Family Grave Yard (MH)—Baldwin, Maine
Entered Service at: Gorham, Cumberland County, Maine
Unit: 5th Battery, Maine Light Artillery
Battle or Place of Action: Fisher's Hill, Virginia
Date of Action: 22 September 1864
Date of Issue: 13 January 1892
Citation: While acting as assistant adjutant general, Artillery Brigade, 6th Army Corps, went over the enemy's works, mounted, with the assaulting column, to gain quicker possession of the guns and to turn them upon the enemy.

1457 ◆ WIDICK, ANDREW J.

Rank: Private
Service: U.S. Army
Birthday: 27 March 1842
Place of Birth: Macon County, Illinois
Date of Death: 24 January 1929
Place of Death: Bertrand, Nebraska
Cemetery: Bertrand Cemetery (MH)—Bertrand, Nebraska
Entered Service at: Decatur, Macon County, Illinois
Unit: Company B, 116th Illinois Infantry
Battle or Place of Action: Vicksburg, Mississippi
Date of Action: 22 May 1863
Date of Issue: 11 August 1894
Citation: Gallantry in the charge of the "volunteer storming party."

1458 ◆ WILCOX, FRANKLIN L.

Rank: Ordinary Seaman
Service: U.S. Navy
Birthday: November 1830
Place of Birth: Paris, Oneida County, New York
Date of Death: 16 November 1898
Place of Death: Grand Rapids (Soldier's Home), Michigan
Cemetery: Michigan Veterans Cemetery—Grand Rapids, Michigan
Entered Service at: New York
Unit: U.S.S. *Minnesota*
Battle or Place of Action: Fort Fisher, North Carolina
Date of Action: 15 January 1865
G.O. Number, Date: 59, 22 June 1865
Citation: On board the U.S.S. *Minnesota* in action during the assault on Fort Fisher, 15 January 1865. Landing on the beach with the assaulting party from his ship, Wilcox advanced to the top of the sandhill and partly through the breach in the palisades, despite enemy fire which killed and wounded many officers and men. When more than two-thirds of the men became seized with panic and retreated on the run, he remained with the party until dark when it came safely away, bringing its wounded, its arms and its colors.

1459 ◆ WILCOX, WILLIAM H.

Rank: Sergeant
Service: U.S. Army
Birthday: 12 November 1840
Place of Birth: Lempster, Sullivan County, New Hampshire
Date of Death: 27 October 1913
Place of Death: Kalamazoo, Michigan
Cemetery: Lake View Cemetery—South Haven, Michigan
Entered Service at: Lempster, Sullivan County, New Hampshire
Unit: Company G, 9th New Hampshire Infantry
Battle or Place of Action: Spotsylvania, Virginia
Date of Action: 12 May 1864
Date of Issue: 28 July 1896
Citation: Took command of his company, deployed as skirmishers, after the officers in the command of the skirmish line had both been wounded, conducting himself gallantly; afterwards, becoming separated from command, he asked and obtained permission to fight in another company.

1460 ◆ *WILEY, JAMES

Rank: Sergeant
Service: U.S. Army
Birthday: 1835
Place of Birth: Ohio
Date of Death: 7 February 1865
Place of Death: Andersonville, Georgia
Cemetery: Andersonville National Historical Site (H-10607) (MH)—Andersonville, Georgia
Entered Service at: Bellville, Richland County, Ohio
Unit: Company B, 59th New York Infantry
Battle or Place of Action: Gettysburg, Pennsylvania
Date of Action: 3 July 1863
Date of Issue: 1 December 1864
Citation: Capture of flag of a Georgia regiment.

1461 ◆ WILHELM, GEORGE

Rank: Captain (highest rank: Lieutenant Colonel)
Service: U.S. Army
Birthday: 2 April 1829
Place of Birth: Scioto County, Ohio
Date of Death: 20 August 1920
Place of Death: Dayton, Ohio
Cemetery: Greenville Cemetery—Greenville, Mississippi
Entered Service at: Lancaster, Fairfield County, Ohio
Unit: Company F, 56th Ohio Infantry
Battle or Place of Action: Champion Hill or Baker's Creek, Mississippi
Date of Action: 16 May 1863
Date of Issue: 17 November 1887
Citation: Having been badly wounded in the breast and captured, he made a prisoner of his captor and brought him into camp.

1462 ◆ WILKES, HENRY

Rank: Landsman
Service: U.S. Navy

Birthday: 1845
Place of Birth: New York, New York
Date of Death: 3 March 1888
Place of Death: Rensselaer, New York
Cemetery: Beverwyck Cemetery (MH)—Rensselaer, New York
Entered Service at: New York, New York
Unit: U.S. Picket Boat No. 1
Battle or Place of Action: Plymouth, North Carolina
Date of Action: 27 October 1864
G.O. Number, Date: 45, 31 December 1864
Citation: Wilkes served on board the U.S. Picket Boat No. 1 in action, 27 October 1864, against the Confederate ram, *Albemarle*, which had resisted repeated attacks by our steamers and had kept a large force of vessels employed in watching her. The picket boat, equipped with a spar torpedo, succeeded in passing the enemy pickets within 20 yards without being discovered and then made for the *Albemarle* under a full head of steam. Immediately taken under fire by the ram, the small boat plunged on, jumped the log boom which encircled the target and exploded its torpedo under the port bow of the ram. The picket boat was destroyed by enemy fire and almost the entire crew taken prisoner or lost.
Notes: POW

1463 ◆ WILKES, PERRY

Rank: Pilot
Service: U.S. Navy
Birthday: 6 June 1830
Place of Birth: Indiana
Date of Death: 19 March 1889
Place of Death: Louisville, Kentucky
Cemetery: Cave Hill Cemetery South One-Half-866 Section P, (MH)—Louisville, Kentucky
Entered Service at: Jeffersonville, Clark County, Indiana
Unit: U.S.S. *Signal*
Battle or Place of Action: Red River, Louisiana
Date of Action: 5 May 1864
G.O. Number, Date: 45, 31 December 1864
Citation: Served as pilot on board the U.S.S. *Signal*, Red River, 5 May 1864. Proceeding up the Red River, the U.S.S. *Signal* engaged a large force of enemy field batteries and sharpshooters, returning their fire until the ship was totally disabled, at which time the white flag was ordered raised. Acting as pilot throughout the battle, Wilkes stood by his wheel until it was disabled in his hands by a bursting enemy shell.

1464 ◆ WILKINS, LEANDER A.

Rank: Sergeant
Service: U.S. Army
Place of Birth: Lancaster, Coos County, New Hampshire
Entered Service at: Northumberland, New Hampshire
Unit: Company H, 9th New Hampshire Infantry
Battle or Place of Action: Petersburg, Virginia
Date of Action: 30 July 1864
Date of Issue: 1 December 1864
Citation: Recaptured the colors of 21st Massachusetts Infantry in a hand-to-hand encounter.

1465 ◆ WILLCOX, ORLANDO BOLIVAR

Rank: Colonel (highest rank: Major General)
Service: U.S. Army
Birthday: 16 April 1823
Place of Birth: Detroit, Wayne County, Michigan
Date of Death: 10 May 1907
Place of Death: Ontario, Canada
Cemetery: Arlington National Cemetery (1-18)—Arlington, Virginia
Entered Service at: Detroit, Wayne County, Michigan
Unit: 1st Michigan Infantry
Battle or Place of Action: Bull Run, Virginia
Date of Action: 21 July 1861
Date of Issue: 2 March 1895
Citation: Led repeated charges until wounded and taken prisoner.
Notes: POW

1466 ◆ WILLIAMS, ANTHONY

Rank: Sailmaker's Mate
Service: U.S. Navy
Birthday: 1822
Place of Birth: Plymouth, Plymouth County, Massachusetts
Entered Service at: Portsmouth, Maine
Unit: U.S.S. *Pontoosuc*
Battle or Place of Action: Fort Fisher and Wilmington, North Carolina
Date of Action: 24 December 1864
G.O. Number, Date: 59, 22 June 1865
Citation: Served as sailmaker's mate on board the U.S.S. *Pontoosuc* during the capture of Fort Fisher and Wilmington, 24 December 1864 to 22 February 1865. Carrying out his duties faithfully throughout this period, Williams was recommended for gallantry and skill and for his cool courage while under the fire of the enemy throughout these various actions.

1467 ◆ WILLIAMS, AUGUSTUS

Rank: Seaman
Service: U.S. Navy
Birthday: 1842
Place of Birth: Kristiansand, Norway
Entered Service at: Massachusetts
Unit: U.S.S. *Santiago de Cuba*
Battle or Place of Action: Fort Fisher, North Carolina
Date of Action: 15 January 1865
G.O. Number, Date: 59, 22 June 1865
Citation: On board the U.S.S. *Santiago de Cuba* during the assault by the fleet on Fort Fisher, 15 January 1865. When the landing party to which he was attached charged on the fort with a cheer, and with determination to plant their colors on the ramparts, Williams remained steadfast when they reached the foot of the fort and more than two-thirds of the marines and sailors fell back in panic. Taking cover when the enemy concentrated his fire on the remainder of the group, he alone remained with his executive officer, subsequently withdrawing from the field after dark.

1468 ♦ WILLIAMS, ELWOOD N.

Rank: Private
Service: U.S. Army
Birthday: 11 November 1842
Place of Birth: Philadelphia, Philadelphia County, Pennsylvania
Date of Death: 8 March 1921
Place of Death: Philadelphia, Pennsylvania
Entered Service at: Havana, Mason County, Illinois
Unit: Company A, 28th Illinois Infantry
Battle or Place of Action: Shiloh, Tennessee
Date of Action: 6 April 1862
Date of Issue: 28 September 1897
Citation: A box of ammunition having been abandoned between the lines, this soldier voluntarily went forward with one companion, under a heavy fire from both armies, secured the box, and delivered it within the lines of his regiment, his companion being mortally wounded.

1469 ♦ WILLIAMS, GEORGE C.

Rank: Quartermaster Sergeant
Service: U.S. Army
Birthday: 9 December 1839
Place of Birth: England
Date of Death: 14 November 1926
Place of Death: New London, Connecticut
Cemetery: Cedar Grove Cemetery (MH)—New London, Connecticut
Entered Service at: New London, New London County, Connecticut
Unit: 14th U.S. Infantry, 1st Battalion
Battle or Place of Action: Gaines' Mill, Virginia
Date of Action: 27 June 1862
Date of Issue: 28 August 1897
Citation: While on duty with the wagon train as quartermaster sergeant he voluntarily left his place of safety in the rear, joined a company, and fought with distinguished gallantry through the action.

1470 ♦ WILLIAMS, JOHN

Rank: Captain of the Maintop (highest rank: Master's Mate)
Service: U.S. Navy
Birthday: 1828
Place of Birth: New Orleans, Orleans County, Louisiana
Entered Service at: Louisiana
Unit: U.S.S. *Pawnee*
Battle or Place of Action: Matthias Point, Virginia
Date of Action: 26 June 1861
G.O. Number, Date: 11, 3 April 1863
Citation: Served as captain of the maintop of the U.S.S. *Pawnee* in the attack upon Mathias Point, 26 June 1861, Williams told his men, while lying off in the boat, that every man must die on his thwart sooner than leave a man behind. Although wounded by a musket ball in the thigh he retained the charge of his boat; and when the staff was shot away, held the stump in his hand, with the flag, until alongside the *Freeborn*.

1471 ♦ WILLIAMS, JOHN

Rank: Seaman
Service: U.S. Navy
Birthday: 1832
Place of Birth: Blair County, Pennsylvania
Entered Service at: Pennsylvania
Unit: U.S.S. *Commodore Perry*
Battle or Place of Action: Franklin, Virginia
Date of Action: 3 October 1862
G.O. Number, Date: 11, 3 April 1863
Citation: On board the U.S.S. *Commodore Perry* in the attack upon Franklin, Va., 3 October 1862. With enemy fire raking the deck of his ship and blockades thwarting her progress, Williams remained at his post and performed his duties with skill and courage as the *Commodore Perry* fought a gallant battle to silence many rebel batteries as she steamed down the Blackwater River.

1472 ♦ WILLIAMS II, JOHN

Rank: Boatswain's Mate
Service: U.S. Navy
Place of Birth: Elizabethtown, New Jersey
Entered Service at: New York
Unit: U.S.S. *Mohican*
Battle or Place of Action: Hilton Head, South Carolina
Date of Action: 7 November 1861
G.O. Number, Date: 17, 10 July 1863
Citation: Captain of an 11-inch gun aboard the U.S.S. *Mohican* during action of the main squadron of ships against the heavily defended Forts Beauregard and Walker on Hilton Head, and against ships of the Confederate fleet, 7 November 1861. Cool and courageous at his battle station, Williams maintained steady fire against the enemy while under the fort batteries during a four-hour engagement which resulted in silencing the batteries of the forts and in the rout of the rebel steamers.

1473 ♦ WILLIAMS, LEROY

Rank: Sergeant (highest rank: First Lieutenant)
Service: U.S. Army
Birthday: 18 August 1845
Place of Birth: Oswego, Oswego County, New York
Date of Death: 14 February 1930
Place of Death: Cleveland, Ohio
Cemetery: Oakwood Cemetery (MH)—Niagara Falls, New York
Entered Service at: Batavia, Genesee County, New York
Unit: Company G, 8th New York Heavy Artillery
Battle or Place of Action: Cold Harbor, Virginia
Date of Action: 3 June 1864
Date of Issue: 1 April 1898
Citation: Voluntarily exposed himself to the fire of the enemy's sharpshooters and located the body of his colonel who had been killed close to the enemy's lines. Under cover of darkness, with four companions, he recovered the body and brought it within the Union lines, having approached within a few feet of the Confederate pickets while so engaged.

1474 ◆ WILLIAMS, PETER

Rank: Seaman (highest rank: Quartermaster)
Service: U.S. Navy
Birthday: 1831
Place of Birth: Norway
Entered Service at: Pennsylvania
Unit: U.S. Ironclad Steamer *Monitor*
Battle or Place of Action: Hampton Roads, Virginia
Date of Action: 9 March 1862
G.O. Number, Date: 11, 3 April 1863
Citation: Served on board the U.S. Ironclad Steamer *Monitor*, at Hampton Roads, 9 March 1862. During the engagement between the U.S.S. *Monitor* and the C.S.S. *Merrimack*, Williams gallantly served throughout the engagement as quartermaster, piloting the *Monitor* throughout the battle in which the *Merrimack*, after being damaged, retired from the scene of the battle.

1475 ◆ WILLIAMS, ROBERT

Rank: Signal Quartermaster
Service: U.S. Navy
Birthday: 1837
Place of Birth: New York, New York
Entered Service at: New York
Unit: U.S.S. *Benton*
Battle or Place of Action: Drumgould's Bluff, Mississippi
Date of Action: 27 December 1862
G.O. Number, Date: 11, 3 April 1863
Date of Presentation: 15 May 1863
Place of Presentation: Brooklyn Navy Yard, New York, on board the U.S.S. *North Carolina*, presented by Capt. Richard Meade
Citation: Served as quartermaster on board the U.S.S. *Benton* during the Yazoo River Expedition, 23 to 27 December 1862. Taking part in the hour-and-a-half engagement with the enemy at Drumgould's Bluff, 27 December, Williams served courageously throughout that battle against hostile forces in which the enemy had the dead-range of the vessel and were punishing her with heavy fire and various other action in which he took part during the Yazoo River Expedition.

1476 ◆ WILLIAMS, WILLIAM

Rank: Landsman
Service: U.S. Navy
Birthday: 1840
Place of Birth: Ireland
Entered Service at: Pennsylvania
Unit: U.S.S. *Lehigh*
Battle or Place of Action: Charleston Harbor, South Carolina
Date of Action: 16 November 1863
G.O. Number, Date: 32, 16 April 1864
Citation: On board the U.S.S. *Lehigh*, Charleston Harbor, 16 November 1863, during the hazardous task of freeing the *Lehigh*, which had been grounded, and was under heavy enemy fire from Fort Moultrie. After several previous attempts had been made, Williams succeeded in passing in a small boat from the *Lehigh* to the *Nahant* with a line bent on a hawser. This courageous action while under severe enemy fire enabled the *Lehigh* to be freed from her helpless position.

1477 ◆ WILLIAMS, WILLIAM HALIDAY

Rank: Private
Service: U.S. Army
Birthday: 13 December 1845
Place of Birth: Williamstown, Hancock County, Ohio
Date of Death: 1 September 1916
Place of Death: Schuyler, Nebraska
Cemetery: Schuyler Cemetery (MH)—Schuyler, Nebraska
Entered Service at: Lima, Allen County, Ohio
Unit: Company C, 82d Ohio Infantry
Battle or Place of Action: Peach Tree Creek, Georgia
Date of Action: 20 July 1864
Date of Issue: 19 June 1894
Citation: Voluntarily went beyond the lines to observe the enemy; also aided a wounded comrade.

1478 ◆ WILLIAMSON, JAMES ALEXANDER

Rank: Colonel (highest rank: Brevet Major General U.S. Volunteers)
Service: U.S. Army
Birthday: 8 February 1829
Place of Birth: Columbia, Adair County, Kentucky
Date of Death: 7 September 1902
Place of Death: Jamestown, Rhode Island
Cemetery: Rock Creek Cemetery—Washington, D.C.
Entered Service at: Des Moines, Polk County, Iowa
Unit: 4th Iowa Infantry
Battle or Place of Action: Chickasaw Bayou, Mississippi
Date of Action: 29 December 1862
Date of Issue: 17 January 1895
Citation: Led his regiment against a superior force, strongly entrenched, and held his ground when all support had been withdrawn.

1479 ◆ WILLIS, RICHARD

Rank: Coxswain (highest rank: Quartermaster)
Service: U.S. Navy
Birthday: 1826
Place of Birth: England
Entered Service at: Philadelphia, Philadelphia County, Pennsylvania
Unit: U.S.S. *New Ironsides*
Battle or Place of Action: Fort Fisher, North Carolina
Date of Action: 24-25 December 1864 & 13-15 January 1865
G.O. Number, Date: 59, 22 June 1865
Citation: Willis served on board the U.S.S. *New Ironsides* during action in several attacks on Fort Fisher, 24 and 25 December 1864; and 13, 14 and 15 January 1865. The ship steamed in and took the lead in the ironclad division close inshore and immediately opened its starboard battery in a barrage of well-directed fire to cause several fires and explosions and dismount several guns during the first two days of fighting. Taken under fire as she steamed into position on 13

January, the *New Ironsides* fought all day and took on ammunition at night, despite severe weather conditions. When the enemy troops came out of their bombproofs to defend the fort against the storming party, the ship's battery disabled nearly every gun on the fort facing the shore before the cease-fire order was given by the flagship.

1480 ◆ WILLISTON, EDWARD BANCROFT

Rank: First Lieutenant (highest rank: Brigadier General)
Service: U.S. Army
Birthday: 15 July 1836
Place of Birth: Norwich, Windsor County, Vermont
Date of Death: 24 April 1920
Cemetery: Arlington National Cemetery (1-422) (MH)—Arlington, Virginia
Entered Service at: San Francisco, San Francisco County, California
Unit: Horse Battery D, 2d U.S. Artillery
Served as: Commanding Officer
Battle or Place of Action: Trevilian Station, Virginia
Date of Action: 12 June 1864
Date of Issue: 6 April 1892
Citation: Distinguished gallantry.

1481 ◆ WILSON, CHARLES E.

Rank: Sergeant (highest rank: First Lieutenant)
Service: U.S. Army
Birthday: 1840
Place of Birth: Bucks County, Pennsylvania
Date of Death: 15 August 1915
Place of Death: Trenton, New Jersey
Cemetery: Highland Cemetery (MH)—Hopewell Township, New Jersey
Entered Service at: Hatborough, Montgomery County, New Jersey
Unit: Company A, 1st New Jersey Cavalry
Battle or Place of Action: Deatonsville (Sailor's Creek), Virginia
Date of Action: 6 April 1865
Date of Issue: 3 July 1865
Citation: Charged the enemy's works, colors in hand, and had two horses shot from under him.

1482 ◆ WILSON, CHRISTOPHER W.

Rank: Private
Service: U.S. Army
Birthday: 1846
Place of Birth: Ireland
Date of Death: 12 September 1916
Place of Death: Seacliff, New York
Cemetery: The Evergreen Cemetery (MH)—Brooklyn, New York
Entered Service at: West Meriden, New Haven County, Connecticut
Unit: Company E, 73d New York Infantry
Battle or Place of Action: Spotsylvania, Virginia
Date of Action: 12 May 1864
Date of Issue: 30 December 1898
Citation: Took the flag from the wounded color bearer and carried it in the charge over the Confederate works, in which charge he also captured the colors of the 56th Virginia (C.S.A.) bringing off both flags in safety.

1483 ◆ WILSON, FRANCIS A.

Rank: Corporal
Service: U.S. Army
Birthday: 1840
Place of Birth: Philadelphia, Philadelphia County, Pennsylvania
Date of Death: 11 July 1888
Cemetery: Mount Moriah Cemetery (No marker.)—Philadelphia, Pennsylvania
Entered Service at: Philadelphia, Philadelphia County, Pennsylvania
Unit: Company B, 95th Pennsylvania Infantry
Battle or Place of Action: Petersburg, Virginia
Date of Action: 2 April 1865
Date of Issue: 25 June 1880
Citation: Was among the first to penetrate the enemy's lines and himself captured a gun of the two batteries captured.

1484 ◆ WILSON, JOHN

Rank: Sergeant
Service: U.S. Army
Place of Birth: England
Entered Service at: Jersey City, Hudson County, New Jersey
Unit: Company L, 1st New Jersey Cavalry
Battle or Place of Action: Chamberlains Creek, Virginia
Date of Action: 31 March 1865
Date of Issue: 3 July 1865
Citation: With the assistance of one comrade, headed off the advance of the enemy, shooting two of his color bearers; also posted himself between the enemy and the lead horses of his own command, thus saving the herd from capture.

1485 ◆ WILSON, JOHN ALFRED

Rank: Private (highest rank: Corporal)
Service: U.S. Army
Birthday: 25 July 1833
Place of Birth: Columbus, Franklin County, Ohio
Date of Death: 28 March 1904
Cemetery: Union Hill Cemetery (MH)—Bowling Green, Ohio
Entered Service at: Perrysburg, Wood County, Ohio
Unit: Company C, 21st Ohio Infantry
Battle or Place of Action: Georgia
Date of Action: April 1862
Date of Issue: September 1863
Citation: One of 19 of 24 men (including two civilians) who, by direction of Gen. Ormsby M. Mitchell, penetrated

nearly 200 miles south into enemy territory and captured a railroad train at Big Shanty, Ga., in an attempt to destroy the bridges and track between Chattanooga and Atlanta.
Notes: POW

1486 ◆ WILSON, JOHN MOULDER

Rank: First Lieutenant (highest rank: Brigadier General)
Service: U.S. Army
Birthday: 8 October 1837
Place of Birth: Washington, D.C.
Date of Death: 1 February 1919
Place of Death: Washington, D.C.
Cemetery: U.S. Military Academy Cemetery (K-9)—West Point, New York
Entered Service at: Olympia, Thurston County, Washington Territory
Unit: U.S. Engineers
Battle or Place of Action: Malvern Hill, Virginia
Date of Action: 6 August 1862
Date of Issue: 3 July 1897
Citation: Remained on duty, while suffering from an acute illness and very weak, and participated in the action of that date. A few days previous he had been transferred to a staff corps, but preferred to remain until the close of the campaign, taking part in several actions.

1487 ◆ WINEGAR, WILLIAM W.

Rank: First Lieutenant (highest rank: Brevet Captain)
Service: U.S. Army
Birthday: 20 October 1844
Place of Birth: Springport, New York
Date of Death: 3 September 1916
Place of Death: Bath, New York
Cemetery: Nondago Cemetery (MH)—Bath, New York
Entered Service at: Mount Morris, Livingston County, New York
Unit: Company B, 19th New York Cavalry (1st New York Dragoons)
Battle or Place of Action: Five Forks, Virginia
Date of Action: 1 April 1865
Date of Issue: 3 May 1865
Citation: While advancing in front of his company and alone, he found himself surrounded by the enemy. He accosted a nearby enemy flag-bearer demanding the surrender of the group. His effective firing of one shot so demoralized the unit that it surrendered with flag.

1488 ◆ WISNER, LEWIS S.

Rank: First Lieutenant (highest rank: Captain)
Service: U.S. Army
Birthday: 11 August 1841
Place of Birth: Wallkill, Ulster County, New York
Date of Death: 6 October 1906
Place of Death: Middletown, New York
Cemetery: Hillside Cemetery (MH)—Middletown, New York
Entered Service at: Wallkill, Ulster County, New York
Unit: Company K, 124th New York Infantry
Served as: Engineer Officer
Battle or Place of Action: Spotsylvania, Virginia
Date of Action: 12 May 1864
Date of Issue: 2 January 1895
Citation: While serving as an engineer officer voluntarily exposed himself to the enemy's fire.

1489 ◆ WITHINGTON, WILLIAM HERBERT

Rank: Captain (highest rank: Brevet Brigadier General)
Service: U.S. Army
Birthday: 1 February 1835
Place of Birth: Dorchester, Suffolk County, Massachusetts
Date of Death: 27 June 1903
Place of Death: Jackson, Michigan
Cemetery: Mount Evergreen Cemetery (MH)—Jackson, Michigan
Entered Service at: Jackson, Jackson County, Michigan
Unit: Company B, 1st Michigan Infantry
Battle or Place of Action: Bull Run, Virginia
Date of Action: 21 July 1861
Date of Issue: 7 January 1895
Citation: Remained on the field under heavy fire to succor his superior officer.

1490 ◆ WOLLAM, JOHN

Rank: Private
Service: U.S. Army
Birthday: 1838
Place of Birth: Hamilton, Butler County, Ohio
Date of Death: 26 September 1890
Cemetery: Fairmount Cemetery—Jackson, Ohio
Entered Service at: Jackson, Jackson County, Ohio
Unit: Company C, 33d Ohio Infantry
Battle or Place of Action: Georgia
Date of Action: April 1862
Date of Issue: 20 July 1864
Citation: One of 19 of 24 men (including two civilians) who, by direction of Gen. Ormsby M. Mitchell, penetrated nearly 200 miles south into enemy territory and captured a railroad train at Big Shanty, Ga., in an attempt to destroy the bridges and track between Chattanooga and Atlanta.
Notes: POW

1491 ◆ WOOD, HENRY CLAY

Rank: First Lieutenant (highest rank: Brigadier General)
Service: U.S. Army
Birthday: 26 May 1832
Place of Birth: Winthrop, Kennebec County, Maine
Date of Death: 29 August 1918
Cemetery: Arlington National Cemetery (1-80-A) (MH)—Arlington, Virginia
Entered Service at: Winthrop, Kennebec County, Maine
Unit: 11th U.S. Infantry
Battle or Place of Action: Wilson's Creek, Missouri

Date of Action: 10 August 1861
Date of Issue: 28 October 1893
Citation: Distinguished gallantry.

1492 ◆ WOOD, MARK

Rank: Private
Service: U.S. Army
Birthday: 1839
Place of Birth: England
Date of Death: 11 July 1866
Cemetery: Forest Cemetery—Toledo, Ohio
Entered Service at: Portage, Wood County, Ohio
Unit: Company C, 21st Ohio Infantry
Battle or Place of Action: Georgia
Date of Action: April 1862
Date of Issue: September 1863
Citation: One 19 of 24 men (including two civilians) who, by direction of Gen. Ormsby M. Mitchell, penetrated nearly 200 miles south into enemy territory and captured a railroad train at Big Shanty, Ga., in an attempt to destroy the bridges and track between Chattanooga and Atlanta.
Notes: POW

1493 ◆ WOOD, RICHARD H.

Rank: Captain
Service: U.S. Army
Birthday: 15 November 1833
Place of Birth: Canton, New Jersey
Date of Death: 8 March 1903
Cemetery: Woodburn Cemetery (MH)—Bunker Hill, Illinois
Entered Service at: Woodburn, Macoupin County, Illinois
Unit: Company A, 97th Illinois Infantry
Battle or Place of Action: Vicksburg, Mississippi
Date of Action: 22 May 1863
Date of Issue: 12 December 1895
Citation: Led the "volunteer storming party," which made a most gallant assault upon the enemy's works.

1494 ◆ WOOD, ROBERT B.

True Name: Woods, Robert B.
Rank: Coxswain
Service: U.S. Navy
Place of Birth: New Garden, Ohio
Date of Death: 1 July 1878
Place of Death: Columbus, Ohio
Entered Service at: Ohio
Unit: attached to the U.S.S. *Minnesota* & temporarily serving on the U.S.S. *Mount Washington*
Battle or Place of Action: Nansemond River, Virginia
Date of Action: 14 April 1863
G.O. Number, Date: 17, 10 July 1863
Citation: Attached to the U.S.S. *Minnesota* and temporarily served on the U.S.S. *Mount Washington* during action against the enemy in the Nansemond River, 14 April 1863. When the U.S.S. *Mount Washington* drifted against the bank and all men were driven from the decks by escaping steam following several successive hits which struck her boilers and stopped her engines, Wood boarded the stricken vessel and, despite a strike on the head by a spent ball, continued at his gun for six hours as fierce artillery and musketry continued to rake her decks.

1495 ◆ WOODALL, WILLIAM H.

Rank: Scout
Service: U.S. Army
Place of Birth: Lynchburg, Lynchburg County, Virginia
Entered Service at: Winchester, Frederic County, Virginia
Battle or Place of Action: Deatonsville (Sailor's Creek), Virginia
Date of Action: 29 March-9 April 1865
Date of Issue: 3 May 1865
Citation: Capture of flag.

1496 ◆ WOODBURY, ERI DAVIDSON

Rank: Sergeant (highest rank: Brevet Captain)
Service: U.S. Army
Birthday: 30 May 1837
Place of Birth: Francistown, Hillsborough County, New Hampshire
Date of Death: 14 April 1928
Place of Death: Cheshire, Connecticut
Cemetery: St. Peter's Episcopal Cemetery (MH)—Cheshire, Connecticut
Entered Service at: St. Johnsbury, Caledonia County, Vermont
Unit: Company E, 1st Vermont Cavalry
Battle or Place of Action: Cedar Creek, Virginia
Date of Action: 19 October 1864
Date of Issue: 26 October 1864
Citation: During the regiment's charge when the enemy was in retreat, Sgt. Woodbury encountered four Confederate infantrymen retreating. He drew his saber and ordered them to surrender, overcoming by his determined actions their willingness to further resist. They surrendered to him together with their rifles and 12th North Carolina (C.S.A.) regimental flag.

1497 ◆ WOODRUFF, ALONZO

Rank: Sergeant
Service: U.S. Army
Birthday: 31 March 1839
Place of Birth: Ionia, Ionia County, Michigan
Date of Death: 10 February 1917
Cemetery: Valley Cemetery—Luther, Michigan
Entered Service at: Ionia, Ionia County, Michigan
Unit: Company I, 1st U.S. Sharpshooters
Battle or Place of Action: Hatcher's Run, Virginia
Date of Action: 27 October 1864
Date of Issue: 29 January 1896
Citation: Went to the assistance of a wounded and overpowered comrade, and in a hand-to-hand encounter effected his rescue.

1498 ◆ WOODRUFF, CARLE AUGUSTUS

Rank: First Lieutenant (highest rank: Brigadier General)
Service: U.S. Army

Birthday: 8 August 1841
Place of Birth: Buffalo, Erie County, New York
Date of Death: 20 July 1913
Place of Death: Raleigh, North Carolina
Cemetery: Oakwood Cemetery (MH)—Raleigh, North Carolina
Entered Service at: Washington, D.C.
Unit: Horse Battery M, 2d U.S. Artillery
Battle or Place of Action: Newbys Crossroads, Virginia
Date of Action: 24 July 1863
Date of Issue: 1 September 1893
Citation: While in command of a section of a battery constituting a portion of the rear guard of a division then retiring before the advance of a corps of Infantry, Woodruff was attacked by the enemy and ordered to abandon his guns. Lt. Woodruff disregarded the orders received and aided in repelling the attack and saving the guns.

1499 ◆ WOODS, DANIEL A. (WOOD)

True Name: Wood, Daniel A.
Rank: Private
Service: U.S. Army
Birthday: 1843
Place of Birth: Ohio County, West Virginia
Date of Death: 10 August 1894
Place of Death: Wheeling, West Virginia
Cemetery: Greenwood Cemetery (MH)—Wheeling, West Virginia
Entered Service at: Wheeling, Ohio County, West Virginia
Unit: Company K, 1st West Virginia Cavalry
Battle or Place of Action: Deatonsville (Sailor's Creek), Virginia
Date of Action: 6 April 1865
Date of Issue: 3 May 1865
Citation: Capture of flag, 18th Florida Infantry (C.S.A.)

1500 ◆ WOODS, SAMUEL

Rank: Seaman (highest rank: Boatswain's Mate)
Service: U.S. Navy
Birthday: 1838
Place of Birth: San Francisco, San Francisco County, California
Date of Death: 23 May 1885
Place of Death: Portsmouth, Virginia
Cemetery: Oak Grove Cemetery (MH)—Portsmouth, Virginia
Entered Service at: California
Unit: U.S.S. *Mount Washington*
Battle or Place of Action: Nansemond River, Virginia
Date of Action: 14 April 1863
G.O. Number, Date: 17, 10 July 1863
Citation: As captain of the gun, served temporarily on board the U.S.S. *Mount Washington* during the Nansemond River action, 14 April 1863. When one of his comrades was struck by a bullet and knocked overboard, Woods fearlessly jumped into the water and swam after him. Before he reached him, the man sank beneath the surface and Woods promptly swam back to the vessel, went to his gun, and fought it to the close of the action. At the close of the battle, he tirelessly cared for the wounded.

1501 ◆ WOODWARD, EVAN M.

Rank: First Lieutenant & Adjutant (highest rank: Brevet Major)
Service: U.S. Army
Birthday: 11 March 1838
Place of Birth: Philadelphia Philadelphia County, Pennsylvania
Date of Death: 15 August 1904
Place of Death: Trenton, New Jersey
Cemetery: Riverview Cemetery—Trenton, New Jersey
Entered Service at: Sandy Hook, Maryland
Unit: 2d Pennsylvania Reserve Infantry
Battle or Place of Action: Fredericksburg, Virginia
Date of Action: 13 December 1862
Date of Issue: 14 December 1894
Citation: Advanced between the lines, demanded and received the surrender of the 19th Georgia Infantry (C.S.A.) and captured their battle flag.

1502 ◆ WOON, JOHN

Rank: Boatswain's Mate
Service: U.S. Navy
Birthday: 1823
Place of Birth: England
Entered Service at: New York, New York
Unit: U.S.S. *Pittsburgh*
Battle or Place of Action: Grand Gulf, Mississippi River, Mississippi
Date of Action: 29 April 1863
G.O. Number, Date: 17, 10 July 1863
Citation: Serving on board the U.S.S. *Pittsburgh*, Mississippi River, 29 April 1863. Engaging the enemy batteries at Grand Gulf, the U.S.S. *Pittsburgh*, although severely damaged and suffering many personnel casualties, continued to fire her batteries until ordered to withdraw. Taking part in a similar action after nightfall, the U.S.S. *Pittsburgh* received further damage, but received no personnel casualties in the latter action. Woon showed courage and devotion to duty throughout these bitter engagements.

1503 ◆ WORAM, CHARLES B.

Rank: Seaman (highest rank: Landsman)
Service: U.S. Navy
Birthday: 29 March 1845
Place of Birth: New York, New York
Date of Death: 1 November 1897
Place of Death: New York, New York
Cemetery: Woodlawn Cemetery—Bronx, New York
Entered Service at: New York, New York
Unit: U.S.S. *Oneida*
Battle or Place of Action: Mobile Bay, Alabama
Date of Action: 5 August 1864
G.O. Number, Date: 45, 31 December 1864

Citation: Served on board the U.S.S. *Oneida* in the engagement at Moblie Bay, 5 August 1864. Acting as an aid to the executive officer, Woram carried orders intelligently and correctly, distinguishing himself by his cool courage throughout the battle which resulted in the capture of the rebel ram *Tennessee* and the damaging of Fort Morgan.

1504 ◆ WORTICK, JOSEPH

True Name: Wertick, Joseph
Rank: Private
Service: U.S. Army
Birthday: 1838
Place of Birth: Fayette County, Pennsylvania
Place of Death: Leon, Kansas
Cemetery: Leon Cemetery (MH)—Leon, Kansas
Entered Service at: Hannibal, Marion County, Missouri
Unit: Company A, 6th Missouri Infantry
Battle or Place of Action: Vicksburg, Mississippi
Date of Action: 22 May 1863
Date of Issue: 14 July 1894
Citation: Gallantry in the charge of the "volunteer storming party."

1505 ◆ WRAY, WILLIAM J.

Rank: Sergeant
Service: U.S. Army
Birthday: 16 May 1845
Place of Birth: Philadelphia, Philadelphia County, Pennsylvania
Date of Death: 2 June 1919
Place of Death: Philadelphia, Pennsylvania
Cemetery: Philadelphia Memorial Park—Frazier, Pennsylvania
Entered Service at: Philadelphia, Philadelphia County, Pennsylvania
Unit: Company K, 1st Veterans Reserve Corps
Battle or Place of Action: Fort Steven's, Washington, D.C.
Date of Action: 12 July 1864
Date of Issue: 15 December 1892
Citation: Rallied the company at a critical moment during a change of position under fire.

1506 ◆ WRIGHT, ALBERT D.

Rank: Captain
Service: U.S. Army
Birthday: 10 December 1842
Place of Birth: Elkland, Tioga County, Pennsylvania
Date of Death: 15 February 1926
Place of Death: Tampa, Florida
Cemetery: Greenwood Cemetery (MH)—Eustis, Florida
Entered Service at: Wellsboro, Tioga County, Pennsylvania
Unit: Company G, 43d U.S. Colored Troops
Battle or Place of Action: Petersburg, Virginia
Date of Action: 30 July 1864
Date of Issue: 1 May 1893
Citation: Advanced beyond the enemy's lines, capturing a stand of colors and its color guard; was severely wounded.

1507 ◆ WRIGHT, EDWARD

Rank: Quartermaster
Service: U.S. Navy
Birthday: 1829
Place of Birth: New York, New York
Date of Death: 17 February 1901
Place of Death: New York, New York
Cemetery: Maple Grove Cemetery—Kew Gardens, New York
Entered Service at: New York, New York
Unit: U.S.S. *Cayuga*
Battle or Place of Action: Fts. St. Philip & Jackson and New Orleans, Louisiana
Date of Action: 24-25 April 1862
G.O. Number, Date: 11, 3 April 1863
Citation: On board the U.S.S. *Cayuga* during the capture of Forts St. Philip and Jackson and the taking of New Orleans, 24 and 25 April 1862. As his ship led the advance column toward the barrier and both forts opened fire simultaneously, striking the vessel from stem to stern, Wright conscientiously performed his duties throughout the action in which the attempts of three rebel steamers to butt and board were repelled, and the ships driven off or forced to surrender. Eleven gunboats were successfully engaged and garrisons captured during this battle in which the *Cayuga* sustained 46 hits.

1508 ◆ WRIGHT, ROBERT

Rank: Private
Service: U.S. Army
Birthday: 1828
Place of Birth: Ireland
Date of Death: 22 October 1885
Cemetery: Cedar Lawn Cemetery (MH)—Patterson, New Jersey
Entered Service at: Woodstock, Windham County, Connecticut
Unit: Company G, 14th U.S. Infantry
Battle or Place of Action: Chapel House Farm, Virginia
Date of Action: 1 October 1864
Date of Issue: 25 November 1869
Citation: Gallantry in action.

1509 ◆ WRIGHT, SAMUEL

Rank: Corporal
Service: U.S. Army
Birthday: 20 January 1828
Place of Birth: Indiana
Date of Death: 7 July 1918
Place of Death: Tribune, Kansas
Cemetery: Maple Grove Cemetery (MH)—Wichita, Kansas
Entered Service at: Mankato, Blue Earth County, Minnesota
Unit: Company H, 2d Minnesota Infantry
Battle or Place of Action: Nolensville, Tennessee
Date of Action: 15 February 1863

Date of Issue: 11 September 1897
Citation: Was one of a detachment of 16 men who heroically defended a wagon train against the attack of 125 cavalry, repulsed the attack, and saved the train.

1510 ◆ WRIGHT, SAMUEL COLE

Rank: Private (highest rank: Sergeant)
Service: U.S. Army
Birthday: 7 September 1842
Place of Birth: Plympton, Plymouth County, Massachusetts
Date of Death: 6 July 1906
Place of Death: Plympton, Massachusetts
Cemetery: Oak Grove Cemetery (MH)—Plymouth, Massachusetts
Entered Service at: Plympton, Plymouth County, Massachusetts
Unit: Company E, 29th Massachusetts Infantry
Battle or Place of Action: Antietam, Maryland
Date of Action: 17 September 1862
Date of Issue: 29 January 1896
Citation: Voluntarily advanced under a destructive fire and removed a fence which would have impeded a contemplated charge.

1511 ◆ WRIGHT, WILLIAM

Rank: Yeoman
Service: U.S. Navy
Birthday: 1835
Place of Birth: London, England
Entered Service at: Baltimore, Baltimore County, Maryland
Unit: U.S.S. *Monticello*
Battle or Place of Action: Wilmington, North Carolina
Date of Action: 23-25 June 1864
G.O. Number, Date: 45, 31 December 1864
Citation: Served as yeoman on board the U.S.S. *Monticello* during the reconnaissance of the harbor and water defenses of Wilmington, N.C., 23 to 25 June 1864. Taking part in a reconnaissance of enemy defenses which covered a period of two days and nights, Wright courageously carried out his cutting of a telegraph wire and the capture of a large group of prisoners. Although in immediate danger from the enemy at all times, Wright showed gallantry and coolness throughout this action which resulted in the gaining of much vital information on the rebel defenses.

1512 ◆ YEAGER, JACOB F.

Rank: Private
Service: U.S. Army
Birthday: 27 January 1841
Place of Birth: New Texas, Lehigh County, Pennsylvania
Date of Death: 13 November 1909
Cemetery: Greenlawn Cemetery (MH)—Tiffin, Ohio
Entered Service at: Tiffin, Seneca County, Ohio
Unit: Company H, 101st Ohio Infantry
Battle or Place of Action: Buzzard's Roost, Georgia
Date of Action: 11 May 1864

Date of Issue: 3 August 1897
Citation: Seized a shell with fuse burning that had fallen in the ranks of his company and threw it into a stream, thereby probably saving his comrades from injury.
Notes: POW

1513 ◆ YOUNG, ANDREW J.

Rank: Sergeant
Service: U.S. Army
Birthday: 28 December 1837
Place of Birth: Greene County, Pennsylvania
Date of Death: 27 January 1910
Place of Death: Jefferson, Pennsylvania
Cemetery: Jefferson Cemetery—Jefferson, Pennsylvania
Entered Service at: Carmichaels, Greene County, Pennsylvania
Unit: Company F, 1st Pennsylvania Cavalry
Battle or Place of Action: Paines Crossroads, Virginia
Date of Action: 5 April 1865
Date of Issue: 3 May 1865
Citation: Capture of flag.

1514 ◆ YOUNG, BENJAMIN F.

Rank: Corporal
Service: U.S. Army
Birthday: 1841
Place of Birth: Canada
Date of Death: 27 January 1927
Place of Death: Los Angeles, California
Cemetery: Odd Fellow Cemetery—Los Angeles, California
Entered Service at: Detroit, Wayne County, Michigan
Unit: 1st Michigan Sharpshooters
Battle or Place of Action: Petersburg, Virginia
Date of Action: 17 June 1864
Date of Issue: 1 December 1864
Citation: Capture of flag of 35th North Carolina Infantry (C.S.A.).
Notes: POW

1515 ◆ YOUNG, CALVARY MORRIS

Rank: Sergeant
Service: U.S. Army
Birthday: 12 March 1840
Place of Birth: Washington County, Ohio
Date of Death: 11 July 1909
Place of Death: Ludlow, Kentucky
Cemetery: Highland Cemetery (MH)—Fort Mitchell, Kentucky
Entered Service at: Hopeville, Clark County, Iowa
Unit: Company L, 3d Iowa Cavalry
Battle or Place of Action: Osage, Kansas
Date of Action: 25 October 1864
Date of Issue: 4 April 1865
Citation: Gallantry in capturing Brig. Gen. William Lewis Cabell, (C.S.A.).

1516 ◆ YOUNG, EDWARD B.

Rank: Coxswain (highest rank: Wardroom Steward)
Service: U.S. Navy
Birthday: 1835
Place of Birth: Bergen, Hudson County, New Jersey
Date of Death: 24 February 1867
Place of Death: Philadelphia, Pennsylvania
Cemetery: Lafayette Cemetery—Philadelphia, Pennsylvania
Entered Service at: New Jersey
Unit: U.S.S. *Galena*
Battle or Place of Action: Mobile Bay, Alabama
Date of Action: 5 August 1864
G.O. Number, Date: 59, 22 June 1865
Citation: On board the U.S.S. *Galena* during the attack on enemy forts at Mobile Bay, 5 August 1864. Securely lashed to the side of the *Oneida*, which had suffered the loss of her steering apparatus and an explosion of her boiler from enemy fire, the *Galena* aided the stricken vessel past the enemy forts to safety. Despite heavy damage to his ship from raking enemy fire, Young performed his duties with skill and courage throughout the action.

1517 ◆ YOUNG, HORATIO NELSON

Rank: Seaman
Service: U.S. Navy
Birthday: 19 July 1845
Place of Birth: Calais, Washington County, Maine
Date of Death: 3 July 1913
Place of Death: Calais (Red Beach), Maine
Cemetery: The Rural Cemetery (MH)—St. Stephen, New Brunswick, Canada
Entered Service at: Boston, Suffolk County, Massachusetts
Unit: U.S.S. *Lehigh*
Battle or Place of Action: Charleston Harbor, South Carolina
Date of Action: 16 November 1863
G.O. Number, Date: 32, 16 April 1864
Citation: On board the U.S.S. *Lehigh*, Charleston Harbor, 16 November 1863, during the hazardous task of freeing the *Lehigh*, which had grounded and was under heavy enemy fire from Fort Moultrie. After several previous attempts had been made, Young succeeded in passing in a small boat from the *Lehigh* to the *Nahant* with a line bent on a hawser. This courageous action while under severe enemy fire enabled the *Lehigh* to be freed from her helpless position.

1518 ◆ YOUNG, JAMES MARVIN

Rank: Private
Service: U.S. Army
Birthday: 2 December 1843
Place of Birth: Ellicott, Erie County, New York
Date of Death: 30 November 1913
Place of Death: Jamestown, New York
Cemetery: Lake View Cemetery—Jamestown, New York
Entered Service at: Chautauqua County, New York
Unit: Company B, 72d New York Infantry
Battle or Place of Action: Wilderness Campaign, Virginia
Date of Action: 6 May 1864
Date of Issue: 2 April 1898
Citation: With two companions, voluntarily went forward in the forest to reconnoiter the enemy's position; was fired upon and one of his companions disabled. Pvt. Young took the wounded man upon his back and, under fire, carried him to within the Union lines.

1519 ◆ YOUNG, WILLIAM

Rank: Boatswain's Mate
Service: U.S. Navy
Birthday: 1835
Place of Birth: New York
Entered Service at: New York, New York
Unit: U.S.S. *Cayuga*
Battle or Place of Action: Fts. St. Philip & Jackson and New Orleans, Louisiana
Date of Action: 24-25 April 1862
G.O. Number, Date: 11, 3 April 1863
Citation: On board the U.S.S. *Cayuga* during the capture of Forts St. Philip and Jackson and the taking of New Orleans, 24 and 25 April 1862. As his ship led the advance column toward the barrier and both forts opened fire simultaneously, striking the vessel from stem to stern, Young calmly manned a Parrot gun throughout the action in which attempts by three rebel steamers to butt and board were thwarted and the ships driven off or captured, 11 gunboats were successfully engaged, and garrisons forced to surrender. During the battle, the *Cayuga* sustained 46 hits.

1520 ◆ YOUNKER, JOHN L.

Rank: Private
Service: U.S. Army
Birthday: 16 November 1836
Place of Birth: Wurttemberg, Germany
Date of Death: 18 May 1911
Place of Death: Logan, Ohio
Cemetery: Oak Grove Cemetery—Logan, Ohio
Entered Service at: Lancaster, Fairfield County, Ohio
Unit: Company A, 12th U.S. Infantry
Battle or Place of Action: Cedar Mountain, Virginia
Date of Action: 9 August 1862
Date of Issue: 1 November 1893

INTERIM 1865–1870

1521 ◆ **BATES, RICHARD**

Rank: Seaman
Service: U.S. Navy
Birthday: 1829
Place of Birth: Wales
Entered Service at: New York
Unit: U.S.S. *Winooski*
Battle or Place of Action: off Eastport, Maine
Date of Action: 10 May 1866
G.O. Number, Date: 77, 1 August 1866
Citation: For heroic conduct in rescuing from drowning James Rose and John Russell, seamen of the U.S.S. *Winooski*, off Eastport, Maine, 10 May 1866.

1522 ◆ **BROWN, JOHN**

Rank: Captain of the Afterguard
Service: U.S. Navy
Birthday: 1838
Place of Birth: Denmark
Entered Service at: Maryland
Unit: U.S.S. *Winooski*
Battle or Place of Action: off Eastport, Maine
Date of Action: 10 May 1866
G.O. Number, Date: 77, 1 August 1866
Citation: For heroic conduct with two comrades, in rescuing from drowning James Rose and John Russell, seamen of the U.S.S. *Winooski*, off Eastport, Maine, 10 May 1866.

1523 ◆ **BURKE, THOMAS**

Rank: Seaman
Service: U.S. Navy
Birthday: 1833
Place of Birth: Ireland
Entered Service at: New York
Unit: U.S.S. *Winooski*
Battle or Place of Action: off Eastport, Maine
Date of Action: 10 May 1866
G.O. Number, Date: 77, 1 August 1866
Citation: For heroic conduct with two comrades, in rescuing from drowning James Rose and John Russell, seamen of the U.S.S. *Winooski*, off Eastport, Maine, 10 May 1866.

1524 ◆ **CAREY, JAMES**

Rank: Seaman
Service: U.S. Navy
Birthday: 1844
Place of Birth: Ireland
Entered Service at: New York
Unit: U.S.S. *Huron*
Citation: Seaman on board the U.S.S. *Huron*, for saving three shipmates from drowning.

1525 ◆ **COOPER, JOHN✛**

True Name: Mather, John Laver
Rank: Quartermaster
Service: U.S. Navy
Birthday: 24 July 1828
Place of Birth: Dublin, Ireland
Date of Death: 22 August 1891
Cemetery: Cypress Hills National Cemetery (2-5022) (MH)—Brooklyn, New York
Entered Service at: New York, New York
Unit: on Acting Rear Adm. Thatcher's staff
Battle or Place of Action: Mobile, Alabama
Date of Action: 26 April 1865
G.O. Number, Date: 62, 29 June 1865
Citation: **Second Award** Served as quartermaster on Acting Rear Adm. Thatcher's staff. During the terrific fire at Mobile, on 26 April 1865, at the risk of being blown to pieces by exploding shells, Cooper advanced through the burning locality, rescued a wounded man from certain death, and bore him on his back to a place of safety.
Notes: ✛Double Awardee: *see also* Civil War

1526 ◆ **DU MOULIN, FRANK**

Rank: Apprentice
Service: U.S. Navy
Birthday: 1850
Place of Birth: Philadelphia, Philadelphia County, Pennsylvania
Entered Service at: Pennsylvania
Unit: U.S.S. *Sabine*
Battle or Place of Action: in New London Harbor, Connecticut
Date of Action: 5 September 1867
G.O. Number, Date: 84, 3 October 1867
Citation: On 5 September 1867, Du Moulin jumped overboard and saved from drowning Apprentice D'Orsay, who had fallen from the mizzen topmast rigging of the *Sabine*, in New London Harbor and was rendered helpless by striking the mizzen rigging and boat davit in the fall.

1527 ◆ GERBER, FREDERICK WILLIAM

Rank: Sergeant Major
Service: U.S. Army
Birthday: 1813
Place of Birth: Dresden, Germany
Date of Death: 10 November 1875
Cemetery: Cypress Hills National Cemetery (2-6101) (MH)—Brooklyn, New York
Entered Service at: Brooklyn, Kings County, New York
Unit: U.S. Engineers
Date of Action: 1839—1871
Date of Issue: 8 November 1871
Citation: Distinguished gallantry in many actions and in recognition of long, faithful, and meritorious services covering a period of 32 years.

1528 ◆ HALFORD, WILLIAM

Rank: Coxswain (highest rank: Lieutenant)
Service: U.S. Navy
Birthday: 18 August 1841
Place of Birth: Gloucester, Gloucestershire, England
Date of Death: 17 February 1919
Place of Death: Vallejo, California
Cemetery: Mare Island Shipyard Cemetery (MH)—Vallejo, California
Entered Service at: San Francisco, San Francisco County, California
Unit: U.S.S. *Saginaw*
Battle or Place of Action: Sandwich Islands
Date of Action: October 1870
G.O. Number, Date: 169, 8 February 1872
Citation: Halford was sole survivor of the boat's crew sent to the Sandwich Islands for assistance after the wreck of the *Saginaw*, October 1870. Promoted to acting gunner.

1529 ◆ MULLEN, PATRICK✣

Rank: Boatswain's Mate
Service: U.S. Navy
Birthday: 6 May 1844
Place of Birth: Ireland
Date of Death: 14 February 1897
Cemetery: New Cathedral Cemetery—Baltimore, Maryland
Entered Service at: Baltimore, Baltimore County, Maryland
Unit: U.S.S. *Don*
Battle or Place of Action: off the coast of Virginia
Date of Action: 1 May 1865
G.O. Number, Date: 62, 29 June 1865
Citation: Second Award Served as boatswain's mate on board the U.S.S. *Don*, 1 May 1865. Engaged in picking up the crew of Picket Launch No. 6, which had swamped. Mullen, seeing an officer who at that time was no longer able to keep up and was below the surface of the water, jumped overboard and brought the officer to the boat, thereby rescuing him from drowning, which brave action entitled him to wear a bar on the medal he had already received at Mattox Creek, 17 March 1865.
Notes: ✣Double Awardee: *see also* Civil War

1530 ◆ ROBINSON, JOHN

Rank: Captain of the Hold
Service: U.S. Navy
Birthday: 1840
Place of Birth: Cuba
Entered Service at: Maine
Unit: U.S.S. *Yucca*
Battle or Place of Action: in Pensacola Bay, Florida
Date of Action: 19 January 1867
G.O. Number, Date: 82, 23 February 1867
Citation: With Acting Ens. James H. Bunting, during the heavy gale which occurred in Pensacola Bay on the night of 19 January 1867, Robinson swam ashore with a line for the purpose of sending off a blowcock, which would facilitate getting upsteam and prevent the vessel from stranding, thus voluntarily periling his life to save the vessel and the lives of others.

1531 ◆ ROBINSON, THOMAS

Rank: Captain of the Afterguard
Service: U.S. Navy
Birthday: 17 May 1837
Place of Birth: Norway
Date of Death: 12 May 1915
Cemetery: Lakewood Cemetery (no marker on grave)—Minneapolis, Minnesota
Entered Service at: New York
Unit: U.S.S. *Tallapoosa*
Battle or Place of Action: off New Orleans, Louisiana
Date of Action: 15 July 1866
G.O. Number, Date: 77, 1 August 1866
Citation: For heroic efforts to save from drowning Wellington Brocar, landsman, of the *Tallapoosa*, off New Orleans, 15 July 1866.

1532 ◆ STACY, WILLIAM BRADFORD

Rank: Seaman
Service: U.S. Navy
Birthday: 4 March 1838
Place of Birth: Fall River, Bristol County, Massachusetts
Date of Death: 3 May 1921
Place of Death: Haswell, Colorado
Cemetery: Highland Cemetery—Iola, Kansas
Entered Service at: New Bedford, Bristol County, Massachusetts
Unit: U.S.S. *Rhode Island*
Battle or Place of Action: in the harbor, Cape Haiten, Haiti
G.O. Number, Date: 71, 15 January 1866
Citation: While coaling ship in the harbor of Cape Haiten, one of the crew of the U.S.S. *Rhode Island* fell overboard,

and, after catching a rope, had been forced by exhaustion to relinquish his hold. Although the sea was running high at the time, Stacy, at the peril of his life, jumped overboard, secured the rope around his shipmate, and thus saved him from drowning.

1533 ◆ TAYLOR, JOHN

Rank: Seaman
Service: U.S. Navy
Battle or Place of Action: New York Navy Yard
Date of Action: 9 September 1865
G.O. Number, Date: 71, 15 January 1866
Citation: Seaman in charge of the picket boat attached to the Navy Yard, New York, 9 September 1865. Acting with promptness, coolness, and good judgment, Taylor rescued from drowning Comdr. S.D. Trenchard of the U.S. Navy, who fell overboard in attempting to get on a ferryboat which had collided with an English steamer and who needed immediate assistance.

INDIAN CAMPAIGNS

1534 ◆ ALBEE, GEORGE EMERSON
Rank: First Lieutenant (highest rank: Captain)
Service: U.S. Army
Birthday: 27 January 1845
Place of Birth: Lisbon, Grafton County, New Hampshire
Date of Death: 24 March 1918
Place of Death: Laurel, Maryland
Cemetery: Arlington National Cemetery (2-850)—Arlington, Virginia
Entered Service at: Owatonna, Steele County, Minnesota
Unit: Company L, 41st U.S. Infantry
Battle or Place of Action: Brazos River, Texas
Date of Action: 28 October 1869
Date of Issue: 18 January 1894
Citation: Attacked with two men a force of 11 Indians, drove them from the hills, and reconnoitered the country beyond.

1535 ◆ ALCHESAY, WILLIAM
Rank: Sergeant
Service: U.S. Army
Birthday: 17 May 1853
Place of Birth: Arizona
Date of Death: 6 August 1928
Cemetery: Fort Apache Indian Reservation near Little Round Top Peak—White River, Arizona
Entered Service at: Camp Verde, Yavapai County, Arizona Territory
Unit: Indian Scouts
Battle or Place of Action: Apache Campaigns
Date of Action: winter 1872-73
Date of Presentation: 12 April 1875
Place of Presentation: Fort Apache, Arizona, presented by Gen. Crook
Citation: Gallant conduct during campaigns and engagements with Apaches.

1536 ◆ ALLEN, WILLIAM
Rank: First Sergeant (highest rank: First Lieutenant)
Service: U.S. Army
Birthday: 1846
Place of Birth: Philadelphia, Philadelphia County, Pennsylvania
Date of Death: 8 January 1892
Cemetery: San Francisco National Cemetery (OS-48-2)—San Francisco, California
Entered Service at: Philadelphia, Philadelphia County, Pennsylvania
Unit: Company I, 23d U.S. Infantry
Battle or Place of Action: Turret Mountain, Arizona Territory
Date of Action: 27 March 1873
Date of Issue: 12 April 1875
Citation: Gallantry in action.

1537 ◆ ANDERSON, JAMES
True Name: Smyth, James
Rank: Private (highest rank: Sergeant)
Service: U.S. Army
Birthday: 28 May 1849
Place of Birth: Canada East
Date of Death: 31 May 1918
Cemetery: St. Peter & Paul Cemetery—St. Louis, Missouri
Entered Service at: St. Louis, St. Louis County, Missouri
Unit: Company M, 6th U.S. Cavalry
Battle or Place of Action: Wichita River, Texas
Date of Action: 5 October 1870
Date of Issue: 19 November 1870
Citation: Gallantry during the pursuit and fight with Indians.

1538 ◆ ASTON, EDGAR R.
Rank: Private
Service: U.S. Army
Birthday: 1846
Place of Birth: Clermont County, Ohio
Date of Death: 14 April 1932
Cemetery: Tate Township Cemetery—Bethel, Ohio
Entered Service at: Cincinnati, Hamilton County, Ohio
Unit: Company L, 8th U.S. Cavalry
Battle or Place of Action: San Carlos, Arizona
Date of Action: 30 May 1868
Date of Issue: 28 July 1868
Citation: With two other men he volunteered to search for a wagon passage out of a 4,000-foot valley wherein an infantry column was immobile. This small group passed six miles through hostile Apache terrain, finding the sought passage. On their return trip down the canyon they were attacked by Apaches, who were successfully held at bay.

1539 ◆ AUSTIN, WILLIAM GRAFTON
Rank: Sergeant
Service: U.S. Army
Birthday: 6 January 1868

Place of Birth: Galveston, Galveston County, Texas
Date of Death: 15 July 1929
Place of Death: Los Altos, California
Cemetery: Cypress Lawn Cemetery—Colma, California
Entered Service at: New York, New York
Unit: Company E, 7th U.S. Cavalry
Battle or Place of Action: Wounded Knee Creek, South Dakota
Date of Action: 29 December 1890
Date of Issue: 27 June 1891
Citation: While the Indians were concealed in a ravine, assisted men on the skirmish line, directing their fire, etc., and using every effort to dislodge the enemy.

1540 ◆ AYERS, JAMES F.

Rank: Private
Service: U.S. Army
Birthday: 1847
Place of Birth: Collinstown, Henry County, Virginia
Date of Death: 18 January 1895
Place of Death: Fort Reily, Kansas
Cemetery: Post Cemetery (F-27) (MH)—Fort Riley, Kansas
Entered Service at: Richmond, Richmond County, Virginia
Unit: Company H, 6th U.S. Cavalry
Battle or Place of Action: Sappa Creek, Kansas
Date of Action: 23 April 1875
Date of Issue: 16 November 1876
Citation: Rapid pursuit, gallantry, energy, and enterprise in an engagement with Indians.

1541 ◆ BABCOCK, JOHN BRECKINRIDGE

True Name: Breckenridge, John
Rank: First Lieutenant (highest rank: Brigadier General U.S. Vols.)
Service: U.S. Army
Birthday: 7 February 1847
Place of Birth: New Orleans, Orleans County, Louisiana
Date of Death: 26 April 1909
Cemetery: Evergreen Cemetery (MH)—Stonington, Connecticut
Entered Service at: Stonington, New London County, Connecticut
Unit: 5th U.S. Cavalry
Battle or Place of Action: Spring Creek, Nebraska
Date of Action: 16 May 1869
Date of Issue: 18 September 1897
Citation: While serving with a scouting column, this officer's troop was attacked by a vastly superior force of Indians. Advancing to high ground, he dismounted his men, remaining mounted himself to encourage them, and there fought the Indians until relieved, his horse being wounded.

1542 ◆ BAILEY, JAMES E.

Rank: Sergeant
Service: U.S. Army
Place of Birth: Dexter, Penobscot County, Maine
Entered Service at: Boston, Suffolk County, Massachusetts
Unit: Company E, 5th U.S. Cavalry
Battle or Place of Action: Apache campaigns
Date of Action: 1872—1873
Date of Issue: 12 April 1875
Citation: Gallant conduct during campaigns and engagements with Apaches.

1543 ◆ BAIRD, GEORGE WILLIAM

Rank: First Lieutenant, Adjutant (highest rank: Major General)
Service: U.S. Army
Birthday: 13 December 1839
Place of Birth: Milford, New Haven County, Connecticut
Date of Death: 28 November 1906
Place of Death: Ashville, North Carolina
Cemetery: Old Milford Cemetery (MH)—Milford, Connecticut
Entered Service at: Milford, New Haven County, Connecticut
Unit: 5th U.S. Infantry
Battle or Place of Action: Bear Paw Mountain, Montana
Date of Action: 30 September 1877
Date of Issue: 27 November 1894
Citation: Most distinguished gallantry in action with the Nez Perce Indians.

1544 ◆ BAKER, JOHN

Rank: Musician
Service: U.S. Army
Birthday: 1853
Place of Birth: Hessen, Germany
Entered Service at: Brooklyn, Kings County, New York
Unit: Company D, 5th U.S. Infantry
Battle or Place of Action: Cedar Creek, etc., Montana
Date of Action: October 1876—January 1877
Date of Issue: 27 April 1877
Citation: Gallantry in engagements.

1545 ◆ BALDWIN, FRANK DWIGHT✛

Rank: First Lieutenant (highest rank: Major General)
Service: U.S. Army
Birthday: 26 June 1842
Place of Birth: Manchester, Washtenaw County, Michigan
Date of Death: 22 April 1923
Cemetery: Arlington National Cemetery (3-1894)—Arlington, Virginia
Entered Service at: Constantine, St. Joseph County, Michigan
Unit: 5th U.S. Infantry
Battle or Place of Action: McClellans Creek, Texas
Date of Action: 8 November 1874
Date of Issue: 3 December 1891
Citation: **Second Award** Rescued, with two companies, two white girls by a voluntary attack upon Indians whose superior numbers and strong position would have warranted delay for

reinforcements, but which delay would have permitted the Indians to escape and kill their captives.
Notes: ✢Double Awardee: *see also* Civil War

1546 ◆ BANCROFT, NEIL

Rank: Private
Service: U.S. Army
Birthday: 1846
Place of Birth: Oswego, Oswego County, New York
Entered Service at: Chicago, Cook County, Illinois
Unit: Company A, 7th U.S. Cavalry
Battle or Place of Action: Little Big Horn, Montana
Date of Action: 25 June 1876
Date of Issue: 5 October 1878
Citation: Brought water for the wounded under a most galling fire.

1547 ◆ BARNES, WILL CROFT

Rank: Private First Class
Service: U.S. Army
Birthday: 21 June 1858
Place of Birth: San Francisco, San Francisco County, California
Date of Death: 17 December 1936
Place of Death: Phoenix, Arizona
Cemetery: Arlington National Cemetery (6-9754)—Arlington, Virginia
Entered Service at: Washington, D.C.
Unit: U.S. Army, Signal Corps
Battle or Place of Action: Arizona
Date of Action: 1 September 1881
Date of Issue: 8 November 1882
Citation: Bravery in action.

1548 ◆ BARRETT, RICHARD

Rank: First Sergeant
Service: U.S. Army
Birthday: 1838
Date of Birth: County Mayo, Ireland
Date of Death: 20 March 1898
Cemetery: Soldiers Home National Cemetery (K-6765) (MH)—Washington, D.C.,
Entered Service at: Buffalo, Erie County, New York
Unit: Company A, 1st U.S. Cavalry
Battle or Place of Action: Sycamore Canyon, Arizona
Date of Action: 23 May 1872
Date of Issue: 12 April 1875
Citation: Conspicuous gallantry in a charge upon the Tonto Apaches.

1549 ◆ BEAUFORD, CLAY

True Name: Bridwell, Welford Chapman
Rank: First Sergeant
Service: U.S. Army
Birthday: 1847
Place of Birth: Washington County, Maryland
Date of Death: 1 February 1905
Cemetery: Rosedale Cemetery—Los Angeles, California
Entered Service at: Nashville, Davidson County, Tennessee
Unit: Company B, 5th U.S. Cavalry
Battle or Place of Action: Apache campaigns
Date of Action: 1872-73
Date of Issue: 12 April 1875
Citation: Gallant conduct during campaigns and engagements with Apaches.

1550 ◆ BELL, JAMES

Rank: Private (highest rank: Sergeant)
Service: U.S. Army
Birthday: 1845
Place of Birth: County Antrim, Ireland
Date of Death: 1 July 1901
Place of Death: Chicago, Illinois
Cemetery: Mount Olivet Cemetery—Chicago, Illinois
Entered Service at: Troy, Rensselaer County, New York
Unit: Company E, 7th U.S. Infantry
Battle or Place of Action: Big Horn, Montana
Date of Action: 9 July 1876
Date of Issue: 2 December 1876
Citation: Carried dispatches to Gen. Crook at the imminent risk of his life.

1551 ◆ BERGENDAHL, FREDERICK

Rank: Private (highest rank: Sergeant)
Service: U.S. Army
Birthday: 26 February 1858
Place of Birth: Gothenburg, Sweden
Date of Death: 15 December 1889
Place of Death: Gothenburg, Sweden
Cemetery: The Cast Cemetery, Ostra Kyrkcogardco—Gothenburg, Sweden
Entered Service at: Boston, Suffolk County, Massachusetts
Unit: Band, 4th U.S. Cavalry
Battle or Place of Action: Staked Plains, Texas
Date of Action: 8 December 1874
Date of Issue: 13 October 1875
Citation: Gallantry in a long chase after Indians.

1552 ◆ BERTRAM, HEINRICH

Rank: Corporal
Service: U.S. Army
Birthday: 1842
Place of Birth: Brunswick, Germany
Entered Service at: Cincinnati, Hamilton County, Ohio
Unit: Company B, 8th U.S. Cavalry
Battle or Place of Action: Arizona
Date of Action: 1868
Date of Issue: 24 July 1869
Citation: Bravery in scouts and actions against Indians.

1553 ◆ BESSEY, CHARLES ALBERT

Rank: Corporal (highest rank: Chief Musician-Ret.)
Service: U.S. Army
Birthday: 6 November 1848
Place of Birth: Reading, Middlesex County, Massachusetts
Date of Death: 4 June 1909
Place of Death: Biloxi, Mississippi
Cemetery: Old Biloxi Cemetery—Biloxi, Mississippi
Entered Service at: Boston, Suffolk County, Massachusetts
Unit: Company A, 3d U.S. Cavalry
Battle or Place of Action: Elkhorn Creek, Wyoming
Date of Action: 13 January 1877
Date of Issue: 15 May 1890
Citation: While scouting with four men and being attacked in ambush by 14 hostile Indians, held his ground, two of his men being wounded, and kept up the fight until himself wounded in the side, and then went to the assistance of his wounded comrades.

1554 ◆ BISHOP, DANIEL

Rank: Sergeant
Service: U.S. Army
Birthday: 1846
Place of Birth: Monroe County, Ohio
Date of Death: 23 May 1891
Place of Death: Bellaire, Ohio
Cemetery: Greenwood Cemetery—Bellaire, Ohio
Entered Service at: Wheeling, Ohio County, West Virginia
Unit: Company A, 5th U.S. Cavalry
Battle or Place of Action: Turret Mountain, Arizona Territory
Date of Action: 25 March 1873
Date of Issue: 12 April 1875
Citation: Gallantry in engagements.

1555 ◆ BLAIR, JAMES

Rank: First Sergeant
Service: U.S. Army
Birthday: 1841
Place of Birth: Schuyler County, Pennsylvania
Entered Service at: Camp Winfield Scott, Humbolt County, Nevada
Unit: Company I, 1st U.S. Cavalry
Battle or Place of Action: Apache campaigns
Date of Action: 1872-73
Date of Issue: 12 April 1875
Citation: Gallant conduct during campaigns and engagements with Apaches.

1556 ◆ BLANQUET

Rank: Indian Scout
Service: U.S. Army
Place of Birth: Arizona
Unit: Indian Scouts
Battle or Place of Action: Apache campaigns
Date of Action: 1872-73
Date of Issue: 12 April 1875
Citation: Gallant conduct during campaigns and engagements with Apaches.

1557 ◆ BOWDEN, SAMUEL

Rank: Corporal
Service: U.S. Army
Birthday: 1846
Place of Birth: Salem, Essex County, Massachusetts
Entered Service at: Boston, Suffolk County, Massachusetts
Unit: Company M, 6th U.S. Cavalry
Battle or Place of Action: Wichita River, Texas
Date of Action: 5 October 1870
Date of Issue: 19 November 1870
Citation: Gallantry in pursuit of and fight with Indians.

1558 ◆ BOWMAN, ALONZO

Rank: Sergeant
Service: U.S. Army
Birthday: 15 June 1848
Place of Birth: Washington Township, Knox County, Maine
Date of Death: 4 October 1885
Place of Death: Fort Bayard, New Mexico
Cemetery: Fort Bayard National Cemetery (A-1-31)—Fort Bayard, New Mexico
Entered Service at: Boston, Suffolk County, Massachusetts
Unit: Company D, 6th U.S. Cavalry
Battle or Place of Action: Cibicu Creek, Arizona
Date of Action: 30 August 1881
Date of Issue: 4 November 1882
Citation: Conspicuous and extraordinary bravery in attacking mutinous scouts.

1559 ◆ BOYNE, THOMAS

Rank: Sergeant
Service: U.S. Army
Birthday: 1849
Place of Birth: Prince Georges County, Maryland
Date of Death: 21 April 1896
Place of Death: Washington, D.C.
Cemetery: Soldiers Home National Cemetery (J-5859) (MH)—Washington, D.C.,
Entered Service at: Norfolk, Norfolk County, Virginia
Unit: Company C, 9th U.S. Cavalry
Battle or Place of Action: Cuchillo Negro River & Mimbres Mountains, New Mexico
Date of Action: 29 May & 27 September 1879
Date of Issue: 6 January 1882
Citation: Bravery in action.

1560 ◆ BRADBURY, SANFORD

Rank: First Sergeant
Service: U.S. Army

1561 ◆ BRANAGAN, EDWARD

Birthday: 1840
Place of Birth: Newton, Sussex County, New Jersey
Date of Death: 7 December 1911
Cemetery: Arlington National Cemetery (3-2162WS)—Arlington, Virginia
Entered Service at: Washington, D.C.
Unit: Company L, 8th U.S. Cavalry
Battle or Place of Action: Hell Canyon, Arizona
Date of Action: 3 July 1869
Date of Issue: 3 March 1870
Citation: Conspicuous gallantry in action.

1561 ◆ BRANAGAN, EDWARD

Rank: Private
Service: U.S. Army
Birthday: 1846
Place of Birth: County Louth, Ireland
Cemetery: Fort Concho National Historic Landmark (MH) (Marker Only)—San Angelo, Texas
Entered Service at: New York, New York
Unit: Company F, 4th U.S. Cavalry
Battle or Place of Action: Red River, Texas
Date of Action: 29 September 1872
Date of Issue: 19 November 1872
Citation: Gallantry in action.

1562 ◆ *BRANT, ABRAM B.

Rank: Private
Service: U.S. Army
Birthday: 1849
Place of Birth: New York, New York
Date of Death: 4 October 1878
Place of Death: near Camp Ruhlen, Dakota Territory
Cemetery: Fort Meade National Cemetery—Fort Meade, South Dakota (as unknown)
Entered Service at: St. Louis, St. Louis County, Missouri
Unit: Company D, 7th U.S. Cavalry
Battle or Place of Action: Little Big Horn, Montana
Date of Action: 25 June 1876
Date of Issue: 5 October 1878
Citation: Brought water for the wounded under a most galling fire.

1563 ◆ *BRATLING, FRANK

Rank: Corporal
Service: U.S. Army
Birthday: 1845
Place of Birth: Bavaria, Germany
Date of Death: 13 July 1873
Place of Death: near Canada Alamos, New Mexico
Cemetery: Post Cemetery—Fort McRae, New Mexico; Fort Bliss National Cemetery (MH)(marker only)—Fort Bliss, Texas
Entered Service at: Louisville, Jefferson County, Kentucky
Unit: Company C, 8th U.S. Cavalry
Battle or Place of Action: Fort Selden, New Mexico
Date of Action: 8-11 July 1873
Date of Issue: 12 August 1875
Citation: Services against hostile Indians.

1564 ◆ BRETT, LLOYD MILTON

Rank: Second Lieutenant (highest rank: Brigadier General-Ret.)
Service: U.S. Army
Birthday: 22 February 1856
Place of Birth: Dead River, Maine
Date of Death: 23 September 1927
Place of Death: Washington, D.C.
Cemetery: Arlington National Cemetery {6-8367)—Arlington, Virginia
Entered Service at: Malden, Middlesex County, Massachusetts
Unit: 2d U.S. Cavalry
Battle or Place of Action: O'Fallons Creek, Montana
Date of Action: 1 April 1880
Date of Issue: 7 February 1895
Citation: Fearless exposure and dashing bravery in cutting off the Indians' pony herd, thereby greatly crippling the hostiles.

1565 ◆ BROGAN, JAMES

True Name: Brogan, Edward James
Rank: Sergeant
Service: U.S. Army
Birthday: 1834
Place of Birth: County Donegal, Ireland
Date of Death: 30 October 1908
Place of Death: Summit Hill, Pennsylvania
Cemetery: Saint Joseph's Cemetery (MH)—Summit Hill, Pennsylvania
Entered Service at: Harrisburg, Dauphin County, Pennsylvania
Unit: Company G, 6th U.S. Cavalry
Battle or Place of Action: Simon Valley, Arizona
Date of Action: 14 December 1877
Date of Issue: 9 January 1880
Citation: Engaged singlehandedly two renegade Indians until his horse was shot under him and then pursued them so long as he was able.

1566 ◆ BROPHY, JAMES

Rank: Private
Service: U.S. Army
Birthday: 20 May 1846
Place of Birth: Kilkenny, Ireland
Date of Death: 7 August 1929
Cemetery: Soldiers Home National Cemetery (L-9086) (MH)—Washington, D.C.
Entered Service at: Stockton, San Joaquin County, California
Unit: Company B, 8th U.S. Cavalry
Battle or Place of Action: Arizona

Date of Action: 1868
Date of Issue: 24 July 1869
Citation: Bravery in scouts and actions against Indians.

1567 ◆ BROWN, BENJAMIN

Rank: Sergeant
Service: U.S. Army
Birthday: 1859
Place of Birth: Spotsylvania County, Virginia
Date of Death: 5 September 1910
Place of Death: Washington, D.C.
Cemetery: Soldier's Home National Cemetery (K-7519) (MH)—Washington, D.C.
Entered Service at: Harrisburg, Dauphin County, Pennsylvania
Unit: Company C, 24th U.S. Infantry
Battle or Place of Action: Arizona
Date of Action: 11 May 1889
Date of Issue: 19 February 1890
Citation: Although shot in the abdomen, in a fight between a paymaster's escort and robbers, did not leave the field until again wounded through both arms.

1568 ◆ BROWN, JAMES

Rank: Sergeant
Service: U.S. Army
Birthday: 1847
Place of Birth: Wexford, Ireland
Entered Service at: New York, New York
Unit: Company F, 5th U.S. Cavalry
Battle or Place of Action: Davidson Canyon, Arizona
Date of Action: 27 August 1872
Date of Issue: 4 December 1874
Citation: In command of a detachment of four men, defeated a superior force.

1569 ◆ BROWN, LORENZO DOW

Rank: Private
Service: U.S. Army
Birthday: December 1851
Place of Birth: Davidson County, North Carolina
Date of Death: 17 April 1906
Place of Death: near Jonesboro, Arkansas
Entered Service at: Indianapolis, Marion County, Indiana
Unit: Company A, 7th U.S. Infantry
Battle or Place of Action: Big Hole, Montana
Date of Action: 9 August 1877
Date of Issue: 8 May 1878
Citation: After having been severely wounded in right shoulder, continued to do duty in a most courageous manner.

1570 ◆ BRYAN, WILLIAM C.

Rank: Hospital Steward
Service: U.S. Army
Birthday: 9 September 1852
Place of Birth: Zanesville, Muskingum County, Ohio
Date of Death: 27 March 1933
Place of Death: Santa Monica, California
Cemetery: Forest Lawn Cemetery (MH)—Los Angeles, California
Entered Service at: St. Louis, St. Louis County, Missouri
Unit: U.S. Army
Battle or Place of Action: Powder River, Wyoming
Date of Action: 17 March 1876
Date of Issue: 15 June 1899
Citation: Accompanied a detachment of cavalry in a charge on a village of hostile Indians and fought through the engagements, having his horse killed under him. He continued to fight on foot, and under severe fire and without assistance conveyed two wounded comrades to places of safety, saving them from capture.

1571 ◆ BURKARD, OSCAR R.

Rank: Private (highest rank: Major, Medical Corps)
Service: U.S. Army
Birthday: 21 December 1877
Place of Birth: Baden Achern, Germany
Date of Death: 18 February 1950
Place of Death: Rome, New York
Cemetery: Rome Cemetery (MH)—Rome, New York
Entered Service at: Fort Snelling, St. Paul County, Minnesota
Unit: U.S. Army, Hospital Corps
Served as: Medic
Battle or Place of Action: Leech Lake, Minnesota
Date of Action: 5 October 1898
Date of Issue: 21 August 1899
Citation: For distinguished bravery in action against hostile Indians.
Notes: This, the last Medal of Honor won in an Indian campaign, was awarded for an action during the uprising of Chippewa Indians, on Lake Leech, northern Minn., 5 October 1898.

1572 ◆ BURKE, PATRICK J.

Rank: Farrier
Service: U.S. Army
Birthday: 1835
Place of Birth: Kilkenny, Ireland
Entered Service at: Vallejo, Solano County, California
Unit: Company B, 8th U.S. Cavalry
Battle or Place of Action: Arizona
Date of Action: 1868
Date of Issue: 24 July 1869
Citation: Bravery in scouts and actions against Indians.

1573 ◆ BURKE, RICHARD

Rank: Private
Service: U.S. Army
Birthday: 1847
Place of Birth: Tipperary, Ireland

Entered Service at: New York, New York
Unit: Company G., 5th U.S. Infantry
Battle or Place of Action: Cedar Creek, etc., Montana
Date of Action: October 1876—January 1877
Date of Issue: 27 April 1877
Citation: Gallantry in engagements.

1574 ◆ BURNETT, GEORGE RITTER

Rank: Second Lieutenant (highest rank: First Lieutenant)
Service: U.S. Army
Birthday: 21 April 1858
Place of Birth: Lower Providence Township, Pennsylvania
Date of Death: 1 November 1908
Place of Death: Lincoln, Nebraska
Cemetery: Arlington National Cemetery (3-2193WS)—Arlington, Virginia
Entered Service at: Spring Mills, Centre County, Pennsylvania
Unit: 9th U.S. Cavalry
Battle or Place of Action: Cuchillo Negro Mountains, New Mexico
Date of Action: 16 August 1881
Date of Issue: 23 July 1897
Citation: Saved the life of a dismounted soldier, who was in imminent danger of being cut off, by alone galloping quickly to his assistance under heavy fire and escorting him to a place of safety, his horse being twice shot in this action.

1575 ◆ BUTLER, EDMOND THOMAS

Rank: Captain (highest rank: Lieutenant Colonel)
Service: U.S. Army
Birthday: 19 March 1827
Place of Birth: Clonmel, County Tipperary, Ireland
Date of Death: 21 August 1895
Place of Death: Paris, France
Cemetery: Holy Sepulchre Cemetery (MH)—Omaha, Nebraska
Entered Service at: Brooklyn, Kings County, New York
Unit: 5th U.S. Infantry
Battle or Place of Action: Wolf Mountain, Montana
Date of Action: 8 January 1877
Date of Issue: 27 April 1877
Citation: Most distinguished gallantry in action with hostile Indians.

1576 ◆ BYRNE, DENIS

Rank: Sergeant
Service: U.S. Army
Birthday: 1833
Place of Birth: Wexford, Ireland
Date of Death: 31 December 1905
Place of Death: Birds Island, Minnesota
Entered Service at: New York, New York
Unit: Company G, 5th U.S. Infantry
Battle or Place of Action: Cedar Creek, etc., Montana
Date of Action: October 1876—January 1877
Date of Issue: 27 April 1877
Citation: Gallantry in engagements.

1577 ◆ CABLE, JOSEPH A.

Rank: Private (highest rank: Corporal)
Service: U.S. Army
Birthday: 1848
Place of Birth: Cape Girardeau, Cape Girardeau County, Missouri
Date of Death: 15 October 1877
Place of Death: Bear Paw Mountain, Montana
Cemetery: Custer Battlefield National Cemetery—Crow Agency, Montana
Entered Service at: Madison, Dane County, Wisconsin
Unit: Company I, 5th U.S. Infantry
Battle or Place of Action: Cedar Creek, etc., Montana
Date of Action: October 1876—January 1877
Date of Issue: 27 April 1877
Citation: Gallantry in action.

1578 ◆ CALLEN, THOMAS JOSEPH

True Name: Callan, Thomas Joseph
Rank: Private
Service: U.S. Army
Birthday: 13 July 1853
Place of Birth: County Louth, Ireland
Date of Death: 5 March 1908
Cemetery: Holy Sepulchre Cemetery (MH)—East Orange, New Jersey
Entered Service at: Boston, Suffolk County, Massachusetts
Unit: Company B, 7th U.S. Cavalry
Battle or Place of Action: Little Big Horn, Montana
Date of Action: 25-26 June 1876
Date of Issue: 24 October 1896
Citation: Volunteered and succeeded in obtaining water for the wounded of the command; also displayed conspicuously good conduct in assisting to drive away the Indians.

1579 ◆ CALVERT, JAMES SPENCER

Rank: Private (highest rank: Regimental Quartermaster Sergeant)
Service: U.S. Army
Birthday: 27 June 1852
Place of Birth: Athens County, Ohio
Date of Death: 26 February 1929
Place of Death: Washington, D.C.
Cemetery: Arlington National Cemetery (3-2490)—Arlington, Virginia
Entered Service at: Springfield, Sangamon County, Illinois
Unit: Company C, 5th U.S. Infantry
Battle or Place of Action: Cedar Creek, etc., Montana
Date of Action: October 1876—January 1877
Date of Issue: 27 April 1877
Citation: Gallantry in action.

1580 ◆ CANFIELD, HETH

Rank: Private
Service: U.S. Army
Birthday: 1849
Place of Birth: New Milford, Litchfield County, Connecticut
Date of Death: 16 December 1913
Place of Death: St. Augustine, Florida
Cemetery: Evergreen Cemetery (MH)—St. Augustine, Florida
Entered Service at: Carlisle, Cumberland County, Pennsylvania
Unit: Company C, 2d U.S. Cavalry
Battle or Place of Action: Little Blue, Nebraska
Date of Action: 15 May 1870
Date of Issue: 22 June 1870
Citation: Gallantry in action.

1581 ◆ CARPENTER, LOUIS HENRY

Rank: Captain (highest rank: Brigadier General Ret.)
Service: U.S. Army
Birthday: 11 February 1839
Place of Birth: Glassboro, Gloucester County, New Jersey
Date of Death: 21 January 1916
Place of Death: Philadelphia, Pennsylvania
Cemetery: Trinity Church Cemetery—Swedesboro, New Jersey
Entered Service at: Philadelphia, Philadelphia County, Pennsylvania
Unit: Company H, 10th U.S. Cavalry
Battle or Place of Action: Indian Campaigns, Kansas and Colorado
Date of Action: September, October 1868
Date of Issue: 8 April 1898
Citation: Was gallant and meritorious throughout the campaigns, especially in the combat of October 15 and in the forced march on September 23, 24 and 25 to the relief of Forsyth's Scouts, who were known to be in danger of annihilation by largely superior forces of Indians.

1582 ◆ CARR, JOHN

Rank: Private (highest rank: Corporal)
Service: U.S. Army
Birthday: 1847
Place of Birth: Columbus, Franklin County, Ohio
Date of Death: 15 July 1891
Place of Death: Columbian Arsenel, Tennessee
Cemetery: Nashville National Cemetery (A-16550) (MH)—Nashville, Tennessee
Entered Service at: San Jose, Santa Clara County, California
Unit: Company G, U.S. Cavalry
Battle or Place of Action: Chiricahua Mountains, Arizona Territory
Date of Action: 29 October 1869
Date of Issue: 14 February 1870
Citation: Gallantry in action.

1583 ◆ CARROLL, THOMAS

Rank: Private
Service: U.S. Army
Birthday: 1842
Place of Birth: Kilkenny, Ireland
Entered Service at: Chicago, Cook County, Illinois
Unit: Company L, 8th U.S. Cavalry
Battle or Place of Action: Arizona
Date of Action: August-October 1868
Date of Issue: 24 July 1869
Citation: Bravery in scouts and actions against Indians.

1584 ◆ CARTER, GEORGE

Rank: Private
Service: U.S. Army
Birthday: 1839
Place of Birth: Dublin, Ireland
Entered Service at: Vallejo, Solano County, California
Unit: Company B, 8th U.S. Cavalry
Battle or Place of Action: Arizona
Date of Action: August-October 1868
Date of Issue: 24 July 1869
Citation: Bravery in scouts and actions against Indians.

1585 ◆ CARTER, MASON

Rank: First Lieutenant (highest rank: Brevet Major)
Service: U.S. Army
Birthday: 26 January 1834
Place of Birth: Augusta, Richmond County, Georgia
Date of Death: 11 December 1909
Cemetery: Fort Rosecrans National Cemetery (PS-4-102)—San Diego, California
Entered Service at: Augusta, Richmond County, Georgia
Unit: 5th U.S. Infantry
Battle or Place of Action: Bear Paw Mountain, Montana
Date of Action: 30 October 1877
Date of Issue: 27 November 1894
Citation: Led a charge under a galling fire, in which he inflicted great loss upon the enemy.

1586 ◆ CARTER, ROBERT GOLDTHWAITE

Rank: Second Lieutenant (highest rank: Brevet Captain)
Service: U.S. Army
Birthday: 18 April 1847
Place of Birth: Bridgton, Cumberland County, Maine
Date of Death: 4 January 1936
Place of Death: Walter Reed Hospital, Washington, D.C.
Cemetery: Arlington National Cemetery (1-106A)—Arlington, Virginia
Entered Service at: Bradford, Essex County, Massachusetts
Unit: 4th U.S. Cavalry

Battle or Place of Action: Brazos River, Texas
Date of Action: 10 October 1871
Date of Issue: 27 February 1900
Citation: Held the left of the line with a few men during the charge of a large body of Indians, after the right of the line had retreated, and by delivering a rapid fire, succeeded in checking the enemy until other troops came to the rescue.

1587 ◆ CARTER, WILLIAM HARDING

Rank: First Lieutenant (highest rank: Major General)
Service: U.S. Army
Birthday: 19 November 1851
Place of Birth: Nashville, Davidson County, Tennessee
Date of Death: 24 May 1925
Place of Death: Washington, D.C.
Cemetery: Arlington National Cemetery (1-443-WS)—Arlington, Virginia
Entered Service at: New York, New York
Unit: 6th U.S. Cavalry
Battle or Place of Action: Cibicu, Arizona
Date of Action: 30 August 1881
Date of Issue: 17 October 1891
Citation: Rescued, with the voluntary assistance of two soldiers, the wounded from under a heavy fire.

1588 ◆ CASEY, JAMES SEAMAN

Rank: Captain (highest rank: Colonel-USA-Ret.)
Service: U.S. Army
Birthday: 28 January 1833
Place of Birth: Philadelphia, Philadelphia County, Pennsylvania
Date of Death: 24 December 1899
Place of Death: New York, New York
Cemetery: Vale Cemetery—Schenectady, New York
Entered Service at: New York, New York
Unit: 5th U.S. Infantry
Battle or Place of Action: Wolf Mountain, Montana
Date of Action: 8 January 1877
Date of Issue: 27 November 1894
Citation: Led his command in a successful charge against superior numbers of the enemy strongly posted.

1589 ◆ CHAPMAN, AMOS

Rank: Scout (Civilian)
Service: U.S. Army
Birthday: 15 March 1839
Place of Birth: Kalamazoo, Kalamazoo County, Michigan
Date of Death: 18 July 1925
Cemetery: Bromfield Cemetery—Seiling, Oklahoma
Entered Service at: Fort Supply, Indian Territory (Oklahoma)
Unit: 6th U.S. Cavalry (Assigned)
Battle or Place of Action: Washita River, Texas
Date of Action: 12 September 1874
Date of Issue: 7 November 1874
Citation: Gallantry in action.

1590 ◆ CHEEVER JR., BENJAMIN HARRISON

Rank: First Lieutenant (highest rank: Colonel)
Service: U.S. Army
Birthday: 7 June 1850
Place of Birth: Washington, D.C.
Date of Death: 21 October 1930
Place of Death: Atlantic City, New Jersey
Cemetery: Arlington National Cemetery (1-421) (MH)—Arlington, Virginia
Entered Service at: Washington, D.C.
Unit: 6th U.S. Cavalry
Battle or Place of Action: White River, South Dakota
Date of Action: 1 January 1891
Date of Issue: 25 April 1891
Citation: Headed the advance across White River, partly frozen, in a spirited movement to the effective assistance of Troop K, 6th U.S. Cavalry.

1591 ◆ CHIQUITO

Rank: Scout
Service: U.S. Army
Place of Birth: Arizona
Entered Service at: San Carlos, Gila County, Arizona
Unit: Indian Scouts
Battle or Place of Action: Arizona
Date of Action: winter 1872-73
Date of Issue: 12 April 1875
Citation: Gallant conduct during campaigns and engagements with Apaches.

1592 ◆ CLANCY, JOHN E.

Rank: Musician (highest rank: First Sergeant Ret.)
Service: U.S. Army
Birthday: 25 October 1869
Place of Birth: New York, New York
Date of Death: 11 July 1932
Cemetery: Fort Riley Post Cemetery (I-5) (MH)—Fort Riley, Kansas
Entered Service at: Vancouver Barracks, Clark County, Washington
Unit: Company E, 1st U.S. Artillery
Battle or Place of Action: Wounded Knee Creek, South Dakota
Date of Action: 29 December 1890
Date of Issue: 23 January 1892
Citation: Twice voluntarily rescued wounded comrades under fire of the enemy.

1593 ◆ CLARK, WILFRED

Rank: Private
Service: U.S. Army
Birthday: 1841
Place of Birth: Philadelphia, Philadelphia County, Pennsylvania
Entered Service at: Philadelphia, Philadelphia County, Pennsylvania

Unit: Company L, 2d U.S. Cavalry
Battle or Place of Action: Big Hole, Montana-Camas Meadows, Idaho
Date of Action: 9-20 August 1877
Date of Issue: 28 February 1878
Citation: Conspicuous gallantry; especial skill as sharpshooter.

1594 ◆ CLARKE, POWHATAN HENRY

Rank: Second Lieutenant
Service: U.S. Army
Birthday: 9 October 1862
Place of Birth: Alexandria, Rapides County, Louisiana
Date of Death: 21 July 1893
Place of Death: Little Big Horn River, Montana
Cemetery: Calvary Cemetery—St.Louis, Missouri
Entered Service at: Baltimore, Baltimore County, Maryland
Unit: 10th U.S. Cavalry
Battle or Place of Action: Pinito Mountains, Sonora, Mexico
Date of Action: 3 May 1886
Date of Issue: 12 March 1891
Citation: Rushed forward to the rescue of a soldier who was severely wounded and lay, disabled, exposed to the enemy's fire, and carried him to a place of safety.

1595 ◆ CODY, WILLIAM FREDERICK "BUFFALO BILL"

Rank: Guide (Civilian)
Service: U.S. Army
Birthday: 16 February 1846
Place of Birth: Scott County, Iowa
Date of Death: 10 January 1917
Place of Death: Denver, Colorado
Cemetery: Lookout Mountain (MH)—Golden, Colorado
Entered Service at: Fort McPherson, Nebraska
Unit: Indian Scouts attached to 3d U.S. Cavalry
Battle or Place of Action: Loupe Fork of the Platte River, Nebraska
Date of Action: 26 April 1872
Date of Issue: 22 May 1872
Citation: Gallantry in action.

1596 ◆ COMFORT, JOHN W.

Rank: Corporal
Service: U.S. Army
Birthday: 1844
Place of Birth: Philadelphia, Philadelphia County, Pennsylvania
Date of Death: 29 November 1893
Place of Death: Philadelphia, Pennsylvania
Cemetery: Mount Peace Cemetery—Rockledge, Pennsylvania
Entered Service at: Philadelphia, Philadelphia County, Pennsylvania
Unit: Company A, 4th U.S. Cavalry
Battle or Place of Action: Staked Plains, Texas
Date of Action: 5 November 1874
Date of Issue: 13 October 1875
Citation: Ran down and killed an Indian.

1597 ◆ CONNOR, JOHN

Rank: Corporal (highest rank: Sergeant Ret.)
Service: U.S. Army
Birthday: 1845
Place of Birth: Galway, Ireland
Date of Death: 5 February 1907
Place of Death: Washington, D.C.
Cemetery: Soldier's Home National Cemetery (K-7258) (MH)—Washington, D.C.
Entered Service at: Jefferson, Marion County, Texas
Unit: Company H, 6th U.S. Cavalry
Battle or Place of Action: Wichita River, Texas
Date of Action: 12 July 1870
Date of Issue: 25 August 1870
Citation: Gallantry in action.

1598 ◆ COONROD, AQUILLA

Rank: Sergeant (highest rank: First Sergeant)
Service: U.S. Army
Birthday: 1831
Place of Birth: Williams County, Ohio
Date of Death: 14 May 1884
Cemetery: Custer Battlefield National Monument (A-372)—Crow Agency, Montana
Entered Service at: Bryan, Williams County, Ohio
Unit: Company C, 5th U.S. Infantry
Battle or Place of Action: Cedar Creek, etc., Montana
Date of Action: October 1876—January 1877
Date of Issue: 27 April 1877
Citation: Gallantry in action.

1599 ◆ CORCORAN, MICHAEL

Rank: Corporal
Service: U.S. Army
Birthday: 1847
Place of Birth: Philadelphia, Philadelphia County, Pennsylvania
Date of Death: 3 October 1919
Cemetery: Calvary Cemetery—Cleveland, Ohio
Entered Service at: Wheeling, Ohio County, West Virginia
Unit: Company E, 8th U.S. Cavalry
Battle or Place of Action: Agua Fria River, Arizona
Date of Action: 25 August 1869
Date of Issue: 3 March 1870
Citation: Gallantry in action.

1600 ◆ CO-RUX-TE-CHOD-ISH (MAD BEAR)

Rank: Sergeant
Service: U.S. Army
Place of Birth: Nebraska

Entered Service at: Columbus, Platte County, Nebraska
Unit: U.S. Army
Battle or Place of Action: Republican River, Kansas
Date of Action: 8 July 1869
Date of Issue: 24 August 1869
Citation: Ran out from the command in pursuit of a dismounted Indian; was shot down and badly wounded by a bullet from his own command.

1601 ◆ CRAIG, SAMUEL HENRY

Rank: Sergeant (highest rank: First Sergeant)
Service: U.S. Army
Birthday: 31 October 1863
Place of Birth: New Market, Rockingham County, New Hampshire
Date of Death: 1 June 1929
Place of Death: Kittery, Maine
Cemetery: Laurel Hill Cemetery (MH)—Saco, Maine
Entered Service at: Chicago, Cook County, Illinois
Unit: Company D, 4th U.S. Cavalry
Battle or Place of Action: Santa Cruz Mountains, Mexico
Date of Action: 15 May 1886
Date of Issue: 27 April 1887
Citation: Conspicuous gallantry during an attack on a hostile Apache Indian camp; seriously wounded.

1602 ◆ CRANDALL, CHARLES

Rank: Private
Service: U.S. Army
Birthday: 1847
Place of Birth: Worcester, Worcester County, Massachusetts
Entered Service at: Philadelphia, Philadelphia County, Pennsylvania
Unit: Company B, 8th U.S. Cavalry
Battle or Place of Action: Arizona
Date of Action: August–October 1868
Date of Issue: 24 July 1869
Citation: Bravery in scouts and actions against Indians.

1603 ◆ CRIST, JOHN

Rank: Sergeant
Service: U.S. Army
Birthday: 1845
Place of Birth: Baltimore, Baltimore County, Maryland
Entered Service at: Baltimore, Baltimore County, Maryland
Unit: Company L, 8th U.S. Cavalry
Battle or Place of Action: Arizona
Date of Action: 26 November 1869
Date of Issue: 3 March 1870
Citation: Gallantry in action.

1604 ◆ CRISWELL, BENJAMIN C.

Rank: Sergeant (highest rank: First Sergeant)
Service: U.S. Army
Birthday: 9 February 1849
Place of Birth: Moundsville, Marshall County, West Virginia
Date of Death: 17 October 1921
Place of Death: Eldorado, Oklahoma
Entered Service at: Cincinnati, Hamilton County, Ohio
Unit: Company B, 7th U.S. Cavalry
Battle or Place of Action: Little Big Horn River, Montana
Date of Action: 25 June 1876
Date of Issue: 5 October 1878
Citation: Rescued the body of Lt. Hodgson from within the enemy's lines; brought up ammunition and encouraged the men in the most exposed positions under heavy fire.

1605 ◆ CRUSE, THOMAS

Rank: Second Lieutenant (highest rank: Brigadier General)
Service: U.S. Army
Birthday: 29 December 1857
Place of Birth: Owensboro, Daviess County, Kentucky
Date of Death: 8 June 1943
Cemetery: Arlington National Cemetery (3-1763)—Arlington, Virginia
Entered Service at: Owensboro, Daviess County, Kentucky
Unit: 6th U.S. Cavalry
Battle or Place of Action: Big Dry Fork (Chevelon's Fork), Arizona
Date of Action: 17 July 1882
Date of Issue: 12 July 1892
Citation: Gallantly charged hostile Indians and with his carbine compelled a party of them to keep under cover of their breastworks, thus being enabled to recover a severely wounded soldier.

1606 ◆ CUBBERLY, WILLIAM G.

Rank: Private
Service: U.S. Army
Birthday: 26 November 1847
Place of Birth: Butler County, Ohio
Date of Death: 27 July 1919
Cemetery: Union Cemetery—Lyonsville, Indiana
Entered Service at: Cincinnati, Hamilton County, Ohio
Unit: Company L, 8th U.S. Cavalry
Battle or Place of Action: San Carlos, Arizona
Date of Action: 30 May 1868
Date of Issue: 28 July 1868
Citation: With two other men he volunteered to search for a wagon passage out of a 4,000-foot valley wherein an infantry column was immobile. This small group passed six miles among hostile Apache terrain finding the sought passage. On their return trip down the canyon they were attacked by Apache, who were successfully held at bay.

1607 ◆ CUNNINGHAM, CHARLES

Rank: Corporal
Service: U.S. Army
Birthday: 1845
Place of Birth: Hudson, Columbia County, New York

Entered Service at: New York, New York
Unit: Company B, 7th U.S. Cavalry
Battle or Place of Action: Little Big Horn River, Montana
Date of Action: 25 June 1876
Date of Issue: 5 October 1878
Citation: Declined to leave the line when wounded in the neck during heavy fire and fought bravely all next day.

1608 ◆ DAILY, CHARLES

Rank: Private
Service: U.S. Army
Birthday: 1841
Place of Birth: Mallow, County Cork, Ireland
Entered Service at: Philadelphia, Philadelphia County, Pennsylvania
Unit: Company B, 8th U.S. Cavalry
Battle or Place of Action: Arizona
Date of Action: August-October 1868
Date of Issue: 24 July 1869
Citation: Bravery in scouts and actions against Indians.

1609 ◆ DANIELS, JAMES THOMAS

Rank: Sergeant
Service: U.S. Army
Birthday: 1860
Place of Birth: Richland County, Illinois
Date of Death: 2 January 1933
Place of Death: Richmond, Virginia
Cemetery: Riverview Cemetery—Richmond, Virginia
Entered Service at: Fort Leavenworth, Leavenworth County, Kansas
Unit: Company L, 4th U.S. Cavalry
Battle or Place of Action: Arizona
Date of Action: 7 March 1890
Date of Issue: 15 May 1890
Citation: Untiring energy and cool gallantry under fire in an engagement with Apache Indians.

1610 ◆ DAWSON, MICHAEL

Rank: Trumpeter (highest rank: Musician)
Service: U.S. Army
Birthday: 1845
Place of Birth: Boston, Suffolk County, Massachusetts
Entered Service at: New York, New York
Unit: Company H, 6th U.S. Cavalry
Battle or Place of Action: Sappa Creek, Kansas
Date of Action: 23 April 1875
Date of Issue: 16 November 1876
Citation: Gallantry in action.

1611 ◆ DAY, MATTHIAS WALTER

Rank: Second Lieutenant (highest rank: Colonel Ret.)
Service: U.S. Army
Birthday: 8 August 1853
Place of Birth: Mansfield, Richland County, Ohio
Date of Death: 12 September 1927
Place of Death: Los Angeles, California
Cemetery: San Francisco National Cemetery OS-2-11—San Francisco, California
Entered Service at: Oberlin, Lorain County, Ohio
Unit: 9th U.S. Cavalry
Battle or Place of Action: Las Animas Canyon, New Mexico
Date of Action: 18 September 1879
Date of Issue: 7 May 1890
Citation: Advanced alone into the enemy's lines and carried off a wounded soldier of his command under a hot fire and after he had been ordered to retreat.

1612 ◆ DAY, WILLIAM L.

Rank: First Sergeant
Service: U.S. Army
Birthday: 1837
Place of Birth: Barron County, Kentucky
Entered Service at: Louisville, Jefferson County, Kentucky
Unit: Company E, 5th U.S. Cavalry
Battle or Place of Action: Apache campaigns
Date of Action: 1872-73
Date of Issue: 12 April 1875
Citation: Gallant conduct during campaigns and engagements with Apaches.

1613 ◆ *DE ARMOND, WILLIAM

Rank: Sergeant
Service: U.S. Army
Birthday: 1838
Place of Birth: Butler County, Ohio
Date of Death: 9 September 1874
Cemetery: San Antonio National Cemetery (MH)—San Antonio, Texas
Entered Service at: New York, New York
Unit: Company I, 5th U.S. Infantry
Battle or Place of Action: Upper Washita, Texas
Date of Action: 9-11 September 1874
Date of Issue: 23 April 1875
Citation: Gallantry in action.

1614 ◆ DEARY, GEORGE

Rank: Sergeant
Service: U.S. Army
Birthday: 1845
Place of Birth: Philadelphia, Philadelphia County, Pennsylvania
Date of Death: 26 September 1901
Place of Death: Philadelphia, Pennsylvania
Cemetery: Mount Moriah Cemetery—Philadelphia, Pennsylvania
Entered Service at: Philadelphia, Philadelphia County, Pennsylvania
Unit: Company L, 5th U.S. Cavalry

Battle or Place of Action: Apache Creek, Arizona
Date of Action: 2 April 1874
Date of Issue: 12 April 1875
Citation: Gallantry in action.

1615 ◆ DEETLINE, FREDERICK

Rank: Private (highest rank: Quartermaster Sergeant)
Service: U.S. Army
Birthday: 1846
Place of Birth: Offenheim, Germany
Date of Death: 13 December 1910
Cemetery: San Antonio National Cemetery (F-921) (MH)—San Antonio, Texas
Entered Service at: Baltimore, Baltimore County, Maryland
Unit: Company D, 7th U.S. Cavalry
Battle or Place of Action: Little Big Horn, Montana
Date of Action: 25 June 1876
Date of Issue: 15 October 1878
Citation: Voluntarily brought water to wounded under fire.

1616 ◆ DENNY, JOHN

Rank: Sergeant
Service: U.S. Army
Birthday: 1846
Place of Birth: Big Flats, Chemung County, New York
Date of Death: 28 November 1901
Place of Death: Washington, D.C.
Cemetery: Soldier's Home Cemetery (K-7020) (MH)—Washington, D.C.
Entered Service at: Elmira, Chemung County, New York
Unit: Company C, 9th U.S. Cavalry
Battle or Place of Action: Las Animas Canyon, New Mexico
Date of Action: 18 September 1879
Date of Issue: 27 November 1894
Citation: Removed a wounded comrade, under a heavy fire, to a place of safety.

1617 ◆ DICKENS, CHARLES H.

Rank: Corporal
Service: U.S. Army
Place of Birth: Dublin, Ireland
Date of Death: 1 March 1880
Cemetery: St. John's Cemetery—Worcester, Massachusetts
Entered Service at: San Francisco, San Francisco County, California
Unit: Company G, 8th U.S. Cavalry
Battle or Place of Action: Chiricahua Mountains, Arizona Territory
Date of Action: 20 October 1869
Date of Issue: 14 February 1870
Citation: Gallantry in action.

1618 ◆ DIXON, WILLIAM "BILLY"

Rank: Scout (Civilian)
Service: U.S. Army
Birthday: 25 September 1850
Place of Birth: Ohio County, West Virginia
Date of Death: 9 March 1913
Place of Death: Cimmarron County, Oklahoma
Cemetery: Adobe Walls Battlefield Site (MH)—Adobe Walls, Texas
Entered Service at: Indian Territory
Unit: Indian Scouts
Battle or Place of Action: Washita River, Texas
Date of Action: 12 September 1874
Date of Issue: 7 November 1874
Citation: Gallantry in action.

1619 ◆ DODGE, FRANCIS SAFFORD

Rank: Captain (highest rank: Brigadier General)
Service: U.S. Army
Birthday: 9 November 1842
Place of Birth: Danvers, Essex County, Massachusetts
Date of Death: 19 February 1908
Cemetery: Arlington National Cemetery (3-1874)—Arlington, Virginia
Entered Service at: Danvers, Essex County, Massachusetts
Unit: Troop D, 9th U.S. Cavalry
Battle or Place of Action: White River Agency, Colorado
Date of Action: 29 September 1879
Date of Issue: 2 April 1898
Citation: With a force of 40 men rode all night to the relief of a command that had been defeated and was besieged by an overwhelming force of Indians, reached the field at daylight, joined in the action, and fought for three days.

1620 ◆ DONAHUE, JOHN L.

True Name: Donohue, John L.
Rank: Private
Service: U.S. Army
Birthday: 1847
Place of Birth: Baltimore County, Maryland
Date of Death: 16 March 1900
Cemetery: Arlington National Cemetery (13-14045)—Arlington, Virginia
Entered Service at: Baltimore, Baltimore County, Maryland
Unit: Company G, 8th U.S. Cavalry
Battle or Place of Action: Chiricahua Mountains, Arizona Territory
Date of Action: 20 October 1869
Date of Issue: 14 February 1870
Citation: Gallantry in action.

1621 ◆ DONAVAN, CORNELIUS

True Name: Donovan, Cornelius
Rank: Sergeant
Service: U.S. Army
Birthday: 1839
Place of Birth: County Cork, Ireland
Entered Service at: New York, New York
Unit: Company E, 8th U.S. Cavalry

Battle or Place of Action: Agua Fria River, Arizona
Date of Action: 25 August 1869
Date of Issue: 3 March 1870
Citation: Gallantry in action.

1622 ◆ DONELLY, JOHN S.

True Name: Donnelly, John S.
Rank: Private
Service: U.S. Army
Birthday: 1850
Place of Birth: County Kerry, Ireland
Entered Service at: Jersey City, Hudson County, New Jersey
Unit: Company G, 5th U.S. Infantry
Battle or Place of Action: Cedar Creek, etc., Montana
Date of Action: October 1876—January 1877
Date of Issue: 27 April 1877
Citation: Gallantry in action.

1623 ◆ DOUGHERTY, WILLIAM

Rank: Blacksmith
Service: U.S. Army
Birthday: 1841
Place of Birth: Detroit, Wayne County, Michigan
Entered Service at: Philadelphia, Philadelphia County, Pennsylvania
Unit: Company B, 8th U.S. Cavalry
Battle or Place of Action: Arizona
Date of Action: August-October 1868
Date of Issue: 24 July 1869
Citation: Bravery in scouts and actions against Indians.

1624 ◆ DOWLING, JAMES

Rank: Corporal (highest rank: Sergeant)
Service: U.S. Army
Birthday: August 1846
Place of Birth: County Meath, Ireland
Date of Death: 26 December 1891
Place of Death: Washington, D.C.
Cemetery: Soldier's Home National Cemetery (J-6352) (MH)—Washington, D.C.
Entered Service at: Cleveland, Cuyahoga County, Ohio
Unit: Company B, 8th U.S. Cavalry
Battle or Place of Action: Arizona
Date of Action: August-October 1868
Date of Issue: 24 July 1869
Citation: Bravery in scouts and actions against Indians.

1625 ◆ DOZIER, JAMES B.

True Name: Dosher, James B.
Rank: Civilian Guide
Service: U.S. Army
Birthday: 2 May 1820
Place of Birth: Warren County, Tennessee
Date of Death: Early 1900's
Place of Death: Jacksboro, Texas
Cemetery: Bottom Cemetery (MH)—Jack County, Texas
Entered Service at: Fort Richardson, Texas
Unit: Indian Scouts
Battle or Place of Action: Wichita River, Texas
Date of Action: 5 October 1870
Date of Issue: 19 November 1870
Citation: Gallantry in action and on the march.

1626 ◆ EDWARDS, WILLIAM D.

Rank: First Sergeant
Service: U.S. Army
Birthday: 1849
Place of Birth: Brooklyn, Kings County, New York
Date of Death: 24 January 1903
Place of Death: Washington, D.C.
Cemetery: Soldier's Home National Cemetery (K-7023) (MH)—Washington, D.C.
Entered Service at: Brooklyn, Kings County, New York
Unit: Company F, 7th U.S. Infantry
Battle or Place of Action: Big Hole, Montana
Date of Action: 9 August 1877
Date of Issue: 2 December 1878
Citation: Bravery in action.

1627 ◆ ELDRIDGE, GEORGE H.

Rank: Sergeant
Service: U.S. Army
Birthday: 12 May 1846
Place of Birth: Sackets Harbor, Jefferson County, New York
Date of Death: 20 November 1918
Place of Death: Los Angeles, California
Cemetery: Los Angeles National Cemetery (37-B-1) (MH)—Los Angeles, California
Entered Service at: Detroit, Wayne County, Michigan
Unit: Company C, 6th U.S. Cavalry
Battle or Place of Action: Wichita River, Texas
Date of Action: 12 July 1870
Date of Issue: 25 August 1870
Citation: Gallantry in action.

1628 ◆ ELSATSOOSH

Rank: Corporal
Service: U.S. Army
Place of Birth: Arizona Territory
Unit: Indian Scouts
Battle or Place of Action: Apache campaigns
Date of Action: winter 1872-73
Date of Issue: 12 April 1875
Citation: Gallant conduct during campaigns and engagements with Apaches.

1629 ◆ ELWOOD, EDWIN L.

Rank: Private
Service: U.S. Army

Birthday: 1847
Place of Birth: St. Louis, St Louis County, Missouri
Date of Death: 13 September 1907
Cemetery: Santa Fe National Cemetery (H-705) (MH)—Santa Fe, New Mexico
Entered Service at: San Jose, Santa Clara County, California
Unit: Company G, 8th U.S. Cavalry
Battle or Place of Action: Chiricahua Mountains, Arizona Territory
Date of Action: 20 October 1869
Date of Issue: 14 February 1870
Citation: Gallantry in action.

1630 ◆ EMMET, ROBERT TEMPLE

Rank: Second Lieutenant (highest rank: Colonel)
Service: U.S. Army
Birthday: 13 December 1854
Place of Birth: New York, New York
Date of Death: 25 October 1936
Place of Death: Ashfield, Massachusetts
Cemetery: Beechwoods Cemetery—New Rochelle, New York
Entered Service at: New York, New York
Unit: 9th U.S. Cavalry
Battle or Place of Action: Las Animas Canyon, New Mexico
Date of Action: 18 September 1879
Date of Issue: 24 August 1899
Citation: Lt. Emmet was in G Troop, which was sent to relieve a detachment of soldiers under attack by hostile Apaches. During a flank attack on the Indian camp, made to divert the hostiles, Lt. Emmet and five of his men became surrounded when the Indians returned to defend their camp. Finding that the Indians were making for a position from which they could direct their fire on the retreating troop, the lieutenant held his point with his party until the soldiers reached the safety of a canyon. Lt. Emmet then continued to hold his position while his party recovered their horses. The enemy force consisted of approximately 200.

1631 ◆ EVANS, WILLIAM

Rank: Private
Service: U.S. Army
Birthday: 1851
Place of Birth: Annagh, Ireland
Date of Death: 27 August 1881
Place of Death: St. Louis, Missouri
Cemetery: Bellefontaine Cemetery (MH)—St. Louis, Missouri
Entered Service at: St. Louis, St. Louis County, Missouri
Unit: Company E, 7th U.S. Infantry
Battle or Place of Action: Big Horn, Montana
Date of Action: 9 July 1876
Date of Issue: 9 July 1876
Citation: Carried dispatches to Brig. Gen. Crook through a country occupied by Sioux.

1632 ◆ FACTOR, POMPEY

Rank: Private
Service: U.S. Army
Birthday: 1849
Place of Birth: Arkansas
Date of Death: 29 March 1928
Cemetery: Seminole Indian Scout Cemetery (MH)—Brackettsville, Texas
Entered Service at: Fort Duncan, Texas
Unit: Indian Scouts
Battle or Place of Action: Pecos River, Texas
Date of Action: 25 April 1875
Date of Issue: 28 May 1875
Citation: With three other men, he participated in a charge against 25 hostiles while on a scouting patrol.

1633 ◆ FALCOTT, HENRY

Rank: Sergeant (highest rank: First Sergeant)
Service: U.S. Army
Birthday: 1835
Place of Birth: Champagne, France
Date of Death: 2 December 1910
Place of Death: San Antonio, Texas
Cemetery: San Antonio National Cemetery (F-918) (MH)—San Antonio, Texas
Entered Service at: San Francisco, San Francisco County, California
Unit: Company L, 8th U.S. Cavalry
Battle or Place of Action: Arizona
Date of Action: August-October 1868
Date of Issue: 24 July 1869
Citation: Bravery in scouts and actions against Indians.

1634 ◆ FARREN, DANIEL

Rank: Private
Service: U.S. Army
Birthday: 1848
Place of Birth: County Derry, Ireland
Entered Service at: Philadelphia, Philadelphia County, Pennsylvania
Unit: Company B, 8th U.S. Cavalry
Battle or Place of Action: Arizona
Date of Action: August-October 1868
Date of Issue: 24 July 1869
Citation: Bravery in scouts and actions against Indians.

1635 ◆ FEASTER, MOSHEIM

Rank: Private
Service: U.S. Army
Birthday: 27 May 1867
Place of Birth: Schellsburg, Bedford County, Pennsylvania
Date of Death: 18 March 1950
Cemetery: Golden Gate National Cemetery (0-319)—San Bruno, California

Entered Service at: Cleveland, Cuyahoga County, Ohio
Unit: Company E, 7th U.S. Cavalry
Battle or Place of Action: Wounded Knee Creek, South Dakota
Date of Action: 29 December 1890
Date of Issue: 23 June 1891
Citation: Extraordinary gallantry.

1636 ◆ FEGAN, JAMES

Rank: Sergeant
Service: U.S. Army
Birthday: 1827
Place of Birth: Athlone, County Westmeath, Ireland
Date of Death: 25 June 1886
Cemetery: Custer Battlefield National Monument (A-749)—Crow Agency, Montana
Entered Service at: New York, New York
Unit: Company H, 3d U.S. Infantry
Battle or Place of Action: Plum Creek, Kansas
Date of Action: March 1868
Date of Issue: 19 October 1878
Citation: While in charge of a powder train en route from Fort Harker to Fort Dodge, Kan., was attacked by a party of desperadoes, who attempted to rescue a deserter in his charge and to fire the train. Sgt. Fegan, singlehandedly, repelled the attacking party, wounding two of them, and brought his train through in safety.

1637 ◆ FERRARI, GEORGE

Rank: Corporal
Service: U.S. Army
Birthday: 1845
Place of Birth: New York, New York
Entered Service at: Cleveland, Cuyahoga County, Ohio
Unit: Company D, 8th U.S. Cavalry
Battle or Place of Action: Red Creek, Arizona
Date of Action: 23 September 1869
Date of Issue: 23 November 1869
Citation: Gallantry in action.

1638 ◆ FICHTER, HERMANN EMIL

Rank: Private (highest rank: Corporal)
Service: U.S. Army
Birthday: 30 March 1845
Place of Birth: Baden, Germany
Date of Death: 5 August 1912
Place of Death: Quincy, Illinois
Cemetery: St. Boniface Cemetery (MH)—Quincy, Illinois
Entered Service at: New York, New York
Unit: Company F, 3d U.S. Cavalry
Battle or Place of Action: Whetstone Mountains, Arizona Territory
Date of Action: 5 May 1871
Date of Issue: 13 November 1871
Citation: Gallantry in action.

1639 ◆ FOLEY, JOHN H.

Rank: Sergeant
Service: U.S. Army
Birthday: 1839
Place of Birth: Cork, Ireland
Date of Death: 18 November 1874
Place of Death: Benicia Barracks, California
Cemetery: Post Cemetery as Unknown—Benicia Barracks, California
Entered Service at: Boston, Suffolk County, Massachusetts
Unit: Company B, 3d U.S. Cavalry
Battle or Place of Action: Loupe Fork of the Platte River, Nebraska
Date of Action: 26 April 1872
Date of Issue: 22 May 1872
Citation: Gallantry in action.

1640 ◆ FOLLY, WILLIAM H.

Rank: Private
Service: U.S. Army
Birthday: 1845
Place of Birth: Bergen County, New Jersey
Entered Service at: New York, New York
Unit: Company B, 8th U.S. Cavalry
Battle or Place of Action: Arizona
Date of Action: August-October 1868
Citation: Bravery in scouts and actions against Indians.

1641 ◆ FORAN, NICHOLAS

Rank: Private (highest rank: Sergeant)
Service: U.S. Army
Birthday: 3 June 1844
Place of Birth: County Waterford, Ireland
Date of Death: 29 September 1927
Place of Death: Prescott, Arizona
Cemetery: Prescott National Cemetery (1-2-54) (MH)—Prescott, Arizona
Entered Service at: St. Louis, St. Louis County, Missouri
Unit: Company L, 8th U.S. Cavalry
Battle or Place of Action: Arizona
Date of Action: August-October 1868
Date of Issue: 24 July 1869
Citation: Bravery in scouts and actions against Indians.

1642 ◆ FORSYTH, THOMAS HALL

Rank: First Sergeant (highest rank: Commissary Sergeant Ret.)
Service: U.S. Army
Birthday: 17 December 1842
Place of Birth: Hartford, Hartford County, Connecticut
Date of Death: 22 March 1908
Place of Death: San Diego, California
Cemetery: Mount Hope Cemetery (MH)—San Diego, California

Entered Service at: St. Louis, St. Louis County, Missouri
Unit: Company M, 4th U.S. Cavalry
Battle or Place of Action: Powder River, Wyoming
Date of Action: 25 November 1876
Date of Issue: 14 July 1891
Citation: Though dangerously wounded, he maintained his ground with a small party against a largely superior force after his commanding officer had been shot down during a sudden attack and rescued that officer and a comrade from the enemy.

1643 ◆ FOSTER, WILLIAM

Rank: Sergeant
Service: U.S. Army
Birthday: 1832
Place of Birth: Somerset County, England
Date of Death: 16 July 1880
Place of Death: Presido of San Francisco, California
Cemetery: San Francisco National Cemetery (WS-187) (MH)—San Francisco, California
Entered Service at: Bakersville, Maryland
Unit: Company F, 4th U.S. Cavalry
Battle or Place of Action: Red River, Texas
Date of Action: 29 September 1872
Date of Issue: 19 November 1872
Citation: Gallantry in action.

1644 ◆ FREEMEYER, CHRISTOPHER

Rank: Private
Service: U.S. Army
Birthday: 1838
Place of Birth: Bavaria, Germany
Date of Death: 14 October 1894
Cemetery: Cypress Hills National Cemetery (2-5259) (MH)—Brooklyn, New York
Entered Service at: New York, New York
Unit: Company D, 5th U.S. Infantry
Battle or Place of Action: Cedar Creek, etc., Montana
Date of Action: 21 October 1876—8 January 1877
Date of Issue: 27 April 1877
Citation: Gallantry in action.

1645 ◆ GARDINER, PETER W.

Rank: Private
Service: U.S. Army
Birthday: 1841
Place of Birth: Carlisle, Schoharie County, New York
Date of Death: 1883
Place of Death: Fort Lowell, Arizona
Entered Service at: New York, New York
Unit: Company H, 6th U.S. Cavalry
Battle or Place of Action: Sappa Creek, Kansas
Date of Action: 23 April 1875
Date of Issue: 16 November 1876
Citation: With five other men he waded in mud and water up the creek to a position directly behind an entrenched Cheyenne position, who were using natural bank pits to good advantage against the main column. This surprise attack from the enemy rear broke their resistance.

1646 ◆ GARDNER, CHARLES

True Name: Suhler, Simon
Rank: Private
Service: U.S. Army
Birthday: 1844
Place of Birth: Bavaria, Germany
Date of Death: 16 May 1895
Cemetery: San Antonio National Cemetery (I-1610) (MH)—San Antonio, Texas
Entered Service at: San Francisco, San Francisco County, California
Unit: Company B, 8th U.S. Cavalry
Battle or Place of Action: Arizona
Date of Action: August-October 1868
Date of Issue: 24 July 1869
Citation: Bravery in scouts and actions against Indians.
Notes: POW—Civil War

1647 ◆ GARLAND, HARRY

Rank: Corporal (highest rank: Hospital Steward)
Service: U.S. Army
Birthday: 1844
Place of Birth: Boston, Suffolk County, Massachusetts
Date of Death: 7 May 1883
Cemetery: unknown gravesite, Fort Ellis, Wyoming
Entered Service at: Indianapolis, Marion County, Indiana
Unit: Company L, 2d U.S. Cavalry
Battle or Place of Action: Little Muddy Creek, Montana & Camas Meadows, Idaho
Date of Action: 7 May & 29 August 1877
Date of Issue: 28 February 1878
Citation: Gallantry in action with hostile Sioux at Little Muddy Creek, Mont.; having been wounded in the hip so as to be unable to stand, at Camas Meadows, Idaho, he still continued to direct the men under his charge until the enemy withdrew.

1648 ◆ GARLINGTON, ERNEST ALBERT

Rank: First Lieutenant (highest rank: Brigadier General)
Service: U.S. Army
Birthday: 20 February 1853
Place of Birth: Newberry Hill, Newberry County, South Carolina
Date of Death: 16 October 1934
Place of Death: California
Cemetery: Arlington National Cemetery (3-1735-B)—Arlington, Virginia
Entered Service at: Athens, Clarke County, Georgia
Unit: 7th U.S. Cavalry
Battle or Place of Action: Wounded Knee Creek, South Dakota
Date of Action: 29 December 1890
Date of Issue: 26 September 1893
Citation: Distinguished gallantry.

1649 ◆ GATES, GEORGE

Rank: Bugler (highest rank: Blacksmith)
Service: U.S. Army
Birthday: 30 July 1844
Place of Birth: Delaware County, Ohio
Date of Death: 18 March 1915
Place of Death: Quincy, Illinois
Cemetery: Illinois Veteran Home Sunset Cemetery (MH)—Quincy, Illinois
Entered Service at: Dubuque, Dubuque County, Iowa
Unit: 8th U.S. Cavalry
Battle or Place of Action: Picacho Mountain, Arizona Territory
Date of Action: 4 June 1869
Date of Issue: 3 March 1870
Citation: Killed an Indian warrior and captured his arms.

1650 ◆ GAY, THOMAS H.

Rank: Private (highest rank: Sergeant)
Service: U.S. Army
Birthday: 8 June 1848
Place of Birth: Prince Edward Island, Canada
Date of Death: 28 February 1895
Place of Death: Attleboro, Massachusetts
Cemetery: Woodlawn Cemetery (MH)—Attleboro, Massachusetts
Entered Service at: Boston, Suffolk County, Massachusetts
Unit: Company B, 8th U.S. Cavalry
Battle or Place of Action: Arizona
Date of Action: August-October 1868
Date of Issue: 24 July 1869
Citation: Bravery in scouts and actions against Indians.

1651 ◆ GEIGER, GEORGE

Rank: Sergeant
Service: U.S. Army
Birthday: 1843
Place of Birth: Cincinnati, Hamilton County, Ohio
Date of Death: 23 January 1904
Place of Death: Dayton, Ohio
Cemetery: Dayton National Cemetery (N-20-47) (MH)—Dayton, Ohio
Entered Service at: St. Louis, St. Louis County, Missouri
Unit: Company H, 7th U.S. Cavalry
Battle or Place of Action: Little Big Horn River, Montana
Date of Action: 25 June 1876
Date of Issue: 5 October 1878
Citation: With three comrades during the entire engagement courageously held a position that secured water for the command.

1652 ◆ GEORGIAN, JOHN

Rank: Private
Service: U.S. Army
Birthday: 1842
Place of Birth: Germany
Entered Service at: Buffalo, Erie County, New York
Unit: Company G, 8th U.S. Cavalry
Battle or Place of Action: Chiricahua Mountains, Arizona Territory
Date of Action: 20 October 1869
Date of Issue: 14 February 1870
Citation: Bravery in action.

1653 ◆ *GIVEN, JOHN J.

Rank: Corporal
Service: U.S. Army
Birthday: 1840
Place of Birth: Daviess County, Kentucky
Date of Death: 12 July 1870
Cemetery: San Antonio National Cemetery (MH)—San Antonio, Texas
Entered Service at: Cincinnati, Hamilton County, Ohio
Unit: Company K, 6th U.S. Cavalry
Battle or Place of Action: Wichita River, Texas
Date of Action: 12 July 1870
Date of Issue: 25 August 1870
Citation: Bravery in action.

1654 ◆ GLAVINSKI, ALBERT

True Name: Glawinski, Albert
Rank: Blacksmith
Service: U.S. Army
Birthday: 1852
Place of Birth: Germany (Prussia)
Entered Service at: Pittsburgh, Allegheny County, Pennsylvania
Unit: Company M, 3d U.S. Cavalry
Battle or Place of Action: Powder River, Montana
Date of Action: 17 March 1876
Date of Issue: 16 October 1877
Citation: During a retreat he selected exposed positions; he was part of the rear guard.

1655 ◆ GLOVER, THADDEUS BROWN

Rank: Sergeant (highest rank: Major, Quartermaster Corps)
Service: U.S. Army
Birthday: 2 January 1852
Place of Birth: New York, New York
Date of Death: 18 December 1932
Place of Death: Buffalo, New York
Cemetery: Willow Mill Cemetery—Southold, New York
Entered Service at: New York, New York
Unit: Troop B, 2d U.S. Cavalry
Battle or Place of Action: Mizpah & Pumpkin Creek, Montana
Date of Action: 10 April 1879 & 10 February 1880
Date of Issue: 20 November 1897
Citation: While in charge of small scouting parties, fought, charged, surrounded, and captured war parties of Sioux Indians.

1656 ◆ GLYNN, MICHAEL

Rank: Private
Service: U.S. Army
Birthday: 1845
Place of Birth: Galway, Ireland
Entered Service at: New York, New York
Unit: Company F, 5th U.S. Cavalry
Battle or Place of Action: Whetstone Mountains, Arizona Territory
Date of Action: 13 July 1872
Date of Issue: 4 December 1874
Citation: Drove off, singlehandedly, eight hostile Indians, killing and wounding five.

1657 ◆ GODFREY, EDWARD SETTLE

Rank: Captain (highest rank: Brigadier General)
Service: U.S. Army
Birthday: 9 October 1843
Place of Birth: Kalida, Putnam County, Ohio
Date of Death: 1 April 1932
Place of Death: Mount Holly, New Jersey
Cemetery: Arlington National Cemetery (3-4175-E)—Arlington, Virginia
Entered Service at: Ottawa, Putnam County, Ohio
Unit: 7th U.S. Cavalry
Battle or Place of Action: Bear Paw Mountain, Montana
Date of Action: 30 September 1877
Date of Issue: 27 November 1894
Citation: Led his command into action when he was severely wounded.

1658 ◆ GOLDEN, PATRICK

Rank: Sergeant
Service: U.S. Army
Birthday: 1836
Place of Birth: County Sligo, Ireland
Date of Death: 25 May 1872
Place of Death: Fort Columbus, New York
Cemetery: Cypress Hills National Cemetery (2-4316) (MH)—Brooklyn, New York
Entered Service at: San Francisco, San Francisco County, California
Unit: Company B, 8th U.S. Cavalry
Battle or Place of Action: Arizona
Date of Action: August-October 1868
Date of Issue: 24 July 1869
Citation: Bravery in scouts and actions against Indians.

1659 ◆ GOLDIN, THEODORE W. B.

Rank: Private
Service: U.S. Army
Birthday: 25 July 1858
Place of Birth: Avon, Rock County, Wisconsin
Date of Death: 15 February 1935
Place of Death: Waupaca, Wisconsin
Cemetery: King Veterans Memorial Cemetery (MH)—Waupaca, Wisconsin
Entered Service at: Chicago, Cook County, Illinois
Unit: Troop G, 7th U.S. Cavalry
Battle or Place of Action: Little Big Horn, Montana
Date of Action: 26 June 1876
Date of Issue: 21 December 1895
Citation: One of a party of volunteers who, under a heavy fire from the Indians, went for and brought water to the wounded.

1660 ◆ GOODMAN, DAVID

Rank: Private
Service: U.S. Army
Birthday: 1846
Place of Birth: Paxton, Worcester County, Massachusetts
Entered Service at: Boston, Suffolk County, Massachusetts
Unit: Company L, 8th U.S. Cavalry
Battle or Place of Action: Lyry Creek, Arizona Territory
Date of Action: 14 October 1869
Date of Issue: 3 March 1870
Citation: Bravery in action.

1661 ◆ GRANT, GEORGE

Rank: Sergeant
Service: U.S. Army
Birthday: 1834
Place of Birth: Raleigh, Shelby County, Tennessee
Date of Death: 1 September 1876
Cemetery: Arbor Cemetery—Stockville, Nebraska
Entered Service at: Indianapolis, Marion County, Indiana
Unit: Company E, 18th U.S. Infantry
Battle or Place of Action: Ft. Phil Kearny to Ft. C. F. Smith, Dakota Territory
Date of Action: February 1867
Date of Issue: 6 May 1871
Citation: Bravery, energy and perseverance, involving much suffering and privation through attacks by hostile Indians, deep snows, etc., while voluntarily carrying dispatches.

1662 ◆ GREAVES, CLINTON

Rank: Corporal
Service: U.S. Army
Birthday: 12 August 1855
Place of Birth: Madison County, Virginia
Date of Death: 18 August 1906
Cemetery: Greenlawn Cemetery—Columbus, Ohio
Entered Service at: Baltimore, Baltimore County, Maryland
Unit: Company C, 9th U.S. Cavalry
Battle or Place of Action: Florida Mountains, New Mexico
Date of Action: 24 January 1877
Date of Issue: 26 June 1879
Citation: While part of a small detachment to persuade a band of renegade Apache Indians to surrender, his group was

surrounded. Cpl. Greaves in the center of the savage hand-to-hand fighting, managed to shoot and bash a gap through the swarming Apaches, permitting his companions to break free.

1663 ◆ GREEN, FRANCIS C.
Rank: Sergeant
Service: U.S. Army
Birthday: 4 September 1835
Place of Birth: Mount Vernon, Posey County, Indiana
Date of Death: 13 March 1905
Cemetery: Nicolas Graveyard—Erin, Tennessee
Entered Service at: Sacramento, Sacramento County, California
Unit: Company K, 8th U.S. Cavalry
Battle or Place of Action: Arizona
Date of Action: 1868 & 1869
Date of Issue: 6 September 1869
Citation: Bravery in action.

1664 ◆ GREEN, JOHN
Rank: Major (highest rank: Brevet Brigadier General)
Service: U.S. Army
Birthday: 20 November 1825
Place of Birth: Wurttemberg, Germany
Date of Death: 22 November 1908
Cemetery: Morris Hill Cemetery (MH)—Boise, Idaho
Entered Service at: Columbus, Franklin County, Ohio
Unit: 1st U.S. Cavalry
Battle or Place of Action: Lava Beds, California
Date of Action: 17 January 1873
Date of Issue: 18 November 1897
Citation: In order to reassure his command, this officer, in the most fearless manner and exposed to very great danger, walked in front of the line; the command, thus encouraged, advanced over the lava upon the Indians who were concealed among the rocks.

1665 ◆ GRESHAM, JOHN CHOWNING
Rank: First Lieutenant (highest rank: Colonel)
Service: U.S. Army
Birthday: 25 September 1851
Place of Birth: Virginia
Date of Death: 2 September 1926
Place of Death: San Diego, California
Cemetery: San Francisco National Cemetery (OS-4P5)—San Francisco, California
Entered Service at: Lancaster Courthouse, Lancaster County, Virginia
Unit: 7th U.S. Cavalry
Battle or Place of Action: Wounded Knee Creek, South Dakota
Date of Action: 29 December 1890
Date of Issue: 26 March 1895
Citation: Voluntarily led a party into a ravine to dislodge Sioux Indians concealed therein. He was wounded during this action.

1666 ◆ GRIMES, EDWARD P.
Rank: Sergeant (highest rank: First Sergeant)
Service: U.S. Army
Birthday: 18 May 1848
Place of Birth: Dover, Strafford County, New Hampshire
Date of Death: 17 June 1913
Cemetery: Cypress Hills National Cemetery (2-7210) (MH)—Brooklyn, New York
Entered Service at: Boston, Suffolk County, Massachusetts
Unit: Company F, 5th U.S. Cavalry
Battle or Place of Action: Milk River, Colorado
Date of Action: 29 September-5 October 1879
Date of Issue: 27 January 1880
Citation: The command being almost out of ammunition and surrounded on three sides by the enemy, he voluntarily brought up a supply under heavy fire at almost point-blank range.

1667 ◆ GUNTHER, JACOB
True Name: Guenther, Jacob
Rank: Corporal
Service: U.S. Army
Birthday: 13 November 1844
Place of Birth: Schuylkill County, Pennsylvania
Date of Death: 29 March 1871
Place of Death: Fort Wingate (near Gallup), New Mexico
Cemetery: Santa Fe National Cemetery (A3-1055) (MH)—Santa Fe, New Mexico
Entered Service at: Philadelphia, Philadelphia County, Pennsylvania
Unit: Company E, 8th U.S. Cavalry
Battle or Place of Action: Arizona
Date of Action: 1868-1869
Date of Issue: 6 September 1869
Citation: Bravery in scouts and actions against Indians.

1668 ◆ *HADDOO, JOHN
True Name: Haddo Jr., John
Rank: Corporal
Service: U.S. Army
Birthday: 13 August 1851
Place of Birth: Hooksett, Merrimack County, New Hampshire
Date of Death: 30 September 1877
Place of Death: Bear Paw Mountain, Montana
Cemetery: Custer Battlefield National Cemetery—Crow Agency, Montana
Entered Service at: Columbus, Cherokee County, Kansas
Unit: Company B, 5th U.S. Infantry
Battle or Place of Action: Cedar Creek, etc., Montana
Date of Action: October 1876—8 January 1877
Date of Issue: 18 July 1877
Citation: Gallantry in action.

1669 ◆ HALL, JOHN

Rank: Private
Service: U.S. Army
Birthday: 1834
Place of Birth: Logan County, Illinois
Entered Service at: Sacramento, Sacramento County, California
Unit: Company B, 8th U.S. Cavalry
Battle or Place of Action: Arizona
Date of Action: August-October 1868
Date of Issue: 24 July 1869
Citation: Bravery in scouts and actions against Indians.

1670 ◆ HALL, WILLIAM PREBLE

Rank: First Lieutenant (highest rank: Brigadier General)
Service: U.S. Army
Birthday: 11 June 1848
Place of Birth: Randolph County, Missouri
Date of Death: 14 December 1927
Place of Death: Washington, D.C.
Cemetery: Arlington National Cemetery (1-653)—Arlington, Virginia
Entered Service at: Huntsville, Randolph County, Missouri
Unit: 5th U.S. Cavalry
Battle or Place of Action: near Camp, White River, Colorado
Date of Action: 20 October 1879
Date of Issue: 18 September 1897
Citation: With a reconnoitering party of three men, was attacked by 35 Indians and several times exposed himself to draw the fire of the enemy, giving his small party opportunity to reply with much effect.

1671 ◆ HAMILTON, FRANK

Rank: Private
Service: U.S. Army
Birthday: 1840
Place of Birth: County Tyrone, Ireland
Entered Service at: Sacramento, Sacramento County, California
Unit: Company E, 8th U.S. Cavalry
Battle or Place of Action: Agua Fria River, Arizona
Date of Action: 25 August 1869
Date of Issue: 3 March 1870
Citation: Gallantry in action.

1672 ◆ HAMILTON, MATHEW H.

Rank: Private
Service: U.S. Army
Birthday: 1865
Place of Birth: Hobart, Australia
Entered Service at: New York, New York
Unit: Company G, 7th U.S. Cavalry
Battle or Place of Action: Wounded Knee Creek, South Dakota
Date of Action: 29 December 1890
Date of Issue: 25 May 1891
Citation: Bravery in action.

1673 ◆ HANLEY, RICHARD P.

Rank: Sergeant
Service: U.S. Army
Birthday: 1843
Place of Birth: Boston, Suffolk County, Massachusetts
Entered Service at: Cincinnati, Hamilton County, Ohio
Unit: Company C, 7th U.S. Cavalry
Battle or Place of Action: Little Big Horn River, Montana
Date of Action: 25 June 1876
Date of Issue: 5 October 1878
Citation: Recaptured, singlehandedly, and without orders, within the enemy's lines and under a galling fire lasting some 20 minutes, a stampeded pack mule loaded with ammunition.

1674 ◆ HARDING, MOSHER A.

Rank: Blacksmith
Service: U.S. Army
Birthday: 2 May 1847
Place of Birth: Canada West
Date of Death: 10 May 1931
Place of Death: Denison, Iowa
Cemetery: Oakland Cemetery—Denison, Iowa
Entered Service at: St. Louis, St. Louis County, Missouri
Unit: Company G, 8th U.S. Cavalry
Battle or Place of Action: Chiricahua Mountains, Arizona Territory
Date of Action: 20 October 1869
Date of Issue: 14 February 1870
Citation: Gallantry in action.

1675 ◆ HARRINGTON, JOHN

Rank: Private (highest rank: Sergeant)
Service: U.S. Army
Birthday: 1848
Place of Birth: Detroit, Wayne County, Michigan
Date of Death: 3 January 1905
Cemetery: San Antonio National Cemetery (F-1012) (MH)—San Antonio, Texas
Entered Service at: Cleveland, Cuyahoga County, Ohio
Unit: Company H, 6th U.S. Cavalry
Battle or Place of Action: Washita River, Texas
Date of Action: 12 September 1874
Date of Issue: 4 November 1874
Citation: While carrying dispatches was attacked by 125 hostile Indians, whom he and his comrades fought throughout the day. He was severely wounded in the hip and unable to move. He continued to fight, defending an exposed dying man.

1676 ◆ HARRIS, CHARLES D.

Rank: Sergeant
Service: U.S. Army
Birthday: 1845

Place of Birth: Albion, Orleans County, New York
Entered Service at: Rochester, Monroe County, New York
Unit: Company D, 8th U.S. Cavalry
Battle or Place of Action: Red Creek, Arizona
Date of Action: 23 September 1869
Date of Issue: 23 November 1869
Citation: Gallantry in action.

1677 ◆ HARRIS, DAVID W.

Rank: Private
Service: U.S. Army
Birthday: 1851
Place of Birth: Indianapolis, Marion County, Indiana
Entered Service at: Cincinnati, Hamilton County, Ohio
Unit: Company A, 7th U.S. Cavalry
Battle or Place of Action: Little Big Horn River, Montana
Date of Action: 25 June 1876
Date of Issue: 5 October 1878
Citation: Brought water to the wounded, at great danger to his life, under a most galling fire from the enemy.

1678 ◆ HARRIS, WILLIAM M.

Rank: Private
Service: U.S. Army
Birthday: 1850
Place of Birth: Madison County, Kentucky
Entered Service at: Mount Vernon, Rockcastle County, Kentucky
Unit: Company D, 7th U.S. Cavalry
Battle or Place of Action: Little Big Horn River, Montana
Date of Action: 25 June 1876
Date of Issue: 5 October 1878
Citation: Voluntarily brought water to the wounded under fire of the enemy.

1679 ◆ HARTZOG, JOSHUA B.

Rank: Private (highest rank: Sergeant)
Service: U.S. Army
Birthday: 3 February 1866
Place of Birth: Paulding County, Ohio
Date of Death: 27 May 1939
Place of Death: Beebe, Arkansas
Cemetery: Gum Springs Cemetery (MH)—Searcy, Arkansas
Entered Service at: Detroit, Wayne County, Michigan
Unit: Company E, 1st U.S. Artillery
Battle or Place of Action: Wounded Knee Creek, South Dakota
Date of Action: 29 December 1890
Date of Issue: 24 March 1891
Citation: Went to the rescue of the commanding officer who had fallen severely wounded, picked him up, and carried him out of range of the hostile guns.

1680 ◆ HAUPT, PAUL

Rank: Corporal
Service: U.S. Army
Birthday: 1842
Place of Birth: Germany (Prussia)
Entered Service at: Baltimore, Baltimore County, Maryland
Unit: Company L, 8th U.S. Cavalry
Battle or Place of Action: Hell Canyon, Arizona
Date of Action: 3 July 1869
Date of Issue: 3 March 1870
Citation: Gallantry in action.

1681 ◆ HAWTHORNE, HARRY LEROY

Rank: Second Lieutenant (highest rank: Colonel)
Service: U.S. Army
Birthday: 27 November 1859
Place of Birth: Minnesota
Date of Death: 9 April 1948
Place of Death: Pasadena, California
Cemetery: Arlington National Cemetery (3-1952) (MH)—Arlington, Virginia
Entered Service at: Kentucky
Unit: 2d U.S. Artillery
Battle or Place of Action: Wounded Knee Creek, South Dakota
Date of Action: 29 December 1890
Date of Issue: 11 October 1892
Citation: Distinguished conduct in battle with hostile Indians.

1682 ◆ HAY, FRED STEWART

True Name: Schwabe, Frederick H.
Rank: Sergeant (highest rank: Drum Major U.S.A. ret.)
Service: U.S. Army
Birthday: 1850
Place of Birth: Stirlingshire, Scotland
Date of Death: 14 January 1914
Place of Death: Highlands, New Jersey
Cemetery: Bayview Cemetery—Leonardo, New Jersey
Entered Service at: Fort Leavenworth, Leavenworth County, Kansas
Unit: Company I, 5th U.S. Infantry
Battle or Place of Action: Upper Wichita River, Texas
Date of Action: 9 September 1874
Date of Issue: 23 April 1875
Citation: Gallantry in action.

1683 ◆ HEARTERY, RICHARD

Rank: Private
Service: U.S. Army
Birthday: 1847
Place of Birth: Ireland
Date of Death: 7 June 1912
Place of Death: Chicago, Illinois
Cemetery: Mount Carmel Cemetery—Hillside, Illinois
Entered Service at: San Francisco, San Francisco County, California
Unit: Company D, 6th U.S. Cavalry
Battle or Place of Action: Cibicu, Arizona
Date of Action: 30 August 1881

Date of Issue: 20 July 1888
Citation: Bravery in action.

1684 ◆ HEISE, CLAMOR

Rank: Private (highest rank: Quartermaster Sergeant)
Service: U.S. Army
Birthday: 12 December 1844
Place of Birth: Germany
Date of Death: October 1921
Cemetery: Heise Hot Springs Cemetery (MH)—Heise, Idaho
Entered Service at: New York, New York
Unit: Company B, 8th U.S. Cavalry
Battle or Place of Action: Arizona
Date of Action: August-October 1868
Date of Issue: 24 July 1869
Citation: Bravery in scouts and actions against Indians.

1685 ◆ HERRON, LEANDER

Rank: Corporal
Service: U.S. Army
Birthday: 29 December 1846
Place of Birth: Bucks County, Pennsylvania
Date of Death: 5 April 1937
Place of Death: St. Paul, Nebraska
Cemetery: Elmwood Cemetery (MH)—St. Paul, Nebraska
Entered Service at: Pittsburgh, Allegheny County, Pennsylvania
Unit: Company A, 3d U.S. Infantry
Battle or Place of Action: Fort Dodge, Kansas
Date of Action: 2 September 1868
Citation: While detailed as mail courier from the fort, voluntarily went to the assistance of a party of four enlisted men, who were attacked by about 50 Indians at some distance from the fort and remained with them until the party was relieved.

1686 ◆ HEYL, CHARLES PETTIT HEATH

Rank: Second Lieutenant (highest rank: Colonel)
Service: U.S. Army
Birthday: 22 July 1849
Place of Birth: Philadelphia, Philadelphia County, Pennsylvania
Date of Death: 12 October 1926
Cemetery: Arlington National Cemetery (1-135-B-WH) (MH)—Arlington, Virginia
Entered Service at: Camden, Camden County, New Jersey
Unit: 23d U.S. Infantry
Battle or Place of Action: Fort Hartsuff, Nebraska
Date of Action: 28 April 1876
Date of Issue: 26 October 1897
Citation: Voluntarily, and with most conspicuous gallantry, charged with three men upon six Indians who were entrenched upon a hillside.

1687 ◆ HIGGINS, THOMAS P.

Rank: Private
Service: U.S. Army
Birthday: 1839
Place of Birth: Longford, Ireland
Entered Service at: Napa, Napa County, California
Unit: Company B, 8th U.S. Cavalry
Battle or Place of Action: Arizona
Date of Action: August-October 1868
Date of Issue: 24 July 1869
Citation: Bravery in scouts and actions against Indians.

1688 ◆ HILL, FRANK E.

Rank: Sergeant (highest rank: First Sergeant)
Service: U.S. Army
Birthday: 1849
Place of Birth: Mayfield, Wisconsin
Date of Death: 20 March 1906
Place of Death: Manhattan, Nevada
Cemetery: San Francisco Columbarium—San Francisco, California
Entered Service at: St. Louis, St. Louis County, Missouri
Unit: Company E, 5th U.S. Cavalry
Battle or Place of Action: Date Creek, Arizona
Date of Action: 8 September 1872
Date of Issue: 12 August 1875
Citation: Secured the person of a hostile Apache chief, although while holding the chief he was severely wounded in the back by another Indian.

1689 ◆ HILL, JAMES MADISON

Rank: First Sergeant (highest rank: Commissary Sergeant)
Service: U.S. Army
Birthday: 25 April 1845
Place of Birth: Washington County, Pennsylvania
Date of Death: 17 September 1919
Place of Death: Vancouver, Washington
Cemetery: Vancouver Barracks Post Cemetery (4-W-650) (MH)—Vancouver, Washington
Entered Service at: Cincinnati, Hamilton County, Ohio
Unit: Company A, 5th U.S. Cavalry
Battle or Place of Action: Turret Mountain, Arizona Territory
Date of Action: 25 March 1873
Date of Issue: 12 August 1875
Citation: Gallantry in action.

1690 ◆ HILLOCK, MARVIN C.

Rank: Private
Service: U.S. Army
Birthday: 1868
Place of Birth: Port Huron, St. Clair County, Michigan
Entered Service at: Detroit, Wayne County, Michigan
Unit: Company B, 7th U.S. Cavalry
Battle or Place of Action: Wounded Knee Creek, South Dakota
Date of Action: 29 December 1890
Date of Issue: 16 April 1891
Citation: Distinguished bravery.

1691 ◆ HIMMELSBACK, MICHAEL

Rank: Private
Service: U.S. Army
Birthday: 1849
Place of Birth: Allegheny County, Pennsylvania
Date of Death: 5 January 1881
Place of Death: Fort Ellis, Montana
Entered Service at: Harrisburg, Dauphin County, Pennsylvania
Unit: Company C, 2d U.S. Cavalry
Battle or Place of Action: Little Blue, Nebraska
Date of Action: 15 May 1870
Date of Issue: 22 June 1870
Citation: Gallantry in action.

1692 ◆ HINEMANN, LEHMANN

Rank: Sergeant
Service: U.S. Army
Birthday: 1844
Place of Birth: Lanback, Germany
Date of Death: 11 November 1920
Place of Death: Newport, Kentucky
Cemetery: St. Stephen's Cemetery—Fort Thomas, Kentucky
Entered Service at: Baltimore, Baltimore County, Maryland
Unit: Company L, 1st U.S. Cavalry
Battle or Place of Action: Arizona
Date of Action: winter 1872-73
Date of Issue: 12 August 1875
Citation: Gallant conduct during campaigns and engagements with Apaches.

1693 ◆ HOBDAY, GEORGE

Rank: Private
Service: U.S. Army
Birthday: 1842
Place of Birth: Pulaski County, Illinois
Date of Death: 22 November 1891
Cemetery: Jefferson Barracks National Cemetery—St. Louis, Missouri
Entered Service at: Memphis, Shelby County, Tennessee
Unit: Company A, 7th U.S. Cavalry
Battle or Place of Action: Wounded Knee Creek, South Dakota
Date of Action: 29 December 1890
Date of Issue: 23 June 1891
Citation: Conspicuous and gallant conduct in battle.

1694 ◆ HOGAN, HENRY✢

Rank: Private (highest rank: Corporal)
Service: U.S. Army
Birthday: 8 March 1840
Place of Birth: County Clare, Ireland
Date of Death: 20 April 1916
Cemetery: Custer County Cemetery (MH)—Miles City, Montana
Entered Service at: New York, New York
Unit: Company G, 5th U.S. Infantry
Battle or Place of Action: Cedar Creek, etc., Montana; at Bear Paw Mountain, Montana
Date of Action: 21 October 1876—8 January 1877; 30 September 1877
Date of Issue: 26 June 1894
Citation: **First Award** Gallantry in actions. **Second Award** Carried Lt. Romeyn, who was severely wounded, off the field of battle under heavy fire.
Notes: ✢Double Awardee

1695 ◆ HOLDEN, HENRY

Rank: Private (highest rank: Corporal)
Service: U.S. Army
Birthday: 1836
Place of Birth: Brighton, Sussex County, England
Date of Death: 14 December 1905
Place of Death: Brighton, England
Cemetery: Brighton & Preston Cemetery (MH)—Brighton, England
Entered Service at: Boston, Suffolk County, Massachusetts
Unit: Company D, 7th U.S. Cavalry
Battle or Place of Action: Little Big Horn River, Montana
Date of Action: 25 June 1876
Date of Issue: 5 October 1878
Citation: Brought up ammunition under a galling fire from the enemy.

1696 ◆ HOLLAND, DAVID

Rank: Corporal (highest rank: Sergeant)
Service: U.S. Army
Birthday: 1839
Place of Birth: Dearborn, Wayne County, Michigan
Entered Service at: Fort Leavenworth, Leavenworth County, Kansas
Unit: Company A, 5th U.S. Infantry
Battle or Place of Action: Cedar Creek, etc., Montana
Date of Action: 21 October 1876—8 January 1877
Date of Issue: 27 April 1877
Citation: Gallantry in actions.

1697 ◆ *HOOKER, GEORGE

Rank: Private
Service: U.S. Army
Birthday: 1847
Place of Birth: Frederick, Frederick County, Maryland
Date of Death: 22 January 1873
Place of Death: Tonto Creek, Arizona
Cemetery: Fort Bliss National Cemetery (MH)—Fort Bliss, Texas
Entered Service at: Washington, D.C.
Unit: Company K, 5th U.S. Cavalry
Battle or Place of Action: Tonto Creek, Arizona
Date of Action: 22 January 1873
Date of Issue: 12 August 1875
Citation: Gallantry in action in which he was killed.

1698 ◆ HOOVER, SAMUEL

Rank: Bugler
Service: U.S. Army
Birthday: 1851
Place of Birth: Dauphin County, Pennsylvania
Entered Service at: Harrisburg, Dauphin County, Pennsylvania
Unit: Company A, 1st U.S. Cavalry
Battle or Place of Action: Santa Maria Mountains, Arizona
Date of Action: 6 May 1873
Date of Issue: 12 August 1875
Citation: Gallantry in action; also services as trailer in May 1872.

1699 ◆ HORNADAY, ELISHA SIMPSON

Rank: Private (highest rank: First Sergeant)
Service: U.S. Army
Birthday: 24 March 1851
Place of Birth: Hendricks County, Indiana
Date of Death: 9 July 1923
Place of Death: San Diego, California
Cemetery: Greenwood Cemetery—San Diego, California
Entered Service at: Des Moines, Polk County, Iowa
Unit: Company H, 6th U.S. Cavalry
Battle or Place of Action: Sappa Creek, Kansas
Date of Action: 23 April 1875
Date of Issue: 16 November 1876
Citation: With five other men he waded in mud and water up the creek to a position directly behind an entrenched Cheyenne position, who were using natural bank pits to good advantage against the main column. This surprise attack from the enemy rear broke their resistance.

1700 ◆ HOWZE, ROBERT LEE

Rank: Second Lieutenant (highest rank: Major General)
Service: U.S. Army
Birthday: 22 August 1864
Place of Birth: Overton, Rusk County, Texas
Date of Death: 19 September 1926
Place of Death: Columbus, Ohio
Cemetery: U.S. Military Academy Cemetery (I-14)—West Point, New York
Entered Service at: Overton, Rusk County, Texas
Unit: Company K, 6th U.S. Cavalry
Battle or Place of Action: White River, South Dakota
Date of Action: 1 January 1891
Date of Issue: 25 July 1891
Citation: Bravery in action.

1701 ◆ HUBBARD, THOMAS H.

Rank: Private
Service: U.S. Army
Birthday: 1848
Place of Birth: Philadelphia, Philadelphia County, Pennsylvania
Date of Death: 19 September 1889
Place of Death: Philadelphia, Pennsylvania
Entered Service at: Philadelphia, Philadelphia County, Pennsylvania
Unit: Company C, 2d U.S. Cavalry
Battle or Place of Action: Little Blue, Nebraska
Date of Action: 15 May 1870
Date of Issue: 22 June 1870
Citation: Gallantry in action.

1702 ◆ HUFF, JAMES W.

Rank: Private (highest rank: Sergeant)
Service: U.S. Army
Birthday: 7 February 1840
Place of Birth: Washington, Washington County, Pennsylvania
Date of Death: 30 November 1927
Place of Death: Port Richey, Florida
Cemetery: Pine Hill Cemetery—New Port Richey, Florida
Entered Service at: Vanburan, Pennsylvania
Unit: Company L, 1st U.S. Cavalry
Battle or Place of Action: Arizona
Date of Action: winter 1872-73
Date of Issue: 12 April 1875
Citation: Gallant conduct during campaigns and engagements with Apaches.

1703 ◆ HUGGINS, ELI LUNDY

Rank: Captain (highest rank: Brigadier General)
Service: U.S. Army
Birthday: 1 August 1842
Place of Birth: Schuyler County, Illinois
Date of Death: 22 October 1929
Cemetery: Mountview View Cemetery—Oakland, California
Entered Service at: Minnesota
Unit: 2d U.S. Cavalry
Battle or Place of Action: O'Fallons Creek, Montana
Date of Action: 1 April 1880
Date of Issue: 27 November 1894
Citation: Surprised the Indians in their strong position and fought them until dark with great boldness.

1704 ◆ HUMPHREY, CHARLES FREDERIC

Rank: First Lieutenant (highest rank: Major General)
Service: U.S. Army
Birthday: 2 September 1844
Place of Birth: Cortland, Cortland County, New York
Date of Death: 4 June 1926
Place of Death: Washington, D.C.
Cemetery: Arlington National Cemetery (4-3115)—Arlington, Virginia
Entered Service at: Buffalo, Erie County, New York
Unit: 4th U.S. Artillery
Battle or Place of Action: Clearwater, Idaho
Date of Action: 11 July 1877
Date of Issue: 2 March 1897
Citation: Voluntarily and successfully conducted, in the face of a withering fire, a party which recovered possession of an abandoned howitzer and two Gatling guns lying between the lines a few yards from the Indians.

1705 ◆ HUNT, FREDERICK O.

Rank: Private (highest rank: Corporal)
Service: U.S. Army
Birthday: 31 January 1848
Place of Birth: London, England
Date of Death: 21 July 1918
Place of Death: Columbia Falls, Montana
Cemetery: Soldier's Home Cemetery (MH)—Columbia Falls, Montana
Entered Service at: Fort Leavenworth, Leavenworth County, Kansas
Unit: 5th U.S. Infantry
Battle or Place of Action: Cedar Creek, etc., Montana
Date of Action: 21 October 1876—8 January 1877
Date of Issue: 27 April 1877
Citation: Gallantry in action.

1706 ◆ HUTCHINSON, RUFUS D.

Rank: Sergeant
Service: U.S. Army
Birthday: 1850
Place of Birth: Butlerville, Ohio
Entered Service at: Cincinnati, Hamilton County, Ohio
Unit: Company B, 7th U.S. Cavalry
Battle or Place of Action: Little Big Horn River, Montana
Date of Action: 25 June 1876
Date of Issue: 5 October 1878
Citation: Guarded and carried the wounded, brought water for the same, and posted and directed the men in his charge under galling fire from the enemy.

1707 ◆ HYDE, HENRY J.

Rank: Sergeant
Service: U.S. Army
Birthday: 11 February 1846
Place of Birth: Bangor, Penobscot County, Maine
Date of Death: 25 July 1893
Place of Death: Marion, Indiana
Cemetery: Marion National Cemetery (I-97) (MH)—Marion, Indiana
Entered Service at: New York, New York
Unit: Company M, 1st U.S. Cavalry
Battle or Place of Action: Arizona
Date of Action: winter 1872-73
Date of Issue: 12 August 1875
Citation: Gallant conduct during campaigns and engagements with Apaches.

1708 ◆ IRWIN, BERNARD JOHN DOWLING

Rank: Assistant Surgeon (highest rank: Brigadier General)
Service: U.S. Army
Birthday: 24 June 1830
Place of Birth: Ireland
Date of Death: 15 December 1927
Place of Death: Cobourg, Ontario, Canada
Cemetery: U.S. Military Academy Cemetery (D-17) (MH)—West Point, New York
Entered Service at: New York, New York
Unit: 7th U.S. Infantry
Battle or Place of Action: Apache Pass, Arizona
Date of Action: 13 February 1861
Date of Issue: 24 January 1894
Citation: Voluntarily took command of troops and attacked and defeated hostile Indians he met on the way. Surg. Irwin volunteered to go to the rescue of 2d Lt. George N. Bascom, 7th Infantry, who with 60 men was trapped by Chiricahua Apaches under Cochise. Irwin and 14 men, not having horses, began the 100-mile march riding mules. After fighting and capturing Indians, recovering stolen horses and cattle, he reached Bascom's column and helped break his siege.

1709 ◆ JACKSON, JAMES

Rank: Captain (highest rank: Brigadier General)
Service: U.S. Army
Birthday: 21 November 1833
Place of Birth: New Jersey
Date of Death: 21 October 1916
Place of Death: Portland, Oregon
Cemetery: Riverside Cemetery—Portland, Oregon
Entered Service at: New Jersey
Unit: 1st U.S. Cavalry
Battle or Place of Action: Camas Meadows, Idaho
Date of Action: 20 August 1877
Date of Issue: 17 April 1896
Citation: Dismounted from his horse in the face of a heavy fire from pursuing Indians and, with the assistance of one or two of the men of his command, secured to a place of safety the body of his trumpeter, who had been shot and killed.

1710 ◆ JAMES, JOHN

Rank: Corporal
Service: U.S. Army
Birthday: 1838
Place of Birth: Manchester, Greater Manchester County, England
Date of Death: 23 May 1902
Place of Death: Washington, D.C.
Cemetery: Soldier's Home National Cemetery (K-6991) (MH)—Washington, D.C.
Entered Service at: Albany, Albany County, New York
Unit: Company I, 5th U.S. Infantry
Battle or Place of Action: Upper Washita River, Texas
Date of Action: 9-11 September 1874
Date of Issue: 23 May 1875
Citation: Gallantry in action.

1711 ◆ JARVIS, FREDERICK

Rank: Sergeant
Service: U.S. Army
Birthday: 1841
Place of Birth: Essex County, New York
Date of Death: 8 April 1894
Place of Death: Salt Lake City, Utah

INDIAN CAMPAIGNS

Cemetery: City Cemetery (MH)—Salt Lake City, Utah
Entered Service at: Hudson, Lenawee County, Michigan
Unit: Company G, 1st U.S. Cavalry
Battle or Place of Action: Chiricahua Mountains, Arizona Territory
Date of Action: 20 October 1869
Date of Issue: 14 February 1870
Citation: Gallantry in action.

1712 ◆ JETTER, BERNHARD

Rank: Sergeant (highest rank: First Sergeant)
Service: U.S. Army
Birthday: 1862
Place of Birth: Wurttemberg, Germany
Date of Death: 23 August 1927
Cemetery: Cypress Hills National Cemetery (5-1) (MH)—Brooklyn, New York
Entered Service at: New York, New York
Unit: Company K, 7th U.S. Cavalry
Battle or Place of Action: Sioux Campaign, South Dakota
Date of Action: 29 December 1890
Date of Issue: 24 April 1891
Citation: Distinguished bravery.

1713 ◆ JIM

Rank: Sergeant
Service: U.S. Army
Birthday: 1850
Place of Birth: Arizona Territory
Date of Death: 1889
Place of Death: Ash Flats, Arizona
Entered Service at: Camp Verde, Yavapia County, Arizona Territory
Unit: Indian Scouts
Battle or Place of Action: Arizona
Date of Action: winter 1872-73
Date of Issue: 12 April 1875
Citation: Gallant conduct during campaigns and engagements with Apaches.

1714 ◆ JOHNSON, HENRY

Rank: Sergeant
Service: U.S. Army
Birthday: 11 June 1850
Place of Birth: Boydton, Mecklenburg County, Virginia
Date of Death: 31 January 1904
Place of Death: Washington, D.C.
Cemetery: Arlington National Cemetery (23-16547) (MH)—Arlington, Virginia
Entered Service at: Detroit, Wayne County, Michigan
Unit: Company D, 9th U.S. Cavalry
Battle or Place of Action: Milk River, Colorado
Date of Action: 2-5 October 1879
Date of Issue: 22 September 1890
Citation: Voluntarily left fortified shelter and under heavy fire at close-range made the rounds of the pits to instruct the guards; fought his way to the creek and back to bring water to the wounded.

1715 ◆ JOHNSTON, EDWARD

Rank: Corporal (highest rank: Sergeant)
Service: U.S. Army
Birthday: 8 February 1844
Place of Birth: Pen Yan, Yates County, New York
Date of Death: 20 January 1920
Cemetery: Lakeview Cemetery (MH)—Penn Yan, New York
Entered Service at: Chicago, Cook County, Illinois
Unit: 5th U.S. Infantry
Battle or Place of Action: Cedar Creek, etc., Montana
Date of Action: 21 October 1876—8 January 1877
Date of Issue: 27 April 1877
Citation: Gallantry in action.

1716 ◆ JONES, WILLIAM H.

Rank: Farrier (highest rank: Blacksmith)
Service: U.S. Army
Birthday: 1842
Place of Birth: Davidson County, North Carolina
Date of Death: 23 December 1911
Cemetery: Efland Methodist Church Cemetery (MH)—Efland, North Carolina
Entered Service at: Louisville, Jefferson County, Kentucky
Unit: Company L, 2d U.S. Cavalry
Battle or Place of Action: Little Muddy Creek, Montana
Date of Action: 7 May 1877
Date of Issue: 28 February 1878
Citation: Gallantry in the attack against hostile Sioux Indians 7 May 1877 at Muddy Creek, Mont., and in the engagement with Nez Perce Indians at Camas Meadows, Idaho, 20 August 1877, in which he sustained a painful knee wound.

1717 ◆ JORDAN, GEORGE

Rank: Sergeant
Service: U.S. Army
Birthday: 1847
Place of Birth: Williamson County, Tennessee
Date of Death: 24 October 1904
Cemetery: Fort McPherson National Cemetery (F-1131) (MH)—Maxwell, Nebraska
Entered Service at: Nashville, Davidson County, Tennessee
Unit: Company K, 9th U.S. Cavalry
Battle or Place of Action: Fort Tularosa & Carrizo Canyon, New Mexico
Date of Action: 14 May 1880 & 12 August 1881
Date of Issue: 7 May 1890
Citation: While commanding a detachment of 25 men at Fort Tularosa, N. Mex., repulsed a force of more than 100 Indians. At Carrizo Canyon, N. Mex., while commanding the right of a detachment of 19 men, 12 August 1881, he stubbornly held his ground in an extremely exposed position and gallantly forced back a much superior number of the enemy, preventing them from surrounding the command.

1718 ◆ KAY, JOHN

Rank: Private
Service: U.S. Army
Birthday: 1846
Place of Birth: Lancashire, England
Entered Service at: Philadelphia, Philadelphia County, Pennsylvania
Unit: Company L, 8th U.S. Cavalry
Battle or Place of Action: Arizona
Date of Action: 21 October 1868
Date of Issue: 3 March 1870
Citation: Brought a comrade, severely wounded, from under the fire of a large party of the enemy.

1719 ◆ KEATING, DANIEL

Rank: Corporal (highest rank: Sergeant)
Service: U.S. Army
Birthday: 1846
Place of Birth: County Cork, Ireland
Date of Death: 20 June 1912
Place of Death: East Boston, Massachusetts
Cemetery: Holy Cross Cemetery (MH)—Malden, Massachusetts
Entered Service at: Boston, Suffolk County, Massachusetts
Unit: Company M, 6th U.S. Cavalry
Battle or Place of Action: Wichita River, Texas
Date of Action: 5 October 1870
Date of Issue: 5 October 1870
Citation: Gallantry in action and in pursuit of Indians.

1720 ◆ KEENAN, BARTHOLOMEW T.

Rank: Trumpeter
Service: U.S. Army
Birthday: 1843
Place of Birth: Brooklyn, Kings County, New York
Entered Service at: Cincinnati, Hamilton County, Ohio
Unit: Company G, 1st U.S. Cavalry
Battle or Place of Action: Chiricahua Mountains, Arizona Territory
Date of Action: 20 October 1869
Date of Issue: 14 February 1870
Citation: Gallantry in action.

1721 ◆ KEENAN, JOHN

Rank: Private
Service: U.S. Army
Birthday: 1843
Place of Birth: Tubbercurry, County Sligo, Ireland
Date of Death: 18 March 1906
Place of Death: McIntyre, Iowa
Entered Service at: San Francisco, San Francisco County, California
Unit: 8th U.S. Cavalry
Battle or Place of Action: Arizona
Date of Action: August-October 1868
Date of Issue: 24 July 1869
Citation: Bravery in scouts and actions against Indians.

1722 ◆ KELLEY, CHARLES

Rank: Private
Service: U.S. Army
Birthday: 1840
Place of Birth: County Clare, Ireland
Entered Service at: New York, New York
Unit: U.S. Cavalry
Battle or Place of Action: Chiricahua Mountains, Arizona Territory
Date of Action: 20 October 1869
Date of Issue: 14 February 1870
Citation: Gallantry in action.

1723 ◆ KELLY, JOHN J. H.

Rank: Corporal (highest rank: Ordnance Sergeant)
Service: U.S. Army
Birthday: 1851
Place of Birth: Schuyler County, Illinois
Date of Death: 4 February 1907
Cemetery: Oak Ridge Cemetery—Springfield, Illinois
Entered Service at: Springfield, Sangamon County, Illinois
Unit: Company I, 5th U.S. Infantry
Battle or Place of Action: Upper Wichita River, Texas
Date of Action: 9 September 1874
Date of Issue: 23 April 1875
Citation: Gallantry in action.

1724 ◆ KELLY, THOMAS

Rank: Private
Service: U.S. Army
Birthday: June 1837
Place of Birth: County Mayo, Ireland
Date of Death: 25 March 1919
Place of Death: Leavenworth, Kansas
Cemetery: Mount Calvary Cemetery (MH)—Leavenworth, Kansas
Entered Service at: New York, New York
Unit: Company I, 5th U.S. Infantry
Battle or Place of Action: Upper Wichita River, Texas
Date of Action: 9 September 1874
Date of Issue: 23 April 1875
Citation: Gallantry in action.

1725 ◆ KELSAY

Rank: Scout
Service: U.S. Army
Place of Birth: Arizona Territory
Entered Service at: Arizona Territory
Unit: Indian Scouts
Battle or Place of Action: Arizona Territory
Date of Action: winter 1872-73
Date of Issue: 23 April 1875

Citation: Gallant conduct during campaigns and engagements with Apaches.

1726 ◆ *KENNEDY, PHILIP

Rank: Private
Service: U.S. Army
Birthday: 1841
Place of Birth: County Galway, Ireland
Date of Death: 3 November 1883
Place of Death: Cincinnati, Ohio
Entered Service at: Evansville, Randolph County, Illinois
Unit: Company C, 5th U.S. Infantry
Battle or Place of Action: Cedar Creek, etc., Montana
Date of Action: 21 October 1876—8 January 1877
Date of Issue: 27 April 1887
Citation: Gallantry in action.

1727 ◆ KERR, JOHN BROWN

Rank: Captain (highest rank: Brigadier General)
Service: U.S. Army
Birthday: 12 March 1847
Place of Birth: Lexington, Fayette County, Kentucky
Date of Death: 27 February 1928
Place of Death: Washington, D.C.
Cemetery: Arlington National Cemetery (3-1950-SH)—Arlington, Virginia
Entered Service at: Hutchison Station, Bourbon County, Kentucky
Unit: 6th U.S. Cavalry
Battle or Place of Action: White River, South Dakota
Date of Action: 1 January 1891
Date of Issue: 25 April 1891
Citation: For distinguished bravery while in command of his troop in action against hostile Sioux Indians on the north bank of the White River, near the mouth of Little Grass Creek, S. Dak., where he defeated a force of 300 Brule Sioux warriors, and turned the Sioux tribe, which was endeavoring to enter the Bad Lands, back into the Pine Ridge Agency.

1728 ◆ KERRIGAN, THOMAS

Rank: Sergeant
Service: U.S. Army
Birthday: 1845
Place of Birth: County Tipperary, Ireland
Entered Service at: New York, New York
Unit: Company H, 6th U.S. Cavalry
Battle or Place of Action: Wichita River, Texas
Date of Action: 12 July 1870
Date of Issue: 25 August 1870
Citation: Gallantry in action.

1729 ◆ KILMARTIN, JOHN

True Name: Gilmartin, John
Rank: Private
Service: U.S. Army
Birthday: 20 February 1850
Place of Birth: Montreal, Canada
Date of Death: 23 March 1890
Place of Death: Toledo, Ohio
Cemetery: Calvary Cemetery—Toledo, Ohio
Entered Service at: Philadelphia, Philadelphia County, Pennsylvania
Unit: Company F, 3d U.S. Cavalry
Battle or Place of Action: Whetstone Mountains, Arizona Territory
Date of Action: 5 May 1871
Date of Issue: 13 November 1871
Citation: Gallantry in action.

1730 ◆ KIRK, JOHN

Rank: First Sergeant (highest rank: Sergeant Major)
Service: U.S. Army
Birthday: 20 November 1846
Place of Birth: York, York County, Pennsylvania
Date of Death: 2 March 1920
Place of Death: New Cumberland, Pennsylvania
Cemetery: Mount Olivet Cemetery—New Cumberland, Pennsylvania
Entered Service at: Harrisburg, Dauphin County, Pennsylvania
Unit: Company L, 6th U.S. Cavalry
Battle or Place of Action: Wichita River, Texas
Date of Action: 12 July 1870
Date of Issue: 25 August 1870
Citation: Gallantry in action.

1731 ◆ KIRKWOOD, JOHN A.

Rank: Sergeant
Service: U.S. Army
Birthday: 29 October 1851
Place of Birth: Allegheny City, Allegheny County, Pennsylvania
Date of Death: 10 May 1930
Place of Death: Washington, D.C.
Cemetery: Soldier's Home National Cemetery (L-9102) (MH)—Washington, D.C.
Entered Service at: North Platte Barracks, Lincoln County, Nebraska
Unit: Company M, 3d U.S. Cavalry
Battle or Place of Action: Slim Butts, Dakota Territory
Date of Action: 9 September 1876
Date of Issue: 16 October 1877
Citation: Bravely endeavored to dislodge some Sioux Indians secreted in a ravine.

1732 ◆ KITCHEN, GEORGE KRAUSE

Rank: Sergeant (highest rank: First Sergeant)
Service: U.S. Army
Birthday: 5 October 1844
Place of Birth: Lebanon County, Pennsylvania
Date of Death: 22 November 1922

Place of Death: San Antonio, Texas
Cemetery: St. Mary's Cemetery (MH)—San Antonio, Texas
Entered Service at: Harrisburg, Dauphin County, Pennsylvania
Unit: Company H, 6th U.S. Cavalry
Battle or Place of Action: Upper Wichita River, Texas
Date of Action: 9 September 1874
Date of Issue: 23 April 1875
Citation: Gallantry in action.

1733 ◆ KNAAK, ALBERT

Rank: Private (highest rank: Ordnance Sergeant)
Service: U.S. Army
Birthday: 1840
Place of Birth: Luxenburg, Switzerland
Date of Death: 7 April 1897
Cemetery: Fort Meade National Cemetery (2-101) (MH)—Sturgis, South Dakota
Entered Service at: Cincinnati, Hamilton County, Ohio
Unit: Company B, 8th U.S. Cavalry
Battle or Place of Action: Arizona
Date of Action: August-October 1868
Date of Issue: 24 July 1869
Citation: Bravery in scouts and actions against Indians.

1734 ◆ KNIGHT, JOSEPH F.

Rank: Sergeant
Service: U.S. Army
Birthday: 23 November 1863
Place of Birth: Danville, Vermilion County, Illinois
Date of Death: 24 May 1940
Cemetery: City of Lubbock Cemetery (MH)—Lubbock, Texas
Entered Service at: Denver, Denver County, Colorado
Unit: Troop F, 6th U.S. Cavalry
Battle or Place of Action: White River, South Dakota
Date of Action: 1 January 1891
Date of Issue: 1 May 1891
Citation: Led the advance in a spirited movement to the assistance of Troop K, 6th U.S. Cavalry.

1735 ◆ KNOX, JOHN W.

Rank: Sergeant
Service: U.S. Army
Birthday: 1851
Place of Birth: Burlington, Des Moines County, Iowa
Date of Death: 1895
Place of Death: Philadelphia, Pennsylvania
Entered Service at: Fort Leavenworth, Leavenworth County, Kansas
Unit: Company I, 5th U.S. Infantry
Battle or Place of Action: Upper Wichita River, Texas
Date of Action: 9 September 1874
Date of Issue: 23 April 1875
Citation: Gallantry in action.

1736 ◆ KOELPIN, WILLIAM

Rank: Sergeant
Service: U.S. Army
Birthday: 5 October 1845
Place of Birth: Stetten, Prussia
Date of Death: 2 January 1912
Place of Death: Brooklyn, New York
Cemetery: Lutheran Cemetery—Middle Village, New York
Entered Service at: Brooklyn, Kings County, New York
Unit: Company I, 5th U.S. Infantry
Battle or Place of Action: Upper Wichita River, Texas
Date of Action: 9 September 1874
Date of Issue: 23 April 1875
Citation: Gallantry in action.

1737 ◆ KOSOHA

Rank: Scout
Service: U.S. Army
Place of Birth: Arizona Territory
Unit: Indian Scouts
Battle or Place of Action: Arizona Territory
Date of Action: winter 1872-73
Date of Issue: 12 April 1875
Citation: Gallant conduct during campaigns and engagements with Apaches.

1738 ◆ *KREHER, WENDELIN

Rank: First Sergeant
Service: U.S. Army
Birthday: 1846
Place of Birth: Stetten, Prussia
Date of Death: 17 March 1877
Place of Death: Tongue River, Montana
Cemetery: Custer Battlefield National Monument (A-466)—Crow Agency, Montana
Entered Service at: Philadelphia, Philadelphia County, Pennsylvania
Unit: Company C, 5th U.S. Infantry
Battle or Place of Action: Cedar Creek, etc., Montana
Date of Action: 21 October 1876
Date of Issue: 27 April 1877
Citation: Gallantry in action.

1739 ◆ KYLE, JOHN

Rank: Corporal
Service: U.S. Army
Birthday: 1846
Place of Birth: Cincinnati, Hamilton County, Ohio
Date of Death: 18 July 1870
Place of Death: Fort Hays, Kansas
Cemetery: Fort Leavenworth National Cemetery (H-3341)—Fort Leavenworth, Kansas
Entered Service at: Nashville, Davidson County, Tennessee
Unit: Company M, 5th U.S. Cavalry
Battle or Place of Action: Republican River, Kansas

Date of Action: 8 July 1869
Date of Issue: 24 August 1869
Citation: This soldier and two others were attacked by eight Indians, but beat them off and badly wounded two of them.

1740 ◆ LARKIN, DAVID

Rank: Farrier
Service: U.S. Army
Birthday: 1845
Place of Birth: Cork, Ireland
Date of Death: 8 May 1905
Cemetery: St. Paul's Cemetery (MH)—Arlington, Massachusetts
Entered Service at: Boston, Suffolk County, Massachusetts
Unit: Company F, 4th U.S. Cavalry
Battle or Place of Action: Red River, Texas
Date of Action: 29 September 1872
Date of Issue: 19 November 1872
Citation: Gallantry in action.

1741 ◆ LAWRENCE, JAMES

Rank: Private
Service: U.S. Army
Birthday: 1832
Place of Birth: Aberdeen, Scotland
Entered Service at: Sacramento, Sacramento County, California
Unit: Company B, 8th U.S. Cavalry
Battle or Place of Action: Arizona
Date of Action: August-October 1868
Date of Issue: 24 July 1869
Citation: Bravery in scouts and actions against Indians.

1742 ◆ LAWTON, JOHN STERLING

Rank: Sergeant
Service: U.S. Army
Birthday: 13 May 1858
Place of Birth: Bristol, Bristol County, Rhode Island
Date of Death: 12 June 1909
Place of Death: Presido of San Francisco, California
Cemetery: San Francisco National Cemetery (WS-1392)—San Francisco, California
Entered Service at: Boston, Suffolk County, Massachusetts
Unit: Company D, 5th U.S. Cavalry
Battle or Place of Action: Milk River, Colorado
Date of Action: 29 October 1879
Date of Issue: 7 June 1880
Citation: Coolness and steadiness under fire; volunteered to accompany a small detachment on a very dangerous mission.

1743 ◆ LENIHAN, JAMES

Rank: Private
Service: U.S. Army
Birthday: 1846
Place of Birth: County Kerry, Ireland
Entered Service at: Washington, D.C.
Unit: Company K, 5th U.S. Cavalry
Battle or Place of Action: Clear Creek, Arizona
Date of Action: 2 January 1873
Date of Issue: 12 April 1875
Citation: Gallantry in action.

1744 ◆ LEONARD, PATRICK JAMES

Rank: Sergeant (highest rank: First Sergeant)
Service: U.S. Army
Birthday: 19 May 1847
Place of Birth: County Meath, Ireland
Date of Death: 24 January 1899
Place of Death: Kansas City, Missouri
Cemetery: St. Joseph's Cemetery (MH)—New Almelo, Kansas
Entered Service at: Cincinnati, Hamilton County, Ohio
Unit: Company C, 2d U.S. Cavalry
Battle or Place of Action: Little Blue, Nebraska
Date of Action: 15 May 1870
Date of Issue: 22 June 1870
Citation: Gallantry in action.

1745 ◆ LEONARD, PATRICK THOMAS

Rank: Corporal (highest rank: Sergeant)
Service: U.S. Army
Birthday: 1828
Place of Birth: County Clare, Ireland
Date of Death: 1 March 1905
Place of Death: Leavenworth, Kansas
Cemetery: Mount Calvary Cemetery (MH)—Leavenworth, Kansas
Entered Service at: New York, New York
Unit: Company A, 23d U.S. Infantry
Battle or Place of Action: Fort Hartsuff (Grace Creek), Nebraska
Date of Action: 28 April 1876
Date of Issue: 26 August 1876
Citation: Gallantry in charge on hostile Sioux.

1746 ◆ LEONARD, WILLIAM

Rank: Private
Service: U.S. Army
Birthday: 14 July 1855
Place of Birth: Ypsilanti, Washtenaw County, Michigan
Date of Death: 15 September 1923
Place of Death: White Sulphur Springs, Montana
Cemetery: Main Cemetery (MH)—White Sulphur Springs, Montana
Entered Service at: Detroit, Wayne County, Michigan
Unit: Company L, 2d U.S. Cavalry
Battle or Place of Action: Muddy Creek, Montana
Date of Action: 7 May 1877
Date of Issue: 8 August 1877
Citation: Bravery in action.

1747 ◆ LEWIS, WILLIAM B.

Rank: Sergeant
Service: U.S. Army
Birthday: 1847
Place of Birth: Boston, Suffolk County, Massachusetts
Date of Death: 1 November 1900
Place of Death: Mamaroneck, New York
Cemetery: Beechwoods Cemetery—New Rochelle, New York
Entered Service at: Boston, Suffolk County, Massachusetts
Unit: Company B, 3d U.S. Cavalry
Battle or Place of Action: Bluff Station, Wyoming
Date of Action: 20-22 January 1879
Date of Issue: 28 March 1879
Citation: Bravery in skirmish.

1748 ◆ LITTLE, THOMAS

Rank: Bugler
Service: U.S. Army
Birthday: 1830
Place of Birth: Barbados, West Indians
Date of Death: 11 February 1880
Place of Death: Washington, D.C.
Cemetery: Soldier's Home National Cemetery (I-5627) (MH)—Washington, D.C.
Entered Service at: New York, New York
Unit: Company B, 8th U.S. Cavalry
Battle or Place of Action: Arizona
Date of Action: August-October 1868
Date of Issue: 24 July 1869
Citation: Bravery in scouts and actions against Indians.

1749 ◆ LLOYD, GEORGE

True Name: Loyd, George
Rank: Sergeant (highest rank: First Sergeant)
Service: U.S. Army
Birthday: 1843
Place of Birth: County Tyrone, Ireland
Date of Death: 17 December 1892
Place of Death: Fort Riley, Kansas
Cemetery: Post Cemetery (MH)—Fort Riley, Kansas
Entered Service at: Canton, Van Zandt County, Texas
Unit: Company I, 7th U.S. Cavalry
Battle or Place of Action: Wounded Knee Creek, South Dakota
Date of Action: 29 December 1890
Date of Issue: 16 April 1891
Citation: Bravery, especially after having been severely wounded through the lung.

1750 ◆ LOHNES, FRANK W.

True Name: Lohnas, Frank W.
Rank: Private
Service: U.S. Army
Birthday: 1840
Place of Birth: Oneida County, New York
Date of Death: 18 September 1889
Place of Death: Near Shubert, Nebraska
Cemetery: Maple Grove Cemetery (MH)—Shubert, Nebraska
Entered Service at: Omaha, Douglas County, Nebraska
Unit: Company H, 1st Nebraska Veteran Cavalry
Battle or Place of Action: Gilmans Ranch, Nebraska
Date of Action: 12 May 1865
Date of Issue: 24 July 1865
Citation: Gallantry in defending Government property against Indians.

1751 ◆ LONG, OSCAR FITZALAN

Rank: Second Lieutenant (highest rank: Brigadier General Ret.)
Service: U.S. Army
Birthday: 16 June 1852
Place of Birth: Utica, Oneida County, New York
Date of Death: 23 December 1928
Place of Death: Piedmont, California
Cemetery: Mountain View Cemetery—Oakland, California
Entered Service at: Utica, Oneida County, New York
Unit: 5th U.S. Infantry
Battle or Place of Action: Bear Paw Mountain, Montana
Date of Action: 30 September 1877
Date of Issue: 22 March 1895
Citation: Having been directed to order a troop of cavalry to advance, and finding both its officers killed, he voluntarily assumed command, and under a heavy fire from the Indians advanced the troop to its proper position.

1752 ◆ LOWTHERS, JAMES

Rank: Private
Service: U.S. Army
Birthday: 1852
Place of Birth: Boston, Suffolk County, Massachusetts
Entered Service at: Boston, Suffolk County, Massachusetts
Unit: Company H, 6th U.S. Cavalry
Battle or Place of Action: Sappa Creek, Kansas
Date of Action: 23 April 1875
Date of Issue: 16 November 1876
Citation: With five other men he waded in mud and water up the creek to a position directly behind an entrenched Cheyenne position, who were using natural bank pits to good advantage against the main column. This surprise attack from the enemy rear broke their resistance.

1753 ◆ LYTLE, LEONIDAS S.

Rank: Sergeant (highest rank: First Sergeant)
Service: U.S. Army
Birthday: 4 September 1846
Place of Birth: Warren County, Pennsylvania
Date of Death: 23 January 1924
Place of Death: Silver City, New Mexico
Cemetery: Memory Lane Cemetery (MH)—Silver City, New Mexico

Entered Service at: Cleveland, Cuyahoga County, Ohio
Unit: Company C, 8th U.S. Cavalry
Battle or Place of Action: Fort Selden, New Mexico
Date of Action: 8-11 July 1873
Date of Issue: 12 April 1875
Citation: Services against hostile Indians.

1754 ◆ LYTTON, JEPTHA L.

Rank: Corporal (highest rank: Sergeant)
Service: U.S. Army
Birthday: 18 November 1849
Place of Birth: Lawrence County, Indiana
Date of Death: 27 December 1932
Place of Death: Washington, D.C.
Cemetery: Soldier's Home National Cemetery (M-9370) (MH)—Washington, D.C.
Entered Service at: San Francisco, San Francisco County, California
Unit: Company A, 23d U.S. Infantry
Battle or Place of Action: Fort Hartsuff, Nebraska
Date of Action: 28 April 1876
Date of Issue: 26 August 1876
Citation: Gallantry in charge on hostile Sioux.

1755 ◆ MACHOL

Rank: Private
Service: U.S. Army
Place of Birth: Arizona Territory
Unit: Indian Scouts
Battle or Place of Action: Arizona Territory
Date of Action: 1872-73
Date of Issue: 12 April 1875
Citation: Gallant conduct during campaign and engagements with Apaches.

1756 ◆ MAHERS, HERBERT

Rank: Private
Service: U.S. Army
Birthday: 1846
Place of Birth: Canada
Entered Service at: Wilmington, Los Angeles County, California
Unit: Company F, 8th U.S. Cavalry
Battle or Place of Action: Seneca Mountain, Arizona
Date of Action: 25 August 1869
Date of Issue: 3 March 1870
Citation: Gallantry in action.

1757 ◆ MAHONEY, GREGORY

Rank: Private
Service: U.S. Army
Birthday: 1850
Place of Birth: Pettypool, South Wales
Cemetery: Fort Concho National Historic Landmark (MH) (Marker Only)—San Angelo, Texas
Entered Service at: Boston, Suffolk County, Massachusetts
Unit: Company E, 4th U.S. Cavalry
Battle or Place of Action: Red River, Texas
Date of Action: 26-28 September 1874
Date of Issue: 13 October 1875
Citation: Gallantry in attack on a large party of Cheyennes.

1758 ◆ MARTIN, PATRICK

Rank: Sergeant
Service: U.S. Army
Birthday: 1846
Place of Birth: County Offaly, Ireland
Date of Death: 12 December 1895
Entered Service at: New York, New York
Unit: Company G, 5th U.S. Cavalry
Battle or Place of Action: Castle Dome and Santa Maria Mountains, Arizona
Date of Action: June-July 1873
Date of Issue: 12 April 1875
Citation: Gallant services in operations of Capt. James Burns, 5th U.S. Cavalry.

1759 ◆ MATTHEWS, DAVID A.

Rank: Corporal (highest rank: First Sergeant)
Service: U.S. Army
Birthday: 7 March 1847
Place of Birth: Boston, Suffolk County, Massachusetts
Date of Death: 12 September 1923
Cemetery: St. John's Cemetery—Worcester, Massachusetts
Entered Service at: Boston, Suffolk County, Massachusetts
Unit: Company E, 8th U.S. Cavalry
Battle or Place of Action: Arizona Territory
Date of Action: 1868 & 1869
Date of Issue: 6 September 1869
Citation: Bravery in scouts and actions against Indians.

1760 ◆ MAUS, MARION PERRY

Rank: First Lieutenant (highest rank: Brigadier General-USA-Ret.)
Service: U.S. Army
Birthday: 25 August 1850
Place of Birth: Burnt Mills, Montgomery County, Maryland
Date of Death: 9 February 1930
Place of Death: New Windsor, Maryland
Cemetery: Arlington National Cemetery (3-3886-B)—Arlington, Virginia
Entered Service at: Tennallytown, Montgomery County, Maryland
Unit: 1st U.S. Infantry
Battle or Place of Action: Rio Aros, Sierra Madre Mountains, Mexico
Date of Action: 11 January 1886
Date of Issue: 27 November 1894
Citation: Most distinguished gallantry in action with hostile Apaches led by Geronimo and Natchez.

1761 ◆ MAY, JOHN
Rank: Sergeant
Service: U.S. Army
Birthday: 1839
Place of Birth: Wurttemberg, Germany
Date of Death: 19 March 1886
Place of Death: La Junta, Colorado
Cemetery: Fairview Cemetery (MH)—La Junta, Colorado
Entered Service at: Philadelphia, Philadelphia County, Pennsylvania
Unit: Company L, 6th U.S. Cavalry
Battle or Place of Action: Wichita River, Texas
Date of Action: 12 July 1870
Date of Issue: 25 August 1870
Citation: Gallantry in action.

1762 ◆ MAYS, ISAIAH
Rank: Corporal
Service: U.S. Army
Birthday: 16 February 1858
Place of Birth: Carters Bridge, Virginia
Date of Death: 2 May 1925
Place of Death: Phoenix, Arizona
Cemetery: Arizona State Hospital Cemetery (MH)—Phoenix, Arizona
Entered Service at: Columbus Barracks, Franklin County, Ohio
Unit: Company B, 24th U.S. Infantry
Battle or Place of Action: Cedar Springs, Arizona Territory
Date of Action: 11 May 1889
Date of Issue: 19 February 1890
Citation: Gallantry in the fight between Paymaster Wham's escort and robbers. Mays walked and crawled two miles to a ranch for help.

1763 ◆ McBRIDE, BERNARD
Rank: Private
Service: U.S. Army
Birthday: 1845
Place of Birth: Brooklyn, Kings County, New York
Entered Service at: Washington, D.C.
Unit: Company B, 8th U.S. Cavalry
Battle or Place of Action: Arizona Territory
Date of Action: August-October 1868
Date of Issue: 24 July 1869
Citation: Bravery in scouts and actions against Indians.

1764 ◆ McBRYAR, WILLIAM
Rank: Sergeant (highest rank: First Lieutenant)
Service: U.S. Army
Birthday: 14 February 1861
Place of Birth: Elizabethtown, Bladen County, North Carolina
Date of Death: 8 March 1941
Place of Death: Philadelphia, Pennsylvania
Cemetery: Arlington National Cemetery (4-2738-B) (MH)—Arlington, Virginia
Entered Service at: New York, New York
Unit: 10th U.S. Cavalry
Battle or Place of Action: Arizona Territory
Date of Action: 7 March 1890
Date of Issue: 15 May 1890
Citation: Distinguished himself for coolness, bravery, and marksmanship while his troop was in pursuit of hostile Apache Indians.

1765 ◆ McCABE, WILLIAM
Rank: Private
Service: U.S. Army
Birthday: 1848
Place of Birth: Belfast, County Antrim, Ireland
Cemetery: Fort Concho National Historic Landmark (MH) (Marker Only)—San Angelo, Texas
Entered Service at: Fort Duncan, Texas
Unit: Company E, 4th U.S. Cavalry
Battle or Place of Action: Red River, Texas
Date of Action: 26-28 September 1874
Date of Issue: 13 October 1875
Citation: Gallantry in attack on a large party of Cheyennes.

1766 ◆ *McCANN, BERNARD
Rank: Private
Service: U.S. Army
Birthday: 1850
Place of Birth: County Roscommon, Ireland
Date of Death: 12 January 1877
Cemetery: Custer Battlefield National Monument (A-859)—Crow Agency, Montana
Entered Service at: New York, New York
Unit: Company F, 22d U.S. Infantry
Battle or Place of Action: Cedar Creek, etc., Montana
Date of Action: 21 October 1876—8 January 1877
Date of Issue: 27 April 1877
Citation: Gallantry in action.

1767 ◆ McCARTHY, MICHAEL
Rank: First Sergeant (highest rank: Colonel–WAANG)
Service: U.S. Army
Birthday: 19 April 1845
Place of Birth: St. John's, Newfoundland, Canada
Date of Death: 15 January 1914
Cemetery: Mountain View Cemetery (IOOF Section)—Walla Walla, Washington
Entered Service at: New York, New York
Unit: Troop H, 1st U.S. Cavalry
Battle or Place of Action: White Bird Canyon, Idaho
Date of Action: June 1876—January 1877
Date of Issue: 20 November 1897
Citation: Was detailed with six men to hold a commanding position and held it with great gallantry until the troops fell back. He then fought his way through the Indians, rejoined a

portion of his command, and continued the fight in retreat. He had two horses shot from under him and was captured, but escaped and reported for duty after three days' hiding and wandering in the mountains.

1768 ◆ McCLERNAND, EDWARD JOHN

Rank: Second Lieutenant (highest rank: Brigadier General)
Service: U.S. Army
Birthday: 29 December 1848
Place of Birth: Jacksonville, Morgan County, Illinois
Date of Death: 9 February 1926
Place of Death: Washington, D.C.
Cemetery: Arlington National Cemetery (3-1931-SW)—Arlington, Virginia
Entered Service at: Springfield, Sangamon County, Illinois
Unit: 2d U.S. Cavalry
Battle or Place of Action: Bear Paw Mountain, Montana
Date of Action: 30 September 1877
Date of Issue: 27 November 1894
Citation: Gallantly attacked a band of hostiles and conducted the combat with excellent skill and boldness.

1769 ◆ McCORMICK, MICHAEL P.

Rank: Private (highest rank: First Sergeant Ret.)
Service: U.S. Army
Birthday: 23 January 1848
Place of Birth: Rutland, Rutland County, Vermont
Date of Death: 27 March 1909
Place of Death: Rutland, Vermont
Cemetery: Calvary Cemetery—Rutland, Vermont
Entered Service at: Harrisburg, Dauphin County, Pennsylvania
Unit: Company G, 5th U.S. Infantry
Battle or Place of Action: Cedar Creek, etc., Montana
Date of Action: 21 October 1876—8 January 1877
Date of Issue: 27 April 1877
Citation: Gallantry in action.

1770 ◆ McDONALD, FRANKLIN M.

Rank: Private
Service: U.S. Army
Birthday: 1850
Place of Birth: Bowling Green, Warren County, Kentucky
Entered Service at: Fort Griffin, Texas
Unit: Company G, 11th U.S. Infantry
Battle or Place of Action: Fort Griffin, Texas
Date of Action: 5 August 1872
Date of Issue: 31 August 1872
Citation: Gallantry in defeating Indians who attacked the mail.

1771 ◆ McDONALD, JAMES

Rank: Corporal (highest rank: Sergeant)
Service: U.S. Army
Birthday: 1834
Place of Birth: Edinburgh, Scotland
Entered Service at: Chicago, Cook County, Illinois
Unit: Company B, 8th U.S. Cavalry
Battle or Place of Action: Arizona Territory
Date of Action: August-October 1868
Date of Issue: 24 July 1869
Citation: Bravery in scouts and actions against Indians.

1772 ◆ McDONALD, ROBERT

Rank: First Lieutenant (highest rank: Captain)
Service: U.S. Army
Birthday: 12 May 1822
Place of Birth: Erie County, New York
Date of Death: 21 May 1901
Place of Death: San Francisco, California
Cemetery: Lone Tree Cemetery—Hayward, California
Entered Service at: Newport, Campbell County, Kentucky
Unit: 5th U.S. Infantry
Battle or Place of Action: Wolf Mountain, Montana
Date of Action: 8 January 1877
Date of Issue: 27 November 1894
Citation: Led his command in a successful charge against superior numbers of hostile Indians, strongly posted.

1773 ◆ McGANN, MICHAEL A.

Rank: First Sergeant (highest rank: Sergeant Major, Ordnance Corps)
Service: U.S. Army
Birthday: 1846
Place of Birth: County Roscommon, Ireland
Date of Death: 27 September 1918
Place of Death: Los Angeles, California
Cemetery: Calvary Cemetery—Los Angeles, California
Entered Service at: St. Louis, St. Louis County, Missouri
Unit: Company F, 3d U.S. Cavalry
Battle or Place of Action: Rosebud River, Montana
Date of Action: 17 June 1876
Date of Issue: 9 September 1880
Citation: Gallantry in action.

1774 ◆ McGAR, OWEN

Rank: Private
Service: U.S. Army
Birthday: 1851
Place of Birth: North Attleboro, Bristol County, Massachusetts
Date of Death: 5 November 1899
Cemetery: St. Francis Cemetery (MH)—Pawtucket, Rhode Island
Entered Service at: Providence, Providence County, Rhode Island
Unit: Company C, 5th U.S. Infantry
Battle or Place of Action: Cedar Creek, etc., Montana
Date of Action: 21 October 1876—8 January 1877
Date of Issue: 27 April 1877
Citation: Gallantry in action.

1775 ◆ McHUGH, JOHN

Rank: Private
Service: U.S. Army
Birthday: 1844
Place of Birth: Syracuse, Onondaga County, New York
Entered Service at: New York, New York
Unit: Company A, 5th U.S. Infantry
Battle or Place of Action: Cedar Creek, etc., Montana
Date of Action: 21 October 1876—8 January 1877
Date of Issue: 27 April 1877
Citation: Gallantry in action.

1776 ◆ McKINLEY, DANIEL

Rank: Private
Service: U.S. Army
Birthday: 1845
Place of Birth: Boston, Suffolk County, Massachusetts
Entered Service at: San Francisco, San Francisco County, California
Unit: Company B, 8th U.S. Cavalry
Battle or Place of Action: Arizona Territory
Date of Action: August-October 1868
Date of Issue: 24 July 1869
Citation: Bravery in scouts and actions against Indians.

1777 ◆ McLENNON, JOHN

Rank: Musician (highest rank: Sergeant)
Service: U.S. Army
Birthday: 1855
Place of Birth: Fort Belknap, Texas
Date of Death: 14 May 1888
Cemetery: St. Joseph's Catholic Cemetary (MH)—Rock Springs, Wyoming
Entered Service at: Fort Ellis, Montana
Unit: Company A, 7th U.S. Infantry
Battle or Place of Action: Big Hole, Montana
Date of Action: 9 August 1877
Date of Issue: 2 December 1878
Citation: Gallantry in action.

1778 ◆ McLOUGHLIN, MICHAEL

Rank: Sergeant
Service: U.S. Army
Birthday: 4 January 1840
Place of Birth: County Sligo, Ireland
Date of Death: 8 June 1921
Place of Death: Orting, Washington
Cemetery: Calvary Cemetery—Tacoma, Washington
Entered Service at: Louisville, Jefferson County, Kentucky
Unit: Company A, 5th U.S. Infantry
Battle or Place of Action: Cedar Creek, etc., Montana
Date of Action: 21 October 1876—8 January 1877
Date of Issue: 27 April 1877
Citation: Gallantry in action.

1779 ◆ *McMASTERS, HENRY A.

Rank: Corporal
Service: U.S. Army
Birthday: 1845
Place of Birth: Augusta, Kennebec County, Maine
Date of Death: 11 November 1872
Place of Death: Fort Griffin, Texas
Cemetery: San Antonio National Cemetery (D-729) (MH)—San Antonio, Texas
Entered Service at: Augusta, Kennebec County, Maine
Unit: Company A, 4th U.S. Cavalry
Battle or Place of Action: Red River, Texas
Date of Action: 29 September 1872
Date of Issue: 19 November 1872
Citation: Gallantry in action.

1780 ◆ McMILLIAN, ALBERT WALTER

Rank: Sergeant
Service: U.S. Army
Birthday: 13 October 1862
Place of Birth: Stillwater, Washington County, Minnesota
Date of Death: 2 October 1948
Place of Death: St. Paul, Minnesota
Cemetery: Oakland Cemetery—St. Paul, Minnesota
Entered Service at: Jefferson Barracks, Missouri
Unit: Company E, 7th U.S. Cavalry
Battle or Place of Action: Wounded Knee Creek, South Dakota
Date of Action: 29 December 1890
Date of Issue: 23 June 1891
Citation: While engaged with Indians concealed in a ravine, he assisted the men on the skirmish line, directed their fire, encouraged them by example, and used every effort to dislodge the enemy.

1781 ◆ McNALLY, JAMES

Rank: First Sergeant
Service: U.S. Army
Birthday: 1839
Place of Birth: County Monaghan, Ireland
Date of Death: 26 November 1904
Place of Death: Kingston, New Mexico
Entered Service at: Albany, Albany County, New York
Unit: Company E, 8th U.S. Cavalry
Battle or Place of Action: Arizona Territory
Date of Action: 1868 & 1869
Date of Issue: 6 September 1869
Citation: Bravery in scouts and actions against Indians.

1782 ◆ McNAMARA, WILLIAM

Rank: First Sergeant
Service: U.S. Army
Birthday: 1835
Place of Birth: County Cork, Ireland
Date of Death: 6 March 1912

Cemetery: Calvary Cemetery—Woodside, New York
Entered Service at: Baltimore, Baltimore County, Maryland
Unit: Company F, 4th U.S. Cavalry
Battle or Place of Action: Red River, Texas
Date of Action: 29 September 1872
Date of Issue: 19 November 1872
Citation: Gallantry in action.

1783 ◆ McPHELAN, ROBERT

Rank: Sergeant
Service: U.S. Army
Birthday: 1837
Place of Birth: County Laois, Ireland
Date of Death: 1 February 1884
Cemetery: Mount Calvary Cemetery (MH)—Leavenworth, Kansas
Entered Service at: New York, New York
Unit: Company E, 5th U.S. Infantry
Battle or Place of Action: Cedar Creek, etc., Montana
Date of Action: 21 October 1876—8 January 1877
Date of Issue: 27 April 1877
Citation: Gallantry in action.

1784 ◆ McVEAGH, CHARLES H.

Rank: Private
Service: U.S. Army
Birthday: 1833
Place of Birth: New York, New York
Entered Service at: San Francisco, San Francisco County, California
Unit: Company B, 8th U.S. Cavalry
Battle or Place of Action: Arizona
Date of Action: August-October 1868
Date of Issue: 24 July 1869
Citation: Bravery in scouts and actions against Indians.

1785 ◆ MEAHER, NICHOLAS

Rank: Corporal (highest rank: Sergeant)
Service: U.S. Army
Birthday: 1845
Place of Birth: Perry County, Ohio
Entered Service at: Cincinnati, Hamilton County, Ohio
Unit: Company G, 1st U.S. Cavalry
Battle or Place of Action: Chiricahua Mountains, Arizona Territory
Date of Action: 20 October 1869
Date of Issue: 14 February 1870
Citation: Gallantry in action.

1786 ◆ MECHLIN, HENRY W.B.

True Name: Mechling, Henry W.B.
Rank: Blacksmith
Service: U.S. Army
Birthday: 14 October 1851
Place of Birth: Mount Pleasant, Westmoreland County, Pennsylvania
Date of Death: 10 April 1926
Place of Death: Washington, D.C.
Cemetery: Soldier's Home National Cemetery (L-8861) (MH)—Washington, D.C.
Entered Service at: Pittsburgh, Allegheny County, Pennsylvania
Unit: Company H, 7th U.S. Cavalry
Battle or Place of Action: Little Big Horn, Montana
Date of Action: 25 June 1876
Date of Issue: 29 August 1878
Citation: With three comrades during the entire engagement courageously held a position that secured water for the command.

1787 ◆ MERRILL, JOHN MITCHELL

Rank: Sergeant
Service: U.S. Army
Birthday: 1846
Place of Birth: New York, New York
Date of Death: 10 June 1883
Place of Death: Fort D.A. Russell, Wyoming
Cemetery: Olivet Catholic Cemetery—Cheyenne, Wyoming
Entered Service at: New York, New York
Unit: Company F, 5th U.S. Cavalry
Battle or Place of Action: Milk River, Colorado
Date of Action: 29 September 1879
Date of Issue: 7 June 1880
Citation: Though painfully wounded, he remained on duty and rendered gallant and valuable service.

1788 ◆ MILLER, DANIEL H.

Rank: Private
Service: U.S. Army
Birthday: 1841
Place of Birth: Fairfield County, Ohio
Date of Death: 6 October 1874
Cemetery: Fort McPherson National Cemetery (A-380) (MH)—Maxwell, Nebraska
Entered Service at: Columbus, Franklin County, Ohio
Unit: Company F, 3d U.S. Cavalry
Battle or Place of Action: Whetstone Mountains, Arizona Territory
Date of Action: 5 May 1871
Date of Issue: 13 November 1871
Citation: Gallantry in action.

1789 ◆ MILLER, GEORGE

Rank: Corporal
Service: U.S. Army
Birthday: 1851
Place of Birth: Brooklyn, Kings County, New York
Date of Death: 10 June 1888

Place of Death: Sheridan, Kansas
Cemetery: Red Top Cemetery (MH)—Baker Township, Kansas
Entered Service at: Boston, Suffolk County, Massachusetts
Unit: Company H, 5th U.S. Infantry
Battle or Place of Action: Cedar Creek, etc., Montana
Date of Action: 21 October 1876—8 January 1877
Date of Issue: 27 April 1877
Citation: Gallantry in action.

1790 ◆ MILLER, GEORGE W.
Rank: Private
Service: U.S. Army
Birthday: 1839
Place of Birth: Philadelphia, Philadelphia County, Pennsylvania
Date of Death: 29 September 1869
Place of Death: Wickensburg, Arizona
Entered Service at: Philadelphia, Philadelphia County, Pennsylvania
Unit: Company B, 8th U.S. Cavalry
Battle or Place of Action: Arizona
Date of Action: August-October 1868
Date of Issue: 24 July 1869
Citation: Bravery in scouts and actions against Indians.

1791 ◆ MITCHELL, JOHN
Rank: First Sergeant (highest rank: Ordnance Sergeant)
Service: U.S. Army
Birthday: 1846
Place of Birth: Dublin, Ireland
Date of Death: 1 May 1904
Cemetery: San Francisco National Cemetery (NAWS-411-Row 51) (MH)—San Francisco, California
Entered Service at: Peoria, Peoria County, Illinois
Unit: Company I, 5th U.S. Infantry
Battle or Place of Action: Upper Washita, Texas
Date of Action: 9-11 September 1874
Date of Issue: 23 April 1875
Citation: Gallantry in engagement with Indians.

1792 ◆ MITCHELL, JOHN JAMES
Rank: Corporal
Service: U.S. Army
Birthday: 1846
Place of Birth: County Tyrone, Ireland
Date of Death: 15 May 1898
Place of Death: Tucson, Arizona
Entered Service at: Philadelphia, Philadelphia County, Pennsylvania
Unit: Company L, 8th U.S. Cavalry
Battle or Place of Action: Hell Canyon, Arizona
Date of Action: 3 July 1869
Date of Issue: 3 March 1870
Citation: Gallantry in action.

1793 ◆ MONTROSE, CHARLES H.
True Name: Munson, Alexander D.
Rank: Private
Service: U.S. Army
Birthday: 1853
Place of Birth: St. Paul, Ramsey County, Minnesota
Entered Service at: New York, New York
Unit: Company I, 5th U.S. Infantry
Battle or Place of Action: Cedar Creek, etc., Montana
Date of Action: 21 October 1876—8 January 1877
Date of Issue: 27 April 1877
Citation: Gallantry in action.

1794 ◆ MOQUIN, GEORGE
Rank: Corporal
Service: U.S. Army
Birthday: 1855
Place of Birth: New York, New York
Entered Service at: Brooklyn, Kings County, New York
Unit: Company F, 5th U.S. Cavalry
Battle or Place of Action: Milk River, Colorado
Date of Action: 29 September-5 October 1879
Date of Issue: 27 January 1880
Citation: Gallantry in action.

1795 ◆ MORAN, JOHN
Rank: Private
Service: U.S. Army
Birthday: 1842
Place of Birth: Lyon, France
Entered Service at: Marysville, Yuba County, California
Unit: Company F, 8th U.S. Cavalry
Battle or Place of Action: Seneca Mountain, Arizona
Date of Action: 25 August 1869
Date of Issue: 3 March 1870
Citation: Gallantry in action.

1796 ◆ MORGAN, GEORGE HORACE
Rank: Second Lieutenant (highest rank: Colonel)
Service: U.S. Army
Birthday: 1 January 1855
Place of Birth: St. Catherines, Canada
Date of Death: 14 February 1948
Place of Death: Washington, D.C.
Cemetery: Arlington National Cemetery (3-2053)—Arlington, Virginia
Entered Service at: Minneapolis, Hennepin County, Minnesota
Unit: 3d U.S. Cavalry
Battle or Place of Action: Big Dry Fork, Arizona
Date of Action: 17 July 1882
Date of Issue: 15 July 1892
Citation: Gallantly held his ground at a critical moment and

fired upon the advancing enemy (hostile Indians) until he was disabled by a shot.

1797 ◆ MORIARITY, JOHN

Rank: Sergeant
Service: U.S. Army
Birthday: 10 March 1846
Place of Birth: Huddersfield, Yorkshire, England
Date of Death: 12 October 1913
Place of Death: Yountville, California
Cemetery: Veterans Home of California Cemetery (MH)—Yountville, California
Entered Service at: Boston, Suffolk County, Massachusetts
Unit: Company E, 8th U.S. Cavalry
Battle or Place of Action: Arizona Territory
Date of Action: 1868 & 1869
Date of Issue: 6 September 1869
Citation: Bravery in scouts and actions against Indians.

1798 ◆ MORRIS, JAMES L.

Rank: First Sergeant
Service: U.S. Army
Birthday: 1844
Place of Birth: County Kerry, Ireland
Date of Death: 9 February 1903
Cemetery: Fairview Memorial Park (MH)—Albuquerque, New Mexico
Entered Service at: Philadelphia, Philadelphia County, Pennsylvania
Unit: Company C, 8th U.S. Cavalry
Battle or Place of Action: Fort Selden, New Mexico
Date of Action: 8-11 July 1873
Date of Issue: 12 August 1875
Citation: Services against hostile Indians.

1799 ◆ MORRIS, WILLIAM W.

Rank: Corporal
Service: U.S. Army
Birthday: 1843
Place of Birth: Stewart County, Tennessee
Entered Service at: Louisville, Jefferson County, Kentucky
Unit: Company H, 6th U.S. Cavalry
Battle or Place of Action: Upper Washita, Texas
Date of Action: 9-11 September 1874
Date of Issue: 23 April 1875
Citation: Gallantry in engagement with Indians.

1800 ◆ MOTT, JOHN

True Name: McMahan, John Mott
Rank: Sergeant (highest rank: Quartermaster Sergeant)
Service: U.S. Army
Birthday: 25 August 1842
Place of Birth: Fifeshire, Scotland
Date of Death: 30 August 1917
Place of Death: Omaha, Nebraska
Cemetery: Forest Lawn Cemetery—Omaha, Nebraska
Entered Service at: Baltimore, Baltimore County, Maryland
Unit: Company F, 3d U.S. Cavalry
Battle or Place of Action: Whetstone Mountains, Arizona Territory
Date of Action: 5 May 1871
Date of Issue: 13 November 1871
Citation: Gallantry in action.

1801 ◆ MOYLAN, MYLES

Rank: Captain (highest rank: Major)
Service: U.S. Army
Birthday: 17 December 1838
Place of Birth: Amesbury, Essex County, Massachusetts
Date of Death: 11 December 1909
Place of Death: San Diego, California
Cemetery: Greenwood Cemetery—San Diego, California
Entered Service at: Essex, Essex County, Massachusetts
Unit: 7th U.S. Cavalry
Battle or Place of Action: Bear Paw Mountain, Montana
Date of Action: 30 September 1877
Date of Issue: 27 November 1894
Citation: Gallantly led his command in action against Nez Perce Indians until he was severely wounded.

1802 ◆ MURPHY, EDWARD

Rank: Private (highest rank: Sergeant)
Service: U.S. Army
Birthday: 1845
Place of Birth: County Cork, Ireland
Date of Death: 27 January 1924
Place of Death: Los Angeles, California
Cemetery: Los Angeles National Cemetery (44-I-22) (MH)—Los Angeles, California
Entered Service at: New York, New York
Unit: Company G, 1st U.S. Cavalry
Battle or Place of Action: Chiricahua Mountains, Arizona Territory
Date of Action: 20 October 1869
Citation: Gallantry in action.

1803 ◆ MURPHY, EDWARD F.

Rank: Corporal
Service: U.S. Army
Birthday: 16 July 1850
Place of Birth: Wayne County, Pennsylvania
Date of Death: 20 April 1908
Place of Death: Philadelphia, Pennsylvania
Cemetery: Old Cathedral Cemetery—Philadelphia, Pennsylvania
Entered Service at: Philadelphia, Philadelphia County, Pennsylvania
Unit: Company D, 5th U.S. Cavalry
Battle or Place of Action: Milk River, Colorado
Date of Action: 29 September 1879

Date of Issue: 23 April 1880
Citation: Gallantry in action.

1804 ◆ MURPHY, JEREMIAH J.

Rank: Private
Service: U.S. Army
Birthday: 2 February 1858
Place of Birth: County Cork, Ireland
Date of Death: 12 May 1932
Place of Death: Detroit, Michigan
Cemetery: Mount Olivet Cemetery—Washington, D.C.
Entered Service at: Boston, Suffolk County, Massachusetts
Unit: Company M, 3d U.S. Cavalry
Battle or Place of Action: Powder River, Montana
Date of Action: 17 March 1876
Date of Issue: 16 October 1877
Citation: Being the only member of his picket not disabled, he attempted to save a wounded comrade.

1805 ◆ MURPHY, PHILIP

Rank: Corporal
Service: U.S. Army
Birthday: 1 November 1844
Place of Birth: County Killkenny, Ireland
Date of Death: 12 February 1923
Place of Death: Freewater, Oregon
Cemetery: Mountain View Cemetery—Walla Walla, Washington
Entered Service at: Chicago, Cook County, Illinois
Unit: Company F, 8th U.S. Cavalry
Battle or Place of Action: Seneca Mountain, Arizona
Date of Action: 25 August 1869
Date of Issue: 3 March 1870
Citation: Gallantry in action.

1806 ◆ MURPHY, THOMAS

Rank: Corporal
Service: U.S. Army
Birthday: 1836
Place of Birth: County Kerry, Ireland
Entered Service at: San Francisco, San Francisco County, California
Unit: Company F, 8th U.S. Cavalry
Battle or Place of Action: Seneca Mountain, Arizona
Date of Action: 25 August 1869
Date of Issue: 3 March 1870
Citation: Gallantry in action.

1807 ◆ MURRAY, THOMAS

Rank: Sergeant
Service: U.S. Army
Birthday: 1836
Place of Birth: County Monaghan, Ireland
Date of Death: 4 August 1888
Cemetery: Soldier's Home National Cemetery (K-6502) (MH)—Washington, D.C.
Entered Service at: New York, New York
Unit: Company B, 7th U.S. Cavalry
Battle or Place of Action: Little Big Horn, Montana
Date of Action: 25 June 1876
Date of Issue: 5 October 1878
Citation: Brought up the pack train, and on the second day the rations, under a heavy fire from the enemy.

1808 ◆ MYERS, FRED

Rank: Sergeant
Service: U.S. Army
Birthday: 1848
Place of Birth: Brunswick, Germany
Date of Death: 5 May 1900
Cemetery: Arlington National Cemetery (13-14034) (MH)—Arlington, Virginia
Entered Service at: St. Louis, St. Louis County, Missouri
Unit: Company K, 6th U.S. Cavalry
Battle or Place of Action: White River, South Dakota
Date of Action: 1 January 1891
Date of Issue: 4 February 1891
Citation: With five men repelled a superior force of the enemy and held his position against their repeated efforts to recapture it.

1809 ◆ NANNASADDIE

Rank: Scout
Service: U.S. Army
Place of Birth: Arizona Territory
Unit: Indian Scouts
Battle or Place of Action: Arizona Territory
Date of Action: 1872-73
Date of Issue: 12 April 1875
Citation: Gallant conduct during campaigns and engagements with Apaches.

1810 ◆ NANTAJE (NANTAHE)

Rank: Scout
Service: U.S. Army
Place of Birth: Arizona Territory
Unit: Indian Scouts
Battle or Place of Action: Arizona Territory
Date of Action: 1872-73
Date of Issue: 12 April 1875
Citation: Gallant conduct during campaigns and engagements with Apaches.

1811 ◆ NEAL, SOLON D.

Rank: Private (highest rank: Sergeant)
Service: U.S. Army
Birthday: 1846
Place of Birth: Hanover, Grafton County, New Hampshire
Date of Death: 1 November 1920
Cemetery: San Antonio National Cemetery (G-1323) (MH)—San Antonio, Texas

Entered Service at: Boston, Suffolk County, Massachusetts
Unit: Company L, 6th U.S. Cavalry
Battle or Place of Action: Wichita River, Texas
Date of Action: 12 July 1870
Date of Issue: 25 August 1870
Citation: Gallantry in action.

1812 ◆ NEDER, ADAM

Rank: Corporal
Service: U.S. Army
Birthday: 1865
Place of Birth: Bavaria, Germany
Date of Death: 17 September 1910
Place of Death: Manila, Philippine Islands
Cemetery: San Francisco National Cemetery (NAWS-1805) (MH)—San Francisco, California
Entered Service at: St. Louis, St. Louis County, Missouri
Unit: Company A, 7th U.S. Cavalry
Battle or Place of Action: Sioux Campaign
Date of Action: December 1890
Date of Issue: 25 April 1891
Citation: Distinguished bravery.

1813 ◆ NEILON, FREDERICK S.

Rank: Sergeant
Service: U.S. Army
Birthday: 22 June 1846
Place of Birth: Boston, Suffolk County, Massachusetts
Date of Death: 13 September 1916
Place of Death: Somerville, Massachusetts
Cemetery: St. Paul's Cemetery (MH)—Arlington, Massachusetts
Entered Service at: Watertown, Middlesex County, Massachusetts
Unit: Company A, 6th U.S. Cavalry
Battle or Place of Action: Upper Washita, Texas
Date of Action: 9-11 September 1874
Date of Issue: 23 April 1875
Citation: Gallantry in action.

1814 ◆ NEWMAN, HENRY

Rank: First Sergeant
Service: U.S. Army
Birthday: 1845
Place of Birth: Hanover, Germany
Date of Death: 13 July 1915
Cemetery: Loudon Park National Cemetery (PS-739)—Baltimore, Maryland
Entered Service at: Cincinnati, Hamilton County, Ohio
Unit: Company F, 5th U.S. Cavalry
Battle or Place of Action: Whetstone Mountains, Arizona Territory
Date of Action: 13 July 1872
Date of Issue: 4 December 1874
Citation: He and two companions covered the withdrawal of wounded comrades from the fire of an Apache band well concealed among rocks.

1815 ◆ NIHILL, JOHN

Rank: Private (highest rank: Sergeant)
Service: U.S. Army
Birthday: 25 May 1850
Place of Birth: Nenagh, County Tipperary, Ireland
Date of Death: 29 May 1908
Cemetery: Cypress Hills National Cemetery (2-6640) (MH)—Brooklyn, New York
Entered Service at: Brooklyn, Kings County, New York
Unit: Company F, 5th U.S. Cavalry
Battle or Place of Action: Whetstone Mountains, Arizona Territory
Date of Action: 13 July 1872
Date of Issue: 4 December 1874
Citation: Fought and defeated four hostile Apaches located between him and his comrades.

1816 ◆ NOLAN, RICHARD J.

Rank: Farrier
Service: U.S. Army
Birthday: 1848
Place of Birth: Ireland
Date of Death: 26 August 1905
Place of Death: Washington, D.C.
Cemetery: Soldier's Home National Cemetery (K-7179) (MH)—Washington, D.C.
Entered Service at: Milwaukee, Milwaukee County, Wisconsin
Unit: Company I, 7th U.S. Cavalry
Battle or Place of Action: White Clay Creek, South Dakota
Date of Action: 30 December 1890
Date of Issue: 1 April 1891
Citation: Bravery.

1817 ◆ O'CALLAGHAN, JOHN

Rank: Sergeant
Service: U.S. Army
Birthday: 1838
Place of Birth: New York, New York
Entered Service at: San Francisco, San Francisco County, California
Unit: Company B, 8th U.S. Cavalry
Battle or Place of Action: Arizona
Date of Action: August-October 1868
Date of Issue: 24 July 1869
Citation: Bravery in scouts and actions against Indians.

1818 ◆ OLIVER, FRANCIS

Rank: First Sergeant
Service: U.S. Army

Birthday: 1832
Place of Birth: Baltimore, Baltimore County, Maryland
Date of Death: 28 July 1880
Place of Death: Lewiston, Idaho
Cemetery: Normal Hill Cemetery (MH)—Lewiston, Idaho
Entered Service at: Fort Filmore, New Mexico
Unit: Company G, 1st U.S. Cavalry
Battle or Place of Action: Chiricahua Mountains, Arizona Territory
Date of Action: 20 October 1869
Date of Issue: 14 February 1870
Citation: Bravery in action.

1819 ◆ O'NEILL, WILLIAM

Rank: Corporal
Service: U.S. Army
Birthday: 1848
Place of Birth: Tariffville, Hartford County, Connecticut
Cemetery: Fort Concho National Historic Landmark (MH) (Marker Only)—San Angelo, Texas
Entered Service at: New York, New York
Unit: Company I, 4th U.S. Cavalry
Battle or Place of Action: Red River, Texas
Date of Action: 29 September 1872
Date of Issue: 19 November 1872
Citation: Bravery in action.

1820 ◆ O'REGAN, MICHAEL

Rank: Private
Service: U.S. Army
Birthday: 1846
Place of Birth: Fall River, Bristol County, Massachusetts
Entered Service at: Boston, Suffolk County, Massachusetts
Unit: Company B, 8th U.S. Cavalry
Battle or Place of Action: Arizona
Date of Action: August-October 1868
Date of Issue: 24 July 1869
Citation: Bravery in scouts and actions against Indians.

1821 ◆ ORR, MOSES

Rank: Private
Service: U.S. Army
Birthday: 1840
Place of Birth: County Tyrone, Ireland
Date of Death: 1897
Place of Death: Philadelphia, Pennsylvania
Entered Service at: Philadelphia, Philadelphia County, Pennsylvania
Unit: Company A, 1st U.S. Cavalry
Battle or Place of Action: Apache campaigns
Date of Action: winter 1872-73
Date of Issue: 12 April 1875
Citation: Gallant conduct during campaigns and engagements with Apaches.

1822 ◆ OSBORNE, WILLIAM

True Name: Osborn, William
Rank: Sergeant
Service: U.S. Army
Birthday: 1837
Place of Birth: Boston, Suffolk County, Massachusetts
Date of Death: 17 May 1876
Place of Death: Washington, D.C.
Cemetery: Soldier's Home National Cemetery (K-6512)—Washington, D.C.
Entered Service at: Boston, Suffolk County, Massachusetts
Unit: Company M, 1st U.S. Cavalry
Battle or Place of Action: Apache campaigns
Date of Action: winter 1872-73
Date of Issue: 12 April 1875
Citation: Gallant conduct during campaigns and engagements with Apaches.

1823 ◆ O'SULLIVAN, JOHN FRANCIS

Rank: Private
Service: U.S. Army
Birthday: 1850
Place of Birth: County Kerry, Ireland
Date of Death: 19 May 1907
Place of Death: New York, New York
Cemetery: Calvary Cemetery—Woodside, New York
Entered Service at: New York, New York
Unit: Company I, 4th U.S. Cavalry
Battle or Place of Action: Staked Plains, Texas
Date of Action: 8 December 1874
Date of Issue: 13 October 1875
Citation: Gallantry in a long chase after Indians.

1824 ◆ PAINE, ADAM

True Name: Payne, Adan
Rank: Private
Service: U.S. Army
Birthday: 1843
Place of Birth: Florida
Date of Death: 1 January 1877
Cemetery: Seminole Indian Scout Cemetery (MH)—Brackettville, Texas
Entered Service at: Fort Duncan, Texas
Unit: Indian Scouts
Battle or Place of Action: Canyon Blanco tributary of the Red River, Texas
Date of Action: 26-27 September 1874
Date of Issue: 13 October 1875
Citation: Rendered invaluable service to Col. R.S. Mackenzie, 4th U.S. Cavalry, during this engagement.

1825 ◆ PARNELL, WILLIAM RUSSELL

Rank: First Lieutenant (highest rank: Colonel)
Service: U.S. Army

1826 ◆ PAYNE, ISAAC

Birthday: 13 August 1836
Place of Birth: Dublin, Ireland
Date of Death: 20 August 1910
Cemetery: San Francisco National Cemetery (OS-68 Row 54)—San Francisco, California
Entered Service at: Brooklyn, Kings County, New York
Unit: 1st U.S. Cavalry
Battle or Place of Action: White Bird Canyon, Idaho
Date of Action: 17 June 1877
Date of Issue: 16 September 1897
Citation: With a few men, in the face of a heavy fire from pursuing Indians and in imminent peril, returned and rescued a soldier whose horse had been killed and who had been left behind in the retreat.

1826 ◆ PAYNE, ISAAC

Rank: Trumpeter
Service: U.S. Army
Birthday: 1854
Place of Birth: Mexico
Date of Death: 12 January 1904
Cemetery: Seminole Indian Scout Cemetery (MH)—Brackettville, Texas
Entered Service at: Fort Duncan, Texas
Unit: Indian Scouts
Battle or Place of Action: Pecos River, Texas
Date of Action: 25 April 1875
Date of Issue: 28 May 1875
Citation: With three other men, he participated in a charge against 25 hostiles while on a scouting patrol.

1827 ◆ PENGALLY, EDWARD

Rank: Private
Service: U.S. Army
Birthday: 1824
Place of Birth: Devonshire, England
Date of Death: 25 November 1874
Place of Death: Fort Supply, Oklahoma
Cemetery: Fort Leavenworth National Cemetery (G-3032 (MH)—Leavenworth, Kansas
Entered Service at: Albany, Albany County, New York
Unit: Company B, 8th U.S. Cavalry
Battle or Place of Action: Chiricahua Mountains, Arizona Territory
Date of Action: 20 October 1869
Date of Issue: 14 February 1870
Citation: Gallantry in action.

1828 ◆ PENNSYL, JOSIAH

Rank: Sergeant
Service: U.S. Army
Birthday: 15 September 1850
Place of Birth: Frederick County, Maryland
Date of Death: 22 January 1920
Place of Death: Pima, Arizona
Cemetery: Pima Cemetery (MH)—Pima, Arizona
Entered Service at: Carlisle, Cumberland County, Pennsylvania
Unit: Company M, 6th U.S. Cavalry
Battle or Place of Action: Upper Washita, Texas
Date of Action: 11 September 1874
Date of Issue: 23 April 1875
Citation: Gallantry in action.

1829 ◆ PHIFE, LEWIS

True Name: Pheiff, Louis
Rank: Sergeant
Service: U.S. Army
Birthday: 31 October 1841
Place of Birth: Des Moines County, Iowa
Date of Death: 31 January 1913
Place of Death: Wever, Iowa
Cemetery: Tierney Cemetery—Wever, Iowa
Entered Service at: Marion, Marion County, Oregon
Unit: Company B, 8th U.S. Cavalry
Battle or Place of Action: Arizona Territory
Date of Action: August-October 1868
Date of Issue: 24 July 1869
Citation: Bravery in scouts and actions against Indians.

1830 ◆ PHILIPSEN, WILHELM O.

Rank: Blacksmith
Service: U.S. Army
Birthday: 1852
Place of Birth: Schleswig, Germany
Entered Service at: Baltimore, Baltimore County, Maryland
Unit: Troop D, 5th U.S. Cavalry
Battle or Place of Action: Milk Creek, Colorado
Date of Action: 29 September 1879
Date of Issue: 12 December 1894
Citation: With nine others voluntarily attacked and captured a strong position held by Indians.

1831 ◆ PHILLIPS, SAMUEL D.

Rank: Private
Service: U.S. Army
Birthday: 28 January 1845
Place of Birth: Butler County, Ohio
Date of Death: 12 November 1915
Cemetery: Oakland Cemetery—St. Paul, Minnesota
Entered Service at: St. Louis, St. Louis County, Missouri
Unit: Company H, 2d U.S. Cavalry
Battle or Place of Action: Muddy Creek, Montana
Date of Action: 7 May 1877
Date of Issue: 8 August 1877
Citation: Gallantry in action.

1832 ◆ PHOENIX, EDWIN

Rank: Corporal
Service: U.S. Army
Birthday: 1846
Place of Birth: St. Louis, St. Louis County, Missouri

Date of Death: 26 September 1932
Place of Death: Los Angeles, California
Cemetery: Los Angeles National Cemetery (67-H-22) (MH)—Los Angeles, California
Entered Service at: St. Louis, St. Louis County, Missouri
Unit: Company E, 4th U.S. Cavalry
Battle or Place of Action: Red River, Texas
Date of Action: 26-28 September 1874
Date of Issue: 13 October 1875
Citation: Gallantry in action.

1833 ◆ PLATTEN, FREDERICK

Rank: Sergeant (highest rank: First Sergeant)
Service: U.S. Army
Birthday: 1849
Place of Birth: Torbeck, Ireland
Date of Death: 2 March 1939
Cemetery: Williams Cemetery—Williams, Arizona
Entered Service at: New York, New York
Unit: Company H, 6th U.S. Cavalry
Battle or Place of Action: Sappa Creek, Kansas
Date of Action: 23 April 1875
Date of Issue: 16 November 1876
Citation: With five other men he waded in mud and water up the creek to a position directly behind an entrenched Cheyenne position, who were using natural bank pits to good advantage against the main column. This surprise attack from the enemy rear broke their resistance.

1834 ◆ POPPE, JOHN A.

Rank: Sergeant
Service: U.S. Army
Birthday: 1854
Place of Birth: Cincinnati, Hamilton County, Ohio
Entered Service at: Fort Dodge, Ford County, Kansas
Unit: Company F, 5th U.S. Cavalry
Battle or Place of Action: Milk River, Colorado
Date of Action: 29 September-5 October 1879
Date of Issue: 27 January 1880
Citation: Gallantry in action.

1835 ◆ PORTER, SAMUEL

Rank: Farrier
Service: U.S. Army
Birthday: 5 December 1843
Place of Birth: Montgomery County, Maryland
Date of Death: 17 April 1920
Place of Death: Los Angeles, California
Cemetery: Los Angeles National Cemetery (40-E-6) (MH)—Los Angeles, California
Entered Service at: Washington, D.C.
Unit: Company L, 6th U.S. Cavalry
Battle or Place of Action: Wichita River, Texas
Date of Action: 12 July 1870
Date of Issue: 25 August 1870
Citation: Gallantry in action.

1836 ◆ POWERS, THOMAS

Rank: Corporal
Service: U.S. Army
Birthday: 1841
Place of Birth: New York, New York
Date of Death: 8 December 1884
Place of Death: Vience, Michigan
Entered Service at: Detroit, Wayne County, Michigan
Unit: Company G, 1st U.S. Cavalry
Battle or Place of Action: Chiricahua Mountains, Arizona Territory
Date of Action: 20 October 1869
Date of Issue: 14 February 1870
Citation: Gallantry in action.

1837 ◆ PRATT, JAMES N.

Rank: Blacksmith
Service: U.S. Army
Birthday: 12 September 1852
Place of Birth: Bellefontaine, Logan County, Ohio
Date of Death: 13 October 1903
Place of Death: Bellefontaine, Ohio
Cemetery: Bellefontaine Cemetery (MH)—Bellefontaine, Ohio
Entered Service at: Bellefontaine, Logan County, Ohio
Unit: Company I, 4th U.S. Cavalry
Battle or Place of Action: Red River, Texas
Date of Action: 29 September 1872
Date of Issue: 19 November 1872
Citation: Gallantry in action.

1838 ◆ PYM, JAMES

Rank: Private
Service: U.S. Army
Birthday: 1852
Place of Birth: Oxfordshire, England
Date of Death: 6 December 1893
Cemetery: Custer County Cemetery (MH)—Miles City, Missouri
Entered Service at: Boston, Suffolk County, Massachusetts
Unit: Company B, 7th U.S. Cavalry
Battle or Place of Action: Little Big Horn River, Montana
Date of Action: 25 June 1876
Date of Issue: 5 October 1878
Citation: Voluntarily went for water and secured the same under heavy fire.

1839 ◆ RAERICK, JOHN

Rank: Private
Service: U.S. Army
Birthday: 1844
Place of Birth: Baden, Germany
Entered Service at: Cincinnati, Hamilton County, Ohio
Unit: Company L, 8th U.S. Cavalry
Battle or Place of Action: Lyry Creek, Arizona Territory

Date of Action: 14 October 1869
Date of Issue: 3 March 1870
Citation: Gallantry in action with Indians.

1840 ◆ RAGNAR, THEODORE

True Name: Ling-Vannerus, Ragnar Theodor
Rank: First Sergeant
Service: U.S. Army
Birthday: 1 June 1856
Place of Birth: Linkoping, Sweden
Date of Death: 2 November 1943
Place of Death: Gothenburg, Sweden
Cemetery: St. Elius Cemetery—Skorde, Sweden
Entered Service at: New York, New York
Unit: Company K, 7th U.S. Cavalry
Battle or Place of Action: White Clay Creek, South Dakota
Date of Action: 30 December 1890
Date of Issue: 13 April 1891
Citation: Bravery.

1841 ◆ RANKIN, WILLIAM

Rank: Private (highest rank: Farrier-USA-Ret.)
Service: U.S. Army
Birthday: 1836
Place of Birth: Lewistown, Mifflin County, Pennsylvania
Date of Death: 2 February 1916
Place of Death: Lewiston, Pennsylvania
Cemetery: St. Mark's Episcopal Cemetery—Lewiston, Pennsylvania
Entered Service at: Harrisburg, Dauphin County, Pennsylvania
Unit: Company F, 4th U.S. Cavalry
Battle or Place of Action: Red River, Texas
Date of Action: 29 September 1872
Date of Issue: 19 November 1872
Citation: Gallantry in action with Indians.

1842 ◆ REED, JAMES C.

Rank: Private
Service: U.S. Army
Birthday: 1833
Place of Birth: Kilkenny, Ireland
Entered Service at: San Francisco, San Francisco County, California
Unit: Company A, 8th U.S. Cavalry
Battle or Place of Action: Arizona Territory
Date of Action: 29 April 1868
Date of Issue: 24 July 1869
Citation: Defended his position (with three others) against a party of 17 hostile Indians under heavy fire at close quarters, the entire party except himself being severely wounded.

1843 ◆ RICHMAN, SAMUEL

Rank: Private
Service: U.S. Army
Birthday: 1845
Place of Birth: Cleveland, Cuyahoga County, Ohio
Entered Service at: Cleveland, Cuyahoga County, Ohio
Unit: Company E, 8th U.S. Cavalry
Battle or Place of Action: Arizona Territory
Date of Action: 1868 & 1869
Date of Issue: 6 September 1869
Citation: Bravery in actions with Indians.

1844 ◆ ROACH, HAMPTON MITCHELL

Rank: Corporal (highest rank: Second Lieutenant)
Service: U.S. Army
Birthday: 1854
Place of Birth: Concord, Louisiana
Date of Death: 24 January 1923
Cemetery: Arlington National Cemetery (3-2393-WS) (MH)—Arlington, Virginia
Entered Service at: Fort Dodge, Ford County, Kansas
Unit: Company F, 5th U.S. Cavalry
Battle or Place of Action: Milk River, Colorado
Date of Action: 29 September-5 October 1879
Date of Issue: 27 January 1880
Citation: Erected breastworks under fire; also kept the command supplied with water three consecutive nights while exposed to fire from ambushed Indians at close-range.

1845 ◆ ROBBINS, MARCUS M.

Rank: Private (highest rank: Sergeant)
Service: U.S. Army
Birthday: 25 July 1851
Place of Birth: Elba, Dodge County, Wisconsin
Date of Death: 21 June 1924
Cemetery: Pittsfield Cemetery (MH)—Pittsfield, Massachusetts
Entered Service at: Boston, Suffolk County, Massachusetts
Unit: Company H, 6th U.S. Cavalry
Battle or Place of Action: Sappa Creek, Kansas
Date of Action: 23 April 1875
Date of Issue: 16 November 1876
Citation: With five other men he waded in mud and water up the creek to a position directly behind an entrenched Cheyenne position, who were using natural bank pits to good advantage against the main column. This suprise attack from the enemy rear broke their resistance.

1846 ◆ ROBINSON, JOSEPH

Rank: First Sergeant
Service: U.S. Army
Birthday: 12 October 1845
Place of Birth: Montreal, Canada
Date of Death: 18 December 1917
Cemetery: Fort Leavenworth National Cemetery (D-1269-D) (MH)—Fort Leavenworth, Kansas
Entered Service at: Boston, Suffolk County, Massachusetts
Unit: Company D, 3d U.S. Cavalry

Battle or Place of Action: Rosebud River, Montana
Date of Action: 17 June 1876
Date of Issue: 23 January 1880
Citation: Discharged his duties while in charge of the skirmish line under fire with judgment and great coolness and brought up the lead horses at a critical moment.

1847 ◆ ROCHE, DAVID

Rank: First Sergeant
Service: U.S. Army
Birthday: 1 May 1838
Place of Birth: County Kerry, Ireland
Date of Death: 19 November 1914
Place of Death: Worcester, Massachusetts
Cemetery: Hope Cemetery (MH)—Worcester, Massachusetts
Entered Service at: New York, New York
Unit: Company A, 5th U.S. Infantry
Battle or Place of Action: Cedar Creek, etc., Montana
Date of Action: 21 October 1876—8 January 1877
Date of Issue: 27 April 1877
Citation: Gallantry in action.

1848 ◆ RODENBURG, HENRY

Rank: Private (highest rank: Corporal)
Service: U.S. Army
Birthday: 1851
Place of Birth: Germany
Date of Death: 13 December 1899
Place of Death: Fort Columbus, New York
Cemetery: Cypress Hills National Cemetery (2-5825) (MH)—Brooklyn, New York
Entered Service at: Fort Leavenworth, Leavenworth County, Kansas
Unit: Company A, 5th U.S. Infantry
Battle or Place of Action: Cedar Creek, etc., Montana
Date of Action: 21 October 1876—8 January 1877
Date of Issue: 27 April 1877
Citation: Gallantry in action.

1849 ◆ ROGAN, PATRICK

Rank: Sergeant (highest rank: First Sergeant)
Service: U.S. Army
Birthday: 1847
Place of Birth: County Leitrim, Ireland
Date of Death: 27 December 1912
Place of Death: Rock Springs, Wyoming
Cemetery: St. Joseph's Catholic Cemetary (MH)—Rock Springs, Wyoming
Entered Service at: Reading, Berks County, Pennsylvania
Unit: Company A, 7th U.S. Infantry
Battle or Place of Action: Big Hole, Montana
Date of Action: 9 August 1877
Date of Issue: 2 December 1878
Citation: Verified and reported the company while subjected to a galling fire from the enemy.

1850 ◆ ROMEYN, HENRY

Rank: First Lieutenant (highest rank: Major)
Service: U.S. Army
Birthday: 1 June 1833
Place of Birth: Galen, Wayne County, New York
Date of Death: 21 February 1913
Cemetery: Arlington National Cemetery (3-1750)—Arlington, Virginia
Entered Service at: Michigan
Unit: 5th U.S. Infantry
Battle or Place of Action: Bear Paw Mountain, Montana
Date of Action: 30 September 1877
Date of Issue: 27 November 1894
Citation: Led his command into close-range of the enemy, there maintained his position, and vigorously prosecuted the fight until he was severely wounded.

1851 ◆ ROONEY, EDWARD

Rank: Private (highest rank: First Sergeant)
Service: U.S. Army
Birthday: 1847
Place of Birth: Poughkeepsie, Dutchess County, New York
Entered Service at: Poughkeepsie, Dutchess County, New York
Unit: Company D, 5th U.S. Infantry
Battle or Place of Action: Cedar Creek, etc., Montana
Date of Action: 21 October 1876—8 January 1877
Date of Issue: 27 April 1877
Citation: Gallantry in action.

1852 ◆ ROTH, PETER PAUL

Rank: Private
Service: U.S. Army
Birthday: 1849
Place of Birth: Wurttemberg, Germany
Date of Death: 18 January 1907
Cemetery: Rottenmunster Cemetery—Rottenmunster, Germany
Entered Service at: Brooklyn, Kings County, New York
Unit: Company A, 6th U.S. Cavalry
Battle or Place of Action: Washita River, Texas
Date of Action: 12 September 1874
Date of Issue: 4 November 1874
Citation: While carrying dispatches was attacked by 125 hostile Indians, whom he and his comrades fought throughout the day.

1853 ◆ ROWALT, JOHN F.

Rank: Private
Service: U.S. Army
Birthday: 1847
Place of Birth: Belleville, Richland County, Ohio
Entered Service at: Cincinnati, Hamilton County, Ohio
Unit: Company L, 8th U.S. Cavalry

Battle or Place of Action: Lyry Creek, Arizona Territory
Date of Action: 14 October 1869
Date of Issue: 3 March 1870
Citation: Gallantry in action with Indians.

1854 ◆ ROWDY

Rank: Sergeant
Service: U.S. Army
Place of Birth: Arizona Territory
f Death: 29 March 1893
Cemetery: Santa Fe National Cemetery (A-894) (MH)—Santa Fe, New Mexico
Entered Service at: San Carlos, Gila County, Arizona
Unit: Company A, Indian Scouts
Battle or Place of Action: Arizona Territory
Date of Action: 7 March 1890
Date of Issue: 15 May 1890
Citation: Bravery in action with Apache Indians.

1855 ◆ ROY, STANISLAUS

True Name: Roy, Stanilas
Rank: Sergeant (highest rank: Color Sergeant)
Service: U.S. Army
Birthday: 12 November 1846
Place of Birth: France
Date of Death: 10 February 1913
Cemetery: Columbus Barracks, Green Lawn Cemetery–Post Cemetery (51-A-1A3) (MH)—Columbus, Ohio
Entered Service at: Cincinnati, Hamilton County, Ohio
Unit: Company A, 7th U.S. Cavalry
Battle or Place of Action: Little Big Horn, Montana
Date of Action: 25 June 1876
Date of Issue: 5 October 1878
Citation: Brought water to the wounded at great danger to life and under a most galling fire of the enemy.

1856 ◆ RUSSELL, JAMES

Rank: Private
Service: U.S. Army
Birthday: 1846
Place of Birth: New York, New York
Entered Service at: New York, New York
Unit: Company G, 1st U.S. Cavalry
Battle or Place of Action: Chiricahua Mountains, Arizona Territory
Date of Action: 20 October 1869
Date of Issue: 14 February 1870
Citation: Gallantry in action with Indians.

1857 ◆ RYAN, DAVID

Rank: Private (highest rank: Sergeant)
Service: U.S. Army
Birthday: 1836
Place of Birth: County Kilkenny, Ireland
Date of Death: 8 September 1896
Place of Death: St. Louis, Missouri
Cemetery: Jefferson Barracks National Cemetery (59-11715) (MH)—St. Louis, Missouri
Entered Service at: Philadelphia, Philadelphia County, Pennsylvania
Unit: Company G, 5th U.S. Infantry
Battle or Place of Action: Cedar Creek, etc., Montana
Date of Action: 21 October 1876—8 January 1877
Date of Issue: 27 April 1877
Citation: Gallantry in action.

1858 ◆ RYAN, DENIS

Rank: First Sergeant
Service: U.S. Army
Birthday: 1848
Place of Birth: Cork, Ireland
Entered Service at: New York, New York
Unit: Company I, 6th U.S. Cavalry
Battle or Place of Action: Gageby Creek, Indian Territory
Date of Action: 2 December 1874
Date of Issue: 23 April 1875
Citation: Courage while in command of a detachment.

1859 ◆ SALE, ALBERT

Rank: Private (highest rank: Corporal)
Service: U.S. Army
Birthday: 1850
Place of Birth: Broome County, New York
Date of Death: 29 November 1874
Place of Death: Fort Union, New Mexico
Entered Service at: Dubuque, Dubuque County, Iowa
Unit: Company F, 8th U.S. Cavalry
Battle or Place of Action: Santa Maria River, Arizona
Date of Action: 29 June 1869
Date of Issue: 3 March 1870
Citation: Gallantry in killing an Indian warrior and capturing pony and effects.

1860 ◆ SCHNITZER, JOHN

Rank: Wagoner
Service: U.S. Army
Birthday: 1854
Place of Birth: Kempten, Bavaria, Germany
Date of Death: 26 October 1904
Cemetery: Fort Bayard Post Cemetery (A-O-43) (MH)—Fort Bayard, New Mexico
Entered Service at: New York, New York
Unit: Troop G, 4th U.S. Cavalry
Battle or Place of Action: Horseshoe Canyon, New Mexico
Date of Action: 23 April 1882
Date of Issue: 17 August 1896
Citation: Assisted, under a heavy fire, in rescuing a wounded comrade.

1861 ◆ SCHOU, JULIUS ALEXIS

Rank: Corporal (highest rank: Sergeant)
Service: U.S. Army
Birthday: 17 July 1849
Place of Birth: Copenhagen, Denmark
Date of Death: 19 November 1929
Place of Death: Washington, D.C.
Cemetery: Arlington National Cemetery (17-21482) (MH)—Arlington, Virginia
Entered Service at: Brooklyn, Kings County, New York
Unit: Company I, 22d U.S. Infantry
Battle or Place of Action: Sioux Campaign
Date of Action: 1870
Date of Issue: 19 November 1884
Citation: Carried dispatches to Fort Buford.

1862 ◆ SCHROETER, CHARLES

Rank: Private (highest rank: Sergeant)
Service: U.S. Army
Birthday: 1839
Place of Birth: Lindberg, Hanover, Germany
Entered Service at: St. Louis, St. Louis County, Missouri
Unit: Company G, 8th U.S. Cavalry
Battle or Place of Action: Chiricahua Mountains, Arizona Territory
Date of Action: 20 October 1869
Date of Issue: 14 February 1870
Citation: Gallantry in action.

1863 ◆ SCOTT, GEORGE D.

Rank: Private
Service: U.S. Army
Birthday: 1850
Place of Birth: Lancaster, Garrard County, Kentucky
Entered Service at: Mount Vernon, Rockcastle County, Kentucky
Unit: Company D, 7th U.S. Cavalry
Battle or Place of Action: Little Big Horn, Montana
Date of Action: 25-26 June 1876
Date of Issue: 5 October 1878
Citation: Voluntarily brought water to the wounded under fire.

1864 ◆ SCOTT, ROBERT B.

Rank: Private
Service: U.S. Army
Birthday: 1845
Place of Birth: Washington County, New York
Date of Death: 3 March 1908
Place of Death: Argyle, New York
Cemetery: Prospect Hill Cemetery—Argyle, New York
Entered Service at: St. Louis, St. Louis County, Missouri
Unit: Company G, 8th U.S. Cavalry
Battle or Place of Action: Chiricahua Mountains, Arizona Territory
Date of Action: 20 October 1869
Date of Issue: 14 February 1870
Citation: Gallantry in action.

1865 ◆ SEWARD, GRIFFIN

Rank: Wagoner
Service: U.S. Army
Birthday: 8 October 1842
Place of Birth: Dover, Kent County, Delaware
Date of Death: 10 September 1908
Place of Death: Los Angeles, California
Cemetery: Los Angeles National Cemetery (15-D-10) (MH)—Los Angeles, California
Entered Service at: Philadelphia, Philadelphia County, Pennsylvania
Unit: Company G, 8th U.S. Cavalry
Battle or Place of Action: Chiricahua Mountains, Arizona Territory
Date of Action: 20 October 1869
Date of Issue: 14 February 1870
Citation: Gallantry in action.

1866 ◆ SHAFFER, WILLIAM

True Name: Schaffer, William
Rank: Private
Service: U.S. Army
Birthday: 1841
Place of Birth: Bavaria, Germany
Date of Death: 2 January 1910
Place of Death: Los Angeles, California
Cemetery: I.O.O.F. Cemetery—Los Angeles, California
Entered Service at: Cincinnati, Hamilton County, Ohio
Unit: Company B, 8th U.S. Cavalry
Battle or Place of Action: Arizona Territory
Date of Action: August-October 1868
Date of Issue: 24 July 1869
Citation: Bravery in scouts and actions against Indians.

1867 ◆ SHARPLESS, EDWARD CLAY

Rank: Corporal
Service: U.S. Army
Birthday: 10 August 1853
Place of Birth: Marion County, Ohio
Date of Death: 12 January 1934
Place of Death: Mountainair, New Mexico
Cemetery: Mountainair Cemetery (MH)—Mountainair, New Mexico
Entered Service at: Columbus, Franklin County, Ohio
Unit: Company H, 6th U.S. Cavalry
Battle or Place of Action: Upper Washita River, Texas
Date of Action: 9-11 September 1874
Date of Issue: 23 April 1875
Citation: While carrying dispatches was attacked by 125 hostile Indians, whom he (and a comrade) fought throughout the day.

1868 ◆ SHAW, THOMAS
Rank: Sergeant (highest rank: First Sergeant)
Service: U.S. Army
Birthday: 1846
Place of Birth: Covington, Kenton County, Kentucky
Date of Death: 23 June 1895
Place of Death: Washington, D.C.
Cemetery: Arlington National Cemetery (27-952-B) (MH)—Arlington, Virginia
Entered Service at: Baton Rouge, Baton Rouge County, Louisiana
Unit: Company K, 9th U.S. Cavalry
Battle or Place of Action: Carrizo Canyon, New Mexico
Date of Action: 12 August 1881
Date of Issue: 7 December 1890
Citation: Forced the enemy back after stubbornly holding his ground in an extremely exposed position and prevented the enemy's superior numbers from surrounding his command.

1869 ◆ SHEERIN, JOHN
Rank: Blacksmith
Service: U.S. Army
Birthday: 1841
Place of Birth: Camden County, New Jersey
Entered Service at: Baltimore, Baltimore County, Maryland
Unit: Company C, 8th U.S. Cavalry
Battle or Place of Action: Fort Selden, New Mexico
Date of Action: 8-11 July 1873
Date of Issue: 12 August 1875
Citation: Services against hostile Indians.

1870 ◆ SHEPPARD, CHARLES
Rank: Private
Service: U.S. Army
Birthday: 27 November 1850
Place of Birth: Rocky Hill, Hartford County, Connecticut
Entered Service at: St. Louis, St. Louis County, Missouri
Unit: Company A, 5th U.S. Infantry
Battle or Place of Action: Cedar Creek, etc, Montana
Date of Action: 21 October 1876—8 January 1877
Date of Issue: 27 April 1877
Citation: Bravery in action with Sioux.

1871 ◆ SHINGLE, JOHN HENRY
Rank: First Sergeant
Service: U.S. Army
Birthday: 25 November 1842
Place of Birth: Philadelphia, Philadelphia County, Pennsylvania
Date of Death: 29 July 1907
Place of Death: Leavenworth, Kansas
Cemetery: Leavenworth National Cemetery (22-4-2) (MH)—Leavenworth, Kansas
Entered Service at: St. Louis, St. Louis County, Missouri
Unit: Troop I, 3d U.S. Cavalry
Battle or Place of Action: Rosebud River, Montana
Date of Action: 17 June 1876
Date of Issue: 1 June 1880
Citation: Gallantry in action.

1872 ◆ SKINNER, JOHN OSCAR
Rank: Contract Surgeon (highest rank: Lieutenant Colonel)
Service: U.S. Army
Birthday: 4 May 1845
Place of Birth: Baltimore, Baltimore County, Maryland
Date of Death: 12 September 1932
Cemetery: Arlington National Cemetery (3-1662)—Arlington, Virginia
Entered Service at: Maryland
Unit: U.S. Army
Battle or Place of Action: Lava Beds, California
Date of Action: 17 January 1873
Date of Issue: 6 April 1915
Citation: Rescued a wounded soldier who lay under a close and heavy fire during the assault on the Modoc stronghold after two soldiers had unsuccessfully attempted to make the rescue and both had been wounded in doing so.

1873 ◆ SMITH, ANDREW J.
Rank: Sergeant
Service: U.S. Army
Birthday: 1848
Place of Birth: Baltimore, Baltimore County, Maryland
Entered Service at: Baltimore, Baltimore County, Maryland
Unit: Company G, 8th U.S. Cavalry
Battle or Place of Action: Chiricahua Mountains, Arizona Territory
Date of Action: 20 October 1869
Date of Issue: 14 February 1870
Citation: Gallantry in action.

1874 ◆ SMITH, CHARLES E.
Rank: Corporal
Service: U.S. Army
Birthday: 1844
Place of Birth: Auburn, Cayuga County, New York
Entered Service at: St. Louis, St. Louis County, Missouri
Unit: Company H, 6th U.S. Cavalry
Battle or Place of Action: Wichita River, Texas
Date of Action: 12 July 1870
Date of Issue: 25 August 1870
Citation: Gallantry in action.

1875 ◆ SMITH, CORNELIUS COLE
Rank: First Sergeant (highest rank: Colonel U.S. Army Ret.)
Service: U.S. Army
Birthday: 7 April 1869
Place of Birth: Tucson, Pima County, Arizona
Date of Death: 10 January 1936

Cemetery: Evergreen Memorial Park (MH)—Riverside, California
Entered Service at: Helena, Lewis & Clark County, Montana
Unit: Company K, 6th U.S. Cavalry
Battle or Place of Action: White River, South Dakota
Date of Action: 1 January 1891
Date of Issue: 4 February 1891
Citation: With four men of his troop drove off a superior force of the enemy and held his position against their repeated efforts to recapture it, and subsequently pursued them a great distance.

1876 ◆ *SMITH, GEORGE W.

Rank: Private
Service: U.S. Army
Birthday: 1848
Place of Birth: Greenfield, Saratoga County, New York
Date of Death: 13 September 1874
Place of Death: Buffalo Wallow Battlegrounds remains not recovered, Texas
Cemetery: San Antonio National Cemetery (marker only) (MH)—San Antonio, Texas
Entered Service at: New York, New York
Unit: Company M, 6th U.S. Cavalry
Battle or Place of Action: Washita River, Texas
Date of Action: 12 September 1874
Date of Issue: 4 November 1874
Citation: While carrying dispatches was attacked by 125 hostile Indians, whom he and his comrades fought throughout the day. Pvt. Smith was mortally wounded during the engagement and died early the next day.

1877 ◆ SMITH, OTTO

Rank: Private
Service: U.S. Army
Birthday: 1840
Place of Birth: Baltimore, Baltimore County, Maryland
Entered Service at: Sacramento, Sacramento County, California
Unit: Company K, 8th U.S. Cavalry
Battle or Place of Action: Arizona Territory
Date of Action: 1868 & 1869
Date of Issue: 6 September 1869
Citation: Bravery in scouts and actions against Indians.

1878 ◆ SMITH, ROBERT

Rank: Private
Service: U.S. Army
Birthday: 1851
Place of Birth: Philadelphia, Philadelphia County, Pennsylvania
Entered Service at: Philadelphia, Philadelphia County, Pennsylvania
Unit: Company M, 3d U.S. Cavalry
Battle or Place of Action: Slim Buttes, Montana
Date of Action: 9 September 1876

Date of Issue: 16 October 1877
Citation: Special bravery in endeavoring to dislodge Indians secreted in a ravine.

1879 ◆ SMITH, THEODORE F.

Rank: Private (highest rank: Corporal)
Service: U.S. Army
Birthday: 6 September 1852
Place of Birth: Rahway, Union County, New Jersey
Date of Death: 6 June 1925
Place of Death: Washington, D.C.
Cemetery: Arlington Cemetery—Drexel Hill, Pennsylvania
Entered Service at: Harrisburg, Dauphin County, Pennsylvania
Unit: Company G, 1st U.S. Cavalry
Battle or Place of Action: Chiricahua Mountains, Arizona Territory
Date of Action: 20 October 1869
Date of Issue: 14 February 1879
Citation: Gallantry in action.

1880 ◆ SMITH, THOMAS

Rank: Private
Service: U.S. Army
Birthday: 4 July 1847
Place of Birth: Boston, Suffolk County, Massachusetts
Date of Death: 1 September 1909
Place of Death: Washington, D.C.
Cemetery: Soldier's Home National Cemetery (K-7492) (MH)—Washington, D.C.
Entered Service at: Fort Adams, Rhode Island
Unit: Company G, 1st U.S. Cavalry
Battle or Place of Action: Chiricahua Mountains, Arizona Territory
Date of Action: 20 October 1869
Date of Issue: 14 February 1870
Citation: Gallantry in action.

1881 ◆ SMITH, THOMAS J.

True Name: Smith, Thomas J.
Rank: Private
Service: U.S. Army
Birthday: 1833
Place of Birth: Liverpool, Merseyside County, England
Entered Service at: New York, New York
Unit: Company G, 1st U.S. Cavalry
Battle or Place of Action: Chiricahua Mountains, Arizona Territory
Date of Action: 20 October 1869
Date of Issue: 14 February 1870
Citation: Gallantry in action.

1882 ◆ SMITH, WILLIAM

Rank: Private
Service: U.S. Army

Birthday: 1848
Place of Birth: Bath, Sagadahoc County, Maine
Entered Service at: San Francisco, San Francisco County, California
Unit: Company G, 8th U.S. Cavalry
Battle or Place of Action: Chiricahua Mountains, Arizona Territory
Date of Action: 20 October 1869
Date of Issue: 14 February 1870
Citation: Gallantry in action.

1883 ◆ SMITH, WILLIAM H.

Rank: Private
Service: U.S. Army
Birthday: 1847
Place of Birth: Lapeer, Lapeer County, Michigan
Entered Service at: Cincinnati, Hamilton County, Ohio
Unit: Company G, 1st U.S. Cavalry
Battle or Place of Action: Chiricahua Mountains, Arizona Territory
Date of Action: 20 October 1869
Date of Issue: 14 February 1870
Citation: Gallantry in action.

1884 ◆ SNOW, ELMER A.

Rank: Trumpeter
Service: U.S. Army
Birthday: 1851
Place of Birth: Hardwick, Worcester County, Massachusetts
Date of Death: 21 January 1892
Cemetery: Highland Cemetery (MH)—Athol, Massachusetts
Entered Service at: Chicago, Cook County, Illinois
Unit: Company M, 3d U.S. Cavalry
Battle or Place of Action: Rosebud Creek, Montana
Date of Action: 17 June 1876
Date of Issue: 16 October 1877
Citation: Bravery in action; was wounded in both arms.

1885 ◆ SPENCE, ORIZOBA

True Name: Spence, Orisoba
Rank: Private
Service: U.S. Army
Birthday: 1847
Place of Birth: Forest County, Pennsylvania
Date of Death: 7 April 1876
Cemetery: Post Cemetery (Sec. E-16 Grave #58)—Fort Bowie, Arizona
Entered Service at: Cincinnati, Hamilton County, Ohio
Unit: Company G, 8th U.S. Cavalry
Battle or Place of Action: Chiricahua Mountains, Arizona Territory
Date of Action: 20 October 1869
Date of Issue: 14 February 1870
Citation: Gallantry in action.

1886 ◆ SPRINGER, GEORGE

Rank: Private
Service: U.S. Army
Birthday: 7 May 1848
Place of Birth: York County, Pennsylvania
Date of Death: 11 June 1931
Cemetery: Mount Olivet Cemetery—New Cumberland, Pennsylvania
Entered Service at: Harrisburg, Dauphin County, Pennsylvania
Unit: Company G, 1st U.S. Cavalry
Battle or Place of Action: Chiricahua Mountains, Arizona Territory
Date of Action: 20 October 1869
Date of Issue: 14 February 1870
Citation: Gallantry in action.

1887 ◆ STANCE, EMANUEL

Rank: Sergeant (highest rank: First Sergeant)
Service: U.S. Army
Birthday: 1843
Place of Birth: Carroll Parish, Louisiana
Date of Death: 25 December 1887
Place of Death: Fort Robinson, Nebraska
Cemetery: Fort McPherson National Cemetery (F-1040) (MH)—Maxwell, Nebraska
Entered Service at: East Carroll Parish, Louisiana
Unit: Company F, 9th U.S. Cavalry
Battle or Place of Action: Kickapoo Springs, Texas
Date of Action: 20 May 1870
Date of Issue: 28 June 1870
Citation: Gallantry on scout after Indians.

1888 ◆ STANLEY, EBEN

Rank: Private
Service: U.S. Army
Birthday: 1844
Place of Birth: Decatur County, Iowa
Date of Death: 19 November 1904
Place of Death: Hillsboro, New Mexico
Cemetery: Hillsboro Cemetery—Hillsboro, New Mexico
Entered Service at: Santa Fe, Santa Fe County, New Mexico
Unit: Company A, 5th U.S. Cavalry
Battle or Place of Action: Turret Mountain, Arizona Territory
Date of Action: 25, 27 March 1873
Date of Issue: 12 April 1875
Citation: Gallantry in action.

1889 ◆ STANLEY, EDWARD

Rank: Corporal
Service: U.S. Army
Birthday: 1846
Place of Birth: New York, New York
Entered Service at: San Francisco, San Francisco County, California

Unit: Company F, 8th U.S. Cavalry
Battle or Place of Action: Seneca Mountain, Arizona
Date of Action: 26 August 1869
Date of Issue: 3 March 1870
Citation: Gallantry in action.

1890 ◆ STAUFFER, RUDOLPH

Rank: First Sergeant
Service: U.S. Army
Birthday: 27 November 1836
Place of Birth: Berne, Switzerland
Date of Death: 9 June 1918
Place of Death: Washington, D.C.
Cemetery: Soldier's Home National Cemetery (K-8132) (MH)—Washington, D.C.
Entered Service at: Cincinnati, Hamilton County, Ohio
Unit: Company K, 5th U.S. Cavalry
Battle or Place of Action: Camp Hualpai, Arizona Territory
Date of Action: 1872
Date of Issue: 30 July 1875
Citation: Gallantry on scouts after Indians.

1891 ◆ STEINER, CHRISTIAN

Rank: Saddler
Service: U.S. Army
Birthday: 1833
Place of Birth: Wurttemberg, Germany
Date of Death: 5 August 1880
Place of Death: Hot Springs, Arkansas
Entered Service at: St. Louis, St. Louis County, Missouri
Unit: Company G, 8th U.S. Cavalry
Battle or Place of Action: Chiricahua Mountains, Arizona Territory
Date of Action: 20 October 1869
Date of Issue: 14 February 1870
Citation: Gallantry in action.

1892 ◆ STEVERS, THOMAS W.

True Name: Stivers, Thomas W.
Rank: Private
Service: U.S. Army
Birthday: 1850
Place of Birth: Madison County, Kentucky
Entered Service at: Mount Vernon, Rockcastle County, Kentucky
Unit: Company D, 7th U.S. Cavalry
Battle or Place of Action: Little Big Horn, Montana
Date of Action: 25-26 June 1876
Date of Issue: 5 October 1878
Citation: Voluntarily brought water to the wounded under fire.

1893 ◆ STEWART, BENJAMIN F.

Rank: Private
Service: U.S. Army
Birthday: 1851
Place of Birth: Norfolk, Norfolk County, Virginia
Entered Service at: Boston, Suffolk County, Massachusetts
Unit: Company E, 7th U.S. Infantry
Battle or Place of Action: Big Horn River, Montana
Date of Action: 9 July 1876
Date of Issue: 2 December 1876
Citation: Carried dispatches to Gen. Crook at imminent risk of his life.

1894 ◆ STICKOFFER, JULIUS HENRY

Rank: Saddler (highest rank: First Sergeant)
Service: U.S. Army
Birthday: 1845
Place of Birth: Switzerland
Date of Death: 3 September 1925
Place of Death: Yountville, California
Cemetery: Veterans Home of California Cemetery (MH)—Yountville, California
Entered Service at: Cincinnati, Hamilton County, Ohio
Unit: Company L, 8th U.S. Cavalry
Battle or Place of Action: Cienaga Springs, Utah
Date of Action: 11 November 1868
Date of Issue: 3 March 1870
Citation: Gallantry in action.

1895 ◆ STOKES, ALONZO

Rank: First Sergeant
Service: U.S. Army
Birthday: 1837
Place of Birth: Logan County, Ohio
Date of Death: 4 July 1876
Place of Death: St. Louis, Missouri
Cemetery: Jefferson Barracks National Cemetery (63-114-50) (MH)—St. Louis, Missouri
Entered Service at: Cincinnati, Hamilton County, Ohio
Unit: Company H, 6th U.S. Cavalry
Battle or Place of Action: Wichita River, Texas
Date of Action: 12 July 1870
Date of Issue: 25 August 1870
Citation: Gallantry in action.

1896 ◆ STRAYER, WILLIAM H.

Rank: Private (highest rank: Sergeant)
Service: U.S. Army
Birthday: 1847
Place of Birth: Maytown, Lancaster County, Pennsylvania
Entered Service at: Carlisle, Cumberland County, Pennsylvania
Unit: Company B, 3d U.S. Cavalry
Battle or Place of Action: Loupe Fork of the Platte River, Nebraska
Date of Action: 26 April 1872
Date of Issue: 22 May 1872
Citation: Gallantry in action.

1897 ◆ STRIVSON, BENONI
True Name: Stinson, Benoni
Rank: Private
Service: U.S. Army
Birthday: 1831
Place of Birth: Overton, Tennessee
Entered Service at: Sacramento, Sacramento County, California
Unit: Company B, 8th U.S. Cavalry
Battle or Place of Action: Arizona
Date of Action: August–October 1868
Date of Issue: 24 July 1869
Citation: Bravery in scouts and actions against Indians.

1898 ◆ SULLIVAN, THOMAS
Rank: Private (highest rank: First Sergeant)
Service: U.S. Army
Birthday: 20 April 1859
Place of Birth: County Meath, Ireland
Date of Death: 10 January 1940
Cemetery: Holy Sepulchre Cemetery—East Orange, New Jersey
Entered Service at: Newark, Essex County, New Jersey
Unit: Company E, 7th U.S. Cavalry
Battle or Place of Action: Wounded Knee Creek, South Dakota
Date of Action: 29 December 1890
Date of Issue: 17 December 1891
Citation: Conspicuous bravery in action against Indians concealed in a ravine.

1899 ◆ SULLIVAN, THOMAS
Rank: Private
Service: U.S. Army
Birthday: 1847
Place of Birth: Covington, Kenton County, Kentucky
Entered Service at: Cincinnati, Hamilton County, Ohio
Unit: Company G, 1st U.S. Cavalry
Battle or Place of Action: Chiricahua Mountains, Arizona Territory
Date of Action: 20 October 1869
Date of Issue: 14 February 1870
Citation: Gallantry in action against Indians concealed in a ravine.

1900 ◆ SUMNER, JAMES
Rank: Private
Service: U.S. Army
Birthday: 1840
Place of Birth: London, England
Date of Death: 5 July 1912
Place of Death: Ventura, California
Cemetery: Ventura Cemetery (MH)—Ventura, California
Entered Service at: Chicago, Cook County, Illinois
Unit: Company G, 1st U.S. Cavalry
Battle or Place of Action: Chiricahua Mountains, Arizona Territory
Date of Action: 20 October 1869
Date of Issue: 14 February 1870
Citation: Gallantry in action.

1901 ◆ SUTHERLAND, JOHN ALEXANDER
Rank: Corporal
Service: U.S. Army
Birthday: 19 February 1849
Place of Birth: Harrodsburg, Monroe County, Indiana
Date of Death: 2 December 1891
Cemetery: El Reno Cemetery (PM)—El Reno, Oklahoma
Entered Service at: Indianapolis, Marion County, Indiana
Unit: Company L, 8th U.S. Cavalry
Battle or Place of Action: Arizona Territory
Date of Action: August–October 1868
Date of Issue: 24 July 1869
Citation: Bravery in scouts and actions against Indians.

1902 ◆ *TAYLOR, BERNARD
Rank: Sergeant
Service: U.S. Army
Birthday: 1844
Place of Birth: St. Louis, St. Louis County, Missouri
Date of Death: 14 April 1875
Cemetery: San Francisco National Cemetery (WS-1090)—San Francisco, California
Entered Service at: Washington, D.C.
Unit: Company A, 5th U.S. Cavalry
Battle or Place of Action: Sunset Pass, Arizona Territory
Date of Action: 1 November 1874
Date of Issue: 12 April 1875
Citation: Bravery in rescuing Lt. Charles King, 5th U.S. Cavalry, from Indians.

1903 ◆ TAYLOR, CHARLES
Rank: First Sergeant
Service: U.S. Army
Birthday: 1840
Place of Birth: Baltimore, Baltimore County, Maryland
Date of Death: 3 August 1899
Place of Death: Washington, D.C.
Cemetery: Soldier's Home National Cemetery (K-0851) (MH)—Washington, D.C.
Entered Service at: St. Louis, St. Louis County, Missouri
Unit: Company D, 3d U.S. Cavalry
Battle or Place of Action: Big Dry Wash, Arizona Territory
Date of Action: 17 July 1882
Date of Issue: 16 December 1882
Citation: Gallantry in action.

1904 ◆ TAYLOR, WILBUR NELSON
Rank: Corporal (highest rank: Sergeant)
Service: U.S. Army

Birthday: 2 December 1846
Place of Birth: Hampden, Penobscot County, Maine
Date of Death: 20 November 1903
Place of Death: Minneapolis, Minnesota
Cemetery: Lakewood Cemetery—Minneapolis, Minnesota
Entered Service at: Boston, Suffolk County, Massachusetts
Unit: Company K, 8th U.S. Cavalry
Battle or Place of Action: Arizona Territory
Date of Action: 1868 & 1869
Date of Issue: 6 September 1869
Citation: Bravery in actions with Indians.

1905 ◆ TEA, RICHARD LONGSTREET

Rank: Sergeant
Service: U.S. Army
Birthday: February 1842
Place of Birth: Philadelphia, Philadelphia County, Pennsylvania
Date of Death: 14 September 1911
Place of Death: Fort Whipple, Arizona
Cemetery: Mountain View Cemetery (MH)—Prescott, Arizona
Entered Service at: Philadelphia, Philadelphia County, Pennsylvania
Unit: Company H, 6th U.S. Cavalry
Battle or Place of Action: Sappa Creek, Kansas
Date of Action: 23 April 1875
Date of Issue: 16 November 1876
Citation: With five other men he waded in mud and water up the creek to a position directly behind an entrenched Cheyenne position, who were using natural bank pits to good advantage against the main column. This surprise attack from the enemy rear broke their resistance.

1906 ◆ *THOMAS, CHARLES L.

Rank: Sergeant
Service: U.S. Army
Birthday: 12 February 1843
Place of Birth: Philadelphia, Philadelphia County, Pennsylvania
Date of Death: 24 February 1893
Place of Death: Dwight, Kansas
Cemetery: Dwight-Morris Cemetery (MH)—Dwight, Kansas
Entered Service at: Cincinnati, Hamilton County, Ohio
Unit: Company E, 11th Ohio Cavalry
Battle or Place of Action: Powder River Expedition, Dakota Territory
Date of Action: 17 September 1865
Date of Issue: 24 August 1894
Citation: Carried a message through a country infested with hostile Indians and saved the life of a comrade en route.

1907 ◆ THOMPSON, GEORGE WASHINGTON

Rank: Private
Service: U.S. Army
Birthday: 1847
Place of Birth: Victory, Cayuga County, New York
Entered Service at: Syracuse, Onondaga County, New York
Unit: Company C, 2d U.S. Cavalry
Battle or Place of Action: Little Blue, Nebraska
Date of Action: 15 May 1870
Date of Issue: 22 June 1870
Citation: Gallantry in action.

1908 ◆ THOMPSON, JOHN

Rank: Sergeant
Service: U.S. Army
Birthday: 1842
Place of Birth: Glasgow, Scotland
Entered Service at: Chicago, Cook County, Illinois
Unit: Company G, 1st U.S. Cavalry
Battle or Place of Action: Chiricahua Mountains, Arizona Territory
Date of Action: 20 October 1869
Date of Presentation: 24 February 1870
Place of Presentation: Fort Camp Bowie, Arizona
Citation: Bravery in action with Indians.

1909 ◆ THOMPSON, PETER

Rank: Private
Service: U.S. Army
Birthday: 28 December 1854
Place of Birth: Scotland
Date of Death: 4 December 1928
Place of Death: Hot Springs, South Dakota
Cemetery: West Lead Cemetery (MH)—Hot Springs, South Dakota
Entered Service at: Pittsburgh, Allegheny County, Pennsylvania
Unit: Company C, 7th U.S. Cavalry
Battle or Place of Action: Little Big Horn, Montana
Date of Action: 25 June 1876
Date of Issue: 5 October 1878
Citation: After having voluntarily brought water to the wounded, during which effort he was shot through the head, he made two successful trips for the same purpose, notwithstanding remonstrances of his sergeant.

1910 ◆ TILTON, HENRY REMSEN

Rank: Major and Surgeon (highest rank: Colonel)
Service: U.S. Army
Birthday: 1 February 1836
Place of Birth: Barnegat, Ocean County, New Jersey
Date of Death: 25 June 1906
Cemetery: Arlington National Cemetery (1-392)—Arlington, Virginia
Entered Service at: Jersey City, Hudson County, New Jersey
Unit: U.S. Army
Battle or Place of Action: Bear Paw Mountain, Montana
Date of Action: 30 September 1877

Date of Issue: 22 March 1895
Citation: Fearlessly risked his life and displayed great gallantry in rescuing and protection the wounded men.

1911 ◆ TOLAN, FRANK

Rank: Private
Service: U.S. Army
Birthday: 1854
Place of Birth: Malone, Franklin County, New York
Entered Service at: Boston, Suffolk County, Massachusetts
Unit: Company D, 7th U.S. Cavalry
Battle or Place of Action: Little Big Horn, Montana
Date of Action: 25 June 1876
Date of Issue: 5 October 1878
Citation: Voluntarily brought water to the wounded under fire.

1912 ◆ TOY, FREDERICK ERNEST

Rank: First Sergeant (highest rank: Captain)
Service: U.S. Army
Birthday: 1866
Place of Birth: Buffalo, Erie County, New York
Date of Death: 5 August 1933
Place of Death: Youngstown, New York
Cemetery: Riverdale Cemetery—Lewiston, New York
Entered Service at: Chicago, Cook County, Illinois
Unit: Company G, 7th U.S. Cavalry
Battle or Place of Action: Wounded Knee Creek, South Dakota
Date of Action: 29 December 1890
Date of Issue: 26 May 1891
Citation: Bravery.

1913 ◆ TRACY, JOHN

True Name: Nabers, Henry G.
Rank: Private
Service: U.S. Army
Birthday: 28 December 1848
Place of Birth: Dublin, Ireland
Date of Death: 29 May 1918
Place of Death: St. Louis, Missouri
Cemetery: Calvary Cemetery—St. Louis, Missouri
Entered Service at: Chicago, Cook County, Illinois
Unit: Company G, 8th U.S. Cavalry
Battle or Place of Action: Chiricahua Mountains, Arizona Territory
Date of Action: 20 October 1869
Date of Issue: 14 February 1870
Citation: Bravery in action with Indians.

1914 ◆ TRAUTMAN, JACOB

Rank: First Sergeant
Service: U.S. Army
Birthday: 1840
Place of Birth: Hamburg, Germany
Date of Death: 7 November 1898
Cemetery: Southside Cemetery (MH)—Pittsburgh, Pennsylvania
Entered Service at: Pittsburgh, Allegheny County, Pennsylvania
Unit: Company I, 7th U.S. Cavalry
Battle or Place of Action: Wounded Knee Creek, South Dakota
Date of Action: 29 December 1890
Date of Issue: 27 March 1891
Citation: Killed a hostile Indian at close quarters, and, although entitled to retirement from service, remained to the close of the campaign.

1915 ◆ TURPIN, JAMES H.

Rank: First Sergeant
Service: U.S. Army
Birthday: 1846
Place of Birth: Easton, Bristol County, Massachusetts
Date of Death: 30 May 1893
Place of Death: Denver, Colorado
Cemetery: Fairmount Cemetery (MH)—Denver, Colorado
Entered Service at: Boston, Suffolk County, Massachusetts
Unit: Company L, 5th U.S. Cavalry
Battle or Place of Action: Arizona Territory
Date of Action: 1872-74
Date of Issue: 12 April 1875
Citation: Gallantry in actions with Apaches.

1916 ◆ VARNUM, CHARLES ALBERT

Rank: Captain (highest rank: Colonel)
Service: U.S. Army
Birthday: 21 June 1849
Place of Birth: Troy, Rensselaer County, New York
Date of Death: 26 February 1936
Cemetery: San Francisco National Cemetery (OS-3-3A) (MH)—San Francisco, California
Entered Service at: Pensacola, Escambia County, Florida
Unit: Company B, 7th U.S. Cavalry
Battle or Place of Action: White Clay Creek, South Dakota
Date of Action: 30 December 1890
Date of Issue: 22 September 1897
Citation: While executing an order to withdraw, seeing that a continuance of the movement would expose another troop of his regiment to being cut off and surrounded, he disregarded orders to retire, placed himself in front of his men, led a charge upon the advancing Indians, regained a commanding position that had just been vacated, and thus insured a safe withdrawal of both detachments without further loss.

1917 ◆ VEUVE, ERNEST

Rank: Farrier (highest rank: Sergeant)
Service: U.S. Army
Birthday: 19 March 1843

Place of Birth: New Castle, Switzerland
Date of Death: 17 June 1916
Place of Death: Missoula, Montana
Cemetery: Missoula Cemetery—Missoula, Montana
Entered Service at: Jackson Barracks, Louisanna
Unit: Company A, 4th U.S. Cavalry
Battle or Place of Action: Staked Plains, Texas
Date of Action: 3 November 1874
Date of Issue: 13 October 1875
Citation: Gallant manner in which he faced a desperate Indian.

1918 ◆ VOIT, OTTO EMIL

Rank: Saddler
Service: U.S. Army
Birthday: 5 February 1845
Place of Birth: Baden, Germany
Date of Death: 1 June 1906
Place of Death: Louisville, Kentucky
Cemetery: St. Stephen's Cemetery—Louisville, Kentucky
Entered Service at: Louisville, Jefferson County, Kentucky
Unit: Company H, 7th U.S. Cavalry
Battle or Place of Action: Little Big Horn, Montana
Date of Action: 25 June 1876
Date of Issue: 5 October 1878
Citation: Volunteered with George Geiger, Charles Windolph, and Henry Mechlin to hold an exposed position standing erect on the brow of the hill facing the Little Big Horn River. They fired constantly in this manner for more than 20 minutes diverting fire and attention from another group filling canteens of water that were desperately needed.

1919 ◆ VOKES, LEROY H.

Rank: First Sergeant
Service: U.S. Army
Birthday: 12 November 1849
Place of Birth: Lake County, Illinois
Entered Service at: St. Louis, St. Louis County, Missouri
Unit: Company B, 3d U.S. Cavalry
Battle or Place of Action: Loupe Fork of the Platte River, Nebraska
Date of Action: 26 April 1872
Date of Issue: 22 May 1872
Citation: Gallantry in action.

1920 ◆ VON MEDEM, RUDOLPH

Rank: Sergeant
Service: U.S. Army
Birthday: 1846
Place of Birth: Germany (Prussia)
Entered Service at: New York, New York
Unit: Company A, 5th U.S. Cavalry
Battle or Place of Action: Apache campaigns
Date of Action: 1872-73
Date of Issue: 12 April 1875
Citation: Gallantry in actions and campaigns.

1921 ◆ WALKER, ALLEN

Rank: Private (highest rank: Captain)
Service: U.S. Army
Birthday: 19 January 1866
Place of Birth: Patriot, Switzerland County, Indiana
Date of Death: 11 September 1953
Cemetery: Catholic Cemetery (MH)—Laredo, Texas
Entered Service at: Cincinnati, Hamilton County, Ohio
Unit: Company C, 3d U.S. Cavalry
Battle or Place of Action: Texas
Date of Action: 30 December 1891
Date of Issue: 25 April 1892
Citation: While carrying dispatches, he attacked a party of three armed men and secured papers valuable to the United States.

1922 ◆ WALKER, JOHN

Rank: Private
Service: U.S. Army
Birthday: 1845
Place of Birth: Leon, France
Entered Service at: Detroit, Wayne County, Michigan
Unit: Company D, 8th U.S. Cavalry
Battle or Place of Action: Red Creek, Arizona Territory
Date of Action: 23 September 1869
Date of Issue: 23 November 1869
Citation: Gallantry in action with Indians.

1923 ◆ WALLACE, WILLIAM

True Name: Wallace, John A.
Rank: Sergeant
Service: U.S. Army
Birthday: 31 October 1847
Place of Birth: County Donegal, Ireland
Date of Death: 9 January 1928
Place of Death: Walnut, Kansas
Cemetery: Walnut Cemetery—Walnut, Kansas
Entered Service at: New York, New York
Unit: Company C, 5th U.S. Infantry
Battle or Place of Action: Cedar Creek, etc., Montana
Date of Action: 21 October 1876—8 January 1877
Date of Issue: 27 April 1877
Citation: Gallantry in action.

1924 ◆ WALLEY, AUGUSTUS

Rank: Private (highest rank: First Sergeant)
Service: U.S. Army
Birthday: 10 March 1856
Place of Birth: Reistertown, Baltimore County, Maryland
Date of Death: 9 April 1938
Place of Death: Baltimore, Maryland
Cemetery: St. Luke's Cemetery (MH)—Reistertown, Maryland
Entered Service at: Baltimore, Baltimore County, Maryland
Unit: Company I, 9th U.S. Cavalry
Battle or Place of Action: Cuchillo Negro Mountains, New Mexico

Date of Action: 16 August 1881
Date of Issue: 1 October 1890
Citation: Bravery in action with hostile Apaches.

1925 ◆ WARD, CHARLES H.

Rank: Private
Service: U.S. Army
Birthday: 1845
Place of Birth: Bradford, England
Entered Service at: Philadelphia, Philadelphia County, Pennsylvania
Unit: Company G, 1st U.S. Cavalry
Battle or Place of Action: Chiricahua Mountains, Arizona Territory
Date of Action: 20 October 1869
Date of Issue: 14 February 1870
Citation: Gallantry in action with Indians.

1926 ◆ WARD, JAMES

Rank: Sergeant
Service: U.S. Army
Birthday: 6 December 1858
Place of Birth: Quincy, Norfolk County, Massachusetts
Date of Death: 11 March 1901
Place of Death: Boston, Massachusetts
Cemetery: New Calvary Cemetery (MH)—Boston, Massachusetts
Entered Service at: Boston, Suffolk County, Massachusetts
Unit: Company B, 7th U.S. Cavalry
Battle or Place of Action: Wounded Knee Creek, South Dakota
Date of Action: 29 December 1890
Date of Issue: 16 April 1891
Citation: Continued to fight after being severely wounded.

1927 ◆ WARD, JOHN

True Name: Warrior, John
Rank: Sergeant
Service: U.S. Army
Birthday: 1847
Place of Birth: Arkansas
Date of Death: 24 May 1911
Cemetery: Seminole Indian Scout Cemetery (MH)—Brackettville, Texas
Entered Service at: Fort Duncan, Texas
Unit: 24th U.S. Infantry, Indian Scouts
Battle or Place of Action: Pecos River, Texas
Date of Action: 25 April 1875
Date of Issue: 28 May 1875
Citation: With three other men, he participated in a charge against 25 hostiles while on a scouting patrol.

1928 ◆ WARRINGTON, LEWIS

Rank: First Lieutenant
Service: U.S. Army
Place of Birth: Washington, D.C.
Date of Death: 5 January 1879
Place of Death: San Antonio, Texas
Cemetery: San Antonio National Cemetery (A-60) (MH)—San Antonio, Texas
Entered Service at: Washington, D.C.
Unit: 4th U.S. Cavalry
Battle or Place of Action: Muchague Valley, Texas
Date of Action: 8 December 1874
Date of Issue: 12 April 1875
Citation: Gallantry in combat with five Indians.

1929 ◆ WATSON, JAMES C.

Rank: Corporal (highest rank: Sergeant)
Service: U.S. Army
Birthday: 1842
Place of Birth: Cochecton, Sullivan County, New York
Date of Death: 7 January 1890
Place of Death: Chicago, Illinois
Cemetery: Rose Hill Cemetery—Chicago, Illinois
Entered Service at: Philadelphia, Philadelphia County, Pennsylvania
Unit: Company L, 6th U.S. Cavalry
Battle or Place of Action: Wichita River, Texas
Date of Action: 12 July 1870
Date of Issue: 25 August 1870
Citation: Gallantry in action.

1930 ◆ WATSON, JOSEPH

Rank: Private
Service: U.S. Army
Birthday: 1846
Place of Birth: Union City, Branch County, Michigan
Entered Service at: Chicago, Cook County, Illinois
Unit: Company F, 8th U.S. Cavalry
Battle or Place of Action: Picacho Mountain, Arizona Territory
Date of Action: 4 June 1869
Date of Issue: 3 March 1870
Citation: Killed an Indian warrior and captured his arms.

1931 ◆ WEAHER, ANDREW J.

True Name: Weaber, Andrew J.
Rank: Private
Service: U.S. Army
Birthday: 22 May 1842
Place of Birth: Philadelphia, Philadelphia County, Pennsylvania
Date of Death: 27 August 1920
Place of Death: Phoenix, Arizona
Cemetery: Greenwood Memorial Park—Phoenix, Arizona
Entered Service at: Philadelphia, Philadelphia County, Pennsylvania
Unit: Company B, 8th U.S. Cavalry
Battle or Place of Action: Arizona Territory
Date of Action: August-October 1868

Date of Issue: 24 July 1869
Citation: Bravery in scouts and against Indians.

1932 ◆ WEINERT, PAUL H.
Rank: Corporal (highest rank: Sergeant)
Service: U.S. Army
Birthday: 15 July 1869
Place of Birth: Frankfort, Germany
Date of Death: 19 January 1919
Place of Death: Mattapan, Massachusetts
Cemetery: Milton Cemetery (MH)—Milton, Massachusetts
Entered Service at: Baltimore, Baltimore County, Maryland
Unit: Battery E, 1st U.S. Artillery
Battle or Place of Action: Wounded Knee Creek, South Dakota
Date of Action: 29 December 1890
Date of Issue: 24 March 1891
Citation: Taking the place of his commanding officer, who had fallen severely wounded, he gallantly served his piece, after each fire advancing it to a better position.

1933 ◆ WEISS, ENOCH R.
Rank: Private
Service: U.S. Army
Birthday: 13 February 1848
Place of Birth: Kosciusko County, Indiana
Date of Death: 29 December 1917
Cemetery: South Bend Cemetery—South Bend, Indiana
Entered Service at: St. Louis, St. Louis County, Missouri
Unit: Company G, 1st U.S. Cavalry
Battle or Place of Action: Chiricahua Mountains, Arizona Territory
Date of Action: 20 October 1869
Date of Issue: 14 February 1870
Citation: Gallantry in action with Indians.

1934 ◆ WELCH, CHARLES H.
Rank: Sergeant
Service: U.S. Army
Birthday: 16 March 1845
Place of Birth: New York, New York
Date of Death: 22 June 1915
Place of Death: LaSalle, Colorado
Cemetery: Evans Cemetery (MH)—Evans, Colorado
Entered Service at: Fort Snelling, St. Paul County, Minnesota
Unit: Company D, 7th U.S. Cavalry
Battle or Place of Action: Little Big Horn, Montana
Date of Action: 25-26 June 1876
Date of Issue: 5 October 1878
Citation: Voluntarily brought water to the wounded, under fire.

1935 ◆ WELCH, MICHAEL
Rank: Sergeant
Service: U.S. Army
Birthday: 1843
Place of Birth: Poughkeepsie, Dutchess County, New York
Entered Service at: New York, New York
Unit: Company M, 6th U.S. Cavalry
Battle or Place of Action: Wichita River, Texas
Date of Action: 5 October 1870
Date of Issue: 19 November 1870
Citation: Gallantry in action.

1936 ◆ WEST, FRANK
Rank: First Lieutenant (highest rank: Colonel)
Service: U.S. Army
Birthday: 26 September 1850
Place of Birth: Mohawk, Herkimer County, New York
Date of Death: 26 August 1923
Place of Death: Mohawk, New York
Cemetery: Arlington National Cemetery (1-549)—Arlington, Virginia
Entered Service at: Mohawk, Herkimer County, New York
Unit: 6th U.S. Cavalry
Battle or Place of Action: Big Dry Wash, Arizona
Date of Action: 17 July 1882
Date of Issue: 12 July 1892
Citation: Rallied his command and led it in the advance against the enemy's fortified position.

1937 ◆ WHITEHEAD, PATTON G.
True Name: Whited, Patton G.
Rank: Private (highest rank: Corporal)
Service: U.S. Army
Birthday: 25 September 1840
Place of Birth: Russell County, Virginia
Date of Death: 8 December 1900
Place of Death: Los Angeles, California
Cemetery: New Calvary Cemetery—Los Angeles, California
Entered Service at: Louisville, Jefferson County, Kentucky
Unit: Company C, 5th U.S. Infantry
Battle or Place of Action: Cedar Creek, etc., Montana
Date of Action: 21 October 1876—8 January 1877
Date of Issue: 27 April 1877
Citation: Gallantry in action.

1938 ◆ WIDMER, JACOB
Rank: First Sergeant
Service: U.S. Army
Birthday: 1845
Place of Birth: Wurttemberg, Germany
Date of Death: 5 July 1880
Place of Death: Fort Niobrara, Nebraska
Cemetery: Fort Leavenworth National Cemetery (G-3529) (MH)—Fort Leavenworth, Kansas
Entered Service at: Philadelphia, Philadelphia County, Pennsylvania
Unit: Company D, 5th U.S. Cavalry
Battle or Place of Action: Milk River, Colorado
Date of Action: 29 September 1879
Date of Issue: 4 May 1880

Citation: Volunteered to accompany a small detachment on a very dangerous mission.

1939 ◆ WILDER, WILBER ELLIOTT

Rank: First Lieutenant (highest rank: Brigadier General)
Service: U.S. Army
Birthday: 16 August 1857
Place of Birth: Atlas, Genesee County, Michigan
Date of Death: 30 January 1952
Place of Death: Governors Island, New York
Cemetery: Fairlawn Cemetery—Ridgefield, Connecticut
Entered Service at: Detroit, Wayne County, Michigan
Unit: 4th U.S. Cavalry
Battle or Place of Action: Horseshoe Canyon, New Mexico
Date of Action: 23 April 1882
Date of Issue: 17 August 1896
Citation: Assisted, under a heavy fire, in rescuing a wounded comrade.

1940 ◆ WILKENS, HENRY

Rank: First Sergeant (highest rank: Ordnance Sergeant)
Service: U.S. Army
Birthday: 1855
Place of Birth: Germany
Date of Death: 2 August 1895
Cemetery: Cypress Hills National Cemetery (2-5325)—Brooklyn, New York
Entered Service at: Pittsburgh, Allegheny County, Pennsylvania
Unit: Company L, 2d U.S. Cavalry
Battle or Place of Action: Little Muddy Creek, Montana; Camas Meadows, Idaho
Date of Action: 7 May & 20 August 1877
Date of Issue: 28 February 1878
Citation: Bravery in actions with Indians.

1941 ◆ WILLIAMS, MOSES

Rank: First Sergeant (highest rank: Ordnance Sergeant)
Service: U.S. Army
Birthday: 1845
Place of Birth: Carrollton, Orleans Parish, Louisiana
Date of Death: 23 August 1899
Cemetery: Vancouver Barracks National Cemetery (8-W-393) (MH)—Vancouver, Washington
Entered Service at: East Carroll Parish, Louisiana
Unit: Company I, 9th U.S. Cavalry
Battle or Place of Action: foothills of the Cuchillo Negro Mountains, New Mexico
Date of Action: 16 August 1881
Date of Issue: 12 November 1896
Citation: Rallied a detachment, skillfully conducted a running fight of three or four hours, and by his coolness, bravery, and unflinching devotion to duty in standing by his commanding officer in an exposed position under a heavy fire from a large party of Indians saved the lives of at least three of his comrades.

1942 ◆ WILLS, HENRY

Rank: Private (highest rank: Sergeant)
Service: U.S. Army
Birthday: 1842
Place of Birth: Gracon, Virginia
Entered Service at: St. Louis, St. Louis County, Missouri
Unit: Company C, 8th U.S. Cavalry
Battle or Place of Action: Fort Selden, New Mexico
Date of Action: 8-11 July 1873
Date of Issue: 12 August 1875
Citation: Services against hostile Indians.

1943 ◆ WILSON, BENJAMIN

Rank: Private
Service: U.S. Army
Birthday: 1843
Place of Birth: Pittsburgh, Allegheny County, Pennsylvania
Entered Service at: Cincinnati, Hamilton County, Ohio
Unit: Company M, 6th U.S. Cavalry
Battle or Place of Action: Wichita River, Texas
Date of Action: 5 October 1870
Date of Issue: 19 November 1870
Citation: Gallantry in action.

1944 ◆ WILSON, CHARLES

Rank: Corporal (highest rank: Sergeant)
Service: U.S. Army
Birthday: 1852
Place of Birth: Petersburg, Menard County, Illinois
Date of Death: 16 February 1943
Place of Death: Los Angeles, California
Cemetery: Inglewood Park Cemetery—Inglewood, California
Entered Service at: Springfield, Sangamon County, Illinois
Unit: Company H, 5th U.S. Infantry
Battle or Place of Action: Cedar Creek, etc., Montana
Date of Action: 21 October 1876—8 January 1877
Date of Issue: 27 April 1877
Citation: Gallantry in action.

1945 ◆ WILSON, MILDEN H.

Rank: Sergeant (highest rank: Ordnance Sergeant)
Service: U.S. Army
Birthday: 25 July 1847
Place of Birth: Huron County, Ohio
Date of Death: 6 February 1924
Entered Service at: Newark, Licking County, Ohio
Unit: Company I, 7th U.S. Infantry
Battle or Place of Action: Big Hole, Montana
Date of Action: 9 August 1877

Date of Issue: 2 December 1878
Citation: Gallantry in forming company from line of skirmishers and deploying again under a galling fire, and in carrying dispatches at the imminent risk of his life.

1946 ◆ WILSON, WILLIAM✢

Rank: Sergeant
Service: U.S. Army
Birthday: 1847
Place of Birth: Philadelphia, Philadelphia County, Pennsylvania
Date of Death: 22 December 1895
Cemetery: San Francisco National Cemetery (WS-527-Row 28) (MH)—San Francisco, California
Entered Service at: Philadelphia, Philadelphia County, Pennsylvania
Unit: Company I, 4th U.S. Cavalry
Battle or Place of Action: Colorado Valley and Red River, Texas
Date of Action: 28 March 1872; 29 September 1872
Date of Issue: 27 April 1872
Citation: **First Award** In pursuit of a band of cattle thieves from New Mexico. **Second Award** Distinguished conduct in action with Indians.
Notes: ✢Double Awardee

1947 ◆ WILSON, WILLIAM O.

Rank: Corporal
Service: U.S. Army
Birthday: 1867
Place of Birth: Hagerstown, Washington County, Maryland
Date of Death: 18 January 1928
Place of Death: Washington County, Maryland
Cemetery: Jewish Cemetery—Halfway, Maryland
Entered Service at: St. Paul, Ramsey County, Minnesota
Unit: Company I, 9th U.S. Cavalry
Battle or Place of Action: Sioux Campaign
Date of Action: 1890
Date of Issue: 17 September 1891
Citation: Bravery.

1948 ◆ WINDOLPH, CHARLES

Rank: Private (highest rank: First Sergeant)
Service: U.S. Army
Birthday: 9 December 1851
Place of Birth: Bergen, Germany
Date of Death: 11 March 1950
Place of Death: Lead, South Dakota
Cemetery: Black Hills National Cemetery (A-239) (MH)—Sturgis, South Dakota
Entered Service at: Brooklyn, Kings County, New York
Unit: Company H, 7th U.S. Cavalry
Battle or Place of Action: Little Big Horn, Montana
Date of Action: 25-26 June 1876
Date of Issue: 5 October 1878

Citation: With three comrades, during the entire engagement, courageously held a position that secured water for the command.

1949 ◆ WINDUS, CLARON

Rank: Bugler (highest rank: Captain)
Service: U.S. Army
Birthday: 10 January 1850
Place of Birth: Janesville, Rock County, Wisconsin
Date of Death: 18 October 1927
Place of Death: Fort Sam Houston, Texas
Cemetery: Masonic Cemetery (MH)—Brackettville, Texas
Entered Service at: Indianapolis, Marion County, Indiana
Unit: Company L, 6th U.S. Cavalry
Battle or Place of Action: Wichita River, Texas
Date of Action: 12 July 1870
Date of Issue: 25 August 1870
Citation: Gallantry in action.

1950 ◆ WINTERBOTTOM, WILLIAM

Rank: Sergeant
Service: U.S. Army
Birthday: 1847
Place of Birth: Manchester, Greater Manchester County, England
Date of Death: 4 April 1932
Cemetery: Bayview Cemetery (MH)—Jersey City, New Jersey
Entered Service at: Boston, Suffolk County, Massachusetts
Unit: Company A, 6th U.S. Cavalry
Battle or Place of Action: Wichita River, Texas
Date of Action: 12 July 1870
Date of Issue: 25 August 1870
Citation: Gallantry in action.

1951 ◆ WITCOME, JOSEPH

Rank: Private
Service: U.S. Army
Birthday: 1846
Place of Birth: Mechanicsburg, Cumberland County, Pennsylvania
Date of Death: 7 October 1869
Place of Death: Ash Creek, Arizona
Entered Service at: Carlisle, Cumberland County, Pennsylvania
Unit: Company B, 8th U.S. Cavalry
Battle or Place of Action: Arizona Territory
Date of Action: August-October 1868
Date of Issue: 24 July 1869
Citation: Bravery in scouts and actions against Indians.

1952 ◆ WOOD, LEONARD

Rank: Assistant Surgeon (highest rank: Major General)
Service: U.S. Army

Birthday: 9 October 1860
Place of Birth: Winchester, Cheshire County, New Hampshire
Date of Death: 7 August 1927
Place of Death: Boston, Massachusetts
Cemetery: Arlington National Cemetery (21-S-10)—Arlington, Virginia
Entered Service at: Boston, Suffolk County, Massachusetts
Unit: U.S. Army
Served as: Assistant Surgeon
Battle or Place of Action: Apache Campaign, Arizona Territory
Date of Action: summer 1886
Date of Issue: 8 April 1898
Citation: Voluntarily carried dispatches through a region infested with hostile Indians, making a journey of 70 miles in one night and walking 30 miles the next day. Also for several weeks, while in close pursuit of Geronimo's band and constantly expecting an encounter, commanded a detachment of infantry, which was then without an officer and to the command of which he was assigned upon his own request.

1953 ◆ WOODALL, ZACHARIAH

True Name: Woodall, Zachery T.
Rank: Sergeant (highest rank: Ordnance Sergeant)
Service: U.S. Army
Birthday: 1850
Place of Birth: Alexandria, Alexandria County, Virginia
Date of Death: 12 September 1899
Place of Death: Havana, Cuba
Cemetery: Arlington National Cemetery (22-15788) (MH)—Arlington, Virginia
Entered Service at: Carlisle, Cumberland County, Pennsylvania
Unit: Company I, 6th U.S. Cavalry
Battle or Place of Action: Washita River, Texas
Date of Action: 12 September 1874
Date of Issue: 7 November 1874
Citation: While in command of five men and carrying dispatches, was attacked by 125 Indians, whom he with his command fought throughout the day, he being severely wounded.

1954 ◆ WOODS, BRENT

Rank: Sergeant
Service: U.S. Army
Birthday: 1850
Place of Birth: Pulaski County, Kentucky
Date of Death: 31 March 1906
Cemetery: Mill Springs National Cemetery (A-930) (MH)—Nancy, Kentucky
Entered Service at: Louisville, Jefferson County, Kentucky
Unit: Company B, 9th U.S. Cavalry
Battle or Place of Action: New Mexico
Date of Action: 19 August 1881
Date of Issue: 12 July 1894
Citation: Saved the lives of his comrades and citizens of the detachment.

1955 ◆ WORTMAN, GEORGE G.

Rank: Sergeant (highest rank: Quartermaster Sergeant)
Service: U.S. Army
Birthday: 15 August 1841
Place of Birth: Monckton, New Brunswick, Canada
Date of Death: 19 May 1913
Cemetery: Crown Hill Cemetery (MH)—Denver, Colorado
Entered Service at: Boston, Suffolk County, Massachusetts
Unit: Company B, 8th U.S. Cavalry
Battle or Place of Action: Arizona Territory
Date of Action: August-October 1868
Date of Issue: 24 July 1869
Citation: Bravery in scouts and actions against Indians.

1956 ◆ YOUNT, JOHN P.

Rank: Private
Service: U.S. Army
Birthday: 1849
Place of Birth: Putnam County, Indiana
Date of Death: 11 December 1872
Place of Death: Fort McPherson, Nebraska
Entered Service at: Sacramento, Sacramento County, California
Unit: Company F, 3d U.S. Cavalry
Battle or Place of Action: Whetstone Mountains, Arizona Territory
Date of Action: 5 May 1871
Date of Issue: 13 November 1871
Citation: Gallantry in action with Indians.

1957 ◆ ZIEGNER, HERMAN

Rank: Private
Service: U.S. Army
Birthday: 1864
Place of Birth: Aploda, Germany
Date of Death: 9 September 1898
Cemetery: Calvary Cemetery—Woodside, New York
Entered Service at: Baltimore, Baltimore County, Maryland
Unit: Company E, 7th U.S. Cavalry
Battle or Place of Action: South Dakota Wounded Knee Creek and White Clay Creek
Date of Action: 29-30 December 1890
Date of Issue: 23 June 1891
Citation: Conspicuous bravery.

KOREAN CAMPAIGN 1871

1958 ◆ ANDREWS, JOHN
Rank: Ordinary Seaman
Service: U.S. Navy
Birthday: 1821
Place of Birth: York County, Pennsylvania
Entered Service at: Maryland
Unit: U.S.S. *Benicia*
Battle or Place of Action: Korean Forts
Date of Action: 9-10 June 1871
G.O. Number, Date: 176, 9 July 1872
Citation: On board the U.S.S. *Benicia* in action against Korean forts on 9 and 10 June 1871. Stationed at the lead in passing the forts, Andrews stood on the gunwale on the *Benicia*'s launch, lashed to the ridgerope. He remained unflinchingly in this dangerous position and gave his soundings with coolness and accuracy under a heavy fire.

1959 ◆ BROWN, CHARLES
Rank: Corporal
Service: U.S. Marine Corps
Place of Birth: New York, New York
Enlisted at: Hong Kong
Unit: U.S.S. *Colorado*
Battle or Place of Action: Korean Forts
Date of Action: 11 June 1871
G.O. Number, Date: 169, 8 February 1872
Citation: On board the U.S.S. *Colorado* in action against a Korean fort, 11 June 1871. Assisted in capturing the Korean standard in the center of the citadel of the fort.

1960 ◆ COLEMAN, JOHN
Rank: Private
Service: U.S. Marine Corps
Birthday: 9 October 1847
Place of Birth: County Cork, Ireland
Entered Service at: California
Unit: U.S.S. *Colorado*
Battle or Place of Action: Korean Forts
Date of Action: 11 June 1871
G.O. Number, Date: 169, 8 February 1872
Citation: On board the U.S.S. *Colorado* in action at Korea, 11 June 1871. Fighting hand-to-hand with the enemy, Coleman succeeded in saving the life of Alexander McKenzie.

1961 ◆ DOUGHERTY, JAMES
Rank: Private
Service: U.S. Marine Corps
Birthday: 16 November 1839
Place of Birth: Langhash, Ireland
Date of Death: 25 November 1897
Cemetery: Cypress Hills National Cemetery (6-12374) (MH)—Brooklyn, New York
Entered Service at: Pennsylvania
Unit: U.S.S. *Benicia*
Battle or Place of Action: Korean Forts
Date of Action: 11 June 1871
G.O. Number, Date: 169, 8 February 1872
Citation: On board the U.S.S. *Carondelet* in various actions of that vessel. Wounded several times, Dougherty invariably returned to duty, presenting an example of constancy and devotion to the flag.

1962 ◆ FRANKLIN, FREDERICK H.
Rank: Quartermaster
Service: U.S. Navy
Birthday: 1840
Place of Birth: Portsmouth, Rockingham County, New Hampshire
Date of Death: 10 May 1873
Cemetery: Proprietors Cemetery (MH)—Portsmouth, New Hampshire
Entered Service at: New Hampshire
Unit: Ship's Company D, U.S.S. *Colorado*
Battle or Place of Action: Korean Forts
Date of Action: 11 June 1871
G.O. Number, Date: 169, 8 February 1872
Citation: On board the U.S.S. *Colorado* during the attack and capture of the Korean forts, 11 June 1871. Assuming command of Company D, after Lt. McKee was wounded, Franklin handled the company with great credit until relieved.

1963 ◆ GRACE, PATRICK HENRY
True Name: Grace, Henry Patrick
Rank: Chief Quartermaster
Service: U.S. Navy
Birthday: 1832
Place of Birth: Ireland
Date of Death: 24 February 1896
Place of Death: Dorchester, Massachusetts

Entered Service at: Pennsylvania
Unit: U.S.S. *Benicia*
Battle or Place of Action: Korean Forts
Date of Action: 10-11 June 1871
G.O. Number, Date: 177, 4 December 1915
Citation: On board the U.S.S. *Benicia* during the attack on Korean forts, 10 and 11 June 1871. Carrying out his duties with coolness, Grace set forth gallant and meritorious conduct throughout this action.

1964 ◆ HAYDEN, CYRUS

Rank: Carpenter
Service: U.S. Navy
Birthday: 1843
Place of Birth: York, York County, Maine
Entered Service at: Maine
Unit: U.S.S. *Colorado*
Served as: Color Bearer
Battle or Place of Action: Korean Forts
Date of Action: 11 June 1871
G.O. Number, Date: 169, 8 February 1872
Citation: On board the U.S.S. *Colorado* during the attack and capture of the Korean forts, 11 June 1871. Serving as color bearer of the battalion, Hayden planted his flag on the ramparts of the citadel and protected it under a heavy fire from the enemy.

1965 ◆ LUKES, WILLIAM F.

Rank: Landsman (highest rank: Seaman)
Service: U.S. Navy
Birthday: 19 February 1847
Place of Birth: Niderbergdorf, Bohemia
Date of Death: 17 December 1923
Place of Death: Los Angeles, California
Cemetery: Los Angeles National Cemetery (7-F-19) (MH)—Los Angeles, California
Entered Service at: Enlisted in Tientsin, China
Unit: Company D, U.S.S. *Colorado*
Battle or Place of Action: Korean Forts
Date of Action: 9-10 June 1871
G.O. Number, Date: 180, 10 October 1872
Citation: Served with Company D during the capture of the Korean forts, 9 and 10 June 1871. Fighting the enemy inside the fort, Lukes received a severe cut over the head.

1966 ◆ McKENZIE, ALEXANDER

Rank: Boatswain's Mate
Service: U.S. Navy
Birthday: 1837
Place of Birth: Glasgow, Scotland
Entered Service at: New York
Unit: U.S.S. *Colorado*
Battle or Place of Action: Korean Forts
Date of Action: 11 June 1871
G.O. Number, Date: 169, 8 February 1872
Citation: On board the U.S.S. *Colorado* during the capture of the Korean forts, 11 June 1871. Fighting at the side of Lt. McKee during this action, McKenzie was struck by a sword and received a severe cut in the head from the blow.

1967 ◆ McNAMARA, MICHAEL

Rank: Private
Service: U.S. Marine Corps
Birthday: 1841
Place of Birth: Clure, Ireland
Entered Service at: New York
Unit: U.S.S. *Benicia*
Battle or Place of Action: Korean Forts
Date of Action: 11 June 1871
G.O. Number, Date: 169, 8 February 1872
Citation: On board the U.S.S. *Benicia* during the capture of the Korean forts, 11 June 1871. Advancing to the parapet, McNamara wrenched the matchlock from the hands of an enemy and killed him.

1968 ◆ MERTON, JAMES F.

Rank: Landsman (highest rank: Carpenter)
Service: U.S. Navy
Birthday: 1845
Place of Birth: Cheshire, England
Entered Service at: Portsmouth, Rockingham County, New Hampshire
Unit: Ship's Company D, U.S.S. *Colorado*
Battle or Place of Action: Korean Forts
Date of Action: 9-10 June 1871
G.O. Number, Date: 180, 10 October 1872
Citation: Landsman and member of Company D during the capture of the Korean forts, 9 and 10 June 1871. Merton was severely wounded in the arm while trying to force his way into the fort.

1969 ◆ OWENS, MICHAEL

Rank: Private
Service: U.S. Marine Corps
Birthday: 6 February 1837
Place of Birth: New York, New York
Date of Death: 8 December 1890
Entered Service at: New York
Unit: U.S.S. *Colorado*
Battle or Place of Action: Korean Forts
Date of Action: 11 June 1871
G.O. Number, Date: 169, 8 February 1872
Citation: On board the U.S.S. *Colorado* during the capture of the Korean forts, 11 June 1871. Fighting courageously in hand-to-hand combat, Owens was badly wounded by the enemy during this action.

1970 ◆ PURVIS, HUGH

Rank: Private
Service: U.S. Marine Corps
Birthday: 5 March 1846

Place of Birth: Philadelphia, Philadelphia County, Pennsylvania
Date of Death: 12 February 1922
Place of Death: Annapolis, Maryland
Cemetery: Cedar Bluff Cemetery (MH)—Annapolis, Maryland
Entered Service at: Pennsylvania
Unit: U.S.S. *Alaska*
Battle or Place of Action: Korean Forts
Date of Action: 11 June 1871
G.O. Number, Date: 169, 8 February 1872
Citation: On board the U.S.S. *Alaska* during the attack on and capture of the Korean forts, 11 June 1871. Braving the enemy fire, Purvis was the first to scale the walls of the fort and capture the flag of the Korean forces.

1971 ◆ ROGERS, SAMUEL F.

Rank: Quartermaster
Service: U.S. Navy
Birthday: 1845
Place of Birth: Buffalo, Erie County, New York
Date of Death: 1 November 1905
Cemetery: Forest Homes Cemetery—Forest Park, Illinois
Entered Service at: New York
Unit: U.S.S. *Colorado*
Battle or Place of Action: Korean Forts
Date of Action: 11 June 1871
G.O. Number, Date: 169, 8 February 1872
Citation: On board the U.S.S. *Colorado* during the attack and capture of the Korean forts, 11 June 1871. Fighting courageously at the side of Lt. McKee during this action, Rogers was wounded by the enemy.

1972 ◆ TROY, WILLIAM

Rank: Ordinary Seaman
Service: U.S. Navy
Birthday: 1848
Place of Birth: Boston, Suffolk County, Massachusetts
Date of Death: 8 March 1907
Cemetery: Stockton State Hospital Cemetery—Stockton, California
Entered Service at: Massachusetts
Unit: U.S.S. *Colorado*
Battle or Place of Action: Korean Forts
Date of Action: 11 June 1871
G.O. Number, Date: 169, 8 February 1872
Citation: On board the U.S.S. *Colorado* during the capture of the Korean forts, 11 June 1871. Fighting at the side of Lt. McKee, by whom he was especially commended, Troy was badly wounded by the enemy.

INTERIM 1871–1898

1973 ◆ AHERN, WILLIAM
Rank: Watertender
Service: U.S. Navy
Birthday: 1861
Place of Birth: Ireland
Entered Service at: New York
Unit: U.S.S. *Puritan*
Battle or Place of Action: U.S.S. *Puritan*
Date of Action: 1 July 1897
G.O. Number, Date: 482, 1 November 1897
Citation: On board the U.S.S. *Puritan* at the time of the collapse of one of the crown sheets of boiler E of that vessel, 1 July 1897. Wrapped in wet cloths to protect his face and arms, Ahern entered the fireroom, crawled over the tops of the boilers and closed the auxiliary stop valve, disconnecting boiler E and removing the danger of disabling the other boilers.

1974 ◆ ANDERSON, WILLIAM
Rank: Coxswain
Service: U.S. Navy
Birthday: 1852
Place of Birth: Sweden
Entered Service at: New York
Unit: U.S.S. *Powhatan*
Battle or Place of Action: U.S.S. *Powhatan*
Date of Action: 28 June 1878
Citation: On board the U.S.S. *Powhatan*, 28 June 1878. Acting courageously, Anderson rescued from drowning W.H. Moffatt, first class boy.

1975 ◆ ATKINS, DANIEL
Rank: Ship's Cook First Class (highest rank: Chief Commissary Steward)
Service: U.S. Navy
Birthday: 18 November 1866
Place of Birth: Brunswick, Virginia
Date of Death: 11 May 1923
Place of Death: Portsmouth, Virginia
Cemetery: U.S. Navy Hospital Cemetery (MH)—Portsmouth, Virginia
Entered Service at: Virginia
Unit: U.S.S. *Cushing*
Battle or Place of Action: U.S.S. *Cushing*
Date of Action: 11 February 1898
G.O. Number, Date: 489, 20 May 1898
Citation: On board the U.S.S. *Cushing*, 11 February 1898. Showing gallant conduct, Atkins attempted to save the life of the late Ens. Joseph C. Breckenridge, U.S. Navy, who fell overboard at sea from that vessel on this date.

1976 ◆ AUER, JOHN F.
Rank: Ordinary Seaman Apprentice
Service: U.S. Navy
Birthday: 1866
Place of Birth: New York
Entered Service at: New York
Unit: U.S.S. *Lancaster*
Battle or Place of Action: Marseille, France
Date of Action: 20 November 1883
Citation: On board the U.S.S. *Lancaster*, Marseille, France, 20 November 1883. Jumping overboard, Auer rescued from drowning a French lad who had fallen into the sea from a stone pier astern of the ship.

1977 ◆ BARRETT, EDWARD
Rank: Second Class Fireman
Service: U.S. Navy
Birthday: 1855
Place of Birth: Philadelphia, Philadelphia County, Pennsylvania
Entered Service at: Pennsylvania
Unit: U.S.S. *Alaska*
Battle or Place of Action: Callao Bay, Peru
Date of Action: 14 September 1881
G.O. Number, Date: 326, 18 October 1884
Citation: On board the U.S.S. *Alaska* at Callao Bay, Peru, 14 September 1881. Following the rupture of the stop-valve chamber, Barrett courageously hauled the fires from under the boiler of that vessel.

1978 ◆ BELPITT, WILLIAM HENRY
Rank: Captain of the Afterguard
Service: U.S. Navy
Birthday: 3 May 1860
Place of Birth: Ryde, Australia
Unit: U.S.S. *Monocacy*
Battle or Place of Action: Foochow, China
Date of Action: 7 October 1884
G.O. Number, Date: Letter No. 126 LCDR Iverson, U.S. Navy; 27 October 1884
Citation: On board the U.S.S. *Monocacy*, Foochow, China, 7 October 1884. Jumping overboard from that vessel on the morning of this date, Belpitt sustained, until picked up, a

Chinaman who had been thrown into the water by the capsizing of a canoe.

1979 ◆ BENSON, JAMES

Rank: Seaman
Service: U.S. Navy
Birthday: 1842
Place of Birth: Denmark
Date of Death: 4 August 1890
Place of Death: Boston Harbor, Massachusetts
Enlisted at: Yokohama, Japan
Unit: U.S.S. *Ossipee*
Battle or Place of Action: at sea
Date of Action: 20 June 1872
G.O. Number, Date: 180, 10 October 1872
Date of Issue: 1872
Citation: On board the U.S.S. *Ossipee*, 20 June 1872. Risking his life, Benson leaped into the sea while the ship was going at a speed of four knots and endeavored to save John K. Smith, landsman, of the same vessel, from drowning.

1980 ◆ BRADLEY, ALEXANDER

Rank: Landsman
Service: U.S. Navy
Birthday: 19 September 1851
Place of Birth: Boston, Suffolk County, Massachusetts
Date of Death: 6 March 1925
Place of Death: Akron, Ohio
Cemetery: Holy Cross Cemetery—Akron, Ohio
Entered Service at: Massachusetts
Unit: U.S.S. *Wachusett*
Battle or Place of Action: off Cowes, Isle of Wight, England
Date of Action: 7 August 1872
G.O. Number, Date: 180, 10 October 1872
Citation: On board the U.S.S. *Wachusett* off Cowes, 7 August 1872. Jumping overboard into a strong tideway, Bradley attempted to save Philip Cassidy, landsman, of the U.S.S. *Wabash*, from drowning.

1981 ◆ BUCHANAN, DAVID M.

Rank: Apprentice
Service: U.S. Navy
Birthday: 1862
Place of Birth: Philadelphia, Philadelphia County, Pennsylvania
Entered Service at: Pennsylvania
Unit: U.S.S. *Saratoga*
Battle or Place of Action: off The Battery, New York Harbor, New York
Date of Action: 15 July 1879
G.O. Number, Date: 246, 22 July 1879
Citation: On board the U.S.S. *Saratoga* off Battery, New York Harbor, 15 July 1879. On the morning of this date, Robert Lee Robey, apprentice, fell overboard from the after part of the ship into the tide which was running strong ebb at the time and, not being an expert swimmer, was in danger of drowning. Instantly springing over the rail after him, Buchanan never hesitated for an instant to remove even a portion of his clothing. Both men were picked up by the ship's boat following this act of heroism.

1982 ◆ CAVANAUGH, THOMAS

Rank: Fireman First Class
Service: U.S. Navy
Birthday: 10 May 1869
Place of Birth: Ireland
Entered Service at: New York
Unit: U.S.S. *Potomac*
Served as: Fireman
Battle or Place of Action: at sea between Cat Island and Nassau
Date of Action: 14 November 1898
G.O. Number, Date: 503, 12 December 1898
Citation: On board the U.S.S. *Potomac* during the passage of that vessel from Cat Island to Nassau, 14 November 1898. Volunteering to enter the fireroom, which was filled with steam, Cavanaugh, after repeated attempts, succeeded in reaching the auxiliary valve and opening it, thereby relieving the vessel from further danger.

1983 ◆ CHANDRON, AUGUST

Rank: Seaman Apprentice Second Class
Service: U.S. Navy
Birthday: 1866
Place of Birth: France
Entered Service at: New York
Unit: U.S.S. *Quinnebaug*
Battle or Place of Action: Alexandria, Egypt
Date of Action: 21 November 1885
G.O. Number, Date: Letter, Capt. N. Judlow, U.S. Navy, No. 8326B; 21 November 1885
Citation: On board the U.S.S. *Quinnebaug*, Alexandria, Egypt, on the morning of 21 November 1885. Jumping overboard from that vessel, Chandron, with the aid of Hugh Miller, boatswain's mate, rescued William Evans, ordinary seaman, from drowning.

1984 ◆ CONNOLLY, MICHAEL

Rank: Ordinary Seaman
Service: U.S. Navy
Birthday: 1855
Place of Birth: Boston, Suffolk County, Massachusetts
Entered Service at: Massachusetts
Unit: U.S.S. *Plymouth*
Battle or Place of Action: Halifax Harbor, Nova Scotia, Canada
Date of Action: 7 August 1876
G.O. Number, Date: 218, 24 August 1876
Citation: On board the U.S.S. *Plymouth*, Halifax Harbor, Nova Scotia, 7 August 1876. Acting gallantly, Connolly succeeded in rescuing a citizen from drowning on this date.

1985 ◆ COREY, WILLIAM

Rank: Landsman
Service: U.S. Navy
Birthday: 1853
Place of Birth: New York, New York
Entered Service at: New York
Unit: U.S.S. *Plymouth*
Battle or Place of Action: Navy Yard, New York
Date of Action: 26 July 1876
G.O. Number, Date: 215, 9 August 1876
Citation: On board the U.S.S. *Plymouth*, Navy Yard, New York, 26 July 1876. Showing heroic conduct, Corey endeavored to save the life of one of the crew of that ship who had fallen overboard from aloft.

1986 ◆ COSTELLO, JOHN

Rank: Ordinary Seaman
Service: U.S. Navy
Birthday: 1850
Place of Birth: Rouses Point, Clinton County, New York
Entered Service at: New York
Unit: U.S.S. *Hartford*
Battle or Place of Action: Philadelphia, Pennsylvania
Date of Action: 16 July 1876
G.O. Number, Date: 214, 27 July 1876
Citation: On board the U.S.S. *Hartford*, Philadelphia, Pa., 16 July 1876. Showing gallantry, Costello rescued from drowning a landsman of that vessel.

1987 ◆ COURTNEY, HENRY C.

Rank: Seaman
Service: U.S. Navy
Birthday: 1856
Place of Birth: Springfield, Sangamon County, Illinois
Entered Service at: Illinois
Unit: U.S. Training Ship *Portsmouth*
Battle or Place of Action: Navy Yard, Washington, D.C.
Date of Action: 7 February 1882
G.O. Number, Date: 326, 18 October 1884
Citation: On board the U.S. training ship *Portsmouth*, Washington Navy Yard, 7 February 1882. Jumping overboard from that vessel, Courtney assisted in rescuing Charles Taliaferro, jack-of-the-dust, from drowning.

1988 ◆ CRAMEN, THOMAS

Rank: Boatswain's Mate
Service: U.S. Navy
Birthday: 1848
Place of Birth: Ireland
Entered Service at: Massachusetts
Unit: U.S.S. *Portsmouth*
Battle or Place of Action: Navy Yard, Washington, D.C.
Date of Action: 7 February 1882
G.O. Number, Date: 326, 18 October 1884
Citation: On board the U.S.S. *Portsmouth*, Washington Navy Yard, 7 February 1882. Jumping overboard from that vessel, Cramen rescued Charles Taliaferro, jack-of-the-dust, from drowning.

1989 ◆ CREELMAN, WILLIAM JAMES

Rank: Landsman (highest rank: Chief Gunner)
Service: U.S. Navy
Birthday: 3 August 1874
Place of Birth: Brooklyn, Kings County, New York
Date of Death: 24 March 1928
Place of Death: Brooklyn, New York
Cemetery: 1st Calvary Cemetery—Woodside, New York
Entered Service at: New York
Unit: U.S.S. *Maine*
Battle or Place of Action: at Sea
Date of Action: 7 February 1897
Citation: Attached to the U.S.S. *Maine*, 6 February 1897. Distinguishing himself, Creelman showed extraordinary heroism in the line of his profession during an attempt to save life at sea.

1990 ◆ CUTTER, GEORGE W.

Rank: Landsman
Service: U.S. Navy
Birthday: 1849
Place of Birth: Philadelphia, Philadelphia County, Pennsylvania
Entered Service at: Pennsylvania
Unit: U.S.S. *Powhatan*
Battle or Place of Action: Norfolk, Virginia
Date of Action: 27 May 1872
G.O. Number, Date: 176, 9 July 1872
Citation: On board the U.S.S. *Powhatan*, Norfolk, Va., 27 May 1872. Jumping overboard on this date, Cutter aided in saving one of the crew of that vessel from drowning.

1991 ◆ DAVIS, JOHN

Rank: Ordinary Seaman
Service: U.S. Navy
Birthday: 1854
Place of Birth: Kingston, Jamaica
Date of Death: 19 August 1903
Place of Death: Hampton, Virginia
Cemetery: Hampton National Cemetery (C-8534) (MH)—Hampton, Virginia
Unit: U.S.S. *Trenton*
Battle or Place of Action: Toulon, France
Date of Action: February 1881
G.O. Number, Date: 326, 18 October 1884
Citation: On board the U.S.S. *Trenton*, Toulon, France, February 1881. Jumping overboard, Davis rescued Augustus Ohlensen, coxswain, from drowning.

1992 ◆ DAVIS, JOSEPH H.

Rank: Landsman
Service: U.S. Navy

Birthday: 22 July 1860
Place of Birth: Philadelphia, Philadelphia County, Pennsylvania
Entered Service at: Philadelphia, Philadelphia County, Pennsylvania
Unit: U.S. Receiving Ship *Dale*
Battle or Place of Action: off the wharf, Norfolk, Virginia
Date of Action: 22 January 1886
G.O. Number, Date: Letter Mate J.W. Baxter, U.S Navy, No. 8985; 25 January 1886
Citation: On board the U.S. receiving ship *Dale* off the Wharf at Norfolk, Va., 22 January 1886. Jumping overboard from the ferryboat, Davis rescued from drowning John Norman, ordinary seaman.

1993 ◆ DEMPSEY, JOHN

Rank: Seaman
Service: U.S. Navy
Birthday: 1848
Place of Birth: Ireland
Entered Service at: Boston, Suffolk County, Massachusetts
Unit: U.S.S. *Kearsarge*
Battle or Place of Action: Shanghai, China
Date of Action: 23 January 1875
Citation: On board the U.S.S. *Kearsarge* at Shanghai, China, 23 January 1875. Displaying gallant conduct, Dempsey jumped overboard from the *Kearsarge* and rescued from drowning one of the crew of that vessel.

1994 ◆ DENEEF, MICHAEL

Rank: Captain of the Top
Service: U.S. Navy
Birthday: 1851
Place of Birth: Massachusetts
Entered Service at: Massachusetts
Unit: U.S.S. *Swatara*
Battle or Place of Action: Para, Brazil
Date of Action: 1 December 1875
G.O. Number, Date: 201, 18 January 1876
Citation: On board the U.S.S. *Swatara* at Para, Brazil, 1 December 1875. Displaying gallant conduct, Deneef jumped overboard and rescued one of the crew of that vessel from drowning.

1995 ◆ DENHAM, AUSTIN

Rank: Seaman
Service: U.S. Navy
Birthday: 29 September 1850
Place of Birth: England
Date of Death: 2 June 1948
Place of Death: Los Angeles, California
Cemetery: Calvary Cemetery—Los Angeles, California
Entered Service at: New York
Unit: U.S.S. *Kansas*
Battle or Place of Action: near Greytown, Nicaragua
Date of Action: 12 April 1872
G.O. Number, Date: 176, 9 July 1872
Citation: On board the U.S.S. *Kansas* near Greytown, Nicaragua, 12 April 1872. Displaying great coolness and self-possession at the time Comdr. A.F. Crosman and others were drowned, Denham, by heroism and personal exertion, prevented greater loss of life.

1996 ◆ EILERS, HENRY A.

Rank: Gunner's Mate (highest rank: Gunner)
Service: U.S. Navy
Birthday: 11 August 1870
Place of Birth: Newark, Essex County, New Jersey
Date of Death: 30 June 1901
Entered Service at: New Jersey
Unit: U.S.S. *Philadelphia*
Battle or Place of Action: Fort McHenry, Baltimore, Maryland
Date of Action: 17 September 1892
G.O. Number, Date: 404, 22 November 1892
Citation: On board the U.S.S. *Philadelphia* during the sham attack on Fort McHenry, Baltimore, Md., 17 September 1892. Displaying extraordinary heroism in the line of his profession on this occasion, Eilers remained at his post in the magazine and stamped out the burning particles of a prematurely exploded cartridge which had blown down the chute.

1997 ◆ ELMORE, WALTER

Rank: Landsman
Service: U.S. Navy
Birthday: 1857
Place of Birth: England
Entered Service at: Toulon, France
Unit: U.S.S. *Gettysburg*
Battle or Place of Action: Latitude 36 degrees 58 minutes north, longitude 3 degrees 44 minutes east.
Date of Action: 1 October 1878
Citation: On board the U.S.S. *Gettysburg*, for jumping overboard and saving from drowning Wallace Febrey, landsman, while that vessel was under way at sea in latitude 36 degrees 58 minutes north, longitude three degrees 44 minutes east, 1 October 1878.

1998 ◆ ENRIGHT, JOHN

Rank: Landsman
Service: U.S. Navy
Birthday: 2 July 1864
Place of Birth: Lynn, Essex County, Massachusetts
Date of Death: 19 February 1898
Place of Death: at Sea
Cemetery: Buried at sea
Entered Service at: Massachusetts
Unit: U.S.S. *Ranger*
Battle or Place of Action: off Ensenada, Mexico
Date of Action: 18 January 1886
Citation: On board the U.S.S. *Ranger* off Ensenada, Mexico, 18 January 1886. Jumping overboard from that ves-

sel, Enright rescued John Bell, ordinary seaman, and George Svensson, ordinary seaman, from drowning.

1999 ◆ EVERETTS, JOHN

Rank: Gunner's Mate Third Class
Service: U.S. Navy
Birthday: 25 August 1873
Place of Birth: Thorold, Canada
Date of Death: 12 September 1956
Cemetery: Long Island National Cemetery (DSS-36) (MH)—Farmingdale, New York
Entered Service at: New York
Unit: U.S.S. *Cushing*
Battle or Place of Action: at Sea
Date of Action: 11 February 1898
G.O. Number, Date: 489, 20 May 1898
Citation: Serving on board the U.S.S. *Cushing*, 11 February 1898, Everetts displayed gallant conduct in attempting to save the life of the late Ens. Joseph C. Breckenridge, U.S. Navy, who fell overboard at sea from that vessel.

2000 ◆ FASSEUR, ISAAC L.

Rank: Ordinary Seaman
Service: U.S. Navy
Birthday: 1860
Place of Birth: Flushing, Holland
Entered Service at: Valparaiso, Chile
Unit: U.S.S. *Lackawanna*
Battle or Place of Action: Callao, Peru
Date of Action: 13 June 1884
Citation: Serving on board the U.S.S. *Lackawanna*, 13 June 1884, at Callao, Peru, Fasseur rescued William Cruise, who had fallen overboard, from drowning.

2001 ◆ FLANNAGAN, JOHN

Rank: Boatswain's Mate
Service: U.S. Navy
Birthday: 1852
Place of Birth: Ireland
Entered Service at: New York
Unit: U.S.S. *Supply*
Battle or Place of Action: Le Havre, France
Date of Action: 26 October 1878
Citation: Serving on board the U.S.S. *Supply*, Flannagan rescued from drowning David Walsh, seaman, off Le Havre, France, 26 October 1878.

2002 ◆ FOWLER, CHRISTOPHER

Rank: Quartermaster
Service: U.S. Navy
Birthday: 1850
Place of Birth: New York
Entered Service at: New York
Unit: U.S.S. *Fortune*
Battle or Place of Action: off Point Zapotitlan, Mexico
Date of Action: 11 May 1874
Citation: Served on board the U.S.S. *Fortune* off Point Zapotitlan, Mexico, 11 May 1874. On the occasion of the capsizing of one of the boats of the *Fortune* and the drowning of a portion of the boat's crew, Fowler displayed gallant conduct.

2003 ◆ GIDDING, CHARLES

Rank: Seaman
Service: U.S. Navy
Birthday: 1853
Place of Birth: Bangor, Penobscot County, Maine
Entered Service at: Maine
Unit: U.S.S. *Plymouth*
Battle or Place of Action: Navy Yard, New York
Date of Action: 26 July 1876
G.O. Number, Date: 215, 9 August 1876
Citation: Serving on board the U.S.S. *Plymouth*, Gidding showed heroic conduct in trying to save the life of one of the crew of that ship, who had fallen overboard from aloft at the Navy Yard, New York, 26 July 1876.

2004 ◆ GILLICK, MATTHEW

Rank: Boatswain's Mate
Service: U.S. Navy
Birthday: 1852
Place of Birth: Providence, Providence County, Rhode Island
Entered Service at: Rhode Island
Unit: U.S.S. *Lancaster*
Battle or Place of Action: Marseille, France
Date of Action: 20 November 1883
G.O. Number, Date: 326, 18 October 1884
Citation: Serving on board the U.S.S. *Lancaster* at Marseille, France, 20 November 1883. Jumping overboard from the *Lancaster*, Gillick rescued from drowning a French lad who had fallen into the sea from a stone pier astern of the ship.

2005 ◆ HANDRAN, JOHN

Rank: Seaman
Service: U.S. Navy
Birthday: 1852
Place of Birth: Massachusetts
Entered Service at: Massachusetts
Unit: U.S.S. *Franklin*
Battle or Place of Action: Lisbon, Portugal
Date of Action: 9 January 1876
G.O. Number, Date: 206, 15 February 1876
Citation: For gallant conduct while serving on board the U.S.S. *Franklin* at Lisbon, Portugal, 9 January 1876. Jumping overboard, Handran rescued from drowning one of the crew of that vessel.

2006 ◆ HARRINGTON, DAVID

Rank: First Class Fireman
Service: U.S. Navy

Birthday: 4 April 1856
Place of Birth: Washington, D.C.
Date of Death: 20 September 1945
Cemetery: Arlington National Cemetery (17-23162-D) (MH)—Arlington, Virginia
Entered Service at: Washington, D.C.
Unit: U.S.S. *Tallapoosa*
Date of Action: 21 August 1884
G.O. Number, Date: 326, 18 October 1884
Citation: Served on board the U.S.S. *Tallapoosa* at the time of the sinking of that vessel, on the night of 21 August 1884. Remaining at his post of duty in the fireroom until the fires were put out by the rising waters, Harrington opened the safety valves when the water was up to his waist.

2007 ◆ HAYDEN, JOHN

Rank: Apprentice
Service: U.S. Navy
Birthday: 1863
Place of Birth: Washington, D.C.
Entered Service at: Washington, D.C.
Unit: U.S. Training Ship *Saratoga*
Battle or Place of Action: off The Battery, New York Harbor, New York
Date of Action: 15 July 1879
G.O. Number, Date: 246, 22 July 1879
Citation: On board the U.S. training ship *Saratoga*. On the morning of 15 July 1879, while the *Saratoga* was anchored off The Battery, in New York Harbor, R.L. Robey, apprentice, fell overboard. As the tide was running strong ebb, the man, not being an expert swimmer, was in danger of drowning. David M. Buchanan, apprentice, instantly, without removing any of his clothing, jumped after him. Stripping himself, Hayden stood coolly watching the two in the water, and when he thought his services were required, he made a dive from the rail and came up alongside them and rendered assistance until all three were picked up by a boat from the ship.

2008 ◆ HILL, GEORGE

Rank: Chief Quarter Gunner
Service: U.S. Navy
Birthday: 1844
Place of Birth: England
Entered Service at: New York, New York
Unit: U.S.S. *Kansas*
Battle or Place of Action: near Greytown, Nicaragua
Date of Action: 12 April 1872
G.O. Number, Date: 176, 9 July 1872
Citation: Serving on board the U.S.S. *Kansas*, Hill displayed great coolness and self-possession at the time Comdr. A.F. Crosman and others were drowned, near Greytown, Nicaragua, 12 April 1872, and by extraordinary heroism and personal exertion, prevented greater loss of life.

2009 ◆ HILL, WILLIAM LOWELL

Rank: Captain of the Top (highest rank: Chief Boatswain's Mate)

Service: U.S. Navy
Birthday: 12 October 1855
Place of Birth: Brooklyn, Kings County, New York
Date of Death: 2 August 1922
Cemetery: Lindenwood Cemetery (Lot 939 Gr.2) (MH)—Stoneham, Massachusetts
Entered Service at: New York
Unit: U.S. Training Ship *Minnesota*
Battle or Place of Action: Newport, Rhode Island
Date of Action: 22 June 1881
G.O. Number, Date: 326, 18 October 1884
Citation: Serving on board the U.S. training ship *Minnesota* at Newport, R.I., 22 June 1881, Hill jumped overboard and sustained William Mulcahy, third class boy, who had fallen overboard, until picked up by a steam launch.

2010 ◆ HOLT, GEORGE

Rank: Quarter Gunner
Service: U.S. Navy
Birthday: 1840
Place of Birth: Kentucky
Entered Service at: Kentucky
Unit: U.S.S. *Plymouth*
Battle or Place of Action: Hamburg Harbor, Germany
Date of Action: 3 July 1871
G.O. Number, Date: 180, 10 October 1872
Citation: On board the U.S.S. *Plymouth*, Hamburg Harbor, 3 July 1871. Jumping overboard at the imminent risk of his life, Holt, with a comrade, rescued from drowning one of a party who was thrown from a shore boat into a four-knot running tide while the boat was coming alongside the ship.

2011 ◆ HORTON, JAMES

Rank: Captain of the Top
Service: U.S. Navy
Birthday: 1850
Place of Birth: Boston, Suffolk County, Massachusetts
Entered Service at: Massachusetts
Unit: U.S.S. *Constitution*
Battle or Place of Action: at sea, northeast Atlantic, west of the English Channel
Date of Action: 13 February 1879
G.O. Number, Date: 326, 18 October 1884
Date of Presentation: 7 September 1879
Place of Presentation: On board the U.S.S. *Constitution* at the New York Navy Yard, presented by Lt. Commander Theodore F. Jewell, executive officer
Citation: Serving on board the U.S.S. *Constitution*, at sea, 13 February 1879, Horton showed courageous conduct in going over the stern during a heavy gale and cutting the fastenings of the ship's rudder chains.

2012 ◆ JARDINE, ALEXANDER

Rank: Fireman 1st Class
Service: U.S. Navy
Birthday: 19 March 1873
Place of Birth: Inverness, Scotland

Date of Death: 22 February 1949
Cemetery: Arlington National Cemetery (12-4280) (MH)—Arlington, Virginia
Entered Service at: Ohio
Unit: U.S.S. *Potomac*
Battle or Place of Action: at see between Cat Island and Nassau
Date of Action: 14 November 1898
G.O. Number, Date: 503, 13 December 1898
Citation: On board the U.S.S. *Potomac* during the passage of that vessel from Cat Island to Nassau, 14 November 1898. Volunteering to enter the fireroom, which was filled with steam, Jardine, after repeated attempts, succeeded in reaching the auxiliary valve and opening it, thereby relieving the vessel from further danger.

2013 ◆ JOHNSON, JOHN

Rank: Seaman
Service: U.S. Navy
Birthday: 1839
Place of Birth: Philadelphia, Philadelphia County, Pennsylvania
Entered Service at: Pennsylvania
Unit: U.S.S. *Kansas*
Battle or Place of Action: near Greytown, Nicaragua
Date of Action: 12 April 1872
G.O. Number, Date: 176, 9 July 1872
Citation: Serving on board the U.S.S. *Kansas*, near Greytown, Nicaragua, 12 April 1872, Johnson displayed great coolness and self-possession at the time Comdr. A.F. Crosman and others were drowned and, by extraordinary heroism and personal exertion, prevented greater loss of life.

2014 ◆ JOHNSON, WILLIAM

Rank: Cooper
Service: U.S. Navy
Birthday: 1855
Place of Birth: St. Vincent, West Indies
Date of Death: 20 May 1903
Cemetery: Arlington National Cemetery (23-16648-32) (MH)—Arlington, Virginia
Entered Service at: New York
Unit: U.S.S. *Adams*
Battle or Place of Action: Navy Yard, Mare Island, California
Date of Action: 14 November 1879
G.O. Number, Date: 326, 18 October 1884
Citation: Serving on board the U.S.S. *Adams* at the Navy Yard, Mare Island, Cal., 14 November 1879, Johnson rescued Daniel W. Kloppen, a workman, from drowning.

2015 ◆ KERSEY, THOMAS JOSEPH

Rank: Ordinary Seaman
Service: U.S. Navy
Birthday: 1847
Place of Birth: St. Johns, Newfoundland, Canada
Date of Death: 16 April 1888
Place of Death: Chelsea, Massachusetts
Cemetery: Woodlawn Cemetery—Everett, Massachusetts
Entered Service at: Massachusetts
Unit: U.S.S. *Plymouth*
Battle or Place of Action: Navy Yard, New York
Date of Action: 26 July 1876
G.O. Number, Date: 215, 9 August 1876
Citation: Serving on board the U.S.S. *Plymouth* at the Navy Yard, New York, 26 July 1876, Kersey displayed bravery and presence of mind in rescuing from drowning one of the crew of that vessel.

2016 ◆ KING, HUGH

Rank: Ordinary Seaman
Service: U.S. Navy
Birthday: 1845
Place of Birth: Ireland
Entered Service at: New York
Unit: U.S.S. *Iroquois*
Battle or Place of Action: Delaware River
Date of Action: 7 September 1871
G.O. Number, Date: 176, 9 July 1872
Citation: On board the U.S.S. *Iroquois*, Delaware River, 7 September 1871. Jumping overboard at the imminent risk of his life, King rescued one of the crew of that vessel from drowning.

2017 ◆ KYLE, PATRICK J.

Rank: Landsman
Service: U.S. Navy
Birthday: 4 November 1854
ace of Birth: Ireland
Date of Death: 28 October 1929
Place of Death: Charlestown, Massachusetts
Cemetery: Old Calvary Cemetery (MH)—Roslindas (Boston), Massachusetts
Entered Service at: Massachusetts
Unit: U.S.S. *Quinnebaug*
Battle or Place of Action: Port Mahon, Minorca, Spain
Date of Action: 13 March 1879
Citation: For rescuing from drowning a shipmate from the U.S.S. *Quinnebaug*, at Port Mahon, Minorca, 13 March 1879.

2018 ◆ LAKIN, THOMAS

Rank: Seaman
Service: U.S. Navy
Birthday: 1840
Place of Birth: New York
Entered Service at: New York
Unit: U.S.S. *Narragansett*
Battle or Place of Action: Navy Yard, Mare Island, California
Date of Action: November 1874
Citation: Serving on board the U.S.S. *Narragansett* at the Navy Yard, Mare Island, Cal., November 1874. Jumping overboard, Lakin displayed gallant conduct by rescuing two men of that ship from drowning.

2019 ◆ LAVERTY, JOHN✝

Rank: First Class Fireman
Service: U.S. Navy
Birthday: June 1845
Place of Birth: County Tyrone, Ireland
Date of Death: 13 November 1903
Place of Death: Philadelphia, Pennsylvania
Cemetery: Mount Moriah Cemetery (3-3-17 VA Plot)—Philadelphia, Pennsylvania
Entered Service at: California
Unit: U.S.S. *Alaska*
Battle or Place of Action: Callao Bay, Peru
Date of Action: 14 September 1881
G.O. Number, Date: 326, 18 October 1884
Citation: Second Award Serving on board the U.S.S. *Alaska* at Callao Bay, Peru, 14 September 1881. Following the rupture of the stop-valve chamber on that vessel, Laverty hauled the fires from under the boiler.
Notes: ✝Double Awardee: *see also* Civil War in which he served under the name John Lafferty

2020 ◆ LEJEUNE, EMILE

Rank: Seaman
Service: U.S. Navy
Birthday: 1853
Place of Birth: France
Entered Service at: New York
Unit: U.S.S. *Plymouth*
Battle or Place of Action: Port Royal, South Carolina
Date of Action: 6 June 1876
G.O. Number, Date: 212, 9 June 1876
Citation: Serving on board the U.S.S. *Plymouth*, Lejeune displayed gallant conduct in rescuing a citizen from drowning at Port Royal, S.C., 6 June 1876.

2021 ◆ LOW, GEORGE

True Name: Evatt, George L.
Rank: Seaman
Service: U.S. Navy
Birthday: 1847
Place of Birth: Canada
Entered Service at: New York
Unit: U.S.S. *Tennessee*
Battle or Place of Action: New Orleans, Louisiana
Date of Action: 15 February 1881
G.O. Number, Date: 326, 18 October 1884
Citation: For jumping overboard from the U.S.S. *Tennessee* at New Orleans, La., 15 February 1881, and sustaining, until picked up by a boat's crew, N.P. Petersen, gunner's mate, who had fallen overboard.

2022 ◆ LUCY, JOHN

Rank: Second Class Boy
Service: U.S. Navy
Birthday: 1859
Place of Birth: New York, New York
Entered Service at: New York
Unit: U.S. Training Ship *Minnesota*
Battle or Place of Action: Castle Garden, New York City, New York
Date of Action: 9 July 1876
G.O. Number, Date: 214, 27 July 1876
Citation: Displayed heroic conduct while serving on board the U.S. training ship *Minnesota* on the occasion of the burning of Castle Garden at New York, 9 July 1876.

2023 ◆ MADDIN, EDWARD

True Name: Madden, Edward
Rank: Ordinary Seaman
Service: U.S. Navy
Birthday: 15 May 1852
Place of Birth: Newfoundland, Canada
Entered Service at: Massachusetts
Unit: U.S.S. *Franklin*
Battle or Place of Action: Lisbon, Portugal
Date of Action: 9 January 1876
G.O. Number, Date: 206, 15 February 1876
Citation: Served on board the U.S.S. *Franklin* at Lisbon, Portugal, 9 January 1876. Displaying gallant conduct, Maddin jumped overboard and rescued one of the crew of that vessel from drowning.

2024 ◆ MAGEE, JOHN W.

Rank: Second Class Fireman
Service: U.S. Navy
Birthday: 1859
Place of Birth: Maryland
Entered Service at: Maryland
Unit: U.S.S. *Tallapoosa*
Date of Action: 21 August 1884
G.O. Number, Date: 326, 18 October 1884
Citation: Serving on board the U.S.S. *Tallapoosa* during the sinking of that vessel on the night of 21 August 1884. During this period, Magee remained at his post of duty in the fireroom until the fires were put out by the rising waters.

2025 ◆ MANNING, HENRY J.

Rank: Quartermaster
Service: U.S. Navy
Birthday: 1859
Place of Birth: New Haven, New Haven County, Connecticut
Entered Service at: Connecticut
Unit: U.S. Training Ship *New Hampshire*
Battle or Place of Action: off Coasters Harbor Island, Newport, Rhode Island
Date of Action: 4 January 1882
G.O. Number, Date: 326, 18 October 1884
Citation: Serving on board the U.S. training ship *New Hampshire*, off Newport, R.I., 4 January 1882. Jumping overboard, Manning endeavored to rescue Jabez Smith, second class musician, from drowning.

2026 ♦ MATTHEWS, JOSEPH

Rank: Captain of the Top
Service: U.S. Navy
Birthday: 1849
Place of Birth: Malta
Entered Service at: Pennsylvania
Unit: U.S.S. *Constitution*
Battle or Place of Action: at sea, northeast Atlantic, west of the English Channel
Date of Action: 13 February 1879
G.O. Number, Date: 326, 18 October 1884
Date of Presentation: 7 September 1879
Place of Presentation: On board the U.S.S. *Constitution* at the New York Navy Yard, presented by Lt. Commander Theodore F. Jewell, executive officer
Citation: For courageous conduct in going over the stern of the U.S.S. *Constitution* at sea, 13 February 1879, during a heavy gale, and cutting the fastenings of the ship's rudder chains.

2027 ♦ McCARTON, JOHN

Rank: Ship's Printer
Service: U.S. Navy
Birthday: 1847
Place of Birth: Brooklyn, Kings County, New York
Entered Service at: New York
Unit: U.S. Training Ship *New Hampshire*
Battle or Place of Action: off Coasters Harbor Island, Newport, Rhode Island
Date of Action: 4 January 1882
G.O. Number, Date: 326, 18 October 1884
Citation: For jumping overboard from the U.S. training ship *New Hampshire* off Coasters Harbor Island, near Newport, R.I., 4 January 1882, and endeavoring to rescue Jabez Smith, second class musician, from drowning.

2028 ♦ MILLER, HUGH

Rank: Boatswain's Mate
Service: U.S. Navy
Birthday: 1859
Place of Birth: Philadelphia, Philadelphia County, Pennsylvania
Entered Service at: Pennsylvania
Unit: U.S.S. *Quinnebaug*
Battle or Place of Action: Alexandria, Egypt
Date of Action: 21 November 1885
Citation: For jumping overboard from the U.S.S. *Quinnebaug*, at Alexandria, Egypt, on the morning of 21 November 1885 and assisting in saving a shipmate from drowning.

2029 ♦ MILLMORE, JOHN

Rank: Ordinary Seaman
Service: U.S. Navy
Birthday: 1860
Place of Birth: New York, New York
Entered Service at: New York
Unit: U.S.S. *Essex*
Battle or Place of Action: Monrovia, Liberia
Date of Action: 31 October 1877
G.O. Number, Date: 326, 18 October 1884
Citation: Serving on board the U.S.S. *Essex*, Millmore rescued from drowning John W. Powers, ordinary seaman, serving on the same vessel with him, at Monrovia, Liberia, 31 October 1877.

2030 ♦ MITCHELL, THOMAS

Rank: Landsman
Service: U.S. Navy
Birthday: 1857
Place of Birth: New York, New York
Date of Death: 18 July 1942
Cemetery: Long Island National Cemetery (M-27661)—Farmingdale, New York
Entered Service at: New York
Unit: U.S.S. *Richmond*
Battle or Place of Action: Shanghai, China
Date of Action: 17 November 1879
G.O. Number, Date: 326, 18 October 1884
Citation: Serving on board the U.S.S. *Richmond*, Mitchell rescued from drowning, M.F. Caulan, first class boy, serving with him on the same vessel, at Shanghai, China, 17 November 1879.

2031 ♦ MOORE, FRANCIS

Rank: Boatswain's Mate
Service: U.S. Navy
Birthday: 1858
Place of Birth: New York
Entered Service at: New York
Unit: U.S. Training Ship *Portsmouth*
Battle or Place of Action: Navy Yard, Washington, D.C.
Date of Action: 23 January 1882
G.O. Number, Date: 326, 18 October 1884
Citation: For jumping overboard from the U.S. training ship *Portsmouth*, at the Washington Navy Yard, 23 January 1882, and endeavoring to rescue Thomas Duncan, carpenter and caulker, who had fallen overboard.

2032 ♦ MOORE, PHILIP

Rank: Seaman
Service: U.S. Navy
Birthday: 1853
Place of Birth: Newfoundland, Canada
Entered Service at: Rhode Island
Unit: U.S.S. *Trenton*
Battle or Place of Action: Genoa, Italy
Date of Action: 21 September 1880
G.O. Number, Date: 326, 18 October 1884
Citation: For jumping overboard from the U.S.S. *Trenton*,

at Genoa, Italy, 21 September 1880, and rescuing from drowning Hans Paulsen, ordinary seaman.

2033 ◆ MORRIS, JOHN

Rank: Corporal
Service: U.S. Marine Corps
Birthday: 25 January 1855
Place of Birth: New York
Entered Service at: New York
Unit: U.S.S. *Lancaster*
Battle or Place of Action: Villefranche, France
Date of Action: 25 December 1881
G.O. Number, Date: 326, 18 October 1884
Citation: For leaping overboard from the U.S. flagship *Lancaster*, at Villefranche, France, 25 December 1881, and rescuing from drowning Robert Blizzard, ordinary seaman, a prisoner, who had jumped overboard.

2034 ◆ MORSE, WILLIAM

Rank: Seaman
Service: U.S. Navy
Birthday: 1852
Place of Birth: Germany
Entered Service at: New York
Unit: U.S.S. *Shenandoah*
Battle or Place of Action: Rio de Janeiro, Brazil
Date of Action: 19 September 1880
G.O. Number, Date: 326, 18 October 1884
Citation: For jumping overboard from the U.S.S. *Shenandoah* at Rio de Janeiro, Brazil, 19 September 1880, and rescuing from drowning James Grady, first class fireman.

2035 ◆ NOIL, JOSEPH B.

Rank: Seaman
Service: U.S. Navy
Birthday: 1841
Place of Birth: Nova Scotia, Canada
Entered Service at: New York
Unit: U.S.S. *Powhatan*
Battle or Place of Action: Norfolk, Virginia
Date of Action: 26 December 1872
Citation: Serving on board the U.S.S. *Powhatan* at Norfolk, 26 December 1872, Noil saved Boatswain J.C. Walton from drowning.

2036 ◆ NORRIS, J. W.

Rank: Landsman
Service: U.S. Navy
Birthday: 1862
Place of Birth: England
Entered Service at: New York
Unit: U.S.S. *Jamestown*
Battle or Place of Action: Navy Yard, New York
Date of Action: 20 December 1883
G.O. Number, Date: 326, 18 October 1884
Citation: Serving on board the U.S.S. *Jamestown*, New York Navy Yard, 20 December 1883, Norris rescued from drowning A.A. George, who had fallen overboard.

2037 ◆ O'CONNER, JAMES FRANCIS

True Name: O'Connor, James Francis
Rank: Landsman, Engineer's Force
Service: U.S. Navy
Birthday: 28 November 1861
Place of Birth: Portsmouth, Portsmouth County, Virginia
Date of Death: 17 September 1940
Place of Death: Portsmouth, Virginia
Cemetery: Oak Grove Cemetery (MH)—Portsmouth, Virginia
Entered Service at: Virginia
Unit: U.S.S. *Jean Sands*
Battle or Place of Action: opposite the Navy Yard, Norfolk, Virginia
Date of Action: 15 June 1880
G.O. Number, Date: 326, 18 October 1884
Citation: For jumping overboard from the U.S.S. *Jean Sands*, opposite the Norfolk Navy Yard, on the night of 15 June 1880, and rescuing from drowning a young girl who had fallen overboard.

2038 ◆ OHMSEN, AUGUST

Rank: Master-at-Arms (highest rank: Lieutenant)
Service: U.S. Navy
Birthday: 15 March 1854
Place of Birth: Lubeck, Germany
Date of Death: 13 February 1938
Place of Death: Portsmouth, Virginia
Cemetery: St. Paul's Catholic Cemetery (PM)—Portsmouth, Virginia
Entered Service at: New York
Unit: U.S.S. *Tallapoosa*
Battle or Place of Action: off Woods Hole, Massachusetts
Date of Action: 21 August 1884
G.O. Number, Date: 326, 18 October 1884
Citation: On board the U.S.S. *Tallapoosa* at the time of the sinking of that vessel, on the night of 21 August 1884. Clearing the berth deck, Ohmsen remained there until the water was waist deep, wading about with outstretched arms, rousing the men out of their hammocks. Then, going on deck, he assisted in lowering the first cutter and then the dinghy, of which he took charge.

2039 ◆ O'NEAL, JOHN

Rank: Boatswain's Mate
Service: U.S. Navy
Birthday: 1841
Place of Birth: Ireland
Entered Service at: Pennsylvania
Unit: U.S.S. *Kansas*
Battle or Place of Action: Greytown, Nicaragua
Date of Action: 12 April 1872

G.O. Number, Date: 179, 9 July 1872
Citation: Serving on board the U.S.S. *Kansas*, O'Neal displayed great coolness and self-possession at the time Comdr. A.F. Crosman and others were drowned near Greytown, Nicaragua, 12 April 1872, and by personal exertion prevented greater loss of life.

2040 ◆ OSBORNE, JOHN

Rank: Seaman
Service: U.S. Navy
Birthday: 1844
Place of Birth: New Orleans, Orleans County, Louisiana
Date of Death: 23 April 1920
Cemetery: Arlington National Cemetery (17-19689) (MH)—Arlington, Virginia
Entered Service at: Louisiana
Unit: U.S.S. *Juniata*
Battle or Place of Action: Philadelphia, Pennsylvania
Date of Action: 21 August 1876
G.O. Number, Date: 218, 24 August 1876
Citation: Serving on board the U.S.S. *Juniata*, Osborne displayed gallant conduct in rescuing from drowning an enlisted boy of that vessel, at Philadelphia, Pa., 21 August 1876.

2041 ◆ OSEPINS, CHRISTIAN

Rank: Seaman
Service: U.S. Navy
Birthday: 1858
Place of Birth: Holland
Entered Service at: New York
Unit: U.S. Tug *Fortune*
Battle or Place of Action: Hampton Roads, Virginia
Date of Action: 7 May 1882
G.O. Number, Date: 326, 18 October 1884
Citation: For jumping overboard from the U.S. Tug *Fortune*, 7 May 1882, at Hampton Roads, Va., and rescuing from drowning James Walters, gunner's mate.

2042 ◆ PARKER, ALEXANDER

Rank: Boatswain's Mate
Service: U.S. Navy
Birthday: 1832
Place of Birth: Kensington, New Jersey
Entered Service at: New Jersey
Battle or Place of Action: Mare Island Navy Yard, California
Date of Action: 25 July 1876
G.O. Number, Date: 215, 9 August 1876
Citation: For gallant conduct in attempting to save a shipmate from drowning at the Navy Yard, Mare Island, Cal., on 25 July 1876.

2043 ◆ PILE, RICHARD

Rank: Ordinary Seaman
Service: U.S. Navy
Birthday: 1849
Place of Birth: West Indies
Entered Service at: Massachusetts
Unit: U.S.S. *Kansas*
Battle or Place of Action: Greytown, Nicaragua
Date of Action: 12 April 1872
G.O. Number, Date: 179, 9 July 1872
Citation: Serving on board the U.S.S. *Kansas*, Pile displayed great coolness and self-possession at the time Comdr. A.F. Crosman and others were drowned near Greytown, Nicaragua, 12 April 1872, and by his extraordinary heroism and personal exertion prevented greater loss of life.

2044 ◆ REGAN, PATRICK

Rank: Ordinary Seaman
Service: U.S. Navy
Birthday: 1852
Place of Birth: Queenstown, County Cork, Ireland
Entered Service at: New York
Unit: U.S.S. *Pensacola*
Battle or Place of Action: in the harbor of Coquimbo, Chile
Date of Action: 30 July 1873
Citation: Serving on board the U.S.S. *Pensacola*, Regan displayed gallant conduct in the harbor of Coquimbo, Chile, 30 July 1873.

2045 ◆ ROUNING, JOHANNES

Rank: Ordinary Seaman
Service: U.S. Navy
Unit: U.S. Tug *Fortune*
Battle or Place of Action: Hampton Roads, Virginia
Date of Action: 7 May 1882
G.O. Number, Date: 326, 18 October 1884
Citation: For jumping overboard from the U.S. tug *Fortune*, 7 May 1882, at Hampton Roads, Va., and rescuing from drowning James Walters, gunner's mate.

2046 ◆ RUSSELL, JOHN

Rank: Seaman
Service: U.S. Navy
Birthday: 1852
Place of Birth: New York, New York
Entered Service at: New York
Unit: U.S.S. *Trenton*
Battle or Place of Action: Genoa, Italy
Date of Action: 21 September 1880
G.O. Number, Date: 326, 18 October 1884
Citation: For jumping overboard from the U.S.S. *Trenton*, at Genoa, Italy, 21 September 1880, and rescuing from drowning Hans Paulsen, ordinary seaman.

2047 ◆ RYAN, RICHARD

Rank: Ordinary Seaman
Service: U.S. Navy

Birthday: 1851
Place of Birth: Connecticut
Entered Service at: Connecticut
Unit: U.S.S. *Hartford*
Battle or Place of Action: Norfolk, Virginia
Date of Action: 4 March 1876
G.O. Number, Date: 207, 23 March 1876
Citation: Serving on board the U.S.S. *Hartford*, Ryan displayed gallant conduct in jumping overboard at Norfolk, Va., and rescuing from drowning one of the crew of that vessel, 4 March 1876.

2048 ◆ SADLER, WILLIAM

Rank: Captain of the Top
Service: U.S. Navy
Birthday: 1854
Place of Birth: Boston, Suffolk County, Massachusetts
Entered Service at: Massachusetts
Unit: U.S.S. *Saratoga*
Battle or Place of Action: off Coasters Harbor Island, Newport, Rhode Island
Date of Action: 25 June 1881
G.O. Number, Date: 326, 18 October 1884
Citation: For jumping overboard from the U.S.S. *Saratoga*, off Coasters Harbor Island, R.I., 25 June 1881, and sustaining until picked up by a boat from the ship, Frank Gallagher, second class boy, who had fallen overboard.

2049 ◆ SAPP, ISAAC

Rank: Seaman, Engineer's Force
Service: U.S. Navy
Birthday: 1844
Place of Birth: Philadelphia, Philadelphia County, Pennsylvania
Entered Service at: Pennsylvania
Unit: U.S.S. *Shenandoah*
Battle or Place of Action: Villefranche, France
Date of Action: 15 December 1871
G.O. Number, Date: 169, 8 February 1872
Citation: On board the U.S.S. *Shenandoah* during the rescue of a shipmate at Villefranche, 15 December 1871. Jumping overboard, Sapp gallantly assisted in saving Charles Prince, seaman, from drowning.

2050 ◆ SIMPSON, D. HENRY LAKIN

True Name: Simpson, Henry
Rank: Fireman First Class
Service: U.S. Navy
Birthday: 1859
Place of Birth: London, England
Entered Service at: New York
Unit: U.S.S. *Essex*
Battle or Place of Action: Monrovia, Liberia
Date of Action: 31 October 1877
G.O. Number, Date: 326, 18 October 1884
Citation: For rescuing from drowning John W. Powers, ordinary seaman on board the U.S.S. *Essex*, at Monrovia, Liberia, 31 October 1877.

2051 ◆ SMITH, JAMES

Rank: Seaman
Service: U.S. Navy
Birthday: 1838
Place of Birth: Hawaiian Islands
Entered Service at: New York
Unit: U.S.S. *Kansas*
Battle or Place of Action: Greytown, Nicaragua
Date of Action: 12 April 1872
G.O. Number, Date: 176, 9 July 1872
Citation: Serving on board the U.S.S. *Kansas*, Smith displayed great coolness and self-possession at the time Comdr. A. F. Crosman and others were drowned near Greytown, Nicaragua, 12 April 1872, and by extraordinary heroism and personal exertion, prevented greater loss of life.

2052 ◆ SMITH, JOHN

Rank: Seaman
Service: U.S. Navy
Birthday: 1854
Place of Birth: Bermuda
Entered Service at: New York
Unit: U.S.S. *Shenandoah*
Battle or Place of Action: Rio de Janeiro, Brazil
Date of Action: 19 September 1880
G.O. Number, Date: 326, 18 October 1884
Citation: For jumping overboard from the U.S.S. *Shenandoah*, at Rio de Janeiro, Brazil, 19 September 1880, and rescuing from drowning James Grady, first class fireman.

2053 ◆ SMITH, THOMAS

Rank: Seaman
Service: U.S. Navy
Birthday: 1856
Place of Birth: Ireland
Entered Service at: Virginia
Unit: U.S.S. *Enterprise*
Battle or Place of Action: off Para, Brazil
Date of Action: 1 October 1878
Citation: For rescuing from drowning William Kent, coxswain of the U.S.S. *Enterprise*, off Para, Brazil, 1 October 1878.

2054 ◆ STEWART, JAMES A.

Rank: Corporal (highest rank: Sergeant)
Service: U.S. Marine Corps
Birthday: 1839
Place of Birth: Philadelphia, Philadelphia County, Pennsylvania
Entered Service at: Pennsylvania
Unit: U.S.S. *Plymouth*
Battle or Place of Action: Villefranche Harbor, France

Date of Action: 1 February 1872
G.O. Number, Date: 180, 10 October 1872
Citation: Serving on board the U.S.S. *Plymouth*, Stewart jumped overboard in the harbor of Villefranche, France, 1 February 1872 and saved Midshipman Osterhaus from drowning.

2055 ◆ SULLIVAN, JAMES F.

Rank: Boatswain's Mate
Service: U.S. Navy
Birthday: 1857
Place of Birth: Lowell, Middlesex County, Massachusetts
Entered Service at: Massachusetts
Unit: U.S. Training Ship *New Hampshire*
Battle or Place of Action: Newport, Rhode Island
Date of Action: 21 April 1882
G.O. Number, Date: 326, 18 October 1884
Citation: For jumping overboard from the U.S. training ship *New Hampshire*, at Newport, R.I., 21 April 1882, and rescuing from drowning Francis T. Price, third class boy.

2056 ◆ SWEENEY, ROBERT AUGUSTUS✛

Rank: Ordinary Seaman
Service: U.S. Navy
Birthday: 20 February 1853
Place of Birth: Montserrat, West Indies
Date of Death: 19 December 1890
Cemetery: Calvary Cemetery (unknown grave)—Woodside, New York
Entered Service at: New Jersey
Unit: U.S.S. *Kearsarge*—U.S.S. *Yantic*
Battle or Place of Action: Hampton Roads, Virginia & Navy Yard, New York
Date of Action: 26 October 1881 & 20 December 1883
G.O. Number, Date: 326, 18 October 1884
Citation: **First Award** Serving on board the U.S.S. *Kearsarge*, at Hampton Roads, Va., 26 October 1881, Sweeney jumped overboard and assisted in saving from drowning a shipmate who had fallen overboard into a strongly running tide. **Second Award** Serving on board the U.S.S. *Yantic*, at the Navy Yard, New York, 20 December 1883, Sweeney rescued from drowning A.A. George, who had fallen overboard from the U.S.S. *Jamestown*.
Notes: ✛Double Awardee

2057 ◆ SWEENEY, WILLIAM

Rank: Landsman, Engineer's Force
Service: U.S. Navy
Birthday: 1856
Place of Birth: Boston, Suffolk County, Massachusetts
Entered Service at: Massachusetts
Unit: U.S.S. *Jean Sands*
Battle or Place of Action: opposite the Navy Yard, Norfolk, Virginia
Date of Action: 15 June 1880
G.O. Number, Date: 326, 18 October 1884
Citation: For jumping overboard from the U.S.S. *Jean Sands*, opposite the Navy Yard, Norfolk, Va., on the night of 15 June 1880, and rescuing from drowning a young girl who had fallen overboard.

2058 ◆ TAYLOR, RICHARD HAMILTON

Rank: Quartermaster (highest rank: Schoolmaster)
Service: U.S. Navy
Birthday: 8 September 1870
Place of Birth: Staunton, Staunton County, Virginia
Date of Death: 24 March 1956
Place of Death: Holy Ghost Hospital, Cambridge, Massachusetts
Cemetery: Evergreen Cemetery—Boston, Massachusetts
Entered Service at: Virginia
Unit: U.S.S. *Nipsic*
Battle or Place of Action: Apia, Samoa
Date of Action: 19 March 1889
G.O. Number, Date: 157, 20 April 1904
Place of Presentation: The White House, presented by Pres. Theodore Roosevelt
Citation: Serving on board the U.S.S. *Nipsic*, Taylor displayed gallantry during the hurricane at Apia, Samoa, 16 March 1889.

2059 ◆ THAYER, JAMES

Rank: Ship's Corporal
Service: U.S. Navy
Birthday: 1853
Place of Birth: Ireland
Entered Service at: Pennsylvania
Unit: U.S.S. *Constitution*
Battle or Place of Action: Navy Yard, Norfolk, Virginia
Date of Action: 16 November 1879
G.O. Number, Date: 326, 18 October 1884
Citation: For rescuing from drowning a boy serving with him on the U.S.S. *Constitution*, at the Navy Yard, Norfolk, Va., 16 November 1879.

2060 ◆ THOMPSON, HENRY

Rank: Seaman
Service: U.S. Navy
Battle or Place of Action: Mare Island, California
Date of Action: 27 June 1878
Citation: For rescuing a man from drowning at Mare Island, Cal., 27 June 1878.

2061 ◆ THORNTON, MICHAEL

Rank: Seaman
Service: U.S. Navy
Birthday: 1856
Place of Birth: Ireland
Entered Service at: Pennsylvania
Unit: U.S. Tug *Leyden*
Battle or Place of Action: near Boston, Massachusetts

Date of Action: 26 August 1881
G.O. Number, Date: 326, 18 October 1884
Citation: For jumping overboard from the U.S. Tug *Leyden*, near Boston, Mass., 26 August 1881, and sustaining until picked up Michael Drennan, landsman, who had jumped overboard while temporarily insane.

2062 ◆ TOBIN, PAUL

Rank: Landsman
Service: U.S. Navy
Place of Birth: Plybin, France
Entered Service at: Brest, France
Unit: U.S.S. *Plymouth*
Battle or Place of Action: Hamburg Harbor, Germany
Date of Action: 3 July 1871
G.O. Number, Date: 180, 10 October 1872
Citation: On board the U.S.S. *Plymouth*, Hamburg Harbor, 3 July 1871. Jumping overboard at the imminent risk of his life, Tobin, with a comrade, rescued from drowning one of a party who was thrown from a shore boat into a four-knot running tide while the boat was coming alongside the ship.

2063 ◆ TROUT, JAMES M.

Rank: Fireman Second Class
Service: U.S. Navy
Birthday: 1850
Place of Birth: Philadelphia, Philadelphia County, Pennsylvania
Entered Service at: Pennsylvania
Unit: U.S.S. *Frolic*
Battle or Place of Action: Montevideo, Uruguay
Date of Action: 20 April 1877
Citation: Serving on board the U.S.S. *Frolic*, Trout displayed gallant conduct in endeavoring to save the life of one of the crew of that vessel who had fallen overboard at Montevideo, 20 April 1877.

2064 ◆ TROY, JEREMIAH

Rank: Chief Boatswain's Mate
Service: U.S. Navy
Birthday: 1845
Place of Birth: New York, New York
Entered Service at: New York
Unit: U.S. Training Ship *New Hampshire*
Battle or Place of Action: Newport, Rhode Island
Date of Action: 21 April 1882
G.O. Number, Date: 326, 18 October 1884
Citation: For jumping overboard from the U.S. training ship *New Hampshire*, at Newport, R.I., 21 April 1882, and rescuing from drowning Francis T. Price, third class boy.

2065 ◆ TURVELIN, ALEXANDER HAURE

Rank: Seaman
Service: U.S. Navy
Birthday: 1847
Place of Birth: Russia
Unit: U.S.S. *Trenton*
Battle or Place of Action: Toulon, France
Date of Action: February 1881
G.O. Number, Date: 326, 18 October 1884
Citation: For jumping overboard from the U.S.S. *Trenton*, at Toulon, France, February 1881, and rescuing from drowning Augustus Ohlensen, coxswain.

2066 ◆ WEISBOGEL, ALBERT✛

Rank: Captain of the Mizzen Top (highest rank: Petty Officer)
Service: U.S. Navy
Birthday: 1844
Place of Birth: New Orleans, Orleans County, Louisiana
Entered Service at: Louisiana
Unit: U.S.S. *Benicia*—U.S.S. *Plymouth*
Battle or Place of Action: at Sea
Date of Action: 11 January 1874 & 27 April 1876
G.O. Number, Date: 207, 23 March 1876 & 212, 9 June 1876
Citation: **First Award** For gallant conduct in jumping overboard from the U.S.S. *Benicia*, at sea, and rescuing from drowning one of the crew of that vessel, 11 January 1874. **Second Award** For gallant conduct in jumping overboard from the U.S.S. *Plymouth*, at sea, and rescuing from drowning one of the crew of that vessel on 27 April 1876.
Notes: ✛Double Awardee

2067 ◆ WEISSEL, ADAM

Rank: Ship's Cook
Service: U.S. Navy
Birthday: 1854
Place of Birth: Germany
Date of Death: 10 December 1928
Place of Death: Berkeley, California
Cemetery: Mountain View Cemetery—Oakland, California
Entered Service at: New York
Unit: U.S. Training Ship *Minnesota*
Battle or Place of Action: Newport, Rhode Island
Date of Action: 26 August 1881
G.O. Number, Date: 326, 18 October 1884
Citation: For jumping overboard from the U.S. training ship *Minnesota*, Newport, R.I., 26 August 1881, and sustaining until picked up by a boat from the ship, C. Lorenze, captain of the forecastle, who had fallen overboard.

2068 ◆ WILLIAMS, ANTONIO

Rank: Seaman
Service: U.S. Navy
Birthday: 1825
Place of Birth: Malta
Unit: U.S.S. *Huron*
Date of Action: 24 November 1877
Citation: For courage and fidelity displayed in the loss of the U.S.S. *Huron*, 24 November 1877.

2069 ◆ WILLIAMS, HENRY

Rank: Carpenter's Mate (highest rank: Carpenter)
Service: U.S. Navy
Birthday: 6 February 1834
Place of Birth: Canada
Date of Death: 17 October 1917
Place of Death: Wildwood Crest, New Jersey
Cemetery: West Laurel Cemetery—Bala-Cynwyd, Pennsylvania
Entered Service at: Pennsylvania
Unit: U.S.S. *Constitution*
Battle or Place of Action: at sea, northeast Atlantic, west of the English Channel
Date of Action: 13 February 1879
G.O. Number, Date: 326, 18 October 1884
Date of Presentation: 7 September 1879
Place of Presentation: On board the U.S.S. *Constitution* at the New York Navy Yard, presented by Lt. Commander Theodore F. Jewell, executive officer
Citation: For going over the stern of the U.S.S. *Constitution*, at sea, 13 February 1879, during a heavy gale, and performing important carpenter's work upon her rudder.

2070 ◆ WILLIAMS, LOUIS✛

True Name: Olsen, Ludwig Andreas
Rank: Captain of the Hold
Service: U.S. Navy
Birthday: 1845
Place of Birth: Christiana (now Oslo), Norway
Date of Death: 20 February 1886
Cemetery: Cypress Hills National Cemetery (G-42616) (MH)—Brooklyn, New York
Entered Service at: California
Unit: U.S.S. *Lackawanna*
Battle or Place of Action: Honolulu, Territory of Hawaii & Callao, Peru
Date of Action: 16 March 1883 & 13 June 1884
G.O. Number, Date: 326, 18 October 1884 (2nd award)
Citation: **First Award** For jumping overboard from the U.S.S. *Lackawanna*, 16 March 1883, at Honolulu, T.H., and rescuing from drowning Thomas Moran, landsman. **Second Award** Serving on board the U.S.S. *Lackawanna*, Williams rescued from drowning William Cruise, who had fallen overboard at Callao, Peru, 13 June 1884.
Notes: ✛Double Awardee

2071 ◆ WILLIS, GEORGE

Rank: Coxswain
Service: U.S. Navy
Birthday: 1839
Place of Birth: Boston, Suffolk County, Massachusetts
Entered Service at: Massachusetts
Unit: U.S.S. *Tigress*
Battle or Place of Action: off the coast of Greenland
Date of Action: 22 September 1873
Citation: Serving on board the U.S.S. *Tigress*, Willis displayed gallant and meritorious conduct on the night of 22 September 1873 off the coast of Greenland.

2072 ◆ WILSON, AUGUST

Rank: Boilermaker
Service: U.S. Navy
Birthday: 1864
Place of Birth: Danzig, Germany
Entered Service at: New York
Unit: U.S.S. *Puritan*
Date of Action: 1 July 1897
G.O. Number, Date: 482, 1 November 1897
Citation: For gallant conduct while serving on board the U.S.S. *Puritan* and at the time of the collapse of one of the crown sheets of boiler E on that vessel, 1 July 1897. Wrapping wet cloths about his face and arms, Wilson entered the fireroom and opened the safety valve, thus removing the danger of disabling the other boilers.

SPANISH-AMERICAN WAR

2073 ♦ BAKER, BENJAMIN F.
Rank: Coxswain (highest rank: Chief Master-at-Arms)
Service: U.S. Navy
Birthday: 12 March 1862
Place of Birth: Dennis Port, Barnstable County, Massachusetts
Date of Death: 19 May 1927
Place of Death: Dennisport, Massachusetts
Cemetery: Old Swan Lake Cemetery (MH)—Dennisport, Massachusetts
Unit: U.S.S. *Nashville*
Battle or Place of Action: Cienfuegos, Cuba
Date of Action: 11 May 1898
G.O. Number, Date: 521, 7 July 1899
Citation: On board the U.S.S. *Nashville* during the cutting of the cable leading from Cienfuegos, Cuba, 11 May 1898. Facing the heavy fire of the enemy, Baker set an example of extraordinary bravery and coolness throughout this action.

2074 ♦ BAKER JR., EDWARD LEE
Rank: Sergeant Major (highest rank: Captain)
Service: U.S. Army
Birthday: 28 December 1865
Place of Birth: Platte River, Laramie County, Wyoming
Date of Death: 26 August 1913
Place of Death: Presido of San Francisco, California
Cemetery: Rosedale Cemetery—Los Angeles, California
Entered Service at: Cincinnati, Hamilton County, Ohio
Unit: 10th U.S. Cavalry
Battle or Place of Action: Santiago, Cuba
Date of Action: 1 July 1898
Date of Issue: 3 July 1902
Citation: Left cover and, under fire, rescued a wounded comrade from drowning.

2075 ♦ BARROW, DAVID DUFFY
Rank: Seaman (highest rank: Coxswain)
Service: U.S. Navy
Birthday: 22 July 1876
Place of Birth: Reelsboro, North Carolina
Date of Death: 6 December 1948
Place of Death: Richmond, Virginia
Cemetery: Evergreen Memorial Cemetery (MH)—Portsmouth, Virginia
Entered Service at: Norfolk, Norfolk County, Virginia
Unit: U.S.S. *Nashville*
Battle or Place of Action: Cienfuegos, Cuba
Date of Action: 11 May 1898
G.O. Number, Date: 521, 7 July 1899
Citation: On board the U.S.S. *Nashville* during the cutting of the cable leading from Cienfuegos, Cuba, 11 May 1898. Facing the heavy fire of the enemy, Barrow set an example of extraordinary bravery and coolness throughout this action.

2076 ♦ BELL, DENNIS
Rank: Private
Service: U.S. Army
Birthday: 28 December 1866
Place of Birth: Washington, D.C.
Date of Death: 25 September 1953
Place of Death: Washington, D.C.
Cemetery: Arlington National Cemetery (31-349) (MH)—Arlington, Virginia
Entered Service at: Washington, D.C.
Unit: Troop H, 10th U.S. Cavalry
Battle or Place of Action: Tayabacoa, Cuba
Date of Action: 30 June 1898
Date of Issue: 23 June 1899
Citation: Voluntarily went ashore in the face of the enemy and aided in the rescue of his wounded comrades; this after several previous attempts at rescue had been frustrated.

2077 ♦ BENNETT, JAMES HARVEY
Rank: Chief Boatswain's Mate
Service: U.S. Navy
Birthday: 5 April 1851
Place of Birth: Haverstraw, Rockland County, New York
Entered Service at: New York
Unit: U.S.S. *Marblehead*
Battle or Place of Action: Cienfuegos, Cuba
Date of Action: 11 May 1898
G.O. Number, Date: 521, 7 July 1899
Citation: On board the U.S.S. *Marblehead* during the cutting of the cable leading from Cienfuegos, Cuba, 11 May 1898. Facing the heavy fire of the enemy, Bennett set an example of extraordinary bravery and coolness throughout this action.

2078 ♦ BERG, GEORGE FRANCIS
Rank: Private (highest rank: Master Sergeant Ret.)
Service: U.S. Army
Birthday: 2 December 1868

Place of Birth: Mount Erie, Wayne County, Illinois
Date of Death: 27 November 1945
Place of Death: Washington, D.C.
Cemetery: Mount Pleasant Cemetery (MH)—South Portland, Maine
Entered Service at: Fort Omaha, Douglas County, Nebraska
Unit: Company C, 17th U.S. Infantry
Battle or Place of Action: El Caney, Cuba
Date of Action: 1 July 1898
Date of Issue: 17 October 1927
Citation: Gallantly assisted in the rescue of the wounded from in front of the lines and while under heavy fire of the enemy.

2079 ◆ BEYER, ALBERT

Rank: Coxswain (highest rank: Chief Master-of-Arms)
Service: U.S. Navy
Birthday: 13 June 1859
Place of Birth: Hanover, Germany
Date of Death: 29 October 1929
Place of Death: Philadelphia, Pennsylvania
Cemetery: Mount Moriah Cemetery (VA Plot USN-1-9-2) (MH)—Philadelphia, Pennsylvania
Entered Service at: Boston, Suffolk County, Massachusetts
Unit: U.S.S. *Nashville*
Battle or Place of Action: Cienfuegos, Cuba
Date of Action: 11 May 1898
G.O. Number, Date: 521, 7 July 1899
Citation: On board the U.S.S. *Nashville* during the cutting of the cable leading from Cienfuegos, Cuba, 11 May 1898. Facing the heavy fire of the enemy, Beyer set an example of extraordinary bravery and coolness throughout this action.

2080 ◆ BLUME, ROBERT

Rank: Seaman (highest rank: Chief Boatswain's Mate)
Service: U.S. Navy
Birthday: 19 November 1868
Place of Birth: Pittsburgh, Allegheny County, Pennsylvania
Date of Death: 16 September 1937
Cemetery: Arlington National Cemetery (6-9752-SS) (MH)—Arlington, Virginia
Entered Service at: New Jersey
Unit: U.S.S. *Nashville*
Battle or Place of Action: Cienfuegos, Cuba
Date of Action: 11 May 1898
G.O. Number, Date: 521, 7 July 1899
Citation: On board the U.S.S. *Nashville* during the cutting of the cable leading from Cienfuegos, Cuba, 11 May 1898. Facing the heavy fire of the enemy, Blume set an example of extraordinary bravery and coolness throughout this action.

2081 ◆ BRADY, GEORGE F.

Rank: Chief Gunner's Mate
Service: U.S. Navy
Birthday: 7 September 1867
Place of Birth: Ireland
Entered Service at: New York
Unit: U.S.S. *Winslow*
Battle or Place of Action: Cardenas, Cuba
Date of Action: 11 May 1898
G.O. Number, Date: 497, 3 September 1899
Citation: On board the torpedo Boat *Winslow* during the actions at Cardenas, Cuba, 11 May 1989. Conspicuously gallant during this period, Brady, by his energy in assisting to sustain fire, his efforts to repair the steering gear and his promptness in maintaining watertight integrity, was largely instrumental in saving the vessel.

2082 ◆ BRIGHT, GEORGE WASHINGTON

Rank: Coal Passer
Service: U.S. Navy
Birthday: 27 December 1874
Place of Birth: Norfolk, Norfolk County, Virginia
Date of Death: 20 March 1949
Place of Death: Richmond, Virginia
Cemetery: Blanford Cemetery—Petersburg, Virginia
Entered Service at: Virginia
Unit: U.S.S. *Nashville*
Battle or Place of Action: Cienfuegos, Cuba
Date of Action: 11 May 1898
G.O. Number, Date: 521, 7 July 1899
Citation: On board the U.S.S. *Nashville* during the cutting of the cable leading from Cienfuegos, Cuba, 11 May 1898. Facing the heavy fire of the enemy, Bright set an example of extraordinary bravery and coolness throughout this action.

2083 ◆ BROOKIN, OSCAR

True Name: Brookins, Oscar
Rank: Private
Service: U.S. Army
Birthday: 19 July 1869
Place of Birth: Byron, Fond Du Lac County, Wisconsin
Date of Death: 18 August 1938
Cemetery: Sunset Cemetery (MH)—Galloway, Ohio
Entered Service at: Green County, Ohio
Unit: Company C, 17th U.S. Infantry
Battle or Place of Action: El Caney, Cuba
Date of Action: 1 July 1898
Date of Issue: 21 June 1899
Citation: Gallantly assisted in the rescue of the wounded from in front of the lines and under heavy fire from the enemy.

2084 ◆ BUZZARD, ULYSSES G.

Rank: Private (highest rank: Sergeant)
Service: U.S. Army
Birthday: 31 January 1865
Place of Birth: Armstrong, Pennsylvania
Date of Death: 2 August 1939
Place of Death: Philippine Islands
Cemetery: San Nicolas Cemetery American Lot—Cebu City, Philippine Islands

Entered Service at: Pittsburgh, Allegheny County, Pennsylvania
Unit: Company C, 17th U.S. Infantry
Battle or Place of Action: El Caney, Cuba
Date of Action: 1 July 1898
Date of Issue: 24 June 1899
Citation: Gallantly assisted in the rescue of the wounded from in front of the lines and under heavy fire from the enemy.

2085 ◆ CAMPBELL, DANIEL J.

Rank: Private
Service: U.S. Marine Corps
Birthday: 26 December 1874
Place of Birth: Prince Edward Island, Canada
Date of Death: 28 April 1955
Cemetery: Mount Hope Cemetery (MH)—Mattapan, Massachusetts
Entered Service at: Boston, Suffolk County, Massachusetts
Unit: U.S.S. *Marblehead*
Battle or Place of Action: Cienfuegos, Cuba
Date of Action: 11 May 1898
G.O. Number, Date: 521, 7 July 1899
Citation: On board the U.S.S. *Marblehead* during the cutting of the cable leading from Cienfuegos, Cuba, 11 May 1898. Facing the heavy fire of the enemy, Campbell set an example of extraordinary bravery and coolness throughout this action.

2086 ◆ CANTRELL, CHARLES P.

Rank: Private
Service: U.S. Army
Birthday: 13 February 1874
Place of Birth: Smithville, Dekalb County, Tennessee
Date of Death: 3 August 1948
Cemetery: Nashville National Cemetery (I-132) (MH)—Madison, Tennessee
Entered Service at: Nashville, Davidson County, Tennessee
Unit: Company F, 10th U.S. Infantry
Battle or Place of Action: Santiago, Cuba
Date of Action: 1 July 1898
Citation: Gallantly assisted in the rescue of the wounded from in front of the lines and under heavy fire from the enemy.

2087 ◆ CARTER, JOSEPH EDWARD

Rank: Blacksmith
Service: U.S. Navy
Birthday: 15 August 1875
Place of Birth: Manchester, Greater Manchester County, England
Date of Death: 19 June 1950
Cemetery: Arlington National Cemetery (34-2631-1) (MH)—Arlington, Virginia
Entered Service at: North Dakota
Unit: U.S.S. *Marblehead*
Battle or Place of Action: Cienfuegos, Cuba
Date of Action: 11 May 1898
G.O. Number, Date: 521, 7 July 1899
Citation: On board the U.S.S. *Marblehead* during the operation of cutting the cable leading from Cienfuegos, Cuba, 11 May 1898. Facing the heavy fire of the enemy, Carter set an example of extraordinary bravery and coolness throughout this action.

2088 ◆ CHADWICK, LEONARD B.

Rank: Apprentice First Class (highest rank: Gunner's Mate Third Class)
Service: U.S. Navy
Birthday: 24 November 1878
Place of Birth: Middletown, New Castle County, Delaware
Date of Death: 18 May 1940
Place of Death: Boston, Massachusetts
Cemetery: Mount Hope Cemetery (MH)—Mattapan, Massachusetts
Entered Service at: Delaware
Unit: U.S.S. *Marblehead*
Battle or Place of Action: Cienfuegos, Cuba
Date of Action: 11 May 1898
G.O. Number, Date: 521, 7 July 1899
Citation: On board the U.S.S. *Marblehead* during the operation of cutting the cable leading from Cienfuegos, Cuba, 11 May 1898. Facing the heavy fire of the enemy, Chadwick set an example of extraordinary bravery and coolness throughout this period.

2089 ◆ CHARETTE, GEORGE

Rank: Gunner's Mate First Class (highest rank: Lieutenant)
Service: U.S. Navy
Birthday: 6 June 1867
Place of Birth: Lowell, Middlesex County, Massachusetts
Date of Death: 7 February 1938
Cemetery: Arlington National Cemetery (7-10222)—Arlington, Virginia
Entered Service at: Lowell, Middlesex County, Massachusetts
Unit: U.S.S. *Merrimac*—assigned to the U.S.S. *New York*
Battle or Place of Action: harbor entrance, Santiago de Cuba, Cuba
Date of Action: 3 June 1898
G.O. Number, Date: 529, 2 November 1899
Citation: In connection with the sinking of the U.S.S. *Merrimac* at the entrance to the harbor of Santiago de Cuba, 2 June 1898. Despite heavy fire from the Spanish batteries, Charette displayed extraordinary heroism throughout this operation.
Notes: POW

2090 ◆ CHURCH, JAMES ROBB

Rank: Assistant Surgeon (highest rank: Colonel)
Service: U.S. Army
Birthday: 1866
Place of Birth: Chicago, Cook County, Illinois

Date of Death: 18 May 1923
Cemetery: Arlington National Cemetery (3-1409A)—Arlington, Virginia
Entered Service at: Washington, D.C.
Unit: 1st U.S. Volunteer Cavalry
Battle or Place of Action: Las Guasimas, Cuba
Date of Action: 24 June 1898
Date of Presentation: 10 January 1906
Place of Presentation: The White House, presented by Pres. Theodore Roosevelt
Citation: In addition to performing gallantly the duties pertaining to his position, voluntarily and unaided carried several seriously wounded men from the firing line to a secure position in the rear, in each instance being subjected to a very heavy fire and great exposure and danger.

2091 ♦ CLAUSEN, CLAUS KRISTIAN RANDOLPH

Rank: Coxswain (highest rank: Lieutenant)
Service: U.S. Navy
Birthday: 9 December 1869
Place of Birth: Denmark
Date of Death: 23 December 1958
Place of Death: St. Albans, New York
Cemetery: U.S. Columbarium—Middle Village, New York
Entered Service at: New York
Unit: U.S.S. *Merrimac*—assigned to the U.S.S. *New York*
Battle or Place of Action: harbor entrance, Santiago de Cuba, Cuba
Date of Action: 3 June 1898
G.O. Number, Date: 529, 2 November 1899
Citation: In connection with the sinking of the U.S.S. *Merrimac* at the entrance to the harbor of Santiago de Cuba, 2 June 1898. Despite heavy fire from the Spanish batteries, Clausen displayed extraordinary heroism throughout this operation.
Notes: POW

2092 ♦ COONEY, THOMAS C.

Rank: Chief Machinist (highest rank: Chief Carpenter)
Service: U.S. Navy
Birthday: 18 July 1853
Place of Birth: Westport, Nova Scotia, Canada
Date of Death: 8 January 1907
Place of Death: Norfolk, Virginia
Cemetery: U.S. Naval Academy Cemetery (Lot 254)—Annapolis, Maryland
Entered Service at: New Jersey
Unit: U.S. Torpedo Boat *Winslow*
Battle or Place of Action: Cardenas, Cuba
Date of Action: 11 May 1898
G.O. Number, Date: 497, 3 September 1898
Citation: On board the U.S. torpedo boat *Winslow* during the actions at Cardenas, Cuba, 11 May 1898. Following the piercing of the boiler by an enemy shell, Cooney, by his gallantry and promptness in extinguishing the resulting flames, saved the boiler tubes from burning out.

2093 ♦ CROUSE, WILLIAM ADOLPHUS

Rank: Watertender (highest rank: Chief Commissary Steward)
Service: U.S. Navy
Birthday: 22 October 1866
Place of Birth: Tannettsburg, Franklin County, Pennsylvania
Date of Death: 27 June 1941
Place of Death: Harrisburg, Pennsylvania
Cemetery: Arlington Cemetery—Drexel Hill, Pennsylvania
Entered Service at: Pennsylvania
Unit: U.S.S. *Concord*
Battle or Place of Action: off Cavite, Manila Bay, Philippine Islands
Date of Action: 21 May 1898
G.O. Number, Date: 502, 14 December 1898
Citation: On board the U.S.S. *Concord* off Cavite, Manila Bay, P.I., 21 May 1898. Following the blowing-out of a lower manhole plate joint on boiler B of that vessel, Crouse hauled the fires in the hot, vapor-filled atmosphere, which necessitated the playing of water into the fireroom from a hose.

2094 ♦ CUMMINS, ANDREW JOHNSON

Rank: Sergeant
Service: U.S. Army
Birthday: 1868
Place of Birth: Alexandria, Madison County, Indiana
Date of Death: 15 September 1923
Cemetery: Lewiston Cemetery—Lewiston, Montana
Entered Service at: Alexandria, Madison County, Indiana
Unit: Company F, 10th U.S. Infantry
Battle or Place of Action: Santiago, Cuba
Date of Action: 1 July 1898
Date of Issue: 22 June 1899
Citation: Gallantly assisted in the rescue of the wounded from in front of the lines and under heavy fire from the enemy.

2095 ♦ DAVIS, JOHN

Rank: Gunner's Mate Third Class (highest rank: Captain)
Service: U.S. Navy
Birthday: 28 October 1877
Place of Birth: Germany
Date of Death: 9 June 1970
Place of Death: St. Petersburg, Florida
Cemetery: Arlington National Cemetery (11-639-SS) (MH)—Arlington, Virginia
Entered Service at: New York, New York
Unit: U.S.S. *Marblehead*
Battle or Place of Action: Cienfuegos, Cuba
Date of Action: 11 May 1898
G.O. Number, Date: 521, 7 July 1899
Citation: On board the U.S.S. *Marblehead* during the operation of cutting the cable leading from Cienfuegos, Cuba, 11 May 1898. Facing the heavy fire of the enemy, Davis set an example of extraordinary bravery and coolness throughout this action.

2096 ◆ DEIGNAN, OSBORN WARREN

Rank: Coxswain (highest rank: Boatswain)
Service: U.S. Navy
Birthday: 24 February 1877
Place of Birth: Stuart, Guthrie County, Iowa
Date of Death: 16 April 1916
Place of Death: Cannon City, Colorado
Cemetery: Forest Lawn Memorial Park—Glendale, California
Entered Service at: Iowa
Unit: U.S.S. *Merrimac*
Battle or Place of Action: harbor entrance, Santiago de Cuba, Cuba
Date of Action: 3 June 1898
G.O. Number, Date: 529, 2 November 1899
Citation: In connection with the sinking of the U.S.S. *Merrimac* at the entrance to the harbor of Santiago de Cuba, 2 June 1898. Despite heavy fire from the Spanish batteries, Deignan displayed extraordinary heroism throughout this operation.
Notes: POW

2097 ◆ DESWAN, JOHN FRANCIS

Rank: Private
Service: U.S. Army
Birthday: 13 January 1876
Place of Birth: Philadelphia, Philadelphia County, Pennsylvania
Date of Death: 1 December 1956
Cemetery: Golden Gate National Cemetery (R-195-A)—San Bruno, California
Entered Service at: Philadelphia, Philadelphia County, Pennsylvania
Unit: Company H, 21st U.S. Infantry
Battle or Place of Action: Santiago, Cuba
Date of Action: 1 July 1898
Date of Issue: 22 June 1899
Citation: Gallantly assisted in the rescue of the wounded from in front of the lines and under heavy fire from the enemy.

2098 ◆ DOHERTY, THOMAS M.

Rank: Corporal (highest rank: Drum Major)
Service: U.S. Army
Birthday: 11 May 1869
Place of Birth: Mitchelstown, County Cork, Ireland
Date of Death: 21 September 1906
Place of Death: Fort Thomas, Kentucky
Cemetery: Evergreen Cemetery (U.S. Government Sec.)(MH)—Southgate, Kentucky
Entered Service at: Newcastle, Lincoln County, Maine
Unit: Company H, 21st U.S. Infantry
Battle or Place of Action: Santiago de Cuba, Cuba
Date of Action: 1 July 1898
Date of Issue: 22 June 1899
Citation: Gallantly assisted in the rescue of the wounded from in front of the lines and while under heavy fire from the enemy.

2099 ◆ DORAN, JOHN JAMES

Rank: Boatswain's Mate Second Class (highest rank: Chief Master-At-Arms)
Service: U.S. Navy
Birthday: 6 July 1864
Place of Birth: Boston, Suffolk County, Massachusetts
Date of Death: 16 February 1904
Place of Death: Santiago, Cuba
Cemetery: St. Patrick's Cemetery (MH)—Fall River, Massachusetts
Entered Service at: Massachusetts
Unit: U.S.S. *Marblehead*
Battle or Place of Action: Cienfuegos, Cuba
Date of Action: 11 May 1898
G.O. Number, Date: 521, 7 July 1899
Citation: On board the U.S.S. *Marblehead* during the operation of cutting the cable leading from Cienfuegos, Cuba, 11 May 1898. Facing the heavy fire of the enemy, Doran set an example of extraordinary bravery and coolness throughout this action.

2100 ◆ DURNEY, AUSTIN JOSEPH

Rank: Blacksmith
Service: U.S. Navy
Birthday: 26 November 1867
Place of Birth: Philadelphia, Philadelphia County, Pennsylvania
Date of Death: 17 November 1926
Place of Death: Ridgely, Maryland
Cemetery: St. Joseph's R.C. Cemetery—Cordova, Maryland
Entered Service at: Woodland, Maryland
Unit: U.S.S. *Nashville*
Battle or Place of Action: Cienfuegos, Cuba
Date of Action: 11 May 1898
G.O. Number, Date: 521, 7 July 1899
Citation: On board the U.S.S. *Nashville* during the operation of cutting the cable leading from Cienfuegos, Cuba, 11 May 1898. Facing the heavy fire of the enemy, Durney set an example of extraordinary bravery and coolness throughout this action.

2101 ◆ EGLIT, JOHN

Rank: Seaman
Service: U.S. Navy
Birthday: 17 October 1874
Place of Birth: Finland
Entered Service at: New York
Unit: U.S.S. *Nashville*
Battle or Place of Action: Cienfuegos, Cuba
Date of Action: 11 May 1898
G.O. Number, Date: 521, 7 July 1899
Citation: On board the U.S.S. *Nashville* during the operation of cutting the cable leading from Cienfuegos, Cuba, 11 May 1898. Facing the heavy fire of the enemy, Eglit set an example of extraordinary bravery and coolness throughout this action.

2102 ◆ EHLE, JOHN WALTER

Rank: Fireman First Class
Service: U.S. Navy
Birthday: 11 May 1873
Place of Birth: Kearney, Buffalo County, Nebraska
Date of Death: 25 July 1927
Place of Death: Presido of San Francisco, California
Cemetery: St. Mary's Cemetery—Oakland, California
Entered Service at: Nebraska
Unit: U.S.S. *Concord*
Battle or Place of Action: off Cavite, Manila Bay, Philippine Islands
Date of Action: 21 May 1898
G.O. Number, Date: 502, 14 December 1898
Citation: On board the U.S.S. *Concord* off Cavite, Manila Bay, P.I., 21 May 1898. Following the blowing-out of a lower manhole plate joint on boiler B of that vessel, Ehle assisted in hauling the fires in the hot, vapor-filled atmosphere, which necessitated the playing of water into the fireroom from a hose.

2103 ◆ ERICKSON, NICHOLAS

Rank: Coxswain
Service: U.S. Navy
Birthday: 18 July 1870
Place of Birth: Finland
Date of Death: 21 June 1931
Place of Death: New York, New York
Cemetery: Woodlawn Cemetery—Bronx, New York
Entered Service at: New York
Unit: U.S.S. *Marblehead*
Battle or Place of Action: Cienfuegos, Cuba
Date of Action: 11 May 1898
G.O. Number, Date: 521, 7 July 1899
Citation: On board the U.S.S. *Marblehead* during the operation of cutting the cable leading from Cienfuegos, Cuba, 11 May 1898. Facing the heavy fire of the enemy, Erickson set an example of extraordinary bravery and coolness throughout this action.

2104 ◆ FIELD, OSCAR WADSWORTH

Rank: Private (highest rank: Quartermaster Sergeant)
Service: U.S. Marine Corps
Birthday: 6 October 1873
Place of Birth: Jersey City, Hudson County, New Jersey
Date of Death: 5 January 1912
Cemetery: Dayton National Cemetery (0-Q-A9) (MH)—Dayton, Ohio
Entered Service at: New York
Unit: U.S.S. *Nashville*
Battle or Place of Action: Cienfuegos, Cuba
Date of Action: 11 May 1898
G.O. Number, Date: 521, 7 July 1899
Date of Issue: 19 August 1899
Citation: On board the U.S.S. *Nashville* during the operation of cutting the cable leading from Cienfuegos, Cuba, 11 May 1898. Facing the heavy fire of the enemy, Field set an example of extraordinary bravery and coolness throughout this action.

2105 ◆ FITZGERALD, JOHN

Rank: Private (highest rank: Gunnery Sergeant)
Service: U.S. Marine Corps
Birthday: 17 March 1873
Place of Birth: Limerick, Ireland
Date of Death: 19 April 1948
Cemetery: Holy Cross Cemetery—Brooklyn, New York
Entered Service at: New York
Battle or Place of Action: Cuzco, Cuba
Date of Action: 14 June 1898
G.O. Number, Date: 92, 8 December 1910
Citation: For heroism and gallantry in action at Cuzco, Cuba, 14 June 1898.

2106 ◆ FOSS, HERBERT LOUIS

Rank: Seaman
Service: U.S. Navy
Birthday: 12 October 1871
Place of Birth: Belfast, Waldo County, Maine
Date of Death: 1 September 1937
Cemetery: Forest Hill Cemetery (MH)—Hingman, Massachusetts
Entered Service at: Maine
Unit: U.S.S. *Marblehead*
Battle or Place of Action: Cienfuegos, Cuba
Date of Action: 11 May 1898
G.O. Number, Date: 521, 7 July 1899
Citation: On board the U.S.S. *Marblehead* during the operation of cutting the cable leading from Cienfuegos, Cuba, 11 May 1898. Facing the heavy fire of the enemy, Foss set an example of extraordinary bravery and coolness throughout this action.

2107 ◆ FOURNIA, FRANK OTTIS

Rank: Private
Service: U.S. Army
Birthday: January 1873
Place of Birth: Rome, Oneida County, New York
Entered Service at: Plattsburgh, Clinton County, New York
Unit: Company H, 21st U.S. Infantry
Battle or Place of Action: Santiago, Cuba
Date of Issue: 22 June 1899
Citation: Gallantly assisted in the rescue of the wounded from in front of the lines and while under heavy fire of the enemy.

2108 ◆ FRANKLIN, JOSEPH JOHN

Rank: Private (highest rank: Marine Gunner)
Service: U.S. Marine Corps
Birthday: 18 June 1870
Place of Birth: Buffalo, Erie County, New York

Date of Death: 28 April 1940
Place of Death: Philadelphia, Pennsylvania
Cemetery: Cypress Hills Cemetery—Brooklyn, New York
Entered Service at: New York
Unit: U.S.S. *Nashville*
Battle or Place of Action: Cienfuegos, Cuba
Date of Action: 11 May 1898
G.O. Number, Date: 521, 7 July 1899
Citation: On board the U.S.S. *Nashville* during the operation of cutting the cable leading from Cienfuegos, Cuba, 11 May 1898. Facing the heavy fire of the enemy, Franklin set an example of extraordinary bravery and coolness throughout this action.

2109 ◆ GAUGHAN, PHILIP

Rank: Sergeant (highest rank: First Sergeant)
Service: U.S. Marine Corps
Birthday: 17 March 1865
Place of Birth: Belmullet, County Mayo, Ireland
Date of Death: 31 December 1913
Place of Death: Philadelphia, Pennsylvania
Cemetery: Holy Cross Cemetery (MH)—Yeadon, Pennsylvania
Entered Service at: Pennsylvania
Unit: U.S.S. *Nashville*
Battle or Place of Action: Cienfuegos, Cuba
Date of Action: 11 May 1898
G.O. Number, Date: 521, 7 July 1899
Citation: On board the U.S.S. *Nashville* during the operation of cutting the cable leading from Cienfuegos, Cuba, 11 May 1898. Facing the heavy fire of the enemy, Gaughan set an example of extraordinary bravery and coolness throughout this action.

2110 ◆ GIBBONS, MICHAEL

Rank: Oiler (highest rank: Fireman First Class)
Service: U.S. Navy
Birthday: 15 November 1866
Place of Birth: Ireland
Date of Death: 27 February 1933
Place of Death: Rosow, Kilmeena, Westport, County Mayo, Ireland
Entered Service at: New York
Unit: U.S.S. *Nashville*
Battle or Place of Action: Cienfuegos, Cuba
Date of Action: 11 May 1898
G.O. Number, Date: 521, 7 July 1899
Citation: On board the U.S.S. *Nashville* during the operation of cutting the cable leading from Cienfuegos, Cuba, 11 May 1898. Facing the heavy fire of the enemy, Gibbons set an example of extraordinary bravery and coolness throughout this action.

2111 ◆ GILL, FREEMAN

Rank: Gunner's Mate First Class
Service: U.S. Navy
Birthday: 5 September 1851
Place of Birth: Boston, Suffolk County, Massachusetts
Date of Death: 8 April 1905
Place of Death: Chelsea, Massachusetts
Cemetery: Woodlawn Cemetery (MH)—Everett, Massachusetts
Entered Service at: Massachusetts
Unit: U.S.S. *Marblehead*
Battle or Place of Action: Cienfuegos, Cuba
Date of Action: 11 May 1898
G.O. Number, Date: 55, 19 July 1901
Citation: On board the U.S.S. *Marblehead* during the operation of cutting the cable leading from Cienfuegos, Cuba, 11 May 1898. Facing the heavy fire of the enemy, Gill set an example of extraordinary bravery and coolness throughout this action.

2112 ◆ GRAVES, THOMAS J.

Rank: Private (highest rank: Quartermaster Sergeant)
Service: U.S. Army
Birthday: 29 September 1866
Place of Birth: Milton, Wayne County, Indiana
Date of Death: 27 January 1944
Cemetery: Zion Lutheran Cemetery—Pershing, Indiana
Entered Service at: Millville, Indiana
Unit: Company C, 17th U.S. Infantry
Battle or Place of Action: El Caney, Cuba
Date of Action: 1 July 1898
Date of Issue: 22 June 1899
Citation: Gallantly assisted in the rescue of the wounded from in front of the lines and under heavy fire from the enemy.

2113 ◆ HARDAWAY, BENJAMIN FRANKLIN

Rank: First Lieutenant (highest rank: Colonel)
Service: U.S. Army
Birthday: 17 July 1865
Place of Birth: Benleyville, Kentucky
Date of Death: 9 July 1955
Cemetery: Arlington National Cemetery (2-1044-1)—Arlington, Virginia
Entered Service at: Fort Totten, Benson County, Dakota Territory
Unit: 17th U.S. Infantry
Battle or Place of Action: El Caney, Cuba
Date of Action: 1 July 1898
Date of Issue: 21 June 1899
Citation: Gallantly assisted in the rescue of the wounded from in front of the lines and under heavy fire from the enemy.

2114 ◆ HART, WILLIAM

Rank: Machinist First Class
Service: U.S. Navy
Birthday: 9 June 1866
Place of Birth: Massachusetts

Date of Death: 6 February 1899
Cemetery: The Green Wood Cemetery—Brooklyn, New York
Entered Service at: Massachusetts
Unit: U.S.S. *Marblehead*
Battle or Place of Action: Cienfuegos, Cuba
Date of Action: 11 May 1898
G.O. Number, Date: 521, 7 July 1899
Citation: On board the U.S.S. *Marblehead* during the operation of cutting the cable leading from Cienfuegos, Cuba, 11 May 1898. Facing the heavy fire of the enemy, Hart set an example of extraordinary bravery and coolness throughout this action.

2115 ◆ HEARD, JOHN WILLIAM

Rank: First Lieutenant (highest rank: Brigadier General)
Service: U.S. Army
Birthday: 27 March 1860
Place of Birth: Woodstock, Mississippi
Date of Death: 4 February 1922
Place of Death: New Orleans, Louisiana
Cemetery: U.S. Military Academy Cemetery (8-39)—West Point, New York
Entered Service at: Mississippi
Unit: 3d U.S. Cavalry
Battle or Place of Action: at mouth of Manimani River, west of Bahia Honda, Cuba
Date of Action: 23 July 1898
Date of Issue: 21 June 1899
Citation: After two men had been shot down by Spaniards while transmitting orders to the engine-room on the *Wanderer*, the ship having become disabled, this officer took the position held by them and personally transmitted the orders, remaining at his post until the ship was out of danger.

2116 ◆ HENDRICKSON, HENRY

Rank: Seaman
Service: U.S. Navy
Birthday: 12 March 1862
Place of Birth: Germany
Unit: U.S.S. *Marblehead*
Battle or Place of Action: Cienfuegos, Cuba
Date of Action: 11 May 1898
G.O. Number, Date: 521, 7 July 1899
Citation: On board the U.S.S. *Marblehead* during the operation of cutting the cable leading from Cienfuegos, Cuba, 11 May 1898. Facing the heavy fire of the enemy, Hendrickson displayed extraordinary bravery and coolness throughout this action.

2117 ◆ HILL, FRANK

Rank: Private
Service: U.S. Marine Corps
Birthday: 13 August 1864
Place of Birth: Hartford, Hartford County, Connecticut
Entered Service at: Connecticut
Unit: U.S.S. *Nashville*
Battle or Place of Action: Cienfuegos, Cuba
Date of Action: 11 May 1898
G.O. Number, Date: 521, 7 July 1899
Date of Issue: 15 August 1899
Citation: On board the U.S.S. *Nashville* during the operation of cutting the cable leading from Cienfuegos, Cuba, 11 May 1898. Facing the heavy fire of the enemy, Hill displayed extraordinary bravery and coolness throughout this action.

2118 ◆ HOBAN, THOMAS

Rank: Coxswain
Service: U.S. Navy
Birthday: 11 September 1872
Place of Birth: New York, New York
Entered Service at: New York
Unit: U.S.S. *Nashville*
Battle or Place of Action: Cienfuegos, Cuba
Date of Action: 11 May 1898
G.O. Number, Date: 521, 7 July 1899
Citation: On board the U.S.S. *Nashville* during the operation of cutting the cable leading from Cienfuegos, Cuba, 11 May 1898. Facing the heavy fire of the enemy, Hobin displayed extraordinary bravery and coolness throughout this action.

2119 ◆ HOBSON, RICHMOND PEARSON

Rank: Lieutenant (highest rank: Rear Admiral)
Service: U.S. Navy
Birthday: 17 August 1870
Place of Birth: Greensboro, Hale County, Alabama
Date of Death: 16 March 1937
Place of Death: New York, New York
Cemetery: Arlington National Cemetery (6-5014)—Arlington, Virginia
Entered Service at: New York
Unit: U.S.S. *Merrimac*
Battle or Place of Action: harbor entrance, Santiago de Cuba, Cuba
Date of Action: 3 June 1898
Date of Presentation: 29 April 1933
Place of Presentation: Presented by Pres. Franklin D. Roosevelt
Citation: In connection with the sinking of the U.S.S. *Merrimac* at the entrance to the fortified harbor of Santiago de Cuba, 3 June 1898. Despite persistent fire from the enemy fleet and fortifications onshore, Lt. Hobson distinguished himself by extraordinary courage and carried out this operation at the risk of his own personal safety.
Notes: POW

2120 ◆ HULL, JAMES LOTT

Rank: Fireman First Class
Service: U.S. Navy
Birthday: 27 November 1873
Place of Birth: Patoka, Marion County, Illinois

Date of Death: 25 July 1928
Cemetery: Haven Hill Cemetery—Olney, Illinois
Entered Service at: Illinois
Unit: U.S.S. *Concord*
Battle or Place of Action: off Cavite, Manila Bay, Philippine Islands
Date of Action: 21 May 1898
G.O. Number, Date: 502, 14 December 1898
Citation: On board the U.S.S. *Concord* off Cavite, Manila Bay, P.I., 21 May 1898. Following the blowing-out of a lower manhole plate joint on boiler B of that vessel, Hull assisted in hauling the fires in the hot, vapor-filled atmosphere, which necessitated the playing of water into the fireroom from a hose.

2121 ◆ ITRICH, FRANZ ANTON

Rank: Chief Carpenter's Mate (highest rank: Chief Gunner)
Service: U.S. Navy
Birthday: 26 November 1853
Place of Birth: Gross Katz, Germany
Date of Death: 11 June 1933
Cemetery: San Francisco National Cemetery (OSA-83-5)—San Francisco, California
Entered Service at: California
Unit: U.S.S. *Petrel*
Battle or Place of Action: Manila, Philippine Islands
Date of Action: 1 May 1898
G.O. Number, Date: 13, 5 December 1900
Citation: On board the U.S.S. *Petrel*, Manila, Philippine Islands, 1 May 1898. Serving in the presence of the enemy, Itrich displayed heroism during the action.

2122 ◆ JOHANSON, JOHN PETER

Rank: Seaman (highest rank: Chief Boatswain's Mate)
Service: U.S. Navy
Birthday: 22 January 1865
Place of Birth: Oskarshamn, Sweden
Date of Death: 14 December 1937
Cemetery: Arlington National Cemetery (6-9768) (MH)—Arlington, Virginia
Entered Service at: Maryland
Unit: U.S.S. *Marblehead*
Battle or Place of Action: Cienfuegos, Cuba
Date of Action: 11 May 1898
G.O. Number, Date: 529, 21 November 1899
Citation: On board the U.S.S. *Marblehead* during the operation of cutting the cable leading from Cienfuegos, Cuba, 11 May 1898. Facing the heavy fire of the enemy, Johanson set an example of extraordinary bravery and coolness throughout this action.

2123 ◆ JOHANSSON, JOHAN J.

Rank: Ordinary Seaman
Service: U.S. Navy
Birthday: 12 May 1870

Place of Birth: Sweden
Date of Death: 4 December 1948
Cemetery: Arlington National Cemetery (13-720) (MH)—Arlington, Virginia
Entered Service at: New York
Unit: U.S.S. *Nashville*
Battle or Place of Action: Cienfuegos, Cuba
Date of Action: 11 May 1898
G.O. Number, Date: 521, 7 July 1899
Citation: On board the U.S.S. *Nashville* during the operation of cutting the cable leading from Cienfuegos, Cuba, 11 May 1898. Facing the heavy fire of the enemy, Johansson set an example of extraordinary bravery and coolness throughout this action.

2124 ◆ JOHNSEN, HANS

Rank: Chief Machinist (highest rank: Lieutenant)
Service: U.S. Navy
Birthday: 3 January 1865
Place of Birth: Sandnes, Norway
Date of Death: 17 June 1920
Cemetery: Bayview Cemetery (MH)—Jersey City, New Jersey
Entered Service at: Pennsylvania
Unit: U.S. Torpedo Boat *Winslow*
Battle or Place of Action: Cardenas, Cuba
Date of Action: 11 May 1898
G.O. Number, Date: 497, 3 September 1899
Citation: On board the torpedo boat *Winslow* during the actions at Cardenas, Cuba, 11 May 1898. Showing great presence of mind, Johnsen turned off the steam from the engine which had been wrecked by a shell bursting in the cylinder.

2125 ◆ JOHNSON, PETER

Rank: Fireman First Class
Service: U.S. Navy
Birthday: 29 December 1857
Place of Birth: Sumerland, England
Entered Service at: Pennsylvania
Unit: U.S.S. *Vixen*
Date of Action: 28 May 1898
G.O. Number, Date: 167, 27 August 1904
Citation: On board the U.S.S. *Vixen* on the night of 28 May 1898. Following the explosion of the lower front manhole gasket of boiler A of the vessel, Johnson displayed great coolness and self-possession in entering the fireroom.

2126 ◆ KEARNEY, MICHAEL

Rank: Private (highest rank: Captain)
Service: U.S. Marine Corps
Birthday: 4 October 1874
Place of Birth: Newmarket, County Cork, Ireland
Date of Death: 31 October 1937
Place of Death: Brooklyn, New York
Cemetery: Holy Cross Cemetery—Brooklyn, New York

Entered Service at: Massachusetts
Unit: U.S.S. *Nashville*
Battle or Place of Action: Cienfuegos, Cuba
Date of Action: 11 May 1898
G.O. Number, Date: 521, 7 July 1899
Citation: On board the U.S.S. *Nashville* during the operation of cutting the cable leading from Cienfuegos, Cuba, 11 May 1898. Facing the heavy fire of the enemy, Kearney set an example of extraordinary bravery and coolness throughout this action.

2127 ◆ KEEFER, PHILIP BOGAN

Rank: Coppersmith
Service: U.S. Navy
Birthday: 4 September 1875
Place of Birth: Washington, D.C.
Date of Death: 15 January 1949
Cemetery: Arlington National Cemetery (11-527-SH) (MH)—Arlington, Virginia
Entered Service at: Washington, D.C.
Unit: U.S.S. *Iowa*
Battle or Place of Action: Santiago de Cuba, Cuba
Date of Action: 20 July 1898
G.O. Number, Date: 501, 14 December 1898
Citation: On board the U.S.S. *Iowa* off Santiago de Cuba, 20 July 1898. Following the blow-out of a manhole gasket of that vessel which caused the fireroom to be filled with live steam and the floor plates to be covered with boiling water, Keefer showed courageous and zealous conduct in hauling fires from two furnaces of boiler B.

2128 ◆ KELLER, WILLIAM G.

Rank: Private (highest rank: Corporal)
Service: U.S. Army
Birthday: 19 April 1876
Place of Birth: Buffalo, Erie County, New York
Date of Death: 20 September 1963
Place of Death: Sarasota, Florida
Cemetery: Lakeview Cemetery—Cleveland, Ohio
Entered Service at: Buffalo, Erie County, New York
Unit: Company F, 10th U.S. Infantry
Battle or Place of Action: Santiago de Cuba, Cuba
Date of Action: 1 July 1898
Date of Issue: 22 June 1899
Citation: Gallantly assisted in the rescue of the wounded from in front of the lines and under heavy fire of the enemy.

2129 ◆ KELLY, FRANCIS

Rank: Watertender (highest rank: Chief Machinist's Mate)
Service: U.S. Navy
Birthday: 5 July 1860
Place of Birth: Boston, Suffolk County, Massachusetts
Date of Death: 19 May 1938
Place of Death: Glasgow, Scotland
Cemetery: Sandymount Cemetery—Glasgow, Scotland
Entered Service at: Massachusetts
Unit: U.S.S. *Merrimac*
Battle or Place of Action: harbor entrance, Santiago de Cuba, Cuba
Date of Action: 3 June 1898
G.O. Number, Date: 529, 2 November 1899
Citation: In connection with the sinking of the U.S.S. *Merrimac* at the entrance to the harbor of Santiago de Cuba, 3 June 1898. Despite heavy fire from the Spanish batteries, Kelly displayed extraordinary heroism throughout this operation.
Notes: POW

2130 ◆ KELLY, THOMAS

Rank: Private
Service: U.S. Army
Place of Birth: Ireland
Date of Death: 17 December 1920
Cemetery: Post Barracks Cemetery (Q6) (MH)—Plattsburg, New York
Entered Service at: New York
Unit: Company H, 21st U.S. Infantry
Battle or Place of Action: Santiago de Cuba, Cuba
Date of Action: 1 July 1898
Date of Issue: 22 June 1899
Citation: Gallantly assisted in the rescue of the wounded from in front of the lines and while under heavy fire from the enemy.

2131 ◆ KRAMER, FRANZ

Rank: Seaman
Service: U.S. Navy
Birthday: 20 January 1865
Place of Birth: Nierstein, Germany
Date of Death: 18 April 1924
Place of Death: New York, New York
Cemetery: Calvary Cemetery—Woodside, New York
Entered Service at: Massachusetts
Unit: U.S.S. *Marblehead*
Battle or Place of Action: Cienfuegos, Cuba
Date of Action: 11 May 1898
G.O. Number, Date: 521, 7 July 1899
Citation: On board the U.S.S. *Marblehead* during the operation of cutting the cable leading from Cienfuegos, Cuba, 11 May 1898. Facing the heavy fire of the enemy, Kramer set an example of extraordinary bravery and coolness throughout this action.

2132 ◆ KRAUSE, ERNEST

Rank: Coxswain (highest rank: Gunner's Mate)
Service: U.S. Navy
Birthday: 3 July 1866
Place of Birth: Lubeck, Germany
Entered Service at: New York
Unit: U.S.S. *Nashville*
Battle or Place of Action: Cienfuegos, Cuba
Date of Action: 11 May 1898

G.O. Number, Date: 521, 7 July 1899
Citation: On board the U.S.S. *Nashville* during the operation of cutting the cable leading from Cienfuegos, Cuba, 11 May 1898. Facing the heavy fire of the enemy, Krause displayed extraordinary bravery and coolness throughout this action.

2133 ◆ KUCHNEISTER, HERMANN WILHELM

Rank: Private (highest rank: Corporal)
Service: U.S. Marine Corps
Birthday: 16 October 1877
Place of Birth: Hamburg, Germany
Date of Death: 1 February 1923
Cemetery: Winthrop Cemetery (MH)—Winthrop, Massachusetts
Entered Service at: New York
Unit: U.S.S. *Marblehead*
Battle or Place of Action: Cienfuegos, Cuba
Date of Action: 11 May 1898
G.O. Number, Date: 521, 7 July 1899
Citation: On board the U.S.S. *Marblehead* during the operation of cutting the cable leading from Cienfuegos, Cuba, 11 May 1898. Facing the heavy fire of the enemy, Kuchneister displayed extraordinary bravery and coolness throughout this action.

2134 ◆ LEE, FITZ

Rank: Private
Service: U.S. Army
Birthday: June 1866
Place of Birth: Dinwiddie County, Virginia
Date of Death: 14 September 1899
Place of Death: Leavenworth, Kansas
Cemetery: Leavenworth National Cemetery (G-3183) (MH)—Leavenworth, Kansas
Entered Service at: Philadelphia, Philadelphia County, Pennsylvania
Unit: Troop M, 10th U.S. Cavalry
Battle or Place of Action: Tayabacoa, Cuba
Date of Action: 30 June 1898
Date of Issue: 23 June 1899
Citation: Voluntarily went ashore in the face of the enemy and aided in the rescue of his wounded comrades; this after several previous attempts had been frustrated.

2135 ◆ LEVERY, WILLIAM

Rank: Apprentice First Class
Service: U.S. Navy
Birthday: 30 June 1879
Place of Birth: Philadelphia, Philadelphia County, Pennsylvania
Entered Service at: Pennsylvania
Unit: U.S.S. *Marblehead*
Battle or Place of Action: Cienfuegos, Cuba
Date of Action: 11 May 1898
G.O. Number, Date: 521, 7 July 1899
Citation: On board the U.S.S. *Marblehead* during the operation of cutting the cable leading from Cienfuegos, Cuba, 11 May 1989. Facing the heavy fire of the enemy, Levery displayed extraordinary bravery and coolness throughout this action.

2136 ◆ MACNEAL, HARRY LEWIS

Rank: Private (highest rank: Corporal)
Service: U.S. Marine Corps
Birthday: 22 March 1879
Place of Birth: Philadelphia, Philadelphia County, Pennsylvania
Date of Death: 13 March 1950
Cemetery: East Ridge Lawn Cemetery (MH)—Delawanna, New Jersey
Entered Service at: Pennsylvania
Unit: U.S.S. *Brooklyn*
Battle or Place of Action: Santiago de Cuba, Cuba
Date of Action: 3 July 1898
G.O. Number, Date: 526, 9 August 1899
Citation: On board the U.S.S. *Brooklyn* during action at the Battle of Santiago de Cuba, 3 July 1898. Braving the fire of the enemy, MacNeal displayed gallantry throughout this action.

2137 ◆ MAGER, GEORGE FREDERICK

Rank: Apprentice First Class
Service: U.S. Navy
Birthday: 23 February 1875
Place of Birth: Phillipsburg, Warren County, New Jersey
Date of Death: 12 April 1938
Cemetery: Greenwood Cemetery—Trenton, New Jersey
Entered Service at: New Jersey
Unit: U.S.S. *Marblehead*
Battle or Place of Action: Cienfuegos, Cuba
Date of Action: 11 May 1898
G.O. Number, Date: 529, 2 November 1899
Citation: On board the U.S.S. *Marblehead* during the operation of cutting the cable leading from Cienfuegos, Cuba, 11 May 1898. Facing the heavy fire of the enemy, Mager displayed extraordinary bravery and coolness throughout this action.

2138 ◆ MAHONEY, GEORGE

Rank: Fireman First Class
Service: U.S. Navy
Birthday: 15 January 1865
Place of Birth: Worcester, Worcester County, Massachusetts
Entered Service at: Pennsylvania
Unit: U.S.S. *Vixen*
Date of Action: 28 May 1898
G.O. Number, Date: 167, 27 August 1904
Citation: On board the U.S.S. *Vixen* on the night of 28 May 1898. Following the explosion of the lower front manhole gasket of boiler A of the vessel, Mahoney displayed great coolness and self-possession in entering the fireroom.

2139 ◆ MAXWELL, JOHN

Rank: Fireman Second Class (highest rank: Oiler)
Service: U.S. Navy
Birthday: 26 June 1874
Place of Birth: Brooklyn, Kings County, New York
Date of Death: 13 November 1931
Place of Death: Westbury, New York
Cemetery: Friends Cemetery—Westbury, New York
Entered Service at: New York
Unit: U.S.S. *Marblehead*
Battle or Place of Action: Cienfuegos, Cuba
Date of Action: 11 May 1898
G.O. Number, Date: 521, 7 July 1899
Citation: On board the U.S.S. *Marblehead* during the operation of cutting the cable leading from Cienfuegos, Cuba, 11 May 1898. Facing the heavy fire of the enemy, Maxwell displayed extraordinary bravery and coolness throughout this action.

2140 ◆ MEREDITH, JAMES

True Name: Ford Jr., Patrick F.
Rank: Private (highest rank: Sergeant)
Service: U.S. Marine Corps
Birthday: 11 April 1872
Place of Birth: Omaha, Douglas County, Nebraska
Date of Death: 18 January 1915
Cemetery: St. Mary's Cemetery—South Omaha, Nebraska
Entered Service at: Boston, Suffolk County, Massachusetts
Unit: U.S.S. *Marblehead*
Battle or Place of Action: Cienfuegos, Cuba
Date of Action: 11 May 1898
G.O. Number, Date: 521, 7 July 1899
Date of Issue: 15 August 1899
Citation: On board the U.S.S. *Marblehead* during the operation of cutting the cable leading from Cienfuegos, Cuba, 11 May 1898. Facing the heavy fire of the enemy, Meredith displayed extraordinary bravery and coolness throughout this action.

2141 ◆ MEYER, WILLIAM

Rank: Carpenter's Mate Third Class (highest rank: Carpenter Third Class)
Service: U.S. Navy
Birthday: 22 June 1863
Place of Birth: Germany
Date of Death: 6 September 1926
Place of Death: Chicago, Illinois
Cemetery: Forest Home Cemetery—Chicago, Illinois
Entered Service at: Illinois
Unit: U.S.S. *Nashville*
Battle or Place of Action: Cienfuegos, Cuba
Date of Action: 11 May 1898
G.O. Number, Date: 521, 7 July 1899
Citation: On board the U.S.S. *Nashville* during the operation of cutting the cable leading from Cienfuegos, Cuba, 11 May 1898. Facing the heavy fire of the enemy, Meyer displayed extraordinary bravery and coolness throughout this action.

2142 ◆ MILLER, HARRY HERBERT

Rank: Seaman (highest rank: Quartermaster Third Class)
Service: U.S. Navy
Birthday: 4 May 1879
Place of Birth: Noel Shore, Hants County, Nova Scotia, Canada
Date of Death: 12 March 1968
Place of Death: Costa Rica
Cemetery: Central Cemetery (MH)—Tres De Rios, Costa Rica
Entered Service at: Massachusetts
Unit: U.S.S. *Nashville*
Battle or Place of Action: Cienfuegos, Cuba
Date of Action: 11 May 1898
G.O. Number, Date: 521, 7 July 1899
Citation: On board the U.S.S. *Nashville* during the operation of cutting the cable leading from Cienfuegos, Cuba, 11 May 1898. Facing the heavy fire of the enemy, Miller displayed extraordinary bravery and coolness throughout this action.

2143 ◆ MILLER, WILLARD D.

Rank: Seaman
Service: U.S. Navy
Birthday: 5 June 1877
Place of Birth: Noel Shore, Hants County, Nova Scotia, Canada
Date of Death: 19 February 1959
Cemetery: Arlington National Cemetery (46-15) (MH)—Arlington, Virginia
Entered Service at: Massachusetts
Unit: U.S.S. *Nashville*
Battle or Place of Action: Cienfuegos, Cuba
Date of Action: 11 May 1898
G.O. Number, Date: 521, 7 July 1899
Citation: On board the U.S.S. *Nashville* during the operation of cutting the cable leading from Cienfuegos, Cuba, 11 May 1898. Facing the heavy fire of the enemy, Miller displayed extraordinary bravery and coolness throughout this action.

2144 ◆ MILLS, ALBERT LEOPOLD

Rank: Captain & Assistant Adjutant General (highest rank: Major General)
Service: U.S. Army
Birthday: 7 May 1854
Place of Birth: New York City (Washington Heights), New York
Date of Death: 18 September 1916
Place of Death: Washington, D.C.
Cemetery: U.S. Military Academy Cemetery (4-7)—West Point, New York
Entered Service at: New York, New York

Unit: U.S. Volunteers
Battle or Place of Action: near Santiago, Cuba
Date of Action: 1 July 1898
Date of Issue: 9 July 1902
Citation: Distinguished gallantry in encouraging those near him by his bravery and coolness after being shot though the head and entirely without sight.

2145 ◆ MONTAGUE, DANIEL

Rank: Chief Master-at-Arms (highest rank: Chief Boatswain)
Service: U.S. Navy
Birthday: 22 October 1867
Place of Birth: Wicklow, Ireland
Date of Death: 4 February 1912
Cemetery: U.S. Naval Academy Cemetery (275)—Annapolis, Maryland
Unit: U.S.S. *Merrimac*—assigned to the U.S.S. *New York*
Battle or Place of Action: harbor entrance, Santiago de Cuba, Cuba
Date of Action: 3 June 1898
G.O. Number, Date: 529, 2 November 1899
Citation: In connection with the sinking of the U.S.S. *Merrimac* at the entrance to the harbor of Santiago de Cuba, 3 June 1898. Despite heavy fire from the Spanish batteries, Montague displayed extraordinary heroism throughout this operation.
Notes: POW

2146 ◆ MORIN, WILLIAM HENRY

Rank: Boatswain's Mate Second Class (highest rank: Boatswain)
Service: U.S. Navy
Birthday: 23 May 1868
Place of Birth: Birmingham, West Midlands County, England
Date of Death: 29 August 1935
Place of Death: Staten Island, New York
Cemetery: St. John's Cemetery—Middle Village, New York
Entered Service at: New York
Unit: U.S.S. *Marblehead*
Battle or Place of Action: approaches to Caimanera, Guantanamo Bay, Cuba
Date of Action: 26-27 July 1898
G.O. Number, Date: 500, 14 December 1898
Citation: On board the U.S.S. *Marblehead* at the approaches to Caimanera, Guantanamo Bay, Cuba, 26 and 27 July 1898. Displaying heroism, Morin took part in the perilous work of sweeping for and disabling 27 contact mines during this period.

2147 ◆ MULLER, FREDERICK

Rank: Mate (highest rank: Lieutenant Commander)
Service: U.S. Navy
Birthday: 29 March 1861
Place of Birth: Copenhagen, Denmark
Date of Death: 9 June 1946
Cemetery: Arlington National Cemetery (8-6035)—Arlington, Virginia
Entered Service at: Massachusetts
Unit: U.S.S. *Wompatuck*
Battle or Place of Action: Manzanillo, Cuba
Date of Action: 30 June 1898
G.O. Number, Date: 45, 30 April 1901
Citation: On board the U.S.S. *Wompatuck*, Manzanillo, Cuba, 30 June 1898. Serving under the fire of the enemy, Muller displayed heroism and gallantry during this period.

2148 ◆ MURPHY, JOHN EDWARD

Rank: Coxswain
Service: U.S. Navy
Birthday: 3 May 1869
Place of Birth: Ireland
Date of Death: 9 April 1941
Cemetery: Fort Rosecrans National Cemetery (OS-363) (MH)—San Diego, California
Entered Service at: New York
Unit: U.S.S. *Merrimac*—assigned to the U.S.S. *Iowa*
Battle or Place of Action: harbor entrance, Santiago de Cuba, Cuba
Date of Action: 3 June 1898
G.O. Number, Date: 529, 2 November 1899
Citation: In connection with the sinking of the U.S.S. *Merrimac* at the entrance to the harbor of Santiago de Cuba, 3 June 1898. Despite heavy fire from the Spanish shore batteries, Murphy displayed extraordinary heroism throughout this operation.
Notes: POW

2149 ◆ NASH, JAMES J.

Rank: Private (highest rank: First Sergeant)
Service: U.S. Army
Birthday: 1875
Place of Birth: Louisville, Jefferson County, Kentucky
Date of Death: 11 June 1927
Cemetery: San Antonio National Cemetery (T-1461-A) (MH)—San Antonio, Texas
Entered Service at: Louisville, Jefferson County, Kentucky
Unit: Company F, 10th U.S. Infantry
Battle or Place of Action: Santiago, Cuba
Date of Action: 1 July 1898
Date of Issue: 22 June 1899
Citation: Gallantly assisted in the rescue of the wounded from in front of the lines and under heavy fire from the enemy.

2150 ◆ NEE, GEORGE HENRY

Rank: Private (highest rank: Sergeant)
Service: U.S. Army
Birthday: 12 March 1876
Place of Birth: Boston, Suffolk County, Massachusetts
Date of Death: 4 March 1952
Place of Death: Boston, Massachusetts

Cemetery: Forest Hills Cemetery—Boston, Massachusetts
Entered Service at: Boston, Suffolk County, Massachusetts
Unit: Company H, 21st U.S. Infantry
Battle or Place of Action: Santiago, Cuba
Date of Action: 1 July 1898
Date of Issue: 22 June 1899
Citation: Gallantly assisted in the rescue of the wounded from in front of the lines and under heavy fire from the enemy.

2151 ◆ NELSON, LAURITZ

Rank: Sailmaker's Mate (highest rank: Chief Boatswain's Mate)
Service: U.S. Navy
Birthday: 26 March 1860
Place of Birth: Norway
Date of Death: 19 September 1941
Cemetery: Long Island National Cemetery (DSS-2) (MH)—Farmingdale, New York
Unit: U.S.S. *Nashville*
Battle or Place of Action: Cienfuegos, Cuba
Date of Action: 11 May 1898
G.O. Number, Date: 521, 7 July 1899
Citation: On board the U.S.S. *Nashville* during the operation of cutting the cable leading from Cienfuegos, Cuba, 11 May 1898. Facing the heavy fire of the enemy, Nelson displayed extraordinary bravery and coolness throughout this action.

2152 ◆ OAKLEY, WILLIAM

Rank: Gunner's Mate Second Class
Service: U.S. Navy
Birthday: 25 August 1860
Place of Birth: Colchester, Essex County, England
Entered Service at: New York
Unit: U.S.S. *Marblehead*
Battle or Place of Action: Cienfuegos, Cuba
Date of Action: 11 May 1898
G.O. Number, Date: 521, 7 July 1899
Citation: On board the U.S.S. *Marblehead* during the operation of cutting the cable leading from Cienfuegos, Cuba, 11 May 1898. Facing the heavy fire of the enemy, Oakley displayed extraordinary bravery and coolness throughout this period.

2153 ◆ OLSEN, ANTON

Rank: Ordinary Seaman (highest rank: Quartermaster Third Class)
Service: U.S. Navy
Birthday: 13 July 1873
Place of Birth: Christiana (now Oslo), Norway
Date of Death: 23 June 1924
Cemetery: Cypress Hills National Cemetery (2-9158) (MH)—Brooklyn, New York
Entered Service at: Massachusetts
Unit: U.S.S. *Marblehead*
Battle or Place of Action: Cienfuegos, Cuba
Date of Action: 11 May 1898
G.O. Number, Date: 529, 2 November 1899
Citation: On board the U.S.S. *Marblehead* during the operation of cutting the cable leading from Cienfuegos, Cuba, 11 May 1898. Facing the heavy fire of the enemy, Olsen displayed extraordinary bravery and coolness throughout this period.

2154 ◆ PARKER, POMEROY

Rank: Private
Service: U.S. Marine Corps
Birthday: 17 March 1874
Place of Birth: Gates County, North Carolina
Date of Death: 30 December 1946
Place of Death: Savannah, Georgia
Cemetery: Roxobel-Kelford Cemetery (MH)—Bertie County, North Carolina
Entered Service at: North Carolina
Unit: U.S.S. *Nashville*
Battle or Place of Action: Cienfuegos, Cuba
Date of Action: 11 May 1898
G.O. Number, Date: 521, 7 July 1899
Citation: On board the U.S.S. *Nashville* during the operation of cutting the cable leading from Cienfuegos, Cuba, 11 May 1898. Facing the heavy fire of the enemy, Parker displayed extraordinary bravery and coolness throughout this action.

2155 ◆ PENN, ROBERT

Rank: Fireman First Class
Service: U.S. Navy
Birthday: 10 October 1872
Place of Birth: City Point, Virginia
Date of Death: 8 June 1912
Place of Death: Las Animas, Colorado
Cemetery: unknown cemetery—Philadelphia, Pennsylvania
Entered Service at: Virginia
Unit: U.S.S. *Iowa*
Battle or Place of Action: Santiago de Cuba, Cuba
Date of Action: 20 July 1898
G.O. Number, Date: 501, 14 December 1898
Citation: On board the U.S.S. *Iowa* off Santiago de Cuba, 20 July 1898. Performing his duty at the risk of serious scalding at the time of the blowing-out of the manhole gasket on board the vessel, Penn hauled the fire while standing on a board thrown across a coal bucket one foot above the boiling water which was still blowing from the boiler.

2156 ◆ PFISTERER, HERMAN

Rank: Musician
Service: U.S. Army
Birthday: 1 April 1866
Place of Birth: Brooklyn, Kings County, New York
Date of Death: 6 August 1905
Cemetery: Vancouver Barracks, Post Cemetery (4-E-448) (MH)—Vancouver, Washington

Entered Service at: New York, New York
Unit: Company H, 21st U.S. Infantry
Battle or Place of Action: Santiago, Cuba
Date of Action: 1 July 1898
Date of Issue: 22 June 1899
Citation: Gallantly assisted in the rescue of the wounded from in front of the lines and under heavy fire from the enemy.

2157 ◆ PHILLIPS, GEORGE FREDERICK

Rank: Machinist First Class (highest rank: Chief Machinist)
Service: U.S. Navy
Birthday: 8 March 1862
Place of Birth: St. John, New Brunswick, Canada
Date of Death: 4 June 1904
Place of Death: Cambridge, Massachusetts
Cemetery: Fernhill Cemetery (MH)—St. John, New Brunswick, Canada
Entered Service at: Galveston, Galveston County, Texas
Unit: U.S.S. *Merrimac*
Battle or Place of Action: harbor entrance, Santiago de Cuba, Cuba
Date of Action: 3 June 1898
G.O. Number, Date: 529, 2 November 1899
Citation: In connection with the sinking of the U.S.S. *Merrimac* at the entrance to the harbor of Santiago de Cuba, 3 June 1898. Despite heavy fire from the Spanish shore batteries, Phillips displayed extraordinary heroism throughout this operation.
Notes: POW

2158 ◆ POLOND, ALFRED

Rank: Private (highest rank: Sergeant)
Service: U.S. Army
Birthday: 29 February 1872
Place of Birth: Lapeer, Lapeer County, Michigan
Date of Death: 26 March 1956
Cemetery: Riverside Cemetery—Kalamazoo, Michigan
Entered Service at: Lapeer, Lapeer County, Michigan
Unit: Company F, 10th U.S. Infantry
Battle or Place of Action: Santiago, Cuba
Date of Action: 1 July 1898
Date of Issue: 22 June 1899
Citation: Gallantly assisted in the rescue of the wounded from in front of the lines and while under heavy fire from the enemy.

2159 ◆ QUICK, JOHN HENRY

Rank: Sergeant (highest rank: Sergeant Major)
Service: U.S. Marine Corps
Birthday: 20 June 1870
Place of Birth: Charleston, Kanawha County, West Virginia
Date of Death: 9 September 1922
Place of Death: St. Louis, Missouri
Cemetery: Memorial Park Cemetery (MH)—St. Louis, Missouri
Entered Service at: Pennsylvania
Battle or Place of Action: Cuzco, Cuba
Date of Action: 14 June 1898
G.O. Number, Date: 504, 13 December 1898
Citation: In action during the battle of Cuzco, Cuba, 14 June 1898. Distinguishing himself during this action, Quick signaled the U.S.S. *Dolphin* on three different occasions while exposed to a heavy fire from the enemy.

2160 ◆ QUINN, ALEXANDER M.

Rank: Sergeant (highest rank: Color Sergeant)
Service: U.S. Army
Birthday: 1866
Place of Birth: Passaic, Passaic County, New Jersey
Date of Death: 4 May 1906
Place of Death: Philippine Islands (Killed in Action)
Cemetery: Holy Sepulchre Cemetery (MH)—Totowa, New Jersey
Entered Service at: Philadelphia, Philadelphia County, Pennsylvania
Unit: Company A, 13th U.S. Infantry
Battle or Place of Action: Santiago, Cuba
Date of Action: 1 July 1898
Date of Issue: 22 June 1899
Citation: Gallantly assisted in the rescue of the wounded from in front of the lines and under heavy fire from the enemy.

2161 ◆ RESSLER, NORMAN W.

Rank: Corporal (highest rank: Master Gunner)
Service: U.S. Army
Birthday: 27 May 1873
Place of Birth: Dalmatia, Northumberland County, Pennsylvania
Date of Death: 29 September 1914
Cemetery: San Francisco National Cemetery (WS-134-A)—San Francisco, California
Entered Service at: Dalmatia, Northumberland County, Pennsylvania
Unit: Company D, 17th U.S. Infantry
Battle or Place of Action: El Caney, Cuba
Date of Action: 1 July 1898
Date of Issue: 21 August 1899
Citation: Gallantly assisted in the rescue of the wounded from in front of the lines and under heavy fire of the enemy.

2162 ◆ RILLEY, JOHN PHILLIP

Rank: Landsman
Service: U.S. Navy
Birthday: 22 January 1877
Place of Birth: Allentown, Lehigh County, Pennsylvania
Date of Death: 16 November 1950
Cemetery: Greenlawn Cemetery (MH)—Salem, Massachusetts
Entered Service at: Massachusetts
Unit: U.S.S. *Nashville*

Battle or Place of Action: Cienfuegos, Cuba
Date of Action: 11 May 1898
G.O. Number, Date: 521, 7 July 1899
Citation: On board the U.S.S. *Nashville* during the operation of cutting the cable leading from Cienfuegos, Cuba, 11 May 1898. Facing the heavy fire of the enemy, Rilley displayed extraordinary bravery and coolness throughout this action.

2163 ◆ ROBERTS, CHARLES DUVAL

Rank: Second Lieutenant (highest rank: Brigadier General)
Service: U.S. Army
Birthday: 18 June 1873
Place of Birth: Cheyenne Agency, Dakota
Date of Death: 24 October 1966
Place of Death: Silver Springs, Maryland
Cemetery: Arlington National Cemetery (2-3671)—Arlington, Virginia
Entered Service at: Fort D.A. Russell, Wyoming
Unit: 17th U.S. Infantry
Battle or Place of Action: El Caney, Cuba
Date of Action: 1 July 1898
Date of Issue: 21 June 1899
Citation: Gallantly assisted in the rescue of the wounded from in front of the lines under heavy fire of the enemy.

2164 ◆ RUSSELL, HENRY PETER

Rank: Landsman (highest rank: Captain U.S. Army Ret.)
Service: U.S. Navy
Birthday: 10 June 1878
Place of Birth: Quebec, Canada
Date of Death: 1 December 1956
Cemetery: Arlington National Cemetery (31-6377) (MH)—Arlington, Virginia
Entered Service at: New York
Unit: U.S.S. *Marblehead*
Battle or Place of Action: Cienfuegos, Cuba
Date of Action: 11 May 1898
G.O. Number, Date: 521, 7 July 1899
Citation: On board the U.S.S. *Marblehead* during the operation of cutting the cable leading from Cienfuegos, Cuba, 11 May 1898. Facing the heavy fire of the enemy, Russell displayed extraordinary bravery and coolness throughout this action.

2165 ◆ SCOTT, JOSEPH FRANCIS

Rank: Private (highest rank: Corporal)
Service: U.S. Marine Corps
Birthday: 4 June 1866
Place of Birth: Boston, Suffolk County, Massachusetts
Date of Death: 28 February 1941
Place of Death: Cambridge, Massachusetts
Cemetery: Cambridge Cemetery (MH)—Cambridge, Massachusetts
Entered Service at: Cambridge, Middlesex County, Massachusetts
Unit: U.S.S. *Nashville*
Battle or Place of Action: Cienfuegos, Cuba
Date of Action: 11 May 1898
G.O. Number, Date: 521, 7 July 1899
Citation: On board the U.S.S. *Nashville* during the operation of cutting the cable leading from Cienfuegos, Cuba, 11 May 1898. Facing the heavy fire of the enemy, Scott displayed extraordinary bravery and coolness throughout this action.

2166 ◆ SHEPHERD, WARREN JULIUS

Rank: Corporal
Service: U.S. Army
Birthday: 28 September 1871
Place of Birth: Cherry Tree, Indiana County, Pennsylvania
Date of Death: 24 April 1942
Cemetery: Inglewood Cemetery—Inglewood, California
Entered Service at: Westover, Clearfield County, Pennsylvania
Unit: Company D, 17th U.S. Infantry
Battle or Place of Action: El Caney, Cuba
Date of Action: 1 July 1898
Date of Issue: 21 August 1899
Citation: Gallantly assisted in the rescue of the wounded from in front of the lines under heavy fire from the enemy.

2167 ◆ SPICER, WILLIAM

Rank: Gunner's Mate First Class (highest rank: Chief Gunner's Mate)
Service: U.S. Navy
Birthday: 28 May 1864
Place of Birth: Liverpool, Merseyside County, England
Date of Death: 14 December 1949
Place of Death: Long Beach, California
Entered Service at: New York
Unit: U.S.S. *Marblehead*
Battle or Place of Action: approaches to Caimanera, Guantanamo Bay, Cuba
Date of Action: 26-27 July 1898
G.O. Number, Date: 500, 14 December 1898
Citation: On board the U.S.S. *Marblehead* at the approaches to Caimanera, Guantanamo Bay, Cuba, 26 and 27 July 1898. Displaying heroism, Spicer took part in the perilous work of sweeping for and disabling 27 contact mines during this period.

2168 ◆ SULLIVAN, EDWARD

Rank: Private (highest rank: Corporal)
Service: U.S. Marine Corps
Birthday: 16 May 1870
Place of Birth: Cork, Ireland
Date of Death: 11 March 1955
Place of Death: Grafton, Massachusetts
Cemetery: Prospect Hill Cemetery (MH)—Oxbridge, Massachusetts
Entered Service at: Massachusetts

Unit: U.S.S. *Marblehead*
Battle or Place of Action: Cienfuegos, Cuba
Date of Action: 11 May 1898
G.O. Number, Date: 521, 7 July 1899
Date of Issue: 15 August 1899
Citation: On board the U.S.S. *Marblehead* during the operation of cutting the cable leading from Cienfuegos, Cuba, 11 May 1898. Facing the heavy fire of the enemy, Sullivan displayed extraordinary bravery and coolness throughout this action.

2169 ◆ SUNDQUIST, AXEL LEOHARD

Rank: Chief Carpenter's Mate (highest rank: Carpenter)
Service: U.S. Navy
Birthday: 26 May 1867
Place of Birth: Finland
Date of Death: 22 December 1910
Place of Death: on board the U.S.S. *Alliance*, Culebra, Puerto Rico
Cemetery: Braman Cemetery—Newport, Rhode Island
Entered Service at: Pennsylvania
Unit: U.S.S. *Marblehead*
Battle or Place of Action: approaches to Caimanera, Guantanamo Bay, Cuba
Date of Action: 26-27 July 1898
G.O. Number, Date: 500, 14 December 1898
Citation: On board the U.S.S. *Marblehead* at the approaches to Caimanera, Guantanamo Bay, Cuba, 26 and 27 July 1898. Displaying heroism, Sundquist took part in the perilous work of sweeping for and disabling 27 contact mines during this period.

2170 ◆ SUNDQUIST, GUSTAV ADOLF

Rank: Ordinary Seaman (highest rank: Chief Special Mechanic)
Service: U.S. Navy
Birthday: 4 June 1879
Place of Birth: Sweden
Date of Death: 25 August 1918
Place of Death: Drowned at Cape Ferret, Gironne, France. Body not recovered.
Entered Service at: New York
Unit: U.S.S. *Nashville*
Battle or Place of Action: Cienfuegos, Cuba
Date of Action: 11 May 1898
G.O. Number, Date: 529, 2 November 1899
Citation: On board the U.S.S. *Nashville* during the operation of cutting the cable leading from Cienfuegos, Cuba, 11 May 1898. Facing the heavy fire of the enemy, Sundquist displayed extraordinary bravery and coolness throughout this action.

2171 ◆ THOMPKINS, WILLIAM H.

Rank: Private (highest rank: Sergeant)
Service: U.S. Army
Birthday: 3 October 1872
Place of Birth: Paterson, Passaic County, New Jersey
Date of Death: 24 September 1916
Cemetery: San Francisco National Cemetery (WS-1036-A Row 11) (MH)—San Francisco, California
Entered Service at: Paterson, Passaic County, New Jersey
Unit: Troop G, 10th U.S. Cavalry
Battle or Place of Action: Tayabacoa, Cuba
Date of Action: 30 June 1898
Date of Issue: 23 June 1899
Citation: Voluntarily went ashore in the face of the enemy and aided in the rescue of his wounded comrades; this after several previous attempts at rescue had been frustrated.

2172 ◆ TRIPLETT, SAMUEL S.

Rank: Ordinary Seaman (highest rank: Chief Gunner)
Service: U.S. Navy
Birthday: 18 December 1869
Place of Birth: Cherokee, Crawford County, Kansas
Date of Death: 25 August 1957
Cemetery: North Edna Cemetery (MH)—Edna, Kansas
Entered Service at: New York
Unit: U.S.S. *Marblehead*
Battle or Place of Action: approaches to Caimanera, Guantanamo Bay, Cuba
Date of Action: 26-27 July 1898
G.O. Number, Date: 500, 14 December 1898
Citation: On board the U.S.S. *Marblehead* at the approaches to Caimanera, Guantanamo Bay, Cuba, 26 and 27 July 1898. Displaying heroism, Triplett took part in the perilous work of sweeping for and disabling 27 contact mines during this period.

2173 ◆ VADAS, ALBERT

True Name: Wadas, Albert
Rank: Seaman
Service: U.S. Navy
Birthday: 26 March 1877
Place of Birth: Austria-Hungary
Date of Death: 3 October 1946
Place of Death: Camp Kilmer, New Jersey
Cemetery: Weehawken Cemetery (MH)—North Bergen, New Jersey
Entered Service at: New York
Unit: U.S.S. *Marblehead*
Battle or Place of Action: Cienfuegos, Cuba
Date of Action: 11 May 1898
G.O. Number, Date: 521, 7 July 1899
Citation: On board the U.S.S. *Marblehead* during the operation of cutting the cable leading from Cienfuegos, Cuba, 11 May 1898. Facing the heavy fire of the enemy, Vadas displayed extraordinary bravery and coolness throughout this period.

2174 ◆ VAN ETTEN, HUDSON

Rank: Seaman (highest rank: Chief Watertender)
Service: U.S. Navy

Birthday: 17 May 1874
Place of Birth: Port Jervis, Orange County, New York
Date of Death: 27 October 1941
Place of Death: Kittery, Maine
Cemetery: Prospect Cemetery (MH)—Greenland, New Hampshire
Entered Service at: New Jersey
Unit: U.S.S. *Nashville*
Battle or Place of Action: Cienfuegos, Cuba
Date of Action: 11 May 1898
G.O. Number, Date: 521, 7 July 1899
Citation: On board the U.S.S. *Nashville* during the operation of cutting the cable leading from Cienfuegos, Cuba, 11 May 1898. Facing the heavy fire of the enemy, Van Etten displayed extraordinary bravery and coolness throughout this period.

2175 ◆ VOLZ, ROBERT

Rank: Seaman (highest rank: Gunner's Mate First Class)
Service: U.S. Navy
Birthday: 31 January 1875
Place of Birth: San Francisco, San Francisco County, California
Entered Service at: Virginia
Unit: U.S.S. *Nashville*
Battle or Place of Action: Cienfuegos, Cuba
Date of Action: 11 May 1898
G.O. Number, Date: 521, 7 July 1899
Citation: On board the U.S.S. *Nashville* during the operation of cutting the cable leading from Cienfuegos, Cuba, 11 May 1989. Facing the heavy fire of the enemy, Volz displayed extraordinary bravery and coolness thoughout this period.

2176 ◆ WANTON, GEORGE HENRY

Rank: Private (highest rank: Master Sergeant)
Service: U.S. Army
Birthday: 15 May 1868
Place of Birth: Paterson, Passaic County, New Jersey
Date of Death: 27 November 1940
Place of Death: Washington, D.C.
Cemetery: Arlington National Cemetery (4-2749) (MH)—Arlington, Virginia
Entered Service at: Paterson, Passaic County, New Jersey
Unit: Troop M, 10th U.S. Cavalry
Battle or Place of Action: Tayabacoa, Cuba
Date of Action: 30 June 1898
Date of Issue: 23 June 1899
Citation: Voluntarily went ashore in the face of the enemy and aided in the rescue of his wounded comrades; this after several previous attempts at rescue had been frustrated.

2177 ◆ WELBORN, IRA CLINTON

Rank: Second Lieutenant (highest rank: Colonel)
Service: U.S. Army
Birthday: 13 February 1874
Place of Birth: Mico, Mississippi
Date of Death: 13 July 1956
Cemetery: Biloxi National Cemetery (12-4-12)—Biloxi, Mississippi
Entered Service at: Mico, Mississippi
Unit: 9th U.S. Infantry
Battle or Place of Action: Santiago, Cuba
Date of Action: 2 July 1898
Date of Issue: 21 June 1899
Citation: Voluntarily left shelter and went, under fire, to the aid of a private of his company who was wounded.

2178 ◆ WENDE, BRUNO

Rank: Private
Service: U.S. Army
Birthday: 17 April 1859
Place of Birth: Germany
Date of Death: 27 December 1929
Cemetery: Spring Grove Cemetery—Cincinnati, Ohio
Entered Service at: Canton, Stark County, Ohio
Unit: Company C, 17th U.S. Infantry
Battle or Place of Action: El Caney, Cuba
Date of Action: 1 July 1898
Date of Issue: 22 June 1899
Citation: Gallantly assisted in the rescue of the wounded from in front of the lines and under heavy fire from the enemy.

2179 ◆ WEST, WALTER SCOTT

Rank: Private
Service: U.S. Marine Corps
Birthday: 13 March 1872
Place of Birth: Bradford, Merrimack County, New Hampshire
Date of Death: 14 September 1943
Cemetery: Forest Hill Cemetery—Boston, Massachusetts
Entered Service at: New Hampshire
Unit: U.S.S. *Marblehead*
Battle or Place of Action: Cienfuegos, Cuba
Date of Action: 11 May 1898
G.O. Number, Date: 521, 7 July 1899
Citation: On board the U.S.S. *Marblehead* during the operation of cutting the cable leading from Cienfuegos, Cuba, 11 May 1898. Facing the heavy fire of the enemy, West displayed extraordinary bravery and coolness throughout this action.

2180 ◆ WILKE, JULIUS AUGUST ROBERT

Rank: Boatswain's Mate First Class
Service: U.S. Navy
Birthday: 14 November 1860
Place of Birth: Germany
Entered Service at: New York
Unit: U.S.S. *Marblehead*
Battle or Place of Action: Cienfuegos, Cuba
Date of Action: 11 May 1898
G.O. Number, Date: 521, 7 July 1899

Citation: On board the U.S.S. *Marblehead* during the operation of cutting the cable leading from Cienfuegos, Cuba, 11 May 1989. Facing the heavy fire of the enemy, Wilke displayed extraordinary bravery and coolness throughout this action.

2181 ◆ WILLIAMS, FRANK

Rank: Seaman
Service: U.S. Navy
Birthday: 19 October 1871
Place of Birth: Danzig, Germany
Entered Service at: New York
Unit: U.S.S. *Marblehead*
Battle or Place of Action: Cienfuegos, Cuba
Date of Action: 11 May 1898
G.O. Number, Date: 521, 7 July 1899
Citation: On board the U.S.S. *Marblehead* during the operation of cutting the cable leading from Cienfuegos, Cuba, 11 May 1989. Facing the heavy fire of the enemy, Williams displayed extraordinary bravery and coolness throughout this period.

SAMOA CAMPAIGN

2182 ◆ FISHER, FREDERICK THOMAS

Rank: Gunner's Mate First Class
Service: U.S. Navy
Birthday: 3 June 1872
Place of Birth: England
Date of Death: 15 April 1906
Cemetery: Naval Cemetery—Guantanamo Bay, Cuba
Entered Service at: California
Unit: U.S.S. *Philadelphia*
Battle or Place of Action: Samoa
Date of Action: 1 April 1899
G.O. Number, Date: 55, 19 July 1901
Citation: Served on board the U.S.S. *Philadelphia*, Samoa, 1 April 1899. Serving in the presence of the enemy on this date, Fisher distinguished himself by his conduct.

2183 ◆ FORSTERER, BRUNO ALBERT

Rank: Sergeant
Service: U.S. Marine Corps
Birthday: 14 July 1869
Place of Birth: Koenigsberg, Germany
Date of Death: 13 June 1957
Cemetery: Arlington National Cemetery (53-2757) (MH)—Arlington, Virginia
Entered Service at: Massachusetts
Battle or Place of Action: near Tagalli, Samoa
Date of Action: 1 April 1899
G.O. Number, Date: 55, 19 July 1901
Citation: For distinguished conduct in the presence of the enemy at Samoa, 1 April 1899.

2184 ◆ HULBERT, HENRY LEWIS

Rank: Private (highest rank: First Lieutenant)
Service: U.S. Marine Corps
Birthday: 12 January 1867
Place of Birth: Kingston upon Hull, Humberside County, England
Date of Death: 4 October 1918
Place of Death: near Mont Blanc, France (WWI)
Cemetery: Arlington National Cemetery (3-4309)—Arlington, Virginia
Entered Service at: California
Unit: Marine guard, U.S.S. *Philadelphia*
Battle or Place of Action: Samoa
Date of Action: 1 April 1899
G.O. Number, Date: 55, 19 July 1901
Citation: For distinguished conduct in the presence of the enemy at Samoa, 1 April 1899.

2185 ◆ McNALLY, MICHAEL JOSEPH

Rank: Sergeant
Service: U.S. Marine Corps
Birthday: 29 June 1860
Place of Birth: New York, New York
Entered Service at: California
Battle or Place of Action: Samoa
Date of Action: 1 April 1899
G.O. Number, Date: 55, 19 July 1901
Citation: For distinguished conduct in the presence of the enemy at Samoa, 1 April 1899.

PHILIPPINE INSURRECTION

2186 ◆ ANDERS, FRANK LAFAYETTE

Rank: Corporal (highest rank: Major)
Service: U.S. Army
Birthday: 10 November 1875
Place of Birth: Fort Lincoln, Dakota Territory
Date of Death: 20 January 1966
Cemetery: Hill Side Cemetery—Ripon, Wisconsin
Entered Service at: Fargo, Cass County, North Dakota
Unit: Company B, 1st North Dakota Volunteer Infantry
Battle or Place of Action: San Miguel de Mayumo, Luzon, Philippine Islands
Date of Action: 13 May 1899
Date of Issue: 3 March 1906
Citation: With 11 other scouts, without waiting for the supporting battalion to aid them or to get into a position to do so, charged over a distance of about 150 yards and completely routed about 300 of the enemy who were in line and in a position that could only be carried by a frontal attack.

2187 ◆ BATSON, MATTHEW ARLINGTON

Rank: First Lieutenant (highest rank: Captain)
Service: U.S. Army
Birthday: 24 April 1866
Place of Birth: Anna, Union County, Illinois
Date of Death: 13 January 1917
Cemetery: Arlington National Cemetery (2-3604-WS) (MH)—Arlington, Virginia
Entered Service at: Carbondale, Jackson County, Illinois
Unit: 4th U.S. Cavalry
Battle or Place of Action: Calamba, Luzon, Philippine Islands
Date of Action: 26 July 1899
Date of Issue: 8 March 1902
Citation: Swam the San Juan River in the face of the enemy's fire and drove him from his entrenchments.

2188 ◆ BEARSS, HIRAM IDDINGS

Rank: Colonel (highest rank: Brigadier General)
Service: U.S. Marine Corps
Birthday: 13 April 1875
Place of Birth: Peru, Miami County, Indiana
Date of Death: 26 August 1938
Place of Death: Peru, Indiana
Cemetery: Mount Hope Cemetery (MH)—Peru, Indiana
Entered Service at: Indiana
Unit: 1st Marine Brigade
Battle or Place of Action: Cadaean & Sohoton Rivers Junction, Samar, Philippine Islands
Date of Action: 17 November 1901
Date of Presentation: 5 April 1934
Place of Presentation: Presented by Pres. Franklin D. Roosevelt
Citation: For extraordinary heroism and eminent and conspicuous conduct in battle at the junction of the Cadacan and Sohoton Rivers, Samar, Philippine Islands, 17 November 1901. Col. Bearss (then Capt.), second in command of the columns upon their uniting ashore in the Sohoton River region, made a surprise attack on the fortified cliffs and completely routed the enemy, killing 30 and capturing and destroying the powder magazine, 40 lantacas (guns), rice, food and cuartels. Due to his courage, intelligence, discrimination, and zeal, he successfully led his men up the cliffs by means of bamboo ladders to a height of 200 feet. The cliffs were of soft stone of volcanic origin, in the nature of pumice, and were honeycombed with caves. Tons of rocks were suspended in platforms held in position by vine cables (known as bejuco) in readiness to be precipitated upon people below. After driving the insurgents from their position, which was almost impregnable, being covered with numerous trails lined with poison spears, pits, etc., he led his men across the river, scaled the cliffs on the opposite side, and destroyed the camps there. Col. Bearss and the men under his command overcame incredible difficulties and dangers in destroying positions which, according to reports from old prisoners, had taken three years to perfect, were held as a final rallying point, and were never before penetrated by white troops. Col. Bearss also rendered distinguished public service in the presence of the enemy at Quinapundan River, Samar, Philipine Islands, on 19 January 1902.

2189 ◆ BELL, HARRY

Rank: Captain
Service: U.S. Army
Birthday: 21 September 1860
Place of Birth: Milwaukee, Milwaukee County, Wisconsin
Date of Death: 10 November 1938
Cemetery: Fort Leavenworth National Cemetery (OFF-167) (MH)—Fort Leavenworth, Kansas
Entered Service at: Minneapolis, Hennepin County, Minnesota
Unit: 36th Infantry, U.S. Volunteers
Battle or Place of Action: near Porac, Luzon, Philippine Islands

Date of Action: 17 October 1899
Date of Issue: 8 March 1902
Citation: Led a successful charge against a superior force, capturing, and dispersing the enemy and relieving other members of his regiment from a perilous position.

2190 ◆ BELL, JAMES FRANKLIN

Rank: Colonel (highest rank: Major General)
Service: U.S. Army
Birthday: 9 January 1856
Place of Birth: Shelbyville, Shelby County, Kentucky
Date of Death: 8 January 1919
Place of Death: New York, New York
Cemetery: Arlington National Cemetery (3-1735-4)—Arlington, Virginia
Entered Service at: Shelbyville, Shelby County, Kentucky
Unit: 36th Infantry, U.S. Volunteers
Battle or Place of Action: near Porac, Luzon, Philippine Islands
Date of Action: 9 September 1899
Date of Issue: 11 December 1899
Citation: While in advance of his regiment, charged seven insurgents with his pistol and compelled the surrender of the captain and two privates under a close fire from the remaining insurgents concealed in a bamboo thicket.

2191 ◆ BICKHAM, CHARLES GOODWIN

Rank: First Lieutenant (highest rank: Captain)
Service: U.S. Army
Birthday: 12 August 1867
Place of Birth: Dayton, Montgomery County, Ohio
Date of Death: 14 December 1944
Cemetery: Woodlawn Cemetery (MH)—Dayton, Ohio
Entered Service at: Dayton, Montgomery County, Ohio
Unit: 27th U.S. Infantry
Battle or Place of Action: Bayong, near Lake Lanao, Mindanao, Philippine Islands
Date of Action: 2 May 1902
G.O. Number, Date: 165, W.D. 7 August 1909
Date of Issue: 29 April 1904
Citation: Crossed a fire-swept field, in close-range of the enemy, and brought a wounded soldier to a place of shelter.

2192 ◆ BIEGLER, GEORGE WESLEY

Rank: Captain (highest rank: Lieutenant Colonel)
Service: U.S. Army
Birthday: 31 May 1868
Place of Birth: Terre Haute, Vigo County, Indiana
Date of Death: 2 April 1929
Place of Death: Presidio of San Francisco, California
Cemetery: The Hollywood Cemetery—Hollywood, California
Entered Service at: Terre Haute, Vigo County, Indiana
Unit: 28th Infantry, U.S. Volunteers
Battle or Place of Action: near Loac, Luzon, Philippine Islands
Date of Action: 21 October 1900
Date of Issue: 11 March 1902
Citation: With but 19 men resisted and at close quarters defeated 300 of the enemy.

2193 ◆ BIRKHIMER, WILLIAM EDWARD

Rank: Captain (highest rank: Brigadier General U.S.A. Ret.)
Service: U.S. Army
Birthday: 1 March 1848
Place of Birth: Somerset, Perry County, Ohio
Date of Death: 10 June 1914
Place of Death: Washington, D.C.
Cemetery: Arlington National Cemetery (1-339-WD)—Arlington, Virginia
Entered Service at: Iowa
Unit: 3d U.S. Artillery
Battle or Place of Action: San Miguel de Mayumo, Luzon, Philippine Islands
Date of Action: 13 May 1899
Date of Issue: 15 July 1902
Citation: With 12 men charged and routed 300 of the enemy.

2194 ◆ BOEHLER, OTTO A.

Rank: Private
Service: U.S. Army
Birthday: 15 October 1873
Place of Birth: Germany
Date of Death: 15 October 1910
Cemetery: St. Mary's Catholic Cemetery (MH)—Breckenridge, Minnesota
Entered Service at: Wahpeton, Richland County, North Dakota
Unit: Company I, 1st North Dakota Volunteer Infantry
Battle or Place of Action: near San Isidro, Luzon, Philippine Islands
Date of Action: 16 May 1899
Date of Issue: 17 May 1906
Citation: With 21 other scouts charged across a burning bridge, under heavy fire, and completely routed 600 of the enemy who were entrenched in a strongly fortified position.

2195 ◆ BUCKLEY, HOWARD MAJOR

Rank: Private (highest rank: Gunnery Sergeant)
Service: U.S. Marine Corps
Birthday: 23 January 1862
Place of Birth: Croton Falls, Westchester County, New York
Date of Death: 2 July 1941
Place of Death: Bath, New York
Cemetery: Wheeler Cemetery—Wheeler, New York
Entered Service at: New York
Battle or Place of Action: with the Eighth Army Corps
Date of Action: 25, 27, 29 March 1899 & 4 April 1899
G.O. Number, Date: 55, 19 July 1901
Citation: For distinguished conduct in the presence of the

enemy in battle, while with the 8th Army Corps on 25, 27, 29 March, and 4 April 1899.

2196 ◆ BYRNE, BERNARD ALBERT

Rank: Captain (highest rank: Lieutenant Colonel)
Service: U.S. Army
Birthday: 19 October 1853
Place of Birth: Newport Barracks, Giles County, Virginia
Date of Death: 29 February 1910
Cemetery: Arlington National Cemetery (1-707)—Arlington, Virginia
Entered Service at: Washington, D.C.
Unit: 6th U.S. Infantry
Battle or Place of Action: Bobong, Negros, Philippine Islands
Date of Action: 19 July 1899
Date of Issue: 15 July 1902
Citation: Most distinguished gallantry in rallying his men on the bridge after the line had been broken and pushed back.

2197 ◆ CARSON, ANTHONY J.

Rank: Corporal
Service: U.S. Army
Birthday: 23 April 1869
Place of Birth: Boston, Suffolk County, Massachusetts
Date of Death: 25 April 1943
Place of Death: Dorchester, Massachusetts
Cemetery: Calvary Cemetery—Boston, Massachusetts
Entered Service at: Malden, Middlesex County, Massachusetts
Unit: Company H, 43d Infantry, U.S. Volunteers
Battle or Place of Action: Catubig, Samar, Philippine Islands
Date of Action: 15-19 April 1900
Date of Issue: 4 January 1906
Citation: Assumed command of a detachment of the company which had survived an overwhelming attack of the enemy, and by his bravery and untiring efforts and the exercise of extraordinary good judgment in the handling of his men, successfully withstood for two days the attacks of a large force of the enemy, thereby saving the lives of the survivors and protecting the wounded until relief came.

2198 ◆ CAWETZKA, CHARLES

Rank: Private
Service: U.S. Army
Birthday: 1 March 1877
Place of Birth: Detroit, Wayne County, Michigan
Date of Death: 23 October 1951
Cemetery: Romulus Cemetery—Romulus, Michigan
Entered Service at: Wayne, Wayne County, Michigan
Unit: Company F, 30th Infantry, U.S. Volunteers
Battle or Place of Action: near Sariaya, Luzon, Philippine Islands
Date of Action: 23 August 1900
Date of Issue: 14 March 1902
Citation: Singlehanded he defended a disabled comrade against a greatly superior force of the enemy.

2199 ◆ CECIL, JOSEPH SAMUEL

Rank: First Lieutenant (highest rank: Colonel)
Service: U.S. Army
Birthday: 11 January 1878
Place of Birth: New River, Tennessee
Date of Death: 20 August 1940
Cemetery: Arlington National Cemetery (6-5718)—Arlington, Virginia
Entered Service at: New River, Tennessee
Unit: 19th U.S. Infantry
Battle or Place of Action: Bud-Dajo, Jolo, Philippine Islands
Date of Action: 7 March 1906
G.O. Number, Date: 7, W.D. 3 February 1913
Date of Issue: 23 January 1913
Citation: While at the head of the column about to assault the first cotta under a superior fire at short-range, personally carried to a sheltered position a wounded man and the body of one who was killed beside him.

2200 ◆ CONDON, CLARENCE MILVILLE

Rank: Sergeant (highest rank: Lieutenant Colonel)
Service: U.S. Army
Birthday: 12 August 1875
Place of Birth: South Brooksville, Hancock County, Maine
Date of Death: 20 July 1916
Cemetery: Arlington National Cemetery (2-3834)—Arlington, Virginia
Entered Service at: St. Augustine, St. Johns County, Florida
Unit: Battery G, 3d U.S. Artillery
Battle or Place of Action: near Calulut, Luzon, Philippine Islands
Date of Action: 5 November 1899
Date of Issue: 11 March 1902
Citation: While in command of a detachment of four men, charged and routed 40 entrenched insurgents, inflicting on them heavy loss.

2201 ◆ DAVIS, CHARLES P.

Rank: Private
Service: U.S. Army
Birthday: 5 June 1872
Place of Birth: Long Prairie, Todd County, Minnesota
Date of Death: 28 May 1943
Cemetery: Hillside Cemetery (MH)—Valley City, North Dakota
Entered Service at: Valley City, Barnes County, North Dakota
Unit: Company G, 1st North Dakota Volunteer Infantry
Battle or Place of Action: near San Isidro, Luzon, Philippine Islands

Date of Action: 16 May 1899
Date of Issue: 28 April 1906
Citation: With 21 other scouts charged across a burning bridge, under heavy fire, and completely routed 600 of the enemy who were entrenched in a strongly fortified position.

2202 ◆ DOWNS, WILLIS H.

Rank: Private (highest rank: Wagoneer)
Service: U.S. Army
Birthday: 1 June 1870
Place of Birth: Mount Carmel, Connecticut
Date of Death: 15 September 1929
Cemetery: Highland Home Cemetery (MH)—Jamestown, North Dakota
Entered Service at: Jamestown, Stutsman County, North Dakota
Unit: Company H, 1st North Dakota Volunteer Infantry
Battle or Place of Action: San Miguel de Mayumo, Luzon, Philippine Islands
Date of Action: 13 May 1899
Date of Issue: 16 February 1906
Citation: With 11 other scouts, without waiting for the supporting battalion to aid them or to get into a position to do so, charged over a distance of about 150 yards and completely routed about 300 of the enemy who were in line and in a position that could only be carried by a frontal attack.

2203 ◆ EPPS, JOSEPH L.

Rank: Private
Service: U.S. Army
Birthday: 16 May 1870
Place of Birth: Jamestown, Moniteau County, Missouri
Date of Death: 20 June 1952
Cemetery: Green Hill Cemetery—Muskogee, Oklahoma
Entered Service at: Oklahoma Indian Territory
Unit: Company B, 33d Infantry, U.S. Volunteers
Battle or Place of Action: Vigan, Luzon, Philippine Islands
Date of Action: 4 December 1899
Date of Issue: 7 February 1902
Citation: Discovered a party of insurgents inside a wall, climbed to the top of the wall, covered them with his gun, and forced them to stack arms and surrender.

2204 ◆ FERGUSON, ARTHUR MEDWORTH

Rank: First Lieutenant (highest rank: Lieutenant Colonel)
Service: U.S. Army
Birthday: 11 December 1877
Place of Birth: Coffey County, Kansas
Date of Death: 20 February 1923
Cemetery: Arlington National Cemetery (3-4016)—Arlington, Virginia
Entered Service at: Burlington, Coffey County, Kansas
Unit: 36th Infantry, U.S. Volunteers
Battle or Place of Action: near Porac, Luzon, Philippine Islands
Date of Action: 28 September 1899
Date of Issue: 8 March 1902
Citation: Charged alone a body of the enemy and captured a captain.

2205 ◆ FITZ, JOSEPH

Rank: Ordinary Seaman
Service: U.S. Navy
Birthday: 24 May 1886
Place of Birth: Austria
Date of Death: 24 February 1945
Cemetery: Glendale Cemetery—Des Moines, Iowa
Entered Service at: Des Moines, Polk County, Iowa
Unit: U.S.S. *Pampanga*
Battle or Place of Action: Mount Dajo Jolo, Philippine Islands
Date of Action: 8 March 1906
G.O. Number, Date: 19, 1 May 1906
Citation: On board the U.S.S. *Pampanga*, Mount Dajo Jolo, Philippine Islands, 8 March 1906. Serving in the presence of the enemy on this date, Fitz displayed bravery and extraordinary heroism.

2206 ◆ FORBECK, ANDREW PETER

Rank: Seaman
Service: U.S. Navy
Birthday: 29 August 1881
Place of Birth: New York
Date of Death: 25 April 1924
Cemetery: Erie Cemetery—Erie, Pennsylvania
Entered Service at: New York
Unit: U.S.S. *Pampanga*
Battle or Place of Action: Katbalogan, Samar, Philippine Islands
Date of Action: 16 July 1900
G.O. Number, Date: 55, 19 July 1901
Citation: For distinguished conduct in the presence of the enemy during the battle of Katbalogan, Samar, Philippine Islands, 16 July 1900.

2207 ◆ FUNSTON SR., FREDERICK

Rank: Colonel (highest rank: Major General U.S.A.)
Service: U.S. Army
Birthday: 9 November 1865
Place of Birth: New Carlisle, Clark County, Ohio
Date of Death: 19 February 1917
Place of Death: Fort Sam Houston, Texas
Cemetery: San Francisco National Cemetery (OS-68-3) (MH)—San Francisco, California
Entered Service at: Iola, Allen County, Kansas
Unit: 20th Kansas Volunteer Infantry
Battle or Place of Action: Rio Grande de la Pampanga, Luzon, Philippine Islands
Date of Action: 27 April 1899
Date of Issue: 14 February 1900
Citation: Crossed the river on a raft and by his skill and daring enabled the general commanding to carry the enemy's entrenched position on the north bank of the river and to drive him with great loss from the important strategic position of Calumpit.

2208 ◆ GALBRAITH, ROBERT

Rank: Gunner's Mate Third Class
Service: U.S. Navy
Birthday: 18 February 1878
Place of Birth: Brooklyn, Kings County, New York
Date of Death: 13 May 1949
Cemetery: Long Island National Cemetery (DSS-17) (MH)—Farmingdale, New York
Entered Service at: New York
Battle or Place of Action: at El pardo, Cebu, Philippine Islands
Date of Action: 12-13 September 1899
G.O. Number, Date: 531, 21 November 1900r
Citation: For extraordinary heroism and gallantry while under fire of the enemy at El Pardo, Cebu, Philippine Islands, 12 and 13 September 1899.

2209 ◆ GALT, STERLING ARCHIBALD

Rank: Artificer (highest rank: Battalion Sergeant Major)
Service: U.S. Army
Birthday: October 1866
Place of Birth: Taneytown, Carroll County, Maryland
Date of Death: 21 October 1908
Place of Death: Kansas City, Missouri
Cemetery: Orient Cemetery (MH)—Harrisonville, Missouri
Entered Service at: Taneytown, Carroll County, Maryland
Unit: Company F, 36th Infantry, U.S. Volunteers
Battle or Place of Action: Bamban, Luzon, Philippine Islands
Date of Action: 9 November 1899
Date of Issue: 30 April 1902
Citation: Distinguished bravery and conspicuous gallantry in action against insurgents.

2210 ◆ GAUJOT, ANTOINE AUGUST

Rank: Corporal
Service: U.S. Army
Birthday: 1879
Place of Birth: Keweenaw, Baraga County, Michigan
Date of Death: 14 April 1936
Cemetery: Fairview Cemetery—Williamson, West Virginia
Entered Service at: Williamson, Mingo County, West Virginia
Unit: Company M, 27th Infantry, U.S. Volunteers
Battle or Place of Action: at San Mateo, Philippine Islands
Date of Action: 19 December 1899
Date of Presentation: 15 February 1911
Place of Presentation: The White House, presented by Pres. William H. Taft
Citation: Attempted under a heavy fire of the enemy to swim a river for the purpose of obtaining and returning with a canoe.

2211 ◆ GEDEON, LOUIS

Rank: Private (highest rank: Sergeant)
Service: U.S. Army
Birthday: 19 September 1878
Place of Birth: Pittsburgh, Allegheny County, Pennsylvania
Date of Death: 11 October 1950
Place of Death: Washington, D.C.
Cemetery: Soldier's Home National Cemetery (O-25) (MH)—Washington, D.C.
Entered Service at: Pittsburgh, Allegheny County, Pennsylvania
Unit: Company G, 19th U.S. Infantry
Battle or Place of Action: at Mount Amia, Cebu, Philippine Islands
Date of Action: 4 February 1900
Date of Issue: 10 March 1902
Citation: Singlehanded defended his mortally wounded captain from an overwhelming force of the enemy.

2212 ◆ GIBSON, EDWARD HERRICK

Rank: Sergeant
Service: U.S. Army
Birthday: 4 July 1872
Place of Birth: Boston, Suffolk County, Massachusetts
Date of Death: 25 April 1942
Cemetery: Golden Gate National Cemetery (L-5-7791)—San Bruno, California
Entered Service at: Boston, Suffolk County, Massachusetts
Unit: Company M, 27th Infantry, U.S. Volunteers
Battle or Place of Action: San Mateo, Philippine Islands
Date of Action: 19 December 1899
Date of Issue: 5 April 1911
Citation: Attempted under a heavy fire of the enemy to swim a river for the purpose of obtaining and returning with a canoe.

2213 ◆ GILLENWATER, JAMES ROBERT LEE

Rank: Corporal
Service: U.S. Army
Birthday: 28 October 1871
Place of Birth: Rye Cove, Virginia
Date of Death: 19 January 1946
Cemetery: Payne Cemetery (MH)—Rogersville, Tennessee
Entered Service at: Rye Cove, Virginia
Unit: Company A, 36th Infantry, U.S. Volunteers
Battle or Place of Action: near Porac, Luzon, Philippine Islands
Date of Action: 3 September 1899
Date of Issue: 15 March 1902
Citation: While on a scout drove off a superior force of insurgents and with the assistance of one comrade brought from the field of action the bodies of two comrades, one killed and the other severely wounded.

2214 ◆ GREER, ALLEN JAMES

Rank: Second Lieutenant (highest rank: Lieutenant Colonel)
Service: U.S. Army
Birthday: 11 August 1878

Place of Birth: Memphis, Shelby County, Tennessee
Date of Death: 16 March 1964
Cemetery: Arlington National Cemetery (1-701-B) (MH)—Arlington, Virginia
Entered Service at: Memphis, Shelby County, Tennessee
Unit: 4th U.S. Infantry
Battle or Place of Action: near Majada, Laguna Province, Philippine Islands
Date of Action: 2 July 1901
Date of Issue: 10 March 1902
Citation: Charged alone an insurgent outpost with his pistol, killing one, wounding two, and capturing three insurgents with their rifles and equipment.

2215 ◆ GROVE, WILLIAM REMSBURG

Rank: Lieutenant Colonel (highest rank: Colonel)
Service: U.S. Army
Birthday: 16 May 1872
Place of Birth: Montezuma, Poweshiek County, Iowa
Date of Death: 6 August 1952
Cemetery: Manasota Memorial Park—Sarasota, Florida
Entered Service at: Denver, Denver County, Colorado
Unit: 36th Infantry, U.S. Volunteers
Battle or Place of Action: near Porac, Luzon, Philippine Islands
Date of Action: 9 September 1899
Date of Issue: 16 July 1902
Citation: In advance of his regiment, rushed to the assistance of his colonel, charging, pistol in hand, seven insurgents, and compelling surrender of all not killed or wounded.

2216 ◆ HARVEY, HARRY

Rank: Sergeant
Service: U.S. Marine Corps
Birthday: 4 June 1873
Place of Birth: New York, New York
Date of Death: 5 April 1929
Cemetery: Los Angeles National Cemetery (60-E-4) (MH)—Los Angeles, California
Entered Service at: New Jersey
Battle or Place of Action: Benefictican, Philippine Islands
Date of Action: 16 February 1900
G.O. Number, Date: 55, 19 July 1901
Date of Issue: 24 January 1902
Citation: Served in battle against the enemy at Benefictican, 16 February 1900. Throughout this action and in the presence of the enemy, Harvey distinguished himself by meritorious conduct.

2217 ◆ HAYES, WEBB COOK

Rank: Lieutenant Colonel (highest rank: Colonel)
Service: U.S. Army
Birthday: 20 March 1856
Place of Birth: Cincinnati, Hamilton County, Ohio
Date of Death: 26 July 1934
Cemetery: Spiegal Grove Estate Park—Freemont, Ohio
Entered Service at: Fremont, Sandusky County, Ohio
Unit: 31st Infantry, U.S. Volunteers
Battle or Place of Action: Vigan, Luzon, Philippine Islands
Date of Action: 4 December 1899
Date of Issue: 17 December 1902
Citation: Pushed through the enemy's lines alone, during the night, from the beach to the beleaguered force at Vigan, and returned the following morning to report the condition of affairs to the Navy and secure assistance.

2218 ◆ HENDERSON, JOSEPH

Rank: Sergeant (highest rank: First Sergeant)
Service: U.S. Army
Birthday: December 1869
Place of Birth: Leavenworth, Leavenworth County, Kansas
Date of Death: 19 December 1938
Cemetery: Arlington National Cemetery (20-50042) (MH)—Arlington, Virginia
Entered Service at: Leavenworth, Leavenworth County, Kansas
Unit: Troop B, 6th U.S. Cavalry
Battle or Place of Action: Patian Island, Philippine Islands
Date of Action: 2 July 1909
Date of Presentation: 23 November 1912
Place of Presentation: Presented by Pres. William H. Taft
Citation: While in action against hostile Moros, voluntarily advanced alone, in the face of a heavy fire, to within about 15 yards of the hostile position and refastened to a tree a block and tackle used in checking the recoil of a mountain gun.

2219 ◆ HIGH, FRANK CHARLES

Rank: Private
Service: U.S. Army
Birthday: 7 June 1875
Place of Birth: Dunningham, Yolo County, California
Date of Death: 13 December 1966
Place of Death: Ashland, Oregon
Cemetery: Memory Gardens Cemetery—Medford, Oregon
Entered Service at: Ashland, Jackson County, Oregon
Unit: Company G, 2d Oregon Volunteer Infantry
Battle or Place of Action: near San Isidro, Luzon, Philippine Islands
Date of Action: 16 May 1899
Date of Issue: 4 April 1906
Citation: With 21 other scouts charged across a burning bridge, under heavy fire, and completely routed 600 of the enemy who were entrenched in a strongly fortified position.

2220 ◆ HUNTSMAN, JOHN A.

Rank: Sergeant (highest rank: Second Lieutenant)
Service: U.S. Army
Place of Birth: Oskaloosa, Mahaska County, Iowa
Entered Service at: Lawrence, Douglas County, Kansas
Unit: Company E, 36th Infantry, U.S. Volunteers
Battle or Place of Action: Bamban, Luzon, Philippine Islands

Date of Action: 9 November 1899
Date of Issue: 26 March 1902
Citation: For distinguished bravery and conspicuous gallantry in action against insurgents.

2221 ◆ JENSEN, GOTFRED

Rank: Private
Service: U.S. Army
Birthday: 20 November 1872
Place of Birth: Denmark
Date of Death: 26 December 1945
Cemetery: Washington Soldier's Home Cemetery (MH)—Retsil, Washington
Entered Service at: Devils Lake, Ramsey County, North Dakota
Unit: Company D, 1st North Dakota Volunteer Infantry
Battle or Place of Action: San Miguel de Mayumo, Luzon, Philippine Islands
Date of Action: 13 May 1899
Date of Issue: 6 June 1906
Citation: With 11 other scouts, without waiting for the supporting battalion to aid them or to get into a position to do so, charged over a distance of about 150 yards and completely routed about 300 of the enemy, who were in line and in a position that could only be carried by a frontal attack.

2222 ◆ JOHNSTON, GORDON

Rank: First Lieutenant (highest rank: Colonel)
Service: U.S. Army
Birthday: 25 May 1874
Place of Birth: Charlotte, Mecklenburg County, North Carolina
Date of Death: 8 March 1934
Cemetery: Arlington National Cemetery (7-10092)—Arlington, Virginia
Entered Service at: Birmingham, Jefferson County, Alabama
Unit: U.S. Signal Corps
Battle or Place of Action: Mount Bud Dajo, Jolo, Philippine Islands
Date of Action: 7 March 1906
G.O. Number, Date: 207
Date of Presentation: 7 November 1910
Place of Presentation: The White House, presented by Pres. William H. Taft
Citation: Voluntarily took part in and was dangerously wounded during an assault on the enemy's works.

2223 ◆ KENNEDY, JOHN THOMAS

Rank: Second Lieutenant (highest rank: Brigadier General)
Service: U.S. Army
Birthday: 22 July 1885
Place of Birth: Hendersonville, South Carolina
Date of Death: 26 September 1969
Place of Death: Columbia, South Carolina
Cemetery: Arlington National Cemetery (7-10076)—Arlington, Virginia
Entered Service at: Orangeburg, Orangeburg County, South Carolina
Unit: 6th U.S. Cavalry
Battle or Place of Action: at Patian Island, Philippine Islands
Date of Action: 4 July 1909
Date of Presentation: 23 November 1912
Place of Presentation: Presented by Pres. William H. Taft
Citation: While in action against hostile Moros, he entered with a few enlisted men the mouth of a cave occupied by a desperate enemy, this act having been ordered after he had volunteered several times. In this action 2d Lt. Kennedy was severely wounded.

2224 ◆ KILBOURNE JR., CHARLES EVANS

Rank: First Lieutenant (highest rank: Major General)
Service: U.S. Army
Birthday: 23 December 1872
Place of Birth: Fort Myer, Arlington County, Virginia
Date of Death: 12 November 1963
Cemetery: Arlington National Cemetery (3-1705)—Arlington, Virginia
Entered Service at: Portland, Multnomah County, Oregon
Unit: U.S. Volunteer Signal Corps
Battle or Place of Action: Paco Bridge, Philippine Islands
Date of Action: 5 February 1899
Date of Issue: 6 May 1905
Citation: Within a range of 250 yards of the enemy and in the face of a rapid fire climbed a telegraph pole at the east end of the bridge and in full view of the enemy coolly and carefully repaired a broken telegraph wire, thereby reestablishing telegraphic communication to the front.

2225 ◆ KINNE, JOHN BAXTER

Rank: Private (highest rank: Captain U.S. Medical Corps WWI)
Service: U.S. Army
Birthday: 3 October 1877
Place of Birth: Beloit, Rock County, Wisconsin
Date of Death: 19 June 1943
Cemetery: Fern Hill Cemetery—Aberdeen, Washington
Entered Service at: Fargo, Cass County, North Dakota
Unit: Company B, 1st North Dakota Volunteer Infantry
Battle or Place of Action: near San Isidro, Luzon, Philippine Islands
Date of Action: 16 May 1899
Date of Issue: 17 May 1906
Citation: With 21 other scouts charged across a burning bridge, under heavy fire, and completely routed 600 of the enemy who were entrenched in a strongly fortified position.

2226 ◆ *LEAHY, CORNELIUS J.

Rank: Private
Service: U.S. Army
Birthday: June 1872
Place of Birth: Limerick, Ireland

Date of Death: 1 December 1900
Place of Death: Philippine Islands (Killed in Action)
Cemetery: San Francisco National Cemetery (ADD-NA-970)—San Francisco, California
Entered Service at: San Francisco, San Francisco County, California
Unit: Company A, 36th Infantry, U.S. Volunteers
Battle or Place of Action: near Porac, Luzon, Philippine Islands
Date of Action: 3 September 1899
Date of Issue: 3 May 1902
Citation: Distinguished gallantry in action in driving off a superior force, and with the assistance of one comrade, brought from the field of action the bodies of two comrades, one killed and the other severely wounded, this while on a scout.

2227 ◆ LEONARD, JOSEPH H.

Rank: Private (highest rank: Sergeant)
Service: U.S. Marine Corps
Birthday: 28 August 1876
Place of Birth: Cohoes, Albany County, New York
Date of Death: 23 September 1946
Place of Death: Yountville, California
Cemetery: Veterans Home of California Cemetery (MH)—Yountville, California
Entered Service at: New York, New York
Battle or Place of Action: with the Eighth Army Corps
Date of Action: 25, 27, 29 March & 4 April 1899
G.O. Number, Date: 55, 19 July 1901
Citation: For distinguished conduct in the presence of the enemy in battles, while with the 8th Army Corps on 25, 27, 29 March, and 4 April 1899.

2228 ◆ *LOGAN JR., JOHN ALEXANDER

Rank: Major
Service: U.S. Army
Birthday: 24 July 1865
Place of Birth: Carbondale, Jackson County, Illinois
Date of Death: 11 November 1899
Place of Death: At San Jacinto, Philippine Islands
Cemetery: Oak Hill Cemetery (MH)—Youngstown, Ohio
Entered Service at: Youngstown, Mahoning County, Ohio
Unit: 33d Infantry, U.S. Volunteers
Battle or Place of Action: at San Jacinto, Philippine Islands
Date of Action: 11 November 1899
Date of Issue: 3 May 1902
Citation: For most distinguished gallantry in leading his battalion upon the entrenchments of the enemy, on which occasion he fell mortally wounded.

2229 ◆ LONGFELLOW, RICHARD MOSES

Rank: Private
Service: U.S. Army
Birthday: 24 June 1867
Place of Birth: Logan County, Illinois
Date of Death: 17 May 1951
Cemetery: Norman Hill Cemetery (MH)—Lewiston, Idaho
Entered Service at: Mandan, Morton County, North Dakota
Unit: Company A, 1st North Dakota Volunteer Infantry
Battle or Place of Action: near San Isidro, Luzon, Philippine Islands
Date of Action: 16 May 1899
Date of Issue: 4 April 1906
Citation: With 21 other scouts charged across a burning bridge, under heavy fire, and completely routed 600 of the enemy who were entrenched in a strongly fortified position.

2230 ◆ LYON, EDWARD EUGENE

Rank: Private
Service: U.S. Army
Birthday: 8 August 1871
Place of Birth: Hixton, Jackson County, Wisconsin
Date of Death: 18 November 1931
Place of Death: Los Angeles, California
Cemetery: Hollywood Cemetery—Hollywood, California
Entered Service at: Amboy, Clark County, Washington
Unit: Company B, 2d Oregon Volunteer Infantry
Battle or Place of Action: San Miguel de Mayumo, Luzon, Philippine Islands
Date of Action: 13 May 1899
Date of Issue: 24 January 1906
Citation: With 11 other scouts without waiting for the supporting battalion to aid them or to get into a position to do so, charged over a distance of about 150 yards and completely routed about 300 of the enemy, who were in line and in a position that could only be carried by a frontal attack.

2231 ◆ MACLAY, WILLIAM PALMER

Rank: Private (highest rank: First Lieutenant)
Service: U.S. Army
Birthday: 1877
Place of Birth: Spruce Creek, Huntingdon County, Pennsylvania
Date of Death: 31 July 1943
Cemetery: Arlington National Cemetery (7-9008-F) (MH)—Arlington, Virginia
Entered Service at: Altoona, Blair County, Pennsylvania
Unit: Company A, 43d Infantry, U.S. Volunteers
Battle or Place of Action: Hilongas, Leyte, Philippine Islands
Date of Action: 6 May 1900
Date of Issue: 11 March 1902
Citation: Charged an occupied bastion, saving the life of an officer in a hand-to-hand combat and destroying the enemy.

2232 ◆ MATHEWS, GEORGE WILLIAM

Rank: Captain Assistant Surgeon (highest rank: Major Surgeon)
Service: U.S. Army
Birthday: 1874

Place of Birth: Worcester, Worcester County, Massachusetts
Date of Death: 31 July 1943
Cemetery: St. John's Cemetery—Worcester, Massachusetts
Entered Service at: Worcester, Worcester County, Massachusetts
Unit: 36th Infantry, U.S. Volunteers
Battle or Place of Action: near Labo, Luzon, Philippine Islands
Date of Action: 29 October 1899
Date of Issue: 14 March 1902
Citation: While in attendance upon the wounded and under a severe fire from the enemy, seized a carbine and beat off an attack upon wounded officers and men under his charge.

2233 ◆ McCONNELL, JAMES

Rank: Private
Service: U.S. Army
Birthday: 1878
Place of Birth: Syracuse, Onondaga County, New York
Date of Death: 23 July 1918
Cemetery: Arlington National Cemetery (7-8317) (MH)—Arlington, Virginia
Entered Service at: Detroit, Wayne County, Michigan
Unit: Company B, 33d Infantry, U.S. Volunteers
Battle or Place of Action: Vigan, Luzon, Philippine Islands
Date of Action: 4 December 1899
Date of Issue: 1 October 1902
Citation: Fought for hours lying between two dead comrades, notwithstanding his hat was pierced, his clothing plowed through by bullets, and his face cut and bruised by flying gravel.

2234 ◆ *McGRATH, HUGH JOCELYN

Rank: Captain (highest rank: Major)
Service: U.S. Army
Birthday: 8 April 1856
Place of Birth: Fond Du Lac, Fond Du Lac County, Wisconsin
Date of Death: 7 November 1899
Place of Death: Philippine Islands
Cemetery: Arlington National Cemetery (1-315-ES)—Arlington, Virginia
Entered Service at: Eau Claire, Eau Claire County, Wisconsin
Unit: 4th U.S. Cavalry
Battle or Place of Action: Calamba, Luzon, Philippine Islands
Date of Action: 26 July 1899
Date of Issue: 29 April 1902
Citation: Swam the San Juan River in the face of the enemy's fire and drove him from his entrenchments.

2235 ◆ MILLER, ARCHIE

Rank: First Lieutenant (highest rank: Lieutenant Colonel)
Service: U.S. Army
Birthday: 1878
Place of Birth: Fort Sheridan, Lake County, Illinois
Date of Death: 28 May 1921
Cemetery: Arlington National Cemetery (1-300-A)—Arlington, Virginia
Entered Service at: St. Louis, St. Louis County, Missouri
Unit: 6th U.S. Cavalry
Battle or Place of Action: Patian Island, Philippine Islands
Date of Action: 2 July 1909
Date of Issue: 23 November 1912
Citation: While in action against hostile Moros, when the machine-gun detachment, having been driven from its position by a heavy fire, one member being killed, did, with the assistance of an enlisted man, place the machine gun in advance of its former position at a distance of about 20 yards from the enemy, in accomplishing which he was obliged to splice a piece of timber to one leg of the gun tripod, all the while being under a heavy fire, and the gun tripod being several times struck by bullets.

2236 ◆ MORAN, JOHN E.

Rank: Captain
Service: U.S. Army
Birthday: 13 August 1856
Place of Birth: Vernon, Windham County, Vermont
Date of Death: 7 November 1930
Cemetery: Highlands Cemetery (MH)—Great Falls, Montana
Entered Service at: Cascade County, Montana
Unit: Company L, 37th Infantry, U.S. Volunteers
Battle or Place of Action: near Mabitac, Laguna, Luzon, Philippine Islands
Date of Action: 17 September 1900
Date of Issue: 10 June 1910
Citation: After the attacking party had become demoralized, fearlessly led a small body of troops under a severe fire and through water waist deep in the attack against the enemy.

2237 ◆ MOSHER, LOUIS C.

Rank: Second Lieutenant (highest rank: First Lieutenant)
Service: U.S. Army
Birthday: 26 April 1880
Place of Birth: Westport, Bristol County, Massachusetts
Date of Death: 29 September 1958
Cemetery: San Francisco National Cemetery (NA-1408) (MH)—San Francisco, California
Entered Service at: Brockton, Plymouth County, Massachusetts
Unit: Philippine Scouts
Battle or Place of Action: Gagsak Mountain, Jolo, Philippine Islands
Date of Action: 11 June 1913
Date of Issue: 4 March 1914
Citation: Voluntarily entered a cleared space within about 20 yards of the Moro trenches under a furious fire from them and carried a wounded soldier of his company to safety at the risk of his own life.

2238 ◆ NOLAN, JOSEPH A.

Rank: Artificer
Service: U.S. Army
Birthday: 20 January 1857
Place of Birth: Elkhart, Elkhart County, Indiana
Date of Death: 19 August 1921
Cemetery: Silverbrook Cemetery (MH)—Niles, Michigan
Entered Service at: South Bend, St. Joseph County, Indiana
Unit: Company B, 45th Infantry, U.S. Volunteers
Battle or Place of Action: Labo, Luzon, Philippine Islands
Date of Action: 29 May 1900
Date of Issue: 14 March 1902
Citation: Voluntarily left shelter and at great personal risk passed the enemy's lines and brought relief to besieged comrades.

2239 ◆ PARKER, JAMES

Rank: Lieutenant Colonel (highest rank: Major General)
Service: U.S. Army
Birthday: 20 February 1854
Place of Birth: Newark, Essex County, New Jersey
Date of Death: 2 June 1934
Place of Death: New York, New York
Cemetery: St. Mary's Episcopal Cemetery—Portsmouth, Rhode Island
Entered Service at: Newark, Essex County, New Jersey
Unit: 45th Infantry, U.S. Volunteers
Battle or Place of Action: Vigan, Luzon, Philippine Islands
Date of Action: 4 December 1899
Date of Issue: 8 March 1902
Citation: While in command of a small garrison repulsed a savage night attack by overwhelming numbers of the enemy, fighting at close quarters in the dark for several hours.

2240 ◆ PIERCE, CHARLES H.

Rank: Private (highest rank: First Sergeant)
Service: U.S. Army
Birthday: 22 February 1875
Place of Birth: Cecil County, Maryland
Date of Death: 2 March 1944
Cemetery: Valhalla Memorial Park—North Hollywood, California
Entered Service at: Delaware City, New Castle County, Delaware
Unit: Company I, 22d U.S. Infantry
Battle or Place of Action: San Isidro, Luzon, Philippine Islands
Date of Action: 19 October 1899
Date of Issue: 10 March 1902
Citation: Held a bridge against a superior force of the enemy and fought, though severely wounded, until the main body came up to cross.

2241 ◆ PORTER, DAVID DIXON

Rank: Colonel (highest rank: Major General)
Service: U.S. Marine Corps
Birthday: 29 April 1877
Place of Birth: Washington, D.C.
Date of Death: 25 February 1944
Place of Death: Philadelphia, Pennsylvania
Cemetery: Arlington National Cemetery (2-3479) (MH)—Arlington, Virginia
Entered Service at: Washington, D.C.
Battle or Place of Action: Cadacan & Sohoton rivers junction, Samar, Philippine Islands
Date of Action: 17 November 1901
Date of Presentation: 25 April 1934
Place of Presentation: Presented by Pres. Franklin D. Roosevelt
Citation: For extraordinary heroism and eminent and conspicuous conduct in battle at the junction of the Cadacan and Sohoton Rivers, Samar, Philippine Islands, 17 November 1901. In command of the columns upon their uniting ashore in the Sohoton Region, Col. Porter (then Capt.) made a surprise attack on the fortified cliffs and completely routed the enemy, killing 30 and capturing and destroying the powder magazine, 40 lantacas (guns), rice, food and cuartels. Due to his courage, intelligence, discrimination, and zeal, he successfully led his men up the cliffs by means of bamboo ladders to a height of 200 feet. The cliffs were of soft stone of volcanic origin, in the nature of pumice, and were honeycombed with caves. Tons of rocks were suspended in platforms held in position by vine cables (known as bejuco) in readiness to be precipitated upon people below. After driving the insurgents from their position, which was almost impregnable, being covered with numerous trails lined with poison spears, pits, etc., Col. Porter led his men across the river, scaled the cliffs on the opposite side, and destroyed the camps there. He and the men under his command overcame incredible difficulties and dangers in destroying positions which, according to reports from old prisoners, had taken three years to perfect, were held as a final rallying post, and had never before been penetrated by white troops. Col. Porter also rendered distinguished public service in the presence of the enemy at Quinapundan River, Samar, Philippine Islands, 26 October 1901.

2242 ◆ PRENDERGAST, THOMAS FRANCIS

Rank: Corporal (highest rank: Sergeant)
Service: U.S. Marine Corps
Birthday: 2 April 1871
Place of Birth: Waterford, Ireland
Date of Death: 26 April 1913
Place of Death: Philadelphia, Pennsylvania
Cemetery: Greenwood Cemetery—Philadelphia, Pennsylvania
Entered Service at: Massachusetts
Battle or Place of Action: with the Eighth Army Corps
Date of Action: 25, 27, 29 March & 5 April 1899
Date of Issue: 19 July 1901
Citation: For distinguished conduct in the presence of the enemy in battle, while with the 8th Army Corps on 25, 27, 29 March, and 5 April 1899.

2243 ◆ QUINN, PETER H.

Rank: Private (highest rank: Trumpeter)
Service: U.S. Army
Birthday: May 1873
Place of Birth: San Francisco, San Francisco County, California
Date of Death: 19 April 1934
Cemetery: Arlington National Cemetery (6-9749-SH) (MH)—Arlington, Virginia
Entered Service at: San Francisco, San Francisco County, California
Unit: Company L, 4th U.S. Cavalry
Battle or Place of Action: San Miguel de Mayumo, Luzon, Philippine Islands
Date of Action: 13 May 1899
Date of Issue: 14 June 1906
Citation: With 11 other scouts, without waiting for the supporting battalion to aid them or to get into a position to do so, charged over a distance of about 150 yards and completely routed about 300 of the enemy, who were in line and in a position that could only be carried by a frontal attack.

2244 ◆ RAY, CHARLES W.

Rank: Sergeant
Service: U.S. Army
Birthday: 6 August 1872
Place of Birth: Pensacola, Yancey County, North Carolina
Date of Death: 23 March 1959
Place of Death: Grandfield, Oklahoma
Cemetery: Grandfield Memorial Cemetery—Grandfield, Oklahoma
Entered Service at: St. Louis, St. Louis County, Missouri
Unit: Company I, 22d U.S. Infantry
Battle or Place of Action: near San Isidro, Luzon, Philippine Islands
Date of Action: 19 October 1899
Date of Issue: 18 April 1902
Citation: Most distinguished gallantry in action. Captured a bridge with the detachment he commanded and held it against a superior force of the enemy, thereby enabling an army to come up and cross.

2245 ◆ ROBERTSON, MARCUS WILLIAM

Rank: Private
Service: U.S. Army
Birthday: 12 February 1870
Place of Birth: Flintville, Wisconsin
Date of Death: 24 May 1948
Place of Death: Portland, Oregon
Cemetery: Cremated at Lincoln Memorial Park—Portland, Oregon
Entered Service at: Hood River, Hood River County, Oregon
Unit: Company B, 2d Oregon Volunteer Infantry
Battle or Place of Action: near San Isidro, Luzon, Philippine Islands
Date of Action: 16 May 1899
Date of Issue: 28 April 1906
Citation: With 21 other scouts charged across a burning bridge, under heavy fire, and completely routed 600 of the enemy who were entrenched in a strongly fortified position.

2246 ◆ ROSS, FRANK FULTON

Rank: Private
Service: U.S. Army
Birthday: 2 December 1867
Place of Birth: Avon, Fulton County, Illinois
Date of Death: 29 January 1936
Place of Death: San Bernandino, California
Cemetery: Bellevue Cemetery—Ontario, California
Entered Service at: Langdon, Cavalier County, North Dakota
Unit: Company H, 1st North Dakota Volunteer Infantry
Battle or Place of Action: near San Isidro, Luzon, Philippine Islands
Date of Action: 16 May 1899
Date of Issue: 6 June 1906
Citation: With 21 other scouts charged across a burning bridge, under heavy fire, and completely routed 600 of the enemy who were entrenched in a strongly fortified position.

2247 ◆ SAGE, WILLIAM HAMPDEN

Rank: Captain (highest rank: Brigadier General)
Service: U.S. Army
Birthday: 6 April 1858
Place of Birth: Centerville, Allegany County, New York
Date of Death: 4 June 1922
Place of Death: Omaha, Nebraska
Cemetery: Arlington National Cemetery (2-913)—Arlington, Virginia
Entered Service at: Binghamton, Broome County, New York
Unit: 23d U.S. Infantry
Battle or Place of Action: near Zapote River, Luzon, Philippine Islands
Date of Action: 13 June 1899
Date of Issue: 24 July 1902
Citation: With nine men volunteered to hold an advanced position and held it against a terrific fire of the enemy estimated at 1,000 strong. Taking a rifle from a wounded man, and cartridges from the belts of others, Capt. Sage himself killed five of the enemy.

2248 ◆ SCHROEDER, HENRY FRANK

Rank: Sergeant (highest rank: Captain)
Service: U.S. Army
Birthday: 7 December 1874
Place of Birth: Chicago, Cook County, Illinois
Date of Death: 26 January 1959
Cemetery: Fort Rosecrans National Cemetery (S-854)—San Diego, California
Entered Service at: Chicago, Cook County, Illinois
Unit: Company L, 16th U.S. Infantry

Battle or Place of Action: Carig, Philippine Islands
Date of Action: 14 September 1900
Date of Issue: 10 March 1902
Citation: With 22 men defeated 400 insurgents, killing 36 and wounding 90.

2249 ◆ SHAW, GEORGE CLYMER

Rank: First Lieutenant (highest rank: Brigadier General)
Service: U.S. Army
Birthday: 6 March 1866
Place of Birth: Pontiac, Oakland County, Michigan
Date of Death: 10 February 1960
Cemetery: Arlington National Cemetery (3-4247)—Arlington, Virginia
Entered Service at: Washington, D.C.
Unit: Company C, 27th U.S. Infantry
Served as: Commanding Officer
Battle or Place of Action: Fort Pitacus, Lake Lanao, Mindanao, Philippine Islands
Date of Action: 4 May 1903
Date of Issue: 9 June 1904
Citation: For distinguished gallantry in leading the assault and, under a heavy fire from the enemy, maintaining alone his position on the parapet after the first three men who followed him there had been killed or wounded, until a foothold was gained by others and the capture of the place assured.

2250 ◆ SHELTON, GEORGE MATHEWS

Rank: Private (highest rank: Major)
Service: U.S. Army
Birthday: 23 December 1877
Place of Birth: Brownwood, Brown County, Texas
Date of Death: 18 January 1949
Place of Death: Presidio of San Francisco, California
Cemetery: San Francisco National Cemetery (OSD-799)—San Francisco, California
Entered Service at: Bellington, Texas
Unit: Company I, 23d U.S. Infantry
Battle or Place of Action: La Paz, Leyte, Philippine Islands
Date of Action: 26 April 1900
Date of Issue: 10 March 1902
Citation: Advanced alone under heavy fire of the enemy and rescued a wounded comrade.

2251 ◆ SHIELS, GEORGE FRANKLIN

Rank: Major Surgeon
Service: U.S. Army
Birthday: 13 April 1863
Place of Birth: California
Date of Death: 26 October 1943
Place of Death: Palo Alto, California
Cemetery: Cypress Lawn Cemetery—Colma, California
Entered Service at: California
Unit: U.S. Volunteers
Battle or Place of Action: at Tuliahan River, Philippine Islands
Date of Action: 25 March 1899
Date of Issue: 22 November 1906
Citation: Voluntarily exposed himself to the fire of the enemy and went with four men to the relief of two native Filipinos lying wounded about 150 yards in front of the lines and personally carried one of them to a place of safety.

2252 ◆ SLETTELAND, THOMAS

Rank: Private
Service: U.S. Army
Birthday: 1871
Place of Birth: Bergen, Norway
Date of Death: 1915
Cemetery: Evergreen Cemetery (MH)—Everett, Washington
Entered Service at: Grafton, Walsh County, North Dakota
Unit: Company C, 1st North Dakota Infantry
Battle or Place of Action: near Paete, Luzon, Philippine Islands
Date of Action: 12 April 1899
Date of Issue: 11 March 1902
Citation: Singlehanded and alone defended his dead and wounded comrades against a greatly superior force of the enemy.

2253 ◆ STEWART, GEORGE EVANS

Rank: Second Lieutenant (highest rank: Colonel)
Service: U.S. Army
Birthday: 2 August 1872
Place of Birth: New South Wales, Australia
Date of Death: 2 March 1946
Place of Death: Portland, Texas
Cemetery: Arlington National Cemetery (2-3408-A-RH)—Arlington, Virginia
Entered Service at: New York, New York
Unit: 19th U.S. Infantry
Battle or Place of Action: Passi, Island of Panay, Philippine Islands
Date of Action: 26 November 1899
Date of Issue: 26 June 1900
Citation: While crossing a river in the face of the enemy, this officer plunged in and at the imminent risk of his own life saved from drowning an enlisted man of his regiment.

2254 ◆ STOLTENBERG, ANDREW VINCENT

Rank: Gunner's Mate Second Class (highest rank: Chief Gunner's Mate)
Service: U.S. Navy
Birthday: 25 January 1866
Place of Birth: Bodo, Norway
Date of Death: 25 December 1941
Cemetery: San Francisco National Cemetery (A-242)—San Francisco, California
Entered Service at: California
Unit: U.S.S. *Panay*
Battle or Place of Action: Katbalogan, Samar, Philippine Islands

Date of Action: 16 July 1900
G.O. Number, Date: 55, 29 July 1899
Citation: For distinguished conduct in the presence of the enemy in battle at Katbalogan, Samar, Philippine Islands, 16 July 1900.

2255 ◆ STRAUB, PAUL FREDERICK

Rank: Major Surgeon
Service: U.S. Army
Birthday: 5 January 1865
Place of Birth: Baden, Germany
Date of Death: 25 November 1937
Cemetery: Forest Home Cemetery—Mount Pleasant, Iowa
Entered Service at: Mount Pleasant, Henry County, Iowa
Unit: 36th Infantry, U.S. Volunteers
Battle or Place of Action: at Alos Zambales, Luzon, Philippine Islands
Date of Action: 21 December 1899
Date of Issue: 3 October 1906
Citation: Voluntarily exposed himself to a hot fire from the enemy in repelling with pistol fire an insurgent attack and at great risk of his own life went under fire to the rescue of a wounded officer and carried him to a place of safety.

2256 ◆ THORDSEN, WILLIAM GEORGE

Rank: Coxswain (highest rank: Chief Gunner's Mate)
Service: U.S. Navy
Birthday: 2 April 1879
Place of Birth: Fredericstadt, Germany
Date of Death: 8 May 1932
Cemetery: Arlington National Cemetery (1-69-W) (MH)—Arlington, Virginia
Entered Service at: New York
Unit: U.S.S. *Pampanga*
Battle or Place of Action: Hilongas, Philippine Islands
Date of Action: 6 May 1900
G.O. Number, Date: 6, 15 August 1900
Citation: For heroism and gallantry under fire of the enemy at Hilongas, Philippine Islands, 6 May 1900.

2257 ◆ TREMBLEY, WILLIAM BEATTIE

Rank: Private
Service: U.S. Army
Birthday: 1877
Place of Birth: Johnson, Stanton County, Kansas
Date of Death: 13 January 1952
Place of Death: Pharr, Texas
Cemetery: Monticello Methodist Church Cemetery—Olathe, Kansas
Entered Service at: Kansas City, Wyandotte County, Kansas
Unit: Company B, 20th Kansas Volunteer Infantry
Battle or Place of Action: at Calumpit, Luzon, Philippine Islands
Date of Action: 27 April 1899
Date of Issue: 11 March 1902
Citation: Swam the Rio Grande de Pampanga in the face of the enemy's fire and fastened a rope to the occupied trenches, thereby enabling the crossing of the river and the driving of the enemy from his fortified position.

2258 ◆ VAN SCHAICK, LOUIS JOSEPH

Rank: First Lieutenant (highest rank: Colonel)
Service: U.S. Army
Birthday: 1 July 1875
Place of Birth: Cobleskill, Schoharie County, New York
Date of Death: 14 February 1945
Place of Death: Philippine Islands
Cemetery: Santo Tomas Cemetery—Manila, Philippine Islands
Entered Service at: Cobleskill, Schoharie County, New York
Unit: 4th U.S. Infantry
Battle or Place of Action: near Nasugbu, Batangas, Philippine Islands
Date of Action: 23 November 1901
G.O. Number, Date: 33 1913
Date of Presentation: 19 May 1913
Place of Presentation: Presented by Pres. Woodrow Wilson
Citation: While in pursuit of a band of insurgents, was the first of his detachment to emerge from a canyon and, seeing a column of insurgents and fearing they might turn and dispatch his men as they emerged one by one from the canyon, galloped forward and closed with the insurgents, thereby throwing them into confusion until the arrival of others of the detachment.

2259 ◆ WALKER, FRANK T. O.

Rank: Private
Service: U.S. Army
Birthday: 6 October 1878
Place of Birth: South Boston, Suffolk County, Massachusetts
Date of Death: 29 October 1904
Cemetery: North Burial Cemetery (MH)—Bristol, Rhode Island
Entered Service at: Burlington, Middlesex County, Massachusetts
Unit: Company F, 46th Infantry, U.S. Volunteers
Battle or Place of Action: near Taal, Luzon, Philippine Islands
Date of Action: 18 January 1900
Date of Issue: 11 March 1902
Citation: Under heavy fire of the enemy he rescued a dying comrade who was sinking beneath the water.

2260 ◆ WALLACE, GEORGE WEED

Rank: Second Lieutenant (highest rank: Lieutenant Colonel)
Service: U.S. Army
Birthday: 25 May 1872
Place of Birth: Fort Riley, Geary County, Kansas
Date of Death: 22 May 1946
Cemetery: San Francisco National Cemetery (OS-319-A)—

San Francisco, California
Entered Service at: Denver, Denver County, Colorado
Unit: 9th U.S. Infantry
Battle or Place of Action: Tinuba, Luzon, Philippine Islands
Date of Action: 4 March 1900
Date of Issue: 25 June 1900
Citation: With another officer and a native Filipino, was shot at from an ambush, the other officer falling severely wounded. Second Lt. Wallace fired in the direction of the enemy, put them to rout, removed the wounded officer from the path, returned to the town, a mile distant, and summoned assistance from his command.

2261 ◆ WEAVER, AMOS

Rank: Sergeant
Service: U.S. Army
Birthday: 13 June 1869
Place of Birth: Niles Township, Delaware County, Indiana
Date of Death: 12 November 1937
Cemetery: Gaines Cemetery—Gaines, Michigan
Entered Service at: San Francisco, San Francisco County, California
Unit: Company F, 36th Infantry, U.S. Volunteers
Battle or Place of Action: Between Calubud & Malalong, Philippine Islands
Date of Action: 5 November 1899
Date of Issue: 15 March 1902
Citation: Alone and unaided, charged a body of 15 insurgents, dislodging them, killing four and wounding several.

2262 ◆ WELD, SETH LATHROP

Rank: Corporal (highest rank: Colonel)
Service: U.S. Army
Birthday: 19 February 1879
Place of Birth: Sandy Hook, Maryland
Date of Death: 20 December 1958
Cemetery: Fort Sam Houston National Cemetery (A-H-189) (MH)—San Antonio, Texas
Entered Service at: Altamont, Grundy County, Tennessee
Unit: Company L, 8th U.S. Infantry
Battle or Place of Action: La Paz, Leyte, Philippine Islands
Date of Action: 5 December 1906
Date of Issue: 10 October 1908
Citation: With his right arm cut open with a bolo, went to the assistance of a wounded constabulary officer and a fellow soldier who were surrounded by about 40 Pulajanes, and, using his disabled rifle as a club, beat back the assailants and rescued his party.

2263 ◆ *WETHERBY, JOHN C.

Rank: Private
Service: U.S. Army
Birthday: 2 July 1880
Place of Birth: Morgan County, Indiana
Date of Death: 29 November 1899
Place of Death: Luzon, Philippine Islands
Cemetery: Frye Cemetery—Martinsville, Indiana
Entered Service at: Martinsville, Morgan County, Indiana
Unit: Company L, 4th U.S. Infantry
Battle or Place of Action: near Imus, Luzon, Philippine Islands
Date of Action: 20 November 1899
Date of Issue: 25 April 1902
Citation: While carrying important orders on the battlefield, was desperately wounded and, being unable to walk, crawled far enough to deliver his orders.

2264 ◆ WHITE, EDWARD

Rank: Private
Service: U.S. Army
Birthday: 15 January 1877
Place of Birth: Seneca, Nemaha County, Kansas
Date of Death: 3 December 1908
Place of Death: Kansas City, Kansas
Cemetery: Mount Calvary Cemetery (MH)—Kansas City, Kansas
Entered Service at: Kansas City, Wyandotte County, Kansas
Unit: Company B, 20th Kansas Volunteer Infantry
Battle or Place of Action: at Calumpit, Luzon, Philippine Islands
Date of Action: 27 April 1899
Date of Issue: 11 March 1902
Citation: Swam the Rio Grande de Pampanga in the face of the enemy's fire and fastened a rope to the occupied trenches, thereby enabling the crossing of the river and the driving of the enemy from his fortified position.

2265 ◆ WILSON, ARTHUR HARRISON

Rank: Second Lieutenant (highest rank: Colonel)
Service: U.S. Army
Birthday: 17 August 1881
Place of Birth: Springfield, Sangamon County, Illinois
Date of Death: 15 December 1953
Place of Death: Port Isabel, Texas
Cemetery: Oakridge Cemetery—Springfield, Illinois
Entered Service at: Springfield, Sangamon County, Illinois
Unit: 6th U.S. Cavalry
Battle or Place of Action: Patian Island, Philippine Islands
Date of Action: 4 July 1909
Date of Issue: 23 November 1912
Citation: While in action against hostile Moros, when, it being necessary to secure a mountain gun in position by rope and tackle, voluntarily and with the assistance of an enlisted man, carried the rope forward and fastened it, being all the time under heavy fire of the enemy at short-range.

CHINA RELIEF EXPEDITION

2266 ◆ ADAMS, JOHN MAPES

Rank: Sergeant
Service: U.S. Marine Corps
Birthday: 11 October 1871
Place of Birth: Haverhill, Essex County, Massachusetts
Date of Death: 6 January 1921
Cemetery: Cypress Hills National Cemetery (2-8262) (MH)—Brooklyn, New York
Entered Service at: Massachusetts
Battle or Place of Action: Tientsin, China
Date of Action: 19 July 1900
G.O. Number, Date: 55, 19 July 1901
Citation: In the presence of the enemy during the battle near Tientsin, China, 13 July 1900, Adams distinguished himself by meritorious conduct.

2267 ◆ ADRIANCE, HARRY CHAPMAN

Rank: Corporal (highest rank: Sergeant)
Service: U.S. Marine Corps
Birthday: 27 October 1864
Place of Birth: Oswego, Oswego County, New York
Date of Death: 25 January 1934
Place of Death: Brooklyn, New York
Entered Service at: Massachusetts
Battle or Place of Action: Tientsin, China
Date of Action: 13 July 1900
G.O. Number, Date: 55, 19 July 1901
Citation: In the presence of the enemy during the battle near Tientsin, China, 13 July 1900, Adriance distinguished himself by meritorious conduct.

2268 ◆ ALLEN, EDWARD G.

Rank: Boatswain's Mate First Class (highest rank: Chief Boatswain)
Service: U.S. Navy
Birthday: 4 December 1859
Place of Birth: Amsterdam, Holland
Date of Death: 16 April 1917
Place of Death: Brooklyn, New York
Cemetery: The Evergreen Cemetery—Brooklyn, New York
Entered Service at: New York
Unit: U.S.S. *Newark*
Battle or Place of Action: China
Date of Action: 22 June 1900
G.O. Number, Date: 55, 19 July 1901
Citation: Fighting with the relief expedition of the Allied forces, 13, 20, 21, and 22 June 1900, Allen distinguished himself by meritorious conduct.

2269 ◆ APPLETON, EDWIN NELSON

Rank: Corporal (highest rank: Captain U.S.A.)
Service: U.S. Marine Corps
Birthday: 28 August 1877
Place of Birth: Brooklyn, Kings County, New York
Date of Death: 26 September 1937
Cemetery: The Green Wood Cemetery—Brooklyn, New York
Entered Service at: New York
Battle or Place of Action: Tientsin, China
Date of Action: 20 June 1900
G.O. Number, Date: 84, 22 March 1902
Citation: In action against the enemy at Tientsin, China, 20 June 1900. Crossing the river in a small boat while under heavy enemy fire, Appleton assisted in destroying buildings occupied by the enemy.

2270 ◆ BOYDSTON, ERWIN JAY

Rank: Private
Service: U.S. Marine Corps
Birthday: 22 April 1875
Place of Birth: Deer Creek, Colorado
Date of Death: 19 May 1957
Cemetery: National Memorial Cemetery of the Pacific (G-703) (MH)—Honolulu, Hawaii
Entered Service at: California
Battle or Place of Action: Peking, China
Date of Action: 19 July-17 August 1900
G.O. Number, Date: 55, 19 July 1901
Citation: In the presence of the enemy at Peking, China, 21 July to 17 August 1900. Under a heavy fire from the enemy during this period, Boydston assisted in the erection of barricades.

2271 ◆ BREWSTER, ANDRE WALKER

Rank: Captain (highest rank: Major General)
Service: U.S. Army
Birthday: 9 December 1862
Place of Birth: Hoboken, Hudson County, New Jersey
Date of Death: 27 March 1942
Cemetery: Arlington National Cemetery (2-1130) (MH)—Arlington, Virginia
Entered Service at: Philadelphia, Philadelphia County, Pennsylvania

Unit: 9th U.S. Infantry
Battle or Place of Action: Tientsin, China
Date of Action: 13 July 1900
Date of Issue: 15 September 1903
Citation: While under fire rescued two of his men from drowning.

2272 ◆ BURNES, JAMES

Rank: Private
Service: U.S. Marine Corps
Birthday: 14 January 1870
Place of Birth: Worcester, Worcester County, Massachusetts
Entered Service at: California
Battle or Place of Action: Tientsin, China
Date of Action: 20 June 1900
G.O. Number, Date: 84, 22 March 1902
Date of Issue: 21 April 1902
Citation: In action against the enemy at Tientsin, China, 20 June 1900. Crossing the river in a small boat with three other men while under a heavy fire from the enemy, Burnes assisted in destroying buildings occupied by hostile forces.

2273 ◆ CAMPBELL, ALBERT RALPH

Rank: Private (highest rank: Corporal)
Service: U.S. Marine Corps
Birthday: 8 April 1875
Place of Birth: Williamsport, Lycoming County, Pennsylvania
Date of Death: 4 December 1925
Cemetery: Forest Lawn Memorial Park—Glendale, California
Entered Service at: Pennsylvania
Battle or Place of Action: Tientsin, China
Date of Action: 21 June 1900
G.O. Number, Date: 55, 19 July 1901
Date of Issue: 24 March 1902
Citation: In action at Tientsin, China, 21 June 1900. During the advance on Tientsin, Campbell distinguished himself by his conduct.

2274 ◆ CARR, WILLIAM LOUIS

Rank: Private (highest rank: Corporal)
Service: U.S. Marine Corps
Birthday: 1 April 1878
Place of Birth: Peabody, Essex County, Massachusetts
Date of Death: 14 April 1921
Place of Death: Sandusky, Ohio
Cemetery: Ohio Veteran's Home Cemetery (MH)—Sandusky, Ohio
Entered Service at: Boston, Suffolk County, Massachusetts
Battle or Place of Action: Peking, China
Date of Action: 21 July–17 August 1900
G.O. Number, Date: 55, 19 July 1901
Date of Issue: 11 December 1901
Citation: In action at Peking, China, 21 July to 17 August 1900. Throughout this action and in the presence of the enemy, Carr distinguished himself by his conduct.

2275 ◆ CHATHAM, JOHN PURNESS

Rank: Gunner's Mate Second Class
Service: U.S. Navy
Birthday: 2 July 1872
Place of Birth: Warchester, Maryland
Date of Death: 3 October 1914
Place of Death: Salisbury, Maryland
Cemetery: Parsons Cemetery—Salisbury, Maryland
Entered Service at: Maryland
Unit: U.S.S. *Newark*
Battle or Place of Action: China
Date of Action: 13, 20-22 June 1900
G.O. Number, Date: 55, 19 July 1901
Citation: In action with the relief expedition of the Allied forces in China, 13, 20, 21, and 22 June 1900. During this period and in the presence of the enemy, Chatham distinguished himself by his conduct.

2276 ◆ CLANCY, JOSEPH

Rank: Chief Boatswain's Mate (highest rank: Lieutenant)
Service: U.S. Navy
Birthday: 29 September 1863
Place of Birth: New York, New York
Date of Death: 2 February 1929
Cemetery: Arlington National Cemetery (7-8145) (MH)—Arlington, Virginia
Unit: U.S.S. *Newark*
Battle or Place of Action: China
Date of Action: 13, 20-22 June 1900
G.O. Number, Date: 55, 19 July 1901
Citation: In action with the relief expedition of the Allied forces in China, 13, 20, 21, and 22 June 1900. During this period and in the presence of the enemy, Clancy distinguished himself by his conduct.

2277 ◆ COONEY, JAMES

Rank: Private (highest rank: Corporal)
Service: U.S. Marine Corps
Birthday: 27 July 1860
Place of Birth: Limerick, Ireland
Date of Death: 14 March 1903
Cemetery: Mare Island Cemetery (10-93) (MH)—Vallejo, California
Entered Service at: Massachusetts
Battle or Place of Action: Tientsin, China
Date of Action: 13 July 1900
G.O. Number, Date: 55, 19 July 1901
Date of Issue: 11 December 1901
Citation: In the presence of the enemy during the battle near Tientsin, China, 13 July 1900, Cooney distinguished himself by meritorious conduct.

2278 ◆ DAHLGREN, JOHN OLOF

Rank: Corporal
Service: U.S. Marine Corps
Birthday: 14 September 1872
Place of Birth: Kahliwar, Sweden
Date of Death: 11 February 1963
Cemetery: Golden Gate National Cemetery (Z-1950)—San Bruno, California
Entered Service at: California
Battle or Place of Action: Peking, China
Date of Action: 20 June & 16 July 1900
G.O. Number, Date: 55, 19 July 1901
Citation: In the presence of the enemy during the battle of Peking, China, 20 June to 16 July 1900, Dahlgren distinguished himself by meritorious conduct.

2279 ◆ DALY, DANIEL JOSEPH✢

Rank: Private (highest rank: Sergeant Major)
Service: U.S. Marine Corps
Birthday: 11 November 1873
Place of Birth: Glen Cove, Nassau County, New York
Date of Death: 27 April 1937
Place of Death: Glendale, New York
Cemetery: Cypress Hills National Cemetery (5-70) (MH)—Brooklyn, New York
Entered Service at: New York
Unit: Capt. Newt H. Hall's Marine Detachment, U.S.S. *Newark*
Battle or Place of Action: Peking, China
Date of Action: 14 August 1900
G.O. Number, Date: 55, 19 July 1901
Date of Issue: 11 December 1901
Citation: **First Award** In the presence of the enemy during the battle of Peking, China, 14 August 1900, Daly distinguished himself by meritorious conduct.
Notes: ✢Double Awardee: *see also* Haitian Campaign, 1915

2280 ◆ *FISHER, HARRY

True Name: Phillips, Franklin J.
Rank: Private
Service: U.S. Marine Corps
Birthday: 20 October 1874
Place of Birth: McKeesport, Allegheny County, Pennsylvania
Date of Death: 16 July 1900
Place of Death: Peking, China
Cemetery: Versailles Cemetery (MH)—McKeesport, Pennsylvania
Entered Service at: Pennsylvania
Battle or Place of Action: Peking, China
Date of Action: 20 June-16 July 1900
G.O. Number, Date: 55, 19 July 1901
Citation: Served in the presence of the enemy at the battle of Peking, China, 20 June to 16 July 1900. Assisting in the erection of barricades during the action, Fisher was killed by the heavy fire of the enemy.

2281 ◆ FOLEY, ALEXANDER JOSEPH

Rank: Sergeant (highest rank: First Sergeant)
Service: U.S. Marine Corps
Birthday: 19 February 1866
Place of Birth: Heckersville, Pennsylvania
Date of Death: 14 January 1910
Cemetery: Culebra Naval Station Cemetery—Culebra, Puerto Rico
Entered Service at: Pennsylvania
Unit: U.S.S. *Monadnock*
Battle or Place of Action: near Tientsin, China
Date of Action: 21 June 1900
G.O. Number, Date: 55, 19 July 1901
Citation: In the presence of the enemy during the battle near Tientsin, China, 13 July 1900, Foley distinguished himself by meritorious conduct.

2282 ◆ FRANCIS, CHARLES ROBERT

Rank: Private (highest rank: Second Lieutenant)
Service: U.S. Marine Corps
Birthday: 19 May 1875
Place of Birth: Doylestown, Bucks County, Pennsylvania
Date of Death: 15 July 1946
Place of Death: Santa Monica, California
Cemetery: Hollywood Cemetery—Hollywood, California
Entered Service at: Philadelphia, Philadelphia County, Pennsylvania
Battle or Place of Action: Tientsin, China
Date of Action: 21 June 1900
G.O. Number, Date: 55, 19 July 1901
Citation: In the presence of the enemy during the battle near Tientsin, China, 13 July 1900, Francis distinguished himself by meritorious conduct.

2283 ◆ GAIENNIE, LOUIS RENE

Rank: Private
Service: U.S. Marine Corps
Birthday: 9 June 1878
Place of Birth: St. Louis, St. Louis County, Missouri
Date of Death: 25 November 1942
Cemetery: Calvary Cemetery—St. Louis, Missouri
Entered Service at: St. Louis, St. Louis County, Missouri
Battle or Place of Action: Peking, China
Date of Action: 21 July-17 August 1900
G.O. Number, Date: 55, 19 July 1901
Date of Issue: 11 December 1901
Citation: In the presence of the enemy during the action at Peking, China, 21 July to 17 August 1900, Gaiennie distinguished himself by meritorious conduct.

2284 ◆ HAMBERGER, WILLIAM FRANCIS

Rank: Chief Carpenter's Mate (highest rank: Lieutenant Commander)
Service: U.S. Navy

Birthday: 5 January 1871
Place of Birth: Newark, Essex County, New Jersey
Date of Death: 1 September 1937
Cemetery: Arlington National Cemetery (6-9164)—Arlington, Virginia
Entered Service at: New Jersey
Unit: U.S.S. *Newark*
Battle or Place of Action: China
Date of Action: 13, 20-22 June 1900
G.O. Number, Date: 55, 19 July 1901
Citation: Fighting with the relief expedition of the Allied forces on 13, 20, 21, and 22 June 1900, Hamberger distinguished himself by meritorious conduct.

2285 ◆ HANFORD, BURKE

Rank: Machinist First Class (highest rank: Chief Machinist)
Service: U.S. Navy
Birthday: 17 December 1872
Place of Birth: Toledo, Lucas County, Ohio
Date of Death: 11 April 1928
Cemetery: Greenwood Memorial Park—San Diego, California
Entered Service at: Ohio
Unit: U.S.S. *Newark*
Battle or Place of Action: China
Date of Action: 13, 20-22 June 1900
G.O. Number, Date: 55, 19 July 1901
Citation: Served with the relief expedition of the Allied forces in China on 13, 20, 21, and 22 June 1900. In the presence of the enemy during this period, Hanford distinguished himself by meritorious conduct.

2286 ◆ HANSEN, HANS ANTON

Rank: Seaman
Service: U.S. Navy
Birthday: 16 April 1872
Place of Birth: Germany
Date of Death: 9 May 1915
Cemetery: Arlington National Cemetery (17-18576) (MH)—Arlington, Virginia
Entered Service at: California
Unit: U.S.S. *Newark*
Battle or Place of Action: China
Date of Action: 13, 20-22 June 1900
G.O. Number, Date: 55, 19 July 1901
Citation: Served with the relief expedition of the Allied forces in China on 13, 20, 21, and 22 June 1900. In the presence of the enemy during this period, Hansen distinguished himself by meritorious conduct.

2287 ◆ HEISCH, HENRY WILLIAM

Rank: Private
Service: U.S. Marine Corps
Birthday: 10 June 1872
Place of Birth: Latendorf, Germany
Date of Death: 10 July 1941
Place of Death: Napa, California
Cemetery: Tulocay Cemetery—Napa, California
Entered Service at: California
Battle or Place of Action: Tientsin, China
Date of Action: 20 June 1900
G.O. Number, Date: 84, 22 March 1902
Citation: In action against the enemy at Tientsin, China, 20 June 1900. Crossing the river in a small boat while under heavy fire, Heisch assisted in destroying buildings occupied by the enemy.

2288 ◆ HOLYOKE, WILLIAM EDWARD

Rank: Boatswain's Mate First Class
Service: U.S. Navy
Birthday: 13 March 1868
Place of Birth: Groveton, Coos County, New Hampshire
Date of Death: 3 April 1934
Cemetery: Charles Evans Cemetery (MH)—Reading, Pennsylvania
Entered Service at: Illinois
Unit: U.S.S. *Newark*
Battle or Place of Action: China
Date of Action: 13, 20-22 June 1900
G.O. Number, Date: 55, 19 July 1901
Citation: In action with the relief expedition of the Allied forces in China, 13, 20, 21, and 22 June 1900. During this period and in the presence of the enemy, Holyoke distinguished himself by meritorious conduct.

2289 ◆ HORTON, WILLIAM M. CHARLIE

Rank: Private (highest rank: Sergeant)
Service: U.S. Marine Corps
Birthday: 21 July 1876
Place of Birth: Chicago, Cook County, Illinois
Date of Death: 14 February 1969
Cemetery: Evergreen-Washelli Memorial Park—Seattle, Washington
Entered Service at: Philadelphia, Philadelphia County, Pennsylvania
Unit: U.S.S. *Oregon*
Battle or Place of Action: Peking, China
Date of Action: 21 July-17 August 1900
G.O. Number, Date: 55, 19 July 1901
Date of Issue: 5 January 1902
Citation: In action against the enemy at Peking, China, 21 July to 17 August 1900. Although under heavy fire from the enemy, Horton assisted in the erection of barricades.

2290 ◆ HUNT, MARTIN

Rank: Private (highest rank: Corporal)
Service: U.S. Marine Corps
Birthday: 9 July 1873
Place of Birth: County Mayo, Ireland
Date of Death: 22 July 1938

Place of Death: Pasay Rizal, Philippine Islands
Entered Service at: Boston, Suffolk County, Massachusetts
Battle or Place of Action: Peking, China
Date of Action: 20 June-16 July 1900
G.O. Number, Date: 55, 19 July 1901
Date of Issue: 2 July 1915
Citation: In the presence of the enemy during the battle of Peking, China, 20 June to 16 July 1900, Hunt distinguished himself by meritorious conduct.

2291 ◆ KATES, THOMAS WILBUR

Rank: Private (highest rank: Sergeant)
Service: U.S. Marine Corps
Birthday: 7 May 1865
Place of Birth: Shelby Center, New York
Entered Service at: New York
Battle or Place of Action: Tientsin, China
Date of Action: 21 June 1900
G.O. Number, Date: 55, 19 July 1901
Citation: In presence of the enemy during the advance on Tientsin, China, 21 June 1900, Kates distinguished himself by meritorious conduct.

2292 ◆ KILLACKEY, JOSEPH

Rank: Landsman (highest rank: Gunner's Mate Third Class)
Service: U.S. Navy
Birthday: 21 January 1879
Place of Birth: County Cork, Ireland
Date of Death: 8 September 1946
Cemetery: Mount Moriah VA plot (4-3-23) (MH)—Philadelphia, Pennsylvania
Entered Service at: Pennsylvania
Unit: U.S.S. *Newark*
Battle or Place of Action: China
Date of Action: 13, 20-22 June 1900
G.O. Number, Date: 55, 19 July 1901
Citation: In action with the relief expedition of the Allied forces in China, 13, 20, 21, and 22 June 1900. During this period and in the presence of the enemy, Killackey distinguished himself by meritorious conduct.

2293 ◆ LAWTON, LOUIS BOWEM

Rank: First Lieutenant (highest rank: Major)
Service: U.S. Army
Birthday: 1872
Place of Birth: Independence, Buchanan County, Iowa
Date of Death: 9 July 1949
Cemetery: Fort Hill Cemetery—Auburn, New York
Entered Service at: Auburn, Cayuga County, New York
Unit: 9th U.S. Infantry
Battle or Place of Action: Tientsin, China
Date of Action: 13 July 1900
Date of Issue: 11 March 1902
Citation: Carried a message and guided reinforcements across a wide and fire-swept space, during which he was thrice wounded.

2294 ◆ MATHIAS, CLARENCE EDWARD

Rank: Private (highest rank: Sergeant Major)
Service: U.S. Marine Corps
Birthday: 12 December 1876
Place of Birth: Royalton, Dauphin County, Pennsylvania
Date of Death: 9 December 1935
Cemetery: Arlington National Cemetery (6-8681) (MH)—Arlington, Virginia
Entered Service at: Pennsylvania
Unit: U.S.S. *Solace*
Battle or Place of Action: Tientsin, China
Date of Action: 13 July 1900
G.O. Number, Date: 84, 22 March 1902
Citation: In the presence of the enemy during the advance on Tientsin, China, 13 July 1900, Mathias distinguished himself by meritorious conduct.

2295 ◆ McALLISTER, SAMUEL

Rank: Ordinary Seaman
Service: U.S. Navy
Birthday: 23 January 1869
Place of Birth: Belfast, County Antrim, Ireland
Date of Death: 13 December 1903
Place of Death: Died on active duty U.S.S. *Wisconsin*
Cemetery: Buried at sea between Japan and Hawaii
Entered Service at: California
Unit: U.S.S. *Newark*
Battle or Place of Action: Tientsin, China
Date of Action: 20 June 1900
G.O. Number, Date: 84, 22 March 1902
Citation: In action against the enemy at Tientsin, China, 20 June 1900. Crossing the river in a small boat while under heavy enemy fire, McAllister assisted in destroying buildings occupied by the enemy.

2296 ◆ McCLOY, JOHN✠

Rank: Coxswain (highest rank: Lieutenant Commander)
Service: U.S. Navy
Birthday: 3 January 1876
Place of Birth: Brewster, Putnam County, New York
Date of Death: 25 May 1945
Cemetery: Arlington National Cemetery (8-5246)—Arlington, Virginia
Entered Service at: New York
Unit: U.S.S. *Newark*
Battle or Place of Action: Wu-Tsing-Hune and near Peh-Tsang, China
Date of Action: 13, 20-22 June 1900
G.O. Number, Date: 55, 19 July 1901
Citation: First Award In action with the relief expedition of the Allied forces in China, 13, 20, 21 and 22 June 1900. During this period and in the presence of the enemy,

Coxswain McCloy distinguished himself by meritorious conduct.
Notes: ✢Double Awardee: *see also* Mexican Campaign (Vera Cruz)

2297 ◆ MITCHELL, JOSEPH ANDREW

Rank: Gunner's Mate First Class (highest rank: Lieutenant)
Service: U.S. Navy
Birthday: 27 November 1876
Place of Birth: Philadelphia, Philadelphia County, Pennsylvania
Date of Death: 9 June 1925
Place of Death: Philadelphia, Pennsylvania
Cemetery: St. Paul's Catholic Cemetery (MH)—Portsmouth, Virginia
Entered Service at: Pennsylvania
Unit: U.S.S. *Newark*
Battle or Place of Action: Peking, China
Date of Action: 12 July 1900
G.O. Number, Date: 55, 19 July 1901
Citation: In the presence of the enemy during the battle of Peking, China, 12 July 1900, Mitchell distinguished himself by meritorious conduct.

2298 ◆ MOORE, ALBERT

Rank: Private (highest rank: First Sergeant U.S. Army Retired)
Service: U.S. Marine Corps
Birthday: 25 December 1862
Place of Birth: Merced, Merced County, California
Date of Death: 14 September 1916
Place of Death: Port Mason, California
Cemetery: San Francisco National Cemetery (WS-1032-A)—San Francisco, California
Entered Service at: California
Battle or Place of Action: Peking, China
Date of Action: 21 July-17 August 1900
G.O. Number, Date: 55, 19 July 1901
Citation: In the presence of the enemy during the battle of Peking, China, 21 July to 17 August 1900. Although under a heavy fire from the enemy, Moore assisted in the erection of barricades.

2299 ◆ MURPHY, JOHN ALPHONSUS

Rank: Drummer
Service: U.S. Marine Corps
Birthday: 26 February 1881
Place of Birth: New York, New York
Date of Death: 29 November 1935
Place of Death: New York, New York
Entered Service at: Washington, D.C.
Battle or Place of Action: Peking, China
Date of Action: 21 July-17 August 1900
G.O. Number, Date: 55, 19 July 1901
Citation: In the presence of the enemy during the action at Peking, China, 21 July to 17 August 1900, Murphy distinguished himself by meritorious conduct.

2300 ◆ MURRAY, WILLIAM HENRY

True Name: Served as Davis, Henry W.
Rank: Private
Service: U.S. Marine Corps
Birthday: 3 June 1876
Place of Birth: Brooklyn, Kings County, New York
Date of Death: 12 October 1923
Place of Death: Rutland, Massachusetts
Cemetery: Oak Grove Cemetery (MH)—Medford, Massachusetts
Entered Service at: Brooklyn, Kings County, New York
Battle or Place of Action: Peking, China
Date of Action: 21 July-17 August 1900
G.O. Number, Date: 55, 19 July 1901
Citation: In the presence of the enemy during the action at Peking, China, 21 July to 17 August 1900. During this period, Murray distinguished himself by meritorious conduct.

2301 ◆ ORNDOFF, HARRY WESTLEY

True Name: Orndof, Harry Westley
Rank: Private
Service: U.S. Marine Corps
Birthday: 8 November 1875
Place of Birth: Sandusky, Erie County, Ohio
Date of Death: 14 July 1938
Cemetery: Highland Park Cemetery (MH)—Cleveland, Ohio
Entered Service at: California
Battle or Place of Action: China
Date of Action: 13, 20-22 June 1900
G.O. Number, Date: 55, 19 July 1901
Date of Issue: 10 December 1901
Citation: In action with the relief expedition of the Allied forces in China, 13, 20, 21, and 22 June 1900. During this period and in the presence of the enemy, Orndoff distinguished himself by meritorious conduct.

2302 ◆ PETERSEN, CARL EMIL

Rank: Chief Machinist
Service: U.S. Navy
Birthday: 24 August 1875
Place of Birth: Hamburg, Germany
Date of Death: 17 November 1971
Place of Death: Edison, New Jersey
Cemetery: Cloverleaf Park Cemetery (MH)—Woodbridge, New Jersey
Entered Service at: New Jersey
Unit: U.S.S. *Newark*
Battle or Place of Action: Peking, China
Date of Action: 28 June-17 August 1900
G.O. Number, Date: 55, 19 July 1901
Citation: In the presence of the enemy during the action at Peking, China, 28 June to 17 August 1900. During this peri-

od Chief Machinist Petersen distinguished himself by meritorious conduct.

2303 ◆ PHILLIPS, REUBEN JASPER

Rank: Corporal (highest rank: Sergeant)
Service: U.S. Marine Corps
Birthday: 28 July 1874
Place of Birth: Cambria, San Luis Obispo County, California
Date of Death: 8 February 1936
Cemetery: San Francisco National Cemetery (OS-D-3 Row 118) (MH)—San Francisco, California
Entered Service at: California
Battle or Place of Action: China
Date of Action: 13, 20-22 June 1900
G.O. Number, Date: 55, 19 July 1901
Citation: In action with the relief expedition of the Allied forces in China during the battles of 13, 20, 21, and 22 June 1900. Throughout this period and in the presence of the enemy, Phillips distinguished himself by meritorious conduct.

2304 ◆ PRESTON, HERBERT IRVING

Rank: Private
Service: U.S. Marine Corps
Birthday: 6 August 1876
Place of Birth: Berkeley, Union County, New Jersey
Entered Service at: New Jersey
Battle or Place of Action: Peking, China
Date of Action: 21 July-17 August 1900
G.O. Number, Date: 55, 19 July 1901
Citation: In the presence of the enemy during the action at Peking, China, 21 July to 17 August 1900. Throughout this period, Preston distinguished himself by meritorious conduct.

2305 ◆ ROSE, GEORGE HARRY

Rank: Seaman (highest rank: Lieutenant Commander)
Service: U.S. Navy
Birthday: 28 February 1880
Place of Birth: Stamford, Fairfield County, Connecticut
Date of Death: 7 December 1932
Place of Death: Newark, New Jersey
Cemetery: Arlington National Cemetery (7-9978-ES) (MH)—Arlington, Virginia
Entered Service at: Connecticut
Unit: U.S.S. *Newark*
Battle or Place of Action: Peking, China
Date of Action: 13, 20-22 June 1900
G.O. Number, Date: 55, 19 July 1901
Citation: In the presence of the enemy during the battles at Peking, China, 13, 20, 21, and 22 June 1900. Throughout this period, Rose distinguished himself by meritorious conduct. While stationed as a crewmember of the U.S.S. *Newark*, he was part of its landing force that went ashore off Taku, China. On 31 May 1900, he was in a party of six under John McCloy (MH) which took ammunition from the *Newark* to Tientsin. On 10 June 1900, he was one of a party that carried dispatches from LaFa to Yongstsum at night. On the 13th, he was one of a few who fought off a large force of the enemy, saving the main baggage train from destruction. On the 20th and 21st he was engaged in heavy fighting against the Imperial Army, being always in the first rank. On the 22d he showed gallantry in the capture of the Siku Arsenal. He volunteered to go to the nearby village which was occupied by the enemy to secure medical supplies urgently required. The party brought back the supplies carried by newly taken prisoners

2306 ◆ RYAN, FRANCIS THOMAS

True Name: Gallagher, Frank
Rank: Coxswain (highest rank: Ship's Cook First Class Retired)
Service: U.S. Navy
Birthday: 6 April 1862
Place of Birth: Massachusetts
Date of Death: 14 June 1927
Place of Death: Philadelphia, Pennsylvania
Cemetery: Arlington National Cemetery (17-21008) (MH)—Arlington, Virginia
Entered Service at: Massachusetts
Unit: U.S.S. *Newark*
Battle or Place of Action: China
Date of Action: 13, 20-22 June 1900
G.O. Number, Date: 55, 19 July 1901
Citation: In action with the relief expediton of the Allied forces in China during the battles of 13, 20 21, and 22 June 1900. Throughout this period and in the presence of the enemy, Ryan distinguished himself by meritorious conduct.

2307 ◆ SCANNELL, DAVID JOHN

Rank: Private
Service: U.S. Marine Corps
Birthday: 30 March 1875
Place of Birth: Boston, Suffolk County, Massachusetts
Date of Death: 7 May 1923
Place of Death: Togus, Maine
Cemetery: Togus National Cemetery (3955-W-2-42) (MH)—Togus, Maine
Entered Service at: Boston, Suffolk County, Massachusetts
Battle or Place of Action: Peking, China
Date of Action: 21 July-17 August 1900
G.O. Number, Date: 55, 19 July 1901
Citation: In the presence of the enemy during the action at Peking, China, 21 July to 17 August 1900. Throughout this period, Scannell distinguished himself by meritorious conduct.

2308 ◆ SEACH, WILLIAM

Rank: Ordinary Seaman (highest rank: Lieutenant)
Service: U.S. Navy
Birthday: 23 May 1877
Place of Birth: London, England
Date of Death: 24 October 1978

Place of Death: Brockton, Massachusetts
Cemetery: Arlington National Cemetery (11-334-2) (MH)—Arlington, Virginia
Entered Service at: Massachusetts
Unit: U.S.S. *Newark*
Battle or Place of Action: China
Date of Action: 13, 20-22 June 1900
G.O. Number, Date: 55, 19 July 1901
Date of Issue: 1903
Citation: In action with the relief expedition of the Allied forces in China during the battles of 13, 20, 21, and 22 June 1900. June 13: Seach and six others were cited for their courage in repulsing an attack by 300 Chinese Imperialist soldiers and Boxer militants with a bayonet charge, thus thwarting a planned massive attack on the entire force. June 20: During a day-long battle, Seach ran across an open clearing, gained cover, and cleaned out nests of Chinese snipers. June 21: During a surprise saber attack by Chinese cavalrymen, Seach was cited for defending gun emplacements. June 22: Seach and others breached the wall of a Chinese fort, fought their way to the enemy's guns, and turned the cannon upon the defenders of the fort. Throughout this period and in the presence of the enemy, Seach distinguished himself by meritorious conduct.

2309 ◆ SILVA, FRANCE

Rank: Private
Service: U.S. Marine Corps
Birthday: 8 May 1876
Place of Birth: Hayward, Alameda County, California
Date of Death: 10 April 1951
Place of Death: Red Bluff, California
Cemetery: Sunset Hill Cemetery (MH)—Corning, California
Entered Service at: San Francisco, San Francisco County, California
Unit: U.S.S. *Newark*
Battle or Place of Action: Peking, China
Date of Action: 28 June-17 August 1900
G.O. Number, Date: 55, 19 July 1901
Citation: In the presence of the enemy during the action at Peking, China, 28 June to 17 August 1900. Throughout this period, Silva distinguished himself by meritorious conduct.

2310 ◆ SMITH, FRANK ELMER

Service: U.S. Navy
Birthday: 22 August 1864
Place of Birth: Boston, Suffolk County, Massachusetts
Entered Service at: Virginia
Unit: U.S.S. *Newark*
Battle or Place of Action: China
Date of Action: 13, 20-22 June 1900
G.O. Number, Date: 55, 19 July 1901
Citation: In action with the relief expedition of the Allied forces in China during the battles of 13, 20, 21, and 22 June 1900. Throughout this period and in the presence of the enemy, Smith distinguished himself by meritorious conduct.

2311 ◆ SMITH, JAMES A.

Rank: Landsman
Service: U.S. Navy
Birthday: 2 September 1880
Place of Birth: New York
Entered Service at: New York
Unit: U.S.S. *Newark*
Battle or Place of Action: near Tientsin, China
Date of Action: 13, 20-22 June 1900
G.O. Number, Date: 55, 19 July 1901
Citation: In action with the relief expedition of the Allied forces in China during the battles of 13, 20, 21, and 22 June 1900. Throughout this period and in the presence of the enemy, Smith distinguished himself by meritorious conduct.

2312 ◆ STANLEY, ROBERT HENRY

Rank: Hospital Apprentice (highest rank: Chief Pharmacist)
Service: U.S. Navy
Birthday: 2 May 1881
Place of Birth: Brooklyn, Kings County, New York
Date of Death: 15 July 1942
Place of Death: Pensacola, Florida
Cemetery: Arlington National Cemetery (7-8348)—Arlington, Virginia
Entered Service at: aboard U.S.S. *Vermont*
Unit: U.S.S. *Newark*
Battle or Place of Action: Peking, China
Date of Action: 13, 20-22 June 1900
G.O. Number, Date: 55, 19 July 1901
Place of Presentation: On board the U.S.S. *Brooklyn*
Citation: For distinguished conduct in the presence of the enemy in volunteering and carrying messages under fire at Peking, China, 12 July 1900.

2313 ◆ STEWART, PETER

Rank: Gunnery Sergeant
Service: U.S. Marine Corps
Birthday: 17 February 1858
Place of Birth: Airdrie, Scotland
Date of Death: 17 June 1914
Cemetery: Cypress Hills National Cemetery (2-7303) (MH)—Brooklyn, New York
Entered Service at: Washington, D.C.
Unit: Marine Guard, U.S.S. *Newark*
Battle or Place of Action: China
Date of Action: 13, 20-22 June 1900
G.O. Number, Date: 55, 19 July 1901
Citation: In action with the relief expedition of the Allied forces in China during the battles of 13, 20, 21, and 22 June 1900. Throughout this period and in the presence of the enemy, Stewart distinguished himself by meritorious conduct.

2314 ◆ SUTTON, CLARENCE EDWIN

Rank: Sergeant (highest rank: First Sergeant)
Service: U.S. Marine Corps

Birthday: 18 February 1871
Place of Birth: Urbanna, Middlesex County, Virginia
Date of Death: 9 October 1916
Cemetery: Arlington National Cemetery (17-18847) (MH)—Arlington, Virginia
Entered Service at: Washington, D.C.
Battle or Place of Action: Tientsin, China
Date of Action: 13 July 1900
G.O. Number, Date: 55, 19 July 1901
Citation: In action during the battle near Tientsin, China, 13 July 1900. Although under heavy fire from the enemy, Sutton assisted in carrying a wounded officer from the field of battle.

2315 ◆ THOMAS, KARL

Rank: Coxswain
Service: U.S. Navy
Birthday: 17 March 1871
Place of Birth: Germany
Entered Service at: New York
Unit: U.S.S. *Newark*
Battle or Place of Action: China
Date of Action: 13, 20-22 June 1900
G.O. Number, Date: 55, 19 July 1901
Citation: In action with the relief expedition of the Allied forces in China, 13, 20, 21, and 22 June 1900. During this period and in the presence of the enemy, Thomas distinguished himself by meritorious conduct.

2316 ◆ TITUS, CALVIN PEARL

Rank: Musician (highest rank: Lieutenant Colonel)
Service: U.S. Army
Birthday: 22 September 1879
Place of Birth: Vinton, Benton County, Iowa
Date of Death: 27 May 1966
Place of Death: San Fernando, California
Cemetery: Forest Lawn Memorial Park—Hollywood, California
Entered Service at: Iowa
Unit: Company E, 14th U.S. Infantry
Battle or Place of Action: Peking, China
Date of Action: 14 August 1900
Date of Issue: 11 March 1902
Citation: Gallant and daring conduct in the presence of his colonel and other officers and enlisted men of his regiment; was first to scale the wall of the city.

2317 ◆ TORGERSON, MARTIN TORINUS

Rank: Gunner's Mate Third Class
Service: U.S. Navy
Birthday: 7 November 1875
Place of Birth: Oleesen, Norway
Date of Death: 12 June 1935
Place of Death: Rosedale, New York
Cemetery: Arlington National Cemetery (6-8680)—Arlington, Virginia
Entered Service at: Virginia
Unit: U.S.S. *Newark*
Battle or Place of Action: China
Date of Action: 13, 20-22 June 1900
G.O. Number, Date: 55, 19 July 1901
Citation: In action with the relief expedition of the Allied forces in China, 13, 20, 21, and 22 June 1900. During this period and in the presence of the enemy, Torgerson distinguished himself by meritorious conduct.

2318 ◆ UPHAM, OSCAR JEFFERSON

Rank: Private
Service: U.S. Marine Corps
Birthday: 11 January 1871
Place of Birth: Toledo, Lucas County, Ohio
Date of Death: 18 February 1949
Place of Death: Guthrie, Oklahoma
Cemetery: Summit View Cemetery—Guthrie, Oklahoma
Entered Service at: Illinois
Unit: Marine Guard, U.S.S. *Oregon*
Battle or Place of Action: Peking, China
Date of Action: 21 July-17 August 1900
G.O. Number, Date: 55, 19 July 1901
Citation: In the presence of the enemy at Peking, China, 21 July to 17 August 1900. Although under a heavy fire from the enemy during this period, Upham assisted in the erection of barricades.

2319 ◆ VON SCHLICK, ROBERT H.

Rank: Private
Service: U.S. Army
Birthday: 2 January 1875
Place of Birth: Germany
Date of Death: 1 July 1941
Cemetery: Los Angeles National Cemetery (81-G-20) (MH)—Los Angeles, California
Entered Service at: San Francisco, San Francisco County, California
Unit: Company C, 9th U.S. Infantry
Battle or Place of Action: Tientsin, China
Date of Action: 13 July 1900
Date of Issue: 3 September 1903
Citation: Although previously wounded while carrying a wounded comrade to a place of safety, Von Schlick rejoined his command which partly occupied an exposed position upon a dike, remaining there after his command had been withdrawn, singly keeping up the fire, and obliviously presenting himself as a conspicuous target until he was literally shot off his position by the enemy.

2320 ◆ WALKER, EDWARD ALEXANDER

Rank: Sergeant
Service: U.S. Marine Corps
Birthday: 2 October 1864
Place of Birth: Huntley, Scotland
Date of Death: 24 October 1946

Cemetery: Oak Hill Mausoleum—San Jose, California
Entered Service at: Brooklyn, Kings County, New York
Battle or Place of Action: Peking, China
Date of Action: 20 June-16 July 1900
G.O. Number, Date: 55, 19 July 1901
Citation: In the presence of the enemy during the battle of Peking, China, 20 June to 16 July 1900. Throughout this period, Walker distinguished himself by meritorious conduct.

2321 ◆ WESTERMARK, AXEL

Rank: Seaman (highest rank: Gunner's Mate First Class)
Service: U.S. Navy
Birthday: 8 April 1875
Place of Birth: Bergo, Finland
Date of Death: 7 May 1911
Place of Death: Puget Sound, Washington
Cemetery: San Francisco National Cemetery (A-32)—San Francisco, California
Entered Service at: California
Unit: U.S.S. *Newark*
Battle or Place of Action: Peking, China
Date of Action: 28 June-17 August 1900
G.O. Number, Date: 55, 19 July 1901
Citation: In the presence of the enemy during the battle of Peking, China, 28 June to 17 August 1900. Throughout this period, Westermark distinguished himself by meritorious conduct.

2322 ◆ WILLIAMS, JAY P.

Rank: Coxswain
Service: U.S. Navy
Birthday: 23 September 1872
Place of Birth: Orland, Steuben County, Indiana
Date of Death: 4 July 1938
Cemetery: Woodlawn Cemetery (MH)—Norwalk, Ohio
Entered Service at: Ohio
Unit: U.S.S. *Newark*
Battle or Place of Action: China
Date of Action: 13, 20-22 June 1900
G.O. Number, Date: 55, 19 July 1901
Citation: In action with the relief expedition of the Allied forces in China, 13, 20, 21, and 22 June 1900. During this period and in the presence of the enemy, Williams distinguished himself by meritiorious conduct.

2323 ◆ YOUNG, FRANK ALBERT

Rank: Private (highest rank: Sergeant Major)
Service: U.S. Marine Corps
Birthday: 22 June 1876
Place of Birth: Milwaukee, Milwaukee County, Wisconsin
Date of Death: 3 April 1941
Place of Death: Mare Island Shipyard, California
Cemetery: Arlington National Cemetery (17-18979-D) (MH)—Arlington, Virginia
Entered Service at: Wisconsin
Battle or Place of Action: Peking, China
Date of Action: 20 June-16 July 1900
G.O. Number, Date: 55, 19 July 1901
Citation: In the presence of the enemy during the battle of Peking, China, 20 June to 16 July 1900. Throughout this period, Young distinguished himself by meritorious conduct.

2324 ◆ ZION, WILLIAM F.

Rank: Private (highest rank: First Lieutenant U.S. Army)
Service: U.S. Marine Corps
Birthday: 23 October 1872
Place of Birth: Knightstown, Henry County, Indiana
Date of Death: 25 March 1919
Cemetery: Chattanooga National Cemetery (U-40) (MH)—Chattanooga, Tennessee
Entered Service at: California
Battle or Place of Action: Peking, China
Date of Action: 21 July-17 August 1900
G.O. Number, Date: 55, 19 July 1901
Citation: In the presence of the enemy during the battle of Peking, China, 21 July to 17 August 1900. Throughout this period, Zion distinguished himself by meritorious conduct.

INTERIM 1899–1910

2325 ◆ BEHNE, FREDERICK

Rank: Fireman First Class
Service: U.S. Navy
Birthday: 3 October 1873
Place of Birth: Lodi, Bergen County, New Jersey
Date of Death: 11 February 1918
Entered Service at: New Jersey
Unit: U.S.S. *Iowa*
Battle or Place of Action: U.S.S. *Iowa*
Date of Action: 25 January 1905
G.O. Number, Date: 182, 20 March 1905
Citation: On board the U.S.S. *Iowa*, 25 January 1905. Following the blowing-out of the manhole plate of boiler D of that vessel, Behne displayed extraordinary heroism in the resulting action.

2326 ◆ BEHNKE, HEINRICH

Rank: Seaman First Class
Service: U.S. Navy
Birthday: 10 April 1882
Place of Birth: Germany
Date of Death: 19 June 1952
Cemetery: Long Island National Cemetery (DSS-20-A) (MH)—Farmingdale, New York
Entered Service at: Washington, D.C.
Unit: U.S.S. *Iowa*
Battle or Place of Action: U.S.S. *Iowa*
Date of Action: 25 January 1905
G.O. Number, Date: 182, 20 March 1905
Citation: While serving aboard the U.S.S. *Iowa*, Behnke displayed extraordinary heroism at the time of the blowing-out of the manhole plate of boiler D on board that vessel, 25 January 1905.

2327 ◆ BJORKMAN, ERNEST H.

Rank: Ordinary Seaman
Service: U.S. Navy
Birthday: 25 April 1881
Place of Birth: Malmo, Sweden
Date of Death: 16 September 1912
Place of Death: Edgewater, Colorado
Cemetery: Crown Hill Cemetery (MH)—Edgewater, Colorado
Entered Service at: New York
Unit: U.S.S. *Leyden*
Battle or Place of Action: on the rocks of Block Island, Rhode Island
Date of Action: 21 January 1903
G.O. Number, Date: 145, 26 December 1903
Citation: On board the U.S.S. *Leyden*, 21 January 1903, Bjorkman displayed heroism at the time of the wreck of that vessel.

2328 ◆ BOERS, EDWARD WILLIAM

Rank: Seaman
Service: U.S. Navy
Birthday: 10 March 1884
Place of Birth: Cincinnati, Hamilton County, Ohio
Date of Death: 2 April 1929
Place of Death: Cincinnati, Ohio
Cemetery: Vine Street Hill Cemetery—Cincinnati, Ohio
Entered Service at: Kentucky
Unit: U.S.S. *Bennington*
Battle or Place of Action: U.S.S. *Bennington*
Date of Action: 21 July 1905
G.O. Number, Date: 13, 5 January 1906
Citation: On board the U.S.S. *Bennington*, 21 July 1905. Following the explosion of a boiler of that vessel, Boers displayed extraordinary heroism in the resulting action.

2329 ◆ BONNEY, ROBERT EARL

Rank: Chief Watertender (highest rank: Chief Machinist–Warrant Officer)
Service: U.S. Navy
Birthday: 23 November 1882
Place of Birth: Maryville, Blount County, Tennessee
Date of Death: 22 November 1967
Cemetery: Acacia Memorial Park (MH)—Seattle, Washington
Entered Service at: Nashville, Davidson County, Tennessee
Unit: U.S.S. *Hopkins*
Battle or Place of Action: U.S.S. *Hopkins*
Date of Action: 14 February 1910
Citation: While serving on board the U.S.S. *Hopkins*, Bonney displayed extraordinary heroism in the line of his profession on the occasion of the accident to one of the boilers of that vessel, 14 February 1910.

2330 ◆ BREEMAN, GEORGE

Rank: Seaman (highest rank: Chief Turret Captain)
Service: U.S. Navy
Birthday: 15 September 1880
Place of Birth: Passaic, Passaic County, New Jersey
Date of Death: 10 April 1937

Place of Death: Passaic, New Jersey
Cemetery: Arlington National Cemetery (6-9743-SH)—Arlington, Virginia
Entered Service at: New Jersey
Unit: U.S.S. *Kearsarge*
Battle or Place of Action: U.S.S. *Kearsarge*
G.O. Number, Date: 21, 5 May 1906
Citation: Breeman displayed heroism in the line of his profession while serving on board the U.S.S. *Kearsarge* at the time of the accidental ignition of powder charges in the forward 13-inch turret.

2331 ◆ BRESNAHAN, PATRICK FRANCIS

Rank: Watertender
Service: U.S. Navy
Birthday: 1 May 1872
Place of Birth: Peabody, Essex County, Massachusetts
Date of Death: 29 January 1940
Cemetery: St. Mary's Cemetery (MH)—Salem, Massachusetts
Entered Service at: Vermont
Unit: U.S.S. *Iowa*
Battle or Place of Action: U.S.S. *Iowa*
Date of Action: 25 January 1905
G.O. Number, Date: 182, 20 March 1905
Citation: Serving on board the U.S.S. *Iowa* for extraordinary heroism at the time of the blowing-out of the manhole plate of boiler D on board that vessel, 25 January 1905.

2332 ◆ BROCK, GEORGE F.

Rank: Carpenter's Mate Second Class
Service: U.S. Navy
Birthday: 18 October 1872
Place of Birth: Cleveland, Montgomery County, Ohio
Entered Service at: California
Unit: U.S.S. *Bennington*
Battle or Place of Action: U.S.S. *Bennington*
Date of Action: 21 July 1905
G.O. Number, Date: 13, 5 January 1906
Citation: Serving on board the U.S.S. *Bennington* for extraordinary heroism displayed at the time of the explosion of that vessel at San Diego, Cal., 21 July 1905.

2333 ◆ CAHEY, THOMAS

Rank: Seaman (highest rank: Chief Gunner's Mate)
Service: U.S. Navy
Birthday: 13 April 1870
Place of Birth: Belfast, County Antrim, Ireland
Date of Death: 5 January 1935
Cemetery: Arlington National Cemetery (6-8667)—Arlington, Virginia
Entered Service at: New York
Unit: U.S.S. *Petrel*
Battle or Place of Action: U.S.S. *Petrel*
Date of Action: 31 March 1901
G.O. Number, Date: 59, 23 March 1910
Citation: On board the U.S.S. *Petrel* for heroism and gallantry, fearlessly exposing his own life to danger in saving others on the occasion of the fire on board that vessel, 31 March 1901.

2334 ◆ CLARY, EDWARD ALVIN

Rank: Watertender
Service: U.S. Navy
Birthday: 6 May 1883
Place of Birth: Foxport, Kentucky
Date of Death: 30 April 1939
Cemetery: Sante Fe National Cemetery (O-335)—Sante Fe, New Mexico
Entered Service at: Kentucky
Unit: U.S.S. *Hopkins*
Battle or Place of Action: U.S.S. *Hopkins*
Date of Action: 14 February 1910
G.O. Number, Date: 59, 23 March 1910
Citation: On board the U.S.S. *Hopkins* for extraordinary heroism in the line of his profession on the occasion of the accident to one of the boilers of that vessel, 14 February 1910.

2335 ◆ CLAUSEY, JOHN JOSEPH

Rank: Chief Gunner's Mate (highest rank: Lieutenant)
Service: U.S. Navy
Birthday: 16 May 1875
Place of Birth: San Francisco, San Francisco County, California
Date of Death: 9 September 1951
Cemetery: Golden Gate National Cemetery (C-121-B) (MH)—San Bruno, California
Entered Service at: California
Unit: U.S.S. *Bennington*
Battle or Place of Action: U.S.S. *Bennington*
Date of Action: 21 July 1905
G.O. Number, Date: 13, 5 January 1906
Citation: On board the U.S.S. *Bennington* for extraordinary heroism displayed at the time of the explosion of a boiler of that vessel at San Diego, Cal., 21 July 1905.

2336 ◆ CORAHORGI, DEMETRI

Rank: Fireman First Class
Service: U.S. Navy
Birthday: 3 January 1880
Place of Birth: Trieste, Austria
Date of Death: 15 October 1973
Cemetery: Mount Pleasant Cemetery—Seattle, Washington
Entered Service at: New York
Unit: U.S.S. *Iowa*
Battle or Place of Action: U.S.S. *Iowa*
Date of Action: 25 January 1905
G.O. Number, Date: 182, 20 March 1905
Citation: Serving on board the U.S.S. *Iowa* for extraordinary heroism at the time of the blowing-out of the manhole plate of boiler D on board that vessel, 25 January 1905.

2337 ◆ COX, ROBERT EDWARD

Rank: Chief Gunner
Service: U.S. Navy
Birthday: 22 December 1876
Place of Birth: St. Albans, Kanawha County, West Virginia
Date of Death: 24 April 1937
Place of Death: Philadelphia, Pennsylvania
Cemetery: Rose Hill Cemetery (MH)—Altoona, Pennsylvania
Entered Service at: West Virginia
Unit: U.S.S. *Missouri*
Battle or Place of Action: U.S.S. *Missouri*
Date of Action: 13 April 1904
G.O. Number, Date: 43, 14 April 1921
Place of Presentation: The White House, presented by Pres. Warren G. Harding
Citation: For extraordinary heroism on U.S.S. *Missouri* 13 April 1904. While at target practice off Pensacola, Fla., an accident occurred in the after turret of the *Missouri* whereby the lives of five officers and 28 men were lost. The ship was in imminent danger of destruction by explosion, and the prompt action of C.G. Cox and two gunners' mates caused the fire to be brought under control, and the loss of the *Missouri*, together with her crew, was averted.

2338 ◆ CRONAN, WILLIAM S. (WILLIE)

Rank: Boatswain's Mate
Service: U.S. Navy
Birthday: 18 October 1883
Place of Birth: Chicago, Cook County, Illinois
Date of Death: 22 October 1959
Cemetery: Fort Rosecrans National Cemetery (T-534) (MH)—San Diego, California
Entered Service at: Illinois
Unit: U.S.S. *Bennington*
Battle or Place of Action: U.S.S. *Bennington*
Date of Action: 21 July 1905
G.O. Number, Date: 13, 5 January 1906
Citation: Serving on board the U.S.S. *Bennington*, for extraordinary heroism displayed at the time of the explosion of a boiler of that vessel at San Diego, Cal., 21 July 1905.

2339 ◆ DAVIS, RAYMOND ERWIN

Rank: Quartermaster Third Class
Service: U.S. Navy
Birthday: 19 September 1885
Place of Birth: Mankato, Blue Earth County, Minnesota
Date of Death: 9 September 1965
Cemetery: Calvary Cemetery—Seattle, Washington
Entered Service at: Puget Sound, Washington
Unit: U.S.S. *Bennington*
Battle or Place of Action: U.S.S. *Bennington*
Date of Action: 21 July 1905
G.O. Number, Date: 13, 5 January 1906
Citation: Serving on board the U.S.S. *Bennington*, for extraordinary heroism displayed at the time of the explosion of a boiler of that vessel at San Diego, Cal., 21 July 1905.

2340 ◆ FADDEN, HARRY DELMAR

Rank: Coxswain
Service: U.S. Navy
Birthday: 17 September 1882
Place of Birth: The Dalles, Wasco County, Oregon
Date of Death: 2 February 1955
Cemetery: Evergreen-Washelli Memorial Park—Seattle, Washington
Entered Service at: Washington
Unit: U.S.S. *Adams*
Battle or Place of Action: off the California coast
Date of Action: 30 June 1903
G.O. Number, Date: 138, 31 July 1903
Citation: On board the U.S.S. *Adams*, for gallantry, rescuing O.C. Hawthorne, landsman for training, from drowning at sea, 30 June 1903.

2341 ◆ FLOYD, EDWARD

Rank: Boilermaker
Service: U.S. Navy
Birthday: 21 February 1850
Place of Birth: Ireland
Date of Death: 16 January 1923
Cemetery: St. Lawrence Cemetery (MH)—Charleston, South Carolina
Entered Service at: South Carolina
Unit: U.S.S. *Iowa*
Battle or Place of Action: U.S.S. *Iowa*
Date of Action: 25 January 1905
G.O. Number, Date: 182, 20 March 1905
Citation: Serving on board the U.S.S. *Iowa*, for extraordinary heroism at the time of the blowing-out of the manhole plate of boiler D on board that vessel, 25 January 1905.

2342 ◆ FREDERICKSEN, EMIL

Rank: Watertender
Service: U.S. Navy
Date of Death: 1960
Unit: U.S.S. *Bennington*
Battle or Place of Action: U.S.S. *Bennington*
Date of Action: 21 July 1905
G.O. Number, Date: 13, 5 January 1906
Citation: Serving on board the U.S.S. *Bennington*, for extraordinary heroism displayed at the time of the explosion of a boiler of that vessel at San Diego, Cal., 21 July 1905.

2343 ◆ GIRANDY, ALPHONSE

Rank: Seaman
Service: U.S. Navy
Birthday: 21 January 1868
Place of Birth: Guadaloupe, West Indies
Date of Death: 3 April 1941
Cemetery: Philadelphia National Cemetery (N-66) (MH)—Philadelphia, Pennsylvania

Entered Service at: Pennsylvania
Unit: U.S.S. *Petrel*
Battle or Place of Action: U.S.S. *Petrel*
Date of Action: 31 March 1901
G.O. Number, Date: 85, 22 March 1902
Citation: Serving on board the U.S.S. *Petrel*, for heroism and gallantry, fearlessly exposing his own life to danger for the saving of others, on the occasion of the fire on board that vessel, 31 March 1901.

2344 ♦ GOWAN, WILLIAM HENRY

Rank: Boatswain's Mate
Service: U.S. Navy
Birthday: 2 June 1884
Place of Birth: Rye, Westchester County, New York
Date of Death: 22 May 1957
Place of Death: Brooklyn, New York
Cemetery: Long Island National Cemetery (DSS-7) (MH)—Farmingdale, New York
Entered Service at: New York
Battle or Place of Action: Coquimbo, Chile
Date of Action: 20 January 1909
G.O. Number, Date: 18, 19 March 1909
Citation: For bravery and extraordinary heroism displayed by him during a conflagration in Coquimbo, Chile, 20 January 1909.

2345 ♦ GRBITCH, RADE

Rank: Seaman
Service: U.S. Navy
Birthday: 24 December 1870
Place of Birth: Austria
Date of Death: 5 March 1910
Cemetery: San Francisco National Cemetery (A-44)—San Francisco, California
Entered Service at: Illinois
Unit: U.S.S. *Bennington*
Battle or Place of Action: U.S.S. *Bennington*
Date of Action: 21 July 1905
G.O. Number, Date: 13, 5 January 1906
Citation: On board the U.S.S. *Bennington*, for extraordinary heroism displayed at the time of the explosion of a boiler of that vessel at San Diego, Cal., 21 July 1905.

2346 ♦ HALLING, LUOVI

Rank: Boatswain's Mate First Class
Service: U.S. Navy
Birthday: 7 August 1867
Place of Birth: Stockholm, Sweden
Date of Death: 22 March 1928
Cemetery: St. Michael's Cemetery—Astoria, New York
Entered Service at: New York
Unit: U.S.S. *Missouri*
Battle or Place of Action: off Martha's Vineyard, Massachusetts
Date of Action: 15 September 1904
G.O. Number, Date: 172, 4 October 1904
Citation: Serving on board the U.S.S. *Missouri*, for heroism in attempting to rescue from drowning Cecil C. Young, ordinary seaman, 15 September 1904.

2347 ♦ HELMS, JOHN HENRY

Rank: Sergeant
Service: U.S. Marine Corps
Birthday: 16 March 1874
Place of Birth: Chicago, Cook County, Illinois
Date of Death: 17 February 1919
Cemetery: Mound Grove Cemetery (MH)—Kankakee, Illinois
Entered Service at: Illinois
Unit: U.S.S. *Chicago*
Battle or Place of Action: Montevideo, Uruguay
Date of Action: 10 January 1901
G.O. Number, Date: 35, 23 March 1901
Citation: Serving on board the U.S.S. *Chicago*, for heroism in rescuing Ishi Tomizi, ship's cook, from drowning at Montevideo, Uruguay, 10 January 1901.

2348 ♦ HILL, FRANK EBENEZER

Rank: Ship's Cook First Class (highest rank: First Lieutenant U.S. Army WWI)
Service: U.S. Navy
Birthday: 31 July 1880
Place of Birth: La Grange, La Grange County, Indiana
Date of Death: 23 September 1932
Cemetery: unknown cemetery—St. Cloud, Florida
Entered Service at: Indiana
Unit: U.S.S. *Bennington*
Battle or Place of Action: San Diego, California
Date of Action: 21 July 1905
G.O. Number, Date: 13, 5 January 1906
Citation: On board the U.S.S. *Bennington*, for extraordinary heroism displayed at the time of the explosion of a boiler of that vessel at San Diego, Cal., 21 July 1905.

2349 ♦ HOLTZ, AUGUST

Rank: Chief Watertender
Service: U.S. Navy
Birthday: 12 February 1871
Place of Birth: St. Louis, St. Louis County, Missouri
Date of Death: 5 March 1938
Cemetery: Long Island National Cemetery (F-916) (MH)—Farmingdale, New York
Entered Service at: St. Louis, St. Louis County, Missouri
Unit: U.S.S. *North Dakota*
Battle or Place of Action: U.S.S. *North Dakota*
Date of Action: 8 September 1910
G.O. Number, Date: 83, 4 October 1910
Citation: On board the U.S.S. *North Dakota*, for extraordi-

nary heroism in the line of his profession during the fire on board that vessel, 8 September 1910.

2350 ◆ JOHANNESSEN, JOHANNES J.

Rank: Chief Watertender
Service: U.S. Navy
Birthday: 13 May 1872
Place of Birth: Bodo, Norway
Date of Death: 14 November 1915
Cemetery: Cypress Hills National Cemetery (2-7425) (MH)—Brooklyn, New York
Enlisted at: Yokohama, Japan
Unit: U.S.S. *Iowa*
Battle or Place of Action: U.S.S. *Iowa*
Date of Action: 25 January 1905
G.O. Number, Date: 182, 20 March 1905
Citation: Serving on board the U.S.S. *Iowa* for extraordinary heroism at the time of the blowing out of the manhole plate of Boiler D on board that vessel, 25 January 1905.

2351 ◆ KING, JOHN✢

Rank: Watertender (highest rank: Chief Watertender)
Service: U.S. Navy
Birthday: 7 February 1862
Place of Birth: County Mayo, Ireland
Date of Death: 20 May 1938
Cemetery: Calvary Cemetery (MH)—Hot Springs, Arkansas
Entered Service at: New York
Unit: U.S.S. *Vicksburg*; U.S.S. *Salem*
Served as: Watertender
Battle or Place of Action: U.S.S. *Vicksburg*; U.S.S. *Salem*
Date of Action: 29 May 1901; 13 September 1909
G.O. Number, Date: 72, 6 December 1901; 40, 19 October 1909
Citation: **First Award** On board the U.S.S. *Vicksburg*, for heroism in the line of his profession at the time of the accident to the boiler, 29 May 1901. **Second Award** Watertender, serving on board the U.S.S. *Salem*, for extraordinary heroism in the line of his profession on the occasion of the accident to one of the boilers of that vessel, 13 September 1909.
Notes: ✢Double Awardee

2352 ◆ KLEIN, ROBERT

Rank: Chief Carpenter's Mate
Service: U.S. Navy
Birthday: 11 November 1848
Place of Birth: Gerdonen, Germany
Date of Death: 29 November 1931
Place of Death: Shanghi, China
Cemetery: Bubbling Well Cemetery—Shanghi, China
Enlisted at: Marseilles, France
Unit: U.S.S. *Raleigh*
Battle or Place of Action: Olongapo, Philippine Island
Date of Action: 25 January 1904
G.O. Number, Date: 173, 6 October 1904
Citation: Serving on board the U.S.S. *Raleigh*, for heroism in rescuing shipmates overcome in double bottoms by fumes of turpentine, 25 January 1904.

2353 ◆ LIPSCOMB, HARRY

Rank: Watertender (highest rank: Chief Watertender)
Service: U.S. Navy
Birthday: 2 April 1878
Place of Birth: Washington, D.C.
Date of Death: 7 September 1926
Cemetery: Arlington National Cemetery (3-2481-WS)—Arlington, Virginia
Entered Service at: Washington, D.C.
Unit: U.S.S. *North Dakota*
Battle or Place of Action: U.S.S. *North Dakota*
Date of Action: 8 September 1910
G.O. Number, Date: 83, 4 October 1910
Citation: On board the U.S.S. *North Dakota*, for extraordinary heroism in the line of his profession during the fire on board that vessel, 8 September 1910.

2354 ◆ MONSSEN, MONS

Rank: Chief Gunner's Mate (highest rank: lieutenant)
Service: U.S. Navy
Birthday: 20 January 1867
Place of Birth: Bergen, Norway
Date of Death: 10 February 1930
Cemetery: Cypress Hills National Cemetery (OS-190) (MH)—Brooklyn, New York
Unit: U.S.S. *Missouri*
Battle or Place of Action: U.S.S. *Missouri*
Date of Action: 13 April 1904
G.O. Number, Date: 160, 26 May 1904
Citation: Serving on board the U.S.S. *Missouri*, for extraordinary heroism in entering a burning magazine through the scuttle and endeavoring to extinguish the fire by throwing water with his hands until a hose was passed to him, 13 April 1904.

2355 ◆ MULLIN, HUGH PATRICK

Rank: Seaman
Service: U.S. Navy
Birthday: 20 March 1878
Place of Birth: Richmond, McHenry County, Illinois
Date of Death: 9 June 1948
Cemetery: Golden Gate National Cemetery (A-2-294)—San Bruno, California
Entered Service at: Chicago, Cook County, Illinois
Unit: U.S.S. *Texas*
Battle or Place of Action: Hampton Roads, Virginia
Date of Action: 11 November 1899
G.O. Number, Date: 537, 8 January 1900
Citation: On board the U.S.S. *Texas* during the coaling of that vessel at Hampton Roads, Va., 11 November 1899. Jumping overboard while wearing a pair of heavy rubber

boots and at great risk to himself, Mullin rescued Alfred Kosminski, apprentice, second class, who fell overboard, by supporting him until he was safely hauled from the water.

2356 ◆ NELSON, OSCAR FREDERICK
Rank: Machinist's Mate First Class
Service: U.S. Navy
Birthday: 5 November 1881
Place of Birth: Minneapolis, Hennepin County, Minnesota
Date of Death: 26 September 1951
Cemetery: Fort Snelling National Cemetery (DS-64-N) (MH)—Minneapolis, Minnesota
Entered Service at: Minnesota
Unit: U.S.S. *Bennington*
Battle or Place of Action: U.S.S. *Bennington*
Date of Action: 21 July 1905
G.O. Number, Date: 13, 5 January 1906
Citation: Serving on board the U.S.S. *Bennington*, for extraordinary heroism displayed at the time of the explosion of a boiler of that vessel at San Diego, Cal., 21 July 1905.

2357 ◆ NORDSTROM, ISADOR A.
Rank: Chief Boatswain (highest rank: Lieutenant)
Service: U.S. Navy
Birthday: 24 May 1876
Place of Birth: Goteborg, Sweden
Date of Death: 6 March 1930
Cemetery: Arlington National Cemetery (7-8273)—Arlington, Virginia
Entered Service at: New York
Unit: U.S.S. *Kearsarge*
Battle or Place of Action: U.S.S. *Kearsarge*
Date of Action: 13 April 1906
G.O. Number, Date: 142, 4 December 1924
Citation: For gallant conduct upon the occasion of the disastrous fire of accidentally ignited powder charges, which occurred in the forward turret of the U.S.S. *Kearsarge* during target practice on 13 April 1906. Chief Boatswain Nordstrom, then chief boatswain's mate, was among the first to enter the turret in order to assist in bringing out the injured.

2358 ◆ PETERS, ALEXANDER
Rank: Boatswain's Mate First Class (highest rank: Chief Gunner's Mate)
Service: U.S. Navy
Birthday: 16 November 1869
Place of Birth: Russia
Date of Death: 11 June 1951
Place of Death: Martha's Vineyard, Massachusetts
Cemetery: Arlington National Cemetery (8-5300-A) (MH)—Arlington, Virginia
Entered Service at: Pennsylvania
Unit: U.S.S. *Missouri*
Battle or Place of Action: off Martha's Vineyard, Massachusetts
Date of Action: 15 September 1904
G.O. Number, Date: 172, 4 October 1904
Citation: For heroism in attempting to rescue from drowning Cecil C. Young, ordinary seaman, 15 September 1904, while serving on board the U.S.S. *Missouri*.

2359 ◆ PFEIFER, LOUIS FRED
Rank: Private
Service: U.S. Marine Corps
Birthday: 19 June 1876
Place of Birth: Philadelphia, Philadelphia County, Pennsylvania
Entered Service at: New Jersey
Unit: U.S.S. *Petrel*
Battle or Place of Action: U.S.S. *Petrel*
Date of Action: 31 March 1901
G.O. Number, Date: 85, 22 March 1902
Citation: Serving on board the U.S.S. *Petrel*; for heroism and gallantry, fearlessly exposing his own life to danger for the saving of the others on the occasion of the fire on board that vessel, 31 March 1901.

2360 ◆ QUICK, JOSEPH
Rank: Coxswain
Service: U.S. Navy
Birthday: 1877
Place of Birth: New York
Date of Death: 27 June 1969
Place of Death: Tampa, Florida
Cemetery: The Evergreen Cemetery—Brooklyn, New York
Entered Service at: New York
Unit: U.S.S. *Yorktown*
Battle or Place of Action: Yokohama, Japan
Date of Action: 27 April 1902
G.O. Number, Date: 93, 7 July 1902
Citation: For heroism in rescuing Walenty Wisnieroski, Machinist Second Class, from drowning at Yokohama, Japan, 27 April 1902, while serving on board the U.S.S. *Yorktown*.

2361 ◆ REID, PATRICK
Rank: Chief Watertender
Service: U.S. Navy
Birthday: 17 June 1875
Place of Birth: Dublin, Ireland
Entered Service at: New York
Unit: U.S.S. *North Dakota*
Battle or Place of Action: U.S.S. *North Dakota*
Date of Action: 8 September 1910
G.O. Number, Date: 83, 4 October 1910
Citation: For extraordinary heroism in the line of his profession during the fire on board the U.S.S. *North Dakota* where Reid was serving, 8 September 1910.

2362 ◆ ROBERTS, CHARLES CHURCH
Rank: Machinist's Mate First Class
Service: U.S. Navy

Birthday: 6 March 1882
Place of Birth: Newton, Middlesex County, Massachusetts
Date of Death: 8 March 1957
Cemetery: Prospect Hill Cemetery (MH)—Millis, Massachusetts
Entered Service at: Illinois
Unit: U.S.S. *North Dakota*
Battle or Place of Action: U.S.S. *North Dakota*
Date of Action: 8 September 1910
G.O. Number, Date: 83, 4 October 1910
Citation: Serving on board the U.S.S. *North Dakota*; for extraordinary heroism in the line of his profession during the fire on board that vessel, 8 September 1910.

2363 ◆ SCHEPKE, CHARLES STEPHEN

Rank: Gunner's Mate First Class (highest rank: Lieutenant)
Service: U.S. Navy
Birthday: 26 December 1878
Place of Birth: New York, New York
Date of Death: 27 February 1933
Place of Death: Brooklyn, New York
Cemetery: The Lutheran Cemetery—Middle Village, New York
Entered Service at: New York
Unit: U.S.S. *Missouri*
Battle or Place of Action: U.S.S. *Missouri*
Date of Action: 13 April 1904
G.O. Number, Date: 160, 26 May 1904
Citation: For extraordinary heroism while serving on the U.S.S. *Missouri* in remaining by a burning magazine and assisting in extinguishing the fire, 13 April 1904.

2364 ◆ SCHMIDT, OTTO DILLER

Rank: Seaman
Service: U.S. Navy
Birthday: 10 August 1883
Place of Birth: Blair, Washington County, Nebraska
Date of Death: 9 February 1963
Cemetery: Prospect Hill Cemetery (MH)—Norfolk, Nebraska
Entered Service at: Nebraska
Unit: U.S.S. *Bennington*
Battle or Place of Action: U.S.S. *Bennington*
Date of Action: 21 July 1905
G.O. Number, Date: 13, 5 January 1906
Citation: While serving on board the U.S.S. *Bennington* for extraordinary heroism displayed at the time of the explosion of a boiler of that vessel at San Diego, Cal., 21 July 1905.

2365 ◆ SHACKLETTE, WILLIAM SIDNEY

Rank: Hospital Steward
Service: U.S. Navy
Birthday: 17 May 1880
Place of Birth: Delaplane, Fauquier County, Virginia
Date of Death: 12 February 1945
Cemetery: Arlington National Cemetery (10-10688) (MH)—Arlington, Virginia
Entered Service at: Virginia
Unit: U.S.S. *Bennington*
Battle or Place of Action: U.S.S. *Bennington*
Date of Action: 21 July 1905
G.O. Number, Date: 13, 5 January 1906
Citation: For extraordinary heroism while serving on the U.S.S. *Bennington* at the time of the explosion of a boiler of that vessel at San Diego, Cal., 21 July 1905.

2366 ◆ SHANAHAN, PATRICK

Rank: Chief Boatswain's Mate (highest rank: Lieutenant)
Service: U.S. Navy
Birthday: 6 November 1867
Place of Birth: Shanat Castle, County Limerick, Ireland
Date of Death: 7 December 1937
Cemetery: Arlington National Cemetery (7-10295) (MH)—Arlington, Virginia
Entered Service at: New York
Unit: U.S. Training Ship *Alliance*
Battle or Place of Action: off Annapolis, Maryland
Date of Action: 28 May 1899
G.O. Number, Date: 534, 29 November 1899
Citation: On board the U.S.S. *Alliance*, 28 May 1899. Displaying heroism, Shanahan rescued William Steven, quartermaster first class, from drowning.

2367 ◆ SNYDER, WILLIAM ELLSWORTH

Rank: Chief Electrician (highest rank: Lieutenant Commander)
Service: U.S. Navy
Birthday: 24 February 1883
Place of Birth: South Bethlehem, Northampton County, Pennsylvania
Date of Death: 30 December 1944
Cemetery: Arlington National Cemetery (10-10636)—Arlington, Virginia
Entered Service at: Pennsylvania
Unit: U.S.S. *Birmingham*
Battle or Place of Action: U.S.S. *Birmingham*
Date of Action: 4 January 1910
G.O. Number, Date: 58, 2 March 1910
Citation: Serving on board the U.S.S. *Birmingham*, for extraordinary heroism, rescuing G.H. Kephart, seaman, from drowning at Hampton Roads, Va., 4 January 1910.

2368 ◆ STANTON, THOMAS

Rank: Chief Machinist's Mate
Service: U.S. Navy
Birthday: 11 August 1869
Place of Birth: Ireland
Date of Death: 7 May 1950
Cemetery: St. Columbia's Cemetery—Middleton, Rhode Island
Entered Service at: New York
Unit: U.S.S. *North Dakota*
Battle or Place of Action: U.S.S. *North Dakota*

Date of Action: 8 September 1910
G.O. Number, Date: 83, 4 October 1910
Citation: For extraordinary heroism in the line of his profession during the fire on board the U.S.S. *North Dakota*, 8 September 1910.

2369 ◆ STOKES, JOHN S.

Rank: Chief Master-of-Arms (highest rank: Boatswain)
Service: U.S. Navy
Birthday: 12 June 1871
Place of Birth: New York, New York
Date of Death: 14 February 1923
Cemetery: Arlington National Cemetery (17-20184) (MH)—Arlington, Virginia
Entered Service at: New York
Unit: U.S.S. *New York*
Battle or Place of Action: off the coast of Jamaica
Date of Action: 31 March 1899
G.O. Number, Date: 525, 29 July 1899
Citation: On board the U.S.S. *New York* off the coast of Jamaica, 31 March 1899. Showing gallant conduct, Stokes jumped overboard and assisted in the rescue of Peter Mahoney, watertender, U.S. Navy.

2370 ◆ STUPKA, LADDIE

Rank: Fireman First Class
Service: U.S. Navy
Birthday: 4 March 1878
Place of Birth: Cleveland, Cuyahoga County, Ohio
Date of Death: 20 February 1946
Cemetery: Baltimore National Cemetery (DS-1) (MH)—Baltimore, Maryland
Entered Service at: Ohio
Unit: U.S.S. *Leyden*
Battle or Place of Action: on the rocks of Block Island, Rhode Island
Date of Action: 21 January 1903
G.O. Number, Date: 145, 26 December 1903
Citation: Serving on board the U.S.S. *Leyden*; for heroism at the time of the wreck of that vessel, 21 January 1903.

2371 ◆ TEYTAND, AUGUST P.

True Name: Teytard, August P.
Rank: Quartermaster Third Class
Service: U.S. Navy
Birthday: 6 April 1878
Place of Birth: Santa Cruz, West Indies
Date of Death: 4 March 1956
Cemetery: Mount Moriah VA Plot (5-4-5) (MH)—Philadelphia, Pennsylvania
Entered Service at: New Jersey
Unit: U.S.S. *Leyden*
Battle or Place of Action: on the rocks of Block Island, Rhode Island
Date of Action: 21 January 1903

G.O. Number, Date: 145, 26 December 1903
Citation: For heroism while serving on board the U.S.S. *Leyden* at the time of the wreck of that vessel, 21 January 1903.

2372 ◆ WALSH, MICHAEL

Rank: Chief Machinist
Service: U.S. Navy
Birthday: 27 July 1858
Place of Birth: Newport, Newport County, Rhode Island
Date of Death: 29 June 1913
Cemetery: St. Columbia's Cemetery (MH)—Middletown, Rhode Island
Entered Service at: Rhode Island
Unit: U.S.S. *Leyden*
Battle or Place of Action: on the rocks of Block Island, Rhode Island
Date of Action: 21 January 1903
G.O. Number, Date: 145, 26 December 1903
Citation: Serving on board the U.S.S. *Leyden*; for heroism at the time of the wreck of that vessel, 21 January 1903.

2373 ◆ WESTA, KARL

Rank: Chief Machinist's Mate
Service: U.S. Navy
Birthday: 8 April 1875
Place of Birth: Norway
Date of Death: 3 March 1949
Cemetery: Arlington National Cemetery (11-83-SH) (MH)—Arlington, Virginia
Entered Service at: New York
Unit: U.S.S. *North Dakota*
Battle or Place of Action: U.S.S. *North Dakota*
Date of Action: 8 September 1910
G.O. Number, Date: 83, 4 October 1910
Citation: On board the U.S.S. *North Dakota*; for extraordinary heroism in the line of his profession during the fire on board that vessel, 8 September 1910.

2374 ◆ WHEELER, GEORGE HUBER

Rank: Shipfitter First Class (highest rank: Lieutenant)
Service: U.S. Navy
Birthday: 26 September 1881
Place of Birth: Charleston, Charleston County, South Carolina
Date of Death: 20 January 1957
Place of Death: Bethesda, Maryland
Cemetery: Arlington National Cemetery (7-10040-EH)—Arlington, Virginia
Entered Service at: Washington, D.C.
Battle or Place of Action: Coquimbo, Chile
Date of Action: 20 January 1909
G.O. Number, Date: 18, 19 March 1909
Citation: For bravery and extraordinary heroism displayed by him during a conflagration in Coquimbo, Chile, 20 January 1909.

ACTION AGAINST OUTLAWS, PHILIPPINES 1911

2375 ◆ CATHERWOOD, JOHN HUGH

Rank: Ordinary Seaman
Service: U.S. Navy
Birthday: 7 August 1888
Place of Birth: Springfield, Sangamon County, Illinois
Date of Death: 18 December 1930
Cemetery: Camp Butler National Cemetery (MH)—Springfield, Illinois
Entered Service at: Illinois
Unit: U.S.S. *Pampang*
Battle or Place of Action: near the village of Mundang, Basilan Island, Philippine Islands
Date of Action: 24 September 1911
G.O. Number, Date: 138, 13 December 1911
Citation: While attached to the U.S.S. *Pampang*, Catherwood was one of a shore party moving in to capture Mundang, on the island of Basilan, P.I., on the morning of 24 September 1911. Advancing with the scout party to reconnoiter a group of nipa huts close to the trail, Catherwood unhesitatingly entered the open area before the huts, where his party was suddenly taken under point-blank fire and charged by approximately 20 enemy Moros coming out from inside the native huts and from other concealed positions. Struck down almost instantly by the outlaws' deadly fire, Catherwood, although unable to rise, rallied to the defense of his leader and fought desperately to beat off the hostile attack. By his valiant effort under fire and in the face of great odds, Catherwood contributed materially toward the destruction and rout of the enemy.

2376 ◆ HARRISON, BOLDEN REUSH

Rank: Seaman
Service: U.S. Navy
Birthday: 26 April 1886
Place of Birth: Savannah, Hardin County, Tennessee
Date of Death: 26 January 1952
Cemetery: Savannah Cemetery (MH)—Savannah, Tennessee
Entered Service at: Tennessee
Unit: U.S.S. *Pampang*
Battle or Place of Action: near the village of Mundang, Basilan Island, Philippine Islands
Date of Action: 24 September 1911
G.O. Number, Date: 138, 13 December 1911
Citation: While attached to the U.S.S. *Pampang*, Harrison was one of a shore party moving in to capture Mundang, on the island of Basilan, P.I., 24 September 1911. Harrison instantly responded to the calls for help when the advance scout party investigating a group of nipa huts close to the trail was suddenly taken under point-blank fire and rushed by approximately 20 enemy Moros attacking from inside the huts and from other concealed positions. Armed with a double-barreled shotgun, he concentrated his blasting fire on the outlaws, destroying three of the Moros and assisting in the rout of the remainder. By his aggressive charging of the enemy under heavy fire and in the face of great odds, Harrison contributed materially to the success of the engagement.

2377 ◆ HENRECHON, GEORGE FRANCIS

Rank: Machinist's Mate Second Class
Service: U.S. Navy
Birthday: 22 November 1885
Place of Birth: Hartford, Hartford County, Connecticut
Date of Death: 16 August 1929
Cemetery: Mount St. Benedict Cemetery (MH)—Bloomfield, Connecticut
Entered Service at: California
Unit: U.S.S. *Pampang*
Battle or Place of Action: near the village of Mundang, Basilan Island, Philippine Islands
Date of Action: 24 September 1911
G.O. Number, Date: 138, 13 December 1911
Citation: While attached to the U.S.S. *Pampang*, Henrechon was one of a shore party moving in to capture Mundang, on the island of Basilan, P.I., 24 September 1911. Ordered to take station within 100 yards of a group of nipa huts close to the trail, Henrechon advanced and stood guard as the leader, and his scout party first searched the surrounding deep grasses, then moved into the open area before the huts. Instantly enemy Moros opened point-blank fire on the exposed men and approximately 20 Moros rushed the small group from inside the huts and from other concealed positions. Henrechon, responding to the calls for help, was one of the first on the scene. With his rifle jammed after the first shot, he closed in with rifle, using it as a club to break the stock over the head of the nearest Moro and then, drawing his pistol, started in pursuit of the fleeing outlaws. Henrechon's aggressive charging of the enemy under heavy fire and in the face of great odds contributed materially to the success of the engagement.

2378 ◆ McGUIRE, FRED HENRY

Rank: Hospital Apprentice (highest rank: Chief Pharmacist)
Service: U.S. Navy

Birthday: 7 November 1890
Place of Birth: Gordonville, Cape Girardeau County, Missouri
Date of Death: 4 February 1958
Cemetery: Springfield National Cemetery (29-332) (MH)—Springfield, Missouri
Entered Service at: Gordonville, Cape Girardeau County, Missouri
Unit: U.S.S. *Pampanga*
Battle or Place of Action: near the village of Mundang, Basilan Island, Philippine Islands
Date of Action: 24 September 1911
G.O. Number, Date: 138, 13 December 1911
Citation: While attached to the U.S.S. *Pampang*, McGuire was one of a shore party moving in to capture Mundang, on the island of Basilan, P.I., 24 September 1911. Ordered to take station within 100 yards of a group of nipa huts close to the trail, McGuire advanced and stood guard as the leader and his scout party first searched the surrounding deep grasses, then moved into the open area before the huts. Instantly enemy Moros opened point-blank fire on the exposed men, and approximately 20 Moros charged the small group from inside the huts and from other concealed positions. McGuire, responding to the calls for help, was one of the first on the scene. After emptying his rifle into the attackers, he closed in with rifle, using it as a club to wage fierce battle until his comrades arrived on the field, when he rallied to the aid of his dying leader and other wounded. Although himself wounded, McGuire ministered tirelessly and efficiently to those who had been struck down, thereby saving the lives of two who otherwise might have succumbed to enemy-inflicted wounds.

2379 ◆ NISPEROS, JOSE B.

Rank: Private
Service: U.S. Army
Birthday: 30 December 1887
Place of Birth: San Fernandos Union, Philippine Islands
Date of Death: 1 September 1922
Place of Death: San Fernandos Union, Philippine Islands
Cemetery: New Municipal Cemetery—San Fernandos Union, Philippine Islands
Entered Service at: San Fernandos Union, Philippine Islands
Unit: 34th Company, Philippine Scouts
Battle or Place of Action: at Lapurap, Basilan Island, Philippine Islands
Date of Action: 24 September 1911
G.O. Number, Date: 64, 25 November 1912
Date of Presentation: 3 February 1913
Place of Presentation: Manila, Philippine Islands (Parade Grounds), presented by Mrs. J. Franklin Bell (wife of the commanding officer, Maj. Gen. Bell)
Citation: Having been badly wounded (his left arm was broken and lacerated and he had received several spear wounds in the body so he could not stand) continued to fire his rifle with one hand until the enemy was repulsed, thereby aiding materially in preventing the annihilation of his party and the mutilation of their bodies.

2380 ◆ VOLZ, JACOB

Rank: Carpenter's Mate Third Class
Service: U.S. Navy
Birthday: 23 June 1889
Place of Birth: Sutton, Clay County, Nebraska
Date of Death: 22 July 1965
Place of Death: Portland, Oregon
Cemetery: Lincoln Memorial Park—Portland, Oregon
Entered Service at: Nebraska
Unit: U.S.S. *Pampang*
Battle or Place of Action: near the village of Mundang, Basilan Island, Philippine Islands
Date of Action: 24 September 1911
G.O. Number, Date: 138, 13 December 1911
Citation: While attached to the U.S.S. *Pampang*, Volz was one of a shore party moving in to capture Mundang, on the island of Basilan, P.I., on 24 September 1911. Investigating a group of nipa huts close to the trail, the advanced scout party was suddenly taken under point-blank fire and rushed by approximately 20 enemy Moros attacking from inside the huts and from other concealed positions. Volz responded instantly to calls for help and, finding all members of the scout party writhing on the ground but still fighting, he blazed his rifle into the outlaws with telling effect, destroying several of the Moros and assisting in the rout of the remainder. By his aggressive charging of the enemy under heavy fire and in the face of great odds, Volz contributed materially to the success of the engagement.

MEXICAN CAMPAIGN (VERA CRUZ)

2381 ◆ ANDERSON, EDWIN ALEXANDER

Rank: Captain (highest rank: Admiral)
Service: U.S. Navy
Birthday: 16 July 1860
Place of Birth: Wilmington, New Hanover County, North Carolina
Date of Death: 23 September 1933
Cemetery: Arlington National Cemetery (2-3798)—Arlington, Virginia
Entered Service at: Wilmington, New Hanover County, North Carolina
Unit: 2d Regiment of Bluejackets
Served as: Commanding Officer
Battle or Place of Action: Vera Cruz, Mexico
Date of Action: 22 April 1914
G.O. Number, Date: 177, 4 December 1915
Citation: For extraordinary heroism in battle, engagement of Vera Cruz, 22 April 1914, in command of the 2d Seaman Regiment. Marching his regiment across the open space in front of the Naval Academy and other buildings, Capt. Anderson unexpectedly met a heavy fire from riflemen, machine guns and one-pounders, which caused part of his command to break and fall back, many casualties occurring amongst them at the time. His indifference to the heavy fire, to which he himself was exposed at the head of his regiment, showed him to be fearless and courageous in battle.

2382 ◆ BADGER, OSCAR CHARLES

Rank: Ensign (highest rank: Admiral)
Service: U.S. Navy
Birthday: 26 June 1890
Place of Birth: Washington, D.C.
Date of Death: 30 November 1958
Place of Death: Glen Cove, New York
Cemetery: Arlington National Cemetery (2-3760-WS)—Arlington, Virginia
Entered Service at: Washington, D.C.
Battle or Place of Action: Vera Cruz, Mexico
Date of Action: 21-22 April 1914
G.O. Number, Date: 177, 4 December 1915
Citation: For distinguished conduct in battle, engagements of Vera Cruz, 21–22 April 1914. Ens. Badger was in both days' fighting at the head of his company and was eminent and conspicuous in his conduct, leading his men with skill and courage.

2383 ◆ BEASLEY, HARRY C.

Rank: Seaman
Service: U.S. Navy
Birthday: 1 November 1889
Place of Birth: Ohio
Date of Death: 2 July 1931
Cemetery: Cedar Hill Cemetery (MH)—Newark, Ohio
Entered Service at: Ohio
Unit: U.S.S. *Florida*
Battle or Place of Action: Vera Cruz, Mexico
Date of Action: 21 April 1914
G.O. Number, Date: 101, 15 June 1914
Citation: On board the U.S.S. *Florida* for extraordinary heroism in the line of his profession during the seizure of Vera Cruz, Mexico, 21 April 1914.

2384 ◆ BERKELEY, RANDOLPH CARTER

Rank: Major (highest rank: Major General)
Service: U.S. Marine Corps
Birthday: 9 January 1875
Place of Birth: Staunton, Staunton County, Virginia
Date of Death: 31 January 1960
Place of Death: Beaufort, South Carolina
Cemetery: Arlington National Cemetery (3-1767-SH)—Arlington, Virginia
Appointed from: Washington, D.C
Unit: 1st Battalion, 2d Advanced Base Regiment
Served as: Commanding Officer
Battle or Place of Action: Vera Cruz, Mexico
Date of Action: 21-22 April 1914
G.O. Number, Date: 177, 4 December 1915
Citation: For distinguished conduct in battle, engagements of Vera Cruz, 21–22 April 1914. Maj. Berkeley was eminent and conspicuous in command of his battalion, was in the fighting of both days, and exhibited courage and skill in leading his men through action. His cool judgment and courage, and his skill in handling his men in encountering and overcoming the machine-gun and rifle fire down Cinco de Mayo and parallel streets account for the small percentage of the losses of marines under his command.

2385 ◆ BISHOP, CHARLES FRANCIS

Rank: Quartermaster Second Class (highest rank: Chief Quartermaster)
Service: U.S. Navy

Birthday: 2 August 1888
Place of Birth: Pittsburgh, Allegheny County, Pennsylvania
Date of Death: 1 February 1954
Cemetery: Fort Rosecrans National Cemetery (O-4562)—San Diego, California
Entered Service at: Pennsylvania
Unit: U.S.S. *Florida*
Battle or Place of Action: Vera Cruz, Mexico
Date of Action: 21 April 1914
G.O. Number, Date: 101, 15 June 1914
Citation: On board the U.S.S. *Florida* for extraordinary heroism in the line of his profession during the seizure of Vera Cruz, Mexico, 21 April 1914.

2386 ◆ BRADLEY, GEORGE

Rank: Chief Gunner's Mate (highest rank: Lieutenant)
Service: U.S. Navy
Birthday: 5 December 1881
Place of Birth: New York, New York
Date of Death: 9 June 1942
Cemetery: St. Columbia's Cemetery (MH)—Middletown, Rhode Island
Entered Service at: Rhode Island
Unit: U.S.S. *Utah*
Battle or Place of Action: Vera Cruz, Mexico
Date of Action: 21 April 1914
G.O. Number, Date: 117, 13 September 1923
Date of Presentation: 4 October 1923
Place of Presentation: The White House, presented by Pres. Calvin Coolidge
Citation: For meritorious service under fire on the occasion of the landing of the American naval forces at Vera Cruz in 1914. C.G. Bradley was then attached to the U.S.S. *Utah*, as a chief gunner's mate, and was in charge of the ammunition party and special details at Vera Cruz.

2387 ◆ BUCHANAN, ALLEN

Rank: Lieutenant Commander (highest rank: Captain)
Service: U.S. Navy
Birthday: 22 December 1876
Place of Birth: Evansville, Vanderburgh County, Indiana
Date of Death: 12 January 1940
Cemetery: Arlington National Cemetery (9-5845)—Arlington, Virginia
Entered Service at: Indiana
Battle or Place of Action: Vera Cruz, Mexico
Date of Action: 21-22 April 1914
G.O. Number, Date: 177, 4 December 1915
Citation: For distinguished conduct in battle, engagements of Vera Cruz, 21–22 April 1914. In command of the 1st Seaman Regiment, Lt. Comdr. Buchanan was in both days' fighting and almost continually under fire from soon after landing, about noon of the 21st, until we were in possession of the city, about noon of the 22d. His duties required him to be at points of great danger in directing his officers and men, and he exhibited conspicuous courage, coolness, and skill in his conduct of the fighting. Upon his courage and skill depended, in great measure, success or failure. His responsibilities were great, and he met them in a manner worthy of commendation.

2388 ◆ BUTLER, SMEDLEY DARLINGTON✥

Rank: Major (highest rank: Major General)
Service: U.S. Marine Corps
Birthday: 30 July 1881
Place of Birth: West Chester, Chester County, Pennsylvania
Date of Death: 21 June 1940
Place of Death: Philadelphia, Pennsylvania
Cemetery: Oakland Cemetery—West Chester, Pennsylvania
Entered Service at: Pennsylvania
Served as: Battalion Commander
Battle or Place of Action: Vera Cruz, Mexico
Date of Action: 22 April 1914
G.O. Number, Date: 177, 4 December 1915
Citation: **First Award** For distinguished conduct in battle, engagement of Vera Cruz, 22 April 1914. Maj. Butler was eminent and conspicuous in command of his battalion. He exhibited courage and skill in leading his men through the action of the 22d and in the final occupation of the city.
Notes: ✥Double Awardee: *see also* Haitian Campaign 1915

2389 ◆ CASTLE, GUY WILKINSON STUART

Rank: Lieutenant (highest rank: Commander)
Service: U.S. Navy
Birthday: 8 February 1879
Date of Death: 10 August 1919
Place of Death: Brest, France, on board the U.S.S. *Martha Washington*
Cemetery: Arlington National Cemetery (3-4345)—Arlington, Virginia
Appointed from: Wisconsin
Battle or Place of Action: Vera Cruz, Mexico
Date of Action: 21-22 April 1914
G.O. Number, Date: 177, 4 December 1915
Citation: For distinguished conduct in battle, engagements of Vera Cruz, 21–22 April 1914. Eminent and conspicuous in command of his battalion, Lt. Castle was in the fighting of both days, and exhibited courage and skill in leading his men through action. In seizing the customhouse, he encountered for many hours the heaviest and most pernicious concealed fire of the entire day, but his courage and coolness under trying conditions were marked.

2390 ◆ CATLIN, ALBERTUS WRIGHT

Rank: Major (highest rank: Brigadier General)
Service: U.S. Marine Corps
Birthday: 1 December 1868
Place of Birth: Gowanda, Cattaraugus County, New York
Date of Death: 31 May 1933
Place of Death: Culpeper, Virginia
Cemetery: Arlington National Cemetery (7-10038)—Arlington, Virginia
Appointed from: Minnesota

Unit: 3d Marines
Served as: Commanding Officer
Battle or Place of Action: Vera Cruz, Mexico
Date of Action: 22 April 1914
G.O. Number, Date: 177, 4 December 1915
Citation: For distinguished conduct in battle, engagement of Vera Cruz, 22 April 1914. Eminent and conspicuous in command of his battalion, Maj. Catlin exhibited courage and skill in leading his men through the action of the 22d and in the final occupation of the city.

2391 ◆ COURTS, GEORGE MCCALL

Rank: Lieutenant (j.g.) (highest rank: Commander)
Service: U.S. Navy
Birthday: 16 February 1888
Place of Birth: Washington, D.C.
Date of Death: 1 August 1932
Place of Death: Newport, Rhode Island
Cemetery: Arlington National Cemetery (7-9874)—Arlington, Virginia
Entered Service at: Washington, D.C.
Battle or Place of Action: Vera Cruz, Mexico
Date of Action: 21-22 April 1914
G.O. Number, Date: 177, 4 December 1915
Citation: For distinguished conduct in battle, engagements of Vera Cruz, 21–22 April 1914. Under fire, Lt. (j.g.) Courts was eminent and conspicuous in the performance of his duties. He had well qualified himself by thorough study during his years of duty in Mexico to deal with the conditions of this engagement, and his services were of great value. He twice volunteered and passed in an open boat through the zone of fire to convey important orders to the *Chester*, then under a severe fire.

2392 ◆ CREGAN, GEORGE

Rank: Coxswain (highest rank: Commander)
Service: U.S. Navy
Birthday: 11 December 1886
Place of Birth: New York, New York
Date of Death: 30 June 1969
Place of Death: Manasquan, New Jersey
Cemetery: Arlington National Cemetery (46-10666) (MH)—Arlington, Virginia
Entered Service at: New York
Unit: U.S.S. *Florida*
Battle or Place of Action: Vera Cruz, Mexico
Date of Action: 21 April 1914
G.O. Number, Date: 101, 15 June 1914
Citation: On board the U.S.S. *Florida*, for extraordinary heroism in the line of his profession during the seizure of Vera Cruz, Mexico, 21 April 1914. Cregan was ashore when he volunteered for an assault detail under Ens. George Maus Lowry on the Vera Cruz customhouse under enemy fire both in the alley between the customhouse and warehouse and the assault over the objective's walls. During the move up the alley, he tended a wounded comrade, J.F. Schumaker, holding a compress with one hand and firing with the other.

2393 ◆ DECKER, PERCY A.

Rank: Boatswain's Mate Second Class (highest rank: Lieutenant)
Service: U.S. Navy
Birthday: 4 August 1890
Place of Birth: New York, New York
Date of Death: 18 August 1936
Cemetery: Arlington National Cemetery (7-10302) (MH)—Arlington, Virginia
Entered Service at: New York
Unit: U.S.S. *Florida*
Battle or Place of Action: Vera Cruz, Mexico
Date of Action: 21 April 1914
G.O. Number, Date: 101, 15 June 1914
Citation: On board the U.S.S. *Florida* during the seizure of Vera Cruz, Mexico, 21 April 1914; for extraordinary heroism in the line of his profession during the seizure of Vera Cruz, Mexico.

2394 ◆ DESOMER, ABRAHAM

Rank: Lieutenant (highest rank: Lieutenant Commander, Ret.)
Service: U.S. Navy
Birthday: 29 December 1884
Place of Birth: Milwaukee, Milwaukee County, Wisconsin
Date of Death: 31 August 1974
Cemetery: San Francisco National Cemetery (MA-15)—San Francisco, California
Entered Service at: Wisconsin
Unit: U.S.S. *Utah*
Battle or Place of Action: U.S.S. *Utah* off the coast of Vera Cruz, Mexico
Date of Action: 21-22 April 1914
Place of Presentation: 8 January 1915
Citation: On board the U.S.S. *Utah*, for extraordinary heroism in the line of his profession during the seizure of Vera Cruz, Mexico, 21–22 April 1914.

2395 ◆ DRUSTRUP, NIELS

Rank: Lieutenant (highest rank: Lieutenant Commander)
Service: U.S. Navy
Birthday: 17 October 1876
Place of Birth: Denmark
Date of Death: 15 March 1957
Cemetery: Arlington National Cemetery (3-4378-RH) (MH)—Arlington, Virginia
Entered Service at: Pennsylvania
Unit: U.S.S. *Utah*
Battle or Place of Action: Vera Cruz, Mexico
Date of Action: 21 April 1914
G.O. Number, Date: 131, 17 July 1924
Citation: For meritorious service under fire on the occasion of the landing of the naval forces at Vera Cruz, Mexico, 21 April 1914. For several hours Lt. Drustrup was in charge of an advanced barricade under a heavy fire, and not only dis-

played utmost ability as a leader of men but also exerted a great steadying influence on the men around him. Lt. Drustrup was then attached to the U.S.S. *Utah* as a chief turret captain.

2396 ◆ DYER, JESSE FARLEY

Rank: Captain (highest rank: Brigadier General)
Service: U.S. Marine Corps
Birthday: 2 December 1877
Place of Birth: St. Paul, Ramsey County, Minnesota
Date of Death: 31 March 1955
Cemetery: Fort Rosecrans National Cemetery (P-1606)—San Diego, California
Appointed from: Minnesota
Served as: Company Commander
Battle or Place of Action: Vera Cruz, Mexico
Date of Action: 21-22 April 1914
G.O. Number, Date: 177, 4 December 1915
Citation: For distinguished conduct in battle, engagements of Vera Cruz, 21–22 April 1914; was in both days' fighting at the head of his company, and was eminent and conspicuous in his conduct, leading his men with skill and courage.

2397 ◆ ELLIOTT, MIDDLETON STUART

Rank: Surgeon
Service: U.S. Navy
Birthday: 16 October 1872
Place of Birth: Beauford, Beauford County, South Carolina
Date of Death: 29 October 1952
Place of Death: Long Beach, California
Cemetery: Fort Rosecrans National Cemetery (P-2628) (MH)—San Diego, California
Entered Service at: South Carolina
Served as: Surgeon
Battle or Place of Action: Vera Cruz, Mexico
Date of Action: 21-22 April 1914
G.O. Number, Date: 177, 4 December 1915
Citation: For distinguished conduct in battle, engagements of Vera Cruz, 21–22 April 1914. Surg. Elliott was eminent and conspicuous in the efficient establishment and operation of the base hospital, and in his cool judgment and courage in supervising first-aid stations on the firing line and removing the wounded.

2398 ◆ FLETCHER, FRANK FRIDAY

Rank: Rear Admiral
Service: U.S. Navy
Birthday: 23 November 1855
Place of Birth: Oskaloosa, Mahaska County, Iowa
Date of Death: 28 November 1928
Cemetery: Arlington National Cemetery (3-1933)—Arlington, Virginia
Entered Service at: Iowa
Battle or Place of Action: Vera Cruz, Mexico
Date of Action: 21-22 April 1914
G.O. Number, Date: 177, 4 December 1915
Citation: For distinguished conduct in battle, engagements of Vera Cruz, 21–22 April 1914. Under fire, Rear Adm. Fletcher was eminent and conspicuous in the performance of his duties; was senior officer present at Vera Cruz, and the landing and the operations of the landing force were carried out under his orders and directions. In connection with these operations, he was at times onshore and under fire.

2399 ◆ FLETCHER, FRANK JACK

Rank: Lieutenant (highest rank: Admiral)
Service: U.S. Navy
Birthday: 29 April 1885
Place of Birth: Marshalltown, Marshall County, Iowa
Date of Death: 25 April 1973
Place of Death: Bethesda, Maryland
Cemetery: Arlington National Cemetery (2-4736-E) (MH)—Arlington, Virginia
Entered Service at: Iowa
Battle or Place of Action: Vera Cruz, Mexico
Date of Action: 21-22 April 1914
G.O. Number, Date: 177, 4 December 1915
Citation: For distinguished conduct in battle, engagements of Vera Cruz, 21–22 April 1914. Under fire, Lt. Fletcher was eminent and conspicuous in performance of his duties. He was in charge of the *Esperanze* and succeeded in getting on board over 350 refugees, many of them after the conflict had commenced. Although the ship was under fire, being struck more than 30 times, he succeeded in getting all the refugees placed in safety. Lt. Fletcher was later placed in charge of the train conveying refugees under a flag of truce. This was hazardous duty, as it was believed that the track was mined, and a small error in dealing with the Mexican guard of soldiers might readily have caused a conflict, such a conflict at one time being narrowly averted. It was greatly due to his efforts in establishing friendly relations with the Mexican soldiers that so many refugees succeeded in reaching Vera Cruz from the interior.

2400 ◆ FOSTER, PAUL FREDERICK

Rank: Ensign (highest rank: Vice Admiral)
Service: U.S. Navy
Birthday: 25 March 1889
Place of Birth: Wichita, Sedgwick County, Kansas
Date of Death: 30 January 1972
Place of Death: Virginia Beach, Virginia
Cemetery: Arlington National Cemetery (5-106) (MH)—Arlington, Virginia
Entered Service at: Kansas
Battle or Place of Action: Vera Cruz, Mexico
Date of Action: 21-22 April 1914
G.O. Number, Date: 177, 4 December 1915
Citation: For distinguished conduct in battle, engagements of Vera Cruz, 21–22 April 1914. In both days' fighting at the head of his company, Ens. Foster was eminent and conspicuous in his conduct, leading his men with skill and courage.

2401 ◆ FRAZER, HUGH CARROLL

Rank: Ensign (highest rank: Commander)
Service: U.S. Navy
Birthday: 22 February 1891
Place of Birth: Martinsburg, Berkeley County, West Virginia
Date of Death: 9 July 1975
Place of Death: Washington, D.C.
Cemetery: Arlington National Cemetery (46-282) (MH)—Arlington, Virginia
Entered Service at: West Virginia
Battle or Place of Action: Vera Cruz, Mexico
Date of Action: 22 April 1914
G.O. Number, Date: 177, 4 December 1915
Citation: For extraordinary heroism in battle, engagement of Vera Cruz, 22 April 1914. During this engagement, Ens. Frazer ran forward to rescue a wounded man, exposing himself to hostile fire and that of his own men. Having accomplished the mission, he returned at once to his position in line.

2402 ◆ FRYER, ELI THOMPSON

Rank: Captain (highest rank: Brigadier General)
Service: U.S. Marine Corps
Birthday: 22 August 1878
Place of Birth: Hightstown, Mercer County, New Jersey
Date of Death: 6 June 1963
Cemetery: Arlington National Cemetery (34-102-A) (MH)—Arlington, Virginia
Appointed from: New Jersey
Unit: 2d Advanced Base Regiment
Battle or Place of Action: Vera Cruz, Mexico
Date of Action: 21-22 April 1914
G.O. Number, Date: 177, 4 December 1915
Citation: For distinguished conduct in battle, engagements of Vera Cruz, 21–22 April 1914. In both days' fighting at the head of his company, Capt. Fryer was eminent and conspicuous in his conduct, leading his men with skill and courage.

2403 ◆ GAUJOT, JULIEN EDMUND

Rank: Captain (highest rank: Colonel)
Service: U.S. Army
Birthday: 22 October 1874
Place of Birth: Keweenaw, Baraga County, Michigan
Date of Death: 7 April 1938
Cemetery: Arlington National Cemetery (6-8423-NH) (MH)—Arlington, Virginia
Entered Service at: Williamson, Mingo County, West Virginia
Unit: Troop K, 1st U.S. Cavalry
Battle or Place of Action: Aqua Prieta, Mexico
Date of Action: 13 April 1911
Date of Presentation: 23 November 1912
Place of Presentation: The White House, presented by Pres. William H. Taft
Citation: Crossed the field of fire to obtain the permission of the rebel commander to receive the surrender of the surrounded forces of Mexican Federals and escort such forces, together with five Americans held as prisoners, to the American line.
Notes: Pre-Vera Cruz

2404 ◆ GISBURNE, EDWARD ALLEN

Rank: Electrician Third Class (highest rank: Lieutenant)
Service: U.S. Navy
Birthday: 14 June 1892
Place of Birth: Providence, Providence County, Rhode Island
Date of Death: 29 June 1955
Cemetery: Milton Cemetery (MH)—Milton, Massachusetts
Entered Service at: Massachusetts
Unit: U.S.S. *Florida*
Battle or Place of Action: Vera Cruz, Mexico
Date of Action: 21-22 April 1914
G.O. Number, Date: 101, 15 June 1914
Citation: On board the U.S.S. *Florida* during the seizure of Vera Cruz, Mexico, 21–22 April 1914, and for extraordinary heroism in the line of his profession during this action.

2405 ◆ GRADY, JOHN

Rank: Lieutenant (highest rank: Captain)
Service: U.S. Navy
Birthday: 25 December 1872
Place of Birth: New Brunswick, Canada
Date of Death: 9 December 1956
Cemetery: Arlington National Cemetery (4-2723-2-RH)(MH)—Arlington, Virginia
Entered Service at: Massachusetts
Battle or Place of Action: Vera Cruz, Mexico
Date of Action: 22 April 1914
G.O. Number, Date: 177, 4 December 1915
Citation: For distinguished conduct in battle, engagement of Vera Cruz, 22 April 1914. During the second day's fighting, the service performed by Lt. Grady, in command of the 2d Regiment, Artillery, was eminent and conspicuous. From necessarily exposed positions, he shelled the enemy from the strongest position.

2406 ◆ HARNER, JOSEPH GABRIEL

Rank: Boatswain's Mate Second Class
Service: U.S. Navy
Birthday: 19 February 1889
Place of Birth: Louisville, Stark County, Ohio
Date of Death: 5 March 1958
Cemetery: Arlington National Cemetery (17-21199-B-2) (MH)—Arlington, Virginia
Entered Service at: Ohio
Unit: U.S.S. *Florida*
Battle or Place of Action: Vera Cruz, Mexico
Date of Action: 21 April 1914
G.O. Number, Date: 101, 15 June 1914
Citation: On board the U.S.S. *Florida*, for extraordinary heroism in the line of his profession during the seizure of Vera Cruz, Mexico, 21 April 1914.

2407 ◆ HARRISON, WILLIAM KELLY

Rank: Commander
Service: U.S. Navy
Birthday: 30 July 1870
Place of Birth: Waco, McLennan County, Texas
Date of Death: 15 August 1928
Cemetery: Arlington National Cemetery (2-1080)—Arlington, Virginia
Entered Service at: Texas
Unit: U.S.S. *Chester*
Battle or Place of Action: Vera Cruz, Mexico
Date of Action: 21-22 April 1914
G.O. Number, Date: 177, 4 December 1915
Citation: For distinguished conduct in battle, engagements of Vera Cruz, 21–22 April 1914. During this period, Comdr. Harrison brought his ship into the inner harbor during the nights of the 21st and 22d without the assistance of a pilot or navigational lights, and was in a position on the morning of the 22d to use his guns with telling effect at a critical time.

2408 ◆ HARTIGAN, CHARLES CONWAY

Rank: Lieutenant (highest rank: Rear Admiral)
Service: U.S. Navy
Birthday: 13 September 1882
Place of Birth: Middletown, Orange County, New York
Date of Death: 25 February 1944
Cemetery: Arlington National Cemetery (3-2194-B)—Arlington, Virginia
Entered Service at: Norwich, Chenango County, New York
Battle or Place of Action: Vera Cruz, Mexico
Date of Action: 22 April 1914
G.O. Number, Date: 177, 4 December 1915
Citation: For distinguished conduct in battle, engagement of Vera Cruz, 22 April 1914. During the second day's fighting the service performed by him was eminent and conspicuous. He was conspicuous for the skillful handling of his company under heavy rifle and machine-gun fire, for which conduct he was commended by his battalion commander.

2409 ◆ HILL, WALTER NEWELL

Rank: Captain (highest rank: Brigadier General)
Service: U.S. Marine Corps
Birthday: 29 September 1881
Place of Birth: Haverhill, Essex County, Massachusetts
Date of Death: 29 June 1955
Place of Death: St. Albans, New York
Cemetery: Arlington National Cemetery (6-9646-C)—Arlington, Virginia
Appointed from: Massachusetts
Served as: Company Commander
Battle or Place of Action: Vera Cruz, Mexico
Date of Action: 21-22 April 1914
G.O. Number, Date: 177, 4 December 1915
Citation: For distinguished conduct in battle, engagements of Vera Cruz, 21–22 April 1914. Capt. Hill was in both days' fighting at the head of his company, and was eminent and conspicuous in his conduct, leading his men with skill and courage.

2410 ◆ HUGHES, JOHN ARTHUR

Rank: Captain (highest rank: Colonel)
Service: U.S. Marine Corps
Birthday: 2 November 1880
Place of Birth: New York, New York
Date of Death: 25 May 1942
Place of Death: St. Petersburg, Florida
Cemetery: Arlington National Cemetery (8-5265)—Arlington, Virginia
Entered Service at: New York
Served as: Company Commander
Battle or Place of Action: Vera Cruz, Mexico
Date of Action: 21-22 April 1914
G.O. Number, Date: 177, 4 December 1915
Citation: For distinguished conduct in battle, engagements of Vera Cruz, 21–22 April 1914. Capt. Hughes was in both days' fighting at the head of his company, and was eminent and conspicuous in his conduct, leading his men with skill and courage.

2411 ◆ HUSE, HENRY MCLAREN PINCKNEY

Rank: Captain (highest rank: Vice Admiral)
Service: U.S. Navy
Birthday: 8 December 1858
Place of Birth: USMA, West Point, Orange County, New York
Date of Death: 14 May 1942
Place of Death: Bethesda, Maryland
Cemetery: Arlington National Cemetery (2-4889)—Arlington, Virginia
Appointed from: New York
Battle or Place of Action: Vera Cruz, Mexico
Date of Action: 21-22 April 1914
G.O. Number, Date: 177, 4 December 1915
Date of Issue: 24 January 1916
Citation: For distinguished conduct in battle, engagements of Vera Cruz, 21–22 April 1914. Under fire, Capt. Huse was eminent and conspicuous in the performance of his duties; was indefatigable in his labors of a most important character, both with the division commander in directing affairs and in his efforts onshore to get in communication with the Mexican authorities to avoid needlessly prolonging the conflict.

2412 ◆ INGRAM, JONAS HOWARD

Rank: Lieutenant (j.g.) (highest rank: Admiral)
Service: U.S. Navy
Birthday: 15 October 1887
Place of Birth: Jeffersonville, Clark County, Indiana
Date of Death: 10 September 1952
Cemetery: Arlington National Cemetery (30-643-RH)—Arlington, Virginia
Entered Service at: Indiana
Battle or Place of Action: Vera Cruz, Mexico

Date of Action: 22 April 1914
G.O. Number, Date: 177, 4 December 1915
Citation: For distinguished conduct in battle, engagement of Vera Cruz, 22 April 1914. During the second day's fighting the service performed by him was eminent and conspicuous. He was conspicuous for skillful and efficient handling of the artillery and machine guns of the Arkansas battalion, for which he was specially commended in reports.

2413 ◆ JARRETT, BERRIE HENRY

Rank: Seaman (highest rank: Gunner)
Service: U.S. Navy
Birthday: 10 June 1894
Place of Birth: Baltimore, Baltimore County, Maryland
Date of Death: 14 August 1927
Cemetery: Lorraine Park Cemetery—Baltimore, Maryland
Entered Service at: Maryland
Unit: U.S.S. *Florida*
Battle or Place of Action: Vera Cruz, Mexico
Date of Action: 21 April 1914
G.O. Number, Date: 116, 19 August 1914
Citation: On board the U.S.S. *Florida* Jarrett displayed extraordinary heroism in the line of his profession during the seizure of Vera Cruz, Mexico, 21 April 1914.

2414 ◆ JOHNSTON JR., RUFUS ZENAS

Rank: Lieutenant Commander (highest rank: Rear Admiral)
Service: U.S. Navy
Birthday: 7 June 1874
Place of Birth: Lincolnton, Lincoln County, North Carolina
Date of Death: 4 July 1959
Place of Death: Newport, Rhode Island
Cemetery: Arlington National Cemetery (2-3645-RH) (MH)—Arlington, Virginia
Entered Service at: North Carolina
Battle or Place of Action: Vera Cruz, Mexico
Date of Action: 22 April 1914
G.O. Number, Date: 177, 4 December 1915
Citation: For distinguished conduct in battle, engagement of Vera Cruz, 22 April 1914; was regimental adjutant, and eminent and conspicuous in his conduct. He exhibited courage and skill in leading his men through the action of the 22d and in the final occupation of the city.

2415 ◆ LANGHORNE, CARY DEVALL

Rank: Surgeon (highest rank: Commander)
Service: U.S. Navy
Birthday: 14 May 1873
Place of Birth: Lynchburg, Lynchburg County, Virginia
Date of Death: 25 April 1948
Cemetery: Arlington National Cemetery (11-868)—Arlington, Virginia
Entered Service at: Virginia
Battle or Place of Action: Vera Cruz, Mexico
Date of Action: 22 April 1914
G.O. Number, Date: 177, 4 December 1915

Citation: For extraordinary heroism in battle, engagement of Vera Cruz, 22 April 1914. Surg. Langhorne carried a wounded man from the front of the Naval Academy while under heavy fire.

2416 ◆ LANNON, JAMES PATRICK

Rank: Lieutenant (highest rank: Rear Admiral)
Service: U.S. Navy
Birthday: 12 October 1878
Place of Birth: Alexandria, Alexandria County, Virginia
Date of Death: 13 March 1953
Cemetery: Arlington National Cemetery (8-6410-B)—Arlington, Virginia
Entered Service at: Virginia
Battle or Place of Action: Vera Cruz, Mexico
Date of Action: 22 April 1914
G.O. Number, Date: 177, 4 December 1915
Citation: For extraordinary heroism in battle, engagement of Vera Cruz, 22 April 1914. Lt. Lannon assisted a wounded man under heavy fire, and after returning to his battalion, was himself desperately wounded.

2417 ◆ LOWRY, GEORGE MAUS

Rank: Ensign (highest rank: Rear Admiral)
Service: U.S. Navy
Birthday: 27 October 1889
Place of Birth: Erie, Erie County, Pennsylvania
Date of Death: 25 September 1981
Place of Death: Carmel, California
Cemetery: Ashes scattered at sea
Entered Service at: Pennsylvania
Battle or Place of Action: Vera Cruz, Mexico
Date of Action: 21-22 April 1914
G.O. Number, Date: 177, 4 December 1915
Citation: For distinguished conduct in battle, engagements of Vera Cruz, 21–22 April 1914; Ens. Lowry was in both days' fighting at the head of his company, and was eminent and conspicuous in his conduct, leading his men with skill and courage.

2418 ◆ McCLOY, JOHN✝

Rank: Chief Boatswain (highest rank: Lieutenant Commander)
Service: U.S. Navy
Birthday: 3 January 1876
Place of Birth: Brewster, Putnam County, New York
Date of Death: 25 May 1945
Cemetery: Arlington National Cemetery (8-5246)—Arlington, Virginia
Entered Service at: New York
Battle or Place of Action: Vera Cruz, Mexico
Date of Action: 22 April 1914
G.O. Number, Date: 177, 4 December 1915
Citation: Second Award For heroism in leading three picket launches along Vera Cruz sea front, drawing Mexican fire and enabling cruisers to save our men onshore, 22 April

1914. Though wounded, he gallantly remained at his post.
Notes: ✛Double Awardee: *see also* China Relief Expedition

2419 ♦ McDONNELL, EDWARD ORRICK

Rank: Ensign (highest rank: Vice Admiral)
Service: U.S. Navy
Birthday: 13 November 1891
Place of Birth: Baltimore, Baltimore County, Maryland
Date of Death: 6 January 1960
Place of Death: North Carolina
Cemetery: Arlington National Cemetery (2-4955-4)—Arlington, Virginia
Entered Service at: Maryland
Battle or Place of Action: Vera Cruz, Mexico
Date of Action: 21-22 April 1914
G.O. Number, Date: 177, 4 December 1915
Citation: For extraordinary heroism in battle, engagements of Vera Cruz, 21–22 April 1914. Posted on the roof of the Terminal Hotel and landing, Ens. McDonnell established a signal station there day and night, maintaining communication between troops and ships. At this exposed post he was continually under fire. One man was killed and three wounded at his side during the two days' fighting. He showed extraordinary heroism and striking courage and maintained his station in the highest degree of efficiency. All signals got through, largely due to his heroic devotion to duty.

2420 ♦ McNAIR JR., FREDERICK VALLETTE

Rank: Lieutenant (highest rank: Captain)
Service: U.S. Navy
Birthday: 13 March 1882
Place of Birth: Maryland
Date of Death: 2 September 1962
Cemetery: U.S. Naval Academy Cemetery (Lot 406)—Annapolis, Maryland
Appointed from: Appointed at large
Battle or Place of Action: Vera Cruz, Mexico
Date of Action: 22 April 1914
G.O. Number, Date: 177, 4 December 1915
Citation: For distinguished conduct in battle engagement of Vera Cruz, 22 April 1914. Lt. McNair was eminent and conspicuous in command of his battalion. He exhibited courage and skill in leading his men through the action of the 22d and in the final occupation of the city.

2421 ♦ MOFFETT, WILLIAM ADGER

Rank: Commander (highest rank: Rear Admiral)
Service: U.S. Navy
Birthday: 31 October 1869
Place of Birth: Charleston, Charleston County, South Carolina
Date of Death: 4 April 1933
Cemetery: Arlington National Cemetery (3-1655-A)—Arlington, Virginia
Entered Service at: Charleston, Charleston County, South Carolina
Unit: U.S.S. *Chester*
Battle or Place of Action: Vera Cruz, Mexico
Date of Action: 21-22 April 1914
G.O. Number, Date: 177, 4 December 1915
Citation: For distinguished conduct in battle, engagements of Vera Cruz, 21–22 April 1914. Comdr. Moffett brought his ship into the inner harbor during the nights of the 21st and 22d without the assistance of a pilot or navigational lights, and was in a position on the morning of the 22d to use his guns at a critical time with telling effect. His skill in mooring his ship at night was especially noticeable. He placed her nearest to the enemy and did most of the firing and received most of the hits.

2422 ♦ NEVILLE, WENDELL CUSHING

Rank: Lieutenant Colonel (highest rank: Major General)
Service: U.S. Marine Corps
Birthday: 12 May 1870
Place of Birth: Portsmouth, Portsmouth County, Virginia
Date of Death: 8 July 1930
Place of Death: Edgewater Beach, Maryland
Cemetery: Arlington National Cemetery (6-8409)—Arlington, Virginia
Appointed from: Virginia
Unit: 2d Marine Regiment
Served as: Commanding Officer
Battle or Place of Action: Vera Cruz, Mexico
Date of Action: 21-22 April 1914
G.O. Number, Date: 177, 4 December 1915
Citation: For distinguished conduct in battle engagements of Vera Cruz, 21–22 April 1914. In command of the 2d Regiment Marines, Lt. Col. Neville was in both days' fighting and almost continually under fire from soon after landing, about noon on the 21st, until we were in possession of the city, about noon of the 22d. His duties required him to be at points of great danger in directing his officers and men, and he exhibited conspicuous courage, coolness, and skill in his conduct of the fighting. Upon his courage and skill depended, in great measure, success or failure. His responsibilities were great, and he met them in a manner worthy of commendation.

2423 ♦ NICKERSON, HENRY NEHEMIAH

Rank: Boatswain's Mate Second Class
Service: U.S. Navy
Birthday: 2 December 1888
Place of Birth: Edgewood, West Virginia
Date of Death: 2 May 1979
Cemetery: Greenwood Cemetery (MH)—Wheeling, West Virginia
Entered Service at: West Virginia
Unit: U.S.S. *Utah*
Battle or Place of Action: Vera Cruz, Mexico
Date of Action: 21 April 1914
Citation: On board the U.S.S. *Utah*, Nickerson showed extraordinary heroism in the line of his profession during the seizure of Vera Cruz, Mexico, 21 April 1914.

2424 ◆ NORDSIEK, CHARLES LUERS

Rank: Ordinary Seaman (highest rank: lieutenant)
Service: U.S. Navy
Birthday: 19 April 1896
Place of Birth: New York, New York
Date of Death: 9 March 1937
Cemetery: Arlington National Cemetery (7-10230-SS) (MH)—Arlington, Virginia
Entered Service at: New York
Unit: U.S.S. *Florida*
Battle or Place of Action: Vera Cruz, Mexico
Date of Action: 21-22 April 1914
G.O. Number, Date: 101, 15 June 1914
Citation: On board the U.S.S. *Florida*, Nordsiek showed extraordinary heroism in the line of his profession during the seizure of Vera Cruz, Mexico, 21–22 April 1914.

2425 ◆ REID, GEORGE CROGHAN

Rank: Major (highest rank: Brigadier General)
Service: U.S. Marine Corps
Birthday: 9 December 1876
Place of Birth: Lorain, Lorain County, Ohio
Date of Death: 19 February 1961
Place of Death: Harlingen, Texas
Cemetery: Arlington National Cemetery (2-1096-A-LH)(MH)—Arlington, Virginia
Appointed from: Ohio
Served as: Division Marine Officer of the Atlantic Fleet
Battle or Place of Action: Vera Cruz, Mexico
Date of Action: 21-22 April 1914
G.O. Number, Date: 177, 4 December 1915
Citation: For distinguished conduct in battle, engagements of Vera Cruz, 21–22 April 1914; was eminent and conspicuous in command of his battalion; was in the fighting of both days and exhibited courage and skill in leading his men through action. His cool judgment and courage and his skill in handling his men in encountering and overcoming the machine-gun and rifle fire down Cinco de Mayo and parallel streets account for the small percentage of the losses of marines under his command.

2426 ◆ RUSH, WILLIAM REES

Rank: Captain
Service: U.S. Navy
Birthday: 19 September 1857
Place of Birth: Philadelphia, Philadelphia County, Pennsylvania
Date of Death: 2 August 1940
Place of Death: Pallanza, Italy
Cemetery: Arlington National Cemetery (3-3977)—Arlington, Virginia
Entered Service at: Pennsylvania
Battle or Place of Action: Vera Cruz, Mexico
Date of Action: 21-22 April 1914
G.O. Number, Date: 177, 4 December 1915
Citation: For distinguished conduct in battle, engagements of Vera Cruz, 21–22 April 1914. In command of the naval brigade, Capt. Rush was in both days' fighting and almost continually under fire from soon after landing, about noon on the 21st, until we were in possession of the city, about noon of the 22d. His duties required him to be at points of great danger in directing his officers and men, and he exhibited conspicuous courage, coolness and skill in his conduct of the fighting. Upon his courage and skill depended in great measure success or failure. His responsibilities were great, and he met them in a manner worthy of commendation.

2427 ◆ SCHNEPEL, FRED JURGEN

Rank: Ordinary Seaman (highest rank: Chief Quartermaster)
Service: U.S. Navy
Birthday: 24 February 1892
Place of Birth: New York, New York
Date of Death: 7 February 1948
Cemetery: Arlington National Cemetery (11-825) (MH)—Arlington, Virginia
Entered Service at: New York
Unit: U.S.S. *Florida*
Battle or Place of Action: Vera Cruz, Mexico
Date of Action: 21-22 April 1914
G.O. Number, Date: 101, 15 June 1914
Citation: On board the U.S.S. *Florida*, Schnepel showed extraordinary heroism in the line of his profession during the seizure of Vera Cruz, Mexico, 21–22 April 1914.

2428 ◆ SEMPLE, ROBERT

Rank: Chief Gunner (highest rank: Lieutenant Commander)
Service: U.S. Navy
Birthday: 18 August 1887
Place of Birth: Pittsburgh, Allegheny County, Pennsylvania
Date of Death: 13 May 1943
Cemetery: Fort Rosecrans National Cemetery (OS-A-192)—San Diego, California
Entered Service at: Pennsylvania
Unit: U.S.S. *Florida*
Battle or Place of Action: Vera Cruz, Mexico
Date of Action: 21 April 1914
G.O. Number, Date: 120, 10 January 1924
Citation: For meritorious service under fire on the occasion of the landing of the American naval forces at Vera Cruz on 21 April 1914. C.G. Semple was then attached to the U.S.S. *Florida* as a chief turret captain.

2429 ◆ SINNETT, LAWRENCE CLINTON

Rank: Seaman
Service: U.S. Navy
Birthday: 4 April 1888
Place of Birth: Burnt House, West Virginia
Date of Death: 11 June 1962
Cemetery: I.O.O.F. Cemetery—Harrisville, West Virginia
Entered Service at: Pennsylvania
Unit: U.S.S. *Florida*
Battle or Place of Action: Vera Cruz, Mexico

Date of Action: 21 April 1914
G.O. Number, Date: 101, 15 June 1914
Citation: On board the U.S.S. *Florida*, Sinnett showed extraordinary heroism in the line of his profession during the seizure of Vera Cruz, Mexico, 21 April 1914.

2430 ◆ STATON, ADOLPHUS

Rank: Lieutenant (highest rank: Rear Admiral)
Service: U.S. Navy
Birthday: 28 August 1879
Place of Birth: Tarboro, Edgecombe County, North Carolina
Date of Death: 4 June 1964
Cemetery: Arlington National Cemetery (4-280-A)—Arlington, Virginia
Entered Service at: North Carolina
Battle or Place of Action: Vera Cruz, Mexico
Date of Action: 22 April 1914
Date of Issue: 1915
Citation: For distinguished conduct in battle, engagement of Vera Cruz, 22 April 1914; was eminent and conspicuous in command of his battalion. He exhibited courage and skill in leading his men through the action of the 22d and in the final occupation of the city.

2431 ◆ STICKNEY, HERMAN OSMAN

Rank: Commander (highest rank: Rear Admiral)
Service: U.S. Navy
Birthday: 10 December 1867
Place of Birth: Pepperell, Middlesex County, Massachusetts
Date of Death: 13 September 1936
Cemetery: Arlington National Cemetery (3-1821)—Arlington, Virginia
Entered Service at: Massachusetts
Battle or Place of Action: Vera Cruz, Mexico
Date of Action: 21-22 April 1914
G.O. Number, Date: 177, 4 December 1915
Citation: For distinguished conduct in battle, engagements of Vera Cruz, 21–22 April 1914. Comdr. Stickney covered the landing of the 21st with the guns of the U.S.S. *Prairie*, and throughout the attack and occupation, rendered important assistance to our forces onshore with his 3-inch battery.

2432 ◆ TOWNSEND, JULIUS CURTIS

Rank: Lieutenant (highest rank: Rear Admiral)
Service: U.S. Navy
Birthday: 22 February 1881
Place of Birth: Athens, Missouri
Date of Death: 28 December 1939
Place of Death: Brooklyn, New York
Cemetery: Arlington National Cemetery (6-8590)—Arlington, Virginia
Entered Service at: Athens, Missouri
Battle or Place of Action: Vera Cruz, Mexico
Date of Action: 22 April 1914
G.O. Number, Date: 177, 4 December 1915
Citation: For distinguished conduct in battle, engagement of Vera Cruz, 22 April 1914. Lt. Townsend was eminent and conspicuous in command of his battalion. He exhibited courage and skill in leading his men through the action of the 22d and in the final occupation of the city.

2433 ◆ WAINWRIGHT JR., RICHARD

Rank: Lieutenant (highest rank: Lieutenant Commander)
Service: U.S. Navy
Birthday: 15 September 1881
Place of Birth: Washington, D.C.
Date of Death: 28 March 1944
Place of Death: Annapolis, Maryland
Cemetery: U.S. Naval Academy Cemetery—Annapolis, Maryland
Entered Service at: Washington, D.C.
Battle or Place of Action: Vera Cruz, Mexico
Date of Action: 21-22 April 1914
G.O. Number, Date: 177, 4 December 1915
Citation: For distinguished conduct in battle, engagements of Vera Cruz, 21–22 April 1914. Lt. Wainwright was eminent and conspicuous in command of his battalion; was in the fighting of both days, and exhibited courage and skill in leading his men through action. In seizing the customhouse, he encountered for many hours the heaviest and most pernicious concealed fire of the entire day, but his courage and coolness under trying conditions were marked.

2434 ◆ WALSH, JAMES ALOYSIUS

Rank: Seaman
Service: U.S. Navy
Birthday: 24 July 1897
Place of Birth: New York, New York
Date of Death: 29 May 1960
Cemetery: Long Island National Cemetery (DSS-47-A)(MH)—Farmingdale, New York
Entered Service at: New York, New York
Unit: U.S.S. *Florida*
Battle or Place of Action: Vera Cruz, Mexico
Date of Action: 21-22 April 1914
G.O. Number, Date: 101, 15 June 1914
Citation: On board the U.S.S. *Florida*; for extrordinary heroism in the line of his profession during the seizure of Vera Cruz, Mexico, 21 and 22 April 1914.

2435 ◆ WILKINSON JR., THEODORE STARK

Rank: Ensign (highest rank: Vice Admiral)
Service: U.S. Navy
Birthday: 22 December 1888
Place of Birth: Annapolis, Anne Arundel County, Maryland
Date of Death: 21 February 1946
Cemetery: Arlington National Cemetery (2-3645)—Arlington, Virginia
Appointed from: Louisiana
Unit: U.S.S. *Floria*
Battle or Place of Action: Vera Cruz, Mexico

Date of Action: 21-22 April 1914
G.O. Number, Date: 177, 4 December 1915
Citation: For distinguished conduct in battle, engagements of Vera Cruz, 21–22 April 1914. Ens. Wilkinson was in both days' fighting at the head of his company and was eminent and conspicuous in his conduct, leading his men with skill and courage.

2436 ◆ ZUIDERVELD, WILLIAM

Rank: Hospital Apprentice First Class (highest rank: Lieutenant)
Service: U.S. Navy
Birthday: 24 January 1888
Place of Birth: Michigan
Date of Death: 5 February 1978
Cemetery: Fort Rosecrans National Cemetery (A-1-9-13) (MH)—San Diego, California
Entered Service at: Michigan
Unit: U.S.S. *Florida*
Battle or Place of Action: Vera Cruz, Mexico
Date of Action: 21 April 1914
G.O. Number, Date: 116, 19 August 1914
Citation: On board the U.S.S. *Florida*, Zuiderveld showed extraordinary heroism in the line of his profession during the seizure of Vera Cruz, Mexico, 21 April 1914.

HAITIAN CAMPAIGN 1915

2437 ◆ BUTLER, SMEDLEY DARLINGTON✛

Rank: Major (highest rank: Major General)
Service: U.S. Marine Corps
Birthday: 30 July 1881
Place of Birth: West Chester, Chester County, Pennsylvania
Date of Death: 21 June 1940
Place of Death: Philadelphia, Pennsylvania
Cemetery: Oakland Cemetery—West Chester, Pennsylvania
Appointed from: Pennsylvania
Unit: U.S.S. *Connecticut*
Served as: Commanding Officer of Marines & Seaman
Battle or Place of Action: Fort Riviere, Haiti
Date of Action: 17 November 1915
Date of Issue: 1916
Citation: Second Award As commanding officer of detachments from the 5th, 13th, 23d Companies and the marine and sailor detachment from the U.S.S. *Connecticut*, Maj. Butler led the attack on Fort Riviere, Haiti, 17 November 1915. Following a concentrated drive, several different detachments of marines gradually closed in on the old French bastion fort in an effort to cut off all avenues of retreat for the Caco bandits. Reaching the fort on the southern side where there was a small opening in the wall, Maj. Butler gave the signal to attack and marines from the 15th Company poured through the breach, engaged the Cacos in hand-to-hand combat, took the bastion and crushed the Caco resistance. Throughout this perilous action, Maj. Butler was conspicuous for his bravery and forceful leadership.
Notes: ✛Double Awardee: *see also* Mexican Campaign (Vera Cruz)

2438 ◆ DALY, DANIEL JOSEPH✛

Rank: Gunnery Sergeant (highest rank: Sergeant Major)
Service: U.S. Marine Corps
Birthday: 11 November 1873
Place of Birth: Glen Cove, Nassau County, New York
Date of Death: 27 April 1937
Place of Death: Glendale, New York
Cemetery: Cypress Hills National Cemetery (5-70) (MH)—Brooklyn, New York
Entered Service at: New York
Unit: 15th Company, 2d Regiment
Battle or Place of Action: Fort Dipitie, Haiti
Date of Action: 24 October 1915
Citation: Second Award Serving with the 15th Company of Marines on 22 October 1915, G/Sgt. Daly was one of the company to leave Fort Liberte, Haiti, for a six-day reconnaissance. After dark on the evening of 24 October, while crossing the river in a deep ravine, the detachment was suddenly fired upon from three sides by about 400 Cacos concealed in bushes about 100 yards from the fort. The marine detachment fought its way forward to a good position, which it maintained during the night, although subjected to a continuous fire from the Cacos. At daybreak the marines, in three squads, advanced in three different directions, surprising and scattering the Cacos in all directions. G/Sgt. Daly fought with exceptional gallantry against heavy odds throughout this action.
Notes: ✛Double Awardee: *see also* China Relief Expedition

2439 ◆ GROSS, SAMUEL

True Name: Marguilies, Samuel
Rank: Private (highest rank: Corporal)
Service: U.S. Marine Corps
Birthday: 9 May 1891
Place of Birth: Philadelphia, Philadelphia County, Pennsylvania
Date of Death: 13 September 1934
Place of Death: Coatesville, Pennsylvania
Cemetery: Har-Nebo Jewish Cemetery (MH)—Philadelphia, Pennsylvania
Entered Service at: Pennsylvania
Unit: 23d Company
Battle or Place of Action: Fort Riviere, Haiti
Date of Action: 17 November 1915
Place of Presentation: Presented by Maj. Gen. George Barnett, Commandant U.S.M.C
Citation: In company with members of the 5th, 13th, 23d Companies and the marine and sailor detachment from the U.S.S. *Connecticut*, Gross participated in the attack on Fort Riviere, Haiti, 17 November 1915. Following a concentrated drive, several different detachments of marines gradually closed in on the old French bastion fort in an effort to cut off all avenues of retreat for the Caco bandits. Approaching a breach in the wall which was the only entrance to the fort, Gross was the second man to pass through the breach in the face of constant fire from the Cacos and, thereafter, for a 10-minute period, engaged the enemy in desperate hand-to-hand combat until the bastion was captured and Caco resistance neutralized.

2440 ◆ IAMS, ROSS LINDSEY

Rank: Sergeant
Service: U.S. Marine Corps

Birthday: 5 May 1881
Place of Birth: Graysville, Greene County, Pennsylvania
Date of Death: 29 March 1952
Cemetery: Fort Rosecrans National Cemetery (P-2930) (MH)—San Diego, California
Entered Service at: Pennsylvania
Unit: 5th Company
Battle or Place of Action: Fort Riviere, Haiti
Date of Action: 17 November 1915
Citation: In company with members of the 5th, 13th, and 23d Companies and marine and sailor detachment from the U.S.S. *Connecticut*, Sgt. Iams participated in the attack on Fort Riviere, Haiti, 17 November 1915. Following a concentrated drive, several different detachments of marines gradually closed in on the old French bastion fort in an effort to cut off all avenues of retreat for the Caco bandits. Approaching a breach in the wall which was the only entrance to the fort, Sgt. Iams unhesitatingly jumped through the breach despite constant fire from the Cacos and engaged the enemy in a desperate hand-to-hand combat until the bastion was captured and Caco resistance neutralized.

2441 ◆ OSTERMANN, EDWARD ALBERT

Rank: First Lieutenant (highest rank: Major General)
Service: U.S. Marine Corps
Birthday: 23 November 1882
Place of Birth: Columbus, Franklin County, Ohio
Date of Death: 18 May 1969
Place of Death: Fairfax, Virginia
Cemetery: Arlington National Cemetery (46-521) (MH)—Arlington, Virginia
Entered Service at: Ohio
Unit: 15th Company of Marines (Mounted)
Battle or Place of Action: Fort Dipitie, Haiti
Date of Action: 24 October 1915
Date of Issue: 1917
Citation: In company with members of the 15th Company of Marines, all mounted, 1st Lt. Ostermann left Fort Liberte, Haiti, for a six-day reconnaissance. After dark on the evening of 24 October 1915, while crossing the river in a deep ravine, the detachment was suddenly fired upon from three sides by about 400 Cacos concealed in bushes about 100 yards from the fort. The marine detachment fought its way forward to a good position, which it maintained during the night, although subjected to a continuous fire from the Cacos. At daybreak, 1st Lt. Ostermann, in command of one of the three squads which advanced in three different directions, led his men forward, surprising and scattering the Cacos, and aiding in the capture of Fort Dipitie.

2442 ◆ UPSHUR, WILLIAM PETERKIN

Rank: Captain (highest rank: Major General)
Service: U.S. Marine Corps
Birthday: 28 October 1881
Place of Birth: Richmond, Richmond County, Virginia
Date of Death: 21 July 1943
Place of Death: Sitka, Alaska
Cemetery: U.S. Naval Academy Cemetery (Lot 250-A)—Annapolis, Maryland
Appointed from: Virginia
Unit: 15th Company, 2d Marine Regiment
Served as: Commanding Officer
Battle or Place of Action: Fort Dipitie, Haiti
Date of Action: 24 October 1915
Citation: In company with members of the 15th Company of Marines, all mounted, Capt. Upshur left Fort Liberte, Haiti, for a six-day reconnaissance. After dark on the evening of 24 October 1915, while crossing the river in a deep ravine, the detachment was suddenly fired upon from three sides by about 400 Cacos concealed in bushes about 100 yards from the fort. The marine detachment fought its way forward to a good position, which it maintained during the night, although subjected to a continuous fire from the Cacos. At daybreak, Capt. Upshur, in command of one of the three squads which advanced in three different directions, led his men forward, surprising and scattering the Cacos, and aiding in the capture of Fort Dipitie.

INTERIM 1915–1916

2443 ♦ CARY, ROBERT WEBSTER

Rank: Lieutenant Commander (highest rank: Rear Admiral)
Service: U.S. Navy
Birthday: 18 August 1890
Place of Birth: Kansas City, Clay County, Missouri
Date of Death: 15 July 1967
Place of Death: Toledo, Ohio
Cemetery: Arlington National Cemetery (6-5695-G)—Arlington, Virginia
Entered Service at: Bunceton, Cooper County, Missouri
Unit: U.S.S. *San Diego*
Battle or Place of Action: U.S.S. *San Diego*
Date of Action: 21 January 1915
Date of Issue: 23 May 1934
Citation: For extraordinary heroism in the line of his profession on the occasion of an explosion on board the U.S.S. *San Diego* 21 January 1915. Lt. Comdr. Cary (then Ens.), U.S. Navy, an observer on duty in the firerooms of the U.S.S. *San Diego*, commenced to take the half-hourly readings of the steam pressure at every boiler. He had read the steam and air pressure on No. 2 boiler and was just stepping through the electric watertight door into No. 1 fireroom when the boilers in No. 2 fireroom exploded. Ens. Cary stopped and held open the doors which were being closed electrically from the bridge, and yelled to the men in No. 2 fireroom to escape through these doors, which three of them did. Ens. Cary's action undoubtedly saved the lives of these men. He held the doors probably a minute with the escaping steam from the ruptured boilers around him. His example of coolness did much to keep the men in No. 1 fireroom at their posts hauling fires, although five boilers in their immediate vicinity had exploded and boilers Nos. 1 and 3 apparently had no water in them and were likely to explode any instant. When these fires were hauled under Nos. 1 and 3 boilers, Ens. Cary directed the men in this fireroom into the bunker, for they well knew the danger of these two boilers exploding. During the entire time Ens. Cary was cool and collected and showed an abundance of nerve under the most trying circumstances. His action on this occasion was above and beyond the call of duty.

2444 ♦ CRILLEY, FRANK WILLIAM

Rank: Chief Gunner's Mate (highest rank: Ensign)
Service: U.S. Navy
Birthday: 13 September 1883
Place of Birth: Trenton, Mercer County, New Jersey
Date of Death: 23 November 1947
Cemetery: Arlington National Cemetery (8-6430)—Arlington, Virginia
Entered Service at: Pennsylvania
Unit: Navy's Experimental Diving Team
Served as: Diver
Battle or Place of Action: off Honolulu, Territory of Hawaii
Date of Action: 17 April 1915
Date of Presentation: 15 February 1929
Citation: For display of extraordinary heroism in the line of his profession above and beyond the call of duty during the diving operations in connection with the sinking in a depth of water 304 feet of the U.S.S. *F-4* with all on board, as a result of loss of depth control, which occurred off Honolulu, T.H., 25 March 1915. On 17 April 1915, William F. Loughman, chief gunner's mate, U.S. Navy, who had descended to the wreck and had examined one of the wire hawsers attached to it, upon starting his ascent, and when at a depth of 250 feet beneath the surface of the water, had his lifeline and air hose so badly fouled by this hawser that he was unable to free himself; he could neither ascend nor descend. On account of the length of time that Loughman had already been subjected to the great pressure due to the depth of water, and of the uncertainty of the additional time he would have to be subjected to this pressure before he could be brought to the surface, it was imperative that steps be taken at once to clear him. Instantly, realizing the desperate case of his comrade, Crilley volunteered to go to his aid, immediately donned a diving suit and descended. After a lapse of time of two hours and 11 minutes, Crilley was brought to the surface, having by a superb exhibition of skill, coolness, endurance, and fortitude, untangled the snarl of lines and cleared his imperiled comrade, so that he was brought, still alive, to the surface.

2445 ♦ JONES, CLAUD ASHTON

Rank: Commander (rank at time of action: Lieutenant) (highest rank: Rear Admiral)
Service: U.S. Navy
Birthday: 7 October 1885
Place of Birth: Fire Creek, West Virginia
Date of Death: 8 August 1948
Cemetery: Arlington National Cemetery (11-546-SS)—Arlington, Virginia
Entered Service at: West Virginia
Unit: U.S.S. *Memphis*
Battle or Place of Action: off Santo Domingo City, Santo Domingo
Date of Action: 29 August 1916
Citation: For extraordinary heroism in the line of his profes-

sion as a senior engineer officer on board the U.S.S. *Memphis*, at a time when the vessel was suffering total destruction from a hurricane while anchored off Santo Domingo City, 29 August 1916. Lt. Jones did everything possible to get the engines and boilers ready, and if the elements that burst upon the vessel had delayed for a few minutes, the engines would have saved the vessel. With boilers and steampipes bursting about him in clouds of scalding steam, with thousands of tons of water coming down upon him and in almost complete darkness, Lt. Jones nobly remained at his post as long as the engines would turn over, exhibiting the most supreme unselfish heroism which inspired the officers and men who were with him. When the boilers exploded, Lt. Jones, accompanied by two of his shipmates, rushed into the firerooms and drove the men there out, dragging some, carrying others to the engineroom, where there was air to be breathed instead of steam. Lt. Jones' action on this occasion was above and beyond the call of duty.

2446 ◆ *RUD, GEORGE WILLIAM

Rank: Chief Machinist's Mate
Service: U.S. Navy
Birthday: 7 October 1883
Place of Birth: Minneapolis, Hennepin County, Minnesota
Date of Death: 29 August 1916
Cemetery: Crystal Lake Cemetery—Minneapolis, Minnesota
Entered Service at: Minnesota
Unit: U.S.S. *Memphis*
Battle or Place of Action: off Santo Domingo City, Santo Domingo
Date of Action: 29 August 1916
Citation: For extraordinary heroism in the line of his profession while attached to the U.S.S. *Memphis*, at a time when that vessel was suffering total destruction from a hurricane while anchored off Santo Domingo City, 29 August 1916. C.M.M. Rud took his station in the engineroom and remained at his post amidst scalding steam and the rushing of thousands of tons of water into his cepartment, receiving serious burns from which he immediately died.

2447 ◆ SMITH, EUGENE P.

Rank: Chief Watertender
Service: U.S. Navy
Birthday: 8 August 1871
Place of Birth: Illinois
Date of Death: 24 March 1918
Cemetery: Cypress Hills National Cemetery (2-7742) (MH)—Brooklyn, New York
Entered Service at: California
Unit: U.S.S. *Decatur*
Battle or Place of Action: U.S.S. *Decatur*
Date of Action: 9 September 1915
G.O. Number, Date: 189, 8 February 1916
Citation: Attached to U.S.S. *Decatur*; for several times entering compartments on board of *Decautur* immediately following an explosion on board that vessel, 9 September 1915, and locating and rescuing injured shipmates.

2448 ◆ SMITH, WILHELM

Rank: Gunner's Mate First Class
Service: U.S. Navy
Birthday: 10 April 1870
Place of Birth: Germany
Date of Death: 30 October 1925
Cemetery: Cypress Hills National Cemetery (2-9493) (MH)—Brooklyn, New York
Entered Service at: New York
Unit: U.S.S. *New York*
Battle or Place of Action: U.S.S. *New York*
Date of Action: 24 January 1916
G.O. Number, Date: 202, 6 April 1916
Citation: On board the U.S.S. *New York*; for entering a compartment filled with gases and rescuing a shipmate on 24 January 1916.

2449 ◆ TRINIDAD, TELESFORO DE LA CRUZ

Rank: Fireman Second Class
Service: U.S. Navy
Birthday: 25 November 1890
Place of Birth: New Washington, Capig, Philippine Islands
Date of Death: 8 May 1968
Place of Death: Cavite Navy Yard, Philippine Islands
Cemetery: Imus Cemetery—Imus, Cavite, Philippine Islands
Entered Service at: Philippine Islands
Unit: U.S.S. *San Diego*
Battle or Place of Action: U.S.S. *San Diego*
Date of Action: 21 January 1915
G.O. Number, Date: 142, 1 April 1915
Date of Issue: August 1915
Citation: For extraordinary heroism in the line of his profession at the time of the boiler explosion on board the U.S.S. *San Diego*, 21 January 1915. Trinidad was driven out of fireroom No. 2 by the explosion, but at once returned and picked up R.E. Daly, fireman second class, whom he saw injured, and proceeded to bring him out. While coming into No. 4 fireroom, Trinidad was just in time to catch the explosion in No. 3 fireroom, but without consideration for his own safety, passed Daly on and then assisted in rescuing another injured man from No. 3 fireroom. Trinidad was himself burned about the face by the blast from the explosion in No. 3 fireroom.

2450 ◆ WILLEY, CHARLES H.

Rank: Machinist
Service: U.S. Navy
Birthday: 31 March 1889
Place of Birth: East Boston, Suffolk County, Massachusetts
Date of Death: 11 September 1977
Place of Death: Manchester, New Hampshire
Cemetery: Blossom Hill Cemetery (MH)—Concord, New Hampshire
Entered Service at: Massachusetts
Unit: U.S.S. *Memphis*

WILLEY, CHARLES H.

Battle or Place of Action: off Santo Domingo City, Santo Domingo
Date of Action: 29 August 1916
G.O. Number, Date: 1 August 1932
Citation: For extraordinary heroism in the line of his profession while serving on board the U.S.S. *Memphis*, at a time when that vessel was suffering total destruction from a hurricane while anchored off Santo Domingo City, 29 August 1916. Machinist Willey took his station in the engineer's department and remained at his post of duty amidst scalding steam and the rush of thousands of tons of water into his department as long as the engines would turn, leaving only when ordered to leave. When the boilers exploded, he assisted in getting the men out of the fireroom and carrying them into the engineroom, where there was air instead of steam to breathe. Machinist Willey's conduct on this occasion was above and beyond the call of duty.

DOMINICAN CAMPAIGN

2451 ◆ GLOWIN, JOSEPH ANTHONY

Rank: Corporal
Service: U.S. Marine Corps
Birthday: 14 March 1892
Place of Birth: Detroit, Wayne County, Michigan
Date of Death: 23 August 1952
Cemetery: Mount Olivet Cemetery—Detroit, Michigan
Entered Service at: Michigan
Battle or Place of Action: Guayacanas, Dominican Republic
Date of Action: 3 July 1916
G.O. Number, Date: 244, 2 November 1916
Citation: During an engagement at Guayacanas on 3 July 1916, Cpl. Glowin participated in action against a considerable force of rebels on the line of march.

2452 ◆ WILLIAMS, ERNEST CALVIN

Rank: First Lieutenant (highest rank: Lieutenant Colonel)
Service: U.S. Marine Corps
Birthday: 2 August 1887
Place of Birth: Broadwell, Elkhart County, Illinois
Date of Death: 31 July 1940
Cemetery: Woodlawn Cemetery—Indianola, Illinois
Entered Service at: Illinois
Battle or Place of Action: San Francisco de Macoris, Dominican Republic
Date of Action: 29 November 1916
G.O. Number, Date: 289, 27 April 1917
Citation: In action against hostile forces at San Francisco de Macoris, Dominican Republic, 29 November 1916. With only a dozen men available, 1st Lt. Williams rushed the gate of the fortress. With eight of his party wounded by rifle fire of the defenders, he pressed on with the four remaining men, threw himself against the door just as it was being closed by the Dominicans, and forced an entry. Despite a narrow escape from death at the hands of a rifleman, he and his men disposed of the guards and within a few minutes had gained control of the fort and the hundred prisoners confined there.

2453 ◆ WINANS, ROSWELL

Rank: First Sergeant (highest rank: Brigadier General)
Service: U.S. Marine Corps
Birthday: 9 December 1887
Place of Birth: Brookville, Franklin County, Indiana
Date of Death: 7 April 1968
Cemetery: Cypress View Mausoleum—San Diego, California
Entered Service at: Washington
Battle or Place of Action: Guayacanas, Dominican Republic
Date of Action: 3 July 1916
G.O. Number, Date: 244, 2 November 1916
Citation: During an engagement at Guayacanas on 3 July 1916, 1st Sgt. Winans participated in action against a considerable force of rebels on the line of march. During a running fight of 1,200 yards, our forces reached the enemy entrenchments and Cpl. Joseph A. Gowin, USMC, placed the machine gun, of which he had charge, behind a large log across the road and immediately opened fire on the trenches. He was struck once but continued firing his gun, but a moment later he was again struck and had to be dragged out of the position into cover. First Sgt. Winans, USMC, then arrived with a Colt's gun which he placed in a most exposed position, coolly opened fire on the trenches and when the gun jammed, stood up and repaired it under fire. All the time Glowin and Winans were handling their guns they were exposed to a very heavy fire which was striking into the logs and around the men, seven men being wounded and one killed within 20 feet. First Sgt. Winans continued firing his gun until the enemy had abandoned the trenches.

WORLD WAR I

2454 ◆ ADKINSON, JOSEPH B.

Rank: Sergeant
Service: U.S. Army
Birthday: 4 January 1892
Place of Birth: Egypt, Tennessee
Date of Death: 23 May 1965
Cemetery: Salem Cemetery—Atoka, Tennessee
Entered Service at: Memphis, Shelby County, Tennessee
Unit: Company C, 119th Infantry, 30th Division
Battle or Place of Action: near Bellicourt, France
Date of Action: 29 September 1918
G.O. Number, Date: 59, W.D. 3 May 1919
Citation: When murderous machine-gun fire at a range of 50 yards had made it impossible for his platoon to advance and had caused the platoon to take cover, Sgt. Adkinson alone, with the greatest intrepidity, rushed across the 50 yards of open ground directly into the face of the hostile machine gun, kicked the gun from the parapet into the enemy trench, and at the point of the bayonet captured the three men manning the gun. The gallantry and quick decision of this soldier enabled the platoon to resume its advance.

2455 ◆ ALLEX, JAKE

True Name: Mandushich, Jake Allex
Rank: Corporal
Service: U.S. Army
Birthday: 13 July 1887
Place of Birth: Streska, near Prizren, Serbia
Date of Death: 28 August 1959
Place of Death: Chicago, Illinois
Cemetery: St. Sava Cemetery—Libertyville, Illinois
Entered Service at: Chicago, Cook County, Illinois
Unit: Company H, 131st Infantry, 33d Division
Battle or Place of Action: at Chipilly Ridge, France
Date of Action: 9 August 1918
G.O. Number, Date: 44, W.D. 2 April 1919
Citation: At a critical point in the action, when all the officers of his platoon had become casualties, Cpl. Allex took command of the platoon and led it forward until the advance was stopped by fire from a machine-gun nest. He then advanced alone for about 30 yards in the face of intense fire and attacked the nest. With his bayonet he killed five of the enemy, and when it was broken, used the butt of his rifle, capturing 15 prisoners.

2456 ◆ ALLWORTH, EDWARD C.

Rank: Captain
Service: U.S. Army
Birthday: 6 July 1887
Place of Birth: Crawford, Washington
Date of Death: 25 June 1966
Cemetery: Crystal Lake Cemetery—Corvallis, Oregon
Entered Service at: Corvallis, Benton County, Oregon
Unit: 60th Infantry, 5th Division
Battle or Place of Action: at Clery-le-Petit, France
Date of Action: 5 November 1918
G.O. Number, Date: 16, W.D. 22 January 1919
Citation: While his company was crossing the Meuse River and canal at a bridgehead opposite Clery-le-Petit, the bridge over the canal was destroyed by shell fire and Capt. Allworth's command became separated, part of it being on the east bank of the canal and the remainder on the west bank. Seeing his advance units making slow headway up the steep slope ahead, this officer mounted the canal bank and called for his men to follow. Plunging in he swam across the canal under fire from the enemy, followed by his men. Inspiring his men by his example of gallantry, he led them up the slope, joining his hard-pressed platoons in front. By his personal leadership he forced the enemy back for more than a kilometer, overcoming machine-gun nests and capturing 100 prisoners, whose number exceeded that of the men in his command. The exceptional courage and leadership displayed by Capt. Allworth made possible the reestablishment of a bridgehead over the canal and the successful advance of other troops.

2457 ◆ ANDERSON, JOHANNES SEIGFRIED

Rank: First Sergeant
Service: U.S. Army
Birthday: 20 July 1887
Place of Birth: Bjoroky, Finland
Date of Death: 3 April 1950
Cemetery: Acacia Cemetery—Chicago, Illinois
Entered Service at: Chicago, Cook County, Illinois
Unit: Company B, 132d Infantry, 33d Infantry Division
Battle or Place of Action: at Consenvoye, France
Date of Action: 8 October 1918
G.O. Number, Date: 16, W.D. 22 January 1919
Date of Presentation: 17 February 1919
Place of Presentation: Chaumont, France, presented by Gen. John J. Pershing
Citation: While his company was being held up by intense

artillery and machine-gun fire, 1st Sgt. Anderson, without aid, voluntarily left the company and worked his way to the rear of the nest that was offering the most stubborn resistance. His advance was made through an open area and under constant hostile fire, but the mission was successfully accomplished, and he not only silenced the gun and captured it, but also brought back with him 23 prisoners.

2458 ◆ *BAESEL, ALBERT E.

Rank: Second Lieutenant
Service: U.S. Army
Birthday: 21 March 1890
Place of Birth: Berea, Cuyahoga County, Ohio
Date of Death: 27 September 1918
Cemetery: Woodvale Union Cemetery (MH)—Cleveland, Ohio
Entered Service at: Berea, Cuyahoga County, Ohio
Unit: Company B, 148th Infantry, 37th Division
Battle or Place of Action: near Ivry, France
Date of Action: 27 September 1918
G.O. Number, Date: 43, W.D. 23 October 1922
Citation: Upon hearing that a squad leader of his platoon had been severely wounded while attempting to capture an enemy machine-gun nest about 200 yards in advance of the assault line and somewhat to the right, 2d Lt. Baesel requested permission to go to the rescue of the wounded corporal. After thrice repeating his request and permission having been reluctantly given, due to the heavy artillery, rifle, and machine-gun fire, and heavy deluge of gas in which the company was at the time, accompanied by a volunteer, he worked his way forward, and reaching the wounded man, placed him upon his shoulders and was instantly killed by enemy fire.

2459 ◆ BALCH, JOHN HENRY

Rank: Pharmacist's Mate First Class (highest rank: Commander)
Service: U.S. Navy
Birthday: 2 January 1896
Place of Birth: Edgerton, Johnson County, Kansas
Date of Death: 15 October 1980
Place of Death: Sun City, California
Cemetery: Riverside National Cemetery (2-1925) (MH)—Riverside, California
Entered Service at: Kansas City, Clay County, Missouri
Unit: 6th Regiment, U.S. Marines
Battle or Place of Action: Vierzy & Somme-Py, France
Date of Action: 19 July & 5 October 1918
Date of Presentation: September 1919
Place of Presentation: Great Lakes Naval Station, presented by Adm. William A. Moffett
Citation: For gallantry and intrepidity at the risk of his life above and beyond the call of duty, with the 6th Regiment, U.S. Marines, in action at Vierzy, on 19 July 1918. Balch unhesitatingly and fearlessly exposed himself to terrific machine-gun and high-explosive fire to succor the wounded as they fell in the attack, leaving his dressing station voluntarily and keeping up the work all day and late into the night unceasingly for 16 hours. Also in the action at Somme-Py on 5 October 1918, he exhibited exceptional bravery in establishing an advanced dressing station under heavy shellfire.

2460 ◆ BARGER, CHARLES DENVER

Rank: Private First Class
Service: U.S. Army
Birthday: 1892
Place of Birth: Mount Vernon, Lawrence County, Missouri
Date of Death: 25 November 1936
Place of Death: Kansas City, Missouri
Cemetery: Blue Springs Cemetery (MH)—Blue Springs, Missouri
Entered Service at: Stotts City, Lawrence County, Missouri
Unit: Company L, 354th Infantry, 89th Division
Battle or Place of Action: near Bois-de-Bantheville, France
Date of Action: 31 October 1918
G.O. Number, Date: 20, W.D. 30 January 1919
Citation: Learning that two daylight patrols had been caught out in No Man's Land and were unable to return, Pfc. Barger and another stretcher bearer upon their own initiative made two trips 500 yards beyond our lines, under constant machine-gun fire, and rescued two wounded officers.

2461 ◆ *BARKELEY, DAVID B.

True Name: Barkley, David Bennes
Rank: Private
Service: U.S. Army
Birthday: 31 March 1899
Place of Birth: Laredo, Webb County, Texas
Date of Death: 9 November 1918
Cemetery: San Antonio National Cemetery (G-1302) (MH)—San Antonio, Texas
Entered Service at: San Antonio, Bexar County, Texas
Unit: Company A, 356th Infantry, 89th Division
Battle or Place of Action: near Pouilly, France
Date of Action: 9 November 1918
G.O. Number, Date: 20, W.D. 30 January 1919
Date of Presentation: 1919
Place of Presentation: San Antonio, presented to his Mother at her home
Citation: When information was desired as to the enemy's position on the opposite side of the Meuse River, Pvt. Barkeley, with another soldier, volunteered without hesitation and swam the river to reconnoiter the exact location. He succeeded in reaching the opposite bank, despite the evident determination of the enemy to prevent a crossing. Having obtained his information, he again entered the water for his return, but before his goal was reached, he was seized with cramps and drowned.

2462 ◆ BARKLEY, JOHN LEWIS

Rank: Private First Class
Service: U.S. Army

Birthday: 28 August 1895
Place of Birth: Blairstown, Henry County, Missouri
Date of Death: 14 April 1966
Cemetery: Forest Hills Cemetery—Kansas City, Missouri
Entered Service at: Blairstown, Henry County, Missouri
Unit: Company K, 4th Infantry, 3d Division
Battle or Place of Action: near Cunel, France
Date of Action: 7 October 1918
G.O. Number, Date: 44, W.D. 2 April 1919
Citation: Pfc. Barkley, who was stationed in an observation post half a kilometer from the German line, on his own initiative repaired a captured enemy machine gun and mounted it in a disabled French tank near his post. Shortly afterward, when the enemy launched a counterattack against our forces, Pfc. Barkley got into the tank, waited under the hostile barrage until the enemy line was abreast of him and then opened fire, completely breaking up the counterattack and killing and wounding a large number of the enemy. Five minutes later an enemy 77-millimeter gun opened fire on the tank point-blank. One shell struck the drive wheel of the tank, but this soldier nevertheless remained in the tank and after the barrage ceased broke up a second enemy counterattack, thereby enabling our forces to gain and hold Hill 25.

2463 ◆ BART, FRANK J.

Rank: Private
Service: U.S. Army
Birthday: 15 April 1883
Place of Birth: New York, New York
Date of Death: 31 March 1961
Cemetery: Flower Hill Cemetery (MH)—North Bergen, New Jersey
Entered Service at: Newark, Essex County, New Jersey
Unit: Company C, 9th Infantry, 2d Division
Battle or Place of Action: near Medeah Ferme, France
Date of Action: 3 October 1918
G.O. Number, Date: 16, W.D. 22 January 1919
Citation: Pvt. Bart, being on duty as a company runner, when the advance was held up by machine-gun fire voluntarily picked up an automatic rifle, ran out ahead of the line, and silenced a hostile machine-gun nest, killing the German gunners. The advance then continued, and when it was again hindered shortly afterward by another machine-gun nest this courageous soldier repeated his bold exploit by putting the second machine gun out of action.

2464 ◆ *BLACKWELL, ROBERT LESTER

Rank: Private
Service: U.S. Army
Birthday: 4 October 1895
Place of Birth: Person County, North Carolina
Date of Death: 11 October 1918
Cemetery: Somme Cemetery (D-20-2) (MH)—Bony Aisne, France
Entered Service at: Hurdle Mills, Person County, North Carolina
Unit: Company K, 119th Infantry, 30th Division
Battle or Place of Action: near St. Souplet, France
Date of Action: 11 October 1918
G.O. Number, Date: 13, W.D. 18 January 1919
Citation: When his platoon was almost surrounded by the enemy and his platoon commander asked for volunteers to carry a message calling for reinforcements, Pvt. Blackwell volunteered for this mission, well knowing the extreme danger connected with it. In attempting to get through the heavy shell and machine-gun fire this gallant soldier was killed.

2465 ◆ *BLECKLEY, ERWIN RUSSELL

Rank: Second Lieutenant
Service: U.S. Army Air Service
Birthday: 30 December 1894
Place of Birth: Wichita, Sedgwick County, Kansas
Date of Death: 6 October 1918
Cemetery: Meuse-Argonne Cemetery (F-25-33) (MH)—Romagne Meuse, France
Entered Service at: Wichita, Sedgwick County, Kansas
Unit: 50th Aero Squadron, 130th Field Artillery, Air Service
Served as: DH-4 Observer
Battle or Place of Action: near Binarville, France
Date of Action: 6 October 1918
G.O. Number, Date: 56, W.D. 30 December 1922
Citation: Second Lt. Bleckley, with his pilot, 1st Lt. Harold E. Goettler, Air Service, left the airdrome late in the afternoon on their second trip to drop supplies to a battalion of the 77th Division, which had been cut off by the enemy in the Argonne Forest. Having been subjected on the first trip to violent fire from the enemy, they attempted on the second trip to come still lower in order to get the packages even more precisely on the designated spot. In the course of his mission the plane was brought down by enemy rifle and machine-gun fire from the ground, resulting in fatal wounds to 2d Lt. Bleckley, who died before he could be taken to a hospital. In attempting and performing this mission 2d Lt. Bleckley showed the highest possible contempt of personal danger, devotion to duty, courage, and valor.

2466 ◆ BOONE, JOEL THOMPSON

Rank: Lieutenant (highest rank: Vice Admiral)
Service: U.S. Navy
Birthday: 29 August 1889
Place of Birth: St. Clair, Schuylkill County, Pennsylvania
Date of Death: 2 April 1974
Place of Death: Bethesda, Maryland
Cemetery: Arlington National Cemetery (11-137-2)—Arlington, Virginia
Entered Service at: St. Clair, Schuylkill County, Pennsylvania
Unit: 6th Regiment, U.S. Marines
Served as: Surgeon (Medical Corps)
Battle or Place of Action: vicinity of Vierzy, France
Date of Action: 19 July 1918
Citation: For extraordinary heroism, conspicuous gallantry, and intrepidity while serving with the 6th Regiment, U.S. Marines, in actual conflict with the enemy. With absolute dis-

regard for personal safety, ever conscious and mindful of the suffering fallen, Surg. Boone, leaving the shelter of a ravine, went forward onto the open field where there was no protection and despite the extreme enemy fire of all calibers, through a heavy mist of gas, applied dressings and first aid to wounded marines. This occurred southeast of Vierzy, near the cemetery, and on the road south from the town. When the dressings and supplies had been exhausted, he went through a heavy barrage of large-caliber shells, both high-explosive and gas, to replenish these supplies, returning quickly with a sidecar load, and administered them in saving the lives of the wounded. A second trip, under the same conditions and for the same purpose, was made by Surg. Boone later that day.

2467 ◆ BRADLEY JR., WILLIS WINTER

Rank: Commander (highest rank: Captain)
Service: U.S. Navy
Birthday: 28 June 1884
Place of Birth: Ransomville, Niagara County, New York
Date of Death: 27 August 1954
Cemetery: Fort Rosecrans National Cemetery (O-2925) (MH)—San Diego, California
Entered Service at: North Dakota
Unit: U.S.S. *Pittsburgh*
Battle or Place of Action: U.S.S. *Pittsburgh*
Date of Action: 23 June 1917
Citation: For extraordinary heroism and devotion to duty while serving on the U.S.S. *Pittsburgh*, at the time of an accidental explosion of ammunition on that vessel. On 23 July 1917, some saluting cartridge cases were being reloaded in the after casemate: through an accident an explosion occurred. Comdr. Bradley (then lieutenant), who was about to enter the casemate, was blown back by the explosion and rendered momentarily unconscious, but while still dazed, crawled into the casemate to extinguish burning materials in dangerous proximity to a considerable amount of powder, thus preventing further explosions.

2468 ◆ BRONSON, DEMING

Rank: First Lieutenant
Service: U.S. Army
Birthday: 8 July 1894
Place of Birth: Rhinelander, Oneida County, Wisconsin
Date of Death: 29 May 1957
Place of Death: Roseburg, Oregon
Cemetery: Arlington National Cemetery (30-500-2) (MH)—Arlington, Virginia
Entered Service at: Seattle, King County, Washington
Unit: Company H, 364th Infantry, 91st Division
Battle or Place of Action: near Eclisfontaine, France
Date of Action: 26-27 September 1918
G.O. Number, Date: 12, W.D. 27 June 1929
Date of Presentation: 1929
Place of Presentation: Presented by Pres. Herbert Hoover
Citation: For conspicuous gallantry and intrepidity above and beyond the call of duty in action with the enemy. On the morning of 26 September, during the advance of the 364th Infantry, 1st Lt. Bronson was struck by an exploding enemy hand grenade, receiving deep cuts on his face and back of his head. He nevertheless participated in the action which resulted in the capture of an enemy dugout from which a great number of prisoners were taken. This was effected with difficulty and under extremely hazardous conditions because it was necessary to advance without the advantage of cover and, from an exposed position, throw hand grenades and phosphorous bombs to compel the enemy to surrender. On the afternoon of the same day he was painfully wounded in the left arm by an enemy rifle bullet, and after receiving first-aid treatment he was directed to the rear. Disregarding these instructions, 1st Lt. Bronson remained on duty with his company through the night although suffering from severe pain and shock. On the morning of the 27 September, his regiment resumed its attack, the object being the village of Eclisfontaine. Company H, to which 1st Lt. Bronson was assigned, was left in support of the attacking line, Company E being in the line. He gallantly joined that company in spite of his wounds and engaged with it in the capture of the village. After the capture he remained with Company E and participated with it in the capture of an enemy machine gun, he himself killing the enemy gunner. Shortly after this encounter the company was compelled to retire due to the heavy enemy artillery barrage. During this retirement 1st Lt. Bronson, who was the last man to leave the advanced position, was again wounded in both arms by an enemy high-explosive shell. He was then assisted to cover by another officer who applied first aid. Although bleeding profusely and faint from loss of blood, 1st Lt. Bronson remained with the survivors of the company throughout the night of the second day, refusin
g to go to the rear for treatment. His conspicuous gallantry and spirit of self-sacrifice were a source of great inspiration to the members of the entire command.

2469 ◆ CALL, DONALD MARSHALL

Rank: Corporal
Service: U.S. Army
Birthday: 29 November 1892
Place of Birth: New York, New York
Date of Death: 19 March 1984
Place of Death: Bethesda, Maryland
Cemetery: Cremated Ashes in Flower Garden—Bethesda, Maryland
Entered Service at: France
Unit: 344th Battalion, Tank Corps
Battle or Place of Action: near Varennes, France
Date of Action: 26 September 1918
G.O. Number, Date: 13, W.D. 18 January 1919
Citation: During an operation against enemy machine-gun nests west of Varennes, Cpl. Call was in a tank with an officer when half of the turret was knocked off by a direct artillery hit. Choked by gas from the high-explosive shell, he left the tank and took cover in a shellhole 30 yards away. Seeing that the officer did not follow, and thinking that he might be alive, Cpl. Call returned to the tank under intense machine-gun and shell fire and carried the officer over a mile under machine-gun and sniper fire to safety.

2470 ◆ CANN, TEDFORD HARRIS

Rank: Seaman (highest rank: Ensign)
Service: U.S. Navy
Birthday: 3 September 1897
Place of Birth: Bridgeport, Fairfield County, Connecticut
Date of Death: 26 January 1963
Place of Death: Port Chester, New York
Cemetery: Arlington National Cemetery (7-10118-SS) (MH)—Arlington, Virginia
Entered Service at: New York
Unit: U.S.S. *May*
Battle or Place of Action: between Bermuda & the Azores
Date of Action: 5 November 1917
G.O. Number, Date: 366, W.D. 1918
Place of Presentation: Brest, France, presented by Adm. Newton A. McCully
Citation: For courageous conduct while serving on board the U.S.S. *May*, 5 November 1917. Cann found a leak in a flooded compartment and closed it at the peril of his life, thereby unquestionably saving the ship.

2471 ◆ *CHILES, MARCELLUS HOLMES

Rank: Captain
Service: U.S. Army
Birthday: 5 February 1895
Place of Birth: Eureka Springs, Carroll County, Arkansas
Date of Death: 5 November 1918
Cemetery: Meuse-Argonne Cemetery (C-31-23) (MH)—Romagne Meuse, France
Entered Service at: Denver, Denver County, Colorado
Unit: Company A, 356th Infantry, 89th Division
Served as: Battalion Commander
Battle or Place of Action: near Le Champy Bas, France
Date of Action: 3 November 1918
G.O. Number, Date: 20, W.D. 30 January 1919
Date of Issue: 15 April 1919
Citation: When his battalion, of which he had just taken command, was halted by machine-gun fire from the front and left flank, he picked up the rifle of a dead soldier and, calling on his men to follow, led the advance across a stream, waist deep, in the face of the machine-gun fire. Upon reaching the opposite bank this gallant officer was seriously wounded in the abdomen by a sniper, but before permitting himself to be evacuated he made complete arrangements for turning over his command to the next senior officer, and under the inspiration of his fearless leadership, his battalion reached its objective. Capt. Chiles died shortly after reaching the hospital.

2472 ◆ *COLYER, WILBUR E.

Rank: Sergeant
Service: U.S. Army
Birthday: 5 March 1898
Place of Birth: Brooklyn, Kings County, New York
Date of Death: 10 October 1918
Cemetery: Cypress Hills National Cemetery (2-8588)—Brooklyn, New York
Entered Service at: South Ozone, Queens County, New York
Unit: Company A, 1st Engineers, 1st Division
Battle or Place of Action: near Verdun, France
Date of Action: 9 October 1918
G.O. Number, Date: 20, W.D. 30 January 1919
Citation: Volunteering with two other soldiers to locate machine-gun nests, Sgt. Colyer advanced on the hostile positions to a point where he was half surrounded by the nests, which were in ambush. He killed the gunner of one gun with a captured German grenade and then turned this gun on the other nests, silencing all of them before he returned to his platoon. He was later killed in action.

2473 ◆ *COSTIN, HENRY G.

Rank: Private
Service: U.S. Army
Birthday: 15 June 1898
Place of Birth: Baltimore, Baltimore County, Maryland
Date of Death: 8 October 1918
Cemetery: Loudon Park National Cemetery (B-460)—Baltimore, Maryland
Entered Service at: Baltimore, Baltimore County, Maryland
Unit: Company H, 115th Infantry, 29th Division
Battle or Place of Action: near Bois-de-Consenvoye, France
Date of Action: 8 October 1918
G.O. Number, Date: 34, W.D. 7 March 1919
Citation: When the advance of his platoon had been held up by machine-gun fire and a request was made for an automatic rifle team to charge the nest, Pvt. Costin was the first to volunteer. Advancing with his team, under terrific fire of enemy artillery, machine guns, and trench mortars, he continued after all his comrades had become casualties and he himself had been seriously wounded. He operated his rifle until he collapsed. His act resulted in the capture of about 100 prisoners and several machine guns. He succumbed to the effects of his wounds shortly after the accomplishment of his heroic deed.

2474 ◆ COVINGTON, JESSE WHITFIELD

Rank: Ship's Cook Third Class (highest rank: Chief Steward)
Service: U.S. Navy
Birthday: 16 September 1889
Place of Birth: Haywood, Tennessee
Date of Death: 21 November 1966
Place of Death: Richmond, Virginia
Cemetery: Oak Grove Cemetery (PM)—Portsmouth, Virginia
Entered Service at: California
Unit: U.S.S. *Stewart*
Battle or Place of Action: at Sea
Date of Action: 17 April 1918
G.O. Number, Date: 403, W.D. 1918
Date of Issue: 1919
Citation: For extraordinary heroism following internal explosion of the *Florence H*. The sea in the vicinity of wreck-

age was covered by a mass of boxes of smokeless powder, which were repeatedly exploding. Jesse W. Covington, of the U.S.S. *Stewart*, plunged overboard to rescue a survivor who was surrounded by powder boxes and too exhausted to help himself, fully realizing that similar powder boxes in the vicinity were continually exploding and that he was thereby risking his life in saving the life of this man.

2475 ◆ CUKELA, LOUIS ✣

Rank: Sergeant (highest rank: Major)
Service: U.S. Marine Corps
Birthday: 1 May 1888
Place of Birth: Spalato, Yugoslavia
Date of Death: 19 March 1956
Place of Death: Bethesda, Maryland
Cemetery: Arlington National Cemetery (1-427-A)—Arlington, Virginia
Entered Service at: Minneapolis, Hennepin County, Minnesota
Unit: 66th Rifle Company, 5th Regiment, 2d Division
Battle or Place of Action: near Villers-Cotterets, France
Date of Action: 18 July 1918
G.O. Number, Date: 34, W.D. 7 March 1919
Citation: **Army Medal of Honor** When his company, advancing through a wood, met with strong resistance from an enemy strong point, Sgt. Cukela crawled out from the flank and made his way toward the German lines in the face of heavy fire, disregarding the warnings of his comrades. He succeeded in getting behind the enemy position and rushed a machine-gun emplacement, killing or driving off the crew with his bayonet. With German hand grenades he then bombed out the remaining portion of the strong point, capturing four men and two damaged machine guns. **Navy Medal of Honor** For extraordinary heroism while serving with the 66th Company, 5th Regiment, during action in the Forest de Retz, near Viller-Cotterres, France, 18 July 1918. Sgt. Cukela advanced alone against an enemy strong point that was holding up his line. Disregarding the warnings of his comrades, he crawled out from the flank in the face of heavy fire and worked his way to the rear of the enemy position. Rushing a machine-gun emplacement, he killed or drove off the crew with his bayonet, bombed out the remaining part of the strong point with German hand grenades, and captured two machine guns and four men.
Notes: Received both the Army and Navy Medal of Honor for the same deed.

2476 ◆ *DILBOY, GEORGE

Rank: Private First Class
Service: U.S. Army
Birthday: 5 February 1896
Place of Birth: Greece
Date of Death: 18 July 1918
Cemetery: Arlington National Cemetery (18-4574) (MH)—Arlington, Virginia
Entered Service at: Keene, Cheshire County, New Hampshire
Unit: Company H, 103d Infantry, 26th Division
Battle or Place of Action: near Belleau, France
Date of Action: 18 July 1918
G.O. Number, Date: 13, W.D. 18 January 1919
Citation: After his platoon had gained its objective along a railroad embankment, Pfc. Dilboy, accompanying his platoon leader to reconnoiter the ground beyond, was suddenly fired upon by an enemy machine gun from 100 yards. From a standing position on the railroad track, fully exposed to view, he opened fire at once, but failing to silence the gun, rushed forward with his bayonet fixed, through a wheat field toward the gun emplacement, falling within 25 yards of the gun with his right leg nearly severed above the knee and with several bullet holes in his body. With undaunted courage he continued to fire into the emplacement from a prone position, killing two of the enemy and dispersing the rest of the crew.

2477 ◆ DONALDSON, MICHAEL ALOYISIUS

Rank: Sergeant
Service: U.S. Army
Birthday: 16 January 1887
Place of Birth: Haverstraw, Rockland County, New York
Date of Death: 12 April 1970
Place of Death: Montrose, New York
Cemetery: St. Peter's Cemetery (MH)—Haverstraw, New York
Entered Service at: Haverstraw, Rockland County, New York
Unit: Company I, 165th Infantry, 42d Division
Battle or Place of Action: road between Sommerance and Landres-et St. Georges, France
Date of Action: 14 October 1918
G.O. Number, Date: 9, W.D. 23 March 1923
Citation: The advance of his regiment having been checked by intense machine-gun fire of the enemy, who were entrenched on the crest of a hill before Landres-et-St.-Georges, his company retired to a sunken road to reorganize their position, leaving several of their number wounded near the enemy lines. Of his own volition, in broad daylight and under direct observation of the enemy and with utter disregard for his own safety, he advanced to the crest of the hill, rescued one of his wounded comrades, and returned under withering fire to his own lines, repeating his splendidly heroic act until he had brought in all the men, six in number.

2478 ◆ DONOVAN, WILLIAM JOSEPH "WILD BILL"

Rank: Lieutenant Colonel (highest rank: Major General)
Service: U.S. Army
Birthday: 1 January 1883
Place of Birth: Buffalo, Erie County, New York
Date of Death: 8 February 1959
Place of Death: Washington, D.C.
Cemetery: Arlington National Cemetery (2-4874) (MH)—Arlington, Virginia
Entered Service at: Buffalo, Erie County, New York
Unit: 165th Infantry, 42d Division

Battle or Place of Action: near Landres-et-St. Georges, France
Date of Action: 14-15 October 1918
G.O. Number, Date: 56, W.D. 30 December 1922
Citation: Lt. Col. Donovan personally led the assaulting wave in an attack upon a very strongly organized position, and when our troops were suffering heavy casualties he encouraged all near him by his example, moving among his men in exposed positions, reorganizing decimated platoons, and accompanying them forward in attacks. When he was wounded in the leg by machine-gun bullets, he refused to be evacuated and continued with his unit until it withdrew to a less exposed position.

2479 ◆ DOZIER, JAMES C.

Rank: First Lieutenant (highest rank: Lieutenant General SCARNG)
Service: U.S. Army
Birthday: 17 February 1885
Place of Birth: Galivants Ferry, Horry County, South Carolina
Date of Death: 24 October 1974
Cemetery: Elmwood Cemetery (MH)—Columbia, South Carolina
Entered Service at: Rock Hill, York County, South Carolina
Unit: Company G, 118th Infantry, 30th Division
Battle or Place of Action: near Montbrehain, France
Date of Action: 8 October 1918
G.O. Number, Date: 16, W.D. 22 January 1919
Date of Presentation: 21 January 1919
Place of Presentation: Southwest of Teille, France, presented By Gen. John J. Pershing
Citation: In command of two platoons, 1st Lt. Dozier was painfully wounded in the shoulder early in the attack, but he continued to lead his men, displaying the highest bravery and skill. When his command was held up by heavy machine-gun fire, he disposed his men in the best cover available and with a soldier continued forward to attack a machine-gun nest. Creeping up to the position in the face of intense fire, he killed the entire crew with hand grenades and his pistol and a little later captured a number of Germans who had taken refuge in a dugout nearby.

2480 ◆ *DUNN, PARKER F.

Rank: Private First Class
Service: U.S. Army
Place of Birth: Albany, Albany County, New York
Date of Death: 23 October 1918
Cemetery: St. Agnes Cemetery—Albany, New York
Entered Service at: Albany, Albany County, New York
Unit: Company A, 312th Infantry, 78th Division
Battle or Place of Action: near Grand-Pre, France
Date of Action: 23 October 1918
G.O. Number, Date: 49, W.D. 25 November 1922
Citation: When his battalion commander found it necessary to send a message to a company in the attacking line and hesitated to order a runner to make the trip because of the extreme danger involved, Pfc. Dunn, a member of the intelligence section, volunteered for the mission. After advancing but a short distance across a field swept by artillery and machine-gun fire, he was wounded, but continued on and fell wounded a second time. Still undaunted, he persistently attempted to carry out his mission until he was killed by a machine-gun bullet before reaching the advance line.

2481 ◆ EDWARDS, DANIEL RICHMOND

Rank: Private First Class (highest rank: Major)
Service: U.S. Army
Birthday: 9 April 1888
Place of Birth: Mooreville, Texas
Date of Death: 21 October 1967
Cemetery: Cunningham Cemetery (MH)—Hot Springs, Arkansas
Entered Service at: Bruceville, McLennan County, Texas
Unit: Company C, 3d Machine Gun Battalion, 1st Division
Battle or Place of Action: near Soissons, France
Date of Action: 18 July 1918
G.O. Number, Date: 14, W.D. 4 April 1923
Citation: Reporting for duty from the hospital where he had been for several weeks under treatment for numerous and serious wounds and although suffering intense pain from a shattered arm, he crawled alone into an enemy trench for the purpose of capturing or killing enemy soldiers known to be concealed therein. He killed four of the men and took the remaining four men prisoners; while conducting them to the rear, one of the enemy was killed by a high-explosive enemy shell which also completely shattered one of Pfc. Edwards' legs, causing him to be immediately evacuated to the hospital. The bravery of Pfc. Edwards, now a tradition in his battalion because of his previous gallant acts, again caused the morale of his comrades to be raised to high pitch.

2482 ◆ EGGERS, ALAN LOUIS

Rank: Sergeant
Service: U.S. Army
Birthday: 2 November 1895
Place of Birth: Saranac Lake, Franklin County, New York
Date of Death: 3 October 1968
Cemetery: Arlington National Cemetery (2-3389-A) (MH)—Arlington, Virginia
Entered Service at: Summit, Union County, New Jersey
Unit: 3d Platoon, Machine Gun Company, 107th Infantry, 27th Division
Battle or Place of Action: near Le Catelet, France
Date of Action: 29 September 1918
G.O. Number, Date: 20, W.D. 30 January 1919
Date of Presentation: 4 February 1919
Place of Presentation: Chaumont, France, presented by Gen. John J. Pershing
Citation: Becoming separated from their platoon by a smoke barrage, Sgt. Eggers, Sgt. John C. Latham and Cpl. Thomas E. O'Shea took cover in a shell hole well within the enemy's lines. Upon hearing a call for help from an American tank, which had become disabled 30 yards from them, the

three soldiers left their shelter and started towards the tank, under heavy fire from German machine guns and trench mortars. In crossing the fire-swept area Cpl. O'Shea was mortally wounded, but his companions, undeterred, proceeded to the tank, rescued a wounded officer, and assisted two wounded soldiers to cover in a sap of a nearby trench. Sgt. Eggers and Sgt. Latham then returned to the tank in the face of the violent fire, dismounted a Hotchkiss gun, and took it back to where the wounded men were, keeping off the enemy all day by effective use of the gun and later bringing it, with the wounded men, back to our lines under cover of darkness.

2483 ◆ ELLIS, MICHAEL B.

Rank: Sergeant
Service: U.S. Army
Birthday: 28 October 1894
Place of Birth: St. Louis, St. Louis County, Missouri
Date of Death: 9 December 1937
Place of Death: Chicago, Illinois
Cemetery: Arlington National Cemetery (6-9520) (MH)—Arlington, Virginia
Entered Service at: East St. Louis, St. Clair County, Illinois
Unit: Company C, 28th Infantry, 1st Division
Battle or Place of Action: near Exermont, France
Date of Action: 5 October 1918
G.O. Number, Date: 74, W.D. 7 June 1919
Citation: During the entire day's engagement he operated far in advance of the first wave of his company, voluntarily undertaking most dangerous missions and singlehandedly attacking and reducing machine-gun nests. Flanking one emplacement, he killed two of the enemy with rifle fire and captured 17 others. Later he singlehandedly advanced under heavy fire and captured 27 prisoners, including two officers and six machine guns, which had been holding up the advance of the company. The captured officers indicated the locations of four other machine guns, and he in turn captured these, together with their crews, at all times showing marked heroism and fearlessness.

2484 ◆ FORREST, ARTHUR J.

Rank: Sergeant
Service: U.S. Army
Birthday: 1896
Place of Birth: St. Louis, St. Louis County, Missouri
Date of Death: 30 November 1964
Place of Death: St. Louis, Missouri
Cemetery: Grand View Burial Park (MH)—Hannibal, Missouri
Entered Service at: Hannibal, Marion County, Missouri
Unit: Company D, 354th Infantry, 89th Division
Battle or Place of Action: near Remonville, France
Date of Action: 1 November 1919
G.O. Number, Date: 50, W.D. 12 April 1919
Citation: When the advance of his company was stopped by bursts of fire from a nest of six enemy machine guns, without being discovered, he worked his way singlehandedly to a point within 50 yards of the machine-gun nest. Charging, singlehandedly, he drove out the enemy in disorder, thereby protecting the advance platoon from annihilating fire, and permitting the resumption of the advance of his company.

2485 ◆ FOSTER, GARY EVANS

Rank: Sergeant
Service: U.S. Army
Birthday: 6 November 1894
Place of Birth: Spartanburg, Spartanburg County, South Carolina
Date of Death: 22 July 1951
Cemetery: New Prospect Cemetery—Boiling Springs, South Carolina
Entered Service at: Inman, Spartanburg County, South Carolina
Unit: Company F, 118th Infantry, 30th Division
Battle or Place of Action: near Montbrehain, France
Date of Action: 8 October 1918
G.O. Number, Date: 16, W.D. 22 January 1919
Citation: When his company was held up by violent machine-gun fire from a sunken road, Sgt. Foster with an officer went forward to attack the hostile machine-gun nests. The officer was wounded, but Sgt. Foster continued on alone in the face of the heavy fire and by effective use of hand grenades and his pistol killed several of the enemy and captured 18.

2486 ◆ FUNK, JESSE N.

Rank: Private First Class
Service: U.S. Army
Birthday: 20 August 1888
Place of Birth: New Hampton, Harrison County, Missouri
Date of Death: 21 March 1933
Cemetery: Calhan Cemetery (MH)—Calhan, Colorado
Entered Service at: Calhan, El Paso County, Colorado
Unit: Company L, 354th Infantry, 89th Division
Battle or Place of Action: near Bois-de-Bantheville, France
Date of Action: 31 October 1918
G.O. Number, Date: 20, W.D. 30 January 1919
Citation: Learning that two daylight patrols had been caught out in No Man's Land and were unable to return, Pfc. Funk and another stretcher bearer, upon their own initiative, made two trips 500 yards beyond our lines, under constant machine-gun fire, and rescued two wounded officers.

2487 ◆ FURLONG, HAROLD ARTHUR

Rank: First Lieutenant (highest rank: Colonel)
Service: U.S. Army
Birthday: 1 August 1895
Place of Birth: Pontiac, Oakland County, Michigan
Date of Death: 27 July 1987
Cemetery: Oak Hill Cemetery—Pontiac, Michigan
Entered Service at: Detroit, Wayne County, Michigan
Unit: Company M, 353d Infantry, 89th Division
Battle or Place of Action: near Bantheville, France
Date of Action: 1 November 1918

G.O. Number, Date: 16, W.D. 22 January 1919
Date of Presentation: 9 February 1919
Place of Presentation: Chaumont, France, presented by Gen.John J. Pershing
Citation: Immediately after the opening of the attack in the Bois-de-Bantheville, when his company was held up by severe machine-gun fire from the front, which killed his company commander and several soldiers, 1st Lt. Furlong moved out in advance of the line with great courage and coolness, crossing an open space several hundred yards wide. Taking up a position behind the line of the machine guns, he closed in on them, one at a time, killing a number of the enemy with his rifle, putting four machine-gun nests out of action, and driving 20 German prisoners into our lines.

2488 ◆ GAFFNEY, FRANK J.

Rank: Private First Class
Service: U.S. Army
Birthday: 16 December 1883
Place of Birth: Buffalo, Erie County, New York
Date of Death: 25 May 1948
Place of Death: Niagara Falls, New York
Cemetery: United German & French RC Cemetery (MH)—Buffalo, New York
Entered Service at: Niagara Falls, Niagara County, New York
Unit: Company G, 108th Infantry, 27th Division
Served as: Automatic Rifleman
Battle or Place of Action: near Ronssoy, France
Date of Action: 29 September 1918
G.O. Number, Date: 20, W.D. 30 January 1919
Citation: Pfc. Gaffney, an automatic rifleman, pushing forward alone, after all the other members of his squad had been killed, discovered several Germans placing a heavy machine gun in position. He killed the crew, captured the gun, bombed several dugouts, and, after killing four more of the enemy with his pistol, held the position until reinforcements came up, when 80 prisoners were captured.

2489 ◆ *GOETTLER, HAROLD ERNEST

Rank: First Lieutenant
Service: U.S. Army Air Service
Birthday: 21 July 1890
Place of Birth: Chicago, Cook County, Illinois
Date of Death: 6 October 1918
Cemetery: Graceland Cemetery—Chicago, Illinois
Entered Service at: Chicago, Cook County, Illinois
Unit: 50th Aero Squadron, Air Service
Served as: DH-4 Pilot
Battle or Place of Action: near Binarville, France
Date of Action: 6 October 1918
G.O. Number, Date: 56, W.D. 1922
Citation: First Lt. Harold E. Goettler, with his observer, 2d Lt. Erwin R. Bleckley, 130th Field Artillery, left the airdrome late in the afternoon on their second trip to drop supplies to a battalion of the 77th Division which had been cut off by the enemy in the Argonne Forest. Having been subjected on the first trip to violent fire from the enemy, they attempted on the second trip to come still lower in order to get the packages even more precisely on the designated spot. In the course of his mission the plane was brought down by enemy rifle and machine-gun fire from the ground, resulting in the instant death of 1st Lt. Goettler. In attempting and performing this mission 1st Lt. Goettler showed the highest possible contempt of personal danger, devotion to duty, courage, and valor.

2490 ◆ GRAVES, ORA

Rank: Seaman
Service: U.S. Navy
Birthday: 26 July 1896
Place of Birth: Las Animas, Bent County, Colorado
Date of Death: 28 September 1961
Cemetery: Fort Rosecrans National Cemetery (W-1208)—San Diego, California
Entered Service at: Nebraska
Unit: U.S.S. *Pittsburgh*
Battle or Place of Action: at Sea aboard the U.S.S. *Pittsburgh*
Date of Action: 23 July 1917
G.O. Number, Date: 366, W.D. 1918
Citation: For extraordinary heroism on 23 July 1917, while the U.S.S. *Pittsburgh* was proceeding to Buenos Aires, Argentina. A 3-inch saluting charge exploded, causing the death of C.T. Lyles, seaman. Upon the explosion, Graves was blown to the deck, but soon recovered and discovered burning waste on the deck. He put out the burning waste while the casemate was filled with clouds of smoke, knowing that there was more powder there which might explode.

2491 ◆ GREGORY, EARL D.

Rank: Sergeant
Service: U.S. Army
Birthday: 18 October 1897
Place of Birth: Chase City, Mecklenburg County, Virginia
Date of Death: 6 January 1972
Place of Death: Birmingham, Alabama
Cemetery: Tuscaloosa Memorial Park Corp.—Tuscaloosa, Alabama
Entered Service at: Chase City, Mecklenburg County, Virginia
Unit: Headquarters Company, 116th Infantry, 29th Division
Battle or Place of Action: at Bois-de-Consenvoye, France
Date of Action: 8 October 1918
G.O. Number, Date: 34, W.D. 7 March 1919
Citation: With the remark "I will get them," Sgt. Gregory seized a rifle and a trench mortar shell, which he used as a hand grenade, left his detachment of the trench-mortar platoon, and advancing ahead of the infantry, captured a machine gun and three of the enemy. Advancing still farther from the machine-gun nest, he captured a 7.5 centimeter mountain howitzer and, entering a dugout in the immediate vicinity, singlehandedly captured 19 of the enemy.

2492 ◆ GUMPERTZ, SYDNEY G.

Rank: First Sergeant (highest rank: Captain)
Service: U.S. Army
Birthday: 24 October 1879
Place of Birth: San Raphael, Marin County, California
Date of Death: 16 February 1971
Cemetery: Long Island National Cemetery (DSS-65) (MH)—Farmingdale, New York
Entered Service at: Chicago, Cook County, Illinois
Unit: Company E, 132d Infantry, 33d Division
Battle or Place of Action: in the Bois-de-Forges, France
Date of Action: 29 September 1918
G.O. Number, Date: 16, W.D. 22 January 1919
Citation: When the advancing line was held up by machine-gun fire, 1st Sgt. Gumpertz left the platoon of which he was in command and started with two other soldiers through a heavy barrage toward the machine-gun nest. His two companions soon became casualties from bursting shells, but 1st Sgt. Gumpertz continued on alone in the face of direct fire from the machine gun, jumped into the nest, and silenced the gun, capturing nine of the crew.

2493 ◆ *HALL, THOMAS LEE

Rank: Sergeant
Service: U.S. Army
Place of Birth: Fort Mill, York County, South Carolina
Date of Death: 8 October 1918
Cemetery: Unity Cemetery (MH)—Fort Mill, South Carolina
Entered Service at: Fort Mill, York County, South Carolina
Unit: Company G, 118th Infantry, 30th Division
Battle or Place of Action: near Montbrehain, France
Date of Action: 8 October 1918
G.O. Number, Date: 50, W.D. 12 April 1919
Citation: Having overcome two machine-gun nests under his skillful leadership, Sgt. Hall's platoon was stopped 800 yards from its final objective by machine-gun fire of particular intensity. Ordering his men to take cover in a sunken road, he advanced alone on the enemy machine-gun post and killed five members of the crew with his bayonet and thereby made possible the further advance of the line. While attacking another machine-gun nest later in the day this gallant soldier was mortally wounded.

2494 ◆ HAMMANN, CHARLES HAZELTINE

Rank: Ensign
Service: U.S. Naval Reserve Fleet
Birthday: 16 March 1892
Place of Birth: Baltimore, Baltimore County, Maryland
Date of Death: 14 June 1919
Place of Death: Hampton, Virginia
Cemetery: Oak Lawn Cemetery (MH)—Baltimore, Maryland
Entered Service at: Maryland
Served as: Pilot (Seaplane)
Battle or Place of Action: off Pola, Austria
Date of Action: 21 August 1918
Citation: For extraordinary heroism as a pilot of a seaplane on 21 August 1918, when with three other planes Ens. Hammann took part in a patrol and attacked a superior force of enemy land planes. In the course of the engagement which followed, the plane of Ens. George M. Ludlow was shot down and fell in the water five miles off Pola. Ens. Hammann immediately dived down and landed on the water close alongside the disabled machine, where he took Ludlow on board. Although his machine was not designed for the double load to which it was subjected, and although there was danger of attack by Austrian planes, he made his way to Porto Corsini.

2495 ◆ HATLER, M. WALDO

Rank: Sergeant
Service: U.S. Army
Birthday: 6 January 1894
Place of Birth: Bolivar, Polk County, Missouri
Date of Death: 31 August 1967
Cemetery: Grand Army of the Republic Cemetery—Sulphur Springs, Arkansas
Entered Service at: Neosho, Newton County, Missouri
Unit: Company B, 356th Infantry, 89th Division
Battle or Place of Action: near Pouilly, France
Date of Action: 8 November 1918
G.O. Number, Date: 74, W.D. 7 June 1919
Citation: When volunteers were called for to secure information as to the enemy's position on the opposite bank of the Meuse River, Sgt. Hatler was the first to offer his services for the dangerous mission. Swimming across the river, he succeeded in reaching the German lines after another soldier, who had started with him, had been seized with cramps and drowned in midstream. Alone he carefully and courageously reconnoitered the enemy's positions, which were held in force, and again successfully swam the river, bringing back information of great value.

2496 ◆ HAYDEN, DAVID EPHRAIM

Rank: Hospital Apprentice First Class (highest rank: Pharmacist's Mate Third Class)
Service: U.S. Navy
Birthday: 2 October 1897
Place of Birth: Florence, Williamson County, Texas
Date of Death: 18 March 1974
Cemetery: Arlington National Cemetery (35-1864) (MH)—Arlington, Virginia
Entered Service at: Texas
Unit: 2d Battalion, 6th Regiment, U.S. Marines
Battle or Place of Action: Thiaucourt, France
Date of Action: 15 September 1918
Citation: For gallantry and intrepidity at the risk of his life above and beyond the call of duty. During the advance, when Cpl. Creed was mortally wounded while crossing an open field swept by machine-gun fire, Hayden unhesitatingly ran to his assistance and, finding him so severely wounded as to require immediate attention, disregarded his own personal safety to dress the wound under intense machine-gun fire, and then carried the wounded man back to a place of safety.

2497 ◆ HAYS, GEORGE PRICE

Rank: First Lieutenant (highest rank: Lieutenant General)
Service: U.S. Army
Birthday: 27 September 1892
Place of Birth: Chee Foo, China
Date of Death: 7 September 1978
Place of Death: Pinehurst, North Carolina
Cemetery: Arlington National Cemetery (11-540-2) (MH)—Arlington, Virginia
Entered Service at: Okarche, Kingfisher County, Oklahoma
Unit: 10th Field Artillery, 3d Division
Battle or Place of Action: near Greves Farm, France
Date of Action: 14-15 July 1918
G.O. Number, Date: 34, W.D. 7 March 1919
Date of Issue: 17 March 1919
Citation: At the very onset of the unprecedented artillery bombardment by the enemy, his line of communication was destroyed beyond repair. Despite the hazard attached to the mission of runner, he immediately set out to establish contact with the neighboring post of command and further establish liaison with French batteries, visiting their position so frequently that he was mainly responsible for the accurate fire therefrom. While thus engaged, seven horses were shot under him and he was severely wounded. His activity under most severe fire was an important factor in checking the advance of the enemy.

2498 ◆ *HERIOT, JAMES DAVIDSON

Rank: Corporal
Service: U.S. Army
Birthday: 2 November 1890
Place of Birth: Providence, South Carolina
Date of Death: 12 October 1918
Place of Death: France
Cemetery: Rembert Church Cemetery—Rembert, South Carolina
Entered Service at: Providence, South Carolina
Unit: Company I, 118th Infantry, 30th Division
Battle or Place of Action: at Vaux-Andigny, France
Date of Action: 12 October 1918
G.O. Number, Date: 13, W.D. 18 January 1919
Citation: Cpl. Heriot, with four other soldiers, organized a combat group and attacked an enemy machine-gun nest which had been inflicting heavy casualties on his company. In the advance two of his men were killed, and because of the heavy fire from all sides the remaining two sought shelter. Unmindful of the hazard attached to his mission, Cpl. Heriot, with fixed bayonet, alone charged the machine gun, making his way through the fire for a distance of 30 yards and forcing the enemy to surrender. During this exploit he received several wounds in the arm, and later in the same day, while charging another nest, he was killed.

2499 ◆ HILL, RALYN M.

Rank: Corporal
Service: U.S. Army
Birthday: 6 May 1899
Place of Birth: Lindenwood, Ogle County, Illinois
Date of Death: 25 March 1977
Cemetery: Abilene Cemetery (MH)—Abilene, Kansas
Entered Service at: Oregon, Ogle County, Illinois
Unit: Company H, 129th Infantry, 33d Division
Battle or Place of Action: near Donnevoux, France
Date of Action: 7 October 1918
G.O. Number, Date: 34, W.D. 7 March 1919
Citation: Seeing a French airplane fall out of control on the enemy side of the Meuse River with its pilot injured, Cpl. Hill voluntarily dashed across the footbridge to the side of the wounded man and, taking him on his back, started back to his lines. During the entire exploit he was subjected to murderous fire of enemy machine guns and artillery, but he successfully accomplished his mission and brought his man to a place of safety, a distance of several hundred yards.

2500 ◆ HILTON, RICHMOND HOBSON

Rank: Sergeant
Service: U.S. Army
Birthday: 8 October 1898
Place of Birth: Westville, Kershaw County, South Carolina
Date of Death: 13 August 1933
Cemetery: Quaker Cemetery—Camden, South Carolina
Entered Service at: Westville, Kershaw County, South Carolina
Unit: Company M, 118th Infantry, 30th Division
Battle or Place of Action: at Brancourt, France
Date of Action: 11 October 1918
G.O. Number, Date: 16, W.D. 22 January 1919
Citation: While Sgt. Hilton's company was advancing through the village of Brancourt it was held up by intense enfilading fire from a machine gun. Discovering that this fire came from a machine-gun nest among shell holes at the edge of the town, Sgt. Hilton, accompanied by a few other soldiers, but well in advance of them, pressed on toward this position, firing with his rifle until his ammunition was exhausted, and then with his pistol, killing six of the enemy and capturing 10. In the course of this daring exploit he received a wound from a bursting shell, which resulted in the loss of his arm.

2501 ◆ HOFFMAN, CHARLES F. ✚

True Name: Janson, Ernest August
Rank: Gunnery Sergeant (highest rank: Sergeant Major)
Service: U.S. Marine Corps
Birthday: 17 August 1878
Place of Birth: New York, New York
Date of Death: 14 May 1940
Cemetery: Evergreen Cemetery—Brooklyn, New York
Entered Service at: Brooklyn, Kings County, New York
Unit: 49th Company, 5th Regiment, 2d Division
Battle or Place of Action: near Chateau-Thierry, France
Date of Action: 6 June 1918
G.O. Number, Date: 34, W.D. 7 March 1919
Citation: **Army Medal of Honor:** Immediately after the

company to which he belonged had reached its objective on Hill 142, several hostile counterattacks were launched against the line before the new position had been consolidated. G/Sgt. Hoffman was attempting to organize a position on the north slope of the hill when he saw 12 of the enemy, armed with five light machine guns, crawling toward his group. Giving the alarm, he rushed the hostile detachment, bayoneted the two leaders, and forced the others to flee, abandoning their guns. His quick action, initiative, and courage drove the enemy from a position from which they could have swept the hill with machine-gun fire and forced the withdrawal of our troops. **Navy Medal of Honor**: For conspicuous gallantry and intrepidity above and beyond the call of duty in action with the enemy near Chateau-Thierry, France, 6 June 1918. Immediately after the company to which G/Sgt. Janson belonged had reached its objective on Hill 142, several hostile counterattacks were launched against the line before the new position had been consolidated. G/Sgt. Janson was attempting to organize a position on the north slope of the hill when he saw 12 of the enemy, armed with five light machine guns, crawling toward his group. Giving the alarm, he rushed the hostile detachment, bayoneted the two leaders, and forced the others to flee, abandoning their guns. His quick action, initiative, and courage drove the enemy from a position from which they could have swept the hill with machine-gun fire and forced the withdrawal of our troops.
Notes: ✣Received both the Army and Navy Medal of Honor for the same deed.

2502 ◆ HOLDERMAN, NELSON MILES

Rank: Captain (highest rank: Colonel)
Service: U.S. Army
Birthday: 10 November 1885
Place of Birth: Trumbull, Clay County, Nebraska
Date of Death: 3 September 1953
Cemetery: Golden Gate National Cemetery (R-17)—San Bruno, California
Entered Service at: Santa Ana, Orange County, California
Unit: 307th Infantry, 77th Division
Battle or Place of Action: northeast of Binarville, in the Argonne Forest, France
Date of Action: 2-8 October 1918
G.O. Number, Date: 11, W.D. 12 March 1921
Citation: Capt. Holderman commanded a company of a battalion which was cut off and surrounded by the enemy. He was wounded on 4, 5, and 7 October, but throughout the entire period, suffering great pain and subjected to fire of every character, he continued personally to lead and encourage the officers and men under his command with unflinching courage and with distinguished success. On 6 October, in a wounded condition, he rushed through enemy machine-gun and shell fire and carried two wounded men to a place of safety.

2503 ◆ *INGRAM, OSMOND KELLY

Rank: Gunner's Mate First Class
Service: U.S. Navy
Birthday: 4 August 1887
Place of Birth: Alabama
Date of Death: 15 October 1917
Place of Death: at Sea
Cemetery: A.B.M.C. Wall of the Missing—Brookwood, Surrey, England
Entered Service at: Alabama
Unit: U.S.S. *Cassin*
Battle or Place of Action: at sea 20 miles south of Mind Head, Ireland
Date of Action: 15 October 1917
Citation: For extraordinary heroism in the presence of the enemy on the occasion of the torpedoing of the *Cassin*, 15 October 1917. While the Cassin was searching for the submarine, Ingram sighted the torpedo coming, and realizing that it might strike the ship aft in the vicinity of the depth charges, ran aft with the intention of releasing the depth charges before the torpedo could reach the *Cassin*. The torpedo struck the ship before he could accomplish his purpose, and Ingram was killed by the explosion. The depth charges exploded immediately afterward. His life was sacrificed in an attempt to save the ship and his shipmates, as the damage to the ship would have been much less if he had been able to release the depth charges.

2504 ◆ IZAC, EDOUARD VICTOR MICHEL

Rank: Lieutenant
Service: U.S. Navy
Birthday: 18 December 1889
Place of Birth: Cresco, Howard County, Iowa
Date of Death: 18 January 1990
Cemetery: Arlington National Cemetery (3-4222-16 (MH)—Arlington, Virginia
Entered Service at: Illinois
Unit: U.S.S. *President Lincoln*
Battle or Place of Action: aboard German submarine U-90 as prisoner of war
Date of Action: 21 May 1918
Date of Presentation: 11 November 1920
Place of Presentation: The Washington Navy Yard, presented by Under Secretary of the Navy Franklin D. Roosevelt
Citation: When the U.S.S. *President Lincoln* was attacked and sunk by the German submarine *U-90*, 21 May 1918, Lt. Izac was captured and held as a prisoner on board the *U-90* until the return of the submarine to Germany, when he was confined in the prison camp. During his stay on the *U-90* he obtained information of the movements of German submarines which was so important that he determined to escape, with a view to making this information available to the U.S. and Allied Naval authorities. In attempting to carry out this plan, he jumped through the window of a rapidly moving train at the imminent risk of death, not only from the nature of the act itself but from the fire of the armed German soldiers who were guarding him. Having been recaptured and reconfined, Lt. Izac made a second and successful attempt to escape, breaking his way through barbed-wire fences and deliberately drawing the fire of the armed guards in the hope of permitting others to escape during the confusion. He made

his way through the mountains of southwestern Germany, having only raw vegetables for food, and at the end, swam the river Rhine during the night in the immediate vicinity of German sentries.

2505 ◆ JOHNSTON, HAROLD IRVING

Rank: Sergeant (rank at time of action: Private First Class) (highest rank: Major A.A.C. WWII)
Service: U.S. Army
Birthday: 9 March 1892
Place of Birth: Kendall, Hamilton County, Kansas
Date of Death: 28 August 1949
Cemetery: Fairmount Cemetery (MH)—Denver, Colorado
Entered Service at: Chicago, Cook County, Illinois
Unit: Company A, 356th Infantry, 89th Division
Battle or Place of Action: near Pouilly, France
Date of Action: 9 November 1918
G.O. Number, Date: 20, W.D. 30 January 1919
Citation: When information was desired as to the enemy's position on the opposite side of the Meuse River, Sgt. Johnston, with another soldier, volunteered without hesitation and swam the river to reconnoiter the exact location of the enemy. He succeeded in reaching the opposite bank, despite the evident determination of the enemy to prevent a crossing. Having obtained his information, he again entered the water for his return. This was accomplished after a severe struggle which so exhausted him that he had to be assisted from the water, after which he rendered his report of the exploit.

2506 ◆ KARNES, JAMES ERNEST

Rank: Sergeant
Service: U.S. Army
Birthday: 20 July 1889
Place of Birth: Arlington, Shelby County, Tennessee
Date of Death: 8 July 1966
Cemetery: Greenwood Cemetery—Knoxville, Tennessee
Entered Service at: Knoxville, Knox County, Tennessee
Unit: Company D, 117th Infantry, 30th Division
Battle or Place of Action: near Estrees, France
Date of Action: 8 October 1918
G.O. Number, Date: 50, W.D. 12 April 1919
Citation: During the advance, his company was held up by a machine gun, which was enfilading the line. Accompanied by another soldier, he advanced against this position and succeeded in reducing the nest by killing three and capturing seven of the enemy and their guns.

2507 ◆ KATZ, PHILLIP CARL

Rank: Sergeant
Service: U.S. Army
Birthday: 12 December 1889
Place of Birth: San Francisco, San Francisco County, California
Date of Death: 29 October 1987
Place of Death: San Francisco, California
Cemetery: Cypress Lawn Cemetery—Colma, California
Entered Service at: San Francisco, San Francisco County, California
Unit: Company C, 363d Infantry, 91st Division
Battle or Place of Action: near Eclisfontaine, France
Date of Action: 26 September 1918
G.O. Number, Date: 16, W.D. 22 January 1919
Citation: After his company had withdrawn for a distance of 200 yards on a line with the units on its flanks, Sgt. Katz learned that one of his comrades had been left wounded in an exposed position at the point from which the withdrawal had taken place. Voluntarily crossing an area swept by heavy machine-gun fire, he advanced to where the wounded soldier lay and carried him to a place of safety.

2508 ◆ KAUFMAN, BENJAMIN

Rank: First Sergeant
Service: U.S. Army
Birthday: 10 March 1894
Place of Birth: Buffalo, Erie County, New York
Date of Death: 5 February 1981
Cemetery: Fountain Lawn Memorial Park (MH)—Trenton, New Jersey
Entered Service at: Brooklyn, Kings County, New York
Unit: Company K, 308th Infantry, 77th Division
Battle or Place of Action: in Argonne Forest, France
Date of Action: 4 October 1918
G.O. Number, Date: 50, W.D. 12 April 1919
Citation: He took out a patrol for the purpose of attacking an enemy machine gun which had checked the advance of his company. Before reaching the gun he became separated from his patrol and a machine-gun bullet shattered his right arm. Without hesitation he advanced on the gun alone, throwing grenades with his left hand and charging with an empty pistol, taking one prisoner and scattering the crew, bringing the gun and prisoner back to the first-aid station.

2509 ◆ KELLY, JOHN JOSEPH✣

Rank: Private
Service: U.S. Marine Corps
Birthday: 24 June 1898
Place of Birth: Chicago, Cook County, Illinois
Date of Death: 20 November 1957
Place of Death: Florida
Cemetery: All Saints Cemetery—Des Plaines, Illinois
Entered Service at: Chicago, Cook County, Illinois
Unit: 78th Company, 6th Regiment, 2d Division
Battle or Place of Action: at Blanc Mont Ridge, France
Date of Action: 3 October 1918
G.O. Number, Date: 16, W.D. 22 January 1919
Date of Presentation: 17 March 1919
Place of Presentation: Coblenz, France, presented by Gen. John J. Pershing
Citation: **Army Medal of Honor** Pvt. Kelly ran through our own barrage 100 yards in advance of the front line and attacked an enemy machine-gun nest, killing the gunner with a grenade, shooting another member of the crew with his pis-

tol, and returning through the barrage with eight prisoners.
Navy Medal of Honor For conspicuous gallantry and intrepidity above and beyond the call of duty while serving with the 78th Company, 6th Regiment, 2d Division, in action with the enemy at Blanc Mont Ridge, France, 3 October 1918. Pvt. Kelly ran through our own barrage a hundred yards in advance of the front line and attacked an enemy machine-gun nest, killing the gunner with a grenade, shooting another member of the crew with his pistol, and returning through the barrage with eight prisoners.
Notes: ✣Double Awardee: received both the Army and Navy Medal of Honor for the same deed

2510 ◆ *KOCAK, MATEJ✣

Rank: Sergeant
Service: U.S. Marine Corps
Birthday: 31 December 1882
Place of Birth: Gbely (Slovakia), Austria
Date of Death: 4 October 1918
Place of Death: Blanc Mont Ridge, France
Cemetery: Meuse Argonne Cemetery (D-41-32) (MH)—Romagne Meuse, France
Entered Service at: New York, New York
Unit: 66th Company, 5th Regiment, 2d Division
Battle or Place of Action: Soissons, France
Date of Action: 18 July 1918
G.O. Number, Date: 34, W.D. 7 March 1919
Date of Issue: Army: 18 February 1919 Navy: 11 November 1920
Citation: **Army Medal of Honor** When the advance of his battalion was checked by a hidden machine-gun nest, he went forward alone, unprotected by covering fire from his own men, and worked in between the German positions in the face of fire from enemy covering detachments. Locating the machine-gun nest, he rushed it and with his bayonet and drove off the crew. Shortly after this he orgnaized 25 French colonial soldiers who had become separated from their company and led them in attacking another machine-gun nest, which was also put out of action. **Navy Medal of Honor** For extraordinary heroism while serving with the 66th Company, 5th Regiment, 2d Division, in action in the Viller-Cottertes section, south of Soissons, France, 18 July 1918. When a hidden machine-gun nest halted the advance of his battalion, Sgt. Kocak went forward alone unprotected by covering fire and worked his way in between the German positions in the face of heavy enemy fire. Rushing the enemy position with his bayonet, he drove off the crew. Later the same day, Sgt. Kocak organized French colonial soldiers who had become separated from their company and led them in an attack on another machine-gun nest which was also put out of action.
Notes: ✣Double Awardee: received both the Army and Navy Medal of Honor for the same deed

2511 ◆ LATHAM, JOHN CRIDLAND

Rank: Sergeant [highest rank: Warrant Officer (j.g.)]
Service: U.S. Army
Birthday: 3 March 1888
Place of Birth: Windemere, Cumbria County, England
Date of Death: 2 November 1975
Place of Death: Stanford, Connecticut
Cemetery: Arlington National Cemetery (35-1127) (MH)—Arlington, Virginia
Entered Service at: Rutherford, Bergen County, New Jersey
Unit: 3d Platoon, Machine Gun Company, 107th Infantry, 27th Division
Battle or Place of Action: near Le Catelet, France
Date of Action: 29 September 1918
G.O. Number, Date: 20, W.D. 30 January 1919
Date of Presentation: 4 February 1919
Place of Presentation: Chaumont, France, presented by Gen. John J. Pershing
Citation: Becoming separated from their platoon by a smoke barrage, Sgt. Latham, Sgt. Alan L. Eggers, and Cpl. Thomas E. O'shea took cover in a shellhole well within the enemy lines. Upon hearing a call for help from an American tank which had became disabled 30 yards from them, the three soldiers left their shelter and started toward the tank under heavy fire from German machine guns and trench mortars. In crossing the fire-swept area, Cpl. O'Shea was mortally wounded, but his companions, undeterred, proceeded to the tank, rescued a wounded officer, and assisted two wounded soldiers to cover in the sap of a trench nearby. Sgts. Latham and Eggers then returned to the tank in the face of violent fire, dismounted a Hotchkiss gun, and took it back where the wounded men were, keeping off the enemy all day by effective use of the gun, and later bringing it with the wounded men back to our lines under cover of darkness.

2512 ◆ *LEMERT, MILO

Rank: First Sergeant
Service: U.S. Army
Birthday: 25 March 1890
Place of Birth: Marshalltown, Marshall County, Iowa
Date of Death: 29 September 1918
Place of Death: France
Cemetery: Crossville City Cemetery (MH)—Crossville, Tennessee
Entered Service at: Crossville, Cumberland County, Tennessee
Unit: Company G, 119th Infantry, 30th Division
Battle or Place of Action: near Bellicourt, France
Date of Action: 29 September 1918
G.O. Number, Date: 59, W.D. 3 May 1919
Citation: Seeing that the left flank of his company was held up, he located the enemy machine-gun emplacement, which had been causing heavy casualties. In the face of heavy fire he rushed it singlehandedly, killing the entire crew with grenades. Continuing along the enemy trench in advance of the company, he reached another emplacement, which he also charged, silencing the gun with grenades. A third machine-gun emplacement opened up on him from the left and with similar skill and bravery he destroyed this also. Later, in company with another sergeant, he attacked a fourth machine-gun nest, being killed as he reached the parapet of the emplace-

ment. His courageous action in destroying in turn four enemy machine-gun nests prevented many casualties among his company and very materially aided in achieving the objective.

2513 ◆ LOMAN, BERGER HOLTON

Rank: Private (highest rank: Corporal)
Service: U.S. Army
Birthday: 24 August 1886
Place of Birth: Bergen, Norway
Date of Death: 9 May 1968
Cemetery: Arlington National Cemetery (37-4909) (MH)—Arlington, Virginia
Entered Service at: Chicago, Cook County, Illinois
Unit: Company H, 132d Infantry, 33d Division
Battle or Place of Action: near Consenvoye, France
Date of Action: 9 October 1918
G.O. Number, Date: 16, W.D. 22 January 1919
Citation: When his company had reached a point within 100 yards of its objective, to which it was advancing under terrific machine-gun fire, Pvt. Loman voluntarily and unaided made his way forward after all others had taken shelter from the direct fire of an enemy machine gun. He crawled to a flank position of the gun and, after killing or capturing the entire crew, turned the machine gun on the retreating enemy.

2514 ◆ *LUKE JR., FRANK

Rank: Second Lieutenant
Service: U.S. Army Air Service
Birthday: 19 May 1897
Place of Birth: Phoenix, Maricopa County, Arizona
Date of Death: 29 September 1918
Place of Death: near Murvaux, France
Cemetery: Meuse-Argonne Cemetery (A-26-13) (MH)—Romagne Meuse, France
Entered Service at: Phoenix, Maricopa County, Arizona
Unit: 27th Aero Squadron, 1st Pursuit Group, Air Service
Served as: Pilot of a SPAD
Battle or Place of Action: near Murvaux, France
Date of Action: 29 September 1918
G.O. Number, Date: 59, W.D. 3 May 1919
Date of Presentation: 29 May 1919
Place of Presentation: Phoenix, Arizona, presented by Brig. Gen. Howard R. Hickok to his Father
Citation: After having previously destroyed a number of enemy aircraft within 17 days, he voluntarily started on a patrol after German observation balloons. Though pursued by eight German planes which were protecting the enemy balloon line, he unhesitatingly attacked and shot down in flames three German balloons, being himself under heavy fire from ground batteries and the hostile planes. Severely wounded, he descended to within 50 meters of the ground, and flying at this low altitude near the town of Murvaux opened fire upon enemy troops, killing six and wounding as many more. Forced to make a landing and surrounded on all sides by the enemy, who called upon him to surrender, he drew his automatic pistol and defended himself gallantly until he fell dead from a wound in the chest.

2515 ◆ LYLE, ALEXANDER GORDON

Rank: Lieutenant Commander (highest rank: Vice Admiral)
Service: U.S. Navy
Birthday: 12 November 1889
Place of Birth: Gloucester, Essex County, Massachusetts
Date of Death: 15 July 1955
Cemetery: Arlington National Cemetery (2-1114-1)—Arlington, Virginia
Entered Service at: Massachusetts
Unit: Dental Corps serving with the 5th Regiment U.S.M.C.
Battle or Place of Action: the French Front, France
Date of Action: 23 April 1919
Date of Issue: 11 December 1919
Citation: For extraordinary heroism and devotion to duty while serving with the 5th Regiment, U.S. Marine Corps. Under heavy shellfire, 23 April 1918, on the French front, Lt. Comdr. Lyle rushed to the assistance of Cpl. Thomas Regan, who was seriously wounded, and administered such effective surgical aid while bombardment was still continuing as to save the life of Cpl. Regan.

2516 ◆ MacKENZIE, JOHN

Rank: Chief Boatswain's Mate
Service: U.S. Navy
Birthday: 7 July 1886
Place of Birth: Bridgeport, Fairfield County, Connecticut
Date of Death: 26 December 1933
Cemetery: Foresdale Cemetery (MH)—Holyoke, Massachusetts
Entered Service at: Massachusetts
Unit: U.S.S. *Remlik*
Battle or Place of Action: at Sea
Date of Action: 17 December 1917
G.O. Number, Date: 391, W.D. 1918
Citation: For extraordinary heroism while serving on board the U.S.S. *Remlik*, on the morning of 17 December 1917, when the *Remlik* encountered a heavy gale. During this gale, there was a heavy sea running. The depth charge box on the taffrail aft, containing a Sperry depth charge, was washed overboard, the depth charge itself falling inboard and remaining on deck. MacKenzie, on his own initiative, went aft and sat down on the depth charge, as it was impracticable to carry it to safety until the ship was headed up into the sea. In acting as he did, MacKenzie exposed his life and prevented a serious accident to the ship and probable loss of the ship and the entire crew.

2517 ◆ MADISON, JAMES JONAS

Rank: Lieutenant Commander
Service: U.S. Naval Reserve Force
Birthday: 20 May 1884
Place of Birth: Jersey City, Hudson County, New Jersey
Date of Death: 25 December 1922
Cemetery: Fairview Cemetery—Fairview, New Jersey
Entered Service at: Mississippi
Unit: U.S.S. *Ticonderoga*
Served as: Commanding Officer

Battle or Place of Action: at Sea
Date of Action: 4 October 1918
Citation: For exceptionally heroic service in a position of great responsibility as commanding officer of the U.S.S. *Ticonderoga*, when, on 4 October 1918, that vessel was attacked by an enemy submarine and was sunk after a prolonged and gallant resistance. The submarine opened fire at a range of 500 yards, the first shots taking effect on the bridge and forecastle, one of the two forward guns of the *Ticonderoga* being disabled by the second shot. The fire was returned and the fight continued for nearly two hours. Lt. Comdr. Madison was severely wounded early in the fight, but caused himself to be placed in a chair on the bridge and continued to direct the fire and to maneuver the ship. When the order was finally given to abandon the sinking ship, he became unconscious from loss of blood, but was lowered into a lifeboat and was saved, with 31 others, out of a total number of 236 on board.

2518 ◆ MALLON, GEORGE H.

Rank: Captain
Service: U.S. Army
Birthday: 15 June 1877
Place of Birth: Ogden, Riley County, Kansas
Date of Death: 2 August 1934
Place of Death: St. Cloud, Minnesota
Cemetery: Fort Snelling National Cemetery (DS-1-S) (MH)—St. Paul, Minnesota
Entered Service at: Minneapolis, Hennepin County, Minnesota
Unit: Company E, 132d Infantry Regiment, 33d Division
Served as: Company Commander
Battle or Place of Action: in the Bois-de-Forges, France
Date of Action: 26 September 1918
G.O. Number, Date: 16, W.D. 22 January 1919
Date of Presentation: 9 February 1919
Place of Presentation: Chaumont, France, presented by Gen. John J. Pershing
Citation: Becoming separated from the balance of his company because of fog, Capt. Mallon, with nine soldiers, pushed forward and attacked nine active and hostile machine guns, capturing all of them without the loss of a man. Continuing on through the woods, he led his men in attacking a battery of four 155-millimeter howitzers, which were in action, rushing the position and capturing the battery and its crews. In this encounter Capt. Mallon personally attacked one of the enemy with his fists. Later, when the party came upon two more machine guns, this officer sent men to the flanks while he rushed forward directly in the face of the fire and silenced the guns, being the first one of the party to reach the nest. The exceptional gallantry and determination displayed by Capt. Mallon resulted in the capture of 100 prisoners, 11 machine guns, four 155-millimeter howitzers, and one antiaircraft gun.

2519 ◆ MANNING, SIDNEY E.

Rank: Corporal
Service: U.S. Army
Birthday: 17 July 1892
Place of Birth: Butler County, Alabama
Date of Death: 15 December 1960
Cemetery: Little Escombia Cemetery (MH)—Flomaton, Alabama
Entered Service at: Flomaton, Escambia County, Alabama
Unit: Company G, 167th Infantry, 42d Division
Battle or Place of Action: near Breuvannes, France
Date of Action: 28 July 1918
G.O. Number, Date: 44, W.D. 2 April 1919
Citation: When his platoon commander and platoon sergeant had both become casualties soon after the beginning of an assault on strongly fortified heights overlooking the Ourcq River, Cpl. Manning took command of his platoon, which was near the center of the attacking line. Though himself severely wounded he led forward the 35 men remaining in the platoon and finally succeeded in gaining a foothold on the enemy's position, during which time he had received more wounds and all but seven of his men had fallen. Directing the consolidation of the position, he held off a large body of the enemy only 50 yards away by fire from his automatic rifle. He declined to take cover until his line had been entirely consolidated with the line of the platoon on the front when he dragged himself to shelter, suffering from nine wounds in all parts of the body.

2520 ◆ McGUNIGAL, PATRICK

Rank: Shipfitter First Class (highest rank: Carpenter)
Service: U.S. Navy
Birthday: 30 May 1876
Place of Birth: Hubbard, Trumbull County, Ohio
Date of Death: 19 January 1936
Cemetery: Arlington National Cemetery (6-8674) (MH)—Arlington, Virginia
Entered Service at: Ohio
Unit: U.S.S. *Huntington*
Battle or Place of Action: at Sea
Date of Action: 17 September 1917
G.O. Number, Date: 341, W.D. 7 November 1917
Citation: For extraordinary heroism while attached to the U.S.S. *Huntington*. On the morning of 17 September 1917, while the U.S.S. *Huntington* was passing through the war zone, a kite balloon was sent up with Lt. (j.g.) H.W. Hoyt, U.S. Navy, as observer. When the balloon was about 400 feet in the air, the temperature suddenly dropped, causing the balloon to descend about 200 feet, when it was struck by a squall. The balloon was hauled to the ship's side, but the basket trailed in the water and the pilot was submerged. McGunigal, with great daring, climbed down the side of the ship, jumped to the ropes leading to the basket, and cleared the tangle enough to get the pilot out of them. He then helped the pilot to get clear, put a bowline around him, and enabled him to be hauled to the deck. A bowline was lowered to McGunigal and he was taken safely aboard.

2521 ◆ McMURTRY, GEORGE G.

Rank: Captain (highest rank: Major)
Service: U.S. Army
Birthday: 6 November 1876

2522 ◆ *MESTROVITCH, JAMES I.

Place of Birth: Pittsburgh, Allegheny County, Pennsylvania
Date of Death: 22 November 1958
Place of Death: New York, New York
Cemetery: Ledge Lawn Cemetery—Bar Harbor, Maine
Entered Service at: New York, New York
Unit: 308th Infantry, 77th Division
Battle or Place of Action: in the Argonne Forest, at Charlevaux, France
Date of Action: 2-8 October 1918
G.O. Number, Date: 118, W.D. 2 December 1918
Citation: Commanded a battalion which was cut off and surrounded by the enemy and although wounded in the knee by shrapnel on 4 October and suffering great pain, he continued throughout the entire period to encourage his officers and men with a resistless optimism that contributed largely toward preventing panic and disorder among the troops, who were without food, cut off from communication with our lines. On 4 October during a heavy barrage, he personally directed and supervised the moving of the wounded to shelter before himself seeking shelter. On 6 October he was again wounded in the shoulder by a German grenade, but continued personally to organize and direct the defense against the German attack on the position until the attack was defeated. He continued to direct and command his troops, refusing relief, and personally led his men out of the position after assistance arrived before permitting himself to be taken to the hospital on 8 October. During this period the successful defense of the position was due largely to his efforts.

2522 ◆ *MESTROVITCH, JAMES I.

Rank: Sergeant
Service: U.S. Army
Birthday: 22 May 1894
Place of Birth: Crna Cora, Yugoslavia
Date of Death: 4 November 1918
Place of Death: France
Cemetery: Cemetery near Sveti Jovan Church—Crna Gora, Yugoslavia
Entered Service at: Pittsburgh, Allegheny County, Pennsylvania
Unit: Company C, 111th Infantry, 28th Division
Battle or Place of Action: at Fismette, France
Date of Action: 10 August 1918
G.O. Number, Date: 20, W.D. 30 January 1919
Date of Issue: 1922
Citation: Seeing his company commander lying wounded 30 yards in front of the line after his company had withdrawn to a sheltered position behind a stone wall, Sgt. Mestrovitch voluntarily left cover and crawled through heavy machine-gun and shell fire to where the officer lay. He took the officer upon his back and crawled to a place of safety, where he administered first-aid treatment, his exceptional heroism saving the officer's life.

2523 ◆ MILES, LOUIS WARDLAW

Rank: Captain
Service: U.S. Army
Birthday: 23 March 1873
Place of Birth: Baltimore, Baltimore County, Maryland
Date of Death: 27 June 1944
Cemetery: Greenmount Cemetery—Baltimore, Maryland
Entered Service at: Princeton, Mercer County, New Jersey
Unit: 308th Infantry, 77th Division
Battle or Place of Action: near Revillon, France
Date of Action: 14 September 1918
G.O. Number, Date: 44, W.D. 2 April 1919
Citation: Volunteered to lead his company in a hazardous attack on a commanding trench position near the Aisne Canal, which other troops had previously attempted to take without success. His company immediately met with intense machine-gun fire, against which it had no artillery assistance, but Capt. Miles preceded the first wave and assisted in cutting a passage through the enemy's wire entanglements. In so doing he was wounded five times by machine-gun bullets, both legs and one arm being fractured, whereupon he ordered himself placed on a stretcher and had himself carried forward to the enemy trench in order that he might encourage and direct his company, which by this time had suffered numerous casualties. Under the inspiration of this officer's indomitable spirit his men held the hostile position and consolidated the front line after an action lasting two hours, at the conclusion of which Capt. Miles was carried to the aid station against his will.

2524 ◆ *MILLER, OSCAR F.

Rank: Major
Service: U.S. Army
Place of Birth: Franklin County, Arkansas
Date of Death: 30 September 1918
Place of Death: France
Cemetery: Meuse-Argonne Cemetery (F-10-36) (MH)—Romagne Meuse, France
Entered Service at: Los Angeles, Los Angeles County, California
Unit: 361st Infantry, 91st Division
Battle or Place of Action: near Gesnes, France
Date of Action: 28 September 1918
G.O. Number, Date: 16, W.D. 22 January 1919
Citation: After two days of intense physical and mental strain, during which Maj. Miller had led his battalion in the front line of the advance through the Argonne Forest, the enemy was met in a prepared position south of Gesnes. Though almost exhausted, he energetically reorganized his battalion and ordered an attack. Upon reaching open ground the advancing line began to waver in the face of machine-gun fire from the front and flanks and direct artillery fire. Personally leading his command group forward between his front-line companies, Maj. Miller inspired his men by his personal courage, and they again pressed on toward the hostile position. As this officer led the renewed attack he was shot in the right leg, but he nevertheless staggered forward at the head of his command. Soon afterwards he was again shot in the right arm, but he continued the charge, personally cheering his troops on through the heavy machine-gun fire. Just before the objective was reached he received a wound in the

abdomen, which forced him to the ground, but he continued to urge his men on, telling them to push on to the next ridge and leave him where he lay. He died from his wounds a few days later.

2525 ◆ MORELOCK, STERLING LEWIS

Rank: Private
Service: U.S. Army
Birthday: 5 June 1890
Place of Birth: Silver Run, Maryland
Date of Death: 1 September 1964
Cemetery: Arlington National Cemetery (35-1824) (MH)—Arlington, Virginia
Entered Service at: Oquawka, Henderson County, Illinois
Unit: Company M, 28th Infantry, 1st Division
Battle or Place of Action: near Exermont, France
Date of Action: 4 October 1918
G.O. Number, Date: 43, W.D. 23 October 1919
Citation: While his company was being held up by heavy enemy fire, Pvt. Morelock, with three other men who were acting as runners at company headquarters, voluntarily led them as a patrol in advance of his company's front line through intense rifle, artillery, and machine-gun fire and penetrated a woods which formed the German front line. Encountering a series of five hostile machine-gun nests, containing from one to five machine guns each, with his patrol he cleaned them all out, gained and held complete mastery of the situation until the arrival of his company commander with reinforcements, even though his entire party had become casualties. He rendered first aid to the injured and evacuated them by using stretcher bearers 10 German prisoners whom he had captured. Soon thereafter his company commander was wounded and while dressing his wound Pvt. Morelock was very seriously wounded in the hip, which forced his evacuation. His heroic action and devotion to duty were an inspiration to the entire regiment.

2526 ◆ NEIBAUR, THOMAS CROFT

Rank: Private (highest rank: Private First Class)
Service: U.S. Army
Birthday: 17 May 1898
Place of Birth: Sharon, Idaho
Date of Death: 23 December 1942
Cemetery: Sugar City Cemetery (MH)—Sugar City, Idaho
Entered Service at: Sugar City, Madison County, Idaho
Unit: Company M, 107th Infantry, 42d Division
Battle or Place of Action: near Landres-et-St. Georges, France
Date of Action: 16 October 1918
G.O. Number, Date: 118, W.D. 2 December 1919
Citation: On the afternoon of 16 October 1918, when the Cote-de-Chatillion had just been gained after bitter fighting and the summit of the strong bulwark in the *Kriemhilde Stellung* was being organized, Pvt. Neibaur was sent out on patrol with his automatic rifle squad to enfilade enemy machine-gun nests. As he gained the ridge, he set up his automatic rifle and was directly thereafter wounded in both legs by fire from a hostile machine gun on his flank. The advance wave of the enemy troops, counterattacking, had about gained the ridge, and although practically cut off and surrounded, the remainder of his detachment being killed or wounded, this gallant soldier kept his automatic rifle in operation to such effect that by his own efforts and by fire from the skirmish line of his company, at least 100 yards in his rear, the attack was checked. The enemy wave being halted and lying prone, four of the enemy attacked Pvt. Neibaur at close quarters. These he killed. He then moved alone among the enemy lying on the ground about him, in the midst of the fire from his own lines, and by coolness and gallantry captured 11 prisoners at the point of his pistol and, although painfully wounded, brought them back to our lines. The counterattack in full force was arrested to a large extent by the single efforts of this soldier, whose heroic exploits took place against the skyline in full view of his entire battalion.

2527 ◆ O'NEILL, RICHARD WILLIAM

Rank: Sergeant (highest rank: First Lieutenant)
Service: U.S. Army
Birthday: 28 August 1898
Place of Birth: New York, New York
Date of Death: 9 April 1982
Place of Death: Hawthorne, New York
Cemetery: Gate of Heaven Cemetery—Hawthorne, New York
Entered Service at: New York, New York
Unit: Company D, 165th Infantry, 42d Division
Battle or Place of Action: on the Ourcq River, France
Date of Action: 30 July 1918
G.O. Number, Date: 30, W.D. 15 July 1921
Citation: In advance of an assaulting line, he attacked a detachment of about 25 of the enemy. In the ensuing hand-to-hand encounter he sustained pistol wounds, but heroically continued in the advance, during which he received additional wounds; but, with great physical effort, he remained in active command of his detachment. Being again wounded, he was forced by weakness and loss of blood to be evacuated, but insisted upon being taken first to the battalion commander in order to transmit to him valuable information relative to enemy positions and the disposition of our men.

2528 ◆ ORMSBEE JR., FRANCIS EDWARD

Rank: Chief Machinist's Mate (highest rank: Chief Aviation Pilot)
Service: U.S. Navy
Birthday: 30 April 1892
Place of Birth: Providence, Providence County, Rhode Island
Date of Death: 24 October 1936
Place of Death: Ardmore, Oklahoma
Cemetery: St. Francis Cemetery—Newport, Rhode Island
Entered Service at: Florida
Battle or Place of Action: Pensacola, Florida
Date of Action: 25 September 1918
G.O. Number, Date: 436, W.D. 1918

Citation: For extraordinary heroism while attached to the Naval Air Station, Pensacola, Fla., 25 September 1918. While flying with Ens. J.A. Jova, Ormsbee saw a plane go into a tailspin and crash about three-quarters of a mile to the right. Having landed nearby, Ormsbee lost no time in going overboard and made for the wreck, which was all under water except the two wing tips. He succeeded in partially extricating the gunner so that his head was out of the water, and held him in this position until the speedboat arrived. Ormsbee then made a number of desperate attempts to rescue the pilot, diving into the midst of the tangled wreckage although cut about the hands, but was too late to save his life.

2529 ◆ *OSBORNE, WEEDON EDWARD

Rank: Lieutenant (j.g.)
Service: U.S. Navy
Birthday: 13 November 1892
Place of Birth: Chicago, Cook County, Illinois
Date of Death: 6 June 1918
Place of Death: France
Cemetery: Aisne-Marne Cemetery (A-3-39) (MH)—Belleau Aisne, France
Entered Service at: Illinois
Unit: Dental Corps, attached to U.S. Marines, 6th Regiment
Battle or Place of Action: Bouresche, France
Date of Action: 6 June 1918
Citation: For extraordinary heroism while attached to the 6th Regiment, U.S. Marines, in actual conflict with the enemy and under fire during the advance on Bouresche, France, on 6 June 1918. In the hottest of the fighting when the marines made their famous advance on Bouresche at the southern edge of Belleau Wood, Lt. (j.g.) Osborne threw himself zealously into the work of rescuing the wounded. Extremely courageous in the performance of this perilous task, he was killed while carrying a wounded officer to a place of safety.

2530 ◆ *O'SHEA, THOMAS E.

Rank: Corporal
Service: U.S. Army
Birthday: 18 April 1895
Place of Birth: New York, New York
Date of Death: 29 September 1918
Place of Death: France
Cemetery: Somme Cemetery (B-16-14) (MH)—Bony Aisne, France
Entered Service at: Summit, Union County, New Jersey
Unit: 3d Platoon, Machine Gun Company, 107th Infantry, 27th Division
Battle or Place of Action: near Le Catelet, France
Date of Action: 29 September 1918
G.O. Number, Date: 20, W.D. 30 January 1919
Citation: Becoming separated from their platoon by a smoke barrage, Cpl. O'Shea, with two other soldiers, took cover in a shell hole well within the enemy's lines. Upon hearing a call for help from an American tank, which had become disabled 30 yards from them, the three soldiers left their shelter and started toward the tank under heavy fire from German machine guns and trench mortars. In crossing the fire-swept area Cpl. O'Shea was mortally wounded and died of his wounds shortly afterwards.

2531 ◆ PARKER, SAMUEL IREDELL

Rank: Second Lieutenant
Service: U.S. Army
Birthday: 17 October 1891
Place of Birth: Monroe, Union County, North Carolina
Date of Death: 1 December 1975
Cemetery: Oakwood Cemetery (MH)—Concord, North Carolina
Entered Service at: Monroe, Union County, North Carolina
Unit: Company K, 28th Infantry, 1st Division
Served as: Platoon Leader
Battle or Place of Action: near Soissons, France
Date of Action: 18-19 July 1918
G.O. Number, Date: 1, W.D. 1937
Place of Presentation: The White House, presented by Pres. Franklin D. Roosevelt
Citation: For conspicuous gallantry and intrepidity above and beyond the call of duty. During the attack the 2d and 3d Battalions of the 28th Infantry were merged, and after several hours of severe fighting, successfully established a frontline position. In so doing, a gap was left between the right flank of the French 153d Division on their left and the left flank of the 28th Infantry, exposing the left flank to a terrific enfilade fire from several enemy machine guns located in a rock quarry on high ground. Second Lt. Parker, observing this serious situation, ordered his depleted platoon to follow him in an attack upon the strong point. Meeting a disorganized group of French Colonials wandering leaderlessly about, he persuaded them to join his platoon. This consolidated group followed 2d Lt. Parker through direct enemy rifle and machine-gun fire to the crest of the hill, and rushing forward, took the quarry by storm, capturing six machine guns and about 40 prisoners. The next day when the assault was continued, 2d Lt. Parker in command of the merged 2d and 3d Battalions was in support of the 1st Battalion. Although painfully wounded in the foot, he refused to be evacuated and continued to lead his command until the objective was reached. Seeing that the assault battalion was subjected to heavy enfilade fire due to a gap between it and the French on its left, 2d Lt. Parker led his battalion through this heavy fire up on the line to the left of the 1st Battalion and thereby closed the gap, remaining in command of his battalion until the newly established lines of the 28th Infantry were thoroughly consolidated. In supervising the consolidation of the new position, 2d Lt. Parker was compelled to crawl about on his hands and knees on account of his painful wound. His conspicuous gallantry and spirit of self-sacrifice were a source of great inspiration to the members of the entire command.

2532 ◆ PECK, ARCHIE A.

Rank: Private (highest rank: First Sergeant)
Service: U.S. Army

Birthday: 22 November 1894
Place of Birth: Tyrone, Schuyler County, New York
Date of Death: 15 September 1978
Place of Death: Jamestown, New York
Cemetery: Evergreen Cemetery (MH)—Sinclairville, New York
Entered Service at: Hornell, Steuben County, New York
Unit: Company A, 307th Infantry, 77th Division
Served as: Rifleman
Battle or Place of Action: in the Argonne Forest, France
Date of Action: 6 October 1918
G.O. Number, Date: 16, W.D. 22 January 1919
Date of Presentation: 9 February 1919
Place of Presentation: Chaumont, France, presented by Gen. John J. Pershing
Citation: While engaged with two other soldiers on patrol duty, he and his comrades were subjected to the direct fire of an enemy machine gun, at which time both his companions were wounded. Returning to his company, he obtained another soldier to accompany him to assist in bringing in the wounded men. His assistant was killed in the exploit, but he continued on, twice returning safely, bringing in both men, being under terrific machine-gun fire during the entire journey.

2533 ◆ *PERKINS, MICHAEL J.

Rank: Private First Class
Service: U.S. Army
Birthday: 1899
Place of Birth: Boston, Suffolk County, Massachusetts
Date of Death: 28 October 1918
Place of Death: France
Cemetery: New Calvary Cemetery (MH)—Mattapan, Massachusetts
Entered Service at: Boston, Suffolk County, Massachusetts
Unit: Company D, 101st Infantry, 26th Division
Battle or Place of Action: at Belieu Bois, France
Date of Action: 27 October 1918
G.O. Number, Date: 34, W.D. 7 March 1919
Citation: He, voluntarily and alone, crawled to a German "pill box" machine-gun emplacement, from which grenades were being thrown at his platoon. Awaiting his opportunity, when the door was again opened and another grenade thrown, he threw a bomb inside, bursting the door open, and then, drawing his trench knife, rushed into the emplacement. In a hand-to-hand struggle he killed or wounded several of the occupants and captured about 25 prisoners, at the same time silencing seven machine guns.

2534 ◆ PETTY, ORLANDO HENDERSON

Rank: Lieutenant
Service: U.S. Naval Reserve Forces
Birthday: 20 February 1874
Place of Birth: Harrison, Hamilton County, Ohio
Date of Death: 2 June 1932
Cemetery: St. Timothy's Church Yard Cemetery—Roxborough, Pennsylvania
Entered Service at: Pennsylvania
Unit: Medical Corps, attached to the 5th Regiment, U.S. Marines
Battle or Place of Action: Boise de Belleau, France
Date of Action: 11 June 1918
Citation: For extraordinary heroism while serving with 5th Regiment, U.S. Marines, in France during the attack in the Bois de Belleau, 11 June 1918. While under heavy fire of high-explosive and gas shells in the town of Lucy, where his dressing station was located, Lt. Petty attended to and evacuated the wounded under most trying conditions. Having been knocked to the ground by an exploding gas shell which tore his mask, Lt. Petty discarded the mask and courageously continued his work. His dressing station being hit and demolished, he personally helped carry Capt. Williams, wounded, through the shellfire to a place of safety.

2535 ◆ *PIKE, EMORY JENISON

Rank: Lieutenant Colonel
Service: U.S. Army
Birthday: 17 December 1876
Place of Birth: Columbus City, Louisa County, Iowa
Date of Death: 16 September 1918
Place of Death: France
Cemetery: Woodland Cemetery—Des Moines, Iowa
Entered Service at: Sigourney, Keokuk County, Iowa
Unit: Division Machine-gun Officer, 82d Division
Battle or Place of Action: near Vandieres, France
Date of Action: 15 September 1918
G.O. Number, Date: 16, W.D. 22 January 1919
Citation: Having gone forward to reconnoiter new machine-gun positions, Lt. Col. Pike offered his assistance in reorganizing advanced infantry units which had become disorganized during a heavy artillery shelling. He succeeded in locating only about 20 men, but these he advanced and when later joined by several infantry platoons rendered inestimable service in establishing outposts, encouraging all by his cheeriness, in spite of the extreme danger of the situation. When a shell had wounded one of the men in the outpost, Lt. Col. Pike immediately went to his aid and was severely wounded himself when another shell burst in the same place. While waiting to be brought to the rear, Lt. Col. Pike continued in command, still retaining his jovial manner of encouragement, directing the reorganization until the position could be held. The entire operation was carried on under terrific bombardment, and the example of courage and devotion to duty, as set by Lt. Col. Pike, established the highest standard of morale and confidence to all under his charge. The wounds he received were the cause of his death.

2536 ◆ POPE, THOMAS A.

Rank: Corporal
Service: U.S. Army
Birthday: 15 December 1894
Place of Birth: Chicago, Cook County, Illinois
Date of Death: 14 June 1989
Place of Death: Maywood, Illinois

Cemetery: Arlington National Cemetery (35-3157) (MH)—Arlington, Virginia
Entered Service at: Chicago, Cook County, Illinois
Unit: 1st Platoon, Company E, 131st Infantry, 33d Division
Battle or Place of Action: at Hamel, France
Date of Action: 4 July 1918
G.O. Number, Date: 44, W.D. 2 April 1919
Date of Presentation: 22 April 1919
Place of Presentation: Chaumont, France, presented by Gen. John J. Pershing
Citation: His company was advancing behind the tanks when it was halted by hostile machine-gun fire. Going forward alone, he rushed a machine-gun nest, killed several of the crew with his bayonet, and, standing astride his gun, held off the others until reinforcements arrived and captured them.

2537 ◆ *PRUITT, JOHN HENRY✚

Rank: Corporal
Service: U.S. Marine Corps
Birthday: 4 October 1896
Place of Birth: Fayetteville, Washington County, Arkansas
Date of Death: 4 October 1918
Place of Death: France
Cemetery: Arlington National Cemetery (18-2453) (MH)—Arlington, Virginia
Entered Service at: Phoenix, Maricopa County, Arizona
Unit: 78th Company, 6th Regiment, 2d Division
Battle or Place of Action: at Blanc Mont Ridge, France
Date of Action: 3 October 1918
G.O. Number, Date: 62, W.D. 10 May 1919
Citation: **Army Medal of Honor** Cpl. Pruitt singlehandedly attacked two machine guns, capturing them and killing two of the enemy. He then captured 40 prisoners in a dugout nearby. This gallant soldier was killed soon afterwards by shellfire while he was sniping at the enemy. **Navy Medal of Honor** For extraordinary gallantry and intrepidity above and beyond the call of duty while serving with the 78th Company, 6th Regiment, 2d Division, in action with the enemy at Blanc Mont Ridge, France, 3 October 1918. Cpl. Pruitt, singlehandedly attacked two machine guns, capturing them and killing two of the enemy. He then captured 40 prisoners in a dugout nearby. This gallant soldier was killed soon afterward by shellfire while he was sniping at the enemy.
Notes: ✚Double Awardee: received both the Army and Navy Medal of Honor for the same deed

2538 ◆ REGAN, PATRICK J.

Rank: Second Lieutenant
Service: U.S. Army
Birthday: 25 March 1882
Place of Birth: Middleboro, Plymouth County, Massachusetts
Date of Death: 30 October 1943
Cemetery: Mount Olivet Cemetery (MH)—Bloomfield, New Jersey
Entered Service at: Los Angeles, Los Angeles County, California
Unit: 115th Infantry, 29th Division
Battle or Place of Action: at the Bois-de-Consenvoye, France
Date of Action: 8 October 1918
G.O. Number, Date: 50, W.D. 12 April 1919
Citation: While leading his platoon against a strong enemy machine-gun nest which had held up the advance of two companies, 2d Lt. Regan divided his men into three groups, sending one group to either flank, and he himself attacking with an automatic rifle team from the front. Two of the team were killed outright, while 2d Lt. Regan and the third man were seriously wounded, the latter unable to advance. Although seriously wounded, 2d Lt. Regan dashed with empty pistol into the machine-gun nest, capturing 30 Austrian gunners and four machine guns. This gallant deed permitted the companies to advance, avoiding a terrific enemy fire. Despite his wounds, he continued to lead his platoon forward until ordered to the rear by his commanding officer.

2539 ◆ RICKENBACKER, EDWARD VERNON

Rank: First Lieutenant (highest rank: Captain)
Service: U.S. Army Air Service
Birthday: 8 October 1890
Place of Birth: Columbus, Franklin County, Ohio
Date of Death: 23 July 1973
Place of Death: Zurich, Switzerland
Cemetery: Greenlawn Cemetery—Columbus, Ohio
Entered Service at: Columbus, Franklin County, Ohio
Unit: 94th Aero Squadron, Air Service
Served as: Commanding Officer/Pilot of a SPAD
Battle or Place of Action: near Billy, France
Date of Action: 25 September 1918
G.O. Number, Date: 2, W.D. 23 January 1931
Date of Presentation: 6 November 1930
Place of Presentation: Bolling Field near Washington, D.C., presented by Pres. Herbert Hoover
Citation: For conspicuous gallantry and intrepidity above and beyond the call of duty in action against the enemy near Billy, France, 25 September 1918. While on a voluntary patrol over the lines, 1st Lt. Rickenbacker attacked seven enemy planes (five type Fokker, protecting two type Halberstadt). Disregarding the odds against him, he dived on them and shot down one of the Fokkers out of control. He then attacked one of the Halberstadts and sent it down also.

2540 ◆ ROBB, GEORGE SEANOR

Rank: First Lieutenant
Service: U.S. Army
Birthday: 18 May 1887
Place of Birth: Assaria, Saline County, Kansas
Date of Death: 14 May 1972
Place of Death: Topeka, Kansas
Cemetery: Gypsum Hill Cemetery—Salina, Kansas
Entered Service at: Salina, Saline County, Kansas
Unit: 369th Infantry, 93d Division
Battle or Place of Action: near Sechault, France
Date of Action: 29-30 September 1918

G.O. Number, Date: 16, W.D. 22 January 1919
Citation: While leading his platoon in the assault, 1st Lt. Robb was severely wounded by machine-gun fire, but rather than go to the rear for proper treatment he remained with his platoon until ordered to the dressing station by his commanding officer. Returning within 45 minutes, he remained on duty throughout the entire night, inspecting his lines and establishing outposts. Early the next morning he was again wounded, once again displaying his remarkable devotion to duty by remaining in command of his platoon. Later the same day a bursting shell added two more wounds, the same shell killing his commanding officer and two officers of his company. He then assumed command of the company and organized its position in the trenches. Displaying wonderful courage and tenacity at the critical times, he was the only officer of his battalion who advanced beyond the town, and by clearing machine-gun and sniping posts contributed largely to the aid of his battalion in holding their objective. His example of bravery and fortitude and his eagerness to continue with his mission despite severe wounds set before the enlisted men of his command a most wonderful standard of morale and self-sacrifice.

2541 ◆ *ROBERTS, HAROLD W.

Rank: Corporal
Service: U.S. Army
Place of Birth: San Francisco, San Francisco County, California
Date of Death: 4 October 1918
Place of Death: France
Cemetery: Meuse-Argonne Cemetery (B-45-36) (MH)—Romagne Meuse, France
Entered Service at: San Francisco, San Francisco County, California
Unit: Company A, 344th Battalion, Tank Corps
Served as: Tank Driver
Battle or Place of Action: in the Montrebeau Woods, France
Date of Action: 4 October 1918
G.O. Number, Date: 16, W.D. 22 January 1919
Citation: Cpl. Roberts, a tank driver, was moving his tank into a clump of bushes to afford protection to another tank which had become disabled. The tank slid into a shell hole, 10 feet deep, filled with water, and was immediately submerged. Knowing that only one of the two men in the tank could escape, Cpl. Roberts said to the gunner, "Well only one of us can get out, and out you go," whereupon he pushed his companion through the back door of the tank and was himself drowned.

2542 ◆ ROBINSON, ROBERT GUY

Rank: Gunnery Sergeant (highest rank: First Lieutenant)
Service: U.S. Marine Corps
Birthday: 30 April 1896
Place of Birth: New York, New York
Date of Death: 5 October 1974
Cemetery: Arlington National Cemetery (46-390) (MH)—Arlington, Virginia
Entered Service at: Chicago, Cook County, Illinois
Unit: 1st Marine Aviation Force
Served as: Observer/Gunner
Battle or Place of Action: Pittham, Belgium
Date of Action: 14 October 1918
Citation: For extraordinary heroism as observer in the 1st Marine Aviation Force at the front in France. In company with planes from Squadron 218, Royal Air Force, conducting an air raid on 8 October 1918, G/Sgt. Robinson's plane was attacked by nine enemy scouts. In the fight which followed, he shot down one of the enemy planes. In a later air raid over Pittham, Belgium, on 14 October 1918, his plane and one other became separated from their formation on account of motor trouble and were attacked by 12 enemy scouts. Acting with conspicuous gallantry and intrepidity in the fight which ensued, G/Sgt. Robinson, after shooting down one of the enemy planes, was struck by a bullet which carried away most of his elbow. At the same time his gun jammed. While his pilot maneuvered for position, he cleared the jam with one hand and returned to the fight. Although his left arm was useless, he fought off the enemy scouts until he collapsed after receiving two more bullet wounds, one in the stomach and one in the thigh.

2543 ◆ SAMPLER, SAMUEL M.

Rank: Corporal
Service: U.S. Army
Birthday: 27 January 1895
Place of Birth: Decatur, Wise County, Texas
Date of Death: 19 November 1979
Cemetery: Memorial Gardens Cemetery—Fort Myers, Florida
Entered Service at: Altus, Jackson County, Oklahoma
Unit: Company H, 142d Infantry, 36th Division
Battle or Place of Action: near St. Etienne, France
Date of Action: 8 October 1918
G.O. Number, Date: 59, W.D. 3 May 1919
Citation: His company, having suffered severe casualties during an advance under machine-gun fire, was finally stopped. Cpl. Sampler detected the position of the enemy machine guns on an elevation. Armed with German hand grenades, which he had picked up, he left the line and rushed forward in the face of heavy fire until he was near the hostile nest, where he grenaded the position. His third grenade landed among the enemy, killing two, silencing the machine guns, and causing the surrender of 28 Germans, whom he sent to the rear as prisoners. As a result of his act the company was immediately enabled to resume the advance.

2544 ◆ SANDLIN, WILLIE

Rank: Sergeant
Service: U.S. Army
Birthday: 1 January 1890
Place of Birth: Jackson, Breathitt County, Kentucky
Date of Death: 29 May 1949
Cemetery: Zachary Taylor National Cemetery (E-10-A) (MH)—Louisville, Kentucky

Entered Service at: Hyden, Leslie County, Kentucky
Unit: Company A, 132d Infantry, 33d Division
Battle or Place of Action: at Bois-de-Forges, France
Date of Action: 26 September 1918
G.O. Number, Date: 16, W.D. 22 January 1919
Citation: He showed conspicuous gallantry in action by advancing alone directly on a machine-gun nest which was holding up the line with its fire. He killed the crew with a grenade and enabled the line to advance. Later in the day he attacked alone and put out of action two other machine-gun nests, setting a splendid example of bravery and coolness to his men.

2545 ◆ *SAWELSON, WILLIAM

Rank: Sergeant
Service: U.S. Army
Birthday: 5 August 1895
Place of Birth: Newark, Essex County, New Jersey
Date of Death: 26 October 1918
Place of Death: France
Cemetery: Meuse-Argonne Cemetery (C-9-33) (MH)—Romagne Meuse, France
Entered Service at: Harrison, Hudson County, New Jersey
Unit: Company M, 312th Infantry, 78th Division
Battle or Place of Action: at Grand-Pre, France
Date of Action: 26 October 1918
G.O. Number, Date: 16, W.D. 22 January 1919
Citation: Hearing a wounded man in a shell hole some distance away calling for water, Sgt. Sawelson, upon his own initiative, left shelter and crawled through heavy machine-gun fire to where the man lay, giving him what water he had in his canteen. He then went back to his own shell hole, obtained more water, and was returning to the wounded man when he was killed by a machine-gun bullet.

2546 ◆ SCHAFFNER, DWITE H.

Rank: First Lieutenant
Service: U.S. Army
Birthday: 5 November 1889
Place of Birth: Arroya, Pennsylvania
Date of Death: 22 November 1955
Cemetery: Rose Hill Cemetery—Akron, Ohio
Entered Service at: Falls Creek, Jefferson County, Pennsylvania
Unit: Company K, 306th Infantry, 77th Division
Served as: Company Commander
Battle or Place of Action: near St. Hubert's Pavillion, Boureuilles, France
Date of Action: 28 September 1918
G.O. Number, Date: 15, W.D. 5 April 1923
Citation: He led his men in an attack on St. Hubert's Pavillion through terrific enemy machine-gun, rifle, and artillery fire and drove the enemy from a strongly held entrenched position after hand-to-hand fighting. His bravery and contempt for danger inspired his men, enabling them to hold fast in the face of three determined enemy counterattacks. His company's position being exposed to enemy fire from both flanks, he made three efforts to locate an enemy machine gun which had caused heavy casualties. On his third reconnaissance he discovered the gun position and personally silenced the gun, killing or wounding the crew. The third counterattack made by the enemy was initiated by the appearance of a small detachment in advance of the enemy attacking wave. When almost within reach of the American front line, the enemy appeared behind them, attacking vigorously with pistols, rifles, and hand grenades, causing heavy casualties in the American platoon. First Lt. Schaffner mounted the parapet of the trench and used his pistol and grenades, killing a number of the enemy soldiers, finally reaching the enemy officer leading the attack forces, a captain, shooting and mortally wounding the latter with his pistol, and dragging the captured officer back to the company's trench, securing from him valuable information as to the enemy's strength and position. The information enabled 1st Lt. Schaffner to maintain for five hours the advanced position of his company despite the fact that it was surrounded on three sides by strong enemy forces. The undaunted bravery, gallant soldierly conduct, and leadership displayed by 1st Lt. Schaffner undoubtedly saved the survivors of the company from death or capture.

2547 ◆ SCHMIDT JR., OSCAR

Rank: Chief Gunner's Mate
Service: U.S. Navy
Birthday: 25 March 1896
Place of Birth: Philadelphia, Philadelphia County, Pennsylvania
Date of Death: 24 March 1973
Place of Death: Sommers Point, New Jersey
Cemetery: Arlington National Cemetery (11-116-LH) (MH)—Arlington, Virginia
Entered Service at: Pennsylvania
Unit: U.S.S. *Chestnut Hill*
Battle or Place of Action: at Sea
Date of Action: 9 October 1918
G.O. Number, Date: 450, W.D. 1919
Citation: For gallant conduct and extraordinary heroism while attached to the U.S.S. *Chestnut Hill*, on the occasion of the explosion and subsequent fire on board the U.S. submarine chaser *219*. Schmidt, seeing a man, whose legs were partly blown off, hanging on a line from the bow of the *219*, jumped overboard, swam to the sub chaser and carried him from the bow to the stern where a member of the *219*'s crew helped him land the man on the afterdeck of the submarine. Schmidt then endeavored to pass through the flames amidships to get another man who was seriously burned. This he was unable to do, but when the injured man fell overboard and drifted to the stern of the chaser Schmidt helped him aboard.

2548 ◆ SEIBERT, LLOYD MARTIN

Rank: Sergeant (highest rank: Chief Warrant Officer)
Service: U.S. Army
Birthday: 23 May 1889

Place of Birth: Caledonia, Kent County, Michigan
Date of Death: 15 October 1972
Cemetery: San Francisco National Cemetery (OS-10-128-31) (MH)—San Francisco, California
Entered Service at: Salinas, Monterey County, California
Unit: Company F, 364th Infantry, 91st Division
Battle or Place of Action: near Epinonville, France
Date of Action: 26 September 1918
G.O. Number, Date: 445, W.D. 1919
Citation: Suffering from illness, Sgt. Seibert remained with his platoon and lead his men with the highest courage and leadership under heavy shell and machine-gun fire. With two other soldiers he charged a machine-gun emplacement in advance of their company, he himself killing one of the enemy with a shotgun and capturing two others. In this encounter he was wounded, but he nevertheless continued in action, and when a withdrawal was ordered he returned with the last unit, assisting a wounded comrade. Later in the evening he volunteered and carried in wounded until he fainted from exhaustion.

2549 ◆ SIEGEL, JOHN OTTO

Rank: Boatswain's Mate Second Class
Service: U.S. Navy
Birthday: 21 April 1890
Place of Birth: Milwaukee, Milwaukee County, Wisconsin
Entered Service at: New Jersey
Unit: U.S.S. *Mohawk*
Date of Action: 1 November 1918
Citation: For extraordinary heroism while serving on board the *Mohawk* in performing a rescue mission aboard the schooner *Hjeltenaes* which was in flames on 1 November 1918. Going aboard the blazing vessel, Siegel rescued two men from the crew's quarters and went back the third time. Immediately after he had entered the crew's quarters, a steam pipe over the door burst, making it impossible for him to escape. Siegel was overcome with smoke and fell to the deck, being finally rescued by some of the crew of the *Mohawk* who carried him out and rendered first aid.

2550 ◆ *SKINKER, ALEXANDER RIVES

Rank: Captain
Service: U.S. Army
Birthday: 13 October 1883
Place of Birth: St. Louis, St. Louis County, Missouri
Date of Death: 26 September 1918
Place of Death: Cheppy, France
Cemetery: Bellafontaine Cemetery—St. Louis, Missouri
Entered Service at: St. Louis, St. Louis County, Missouri
Unit: Company I, 138th Infantry, 35th Division
Served as: Company Commander
Battle or Place of Action: at Cheppy, France
Date of Action: 26 September 1918
G.O. Number, Date: 13, W.D. 18 January 1919
Citation: Unwilling to sacrifice his men when his company was held up by terrific machine-gun fire from iron pill boxes in the Hindenburg Line, Capt. Skinker personally led an automatic rifleman and a carrier in an attack on the machine guns. The carrier was killed instantly, but Capt. Skinker seized the ammunition and continued through an opening in the barbed wire, feeding the automatic rifle until he too, was killed.

2551 ◆ SLACK, CLAYTON KIRK

Rank: Private
Service: U.S. Army
Birthday: 23 February 1896
Place of Birth: Plover, Portage County, Wisconsin
Date of Death: 1 March 1976
Cemetery: Arlington National Cemetery (34-59) (MH)—Arlington, Virginia
Entered Service at: Madison, Dane County, Wisconsin
Unit: Company D, 124th Machine Gun Battalion, 33d Division
Battle or Place of Action: near Consenvoye, France
Date of Action: 8 October 1918
G.O. Number, Date: 16, W.D. 22 January 1919
Citation: Observing German soldiers under cover 50 yards away on the left flank, Pvt. Slack, upon his own initiative, rushed them with his rifle and, singlehandedly, captured 10 prisoners and two heavy-type machine guns, thus saving his company and neighboring organizations from heavy casualties.

2552 ◆ *SMITH, FRED E.

Rank: Lieutenant Colonel
Service: U.S. Army
Birthday: 29 March 1873
Place of Birth: Rockford, Winnebago County, Illinois
Date of Death: 29 September 1918
Place of Death: France
Cemetery: Meuse-Argonne Cemetery (A-7-18) (MH)—Romagne Meuse, France
Entered Service at: Bartlett, North Dakota
Unit: 308th Infantry, 77th Division
Battle or Place of Action: near Binarville, France
Date of Action: 29 September 1918
G.O. Number, Date: 49, W.D. 25 November 1922
Citation: When communication from the forward regimental post of command to the battalion leading the advance had been interrupted temporarily by the infiltration of small parties of the enemy armed with machine guns, Lt. Col. Smith personally led a party of two other officers and 10 soldiers, and went forward to reestablish runner posts and carry ammunition to the front line. The guide became confused and the party strayed to the left flank beyond the outposts of supporting troops, suddenly coming under fire from a group of enemy machine guns only 50 yards away. Shouting to the other members of his party to take cover, this officer, in disregard of his danger, drew his pistol and opened fire on the German gun crew. About this time he fell, severely wounded in the side, but regaining his footing, he continued to fire on the enemy until most of the men in his party were out of danger. Refusing first-aid treatment, he then made his way in plain view of the enemy to a hand grenade dump and returned under continued heavy machine-gun fire for the pur-

pose of making another attack on enemy emplacements. As he was attempting to ascertain the exact location of the nearest nest, he again fell, mortally wounded.

2553 ◆ *STOCKHAM, FRED WILLIAM

Rank: Gunnery Sergeant
Service: U.S. Marine Corps
Birthday: 16 March 1881
Place of Birth: Detroit, Wayne County, Michigan
Date of Death: 22 June 1918
Place of Death: France
Cemetery: Hollywood Cemetery (MH)—Union, New Jersey
Entered Service at: New York, New York
Unit: 96th Company, 2d Battalion, 6th Regiment, 4th Brigade, 2d Division
Battle or Place of Action: in Bois-de-Belleau, France
Date of Action: 13-14 June 1918
G.O. Number, Date: W.D. 15 July 1939
Date of Presentation: 21 December 1939
Place of Presentation: Smithsonian Institute, Washington, D.C., later presented to American Legion Post named in his honor in St. Louis, Mo
Citation: **Army Medal of Honor** During an intense enemy bombardment with high-explosive and gas shells which wounded or killed many members of the company, G/Sgt. Stockham, upon noticing that the gas mask of a wounded comrade was shot away, without hesitation, removed his own gas mask and insisted upon giving it to the wounded man, well knowing that the effects of the gas would be fatal to himself. He continued with undaunted courage and valor to direct and assist in the evacuation of the wounded, until he himself collapsed from the effects of gas, dying as a result thereof a few days later. His courageous conduct undoubtedly saved the lives of many of his wounded comrades, and his conspicuous gallantry and spirit of self-sacrifice were a source of great inspiration to all who served with him.
Notes: This marine received only the Army Medal of Honor, whereas five other Marines in the 2d Division who received the Medal received both the Army and Navy Medal of Honor

2554 ◆ *STOWERS, FREDDIE

Rank: Corporal
Service: U.S. Army
Birthday: 1896
Place of Birth: Sandy Springs, Anderson County, South Carolina
Date of Death: 28 September 1918
Place of Death: Champagne Marne Sector, France
Cemetery: A.B.M.C. Meuse-Argonne Cemetery—Meuse, France
Entered Service at: Anderson County, South Carolina
Unit: Company C, 371st Infantry Regiment, 93d Division
Served as: Squad Leader
Battle or Place of Action: Hill 188, Champagne Marne Sector, France
Date of Action: 28 September 1918
Date of Presentation: 24 April 1991
Place of Presentation: The White House, presented by Pres. George Bush to his sisters
Citation: Cpl. Freddie Stowers distinguished himself by exceptional heroism on 28 September 1918 while serving as a squad leader in Company C, 371st Infantry Regiment, 93d Infantry Division. His company was the lead company during the attack on Hill 188, Champagne Marne Sector, France, during World War I. A few minutes after the attack began, the enemy ceased firing and began climbing up onto the parapets of the trenches, holding up their arms as if wishing to surrender. The enemy's actions caused the American forces to cease fire and to come out into the open. As the company started forward and when within about 100 meters of the trench line, the enemy jumped back into their trenches and greeted Cpl. Stowers' company with interlocking bands of machine-gun fire and mortar fire causing well over fifty percent casualties. Faced with incredible enemy resistance, Cpl. Stowers took charge, setting such a courageous example of personal bravery and leadership that he inspired his men to follow him in the attack. With extraordinary heroism and complete disregard of personal danger under devastating fire, he crawled forward, leading his squad toward an enemy machine-gun nest which was causing heavy casualties to his company. After fierce fighting, the machine-gun position was destroyed and the enemy soldiers were killed. Displaying great courage and intrepidity Cpl. Stowers continued to press the attack against a determined enemy. While crawling forward and urging his men to continue the attack on a second trench line, he was gravely wounded by machine-gun fire. Although Cpl. Stowers was mortally wounded, he pressed forward, urging on the members of his squad, until he died. Inspired by the heroism and display of bravery of Cpl. Stowers, his company continued the attack against incredible odds, contributing to the capture of Hill 188 and causing heavy enemy casualties. Cpl. Stowers' conspicuous gallantry, extraordinary heroism, and supreme devotion to his men were well above and beyond the call of duty, follow the finest traditions of military service, and reflect the utmost credit on him and the United States Army.

2555 ◆ SULLIVAN, DANIEL AUGUSTUS JOSEPH

Rank: Ensign (highest rank: lieutenant Commander)
Service: U.S. Naval Reserve Force
Birthday: 31 July 1884
Place of Birth: Charleston, Charleston County, South Carolina
Date of Death: 27 January 1941
Cemetery: Arlington National Cemetery (8-5327-A)—Arlington, Virginia
Entered Service at: South Carolina
Unit: U.S.S. *Cristabel*
Battle or Place of Action: at Sea
Date of Action: 21 May 1918
Citation: For extraordinary heroism as an officer of the U.S.S. *Christabel* in conflict with an enemy submarine on 21

May 1918. As a result of the explosion of a depth bomb dropped near the submarine, the *Christabel* was so badly shaken that a number of depth charges which had been set for firing were thrown about the deck and there was imminent danger that they would explode. Ens. Sullivan immediately fell on the depth charges and succeeded in securing them, thus saving the ship from disaster, which would inevitably have caused great loss of life.

2556 ◆ *TALBOT, RALPH

Rank: Second Lieutenant
Service: U.S. Marine Corps
Birthday: 6 January 1897
Place of Birth: South Weymouth, Norfolk County, Massachusetts
Date of Death: 25 October 1918
Cemetery: Mount Wollaston Cemetery (MH)—Quincy, Massachusetts
Entered Service at: Connecticut
Unit: Squadron C, 1st Marine Aviation Force
Battle or Place of Action: France
Date of Action: 8, 14 October 1918
Citation: For exceptionally meritorious service and extraordinary heroism while attached to Squadron C, 1st Marine Aviation Force, in France. Second Lt. Talbot participated in numerous air raids into enemy territory. On 8 October 1918, while on such a raid, he was attacked by nine enemy scouts, and in the fight that followed shot down an enemy plane. Also, on 14 October 1918, while on a raid over Pittham, Belgium, 2d Lt. Talbot and another plane became detached from the formation on account of motor trouble and were attacked by 12 enemy scouts. During the severe fight that followed, his plane shot down one of the enemy scouts. His observer was shot through the elbow and his gun jammed. Second Lt. Talbot maneuvered to gain time for his observer to clear the jam with one hand, and then returned to the fight. The observer fought until shot twice, once in the stomach and once in the hip, and then collapsed. Second Lt. Talbot attacked the nearest enemy scout with his front guns and shot him down. With his observer unconscious and his motor failing, he dived to escape the balance of the enemy and crossed the German trenches at an altitude of 50 feet, landing at the nearest hospital to leave his observer, and then returning to his aerodrome.

2557 ◆ TALLEY, EDWARD R.

Rank: Sergeant
Service: U.S. Army
Birthday: 6 September 1890
Place of Birth: Russellville, Hamblen County, Tennessee
Date of Death: 14 December 1950
Cemetery: Bent Creek Cemetery—Whitesburg, Tennessee
Entered Service at: Russellville, Hamblen County, Tennessee
Unit: Company L, 117th Infantry, 30th Division
Battle or Place of Action: near Ponchaux, France
Date of Action: 7 October 1918
G.O. Number, Date: 50, W.D. 12 April 1919
Citation: Undeterred by seeing several comrades killed in attempting to put a hostile machine-gun nest out of action, Sgt. Talley attacked the position singlehandedly. Armed only with a rifle, he rushed the nest in the face of intense enemy fire, killed or wounded at least six of the crew, and silenced the gun. When the enemy attempted to bring forward another gun and ammunition he drove them back by effective fire from his rifle.

2558 ◆ THOMPSON, JOSEPH HENRY

Rank: Major (highest rank: Colonel)
Service: U.S. Army
Birthday: 26 September 1871
Place of Birth: Kilkeel, County Down, Ireland
Date of Death: 1 February 1928
Cemetery: Beaver Falls Cemetery & Memorial Park (MH)—Beaver Falls, Pennsylvania
Entered Service at: Beaver Falls, Beaver County, Pennsylvania
Unit: 110th Infantry, 28th Division
Battle or Place of Action: near Apremont, France
Date of Action: 1 October 1918
G.O. Number, Date: 21, W.D. 5 October 1925
Citation: Counterattacked by two regiments of the enemy, Maj. Thompson encouraged his battalion in the front line by constantly braving the hazardous fire of machine guns and artillery. His courage was mainly responsible for the heavy repulse of the enemy. Later in the action, when the advance of his assaulting companies was held up by fire from a hostile machine-gun nest and all but one of the six assaulting tanks were disabled, Maj. Thompson, with great gallantry and coolness, rushed forward on foot three separate times in advance of the assaulting line, under heavy machine-gun and antitank-gun fire, and led the one remaining tank to within a few yards of the enemy machine-gun nest, which it succeeded in reducing, thereby making it possible for the infantry to advance.

2559 ◆ TURNER, HAROLD LEO

Rank: Corporal (highest rank: Second Lieutenant)
Service: U.S. Army
Birthday: 5 May 1898
Place of Birth: Aurora, Lawrence County, Missouri
Date of Death: 12 March 1933
Place of Death: Caddo Lake, Texas
Cemetery: Little Cemetery (MH)—Little, Oklahoma
Entered Service at: Seminole, Seminole County, Oklahoma
Unit: Company F, 142d Infantry, 36th Division
Battle or Place of Action: near St. Etienne, France
Date of Action: 8 October 1918
G.O. Number, Date: 59, W.D. 3 May 1919
Date of Presentation: 2 May 1919
Place of Presentation: Cheney, France, presented by Gen. William R. Smith
Citation: After his platoon had started the attack, Cpl. Turner assisted in organizing a platoon consisting of the battalion scouts, runners, and a detachment of Signal Corps. As

second in command of this platoon he fearlessly led them forward through heavy enemy fire, continually encouraging the men. Later he encountered deadly machine-gun fire which reduced the strength of his command to but four men, and these were obliged to take shelter. The enemy machine-gun emplacement, 25 yards distant, kept up a continual fire from four machine guns. After the fire had shifted momentarily, Cpl. Turner rushed forward with fixed bayonet and charged the position alone, capturing the strong point with a complement of 50 Germans and four machine guns. His remarkable display of courage and fearlessness was instrumental in destroying the strong point, the fire from which had blocked the advance of his company.

2560 ◆ *TURNER, WILLIAM BRADFORD

Rank: First Lieutenant
Service: U.S. Army
Birthday: 1892
Place of Birth: Dorchester, Suffolk County, Massachusetts
Date of Death: 27 September 1918
Place of Death: Near Ronssoy, France
Cemetery: Somme Cemetery (B-13-1) (MH)—Bony, Aisne, France
Entered Service at: Garden City, Nassau County, New York
Unit: Company M, 105th Infantry, 27th Division
Battle or Place of Action: near Ronssoy, France
Date of Action: 27 September 1918
G.O. Number, Date: 81, W.D. 26 June 1919
Citation: He led a small group of men to the attack, under terrific artillery and machine-gun fire, after they had become separated from the rest of the company in the darkness. Singlehandedly he rushed an enemy machine gun which had suddenly opened fire on his group and killed the crew with his pistol. He then pressed forward to another machine-gun post 25 yards away and had killed one gunner himself by the time the remainder of his detachment arrived and put the gun out of action. With the utmost bravery he continued to lead his men over three lines of hostile trenches, cleaning up each one as they advanced, regardless of the fact that he had been wounded three times, and killed several of the enemy in hand-to-hand encounters. After his pistol ammunition was exhausted, this gallant officer seized the rifle of a dead soldier, bayoneted several members of a machine-gun crew, and shot the other. Upon reaching the fourth-line trench, which was his objective, 1st Lt. Turner captured it with the nine men remaining in his group and resisted a hostile counterattack until he was finally surrounded and killed.

2561 ◆ UPTON, FRANK MONROE

Rank: Quartermaster (highest rank: Ensign)
Service: U.S. Navy
Birthday: 29 April 1896
Place of Birth: Loveland, Larimer County, Colorado
Date of Death: 25 June 1962
Cemetery: Arlington National Cemetery (8-55-A) (MH)—Arlington, Virginia
Entered Service at: Colorado
Unit: U.S.S. *Stewart*
Battle or Place of Action: at Sea
Date of Action: 17 April 1918
G.O. Number, Date: 403, W.D. 1918
Citation: For extraordinary heroism following internal explosion of the *Florence H*, on 17 April 1918. The sea in the vicinity of wreckage was covered by a mass of boxes of smokeless powder, which were repeatedly exploding. Frank M. Upton, of the U.S.S. *Stewart*, plunged overboard to rescue a survivor who was surrounded by powder boxes and too exhausted to help himself. Fully realizing the danger from continual explosion of similar powder boxes in the vicinity, he risked his life to save the life of this man.

2562 ◆ VALENTE, MICHAEL

Rank: Private
Service: U.S. Army
Birthday: 5 February 1895
Place of Birth: Cassino, Italy
Date of Death: 10 January 1976
Place of Death: Long Beach, New York
Cemetery: Long Island National Cemetery (DSS-60-A) (MH)—Farmingdale, New York
Entered Service at: Ogdensburg, St. Lawrence County, New York
Unit: Company D, 107th Infantry, 27th Division
Battle or Place of Action: Hindenburg Line, east of Ronssoy, France
Date of Action: 29 September 1918
G.O. Number, Date: 16, W.D. 26 September 1919
Date of Presentation: 27 September 1929
Place of Presentation: The White House (lawn), presented by Pres. Herbert Hoover
Citation: For conspicuous gallantry and intrepidity above and beyond the call of duty in action with the enemy during the operations against the Hindenburg line, east of Ronssoy, France, 29 September 1918. Finding the advance of his organization held up by a withering enemy machine-gun fire, Pvt. Valente volunteered to go forward. With utter disregard of his own personal danger, accompanied by another soldier, Pvt. Valente rushed forward through an intense machine-gun fire directly upon the enemy nest, killing two and capturing five of the enemy and silencing the gun. Discovering another machine-gun nest close by which was pouring a deadly fire on the American forces, preventing their advance, Pvt. Valente and his companion charged upon this strong point, killing the gunner and putting this machine gun out of action. Without hesitation they jumped into the enemy's trench, killed two and captured 16 German soldiers. Pvt. Valente was later wounded and sent to the rear.

2563 ◆ VAN IERSEL, LUDOVICUS M.M.

True Name: Changed name to: Van Iersel, Louis M.M.
Rank: Sergeant
Service: U.S. Army
Birthday: 19 October 1893
Place of Birth: Dussen, Holland

Date of Death: 9 June 1987
Place of Death: Roseburg, Oregon
Cemetery: Arlington National Cemetery (42-1770) (MH)—Arlington, Virginia
Entered Service at: Glen Rock, Bergen County, New Jersey
Unit: Company M, 9th Infantry, 2d Division
Battle or Place of Action: at Mouzon, France
Date of Action: 9 November 1918
G.O. Number, Date: 34, W.D. 7 March 1919
Citation: While a member of a reconnaissance patrol, sent out at night to ascertain the condition of a damaged bridge, Sgt. Van Iersel volunteered to lead a party across the bridge in the face of heavy machine-gun and rifle fire from a range of only 75 yards. Crawling alone along the debris of the ruined bridge, he came upon a trap, which gave way and precipitated him into the water. In spite of the swift current he succeeded in swimming across the stream and found a lodging place among the timbers on the opposite bank. Disregarding the enemy fire, he made a careful investigation of the hostile position by which the bridge was defended and then returned to the other bank of the river, reporting this valuable information to the battalion commander.

2564 ◆ VILLEPIGUE, JOHN CANTEY

Rank: Corporal
Service: U.S. Army
Birthday: 29 March 1896
Place of Birth: Camden, Kershaw County, South Carolina
Date of Death: 18 April 1943
Cemetery: Quaker Cemetery—Camden, South Carolina
Entered Service at: Camden, Kershaw County, South Carolina
Unit: Company M, 118th Infantry, 30th Division
Battle or Place of Action: at Vaux-Andigny, France
Date of Action: 15 October 1918
G.O. Number, Date: 16, W.D. 22 January 1919
Citation: Having been sent out with two other soldiers to scout through the village of Vaux-Andigny, he met with strong resistance from enemy machine-gun fire, which killed one of his men and wounded the other. Continuing his advance without aid 500 yards in advance of his platoon and in the face of machine-gun and artillery fire, he encountered four of the enemy in a dugout, whom he attacked and killed with a hand grenade. Crawling forward to a point 150 yards in advance of his first encounter, he rushed a machine-gun nest, killing four and capturing six of the enemy and taking two light machine guns. After being joined by his platoon he was severely wounded in the arm.

2565 ◆ WAALER, REIDAR

Rank: Sergeant
Service: U.S. Army
Birthday: 12 February 1894
Place of Birth: Christiana, now Oslo, Norway
Date of Death: 5 February 1979
Cemetery: Forest Hills Memorial Park—Palm City, Florida
Entered Service at: New York, New York
Unit: Company A, 105th Machine-Gun Battalion, 27th Division
Battle or Place of Action: near Ronssoy, France
Date of Action: 27 September 1918
G.O. Number, Date: 20, W.D. 30 January 1919
Date of Presentation: 4 February 1919
Place of Presentation: Chaumont, France, presented by Gen. John J. Pershing
Citation: In the face of heavy artillery and machine-gun fire, he crawled forward to a burning British tank, in which some of the crew were imprisoned, and succeeded in rescuing two men. Although the tank was then burning fiercely and contained ammunition which was likely to explode at any time, this soldier immediately returned to the tank and, entering it, made a search for the other occupants, remaining until he satisfied himself that there were no more living men in the tank.

2566 ◆ WARD, CALVIN JOHN

Rank: Private (highest rank: Private First Class)
Service: U.S. Army
Birthday: 30 October 1899
Place of Birth: Green County, Tennessee
Date of Death: 15 December 1967
Place of Death: Morristown, Tennessee
Cemetery: Glenwood Cemetery—Bristol, Tennessee
Entered Service at: Morristown, Hamblen County, Tennessee
Unit: Company D, 117th Infantry, 30th Division
Battle or Place of Action: near Estrees, France
Date of Action: 8 October 1918
G.O. Number, Date: 16, W.D. 22 January 1919
Citation: During an advance, Pvt. Ward's company was held up by a machine gun, which was enfilading the line. Accompanied by a noncommissioned officer, he advanced against this post and succeeded in reducing the nest by killing three and capturing seven of the enemy and their guns.

2567 ◆ WEST, CHESTER HOWARD

Rank: First Sergeant
Service: U.S. Army
Birthday: 3 January 1888
Place of Birth: Fort Collins, Larimer County, Colorado
Date of Death: 20 May 1935
Place of Death: Gallipolis, Ohio
Cemetery: Pine Grove Cemetery—Pliny, West Virginia
Entered Service at: Los Banos, Merced County, California
Unit: Company D, 363d Infantry, 91st Division
Battle or Place of Action: near Bois-de-Cheppy, France
Date of Action: 26 September 1918
G.O. Number, Date: 34, W.D. 7 March 1919
Citation: While making his way through a thick fog with his automatic rifle section, his advance was halted by direct and unusual machine-gun fire from two guns. Without aid, he at once dashed through the fire and, attacking the nest, killed two of the gunners, one of whom was an officer. This prompt

and decisive hand-to-hand encounter on his part enabled his company to advance farther without the loss of a man.

2568 ♦ WHITTLESEY, CHARLES WHITE

Rank: Major (highest rank: Lieutenant Colonel
Service: U.S. Army
Birthday: 20 January 1884
Place of Birth: Florence, Florence County, Wisconsin
Date of Death: 27 November 1921
Place of Death: at sea between New York & Cuba
Cemetery: Atlantic Ocean (lost at sea)
Entered Service at: Pittsfield, Berkshire County, Massachusetts
Unit: 1st Battalion, 308th Infantry, 77th Division
Served as: Battalion Commander
Battle or Place of Action: northeast of Binarville, in the Argonne Forest, France
Date of Action: 2-7 October 1918
G.O. Number, Date: 118, W.D. 2 December 1918
Date of Presentation: 25 December 1918
Place of Presentation: Boston Common, Massachusetts
Citation: Although cut off for five days from the remainder of his division, Maj. Whittlesey maintained his position, which he had reached under orders received for an advance, and held his command, consisting originally of 46 officers and men of the 308th Infantry and of Company K, of the 307th Infantry, together in the face of superior numbers of the enemy during the five days. Maj. Whittlesey and his command were cut off, and no rations or other supplies reached him, in spite of determined efforts which were made by his division. On the fourth day Maj. Whittlesey received from the enemy a written proposition to surrender, which he treated with contempt, although he was at the time out of rations and had suffered a loss of about 50 percent in killed and wounded of his command and was surrounded by the enemy.

2569 ♦ *WICKERSHAM, J. HUNTER

Rank: Second Lieutenant
Service: U.S. Army
Place of Birth: New York, New York
Date of Death: 12 September 1918
Place of Death: France
Cemetery: St. Mihiel Cemetery (B-19-12) (MH)—Thiaucourt, France
Entered Service at: Denver, Denver County, Colorado
Unit: 353d Infantry, 89th Division
Battle or Place of Action: near Limey, France
Date of Action: 12 September 1918
G.O. Number, Date: 16, W.D. 22 January 1919
Citation: Advancing with his platoon during the St. Mihiel offensive, he was severely wounded in four places by the bursting of a high-explosive shell. Before receiving any aid for himself, he dressed the wounds of his orderly, who was wounded at the same time. He then ordered and accompanied the further advance of his platoon, although weakened by the loss of blood. His right hand and arm being disabled by wounds, he continued to fire his revolver with his left hand until, exhausted by loss of blood, he fell and died from his wounds before aid could be administered.

2570 ♦ *WOLD, NELS T.

Rank: Private
Service: U.S. Army
Birthday: 24 December 1895
Place of Birth: Winger, Polk County, Minnesota
Date of Death: 26 September 1918
Place of Death: France
Cemetery: Elim Cemetery (MH)—Winger, Minnesota
Entered Service at: Minnewaukan, Benson County, North Dakota
Unit: Company I, 138th Infantry, 35th Division
Battle or Place of Action: near Cheppy, France
Date of Action: 26 September 1918
G.O. Number, Date: 16, W.D. 22 January 1919
Citation: He rendered most gallant service in aiding the advance of his company, which had been held up by machine-gun nests, advancing, with one other soldier, and silencing the guns, bringing with him, upon his return, 11 prisoners. Later the same day he jumped from a trench and rescued a comrade who was about to be shot by a German officer, killing the officer during the exploit. His actions were entirely voluntary, and it was while attempting to rush a fifth machine-gun nest that he was killed. The advance of his company was mainly due to his great courage and devotion to duty.

2571 ♦ WOODFILL, SAMUEL

Rank: First Lieutenant (highest rank: Major)
Service: U.S. Army
Birthday: 6 January 1883
Place of Birth: Jefferson County, Indiana
Date of Death: 10 August 1951
Cemetery: Arlington National Cemetery (34-642-A) (MH)—Arlington, Virginia
Entered Service at: Bryantsburg, Indiana
Unit: Company M, 60th Infantry, 5th Division
Served as: Company Commander
Battle or Place of Action: at Cunel, France
Date of Action: 12 October 1918
G.O. Number, Date: 16, W.D. 22 January 1919
Citation: While he was leading his company against the enemy, his line came under heavy machine-gun fire, which threatened to hold up the advance. Followed by two soldiers at 25 yards, this officer went out ahead of his first line toward a machine-gun nest and worked his way around its flank, leaving the two soldiers in front. When he got within 10 yards of the gun it ceased firing, and four of the enemy appeared, three of whom were shot by 1st Lt. Woodfill. The fourth, an officer, rushed at 1st Lt. Woodfill, who attempted to club the officer with his rifle. After a hand-to-hand struggle, 1st Lt. Woodfill killed the officer with his pistol. His company thereupon continued to advance, until shortly afterwards another machine-gun nest was encountered. Calling on his men to follow, 1st Lt. Woodfill rushed ahead of his line in the face of

heavy fire from the nest, and when several of the enemy appeared above the nest, he shot them, capturing three other members of the crew and silencing the gun. A few minutes later this officer for a third time demonstrated conspicuous daring by charging another machine-gun position, killing five men in one machine-gun pit with his rifle. He then drew his revolver and started to jump into the pit, when two other gunners only a few yards away turned their guns on him. Failing to kill them with his revolver, he grabbed a pick lying nearby and killed both of them. Inspired by the exceptional courage displayed by this officer, his men pressed on to their objective under severe shell and machine-gun fire.

2572 ◆ YORK, ALVIN CULLIUM

Rank: Corporal (highest rank: Sergeant)
Service: U.S. Army
Birthday: 13 December 1887
Place of Birth: Fentress County, Tennessee
Date of Death: 2 September 1964
Place of Death: Nashville, Tennessee
Cemetery: Wolf River Cemetery—Jamestown, Tennessee
Entered Service at: Pall Mall, Fentress County, Tennessee
Unit: Company G, 2d Battalion, 328th Infantry, 82d Division
Served as: Squad Leader
Battle or Place of Action: near Chatel-Chehery, France
Date of Action: 8 October 1918
G.O. Number, Date: 59, W.D. 3 May 1919
Place of Presentation: France, presented by Maj. Gen. Duncan, commanding general 82nd Division
Citation: After his platoon had suffered heavy casualties and three other noncommissioned officers had become casualties, Cpl. York assumed command. Fearlessly leading seven men, he charged with great daring a machine-gun nest which was pouring deadly and incessant fire upon his platoon. In his heroic feat the machine-gun nest was taken, together with four officers and 128 men and several guns.

HAITIAN CAMPAIGN 1919–1920

2573 ◆ BUTTON, WILLIAM ROBERT

Rank: Corporal
Service: U.S. Marine Corps
Birthday: 3 December 1895
Place of Birth: St. Louis, St. Louis County, Missouri
Date of Death: 15 April 1921
Place of Death: Cape Haitien, Haiti
Cemetery: Valhalla Cemetery—St. Louis, Missouri
Entered Service at: St. Louis, St. Louis County, Missouri
Unit: Gendarmerie d'Haiti
Battle or Place of Action: near Grande Riviere, Republic of Haiti
Date of Action: 31 October-1 November 1919
G.O. Number, Date: 536, 10 June 1920
Date of Presentation: 1 July 1920
Place of Presentation: Washington, D.C., presented by Gen. John A. Lejeune
Citation: For extraordinary heroism and conspicuous gallantry and intrepidity in actual conflict with the enemy near Grande Riviere, Republic of Haiti, on the night from 31 October to 1 November 1919, resulting in the death of Charlemagne Peralte, the supreme bandit chief in the Republic of Haiti, and the killing, capture, and dispersal of about 1,200 of his outlaw followers. Cpl. William R. Button not only distinguished himself by his excellent judgment and leadership but also unhesitatingly exposed himself to great personal danger when the slightest error would have forfeited not only his life but the lives of the detachments of Gendarmerie under his command. The successful termination of his mission will undoubtedly prove of untold value to the Republic of Haiti.

2574 ◆ HANNEKEN, HERMAN HENRY

Rank: Second Lieutenant (highest rank: Brigadier General)
Service: U.S. Marine Corps
Birthday: 23 June 1893
Place of Birth: St. Louis, St. Louis County, Missouri
Date of Death: 23 August 1986
Place of Death: Lanolla, California
Cemetery: Fort Rosecrans National Cemetery (C-1166-D)—San Diego, California
Entered Service at: St. Louis, St. Louis County, Missouri
Unit: Gendarmerie d'Haiti
Battle or Place of Action: near Grande Riviere, Republic of Haiti
Date of Action: 31 October-1 November 1919
G.O. Number, Date: 536, 10 June 1920
Date of Presentation: 1 July 1920
Place of Presentation: Washington, D.C., presented by Gen. John A. Lejeune
Citation: For extraordinary heroism and conspicuous gallantry and intrepidity in actual conflict with the enemy near Grande Riviere, Republic of Haiti, on the night from 31 October to 1 November 1919, resulting in the death of Charlemagne Peralte, the supreme bandit chief in the Republic of Haiti, and the killing, capture, and dispersal of about 1,200 of his outlaw followers. Second Lt. Hanneken not only distinguished himself by his excellent judgment and leadership but also unhesitatingly exposed himself to great personal danger when the slightest error would have forfeited not only his life but the lives of the detachments of Gendarmerie under his command. The successful termination of his mission will undoubtedly prove of untold value to the Republic of Haiti.

SECOND NICARAGUAN CAMPAIGN

2575 ◆ SCHILT, CHRISTIAN FRANKLIN

Rank: First Lieutenant (highest rank: General)
Service: U.S. Marine Corps
Birthday: 18 March 1895
Place of Birth: Richland County, Illinois
Date of Death: 8 January 1987
Place of Death: Norfolk, Virginia
Cemetery: Arlington National Cemetery (2E-151-2) (MH)—Arlington, Virginia
Entered Service at: Illinois
Unit: Observation Squadron 7-M
Battle or Place of Action: Quilali, Nicaragua
Date of Action: 6-8 January 1928
Citation: During the progress of an insurrection at Quilali, Nicaragua, 6, 7, and 8 January 1928, 1st Lt. Schilt, then a member of a Marine expedition which had suffered severe losses in killed and wounded, volunteered under almost impossible conditions to evacuate the wounded by air and to transport a relief commanding officer to assume charge of a very serious situation. First Lt. Schilt bravely undertook this dangerous and important task and, by taking off a total of ten times in the rough, rolling street of a partially burning village, under hostile infantry fire on each occasion, succeeded in accomplishing his mission, thereby actually saving three lives and bringing supplies and aid to others in desperate need.

2576 ◆ TRUESDELL, DONALD LEROY

True Name: Name Changed to: Truesdale, Donald Leroy
Rank: Corporal (highest rank: Chief Warrent Officer 2)
Service: U.S. Marine Corps
Birthday: 8 August 1906
Place of Birth: Lugoff, Kershaw County, South Carolina
Date of Death: 21 September 1993
Place of Death: Lugoff, South Carolina
Entered Service at: South Carolina
Battle or Place of Action: vicinity of Constancia, near Coco River, northern Nicaragua
Date of Action: 24 April 1932
Place of Presentation: Presented by Brig. Gen. Randolph C. Berkeley
Citation: Cpl. Truesdale was second in command of a Guardia Nacional Patrol in active operations against armed bandit forces in the vicinity of Constancia, near Coco River, northern Nicaragua, on 24 April 1932. While the patrol was in formation on the trail searching for a bandit group with which contact had just previously been made, a rifle grenade fell from its carrier and struck a rock, igniting the detonator. Several men close to the grenade at the time were in danger. Cpl. Truesdale, who was several yards away, could easily have sought cover and safety for himself. Knowing full well the grenade would explode within two or three seconds, he rushed for the grenade, grasped it in his right hand, and attempted to throw it away from the patrol. The grenade exploded in his hand, blowing it off and inflicting serious multiple wounds about his body. Cpl. Truesdale, in taking the full shock of the explosion himself, saved the members of the patrol from loss of life or serious injury.

INTERIM 1920–1940

2577 ◆ BADDERS, WILLIAM

Rank: Chief Machinist's Mate
Service: U.S. Navy
Birthday: 15 September 1900
Place of Birth: Harrisburg, Saline County, Illinois
Date of Death: 23 November 1986
Cemetery: San Francisco National Cemetery (A-788A) (MH)—San Francisco, California
Entered Service at: Indianapolis, Marion County, Indiana
Unit: Submarine Rescue & Salvage Unit, U.S.S. *Falcon*
Battle or Place of Action: Portsmouth, southeast off the Isle of Shoals, New Hampshire
Date of Action: 23 May 1939
Date of Presentation: 19 January 1940
Place of Presentation: Washington, D.C., presented by Sec. of the Navy Charles Edison
Citation: For extraordinary heroism in the line of his profession during the rescue and salvage operations following the sinking of the U.S.S. *Squalus* on 23 May 1939. During the rescue operations, Badders, as senior member of the rescue chamber crew, made the last extremely hazardous trip of the rescue chamber to attempt to rescue any possible survivors in the flooded afterportion of the *Squalus*. He was fully aware of the great danger involved in that if he and his assistant became incapacitated, there was no way in which either could be rescued. During the salvage operations, Badders made important and difficult dives under the most hazardous conditions. His outstanding performance of duty contributed much to the success of the operations and characterizes conduct far above and beyond the ordinary call of duty.

2578 ◆ BENNETT, FLOYD

Rank: Machinist (highest rank: Chief Aviation Machinist Mate)
Service: U.S. Navy
Birthday: 25 October 1890
Place of Birth: Warrensburg, Warren County, New York
Date of Death: 25 April 1928
Place of Death: Quebec, Canada
Cemetery: Arlington National Cemetery (3-1852-B)—Arlington, Virginia
Entered Service at: New York
Served as: Co-Pilot/Radio Operator
Battle or Place of Action: Spitsbergen, Norway to the North Pole
Date of Action: 9 May 1926
Date of Presentation: 25 February 1927
Place of Presentation: The White House, presented by Pres. Calvin Coolidge
Citation: For distinguishing himself conspicuously by courage and intrepidity at the risk of his life as a member of the Byrd Arctic Expedition and thus contributing largely to the success of the first heavier-than-air flight to the North Pole and return.

2579 ◆ BREAULT, HENRY

Rank: Torpedoman Second Class
Service: U.S. Navy
Birthday: 14 October 1900
Place of Birth: Putnam, Windham County, Connecticut
Date of Death: 5 December 1941
Place of Death: Newport, Rhode Island
Cemetery: St. Mary's Cemetery (MH)—Putnam, Connecticut
Entered Service at: Vermont
Unit: U.S. Submarine *0-5*
Battle or Place of Action: Limon Bay, Canal Zone, Panama
Date of Action: 28 October 1923
G.O. Number, Date: 125, 20 February 1924
Date of Presentation: 8 March 1924
Place of Presentation: The White House, presented by Pres. Calvin Coolidge
Citation: For heroism and devotion to duty while serving on board the U.S. submarine *0-5* at the time of the sinking of that vessel. On the morning of 28 October 1923, the *0-5* collided with the steamship *Abangarez* and sank in less than a minute. When the collision occurred, Breault was in the torpedo room. Upon reaching the hatch, he saw that the boat was rapidly sinking. Instead of jumping overboard to save his own life, he returned to the torpedo room to the rescue of a shipmate who he knew was trapped in the boat, closing the torpedo room hatch on himself. Breault and Brown remained trapped in this compartment until rescued by the salvage party 31 hours later.

2580 ◆ BYRD JR., RICHARD EVELYN

Rank: Commander (highest rank: Rear Admiral)
Service: U.S. Navy
Birthday: 25 October 1888
Place of Birth: Winchester, Frederick County, Virginia
Date of Death: 11 March 1957
Place of Death: Boston, Massachusetts
Cemetery: Arlington National Cemetery (2-4969-1) (MH)—Arlington, Virginia

Entered Service at: Virginia
Served as: Pilot
Battle or Place of Action: Spitsbergen, Norway to the North Pole
 of Action: 9 May 1926
Date of Presentation: 25 February 1927
Place of Presentation: The White House, presented by Pres. Calvin Coolidge
Citation: For distinguishing himself conspicuously by courage and intrepidity at the risk of his life, in demonstrating that it is possible for aircraft to travel in continuous flight from a now inhabited portion of the earth over the North Pole and return.

2581 ◆ *CHOLISTER, GEORGE ROBERT

Rank: Boatswain's Mate First Class
Service: U.S. Navy
Birthday: 18 December 1898
Place of Birth: Camden, Camden County, New Jersey
Date of Death: 21 October 1924
Cemetery: Colestown Cemetery—Cherry Hill, New Jersey
Entered Service at: New Jersey
Unit: U.S.S. *Trenton*
Battle or Place of Action: U.S.S. *Trenton*
Date of Action: 20 October 1924
Date of Issue: 3 February 1933
Citation: For extraordinary heroism in the line of his profession on the occasion of a fire on board the U.S.S. *Trenton*. At 3:35 on the afternoon of 20 October 1924, while the *Trenton* was preparing to fire trial installation shots from the two 6-inch guns in the forward twin mount of that vessel, two charges of powder ignited. Twenty men were trapped in the twin mount. Four died almost immediately and 10 later from burns and inhalation of flames and gases. The six others were severely injured. Cholister, without thought of his own safety, on seeing that the charge of powder from the left gun was ignited, jumped for the right charge and endeavored to put it in the immersion tank. The left charge burst into flame and ignited the right charge before Cholister could accomplish his purpose. He fell unconscious while making a supreme effort to save his shipmates and died the following day.

2582 ◆ *CORRY JR., WILLIAM MERRILL

Rank: Lieutenant Commander
Service: U.S. Navy
Birthday: 5 October 1889
Place of Birth: Quincy, Gadsden County, Florida
Date of Death: 6 October 1920
Place of Death: Hartford, Connecticut
Cemetery: Eastern Cemetery—Quincy, Florida
Entered Service at: Florida
Battle or Place of Action: near Hartford, Connecticut
Date of Action: 2 October 1920
Citation: For heroic service in attempting to rescue a brother officer from a flame-enveloped airplane. On 2 October 1920, an airplane in which Lt. Comdr. Corry was a passenger crashed and burst into flames. He was thrown 30 feet clear of the plane and, though injured, rushed back to the burning machine and endeavored to release the pilot. In so doing he sustained serious burns, from which he died four days later.

2583 ◆ CRANDALL, ORSON LEON

Rank: Chief Boatswain's Mate (highest rank: Lieutenant)
Service: U.S. Navy
Birthday: 2 February 1903
Place of Birth: St. Joseph, Buchanan County, Missouri
Date of Death: 10 May 1960
Place of Death: St. Petersburg, Florida
Cemetery: Arlington National Cemetery (48-2004) (MH)—Arlington, Virginia
Entered Service at: Connecticut
Unit: Submarine Rescue & Salvage Unit, U.S.S. *Falcon*
Served as: Master Diver
Battle or Place of Action: Portsmouth, southeast off the Isle of Shoals, New Hampshire
Date of Action: 23 May 1939
Date of Presentation: 19 January 1940
Place of Presentation: Washington, D.C., presented by Sec. of the Navy Charles Edison
Citation: For extraordinary heroism in the line of his profession as a master diver throughout the rescue and salvage operations following the sinking of the U.S.S. *Squalus* on 23 May 1939. His leadership and devotion to duty in directing diving operations and in making important and difficult dives under the most hazardous conditions characterize conduct far above and beyond the ordinary call of duty.

2584 ◆ *DREXLER, HENRY CLAY

Rank: Ensign
Service: U.S. Navy
Birthday: 7 August 1901
Place of Birth: Braddock, Allegheny County, Pennsylvania
Date of Death: 20 October 1924
Place of Death: on board U.S.S. Trenton
Cemetery: Arlington National Cemetery (4-3051)—Arlington, Virginia
Entered Service at: Pennsylvania
Unit: U.S.S. *Trenton*
Battle or Place of Action: U.S.S. *Trenton*
Date of Action: 20 October 1924
Date of Issue: 3 February 1933
Citation: For extraordinary heroism in the line of his profession on the occasion of a fire on board the U.S.S. *Trenton*. At 3:35 on the afternoon of 20 October 1924, while the Trenton was preparing to fire trial installation shots from the two 6-inch guns in the forward twin mount of that vessel, two charges of powder ignited. Twenty men were trapped in the twin mount. Four died almost immediately and 10 later from burns and inhalation of flames and gases. The six others were severely injured. Ens. Drexler, without thought of his own safety, on seeing that the charge of powder from the left gun was ignited, jumped for the right charge and endeavored to put it in the immersion tank. The left charge burst into

flame and ignited the right charge before Ens. Drexler could accomplish his purpose. He met his death while making a supreme effort to save his shipmates.

2585 ◆ EADIE, THOMAS

Rank: Chief Gunner's Mate
Service: U.S. Navy
Birthday: 7 April 1887
Place of Birth: Scotland
Date of Death: 14 November 1974
Place of Death: Brockton, Massachusetts
Cemetery: Island Cemetery Annex—Newport, Rhode Island
Entered Service at: Newport, Newport County, Rhode Island
Served as: Diver
Battle or Place of Action: off Provincetown, Massachusetts
Date of Action: 18 December 1927
Place of Presentation: Presented by Pres. Calvin Coolidge
Citation: For display of extraordinary heroism in the line of his profession above and beyond the call of duty on 18 December 1927, during the diving operations in connection with the sinking of the U.S.S. *S-4* with all on board, as a result of a collision off Provincetown, Mass. On this occasion when Michels, chief torpedoman, U.S. Navy, while attempting to connect an air line to the submarine at a depth of 102 feet became seriously fouled, Eadie, under the most adverse diving conditions, deliberately, knowingly, and willingly took his own life in his hands by promptly descending to the rescue in response to the desperate need of his companion diver. After two hours of extremely dangerous and heartbreaking work, by his cool, calculating, and skillful labors, he succeeded in his mission and brought Michels safely to the surface.

2586 ◆ EDWARDS, WALTER ATLEE

Rank: Lieutenant Commander
Service: U.S. Navy
Birthday: 8 November 1886
Place of Birth: Philadelphia, Philadelphia County, Pennsylvania
Date of Death: 15 January 1928
Cemetery: Arlington National Cemetery (4-3183)—Arlington, Virginia
Entered Service at: Pennsylvania
Unit: U.S.S. *Bainbridge*
Battle or Place of Action: Sea of Marmora, Turkey
Date of Action: 16 December 1922
G.O. Number, Date: 123, 4 February 1924
Date of Presentation: 2 February 1924
Place of Presentation: The White House, presented by Pres. Calvin Coolidge
Citation: For heroism in rescuing 482 men, women, and children from the French military transport *Vinh-Long*, destroyed by fire in the Sea of Marmora, Turkey, on 16 December 1922. Lt. Comdr. Edwards, commanding the U.S.S. *Bainbridge*, placed his vessel alongside the bow of the transport and, in spite of several violent explosions which occurred on the burning vessel, maintained his ship in that position until all who were alive were taken on board. Of a total of 495 on board, 482 were rescued by his coolness, judgment, and professional skill, which were combined with a degree of heroism that must reflect new glory on the U.S. Navy.

2587 ◆ GREELY, ADOLPHUS WASHINGTON

Rank: Major General
Service: U.S. Army Ret.
Birthday: 27 March 1844
Place of Birth: Newburyport, Essex County, Massachusetts
Date of Death: 20 October 1935
Place of Death: Washington, D.C.
Cemetery: Arlington National Cemetery (1-129)—Arlington, Virginia
Entered Service at: Louisiana
Served as: Commander
Date of Action: 26 July 1861-10 February 1906
G.O. Number, Date: 3 W.D. 1935 Act of Congress, 21 March 1935
Date of Issue: 27 March 1935
Citation: For his life of splendid public service, begun on 27 March 1844, having enlisted as a private in the U.S. Army on 26 July 1861, and by successive promotions was commissioned as major general 10 February 1906, and retired by operation of the law on his 64th birthday.

2588 ◆ HUBER, WILLIAM RUSSELL

Rank: Machinist's Mate (highest rank: Lieutenant)
Service: U.S. Navy
Birthday: 16 July 1902
Place of Birth: Harrisburg, Dauphin County, Pennsylvania
Date of Death: 25 January 1982
Place of Death: San Mateo, California
Cemetery: Golden Gate National Cemetery (2-B-4085)—San Bruno, California
Entered Service at: Pennsylvania
Unit: U.S.S. *Bruce*
Battle or Place of Action: Navy Yard, Norfolk, Virginia
Date of Action: 11 June 1928
Date of Presentation: 15 December 1928
Place of Presentation: The White House, presented by Pres. Calvin Coolidge
Citation: For display of extraordinary heroism in the line of his profession on 11 June 1928, after a boiler accident on the U.S.S. *Bruce*, then at the Naval Shipyard, Norfolk, Va. Immediately on becoming aware of the accident, Huber without hesitation and in complete disregard of his own safety, entered the steam-filled fireroom and at grave risk to his life succeeded by almost superhuman efforts in carrying Charles H. Byran to safety. Although having received severe and dangerous burns about the arms and neck, he descended with a view toward rendering further assistance. The great courage,

grit, and determination displayed by Huber on this occasion characterized conduct far above and beyond the call of duty.

2589 ◆ *HUTCHINS, CARLTON BARMORE

Rank: Lieutenant
Service: U.S. Navy
Birthday: 12 September 1904
Place of Birth: Albany, Albany County, New York
Date of Death: 2 February 1938
Place of Death: at Sea Pacific Ocean
Cemetery: Remains not recovered.
Entered Service at: New York
Unit: U.S. Navy Seaplane PBY-2 No. 0463 (11-P-3)
Battle or Place of Action: off California Coast
Date of Action: 2 February 1938
Citation: For extraordinary heroism as the pilot of the U.S. Navy seaplane PBY-2 No.0463 (11-P-3) while engaged in tactical exercises with the U.S. Fleet on 2 February 1938. Although his plane was badly damaged, Lt. Hutchins remained at the controls endeavoring to bring the damaged plane to a safe landing and to afford an opportunity for his crew to escape by parachutes. His cool, calculated conduct contributed principally to the saving of the lives of all who survived. His conduct on this occasion was above and beyond the call of duty.

2590 ◆ LINDBERGH JR., CHARLES AUGUSTUS

Rank: Captain (highest rank: Brigadier General)
Service: U.S. Army Air Corps Reserve
Birthday: 4 February 1902
Place of Birth: Detroit, Wayne County, Michigan
Date of Death: 26 August 1974
Cemetery: Kipahulu Church Cemetery—Maui, Hawaii
Entered Service at: Little Falls, Morrison County, Minnesota
Served as: Pilot, Navigator
Battle or Place of Action: from New York City to Paris, France
Date of Action: 20-21 May 1927
G.O. Number, Date: 5, W.D. 1928; Act of Congress: 14 December 1927
Citation: For displaying heroic courage and skill as a navigator, at the risk of his life, by his nonstop flight in his airplane, the *Spirit of St. Louis*, from New York City to Paris, France, 20–21 May 1927, by which Capt. Lindbergh not only achieved the greatest individual triumph of any American citizen but demonstrated that travel across the ocean by aircraft was possible.

2591 ◆ McDONALD, JAMES HARPER

Rank: Chief Metalsmith (highest rank: Lieutenant)
Service: U.S. Navy
Birthday: 15 July 1900
Place of Birth: near Newmand, Scotland
Date of Death: 29 December 1973
Cemetery: Fishing Creek Cemetery—Roulette, Pennsylvania
Entered Service at: Washington, D.C.
Served as: Master Diver
Battle or Place of Action: Portsmouth, southeast off the Isle of Shoals, New Hampshire
Date of Action: 23 May 1939
Date of Presentation: 19 January 1940
Place of Presentation: Washington, D.C., presented by Sec. of the Navy Charles Edison
Citation: For extraordinary heroism in the line of his profession as a master diver throughout the rescue and salvage operations following the sinking of the U.S.S. *Squalus* on 23 May 1939. His leadership, masterly skill, general efficiency, and untiring devotion to duty in directing diving operations and in making important and difficult dives under the most hazardous conditions, characterize conduct far above and beyond the ordinary call of duty.

2592 ◆ MIHALOWSKI, JOHN

Rank: Torpedoman First Class (highest rank: Lieutenant Commander)
Service: U.S. Navy
Birthday: 12 August 1910
Place of Birth: Worcester, Worcester County, Massachusetts
Date of Death: 29 October 1993
Place of Death: Largo, Florida
Cemetery: Serenity Gardens Memorial Park (MH)—Largo, Florida
Entered Service at: Massachusetts
Unit: Submarine Rescue & Salvage Unit, U.S.S. *Falcon*
Served as: Diver
Battle or Place of Action: Portsmouth, southeast off the Isle of Shoals, New Hampshire
Date of Action: 23 May 1939
Date of Presentation: 19 January 1940
Place of Presentation: Washington, D.C., presented by Sec. of the Navy Charles Edison
Citation: For extraordinary heroism in the line of his profession during the rescue and salvage operations following the sinking of the U.S.S. *Squalus* on 23 May 1939. Mihalowski, as a member of the rescue chamber crew, made the last extremely hazardous trip of the rescue chamber to attempt the rescue of any possible survivors in the flooded afterportion of the *Squalus*. He was fully aware of the great danger involved, in that, if he and the other member of the crew became incapacitated, there was no way in which either could be rescued. During the salvage operations Mihalowski made important and difficult dives under the most hazardous conditions. His outstanding performance of duty contributed much to the success of the operations and characterizes conduct far above and beyond the ordinary call of duty.

2593 ◆ RYAN JR., THOMAS JOHN

Rank: Ensign (highest rank: Rear Admiral)
Service: U.S. Navy

Birthday: 5 August 1901
Place of Birth: New Orleans, Orleans County, Louisiana
Date of Death: 28 January 1970
Place of Death: New Orleans, Louisiana
Cemetery: Arlington National Cemetery (34-80-A-1) (MH)—Arlington, Virginia
Entered Service at: Louisiana
Battle or Place of Action: Yokohama, Japan
Date of Action: 1 September 1923
Date of Presentation: 15 March 1924
Place of Presentation: The White House, by Pres. Calvin Coolidge
Citation: For heroism in effecting the rescue of a woman from the burning Grand Hotel, Yokohama, Japan, on 1 September 1923. Following the earthquake and fire which occurred in Yokohama on 1 September, Ens. Ryan, with complete disregard for his own life, extricated a woman from the Grand Hotel, thus saving her life. His heroic conduct upon this occasion reflects the greatest credit on himself and on the U.S. Navy, of which he is part.

2594 ◆ SMITH, ALBERT JOSEPH

Rank: Private (highest rank: Sergeant)
Service: U.S. Marine Corps
Birthday: 31 July 1898
Place of Birth: Calumet, Houghton County, Michigan
Date of Death: 27 March 1973
Cemetery: Grand Lawn Cemetery—Detroit, Michigan
Entered Service at: Michigan
Served as: Sentry
Battle or Place of Action: Marine Barracks, Naval Air Station, Pensacola, Florida
Date of Action: 11 February 1921
G.O. Number, Date: 72, 29 September 1921
Date of Presentation: 17 October 1921
Place of Presentation: Santo Domingo, Dominican Republic, presented by Brig. Gen. Harry Lee
Citation: At about 7:30 A.M. on the morning of 11 February 1921, Pvt. Smith, while on duty as a sentry, rescued Plen M. Phelps, late machinist's mate second class, U.S. Navy, from a burning seaplane which had fallen near his post, gate No. 1, Marine Barracks, Naval Air Station, Pensacola, Fla. Despite the explosion of the gravity gasoline tank, with total disregard of personal safety, he pushed himself to a position where he could reach Phelps, who was pinned beneath the burning wreckage, and rescued him from the burning plane, in the performance of which he sustained painful burns about the head, neck, and both hands.

MEDAL OF HONOR RECIPIENTS 1863–1994

Volume II
World War II to Somalia

MEDAL OF HONOR RECIPIENTS 1863–1994

Volume II
World War II to Somalia

Compiled by George Lang, M.H.,
Raymond L. Collins and
Gerard F. White

Medal of Honor Recipients 1863–1994

Copyright © 1995 by George Lang, Raymond L. Collins and Gerard F. White

All rights reserved. No part of this book may be reproduced or utilized
in any form or by any means, electronic or mechanical, including photocopying,
recording, or by any information storage or retrieval systems, without permission
in writing from the publisher. For information contact:

Facts On File, Inc.
460 Park Avenue South
New York, NY 10016

Library of Congress Cataloging-in-Publication Data

Lang, George.
    Medal of Honor recipients, 1863–1994 / compiled by George Lang,
Raymond L. Collins, and Gerard F. White
      p. cm.
    Includes bibliographical references and index.
    ISBN 0-8160-3259-9 (set)
    ISBN 0-8160-3260-2 (vol. 1)
    ISBN 0-8160-3261-0 (vol. 2)
    1. Medal of Honor. 2. United States—Armed Forces—Biography.
I. Collins, Raymond L. (Raymond Luther) II. White, Gerard F.
III. Title.
UB433.L36 1995
355.1'342—dc20   95-12529

Facts On File books are available at special discounts when purchased in bulk quantities
for businesses, associations, institutions or sales promotions. Please call our Special Sales
Department in New York at 212/683-2244 or 800/322-8755.

This book is printed on acid-free paper.

Printed in the United States of America

VB CC 10 9 8 7 6 5 4 3 2 1

TABLE OF CONTENTS

Acknowledgments	vii
Introduction	ix
Methodology	xi
The History of the Medal of Honor	xiii
VOLUME I	
Civil War	1
Interim 1865–1870	251
Indian Campaigns	254
Korean Campaign 1871	315
Interim 1871–1898	318
Spanish-American War	333
Samoa Campaign	352
Philippine Insurrection	353
China Relief Expedition	367
Interim 1899–1910	377
Action Against Outlaws, Philippines 1911	385
Mexican Campaign	387
Haitian Campaign 1915	398
Interim 1915–1916	400
Dominican Campaign	403
World War I	404
Haitian Campaign 1919–1924	434
Second Nicaraguan Campaign	435
Interim 1920–1940	436
VOLUME II	
World War II	441
Korean War	605
Vietnam War	656
Somalia	761
Medals of Honor Awarded to Unknowns	763
Appendixes	765
Abbreviations	766
Recipients by State of Enlistment & Birth	767
Foreign-born Recipients	842
Table of Medal Recipients	851
A Select Medal of Honor Bibliography	852
Index	865

MEDAL OF HONOR RECIPIENTS 1863–1994

Volume II
World War II to Somalia

WORLD WAR II

2595 ◆ ADAMS, LUCIAN
Rank: Staff Sergeant
Service: U.S. Army
Birthday: 26 October 1922
Place of Birth: Port Arthur, Jefferson County, Texas
Entered Service at: Port Arthur, Jefferson County, Texas
Unit: Company I, 3d Battalion, 30th Infantry, 3d Infantry Division
Served as: Squad Leader
Battle or Place of Action: near St. Die, France
Date of Action: 28 October 1944
G.O. Number, Date: 20, 29 March 1945
Date of Presentation: 23 April 1945
Place of Presentation: Zepman Stadium, Nuremberg, Germany, presented by Lt. Gen. Alexander M. Patch III
Citation: For conspicuous gallantry and intrepidity at risk of his life above and beyond the call of duty on 28 October 1944, near St. Die, France. When his company was stopped in its effort to drive through the Mortagne Forest to reopen the supply line to the isolated third battalion, S/Sgt. Adams braved the concentrated fire of machine guns in a lone assault on a force of German troops. Although his company had progressed less than 10 yards and had lost three killed and six wounded, S/Sgt. Adams charged forward dodging from tree to tree firing a borrowed BAR from the hip. Despite intense machine-gun fire which the enemy directed at him and rifle grenades which struck the trees over his head, showering him with broken twigs and branches, S/Sgt. Adams made his way to within 10 yards of the closest machine gun and killed the gunner with a hand grenade. An enemy soldier threw hand grenades at him from a position only 10 yards distant; however, S/Sgt. Adams dispatched him with a single burst of BAR fire. Charging into the vortex of the enemy fire, he killed another machine gunner at 15 yards' range with a hand grenade and forced the surrender of two supporting infantrymen. Although the remainder of the German group concentrated the full force of its automatic-weapon fire in a desperate effort to knock him out, he proceeded through the woods to find and exterminate five more of the enemy. Finally, when the third German machine gun opened up on him at a range of 20 yards, S/Sgt. Adams killed the gunner with BAR fire. In the course of the action, he personally killed nine Germans, eliminated three enemy machine guns, vanquished a specialized force which was armed with automatic weapons, and grenade launchers, cleared the woods of hostile elements and reopened the severed supply lines to the assault companies of his battalion.

2596 ◆ *AGERHOLM, HAROLD CHRIST
Rank: Private First Class
Service: U.S. Marine Corps Reserve
Birthday: 29 January 1925
Place of Birth: Racine, Wisconsin
Date of Death: 7 July 1944
Place of Death: Saipan, Marianas Islands
Cemetery: Mound Cemetery—Racine, Wisconsin
Entered Service at: Wisconsin
Unit: 4th Battalion, 10th Marines, 2d Marine Division
Battle or Place of Action: Saipan, Marianas Islands
Date of Action: 7 July 1944
Citation: For conspicuous gallantry and intrepidity at the risk of his life above and beyond the call of duty while serving with the 4th Battalion, 10th Marines, 2d Marine Division, in action against enemy Japanese forces on Saipan, Marianas Islands, 7 July 1944. When the enemy launched a fierce, determined counterattack against our positions and overran a neighboring artillery battalion, Pfc. Agerholm immediately volunteered to assist in the efforts to check the hostile attack and evacuate our wounded. Locating and appropriating an abandoned ambulance jeep, he repeatedly made extremely perilous trips under heavy rifle and mortar fire and single-handedly loaded and evacuated approximately 45 casualties, working tirelessly and with utter disregard for his own safety during a grueling period of more than three hours. Despite intense, persistent enemy fire, he ran out to aid two men whom he believed to be wounded marines, but was himself mortally wounded by a Japanese sniper while carrying out his hazardous mission. Pfc. Agerholm's brilliant initiative, great personal valor, and self-sacrificing efforts in the face of almost certain death reflect the highest credit upon himself and the U.S. Naval Service. He gallantly gave his life for his country.

2597 ◆ ANDERSON, BEAUFORD THEODORE
Rank: Technical Sergeant (highest rank: First Lieutenant)
Service: U.S. Army
Birthday: 6 July 1922
Place of Birth: Eagle, Waukesha County, Wisconsin
Entered Service at: Soldiers Grove, Crawford County, Wisconsin
Unit: Weapons Platoon, Company A, 1st Battalion, 381st Infantry, 96th Infantry Division

2598 ◆ *ANDERSON, RICHARD BEATTY

Served as: Mortar Section Sergeant
Battle or Place of Action: Okinawa, Ryukyu Islands
Date of Action: 13 April 1945
G.O. Number, Date: 63, 27 June 1946
Date of Presentation: 14 June 1946
Place of Presentation: The White House, Presented by Pres. Harry S. Truman
Citation: He displayed conspicuous gallantry and intrepidity above and beyond the call of duty. When a powerfully conducted predawn Japanese counterattack struck his unit's flank, he ordered his men to take cover in an old tomb, and then, armed only with a carbine, faced the onslaught alone. After emptying one magazine at point-blank range into the screaming attackers, he seized an enemy mortar dud and threw it back among the charging Japs, killing several as it burst. Securing a box of mortar shells, he extracted the safety pins, banged the bases upon a rock to arm them and proceeded alternately to hurl shells and fire his piece among the fanatical foe, finally forcing them to withdraw. Despite the protests of his comrades, and bleeding profusely from a severe shrapnel wound, he made his way to his company commander to report the action. T/Sgt. Anderson's intrepid conduct in the face of overwhelming odds accounted for 25 enemy killed and several machine guns and knee mortars destroyed, thus singlehandedly removing a serious threat to the company's flank.

2598 ◆ *ANDERSON, RICHARD BEATTY

Rank: Private First Class
Service: U.S. Marine Corps
Birthday: 26 June 1921
Place of Birth: Tacoma, Pierce County, Washington
Date of Death: 1 February 1944
Place of Death: Roi Island, Marshall Islands
Cemetery: New Tacoma Cemetery—Tacoma, Washington
Entered Service at: Washington
Unit: Company E, 2d Battalion, 23d Marines, 4th Marine Division
Battle or Place of Action: Roi Island, Kwajalein Atoll, Marshall Islands
Date of Action: 1 February 1944
Place of Presentation: Seattle, WA, presented by Rear Adm. J.A. Taffinder, Commandandant, 13th Naval District to his parents
Citation: For conspicuous gallantry and intrepidity at the risk of his life above and beyond the call of duty while serving with the 4th Marine Division during action against enemy Japanese forces on Roi Island, Kwajalein Atoll, Marshall Islands, 1 February 1944. Entering a shell crater occupied by three other marines, Pfc. Anderson was preparing to throw a grenade at an enemy position when it slipped from his hands and rolled toward the men at the bottom of the hole. With insufficient time to retrieve the armed weapon and throw it, Pfc. Anderson fearlessly chose to sacrifice himself and save his companions by hurling his body upon the grenade and taking the full impact of the explosion. His personal valor and exceptional spirit of loyalty in the face of almost certain death were in keeping with the highest traditions of the U.S. Naval Service. He gallantly gave his life for his country.

2599 ◆ *ANTOLAK, SYLVESTER

Rank: Sergeant
Service: U.S. Army
Place of Birth: Clairsville, Ohio
Date of Death: 24 May 1944
Place of Death: Near Cisterna di Littoria, Italy
Cemetery: A.B.M.C. Sicily-Rome Cemetery (C-12-13)—Nettuno, Italy
Entered Service at: Clairsville, Ohio
Unit: Company B, 15th Infantry, 3d Infantry Division
Battle or Place of Action: near Cisterna di Littoria, Italy
Date of Action: 24 May 1944
G.O. Number, Date: 89, 19 October 1945
Citation: Near Cisterna di Littoria, Italy, he charged 200 yards over flat, coverless terrain to destroy an enemy machine-gun nest during the second day of the offensive which broke through the German cordon of steel around the Anzio beachhead. Fully 30 yards in advance of his squad, he ran into withering enemy machine-gun, machine-pistol and rifle fire. Three times he was struck by bullets and knocked to the ground, but each time he struggled to his feet to continue his relentless advance. With one shoulder deeply gashed and his right arm shattered, he continued to rush directly into the enemy fire concentration with his submachine gun wedged under his uninjured arm until within 15 yards of the enemy strongpoint, where he opened fire at deadly close range, killing two Germans and forcing the remaining 10 to surrender. He reorganized his men and, refusing to seek medical attention so badly needed, chose to lead the way toward another strongpoint 100 yards distant. Utterly disregarding the hail of bullets concentrated upon him, he had stormed ahead nearly three-fourths of the space between strongpoints when he was instantly killed by hostile enemy fire. Inspired by his example, his squad went on to overwhelm the enemy troops. By his supreme sacrifice, superb fighting courage, and heroic devotion to the attack, Sgt. Antolak was directly responsible for eliminating 20 Germans, capturing an enemy machine gun, and clearing the path for his company to advance.

2600 ◆ ANTRIM, RICHARD NOTT

Rank: Commander (rank at time of action: Lieutenant) (highest rank: Rear Admiral)
Service: U.S. Navy
Birthday: 17 December 1907
Place of Birth: Peru, Miami County, Indiana
Date of Death: 8 March 1969
Place of Death: Mountain Home, Arkansas
Cemetery: Arlington National Cemetery (35-2613) (MH)—Arlington, Virginia
Entered Service at: Indiana
Unit: U.S.S. *Pope*
Served as: Executive Officer
Battle or Place of Action: Macassar, Celebes, Netherlands East Indies
Date of Action: April 1942
Date of Presentation: 30 January 1947

Place of Presentation: The White House, presented by Pres. Harry S. Truman
Citation: For conspicuous gallantry and intrepidity at the risk of his life above and beyond the call of duty while interned as a prisoner of war of the enemy Japanese in the city of Macassar, Celebes, Netherlands East Indies, in April 1942. Acting instantly on behalf of a naval officer who was subjected to a vicious clubbing by a frenzied Japanese guard venting his insane wrath upon the helpless prisoner, Comdr. (then Lt.) Antrim boldly intervened, attempting to quiet the guard and finally persuading him to discuss the charges against the officer. With the entire Japanese force assembled and making extraordinary preparations for the threatened beating, and with the tension heightened by 2,700 Allied prisoners rapidly closing in, Comdr. Antrim courageously appealed to the fanatic enemy, risking his own life in a desperate effort to mitigate the punishment. When the other had been beaten unconscious by 15 blows of a hawser and was repeatedly kicked by three soldiers to a point beyond which he could not survive, Comdr. Antrim gallantly stepped forward and indicated to the perplexed guards that he would take the remainder of the punishment, throwing the Japanese completely off balance in their amazement and eliciting a roar of acclaim from the suddenly inspired Allied prisoners. By his fearless leadership and valiant concern for the welfare of another, he not only saved the life of a fellow officer and stunned the Japanese into sparing his own life but also brought about a new respect for American officers and men and a great improvement in camp living conditions. His heroic conduct throughout reflects the highest credit upon Comdr. Antrim and the U.S. Naval Service.

2601 ◆ ATKINS, THOMAS E.

Rank: Private First Class
Service: U.S. Army
Birthday: 5 February 1921
Place of Birth: Campobello, Spartanburg County, South Carolina
Entered Service at: Campobello, Spartanburg County, South Carolina
Unit: Company A, 127th Infantry, 32d Infantry Division
Battle or Place of Action: Villa Verde Trail, Luzon, Philippine Islands
Date of Action: 10 March 1945
G.O. Number, Date: 95, 30 October 1945
Date of Presentation: 12 October 1945
Place of Presentation: The White House, presented by Pres. Harry S. Truman
Citation: He fought gallantly on the Villa Verde Trail, Luzon, Philippine Islands. With two companions he occupied a position on a ridge outside the perimeter defense established by the 1st Platoon on a high hill. At about 0300 hours, two companies of Japanese attacked with rifle and machine-gun fire, grenades, TNT charges and land mines, severely wounding Pfc. Atkins and killing his two companions. Despite the intense hostile fire and pain from his deep wound, he held his ground and returned heavy fire. After the attack was repulsed, he remained in his precarious position to repel any subsequent assaults instead of returning to the American lines for medical treatment. An enemy machine gun, set up within 20 yards of his foxhole, vainly attempted to drive him off or silence his gun. The Japanese repeatedly made fierce attacks, but for four hours Pfc. Atkins determinedly remained in his foxhole, bearing the brunt of each assault and maintaining steady and accurate fire until each charge was repulsed. At 7:00 A.M., 13 enemy dead lay in front of his position; he had fired 400 rounds, all he and his two dead companions possessed, and had used three rifles until each had jammed too badly for further operation. He withdrew during a lull to secure a rifle and more ammunition, and was persuaded to remain for medical treatment. While waiting, he saw a Japanese within the perimeter and, seizing a nearby rifle, killed him. A few minutes later, while lying on a litter, he discovered an enemy group moving up behind the platoon's lines. Despite his severe wounds he sat up, delivered heavy rifle fire against the group, and forced them to withdraw. Pfc. Atkins' superb bravery and his fearless determination to hold his post against the main force of repeated enemy attacks, even though painfully wounded, were major factors in enabling his comrades to maintain their lines against a numerically superior enemy force.

2602 ◆ *BAILEY, KENNETH DILLON

Rank: Major
Service: U.S. Marine Corps
Birthday: 21 October 1910
Place of Birth: Pawnee, Pawnee County, Oklahoma
Date of Death: 27 September 1942
Cemetery: Spring Hill Cemetery (MH)—Danville, Illinois
Entered Service at: Illinois
Unit: Company C, 1st Marine Raider Battalion
Served as: Commanding Officer
Battle or Place of Action: Henderson Field, Guadalcanal, Solomon Islands
Date of Action: 12-13 September 1942
Citation: For extraordinary courage and heroic conduct above and beyond the call of duty as commanding officer of Company C, 1st Marine Raider Battalion, during the enemy Japanese attack on Henderson Field, Guadalcanal, Solomon Islands, 12–13 September 1942. Completely reorganized following the severe engagement of the night before, Maj. Bailey's company, within an hour after taking its assigned position as reserve battalion between the main line and the coveted airport, was threatened on the right flank by the penetration of the enemy into a gap in the main line. In addition to repulsing this threat, while steadily improving his own desperately held position, he used every weapon at his command to cover the forced withdrawal of the main line before a hammering assault by superior enemy forces. After rendering invaluable service to the battalion commander in stemming the retreat, reorganizing the troops, and extending the reverse position to the left, Maj. Bailey, despite a severe head wound, repeatedly led his troops in fierce hand-to-hand combat for a period of 10 hours. His great personal valor while exposed to constant and merciless enemy fire and his indomitable fighting spirit inspired his troops to heights of heroic endeavor

which enabled them to repulse the enemy and hold Henderson Field. He gallantly gave his life in the service of his country.

2603 ◆ *BAKER, ADDISON EARL

Rank: Lieutenant Colonel
Service: U.S. Army Air Corps
Birthday: 1 January 1907
Place of Birth: Chicago, Cook County, Illinois
Date of Death: 1 August 1943
Place of Death: Ploesti, Rumania
Cemetery: A.B.M.C. Florence Cemetery (Wall of the Missing)—Florence, Italy
Entered Service at: Akron, Summit County, Ohio
Unit: 328th Bombardment Squadron, 93d Heavy Bombardment Group, 8th Air Force
Served as: Pilot of a B-24, Squadron Commander
Battle or Place of Action: Ploesti, Rumania
Date of Action: 1 August 1943
G.O. Number, Date: 20, 11 March 1944
Date of Presentation: 1944
Place of Presentation: Akron, Ohio
Citation: For conspicuous gallantry and intrepidity above and beyond the call of duty in action with the enemy on 1 August 1943. On this date he led his command, the 93d Heavy Bombardment Group, on a daring low-level attack against enemy oil refineries and installations at Ploesti, Rumania. Approching the target, his aircraft was hit by a large-caliber antiaircraft shell, seriously damaged, and set on fire. Ignoring the fact he was flying over terrain suitable for safe landing, he refused to jeopardize the mission by breaking up the lead formation and continued unswervingly to lead his group to the target upon which he dropped his bombs with devastating effect. Only then did he leave formation, but his valiant attempts to gain sufficient altitude for the crew to escape by parachute were unavailing and his aircraft crashed in flames after his successful efforts to avoid other planes in formation. By extraordinary flying skill, gallant leadership, and intrepidity, Lt. Col. Baker rendered outstanding, distinguished, and valorous service to our nation.

2604 ◆ *BAKER JR., THOMAS ALEXANDER

Rank: Sergeant (rank at time of action: Private)
Service: U.S. Army
Birthday: 25 June 1916
Place of Birth: Troy, Rensselaer County, New York
Date of Death: 12 July 1944
Cemetery: National Memorial Cemetery of the Pacific (F-162) (MH)—Honolulu, Hawaii
Entered Service at: Troy, Rensselaer County, New York
Unit: Company A, 105th Infantry, 27th Infantry Division
Battle or Place of Action: Saipan, Mariana Islands
Date of Action: 19 June-7 July 1944
G.O. Number, Date: 35, 9 May 1945
Citation: For conspicuous gallantry and intrepidity at the risk of his life above and beyond the call of duty at Saipan, Mariana Islands, 19 June to 7 July 1944. When his entire company was held up by fire from automatic-weapon and small-arms fire from strongly fortified enemy positions that commanded the view of the company, Sgt. (then Pvt.) Baker voluntarily took a bazooka and dashed alone to within 100 yards of the enemy. Through heavy rifle and machine-gun fire that was directed at him by the enemy, he knocked out the strongpoint, enabling his company to assault the ridge. Some days later while his company advanced across the open field flanked with obstructions and places of concealment for the enemy, Sgt. Baker again voluntarily took up a position in the rear to protect the company against surprise attack and came upon two heavily fortified enemy pockets manned by two officers and 10 enlisted men which had been bypassed. Without regard for such superior numbers, he unhesitatingly attacked and killed all of them. Five hundred yards farther, he discovered six men of the enemy who had concealed themselves behind our lines and destroyed all of them. On 7 July 1944, the perimeter of which Sgt. Baker was a part was attacked from three sides by from 3,000 to 5,000 Japanese. During the early stages of this attack, Sgt. Baker was seriously wounded, but he insisted on remaining in the line and fired at the enemy at ranges sometimes as close as five yards until his ammunition ran out. Without ammunition and with his own weapon battered to uselessness from hand-to-hand combat, he was carried about 50 yards to the rear by a comrade, who was then himself wounded. At this point Sgt. Baker refused to be moved any farther, stating that he preferred to be left to die rather than risk the lives of any more of his friends. A short time later, at his request, he was placed in a sitting position against a small tree. Another comrade, withdrawing, offered assistance. Sgt. Baker refused, insisting that he be left alone and given a soldier's pistol with its remaining eight rounds of ammunition. When last seen alive, Sgt. Baker was propped against a tree, pistol in hand, calmly facing the foe. Later Sgt. Baker's body was found in the same position, gun empty, with eight Japanese lying dead before him. His deeds were in keeping with the highest traditions of the U.S. Army.

2605 ◆ BARFOOT, VAN THOMAS

Rank: Second Lieutenant (rank at time of action: Technical Sergeant) (highest rank: Colonel)
Service: U.S. Army
Birthday: 15 June 1919
Place of Birth: Edinburg, Leake County, Mississippi
Entered Service at: Carthage, Leake County, Mississippi
Unit: 3d Platoon, Company L 3d Battalion, 157th Infantry, 45th Infantry Division
Served as: Platoon Sergeant
Battle or Place of Action: near Carano, Italy
Date of Action: 23 May 1944
G.O. Number, Date: 79, 4 October 1944
Date of Presentation: 28 September 1944
Place of Presentation: Epinal, France, presented by Lt. Gen. Alexander M. Patch III
Citation: For conspicuous gallantry and intrepidity at the risk of life above and beyond the call of duty on 23 May 1944, near Carano, Italy. With his platoon heavily engaged

during an assault against forces well-entrenched on commanding ground, 2d Lt. Barfoot (then T/Sgt.) moved off alone upon the enemy left flank. He crawled to the proximity of one machine-gun nest and made a direct hit on it with a hand grenade, killing two and wounding three Germans. He continued along the German defense line to another machine-gun emplacement, and with his tommy gun killed two and captured three soldiers. Members of another enemy machine-gun crew then abandoned their position and gave themselves up to Sgt. Barfoot. Leaving the prisoners for his support squad to pick up, he proceeded to mop up positions in the immediate area, capturing more prisoners, and bringing his total count to 17. Later that day, after he had reorganized his men and consolidated the newly captured ground, the enemy launched a fierce armored counterattack directly at his platoon positions. Securing a bazooka, Sgt. Barfoot took up an exposed position directly in front of three advancing Mark VI tanks. From a distance of 75 yards his first shot destroyed the track of the leading tank, effectively disabling it, while the other two changed direction toward the flank. As the crew of the disabled tank dismounted, Sgt. Barfoot killed three of them with his tommy gun. He continued onward into enemy terrain and destroyed a recently abandoned German fieldpiece with a demolition charge placed in the breech. While returning to his platoon position, Sgt. Barfoot, though greatly fatigued by his herculean efforts, assisted two of his seriously wounded men 1,700 yards to a position of safety. Sgt. Barfoot's extraordinary heroism, demonstration of magnificent valor, and aggressive determination in the face of point-blank fire are a perpetual inspiration to his fellow soldiers.

2606 ◆ BARRETT, CARLTON WILLIAM

Rank: Private (highest rank: Technical Sergeant)
Service: U.S. Army
Birthday: 24 November 1919
Place of Birth: Fulton, Oswego County, New York
Date of Death: 3 March 1986
Place of Death: Yountville, California
Cemetery: Napa Valley Memorial Gardens (MH)—Napa, California
Entered Service at: Albany, Albany County, New York
Unit: 18th Infantry, 1st Infantry Division
Battle or Place of Action: in the vicinity of St. Laurent-sur-Mer, France
Date of Action: 6 June 1944
G.O. Number, Date: 78, 2 October 1944
Citation: For gallantry and intrepidity at the risk of his life above and beyond the call of duty on 6 June 1944, in the vicinity of St. Laurent-sur-Mer, France. On the morning of D-day, Pvt. Barrett, landing in the face of extremely heavy enemy fire, was forced to wade ashore through neck-deep water. Disregarding the personal danger, he returned to the surf again and again to assist his floundering comrades and save them from drowning. Refusing to remain pinned down by the intense barrage of small-arms and mortar fire poured at the landing points, Pvt. Barrett, working with fierce determination, saved many lives by carrying casualties to an evacuation boat lying offshore. In addition to his assigned mission as guide, he carried dispatches the length of the fire-swept beach; he assisted the wounded; he calmed the shocked; he arose as a leader in the stress of the occasion. His coolness and his dauntless daring courage while constantly risking his life during a period of many hours had an inestimable effect on his comrades and is in keeping with the highest traditions of the U.S. Army.

2607 ◆ BASILONE, JOHN "MANILA JONN"

Rank: Sergeant (highest rank: Gunnery Sergeant)
Service: U.S. Marine Corps
Birthday: 4 November 1916
Place of Birth: Buffalo, Erie County, New York
Date of Death: 19 February 1945
Place of Death: Iwo Jima, Volcano Islands
Cemetery: Arlington National Cemetery (12-384) (MH)—Arlington, Virginia
Entered Service at: New Jersey
Unit: 1st Battalion, 7th Marines, 1st Marine Division
Battle or Place of Action: Lunga Area, Guadalcanal, Solomon Islands
Date of Action: 24-25 October 1942
Date of Presentation: 21 May 1943
Place of Presentation: Balcombe, Australia, presented by Maj. Gen. Alexander A. Vandegrift, Commanding Gen. 1st Marine Division
Citation: For extraordinary heroism and conspicuous gallantry in action against enemy Japanese forces, above and beyond the call of duty, while serving with the 1st Battalion, 7th Marines, 1st Marine Division in the Lunga area, Guadalcanal, Solomon Islands, on 24 and 25 October 1942. While the enemy was hammering at the Marines' defensive positions, Sgt. Basilone, in charge of two sections of heavy machine guns, fought valiantly to check the savage and determined assault. In a fierce frontal attack with the Japanese blasting his guns with grenades and mortar fire, one of Sgt. Basilone's sections, with its guncrews, was put out of action, leaving only two men able to carry on. Moving an extra gun into position, he placed it in action, then, under continual fire, repaired another and personally manned it, gallantly holding his line until replacements arrived. A little later, with ammunition critically low and the supply lines cut off, Sgt. Basilone, at great risk of his life and in the face of continued enemy attack, battled his way through hostile lines with urgently needed shells for his gunners, thereby contributing in large measure to the virtual annihilation of a Japanese regiment. His great personal valor and courageous initiative were in keeping with the highest traditions of the U.S. Naval Service.

2608 ◆ *BAUER, HAROLD WILLIAM "INDIAN JOE"

Rank: Lieutenant Colonel
Service: U.S. Marine Corps
Birthday: 20 November 1908
Place of Birth: Woodruff, Kansas
Date of Death: 16 November 1942

Place of Death: 15 miles north of Russell Island, Solomon Islands
Cemetery: A.B.M.C. Manila Cemetery (Wall of the Missing)—Manila, Plilippine Islands
Entered Service at: Nebraska
Unit: Marine Fighting Squadron 212
Served as: Squadron Commander/Pilot of F4F Grumman Wildcat
Battle or Place of Action: Guadalcanal, Solomon Islands
Date of Action: 10 May-14 November 1942
Date of Issue: 11 May 1946
Citation: For extraordinary heroism and conspicuous courage as Squadron Commander of Marine Fighting Squadron 212 in the South Pacific area during the period from 10 May to 14 November 1942. Volunteering to pilot a fighter plane in defense of our positions on Guadalcanal, Lt. Col. Bauer participated in two air battles against enemy bombers and fighters outnumbering our force more than two to one, boldly engaged the enemy, and destroyed one Japanese bomber in the engagement of 28 September, and shot down four enemy fighter planes in flames on 3 October, leaving a fifth smoking badly. After successfully leading 26 planes on an over-water ferry flight of more than 600 miles on 16 October, Lt. Col. Bauer, while circling to land, sighted a squadron of enemy planes attacking the U.S.S. *McFarland*. Undaunted by the formidable opposition and with valor above and beyond the call of duty, he engaged the entire squadron and, although alone and his fuel supply nearly exhausted, fought his plane so brilliantly that four of the Japanese planes were destroyed before he was forced down by lack of fuel. His intrepid fighting spirit and distinctive ability as a leader and an airman, exemplified in his splendid record of combat achievement, were vital factors in the successful operations in the South Pacific area.
Notes: MIA

2609 ◆ *BAUSELL, LEWIS KENNETH

Rank: Corporal
Service: U.S. Marine Corps
Birthday: 17 April 1924
Place of Birth: Pulaski, Montgomery County, Virginia
Date of Death: 18 September 1944
Cemetery: A.B.M.C. Manila Cemetery (Wall of the Missing)—Manila, Philippine Islands
Entered Service at: Washington, D.C.
Unit: 1st Battalion, 5th Marines, 1st Marine Division
Battle or Place of Action: Peleliu Island, Palau Group
Date of Action: 15 September 1944
Citation: For conspicuous gallantry and intrepidity at the risk of his life above and beyond the call of duty while serving with the 1st Battalion, 5th Marines, 1st Marine Division, during action against enemy Japanese forces on Peleliu Island, Palau Group, 15 September 1944. Valiantly placing himself at the head of his squad, Cpl. Bausell led the charge forward against a hostile pillbox which was covering a vital sector of the beach and, as the first to reach the emplacement, immediately started firing his automatic into the aperture while the remainder of his men closed in on the enemy. Swift to act, as a Japanese grenade was hurled into their midst, Cpl. Bausell threw himself on the deadly weapon, taking the full blast of the explosion and sacrificing his own life to save his men. His unwavering loyalty and inspiring courage reflect the highest credit upon Cpl. Bausell and the U.S. Naval Service. He gallantly gave his life for his country.

2610 ◆ *BEAUDOIN, RAYMOND OVILA

Rank: First Lieutenant
Service: U.S. Army
Birthday: 15 July 1918
Place of Birth: Holyoke, Hampden County, Massachusetts
Date of Death: 6 April 1945
Cemetery: Notre Dame Cemetery (MH)—South Hadley, Massachusetts
Entered Service at: Holyoke, Hampden County, Massachusetts
Unit: Company F, 119th Infantry, 30th Infantry Division
Served as: Platoon Leader
Battle or Place of Action: Hamelin, Germany
Date of Action: 6 April 1945
G.O. Number, Date: 9, 25 January 1946
Citation: He was leading the 2d Platoon of Company F over flat, open terrain to Hamelin, Germany, when the enemy went into action with machine guns and automatic weapons, laying down a devastating curtain of fire which pinned his unit to the ground. By rotating men in firing positions he made it possible for his entire platoon to dig in, defying all the while the murderous enemy fire to encourage his men and to distribute ammunition. He then dug in himself at the most advanced position, where he kept up a steady fire, killing six hostile soldiers and directing his men in inflicting heavy casualties on the numerically superior opposing force. Despite these defensive measures, however, the position of the platoon became more precarious, for the enemy had brought up strong reinforcements and was preparing a counterattack. Three men, sent back at intervals to obtain ammunition and reinforcements, were killed by sniper fire. To relieve his command from the desperate situation, 1st Lt. Beaudoin decided to make a one-man attack on the most damaging enemy sniper nest 90 yards to the right flank, and thereby divert attention from the runner who would attempt to pierce the enemy's barrier of bullets and secure help. Crawling over completely exposed ground, he relentlessly advanced, undeterred by eight rounds of bazooka fire which threw mud and stones over him or by rifle fire which ripped his uniform. Ten yards from the enemy position he stood up and charged. At point-blank range he shot and killed two occupants of the nest; a third, who tried to bayonet him, he overpowered and killed with the butt of his carbine; and the fourth adversary was cut down by the platoon's rifle fire as he attempted to flee. He continued his attack by running toward a dugout, but there he was struck and killed by a burst from a machine gun. By his intrepidity, great fighting skill, and supreme devotion to his responsibility for the well-being of his platoon, 1st Lt. Beaudoin singlehandedly accomplished a mission that enabled a messenger to secure help which saved

the stricken unit and made possible the decisive defeat of the German forces.

2611 ◆ BELL, BERNARD PIOUS

Rank: Technical Sergeant
Service: U.S. Army
Birthday: 29 December 1911
Place of Birth: Grantsville, Calhoun County, West Virginia
Date of Death: 11 January 1971
Place of Death: Delano, Florida
Cemetery: Arlington National Cemetery (25-3840) (MH)—Arlington, Virginia
Entered Service at: New York, New York
Unit: Company I, 142d Infantry, 36th Infantry Division
Battle or Place of Action: Mittelwihr, France
Date of Action: 18 December 1944
G.O. Number, Date: 73, 30 August 1945
Date of Presentation: 23 August 1945
Place of Presentation: The White House, presented by Pres. Harry S. Truman
Citation: For fighting gallantly at Mittelwihr, France. On the morning of 18 December 1944, he led a squad against a schoolhouse held by enemy troops. While his men covered him, he dashed toward the building, surprised two guards at the door, and took them prisoner without firing a shot. He found that other Germans were in the cellar. These he threatened with hand grenades, forcing 26 in all to emerge and surrender. His squad then occupied the building and prepared to defend it against powerful enemy action. The next day, the enemy poured artillery and mortar barrages into the position, disrupting communications which T/Sgt. Bell repeatedly repaired under heavy small-arms fire as he crossed dangerous terrain to keep his company commander informed of his squad's situation. During the day, several prisoners were taken and other Germans killed when hostile forces were attracted to the schoolhouse by the sound of captured German weapons fired by the Americans. At dawn the next day the enemy prepared to assault the building. A German tank fired round after round into the structure, partially demolishing the upper stories. Despite this heavy fire, T/Sgt. Bell climbed to the second floor and directed artillery fire which forced the hostile tank to withdraw. He then adjusted mortar fire on large forces of enemy foot soldiers attempting to reach the American position and, when this force broke and attempted to retire, he directed deadly machine-gun and rifle fire into their disorganized ranks. Calling for armored support to blast out the German troops hidden behind a wall, he unhesitatingly exposed himself to heavy small-arms fire to stand beside a friendly tank and tell its occupants where to rip holes in walls protecting approaches to the school building. He then trained machine guns on the gaps and mowed down all hostile troops attempting to cross the openings to get closer to the school building. By his intrepidity and bold, aggressive leadership, T/Sgt. Bell enabled his eight-man squad to drive back approximately 150 of the enemy, killing at least 87 and capturing 42. Personally, he killed more than 20 and captured 33 prisoners.

2612 ◆ BENDER, STANLEY

Rank: Staff Sergeant (highest rank: Technical Sergeant)
Service: U.S. Army
Birthday: 31 October 1909
Place of Birth: Carlisle, West Virginia
Date of Death: 22 June 1994
Place of Death: Thacker, West Virginia
Cemetery: High Lawn Memorial Park (MH)—Oak Hill, West Virginia
Entered Service at: Chicago, Cook County, Illinois
Unit: Company E, 7th Infantry, 3d Infantry Division
Battle or Place of Action: La Lande, France
Date of Action: 17 August 1944
G.O. Number, Date: 7, 1 February 1945
Date of Presentation: 21 January 1945
Place of Presentation: France, presented by Lt. Gen. Alexander M. Patch III
Citation: For conspicuous gallantry and intrepidity at risk of life above and beyond the call of duty. On 17 August 1944, near La Lande, France, he climbed on top of a knocked-out tank, in the face of withering machine-gun fire which had halted the advance of his company, in an effort to locate the source of this fire. Although bullets ricocheted off the turret at his feet, he nevertheless remained standing upright in full view of the enemy for over two minutes. Locating the enemy machine guns on a knoll 200 yards away, he ordered two squads to cover him and led his men down an irrigation ditch, running a gauntlet of intense machine-gun fire, which completely blanketed 50 yards of his advance and wounded four of his men. While the Germans hurled hand grenades at the ditch, he stood his ground until his squad caught up with him, then advanced alone, in a wide flanking approach, to the rear of the knoll. He walked deliberately a distance of 40 yards, without cover, in full view of the Germans and under a hail of both enemy and friendly fire, to the first machine gun and knocked it out with a single short burst. Then he made his way through the strongpoint, despite bursting hand grenades, toward the second machine gun, 25 yards distant, whose two-man crew swung the machine gun around and fired two bursts at him, but he walked calmly through the fire and, reaching the edge of the emplacement, dispatched the crew. Signaling his men to rush the rifle pits, he then walked 35 yards further to kill an enemy rifleman and returned to lead his squad in the destruction of the eight remaining Germans in the strongpoint. His audacity so inspired the remainder of the assault company that the men charged out of their positions, shouting and yelling, to overpower the enemy roadblock and sweep into town, knocking out two antitank guns, killing 37 Germans, and capturing 26 others. He had sparked and led the assault company in an attack which overwhelmed the enemy, destroying a road block, taking a town, seizing intact three bridges over the Maravenne River, and capturing commanding terrain which dominated the area.

2613 ◆ *BENJAMIN JR., GEORGE

Rank: Private First Class
Service: U.S. Army

Birthday: 24 April 1919
Place of Birth: Philadelphia, Philadelphia County, Pennsylvania
Date of Death: 21 December 1944
Cemetery: A.B.M.C. Manila Cemetery (B-7-156)—Manila, Plilippine Islands
Entered Service at: Carney's Point, Salem County, New Jersey
Unit: Company A, 306th Infantry, 77th Infantry Division
Served as: Radio Operator
Battle or Place of Action: Leyte, Philippine Islands
Date of Action: 21 December 1944
G.O. Number, Date: 49, 28 June 1945
Place of Presentation: Presented by Brig. Gen. Ralph K. Robertson to his Widow
Citation: He was a radio operator, advancing in the rear of his company as it engaged a well-defended Japanese strongpoint holding up the progress of the entire battalion. When a rifle platoon supporting a light tank hesitated in its advance, he voluntarily and with utter disregard for personal safety left his comparatively secure position and ran across bullet-whipped terrain to the tank, waving and shouting to the men of the platoon to follow. Carrying his bulky radio and armed only with a pistol, he fearlessly penetrated intense machine-gun and rifle fire to the enemy position, where he killed one of the enemy in a foxhole and moved to annihilate the crew of a light machine gun. Heedless of the terrific fire now concentrated on him, he continued to spearhead the assault, killing two more of the enemy and exhorting the other men to advance, until he fell mortally wounded. After being evacuated to an aid station, his first thought was still of the American advance. Overcoming great pain he called for the battalion operations officer to report the location of enemy weapons and valuable tactical information he had secured in his heroic charge. The unwavering courage, the unswerving devotion to the task at hand, the aggressive leadership of Pfc. Benjamin were a source of great and lasting inspiration to his comrades and were to a great extent responsible for the success of the battalion's mission.

2614 ◆ BENNETT, EDWARD ANDREW

Rank: Corporal (highest rank: Major)
Service: U.S. Army
Birthday: 11 February 1920
Place of Birth: Middleport, Meigs County, Ohio
Date of Death: 2 May 1983
Place of Death: Campbell, California
Cemetery: Golden Gate National Cemetery (2-B-10714) (MH)—San Bruno, California
Entered Service at: Middleport, Meigs County, Ohio
Unit: Company B, 1st Battalion, 358th Infantry, 90th Infantry Division
Battle or Place of Action: Heckhuscheid, Germany
Date of Action: 1 February 1945
G.O. Number, Date: 95, 30 October 1945
Date of Presentation: 12 October 1945
Place of Presentation: The White House (Rose Garden), presented by Pres. Harry S. Truman
Citation: He was advancing with Company B across open ground to assault Heckhuscheid, Germany, just after dark when vicious enemy machine-gun fire from a house on the outskirts of the town pinned down the group and caused several casualties. He began crawling to the edge of the field in an effort to flank the house, persisting in this maneuver even when the hostile machine gunners located him by the light of burning buildings and attempted to cut him down as he made for the protection of some trees. Reaching safety, he stealthily made his way by a circuitous route to the rear of the buildings occupied by the German gunners. With his trench knife he killed a sentry on guard there and then charged into the darkened house. In a furious hand-to-hand struggle he stormed about a single room which harbored seven Germans. Three he killed with rifle fire, another he clubbed to death with the butt of his gun, and the three others he dispatched with his .45-caliber pistol. The fearless initiative, stalwart combat ability, and outstanding gallantry of Cpl. Bennett eliminated the enemy fire which was decimating his company's ranks and made it possible for the Americans to sweep all resistance from the town.

2615 ◆ *BENNION, MERVYN SHARP

Rank: Captain
Service: U.S. Navy
Birthday: 5 May 1887
Place of Birth: Vernon, Tooele County, Utah
Date of Death: 7 December 1941
Place of Death: Ohau, Territory of Hawaii
Cemetery: City Cemetery (MH)—Salt Lake City, Utah
Entered Service at: Utah
Unit: U.S.S. *West Virginia*
Served as: Commanding Officer
Battle or Place of Action: Pearl Harbor, Ohau, Territory of Hawaii
Date of Action: 7 December 1941
Citation: For conspicuous devotion to duty, extraordinary courage, and complete disregard of his own life, above and beyond the call of duty, during the attack on the Fleet in Pearl Harbor, by Japanese forces on 7 December 1941. As commanding officer of the U.S.S. *West Virginia*, after being mortally wounded, Capt. Bennion evidenced apparent concern only in fighting and saving his ship, and strongly protested against being carried from the bridge.

2616 ◆ *BERRY, CHARLES JOSEPH

Rank: Corporal
Service: U.S. Marine Corps
Birthday: 10 July 1923
Place of Birth: Lorain, Lorain County, Ohio
Date of Death: 3 March 1945
Place of Death: Iwo Jima, Volcano islands
Cemetery: Elmwood Cemetery (MH)—Lorain, Ohio
Entered Service at: Ohio
Unit: 1st Battalion, 26th Marines, 5th Marine Division
Served as: Machine Gunner
Battle or Place of Action: Iwo Jima, Volcano Islands

Date of Action: 3 March 1945
Citation: For conspicuous gallantry and intrepidity at the risk of his life above and beyond the call of duty as a member of a machine-gun crew, serving with the 1st Battalion, 26th Marines, 5th Marine Division, in action against enemy Japanese forces during the seizure of Iwo Jima in the Volcano Islands, on 3 March 1945. Stationed in the front lines, Cpl. Berry manned his weapon with alert readiness as he maintained a constant vigil with other members of his guncrew during the hazardous night hours. When infiltrating Japanese soldiers launched a surprise attack shortly after midnight in an attempt to overrun his position, he engaged in a pitched hand-grenade duel, returning the dangerous weapons with prompt and deadly accuracy until an enemy grenade landed in the foxhole. Determined to save his comrades, he unhesitatingly chose to sacrifice himself and immediately dived on the deadly missile, absorbing the shattering violence of the exploding charge in his own body and protecting the others from serious injury. Stouthearted and indomitable, Cpl. Berry fearlessly yielded his own life that his fellow marines might carry on the relentless battle against a ruthless enemy, and his superb valor and unfaltering devotion to duty in the face of certain death reflect the highest credit upon himself and upon the U.S. Naval Service. He gallantly gave his life for his country.

2617 ◆ BERTOLDO, VITO R.

Rank: Master Sergeant
Service: U.S. Army
Birthday: 1 December 1916
Place of Birth: Decatur, Macon County, Illinois
Date of Death: 23 July 1966
Cemetery: Golden Gate National Cemetery (C-52-A) (MH)—San Bruno, California
Entered Service at: Decatur, Macon County, Illinois
Unit: Company A, 242d Infantry, 42d Infantry Division
Battle or Place of Action: Hatten, France
Date of Action: 9-10 January 1945
G.O. Number, Date: 5, 10 January 1946
Citation: He fought with extreme gallantry while guarding two command posts against the assault of powerful infantry and armored forces which had overrun the battalion's main line of resistance. On the close approach of enemy soldiers, he left the protection of the building he defended and set up his gun in the street, there to remain for almost 12 hours driving back attacks while in full view of his adversaries and completely exposed to 88-mm, machine-gun, and small-arms fire. He moved back inside the command post, strapped his machine gun to a table, and covered the main approach to the building by firing through a window, remaining steadfast even in the face of 88-mm fire from tanks only 75 yards away. One shell blasted him across the room, but he returned to his weapon. When two enemy personnel carriers led by a tank moved toward his position, he calmly waited for the troops to dismount and then, with the tank firing directly at him, leaned out of the window and mowed down the entire group of more than 20 Germans. Some time later, removal of the command post to another building was ordered. M/Sgt. Bertoldo voluntarily remained behind, covering the withdrawal of his comrades and maintaining his stand all night. In the morning he carried his machine gun to an adjacent building used as the command post of another battalion and began a day-long defense of that position. He broke up a heavy attack, launched by a self-propelled 88-mm gun covered by a tank and about 15 infantrymen. Soon afterward another 88-mm weapon moved up to within a few feet of his position, and, placing the muzzle of its gun almost inside the building, fired into the room, knocking him down and seriously wounding others. An American bazooka team set the German weapon afire, and M/Sgt. Bertoldo went back to his machine gun dazed as he was and killed several of the hostile troops as they attempted to withdraw. It was decided to evacuate the command post under the cover of darkness, but before the plan could be put into operation the enemy began an intensive assault supported by fire from their tanks and heavy guns. Disregarding the devastating barrage, he remained at his post and hurled white phosphorous grenades into the advancing enemy troops until they broke and retreated. A tank less than 50 yards away fired at his stronghold, destroyed the machine gun, and blew him across the room again, but he once more returned to the bitter fight and, with a rifle, singlehandedly covered the withdrawal of his fellow soldiers when the post was finally abandoned. With inspiring bravery and intrepidity M/Sgt. Bertoldo withstood the attack of vastly superior forces for more than 48 hours without rest or relief, time after time escaping death only by the slightest margin while killing at least 40 hostile soldiers and wounding many more during his grim battle against the enemy hordes.

2618 ◆ BEYER, ARTHUR O.

Rank: Corporal
Service: U.S. Army
Birthday: 20 May 1909
Place of Birth: Rock Township, Mitchell County, Iowa
Date of Death: 17 February 1965
Place of Death: Near Buffalo, North Dakota
Cemetery: Immanuel Lutheran Church Cemetery—St. Ansgar, Iowa
Entered Service at: St. Ansgar, Mitchell County, Iowa
Unit: Company C, 603d Tank Destroyer Battalion
Battle or Place of Action: near Arloncourt, Belgium
Date of Action: 15 January 1945
G.O. Number, Date: 73, 30 August 1945
Date of Presentation: 23 August 1945
Place of Presentation: The White House, presented by Pres. Harry S. Truman
Citation: He displayed conspicuous gallantry in action. His platoon, in which he was a tank-destroyer gunner, was held up by antitank, machine-gun, and rifle fire from enemy troops dug in along a ridge about 200 yards to the front. Noting a machine-gun position in this defense line, he fired upon it with his 76-mm gun killing one man and silencing the weapon. He dismounted from his vehicle and, under direct enemy observation, crossed open ground to capture the two remaining members of the crew. Another machine gun, about 250 yards to the left, continued to fire on him. Through withering fire, he advanced on the position. Throwing a

grenade into the emplacement, he killed one crew member and again captured the two survivors. He was subjected to concentrated small-arms fire but, with great bravery, he worked his way a quarter mile along the ridge, attacking hostile soldiers in their foxholes with his carbine and grenades. When he had completed his self-imposed mission against powerful German forces, he had destroyed two machine-gun positions, killed eight of the enemy, and captured 18 prisoners, including two bazooka teams. Cpl. Beyer's intrepid action and unflinching determination to close with and destroy the enemy eliminated the German defense line and enabled his task force to gain its objective.

2619 ◆ *BIANCHI, WILLIBALD CHARLES

Rank: First Lieutenant (highest rank: Captain)
Service: U.S. Army
Birthday: 12 March 1915
Place of Birth: New Ulm, Brown County, Minnesota
Date of Death: 9 January 1945
Place of Death: At Sea POW ship sunk by A.A.C. Attack.
Cemetery: National Memorial Cemetery of the Pacific (MA-39) (MH)—Honolulu, Hawaii (marker only)
Entered Service at: New Ulm, Brown County, Minnesota
Unit: Philippine Scouts, 45th Infantry
Served as: Platoon Leader
Battle or Place of Action: near Bagac, Bataan Province, Philippine Islands
Date of Action: 3 February 1942
G.O. Number, Date: 11, 5 March 1942
Place of Presentation: Presented by Gen. Douglas MacArthur
Citation: For conspicuous gallantry and intrepidity above and beyond the call of duty in action with the enemy on 3 February 1942, near Bagac, Province of Bataan, Philippine Islands. When the rifle platoon of another company was ordered to wipe out two strong enemy machine-gun nests, 1st Lt. Bianchi, voluntarily and of his own initiative, advanced with the platoon leading part of the men. When wounded early in the action by two bullets through the left hand, he did not stop for first aid but discarded his rifle and began firing a pistol. He located a machine-gun nest and personally silenced it with grenades. When wounded the second time by two machine-gun bullets through the chest muscles, 1st Lt. Bianchi climbed to the top of an American tank, manned its antiaircraft machine gun, and fired into strongly held enemy position until knocked completely off the tank by a third severe wound.

2620 ◆ BIDDLE, MELVIN EARL

Rank: Private First Class
Service: U.S. Army
Birthday: 28 November 1923
Place of Birth: Daleville, Delaware County, Indiana
Entered Service at: Anderson, Madison County, Indiana
Unit: 1st Squad, 2d Platoon, Company B, 1st Battalion, 517th Parachute Infantry Regiment
Served as: Lead Scout/Rifleman
Battle or Place of Action: between Soy and Hotton, Belgium
Date of Action: 23-24 December 1944
G.O. Number, Date: 95, 30 October 1945
Date of Presentation: 12 October 1945
Place of Presentation: The White House, presented by Pres. Harry S. Truman
Citation: He displayed conspicuous gallantry and intrepidity in action against the enemy near Soy, Belgium, on 23 and 24 December 1944. Serving as lead scout during an attack to relieve the enemy-encircled town of Hotton, he aggressively penetrated a densely wooded area, advanced 400 yards until he came within range of intense enemy rifle fire, and within 20 yards of enemy positions killed three snipers with unerring marksmanship. Courageously continuing his advance an additional 200 yards, he discovered a hostile machine-gun position and dispatched its two occupants. He then located the approximate position of a well-concealed enemy machine-gun nest, and crawling forward threw hand grenades which killed two Germans and fatally wounded a third. After signaling his company to advance, he entered a determined line of enemy defense, cooly and deliberately shifted his position, and shot three more enemy soldiers. Undaunted by enemy fire, he crawled within 20 yards of a machine-gun nest, tossed his last hand grenade into the position, and after the explosion charged the emplacement firing his rifle. When night fell, he scouted enemy positions alone for several hours and returned with valuable information which enabled our attacking infantry and armor to knock out two enemy tanks. At daybreak he again led the advance and, when flanking elements were pinned down by enemy fire, without hesitation made his way toward a hostile machine-gun position and from a distance of 50 yards killed the crew and two supporting riflemen. The remainder of the enemy, finding themselves without automatic-weapon support, fled panic-stricken. Pfc. Biddle's intrepid courage and superb daring during his 20-hour action enabled his battalion to break the enemy grasp on Hotton with a minimum of casualties.

2621 ◆ *BIGELOW, ELMER CHARLES

Rank: Watertender First Class
Service: U.S. Naval Reserve
Birthday: 12 July 1920
Place of Birth: Hebron, McHenry County, Illinois
Date of Death: 15 February 1945
Cemetery: Linn-Hebron Cemetery—Hebron, Illinois
Entered Service at: Illinois
Unit: U.S.S. *Fletcher*
Served as: Watertender
Battle or Place of Action: off Corregidor Island, Philippine Islands
Date of Action: 14 February 1945
Place of Presentation: Great Lakes Naval Base, Illinois, presented by Vice Adm. A. S. Carpender, Commandant, Ninth Naval District to his mother, Mrs. Verna Perry
Citation: For conspicuous gallantry and intrepidity at the risk of his life above and beyond the call of duty while serving on board the U.S.S. *Fletcher* during action against enemy

Japanese forces off Corregidor Island in the Philippines, 14 February 1945. Standing topside when an enemy shell struck the *Fletcher*, Bigelow, acting instantly as the deadly projectile exploded into fragments which penetrated the No. 1 gun magazine and set fire to several powder cases, picked up a pair of fire extinguishers and rushed below in a resolute attempt to quell the raging flames. Refusing to waste the precious time required to don rescue-breathing apparatus, he plunged through the blinding smoke billowing out of the magazine hatch and dropped into the blazing compartment. Despite the acrid, burning powder smoke which seared his lungs with every agonizing breath, he worked rapidly and with instinctive sureness and succeeded in quickly extinguishing the fires and in cooling the cases and bulkheads, thereby preventing further damage to the stricken ship. Although he succumbed to his injuries on the following day, Bigelow, by his dauntless valor, unfaltering skill and prompt action in the critical emergency, had averted a magazine explosion which undoubtedly would have left the ship wallowing at the mercy of the furiously pounding Japanese guns on Corregidor, and his heroic spirit of self-sacrifice in the face of almost certain death enhanced and sustained the highest traditions of the U.S. Naval Service. He gallantly gave his life in the service of his country.

2622 ◆ BJORKLUND, ARNOLD L.

Rank: First Lieutenant
Service: U.S. Army
Birthday: 14 April 1918
Place of Birth: Clinton, Island County, Washington
Date of Death: 28 November 1979
Cemetery: Williamette National Cemetery (0-3446) (MH)—Portland, Oregon
Entered Service at: Seattle, King County, Washington
Unit: 142d Infantry Regiment, 36th Infantry Division
Served as: Platoon Leader
Battle or Place of Action: Altavilla, Italy
Date of Action: 13 September 1943
G.O. Number, Date: 73, 6 September 1944
Date of Presentation: 31 August 1944
Place of Presentation: The White House (Oval Office), presented by Pres. Franklin D. Roosevelt
Citation: For conspicuous gallantry and intrepidity at the risk of his life above and beyond the call of duty in action with the enemy near Altavilla, Italy, 13 September 1943. When his company attacked a German position on Hill 424, the first platoon led by 1st Lt. Bjorklund, moved forward on the right flank to the slope of the hill where it was pinned down by a heavy concentration of machine-gun and rifle fire. Ordering his men to give covering fire, with only three hand grenades, he crept and crawled forward to a German machine-gun position located on a terrace along the forward slope. Approaching within a few yards of the position, and while continuously exposed to enemy fire, he hurled one grenade into the nest, destroyed the gun, and killed three Germans. Discovering a second machine gun 20 yards to the right on a higher terrace, he moved under intense enemy fire to a point within a few yards and threw a second grenade into this position, destroying it and killing two more Germans. The first platoon was then able to advance 150 yards further up the slope to the crest of the hill, but was again stopped by the fire from a heavy enemy mortar on the reverse slope. First Lt. Bjorklund located the mortar and worked his way under little cover to within ten yards of its position and threw his third grenade, destroying the mortar, killing two of the Germans, and forcing the remaining three to flee. His actions permitted the platoon to take its objective.

2623 ◆ BLOCH, ORVILLE EMIL

Rank: First Lieutenant (highest rank: Colonel)
Service: U.S. Army
Birthday: 10 February 1915
Place of Birth: Big Falls, Waupaca County, Wisconsin
Date of Death: 28 May 1983
Place of Death: Manson, Washington
Cemetery: Evergreen Washelli Memorial Park (MH)—Seattle, Washington
Entered Service at: Streeter, Stutsman County, North Dakota
Unit: Company E, 338th Infantry, 85th Infantry Division
Served as: Platoon Leader
Battle or Place of Action: near Firenzuola, Italy
Date of Action: 22 September 1944
G.O. Number, Date: 9, 10 February 1945
Date of Presentation: 6 February 1945
Place of Presentation: Firenzuloa, Italy, presented by Gen. Mark Clark
Citation: For conspicuous gallantry and intrepidity at the risk of life above and beyond the call of duty. First Lt. Bloch undertook the task of wiping out five enemy machine-gun nests that had held up the advance in that particular sector for one day. Gathering three volunteers from his platoon, the patrol snaked their way to a big rock, behind which a group of three buildings and five machine-gun nests were located. Leaving the three men behind the rock, he attacked the first machine-gun nest alone charging into furious automatic fire, kicking over the machine gun and capturing the machine-gun crew of five. Pulling the pin from a grenade, he held it ready in his hand and dashed into the face of withering automatic fire toward this second machine-gun nest located at the corner of an adjacent building 15 yards distant. When within 20 feet of the machine gun he hurled the grenade, wounding the machine gunner, the other two members of the crew fleeing into a door of the house. Calling one of his volunteer group to accompany him, they advanced to the opposite end of the house, there contacting a machine-gun crew of five running toward this house. First Lt. Bloch and his men opened fire on the enemy crew, forcing them to abandon this machine gun and ammunition and flee into the same house. Without a moment's hesitation, 1st Lt. Bloch, unassisted, rushed through the door into a hail of small-arms fire, firing his carbine from the hip, and captured the seven occupants, wounding three of them. First Lt. Bloch with his men then proceeded to a third house where they discovered an abandoned enemy machine gun and detected another enemy machine-gun nest at the next corner of the building. The crew of six

spotted 1st Lt. Bloch the instant he saw them. Without a moment's hesitation he dashed toward them. The enemy fired pistols wildly in his direction and vanished through a door of the house, 1st Lt. Bloch following them through the door, firing his carbine from the hip, wounding two of the enemy and capturing six. Altogether 1st Lt. Bloch had singlehandedly captured 19 prisoners, wounding six of them and eliminating a total of five enemy machine-gun nests. His gallant and heroic actions saved his company many casualties and permitted them to continue the attack with new inspiration and vigor.

2624 ◆ BOLDEN, PAUL LUTHER

Rank: Staff Sergeant (highest rank: Master Sergeant)
Service: U.S. Army
Birthday: 15 June 1922
Place of Birth: Hobbes Island, Alabama
Date of Death: 21 May 1979
Cemetery: Moons Cemetery (MH)—Owens Crossroads, Alabama
Entered Service at: Madison, Madison County, Alabama
Unit: Company I, 120th Infantry, 30th Infantry Division
Battle or Place of Action: Petit-Coo, Belgium
Date of Action: 23 December 1944
G.O. Number, Date: 73, 30 August 1945
Place of Presentation: The White House, presented by Pres. Harry S. Truman
Citation: He voluntarily attacked a formidable enemy strongpoint in Petit-Coo, Belgium, on 23 December 1944, when his company was pinned down by extremely heavy automatic and small-arms fire coming from a house 200 yards to the front. Mortar and tank artillery shells pounded the unit, when S/Sgt. Bolden and a comrade, on their own initiative, moved forward in a hail of bullets to eliminate the ever-increasing fire from the German position. Crawling ahead to close with what they knew was a powerfully armed, vastly superior force, the pair reached the house and took up assault positions, S/Sgt. Bolden under a window, his comrade across the street where he could deliver covering fire. In rapid succession, S/Sgt. Bolden hurled a fragmentation grenade and a white phosphorous grenade into the building; and then, fully realizing that he faced tremendous odds, rushed to the door, threw it open, and fired into 35 SS troopers who were trying to reorganize themselves after the havoc wrought by the grenades. Twenty Germans died under fire of his submachine gun before he was struck in the shoulder, chest, and stomach by part of a burst which killed his comrade across the street. He withdrew from the house, waiting for the surviving Germans to come out and surrender. When none appeared in the doorway, he summoned his ebbing strength, overcame the extreme pain he suffered, and boldly walked back into the house, firing as he went. He had killed the remaining 15 enemy soldiers when his ammunition ran out. S/Sgt. Bolden's heroic advance against great odds, his fearless assault, and his magnificent display of courage in reentering the building where he had been severely wounded cleared the path for his company and insured the success of its mission.

2625 ◆ BOLTON, CECIL HAMILTON

Rank: First Lieutenant
Service: U.S. Army
Birthday: 7 October 1908
Place of Birth: Crawfordville, Wakulla County, Florida
Date of Death: 22 January 1965
Cemetery: Fort Sam Houston National Cemetery (P-C-22-J) (MH)—San Antonio, Texas
Entered Service at: Huntsville, Madison County, Alabama
Unit: Company E, 413th Infantry, 104th Infantry Division
Battle or Place of Action: Mark River, Holland
Date of Action: 2 November 1944
G.O. Number, Date: 74, 1 September 1945
Date of Presentation: 23 August 1945
Place of Presentation: The White House, presented by Pres. Harry S. Truman
Citation: As leader of the weapons platoon of Company E, 413th Infantry, on the night of 2 November 1944, he fought gallantly in a pitched battle which followed the crossing of the Mark River in Holland. When two machine guns pinned down his company, he tried to eliminate, with mortar fire, their grazing fire which was inflicting serious casualties and preventing the company's advance from an area rocked by artillery shelling. In the moonlight it was impossible for him to locate accurately the enemy's camouflaged positions; but he continued to direct fire until wounded severely in the legs and rendered unconscious by a German shell. When he recovered consciousness he instructed his unit and then crawled to the forward rifle platoon positions. Taking a two-man bazooka team on his voluntary mission, he advanced chest-deep in chilling water along a canal toward one enemy machine gun. While the bazooka team covered him, he approached alone to within 15 yards of the hostile emplacement in a house. He charged the remaining distance and killed the two gunners with hand grenades. Returning to his men he led them through intense fire over open ground to assault the second German machine gun. An enemy sniper who tried to block the way was dispatched, and the trio pressed on. When discovered by the machine-gun crew and subjected to direct fire, 1st Lt. Bolton killed one of the three gunners with carbine fire, and his two comrades shot the others. Continuing to disregard his wounds, he led the bazooka team toward an 88-mm artillery piece which was having telling effect on the American ranks, and approached once more through icy canal water until he could dimly make out the gun's silhouette. Under his fire direction, the two soldiers knocked out the enemy weapon with rockets. On the way back to his own lines he was again wounded. To prevent his men being longer subjected to deadly fire, he refused aid and ordered them back to safety, painfully crawling after them until he reached his lines, where he collapsed. First Lt. Bolton's heroic assaults in the face of vicious fire, his inspiring leadership, and continued aggressiveness even through suffering from serious wounds contributed in large measure to overcoming strong enemy resistance and made it possible for his battalion to reach its objective.

2626 ◆ BONG, RICHARD IRA

Rank: Major
Service: U.S. Army Air Corps
Birthday: 24 September 1920
Place of Birth: Superior, Douglas County, Wisconsin
Date of Death: 6 August 1945
Place of Death: Burbank, California
Cemetery: Poplar Cemetery (MH)—Poplar, Wisconsin
Entered Service at: Poplar, Douglas County, Wisconsin
Unit: 49th Fighter Group, 5th Fighter Command, 5th Air Force
Served as: Fighter Pilot of a P-38
Battle or Place of Action: over Borneo and Leyte, Philippine Islands
Date of Action: 10 October-15 November 1944
G.O. Number, Date: 90, 8 December 1944
Date of Presentation: 12 December 1944
Place of Presentation: Tacloban air strip, Leyte, Philippine Islands, presented by Gen. Douglas MacArthur
Citation: For conspicuous gallantry and intrepidity in action above and beyond the call of duty in the southwest Pacific area from 10 October to 15 November 1944. Though assigned to duty as gunnery instructor and neither required nor expected to perform combat duty, Maj. Bong voluntarily and at his own urgent request engaged in repeated combat missions, including unusually hazardous sorties over Balikpapan, Borneo, and in the Leyte area of the Philippines. His aggressiveness and daring resulted in his shooting down eight enemy airplanes during this period.

2627 ◆ *BONNYMAN JR., ALEXANDER "SANDY"

Rank: First Lieutenant
Service: U.S. Marine Corps Reserve
Birthday: 2 May 1910
Place of Birth: Atlanta, Fulton County, Georgia
Date of Death: 22 November 1943
Cemetery: Santa Fe National Cemetery (MA-84) (MH) ('In Memory' marker)—Santa Fe, New Mexico; National Memorial Cemetery of the Pacific (Wall of the Missing)—Honolulu, Hawaii
Entered Service at: New Mexico
Unit: 2d Battalion Shore Party, 8th Marines, 2d Marine Division
Served as: Executive Officer
Battle or Place of Action: Betio Island, Tarawa Atoll, Gilbert Islands
Date of Action: 20-22 November 1943
Citation: For conspicuous gallantry and intrepidity at the risk of his life above and beyond the call of duty as executive officer of the 2d Battalion Shore Party, 8th Marines, 2d Marine Division, during the assault against enemy Japanese-held Tarawa in the Gilbert Islands, 20–22 November 1943. Acting on his own initiative when assault troops were pinned down at the far end of Betio Pier by the overwhelming fire of Japanese shore batteries, 1st Lt. Bonnyman repeatedly defied the blasting fury of the enemy bombardment to organize and lead the besieged men over the long, open pier to the beach and then, voluntarily obtaining flamethrowers and demolitions, organized his pioneer shore party into assault demolitionists and directed the blowing of several hostile installations before the close of D-day. Determined to effect an opening in the enemy's strongly organized defense line the following day, he voluntarily crawled approximately 40 yards forward of our lines and placed demolitions in the entrance of a large Japanese emplacement as the initial move in his planned attack against the heavily garrisoned, bombproof installation which was stubbornly resisting despite the destruction early in the action of a large number of Japanese who had been inflicting heavy casualties on our forces and holding up our advance. Withdrawing only to replenish his ammunition, he led his men in a renewed assault, fearlessly exposing himself to the merciless slash of hostile fire as he stormed the formidable bastion, directed the placement of demolition charges in both entrances, and seized the top of the bombproof position, flushing more than 100 of the enemy who were instantly cut down and effecting the annihilation of approximately 150 troops inside the emplacement. Assailed by additional Japanese after he had gained his objective, he made a heroic stand on the edge of the structure, defending his strategic position with indomitable determination in the face of the desperate charge and killing three of the enemy before he fell, mortally wounded. By his dauntless fighting spirit, unrelenting aggressiveness and forceful leadership throughout three days of unremitting, violent battle, 1st Lt. Bonnyman had inspired his men to heroic effort, enabling them to beat off the counterattack and break the back of hostile resistance in that sector for an immediate gain of 400 yards with no further casualties to our forces in this zone. He gallantly gave his life for his country.

2628 ◆ *BOOKER, ROBERT D.

Rank: Private
Service: U.S. Army
Birthday: 11 July 1920
Place of Birth: Callaway, Custer County, Nebraska
Date of Death: 9 April 1943
Cemetery: Rose Hill Cemetery—Callaway, Nebraska
Entered Service at: Callaway, Custer County, Nebraska
Unit: Company B, 133d Infantry, 34th Infantry Division
Battle or Place of Action: near Fondouk, Tunisia
Date of Action: 9 April 1943
G.O. Number, Date: 34, 25 April 1944
Citation: For conspicuous gallantry and intrepidity at the risk of life above and beyond the call of duty in action. On 9 April 1943 in the vicinity of Fondouk, Tunisia, Pvt. Booker, while engaged in action against the enemy, carried a light machine gun and a box of ammunition over 200 yards of open ground. He continued to advance despite the fact that two enemy machine guns and several mortars were using him as an individual target. Although enemy artillery also began to register on him, upon reaching his objective he immediately commenced firing. After being wounded he silenced one enemy machine gun and was beginning to fire at the other when he received a second mortal wound. With his last

remaining strength he encouraged the members of his squad and directed their fire. Pvt. Booker acted without regard for his own safety. His initiative and courage against insurmountable odds are an example of the highest standard of self-sacrifice and fidelity to duty.

2629 ◆ *BORDELON, WILLIAM JAMES

Rank: Staff Sergeant
Service: U.S. Marine Corps
Birthday: 25 December 1920
Place of Birth: San Antonio, Bexar County, Texas
Date of Death: 20 November 1943
Cemetery: National Memorial Cemetery of the Pacific (A-481) (MH)—Honolulu, Hawaii
Entered Service at: Texas
Unit: 1st Battalion, 18th Marines, tactically attached to the 2d Marine Division
Battle or Place of Action: Tarawa, Gilbert Islands
Date of Action: 20 November 1943
Date of Presentation: June 1944
Place of Presentation: Alamo Stadium, Texas, presented by Pres. Franklin D. Roosevelt to his parents
Citation: For valorous and gallant conduct above and beyond the call of duty as a member of an assault engineer platoon of the 1st Battalion, 18th Marines, tactically attached to the 2d Marine Division, in action against the Japanese-held atoll of Tarawa in the Gilbert Islands, 20 November 1943. Landing in the assault waves under withering enemy fire which killed all but four of the men in his tractor, S/Sgt. Bordelon Hurriedly made demolition charges and personally put two pillboxes out of action. Hit by enemy machine-gun fire just as a charge exploded in his hand while assaulting a third position, he courageously remained in action and, although out of demolition, provided himself with a rifle and furnished fire coverage for a group of men scaling the seawall. Disregarding his own serious condition, he unhesitatingly went to the aid of one of his demolition men, wounded and calling for help in the water, rescuing this man and another who had been hit by enemy fire while attempting to make the rescue. Still refusing first aid for himself, he again made up demolition charges and singlehandedly assaulted a fourth Japanese machine-gun position, but was instantly killed when caught in a final burst of fire from the enemy. S/Sgt. Bordelon's great personal valor during a critical phase of securing the limited beachhead was a contributing factor in the ultimate occupation of the island, and his heroic determination throughout three days of violent battle reflects the highest credit upon the U.S. Naval Service. He gallantly gave his life for his country.

2630 ◆ *BOYCE JR., GEORGE W. G.

Rank: Second Lieutenant
Service: U.S. Army
Place of Birth: New York, New York
Date of Death: 23 July 1944
Cemetery: A.B.M.C. Manila Cemetery (A-4-189)—Manila, Philippine Islands
Entered Service at: Cornwall, Orange County, New York
Unit: Troop A, 112th Cavalry Regimental Combat Team
Battle or Place of Action: near Afua, New Guinea
Date of Action: 23 July 1944
G.O. Number, Date: 25, 7 April 1945
Date of Issue: 12 February 1945
Citation: For conspicuous gallantry and intrepidity at the risk of his life above and beyond the call of duty near Afua, New Guinea, on 23 July 1944. 2d Lt. Boyce's troop, having been ordered to the relief of another unit surrounded by superior enemy forces, moved out, and upon gaining contact with the enemy, the two leading platoons deployed and built up a firing line. 2d Lt. Boyce was ordered to attack with his platoon and make the main effort on the right of his troop. He launched his attack but after a short advance encountered such intense rifle, machine-gun, and mortar fire that the forward movement of his platoon was temporarily halted. A shallow depression offered a route of advance, and he worked his squad up this avenue of approach in order to close with the enemy. He was promptly met by a volley of hand grenades, one falling between himself and the men immediately following. Realizing at once that the explosion would kill or wound several of his men, he promptly threw himself upon the grenade and smothered the blast with his own body. By thus deliberately sacrificing his life to save those of his men, this officer exemplified the highest traditions of the U.S. Armed Forces.

2631 ◆ BOYINGTON, GREGORY "PAPPY"

Rank: Major (highest rank: Colonel Ret.)
Service: U.S. Marine Corps Reserve
Birthday: 4 December 1912
Place of Birth: Coeur D'Alene, Kootenai County, Idaho
Date of Death: 11 January 1988
Place of Death: Fresno, California
Cemetery: Arlington National Cemetery (7A-150) (MH)—Arlington, Virginia
Entered Service at: Washington
Unit: Marine Squadron 214, Marine Air Group 11, 1st Marine Air Wing
Served as: Commanding Officer
Battle or Place of Action: Central Solomons area
Date of Action: 12 September 1943—3 January 1944
Date of Presentation: March 1944 (received 5 October 1945)
Place of Presentation: The White House, by Pres. Franklin D. Roosevelt to his Mother; presented by Pres. Harry S. Truman in 1945 to him
Citation: For extraordinary heroism and valiant devotion to duty as commanding officer of Marine Fighting Squadron 214 in action against enemy Japanese forces in the central Solomons area from 12 September 1943 to 3 January 1944. Consistently outnumbered throughout successive hazardous flights over heavily defended hostile territory, Maj. Boyington struck at the enemy with daring and courageous persistence, leading his squadron into combat with devastating results to Japanese shipping, shore installations, and aerial forces. Resolute in his efforts to inflict crippling damage on the

enemy, Maj. Boyington led a formation of 24 fighters over Kahili on 17 October and, persistently circling the airdrome where 60 hostile aircraft were grounded, boldly challenged the Japanese to send up planes. Under his brilliant command, our fighters shot down 20 enemy craft in the ensuing action without the loss of a single ship. A superb airman and determined fighter against overwhelming odds, Maj. Boyington personally destroyed 26 of the many Japanese planes shot down by his squadron and, by his forceful leadership, developed the combat readiness in his command, which was a distinctive factor in the Allied aerial achievements in this vitally strategic area.
Notes: POW

2632 ◆ BRILES, HERSCHEL FLOYD "PETE"

Rank: Staff Sergeant (highest rank: First Sergeant)
Service: U.S. Army
Birthday: 7 February 1914
Place of Birth: Colfax, Jasper County, Iowa
Date of Death: 17 July 1994
Place of Death: Mitchellville, Iowa
Cemetery: Waveland Cemetery (MH)—Prairie City, Iowa
Entered Service at: Fort Des Moines, Polk County, Iowa
Unit: Company C, 899th Tank Destroyer Battalion, attached to the 9th Infantry Division
Served as: Squad Leader
Battle or Place of Action: Scherpenseel, Germany
Date of Action: 20 November 1944
G.O. Number, Date: 77, 10 September 1945
Date of Presentation: 23 August 1945
Place of Presentation: The White House, presented by Pres. Harry S. Truman
Citation: He was leading a platoon of destroyers across an exposed slope near Scherpenseel, Germany, on 20 November 1944, when they came under heavy enemy artillery fire. A direct hit was scored on one of the vehicles, killing one man, seriously wounding two others, and setting the destroyer afire. With a comrade, S/Sgt. Briles left the cover of his own armor and raced across ground raked by artillery and small-arms fire to the rescue of the men in the shattered destroyer. Without hesitation, he lowered himself into the burning turret, removed the wounded, and then extinguished the fire. From a position he assumed the next morning, he observed hostile infantrymen advancing. With his machine gun, he poured such deadly fire into the enemy ranks that an entire pocket of 55 Germans surrendered, clearing the way for a junction between American units which had been held up for two days. Later that day, when another of his destroyers was hit by a concealed enemy tank, he again left protection to give assistance. With the help of another soldier, he evacuated two wounded under heavy fire and, returning to the burning vehicle, braved death from exploding ammunition to put out the flames. By his heroic initiative and complete disregard for personal safety, S/Sgt. Briles was largely responsible for causing heavy enemy casualties, forcing the surrender of 55 Germans, making possible the salvage of our vehicles, and saving the lives of wounded comrades.

2633 ◆ BRITT, MAURICE LEE (FOOTSIE)

Rank: Captain (rank at time of action: Lieutenant) (highest rank: Captain)
Service: U.S. Army
Birthday: 29 June 1919
Place of Birth: Carlisle, Lonoke County, Arkansas
Entered Service at: Lonoke, Lonoke County, Arkansas
Unit: Company L, 3d Battalion, 30th Infantry, 3d Infantry Division
Served as: Company Commander
Battle or Place of Action: North of Mignano, Italy
Date of Action: 10 November 1943
G.O. Number, Date: 23, 24 March 1944
Date of Presentation: 7 June 1944
Place of Presentation: University of Arkansas, Little Rock, Arkansas, presented by Gen. Harry Collins
Citation: For conspicuous gallantry and intrepidity at the risk of his life above and beyond the call of duty. Disdaining enemy hand grenades and close-range machine pistols, machine guns, and rifles, Lt. Britt inspired and led a handful of his men in repelling a bitter counterattack by approximately 100 Germans against his company positions north of Mignano, Italy, on the morning of 10 November 1943. During the intense firefight, Lt. Britt's canteen and field glasses were shattered; a bullet pierced his side; his chest, face, and hands were covered with grenade wounds. Despite his wounds, for which he refused to accept medical attention until ordered to do so by his battalion commander following the battle, he personally killed five and wounded an unknown number of Germans, wiped out one enemy machine-gun crew, fired five clips of carbine and an undetermined amount of M-1 rifle ammunition, and threw 32 fragmentation grenades. His bold, aggressive actions, utterly disregarding superior enemy numbers, resulted in capture of four Germans, two of them wounded, and enabled several captured Americans to escape. Lt. Britt's undaunted courage and prowess in arms were largely responsible for repulsing a German counterattack which, if successful, would have isolated his battalion and destroyed his company.

2634 ◆ *BROSTROM, LEONARD C.

Rank: Private First Class
Service: U.S. Army
Birthday: 23 November 1919
Place of Birth: Preston, Franklin County, Idaho
Date of Death: 28 October 1944
Cemetery: Preston Cemetery District (MH)—Preston, Idaho
Entered Service at: Preston, Franklin County, Idaho
Unit: Company F, 17th Infantry Regiment, 7th Infantry Division
Served as: Rifleman
Battle or Place of Action: near Dagami, Leyte, Philippine Islands
Date of Action: 28 October 1944
G.O. Number, Date: 104, 15 November 1945
Date of Presentation: 29 November 1945

Place of Presentation: Preston, Idaho, presented by Brig. Gen. Robert M. Hardaway to his Father
Citation: He was a rifleman with an assault platoon which ran into powerful resistance near Dagami, Leyte, Philippine Islands, on 28 October 1944. From pillboxes, trenches, and spider holes so well-camouflaged that they could be detected at no more than 20 yards, the enemy poured machine-gun and rifle fire, causing severe casualties in the platoon. Realizing that a key pillbox in the center of the strongpoint would have to be knocked out if the company were to advance, Pfc. Brostrom, without orders and completely ignoring his own safety, ran forward to attack the pillbox with grenades. He immediately became the prime target for all the riflemen in the area, as he rushed to the rear of the pillbox and tossed grenades through the entrance. Six enemy soldiers left a trench in a bayonet charge against the heroic American, but he killed one and drove the others off with rifle fire. As he threw more grenades from his completely exposed position he was wounded several times in the abdomen and knocked to the ground. Although suffering intense pain and rapidly weakening from loss of blood, he slowly rose to his feet and once more hurled his deadly missiles at the pillbox. As he collapsed, the enemy began fleeing from the fortification and were killed by riflemen of his platoon. Pfc. Brostrom died while being carried from the battlefield, but his intrepidity and unhesitating willingness to sacrifice himself in a one-man attack against overwhelming odds enabled his company to reorganize against attack and annihilate the entire enemy position.

2635 ◆ BROWN JR., BOBBIE EVAN

Rank: Captain
Service: U.S. Army
Birthday: 2 September 1903
Place of Birth: Dublin, Laurens County, Georgia
Date of Death: 8 November 1971
Place of Death: Highland Falls, New York
Cemetery: Arlington National Cemetery (46-1021-17) (MH)—Arlington, Virginia
Entered Service at: Atlanta, Fulton County, Georgia
Unit: Company C, 18th Infantry, 1st Infantry Division
Served as: Company Commander
Battle or Place of Action: Crucifix Hill, Aachen, Germany
Date of Action: 8 October 1944
G.O. Number, Date: 74, 1 September 1945
Date of Presentation: 23 August 1945
Place of Presentation: The White House, presented by Pres. Harry S. Truman
Citation: He commanded Company C, 18th Infantry Regiment, on 8 October 1944, when it, with the Ranger Platoon of the 1st Battalion, attacked Crucifix Hill, a key point in the enemy's defense of Aachen, Germany. As the leading rifle platoon assaulted the first of many pillboxes studding the rising ground, heavy fire from a flanking emplacement raked it. An intense artillery barrage fell on the American troops which had been pinned down in an exposed position. Seeing that the pillboxes must be neutralized to prevent the slaughter of his men, Capt. Brown obtained a pole charge and started forward alone toward the first pillbox, about 100 yards away. Hugging the ground while enemy bullets whipped around him, he crawled and then ran toward the aperture of the fortification, rammed his explosive inside and jumped back as the pillbox and its occupants were blown up. He rejoined the assault platoon, secured another pole charge, and led the way toward the next pillbox under continuous artillery mortar, automatic and small-arms fire. He again ran forward and placed his charge in the enemy fortification, knocking it out. He then found that fire from a third pillbox was pinning down his company; so he returned to his men, secured another charge, and began to creep and crawl toward the hostile emplacement. With heroic bravery he disregarded opposing fire and worked ahead in the face of bullets streaming from the pillbox. Finally reaching his objective, he stood up and inserted his explosive, silencing the enemy. He was wounded by a mortar shell but refused medical attention and, despite heavy hostile fire, moved swiftly among his troops exhorting and instructing them in subduing powerful opposition. Later, realizing the need for information of enemy activity beyond the hill, Capt. Brown went out alone to reconnoiter. He observed possible routes of enemy approach and several times deliberately drew enemy fire to locate gun emplacements. Twice more, on this self-imposed mission, he was wounded; but he succeeded in securing information which led to the destruction of several enemy guns and enabled his company to throw back two powerful counterattacks with heavy losses. Only when Company C's position was completely secure did he permit treatment of his three wounds. By his indomitable courage, fearless leadership, and outstanding skill as a soldier, Capt. Brown contributed in great measure to the taking of Crucifix Hill, a vital link in the American line encircling Aachen.

2636 ◆ BULKELEY, JOHN DUNCAN

Rank: Lieutenant Commander (highest rank: Vice Admiral)
Service: U.S. Navy
Birthday: 19 August 1911
Place of Birth: San Antonio, Bexar County, Texas
Entered Service at: Texas
Unit: Motor Torpedo Boat Squadron 3
Served as: Commanding Officer
Battle or Place of Action: Philippine Waters
Date of Action: 7 December 1941—10 April 1942
Date of Presentation: 4 August 1942
Place of Presentation: The White House, presented by Pres. Franklin D. Roosevelt
Citation: For extraordinary heroism, distinguished service, and conspicuous gallantry above and beyond the call of duty as commander of Motor Torpedo Boat Squadron 3, in Philippine waters during the period from 7 December 1941 to 10 April 1942. The remarkable achievement of Lt. Comdr. Bulkeley's command in damaging or destroying a notable number of Japanese enemy planes, surface combatant and merchant ships, and in dispersing landing parties and land-based enemy forces during the four months and eight days of operation without benefit of repairs, overhaul, or maintenance

facilities for his squadron, is believed to be without precedence in this type of warfare. His dynamic forcefulness and daring in offensive action, his brilliantly planned and skillfully executed attacks, supplemented by a unique resourcefullness and ingenuity, characterize him as an outstanding leader of men and a gallant and intrepid seaman. These qualities coupled with a complete disregard for his own personal safety reflect great credit upon him and the Naval Service.

2637 ◆ BURKE, FRANCIS XAVIER

Rank: First Lieutenant
Service: U.S. Army
Birthday: 29 September 1918
Place of Birth: New York, New York
Date of Death: 6 September 1988
Cemetery: Veterans Memorial Cemetery (KN-1894) (MH)—Arneytown, New Jersey
Entered Service at: Jersey City, Hudson County, New Jersey
Unit: Company D, 1st Battalion, 15th Infantry, 3d Infantry Division
Served as: Battalion Transportation Officer
Battle or Place of Action: Nuremberg, Germany
Date of Action: 17 April 1945
G.O. Number, Date: 4, 9 January 1946
Date of Presentation: 18 December 1945
Place of Presentation: The White House, presented by Pres. Harry S. Truman
Citation: He fought with extreme gallantry in the streets of war-torn Nuremberg, Germany, where the 1st Battalion, 15th Infantry, was engaged in rooting out fanatical defenders of the citadel of Nazism. As battalion transportation officer he had gone forward to select a motor-pool site, when, in a desire to perform more than his assigned duties and participate in the fight, he advanced beyond the lines of the forward riflemen. Detecting a group of about 10 Germans making preparations for a local counterattack, he rushed back to a nearby American company, secured a light machine gun with ammunition, and daringly opened fire on this superior force, which deployed and returned his fire with machine pistols, rifles, and rocket launchers. From another angle a German machine gun tried to blast him from his emplacement, but 1st Lt. Burke killed this guncrew and drove off the survivors of the unit he had originally attacked. Giving his next attention to enemy infantrymen in ruined buildings, he picked up a rifle and dashed more than 100 yards through intense fire and engaged the Germans from behind an abandoned tank. A sniper nearly hit him from a cellar only 20 yards away, but he dispatched this adversary by running directly to the basement window, firing a full clip into it and then plunging through the darkened aperture to complete the job. He withdrew from the fight only long enough to replace his jammed rifle and secure grenades, then reengaged the Germans. Finding his shots ineffective, he pulled the pins from two grenades, and, holding one in each hand, rushed the enemy-held building, hurling his missiles just as the enemy threw a potato-masher grenade at him. In the triple explosion the Germans were wiped out and 1st Lt. Burke was dazed; but he emerged from the shower of debris that engulfed him, recovered his rifle, and went on to kill three more Germans and meet the charge of a machine pistolman, whom he cut down with three calmly delivered shots. He then retired toward the American lines and there assisted a platoon in a raging, 30-minute fight against formidable armed hostile forces. This enemy group was repulsed, and the intrepid fighter moved to another friendly group which broke the power of a German unit armed with a 20-mm gun in a fierce firefight. In four hours of heroic action, 1st Lt. Burke singlehandedly killed 11 and wounded three enemy soldiers and took a leading role in engagements in which an additional 29 enemy were killed or wounded. His extraordinary bravery and superb fighting skill were an inspiration to his comrades, and his entirely voluntary mission into exremely dangerous territory hastened the fall of Nuremberg, in his battalion's sector.

2638 ◆ *BURR, ELMER J.

Rank: First Sergeant
Service: U.S. Army
Birthday: 11 May 1908
Place of Birth: Neenah, Winnebago County, Wisconsin
Date of Death: 24 December 1942
Cemetery: Oak Hill Cemetery—Neenah, Wisconsin
Entered Service at: Menasha, Winnebago County, Wisconsin
Unit: Company I, 127th Infantry, 32d Infantry Division
Battle or Place of Action: Buna, New Guinea
Date of Action: 24 December 1942
G.O. Number, Date: 66, 11 October 1943
Citation: For conspicuous gallantry and intrepidity in action above and beyond the call of duty. During an attack near Buna, New Guinea, on 24 December 1942, 1st Sgt. Burr saw an enemy grenade strike near his company commander. Instantly and with heroic self-sacrifice he threw himself upon it, smothering the explosion with his body. 1st Sgt. Burr thus gave his life in saving that of his commander.

2639 ◆ BURR, HERBERT HOOVER

Rank: Staff Sergeant (rank at time of action: Private First Class)
Service: U.S. Army
Birthday: 13 September 1920
Place of Birth: St. Joseph, Buchanan County, Missouri
Date of Death: 8 February 1990
Cemetery: Mount Washington Cemetery (MH)—Independence, Missouri
Entered Service at: Kansas City, Clay County, Missouri
Unit: Company C, 41st Tank Battalion, 11th Armored Division
Served as: Bow Gunner
Battle or Place of Action: Dorrmoschel, Germany
Date of Action: 19 March 1945
G.O. Number, Date: 73, 30 August 1945
Date of Presentation: 23 August 1945
Place of Presentation: The White House, presented by Pres. Harry S. Truman

Citation: He displayed conspicuous gallantry during action when the tank in which he was bow gunner was hit by an enemy rocket, which severely wounded the platoon sergeant and forced the remainder of the crew to abandon the vehicle. Deafened, but otherwise unhurt, S/Sgt. Burr immediately climbed into the driver's seat and continued on the mission of entering the town to reconnoiter road conditions. As he rounded a turn he encountered an 88-mm antitank gun at point-blank range. Realizing that he had no crew, no one to man the tank's guns, he heroically chose to disregard his personal safety in a direct charge on the German weapon. At considerable speed he headed straight for the loaded gun, which was fully manned by enemy troops who had only to pull the lanyard to send a shell into his vehicle. So unexpected and daring was his assault that he was able to drive his tank completely over the gun, demolishing it and causing its crew to flee in confusion. He then skillfully sideswiped a large truck, overturned it, and wheeling his lumbering vehicle, returned to his company. When medical personnel who had been summoned to treat the wounded sergeant could not locate him, the valiant soldier ran through a hail of sniper fire to direct them to his stricken comrade. The bold, fearless determination of S/Sgt. Burr, his skill and courageous devotion to duty, resulted in the completion of his mission in the face of seemingly impossible odds.

2640 ◆ BURT, JAMES MONTROSS

Rank: Captain
Service: U.S. Army
Birthday: 18 July 1917
Place of Birth: Hinsdale, Berkshire County, Massachusetts
Entered Service at: Lee, Berkshire County, Massachusetts
Unit: Company B, 3d Battalion (Burt's Knights), 66th Armored Regiment, 2d Armored Division
Served as: Company Commander
Battle or Place of Action: Wurselen, Germany
Date of Action: 13 October 1944
G.O. Number, Date: 95, 30 October 1945
Date of Presentation: 12 October 1945
Place of Presentation: The White House, presented by Pres. Harry S. Truman
Citation: Capt. James M. Burt was in command of Company B, 66th Armored Regiment on the western outskirts of Wurselen, Germany on 13 October 1944, when his organization participated in a coordinated infantry-tank attack destined to isolate the large German garrision which was tenaciously defending the city of Aachen. In the first day's action, when infantrymen ran into murderous small-arms and mortar fire, Capt. Burt dismounted from his tank about 200 yards to the rear and moved forward on foot beyond the infantry positions, where, as the enemy concentrated a tremendous volume of fire upon him, he calmly motioned his tanks into good firing positions. As our attack gained momentum, he climbed aboard his tank and directed the action from the rear deck, exposed to hostile volleys which finally wounded him painfully in the face and neck. He maintained his dangerous post despite point-blank self-propelled gunfire until friendly artillery knocked out these enemy weapons, and then proceeded to the advanced infantry scout's positions to deploy his tanks for the defense of the gains which had been made. The next day, when the enemy counterattacked, he left cover and went 75 yards through heavy fire to assist the infantry battalion commander who was seriously wounded. For the next eight days, through rainy, miserable weather and under constant, heavy shelling, Capt. Burt held the combined forces together, dominating and controlling the critical situation through the sheer force of his heroic example. To direct artillery fire, on 15 October, he took his tank 300 yards into the enemy lines, where he dismounted and remained for one hour giving accurate data to friendly gunners. Twice more on that day he went into enemy territory under deadly fire on reconnaissance. In succeeding days he never faltered in his determination to defeat the strong German forces opposing him. Twice the tank in which he was riding was knocked out by enemy action, and each time he climbed aboard another vehicle and continued the fight. He took great risks to rescue wounded comrades and inflicted prodigious destruction on enemy personnel and material even though suffering from the wounds he received in the battle's opening phase. Capt. Burt's intrepidity and disregard for personal safety were so complete that his own men and the infantry who attached themselves to him were inspired to overcome the wretched and extremely hazardous conditions which accompanied one of the most bitter local actions of the war. The victory achieved closed the Aachen gap.

2641 ◆ BUSH, RICHARD EARL

Rank: Corporal (highest rank: Gunnery Sergeant)
Service: U.S. Marine Corps Reserve
Birthday: 23 December 1923
Place of Birth: Glasgow, Barren County, Kentucky
Entered Service at: Kentucky
Unit: 3d Squad, 3d Platoon, Company C, 1st Battalion, 4th Marines, 6th Marine Division
Served as: Squad Leader
Battle or Place of Action: Mount Yaetake, Okinawa, Ryukyu Islands
Date of Action: 16 April 1945
Date of Presentation: 5 October 1945
Place of Presentation: The White House, presented by Pres. Harry S. Truman
Citation: For conspicuous gallantry and intrepidity at the risk of his life above and beyond the call of duty as a squad leader serving with the 1st Battalion, 4th Marines, 6th Marine Division, in action against enemy Japanese forces, during the final assault against Mount Yaetake on Okinawa, Ryukyu Islands, 16 April 1945. Rallying his men forward with indomitable determination, Cpl. Bush boldly defied the slashing fury of concentrated Japanese artillery fire pouring down from the gun-studded mountain fortress to lead his squad up the face of the rocky precipice, sweep over the ridge, and drive the defending troops from their deeply entrenched position. With his unit, the first to break through the inner defense of Mount Yaetake, he fought relentlessly in the forefront of the action until seriously wounded and evacuated with others under protecting rocks. Although prostrate under

medical treatment when a Japanese hand grenade landed in the midst of the group, Cpl. Bush, alert and courageous in extremity as in battle, unhesitatingly pulled the deadly missile to himself and absorbed the shattering violence of the exploding charge in his body, thereby saving his fellow marines from severe injury or death despite the certain peril to his own life. By his valiant leadership and aggressive tactics in the face of savage opposition, Cpl. Bush contributed materially to the success of the sustained drive toward the conquest of this fiercely defended outpost of the Japanese Empire. His constant concern for the welfare of his men, his resolute spirit of self-sacrifice, and his unwavering devotion to duty throughout the bitter conflict enhance and sustain the highest traditions of the U.S. Naval Service.

2642 ◆ BUSH, ROBERT EUGENE

Rank: Hospital Apprentice First Class
Service: U.S. Navy Reserve
Birthday: 4 October 1926
Place of Birth: Tacoma, Pierce County, Washington
Entered Service at: Washington
Unit: 3d Platoon, Company G, 2d Battalion, 5th Marines, 1st Marine Division
Served as: Medical Corpsman
Battle or Place of Action: Okinawa Jima, Ryukyu Islands
Date of Action: 2 May 1945
Date of Presentation: 5 October 1945
Place of Presentation: The White House, presented by Pres. Harry S. Truman
Citation: For conspicuous gallantry and intrepidity at the risk of life above and beyond the call of duty while serving as medical corpsman with a rifle company, in action against enemy Japanese forces on Okinawa Jima, Ryukyu Islands, 2 May 1945. Fearlessly braving the fury of artillery, mortar, and machine-gun fire from strongly entrenched hostile positions, Bush constantly and unhesitatingly moved from one casualty to another to attend the wounded falling under the enemy's murderous barrages. As the attack passed over a ridge top, Bush was advancing to administer blood plasma to a marine officer lying wounded on the skyline when the Japanese launched a savage counterattack. In this perilously exposed position, he resolutely maintained the flow of lifegiving plasma. With the bottle held high in one hand, Bush drew his pistol with the other and fired into the enemy ranks until his ammunition was expended. Quickly seizing a discarded carbine, he trained his fire on the Japanese charging point-blank over the hill, accounting for six of the enemy despite his own serious wounds and the loss of one eye suffered during his desperate battle in defense of the helpless man. With the hostile force finally routed, he calmly disregarded his own critical condition to complete his mission, valiantly refusing medical treatment for himself until his officer patient had been evacuated, and collapsing only after attempting to walk to the battle aid station. His daring initiative, great personal valor, and heroic spirit of self-sacrifice in service of others reflect great credit upon Bush and enhance the finest traditions of the U.S. Naval Service.

2643 ◆ *BUTTS, JOHN EDWARD

Rank: Second Lieutenant
Service: U.S. Army
Birthday: 8 August 1922
Place of Birth: Medina, Orleans County, New York
Date of Death: 23 June 1944
Cemetery: St. Mary's Cemetery (MH)—Medina, New York
Entered Service at: Buffalo, Erie County, New York
Unit: Company E, 60th Infantry, 9th Infantry Division
Battle or Place of Action: Normandy, France
Date of Action: 14, 16, 23 June 1944
G.O. Number, Date: 58, 19 July 1945
Citation: Heroically led his platoon against an enemy in Normandy, France, on 14, 16, and 23 June 1944. Although painfully wounded on the 14th near Orglandes and again on the 16th while spearheading an attack to establish a bridgehead across the Douve River, he refused medical aid and remained with his platoon. A week later, near Flottemanville Hague, he led an assault on a tactically important and stubbornly defended hill studded with tanks, antitank guns, pillboxes, and machine-gun emplacements and protected by concentrated artillery and mortar fire. As the attack was launched, 2d Lt. Butts, at the head of his platoon, was critically wounded by German machine-gun fire. Although weakened by his injuries, he rallied his men and directed one squad to make a flanking movement while he alone made a frontal assault to draw the hostile fire upon himself. Once more he was struck, but by grim determination and sheer courage continued to crawl ahead. When within 10 yards of his objective, he was killed by direct fire. By his superb courage, unflinching valor, and inspiring actions, 2d Lt. Butts enabled his platoon to take a formidable strongpoint and contributed greatly to the success of his battalion's mission.

2644 ◆ *CADDY, WILLIAM ROBERT

Rank: Private First Class
Service: U.S. Marine Corps Reserve
Birthday: 8 August 1925
Place of Birth: Quincy, Norfolk County, Massachusetts
Date of Death: 3 March 1945
Cemetery: National Memorial Cemetery of the Pacific (C-81) (MH)—Honolulu, Hawaii
Entered Service at: Massachusetts
Unit: Company I, 3d Battalion, 26th Marines, 5th Marine Division
Served as: Rifleman
Battle or Place of Action: Iwo Jima, Volcano Islands
Date of Action: 3 March 1945
Date of Presentation: 8 September 1946
Citation: For conspicuous gallantry and intrepidity at the risk of his life above and beyond the call of duty while serving as a rifleman with Company I, 3d Battalion, 26th Marines, 5th Marine Division, in action against enemy Japanese forces during the seizure of Iwo Jima in the Volcano Islands, 3 March 1945. Consistently aggressive, Pfc. Caddy boldly defied shattering Japanese machine-gun and small-arms fire to move forward with his platoon leader and another marine

during the determined advance of his company through an isolated sector and, gaining the comparative safety of a shell hole, took temporary cover with his comrades. Immediately pinned down by deadly sniper fire from a well-concealed position, he made several unsuccessful attempts to again move forward and then, joined by his platoon leader, engaged the enemy in a fierce exchange of hand grenades until a Japanese grenade fell beyond reach in the shell hole. Fearlessly disregarding all personal danger, Pfc. Caddy instantly dived on the deadly missile, absorbing the exploding charge in his own body and protecting the others from serious injury. Stouthearted and indomitable, he unhesitatingly yielded his own life that his fellow marines might carry on the relentless battle against a fanatic enemy. His dauntless courage and valiant spirit of self-sacrifice in the face of certain death reflect the highest credit upon Pfc. Caddy and upon the U.S. Naval Service. He gallantly gave his life for his comrades.

2645 ◆ *CALLAGHAN, DANIEL JUDSON

Rank: Rear Admiral
Service: U.S. Navy
Birthday: 26 July 1890
Place of Birth: San Francisco, San Francisco County, California
Date of Death: 13 November 1942
Place of Death: Buried at Sea
Cemetery: A.B.M.C. Manila Cemetery (Wall of the Missing)—Manila, Philippine Islands
Entered Service at: Oakland, Alameda County, California
Unit: U.S.S. *San Francisco* (flagship)
Served as: Fleet Commander
Battle or Place of Action: Iron Bottom Sound off Savo Island, Solomon Islands
Date of Action: 12-13 November 1942
Date of Presentation: 9 December 1942
Place of Presentation: The White House, presented by Pres. Franklin D. Roosevelt to his Son
Citation: For extraordinary heroism and conspicuous intrepidity above and beyond the call of duty during action against enemy Japanese forces off Savo Island on the night of 12 to 13 November 1942. Although outbalanced in strength and numbers by a desperate and determined enemy, Rear Adm. Callaghan, with ingenious tactical skill and superb coordination of the units under his command, led his forces into battle against tremendous odds, thereby contributing decisively to the rout of a powerful invasion fleet, and to the consequent frustration of a formidable Japanese offensive. While faithfully directing close-range operations in the face of furious bombardment by superior enemy firepower, he was killed on the bridge of his flagship. His courageous initiative, inspiring leadership, and judicious foresight in a crisis of grave responsibility were in keeping with the finest traditions of the U.S. Naval Service. He gallantly gave his life in the defense of his country.

2646 ◆ CALUGAS, JOSE

Rank: Sergeant (highest rank: Captain)
Service: U.S. Army
Birthday: 29 December 1907
Place of Birth: Barrio Tagsing, Leon, Iloilo, Philippine Islands
Entered Service at: Fort Stotsenburg, Philippine Islands
Unit: Philippine Scouts, Battery B, 1st Battalion, 88th Field Artillery, 23d Division
Served as: Mess Sergeant
Battle or Place of Action: Culis, Bataan Province, Philippine Islands
Date of Action: 16 January 1942
G.O. Number, Date: 10, 24 February 1942
Date of Presentation: 30 April 1945
Place of Presentation: Pampanga, Camp Olivas, Philippine Islands, presented by Gen. George C. Marshall
Citation: The action for which the award was made took place near Culis, Bataan Province, Philippine Islands, on 16 January 1942. A battery gun position was bombed and shelled by the enemy until one gun was put out of commission and all the cannoneers were killed or wounded. Sgt. Calugas, a mess sergeant of another battery, voluntarily and without orders ran 1,000 yards across the shell-swept area to the gun position. There he organized a volunteer squad which placed the gun back in commission and fired effectively against the enemy, although the position remained under constant and heavy Japanese artillery fire.
Notes: POW

2647 ◆ *CANNON, GEORGE HAM

Rank: First Lieutenant
Service: U.S. Marine Corps
Birthday: 5 November 1915
Place of Birth: Webster Groves, St. Louis County, Missouri
Date of Death: 7 December 1941
Place of Death: Sand Island, Midway Islands
Cemetery: National Memorial Cemetery of the Pacific (C-1644) (MH)—Honolulu, Hawaii
Entered Service at: Michigan
Unit: Battery H, 6th Defense Battalion, Fleet Marine Force
Served as: Battery Commander
Battle or Place of Action: Sand Island, Midway Islands
Date of Action: 7 December 1941
Citation: For distinguished conduct in the line of his profession, extraordinary courage, and disregard for his own condition during the bombardment of Sand Island, Midway Islands, by Japanese forces on 7 December 1941. 1st Lt. Cannon, Battery Commander of Battery H, 6th Defense Battalion, Fleet Marine Force, U.S. Marine Corps, was at his command post when he was mortally wounded by enemy shellfire. He refused to be evacuated from his post until after his men who had been wounded by the same shell were evacuated and directed the reorganization of his command post until forcibly removed. As a result of his utter disregard of his own condition he died from loss of blood.

2648 ◆ *CAREY, ALVIN P.

Rank: Staff Sergeant
Service: U.S. Army

Birthday: 16 August 1916
Place of Birth: Lycippus, Pennsylvania
Date of Death: 23 August 1944
Cemetery: Ligonier Valley Cemetery—Ligonier, Pennsylvania
Entered Service at: Laughlintown, Westmoreland County, Pennsylvania
Unit: 38th Infantry, 2d Infantry Division
Served as: Section Leader
Battle or Place of Action: near Plougastel, Brittany, France
Date of Action: 23 August 1944
G.O. Number, Date: 37, 11 May 1945
Citation: For conspicuous gallantry and intrepidity at the risk of his life, above and beyond the call of duty, 23 August 1944. S/Sgt. Carey, leader of a machine-gun section, was advancing with his company in the attack on the strongly held enemy hill 154, near Plougastel, Brittany, France. The advance was held up when the attacking units were pinned down by intense enemy machine-gun fire from a pillbox 200 yards up the hill. From his position covering the right flank, S/Sgt. Carey displaced his guns to an advanced position and then, upon his own initiative, armed himself with as many hand grenades as he could carry and without regard for his personal safety started alone up the hill toward the pillbox. Crawling forward under its withering fire, he proceeded 150 yards when he met a German rifleman whom he killed with his carbine. Continuing his steady forward movement until he reached grenade-throwing distance, he hurled his grenades at the pillbox-opening in the face of intense enemy fire which wounded him mortally. Undaunted, he gathered his strength and continued his grenade attack until one entered and exploded within the pillbox, killing the occupants and putting their guns out of action. Inspired by S/Sgt. Carey's heroic act, the riflemen quickly occupied the position and overpowered the remaining enemy resistance in the vicinity.

2649 ♦ *CAREY JR., CHARLES F.

Rank: Technical Sergeant
Service: U.S. Army
Place of Birth: Canadian, Pittsburg County, Oklahoma
Cemetery: A.B.M.C. Ardennes Cemetery (C-29-12)—Neville-En-Condroz, Belgium
Entered Service at: Cheyenne, Laramie County, Wyoming
Unit: 397th Infantry, 100th Infantry Division
Served as: Platoon Commander
Battle or Place of Action: Rimling, France
Date of Action: 8-9 January 1945
G.O. Number, Date: 53, July 1945
Citation: He was in command of a antitank platoon when about 200 enemy infantrymen and 12 tanks attacked his battalion, overrunning part of its position. After losing his guns, T/Sgt. Carey, acting entirely on his own initiative, organized a patrol and rescued two of his squads from a threatened sector, evacuating those who had been wounded. He organized a second patrol and advanced against an enemy-held house from which vicious fire issued, preventing the free movement of our troops. Covered by fire from his patrol, he approached the house, killed two snipers with his rifle, and threw a grenade in the door. He entered alone and a few minutes later emerged with 16 prisoners. Acting on information he furnished, the American forces were able to capture an additional 41 Germans in adjacent houses. He assembled another patrol, and, under covering fire, moved to within a few yards of an enemy tank and damaged it with a rocket. As the crew attempted to leave their burning vehicle, he calmly shot them with his rifle, killing three and wounding a fourth. Early in the morning of 9 January, German infantry moved into the western part of the town and encircled a house in which T/Sgt. Carey had previously posted a squad. Four of the group escaped to the attic. By maneuvering an old staircase against the building, T/Sgt. Carey was able to rescue these men. Later that day, when attempting to reach an outpost, he was struck down by sniper fire. The fearless and aggressive leadership of T/Sgt. Carey, his courage in the face of heavy fire from superior enemy forces, provided an inspiring example for his comrades and materially helped his battalion to withstand the German onslaught.

2650 ♦ CARR, CHRIS

True Name: Legally changed from Christos H. Karaberis, under which name the medal was awarded
Rank: Sergeant (highest rank: Sergeant First Class)
Service: U.S. Army
Birthday: 6 April 1914
Place of Birth: Manchester, Hillsborough County, New Hampshire
Date of Death: 16 September 1970
Cemetery: Los Angeles National Cemetery (275-G-15) (MH)—Los Angeles, California
Entered Service at: Manchester, Hillsborough County, New Hampshire
Unit: Company L, 337th Infantry, 85th Infantry Division
Served as: Squad Leader
Battle or Place of Action: near Guignola, Italy
Date of Action: 1-2 October 1944
G.O. Number, Date: 97, 1 November 1945
Date of Presentation: 12 October 1945
Place of Presentation: The White House, presented by Pres. Harry S. Truman
Citation: Leading a squad of Company L, he gallantly cleared the way for his company's approach along a ridge toward its objective, the Casoni di Remagna. When his platoon was pinned down by heavy fire from enemy mortars, machine gun, machine pistols, and rifles, he climbed in advance of his squad on a maneuver around the left flank to locate and eliminate the enemy gun positions. Undeterred by deadly fire that ricocheted off the barren rocky hillside, he crept to the rear of the first machine gun and charged, firing his submachine gun. In this surprise attack he captured eight prisoners and turned them over to his squad before striking out alone for a second machine gun. Discovered in his advance and subjected to direct fire from hostile weapons, he leaped to his feet and ran forward, weaving and crouching, pouring automatic fire into the emplacement that killed four of its defenders and forced the surrender of a lone survivor. He again moved forward through heavy fire to attack a third

machine gun. When close to the emplacement, he closed with a nerve-shattering shout and burst of fire. Paralyzed by his whirlwind attack, all four gunners immediately surrendered. Once more advancing aggressively in the face of a thoroughly alerted enemy, he approached a point of high ground occupied by two machine guns which were firing on his company on the slope below. Charging the first of these weapons, he killed four of the crew and captured three more. The six defenders of the adjacent position, cowed by the savagery of his assault, immediately gave up. By his one-man attack, heroically and voluntarily undertaken in the face of tremendous risks, Sgt. Carr captured five enemy machine-gun positions, killed eight Germans, took 22 prisoners, cleared the ridge leading to his company's objective, and drove a deep wedge into the enemy line, making it possible for his battalion to occupy important, commanding ground.

2651 ◆ *CARSWELL JR., HORACE SEAVER

Rank: Major
Service: U.S. Army Air Corps
Birthday: 16 July 1916
Place of Birth: Fort Worth, Tarrant County, Texas
Date of Death: 26 October 1944
Place of Death: Asiatic Area
Cemetery: Oakwood Cemetery—Fort Worth, Texas
Entered Service at: San Angelo, Tom Green County, Texas
Unit: 374th Bombardment Squadron, 308th Bombardment Group, 14th Air Force
Served as: Pilot of a B-24 Bomber
Battle or Place of Action: Over the South China Sea, near Tungchen, China
Date of Action: 26 October 1944
G.O. Number, Date: 14, 4 February 1946
Citation: He piloted a B-24 bomber in a one-plane strike against a Japanese convoy in the South China Sea on the night of 26 October 1944. Taking the enemy force of 12 ships escorted by at least two destroyers by surprise, he made one bombing run at 600 feet, scoring a near miss on one warship and escaping without drawing fire. He circled and, fully realizing that the convoy was thoroughly alerted and would meet his next attack with a barrage of anitaircraft fire, began a second low-level run which culminated in two direct hits on a large tanker. A hail of steel from Japanese guns riddled the bomber, knocking out two engines, damaging a third, crippling the hydraulic system, puncturing one gasoline tank, ripping uncounted holes in the aircraft, and wounding the copilot; but by a magnificent display of flying skill, Maj. Carswell controlled the plane's plunge toward the sea and carefully forced it into a halting climb in the direction of the China shore. On reaching land, where it would have been possible to abandon the staggering bomber, one of the crew discovered that his parachute had been ripped by flak and rendered useless; the pilot, hoping to cross mountainous terrain and reach a base, continued onward until the third engine failed. He ordered the crew to bail out while he struggled to maintain altitude, and, refusing to save himself, chose to remain with his comrade and attempt a crash landing. He died when the plane struck a mountainside and burned. With consummate gallantry and intrepidity, Maj. Carswell gave his life in a supreme effort to save all members of his crew. His sacrifice, far beyond that required of him, was in keeping with the traditional bravery of America's war heroes.

2652 ◆ CASAMENTO, ANTHONY

Rank: Corporal
Service: U.S. Marine Corps
Birthday: 16 November 1920
Place of Birth: New York, New York
Date of Death: 18 July 1987
Place of Death: Northport, N.Y.
Cemetery: Long Island National Cemetery (DSS-79-A) (MH)—Farmingdale, New York
Entered Service at: New York, New York
Unit: Company D, 1st Battalion, 5th Marines, 1st Marine Division
Served as: Section Leader
Battle or Place of Action: Guadalcanal, Solomon Islands
Date of Action: 1 November 1942
of Presentation: 12 September 1980
Place of Presentation: The White House, presented by Pres. Jimmy Carter
Citation: For conspicuous gallantry and intrepidity at the risk of his life above and beyond the call of duty while serving with Company D, First Battalion, Fifth Marines, First Marine Division on Guadalcanal, British Solomon Islands, in action against the enemy Japanese forces on 1 November 1942. Serving as a leader of a machine gun section, Cpl. Casamento directed his unit to advance along a ridge near the Matanikau River where they engaged the enemy. He positioned his section to provide covering fire for two flanking units and to provide direct support for the main force of his company which was behind him. During the course of this engagement, all members of his section were either killed or severely wounded and he himself suffered multiple, grievous wounds. Nonetheless, Cpl. Casamento continued to provide critical supporting fire for the attack and in defense of his position. Following the loss of all effective personnel, he set up, loaded, and manned his unit's machine gun, tenaciously holding the enemy forces at bay. Cpl. Casamento singlehandedly engaged and destroyed one machine gun emplacement to his front and took under fire the other emplacement on the flank. Despite the heat and ferocity of the engagement, he continued to man his weapon and repeatedly repulsed multiple assaults by the enemy forces, thereby protecting the flanks of the adjoining companies and holding his position until the arrival of his main attacking force. Cpl. Casamento's courageous fighting spirit, heroic conduct, and unwavering dedication to duty reflected great credit upon himself and were in keeping with the highest traditions of the Marine Corps and the U.S. Naval Service.

2653 ◆ *CASTLE, FREDERICK WALKER

Rank: Brigadier General
Service: U.S. Army Air Corps
Birthday: 14 October 1908

Place of Birth: Manila, Philippine Island
Date of Death: 24 December 1944
Place of Death: Over Liege, Belgium
Cemetery: A.B.M.C. Henri-Chapelle Cemetery (D-13-53)—Henri-Chapelle, Belgium
Entered Service at: Mountain Lakes, Morris County, New Jersey
Unit: 4th Bombardment Wing, 8th Air Force
Served as: Wing Commander/Pilot of a B-17
Battle or Place of Action: Germany
Date of Action: 24 December 1944
G.O. Number, Date: 22, 28 February 1946
Place of Presentation: Mountain Lakes, New Jersey, pressented by Gen. Ira Eaker to his Mother
Citation: He was air commander and leader of more than 2,000 heavy bombers in a strike against German airfields on 24 December 1944. En route to the target, the failure of one engine forced him to relinquish his place at the head of the formation. In order not to endanger friendly troops on the ground below, he refused to jettison his bombs to gain speed maneuverability. His lagging, unescorted aircraft became the target of numerous enemy fighters which ripped the left wing with cannon shells, set the oxygen system afire, and wounded two members of the crew. Repeated attacks started fires in two engines, leaving the Flying Fortress in imminent danger of exploding. Realizing the hopelessness of the situation, the bail-out order was given. Without regard for his personal safety he gallantly remained alone at the controls to afford all other crewmembers an opportunity to escape. Still another attack exploded gasoline tanks in the right wing, and the bomber plunged earthward, carrying Gen. Castle to his death. His intrepidity and willing sacrifice of his life to save the members of his crew were in keeping with the highest traditions of the military service.

2654 ◆ CHAMBERS, JUSTICE MARION

Rank: Colonel (rank at time of action: Lieutenant Colonel)
Service: U.S. Marine Corps Reserve
Birthday: 2 February 1908
Place of Birth: Huntington, Cabell County, West Virginia
Date of Death: 29 July 1982
Cemetery: Arlington National Cemetery (6-5813-A-9) (MH)—Arlington, Virginia
Entered Service at: Washington, D.C.
Unit: 3d Assault Battalion Landing Team, 25th Marines, 4th Marine Division
Served as: Commanding Officer
Battle or Place of Action: Iwo Jima, Volcano Islands
Date of Action: 19-22 February 1945
Date of Presentation: 1 November 1950
Place of Presentation: The White House, presented by Pres. Harry S. Truman
Citation: For conspicuous gallantry and intrepidity at the risk of his life above and beyond the call of duty as commanding officer of the 3d Assault Battalion Landing Team, 25th Marines, 4th Marine Division, in action against enemy Japanese forces on Iwo Jima, Volcano Islands, from 19-22 February 1945. Under a furious barrage of enemy machine-gun and small-arms fire from the commanding cliffs on the right, Col. Chambers (then Lt. Col.) landed immediately after the initial assault waves of his battalion on D-day to find the momentum of the assault threatened by heavy casualties from withering Japanese artillery, mortar rockets, machine-gun, and rifle fire. Exposed to relentless hostile fire, he coolly reorganized his battle-weary men, inspiring them to heroic efforts by his own valor and leading them in an attack on the critical, impregnable high ground from which the enemy was pouring an increasing volume of fire directly onto troops ashore as well as amphibious craft in succeeding waves. Constantly in the front lines encouraging his men to push forward against the enemy's savage resistance, Col. Chambers led an eight-hour battle to carry the flanking ridge top and reduce the enemy's fields of aimed fire, thus protecting the vital foothold gained. In constant defiance of hostile fire while reconnoitering the entire regimental combat team zone of action, he maintained contact with adjacent units and forwarded vital information to the regimental commander. His zealous fighting spirit undiminished despite terrific casualties and the loss of most of his key officers, he again reorganized troops for renewed attack against the enemy's main line of resistance and was directing the fire of the rocket platoon when he fell, critically wounded. Evacuated under heavy Japanese fire, Col. Chambers, by forceful leadership, courage, and fortitude in the face of staggering odds, was directly instrumental in insuring the success of subsequent operations of the 5th Amphibious Corps on Iwo Jima, thereby sustaining and enhancing the finest traditions of the U.S. Naval Service.

2655 ◆ *CHELI, RALPH

Rank: Major
Service: U.S. Army Air Corps
Birthday: 29 October 1919
Place of Birth: San Francisco, San Francisco County, California
Date of Death: 6 March 1944
Cemetery: Jefferson Barracks National Cemetery (Group burial with 20 others) (78-930-934)—St. Louis, Missouri
Entered Service at: Brooklyn, Kings County, New York
Unit: 405th Bombardment Squadron, 38th Bombardment Group, 5th Air Force
Served as: Squadron Leader/Pilot of a B-25
Battle or Place of Action: near Wewak, New Guinea
Date of Action: 18 August 1943
G.O. Number, Date: 72, 28 October 1943
Citation: For conspicuous gallantry and intrepidity above and beyond the call of duty in action with the enemy. While Maj. Cheli was leading his squadron in a dive to attack the heavily defended Dagua airdrome, intercepting enemy aircraft centered their fire on his plane, causing it to burst into flames while still two miles from the objective. His speed would have enabled him to gain necessary altitude to parachute to safety, but this action would have resulted in his formation becoming disorganized and exposed to the enemy. Although a crash was inevitable, he courageously elected to continue leading the attack in his blazing plane. From a minimum altitude, the squadron made a devastating bombing and strafing attack on

the target. The mission completed, Maj. Cheli instructed his wingman to lead the formation and crashed into the sea.

2656 ◆ CHILDERS, ERNEST "CHIEF"

Rank: Second Lieutenant (highest rank: Colonel)
Service: U.S. Army
Birthday: 1 February 1918
Place of Birth: Broken Arrow, Tulsa County, Oklahoma
Entered Service at: Tulsa, Tulsa County, Oklahoma
Unit: Company C, 180th Infantry, 45th Infantry Division
Served as: Platoon Leader
Battle or Place of Action: Oliveto, Italy
Date of Action: 22 September 1943
G.O. Number, Date: 30, 8 April 1944
Date of Presentation: 22 April 1944
Place of Presentation: Naples, Italy, presented by Lt. Gen. Jacob L. Devers on battlefield
Citation: For conspicuous gallantry and intrepidity at risk of life above and beyond the call of duty in action on 22 September 1943, at Oliveto, Italy. Although 2d Lt. Childers previously had just suffered a fractured instep, he, with eight enlisted men, advanced up a hill toward enemy machine-gun nests. The group advanced to a rock wall overlooking a cornfield and 2d Lt. Childers ordered a base of fire laid across the field so that he could advance. When he was fired upon by two enemy snipers from a nearby house he killed both of them. He moved behind the machine-gun nests and killed all occupants of the nearer one. He continued toward the second one and threw rocks into it. When the two occupants of the nest raised up, he shot one. The other was killed by one of the eight enlisted men. 2d Lt. Childers continued his advance toward a house farther up the hill, and singlehandedly, captured an enemy mortar observer. The exceptional leadership, initiative, calmness under fire, and conspicuous gallantry displayed by 2d Lt. Childers were an inspiration to his men.

2657 ◆ CHOATE, CLYDE LEE

Rank: Staff Sergeant
Service: U.S. Army
Birthday: 28 June 1920
Place of Birth: West Frankfort, Franklin County, Illinois
Entered Service at: Anna, Union County, Illinois
Unit: 2d Platoon, Company C, 601st Tank Destroyer Battalion, 3d Infantry Division
Served as: Platoon Sergeant
Battle or Place of Action: Bruyeres, France
Date of Action: 25 October 1944
G.O. Number, Date: 75, 5 September 1945
Date of Presentation: 23 August 1945
Place of Presentation: The White House, presented by Pres. Harry S. Truman
Citation: He commanded a tank destroyer near Bruyeres, France, on 25 October 1944. Our infantry occupied a position on a wooded hill when, at dusk, an enemy Mark IV tank and a company of infantry attacked, threatening to overrun the American position and capture a command post 400 yards to the rear. S/Sgt. Choate's tank destroyer, the only weapon available to oppose the German armor, was set afire by two hits. Ordering his men to abandon the destroyer, S/Sgt. Choate reached comparative safety. He returned to the burning destroyer to search for comrades possibly trapped in the vehicle, risking instant death in an explosion which was imminent and braving enemy fire which ripped his jacket and tore the helmet from his head. Completing the search and seeing the tank and its supporting infantry overrunning our infantry in their shallow foxholes, he secured a bazooka and ran after the tank dodging from tree to tree and passing through the enemy's loose skirmish line. He fired a rocket from a distance of 20 yards, immobilizing the tank but leaving it able to spray the area with cannon and machine-gun fire. Running back to our infantry through vicious fire, he secured another rocket, and, advancing against a hail of machine-gun and small-arms fire reached a position 10 yards from the tank. His second shot shattered the turret. With his pistol he killed two of the crew as they emerged from the tank; and then running to the crippled Mark IV while enemy infantry sniped at him, he dropped a grenade inside the tank and completed its destruction. With their armor gone, the enemy infantry became disorganized and was driven back. S/Sgt. Choate's great daring in assaulting an enemy tank singlehandedly, his determination to follow the vehicle after it had passed his position, and his skill and crushing thoroughness in the attack prevented the enemy from capturing a battalion command post and turned a probable defeat into tactical success.

2658 ◆ *CHRISTENSEN, DALE ELDON

Rank: Second Lieutenant
Service: U.S. Army
Birthday: 31 May 1920
Place of Birth: Cameron Township, Audubon County, Iowa
Date of Death: 4 August 1944
Place of Death: near Afua, Dutch New Guinea
Cemetery: A.B.M.C. Manila Cemetery (A-12-200)—Manila, Philippine Islands
Entered Service at: Gray, Audubon County, Iowa
Unit: Troop E, 112th Cavalry Regiment
Served as: Platoon Leader
Battle or Place of Action: Driniumor River, New Guinea
Date of Action: 16-19 July 1944
G.O. Number, Date: 36, 10 May 1945
Citation: For conspicuous gallantry and intrepidity at the risk of his life above and beyond the call of duty along the Driniumor River, New Guinea, from 16-19 July 1944. 2d Lt. Christensen repeatedly distinguished himself by conspicuous gallantry above and beyond the call of duty in the continuous heavy fighting which occurred in this area from 16-19 July. On 16 July, his platoon engaged in a savage fire fight in which much damage was caused by one enemy machine gun effectively placed. 2d Lt. Christensen ordered his men to remain under cover, crept forward under fire, and at a range of 15 yards put the gun out of action with hand grenades. Again, on 19 July, while attacking an enemy position strong in mortars and machine guns, his platoon was pinned to the ground by intense fire. Ordering his men to remain under

cover, he crept forward alone to locate definitely the enemy automatic weapons and the best direction from which to attack. Although his rifle was struck by enemy fire and knocked from his hands he continued his reconnaissance, locating five enemy machine guns, destroyed one with hand grenades, and rejoined his platoon. He then led his men to the point selected for launching the attack and, calling encouragement, led the charge. This assault was successful and the enemy was driven from the positions with a loss of four mortars and 10 machine guns and leaving many dead on the field. On 4 August 1944, near Afua, Duch New Guinea, 2d Lt. Christensen was killed in action about two yards from his objective while leading his platoon in an attack on an enemy machine-gun position. 2d Lt. Christenson's leadership, intrepidity, and repeatedly demonstrated gallantry in action at the risk of his life, above and beyond the call of duty, exemplify the highest traditions of the U.S. Armed Forces.

2659 ◆ *CHRISTIAN, HERBERT F.

Rank: Private
Service: U.S. Army
Birthday: 18 June 1912
Place of Birth: Byesville, Guernsey County, Ohio
Date of Death: 3 June 1944
Cemetery: Greenwood Cemetery—Byesville, Ohio
Entered Service at: Steubenville, Jefferson County, Ohio
Unit: Battle Patrol, Company E, 15th Infantry, 3d Infantry Division
Battle or Place of Action: near Valmontone, Italy
Date of Action: 2-3 June 1944
G.O. Number, Date: 43, 30 May 1945
Citation: For conspicuous gallantry and intrepidity at the risk of life above and beyond the call of duty. On 2–3 June 1944, at 1:00 A.M., Pvt. Christian elected to sacrifice his life in order that his comrades might extricate themselves from an ambush. Braving massed fire of about 60 riflemen, three machine guns, and three tanks from positions only 30 yards distant, he stood erect and signaled to the patrol to withdraw. The whole area was brightly illuminated by enemy flares. Although his right leg was severed above the knee by cannon fire, Pvt. Christian advanced on his left knee and the bloody stump of his right thigh, firing his submachine gun. Despite excruciating pain, Pvt. Christian continued on his self-assigned mission. He succeeded in distracting the enemy and enabled his 12 comrades to escape. He killed three enemy soldiers almost at once. Leaving a trail of blood behind him, he made his way forward 20 yards, halted at a point within 10 yards of the enemy, and despite intense fire killed a machine-pistol man. Reloading his weapon, he fired directly into the enemy position. The enemy appeared enraged at the success of his ruse, concentrated 20-mm machine-gun, machine-pistol and rifle fire on him, yet he refused to seek cover. Maintaining his erect position, Pvt. Christian fired his weapon to the very last. Just as he emptied his submachine gun, the enemy bullets found their mark and Pvt. Christian slumped forward dead. The courage and spirit of self-sacrifice displayed by this soldier were an inspiration to his comrades and are keeping with the highest traditions of the Armed Forces.

2660 ◆ *CICCHETTI, JOSEPH J.

Rank: Private First Class
Service: U.S. Army
Birthday: 8 June 1923
Place of Birth: Waynesburg, Stark County, Ohio
Date of Death: 9 February 1945
Cemetery: Sandy Valley Cemetery (MH)—Waynesburg, Ohio
Entered Service at: Waynesburg, Stark County, Ohio
Unit: Company A, 148th Infantry, 37th Infantry Division
Battle or Place of Action: South Manila, Luzon, Philippine Islands
Date of Action: 9 February 1945
G.O. Number, Date: 115, 8 December 1945
Citation: He was with troops assaulting the first important line of enemy defenses. The Japanese had converted the partially destroyed Manila Gas Works and adjacent building into a formidable system of mutually supporting strongpoints from which they were concentrating machine-gun, mortar, and heavy artillery fire on the American forces. Casualties rapidly mounted, and the medical aidmen, finding it increasingly difficult to evacuate the wounded, called for volunteer litter bearers. Pfc. Cicchetti immediately responded, organized a litter team, and skillfully led it for more than four hours in rescuing 14 wounded men, constantly passing back and forth over a 400-yard route which was the impact area for a tremendous volume of the most intense enemy fire. On one return trip the path was blocked by machine-gun fire, but Pfc. Cicchetti deliberately exposed himself to draw the automatic fire which he neutralized with his own rifle while ordering the rest of the team to rush past to safety with the wounded. While gallantly continuing his work, he noticed a group of wounded and helpless soldiers some distance away and ran to their rescue although the enemy fire had increased to new fury. As he approached the casualties, he was struck in the head by a shell fragment, but with complete disregard for his gaping wound he continued to his comrades, lifted one and carried him on his shoulders 50 yards to safety. He then collapsed and died. By his skilled leadership, indomitable will, and dauntless courage, Pfc. Cicchetti saved the lives of many of his fellow soldiers at the cost of his own.

2661 ◆ CLARK, FRANCIS J.

Rank: Technical Sergeant
Service: U.S. Army
Birthday: 22 April 1912
Place of Birth: Whitehall, Washington County, New York
Date of Death: 20 October 1981
Cemetery: Evergreen Cemetery—Salem Township, New York
Entered Service at: Salem, New York
Unit: 3d Platoon, Company K, 109th Infantry, 28th Infantry Division
Served as: Squad Leader
Battle or Place of Action: near Kalborn, Luxembourg; near Sevenig, Germany
Date of Action: 12, 17 September 1944

2662 ◆ COLALILLO, MICHAEL "MIKE"

G.O. Number, Date: 77, 10 September 1945
Date of Presentation: 23 August 1945
Place of Presentation: The White House, presented by Pres. Harry S. Truman
Citation: He fought gallantly in Luxembourg and Germany. On 12 September 1944, Company K began fording the Our River near Kalborn, Luxembourg, to take high ground on the opposite bank. Covered by early morning fog, the 3d Platoon, in which T/Sgt. Clark was squad leader, successfully negotiated the crossing; but when the 2d Platoon reached the shore, withering automatic and small-arms fire ripped into it, eliminating the platoon leader and platoon sergeant and pinning down the troops in the open. From his comparatively safe position, T/Sgt. Clark crawled alone across a field through a hail of bullets to the stricken troops. He led the platoon to safety and then unhesitatingly returned to the fire-swept area to rescue a wounded soldier, carrying him to the American line while hostile gunners tried to cut him down. Later, he led his squad and men of the 2d Platoon in dangerous sorties against strong enemy positions to weaken them by lightning-like jabs. He assaulted an enemy machine gun with hand grenades, killing two Germans. He roamed the front and flanks, dashing toward hostile weapons, killing and wounding an undetermined number of the enemy, scattering German patrols and, eventually, forcing the withdrawal of a full company of Germans heavily armed with automatic weapons. On 17 September, near Sevenig, Germany, he advanced alone against an enemy machine gun, killed the gunner and forced the assistant to flee. The Germans counterattacked, and heavy casualties were suffered by Company K. Seeing that two platoons lacked leadership, T/Sgt. Clark took over their command and moved among the men to give encouragement. Although wounded on the morning of 18 September, he refused to be evacuated and took up a position in a pillbox when night came. Emerging at daybreak, he killed a German soldier setting up a machine gun not more than five yards away. When he located another enemy gun, he moved up unobserved and killed two Germans with rifle fire. Later that day he voluntarily braved small-arms fire to take food and water to members of an isolated platoon. T/Sgt. Clark's actions in assuming command when leadership was desperately needed, in launching attacks and beating off counterattacks, in aiding his stranded comrades, and in fearlessly facing powerful enemy fire, were strikingly heroic examples and put fighting heart into the hard-pressed men of Company K.

2662 ◆ COLALILLO, MICHAEL "MIKE"

Rank: Private First Class (highest rank: Staff Sergeant)
Service: U.S. Army
Birthday: 11 December 1925
Place of Birth: Hibbing, St. Louis County, Minnesota
Entered Service at: Duluth, St. Louis County, Minnesota
Unit: 2d Squad, 2d Platoon, Company C, 1st Battalion, 398th Infantry, 100th Infantry Division
Served as: Rifleman
Battle or Place of Action: near Untergriesheim, Germany
Date of Action: 7 April 1945

G.O. Number, Date: 4, 9 January 1945
Date of Presentation: 18 December 1945
Place of Presentation: The White House, presented by Pres. Harry S. Truman
Citation: He was pinned down with other members of his company during an attack against strong enemy positions in the vicinity of Untergriesheim, Germany. Heavy artillery, mortar, and machine-gun fire made any move hazardous, when he stood up, shouted to the company to follow, and ran forward in the wake of a supporting tank, firing his machine pistol. Inspired by his example, his comrades advanced in the face of savage enemy fire. When his weapon was struck by shrapnel and rendered useless, he climbed the deck of the friendly tank, manned an exposed machine gun on the turret of the vehicle, and, while bullets rattled about him, fired at an enemy emplacement with such devastating accuracy that he killed or wounded at least 10 hostile soldiers and destroyed their machine gun. Maintaining his extremely dangerous post as the tank forged ahead, he blasted three more positions, destroyed another machine-gun emplacement, and silenced all resistance in his area, killing at least three and wounding an undetermined number of riflemen as they fled. His machine gun eventually jammed; so he secured a submachine gun from the tank crew to continue his attack on foot. When our armored forces exhausted their ammunition and the order to withdraw was given, he remained behind to help a seriously wounded comrade over several hundred yards of open terrain rocked by an intense enemy artillery and mortar barrage. By his intrepidity and inspiring courage Pfc. Colalillo gave tremendous impetus to his company's attack, killed or wounded 25 of the enemy in bitter fighting, and assisted a wounded soldier in reaching the American lines at great risk to his own life.

2663 ◆ *COLE, DARIL SAMUEL

Rank: Sergeant
Service: U.S. Marine Corps Reserve
Birthday: 20 July 1920
Place of Birth: Flat River, San Francois County, Missouri
Date of Death: 19 February 1945
Cemetery: Park View Cemetery (MH)—Farmington, Missouri
Entered Service at: Esther, San Francois County, Missouri
Unit: Company B, 1st Battalion, 23d Marines, 4th Marine Division
Served as: Section Leader
Battle or Place of Action: Iwo Jima, Volcano Islands
Date of Action: 19 February 1945
Citation: For conspicuous gallantry and intrepidity at the risk of his life above and beyond the call of duty while serving as leader of a machine-gun section of Company B, 1st Battalion, 23d Marines, 4th Marine Division, in action against enemy Japanese forces during the assault on Iwo Jima in the Volcano Islands, 19 February 1945. Assailed by a tremendous volume of small-arms, mortar, and artillery fire as he advanced with one squad of his section in the initial assault wave, Sgt. Cole boldly led his men up the sloping beach toward Airfield No. 1 despite the blanketing curtain of flying shrapnel and,

personally destroying with hand grenades two hostile emplacements which menaced the progress of his unit, continued to move forward until a merciless barrage of fire emanating from three Japanese pillboxes halted the advance. Instantly placing his one remaining machine gun in action, he delivered a shattering fusillade and succeeded in silencing the nearest and most threatening emplacement before his weapon jammed and the enemy, reopening fire with knee mortars and grenades, pinned down his unit for a second time. Shrewdly gauging the tactical situation and evolving a daring plan of counterattack, Sgt. Cole, armed solely with a pistol and one grenade, coolly advanced alone to the hostile pillboxes. Hurling his one grenade at the enemy in sudden, swift attack, he quickly withdrew, returned to his own lines for additional grenades and again advanced, attacked, and withdrew. With enemy guns still active, he ran the gauntlet of slashing fire a third time to complete the total destruction of the Japanese strongpoint and the annihilation of the defending garrison in this final assault. Although instantly killed by an enemy grenade as he returned to his squad, Sgt. Cole had eliminated a formidable Japanese position, thereby enabling his company to storm the remaining fortifications, continue the advance, and seize the objective. By his dauntless initiative, unfaltering courage, and indomitable determination during a critical period of action, Sgt. Cole served as an inspiration to his comrades, and his stouthearted leadership in the face of almost certain death sustained and enhanced the highest tradition of the U.S. Naval Service. He gallantly gave his life for his country.

2664 ◆ *COLE, ROBERT GEORGE

Rank: Lieutenant Colonel
Service: U.S. Army
Birthday: 19 March 1915
Place of Birth: Fort Sam Houston, Bexar County, Texas
Date of Death: 18 September 1944
Cemetery: A.B.M.C. Netherlands Cemetery (B-15-27)—Margraten, Holland
Entered Service at: San Antonio, Bexar County, Texas
Unit: 3d Battalion, 502d Parachute Infantry Regiment, 101st Airborne Division
Served as: Battalion Commander
Battle or Place of Action: near Carentan, France
Date of Action: 11 June 1944
G.O. Number, Date: 79, 4 October 1944
Date of Presentation: 30 October 1944
Place of Presentation: Fort Sam Houston, Texas, presented by Major Gen. Jonathan W. Anderson to his mother, Mrs. Clara Hoff Cole
Citation: For gallantry and intrepidity at the risk of his own life above and beyond the call of duty on 11 June 1944, in France. Lt. Col. Cole was personally leading his battalion in forcing the last four bridges on the road to Carentan when his entire unit was suddenly pinned down to the ground by intense and withering enemy rifle, machine-gun, mortar, and artillery fire placed upon them from well-prepared and heavily fortified positions within 150 yards of the foremost elements. After the devastating and unceasing enemy fire had for over one hour prevented any move and inflicted numerous casualties, Lt. Col. Cole, observing this almost hopeless situation, courageously issued orders to assault the enemy positions with fixed bayonets. With utter disregard for his own safety and completely ignoring the enemy fire, he rose to his feet in front of his battalion and with drawn pistol shouted to his men to follow him in the assault. Catching up a fallen man's rifle and bayonet, he charged on and led the remnants of his battalion across the bullet-swept open ground and into the enemy position. His heroic and valiant action in so inspiring his men resulted in the complete establishment of our bridgehead across the Douve River. The cool fearlessness, personal bravery, and outstanding leadership displayed by Lt. Col. Cole reflect great credit upon himself and are worthy of the highest praise in the military service.

2665 ◆ CONNOR, JAMES PHILLIP

Rank: Sergeant
Service: U.S. Army
Birthday: 12 January 1919
Place of Birth: Wilmington, New Castle County, Delaware
Date of Death: 27 July 1994
Cemetery: Delaware Memorial Veteran Cemetery—Bear, Delaware
Entered Service at: Wilmington, New Castle County, Delaware
Unit: Battle Patrol, 7th Infantry, 3d Infantry Division
Served as: Squad Leader
Battle or Place of Action: Cape Cavalaire, Southern France
Date of Action: 15 August 1944
G.O. Number, Date: 18, 15 March 1945
Date of Presentation: 7 May 1945
Place of Presentation: France, presented by Lt. Gen. Alexander M. Patch III
Citation: For conspicuous gallantry and intrepidity at risk of life above and beyond the call of duty. On 15 August 1944 Sgt. Connor, through sheer grit and determination, led his platoon in clearing an enemy vastly superior in numbers and firepower from strongly entrenched positions on Cape Cavalaire, removing a grave enemy threat to his division during the amphibious landing in southern France, and thereby insured safe and uninterrupted landings for the huge volume of men and material which followed. His battle patrol landed on "Red Beach" with the mission of destroying the strongly fortified enemy positions on Cape Cavalaire with utmost speed. From the penninsula the enemy had commanding observation and seriously menaced the vast landing operations taking place. Though knocked down and seriously wounded in the neck by a hanging mine which killed his platoon lieutenant, Sgt. Connor refused medical aid and with his driving spirit practically carried the platoon across several thousand yards of mine-saturated beach through intense fire from mortars, 20-mm flak guns, machine guns, and snipers. En route to the cape he personally shot and killed two snipers. The platoon sergeant was killed and Sgt. Connor became platoon leader. Receiving a second wound, which lacerated his shoulder and back, he again refused evacuation, expressing determination to carry on until physically unable to continue. He

reassured and prodded the hesitating men of his decimated platoon forward through almost impregnable mortar concentrations. Again emphasizing the prevalent urgency of the mission, he impelled his men toward a group of buildings honeycombed with enenmy snipers and machine guns. Here he received his third grave wound, this time in the leg, felling him in his tracks. Still resolved to carry on, he relinquished command only after his attempts proved that it was physically impossible to stand. Nevertheless, from his prone position, he gave the orders and directed his men in assualting the enemy. Infused with Sgt. Connor's dogged determination, the platoon, though reduced to less than one-third of its original 36 men, outflanked and rushed the enemy with such furiousness that they killed seven, captured 40, seized three machine guns and considerable other material, and took all their assigned objectives, successfully completing their mission. By his repeated examples of tenaciousess and indomitable spirit Sgt. Connor transmitted his heroism to his men until they became a fighting team which could not be stopped.

2666 ◆ COOLEY, RAYMOND HENRY

Rank: Staff Sergeant
Service: U.S. Army
Birthday: 7 May 1914
Place of Birth: Dunlap, Sequatchie County, Tennessee
Date of Death: 12 March 1947
Cemetery: Cumberland View Cemetery (MH)—Jasper, Tennessee
Entered Service at: Richard City, Tennessee
Unit: Company B, 27th Infantry, 25th Infantry Division
Served as: Platoon Guide
Battle or Place of Action: near Lumboy, Luzon, Philippine Islands
Date of Action: 24 February 1945
G.O. Number, Date: 77, 10 September 1945
Date of Presentation: 23 August 1945
Place of Presentation: The White House, presented by Pres. Harry S. Truman
Citation: He was a platoon guide in an assault on a camouflaged entrenchment defended by machine guns, rifles, and mortars. When his men were pinned down by two enemy machine guns, he voluntarily advanced under heavy fire to within 20 yards of one of the guns and attacked it with a hand grenade. The enemy, however, threw the grenade back at him before it could explode. Arming a second grenade, he held it for several seconds of the safe period and then hurled it into the enemy position, where it exploded instantaneously, destroying the gun and crew. He then moved toward the remaining gun, throwing grenades into enemy foxholes as he advanced. Inspired by his actions, one squad of his platoon joined him. After he had armed another grenade and was preparing to throw it into the second machine-gun position, six enemy soldiers rushed at him. Knowing he could not dispose of the armed grenade without injuring his comrades, because of the intermingling in close combat of the men of his platoon and the enemy in the melee which ensued, he deliberately covered the grenade with his body and was severely wounded as it exploded. By his heroic actions, S/Sgt. Cooley not only silenced a machine gun and so inspired his fellow soldiers that they pressed the attack and destroyed the remaining enemy emplacements, but also, in complete disregard of his own safety, accepted certain injury and possible loss of life to avoid wounding his comrades.

2667 ◆ COOLIDGE, CHARLES HENRY

Rank: Technical Sergeant
Service: U.S. Army
Birthday: 4 August 1921
Place of Birth: Signal Mountain, Hamilton County, Tennessee
Entered Service at: Signal Mountain, Hamilton County, Tennessee
Unit: 2d Platoon, Company M, 3d Battalion, 141st Infantry, 36th Infantry Division
Served as: Machine Gunner
Battle or Place of Action: east of Belmont sur Buttant, France
Date of Action: 24-27 October 1944
G.O. Number, Date: 53, July 1945
Date of Presentation: 18 June 1945
Place of Presentation: near Ulm, Germany, presented by Maj. Gen. Frederick Haislip
Citation: Leading a section of heavy machine guns supported by one platoon of Company K, he took a position near Hill 623, east of Belmont-sur-Buttant, France, 24 October 1944, with the mission of covering the right flank of the 3d Battalion and supporting its action. T/Sgt. Coolidge went forward with a sergeant of Company K to reconnoiter positions for coordinating the fires of the light and heavy machine guns. They ran into an enemy force in the woods estimated to be an infantry company. T/Sgt. Coolidge, attempting to bluff the Germans by a show of assurnace and boldness, called upon them to surrender, whereupon the enemy opened fire. With his carbine, T/Sgt. Coolidge wounded two of them. There being no officer present with the force, T/Sgt. Coolidge at once assumed command. Many of the men were replacements recently arrived; this was their first experience under fire. T/Sgt. Coolidge, unmindful of the enemy fire delivered at close range, walked along the position, calming and encouraging his men and directing their fire. The attack was thrown back. Through 24 and 26 October the enemy launched repeated attacks against the position of this combat group but each was repulsed due to T/Sgt. Coolidge's able leadership. On 27 October, German infantry, supported by two tanks, made a determined attack on the position. The area was swept by enemy small-arms, machine-gun, and tank fire. T/Sgt. Coolidge armed himself with a bazooka and advanced within 25 yards of the tanks. His bazooka failed to function and he threw it aside. Securing all the hand grenades he could carry, he crawled forward and inflicted heavy casualties on the advancing enemy. Finally it became apparent that the enemy, in greatly superior force, supported by tanks, would overrun the position. T/Sgt. Coolidge, displaying great coolness and courage, directed and conducted an orderly withdrawal, being himself the last to leave the position. As a result of T/Sgt. Coolidge's heroic and superior leadership,

the mission of his combat group was accomplished throughout four days of continuous fighting against numerically superior enemy troops in rain and cold and amid dense woods.

2668 ◆ *COURTNEY JR., HENRY ALEXIUS

Rank: Major
Service: U.S. Marine Corps Reserve
Birthday: 6 January 1916
Place of Birth: Duluth, St. Louis County, Minnesota
Date of Death: 15 May 1945
Cemetery: Calvary Cemetery (MH)—Duluth, Minnesota
Entered Service at: Minnesota
Unit: 2d Battalion, 22d Marines, 6th Marine Division
Served as: Executive Officer
Battle or Place of Action: Sugar Loaf Hill, Okinawa Shima, Ryukyu Islands
Date of Action: 14-15 May 1945
Citation: For conspicuous gallantry and intrepidity at the risk of his life above and beyond the call of duty as executive officer of the 2d Battalion, 22d Marines, 6th Marine Division, in action against enemy Japanese forces on Okinawa Shima, in the Ryukyu Islands, 14 and 15 May 1945. Ordered to hold for the night in static defense behind Sugar Loaf Hill after leading the forward elements of his command in a prolonged firefight, Maj. Courtney weighed the effect of a hostile night counterattack against the tactical value of an immediate marine assault, resolved to initiate the assault, and promptly obtained permission to advance and seize the forward slope of the hill. Quickly explaining the situation to his small remaining force, he declared his personal intention of moving forward and then proceeded on his way, boldly blasting nearby cave positions and neutralizing enemy guns as he went. Inspired by his courage, every man followed him without hesitation, and together the intrepid marines braved a terrific concentration of Japanese gunfire to skirt the hill on the right and reach the reverse slope. Temporarily halting, Maj. Courtney sent guides to the rear for more ammunition and possible replacements. Subsequently reinforced by 26 men and an LVT load of grenades, he determined to storm the crest of the hill and crush any planned counterattack before it could gain sufficient momentum to effect a breakthrough. Leading his men by example rather than by command, he pushed ahead with unrelenting aggressiveness, hurling grenades into cave openings on the slope with devastating effect. Upon reaching the crest and observing large numbers of Japanese forming for action less than 100 yards away, he instantly attacked, waged a furious battle, and succeeded in killing many of the enemy and in forcing the remainder to take cover in the caves. Determined to hold, he ordered his men to dig in and, coolly disregarding the continuous hail of flying enemy shrapnel, to rally his weary troops, tirelessly aided casualties and assigned his men to more advantageous positions. Although instantly killed by a hostile mortar burst while moving among his men, Maj. Courtney, by his astute military acumen, indomitable leadership, and decisive action in the face of overwhelming odds, had contributed essentially to the success of the Okinawa campaign. His great personal valor throughout sustained and enhanced the highest traditions of the U.S. Naval Service. He gallantly gave his life for his country.

2669 ◆ *COWAN, RICHARD ELLER

Rank: Private First Class
Service: U.S. Army
Birthday: 5 December 1922
Place of Birth: Lincoln, Lancaster County, Nebraska
Date of Death: 18 December 1944
Cemetery: Wichita Park Cemetery—Wichita, Kansas
Entered Service at: Wichita, Sedgwick County, Kansas
Unit: Company M, 23d Infantry, 2d Infantry Division
Served as: Heavy Machine Gunner
Battle or Place of Action: near Krinkelter Wald, Belgium
Date of Action: 17 December 1944
G.O. Number, Date: 48, 23 June 1945
Citation: He was a heavy machine gunner in a section attached to Company I in the vicinity of Krinkelter Wald, Belgium, 17 December 1944, when that company was attacked by a numerically superior force of German infantry and tanks. The first six waves of hostile infantrymen were repulsed with heavy casualties, but a seventh drive with tanks killed or wounded all but three of his section, leaving Pvt. Cowan to man his gun, supported by only 15 to 20 riflemen of Company I. He maintained his position, holding off the Germans until the rest of the shattered force had set up a new line along a firebreak. Then, unaided, he moved his machine gun and ammunition to the second position. At the approach of a Royal Tiger tank, he held his fire until about 80 enemy infantrymen supporting the tank appeared at a distance of about 150 yards. His first burst killed or wounded about half of these infantrymen. His position was rocked by an 88-mm shell when the tank opened fire, but he continued to man his gun, pouring deadly fire into the Germans when they again advanced. He was barely missed by another shell. Fire from three machine guns and innumerable small arms struck all about him; an enemy rocket shook him badly, but did not drive him from his gun. Infiltration by the enemy had by this time made the position untenable, and the order was given to withdraw. Pvt. Cowan was the last man to leave, voluntarily covering the withdrawal of his remaining comrades. His heroic actions were entirely responsible for allowing the remaining men to retire successfully from the scene of their last-ditch stand.

2670 ◆ CRAFT, CLARENCE BYRLE

Rank: Private First Class (highest rank: Corporal)
Service: U.S. Army
Birthday: 23 September 1921
Place of Birth: San Bernardino, San Bernardino County, California
Entered Service at: Santa Ana, Orange County, California
Unit: Company G, 2d Battalion, 382d Infantry, 96th Infantry Division
Served as: Rifleman

Battle or Place of Action: Hen Hill, Okinawa, Ryukyu Islands
Date of Action: 31 May 1945
G.O. Number, Date: 97, 1 November 1945
Date of Presentation: 12 October 1945
Place of Presentation: The White House, presented by Pres. Harry S. Truman
Citation: He was a rifleman when his platoon spearheaded an attack on Hen Hill, the tactical position on which the entire Naha-Shuri-Yonaburu line of Japanese defense on Okinawa, Ryukyu Islands, was hinged. For 12 days our forces had been stalled, and repeated, heavy assaults by one battalion and then another had been thrown back by the enemy with serious casualties. With five comrades, Pfc. Craft was dispatched in advance of Company G to feel out the enemy resistance. The group had proceeded only a short distance up the slope when rifle and machine-gun fire, coupled with a terrific barrage of grenades, wounded three and pinned down the others. Against odds that appeared suicidal, Pfc. Craft launched a remarkable one-man attack. He stood up in full view of the enemy and began shooting with deadly marksmanship wherever he saw a hostile movement. He steadily advanced up the hill, killing Japanese soldiers with rapid fire, driving others to cover in their strongly disposed trenches, unhesitatingly facing alone the strength that had previously beaten back attacks in battalion strength. He reached the crest of the hill, where he stood silhouetted against the sky while quickly throwing grenades at extremely short range into the enemy positions. His extraordinary assault lifted the pressure from his company for the moment, allowing members of his platoon to comply with his motions to advance and pass him more grenades. With a chain of his comrades supplying him while he stood atop the hill, he furiously hurled a total of two cases of grenades into a main trench and other positions on the reverse slope of Hen Hill, meanwhile directing the aim of his fellow soldiers who threw grenades from the slope below him. He left his position, where grenades from both sides were passing over his head and bursting on either slope, to attack the main enemy trench as confusion and panic seized the defenders. Straddling the excavation, he pumped rifle fire into the Japanese at point-blank range, killing many and causing the others to flee down the trench. Pursuing them, he came upon a heavy machine gun which was still creating havoc in the American ranks. With rifle fire and a grenade he wiped out this position. By this time the Japanese were in complete rout and American forces were swarming over the hill. Pfc. Craft continued down the central trench to the mouth of a cave where many of the enemy had taken cover. A satchel charge was brought to him, and he tossed it into the cave. It failed to explode. With great daring, the intrepid fighter retrieved the charge from the cave, relighted the fuse, and threw it back, sealing up the Japs in a tomb. In the local action, against tremendously superior forces heavily armed with rifles, machine guns, mortars, and grenades, Pfc. Craft killed at least 25 of the enemy; but his contribution to the campaign on Okinawa was of much more far-reaching consequence, for Hen Hill was the key to the entire defense line, which rapidly crumbled after his utterly fearless and heroic attack.

2671 ◆ *CRAIG, ROBERT

Rank: Second Lieutenant
Service: U.S. Army
Birthday: 1919
Place of Birth: Scotland
Date of Death: 11 July 1943
Cemetery: Toledo Memorial Park—Sylvania, Ohio
Entered Service at: Toledo, Lucas County, Ohio
Unit: Company L, 15th Infantry, 3d Infantry Division
Served as: Platoon Leader
Battle or Place of Action: near Favoratta, Sicily
Date of Action: 11 July 1943
G.O. Number, Date: 41, 26 May 1944
Citation: For conspicuous gallantry and intrepidity at the risk of his life above and beyond the call of duty, on 11 July 1943, at Favoratta, Sicily. Second Lt. Craig voluntarily undertook the perilous task of locating and destroying a hidden enemy machine gun which had halted the advance of his company. Attempts by three other officers to locate the weapon had resulted in failure, with each officer receiving wounds. Second Lt. Craig located the gun and snaked his way to a point within 35 yards of the hostile position before being discovered. Charging headlong into the furious automatic fire, he reached the gun, stood over it, and killed the three crew members with his carbine. With this obstacle removed, his company continued its advance. Shortly thereafter, while advancing down the forward slope of a ridge, 2d Lt. Craig and his platoon, in a position devoid of cover and concealment, encountered the fire of approximately 100 enemy soldiers. Electing to sacrifice himself so that his platoon might carry on the battle, he ordered his men to withdraw to the cover of the crest while he drew the enemy fire to himself. With no hope of survival, he charged toward the enemy unitl he was within 25 yards of them. Assuming a kneeling position, he killed five and wounded three enemy soldiers. While the hostile force concentrated fire on him, his platoon reached the cover of the crest. Second Lt. Craig was killed by enemy fire, but his intrepid action so inspired his men that they drove the enemy from the area, inflicting heavy casualties on the hostile force.

2672 ◆ *CRAIN, MORRIS E.

Rank: Technical Sergeant
Service: U.S. Army
Birthday: 7 October 1924
Place of Birth: Bandana, Ballard County, Kentucky
Date of Death: 13 March 1945
Cemetery: Mount Pleasant Cemetery (MH)—LaCenter, Kentucky
Entered Service at: Paducah, McCracken County, Kentucky
Unit: Company E, 141st Infantry, 36th Infantry Division
Battle or Place of Action: Haguenau, France
Date of Action: 13 March 1945
G.O. Number, Date: 18, 13 February 1946
Citation: He led his platoon against powerful German forces during the struggle to enlarge the bridgehead across the Moder River. With great daring and aggressiveness he spear-

headed the platoon in killing 10 enemy soldiers, capturing 12 more and securing its objective near an important road junction. Although heavy concentrations of artillery, mortar, and self-propelled gunfire raked the area, he moved about among his men during the day, exhorting them to great efforts and encouraging them to stand firm. He carried ammunition and maintained contact with the company command post, exposing himself to deadly enemy fire. At nightfall the enemy barrage became more intense and tanks entered the fray to cover foot troops while they bombarded our positions with grenades and rockets. As buildings were blasted by the Germans, the Americans fell back from house to house. T/Sgt. Crain deployed another platoon which had been sent to his support and then rushed through murderous tank and small-arms fire to the foremost house, which was being defended by five of his men. With the enemy attacking from an adjoining room and a tank firing point-blank at the house, he ordered the men to withdraw while he remained in the face of almost certain death to hold the position. Although shells were crashing through the walls and bullets were hitting all around him, he held his ground and with accurate fire from his submachine gun killed three Germans. He was killed when the building was destroyed by the enemy. T/Sgt. Crain's outstanding valor and intrepid leadership enabled his platoon to organize a new defense, repel the attack, and preserve the hard-won bridgehead.

2673 ◆ *CRAW, DEMAS THURLOW

Rank: Colonel
Service: U.S. Army Air Corps
Birthday: 9 April 1900
Place of Birth: Traverse City, Grand Traverse County, Michigan
Date of Death: 8 November 1942
Place of Death: Near Port Lyautey, French Morocco
Cemetery: Cremated—ashes scattered over Weisbaden, Germany, 24 June 1949
Entered Service at: Michigan
Unit: XII Ground Air Support Command, U.S.A.A.C.
Battle or Place of Action: near Port Lyautey, French Morocco
Date of Action: 8 November 1942
G.O. Number, Date: 11, 4 March 1943
Citation: For conspicuous gallantry and intrepidity in action above and beyond the call of duty. On 8 November 1942, near Port Lyautey, French Morocco, Col. Craw volunteered to accompany the leading wave of assault boats to the shore and pass through the enemy lines to locate the French commander with a view of suspending hostilities. This request was first refused as being too dangerous, but upon the officer's insistence that he was qualified to undertake and accomplish the mission he was allowed to go. Encountering heavy fire while in the landing boat and unable to dock in the river because of shellfire from shore batteries, Col. Craw, accompanied by one officer and one soldier, succeeded in landing on the beach at Mehdia Plage under constant low-level strafing from three enemy planes. Riding in a bantam truck toward French headquarters, progress of the party was hindered by fire from our own naval guns. Nearing Port Lyautey, Col. Craw was instantly killed by a sustained burst of machine-gun fire at point-blank range from a concealed position near the road.

2674 ◆ CRAWFORD, WILLIAM JOHN

Rank: Private (highest rank: Master Sergeant)
Service: U.S. Army
Birthday: 19 May 1918
Place of Birth: Pueblo, Pueblo County, Colorado
Entered Service at: Pueblo, Pueblo County, Colorado
Unit: 3d Platoon, Company I, 3d Battalion, 142d Infantry, 36th Infantry Division
Served as: Squad Scout/Rifleman
Battle or Place of Action: near Altavilla, Italy
Date of Action: 13 September 1943
G.O. Number, Date: 57, 20 July 1944
Date of Presentation: 11 May 1944 & 30 May 1984
Place of Presentation: Camp Carson, Colorado, presented posthumously by Maj. Gen. Terry Allen to his Father 1944. U.S. Air Force Academy, Colorado Springs Colorado; medal presented by Pres. Ronald Reagan to William J. Crawford 30 May 1984
Citation: For conspicuous gallantry and intrepidity at risk of life above and beyond the call of duty in action with the enemy near Altavilla, Italy, 13 September 1943. When Company I attacked an enemy-held position on Hill 424, the 3d Platoon, in which Pvt. Crawford was a squad scout, attacked as base platoon for the company. After reaching the crest of a hill, the platoon was pinned down by intense enemy machine-gun and small-arms fire. Locating one of these guns, which was dug in on a terrace on his immediate front, Pvt. Crawford, without orders and on his own initiative moved over the hill under enemy fire to a point within a few yards of the gun emplacement and singlehandedly destroyed the machine gun and killed three of the crew with a hand grenade, thus enabling his platoon to continue its advance. When the platoon, after reaching the crest, was once more delayed by enemy fire, Pvt. Crawford again, in the face of intense fire, advanced directly to the front midway between two hostile machine-gun nests located on a higher terrace and emplaced in a small ravine. Moving first to the left, with a grenade he destroyed one gun emplacement and killed the crew; he then worked his way, under continuous fire, to the other and with one grenade and the use of his rifle, killed one enemy and forced the remainder to flee. Seizing the enemy machine gun, he fired on the withdrawing Germans and facilitated his company's advance.
Notes: POW

2675 ◆ CREWS, JOHN R.

Rank: Staff Sergeant
Service: U.S. Army
Birthday: 8 March 1923
Place of Birth: Golden, McCurtain County, Oklahoma
Entered Service at: Bowlegs, Seminole County, Oklahoma
Unit: 2d Platoon, Company F, 2d Battalion, 253d Infantry, 63d Infantry Division

Served as: Squad Leader
Battle or Place of Action: Lobenbacherhof, Germany
Date of Action: 8 April 1945
Date of Presentation: 25 June 1948
Place of Presentation: The White House (Rose Garden), presented by Pres. Harry S. Truman
Citation: He displayed conspicous gallantry and intrepidity at the risk of life above and beyond the call of duty on 8 April 1945 near Lobenbacherhof, Germany. As his company was advancing toward the village under heavy fire, an enemy machine gun and automatic rifle with rifle support opened up on it from a hill on the right flank. Seeing that his platoon leader had been wounded by their fire, S/Sgt. Crews, acting upon his own initiative, rushed the strongpoint with two men of his platoon. Despite the fact that one of these men was killed and the other was badly wounded, he continued his advance up the hill in the face of terrific enemy fire. Storming the well dug-in position singlehandedly, he killed two of the crew of the machine gun at point-blank range with his M1 rifle and wrested the gun from the hands of a German whom he had already wounded. He then with his rifle charged the strongly emplaced automatic rifle. Although badly wounded in the thigh by crossfire from the remaining enemy, he kept on and silenced the entire position with his accurate and deadly rifle fire. His actions so unnerved the remaining enemy soldiers that seven of them surrendered and the others fled. His heroism caused the enemy to concentrate on him and permitted the company to move forward into the village.

2676 ◆ *CROMWELL, JOHN PHILIP

Rank: Captain
Service: U.S. Navy
Birthday: 11 September 1901
Place of Birth: Henry, Marshall County, Illinois
Date of Death: 19 November 1943
Cemetery: National Memorial Cemetery of the Pacific (Wall of the Missing)—Honolulu, Hawaii
Entered Service at: Illinois
Unit: U.S.S. *Sculpin*
Served as: Group Commander
Battle or Place of Action: off Truk Island
Date of Action: 19 November 1943
Date of Presentation: 24 April 1946
Place of Presentation: San Francisco, California, presented to his Widow and Son
Citation: For conspicuous gallantry and intrepidity at the risk of his life above and beyond the call of duty as commander of a submarine coordinated attack group with flag in the U.S.S. *Sculpin*, during the 9th war patrol of that vessel in enemy-controlled waters off Truk Island, 19 November 1943. Undertaking this patrol prior to the launching of our first large-scale offensive in the Pacific, Capt. Cromwell, alone of the entire Task Group, possessed secret intelligence information of our submarine strategy and tactics, scheduled Fleet movements, and specific attack plans. Constantly vigilant and precise in carrying out his secret orders, he moved his undersea flotilla inexorably forward despite savage opposition and established a line of submarines to southeastward of the main Japanese stronghold at Truk. Cool and undaunted as the submarine, rocked and battered by Japanese depth charges, sustained terrific battle damage and sank to an excessive depth, he authorized the *Sculpin* to surface and engage the enemy in a gunfight, thereby providing an opportunity for the crew to abandon ship. Determined to sacrifice himself rather than risk capture and subsequent danger of revealing plans under Japanese torture or use of drugs, he stoically remained aboard the mortally wounded vessel as she plunged to her death. Preserving the security of his mission, at the cost of his own life, he had served his country as he had served the Navy, with deep integrity and an uncompromising devotion to duty. His great moral courage in the face of certain death adds new luster to the traditions of the U.S. Naval Service. He gallantly gave his life for his country.

2677 ◆ CURREY, FRANCIS SHERMAN "FRANK"

Rank: Private First Class (highest rank: Technical Sergeant)
Service: U.S. Army
Birthday: 29 June 1925
Place of Birth: Loch Sheldrake, Sullivan County, New York
Entered Service at: Hurleyville, Sullivan County, New York
Unit: 3d Platoon, Company K, 3d Battalion, 120th Infantry, 30th Infantry Division
Served as: Automatic Rifleman
Battle or Place of Action: Malmedy, Belgium
Date of Action: 21 December 1944
G.O. Number, Date: 69, 17 August 1945
Date of Presentation: 27 July 1945
Place of Presentation: Reims France, presented by Maj. Gen. Leland S. Hobbs
Citation: He was an automatic rifleman with the 3d Platoon defending a strongpoint near Malmedy, Belgium, on 21 December 1944, when the enemy launched a powerful attack. Overrunning tank destroyers and antitank guns located near the strongpoint, German tanks advanced to the 3d Platoon's position, and, after prolonged fighting, forced the withdrawal of this group to a nearby factory. Sgt. Currey found a bazooka in the building and crossed the street to secure rockets, meanwhile enduring intense fire from enemy tanks and hostile infantrymen who had taken up a position at a house a short distance away. In the face of small-arms, machine-gun, and artillery fire, he, with a companion, knocked out a tank with one shot. Moving to another position, he observed three Germans in the doorway of an enemy-held house. He killed or wounded all three with his automatic rifle. He emerged from cover and advanced alone to within 50 yards of the house, intent on wrecking it with rockets. Covered by friendly fire, he stood erect and fired a shot which knocked down half of one wall. While in this forward position, he observed five Americans who had been pinned down for hours by fire from the house and three tanks. Realizing that they could not escape until the enemy tank and infantry guns had been silenced, Sgt. Currey crossed the street to a vehicle, where he procured an armful of antitank grenades. These he launched while under heavy enemy fire, driving tankmen from the vehicles into the house. He then climbed onto a half-track in full

view of the Germans and fired a machine gun at the house. Once again changing his position, he manned another machine gun whose crew had been killed; under covering fire the five soldiers were able to retire to safety. Deprived of tanks and with heavy infantry casualties, the enemy was forced to withdraw. Through his extensive knowledge of weapons and by his heroic and repeated braving of murderous heavy fire, Sgt. Currey was greatly responsible for inflicting heavy losses in men and material on the enemy, for rescuing five comrades, two of whom were wounded, and for stemming an attack which threatened to flank his battalion's position.

2678 ◆ DAHLGREN, EDWARD CARL

Rank: Second Lieutenant (rank at time of action: Sergeant)
Service: U.S. Army
Birthday: 14 March 1916
Place of Birth: Perham, Aroostook County, Maine
Entered Service at: Caribou, Aroostook County, Maine
Unit: 3d Platoon, Company E, 2d Battalion, 142d Infantry, 36th Infantry Division
Served as: Platoon Sergeant
Battle or Place of Action: Oberhoffen, France
Date of Action: 11 February 1945
G.O. Number, Date: 77, 10 September 1945
Date of Presentation: 23 August 1945
Place of Presentation: The White House, presented by Pres. Harry S. Truman
Citation: He led the 3d Platoon to the rescue of a similar unit which had been surrounded in an enemy counterattack at Oberhoffen, France. As he advanced along a street, he observed several Germans crossing a field about 100 yards away. Running into a barn, he took up a position in a window and swept the hostile troops with submachine-gun fire, killing six, wounding others, and completely disorganizing the group. His platoon then moved forward through intermittent sniper fire and made contact with the besieged Americans. When the two platoons had been reorganized, Sgt. Dahlgren continued to advance along the street until he drew fire from an enemy-held house. In the face of machine-pistol and rifle fire, he ran toward the building, hurled a grenade through the door, and blasted his way inside with his gun. This aggressive attack so rattled the Germans that all eight men who had held the strongpoint immediately surrendered. As Sgt. Dahlgren started toward the next house, hostile machine-gun fire drove him to cover. He secured rifle grenades, stepped to an exposed position, and calmly launched his missles from a difficult angle until he had destroyed the machine gun and killed its two operators. He moved to the rear of the house and suddenly came under the fire of a machine gun emplaced in a barn. Throwing a grenade into the structure, he rushed the position, firing his weapon as he ran; within, he overwhelmed five Germans. After reorganizing his unit he advanced to clear hostile riflemen from the building where he had destroyed the machine gun. He entered the house by a window and trapped the Germans in the cellar, where he tossed grenades into their midst, wounding several and forcing 10 more to surrender.

While reconnoitering another street with a comrade, he heard German voices in a house. An attack with rifle grenades drove the hostile troops to the cellar. Sgt. Dahlgren entered the building, kicked open the cellar door, and, firing several bursts down the stairway, called for the trapped enemy to surrender. Sixteen soldiers filed out with their hands in the air. The bold leadership and magnificent courage displayed by Sgt. Dahlgren in his heroic attacks were in a large measure responsible for repulsing an enemy counterattack and saving an American platoon from great danger.

2679 ◆ DALESSONDRO, PETER JOSEPH

Rank: Technical Sergeant
Service: U.S. Army
Birthday: 19 May 1921
Place of Birth: Watervliet, Albany County, New York
Entered Service at: Watervliet, Albany County, New York
Unit: 1st Platoon, Company E, 1st Battalion, 39th Infantry, 9th Infantry Division
Served as: Platoon Sergeant
Battle or Place of Action: Kalterherberg, Germany
Date of Action: 22 December 1944
G.O. Number, Date: 73, 30 August 1945
Date of Presentation: 23 August 1945
Place of Presentation: The White House, presented by Pres. Harry S. Truman
Citation: He was with the 1st Platoon holding an important road junction on high ground near Kalterherberg, Germany, 22 December 1944. In the early morning hours, the enemy, after laying down an intense artillery and mortar barrage, followed through with an all-out attack that threatened to overwhelm the position. T/Sgt. Dalessondro, seeing that his men were becoming disorganized, braved the intense fire to move among them with words of encouragement. Advancing to a fully exposed observation post, he adjusted mortar fire upon the attackers, meanwhile firing upon them with his rifle and encouraging his men in halting and repulsing the attack. Later in the day the enemy launched a second determined attack. Once again, T/Sgt. Dalessondro, in the face of imminent death, rushed to his forward position and immediately called for mortar fire. After exhausting his rifle ammunition, he crawled 30 yards over exposed ground to secure a light machine gun, returned to his position, and fired upon the enemy at almost point-blank range until the gun jammed. He managed to get the gun to fire one more burst, which used up his last round, but with these bullets he killed four German soldiers who were on the verge of murdering an aidman and two wounded soldiers in a nearby foxhole. When the enemy had almost surrounded him, he remained alone, steadfastly facing almost certain death or capture, hurling grenades and calling for mortar fire closer and closer to his outpost as he covered the withdrawal of his platoon to a second line of defense. As the German hordes swarmed about him, he was last heard calling for a barrage, saying, "OK, mortars, let me have it—right in this position!" The gallantry and intrepidity shown by T/Sgt. Dalessondro against an overwhelming enemy attack saved his company from complete rout.

2680 ◆ DALY, MICHAEL JOSEPH

Rank: Captain (rank at time of action: Lieutenant)
Service: U.S. Army
Birthday: 15 September 1924
Place of Birth: New York, New York
Entered Service at: Southport, Fairfield County, Connecticut
Unit: Company A, 1st Battalion, 15th Infantry, 3d Infantry Division
Served as: Company Commander
Battle or Place of Action: Nuremberg, Germany
Date of Action: 18 April 1945
G.O. Number, Date: 77, 10 September 1945
Date of Presentation: 23 August 1945
Place of Presentation: The White House, presented by Pres. Harry S. Truman
Citation: Early in the morning of 18 April 1945, he led his company through the shell-battered, sniper-infested wreckage of Nuremberg, Germany. When blistering machine-gun fire caught his unit in an exposed position, he ordered his men to take cover, dashed forward alone, and, as bullets whined about him, shot the three-man gun-crew with his carbine. Continuing the advance at the head of his company, he located an enemy patrol armed with rocket launchers which threatened friendly armor. He again went forward alone, secured a vantage point, and opened fire on the Germans. Immediately he became the target for concentrated machine-pistol and rocket fire, which blasted the rubble about him. Calmly, he continued to shoot at the patrol until he had killed all six enemy infantrymen. Continuing boldly far in front of his company, he entered a park, where as his men advanced, a German machine gun opened up on them without warning. With his carbine, he killed the gunner; and then, from a completely exposed position, he directed machine-gun fire on the remainder of the crew until all were dead. In a final duel, he wiped out a third machine-gun emplacement with rifle fire at a range of 10 yards. By fearlessly engaging in four singlehanded firefights with a desperate, powerfully armed enemy, Lt. Daly, voluntarily taking all major risks himself and protecting his men at every opportunity, killed 15 Germans, silenced three enemy machine guns, and wiped out an entire enemy patrol. His heroism during the lone bitter struggle with fanatical enemy forces was an inspiration to the valiant Americans who took Nuremberg.

2681 ◆ *DAMATO, ANTHONY PETER

Rank: Corporal
Service: U.S. Marine Corps
Birthday: 28 March 1922
Place of Birth: Shenandoah, Schuylkill County, Pennsylvania
Date of Death: 20 February 1944
Cemetery: National Memorial Cemetery of the Pacific (A-334) (MH)—Honolulu, Hawaii
Entered Service at: Pennsylvania
Battle or Place of Action: Engebi Island, Eniwetok Atoll, Marshall Islands
Date of Action: 19-20 February 1944
Date of Presentation: 9 April 1945
Place of Presentation: Lincoln School, Shenandoah, Pennsylvania, presented to his Mother
Citation: For conspicuous gallantry and intrepidity at the risk of his life above and beyond the call of duty while serving with an assault company in action against enemy Japanese forces on Engebi Island, Eniwetok Atoll, Marshall Islands, on the night of 19–20 February 1944. Highly vulnerable to sudden attack by small, fanatical groups of Japanese still at large despite the efficient and determined efforts of our forces to clear the area, Cpl. Damato lay with two comrades in a large foxhole in his company's defense perimeter which had been dangerously thinned by the forced withdrawal of nearly half of the available men. When one of the enemy approached the foxhole undetected and threw in a hand grenade, Cpl. Damato desperately groped for it in the darkness. Realizing the imminent peril to all three and fully aware of the consequences of his act, he unhesitatingly flung himself on the grenade and, although instantly killed as his body absorbed the explosion, saved the lives of his two companions. Cpl. Damato's splendid initiative, fearless conduct, and valiant sacrifice reflect great credit upon himself and the U.S. Naval Service. He gallantly gave his life for his comrades.

2682 ◆ *DAVID, ALBERT LEROY

Rank: Lieutenant [rank at time of action: Lieutenant (j.g.)]
Service: U.S. Navy
Birthday: 18 July 1902
Place of Birth: Maryville, Nodaway County, Missouri
Date of Death: 17 September 1945
Place of Death: San Diego, California
Cemetery: Fort Rosecrans National Cemetery (OS-125A) (MH)—San Diego, California
Entered Service at: Missouri
Unit: U.S.S. *Pillsbury* DE 133
Served as: Engineering Officer
Battle or Place of Action: off the coast of French West Africa
Date of Action: 4 June 1944
Date of Presentation: 5 October 1945
Place of Presentation: The White House, presented by Pres. Harry S. Truman to his Widow
Citation: For conspicuous gallantry and intrepidity at the risk of his life above and beyond the call of duty while attached to the U.S.S. *Pillsbury* during the capture of an enemy German submarine off French West Africa, 4 June 1944. Taking a vigorous part in the skillfully coordinated attack on the German U-505 which climaxed a prolonged search by the Task Group, Lt. (then Lt. [jg]) David boldly led a party from the *Pillsbury* in boarding the hostile submarine as it circled erratically at five or six knots on the surface. Fully aware that the U-boat might momentarily sink or be blown up by exploding demolition and scuttling charges, he braved the added danger of enemy gunfire to plunge through the conning tower hatch and, with his small party, exerted every effort to keep the ship afloat and to assist the succeeding and more fully equipped salvage parties in making the U-

505 seaworthy for the long tow across the Atlantic to a U.S. port. By his valiant service during the first successful boarding and capture of an enemy man-o-war on the high seas by the U.S. Navy since 1815, Lt. David contributed materially to the effectiveness of our Battle of the Atlantic and upheld the highest traditions of the U.S. Naval Service.

2683 ◆ DAVIS, CHARLES WILLIS

Rank: Major (rank at time of action: Captain) (highest rank: Colonel)
Service: U.S. Army
Birthday: 21 February 1917
Place of Birth: Gordo, Pickens County, Alabama
Date of Death: 18 January 1991
Place of Death: San Francisco, California
Cemetery: Arlington National Cemetery (7-A-170) (MH)—Arlington, Virginia
Entered Service at: Montgomery, Montgomery County, Alabama
Unit: 2d Battalion, 27th Infantry Regiment, 25th Infantry Division
Served as: Battalion Executive Officer
Battle or Place of Action: Guadalcanal, Solomon Islands
Date of Action: 12 January 1943
G.O. Number, Date: 40, 17 July 1943
Date of Presentation: 30 July 1943
Place of Presentation: Guadalcanal, Solomon Islands, presented by Lt. Gen. Millard F. Harmon
Citation: For distinguishing himself conspicuously by gallantry and intrepidity at the risk of his life above and beyond the call of duty in action with the enemy on Guadalcanal Island. On 12 January 1943, Maj. Davis (then Capt.), executive officer of an infantry battalion, volunteered to carry instructions to the leading companies of his battalion which had been caught in crossfire from Japanese machine guns. With complete disregard for his own safety, he made his way to the trapped units, delivered the instructions, supervised their execution, and remained overnight in this exposed position. On the following day, Maj. Davis again volunteered to lead an assault on the Japanese position which was holding up the advance. When his rifle jammed at its first shot, he drew his pistol and, waving his men on, led the assault over the top of the hill. Electrified by this action, another body of soldiers followed and seized the hill. The capture of this position broke Japanese resistance and the battalion was then able to proceed and secure the corps' objective. The courage and leadership displayed by Maj. Davis inspired the entire battalion and unquestionably led to the success of its attack.

2684 ◆ *DAVIS, GEORGE FLEMING

Rank: Commander
Service: U.S. Navy
Birthday: 23 March 1911
Place of Birth: Manila, Philippine Islands
Date of Death: 6 January 1945
Cemetery: A.B.M.C. Manila Cemetery (Wall of the Missing)—Manila, Philippine Islands
Entered Service at: Philippine Islands
Unit: U.S.S. *Walke*
Served as: Commanding Officer
Battle or Place of Action: Lingayen Gulf, Luzon, Philippine Islands
Date of Action: 6 January 1945
Date of Presentation: 15 November 1945
Place of Presentation: Washington, D.C., presented by Sec. of the Navy James Forrestal to his Widow
Citation: For conspicuous gallantry and intrepidity at the risk of his life above and beyond the call of duty as commanding officer of the U.S.S. *Walke* engaged in a detached mission in support of minesweeping operations to clear the waters for entry of our heavy surface and amphibious forces preparatory to the invasion of Lingayen Gulf, Luzon, Philippine Islands, 6 January 1945. Operating without gun support of other surface ships when four Japanese suicide planes were detected flying low overland to attack simultaneously, Comdr. Davis boldly took his position in the exposed wings of the bridge and directed control to pick up the leading plane and open fire. Alert and fearless as the *Walke*'s deadly fire sent the first target crashing into the water and caught the second as it passed close over the bridge to plunge into the sea of portside, he remained steadfast in the path of the third plane plunging swiftly to crash the after end of the bridge structure. Seriously wounded when the craft struck, drenched with gasoline and immediately enveloped in flames, he conned the *Walke* in the midst of the wreckage; he rallied his command to heroic efforts; he exhorted his officers and men to save the ship and, still on his feet, saw the barrage from his guns destroy the fourth suicide bomber. With the fires under control and the safety of the ship assured, he consented to be carried below. Succumbing several hours later, Comdr. Davis by his example of valor and his unhesitating self-sacrifice, steeled the fighting spirit of his command into unyielding purpose in completing a vital mission. He gallantly gave his life in the service of his country.

2685 ◆ *DEALEY, SAMUEL DAVID

Rank: Commander
Service: U.S. Navy
Birthday: 13 September 1906
Place of Birth: Dallas, Collin County, Texas
Date of Death: 24 August 1944 (6th war patrol)
Cemetery: A.B.M.C. Manila Cemetery (Wall of the Missing)—Manila, Philippine Islands
Entered Service at: Texas
Unit: U.S.S. *Harder*
Served as: Commanding Officer
Battle or Place of Action: off Tawi Tawi, Sulu Archipelago
Date of Action: 26 May-3 July 1944 (5th war patrol)
Date of Presentation: 15 November 1945
Place of Presentation: The White House, presented by Pres. Harry S. Truman to his Widow
Citation: For conspicuous gallantry and intrepidity at the risk of his life above and beyond the call of duty as commanding officer of the U.S.S. *Harder* during her 5th war patrol in Japanese-controlled waters. Floodlighted by a bright moon

and disclosed to an enemy destroyer escort which bore down with intent to attack. Comdr. Dealey quickly dived to periscope depth and waited for the pursuer to close range, then opened fire, sending the target and all aboard down in flames with his third torpedo. Plunging deep to avoid fierce depth charges, he again surfaced and, within nine minutes after sighting another destroyer, had sent the enemy down tail first with a hit directly amidship. Evading detection, he penetrated the confined waters off Tawi Tawi with the Japanese Fleet base six miles away and scored death blows on two patrolling destroyers in quick succession. With his ship heeled over by concussion from the first exploding target and the second vessel nose-diving in a blinding detonation, he cleared the area at high speed. Sighted by a large hostile fleet force on the following day, he swung his bow toward the lead destroyer for another "down-the-throat" shot, fired three bow tubes, and promptly crash-dived to be terrifically rocked seconds later by the exploding ship as the *Harder* passed beneath. This remarkable record of five vital Japanese destroyers sunk in five short-range torpedo attacks attests the valiant fighting spirit of Comdr. Dealey and his indomitable command.

2686 ◆ DEBLANC, JEFFERSON JOSEPH

Rank: Captain (highest rank: Colonel)
Service: U.S. Marine Corps Reserve
Birthday: 15 February 1921
Place of Birth: Lockport, Lafourche County, Louisiana
Entered Service at: Lockport, Lafourche County, Louisiana
Unit: Marine Fighting Squadron 112, Marine Air Group 11, 1st Marine Air Wing
Served as: Fighter Pilot of a Grumman Wildcat
Battle or Place of Action: Kolombangara Island, Solomon Islands
Date of Action: 31 January 1943
Date of Presentation: 6 December 1946
Place of Presentation: The White House, presented by Pres. Harry S. Truman
Citation: For conspicuous gallantry and intrepidity at the risk of his life above and beyond the call of duty as leader of a section of six fighter planes in Marine Fighting Squadron 112, during aerial operations against enemy Japanese forces off Kolombangara Island in the Solomon group, 31 January 1943. Taking off with his section as escort for a strike force of dive bombers ordered to attack Japanese surface vessels, 1st Lt. DeBlanc led his flight directly to the target area where, at 14,000 feet, our strike force encountered a large number of Japanese Zeros protecting the enemy's surface craft. In company with the other fighters, 1st Lt. DeBlanc instantly engaged the hostile planes and aggressively countered their repeated attempts to drive off our bombers, persevering in his efforts to protect the diving planes and waging fierce combat until, picking up a call for assistance from the dive bombers, under attack by enemy float planes at 1,000 feet, he broke off his engagement with the Zeros, plunged into the formation of float planes and disrupted the savage attack, enabling our dive bombers to complete their runs on the Japanese surface disposition and withdraw without further incident. Although his escort mission was fulfilled upon the safe retirement of the bombers, 1st Lt. DeBlanc courageously remained on the scene despite a rapidly diminishing fuel supply and, boldly challenging the enemy's superior number of float planes, fought a valiant battle against terrific odds, seizing the tactical advantage and striking repeatedly to destroy three of the hostile aircraft (two float planes and one Zero) and to disperse the remainder. Prepared to maneuver his damaged plane back to base, he had climbed aloft and set his course when he discovered two Zeros closing in behind. Undaunted, he opened fire and blasted both Zeros from the sky in a short, bitterly fought action which resulted in such hopeless damage to his own plane that other Zeros entering the fight set his aircraft on fire forcing him to bail out over enemy waters between Vella Lavella and enemy-held Kolombangara. A gallant officer, a superb airman, and an indomitable fighter, 1st Lt. DeBlanc had rendered decisive assistance during a critical stage of operations, and his unwavering fortitude in the face of overwhelming opposition reflects the highest credit upon himself and adds new luster to the traditions of the U.S. Naval Service.

2687 ◆ *DEFRANZO, ARTHUR FREDERICK

Rank: Staff Sergeant
Service: U.S. Army
Birthday: 20 March 1919
Place of Birth: Saugus, Essex County, Massachusetts
Date of Death: 10 June 1944
Cemetery: Riverside Cemetery (MH)—Saugus, Massachusetts
Entered Service at: Saugus, Essex County, Massachusetts
Unit: 18th Infantry, 1st Infantry Division
Battle or Place of Action: near Vaubadon, France
Date of Action: 10 June 1944
G.O. Number, Date: 1, 4 January 1945
Citation: For conspicuous gallantry and intrepidity at the risk of his life above and beyond the call of duty on 10 June 1944, near Vaubadon, France. As scouts were advancing across an open field, the enemy suddenly opened fire with several machine guns and hit one of the men. S/Sgt. DeFranzo courageously moved out in the open to the aid of the wounded scout and was himself wounded but brought the man to safety. Refusing aid, S/Sgt. DeFranzo reentered the open field and led the advance upon the enemy. There were always at least two machine-guns bringing unrelenting fire upon him, but S/Sgt. DeFranzo kept going forward, firing into the enemy and one by one the enemy emplacements became silent. While advancing he was again wounded, but continued on until he was within 100 yards of the enemy position and even as he fell, he kept firing his rifle and waving his men forward. When his company came up behind him, S/Sgt. DeFranzo, despite his many severe wounds, suddenly raised himself and once more moved forward in the lead of his men until he was again hit by enemy fire. In a final gesture of indomitable courage, he threw several grenades at the enemy machine-gun position and completely destroyed the gun. In this action S/Sgt. DeFranzo lost his life, but by bearing the brunt of the enemy fire in leading the attack, he pre-

vented a delay in the assault which would have been of considerable benefit to the foe, and he made possible his company's advance with a minimum of casualties. The extraordinary heroism and magnificent devotion to duty displayed by S/Sgt. DeFranzo was a great inspiration to all about him and is in keeping with the highest traditions of the Armed Forces.

2688 ◆ *DEGLOPPER, CHARLES N.

Rank: Private First Class
Service: U.S. Army
Birthday: 30 November 1921
Place of Birth: Grand Island, Erie County, New York
Date of Death: 9 June 1944
Cemetery: Maple Grove Cemetery—Grand Island, New York
Entered Service at: Grand Island, Erie County, New York
Unit: Company C, 325th Glider Infantry, 82d Airborne Division
Served as: Automatic Rifleman
Battle or Place of Action: Merderet River at La Fiere, France
Date of Action: 9 June 1944
G.O. Number, Date: 22, 28 February 1946
Citation: He was a member of Company C, 325th Glider Infantry, on 9 June 1944 advancing with the forward platoon to secure a bridgehead across the Merderet River at La Fiere, France. At dawn the platoon had penetrated an outer line of machine guns and riflemen, but in so doing had become cut off from the rest of the company. Vastly superior forces began a decimation of the stricken unit and put in motion a flanking maneuver which would have completely exposed the American platoon in a shallow roadside ditch where it had taken cover. Detecting this danger, Pfc. DeGlopper volunteered to support his comrades by fire from his automatic rifle while they attempted a withdrawal through a break in a hedgerow 40 yards to the rear. Scorning a concentration of enemy automatic-weapons and rifle fire, he walked from the ditch onto the road in full view of the Germans and sprayed the hostile positions with assault fire. He was wounded, but he continued firing. Struck again, he started to fall; and yet his grim determination and valiant fighting spirit could not be broken. Kneeling in the roadway, weakened by his grievous wounds, he leveled his heavy weapon against the enemy and fired burst after burst until killed outright. He was successful in drawing the enemy action away from his fellow soldiers, who continued the fight from a more advantageous position and established the first bridgehead over the Merderet. In the area where he made his intrepid stand his comrades later found the ground strewn with dead Germans and many machine guns and automatic weapons which he had knocked out of action. Pfc. DeGlopper's gallant sacrifice and unflinching heroism while facing unsurmountable odds were in great measure responsible for a highly important tactical victory in the Normandy Campaign.

2689 ◆ *DELEAU JR., EMILE

Rank: Sergeant
Service: U.S. Army
Birthday: 28 June 1923
Place of Birth: Lansing, Belmont County, Ohio
Date of Death: 2 February 1945
Cemetery: Linwood Cemetery—Blaine, Ohio
Entered Service at: Blaine, Belmont County, Ohio
Unit: Company A, 142d Infantry, 36th Infantry Division
Served as: Squad Leader
Battle or Place of Action: Oberhoffen, France
Date of Action: 1-2 February 1945
G.O. Number, Date: 60, 25 July 1945
Citation: He led a squad in the night attack on Oberhoffen, France, where fierce house-to-house fighting took place. After clearing one building of opposition, he moved his men toward a second house from which heavy machine-gun fire came. He courageously exposed himself to hostile bullets and, firing his submachine gun as he went, advanced steadily toward the enemy position until close enough to hurl grenades through a window, killing three Germans and wrecking their gun. His progress was stopped by heavy rifle and machine-gun fire from another house. Sgt. Deleau dashed through the door with his gun blazing. Within, he captured 10 Germans. The squad then took up a position for the night and awaited daylight to resume the attack. At dawn of 2 February, Sgt. Deleau pressed forward with his unit, killing two snipers as he advanced to a point where machine-gun fire from a house barred the way. Despite vicious small-arms fire, Sgt. Deleau ran across an open area to reach the rear of the building, where he destroyed one machine gun and killed its two operators with a grenade. He worked to the front of the structure and located a second machine gun. Finding it impossible to toss a grenade into the house from his protected position, he fearlessly moved away from the building and was about to hurl his explosive when he was instantly killed by a burst from the gun he sought to knock out. With magnificent courage and daring aggressiveness, Sgt. Deleau cleared four well-defended houses of Germans, inflicted severe losses on the enemy, and at the sacrifice of his own life aided his battalion to reach its objective with a minimum of casualties.

2690 ◆ DERVISHIAN, ERNEST HERBERT

Rank: Second Lieutenant (rank at time of action: Technical Sergeant) (highest rank: Colonel)
Service: U.S. Army
Birthday: 10 August 1916
Place of Birth: Richmond, Richmond County, Virginia
Date of Death: 20 May 1984
Place of Death: Richmond, Virginia
Cemetery: West Hampton Memorial Park—Richmond, Virginia
Entered Service at: Richmond, Richmond County, Virginia
Unit: Company B, 133d Infantry, 34th Infantry Division
Battle or Place of Action: near Cisterna, Italy
Date of Action: 23 May 1944
G.O. Number, Date: 3, 8 January 1945
Date of Presentation: 12 January 1945
Place of Presentation: Piamaggio, Italy, presented by Gen. Mark Clark

Citation: For conspicuous gallantry and intrepidity at the risk of life above and beyond the call of duty on 23 May 1944, in the vicinity of Cisterna, Italy. Second Lt. Dervishian (then T/Sgt.) and four members of his platoon found themselves far ahead of their company after an aggressive advance in the face of enemy artillery and sniper fire. Approaching a railroad embankment, they observed a force of German soldiers hiding in dugouts. Second Lt. Dervishian, directing his men to cover him, boldly moved forward and, firing his carbine, forced 10 Germans to surrender. His men then advanced and captured 15 more Germans occupying adjacent dugouts. The prisoners were returned to the rear to be picked up by advancing units. From the railroad embankment, 2d Lt. Dervishian and his men then observed nine Germans who were fleeing across a ridge. He and his men opened fire and three of the enemy were wounded. As his men were firing, 2d Lt. Dervishian, unnoticed, fearlessly dashed forward alone and captured all of the fleeing enemy before his companions joined him on the ridge. At this point four other men joined 2d Lt. Dervishian's group. An attempt was made to send the four newly arrived men along the left flank of a large, dense vineyard that lay ahead, but murderous machine-gun fire forced them back. Deploying his men, 2d Lt. Dervishian moved to the front of his group and led the advance into the vineyard. He and his men suddenly became pinned down by a machine gun firing at them at a distance of 15 yards. Feigning death while the hostile weapon blazed away at him, 2d Lt. Dervishian assaulted the position during a halt in the firing, using a hand-grenade and carbine fire, and forced the four German crewmembers to surrender. The four men on the left flank were now ordered to enter the vineyard but encountered machine-gun fire which killed one soldier and wounded another. At this moment the enemy intensified the fight by throwing potato-masher grenades at the valiant band of American soldiers within the vineyard. Second Lt. Dervishian ordered his men to withdraw; but instead of following, jumped into the machine-gun position he had just captured and opened fire with the enemy weapon in the direction of the second hostile machine-gun nest. Observing movement in a dugout two or three yards to the rear, 2d Lt. Dervishian seized a machine-pistol. Simultaneously blazing away at the entrance to the dugout to prevent its occupants from firing and firing his machine gun at the other German nest, he forced five Germans in each position to surrender. Determined to rid the area of all Germans, 2d Lt. Dervishian continued his advance alone. Noticing another machine-gun position beside a house, he picked up an abandoned machine-pistol and forced six more Germans to surrender by spraying their position with fire. Unable to locate additional targets in the vicinity, 2d Lt. Dervishian conducted these prisoners to the rear. The prodigous courage and combat skill exhibited by 2d Lt. Dervishian are exemplary of the finest traditions of the U.S. Armed Forces.

2691 ◆ *DIAMOND, JAMES H.

Rank: Private First Class
Service: U.S. Army
Birthday: 22 April 1925
Place of Birth: New Orleans, Orleans County, Louisiana
Date of Death: 14 May 1945
Cemetery: Evergreen Cemetery (MH)—Gulfport, Mississippi
Entered Service at: Gulfport, Harrison County, Mississippi
Unit: Company D, 21st Infantry, 24th Infantry Division
Battle or Place of Action: Mintal, Mindanao, Philippine Islands
Date of Action: 8 to 14 May 1945
G.O. Number, Date: 23, 6 March 1946
Citation: As a member of the machine-gun section, he displayed extreme gallantry and intrepidity above and beyond the call of duty. When a Japanese sniper rose from his foxhole to throw a grenade into their midst, this valiant soldier charged and killed the enemy with a burst from his submachine-gun; then, by delivering sustained fire from his personal arm and simultaneously directing the fire of 105-mm and .50-caliber weapons upon the enemy pillboxes, immobilizing this and another machine-gun section, he enabled them to put their guns into action. When two infantry companies established a bridgehead, he voluntarily assisted in evacuating the wounded under heavy fire; and then, securing an abandoned vehicle, transported casualties to the rear through mortar and artillery fire so intense as to render the vehicle inoperative and despite the fact he was suffering from a painful wound. The following day he again volunteered, this time for the hazardous job of repairing a bridge under heavy enemy fire. On 14 May 1945, when leading a patrol to evacuate casualties from his battalion, which was cut off, he ran through a virtual hail of Japanese fire to secure an abandoned machine gun. Though mortally wounded as he reached the gun, he succeeded in drawing sufficient fire upon himself so that the remaining members of the patrol could reach safety. Pfc. Diamond's indomitable spirit, constant disregard of danger, and eagerness to assist his comrades, will ever remain a symbol of selflessness and heroic sacrifice to those for whom he gave his life.

2692 ◆ *DIETZ, ROBERT H.

Rank: Staff Sergeant
Service: U.S. Army
Place of Birth: Kingston, Ulster County, New York
Date of Death: 29 March 1945
Cemetery: Wiltwych Rural Cemetery—Kingston, New York
Entered Service at: Kingston, Ulster County, New York
Unit: Company A, 38th Armored Infantry Battalion, 7th Armored Division
Served as: Squad Leader
Battle or Place of Action: Kirchain, Germany
Date of Action: 29 March 1945
G.O. Number, Date: 119, 17 December 1945
Citation: He was a squad leader when the task force to which his unit was attached encountered resistance in its advancing on Kirchain, Germany. Between the town's outlying buildings 300 yards distant and the stalled armored column were a minefield and two bridges defended by German rocket-launching teams and riflemen. From the town itself came heavy small-arms fire. Moving forward with his men to

protect engineers while they removed the minefield and the demolition charges attached to the bridges, S/Sgt. Dietz came under intense fire. On his own initiative he advanced alone, scorning the bullets which struck all around him, until he was able to kill the bazooka team defending the first bridge. He continued ahead and had killed another bazooka team, bayoneted an enemy soldier armed with a panzerfaust, and shot two Germans when he was knocked to the ground by another blast of another panzerfaust. He quickly recovered, killed the man who had fired at him, and then jumped into waist-deep water under the second bridge to disconnect the demolition charges. His work was completed; but as he stood up to signal that the route was clear he was killed by another enemy volley from the left flank. S/Sgt. Dietz by his intrepidity and valiant effort on his self-imposed mission, singlehandedly opened the road for the capture of Kirchain and left with his comrades an inspiring example of gallantry in the face of formidable odds.

2693 ◆ DOOLITTLE, JAMES HAROLD

Rank: Brigadier General (highest rank: General)
Service: U.S. Army Air Corps/U.S. Air Force
Birthday: 14 December 1896
Place of Birth: Alameda, Alameda County, California
Date of Death: 27 September 1993
Place of Death: Pebble Beach, California
Cemetery: Arlington National Cemetery (7A-110)—Arlington, Virginia
Entered Service at: Berkeley, Alameda County, California
Unit: Army Air Force Headquarters, Washington, D.C.
Served as: Commanding Officer/Pilot of a B-25
Battle or Place of Action: over Tokyo, Japan
Date of Action: 18 April 1942
G.O. Number, Date: 29, 9 June 1942
Date of Presentation: 20 May 1942
Place of Presentation: The White House, presented by Pres. Franklin D. Roosevelt
Citation: For conspicuous leadership above the call of duty, involving personal valor and intrepidity at an extreme hazard to life. With the apparent certainty of being forced to land in enemy territory or to perish at sea, Gen. Doolittle personally led a squadron of Army bombers, manned by volunteer crews, in a highly destructive raid on the Japanese mainland.

2694 ◆ DOSS, DESMOND THOMAS

Rank: Private First Class (highest rank: Corporal)
Service: U.S. Army
Birthday: 7 February 1919
Place of Birth: Lynchburg, Lynchburg County, Virginia
Entered Service at: Lynchburg, Lynchburg County, Virginia
Unit: 307th Infantry, Medical Detachment, 77th Infantry Division
Served as: Medical Aidman
Battle or Place of Action: Urasoe-Mura, Okinawa, Ryukyu Islands
Date of Action: 29 April-21 May 1945
G.O. Number, Date: 97, 1 November 1945
Date of Presentation: 12 October 1945
Place of Presentation: The White House, presented by Pres. Harry S. Truman
Citation: He was a company aidman when the 1st Battalion assaulted a jagged escarpment 400 feet high. As our troops gained the summit, a heavy concentration of artillery, mortar, and machine-gun fire crashed into them, inflicting approximately 75 casualties and driving the others back. Pfc. Doss refused to seek cover and remained in the fire-swept area with the many stricken, carrying them one by one to the edge of the escarpment and there lowering them on a rope-supported litter down the face of a cliff to friendly hands. On 2 May, he exposed himself to heavy rifle and mortar fire in rescuing a wounded man 200 yards forward of the lines on the same escarpment; and two days later he treated four men who had been cut down while assaulting a strongly defended cave, advancing through a shower of grenades to within eight yards of enemy forces in a cave's mouth, where he dressed his comrades' wounds before making four separate trips under fire to evacuate them to safety. On 5 May, he unhesitatingly braved enemy shelling and small-arms fire to assist an artillery officer. He applied bandages, moved his patient to a spot that offered protection from small-arms fire, and, while artillery and mortar shells fell close by, painstakingly administered plasma. Later that day, when an American was severely wounded by fire from a cave, Pfc. Doss crawled to him where he had fallen 25 feet from the enemy position, rendered aid, and carried him 100 yards to safety while continually exposed to enemy fire. On 21 May, in a night attack on high ground near Shuri, he remained in exposed territory while the rest of his company took cover, fearlessly risking the chance that he would be mistaken for an infiltrating Japanese and giving aid to the injured until he was himself seriously wounded in the legs by the explosion of a grenade. Rather than call another aidman from cover, he cared for his own injuries and waited five hours before litter bearers reached him and started carrying him to cover. The trio was caught in an enemy tank attack and Pfc. Doss, seeing a more critically wounded man nearby, crawled off the litter and directed the bearers to give their first attention to the other man. Awaiting the litter bearers' return, he was again struck, this time suffering a compound fracture of one arm. With magnificent fortitude he bound a rifle stock to his shattered arm as a splint and then crawled 300 yards over rough terrain to the aid station. Through his outstanding bravery and unflinching determination in the face of desperately dangerous conditions Pfc. Doss saved the lives of many soldiers. His name became a symbol throughout the 77th Infantry Division for outstanding gallantry far above and beyond the call of duty.

2695 ◆ DROWLEY, JESSE RAY

Rank: Staff Sergeant
Service: U.S. Army
Birthday: 13 September 1919
Place of Birth: St. Charles, Saginaw County, Michigan
Entered Service at: Wayne County, Michigan
Unit: Weapons Platoon, Company B, 1st Battalion, 132d Infantry, Americal Division

Served as: Squad Leader
Battle or Place of Action: Bougainville, Solomon Islands
Date of Action: 30 January 1944
G.O. Number, Date: 73, 6 September 1944
Date of Presentation: 30 August 1944
Place of Presentation: The White House, presented by Pres. Franklin D. Roosevelt
Citation: For gallantry and intrepidity at the risk of his life above and beyond the call of duty in action with the enemy at Bougainville Island, Solomon Islands, 30 January 1944. S/Sgt. Drowley, a squad leader in a platoon whose mission during an attack was to remain under cover while holding the perimeter defense and acting as a reserve for assaulting echelon, saw three members of the assault company fall badly wounded. When intense hostile fire prevented aid from reaching the casualties, he fearlessly rushed forward to carry the wounded to cover. After rescuing two men, S/Sgt. Drowley discovered an enemy pillbox undetected by assaulting tanks that was inflicting heavy casualties upon the attacking force and was a chief obstacle to the success of the advance. Delegating the rescue of the third man to an assistant, he ran across open terrain to one of the tanks. Signaling to the crew, he climbed to the turret, exchanged his weapon for a submachine gun and voluntarily rode the deck of the tank directing it toward the pillbox by tracer fire. The tank, under constant heavy enemy fire, continued to within 20 feet of the pillbox where S/Sgt. Drowley received a severe bullet wound in the chest. Refusing to return for medical treatment, he remained on the tank and continued to direct its progress until the enemy box was definitely located by the crew. At this point he again was wounded by small-arms fire, losing his left eye and falling to the ground. He remained alongside the tank until the pillbox had been completely demolished and another directly behind the first destroyed. S/Sgt. Drowley, his voluntary mission successfully accomplished, returned alone for medical treatment.

2696 ◆ DUNHAM, RUSSELL

Rank: Technical Sergeant
Service: U.S. Army
Birthday: 23 February 1920
Place of Birth: East Carondelet, St. Clair County, Illinois
Entered Service at: Brighton, Jersey County, Illinois
Unit: 2d Platoon, Company I, 3d Battalion, 30th Infantry, 3d Infantry Division
Served as: Platoon Sergeant
Battle or Place of Action: Kaysersberg, France
Date of Action: 8 January 1945
G.O. Number, Date: 37, 11 May 1945
Date of Presentation: 23 April 1945
Place of Presentation: Zepman Stadium, Nuremberg, Germany, presented by Lt. Gen. Alexander M. Patch III
Citation: For conspicuous gallantry and intrepidity at risk of life above and beyond the call of duty. At about 1430 hours on 8 January 1945, during an attack on Hill 616, near Kaysersberg, France, T/Sgt. Dunham singlehandedly assaulted three enemy machine guns. Wearing a white robe made of a mattress cover, carrying 12 carbine magazines and with a dozen hand grenades snagged in his belt, suspenders, and buttonholes, T/Sgt. Dunham advanced in the attack up a snow-covered hill under fire from two machine guns and supporting riflemen. His platoon 35 yards behind him, T/Sgt. Dunham crawled 75 yards under heavy direct fire toward the timbered emplacement shielding the left machine gun. As he jumped to his feet 10 yards from the gun and charged forward, machine-gun fire tore through his camouflage robe and a rifle bullet seared a 10-inch gash across his back sending him spinning 15 yards downhill into the snow. When the indomitable sergeant sprang to his feet to renew his one-man assault, a German egg grenade landed beside him. He kicked it aside, and as it exploded five yards away, shot and killed the German machine gunner and assistant gunner. His carbine empty, he jumped into the emplacement and hauled out the third member of the gun crew by the collar. Although his back wound was causing him excruciating pain and blood was seeping through his white coat, T/Sgt. Dunham proceeded 50 yards through a storm of automatic and rifle fire to attack the second machine gun. Twenty-five yards from the emplacement he hurled two grenades, destroying the gun and its crew; then fired down into the supporting foxholes with his carbine, dispatching and dispersing the enemy riflemen. Although his coat was so thoroughly blood-soaked that he was a conspicuous target against the white landscape, T/Sgt. Dunham again advanced ahead of his platoon in an assault on enemy positions farther up the hill. Coming under machine-gun fire from 65 yards to his front, while rifle grenades exploded 10 yards from his position, he hit the ground and crawled forward. At 15 yards' range, he jumped to his feet, staggered a few paces toward the timbered machine-gun emplacement, and killed the crew with hand grenades. An enemy rifleman fired at point-blank range, but missed him. After killing the rifleman, T/Sgt. Dunham drove others from their foxholes with grenades and carbine fire. Killing nine Germans—wounding seven and capturing two—firing about 175 rounds of carbine ammunition, and expending 11 grenades, T/Sgt. Dunham, despite a painful wound, spearheaded a spectacular and successful diversionary attack.

2697 ◆ DUNLAP, ROBERT HUGO

Rank: Captain (highest rank: Major)
Service: U.S. Marine Corps Reserve
Birthday: 19 October 1920
Place of Birth: Abingdon, Knox County, Illinois
Entered Service at: Monmouth, Warren County, Illinois
Unit: Company C, 1st Battalion, 26th Marines, 5th Marine Division
Served as: Commanding Officer
Battle or Place of Action: Iwo Jima, Volcano Islands
Date of Action: 20-21 February 1945
Date of Presentation: 18 December 1945
Place of Presentation: The White House, presented by Pres. Harry S. Truman
Citation: For conspicuous gallantry and intrepidity at the risk of his life above and beyond the call of duty as commanding officer of Company C, 1st Battalion, 26th Marines, 5th Marine division, in action against enemy Japanese forces dur-

ing the seizure of Iwo Jima in the Volcano Islands on 20 and 21 February, 1945. Defying uninterrupted blasts of Japanese artillery, mortar, rifle, and machine-gun fire, Capt. Dunlap led his troops in a determined advance from low ground uphill toward the steep cliffs from which the enemy poured a devastating rain of shrapnel and bullets, steadily inching forward until the tremendous volume of enemy fire from the caves located high to his front temporarily halted his progress. Determined not to yield, he crawled alone approximately 200 yards forward of his front lines, took observation at the base of the cliff 50 yards from Japanese lines, located the enemy gun positions, and returned to his own lines where he relayed the vital information to supporting artillery and naval gunfire units. Persistently disregarding his own personal safety, he then placed himself in an exposed vantage point to direct more accurately the supporting fire and, working without respite for two days and two nights under constant enemy fire, skillfully directed a smashing bombardment against the almost impregnable Japanese positions despite numerous obstacles and heavy marine casualties. A brilliant leader, Capt. Dunlap inspired his men to heroic efforts during this critical phase of the battle and by his cool decision, indomitable fighting spirit, and daring tactics in the face of fanatic opposition greatly accelerated the final decisive defeat of Japanese countermeasures in his sector and materially furthered the continued advance of his company. His great personal valor and gallant spirit of self-sacrifice throughout the bitter hostilities reflect the highest credit upon Capt. Dunlap and the U.S. Naval Service.

2698 ◆ *DUTKO, JOHN W.

Rank: Private First Class
Service: U.S. Army
Birthday: 24 October 1916
Place of Birth: Dilltown, Indiana County, Pennsylvania
Date of Death: 23 May 1944
Cemetery: Beverley National Cemetery (DS-1) (MH)—Beverley, New Jersey
Entered Service at: Riverside, Burlington County, New Jersey
Unit: Company A, 30th Infantry, 3d Infantry Division
Battle or Place of Action: near Ponte Rotto, Italy
Date of Action: 23 May 1944
G.O. Number, Date: 80, 5 October 1944
Citation: For conspicuous gallantry and intrepidity at risk of life above and beyond the call of duty, 23 May 1944, near Ponte Rotto, Italy. Pfc. Dutko left the cover of an abandoned enemy trench at the height of an artillery concentration in a singlehanded attack upon three enemy machine-guns and an 88-mm mobile gun. Despite the intense fire of these four weapons which were aimed directly at him, Pfc. Dutko ran 100 yards through the impact area, paused momentarily in a shell crater, and then continued his one-man assault. Although machine-gun bullets kicked up the dirt at his heels, and 88-mm shells exploded within 30 yards of him, Pfc. Dutko nevertheless made his way to a point within 30 yards of the first enemy machine gun and killed both gunners with a hand grenade. Although the second machine gun wounded him, knocking him to the ground, Pfc. Dutko regained his feet and advanced on the 88-mm gun, firing his Browning automatic rifle from the hip. When he came within 10 yards of this weapon he killed its five-man crew with one long burst of fire. Wheeling on the machine gun which had wounded him, Pfc. Dutko killed the gunner and his assistant. The third German machine gun fired on Pfc. Dutko from a position 20 yards distant wounding him a second time as he proceeded toward the enemy weapon in a half run. He killed both members of its crew with a single burst from his Browning automatic rifle, continued toward the gun and died, his body falling across the dead German crew.

2699 ◆ *DYESS, AQUILLA JAMES

Rank: Lieutenant Colonel
Service: U.S. Marine Corps Reserve
Birthday: 11 January 1909
Place of Birth: Augusta, Richmond County, Georgia
Date of Death: 2 February 1944
Place of Death: Namur Island, Marshall Islands
Cemetery: Westover Memorial Park—Augusta, Georgia
Entered Service at: Georgia
Unit: 1st Battalion, 24th Marines, 4th Marine Division (Rein)
Served as: Commanding Officer
Battle or Place of Action: Namur Island, Kwajalein Atoll, Marshall Islands
Date of Action: 1-2 February 1944
Citation: For conspicuous gallantry and intrepidity at the risk of his life above and beyond the call of duty as commanding officer of the 1st Battalion, 24th Marines (Rein), 4th Marine Division, in action against enemy Japanese forces during the assault on Namur Island, Kwajalein Atoll, Marshall Islands, 1 and 2 February 1944. Undaunted by severe fire from automatic Japanese weapons, Lt. Col. Dyess launched a powerful final attack on the second day of the assault, unhesitatingly posting himself between the opposing lines to point out objectives and avenues of approach and personally leading the advancing troops. Alert and determined to quicken the pace of the offensive against increased enemy fire, he was constantly at the head of advance units, inspiring his men to push forward until the Japanese had been driven back to a small center of resistance and victory assured. While standing on the parapet of the antitank trench directing a group of infantry in a flanking attack against the last enemy position, Lt. Col. Dyess was killed by a burst of enemy machine-gun fire. His daring and forceful leadership and his valiant fighting spirit in the face of terrific opposition were in keeping with the highest traditions of the U.S. Naval Service. He gallantly gave his life for his country.

2700 ◆ EDSON, MERRITT AUSTIN

Rank: Colonel (highest rank: Major General)
Service: U.S. Marine Corps
Birthday: 25 April 1897
Place of Birth: Rutland, Rutland County, Vermont
Date of Death: 14 August 1955

Place of Death: Washington, D.C.
Cemetery: Arlington National Cemetery (2-4960-2)—Arlington, Virginia
Entered Service at: Vermont
Unit: 1st Marine Raider Battalion
Served as: Commanding Officer
Battle or Place of Action: Guadalcanal, Solomon Islands
Date of Action: 13-14 September 1942
Date of Presentation: 21 May 1943
Place of Presentation: Balcombe, Australia, presented by Maj. Gen. Alexander A. Vandegrift
Citation: For extraordinary heroism and conspicuous intrepidity above and beyond the call of duty as commanding officer of the 1st Marine Raider Battalion, with Parachute Battalion attached, during action against enemy Japanese forces in the Solomon Islands on the night of 13–14 September 1942. After the airfield on Guadalcanal had been seized from the enemy on 8 August, Col. Edson, with a force of 800 men, was assigned to the occupation and defense of a ridge dominating the jungle on either side of the airport. Facing a formidable Japanese attack which, augmented by infiltration, had crashed through our front lines, he, by skillful handling of his troops, successfully withdrew his forward units to a reserve line with minimum casualties. When the enemy, in a subsequent series of violent assaults, engaged our force in desperate hand-to-hand combat with bayonets, rifles, pistols, grenades, and knives, Col. Edson, although continuously exposed to hostile fire throughout the night, personally directed defense of the reserve position against a fanatical foe of greatly superior numbers. By his astute leadership and gallant devotion to duty, he enabled his men, despite severe losses, to cling tenaciously to their position on the vital ridge, thereby retaining command not only of the Guadalcanal airfield, but also of the 1st Division's entire offensive installations in the surrounding area.

2701 ◆ EHLERS, WALTER DAVID

Rank: Staff Sergeant (highest rank: Second Lieutenant)
Service: U.S. Army
Birthday: 7 May 1921
Place of Birth: Junction City, Geary County, Kansas
Entered Service at: Manhattan, Riley County, Kansas
Unit: 3d Squad, 3d Platoon, Company L, 3d Battalion, 18th Infantry, 1st Infantry Division
Served as: Squad Leader
Battle or Place of Action: near Goville, France
Date of Action: 9-10 June 1944
G.O. Number, Date: 91, 19 December 1944
Date of Presentation: 19 December 1944
Place of Presentation: Paris, France, presented by Lt. Gen. John C.H. Lee
Citation: For conspicuous gallantry and intrepidity at the risk of his life above and beyond the call of duty on 9–10 June 1944 near Goville, France. S/Sgt. Ehlers, always acting as the spearhead of the attack, repeatedly led his men against heavily defended enemy strongpoints, exposing himself to deadly hostile fire whenever the situation required heroic and courageous leadership. Without waiting for an order, S/Sgt. Ehlers, far ahead of his men, led his squad against a strongly defended enemy strongpoint, personally killing four of an enemy patrol who attacked him en route. Then crawling forward under withering machine-gun fire, he pounced upon the gun-crew and put it out of action. Turning his attention to two mortars protected by the crossfire of two machine guns, S/Sgt. Ehlers led his men through this hail of bullets to kill or put to flight the enemy of the mortar section, killing three men himself. After mopping up the mortar positions, he again advanced on a machine gun, his progress effectively covered by his squad. When he was almost on top of the gun he leaped to his feet and, although greatly outnumbered, he knocked out the position singlehandedly. The next day, having advanced deep into enemy territory, the platoon of which S/Sgt. Ehlers was a member finding itself in an untenable position as the enemy brought increased mortar, machine-gun, and small-arms fire to bear on it, was ordered to withdraw. S/Sgt. Ehlers, after his squad had covered the withdrawal of the remainder of the platoon, stood up and by continuous fire at the semicircle of enemy placements, diverted the bulk of the heavy hostile fire on himself, thus permitting the members of his own squad to withdraw. At this point, though wounded himself, he carried his wounded automatic rifleman to safety and then returned fearlessly over the shell-swept field to retrieve the automatic rifle which he was unable to carry previously. After having his wound treated, he refused to be evacuated, and returned to lead his squad. The intrepid leadership, indomitable courage, and fearless aggressiveness displayed by S/Sgt. Ehlers in the face of overwhelming enemy forces serve as an inspiration to others.

2702 ◆ *ELROD, HENRY TALMAGE

Rank: Captain (highest rank: Major)
Service: U.S. Marine Corps
Birthday: 27 September 1905
Place of Birth: Rebecca, Turner County, Georgia
Date of Death: 23 December 1941
Cemetery: Arlington National Cemetery (12-3246) (MH)—Arlington, Virginia
Entered Service at: Ashburn, Turner County, Georgia
Unit: Marine Fighting Squadron 211
Served as: Pilot of an F4F-3 Grumman Wildcat
Battle or Place of Action: Wake Island
Date of Action: 8-23 December 1941
Citation: For conspicuous gallantry and intrepidity at the risk of his life above and beyond the call of duty while attached to Marine Fighting Squadron 211, during action against enemy Japanese land, surface and aerial units at Wake Island, 8-23 December 1941. Engaging vastly superior forces of enemy bombers and warships on 9 and 12 December, Capt. Elrod shot down two of a flight of 22 hostile planes and, executing repeated bombing and strafing runs at extremely low altitude and close range, succeeded in inflicting deadly damage upon a large Japanese vessel, thereby sinking the first major warship to be destroyed by small-caliber bombs delivered from a fighter-type aircraft. When his plane was disabled by hostile fire and no other ships were operative, Capt. Elrod assumed command of one flank of the line set up

in defiance of the enemy landing and, conducting a brilliant defense, enabled his men to hold their positions and repulse intense hostile fusillades to provide covering fire for unarmed ammunition carriers. Capturing an automatic weapon during one enemy rush in force, he gave his own firearm to one of his men and fought on vigorously against the Japanese. Responsible in a large measure for the strength of his sector's gallant resistance, on 23 December, Capt. Elrod led his men with bold aggressiveness until he fell, mortally wounded. His superb skill as a pilot, daring leadership, and unswerving devotion to duty distinguished him among the defenders of Wake Island, and his valiant conduct reflects the highest credit upon himself and the U.S. Naval Service. He gallantly gave his life for his country.

2703 ◆ *ENDL, GERALD LEON

Rank: Staff Sergeant
Service: U.S. Army
Birthday: 20 August 1915
Place of Birth: Fort Atkinson, Jefferson County, Wisconsin
Date of Death: 11 July 1944
Cemetery: St. Joseph's Cemetery—Fort Atkinson, Wisconsin
Entered Service at: Janesville, Rock County, Wisconsin
Unit: 32d Infantry Division
Battle or Place of Action: near Anamo, New Guinea
Date of Action: 11 July 1944
G.O. Number, Date: 17, 13 March 1945
Citation: For conspicuous gallantry and intrepidity at the risk of his life above and beyond the call of duty near Anamo, New Guinea, 11 July 1944. S/Sgt. Endl was at the head of the leading platoon of his company advancing along a jungle trail when enemy troops were encountered and a firefight developed. The enemy attacked in force under heavy rifle, machine-gun, and grenade fire. His platoon leader wounded, S/Sgt. Endl immediately assumed command and deployed his platoon on a firing line at the fork in the trail toward which the enemy attack was directed. The dense jungle terrain greatly restricted vision and movement, and he endeavored to penetrate down the trail toward an open clearing of kunai grass. As he advanced, he detected the enemy, supported by at least six light and two heavy machine guns, attempting an enveloping movement around both flanks. His commanding officer sent a second platoon to move up on the left flank of the position, but the enemy closed in rapidly, placing our force in imminent danger of being isolated and annihilated. Twelve members of his platoon were wounded, seven being cut off by the enemy. Realizing that if his platoon were forced farther back, these seven men would be hopelessly trapped and at the mercy of a vicious enemy, he resolved to advance at all cost, knowing it meant almost certain death, in an effort to rescue his comrades. In the face of extremely heavy fire he went forward alone and for a period of approximately 10 minutes engaged the enemy in a heroic close-range fight, holding them off while his men crawled forward under cover to evacuate the wounded and to withdraw. Courageously refusing to abandon four more wounded men who were lying along the trail, one by one he brought them back to safety. As he was carrying the last man in his arms he was struck by a heavy burst of automatic-weapon fire and was killed. By his persistent and daring self-sacrifice and on behalf of his comrades, S/Sgt. Endl made possible the successful evacuation of all but one man, and enabled the two platoons to withdraw with their wounded and to reorganize with the rest of the company.

2704 ◆ *EPPERSON, HAROLD GLENN

Rank: Private First Class
Service: U.S. Marine Corps Reserve
Birthday: 14 July 1923
Place of Birth: Akron, Summit County, Ohio
Date of Death: 25 June 1944
Cemetery: Town Cemetery (MH)—Winchester, Kentucky
Entered Service at: Ohio
Unit: 1st Battalion, 6th Marines, 2d Marine Division
Served as: Machine Gunner
Battle or Place of Action: Saipan Island, Mariana Islands
Date of Action: 25 June 1944
Citation: For conspicuous gallantry and intrepidity at the risk of his life above and beyond the call of duty while serving with the 1st Battalion, 6th Marines, 2d Marine Division, in action against enemy Japanese forces on the island of Saipan in the Marianas, 25 June 1944. With his machine-gun emplacement bearing the full brunt of a fanatic assault initiated by the Japanese under cover of predawn darkness, Pfc. Epperson manned his weapon with determined aggressiveness, fighting furiously in the defense of his battalion's position and maintaining a steady stream of devastating fire against rapidly infiltrating hostile troops to aid materially in annihilating several of the enemy and in breaking the abortive attack. Suddenly a Japanese soldier, assumed to be dead, sprang up and hurled a powerful hand grenade into the emplacement. Determined to save his comrades, Pfc. Epperson unhesitatingly chose to sacrifice himself and, diving upon the deadly missile, absorbed the shattering violence of the exploding charge in his own body. Stouthearted and indomitable in the face of certain death, Pfc. Epperson fearlessly yielded his own life that his able comrades might carry on the relentless battle against a ruthless enemy. His superb valor and unfaltering devotion to duty throughout reflect the highest credit upon himself and upon the U.S. Naval Service. He gallantly gave his life for his country.

2705 ◆ ERWIN, HENRY EUGENE "RED"

Rank: Staff Sergeant (highest rank: Master Sergeant)
Service: U.S. Army Air Corps
Birthday: 8 May 1921
Place of Birth: Adamsville, Jefferson County, Alabama
Entered Service at: Bessemer, Jefferson County, Alabama
Unit: 52d Bombardment Squadron, 29th Bombardment Group, 314th Bombardment Wing, 20th Air Force
Served as: Radio Operator on a B-29
Battle or Place of Action: Koriyama, Japan
Date of Action: 12 April 1945
G.O. Number, Date: 44, 6 June 1945
Date of Presentation: 19 April 1945

Place of Presentation: Fleet Hospital 103, Guam, presented by Gen. Curtis LeMay
Citation: He was the radio operator of a B-29 airplane leading a group formation to attack Koriyama, Japan. He was charged with the additional duty of dropping phosphorus smoke bombs to aid in assembling the group when the launching point was reached. Upon entering the assembly area, aircraft fire and enemy fighter opposition was encountered. Among the phosphorus bombs launched by S/Sgt. Erwin, one proved faulty, exploding in the launching chute, and shot back into the interior of the aircraft, striking him in the face. The burning phosphorus obliterated his nose and completely blinded him. Smoke filled the plane, obscuring the vision of the pilot. S/Sgt. Erwin realized that the aircraft and crew would be lost if the burning bomb remained in the plane. Without regard for his own safety, he picked it up and feeling his way, instictively, crawled around the gun turret and headed for the copilot's window. He found the navigator's table obstructing his passage. Grasping the burning bomb between his forearm and body, he unleashed the spring lock and raised the table. Struggling through the narrow passage he stumbled forward into the smoke-filled pilot's compartment. Groping with his burning hands, he located the window and threw the bomb out. Completely aflame, he fell back upon the floor. The smoke cleared, the pilot, at 300 feet, pulled the plane out of its dive. S/Sgt. Erwin's gallantry and heroism above and beyond the call of duty saved the lives of his comrades.

2706 ◆ *EUBANKS, RAY E.

Rank: Sergeant
Service: U.S. Army
Birthday: 6 February 1922
Place of Birth: Snow Hill, Greene County, North Carolina
Date of Death: 23 July 1944
Cemetery: West View Cemetery (MH)—Kinston, North Carolina
Entered Service at: LaGrange, Lenoir County, North Carolina
Unit: Company D, 503d Parachute Infantry
Battle or Place of Action: Noemfoor Island, Dutch New Guinea
Date of Action: 23 July 1944
G.O. Number, Date: 20, 29 March 1945
Citation: For conspicuous gallantry and intrepidity at the risk of his life above and beyond the call of duty at Noemfoor Island, Dutch New Guinea, 23 July 1944. While moving to the relief of a platoon isolated by the enemy, his company encountered a strong enemy position supported by machine-gun, rifle, and mortar fire. Sgt. Eubanks was ordered to make an attack with one squad to neutralize the enemy by fire in order to assist the advance of his company. He maneuvered his squad to within 30 yards of the enemy where heavy fire checked his advance. Directing his men to maintain their fire, he and two scouts worked their way forward up a shallow depression to within 25 yards of the enemy. Directing the scouts to remain in place, Sgt. Eubanks armed himself with an automatic rifle and worked himself forward over terrain swept by intense fire to within 15 yards of the enemy position when he opened fire with telling effect. The enemy, having located his position, concentrated their fire, with the result that he was wounded and a bullet rendered his rifle useless. In spite of his painful wounds he immediately charged the enemy and using his weapon as a club killed four of the enemy before he was himself again hit and killed. Sgt. Eubanks' heroic action, courage, and example in leadership so inspired his men that their advance was successful. They killed 45 of the enemy and drove the remainder from the position, thus effecting the relief of our beleaguered troops.

2707 ◆ *EVANS, ERNEST EDWIN "CHIEF"

Rank: Commander
Service: U.S. Navy
Birthday: 13 August 1908
Place of Birth: Pawnee, Pawnee County, Oklahoma
Date of Death: 25 October 1944
Cemetery: A.B.M.C. Manila Cemetery (Wall of the Missing)—Manila, Philippine Islands
Entered Service at: Oklahoma
Unit: U.S.S. *Johnston*
Served as: Commanding Officer
Battle or Place of Action: off Samar, Philippine Islands
Date of Action: 25 October 1944
Date of Issue: 28 September 1945
Citation: For conspicuous gallantry and intrepidity at the risk of his life above and beyond the call of duty as commanding officer of the U.S.S. *Johnston* in action against major units of the Japanese fleet during the battle off Samar on 25 October 1944. The first to lay a smoke screen and to open fire as an enemy task force, vastly superior in number, firepower, and armor, rapidly approached, Comdr. Evans gallantly diverted the powerful blasts of hostile guns from the lightly armed and armored carriers under his protection, launching the first torpedo attack when the *Johnston* came under straddling Japanese shellfire. Undaunted by damage sustained under the terrific volume of fire, he unhesitatingly joined others of his group to provide fire support during subsequent torpedo attacks against the Japanese and, outshooting and outmaneuvering the enemy as he consistently interposed his vessel between the hostile fleet units and our carriers despite the crippling loss of engine power and communications with steering aft, shifted command to the fantail, shouted steering orders through an open hatch to men turning the rudder by hand, and battled furiously until the *Johnston*, burning and shuddering from a mortal blow, lay dead in the water after three hours of fierce combat. Seriously wounded early in the engagement, Comdr. Evans, by his indomitable courage and brilliant professional skill, aided materially in turning back the enemy during a critical phase of the action. His valiant fighting spirit throughout this historic battle will venture as an inspiration to all who served with him.

2708 ◆ EVERHART SR., FORREST EUGENE

Rank: Technical Sergeant
Service: U.S. Army

Birthday: 28 August 1921
Place of Birth: Bainbridge, Ross County, Ohio
Date of Death: 30 August 1986
Place of Death: Philadelphia, Pennsylvania
Cemetery: Arlington National Cemetery (60-7516) (MH)—Arlington, Virginia
Entered Service at: Texas City, Galveston County, Texas
Unit: Company H, 359th Infantry, 90th Infantry Division
Battle or Place of Action: near Kerling, France
Date of Action: 12 November 1944
G.O. Number, Date: 77, 10 September 1945
Date of Presentation: 23 August 1945
Place of Presentation: The White House, presented by Pres. Harry S. Truman
Citation: He commanded a platoon that bore the brunt of a desperate enemy counterattack near Korling, France, before dawn on 12 November 1944. When German tanks and self-propelled guns penetrated his left flank and overwhelming infantry forces threatened to overrun the one remaining machine-gun in that section, he ran 400 yards through woods churned by artillery and mortar concentrations to strengthen the defense. With the one remaining gunner, he directed furious fire into the advancing hordes until they swarmed close to the position. He left the gun, boldly charged the attackers, and, after a 15-minute exchange of hand grenades, forced them to withdraw leaving 30 dead behind. He recrossed the fire-swept terrain to his then threatened right flank, exhorted his men and directed murderous fire from the single machine-gun at that position. There, in the light of bursting mortar shells, he again closed with the enemy in a hand-grenade duel and, after a fierce 30-minute battle, forced the Germans to withdraw leaving another 20 dead. The gallantry and intrepidity of T/Sgt. Everhart in rallying his men and refusing to fall back in the face of terrible odds were highly instrumental in repelling the fanatical enemy counterattack directed at the American bridgehead across the Moselle River.

2709 ◆ *FARDY, JOHN PETER

Rank: Corporal
Service: U.S. Marine Corps
Birthday: 15 August 1922
Place of Birth: Chicago, Cook County, Illinois
Date of Death: 7 May 1945
Cemetery: Holy Sepulchre Cemetery—Worth, Illinois
Entered Service at: Illinois
Unit: Company C, 1st Battalion, 1st Marines, 1st Marine Division
Served as: Squad Leader
Battle or Place of Action: Okinawa Shima, Ryukyu Islands
Date of Action: 7 May 1945
Citation: For conspicuous gallantry and intrepidity at the risk of his life above and beyond the call of duty as a squad leader, serving with Company C, 1st Battalion, 1st Marines, 1st Marine Division, in action against enemy Japanese forces on Okinawa Shima in the Ryukyu Islands, 7 May 1945. When his squad was suddenly assailed by extremely heavy small-arms fire from the front during a determined advance against strongly fortified, fiercely defended Japanese positions, Cpl. Fardy temporarily deployed his men along a nearby drainage ditch. Shortly thereafter, an enemy grenade fell among the marines in the ditch. Instantly throwing himself upon the deadly missile, Cpl. Fardy absorbed the exploding blast in his own body, thereby protecting his comrades from certain and perhaps fatal injuries. Concerned solely for the welfare of his men, he willingly relinquished his own hope of survival that his fellow marines might live to carry on the fight against a fanatic enemy. A stouthearted leader and indomitable fighter, Cpl. Fardy, by his prompt decision and resolute spirit of self-sacrifice in the face of certain death, had rendered valiant service, and his conduct throughout reflects the highest credit upon himself and the U.S. Naval Service. He gallantly gave his life for his country.

2710 ◆ *FEMOYER, ROBERT EDWARD

Rank: Second Lieutenant
Service: U.S. Army Air Corps
Birthday: 31 October 1921
Place of Birth: Huntington, Cabell County, West Virginia
Date of Death: 2 November 1944
Cemetery: Greenlawn Cemetery (MH)—Jacksonville, Florida
Entered Service at: Jacksonville, Duval County, Florida
Unit: 711th Bombardment Squadron, 447th Bombardment Group, 8th Air Force
Served as: Navigator of a B-17
Battle or Place of Action: over Merseburg, Germany
Date of Action: 2 November 1944
G.O. Number, Date: 35, 9 May 1945
Citation: For conspicuous gallantry and intrepidity at the risk of his life above and beyond the call of duty near Merseburg, Germany on 2 November 1944. While on a mission, the bomber, of which 2d Lt. Femoyer was a navigator, was struck by three enemy antiaircraft shells. The plane suffered serious damage and 2d Lt. Femoyer was severely wounded in the side and back by shell fragments which penetrated his body. In spite of extreme pain and great loss of blood he refused an offered injection of morphine. He was determined to keep his mental faculties clear in order that he might direct his plane out of danger and so save his comrades. Not being able to arise from the floor, he asked to be propped up in order to enable him to see his charts and instruments. He successfully directed the navigation of his lone bomber for 2 1/2 hours so well it avoided enemy flak and returned to the field without further damage. Only when the plane had arrived in the safe area over the English Channel did he feel that he had accomplished his objective; then, and only then, he permitted an injection of a sedative. He died shortly after being moved from the plane. The heroism and self-sacrifice of 2d Lt. Femoyer are in keeping with the highest traditions of the U.S. Army.

2711 ◆ FIELDS, JAMES H.

Rank: First Lieutenant
Service: U.S. Army
Birthday: 26 June 1920

Place of Birth: Caddo, Stephens County, Texas
Date of Death: 17 June 1970
Cemetery: Houston National Cemetery (HB-6) (MH)—Houston, Texas
Entered Service at: Houston, Harris County, Texas
Unit: 10th Armored Infantry, 4th Armored Division
Served as: Platoon Leader
Battle or Place of Action: Rechicourt, France
Date of Action: 27 September 1944
G.O. Number, Date: 13, 27 February 1945
Date of Presentation: 22 February 1945
Place of Presentation: Luxembourg, Belgium, presented by Gen. George S. Patton
Citation: For conspicuous gallantry and intrepidity at the risk of life above and beyond the call of duty, at Rechicourt, France. On 27 September 1944, during a sharp action with the enemy infantry and tank forces, 1st Lt. Fields personally led his platoon in a counterattack on the enemy position. Although his platoon had been seriously depleted, the zeal and fervor of his leadership was such as to inspire his small force to accomplish their mission in the face of overwhelming enemy opposition. Seeing that one of the men had been wounded, he left his slit trench and with complete disregard for his personal safety attended the wounded man and administered first aid. While returning to his slit trench he was seriously wounded by a shell burst, the fragments of which cut through his face and head, tearing his teeth, gums, and nasal passage. Although rendered speechless by his wounds, 1st Lt. Fields refused to be evacuated and continued to lead his platoon by the use of hand signals. On one occasion, when two enemy machine guns had a portion of his unit under deadly crossfire, he left his hole, wounded as he was, ran to a light machine gun, whose crew had been knocked out, picked up the gun, and fired it from the hip with such deadly accuracy that both the enemy gun positions were silenced. His action so impressed his men that they found new courage to take up the firefight, increasing their firepower and exposing themselves more than ever to harass the enemy with additional bazooka and machine-gun fire. Only when his objective had been taken and the enemy scattered did 1st Lt. Fields consent to be evacuated to the battalion command post. At this point he refused to move further back until he had explained to his battalion commander by drawing on paper the position of his men and the disposition of the enemy forces. The dauntless and gallant heroism displayed by 1st Lt. Fields were largely responsible for the repulse of the enemy forces and contributed in a large measure to the successful capture of his battalion objective during this action. His eagerness and determination to close with the enemy and to destroy him were an inspiration to the entire command, and are in the highest traditions of the U.S. Armed Forces.

2712 ◆ FINN, JOHN WILLIAM

Rank: Lieutenant (rank at time of action: Aviation Chief Ordnance Man)
Service: U.S. Navy
Birthday: 24 July 1909
Place of Birth: Los Angeles, Los Angeles County, California
Entered Service at: Belle Vernon Acres, California
Unit: VP-14 Squadron (Patrol Planes Squadron)
Served as: Senior Chief Ordnance Man
Battle or Place of Action: Kaneohe Bay, Territory of Hawaii
Date of Action: 7 December 1941
Date of Presentation: 15 September 1942
Place of Presentation: on board the U.S.S. *Enterprise*, Pearl Harbor, Territory of Hawaii, presented by Adm. Chester W. Nimitz
Citation: For extraordinary heroism distinguished service, and devotion above and beyond the call of duty. During the first attack by Japanese airplanes on the Naval Air Station, Kaneohe Bay, on 7 December 1941, Lt. (then A.C.O.M.) Finn promptly secured and manned a .50-caliber machine gun mounted on an instruction stand in a completely exposed section of the parking ramp, which was under heavy enemy machine-gun strafing fire. Although painfully wounded many times, he continued to man this gun and to return the enemy's fire vigorously and with telling effect throughout the enemy strafing and bombing attacks and with complete disregard for his own personal safety. It was only by specific orders that he was persuaded to leave his post to seek medical attention. Following first-aid treatment, although obviously suffering much pain and moving with great difficulty, he returned to the squadron area and actively supervised the rearming of returning planes. His extraordinary heroism and conduct in this action were in keeping with the highest traditions of the U.S. Naval Service.

2713 ◆ FISHER, ALMOND EDWARD

Rank: Second Lieutenant (highest rank: Lieutenant Colonel)
Service: U.S. Army
Birthday: 28 January 1913
Place of Birth: Hume, Allegany County, New York
Date of Death: 7 January 1982
Place of Death: Concord Township, Ohio
Cemetery: Arlington National Cemetery (6-8751-2)—Arlington, Virginia
Entered Service at: Brooklyn, Kings County, New York
Unit: Company E, 157th Infantry, 45th Infantry Division
Served as: Platoon Leader
Battle or Place of Action: near Grammont, France
Date of Action: 12-13 September 1944
G.O. Number, Date: 32, 23 April 1945
Date of Issue: 23 May 1945
Citation: For conspicuous gallantry and intrepidity at the risk of his life above and beyond the call of duty on the night of 12–13 September 1944, near Grammont, France. In the darkness of the early morning 2d Lt. Fisher was leading a platoon of Company E, 157th Infantry, in single column to the attack of a strongly defended hill position. At 2:30 A.M., the forward elememts were brought under enemy machine-gun fire from a distance of not more than 20 yards. Working his way alone to within 20 feet of the gun emplacement, he opened fire with his carbine and killed the entire guncrew. A few minutes after the advance was resumed, heavy machine-gun fire was encountered from the left flank. Again crawling

forward alone under withering fire, he blasted the gun and crew from their positions with hand grenades. After a halt to replenish ammunition, the advance was again resumed and continued for one hour before being stopped by intense machine-gun and rifle fire. Through the courageous and skillful leadership of 2d Lt. Fisher, the pocket of determined enemy resistance was rapidly obliterated. Spotting an emplaced machine pistol a short time later, with one of his men he moved forward and destroyed the position. As the advance continued the firefight became more intense. When a bypassed German climbed from his foxhole and attempted to tear an M-1 rifle from the hands of one of his men, 2d Lt. Fisher whirled and killed the enemy with a burst from his carbine. About 30 minutes later the platoon came under heavy fire from machine guns from across an open field. Second Lt. Fisher, disregarding the terrific fire, moved across the field with no cover or concealment to within range, knocked the gun from the position, and killed or wounded the crew. Still under heavy fire he returned to his platoon and continued the advance. Once again heavy fire was encountered from a machine gun directly in front. Calling for hand grenades, he found only two remaining in the entire platoon. Pulling the pins and carrying a grenade in each hand, he crawled toward the gun emplacement, moving across areas devoid of cover and under intense fire to within 15 yards when he threw the grenades, demolished the gun, and killed the guncrew. With ammunition low and daybreak near, he ordered his men to dig in and hold the ground already won. Under constant fire from the front and from both flanks, he moved among them directing the preparations for the defense. Shortly after the ammunition supply was replenished, the Germans launched a last determined effort against the depleted group. Attacked by superior numbers from the front, right, and left flank, and even from the rear, the platoon, in bitter hand-to-hand engagements, drove back the enemy at every point. Wounded in both feet by close-range machine pistol fire early in the battle, 2d Lt. Fisher refused medical attention. Unable to walk, he crawled from man to man encouraging them and checking each position. Only after the fighting had subsided did 2d Lt. Fisher crawl 300 yards to the aid station from which he was evacuated. His extraordinary heroism, magnificent valor, and aggressive determination in the face of point-blank enemy fire is an inspiration to his organization and reflects the finest traditions of the U.S. Armed Forces.

2714 ◆ *FLAHERTY, FRANCIS CHARLES

Rank: Ensign
Service: U.S. Naval Reserve
Birthday: 15 March 1919
Place of Birth: Charlotte, Eaton County, Michigan
Date of Death: 7 December 1941
Place of Death: Pearl Harbor, Territory of Hawaii
Cemetery: National Memorial Cemetery of the Pacific (Wall of the Missing)—Honolulu, Hawaii; Maple Hill Cemetery ('In Memory' marker)—Charlotte, Michigan
Entered Service at: Michigan
Unit: U.S.S. *Oklahoma*
Battle or Place of Action: Pearl Harbor, Territory of Hawaii
Date of Action: 7 December 1941
Date of Presentation: 6 March 1946
Place of Presentation: Presented to his Brother
Citation: For conspicuous devotion to duty and extraordinary courage and complete disregard of his own life, above and beyond the call of duty, during the attack on the Fleet in Pearl Harbor, by Japanese forces on 7 December 1941. When it was seen that the U.S.S. *Oklahoma* was going to capsize and the order was given to abandon ship, Ens. Flaherty remained in a turret, holding a flashlight so the remainder of the turret crew could see to escape, thereby sacrificing his own life.

2715 ◆ *FLEMING, RICHARD EUGENE

Rank: Captain
Service: U.S. Marine Corps Reserve
Birthday: 2 November 1917
Place of Birth: St. Paul, Ramsey County, Minnesota
Date of Death: 5 June 1942
Cemetery: National Memorial Cemetery of the Pacific (Wall of the Missing)—Honolulu, Hawaii
Entered Service at: Minnesota
Unit: Marine Scout-Bombing Squadron 241
Served as: Flight Officer
Battle or Place of Action: Midway Island
Date of Action: 4-5 June 1942
Citation: For extraordinary heroism and conspicuous intrepidity above and beyond the call of duty as flight officer, Marine Scout-Bombing Squadron 241, during action against enemy Japanese forces in the battle of Midway on 4 and 5 June 1942. When his squadron commander was shot down during the initial attack upon an enemy aircraft carrier, Capt. Fleming led the remainder of the division with such fearless determination that he dived his own plane to the perilously low altitude of 400 feet before releasing his bomb. Although his craft was riddled by 179 hits in the blistering hail of fire that burst upon him from Japanese fighter guns and antiaircraft batteries, he pulled out with only two minor wounds inflicted upon himself. On the night of 4 June, when the squadron commander lost his way and became separated from the others, Capt. Fleming brought his own plane in for a safe landing at its base despite hazardous weather conditions and total darkness. The following day, after less than four hours' sleep, he led the second division of his squadron in a coordinated glide-bombing and dive-bombing assault upon a Japanese battleship. Undeterred by a fateful approach glide, during which his ship was struck and set afire, he grimly pressed home his attack to an altitude of 500 feet, released his bomb to score a near miss on the stern of his target, then crashed to the sea in flames. His dauntless perseverance and unyielding devotion to duty were in keeping with the highest traditions of the U.S. Naval Service.

2716 ◆ FLUCKEY, EUGENE BENNETT

Rank: Commander (highest rank: Rear Admiral)
Service: U.S. Navy
Birthday: 5 October 1913

Place of Birth: Washington, D.C.
Entered Service at: Neoga, Cumberland County, Illinois
Unit: U.S.S. *Barb*–SS220
Served as: Commanding Officer
Battle or Place of Action: Namkwan Harbor, along coast of China
Date of Action: 19 December 1944—15 February 1945
Date of Presentation: 23 March 1945
Place of Presentation: Washington, D.C., presented by the Sec. of the Navy James V. Forrestal
Citation: For conspicuous gallantry and intrepidity at the risk of his life above and beyond the call of duty as commanding officer of the U.S.S. *Barb* during her 11th war patrol along the east coast of China from 19 December 1944 to 15 February 1945. After sinking a large enemy ammunition ship and damaging additional tonnage during a running two-hour night battle on 8 January, Comdr. Fluckey, in an exceptional feat of brilliant deduction and bold tracking on 25 January, located a concentration of more than 30 enemy ships in the lower reaches of Nankuan Chiang (Mamkwan Harbor). Fully aware that a safe retirement would necessitate an hour's run at full speed through the uncharted, mined, and rock-obstructed waters, he bravely ordered, "Battle station—torpedoes!" In a daring penetration of the heavy enemy screen, and riding in five fathoms of water, he launched the *Barb*'s last forward torpedoes at 3,000-yard range. Quickly bringing the ship's stern tubes to bear, he turned loose four more torpedoes into the enemy, obtaining eight direct hits on six of the main targets to explode a large ammunition ship and cause inestimable damage by the resultant flying shells and other pyrotechnics. Clearing the treacherous area at high speed, he brought the *Barb* through to safety, and four days later sank a large Japanese freighter to complete a record of heroic combat achievement, reflecting the highest credit upon Comdr. Fluckey, his gallant officers and men, and the U.S. Naval Service.

2717 ◆ FOSS, JOSEPH JACOB

Rank: Captain (highest rank: Brigadier General)
Service: U.S. Marine Corps Reserve
Birthday: 17 April 1915
Place of Birth: Sioux Falls, Minnehaha County, South Dakota
Entered Service at: Sioux Falls, Minnehaha County, South Dakota
Unit: Marine Fighting Squadron 121, Marine Air Group 11, 1st Marine Aircraft Wing
Served as: Squadron Executive Officer/Pilot of a Grumman F-4F Wildcat
Battle or Place of Action: over Guadalcanal, Solomon Islands
Date of Action: 9 October-19 November 1942; 15, 23 January 1943
Date of Presentation: 18 May 1943
Place of Presentation: The White House (Oval Office), presented by Pres. Franklin D. Roosevelt
Citation: For outstanding heroism and courage above and beyond the call of duty as executive officer of Marine Fighting Squadron 121, 1st Marine Aircraft Wing, at Guadalcanal. Engaging in almost daily combat with the enemy from 9 October to 19 November 1942, Capt. Foss personally shot down 23 Japanese planes and damaged others so severely that their destruction was extremely probable. In addition, during this period, he successfully led a large number of escort missions, skillfully covering reconnaissance, bombing, and photographic planes as well as surface craft. On 15 January 1943, he added three more enemy planes to his already brilliant successes for a record of aerial combat achievement unsurpassed in this war. Boldly searching out an approaching enemy force on 25 January, Capt. Foss led his eight F4F Marine planes and four Army P-38s into action and, undaunted by tremendously superior numbers, intercepted and struck with such force that four Japanese fighters were shot down and the bombers were turned back without releasing a single bomb. His remarkable flying skill, inspiring leadership, and indomitable fighting spirit were distinctive factors in the defense of strategic American positions on Guadalcanal.

2718 ◆ *FOSTER, WILLIAM ADELBERT

Rank: Private First Class
Service: U.S. Marine Corps Reserve
Birthday: 17 February 1915
Place of Birth: Cleveland, Cuyahoga County, Ohio
Date of Death: 2 May 1945
Place of Death: Okinawa Shima, Ryukyu Islands
Cemetery: Calvary Cemetery (MH)—Cleveland, Ohio
Entered Service at: Ohio
Unit: Company K, 3d Battalion, 1st Marines, 1st Marine Division
Served as: Rifleman
Battle or Place of Action: Okinawa Shima, Ryukyu Islands
Date of Action: 2 May 1945
Date of Presentation: 19 August 1945
Place of Presentation: Mayor's office, Cleveland, Ohio, presented by Gen. Alexander A. Vandergrift to his parents
Citation: For conspicuous gallantry and intrepidity at the risk of his life above and beyond the call of duty while serving as a rifleman with the 3d Battalion, 1st Marines, 1st Marine Division, in action against enemy Japanese forces on Okinawa Shima in the Ryukyu Chain, 2 May 1945. Dug in with another marine on the point of the perimeter defense after waging a furious assault against a strongly fortified Japanese position, Pfc. Foster and his comrade engaged in a fierce hand-grenade duel with infiltrating enemy soldiers. Suddenly an enemy grenade landed beyond reach of the foxhole. Instantly diving on the deadly missile, Pfc. Foster absorbed the exploding charge in his own body, thereby protecting the other marine from serious injury. Although mortally wounded as a result of his heroic action, he quickly rallied, handed his own two remaining grenades to his comrade and said, "Make them count." Stouthearted and indomitable, he had unhesitatingly relinquished his own chance of survival that his fellow marine might carry on the relentless fight against a fanatic enemy, and his dauntless determination, cool decision, and valiant spirit of self-sacrifice in the face of certain death reflect the

highest credit upon Pfc. Foster and upon the U.S. Naval Service. He gallantly gave his life in the service of his country.

2719 ◆ *FOURNIER, WILLIAM GRANT

Rank: Sergeant
Service: U.S. Army
Birthday: 21 June 1913
Place of Birth: Norwich, New London County, Connecticut
Date of Death: 10 January 1943
Cemetery: National Memorial Cemetery of the Pacific (L-462) (MH)—Honolulu, Hawaii
Entered Service at: Winterport, Waldo County, Maine
Unit: Company M, 35th Infantry, 25th Infantry Division
Served as: Section Leader
Battle or Place of Action: Mount Austen, Guadalcanal, Solomon Islands
Date of Action: 10 January 1943
G.O. Number, Date: 28, 5 June 1943
Citation: For gallantry and intrepidity above and beyond the call of duty. As leader of a machine-gun section charged with the protection of other battalion units, his group was attacked by a superior number of Japanese, his gunner killed, his assistant gunner wounded, and an adjoining guncrew put out of action. Ordered to withdraw from this hazardous position, Sgt. Fournier refused to retire but rushed forward to the idle gun and, with the aid of another soldier who joined him, held up the machine gun by the tripod to increase its field of action. They opened fire and inflicted heavy casualties upon the enemy. While so engaged both these gallant soldiers were killed, but their sturdy defensive action was a decisive factor in the following success of the attacking battalion.

2720 ◆ *FOWLER, THOMAS WELDON

Rank: Second Lieutenant
Service: U.S. Army
Birthday: 31 October 1921
Place of Birth: Wichita Falls, Wichita County, Texas
Date of Death: 3 June 1944
Cemetery: Crestview Memorial Park (MH)—Wichita Falls, Texas
Entered Service at: Wichita Falls, Wichita County, Texas
Unit: 1st Armored Division
Battle or Place of Action: near Carano, Italy
Date of Action: 23 May 1944
G.O. Number, Date: 84, 28 October 1944
Place of Presentation: Fort Sill, Oklahoma, presented by Maj. Gen. Ralph McT. Pennel to his family
Citation: For conspicuous gallantry and intrepidity at the risk of his life above and beyond the call of duty on 23 May 1944, in the vicinity of Carano, Italy. In the midst of a full-scale armored-infantry attack, 2d Lt. Fowler, while on foot, came upon two completely disorganized infantry platoons held up in their advance by an enemy minefield. Although a tank officer, he immediately reorganized the infantry. He then made a personal reconnaissance through the minefield, clearing a path as he went, by lifting the antipersonnel mines out of the ground with his hands. After he had gone through the 75-yard belt of deadly explosives, he returned to the infantry and led them through the minefield, a squad at a time. As they deployed, 2d Lt. Fowler, despite small-arms fire and the constant danger of antipersonnel mines, made a reconnaissance into enemy territory in search of a route to continue the advance. He then returned through the minefield and, on foot, he led the tanks through the mines into a position from which they could best support the infantry. Acting as scout 300 yards in front of the infantry, he led the two platoons forward until he had gained his objective, where he came upon several dug-in enemy infantrymen. Having taken them by surprise, 2d Lt. Fowler dragged them out of their foxholes and sent them to the rear; twice, when they resisted, he threw hand grenades into their dugouts. Realizing that a dangerous gap existed between his company and the unit on his right, 2d Lt. Fowler decided to continue his advance until the gap was filled. He reconnoitered to his front, brought the infantry into position where they dug in, and, under heavy mortar and small-arms fire, brought his tanks forward. A few minutes later, the enemy began an armored counterattack. Several Mark VI tanks fired their cannons directly on 2d Lt. Fowler's position. One of his tanks was set afire. With utter disregard for his own life, with shells bursting near him, he ran directly into the enemy tank fire to reach the burning vehicle. For a half-hour, under intense strafing from the advancing tanks, although all other elements had withdrawn, he remained in his forward position, attempting to save the lives of the wounded tank crew. Only when the enemy tanks had almost overrun him, did he withdraw a short distance where he personally rendered first aid to nine wounded infantrymen in the midst of the relentless incoming fire. Second Lt. Fowler's courage, his ability to estimate the situation and to recognize his full responsibility as an officer in the Army of the United States, exemplify the high traditions of the military service for which he later gave his life.

2721 ◆ *FRYAR, ELMER E.

Rank: Private
Service: U.S. Army
Place of Birth: Denver, Denver County, Colorado
Date of Death: 8 December 1944
Cemetery: A.B.M.C. Manila Cemetery (Wall of the Missing)—Manila, Philippine Islands
Entered Service at: Denver, Denver County, Colorado
Unit: Company E, 511th Parachute Infantry, 11th Airborne Division
Battle or Place of Action: Leyte, Philippine Islands
Date of Action: 8 December 1944
G.O. Number, Date: 35, 9 May 1945
Citation: For conspicuous gallantry and intrepidity at the risk of his life above and beyond the call of duty. Pvt. Fryar's battalion encountered the enemy strongly entrenched in a position supported by mortars and automatic weapons. The battalion attacked, but in spite of repeated efforts was unable to take the position. Pvt. Fryar's company was ordered to cover the battalion's withdrawal to a more suitable point from which to attack, but the enemy launched a strong counterat-

tack which threatened to cut off the company. Seeing an enemy platoon moving to outflank his company, he moved to higher ground and opened heavy and accurate fire. He was hit, and wounded, but continuing his attack he drove the enemy back with a loss of 27 killed. While withdrawing to overtake his squad, he found a seriously wounded comrade, helped him to the rear, and soon overtook his platoon leader, who was assisting another wounded. While these four were moving to rejoin their platoon, an enemy sniper appeared and aimed his weapon at the platoon leader. Pvt. Fryar instantly sprang forward, received the full burst of automatic fire in his own body and fell mortally wounded. With his remaining strength he threw a hand grenade and killed the sniper. Pvt. Fryar's indomitable fighting spirit and extraordinary gallantry above and beyond the call of duty contributed outstandingly to the success of the battalion's withdrawal and its subsequent attack and defeat of the enemy. His heroic action in unhesitatingly giving his own life for his comrade in arms exemplifies the highest tradition of the U.S. Armed Forces.

2722 ◆ FUNK JR., LEONARD ALFRED

Rank: First Sergeant
Service: U.S. Army
Birthday: 27 August 1916
Place of Birth: Braddock Township, Allegheny County, Pennsylvania
Date of Death: 20 November 1992
Place of Death: McKeesport, Pennsylvania
Cemetery: Arlington National Cemetery (35-2373-4)—Arlington, Virginia
Entered Service at: Wilkinsburg, Allegheny County, Pennsylvania
Unit: Company C, 1st Battalion, 508th Parachute Infantry, 82d Airborne Division
Served as: Company First Sergeant
Battle or Place of Action: Holzheim, Belgium
Date of Action: 29 January 1945
G.O. Number, Date: 75, 5 September 1945
Date of Presentation: 23 August 1945
Place of Presentation: The White House, presented by Pres. Harry S. Truman
Citation: He distinguished himself by gallant, intrepid actions against the enemy. After advancing 15 miles in a driving snowstorm, the American force prepared to attack through waist-deep drifts. The company executive officer became a casualty, and 1st Sgt. Funk immediately assumed his duties, forming headquarters soldiers into a combat unit for an assault in the face of direct artillery shelling and harassing fire from the right flank. Under his skillful and courageous leadership, this miscellaneous group and the 3d Platoon attacked 15 houses, cleared them, and took 30 prisoners without suffering a casualty. The fierce drive of Company C quickly overran Holzheim, netting some 80 prisoners, who were placed under a four-man guard, all that could be spared, while the rest of the understrength unit went about mopping up isolated points of resistance. An enemy patrol, by means of a ruse, succeeded in capturing the guards and freeing the prisoners, and had begun preparations to attack Company C from the rear when 1st Sgt. Funk walked around the building and into their midst. He was ordered to surrender by a German officer who pushed a machine pistol into his stomach. Although overwhelmingly outnumbered and facing almost certain death, 1st Sgt. Funk, pretending to comply with the order, began slowly to unsling his submachine-gun from his shoulder and then, with lightning motion, brought the muzzle into line and riddled the German officer. He turned upon the other Germans, firing and shouting to the other Americans to seize the enemy's weapons. In the ensuing fight 21 Germans were killed, many wounded, and the remainder captured. First Sgt. Funk's bold action and heroic disregard for his own safety were directly responsible for the recapture of a vastly superior enemy force, which, if allowed to remain free, could have taken the widespread units of Company C by surprise and endangered the entire attack plan.

2723 ◆ FUQUA, SAMUEL GLENN

Rank: Captain (rank at time of action: Lieutenant Commander) (highest rank: Rear Admiral)
Service: U.S. Navy
Birthday: 15 October 1899
Place of Birth: Laddonia, Audrain County, Missouri
Date of Death: 27 January 1987
Cemetery: Arlington National Cemetery (59-485) (MH)—Arlington, Virginia
Entered Service at: Laddonia, Audrain County, Missouri
Unit: U.S.S. *Arizona*
Battle or Place of Action: Pearl Harbor, Territory Of Hawaii
Date of Action: 7 December 1941
Date of Presentation: 19 March 1942
Citation: For distinguished conduct in action, outstanding heroism, and utter disregard of his own safety above and beyond the call of duty during the attack on the Fleet in Pearl Harbor, by Japanese forces on 7 December 1941. Upon the commencement of the attack, Lt. Comdr. Fuqua rushed to the quarterdeck of the U.S.S. *Arizona*, to which he was attached, where he was stunned and knocked down by the explosion of a large bomb which hit the quarterdeck, penetrated several decks, and started a severe fire. Upon regaining consciousness, he began to direct the fighting of the fire and the rescue of the wounded and injured personnel. Almost immediately there was a tremendous explosion forward, which made the ship appear to rise out of the water, shudder, and settle down by the bow rapidly. The whole forward part of the ship was enveloped in flames which were spreading rapidly, and wounded and burned men were pouring out of the ship to the quarterdeck. Despite these conditions, his harrowing experience, and severe enemy bombing and strafing at the time, Lt. Comdr. Fuqua continued to direct the fighting of the fires in order to check them while the wounded and burned could be taken from the ship, and supervised the rescue of these men in such an amazingly calm and cool manner and with such excellent judgment that it inspired everyone who saw him and undoubtedly resulted in the saving of many lives. After realizing the ship could not be saved and that he

was the senior surviving officer aboard, he directed it to be abandoned, but continued to remain on the quarterdeck and directed abandoning ship and rescue of personnel until satisfied that all personnel that could be had been saved, after which he left his ship with the boatload. The conduct of Lt. Comdr. Fuqua was not only in keeping with the highest traditions of the Naval Service but characterizes him as an outstanding leader of men.

2724 ◆ GALER, ROBERT EDWARD

Rank: Major (highest rank: Brigadier General)
Service: U.S. Marine Corps
Birthday: 23 October 1913
Place of Birth: Seattle, King County, Washington
Entered Service at: Seattle, King County, Washington
Unit: Marine Fighter Squadron 224, Marine Aviation Group 21
Served as: Squadron Commander
Battle or Place of Action: Guadalcanal, Solomon Islands
Date of Action: 1 October 1942
Date of Presentation: 24 March 1943
Place of Presentation: The White House, presented by Pres. Franklin D. Roosevelt
Citation: For conspicuous heroism and courage above and beyond the call of duty as leader of a marine fighter squadron in aerial combat with enemy Japanese forces in the Solomon Islands area. Leading his squadron repeatedly in daring and aggressive raids against Japanese aerial forces, vastly superior in numbers, Maj. Galer availed himself of every favorable attack opportunity, individually shooting down 11 enemy bomber and fighter aircraft over a period of 29 days. Though suffering the extreme physical strain attendant upon protracted fighter operations at an altitude above 25,000 feet, the squadron under his zealous and inspiring leadership shot down a total of 27 Japanese planes. His superb airmanship, his outstanding skill, and personal valor reflect great credit upon Maj. Galer's gallant fighting spirit and upon the U.S. Naval Service.

2725 ◆ *GALT, WILLIAM WYLIE

Rank: Captain
Service: U.S. Army
Birthday: 19 December 1919
Place of Birth: Geyser, Judith Basin County, Montana
Date of Death: 29 May 1944
Cemetery: Mount Olivet Cemetery—Great Falls, Montana
Entered Service at: Stanford, Judith Basin County, Montana
Unit: 1st Battalion, 168th Infantry, 34th Infantry Division
Served as: S-3 Officer
Battle or Place of Action: at Villa Crocetta, Italy
Date of Action: 29 May 1944
G.O. Number, Date: 7, 1 February 1945
Citation: For conspicuous gallantry and intrepidity above and beyond the call of duty. Capt. Galt, Battalion S-3, at a particularly critical period following two unsuccessful attacks by his battalion, of his own volition went forward and ascertained just how critical the situation was. He volunteered, at the risk of his life, personally to lead the battalion against the objective. When the lone remaining tank destroyer refused to go forward, Capt. Galt jumped on the tank destroyer and ordered it to precede the attack. As the tank destroyer moved forward, followed by a company of riflemen, Capt. Galt manned the .30-caliber machine gun in the turret of the tank destroyer, located and directed fire on an enemy 77-mm antitank gun, and destroyed it. Nearing the enemy positions, Capt. Galt stood fully exposed in the turret, ceaselessly firing his machine gun and tossing hand grenades into the enemy zigzag series of trenches despite the hail of sniper and machine-gun bullets ricocheting off the tank destroyer. As the tank destroyer moved, Capt. Galt so maneuvered it that 40 of the enemy were trapped in one trench. When they refused to surrender, Capt. Galt pressed the trigger of the machine gun and dispatched every one of them. A few minutes later an 88-mm shell struck the tank destroyer and Capt. Galt fell mortally wounded across his machine gun. He had personally killed 40 Germans and wounded many more. Capt. Galt pitted his judgment and superb courage against overwhelming odds, exemplifying the highest measure of devotion to his country and the finest traditions of the U.S. Army.

2726 ◆ *GAMMON, ARCHER T.

Rank: Staff Sergeant
Service: U.S. Army
Birthday: 11 September 1918
Place of Birth: Chatham, Pittsylvania County, Virginia
Date of Death: 11 January 1945
Cemetery: Mountain View Cemetery—Danville, Virginia
Entered Service at: Roanoke, Roanoke County, Virginia
Unit: Company A, 9th Armored Infantry Battalion, 6th Armored Division
Served as: Squad Leader
Battle or Place of Action: near Bastogne, Belgium
Date of Action: 11 January 1945
G.O. Number, Date: 18, 13 February 1946
Citation: He charged 30 yards through hip-deep snow to knock out a machine gun and its three-man crew with grenades, saving his platoon from being decimated and allowing it to continue its advance from an open field into some nearby woods. The platoon's advance through the woods had only begun when a machine gun supported by riflemen opened fire and a Tiger Royal tank sent 88-mm shells screaming at the unit from the left flank. S/Sgt. Gammon, disregarding all thoughts of personal safety, rushed forward, then cut to the left, crossing the width of a platoon's skirmish line in an attempt to get within grenade range of the tank and its protecting foot troops. Intense fire was concentrated on him by riflemen and the machine gun emplaced near the tank. He charged the automatic weapon, wiped out its crew of four with grenades, and, with supreme daring, advanced to within 25 yards of the armored vehicle, killing two hostile infantrymen with rifle fire as he moved forward. The tank had started to withdraw, backing a short distance, then firing, backing some more, and then stopping to blast out another round, when the man whose singlehanded relentless attack had put

the ponderous machine on the defensive was struck and instantly killed by a direct hit from the Tiger Royal's heavy gun. By his intrepidity and extreme devotion to the task of driving the enemy back no matter what the odds, S/Sgt. Gammon cleared the woods of German forces, for the tank continued to withdraw, leaving open the path for the gallant squad leader's platoon.

2727 ◆ GARCIA, MARCARIO

Rank: Staff Sergeant (rank at time of action: Private)
Service: U.S. Army
Birthday: 2 January 1920
Place of Birth: Villa de Castano, Mexico
Date of Death: 24 December 1972
Cemetery: Houston National Cemetery (HA-1) (MH)—Houston, Texas
Entered Service at: Sugar Land, Fort Bend County, Texas
Unit: Company B, 22d Infantry, 4th Infantry Division
Served as: Squad Leader
Battle or Place of Action: near Grosshau, Germany
Date of Action: 27 November 1944
G.O. Number, Date: 74, 1 September 1945
Date of Presentation: 23 August 1945
Place of Presentation: The White House, presented by Pres. Harry S. Truman
Citation: While an acting squad leader of Company B, 22d Infantry, on 27 November 1944, near Grosshau, Germany, he singlehandedly assaulted two enemy machine-gun emplacements. Attacking prepared positions on a wooded hill, which could be approached only through meager cover, his company was pinned down by intense machine-gun fire and subjected to a concentrated artillery and mortar barrage. Although painfully wounded, he refused to be evacuated and on his own initiative crawled forward alone until he reached a position near an enemy emplacement. Hurling grenades, he boldly assaulted the position, destroyed the gun, and with his rifle killed three of the enemy who attempted to escape. When he rejoined his company, a second machine gun opened fire and again the intrepid soldier went forward, utterly disregarding his own safety. He stormed the position and destroyed the gun, killed three more Germans, and captured four prisoners. He fought on with his unit until the objective was taken and only then did he permit himself to be removed for medical care. S/Sgt. (then Pvt.) Garcia's conspicuous heroism, his inspiring, courageous conduct, and his complete disregard for his personal safety wiped out two enemy emplacements and enabled his company to advance and secure its objective.

2728 ◆ GARMAN, HAROLD ALVA

Rank: Private (highest rank: Technician Fifth Grade)
Service: U.S. Army
Birthday: 26 February 1918
Place of Birth: Fairfield, Wayne County, Illinois
Date of Death: 13 August 1992
Place of Death: Albion, Illinois
Cemetery: Samaria Baptist Church Cemetery—Albion, Illinois
Entered Service at: Albion, Edwards County, Illinois
Unit: Company B, 5th Medical Battalion, 10th Infantry, 5th Infantry Division
Served as: Litter Bearer
Battle or Place of Action: near Montereau, France
Date of Action: 25 August 1944
G.O. Number, Date: 20, 29 March 1945
Date of Presentation: 6 April 1945
Place of Presentation: Munetx, Germany, presented by Gen. George S. Patton
Citation: For conspicuuus gallantry and intrepidity at the risk of his life above and beyond the call of duty. On 25 August 1944, in the vicinity of Montereau, France, the enemy was sharply contesting any enlargement of the bridgehead which our forces had established on the northern bank of the Seine River in this sector. Casualties were being evacuated to the southern shore in assault boats paddled by litter bearers from a medical battalion. Pvt. Garman, also a litter bearer in this battalion, was working on the friendly shore carrying the wounded from the boats to waiting ambulances. As one boatload of wounded reached midstream, a German machine gun suddenly opened fire upon it from a commanding position on the northern bank 100 yards away. All of the men in the boat immediately took to the water except one man who was so badly wounded he could not rise from his litter. Two other patients who were unable to swim because of their wounds clung to the sides of the boat. Seeing the extreme danger of these patients, Pvt. Garman without a moment's hesitation plunged into the Seine. Swimming directly into a hail of machine-gun bullets, he rapidly reached the assault boat and then while still under accurately aimed fire towed the boat with great effort to the southern shore. This soldier's moving heroism not only saved the lives of the three patients but so inspired his comrades that additional assault boats were immediately procured and the evacuation of the wounded resumed. Pvt. Garman's great courage and his heroic devotion to the highest tenets of the Medical Corps may be written with great pride in the annals of the corps.

2729 ◆ GARY, DONALD ARTHUR

Rank: Lieutenant (j.g.) (highest rank: Commander)
Service: U.S. Navy
Birthday: 23 July 1903
Place of Birth: Findlay, Hancock County, Ohio
Date of Death: 9 April 1977
Place of Death: Long Beach, California
Cemetery: Fort Rosecrans National Cemetery (A-13-B) (MH)—San Diego, California
Entered Service at: Ohio
Unit: U.S.S. *Franklin*
Served as: Engineering Officer
Battle or Place of Action: near Kobe, Japan
Date of Action: 19 March 1945
Date of Presentation: 23 January 1946
Place of Presentation: The White House, presented By Pres. Harry S. Truman

Citation: For conspicuous gallantry and intrepidity at the risk of life above and beyond the call of duty as an engineering officer attached to the U.S.S. Franklin when that vessel was fiercely attacked by enemy aircraft during operations against the Japanese Home Islands near Kobe, Japan, 19 March 1945. Stationed on the third deck when the ship was rocked by a series of violent explosions set off in her own ready bombs, rockets and ammunition by the hostile attack, Lt. Gary unhesitantingly risked his life to assist several hundred men trapped in a messing compartment filled with smoke, and with no apparent egress. As the imperiled men below decks became increasingly panic stricken under the raging fury of incessant explosions, he confidently assured them he would find a means of effecting their release and groping through the dark, debris-filled corridors, ultimately discovered an escapeway. Staunchly determined, he struggled back to the messing compartment three despite menacing flames, flooding water, and the ominous threat of sudden additional explosions, on each occasion calmly leading his men through the blanketing pall of smoke until the lst one had been saved. Selfless in his concern for his ship and his fellows, he constantly rallied others about him, repeatedly organized and led firefighting parties into the blazing inferno on the flight deck, and, when firerooms 1 and 2 were found to be inoperable, entered No. 3 fireroom and directed the raising of steam in one boiler in the face of extreme difficulty and hazard. An inspiring and courageous leader, Lt. Gary rendered self-sacrificing service under the most perilous conditions and, by his heroic initiative, fortitude, and valor, was responsible for the saving of several hundred lives. His conduct throughout reflects the highest credit upon himself and upon the U.S. Naval Service.

2730 ✷ GERSTUNG, ROBERT E.

Rank: Technical Sergeant
Service: U.S. Army
Birthday: 6 August 1915
Place of Birth: Chicago, Cook County, Illinois
Date of Death: 17 June 1979
Cemetery: Arlington National Cemetery (66-6152) (MH)—Arlington, Virginia
Entered Service at: Chicago, Cook County, Illinois
Unit: Company H, 313th Infantry, 79th Infantry Division
Served as: Squad Leader
Battle or Place of Action: Siegfried Line, near Berg, Germany
Date of Action: 19 December 1944
G.O. Number, Date: 75, 5 September 1945
Date of Presentation: 23 August 1945
Place of Presentation: The White House, presented by Pres. Harry S. Truman
Citation: On 19 December 1944 he was ordered with his heavy machine-gun squad to the support of an infantry company attacking the outer defenses of the Siegfried line near Berg, Germany. For eight hours he maintained a position made almost untenable by the density of artillery and mortar fire concentrated upon it and the proximity of enemy troops who threw hand grenades into the emplacement. While all other members of his squad became casualties, he remained at his gun. When he ran out of ammunition, he fearlessly dashed across bullet-swept, open terrain to secure a new supply from a disabled friendly tank. A fierce barrage pierced the water jacket of his gun, but he continued to fire until the weapon overheated and jammed. Instead of withdrawing, he crawled 50 yards across coverless ground to another of his company's machine guns which had been silenced when its entire crew was killed. He continued to man this gun, giving support vitally needed by the infantry. At one time he came under direct fire from a hostile tank, which shot the glove from his hand with an armor-piercing shell but could not drive him from his position or stop his shooting. When the American forces were ordered to retire to their original positions, he remained at his gun, giving the only covering fire. Finally withdrawing, he cradled the heavy weapon in his left arm, slung a belt of ammunition over his shoulder, and walked to the rear, loosing small bursts at the enemy as he went. One hundred yards from safety, he was struck in the leg by a mortar shell; but, with a supreme effort, he crawled the remaining distance, dragging along the gun which had served him and his comrades so well. By his remarkable perseverance, indomitable courage, and heroic devotion to his task in the face of devastating fire, T/Sgt. Gerstung gave his fellow soldiers powerful support in their encounter with formidable enemy forces.

2731 ◆ *GIBSON, ERIC GUNNAR

Rank: Technician Fifth Grade
Service: U.S. Army
Birthday: 3 October 1919
Place of Birth: Nysund, Sweden
Date of Death: 28 January 1944
Cemetery: Nora Cemetery—Rice Lake, Wisconsin
Entered Service at: Chicago, Cook County, Illinois
Unit: Company I, 30th Infantry, 3d Infantry Division
Served as: Company Cook
Battle or Place of Action: near Isola Bella, Italy
Date of Action: 28 January 1944
G.O. Number, Date: 74, 11 September 1944
Date of Presentation: 15 September 1944
Place of Presentation: Camp McCoy, Wisconsin, presented to his parents
Citation: For conspicuous gallantry and intrepidity at the risk of life above and beyond the call of duty. On 28 January 1944, near Isola Bella, Italy, Tech. 5th Grade Gibson, company cook, led a squad of replacements through their initial baptism of fire, destroyed four enemy positions, killed five, and captured two German soldiers, and secured the left flank of his company during an attack on a strongpoint. Placing himself 50 yards in front of his new men, Gibson advanced down the wide stream ditch known as the Fossa Femminamorta, keeping pace with the advance of his company. An enemy soldier allowed Tech. 5th Grade Gibson to come within 20 yards of his concealed position and then opened fire on him with a machine pistol. Despite the stream of automatic fire which barely missed him, Gibson charged the position, firing his submachine gun every few steps.

Reaching the position, Gibson fired point-blank at his opponent, killing him. An artillery concentration fell in and around the ditch; the concussion from one shell knocked him flat. As he got to his feet Gibson was fired on by two soldiers armed with a machine pistol and a rifle from a position only 75 yards distant. Gibson immediately raced toward the foe. Halfway to the position a machine gun opened fire on him. Bullets came within inches of his body, yet Gibson never paused in his forward movement. He killed one and captured the other soldier. Shortly after, when he was fired upon by a heavy machine gun 200 yards down the ditch, Gibson crawled back to his squad and ordered it to lay down a base of fire while he flanked the emplacement. Despite all warnings, Gibson crawled 125 yards through an artillery concentration and the crossfire of two machine guns which showered dirt over his body, threw two hand grenades into the emplacement, and charged it with his submachine gun, killing two of the enemy and capturing a third. Before leading his men around a bend in the stream ditch, Gibson went forward alone to reconnoiter. Hearing an exchange of machine pistol and submachine-gun fire, Gibson's squad went forward to find that its leader had run 35 yards toward an outpost, killed the machine pistol man, and had himself been killed while firing at the Germans.

2732 ◆ *GILMORE, HOWARD WALTER

Rank: Commander
Service: U.S. Navy
Birthday: 29 September 1902
Place of Birth: Selma, Dallas County, Alabama
Date of Death: 7 February 1943
Cemetery: A.B.M.C. Manila Cemetery (Wall of the Missing)—Manila, Philippine Islands
Entered Service at: Louisiana
Unit: U.S.S. *Growler*
Served as: Commanding Officer
Battle or Place of Action: Southwest Pacific
Date of Action: 10 January–7 February 1943
Date of Presentation: 13 July 1943
Place of Presentation: New Orleans, Louisiana, presented by Rear Adm. A.C. Bennett to his Widow
Citation: For distinguished gallantry and valor above and beyond the call of duty as commanding officer of the U.S.S. *Growler* during her fourth war patrol in the southwest Pacific from 10 January to 7 February 1943. Boldly striking at the enemy in spite of continuous hostile air and anti-submarine patrols, Comdr. Gilmore sank one Japanese freighter and damaged another by torpedo fire, successfully evading severe depth charges following each attack. In the darkness of night on 7 February, an enemy gunboat closed range and prepared to ram the *Growler*. Comdr. Gilmore daringly maneuvered to avoid the crash and rammed the attacker instead, ripping into her port side at 17 knots and bursting wide her plates. In the terrific fire of the sinking gunboat's heavy machine guns, Comdr. Gilmore calmly gave the order to clear the bridge, and refusing safety for himself, remained on deck while his men preceded him below. Struck down by the fusillade of bullets and having done his utmost against the enemy, in his final living moments, Comdr. Gilmore gave his last order to the officer of the deck, "Take her down." The *Growler* dived; seriously damaged but under control, she was brought safely to port by her well-trained crew inspired by the courageous fighting spirit of their dead captain.

2733 ◆ *GONSALVES, HAROLD

Rank: Private First Class
Service: U.S. Marine Corps Reserve
Birthday: 28 January 1926
Place of Birth: Alameda, Alameda County, California
Date of Death: 15 April 1945
Place of Death: Okinawa Shima, Ryukyu Islands
Cemetery: Golden Gate National Cemetery (B-61) (MH)—San Bruno, California
Entered Service at: California
Unit: Battery L, 4th Battalion, 15th Marines, 6th Marine Division
Served as: Acting Scout Sergeant
Battle or Place of Action: Okinawa Shima, Ryukyu Islands
Date of Action: 15 April 1945
Citation: For conspicuous gallantry and intrepidity at the risk of his life above and beyond the call of duty while serving as acting scout sergeant with the 4th Battalion, 15th Marines, 6th Marine Division, during action against enemy Japanese forces on Okinawa Shima in the Ryukyu Chain, 15 April 1945. Undaunted by the powerfully organized opposition encountered on Motobu Peninsula during the fierce assault waged by his battalion against the Japanese stronghold at Mount Yaetake, Pfc. Gonsalves repeatedly braved the terrific enemy bombardment to aid his forward observation team in directing well-placed artillery fire. When his commanding officer determined to move into the front lines in order to register a more effective bombardment in the enemy's defensive position, he unhesitatingly advanced uphill with the officer and another marine despite a slashing barrage of enemy mortar and rifle fire. As they reached the front and a Japanese grenade fell close within the group, instantly Pfc. Gonsalves dived on the deadly missile, absorbing the exploding charge in his own body and thereby protecting the others from serious and perhaps fatal wounds. Stouthearted and indomitable, Pfc. Gonsalves readily yielded his own chances of survival that his fellow marines might carry on the relentless battle against a fanatic enemy, and his cool decision, prompt action, and valiant spirit of self-sacrifice in the face of certain death reflect the highest credit upon himself and upon the U.S. Naval Service.

2734 ◆ *GONZALES, DAVID M.

Rank: Private First Class
Service: U.S. Army
Birthday: 9 June 1923
Place of Birth: Pacoima, Los Angeles County, California
Date of Death: 25 April 1945
Cemetery: Calvary Cemetery—Los Angeles, California
Entered Service at: Pacoima, Los Angeles County, California
Unit: Company A, 127th Infantry, 32d Infantry Division

Battle or Place of Action: Hill 507, Villa Verde Trail, Luzon, Philippine Islands
Date of Action: 25 April 1945
G.O. Number, Date: 115, 8 December 1945
Citation: He was pinned down with his company. As enemy fire swept the area, making any movement extremely hazardous, a 500-pound bomb smashed into the company's perimeter, burying five men with its explosion. Pfc. Gonzales, without hesitation, seized an entrenching tool and under a hail of fire crawled 15 yards to his entombed comrades, where his commanding officer, who had also rushed forward, was beginning to dig the men out. Nearing his goal, he saw the officer struck and instantly killed by machine-gun fire. Undismayed, he set to work swiftly and surely with his hands and entrenching tool while enemy sniper and machine-gun bullets struck all about him. He succeeded in digging one of the men out of the pile of rock and sand. To dig faster he stood up regardless of the greater danger from so exposing himself. He extricated a second man, and then another. As he completed the liberation of the third, he was hit and mortally wounded, but the comrades for whom he so gallantly gave his life were safely evacuated. Pfc. Gonzales' valiant and intrepid conduct exemplifies the highest traditions of the military service.

2735 ◆ GORDON, NATHAN GREEN

Rank: Lieutenant (highest rank: Lieutenant Commander)
Service: U.S. Navy
Birthday: 4 September 1916
Place of Birth: Morrilton, Conway County, Arkansas
Entered Service at: Morrilton, Conway County, Arkansas
Unit: Patrol Squadron 34 (VPB-34), Naval Air Base, Samari Island, New Guinea
Served as: Commander/Pilot of a Catalina Patrol Plane
Battle or Place of Action: Kavieng Harbor, New Ireland, Bismark Sea, southwestern Pacific
Date of Action: 15 February 1944
Date of Presentation: 13 July 1944
Place of Presentation: Brisbane, Australia, presented by Vice Adm. Thomas C. Kincaid
Citation: For extraordinary heroism above and beyond the call of duty as commander of a Catalina patrol plane in rescuing personnel of the U.S. Army 5th Air Force shot down in combat over Kavieng Harbor in the Bismarck Sea, 15 February 1944. On air alert in the vicinity of Vitu Islands, Lt. (then Lt. [jg]) Gordon unhesitatingly responded to a report of the crash and flew boldly into the harbor, defying close-range fire from enemy shore guns to make three separate landings in full view of the Japanese and pick up nine men, several of them injured. With his cumbersome flying boat dangerously overloaded, he made a brilliant takeoff despite heavy swells and almost total absence of wind and set a course for base, only to receive the report of another group stranded in a rubber liferaft 600 yards from the enemy shore. Promptly turning back, he again risked his life to set his plane down under direct fire of the heaviest defenses of Kavieng and take aboard six more survivors, cooly making his fourth dexterous takeoff with 15 rescued officers and men. By his exceptional daring, personal valor, and incomparable airmanship under most perilous conditions, Lt. Gordon prevented certain death or capture of our airmen by the Japanese.

2736 ◆ *GOTT, DONALD JOSEPH

Rank: First Lieutenant
Service: U.S. Army Air Corps
Birthday: 3 June 1923
Place of Birth: Arnett, Ellis County, Oklahoma
Date of Death: 9 November 1944
Place of Death: Near Saarbrucken, Germany
Cemetery: Harmon Cemetery—Harmon, Oklahoma
Entered Service at: Arnett, Ellis County, Oklahoma
Unit: 729th Bombardment Squadron, 452d Bombardment Group, 8th Air Force
Served as: Pilot of a B-17
Battle or Place of Action: Saarbrucken, Germany
Date of Action: 9 November 1944
G.O. Number, Date: 38, 16 May 1945
Citation: On a bombing run upon the marshaling yards at Saarbrucken, a B-17 aircraft piloted by 1st Lt. Gott was seriously damaged by antiaircraft fire. Three of the aircraft's engines were damaged beyond control and on fire; dangerous flames from the No. 4 engine were leaping back as far as the tail assembly. Flares in the cockpit were ignited and a fire raged therein, which was further increased by free-flowing fluid from two damaged hydraulic lines. The interphone system was rendered useless. In addition to these serious mechanical difficulties the engineer was wounded in the leg and the radio operator's arm was severed below the elbow. Suffering from intense pain, despite the application of a tourniquet, the radio operator fell unconscious. Faced with the imminent explosion of his aircraft and death to his entire crew, mere seconds before bombs away on the target, 1st Lt. Gott and his copilot conferred. Something had to be done immediately to save the life of the wounded radio operator. The lack of a static line and the thought that his unconscious body striking the ground in unknown territory would not bring immediate medical attention forced a quick decision. First Lt. Gott and his copilot decided to fly the flaming aircraft to friendly territory and then attempt to crash land. Bombs were released on the target and the crippled aircraft proceeded alone to Allied-controlled territory. When that had been reached, 1st Lt. Gott had the copilot personally inform all crewmembers to bail out. The copilot chose to remain with 1st Lt. Gott in order to assist in landing the bomber. With only one normally functioning engine, and with the danger of explosion much greater, the aircraft banked into an open field, and when it was at an altitude of 100 feet it exploded, crashed, exploded again, and then disintegrated. All three crew members were instantly killed. First Lt. Gott's loyalty to his crew, his determination to accomplish the task set forth to him, and his deed of knowingly performing what may have been his last service to his country was an example of valor at its highest.

2737 ◆ *GRABIARZ, WILLIAM J.

Rank: Private First Class
Service: U.S. Army

Birthday: 1925
Place of Birth: Buffalo, Erie County, New York
Date of Death: 23 February 1945
Place of Death: Manila, Philippine Islands
Cemetery: St. Stanislaws Cemetery—Cheektowaga, New York
Entered Service at: Buffalo, Erie County, New York
Unit: Troop E, 5th Cavalry, 1st Cavalry Division
Served as: Scout
Battle or Place of Action: Manila, Luzon, Philippine Islands
Date of Action: 23 February 1945
G.O. Number, Date: 115, 8 December 1945
Citation: He was a scout when the unit advanced with tanks along a street in Manila, Luzon, Philippine Islands. Without warning, enemy machine guns and rifle fire from concealed positions in the Customs building swept the street, striking down the troop commander and driving his men to cover. As the officer lay in the open road, unable to move and completely exposed to the point-blank enemy fire, Pfc. Grabiarz voluntarily ran from behind a tank to carry him to safety, but was himself wounded in the shoulder. Ignoring both the pain in his injured, useless arm and his comrades' shouts to seek the cover which was only a few yards distant, the valiant rescuer continued his efforts to drag his commander out of range. Finding this impossible, he rejected the opportunity to save himself and deliberately covered the officer with his own body to form a human shield, calling as he did so for a tank to maneuver into position between him and the hostile emplacement. The enemy riddled him with concentrated fire before the tank could interpose itself. Our troops found that he had been successful in preventing bullets from striking his leader, who survived. Through his magnificent sacrifice in gallantly giving his life to save that of his commander, Pfc. Grabiarz provided an outstanding and lasting inspiration to his fellow soldiers.

2738 ◆ *GRAY, ROSS FRANKLIN

Rank: Sergeant
Service: U.S. Marine Corps Reserve
Birthday: 1 August 1920
Place of Birth: Marvel Valley, Alabama
Date of Death: 27 February 1945
Cemetery: Ada Chapel Cemetery (MH)—West Blocton, Alabama
Entered Service at: Alabama
Unit: Company A, 1st Battalion, 25th Marines, 4th Marine Division
Served as: Platoon Sergeant
Battle or Place of Action: Iwo Jima, Volcano Islands
Date of Action: 21 February 1945
Citation: For conspicuous gallantry and intrepidity at the risk of his life above and beyond the call of duty as a platoon sergeant attached to Company A, 1st Battalion, 25th Marines, 4th Marine Division, in action against enemy Japanese forces on Iwo Jima, Volcano Islands, 21 February 1945. Shrewdly gaging the tactical situation when his platoon was held up by a sudden barrage of hostile grenades while advancing toward the high ground northeast of Airfield No. 1, Sgt. Gray promptly organized the withdrawal of his men from enemy grenade range, quickly moved forward alone to reconnoiter, and discovered a heavily mined area extending along the front of a strong network of emplacements joined by covered trenches. Although assailed by furious gunfire, he cleared a path leading through the minefield to one of the fortifications, then returned to the platoon position and, informing his leader of the serious situation, volunteered to initiate an attack under cover of three fellow marines. Alone and unarmed but carrying a huge satchel charge, he crept up on the Japanese emplacement, boldly hurled the short-fused explosive, and sealed the entrance. Instantly taken under machine-gun fire from a second entrance to the same position, he unhesitatingly braved the increasingly vicious fusillades to crawl back for another charge, returned to his objective, and blasted the second opening, thereby demolishing the position. Repeatedly covering the ground between the savagely defended enemy fortifications and his platoon area, he systematically approached, attacked, and withdrew under blanketing fire to destroy a total of six Japanese positions, more than 25 troops, and a quantity of vital ordnance gear and ammunition. Stouthearted and indomitable, Sgt. Gray had singlehandedly overcome a strong enemy garrison and had completely disarmed a large minefield before finally rejoining his unit. By his great personal valor, daring tactics, and tenacious perseverance in the face of extreme peril, he had contributed materially to the fulfillment of his company's mission. His gallant conduct throughout enhanced and sustained the highest traditions of the U.S. Naval Service.

2739 ◆ GREGG, STEPHEN RAYMOND

Rank: Second Lieutenant (rank at time of action: Technical Sergeant)
Service: U.S. Army
Birthday: 1 September 1914
Place of Birth: New York, New York
Entered Service at: Bayonne, Hudson County, New Jersey
Unit: Weapons Platoon, Company L, 143d Infantry, 36th Infantry Division
Served as: Platoon Sergeant
Battle or Place of Action: near Montelimar, France
Date of Action: 27 August 1944
G.O. Number, Date: 31, 17 April 1945
Date of Presentation: 14 March 1945
Place of Presentation: Berholsheim, France, presented by Lt. Gen. Alexander M. Patch III
Citation: For conspicuous gallantry and intrepidity at risk of life above and beyond the call of duty on 27 August 1944, in the vicinity of Montelimar, France. As his platoon advanced upon the enemy positions, the leading scout was fired upon and 2d Lt. Gregg (then a T/Sgt.) immediately put his machine guns into action to cover the advance of the riflemen. The Germans, who were at close range, threw hand grenades at the riflemen, killing some and wounding seven. Each time a medical aidman attempted to reach the wounded, the Germans fired at him. Realizing the seriousness of the situation, 2d Lt. Gregg took one of the light .30-caliber machine guns and, firing from the hip, started boldly up the

hill with the medical aidman following him. Although the enemy was throwing hand grenades at him, 2d Lt. Gregg remained and fired into the enemy positions while the medical aidman removed the seven wounded men to safety. When 2d Lt. Gregg had expended all his ammunition, he was covered by four Germans who ordered him to surrender. Since the attention of most of the Germans had been diverted by watching this action, friendly riflemen were able to maneuver into firing positions. One, seeing 2d Lt. Gregg's situation, opened fire on his captors. The four Germans hit the ground and thereupon 2d Lt. Gregg recovered a machine pistol from one of the Germans and managed to escape to his other machine-gun positions. He manned a gun, firing at his captors, killed one of them and wounded the other. This action so discouraged the Germans that the platoon was able to continue its advance up the hill to achieve its objective. The following morning, just prior to daybreak, the Germans launched a strong attack, supported by tanks, in an attempt to drive Company L from the hill. As these tanks moved along the valley and their foot troops advanced up the hill, 2d Lt. Gregg immediately ordered his mortars into action. During the day, by careful observation, he was able to direct effective fire on the enemy, inflicting heavy casualties. By late afternoon he had directed 600 rounds when his communication to the mortars was knocked out. Without hesitation he started checking his wires, although the area was under heavy enemy small-arms and artillery fire. When he was within 100 yards of his mortar position, one of his men informed him that the section had been captured and the Germans were using the mortars to fire on the company. Second Lt. Gregg with this man and another nearby rifleman started for the gun position where he could see five Germans firing his mortars. He ordered the two men to cover him, crawled up, threw a hand grenade into the position, and then charged it. The hand grenade killed one, injured two; 2d Lt. Gregg took the other two prisoners, and put his mortars back into action.

2740 ◆ *GRUENNERT, KENNETH E.

Rank: Sergeant
Service: U.S. Army
Birthday: 19 November 1922
Place of Birth: Helenville, Jefferson County, Wisconsin
Date of Death: 24 December 1942
Place of Death: near Buna, New Guinea
Cemetery: Evergreen Lutheran Cemetery—Helenville, Wisconsin
Entered Service at: Helenville, Jefferson County, Wisconsin
Unit: Company L, 127th Infantry, 32d Infantry Division
Battle or Place of Action: near Buna, New Guinea
Date of Action: 24 December 1942
G.O. Number, Date: 66, 11 October 1943
Place of Presentation: The Medal was sent to the parents at their request in the mail
Citation: For conspicuous gallantry and intrepidity in action above and beyond the call of duty. On 24 December 1942, near Buna, New Guinea, Sgt. Gruennert was second in command of a platoon with a misssion to drive through the enemy lines to the beach 600 yards ahead. Within 150 yards of the objective, the platoon encountered two hostile pillboxes. Sgt. Gruennert advanced alone on the first and put it out of action with hand grenades and rifle fire, killing three of the enemy. Seriously wounded in the shoulder, he bandaged his wound under cover of the pillbox, refusing to withdraw to the aid station and leave his men. He then, with undiminished daring, and under extremely heavy fire, attacked the second pillbox. As he neared it he threw grenades which forced the enemy out where they were easy targets for his platoon. Before the leading elements of his platoon could reach him he was shot by enemy snipers. His inspiring valor cleared the way for his platoon which was the first to attain the beach in this successful effort to split the enemy position.

2741 ◆ *GURKE, HENRY

Rank: Private First Class
Service: U.S. Marine Corps
Birthday: 6 November 1922
Place of Birth: Neche, Pembina County, North Dakota
Date of Death: 9 November 1943
Cemetery: Neche Union Cemetery (MH)—Neche, North Dakota
Entered Service at: North Dakota
Unit: 3d Marine Raider Battalion
Battle or Place of Action: near Empress Augusta Bay, Bougainville, Solomon Islands
Date of Action: 9 November 1943
Citation: For extraordinary heroism and courage above and beyond the call of duty while attached to the 3d Marine Raider Battalion during action against enemy Japanese forces in the Solomon Islands area on 9 November 1943. While his platoon was engaged in the defense of a vital road block near Empress Augusta Bay on Bougainville Island, Pfc. Gurke, in company with another marine, was delivering a fierce stream of fire against the main vanguard of the Japanese. Concluding from the increasing ferocity of grenade barrages that the enemy was determined to annihilate their small, two-man foxhole, he resorted to a bold and desperate measure for holding out despite the torrential hail of shells. When a Japanese grenade dropped squarely into the foxhole, Pfc. Gurke, mindful that his companion manned an automatic weapon of superior firepower and therefore could provide more effective resistance, thrust him roughly aside and flung his own body over the missile to smother the explosion. With unswerving devotion to duty and superb valor, Pfc. Gurke sacrificed himself in order that his comrade might live to carry on the fight. He gallantly gave his life in the service of his country.

2742 ◆ HALL, GEORGE JOHN

Rank: Staff Sergeant
Service: U.S. Army
Birthday: 9 January 1920
Place of Birth: Stoneham, Middlesex County, Massachusetts
Date of Death: 16 February 1946
Place of Death: West Roxbury, Massachusetts
Cemetery: St. Patrick's Cemetery (MH)—Stoneham, Massachusetts

2743 ◆ *HALL, LEWIS R.

Entered Service at: Boston, Suffolk County, Massachusetts
Unit: Company B, 135th Infantry, 34th Infantry Division
Battle or Place of Action: near Anzio, Italy
Date of Action: 23 May 1944
G.O. Number, Date: 24, 6 April 1945
Date of Presentation: 13 April 1945
Place of Presentation: Boston Common, Massachusetts, presented by Maj. Gen. Sherman Miles
Citation: For conspicuous gallantry and intrepidity at risk of life above and beyond the call of duty. Attacking across flat, open terrain under direct enemy observation, S/Sgt. Hall's company was pinned down by grazing fire from three enemy machine guns and harassing sniper fire. S/Sgt. Hall volunteered to eliminate these obstacles in the path of advance. Crawling along a plowed furrow through furious machine-gun fire, he made his way to a point within hand-grenade range of one of the enemy positions. He pounded the enemy with four hand grenades, and when the smoke had died away, S/Sgt. Hall and two dead Germans occupied the position, while four of the enemy were crawling back to our lines as prisoners. Discovering a quantity of German potato-masher grenades in the position, S/Sgt. Hall engaged the second enemy nest in a deadly exchange of grenades. Each time he exposed himself to throw a grenade the Germans fired machine-gun bursts at him. The vicious duel finally ended in S/Sgt. Hall's favor with five of the enemy surrendered and five others lay dead. Turning his attention to the third machine gun, S/Sgt. Hall left his position and crawled along a furrow, the enemy firing frantically in a effort to halt him. As he neared his final objective, an enemy artillery concentration fell on the area, and S/Sgt. Hall's right leg was severed by a shell burst. With two enemy machine guns eliminated, his company was able to flank the third and continue its advance without incurring excessive casualties. S/Sgt. Hall's fearlessness, his determined fighting spirit, and his prodigious combat skill exemplify the heroic tradition of the American infantryman.

2743 ◆ *HALL, LEWIS R.

Rank: Technician Fifth Grade
Service: U.S. Army
Birthday: 2 March 1895
Place of Birth: Bloom, Ohio
Date of Death: 10 January 1943
Place of Death: Guadalcanal, Mount Austen, Solomon Islands
Cemetery: Glenrest Memorial Estate (MH)—Reynoldsburg, Ohio
Entered Service at: Columbus, Franklin County, Ohio
Unit: Company M, 35th Infantry, 25th Infantry Division
Served as: Squad Leader
Battle or Place of Action: Mount Austen, Guadalcanal, Solomon Islands
Date of Action: 10 January 1943
G.O. Number, Date: 28, 5 June 1943
Citation: For gallantry and intrepidity above and beyond the call of duty. As leader of a machine-gun squad charged with the protection of other battalion units, his group was attacked by a superior number of Japanese, his gunner killed, his assistant gunner wounded, and an adjoining guncrew put out of action. Ordered to withdraw from his hazardous position, he refused to retire but rushed forward to the idle gun and with the aid of another soldier who joined him and held up the machine gun by the tripod to increase its field of action he opened fire and inflicted heavy casualties upon the enemy. While so engaged both these gallant soldiers were killed, but their sturdy defense was a decisive factor in the following success of the attacking battalion.

2744 ◆ HALL, WILLIAM EDWARD

Rank: Lieutenant (j.g.) (highest rank: Lieutenant Commander)
Service: U.S. Navy
Birthday: 31 October 1913
Place of Birth: Storrs, Carbon County, Utah
Entered Service at: Mohrland, Emery County, Utah
Unit: Scouting Squadron 2, Air Group 2, U.S.S. *Lexington*
Served as: Pilot of a Douglas Dauntless
Battle or Place of Action: Coral Sea
Date of Action: 7-8 May 1942
Date of Presentation: 22 November 1942
Place of Presentation: San Diego, California, presented by Vice Adm. Ephraim P. Holmes
Citation: For extreme courage and conspicuous heroism in combat above and beyond the call of duty as pilot of a scouting plane in action against enemy Japanese forces in the Coral Sea on 7 and 8 May 1942. In a resolute and determined attack on 7 May, Lt. (j.g.) Hall dived his plane at an enemy Japanese aircraft carrier, contributing materially to the destruction of that vessel. On 8 May, facing heavy and fierce fighter opposition, he again displayed extraordinary skill as an airman and the aggressive spirit of a fighter in repeated and effectively executed counterattacks against a superior number of enemy planes in which three enemy aircraft were destroyed. Though seriously wounded in this engagement, Lt. (j.g.) Hall, maintaining the fearless and indomitable tactics pursued throughout these actions, succeeded in landing his plane safely.

2745 ◆ *HALLMAN, SHERWOOD H.

Rank: Staff Sergeant
Service: U.S. Army
Birthday: 29 October 1913
Place of Birth: Spring City, Chester County, Pennsylvania
Date of Death: 14 September 1944
Cemetery: A.B.M.C. Brittany Cemetery (M-5-11)—St. James, France
Entered Service at: Spring City, Chester County, Pennsylvania
Unit: Company F, 2d Battalion, 175th Infantry, 29th Infantry Division
Served as: Squad Leader
Battle or Place of Action: Brest, Brittany, France
Date of Action: 13 September 1944
G.O. Number, Date: 31, 17 April 1945

Citation: For conspicuous gallantry and intrepidity at risk of his life above and beyond the call of duty. On 13 September 1944, in Brittany, France, the 2d Battalion in its attack on the fortified city of Brest was held up by a strongly defended enemy position which had prevented its advance despite repeated attacks extending over a three-day period. Finally, Company F advanced to within several hundred yards of the enemy position but was again halted by intense fire. Realizing that the position must be neutralized without delay, S/Sgt. Hallman ordered his squad to cover his movements with fire while he advanced alone to a point from which he could make the assault. Without hesitating, S/Sgt. Hallman leaped over a hedgerow into a sunken road, the central point of the German defenses which was known to contain an enemy machine-gun position and at least 30 enemy riflemen. Firing his carbine and hurling grenades, S/Sgt. Hallman, unassisted, killed or wounded four of the enemy, then ordered the remainder to surrender. Immediately, 12 of the enemy surrendered and the position was shortly secured by the remainder of his company. Seeing the surrender of this position, about 75 of the enemy in the vicinity surrendered, yielding a defensive organization which the battalion with heavy supporting fires had been unable to take. This single heroic act on the part of S/Sgt. Hallman resulted in the immediate advance of the entire battalion for a distance of 2,000 yards to a position from which Fort Keranroux was captured later the same day. S/Sgt. Hallman's fighting determination and intrepidity in battle exemplify the highest tradition of the U.S. Armed Forces.

2746 ◆ *HALYBURTON JR., WILLIAM DAVID

Rank: Pharmacist's Mate Second Class
Service: U.S. Naval Reserve
Birthday: 2 August 1924
Place of Birth: Canton, Haywood County, North Carolina
Date of Death: 10 May 1945
Place of Death: Okinawa Shima, Ryukyu Islands
Cemetery: National Memorial Cemetery of the Pacific (0-274) (MH)—Honolulu, Hawaii
Entered Service at: North Carolina
Unit: 2d Battalion, 5th Marines, 1st Marine Division
Served as: Medical Corpsman
Battle or Place of Action: Okinawa Shima, Ryukyu Islands
Date of Action: 10 May 1945
Citation: For conspicuous gallantry and intrepidity at risk of his life above and beyond the call of duty while serving with a Marine Rifle Company in the 2d Battalion, 5th Marines, 1st Marine Division, during action against enemy Japanese forces on Okinawa Shima in the Ryukyu Chain, 10 May 1945. Undaunted by the deadly accuracy of Japanese counterfire as his unit pushed the attack through a strategically important draw, Halyburton unhesitatingly dashed across the draw and up the hill into an open fire-swept field where the company advance squad was suddenly pinned down under a terrific concentration of mortar, machine-gun, and sniper fire with resultant severe casualties. Moving steadily forward despite the enemy's merciless barrage, he reached the wounded marine who lay farthest away and was rendering first aid when his patient was struck for a second time by a Japanese bullet. Instantly placing himself in the direct line of fire, he shielded the fallen fighter with his own body and staunchly continued his ministrations although constantly menaced by the slashing fury of shrapnel and bullets falling on all sides. Alert, determined, and completely unselfish in his concern for the helpless marine, he persevered in his efforts until he himself sustained mortal wounds and collapsed, heroically sacrificing himself that his comrade might live. By his outstanding valor and unwavering devotion to duty in the face of tremendous odds, Halyburton sustained and enhanced the highest traditions of the U.S. Naval Service. He gallantly gave his life in the service of his country.

2747 ◆ HAMILTON, PIERPONT MORGAN

Rank: Major (highest rank: Major General)
Service: U.S. Army Air Corps
Birthday: 3 August 1898
Place of Birth: Tuxedo Park, Orange County, New York
Date of Death: 4 March 1982
Place of Death: Los Angeles, California
Cemetery: Santa Barbara Cemetery—Santa Barbara, California
Entered Service at: New York, New York
Unit: Western Task Force
Served as: Assistant Chief of Staff for Intelligence
Battle or Place of Action: near Port Lyautey, French Morocco
Date of Action: 8 November 1942
G.O. Number, Date: 4, 23 January 1943
Citation: For conspicuous gallantry and intrepidity in action above and beyond the call of duty. On 8 November 1942, near Port Lyautey, French Morocco, Lt. Col. Hamilton volunteered to accompany Col. Demas Craw on a dangerous mission to the French commander, designed to bring about a cessation of hostilities. Driven away from the mouth of the Sebou River by heavy shelling from all sides, the landing boat was finally beached at Mehdia Plage despite continuous machine-gun fire from three low-flying hostile planes. Driven in a light truck toward French headquarters, this courageous mission encountered intermittent firing, and as it neared Port Lyautey a heavy burst of machine-gun fire was delivered upon the truck from point-blank range, killing Col. Craw instantly. Although captured immediately after this incident, Lt. Col. Hamilton completed the mission.

2748 ◆ *HAMMERBERG, OWEN FRANCIS PATRICK

Rank: Boatswain's Mate Second Class
Service: U.S. Navy
Birthday: 31 May 1920
Place of Birth: Daggett, Menominee County, Michigan
Date of Death: 17 February 1945
Place of Death: Pearl Harbor, Territory of Hawaii
Cemetery: Holy Sepulchre Cemetery (MH)—Southfield, Michigan
Entered Service at: Michigan

Served as: Diver
Battle or Place of Action: Pearl Harbor, Territory of Hawaii
Date of Action: 17 February 1945
Citation: For conspicuous gallantry and intrepidity at risk of his life above and beyond the call of duty as a diver engaged in rescue operations at West Loch, Pearl Harbor, 17 February 1945. Aware of the danger when two fellow divers were hopelessly trapped in a cave-in of steel wreckage while tunneling with jet nozzles under an LST sunk in 40 feet of water and 20 feet of mud, Hammerberg unhesitatingly went overboard in a valiant attempt to effect their rescue despite the certain hazard of additional cave-ins and the risk of fouling his lifeline on jagged pieces of steel imbedded in the shifting mud. Washing a passage through the original excavation, he reached the first of the trapped men, freed him from the wreckage, and, working desperately in pitch-black darkness, finally effected his release from fouled lines, thereby enabling him to reach the surface. Wearied but undaunted after several hours of arduous labor, Hammerberg resolved to continue his struggle to wash through the oozing submarine, subterranean mud in a determined effort to save the second diver. Venturing still farther under the buried hulk, he held tenaciously to his purpose, reaching a place immediately above the other man just as another cave-in occurred and a heavy piece of steel pinned him crosswise over his shipmate in a position which protected the man beneath from further injury while placing the full brunt of terrific presure on himself. Although he succumbed in agony 18 hours after he had gone to the aid of his fellow divers, Hammerberg, by his cool judgment, unfaltering professional skill, and consistent disregard of all personal danger in the face of tremendous odds, had contributed effectively to the saving of his two comrades. His heroic spirit of self-sacrifice throughout enhanced and sustained the highest traditions of the U.S. Naval Service. He gallantly gave his life in the service of his country.

2749 ◆ *HANSEN, DALE MERLIN

Rank: Private
Service: U.S. Marine Corps
Birthday: 13 December 1922
Place of Birth: Wisner, Cuming County, Nebraska
Date of Death: 11 May 1945
Cemetery: Wisner Cemetery (MH)—Wisner, Nebraska
Entered Service at: Nebraska
Unit: Company E, 2d Battalion, 1st Marines, 1st Marine Division
Battle or Place of Action: Okinawa Shima, Ryukyu Islands
Date of Action: 7 May 1945
Citation: For conspicuous gallantry and intrepidity at risk of his life above and beyond the call of duty while serving with Company E, 2d Battalion, 1st Marines, 1st Marine Division, in action against enemy Japanese forces on Okinawa Shima in the Ryukyu Chain, 7 May 1945. Cool and courageous in combat, Pvt. Hansen unhesitatingly took the initiative during a critical stage of the action and, armed with a rocket launcher, crawled to an exposed position where he attacked and destroyed a strategically located hostile pillbox. With his weapon subsequently destroyed by enemy fire, he seized a rifle and continued his one-man assault. Reaching the crest of a ridge, he leaped across, opened fire on six Japanese, and killed four before his rifle jammed. Attacked by the remaining two Japanese, he beat them off with the butt of his rifle and then climbed back to cover. Promptly returning with another weapon and supply of grenades, he fearlessly advanced, destroyed a strong mortar position, and annihilated eight more of the enemy. In the forefront of battle throughout this bitterly waged engagement, Pvt. Hansen, by his indomitable determination, bold tactics, and complete disregard of all personal danger, contributed essentially to the success of his company's mission and to the ultimate capture of this fiercely defended outpost of the Japanese Empire. His great personal valor in the face of extreme peril reflects the highest credit upon himself and the U.S. Naval Service.

2750 ◆ *HANSON, ROBERT MURRAY

Rank: First Lieutenant (highest rank: Captain)
Service: U.S. Marine Corps Reserve
Birthday: 4 February 1920
Place of Birth: Lucknow, India
Date of Death: 3 February 1944
Cemetery: Newton Cemetery (MH) (Marker Only)—Newton Center, Massachusetts; A.B.M.C. Manila Cemetery (Wall of the Missing)—Manila, Philippine Islands
Entered Service at: Massachusetts
Unit: Marine Fighting Squadron 215
Served as: Fighter Pilot
Battle or Place of Action: Bougainville Island, Soloman Islands & New Britain Island, Bismarck Archipelago
Date of Action: 1 November 1943—24 January 1944
Date of Presentation: 19 August 1944
Place of Presentation: Boston, Massachusetts by Maj. Gen. Lewis G. Merrit to his Mother
Citation: For conspicuous gallantry and intrepidity at risk of his life above and beyond the call of duty as fighter pilot attached to Marine Fighting Squadron 215 in action against enemy Japanese forces at Bougainville Island, 1 November 1943; and New Britain Island, 24 January 1944. Undeterred by fierce opposition, and fearless in the face of overwhelming odds, 1st Lt. Hanson fought the Japanese boldly and with daring aggressiveness. On 1 November, while flying cover for our landing operations at Empress Augusta Bay, he dauntlessly attacked six enemy torpedo bombers, forcing them to jettison their bombs and destroying one Japanese plane during the action. Cut off from his division while deep in enemy territory during a high cover flight over Simpson Harbor on 24 January, 1st Lt. Hanson waged a lone and gallant battle against hostile interceptors as they were orbiting to attack our bombers and, striking with devastating fury, brought down four Zeros and probably a fifth. Handling his plane superbly in both pursuit and attack measures, he was a master of individual air combat, accounting for a total of 25 Japanese aircraft in this theater of war. His great personal valor and invincible fighting spirit were in keeping with the highest traditions of the U.S. Naval Service.

2751 ◆ *HARMON, ROY W.

Rank: Sergeant
Service: U.S. Army
Place of Birth: Talala, Rogers County, Oklahoma
Date of Death: 12 July 1944
Place of Death: Near Casaglia, Italy
Cemetery: A.B.M.C. Florence Cemetery (A-4-37)—Florence, Italy
Entered Service at: Pixley, Tulare County, California
Unit: Company C, 362d Infantry, 91st Infantry Division
Served as: Squad Leader
Battle or Place of Action: near Casaglia, Italy
Date of Action: 12 July 1944
G.O. Number, Date: 83, 2 October 1945
Citation: He was an acting squad leader when heavy machine-gun fire from enemy positions, well dug-in on commanding ground and camouflaged by haystacks, stopped his company's advance and pinned down one platoon where it was exposed to almost certain annihilation. Ordered to rescue the beleaguered platoon by neutralizing the German automatic fire, he led his squad forward along a draw to the right of the trapped unit against three key positions which poured murderous fire into his helpless comrades. When within range, his squad fired tracer bullets in an attempt to set fire to the three haystacks which were strung out in a loose line directly to the front, 75, 150, and 250 yards away. Realizing that this attack was ineffective, Sgt. Harmon ordered his squad to hold their position and voluntarily began a one-man assault. Carrying white phosphorus grenades and a submachine gun, he skillfully took advantage of what little cover the terrain afforded and crept to within 25 yards of the first position. He set the haystack afire with a grenade, and when two of the enemy attempted to flee from the inferno, he killed them with his submachine gun. Crawling toward the second machine-gun emplacement, he attracted fire and was wounded; but he continued to advance and destroyed the position with hand grenades, killing the occupants. He then attacked the third machine gun, running to a small knoll, then crawling over ground which offered no concealment or cover. About halfway to his objective, he was again wounded. But he struggled ahead until within 20 yards of the machine-gun nest, where he raised himself to his knees to throw a grenade. He was knocked down by direct enemy fire. With a final, magnificent effort, he again arose, hurled the grenade and fell dead, riddled by bullets. His missile fired the third position, destroying it. Sgt. Harmon's extraordinary heroism, gallantry, and self-sacrifice saved a platoon from being wiped out, and made it possible for his company to advance against powerful enemy resistance.

2752 ◆ *HARR, HARRY R.

Rank: Corporal
Service: U.S. Army
Birthday: 22 February 1921
Place of Birth: Pine Croft, Pennsylvania
Date of Death: 5 June 1945
Place of Death: Near Maglamin, Philippine Islands
Cemetery: Alto-Reste Park Cemetery (MH)—Altoona, Pennsylvania
Entered Service at: East Freedom, Blair County, Pennsylvania
Unit: Company D, 124th Infantry, 31st Infantry Division
Battle or Place of Action: near Maglamin, Mindanao, Philippine Islands
Date of Action: 5 June 1945
G.O. Number, Date: 28, 28 March 1946
Citation: He displayed conspicuous gallantry and intrepidity. In a fierce counterattack, the Japanese closed in on his machine-gun emplacement, hurling grenades, one of which exploded under the gun, putting it out of action and wounding two of the crew. While the remaining gunners were desperately attempting to repair their weapon, another grenade landed squarely in the emplacement. Quickly realizing he could not safely throw the unexploded missile from the crowded position, Cpl. Harr unhesitatingly covered it with his body to smother the blast. His supremely courageous act, which cost him his life, saved four of his comrades and enabled them to continue their mission.

2753 ◆ HARRELL, WILLIAM GEORGE

Rank: Sergeant
Service: U.S. Marine Corps
Birthday: 26 June 1922
Place of Birth: Rio Grande City, Starr County, Texas
Date of Death: 9 August 1964
Place of Death: San Antonio, Texas
Cemetery: Fort Sam Houston National Cemetery (W-3247) (MH)—San Antonio, Texas
Entered Service at: Mercedes, Hidalgo County, Texas
Unit: Company A, 1st Battalion, 28th Marines, 5th Marine Division
Battle or Place of Action: Iwo Jima, Volcano Islands
Date of Action: 3 March 1945
Date of Presentation: 5 October 1945
Place of Presentation: The White House, presented by Pres. Harry S. Truman
Citation: For conspicuous gallantry and intrepidity at risk of his life above and beyond the call of duty as leader of an assault group attached to the 1st Battalion, 28th Marines, 5th Marine Division during hand-to-hand combat with enemy Japanese at Iwo Jima, Volcano Islands on 3 March 1945. Standing watch alternately with another marine in a terrain studded with caves and ravines, Sgt. Harrell was holding a position in a perimeter defense around the company command post when Japanese troops infiltrated our lines in the early hours of dawn. Awakened by a sudden attack, he quickly opened fire with his carbine and killed two of the enemy as they emerged from a ravine in the light of a star shell burst. Unmindful of his danger as hostile grenades fell closer, he waged a fierce lone battle until an exploding missile tore off his left hand and fractured his thigh. He was vainly attempting to reload the carbine when his companion returned from the command post with another weapon. Wounded again by a Japanese who rushed the foxhole wielding a saber in the

darkness, Sgt. Harrell succeeded in drawing his pistol and killing his opponent and then ordered his wounded companion to a place of safety. Exhausted by profuse bleeding but still unbeaten, he fearlessly met the challenge of two more enemy troops who charged his position and placed a grenade near his head. Killing one man with his pistol, he grasped the sputtering grenade with his good right hand, and, pushing it painfully toward the crouching soldier, saw his remaining assailant destroyed but his own hand severed in the explosion. At dawn Sgt. Harrell was evacuated from a position hedged by the bodies of 12 dead Japanese, at least five of whom he had personally destroyed in his self-sacrificing defense of the command post. His grim fortitude, exceptional valor, and indomitable fighting spirit against almost insurmountable odds reflect the highest credit upon himself and enhance the finest traditions of the U.S. Naval Servic e.

2754 ◆ *HARRIS, JAMES LINDELL

Rank: Second Lieutenant
Service: U.S. Army
Birthday: 27 June 1916
Place of Birth: Hillsboro, Hill County, Texas
Date of Death: 7 October 1944
Place of Death: At Vagney, France
Cemetery: Ridge Park Cemetery—Hillsboro, Texas
Entered Service at: Hillsboro, Hill County, Texas
Unit: Company A, 756th Tank Battalion, 3d Infantry Division
Served as: Tank Commander
Battle or Place of Action: at Vagney, France
Date of Action: 7 October 1944
G.O. Number, Date: 32, 23 April 1945
Citation: For conspicuous gallantry and intrepidity at risk of life above and beyond the call of duty on 7 October 1944, in Vagney, France. At 9 P.M. an enemy raiding party, comprising a tank and two platoons of infantry, infiltrated through the lines under cover of mist and darkness and attacked an infantry battalion command post with hand grenades, retiring a short distance to an ambush position on hearing the approach of the M-4 tank commanded by 2d Lt. Harris. Realizing the need for bold aggressive action, 2d Lt. Harris ordered his tank to halt while he proceeded on foot, fully 10 yards ahead of his six-man patrol and armed only with a service pistol, to probe the darkness for the enemy. Although struck down and mortally wounded by machine-gun bullets which penetrated his solar plexus, he crawled back to his tank, leaving a trail of blood behind him, and, too weak to climb inside it, issued fire orders while lying on the road between the two contending armored vehicles. Although the tank which he commanded was destroyed in the course of the firefight, he stood the enemy off until friendly tanks, preparing to come to his aid, caused the enemy to withdraw and thereby lose an opportunity to kill or capture the entire battalion command personnel. Suffering a second wound, which severed his leg at the hip, in the course of this tank duel, 2d Lt. Harris refused aid until after a wounded member of his crew had been carried to safety. He died before he could be given medical attention.

2755 ◆ *HASTINGS, JOE R.

Rank: Private First Class
Service: U.S. Army
Birthday: 8 April 1925
Place of Birth: Malvern, Carroll County, Ohio
Date of Death: 16 April 1945
Cemetery: Magnolia Cemetery—Magnolia, Ohio
Entered Service at: Magnolia, Stark County, Ohio
Unit: Company C, 386th Infantry, 97th Infantry Division
Served as: Squad Leader
Battle or Place of Action: Drabenderhohe, Germany
Date of Action: 12 April 1945
G.O. Number, Date: 101, 8 November 1945
Citation: He fought gallantly during an attack against strong enemy forces defending Drabenderhohe, Germany, from the dug-in position on commanding ground. As squad leader of a light machine-gun section supporting the advance of the 1st and 3d Platoons, he braved direct rifle, machine-gun, 20-mm, and mortar fire, some of which repeatedly missed him only by inches, and rushed forward over 350 yards of open, rolling fields to reach a position from which he could fire on the enemy troops. From this vantage point he killed the crew of the 20-mm gun and a machine gun, drove several enemy riflemen from their positions, and so successfully shielded the 1st Platoon that it had time to reorganize and remove its wounded to safety. Observing that the 3d Platoon to his right was being met by very heavy 40-mm and machine-gun fire, he ran 150 yards with his gun to the leading elements of that unit, where he killed the crew of the 40-mm gun. As spearhead of the 3d Platoon's attack, he advanced, firing his gun held at hip height, disregarding the bullets that whipped past him, until the assault had carried 175 yards to the objective. In this charge he and the riflemen he led killed or wounded many of the fanatical enemy and put two machine guns out of action. Pfc. Hastings, by his intrepidity, outstanding leadership, and unrelenting determination to wipe out the formidable German opposition, cleared the path for his company's advance into Drabenderhohe. He was killed four days later while again supporting the 3d Platoon.

2756 ◆ *HAUGE JR., LOUIS JAMES

Rank: Corporal
Service: U.S. Marine Corps Reserve
Birthday: 12 December 1924
Place of Birth: Ada, Norman County, Minnesota
Date of Death: 14 May 1945
Place of Death: Okinawa Shima, Ryukyu Islands
Cemetery: National Memorial Cemetery of the Pacific (Wall of the Missing)—Honolulu, Hawaii; Ada Cemetery (marker only)—Ada, Minnesota
Entered Service at: Minnesota
Unit: Company C, 1st Battalion, 1st Marines, 1st Marine Division
Served as: Squad Leader
Battle or Place of Action: Okinawa Shima, Ryukyu Islands
Date of Action: 14 May 1945
Date of Presentation: 14 June 1946

Place of Presentation: Presented by Col. Norman E. True to his Father

Citation: For conspicuous gallantry and intrepidity at risk of his life above and beyond the call of duty as leader of a machine-gun squad serving with Company C, 1st Battalion, 1st Marines, 1st Marine Division, in action against enemy Japanese forces on Okinawa Shima in the Ryukyu Chain on 14 May 1945. Alert and aggressive during a determined assault against a strongly fortified Japanese hill position, Cpl. Hauge boldly took the initiative when his company's left flank was pinned down under a heavy machine-gun and mortar barrage with resultant severe casualties and, quickly locating the two machine guns which were delivering the uninterrupted stream of enfilade fire, ordered his squad to maintain a covering barrage as he rushed across an exposed area toward the furiously blazing enemy weapons. Although painfully wounded as he charged the first machine gun, he launched a vigorous singlehanded grenade attack, destroyed the entire hostile gun position, and moved relentlessly forward toward the other emplacement despite his wounds and the increasingly heavy Japanese fire. Undaunted by the savage opposition, he again hurled his deadly grenades with unerring aim and succeeded in demolishing the second enemy gun before he fell under the slashing fury of Japanese sniper fire. By his ready grasp of the critical situation and his heroic one-man assault tactics, Cpl. Hauge had eliminated two strategically placed enemy weapons, thereby releasing the besieged troops from an overwhelming volume of hostile fire and enabling his company to advance. His indomitable fighting spirit and decisive valor in the face of almost certain death reflect the highest credit upon Cpl. Hauge and the U.S. Naval Service. He gallantly gave his life in the service of his country.

2757 ◆ HAWK, JOHN DRUSE "BUD"

Rank: Sergeant
Service: U.S. Army
Birthday: 30 May 1924
Place of Birth: San Francisco, San Francisco County, California
Entered Service at: Bremerton, Kitsap County, Washington
Unit: Weapons Platoon, Company E, 2d Battalion, 359th Infantry, 90th Infantry Division
Served as: Machine Gunner
Battle or Place of Action: near Chambois, France
Date of Action: 20 August 1944
G.O. Number, Date: 55, 13 July 1945
Date of Presentation: 21 June 1945
Place of Presentation: Olympia, Washington, presented by Pres. Harry S. Truman

Citation: He manned a light machine gun on 20 August 1944, near Chambois, France, a key point in the encirclement which created the Falaise pocket. During an enemy counterattack, his position was menaced by a strong force of tanks and infantry. His fire forced the infantry to withdraw, but an artillery shell knocked out his gun and wounded him in the right thigh. Securing a bazooka, he and another man stalked the tanks and forced them to retire to a wooded section. In the lull which followed, Sgt. Hawk reorganized two machine-gun squads and, in the face of intense enemy fire, directed the assembly of one workable weapon from two damaged guns. When another enemy assault developed, he was forced to pull back from the pressure of spearheading armor. Two of our tank destroyers were brought up. Their shots were ineffective because of the terrain until Sgt. Hawk, despite his wound, boldly climbed to an exposed position on a knoll where, unmoved by fusillades from the enemy, he became a human aiming-stake for the destroyers. Realizing that his shouted fire directions could not be heard above the noise of battle, he ran back to the destroyers through a concentration of bullets and shrapnel to correct the range. He returned to his exposed position, repeating this performance until two of the tanks were knocked out and a third driven off. Still at great risk, he continued to direct the destroyers' fire into the Germans' wooded position until the enemy came out and surrendered. Sgt. Hawk's fearless initiative and heroic conduct, even while suffering from a painful wound, was in large measure responsible for crushing two desperate attempts of the enemy to escape from the Falaise pocket and for taking more that 500 prisoners.

2758 ◆ *HAWKINS, WILLIAM DEANE

Rank: First Lieutenant
Service: U.S. Marine Corps
Birthday: 19 April 1914
Place of Birth: Fort Scott, Bourbon County, Kansas
Date of Death: 21 November 1943
Place of Death: Tarawa, Gilbert Islands
Cemetery: National Memorial Cemetery of the Pacific (B-646) (MH)—Honolulu, Hawaii
Entered Service at: El Paso, El Paso County, Texas
Unit: Scout Sniper Platoon, 2d Marines, 2d Marine Division
Served as: Commanding Officer
Battle or Place of Action: Tarawa, Gilbert Islands
Date of Action: 20-21 November 1943

Citation: For valorous and gallant conduct above and beyond the call of duty as commanding officer of a Scout Sniper Platoon attached to the Assault Regiment in action against Japanese-held Tarawa in the Gilbert Islands, 20 and 21 November 1943. The first to disembark from the jeep lighter, 1st Lt. Hawkins unhesitatingly moved forward under heavy enemy fire at the end of the Betio Pier, neutralizing emplacements in coverage of troops assaulting the main beach positions. Fearlessly leading his men on to join the forces fighting desperately to gain a beachhead, he repeatedly risked his life throughout the day and night to direct and lead attacks on pillboxes and installations with grenades and demolitions. At dawn on the following day, 1st Lt. Hawkins resumed the dangerous mission of clearing the limited beachhead of Japanese resistance, personally initiating an assault on a hostile position fortified by five enemy machine guns, and, crawling forward in the face of withering fire, boldly fired point-blank into the loopholes and completed the destruction with grenades. Refusing to withdraw after being seriously wounded in the chest during this skirmish, 1st Lt. Hawkins steadfastly carried the fight to the enemy, destroying three more pillboxes before he was caught in a burst of Japanese shellfire and mortally wounded. His relentless fighting spirit in the face of formidable opposition and his exceptionally daring tactics served as an inspiration to his comrades during the most crucial phase of the battle and reflect the highest credit upon the U.S. Naval Service. He gallantly gave his life for his country.

2759 ◆ HAWKS, LLOYD C.

Rank: Private First Class
Service: U.S. Army
Birthday: 13 January 1911
Place of Birth: Becker, Sherburne County, Minnesota
Date of Death: 26 October 1953
Cemetery: Greenwood Cemetery—Park Rapids, Minnesota
Entered Service at: Park Rapids, Hubbard County, Minnesota
Unit: Medical Detachment, Company G, 30th Infantry, 3d Infantry Division
Served as: Medical Aidman
Battle or Place of Action: near Carano, Italy
Date of Action: 30 January 1944
G.O. Number, Date: 5, 15 January 1945
Citation: For conspicuous gallantry and intrepidity at risk of life above and beyond the call of duty. On 30 January 1944, at 3 P.M., near Carano, Italy, Pfc. Hawks braved an enemy counterattack in order to rescue two wounded men who, unable to move, were lying in an exposed position within 30 yards of the enemy. Two riflemen, attempting the rescue, had been forced to return to their fighting holes by extremely severe enemy machine-gun fire, after crawling only 10 yards toward the casualties. An aidman, whom the enemy could plainly identify as such, had been critically wounded in a similar attempt. Pfc. Hawks, nevertheless, crawled 50 yards through a veritable hail of machine-gun bullets and flying mortar fragments to a small ditch, administered first aid to his fellow aidman who had sought cover therein, and continued toward the two wounded men 50 yards distant. An enemy machine-gun bullet penetrated his helmet, knocking it from his head, momentarily stunning him. Thirteen bullets passed through his helmet as it lay on the ground within six inches of his body. Pfc. Hawks crawled to the casualties, administered first aid to the more seriously wounded man, and dragged him to a covered position 25 yards distant. Despite continuous automatic fire from positions only 30 yards away and shells which exploded within 25 yards, Pfc. Hawks returned to the second man and administered first aid to him. As he raised himself to obtain bandages from his medical kit his right hip was shattered by a burst of machine-gun fire and a second burst splintered his left forearm. Displaying dogged determination and extreme self-control, Pfc. Hawks, despite severe pain and his dangling left arm, completed the task of bandaging the remaining casualty and with superhuman effort dragged him to the same depression to which he had brought the first man. Finding insufficient cover for three men at this point, Pfc. Hawks crawled 75 yards in an effort to regain his company, reaching the ditch in which his fellow aidman was lying.

2760 ◆ *HEDRICK, CLINTON M.

Rank: Technical Sergeant
Service: U.S. Army
Birthday: 1 May 1918
Place of Birth: Cherry Grove, West Virginia
Date of Death: 28 March 1945
Place of Death: Near Lembeck, Germany
Cemetery: North Fork Cemetery—Riverton, West Virginia
Entered Service at: Riverton, Pendleton County, West Virginia
Unit: Company I, 194th Glider Infantry, 17th Airborne Division
Battle or Place of Action: near Lembeck, Germany
Date of Action: 27-28 March 1945
G.O. Number, Date: 89, 19 October 1945
Citation: He displayed extraordinary heroism and gallantry in action on 27–28 March 1945, in Germany. Following an airborne landing near Wesel, his unit was assigned as the assault platoon for the assault on Lembeck. Three times the landing elements were pinned down by intense automatic-weapon fire from strongly defended positions. Each time, T/Sgt. Hedrick fearlessly charged through heavy fire, shooting his automatic rifle from his hip. His courageous action so inspired his men that they reduced the enemy positions in rapid succession. When six of the enemy attempted a surprise, flanking movement, he quickly turned and killed the entire party with a burst of fire. Later, the enemy withdrew across a moat into Lembeck Castle. T/Sgt. Hedrick, with utter disregard for his own safety, plunged across the drawbridge alone in pursuit. When a German soldier, with hands upraised, declared the garrison wished to surrender, he entered the castle yard with four of his men to accept the capitulation. The group moved through a sally port, and was met by fire from a German self-propelled gun. Although mortally wounded, T/Sgt. Hedrick fired at the enemy gun and covered the withdrawal of his comrades. He died while being evacuated after the castle was taken. His great personal courage and heroic leadership contributed in large measure to the speedy capture of Lembeck and provided an inspiring example to his comrades.

2761 ◆ HENDRIX, JAMES RICHARD

Rank: Private (highest rank: Master Sergeant)
Service: U.S. Army
Birthday: 20 August 1925
Place of Birth: Lepanto, Poinsett County, Arkansas
Entered Service at: Lepanto, Poinsett County, Arkansas
Unit: 3d Platoon, Company C, 53d Armored Infantry Battalion, 4th Armored Division
Served as: Bazookaman
Battle or Place of Action: near Assenois, Belgium
Date of Action: 26 December 1944
G.O. Number, Date: 74, 1 September 1945
Date of Presentation: 23 August 1945
Place of Presentation: The White House, presented by Pres. Harry S. Truman
Citation: On the night of 26 December 1944, near

Assenois, Belgium, he was with the leading element engaged in the final thrust to break through to the besieged garrison at Bastogne when halted by a fierce combination of artillery and small-arms fire. He dismounted from his half-track and advanced against two 88-mm guns, and, by the ferocity of his rifle fire, compelled the guncrews to take cover and then to surrender. Later in the attack he again left his vehicle, voluntarily, to aid two wounded soldiers, helpless and exposed to intense machine-gun fire. Effectively silencing two hostile machine guns, he held off the enemy by his own fire until the wounded men were evacuated. Pvt. Hendrix again distinguished himself when he hastened to the aid of still another soldier who was trapped in a burning half-track. Braving enemy sniper fire and exploding mines and ammunition in the vehicle, he extricated the wounded man and extinguished his flaming clothing, thereby saving the life of his fellow soldier. Pvt. Hendrix, by his superb courage and heroism, exemplified the highest traditions of the military service.

2762 ◆ *HENRY, ROBERT T.

Rank: Private
Service: U.S. Army
Birthday: 27 November 1923
Place of Birth: Greenville, Washington County, Mississippi
Date of Death: 3 December 1944
Place of Death: Luchem, Germany
Cemetery: Greenville Cemetery—Greenville, Mississippi
Entered Service at: Greenville, Washington County, Mississippi
Unit: 16th Infantry, 1st Infantry Division
Battle or Place of Action: Luchem, Germany
Date of Action: 3 December 1944
G.O. Number, Date: 45, 12 June 1945
Citation: Near Luchem, Germany, he volunteered to attempt the destruction of a nest of five enemy machine guns located in a bunker 150 yards to the flank which had stopped the advance of his platoon. Stripping off his pack, overshoes, helmet, and overcoat, he sprinted alone with his rifle and hand grenades across the open terrain toward the enemy emplacement. Before he had gone half the distance he was hit by a burst of machine-gun fire. Dropping his rifle, he continued to stagger forward until he fell mortally wounded only 10 yards from the enemy emplacement. His singlehanded attack forced the enemy to leave the machine guns. During this break in hostile fire the platoon moved forward and overran the position. Pvt. Henry, by his gallantry and intrepidity and utter disregard for his own life, enabled his company to reach its objective, capturing this key defense and 70 German prisoners.

2763 ◆ HERRERA, SILVESTRE SANTANA

Rank: Private First Class (highest rank: Sergeant)
Service: U.S. Army
Birthday: 17 July 1917
Place of Birth: El Paso, El Paso County, Texas
Entered Service at: Phoenix, Maricopa County, Arizona
Unit: 1st Squad, 1st Platoon, Company E, 2d Battalion, 142d Infantry, 36th Infantry Division
Served as: Acting Squad Leader/Automatic Rifleman
Battle or Place of Action: near Merzwiller, France
Date of Action: 15 March 1945
G.O. Number, Date: 75, 5 September 1945
Date of Presentation: 23 August 1945
Place of Presentation: The White House, presented by Pres. Harry S. Truman
Citation: He advanced with a platoon along a wooded road until stopped by heavy enemy machine-gun fire. As the rest of the unit took cover, he made a one-man frontal assault on a strongpoint and captured eight enemy soldiers. When the platoon resumed its advance and was subjected to fire from a second emplacement beyond an extensive minefield, Pvt. Herrera again moved forward, disregarding the danger of exploding mines, to attack the position. He stepped on a mine and had both feet severed; but, despite intense pain and unchecked loss of blood, he pinned down the enemy with accurate rifle fire while a friendly squad captured the enemy gun by skirting the minefield and rushing in from the flank. The magnificent courage, extraordinary heroism, and willing self-sacrifice displayed by Pvt. Herrera resulted in the capture of two enemy strongpoints and the taking of eight prisoners.

2764 ◆ HERRING, RUFUS GEDDIE

Rank: Lieutenant [rank at time of action: Lieutenant (j.g.)] (highest rank: Lieutenant Commander)
Service: U.S. Navy
Birthday: 11 June 1921
Place of Birth: Roseboro, Sampson County, North Carolina
Entered Service at: Roseboro, Sampson County, North Carolina
Unit: Landing Craft Infantry Gunboat LCI(G)-449, LCI(G) Group 8
Served as: Commanding Officer
Battle or Place of Action: Iwo Jima, Volcano Islands
Date of Action: 17 February 1945
Date of Presentation: 17 September 1945
Place of Presentation: Washington, D.C., presented by Sec. of the Navy James V. Forrestal
Citation: For conspicuous gallantry and intrepidity at the risk of his life above and beyond the call of duty as commanding officer of LCI (G) 449 operating as a unit of LCI (G) Group 8, during the pre-invasion attack on Iwo Jima on 17 February 1945. Boldly closing the strongly fortified shores under the devastating fire of Japanese coastal defense guns, Lt. (then Lt. [jg]) Herring directed shattering barrages of 40-mm and 20-mm gunfire against hostile beaches until struck down by the enemy's savage counterfire which blasted the 449's heavy guns and whipped her decks into sheets of flame. Regaining consciousness despite profuse bleeding he was again critically wounded when a Japanese mortar crashed the conning station, instantly killing or fatally wounding most of the officers and leaving the ship wallowing without navigational control. Upon recovering the second time, Lt. Herring resolutely climbed down to the pilothouse and, fighting against his rapidly waning strength, took over the helm, established communication with the engineroom, and carried on valiantly until relief could be obtained. When no longer

able to stand, he propped himself against empty shell cases and rallied his men to the aid of the wounded; he maintained position in the firing line with his 20-mm guns in action in the face of sustained enemy fire, and conned his crippled ship to safety. His unwavering fortitude, aggressive perseverance, and indomitable spirit against terrific odds reflect the highest credit upon Lt. Herring and uphold the highest traditions of the U.S. Naval Service.

2765 ◆ *HILL, EDWIN JOSEPH

Rank: Chief Boatswain
Service: U.S. Navy
Birthday: 4 October 1895
Place of Birth: Philadelphia, Philadelphia County, Pennsylvania
Date of Death: 7 December 1941
Place of Death: Pearl Harbor, Territory of Hawaii
Cemetery: National Memorial Cemetery of the Pacific (A-895) (MH)—Honolulu, Hawaii
Entered Service at: Pennsylvania
Unit: U.S.S. *Nevada*
Battle or Place of Action: Pearl Harbor, Territory of Hawaii
Date of Action: 7 December 1941
Citation: For distinguished conduct in the line of his profession, extraordinary courage, and disregard of his own safety during the attack on the Fleet in Pearl Harbor, by Japanese forces on 7 December 1941. During the height of the strafing and bombing, Chief Boatswain Hill led his men of the line-handling details of the U.S.S. *Nevada* to the quays, cast off the lines and swam back to his ship. Later, while on the forecastle, attempting to let go the anchors, he was blown overboard and killed by the explosion of several bombs.

2766 ◆ HORNER, FREEMAN VICTOR

Rank: Staff Sergeant (highest rank: Major)
Service: U.S. Army
Birthday: 7 June 1922
Place of Birth: Mount Carmel, Northumberland County, Pennsylvania
Entered Service at: Shamokin, Northumberland County, Pennsylvania
Unit: 2d Platoon, Company K, 2d Battalion, 119th Infantry, 30th Infantry Division
Served as: Acting Platoon Leader
Battle or Place of Action: Wurselen, Germany
Date of Action: 16 November 1944
G.O. Number, Date: 95, 30 October 1945
Date of Presentation: 12 October 1945
Place of Presentation: The White House (Lawn), presented by Pres. Harry S. Truman
Citation: S/Sgt. Horner and other members of his company were attacking Wurselen, Germany, against stubborn resistance on 16 November 1944, when machine-gun fire from houses on the edge of the town pinned the attackers in flat, open terrain 100 yards from their objective. As they lay in the field, enemy artillery observers directed fire upon them, causing serious casualties. Realizing that the machine guns must be eliminated in order to permit the company to advance from its precarious position, S/Sgt. Horner voluntarily stood up with his submachine gun and rushed into the teeth of concentrated fire, burdened by a heavy load of ammunition and hand grenades. Just as he reached a position of seeming safety, he was fired on by a machine gun which had remained silent up until that time. He coolly wheeled in his fully exposed position while bullets barely missed him and killed two hostile gunners with a single, devastating burst. He turned to face the fire of the other two machine guns and, dodging fire as he ran, charged the two positions 50 yards away. Demoralized by their inability to hit the intrepid infantryman, the enemy abandoned their guns and took cover in the cellar of the house they occupied. S/Sgt. Horner burst into the building, hurled two grenades down the cellar stairs, and called for the Germans to surrender. Four men gave up to him. By his extraordinary courage, S/Sgt. Horner destroyed three enemy machine-gun positions, killed or captured seven enemy, and cleared the path for his company's successful assault on Wurselen.

2767 ◆ HOWARD, JAMES HOWELL

Rank: Lieutenant Colonel (rank at time of action: Major) (highest rank: Brigadier General)
Service: U.S. Army Air Corps/U.S. Air Force
thday: 8 April 1913
Place of Birth: Canton, China
Date of Death: 18 march 1995
Place of Death: Belleair Bluffs, Florida
Cemetery: Arlington national Cemetery (34-2571) (MH)—Arlington, Virginia
Entered Service at: St. Louis, St. Louis County, Missouri
Unit: 356th Fighter Squadron, 354th Fighter Group, 9th Air Force
Served as: Group Commander of P-51s
Battle or Place of Action: over Oschersleben, Germany
Date of Action: 11 January 1944
G.O. Number, Date: 45, 5 June 1944
Date of Presentation: 27 June 1944
Place of Presentation: London, England, presented by Lt. Gen. Carl A. Spaatz, Commander of the Air Forces in Europe
Citation: For conspicuous gallantry and intrepidity above and beyond the call of duty in action with the enemy near Oschersleben, Germany on 11 January 1944. On that day Col. Howard was the leader of a group of P-51 aircraft providing support for a heavy bomber formation on a long-range mission deep in enemy territory. As Col. Howard's group met the bombers in the target area the bomber force was attacked by numerous enemy fighters. Col. Howard, with his group, at once engaged the enemy and himself destroyed a German ME. 110. As a result of this attack Col. Howard lost contact with his group, and at once returned to the level of the bomber formation. He then saw that the bombers were being heavily attacked by enemy airplanes and that no other friendly fighters were at hand. While Col. Howard could have waited to attempt to assemble his group before engaging the enemy, he chose instead to attack singlehandedly a formation of more than 30 German airplanes. With utter disregard for his own

safety he immediately pressed home determined attacks for some 30 minutes, during which time he destroyed three enemy airplanes and probably destroyed and damaged others. Toward the end of this engagement three of his guns went out of action and his fuel supply was becoming dangerously low. Despite these handicaps and the almost insuperable odds against him, Col. Howard continued his aggressive action in an attempt to protect the bombers from the numerous fighters. His skill, courage, and intrepidity on this occasion set an example of heroism which will be an inspiration to the U.S. Armed Forces.

2768 ◆ HUFF, PAUL BERT

Rank: Corporal (highest rank: Command Sergeant Major)
Service: U.S. Army
Birthday: 23 June 1918
Place of Birth: Cleveland, Bradley County, Tennessee
Date of Death: 21 September 1994
Place of Death: Clarksville, Tennessee
Cemetery: Hillcrest Cemetery—Cleveland, Tennessee
Entered Service at: Cleveland, Bradley County, Tennessee
Unit: 1st Squad, 1st Platoon, Company A, 509th Parachute Infantry Battalion, 5th Army
Served as: Acting Platoon Sergeant
Battle or Place of Action: near Carano, Italy
Date of Action: 8 February 1944
G.O. Number, Date: 41, 26 May 1944
Date of Presentation: 8 June 1944
Place of Presentation: Rome, Italy, presented by Lt. Gen. Mark W. Clark
Citation: For conspicuous gallantry and intrepidiity at risk of life above and beyond the call of duty, in action on 8 February 1944, near Carano, Italy. Cpl. Huff volunteered to lead a six-man patrol with the mission of determining the location and strength of an enemy unit which was delivering fire on the exposed right flank of his company. The terrain over which he had to travel consisted of exposed, rolling ground, affording the enemy excellent visibility. As the patrol advanced, its members were subjected to small-arms and machine-gun fire and a concentration of mortar fire, shells bursting within 5 to 10 yards of them and bullets striking the ground at their feet. Moving ahead of his patrol, Cpl. Huff drew fire from three enemy machine guns and a 20-mm weapon. Realizing the danger confronting his patrol, he advanced alone under deadly fire through a minefield and arrived at a point within 75 yards of the nearest machine-gun position. Under direct fire from the rear machine gun, he crawled the remaining 75 yards to the closest emplacement, killed the crew with his submachine gun, and destroyed the gun. During this act he fired from a kneeling position which drew fire from other positions, enabling him to estimate correctly the strength and location of the enemy. Still under concentrated fire, he returned to his patrol and led his men to safety. As a result of the information he gained, a patrol in strength sent out that afternoon, one group under the leadership of Cpl. Huff, succeeded in routing an enemy company of 125 men, killing 27 Germans, and capturing 21 others, with a loss of only three patrol members. Cpl. Huff's intrepid leadership and daring combat skill reflect the finest traditions of the American infantryman.

2769 ◆ *HUGHES, LLOYD HERBERT

Rank: Second Lieutenant
Service: U.S. Army Air Corps
Birthday: 12 July 1921
Place of Birth: Alexandria, Rapides County, Louisiana
Date of Death: 1 August 1943
Cemetery: Fort Sam Houston National Cemetery (U-53) (MH)—San Antonio, Texas
Entered Service at: San Antonio, Bexar County, Texas
Unit: 564th Bombardment Squadron, 389th Bombardment Group, 9th Air Force
Served as: Pilot of a B-24
Battle or Place of Action: Ploesti, Rumania
Date of Action: 1 August 1943
G.O. Number, Date: 17, 26 February 1944
Citation: For conspicuous gallantry in action and intrepidity at risk of his life above and beyond the call of duty. On 1 August 1943, 2d Lt. Hughes served in the capacity of pilot of a heavy bombardment aircraft participating in a long and hazardous minimum-altitude attack against the Axis oil refineries of Ploesti, Rumania, launched from the northern shores of Africa. Flying in the last formation to attack the target, he arrived in the target area after previous flights had thoroughly alerted the enemy defenses. Approaching the target through intense and accurate antiaircraft fire and dense balloon barrages at dangerously low altitude, his plane received several direct hits from both large and small caliber antiaircraft guns which seriously damaged his aircraft, causing sheets of escaping gasoline to stream from the bomb bay and from the left wing. This damage was inflicted at a time prior to reaching the target when 2d Lt. Hughes could have made a forced landing in any of the grain fields readily available at the time. The target area was blazing with burning oil tanks and damaged refinery installations from which flames leaped high above the bombing level of the formation. With full knowledge of the consequences of entering this blazing inferno when his airplane was profusely leaking gasoline in two separate locations, 2d Lt. Hughes, motivated only by his high conception of duty which called for the destruction of his assigned target at any cost, did not elect to make a forced landing or turn back from the attack. Instead, rather than jeopardize the formation and the success of the attack, he unhesitatingly entered the blazing area and dropped his bomb load with great precision. After successfully bombing the objective, his aircraft emerged from the conflagration with the left wing aflame. Only then did he attempt a forced landing, but because of the advanced stage of the fire enveloping his aircraft the plane crashed and was consumed. By 2d Lt. Hughes' heroic decisi on to complete his mission regardless of the consequences, in utter disregard of his own life, and by his gallant and valorous execution of this decision, he has rendered a service to our country in the defeat of our enemies which will everlastingly be outstanding in the annals of our nation's history.

2770 ◆ *HUTCHINS, JOHNNIE DAVID

Rank: Seaman First Class
Service: U.S. Naval Reserve
Birthday: 4 August 1922
Place of Birth: Weimer, Colorado County, Texas
Date of Death: 4 September 1943
Place of Death: Lae, New Guinea
Cemetery: Lakeside Cemetery (MH)—Eagle Lake, Texas
Entered Service at: Texas
Unit: U.S.S. Landing Ship Tank LST-473
Battle or Place of Action: Lae, New Guinea
Date of Action: 4 September 1943
Date of Presentation: September 1944
Place of Presentation: Sam Houston Coliseum, Houston, Texas, presented by Rear Adm. A.C. Bennett to his Mother
Citation: For extraordinary heroism and conspicuous valor above and beyond the call of duty while serving on board a landing ship tank, during the assault on Lae, New Guinea, 4 September 1943. As the ship on which Hutchins was stationed approached the enemy-occupied beach under a veritable hail of fire from Japanese shore batteries and aerial bombardment, a hostile torpedo pierced the surf and bore down upon the vessel with deadly accuracy. In the tense split seconds before the helmsman could steer clear of the threatening missile, a bomb struck the pilothouse, dislodged him from his station, and left the stricken ship helplessly exposed. Fully aware of the dire peril of the situation, Hutchins, although mortally wounded by the shattering explosion, quickly grasped the wheel and exhausted the last of his strength in maneuvering the vessel clear of the advancing torpedo. Still clinging to the helm, he eventually succumbed to his injuries, his final thoughts concerned only with the safety of his ship, his final efforts expended toward the security of his mission. He gallantly gave his life in the service of his country.

2771 ◆ *JACHMAN, ISADORE SEIGFREID

Rank: Staff Sergeant
Service: U.S. Army
Birthday: 14 December 1922
Place of Birth: Berlin, Germany
Date of Death: 4 January 1945
Place of Death: Flamierge, Belgium
Cemetery: Adath Israel Anshe Sfard Cemetery—Baltimore, Maryland
Entered Service at: Baltimore, Baltimore County, Maryland
Unit: Company B, 513th Parachute Infantry Regiment, 17th Airborne Division
Battle or Place of Action: Flamierge, Belgium
Date of Action: 4 January 1945
G.O. Number, Date: 25, 9 June 1950
Place of Presentation: Ft. George Meade, Md., presented by Lt. Gen. Leonard Derow to his parents
Citation: For conspicuous gallantry and intrepidity above and beyond the call of duty at Flamierge, Belgium on 4 January 1945, when his company was pinned down by enemy artillery, mortar, and small-arms fire, two hostile tanks attacked the unit, inflicting heavy casualties. S/Sgt. Jachman, seeing the desperate plight of his comrades, left his place of cover and with total disregard for his own safety dashed across open ground through a hail of fire and, seizing a bazooka from a fallen comrade, advanced on the tanks, which concentrated their fire on him. Firing the weapon alone, he damaged one and forced both to retire. S/Sgt. Jachman's heroic action, in which he suffered fatal wounds, disrupted the entire enemy attack, reflecting the highest credit upon himself and the parachute infantry.

2772 ◆ JACKSON, ARTHUR JUNIOR

Rank: Private First Class (highest rank: Captain)
Service: U.S. Marine Corps
Birthday: 18 October 1924
Place of Birth: Cleveland, Cuyahoga County, Ohio
Entered Service at: Portland, Multnomah County, Oregon
Unit: 3d Squad, 2d Platoon, Company I, 3d Battalion, 7th Marines, 1st Marine Division
Served as: Automatic Rifleman
Battle or Place of Action: Peleliu Island, Palau Islands
Date of Action: 18 September 1944
Date of Presentation: 5 October 1945
Place of Presentation: The White House, presented by Pres. Harry S. Truman
Citation: For conspicuous gallantry and intrepidity at the risk of his life above and beyond the call of duty while serving with the 3d Battalion, 7th Marines, 1st Marine Division, in action against enemy Japanese forces on the island of Peleliu in the Palau group, 18 September 1944. Boldly taking the initiative when his platoon's left flank advance was held up by the fire of Japanese troops concealed in strongly fortified positions, Pfc. Jackson unhesitatingly proceeded forward of our lines and, courageously defying the heavy barrages, charged a large pillbox housing approximately 35 enemy soldiers. Pouring his automatic fire into the opening of the fixed installation to trap the occupying troops, he hurled white phosphorus grenades and explosive charges brought up by a fellow marine, demolishing the pillbox and killing all of the enemy. Advancing alone under the continuous fire from other hostile emplacements, he employed similar means to smash two smaller positions in the immediate vicinity. Determined to crush the entire pocket of resistance although harassed on all sides by the shattering blasts of Japanese weapons and covered only by small rifle parties, he stormed one gun position after another, dealing death and destruction to the savagely fighting enemy in his inexorable drive against the remaining defenses, and succeeded in wiping out a total of 12 pillboxes and 50 Japanese soldiers. Stouthearted and indomitable despite the terrific odds, Pfc. Jackson resolutely maintained control of the platoon's left flank movement throughout his valiant one-man assault and, by his cool decision and relentless fighting spirit during a critical situation, contributed essentially to the complete annihilation of the enemy in the southern sector of the island. His gallant initiative and heroic conduct in the face of extreme peril reflect the highest credit upon Pfc. Jackson and the U.S. Naval Service.

2773 ◆ JACOBSON, DOUGLAS THOMAS

Rank: Private First Class (highest rank: Major)
Service: U.S. Marine Corps Reserve

Birthday: 25 November 1925
Place of Birth: Rochester, Monroe County, New York
Entered Service at: New York
Unit: Company L, 3d Battalion, 24th Marines, 4th Marine Division
Served as: Demolition Specialist/Bazooka/Flamethrower
Battle or Place of Action: Hill 382, Iwo Jima, Volcano Islands
Date of Action: 26 February 1945
Date of Presentation: 5 October 1945
Place of Presentation: The White House, presented by Pres. Harry S. Truman
Citation: For conspicuous gallantry and intrepidity at the risk of his life above and beyond the call of duty while serving with the 3d Battalion, 23d Marines, 4th Marine Division, in combat against enemy Japanese forces during the seizure of Iwo Jima in the Volcano Islands, 26 February 1945. Promptly destroying a stubborn 20-mm antiaircraft gun and its crew after assuming the duties of a bazooka man who had been killed, Pfc. Jacobson waged a relentless battle as his unit fought desperately toward the summit of Hill 382 in an effort to penetrate the heart of Japanese cross-island defense. Employing his weapon with ready accuracy when his platoon was halted by overwhelming enemy fire on 26 February, he first destroyed two hostile machine-gun positions, then attacked a large blockhouse, completely neutralizing the fortification before dispatching the five-man crew of a second pillbox and exploding the installation with a terrific demolitions blast. Moving steadily forward, he wiped out an earth-covered rifle emplacement and, confronted by a cluster of similar emplacements which constituted the perimeter of enemy defenses in his assigned sector, fearlessly advanced, quickly reduced all six positions to a shambles, killed 10 of the enemy, and enabled our forces to occupy the strongpoint. Determined to widen the breach thus forced, he volunteered his services to an adjacent assault company, neutralized a pillbox holding up its advance, opened fire on a Japanese tank pouring a steady stream of bullets on one of our supporting tanks, and smashed the enemy tank's gun turret in a brief but furious action culminating in a singlehanded assault against still another blockhouse and the subsequent neutralization of its firepower. By his dauntless skill and valor, Pfc. Jacobson destroyed a total of 16 enemy positions and annihilated approximately 75 Japanese, thereby contributing essentially to the success of his division's operations against this fanatically defended outpost of the Ja panese Empire. His gallant conduct in the face of tremendous odds enhanced and sustained the highest traditions of the U.S. Naval Service.

2774 ◆ *JERSTAD, JOHN LOUIS

Rank: Major
Service: U.S. Army Air Corps
Birthday: 12 February 1918
Place of Birth: Racine, Racine County, Wisconsin
Date of Death: 1 August 1943
Place of Death: near Ploesti, Rumania
Cemetery: A.B.M.C. Ardennes Cemetery (C-24-10)—Neuvile-En-Condroz, Belgium
Entered Service at: Racine, Racine County, Wisconsin
Unit: 201st Provisional Combat Wing, 9th Air Force
Served as: Pilot of a B-24
Battle or Place of Action: Ploesti, Rumania
Date of Action: 1 August 1943
G.O. Number, Date: 72, 28 October 1943
Citation: For conspicuous gallantry and intrepidity above and beyond the call of duty. On 1 August 1943, he served as pilot of the lead aircraft in his group in a daring low-level attack against enemy oil refineries and installations at Ploesti, Rumania. Although he had completed more than his share of missions and was no longer connected with this group, so high was his conception of duty that he volunteered to lead the formation in the correct belief that his participation would contribute materially to the success of this attack. Maj. Jerstad led the formation into attack with full realization of the extreme hazards involved and despite withering fire from heavy and light anitaircraft guns. Three miles from the target his airplane was hit, badly damaged, and set on fire. Ignoring the fact that he was flying over a field suitable for a forced landing, he kept on the course. After the bombs of his aircraft were released on the target, the fire in his ship became so intense as to make further progress impossible and he crashed into the target area. By his voluntary acceptance of a mission he knew was extremely hazardous and his assumption of an intrepid course of action at the risk of life over and above the call of duty, Maj. Jerstad set an example of heroism which will be an inspiration to the U.S. Armed Forces.

2775 ◆ *JOHNSON, ELDEN HARVEY

Rank: Private
Service: U.S. Army
Birthday: 13 February 1921
Place of Birth: Bivale, Cumberland County, New Jersey
Date of Death: 3 June 1944
Cemetery: Union Cemetery (MH)—Scituate, Massachusetts
Entered Service at: East Weymouth, Norfolk County, Massachusetts
Unit: Company H, 15th Infantry, 3d Infantry Division
Battle or Place of Action: near Valmontone, Italy
Date of Action: 3 June 1944
G.O. Number, Date: 38, 16 May 1945
Date of Presentation: 30 May 1945
Place of Presentation: Boston Commons, Boston, Massachusetts, presented by Gen. Sherman Miles to his Mother
Citation: For conspicuous gallantry and intrepidity at the risk of life above and beyond the call of duty. Pvt. Johnson elected to sacrifice his life in order that his comrades might extricate themselves from an ambush. Braving the massed fire of about 60 riflemen, three machine guns, and three tanks from positions only 25 yards distant, he stood erect and signaled his patrol leader to withdraw. The whole area was brightly illuminated by enemy flares. Then, despite 20-mm machine-gun, machine-pistol, and rifle fire directed at him, Pvt. Johnson advanced beyond the enemy in a slow deliberate walk. Firing his automatic rifle from the hip, he succeeded in distracting the enemy and enabled his 12 comrades to escape. Advancing to within five yards of a machine gun, emptying his weapon, Pvt. Johnson killed its crew. Standing in full view

of the enemy, he reloaded and turned on the riflemen to the left, firing directly into their positions. He either killed or wounded four of them. A burst of machine-gun fire tore into Pfc. Johnson and he dropped to his knees. Fighting to the very last, he steadied himself on his knees and sent a final burst of fire crashing into another German. With that he slumped forward dead. Pvt. Johnson had willingly given his life in order that his comrades might live. These acts on the part of Pvt. Johnson were an inspiration to the entire command and are in keeping with the highest traditions of the Armed Forces.

2776 ◆ JOHNSON, LEON WILLIAM

Rank: Colonel (highest rank: General)
Service: U.S. Army Air Corps/U.S. Air Force
Birthday: 13 September 1904
Place of Birth: Columbia, Boone County, Missouri
Entered Service at: Moline, Elk County, Kansas
Unit: 44th Bombardment Group, 2d Bomb Division, 9th Air Force
Served as: Commanding Officer/Pilot of a B-24
Battle or Place of Action: Ploesti, Rumania
Date of Action: 1 August 1943
G.O. Number, Date: 54, 7 September 1943
Date of Presentation: 22 November 1943
Place of Presentation: England, presented by Lt. Gen. Jacob L. Devers
Citation: For conspicuous gallantry in action and intrepidity at the risk of his life above and beyond the call of duty on 1 August 1943. Col. Johnson, as commanding officer of a heavy bombardment group, led the formation of the aircraft of his organization constituting the fourth element of the mass low-level bombing attack of the 9th U.S. Air Force against the vitally important enemy target of the Ploesti oil refineries. While proceeding to the target on this 2,400-mile flight, his element became separated from the leading elements of the mass formation in maintaining the formation of the unit while avoiding dangerous cumulus cloud conditions encountered over mountainous territory. Though temporarily lost, he reestablished contact with the third element and continued on the mission with this reduced force to the prearranged point of attack, where it was discovered that the target assigned to Col. Johnson's group had been attacked and damaged by a preceding element. Though having lost the element of surprise upon which the safety and success of such a daring form of mission in heavy bombardment aircraft so strongly depended, Col. Johnson elected to carry out his planned low-level attack despite the thoroughly alerted defenses, the destructive anitaircraft fire, enemy fighter planes, the imminent danger of exploding delayed-action bombs from the previous element, of oil fires and explosions, and of intense smoke obscuring the target. By his gallant courage, brilliant leadership, and superior flying skill, Col. Johnson so led his formation as to destroy totally the important refining plants and installations which were the object of his mission. Col. Johnson's personal contribution to the success of this historic raid, and the conspicuous gallantry in action and intrepidity at the risk of his life above and beyond the call of duty demonstrated by him on this occasion constitute such deeds of valor and distinguished service as have during our nation's history formed the fi nest traditions of our Armed Forces.

2777 ◆ *JOHNSON, LEROY

Rank: Sergeant
Service: U.S. Army
Place of Birth: Caney Creek, Louisiana
Date of Death: 15 December 1944
Cemetery: A.B.M.C. Mamila Cemetery (C-10-79)—Manila, Philippine Islands
Entered Service at: Oakdale, Allen County, Louisiana
Unit: Company K, 126th Infantry, 32d Infantry Division
Served as: Squad Leader
Battle or Place of Action: near Limon, Leyte, Philippine Islands
Date of Action: 15 December 1944
G.O. Number, Date: 83, 2 October 1945
Citation: He was a squad leader of a nine-man patrol sent to reconnoiter a ridge held by a well-entrenched enemy force. Seeing an enemy machine-gun position, he ordered his men to remain behind while he crawled to within six yards of the gun. One of the enemy crew jumped up and prepared to man the weapon. Quickly withdrawing, Sgt. Johnson rejoined his patrol and reported the situation to his commanding officer. Ordered to destroy the gun, which covered the approaches to several other enemy positions, he chose three other men, armed them with hand grenades, and led them to a point near the objective. After taking partial cover behind a log, the men had knocked out the gun and begun an assault when hostile troops on the flank hurled several grenades. As he started for cover, Sgt. Johnson saw two unexploded grenades which had fallen near his men. Knowing that his comrades would be wounded or killed by the explosion, he deliberately threw himself on the grenades and received their full charge in his body. Fatally wounded by the blast, he died soon afterward. Through his outstanding gallantry in sacrificing his life for his comrades, Sgt. Johnson provided a shining example of the highest traditions of the U.S. Army.

2778 ◆ JOHNSON JR., OSCAR GODFREY

Rank: Sergeant (rank at time of action: Private First Class) (highest rank: Chief Warrant Officer 4)
Service: U.S. Army
Birthday: 25 March 1921
Place of Birth: Foster City, Dickinson County, Michigan
Entered Service at: Foster City, Dickinson County, Michigan
Unit: Weapons Platoon, Company B, 1st Battalion, 363d Infantry, 91st Infantry Division
Served as: Mortar Gunner
Battle or Place of Action: near Scarperia, Italy
Date of Action: 16-18 September 1944
G.O. Number, Date: 58, 19 July 1945
Date of Presentation: 25 June 1945
Place of Presentation: Northern Italy, presented by Gen. Mark W. Clark

Citation: He practically singlehandedly protected the left flank of his company's position in the offensive to break the Germans's Gothic line. Company B was the extreme left assault unit of the corps. The advance was stopped by heavy fire from Monticelli Ridge, and the company took cover behind an embankment. Sgt. Johnson, a mortar gunner, having expended his ammunition, assumed the duties of a rifleman. As leader of a squad of seven men he was ordered to establish a combat post 50 yards to the left of the company to cover its exposed flank. Repeated enemy counterattacks, supported by artillery, mortar, and machine-gun fire from the high ground to his front, had by the afternoon of 16 September killed or wounded all his men. Collecting weapons and ammunition from his fallen comrades, in the face of hostile fire, he held his exposed position and inflicted heavy casualties upon the enemy, who several times came close enough to throw hand grenades. On the night of 16–17 September, the enemy launched his heaviest attack on Company B, putting his greatest pressure against the lone defender of the left flank. In spite of mortar fire which crashed about him and machine-gun bullets which whipped the crest of his shallow trench, Sgt. Johnson stood erect and repulsed the attack with grenades and small-arms fire. He remained awake and on the alert throughout the night, frustrating all attempts at infiltration. On 17 September, 25 German soldiers surrendered to him. Two men, sent to reinforce him that afternoon, were caught in a devastating mortar and artillery barrage. With no thought of his own safety, Sgt. Johnson rushed to the shell hole where they lay half buried and seriously wounded, covered their position by his fire, and assisted a medical corpsman in rendering aid. That night he secured their removal to the rear and remained on watch until his company was relieved. Five companies of a German parachute regiment had been repeatedly committed to the attack on Company B without success. Twenty dead Germans were found in front of his position. By his heroic stand and utter disregard for personal safety, Sgt. Johnson was in a large measure responsible for defeating the enemy's attempts to turn the exposed left flank.

2779 ♦ JOHNSTON SR., WILLIAM JAMES

Rank: Private First Class
Service: U.S. Army
Birthday: 15 August 1918
Place of Birth: Trenton, Mercer County, New Jersey
Date of Death: 29 May 1990
Place of Death: Newington, Connecticut
Cemetery: Connecticut State Veterans Cemetery (MH)—Middletown, Connecticut
Entered Service at: Colchester, New London County, Connecticut
Unit: Company G, 180th Infantry, 45th Infantry Division
Served as: Machine Gunner
Battle or Place of Action: near Padiglione, Italy
Date of Action: 17-19 February 1944
G.O. Number, Date: 73, 6 September 1944
Place of Presentation: The White House, presented by Pres. Franklin D. Roosevelt
Citation: For conspicuous gallantry and intrepidity at the risk of life above and beyond the call of duty in action against the enemy. On 17 February 1944, near Padiglione, Italy, he observed and fired upon an attacking force of approximately 80 Germans, causing at least 25 casualties and forcing withdrawal of the remainder. All that day he manned his gun without relief, subject to mortar, artillery, and sniper fire. Two Germans individually worked so close to his position that his machine gun was ineffective, whereupon he killed one with his pistol, the second with a rifle taken from another soldier. When a rifleman protecting his gun position was killed by a sniper, he immediately moved the body and relocated the machine gun in that spot in order to obtain a better field of fire. He volunteered to cover the platoon's withdrawal and was the last man to leave that night. In his new position he maintained an all-night vigil, the next day causing seven German casualties. On the afternoon of the 18th, the organization on the left flank having been forced to withdraw, he again covered the withdrawal of his own organization. Shortly thereafter, he was seriously wounded over the heart, and a passing soldier saw him trying to crawl up the embankment. The soldier aided him in resuming his position behind the machine gun which was soon heard in action for about 10 minutes. Though reported killed, Pfc. Johnston was seen returning to the American lines on the morning of 19 February slowly and painfully working his way back from his overrun position through enemy lines. He gave valuable information of new enemy dispositions. His heroic determination to destroy the enemy and his disregard of his own safety aided immeasurably in halting a strong enemy attack, caused an enormous amount of enemy casualties, and so inspired his fellow soldiers that they fought for and held a vitally important position against greatly superior forces.

2780 ♦ *JONES, HERBERT CHARPOIT

Rank: Ensign
Service: U.S. Naval Reserve
Birthday: 1 December 1918
Place of Birth: Los Angeles, Los Angeles County, California
Date of Death: 7 December 1941
Place of Death: Pearl Harbor, Territory of Hawaii
Cemetery: Fort Rosecrans National Cemetery (G-7G) (MH)—San Diego, California
Entered Service at: California
Unit: U.S.S. *California*
Battle or Place of Action: Pearl Harbor, Territory of Hawaii
Date of Action: 7 December 1941
Citation: For conspicuous devotion to duty, extraordinary courage, and complete disregard of his own life, above and beyond the call of duty, during the attack on the Fleet in Pearl Harbor, by Japanese forces on 7 December 1941. Ens. Jones organized and led a party which was supplying ammunition to the antiaircraft battery of the U.S.S. *California* after the mechanical hoists were put out of action, when he was fatally wounded by a bomb explosion. When two men attempted to take him from the area which was on fire, he refused to let them do so, saying in words to the effect, "Leave me alone! I am done for. Get out of here before the magazines go off."

2781 ◆ *JULIAN, JOSEPH RODOLPH

Rank: Platoon Sergeant
Service: U.S. Marine Corps Reserve
Birthday: 3 April 1918
Place of Birth: Sturbridge, Worcester County, Massachusetts
Date of Death: 9 March 1945
Cemetery: Long Island National Cemetery (DSS-12) (MH)—Farmingdale, New York
Entered Service at: Massachusetts
Unit: 1st Battalion, 27th Marines, 5th Marine Division
Served as: Platoon Sergeant
Battle or Place of Action: Iwo Jima, Volcano Islands
Date of Action: 9 March 1945
Citation: For conspicuous gallantry and intrepidity at the risk of his life above and beyond the call of duty as a P/Sgt. Serving with the 1st Battalion, 27th Marines, 5th Marine Division, in action against enemy Japanese forces during the seizure of Iwo Jima in the Volcano Islands, 9 March 1945. Determined to force a breakthrough when Japanese troops occupying trenches and fortified positions on the left front laid down a terrific machine-gun and mortar barrage in a desperate effort to halt his company's advance, P/Sgt. Julian quickly established his platoon's guns in strategic supporting positions, and then, acting on his own initiative, fearlessly moved forward to execute a one-man assault on the nearest pillbox. Advancing alone, he hurled deadly demolitions and white phosphorus grenades into the emplacement, killing two of the enemy and driving the remaining five out into the adjoining trench system. Seizing a discarded rifle, he jumped into the trench and dispatched the five before they could make an escape. Intent on wiping out all resistance, he obtained more explosives and, accompanied by another marine, again charged the hostile fortifications and knocked out two more cave positions. Immediately thereafter, he launched a bazooka attack unassisted, firing four rounds into the one remaining pillbox and completely destroying it before he fell, mortally wounded by a vicious burst of enemy fire. Stouthearted and indomitable, P/Sgt. Julian consistently disregarded all personal danger and, by his bold decision, daring tactics, and relentless fighting spirit during a critical phase of the battle, contributed materially to the continued advance of his company and to the success of his division's operations in the sustained drive toward the conquest of this fiercely defended outpost of the Japanese Empire. His outstanding valor and unfaltering spirit of self-sacrifice throughout the bitter conflict sustained and enhanced the highest traditions of the U.S. Naval Service. H e gallantly gave his life for his country.

2782 ◆ *KANDLE, VICTOR LEONARD

Rank: First Lieutenant
Service: U.S. Army
Birthday: 13 June 1921
Place of Birth: Roy, Pierce County, Washington
Date of Death: 31 December 1944
Cemetery: A.B.M.C. Epinal Cemetery (B-14-55)—Epinal, France
Entered Service at: Redwood City, San Mateo County, California
Unit: Company I, 15th Infantry, 3d Infantry Division
Battle or Place of Action: near La Forge, France
Date of Action: 9 October 1944
G.O. Number, Date: 37, 11 May 1945
Place of Presentation: Presidio, San Francisco, CA; presented by Maj. Gen. H.C. Pratt to his Widow and Son
Citation: For conspicuous gallantry and intrepidity at the risk of his life above and beyond the call of duty. On 9 October 1944, at about noon, near La Forge, France, 1st Lt. Kandle, while leading a reconnaissance patrol into enemy territory, engaged in a duel at point-blank range with a German field officer and killed him. Having already taken five enemy prisoners that morning, he led a skeleton platoon of 16 men, reinforced with a light machine-gun squad, through fog and over precipitious mountain terrain to fall on the rear of a German quarry stronghold which had checked the advance of an infantry battalion for two days. Rushing forward, several yards ahead of his assault elements, 1st Lt. Kandle fought his way into the heart of the enemy strongpoint, and by his boldness and audacity, forced the Germans to surrender. Harassed by machine-gun fire from a position which he had bypassed in the dense fog, he moved to within 15 yards of the enemy, killed a German machine gunner with accurate rifle fire and led his men in the destruction of another machine-gun crew and its rifle security elements. Finally, he led his small force against a fortified house held by two German officers and 30 enlisted men. After establishing a base of fire, he rushed forward alone through an open clearing in full view of the enemy, smashed through a barricaded door, and forced all 32 Germans to surrender. His intrepidity and bold leadership resulted in the capture or killing of three enemy officers and 54 enlisted men, the destruction of three enemy strongpoints, and the seizure of enemy positions which had halted a battalion attack.

2783 ◆ KANE, JOHN RILEY

Rank: Colonel
Service: U.S. Army Air Corps/U.S. Air Force
Birthday: 5 January 1907
Place of Birth: McGregor, McLennan County, Texas
Entered Service at: Shreveport, Caddo County, Louisiana
Unit: 98th Bombardment Group, 9th Air Force
Served as: Pilot of a B-24
Battle or Place of Action: Ploesti, Rumania
Date of Action: 1 August 1943
G.O. Number, Date: 54, 9 August 1943
Date of Presentation: 7 September 1943
Place of Presentation: Gezira Sporting Club (Cricket Pitch), Cairo, Egypt, presented by Major Gen. Lewis H. Brereton
Citation: For conspicuous gallantry in action and intrepidity at the risk of his life above and beyond the call of duty, 1 August 1943. On this date he led the third element of heavy bombardment aircraft in a mass low-level bombing attack against the vitally important enemy target of the Ploesti oil refineries. En route to the target, which necessitated a round-trip flight of over 2,400 miles, Col. Kane's element became

separated from the leading portion of the massed formation in avoiding dense and dangerous cumulus cloud conditions over mountainous terrain. Rather than turn back from such a vital mission he elected to proceed to his target. Upon arrival at the target area it was discovered that another group had apparently missed its target and had previously attacked and damaged the target assigned to Col. Kane's element. Despite the thoroughly warned defenses, the intensive antiaircraft fire, enemy fighter airplanes, extreme hazards on a low-level attack of exploding delayed-action bombs from the previous element, of oil fire and explosions and dense smoke over the target area, Col. Kane elected to lead his formation into the attack. By his gallant courage, brilliant leadership, and superior flying skill, he and the formation under his command successfully attacked this vast refinery so essential to our enemies' war effort. Through his conspicuous gallantry in this most hazardous action against the enemy, and by his intrepidity at the risk of his life above and beyond the call of duty, Col. Kane personally contributed vitally to the success of this daring mission and thereby rendered most distinguished service in the furtherance of the defeat of our enemies.

2784 ◆ KEARBY, NEEL ERNEST

Rank: Colonel
Service: U.S. Army Air Corps
Birthday: 5 June 1911
Place of Birth: Wichita Falls, Wichita County, Texas
Date of Death: 5 March 1944
Place of Death: near Wewak, New Guinea
Cemetery: Hillcrest Memorial Park (MH)—Dallas, Texas
Entered Service at: Dallas, Collin County, Texas
Unit: 309th Bombardment Wing, 5th Air Force
Served as: Commanding Officer/Pilot of a P-47
Battle or Place of Action: near Wewak, New Guinea
Date of Action: 11 October 1943
G.O. Number, Date: 3, 6 January 1944
Date of Presentation: 23 January 1944
Place of Presentation: Brisbane, Australia, presented by Gen. Douglas MacArthur
Citation: For conspicuous gallantry and intrepidity above and beyond the call of duty in action with the enemy, Col. Kearby volunteered to lead a flight of four fighters to reconnoiter the strongly defended enemy base at Wewak. Having observed enemy installations and reinforcements at four airfields, and secured important tactical information, he saw an enemy fighter below him, made a diving attack, and shot it down in flames. The small formation then sighted approximately 12 enemy bombers accompanied by 36 fighters. Although his mission had been completed, his fuel was running low, and the numerical odds were 12 to 1, he gave the signal to attack. Diving into the midst of the enemy airplanes he shot down three in quick succession. Observing one of his comrades with two enemy fighters in pursuit, he destroyed both enemy aircraft. The enemy broke off in large numbers to make a multiple attack on his airplane, but despite his peril he made one more pass before seeking cloud protection. Coming into the clear, he called his flight together and led them to a friendly base. Col. Kearby brought down six enemy aircraft in this action, undertaken with superb daring after his mission was completed.

2785 ◆ *KEATHLEY, GEORGE D.

Rank: Staff Sergeant
Service: U.S. Army
Place of Birth: Olney, Young County, Texas
Date of Death: 14 September 1944
Cemetery: A.B.M.C. Florence Cemetery (D-11-26)—Florence, Italy
Entered Service at: Lamesa, Dawson County, Texas
Unit: 1st Platoon, Company B, 85th Infantry Division
Served as: Platoon Guide
Battle or Place of Action: Mount Altuzzo, Italy
Date of Action: 14 September 1944
G.O. Number, Date: 20, 29 March 1945
Date of Presentation: 11 April 1945
Place of Presentation: Camp Walters, Texas, presented by Major Gen. Bruce Magruder to his Widow Geneva
Citation: For conspicuous gallantry and intrepidity at the risk of his life above and beyond the call of duty, in action on the western ridge of Mount Altuzzo, Italy. After bitter fighting his company had advanced to within 50 yards of the objective, where it was held up due to intense enemy sniper, automatic, small-arms, and mortar fire. The enemy launched three desperate counterattacks in an effort to regain their former positions, but all three were repulsed with heavy casualties on both sides. All officers and noncommissioned officers of the 2d and 3d platoons of Company B had become casualties, and S/Sgt. Keathley, guide of the 1st platoon, moved up and assumed command of both the 2d and 3d platoons, reduced to 20 men. The remnants of the two platoons were dangerously low on ammunition, so S/Sgt. Keathley, under deadly small-arms and mortar fire, crawled from one casualty to another, collecting their ammunition and administering first aid. He then visited each man of his two platoons, issuing the precious ammunition he had collected from the dead and wounded, and giving them words of encouragement. The enemy now delivered their fourth counterattack, which was approximately two companies in strength. In a furious charge they attacked from the front and both flanks, throwing hand grenades, firing automatic weapons, and assisted by a terrific mortar barrage. So strong was the enemy counterattack that the company was given up for lost. The remnants of the 2d and 3d platoons of Company B were now looking to S/Sgt. Keathley for leadership. He shouted his orders precisely and with determination and the men responded with all that was in them. Time after time the enemy tried to drive a wedge into S/Sgt. Keathley's position and each time they were driven back, suffering huge casualties. Suddenly an enemy hand grenade hit and exploded near S/Sgt. Keathley, inflicting a mortal wound in his left side. However, hurling defiance at the enemy, he rose to his feet. Taking his left hand away from his wound and using it to steady his rifle, he fired and killed an attacking enemy soldier, and continued shouting orders to his men. His heroic and intrepid action so inspired his men that they fought with incomparable determination

and viciousness. For 15 minutes S/Sgt. Keathley continued leading his men and effectively firing his rifle. He could have sought a sheltered spot and perhaps saved his life, but instead he elected to set an example for his men and make every possible effort to hold his position. Finally, friendly artillery fire helped to force the enemy to withdraw, leaving behind many of their number either dead or seriously wounded. S/Sgt. Keathley died a few moments later. Had it not been for his indomitable courage and incomparable heroism, the remnants of three rifle platoons of Company B might well have been annihilated by the overwhelming enemy attacking force. His actions were in keeping with the highest traditions of the military service.

2786 ◆ *KEFURT, GUS

Rank: Staff Sergeant
Service: U.S. Army
Place of Birth: Greenville, Mercer County, Pennsylvania
Date of Death: 24 December 1944
Cemetery: A.B.M.C. Epinal Cemetery (A-29-37)—Epinal, France
Entered Service at: Youngstown, Mahoning County, Ohio
Unit: Company K, 15th Infantry, 3d Infantry Division
Battle or Place of Action: near Bennwihr, France
Date of Action: 23, 24 December 1944
Citation: He distinguished himself by conspicuous gallantry and intrepidity above and beyond the call of duty on 23 and 24 December 1944, near Bennwihr, France. Early in the attack S/Sgt. Kefurt jumped through an opening in a wall to be confronted by about 15 Germans. Although outnumbered he opened fire, killing 10 and capturing the others. During a seesaw battle which developed he effectively adjusted artillery fire on an enemy tank close to his position although exposed to small-arms fire. When night fell he maintained a three-man outpost in the center of the town in the middle of the German positions and successfully fought off several hostile patrols attempting to penetrate our lines. Assuming command of his platoon the following morning he led it in hand-to-hand fighting through the town until blocked by a tank. Using rifle grenades he forced surrender of its crew and some supporting infantry. He then continued his attack from house to house against heavy machine-gun and rifle fire. Advancing against a strongpoint that was holding up the company, his platoon was subjected to a strong counterattack and infiltration to its rear. Suffering heavy casualties in their exposed position the men remained there due to S/Sgt. Kefurt's personal example of bravery, determination, and leadership. He constantly exposed himself to fire by going from man to man to direct fire. During this time he killed approximately 15 of the enemy at close range. Although severely wounded in the leg he refused first aid and immediately resumed fighting. When the forces to his rear were pushed back three hours later, he refused to be evacuated, but, during several more counterattacks moved painfully about under intense small-arms and mortar fire, stiffening the resistance of his platoon by encouraging individual men and by his own fire until he was killed. As a result of S/Sgt. Kefurt's gallantry the position was maintained.

2787 ◆ *KELLEY, JONAH EDWARD HIGH

Rank: Staff Sergeant
Service: U.S. Army
Birthday: 13 April 1923
Place of Birth: Roda, West Virginia
Date of Death: 31 January 1945
Cemetery: Queens Point Cemetery (MH)—Keyser, West Virginia
Entered Service at: Keyser, Mineral County, West Virginia
Unit: Company E, 311th Infantry, 78th Infantry Division
Served as: Squad Leader
Battle or Place of Action: Kesternich, Germany
Date of Action: 30-31 January 1945
G.O. Number, Date: 77, 10 September 1945
Date of Presentation: 5 September 1945
Place of Presentation: Fort Hayes, Ohio, presented to his Father
Citation: In charge of the leading squad of Company E, he heroically spearheaded the attack in furious house-to-house fighting. Early on 30 January, he led his men through intense mortar and small-arms fire in repeated assaults on barricaded houses. Although twice wounded, once when struck in the back, the second time when a mortar shell fragment passed through his left hand and rendered it practically useless, he refused to withdraw and continued to lead his squad after hasty dressings had been applied. His serious wounds forced him to fire his rifle with one hand, resting it on rubble or over his left forearm. To blast his way forward with hand grenades, he set aside his rifle to pull the pins with his teeth while grasping the missles with his good hand. Despite these handicaps, he created tremendous havoc in the enemy ranks. He rushed one house, killing three of the enemy and clearing the way for his squad to advance. On approaching the next house, he was fired upon from an upstairs window. He killed the sniper with a single shot and similarly accounted for another enemy soldier who ran from the cellar of the house. As darkness came, he assigned his men to defensive positions, never leaving them to seek medical attention. At dawn the next day, the squad resumed the attack, advancing to a point where heavy automatic and small-arms fire stalled them. Despite his wounds, S/Sgt. Kelley moved out alone, located an enemy gunner dug in under a haystack, and killed him with rifle fire. He returned to his men and found that a German machine gun, from a well-protected position in a neighboring house, still held up the advance. Ordering the squad to remain in comparatively safe positions, he valiantly dashed into the open and attacked the positions singlehandedly through a hail of bullets. He was hit several times and fell to his knees when within 25 yards of his objective; but he summoned his waning strength and emptied his rifle into the machine-gun nest, silencing the weapon before he died. The superb courage, aggressiveness, and utter disregard for his own safety displayed by S/Sgt. Kelley inspired the men he led and enabled them to penetrate the last line of defense held by the enemy in the village of Kesternich.

2788 ◆ *KELLEY, OVA ART

Rank: Private
Service: U.S. Army

Birthday: 27 March 1914
Place of Birth: Norwood, Wright County, Missouri
Date of Death: 10 December 1944
Cemetery: Oak Grove Cemetery (MH)—Norwood, Missouri
Entered Service at: Norwood, Wright County, Missouri
Unit: Company A, 382d Infantry, 96th Infantry Division
Battle or Place of Action: Leyte, Philippine Islands
Date of Action: 8 December 1944
G.O. Number, Date: 89, 19 October 1945
Citation: For conspicuous gallantry and intrepidity at the risk of his life above and beyond the call of duty. Before dawn, near the edge of enemy-held Buri airstrip, the company was immobilized by heavy, accurate rifle and machine-gun fire from hostile troops entrenched in bomb craters and a ditch less than 100 yards distant. The company commander ordered a mortar concentration which destroyed one machine gun but failed to dislodge the main body of the enemy. At this critical moment Pvt. Kelley, on his own initiative, left his shallow foxhole with an armload of hand grenades and began a one-man assault on the foe. Throwing his missles with great accuracy, he moved forward, killing or wounding five men, and forced the remainder to flee in a disorganized route. He picked up an M1 rifle and emptied its clip at the running Japanese, killing three. Discarding this weapon, he took a carbine and killed three more of the enemy. Inspired by his example, his comrades followed him in a charge which destroyed the entire enemy force of 34 enlisted men and two officers and captured two heavy and one light machine guns. Pvt. Kelley continued to press the attack onto an airstrip, where sniper fire wounded him so grievously that he died two days later. His outstanding courage, aggressiveness, and initiative in the face of grave danger was an inspiration to his entire company and led to the success of the attack.

2789 ◆ KELLY, CHARLES E.

Rank: Corporal
Service: U.S. Army
Birthday: 23 September 1920
Place of Birth: Pittsburgh, Allegheny County, Pennsylvania
Date of Death: 11 January 1985
Cemetery: Highwood Cemetery (MH)—Pittsburgh, Pennsylvania
Entered Service at: Pittsburgh, Allegheny County, Pennsylvania
Unit: Company L, 3d Battalion, 143d Infantry, 36th Infantry Division
Battle or Place of Action: near Altavilla, Italy
Date of Action: 13 September 1943
G.O. Number, Date: 13, 18 February 1944
Place of Presentation: Presented by Lt. Gen. Mark W. Clark
Citation: For conspicuous gallantry and intrepidity at the risk of life above and beyond the call of duty. On 13 September 1943, near Altavilla, Italy, Cpl. Kelly voluntarily joined a patrol which located and neutralized enemy machine-gun positions. After this hazardous duty he volunteered to establish contact with a battalion of the U.S. infantry which was beleived to be located on Hill 315, a mile distant. He travelled over a route commanded by enemy observation and under sniper, mortar, and artillery fire; and later he returned with the correct information that the enemy occupied Hill 315 in organized positions. Immediately thereafter Cpl. Kelly, again a volunteer patrol member, assisted materially in the destruction of two enemy machine-gun nests under conditions requiring great skill and courage. Having effectively fired his weapon until all the ammunition was exhausted, he secured permission to obtain more at an ammunition dump. Arriving at the dump, which was located near a storehouse on the extreme flank of his regiment's position, Cpl. Kelly found that the Germans were attacking ferociously at this point. He obtained his ammunition and was given the mission of protecting the rear of the storehouse. He held his position throughout the night. The following morning the enemy attack was resumed. Cpl. Kelly took a position at an open window of the storehouse. One machine gunner had been killed at this position and several other soldiers wounded. Cpl. Kelly delivered continuous aimed and effective fire upon the enemy with his automatic rifle until the weapon locked from overheating. Finding another automatic rifle, he again directed effective fire upon the enemy until this weapon also locked. At this critical point, with the enemy threatening to overrun the position, Cpl. Kelly picked up 60-mm mortar shells, pulled the safety pins, and used the shells as grenades, killing at least five of the enemy. When it became imperative that the house be evacuated, Cpl. Kelly, de spite his sergeant's injunctions, volunteered to hold the position until the remainder of the detachment could withdraw. As the detachment moved out, Cpl. Kelly was observed deliberately loading and firing a rocket launcher from the window. He was successful in covering the withdrawl of his unit, and later in joining his own organization. Cpl. Kelly's fighting determination and intrepidity in battle exemplify the highest traditions of the U.S. Armed Forces.

2790 ◆ *KELLY, JOHN D.

Rank: Technical Sergeant (rank at time of action: Corporal)
Service: U.S. Army
Birthday: 8 July 1923
Place of Birth: Venango Township, Crawford County, Pennsylvania
Date of Death: 23 November 1944
Cemetery: A.B.M.C. Epinal Cemetery (A-44-7)—Epinal, France
Entered Service at: Cambridge Springs, Crawford County, Pennsylvania
Unit: Company E, 314th Infantry, 79th Infantry Division
Battle or Place of Action: Fort du Roule, Cherbourg, France
Date of Action: 25 June 1944
G.O. Number, Date: 6, 24 January 1945
Date of Presentation: 9 September 1953
Place of Presentation: Presented by Vice Pres. Richard M. Nixon to his Mother
Citation: For conspicuous gallantry and intrepidity at the risk of his life above and beyond the call of duty. On 25 June 1944, in the vicinity of Fort du Roule, Cherbourg, France, when Cpl. Kelly's unit was pinned down by heavy enemy

machine-gun fire emanating from a deeply entrenched strongpoint on the slope leading up to the fort, Cpl. Kelly volunteered to attempt to neutralize the strongpoint. Armed himself with a pole charge about 10 feet long and with 15 pounds of explosive affixed, he climbed the slope under a withering blast of machine-gun fire and placed the charge at the strongpoint's base. The subsequent blast was ineffective, and again, alone and unhesitatingly, he braved the slope to repeat the operation. This second blast blew off the ends of the enemy guns. Cpl. Kelly then climbed the slope a third time to place a pole charge at the strongpoint's rear entrance. When this had been blown open he hurled grenades inside the position, forcing survivors of the enemy guncrews to come out and surrender. The gallantry, tenacity of purpose, and utter disregard for personal safety displayed by Cpl. Kelly were an incentive to his comrades and worthy of emulation by all.

2791 ◆ KELLY, THOMAS JOSEPH

Rank: Corporal
Service: U.S. Army
Birthday: 9 September 1923
Place of Birth: Brooklyn, Kings County, New York
Date of Death: 2 October 1988
Place of Death: Somers Point, New Jersey
Cemetery: Arlington National Cemetery (7-A-125) (MH)—Arlington, Virginia
Entered Service at: Brooklyn, Kings County, New York
Unit: Medical Detachment, 48th Armored Infantry Battalion, 7th Armored Division
Served as: Medical Aidman
Battle or Place of Action: Alemert, Germany
Date of Action: 5 April 1945
G.O. Number, Date: 97, 1 November 1945
Date of Presentation: 12 October 1945
Place of Presentation: The White House, by Pres. Harry S. Truman
Citation: He was an aidman with the 1st Platoon of Company C during an attack on the town of Alemert, Germany. The platoon, committed in a flanking maneuver, had advanced down a small, open valley overlooked by wooded slopes hiding enemy machine guns and tanks, when the attack was stopped by murderous fire that inflicted heavy casualties in the American ranks. Ordered to withdraw, Cpl. Kelly reached safety with uninjured remnants of his unit, but, on realizing the extent of casualties suffered by the platoon, voluntarily retraced his steps and began evacuating his comrades under direct machine-gun fire. He was forecd to crawl, dragging the injured behind him for most of the 300 yards separating the exposed area from a place of comparative safety. Two other volunteers who attempted to negotiate the hazardous route with him were mortally wounded, but he kept on with his herculean task after dressing their wounds and carrying them to friendly hands. In all, he made 10 separate trips throughout the brutal fire, each time bringing out a man from the death trap. Seven more casualties who were able to crawl by themselves he guided and encouraged in escaping from the hail of fire. After he had completed his heroic, self-imposed task and was near collapse from fatigue, he refused to leave his platoon until the attack had been resumed and the objective taken. Cpl. Kelly's gallantry and intrepidity in face of seemingly certain death saved the lives of many of his fellow soldiers and was an example of bravery under fire.

2792 ◆ *KEPPLER, REINHARDT JOHN

Rank: Boatswain's Mate First Class
Service: U.S. Navy
Birthday: 22 January 1918
Place of Birth: Ralston, Washington
Date of Death: 15 November 1942
Place of Death: Naval Hospital, New Hebrides
Cemetery: Golden Gate National Cemetery (C-379) (MH)—San Bruno, California
Entered Service at: Washington
Unit: U.S.S. *San Francisco*
Battle or Place of Action: Iron Bottom Sound, near Savo Island, Solomon Islands
Date of Action: 12-13 November 1942
Date of Presentation: 17 September 1943
Place of Presentation: Naval District Headquarters, San Francisco, California, presented by Vice Adm. John W. Greensale to his Widow
Citation: For extraordinary heroism and distinguished courage above and beyond the call of duty while serving aboard the U.S.S. *San Francisco* during action against enemy Japanese forces in the Solomon Islands, 12–13 November 1942. When a hostile torpedo plane, during a daylight air raid, crashed on the after machine-gun platform, Keppler promptly assisted in removal of the dead and, by his capable supervision of the wounded, undoubtedly helped save the lives of several shipmates who otherwise might have perished. That night, when the ship's hangar was set afire during the great battle off Savo Island, he bravely led a hose into the starboard side of the stricken area and there, without assistance and despite frequent hits from terrific enemy bombardment, eventually brought the fire under control. Later, although mortally wounded, he labored valiantly in the midst of bursting shells, persistently directing firefighting operations and administering to wounded personnel until he finally collapsed from loss of blood. His great personal valor, maintained with utter disregard of personal safety, was in keeping with the highest traditions of the U.S. Naval Service. He gallantly gave his life for his country.

2793 ◆ KERSTETTER, DEXTER JAMES

Rank: Private First Class
Service: U.S. Army
Birthday: 21 December 1907
Place of Birth: Centralia, Lewis County, Washington
Date of Death: 9 July 1972
Cemetery: Drowned in Hood Canal, Puget Sound, Seabeck, Washington. Body not found
Entered Service at: Centralia, Lewis County, Washington
Unit: Company C, 130th Infantry, 33d Infantry Division
Battle or Place of Action: near Galiano, Luzon, Philippine Islands
Date of Action: 13 April 1945
G.O. Number, Date: 97, 1 November 1945

Date of Presentation: 12 October 1945
Place of Presentation: The White House, by Pres. Harry S. Truman
Citation: He was with his unit in a dawn attack against hill positions appoachable only along a narrow ridge paralleled on each side by steep cliffs which were heavily defended by enemy mortars, machine guns, and rifles in well-camouflaged spider holes and tunnels leading to caves. When the leading element was halted by intense fire that inflicted five casualties, Pfc. Kerstetter passed through the American line with his squad. Placing himself well in advance of his men, he grimly worked his way up the narrow steep hogback, meeting the brunt of enemy action. With well-aimed shots and rifle-grenade fire, he forced the Japs to take cover. He left the trail and, moving down a cliff that offered only precarious footholds, dropped among four Japs at the entrance to a cave, fired his rifle from his hip, and killed them all. Climbing back to the trail, he advanced against heavy enemy machine-gun, rifle, and mortar fire to silence a heavy machine gun by killing its crew of four with rifle fire and grenades. He expended his remaining ammunition and grenades on a group of approximately 20 Japs, scattering them, and returned to his squad for more ammunition and first aid for his left hand, which had been blistered by the heat from his rifle. Resupplied, he guided a fresh platoon into a position from which a concerted attack could be launched, killing three hostile soldiers on the way. In all, he dispatched 16 Japs that day. The hill was taken and held against the enemy's counterattacks, which continued for three days. Pfc. Kerstetter's dauntless and gallant heroism was largely responsible for the capture of this key enemy position, and his fearless attack in the face of great odds was an inspiration to his comrades in their dangerous task.

2794 ◆ *KESSLER, PATRICK L.

Rank: Private First Class
Service: U.S. Army
Birthday: 17 March 1922
Place of Birth: Middletown, Butler County, Ohio
Date of Death: 25 May 1944
Cemetery: Woodside Cemetery—Middletown, Ohio
Entered Service at: Middletown, Butler County, Ohio
Unit: Company K, 30th Infantry, 3d Infantry Division
Battle or Place of Action: near Ponte Rotto, Italy
Date of Action: 23 May 1944
G.O. Number, Date: 1, 4 January 1945
Citation: For conspicuous gallantry and intrepidity at the risk of life above and beyond the call of duty. Pfc. Kessler, acting without orders, raced 50 yards through a hail of machine-gun fire, which had killed five of his comrades and halted the advance of his company, in order to form an assault group to destroy the machine gun. Ordering three men to act as a base of fire, he left the cover of a ditch and snaked his way to a point within 50 yards of the enemy machine gun before he was discovered, whereupon he plunged headlong into the furious chain of automatic fire. Reaching a spot within six feet of the emplacement he stood over it and killed both the gunner and his assistant, jumped into the gun position, overpowered and captured a third German after a short struggle. The remaining member of the crew escaped, but Pfc. Kessler wounded him as he ran. While taking his prisoner to the rear, this soldier saw two of his comrades killed as they assaulted an enemy strongpoint, fire from which had already killed 10 men in the company. Turning his prisoner over to another man, Pfc. Kessler crawled 35 yards to the side of one of the casualties, relieved him of his BAR and ammunition, and continued on toward the strongpoint, 125 yards distant. Although two machine guns concentrated their fire directly on him and shells exploded within 10 yards, bowling him over, Pfc. Kessler crawled 75 yards, passing through an antipersonnel minefield to a point within 50 yards of the enemy and engaged the machine guns in a duel. When an artillery shell burst within a few feet of him, he left the cover of the ditch and advanced upon the position in a slow walk, firing his BAR from the hip. Although the enemy poured heavy machine-gun and small-arms fire at him, Pfc. Kessler succeeded in reaching the edge of their position, killed the gunners, and captured 13 Germans. Then, despite continuous shelling, he started to the rear. After going 25 yards, Pfc. Kessler was fired upon by two snipers only 100 yards away. Several of his prisoners took advantage of this opportunity and attempted to escape; however, Pfc. Kessler hit the ground, fired on either flank of his prisoners, forcing them to cover, and then engaged the two snipers in a firefight and captured them. With this last threat removed, Company K continued its advance, capturing its objective without further opposition. Pfc. Kessler was killed in a subsequent action.

2795 ◆ *KIDD, ISAAC CAMPBELL

Rank: Rear Admiral
Service: U.S. Navy
Birthday: 26 March 1884
Place of Birth: Cleveland, Cuyahoga County, Ohio
Date of Death: 7 December 1941
Place of Death: Pearl Harbor, Territory of Hawaii
Cemetery: U.S.S. *Arizona* (Missing in Action)—Pearl Harbor, Hawaii; National Memorial Cemetery of the Pacific (Wall of the Missing)—Honolulu, Hawaii
Entered Service at: Ohio
Unit: U.S.S. *Arizona*, Battleship Division One
Served as: Commanding Officer
Battle or Place of Action: Pearl Harbor, Territory of Hawaii
Date of Action: 7 December 1941
Citation: For conspicuous devotion to duty, extraordinary courage and complete disregard of his own life, during the attack on the Fleet in Pearl Harbor, by Japanese forces on 7 December 1941. Rear Adm. Kidd immediately went to the bridge and, as Commander Battleship Division One, courageously discharged his duties as senior officer present afloat until the U.S.S. *Arizona*, his flagship, blew up from magazine explosions and a direct bomb hit on the bridge which resulted in the loss of his life.

2796 ◆ *KIMBRO, TRUMAN

Rank: Technician Fourth Grade
Service: U.S. Army
Place of Birth: Madisonville, Madison County, Texas

2797 ◆ *KINER, HAROLD G.

Date of Death: 19 December 1944
Cemetery: A.B.M.C. Henri-Chapelle Cemetery (F-6-28)—Henri-Chapelle, Belgium
Entered Service at: Houston, Harris County, Texas
Unit: Company C, 2d Engineer Combat Battalion, 2d Infantry Division
Served as: Scout
Battle or Place of Action: near Rocherath, Belgium
Date of Action: 19 December 1944
G.O. Number, Date: 42, 24 May 1945
Citation: On 19 December 1944, as scout, he led a squad assigned to the mission of mining a vital crossroads near Rocherath, Belgium. At the first attempt to reach the objective, he discovered it was occupied by an enemy tank and at least 20 infantrymen. Driven back by the withering fire, Technician Fourth Grade Kimbro made two more attempts to lead his squad to the crossroads, but all approaches were covered by intense enemy fire. Although warned by our own infantrymen of the great danger involved, he left his squad in a protected place and, laden with mines, crawled alone toward the crossroads. When nearing his objective he was severely wounded, but he continued to drag himself forward and laid his mines across the road. As he tried to crawl from the objective his body was riddled with rifle and machine-gun fire. The mines laid by his act of indomitable courage delayed the advance of enemy armor and prevented the rear of our withdrawing columns from being attacked by the enemy.

2797 ◆ *KINER, HAROLD G.

Rank: Private
Service: U.S. Army
Birthday: 14 April 1924
Place of Birth: Aline, Alfalfa County, Oklahoma
Date of Death: 2 October 1944
Cemetery: Eastern Star Cemetery—Aline, Oklahoma
Entered Service at: Enid, Garfield County, Oklahoma
Unit: Company F, 117th Infantry, 30th Infantry Division
Battle or Place of Action: near Palenberg, Germany
Date of Action: 2 October 1944
G.O. Number, Date: 48, 23 June 1945
Citation: With four other men, he was leading in a frontal assault 2 October 1944, on a Siegfried line pillbox near Palenberg, Germany. Machine-gun fire from the strongly defended enemy position 25 yards away pinned down the attackers. The Germans threw hand grenades, one of which dropped between Pvt. Kiner and two other men. With no hesitation, Pvt. Kiner hurled himself upon the grenade, smothering the explosion. By his gallant action and voluntary sacrifice of his own life, he saved his two comrades from serious injury or death.

2798 ◆ *KINGSLEY, DAVID RICHARD

Rank: Second Lieutenant
Service: U.S. Army Air Corps
Birthday: 27 June 1918
Place of Birth: Portland, Multnomah County, Oregon
Date of Death: 23 June 1944
Place of Death: near Polesti, Rumania
Cemetery: Arlington National Cemetery (34-4786) (MH)—Arlington, Virginia
Entered Service at: Portland, Multnomah County, Oregon
Unit: 341st Bombardment Squadron, 97th Bombardment Group, 15th Air Force
Served as: Bombardier of a B-17
Battle or Place of Action: Ploesti, Rumania
Date of Action: 23 June 1944
G.O. Number, Date: 26, 9 April 1945
Place of Presentation: Portland, Oregon presented by Major Gen. Ralph P. Cousins to his Brother, Thomas E. Kingsley
Citation: For conspicuous gallantry and intrepidity in action at the risk of life above and beyond the call of duty, 23 June 1944 near Ploesti, Rumania, while flying as bombardier of a B-17 type aircraft. On the bomb run 2d Lt. Kingsley's aircraft was severely damaged by intense flak and forced to drop out of formation, but the pilot proceeded over the target and 2d Lt. Kingsley successfully dropped his bombs, causing severe damage to vital installations. The damaged aircraft, forced to lose altitude and to lag behind the formation, was aggressively attacked by three ME-109 aircraft, causing more damage to the aircraft and severely wounding the tail gunner in the upper arm. The radio operator and engineer notified 2d Lt. Kingsley that the tail gunner had been wounded and that assistance was needed to check the bleeding. Second Lt. Kingsley made his way back to the radio room, skillfully applied first aid to the wound, and succeeded in checking the bleeding. The tail gunner's parachute harness and heavy clothes were removed and he was covered with blankets, making him as comfortable as possible. Eight ME-109 aircraft again aggressively attacked 2d Lt. Kingsley's aircraft and the ball turret gunner was wounded by 20-mm shell fragments. He went forward to the radio room to have 2d Lt. Kingsley administer first aid. A few minutes later when the pilot gave the order to prepare to bail out, 2d Lt. Kingsley immediately began to assist the wounded gunners in putting on their parachute harness. In the confusion, the tail gunner's harness, believed to have been damaged, could not be located in the bundle of blankets and flying clothes which had been removed from the wounded men. With utter disregard for his own means of escape, 2d Lt. Kingsley unhesitatingly removed his parachute harness and adjusted it to the wounded tail gunner. Due to the extensive damage caused by the accurate and concentrated 20-mm fire by the enemy aircraft the pilot gave the order to bail out, as it appeare d that the aircraft would disintegrate at any moment. Second Lt. Kingsley aided the wounded men in bailing out and when last seen by the crewmembers he was standing on the bomb bay catwalk. The aircraft continued to fly on automatic pilot for a short distance, then crashed and burned. His body was later found in the wreckage. Second Lt. Kingsley by his gallant and heroic action was directly responsible for saving the life of the wounded gunner.

2799 ◆ *KINSER, ELBERT LUTHER

Rank: Sergeant
Service: U.S. Marine Corps Reserve

Birthday: 21 October 1922
Place of Birth: Greeneville, Greene County, Tennessee
Date of Death: 4 May 1945
Cemetery: Solomon Lutheran Church Cemetery—Greeneville, Tennessee
Entered Service at: Tennessee
Unit: Company I, 3d Battalion, 1st Marines, 1st Marine Division
Served as: Acting Platoon Leader
Battle or Place of Action: Okinawa Shima, Ryukyu Islands
Date of Action: 4 May 1945
Citation: For conspicuous gallantry and intrepidity at the risk of his life above and beyond the call of duty while acting as leader of a rifle platoon, serving with Company I, 3d Battalion, 1st Marines, 1st Marine Division, in action against Japanese forces on Okinawa Shima in the Ryukyu Chain, 4 May 1945. Taken under sudden, close attack by hostile troops entrenched on the reverse slope while moving up a strategic ridge along which his platoon was holding newly won positions, Sgt. Kinser engaged the enemy in a fierce hand-grenade battle. Quick to act when a Japanese grenade landed in the immediate vicinity, Sgt. Kinser unhesitatingly threw himself on the deadly missile, absorbing the full charge of the shattering explosion in his own body and thereby protecting his men from serious injury and possible death. Stouthearted and indomitable, he had yielded his own chance of survival that his comrades might live to carry on the relentless battle against the fanatic enemy. His courage, cool decision, and valiant spirit of self-sacrifice in the face of certain death sustained and enhanced the highest traditions of the U.S. Naval Service. He gallantly gave his life for his country.

2800 ◆ KISTERS, GERRY HERMAN

Rank: Second Lieutenant (rank at time of action: Sergeant) (highest rank: First Lieutenant)
Service: U.S. Army
Birthday: 3 March 1919
Place of Birth: Salt Lake City, Salt Lake County, Utah
Date of Death: 11 May 1986
Place of Death: Bloomington, Indiana
Cemetery: Rose Hill Cemetery (MH)—Bloomington, Indiana
Entered Service at: Bloomington, Monroe County, Indiana
Unit: Company B, 91st Reconnaisance Squadron (attached to the 1st Infantry Division), 2d Armored Division
Battle or Place of Action: near Gagliano, Sicily
Date of Action: 31 July 1943
G.O. Number, Date: 13, 18 February 1944
Date of Presentation: 8 February 1944
Place of Presentation: The White House, presented by Pres. Franklin D. Roosevelt
Citation: On 31 July 1943, near Gagliano, Sicily, a detachment of one officer and nine enlisted men, including Sgt. Kisters, advancing ahead of the leading elements of U.S. troops to fill a large crater in the only available vehicle route through Gagliano, was taken under fire by two enemy machine guns. Sgt. Kisters and the officer, unaided and in the face of intense small-arms fire, advanced on the nearest machine-gun emplacement and succeeded in capturing the gun and its crew of four. Although the greater part of the remaining small-arms fire was now directed on the captured machine-gun position, Sgt. Kisters voluntarily advanced alone toward the second gun emplacement. While creeping forward, he was struck five times by enemy bullets, receiving wounds in both legs and his right arm. Despite the wounds, he continued to advance on the enemy, and captured the second machine gun after killing three of its crew and forcing the fourth member to flee. The courage of this soldier and his unhesitating willingness to sacrifice his life, if necessary, served as an inspiration to the command.

2801 ◆ KNAPPENBERGER, ALTON W.

Rank: Private First Class (highest rank: Staff Sergeant)
Service: U.S. Army
Birthday: 31 December 1924
Place of Birth: Coopersburg, Lehigh County, Pennsylvania
Entered Service at: Almount, Bucks County, Pennsylvania
Unit: 1st Platoon, Company C, 15th Battalion, 30th Infantry, 3d Infantry Division
Served as: Automatic Rifleman
Battle or Place of Action: near Cisterna di Littoria, Italy
Date of Action: 1 February 1944
G.O. Number, Date: 41, 26 May 1944
Date of Presentation: August 1944
Place of Presentation: Rome, Italy, presented by Lt. Gen. Mark W. Clark
Citation: For conspicuous gallantry and intrepidity at the risk of his life above and beyond the call of duty in action involving actual conflict with the enemy, on 1 February 1944 near Cisterna di Littoria, Italy. When a heavy German counterattack was launched against his battalion, Pfc. Knappenberger crawled to an exposed knoll and went into position with his automatic rifle. An enemy machine gun 85 yards away opened fire, and bullets struck within six inches of him. Raising to a kneeling position, Pfc. Knappenberger opened fire on the hostile crew, knocked out the gun, killed two members of the crew, and wounded the third. While he fired at this hostile position, two Germans crawled to a point within 20 yards of the knoll and threw potato-masher grenades at him, but Pfc. Knappenberger killed them both with one burst from his automatic rifle. Later, a second machine gun opened fire upon his exposed position from a distance of 100 yards, and this weapon was also silenced by his well-aimed shots. Shortly thereafter, an enemy 20-mm antiaircraft gun directed fire at him, and again Pfc. Knappenberger returned fire to wound one member of the hostile crew. Under tank and artillery shellfire, with shells bursting within 15 yards of him, he held his precarious position and fired at all enemy infantrymen armed with machine pistols and machine guns which he could locate. When his ammunition supply became exhausted, he crawled 15 yards forward through steady machine-gun fire, removed rifle clips from the belt of a casualty, returned to his position, and resumed firing to repel an assaulting German platoon armed with automatic weapons. Finally, his ammunition supply being completely exhausted, he rejoined his company. Pfc.

Knappenberger's intrepid action disrupted the enemy attack for over two hours.

2802 ◆ *KNIGHT, JACK LLEWELLYN

Rank: First Lieutenant
Service: U.S. Army
Birthday: 29 May 1917
Place of Birth: Garner, Texas
Date of Death: 2 February 1945
Cemetery: Holders Chapel Cemetery (MH)—Millsap, Texas
Entered Service at: Weatherford, Parker County, Texas
Unit: 124th Cavalry Regiment, Mars Task Force
Battle or Place of Action: near Loi-Kang, Burma
Date of Action: 2 February 1945
G.O. Number, Date: 44, 6 June 1945
Citation: He led his cavalry troop against heavy concentrations of enemy mortar, artillery, and small-arms fire. After taking the troop's objective and while making preparations for a defense, he discovered a nest of Japanese pillboxes and foxholes to the right front. Preceding his men by at least 10 feet, he immediately led an attack. Singlehandedly he knocked out two enemy pillboxes and killed the occupants of several foxholes. While attempting to knock out a third pillbox, he was struck and blinded by an enemy grenade. Although unable to see, he rallied his platoon and continued forward in the assault on the remaining pillboxes. Before the task was completed he fell mortally wounded. First Lt. Knight's gallantry and intrepidity were responsible for the successful elimination of most of the Japs' positions and served as an inspiration to officers and men of his troop.

2803 ◆ *KNIGHT, RAYMOND LARRY

Rank: First Lieutenant
Service: U.S. Army Air Corps
Birthday: 15 June 1922
Place of Birth: Houston, Harris County, Texas
Date of Death: 25 April 1945
Place of Death: Appenine Mountains, Italy
Cemetery: Houston National Cemetery (H-B-11) (MH)—Houston, Texas
Entered Service at: Houston, Harris County, Texas
Unit: 346th Fighter Squadron, 350th Fighter Group, 12th Air Force
Served as: Pilot of a P-47
Battle or Place of Action: Northern Po Valley, Italy
Date of Action: 24-25 April 1945
G.O. Number, Date: 81, 24 September 1945
Citation: He piloted a fighter-bomber aircraft in a series of low-level strafing missions, destroying 14 grounded enemy aircraft and leading attacks which wrecked 10 others during a critical period of the Allied drive in northern Italy. On the morning of 24 April, he volunteered to lead two other aircraft against the strongly defended enemy airdrome at Ghedi. Ordering his fellow pilots to remain aloft, he skimmed the ground through a deadly curtain of anti-aircraft fire to reconnoiter the field, locating eight German aircraft hidden beneath heavy camouflage. He rejoined his flight, briefed them by radio, and then led them with consummate skill through the hail of enemy fire in a low-level attack, destroying five aircraft, while his flight accounted for two others. Returning to his base, he volunteered to lead three other aircraft in reconnaissance of Bergamo airfield, an enemy base near Ghedi, and one known to be equally well-defended. Again ordering his flight to remain out of range of antiaircraft fire, 1st Lt. Knight flew through an exceptionally intense barrage, which heavily damaged his Thunderbolt, to observe the field at minimum altitude. He discovered a squadron of enemy aircraft under heavy camouflage and led his flight to the assault. Returning alone after the strafing, he made 10 deliberate passes against the field despite being hit by antiaircraft fire twice more, destroying six fully loaded enemy twin-engine aircraft and two fighters. His skillfully led attack enabled his flight to destroy four other twin-engine aircraft and a fighter plane. He then returned to his base in his seriously damaged plane. Early the next morning, when he again attacked Bergamo, he sighted an enemy plane on the runway. Again he led three other American pilots in a blistering low-level sweep through vicious antiaircraft fire that damaged his plane so severely that it was virtually nonflyable. Three of the few remaining twin-engine aircraft at that base were destroyed. Realizing the critical need for aircraft in his unit, he declined to parachute to safety over friendly territory and unhesitatingly attempted to return his shattered plane to his home field. With great skill and strength, he flew homeward until caught by treacherous air conditions in the Apennines Mountains, where he crashed and was killed. The gallant action of 1st Lt. Knight eliminated the German aircraft which were poised to wreak havoc on Allied forces pressing to establish the first firm bridgehead across the Po River; his fearless daring and voluntary self-sacrifice averted possible heavy casualties among ground forces, and the resultant slowing on the German drive culminated in the collapse of enemy resistance in Italy.

2804 ◆ *KRAUS, RICHARD EDWARD

Rank: Private First Class
Service: U.S. Marine Corps Reserve
Birthday: 24 November 1925
Place of Birth: Chicago, Cook County, Illinois
Date of Death: 5 October 1944
Cemetery: Fort Snelling National Cemetery (DS-61A) (MH)—St. Paul, Minnesota
Entered Service at: Minnesota
Unit: 8th Amphibious Tractor Battalion, Fleet Marine Force
Served as: Amphibious Tractor Driver
Battle or Place of Action: Peleliu Island, Palau Islands
Date of Action: 5 October 1944
Citation: For conspicuous gallantry and intrepidity at the risk of his life above and beyond the call of duty while serving with the 8th Amphibious Tractor Battalion, Fleet Marine Force, in action against enemy Japanese forces on Peleliu, Palau Islands on 5 October 1944. Unhesitatingly volunteering for the extremely hazardous mission of evacuating a wounded comrade from the front lines, Pfc. Kraus and three companions courageously made their way forward and suc-

cessfully penetrated the lines for some distance before the enemy opened with an intense, devastating barrage of hand grenades which forced the stretcher party to take cover and subsequently abandon the mission. While returning to the rear, they observed two men approaching who appeared to be marines and immediately demanded the password. When, instead of answering, one of the two Japanese threw a hand grenade into the midst of the group, Pfc. Kraus heroically flung himself upon the grenade and, covering it with his body, absorbed the full impact of the explosion and was instantly killed. By his prompt action and great personal valor in the face of almost certain death, he saved the lives of his three companions, and his loyal spirit of self-sacrifice reflects the highest credit upon himself and the U.S. Naval Service. He gallantly gave his life for his comrades.

2805 ◆ *KROTIAK, ANTON L.

Rank: Private First Class
Service: U.S. Army
Birthday: 15 August 1915
Place of Birth: Chicago, Cook County, Illinois
Date of Death: 8 May 1945
Cemetery: Holy Sepulchre Cemetery (MH)—Worth, Illinois
Entered Service at: Chicago, Cook County, Illinois
Unit: Company I, 148th Infantry, 37th Infantry Division
Served as: Acting Squad Leader
Battle or Place of Action: Balete Pass, Luzon, Philippine Islands
Date of Action: 8 May 1945
G.O. Number, Date: 18, 13 February 1946
Citation: He was an acting squad leader, directing his men in consolidating a newly won position on Hill B when the enemy concentrated small-arms fire and grenades upon him and four others, driving them to cover in an abandoned Japanese trench. A grenade thrown from above landed in the center of the group. Instantly pushing his comrades aside and jamming the grenade into the earth with his rifle butt, he threw himself over it, making a shield of his body to protect the other men. The grenade exploded under him, and he died a few minutes later. By his extraordinary heroism and deliberately giving his life to save those of his comrades, Pfc. Krotiak set an inspiring example of utter devotion and self-sacrifice which reflects the highest traditions of the military service.

2806 ◆ *LA BELLE, JAMES DENNIS

Rank: Private First Class
Service: U.S. Marine Corps Reserve
Birthday: 22 November 1925
Place of Birth: Columbia Heights, Hennepin County, Minnesota
Date of Death: 8 March 1945
Cemetery: Fort Snelling National Cemetery (B-1-422-S) (MH)—St. Paul, Minnesota
Entered Service at: Minnesota
Unit: 27th Marines, 5th Marine Division
Battle or Place of Action: Iwo Jima, Volcano Islands
Date of Action: 8 March 1945
Citation: For conspicuous gallantry and intrepidity at the risk of his life above and beyond the call of duty while attached to the 27th Marines, 5th Marine Division, in action against enemy Japanese forces during the seizure of Iwo Jima in the Volcano Islands, 8 March 1945. Filling a gap in the front lines during a critical phase in the battle, Pfc. La Belle had dug into a foxhole with two other marines and, grimly aware of the enemy's persistent attempts to blast a way through our lines with hand grenades, applied himself with steady concentration to maintaining a sharply vigilant watch during the hazardous night hours. Suddenly a hostile grenade landed beyond reach of his foxhole. Quickly estimating the situation, he determined to save the others if possible, shouted a warning, and instantly dived on the deadly missile, absorbing the exploding charge in his own body and thereby protecting his comrades from serious injury. Stouthearted and indomitable, he had unhesitatingly relinquished his own chance of survival that his fellow marines might carry on the relentless fight against a fanatic enemy. His dauntless courage, cool decision, and valiant spirit of self-sacrifice in the face of certain death reflect the highest credit upon Pfc. La Belle and upon the U.S. Naval Service. He gallantly gave his life in the service of his country.

2807 ◆ LAWLEY JR., WILLIAM ROBERT

Rank: First Lieutenant (highest rank: Colonel)
Service: U.S. Army Air Corps/U.S. Air Force
Birthday: 23 August 1920
Place of Birth: Leeds, Jefferson County, Alabama
Entered Service at: Birmingham, Jefferson County, Alabama
Unit: 364th Bombardment Squadron, 305th Bombardment Group, 40th Combat Wing, 1st Air Division, 8th Air Force
Served as: Pilot of a B-17
Battle or Place of Action: over Liepzig, Germany
Date of Action: 20 February 1944
G.O. Number, Date: 64, 8 August 1944
Date of Presentation: 8 August 1944
Place of Presentation: Headquarters U.S. Army Air Forces Europe, High Wycomb, England, presented by Lt. Gen. Carl A. Spaatz
Citation: For conspicuous gallantry and intrepidity in action above and beyond the call of duty, 20 February 1944, while serving as pilot of a B-17 aircraft on a heavy bombardment mission over enemy-occupied continental Europe. Coming off the target he was attacked by approximately 20 enemy fighters, shot out of formation, and his plane severely crippled. Eight crewmembers were wounded; the copilot was killed by a 20-mm shell. One engine was on fire, the controls shot away, and 1st Lt. Lawley seriously and painfully wounded about the face. Forcing the copilot's body off the controls, he brought the plane out of a steep dive, flying with his left hand only. Blood covered the instruments and windshield and visibility was impossible. With a full bomb load the plane was difficult to maneuver and the bombs could not be released because the racks were frozen. After the order to bail out had been given, one of the waist gunners informed the pilot that

two crewmembers were so severely wounded that it would be impossible for them to bail out. With the fire in the engine spreading, the danger of an explosion was imminent. Because of the helpless condition of his wounded crewmembers 1st Lt. Lawley elected to remain with the ship and bring them to safety if it was humanly possible, giving the other crewmembers the option of bailing out. Enemy fighters again attacked but by using masterful evasive action he managed to lose them. One engine again caught on fire and was extinguished by skillful flying. First Lt. Lawley remained at his post, refusing first aid until he collapsed from sheer exhaustion caused by loss of blood, shock, and the energy he had expended in keeping control of his plane. He was revived by the bombardier and again took over the controls. Coming over the English coast one engine ran out of gasoline and had to be feathered. Another engine started to burn and continued to do so until a successful crash landing was made on a small fighter base. Through his heroism and exceptional flying skill 1st Lt. Lawley rendered outstanding distinguished and valorous service to our nation.

2808 ◆ LAWS, ROBERT EARL

Rank: Staff Sergeant
Service: U.S. Army
Birthday: 18 January 1921
Place of Birth: Altoona, Blair County, Pennsylvania
Date of Death: 1 January 1990
Cemetery: Blair Memorial Park (MH)—Bellwood, Pennsylvania
Entered Service at: Altoona, Blair County, Pennsylvania
Unit: Company G, 169th Infantry, 43d Infantry Division
Served as: Squad Leader
Battle or Place of Action: Pangasinan Province, Luzon, Philippine Islands
Date of Action: 12 January 1945
G.O. Number, Date: 77, 10 September 1945
Date of Presentation: 23 August 1945
Place of Presentation: The White House, presented by Pres. Harry S. Truman
Citation: He led the assault squad when Company G attacked enemy hill positions. The enemy force, estimated to be a reinforced infantry company, was well-supplied with machine guns, ammunition, grenades, and blocks of TNT, and could be attacked only across a narrow ridge 70 yards long. At the end of this ridge an enemy pillbox and rifle positions were set in rising ground. Covered by his squad, S/Sgt. Laws traversed the hogback through vicious enemy fire until close to the pillbox, where he hurled grenades at the fortification. Enemy grenades wounded him, but he persisted in his assault until one of his missiles found its mark and knocked out the pillbox. With more grenades, passed to him by members of his squad who had joined him, he led the attack on the entrenched riflemen. In the advance up the hill, he suffered additional wounds in both arms and legs, about the body and in the head, as grenades and TNT charges exploded near him. Three Japs rushed him with fixed bayonets, and he emptied the magazine of his machine pistol at them, killing two. He closed in hand-to-hand combat with the third, seizing the Jap's rifle as he met the onslaught. The two fell to the ground and rolled some 50 or 60 feet down a bank. When the dust cleared the Jap lay dead and the valiant American was climbing up the hill with a large gash across the head. He was given first aid and evacuated from the area his courageous determination in the face of formidable odds and while his squad completed the destruction of the enemy position. S/Sgt. Laws' heroic actions provided great inspiration to his comrades, and his courageous determination, in the face of formidable odds and while suffering from multiple wounds, enabled them to secure an important objective with minimum casualties.

2809 ◆ LEE SR., DANIEL WARNEL

Rank: First Lieutenant (rank at time of action: Second Lieutenant)
Service: U.S. Army
Birthday: 23 June 1919
Place of Birth: Alma, Bacon County, Georgia
Date of Death: 22 January 1985
Cemetery: Rose Hill Cemetery (MH)—Alma, Georgia
Entered Service at: Alma, Bacon County, Georgia
Unit: Troop A, 117th Cavalry Reconnaissance Squadron, 7th Army
Served as: Platoon Leader
Battle or Place of Action: Montreval, France
Date of Action: 2 September 1944
G.O. Number, Date: 14, 4 February 1946
Date of Presentation: 23 January 1946
Place of Presentation: Washington, D.C., presented by Pres. Harry S. Truman
Citation: First Lt. (then 2d Lt.) Daniel W. Lee was leader of Headquarters Platoon, Troop A, 117th Cavalry Reconnaissance Squadron, Mechanized, at Montreval, France, on 2 September 1944, when the Germans mounted a strong counterattack, isolating the town and engaging its outnumbered defenders in a pitched battle. After the fight had raged for hours and our forces had withstood heavy shelling and armor-supported infantry attacks, 2d Lt. Lee organized a patrol to knock out mortars which were inflicting heavy casualties on the beleaguered reconnaissance troops. He led the small group to the edge of the town, sweeping enemy riflemen out of position on a ridge from which he observed seven Germans manning two large mortars near an armored half-track about 100 yards down the reverse slope. Armed with a rifle and grenades, he left his men on the high ground and crawled to within 30 yards of the mortars, where the enemy discovered him and unleashed machine-pistol fire which shattered his right thigh. Scorning retreat, bleeding, and suffering intense pain, he dragged himself relentlessly forward. He killed five of the enemy with rifle fire, and the others fled before he reached their position. Fired on by an armored car, he took cover behind the German half-track and there found a panzerfaust with which to neutralize this threat. Despite his wounds, he inched his way toward the car through withering machine-gun fire, maneuvered into range, and blasted the vehicle with a round from the rocket launcher, forcing it to withdraw. Having cleared the slope of hostile troops, he

struggled back to his men, where he collapsed from pain and loss of blood. Second Lt. Lee's outstanding gallantry, willing risk of life, and extreme tenacity of purpose in coming to grips with the enemy, although suffering from grievous wounds, set an example of bravery and devotion to duty in keeping with the highest traditions of the military service.

2810 ◆ LEIMS, JOHN HAROLD

Rank: Second Lieutenant
Service: U.S. Marine Corps Reserve
Birthday: 8 June 1921
Place of Birth: Chicago, Cook County, Illinois
Date of Death: 28 June 1985
Place of Death: Conroe, Texas
Cemetery: Arlington National Cemetery (2-1132-2) (MH)—Arlington, Virginia
Entered Service at: Chicago, Cook County, Illinois
Unit: Company B, 1st Battalion, 9th Marines, 3d Marine Division
Served as: Commanding Officer
Battle or Place of Action: Iwo Jima, Volcano Islands
Date of Action: 7 March 1945
Date of Presentation: 14 June 1946
Place of Presentation: The White House, presented by Pres. Harry S. Truman
Citation: For conspicuous gallantry and intrepidity at the risk of his life above and beyond the call of duty as commanding officer of Company B, 1st Battalion, 9th Marines, 3d Marine Division, in action against enemy Japanese forces on Iwo Jima in the Volcano Islands, 7 March 1945. Launching a surprise attack against the rock-imbedded fortifications of a dominating Japanese hill position, 2d Lt. Leims spurred his company forward with indomitable determination and, skillfully directing his assault platoons against the cave-emplaced enemy troops and heavily fortified pillboxes, succeeded in capturing the objective in the late afternoon. When it became apparent that his assault platoon were cut off in this newly won position, approximately 400 yards forward of adjacent units, and lacked all communication with the command post, he personally advanced and laid telephone lines across the isolating expanse of open, fire-swept terrain. Ordered to withdraw his command after he had joined his forward platoons he immediately complied, adroitly effecting the withdrawal of his troops without incident. Upon arriving at the rear, he was informed that several casualties had been left at the abandoned ridge position beyond the front lines. Although suffering acutely from the strain and exhaustion of battle, he instantly went forward despite darkness and the slashing fury of hostile machine-gun fire, located and carried to safety one seriously wounded marine, and then, running the gauntlet of enemy fire for the third time that night, again made his tortuous way into the bullet-riddled death trap and rescued another of his wounded men. A dauntless leader, concerned at all times for the welfare of his men, 2d Lt. Leims soundly maintained the coordinated strength of his battle-wearied company under extremely difficult conditions and, by his bold tactics, sustained aggressiveness, and heroic disregard of all personal danger, contributed essentially to the success of his division's

operations against this vital Japanese base. His valiant conduct in the face of fanatic opposition sustains and enhances the highest traditions of the U.S. Naval Service.

2811 ◆ *LEONARD, TURNEY WHITE

Rank: First Lieutenant
Service: U.S. Army
Birthday: 18 June 1921
Place of Birth: Dallas, Collin County, Texas
Date of Death: 7 November 1944
Cemetery: Grove Hill Memorial Park (MH)—Dallas, Texas
Entered Service at: Dallas, Collin County, Texas
Unit: Company C, 893d Tank Destroyer Battalion
Served as: Platoon Leader
Battle or Place of Action: Kommerscheidt, Germany
Date of Action: 4-6 November 1944
G.O. Number, Date: 74, 1 September 1945
Citation: He displayed extraordinary heroism while commanding a platoon of mobile weapons at Kommerscheidt, Germany, on 4, 5, and 6 November 1944. During the fierce three-day engagement, he repeatedly braved overwhelming enemy fire in advance of his platoon to direct the fire of his tank destroyer from exposed, dismounted positions. He went on lone reconnaissance missions to discover what opposition his men faced, and on one occasion, when fired upon by a hostile machine gun, advanced alone and eliminated the enemy emplacement with a hand grenade. When a strong German attack threatened to overrun friendly positions, he moved through withering artillery, mortar, and small-arms fire, reorganized confused infantry units whose leaders had become casualties, and exhorted them to hold firm. Although wounded early in battle, he continued to direct fire from his advanced position until he was disabled by a high-explosive shell which shattered his arm, forcing him to withdraw. He was last seen at a medical aid station which was subsequently captured by the enemy. By his superb courage, inspiring leadership, and indomitable fighting spirit, 1st Lt. Leonard enabled our forces to hold off the enemy attack and was personally responsible for the direction of fire which destroyed six German tanks.

2812 ◆ *LESTER, FRED FAULKNER

Rank: Hospital Apprentice First Class
Service: U.S. Navy
Birthday: 29 April 1926
Place of Birth: Downers Grove, Du Page County, Illinois
Date of Death: 8 June 1945
Cemetery: Clarendon Hills Cemetery—Westmont, Illinois
Entered Service at: Illinois
Unit: Assault Rifle Platoon, 1st Battalion, 22d Marines, 6th Marine Division
Served as: Medical Corpsman
Battle or Place of Action: Okinawa Shima, Ryukyu Islands
Date of Action: 8 June 1945
Citation: For conspicuous gallantry and intrepidity at the risk of his life above and beyond the call of duty while serving as a medical corpsman with an assault rifle platoon, attached

to the 1st Battalion, 22d Marines, 6th Marine Division, during action against enemy Japanese forces on Okinawa Shima in the Ryukyu Chain, 8 June 1945. Quick to spot a wounded marine lying in an open field beyond the front lines following the relentless assault against a strategic Japanese hill position, Lester unhesitatingly crawled toward the casualty under a concentrated barrage from hostile machine guns, rifles, and grenades. Torn by enemy rifle bullets as he inched forward, he stoically disregarded the mounting fury of Japanese fire and his own pain to pull the wounded man toward a covered position. Struck by enemy fire a second time before he reached cover, he exerted tremendous effort and succeeded in pulling his comrade to safety where, too seriously wounded himself to administer aid, he instructed two of his squad in proper medical treatment of the rescued marine. Realizing that his own wounds were fatal, he staunchly refused medical attention for himself and, gathering his fast-waning strength with calm determination, coolly and expertly directed his men in the treatment of two other wounded marines, succumbing shortly thereafter. Completely selfless in his concern for the welfare of his fighting comrades, Lester, by his indomitable spirit, outstanding valor, and competent direction of others, had saved the life of one who otherwise must have perished, and had contributed to the safety of countless others. Lester's fortitude in the face of certain death sustains and enhances the highest traditions of the U.S. Naval Service. He gallantly gave his life for his country.

2813 ◆ *LINDSEY, DARRELL ROBINS

Rank: Captain
Service: U.S. Army Air Corps
Birthday: 30 December 1919
Place of Birth: Jefferson, Greene County, Iowa
Date of Death: 9 August 1944
Place of Death: L'Isle Adam railroad bridge over the Seine, France
Cemetery: A.B.M.C. Ardennes Cemetery (Wall of the Missing)—Neuvile-En-Condroz, Belgium
Entered Service at: Storm Lake, Buena Vista County, Iowa
Unit: 585th Bombardment Squadron, 394th Bombardment Group, 9th Air Force
Served as: Pilot of a B-26 Medium Bomber
Battle or Place of Action: L'Isle Adam railroad bridge over the Seine River, France
Date of Action: 9 August 1944
G.O. Number, Date: 43, 30 May 1945
Citation: On 9 August 1944, Capt. Lindsey led a formation of 30 B-26 medium bombers in a hazardous mission to destroy the strategic enemy-held L'Isle Adam railroad bridge over the Seine in occupied France. With most of the bridges over the Seine destroyed, the heavily fortified L'Isle Adam bridge was of inestimable value to the enemy in moving troops, supplies, and equipment to Paris. Capt. Lindsey was fully aware of the fierce resistance that would be encountered. Shortly after reaching enemy territory the formation was buffeted with heavy and accurate antiaircraft fire. By skillful evasive action, Capt. Lindsey was able to elude much of the enemy flak, but just before entering the bombing run his B-26 was peppered with holes. During the bombing run the enemy fire was even more intense, and Capt. Lindsey's right engine received a direct hit and burst into flames. Despite the fact that his ship was hurled out of formation by the violence of the concussion, Capt. Lindsey brilliantly maneuvered back into the lead position without disrupting the flight. Fully aware that the gasoline tanks might explode at any moment, Capt. Lindsey gallantly elected to continue the perilous bombing run. With fire streaming from his right engine and his right wing half enveloped in flames, he led his formation over the target upon which the bombs were dropped with telling effect. Immediately after the objective was attacked, Capt. Lindsey gave the order for the crew to parachute from the doomed aircraft. With magnificent coolness and superb pilotage, and without regard for his own life, he held the swiftly descending airplane in a steady glide until the members of the crew could jump to safety. With the right wing completely enveloped in flames and an explosion of the gasoline tank imminent, Capt. Lindsey still remained unperturbed. The last man to leave the stricken plane was the bombardier, who offered to lower the wheels so that Capt. Lindsey might escape from the nose. Realizing that this might throw the aircraft into an uncontrollable spin and jeopardize the bombardier's chances to escape, Capt. Lindsey refused the offer. Immediately after the bombardier had bailed out, and before Capt. Lindsey was able to follow, the right gasoline tank exploded. The aircraft sheathed in fire, went into a steep dive and was seen to explode as it crashed. All who are living today from this plane owe their lives to the fact that Capt. Lindsey remained cool and showed supreme courage in this emergency.

2814 ◆ LINDSEY SR., JAKE WILLIAM

Rank: Technical Sergeant (highest rank: Second Lieutenant)
Service: U.S. Army
Birthday: 1 May 1921
Place of Birth: Isney, Alabama
Date of Death: 18 July 1988
Cemetery: White House Cemetery (MH)—Waynesboro, Mississippi
Entered Service at: Lucedale, George County, Mississippi
Unit: Company C, 16th Infantry, 1st Infantry Division
Battle or Place of Action: near Hamich, Germany
Date of Action: 16 November 1944
G.O. Number, Date: 43, 30 May 1945
Date of Presentation: 21 May 1945
Place of Presentation: At a joint session of Congress, Washington, D.C., presented by Pres. Harry S. Truman
Citation: For gallantry and intrepidity in action at the risk of his life above and beyond the call of duty. Technical Sergeant Jake W. Lindsey led a platoon, reduced to six of its original strength of forty, in the attack on an enemy position near Hamich, Germany, 16 November 1944. His men had captured their objective and were digging in when counterattacked by a German infantry company and five tanks. Armed with a rifle and grenades, T/Sgt. Lindsey took position on the left and in advance of the remnant of his platoon, and though exposed to heavy rifle, machine-gun and tank fire,

beat off repeated enemy attacks. Tanks moved to within 50 yards of him but were forced to withdraw because of his accurate rifle and grenade fire. After driving off the tanks, he knocked out two machine guns to his front. Though painfully wounded, T/Sgt. Lindsey continued firing and throwing grenades until his ammunition was expended. An enemy squad attempted to set up a machine gun 50 yards from him. Unmindful of his wounds and enemy fire, he rushed these eight German soldiers, singlehandedly closed with them, killed three with his bayonet, and captured three, the two others escaping. In his fearlessness, inspiring courage and superb leadership, T/Sgt. Lindsey carried on a brilliant defense of his platoon's hard-won ground, securing the position and inflicting heavy casualties on the numerically superior enemy.

2815 ◆ *LINDSTROM, FLOYD K.

Rank: Private First Class
Service: U.S. Army
Birthday: 21 June 1912
Place of Birth: Holdrege, Phelps County, Nebraska
Date of Death: 3 February 1944
Cemetery: Evergreen Cemetery (MH)—Colorado Springs, Colorado
Entered Service at: Colorado Springs, El Paso County, Colorado
Unit: Company H, 7th Infantry Regiment, 3d Infantry Division
Battle or Place of Action: near Mignano, Italy
Date of Action: 11 November 1943
G.O. Number, Date: 32, 20 April 1944
Place of Presentation: Camp Carson, Colorado, presented by Major Gen. Terry Allen, Commanding Gen. 104th Division, to his family
Citation: For conspicuous gallantry and intrepidity at the risk of life above and beyond the call of duty. On 11 November 1943, this soldier's platoon was furnishing machine-gun support for a rifle company attacking a hill near Mignano, Italy, when the enemy counterattacked, forcing the riflemen and half the machine-gun platoon to retire to a defensive position. Pfc. Lindstrom saw that his small section was alone and outnumbered five to one, yet he immediately deployed the few remaining men into position and opened fire with his single gun. The enemy centered fire on him with machine gun, machine pistols, and grenades. Unable to knock out the enemy nest from his original position, Pfc. Lindstrom picked up his own heavy machine gun and staggered 15 yards up the barren, rocky hillside to a new position, completely ignoring enemy small-arms fire which was striking all around him. From this new site, only 10 yards from the enemy machine gun, he engaged it in an intense duel. Realizing that he could not hit the hostile gunners because they were behind a large rock, he charged uphill under a steady stream of fire, killed both gunners with his pistol, and dragged their gun down to his own men, directing them to employ it against the enemy. Disregarding heavy rifle fire, he returned to the enemy machine-gun nest for two boxes of ammunition, came back, and resumed withering fire from his own gun. His spectacular performance completely broke up the German counterattack. Pfc. Lindstrom demonstrated aggressive spirit and complete fearlessness in the face of almost certain death.

2816 ◆ *LLOYD, EDGAR HAROLD

Rank: First Lieutenant
Service: U.S. Army
Birthday: 28 February 1922
Place of Birth: Blytheville, Mississippi County, Arkansas
Date of Death: 16 November 1944
Cemetery: Courthouse Lawn—Blytheville, Arkansas
Entered Service at: Blytheville, Mississippi County, Arkansas
Unit: Company E, 319th Infantry, 80th Infantry Division
Served as: Rifle Platoon Leader
Battle or Place of Action: near Pompey, France
Date of Action: 14 September 1944
G.O. Number, Date: 25, 7 April 1945
Citation: For conspicuous gallantry and intrepidity at the risk of his life above and beyond the call of duty. On 14 September 1944, Company E, 319th Infantry, with which 1st Lt. Lloyd was serving as a rifle platoon leader, was assigned the mission of expelling an estimated enemy force of 200 men from a heavily fortified position near Pompey, France. As the attack progressed, 1st Lt. Lloyd's platoon advanced to within 50 yards of the enemy position where they were caught in a withering machine-gun and rifle crossfire which inflicted heavy casualties and momentarily disorganized the platoon. With complete disregard for his own safety, 1st Lt. Lloyd leaped to his feet and led his men on a run into the raking fire, shouting encouragement to them. He jumped into the first enemy machine-gun position, knocked out the gunner with his fist, dropped a grenade, and jumped out before it exploded. Still shouting encouragement he went from one machine-gun nest to another, pinning the enemy down with submachine-gun fire until he was within throwing distance, and then destroyed them with hand grenades. He personally destroyed five machine guns and many of the enemy, and by his daring leadership and conspicuous bravery inspired his men to overrun the enemy positions and accomplish the objective in the face of seemingly insurmountable odds. His audacious determination and courageous devotion to duty exemplify the highest traditions of the military forces of the United States.

2817 ◆ *LOBAUGH, DONALD RONALD

Rank: Private
Service: U.S. Army
Birthday: 7 February 1925
Place of Birth: Freeport, Armstrong County, Pennsylvania
Date of Death: 22 July 1944
Cemetery: Rimbersburg Cemetery (MH)—Rimbersburg, Pennsylvania
Entered Service at: Freeport, Armstrong County, Pennsylvania
Unit: 127th Infantry, 32d Infantry Division
Battle or Place of Action: near Afua, New Guinea
Date of Action: 22 July 1944

G.O. Number, Date: 31, 17 April 1945
Citation: For conspicuous gallantry and intrepidity at the risk of his life above and beyond the call of duty near Afua, New Guinea, 22 July 1944. While Pvt. Lobaugh's company was withdrawing from its position on 21 July, the enemy attacked and cut off approximately one platoon of our troops. The platoon immediately occupied, organized, and defended a position, which it held throughout the night. Early on 22 July, an attempt was made to effect its withdrawal, but during the preparation therefor, the enemy emplaced a machine gun, protected by the fire of rifles and automatic weapons, which blocked the only route over which the platoon could move. Knowing that it was the key to the enemy position, Pfc. Lobaugh volunteered to attempt to destroy this weapon, even though in order to reach it he would be forced to work his way about 30 yards over ground devoid of cover. When part way across this open space he threw a hand grenade, but exposed himself in the act and was wounded. Heedless of his wound, he boldly rushed the emplacement, firing as he advanced. The enemy concentrated their fire on him, and he was struck repeatedly, but he continued his attack and killed two more before he was himself slain. Pfc. Lobaugh's heroic actions inspired his comrades to press the attack, and to drive the enemy from the position with heavy losses. His fighting determination and intrepidity in battle exemplify the highest traditions of the U.S. Armed Forces.

2818 ◆ LOGAN, JAMES MARION

Rank: Sergeant (highest rank: Technical Sergeant)
Service: U.S. Army
Birthday: 19 December 1920
Place of Birth: McNeil, Travis County, Texas
Entered Service at: Luling, Caldwell County, Texas
Unit: 1st Platoon, Company I, 3d Battalion, 141st Infantry, 36th Infantry Division
Served as: Rifleman
Battle or Place of Action: near Salerno, Italy
Date of Action: 9 September 1943
G.O. Number, Date: 54, 5 July 1944
Date of Presentation: 6 June 1944
Place of Presentation: near Naples, Italy, presented by Lt. Gen. Alexander M. Patch III
Citation: For conspicuous gallantry and intrepidity at the risk of life above and beyond the call of duty in action involving actual conflict on 9 September 1943 in the vicinity of Salerno, Italy. As a rifleman of an infantry company, Sgt. Logan landed with the first wave of the assault echelon on the beaches of the Gulf of Salerno, and after his company had advanced 800 yards inland and taken positions along the forward bank of an irrigation canal, the enemy began a serious counterattack from positions along a rock wall which ran parallel with the canal about 200 yards further inland. Voluntarily exposing himself to the fire of a machine gun located along the rock wall, which sprayed the ground so close to him that he was splattered with dirt and rocks and splinters from the impact of the bullets, Sgt. Logan killed the first three Germans as they came through a gap in the wall. He then attacked the machine gun. As he dashed across the 200 yards of exposed terrain a withering stream of fire followed his advance. Reaching the wall, he crawled along the base, within easy reach of the enemy crouched along the opposite side, until he reached the gun. Jumping up, he shot the two gunners down, hurdled the wall, and seized the gun. Swinging it around, he immediately opened fire on the enemy with the remaining ammunition, raking their flight and inflicting further casualties on them as they fled. After smashing the machine gun over the rocks, Sgt. Logan captured an enemy officer and private who were attempting to sneak away. Later in the morning, Sgt. Logan went after a sniper hidden in a house about 150 yards from the company. Again the intrepid Sergeant ran a gauntlet of fire to reach his objective. Shooting the lock off the door, Sgt. Logan kicked it in and shot the sniper who had just reached the bottom of the stairs. The conspicuous gallantry and intrepidity which characterized Sgt. Logan's exploits proved a constant inspiration to all the men of his company, and aided mate rially in insuring the success of the beachhead at Salerno.

2819 ◆ LOPEZ, JOSE MENDOZA

Rank: Sergeant (highest rank: Sergeant First Class)
Service: U.S. Army
Birthday: 1 June 1912
Place of Birth: Mission, Hidalgo County, Texas
Entered Service at: Brownsville, Cameron County, Texas
Unit: Weapons Platoon, Company M, 3d Battalion, 23d Infantry, 2d Infantry Division
Served as: Machine Gunner
Battle or Place of Action: near Krinkelt, Belgium
Date of Action: 17 December 1944
G.O. Number, Date: 47, 18 June 1945
Date of Presentation: 18 June 1945
Place of Presentation: Zepman Stadium, Nuremberg, Germany, presented by Major Gen. James Van Fleet III
Citation: On his own initiative, he carried his heavy machine gun from Company K's right flank to its left, in order to protect that flank, which was in danger of being overrun by advancing enemy infantry supported by tanks. Occupying a shallow hole offering no protection above the waist, he cut down a group of 10 Germans. Ignoring enemy fire from an advancing tank, he held his position and cut down 25 more enemy infantry attempting to turn his flank. Glancing to his right, he saw a large number of infantry swarming in from the front. Although dazed and shaken from enemy artillery fire which had crashed into the ground only a few yards away, he realized that his position soon would be outflanked. Again, alone, he carried his machine gun to a position to the right rear of the sector; enemy tanks and infantry were forcing a withdrawal. Blown over backwards by the concussion of enemy fire, he immediately reset his gun and continued his fire. Singlehanded he held off the German horde until he was satisfied his company had effected its retirement. Again he loaded his gun on his back and in a hail of small-arms fire he ran to a point where a few of his comrades were attempting to set up another defense against the onrushing enemy. He fired from this position until his ammunition was exhausted. Still carrying his gun, he fell back with his small group to

Krinkelt. Sgt. Lopez's gallantry and intrepidity, on seemingly suicidal missions in which he killed at least 100 of the enemy, were almost solely responsible for allowing Company K to avoid being enveloped, to withdraw successfully, and to give other forces coming up in support time to build a line which repelled the enemy drive.

2820 ◆ LUCAS, JACKLYN HAROLD

Rank: Private First Class
Service: U.S. Marine Corps Reserve
Birthday: 14 February 1928
Place of Birth: Plymouth, Washington County, North Carolina
Entered Service at: Norfolk, Norfolk County, Virginia
Unit: Company C, 1st Battalion, 26th Marines, 5th Marine Division
Served as: Rifleman
Battle or Place of Action: Iwo Jima, Volcano Islands
Date of Action: 20 February 1945
Date of Presentation: 5 October 1945
Place of Presentation: The White House, presented by Pres. Harry S. Truman
Citation: For conspicuous gallantry and intrepidity at the risk of his life above and beyond the call of duty while serving with the 1st Battalion, 26th Marines, 5th Marine Division, during action against enemy Japanese forces on Iwo Jima, Volcano Islands, 20 February 1945. While creeping through a treacherous, twisting ravine which ran in close proximity to a fluid and uncertain front line on D-day plus one, Pfc. Lucas and three other men were suddenly ambushed by a hostile patrol which savagely attacked with rifle fire and grenades. Quick to act when the lives of the small group were endangered by two grenades which landed directly in front of them, Pfc. Lucas unhesitatingly hurled himself over his comrades upon one grenade and pulled the other under him, absorbing the whole blasting forces of the explosions in his own body in order to shield his companions from the concussion and murderous flying fragments. By his inspiring action and valiant spirit of self-sacrifice, he not only protected his comrades from certain injury or possible death but also enabled them to rout the Japanese patrol and continue the advance. His exceptionally courageous initiative and loyalty reflect the highest credit upon Pfc. Lucas and the U.S. Naval Service.

2821 ◆ *LUMMUS, JACK

Rank: First Lieutenant
Service: U.S. Marine Corps Reserve
Birthday: 22 October 1915
Place of Birth: Ennis, Ellis County, Texas
Date of Death: 8 March 1945
Cemetery: Myrtle Cemetery (MH)—Ennis, Texas
Entered Service at: Texas
Unit: Company E, 2d Battalion, 27th Marines, 5th Marine Division
Served as: Rifle Platoon Leader
Battle or Place of Action: Iwo Jima, Volcano Islands
Date of Action: 8 March 1945
Citation: For conspicuous gallantry and intrepidity at the risk of his life above and beyond the call of duty as leader of a rifle platoon attached to the 2d Battalion, 27th Marines, 5th Marine Division, in action against enemy Japanese forces on Iwo Jima in the Volcano Islands, 8 March 1945. Resuming his assault tactics with bold decision after fighting without respite for two days and nights, 1st Lt. Lummus slowly advanced his platoon against an enemy deeply entrenched in a network of mutually supporting positions. Suddenly halted by a terrific concentration of hostile fire, he unhesitatingly moved forward of his front lines in an effort to neutralize the Japanese position. Although knocked to the ground when an enemy grenade exploded close by, he immediately recovered himself and, again moving forward despite the intensified barrage, quickly located, attacked, and destroyed the occupied emplacement. Instantly taken under fire by the garrison of a supporting pillbox and further assailed by the slashing fury of hostile rifle fire, he fell under the impact of a second enemy grenade but, courageously disregarding painful shoulder wounds, staunchly continued his heroic one-man assault and charged the second pillbox, annihilating all the occupants. Subsequently returning to his platoon position, he fearlessly traversed his lines under fire, encouraging his men to advance and directing the fire of supporting tanks against other stubbornly holding Japanese emplacements. Held up again by a devastating barrage, he again moved into the open, rushed a third heavily fortified installation and killed the defending troops. Determined to crush all resistance, he led his men indomitably, personally attacking foxholes and spider traps with his carbine and systematically reducing the fanatic opposition, until, stepping on a land mine, he sustained fatal wounds. By his outstanding valor, skilled tactics, and tenacious perseverance in the face of overwhelming odds, 1st Lt. Lummus had inspired his stouthearted marines to continue the relentless drive northward, thereby contributing materially to the success of his regimental mission. His dauntless leadership and unwavering devotion to duty throughout sustain and enhance the highest traditions of the U.S. Naval Service. He gallantly gave his life in the service of his country.

2822 ◆ MABRY JR., GEORGE LAFAYETTE

Rank: Lieutenant Colonel (highest rank: Major General)
Service: U.S. Army
Birthday: 14 September 1917
Place of Birth: Sumter, Sumter County, South Carolina
Date of Death: 13 July 1990
Cemetery: Holy Cross Episcopal Church Cemetery (MH)—Stateboro, South Carolina
Entered Service at: Sumter, Sumter County, South Carolina
Unit: 2d Battalion, 8th Infantry, 4th Infantry Division
Served as: Battalion Commander
Battle or Place of Action: Hurtgen Forest near Schevenhutte, Germany
Date of Action: 20 November 1944
G.O. Number, Date: 77, September 1945
Date of Presentation: 23 August 1945
Place of Presentation: The White House, presented by Pres. Harry S. Truman

Citation: He was commanding the 2d Battalion, 8th Infantry, in an attack through the Hurtgen Forest near Schevenhutte, Germany, on 20 November 1944. During the early phases of the assault, the leading elements of his battalion were halted by a minefield and immobilized by heavy hostile fire. Advancing alone into the mined area, Col. Mabry established a safe route of passage. He then moved ahead of the foremost scouts, personally leading the attack, until confronted by a booby-trapped double concertina obstacle. With the assistance of the scouts, he disconnected the explosives and cut a path through the wire. Upon moving through the opening, he observed three enemy in foxholes whom he captured at bayonet point. Driving steadily forward he paced the assault against three log bunkers which housed mutually supported automatic weapons. Racing up a slope ahead of his men, he found the initial bunker deserted, then pushed on to a second where he was suddenly confronted by nine onrushing enemy. Using the butt of his rifle, he felled one adversary and bayoneted a second, before his scouts came to his aid and assisted him in overcoming the others in hand-to-hand combat. Accompanied by the riflemen, he charged the third bunker under point-blank small-arms fire and led the way into the fortification from which he prodded six enemy at bayonet point. Following the consolidation of this area, he led his battalion across 300 yards of fire-swept terrain to seize elevated ground upon which he established a defensive position which menaced the enemy on both flanks, and provided his regiment a firm foothold on the approach to the Cologne Plain. Col. Mabry's superlative courage, daring, and leadership in an operation of major importance exemplify the finest characteristics of the military service.

2823 ◆ MacARTHUR, DOUGLAS

Rank: General of the Armies
Service: U.S. Army
Birthday: 26 January 1880
Place of Birth: Little Rock, Pulaski County, Arkansas
Date of Death: 5 April 1964
Cemetery: Old Norfolk City Hall Memorial (PM)—Norfolk, Virginia
Entered Service at: Ashland, Ashland County, Wisconsin
Unit: U.S. Army Forces in the Far East
Served as: Commanding General
Battle or Place of Action: Bataan Peninsula, Philippine Islands
G.O. Number, Date: 16, 1 April 1942
Date of Presentation: 30 June 1942
Place of Presentation: Melborne, Australia, presented by Nelson Trussler Johnson, Minister of Australia
Citation: For conspicuous leadership in preparing the Philippine Islands to resist conquest, for gallantry and intrepidity above and beyond the call of duty in action against invading Japanese forces, and for the heroic conduct of defensive and offensive operations on the Bataan Peninsula. He mobilized, trained, and led an army which has received world acclaim for its gallant defense against a tremendous superiority of enemy forces in men and arms. His utter disregard of personal danger under heavy fire and aerial bombardment, his calm judgement in each crisis, inspired his troops, galvanized the spirit of resistance of the Filipino people, and confirmed the faith of the American people in their Armed Forces.

2824 ◆ MacGILLIVARY, CHARLES ANDREW

Rank: Sergeant (highest rank: Technical Sergeant)
Service: U.S. Army
Birthday: 17 January 1917
Place of Birth: Charlottetown, Prince Edward Island, Canada
Entered Service at: Boston, Suffolk County, Massachusetts
Unit: Company I, 463d Battalion, 71st Infantry, 44th Infantry Division
Served as: Platoon Leader
Battle or Place of Action: near Woelfling, France
Date of Action: 1 January 1945
G.O. Number, Date: 77, 10 September 1945
Date of Presentation: 23 August 1945
Place of Presentation: The White House, presented by Pres. Harry S. Truman
Citation: He led a squad when his unit moved forward in darkness to meet the threat of a breakthrough by elements of the 17th German Panzer Grenadier Division. Assigned to protect the left flank, he discovered hostile troops digging in. As he reported this information, several German machine guns opened fire, stopping the American advance. Knowing the position of the enemy, Sgt. MacGillivary volunteered to knock out one of the guns while another company closed in from the right to assault the remaining strongpoints. He circled from the left through woods and snow, carefully worked his way to the emplacement, and shot the two camouflaged gunners at a range of three feet as other enemy forces withdrew. Early in the afternoon of the same day, Sgt. MacGillivary was dispatched on reconnaissance and found that Company I was being opposed by about six machine guns reinforcing a company of fanatically fighting Germans. His unit began to attack but was pinned down by furious automatic and small-arms fire. With a clear idea of where the enemy guns were placed, he voluntarily embarked on a lone combat patrol. Skillfully taking advantage of all available cover, he stalked the enemy, reached a hostile machine gun, and blasted its crew with a grenade. He picked up a submachine gun from the battlefield and pressed on to within 10 yards of another machine gun, where the enemy crew discovered him and feverishly tried to swing their weapon into line to cut him down. He charged ahead, jumped into the midst of the Germans, and killed them with several bursts. Without hesitation, he moved on to still another machine gun, creeping, crawling, and rushing from tree to tree, until close enough to toss a grenade into the emplacement and close with its defenders. He dispatched this crew also, but was himself seriously wounded. Through his indomitable fighting spirit, great initiative, and utter disregard for personal safety in the face of powerful enemy resistance, Sgt. MacGillivary destroyed four hostile machine guns and immeasurably helped his company to continue on its mission with minimum casualties.

2825 ◆ *MAGRATH, JOHN D.

Rank: Private First Class
Service: U.S. Army
Birthday: 4 July 1924
Place of Birth: East Norwalk, Fairfield County, Connecticut
Date of Death: 14 April 1945
Cemetery: Riverside Cemetery (MH)—Norwalk, Connecticut
Entered Service at: East Norwalk, Fairfield County, Connecticut
Unit: Company G, 85th Infantry, 10th Mountain Division
Served as: Scout
Battle or Place of Action: near Castel d'Aiano, Italy
Date of Action: 14 April 1945
G.O. Number, Date: 71, 17 July 1946
Citation: He displayed conspicuous gallantry and intrepidity above and beyond the call of duty when his company was pinned down by heavy artillery, mortar, and small-arms fire, near Castel d'Aiano, Italy. Volunteering to act as scout, armed with only a rifle, he charged headlong into withering fire, killing two Germans and wounding three in order to capture a machine gun. Carrying this weapon across an open field through heavy fire, he neutralized two more machine-gun nests; he then circled behind four other Germans, killing them with a burst as they were firing on his company. Spotting another dangerous enemy position to his right, he knelt with the machine gun in his arms and exchanged fire with the Germans until he had killed two and wounded three. The enemy now poured increased mortar and artillery fire on the company's newly won position. Pfc. Magrath fearlessly volunteered again to brave the shelling in order to collect a report of casualties. Heroically carrying out this task, he made the supreme sacrifice—a climax to the valor and courage that are in keeping with the highest traditions of the military service.

2826 ◆ *MANN, JOE EUGENE

Rank: Private First Class
Service: U.S. Army
Birthday: 12 July 1922
Place of Birth: Reardan, Lincoln County, Washington
Date of Death: 19 September 1944
Cemetery: Greenwood Cemetery—Spokane, Washington
Entered Service at: Seattle, King County, Washington
Unit: Company H, 502d Parachute Infantry, 101st Airborne Division
Served as: Lead Scout
Battle or Place of Action: Best, Holland
Date of Action: 18 September 1944
G.O. Number, Date: 73, 30 August 1945
Date of Presentation: Spring, 1945
Place of Presentation: Baxter Veterans Hospital, Spokane, WA, preseented by the hospital commanding officer to his Father
Citation: He distinguished himself by conspicuous gallantry above and beyond the call of duty. On 18 September 1944, in the vicinity of Best, Holland, his platoon, attempting to seize the bridge across the Wilhelmina Canal, was surrounded and isolated by an enemy force greatly superior in personnel and firepower. Acting as lead scout, Pfc. Mann boldly crept to within rocket-launcher range of an enemy artillery position and, in the face of heavy enemy fire, destroyed an 88-mm gun and an ammunition dump. Completely disregarding the great danger involved, he remained in his exposed position, and, with his M1 rifle, killed the enemy one by one until he was wounded four times. Taken to a covered position, he insisted on returning to a forward position to stand guard during the night. On the following morning the enemy launched a concerted attack and advanced to within a few yards of the position, throwing hand grenades as they approached. One of these landed within a few feet of Pfc. Mann. Unable to raise his arms, which were bandaged to his body, he yelled "Grenade" and threw his body over the grenade, and as it exploded, died. His outstanding gallantry above and beyond the call of duty and his magnificent conduct were an everlasting inspiration to his comrades for whom he gave his life.

2827 ◆ *MARTIN, HARRY LINN

Rank: First Lieutenant
Service: U.S. Marine Corps Reserve
Birthday: 4 January 1911
Place of Birth: Bucyrus, Crawford County, Ohio
Date of Death: 26 March 1945
Cemetery: Oakwood Cemetery (MH)—Bucyrus, Ohio
Entered Service at: Ohio
Unit: Company C, 5th Pioneer Battalion, 5th Marine Division
Served as: Platoon Leader
Battle or Place of Action: Iwo Jima, Volcano Islands
Date of Action: 26 March 1945
Citation: For conspicuous gallantry and intrepidity at the risk of his life above and beyond the call of duty as platoon leader attached to Company C, 5th Pioneer Battalion, 5th Marine Division, in action against enemy Japanese forces on Iwo Jima, Volcano Islands, 26 March 1945. With his sector of the 5th Pioneer Battalion bivouac area penetrated by a concentrated enemy attack launched a few minutes before dawn, 1st Lt. Martin instantly organized a firing line with the marines nearest his foxhole and succeeded in checking momentarily the headlong rush of the Japanese. Determined to rescue several of his men trapped in positions overrun by the enemy, he defied intense hostile fire to work his way through the Japanese to the surrounded marines. Although sustaining two severe wounds, he blasted the Japanese who attempted to intercept him, located his beleaguered men, and directed them to their own lines. When four of the infiltrating enemy took possession of an abandoned machine-gun pit and subjected his sector to a barrage of hand grenades, 1st Lt. Martin, alone and armed only with a pistol, boldly charged the hostile position and killed all its occupants. Realizing that his few remaining comrades could not repulse another organized attack, he called to his men to follow and then charged into the midst of the strong enemy force, firing his weapon and scattering them until he fell, mortally wounded by a grenade. By his outstanding valor, indomitable fighting spirit, and tenacious determination in the face of overwhelming

odds, 1st Lt. Martin permanently disrupted a coordinated Japanese attack and prevented a greater loss of life in his own and adjacent platoons. His inspiring leadership and unswerving devotion to duty reflect the highest credit upon himself and the U.S. Naval Service. He gallantly gave his life in the service of his country.

2828 ◆ *MARTINEZ, JOE P.

Rank: Private
Service: U.S. Army
Birthday: 27 July 1920
Place of Birth: Taos, Taos County, New Mexico
Date of Death: 26 May 1943
Cemetery: Ault Cemetery (MH)—Ault, Colorado
Entered Service at: Ault, Weld County, Colorado
Unit: Company K, 32d Infantry, 7th Infantry Division
Served as: Automatic Rifleman
Battle or Place of Action: on Attu Island, Aleutian Islands
Date of Action: 26 May 1943
G.O. Number, Date: 71, 27 October 1943
Date of Presentation: 11 November 1943
Place of Presentation: Ault, Colorado, presented by Brigadier Gen. Frank L. Culin Jr. to his family
Citation: For conspicuous gallantry and intrepidity above and beyond the call of duty in action with the enemy. Over a period of several days, repeated efforts to drive the enemy from a key defensive position high in the snow-covered precipitous mountains between east arm of Holtz Bay and Chichogof Harbor had failed. On 26 May 1943, troop dispositions were readjusted and a trial coordinated attack on this position by a reinforced battalion was launched. Initially successful, the attack hesitated. In the face of severe hostile machine-gun, rifle, and mortar fire, Pvt. Martinez, an automatic rifleman, rose to his feet and resumed his advance. Occasionally he stopped to urge his comrades on. His example inspired others to follow. After a most difficult climb, Pvt. Martinez eliminated resistance from part of the enemy position by BAR fire and hand grenades, thus assisting the advance of other attacking elements. This success only partially completed the action. The main Holtz-Chichogof Pass rose about 150 feet higher, flanked by steep rocky ridges and reached a snow-filled defile. Passage was barred by enemy fire from either flank and from tiers of snow trenches in front. Despite these obstacles, and knowing of their existence, Pvt. Martinez again led the troops on and up, personally silencing several trenches with BAR fire and ultimately reaching the pass itself. Here, just below the knifelike rim of the pass, Pvt. Martinez encountered a final enemy-occupied trench and as he was engaged in firing into it he was mortally wounded. The pass, however, was taken and its capture was an important preliminary to the end of organized hostile resistance on the island.

2829 ◆ *MASON, LEONARD FOSTER

Rank: Private First Class
Service: U.S. Marine Corps
Birthday: 2 February 1920
Place of Birth: Middlesboro, Bell County, Kentucky
Date of Death: 22 July 1944
Cemetery: National Memorial Cemetery of the Pacific (Wall of the Missing)—Honolulu, Hawaii
Entered Service at: Ohio
Unit: 2d Battalion, 3d Marines, 3d Marine Division
Served as: Automatic Rifleman
Battle or Place of Action: Asan-Adelup Beachhead, Guam, Marianas Islands
Date of Action: 22 July 1944
Citation: For conspicuous gallantry and intrepidity at the risk of his life above and beyond the call of duty as an automatic rifleman serving with the 2d Battalion, 3d Marines, 3d Marine Division, in action against enemy Japanese forces on the Asan-Adelup Beachhead, Guam, Marianas Islands on 22 July 1944. Suddenly taken under fire by two enemy machine guns not more than 15 yards away while clearing out hostile positions holding up the advance of his platoon through a narrow gully, Pfc. Mason, alone and entirely on his own initiative, climbed out of the gully and moved parallel to it toward the rear of the enemy position. Although fired upon immediately by hostile riflemen from a higher position and wounded repeatedly in the arm and shoulder, Pfc. Mason grimly pressed forward and had just reached his objective when hit again by a burst of enemy machine-gun fire, causing a critical wound to which he later succumbed. With valiant disregard for his own peril, he persevered, clearing out the hostile position, killing five Japanese, wounding another, and then rejoining his platoon to report the results of his action before consenting to be evacuated. His exceptionally heroic act in the face of almost certain death enabled his platoon to accomplish its mission and reflects the highest credit upon Pfc. Mason and the U.S. Naval Service. He gallantly gave his life for his country.

2830 ◆ *MATHIES, ARCHIBALD

Rank: Sergeant
Service: U.S. Army Air Corps
Birthday: 3 June 1918
Place of Birth: Scotland
Date of Death: 20 February 1944
Cemetery: Finleyville Cemetery (MH)—Finleyville, Pennsylvania
Entered Service at: Pittsburgh, Allegheny County, Pennsylvania
Unit: 510th Bombardment Squadron, 351st Bombardment Group, 8th Air Force
Served as: Engineer & Ball Turret Gunner on a B-17
Battle or Place of Action: over Europe
Date of Action: 20 February 1944
G.O. Number, Date: 52, 22 June 1944
Place of Presentation: Presented to his Mother
Citation: For conspicuous gallantry and intrepidity at the risk of life above and beyond the call of duty in action against the enemy in connection with a bombing mission over enemy-occupied Europe on 20 February 1944. The aircraft on which Sgt. Mathies was serving as engineer and ball turret gunner was attacked by a squadron of enemy fighters with the

result that the copilot was killed outright, the pilot wounded and rendered unconscious, the radio operator wounded, and the plane severely damaged. Nevertheless, Sgt. Mathies and other members of the crew managed to right the plane and fly it back to their home station, where they contacted the control tower and reported the situation. Sgt. Mathies and the navigator volunteered to attempt to land the plane. Other members of the crew were ordered to jump, leaving Sgt. Mathies and the navigator aboard. After observing the distressed aircraft from another plane, Sgt. Mathies' commanding officer decided the damaged plane could not be landed by the inexperienced crew and ordered them to abandon it and parachute to safety. Demonstrating unsurpassed courage and heroism, Sgt. Mathies and the navigator replied that the pilot was still alive but could not be moved and they would not desert him. They were then told to attempt a landing. After two unsuccessful efforts, the plane crashed into an open field in a third attempt to land. Sgt. Mathies, the navigator, and the wounded pilot were killed.

2831 ◆ *MATHIS, JACK WARREN

Rank: First Lieutenant
Service: U.S. Army Air Corps
Birthday: 25 September 1921
Place of Birth: San Angelo, Tom Green County, Texas
Date of Death: 18 March 1943
Place of Death: over Vegesack, Germany
Cemetery: Fairmount Cemetery—San Angelo, Texas
Entered Service at: San Angelo, Tom Green County, Texas
Unit: 359th Bombardment Squadron, 303d Bombardment Group, 8th Air Force
Served as: Lead Bombardier of a B-17
Battle or Place of Action: over Vegesack, Germany
Date of Action: 18 March 1943
G.O. Number, Date: 38, 12 July 1943
Date of Presentation: 21 September 1943
Place of Presentation: Goodfellow Field, San Angelo, Texas, presented by Maj. Gen. Barton K. Yount to his Mother
Citation: For conspicuous gallantry and intrepidity above and beyond the call of duty in action with the enemy over Vegesack, Germany on 18 March 1943. First Lt. Mathis, as leading bombardier of his squadron, flying through intense and accurate antiaircraft fire, was just starting his bomb run, upon which the entire squadron depended upon for accurate bombing, when he was hit by the enemy antiaircraft fire. His right arm was shattered above the elbow, a large wound was torn in his side and abdomen, and he was knocked from his bombsight to the rear of the bombardier's compartment. Realizing that the success of the mission depended upon him, 1st Lt. Mathis, by sheer determination and willpower, though mortally wounded, dragged himself back to his sights, released his bombs, then died at his post of duty. As the result of this action the airplanes of his bombardment squadron placed their bombs directly upon the assigned target for a perfect attack against the enemy. First Lt. Mathis' undaunted bravery has been a great inspiration to the officers and men of his unit.

2832 ◆ MAXWELL, ROBERT DALE

Rank: Technician Fifth Grade
Service: U.S. Army
Birthday: 26 October 1920
Place of Birth: Boise, Ada County, Idaho
Entered Service at: Creswell, Larimer County, Colorado
Unit: Wire Section, Communications Platoon, Headquarters Company, 3d Battalion, 7th Infantry Regiment, 3d Infantry Division
Served as: Wireman/Switchboard Operator
Battle or Place of Action: near Besancon, France
Date of Action: 7 September 1944
G.O. Number, Date: 24, 6 April 1945
Date of Presentation: 12 May 1945
Place of Presentation: Denver, Colorado, presented by Gen. Danielson
Citation: For conspicuous gallantry and intrepidity at the risk of life above and beyond the call of duty on 7 September 1944, near Besancon, France. Technician 5th Grade Maxwell and three other soldiers, armed only with .45-caliber automatic pistols, defended the battalion observation post against an overwhelming onslaught by enemy infantrymen in approximately platoon strength, supported by 20-mm flak and machine-gun fire, who had infiltrated through the battalion's forward companies and were attacking the observation post with machine-gun, machine pistol, and grenade fire at ranges as close as 10 yards. Despite a hail of fire from automatic weapons and grenade launchers, Technician 5th Grade Maxwell aggressively fought off advancing enemy elements and, by his calmness, tenacity, and fortitude, inspired his fellows to continue the unequal struggle. When an enemy hand grenade was thrown in the midst of his squad, Technician 5th Grade Maxwell unhesitatingly hurled himself squarely upon it, using his blanket and his unprotected body to absorb the full force of the explosion. This act of instantaneous heroism permanently maimed Technican 5th Grade Maxwell, but saved the lives of his comrades in arms and facilitated maintenance of vital military communications during the temporary withdrawal of the battalion's forward headquarters.

2833 ◆ *MAY, MARTIN O.

Rank: Private First Class
Service: U.S. Army
Birthday: 18 April 1922
Place of Birth: Phillipsburg, Warren County, New Jersey
Date of Death: 21 April 1945
Cemetery: National Memorial Cemetery of the Pacific (N-1242) (MH)—Honolulu, Hawaii
Entered Service at: Phillipsburg, Warren County, New Jersey
Unit: 307th Infantry, 77th Infantry Division
Served as: Heavy Machine Gunner
Battle or Place of Action: Iegusuku-Yama, Ie-shima, Ryukyu Islands
Date of Action: 19-20 April 1945
G.O. Number, Date: 9, 25 January 1946
Citation: He gallantly maintained a three-day stand in the

face of terrible odds when American troops fought for possession of the rugged slopes of Iegusuku-Yama on Ie-shima, Ryukyu Islands. After placing his heavy machine gun in an advantageous yet vulnerable position on a ridge to support riflemen, he became the target of fierce mortar and small-arms fire from the counterattacking Japanese. He repulsed this assault by sweeping the enemy with accurate bursts while explosions and ricocheting bullets threw blinding dust and dirt about him. He broke up a second counterattack by hurling grenades into the midst of the enemy forces, and then refused to withdraw, volunteering to maintain his post and cover the movement of American riflemen as they reorganized to meet any further hostile action. The major effort of the enemy did not develop until the morning of 21 April. It found Pfc. May still supporting the rifle company in the face of devastating rifle, machine-gun, and mortar fire. While many of the friendly troops about him became casualties, he continued to fire his machine gun until he was severely wounded and his gun rendered useless by the burst of a mortar shell. Refusing to withdraw from the violent action, he blasted fanatical Japanese troops with hand grenades until wounded again, this time mortally. By his intrepidity and the extreme tenacity with which he held firm until death against overwhelming forces, Pfc. May killed at least 16 Japanese, was largely responsible for maintaining the American lines, and inspired his comrades to efforts which later resulted in complete victory and seizure of the mountain stronghold.

2834 ◆ MAYFIELD, MELVIN

Rank: Corporal
Service: U.S. Army
Birthday: 12 March 1919
Place of Birth: Salem, Harrison County, West Virginia
Date of Death: 19 June 1990
Cemetery: Frazeysburg Cemetery (MH)—Frazeysburg, Ohio
Entered Service at: Nashport, Muskingum County, Ohio
Unit: Company D, 1st Battalion, 20th Infantry, 6th Infantry Division
Served as: Lineman
Battle or Place of Action: Cordillera Mountains, Luzon, Philippine Islands
Date of Action: 29 July 1945
G.O. Number, Date: 49, 31 May 1946
Citation: He displayed conspicuous gallantry and intrepidity above and beyond the call of duty while fighting in the Cordillera Mountains of Luzon, Philippine Islands. When two Filipino companies were pinned down under a torrent of enemy fire that converged on them from a circular ridge commanding their position, Cpl. Mayfield, in a gallant single-handed effort to aid them, rushed from shell hole to shell hole until he reached four enemy caves atop the barren fire-swept hill. With grenades and his carbine, he assaulted each of the caves while enemy fire pounded about him. However, before he annihilated the last hostile redoubt, a machine-gun bullet destroyed his weapon and slashed his left hand. Disregarding his wound, he secured more grenades and dauntlessly charged again into the face of point-blank fire to help destroy a hostile observation post. By his gallant determination and heroic leadership, Cpl. Mayfield inspired the men to eliminate all remaining pockets of resistance in the area and to press the advance against the enemy.

2835 ◆ McCALL, THOMAS EDWARD

Rank: Staff Sergeant
Service: U.S. Army
Birthday: 9 May 1916
Place of Birth: Burrton, Harvey County, Kansas
Date of Death: 19 September 1965
Place of Death: Darlington, Maryland
Cemetery: Spring Vale Cemetery—Lafayette, Indiana
Entered Service at: Veedersburg, Fountain County, Indiana
Unit: Company F, 143d Infantry, 36th Infantry Division
Served as: Commander of a Machine Gun Section
Battle or Place of Action: near San Angelo, Italy
Date of Action: 22 January 1944
G.O. Number, Date: 31, 17 April 1945
Citation: For conspicuous gallantry and intrepidity at risk of life above and beyond the call of duty. On 22 January 1944, Company F had the mission of crossing the Rapido River in the vicinity of San Angelo, Italy, and attacking the well-prepared German positions to the west. For the defense of these positions the enemy had prepared a network of machine-gun positions covering the terrain to the front with a pattern of withering machine-gun fire, and mortar and artillery positions zeroed in on the defilade areas. S/Sgt. McCall commanded a machine-gun section that was to provide added fire support for the riflemen. Under cover of darkness, Company F advanced to the river-crossing site and under intense enemy mortar, artillery, and machine-gun fire crossed an ice-covered bridge which was continually the target for enemy fire. Many casualties occurred on reaching the west side of the river and reorganization was imperative. Exposing himself to the deadly enemy machine-gun and small-arms fire that swept over the flat terrain, S/Sgt. McCall, with unusual calmness, encouraged and welded his men into an effective fighting unit. He then led them forward across the muddy, exposed terrain. Skillfully he guided his men through a barbed-wire entanglement to reach a road where he personally placed the weapons of his two squads into positions of vantage, covering the battalion's front. A shell landed near one of the positions, wounding the gunner, killing the assistant gunner, and destroying the weapon. Even though enemy shells were falling dangerously near, S/Sgt. McCall crawled across the treacherous terrain and rendered first aid to the wounded man, dragging him into a position of cover with the help of another man. The gunners of the second machine gun had been wounded from the fragments of an enemy shell, leaving S/Sgt. McCall the only remaining member of his machine-gun section. Displaying outstanding aggressiveness, he ran forward with the weapon on his hip, reaching a point 30 yards from the enemy, where he fired two bursts of fire into the nest, killing or wounding all of the crew and putting the gun out of action. A second machine gun now opened fire upon him and he rushed its position, firing his weapon from the hip, killing four of the guncrew. A third machine gun, 50 yards in the rear of the first two, was delivering a tremendous

volume of fire upon our troops. S/Sgt. McCall spotted its position and valiantly went toward it in the face of overwhelming enemy fire. He was last seen courageously moving forward on the enemy position, firing his machine gun from the hip. S/Sgt. McCall's intrepidity and unhesitating willingness to sacrifice his life exemplify the highest traditions of the Armed Forces.

2836 ◆ McCAMPBELL, DAVID

Rank: Commander (highest rank: Captain)
Service: U.S. Navy
Birthday: 16 January 1910
Place of Birth: Bessemer, Jefferson County, Alabama
Entered Service at: West Palm Beach, Palm Beach County, Florida
Unit: Air Group 15, U.S.S. *Essex*
Served as: Air Group Commander/Pilot of a Grumman Hellcat
Battle or Place of Action: Battle of the Philippine Sea & Battle of Leyte Gulf
Date of Action: 19 June & 24-25 October 1944
Date of Presentation: 10 January 1945
Place of Presentation: The White House, presented by Pres. Franklin D. Roosevelt
Citation: For conspicuous gallantry and intrepidity at the risk of his life above and beyond the call of duty as commander, Air Group 15, during combat against enemy Japanese aerial forces in the first and second battles of the Philippine Sea. An inspiring leader, fighting boldly in the face of terrific odds, Comdr. McCampbell led his fighter planes against a force of 80 Japanese carrier-based aircraft bearing down on our fleet on 19 June 1944. Striking fiercely in valiant defense of our surface force, he personally destroyed seven hostile planes during this single engagement in which the outnumbering attack force was utterly routed and vitually annihilated. During a major fleet engagement with the enemy on 24 October, Comdr. McCampbell, assisted by but one plane, intercepted and daringly attacked a formation of 60 hostile land-based craft approaching our forces. Fighting desperately but with superb skill against such overwhelming airpower, he shot down nine Japanese planes and, completely disorganizing the enemy group, forced the remainder to abandon the attack before a single aircraft could reach the fleet. His great personal valor and indomitable spirit of aggression under extremely perilous combat conditions reflect the highest credit upon Comdr. McCampbell and the U.S. Naval Service.

2837 ◆ McCANDLESS, BRUCE

Rank: Commander (highest rank: Rear Admiral)
Service: U.S. Navy
Birthday: 12 August 1911
Place of Birth: Washington, D.C.
Date of Death: 24 January 1968
Cemetery: U.S. Naval Academy Cemetery (Lot 1021)—Annapolis, Maryland
Entered Service at: Colorado
Unit: U.S.S. *San Francisco*
Served as: Commanding Officer
Battle or Place of Action: Iron Bottom Sound, off Savo Island, Solomon Islands
Date of Action: 12-13 November 1942
Date of Presentation: 12 December 1942
Place of Presentation: Onboard the U.S.S. *San Francisco*, San Francisco, California, presented by Adm. Ernest J. King
Citation: For conspicuous gallantry and exceptionally distinguished service above and beyond the call of duty as communication officer of the U.S.S. *San Francisco* in combat with enemy Japanese forces in the battle off Savo Island, 12–13 November 1942. In the midst of a violent night engagement, the fire of a determined and desperate enemy seriously wounded Lt. Comdr. McCandless and rendered him unconscious, killed or wounded the admiral in command, his staff, the captain of the ship, the navigator, and all other personnel on the navigating and signal bridges. Faced with the lack of superior command upon his recovery, and displaying superb initiative, he promptly assumed command of the ship and ordered her course and gunfire against an overwhelmingly powerful force. With his superiors in other vessels unaware of the loss of their admiral, and challenged by his great responsibility, Lt. Comdr. McCandless boldly continued to engage the enemy and to lead our column of following vessels to a great victory. Largely through his brilliant seamanship and great courage, the U.S.S. *San Francisco* was brought back to port, saved to fight again in the service of her country.

2838 ◆ *McCARD, ROBERT HOWARD

Rank: Gunnery Sergeant
Service: U.S. Marine Corps
Birthday: 25 November 1918
Place of Birth: Syracuse, Onondaga County, New York
Date of Death: 16 June 1944
Cemetery: National Memorial Cemetery of the Pacific (B-1024) (MH)—Honolulu, Hawaii
Entered Service at: New York
Unit: Company A, 4th Tank Battalion, 4th Marine Division
Served as: Platoon Sergeant
Battle or Place of Action: Saipan, Marianas Islands
Date of Action: 16 June 1944
Date of Presentation: 10 April 1945
Place of Presentation: Centralia, IL, presented by Rear Adm. Arthur C. Carpender, Commandant, 9th Naval District, tohis widow, Lizette McCard
Citation: For conspicuous gallantry and intrepidity at the risk of his life above and beyond the call of duty while serving as platoon sergeant of Company A, 4th Tank Battalion, 4th Marine Division, during the battle for enemy Japanese-held Saipan, Marianas Islands on 16 June 1944. Cut off from the other units of his platoon when his tank was put out of action by a battery of enemy 77-mm guns, G/Sgt. McCard carried on resolutely, bringing all the tank's weapons to bear on the enemy, until the severity of the hostile fire caused him to order his crew out of the escape hatch while he courageously exposed himself to enemy guns by hurling hand grenades in order to cover the evacuation of his men. Seriously wounded during this action and with his supply of grenades exhausted,

G/Sgt. McCard then dismantled one of the tank's machine guns and faced the Japanese for the second time to deliver vigorous fire into their positions, destroying 16 of the enemy but sacrificing himself to insure the safety of his crew. His valiant fighting spirit and supreme loyalty in the face of almost certain death reflect the highest credit upon G/Sgt. McCard and the U.S. Naval Service. He gallantly gave his life for his country.

2839 ◆ McCARTER, LLOYD G.

Rank: Private
Service: U.S. Army
Birthday: 11 May 1917
Place of Birth: St. Maries, Benewah County, Idaho
Date of Death: 2 February 1956
Cemetery: Woodlawn Cemetery (MH)—St. Maries, Idaho
Entered Service at: Tacoma, Pierce County, Washington
Unit: 503d Parachute Infantry
Served as: Scout
Battle or Place of Action: Corregidor, Philippine Islands
Date of Action: 16-19 February 1945
G.O. Number, Date: 77, 10 September 1945
Date of Presentation: 23 August 1945
Place of Presentation: The White House, presented by Pres. Harry S. Truman
Citation: He was a scout with the regiment which seized the fortress of Corregidor, Philippine Islands. Shortly after the initial parachute assault on 16 February 1945, he crossed 30 yards of open ground under intense enemy fire, and at point-blank range silenced a machine gun with hand grenades. On the afternoon of 18 February he killed six snipers. That evening, when a large force attempted to bypass his company, he voluntarily moved to an exposed area and opened fire. The enemy attacked his position repeatedly throughout the night and was each time repulsed. By two o'clock in the morning, all the men about him had been wounded; but shouting encouragement to his comrades and defiance at the enemy, he continued to bear the brunt of the attack, fearlessly exposing himself to locate enemy soldiers and then pouring heavy fire on them. He repeatedly crawled back to the American line to secure more ammunition. When his submachine gun would no longer operate, he seized an automatic rifle and continued to inflict heavy casualties. This weapon, in turn, became too hot to use and, discarding it, he continued with an M1 rifle. At dawn the enemy attacked with renewed intensity. Completely exposing himself to hostile fire, he stood erect to locate the most dangerous enemy positions. He was seriously wounded; but, though he had already killed more than 30 of the enemy, he refused to evacuate until he had pointed out immediate objectives for attack. Through his sustained and outstanding heroism in the face of grave and obvious danger, Pvt. McCarter made outstanding contributions to the success of his company and the recapture of Corregidor.

2840 ◆ McCARTHY, JOSEPH JEREMIAH

Rank: Captain [highest rank: Brigadier General (hon.)]
Service: U.S. Marine Corps Reserve
Birthday: 10 August 1911
Place of Birth: Chicago, Cook County, Illinois
Entered Service at: Chicago, Cook County, Illinois
Unit: Company G, 2d Battalion, 24th Marines, 4th Marine Division
Served as: Company Commander
Battle or Place of Action: Iwo Jima, Volcano Islands
Date of Action: 21 February 1945
Date of Presentation: 5 October 1945
Place of Presentation: The White House, presented by Pres. Harry S. Truman
Citation: For conspicuous gallantry and intrepidity at the risk of his life above and beyond the call of duty as commanding officer of a rifle company attached to the 2d Battalion, 24th Marines, 4th Marine Division, in action against enemy Japanese forces during the seizure of Iwo Jima, Volcano Islands on 21 February 1945. Determined to break through the enemy's cross-island defenses, Capt. McCarthy acted on his own initiative when his company advance was held up by uninterrupted Japanese rifle, machine-gun, and high-velocity 47-mm fire during the approach to Motoyama Airfield No. 2. Quickly organizing a demolition and flamethrower team to accompany his picked rifle squad, he fearlessly led the way across 75 yards of fire-swept ground, charged a heavily fortified pillbox on the ridge of the front, and, personally hurling hand grenades into the emplacement as he directed the combined operations of his small assault group, completely destroyed the hostile installation. Spotting two Japanese soldiers attempting an escape from the shattered pillbox, he boldly stood upright in full view of the enemy and dispatched both troops before advancing to a second emplacement under greatly intensified fire and then blasted the strong fortifications with a well-planted demolitions attack. Subsequently entering the ruins, he found a Japanese taking aim at one of our men and, with alert presence of mind, jumped the enemy, disarmed, and shot him with his own weapon. Then, intent on smashing through the narrow breach, he rallied the remainder of his company and pressed a full attack with furious aggressiveness until he had neutralized all resistance and captured the ridge. An inspiring leader and indomitable fighter, Capt. McCarthy consistently disregarded all personal danger during the fierce conflict and, by his brilliant professional skill, daring tactics, and tenacious perseverance in the face of overwhelming odds, contributed materially to the success of his division's operations again st the savagely defended outpost of the Japanese Empire. His cool decision and outstanding valor reflect the highest credit upon Capt. McCarthy and enhance the finest traditions of the U.S. Naval Service.

2841 ◆ McCOOL JR., RICHARD MILES

Rank: Lieutenant (highest rank: Captain)
Service: U.S. Navy
Birthday: 4 January 1922
Place of Birth: Tishomingo, Johnston County, Oklahoma
Entered Service at: Oklahoma
Unit: U.S.S. LCS (L) (3) 122
Served as: Commanding Officer
Battle or Place of Action: North of Okinawa

Date of Action: 10-11 June 1945
Date of Presentation: 18 December 1945
Place of Presentation: The White House (Oval Office), presented by Pres. Harry S. Truman
Citation: For conspicuous gallantry and intrepidity at the risk of his life above and beyond the call of duty as commanding officer of the U.S.S. LCS (L) (3) 122 during operations against enemy Japanese forces in the Ryukyu Chain, 10 and 11 June 1945. Sharply vigilant during hostile air raids against Allied ships on radar picket duty off Okinawa on 10 June, Lt. McCool aided materially in evacuating all survivors from a sinking destroyer which had sustained mortal damage under the devastating attacks. When his own craft was attacked simultaneously by two of the enemy's suicide squadron early in the evening of 11 June, he instantly hurled the full power of his gun batteries against the plunging aircraft, shooting down the first and damaging the second before it crashed his station in the conning tower and engulfed the immediate area in a mass of flames. Although suffering from shrapnel wounds and painful burns, he rallied his concussion-shocked crew and initiated vigorous firefighting measures and then proceeded to the rescue of several trapped in a blazing compartment, subsequently carrying one man to safety despite the excruciating pain of additional severe burns. Unmindful of all personal danger, he continued his efforts without respite until aid arrived from other ships and he was evacuated. By his staunch leadership, capable direction, and indomitable determination throughout the crisis, Lt. McCool saved the lives of many who otherwise might have perished and contributed materially to the saving of his ship for further combat service. His valiant spirit of self-sacrifice in the face of extreme peril sustains and enhances the highest traditions of the U.S. Naval Service.

2842 ◆ McGAHA, CHARLES L.

Rank: Master Sergeant (highest rank: Major)
Service: U.S. Army
Birthday: 26 February 1914
Place of Birth: Crosby, Tennessee
Date of Death: 8 August 1984
Place of Death: Columbus, Georgia
Cemetery: Union Cemetery—New Port, Tennessee
Entered Service at: Crosby, Tennessee
Unit: Company G, 35th Infantry, 25th Infantry Division
Battle or Place of Action: near Lupao, Luzon, Philippine Islands
Date of Action: 7 February 1945
G.O. Number, Date: 30, 2 April 1946
Citation: He displayed conspicuous gallantry and intrepidity. His platoon and one other from Company G were pinned down in a roadside ditch by heavy fire from five Japanese tanks supported by 10 machine guns and a platoon of riflemen. When one of his men fell wounded 40 yards away, he unhesitatingly crossed the road under a hail of bullets and moved the man 75 yards to safety. Although he had suffered a deep arm wound, he returned to his post. Finding the platoon leader seriously wounded, he assumed command and rallied his men. Once more he braved the enemy fire to go to the aid of a litter party removing another wounded soldier. A shell exploded in their midst, wounding him in the shoulder and killing two of the party. He picked up the remaining man, carried him to cover, and then moved out in front deliberately to draw the enemy fire while the American forces, thus protected, withdrew to safety. When the last man had gained the new position, he rejoined his command and there collapsed from loss of blood and exhaustion. M/Sgt. McGaha set an example of courage and leadership in keeping with the highest traditions of the service.

2843 ◆ McGARITY, VERNON

Rank: Technical Sergeant
Service: U.S. Army
Birthday: 1 December 1921
Place of Birth: Right, Tennessee
Entered Service at: Model, Tennessee
Unit: 3d Squad, 3d Platoon, Company L, 3d Battalion, 393d Infantry, 99th Infantry Division
Served as: Squad Leader
Battle or Place of Action: near Krinkelt, Belgium
Date of Action: 16 December 1944
G.O. Number, Date: 6, 11 January 1946
Date of Presentation: 12 October 1945
Place of Presentation: The White House, presented by Pres. Harry S. Truman
Citation: He was painfully wounded in an artillery barrage that preceded the powerful counteroffensive launched by the Germans near Krinkelt, Belgium, on the morning of 16 December 1944. He made his way to an aid station, received treatment, and then refused to be evacuated, choosing to return to his hard-pressed men instead. The fury of the enemy's great Western Front offensive swirled about the position held by T/Sgt. McGarity's small force, but so tenaciously did these men fight on orders to stand firm at all costs that they could not be dislodged despite murderous enemy fire and the breakdown of their communications. During the day the heroic squad leader rescued one of his friends who had been wounded in a forward position, and throughout the night he exhorted his comrades to repulse the enemy's attempts of infiltration. When morning came and the Germans attacked with tanks and infantry, he braved heavy fire to run to an advantageous position where he immobilized the enemy's lead tank with a round from a rocket launcher. Fire from his squad drove the attacking infantrymen back, and three supporting tanks withdrew. He rescued, under heavy fire, another wounded American, and then directed devastating fire on a light cannon which had been brought up by the hostile troops to clear resistance from the area. When ammunition began to run low, T/Sgt. McGarity, remembering an old ammunition hole about 100 yards distant in the general direction of the enemy, braved a concentration of hostile fire to replenish his unit's supply. By circuitous route the enemy managed to emplace a machine gun to the rear and flank of the squad's position, cutting off the only escape route. Unhesitatingly, the gallant soldier took it upon himself to destroy this menace singlehandedly. He left cover, and while under steady fire from the enemy, killed or wounded all

the hostile gunners with deadly accurate rifle fire, and prevented all attempts to re-man the gun. Only when his squad's last round ha d been fired was the enemy able to advance and capture the intrepid leader and his men. The extraordinary bravery and extreme devotion to duty of T/Sgt. McGarity supported a remarkable delaying action which provided the time necessary for assembling reserves and forming a line against which the German striking power was shattered.
Notes: POW

2844 ◆ *McGEE, WILLIAM D.

Rank: Private
Service: U.S. Army
Place of Birth: Indianapolis, Marion County, Indiana
Date of Death: 18 March 1945
Cemetery: A.B.M.C. Luxembourg Cemetery—Luxembourg, France
Entered Service at: Indianapolis, Marion County, Indiana
Unit: Medical Detachment, 304th Infantry, 76th Infantry Division
Served as: Medical Aidman
Battle or Place of Action: near Mulheim, Germany
Date of Action: 18 March 1945
G.O. Number, Date: 21, 26 February 1946
Citation: A medical aidman, he made a night crossing of the Moselle River with troops endeavoring to capture the town of Mulheim. The enemy had retreated in the sector where the assault boats landed, but had left the shore heavily strewn with antipersonnel mines. Two men of the first wave attempting to work their way forward detonated mines which wounded them seriously, leaving them bleeding and in great pain beyond the reach of their comrades. Entirely on his own initiative, Pvt. McGee entered the minefield, brought out one of the injured to comparative safety, and had returned to rescue the second victim when he stepped on a mine and was severely wounded in the resulting explosion. Although suffering intensely and bleeding profusely, he shouted orders that none of his comrades was to risk his life by entering the death-sown field to render first aid that might have saved his life. In making the supreme sacrifice, Pvt. McGee demonstrated a concern for the well-being of his fellow soldiers that transcended all considerations for his own safety and a gallantry in keeping with the highest traditions of the military service.

2845 ◆ *McGILL, TROY A.

Rank: Sergeant
Service: U.S. Army
Birthday: 15 July 1914
Place of Birth: Knoxville, Knox County, Tennessee
Date of Death: 4 March 1944
Cemetery: Knoxville National Cemetery (B-6294) (MH)—Knoxville, Tennessee
Entered Service at: Ada, Pontotoc County, Oklahoma
Unit: Troop G, 5th Cavalry, 1st Cavalry Division
Battle or Place of Action: Admiralty Group, Los Negros Islands
Date of Action: 4 March 1944
G.O. Number, Date: 74, 11 September 1944
Citation: For conspicuous gallantry and intrepidity above and beyond the call of duty in action with the enemy at Los Negros Island, Admiralty Group, on 4 March 1944. In the early morning hours Sgt. McGill, with a squad of eight men, occupied a revetment which bore the brunt of a furious attack by approximately 200 drink-crazed enemy troops. Although covered by crossfire from machine guns on the right and left flank he could receive no support from the remainder of our troops stationed at his rear. All members of the squad were killed or wounded except Sgt. McGill and another man, whom he ordered to return to the next revetment. Courageously resolved to hold his position at all costs, he fired his weapon until it ceased to function. Then, with the enemy only five yards away, he charged from his foxhole in the face of certain death and clubbed the enemy with his rifle in hand-to-hand combat until he was killed. At dawn 105 enemy dead were found around his position. Sgt. McGill's intrepid stand was an inspiration to his comrades and a decisive factor in the defeat of a fanatical enemy.

2846 ◆ *McGRAW, FRANCIS XAVIER

Rank: Private First Class
Service: U.S. Army
Place of Birth: Philadelphia, Philadelphia County, Pennsylvania
Date of Death: 19 November 1944
Cemetery: A.B.M.C. Henri-Chapelle Cemetery—Henri-Chapelle, Belgium
Entered Service at: Camden, Camden County, New Jersey
Unit: Company H, 26th Infantry, 1st Infantry Division
Served as: Heavy Machine Gunner
Battle or Place of Action: near Schevenhutte, Germany
Date of Action: 19 November 1944
G.O. Number, Date: 92, 25 October 1945
Citation: He manned a heavy machine gun emplaced in a foxhole near Schevenhutte, Germany, on 19 November 1944, when the enemy launched a fierce counterattack. Braving an intense hour-long preparatory barrage, he maintained his stand and poured deadly accurate fire into the advancing foot troops until they faltered and came to a halt. The hostile forces brought up a machine gun in an effort to dislodge him but were frustrated when he lifted his gun to an exposed but advantageous position atop a log, courageously stood up in his foxhole, and knocked out the enemy weapon. A rocket blasted his gun from position, but he retrieved it and continued firing. He silenced a second machine gun and then made repeated trips over fire-swept terrain to replenish his ammunition supply. Wounded painfully in this dangerous task, he disregarded his injury and hurried back to his post, where his weapon was showered with mud when another rocket barely missed him. In the midst of the battle, with enemy troops taking advantage of his predicament to press forward, he calmly cleaned his gun, put it back into action and drove off the attackers. He continued to fire until his ammunition was expended, when, with a fierce desire to close with the enemy, he picked up a carbine, killed one enemy soldier, wounded

another, and engaged in a desperate fire-fight with a third until he was mortally wounded by a burst from a machine pistol. The extraordinary heroism and intrepidity displayed by Pvt. McGraw inspired his comrades to great efforts and was a major factor in repulsing the enemy attack.

2847 ◆ *McGUIRE JR., THOMAS BUCHANAN

Rank: Major
Service: U.S. Army Air Corps
Birthday: 1 August 1920
Place of Birth: Ridgewood, Bergen County, New Jersey
Date of Death: 7 January 1945
Place of Death: over Los Negros Island
Cemetery: Arlington National Cemetery (11-426-SH) (MH)—Arlington, Virginia
Entered Service at: Sebring, Highlands County, Florida
Unit: 475th Fighter Group, 5th Air Force
Served as: Pilot/Group Operations Officer
Battle or Place of Action: over Luzon, Philippine Islands
Date of Action: 25-26 December 1944
G.O. Number, Date: 24, 7 March 1946
Date of Presentation: 8 May 1946
Place of Presentation: Patterson, New Jersey, presented by Gen. George C. Kenney to his family
Citation: He fought with conspicuous gallantry and intrepidity over Luzon, Philippine Islands. Voluntarily, he led a squadron of 15 P-38s as top cover for heavy bombers striking Mabalacat Airdrome, where his formation was attacked by 20 aggressive Japanese fighters. In the ensuing action he repeatedly flew to the aid of embattled comrades, driving off enemy assaults while himself under attack and at times outnumbered three to one, and even after his guns jammed, continued the fight by forcing a hostile plane into his wingman's line of fire. Before he started back to his base he had shot down three Zeros. The next day he again volunteered to lead escort fighters on a mission to strongly defended Clark Field. During the resultant engagement he again exposed himself to attacks so that he might rescue a crippled bomber. In rapid succession he shot down one aircraft, parried the attack of four enemy fighters, one of which he shot down, singlehandedly engaged three more Japanese, destroying one, and then shot down still another, his 38th victory in aerial combat. On 7 January 1945, while leading a voluntary fighter sweep over Los Negros Island, he risked an extremely hazardous maneuver at low altitude in an attempt to save a fellow flyer from attack, crashed, and was reported missing in action. With gallant initiative, deep and unselfish concern for the safety of others, and heroic determination to destroy the enemy at all costs, Maj. McGuire set an inspiring example in keeping with the highest traditions of the military service.

2848 ◆ McKINNEY, JOHN R.

Rank: Sergeant (rank at time of action: Private)
Service: U.S. Army
Birthday: 26 February 1921
Place of Birth: Woodcliff, Georgia
Entered Service at: Woodcliff, Georgia
Unit: Company A, 123d Infantry Regiment, 33d Infantry Division
Battle or Place of Action: Tayabas Province, Luzon, Philippine Islands
Date of Action: 11 May 1945
G.O. Number, Date: 14, 4 February 1946
Date of Presentation: 23 January 1946
Place of Presentation: The White House, presented by Pres. Harry S. Truman
Citation: He fought with extreme gallantry to defend the outpost which had been established near Dingalan Bay. Just before daybreak approximately 100 Japanese stealthily attacked the perimeter defense, concentrating on a light machine-gun position manned by three Americans. Having completed a long tour of duty at this gun, Pvt. McKinney was resting a few paces away when an enemy soldier dealt him a glancing blow on the head with a saber. Although dazed by the stroke, he seized his rifle, bludgeoned his attacker, and then shot another assailant who was charging him. Meanwhile, one of his comrades at the machine gun had been wounded and his other companion withdrew carrying the injured man to safety. Alone, Pvt. McKinney was confronted by 10 infantrymen who had captured the machine gun with the evident intent of reversing it to fire into the perimeter. Leaping into the emplacement, he shot seven of them at point-blank range and killed three more with his rifle butt. In the melee the machine gun was rendered inoperative, leaving him only his rifle with which to meet the advancing Japanese, who hurled grenades and directed knee mortar shells into the perimeter. He warily changed position, secured more ammunition, and reloading repeatedly, cut down waves of the fanatical enemy with devastating fire or clubbed them to death in hand-to-hand combat. When assistance arrived, he had thwarted the assault and was in complete control of the area. Thirty-eight dead Japanese around the machine gun and two more at the side of a mortar 45 yards distant was the amazing toll he had exacted singlehandedly. By his indomitable spirit, extraordinary fighting ability, and unwavering courage in the face of tremendous odds, Pvt. McKinney saved his company from possible annihilation and set an example of unsurpassed intrepidity.

2849 ◆ *McTUREOUS JR., ROBERT MILLER

Rank: Private
Service: U.S. Marine Corps
Birthday: 26 March 1924
Place of Birth: Altoona, Lake County, Florida
Date of Death: 11 June 1945
Place of Death: Aboard the Hospital Ship U.S.S. *Relief*
Cemetery: Glendale Cemetery (MH)—Umatilla, Florida
Entered Service at: Florida
Unit: Company H, 3d Battalion, 29th Marines, 6th Marine Division
Battle or Place of Action: Okinawa, Ryukyu Islands
Date of Action: 7 June 1945
Citation: For conspicuous gallantry and intrepidity at the risk of his life above and beyond the call of duty, while serv-

ing with the 3d Battalion, 29th Marines, 6th Marine Division, during action against enemy Japanese forces on Okinawa in the Ryukyu Chain, 7 June 1945. Alert and ready for any hostile counteraction following his company's seizure of an important hill objective, Pvt. McTureous was quick to observe the plight of company stretcher bearers who were suddenly assailed by slashing machine-gun fire as they attempted to evacuate wounded at the rear of the newly won position. Determined to prevent further casualties, he quickly filled his jacket with hand grenades and charged the enemy-occupied caves from which the concentrated barrage was emanating. Coolly disregarding all personal danger as he waged his furious one-man assault, he smashed grenades into the cave entrances, thereby diverting the heaviest fire from the stretcher bearers to his own person and, resolutely returning to his own lines under a blanketing hail of rifle and machine-gun fire to replenish his supply of grenades, dauntlessly continued his systematic reduction of Japanese strength until he himself sustained serious wounds after silencing a large number of the hostile guns. Aware of his own critical condition and unwilling to further endanger the lives of his comrades, he stoically crawled a distance of 200 yards to a sheltered position within friendly lines before calling for aid. By his fearless initiative and bold tactics, Pvt. McTureous had succeeded in neutralizing the enemy fire, killing six Japanese troops, and effectively disorganizing the remainder of the savagely defended garrison. His outstanding valor and heroic spirit of self-sacrifice during a critical stage of operations reflect the highest credit upon himself and the U.S. Naval Service.

2850 ◆ *McVEIGH, JOHN J.

Rank: Sergeant
Service: U.S. Army
Place of Birth: Philadelphia, Philadelphia County, Pennsylvania
Date of Death: 29 August 1944
Cemetery: Holy Sepulchre Cemetery—Philadelphia, Pennsylvania
Entered Service at: Philadelphia, Philadelphia County, Pennsylvania
Unit: Company H, 23d Infantry, 2d Infantry Division
Battle or Place of Action: near Brest, France
Date of Action: 29 August 1944
G.O. Number, Date: 24, 6 April 1945
Citation: For conspicuous gallantry and intrepidity at the risk of his life above and beyond the call of duty near Brest, France, on 29 August 1944. Shortly after dusk an enemy counterattack of platoon strength was launched against one platoon of Company G, 23d Infantry. Since the Company G platoon was not dug in and had just begun to assume defensive positions along a hedge, part of the line sagged momentarily under heavy fire from small-arms and two flak guns, leaving a section of heavy machine guns holding a wide frontage without rifle protection. The enemy drive moved so swiftly that German riflemen were soon almost on top of one machine-gun position. Sgt. McVeigh, heedless of a tremendous amount of small-arms and flak fire directed toward him, stood up in full view of the enemy and directed the fire of his squad on the attacking Germans until his position was almost overrun. He then drew his trench knife, and singlehandedly charged several of the enemy. In a savage hand-to-hand struggle, Sgt. McVeigh killed one German with the knife, his only weapon, and was advancing on three more of the enemy when he was shot down and killed with small-arms fire at point-blank range. Sgt. McVeigh's heroic act allowed the two remaining men in his squad to concentrate their machine-gun fire on the attacking enemy and then turn their weapons on the three Germans in the road, killing all three. Fire from this machine gun and the other gun of the section was almost entirely responsible for stopping the enemy assault, and allowing the rifle platoon to which it was attached time to reorganize, assume positions on and hold the high ground gained during the day.

2851 ◆ *McWHORTER, WILLIAM A.

Rank: Private First Class (highest rank: Sergeant)
Service: U.S. Army
Birthday: 7 December 1918
Place of Birth: Liberty, Pickins County, South Carolina
Date of Death: 5 December 1944
Cemetery: West View Cemetery (MH)—Liberty, South Carolina
Entered Service at: Liberty, Pickins County, South Carolina
Unit: Company M, 126th Infantry, 32d Infantry Division
Served as: Machine Gunner
Battle or Place of Action: Leyte, Philippine Islands
Date of Action: 5 December 1944
G.O. Number, Date: 82, 27 September 1945
Citation: He displayed gallantry and intrepidity at the risk of his life above and beyond the call of duty while engaged in operations against the enemy. Pfc. McWhorter, a machine gunner, was emplaced in a defensive position with one assistant when the enemy launched a heavy attack. Manning the gun and opening fire, he killed several members of an advancing demolition squad, when one of the enemy succeeded in throwing a fused demolition charge in the entrenchment. Without hesitation and with complete disregard for his own safety, Pfc. McWhorter picked up the improvised grenade and deliberately held it close to his body, bending over and turning away from his companion. The charge exploded, killing him instantly, but leaving his assistant unharmed. Pfc. McWhorter's outstanding heroism and supreme sacrifice in shielding a comrade reflect the highest traditions of the military service.

2852 ◆ MEAGHER, JOHN WILLIAM

Rank: Technical Sergeant
Service: U.S. Army
Birthday: 5 December 1917
Place of Birth: Jersey City, Hudson County, New Jersey
Entered Service at: Jersey City, Hudson County, New Jersey
Unit: 2d Platoon, Company E, 2d Battalion, 305th Infantry, 77th Infantry Division

Served as: Acting Platoon Leader
Battle or Place of Action: near Ozato, Okinawa, Ryukyu Islands
Date of Action: 19 June 1945
G.O. Number, Date: 60, 26 June 1946
Date of Presentation: 14 June 1946
Place of Presentation: The White House (lawn), presented by Pres. Harry S. Truman
Citation: He displayed conspicuous gallantry and intrepidity above and beyond the call of duty. In the heat of the fight, he mounted an assault tank, and, with bullets splattering about him, designated targets to the gunner. Seeing an enemy soldier carrying an explosive charge dash for the tank treads, he shouted fire orders to the gunner, leaped from the tank, and bayonetted the charging soldier. Knocked unconscious and his rifle destroyed, he regained consciousness, secured a machine gun from the tank, and began a furious one-man assault on the enemy. Firing from his hip, moving through vicious crossfire that ripped through his clothing, he charged the nearest pillbox, killing six. Going on amid the hail of bullets and grenades, he dashed for a second enemy gun, running out of ammunition just as he reached the position. He grasped his empty gun by the barrel and in a violent onslaught killed the crew. By his fearless assault T/Sgt. Meagher singlehandedly broke the enemy resistance, enabling his platoon to take its objective and continue the advance.

2853 ◆ MERLI, GINO JOSEPH

Rank: Private First Class (highest rank: Sergeant)
Service: U.S. Army
Birthday: 13 May 1924
Place of Birth: Scranton, Lackawanna County, Pennsylvania
Entered Service at: Peckville, Lackawanna County, Pennsylvania
Unit: Weapons Platoon, Company H, 2d Battalion, 18th Infantry, 1st Infantry Division
Served as: Machine Gunner
Battle or Place of Action: near Sars la Bruyere, Belgium
Date of Action: 4-5 September 1944
G.O. Number, Date: 64, 4 August 1945
Date of Presentation: 15 June 1945
Place of Presentation: The White House, presented by Pres. Harry S. Truman
Citation: He was serving as a machine gunner in the vicinity of Sars-la-Bruyere, Belgium, on the night of 4–5 September 1944, when his company was attacked by a superior German force. Its position was overrun and he was surrounded when our troops were driven back by overwhelming numbers and firepower. Disregarding the fury of the enemy fire concentrated on him he maintained his position, covering the withdrawal of our riflemen and breaking the force of the enemy pressure. His assistant machine gunner was killed and the position captured; the other eight members of the section were forced to surrender. Pfc. Merli slumped down beside the dead assistant gunner and feigned death. No sooner had the enemy group withdrawn than he was up and firing in all directions. Once more his position was taken and the captors found two apparently lifeless bodies. Throughout the night Pfc. Merli stayed at his weapon. By daybreak the enemy had suffered heavy losses, and as our troops launched an assault, asked for a truce. Our negotiating party, who accepted the German surrender, found Pfc. Merli still at his gun. On the battlefield lay 52 enemy dead, 19 of whom were directly in front of the gun. Pfc. Merli's gallantry and courage, and the losses and confusion that he caused the enemy, contributed materially to our victory.

2854 ◆ *MERRELL, JOSEPH FREDERICK

Rank: Private
Service: U.S. Army
Birthday: 21 August 1926
Place of Birth: Staten Island, Richmond County, New York
Date of Death: 18 April 1945
Cemetery: St. Peter's Cemetery (MH)—Staten Island, New York
Entered Service at: Staten Island, Richmond County, New York
Unit: Company I, 3d Battalion, 15th Infantry, 3d Infantry Division
Battle or Place of Action: near Lohe, Germany
Date of Action: 18 April 1945
G.O. Number, Date: 21, 26 February 1946
Citation: He made a gallant, one-man attack against vastly superior enemy forces near Lohe, Germany. His unit, attempting a quick conquest of hostile hill positions that would open the route to Nuremberg before the enemy could organize his defense of that city, was pinned down by brutal fire from rifles, machine pistols, and two heavy machine guns. Entirely on his own initiative, Pvt. Merrell began a single-handed assault. He ran 100 yards through concentrated fire, barely escaping death at each stride, and at point-blank range engaged four German machine pistolmen with his rifle, killing all of them while their bullets ripped his uniform. As he started forward again, his rifle was smashed by a sniper's bullet, leaving him armed only with three grenades. But he did not hesitate. He zigzagged 200 yards through a hail of bullets to within 10 yards of the first machine gun, where he hurled two grenades and then rushed the position ready to fight with his bare hands if necessary. In the emplacement he seized a Luger pistol and killed what Germans had survived the grenade blast. Rearmed, he crawled toward the second machine gun located 30 yards away, killing four Germans in camouflaged foxholes on the way, but himself receiving a critical wound in the abdomen. And yet he went on, staggering, bleeding, disregarding bullets which tore through the folds of his clothing and glanced off his helmet. He threw his last grenade into the machine-gun nest and stumbled on to wipe out the crew. He had completed this self-appointed task when a machine pistol burst killed him instantly. In his spectacular one-man attack Pvt. Merrell killed six Germans in the first machine-gun emplacement, seven in the next, and an additional 10 infantrymen who were astride his path to the weapons which would have decimated his unit had he not assumed the burden of the assault and stormed the enemy positions with utter fearlessness, intrepidity of the highest order, and a willingness to sacrifice his own life so that his comrades could go on to victory.

2855 ◆ *MESSERSCHMIDT, HAROLD O.

Rank: Sergeant
Service: U.S. Army
Birthday: 1924
Place of Birth: Grier City, Pennsylvania
Date of Death: 17 September 1944
Cemetery: Christ White Church Cemetery—Rush Township, Pennsylvania
Entered Service at: Chester, Delaware County, Pennsylvania
Unit: Company L, 30th Infantry, 3d Infantry Division
Battle or Place of Action: near Radden, France
Date of Action: 17 September 1944
G.O. Number, Date: 71, 17 July 1946
Citation: He displayed conspicuous gallantry and intrepidity above and beyond the call of duty. Braving machine-gun, machine pistol, and rifle fire, he moved fearlessly and calmly from man to man along his 40-yard squad front, encouraging each to hold against the overwhelming assault of a fanatical foe surging up the hillside. Knocked to the ground by a burst from an enemy automatic weapon, he immediately jumped to his feet, and ignoring his grave wounds, fired his submachine gun at the enemy that was now upon them, killing five and wounding many others before his ammunition was spent. Virtually surrounded by a frenzied foe and all of his squad now casualties, he elected to fight alone, using his empty submachine gun as a bludgeon against his assailants. Spotting one of the enemy about to kill a wounded comrade, he felled the German with a blow of his weapon. Seeing friendly reinforcements running up the hill, he continued furiously to wield his empty gun against the foe in a new attack, and it was thus that he made the supreme sacrifice. Sgt. Messerschmidt's sustained heroism in hand-to-hand combat with superior enemy forces was in keeping with the highest traditions of the military service.

2856 ◆ *METZGER JR., WILLIAM EDWARD

Rank: Second Lieutenant
Service: U.S. Army Air Corps
Birthday: 9 February 1922
Place of Birth: Lima, Allen County, Ohio
Date of Death: 9 November 1944
Cemetery: Woodlawn Cemetery—Lima, Ohio
Entered Service at: Lima, Allen County, Ohio
Unit: 729th Bombardment Squadron, 452d Bombardment Group, 8th Air Force
Served as: Copilot of a B-17
Battle or Place of Action: Saarbrucken, Germany
Date of Action: 9 November 1944
G.O. Number, Date: 38, 16 May 1945
Citation: On a bombing run upon the marshaling yards at Saarbrucken, Germany, on 9 November 1944, a B-17 aircraft on which 2d Lt. Metzger was serving as copilot was seriously damaged by antiaircraft fire. Three of the aircraft's engines were damaged beyond control and on fire; dangerous flames from the No. 4 engine were leaping back as far as the tail assembly. Flares in the cockpit were ingited and a fire roared therein which was further increased by free-flowing fluid from damaged hydraulic lines. The interphone system was rendered useless. In addition to these serious mechanical difficulties the engineer was wounded in the leg and the radio operator's arm was severed below the elbow. Suffering from intense pain, despite the application of a tourniquet, the radio operator fell unconscious. Faced with the imminent explosion of his aircraft and death to his entire crew, mere seconds before bombs away on the target, 2d Lt. Metzger and his pilot conferred. Something had to be done immediately to save the life of the wounded radio operator. The lack of a static line and the thought that his unconscious body striking the ground in unknown territory would not bring immediate medical attention forced a quick decision. Second Lt. Metzger and his pilot decided to fly the flaming aircraft to friendly territory and then attempt to crash land. Bombs were released on the target and the crippled aircraft proceeded along to Allied-controlled territory. When that had been reached 2d Lt. Metzger personally informed all crewmembers to bail out upon the suggestion of the pilot, 2d Lt. Metzger chose to remain with the pilot for the crash landing in order to assist him in this emergency. With only one normally functioning engine and with the danger of explosion much greater, the aircraft banked into an open field, and when it was at an altitude of 100 feet it exploded, crashed, exploded again, and then disintegrated. All three crewmembers were instantly killed. Second Lt. Metzger's loyalty to his crew, his determination to accomplish the task set forth to him, and his deed of knowingly performing what may have been his last service to his country was an example of valor at its highest.

2857 ◆ MICHAEL, EDWARD STANLEY

Rank: First Lieutenant (highest rank: Lieutenant Colonel)
Service: U.S. Army Air Corps/U.S. Air Force
Birthday: 2 May 1918
Place of Birth: Chicago, Cook County, Illinois
Date of Death: 10 May 1994
Place of Death: Fairfield, California
Cemetery: Springfield, Utah
Entered Service at: Chicago, Cook County, Illinois
Unit: 364th Bombardment Squadron, 305th Bombardment Group, 40th Combat Wing, 2d Air Division, 8th Air Force
Served as: Aircraft Commander/Pilot of a B-17
Battle or Place of Action: over Stettin, Germany
Date of Action: 11 April 1944
G.O. Number, Date: 5, 15 January 1945
Date of Presentation: 10 January 1945
Place of Presentation: The White House, presented by Pres. Franklin D. Roosevelt
Citation: For conspicuous gallantry and intrepidity above and beyond the call of duty while serving as pilot of a B-17 aircraft on a heavy-bombardment mission to Germany, 11 April 1944. The group in which 1st Lt. Michael was flying was attacked by a swarm of fighters. His plane was singled out and the fighters pressed their attacks home recklessly, completely disregarding the Allied fighter escort and their own intensive flak. His plane was riddled from nose to tail with exploding cannon shells and knocked out of formation, with a large number of fighters following it down, blasting it with

cannon fire as it descended. A cannon shell exploded in the cockpit, wounded the copilot, wrecked the instruments, and blew out the side window. First Lt. Michael was seriously and painfully wounded in the right thigh. Hydraulic fluid filmed over the windshield making visibility impossible, and smoke filled the cockpit. The controls failed to respond and 3,000 feet were lost before he succeeded in leveling off. The radio operator informed him that the whole bomb bay was in flames as a result of the explosion of three cannon shells, which had ignited the incendiaries. With a full load of incendiaries in the bomb bay and a considerable gas load in the tanks, the danger of fire enveloping the plane and the tanks exploding seemed imminent. When the emergency release lever failed to function, 1st Lt. Michael at once gave the order to bail out and seven of the crew left the plane. Seeing the bombardier firing the navigator's gun at the enemy planes, 1st Lt. Michael ordered him to bail out as the plane was liable to explode any minute. When the bombardier looked for his parachute he found that it had been riddled with 20-mm fragments and was useless. First Lt. Michael, seeing the ruined parachute, realized that if the plane was abandoned the bombardier would perish and decided that the only chance would be a crash landing. Completely disregarding his own painful and profusely bleeding wounds , but thinking only of the safety of the remaining crewmembers, he gallantly evaded the enemy using violent evasive action despite the battered condition of his plane. After the plane had been under sustained enemy attack for fully 45 minutes, 1st Lt. Michael finally lost the persisent fighters in a cloud bank. Upon emerging, an accurate barrage of flak caused him to come down to treetop level where flak towers poured a continuous rain of fire on the plane. He continued into France, realizing that at any moment a crash landing might have to be attempted, but trying to get as far as possible to increase the escape possibilities if a safe landing could be achieved. First Lt. Michael flew the plane until he became exhausted from loss of blood, which had formed on the floor in pools, and he lost consciousness. The copilot succeeded in reaching England and sighted an RAF field near the coast. First Lt. Michael finally regained consciousness and insisted upon taking over the controls to land the plane. The undercarriage was useless; the bomb bay doors were jammed open; the hydraulic system and altimeter were shot out. In addition, there was no airspeed indicator, the ball turret was jammed with the guns pointing downward, and the flaps would not respond. Despite these apparently insurmountable obstacles, he landed the plane without mishap.

2858 ◆ *MICHAEL, HARRY J.

Rank: Second Lieutenant
Service: U.S. Army
Birthday: 13 March 1922
Place of Birth: Benton, Indiana
Date of Death: 14 March 1945
Cemetery: Violett Cemetery (MH)—Goshen, Indiana
Entered Service at: Milford, Kosciusko County, Indiana
Unit: Company L, 318th Infantry, 80th Infantry Division
Served as: Platoon Leader
Battle or Place of Action: near Neiderzerf, Germany
Date of Action: 14 March 1945
G.O. Number, Date: 18, 13 February 1946
Citation: He was serving as a rifle platoon leader when his company began an assault on a wooded ridge northeast of the village of Neiderzerf, Germany, early on 13 March 1945. A short distance up the side of the hill, 2d Lt. Michael, at the head of his platoon, heard the click of an enemy machine-gun bolt. Quietly halting the company, he silently moved off into the woods and discovered two enemy machine guns and crews. Executing a sudden charge, he completely surprised the enemy and captured the guns and crews. At daybreak, enemy voices were heard in the thick woods ahead. Leading his platoon in a flanking movement, they charged the enemy with hand grenades and, after a bitter fight, captured 25 members of an SS mountain division, three artillery pieces, and 20 horses. While his company was establishing its position, 2d Lt. Michael made two personal reconnaissance missions of the wood on his left flank. On his first mission he killed two, wounded four, and captured six enemy soldiers singlehandedly. On the second mission he captured seven prisoners. During the afternoon he led his platoon on a frontal assault of a line of enemy pillboxes, successfully capturing the objective, killing 10, and capturing 30 prisoners. The following morning the company was subjected to sniper fire and 2d Lt. Michael, in an attempt to find the hidden sniper, was shot and killed. The inspiring leadership and heroic agressiveness displayed by 2d Lt. Michael upheld the highest traditions of the military service.

2859 ◆ *MILLER, ANDREW

Rank: Staff Sergeant
Service: U.S. Army
Birthday: 11 August 1916
Place of Birth: Manitowoc, Manitowoc County, Wisconsin
Date of Death: 29 November 1944
Cemetery: A.B.M.C. Lorraine Cemetery (A-26-1)—St. Avold, France
Entered Service at: Two Rivers, Manitowoc County, Wisconsin
Unit: Company G, 377th Infantry, 95th Infantry Division
Served as: Squad Leader
Battle or Place of Action: Woippy, France, through Metz to Kerprich Hemmersdorf, Germany
Date of Action: 16-29 November 1944
G.O. Number, Date: 74, 1 September 1945
Citation: For performing a series of heroic deeds from 16 to 29 November 1944, during his company's relentless drive from Woippy, France, through Metz to Kerprich Hemmersdorf, Germany. As he led a rifle squad on 16 November at Woippy, a crossfire from enemy machine guns pinned down his unit. Ordering his men to remain under cover, he went forward alone, entered a building housing one of the guns, and forced five Germans to surrender at bayonet point. He then took the second gun singlehandedly by hurling grenades into the enemy position, killing two, wounding three more, and taking two additional prisoners. At the outskirts of Metz the next day, when his platoon, confused by

heavy explosions and the withdrawal of friendly tanks, retired, he fearlessly remained behind armed with an automatic rifle and exchanged bursts with a German machine gun until he silenced the enemy weapon. His quick action in covering his comrades gave the platoon time to regroup and carry on the fight. On 19 November S/Sgt. Miller led an attack on large enemy barracks. Covered by his squad, he crawled to a barracks window, climbed in, and captured six riflemen occupying the room. His men, and then the entire company, followed through the window, scoured the building, and took 75 prisoners. S/Sgt. Miller volunteered, with three comrades, to capture Gestapo officers who were preventing the surrender of German troops in another building. He ran a gauntlet of machine-gun fire and was lifted through a window. Inside, he found himself covered by a machine pistol, but he persuaded the four Gestapo agents confronting him to surrender. Early the next morning, when strong hostile forces punished his company with heavy fire, S/Sgt. Miller assumed the task of destroying a well-placed machine gun. He was knocked down by a rifle grenade as he climbed an open stairway in a house, but pressed on with a bazooka to find an advantageous spot from which to launch his rocket. He discovered that he could fire only from t he roof, a position where he would draw tremendous enemy fire. Facing the risk, he moved into the open, coolly took aim, and scored a direct hit on the hostile emplacement, wreaking such havoc that the enemy troops became completely demoralized and began surrendering by the score. The following day, in Metz, he captured 12 more prisoners and silenced an enemy machine gun after volunteering for a hazardous mission in advance of his company's position. On 29 November, as Company G climbed a hill overlooking Kerprich Hemmersdorf, enemy fire pinned the unit to the ground. S/Sgt. Miller, on his own initiative, pressed ahead with his squad past the company's leading element to meet the surprise resistance. His men stood up and advanced deliberately, firing as they went. Inspired by S/Sgt. Miller's leadership, the platoon followed, and then another platoon arose and grimly closed with the Germans. The enemy action was smothered, but at the cost of S/Sgt. Miller's life. His tenacious devotion to the attack, his gallant choice to expose himself to enemy action rather than endanger his men, his limitless bravery, assured the success of Company G.

2860 ◆ MILLS, JAMES HENRY

Rank: Private
Service: U.S. Army
Birthday: 2 May 1923
Place of Birth: Fort Meade, Polk County, Florida
Date of Death: 11 November 1973
Cemetery: Oak Hill Burial Park—South Lakeland, Florida
Entered Service at: Fort Meade, Polk County, Florida
Unit: Company F, 15th Infantry, 3d Infantry Division
Battle or Place of Action: near Cisterna di Littoria, Italy
Date of Action: 24 May 1944
G.O. Number, Date: 87, 14 November 1944
Citation: For conspicuous gallantry and intrepidity at the risk of life above and beyond the call of duty. Pvt. Mills, undergoing his baptism of fire, preceded his platoon down a draw to reach a position from which an attack could be launched against a heavily fortified strongpoint. After advancing about 300 yards, Pvt. Mills was fired on by a machine gun only five yards distant. He killed the gunner with one shot and forced the surrender of the assistant gunner. Continuing his advance, he saw a German soldier in a camouflaged position behind a large bush pulling the pin of a potato-masher grenade. Covering the German with his rifle, Pvt. Mills forced him to drop the grenade and captured him. When another enemy soldier attempted to throw a hand grenade into the draw, Pvt. Mills killed him with one shot. Brought under fire by a machine gun, two machine pistols, and three rifles at a range of only 50 feet, he charged headlong into the furious chain of automatic fire, shooting his M1 from the hip. The enemy was completely demoralized by Pvt. Mills' daring charge, and when he reached a point within 10 feet of their position, all six surrendered. As he neared the end of the draw, Pvt. Mills was brought under fire by a machine gunner 20 yards distant. Despite the fact that he had absolutely no cover, Pvt. Mills killed the gunner with one shot. Two enemy soldiers near the machine gunner fired wildly at Pvt. Mills and then fled. Pvt. Mills fired twice, killing one of the enemy. Continuing on to the position, he captured a fourth soldier. When it became apparent that an assault on the strongpoint would in all probability cause heavy casualties on the platoon, Pvt. Mills volunteered to cover the advance down a shallow ditch to a point within 50 yards of the objective. Standing on the bank in full view of the enemy less than 100 yards away, he shouted and fired his rifle directly into the position. His ruse worked exactly as planned. The enemy centered his fire on Pvt. Mills. Trace rs passed within inches of his body, rifle and machine-pistol bullets ricocheted off the rocks at his feet. Yet he stood there firing until his rifle was empty. Intent on covering the movement of his platoon, Pvt. Mills jumped into the draw, reloaded his weapon, climbed out again, and continued to lay down a base of fire. Repeating this action four times, he enabled his platoon to reach the designated spot undiscovered, from which position it assaulted and overwhelmed the enemy, capturing 22 Germans and taking the objective without casualties.

2861 ◆ *MINICK, JOHN W.

Rank: Staff Sergeant
Service: U.S. Army
Birthday: 14 June 1908
Place of Birth: Wall, Allegheny County, Pennsylvania
Date of Death: 21 November 1944
Cemetery: Westminster Cemetery—Carlisle, Pennsylvania
Entered Service at: Carlisle, Cumberland County, Pennsylvania
Unit: Company I, 3d Battalion, 121st Infantry, 8th Infantry Division
Served as: Squad Leader
Battle or Place of Action: near Hurtgen, Germany
Date of Action: 21 November 1944
Citation: He displayed conspicuous gallantry and intrepidity at the risk of his own life, above and beyond the call of duty, in action involving actual conflict with the enemy on 21 November 1944, near Hurtgen, Germany. S/Sgt. Minick's

battalion was halted in its advance by extensive minefields, exposing troops to heavy concentrations of enemy artillery and mortar fire. Further delay in the advance would result in numerous casualties, and a movement through the minefield was essential. Voluntarily, S/Sgt. Minick led four men through hazardous barbed wire and debris, finally making his way through the minefield for a distance of 300 yards. When an enemy machine gun opened fire, he signaled his men to take covered positions, edged his way alone toward the flank of the weapon, and opened fire, killing two members of the guncrew and capturing three others. Moving forward again, he encountered and engaged singlehandedly an entire company killing 20 Germans and capturing 20, and enabling his platoon to capture the remainder of the hostile group. Again moving ahead and spearheading his battalion's advance, he again encountered machine-gun fire. Crawling forward toward the weapon, he reached a point from which he knocked the weapon out of action. Still another minefield had to be crossed. Undeterred, S/Sgt. Minick advanced forward alone through constant enemy fire and while thus moving, detonated a mine and was instantly killed.

2862 ◆ *MINUE, NICHOLAS

Rank: Private
Service: U.S. Army
Birthday: 1899
Place of Birth: Sedden, Poland
Date of Death: 28 April 1943
Cemetery: A.B.M.C. North Africa Cemetery (E-8-4)—Carthage, Tunisia
Entered Service at: Carteret, Middlesex County, New Jersey
Unit: Company A, 6th Armored Infantry, 1st Armored Division
Battle or Place of Action: near Medjez-el-Bab, Tunisia
Date of Action: 28 April 1943
G.O. Number, Date: 24, 25 March 1944
Citation: For distinguishing himself conspicuously by gallantry and intrepidity at the loss of life above and beyond the call of duty in action with the enemy on 28 April 1943, in the vicinity of Medjez-el-Bab, Tunisia. When the advance of the assault elements of Company A was held up by flanking fire from an enemy machine-gun nest, Pvt. Minue voluntarily, alone, and unhesitatingly, with complete disregard of his own welfare, charged the enemy entrenched position with fixed bayonet. Pvt. Minue assaulted the enemy under a withering machine-gun and rifle fire, killing approximately 10 enemy machine gunners and riflemen. After completely destroying this position, Pvt. Minue continued forward, routing enemy riflemen from dugout positions until he was fatally wounded. The courage, fearlessness, and aggressiveness displayed by Pvt. Minue in the face of inevitable death was unquestionably the factor that gave his company the offensive spirit that was necessary for advancing and driving the enemy from the entire sector.

2863 ◆ *MONTEITH JR., JIMMIE W.

Rank: First Lieutenant
Service: U.S. Army
Birthday: 1 July 1917
Place of Birth: Low Moor, Alleghany County, Virginia
Date of Death: 6 June 1944
Cemetery: A.B.M.C. Normandy Cemetery (I-20-12)—St Laurent-sur-Mer, France
Entered Service at: Richmond, Richmond County, Virginia
Unit: 16th Infantry, 1st Infantry Division
Battle or Place of Action: near Colleville-sur-Mer, France
Date of Action: 6 June 1944
G.O. Number, Date: 20, 29 March 1945
Place of Presentation: Richmond, Virginia, presented by Brig. Gen. Frank Dorn to his family
Citation: For conspicuous gallantry and intrepidity above and beyond the call of duty on 6 June 1944, near Colleville-sur-Mer, France. First Lt. Monteith landed with the initial assault waves on the coast of France under heavy enemy fire. Without regard to his own personal safety he continually moved up and down the beach reorganizing men for further assault. He then led the assault over a narrow protective ledge and across the flat, exposed terrain to the comparative safety of a cliff. Retracing his steps across the field to the beach, he moved over to where two tanks were buttoned up and blind under violent enemy artillery and machine-gun fire. Completely exposed to the intense fire, 1st Lt. Monteith led the tanks on foot through a minefield and into firing positions. Under his direction several enemy positions were destroyed. He then rejoined his company and under his leadership his men captured an advantageous position on the hill. Supervising the defense of his newly won position against repeated vicious counterattacks, he continued to ignore his own personal safety, repeatedly crossing the 200 or 300 yards of open terrain under heavy fire to strengthen links in his defensive chain. When the enemy succeeded in completely surrounding 1st Lt. Monteith and his unit and while leading the fight out of the situation, 1st Lt. Monteith was killed by enemy fire. The courage, gallantry, and intrepid leadership displayed by 1st Lt. Monteith is worthy of emulation.

2864 ◆ MONTGOMERY, JACK CLEVELAND

Rank: First Lieutenant
Service: U.S. Army
Birthday: 23 July 1917
Place of Birth: Long, Oklahoma
Entered Service at: Sallisaw, Sequoyah County, Oklahoma
Unit: 1st Platoon, Company I, 3d Battalion, 180th Infantry, 45th Infantry Division
Served as: Platoon Leader
Battle or Place of Action: near Padiglione, Italy
Date of Action: 22 February 1944
G.O. Number, Date: 5, 15 January 1945
Date of Presentation: 10 January 1945
Place of Presentation: The White House (Oval Office), presented by Pres. Franklin D. Roosevelt
Citation: For conspicuous gallantry and intrepidity at the risk of life above and beyond the call of duty on 22 February 1944, near Padiglione, Italy. Two hours before daybreak a strong force of enemy infantry established themselves in three echelons at 50 yards, 100 yards, and 300 yards, respectively, in front of the rifle platoons commanded by 1st Lt.

Montgomery. The closest position, consisting of four machine guns and one mortar, threatened the immediate security of the platoon position. Seizing an M1 rifle and several hand grenades, 1st Lt. Montgomery crawled up a ditch to within hand-grenade range of the enemy. Then climbing boldly onto a little mound, he fired his rifle and threw his grenades so accurately that he killed eight of the enemy and captured the remaining four. Returning to his platoon, he called for artillery fire on a house, in and around which he suspected that the majority of the enemy had entrenched themselves. Arming himself with a carbine, he proceeded along the shallow ditch, as withering fire from the riflemen and machine gunners in the second position was concentrated on him. He attacked this position with such fury that seven of the enemy surrendered to him, and both machine guns were silenced. Three German dead were found in the vicinity later that morning. First Lt. Montgomery continued boldly toward the house, 300 yards from his platoon position. It was now daylight, and the enemy observation was excellent across the flat open terrain which led to 1st Lt. Montgomery's objective. When the artillery barrage had lifted, 1st Lt. Montgomery ran fearlessly toward the strongly defended position. As the enemy started streaming out of the house, 1st Lt. Montgomery, unafraid of treacherous snipers, exposed himself daringly to assemble the surrendering enemy and send them to the rear. His fearless, aggressive, and intrepid actions that morning accounted for a total of 11 enemy dead, 32 prisoners, and an unknown number of wounded. That night, while ai ding an adjacent unit to repulse a counterattack, he was struck by mortar fragments and seriously wounded. The selflessness and courage exhibited by 1st Lt. Montgomery in alone attacking three strong enemy positions inspired his men to a degree beyond estimation.

2865 ◆ *MOON JR., HAROLD HERMAN

Rank: Private
Service: U.S. Army
Birthday: 15 March 1921
Place of Birth: Albuquerque, Bernalillo County, New Mexico
Date of Death: 21 October 1944
Cemetery: Sunset Memorial Park (MH)—Albuquerque, New Mexico
Entered Service at: Gardena, Los Angeles County, California
Unit: Company G, 34th Infantry, 24th Infantry Division
Battle or Place of Action: Pawig, Leyte, Philippine Islands
Date of Action: 21 October 1944
G.O. Number, Date: 104, 15 November 1945
Citation: He fought with conspicuous gallantry and intrepidity when powerful Japanese counterblows were being struck in a desperate effort to annihilate a newly won beachhead. In a forward position, armed with a submachine gun, he met the brunt of a strong, well-supported night attack which quickly enveloped his platoon's flanks. Many men in nearby positions were killed or injured, and Pvt. Moon was wounded as his foxhole became the immediate object of a concentration of mortar and machine-gun fire. Nevertheless, he maintained his stand, poured deadly fire into the enemy, daringly exposed himself to hostile fire time after time to exhort and inspire what American troops were left in the immediate area. A Japanese officer, covered by machine-gun fire and hidden by an embankment, attempted to knock out his position with grenades, but Pvt. Moon, after protracted and skillful maneuvering, killed him. When the enemy advanced a light machine gun to within 20 yards of the shattered perimeter and fired with telling effects on the remnants of the platoon, he stood up to locate the gun and remained exposed, while calling back range corrections to friendly mortars which knocked out the weapon. A little later he killed two Japanese as they charged an aidman. By dawn his position, the focal point of the attack for more than four hours, was virtually surrounded. In a fanatical effort to reduce it and kill its defender, an entire platoon charged with fixed bayonets. Firing from a sitting position, Pvt. Moon calmly emptied his magazine into the advancing horde, killing 18 and repulsing the attack. In a final display of bravery, he stood up to throw a grenade at a machine gun which had opened fire on the right flank. He was hit and instantly killed, falling in the position from which he had not been driven by the fiercest enemy action. Nearly 200 dead Japanese were found within 100 yards of his foxhole. The continued tenacity, combat sagacity, and magnificent heroism with which Pvt. Moon fought on against overwhelming odds contributed in a large measure to breaking up a powerful enemy threat and did much to insure our initial successes during a most important operation.

2866 ◆ MORGAN, JOHN CARY "RED"

Rank: Second Lieutenant (rank at time of action: Flight Officer) (highest rank: Lieutenant Colonel)
Service: U.S. Army Air Corps/U.S. Air Force
Birthday: 24 August 1914
Place of Birth: Vernon, Wilbarger County, Texas
Date of Death: 17 January 1991
Place of Death: Papillton, Nebraska
Cemetery: Arlington National Cemetery (59-351) (MH)—Arlington, Virginia
Entered Service at: London, England
Unit: 326th Bombardment Squadron, 92d Bombardment Group, 8th Air Force
Served as: Copilot of a B-17
Battle or Place of Action: over Kiel, Germany
Date of Action: 28 July 1943
G.O. Number, Date: 85, 17 December 1943
Date of Presentation: 18 December 1943
Place of Presentation: Widewing, England
Citation: For conspicuous gallantry and intrepidity above and beyond the call of duty, while participating on a bombing mission over enemy-occupied continental Europe, 28 July 1943. Prior to reaching the German coast on the way to the target, the B-17 airplane in which 2d Lt. Morgan was serving as copilot was attacked by a large force of enemy fighters, during which the oxygen system to the tail, waist, and radio gun positions was knocked out. A frontal attack placed a cannon shell through the windshield, totally shattering it, and the pilot's skull was split open by a .303-caliber shell, leaving

him in a crazed condition. The pilot fell over the steering wheel, tightly clamping his arms around it. Second Lt. Morgan at once grasped the controls from his side and, by sheer strength, pulled the airplane back into formation despite the frantic struggles of the semiconscious pilot. The interphone had been destroyed, rendering it impossible to call for help. At this time the top turret gunner fell to the floor and down through the hatch with his arms shot off at the shoulder and a gaping wound in his side. The waist, tail, and radio gunners had lost consciousness from lack of oxygen and, hearing no fire from their guns, the copilot believed they had bailed out. The wounded pilot still offered desperate resistance in his crazed attempts to fly the airplane. There remained the prospect of flying to and over the target and back to a friendly base wholly unassisted. In the face of this desperate situation, 2d Lt. Morgan made his decision to continue the flight and protect any members of the crew who might still be in the ship and for two hours he flew in formation with one hand at the controls and the other holding off the struggling pilot before the navigator entered the steering compartment and relieved the situation. The miraculous and heroic performance of 2d Lt. Morgan on this occasion resulted in the successful completion of a vital bombing mission and the safe return of his airplane and crew.
Notes: POW

2867 ◆ *MOSKALA, EDWARD J.

Rank: Private First Class
Service: U.S. Army
Birthday: 6 November 1921
Place of Birth: Chicago, Cook County, Illinois
Date of Death: 9 April 1945
Cemetery: Rock Island National Cemetery (E-293) (MH)—Rock Island, Illinois
Entered Service at: Chicago, Cook County, Illinois
Unit: Company C, 383d Infantry, 96th Infantry Division
Battle or Place of Action: Kakazu Ridge, Okinawa, Ryukyu Islands
Date of Action: 9 April 1945
G.O. Number, Date: 21, 26 February 1946
Citation: He was the leading element when grenade explosions and concentrated machine-gun and mortar fire halted the unit's attack on Kakazu Ridge, Okinawa, Ryukyu Islands. With utter disregard for his personal safety, he charged 40 yards through withering, grazing fire and wiped out two machine-gun nests with well-aimed grenades and deadly accurate fire from his automatic rifle. When strong counterattacks and fierce enemy resistance from other positions forced his company to withdraw, he voluntarily remained behind with eight others to cover the maneuver. Fighting from a critically dangerous position for three hours, he killed more than 25 Japanese before following his surviving companions through screening smoke down the face of the ridge to a gorge where it was discovered that one of the group had been left behind, wounded. Unhesitatingly, Pvt. Moskala climbed the bullet-swept slope to assist in the rescue, and, returning to lower ground, volunteered to protect other wounded while the bulk of the troops quickly took up more favorable positions. He had saved another casualty and killed four enemy infiltrators when he was struck and mortally wounded himself while aiding still another disabled soldier. With gallant initiative, unfaltering courage, and heroic determination to destroy the enemy, Pvt. Moskala gave his life in his complete devotion to his company's mission and his comrades' well-being. His intrepid conduct provided a lasting inspiration for those with whom he served.

2868 ◆ *MOWER, CHARLES E.

Rank: Sergeant
Service: U.S. Army
Birthday: 29 November 1924
Place of Birth: Chippewa Falls, Chippewa County, Wisconsin
Date of Death: 3 November 1944
Cemetery: A.B.M.C. Manila Cemetery (L-2-110)—Manila, Philippine Islands
Entered Service at: Chippewa Falls, Chippewa County, Wisconsin
Unit: Company A, 34th Infantry, 24th Infantry Division
Served as: Assistant Squad Leader
Battle or Place of Action: near Capoocan, Leyte, Philippine Islands
Date of Action: 3 November 1944
G.O. Number, Date: 17, 11 February 1946
Citation: He was assistant squad leader in an attack against strongly defended enemy positions on both sides of a stream running through a wooded gulch. As the squad advanced through concentrated fire, the leader was killed and Sgt. Mower assumed command. In order to bring direct fire upon the enemy, he had started to lead his men across the stream, which by this time was churned by machine-gun and rifle fire, but he was severely wounded before reaching the opposite bank. After signaling his unit to halt, he realized his own exposed position was the most advantageous point from which to direct the attack, and stood fast. Half submerged, gravely wounded, but refusing to seek shelter or accept aid of any kind, he continued to shout and signal to his squad as he directed it in the destruction of two enemy machine guns and numerous riflemen. Discovering that the intrepid man in the stream was largely responsible for the successful action being taken against them, the remaining Japanese concentrated the full force of their firepower upon him, and he was killed while still urging his men on. Sgt. Mower's gallant initiative and heroic determination aided materially in the successful completion of his squad's mission. His magnificent leadership was an inspiration to those with whom he served.

2869 ◆ *MULLER, JOSEPH E.

Rank: Sergeant
Service: U.S. Army
Birthday: 23 June 1908
Place of Birth: Holyoke, Hampden County, Massachusetts
Date of Death: 16 May 1945
Cemetery: National Memorial Cemetery of the Pacific (M-1259) (MH)—Honolulu, Hawaii

Entered Service at: New York, New York
Unit: Company B, 305th Infantry, 77th Infantry Division
Battle or Place of Action: near Ishimmi, Okinawa, Ryukyu Islands
Date of Action: 15-16 May 1945
G.O. Number, Date: 71, 17 July 1946
Citation: He displayed conspicuous gallantry and intrepidity above and beyond the call of duty. When his platoon was stopped by deadly fire from a strongly defended ridge, he directed men to points where they could cover his attack. Then through the vicious machine-gun and automatic fire, crawling forward alone, he suddenly jumped up, hurled his grenades, charged the enemy, and drove them into the open where his squad shot them down. Seeing enemy survivors about to man a machine gun, he fired his rifle at point-blank range, hurled himself upon them, and killed the remaining four. Before dawn the next day, the enemy counterattacked fiercely to retake the position. Sgt. Muller crawled forward through the flying bullets and explosives, then leaping to his feet, hurling grenades, and firing his rifle, he charged the Japs and routed them. As he moved into his foxhole shared with two other men, a lone enemy, who had been feigning death, threw a grenade. Quickly seeing the danger to his companions, Sgt. Muller threw himself over it and smothered the blast with his body. Heroically sacrificing his life to save his comrades, he upheld the highest traditions of the military service.

2870 ◆ *MUNEMORI, SADAO S.

Rank: Private First Class
Service: U.S. Army
Birthday: 17 August 1922
Place of Birth: Los Angeles, Los Angeles County, California
Date of Death: 5 April 1945
Cemetery: Evergreen Cemetery (MH)—Los Angeles, California
Entered Service at: Los Angeles, Los Angeles County, California
Unit: 442d Combat Team, Company A, 100th Infantry Battalion, 34th Infantry Division
Battle or Place of Action: near Seravezza, Italy
Date of Action: 5 April 1945
G.O. Number, Date: 24, 7 March 1946
Date of Issue: 13 March 1946
Citation: He fought with great gallantry and intrepidity near Seravezza, Italy. When his unit was pinned down by grazing fire from the enemy's strong mountain defense and command of the squad devolved on him with the wounding of its regular leader, he made frontal, one-man attacks through direct fire and knocked out two machine guns with grenades. Withdrawing under murderous fire and showers of grenades from other enemy emplacements, he had nearly reached a shell crater occupied by two of his men when an unexploded grenade bounced on his helmet and rolled toward his helpless comrades. He arose into the withering fire, dived for the missile, and smothered its blast with his body. By his swift, supremely heroic action Pfc. Munemori saved two of his men at the cost of his own life and did much to clear the path for his company's victorious advance.

2871 ◆ *MUNRO, DOUGLAS ALBERT

Rank: Signalman First Class
Service: U.S. Coast Guard
Birthday: 11 October 1919
Place of Birth: Vancouver, British Columbia, Canada
Date of Death: 27 September 1942
Cemetery: Laurel Hill Memorial Park (MH)—Cle Elum, Washington
Entered Service at: Washington
Served as: Petty Officer
Battle or Place of Action: Point Cruz, Guadalcanal, Solomon Islands
Date of Action: 27 September 1942
Date of Presentation: 24 May 1943
Place of Presentation: The White House (Oval Office), presented by Pres. Franklin D. Roosevelt to his mother, Edith Munro
Citation: For extraordinary heroism and conspicuous gallantry in action above and beyond the call of duty as petty officer in charge of a group of 24 Higgins boats, engaged in the evacuation of a battalion of marines trapped by enemy Japanese forces at Point Cruz, Guadalcanal on 27 September 1942. After making preliminary plans for the evacuation of nearly 500 beleaguered marines, Munro, under constant strafing by enemy machine guns on the island, and at great risk of his life, daringly led five of his small craft toward the shore. As he closed the beach, he signaled the others to land, and then in order to draw the enemy's fire and protect the heavily loaded boats, he valiantly placed his craft with its two small guns as a shield between the beachhead and the Japanese. When the perilous task of evacuation was nearly completed, Munro was instantly killed by enemy fire, but his crew, two of whom were wounded, carried on until the last boat had loaded and cleared the beach. By his outstanding leadership, expert planning, and dauntless devotion to duty, he and his courageous comrades undoubtedly saved the lives of many who otherwise would have perished. He gallantly gave his life for his country.

2872 ◆ MURPHY, AUDIE LEON

Rank: Second Lieutenant (highest rank: Major)
Service: U.S. Army
Birthday: 20 June 1924
Place of Birth: near Kingston, Hunt County, Texas
Date of Death: 28 May 1971
Place of Death: near Roanoke, Virginia
Cemetery: Arlington National Cemetery (46-366-11)—Arlington, Virginia
Entered Service at: Dallas, Collin County, Texas
Unit: Company B, 1st Battalion, 15th Infantry, 3d Infantry Division
Served as: Company Commander
Battle or Place of Action: near Holtzwihr, France
Date of Action: 26 January 1945
G.O. Number, Date: 65, 9 August 1945
Date of Presentation: 2 June 1945
Place of Presentation: Airfield near Werfen, Austria, presented by Lt. Gen. Alexander M. Patch III

Citation: Second Lt. Murphy commanded Company B, which was attacked by six tanks and waves of infantry. Second Lt. Murphy ordered his men to withdraw to prepared positions in a woods, while he remained forward at his command post and continued to give fire directions to the artillery by telephone. Behind him, to his right, one of our tank destroyers received a direct hit and began to burn. Its crew withdrew to the woods. Second Lt. Murphy continued to direct artillery fire which killed large numbers of the advancing enemy infantry. With the enemy tanks abreast of his position, 2d Lt. Murphy climbed on the burning tank destroyer, which was in danger of blowing up at any moment, and employed its .50-caliber machine gun against the enemy. He was alone and exposed to German fire from three sides, but his deadly fire killed dozens of Germans and caused their infantry attack to waver. The enemy tanks, losing infantry support, began to fall back. For an hour the Germans tried every available weapon to eliminate 2d Lt. Murphy, but he continued to hold his position and wiped out a squad which was trying to creep up unnoticed on his right flank. Germans reached as close as 10 yards, only to be mowed down by his fire. He received a leg wound, but ignored it and continued the singlehanded fight until his ammunition was exhausted. He then made his way to his company, refused medical attention, and organized the company in a counterattack which forced the Germans to withdraw. His directing of artillery fire wiped out many of the enemy; he killed or wounded about 50. Second Lt. Murphy's indomitable courage and his refusal to give an inch of ground saved his company from possible encirclement and destruction, and enabled it to hold the woods which had been the enemy's objective.

2873 ◆ *MURPHY, FREDERICK C.

Rank: Private First Class
Service: U.S. Army
Birthday: 1918
Place of Birth: Boston, Suffolk County, Massachusetts
Date of Death: 18 March 1945
Cemetery: A.B.M.C. Lorraine Cemetery—St. Avold, France
Entered Service at: Weymouth, Norfolk County, Massachusetts
Unit: Medical Detachment, 259th Infantry, 65th Infantry Division
Served as: Medical Aidman
Battle or Place of Action: Siegfried Line at Saarlautern, Germany
Date of Action: 18 March 1945
G.O. Number, Date: 21, 26 February 1946
Date of Presentation: February 1946
Place of Presentation: City Hall, Quincy, Massachusetts, presented by Lt. Gen. O.W. Griswold to his Widow and Daughter
Citation: An aidman, he was wounded in the right shoulder soon after his comrades had jumped off in a dawn attack, 18 March 1945, against the Siegfried Line at Saarlautern, Germany. He refused to withdraw for treatment and continued forward, administering first aid under heavy machine-gun, mortar, and artillery fire. When the company ran into a thickly sown antipersonnel minefield and began to suffer more and more casualties, he continued to disregard his own wound and unhesitatingly braved the danger of exploding mines, moving about through heavy fire and helping the injured until he stepped on a mine which severed one of his feet. In spite of his grievous wounds, he struggled on with his work, refusing to be evacuated and crawling from man to man administering to them while in great pain and bleeding profusely. He was killed by the blast of another mine which he had dragged himself across in an effort to reach still another casualty. With indomitable courage, and unquenchable spirit of self-sacrifice and supreme devotion to duty which made it possible for him to continue performing his tasks while barely able to move, Pfc. Murphy saved many of his fellow soldiers at the cost of his own life.

2874 ◆ MURRAY JR., CHARLES PATRICK "CHUCK"

Rank: First Lieutenant (highest rank: Colonel)
Service: U.S. Army
Birthday: 26 September 1921
Place of Birth: Baltimore, Baltimore County, Maryland
Entered Service at: Wilmington, New Hanover County, North Carolina
Unit: Company C, 1st Battalion, 30th Infantry, 3d Infantry Division
Served as: Company Commander
Battle or Place of Action: near Kaysersberg, France
Date of Action: 16 December 1944
G.O. Number, Date: 63, 1 August 1945
Date of Presentation: 5 July 1945
Place of Presentation: Salzburg, Austria, presented by Lt. Gen. Geoffrey Keyes, Commanding Gen. U.S. II Corps
Citation: For commanding Company C, 30th Infantry, displaying supreme courage and heroic initiative near Kaysersberg, France on 16 December 1944, while leading a reinforced platoon into enemy territory. Descending into a valley beneath hilltop positions held by our troops, he observed a force of 200 Germans pouring deadly mortar, bazooka, machine-gun, and small-arms fire into an American battalion occupying the crest of the ridge. The enemy's position in a sunken road, though hidden from the ridge, was open to a flank attack by 1st Lt. Murray's patrol but he hesitated to commit so small a force to battle with the superior and strongly disposed enemy. Crawling out ahead of his troops to a vantage point, he called by radio for artillery fire. His shells bracketed the German force, but when he was about to correct the range his radio went dead. He returned to his patrol, secured grenades and a rifle to launch them, and went back to his self-appointed outpost. His first shots disclosed his position; the enemy directed heavy fire against him as he methodically fired his missiles into the narrow defile. Again he returned to his patrol. With an automatic rifle and ammunition, he once more moved to his exposed position. Burst after burst he fired into the enemy, killing 20, wounding many others, and completely disorganizing its ranks, which began to withdraw. He prevented the removal of three German mortars by knocking out a truck. By that time a mor-

tar had been brought to his support. First Lt. Murray directed the fire of this weapon, causing further casualties and confusion in the German ranks. Calling on his patrol to follow, he then moved out toward his original objective, possession of a bridge and construction of a roadblock. He captured 10 Germans in foxholes. An eleventh, while pretending to surrender, threw a grenade which knocked him to the ground, inflicting eight wounds. Though suffering and bleeding profusely, he refused to return to the rear until he had chosen the spot for the block and had seen his men correctly deployed. By his singlehanded attack on an overwhelming force and by his intrepid and heroic fighting, 1st Lt. Murray stopped a counterattack, established an advance position against formidable odds, and provided an inspiring example for the men of his command.

2875 ◆ *NELSON, WILLIAM LANCASTER

Rank: Sergeant
Service: U.S. Army
Place of Birth: Dover, Kent County, Delaware
Date of Death: 24 April 1943
Cemetery: Silver Brook Cemetery—Wilmington, Delaware
Entered Service at: Middletown, New Castle County, Delaware
Unit: 60th Infantry, 9th Infantry Division
Served as: Mortar Section Leader
Battle or Place of Action: Djebel Dardys, northwest of Sedjenane, Tunisia
Date of Action: 24 April 1943
G.O. Number, Date: 85, 17 December 1943
Date of Presentation: December 1943
Place of Presentation: Fort Dupont, Delaware, presented to his wife Rebecca by Maj. Gen. Lunsford E. Oliver, CG 5th Armored Division
Citation: For conspicuous gallantry and intrepidity at risk of life, above and beyond the call of duty in action involving actual conflict. On the morning of 24 April 1943, Sgt. Nelson led his section of heavy mortars to a forward position where he placed his guns and men. Under intense enemy artillery, mortar, and small-arms fire, he advanced alone to a chosen observation position from which he directed the laying of a concentrated mortar barrage which successfully halted an initial enemy counterattack. Although mortally wounded in the accomplishment of his mission, and with his duty clearly completed, Sgt. Nelson crawled to a still more advanced observation point and continued to direct the fire of his section. Dying of hand-grenade wounds and only 50 yards from the enemy, Sgt. Nelson encouraged his section to continue their fire and by doing so they took a heavy toll of enemy lives. The skill which Sgt. Nelson displayed in this engagement, his courage, and self-sacrificing devotion to duty and heroism resulting in the loss of his life, was a priceless inspiration to our Armed Forces and were in keeping with the highest traditions of the U.S. Army.

2876 ◆ NEPPEL, RALPH GEORGE

Rank: Sergeant
Service: U.S. Army
Birthday: 31 October 1923
Place of Birth: Willey, Carroll County, Iowa
Date of Death: 27 January 1987
Cemetery: Holy Family Cemetery (MH)—Lidderdale, Iowa
Entered Service at: Glidden, Carroll County, Iowa
Unit: Company M, 329th Infantry, 83d Infantry Division
Served as: Squad Leader
Battle or Place of Action: Birgel, Germany
Date of Action: 14 December 1944
G.O. Number, Date: 77, 10 September 1945
Date of Presentation: 23 August 1945
Place of Presentation: The White House, presented by Pres. Harry S. Truman
Citation: He was a leader of a machine-gun squad defending an approach to the village of Birgel, Germany, on 14 December 1944, when an enemy tank, supported by 20 infantrymen, counterattacked. He held his fire until the Germans were within 100 yards and then raked the foot soldiers beside the tank, killing several of them. The enemy armor continued to press forward, and, at the point-blank range of 30 yards, fired a high-velocity shell into the American emplacement, wounding the entire squad. Sgt. Neppel, blown 10 yards from his gun, had one leg severed below the knee and suffered other wounds. Despite his injuries and the danger from the onrushing tank and infantry, he dragged himself back to his position on his elbows, remounted his gun, and killed the remaining enemy riflemen. Stripped of its infantry protection, the tank was forced to withdraw. By his superb courage and indomitable fighting spirit, Sgt. Neppel inflicted heavy casualties on the enemy and broke a determined counterattack.

2877 ◆ NETT, ROBERT BURTON

Rank: Captain (rank at time of action: First Lieutenant) (highest rank: Colonel)
Service: U.S. Army
Birthday: 13 June 1922
Place of Birth: New Haven, New Haven County, Connecticut
Entered Service at: New Haven, New Haven County, Connecticut
Unit: Company E, 2d Battalion, 305th Infantry, 77th Infantry Division
Served as: Company Commander
Battle or Place of Action: near Cognon, Leyte, Philippine Islands
Date of Action: 14 December 1944
G.O. Number, Date: 16, 8 February 1946
Date of Presentation: 8 February 1946
Place of Presentation: New Haven, Connecticut, presented by Lt. Gen. Oscar W. Griswold
Citation: He commanded Company E in an attack against a reinforced enemy battalion which had held up the American advance for two days from its entrenched positions around a three-story concrete building. With another infantry company and armored vehicles, Company E advanced against heavy machine-gun and other automatic-weapon fire with Lt. Nett spearheading the assault against the strongpoint. During the fierce hand-to-hand encounter which ensued, he killed seven

deeply entrenched Japanese with his rifle and bayonet and, although seriously wounded, gallantly continued to lead his men forward, refusing to relinquish his command. Again he was severely wounded, but, still unwilling to retire, pressed ahead with his troops to assure the capture of the objective. Wounded once more in the final assault, he calmly made all arrangements for the resumption of the advance, turned over his command to another officer, and then walked unaided to the rear for medical treatment. By his remarkable courage in continuing forward through sheer determination despite successive wounds, Lt. Nett provided an inspiring example for his men and was instrumental in the capture of a vital strongpoint.

2878 ◆ *NEW, JOHN DURY

Rank: Private First Class
Service: U.S. Marine Corps
Birthday: 12 August 1924
Place of Birth: Mobile, Mobile County, Alabama
Date of Death: 25 September 1944
Cemetery: Mobile National Cemetery (7-2147) (MH)—Mobile, Alabama
Entered Service at: Alabama
Unit: 2d Battalion, 7th Marines, 1st Marine Division
Battle or Place of Action: Peleliu Island, Palau Islands
Date of Action: 25 September 1944
Citation: For conspicuous gallantry and intrepidity at the risk of his life above and beyond the call of duty while serving with the 2d Battalion, 7th Marines, 1st Marine Division, in action against enemy Japanese forces on Peleliu Island, Palau Group, 25 September 1944. When a Japanese soldier emerged from a cave in a cliff directly below an observation post and suddenly hurled a grenade into the position from which two of our men were directing mortar fire against enemy emplacements, Pfc. New instantly perceived the dire peril to the other marines and, with utter disregard for his own safety, unhesitatingly flung himself upon the grenade and absorbed the full impact of the explosion, thus saving the lives of the two observers. Pfc. New's great personal valor and selfless conduct in the face of almost certain death reflect the highest credit upon himself and the U.S. Naval Service. He gallantly gave his life for his country.

2879 ◆ NEWMAN, BERYL RICHARD

Rank: First Lieutenant (highest rank: Captain)
Service: U.S. Army
Birthday: 2 November 1911
Place of Birth: Baraboo, Sauk County, Wisconsin
Entered Service at: Baraboo, Sauk County, Wisconsin
Unit: 1st Platoon, Company F, 2d Battalion, 133d Infantry, 34th Infantry Division
Served as: Platoon Leader
Battle or Place of Action: near Cisterna, Italy
Date of Action: 26 May 1944
G.O. Number, Date: 5, 15 January 1945
Date of Presentation: 10 January 1945
Place of Presentation: The White House, presented by Pres. Franklin D. Roosevelt
Citation: For conspicuous gallantry and intrepidity above and beyond the call of duty on 26 May 1944. Attacking the strongly held German Anzio-Nettuno defense line near Cisterna, Italy, 1st Lt. Newman, in the lead of his platoon, was suddenly fired upon by two enemy machine guns located on the crest of a hill about 100 yards to his front. The four scouts with him immediately hit the ground, but 1st Lt. Newman remained standing in order to see the enemy positions and his platoon then about 100 yards behind. Locating the enemy nests, 1st Lt. Newman called back to his platoon and ordered one squad to advance to him and the other to flank the enemy to the right. Then, still standing upright in the face of enemy machine-gun fire, 1st Lt. Newman opened up with his tommy gun on the enemy nests. From this range, his fire was not effective in covering the advance of his squads, and one squad was pinned down by the enemy fire. Seeing that his squad was unable to advance, 1st Lt. Newman, in full view of the enemy gunners and in the face of their continuous fire, advanced alone on the enemy nests. He returned their fire with his tommy gun and succeeded in wounding a German in each of the nests. The remaining two Germans fled from the position into a nearby house. Three more enemy soldiers then came out of the house and ran toward a third machine gun. First Lt. Newman, still relentlessly advancing toward them, killed one before he reached the gun, the second before he could fire it. The third fled for his life back into the house. Covering his assault by firing into the doors and windows of the house, 1st Lt. Newman, boldly attacking by himself, called for the occupants to surrender to him. Gaining the house, he kicked in the door and went inside. Although armed with rifles and machine pistols, the 11 Germans there, apparently intimidated, surrendered to the lieutenant without further resistance. 1st Lt. Newman, singlehandedly, had silenced three enemy machine guns, wounded two Germa ns, killed two more, and taken 11 prisoners. This demonstration of sheer courage, bravery, and willingness to close with the enemy even in the face of such heavy odds, instilled into these green troops the confidence of veterans and reflect the highest traditions of the U.S. Armed Forces.

2880 ◆ *NININGER JR., ALEXANDER RAMSEY

Rank: Second Lieutenant
Service: U.S. Army
Birthday: 20 October 1918
Place of Birth: Gainesville, Hall County, Georgia
Date of Death: 12 January 1942
Cemetery: Abucay Church Cemetery (grave 9)—Manila, Philippine Islands
Entered Service at: Fort Lauderdale, Broward County, Florida
Unit: Philippine Scouts, Company A, 1st Battalion, 57th Infantry, U.S. Army
Served as: Platoon Leader
Battle or Place of Action: near Abucay, Bataan, Philippine Islands
Date of Action: 12 January 1942
G.O. Number, Date: 9, 5 February 1942
Date of Presentation: 10 February 1942
Place of Presentation: Third Air Force Headquarters, Tampa, Florida, presented by Maj. Gen. Walter H. Frank

Citation: For conspicuous gallantry and intrepidity above and beyond the call of duty in action with the enemy near Abucay, Bataan, Philippine Islands on 12 January 1942. This officer, though assigned to another company not then engaged in combat, voluntarily attached himself to Company K, same regiment, while that unit was being attacked by enemy forces superior in firepower. Enemy snipers in trees and foxholes had stopped a counterattack to regain part of the position. In the hand-to-hand fighting which followed, 2d Lt. Nininger repeatedly forced his way to and into the hostile position. Though exposed to heavy enemy fire, he continued to attack with rifle and hand grenades and succeeded in destroying several enemy groups in foxholes, and enemy snipers. Although wounded three times, he continued his attacks until he was killed after pushing alone far within the enemy position. When his body was found after recapture of the position, one enemy officer and two enemy soldiers lay dead around him.

2881 ◆ *O'BRIEN, WILLIAM JOSEPH

Rank: Lieutenant Colonel
Service: U.S. Army
Birthday: 1899
Place of Birth: Troy, Rensselaer County, New York
Date of Death: 7 July 1944
Cemetery: St. Peter's Cemetery (MH)—Troy, New York
Entered Service at: Troy, Rensselaer County, New York
it: 1st Battalion, 105th Infantry, 27th Infantry Division
Battle or Place of Action: Saipan, Marianas Islands
Date of Action: 20 June-7 July 1944
G.O. Number, Date: 35, 9 May 1945
Citation: For conspicuous gallantry and intrepidity at the risk of his life above and beyond the call of duty at Saipan, Marianas Islands, from 20 June through 7 July 1944. When assault elements of his platoon were held up by intense enemy fire, Lt. Col. O'Brien ordered three tanks to precede the assault companies in an attempt to knock out the strongpoint. Due to direct enemy fire the tanks' turrets were closed, causing the tanks to lose direction and to fire into our own troops. Lt. Col. O'Brien, with complete disregard for his own safety, dashed into full view of the enemy and ran to the leader's tank and pounded on the tank with his pistol butt to attract two of the tank's crew and, mounting the tank fully exposed to the enemy fire, Lt. Col. O'Brien personally directed the assault until the enemy strongpoint had been liquidated. On 28 June 1944, while his platoon was attempting to take a bitterly defended high ridge in the vicinity of Donnay, Lt. Col. O'Brien arranged to capture the ridge by a double envelopment movement of two large combat battalions. He personally took control of the maneuver. Lt. Col. O'Brien crossed 1,200 yards of sniper-infested underbrush alone to arrive at a point where one of his platoons was being held up by the enemy. Leaving some men to contain the enemy, he personally led four men into a narrow ravine behind, and killed or drove off all the Japanese manning that strongpoint. In this action he captured five machine guns and one 77-mm fieldpiece. Lt. Col. O'Brien then organized the two platoons for night defense and against repeated counterattacks directed them. Meanwhile he managed to hold ground. On 7 July 1944 his battalion and another battalion were attacked by an overwhelming enemy force estimated at between 3,000 and 5,000 Japanese. With bloody hand-to-hand fighting in progress everywhere, their forward positions were finally overrun by the sheer weight of the enemy numbers. With many casualties and ammunition running low, Lt. Col. O'Brien refused to leave the front lines. Striding up and down the lines, he fired at the enemy with a pistol in each hand and his presence there bolstered the spirits of the men, encouraged them in their fight, and sustained them in their heroic stand. Even after he was seriously wounded, Lt. Col. O'Brien refused to be evacuated and after his pistol ammunition was exhausted, he manned a .50-caliber machine gun, mounted on a jeep, and continued firing. When last seen alive he was standing upright firing into the Jap hordes that were enveloping him. Some time later his body was found surrounded by enemy he had killed. His valor was consistent with the highest traditions of the service.

2882 ◆ O'CALLAHAN, JOSEPH TIMOTHY

Rank: Commander (Chaplain Corps)
Service: U.S. Naval Reserve
Birthday: 14 May 1904
Place of Birth: Boston, Suffolk County, Massachusetts
Date of Death: 18 March 1964
Cemetery: Holy Cross College Cemetery—Worcester, Massachusetts
Entered Service at: Massachusetts
Unit: U.S.S. *Franklin*
Served as: Chaplain
Battle or Place of Action: near Kobe, Japan
Date of Action: 19 March 1945
Date of Presentation: 23 January 1946
Place of Presentation: The White House, presented by Pres. Harry S. Truman
Citation: For conspicuous gallantry and intrepidity at the risk of his life above and beyond the call of duty while serving as chaplain on board the U.S.S. *Franklin* when that vessel was fiercely attacked by enemy Japanese aircraft during offensive operations near Kobe, Japan, on 19 March 1945. A valiant and forceful leader, calmly braving the perilous barriers of flame and twisted metal to aid his men and his ship, Lt. Comdr. O'Callahan groped his way through smoke-filled corridors to the open flight deck and into the midst of violently exploding bombs, shells, rockets, and other armament. With the ship rocked by incessant explosions, with debris and fragments raining down and fires raging in ever-increasing fury, he ministered to the wounded and dying, comforting and encouraging men of all faiths; he organized and led firefighting crews into the blazing inferno on the flight deck; he directed the jettisoning of live ammunition and the flooding of the magazine; he manned a hose to cool hot, armed bombs rolling dangerously on the listing deck, continuing his efforts, despite searing, suffocating smoke which forced men to fall back gasping and imperiled others who replaced them. Serving with courage, fortitude, and deep spiritual strength, Lt. Comdr. O'Callahan inspired the gallant officers and men

of the *Franklin* to fight heroically and with profound faith in the face of almost certain death and to return their stricken ship to port.

2883 ◆ OGDEN SR., CARLOS CARNES

Rank: First Lieutenant (highest rank: Major)
Service: U.S. Army
Birthday: 9 May 1917
Place of Birth: Borton, Edgar County, Illinois
Entered Service at: Fairmount, Vermillion County, Illinois
Unit: Company K, 3d Battalion, 314th Infantry, 79th Infantry Division
Served as: Company Commander
Battle or Place of Action: near Fort du Roule, Cherbourg, France
Date of Action: 25 June 1944
G.O. Number, Date: 49, 28 June 1945
Date of Presentation: 30 May 1945
Place of Presentation: Augsburg, Germany, presented by Lt. Gen. Alexander M. Patch III
Citation: On the morning of 25 June 1944, near Fort du Roule, guarding the approaches to Cherbourg, France, 1st Lt. Ogden's company was pinned down by fire from a German 88-mm gun and two machine guns. Arming himself with an M1 rifle, a grenade launcher, and a number of rifle and hand grenades, he left his company in position and advanced alone, under fire, up the slope toward the enemy emplacements. Struck on the head and knocked down by a glancing machine-gun bullet, 1st Lt. Ogden, in spite of his painful wound and enemy fire from close range, continued up the hill. Reaching a vantage point, he silenced the 88-mm gun with a well-placed rifle grenade and then, with hand grenades, knocked out the two machine guns, again being painfully wounded. First Lt. Ogden's heroic leadership and indomitable courage in alone silencing these enemy weapons inspired his men to greater effort and cleared the way for the company to continue the advance and reach its objectives.

2884 ◆ O'HARE, EDWARD HENRY "BUTCH"

Rank: Lieutenant (highest rank: Lieutenant Commander)
Service: U.S. Navy
Birthday: 13 March 1914
Place of Birth: St. Louis, St. Louis County, Missouri
Date of Death: 23 November 1943
Place of Death: South Pacific Area
Cemetery: National Memorial Cemetery of the Pacific (Wall of the Missing)—Honolulu, Hawaii
Entered Service at: St. Louis, St. Louis County, Missouri
Unit: Fighting Squadron 3, U.S.S. *Lexington*
Served as: Section Leader & Pilot
Battle or Place of Action: South Pacific
Date of Action: 20 February 1942
Date of Presentation: 21 April 1942
Place of Presentation: The White House, presented by Pres. Franklin D. Roosevelt
Citation: For conspicuous gallantry and intrepidity in aerial combat, at grave risk of his life above and beyond the call of duty, as section leader and pilot of Fighting Squadron 3 on 20 February 1942. Having lost the assistance of his teammates, Lt. O'Hare interposed his plane between his ship and an advancing enemy formation of nine attacking twin-engined heavy bombers. Without hesitation, alone and unaided, he repeatedly attacked this enemy formation, at close range in the face of intense combined machine-gun and cannon fire. Despite his concentrated opposition, Lt. O'Hare, by his gallant and courageous action, his extremely skillful marksmanship in making the most of every shot of his limited amount of ammunition, shot down five enemy bombers and severely damaged a sixth before they reached the bomb release point. As a result of his gallant action—one of the most daring, if not the most daring, single action in the history of combat aviation—he undoubtedly saved his carrier from serious damage.

2885 ◆ O'KANE, RICHARD HETHERINGTON

Rank: Commander (highest rank: Rear Admiral)
Service: U.S. Navy
Birthday: 2 February 1911
Place of Birth: Dover, Strafford County, New Hampshire
Date of Death: 16 February 1994
Place of Death: Petaluma, California
Cemetery: Arlington National Cemetery—Arlington, Virginia
Entered Service at: Durham, Strafford County, New Hampshire
Unit: U.S.S. *Tang* SS-306
Served as: Commanding Officer
Battle or Place of Action: Vicinity of Formosa Straits, Philippine Islands
Date of Action: 23-24 October 1944
Date of Presentation: 27 March 1946
Place of Presentation: The White House, presented by Pres. Harry S. Truman
Citation: For conspicuous gallantry and intrepidity at the risk of his life above and beyond the call of duty as commanding officer of the U.S.S. *Tang* operating against two enemy Japanese convoys on 23 and 24 October 1944, during her fifth and last war patrol. Boldly maneuvering on the surface into the midst of a heavily escorted convoy, Comdr. O'Kane stood in the fusillade of bullets and shells from all directions to launch smashing hits on three tankers, coolly swung his ship to fire at a freighter and, in a split-second decision, shot out of the path of an onrushing transport, missing it by inches. Boxed in by blazing tankers, a freighter, transport, and several destroyers, he blasted two of the targets with his remaining torpedoes and, with pyrotechnics bursting on all sides, cleared the area. Twenty-four hours later, he again made contact with a heavily escorted convoy steaming to support the Leyte campaign with reinforcements and supplies and with crated planes piled high on each unit. In defiance of the enemy's relentless fire, he closed the concentration of ships and in quick succession sent two torpedoes each into the first and second transports and an adjacent tanker, finding his mark with each torpedo in a series of violent explosions at less than 1,000-yard range. With ships bearing down from all

sides, he charged the enemy at high speed, exploding the tanker in a burst of flame, smashing the transport dead in the water, and blasting the destroyer with a mighty roar which rocked the *Tang* from stem to stern. Expending his last two torpedoes into the remnants of a once powerful convoy before his own ship went down, Comdr. O'Kane, aided by his gallant command, achieved an illustrious record of heroism in combat, enhancing the finest traditions of the U.S. Naval Service.

2886 ◆ *OLSON, ARLO L.

Rank: Captain
Service: U.S. Army
Birthday: 20 April 1918
Place of Birth: Greenville, Clay County, Iowa
Date of Death: 13 October 1943
Cemetery: Toronto Cemetery—Toronto, South Dakota
Entered Service at: Toronto, Deuel County, South Dakota
Unit: 15th Infantry, 3d Infantry Division
Battle or Place of Action: crossing of the Volturno River, Italy
Date of Action: 13 October 1943
G.O. Number, Date: 71, 31 August 1944
Citation: For conspicuous gallantry and intrepidity at the risk of his life above and beyond the call of duty. On 13 October 1943, when the drive across the Volturno River began, Capt. Olson and his company spearheaded the advance of the regiment through 30 miles of mountainous enemy territory in 13 days. Placing himself at the head of his men, Capt. Olson waded into the chest-deep water of the raging Volturno River and despite point-blank machine-gun fire aimed directly at him made his way to the opposite bank and threw two hand grenades into the gun position, killing the crew. When an enemy machine gun 150 yards distant opened fire on his company, Capt. Olson advanced upon the position in a slow, deliberate walk. Although five German soldiers threw hand grenades at him from a range of five yards, Capt. Olson dispatched them all, picked up a machine pistol, and continued toward the enemy. Advancing to within 15 yards of the position he shot it out with the foe, killing nine and seizing the post. Throughout the next 13 days Capt. Olson led combat patrols, acted as company No. 1 scout, and maintained unbroken contact with the enemy. On 27 October 1943, Capt. Olson conducted a platoon in attack on a strongpoint, crawling to within 25 yards of the enemy and then charging the position. Despite continuous machine-gun fire which barely missed him, Capt. Olson made his way to the gun and killed the crew with his pistol. When the men saw their leader make this desperate attack they followed him and overran the position. Continuing the advance, Capt. Olson led his company to the next objective at the summit of Monte San Nicola. Although the company to his right was forced to take cover from the furious automatic and small-arms fire, which was directed upon him and his men with equal intensity, Capt. Olson waved his company into a skirmish line and despite the fire of a machine gun which singled him out as its sole target led the assault which drove the enemy away. While making a reconnaissance for defensive positions, Capt. Olson was fatally wounded. Ignoring his severe pain, this intrepid officer completed his reconnaissance, supervised the location of his men in the best defense positions, refused medical aid until all of his men had been cared for, and died as he was being carried down the mountain.

2887 ◆ *OLSON, TRUMAN O.

Rank: Sergeant
Service: U.S. Army
Birthday: 13 October 1917
Place of Birth: Christiana, Wisconsin
Date of Death: 31 January 1944
Cemetery: West Koshkonong Lutheran Cemetery (MH)—Stoughton, Wisconsin
Entered Service at: Cambridge, Dane County, Wisconsin
Unit: Company B, 7th Infantry, 3d Infantry Division
Served as: Light Machine Gunner
Battle or Place of Action: near Cisterna di Littoria, Italy
Date of Action: 30-31 January 1944
G.O. Number, Date: 6, 24 January 1945
Citation: For conspicuous gallantry and intrepidity above and beyond the call of duty. Sgt. Olson, a light machinegunner, elected to sacrifice his life to save his company from annihilation. On the night of 30 January 1944, after a 16-hour assault on entrenched enemy positions in the course of which over one-third of Company B became casualties, the survivors dug in behind a horseshoe elevation, placing Sgt. Olson and his crew, with the one available machine gun, forward of their lines and in an exposed position to bear the brunt of the expected German counterattack. Although he had been fighting without respite, Sgt. Olson stuck grimly to his post all night while his guncrew was cut down, one by one, by accurate and overwhelming enemy fire. Weary from over 24 hours of continuous battle and suffering from an arm wound, received during the night engagement, Sgt. Olson manned his gun alone, meeting the full force of an all-out enemy assault by approximately 200 men supported by mortar and machine-gun fire which the Germans launched at daybreak on the morning of 31 January. After 30 minutes of fighting, Sgt. Olson was mortally wounded, yet, knowing that only his weapons stood between his company and complete destruction, he refused evacuation. For an hour and a half after receiving his second and fatal wound he continued to fire his machine gun, killing as least 20 of the enemy, wounding many more, and forcing the assaulting German elements to withdraw.

2888 ◆ ORESKO, NICHOLAS

Rank: Master Sergeant
Service: U.S. Army
Birthday: 18 January 1917
Place of Birth: Bayonne, Hudson County, New Jersey
Entered Service at: Bayonne, Hudson County, New Jersey
Unit: 1st Platoon, Company C, 1st Battalion, 302d Infantry, 94th Infantry Division
Served as: Platoon Leader
Battle or Place of Action: near Tettington, Germany

Date of Action: 23 January 1945
G.O. Number, Date: 95, 30 October 1945
Date of Presentation: 12 October 1945
Place of Presentation: The White House, presented by Pres. Harry S. Truman
Citation: M/Sgt. Oresko was a platoon leader with Company C, in an attack against strong enemy positions. Deadly automatic fire from the flanks pinned down his unit. Realizing that a machine gun in a nearby bunker must be eliminated, he swiftly worked ahead alone, braving bullets which struck about him, until close enough to throw a grenade into the German position. He rushed the bunker and, with point-blank rifle fire, killed all the hostile occupants who survived the grenade blast. Another machine gun opened up on him, knocking him down and seriously wounding him in the hip. Refusing to withdraw from the battle, he placed himself at the head of his platoon to continue the assault. As withering machine-gun and rifle fire swept the area, he struck out alone in advance of his men to a second bunker. With a grenade, he crippled the dug-in machine gun defending this position and then wiped out the troops manning it with his rifle, completing his second self-imposed, one-man attack. Although weak from loss of blood, he refused to be evacuated until assured the mission was successfully accomplished. Through quick thinking, indomitable courage, and unswerving devotion to the attack in the face of bitter resistance and while wounded, M/Sgt. Oresko killed 12 Germans, prevented a delay in the assault, and made it possible for Company C to obtain its objective with minimum casualties.

2889 ◆ *OWENS, ROBERT ALLEN

Rank: Sergeant
Service: U.S. Marine Corps
Birthday: 13 September 1920
Place of Birth: Greenville, Greenville County, South Carolina
Date of Death: 1 November 1943
Cemetery: A.B.M.C. Manila Cemetery (N-12-200)—Manila, Philippine Islands
Entered Service at: South Carolina
Battle or Place of Action: Cape Torokina, Bougainville, Solomon Islands
Date of Action: 1 November 1943
Citation: For conspicuous gallantry and intrepidity at the risk of his life above and beyond the call of duty while serving with a marine division, in action against enemy Japanese forces during extremely hazardous landing operations at Cape Torokina, Bougainville Island, Solomon Islands, on 1 November 1943. Forced to pass within disastrous range of a strongly protected, well-camouflaged Japanese 75-mm regimental gun strategically located on the beach, our landing units were suffering heavy losses in casualties and boats while attempting to approach the beach, and the success of the operations was seriously threatened. Observing the ineffectiveness of marine rifle and grenade attacks against the incessant, devastating fire of the enemy weapon and aware of the urgent need for prompt action, Sgt. Owens unhesitatingly determined to charge the gun bunker from the front and, calling on four of his comrades to assist him, carefully placed them to cover the fire of the two adjacent hostile bunkers. Choosing a moment that provided a fair opportunity for passing these bunkers, he immediately charged into the mouth of the steadily firing cannon and entered the emplacement through the fire port, driving the guncrew out of the rear door and insuring their destruction before he himself was wounded. Indomitable and aggressive in the face of almost certain death, Sgt. Owens silenced a powerful gun which was of inestimable value to the Japanese defense and, by his brilliant initiative and heroic spirit of self-sacrifice, contributed immeasurably to the success of the vital landing operations. His valiant conduct throughout reflects the highest credit upon himself and the U.S. Naval Service.

2890 ◆ *OZBOURN, JOSEPH WILLIAM

Rank: Private
Service: U.S. Marine Corps
Birthday: 24 October 1919
Place of Birth: Herrin, Williamson County, Illinois
Date of Death: 28 July 1944
Cemetery: National Memorial Cemetery of the Pacific (F-77) (MH)—Honolulu, Hawaii
Entered Service at: Illinois
Unit: 1st Battalion, 23d Marines, 4th Marine Division
Served as: Browning Automatic Rifleman
Battle or Place of Action: Tinian Island, Marianas Islands
Date of Action: 28 July 1944
Citation: For conspicuous gallantry and intrepidity at the risk of his life above and beyond the call of duty as a Browning automatic rifleman serving with the 1st Battalion, 23d Marines, 4th Marine Division, during the battle for enemy Japanese-held Tinian Island, Marianas Islands, 30 July 1944. As a member of a platoon assigned the mission of clearing the remaining Japanese troops from dugouts and pillboxes along a treeline, Pvt. Ozbourn, flanked by two men on either side, was moving forward to throw an armed hand grenade into a dugout when a terrific blast from the entrance severely wounded the four men and himself. Unable to throw the grenade into the dugout and with no place to hurl it without endangering the other men, Pvt. Ozbourn unhesitatingly grasped it close to his body and fell upon it, sacrificing his own life to absorb the full impact of the explosion, but saving his comrades. His great personal valor and unwavering loyalty reflect the highest credit upon Pvt. Ozbourn and the U.S. Naval Service. He gallantly gave his life for his country.

2891 ◆ PAIGE, MITCHELL

Rank: Platoon Sergeant (highest rank: Colonel)
Service: U.S. Marine Corps
Birthday: 31 August 1918
Place of Birth: Charleroi, Washington County, Pennsylvania
Entered Service at: Pennsylvania
Unit: Company H, 2d Battalion, 7th Marine Regiment, 1st Marine Division
Served as: Platoon Sergeant
Battle or Place of Action: Guadalcanal, Solomon Islands

Date of Action: 26 October 1942
Date of Presentation: 21 May 1943
Place of Presentation: Balcombe, Australia, presented by Major Gen. Alexander A. Vandegrift, Commanding Gen. 1st Marine Division
Citation: For extraordinary heroism and conspicuous gallantry in action above and beyond the call of duty while serving with a company of marines in combat against enemy Japanese forces in the Solomon Islands on 26 October 1942. When the enemy broke through the line directly in front of his position, P/Sgt. Paige, commanding a machine-gun section with fearless determination, continued to direct the fire of his gunners until all his men were either killed or wounded. Alone, against the deadly hail of Japanese shells, he fought with his gun and when it was destroyed, took over another, moving from gun to gun, never ceasing his withering fire against the advancing hordes until reinforcements finally arrived. Then, forming a new line, he dauntlessly and aggressively led a bayonet charge, driving the enemy back and preventing a breakthrough in our lines. His great personal valor and unyielding devotion to duty were in keeping with the highest traditions of the U.S. Naval Service.

2892 ◆ *PARLE, JOHN JOSEPH

Rank: Ensign
Service: U.S. Naval Reserve
Birthday: 26 May 1920
Place of Birth: Omaha, Douglas County, Nebraska
Date of Death: 17 July 1943
Cemetery: Holy Sepulchre Cemetery—Omaha, Nebraska
Entered Service at: Nebraska
Unit: U.S.S. *LST 375*
Battle or Place of Action: Sicily
Date of Action: 9-10 July 1943
Citation: For valor and courage above and beyond the call of duty as officer-in-charge of small boats in the U.S.S. LST 375 during the amphibious assault on the island of Sicily, 9–10 July 1943. Realizing that a detonation of explosives would prematurely disclose to the enemy the assault about to be carried out, and with full knowledge of the peril involved, Ens. Parle unhesitatingly risked his life to extinguish a smoke pot accidentally ignited in a boat carrying charges of high explosives, detonating fuses and ammunition. Undaunted by fire and blinding smoke, he entered the craft, quickly snuffed out a burning fuse, and after failing in his desperate efforts to extinguish the fire pot, finally seized it with both hands and threw it over the side. Although he succumbed a week later from smoke and fumes inhaled, Ens. Parle's heroic self-sacrifice prevented grave damage to the ship and personnel and insured the security of a vital mission. He gallantly gave his life in the service of his country.

2893 ◆ *PARRISH, LAVERNE

Rank: Technician Fourth Grade
Service: U.S. Army
Birthday: 16 July 1918
Place of Birth: Knox City, Montana
Date of Death: 24 January 1945
Cemetery: Mountain View Cemetery—Ronon, Montana
Entered Service at: Ronan, Lake County, Montana
Unit: Medical Detachment, 161st Infantry, 25th Infantry Division
Served as: Medical Aidman
Battle or Place of Action: Binalonan, Luzon, Philippine Islands
Date of Action: 18-24 January 1945
G.O. Number, Date: 55, 13 July 1945
Citation: He was medical aidman with Company C during the fighting in Binalonan, Luzon, Philippine Islands. On the 18th, he observed two wounded men under enemy fire and immediately went to their rescue. After moving one to cover, he crossed 25 yards of open ground to administer aid to the second. In the early hours of the 24th, his company, crossing an open field near San Manuel, encountered intense enemy fire and was ordered to withdraw to the cover of a ditch. While treating casualties, Technician Parrish observed two wounded still in the field. Without hesitation he left the ditch, crawled forward under enemy fire, and in two successive trips brought both men to safety. He next administered aid to 12 casualties in the same field, crossing and recrossing the open area raked by hostile fire. Making successive trips, he then brought three wounded to cover. After treating nearly all of the 37 casualties suffered by his company, he was mortally wounded by mortar fire, and shortly after was killed. The indomitable spirit, intrepidity, and gallantry of Technician Parrish saved many lives at the cost of his own.

2894 ◆ *PEASE JR., HARL

Rank: Captain
Service: U.S. Army Air Corps
Birthday: 10 April 1917
Place of Birth: Plymouth, Grafton County, New Hampshire
Date of Death: 8 October 1942
Place of Death: New Guinea
Cemetery: A.B.M.C. Manila Cemetery (Wall of the Missing)—Manila, Philippine Islands
Entered Service at: Boston, Suffolk County, Massachusetts
Unit: Heavy Bombardment Squadron, 19th Bombardment Group, 509th Bombardment Wing, 5th Air Force
Served as: Pilot of a B-17
Battle or Place of Action: near Rabaul, New Britain, Bismarck Archipelago
Date of Action: 6-7 August 1942
G.O. Number, Date: 59, 4 November 1942
Date of Presentation: 2 December 1942
Place of Presentation: The White House, presented by Pres. Franklin D. Roosevelt to his parents Mr. & Mrs. Harl Pease Sr
Citation: For conspicuous gallantry and intrepidity above and beyond the call of duty in action with the enemy on 6–7 August 1942. When one engine of the bombardment airplane of which he was a pilot failed during a bombing mission over New Guinea, Capt. Pease was forced to return to base in Australia. Knowing that all available airplanes of his group were to participate the next day in an attack on an enemy-held airdrome near Rabaul, New Britain, although he was not

scheduled to take part in this mission, Capt. Pease selected the most serviceable airplane at this base and prepared it for combat, knowing that it had been found and declared unserviceable for combat missions. With the members of his combat crew, who volunteered to accompany him, he rejoined his squadron at Port Moresby, New Guinea, at 1 A.M. on 7 August, after having flown almost continuously since early in the preceding morning. With only three hours' rest, he took off with his squadron for the attack. Throughout the long flight to Rabaul, New Britain, he managed by skillful flying of his unserviceable airplane to maintain his position in the group. When the formation was intercepted by about 30 enemy fighter airplanes before reaching the target, Capt. Pease, on the wing which bore the brunt of the hostile attack, by gallant action and the accurate shooting by his crew, succeeded in destroying several Zeros before dropping his bombs on the hostile base as planned, this in spite of continuous enemy attacks. The fight with the enemy pursuit lasted 25 minutes until the group dived into cloud cover. After leaving the target, Capt. Pease's aircraft fell behind the balance of the group due to unknown difficulties as a result of the combat and was unable to reach this cover before the enemy pursuit succeeded in igniting one of his bomb bay tanks. He was seen to drop the flaming tank. It is believed that Capt. Pease's airplane and crew were subsequently shot down in flames, as they did not return to their base. In voluntarily performing this mission Capt. Pease contributed materially to the success of the group and displayed high devotion to duty, valor, and complete contempt for personal danger. His undaunted bravery has been a great inspiration to the officers and men of his unit.

2895 ◆ *PEDEN, FORREST E.

Rank: Technician Fifth Grade
Service: U.S. Army
Birthday: 3 October 1913
Place of Birth: St. Joseph, Buchanan County, Missouri
Date of Death: 3 February 1945
Cemetery: Mount Olive Cemetery—Troy, Kansas
Entered Service at: Wathena, Doniphan County, Kansas
Unit: Battery C, 10th Field Artillery Battalion, 3d Infantry Division
Served as: Forward Artillery Observer
Battle or Place of Action: near Biesheim, France
Date of Action: 3 February 1945
G.O. Number, Date: 18, 13 February 1946
Citation: He was a forward artillery observer when the group of about 45 infantrymen with whom he was advancing was ambushed in the uncertain light of a waning moon. Enemy forces outnumbering the Americans by four to one poured withering artillery, mortar, machine-gun, and small-arms fire into the stricken unit from the flanks, forcing our men to seek the cover of a ditch which they found already occupied by enemy foot troops. As the opposing infantrymen struggled in hand-to-hand combat, Technician Peden courageously went to the assistance of two wounded soldiers and rendered first aid under heavy fire. With radio cummunications inoperative, he realized that the unit would be wiped out unless help could be secured from the rear. On his own initiative, he ran 800 yards to the battalion command post through a hail of bullets which pierced his jacket, and there secured two light tanks to go to the relief of his hard-pressed comrades. Knowing the terrible risk involved, he climbed upon the hull of the lead tank and guided it into battle. Through a murderous concentration of fire the tank lumbered onward, bullets and shell fragments ricocheting from its steel armor within inches of the completely exposed rider, until it reached the ditch. As it was about to go into action it was turned into a flaming pyre by a direct hit which killed Technican Peden. However, his intrepidity and gallant sacrifice was not in vain. Attracted by the light from the burning tank, reinforcements found the beleaguered Americans and drove off the enemy.

2896 ◆ *PENDLETON, JACK JAMES

Rank: Staff Sergeant
Service: U.S. Army
Birthday: 31 March 1918
Place of Birth: Sentinel Butte, Golden Valley County, North Dakota
Date of Death: 12 October 1944
Cemetery: Tahoma Cemetery—Yakima, Washington
Entered Service at: Yakima, Yakima County, Washington
Unit: Company I, 120th Infantry, 30th Infantry Division
Served as: Squad Leader
Battle or Place of Action: Bardenberg, Germany
Date of Action: 12 October 1944
G.O. Number, Date: 24, 6 April 1945
Citation: For conspicuous gallantry and intrepidity at the risk of his life above and beyond the call of duty on 12 October 1944. When Company I was advancing on the town of Bardenberg, Germany, they reached a point approximately two-thirds of the distance through the town when they were pinned down by fire from a nest of enemy machine guns. This enemy strongpoint was protected by a lone machine gun strategically placed at an intersection and firing down a street which offered little or no cover or concealment for the advancing troops. The elimination of this protecting machine gun was imperative in order that the stronger position it protected could be neutralized. After repeated and unsuccessful attempts had been made to knock out this position, S/Sgt. Pendleton volunteered to lead his squad in an attempt to neutralize this strongpoint. S/Sgt. Pendleton started his squad slowly forward, crawling about 10 yards in front of his men in the advance toward the enemy gun. After advancing approximately 130 yards under the withering fire, S/Sgt. Pendleton was seriously wounded in the leg by a burst from the gun he was assaulting. Disregarding his grievous wound, he ordered his men to remain where they were, and with a supply of hand grenades he slowly and painfully worked his way forward alone. With no hope of surviving the veritable hail of machine-gun fire which he deliberately drew onto himself, he succeeded in advancing within 10 yards of the enemy position when he was instantly killed by a burst from the enemy gun. By deliberately diverting the attention of the enemy machine-gunners upon himself, a second squad was

able to advance, undetected, and with the help of S/Sgt. Pendleton's squad, neutralized the lone machine gun, while another platoon of his company advanced up the intersecting street and knocked out the machine-gun nest which the first gun had been covering. S/Sgt. Pendleton's sacrifice enabled the entire company to continue the advance and complete their missi on at a critical phase of the action.

2897 ◆ *PEREGORY, FRANK D.

Rank: Technical Sergeant
Service: U.S. Army
Birthday: 10 April 1915
Place of Birth: Esmont, Albemarle County, Virginia
Date of Death: 14 June 1944
Cemetery: A.B.M.C. Normandy Cemetery (G-21-7)—St. Laurent-Sur-Mer, France
Entered Service at: Charlottesville, Charlottesville County, Virginia
Unit: Company K, 3d Battalion, 116th Infantry, 29th Infantry Division
Battle or Place of Action: Grandcampe, France
Date of Action: 8 June 1944
G.O. Number, Date: 43, 30 May 1945
Citation: On 8 June 1944, the 3d Battalion of the 116th Infantry was advancing on the strongly held German defenses at Grandcampe, France, when the leading elements were suddenly halted by decimating machine-gun fire from a firmly entrenched enemy force on the high ground overlooking the town. After numerous attempts to neutralize the enemy position by supporting artillery and tank fire had proved ineffective, T/Sgt. Peregory, on his own initiative, advanced up the hill under withering fire and worked his way to the crest, where he discovered an entrenchment leading to the main fortifications 200 yards away. Without hesitating, he leaped into the trench and moved toward the emplacement. Encountering a squad of enemy riflemen, he fearlessly attacked them with hand grenades and bayonet, killed eight, and forced three to surrender. Continuing along the trench, he singlehandedly forced the surrender of 32 more riflemen, captured the machine gunners, and opened the way for the leading elements of the battalion to advance and secure its objective. The extraordinary gallantry and aggressiveness displayed by T/Sgt. Peregory are exemplary of the highest traditions of the Armed Forces.

2898 ◆ *PEREZ JR., MANUEL

Rank: Private First Class
Service: U.S. Army
Birthday: 3 March 1923
Place of Birth: Oklahoma City, Oklahoma County, Oklahoma
Date of Death: 14 March 1945
Cemetery: Fairlawn Cemetery (MH)—Oklahoma City, Oklahoma
Entered Service at: Chicago, Cook County, Illinois
Unit: Company A, 511th Parachute Infantry, 11th Airborne Division
Served as: Scout
Battle or Place of Action: Fort William McKinley, Luzon, Philippine Islands
Date of Action: 13 February 1945
G.O. Number, Date: 124, 27 December 1945
Citation: He was lead scout for Company A, which had destroyed 11 of 12 pillboxes in a strongly fortified sector defending the approach to enemy-held Fort William McKinley on Luzon, Philippine Islands. In the reduction of these pillboxes, he killed five Japanese in the open and blasted others in pillboxes with grenades. Realizing the urgent need for taking the last emplacement, which contained two twin-mount .50-caliber dual-purpose machine guns, he took a circuitous route to within 20 yards of the position, killing four of the enemy in his advance. He threw a grenade into the pillbox, and, as the crew started withdrawing through a tunnel just to the rear of the emplacement, shot and killed four before exhausting his clip. He had reloaded and killed four more when an escaping Jap threw his rifle with fixed bayonet at him. In warding off this thrust, his own rifle was knocked to the ground. Seizing the Jap rifle, he continued firing, killing two more of the enemy. He rushed the remaining Japanese, killed three of them with the butt of the rifle, and entered the pillbox, where he bayoneted the one surviving hostile soldier. Singlehandedly, he killed 18 of the enemy in neutralizing the position that had held up the advance of his entire company. Through his courageous determination and heroic disregard of grave danger, Pfc. Perez made possible the successful advance of his unit toward a valuable objective and provided a lasting inspiration for his comrades.

2899 ◆ *PETERS, GEORGE J.

Rank: Private
Service: U.S. Army
Place of Birth: Cranston, Providence County, Rhode Island
Date of Death: 24 March 1945
Cemetery: A.B.M.C. Netherlands Cemetery (6-17-8)—Margraten, Holland
Entered Service at: Cranston, Providence County, Rhode Island
Unit: Company G, 507th Parachute Infantry, 17th Airborne Division
Served as: Platoon Radio Operator
Battle or Place of Action: near Fluren, Germany
Date of Action: 24 March 1945
G.O. Number, Date: 16, 8 February 1946
Citation: Pvt. Peters, a platoon radio operator with Company G, made a descent into Germany near Fluren, east of the Rhine. With 10 others, he landed in a field about 75 yards from a German machine gun supported by riflemen and was immediately pinned down by heavy, direct fire. The position of the small unit seemed hopeless, with the men struggling to free themselves of their parachutes in a hail of bullets that cut them off from their nearby equipment bundles, when Pvt. Peters stood up without orders and began a one-man charge against the hostile emplacement armed only with a rifle and grenades. His singlehanded assault immediately drew the enemy fire away from his comrades. He had run halfway to his objective, pitting rifle fire against that of the machine gun, when he was struck and knocked to the ground by a

burst. Heroically, he regained his feet and struggled onward. Once more he was torn by bullets, and this time he was unable to rise. With gallant devotion to his self-imposed mission, he crawled directly into the fire that had mortally wounded him until close enough to hurl grenades which knocked out the machine gun, killed two of its operators, and drove protecting riflemen from their positions into the safety of a woods. By his intrepidity and supreme sacrifice, Pvt. Peters saved the lives of many of his fellow soldiers and made it possible for them to reach their equipment, organize, and seize their first objective.

2900 ◆ *PETERSON, GEORGE

Rank: Staff Sergeant
Service: U.S. Army
Place of Birth: Brooklyn, Kings County, New York
Date of Death: 30 March 1945
Cemetery: A.B.M.C. Netherlands Cemetery (D-21-10)—Margraten, Holland
Entered Service at: Brooklyn, Kings County, New York
Unit: Company K, 18th Infantry, 1st Infantry Division
Served as: Acting Platoon Sergeant
Battle or Place of Action: near Eisern, Germany
Date of Action: 30 March 1945
G.O. Number, Date: 88, 17 October 1945
Citation: He was an acting platoon sergeant with Company K, near Eisern, Germany. When his company encountered an enemy battalion and came under heavy small-arms, machine-gun, and mortar fire, the 2d Platoon was given the mission of flanking the enemy positions while the remaining units attacked frontally. S/Sgt. Peterson crept and crawled to a position in the lead and motioned for the 2d Platoon to follow. A mortar shell fell close by and severely wounded him in the legs, but, although bleeding and suffering intense pain, he refused to withdraw and continued forward. Two hostile machine guns went into action at close range. Braving this grazing fire, he crawled steadily toward the guns and worked his way alone to a shallow draw, where, despite the hail of bullets, he raised himself to his knees and threw a grenade into the nearest machine-gun nest, silencing the weapon and killing or wounding all its crew. The second gun was immediately turned on him, but he calmly and deliberately threw a second grenade which rocked the position and killed all four Germans who occupied it. As he continued forward he was spotted by an enemy rifleman, who shot him in the arm. Undeterred, he crawled some 20 yards until a third machine gun opened fire on him. By almost superhuman effort, weak from loss of blood and suffering great pain, he again raised himself to his knees and fired a grenade from his rifle, killing three of the enemy guncrew and causing the remaining one to flee. With the first objective seized, he was being treated by the company aidman when he observed one of his outpost men seriously wounded by a mortar burst. He wrenched himself from the hands of the aidman and began to crawl forward to assist his comrade, whom he had almost reached when he was struck and fatally wounded by an enemy bullet. S/Sgt. Peterson, by his gallant, intrepid actions, unrelenting fighting spirit, and outstanding initiative, silenced three enemy machine guns against great odds and while suffering from severe wounds, enabling his company to advance with minimum casualties.

2901 ◆ *PETERSON, OSCAR VERNER

Rank: Chief Watertender
Service: U.S. Navy
Birthday: 27 August 1899
Place of Birth: Prentice, Price County, Wisconsin
Date of Death: 7 May 1942
Cemetery: A.B.M.C. Manila Cemetery (Wall of the Missing)—Manila, Philippine Islands
Entered Service at: Wisconsin
Unit: U.S.S. *Neosho*
Date of Action: 7 May 1942
Citation: For extraordinary courage and conspicuous heroism above and beyond the call of duty while in charge of a repair party during an attack on the U.S.S. *Neosho* by enemy Japanese aerial forces on 7 May 1942. Lacking assistance because of injuries to the other members of his repair party and severely wounded himself, Peterson, with no concern for his own life, closed the bulkhead stop valves and in so doing received additional burns which resulted in his death. His spirit of self-sacrifice and loyalty, characteristic of a fine seaman, was in keeping with the highest traditions of the U.S. Naval Service. He gallantly gave his life in the service of his country.

2902 ◆ *PETRARCA, FRANK JOSEPH

Rank: Private First Class
Service: U.S. Army
Birthday: 31 July 1918
Place of Birth: Cleveland, Cuyahoga County, Ohio
Date of Death: 31 July 1943
Cemetery: Calvary Cemetery (MH)—Cleveland, Ohio
Entered Service at: Cleveland, Cuyahoga County, Ohio
Unit: Medical Detachment, 145th Infantry, 37th Infantry Division
Served as: Medical Aidman
Battle or Place of Action: Horseshoe Hill, New Georgia, Solomon Islands
Date of Action: 27 July 1943
G.O. Number, Date: 86, 23 December 1943
Citation: For conspicuous gallantry and intrepidity in action above and beyond the call of duty. Pfc. Petrarca advanced with the leading troop element to within 100 yards of the enemy fortifications where mortar and small-arms fire caused a number of casualties. Singling out the most seriously wounded, he worked his way to the aid of Pfc. Scott, lying within 75 yards of the enemy, whose wounds were so serious that he could not even be moved out of the direct line of fire. Pfc. Petrarca fearlessly administered first aid to Pfc. Scott and two other soldiers and shielded the former until his death. On 29 July 1943, Pfc. Petrarca, during an intense mortar barrage, went to the aid of his sergeant who had been partly buried in a foxhole under the debris of a shell explosion, dug him out, restored him to consciousness, and caused his evacuation. On 31 July 1943 and against the warning of a fellow soldier, he went to the aid of a mortar fragment casualty where his path

over the crest of a hill exposed him to enemy observation from only 20 yards distance. A target for intense knee mortar and automatic fire, he resolutely worked his way to within two yards of his objective where he was mortally wounded by hostile mortar fire. Even on the threshold of death he continued to display valor and contempt for the foe; raising himself to his knees, this intrepid soldier shouted defiance at the enemy, made a last attempt to reach his wounded comrade and fell in glorious death.

2903 ◆ PHARRIS, JACKSON CHARLES

Rank: Lieutenant (rank at time of action: Gunner) (highest rank: Lieutenant Commander)
Service: U.S. Navy
Birthday: 26 June 1912
Place of Birth: Columbus, Muscogee County, Georgia
Date of Death: 17 October 1966
Cemetery: Arlington National Cemetery (13-16281) (MH)—Arlington, Virginia
Entered Service at: California
Unit: U.S.S. *California*
Battle or Place of Action: Pearl Harbor, Territory of Hawaii
Date of Action: 7 December 1941
Citation: For conspicuous gallantry and intrepidity at the risk of his life above and beyond the call of duty while attached to the U.S.S. *California* during the surprise enemy Japanese aerial attack on Pearl Harbor, Territory of Hawaii, 7 December 1941. In charge of the ordnance repair party on the third deck when the first Japanese torpedo struck almost directly under his station, Lt. (then Gunner) Pharris was stunned and severely injured by the concussion which hurled him to the overhead and back to the deck. Quickly recovering, he acted on his own initiative to set up a hand-supply ammunition train for the antiaircraft guns. With water and oil rushing in where the port bulkhead had been torn up from the deck, with many of the remaining crewmembers overcome by oil fumes, and the ship without power and listing heavily to port as a result of a second torpedo hit, Lt. Pharris ordered the shipfitters to counterflood. Twice rendered unconscious by the nauseous fumes and handicapped by his painful injuries, he persisted in his desperate efforts to speed up the supply of ammunition and at the same time repeatedly risked his life to enter the flooding compartments and drag to safety unconscious shipmates who were gradually being submerged in oil. By his inspiring leadership, his valiant efforts, and extreme loyalty to his ship and her crew, he saved many of his shipmates from death and was largely responsible for keeping the *California* in action during the attack. His heroic conduct throughout this first eventful engagement of World War II reflects the highest credit upon Lt. Pharris and enhances the finest traditions of the U.S. Naval Service.

2904 ◆ *PHELPS, WESLEY

Rank: Private
Service: U.S. Marine Corps Reserve
Birthday: 12 June 1923
Place of Birth: Neafus, Grayson County, Kentucky
Date of Death: 4 October 1944
Cemetery: Rosine Cemetery (MH)—Rosine, Kentucky
Entered Service at: Kentucky
Unit: 3d Battalion, 7th Marines, 1st Marine Division
Battle or Place of Action: Peleliu Island, Palau Islands
Date of Action: 4 October 1944
Citation: For conspicuous gallantry and intrepidity at the risk of his life above and beyond the call of duty while serving with the 3d Battalion, 7th Marines, 1st Marine Division, in action against enemy Japanese forces on Peleliu Island, Palau Group, during a savage hostile counterattack on the night of 4 October 1944. Stationed with another marine in an advanced position when a Japanese hand grenade landed in his foxhole, Pfc. Phelps instantly shouted a warning to his comrade and rolled over on the deadly bomb, absorbing with his own body the full, shattering impact of the exploding charge. Courageous and indomitable, Pfc. Phelps fearlessly gave his life that another might be spared serious injury, and his great valor and heroic devotion to duty in the face of certain death reflect the highest credit upon himself and the U.S. Naval Service. He gallantly gave his life for his country.

2905 ◆ *PHILLIPS, GEORGE

Rank: Private
Service: U.S. Marine Corps Reserve
Birthday: 14 July 1926
Place of Birth: Rich Hill, Vernon County, Missouri
Date of Death: 14 March 1945
Cemetery: Bethel Cemetery (MH)—Labadie, Missouri
Entered Service at: Labadie, Franklin County, Missouri
Unit: 2d Battalion, 28th Marines, 5th Marine Division
Battle or Place of Action: Iwo Jima, Volcano Islands
Date of Action: 14 March 1945
Citation: For conspicuous gallantry and intrepidity at the risk of his life above and beyond the call of duty while serving with the 2d Battalion, 28th Marines, 5th Marine Division, in action against enemy Japanese forces during the seizure of Iwo Jima in the Volcano Islands on 14 March 1945. Standing the foxhole watch while other members of his squad rested after a night of bitter hand-grenade fighting against infiltrating Japanese troops, Pvt. Phillips was the only member of his unit alerted when an enemy hand grenade was tossed into their midst. Instantly shouting a warning, he unhesitatingly threw himself on the deadly missile, absorbing the shattering violence of the exploding charge in his own body and protecting his comrades from serious injury. Stouthearted and indomitable, Pvt. Phillips willingly yielded his own life that his fellow marines might carry on the relentless battle against a fanatic enemy. His superb valor and unfaltering spirit of self-sacrifice in the face of certain death reflect the highest credit upon himself and upon the U.S. Naval Service. He gallantly gave his life for his country.

2906 ◆ PIERCE, FRANCIS JUNIOR

Rank: Pharmacist's Mate First Class
Service: U.S. Navy
Birthday: 7 December 1924

Place of Birth: Earlville, Delaware County, Iowa
Date of Death: 21 December 1986
Cemetery: Holy Cross Cemetery—Grand Rapids, Michigan
Entered Service at: Iowa
Unit: 2d Battalion, 24th Marines, 4th Marine Division
Served as: Medical Corpsman
Battle or Place of Action: Iwo Jima, Volcano Islands
Date of Action: 15-16 March 1945
Date of Issue: 1948
Citation: For conspicuous gallantry and intrepidity at the risk of his life above and beyond the call of duty while attached to the 2d Battalion, 24th Marines, 4th Marine Division, during the Iwo Jima campaign, 15 and 16 March 1945. Almost continuously under fire while carrying out the most dangerous volunteer assignments, Pierce gained valuable knowledge of the terrain and disposition of troops. Caught in heavy enemy rifle and machine-gun fire which wounded a corpsman and two of the eight stretcher bearers who were carrying two wounded marines to a forward aid station on 15 March, Pierce quickly took charge of the party, carried the newly wounded men to a sheltered position, and rendered first aid. After directing the evacuation of three of the casualties, he stood in the open to draw the enemy's fire and, with his weapon blasting, enabled the litter bearers to reach cover. Turning his attention to the other two casualties, he was attempting to stop the profuse bleeding of one man when a Japanese fired from a cave less than 20 yards away and wounded his patient again. Risking his own life to save his patient, Pierce deliberately exposed himself to draw the attacker from the cave and destroyed him with the last of his ammunition. Then lifting the wounded man to his back, he advanced unarmed through deadly rifle fire across 200 feet of open terrain. Despite exhaustion and in the face of warnings against such a suicidal mission, he again traversed the same fire-swept path to rescue the remaining marine. On the following morning, he led a combat patrol to the sniper nest and, while aiding a stricken marine, was seriously wounded. Refusing aid for himself, he directed treatment for the casualty, at the same time maintaining protective fire for his comrades. Completely fearless, completely devoted to the care of his patients, Pierce inspired the entire battalion. His valor in the face of extreme peril sustains and enhances the finest traditions of the U.S. Naval Service.

2907 ◆ *PINDER JR., JOHN J.

Rank: Technician Fifth Grade
Service: U.S. Army
Birthday: 7 June 1912
Place of Birth: McKees Rocks, Allegheny County, Pennsylvania
Date of Death: 6 June 1944
Cemetery: Grand View Cemetery—Hanover Township, Pennsylvania
Entered Service at: Burgettstown, Washington County, Pennsylvania
Unit: 16th Infantry, 1st Infantry Division
Battle or Place of Action: near Colleville-sur-Mer, France
Date of Action: 6 June 1944
G.O. Number, Date: 1, 4 January 1945
Citation: For conspicuous gallantry and intrepidity above and beyond the call of duty on 6 June 1944, near Colleville-sur-Mer, France. On D-day, Technician Fifth Grade Pinder landed on the coast 100 yards offshore under devastating enemy machine-gun and artillery fire which caused severe casualties among the boatload. Carrying a vitally important radio, he struggled towards shore in waist-deep water. Only a few yards from his craft he was hit by enemy fire and was gravely wounded. Technician Fifth Grade Pinder never stopped. He made shore and delivered the radio. Refusing to take cover afforded, or to accept medical attention for his wounds, Technician Fifth Grade Pinder, though terribly weakened by loss of blood and in fierce pain, on three occasions went into the fire-swept surf to salvage communication equipment. He recovered many vital parts and equipment, including another workable radio. On the third trip he was again hit, suffering machine-gun bullet wounds in the legs. Still this valiant soldier would not stop for rest or medical attention. Remaining exposed to heavy enemy fire, growing steadily weaker, he aided in establishing the vital radio communications on the beach. While so engaged this dauntless soldier was hit for the third time and killed. The indomitable courage and personal bravery of Technician Fifth Grade Pinder was a magnificent inspiration to the men with whom he served.

2908 ◆ POPE, EVERETT PARKER

Rank: Captain (highest rank: Major)
Service: U.S. Marine Corps
Birthday: 16 July 1919
Place of Birth: Milton, Norfolk County, Massachusetts
Entered Service at: Quincy, Norfolk County, Massachusetts
Unit: Company C, 1st Battalion, 1st Marines, 1st Marine Division
Served as: Commanding Officer
Battle or Place of Action: Peleliu Island, Palau Islands
Date of Action: 19 September 1944
Date of Presentation: 15 June 1945
Place of Presentation: The White House, presented by Pres. Harry S. Truman
Citation: For conspicuous gallantry and intrepidity at the risk of his life above and beyond the call of duty while serving as commanding officer of Company C, 1st Battalion, 1st Marines, 1st Marine Division, during action against enemy Japanese forces on Peleliu Island, Palau Group on 19–20 September 1944. Subjected to point-blank cannon fire which caused heavy casualties and badly disorganized his company while assaulting a steep coral hill, Capt. Pope rallied his men and gallantly led them to the summit in the face of machine-gun, mortar, and sniper fire. Forced by widespread hostile attack to deploy the remnants of his company thinly in order to hold the ground won, and with his machine guns out of order and insufficient water and ammunition, he remained on the exposed hill with 12 men and one wounded officer, determined to hold through the night. Attacked continuously with grenades, machine guns, and rifles from three sides, he and his valiant men fiercely beat back or destroyed the enemy,

resorting to hand-to-hand combat as the supply of ammunition dwindled, and still maintaining his lines with his eight remaining riflemen when daylight brought more deadly fire and he was ordered to withdraw. His valiant leadership against devastating odds while protecting the units below from heavy Japanese attack reflects the highest credit upon Capt. Pope and the U.S. Naval Service.

2909 ◆ *POWER, JOHN VINCENT

Rank: First Lieutenant
Service: U.S. Marine Corps
Birthday: 20 November 1918
Place of Birth: Worcester, Worcester County, Massachusetts
Date of Death: 1 February 1944
Cemetery: St. John's Cemetery—Worcester, Massachusetts
Entered Service at: Massachusetts
Unit: 4th Marine Division
Served as: Platoon Leader
Battle or Place of Action: Namur Island, Kwajalein Atoll, Marshall Islands
Date of Action: 1 February 1944
Citation: For conspicuous gallantry and intrepidity at the risk of his life above and beyond the call of duty as platoon leader, attached to the 4th Marine Division, during the landing and battle of Namur Island, Kwajalein Atoll, Marshall Islands, 1 February 1944. Severely wounded in the stomach while setting a demolition charge on a Japanese pillbox, 1st Lt. Power was steadfast in his determination to remain in action. Protecting his wound with his left hand and firing with his right, he courageously advanced as another hostile position was taken under attack, fiercely charging the opening made by the explosion and emptying his carbine into the pillbox. While attempting to reload and continue the attack, 1st Lt. Power was shot again in the stomach and head and collapsed in the doorway. His exceptional valor, fortitude and indomitable fighting spirit in the face of withering enemy fire were in keeping with the highest traditions of the U.S. Naval Service. He gallantly gave his life for his country.

2910 ◆ *POWERS, JOHN JAMES

Rank: Lieutenant
Service: U.S. Navy
Birthday: 13 July 1912
Place of Birth: New York, New York
Date of Death: 8 May 1942
Cemetery: A.B.M.C. Manila Cemetery (Wall of the Missing)—Manila, Philippine Islands
Entered Service at: New York
Unit: Bombing Squadron 5, U.S.S. *Yorktown*
Served as: Pilot
Battle or Place of Action: Coral Sea
Date of Action: 4-8 April 1942
Date of Presentation: 7 September 1942
Place of Presentation: Washington, D.C., presented by Adm. Royal E. Ingersoll to his Mother
Citation: For distinguished and conspicuous gallantry and intrepidity at the risk of his life above and beyond the call of duty, while pilot of a airplane of Bombing Squadron 5, Lt. Powers participated, with his squadron, in five engagements with Japanese forces in the Coral Sea area and adjacent waters during the period from 4 to 8 May 1942. Three attacks were made on enemy objectives at or near Tulagi on 4 May. In these attacks he scored a direct hit which instantly demolished a large enemy gunboat or destroyer and is credited with two close misses, one of which severely damaged a large aircraft tender, the other damaging a 20,000-ton transport. He fearlessly strafed a gunboat, firing all his ammunition into it amid intense antiaircraft fire. This gunboat was then observed to be leaving a heavy oil slick in its wake and later was seen beached on a nearby island. On 7 May, an attack was launched against an enemy airplane carrier and other units of the enemy's invasion force. He fearlessly led his attack section of three Douglas Dauntless dive bombers, to attack the carrier. On this occasion he dived in the face of heavy antiaircraft fire, to an altitude well below the safety altitude, at the risk of his life and almost certain damage to his own plane, in order that he might positively obtain a hit in a vital part of the ship, which would insure her complete destruction. This bomb hit was noted by many pilots and observers to cause a tremendous explosion engulfing the ship in a mass of flame, smoke, and debris. The ship sank soon after. That evening, in his capacity as squadron gunnery officer, Lt. Powers gave a lecture to the squadron on point-of-aim and diving technique. During this discourse he advocated low release point in order to insure greater accuracy; yet he stressed the danger not only from enemy fire and the resultant low pull-out, but from own bomb blast and bomb fragments. Thus his low dive bombing attacks were deliberate and premeditated, since he well knew and realized the dangers of such tactics, but went far beyond the call of duty in order to further the cause which he knew to be right. The next morning, 8 May, as the pilots of the attack group left the ready room to man planes, his indomitable spirit and leadership were well-expressed in his own words, "Remember the folks back home are counting on us. I am going to get a hit if I have to lay it on their flight deck." He led his section of dive bombers down to the target from an altitude of 18,000 feet, through a wall of bursting antiaircraft shells and into the face of enemy fighter planes. Again, completely disregarding the safety altitude and without fear or concern for his safety, Lt. Powers courageously pressed home his attack, almost to the very deck of an enemy carrier and did not release his bomb until he was sure of a direct hit. He was last seen attempting recovery from his dive at the extremely low altitude of 200 feet, and amid a terrific barrage of shell and bomb fragments, smoke, flame, and debris from the stricken vessel.

2911 ◆ POWERS, LEO J.

Rank: Private First Class (highest rank: Sergeant)
Service: U.S. Army
Birthday: 5 April 1909
Place of Birth: Anselmo, Custer County, Nebraska
Date of Death: 16 July 1967
Cemetery: Holy Cross Cemetery (MH)—Butte, Montana
Entered Service at: Alder Gulch, Madison County, Montana

Unit: Company L, 133d Infantry, 34th Infantry Division
Served as: Rifleman
Battle or Place of Action: Hill 175, northwest of Casino, Italy
Date of Action: 3 February 1944
G.O. Number, Date: 5, 15 January 1945
Date of Presentation: 10 January 1945
Place of Presentation: Washington, D.C., presented by Pres. Franklin D. Roosevelt
Citation: For conspicuous gallantry and intrepidity at the risk of his life above and beyond the call of duty. On 3 February 1944, this soldier's company was assigned the mission of capturing Hill 175, the key enemy strongpoint northwest of Cassino, Italy. The enemy, estimated to be at least 50 in strength, supported by machine guns emplaced in three pillboxes and mortar fire from behind the hill, was able to pin the attackers down and inflict eight casualties. The company was unable to advance, but Pfc. Powers, a rifleman in one of the assault platoons, on his own initiative and in the face of terrific fire, crawled forward to assault one of the enemy pillboxes which he had spotted. Armed with two hand grenades and well aware that if the enemy should see him it would mean almost certain death, Pfc. Powers crawled up the hill to within 15 yards of the enemy pillbox. Then standing upright in full view of the enemy gunners in order to throw his grenade into the small opening in the roof, he tossed a grenade into the pillbox. At this close, the grenade entered the pillbox, killed two of the occupants and three or four more fled the position, probably wounded. This enemy gun silenced, the center of the line was able to move forward again, but almost immediately came under machine-gun fire from a second pillbox on the left flank. Pfc. Powers, however, had located this pillbox, and crawled toward it, with absolutely no cover if the enemy should see him. Raising himself in full view of the enemy gunners about 15 feet from the pillbox, Pfc. Powers threw his grenade into the pillbox, silencing the gun, killing another German, and probably wounding three or four more who fled. Pfc. Powers, still acting on his own initiative, commenced crawling toward the third enemy pillbox in the face of heavy machine-pistol and machine-gun fire. Skillfully availing himself of meager cover and concealment, Pfc. Powers crawled up to within 10 yards of this pillbox, fully exposed himself to the enemy gunners, stood upright, and tossed the two grenades into the small opening in the roof of the pillbox. His grenades killed two of the enemy and four more, all wounded, came out and surrendered to Pfc. Powers, who was now unarmed. Pfc. Powers had worked his way over the entire company front, and against tremendous odds had singlehandedly broken the backbone of this heavily defended and strategic enemy position, and enabled his regiment to advance into the city of Cassino. Pfc. Powers' fighting determination and intrepidity in battle exemplify the highest traditions of the U.S. Armed Forces.

2912 ◆ PRESTON, ARTHUR MURRAY

Rank: Lieutenant Commander (rank at time of action: Lieutenant) (highest rank: Commander)
Service: U.S. Naval Reserve
Birthday: 1 November 1913
Place of Birth: Washington, D.C.
Date of Death: 7 January 1968
Cemetery: Arlington National Cemetery (3-1847-A-1)—Arlington, Virginia
Entered Service at: Maryland
Unit: Torpedo Boat Squadron 33
Served as: Commanding Officer
Battle or Place of Action: Wasile Bay, Halmahera Island, Moluccas, Netherlands Indies
Date of Action: 16 September 1944
Date of Presentation: 19 December 1947
Place of Presentation: The White House, presented by Pres. Harry S. Truman
Citation: For conspicuous gallantry and intrepidity at the risk of his life above and beyond the call of duty as commander, Motor Torpedo Boat Squadron 33, while effecting the rescue of a Navy pilot shot down in Wasile Bay, Halmahera Island, less than 200 yards from a strongly defended Japanese dock and supply area, 16 September 1944. Volunteering for a perilous mission unsuccessfully attempted by the pilot's squadron mates and a PBY plane, Lt. Comdr. (then Lt.) Preston led PT-489 and PT-363 through 60 miles of restricted, heavily mined waters. Twice turned back while running the gauntlet of fire from powerful coastal defense guns guarding the 11-mile strait at the entrance to the bay, he was again turned back by furious fire in the immediate area of the downed airman. Aided by an aircraft smoke screen, he finally succeeded in reaching his objective and, under vicious fire delivered at 150-yard range, took the pilot aboard and cleared the area, sinking a small hostile cargo vessel with 40-mm fire during retirement. Increasingly vulnerable when covering aircraft were forced to leave because of insufficient fuel, Lt. Comdr. Preston raced PT boats 489 and 363 at high speed for 20 minutes through shell-splashed water and across minefields to safety. Under continuous fire for 2 1/2 hours, Lt. Comdr. Preston successfully achieved a mission considered suicidal in its tremendous hazards and brought his boats through without personnel casualties and with but superficial damage from shrapnel. His exceptional daring and great personal valor enhance the finest traditions of the U.S. Naval Service.

2913 ◆ *PRUSSMAN, ERNEST W.

Rank: Private First Class
Service: U.S. Army
Place of Birth: Baltimore, Baltimore County, Maryland
Date of Death: 8 September 1944
Cemetery: A.B.M.C. Brittany Cemetery (A-12-14)—St. James, France
Entered Service at: Brighton, Suffolk County, Massachusetts
Unit: 13th Infantry, 8th Infantry Division
Battle or Place of Action: near Les Coates, Brittany, France
Date of Action: 8 September 1944
G.O. Number, Date: 31, 17 April 1945
Citation: For conspicuous gallantry and intrepidity at the risk of life above and beyond the call of duty on 8 September

1944, near Les Coates, Brittany, France. When the advance of flank companies of two battalions was halted by intense enemy mortar, machine-gun, and sniper fire from a fortified position on his left, Pfc. Prussman maneuvered his squad to assault the enemy fortifications. Hurdling a hedgerow, he came upon two enemy riflemen whom he disarmed. After leading his squad across an open field to the next hedgerow, he advanced to a machine-gun position, destroyed the gun, captured its crew and two riflemen. Again advancing ahead of his squad in the assault, he was mortally wounded by an enemy rifleman, but as he fell to the ground he threw a hand grenade, killing his opponent. His superb leadership and heroic action at the cost of his life so demoralized the enemy that resistance at this point collapsed, permitting the two battalions to continue their advance.

2914 ◆ *PUCKET, DONALD DALE

Rank: First Lieutenant
Service: U.S. Army Air Corps
Birthday: 19 December 1915
Place of Birth: Longmont, Boulder County, Colorado
Date of Death: 9 July 1944
Cemetery: Jefferson Barracks National Cemetery (One of six in group burial) (84-270-271-272)—St. Louis, Missouri
Entered Service at: Boulder, Boulder County, Colorado
Unit: 343d Bombardment Squadron, 98th Bombardment Group, 8th Air Force
Served as: Pilot of a B-24
Battle or Place of Action: Ploesti, Rumania
Date of Action: 9 July 1944
G.O. Number, Date: 48, 23 June 1945
Citation: He took part in a highly effective attack against vital oil installations in Ploesti on 9 July 1944. Just after "bombs away," the plane received heavy and direct hits from antiaircraft fire. One crewmember was instantly killed and six others severely wounded. The airplane was badly damaged, two were knocked out, the controls cables cut, the oxygen system on fire, and the bomb bay flooded with gas and hydraulic fluid. Regaining control of his crippled plane, 1st Lt. Pucket turned its direction over to the copilot. He calmed the crew, administered first aid, and surveyed the damage. Finding the bomb bay doors jammed, he used the hand crank to open them to allow the gas to escape. He jettisoned all guns and equipment but the plane continued to lose altitude rapidly. Realizing that it would be impossible to reach friendly territory he ordered the crew to abandon ship. Three of the crew, uncontrollable from fright or shock, would not leave. First Lt. Pucket urged the others to jump. Ignoring their entreaties to follow, he refused to abandon the three hysterical men and was last seen fighting to regain control of the plane. A few moments later the flaming bomber crashed on a mountainside. First Lt. Pucket, unhesitatingly and with supreme sacrifice, gave his life in his courageous attempt to save the lives of three others.

2915 ◆ RAMAGE, LAWSON PATERSON "RED"

Rank: Commander (highest rank: Vice Admiral)
Service: U.S. Navy
Birthday: 19 January 1909
Place of Birth: Monroe Bridge, Franklin County, Massachusetts
Date of Death: 15 April 1990
Place of Death: Bethesda, Maryland
Cemetery: Arlington National Cemetery (7-A-184)—Arlington, Virginia
Entered Service at: Vermont
Unit: U.S.S. *Parche*
Served as: Commanding Officer
Battle or Place of Action: off Taiwan, South China Sea
Date of Action: 31 July 1944
Date of Presentation: 10 January 1945
Place of Presentation: The White House, presented by Pres. Franklin D. Roosevelt
Citation: For conspicuous gallantry and intrepidity at the risk of his life above and beyond the call of duty as commanding officer of the U.S.S. *Parche* in a predawn attack on a Japanese convoy, 31 July 1944. Boldly penetrating the screen of a heavily escorted convoy, Comdr. Ramage launched a perilous surface attack by delivering a crippling stern shot into a freighter and quickly following up with a series of bow and stern torpedoes to sink the leading tanker and damage the second one. Exposed by the light of bursting flares and bravely defiant of terrific shellfire passing close overhead, he struck again, sinking a transport by two forward reloads. In the mounting fury of fire from the damaged and sinking tanker, he calmly ordered his men below, remaining on the bridge to fight it out with an enemy now disorganized and confused. Swift to act as a fast transport closed in to ram, Comdr. Ramage daringly swung the stern of the speeding *Parche* as she crossed the bow of the onrushing ship, clearing by less than 50 feet but placing his submarine in a deadly crossfire from escorts on all sides and with the transport dead ahead. Undaunted, he sent three smashing "down the throat" bow shots to stop the target, then scored a killing hit as a climax to 46 minutes of violent action with the *Parche* and her valiant fighting company retiring victorious and unscathed.

2916 ◆ *RAY, BERNARD JAMES

Rank: First Lieutenant
Service: U.S. Army
Birthday: 9 June 1921
Place of Birth: Brooklyn, Kings County, New York
Date of Death: 17 November 1944
Cemetery: Long Island National Cemetery (DSS-6) (MH)—Farmingdale, New York
Entered Service at: Baldwin, Nassau County, New York
Unit: Company F, 8th Infantry, 4th Infantry Division
Served as: Platoon Leader
Battle or Place of Action: Hurtgen Forest, near Schevenhutte, Germany
Date of Action: 17 November 1944
G.O. Number, Date: 115, 8 December 1945
Citation: He was platoon leader with Company F, 8th Infantry, on 17 November 1944, during the drive through the Hurtgen Forest near Schevenhutte, Germany. The American forces attacked in wet, bitterly cold weather over rough, wooded terrain, meeting brutal resistance from posi-

tions spaced throughout the forest behind minefields and wire obstacles. Small arms, machine-gun, mortar, and artillery fire caused heavy casualties in the ranks when Company F was halted by a concertina-type wire barrier. Under heavy fire, 1st Lt. Ray reorganized his men and prepared to blow a path through the entanglement, a task which appeared impossible of accomplishment and from which others tried to dissuade him. With impacable determination to clear the way, he placed explosive caps in his pockets, obtained several bangalore torpedoes, and then wrapped a length of highly explosive primer cord about his body. He dashed forward under direct fire, reached the barbed wire and prepared his demolition charge as mortar shells, which were being aimed at him alone, came steadily nearer his completely exposed position. He had placed a torpedo under the wire and was connecting it to a charge he carried when he was severely wounded by a bursting mortar shell. Apparently realizing that he would fail in his self-imposed mission unless he completed it in a few moments, he made a supremely gallant decision. With the primer cord still wound around his body and the explosive caps in his pocket, he completed a hasty wiring system and unhesitatingly thrust down on the handle of the charger, destroying himself with the wire barricade in the resulting blast. By the deliberate sacrifice of his life, 1st Lt. Ray enabled his company to continue its attack, the resumption of which was of positive significance in gaining the approaches to the Cologne Plain.

2917 ◆ *REESE, JAMES W.

Rank: Private
Service: U.S. Army
Birthday: 1920
Place of Birth: Chester, Delaware County, Pennsylvania
Date of Death: 5 August 1943
Cemetery: Chester Rural Cemetery—Chester, Pennsylvania
Entered Service at: Chester, Delaware County, Pennsylvania
Unit: 26th Infantry, 1st Infantry Division
Served as: Acting Squad Leader
Battle or Place of Action: at Mount Vassillio, Sicily
Date of Action: 5 August 1943
G.O. Number, Date: 85, 17 December 1943
Date of Presentation: December 1943
Place of Presentation: Fort Dupont, Delaware, presented by Maj. Gen. Lunsford Oliver to his family
Citation: For conspicuous gallantry and intrepidity at the risk of life, above and beyond the call of duty in action involving actual conflict with the enemy. When the enemy launched a counterattack which threatened the position of his company, Pvt. Reese, as the acting squad leader of a 60-mm mortar squad, displayed superior leadership on his own initiative, maneuvered his squad forward to a favorable position from which, by skillfully directing the fire of his weapon, he caused many casualties in the enemy ranks, and aided materially in repulsing the counterattack. When the enemy fire became so severe as to make his position untenable, he ordered the other members of his squad to withdraw to a safer position, but declined to seek safety for himself. So as to bring more effective fire upon the enemy, Pvt. Reese, without assistance, moved his mortar to a new position and attacked an enemy machine-gun nest. He had only three rounds of ammunition but secured a direct hit with his last round, completely destroying the nest and killing the occupants. Ammunition being exhausted, he abandoned the mortar, seized a rifle, and continued to advance, moving into an exposed position overlooking the enemy. Despite a heavy concentration of machine-gun, mortar, and artillery fire, the heaviest experienced by his unit throughout the entire Sicilian campaign, he remained at this position and continued to inflict casualties upon the enemy until he was killed. His bravery, coupled with his gallant and unswerving determination to close with the enemy, regardless of consequences and obstacles which he faced, are a priceless inspiration to our Armed Forces.

2918 ◆ *REESE JR., JOHN N.

Rank: Private First Class
Service: U.S. Army
Birthday: 13 June 1923
Place of Birth: Muskogee, Muskogee County, Oklahoma
Date of Death: 9 February 1945
Cemetery: Fort Gibson National Cemetery (2-1259-E) (MH)—Fort Gibson, Oklahoma
Entered Service at: Pryor, Mayes County, Oklahoma
Unit: Company B, 148th Infantry, 37th Infantry Division
Battle or Place of Action: Paco Railroad Station, Manila, Philippine Islands
Date of Action: 9 February 1945
G.O. Number, Date: 89, 19 October 1945
Citation: He was engaged in the attack on the Paco Railroad Station, which was strongly defended by 300 determined enemy soldiers with machine guns and rifles, supported by several pillboxes, three 20-mm guns, one 37-mm gun, and heavy mortars. While making a frontal assault across an open field, his platoon was halted 100 yards from the station by intense enemy fire. On his own initiative he left the platoon, accompanied by a comrade, and continued forward to a house 60 yards from the objective. Although under constant enemy observation, the two men remained in this position for an hour, firing at targets of opportunity, killing more than 35 Japanese and wounding many more. Moving closer to the station and discovering a group of Japanese replacements attempting to reach pillboxes, they opened heavy fire, killed more than 40 and stopped all subsequent attempts to man the emplacements. Enemy fire became more intense as they advanced to within 20 yards of the station. From that point Pfc. Reese provided effective covering fire and courageously drew enemy fire to himself while his companion killed seven Japanese and destroyed a 20-mm gun and heavy machine gun with hand grenades. With their ammunition running low, the two men started to return to the American lines, alternately providing covering fire for each other as they withdrew. During this movement, Pfc. Reese was killed by enemy fire as he reloaded his rifle. The intrepid team, in 2 1/2 hours of fierce fighting, killed more than 82 Japanese, completely disorganized their defense, and paved the way for subsequent complete defeat of the enemy at this strongpoint. By his gallant determination in the face of tremendous odds, aggressive fighting spirit, and extreme heroism at the cost of his life, Pfc. Reese materially aided the advance of our troops in Manila

and provided a lasting inspiration to all those with whom he served.

2919 ◆ *REEVES, THOMAS JAMES

Rank: Radio Electrician (highest rank: Warrant Officer)
Service: U.S. Navy
Birthday: 9 December 1895
Place of Birth: Thomaston, Litchfield County, Connecticut
Date of Death: 7 December 1941
Cemetery: National Memorial Cemetery of the Pacific (A-884) (MH)—Honolulu, Hawaii
Entered Service at: Connecticut
Unit: U.S.S. *California*
Battle or Place of Action: Pearl Harbor, Territory of Hawaii
Date of Action: 7 December 1941
Citation: For distinguished conduct in the line of his profession, extraordinary courage, and disregard of his own safety during the attack on the Fleet in Pearl Harbor, by Japanese forces on 7 December 1941. After the mechanized ammunition hoists were put out of action on the U.S.S. *California*, Reeves, on his own initiative, in a burning passageway, assisted in the maintenance of an ammunition supply by hand to the antiaircraft guns until he was overcome by smoke and fire, which resulted in his death.

2920 ◆ *RICKETTS, MILTON ERNEST

Rank: Lieutenant
Service: U.S. Navy
Birthday: 5 August 1913
Place of Birth: Baltimore, Baltimore County, Maryland
Date of Death: 8 May 1942
Place of Death: Coral Sea
Cemetery: A.B.M.C. Manila Cemetery (Wall of the Missing)—Manila, Philippine Islands
Entered Service at: Maryland
Unit: U.S.S. *Yorktown*
Served as: Officer-in-Charge of the Engineering Repair Party
Battle or Place of Action: Coral Sea
Date of Action: 8 May 1942
Citation: For extraordinary and distinguished gallantry above and beyond the call of duty as officer-in-charge of the Engineering Repair Party of the U.S.S. *Yorktown* in action against enemy Japanese forces in the Battle of the Coral Sea on 8 May 1942. During the severe bombing of the *Yorktown* by enemy Japanese forces, an aerial bomb passed through and exploded directly beneath the compartment in which Lt. Ricketts' battle station was located, killing, wounding, or stunning all of his men and mortally wounding him. Despite his ebbing strength, Lt. Ricketts promptly opened the valve of a near-by fireplug, partially led out the firehose, and directed a heavy stream of water into the fire before dropping dead beside the hose. His courageous action, which undoubtedly prevented the rapid spread of fire to serious proportions, and his unflinching devotion to duty were in keeping with the highest traditions of the U.S. Naval Service. He gallantly gave his life for his country.

2921 ◆ *RIORDAN, PAUL F.

Rank: Second Lieutenant
Service: U.S. Army
Birthday: 8 November 1920
Place of Birth: Charles City, Floyd County, Iowa
Date of Death: 8 February 1944
Place of Death: Cassino, Italy
Cemetery: Mount Olivet Cemetery (MH)—Kansas City, Missouri
Entered Service at: Kansas City, Clay County, Missouri
Unit: Company L, 133d Infantry, 34th Infantry Division
Served as: Platoon Leader
Battle or Place of Action: near Cassino, Italy
Date of Action: 3-8 February 1944
G.O. Number, Date: 74, 11 September 1944
Date of Presentation: 11 September 1944
Place of Presentation: Kansas City, Missouri, presented to his parents at their home
Citation: For conspicuous gallantry and intrepidity above and beyond the call of duty. In the attack on the approaches to the city of Cassino on 3 February 1944, 2d Lt. Riordan led one of the assault platoons. Attacking Hill 175, his command was pinned down by enemy machine-gun fire from the hill and from a pillbox about 45 yards to the right of the hill. In the face of intense fire, 2d Lt. Riordan moved out in full view of the enemy gunners to reach a position from where he could throw a hand grenade into the pillbox. Then, getting to his knees, he hurled the grenade approximately 45 yards, scoring a direct hit. The grenade killed one and wounded the other two Germans in the nest and silenced the gun. Another soldier then cleaned out the enemy pillboxes on the hill itself, and the company took its objective. Continuing the assault into Cassino itself on 8 February 1944, 2d Lt. Riordan and his platoon were given the mission of taking the city jailhouse, one of the enemy's several strongpoints. Again 2d Lt. Riordan took the lead and managed to get through the ring of enemy fire covering the approaches and reached the building. His platoon, however, could not get through the intense fire and was cut off. Second Lt. Riordan, aware that his men were unable to follow, determined to carry on singlehandedly, but the numerically superior enemy force was too much for him to overcome, and he was killed by enemy small-arms fire after disposing of at least two of the defenders. Second Lt. Riordan's bravery and extraordinary heroism in the face of almost certain death were an inspiration to his men and exemplify the highest traditions of the U.S. Armed Forces.

2922 ◆ *ROAN, CHARLES HOWARD

Rank: Private First Class
Service: U.S. Marine Corps Reserve
Birthday: 16 August 1923
Place of Birth: Claude, Armstrong County, Texas
Date of Death: 18 September 1944
Cemetery: A.B.M.C. Manila Cemetery (Wall of the Missing)—Manila, Philippine Islands; Claude Cemetery ('In Memory' marker)—Claude, Texas
Entered Service at: Texas

Unit: 2d Battalion, 7th Marines, 1st Marine Division
Battle or Place of Action: Peleliu Island, Palau Islands
Date of Action: 18 September 1944
Citation: For conspicuous gallantry and intrepidity at the risk of his life above and beyond the call of duty while serving with the 2d Battalion, 7th Marines, 1st Marine Division, in action against enemy Japanese forces on Peleliu, Palau Islands, 18 September 1944. Shortly after his leader ordered a withdrawal upon discovering that his squad was partly cut off from their company as a result of the rapid advance along an exposed ridge during an aggressive attack on the strongly entrenched enemy, Pfc. Roan and his companions were suddenly engaged in a furious exchange of hand grenades by Japanese forces emplaced in a cave on higher ground and to the rear of the squad. Seeking protection with four other marines in a depression in the rocky, broken terrain, Pfc. Roan was wounded by an enemy grenade which fell close to their position and, immediately realizing the imminent peril to his comrades when another grenade landed in the midst of the group, unhesitatingly flung himself upon it, covering it with his body and absorbing the full impact of the explosion. By his prompt action and selfless conduct in the face of almost certain death, he saved the lives of four men. His great personal valor reflects the highest credit upon himself and the U.S. Naval Service. He gallantly gave his life for his comrades.

2923 ◆ *ROBINSON JR., JAMES E.

Rank: First Lieutenant
Service: U.S. Army
Birthday: 10 July 1918
Place of Birth: Toledo, Lucas County, Ohio
Date of Death: 6 April 1945
Cemetery: Fort Sam Houston National Cemetery (T-98) (MH)—San Antonio, Texas
Entered Service at: Waco, McLennan County, Texas
Unit: Battery A, 861st Field Artillery Battalion, 63d Infantry Division
Served as: Forward Observer
Battle or Place of Action: near Untergriesheim, Germany
Date of Action: 6 April 1945
G.O. Number, Date: 117, 11 December 1945
Citation: He was a field artillery observer attached to Company A, 253d Infantry, near Untergriesheim, Germany, on 6 April 1945. Eight hours of desperate fighting over open terrain swept by German machine-gun, mortar, and small-arms fire had decimated Company A, robbing it of its commanding officer and most of its key enlisted personnel, when 1st Lt. Robinson rallied the 23 remaining uninjured riflemen and a few walking wounded, and, while carrying his heavy radio for communications with American batteries, led them through intense fire in a charge against the objective. Ten German infantrymen in foxholes threatened to stop the assault, but the gallant leader killed them all at point-blank range with rifle and pistol fire and then pressed on with his men to sweep the area of all resistance. Soon afterward he was ordered to seize the defended town of Kressbach. He went to each of the 19 exhausted survivors with cheering words, instilling in them courage and fortitude, before leading the little band forward once more. In the advance he was seriously wounded in the throat by a shell fragment, but, despite great pain and loss of blood, he refused medical attention and continued the attack, directing supporting artillery fire even though he was mortally wounded. Only after the town had been taken and he could no longer speak did he leave the command he had inspired in victory and walk nearly two miles to an aid station where he died from his wounds. By his intrepid leadership 1st Lt. Robinson was directly responsible for Company A's accomplishing its mission against tremendous odds.

2924 ◆ RODRIGUEZ, CLETO L.

Rank: Technical Sergeant (rank at time of action: Private) (highest rank: Master Sergeant)
Service: U.S. Army
Birthday: 26 April 1923
Place of Birth: San Marcos, Hays County, Texas
Date of Death: 7 December 1990
Place of Death: San Antonio, Texas
Cemetery: Fort Sam Houston National Cemetery (MH)—San Antonio, Texas
Entered Service at: San Antonio, Bexar County, Texas
Unit: Company B, 148th Infantry, 37th Infantry Division
Served as: Automatic Rifleman
Battle or Place of Action: Paco Railroad Station, Manila, Philippine Islands
Date of Action: 9 February 1945
G.O. Number, Date: 97, 1 November 1945
Date of Presentation: 12 October 1945
Place of Presentation: The White House, presented by Pres. Harry S. Truman
Citation: He was an automatic rifleman when his unit attacked the strongly defended Paco Railroad Station during the battle for Manila, Philippine Islands. While making a frontal assault across an open field, his platoon was halted 100 yards from the station by intense enemy fire. On his own initiative, he left the platoon, accompanied by a comrade, and continued forward to a house 60 yards from the objective. Although under constant enemy observation, the two men remained in this position for an hour, firing at targets of opportunity, killing more than 35 hostile soldiers, and wounding many more. Moving closer to the station and discovering a group of Japanese replacements attempting to reach pillboxes, they opened heavy fire, killed more than 40, and stopped all subsequent attempts to man the emplacements. Enemy fire became more intense as they advanced to within 20 yards of the station. Then, covered by his companion, Pvt. Rodriguez boldly moved up to the building and threw five grenades through a doorway, killing seven Japanese, destroying a 20-mm gun, and wrecking a heavy machine gun. With their ammunition running low, the two men started to return to the American lines, alternately providing covering fire for each other's withdrawal. During this movement, Pvt. Rodriguez' companion was killed. In 2 1/2 hours of fierce fighting the intrepid team killed more than 82 Japanese, completely disorganized their defense, and paved the way for the subsequent overwhelming defeat of the

Battle or Place of Action: Peleliu Island, Palau Islands
Date of Action: 15 September 1944
Date of Presentation: 15 June 1945
Place of Presentation: The White House, presented by Pres. Harry S. Truman
Citation: For conspicuous gallantry and intrepidity at the risk of his life above and beyond the call of duty while attached to the 1st Battalion, 5th Marines, 1st Marine Division, during action against enemy Japanese forces on Peleliu Island, Palau Group, 15 September 1944. Before permitting his men to use an enemy dugout as a position for an 81-mm mortar observation post, 1st Lt. Rouh made a personal reconnaissance of the pillbox and, upon entering, was severely wounded by Japanese rifle fire from within. Emerging from the dugout, he was immediately assisted by two marines to a less exposed area but, while receiving first aid, was further endangered by an enemy grenade which was thrown into their midst. Quick to act in spite of his weakened condition, he lurched to a crouching position and thrust both men aside, placing his own body between them and the grenade and taking the full blast of the explosion himself. His exceptional spirit of loyalty and self-sacrifice in the face of almost certain death reflects the highest credit upon 1st Lt. Rouh and the U.S. Naval Service.

2931 ◆ RUDOLPH, DONALD EUGENE

Rank: Second Lieutenant (rank at time of action: Technical Sergeant)
Service: U.S. Army
Birthday: 21 February 1921
Place of Birth: South Haven, Wright County, Minnesota
Entered Service at: Minneapolis, Hennepin County, Minnesota
Unit: Weapons Platoon, Company E, 2d Battalion, 20th Infantry, 6th Infantry Division
Served as: Acting Platoon Leader
Battle or Place of Action: Munoz, Luzon, Philippine Islands
Date of Action: 5 February 1945
G.O. Number, Date: 77, 10 September 1945
Date of Presentation: 23 August 1945
Place of Presentation: The White House (Gold Room), presented by Pres. Harry S. Truman
Citation: Second Lt. Rudolph (then T/Sgt.) was acting as platoon leader at Munoz, Luzon, Philippine Islands. While administering first aid on the battlefield, he observed enemy fire issuing from a nearby culvert. Crawling to the culvert with rifle and grenades, he killed three of the enemy concealed there. He then worked his way across open terrain toward a line of enemy pillboxes which had immobilized his company. Nearing the first pillbox, he hurled a grenade through its embrasure and charged the position. With his bare hands he tore away the wood and tin covering, then dropped a grenade through the opening, killing the enemy gunners and destroying their machine gun. Ordering several riflemen to cover his further advance, 2d Lt. Rudolph seized a pick mattock and made his way to a second pillbox. Piercing its top with the mattock, he dropped a grenade through the hole, firing several rounds from his rifle into it, and smothered any surviving enemy by sealing the hole and the embrasure with earth. In quick succession he attacked and neutralized six more pillboxes. Later, when his platoon was attacked by an enemy tank, he advanced under covering fire, climbed to the top of the tank, and dropped a white phosphorus grenade through the turret, destroying the crew. Through his outstanding heroism, superb courage, and leadership, and complete disregard for his own safety, 2d Lt. Rudolph cleared a path for an advance which culminated in one of the most decisive victories of the Philippine campaign.

2932 ◆ *RUHL, DONALD JACK

Rank: Private First Class
Service: U.S. Marine Corps Reserve
Birthday: 2 July 1923
Place of Birth: Columbus, Stillwater County, Montana
Date of Death: 21 February 1945
Cemetery: Hillside Cemetery (MH)—Greybull, Wyoming
Entered Service at: Montana
Unit: Company E, 2d Battalion, 28th Marines, 5th Marine Division
Served as: Rifleman
Battle or Place of Action: Iwo Jima, Volcano Islands
Date of Action: 19-21 February 1945
Citation: For conspicuous gallantry and intrepidity at the risk of his life above and beyond the call of duty while serving as a rifleman in an assault platoon of Company E, 28th Marines, 5th Marine Division, in action against enemy Japanese forces on Iwo Jima, Volcano Islands from 19–21 February 1945. Quick to press the advantage after eight Japanese had been driven from a blockhouse on D-day, Pfc. Ruhl singlehandedly attacked the group, killing one of the enemy with his bayonet and another by rifle fire in his determined attempt to annihilate the escaping troops. Cool and undaunted as the fury of hostile resistance steadily increased throughout the night, he voluntarily left the shelter of his tank trap early in the morning of D-day plus one and moved out under a tremendous volume of mortar and machine-gun fire to rescue a wounded marine lying in an exposed position approximately 40 yards forward of the line. Half pulling and half carrying the wounded man, he removed him to a defiladed position, called for an assistant and a stretcher and, again running the gauntlet of hostile fire, carried the casualty to an aid station some 300 yards distant on the beach. Returning to his platoon, he continued his valiant efforts, volunteering to investigate an apparently abandoned Japanese gun emplacement 75 yards forward of the right flank during consolidation of the front lines, and subsequently occupying the position through the night to prevent the enemy from repossessing the valuable weapon. Pushing forward in the assault against the vast network of fortifications surrounding Mt. Suribachi the following morning, he crawled with his platoon guide to the top of a Japanese bunker to bring fire to bear on enemy troops located on the far side of the bunker. Suddenly a hostile grenade landed between the two marines. Instantly Pfc. Ruhl called a warning to his fellow marine and dived on the deadly missile, absorbing the full impact of the shattering

explosion in his own body and protecting all within range from the danger of flying fragments although he might easily have dropped from his position on the edge of the bunker to the ground below. An indomitable fighter, Pfc. Ruhl rendered heroic service toward the defeat of a ruthless enemy, and his valor, initiative, and unfaltering spirit of self-sacrifice in the face of almost certain death sustain and enhance the highest traditions of the U.S. Naval Service. He gallantly gave his life for his country.

2933 ◆ RUIZ, ALEJANDRO RENTERIA

Rank: Private First Class (highest rank: Sergeant)
Service: U.S. Army
Birthday: 26 June 1924
Place of Birth: Loving, Eddy County, New Mexico
Entered Service at: Carlsbad, Eddy County, New Mexico
Unit: 1st Platoon, Company A, 1st Battalion, 165th Infantry, 27th Infantry Division
Served as: Rifleman
Battle or Place of Action: Okinawa, Ryukyu Islands
Date of Action: 28 April 1945
G.O. Number, Date: 60, 26 June 1946
Date of Presentation: 14 June 1946
Place of Presentation: The White House, presented by Pres. Harry S. Truman
Citation: When his unit was stopped by a skillfully camouflaged enemy pillbox, he displayed conspicuous gallantry and intrepidity above and beyond the call of duty. His squad, suddenly brought under a hail of machine-gun fire and a vicious grenade attack, was pinned down. Jumping to his feet, Pfc. Ruiz seized an automatic rifle and lunged through the flying grenades and rifle and automatic fire for the top of the emplacement. When an enemy soldier charged him, his rifle jammed. Undaunted, Pfc. Ruiz whirled on his assailant and clubbed him down. Then he ran back through bullets and grenades, seized more ammunition and another automatic rifle, and again made for the pillbox. Enemy fire now was concentrated on him, but he charged on, miraculously reaching the position, and in plain view he climbed to the top. Leaping from one opening to another, he sent burst after burst into the pillbox, killing 12 of the enemy and completely destroying the position. Pfc. Ruiz's heroic conduct, in the face of overwhelming odds, saved the lives of many comrades and eliminated an obstacle that long would have checked his unit's advance.

2934 ◆ *SADOWSKI, JOSEPH JOHN

Rank: Sergeant
Service: U.S. Army
Birthday: 7 December 1916
Place of Birth: Perth Amboy, Middlesex County, New Jersey
Date of Death: 14 September 1944
Place of Death: Valhey, France
Cemetery: St. Stephen's Cemetery—Keasby, New Jersey
Entered Service at: Perth Amboy, Middlesex County, New Jersey
Unit: Company A, 37th Tank Battalion, 4th Armored Division
Served as: Tank Commander
Battle or Place of Action: Valhey, France
Date of Action: 14 September 1944
G.O. Number, Date: 32, 23 April 1945
Place of Presentation: Fort George Meade, Maryland, presented by Maj. Gen. Francis B. Melon to his family
Citation: For conspicuous gallantry and intrepidity at the risk of his life above and beyond the call of duty at Valhey, France. On the afternoon of 14 September 1944, Sgt. Sadowski as a tank commander was advancing with the lead elements of Combat Command A, 4th Armored Division, through an intensely severe barrage of enemy fire from the streets and buildings of the town of Valhey. As Sgt. Sadowski's tank advanced through the hail of fire, it was struck by a shell from an 88-mm gun fired at a range of 20 yards. The tank was disabled and burst into flames. The suddenness of the enemy attack caused confusion and hesitation among the crews of the remaining tanks of our forces. Sgt. Sadowski immediately ordered his crew to dismount and take cover in the adjoining buildings. After his crew had dismounted, Sgt. Sadowski discovered that one member of the crew, the bow gunner, had been unable to leave the tank. Although the tank was being subjected to a withering hail of enemy small-arms, bazooka, grenade, and mortar fire from the streets and from the windows of adjacent buildings, Sgt. Sadowski unhesitatingly returned to his tank and endeavored to pry up the bow gunner's hatch. While engaged in this attempt to rescue his comrade from the burning tank, he was cut down by a stream of machine-gun fire which resulted in his death. The gallant and noble sacrifice of his life in the aid of his comrade, undertaken in the face of almost certain death, so inspired the remainder of the tank crews that they pressed forward with greater ferocity and completely destroyed the enemy forces in this town without further loss to themselves. The heroism and selfless devotion to duty displayed by Sgt. Sadowski, which resulted in his death, inspired the remainder of his forces to press forward to victory and reflect the highest traditions of the Armed Forces.

2935 ◆ *SARNOSKI, JOSEPH RAYMOND

Rank: Second Lieutenant
Service: U.S. Army Air Corps
Birthday: 30 January 1915
Place of Birth: Simpson, Lackawanna County, Pennsylvania
Date of Death: 16 June 1943
Place of Death: Over Buka Area, Solomon Islands
Cemetery: National Memorial Cemetery of the Pacific (A-582) (MH)—Honolulu, Hawaii
Entered Service at: Simpson, Lackawanna County, Pennsylvania
Unit: 65th Bombardment Squadron, 43d Bombardment Group, 5th Air Force
Served as: Bombardier of a B-17
Battle or Place of Action: over Buka area, Solomon Islands
Date of Action: 16 June 1943

G.O. Number, Date: 85, 17 December 1943
Place of Presentation: Presented to his Widow
Citation: For conspicuous gallantry and intrepidity in action above and beyond the call of duty. On 16 June 1943, 2d Lt. Sarnoski volunteered as bombardier of a crew on an important photographic mapping mission covering the heavily defended Buka area, Solomon Islands. When the mission was nearly completed, about 20 enemy fighters intercepted. At the nose guns, 2d Lt. Sarnoski fought off the first attackers, making it possible for the pilot to finish the plotted course. When a coordinated frontal attack by the enemy extensively damaged his bomber and seriously injured five of the crew, 2d Lt. Sarnoski though wounded, continued firing and shot down two enemy planes. A 20-millimeter shell which burst in the nose of the bomber knocked him into the catwalk under the cockpit. With indomitable fighting spirit, he crawled back to his post and kept on firing until he collapsed on his guns. Second Lt. Sarnoski, by resolute defense of his aircraft at the price of his life, made possible the completion of a vitally important mission.

2936 ◆ *SAYERS, FOSTER JOSEPH

Rank: Private First Class
Service: U.S. Army
Birthday: 27 April 1924
Place of Birth: Marshalls Creek, Monroe County, Pennsylvania
Date of Death: 12 November 1944
Place of Death: near Thionville, France
Cemetery: Schenck Cemetery (MH)—Howard Township, Pennsylvania
Entered Service at: Howard, Centre County, Pennsylvania
Unit: Company L, 357th Infantry, 90th Infantry Division
Served as: Machine Gunner
Battle or Place of Action: near Thionville, France
Date of Action: 12 November 1944
G.O. Number, Date: 89, 19 October 1945
Citation: He displayed conspicuous gallantry above and beyond the call of duty in combat on 12 November 1944, near Thionville, France. During an attack on strong hostile forces entrenched on a hill he fearlessly ran up the steep approach toward his objective and set up his machine gun 20 yards from the enemy. Realizing it would be necessary to attract full attention of the dug-in Germans while his company crossed an open area and flanked the enemy, he picked up his gun, charged through withering machine-gun and rifle fire to the very edge of the emplacement, and there killed 12 German soldiers with devastating close-range fire. He took up a position behind a log and engaged the hostile infantry from the flank in an heroic attempt to distract their attention while his comrades attained their objective at the crest of the hill. He was killed by the very heavy concentration of return fire; but his fearless assault enabled his company to sweep the hill with a minimum of casualties, killing or capturing every enemy soldier on it. Pfc. Sayers' indomitable fighting spirit, aggressiveness, and supreme devotion to duty live on as an example of the highest traditions of the military service.

2937 ◆ SCHAEFER, JOSEPH EDWARD

Rank: Staff Sergeant
Service: U.S. Army
Birthday: 27 December 1918
Place of Birth: New York, New York
Date of Death: 16 March 1987
Place of Death: Staten Island, New York
Cemetery: Long Island National Cemetery (DSS-80) (MH)—Farmingdale, New York
Entered Service at: Long Island, New York
Unit: 2d Platoon, Company I, 18th Infantry, 1st Infantry Division
Served as: Squad Leader
Battle or Place of Action: near Stolberg, Germany
Date of Action: 24 September 1944
G.O. Number, Date: 71, 22 August 1945
Citation: He was in charge of a squad of the 2d Platoon in the vicinity of Stolberg, Germany, early in the morning of 24 September 1944, when two enemy companies supported by machine guns launched an attack to seize control of an important crossroads which was defended by his platoon. One American squad was forced back, another captured, leaving only S/Sgt. Schaefer's men to defend the position. To shift his squad into a house which would afford better protection, he crawled about under heavy small-arms and machine-gun fire, instructed each individual, and moved to the building. A heavy concentration of enemy artillery fire scored hits on his strongpoint. S/Sgt. Schaefer assigned his men to positions and selected for himself the most dangerous one at the door. With his M1 rifle, he broke the first wave of infantry thrown toward the house. The Germans attacked again with grenades and flamethrowers but were thrown back a second time, S/Sgt. Schaefer killing and wounding several. Regrouped for a final assault, the Germans approached from two directions. One force drove at the house from the front, while a second group advanced stealthily along a hedgerow. Recognizing the threat, S/Sgt. Schaefer fired rapidly at the enemy before him, killing or wounding all six; then, with no cover whatever, dashed to the hedgerow and poured deadly accurate shots into the second group, killing five, wounding two others, and forcing the enemy to withdraw. He scoured the area near his battered stronghold and captured 10 prisoners. By this time the rest of his company had begun a counterattack; he moved forward to assist another platoon to regain its position. Remaining in the lead, crawling and running in the face of heavy fire, he overtook the enemy, and liberated the American squad captured earlier in the battle. In all, single-handed and armed only with his rifle, he killed between 15 and 20 Germans, wounded at least as many more, and took 10 prisoners. S/Sgt. Schaefer's indomitable courage and his determination to hold his position at all costs were responsible for stopping an enemy breakthrough.

2938 ◆ SCHAUER, HENRY

Rank: Private First Class (highest rank: Technical Sergeant)
Service: U.S. Army
Birthday: 9 October 1918

Place of Birth: Clinton, Custer County, Oklahoma
Entered Service at: Scobey, Daniels County, Montana
Unit: Battle Patrol, Company F, 2d Battalion, 15th Infantry Regiment, 3d Infantry Division
Served as: Automatic Rifleman
Battle or Place of Action: near Cisterna di Littoria, Italy
Date of Action: 23-24 May 1944
G.O. Number, Date: 83, 27 October 1944
Date of Presentation: 4 October 1944
Place of Presentation: France, presented by Lt. Gen. Alexander M. Patch III
Citation: For conspicuous gallantry and intrepidity at risk of life above and beyond the call of duty. On 23 May 1944, at 12 noon, Pfc. (now T/Sgt.) Schauer left the cover of a ditch to engage four German snipers who opened fire on the patrol from its rear. Standing erect he walked deliberately 30 yards toward the enemy, stopped amid the fire of four rifles centered on him, and with four bursts from his BAR, each at a different range, killed all of the snipers. Catching sight of a fifth sniper waiting for the patrol behind a house chimney, Pfc. Schauer brought him down with another burst. Shortly after, when a heavy enemy artillery concentration and two machine guns temporarily halted the patrol, Pfc. Schauer again left cover to engage the enemy weapons singlehandedly. While shells exploded within 15 yards, showering dirt over him, and strings of grazing German tracer bullets whipped past him at chest level, Pfc. Schauer knelt, killed the two gunners of the machine gun only 60 yards from him with a single burst from his BAR, and crumpled two other enemy soldiers who ran to man the gun. Inserting a fresh magazine in his BAR, Pfc. Schauer shifted his body to fire at the other weapon 500 yards distant and emptied his weapon into the enemy crew, killing all four Germans. Next morning, when shells from a German Mark VI tank and a machine gun only 100 yards distant again forced the patrol to seek cover, Pfc. Schauer crawled toward the enemy machine gun, stood upright only 80 yards from the weapon as its bullets cut the surrounding ground, and four tank shells fired directly at him burst within 20 yards. Raising his BAR to his shoulder, Pfc. Schauer killed the four members of the German machine-gun crew with one burst of fire.

2939 ◆ SCHONLAND, HERBERT EMERY

Rank: Commander (highest rank: Rear Admiral)
Service: U.S. Navy
Birthday: 7 September 1900
Place of Birth: Portland, Cumberland County, Maine
Date of Death: 13 November 1984
Place of Death: New London, Connecticut
Cemetery: Arlington National Cemetery (7-A-168) (MH)—Arlington, Virginia
Entered Service at: Portland, Cumberland County, Maine
Unit: U.S.S. *San Francisco*
Served as: Damage Control Officer
Battle or Place of Action: Iron Bottom Sound, off Savo Island, Solomon Islands
Date of Action: 12-13 November 1943
Date of Presentation: 5 January 1943
Place of Presentation: The White House (Oval Office), presented by Pres. Franklin D. Roosevelt
Citation: For extreme heroism and courage above and beyond the call of duty as damage control officer of the U.S.S. *San Francisco* in action against greatly superior enemy forces in the battle off Savo Island, 12–13 November 1942. In the same violent night engagement in which all of his superior officers were killed or wounded, Lt. Comdr. Schonland was fighting valiantly to free the *San Francisco* of large quantities of water flooding the second deck compartments through numerous shell holes caused by enemy fire. Upon being informed that he was commanding officer, he ascertained that the conning of the ship was being efficiently handled, then directed the officer who had taken over that task to continue while he himself resumed the vitally important work of maintaining the stability of the ship. In water waist deep, he carried on his efforts in darkness illuminated only by hand lanterns until water in flooded compartments had been drained or pumped off and watertight integrity had again been restored to the *San Francisco*. His great personal valor and gallant devotion to duty at great peril to his own life were instrumental in bringing his ship back to port under her own power, saved to fight again in the service of her country.

2940 ◆ *SCHWAB, ALBERT ERNEST

Rank: Private First Class
Service: U.S. Marine Corps Reserve
Birthday: 17 July 1920
Place of Birth: Washington, D.C.
Date of Death: 7 May 1945
Cemetery: Memorial Park Cemetery (MH)—Tulsa, Oklahoma
Entered Service at: Tulsa, Tulsa County, Oklahoma
: Headquarters Company, 1st Battalion, 5th Marines, 1st Marine Division
Served as: Flamethrower Operator
Battle or Place of Action: Okinawa Shima, Ryukyu Islands
Date of Action: 7 May 1945
Date of Presentation: 31 May 1946
Place of Presentation: Presented by Rear Adm. Joseph J. Clark to his Son
Citation: For conspicuous gallantry and intrepidity at the risk of his life above and beyond the call of duty as a flamethrower operator in action against enemy Japanese forces on Okinawa Shima in the Ryukyu Islands, 7 May 1945. Quick to take action when his company was pinned down in a valley and suffered resultant heavy casualties under blanketing machine-gun fire emanating from a high ridge to the front, Pfc. Schwab, unable to flank the enemy emplacement because of steep cliffs on either side, advanced up the face of the ridge in bold defiance of the intense barrage and, skillfully directing the fire of his flamethrower, quickly demolished the hostile gun position, thereby enabling his company to occupy the ridge. Suddenly a second enemy machine gun opened fire, killing and wounding several marines with its initial bursts. Estimating with split-second decision the tactical difficulties

confronting his comrades, Pfc. Schwab elected to continue his one-man assault despite a diminished supply of fuel for his flamethrower. Cool and indomitable, he moved forward in the face of a direct concentration of hostile fire, relentlessly closed with the enemy position, and attacked. Although severely wounded by a final vicious blast from the enemy weapon, Pfc. Schwab had succeeded in destroying two highly strategic Japanese gun positions during a critical stage of the operation and, by his dauntless, singlehanded efforts, had materially furthered the advance of his company. His aggressive initiative, outstanding valor, and professional skill throughout the bitter conflict sustain and enhance the highest traditions of the U.S. Naval Service.

2941 ◆ *SCOTT, NORMAN

Rank: Rear Admiral
Service: U.S. Navy
Birthday: 10 August 1889
Place of Birth: Indianapolis, Marion County, Indiana
Date of Death: 13 November 1942
Cemetery: A.B.M.C. Manila Cemetery (Wall of the Missing)—Manila, Philippine Islands
Entered Service at: Indiana
Unit: U.S.S. *Atlanta* (flagship)
Served as: Fleet Commander
Battle or Place of Action: Iron Bottom Sound, off Savo Island, Solomon Islands
Date of Action: 12-13 November 1942
Date of Presentation: 9 December 1942
Place of Presentation: The White House, presented by Pres. Franklin D. Roosevelt to his Son
Citation: For extraordinary heroism and conspicuous intrepidity above and beyond the call of duty during action against enemy Japanese forces off Savo Island on the night of 11–12 October and again on the night of 12–13 November 1942. In the earlier action, intercepting a Japanese task force intent upon storming our island positions and landing reinforcements at Guadalcanal, Rear Adm. Scott, with courageous skill and superb coordination of the units under his command, destroyed eight hostile vessels and put the others to flight. Again challenged, a month later, by the return of a stubborn and persistent foe, he led his force into a desperate battle against tremendous odds, directing close-range operations against the invading enemy until he himself was killed in the furious bombardment by their superior firepower. On each of these occasions his dauntless initiative, inspiring leadership, and judicious foresight in a crisis of grave responsibility contributed decisively to the rout of a powerful invasion fleet and to the consequent frustration of a formidable Japanese offensive. He gallantly gave his life in the service of his country.

2942 ◆ *SCOTT, ROBERT RAYMOND

Rank: Machinist's Mate First Class
Service: U.S. Navy
Birthday: 13 July 1915
Place of Birth: Massillon, Stark County, Ohio
Date of Death: 7 December 1941
Cemetery: Arlington National Cemetery (34-3939) (MH)—Arlington, Virginia
Entered Service at: Ohio
Unit: U.S.S. *California*
Battle or Place of Action: Pearl Harbor, Territory of Hawaii
Date of Action: 7 December 1941
Citation: For conspicuous devotion to duty, extraordinary courage, and complete disregard for his own life, above and beyond the call of duty, during the attack on the Fleet in Pearl Harbor by Japanese forces on 7 December 1941. The compartment in the U.S.S. *California* in which the air compressor to which Scott was assigned as his battle station was flooded as the result of a torpedo hit. The remainder of the personnel evacuated that compartment but Scott refused to leave, saying words to the effect "This is my station and I will stay and give them air as long as the guns are going."

2943 ◆ SCOTT, ROBERT SHELDON

Rank: Captain (rank at time of action: 2d Lieutenant) (highest rank: Colonel)
Service: U.S. Army
Birthday: 30 November 1913
Place of Birth: Washington, D.C.
Entered Service at: Santa Fe, Santa Fe County, New Mexico
Unit: 1st Platoon, Company C, 1st Battalion, 17th Infantry, 43d Infantry Division
Served as: Platoon Leader
Battle or Place of Action: near Munda Air Strip, New Georgia, Solomon Islands
Date of Action: 29 July 1943
G.O. Number, Date: 81, 14 October 1944
Date of Presentation: 14 October 1944
Place of Presentation: Aitape, New Guinea, presented by Maj. Gen. Leonard F. (Red) Wing
Citation: For conspicuous gallantry and intrepidity at the risk of his life above and beyond the call of duty near Munda Airstrip, New Georgia, Solomon Islands on 29 July 1943. After 27 days of bitter fighting, the enemy held a hilltop salient which commanded the approach to Munda Airstrip. Our troops were exhausted from prolonged battle and heavy casualties, but Lt. Scott advanced with the leading platoon of his company to attack the enemy position, urging his men forward in the face of enemy rifle and enemy machine-gun fire. He had pushed forward alone to a point midway across the barren hilltop within 75 yards of the enemy when the enemy launched a desperate counterattack, which if successful would have gained undisputed possession of the hill. Enemy riflemen charged out on the plateau, firing and throwing grenades as they moved to engage our troops. The company withdrew, but Lt. Scott, with only a blasted tree stump for cover, stood his ground against the wild enemy assault. By firing his carbine and throwing the grenades in his possession he momentarily stopped the enemy advance, using the brief respite to obtain more grenades. Disregarding small-arms fire and exploding grenades aimed at him, suffering a bullet wound in the left hand and a painful shrapnel wound in the head after his carbine had been shot from his hand, he threw

grenade after grenade with devastating accuracy until the beaten enemy withdrew. Our troops, inspired to renewed effort by Lt. Scott's intrepid stand and incomparable courage, swept across the plateau to capture the hill, and from this strategic position four days later captured Munda Airstrip.

2944 ◆ SHEA, CHARLES WILLIAM

Rank: Second Lieutenant (rank at time of action: Staff Sergeant) (highest rank: Colonel)
Service: U.S. Army
Birthday: 24 August 1921
Place of Birth: Bronx County, New York
Date of Death: 7 April 1994
Place of Death: Plainview, New York
Cemetery: Long Island National Cemetery (DSS 71-A)—Farmingdale, New York
Entered Service at: New York, New York
Unit: 2d Squad, 2d Platoon, Company F, 2d Battalion, 350th Infantry, 88th Infantry Division
Served as: Squad Leader
Battle or Place of Action: near Mount Damiano, Italy
Date of Action: 12 May 1944
G.O. Number, Date: 4, 12 January 1945
Date of Presentation: 1 December 1944
Place of Presentation: Montecatini, Italy, presented by Lt. Gen. Mark Clark
Citation: For conspicuous gallantry and intrepidity at the risk of life above and beyond the call of duty, on 12 May 1944, near Mount Damiano, Italy. As 2d Lt. Shea and his company were advancing toward a hill occupied by the enemy, three enemy machine guns suddenly opened fire, inflicting heavy casualties upon the company and halting its advance. Second Lt. Shea immediately moved forward to eliminate these machine-gun nests in order to enable his company to continue its attack. The deadly hail of machine-gun fire at first pinned him down, but boldly continuing his advance, 2d Lt. Shea crept up to the first nest. Throwing several hand grenades, he forced the four enemy soldiers manning this position to surrender, and disarming them, he sent them to the rear. He then crawled to the second machine-gun position and after a short firefight forced two more German soldiers to surrender. At this time, the third machine gun fired at him, and while deadly small-arms fire pitted the earth around him, 2d Lt. Shea crawled toward the nest. Suddenly he stood up and rushed the emplacement and with well-directed fire from his rifle, he killed all three of the enemy machine gunners. Second Lt. Shea's display of personal valor was an inspiration to the officers and men of his company.

2945 ◆ *SHERIDAN, CARL VERNON

Rank: Private First Class
Service: U.S. Army
Birthday: 5 January 1925
Place of Birth: Baltimore, Baltimore County, Maryland
Date of Death: 26 November 1944
Cemetery: Druid Ridge Cemetery (MH)—Pikesville, Maryland
Entered Service at: Baltimore, Baltimore County, Maryland
Unit: Company K, 2d Battalion, 47th Infantry, 9th Infantry Division
Served as: Bazooka Gunner
Battle or Place of Action: Frenzenberg Castle, Weisweiler, Germany
Date of Action: 26 November 1944
G.O. Number, Date: 43, 30 May 1945
Date of Presentation: June 1945
Place of Presentation: To his parents
Citation: Attached to the 2d Battalion of the 47th Infantry on 26 November 1944, for the attack on Frenzenberg Castle, in the vicinity of Weisweiler, Germany, Company K, after an advance of 1,000 yards through a shattering barrage of enemy artillery and mortar fire, had captured two buildings in the courtyard of the castle but was left with an effective fighting strength of only 35 men. During the advance, Pfc. Sheridan, acting as a bazooka gunner, had braved the enemy fire to stop and procure the additional rockets carried by his ammunition bearer who was wounded. Upon rejoining his company in the captured buildings, he found it in a furious fight with approximately 70 enemy paratroopers occupying the castle gatehouse. This was a solidly built stone structure surrounded by a deep water-filled moat 20 feet wide. The only approach to the heavily defended position was across the courtyard and over a drawbridge leading to a barricaded oaken door. Pfc. Sheridan, realizing that his bazooka was the only available weapon with sufficient power to penetrate the heavy oak planking, with complete disregard for his own safety left the protection of the buildings and in the face of heavy and intense small-arms and grenade fire, crossed the courtyard to the drawbridge entrance where he could bring direct fire to bear against the door. Although handicapped by the lack of an assistant, and a constant target for the enemy fire that burst around him, he skillfully and effectively handled his awkward weapon to place two well-aimed rockets into the structure. Observing that the door was only weakened, and realizing that a gap must be made for a successful assault, he loaded his last rocket, took careful aim, and blasted a hole through the heavy planks. Turning to his company he shouted, "Come on, let's get them!" With his .45 pistol blazing, he charged into the gaping entrance and was killed by the withering fire that met him. The final assault on Frenzenberg Castle was made through the gap which Pfc. Sheridan gave his life to create.

2946 ◆ *SHOCKLEY, WILLIAM RALPH

Rank: Private First Class
Service: U.S. Army
Birthday: 4 December 1918
Place of Birth: Bokoshe, LeFlore County, Oklahoma
Date of Death: 31 March 1945
Place of Death: Villa Verde Trail, Luzon, Philippine Islands
Cemetery: Floral Memorial Park—Selma, California
Entered Service at: Selma, Fresno County, California
Unit: Company L, 128th Infantry, 32d Infantry Division
Battle or Place of Action: Villa Verde Trail, Luzon, Philippine Islands

Date of Action: 31 March 1945
G.O. Number, Date: 89, 19 October 1945
Citation: He was in position with his unit on a hill when the enemy, after a concentration of artillery fire, launched a counterattack. He maintained his position under intense enemy fire and urged his comrades to withdraw, saying that he would "remain to the end" to provide cover. Although he had to clear two stoppages which impeded the reloading of his weapon, he halted one enemy charge. Hostile troops then began moving in on his left flank, and he quickly shifted his gun to fire on them. Knowing that the only route of escape was being cut off by the enemy, he ordered the remainder of his squad to withdraw to safety and deliberately remained at his post. He continued to fire until he was killed during the ensuing enemy charge. Later, four Japanese were found dead in front of his position. Pfc. Shockley, facing certain death, sacrificed himself to save his fellow soldiers, but the heroism and gallantry displayed by him enabled his squad to reorganize and continue its attack.

2947 ◆ SHOMO, WILLIAM ARTHUR

Rank: Major (highest rank: Colonel)
Service: U.S. Army Air Corps/U.S. Air Force
Birthday: 30 May 1918
Place of Birth: Jeannette, Westmoreland County, Pennsylvania
Date of Death: 25 June 1990
Place of Death: Warren, Pennsylvania
Cemetery: St. Clair Cemetery—Greenburg, Pennsylvania
Entered Service at: Westmoreland County, Pennsylvania
Unit: 82d Tactical Reconnaissance Squadron, 71st Reconnaissance Gp., 308th Bombardment Wing, 5th Air Force
Served as: Pilot of a P-51
Battle or Place of Action: over Luzon, Philippine Islands
Date of Action: 11 January 1945
G.O. Number, Date: 25, 7 April 1945
Date of Presentation: 3 April 1945
Place of Presentation: Luzon, Philippine Islands, presented by Maj. Gen. Ennis C. Whitehead
Citation: For conspicuous gallantry and intrepidity at the risk of his life above and beyond the call of duty. Maj. Shomo was lead pilot of a flight of two fighter planes charged with an armed photographic and strafing mission against the Aparri and Laoag airdromes. While en route to the objective, he observed an enemy twin engine bomber, protected by 12 fighters, flying about 2,500 feet above him and in the opposite direction. Although the odds were 13 to 2, Maj. Shomo immediately ordered an attack. Accompanied by his wingman he closed on the enemy formation in a climbing turn and scored hits on the leading plane of the third element, which exploded in midair. Maj. Shomo then attacked the second element from the left side of the formation and shot another fighter down in flames. When the enemy formed for counterattack, Maj. Shomo moved to the other side of the formation and hit a third fighter which exploded and fell. Diving below the bomber, he put a burst into its underside and it crashed and burned. Pulling up from this pass he encountered a fifth plane firing head on and destroyed it. He next dived upon the first element and shot down the lead plane; then diving to 300 feet in pursuit of another fighter he caught it with his initial burst and it crashed in flames. During this action his wingman had shot down three planes, while the three remaining enemy fighters had fled into a cloud bank and escaped. Maj. Shomo's extraordinary gallantry and intrepidity in attacking such a far superior force and destroying seven enemy aircraft in one action is unparalleled in the southwest Pacific area.

2948 ◆ *SHOUP, CURTIS F.

Rank: Staff Sergeant
Service: U.S. Army
Birthday: 11 January 1921
Place of Birth: Napanoch, Ulster County, New York
Date of Death: 7 January 1945
Cemetery: North Scriba Church Cemetery (MH)—Scriba, New York
Entered Service at: Buffalo, Erie County, New York
Unit: Company I, 346th Infantry, 87th Infantry Division
Battle or Place of Action: near Tillet, Belgium
Date of Action: 7 January 1945
G.O. Number, Date: 60, 25 July 1945
Citation: On 7 January 1945, near Tillet, Belgium, his company attacked German troops on rising ground. Intense hostile machine-gun fire pinned down and threatened to annihilate the American unit in an exposed position where frozen ground made it impossible to dig in for protection. Heavy mortar and artillery fire from enemy batteries was added to the storm of destruction falling on the Americans. Realizing that the machine gun must be silenced at all costs, S/Sgt. Shoup, armed with an automatic rifle, crawled to within 75 yards of the enemy emplacement. He found that his fire was ineffective from this position, and completely disregarding his own safety, stood up and grimly strode ahead into the murderous stream of bullets, firing his low-held weapon as he went. He was hit several times and finally was knocked to the ground. But he struggled to his feet and staggered forward until close enough to hurl a grenade, wiping out the enemy machine-gun nest with his dying action. By his heroism, fearless determination, and supreme sacrifice, S/Sgt. Shoup eliminated a hostile weapon which threatened to destroy his company and turned a desperate situation into victory.

2949 ◆ SHOUP, DAVID MONROE

Rank: Colonel (highest rank: General)
Service: U.S. Marine Corps
Birthday: 30 December 1904
Place of Birth: Battle Ground, Tippecanoe County, Indiana
Date of Death: 13 January 1983
Place of Death: Alexandria, Virginia
Cemetery: Arlington National Cemetery (7-A-189) (MH)—Arlington, Virginia
Entered Service at: Indiana
Unit: 2d Marines, 2d Marine Division
Served as: Commanding Officer of all Marines on Betio Island

Battle or Place of Action: Betio Island, Tarawa Atoll, Gilbert Islands
Date of Action: 20-22 November 1943
Date of Presentation: 22 January 1945
Place of Presentation: Presented by Sec. of the Navy James V. Forrestal
Citation: For conspicuous gallantry and intrepidity at the risk of his life above and beyond the call of duty as commanding officer of all Marine Corps troops in action against enemy Japanese forces on Betio Island, Tarawa Atoll, Gilbert Islands from 20–22 November 1943. Although severely shocked by an exploding enemy shell soon after landing at the pier and suffering from a serious, painful leg wound which had become infected, Col. Shoup fearlessly exposed himself to the terrific and relentless artillery, machine-gun, and rifle fire from hostile shore emplacements. Rallying his hesitant troops by his own inspiring heroism, he gallantly led them across the fringing reefs to charge the heavily fortified island and reinforce our hard-pressed, thinly held lines. Upon arrival onshore, he assumed command of all landed troops and, working without rest under constant, withering enemy fire during the next two days, conducted smashing attacks against unbelievably strong and fanatically defended Japanese positions despite innumerable obstacles and heavy casualties. By his brilliant leadership, daring tactics, and selfless devotion to duty, Col. Shoup was largely responsible for the final decisive defeat of the enemy, and his indomitable fighting spirit reflects great credit upon the U.S. Naval Service.

2950 ◆ SIGLER, FRANKLIN EARL

Rank: Private (highest rank: Private First Class)
Service: U.S. Marine Corps Reserve
Birthday: 6 November 1924
Place of Birth: Glen Ridge, Essex County, New Jersey
Date of Death: 20 January 1995
Cemetery: Arlington National Cemetery (12-2799)—Arlington, Virginia
Entered Service at: Little Falls, Passaic County, New Jersey
Unit: 2d Squad, 3d Platoon, Company F, 2d Battalion, 26th Marines, 5th Marine Division
Served as: Squad Leader
Battle or Place of Action: Iwo Jima, Volcano Islands
Date of Action: 14 March 1945
Date of Presentation: 5 October 1945
Place of Presentation: The White House, presented by Pres. Harry S. Truman
Citation: For conspicuous gallantry and intrepidity at the risk of his life above and beyond the call of duty while serving with the 2d Battalion, 26th Marines, 5th Marine Division, in action against enemy Japanese forces during the seizure of Iwo Jima in the Volcano Islands on 14 March 1945. Voluntarily taking command of his rifle squad when the leader became a casualty, Pvt. Sigler fearlessly led a bold charge against an enemy gun installation which had held up the advance of his company for several days and, reaching the position in advance of the others, assailed the emplacement with hand grenades and personally annihilated the entire crew. As additional Japanese troops opened fire from concealed tunnels and caves above, he quickly scaled the rocks leading to the attacking guns, surprised the enemy with a furious one-man assault and, although severely wounded in the encounter, deliberately crawled back to his squad position where he steadfastly refused evacuation, persistently directing heavy machine-gun and rocket barrages on the Japanese cave entrances. Undaunted by the merciless rain of hostile fire during the intensified action, he gallantly disregarded his own painful wounds to aid casualties, carrying three wounded squad members to safety behind the lines and returning to continue the battle with renewed determination until ordered to retire for medical treatment. Stouthearted and indomitable in the face of extreme peril, Pvt. Sigler, by his alert initiative, unfaltering leadership, and daring tactics in a critical situation, effected the release of his besieged company from enemy fire and contributed essentially to its further advance against a savagely fighting enemy. His superb valor, resolute fortitude, and heroic spirit of self-sacrifice throughout reflect the highest credit upon Pvt. Sigler and the U.S. Naval Service.

2951 ◆ SILK, EDWARD A.

Rank: First Lieutenant
Service: U.S. Army
Birthday: 8 June 1916
Place of Birth: Johnstown, Cambria County, Pennsylvania
Date of Death: 19 November 1955
Cemetery: Arlington National Cemetery (30-1045-C) (MH)—Arlington, Virginia
Entered Service at: Johnstown, Cambria County, Pennsylvania
Unit: Company E, 398th Infantry, 100th Infantry Division
Served as: Weapons Platoon Leader
Battle or Place of Action: near St. Pravel, France
Date of Action: 23 November 1944
G.O. Number, Date: 97, 1 November 1945
Date of Presentation: 12 October 1945
Place of Presentation: The White House, presented by Pres. Harry S. Truman
Citation: First Lt. Edward A. Silk commanded the weapons platoon of Company E, 398th Infantry, on 23 November 1944, when the end battalion was assigned the mission of seizing high ground overlooking Moyenmoutier, France, prior to an attack on the city itself. His company jumped off in the lead at dawn and by noon had reached the edge of the woods in the vicinity of St. Pravel where scouts saw an enemy sentry standing guard before a farmhouse in a valley below. One squad, engaged in reconnoitering the area, was immediately pinned down by intense machine-gun and automatic-weapon fire from within the house. Skillfully deploying his light machine-gun section, 1st Lt. Silk answered enemy fire, but when 15 minutes had elapsed with no slackening of resistance, he decided to eliminate the strongpoint by a one-man attack. Running 100 yards across an open field to the shelter of a low stone wall directly in front of the farmhouse, he fired into the door and windows with his carbine; then, in full view of the enemy, vaulted the wall and dashed 50 yards through a hail of bullets to the left side of the house, where he hurled a grenade through a window, silencing a machine gun and

killing two gunners. In attempting to move to the right side of the house he drew fire from a second machine gun emplaced in the woodshed. With magnificent courage he rushed this position in the face of direct fire and succeeded in neutralizing the weapon and killing the two gunners by throwing grenades into the structure. His supply of grenades was by now exhausted, but undaunted, he dashed back to the side of the farmhouse and began to throw rocks through a window, demanding the surrender of the remaining enemy. Twelve Germans, overcome by his relentless assault and confused by his unorthodox methods, gave up to the lone American. By his gallant willingness to assume the full burden of the attack and the intrepidity with which he carried out his extremely hazardous mission, 1st Lt. Silk enabled his battalion to continue its advance and seize its objective.

2952 ◆ SJOGREN, JOHN CARLETON

Rank: Staff Sergeant (highest rank: Major)
Service: U.S. Army
Birthday: 19 August 1916
Place of Birth: Rockford, Kent County, Michigan
Date of Death: 30 August 1987
Cemetery: Rockford Cemetery (MH)—Rockford, Michigan
Entered Service at: Rockford, Kent County, Michigan
Unit: Company I, 160th Infantry, 40th Infantry Division
Battle or Place of Action: near San Jose Hacienda, Negros, Philippine Islands
Date of Action: 23 May 1945
G.O. Number, Date: 97, 1 November 1945
Date of Presentation: 12 October 1945
Place of Presentation: The White House, presented by Pres. Harry S. Truman
Citation: He led an attack against a high precipitous ridge defended by a company of enemy riflemen, who were entrenched in spider holes and supported by well-sealed pillboxes housing automatic weapons with interlocking bands of fire. The terrain was such that only one squad could advance at a time; and from a knoll atop a ridge a pillbox covered the only approach with automatic fire. Against this enemy stronghold, S/Sgt. Sjogren led the first squad to open the assault. Deploying his men, he moved forward and was hurling grenades when he saw that his next in command, at the opposite flank, was gravely wounded. Without hesitation he crossed 20 yards of exposed terrain in the face of enemy fire and exploding dynamite charges, moved the man to cover, and administered first aid. He then worked his way forward and, advancing directly into the enemy fire, killed eight Japanese in spider holes guarding the approach to the pillbox. Crawling to within a few feet of the pillbox while his men concentrated their bullets on the fire port, he began dropping grenades through the narrow firing slit. The enemy immediately threw two or three of these unexploded grenades out, and fragments from one wounded him in the hand and back. However, by hurling grenades through the embrasure faster than the enemy could return them, he succeeded in destroying the occupants. Despite his wounds, he directed his squad to follow him in a systematic attack on the remaining positions, which he eliminated in like manner, taking tremendous risks, overcoming bitter resistance, and never hesitating in his relentless advance. To silence one of the pillboxes, he wrenched a light machine gun out through the embrasure as it was firing before blowing up the occupants with hand grenades. During this action, S/Sgt. Sjogren, by his heroic bravery, aggressiveness, and skill as a soldier, singlehandedly killed 43 enemy soldiers and destroyed nine pillboxes, thereby paving the way for his company's successful advance.

2953 ◆ SKAGGS JR., LUTHER

Rank: Private First Class (highest rank: Corporal)
Service: U.S. Marine Corps Reserve
Birthday: 3 March 1923
Place of Birth: Henderson, Henderson County, Kentucky
Date of Death: 6 April 1976
Place of Death: Sarasota, Florida
Cemetery: Arlington National Cemetery (46-1066-8) (MH)—Arlington, Virginia
Entered Service at: Kentucky
Unit: 3d Battalion, 3d Marines, 3d Marine Division
Served as: Squad Leader
Battle or Place of Action: Asan-Adelup Beachhead, Guam, Mariana Islands
Date of Action: 21-22 July 1944
Date of Presentation: 15 June 1945
Place of Presentation: The White House, presented by Pres. Harry S. Truman
Citation: For conspicuous gallantry and intrepidity at the risk of his life above and beyond the call of duty while serving as a squad leader with a mortar section of a rifle company in the 3d Battalion, 3d Marines, 3d Marine Division, during action against enemy Japanese forces on the Asan-Adelup beachhead, Guam, Mariana Islands, 21–22 July 1944. When the section leader became a casualty under a heavy mortar barrage shortly after landing, Pfc. Skaggs promptly assumed command and led the section through intense fire for a distance of 200 yards to a position from which to deliver effective coverage of the assault on a strategic cliff. Valiantly defending this vital position against strong enemy counterattacks during the night, Pfc. Skaggs was critically wounded when a Japanese grenade lodged in his foxhole and exploded, shattering the lower part of one leg. Quick to act, he applied an improvised tourniquet and, while propped up in his foxhole, gallantly returned the enemy's fire with his rifle and hand grenades for a period of eight hours, later crawling unassisted to the rear to continue the fight until the Japanese had been annihilated. Uncomplaining and calm throughout this critical period, Pfc. Skaggs served as a heroic example of courage and fortitude to other wounded men and, by his courageous leadership and inspiring devotion to duty, upheld the high traditions of the U.S. Naval Service.

2954 ◆ SLATON, JAMES DANIEL

Rank: Corporal
Service: U.S. Army
Birthday: 2 April 1912
Place of Birth: Laurel, Jones County, Mississippi

Date of Death: 25 February 1961
Place of Death: Laurel, Mississippi
Cemetery: Harmony Cemetery—Laurel, Mississippi
Entered Service at: Gulfport, Harrison County, Mississippi
Unit: Company K, 157th Infantry, 45th Infantry Division
Served as: Lead Scout
Battle or Place of Action: near Oliveto, Italy
Date of Action: 23 September 1943
G.O. Number, Date: 44, 30 May 1944
Date of Presentation: 7 June 1944
Place of Presentation: Algiers, presented by Lt. Gen. Jacob S. Devers
Citation: For conspicuous gallantry and intrepidity at the risk of life above and beyond the call of duty in action with the enemy in the vicinity of Oliveto, Italy, on 23 September 1943. Cpl. Slaton was lead scout of an infantry squad which had been committed to a flank to knock out enemy resistance which had succeeded in pinning two attacking platoons to the ground. Working ahead of his squad, Cpl. Slaton crept upon an enemy machine-gun nest and, assaulting it with his bayonet, succeeded in killing the gunner. When his bayonet stuck, he detached it from the rifle and killed another gunner with rifle fire. At that time he was fired upon by a machine gun to his immediate left. Cpl. Slaton then moved over open ground under constant fire to within throwing distance, and on his second try scored a direct hit on the second enemy machine-gun nest, killing two enemy gunners. At that time a third machine gun fired on him 100 yards to his front, and Cpl. Slaton killed both of these enemy gunners with rifle fire. As a result of Cpl. Slaton's heroic action in immobilizing three enemy machine-gun nests with bayonet, grenade, and rifle fire, the two rifle platoons which were receiving heavy casualties from enemy fire were able to withdraw to covered positions and again take the initiative. Cpl. Slaton withdrew under mortar fire on order of his platoon leader at dusk that evening. The heroic actions of Cpl. Slaton were far above and beyond the call of duty and are worthy of emulation.

2955 ◆ *SMITH, FURMAN L.

Rank: Private
Service: U.S. Army
Birthday: 11 May 1925
Place of Birth: Six Mile, Pickins County, South Carolina
Date of Death: 31 May 1944
Cemetery: Pleasant Hill Church Cemetery—Central, South Carolina
Entered Service at: Central, Pickins County, South Carolina
Unit: Company L, 135th Infantry, 34th Infantry Division
Served as: Rifleman
Battle or Place of Action: near Lanuvio, Italy
Date of Action: 31 May 1944
G.O. Number, Date: 6, 24 January 1945
Citation: For conspicuous gallantry and intrepidity at the risk of his life above and beyond the call of duty. In its attack on a strongpoint, an infantry company was held up by intense enemy fire. The group to which Pvt. Smith belonged was far in the lead when attacked by a force of 80 Germans. The squad leader and one other man were seriously wounded and other members of the group withdrew to the company position, but Pvt. Smith refused to leave his wounded comrades. He placed them in the shelter of shell craters and then alone faced a strong enemy counterattack, temporarily checking it by his accurate rifle fire at close range, killing and wounding many of the foe. Against overwhelming odds, he stood his ground until shot down and killed, rifle in hand.

2956 ◆ SMITH, JOHN LUCIAN

Rank: Major (highest rank: Colonel)
Service: U.S. Marine Corps
Birthday: 26 December 1914
Place of Birth: Lexington, Cleveland County, Oklahoma
Date of Death: 9 June 1972
Cemetery: Arlington National Cemetery (3-2503-H-2)—Arlington, Virginia
Entered Service at: Oklahoma
Unit: Marine Fighting Squadron 223
Served as: Commanding Officer
Battle or Place of Action: Guadalcanal, Solomon Islands
Date of Action: August–September 1942
Date of Presentation: 24 February 1943
Place of Presentation: The White House, presented by Pres. Franklin D. Roosevelt
Citation: For conspicuous gallantry and heroic achievement in aerial combat above and beyond the call of duty as commanding officer of Marine Fighting Squadron 233 during operations against enemy Japanese forces in the Solomon Islands area, August–September 1942. Repeatedly risking his life in aggressive and daring attacks, Maj. Smith led his squadron against a determined force, greatly superior in numbers, personally shooting down 16 Japanese planes between 21 August and 15 September 1942. In spite of the limited combat experience of many of the pilots of this squadron, they achieved the notable record of a total of 83 enemy aircraft destroyed in this period, mainly attributable to the thorough training under Maj. Smith and to his intrepid and inspiring leadership. His bold tactics and indomitable fighting spirit, and the valiant and zealous fortitude of the men of his command not only rendered the enemy's attacks ineffective and costly to Japan, but contributed to the security of our advance base. His loyal and courageous devotion to duty sustains and enhances the finest traditions of the U.S. Naval Service.

2957 ◆ SMITH SR., MAYNARD HARRISON

Rank: Sergeant (highest rank: Staff Sergeant)
Service: U.S. Army Air Corps
Birthday: 19 May 1911
Place of Birth: Cairo, Michigan
Date of Death: 11 May 1984
Place of Death: Bay Pines, Florida
Cemetery: Arlington National Cemetery (66-7375) (MH)—Arlington, Virginia
Entered Service at: Cairo, Michigan
Unit: 423d Bombardment Squadron, 306th Bombardment Group, 8th Air Force
Served as: Gunner on a B-17

Battle or Place of Action: Brest, France
Date of Action: 1 May 1943
G.O. Number, Date: 38, 12 July 1943
Place of Presentation: Eighth Army Airfield, England, presented by Sec. of War Henry L. Stimson
Citation: For conspicuous gallantry and intrepidity in action above and beyond the call of duty. The aircraft of which Sgt. Smith was a gunner was subjected to intense enemy antiaircraft fire and determined fighter airplane attacks while returning from a mission over enemy-occupied continental Europe on 1 May 1943. The airplane was hit several times by antiaircraft fire and cannon shells of the fighter airplanes, two of the crew were seriously wounded, the aircraft's oxygen system shot out, and several vital control cables severed when intense fires were ignited simultaneously in the radio compartment and waist sections. The situation became so acute that three of the crew bailed out into the comparative safety of the sea. Sgt. Smith, then on his first combat mission, elected to fight the fire by himself, administered first aid to the wounded tail gunner, manned the waist guns, and fought the intense flames alternately. The escaping oxygen fanned the fire to such intense heat that the ammunition in the radio compartment began to explode, the radio, gun mount, and camera were melted, and the compartment completely gutted. Sgt. Smith threw the exploding ammunition overboard, fought the fire until all the firefighting aids were exhausted, manned the workable guns until the enemy fighter were driven away, further administered first aid to his wounded comrade, and then by wrapping himself in protecting cloth, completely extinguished the fire by hand. This soldier's gallantry in action, undaunted bravery, and loyalty to his aircraft and fellow crewmembers, without regard for his own personal safety, is an inspiration to the U.S Armed Forces.

2958 ◆ SODERMAN, WILLIAM ADOLPH

Rank: Private First Class
Service: U.S. Army
Birthday: 20 March 1912
Place of Birth: West Haven, New Haven County, Connecticut
Date of Death: 20 October 1980
Cemetery: Oak Grove Cemetery (MH)—West Haven, Connecticut
Entered Service at: West Haven, New Haven County, Connecticut
Unit: Company K, 9th Infantry, 2d Infantry Division
Served as: Bazooka Gunner
Battle or Place of Action: near Rocherath, Belgium
Date of Action: 17 December 1944
G.O. Number, Date: 97, 1 November 1945
Date of Presentation: 12 October 1945
Place of Presentation: The White House, presented by Pres. Harry S. Truman
Citation: Armed with a bazooka, he defended a key road junction near Rocherath, Belgium, on 17 December 1944, during the German Ardennes counteroffensive. After a heavy artillery barrage had wounded and forced the withdrawal of his assistant, he heard enemy tanks approaching the position where he calmly waited in the gathering darkness of early evening until the five Mark V tanks which made up the hostile force were within point-blank range. He then stood up, completely disregarding the firepower that could be brought to bear upon him, and launched a rocket into the lead tank, setting it afire and forcing its crew to abandon it as the other tanks pressed on before Pfc. Soderman could reload. The daring bazookaman remained at his post all night under severe artillery, mortar, and machine-gun fire, awaiting the next onslaught, which was made shortly after dawn by five more tanks. Running along a ditch to meet them, he reached an advantageous point and there leaped to the road in full view of the tank gunners, deliberately aimed his weapon and disabled the lead tank. The other vehicles, thwarted by a deep ditch in their attempt to go around the crippled machine, withdrew. While returning to his post Pfc. Soderman, braving heavy fire to attack an enemy infantry platoon from close range, killed at least three Germans and wounded several others with a round from his bazooka. By this time, enemy pressure had made Company K's position untenable. Orders were issued for withdrawal to an assembly area, where Pfc. Soderman was located when he once more heard enemy tanks approaching. Knowing that elements of the company had not completed their disengaging maneuver and were consequently extremely vulnerable to an armored attack, he hurried from his comparatively safe position to meet the tanks. Once more he disabled the lead tank with a single rocket, his last; but before he could reach cover, machine-gun bullets from the tank ripped into his right shoulder. Unarmed and seriously wounded he dragged himself along a ditch to the American lines and was evacuated. Through his unfaltering courage against overwhelming odds, Pfc. Soderman contributed in great measure to the defense of Rocherath, exhibiting to a superlative degree the intrepidity and heroism with which American soldiers met and smashed the savage power of the last great German offensive.

2959 ◆ SORENSON, RICHARD KEITH

Rank: Private (highest rank: First Lieutenant)
Service: U.S. Marine Corps Reserve
Birthday: 28 August 1924
Place of Birth: Anoka, Anoka County, Minnesota
Entered Service at: Anoka, Anoka County, Minnesota
Unit: 1st Squad, 1st Platoon, Company M, 3d Battalion, 24th Marine Regiment, 4th Marine Division
Served as: Machinegun Crewman
Battle or Place of Action: Namur Island, Kwajalein Atoll, Marshall Islands
Date of Action: 1-2 February 1944
Date of Presentation: 19 July 1944
Place of Presentation: Seattle Naval Hospital, Seattle, Washington, presented by Maj. Gen. Joseph C. Fegan
Citation: For conspicuous gallantry and intrepidity at the risk of his life above and beyond the call of duty while serving with an assault battalion attached to the 4th Marine Division during the battle of Namur Island, Kwajalein Atoll, Marshall Islands on 1–2 February 1944. Putting up a brave defense against a particularly violent counterattack by the enemy dur-

ing invasion operations, Pvt. Sorenson and five other marines occupying a shell hole were endangered by a Japanese grenade thrown into their midst. Unhesitatingly, and with complete disregard for his own safety, Pvt. Sorenson hurled himself upon the deadly weapon, heroically taking the full impact of the explosion. As a result of his gallant action, he was severely wounded, but the lives of his comrades were saved. His great personal valor and exceptional spirit of self-sacrifice in the face of almost certain death were in keeping with the highest traditions of the U.S. Naval Service.

2960 ◆ *SPECKER, JOE C.

Rank: Sergeant
Service: U.S. Army
Birthday: 10 January 1921
Place of Birth: Odessa, Lafayette County, Missouri
Date of Death: 7 January 1944
Cemetery: Odessa Cemetery—Odessa, Missouri
Entered Service at: Odessa, Lafayette County, Missouri
Unit: 48th Combat Engineer Battalion
Battle or Place of Action: at Mount Porchia, Italy
Date of Action: 7 January 1944
G.O. Number, Date: 56, 12 July 1944
Citation: For conspicuous gallantry and intrepidity at the risk of life above and beyond the call of duty, in action involving actual conflict. On the night of 7 January 1944, Sgt. Specker, with his company, was advancing up the slope of Mount Porchia, Italy. He was sent forward on reconnaissance and on his return he reported to his company commander the fact that there was an enemy machine-gun nest and several well-placed snipers directly in the path and awaiting the company. Sgt. Specker requested and was granted permission to place one of his machine guns in a position near the enemy machine gun. Voluntarily and alone he made his way up the mountain with a machine gun and a box of ammunition. He was observed by the enemy as he walked along and was severely wounded by the deadly fire directed at him. Though so seriously wounded that he was unable to walk, he continued to drag himself over the jagged edges of rock and rough terrain until he reached the position at which he desired to set up his machine gun. He set up the gun so well and fired so accurately that the enemy machine-gun nest was silenced and the remainder of the snipers forced to retire, enabling his platoon to obtain their objective. Sgt. Specker was found dead at his gun. His personal bravery, self-sacrifice, and determination were an inspiration to his officers and fellow soldiers.

2961 ◆ SPURRIER, JUNIOR JAMES

Rank: Staff Sergeant
Service: U.S. Army
Birthday: 14 December 1922
Place of Birth: Russell County, Kentucky
Date of Death: 25 February 1984
Place of Death: Limestone, Tennessee
Cemetery: Mountain Home National Cemetery (HH-15-8) (MH)—Johnson, Tennessee
Entered Service at: Riggs, Kentucky
Unit: Company G, 134th Infantry, 35th Infantry Division
Served as: Automatic Rifleman
Battle or Place of Action: Achain, France
Date of Action: 13 November 1944
G.O. Number, Date: 18, 15 March 1945
Citation: For conspicuous gallantry and intrepidity at the risk of his life above and beyond the call of duty in action against the enemy at Achain, France, on 13 November 1944. At 2:00 P.M., Company G attacked the village of Achain from the east. S/Sgt. Spurrier armed with a BAR passed around the village and advanced alone. Attacking from the west, he immediately killed three Germans. From this time until dark, S/Sgt. Spurrier, using at different times his BAR and M1 rifle, American and German rocket launchers, a German automatic pistol, and hand grenades, continued his solitary attack against the enemy regardless of all types of small-arms and automatic-weapon fire. As a result of his heroic actions he killed an officer and 24 enlisted men and captured two officers and two enlisted men. His valor has shed fresh honor on the U.S. Armed Forces.

2962 ◆ *SQUIRES, JOHN C.

Rank: Sergeant (rank at time of action: Private First Class)
Service: U.S. Army
Birthday: 19 May 1925
Place of Birth: Louisville, Jefferson County, Kentucky
Date of Death: 23 May 1944
Cemetery: Zachary Taylor National Cemetery (A-1359) (MH)—Louisville, Kentucky
Entered Service at: Louisville, Jefferson County, Kentucky
Unit: Company A, 30th Infantry, 3d Infantry Division
Served as: Platoon Messenger
Battle or Place of Action: near Padiglione, Italy
Date of Action: 23-24 April 1944
G.O. Number, Date: 78, 2 October 1944
Citation: For conspicuous gallantry and intrepidity at the risk of life above and beyond the call of duty. At the start of his company's attack on strongly held enemy positions in and around Spaccasassi Creek, near Padiglione, Italy, on the night of 23-24 April 1944, Pfc. Squires, platoon messenger, participating in his first offensive action, braved intense artillery, mortar, and antitank gun fire in order to investigate the effect of an antitank mine explosion on the leading platoon. Despite shells which burst close to him, Pfc. Squires made his way 50 yards forward to the advance element, noted the situation, reconnoitered a new route of advance, and informed his platoon leader of the casualties sustained and the alternate route. Acting without orders, he rounded up stragglers, organized a group of lost men into a squad and led them forward. When the platoon reached Spaccasassi Creek and established an outpost, Pfc. Squires, knowing that almost all of the noncommissioned officers were casualties, placed eight men in position of his own volition, disregarding enemy machine-gun, machine-pistol, and grenade fire which covered the creek draw. When his platoon had been reduced to 14 men, he brought up reinforcements twice. On each trip he went through barbed wire and across an enemy minefield, under intense artillery and mortar fire. Three times in the early morning the outpost was

counterattacked. Each time Pfc. Squires ignored withering enemy automatic fire and grenades which struck all around him, and fired hundreds of rounds of rifle, Browning automatic rifle, and captured German Spandau machine-gun ammunition at the enemy, inflicting numerous casualties and materially aiding in repulsing the attacks. Following these fights, he moved 50 yards to the south end of the outpost and engaged 21 German soldiers in individual machine-gun duels at point-blank range, forcing all 21 enemy to surrender and capturing 13 more Spandau guns. Learning the function of this weapon by questioning a German officer prisoner, he placed the captured guns in position and instructed other members of his platoon in their operation. The next night when the Germans attacked the outpost again he killed three and wounded more Germans with captured potato-masher grenades and fire from his Spandau gun. Pfc. Squires was killed in a subsequent action.

2963 ◆ *STEIN, TONY

Rank: Corporal
Service: U.S. Marine Corps Reserve
Birthday: 30 September 1921
Place of Birth: Dayton, Montgomery County, Ohio
Date of Death: 1 March 1945
Cemetery: Calvary Cemetery (MH)—Dayton, Ohio
Entered Service at: Ohio
Unit: Company A, 1st Battalion, 28th Marines, 5th Marine Division
Battle or Place of Action: Iwo Jima, Volcano Islands
Date of Action: 19 February 1945
Citation: For conspicuous gallantry and intrepidity at the risk of his life above and beyond the call of duty while serving with Company A, 1st Battalion, 28th Marines, 5th Marine Division, in action against enemy Japanese forces on Iwo Jima, in the Volcano Islands, 19 February 1945. The first man of his unit to be on station after hitting the beach in the initial assault, Cpl. Stein, armed with a personally improvised aircraft-type weapon, provided rapid covering fire as the remainder of his platoon attempted to move into position. When his comrades were stalled by a concentrated machine-gun and mortar barrage, he gallantly stood upright and exposed himself to the enemy's view, thereby drawing the hostile fire to his own person and enabling him to observe the location of the furiously blazing hostile guns. Determined to neutralize the strategically placed weapons, he boldly charged the enemy pillboxes one by one and succeeded in killing 20 of the enemy during the furious singlehanded assault. Cool and courageous under the merciless hail of exploding shells and bullets which fell on all sides, he continued to deliver the fire of his skillfully improvised weapon at a tremendous rate of speed which rapidly exhausted his ammunition. Undaunted, he removed his helmet and shoes to expedite his movements and ran back to the beach for additional ammunition, making a total of eight trips under intense fire and carrying or assisting a wounded man back each time. Despite the unrelenting savagery and confusion of battle, he rendered prompt assistance to his platoon whenever the unit was in position, directing the fire of a half-track against a stubborn pillbox until he had effected the ultimate destruction of the Japanese fortification. Later in the day, although his weapon was twice shot from his hands, he personally covered the withdrawal of his platoon to the company position. Stouthearted and indomitable, Cpl. Stein, by his aggressive initiative, sound judgment, and unwavering devotion to duty in the face of terrific odds, contributed materially to the fulfillment of his mission, and his outstanding valor throughout the bitter hours of conflict sustains and enhances the highest traditions of the U.S. Naval Service.

2964 ◆ STREET III, GEORGE LEVICK

Rank: Commander (highest rank: Captain)
Service: U.S. Navy
Birthday: 27 July 1913
Place of Birth: Richmond, Richmond County, Virginia
Entered Service at: Richmond, Richmond County, Virginia
Unit: U.S.S. *Tirante* SS 420
Served as: Commanding Officer
Battle or Place of Action: harbor of Quelpart Island off the coast of Korea
Date of Action: 14 April 1945
Date of Presentation: 5 October 1945
Place of Presentation: The White House, presented by Pres. Harry S. Truman
Citation: For conspicuous gallantry and intrepidity at the risk of his life above and beyond the call of duty as commanding officer of the U.S.S. *Tirante* during the first war patrol of that vessel against enemy Japanese surface forces in the harbor of Quelpart Island, off the coast of Korea on 14 April 1945. With the crew at surface battle stations, Comdr. (then Lt. Comdr.) Street approached the hostile anchorage from the south within 1,200 yards of the coast to complete a reconnoitering circuit of the island. Leaving the 10-fathom curve far behind, he penetrated the mined and shoal-obstructed waters of the restricted harbor despite numerous patroling vessels and in defiance of five shore-based radar stations and menacing aircraft. Prepared to fight it out on the surface if attacked, Comdr. Street went into action, sending two torpedoes with deadly accuracy into a large Japanese ammunition ship and exploding the target in a mountainous and blinding glare of white flames. With the *Tirante* instantly spotted by the enemy as she stood out plainly in the flare of light, he ordered the torpedo data computer set up while retiring and fired his last two torpedoes to disintegrate in quick succession the leading frigate and a similar flanking vessel. Clearing the gutted harbor at emergency full speed ahead, he slipped undetected along the shoreline, diving deep as a pursuing patrol dropped a pattern of depth charges at the point of submergence. His illustrious record of combat achievement during the first war patrol of the *Tirante* characterizes Comdr. Street as a daring and skillful leader and reflects the highest credit upon himself, his valiant command, and the U.S. Naval Service.

2965 ◆ *STRYKER, STUART S.

Rank: Private First Class
Service: U.S. Army

Birthday: 30 October 1924
Place of Birth: Portland, Multnomah County, Oregon
Date of Death: 24 March 1945
Cemetery: Golden Gate National Cemetery (B-719) (MH)—San Bruno, California
Entered Service at: Portland, Multnomah County, Oregon
Unit: Company E, 513th Parachute Infantry, 17th Airborne Division
Served as: Platoon Runner
Battle or Place of Action: near Wesel, Germany
Date of Action: 24 March 1945
G.O. Number, Date: 117, 11 December 1945
Citation: He was a platoon runner, when the unit assembled near Wesel, Germany, after a descent east of the Rhine. Attacking along a railroad, Company E reached a point about 250 yards from a large building used as an enemy headquarters and manned by a powerful force of Germans with rifles, machine guns, and four field pieces. One platoon made a frontal assault but was pinned down by intense fire from the house after advancing only 50 yards. So badly stricken that it could not return the raking fire, the platoon was at the mercy of the German machine gunners when Pfc. Stryker voluntarily left a place of comparative safety, and, armed with a carbine, ran to the head of the unit. In full view of the enemy and under constant fire, he exhorted the men to get to their feet and follow him. Inspired by his fearlessness, they rushed after him in a desperate charge through an increased hail of bullets. Twenty-five yards from the objective the heroic soldier was killed by the enemy fusillades. His gallant and wholly voluntary action in the face of overwhelming firepower, however, so encouraged his comrades and diverted the enemy's attention that other elements of the company were able to surround the house, capturing more than 200 hostile soldiers and much equipment, besides freeing three members of an American bomber crew held prisoner there. The intrepidity and unhesitating self-sacrifice of Pfc. Stryker were in keeping with the highest traditions of the military service.

2966 ◆ SWETT, JAMES ELMS

Rank: First Lieutenant (highest rank: Colonel)
Service: U.S. Marine Corps Reserve
Birthday: 15 June 1920
Place of Birth: Seattle, King County, Washington
Entered Service at: San Mateo, San Mateo County, California
Unit: Marine Fighting Squadron 221, Marine Aircraft Group 12, 1st Marine Air Wing
Served as: Division Leader
Battle or Place of Action: Solomon Islands area
Date of Action: 7 April 1943
Date of Presentation: 12 October 1943
Place of Presentation: Espirito Santo Island, New Hebrides, presented by Maj. Gen. Ralph Mitchell
Citation: For extraordinary heroism and personal valor above and beyond the call of duty, as division leader of Marine Fighting Squadron 221 with Marine Aircraft Group 12, 1st Marine Aircraft Wing, in action against enemy Japanese aerial forces in the Solomon Islands area, 7 April 1943. In a daring flight to intercept a wave of 150 Japanese planes, 1st Lt. Swett unhesitatingly hurled his four-plane division into action against a formation of 15 enemy bombers and personally exploded three hostile planes in midair with accurate and deadly fire during his dive. Although separated from his division while clearing the heavy concentration of antiaircraft fire, he boldly attacked six enemy bombers, engaged the first four in turn and, unaided, shot down all in flames. Exhausting his ammunition as he closed the fifth enemy Japanese bomber, he relentlessly drove his attack against terrific opposition which partially disabled his engine, shattered the windscreen, and slashed his face. In spite of this, he brought his battered plane down with skillful precision in the water off Tulagi without further injury. The superb airmanship and tenacious fighting spirit which enabled 1st Lt. Swett to destroy seven enemy bombers in a single flight were in keeping with the highest traditions of the U.S. Naval Service.

2967 ◆ *TERRY, SEYMOUR W.

Rank: Captain
Service: U.S. Army
Birthday: 11 December 1918
Place of Birth: Little Rock, Pulaski County, Arkansas
Date of Death: 11 May 1945
Cemetery: Roselawn Cemetery—Little Rock, Arkansas
Entered Service at: Little Rock, Pulaski County, Arkansas
Unit: Company B, 382d Infantry, 96th Infantry Division
Served as: Company Commander
Battle or Place of Action: Zebra Hill, Okinawa, Ryukyu Islands
Date of Action: 11 May 1945
G.O. Number, Date: 23, 6 March 1946
Citation: First Lt. Terry was leading an attack against heavily defended Zebra Hill when devastating fire from five pillboxes halted the advance. He braved the hail of bullets to secure satchel charges and white phosphorus grenades, and then ran 30 yards directly at the enemy with an ignited charge to the first stronghold, demolished it, and moved on to the other pillboxes, bombarding them with his grenades and calmly cutting down their defenders with rifle fire as they attempted to escape. When he had finished this job by sealing the four pillboxes with explosives, he had killed 20 Japanese and destroyed three machine guns. The advance was again held up by an intense grenade barrage which inflicted several casualties. Locating the source of enemy fire in trenches on the reverse slope of the hill, 1st Lt. Terry, burdened by six satchel charges, launched a one-man assault. He wrecked the enemy's defenses by throwing explosives into their positions and he himself accounted for 10 of the hostile troops killed when his men overran the area. Pressing forward again toward a nearby ridge, his two assault platoons were stopped by slashing machine-gun and mortar fire. He fearlessly ran across 100 yards of fire-swept terrain to join the support platoon and urge it on in a flanking maneuver. This thrust, too, was halted by stubborn resistance. First Lt. Terry began another one-man drive, hurling grenades upon the strongly entrenched defenders until they fled in confusion, leaving five dead behind them. Inspired by this bold action, the support pla-

toon charged the retreating enemy and annihilated them. Soon afterward, while organizing his company to repulse a possible counterattack, the gallant company commander was mortally wounded by the burst of an enemy mortar shell. By his indomitable fighting spirit, brilliant leadership, and unwavering courage in the face of tremendous odds, 1st Lt. Terry made possible the accomplishment of his unit's mission and set an example of heroism in keeping with the highest traditions of the military service.

2968 ◆ *THOMAS, HERBERT JOSEPH

Rank: Sergeant
Service: U.S. Marine Corps Reserve
Birthday: 8 February 1918
Place of Birth: Columbus, Franklin County, Ohio
Date of Death: 7 November 1943
Cemetery: Sunset Memorial Park—South Charleston, West Virginia
Entered Service at: West Virginia
Unit: 3d Marines, 3d Marine Division
Battle or Place of Action: Koromokina River, Bougainville Island, Solomon Islands
Date of Action: 7 November 1943
Citation: For extraordinary heroism and conspicuous gallantry above and beyond the call of duty while serving with the 3d Marines, 3d Marine Division, in action against enemy Japanese forces during the battle at the Koromokina River, Bougainville Island, Solomon Islands, on 7 November 1943. Although several of his men were struck by enemy bullets as he led his squad through dense jungle undergrowth in the face of severe hostile machine-gun fire, Sgt. Thomas and his group fearlessly pressed forward into the center of the Japanese position and destroyed the crews of two machine guns by accurate rifle fire and grenades. Discovering a third gun more difficult to approach, he carefully placed his men closely around him in strategic positions from which they were to charge after he had thrown a grenade into the emplacement. When the grenade struck vines and fell back into the midst of the group, Sgt. Thomas deliberately flung himself upon it to smother the explosion, valiantly sacrificing his life for his comrades. Inspired by his selfless action, his men unhesitatingly charged the enemy machine gun and, with fierce determination, killed the crew and several other nearby-defenders. The splendid initiative and extremely heroic conduct of Sgt. Thomas in carrying out his prompt decision with full knowledge of his fate reflect great credit upon himself and the U.S. Naval Service. He gallantly gave his life for his country.

2969 ◆ *THOMAS, WILLIAM H.

Rank: Private First Class
Service: U.S. Army
Birthday: 13 January 1923
Place of Birth: Wynne, Cross County, Arkansas
Date of Death: 22 April 1945
Cemetery: A.B.M.C. Manila Cemetery (F-16-90)—Manila, Philippine Islands
Entered Service at: Ypsilanti, Washtenaw County, Michigan
Unit: 149th Infantry, 38th Infantry Division
Served as: Automatic Rifleman
Battle or Place of Action: Zambales Mountains, Luzon, Philippine Islands
Date of Action: 22 April 1945
G.O. Number, Date: 81, 24 September 1945
Citation: He was a member of the leading squad of Company B, which was attacking along a narrow, wooded ridge. The enemy, strongly entrenched in camouflaged emplacements on the hill beyond, directed heavy fire and hurled explosive charges on the attacking riflemen. Pfc. Thomas, an automatic rifleman, was struck by one of these charges, which blew off both his legs below the knees. He refused medical aid and evacuation, and continued to fire at the enemy until his weapon was put out of action by an enemy bullet. Still refusing aid, he threw his last two grenades. He destroyed three of the enemy after suffering the wounds from which he died later that day. The effective fire of Pfc. Thomas prevented the repulse of his platoon and assured the capture of the hostile position. His magnificent courage and heroic devotion to duty provided a lasting inspiration for his comrades.

2970 ◆ *THOMASON, CLYDE A.

Rank: Sergeant
Service: U.S. Marine Corps Reserve
Birthday: 23 May 1914
Place of Birth: Atlanta, Fulton County, Georgia
Date of Death: 18 August 1942
Place of Death: Makin Island, Gilbert Islands
Cemetery: National Memorial Cemetery of the Pacific (Wall of the Missing)—Honolulu, Hawaii
Entered Service at: Georgia
Unit: 2d Marine Raider Battalion
Battle or Place of Action: Makin Island, Gilbert Islands
Date of Action: 17-18 August 1942
Date of Presentation: 20 January 1943
Place of Presentation: Presented by Sec. of the Navy James Forrestal to stepmother, Mrs. Amy M. Thomason
Citation: For conspicuous heroism and intrepidity above and beyond the call of duty during the Marine Raider Expedition against the Japanese-held island of Makin on 17–18 August 1942. Leading the advance element of the assault echelon, Sgt. Thomason disposed his men with keen judgment and discrimination and, by his exemplary leadership and great personal valor, exhorted them to like fearless efforts. On one occasion, he dauntlessly walked up to a house which concealed an enemy Japanese sniper, forced in the door, and shot the man before he could resist. Later in the action, while leading an assault on an enemy position, he gallantly gave his life in the service of his country. His courage and loyal devotion to duty in the face of grave peril were in keeping with the finest traditions of the U.S. Naval Service.

2971 ◆ THOMPSON, MAX

Rank: Sergeant (highest rank: Technical Sergeant)
Service: U.S. Army

Birthday: 21 July 1922
Place of Birth: Bethel, Pitt County, North Carolina
Entered Service at: Canton, Haywood County, North Carolina
Unit: 3d Squad, 3d Platoon, Company K, 3d Battalion, 18th Infantry, 1st Infantry Division
Served as: Assistant Squad Leader
Battle or Place of Action: near Haaren, Germany
Date of Action: 18 October 1944
G.O. Number, Date: 47, 18 June 1945
Date of Presentation: 18 June 1945
Place of Presentation: near Cheb, Czechoslovakia, presented by Lt. Gen. Clarence R. Hubner
Citation: On 18 October 1944, Company K, 18th Infantry, occupying a position on a hill near Haaren, Germany, was attacked by an enemy infantry battalion supported by tanks. The assault was preceded by an artillery concentration, lasting an hour, which inflicted heavy casualties on the company. While engaged in moving wounded men to cover, Sgt. Thomason observed that the enemy had overrun the positions of the 3d Platoon. He immediately attempted to stem the enemy's advance singlehandedly. He manned an abandoned machine gun and fired on the enemy until a direct hit from a hostile tank destroyed the gun. Shaken and dazed, Sgt. Thomason picked up an automatic rifle and, although alone against the enemy force which was pouring into the gap in our lines, he fired burst after burst, halting the leading elements of the attack and dispersing those following. Throwing aside his automatic rifle, which had jammed, he took up a rocket gun, and fired on a light tank, setting it on fire. By evening the enemy had been driven from the greater part of the captured position but still held three pillboxes. Sgt. Thomason's squad was assigned the task of dislodging the enemy from these emplacements. Darkness having fallen and finding that fire of his squad was ineffective from a distance, Sgt. Thomason crawled forward alone to within 20 yards of one of the pillboxes and fired grenades into it. The Germans holding the emplacement concentrated their fire upon him. Though wounded, he held his position fearlessly, continued his grenade fire, and finally forced the enemy to abandon the blockhouse. Sgt. Thomason's courageous leadership inspired his men and materially contributed to the clearing of the enemy from his last remaining hold on this important hill position.

2972 ◆ *THORNE, HORACE MARVIN

Rank: Corporal
Service: U.S. Army
Birthday: 29 September 1918
Place of Birth: Keansburg, Monmouth County, New Jersey
Date of Death: 21 December 1944
Cemetery: Fairview Cemetery (MH)—Red Bank, New Jersey
Entered Service at: Keyport, Monmouth County, New Jersey
Unit: Troop D, 89th Cavalry Reconnaissance Squadron, 9th Armored Division
Served as: Light Machine Gunner
Battle or Place of Action: near Grufflingen, Belgium
Date of Action: 21 December 1944
G.O. Number, Date: 80, 19 September 1945
Citation: He was the leader of a combat patrol on 21 December 1944, near Grufflingen, Belgium, with the mission of driving German forces from dug-in positions in a heavily wooded area. As he advanced his light machine gun, a German Mark III tank emerged from the enemy position and was quickly immobilized by fire from American light tanks supporting the patrol. Two of the enemy tankmen attempted to abandon their vehicle but were killed by Cpl. Thorne's shots before they could jump to the ground. To complete the destruction of the tank and its crew, Cpl. Thorne left his covered position and crept forward alone through intense machine-gun fire until close enough to toss two grenades into the tank's open turret, killing two more Germans. He returned across the same fire-beaten zone as heavy mortar fire began falling in the area, seized his machine gun, and, without help, dragged it to the knocked-out tank and set it up on the vehicle's rear deck. He fired short rapid bursts into the enemy positions from his advantageous but exposed location, killing or wounding eight. Two enemy machine-gun crews abandoned their positions and retreated in confusion. His gun jammed; but rather than leave his self-chosen post he attempted to clear the stoppage; enemy small-arms fire, concentrated on the tank, killed him instantly. Cpl. Thorne, displaying heroic initiative and intrepid fighting qualities, inflicted costly casualties on the enemy and insured the success of his patrol's mission by the sacrifice of his life.

2973 ◆ *THORSON, JOHN F.

Rank: Private First Class
Service: U.S. Army
Birthday: 10 May 1920
Place of Birth: Armstrong, Emmet County, Iowa
Date of Death: 29 October 1944
Cemetery: Keokuk National Cemetery (D-71) (MH)—Keokuk, Iowa
Entered Service at: Armstrong, Emmet County, Iowa
Unit: Company G, 17th Infantry, 7th Infantry Division
Served as: Automatic Rifleman
Battle or Place of Action: Dagami, Leyte, Philippine Islands
Date of Action: 28 October 1944
G.O. Number, Date: 58, 19 July 1945
Citation: He was an automatic rifleman on 28 October 1944, in the attack on Dagami, Leyte, Philippine Islands. A heavily fortified enemy position consisting of pillboxes and supporting trenches held up the advance of his company. His platoon was ordered to outflank and neutralize the strongpoint. Voluntarily moving well out in front of his group, Pvt. Thorson came upon an enemy fire trench defended by several hostile riflemen and, disregarding the intense fire directed at him, attacked singlehandedly. He was seriously wounded and fell about six yards from the trench. Just as the remaining 20 members of the platoon reached him, one of the enemy threw a grenade into their midst. Shouting a warning and making a final effort, Pvt. Thorson rolled onto the grenade and smothered the explosion with his body. He was instantly

killed, but his magnificent courage and supreme self-sacrifice prevented the injury and possible death of his comrades and remain with them as a lasting inspiration.

2974 ◆ *TIMMERMAN, GRANT FREDERICK

Rank: Sergeant
Service: U.S. Marine Corps
Birthday: 14 February 1919
Place of Birth: Americus, Lyon County, Kansas
Date of Death: 8 July 1944
Cemetery: National Memorial Cemetery of the Pacific (A-844) (MH)—Honolulu, Hawaii
Entered Service at: Kansas
Unit: 2d Battalion, 6th Marines, 2d Marine Division
Served as: Tank Commander
Battle or Place of Action: Saipan, Mariana Islands
Date of Action: 8 July 1944
Citation: For conspicuous gallantry and intrepidity at the risk of his life above and beyond the call of duty as tank commander serving with the 2d Battalion, 6th Marines, 2d Marine Division, during action against enemy Japanese forces on Saipan, Mariana Islands, on 8 July 1944. Advancing with his tank a few yards ahead of the infantry in support of a vigorous attack on hostile positions, Sgt. Timmerman maintained steady fire from his antiaircraft sky-mount machine gun until progress was impeded by a series of enemy trenches and pillboxes. Observing a target of opportunity, he immediately ordered the tank stopped and, mindful of the danger from the muzzle blast as he prepared to open fire with the 75-mm, fearlessly stood up in the exposed turret and ordered the infantry to hit the deck. Quick to act, as a grenade, hurled by the Japanese, was about to drop into the open turret hatch, Sgt. Timmerman unhesitatingly blocked the opening with his body, holding the grenade against his chest and taking the brunt of the explosion. His exceptional valor and loyalty in saving his men at the cost of his own life reflect the highest credit upon Sgt. Timmerman and the U.S. Naval Service. He gallantly gave his life in the service of his country.

2975 ◆ *TOMICH, PETER

Rank: Chief Watertender
Service: U.S. Navy
Birthday: 3 June 1893
Place of Birth: Prolog, Austria
Date of Death: 7 December 1941
Cemetery: National Memorial Cemetery of the Pacific (Wall of the Missing)—Honolulu, Hawaii
Entered Service at: New Jersey
Unit: U.S.S. *Utah*
Served as: Chief Watertender
Battle or Place of Action: Pearl Harbor, Territory of Hawaii
Date of Action: 7 December 1941
Date of Presentation: 4 January 1944
Place of Presentation: U.S.S. *Tomich*, presented to the ship by Rear Adm. Monroe Kelly. When the ship was decommissioned on September 20, 1946, Tomich's Medal of Honor was returned to the Navy Department. (No living relatives could be found.) On May 25, 1947 Uath Gov. Herbert B. Maw formally named Tomich an honorary citizen of Utah, the state in whose honor the battleship on which Tomich gave his life was named. On the occasion Rear Adm. Mahlon S. Tisdale, Commander of the U.S. Navy Base, San Francisco, awarded Tomich's Medal of Honor to the State of Utah as the official guardian of the dead hero. The presentation was made with full military honors in the rotunda of the Utah Capitol
Citation: For distinguished conduct in the line of his profession, and extraordinary courage and disregard of his own safety, during the attack on the Fleet in Pearl Harbor by the Japanese forces on 7 December 1941. Although realizing that the ship was capsizing as a result of enemy bombing and torpedoing, Tomich remained at his post in the engineering plant of the U.S.S. *Utah* until he saw that all boilers were secured and all fireroom personnel had left their stations, and by so doing lost his own life.

2976 ◆ TOMINAC, JOHN JOSEPH

Rank: First Lieutenant (highest rank: Colonel)
Service: U.S. Army
Birthday: 29 April 1922
Place of Birth: Conemaugh, Cambria County, Pennsylvania
Entered Service at: Conemaugh, Cambria County, Pennsylvania
Unit: 3d Platoon, Company I, 3d Battalion, 15th Infantry, 3d Infantry Division
Served as: Platoon Leader
Battle or Place of Action: Saulx de Vesoul, France
Date of Action: 12 September 1944
G.O. Number, Date: 20, 29 March 1945
Date of Presentation: 23 April 1945
Place of Presentation: Zepman Stadium, Nuremberg, Germany, presented by Lt. Gen. Alexander M. Patch III
Citation: For conspicuous gallantry and intrepidity at the risk of life above and beyond the call of duty on 12 September 1944, in an attack on Saulx de Vesoul, France. First Lt. Tominac charged alone over 50 yards of exposed terrain onto an enemy roadblock to dispatch a three-man crew of German machine gunners with a single burst from his Thompson machine gun. After smashing the enemy outpost, he led one of his squads in the annihilation of a second hostile group defended by mortar, machine-gun, automatic-pistol, rifle, and grenade fire, killing about 30 of the enemy. Reaching the suburbs of the town, he advanced 50 yards ahead of his men to reconnoiter a third enemy position which commanded the road with a 77-mm SP gun supported by infantry elements. The SP gun opened fire on his supporting tank, setting it afire with a direct hit. A fragment from the same shell painfully wounded 1st Lt. Tominac in the shoulder, knocking him to the ground. As the crew abandoned the M-4 tank, which was running downhill toward the enemy, 1st Lt. Tominac picked himself up and jumped onto the hull of the burning vehicle. Despite withering enemy machine-gun, mortar, pistol, and sniper fire, which was ricocheting off the hull and turret of the M-4, 1st Lt. Tominac climbed into the turret and gripped the .50-caliber antiaircraft machine gun.

Plainly silhouetted against the sky, painfully wounded, and with the tank burning beneath his feet, he directed bursts of machine-gun fire on the roadblock, the SP gun, and the supporting German infantrymen, and forced the enemy to withdraw from his prepared position. Jumping off the tank before it exploded, 1st Lt. Tominac refused evacuation despite his painful wound. Calling upon a sergeant to extract the shell fragments from his shoulder with a pocketknife, he continued to direct the assault, led his squad in a hand-grenade attack against a fortified position occupied by 32 of the enemy armed with machine guns, machine pistols, and rifles, and compelle d them to surrender. His outstanding heroism and exemplary leadership resulted in the destruction of four successive enemy defensive positions, surrender of a vital sector of the city Saulx de Vesoul, and the death or capture of at least 60 of the enemy.

2977 ◆ *TOWLE, JOHN RODERICK

Rank: Private
Service: U.S. Army
Birthday: 19 October 1924
Place of Birth: Cleveland, Cuyahoga County, Ohio
Date of Death: 21 September 1944
Cemetery: Calvary Cemetery (MH)—Cleveland, Ohio
Entered Service at: Cleveland, Cuyahoga County, Ohio
Unit: Company C, 504th Parachute Infantry, 82d Airborne Division
Served as: Rocket Launcher Gunner
Battle or Place of Action: near Oosterhout, Holland
Date of Action: 21 September 1944
G.O. Number, Date: 18, 15 March 1945
Date of Presentation: 25 March 1945
Place of Presentation: Fort Knox, Kentucky, presented to his parents by Maj. Gen. C.L. Scott
Citation: For conspicuous gallantry and intrepidity at the risk of life above and beyond the call of duty on 21 September 1944, near Oosterhout, Holland. The rifle company in which Pvt. Towle served as rocket launcher gunner was occupying a defensive position in the west sector of the recently established Nijmegen bridgehead when a strong enemy force of approximately 100 infantry supported by two tanks and a half-track formed a counterattack. With full knowledge of the disastrous consequences resulting not only to his company but to the entire bridgehead by an enemy breakthrough, Pvt. Towle immediately and without orders left his foxhole and moved 200 yards in the face of intense small-arms fire to a position on an exposed dike roadbed. From this precarious position Pvt. Towle fired his rocket launcher at and hit both tanks to his immediate front. Armored skirting on both tanks prevented penetration by the projectiles, but both vehicles withdrew slightly damaged. Still under intense fire and fully exposed to the enemy, Pvt. Towle then engaged a nearby house which nine Germans had entered and were using as a strongpoint, and with one round killed all nine. Hurriedly replenishing his supply of ammunition, Pvt. Towle, motivated only by his high conception of duty which called for the destruction of the enemy at any cost, then rushed approximately 125 yards through grazing enemy fire to an exposed position from which he could engage the enemy half-track with his rocket launcher. While in a kneeling position preparatory to firing on the enemy vehicle, Pvt. Towle was mortally wounded by a mortar shell. By his heroic tenacity, at the price of his life, Pvt. Towle saved the lives of many of his comrades and was directly instrumental in breaking up the enemy counterattack.

2978 ◆ TREADWELL, JACK LEMASTER

Rank: Captain (rank at time of action: First Lieutenant) (highest rank: Colonel)
Service: U.S. Army
Birthday: 31 March 1919
Place of Birth: Ashland, Clay County, Alabama
Date of Death: 12 December 1977
Cemetery: Fort Sill Post Cemetery (Y-11-8) (MH)—Fort Sill, Oklahoma
Entered Service at: Snyder, Kiowa County, Oklahoma
Unit: Company F, 180th Infantry, 45th Infantry Division
Served as: Commanding Officer
Battle or Place of Action: near Nieder-Wurzbach, Germany
Date of Action: 18 March 1945
G.O. Number, Date: 79, 14 September 1945
Date of Presentation: 23 August 1945
Place of Presentation: The White House, presented by Pres. Harry S. Truman
Citation: Capt. Treadwell (then 1st Lt.), commanding officer of Company F, near Nieder-Wurzbach, Germany, in the Siegfried line, singlehandedly captured six pillboxes and 18 prisoners. Murderous enemy automatic and rifle fire with intermittent artillery bombardments had pinned down his company for hours at the base of a hill defended by concrete fortifications and interlocking trenches. Eight men sent to attack a single point had all become casualties on the bare slope when Capt. Treadwell, armed with a submachine gun and hand grenades, went forward alone to clear the way for his stalled company. Over the terrain devoid of cover and swept by bullets, he fearlessly advanced, firing at the aperture of the nearest pillbox and, when within range, hurling grenades at it. He reached the pillbox, thrust the muzzle of his gun through the port, and drove four Germans out with their hands in the air. A fifth was found dead inside. Waving these prisoners back to the American lines, he continued under terrible, concentrated fire to the next pillbox and took it in the same manner. In this fort he captured the commander of the hill defenses, whom he sent to the rear with the other prisoners. Never slackening his attack, he then ran across the crest of the hill to a third pillbox, traversing this distance in full view of hostile machine gunners and snipers. He was again successful in taking the enemy position. The Germans quickly fell prey to his further rushes on three more pillboxes in the confusion and havoc caused by his whirlwind assaults and capture of their commander. Inspired by the electrifying performance of their leader, the men of Company F stormed after him and overwhelmed resistance on the entire hill, driving a wedge into the Siegfried line and making it possible for their battalion to take its objective. By his courageous willingness to face nearly impossible odds and by his

overwhelming one-man offensive, Capt. Treadwell reduced a heavily fortified, seemingly impregnable enemy sector.

2979 ◆ *TRUEMPER, WALTER EDWARD

Rank: Second Lieutenant
Service: U.S. Army Air Corps
Birthday: 31 October 1918
Place of Birth: Aurora, Du Page County, Illinois
Date of Death: 20 February 1944
Cemetery: St. Paul's Lutheran Cemetery—Aurora, Illinois
Entered Service at: Aurora, Du Page County, Illinois
Unit: 510th Bombardment Squadron, 351st Bombardment Group, 8th Air Force
Served as: Navigator of a B-17
Battle or Place of Action: over Leipzig, Germany
Date of Action: 20 February 1944
G.O. Number, Date: 52, 22 June 1944
Citation: For conspicuous gallantry and intrepidity at the risk of life above and beyond the call of duty in action against the enemy in connection with a bombing mission over enemy-occupied Europe on 20 February 1944. The aircraft on which 2d Lt. Truemper was serving as navigator was attacked by a squadron of enemy fighters with the result that the copilot was killed outright, the pilot wounded and rendered unconscious, the radio operator wounded, and the plane severely damaged. Nevertheless, 2d Lt. Truemper and other members of his crew managed to right the plane and fly it back to their home station, where they contacted the control tower and reported the situation. Second Lt. Truemper and the engineer volunteered to attempt to land the plane. Other members of the crew were ordered to jump, leaving 2d Lt. Truemper and the engineer aboard. After observing the distressed aircraft from another plane, 2d Lt. Truemper's commanding officer decided the damaged plane could not be landed by the inexperienced crew and ordered them to abandon it and parachute to safety. Demonstrating unsurpassed courage and heroism, 2d Lt. Truemper and the engineer replied that the pilot was still alive but could not be moved and that they would not desert him. They were then told to attempt a landing. After two unsuccessful efforts their plane crashed into an open field in a third attempt to land. Second Lt. Truemper, the engineer, and the wounded pilot were killed.

2980 ◆ *TURNER, DAY G.

Rank: Sergeant
Service: U.S. Army
Place of Birth: Berwick, Columbia County, Pennsylvania
Date of Death: 8 February 1945
Cemetery: A.B.M.C. Luxembourg Cemetery (E-10-72)—Luxembourg City, Luxembourg
Entered Service at: Nescopeck, Luzerne County, Pennsylvania
Unit: Company B, 319th Infantry, 80th Infantry Division
Served as: Squad Leader
Battle or Place of Action: at Dahl, Luxembourg
Date of Action: 8 January 1945
G.O. Number, Date: 49, 28 June 1945
Citation: He commanded a nine-man squad with the mission of holding a critical flank position. When overwhelming numbers of the enemy attacked under cover of withering artillery, mortar, and rocket fire, he withdrew his squad into a nearby house, determined to defend it to the last man. The enemy attacked again and again and were repulsed with heavy losses. Supported by direct tank fire, they finally gained entrance, but the intrepid sergeant refused to surrender although five of his men were wounded and one was killed. He boldly flung a can of flaming oil at the first wave of attackers, dispersing them, and fought doggedly from room to room, closing with the enemy in fierce hand-to-hand encounters. He hurled hand grenade for hand grenade, bayoneted two fanatical Germans who rushed a doorway he was defending, and fought on with the enemy's weapons when his own ammunition was expended. The savage fight raged for four hours, and finally, when only three men of the defending squad were left unwounded, the enemy surrendered. Twenty-five prisoners were taken, 11 enemy dead and a great number of wounded were counted. Sgt. Turner's valiant stand will live on as a constant inspiration to his comrades. His heroic, inspiring leadership, his determination, and courageous devotion to duty exemplify the highest traditions of the military service.

2981 ◆ TURNER, GEORGE BENTON

Rank: Private First Class
Service: U.S. Army
Birthday: 27 June 1899
Place of Birth: Longview, Gregg County, Texas
Date of Death: 29 June 1963
Cemetery: Arlington National Cemetery (41-589) (MH)—Arlington, Virginia
Entered Service at: Los Angeles, Los Angeles County, California
Unit: Battery C, 499th Armored Field Artillery Battalion, 14th Armored Division
Battle or Place of Action: Philippsbourg, France
Date of Action: 3 January 1945
G.O. Number, Date: 79, 14 September 1945
Date of Presentation: 23 August 1945
Place of Presentation: The White House, presented by Pres. Harry S. Truman
Citation: At Philippsbourg, France, he was cut off from his artillery unit by an enemy armored infantry attack. Coming upon a friendly infantry company withdrawing under the vicious onslaught, he noticed two German tanks and approximately 75 supporting foot soldiers advancing down the main street of the village. Seizing a rocket launcher, he advanced under intense small-arms and cannon fire to meet the tanks and, standing in the middle of the road, fired at them, destroying one and disabling the second. From a nearby half-track he then dismounted a machine gun, placed it in the open street and fired into the enemy infantrymen, killing or wounding a great number and breaking up the attack. In the American counterattack which followed, two supporting tanks were disabled by an enemy antitank gun. Firing a light machine gun from the hip, Pfc. Turner held off the enemy so

that the crews of the disabled vehicles could extricate themselves. He ran through a hail of fire to one of the tanks which had burst into flames and attempted to rescue a man who had been unable to escape; but an explosion of the tank's ammunition frustrated his effort and wounded him painfully. Refusing to be evacuated, he remained with the infantry until the following day, driving off an enemy patrol with serious casualties, assisting in capturing a hostile strongpoint, and voluntarily and fearlessly driving a truck through heavy enemy fire to deliver wounded men to the rear aid station. The great courage displayed by Pfc. Turner and his magnificently heroic initiative contributed materially to the defense of the French town and inspired the troops about him.

2982 ♦ URBAN, MATT LOUIS

Rank: Lieutenant Colonel (rank at time of action: Captain)
Service: U.S. Army
Birthday: 25 August 1919
Place of Birth: Buffalo, Erie County, New York
Date of Death: 4 March 1995
Place of Death: Holland, Michigan
Cemetery: Arlington National Cemetery (7A-40) (MH)—Arlington, Virginia
Entered Service at: Fort Bragg, Cumberland County, North Carolina
Unit: Company F, 2d Battalion, 60th Infantry Regiment, 9th Infantry Division
Served as: Company Commander/Battalion Commander
Battle or Place of Action: France & Belgium
Date of Action: 14 June-3 September 1944
Date of Presentation: 19 July 1980
Place of Presentation: The White House, presented by Pres. Jimmy Carter
Citation: Lt. Col. (then Capt.) Matt Urban, 112-22-2414, United States Army, who distinguished himself by a series of bold, heroic actions, exemplified by singularly outstanding combat leadership, personal bravery, and tenacious devotion to duty, during the period from 14 June to 3 September 1944 while assigned to the 2d Battalion, 60th Infantry Regiment, 9th Infantry Division. On 14 June, Capt. Urban's company, attacking at Renouf, France, encountered heavy enemy small-arms and tank fire. The enemy tanks were unmercifully raking his unit's positions and inflicting heavy casualties. Capt. Urban, realizing that his company was in imminent danger of being decimated, armed himself with a bazooka. He worked his way with an ammo carrier through hedgerows, under a continuing barrage of fire, to a point near the tanks. He brazenly exposed himself to the enemy fire and, firing the bazooka, destroyed both tanks. Responding to Capt. Urban's action, his company moved forward and routed the enemy. Later that same day, still in the attack near Orglandes, Capt. Urban was wounded in the leg by direct fire from a 37-mm tank gun. He refused evacuation and continued to lead his company until they moved into defensive positions for the night. At 0500 hours the next day, still in the attack near Orglandes, Capt. Urban, though badly wounded, directed his company in another attack. One hour later he was again wounded. Suffering from two wounds, one serious, he was evacuated to England. In mid-July, while recovering from his wounds, he learned of his unit's severe losses in the hedgerows of Normandy. Realizing his unit's need for battle-tested leaders, he voluntarily left the hospital and hitchhiked his way back to his unit near Saint-Lo, France. Arriving at the 2d Battalion Command Post at 1130 hours on 25 July, he found that his unit had jumped off at 1100 hours in the first attack of "Operation Cobra." Still limping from his leg wound, Capt. Urban made his way forward to retake command of h is company. He found his company held up by strong enemy opposition. Two supporting tanks had been destroyed and another, intact but with no tank commander or gunner, was not moving. He located a lieutenant in charge of the support tanks and directed a plan of attack to eliminate the enemy strongpoint. The lieutenant and a sergeant were immediately killed by the heavy enemy fire when they tried to mount the tank. Capt. Urban, though physically hampered by his leg wound and knowing quick action had to be taken, dashed through the scathing fire and mounted the tank. With enemy bullets ricocheting from the tank, Capt. Urban ordered the tank forward and, completely exposed to the enemy fire, manned the machine gun and placed devastating fire on the enemy. His action, in the face of enemy fire, galvanized the battalion into action and they attacked and destroyed the enemy position. On 2 August, Capt. Urban was wounded in the chest by shell fragments and, disregarding the recommendation of the battalion surgeon, again refused evacuation. On 6 August, Capt. Urban became the commander of the 2d Battalion. On 15 August, he was again wounded but remained with his unit. On 3 September, the 2d Battalion was given the mission of establishing a crossing-point on the Meuse River near Heer, Belgium. The enemy planned to stop the advance of the Allied Army by concentrating heavy forces at the Meuse. The 2d Battalion, attacking toward the crossing-point, encountered fierce enemy artillery, small-arms, and mortar fire which stopped the attack. Capt. Urban quickly moved from his command post to the lead position of the battalion. Reorganizing the attacking elements, he personally led a charge toward the enemy's strongpoint. As the charge moved across the open terrain, Capt. Urban was seriously wounded in the neck. Although unable to talk above a whisper from the paralyzing neck wound, and in danger of losing his life, he refused to be evacuated until the enemy was routed and his battalion had secured the crossing-point on the Meuse River. Capt. Urban's personal leadership, limitless bravery, and repeated extraordinary exposure to enemy fire served as an inspiration to his entire battalion. His valorous and intrepid actions reflect the utmost credit upon him and uphold the noble traditions of the United States Army.

2983 ♦ *VALDEZ, JOSE F.

Rank: Private First Class
Service: U.S. Army
Birthday: 3 January 1925
Place of Birth: Governador, New Mexico
Date of Death: 17 February 1945
Cemetery: Santa Fe National Cemetery (Q-29) (MH)—Santa Fe, New Mexico

Entered Service at: Pleasant Grove, Utah County, Utah
Unit: Company B, 7th Infantry, 3d Infantry Division
Battle or Place of Action: near Rosenkrantz, France
Date of Action: 25 January 1945
G.O. Number, Date: 16, 8 February 1946
Citation: He was on outpost duty with five others when the enemy counterattacked with overwhelming strength. From his position near some woods 500 yards beyond the American lines he observed a hostile tank about 75 yards away, and raked it with automatic rifle fire until it withdrew. Soon afterward he saw three Germans stealthily approaching through the woods. Scorning cover as the enemy soldiers opened up with heavy automatic-weapon fire from a range of 30 yards, he engaged in a firefight with the attackers until he had killed all three. The enemy quickly launched an attack with two full companies of infantrymen, blasting the patrol with murderous concentrations of automatic and rifle fire and beginning an encircling movement which forced the patrol leader to order a withdrawal. Despite the terrible odds, Pfc. Valdez immediately volunteered to cover the maneuver, and as the patrol one by one plunged through a hail of bullets toward the American lines, he fired burst after burst into the swarming enemy. Three of his companions were wounded in their dash for safety and he was struck by a bullet that entered his stomach and, passing through his body, emerged from his back. Overcoming agonizing pain, he regained control of himself and resumed his firing position, delivering a protective screen of bullets until all others of the patrol were safe. By field telephone he called for artillery and mortar fire on the Germans and corrected the range until he had shells falling within 50 yards of his position. For 15 minutes he refused to be dislodged by more than 200 of the enemy; then, seeing that the barrage had broken the counterattack, he dragged himself back to his own lines. He died later as a result of his wounds. Through his valiant, intrepid stand and at the cost of his own life, Pfc. Valdez made it possible for his comrades to escape, and was directly responsible for repulsing an attack by vastly superior enemy forces.

2984 ◆ *VANCE JR., LEON ROBERT

Rank: Lieutenant Colonel
Service: U.S. Army Air Corps
Birthday: 11 August 1916
Place of Birth: Enid, Garfield County, Oklahoma
Date of Death: 26 July 1944
Place of Death: Between Iceland & Newfoundland
Cemetery: A.B.M.C. Cambridge Cemetery (Wall of the Missing)—Cambridge, England
Entered Service at: Garden City, Nassau County, New York
Unit: 489th Bombardment Group, 8th Air Force
Served as: Deputy Group Commander/Pilot of a B-24-H
Battle or Place of Action: over Wimereaux, France
Date of Action: 5 June 1944
G.O. Number, Date: 1, 4 January 1945
Date of Presentation: 11 October 1946
Place of Presentation: Enid Air Force Base, Enid, Oklahoma, presented by Maj. Gen. James P. Hodges to his Widow and Daughter

Citation: For conspicuous gallantry and intrepidity above and beyond the call of duty on 5 June 1944, when he led a Heavy Bombardment Group in an attack against defended enemy coastal positions in the vicinity of Wimereaux, France. Approaching the target, his aircraft was hit repeatedly by anti-aircraft fire which seriously crippled the ship, killed the pilot, and wounded several members of the crew, including Lt. Col. Vance, whose right foot was practically severed. In spite of his injury, and with three engines lost to the flak, he led his formation over the target, bombing it successfully. After applying a tourniquet to his leg with the aid of the radar operator, Lt. Col. Vance, realizing that the ship was approaching a stall altitude with the one remaining engine failing, struggled to a semi-upright position beside the copilot and took over control of the ship. Cutting the power and feathering the last engine he put the aircraft in glide sufficiently steep to maintain his airspeed. Gradually losing altitude, he at last reached the English coast, whereupon he ordered all members of the crew to bail out as he knew they would all safely make land. But he received a message over the interphone system which led him to believe one of the crewmembers was unable to jump due to injuries; so he made the decision to ditch the ship in the channel, thereby giving this man a chance for life. To add further to the danger of ditching the ship in his crippled condition, there was a 500-pound bomb hung up in the bomb bay. Unable to climb into the seat vacated by the copilot, since his foot, hanging on to his leg by a few tendons, had become lodged behind the copilot's seat, he nevertheless made a successful ditching while lying on the floor using only aileron and elevators for control and the side window of the cockpit for visual reference. On coming to rest in the water the aircraft commenced to sink rapidly with Lt. Col. Vance pinned in the cockpit by the upper turret which had crashed in during the landing. As it was settling beneath the waves an explosion occurred which threw Lt. Col. Vance clear of the wreckage. After clinging to a piece of floating wreckage until he could muster enough strength to inflate his life vest, he began searching for the crewmember whom he believed to be aboard. Failing to find anyone he began swimming and was found approximately 50 minutes later by an air-sea rescue craft. By his extraordinary flying skill and gallant leadership, despite his grave injury, Lt. Col. Vance led his formation to a successful bombing of the assigned target and returned the crew to a point where they could bail out with safety. His gallant and valorous decision to ditch the aircraft in order to give the crewmember he believed to be aboard a chance for life exemplifies the highest traditions of the U.S. Armed Forces.

2985 ◆ VANDEGRIFT, ALEXANDER ARCHER

Rank: Major General (highest rank: General)
Service: U.S. Marine Corps
Birthday: 13 March 1887
Place of Birth: Charlottesville, Charlottesville County, Virginia
Date of Death: 8 May 1973
Place of Death: Bethesda, Maryland
Cemetery: Arlington National Cemetery (2-4965-B-RH)—Arlington, Virginia

Entered Service at: Virginia
Unit: 1st Marine Division
Served as: Commanding Officer
Battle or Place of Action: Solomon Islands
Date of Action: 7 August–9 December 1942
Citation: For outstanding and heroic accomplishment above and beyond the call of duty as commanding officer of the 1st Marine Division in operations against enemy Japanese forces in the Solomon Islands during the period from 7 August to 9 December 1942. With the adverse factors of weather, terrain, and disease making his task a difficult and hazardous undertaking, and with his command eventually including sea, land, and air forces of Army, Navy, and Marine Corps, Maj. Gen. Vandegrift achieved marked success in commanding the initial landings of the U.S. forces in the Solomon Islands and in their subsequent occupation. His tenacity, courage, and resourcefulness prevailed against a strong, determined, and experienced enemy, and the gallant fighting spirit of the men under his inspiring leadership enabled them to withstand aerial, land, and sea bombardment, to surmount all obstacles, and leave a disorganized and ravaged enemy. This dangerous but vital mission, accomplished at the constant risk of his life, resulted in securing a valuable base for further operations of our forces against the enemy, and its successful completion reflects great credit upon Maj. Gen. Vandegrift, his command, and the U.S. Naval Service.

2986 ◆ *VAN NOY JR., NATHAN

Rank: Private
Service: U.S. Army
Birthday: 9 August 1924
Place of Birth: Grace, Caribou County, Idaho
Date of Death: 17 October 1943
Cemetery: Grace Cemetery (MH)—Grace, Idaho
Entered Service at: Preston, Franklin County, Idaho
Unit: Headquarters Company, Shore Battalion, 532d Engineer Boat & Shore Regiment
Served as: Machine Gunner
Battle or Place of Action: near Finschafen, New Guinea
Date of Action: 17 October 1943
G.O. Number, Date: 17, 26 February 1944
Date of Presentation: 17 March 1944
Place of Presentation: Preston, Idaho, presented by Col. A.E. Merrill to his Mother
Citation: For conspicuous gallantry and intrepidity above and beyond the call of duty in action with the enemy near Finschafen, New Guinea, on 17 October 1943. When wounded late in September, Pvt. Van Noy declined evacuation and continued on duty. On 17 October 1943 he was gunner in charge of a machine-gun post only five yards from the water's edge when the alarm was given that three enemy barges loaded with troops were approaching the beach in the early morning darkness. One landing barge was sunk by Allied fire, but the other two beached 10 yards from Pvt. Van Noy's emplacement. Despite his exposed position, he poured a withering hail of fire onto the debarking enemy troops. His loader was wounded by a grenade and evacuated. Pvt. Van Noy, also grievously wounded, remained at his post, ignoring calls of nearby soldiers urging him to withdraw, and continued to fire with deadly accuracy. He expended every round and was found, covered with wounds, dead beside his gun. In this action Pvt. Van Noy killed at least half of the 39 enemy taking part in the landing. His heroic tenacity at the price of his life not only saved the lives of many of his comrades, but enabled them to annihilate the attacking detachment.

2987 ◆ *VAN VALKENBURGH, FRANKLIN

Rank: Captain
Service: U.S. Navy
Birthday: 5 April 1888
Place of Birth: Minneapolis, Hennepin County, Minnesota
Date of Death: 7 December 1941
Place of Death: Pearl Harbor, Territory of Hawaii
Cemetery: National Memorial Cemetery of the Pacific (Wall of the Missing)—Honolulu, Hawaii
Entered Service at: Wisconsin
Unit: U.S.S. *Arizona*
Served as: Commanding Officer
Battle or Place of Action: Pearl Harbor, Territory of Hawaii
Date of Action: 7 December 1941
Citation: For conspicuous devotion to duty, extraordinary courage and complete disregard of his own life, during the attack on the Fleet in Pearl Harbor, Territory of Hawaii, by Japanese forces on 7 December 1941. As commanding officer of the U.S.S. *Arizona*, Capt. Van Valkenburgh gallantly fought his ship until the U.S.S. *Arizona* blew up from magazine explosions and a direct bomb hit on the bridge which resulted in the loss of his life.

2988 ◆ *VAN VOORHIS, BRUCE AVERY

Rank: Lieutenant Commander (highest rank: Commander)
Service: U.S. Navy
Birthday: 29 January 1908
Place of Birth: Aberdeen, Grays Harbor County, Washington
Date of Death: 6 July 1943
Place of Death: off Greenwich Island, Solomon Islands
Cemetery: Jefferson Barracks National Cemetery (one of six in a group burial) (79-279-280-281)—St. Louis, Missouri; Arlington National Cemetery (MI-86) (MH)—Arlington, Virginia
Entered Service at: Nevada
Unit: Bombing Squadron 102
Served as: Squadron Commander/Pilot of a PB4Y-1
Battle or Place of Action: Greenwich Island, Solomon Islands
Date of Action: 6 July 1943
Citation: For conspicuous gallantry and intrepidity at the risk of his life above and beyond the call of duty as squadron commander of Bombing Squadron 102 and as plane commander of a PB4Y-1 patrol bomber operating against the enemy on Japanese-held Greenwich Island during the battle of the Solomon Islands, 6 July 1943. Fully aware of the limited chance of surviving an urgent mission, voluntarily undertaken to prevent a surprise Japanese attack against our forces,

Lt. Comdr. Van Voorhis took off in total darkness on a perilous 700-mile flight without escort or support. Successful in reaching his objective despite treacherous and varying winds, low visibility, and difficult terrain, he fought a lone but relentless battle under fierce antiaircraft fire and overwhelming aerial opposition. Forced lower and lower by pursuing planes, he coolly persisted in his mission of destruction. Abandoning all chances of a safe return, he executed six bold, ground-level attacks to demolish the enemy's vital radio station, installations, antiaircraft guns and crews with bombs and machine-gun fire, and to destroy one fighter plane in the air and three on the water. Caught in his own bomb blast, Lt. Comdr. Van Voorhis crashed into the lagoon off the beach, sacrificing himself in a singlehanded fight against almost insuperable odds, to make a distinctive contribution to our continued offensive in driving the Japanese from the Solomons and, by his superb daring, courage, and resoluteness of purpose, enhanced the finest traditions of the U.S. Naval Service. He gallantly gave his life for his country.

2989 ◆ *VIALE, ROBERT M.

Rank: Second Lieutenant
Service: U.S. Army
Birthday: 21 April 1916
Place of Birth: Bayside, Humboldt County, California
Date of Death: 5 February 1945
Cemetery: Ocean View Cemetery (MH)—Eureka, California
Entered Service at: Ukiah, Mendocino County, California
Unit: Company K, 148th Infantry, 37th Infantry Division
Served as: Platoon Leader
Battle or Place of Action: Manila, Luzon, Philippine Islands
Date of Action: 5 February 1945
G.O. Number, Date: 92, 25 October 1945
Citation: He displayed conspicuous gallantry and intrepidity above and beyond the call of duty. Forced by the enemy's detonation of prepared demolitions to shift the course of his advance through the city, he led the 1st platoon toward a small bridge, where heavy fire from three enemy pillboxes halted the unit. With two men he crossed the bridge behind screening grenade smoke to attack the pillboxes. The first he knocked out himself while covered by his men's protecting fire; the other two were silenced by one of his companions and a bazooka team which he had called up. He suffered a painful wound in the right arm during the action. After his entire platoon had joined him, he pushed ahead through mortar fire and encircling flames. Blocked from the only escape route by an enemy machine gun placed at a street corner, he entered a nearby building with his men to explore possible means of reducing the emplacement. In one room he found civilians huddled together, in another, a small window placed high in the wall and reached by a ladder. Because of the relative position of the window, ladder, and enemy emplacement, he decided that he, being left-handed, could better hurl a grenade than one of his men who had made an unsuccessful attempt. Grasping an armed grenade, he started up the ladder. His wounded right arm weakened, and, as he tried to steady himself, the grenade fell to the floor. In the five seconds before the grenade would explode, he dropped down, recovered the grenade and looked for a place to dispose of it safely. Finding no way to get rid of the grenade without exposing his own men or the civilians to injury or death, he turned to the wall, held it close to his body and bent over it as it exploded. Second Lt. Viale died in a few minutes, but his heroic act saved the lives of others.

2990 ◆ *VILLEGAS, YSMAEL R.

Rank: Staff Sergeant
Service: U.S. Army
Birthday: 21 March 1924
Place of Birth: Casa Blanca, California
Date of Death: 20 March 1945
Place of Death: Villa Verde Trail, Philippine Islands
Cemetery: Riverside National Cemetery (5-1178) (MH)—Riverside, California
Entered Service at: Casa Blanca, California
Unit: Company F, 127th Infantry, 32d Infantry Division
Served as: Squad Leader
Battle or Place of Action: Villa Verde Trail, Luzon, Philippine Islands
Date of Action: 20 March 1945
G.O. Number, Date: 89, 19 October 1945
Citation: He was a squad leader when his unit, in a forward position, clashed with an enemy strongly entrenched in connected caves and foxholes on commanding ground. He moved boldly from man to man, in the face of bursting grenades and demolition charges, through heavy machine-gun and rifle fire, to bolster the spirit of his comrades. Inspired by his gallantry, his men pressed forward to the crest of the hill. Numerous enemy riflemen, refusing to flee, continued firing from their foxholes. S/Sgt. Villegas, with complete disregard for his own safety and the bullets which kicked up the dirt at his feet, charged an enemy position and, firing at point-blank range, killed the Japanese in a foxhole. He rushed a second foxhole while bullets missed him by inches and killed one more of the enemy. In rapid succession he charged a third, a fourth, a fifth foxhole, each time destroying the enemy within. The fire against him increased in intensity, but he pressed onward to attack a sixth position. As he neared his goal, he was hit and killed by enemy fire. Through his heroism and indomitable fighting spirit, S/Sgt. Villegas, at the cost of his life, inspired his men to a determined attack in which they swept the enemy from the field.

2991 ◆ VLUG, DIRK JOHN

Rank: Private First Class
Service: U.S. Army
Birthday: 20 August 1916
Place of Birth: Maple Lake, Wright County, Minnesota
Entered Service at: Grand Rapids, Kent County, Michigan
Unit: Headquarters Company, 1st Battalion, 126th Infantry, 32d Infantry Division
Served as: Ammunition Bearer
Battle or Place of Action: near Limon, Leyte, Philippine Islands

Date of Action: 15 December 1944
G.O. Number, Date: 60, 26 June 1946
Date of Presentation: 14 June 1946
Place of Presentation: The White House, presented by Pres. Harry S. Truman
Citation: He displayed conspicuous gallantry and intrepidity above and beyond the call of duty when an American roadblock on the Ormoc Road was attacked by a group of enemy tanks. He left his covered position and, with a rocket launcher and six rounds of ammunition, advanced alone under intense machine-gun and 37-mm fire. Loading singlehandedly, he destroyed the first tank, killing its occupants with a single round. As the crew of the second tank started to dismount and attack him, he killed one of the foe with his pistol, forcing the survivors to return to their vehicle, which he then destroyed with a second round. Three more hostile tanks moved up the road, so he flanked the first and eliminated it, and then, despite a hail of enemy fire, pressed forward again to destroy another. With his last round of ammunition he struck the remaining vehicle, causing it to crash down a steep embankment. Through his sustained heroism in the face of superior forces, Pfc. Vlug alone destroyed five enemy tanks and greatly facilitated successful accomplishment of his battalion's mission.

2992 ◆ VOSLER, FORREST LEE "WOODY"

Rank: Technical Sergeant
Service: U.S. Army Air Corps
Birthday: 29 July 1923
Place of Birth: Lyndonville, Orleans County, New York
Date of Death: 17 February 1992
Place of Death: Titusville, Florida
Cemetery: Arlington National Cemetery (60-4924) (MH)—Arlington, Virginia
Entered Service at: Rochester, Monroe County, New York
Unit: 358th Bombardment Squadron, 303d Bombardment Group, 8th Air Force
Served as: Radio Operator/Gunner on a B-17
Battle or Place of Action: over Bremen, Germany
Date of Action: 20 December 1943
G.O. Number, Date: 73, 6 September 1944
Date of Presentation: 31 August 1944
Place of Presentation: The White House (Oval Office), presented by Pres. Franklin D. Roosevelt
Citation: For conspicuous gallantry in action against the enemy above and beyond the call of duty while serving as a radio operator-air gunner on a heavy bombardment aircraft in a mission over Bremen, Germany, 20 December 1943. After bombing the target, the aircraft in which T/Sgt. Vosler was serving was severely damaged by antiaircraft fire, forced out of formation, and immediately subjected to repeated vicious attacks by enemy fighters. Early in the engagement a 20-mm cannon shell exploded in the radio compartment, painfully wounding T/Sgt. Vosler in the legs and thighs. At about the same time a direct hit on the tail of the ship seriously wounded the tail gunner and rendered the tail guns inoperative. Realizing the great need for firepower in protecting the vulnerable tail of the ship, T/Sgt. Vosler, with grim determination, kept up a steady stream of deadly fire. Shortly thereafter another 20-mm enemy shell exploded, wounding T/Sgt. Vosler in the chest and about the face. Pieces of metal lodged in both eyes, impairing his vision to such extent that he could only distinguish blurred shapes. Displaying remarkable tenacity and courage, he kept firing his guns and declined to take first-aid treatment. The radio equipment had been rendered inoperative during the battle, and when the pilot announced that he would have to ditch, although unable to see and working entirely by touch, T/Sgt. Vosler finally got the set operating and sent out distress signals despite several lapses into unconsciousness. When the ship ditched, T/Sgt. Vosler managed to get out on the wing by himself and hold the wounded tail gunner from slipping off until the other crewmembers could help him into the dinghy. T/Sgt. Vosler's actions on this occasion were an inspiration to all serving with him. The extraordinary courage, coolness, and skill he displayed in the face of great odds, when handicapped by injuries that would have incapacitated the average crewmember, were outstanding.

2993 ◆ WAHLEN, GEORGE EDWARD

Rank: Pharmacist's Mate Second Class (highest rank: Major, USA ret.)
Service: U.S. Navy
Birthday: 8 August 1924
Place of Birth: Ogden, Weber County, Utah
Entered Service at: Ogden, Weber County, Utah
Unit: 1st Platoon, Company F, 2d Battalion, 26th Marines, 5th Marine Division
Served as: Medical Corpsman
Battle or Place of Action: Iwo Jima, Volcano Islands
Date of Action: 3 March 1945
Date of Presentation: 5 October 1945
Place of Presentation: The White House, presented by Pres. Harry S. Truman
Citation: For conspicuous gallantry and intrepidity at the risk of his life above and beyond the call of duty while serving with the 2d Battalion, 26th Marines, 5th Marine Division, during action against enemy Japanese forces on Iwo Jima in the Volcano Group on 3 March 1945. Painfully wounded in the bitter action on 26 February, Wahlen remained on the battlefield, advancing well forward of the front lines to aid a wounded marine and carrying him back to safety despite a terrific concentration of fire. Tireless in his ministrations, he consistently disregarded all danger to attend his fighting comrades as they fell under the devastating rain of shrapnel and bullets, and rendered prompt assistance to various elements of his combat group as required. When an adjacent platoon suffered heavy casualties, he defied the continuous pounding of heavy mortars and deadly fire of enemy rifles to care for the wounded, working rapidly in an area swept by constant fire and treating 14 casualties before returning to his own platoon. Wounded again on 2 March, he gallantly refused evacuation, moving out with his company the following day in a furious assault across 600 yards of open terrain and repeatedly rendering medical aid while exposed to the blasting fury of powerful Japanese guns. Stouthearted and indomitable, he

persevered in his determined efforts as his unit waged fierce battle and, unable to walk after sustaining a third agonizing wound, resolutely crawled 50 yards to administer first aid to still another fallen fighter. By his dauntless fortitude and valor, Wahlen served as a constant inspiration and contributed vitally to the high morale of his company during critical phases of this strategically important engagement. His heroic spirit of self-sacrifice in the face of overwhelming enemy fire upheld the highest traditions of the U.S. Naval Service.

2994 ◆ WAINWRIGHT IV, JONATHAN MAYHEW

Rank: General
Service: U.S. Army
Birthday: 23 August 1883
Place of Birth: Fort Walla Walla, Walla Walla County, Washington
Date of Death: 2 September 1953
Place of Death: San Antonio, Texas
Cemetery: Arlington National Cemetery (1-358-B)—Arlington, Virginia
Entered Service at: Skaneateles, Onondaga County, New York
Unit: U.S. Army
Served as: Commanding General of U.S. Armed Forces in the Philippines
Battle or Place of Action: Philippine Islands
Date of Action: 12 March-7 May 1942
G.O. Number, Date: 80, 19 September 1945
Date of Presentation: 10 September 1945
Place of Presentation: The White House (Rose Garden), presented by Pres. Harry S. Truman
Citation: Distinguished himself by intrepid and determined leadership against greatly superior enemy forces. At the repeated risk of life above and beyond the call of duty in his position, he frequented the firing line of his troops where his presence provided the example and incentive that helped make the gallant efforts of these men possible. The final stand on beleaguered Corregidor, for which he was in an important measure personally responsible, commanded the admiration of the nation's allies. It reflected the high morale of American arms in the face of overwhelming odds. His courage and resolution were a vitally needed inspiration to the then sorely pressed freedom-loving peoples of the world.
Notes: POW

2995 ◆ *WALKER, KENNETH NEWTON

Rank: Brigadier General
Service: U.S. Army Air Corps
Birthday: 17 July 1898
Place of Birth: Cerrillos, Santa Fe County, New Mexico
Date of Death: 5 January 1943
Place of Death: Near Rabaul, New Britain
Cemetery: A.B.M.C. Manila Cemetery (Wall of the Missing)—Manila, Philippine Islands
Entered Service at: Denver, Denver County, Colorado
Unit: 5th Bomber Command, 5th Air Force
Served as: Commanding Officer/Pilot of a B-17
Battle or Place of Action: over Rabaul, New Britain, Bismarck Archipelago
Date of Action: 5 January 1943
G.O. Number, Date: 13, 11 March 1943
Date of Presentation: 25 March 1943
Place of Presentation: The White House, presented by Pres. Franklin D. Roosevelt to his family
Citation: For conspicuous leadership above and beyond the call of duty involving personal valor and intrepidity at an extreme hazard to life. As commander of the 5th Bomber Command during the period from 5 September 1942 to 5 January 1943, Brig. Gen. Walker repeatedly accompanied his units on bombing missions deep into enemy-held territory. From the lessons personally gained under combat conditions, he developed a highly efficient technique for bombing when opposed by enemy fighter airplanes and by antiaircraft fire. On 5 January 1943, in the face of extremely heavy antiaircraft fire and determined opposition by enemy fighters, he led an effective daylight bombing attack against shipping in the harbor at Rabaul, New Britain, which resulted in direct hits on nine enemy vessels. During this action his airplane was disabled and forced down by the attack of an overwhelming number of enemy fighters.

2996 ◆ *WALLACE, HERMAN C.

Rank: Private First Class
Service: U.S. Army
Birthday: 1924
Place of Birth: Marlow, Stephens County, Oklahoma
Date of Death: 27 February 1945
Cemetery: City of Lubbock Cemetery (MH)—Lubbock, Texas
Entered Service at: Lubbock, Lubbock County, Texas
Unit: Company B, 301st Combat Engineer Battalion, 76th Infantry Division
Battle or Place of Action: near Prumzurley, Germany
Date of Action: 27 February 1945
G.O. Number, Date: 92, 25 October 1945
Citation: He displayed conspicuous gallantry and intrepidity. While helping clear enemy mines from a road, he stepped on a well-concealed S-type antipersonnel mine. Hearing the characteristic noise indicating that the mine had been activated and, if he stepped aside, would be thrown upward to explode above the ground and spray the area with fragments, surely killing two comrades directly behind him and endangering other members of his squad, he deliberately placed his other foot on the mine even though his best chance for survival was to fall prone. Pvt. Wallace was killed when the charge detonated, but his supreme heroism at the cost of his life confined the blast to the ground and his own body and saved his fellow soldiers from death or injury.

2997 ◆ WALSH, KENNETH AMBROSE

Rank: First Lieutenant (highest rank: Lieutenant Colonel)
Service: U.S. Marine Corps
Birthday: 24 November 1916

Place of Birth: Brooklyn, Kings County, New York
Entered Service at: Brooklyn, Kings County, New York
Unit: Marine Fighting Squadron 124, Marine Air Group 12, 1st Marine Air Wing
Served as: Flight Leader/Pilot of an F4U Corsair
Battle or Place of Action: Vella Lavella & Kahili, Solomon Islands
Date of Action: 15, 30 August 1943
Date of Presentation: 8 February 1944
Place of Presentation: The White House (Oval Office), presented by Pres. Franklin D. Roosevelt
Citation: For extraordinary heroism and intrepidity above and beyond the call of duty as a pilot in Marine Fighting Squadron 124 in aerial combat against enemy Japanese forces in the Solomon Islands area. Determined to thwart the enemy's attempt to bomb Allied ground forces and shipping at Vella Lavella on 15 August 1943, 1st Lt. Walsh repeatedly dived his plane into an enemy formation outnumbering his own division six to one and, although his plane was hit numerous times, shot down two Japanese dive bombers and one fighter. After developing engine trouble on 30 August during a vital escort mission, 1st Lt. Walsh landed his mechanically disabled plane at Munda, quickly replaced it with another, and proceeded to rejoin his flight over Kahili. Separated from his escort group when he encountered approximately 50 Japanese Zeros, he unhesitatingly attacked, striking with relentless fury in his lone battle against a powerful force. He destroyed four hostile fighters before cannon shellfire forced him to make a dead-stick landing off Vella Lavella where he was later picked up. His valiant leadership and his daring skill as a flier served as a source of confidence and inspiration to his fellow pilots and reflect the highest credit upon the U.S. Naval Service.

2998 ◆ *WALSH, WILLIAM GARY

Rank: Gunnery Sergeant
Service: U.S. Marine Corps Reserve
Birthday: 7 April 1922
Place of Birth: Roxbury, Suffolk County, Massachusetts
Date of Death: 27 February 1945
Cemetery: Arlington National Cemetery (12-487) (MH)—Arlington, Virginia
Entered Service at: Massachusetts
Unit: Company G, 3d Battalion, 27th Marines, 5th Marine Division
Served as: Platoon Leader
Battle or Place of Action: Iwo Jima, Volcano Islands
Date of Action: 27 February 1945
Citation: For extraordinary gallantry and intrepidity at the risk of his life above and beyond the call of duty as leader of an assault platoon, attached to Company G, 3d Battalion, 27th Marines, 5th Marine Division, in action against enemy Japanese forces at Iwo Jima, Volcano Islands, on 27 February 1945. With the advance of his company toward Hill 362 disrupted by vicious machine-gun fire from a forward position which guarded the approaches to this key enemy stronghold, G/Sgt. Walsh fearlessly charged at the head of his platoon against the Japanese entrenched on the ridge above him, utterly oblivious to the unrelenting fury of hostile automatic-weapons fire and hand grenades employed with fanatic desperation to smash his daring assault. Thrown back by the enemy's savage resistance, he once again led his men in a seemingly impossible attack up the steep, rocky slope, boldly defiant of the annihilating streams of bullets which saturated the area. Despite his own casualty losses and the overwhelming advantage held by the Japanese in superior numbers and dominant position, he gained the ridge's top only to be subjected to an intense barrage of hand grenades thrown by the remaining Japanese staging a suicidal last stand on the reverse slope. When one of the grenades fell in the midst of his surviving men, huddled together in a small trench, G/Sgt. Walsh, in a final valiant act of complete self-sacrifice, instantly threw himself upon the deadly bomb, absorbing with his own body the full and terrific force of the explosion. Through his extraordinary initiative and inspiring valor in the face of almost certain death, he saved his comrades from injury and possible loss of life and enabled his company to seize and hold this vital enemy position. He gallantly gave his life for his country.

2999 ◆ *WARD, JAMES RICHARD

Rank: Seaman First Class
Service: U.S. Navy
ay: 10 September 1921
Place of Birth: Springfield, Clark County, Ohio
Date of Death: 7 December 1941
Cemetery: National Memorial Cemetery of the Pacific (Wall of the Missing)—Honolulu, Hawaii; Ferncliff Cemetery ('In Memory' marker)—Springfield, Ohio
Entered Service at: Springfield, Clark County, Ohio
Unit: U.S.S. *Oklahoma*
Battle or Place of Action: Pearl Harbor, Territory of Hawaii
Date of Action: 7 December 1941
Citation: For conspicuous devotion to duty, extraordinary courage, and complete disregard of his life, above and beyond the call of duty, during the attack on the Fleet in Pearl Harbor by Japanese forces on 7 December 1941. When it was seen that the U.S.S. *Oklahoma* was going to capsize and the order was given to abandon ship, Ward remained in a turret holding a flashlight so the remainder of the turret crew could see to escape, thereby sacrificing his own life.

3000 ◆ WARE, KEITH LINCOLN

Rank: Lieutenant Colonel (highest rank: Major General)
Service: U.S. Army
Birthday: 23 November 1915
Place of Birth: Denver, Denver County, Colorado
Date of Death: 13 September 1968
Place of Death: Cambodia
Cemetery: Arlington National Cemetery (30-258-3) (MH)—Arlington, Virginia
Entered Service at: Glendale, Los Angeles County, California
Unit: 1st Battalion, 15th Infantry, 3d Infantry Division
Served as: Battalion Commander

Battle or Place of Action: near Sigolsheim, France
Date of Action: 26 December 1944
G.O. Number, Date: 47, 18 June 1945
Date of Presentation: 23 April 1945
Place of Presentation: Zepman Stadium, Nuremberg, Germany, presented by Lt. Gen. Alexander M. Patch III
Citation: Commanding the 1st Battalion attacking a strongly-held enemy position on a hill near Sigolsheim, France, on 26 December 1944, Lt. Col. Ware found that one of his assault companies had been stopped and forced to dig in by a concentration of enemy artillery, mortar, and machine-gun fire. The company had suffered casualties in attempting to take the hill. Realizing that his men must be inspired to new courage, Lt. Col. Ware went forward 150 yards beyond the most forward elements of his command, and for two hours reconnoitered the enemy positions, deliberately drawing fire upon himself which caused the enemy to disclose his dispositions. Returning to his company, he armed himself with an automatic rifle and boldly advanced upon the enemy, followed by two officers, nine enlisted men, and a tank. Approaching an enemy machine gun, Lt. Col. Ware shot two German riflemen and fired tracers into the emplacement, indicating its position to his tank, which promptly knocked the gun out of action. Lt. Col. Ware turned his attention to a second machine gun, killing two of its supporting riflemen and forcing the others to surrender. The tank destroyed the gun. Having expended the ammunition for the automatic rifle, Lt. Col. Ware took up an M1 rifle, killed a German rifleman, and fired upon a third machine gun 50 yards away. His tank silenced the gun. Upon his approach to a fourth machine gun, its supporting riflemen surrendered and his tank disposed of the gun. During this action Lt. Col. Ware's small assault group was fully engaged in attacking enemy positions that were not receiving his direct and personal attention. Five of his party of 11 were casualties and Lt. Col. Ware was wounded, but refused medical attention until this important hill position was cleared of the enemy and securely occupied by his command.

3001 ◆ *WARNER, HENRY F.

Rank: Corporal
Service: U.S. Army
Birthday: 23 August 1923
Place of Birth: Troy, Montgomery County, North Carolina
Date of Death: 21 December 1944
Cemetery: South Side Cemetery (MH)—Troy, North Carolina
Entered Service at: Troy, Montgomery County, North Carolina
Unit: Antitank Company, 2d Battalion, 26th Infantry, 1st Infantry Division
Served as: 57-mm Antitank Gunner
Battle or Place of Action: near Dom Butgenbach, Belgium
Date of Action: 20-21 December 1944
G.O. Number, Date: 48, 23 June 1945
Citation: Serving as 57-mm antitank gunner with the 2d Battalion, he was a major factor in stopping enemy tanks during heavy attacks against the battalion position near Dom Butgenbach, Belgium, on 20–21 December 1944. In the first attack, launched early in the morning on the 20th, enemy tanks succeeded in penetrating parts of the line. Cpl. Warner, disregarding the concentrated cannon and machine-gun fire from two tanks bearing down on him and ignoring the imminent danger of being overrun by the infantry moving under tank cover, destroyed the first tank and scored a direct and deadly hit upon the second. A third tank approached to within five yards of his position while he was attempting to clear a jammed breach lock. Jumping from his gun pit, he engaged in a pistol duel with the tank commander standing in the turret, killing him and forcing the tank to withdraw. Following a day and night during which our forces were subjected to constant shelling, mortar barrages, and numerous unsuccessful infantry attacks, the enemy struck in great force on the early morning of the 21st. Seeing a Mark IV tank looming out of the mist and heading toward his position, Cpl. Warner scored a direct hit. Disregarding his injuries, he endeavored to finish the loading and again fire at the tank, whose motor was now aflame, when a second machine-gun burst killed him. Cpl. Warner's gallantry and intrepidity at the risk of life above and beyond the call of duty contributed materially to the successful defense against the enemy attacks.

3002 ◆ WATSON, WILSON DOUGLAS

Rank: Private (highest rank: Staff Sergeant)
Service: U.S. Marine Corps Reserve
Birthday: 18 February 1922
Place of Birth: Tuscumbia, Colbert County, Alabama
Date of Death: 19 December 1994
Place of Death: Russellville, Arkansas
Cemetery: Russell Cemetery—Ozone, Arkansas
Entered Service at: Earle, Crittenden County, Arkansas
Unit: 2d Squad, 3d Platoon, Company G, 2d Battalion, 9th Marines, 3d Marine Division
Served as: Automatic Rifleman
Battle or Place of Action: Iwo Jima, Volcano Islands
Date of Action: 26-27 February 1945
Date of Presentation: 5 October 1945
Place of Presentation: The White House, presented by Pres. Harry S. Truman
Citation: For conspicuous gallantry and intrepidity at the risk of his life above and beyond the call of duty as automatic rifleman serving with the 2d Battalion, 9th Marines, 3d Marine Division, during action against enemy Japanese forces on Iwo Jima, Volcano Islands, 26 and 27 February 1945. With his squad abruptly halted by intense fire from enemy fortifications in the high rocky ridges and crags commanding the line of advance, Pvt. Watson boldly rushed one pillbox and fired into the embrasure with his weapon, keeping the enemy pinned down singlehandedly until he was in a position to hurl in a grenade and then running to the rear of the emplacement to destroy the retreating Japanese and enable his platoon to take its objective. Again pinned down at the foot of a small hill, he dauntlessly scaled the jagged incline under fierce mortar and machine-gun barrages and, with his assistant BAR man, charged the crest of the hill, firing from

his hip. Fighting furiously against Japanese troops attacking with grenades and knee mortars from the reverse slope, he stood fearlessly erect in his exposed position to cover the hostile entrenchments and held the hill under savage fire for 15 minutes, killing 60 Japanese before his ammunition was exhausted and his platoon was able to join him. His courageous initiative and valiant fighting spirit against devastating odds were directly responsible for the continued advance of his platoon, and his inspiring leadership throughout this bitterly fought action reflects the highest credit upon Pvt. Watson and the U.S. Naval Service.

3003 ◆ *WAUGH, ROBERT T.

Rank: First Lieutenant
Service: U.S. Army
Place of Birth: Ashton, Rhode Island
Date of Death: 19 May 1944
Cemetery: A.B.M.C. Sicily-Rome Cemetery (H-13-37)—Nettuno, Italy
Entered Service at: Augusta, Kennebec County, Maine
Unit: 339th Infantry, 85th Infantry Division
Served as: Platoon Leader
Battle or Place of Action: near Tremensucli, Italy
Date of Action: 11-14 May 1944
G.O. Number, Date: 79, 4 October 1944
Place of Presentation: Fort Dupont, Delaware, presented by Maj. Gen. Henry Terrell Jr. to his family
Citation: For conspicuous gallantry and intrepidity at the risk of life above and beyond the call of duty in action with the enemy. In the course of an attack upon an enemy-held hill on 11 May, 1st Lt. Waugh personally reconnoitered a heavily mined area before entering it with his platoon. Directing his men to deliver fire on six bunkers guarding this hill, 1st Lt. Waugh advanced alone against them, reached the first bunker, threw phosphorus grenades into it, and, as the defenders emerged, killed them with a burst from his tommy gun. He repeated this process on the five remaining bunkers, killing or capturing the occupants. On the morning of 14 May, 1st Lt. Waugh ordered his platoon to lay a base of fire on two enemy pillboxes located on a knoll which commanded the only trail up the hill. He then ran to the first pillbox, threw several grenades into it, drove the defenders into the open, and killed them. The second pillbox was next taken by this intrepid officer by similar methods. The fearless actions of 1st Lt. Waugh broke the Gustav Line at that point, neutralizing six bunkers and two pillboxes, and he was personally responsible for the death of 30 of the enemy and the capture of 25 others. He was later killed in action in Itri, Italy, while leading his platoon in an attack.

3004 ◆ WAYBUR, DAVID CROWDER

Rank: First Lieutenant
Service: U.S. Army
Place of Birth: Oakland, Alameda County, California
Date of Death: 28 March 1945
Cemetery: A.B.M.C. Lorraine Cemetery (E-22-44) (MH)—St. Avold, France
Entered Service at: Piedmont, Alameda County, California
Unit: 3d Reconnaissance Troop, 3d Infantry Division
Battle or Place of Action: near Agrigento, Sicily
Date of Action: 17 July 1943
G.O. Number, Date: 69, 21 October 1943
Citation: For conspicuous gallantry and intrepidity at the risk of life above and beyond the call of duty in action involving actual conflict with the enemy. Commander of a reconnaissance platoon, 1st Lt. Waybur volunteered to lead a three-vehicle patrol into enemy-held territory to locate an isolated Ranger unit. Proceeding under cover of darkness, over roads known to be heavily mined and strongly defended by road blocks and machine-gun positions, the patrol's progress was halted at a bridge which had been destroyed by enemy troops and was suddenly cut off from its supporting vehicles by four enemy tanks. Although hopelessly outnumbered and outgunned, and himself and his men completely exposed, he quickly dispersed his vehicles and ordered his gunners to open fire with their .30 and .50-caliber machine guns. Then, with ammunition exhausted, three of his men hit, and himself seriously wounded, he seized his .45-caliber Thompson submachine gun and, standing in the bright moonlight directly in the line of fire, alone engaged the leading tank at 30 yards and succeeded in killing the crewmembers, causing the tank to run onto the bridge and crash into the stream bed. After dispatching one of the men for aid, he rallied the rest to cover and withstood the continued fire of the tanks until the arrival of aid the following morning.

3005 ◆ *WEICHT, ELLIS R.

Rank: Sergeant
Service: U.S. Army
Place of Birth: Clearville, Bedford County, Pennsylvania
Date of Death: 3 December 1944
Cemetery: A.B.M.C. Epinal Cemetery (B-42-20) (MH)—Epinal, France
Entered Service at: Bedford, Bedford County, Pennsylvania
Unit: Company F, 142d Infantry, 36th Infantry Division
Served as: Squad Leader
Battle or Place of Action: St. Hippolyte, France
Date of Action: 3 December 1944
G.O. Number, Date: 58, 19 July 1945
Citation: For commanding an assault squad in Company F's attack against the strategically important Alsatian town of St. Hippolyte on 3 December 1944. He aggressively led his men down a winding street, clearing the houses of opposition as he advanced. Upon rounding a bend, the group was suddenly brought under the fire of two machine guns emplaced in the door and window of a house 100 yards distant. While his squad members took cover, Sgt. Weicht moved rapidly forward to a high rock wall and, fearlessly exposing himself to the enemy action, fired two clips of ammunition from his rifle. His fire proving ineffective, he entered a house opposite the enemy gun position, and, firing from a window, killed the two hostile gunners. Continuing the attack, the advance was again halted when two 20-mm guns opened fire on the company. An artillery observer ordered friendly troops to evacuate the area and then directed artillery fire upon the gun posi-

tions. Sgt. Weicht remained in the shelled area and continued to fire on the hostile weapons. When the barrage lifted and the enemy soldiers attempted to remove their gun, he killed two crewmembers and forced the others to flee. Sgt. Weicht continued to lead his squad forward until he spotted a road block approximately 125 yards away. Moving to the second floor of a nearby house and firing from a window, he killed three and wounded several of the enemy. Instantly becoming a target for heavy and direct fire, he disregarded personal safety to continue his fire, with unusual effectiveness, until he was killed by a direct hit from an antitank gun.

3006 ◆ *WETZEL, WALTER C.

Rank: Private First Class
Service: U.S. Army
Place of Birth: Huntington, Cabell County, West Virginia
Date of Death: 3 April 1945
Cemetery: A.B.M.C. Netherlands Cemetery (N-18-10) (MH)—Margraten, Holland
Entered Service at: Roseville, Macomb County, Michigan
Unit: Antitank Company, 13th Infantry, 8th Infantry Division
Served as: Acting Squad Leader
Battle or Place of Action: Birken, Germany
Date of Action: 3 April 1945
G.O. Number, Date: 21, 26 February 1946
Citation: Pfc. Wetzel, an acting squad leader with the Antitank Company of the 13th Infantry, was guarding his platoon's command post in a house at Birken, Germany, during the early morning hours of 3 April 1945, when he detected strong enemy forces moving in to attack. He ran into the house, alerted the occupants, and immediately began defending the post against heavy automatic-weapon fire coming from the hostile troops. Under cover of darkness the Germans forced their way close to the building where they hurled grenades, two of which landed in the room where Pfc. Wetzel and the others had taken up firing positions. Shouting a warning to his fellow soldiers, Pfc. Wetzel threw himself on the grenades and, as they exploded, absorbed their entire blast, suffering wounds from which he died. The supreme gallantry of Pfc. Wetzel saved his comrades from death or serious injury and made it possible for them to continue the defense of the command post and break the power of a dangerous local counterthrust by the enemy. His unhesitating sacrifice of his life was in keeping with the U.S. Army's highest traditions of bravery and heroism.

3007 ◆ WHITELEY, ELI LAMAR

Rank: First Lieutenant
Service: U.S. Army
Birthday: 10 December 1913
Place of Birth: Florence, Williamson County, Texas
Date of Death: 2 December 1986
Cemetery: City Cemetery (MH)—College Station, Texas
Entered Service at: Georgetown, Williamson County, Texas
Unit: Company L, 15th Infantry, 3d Infantry Division
Served as: Platoon Leader
Battle or Place of Action: Sigolsheim, France
Date of Action: 27 December 1944
G.O. Number, Date: 79, 14 September 1945
Date of Presentation: 23 August 1945
Place of Presentation: The White House, presented by Pres. Harry S. Truman
Citation: While leading his platoon on 27 December 1944, in savage house-to-house fighting through the fortress town of Sigolsheim, France, he attacked a building through a street swept by withering mortar and automatic-weapon fire. He was hit and severely wounded in the arm and shoulder; but he charged into the house alone and killed its two defenders. Hurling smoke and fragmentation grenades before him, he reached the next house and stormed inside, killing two and capturing 11 of the enemy. He continued leading his platoon in the extremely dangerous task of clearing hostile troops from strongpoints along the street until he reached a building held by fanatical Nazi troops. Although suffering from wounds which had rendered his left arm useless, he advanced on this strongly defended house and, after blasting out a wall with bazooka fire, charged through a hail of bullets. Wedging his submachine gun under his uninjured arm, he rushed into the house through the hole torn by his rockets, killed five of the enemy, and forced the remaining 12 to surrender. As he emerged to continue his fearless attack, he was again hit and critically wounded. In agony and with one eye pierced by a shell fragment, he shouted for his men to follow him to the next house. He was determined to stay in the fighting and remained at the head of his platoon until forcibly evacuated. By his disregard for personal safety, his aggressiveness while suffering from severe wounds, his determined leadership and superb courage, 1st Lt. Whiteley killed nine Germans, captured 23 more, and spearheaded an attack which cracked the core of enemy resistance in a vital area.

3008 ◆ WHITTINGTON, HULON BROOKE

Rank: Sergeant (highest rank: Major)
Service: U.S. Army
Birthday: 9 July 1921
Place of Birth: Bogalusa, Washington County, Louisiana
Date of Death: 17 January 1969
Cemetery: Arlington National Cemetery (13-8-W)—Arlington, Virginia
Entered Service at: Bastrop, Morehouse County, Louisiana
Unit: 41st Armored Infantry, 2d Armored Division
Served as: Squad Leader
Battle or Place of Action: near Grimesnil, France
Date of Action: 29 July 1944
G.O. Number, Date: 32, 23 April 1945
Citation: For conspicuous gallantry and intrepidity at the risk of life above and beyond the call of duty. On the night of 29 July 1944, near Grimesnil, France, during an enemy armored attack, Sgt. Whittington, a squad leader, assumed command of his platoon when the platoon leader and platoon sergeant became missing in action. He reorganized the defense and, under fire, courageously crawled between gun positions to check the actions of his men. When the advancing enemy attempted to penetrate a roadblock, Sgt.

Whittington, completely disregarding intense enemy action, mounted a tank and, by shouting through the turret, directed it into position to fire point-blank at the leading Mark V German tank. The destruction of this vehicle blocked all movement of the remaining enemy column consisting of over 100 vehicles of a Panzer unit. The blocked vehicles were then destroyed by hand grenades, bazooka, tank, and artillery fire, and large numbers of enemy personnel were wiped out by a bold and resolute bayonet charge inspired by Sgt. Whittington. When the medical aidman had become a casualty, Sgt. Whittington personally administered first aid to his wounded men. The dynamic leadership, the inspiring example, and the dauntless courage of Sgt. Whittington, above and beyond the call of duty, are in keeping with the highest traditions of the military service.

3009 ◆ WIEDORFER, PAUL JOSEPH

Rank: Staff Sergeant (rank at time of action: Private) (highest rank: Master Sergeant)
Service: U.S. Army
Birthday: 17 January 1921
Place of Birth: Baltimore, Baltimore County, Maryland
Entered Service at: Baltimore, Baltimore County, Maryland
Unit: 2d Squad, 2d Platoon, Company G, 2d Battalion, 318th Infantry, 80th Infantry Division
Served as: Rifleman
Battle or Place of Action: near Chaumont, Belgium
Date of Action: 25 December 1944
G.O. Number, Date: 45, 12 June 1945
Date of Presentation: 29 May 1945
Place of Presentation: 137th Gen. Hospital, Ellesmere, Shropshire, England, presented by Brigadier Gen. E. F. Koenig, UK Base Commander
Citation: He alone made it possible for his company to advance until its objective was seized. Company G had cleared a wooded area of snipers, and one platoon was advancing across an open clearing toward another wood when it was met by heavy machine-gun fire from two German positions dug in at the edge of the second wood. These positions were flanked by enemy riflemen. The platoon took cover behind a small ridge approximately 40 yards from the enemy position. There was no other available protection and the entire platoon was pinned down by the German fire. It was about noon and the day was clear, but the terrain extremely difficult due to a three-inch snowfall the night before over ice-covered ground. Pvt. Wiedorfer, realizing that the platoon advance could not continue until the two enemy machine-gun nests were destroyed, voluntarily charged alone across the slippery open ground with no protecting cover of any kind. Running in a crouched position, under a hail of enemy fire, he slipped and fell in the snow, but quickly rose and continued forward with the enemy concentrating automatic and small-arms fire on him as he advanced. Miraculously escaping injury, Pvt. Wiedorfer reached a point some 10 yards from the first machine-gun emplacement and hurled a hand grenade into it. With his rifle he killed the remaining Germans, and, without hesitation, wheeled to the right and attacked the second emplacement. One of the enemy was wounded by his fire and the other six immediately surrendered. This heroic action by one man enabled the platoon to advance from behind its protecting ridge and continue successfully to reach its objective. A few minutes later, when both the platoon leader and the platoon sergeant were wounded, Pvt. Wiedorfer assumed command of the platoon, leading it forward with inspired energy until the mission was accomplished.

3010 ◆ *WIGLE, THOMAS W.

Rank: Second Lieutenant
Service: U.S. Army
Birthday: 18 May 1909
Place of Birth: Indianapolis, Marion County, Indiana
Date of Death: 16 September 1944
Cemetery: Arlington National Cemetery (34-3307) (MH)—Arlington, Virginia
Entered Service at: Detroit, Wayne County, Michigan
Unit: Company K, 135th Infantry, 34th Infantry Division
Served as: Executive Officer
Battle or Place of Action: Monte Frassino, Italy
Date of Action: 14 September 1944
G.O. Number, Date: 8, 7 February 1945
Citation: For conspicuous gallantry and intrepidity at the risk of life above and beyond the call of duty in the vicinity of Monte Frassino, Italy. The 3d Platoon, in attempting to seize a strongly fortified hill position protected by three parallel high terraced stone walls, was twice thrown back by the withering crossfire. Second Lt. Wigle, acting company executive, observing that the platoon was without an officer, volunteered to command it on the next attack. Leading his men up the bare, rocky slopes through intense and concentrated fire, he succeeded in reaching the first of the stone walls. Having himself boosted to the top and perching there in full view of the enemy, he drew and returned their fire while his men helped each other up and over. Following the same method, he successfully negotiated the second. Upon reaching the top of the third wall, he faced three houses which were the key point of the enemy defense. Ordering his men to cover him, he made a dash through a hail of machine-pistol fire to reach the nearest house. Firing his carbine as he entered, he drove the enemy before him out of the back door and into the second house. Following closely on the heels of the foe, he drove them from this house to the third where they took refuge in the cellar. When his men rejoined him, they found him mortally wounded on the cellar stairs which he had started to descend to force the surrender of the enemy. His heroic action resulted in the capture of 36 German soldiers and the seizure of the strongpoint.

3011 ◆ WILBUR, WILLIAM HALE

Rank: Colonel (highest rank: Brigadier General)
Service: U.S. Army
Birthday: 24 September 1888
Place of Birth: Palmer, Hampden County, Massachusetts
Date of Death: 27 December 1979
Place of Death: Sanibel, Florida

Cemetery: U.S. Military Academy Cemetery (7-C-148)—West Point, New York
Entered Service at: Palmer, Hampden County, Massachusetts
Unit: Western Task Force, North Africa
Battle or Place of Action: Fedala, North Africa
Date of Action: 8 November 1942
G.O. Number, Date: 2, 13 January 1943
Date of Presentation: 24 January 1943
Place of Presentation: Casablanca, Algiers, presented by Pres. Franklin D. Roosevelt
Citation: For conspicuous gallantry and intrepidity in action above and beyond the call of duty. Col. Wilbur prepared the plan for making contact with French commanders in Casablanca and obtaining an armistice to prevent unnecessary bloodshed. On 8 November 1942, he landed at Fedala with the leading assault waves where opposition had developed into a firm and continuous defensive line across his route of advance. Commandeering a vehicle, he was driven toward the hostile defenses under incessant fire, finally locating a French officer who accorded him passage through the forward positions. He then proceeded in total darkness through 16 miles of enemy-occupied country intermittently subjected to heavy bursts of fire, and accomplished his mission by delivering his letters to appropriate French officials in Casablanca. Returning toward his command, Col. Wilbur detected a hostile battery firing effectively on our troops. He took charge of a platoon of American tanks and personally led them in an attack and capture of the battery. From the moment of landing until the cessation of hostile resistance, Col. Wilbur's conduct was voluntary and exemplary in its coolness and daring.

3012 ◆ *WILKIN, EDWARD G.

Rank: Corporal
Service: U.S. Army
Birthday: 25 May 1917
Place of Birth: Burlington, Chittenden County, Vermont
Date of Death: 18 April 1945
Cemetery: Longmeadow Cemetery (MH)—Longmeadow, Massachusetts
Entered Service at: Longmeadow, Hampden County, Massachusetts
Unit: Company C, 157th Infantry, 45th Infantry Division
Battle or Place of Action: Siegfried Line, Germany
Date of Action: 18 March 1945
G.O. Number, Date: 119, 17 December 1945
Citation: He spearheaded his unit's assault of the Siegfried line in Germany. Heavy fire from enemy riflemen and camouflaged pillboxes had pinned down his comrades when he moved forward on his own initiative to reconnoiter a route of advance. He cleared the way into an area studded with pillboxes, where he repeatedly stood up and walked into vicious enemy fire, storming one fortification after another with automatic rifle fire and grenades, killing enemy troops, taking prisoners as the enemy defense became confused, and encouraging his comrades by his heroic example. When halted by heavy barbed wire entanglements, he secured bangalore torpedoes and blasted a path toward still more pillboxes, all the time braving bursting grenades and mortar shells and direct rifle and automatic-weapon fire. He engaged in fierce firefights, standing in the open while his adversaries fought from the protection of concrete emplacements, and on one occasion pursued enemy soldiers across an open field and through interlocking trenches, disregarding the crossfire from two pillboxes until he had penetrated the formidable line 200 yards in advance of any American element. That night, although terribly fatigued, he refused to rest and insisted on distributing rations and supplies to his comrades. Hearing that a nearby company was suffering heavy casualties, he secured permission to guide litter bearers and assist them in evacuating the wounded. All that night he remained in the battle area on his mercy missions, and for the following two days he continued to remove casualties, venturing into enemy-held territory, scorning cover, and braving devastating mortar and artillery bombardments. In three days he neutralized and captured six pillboxes singlehandedly, killed at least nine Germans, wounded 13, took 13 prisoners, aided in the capture of 14 others, and saved many American lives by his fearless performance as a litter bearer. Through his superb fighting skill, dauntless courage, and gallant, inspiring actions, Cpl. Wilkin contributed in large measure to his company's success in cracking the Siegfried line. One month later he was killed in action while fighting deep in Germany.

3013 ◆ *WILKINS, RAYMOND HARRELL

Rank: Major
Service: U.S. Army Air Corps
Birthday: 28 September 1917
Place of Birth: Portsmouth, Portsmouth County, Virginia
Date of Death: 2 November 1943
Place of Death: Rabaul, New Britain
Cemetery: A.B.M.C. Manila Cemetery (Wall of the Missing)—Manila, Philippine Islands; Olive Branch Cemetery ('In Memory' marker) (MH)—Portsmouth, Va.
Entered Service at: Portsmouth, Portsmouth County, Virginia
Unit: 89th Bombardment Squadron, 3d Bombardment Group, 5th Air Force
Served as: Squadron Leader/Pilot of a B-25
Battle or Place of Action: near Rabaul, New Britain, Bismarck Archipelago
Date of Action: 2 November 1943
G.O. Number, Date: 23, 24 March 1944
Date of Presentation: 1 December 1944
Place of Presentation: Vandalia, Ohio, presented to his family
Citation: For conspicuous gallantry and intrepidity above and beyond the call of duty in action with the enemy near Rabaul, New Britain, on 2 November 1943. Leading his squadron in an attack on shipping in Simpson Harbor, during which intense antiaircraft fire was expected, Maj. Wilkins briefed his squadron so that his airplane would be in the position of greatest risk. His squadron was the last of three in the group to enter the target area. Smoke from bombs dropped by preceding aircraft necessitated a last-second revision of tactics on his part, which still enabled his squadron to strike vital

shipping targets, but forced it to approach through concentrated fire and increased the danger of Maj. Wilkins' left flank position. His airplane was hit almost immediately, the right wing damaged, and control rendered extremely difficult. Although he could have withdrawn, he held fast and led his squadron into the attack. He strafed a group of small harbor vessels, and then, at low level, attacked an enemy destroyer. His 1,000 pound bomb struck squarely amidships, causing the vessel to explode. Although antiaircraft fire from this vessel had seriously damaged his left vertical stabilizer, he refused to deviate from the course. From below-masthead height he attacked a transport of some 9,000 tons, scoring a hit which engulfed the ship in flames. Bombs expended, he began to withdraw his squadron. A heavy cruiser barred the path. Unhesitatingly, to neutralize the cruiser's guns and attract its fire, he went in for a strafing run. His damaged stabilizer was completely shot off. To avoid swerving into his wing planes he had to turn so as to expose the belly and full wing surfaces of his plane to the enemy fire; it caught and crumpled his left wing. Now past control, the bomber crashed into the sea. In the fierce engagement Maj. Wilkins destroyed two enemy vessels, and his heroic self-sacrifice made possible the safe withdrawal of the remaining planes of his squadron.

3014 ◆ *WILL, WALTER J.

Rank: First Lieutenant
Service: U.S. Army
Place of Birth: Pittsburgh, Allegheny County, Pennsylvania
Date of Death: 30 March 1945
Cemetery: A.B.M.C. Netherlands Cemetery (D-3-32) (MH)—Margraten, Holland
Entered Service at: West Winfield, Herkimer County, New York
Unit: Company K, 18th Infantry, 1st Infantry Division
Battle or Place of Action: near Eisern, Germany
Date of Action: 30 March 1945
G.O. Number, Date: 88, 17 October 1945
Citation: He displayed conspicuous gallantry during an attack on powerful enemy positions. He courageously exposed himself to withering hostile fire to rescue two wounded men and then, although painfully wounded himself, made a third trip to carry another soldier to safety from an open area. Ignoring the profuse bleeding of his wound, he gallantly led men of his platoon forward until they were pinned down by murderous flanking fire from two enemy machine guns. He fearlessly crawled alone to within 30 feet of the first enemy position, killed the crew of four, and silenced the gun with accurate grenade fire. He continued to crawl through intense enemy fire to within 20 feet of the second position where he leaped to his feet, made a lone, ferocious charge, and captured the gun and its nine-man crew. Observing another platoon pinned down by two more German machine guns, he led a squad on a flanking approach and, rising to his knees in the face of direct fire, coolly and deliberately lobbed three grenades at the Germans, silencing one gun and killing its crew. With tenacious aggressiveness, he ran toward the other gun and knocked it out with grenade fire. He then returned to his platoon and led it in a fierce, inspired charge, forcing the enemy to fall back in confusion. First Lt. Will was mortally wounded in this last action, but his heroic leadership, indomitable courage, and unflinching devotion to duty live on as a perpetual inspiration to all those who witnessed his deeds.

3015 ◆ WILLIAMS, HERSHEL WOODROW "WOODY"

Rank: Corporal (highest rank: Chief Warrant Officer 4)
Service: U.S. Marine Corps Reserve
Birthday: 2 October 1923
Place of Birth: Quiet Dell, Marion County, West Virginia
Entered Service at: Fairmont, Marion County, West Virginia
Unit: Headquarters Company, 1st Battalion, 21st Marines, 3d Marine Division
Served as: Demolition Sergeant
Battle or Place of Action: Iwo Jima, Volcano Islands
Date of Action: 23 February 1945
Date of Presentation: 5 October 1945
Place of Presentation: The White House, presented by Pres. Harry S. Truman
Citation: For conspicuous gallantry and intrepidity at the risk of his life above and beyond the call of duty as demolition sergeant serving with the 21st Marines, 3d Marine Division, in action against enemy Japanese forces on Iwo Jima, Volcano Islands, 23 February 1945. Quick to volunteer his services when our tanks were maneuvering vainly to open a lane for the infantry through the network of reinforced concrete pillboxes, buried mines, and black volcanic sands, Cpl. Williams daringly went forward alone to attempt the reduction of devastating machine-gun fire from the unyielding positions. Covered only by four riflemen, he fought desperately for four hours under terrific enemy small-arms fire and repeatedly returned to his own lines to prepare demolition charges and obtain serviced flamethrowers, struggling back, frequently to the rear of hostile emplacements, to wipe out one position after another. On one occasion, he daringly mounted a pillbox to insert the nozzle of his flamethrower through the air vent, killing the occupants, and silencing the gun; on another he grimly charged enemy riflemen who attempted to stop him with bayonets and destroyed them with a burst of flame from his weapon. His unyielding determination and extraordinary heroism in the face of ruthless enemy resistance were directly instrumental in neutralizing one of the most fanatically defended Japanese strongpoints encountered by his regiment and aided vitally in enabling his company to reach its objective. Cpl. Williams' aggressive fighting spirit and valiant devotion to duty throughout this fiercely contested action sustain and enhance the highest traditions of the U.S. Naval Service.

3016 ◆ *WILLIAMS, JACK

Rank: Pharmacist's Mate Third Class
Service: U.S. Naval Reserve
Birthday: 18 October 1924
Place of Birth: Harrison, Boone County, Arkansas

Date of Death: 3 March 1945
Cemetery: Springfield National Cemetery (30-2375) (MH)—Springfield, Missouri
Entered Service at: Arkansas
Unit: 3d Battalion, 28th Marines, 5th Marine Division
Served as: Medical Corpsman
Battle or Place of Action: Iwo Jima, Volcano Islands
Date of Action: 3 March 1945
Citation: For conspicuous gallantry and intrepidity at the risk of his life above and beyond the call of duty while serving with the 3d Battalion, 28th Marines, 5th Marine Division, during the occupation of Iwo Jima, Volcano Islands, 3 March 1945. Gallantly going forward on the front lines under intense enemy small-arms fire to assist a marine wounded in a fierce grenade battle, Williams dragged the man to a shallow depression and was kneeling, using his own body as a screen from the sustained fire as he administered first aid, when struck in the abdomen and groin three times by hostile rifle fire. Momentarily stunned, he quickly recovered and completed his ministration before applying battle dressings to his own multiple wounds. Unmindful of his own urgent need for medical attention, he remained in the perilous fire-swept area to care for another marine casualty. Heroically completing his task despite pain and profuse bleeding, he then endeavored to make his way to the rear in search of adequate aid for himself when struck down by a Japanese sniper bullet which caused his collapse. Succumbing later as a result of his self-sacrificing service to others, Williams, by his courageous determination, unwavering fortitude, and valiant performance of duty, served as an inspiring example of heroism, in keeping with the highest traditions of the U.S. Naval Service. He gallantly gave his life for his country.

3017 ◆ *WILLIS, JOHN HARLAN

Rank: Pharmacist's Mate First Class
Service: U.S. Navy
Birthday: 10 June 1921
Place of Birth: Columbia, Maury County, Tennessee
Date of Death: 28 February 1945
Cemetery: Rose Hill Cemetery—Columbia, Tennessee
Entered Service at: Tennessee
Unit: 3d Battalion, 27th Marines, 5th Marine Division
Served as: Platoon Medical Corpsman
Battle or Place of Action: Iwo Jima, Volcano Islands
Date of Action: 28 February 1945
Citation: For conspicuous gallantry and intrepidity at the risk of his life above and beyond the call of duty as platoon corpsman serving with the 3d Battalion, 27th Marines, 5th Marine Division, during operations against enemy Japanese forces on Iwo Jima, Volcano Islands, 28 February 1945. Constantly imperiled by artillery and mortar fire from strong and mutually supporting pillboxes and caves studding Hill 362 in the enemy cross-island defenses, Willis resolutely administered first aid to the many marines wounded during the furious close-in fighting until he himself was struck by shrapnel and was ordered back to the battle-aid station. Without waiting for official medical release, he quickly returned to his company and, during a savage hand-to-hand enemy counterattack, daringly advanced to the extreme front lines under mortar and sniper fire to aid a marine lying wounded in a shell hole. Completely unmindful of his own danger as the Japanese intensified their attack, Willis calmly continued to administer blood plasma to his patient, promptly returning the first hostile grenade which landed in the shell hole while he was working and hurling back seven more in quick succession before the ninth one exploded in his hand and instantly killed him. By his great personal valor in saving others at the sacrifice of his own life, he inspired his companions, although terrifically outnumbered, to launch a fiercely determined attack and repulse the enemy force. His exceptional fortitude and courage in the performance of duty reflect the highest credit upon Willis and the U.S. Naval Service. He gallantly gave his life for his country.

3018 ◆ *WILSON, ALFRED LEONARD

Rank: Technician Grade Five
Service: U.S. Army
Birthday: 18 September 1918
Place of Birth: Fairchance, Fayette County, Pennsylvania
Date of Death: 8 November 1944
Cemetery: Maple Grove Cemetery (MH)—Fairchance, Pennsylvania
Entered Service at: Fairchance, Fayette County, Pennsylvania
Unit: Medical Detachment, 328th Infantry, 26th Infantry Division
Served as: Medical Aidman
Battle or Place of Action: near Bezange la Petite, France
Date of Action: 8 November 1944
G.O. Number, Date: 47, 18 June 1945
Citation: He volunteered to assist as an aidman a company other than his own, which was suffering casualties from constant artillery fire. He administered to the wounded and returned to his own company when a shell burst injured a number of its men. While treating his comrades he was seriously wounded, but refused to be evacuated by litter bearers sent to relieve him. In spite of great pain and loss of blood, he continued to administer first aid until he was too weak to stand. Crawling from one patient to another, he continued his work until excessive loss of blood prevented him from moving. He then verbally directed unskilled enlisted men in continuing the first aid for the wounded. Still refusing asistance himself, he remained to instruct others in dressing the wounds of his comrades until he was unable to speak above a whisper and finally lapsed into unconsciousness. The effects of his injury later caused his death. By steadfastly remaining at the scene without regard for his own safety, Cpl. Wilson through distinguished devotion to duty and personal sacrifice helped to save the lives of at least 10 wounded men.

3019 ◆ WILSON JR., LOUIS HUGH

Rank: Captain (highest rank: General)
Service: U.S. Marine Corps
Birthday: 11 February 1920
Place of Birth: Brandon, Rankin County, Mississippi

Entered Service at: Mississippi
Unit: Company F, 2d Battalion, 9th Marines, 3d Marine Division
Served as: Commanding Officer
Battle or Place of Action: Fonte Hill, Guam, Mariana Islands
Date of Action: 25-26 July 1944
Date of Presentation: 5 October 1945
Place of Presentation: The White House, presented by Pres. Harry S. Truman
Citation: For conspicuous gallantry and intrepidity at the risk of his life above and beyond the call of duty as commanding officer of a rifle company attached to the 2d Battalion, 9th Marines, 3d Marine Division, in action against enemy Japanese forces at Fonte Hill, Guam, 25–26 July 1944. Ordered to take that portion of the hill within his zone of action, Capt. Wilson initiated his attack in midafternoon, pushed up the rugged, open terrain against terrific machine-gun and rifle fire for 300 yards, and successfully captured the objective. Promptly assuming command of other disorganized units and motorized equipment in addition to his own company and one reinforcing platoon, he organized his night defenses in the face of continuous hostile fire and, although wounded three times during this five-hour period, completed his disposition of men and guns before retiring to the company command post for medical attention. Shortly thereafter, when the enemy launched the first of a series of savage counterattacks lasting all night, he voluntarily rejoined his besieged units and repeatedly exposed himself to the merciless hail of shrapnel and bullets, dashing 50 yards into the open on one occasion to rescue a wounded marine lying helpless beyond the front lines. Fighting fiercely in hand-to-hand encounters, he led his men in furiously waged battle for approximately 10 hours, tenaciously holding his line and repelling the fanatically renewed counterthrusts until he succeeded in crushing the last efforts of the hard-pressed Japanese early the following morning. Then organizing a 17-man patrol, he immediately advanced upon a strategic slope essential to the security of his position and, boldly defying intense mortar, machine-gun, and rifle fire which struck down 13 of his men, drove relentlessly forward with the remnants of his patrol to seize the vital ground. By his indomitable leadership, daring combat tactics, and valor in the face of overwhelming odds, Capt. Wilson succeede d in capturing and holding the strategic high ground in his regimental sector, thereby contributing essentially to the success of his regimental mission and to the annihilation of 350 Japanese troops. His inspiring conduct throughout the critical periods of this decisive action sustains and enhances the highest traditions of the U.S. Naval Service.

3020 ◆ *WILSON, ROBERT LEE

Rank: Private First Class
Service: U.S. Marine Corps
Birthday: 24 May 1921
Place of Birth: Centralia, Marion County, Illinois
Date of Death: 4 August 1944
Cemetery: Hillcrest Memorial Park (MH)—Centralia, Illinois
Entered Service at: Illinois
Unit: 2d Battalion, 6th Marines, 2d Marine Division
Battle or Place of Action: Tinian Island, Mariana Islands
Date of Action: 4 August 1944
Citation: For conspicuous gallantry and intrepidity at the risk of his life above and beyond the call of duty while serving with the 2d Battalion, 6th Marines, 2d Marine Division, during action against enemy Japanese forces at Tinian Island, Marianas Group, on 4 August 1944. As one of a group of marines advancing through heavy underbrush to neutralize isolated points of resistance, Pfc. Wilson daringly preceded his companions toward a pile of rocks where Japanese troops were supposed to be hiding. Fully aware of the danger involved, he was moving forward while the remainder of the squad, armed with automatic rifles, closed together in the rear when an enemy grenade landed in the midst of the group. Quick to act, Pfc. Wilson cried a warning to the men and unhesitatingly threw himself on the grenade, heroically sacrificing his own life that the others might live and fulfill their mission. His exceptional valor, his courageous loyalty and unwavering devotion to duty in the face of grave peril reflect the highest credit upon Pfc. Wilson and the U.S. Naval Service. He gallantly gave his life for his country.

3021 ◆ WISE, HOMER L.

Rank: Staff Sergeant (highest rank: First Sergeant)
Service: U.S. Army
Birthday: 27 February 1917
Place of Birth: Baton Rouge, East Baton Rouge County, Louisiana
Date of Death: 22 April 1974
Place of Death: Springdale, Connecticut
Cemetery: St. John's Cemetery (MH)—Darien, Connecticut
Entered Service at: Baton Rouge, East Baton Rouge County, Louisiana
Unit: Company L, 142d Infantry, 36th Infantry Division
Battle or Place of Action: Magliano, Italy
Date of Action: 14 June 1944
G.O. Number, Date: 90, 8 December 1944
Citation: While his platoon was pinned down by enemy small-arms fire from both flanks, he left his position of comparative safety and assisted in carrying one of his men, who had been seriously wounded and who lay in an exposed position, to a point where he could receive medical attention. The advance of the platoon was resumed, but was again stopped by enemy frontal fire. A German officer and two enlisted men, armed with automatic weapons, threatened the right flank. Fearlessly exposing himself, he moved to a position from which he killed all three with his submachine gun. Returning to his squad, he obtained an M1 rifle and several antitank grenades, then took up a position from which he delivered accurate fire on the enemy holding up the advance. As the battalion moved forward it was again stopped by enemy frontal and flanking fire. He procured an automatic rifle and, advancing ahead of his men, neutralized an enemy machine gun with his fire. When the flanking fire became more intense he ran to a nearby tank and, exposing himself

on the turret, restored a jammed machine gun to operating efficiency and used it so effectively that the enemy fire from the adjacent ridge was materially reduced, thus permitting the battalion to occupy its objective.

3022 ◆ *WITEK, FRANK PETER

Rank: Private First Class
Service: U.S. Marine Corps Reserve
Birthday: 10 December 1921
Place of Birth: Derby, New Haven County, Connecticut
Date of Death: 3 August 1944
Cemetery: Rock Island National Cemetery (E-72) (MH)—Rock Island, Illinois
Entered Service at: Illinois
Unit: 1st Battalion, 9th Marines, 3d Marine Division
Battle or Place of Action: Finegayen, Guam, Mariana Islands
Date of Action: 3 August 1944
Citation: For conspicuous gallantry and intrepidity at the risk of his life above and beyond the call of duty while serving with the 1st Battalion, 9th Marines, 3d Marine Division, during the battle of Finegayen at Guam, Marianas, on 3 August 1944. When his rifle platoon was halted by heavy surprise fire from well-camouflaged enemy positions, Pfc. Witek daringly remained standing to fire a full magazine from his automatic at point-blank range into a depression housing Japanese troops, killing eight of the enemy and enabling the greater part of his platoon to take cover. During his platoon's withdrawal for consolidation of lines, he remained to safeguard a severely wounded comrade, courageously returning the enemy's fire until the arrival of stretcher bearers and then covering the evacuation by sustained fire as he moved backward toward his own lines. With his platoon again pinned down by a hostile machine gun, Pfc. Witek, on his own initiative, moved forward boldly to the reinforcing tanks and infantry, alternately throwing hand grenades and firing as he advanced to within 5 to 10 yards of the enemy position, and destroying the hostile machine-gun emplacement and an additional eight Japanese before he himself was struck down by an enemy rifleman. His valiant and inspiring action effectively reduced the enemy's firepower, thereby enabling his platoon to attain its objective, and reflects the highest credit upon Pfc. Witek and the U.S. Naval Service. He gallantly gave his life for his country.

3023 ◆ *WOODFORD, HOWARD E.

Rank: Staff Sergeant
Service: U.S. Army
Birthday: 21 June 1921
Place of Birth: Barberton, Summit County, Ohio
Date of Death: 6 June 1945
Cemetery: Greenlawn Memorial Park (MH)—Akron, Ohio
Entered Service at: Barberton, Summit County, Ohio
Unit: Company I, 130th Infantry, 33d Infantry Division
Battle or Place of Action: near Tabio, Luzon, Philippine Islands
Date of Action: 6 June 1945
G.O. Number, Date: 14, 4 February 1946
Citation: He volunteered to investigate the delay in a scheduled attack by an attached guerrilla battalion. Reaching the line of departure, he found that the lead company, in combat for the first time, was immobilized by intense enemy mortar, machine-gun, and rifle fire which had caused casualties to key personnel. Knowing that further failure to advance would endanger the flanks of adjacent units as well as delay capture of the objective, he immediately took command of the company, evacuated the wounded, reorganized the unit under fire, and prepared to attack. He repeatedly exposed himself to draw revealing fire from the Japanese strongpoints and then moved forward with a five-man covering force to determine exact enemy positions. Although intense enemy machine-gun fire killed two and wounded his other three men, S/Sgt. Woodford resolutely continued his patrol before returning to the company. Then, against bitter resistance, he guided the guerrillas up a barren hill and captured the objective, personally accounting for two hostile machine gunners and courageously reconnoitering strong defensive positions before directing neutralizing fire. After organizing a perimeter defense for the night, he was given permission by radio to return to his battalion, but, feeling that he was needed to maintain proper control, he chose to remain with the guerrillas. Before dawn the next morning the enemy launched a fierce suicide attack with mortars, grenades, and small-arms fire, and infiltrated through the perimeter. Though wounded by a grenade, S/Sgt. Woodford remained at his post calling for mortar support until bullets knocked out his radio. Then, seizing a rifle he began working his way around the perimeter, encouraging the men until he reached a weak spot where two guerrillas had been killed. Filling the gap himself, he fought off the enemy. At daybreak he was found dead in his foxhole, but 37 enemy dead were lying in and around his position. By his daring, skillful, and inspiring leadership as well as by his gallant determination to search out and kill the enemy, S/Sgt. Woodford led an inexperienced unit in capturing and securing a vital objective and was responsible for the successful continuance of a vitally important general advance.

3024 ◆ YOUNG, CASSIN

Rank: Commander (highest rank: Captain)
Service: U.S. Navy
Birthday: 6 March 1894
Place of Birth: Washington, D.C.
Date of Death: 13 November 1942
Place of Death: At Sea Off Guadalcanal
Cemetery: A.B.M.C. Manila Cemetery (Wall of the Missing)—Manila, Buried at sea; Mt. Pleasant Memorial Park ('In Memory' marker only) (MH)—Mt. Pleasant, South Carolina
Entered Service at: Wisconsin
Unit: U.S.S. *Vestal*
Served as: Commanding Officer
Battle or Place of Action: Pearl Harbor, Territory of Hawaii
Date of Action: 7 December 1941
Date of Presentation: 18 April 1942

Place of Presentation: Pearl Harbor, Territory of Hawaii, presented by Adm. Chester W. Nimitz
Citation: For distinguished conduct in action, outstanding heroism and utter disregard of his own safety, above and beyond the call of duty, as commanding officer of the U.S.S. *Vestal*, during the attack on the Fleet in Pearl Harbor, Territory of Hawaii, by enemy Japanese forces on 7 December 1941. Comdr. Young proceeded to the bridge and later took personal command of the three-inch antiaircraft gun. When blown overboard by the blast of the forward magazine explosion of the U.S.S. *Arizona*, to which the U.S.S. *Vestal* was moored, he swam back to his ship. The entire forward part of the U.S.S. *Arizona* was a blazing inferno with oil afire on the water between the two ships; as a result of several bomb hits, the U.S.S. *Vestal* was afire in several places, was settling and taking on a list. Despite severe enemy bombing and strafing at the time and his shocking experience of having been blown overboard, Comdr. Young, with extreme coolness and calmness, moved his ship to an anchorage distant from the U.S.S. *Arizona*, and subsequently beached the U.S.S. *Vestal* upon determining that such action was required to save his ship.

3025 ◆ *YOUNG, RODGER W.

Rank: Private
Service: U.S. Army
Birthday: 28 April 1918
Place of Birth: Tiffin, Seneca County, Ohio
Date of Death: 31 July 1943
Cemetery: McPherson Cemetery—Clyde, Ohio
Entered Service at: Clyde, Sandusky County, Ohio
Unit: 148th Infantry, 37th Infantry Division
Battle or Place of Action: New Georgia, Solomon Islands
Date of Action: 31 July 1943
G.O. Number, Date: 3, 6 January 1944
Date of Presentation: 17 January 1944
Place of Presentation: Fort Knox, Kentucky, presented by Maj. Gen. Charles Scott to his family
Citation: On 31 July 1943, the infantry company of which Pvt. Young was a member, was ordered to make a limited withdrawal from the battle line in order to adjust the battalion's position for the night. At this time, Pvt. Young's platoon was engaged with the enemy in a dense jungle where observation was very limited. The platoon suddenly was pinned down by intense fire from a Japanese machine gun concealed on higher ground only 75 yards away. The initial burst wounded Pvt. Young. As the platoon started to obey the order to withdraw, Pvt. Young called out that he could see the enemy emplacement, whereupon he started creeping toward it. Another burst from the machine gun wounded him the second time. Despite the wounds, he continued his heroic advance, attracting enemy fire and answering with rifle fire. When he was close enough to his objective, he began throwing hand grenades, and while doing so was hit again and killed. Pvt. Young's bold action in closing with this Japanese pillbox, and thus diverting its fire, permitted his platoon to disengage itself, without loss, and was responsible for several enemy casualties.

3026 ◆ ZEAMER JR., JAY

Rank: Major (rank at time of action: Captain) (highest rank: Lieutenant Colonel)
Service: U.S. Army Air Corps
Birthday: 25 July 1918
Place of Birth: Carlisle, Cumberland County, Pennsylvania
Entered Service at: Machias, Washington County, Maine
Unit: 65th Bombardment Squadron, 43d Bombardment Group, 5th Air Force
Served as: Aircraft Commander/Pilot of a B-17
Battle or Place of Action: over Buka area, Solomon Islands
Date of Action: 16 June 1943
G.O. Number, Date: 14 January 1944
Date of Presentation: 16 January 1944
Place of Presentation: The Pentagon, presented by Gen. Henry H. (Hap) Arnold in his office
Citation: On 16 June 1943, Maj. Zeamer (then Capt.) volunteered as pilot of a bomber on an important photographic mapping mission covering the formidably defended area in the vicinity of Buka, Solomon Islands. While photographing the Buka airdrome, his crew observed about 20 enemy fighters on the field, many of them taking off. Despite the certainty of a dangerous attack by this strong force, Maj. Zeamer proceeded with his mapping run, even after the enemy attack began. In the ensuing engagement, Maj. Zeamer sustained gunshot wounds in both arms and legs, one leg being broken. Despite his injuries, he maneuvered the damaged plane so skillfully that his gunners were able to fight off the enemy during a running flight which lasted 40 minutes. The crew destroyed at least five hostile planes, of which Maj. Zeamer himself shot down one. Although weak from loss of blood, he refused medical aid until the enemy had broken combat. He then turned over the controls, but continued to exercise command despite lapses into unconsciousness, and directed the flight to a base 580 miles away. In this voluntary action, Maj. Zeamer, with superb skill, resolution, and courage, accomplished a mission of great value.

3027 ◆ *ZUSSMAN, RAYMOND

Rank: Second Lieutenant
Service: U.S. Army
Birthday: 23 July 1917
Place of Birth: Hamtramck, Wayne County, Michigan
Date of Death: 21 September 1944
Cemetery: The Machpelah Cemetery—Ferndale, Michigan
Entered Service at: Detroit, Wayne County, Michigan
Unit: Company A, 756th Tank Battalion, 3d Infantry Division
Served as: Tank Commander
Battle or Place of Action: Noroy le Bourg, France
Date of Action: 12 September 1944
G.O. Number, Date: 42, 24 May 1945
Citation: On 12 September 1944, 2d Lt. Zussman was in command of two tanks operating with an infantry company in the attack on enemy forces occupying the town of Noroy-le-bourg, France. At 7:00 P.M., his command tank bogged down. Throughout the ensuing action, armed only with a

carbine, he reconnoitered alone on foot far in advance of his remaining tank and the infantry. Returning only from time to time to designate targets, he directed the action of the tank and turned over to the infantry the numerous German soldiers he had caused to surrender. He located a road block and directed his tanks to destroy it. Fully exposed to fire from enemy positions only 50 yards distant, he stood by his tank directing its fire. Three Germans were killed and eight surrendered. Again he walked before his tank, leading it against an enemy-held group of houses, machine-gun and small-arms fire kicking up dust at his feet. The tank fire broke the resistance and 20 enemy surrendered. Going forward again alone he passed an enemy-occupied house from which Germans fired on him and threw grenades in his path. After a brief firefight, he signaled his tank to come up and fire on the house. Eleven German soldiers were killed and 15 surrendered. Going on alone, he disappeared around a street corner. The fire of his carbine could be heard and in a few minutes he reappeared driving 30 prisoners before him. Under 2d Lt. Zussman's heroic and inspiring leadership, 18 enemy soldiers were killed and 92 captured.

KOREAN WAR

3028 ◆ *ABRELL, CHARLES GENE

Rank: Corporal
Service: U.S. Marine Corps
Birthday: 12 August 1931
Place of Birth: Terre Haute, Vigo County, Indiana
Date of Death: 10 June 1951
Cemetery: Westlawn Cemetery—Farmersburg, Indiana
Entered Service at: Terre Haute, Vigo County, Indiana
Unit: Company E, 2d Battalion, 1st Marines, 1st Marine Division (Rein)
Served as: Fire Team Leader
Battle or Place of Action: Hangnyong, Korea
Date of Action: 10 June 1951
Date of Presentation: 4 September 1952
Place of Presentation: The Pentagon, presented by Sec. of the Navy Dan A. Kimball to his Mother
Citation: For conspicuous gallantry and intrepidity at the risk of his life above and beyond the call of duty while serving as a fire team leader in Company E, in action against enemy aggressor forces. While advancing with his platoon in an attack against well-concealed and heavily fortified enemy hill positions, Cpl. Abrell voluntarily rushed forward through the assaulting squad which was pinned down by a hail of intense and accurate automatic-weapons fire from a hostile bunker situated on commanding ground. Although previously wounded by enemy hand-grenade fragments, he proceeded to carry out a bold, single-handed attack against the bunker, exhorting his comrades to follow him. Sustaining two additional wounds as he stormed toward the emplacement, he resolutely pulled the pin from a grenade clutched in his hand and hurled himself bodily into the bunker with the live missile still in his grasp. Fatally wounded in the resulting explosion which killed the entire enemy gun crew within the stronghold, Cpl. Abrell, by his valiant spirit of self-sacrifice in the face of certain death, served to inspire all his comrades and contributed directly to the success of his platoon in attaining its objective. His superb courage and heroic initiative sustain and enhance the highest traditions of the U.S. Naval Service. He gallantly gave his life for his country.

3029 ◆ ADAMS, STANLEY TAYLOR

Rank: Master Sergeant (rank at time of action: Sergeant First Class) (highest rank: Lieutenant Colonel)
Service: U.S. Army
Birthday: 9 May 1922
Place of Birth: DeSoto, Johnson County, Kansas
Entered Service at: Olathe, Johnson County, Kansas
Unit: 1st Platoon, Company A, 1st Battalion, 19th Infantry Regiment, 24th Infantry Division
Served as: Platoon Sergeant
Battle or Place of Action: Sesim-ni, Korea
Date of Action: 4 February 1951
G.O. Number, Date: 66, 2 August 1951
Date of Presentation: 5 July 1951
Place of Presentation: The White House, presented by Pres. Harry S. Truman
Citation: M/Sgt. Adams, Company A, distinguished himself by conspicuous gallantry and intrepidity above and beyond the call of duty in action against an enemy. At approximately 0100 hours M/Sgt. Adams' platoon, holding an outpost some 200 yards ahead of his company, came under a determined attack by an estimated 250 enemy troops. Intense small-arms, machine-gun, and mortar fire from three sides pressed the platoon back against the main line of resistance. Observing approximately 150 hostile troops silhouetted against the skyline advancing against his platoon, M/Sgt. Adams leaped to his feet, urged his men to fix bayonets, and he, with 13 members of his platoon, charged this hostile force with indomitable courage. Within 50 yards of the enemy M/Sgt. Adams was knocked to the ground when pierced in the leg by an enemy bullet. He jumped to his feet and, ignoring his wound, continued on to close with the enemy when he was knocked down four times from the concussion of grenades which had bounced off his body. Shouting orders he charged the enemy positions and engaged them in hand-to-hand combat where man after man fell before his terrific onslaught with bayonet and rifle butt. After nearly an hour of vicious action M/Sgt. Adams and his comrades routed the fanatical foe, killing over 50 and forcing the remainder to withdraw. Upon receiving orders that his battalion was moving back he provided cover fire while his men withdrew. M/Sgt. Adams' superb leadership, incredible courage, and consummate devotion to duty so inspired his comrades that the enemy attack was completely thwarted, saving his battalion from possible disaster. His sustained personal bravery and indomitable fighting spirit against overwhelming odds reflect the utmost glory upon himself and uphold the finest traditions of the infantry and the military service.

3030 ◆ BARBER, WILLIAM EARL

Rank: Captain (highest rank: Colonel)
Service: U.S. Marine Corps
Birthday: 30 November 1919
Place of Birth: Dehart, Morgan County, Kentucky
Entered Service at: West Liberty, Morgan County, Kentucky

3031 ◆ *BARKER, CHARLES H.

Unit: Company F, 2d Battalion, 7th Marines, 1st Marine Division (Rein)
Served as: Commanding Officer
Battle or Place of Action: Chosin Reservoir, Korea
Date of Action: 2 December 1950
Date of Presentation: 20 August 1952
Place of Presentation: The White House, presented by Pres. Harry S. Truman
Citation: For conspicuous gallantry and intrepidity at the risk of his life above and beyond the call of duty as commanding officer of Company F in action against enemy aggressor forces. Assigned to defend a three-mile mountain pass along the division's main supply line and commanding the only route of approach in the march from Yudam-ni to Hagaru-ri, Capt. Barber took position with his battle-weary troops, and, before nightfall, had dug in and set up a defense along the frozen, snow-covered hillside. When a force of estimated regimental strength savagely attacked during the night, inflicting heavy casualties and finally surrounding his position following a bitterly fought seven-hour conflict, Capt. Barber, after repulsing the enemy, gave assurance that he could hold if supplied by airdrops and requested permission to stand fast when orders were received by radio to fight his way back to a relieving force after two reinforcing units had been driven back under fierce resistance in their attempts to reach the isolated troops. Aware that leaving the position would sever contact with the 8,000 marines trapped at Yudam-ni and jeopardize their chances of joining the 3,000 more awaiting their arrival in Hagaru-ri for the continued drive to the sea, he chose to risk loss of his command rather than sacrifice more men if the enemy seized control and forced a renewed battle to regain the position, or abandon his many wounded who were unable to walk. Although severely wounded in the leg in the early morning of the 29th, Capt. Barber continued to maintain personal control, often moving up and down the lines on a stretcher to direct the defense and consistently encouraging and inspiring his men to supreme efforts despite the staggering opposition. Waging desperate battle throughout five days and six nights of repeated onslaughts launched by the fanatical aggressors, he and his heroic command accounted for approximately 1,000 enemy dead in this epic stand in bitter subzero weather, and when the company was relieved, only 82 of his original 220 men were able to walk away from the position so valiantly defended against insuperable odds. His profound faith and courage, great personal valor, and unwavering fortitude were decisive factors in the successful withdrawal of the division from the deathtrap in the Chosin Reservoir sector and reflect the highest credit upon Capt. Barber, his intrepid officers and men, and the U.S. Naval Service.

3031 ◆ *BARKER, CHALRES H.

Rank: Private First Class
Service: U.S. Army
Birthday: 12 April 1935
Place of Birth: Pickens County, South Carolina
Date of Death: 4 June 1953
Cemetery: National Memorial of the Pacific (Wall of the Missing)—Honolulu, Hawaii
Entered Service at: Pickens County, South Carolina
Unit: Company K, 17th Infantry Regiment, 7th Infantry Division
Served as: Rifleman
Battle or Place of Action: Sokkogae, Korea
Date of Action: 4 June 1953
G.O. Number, Date: 37, 7 June 1955
Citation: Pfc. Barker, a member of Company K, distinguished himself by conspicuous gallantry and indomitable courage above and beyond the call of duty in action against the enemy. While participating in a combat patrol engaged in screening an approach to "Pork-Chop Outpost," Pfc. Barker and his companions surprised and engaged an enemy group digging emplacements on the slope. Totally unprepared, the hostile troops sought cover. After ordering Pfc. Barker and a comrade to lay down a base of fire, the patrol leader maneuvered the remainder of the platoon to a vantage point on higher ground. Pfc. Barker moved to an open area firing his rifle and hurling grenades on the hostile positions. As enemy action increased in volume and intensity, mortar bursts fell on friendly positions, ammunition was in critical supply, and the platoon was ordered to withdraw into a perimeter defense preparatory to moving back to the outpost. Voluntarily electing to cover the retrograde movement, he gallantly maintained a defense and was last seen in close hand-to-hand combat with the enemy. Pfc. Barker's unflinching courage, consummate devotion to duty, and supreme sacrifice enabled the patrol to complete the mission and effect an orderly withdrawal to friendly lines, reflecting lasting glory upon himself and upholding the highest traditions of the military service.
Notes: MIA

3032 ◆ *BAUGH, WILLIAM BERNARD

Rank: Private First Class
Service: U.S. Marine Corps
Birthday: 7 July 1930
Place of Birth: McKinney, Lincoln County, Kentucky
Date of Death: 29 November 1950
Cemetery: Glen Haven Cemetery (MH)—Harrison, Ohio
Entered Service at: Harrison, Hamilton County, Ohio
Unit: Company G, 3d Battalion, 1st Marines, 1st Marine Division (Rein)
Battle or Place of Action: along the road from Koto-ri to Hagaru-ri, Korea
Date of Action: 29 November 1950
Date of Presentation: 27 August 1952
Place of Presentation: Dayton, Ohio, presented to parents
Citation: For conspicuous gallantry and intrepidity at the risk of his life above and beyond the call of duty while serving as a member of an antitank assault squad attached to Company G, during a nighttime enemy attack against a motorized column. Acting instantly when a hostile hand grenade landed in his truck as he and his squad prepared to alight and assist in the repulse of an enemy force delivering intense automatic-weapons and grenade fire from deeply entrenched and well-concealed roadside positions, Pfc. Baugh quickly shouted a warning to the other men in the vehicle and, unmindful of his personal safety, hurled himself upon the deadly missile, thereby saving his comrades from serious injury or possible death. Sustaining severe wounds from

which he died a short time afterward, Pfc. Baugh, by his superb courage and valiant spirit of self-sacrifice, upheld the highest traditions of the U.S. Naval Service. He gallantly gave his life for his country.

3033 ◆ *BENFOLD, EDWARD CLYDE "TED"

Rank: Hospital Corpsman Third Class
Service: U.S. Navy
Birthday: 15 January 1931
Place of Birth: Staten Island, Richmond County, New York
Date of Death: 5 September 1952
Cemetery: Beverly National Cemetery (N-804) (MH)—Beverly, New Jersey
Entered Service at: Philadelphia, Philadelphia County, Pennsylvania
Unit: Attached to a company in the 1st Marine Division
Served as: Medical Corpsman
Battle or Place of Action: Korea
Date of Action: 5 September 1952
Date of Presentation: 16 July 1953
Place of Presentation: Philadelphia Naval Base, Pa., presented by Rear Adm. John H. Brown Jr., Commandant 4th Naval District, to his son Edward Joseph Benfold
Citation: For gallantry and intrepidity at the risk of his life above and beyond the call of duty while serving in operations against enemy aggressor forces. When his company was subjected to heavy artillery and mortar barrages, followed by a determined assault during the hours of darkness by an enemy force estimated at battalion strength, HC3c. Benford resolutely moved from position to position in the face of intense hostile fire, treating the wounded and lending words of encouragement. Leaving the protection of his sheltered position to treat the wounded when the platoon area in which he was working was attacked from both the front and rear, he moved forward to an exposed ridgeline where he observed two marines in a large crater. As he approached the two men to determine their condition, an enemy soldier threw two grenades into the crater while two other enemy charged the position. Picking up a grenade in each hand, HC3c. Benford leaped out of the crater and hurled himself against the onrushing hostile soldiers, pushing the grenades against their chests and killing both the attackers. Mortally wounded while carrying out this heroic act, HC3c. Benford, by his great personal valor and resolute spirit of self-sacrifice in the face of almost certain death, was directly responsible for saving the lives of his two comrades. His exceptional courage reflects the highest credit upon himself and enhances the finest traditions of the U.S. Naval Service. He gallantly gave his life for others.

3034 ◆ *BENNETT, EMORY L.

Rank: Private First Class
Service: U.S. Army
Birthday: 20 December 1929
Place of Birth: New Smyrna Beach, Volusia County, Florida
Date of Death: 24 June 1951
Cemetery: Pine Crest Cemetery—Cocoa, Florida
Entered Service at: Cocoa, Brevard County, Florida
Unit: Company B, 15th Infantry Regiment, 3d Infantry Division
Served as: Automatic Rifleman
Battle or Place of Action: Sobangsan, Korea
Date of Action: 24 June 1951
G.O. Number, Date: 11, 1 February 1952
Date of Presentation: 16 January 1952
Place of Presentation: The Pentagon, presented by the Sec. of Defense Robert Lovett to his Father
Citation: Pfc. Bennett, a member of company B, distinguished himself by conspicuous gallantry and intrepidity at the risk of his life above and beyond the call of duty in action against an armed enemy of the United Nations. At approximately 0200 hours, two enemy battalions swarmed up the ridgeline in a ferocious banzai charge in an attempt to dislodge Pfc. Bennett's company from its defensive positions. Meeting the challenge, the gallant defenders delivered destructive retaliation, but the enemy pressed the assault with fanatical determination and the integrity of the perimeter was imperiled. Fully aware of the odds against him, Pfc. Bennett unhesitatingly left his foxhole, moved through withering fire, stood within full view of the enemy, and, employing his automatic rifle, poured crippling fire into the ranks of the onrushing assailants, inflicting numerous casualties. Although wounded, Pfc. Bennett gallantly maintained his one-man defense and the attack was momentarily halted. During this lull in battle, the company regrouped for counterattack, but the numerically superior foe soon infiltrated into the position. Upon orders to move back, Pfc. Bennett voluntarily remained to provide covering fire for the withdrawing elements, and, defying the enemy, continued to sweep the charging foe with devastating fire until mortally wounded. His willing self-sacrifice and intrepid actions saved the position from being overrun and enabled the company to effect an orderly withdrawal. Pfc. Bennett's unflinching courage and consummate devotion to duty reflect lasting glory on himself and the military service.

3035 ◆ BLEAK, DAVID BRUCE

Rank: Sergeant
Service: U.S. Army
Birthday: 27 February 1932
Place of Birth: Idaho Falls, Bonneville County, Idaho
Entered Service at: Shelley, Bingham County, Idaho
Unit: Medical Company, 2d, Battalion, 223d Infantry Regiment, 40th Infantry Division
Served as: Medical Aidman
Battle or Place of Action: Minari-gol, Korea
Date of Action: 14 June 1952
G.O. Number, Date: 83, 2 November 1953
Date of Presentation: 27 October 1953
Place of Presentation: The White House, presented by Pres. Dwight D. Eisenhower
Citation: Sgt. Bleak, a member of the medical company, distinguished himself by conspicuous gallantry and indomitable courage above and beyond the call of duty in action against the enemy. As a medical aidman, he volunteered to accompany a reconnaissance patrol committed to engage the enemy and capture a prisoner for interrogation. Forging up the

rugged slope of the key terrain, the group was subjected to intense automatic-weapons and small-arms fire and suffered several casualties. After administering to the wounded, he continued to advance with the patrol. Nearing the military crest of the hill, while attempting to cross the fire-swept area to attend the wounded, he came under hostile fire from a small group of the enemy concealed in a trench. Entering the trench he closed with the enemy, killed two with bare hands and a third with his trench knife. Moving from the emplacement, he saw a concussion grenade fall in front of a companion and, quickly shifting his position, shielded the man from the impact of the blast. Later, while ministering to the wounded, he was struck by a hostile bullet but, despite the wound, he undertook to evacuate a wounded comrade. As he moved down the hill with his heavy burden, he was attacked by two enemy soldiers with fixed bayonets. Closing with the aggressors, he grabbed them and smacked their heads together, then carried his helpless comrade down the hill to safety. Sgt. Bleak's dauntless courage and intrepid actions reflect utmost credit upon himself and are in keeping with the honored traditions of the military service.

3036 ◆ *BRITTIN, NELSON VOGEL

Rank: Sergeant First Class
Service: U.S. Army
Birthday: 31 October 1920
Place of Birth: Audubon, Camden County, New Jersey
Date of Death: 7 March 1951
Cemetery: Beverly National Cemetery (OS-2) (MH)—Beverly, New Jersey
Entered Service at: Audubon, Camden County, New Jersey
Unit: Company I, 19th Infantry Regiment
Served as: Squad Leader
Battle or Place of Action: Yonggong-ni, Korea
Date of Action: 7 March 1951
G.O. Number, Date: 12, 1 February 1952
Date of Presentation: 16 January 1952
Place of Presentation: The Pentagon, presented by the Sec. of Defense Robert Lovett to his parents
Citation: Sfc. Brittin, a member of Company I, distinguished himself by conspicuous gallantry and intrepidity above and beyond the call of duty in action. Volunteering to lead his squad up a hill, with meager cover against murderous fire from the enemy, he ordered his squad to give him support and, in the face of withering fire and bursting shells, he tossed a grenade at the nearest enemy position. On returning to his squad, he was knocked down and wounded by an enemy grenade. Refusing medical attention, he replenished his supply of grenades and returned, hurling grenades into hostile positions and shooting the enemy as they fled. When his weapon jammed, he leaped without hesitation into a foxhole and killed the occupants with his bayonet and the butt of his rifle. He continued to wipe out foxholes and, noting that his squad had been pinned down, he rushed to the rear of a machine-gun position, threw a grenade into the nest, and ran around to its front, where he killed all three occupants with his rifle. Less than 100 yards up the hill, his squad again came under vicious fire from another camouflaged, sandbagged, machine-gun nest well-flanked by supporting riflemen. Sfc. Brittin again charged this new position in an aggressive endeavor to silence this remaining obstacle and ran directly into a burst of automatic fire which killed him instantly. In his sustained and driving action, he had killed 20 enemy soldiers and destroyed four automatic weapons. The conspicuous courage, consummate valor, and noble self-sacrifice displayed by Sfc. Brittin enabled his inspired company to attain its objective and reflect the highest glory on himself and the heroic traditions of the military service.

3037 ◆ *BROWN, MELVIN L.

Rank: Private First Class
Service: U.S. Army
Birthday: 22 February 1931
Place of Birth: Mahaffey, Clearfield County, Pennsylvania
Date of Death: 5 September 1950
Cemetery: Mahaffey Cemetery—Mahaffey, Pennsylvania
Entered Service at: Erie, Erie County, Pennsylvania
Unit: Company D, 8th Combat Engineer Battalion, 1st Cavalry Div.
Served as: Rifleman
Battle or Place of Action: Kasan, Korea
Date of Action: 4 September 1950
G.O. Number, Date: 11, 16 February 1951
Date of Presentation: 9 January 1951
Place of Presentation: The White House, presented by Pres. Harry S. Truman to his Father
Citation: Pfc. Brown, Company D, distinguished himself by conspicuous gallantry and intrepidity above and beyond the call of duty in action against the enemy. While his platoon was securing Hill 755 (the Walled City), the enemy, using heavy automatic weapons and small arms, counterattacked. Taking a position on a 50-foot-high wall he delivered heavy rifle fire on the enemy. His ammunition was soon expended and although wounded, he remained at his post and threw his few grenades into the attackers, causing many casualties. When his supply of grenades was exhausted his comrades from nearby foxholes tossed others to him and he left his position, braving a hail of fire, to retrieve and throw them at the enemy. The attackers continued to assault his position and Pfc. Brown, weaponless, drew his entrenching tool from his pack and calmly waited until they one by one peered over the wall, delivering each a crushing blow upon the head. Knocking 10 or 12 enemy from the wall, his daring action so inspired his platoon that they repelled the attack and held their position. Pfc. Brown's extraordinary heroism, gallantry, and intrepidity reflect the highest credit upon himself and was in keeping with the honored traditions of the military service. Reportedly missing in action and officially killed in action, September 5, 1950.

3038 ◆ BURKE, LLOYD LESLIE "SCOOTER"

Rank: First Lieutenant (highest rank: Colonel)
Service: U.S. Army
Birthday: 29 September 1924
Place of Birth: Tichnor, Arkansas County, Arkansas

Entered Service at: Stuttgart, Arkansas County, Arkansas
Unit: Company G, 2d Battalion, 5th Cavalry Regiment, 1st Cavalry Division
Served as: Company Commander
Battle or Place of Action: Chong-dong, Korea
Date of Action: 28 October 1951
G.O. Number, Date: 43
Date of Presentation: 12 April 1952
Place of Presentation: The White House, presented by Pres. Harry S. Truman
Citation: First Lt. Burke, distinguished himself by conspicuous gallantry and outstanding courage above and beyond the call of duty in action against the enemy. Intense enemy fire had pinned down leading elements of his company committed to secure commanding ground when 1st Lt. Burke left the command post to rally and urge the men to follow him toward three bunkers impeding the advance. Dashing to an exposed vantage point he threw several grenades at the bunkers, then, returning for an M1 rifle and adapter, he made a lone assault, wiping out the position and killing the crew. Closing on the center bunker he lobbed grenades through the opening and, with his pistol, killed three of its occupants attempting to surround him. Ordering his men forward he charged the third emplacement, catching several grenades in midair and hurling them back at the enemy. Inspired by his display of valor his men stormed forward, overran the hostile position, but were again pinned down by increased fire. Securing a light machine gun and three boxes of ammunition, 1st Lt. Burke dashed through the impact area to an open knoll, set up his gun, and poured a crippling fire into the ranks of the enemy, killing approximately 75. Although wounded, he ordered more ammunition, reloading and destroying two mortar emplacements and a machine-gun position with his accurate fire. Cradling the weapon in his arms he then led his men forward, killing some 25 more of the retreating enemy and securing the objective. First Lt. Burke's heroic action and daring exploits inspired his small force of 35 troops. His unflinching courage and outstanding leadership reflect the highest credit upon himself, the infantry, and the U.S. Army.

3039 ◆ *BURRIS, TONY K.

Rank: Sergeant First Class
Service: U.S. Army
Birthday: 30 May 1929
Place of Birth: Blanchard, McClain County, Oklahoma
Date of Death: 9 October 1951
Cemetery: Blanchard Cemetery (MH)—Blanchard, Oklahoma
Entered Service at: Blanchard, McClain County, Oklahoma
Unit: Company L, 38th Infantry Regiment, 2d Infantry Division
Battle or Place of Action: Mundung-ni, Korea
Date of Action: 8-9 October 1951
G.O. Number, Date: 84, 5 September 1952
Date of Presentation: 14 August 1952
Place of Presentation: The Pentagon, presented by Gen. Omar N. Bradley to his Mother
Citation: Sfc. Burris, a member of Company L, distinguished himself by conspicuous gallantry and outstanding courage above and beyond the call of duty. On 8 October, when his company encountered intense fire from an entrenched hostile force, Sfc. Burris charged forward alone, throwing grenades into the position and destroying approximately 15 of the enemy. On the following day, spearheading a renewed assault on enemy positions on the next ridge, he was wounded by machine-gun fire but continued the assault, reaching the crest of the ridge ahead of his unit and sustaining a second wound. Calling for a 57-mm recoilless-rifle team, he deliberately exposed himself to draw hostile fire and reveal the enemy position. The enemy machine-gun emplacement was destroyed. The company then moved forward and prepared to assault other positions on the ridgeline. Sfc. Burris, refusing evacuation and submitting only to emergency treatment, joined the unit in its renewed attack but fire from hostile emplacement halted the advance. Sfc. Burris rose to his feet, charged forward and destroyed the first emplacement with its heavy machine gun and crew of six men. Moving out to the next emplacement, and throwing his last grenade, which destroyed this position, he fell mortally wounded by enemy fire. Inspired by his consummate gallantry, his comrades renewed a spirited assault which overran enemy positions and secured Hill 605, a strategic position in the battle for "Heartbreak Ridge." Sfc. Burris' indomitable fighting spirit, outstanding heroism, and gallant self-sacrifice reflect the highest glory upon himself, the infantry, and the U.S. Army.

3040 ◆ CAFFERATA JR., HECTOR ALBERT

Rank: Private
Service: U.S. Marine Corps Reserve
Birthday: 4 November 1929
Place of Birth: New York, New York
Entered Service at: Dover, Morris County, New Jersey
Unit: Company F, 2d Battalion, 7th Marines, 1st Marine Division (Rein)
Served as: Rifleman
Battle or Place of Action: Toktong Pass, Korea
Date of Action: 28 November 1950
Date of Presentation: 24 November 1952
Place of Presentation: The White House, presented by Pres. Harry S. Truman
Citation: For conspicuous gallantry and intrepidity at the risk of his life above and beyond the call of duty while serving as a rifleman with Company F, in action against enemy aggressor forces. When all the other members of his fire team became casualties, creating a gap in the lines, during the initial phase of a vicious attack launched by a fanatical enemy of regimental strength against his company's hill position, Pvt. Cafferata waged a lone battle with grenades and rifle fire as the attack gained momentum and the enemy threatened penetration through the gap and endangered the integrity of the entire defensive perimeter. Making a target of himself under the devastating fire from automatic weapons, rifles, grenades, and mortars, he maneuvered up and down the line and delivered accurate and effective fire against the onrushing force, killing 15, wounding many more, and forcing the others to withdraw so that reinforcements could move up and consoli-

date the position. Again fighting desperately against a renewed onslaught later that same morning when a hostile grenade landed in a shallow entrenchment occupied by wounded marines, Pvt. Cafferata rushed into the gully under heavy fire, seized the deadly missile in his right hand and hurled it free of his comrades before it detonated, severing part of one finger and seriously wounding him in the right hand and arm. Courageously ignoring the intense pain, he stanchly fought on until he was struck by a sniper's bullet and forced to submit to evacuation for medical treatment. Stouthearted and indomitable, Pvt. Cafferata, by his fortitude, great personal valor, and dauntless perseverance in the face of almost certain death, saved the lives of several of his fellow marines and contributed essentially to the success achieved by his company in maintaining its defensive position against tremendous odds. His extraordinary heroism throughout was in keeping with the highest traditions of the U.S. Naval Service.

3041 ◆ *CHAMPAGNE, DAVID BERNARD

Rank: Corporal
Service: U.S. Marine Corps
Birthday: 13 November 1932
Place of Birth: Waterville, Kennebec County, Maine
Date of Death: 28 May 1952
Cemetery: St. Francis de Sales Cemetery (MH)—Waterville, Maine
Entered Service at: Wakefield, Washington County, Rhode Island
Unit: Company A, 1st Battalion, 7th Marines, 1st Marine Division (Rein)
Served as: Fire Team Leader
Battle or Place of Action: Korea
Date of Action: 28 May 1952
Citation: For conspicuous gallantry and intrepidity at the risk of his life above and beyond the call of duty while serving as a fire team leader of Company A, in action against enemy aggressor forces. Advancing with his platoon in the initial assault of the company against a strongly fortified and heavily defended hill position, Cpl. Champagne skillfully led his fire team through a veritable hail of intense enemy machine-gun, small-arms, and grenade fire, overrunning trenches and a series of almost impregnable bunker positions before reaching the crest of the hill and placing his men in defensive positions. Suffering a painful leg wound while assisting in repelling the ensuing hostile counterattack, which was launched under cover of a murderous hail of mortar and artillery fire, he steadfastly refused evacuation and fearlessly continued to control his fire team. When the enemy counterattack increased in intensity, and a hostile grenade landed in the midst of the fire team, Cpl. Champagne unhesitatingly seized the deadly missile and hurled it in the direction of the approaching enemy. As the grenade left his hand, it exploded, blowing off his hand and throwing him out of the trench. Mortally wounded by enemy mortar fire while in this exposed position, Cpl. Champagne, by his valiant leadership, fortitude, and gallant spirit of self-sacrifice in the face of almost certain death, undoubtedly saved the lives of several of his fellow marines. His heroic actions served to inspire all who observed him and reflect the highest credit upon himself and the U.S. Naval Service. He gallantly gave his life for his country.

3042 ◆ CHARETTE, WILLIAM RICHARD

Rank: Hospital Corpsman Third Class (highest rank: Master Chief Hospital Corpsman)
Service: U.S. Navy
Birthday: 29 March 1932
Place of Birth: Ludington, Mason County, Michigan
Entered Service at: Ludington, Mason County, Michigan
Unit: Attached to Company F, 2d Battalion, 7th Marines, 1st Marine Division
Served as: Hospital Corpsman
Battle or Place of Action: Panmunjom Corridor (DMZ), Korea
Date of Action: 27 March 1953
Date of Presentation: 12 January 1954
Place of Presentation: The White House, presented by Pres. Dwight D. Eisenhower
Citation: For conspicuous gallantry and intrepidity at the risk of his life above and beyond the call of duty in action against enemy aggressor forces during the early morning hours. Participating in a fierce encounter with a cleverly concealed and well-entrenched enemy force occupying positions on a vital and bitterly contested outpost far in advance of the main line of resistance, HC3c. Charette repeatedly and unhesitatingly moved about through a murderous barrage of hostile small-arms and mortar fire to render assistance to his wounded comrades. When an enemy grenade landed within a few feet of a marine he was attending, he immediately threw himself upon the stricken man and absorbed the entire concussion of the deadly missile with his body. Although sustaining painful facial wounds and undergoing shock from the intensity of the blast which ripped the helmet and medical aid kit from his person, HC3c. Charette resourcefully improvised emergency bandages by tearing off part of his clothing, and gallantly continued to administer medical aid to the wounded in his own unit and to those in adjacent platoon areas as well. Observing a seriously wounded comrade whose armored vest had been torn from his body by the blast from an exploding shell, he selflessly removed his own battle vest and placed it upon the helpless man although fully aware of the added jeopardy to himself. Moving to the side of another casualty who was suffering excruciating pain from a serious leg wound, HC3c. Charette stood upright in the trench line and exposed himself to a deadly hail of enemy fire in order to lend more effective aid to the victim and to alleviate his anguish while being removed to a position of safety. By his indomitable courage and inspiring efforts in behalf of his wounded comrades, HC3c. Charette was directly responsible for saving many lives. His great personal valor reflects the highest credit upon himself and enhances the finest traditions of the U.S. Naval Service.

3043 ◆ *CHARLTON, CORNELIUS H.

Rank: Sergeant
Service: U.S. Army

Birthday: 24 July 1929
Place of Birth: East Gulf, Raleigh County, West Virginia
Date of Death: 2 June 1951
Place of Death: Chipo-ri, Korea
Cemetery: American Legion Cemetery (MH)—Beckley, West Virginia
Entered Service at: Bronx County, New York
Unit: Company C, 24th Infantry Regiment, 25th Infantry Division
Served as: Platoon Sergeant
Battle or Place of Action: Chipo-ri, Korea
Date of Action: 2 June 1951
G.O. Number, Date: 30, 19 March 1952
Date of Presentation: 12 March 1952
Place of Presentation: The Pentagon, presented by Sec. of the Army Frank C. Pace to his parents
Citation: Sgt. Charlton, a member of Company C, distinguished himself by conspicuous gallantry and intrepidity above and beyond the call of duty in action against the enemy. His platoon was attacking heavily defended hostile positions on commanding ground when the leader was wounded and evacuated. Sgt. Charlton assumed command, rallied the men, and spearheaded the assault against the hill. Personally eliminating two hostile positions and killing six of the enemy with his rifle fire and grenades, he continued up the slope until the unit suffered heavy casualties and became pinned down. Regrouping the men, he led them forward only to be again hurled back by a shower of grenades. Despite a severe chest wound, Sgt. Charlton refused medical attention and led a third daring charge which carried to the crest of the ridge. Observing that the remaining emplacement which had retarded the advance was situated on the reverse slope, he charged it alone, was again hit by a grenade but raked the position with a devastating fire which eliminated it and routed the defenders. The wounds received during his daring exploits resulted in his death, but his indomitable courage, superb leadership, and gallant self-sacrifice reflect the highest credit upon himself, the infantry, and the military service.

3044 ◆ *CHRISTIANSON, STANLEY REUBEN

Rank: Private First Class
Service: U.S. Marine Corps
Birthday: 24 January 1925
Place of Birth: Mindoro, La Crosse County, Wisconsin
Date of Death: 29 September 1950
Cemetery: Wet Coulee Cemetery (MH)—Mindoro, Wisconsin
Entered Service at: Mindoro, La Crosse County, Wisconsin
Unit: Company E, 2d Battalion, 1st Marines, 1st Marine Division (Rein)
Battle or Place of Action: Seoul, Korea
Date of Action: 29 September 1950
Date of Presentation: 30 August 1951
Place of Presentation: The Pentagon, presented by Sec. of the Navy Dan A. Kimball to his parents
Citation: For conspicuous gallantry and intrepidity at the risk of his life above and beyond the call of duty while serving with Company E, in action against enemy aggressor forces at Hill 132, in the early morning hours. Manning one of the several listening posts covering approaches to the platoon area when the enemy commenced the attack, Pfc. Christianson quickly sent another marine to alert the rest of the platoon. Without orders, he remained in his position and, with full knowledge that he would have slight chance of escape, fired relentlessly at oncoming hostile troops attacking furiously with rifles, automatic weapons, and incendiary grenades. Accounting for seven enemy dead in the immediate vicinity before his position was overrun and he himself fatally struck down, Pfc. Christianson, by his superb courage, valiant fighting spirit, and devotion to duty, was responsible for allowing the rest of the platoon time to man positions, build up a stronger defense on that flank, and repel the attack with 41 of the enemy destroyed, many more wounded, and three taken prisoner. His self-sacrificing actions in the face of overwhelming odds sustain and enhance the finest traditions of the U.S. Naval Service. Pfc. Christianson gallantly gave his life for his country.

3045 ◆ *COLLIER, GILBERT GEORGIE

Rank: Sergeant (rank at time of action: Corporal)
Service: U.S. Army
Birthday: 30 December 1930
Place of Birth: Hunter, Woodruff County, Arkansas
Date of Death: 22 July 1953
Cemetery: DeWitt Cemetery—DeWitt, Arkansas
Entered Service at: Tichnor, Arkansas County, Arkansas
Unit: Company F, 223d Infantry Regiment, 40th Infantry Division
Served as: Pointman/Assistant Squad Leader
Battle or Place of Action: Tutayon, Korea
Date of Action: 19-20 July 1953
G.O. Number, Date: 3, 12 January 1955
Citation: Sgt. Collier, a member of Company F, distinguished himself by conspicuous gallantry and indomitable courage above and beyond the call of duty in action against the enemy. Sgt. Collier was point man and assistant leader of a combat patrol committed to make contact with the enemy. As the patrol moved forward through the darkness, he and his commanding officer slipped and fell from a steep, 60-foot cliff and were injured. Incapacitated by a badly sprained ankle which prevented immediate movement, the officer ordered the patrol to return to the safety of friendly lines. Although suffering from a painful back injury, Sgt. Collier elected to remain with his leader, and before daylight they managed to crawl back up and over the mountainous terrain to the opposite valley, where they concealed themselves in the brush until nightfall, then edged toward their company positions. Shortly after leaving the daylight retreat they were ambushed and, in the ensuing firefight, Sgt. Collier killed two hostile soldiers, received painful wounds, and was separated from his companion. Then, ammunition expended, he closed in hand-to-hand combat with four attacking hostile infantrymen, killing, wounding, and routing the foe with his bayonet. He was mortally wounded during this action, but made a valiant attempt to reach and assist his leader in a desperate effort to save his comrade's life without regard for his own personal safety. Sgt.

Collier's unflinching courage, consummate devotion to duty, and gallant self-sacrifice reflect lasting glory upon himself and uphold the noble traditions of the military service.

3046 ◆ *COLLIER, JOHN WALTON

Rank: Corporal
Service: U.S. Army
Birthday: 3 April 1929
Place of Birth: Worthington, Greenup County, Kentucky
Date of Death: 19 September 1950
Cemetery: Arlington National Cemetery (12-4637) (MH)—Arlington, Virginia
Entered Service at: Worthington, Greenup County, Kentucky
Unit: Company C, 27th Infantry Regiment, 25th Infantry Division
Battle or Place of Action: Chindoing-ni, Korea
Date of Action: 19 September 1950
G.O. Number, Date: 86, 2 August 1951
Date of Presentation: 21 June 1951
Place of Presentation: The Pentagon, presented by Gen. Omar N. Bradley to his Father
Citation: Cpl. Collier, Company C, distinguished himself by conspicuous gallantry and intrepidity above and beyond the call of duty in action. While engaged in an assault on a strategic ridge strongly defended by a fanatical enemy, the leading elements of his company encountered intense automatic-weapons and grenade fire. Cpl. Collier and three comrades volunteered and moved forward to neutralize an enemy machine-gun position which was hampering the company's advance, but they were twice repulsed. On the third attempt, Cpl. Collier, despite heavy enemy fire and grenade barrages, moved to an exposed position ahead of his comrades, assaulted and destroyed the machine-gun nest, killing at least four enemy soldiers. As he returned down the rocky, fire-swept hill and joined his squad, an enemy grenade landed in their midst. Shouting a warning to his comrades, he, selflessly and unhesitatingly, threw himself upon the grenade and smothered its explosion with his body. This intrepid action saved his comrades from death or injury. Cpl. Collier's supreme, personal bravery, consummate gallantry, and noble self-sacrifice reflect untold glory upon himself and uphold the honored traditions of the military service.

3047 ◆ COMMISKEY SR., HENRY ALFRED

Rank: First Lieutenant (rank at time of action: Second Lieutenant) (highest rank: Major)
Service: U.S. Marine Corps
Birthday: 10 January 1927
Place of Birth: Hattiesburg, Forrest County, Mississippi
Date of Death: 16 August 1971
Place of Death: Meridian, Mississippi
Cemetery: Cremated, ashes scattered over the Gulf of Mexico
Entered Service at: Hattiesburg, Forrest County, Mississippi
Unit: Company C, 1st Battalion, 1st Marines, 1st Marine Division
Served as: Platoon Leader
Battle or Place of Action: Yongdungp'o, Korea
Date of Action: 20 September 1950
Date of Presentation: 1 August 1951
Place of Presentation: The White House, presented by Pres. Harry S. Truman
Citation: For conspicuous gallantry and intrepidity at the risk of his life above and beyond the call of duty while serving as a platoon leader in Company C, in action against enemy aggressor forces. Directed to attack hostile forces well dug in on Hill 85, 1st Lt. Commiskey spearheaded the assault, charging up the steep slopes on the run. Coolly disregarding the heavy enemy machine-gun and small-arms fire, he plunged on well forward of the rest of his platoon and was the first man to reach the crest of the objective. Armed only with a pistol, he jumped into a hostile machine-gun emplacement occupied by five enemy troops and quickly disposed of four of the soldiers with his automatic pistol. Grappling with the fifth, 1st Lt. Commiskey knocked him to the ground and held him until he could obtain a weapon from another member of his platoon and killed the last of the enemy gun crew. Continuing his bold assault, he moved to the next emplacement, killed two more of the enemy and then led his platoon toward the rear nose of the hill to rout the remainder of the hostile troops and destroy them as they fled from their positions. His valiant leadership and courageous fighting spirit served to inspire the men of his company to heroic endeavor in seizing the objective, and reflect the highest credit upon 1st Lt. Commiskey and the U.S. Naval Service.

3048 ◆ *COURSEN, SAMUEL STREIT

Rank: First Lieutenant
Service: U.S. Army
Birthday: 4 August 1926
Place of Birth: Madison, Morris County, New Jersey
Date of Death: 12 October 1950
Place of Death: Kaesong, Korea
Cemetery: U.S. Military Academy Cemetery (7-230)—West Point, New York
Entered Service at: Madison, Morris County, New Jersey
Unit: Company C, 5th Cavalry Regiment, 1st Cavalry Division
Served as: Platoon Leader
Battle or Place of Action: Kaesong, Korea
Date of Action: 12 October 1950
G.O. Number, Date: 57, 2 August 1951
Date of Presentation: 21 June 1951
Place of Presentation: The Pentagon, presented by Gen. Omar N. Bradley to his Son
Citation: First Lt. Coursen distinguished himself by conspicuous gallantry and intrepidity above and beyond the call of duty in action. While Company C was attacking Hill 174 under heavy enemy small-arms fire, his platoon received enemy fire from close-range. The platoon returned the fire and continued to advance. During this phase, one of his men moved into a well-camouflaged emplacement, which was thought to be unoccupied, and was wounded by the enemy who were hidden within the emplacement. Seeing the soldier

in difficulty, he rushed to the man's aid and, without regard for his personal safety, engaged the enemy in hand-to-hand combat in an effort to protect his wounded comrade until he himself was killed. When his body was recovered after the battle, seven enemy dead were found in the emplacement. As the result of 1st Lt. Coursen's violent struggle several of the enemies' heads had been crushed with his rifle. His aggressive and intrepid actions saved the life of the wounded man, eliminated the main position of the enemy roadblock, and greatly inspired the men in his command. First Lt. Coursen's extraordinary heroism and intrepidity refect the highest credit on himself and are in keeping with the honored traditions of the military service.

3049 ◆ *CRAIG, GORDON MAYNARD

Rank: Corporal
Service: U.S. Army
Birthday: 3 August 1929
Place of Birth: Brockton, Plymouth County, Massachusetts
Date of Death: 10 September 1950
Cemetery: Village Cemetery of Elmwood (MH)—East Bridgewater, Massachusetts
Entered Service at: Brockton, Plymouth County, Massachusetts
Unit: Reconnaissance Company, 1st Cavalry Division
Battle or Place of Action: Kasan, Korea
Date of Action: 10 September 1950
G.O. Number, Date: 23, 25 April 1951
Date of Presentation: 3 April 1951
Place of Presentation: The Pentagon, presented by Gen. Omar N. Bradley to his Mother
Citation: Cpl. Craig, 16th Reconnaissance Company, distinguished himself by conspicuous gallantry and intrepidity above and beyond the call of duty in action against the enemy. During the attack on a strategic enemy-held hill, his company's advance was subjected to intense hostile grenade, mortar, and small-arms fire. Cpl. Craig and four comrades moved forward to eliminate an enemy machine-gun nest that was hampering the company's advance. At that instance an enemy machine gunner hurled a hand grenade at the advancing men. Without hesitating or attempting to seek cover for himself, Cpl. Craig threw himself on the grenade and smothered its burst with his body. His intrepid and selfless act, in which he unhesitatingly gave his life for his comrades, inspired them to attack with such ferocity that they annihilated the enemy machine-gun crew, enabling the company to continue its attack. Cpl. Craig's noble self-sacrifice reflects the highest credit upon himself and upholds the esteemed traditions of the military service.

3050 ◆ CRUMP, JERRY KIRT

Rank: Corporal
Service: U.S. Army
Birthday: 18 February 1933
Place of Birth: Charlotte, Mecklenburg County, North Carolina
Date of Death: 10 January 1977
Place of Death: Lincolnton, North Carolina
Cemetery: Mt. Zion Cemetery (MH)—Cornelius, North Carolina
Entered Service at: Forest City, Rutherford County, North Carolina
Unit: Company L, 7th Infantry Regiment, 3d Infantry Division
Battle or Place of Action: Chorwon, Korea
Date of Action: 6-7 September 1951
G.O. Number, Date: 68, 11 July 1952
Date of Presentation: 27 June 1952
Place of Presentation: The White House (Rose Garden), presented by Pres. Harry S. Truman
Citation: Cpl. Crump, a member of Company L, distinguished himself by conspicuous gallantry and outstanding courage above and beyond the call of duty in action against the enemy. During the night a numerically superior hostile force launched an assault against his platoon on Hill 284, overrunning friendly positions and swarming into the sector. Cpl. Crump repeatedly exposed himself to deliver effective fire into the ranks of the assailants, inflicting numerous casualties. Observing two enemy soldiers endeavoring to capture a friendly machine gun, he charged and killed both with his bayonet, regaining control of the weapon. Returning to his position, now occupied by four of his wounded comrades, he continued his accurate fire into enemy troops surrounding his emplacement. When a hostile soldier hurled a grenade into the position, Cpl. Crump immediately flung himself over the missile, absorbing the blast with his body and saving his comrades from death or serious injury. His aggressive actions had so inspired his comrades that a spirited counterattack drove the enemy from the perimeter. Cpl. Crump's heroic devotion to duty, imdomitable fighting spirit, and willingness to sacrifice himself to save his comrades reflect the highest credit upon himself, the infantry and the U.S. Army.

3051 ◆ *DAVENPORT, JACK ARDEN

Rank: Corporal
Service: U.S. Marine Corps
Birthday: 7 September 1931
Place of Birth: Kansas City, Clay County, Missouri
Date of Death: 21 September 1951
Cemetery: Mount Moriah Cemetery (MH)—Kansas City, Missouri
Entered Service at: Mission, Johnson County, Kansas
Unit: Company G, 3d Battalion, 5th Marines, 1st Marine Division (Rein)
Served as: Squad Leader
Battle or Place of Action: Songnae-dong, Korea
Date of Action: 21 September 1951
Date of Presentation: 7 January 1953
Place of Presentation: The Pentagon, presented by Sec. of the Navy Dan A. Kimball to his Father
Citation: For conspicuous gallantry and intrepidity at the risk of his life above and beyond the call of duty while serving as a squad leader in Company G, in action against enemy aggressor forces early in the morning. While expertly directing the defense of his position during a probing attack by hostile

forces attempting to infiltrate the area, Cpl. Davenport, acting quickly when an enemy grenade fell into the foxhole which he was occupying with another marine, skillfully located the deadly projectile in the dark and, undeterred by the personal risk involved, heroically threw himself over the live missile, thereby saving his companion from serious injury or possible death. His cool and resourceful leadership were contributing factors in the successful repulse of the enemy attack and his superb courage and admirable spirit of self-sacrifice in the face of almost certain death enhance and sustain the highest traditions of the U.S. Naval Service. Cpl. Davenport gallantly gave his life for his country.

3052 ◆ *DAVIS JR., GEORGE ANDREW

Rank: Major (highest rank: Lieutenant Colonel)
Service: U.S. Air Force
Birthday: 1 December 1920
Place of Birth: Dublin, Erath County, Texas
Date of Death: 10 February 1952
Place of Death: Sinuiju-Yalu River area, Korea
Cemetery: National Memorial of the Pacific (Wall of the Missing)—Honolulu, Hawaii; City of Lubbock Cemetery (MH)(Headstone Only)—Lubbock, Texas
Entered Service at: Lubbock, Lubbock County, Texas
Unit: 4th Fighter Group, 334th Fighter Squadron,, 5th Air Force
Served as: Flight Commander/Pilot F-86 Saberjet
Battle or Place of Action: Sinuiju-Yalu River area, Korea
Date of Action: 10 February 1952
Date of Presentation: 14 May 1954
Place of Presentation: Reese Air Force Base, Texas, presented by Gen. Nathan F. Twining to his widow
Citation: Maj. Davis distinguished himself by conspicuous gallantry and intrepidity at the risk of his life above and beyond the call of duty. While leading a flight of four F-86 Saberjets on a combat aerial patrol mission near the Manchurian border, Maj. Davis' element leader ran out of oxygen and was forced to retire from the flight with his wingman accompanying him. Maj. Davis and the remaining F-86s continued the mission and sighted a formation of approximately 12 enemy MIG-15 aircraft speeding southward toward an area where friendly fighter-bombers were conducting low-level operations against the Communist lines of communcations. With selfless disregard for the numerical superiority of the enemy, Maj. Davis positioned his two aircraft, then dove at the MIG formation. While speeding through the formation from the rear, he singled out a MIG-15 and destroyed it with a concentrated burst of fire. Although he was now under continuous fire from the enemy fighters to his rear, Maj. Davis sustained his attack. He fired at another MIG-15 which, bursting into smoke and flames, went into a vertical dive. Rather than maintain his superior speed and evade the enemy fire being concentrated on him, he elected to reduce his speed and sought out still a third MIG-15. During this latest attack his aircraft sustained a direct hit, went out of control, then crashed into a mountain 30 miles south of the Yalu River. Maj. Davis' bold attack completely disrupted the enemy formation, permitting the friendly fighter-bombers to successfully complete their interdiction mission. Maj. Davis, by his indomitable fighting spirit, heroic aggressiveness, and superb courage in engaging the enemy against formidable odds exemplified valor at its highest.
Notes: MIA

3053 ◆ DAVIS, RAYMOND GILBERT

Rank: Lieutenant Colonel (highest rank: General)
Service: U.S. Marine Corps
Birthday: 13 January 1915
Place of Birth: Fitzgerald, Ben Hill County, Georgia
Entered Service at: Atlanta, Fulton County, Georgia
Unit: 1st Battalion, 7th Marines, 1st Marine Division (Rein)
Served as: Battalion Commander
Battle or Place of Action: Hagaru-ri, Korea
Date of Action: 1-4 December 1950
Date of Presentation: 24 November 1952
Place of Presentation: The White House, presented by Pres. Harry S. Truman
Citation: For conspicuous gallantry and intrepidity at the risk of his life above and beyond the call of duty as commanding officer of the 1st Battalion, in action against enemy aggressor forces. Although keenly aware that the operation involved breaking through a surrounding enemy and advancing eight miles along primitive icy trails in the bitter cold with every passage disputed by a savage and determined foe, Lt. Col. Davis boldly led his battalion into the attack in a daring attempt to relieve a beleaguered rifle company and to seize, hold, and defend a vital mountain pass controlling the only route available for two marine regiments in danger of being cut off by numerically superior hostile forces during their redeployment to the port of Hungnam. When the battalion immediately encountered strong opposition from entrenched enemy forces commanding high ground in the path of the advance, he promptly spearheaded his unit in a fierce attack up the steep, ice-covered slopes in the face of withering fire and, personally leading the assault groups in a hand-to-hand encounter, drove the hostile troops from their position, rested his men, and reconnoitered the area under enemy fire to determine the best route for continuing the mission. Always in the thick of the fighting, Lt. Col. Davis led his battalion over three successive ridges in the deep snow in continuous attacks against the enemy and, constantly inspiring and encouraging his men throughout the night, brought his unit to a point within 1,500 yards of the surrounded rifle company by daybreak. Although knocked to the ground when a shell fragment struck his helmet and two bullets pierced his clothing, he arose and fought his way forward at the head of his men until he reached the isolated marines. On the following morning, he bravely led his battalion in securing the vital mountain pass from a strongly entrenched and numerically superior hostile force, carrying all his wounded with him, including 22 litter cases and numerous ambulatory patients. Despite repeated savage and heavy assaults by the enemy, he stubbornly held the vital terrrain until the two regiments of the division had deployed through the pass and, on the morning of 4 December, led his battalion into Hagaru-ri intact. By his superb leadership, outstanding courage, and

brilliant tactical ability, Lt. Col. Davis was directly instrumental in saving the beleaguered rifle company from complete annihilation and enabled the two marine regiments to escape possible destruction. His valiant devotion to duty and unyielding fighting spirit in the face of almost insurmountable odds enhance and sustain the highest traditions of the U.S. Naval Service.

3054 ◆ DEAN SR., WILLIAM FRISHE

Rank: Major General
Service: U.S. Army
Birthday: 1 August 1899
Place of Birth: Carlyle, Clinton County, Illinois
Date of Death: 24 August 1981
Cemetery: San Francisco National Cemetery (353-B) (MH)—San Francisco, California
Entered Service at: California
Unit: 24th Infantry Division
Served as: Commanding General
Battle or Place of Action: Taejon, Korea
Date of Action: 20-21 July 1950
G.O. Number, Date: 7, 16 February 1951
Date of Presentation: 9 January 1951
Place of Presentation: White House, presented by Pres. Harry S. Truman to his Wife
Citation: Maj. Gen. Dean distinguished himself by conspicuous gallantry and intrepidity at the repeated risk of his life above and beyond the call of duty. In command of a unit suddenly relieved from occupation duties in Japan and as yet untried in combat, faced with a ruthless and determined enemy, highly trained and overwhelmingly superior in numbers, he felt it his duty to take action which, to a man of his military experience and knowledge, was clearly apt to result in his death. He personally and alone attacked an enemy tank while armed only with a hand grenade. He also directed the fire of his tanks from an exposed position with neither cover nor concealment while under observed artillery and small-arms fire. When the town of Taejon was finally overrun he refused to ensure his own safety by leaving with the leading elements but remained behind organizing his retreating forces, directing stragglers, and was last seen assisting the wounded to a place of safety. These actions indicate that Maj. Gen. Dean felt it necessary to sustain the courage and resolution of his troops by examples of excessive gallantry committed always at the threatened portions of his front lines. The magnificent response of his unit to this willing and cheerful sacrifice, made with full knowledge of its certain cost, is history. The success of this phase of the campaign is in large measure due to Maj. Gen. Dean's heroic leadership, courageous and loyal devotion to his men, and his complete disregard for personal safety.
Notes: POW

3055 ◆ *DESIDERIO, REGINALD BENJAMIN

Rank: Captain
Service: U.S. Army
Birthday: 12 September 1912
Place of Birth: Clairton, Allegheny County, Pennsylvania
Date of Death: 27 November 1950
Cemetery: San Francisco National Cemetery (OS20-128-30) (MH)—San Francisco, California
Entered Service at: Gilroy, Santa Clara County, California
Unit: Company E, 27th Infantry Regiment, 25th Infantry Division
Served as: Company Commander
Battle or Place of Action: Ipsok, Korea
Date of Action: 27 November 1950
G.O. Number, Date: 58, 2 August 1951
Date of Presentation: 21 June 1951
Place of Presentation: The Pentagon, presented by Gen. Omar N. Bradley to his Widow
Citation: Capt. Desiderio distinguished himself by conspicuous gallantry and intrepidity at the repeated risk of his life above and beyond the call of duty. His company was given the mission of defending the command post of a task force against an enemy breakthrough. After personal reconnaissance during darkness and under intense enemy fire, he placed his men in defensive positions to repel an attack. Early in the action he was wounded, but refused evacuation and despite enemy fire continued to move among his men checking their positions and making sure that each element was prepared to receive the next attack. Again wounded, he continued to direct his men. By his inspiring leadership he encouraged them to hold their position. In the subsequent fighting when the fanatical enemy succeeded in penetrating the position, he personally charged them with carbine, rifle, and grenades, inflicting many casualties until he himself was mortally wounded. His men, spurred on by his intrepid example, repelled this final attack. Capt. Desiderio's heroic leadership, courageous and loyal devotion to duty, and his complete disregard for personal safety reflect the highest honor on him and are in keeping with the esteemed traditions of the U.S. Army.

3056 ◆ *DEWERT, RICHARD DAVID

Rank: Hospital Corpsman
Service: U.S. Navy
Birthday: 17 November 1931
Place of Birth: Taunton, Bristol County, Massachusetts
Date of Death: 5 April 1951
Cemetery: Massachusetts National Cemetery (5-167) (MH)—Bourne, Massachusetts
Entered Service at: Taunton, Bristol County, Massachusetts
Unit: Hospital corpsman attached to Marine Infantry Company, 1st Marine Division
Served as: Medical Corpsman
Battle or Place of Action: Korea
Date of Action: 5 April 1951
Date of Presentation: 27 May 1952
Place of Presentation: Presented by Sec. of the Navy Dan A. Kimball to his Mother
Citation: For conspicuous gallantry and intrepidity at the risk of his life above and beyond the call of duty while serving as an HC, in action against enemy aggressor forces. When a fire team from the point platoon of his company was pinned

down by a deadly barrage of hostile automatic-weapons fire and suffered many casualties, HC Dewert rushed to the assistance of one of the more seriously wounded and, despite a painful leg wound sustained while dragging the stricken marine to safety, steadfastly refused medical treatment for himself and immediately dashed back through the fire-swept area to carry a second wounded man out of the line of fire. Undaunted by the mounting hail of devastating enemy fire, he bravely moved forward a third time and received another serious wound in the shoulder after discovering that a wounded marine had already died. Still persistent in his refusal to submit to first aid, he resolutely answered the call of a fourth stricken comrade and, while rendering medical assistance, was himself mortally wounded by a burst of enemy fire. His courageous initiative, great personal valor, and heroic spirit of self-sacrifice in the face of overwhelming odds reflect the highest credit upon HC Dewert and enhance the finest traditions of the U.S. Naval Service. He gallantly gave his life for his country.

3057 ◆ DEWEY, DUANE EDGAR

Rank: Corporal
Service: U.S. Marine Corps Reserve
Birthday: 16 November 1931
ace of Birth: Grand Rapids, Kent County, Michigan
Entered Service at: Muskegon, Muskegon County, Michigan
Unit: 3d Squad, Weapons Platoon, Company E, 2d Battalion, 5th Marines, 1st Marine Division (Rein)
Served as: Squad Leader/Machine Gunner
Battle or Place of Action: near Panmunjom, Korea
Date of Action: 16 April 1952
Date of Presentation: 12 March 1953
Place of Presentation: The White House (Oval Office), presented by Pres. Dwight D. Eisenhower
Citation: For conspicuous gallantry and intrepidity at the risk of his life above and beyond the call of duty while serving as a gunner in a machine-gun platoon of Company E, in action against enemy aggressor forces. When an enemy grenade landed close to his position while he and his assistant gunner were receiving medical attention for their wounds during a fierce night attack by numerically superior hostile forces, Cpl. Dewey, although suffering intense pain, immediately pulled the corpsman to the ground and, shouting a warning to the other marines around him, bravely smothered the deadly missile with his body, personally absorbing the full force of the explosion to save his comrades from possible injury or death. His indomitable courage, outstanding initiative, and valiant efforts in behalf of others in the face of almost certain death reflect the highest credit upon Cpl. Dewey and enhance the finest traditions of the U.S. Naval Service.

3058 ◆ DODD, CARL HENRY

Rank: First Lieutenant (rank at time of action: Second Lieutenant) (highest rank: Major)
Service: U.S. Army
Birthday: 21 April 1925
Place of Birth: Coats, Harlan County, Kentucky
Entered Service at: Kenvir, Harlan County, Kentucky
Unit: 2d Platoon, Company E, 2d Battalion, 5th Infantry Regiment, 24th Infantry Division
Served as: Platoon Leader
Battle or Place of Action: Subuk, Korea
Date of Action: 30-31 January 1951
G.O. Number, Date: 37, 4 June 1951
Date of Presentation: 19 May 1951
Place of Presentation: Blair House, presented by Pres. Harry S. Truman
Citation: First Lt. Dodd, Company E, distinguished himself by conspicuous gallantry and intrepidity above and beyond the call of duty in action against the enemy. First Lt. Dodd, given the responsibility of spearheading an attack to capture Hill 256, a key terrain feature defended by a well-armed, crafty foe who had withstood several previous assaults, led his platoon forward over hazardous terrain under hostile small-arms, mortar, and artillery fire from well-camouflaged enemy emplacements which reached such intensity that his men faltered. With utter disregard for his safety, 1st Lt. Dodd moved among his men, reorganized and encouraged them, and then singlehandedly charged the first hostile machine-gun nest, killing or wounding all its occupants. Inspired by his incredible courage, his platoon responded magnificiently and, fixing bayonets and throwing grenades, closed on the enemy and wiped out every hostile position as it moved relentlessly onward to its initial objective. Securing the first series of enemy positions, 1st Lt. Dodd again reorganized his platoon and led them across a narrow ridge and onto Hill 256. Firing his rifle and throwing grenades, he advanced at the head of his platoon despite the intense concentrated hostile fire which was brought to bear on their narrow avenue of approach. When his platoon was still 200 yards from the objective he moved ahead and with his last grenade destroyed an enemy mortar, killing the crew. Darkness then halted the advance, but at daybreak 1st Lt. Dodd, again boldly advancing ahead of his unit, led the platoon through a dense fog against the remaining hostile positions. With bayonet and grenades he continued to set pace without regard for the danger to his life, until he and his troops had eliminated the last of the defenders and had secured the final objective. First Lt. Dodd's superb leadership and extraordinary heroism inspired his men to overcome this strong enemy defense reflecting the highest credit upon himself and upholding the esteemed traditions of the military service.

3059 ◆ *DUKE, RAY E.

Rank: Sergeant First Class (highest rank: Master Sergeant)
Service: U.S. Army
Birthday: 9 May 1923
Place of Birth: Whitwell, Marion County, Tennessee
Date of Death: 11 November 1951
Cemetery: Chattanooga National Cemetery (Z-373) (MH)—Chattanooga, Tennessee
Entered Service at: Whitwell, Marion County, Tennessee
Unit: Company C, 21st Infantry Regiment, 24th Infantry Division
Battle or Place of Action: Mugok, Korea
Date of Action: 26 April 1951

G.O. Number, Date: 20, 19 March 1954
Citation: Sfc. Duke, a member of Company C, distinguished himself by conspicuous gallantry and outstanding courage above and beyond the call of duty in action against the enemy. Upon learning that several of his men were isolated and heavily engaged in an area yielded by his platoon when ordered to withdraw, he led a small force in a daring assault which recovered the position and the beleaguered men. Another enemy attack in strength resulted in numerous casualties but Sfc. Duke, although wounded by mortar fragments, calmly moved along his platoon line to coordinate fields of fire and urge his men to hold firm in the bitter encounter. Wounded a second time, he received first aid and returned to his position. When the enemy again attacked shortly after dawn, despite his wounds, Sfc. Duke repeatedly braved withering fire to ensure maximum defense of each position. Threatened with annihilation and with mounting casualties, the platoon was again ordered to withdraw when Sfc. Duke was wounded a third time in both legs and was unable to walk. Realizing that he was impeding the progress of two comrades who were carrying him from the hill, he urged them to leave him and seek safety. He was last seen pouring devastating fire into the ranks of the onrushing assailants. The consummate courage, superb leadership, and heroic actions of Sfc. Duke, displayed during intensive action against overwhelming odds, reflect the highest credit upon himself, the infantry, and the U.S. Army.

3060 ◆ *EDWARDS, JUNIOR DEAN

Rank: Sergeant First Class
Service: U.S. Army
Birthday: 7 October 1926
Place of Birth: Indianola, Warren County, Iowa
Date of Death: 2 January 1951
Cemetery: I.O.O.F. Cemetery (MH)—Indianola, Iowa
Entered Service at: Indianola, Warren County, Iowa
Unit: Company E, 23d Infantry Regiment, 2d Infantry Division
Battle or Place of Action: Changbong-ni, Korea
Date of Action: 2 January 1951
G.O. Number, Date: 13, 1 February 1952
Date of Presentation: 16 January 1952
Place of Presentation: The Pentagon, presented by the Sec. of Defense Robert A. Lovett to his Father
Citation: Sfc. Edwards, Company E, distinguished himself by conspicuous gallantry and intrepidity above and beyond the call of duty in action against the enemy. When his platoon, while assisting in the defense of a strategic hill, was forced out of its position and came under vicious raking fire from an enemy machine gun set up on adjacent high ground, Sfc. Edwards individually charged the hostile emplacement, throwing grenades as he advanced. The enemy withdrew, but returned to deliver devastating fire when he had expended his ammunition. Securing a fresh supply of grenades, he again charged the emplacement, neutralized the weapon, and killed the crew, but was forced back by hostile small-arms fire. When the enemy emplaced another machine gun and resumed fire, Sfc. Edwards again renewed his supply of grenades, rushed a third time through a vicious hail of fire, silenced this second gun, and annihilated its crew. In this third daring assault he was mortally wounded, but his indomitable courage and successful action enabled his platoon to regain and hold the vital strongpoint. Sfc. Edwards' consummate valor and gallant self-sacrifice reflect the utmost glory upon himself and are in keeping with the esteemed traditions of the infantry and military service.

3061 ◆ *ESSEBAGGER JR., JOHN

Rank: Corporal
Service: U.S. Army
Birthday: 29 October 1928
Place of Birth: Holland, Ottawa County, Michigan
Date of Death: 25 April 1951
Cemetery: Pilgrim Home Cemetery—Holland, Michigan
Entered Service at: Holland, Ottawa County, Michigan
Unit: Company A, 7th Infantry Regiment, 3d Infantry Division
Battle or Place of Action: Popsu-dong, Korea
Date of Action: 25 April 1951
G.O. Number, Date: 61, 24 April 1952
Date of Presentation: 26 March 1952
Place of Presentation: The Pentagon, presented by Sec. of the Army Frank C. Pace to his Widow
Citation: Cpl. Essebagger, a member of Company A, distinguished himself by conspicuous gallantry and outstanding courage above and beyond the call of duty in action against the enemy. Committed to effect a delaying action to cover the 3d Battalion's withdrawal through Company A, Cpl. Essebagger, a member of one of two squads maintaining defensive positions in key terrain and defending the company's right flank, had participated in repulsing numerous attacks. In a frenzied banzai charge the numerically superior enemy seriously threatened the security of the planned route of withdrawal and the isolation of the small force. Badly shaken, the grossly outnumbered detachment started to fall back and Cpl. Essebagger, realizing the impending danger, voluntarily remained to provide security for the withdrawal. Gallantly maintaining a one-man stand, Cpl. Essebagger raked the menacing hordes with crippling fire and, with the foe closing on the position, left the comparative safety of his shelter and advanced in the face of overwhelming odds, firing his weapon and hurling grenades to disconcert the enemy and afford time for displacement of friendly elements to more tenable positions. Scorning the withering fire and bursting shells, Cpl. Essebagger continued to move forward, inflicting destruction upon the fanatical foe until he was mortally wounded. Cpl. Essebagger's intrepid action and supreme sacrifice exacted a heavy toll in enemy dead and wounded, stemmed the onslaught, and enabled the retiring squads to reach safety. His valorous conduct and devotion to duty reflected lasting glory upon himself and was in keeping with the noblest traditions of the infantry and the U.S. Army.

3062 ◆ *FAITH JR., DON CARLOS

Rank: Lieutenant Colonel
Service: U.S. Army

Birthday: 26 August 1918
Place of Birth: Washington, Daviess County, Indiana
Date of Death: 1 December 1950
Cemetery: National Memorial of the Pacific (Wall of the Missing)—Honolulu, Hawaii; Arlington National Cemetery (4-3016) ('In Memory' inscription on reverse side of parent's headstone)—Arlington, Virginia
Entered Service at: Washington, Daviess County, Indiana
Unit: 1st Battalion, 32d Infantry Regiment, 7th Infantry Division
Served as: Battalion Commander
Battle or Place of Action: Hagaru-ri, Korea
Date of Action: 27 November-1 December 1950
G.O. Number, Date: 59, 2 August 1951
Date of Presentation: 21 June 1951
Place of Presentation: The Pentagon, presented by Gen. Omar N. Bradley to his Widow
Citation: Lt. Col. Faith, commanding 1st Battalion, distinguished himself conspicuously by gallantry and intrepidity in action above and beyond the call of duty in the area of the Chosin Reservoir. When the enemy launched a fanatical attack against his battalion, Lt. Col. Faith unhesitatingly exposed himself to heavy enemy fire as he moved about directing the action. When the enemy penetrated the positions, Lt. Col. Faith personally led counterattacks to restore the position. During an attack by his battalion to effect a junction with another U.S. unit, Lt. Col. Faith reconnoitered the route for, and personally directed, the first elements of his command across the ice-covered reservoir and then directed the movement of his vehicles, which were loaded with wounded, until all of his command had passed through the enemy fire. Having completed this he crossed the reservoir himself. Assuming command of the force his unit had joined, he was given the mission of attacking to join friendly elements to the south. Lt. Col. Faith, although physically exhausted in the bitter cold, organized and launched an attack which was soon stopped by enemy fire. He ran forward under enemy small-arms and automatic-weapons fire, got his men on their feet, and personally led the fire attack as it blasted its way through the enemy ring. As they came to a hairpin curve, enemy fire from a roadblock again pinned the column down. Lt. Col. Faith organized a group of men and directed their attack on the enemy positions on the right flank. He then placed himself at the head of another group of men and in the face of direct enemy fire led an attack on the enemy roadblock, firing his pistol and throwing grenades. When he had reached a position approximately 30 yards from the roadblock, he was mortally wounded, but continued to direct the attack until the roadblock was overrun. Throughout the five days of action Lt. Col. Faith gave no thought to his safety and did not spare himself. His presence each time in the position of greatest danger was an inspiration to his men. Also, the damage he personally inflicted, firing from his position at the head of his men, was of material assistance on several occasions. Lt. Col. Faith's outstanding gallantry and noble self-sacrifice above and beyond the call of duty reflect the highest honor on him and are in keeping with the highest traditions of the U.S. Army.
Notes: MIA

3063 ◆ *GARCIA, FERNANDO LUIS

Rank: Private First Class
Service: U.S. Marine Corps
Birthday: 14 October 1929
Place of Birth: Utuado, Utuado County, Puerto Rico
Date of Death: 5 September 1952
Cemetery: Puerto Rico National Cemetery ('In Memory' marker only)—Bayamon, Puerto Rico; National Memorial of the Pacific—Honolulu, Hawaii
Entered Service at: San Juan, San Juan County, Puerto Rico
Unit: Company I, 3d Battalion, 5th Marines, 1st Marine Division (Rein)
Battle or Place of Action: Korea
Date of Action: 5 September 1952
Date of Presentation: 25 October 1953
Place of Presentation: City Hall, Utuado, Puerto Rico, presented to parents
Citation: For conspicuous gallantry and intrepidity at the risk of his life above and beyond the call of duty while serving as a member of Company I, in action against enemy aggressor forces. While participating in the defense of a combat outpost located more than one mile forward of the main line of resistance during a savage night attack by a fanatical enemy force employing grenades, mortars, and artillery, Pfc. Garcia, although suffering painful wounds, moved through the intense hail of hostile fire to a supply point to secure more hand grenades. Quick to act when a hostile grenade landed nearby, endangering the life of another marine, as well as his own, he unhesitatingly chose to sacrifice himself and immediately threw his body upon the deadly missile, receiving the full impact of the explosion. His great personal valor and cool decision in the face of almost certain death sustain and enhance the finest traditions of the U.S. Naval Service. He gallantly gave his life for his country.
Notes: MIA

3064 ◆ *GEORGE, CHARLES

Rank: Private First Class
Service: U.S. Army
Birthday: 23 August 1932
Place of Birth: Cherokee, Swain County, North Carolina
Date of Death: 30 November 1952
Cemetery: Yellow Hill Cemetery (MH)—Cherokee, North Carolina
Entered Service at: Whittier, Jackson County, North Carolina
Unit: Company C, 179th Infantry Regiment, 45th Infantry Division
Battle or Place of Action: Songnae-dong, Korea
Date of Action: 30 November 1952
G.O. Number, Date: 19, 18 March 1954
Citation: Pfc. George, a member of Company C, distinguished himself by conspicuous gallantry and outstanding courage above and beyond the call of duty in action against the enemy on the night of 30 November 1952. He was a member of a raiding party committed to engage the enemy and capture a prisoner for interrogation. Forging up the

rugged slope of the key terrain feature, the group was subjected to intense mortar and machine-gun fire and suffered several casualties. Throughout the advance, he fought valiantly and, upon reaching the crest of the hill, leaped into the trenches and closed with the enemy in hand-to-hand combat. When friendly troops were ordered to move back upon completion of the assignment, he and two comrades remained to cover the withdrawal. While in the process of leaving the trenches a hostile soldier hurled a grenade into their midst. Pfc. George shouted a warning to one comrade, pushed the other soldier out of danger, and, with full knowledge of the consequences, unhesitatingly threw himself upon the grenade, absorbing the full blast of the explosion. Although seriously wounded in this display of valor, he refrained from any outcry which would divulge the position of his companions. The two soldiers evacuated him to the forward aid station and shortly thereafter he succumbed to his wound. Pfc. George's indomitable courage, consummate devotion to duty, and willing self-sacrifice reflect the highest credit upon himself and uphold the finest traditions of the military service.

3065 ◆ *GILLILAND, CHARLES L.

Rank: Corporal (rank at time of action: Private First Class)
Service: U.S. Army
Birthday: 24 May 1933
Place of Birth: Mountain Home, Baxter County, Arkansas
Date of Death: 25 April 1951
Cemetery: National Memorial of the Pacific—Honolulu, Hawaii
Entered Service at: Yellville, Marion County, Arkansas
Unit: Company I, 7th Infantry Regiment, 3d Infantry Division
Served as: Automatic Rifleman
Battle or Place of Action: Tongmang-ni, Korea
Date of Action: 25 April 1951
G.O. Number, Date: 2, 11 January 1955
Citation: Cpl. Gilliland, a member of Company I, distinguished himself by conspicuous gallantry and outstanding courage above and beyond the call of duty in action against the enemy. A numerically superior hostile force launched a coordinated assault against his company perimeter, the brunt of which was directed up a defile covered by his automatic rifle. His assistant was killed by enemy fire, but Cpl. Gilliland, facing the full force of the assault, poured a steady fire into the foe, which stemmed the onslaught. When two enemy soldiers escaped his raking fire and infiltrated the sector, he leaped from his foxhole, overtook and killed them both with his pistol. Sustaining a serious head wound in this daring exploit, he refused medical attention and returned to his emplacement to continue his defense of the defile. His unit was ordered back to new defensive positions, but Cpl. Gilliland volunteered to remain to cover the withdrawal and hold the enemy at bay. His heroic actions and indomitable devotion to duty prevented the enemy from completely overrunning his company positions. Cpl. Gilliland's incredible valor and supreme sacrifice reflect lasting glory upon himself and are in keeping with the honored traditions of the military service.
Notes: MIA

3066 ◆ *GOMEZ, EDWARD

Rank: Private First Class
Service: U.S. Marine Corps
Birthday: 10 August 1932
Place of Birth: Omaha, Douglas County, Nebraska
Date of Death: 14 September 1951
Cemetery: St. Mary's Cemetery (MH)—Omaha, Nebraska
Entered Service at: Omaha, Douglas County, Nebraska
Unit: Company E, 2d Battalion, 1st Marines, 1st Marine Division (Rein)
Served as: Ammunition Bearer
Battle or Place of Action: Hill 749, Korea
Date of Action: 14 September 1951
Citation: For conspicuous gallantry and intrepidity at the risk of his life above and beyond the call of duty while serving as an ammunition bearer in Company E, in action against enemy aggressor forces. Boldly advancing with his squad in support of a group of riflemen assaulting a series of strongly fortified and bitterly defended hostile positions on Hill 749, Pfc. Gomez consistently exposed himself to the withering barrage to keep his machine gun supplied with ammunition during the drive forward to seize the objective. As his squad deployed to meet an imminent counterattack, he voluntarily moved down an abandoned trench to search for a new location for the gun and, when a hostile grenade landed between himself and his weapon, shouted a warning to those around him as he grasped the activated charge in his hand. Determined to save his comrades, he unhesitatingly chose to sacrifice himself and, diving into the ditch with the deadly missile, absorbed the shattering violence of the explosion in his body. By his stouthearted courage, incomparable valor, and decisive spirit of self-sacrifice, Pfc. Gomez inspired the others to heroic efforts in subsequently repelling the outnumbering foe, and his valiant conduct throughout sustained and enhanced the finest traditions of the U.S. Naval Service. He gallantly gave his life for his country.

3067 ◆ *GOODBLOOD, CLAIR

Rank: Corporal
Service: U.S. Army
Birthday: 18 September 1929
Place of Birth: Fort Kent, Aroostook County, Maine
Date of Death: 25 April 1951
Cemetery: Chandler Cemetery (MH)—Burham, Maine
Entered Service at: Burnham, Waldo County, Maine
Unit: Company D, 7th Infantry Regiment, 3d Infantry Division
Served as: Machine Gunner
Battle or Place of Action: Popsu-dong, Korea
Date of Action: 24-25 April 1951
G.O. Number, Date: 14, 1 February 1952
Date of Presentation: 16 January 1952
Place of Presentation: The Pentagon, presented by Sec. of Defense Robert A. Lovett to his Mother
Citation: Cpl. Goodblood, a member of Company D, distinguished himself by conspicuous gallantry and intrepidity at the risk of his life above and beyond the call of duty in action

against an armed enemy of the United Nations. Cpl. Goodblood, a machine gunner, was attached to Company B in defensive positions on thickly wooded key terrain under attack by a ruthless foe. In the bitter fighting which ensued, the numerically superior enemy infiltrated the perimeter, rendering the friendly positions untenable. Upon order to move back, Cpl. Goodblood voluntarily remained to cover the withdrawal and, constantly vulnerable to heavy fire, inflicted withering destruction on the assaulting force. Seeing a grenade lobbed at his position, he shoved his assistant to the ground and flinging himself upon the soldier attempted to shield him. Despite his valorous act both men were wounded. Rejecting aid for himself, he ordered the ammunition bearer to evacuate the injured man for medical treatment. He fearlessly maintained his one-man defense, sweeping the onrushing assailants with fire until an enemy banzai charge carried the hill and silenced his gun. When friendly elements regained the commanding ground, Cpl. Goodblood's body was found lying beside his gun and approximately 100 hostile dead lay in the wake of his field of fire. Through his unflinching courage and willing self-sacrifice the onslaught was retarded, enabling his unit to withdraw, regroup, and resecure the strongpoint. Cpl. Goodblood's inspirational conduct and devotion to duty reflect lasting glory on himself and are in keeping with the noble traditions of the military service.

3068 ◆ *GUILLEN, AMBROSIO

Rank: Staff Sergeant
Service: U.S. Marine Corps
Birthday: 7 December 1929
Place of Birth: La Junta, Otero County, Colorado
Date of Death: 25 July 1953
Cemetery: Fort Bliss National Cemetery (E-9171) (MH)—Fort Bliss, Texas
Entered Service at: El Paso, El Paso County, Texas
Unit: Company F, 2d Battalion, 7th Marines, 1st Marine Division (Rein)
Served as: Platoon Sergeant
Battle or Place of Action: Songuch-on, Korea
Date of Action: 25 July 1953
Citation: For conspicuous gallantry and intrepidity at the risk of his life above and beyond the call of duty while serving as a platoon sergeant of Company F in action against enemy aggressor forces. Participating in the defense of an outpost forward of the main line of resistance, S/Sgt. Guillen maneuvered his platoon over unfamiliar terrain in the face of hostile fire and placed his men in fighting positions. With his unit pinned down when the outpost was attacked under cover of darkness by an estimated force of two enemy battalions supported by mortar and artillery fire, he deliberately exposed himself to the heavy barrage and attacks to direct his men in defending their positions and personally supervise the treatment and evacuation of the wounded. Inspired by his leadership, the platoon quickly rallied and engaged the enemy in fierce hand-to-hand combat. Although critically wounded during the course of the battle, S/Sgt. Guillen refused medical aid and continued to direct his men throughout the remainder of the engagement until the enemy was defeated and thrown into disorderly retreat. Succumbing to his wounds within a few hours, S/Sgt. Guillen, by his outstanding courage and indomitable fighting spirit, was directly responsible for the success of his platoon in repelling a numerically superior enemy force. His personal valor reflects the highest credit upon himself and enhances the finest traditions of the U.S. Naval Service. He gallantly gave his life for his country.

3069 ◆ *HAMMOND, FRANCIS COLTON

Rank: Hospitalman
Service: U.S. Navy
Birthday: 9 November 1931
Place of Birth: Alexandria, Alexandria County, Virginia
Date of Death: 26 March 1953
Cemetery: Arlington National Cemetery (33-9011) (MH)—Arlington, Virginia
Entered Service at: Alexandria, Alexandria County, Virginia
Unit: 1st Battalion, 5th Marines (Attached), 1st Marine Division
Served as: Medical Corpsman
Battle or Place of Action: near Sanae-dong, Korea
Date of Action: 26-27 March 1953
Date of Presentation: 29 December 1953
Place of Presentation: The Pentagon, Presented by Sec. of the Navy Robert B. Anderson to his infant Son
Citation: For conspicuous gallantry and intrepidity at the risk of his life above and beyond the call of duty as an HC serving with the 1st Marine Division in action against enemy aggressor forces on the night of 26-27 March 1953. After reaching an intermediate objective during a counterattack against a heavily entrenched and numerically superior hostile force occupying ground on a bitterly contested outpost far in advance of the main line of resistance, HC Hammond's platoon was subjected to a murderous barrage of hostile mortar and artillery fire, followed by a vicious assault by onrushing enemy troops. Resolutely advancing through the veritable curtain of fire to aid his stricken comrades, HC Hammond moved among the stalwart garrison of marines and, although critically wounded himself, valiantly continued to administer aid to the other wounded throughout an exhausting four-hour period. When the unit was ordered to withdraw, he skillfully directed the evacuation of casualties and remained in the fire-swept area to assist the corpsmen of the relieving unit until he was struck by a round of enemy mortar fire and fell, mortally wounded. By his exceptional fortitude, inspiring initiative, and self-sacrificing efforts, HC Hammond undoubtedly saved the lives of many marines. His great personal valor in the face of overwhelming odds enhances and sustains the finest traditions of the U.S. Naval Service. He gallantly gave his life for his country.

3070 ◆ *HAMMOND JR., LESTER

Rank: Corporal
Service: U.S. Army
Birthday: 25 March 1931
Place of Birth: Wayland, Clark County, Missouri

Date of Death: 14 August 1952
Cemetery: Sunset Cemetery (MH)—Quincy, Illinois
Entered Service at: Quincy, Adams County, Illinois
Unit: Company A, 187th Airborne Regimental Combat Team
Served as: Radio Operator
Battle or Place of Action: Kumwha, Korea
Date of Action: 14 August 1952
G.O. Number, Date: 63, 17 August 1953
Date of Presentation: 5 August 1953
Place of Presentation: The Pentagon auditorium, presented by Under Sec. of the Army Earl D. Johnson to his Father
Citation: Cpl. Hammond, a radio operator with Company A, distinguished himself by conspicuous gallantry and outstanding courage above and beyond the call of duty in action against the enemy. Cpl. Hammond was a member of a six man reconnaissance patrol which had penetrated approximately 3,500 yards into enemy-held territory. Ambushed and partially surrounded by a large hostile force, the small group opened fire, then quickly withdrew up a narrow ravine in search of protective cover. Despite a wound sustained in the initial exchange of fire and imminent danger of being overrun by the numerically superior foe, he refused to seek shelter and, remaining in an exposed place, called for artillery fire to support a defensive action. Constantly vulnerable to enemy observation and action, he coordinated and directed crippling fire on the assailants, inflicting heavy casualties and repulsing several attempts to overrun friendly positions. Although wounded a second time, he remained steadfast and maintained his stand until mortally wounded. His indomitable fighting spirit set an inspiring example of valor to his comrades and, through his actions, the onslaught was stemmed, enabling a friendly platoon to reach the beleaguered patrol, evacuate the wounded, and effect a safe withdrawal to friendly lines. Cpl. Hammond's unflinching courage and consummate devotion to duty reflect lasting glory on himself and uphold the finest traditions of the military service.

3071 ◆ *HANDRICH, MELVIN O.

Rank: Master Sergeant
Service: U.S. Army
Birthday: 26 January 1919
Place of Birth: Manawa, Waupaca County, Wisconsin
Date of Death: 26 August 1950
Cemetery: Little Wolf Cemetery (MH)—Manawo, Wisconsin
Entered Service at: Manawa, Waupaca County, Wisconsin
Unit: Company C, 5th Infantry Regiment
Battle or Place of Action: Sobuk San Mountain, Korea
Date of Action: 25-26 August 1950
G.O. Number, Date: 60, 2 August 1951
Date of Presentation: 21 June 1951
Place of Presentation: The Pentagon, presented by Gen. Omar N. Bradley to his Father
Citation: M/Sgt. Handrich, Company C, distinguished himself by conspicuous gallantry and intrepidity above and beyond the call of duty in action. His company was engaged in repulsing an estimated 150 enemy who were threatening to overrun its position. Near midnight on 25 August, a hostile group over 100 strong attempted to infiltrate the company perimeter. M/Sgt. Handrich, despite the heavy enemy fire, voluntarily left the comparative safety of the defensive area and moved to a forward position where he could direct mortar and artillery fire upon the advancing enemy. He remained at this post for eight hours, directing fire against the enemy who often approached to within 50 feet of his position. Again, on the morning of 26 August, another strong hostile force made an attempt to overrun the company's position. With complete disregard for his safety, M/Sgt. Handrich rose to his feet and from this exposed position fired his rifle and directed mortar and artillery fire on the attackers. At the peak of this action he observed elements of his company preparing to withdraw. He perilously made his way across fire-swept terrain to the defense area where, by example and forceful leadership, he reorganized the men to continue the fight. During the action M/Sgt. Handrich was severely wounded. Refusing to take cover or be evacuated, he returned to his forward position and continued to direct the company's fire. Later a determined enemy attack overran M/Sgt. Handrich's position and he was mortally wounded. When the position was retaken, over 70 enemy dead were counted in the area he had so intrepidly defended. M/Sgt. Handrich's sustained personal bravery, consummate courage, and gallant self-sacrifice reflect untold glory upon himself and the heroic traditions of the military service.

3072 ◆ *HANSON, JACK G.

Rank: Private First Class
Service: U.S. Army
Birthday: 18 September 1930
Place of Birth: Escatawpa, Jackson County, Mississippi
Date of Death: 7 June 1951
Cemetery: Robinson Cemetery—Escatawpa, Mississippi
Entered Service at: Galveston, Galveston County, Texas
Unit: Company F, 31st Infantry Regiment
Served as: Machine Gunner
Battle or Place of Action: Pachi-dong, Korea
Date of Action: 7 June 1951
G.O. Number, Date: 15, 1 February 1952
Date of Presentation: 16 January 1952
Place of Presentation: The Pentagon, presented by the Sec. of Defense Robert A. Lovett to his Father
Citation: Pfc. Hanson, a machine gunner with the 1st Platoon, Company F, distinguished himself by conspicuous gallantry and intrepidity at the risk of his life above and beyond the call of duty in action against an armed enemy of the United Nations. The company, in defensive positions on two strategic hills separated by a wide saddle, was ruthlessly attacked at approximately 0300 hours, the brunt of which centered on the approach to the divide within range of Pfc. Hanson's machine gun. In the initial phase of the action, four riflemen were wounded and evacuated, and the numerically superior enemy, advancing under cover of darkness, infiltrated and posed an imminent threat to the security of the command post and weapons platoon. Upon orders to move to key terrain above and to the right of Pfc. Hanson's position,

he voluntarily remained to provide protective fire for the withdrawal. Subsequent to the retiring elements' fighting a rearguard action to the new location, it was learned that Pfc. Hanson's assistant gunner and three riflemen had been wounded and had crawled to safety, and that he was maintaining a lone-man defense. After the 1st Platoon reorganized, counterattacked, and rescued its original positions at approximately 0530 hours, Pfc. Hanson's body was found lying in front of his emplacement, his machine-gun ammunition expended, his empty pistol in his right hand, and a machete with blood on the blade in his left hand, and approximately 22 enemy dead lay in the wake of his action. Pfc. Hanson's consummate valor, inspirational conduct, and willing self-sacrifice enabled the company to contain the enemy and regain the commanding ground, and reflect lasting glory on himself and the noble traditions of the military service.

3073 ◆ *HARTELL, LEE ROSS

Rank: First Lieutenant
Service: U.S. Army
Birthday: 23 August 1923
Place of Birth: Philadelphia, Philadelphia County, Pennsylvania
Date of Death: 27 August 1951
Place of Death: Hill 700, South Korea
Cemetery: St. Peter's Cemetery (MH)—Danbury, Connecticut
Entered Service at: Danbury, Fairfield County, Connecticut
Unit: Battery A, 15th Field Artillery Battalion, 2d Infantry Division
Served as: Forward Observer
Battle or Place of Action: Kobangsan-ni, Korea
Date of Action: 27 August 1951
G.O. Number, Date: 16, 1 February 1952
Date of Presentation: 16 January 1952
Place of Presentation: The Pentagon, presented by the Sec. of Defense Robert A. Lovett to his Widow
Citation: 1st Lt. Hartell, a member of Battery A, distinguished himself by conspicuous gallantry and intrepidity at the risk of his life above and beyond the call of duty in action against an armed enemy of the United Nations. During the darkness of early morning, the enemy launched a ruthless attack against friendly positions on a rugged mountainous ridge. 1st Lt. Hartell, attached to Company B, 9th Infantry Regiment, as forward observer, quickly moved his radio to an exposed vantage on the ridgeline to adjust defensive fires. Realizing the tactical advantage of illuminating the area of approach, he called for flares and then directed crippling fire into the onrushing assailants. At this juncture a large force of hostile troops swarmed up the slope in banzai charge and came within 10 yards of 1st Lt. Hartell's position. 1st Lt. Hartell sustained a severe hand wound in the ensuing encounter, but grasped the microphone with his other hand and maintained his magnificent stand until the front and left flank of the company were protected by a close-in wall of withering fire, causing the fanatical foe to disperse and fall back momentarily. After the numerically superior enemy overran an outpost and was closing on his position, 1st Lt. Hartell, in a final radio call, urged the friendly elements to fire both batteries continuously. Although mortally wounded, 1st Lt. Hartell's intrepid actions contributed significantly to stemming the onslaught and enabled his company to maintain the strategic strongpoint. His consummate valor and unwavering devotion to duty reflect lasting glory on himself and uphold the noble traditions of the military service.

3074 ◆ HARVEY, RAYMOND

Rank: Captain (highest rank: Lieutenant Colonel)
Service: U.S. Army
Birthday: 1 March 1920
Place of Birth: Ford City, Armstrong County, Pennsylvania
Entered Service at: Pasadena, Los Angeles County, California
Unit: Company C, 1st Battalion, 17th Infantry Regiment, 7th Infantry Division
Served as: Company Commander
Battle or Place of Action: vicinity of Taemi-Dong, Korea
Date of Action: 9 March 1951
G.O. Number, Date: 67, 2 August 1951
Date of Presentation: 5 July 1951
Place of Presentation: The White House, presented by Pres. Harry S. Truman
Citation: Capt. Harvey, Company C, distinguished himself by conspicuous gallantry and intrepidity above and beyond the call of duty in action. When his company was pinned down by a barrage of automatic-weapons fire from numerous well-entrenched emplacements, imperiling accomplishment of its mission, Capt. Harvey braved a hail of fire and exploding grenades to advance to the first enemy machine-gun nest, killing its crew with grenades. Rushing to the edge of the next emplacement, he killed its crew with carbine fire. He then moved the 1st Platoon forward until it was again halted by a curtain of automatic fire from well-fortified hostile positions. Disregarding the hail of fire, he personally charged and neutralized a third emplacement. Miraculously escaping death from intense crossfire, Capt. Harvey continued to lead the assault. Spotting an enemy pillbox well-camouflaged by logs, he moved close enough to sweep the emplacement with carbine fire and throw grenades through the openings, annihilating its five occupants. Though wounded he then turned to order the company forward, and, suffering agonizing pain, he continued to direct the reduction of the remaining hostile positions, refusing evacuation until assured that the mission would be accomplished. Capt. Harvey's valorous and intrepid actions served as an inspiration to his company, reflecting the utmost glory upon himself and upholding the heroic traditions of the military service.

3075 ◆ *HENRY, FREDERICK F.

Rank: First Lieutenant
Service: U.S. Army
Place of Birth: Vian, Sequoyah County, Oklahoma
Date of Death: 1 September 1950
Cemetery: National Memorial of the Pacific (Wall of the Missing)—Honolulu, Hawaii
Entered Service at: Clinton, Custer County, Oklahoma
Unit: Company F, 28th Infantry Regiment

Served as: Platoon Leader
Battle or Place of Action: Am-Dong, Korea
Date of Action: 1 September 1950
G.O. Number, Date: 8, 16 February 1951
Date of Presentation: 9 January 1951
Place of Presentation: The White House, presented by Pres. Harry S. Truman to his Widow
Citation: 1st Lt. Henry, Company F, distinguished himself by conspicuous gallantry and intrepidity above and beyond the call of duty in action. His platoon was holding a strategic ridge near the town when they were attacked by a superior enemy force, supported by heavy mortar and artillery fire. Seeing his platoon disorganized by this fanatical assault, he left his foxhole and moving along the line ordered his men to stay in place and keep firing. Encouraged by this heroic action, the platoon reformed a defensive line and rained devastating fire on the enemy, checking its advance. Enemy fire had knocked out all communications and 1st Lt. Henry was unable to determine whether or not the main line of resistance was altered to this heavy attack. On his own initiative, although severely wounded, he decided to hold his position as long as possible and ordered the wounded evacuated and their weapons and ammunition brought to him. Establishing a one-man defensive position, he ordered the platoon's withdrawal and despite his wound and with complete disregard for himself remained behind to cover the movement. When last seen he was singlehandedly firing all available weapons so effectively that he caused an estimated 50 enemy casualties. His ammunition was soon expended and his position overrun, but this intrepid action saved the platoon and halted the enemy's advance until the main line of resistance was prepared to throw back the attack. 1st Lt. Henry's outstanding gallantry and noble self-sacrifice above and beyond the call of duty reflect the highest honor on him and are in keeping with the esteemed traditions of the U.S. Army.
Notes: MIA

3076 ◆ HERNANDEZ, RODOLFO PEREZ

Rank: Corporal
Service: U.S. Army
Birthday: 14 April 1931
Place of Birth: Colton, San Bernardino County, California
Entered Service at: Fowler, Fresno County, California
Unit: 3d Squad, 3d Platoon, Company G, 2d Battalion, 187th Airborne Regimental Combat Team
Served as: Squad Leader
Battle or Place of Action: near Wontong-ni, Korea
Date of Action: 31 May 1951
G.O. Number, Date: 40, 21 April 1952
Date of Presentation: 12 April 1952
Place of Presentation: The White House, presented by Pres. Harry S. Truman
Citation: Cpl. Hernandez, a member of Company G, distinguished himself by conspicuous gallantry and intrepidity above and beyond the call of duty in action against the enemy. His platoon, in defensive positions on Hill 420, came under ruthless attack by a numerically superior and fanatical hostile force, accompanied by heavy artillery, mortar, and machine-gun fire which inflicted numerous casualties on the platoon. His comrades were forced to withdraw due to lack of ammunition, but Cpl. Hernandez, although wounded in an exchange of grenades, continued to deliver deadly fire into the ranks of the onrushing assailants until a ruptured cartridge rendered his rifle inoperative. Immediately leaving his position, Cpl. Hernandez rushed the enemy armed only with rifle and bayonet. Fearlessly engaging the foe, he killed six of the enemy before falling unconscious from grenade, bayonet, and bullet wounds, but his heroic action momentarily halted the enemy advance and enabled his unit to counterattack and retake the lost ground. The indomitable fighting spirit, outstanding courage, and tenacious devotion to duty clearly demonstrated by Cpl. Hernandez reflect the highest credit upon himself, the infantry, and the U.S. Army.

3077 ◆ HUDNER JR., THOMAS JEROME

Rank: Lieutenant (j.g.) (highest rank: Captain)
Service: U.S. Navy
Birthday: 31 August 1924
Place of Birth: Fall River, Bristol County, Massachusetts
Entered Service at: Fall River, Bristol County, Massachusetts
Unit: Fighter Squadron 32, Air Group 3, U.S.S. *Leyte*
Served as: Pilot of a F-4U-4 Corsair
Battle or Place of Action: Chosin Reservoir, Korea
Date of Action: 4 December 1950
Date of Presentation: 13 April 1951
Place of Presentation: The White House, presented by Pres. Harry S. Truman
Citation: For conspicuous gallantry and intrepidity at the risk of his life above and beyond the call of duty as a pilot in Fighter Squadron 32, while attempting to rescue a squadron mate whose plane, struck by antiaircraft fire and trailing smoke, was forced down behind enemy lines. Quickly maneuvering to circle the downed pilot and protect him from enemy troops infesting the area, Lt. (j.g.) Hudner risked his life to save the injured flier who was trapped alive in the burning wreckage. Fully aware of the extreme danger in landing on the rough mountainous terrain, and the scant hope of escape or survival in subzero temperature, he put his plane down skillfully in a deliberate wheels-up landing in the presence of enemy troops. With his bare hands, he packed the fuselage with snow to keep the flames away from the pilot and struggled to pull him free. Unsuccessful in this he returned to his crashed aircraft and radioed other airborne planes, requesting that a helicopter be dispatched with an ax and fire extinguisher. He then remained on the spot despite the continuing danger from enemy action and, with the assistance of the rescue pilot, renewed a desperate but unavailing battle against time, cold, and flames. Lt. (j.g.) Hudner's exceptionally valiant action and selfless devotion to a shipmate sustain and enhance the highest traditions of the U.S. Naval Service.

3078 ◆ INGMAN JR., EINAR HAROLD

Rank: Sergeant (rank at time of action: Corporal) (highest rank: Staff Sergeant)
Service: U.S. Army

Birthday: 6 October 1929
Place of Birth: Milwaukee, Milwaukee County, Wisconsin
Entered Service at: West Bend, Washington County, Wisconsin
Unit: 3d Platoon, Company E, 17th Infantry Regiment, 7th Infantry Division
Served as: Acting Platoon Sergeant
Battle or Place of Action: near Maltari, Korea
Date of Action: 26 February 1951
G.O. Number, Date: 68, 2 August 1951
Date of Presentation: 5 July 1951
Place of Presentation: The White House, presented by Pres. Harry S. Truman
Citation: Sgt. Ingman, a member of Company E, distinguished himself by conspicuous gallantry and intrepidity above and beyond the call of duty in action against the enemy. The two leading squads of the assault platoon of his company, while attacking a strongly fortified ridge held by the enemy, were pinned down by withering fire, and both squad leaders and several men were wounded. Cpl. Ingman assumed command, reorganized, and combined the two squads, then moved from one position to another, designating fields of fire and giving advice and encouragement to the men. Locating an enemy machine-gun position that was raking his men with devastating fire, he charged it alone, threw a grenade into the position, and killed the remaining crew with rifle fire. Another enemy machine gun opened fire approximately 15 yards away and inflicted additional casualties to the group and stopped the attack. When Cpl. Ingman charged the second position he was hit by grenade fragments and a hail of fire which seriously wounded him about the face and neck and knocked him to the ground. With incredible courage and stamina, he arose instantly and, using only his rifle, killed the entire gun crew before falling unconscious from his wounds. As a result of the singular action by Cpl. Ingman, the defense of the enemy was broken, his squad secured its objective, and more than 100 hostile troops abandoned their weapons and fled in disorganized retreat. Cpl. Ingman's indomitable courage, extraordinary heroism, and superb leadership reflect the highest credit on himself and are in keeping with the esteemed traditions of the infantry and the U.S. Army.

3079 ◆ *JECELIN, WILLIAM R.

Rank: Sergeant
Service: U.S. Army
Place of Birth: Baltimore, Baltimore County, Maryland
Date of Death: 19 September 1950
Cemetery: Bohemin National Cemetery—Baltimore, Maryland
Entered Service at: Baltimore, Baltimore County, Maryland
Unit: Company C, 35th Infantry Regiment, 25th Infantry Division
Served as: Platoon Sergeant
Battle or Place of Action: near Saga, Korea
Date of Action: 19 September 1950
G.O. Number, Date: 24, 25 April 1951
Date of Presentation: 3 April 1951
Place of Presentation: The Pentagon, presented by Gen. Omar N. Bradley to his Father
Citation: Sgt. Jecelin, Company C, distinguished himself by conspicuous gallantry and intrepidity above and beyond the call of duty in action against the enemy. His company was ordered to secure a prominent, saw-toothed ridge from a well-entrenched and heavily armed enemy. Unable to capture the objective in the first attempt, a frontal and flanking assault was launched. He led his platoon through heavy enemy fire and bursting shells, across rice fields and rocky terrain, in direct frontal attack on the ridge in order to draw fire away from the flanks. The unit advanced to the base of the cliff, where intense, accurate hostile fire stopped the attack. Realizing that an assault was the only solution, Sgt. Jecelin rose from his position firing his rifle and throwing grenades as he called on his men to follow him. Despite the intense enemy fire this attack carried to the crest of the ridge where the men were forced to take cover. Again he rallied his men and stormed the enemy strongpoint. With fixed bayonets they charged into the face of antitank fire and engaged the enemy in hand-to-hand combat. After clubbing and slashing this force into submission the platoon was forced to take cover from direct frontal fire of a self-propelled gun. Refusing to be stopped he leaped to his feet and through sheer personal courage and fierce determination led his men in a new attack. At this instant a well-camouflaged enemy soldier threw a grenade at the remaining members of the platoon. He immediately lunged and covered the grenade with his body, absorbing the full force of the explosion to save those around him. This incredible courage and willingness to sacrifice himself for his comrades so imbued them with fury that they completely eliminated the enemy force. Sgt. Jecelin's heroic leadership and outstanding gallantry reflect the highest credit upon himself and uphold the esteemed traditions of the military service.

3080 ◆ *JOHNSON, JAMES EDMUND

Rank: Sergeant
Service: U.S. Marine Corps
Birthday: 1 January 1926
Place of Birth: Pocatello, Bannock County, Idaho
Date of Death: 2 November 1953
Cemetery: National Memorial of the Pacific (Wall of the Missing)—Honolulu, Hawaii; Arlington National Cemetery ('In Memory' marker) (451) (MH)—Arlington, Virginia
Entered Service at: Washington, D.C.
Unit: Company J, 3d Battalion, 7th Marines, 1st Marine Division (Rein)
Served as: Squad Leader
Battle or Place of Action: Yudam-ni, Korea
Date of Action: 2 December 1950
Date of Presentation: 29 March 1954
Place of Presentation: Washington, D.C., presented by Sec. of the Navy Robert B. Anderson to his Widow
Citation: For conspicuous gallantry and intrepidity at the risk of his life above and beyond the call of duty while serving as a squad leader in a provisional rifle platoon composed of artillerymen and attached to Company J, in action against

enemy aggressor forces. Vastly outnumbered by a well-entrenched and cleverly concealed enemy force wearing the uniforms of friendly troops and attacking his platoon's open and unconcealed positions, Sgt. Johnson unhesitatingly took charge of his platoon in the absence of the leader and, exhibiting great personal valor in the face of a heavy barrage of hostile fire, coolly proceeded to move about among his men, shouting words of encouragement and inspiration and skillfully directing their fire. Ordered to displace his platoon during the firefight, he immediately placed himself in an extremely hazardous position from which he could provide covering fire for his men. Fully aware that his voluntary action meant either certain death or capture to himself, he courageously continued to provide effective cover for his men and was last observed in a wounded condition single-handedly engaging enemy troops in close hand-grenade and hand-to-hand fighting. By his valiant and inspiring leadership, Sgt. Johnson was directly responsible for the successful completion of the platoon's displacement and the saving of many lives. His dauntless fighting spirit and unfaltering devotion to duty in the face of terrific odds reflect the highest credit upon himself and the U.S. Naval Service.
Notes: MIA

3081 ◆ *JORDON, MACK A.

Rank: Private First Class
Service: U.S. Army
Birthday: 8 December 1928
Place of Birth: Collins, Covington County, Mississippi
Date of Death: 15 November 1951
Cemetery: Station Creek Cemetery—Collins, Mississippi
Entered Service at: Collins, Covington County, Mississippi
Unit: 3d Platoon, Company K, 21st Infantry Regiment, 24th Infantry Division
Served as: Squad Leader
Battle or Place of Action: near Kumsong, Korea
Date of Action: 15 November 1951
G.O. Number, Date: 3, 8 January 1953
Date of Presentation: 7 January 1953
Place of Presentation: The Pentagon, presented by Sec. of the Army Frank C. Pace to his family
Citation: Pfc. Jordan, a member of Company K, distinguished himself by conspicuous gallantry and indomitable courage above and beyond the call of duty in action against the enemy. As a squad leader of the 3d Platoon, he was participating in a night attack on key terrain against a fanatical hostile force when the advance was halted by intense small-arms and automatic-weapons fire and a vicious barrage of hand grenades. Upon orders for the platoon to withdraw and reorganize, Pfc. Jordan voluntarily remained behind to provide covering fire. Crawling toward an enemy machine-gun emplacement, he threw three grenades and neutralized the gun. He then rushed the position delivering a devastating hail of fire, killing several of the enemy and forcing the remainder to fall back to new positions. He courageously attempted to move forward to silence another machine gun but, before he could leave his position, the ruthless foe hurled explosives down the hill and in the ensuing blast both legs were severed. Despite mortal wounds, he continued to deliver deadly fire and held off the assailants until the platoon returned. Pfc. Jordan's unflinching courage and gallant self-sacrifice reflect lasting glory upon himself and uphold the noble traditions of the infantry and the military service.

3082 ◆ *KANELL, BILLIE GENE

Rank: Private
Service: U.S. Army
Birthday: 26 June 1931
Place of Birth: Poplar Bluff, Butler County, Missouri
Date of Death: 7 September 1951
Cemetery: Fairdealing Cemetery—Fairdealing, Missouri
Entered Service at: Poplar Bluff, Butler County, Missouri
Unit: Company I, 35th Infantry Regiment, 25th Infantry Division
Battle or Place of Action: near Pyongyang, Korea
Date of Action: 7 September 1951
G.O. Number, Date: 57, 13 June 1952
Date of Presentation: 26 March 1952
Place of Presentation: The Pentagon, presented by Sec. of the Army Frank C. Pace to his Father
Citation: Pvt. Kanell, a member of Company I, distinguished himself by conspicuous gallantry and outstanding courage above and beyond the call of duty in action against the enemy. A numerically superior hostile force had launched a fanatical assault against friendly positions, supported by mortar and artillery fire, when Pvt. Kanell stood in his emplacement exposed to enemy observation and action and delivered accurate fire into the ranks of the assailants. An enemy grenade was hurled into his emplacement and Pvt. Kanell threw himself upon the grenade, absorbing the blast with his body to protect two of his comrades from serious injury and possible death. A few seconds later another grenade was thrown into the emplacement and, although seriously wounded by the first missile, he summoned his waning strength to roll toward the second grenade and used his body as a shield to again protect his comrades. He was mortally wounded as a result of his heroic actions. His indomitable courage, sustained fortitude against overwhelming odds, and gallant self-sacrifice reflect the highest credit upon himself, the infantry, and the U.S. Army.

3083 ◆ *KAUFMAN, LOREN R.

Rank: Sergeant First Class
Service: U.S. Army
Birthday: 27 July 1923
Place of Birth: The Dalles, Wasco County, Oregon
Date of Death: 10 February 1951
Cemetery: Willamette National Cemetery (G-2812) (MH)—Portland, Oregon
Entered Service at: The Dalles, Wasco County, Oregon
Unit: Company G, 9th Infantry Regiment, 2d Infantry Division
Battle or Place of Action: near Yongsan, Korea
Date of Action: 4-5 September 1950
G.O. Number, Date: 61, 2 August 1951

Date of Presentation: 21 June 1951
Place of Presentation: The Pentagon, presented by Gen. Omar N. Bradley to his Father
Citation: Sfc. Kaufman distinguished himself by conspicuous gallantry and intrepidity above and beyond the call of duty in action. On the night of 4 September the company was in a defensive position on two adjoining hills. His platoon was occupying a strong point two miles away protecting the battalion flank. Early on 5 September the company was attacked by enemy battalion and his platoon was ordered to reinforce the company. As his unit moved along a ridge it encountered a hostile encircling force. Sfc. Kaufman, running forward, bayoneted the lead scout and engaged the column in a rifle and grenade assault. His quick, vicious attack so surprised the enemy that they retreated in confusion. When his platoon joined the company he discovered that the enemy had taken commanding ground and pinned the company down in a draw. Without hesitation Sfc. Kaufman charged the enemy lines firing his rifle and throwing grenades. During the action, he bayoneted two enemy and, seizing an unmanned machine gun, delivered deadly fire on the defenders. Following this encounter the company regrouped and resumed the attack. Leading the assault, he reached the ridge, destroyed a hostile machine-gun position, and routed the remaining enemy. Pursuing the hostile troops, he bayoneted two more and then rushed a mortar position, shooting the gunners. Remnants of the enemy fled to a village and Sfc. Kaufman led a patrol into the town, dispersed them, and burned the buildings. The dauntless courage and resolute intrepid leadership of Sfc. Kaufman were directly responsible for the success of his company in regaining its positions, reflecting distinct credit upon himself and upholding the esteemed traditions of the military service.

3084 ◆ *KELLY, JOHN DORAN

Rank: Private First Class
Service: U.S. Marine Corps
Birthday: 8 July 1928
Place of Birth: Youngstown, Mahoning County, Ohio
Date of Death: 28 May 1952
Cemetery: Jefferson Memorial Cemetery (MH)—Pittsburgh, Pennsylvania
Entered Service at: Homestead, Allegheny County, Pennsylvania
Unit: Company C, 1st Battalion, 7th Marines, 1st Marine Division (Rein)
Served as: Radio Operator
Battle or Place of Action: Korea
Date of Action: 28 May 1952
Date of Presentation: 9 September 1953
Place of Presentation: Washington, D.C., Marine Corps Barracks, presented by Vice Pres. Richard M. Nixon to his Mother
Citation: For conspicuous gallantry and intrepidity at the risk of his life above and beyond the call of duty while serving as a radio operator of Company C, in action against enemy aggressor forces. With his platoon pinned down by a numerically superior enemy force employing intense mortar, artillery, small-arms, and grenade fire, Pfc. Kelly requested permission to leave his radio in the care of another man and to participate in an assault on enemy key positions. Fearlessly charging forward in the face of a murderous hail of machine-gun fire and hand grenades, he initiated a daring attack against a hostile strongpoint and personally neutralized the position, killing two of the enemy. Unyielding in the face of heavy odds, he continued forward and singlehandedly assaulted a machine-gun bunker. Although painfully wounded, he bravely charged the bunker and destroyed it, killing three of the enemy. Courageously continuing his one-man assault, he again stormed forward in a valiant attempt to wipe out a third bunker and boldly delivered point-blank fire into the aperture of the hostile emplacement. Mortally wounded by enemy fire while carrying out this heroic action, Pfc. Kelly, by his great personal valor and aggressive fighting spirit, inspired his comrades to sweep on, overrun and secure the objective. His extraordinary heroism in the face of almost certain death reflects the highest credit upon himself and enhances the finest traditions of the U.S. Naval Service. He gallantly gave his life for his country.

3085 ◆ *KELSO, JACK WILLIAM

Rank: Private First Class
Service: U.S. Marine Corps
Birthday: 23 January 1934
Place of Birth: Madera, Madera County, California
Date of Death: 2 October 1952
Place of Death: Korea
Cemetery: Washington Colony Cemetery (MH)—Fresno, California
Entered Service at: Caruthers, Fresno County, California
Unit: Company I, 3d Battalion, 7th Marines, 1st Marine Division (Rein)
Served as: Rifleman
Battle or Place of Action: Korea
Date of Action: 2 October 1952
Date of Presentation: 9 September 1953
Place of Presentation: Marine Corps Barracks, Washington, D.C., presented by Vice Pres. Richard M. Nixon to his parents
Citation: For conspicuous gallantry and intrepidity at the risk of his life above and beyond the call of duty while serving as a rifleman of Company I, in action against enemy aggressor forces. When both the platoon commander and the platoon sergeant became casualties during the defense of a vital outpost against a numerically superior enemy force attacking at night under cover of intense small-arms, grenade, and mortar fire, Pfc. Kelso bravely exposed himself to the hail of enemy fire in a determined effort to reorganize the unit and to repel the onrushing attackers. Forced to seek cover, along with four other marines, in a nearby bunker which immediately came under attack, he unhesitatingly picked up an enemy grenade which landed in the shelter, rushed out into the open, and hurled it back at the enemy. Although painfully wounded when the grenade exploded as it left his hand, and again forced to seek the protection of the bunker when the hostile fire became more intensified, Pfc. Kelso refused to remain in

his position of comparative safety and moved out into the fire-swept area to return the enemy fire, thereby permitting the pinned-down marines in the bunker to escape. Mortally wounded while providing covering fire for his comrades, Pfc. Kelso, by his valiant fighting spirit, aggressive determination, and self-sacrificing efforts in behalf of others, served to inspire all who observed him. His heroic actions sustain and enhance the highest traditions of the U.S. Naval Service. He gallantly gave his life for his country.

3086 ◆ KENNEMORE, ROBERT SIDNEY

Rank: Staff Sergeant
Service: U.S. Marine Corps
Birthday: 21 June 1920
Place of Birth: Greenville, Greenville County, South Carolina
Date of Death: 26 April 1989
Cemetery: San Francisco National Cemetery (H-CA-404) (MH)—San Francisco, California
Entered Service at: Greenville, Greenville County, South Carolina
Unit: Company E, 2d Battalion, 7th Marines, 1st Marine Division (Rein)
Served as: Section Leader
Battle or Place of Action: north of Yudam-ni, Korea
Date of Action: 27-28 November 1950
Citation: For conspicuous gallantry and intrepidity at the risk of his life above and beyond the call of duty as leader of a machine-gun section in Company E, in action against enemy aggressor forces. With the company's defensive perimeter overrun by a numerically superior hostile force during a savage night attack north of Yudam-ni and his platoon commander seriously wounded, S/Sgt. Kennemore unhesitatingly assumed command, quickly reorganized the unit and directed the men in consolidating the position. When an enemy grenade landed in the midst of a machine-gun squad, he bravely placed his foot on the missile and, in the face of almost certain death, personally absorbed the full force of the explosion to prevent injury to his fellow marines. By his indomitable courage, outstanding leadership, and selfless efforts in behalf of his comrades, S/Sgt. Kennemore was greatly instrumental in driving the enemy from the area and upheld the highest traditions of the U.S. Naval Service.

3087 ◆ *KILMER, JOHN EDWARD

Rank: Hospital Corpsman
Service: U.S. Navy
Birthday: 15 August 1930
Place of Birth: Highland Park, Lake County, Illinois
Date of Death: 13 August 1952
Cemetery: San Jose Burial Park (MH)—San Antonio, Texas
Entered Service at: Houston, Harris County, Texas
Unit: Attached to duty as a medical corpsman with a Marine rifle company in the 1st Marine Division
Served as: Medical Corpsman
Battle or Place of Action: Korea
Date of Action: 13 August 1952
Citation: For conspicuous gallantry and intrepidity at the risk of his life above and beyond the call of duty in action against enemy aggressor forces. With his company engaged in defending a vitally important hill position well forward of the main line of resistance during an assault by large concentrations of hostile troops, HC Kilmer repeatedly braved intense enemy mortar, artillery, and sniper fire to move from one position to another, administering aid to the wounded and expediting their evacuation. Painfully wounded himself when struck by mortar fragments while moving to the aid of a casualty, he persisted in his efforts and inched his way to the side of the stricken marine through a hail of enemy shells falling around him. Undaunted by the devastating hostile fire, he skillfully administered first aid to his comrade and, as another mounting barrage of enemy fire shattered the immediate area, unhesitatingly shielded the wounded man with his body. Mortally wounded by flying shrapnel while carrying out this heroic action, HC Kilmer, by his great personal valor and gallant spirit of self-sacirfice in saving the life of a comrade, served to inspire all who observed him. His unyielding devotion to duty in the face of heavy odds reflects the highest credit upon himself and enhances the finest traditions of the U.S. Naval Service. He gallantly gave his life for another.

3088 ◆ *KNIGHT, NOAH ODELL

Rank: Private First Class
Service: U.S. Army
Birthday: 29 October 1929
Place of Birth: Chesterfield County, South Carolina
Date of Death: 24 November 1951
Cemetery: Union Hill Baptist Church (MH)—Pageland, South Carolina
Entered Service at: Jefferson, Chesterfield County, South Carolina
Unit: Company F, 7th Infantry Regiment, 3d Infantry Division
Battle or Place of Action: near Kowang-San, Korea
Date of Action: 23-24 November 1951
G.O. Number, Date: 2, 7 January 1953
Date of Presentation: 7 January 1953
Place of Presentation: The Pentagon, presented by Sec. of the Army Frank C. Pace to his family
Citation: Pfc. Knight, a member of Company F, distinguished himself by conspicuous gallantry and indomitable courage above and beyond the call of duty in action against the enemy. He occupied a key position in the defense perimeter when waves of enemy troops passed through their own artillery and mortar concentrations and charged the company position. Two direct hits from an enemy emplacement demolished his bunker and wounded him. Disregarding personal safety, he moved to a shallow depression for a better firing vantage. Unable to deliver effective fire from his defilade position, he left his shelter, moved through heavy fire in full view of the enemy and, firing into the ranks of the relentless assailants, inflicted numerous casualties, momentarily stemming the attack. Later during another vicious onslaught, he observed an enemy squad infiltrating the position and, coun-

terattacking, killed or wounded the entire group. Expending the last of his ammunition, he discovered three enemy soldiers entering the friendly position with demolition charges. Realizing the explosives would enable the enemy to exploit the breach, he fearlessly rushed forward and disabled two assailants with the butt of his rifle when the third exploded a demolition charge killing the three enemy soldiers and mortally wounding Pfc. Knight. Pfc. Knight's supreme sacrifice and consummate devotion to duty reflect lasting glory on himself and uphold the noble traditions of the military service.

3089 ◆ *KOELSCH, JOHN KELVIN

Rank: Lieutenant (j.g.)
Service: U.S. Navy
Birthday: 22 December 1925
Place of Birth: London, England
Date of Death: 16 October 1951
Place of Death: Prison Camp, North Korea
Cemetery: Arlington National Cemetery (30-1123-RH) (MH)—Arlington, Virginia
Entered Service at: Los Angeles, Los Angeles County, California
Unit: Navy Helicopter Rescue Unit, U.S.S. *Princeton*
Served as: Helicopter Pilot
Battle or Place of Action: near Wonsan, North Korea
Date of Action: 3 July 1951
Date of Presentation: August 1955
Place of Presentation: The Pentagon, presented by Secretary of the Navy Charles S. Thomas to his mother
Citation: For conspicuous gallantry and intrepidity at the risk of his life above and beyond the call of duty while serving with a Navy helicopter rescue unit. Although darkness was rapidly approaching when information was received that a marine aviator had been shot down and was trapped by the enemy in mountainous terrain deep in hostile territory, Lt. (j.g.) Koelsch voluntarily flew a helicopter to the reported position of the downed airman in an attempt to effect a rescue. With an almost solid overcast concealing everything below the mountain peaks, he descended in his unarmed and vulnerable aircraft without the accompanying fighter escort to an extremely low altitude beneath the cloud level and began a systematic search. Despite the increasingly intense enemy fire, which struck his helicopter on one occasion, he persisted in his mission until he succeeded in locating the downed pilot, who was suffering from serious burns on the arms and legs. While the victim was being hoisted into the aircraft, it was struck again by an accurate burst of hostile fire and crashed on the side of the mountain. Quickly extricating his crewmen and the aviator from the wreckage, Lt. (j.g.) Koelsch led them from the vicinity in an effort to escape from hostile troops, evading the enemy forces for nine days and rendering such medical attention as possible to his severely burned companion until all were captured. Up to the time of his death while still a captive of the enemy, Lt. (j.g.) Koelsch steadfastly refused to aid his captors in any manner and served to inspire his fellow prisoners by his fortitude and consideration for others. His great personal valor and heroic spirit of self-sacrifice throughout sustain and enhance the finest traditions of the U.S. Naval Service.
Notes: POW

3090 ◆ KOUMA, ERNEST RICHARD

Rank: Master Sergeant (rank at time of action: Sergeant First Class)
Service: U.S. Army
Birthday: 23 November 1919
Place of Birth: Dwight, Butler County, Nebraska
Date of Death: 19 December 1993
Place of Death: McDaniels, Kentucky
Cemetery: Fort Knox Post Cemetery (MH)—Fort Knox, Kentucky
Entered Service at: Dwight, Butler County, Nebraska
Unit: 4th Platoon, Company A, 72d Tank Battalion, 2d Infantry Division
Served as: Tank Commander
Battle or Place of Action: vicinity of Agok, Korea
Date of Action: 31 August-1 September 1951
G.O. Number, Date: 38, 4 June 1951
Date of Presentation: 19 May 1951
Place of Presentation: Blair House, presented by Pres. Harry S. Truman
Citation: M/Sgt. Kouma, a tank commander in Company A, distinguished himself by conspicuous gallantry and intrepidity at the risk of his life above and beyond the call of duty in action against the enemy. His unit was engaged in supporting infantry elements on the Naktong River front. Near midnight on 31 August, a hostile force estimated at 500 crossed the river and launched a fierce attack against the infantry positions, inflicting heavy casualties. A withdrawal was ordered and his armored unit was given the mission of covering the movement until a secondary position could be established. The enemy assault overran two tanks, destroyed one, and forced another to withdraw. Suddenly M/Sgt. Kouma discovered that his tank was the only obstacle in the path of the hostile onslaught. Holding his ground, he gave fire orders to his crew and remained in position throughout the night, fighting off repeated enemy attacks. During one fierce assault, the enemy surrounded his tank and he leaped from the armored turret, exposing himself to a hail of hostile fire, manned the .50 caliber machine gun mounted on the rear deck, and delivered point-blank fire into the fanatical foe. His machine gun emptied, he fired his pistol and threw grenades to keep the enemy from his tank. After more than nine hours of constant combat and close-in fighting, he withdrew his vehicle to friendly lines. During the withdrawal through eight miles of hostile territory, M/Sgt. Kouma continued to inflict casualties upon the enemy and exhausted his ammunition in destroying three hostile machine-gun positions. During this action, M/Sgt. Kouma killed an estimated 250 enemy soldiers. His magnificent stand allowed the infantry sufficient time to reestablish defensive positions. Rejoining his company, although suffering intensely from his wounds, he attempted to resupply his tank and return to the battle area. While being evacuated for medical treatment, his courage was again displayed when he requested to return to the front. M/Sgt.

Kouma's superb leadership, heroism, and intense devotion to duty reflect the highest credit on himself and uphold the esteemed traditions of the U.S. Army.

3091 ◆ *KRZYZOWSKI, EDWARD C.

Rank: Captain
Service: U.S. Army
Birthday: 16 January 1914
Place of Birth: Chicago, Cook County, Illinois
Date of Death: 3 September 1951
Cemetery: Resurrection Cemetery—Justice, Illinois
Entered Service at: Cicero, Cook County, Illinois
Unit: Company B, 9th Infantry Regiment, 2d Infantry Division
Served as: Company Commander
Battle or Place of Action: near Tondul, Korea
Date of Action: 31 August-3 September 1951
G.O. Number, Date: 56, 12 June 1952
Date of Presentation: 26 March 1952
Place of Presentation: The Pentagon, presented by Sec. of the Army Frank C. Pace to his Widow
Citation: Capt. Krzyzowski, distinguished himself by conspicuous gallantry and indomitable courage above and beyond the call of duty in action against the enemy as commanding officer of Company B. Spearheading an assault against strongly defended Hill 700, his company came under vicious crossfire and grenade attack from enemy bunkers. Creeping up the fire-swept hill, he personally eliminated one bunker with his grenades and wiped out a second with carbine fire. Forced to retire to more tenable positions for the night, the company, led by Capt. Krzyzowski, resumed the attack the following day, gaining several hundred yards and inflicting numerous casualties. Overwhelmed by the numerically superior hostile force, he ordered his men to evacuate the wounded and move back. Providing protective fire for their safe withdrawal, he was wounded again by grenade fragments, but refused evacuation and continued to direct the defense. On 3 September, he led his valiant unit in another assault which overran several hostile positions, but again the company was pinned down by murderous fire. Courageously advancing alone to an open knoll to plot mortar concentrations against the hill, he was killed instantly by an enemy sniper's fire. Capt. Krzyzowski's consummate fortitude, heroic leadership, and gallant self-sacrifice, so clearly demonstrated throughout three days of bitter combat, reflect the highest credit and lasting glory on himself, the infantry, and the U.S. Army.

3092 ◆ *KYLE, DARWIN K.

Rank: Second Lieutenant
Service: U.S. Army
Birthday: 1 June 1918
Place of Birth: Jenkins, Letcher County, Kentucky
Date of Death: 16 February 1951
Cemetery: Sunset Memorial Park—South Charleston, West Virginia
Entered Service at: Racine, Boone County, West Virginia
Unit: Company K, 7th Infantry Regiment, 3d Infantry Division
Served as: Platoon Leader
Battle or Place of Action: near Kamil-ni, Korea
Date of Action: 16 February 1951
G.O. Number, Date: 17, 1 February 1952
Date of Presentation: 16 January 1952
Place of Presentation: The Pentagon, presented by Sec. of Defense Robert Lovett to his Widow
Citation: 2d Lt. Kyle, distinguished himself by conspicuous gallantry and intrepidity above and beyond the call of duty in action against the enemy. When his platoon had been pinned down by intense fire, he completely exposed himself to move among and encourage his men to continue the advance against enemy forces strongly entrenched on Hill 185. Inspired by his courageous leadership, the platoon resumed the advance but was again pinned down when an enemy machine gun opened fire, wounding six of the men. 2d Lt. Kyle immediately charged the hostile emplacement alone, engaged the crew in hand-to-hand combat, killing all three. Continuing on toward the objective, his platoon suddenly received an intense automatic-weapons fire from a well-concealed hostile position on its right flank. Again leading his men in a daring bayonet charge against this position, firing his carbine and throwing grenades, 2d Lt. Kyle personally destroyed four of the enemy before he was killed by a burst from an enemy submachine gun. The extraordinary heroism and outstanding leadership of 2d Lt. Kyle, and his gallant self-sacrifice, reflect the highest credit upon himself and are in keeping with the esteemed traditions of the military service.

3093 ◆ LEE, HUBERT LOUIS

Rank: Master Sergeant
Service: U.S. Army
Birthday: 2 February 1915
Place of Birth: Arburg, Missouri
Date of Death: 5 November 1982
Place of Death: Jackson, Mississippi
Cemetery: Leland-Stoneville Cemetery (MH)—Stoneville, Mississippi
Entered Service at: Leland, Washington County, Mississippi
Unit: Company I, 23d Infantry Regiment, 2d Infantry Division
Served as: Platoon Sergeant
Battle or Place of Action: near Ip-o-ri, Korea
Date of Action: 1 February 1951
G.O. Number, Date: 21, 5 February 1952
Date of Presentation: 29 January 1952
Place of Presentation: The White House, presented by Pres. Harry S. Truman
Citation: M/Sgt. Lee, a member of Company I, distinguished himself by conspicuous gallantry and intrepidity above and beyond the call of duty in action against the enemy. When his platoon was forced from its position by a numerically superior enemy force, and his platoon leader wounded, M/Sgt. Lee assumed command, regrouped the remnants of his unit, and led them in repeated assaults to regain the position. Within 25 yards of his objective he received a leg wound from grenade fragments, but refused

assistance and continued the attack. Although forced to withdraw five times, each time he regrouped his remaining men and renewed the assault. Moving forward at the head of his small group in the fifth attempt, he was struck by an exploding grenade, knocked to the ground, and seriously wounded in both legs. Still refusing assistance, he advanced by crawling, rising to his knees to fire, and urging his men to follow. While thus directing the final assault, he was wounded a third time, by small-arms fire. Persistently continuing to crawl forward, he directed his men in a final and successful attack which regained the vital objective. His intrepid leadership and determination led to the destruction of 83 of the enemy and withdrawal of the remainder, and was a vital factor in stopping the enemy attack. M/Sgt. Lee's indomitable courage, consummate valor, and outstanding leadership reflect the highest credit upon himself and are in keeping with the finest traditions of the infantry and the U.S. Army.

3094 ◆ *LIBBY, GEORGE DALTON

Rank: Sergeant
Service: U.S. Army
Birthday: 4 December 1919
Place of Birth: Bridgton, Cumberland County, Maine
Date of Death: 20 July 1950
Cemetery: Arlington National Cemetery (34-1317) (MH)—Arlington, Virginia
Entered Service at: Waterbury, New Haven County, Connecticut
Unit: Company C, 3d Combat Engineer Battalion, 24th Infantry Division
Battle or Place of Action: near Taejon, Korea
Date of Action: 20 July 1950
G.O. Number, Date: 62, 2 August 1951
Date of Presentation: 21 June 1951
Place of Presentation: The Pentagon, presented by Gen. Omar N. Bradley to his Sister
Citation: Sgt. Libby distinguished himself by conspicuous gallantry and intrepidity above and beyond the call of duty in action. While breaking through an enemy encirclement, the vehicle in which he was riding approached an enemy roadblock and encountered devastating fire which disabled the truck, killing or wounding all the passengers except Sgt. Libby. Taking cover in a ditch, Sgt. Libby engaged the enemy and despite the heavy fire crossed the road twice to administer aid to his wounded comrades. He then hailed a passing M-5 artillery tractor and helped the wounded aboard. The enemy directed intense small-arms fire at the driver, and Sgt. Libby, realizing that no one else could operate the vehicle, placed himself between the driver and the enemy thereby shielding him while he returned the fire. During this action he received several wounds in the arms and body. Continuing through the town, the tractor made frequent stops and Sgt. Libby helped more wounded aboard. Refusing first aid, he continued to shield the driver and return the fire of the enemy when another roadblock was encountered. Sgt. Libby received additional wounds but held his position until he lost consciousness. Sgt. Libby's sustained, heroic actions enabled his comrades to reach friendly lines. His dauntless courage and gallant self-sacrifice reflect the highest credit upon himself and uphold the esteemed traditions of the U.S. Army.

3095 ◆ *LITTLETON, HERBERT A.

Rank: Private First Class
Service: U.S. Marine Corps Reserve
Birthday: 1 July 1930
Place of Birth: Mena, Polk County, Arkansas
Date of Death: 22 April 1951
Cemetery: Kohler Lawn Cemetery (MH)—Nampa, Idaho
Entered Service at: Black Hawk, Meade County, South Dakota
Unit: Company C, 1st Battalion, 7th Marines, 1st Marine Division
Served as: Radio Operator
Battle or Place of Action: Chungchon, Korea
Date of Action: 22 April 1951
Citation: For conspicuous gallantry and intrepidity at the risk of his life above and beyond the call of duty while serving as a radio operator with an artillery forward observation team of Company C, in action against enemy aggressor forces. Standing watch when a well-concealed and numerically superior enemy force launched a violent night attack from nearby positions against his company, Pfc. Littleton quickly alerted the forward observation team and immediately moved into an advantageous position to assist in calling down artillery fire on the hostile force. When an enemy hand grenade was thrown into his vantage point shortly after the arrival of the remainder of the team, he unhesitatingly hurled himself on the deadly missile, absorbing its full, shattering impact in his body. By his prompt action and heroic spirit of self-sacrifice, he saved the other members of his team from serious injury or death and enabled them to carry on the vital mission which culminated in the repulse of the hostile attack. His indomitable valor in the face of almost certain death reflects the highest credit upon Pfc. Littleton and the U.S. Naval Service. He gallantly gave his life for his country.

3096 ◆ *LONG, CHARLES RICHARD

Rank: Sergeant
Service: U.S. Army
Birthday: 10 December 1923
Place of Birth: Kansas City, Clay County, Missouri
Date of Death: 12 February 1951
Cemetery: Mount Washington Cemetery (MH)—Independence, Missouri
Entered Service at: Kansas City, Clay County, Missouri
Unit: Company M, 38th Infantry Regiment, 2d Infantry Division
Served as: Forward Observer
Battle or Place of Action: near Hoeng-song, Korea
Date of Action: 12 February 1951
G.O. Number, Date: 18, 1 February 1952
Date of Presentation: 16 January 1952
Place of Presentation: The Pentagon, presented by Sec. of Defense Robert Lovett to his Widow
Citation: Sgt. Long, a member of Company M, distin-

guished himself by conspicuous gallantry and intrepidity above and beyond the call of duty in action against an armed enemy of the United Nations. When Company M, in a defensive perimeter on Hill 300, was viciously attacked by a numerically superior hostile force at approximately 0300 hours and ordered to withdraw, Sgt. Long, a forward observer for the mortar platoon, voluntarily remained at his post to provide cover by directing mortar fire on the enemy. Maintaining radio contact with his platoon, Sgt. Long coolly directed accurate mortar fire on the advancing foe. He continued firing his carbine and throwing hand grenades until his position was surrounded and he was mortally wounded. Sgt. Long's inspirational, valorous action halted the onslaught, exacted a heavy toll of enemy casualties, and enabled his company to withdraw, reorganize, counterattack, and regain the hill strongpoint. His unflinching courage and noble self-sacrifice reflect the highest credit on himself and are in keeping with the honored traditions of the military service.

3097 ◆ *LOPEZ, BALDOMERO

Rank: First Lieutenant
Service: U.S. Marine Corps
Birthday: 23 August 1925
Place of Birth: Tampa, Hillsborough County, Florida
Date of Death: 15 September 1950
Cemetery: Centre Adorim Memorial Park (MH)—Tampa, Florida
Entered Service at: Tampa, Hillsborough County, Florida
Unit: Company A, 1st Battalion, 5th Marines, 1st Marine Division (Rein)
Served as: Rifle Platoon Commander
Battle or Place of Action: Inchon, Korea
Date of Action: 15 September 1950
Date of Presentation: 30 August 1951
Place of Presentation: The Pentagon, presented by Sec. of the Navy Dan A. Kimball to his parents
Citation: For conspicuous gallantry and intrepidity at the risk of his life above and beyond the call of duty as a rifle platoon commander of Company A, in action against enemy aggressor forces. With his platoon 1st Lt. Lopez was engaged in the reduction of immediate enemy beach defenses after landing with the assault waves. Exposing himself to hostile fire, he moved forward alongside a bunker and prepared to throw a hand grenade into the next pillbox whose fire was pinning down that sector of the beach. Taken under fire by an enemy automatic weapon and hit in the right shoulder and chest as he lifted his arm to throw, he fell backward and dropped the deadly missile. After a moment, he turned and dragged his body forward in an effort to retrieve the grenade and throw it. In critical condition from pain and loss of blood, and unable to grasp the hand grenade firmly enough to hurl it, he chose to sacrifice himself rather than endanger the lives of his men and, with a sweeping motion of his wounded right arm, cradled the grenade under him and absorbed the full impact of the explosion. His exceptional courage, fortitude, and devotion to duty reflect the highest credit upon 1st Lt. Lopez and the U.S. Naval Service. He gallantly gave his life for his country.

3098 ◆ *LORING JR., CHARLES JOSEPH

Rank: Major
Service: U.S. Air Force
Birthday: 2 October 1918
Place of Birth: Portland, Cumberland County, Maine
Date of Death: 22 November 1952
Cemetery: National Memorial of the Pacific (Wall of the Missing)—Honolulu, Hawaii
Entered Service at: Portland, Cumberland County, Maine
Unit: 80th Fighter-Bomber Squadron, 8th Fighter-Bomber Wing
Served as: Flight Leader/Pilot of a F-80
Battle or Place of Action: near Sniper Ridge, North Korea
Date of Action: 22 November 1952
Date of Presentation: 5 May 1954
Place of Presentation: The White House, presented by Pres. Dwight D. Eisenhower to his Widow
Citation: Maj. Loring distinguished himself by conspicuous gallantry and intrepidity at the risk of his life above and beyond the call of duty. While leading a flight of four F-80 type aircraft on a close support mission, Maj. Loring was briefed by a controller to dive-bomb enemy gun positions which were harassing friendly ground troops. After verifying the location of the target, Maj. Loring rolled into his dive bomb run. Throughout the run, extremely accurate ground fire was directed on his aircraft. Disregarding the accuracy and intensity of the ground fire, Maj. Loring aggressively continued to press the attack until his aircraft was hit. At approximately 4,000 feet, he deliberately altered his course and aimed his diving aircraft at active gun emplacements concentrated on a ridge northwest of the briefed target, turned his aircraft 45 degrees to the left, pulled up in a deliberate, controlled manuever, and elected to sacrifice his life by diving his aircraft directly into the midst of the enemy emplacements. His selfless and heroic action completely destroyed the enemy gun emplacement and eliminated a dangerous threat to United Nations ground forces. Maj. Loring's noble spirit, superlative courage, and conspicuous self-sacrifice in inflicting maximum damage on the enemy exemplified valor of the highest degree, and his actions were in keeping with the finest traditions of the U.S. Air Force.
Notes: POW WWII—MIA Korea

3099 ◆ *LYELL, WILLIAM FRANKLIN

Rank: Corporal
Service: U.S. Army
Birthday: 14 February 1929
Place of Birth: Hickman County, Tennessee
Date of Death: 31 August 1951
Place of Death: Chup'a-ri, Korea
Cemetery: Nashville National Cemetery (1-151) (MH)—Madison, Tennessee
Entered Service at: Old Hickory, Davidson County, Tennessee
Unit: Company F, 17th Infantry Regiment, 7th Infantry Division
Battle or Place of Action: near Chup'a-ri, Korea

Date of Action: 31 August 1951
G.O. Number, Date: 4, 9 January 1953
Date of Presentation: 7 January 1953
Place of Presentation: The Pentagon, presented by Sec. of the Army Frank C. Pace to his family
Citation: Cpl. Lyell, a member of company F, distinguished himself by conspicuous gallantry and outstanding courage above and beyond the call of duty in action against the enemy. When his platoon leader was killed, Cpl. Lyell assumed command and led his unit in an assault on strongly fortified enemy positions located on commanding terrain. When his platoon came under vicious, raking fire which halted the forward movement, Cpl. Lyell seized a 57-mm recoilless rifle and unhesitatingly moved ahead to a suitable firing position from which he delivered deadly accurate fire completely destroying an enemy bunker, killing its occuppants. He then returned to his platoon and was resuming the assault when the unit was again subjected to intense hostile fire from two other bunkers. Disregarding his personal safety, armed with grenades, he charged forward hurling grenades into one of the enemy emplacements, and although painfully wounded in this action he pressed on, destroying the bunker and killing six of the foe. He then continued his attack against a third enemy position, throwing grenades as he ran forward, annihilating four enemy soldiers. He then led his platoon to the north slope of the hill where positions were occupied from which effective fire was delivered against the enemy in support of friendly troops moving up. Fearlessly exposing himself to enemy fire, he continuously moved about, directing and encouraging his men until he was mortally wounded by enemy mortar fire. Cpl. Lyell's extraordinary heroism, indomitable courage, and aggressive leadership reflect great credit on himself and are in keeping with the highest traditions of the military service.

3100 ◆ *MARTINEZ, BENITO

Rank: Corporal
Service: U.S. Army
Birthday: 21 April 1932
Place of Birth: Fort Hancock, Hudspeth County, Texas
Date of Death: 6 September 1952
Cemetery: Fort Bliss National Cemetery (B-366A) (MH)—Fort Bliss, Texas
Entered Service at: Fort Hancock, Hudspeth County, Texas
Unit: Company A, 1st Battalion, 27th Infantry Regiment, 25th Infantry Division
Served as: Machine Gunner
Battle or Place of Action: near Satae-ri, Korea
Date of Action: 6 September 1952
G.O. Number, Date: 96, 29 December 1953
Date of Presentation: 16 December 1953
Citation: Cpl. Martinez, a machine gunner with Company A, distinguished himself by conspicuous gallantry and outstanding courage above and beyond the call of duty in action against the enemy. While manning a listening post forward of the main line of resistance, his position was attacked by a hostile force of reinforced company strength. In the bitter fighting which ensued, the enemy infiltrated the defense perimeter and, realizing that encirclement was imminent, Cpl. Martinez elected to remain at his post in an attempt to stem the onslaught. In a daring defense, he raked the attacking troops with crippling fire, inflicting numerous casualties. Although contacted by sound power phone several times, he insisted that no attempt be made to rescue him because of the danger involved. Soon thereafter, the hostile forces rushed the emplacement, forcing him to make a limited withdrawal with only an automatic rifle and pistol to defend himself. After a courageous six-hour stand and shortly before dawn, he called in for the last time, stating that the enemy was converging on his position. His magnificent stand enabled friendly elements to reorganize, attack, and regain the key terrain. Cpl. Martinez' incredible valor and supreme sacrifice reflect lasting glory upon himself and are in keeping with the honored traditions of the military service.

3101 ◆ *MATTHEWS, DANIEL PAUL

Rank: Sergeant
Service: U.S. Marine Corps
Birthday: 31 December 1931
Place of Birth: Van Nuys, Los Angeles County, California
Date of Death: 28 March 1953
Place of Death: Vegas Hill, Korea
Cemetery: Glen Haven Memorial Park (MH)—San Fernando, California
Entered Service at: Van Nuys, Los Angeles County, California
Unit: Company F, 2d Battalion, 7th Marines, 1st Marine Division (Rein)
Served as: Squad Leader
Battle or Place of Action: Vegas Hill, Korea
Date of Action: 28 March 1953
Date of Issue: 29 March 1954
Citation: For conspicuous gallantry and intrepidity at the risk of his life above and beyond the call of duty while serving as a squad leader of Company F, in action against enemy aggressor forces. Participating in a counterattack against a firmly entrenched and well-concealed hostile force which had repelled six previous assaults on a vital enemy-held outpost far forward of the main line of resistance, Sgt. Matthews fearlessly advanced in the attack until his squad was pinned down by a murderous sweep of fire from an enemy machine gun located on the peak of the outpost. Observing that the deadly fire prevented a corpsman from removing a wounded man lying in an open area fully exposed to the brunt of the devastating gunfire, he worked his way to the base of the hostile machine-gun emplacement, leaped onto the rock fortification surrounding the gun and, taking the enemy by complete surprise, singlehandedly charged the hostile emplacement with his rifle. Although severely wounded when the enemy brought a withering hail of fire to bear upon him, he gallantly continued his valiant one-man assault and, firing his rifle with deadly effectiveness, succeeded in killing two of the enemy, routing a third, and completely silencing the enemy weapon, thereby enabling his comrades to evacuate the stricken marine to a safe position. Succumbing to his wounds before aid could reach him, Sgt. Matthews, by his indomitable fighting spirit,

courageous initiative, and resolute determination in the face of almost certain death, served to inspire all who observed him and was directly instrumental in saving the life of his wounded comrade. His great personal valor reflects the highest credit upon himself and enhances the finest traditions of the U.S. Naval Service. He gallantly gave his life for his country.

3102 ◆ *MAUSERT III, FREDERICK WILLIAM

Rank: Sergeant
Service: U.S. Marine Corps
Birthday: 2 May 1931
Place of Birth: Cambridge, Washington County, New York
Date of Death: 12 September 1951
Cemetery: Arlington National Cemetery (12-5559) (MH)—Arlington, Virginia
Entered Service at: Dresher, Montgomery County, Pennsylvania
Unit: Company B, 1st Battalion, 7th Marines, 1st Marine Division (Rein)
Served as: Squad Leader
Battle or Place of Action: Songnap-yong, Korea
Date of Action: 12 September 1951
Date of Presentation: 4 September 1952
Place of Presentation: The Pentagon, presented by Sec. of the Navy Dan A. Kimball to his Mother
Citation: For conspicuous gallantry and intrepidity at the risk of his life above and beyond the call of duty while serving as a squad leader in Company B, in action against enemy aggressor forces. With his company pinned down and suffering heavy casualties under murderous machine-gun, rifle, artillery, and mortar fire laid down from heavily fortified, deeply entrenched hostile strongholds on Hill 673, Sgt. Mausert unhesitatingly left his covered position and ran through a heavily mined and fire-swept area to bring back two critically wounded men to the comparative safety of the lines. Staunchly refusing evacuation despite a painful head wound sustained during his voluntary act, he insisted on remaining with his squad and, with his platoon ordered into the assault moments later, took the point position and led his men in a furious bayonet charge against the first of a literally impregnable series of bunkers. Stunned and knocked to the ground when another bullet struck his helmet, he regained his feet and resumed his drive, personally silencing the machine gun and leading his men in eliminating several other emplacements in the area. Promptly reorganizing his unit for a renewed fight to the final objective on top of the ridge, Sgt. Mausert boldly left his position when the enemy's fire gained momentum and, making a target of himself, boldly advanced alone into the face of the machine gun, drawing the fire away from his men and enabling them to move into position to assault. Again severely wounded when the enemy's fire found its mark, he still refused aid and continued spearheading the assault to the topmost machine-gun nest and bunkers, the last bulwark of the fanatic aggressors. Leaping into the wall of fire, he destroyed another machine gun with grenades before he was mortally wounded by bursting grenades and machine-gun fire. Stouthearted and indomitable, Sgt. Mausert, by his fortitude, great personal valor, and extraordinary heroism in the face of almost certain death, had inspired his men to sweep on, overrun, and finally secure the objective. His unyielding courage throughout reflects the highest credit upon himself and the U.S. Naval Service. He gallantly gave his life for his country.

3103 ◆ *McGOVERN, ROBERT MILTON

Rank: First Lieutenant
Service: U.S. Army
Birthday: 24 January 1928
Place of Birth: Washington, D.C.
Date of Death: 30 January 1951
Cemetery: Arlington National Cemetery (3-1212-C)—Arlington, Virginia
Entered Service at: Washington, D.C.
Unit: Company A, 5th Cavalry Regiment, 1st Cavalry Division
Served as: Platoon Leader
Battle or Place of Action: near Kamyangjan-ni, Korea
Date of Action: 30 January 1951
G.O. Number, Date: 2, 8 January 1952
Citation: 1st Lt. McGovern, a member of Company A, distinguished himself by conspicuous gallantry and intrepidity at the risk of life above and beyond the call of duty in action against an armed enemy of the United Nations. As 1st Lt. McGovern led his platoon up a slope to engage hostile troops emplaced in bunker-type pillbox with connecting trenches, the unit came under heavy machine-gun and rifle fire from the crest of the hill, approximately 75 yards distant. Despite a wound sustained in this initial burst of withering fire, 1st Lt. McGovern, assured the men of his ability to continue on and urged them forward. Forging up the rocky incline, he fearlessly led the platoon to within several yards of its objective when the ruthless foe threw and rolled a vicious barrage of hand grenades on the group and halted the advance. Enemy fire increased in volume and intensity, and 1st Lt. McGovern, realizing that casualties were rapidly increasing and the morale of his men badly shaken, hurled back several grenades before they exploded. Then, disregarding his painful wound and weakened condition, he charged a machine-gun emplacement which was raking his position with flanking fire. When he was within 10 yards of the position a burst of fire ripped the carbine from his hands, but, undaunted, he continued his one-man assault and, firing his pistol and throwing grenades, killed seven hostile soldiers before falling mortally wounded in front of the gun he had silenced. 1st Lt. McGovern's incredible display of valor imbued his men with indomitable resolution to avenge his death. Fixing bayonets and throwing grenades, they charged with such ferocity that hostile positions were overrun and the enemy routed from the hill. The inspirational leadership, unflinching courage, and intrepid actions of 1st Lt. McGovern reflected utmost glory on himself and the honored tradition of the military services.

3104 ◆ McLAUGHLIN, ALFORD LEE

Rank: Private First Class
Service: U.S. Marine Corps

3105 ◆ *MENDONCA, LEROY A.

Birthday: 18 March 1928
Place of Birth: Leeds, Jefferson County, Alabama
Date of Death: 15 January 1977
Cemetery: Mount Hebron Cemetery (MH)—Leeds, Alabama
Entered Service at: Leeds, Jefferson County, Alabama
Unit: Company L, 3d Battalion, 5th Marines, 1st Marine Division (Rein)
Served as: Machine Gunner
Battle or Place of Action: Outpost Bruce, Korea
Date of Action: 4-5 September 1952
Date of Presentation: 27 October 1953
Place of Presentation: The White House, presented by Pres. Dwight D. Eisenhower
Citation: For conspicuous gallantry and intrepidity at the risk of his life above and beyond the call of duty while serving as a machine gunner of Company L, in action against enemy aggressor forces on the night of 4-5 September 1952. Volunteering for his second continuous tour of duty on a strategic combat outpost far in advance of the main line of resistance, Pfc. McLaughlin, although operating under a barrage of enemy artillery and mortar fire, set up plans for the defense of his position which proved decisive in the successful defense of the outpost. When hostile forces attacked in battalion strength during the night, he maintained a constant flow of devastating fire upon the enemy, alternately employing two machine guns, a carbine, and hand grenades. Although painfully wounded, he bravely fired the machine guns from the hip until his hands became blistered by the extreme heat of the weapons and, placing the guns on the ground to allow them to cool, continued to defend the position with his carbine and grenades. Standing up in full view, he shouted words of encouragement to his comrades above the din of battle and, throughout a series of fanatical enemy attacks, sprayed the surrounding area with deadly fire, accounting for an estimated 150 enemy dead and 50 wounded. By his indomitable courage, superb leadership, and valiant fighting spirit in the face of overwhelming odds, Pfc. McLaughlin served to inspire his fellow marines in their gallant stand against the enemy and was directly instrumental in preventing the vital outpost from falling into the hands of a determined and numerically superior hostile force. His outstanding heroism and unwavering devotion to duty reflect the highest credit upon himself and enhance the finest traditions of the U.S. Naval Service.

3105 ◆ *MENDONCA, LEROY A.

Rank: Sergeant
Service: U.S. Army
Birthday: 2 August 1932
Place of Birth: Honolulu, Honolulu County, Territory of Hawaii
Date of Death: 4 July 1951
Cemetery: National Memorial Cemetery of the Pacific (Q-1408) (MH)—Honolulu, Hawaii
Entered Service at: Honolulu, Honolulu County, Territory of Hawaii
Unit: Company B, 7th Infantry Regiment, 3d Infantry Division

Battle or Place of Action: near Chich-on, Korea
Date of Action: 4 July 1951
G.O. Number, Date: 83, 3 September 1952
Date of Presentation: 14 August 1952
Place of Presentation: The Pentagon, presented by Gen. Omar N. Bradley to his Mother
Citation: Sgt. LeRoy A. Mendonca, distinguished himself by conspicuous gallantry above and beyond the call of duty in action against the enemy. After his platoon, in an exhaustive fight, had captured Hill 586, the newly won positions were assaulted during the night by a numerically superior enemy force. When the 1st Platoon positions were outflanked and under great pressure and the platoon was ordered to withdraw to a secondary line of defense, Sgt. Mendonca voluntarily remained in an exposed position and covered the platoon's withdrawal. Although under murderous enemy fire, he fired his weapon and hurled grenades at the onrushing enemy until his supply of ammunition was exhausted. He fought on, clubbing with his rifle and using his bayonet until he was mortally wounded. After the action it was estimated that Sgt. Mendonca had accounted for 37 enemy casualties. His daring actions stalled the crushing assault, protecting the platoon's withdrawal to secondary positions, and enabling the entire unit to repel the enemy attack and retain possession of the vital hilltop position. Sgt. Mendonca's extraordinary gallantry and exemplary valor are in keeping with the highest traditions of the U.S. Army.

3106 ◆ MILLETT, LEWIS LEE "RED"

Rank: Captain (highest rank: Colonel)
Service: U.S. Army
Birthday: 15 December 1920
Place of Birth: Mechanic Falls, Androscoggin County, Maine
Entered Service at: Mechanic Falls, Androscoggin County, Maine
Unit: Company E, 2d Battalion, 27th Infantry Regiment, 25th Infantry Division
Served as: Company Commander
Battle or Place of Action: vicinity of Hill 180, Soam-Ni, Korea
Date of Action: 7 February 1951
G.O. Number, Date: 69, 2 August 1951
Date of Presentation: 5 July 1951
Place of Presentation: The White House (Rose Garden), presented by Pres. Harry S. Truman
Citation: Capt. Millett, Company E, distinguished himself by conspicuous gallantry and intrepidity above and beyond the call of duty in action. While personally leading his company in an attack against a strongly held position, he noted that the 1st Platoon was pinned down by small-arms, automatic, and antitank fire. Capt. Millett ordered the 3d Platoon forward, placed himself at the head of the two platoons, and, with fixed bayonet, led the assault up the fire-swept hill. In the fierce charge Capt. Millett bayoneted two enemy soldiers and boldly continued on, throwing grenades, clubbing and bayoneting the enemy, while urging his men forward by shouting encouragement. Despite vicious opposing fire, the

whirlwind hand-to-hand assault carried to the crest of the hill. His dauntless leadership and personal courage so inspired his men that they stormed into the hostile position and used their bayonets with such lethal effect that the enemy fled in wild disorder. During this fierce onslaught Capt. Millett was wounded by grenade fragments but refused evacuation until the objective was taken and firmly secured. The superb leadership, conspicuous courage, and consummate devotion to duty demonstrated by Capt. Millett were directly responsible for the successful accomplishment of a hazardous mission and reflect the highest credit on himself and the heroic traditions of the military service.

3107 ◆ *MITCHELL, FRANK NICIAS

Rank: First Lieutenant
Service: U.S. Marine Corps
Birthday: 18 August 1921
Place of Birth: Indian Gap, Hamilton County, Texas
Date of Death: 26 November 1950
Cemetery: National Memorial of the Pacific (Wall of the Missing)—Honolulu, Hawaii; Roaring Springs Cemetery (MH)('In Memory' marker)—Roaring Springs, Texas
Entered Service at: Roaring Springs, Motley County, Texas
Unit: Company A, 1st Battalion, 7th Marines, 1st Marine Division (Rein)
Served as: Platoon Leader
Battle or Place of Action: near Hansan-ni, Korea
Date of Action: 26 November 1950
Place of Presentation: Atlanta, GA, to his widow, Beverly Banks Mitchell and his daughter, Barbara
Citation: For conspicuous gallantry and intrepidity at the risk of his life above and beyond the call of duty as leader of a rifle platoon of Company A, in action against enemy aggressor forces. Leading his platoon in point position during a patrol by his company through a thickly wooded and snow-covered area in the vicinity of Hansan-ni, 1st Lt. Mitchell acted immediately when the enemy suddenly opened fire at point-blank range, pinning down his forward elements and inflicting numerous casualties in his ranks. Boldly dashing to the front under blistering fire from automatic weapons and small arms, he seized an automatic rifle from one of the wounded men and effectively trained it against the attackers and, when his ammunition was expended, picked up and hurled grenades with deadly accuracy, at the same time directing and encouraging his men in driving the outnumbering enemy from his position. Maneuvering to set up a defense when the enemy furiously counterattacked to the front and left flank, 1st Lt. Mitchell, despite wounds sustained early in the action, reorganized his platoon under the devastating fire and spearheaded a fierce hand-to-hand struggle to repulse the onslaught. Asking for volunteers to assist in searching for and evacuating the wounded, he personally led a party of litter bearers through the hostile lines in growing darkness and, although suffering intense pain from multiple wounds, stormed ahead and waged a singlehanded battle against the enemy, successfully covering the withdrawal of his men before he was fatally struck down by a burst of small-arms fire. Stouthearted and indomitable in the face of tremendous odds, 1st Lt. Mitchell, by his fortitude, great personal valor, and extraordinary heroism, saved the lives of several marines and inflicted heavy casualties among the aggressors. His unyielding courage throughout reflects the highest credit upon himself and the U.S. Naval Service. He gallantly gave his life for his country.
Notes: MIA

3108 ◆ MIYAMURA, HIROSHI

Rank: Corporal (highest rank: Staff Sergeant)
Service: U.S. Army
Birthday: 6 October 1925
Place of Birth: Gallup, McKinley County, New Mexico
Entered Service at: Gallup, McKinley County, New Mexico
Unit: Company H, 2d Battalion, 7th Infantry Regiment, 3d Infantry Division
Served as: Squad Leader
Battle or Place of Action: near Taejon-ni, Korea
Date of Action: 24-25 April 1951
G.O. Number, Date: 85, 4 November 1953
Date of Presentation: 27 October 1953
Place of Presentation: The White House, presented by Pres. Dwight D. Eisenhower
Citation: Cpl. Miyamura, a member of Company H, distinguished himself by conspicuous gallantry and intrepidity above and beyond the call of duty in action against the enemy. On the night of 24 April, Company H was occupying a defensive position when the enemy fanatically attacked, threatening to overrun the position. Cpl. Miyamura, a machine-gun squad leader, aware of the imminent danger to his men, unhesitatingly jumped from his shelter wielding his bayonet in close hand-to-hand combat, killing approximately 10 of the enemy. Returning to his position, he administered first aid to the wounded and directed their evacuation. As another savage assault hit the line, he manned his machine gun and delivered withering fire until his ammunition was expended. He ordered the squad to withdraw while he stayed behind to render the gun inoperative. He then bayoneted his way through infiltrated enemy soldiers to a second gun emplacement and assisted in its operation. When the intensity of the attack necessitated the withdrawal of the company Cpl. Miyamura ordered his men to fall back while he remained to cover their movement. He killed more than 50 of the enemy before his ammunition was depleted and he was severely wounded. He maintained his magnificent stand despite his painful wounds, continuing to repel the attack until his position was overrun. When last seen he was fighting ferociously against an overwhelming number of enemy soldiers. Cpl. Miyamura's indomitable heroism and consummate devotion to duty reflect the utmost glory on himself and uphold the illustrious traditions on the military service.
Notes: POW

3109 ◆ MIZE, OLA LEE

Rank: Master Sergeant (rank at time of action: Sergeant) (highest rank: Colonel)
Service: U.S. Army

Birthday: 28 August 1931
Place of Birth: Albertville, Marshall County, Alabama
Entered Service at: Gadsden, Etowah County, Alabama
Unit: 2d Platoon, Company K, 15th Infantry Regiment, 3d Infantry Division
Served as: Assistant Platoon Sergeant
Battle or Place of Action: near Surang-ni, Korea
Date of Action: 10-11 June 1953
G.O. Number, Date: 70, 24 September 1954
Date of Presentation: 7 September 1954
Place of Presentation: Denver Colorado, presented by Pres. Dwight D. Eisenhower
Citation: M/Sgt. Mize, a member of Company K, distinguished himself by conspicuous gallantry and outstanding courage above and beyond the call of duty in action against the enemy. Company K was committed to the defense of "Outpost Harry," a strategically valuable position, when the enemy launched a heavy attack. Learning that a comrade on a friendly listening post had been wounded, he moved through the intense barrage, accompanied by a medical aidman, and rescued the wounded soldier. On returning to the main position he established an effective defense system and inflicted heavy casualties against attacks from determined enemy assault forces which had penetrated into trenches within the outpost area. During his fearless actions he was blown down by artillery and grenade blasts three times, but each time he dauntlessly returned to his position, tenaciously fighting and successfully repelling hostile attacks. When enemy onslaughts ceased, he took his few men and moved from bunker to bunker, firing through apertures and throwing grenades at the foe, neutralizing their positions. When an enemy soldier stepped out behind a comrade, prepared to fire, M/Sgt. Mize killed him, saving the life of his fellow soldier. After rejoining the platoon, moving from man to man, distributing ammunition, and shouting words of encouragement he observed a friendly machine-gun position overrun. He immediately fought his way to the position, killing 10 of the enemy and dispersing the remainder. Fighting back to the command post, and finding several friendly wounded there, he took a position to protect them. Later, securing a radio, he directed friendly artillery fire upon the attacking enemy's routes of approach. At dawn he helped regroup for a counterattack which successfully drove the enemy from the outpost. M/Sgt. Mize's valorous conduct and unflinching courage reflect lasting glory upon himself and uphold the noble traditions of the military service.

3110 ◆ *MONEGAN JR., WALTER CARLETON

Rank: Private First Class
Service: U.S. Marine Corps
Birthday: 25 December 1930
Place of Birth: Melrose, Middlesex County, Massachusetts
Date of Death: 20 September 1950
Cemetery: Arlington National Cemetery (34-4513) (MH)—Arlington, Virginia
Entered Service at: Seattle, King County, Washington
Unit: Company F, 2d Battalion, 1st Marines, 1st Marine Division (Rein)
Served as: Rocket Gunner
Battle or Place of Action: near Sosa-ri, Korea
Date of Action: 17-20 September 1950
Date of Presentation: 8 February 1952
Place of Presentation: The Pentagon, presented by Under Sec. of the Navy Francis P. Whitehair to his Widow
Citation: For conspicuous gallantry and intrepidity at the risk of his life above and beyond the call of duty while serving as a rocket gunner attached to Company F, and in action against enemy aggressor forces. Dug in on a hill overlooking the main Seoul highway when six enemy tanks threatened to break through the battalion position during a predawn attack on 17 September, Pfc. Monegan promptly moved forward with his bazooka, under heavy hostile automatic-weapons fire and engaged the lead tank at a range of less than 50 yards. After scoring a direct hit and killing the sole surviving tankman with his carbine as he came through the escape hatch, he boldly fired two more rounds of ammunition at the oncoming tanks, disorganizing the attack and enabling our tank crews to continue blasting with their 90-mm guns. With his own and an adjacent company's position threatened by annihilation when an overwhelming enemy tank-infantry force bypassed the area and proceeded toward the battalion command post during the early morning of September 20, he seized his rocket launcher and, in total darkness, charged down the slope of the hill where the tanks had broken through. Quick to act when an illuminating shell lit the area, he scored a direct hit on one of the tanks as hostile rifle and automatic-weapons fire raked the area at close-range. Again exposing himself, he fired another round to destroy a second tank and, as the rear tank turned to retreat, stood upright to fire and was fatally struck down by hostile machine-gun fire when another illuminating shell silhouetted him against the sky. Pfc. Monegan's daring initiative, gallant fighting spirit, and courageous devotion to duty were contributing factors in the success of his company in repelling the enemy, and his self-sacrificing efforts throughout sustain and enhance the highest traditions of the U.S. Naval Service. He gallantly gave his life for his country.

3111 ◆ *MORELAND, WHITT LLOYD

Rank: Private First Class
Service: U.S. Marine Corps
Birthday: 7 March 1930
Place of Birth: Waco, McLennan County, Texas
Date of Death: 29 May 1951
Cemetery: Whittington Cemetery (MH)—Mount Ida, Arkansas
Entered Service at: Austin, Travis County, Texas
Unit: Company C, 1st Battalion, 5th Marines, 1st Marine Division (Rein)
Served as: Intelligence Scout
Battle or Place of Action: Kwagch'i-Dong, Korea
Date of Action: 29 May 1951
Date of Presentation: 19 July 1951
Place of Presentation: Austin Texas
Citation: For conspicuous gallantry and intrepidity at the risk of his life above and beyond the call of duty while serving

as an intelligence scout attached to Company C, in action against enemy aggressor forces. Voluntarily accompanying a rifle platoon in a daring assault against a strongly defended enemy hill position, Pfc. Moreland delivered accurate rifle fire on the hostile emplacement and thereby aided materially in seizing the objective. After the position had been secured, he unhesitatingly led a party forward to neutralize an enemy bunker which he had observed some 400 meters beyond, and moving boldly through a fire-swept area, almost reached the hostile emplacement when the enemy launched a volley of hand grenades on his group. Quick to act despite the personal danger involved, he kicked several of the grenades off the ridgeline where they exploded harmlessly and, while attempting to kick away another, slipped and fell near the deadly missile. Aware that the sputtering grenade would explode before he could regain his feet and dispose of it, he shouted a warning to his comrades, covered the missile with his body and absorbed the full blast of the explosion, but in saving his companions from possible injury or death, was mortally wounded. His heroic initiative and valiant spirit of self-sacrifice in the face of certain death reflect the highest credit upon Pfc. Moreland and the U.S. Naval Service. He gallantly gave his life for his country.

3112 ◆ *MOYER, DONALD RAYMOND

Rank: Sergeant First Class
Service: U.S. Army
Birthday: 15 April 1930
Place of Birth: Pontiac, Oakland County, Michigan
Date of Death: 20 May 1951
Cemetery: Perry Mount Park Cemetery (MH)—Pontiac, Michigan
Entered Service at: Keego Harbor, Oakland County, Michigan
Unit: Company E, 35th Infantry Regiment, 25th Infantry Division
Served as: Assistant Platoon Leader
Battle or Place of Action: near Seoul, Korea
Date of Action: 20 May 1951
G.O. Number, Date: 19, 1 February 1952
Date of Presentation: 16 January 1952
Place of Presentation: The Pentagon, presented by Sec. of Defense Robert Lovett to his Father
Citation: Sfc. Moyer, assistant platoon leader, Company E, distinguished himself by conspicuous gallantry and intrepidity at the risk of his life above and beyond the call of duty in action against an armed enemy of the United Nations. Sfc. Moyer's platoon was committed to attack and secure commanding terrain stubbornly defended by a numerically superior hostile force emplaced in well-fortified positions.
Advancing up the rocky hill, the leading elements came under intense automatic-weapons, small-arms, and grenade fire, wounding the platoon leader and platoon sergeant. Sfc. Moyer, realizing the success of the mission was imperiled, rushed to the head of the faltering column, assumed command, and urged the men forward. Inspired by Sfc. Moyer's unflinching courage, the troops responded magnificently, but as they reached the final approaches to the rugged crest of the hill, enemy fire increased in volume and intensity and the fanatical foe showered the platoon with grenades. Undaunted, the valiant group forged ahead, and as they neared the top of the hill, the enemy hurled a grenade into their midst. Sfc. Moyer, fully aware of the odds against him, unhesitatingly threw himself on the grenade, absorbing the full blast of the explosion with his body. Although mortally wounded in this fearless display of valor, Sfc. Moyer's intrepid act saved several of his comrades from death or serious injury, and his inspirational leadership and consummate devotion to duty contributed significantly to the subsequent seizure of the enemy stronghold and reflect lasting glory on himself and the noble traditions of the military service.

3113 ◆ MURPHY, RAYMOND GERALD

Rank: Second Lieutenant (highest rank: Captain)
Service: U.S. Marine Corps
Birthday: 14 January 1930
Place of Birth: Pueblo, Pueblo County, Colorado
Entered Service at: Pueblo, Pueblo County, Colorado
Unit: 1st Platoon, Company A, 1st Battalion, 5th Marines, 1st Marine Division (Rein)
Served as: Platoon Commander
Battle or Place of Action: Ungok Hill, west of Panmunjan, Korea
Date of Action: 3 February 1953
Date of Presentation: 27 October 1953
Place of Presentation: The White House, presented by Pres. Dwight D. Eisenhower
Citation: For conspicuous gallantry and intrepidity at the risk of his life above and beyond the call of duty as a platoon commander of Company A, in action against enemy aggressor forces. Although painfully wounded by fragments from an enemy mortar shell while leading his evacuation platoon in a support of assault units attacking a cleverly concealed and well-entrenched hostile force occupying commanding ground, 2d Lt. Murphy steadfastly refused medical aid and continued to lead his men up a hill through a withering barrage of hostile mortar and small-arms fire, skillfully maneuvering his force from one position to the next and shouting words of encouragement. Undeterred by the increasing intense enemy fire, he immediately located casualties as they fell and made several trips up and down the fire-swept hill to direct evacuation teams to the wounded, personally carrying many of the stricken marines to safety. When reinforcements were needed by the assaulting elements, 2d Lt. Murphy employed part of his unit as support and, during the ensuing battle, personally killed two of the enemy with his pistol. With all the wounded evacuated and the assaulting units beginning to disengage, he remained behind with a carbine to cover the movement of friendly forces off the hill and, though suffering intense pain from his previous wounds, seized an automatic rifle to provide more firepower when the enemy reappeared in the trenches. After reaching the base of the hill, he organized a search party and again ascended the slope for a final check on missing marines, locating and carrying the bodies of a machine-gun crew back down the hill. Wounded a second time while conducting the entire force to the line of depar-

ture through a continuing barrage of enemy small-arms, artillery, and mortar fire, he again refused medical assistance until assured that every one of his men, including all casualties, had preceded him to the main lines. His resolute and inspiring leadership, exceptional fortitude, and great personal valor reflect the highest credit upon 2d Lt. Murphy and enhance the finest traditions of the U.S. Naval Service.

3114 ◆ MYERS, REGINALD RODNEY

Rank: Major (highest rank: Colonel)
Service: U.S. Marine Corps
Birthday: 26 November 1919
Place of Birth: Boise, Ada County, Idaho
Entered Service at: Boise, Ada County, Idaho
Unit: 3d Battalion, 1st Marines, 1st Marine Division (Rein)
Served as: Battalion Executive Officer
Battle or Place of Action: near Hagaru-ri, Korea
Date of Action: 29 November 1950
Date of Presentation: 29 October 1951
Place of Presentation: The White House, presented by Pres. Harry S. Truman
Citation: For conspicuous gallantry and intrepidity at the risk of his life above and beyond the call of duty as executive officer of the 3d Battalion, in action against enemy aggressor forces. Assuming command of a composite unit of Army and Marine service and headquarters elements totaling approximately 250 men, during a critical stage in the vital defense of the strategically important military base at Hagaru-ri, Maj. Myers immediately initiated a determined and aggressive counterattack against a well-entrenched and cleverly concealed enemy force numbering an estimated 4,000. Severely handicapped by a lack of trained personnel and experienced leaders in his valiant efforts to regain maximum ground prior to daylight, he persisted in constantly exposing himself to intense, accurate, and sustained hostile fire in order to direct and supervise the employment of his men and to encourage and spur them on in pressing the attack. Inexorably moving forward up the steep, snow-covered slope with his depleted group in the face of apparently insurmountable odds, he concurrently directed artillery and mortar fire with superb skill and although losing 170 of his men during 14 hours of raging combat in subzero temperature, continued to reorganize his unit and spearhead the attack which resulted in 600 enemy killed and 500 wounded. By his exceptional and valorous leadership throughout, Maj. Myers contributed directly to the success of his unit in restoring the perimeter. His resolute spirit of self-sacrifice and unfaltering devotion to duty enhance and sustain the highest traditions of the U.S. Naval Service.

3115 ◆ *OBREGON, EUGENE ARNOLD

Rank: Private First Class
Service: U.S. Marine Corps
Birthday: 12 November 1930
Place of Birth: Los Angeles, Los Angeles County, California
Date of Death: 26 September 1950
Place of Death: Seoul, Korea
Cemetery: Calvary Cemetery—East Los Angeles, California
Entered Service at: Los Angeles, Los Angeles County, California
Unit: Company G, 3d Battalion, 5th Marines, 1st Marine Division (Rein)
Served as: Ammunition Carrier
Battle or Place of Action: Seoul, Korea
Date of Action: 26 September 1950
Date of Presentation: 30 August 1951
Place of Presentation: The Pentagon, presented by Sec. of the Navy Dan A. Kimball to his parents
Citation: For conspicuous gallantry and intrepidity at the risk of his life above and beyond the call of duty while serving with Company G, in action against enemy aggressor forces. While serving as an ammunition carrier of a machine-gun squad in a marine rifle company which was temporarily pinned down by hostile fire, Pfc. Obregon observed a fellow marine fall wounded in the line of fire. Armed only with a pistol, he unhesitating dashed from his covered position to the side of the casualty. Firing his pistol with one hand as he ran, he grasped his comrade by the arm with his other hand and, despite the great peril to himself dragged him to the side of the road. Still under enemy fire, he was bandaging the man's wounds when hostile troops of approximately platoon strength began advancing toward his position. Quickly seizing the wounded marine's carbine, he placed his own body as a shield in front of him and lay there firing accurately and effectively into the hostile group until he himself was fatally wounded by enemy machine-gun fire. By his courageous fighting spirit, fortitude, and loyal devotion to duty, Pfc. Obregon enabled his fellow marines to rescue the wounded man and aided essentially in repelling the attack, thereby sustaining and enhancing the highest traditions of the U.S. Naval Service. He gallantly gave his life for his country.

3116 ◆ O'BRIEN JR., GEORGE HERMAN

Rank: Second Lieutenant (highest rank: Major)
Service: U.S. Marine Corps Reserve
Birthday: 10 September 1926
Place of Birth: Fort Worth, Tarrant County, Texas
Entered Service at: Big Spring, Howard County, Texas
Unit: 1st Platoon, Company H, 3d Battalion, 7th Marines, 1st Marine Division (Rein)
Served as: Rifle Platoon Commander
Battle or Place of Action: The Hook, Korea
Date of Action: 27 October 1952
Date of Presentation: 27 October 1953
Place of Presentation: The White House, presented by Pres. Dwight D. Eisenhower
Citation: For conspicuous gallantry and intrepidity at the risk of his life above and beyond the call of duty as a rifle platoon commander of Company H, in action against enemy aggressor forces. With his platoon subjected to an intense mortar and artillery bombardment while preparing to assault a vitally important hill position on the main line of resistance which had been overrun by a numerically superior enemy force on the preceding night, 2d Lt. O'Brien leaped from his trench when the attack signal was given and, shouting for his men to follow, raced across an exposed saddle and up the

enemy-held hill through a virtual hail of deadly small-arms, artillery, and mortar fire. Although shot through the arm and thrown to the ground by hostile automatic-weapons fire as he neared the well-entrenched enemy position, he bravely regained his feet, waved his men onward, and continued to spearhead the assault, pausing only long enough to go to the aid of a wounded marine. Encountering the enemy at close-range, he proceeded to hurl hand grenades into the bunkers and, utilizing his carbine to best advantage in savage hand-to-hand combat, succeeded in killing at least three of the enemy. Struck down by the concussion of grenades on three occasions during the subsequent action, he steadfastly refused to be evacuated for medical treatment and continued to lead his platoon in the assault for a period of nearly four hours, repeatedly encouraging his men and maintaining superb direction of the unit. With the attack halted, he set up a defense with his remaining forces to prepare for a counterattack, personally checking each position, attending to the wounded and expediting their evacuation. When a relief of the position was effected by another unit, he remained to cover the withdrawal and to assure that no wounded were left behind. By his exceptionally daring and forceful leadership in the face of overwhelming odds, 2d Lt. O'Brien served as a constant source of inspiration to all who observed him and was greatly instrumental in the recapture of a strategic position on the main line of resistance. His indomitable determination and valiant fighting spirit reflect the highest credit upon himself and enhance the finest traditions of the U.S. Naval Service.

3117 ◆ *OUELLETTE, JOSEPH R.

Rank: Private First Class
Service: U.S. Army
Birthday: 1930
Place of Birth: Lowell, Middlesex County, Massachusetts
Date of Death: 3 September 1950
Cemetery: St. Joseph's Cemetery (MH)—East Chelmsford, Massachusetts
Entered Service at: Lowell, Middlesex County, Massachusetts
Unit: Company H, 9th Infantry Regiment, 2d Infantry Division
Battle or Place of Action: near Yongsan, Korea
Date of Action: 31 August-3 September 1950
G.O. Number, Date: 25, 25 April 1951
Date of Presentation: 3 April 1951
Place of Presentation: The Pentagon, presented by Gen. Omar N. Bradley to his Mother
Citation: Pfc. Ouellette distinguished himself by conspicuous gallantry and intrepidity in action against the enemy in the Makioug-Chang River salient. When an enemy assault cut off and surrounded his unit, he voluntarily made a reconnaissance of a nearby hill under intense enemy fire to locate friendly troop positions and obtain information of the enemy's strength and location. Finding that friendly troops were not on the hill, he worked his way back to his unit under heavy fire. Later, when an airdrop of water was made outside the perimeter, he again braved enemy fire in an attempt to retrieve water for his unit. Finding the dropped cans broken and devoid of water, he returned to his unit. His heroic attempt greatly increased his comrades' morale. When ammunition and grenades ran low, Pfc. Ouellette again slipped out of the perimeter to collect these from the enemy dead. After collecting grenades he was attacked by an enemy soldier. He killed this enemy in hand-to-hand combat, gathered up the ammunition, and returned to his unit. When the enemy attacked on 3 September, they assaulted his position with grenades. On six occasions Pfc. Ouellette leaped from his foxhole to escape exploding grenades. In doing so, he had to face enemy small-arms fire. He continued his resistance, despite a severe wound, until he lost his life. The extraordinary heroism and intrepidity displayed by Pfc. Ouellette reflect the highest credit on himself and are in keeping with the esteemed traditions of the military service.

3118 ◆ *PAGE, JOHN UPSHUR DENNIS

Rank: Lieutenant Colonel
Service: U.S. Army
Birthday: 8 February 1904
Place of Birth: Malahi Island, Luzon, Philippine Islands
Date of Death: 10 December 1950
Cemetery: Arlington National Cemetery (4-2743-A-B)—Arlington, Virginia
Entered Service at: St. Paul, Ramsey County, Minnesota
Unit: Attached to the 52d Transportation Truck Battalion, X Corps Artillery
Served as: Artillery Officer
Battle or Place of Action: near Chosin Reservoir, Korea
Date of Action: 29 November-10 December 1950
G.O. Number, Date: 21, 25 April 1957
Date of Issue: 19 December 1956
Citation: Lt. Col. Page, a member of X Corps Artillery, distinguished himself by conspicuous gallantry and intrepidity in action above and beyond the call of duty in a series of exploits. On 29 November, Lt. Col. Page left X Corps Headquarters at Hamhung with the mission of establishing traffic control on the main supply route to 1st Marine Division positions and those of some Army elements on the Chosin Reservoir plateau. Having completed his mission Lt. Col. Page was free to return to the safety of Hamhung but chose to remain on the plateau to aid an isolated signal station, thus being cut off with elements of the marine division. After rescuing his jeep driver by breaking up an ambush near a destroyed bridge, Lt. Col. Page reached the lines of a surrounded marine garrison at Koto-ri. He then voluntarily developed and trained a reserve force of assorted army troops trapped with the marines. By exemplary leadership and tireless devotion he made an effective tactical unit available. In order that casualties might be evacuated, an airstrip was improvised on frozen ground partly outside of the Koto-ri defense perimeter which was continually under enemy attack. During two such attacks, Lt. Col. Page exposed himself on the airstrip to direct fire on the enemy and twice mounted the rear deck of a tank, manning the machine gun on the turret to drive the enemy back into a no man's land. On 3 December while being flown low over enemy lines in a light

observation plane, Lt. Col. Page dropped hand grenades on Chinese positions and sprayed foxholes with automatic fire from his carbine. After 10 days of constant fighting the marine and army units in the vicinity of the Chosin Reservoir had succeeded in gathering at the edge of the plateau and Lt. Col. Page was flown to Hamhung to arrange for artillery support of the beleaguered troops attempting to break out. Again Lt. Col. Page refused an opportunity to remain in safety and returned to give every assistance to his comrades. As the column slowly moved south Lt. Col. Page joined the rear guard. When it neared the entrance to a narrow pass it came under frequent attacks on both flanks. Mounting an abandoned tank Lt. Col. Page manned the machine gun, braved heavy return fire, and covered the passing vehicles until the danger diminished. Later when another attack threatened his section of the convoy, then in the middle of the pass, Lt. Col. Page took a machine gun to the hillside and delivered effective counterfire, remaining exposed while men and vehicles passed through the ambuscade. On the night of 10 December the convoy reached the bottom of the pass but was halted by a strong enemy force at the front and on both flanks. Deadly small-arms fire poured into the column. Realizing the danger to the column as it lay motionless, Lt. Col. Page fought his way to the head of the column and plunged forward into the heart of the hostile position. His intrepid action so surprised the enemy that their ranks became disordered and suffered heavy casualties. Heedless of his safety, as he had been throughout the preceding 10 days, Lt. Col. Page remained forward, fiercely engaging the enemy singlehandedly until mortally wounded. By his valiant and aggressive spirit Lt. Col. Page enabled friendly forces to stand off the enemy. His outstanding courage, unswerving devotion to duty, and supreme self-sacrifice reflect great credit upon Lt. Col. Page and are in the highest tradition of the military service.

3119 ◆ *PENDLETON, CHARLES F.

Rank: Corporal
Service: U.S. Army
Birthday: 26 September 1931
Place of Birth: Camden, Benton County, Tennessee
Date of Death: 17 July 1953
Cemetery: Laurel Land Memorial Cemetery—Fort Worth, Texas
Entered Service at: Fort Worth, Texas
Unit: Company D, 15th Infantry Regiment, 3d Infantry Division
Served as: Machine Gunner
Battle or Place of Action: near Choo Gung-Dong, Korea
Date of Action: 16-17 July 1953
Citation: Cpl. Pendleton, a machine gunner with Company D, distinguished himself by conspicuous gallantry and indomitable courage above and beyond the call of duty in action against the enemy. After consolidating and establishing a defensive perimeter on a key terrain feature, friendly elements were attacked by a large hostile force. Cpl. Pendleton delivered deadly accurate fire into the approaching troops, killing approximately 15 and disorganizing the remainder with grenades. Unable to protect the flanks because of the narrow confines of the trench, he removed the machine gun from the tripod and, exposed to enemy observation, positioned it on his knee to improve his firing vantage. Observing a hostile infantryman jumping into the position, intent on throwing a grenade at his comrades, he whirled about and killed the attacker, then inflicted such heavy casualties on the enemy force that they retreated to regroup. After reorganizing, a second wave of hostile soldiers moved forward in an attempt to overrun the position and, later, when a hostile grenade landed nearby, Cpl. Pendleton quickly retrieved and hurled it back at the foe. Although he was burned by the hot shells ejecting from his weapon, and he was wounded by a grenade, he refused evacuation and continued to fire on the assaulting force. As enemy action increased in tempo, his machine gun was destroyed by a grenade but, undaunted, he grabbed a carbine and continued his heroic defense until mortally wounded by a mortar burst. Cpl. Pendleton's unflinching courage, gallant self-sacrifice, and consummate devotion to duty reflect lasting glory upon himself and uphold the finest traditions of the military service.

3120 ◆ *PHILLIPS, LEE HUGH

Rank: Corporal
Service: U.S. Marine Corps
Birthday: 3 February 1930
Place of Birth: Stockbridge, Henry County, Georgia
Date of Death: 27 November 1950
Cemetery: National Memorial of the Pacific (Wall of the Missing)—Honolulu, Hawaii; Marietta National Cemetery (B8) ('In Memory' marker)—Marietta, Georgia
Entered Service at: Ben Hill, Fulton County, Georgia
Unit: Company E, 2d Battalion, 7th Marines, 1st Marine Division (Rein)
Served as: Squad Leader
Battle or Place of Action: Korea
Date of Action: 4 November 1950
Citation: For conspicuous gallantry and intrepidity at the risk of his life above and beyond the call of duty while serving as a squad leader of Company E, in action against enemy aggressor forces. Assuming the point position in the attack against a strongly defended and well-entrenched numerically superior enemy force occupying a vital hill position which had been unsuccessfully assaulted on five separate occasions by units of the Marine Corps and other friendly forces, Cpl. Phillips fearlessly led his men in a bayonet charge up the precipitous slope under a deadly hail of hostile mortar, small-arms, and machine-gun fire. Quickly rallying his squad when it was pinned down by heavy and accurate mortar barrage, he continued to lead his men through the bombarded area and, although only five members were left in the casualty-ridden unit, gained the military crest of the hill where he was immediately subjected to an enemy counterattack. Although greatly outnumbered by an estimated enemy squad, Cpl. Phillips boldly engaged the hostile force with hand grenades and rifle fire and, exhorting his gallant group of marines to follow him, stormed forward to completely overwhelm the enemy. With only three men now left in his squad, he proceeded to spearhead an assault on the last remaining strongpoint which was

defended by four of the enemy on a rocky and almost inaccessible portion of the hill position. Using one hand to climb up the extremely hazardous precipice, he hurled grenades with the other and, with two remaining comrades, succeeded in annihilating the pocket of resistance and in consolidating the position. Immediately subjected to a sharp counterattack by an estimated enemy squad, he skillfully directed the fire of his men and employed his own weapon with deadly effectiveness to repulse the numerically superior hostile force. By his valiant leadership, indomitable fighting spirit, and resolute determination in the face of heavy odds, Cpl. Phillips served to inspire all who observed him and was directly responsible for the destruction of the enemy stronghold. His great personal valor refects the highest credit upon himself and enhances and sustains the finest traditions of the U.S. Naval Service.
Notes: MIA

3121 ◆ *PILILAAU, HERBERT K.

Rank: Private First Class
Service: U.S. Army
Birthday: 10 October 1928
Place of Birth: Waianae, Oahu, Territory of Hawaii
Date of Death: 17 September 1951
Cemetery: National Memorial Cemetery of the Pacific (P-127)—Honolulu, Hawaii
Entered Service at: Oahu, Territory of Hawaii
Unit: Company C, 23d Infantry Regiment, 2d Infantry Division
Battle or Place of Action: near Pia-ri, Korea
Date of Action: 17 September 1951
G.O. Number, Date: 58, 18 June 1952
Date of Presentation: 26 March 1952
Place of Presentation: The Pentagon, presented by Sec. of the Army Frank C. Pace to his Father
Citation: Pfc. Pililaau, a member of Company C, distinguished himself by conspicuous gallantry and outstanding courage above and beyond the call of duty in action against the enemy. The enemy sent wave after wave of fanatical troops against his platoon which held a key terrain feature on "Heartbreak Ridge." Valiantly defending its position, the unit repulsed each attack until ammunition became practically exhausted and it was ordered to withdraw to a new position. Voluntarily remaining behind to cover the withdrawal, Pfc. Pililaau fired his automatic weapon into the ranks of the assailants, threw all his grenades, and, with ammunition exhausted, closed with the foe in hand-to-hand combat, courageously fighting with his trench knife and bare fists until finally overcome and mortally wounded. When the position was subsequently retaken, more than 40 enemy dead were counted in the area he had so valiantly defended. His heroic devotion to duty, indomitable fighting spirit, and gallant self-sacrifice reflect the highest credit upon himself, the infantry, and the U.S. Army.

3122 ◆ PITTMAN, JOHN ALBERT

Rank: Sergeant
Service: U.S. Army
Birthday: 15 October 1928
Place of Birth: Carrollton, Carroll County, Mississippi
Date of Death: 8 April 1995
Place of Death: Greenwood, Mississippi
Cemetery: New Hope Church Cemetery—Greenwood Mississippi
Entered Service at: Carrollton, Carroll County, Mississippi
Unit: 1st Platoon, Company C, 1st Battalion, 23d Infantry Regiment, 2d Infantry Division
Served as: Squad Leader
Battle or Place of Action: near Kujang-dong, Korea
Date of Action: 26 November 1950
G.O. Number, Date: 39, 4 June 1951
Date of Presentation: 19 May 1951
Place of Presentation: Blair House, presented by Pres. Harry S. Truman
Citation: Sgt. Pittman distinguished himself by conspicuous gallantry and intrepidity above and beyond the call of duty in action against the enemy. He volunteered to lead his squad in a counterattack to regain commanding terrain lost in an earlier engagement. Moving aggressively forward in the face of intense artillery, mortar, and small-arms fire, he was wounded by mortar fragments. Disregarding his wounds, he continued to lead and direct his men in a bold advance against the hostile strongpoint. During this daring action, an enemy grenade was thrown in the midst of his squad, endangering the lives of his comrades. Without hesitation, Sgt. Pittman threw himself on the grenade and absorbed its burst with his body. When a medical aidman reached him, his first request was to be informed as to how many of his men were hurt. This intrepid and selfless act saved several of his men from death or serious injury and was an inspiration to the entire command. Sgt. Pittman's extraordinary heroism reflects the highest credit upon himself and is in keeping with the esteemed traditions of the military service.

3123 ◆ *POMEROY, RALPH EUGENE

Rank: Private First Class
Service: U.S. Army
Birthday: 26 March 1930
Place of Birth: Quinwood, Greenbrier County, West Virginia
Date of Death: 15 October 1952
Cemetery: At The End Of The Trail Cemetery (MH)—Clintonville, West Virginia
Entered Service at: Quinwood, Greenbrier County, West Virginia
Unit: Company E, 31st Infantry Regiment, 7th Infantry Division
Served as: Machine Gunner
Battle or Place of Action: near Kumhwa, Korea
Date of Action: 15 October 1952
G.O. Number, Date: 97, 30 December 1953
Citation: Pfc. Pomeroy, a machine gunner with Company E, distinguished himself by conspicuous gallantry and indomitable courage above and beyond the call of duty in action against the enemy. While his comrades were consolidating on a key terrain feature, he manned a machine gun at

the end of a communication trench on the forward slope to protect the platoon flank and prevent a surprise attack. When the enemy attacked through a ravine leading directly to his firing posiiton, he immediately opened fire on the advancing troops, inflicting a heavy toll in casualties and blunting the assault. At this juncture the enemy directed intense concentrations of artillery and mortar fire on his position in an attempt to neutralize his gun. Despite withering fire and bursting shells, he maintained his heroic stand and poured crippling fire into the ranks of the hostile force until a mortar burst severely wounded him and rendered the gun mount inoperable. Quickly removing the hot, heavy weapon, he cradled it in his arms and, moving forward with grim determination, raked the attacking forces with a hail of fire. Although wounded a second time he pursued his relentless course until his ammunition was expended to within 10 feet of the foe and then, using the machine gun as a club, he courageously closed with the enemy in hand-to-hand combat until mortally wounded. Pfc. Pomeroy's consummate valor, inspirational actions, and supreme sacrifice enabled the platoon to contain the attack and maintain the integrity of the perimeter, reflecting lasting glory upon himself and upholding the noble traditions of the military service.

3124 ◆ *PORTER, DONN F.

Rank: Sergeant
Service: U.S. Army
Birthday: 1 March 1931
Place of Birth: Sewickley, Allegheny County, Pennsylvania
Date of Death: 7 September 1952
Place of Death: Mundung-ni, Korea
Cemetery: Arlington National Cemetery (33-4357) (MH)—Arlington, Virginia
Entered Service at: Baltimore, Baltimore County, Maryland
Unit: Company G, 14th Infantry Regiment, 25th Infantry Division
Battle or Place of Action: near Mundung-ni, Korea
Date of Action: 7 September 1952
G.O. Number, Date: 64, 18 August 1953
Date of Presentation: 5 August 1953
Place of Presentation: The Pentagon (Auditorium), presented by Under Sec. of the Army Earl D. Johnson to his Father
Citation: Sgt. Porter, a member of Company G, distinguished himself by conspicuous gallantry and outstanding courage above and beyond the call of duty in action against the enemy. Advancing under cover of intense mortar and artillery fire, two hostile platoons attacked a combat outpost commanded by Sgt. Porter, destroyed communications, and killed two of his three-man crew. Gallantly maintaining his position, he poured deadly accurate fire into the ranks of the enemy, killing 15 and dispersing the remainder. After falling back under a hail of fire, the determined foe reorganized and stormed forward in an attempt to overrun the outpost. Without hesitation, Sgt. Porter jumped from his position with bayonet fixed and, meeting the onslaught and in close combat, killed six hostile soldiers and routed the attack. While returning to the outpost, he was killed by an artillery burst, but his courageous actions forced the enemy to break off the engagement and thwarted a surprise attack on the main line of resistance. Sgt. Porter's incredible display of valor, gallant self-sacrifice, and consummate devotion to duty reflect the highest credit upon himself and uphold the noble traditions of the military service.

3125 ◆ *POYNTER, JAMES IRSLEY

Rank: Sergeant
Service: U.S. Marine Corps Reserve
Birthday: 1 December 1916
Place of Birth: Bloomington, McLean County, Illinois
Date of Death: 4 November 1950
Place of Death: Sudong, Korea
Cemetery: Fort Rosecrans National Cemetery (O-729) (MH)—San Diego, California
Entered Service at: Downey, Los Angeles County, California
Unit: Company A, 1st Battalion, 7th Marines, 1st Marine Division (Rein)
Served as: Squad Leader
Battle or Place of Action: near Sudong, Korea
Date of Action: 4 November 1950
Date of Presentation: 4 September 1952
Place of Presentation: The Pentagon, presented by Sec. of the Navy Dan A. Kimball to his Widow
Citation: For conspicuous gallantry and intrepidity at the risk of his life above and beyond the call of duty while serving as a squad leader in a rifle platoon of Company A, in action against enemy aggressor forces during the defense of Hill 532, south of Sudong, Korea. When a vastly outnumbering, well-concealed hostile force launched a sudden, vicious counterattack against his platoon's hasty defensive position, Sgt. Poynter displayed superb skill and courage in leading his squad and directing its fire against the onrushing enemy. With his ranks critically depleted by casualties and he himself critically wounded as the onslaught gained momentum and the hostile force surrounded his position, he seized his bayonet and engaged in bitter hand-to-hand combat as the breakthrough continued. Observing three machine guns closing in at a distance of 25 yards, he dashed from his position and, grasping hand grenades from fallen marines as he ran, charged the emplacements in rapid succession, killing the crews of two and putting the other out of action before he fell, mortally wounded. By his self-sacrificing and valiant conduct, Sgt. Poynter inspired the remaining members of his squad to heroic endeavor in bearing down upon and repelling the disorganized enemy, thereby enabling the platoon to move out of the trap to a more favorable tactical position. His indomitable fighting spirit, fortitude, and great personal valor maintained in the face of overwhelming odds sustain and enhance the finest traditions of the U.S. Naval Service. He gallantly gave his life for his country.

3126 ◆ *RAMER, GEORGE HENRY

Rank: Second Lieutenant
Service: U.S. Marine Corps Reserve
Birthday: 27 March 1927
Place of Birth: Meyersdale, Somerset County, Pennsylvania

Date of Death: 12 September 1951
Place of Death: Korea
Cemetery: Lewisburg Cemetery (MH)—Lewisburg, Pennsylvania
Entered Service at: Lewisburg, Union County, Pennsylvania
Unit: 3d Platoon, Company I, 3d Battalion, 7th Marines, 1st Marine Division (Rein)
Served as: Platoon Leader
Battle or Place of Action: Korea
Date of Action: 12 September 1951
Date of Presentation: 7 January 1953
Place of Presentation: The Pentagon, presented by Sec. of the Navy Dan A. Kimball to his Widow
Citation: For conspicuous gallantry and intrepidity at the risk of his life above and beyond the call of duty as leader of the 3d Platoon in Company I, in action against enemy aggressor forces. Ordered to attack and seize hostile positions atop a hill, vigorously defended by well-entrenched enemy forces delivering massed small-arms mortar, and machine-gun fire, 2d Lt. Ramer fearlessly led his men up the steep slopes and, although he and the majority of his unit were wounded during the ascent, boldly continued to spearhead the assault. With the terrain becoming more precipitous near the summit and the climb more perilous as the hostile forces added grenades to the devastating hail of fire, he staunchly carried the attack to the top, personally annihilated one enemy bunker with grenade and carbine fire and captured the objective with his remaining eight men. Unable to hold the position against an immediate, overwhelming hostile counterattack, he ordered his group to withdraw and singlehandedly fought the enemy to furnish cover for his men and for the evacuation of three fatally wounded marines. Severely wounded a second time, 2d Lt. Ramer refused aid when his men returned to help him and, after ordering them to seek shelter, courageously manned his post until the hostile troops overran his position and he fell mortally wounded. His indomitable fighting spirit, inspiring leadership and unselfish concern for others in the face of death, reflect the highest credit upon 2d Lt. Ramer and the U.S. Naval Service. He gallantly gave his life for his country.

3127 ♦ *RED CLOUD JR., MITCHELL

Rank: Corporal
Service: U.S. Army
Birthday: 2 July 1924
Place of Birth: Hatfield, Wisconsin
Date of Death: 5 November 1950
Place of Death: Chonghyon, Korea
Cemetery: Decorah Cemetery—Komensky, Wisconsin
Entered Service at: Merrillan, Jackson County, Wisconsin
Unit: Company E, 19th Infantry Regiment, 24th Infantry Division
Served as: Automatic Rifleman
Battle or Place of Action: near Chonghyon, Korea
Date of Action: 5 November 1950
G.O. Number, Date: 26, 25 April 1951
Date of Presentation: 3 April 1951
Place of Presentation: The Pentagon, presented by Gen. Omar N. Bradley to his Mother
Citation: Cpl. Red Cloud, Company E, distinguished himself by conspicuous gallantry and intrepidity above and beyond the call of duty in action against the enemy. From his position on the point of a ridge immediately in front of the company command post, he was the first to detect the approach of the Chinese Communist forces and give the alarm as the enemy charged from a brush-covered area less that 100 feet from him. Springing up he delivered devastating point-blank automatic rifle into the advancing enemy. His accurate and intense fire checked this assault and gained time for the company to consolidate its defense. With utter fearlessness he maintained his firing position until severely wounded by enemy fire. Refusing assistance he pulled himself to his feet and wrapping his arm around a tree continued his deadly fire again, until he was fatally wounded. This heroic act stopped the enemy from overrunning his company's position and gained time for reorganization and evacuation of the wounded. Cpl. Red Cloud's dauntless courage and gallant self-sacrifice refects the highest credit upon himself and upholds the esteemed traditions of the U.S. Army.

3128 ♦ *REEM, ROBERT DALE

Rank: Second Lieutenant
Service: U.S. Marine Corps
Birthday: 20 October 1925
Place of Birth: Lancaster, Lancaster County, Pennsylvania
Date of Death: 6 November 1950
Place of Death: Chinhung-ni, Korea
Cemetery: Arlington National Cemetery (6-9376-B) (MH)—Arlington, Virginia
Entered Service at: Elizabethtown, Lancaster County, Pennsylvania
Unit: Company H, 3d Battalion, 7th Marines, 1st Marine Division (Rein)
Served as: Platoon Commander
Battle or Place of Action: vicinity of Chinhung-ni, Korea
Date of Action: 6 November 1950
Date of Presentation: 8 February 1952
Place of Presentation: The Pentagon, presented by Under Sec. of the Navy Francis P. Whitehair to his Widow
Citation: For conspicuous gallantry and intrepidity at the risk of his life above and beyond the call of duty as a platoon commander in Company H, in action against enemy aggressor forces. Grimly determined to dislodge a group of heavy enemy infantry units occupying well-concealed and strongly fortified positions on commanding ground overlooking unprotected terrain, 2d Lt. Reem moved slowly forward up the side of the ridge with his platoon in the face of a veritable hail of shattering hostile machine-gun, grenade, and rifle fire. Three times repulsed by a resolute enemy force in achieving his objective, and pinned down by the continuing fury of hostile fire, he rallied and regrouped the heroic men in his depleted and disorganized platoon in preparation for a fourth attack. Issuing last-minute orders to his non-commissioned officers when an enemy grenade landed in a depression of the rocky ground in which the group was standing, 2d Lt. Reem unhesitatingly chose to sacrifice himself and, springing upon the deadly missile, absorbed the full impact of the explosion

in his body, thus protecting others from serious injury and possible death. Stouthearted and indomitable, he readily yielded his own chance of survival that his subordinate leaders might live to carry on the fight against a fanatic enemy. His superb courage, cool decisiveness, and valiant spirit of self-sacrifice in the face of certain death reflect the highest credit upon 2d Lt. Reem and the U.S. Naval Service. He gallantly gave his life for his country.

3129 ◆ RODRIGUEZ, JOSEPH CHARLES

Rank: Sergeant (rank at time of action: Private First Class) (highest rank: Colonel)
Service: U.S. Army
Birthday: 14 November 1928
Place of Birth: San Bernardino, San Bernardino County, California
Entered Service at: San Bernardino, San Bernardino County, California
Unit: 2d Squad, 2d Platoon, Company F, 2d Battalion, 17th Infantry Regiment, 7th Infantry Division
Served as: Assistant Squad Leader
Battle or Place of Action: near Munye-ri, Korea
Date of Action: 21 May 1951
G.O. Number, Date: 22, 5 February 1952
Date of Presentation: 29 January 1952
Place of Presentation: The White House, presented by Pres. Harry S. Truman
Citation: Sgt. Rodriguez distinguished himself by conspicuous gallantry and intrepidity at the risk of his life above and beyond the call of duty in action against an armed enemy of the Unites Nations. Sgt. Rodriguez, an assistant squad leader of the 2d Platoon, was participating in an attack against a fanatical hostile force occupying well-fortified positions on rugged command terrain, when his squad's advance was halted within approximately 60 yards by a withering barrage of automatic-weapons and small-arms fire from five emplacements directly to the front and right and left flanks, together with grenades which the enemy rolled down the hill toward the advancing troops. Fully aware of the odds against him, Sgt. Rodriguez leaped to his feet, dashed 60 yards up the fire-swept slope, and, after lobbing grenades into the first foxhole with deadly accuracy, ran around the left flank, silenced an automatic weapon with two grenades and continued his whirlwind assault to the top of the peak, wiping out two more foxholes and then, reaching the right flank, he tossed grenades into the remaining emplacement, destroying the gun and annihilating its crew. Sgt. Rodriguez' intrepid actions exacted a toll of 15 enemy dead and, as a result of his incredible display of valor, the defense of the opposition was broken, and the enemy routed, and the strategic strongpoint secured. His unflinching courage under fire and inspirational devotion to duty reflect highest credit on himself and uphold the honored traditions of the military service.

3130 ◆ ROSSER, RONALD EUGENE

Rank: Corporal (highest rank: Sergeant First Class Ret.)
Service: U.S. Army
Birthday: 24 October 1929
Place of Birth: Columbus, Franklin County, Ohio
Entered Service at: Crooksville, Perry County, Ohio
Unit: Headquarters Company (Heavy Mortar), 38th Infantry Regiment, 2d Infantry Division
Served as: Forward Observer
Battle or Place of Action: near Ponggilli, Korea
Date of Action: 12 January 1952
G.O. Number, Date: 67, 7 July 1952
Date of Presentation: 27 June 1952
Place of Presentation: The White House (Rose Garden), presented by Pres. Harry S. Truman
Citation: Cpl. Rosser distinguished himself by conspicuous gallantry above and beyond the call of duty. While assaulting heavily fortified enemy hill positions, Company L, 38th Infantry Regiment, was stopped by fierce automatic-weapons, small-arms, artillery, and mortar fire. Cpl. Rosser, a forward observer was with the lead platoon of Company L, when it came under fire from two directions. Cpl. Rosser turned his radio over to his assistant and, disregarding the enemy fire, charged the enemy positions armed with only carbine and a grenade. At the first bunker, he silenced its occupants with a burst from his weapon. Gaining the top of the hill, he killed two enemy soldiers, and then went down the trench, killing five more as he advanced. He then hurled his grenade into a bunker and shot two other soldiers as they emerged. Having exhausted his ammunition, he returned through the enemy fire to obtain more ammunition and grenades and charged the enemy bunkers. Although those who attempted to join him became casualties, Cpl. Rosser once again exhausted his ammunition, obtained a new supply, and returning to the hilltop a third time hurled grenades into the enemy positions. During this heroic action Cpl. Rosser singlehandedly killed at least 13 of the enemy. After exhausting his ammunition he accompanied the withdrawing platoon, and though himself wounded, made several trips across open terrain still under enemy fire to help remove other men injured more seriously than himself. This outstanding soldier's courageous and selfless devotion to duty is worthy of emulation by all men. He has contributed magnificently to the high traditions of the military service.

3131 ◆ *SCHOONOVER, DAN D.

Rank: Corporal
Service: U.S. Army
Birthday: 8 October 1933
Place of Birth: Boise, Ada County, Idaho
Date of Death: 10 July 1953
Place of Death: Sokkogae, Korea
Cemetery: National Memorial of the Pacific (Wall of the Missing)—Honolulu, Hawaii
Entered Service at: Boise, Ada County, Idaho
Unit: Company A, 13th Combat Engineer Battalion Attached to Company G, 17th Infantry, 7th Infantry Division
Served as: Squad Leader
Battle or Place of Action: Pork Chop Hill, near Sokkogae, Korea
Date of Action: 8-10 July 1953
G.O. Number, Date: 5, 14 January 1955
Date of Presentation: July 1954

Place of Presentation: Presented to his Mother
Citation: Cpl. Schoonover distinguished himself by conspicuous gallantry and outstanding courage above and beyond the call of duty in action against the enemy. He was in charge of an engineer demolition squad attached to an infantry company which was committed to dislodge the enemy from a vital hill. Realizing that the heavy fighting and intense enemy fire made it impossible to carry out his mission, he voluntarily employed his unit as a rifle squad and, forging up the steep barren slope, participated in the assault on hostile positions. When an artillery round exploded on the roof of an enemy bunker, he courageously ran forward and leaped into the position, killing one hostile infantryman and taking another prisoner. Later in the action, when friendly forces were pinned down by vicious fire from another enemy bunker, he dashed through the hail of fire, hurled grenades in the nearest aperture, then ran to the doorway and emptied his pistol, killing the remainder of the enemy. His brave action neutralized the position and enabled friendly troops to continue their advance to the crest of the hill. When the enemy counterattacked he constantly exposed himself to the heavy bombardment to direct the fire of his men and to call in an effective artillery barrage on hostile forces. Although the company was relieved early the following morning, he voluntarily remained in the area, manned a machine gun for several hours, and subsequently joined another assault on enemy emplacements. When last seen he was operating an automatic rifle with devastating effect until mortally wounded by artillery fire. Cpl. Schoonover's heroic leadership during two days of heavy fighting, superb personal bravery, and willing self-sacrifice inspired his comrades and saved many lives, reflecting lasting glory upon himself and upholding the honored traditions of the military service.
Notes: MIA

3132 ◆ SCHOWALTER JR., EDWARD RIGHTOR

Rank: First Lieutenant (highest rank: Colonel)
Service: U.S. Army
Birthday: 24 December 1927
Place of Birth: New Orleans, Orleans County, Louisiana
Entered Service at: Metairie, Jefferson County, Louisiana
Unit: Company A, 1st Battalion, 31st Infantry Regiment, 7th Infantry Division
Served as: Company Commander
Battle or Place of Action: near Kumhwa, Korea
Date of Action: 14 October 1952
G.O. Number, Date: 6, 28 January 1954
Date of Presentation: 12 October 1953
Place of Presentation: The White House, presented by Pres. Dwight D. Eisenhower
Citation: 1st Lt. Schowalter, commanding officer, Company A, distinguished himself by conspicuous gallantry and indomitable courage above and beyond the call of duty in action against the enemy. Committed to attack and occupy a key approach to the primary objective, the 1st Platoon of his company came under heavy vicious small-arms, grenade, and mortar fire within 50 yards of the enemy-held strong-point, halting the advance and inflicting several casualties. The 2d Platoon moved up in support at this juncture, and although wounded, 1st Lt. Schowalter continued to spearhead the assault. Nearing the objective he was severely wounded by a grenade fragment but, refusing medical aid, he led his men into the trenches and began routing the enemy from the bunkers with grenades. Suddenly from a burst of fire from a hidden cove off the trench he was again wounded. Although suffering from his wounds, he refused to relinquish command and continued issuing orders and encouraging his men until the commanding ground was secured and then he was evacuated. 1st Lt. Schowalter's unflinching courage, extraordinary heroism, and inspirational leadership reflect the highest credit upon himself and are in keeping with the highest traditions of the military service.

3133 ◆ *SEBILLE, LOUIS JOSEPH

Rank: Major
Service: U.S. Air Force
Birthday: 21 November 1915
Place of Birth: Harbor Beach, Huron County, Michigan
Date of Death: 5 August 1950
Place of Death: Near Hanchang, Korea
Cemetery: Forest Home Cemetery—Chicago, Illinois
Entered Service at: Chicago, Cook County, Illinois
Unit: 67th Fighter-Bomber Squadron, 18th Fighter-Bomber Group, 5th Air Force
Served as: Pilot of a F-51
Battle or Place of Action: near Hanchang, Korea
Date of Action: 5 August 1950
Date of Presentation: 24 August 1951
Place of Presentation: March AFB, Riverside, California, presented by Gen. Hoyt Sanford Vandenberg to his Widow
Citation: Maj. Sebille distinguished himself by conspicuous gallantry and intrepidity at the risk of his life above and beyond the call of duty. During an attack on a camouflaged area containing a concentration of enemy troops, artillery, and armored vehicles, Maj. Sebille's F-51 aircraft was severely damaged by antiaircraft fire. Although fully cognizant of the short period he could remain airborne, he deliberately ignored the possibility of survival by abandoning the aircraft or by crash landing, and continued his attack against the enemy forces threatening the security of friendly ground troops. In his determination to inflict maximum damage upon the enemy, Maj. Sebille again exposed himself to the intense fire of enemy gun batteries and dived on the target to his death. The superior leadership, daring, and selfless devotion to duty which he displayed in the execution of an extremely dangerous mission were an inspiration to both his subordinates and superiors and reflect the highest credit upon himself, the U.S. Air Force, and the armed forces of the United Nations.

3134 ◆ *SHEA JR., RICHARD THOMAS

Rank: First Lieutenant
Service: U.S. Army
Birthday: 3 January 1927
Place of Birth: Portsmouth, Portsmouth County, Virginia
Date of Death: 8 July 1953

Place of Death: Sokkogae, Korea
Cemetery: Olive Branch Cemetery (MH)—Portsmouth, Virginia
Entered Service at: Portsmouth, Portsmouth County, Virginia
Unit: Company A, 17th Infantry Regiment, 7th Infantry Division
Served as: Executive Officer
Battle or Place of Action: Pork Chop Hill, near Sokkogae, Korea
Date of Action: 7-8 June 1953
G.O. Number, Date: 38, 8 June 1955
Date of Presentation: 16 May 1955
Place of Presentation: Parade Grounds, Ft. Meyers, Va., by the Secretary of the Army Robert T. Stevens to his widow
Citation: 1st Lt. Shea, executive officer, Company A, distinguished himself by conspicuous gallantry and indomitable courage above and beyond the call of duty in action against the enemy. On the night of 6 July, he was supervising the reinforcement of defensive positions when the enemy attacked with great numerical superiority. Voluntarily proceeding to the area most threatened, he organized and led a counterattack and, in the bitter fighting which ensued, closed with and killed two hostile soldiers with his trench knife. Calmly moving among the men, checking positions, steadying and urging the troops to hold firm, he fought side by side with them throughout the night. Despite heavy losses, the hostile force pressed the assault with determination, and at dawn made an all-out attempt to overrun friendly elements. Charging forward to meet the challenge, 1st Lt. Shea and his gallant men drove back the hostile troops. Elements of Company G joined the defense on the afternoon of 7 July, having lost key personnel through casualties. Immediately integrating these troops into his unit, 1st Lt. Shea rallied a group of 20 men and again charged the enemy. Although wounded in this action, he refused evacuation and continued to lead the counterattack. When the assaulting element was pinned down by heavy machine-gun fire, he personally rushed the emplacement and, firing his carbine and lobbing grenades with deadly accuracy, neutralized the weapon and killed three of the enemy. With forceful leadership and by his heroic example, 1st Lt. Shea coordinated and directed a holding action throughout the night and the following morning. On 8 July, the enemy attacked again. Despite additional wounds, he launched a determined counterattack and was last seen in close hand-to-hand combat with the enemy. 1st Lt. Shea's inspirational leadership and unflinching courage set an illustrious example of valor to the men of his regiment, reflecting lasting glory upon himself and upholding the noble traditions of the military service.

3135 ◆ *SHUCK JR., WILLIAM EDWARD

Rank: Staff Sergeant (highest rank: Master Sergeant)
Service: U.S. Marine Corps
Birthday: 16 August 1926
Place of Birth: Cumberland, Allegany County, Maryland
Date of Death: 3 July 1952
Place of Death: Korea
Cemetery: St. Peter's & Paul Cemetery (MH)—Cumberland, Maryland
Entered Service at: Cumberland, Allegany County, Maryland
Unit: Company G, 3d Battalion, 7th Marines, 1st Marine Division (Rein)
Served as: Squad Leader
Battle or Place of Action: Korea
Date of Action: 3 July 1952
Date of Presentation: 9 September 1953
Place of Presentation: Marine Corps Barracks, Washington, D.C., presented by Vice Pres. Richard M. Nixon to his Widow
Citation: For conspicuous gallantry and intrepidity at the risk of his life above and beyond the call of duty while serving as a squad leader of Company G, in action against enemy aggressor forces. When his platoon was subjected to a devastating barrage of enemy small-arms, grenade, artillery, and mortar fire during an assault against strongly fortified hill positions well forward of the main line of resistance, S/Sgt. Shuck, although painfully wounded, refused medical attention and continued to lead his machine-gun squad in the attack. Unhesitatingly assuming command of a rifle squad when the leader became a casualty, he skillfully organized the two squads into an attacking force and led two more daring assaults upon the hostile positions. Wounded a second time, he steadfastly refused evacuation and remained in the foremost position under heavy fire until assured that all dead and wounded were evacuated. Mortally wounded by an enemy sniper bullet while voluntarily assisting in the removal of the last casualty, S/Sgt. Shuck, by his fortitude and great personal valor in the face of overwhelming odds, served to inspire all who observed him. His unyielding courage throughout reflects the highest credit upon himself and the U.S. Naval Service. He gallantly gave his life for his country.

3136 ◆ SIMANEK, ROBERT ERNEST

Rank: Private First Class
Service: U.S. Marine Corps
Birthday: 26 April 1930
Place of Birth: Detroit, Wayne County, Michigan
Entered Service at: Detroit, Wayne County, Michigan
Unit: 2d Squad, 2d Platoon, Company F, 2d Battalion, 5th Marines, 1st Marine Division (Rein)
Served as: Radio Operator
Battle or Place of Action: Outpost Irene, Korea
Date of Action: 17 August 1952
Date of Presentation: 27 October 1953
Place of Presentation: The White House, presented by Pres. Dwight D. Eisenhower
Citation: For conspicuous gallantry and intrepidity at the risk of his life above and beyond the call of duty while serving with Company F, in action against enemy aggressor forces. While accompanying a patrol en route to occupy a combat outpost forward of friendly lines, Pfc. Simanek exhibited a high degree of courage and a resolute spirit of self-sacrifice in protecting the lives of his fellow marines. With his unit ambushed by an intense concentration of enemy mortar and

small-arms fire, and suffering heavy casualties, he was forced to seek cover with the remaining members of the patrol in a nearby trench line. Determined to save his comrades when a hostile grenade was hurled into their midst, he unhesitatingly threw himself on the deadly missile absorbing the shattering violence of the exploding charge in his body and shielding his fellow marines from serious injury or death. Gravely wounded as a result of his heroic action, Pfc. Simanek, by his daring initiative and great personal valor in the face of almost certain death, served to inspire all who observed him and upheld the highest traditions of the U.S. Naval Service.

3137 ◆ *SITMAN, WILLIAM S.

Rank: Sergeant First Class
Service: U.S. Army
Birthday: 9 August 1923
Place of Birth: Bellwood, Blair County, Pennsylvania
Date of Death: 14 February 1951
Place of Death: Chipyong-ni, Korea
Cemetery: Logan Valley Cemetery (MH)—Bellwood, Pennsylvania
Entered Service at: Bellwood, Blair County, Pennsylvania
Unit: Company A, 23d Infantry Regiment, 2d Infantry Division
Served as: Section Leader
Battle or Place of Action: near Chipyong-ni, Korea
Date of Action: 14 February 1951
G.O. Number, Date: 20, 1 February 1952
Date of Presentation: 16 January 1952
Place of Presentation: The Pentagon, presented by Sec. of Defense Robert Lovett to his Widow
Citation: Sfc. Sitman distinguished himself by conspicuous gallantry and intrepidity above and beyond the call of duty in action against an armed enemy of the United Nations. Sfc. Sitman, a machine-gun section leader of Company M, was attached to Company I, under attack by a numerically superior hostile force. During the encounter when an enemy grenade knocked out his machine gun, a squad from Company I immediately emplaced a light machine gun, and Sfc. Sitman and his men remained to provide security for the crew. In the ensuing action, the enemy lobbed a grenade into the position and Sfc. Sitman, fully aware of the odds against him, selflessly threw himself on it, absorbing the full force of the explosion with his body. Although mortally wounded in this fearless display of valor, his intrepid act saved five men from death or serious injury, and enabled them to continue inflicting withering fire on the ruthless foe throughout the attack. Sfc. Sitman's noble self-sacrifice and consummate devotion to duty reflect lasting glory on himself and uphold the honored traditions of the military service.

3138 ◆ SITTER, CARL LEONARD

Rank: Captain (highest rank: Colonel)
Service: U.S. Marine Corps
Birthday: 2 December 1922
Place of Birth: Syracuse, Morgan County, Missouri
Entered Service at: Pueblo, Pueblo County, Colorado
Unit: Company G, 3d Battalion, 1st Marines, 1st Marine Division (Rein)
Served as: Commanding Officer
Battle or Place of Action: Hagaru-ri, Korea
Date of Action: 29-30 November 1950
Date of Presentation: 29 October 1951
Place of Presentation: The White House, presented by Pres. Harry S. Truman
Citation: For conspicuous gallantry and intrepidity at the risk of his life above and beyond the call of duty as commanding officer of Company G, in action against enemy aggressor forces. Ordered to break through enemy-infested territory to reinforce his battalion the morning of 29 November, Capt. Sitter continuously exposed himself to enemy fire as he led his company forward and, despite 25 percent casualties suffered in the furious action, succeeded in driving through to his objective. Assuming the responsibility of attempting to seize and occupy a strategic area occupied by a hostile force of regiment strength deeply entrenched on a snow-covered hill commanding the entire valley southeast of the town, as well as the line of march of friendly troops withdrawing to the south, he reorganized his depleted units the following morning and boldly led them up the steep, frozen hillside under blistering fire, encouraging and redeploying his troops as casualties occurred and directing forward platoons as they continued the drive to the top of the ridge. During the night when a vastly outnumbering enemy launched a sudden, vicious counterattack, setting the hill ablaze with mortar, machine-gun, and automatic-weapons fire and taking a heavy toll in troops, Capt. Sitter visited each foxhole and gun position, coolly deploying and integrating reinforcing units consisting of service personnel unfamiliar with infantry tactics into a coordinated combat team and instilling in every man the will and determination to hold his position at all costs. With the enemy penetrating his lines in repeated counterattacks which often required hand-to-hand combat, and, on one occasion infiltrating to the command post with hand grenades, he fought gallantly with his men in repulsing and killing the fanatic attackers in each encounter. Painfully wounded in the face, arms, and chest by bursting grenades, he staunchly refused to be evacuated and continued to fight on until a successful defense of the area was assured with a loss to the enemy of more than 50 percent dead, wounded, and captured. His valiant leadership, superb tactics, and great personal valor throughout 36 hours of bitter combat reflect the highest credit upon Capt. Sitter and the U.S. Naval Service.

3139 ◆ *SKINNER JR., SHERROD EMERSON

Rank: Second Lieutenant
Service: U.S. Marine Corps Reserve
Birthday: 29 October 1929
Place of Birth: Hartford, Hartford County, Connecticut
Date of Death: 26 October 1952
Place of Death: Korea
Cemetery: Arlington National Cemetery (3-2032-RH) (MH)—Arlington, Virginia
Entered Service at: East Lansing, Ingham County, Michigan

Unit: Battery F, 2d Battalion, 11th Marines, 1st Marine Division (Rein)
Served as: Forward Observer
Battle or Place of Action: Korea
Date of Action: 26 October 1952
Date of Presentation: 9 September 1953
Place of Presentation: Marine Corps Barracks, Washington, D.C., presented by Vice Pres. Richard M. Nixon to his parents
Citation: For conspicuous gallantry and intrepidity at the risk of his life above and beyond the call of duty as an artillery forward observer of Battery F, in action against enemy aggressor forces on the night of 26 October 1952. When his observation post in an extremely critical and vital sector of the main line of resistance was subjected to a sudden and fanatical attack by hostile forces, supported by a devastating barrage of artillery and mortar fire which completely severed communication lines connecting the outpost with friendly firing batteries, 2d Lt. Skinner, in a determined effort to hold his position, immediately organized and directed the surviving personnel in the defense of the outpost, continuing to call down fire on the enemy by means of radio alone until his equipment became damaged beyond repair. Undaunted by the intense hostile barrage and the rapidly-closing attackers, he twice left the protection of his bunker in order to direct accurate machine-gun fire and to replenish the depleted supply of ammunition and grenades. Although painfully wounded on each occasion, he steadfastly refused medical aid until the rest of the men received treatment. As the ground attack reached its climax, he gallantly directed the final defense until the meager supply of ammunition was exhausted and the position overrun. During the three hours that the outpost was occupied by the enemy, several grenades were thrown into the bunker which served as protection for 2d Lt. Skinner and his remaining comrades. Realizing that there was no chance for other than passive resistance, he directed his men to feign death even though the hostile troops entered the bunker and searched their persons. Later, when an enemy grenade was thrown between him and two other survivors, he immediately threw himself on the deadly missile in an effort to protect the others, absorbing the full force of the explosion and sacrificing his life for his comrades. By his indomitable fighting spirit, superb leadership, and great personal valor in the face of tremendous odds, 2d Lt. Skinner served to inspire his fellow marines in their heroic stand against the enemy and upheld the highest traditions of the U.S. Naval Service. He gallantly gave his life for his country.

3140 ◆ *SMITH, DAVID MONROE

Rank: Private First Class
Service: U.S. Army
Birthday: 10 November 1926
Place of Birth: Livingston, Rockcastle County, Kentucky
Date of Death: 1 September 1950
Place of Death: Yongsan, Korea
Cemetery: Smith Cemetery on the Hill Ponder (MH)—Livingston, Kentucky
Entered Service at: Livingston, Rockcastle County, Kentucky
Unit: Company E, 9th Infantry Regiment, 2d Infantry Division
Served as: Mortar Gunner
Battle or Place of Action: near Yongsan, Korea
Date of Action: 1 September 1950
G.O. Number, Date: 78, 21 August 1952
Date of Presentation: 14 August 1952
Place of Presentation: The Pentagon, presented by Gen. Omar N. Bradley to his Mother
Citation: Pfc. Smith distinguished himself by conspicuous gallantry and outstanding courage above and beyond the call of duty in action. Pfc. Smith was a gunner in the mortar section of Company E, emplaced in rugged mountainous terrain and under attack by a numerically superior hostile force. Bitter fighting ensued and the enemy overran forward elements, infiltrated the perimeter, and rendered friendly positions untenable. The mortar section was ordered to withdraw, but the enemy had encircled and closed in on the position. Observing a grenade lobbed at his emplacement, Pfc. Smith shouted a warning to his comrades and, fully aware of the odds against him, flung himself upon it and smothered the explosion with his body. Although mortally wounded in this display of valor, his intrepid act saved five men from death or serious injury. Pfc. Smith's inspirational conduct and supreme sacrifice reflect lasting glory on himself and are in keeping with the noble traditions of the infantry of the U.S. Army.

3141 ◆ *SPEICHER, CLIFTON T.

Rank: Corporal
Service: U.S. Army
Birthday: 25 March 1931
Place of Birth: Gray, Somerset County, Pennsylvania
Date of Death: 14 June 1952
Place of Death: Minarigol, Korea
Cemetery: Beam Cemetery—Jenner Township, Pennsylvania
Entered Service at: Gray, Somerset County, Pennsylvania
Unit: Company F, 223d Infantry Regiment, 40th Infantry Division
Battle or Place of Action: near Minarigol, Korea
Date of Action: 14 June 1952
G.O. Number, Date: 65, 19 August 1953
Date of Presentation: 5 August 1953
Place of Presentation: The Pentagon Auditorium, presented by Under Sec. of the Army Earl D. Johnson to his Father
Citation: Cpl. Speicher distinguished himself by conspicuous gallantry and indomitable courage above and beyond the call of duty in action against the enemy. While participating in an assault to secure a key terrain feature, Cpl. Speicher's squad was pinned down by withering small-arms, mortar, and machine-gun fire. Although already wounded he left the comparative safety of his position, and made a daring charge against the machine-gun emplacement. Within 10 yards of the goal, he was again wounded by small-arms fire but continued on, entered the bunker, killed two hostile soldiers with his rifle, a third with his bayonet, and silenced the machine gun. Inspired by this incredible display of valor, the men quickly moved up and completed the mission. Dazed and

shaken, he walked to the foot of the hill where he collapsed and died. Cpl. Speicher's consummate sacrifice and unflinching devotion to duty reflect lasting glory upon himself and uphold the noble traditions of the military service.

3142 ◆ STONE, JAMES LAMAR

Rank: First Lieutenant (highest rank: Colonel)
Service: U.S. Army
Birthday: 27 December 1922
Place of Birth: Pine Bluff, Jefferson County, Arkansas
Entered Service at: Houston, Harris County, Texas
Unit: 3d Platoon, Company F, 2d Battalion, 8th Cavalry Regiment, 1st Cavalry Division
Served as: Platoon Leader
Battle or Place of Action: near Sokkogae, Korea
Date of Action: 21-22 November 1951
G.O. Number, Date: 82, 20 October 1953
Date of Presentation: 27 October 1953
Place of Presentation: The White House, presented by Pres. Dwight D. Eisenhower
Citation: 1st Lt. Stone distinguished himself by conspicuous gallantry and indomitable courage above and beyond the call of duty in action against the enemy. When his platoon, holding a vital outpost position, was attacked by overwhelming Chinese forces, 1st Lt. Stone stood erect and exposed to the terrific enemy fire calmly directed his men in the defense. A defensive flamethrower failing to function, he personally moved to its location, further exposing himself, and personally repaired the weapon. Throughout a second attack, 1st Lt. Stone, though painfully wounded, personally carried the only remaining light machine gun from place to place in the position in order to bring fire upon the Chinese advancing from two directions. Throughout he continued to encourage and direct his depleted platoon in its hopeless defense. Although again wounded, he continued the fight with his carbine, still exposing himself as an example to his men. When this final overwhelming assault swept over the platoon's position his voice could still be heard faintly urging his men to carry on, until he lost consciousness. Only because of this officer's driving spirit and heroic action was the platoon emboldened to make its brave but hopeless last ditch stand.
Notes: POW

3143 ◆ *STORY, LUTHER H.

Rank: Private First Class
Service: U.S. Army
Birthday: 20 July 1931
Place of Birth: Buena Vista, Marion County, Georgia
Date of Death: 1 September 1950
Place of Death: Agok, Korea
Cemetery: National Memorial Cemetery of the Pacific (Wall of the Missing)—Honolulu, Hawaii; Andersonville National Cemetery ('In Memory' marker)—Andersonville, Georgia
Entered Service at: Georgia
Unit: Company A, 9th Infantry Regiment, 2d Infantry Division
Served as: Weapons Squad Leader
Battle or Place of Action: near Agok, Korea
Date of Action: 1 September 1950
G.O. Number, Date: 70, 2 August 1951
Date of Presentation: 21 June 1951
Place of Presentation: The Pentagon, presented by Gen. Omar N. Bradley to his Father
Citation: Pfc. Story distinguished himself by conspicuous gallantry and intrepidity above and beyond the call of duty in action. A savage daylight attack by elements of three enemy divisions penetrated the thinly held lines of the 9th Infantry. Company A beat off several banzai attacks but was bypassed and in danger of being cut off and surrounded. Pfc. Story, a weapons squad leader, was heavily engaged in stopping the early attacks and had just moved his squad to a position overlooking the Naktong River when he observed a large group of the enemy crossing the river to attack Company A. Seizing a machine gun from his wounded gunner he placed deadly fire on the hostile column killing or wounding an estimated 100 enemy soldiers. Facing certain encirclement, the company commander ordered a withdrawal. During the move Pfc. Story noticed the approach of an enemy truck loaded with troops and towing an ammunition trailer. Alerting his comrades to take cover, he fearlessly stood in the middle of the road, throwing grenades into the truck. Out of grenades, he crawled to his squad, gathered up additional grenades, and again attacked the vehicle. During the withdrawal the company was attacked by such superior numbers that it was forced to deploy in a rice field. Pfc. Story was wounded in this action, but, disregarding his wounds, rallied the men about him and repelled the attack. Realizing that his wounds would hamper his comrades, he refused to retire to the next position but remained to cover the company's withdrawal. When last seen he was firing every weapon available and fighting off another hostile assault. Pvt. Story's extraordinary heroism, aggressive leadership, and supreme devotion to duty reflect the highest credit upon himself and were in keeping with the esteemed traditions of the military service.
Notes: MIA

3144 ◆ *SUDUT, JEROME A.

Rank: Second Lieutenant
Service: U.S. Army
Birthday: 20 October 1930
Place of Birth: Wausau, Marathon County, Wisconsin
Date of Death: 12 September 1951
Place of Death: Kumhwa, Korea
Cemetery: Restlawn Memorial Cemetery—Wausau, Wisconsin
Entered Service at: Wisconsin
Unit: Company B, 27th Infantry Regiment, 25th Infantry Division
Served as: Platoon Leader
Battle or Place of Action: near Kumhwa, Korea
Date of Action: 12 September 1951
G.O. Number, Date: 31, 21 March 1952
Date of Presentation: 13 March 1952
Place of Presentation: Presented by Sec. of the Army Frank C. Pace to his parents

Citation: 2d Lt. Sudut distinguished himself by conspicuous gallantry above and beyond the call of duty in action against the enemy. His platoon, attacking heavily fortified and stategically located hostile emplacements, had been stopped by intense fire from a large bunker containing several firing posts. Armed with submachine gun, pistol, and grenades, 2d Lt. Sudut charged the emplacement alone through vicious hostile fire, killing three of the occupants and dispersing the remainder. Painfully wounded, he returned to reorganize his platoon, refused evacuation, and led his men in a renewed attack. The enemy had returned to the bunker by means of connecting trenches from other emplacements and the platoon was again halted by devastating fire. Accompanied by an automatic-rifleman, 2d Lt. Sudut again charged into close-range fire to eliminate the postion. When the rifleman was wounded, 2d Lt. Sudut seized his weapon and continued alone, killing three of the four remaining occupants. Though mortally wounded and his ammunition exhausted, he jumped into the emplacement and killed the remaining enemy soldier with his trench knife. His singlehanded assaults so inspired his comrades that they continued the attack and drove the enemy from the hill, securing the objective. Second Lt. Sudut's consummate fighting spirit, outstanding leadership, and gallant self-sacrifice are in keeping with the finest traditions of the infantry and the U.S. Army.

3145 ◆ *THOMPSON, WILLIAM HENRY

Rank: Private First Class
Service: U.S. Army
Birthday: 16 August 1927
Place of Birth: New York, New York
Date of Death: 6 August 1950
Place of Death: Haman, Korea
Cemetery: Long Island National Cemetery (DSS-19) (MH)—Farmingdale, New York
Entered Service at: Bronx County, New York
Unit: Company M, 24th Infantry Regiment, 25th Infantry Division
Served as: Machine Gunner
Battle or Place of Action: near Haman, Korea
Date of Action: 6 August 1950
G.O. Number, Date: 63, 2 August 1951
Date of Presentation: 21 June 1951
Place of Presentation: The Pentagon, presented by Gen. Omar Bradley to his Mother
Citation: Pfc. Thompson distinguished himself by conspicuous gallantry and intrepidity above and beyond the call of duty in action against the enemy. While his platoon was reorganizing under cover of darkness, fanatical enemy forces in overwhelming strength launched a surprise attack on the unit. Pfc. Thompson set up his machine gun in the path of the onslaught and swept the enemy with withering fire, pinning them down momentarily, thus permitting the remainder of his platoon to withdraw to a more tenable position. Although hit repeatedly by grenade fragments and small-arms fire, he resisted all efforts of his comrades to induce him to withdraw, steadfastly remained at his machine gun and continued to deliver deadly, accurate fire until mortally wounded by an enemy grenade. Pfc. Thompson's dauntless courage and gallant self-sacrifice reflect the highest credit on himself and uphold the esteemed traditions of military service.

3146 ◆ *TURNER, CHARLES WILLIAM

Rank: Sergeant First Class
Service: U.S. Army
Birthday: 28 May 1921
Place of Birth: Boston, Suffolk County, Massachusetts
Date of Death: 1 September 1950
Place of Death: Yongsan, Korea
Cemetery: Arlington National Cemetery (12-7762) (MH)—Arlington, Virginia
Entered Service at: Massachusetts
Unit: 2d Reconnaissance Company, 2d Infantry Division
Served as: Section Leader
Battle or Place of Action: near Yongsan, Korea
Date of Action: 2 September 1950
G.O. Number, Date: 10, 16 February 1951
Date of Presentation: 9 January 1951
Place of Presentation: The White House, presented by Pres. Harry S. Truman to his Mother
Citation: Sfc. Turner distinguished himself by conspicuous gallantry and intrepidity above and beyond the call of duty in action against the enemy. A large enemy force launched a mortar-and-automatic-weapon-supported assault against his platoon. Sfc. Turner, a section leader, quickly organized his unit for defense and then observed that the attack was directed at the tank section 100 yards away. Leaving his secured section, he dashed through a hail of fire to the threatened position and, mounting a tank, manned the exposed turret machine gun. Disregarding the intense enemy fire he calmly held this position, delivering deadly accurate fire and pointing out targets for the tank's 75-mm gun. His action resulted in the destruction of seven enemy machine-gun nests. Although severely wounded he remained at the gun shouting encouragement to his comrades. During the action the tank received over 50 direct hits; the periscopes and antenna were shot away and three rounds hit the machine-gun mount. Despite this fire he remained at his post until a burst of enemy fire cost his life. This intrepid and heroic performance enabled the platoon to withdraw and later launch an attack which routed the enemy. Sfc. Turner's valor and example reflect the highest credit upon himself and are in keeping with the esteemed traditions of the U.S. Army.

3147 ◆ VAN WINKLE, ARCHIE

Rank: Staff Sergeant (highest rank: Colonel)
Service: U.S. Marine Corps Reserve
Birthday: 17 March 1925
Place of Birth: Juneau, Juneau County, Alaska
Date of Death: 20 May 1986
Place of Death: Ketchikan, Alaska
Cemetery: Cremated, ashes scattered at sea
Entered Service at: Arlington, Snohomish County, Washington
Unit: 3 Platoon, Company B, 1st Battalion, 7th Marines, 1st Marine Division (Rein)
Served as: Platoon Sergeant

Battle or Place of Action: near Sudong, Korea
Date of Action: 2 November 1950
Date of Presentation: 6 February 1951
Place of Presentation: The White House, presented by Pres. Harry S. Truman
Citation: For conspicuous gallantry and intrepidity at the risk of his life above and beyond the call of duty while serving as a platoon sergeant in company B, in action against enemy aggressor forces. Immediately rallying the men in his area after a fanatical and numerically superior enemy force penetrated the center of the line under cover of darkness and pinned down the platoon with a devastating barrage of deadly automatic-weapons and grenade fire, S/Sgt. Van Winkle boldly spearheaded a determined attack through withering fire against hostile frontal positions and, though he and all the others who charged with him were wounded, succeeded in enabling his platoon to gain the fire superiority and the opportunity to reorganize. Realizing that the left-flank squad was isolated from the rest of the unit, he rushed through 40 yards of fierce enemy fire to reunite his troops despite an elbow wound which rendered one of his arms totally useless. Severely wounded a second time when a direct hit in the chest from a hostile hand grenade caused serious and painful wounds, he staunchly refused evacuation and continued to shout orders and words of encouragement to his depleted and battered platoon. Finally carried from his position unconscious from shock and from loss of blood, S/Sgt. Van Winkle served to inspire all who observed him to heroic efforts in successfully repulsing the enemy attack. His superb leadership, valiant fighting spirit, and unfaltering devotion to duty in the face of heavy odds reflect the highest credit upon himself and the U.S. Naval Service.

3148 ◆ *VITTORI, JOSEPH

Rank: Corporal
Service: U.S. Marine Corps Reserve
Birthday: 1 August 1929
Place of Birth: Beverly, Essex County, Massachusetts
Date of Death: 16 September 1951
Place of Death: Hill 749, Korea
Cemetery: St. Mary's Cemetery (MH)—Beverly, Massachusetts
Entered Service at: Beverly, Essex County, Massachusetts
Unit: Company F, 2d Battalion, 1st Marines, 1st Marine Division (Rein)
Served as: Automatic Rifleman
Battle or Place of Action: Hill 749, Korea
Date of Action: 15-16 September 1951
Place of Presentation: The Pentagon, presented by Sec. of the Navy Dan A. Kimball to his family
Citation: For conspicuous gallantry and intrepidity at the risk of his life above and beyond the call of duty while serving as an automatic-rifleman in Company F, in action against enemy aggressor forces. With a forward platoon suffering heavy casualties and forced to withdraw under a vicious enemy counterattack as his company assaulted strong hostile forces entrenched on Hill 749, Cpl. Vittori boldly rushed through the withdrawing troops with two other volunteers from his reserve platoon and plunged directly into the midst of the enemy. Overwhelming them in a fierce hand-to-hand struggle, he enabled his company to consolidate its positions to meet further imminent onslaught. Quick to respond to an urgent call for a rifleman to defend a heavy machine gun positioned on the extreme point of the northern flank and virtually isolated from the remainder of the unit when the enemy again struck in force during the night, he assumed position under the devastating barrage and, fighting a singlehanded battle, leaped from one flank to the other, covering each foxhole in turn as casualties continued to mount, manning a machine gun when the gunner was struck down, and making repeated trips through the heaviest shellfire to replenish ammunition. With the situation becoming extremely critical, reinforcing units to the rear pinned down under the blistering attack, and foxholes left practically void by dead and wounded for a distance of 100 yards, Cpl. Vittori continued his valiant stand, refusing to give ground as the enemy penetrated to within feet of his position, simulating strength in the line and denying the foe physical occupation of the ground. Mortally wounded by the enemy machine-gun and rifle bullets while persisting in his magnificent defense of the sector where approximately 200 enemy dead were found the following morning, Cpl. Vittori, by his fortitude, stouthearted courage, and great personal valor, had kept the point position intact despite the tremendous odds and undoubtedly prevented the entire battalion position from collapsing. His extraordinary heroism throughout the furious nightlong battle reflects the highest credit upon himself and the U.S. Naval Service. He gallantly gave his life for his country.

3149 ◆ *WALMSLEY JR., JOHN SPRINGER

Rank: Captain
Service: U.S. Air Force
Birthday: 7 January 1920
Place of Birth: Baltimore, Baltimore County, Maryland
Date of Death: 14 September 1951
Place of Death: Yangdok, Korea
Cemetery: Honolulu, Hawaii
Entered Service at: Baltimore, Baltimore County, Maryland
Unit: 8th Bombardment Squadron, 3d Bombardment Group
Served as: Pilot of a Douglas B-26
Battle or Place of Action: near Yangdok, Korea
Date of Action: 14 September 1951
Date of Presentation: 12 June 1954
Place of Presentation: Bolling AFB, presented by Sec. of the Air Force Talbott to his Widow
Citation: Capt. Walmsley distinguished himself by conspicuous gallantry and intrepidity at the risk of his life above and beyond the call of duty. While flying a B-26 aircraft on a night combat mission with the objective of developing new tactics, Capt. Walmsley sighted an enemy supply train which had been assigned top priority as a target of opportunity. He immediately attacked, producing a strike which disabled the train, and, when his ammunition was expended, radioed for friendly aircraft in the area to complete destruction of the target. Employing the searchlight mounted on his aircraft, he guided another B-26 aircraft to the target area, meanwhile constantly exposing himself to enemy fire. Directing an

incoming B-26 pilot, he twice boldly aligned himself with the target, his searchlight illuminating the area, in a determined effort to give the attacking aircraft full visibility. As the friendly aircraft prepared for the attack, Capt. Walmsley descended into the valley in a low-level run over the target with searchlight blazing, selflessly exposing himself to vicious enemy antiaircraft fire. In his determination to inflict maximum damage on the enemy, he refused to employ evasive tactics and valiantly pressed forward straight through an intense barrage, thus insuring complete destruction of the enemy's vitally needed war cargo. While he courageously pressed his attack Capt. Walmsley's plane was hit and crashed into the surrounding mountains, exploding upon impact. His heroic initiative and daring aggressiveness in completing this important mission in the face of overwhelming opposition and at the risk of his life, refects the highest credit upon himself and the U.S. Air Force.
Notes: MIA

3150 ◆ *WATKINS, LEWIS GEORGE

Rank: Staff Sergeant
Service: U.S. Marine Corps
Birthday: 6 June 1925
Place of Birth: Seneca, Oconee County, South Carolina
Date of Death: 7 October 1952
Place of Death: Korea
Cemetery: Honolulu, Hawaii
Entered Service at: Seneca, Oconee County, South Carolina
Unit: Company I, 3d Battalion, 7th Marines, 1st Marine Division (Rein)
Battle or Place of Action: Korea
Date of Action: 7 October 1952
Date of Presentation: 9 September 1953
Place of Presentation: Marine Corps Barracks, Washington, D.C., presented by Vice Pres. Richard M. Nixon to his parents
Citation: For conspicuous gallantry and intrepidity at the risk of his life above and beyond the call of duty while serving as a guide of a rifle platoon of Company I, in action against enemy aggressor forces during the hours of darkness on the morning of 7 October 1952. With his platoon assigned the mission of retaking an outpost which had been overrun by the enemy earlier in the night, S/Sgt. Watkins skillfully led his unit in the assault up the designated hill. Although painfully wounded when a well-entrenched hostile force at the crest of the hill engaged the platoon with intense small-arms and grenade fire, he gallantly continued to lead his men. Obtaining an automatic rifle from one of the wounded men, he assisted in pinning down an enemy machine gun holding up the assault. When an enemy grenade landed among S/Sgt. Watkins and several other marines while they were moving forward through a trench on the hill crest, he immediately pushed his companions aside, placed himself in a position to shield them, and picked up the deadly missile in an attempt to throw it outside the trench. Mortally wounded when the grenade exploded in his hand, S/Sgt. Watkins, by his great personal valor in the face of almost certain death, saved the lives of several of his comrades and contributed materially to the success of the mission. His extraordinary heroism, inspiring leadership, and resolute spirit of self-sacrifice reflect the highest credit upon himself and enhance the finest traditions of the U.S. Naval Service. He gallantly gave his life for his country.
Notes: MIA

3151 ◆ *WATKINS, TRAVIS E.

Rank: Master Sergeant
Service: U.S. Army
Birthday: 5 September 1920
Place of Birth: Waldo, Columbia County, Arkansas
Date of Death: 3 September 1950
Place of Death: Yongsan, Korea
Cemetery: Gladewater Memorial Park (PM)—Gladewater, Texas
Entered Service at: Texas
Unit: Company H, 9th Infantry Regiment, 2d Infantry Division
Battle or Place of Action: near Yongsan, Korea
Date of Action: 31 August-3 September 1950
G.O. Number, Date: 9, 16 February 1951
Date of Presentation: 9 January 1951
Place of Presentation: The White House, presented by Pres. Harry S. Truman to his Widow
Citation: M/Sgt. Watkins distinguished himself by conspicuous gallantry and intrepidity above and beyond the call of duty in action against the enemy. When an overwhelming enemy force broke through and isolated 30 men of his unit, he took command, established a perimeter defense and directed action which repelled continuous, fanatical enemy assaults. With his group completely surrounded and cut off, he moved from foxhole to foxhole exposing himself to enemy fire, giving instructions, and offering encouragement to his men. Later when the need for ammunition and grenades became critical he shot two enemy soldiers 50 yards outside the perimeter and went out alone for their ammunition and weapons. As he picked up their weapons he was attacked by three others and wounded. Returning their fire he killed all three and gathering up the weapons of the five enemy dead returned to his amazed comrades. During a later assault, six enemy soldiers gained a defiladed spot and began to throw grenades into the perimeter making it untenable. Realizing the desperate situation and disregarding his wound, he rose from his foxhole to engage them with rifle fire. Although immediately hit by a burst from an enemy machine gun he continued to fire until he had killed the grenade throwers. With this threat eliminated he collapsed and despite being paralyzed from the waist down, encouraged his men to hold on. He refused all food, saving it for his comrades, and when it became apparent that help would not arrive in time to hold the position ordered his men to escape to friendly lines. Refusing evacuation as his hopeless condition would burden his comrades, he remained in his position and cheerfully wished them luck. Through his aggressive leadership and intrepid actions, this small force destroyed nearly 500 of the enemy before abandoning their position. M/Sgt. Watkins' sustained personal bravery and noble self-sacrifice reflect the

highest glory upon himself and is in keeping with the esteemed traditions of the U.S. Army.

3152 ◆ WEST, ERNEST EDISON

Rank: Private First Class
Service: U.S. Army
Birthday: 2 September 1931
Place of Birth: Russell, Greenup County, Kentucky
Entered Service at: Wurtland, Greenup County, Kentucky
Unit: 2d Squad, 3d Platoon, Company L, 3d Battalion, 14th Infantry Regiment, 25th Infantry Division
Served as: Acting Sergeant/Squad Leader
Battle or Place of Action: near Sataeri, Korea
Date of Action: 12 October 1952
G.O. Number, Date: 7, 29 January 1954
Date of Presentation: 12 January 1954
Place of Presentation: The White House, presented by Pres. Dwight D. Eisenhower
Citation: Pfc. West distinguished himself by conspicuous gallantry above and beyond the call of duty in action against the enemy. He voluntarily accompanied a contingent to locate and destroy a reported enemy outpost. Nearing the objective, the patrol was ambushed and suffered numerous casualties. Observing his wounded leader lying in an exposed position, Pfc. West ordered the troops to withdraw, then braved intense fire to reach and assist him. While attempting evacuation, he was attacked by three hostile soldiers employing grenades and small-arms fire. Quickly shifting his body to shelter the officer, he killed the assailants with his rifle, then carried the helpless man to safety. He was critically wounded and lost an eye in this action, but courageously returned through withering fire and bursting shells to assist the wounded. While evacuating two comrades, he closed with and killed three more of the foe. Pfc. West's indomitable spirit, consummate valor, and intrepid actions inspired all who observed him, reflect the highest credit on himself, and uphold the honored traditions of the military service.

3153 ◆ WILSON, BENJAMIN F.

Rank: First Lieutenant (rank at time of action: Master Sergeant) (highest rank: Major)
Service: U.S. Army
Birthday: 2 June 1922
Place of Birth: Vashon, King County, Washington
Date of Death: 1 March 1988
Place of Death: Honolulu, Hawaii
Cemetery: National Memorial Cemetery of the Pacific (A-1060-A) (MH)—Honolulu, Hawaii
Entered Service at: Vashon, King County, Washington
Unit: Company I, 31st Infantry Regiment, 7th Infantry Division
Battle or Place of Action: near Hwach'on-Myon, Korea
Date of Action: 5 June 1951
G.O. Number, Date: 69, 23 September 1954
Date of Presentation: 7 September 1954
Place of Presentation: Army Hospital, Denver, CO, presented by Pres. Dwight D. Eisenhower
Citation: 1st Lt. Wilson distinguished himself by conspicuous gallantry and indomitable courage above and beyond the call of duty in action against the enemy. Company I was committed to attack and secure commanding terrain stubbornly defended by a numerically superior hostile force emplaced in well-fortified positions. When the spearheading element was pinned down by withering hostile fire, he dashed forward and, firing his rifle and throwing grenades, neutralized the position denying the advance, and killed four enemy soldiers manning submachine guns. After the assault platoon moved up, occupied the position, and a base of fire was established, he led a bayonet attack which reduced the objective and killed approximately 27 hostile soldiers. While friendly forces were consolidating the newly won gain, the enemy launched a counterattack and 1st Lt. Wilson, realizing the imminent threat of being overrun, made a determined lone-man charge, killing seven and wounding two of the enemy, and routing the remainder in disorder. After the position was organized, he led an assault carrying to approximately 15 yards of the final objective, when enemy fire halted the advance. He ordered the platoon to withdraw and, although painfully wounded in this action, remained to provide covering fire. During an ensuing counterattack, the commanding officer and 1st Platoon leader became casualties. Unhesitatingly, 1st Lt. Wilson charged the enemy ranks and fought valiantly, killing three enemy soldiers with his rifle before it was wrested from his hands, and annihilating four others with his entrenching tool. His courageous delaying action enabled his comrades to reorganize and effect an orderly withdrawal. While directing evacuation of the wounded, he suffered a second wound, but elected to remain on the position until assured that all of the men had reached safety. 1st Lt. Wilson's sustained valor and intrepid actions reflect utmost credit upon himself and uphold the honored traditions of the military service.

3154 ◆ WILSON, HAROLD EDWARD "SPEEDY"

Rank: Technical Sergeant (highest rank: Chief Warrant Officer 4)
Service: U.S. Marine Corps Reserve
Birthday: 5 December 1921
Place of Birth: Birmingham, Jefferson County, Alabama
Entered Service at: Birmingham, Jefferson County, Alabama
Unit: 3d Platoon, Company G, 3d Battalion, 1st Marines, 1st Marine Division
Served as: Platoon Sergeant
Battle or Place of Action: Korea
Date of Action: 23-24 April 1951
Date of Presentation: 12 April 1952
Place of Presentation: The White House, presented by Pres. Harry S. Truman
Citation: For gallantry and intrepidity at the risk of his life above and beyond the call of duty while serving as platoon sergeant of a rifle platoon attached to Company G, in action against enemy aggressor forces on the night from 23 to 24 April 1951. When the company outpost was overrun by the enemy while his platoon, firing from hastily constructed fox-

holes, was engaged in resisting the brunt of a fierce mortar, machinegun, grenade, and small-arms attack launched by hostile forces from high ground under cover of darkness, T/Sgt. Wilson braved intense fire to assist the survivors back into the line and to direct the treatment of casualties. Although twice wounded by gunfire, in the right arm and the left leg, he refused medical aid for himself and continued to move about among his men, shouting words of encouragement. After receiving further wounds in the head and shoulder as the attack increased in intensity, he again insisted upon remaining with his unit. Unable to use either arm to fire, and with mounting casualties among our forces, he resupplied his men with rifles and ammunition taken from the wounded. Personally reporting to his company commander on several occasions, he requested and received additional assistance when the enemy attack became even more fierce and, after placing the reinforcements in strategic positions in the line, directed effective fire until blown off his feet by the bursting of a hostile mortar round in his face. Dazed and suffering from concussion, he still refused medical aid and, despite weakness from loss of blood, moved from foxhole to foxhole, directing fire, resupplying ammunition, rendering first aid, and encouraging his men. By his heroic actions in the face of almost certain death, when the unit's ability to hold the disadvantageous position was doubtful, he instilled confidence in his troops, inspiring them to rally repeatedly and turn back the furious assaults. At dawn, after the final attack had been repulsed, he personally accounted for each man in his platoon before walking unassisted one-half mile to the aid station where he submitted to treatment. His outstanding courage, initiative, and skilled leadership in the face of overwhelming odds were contributing factors in the success of his company's mission and reflect the highest credit upon T/Sgt. Wilson and the U.S. Naval Service.

3155 ◆ *WILSON, RICHARD G.

Rank: Private First Class
Service: U.S. Army
Birthday: 19 August 1931
Place of Birth: Marion, Williamson County, Illinois
Date of Death: 21 October 1950
Place of Death: Opari, Korea
Cemetery: Cape County Memorial Park—Cape Girardeau, Missouri
Entered Service at: Cape Girardeau, Cape Girardeau County, Missouri
Unit: Medical Company, Company I, 187th Airborne Infantry Regiment
Served as: Medical Aidman
Battle or Place of Action: near Opari, Korea
Date of Action: 21 October 1950
G.O. Number, Date: 64, 2 August 1951
Date of Presentation: 21 June 1951
Place of Presentation: The Pentagon, presented by Gen. Omar N. Bradley to his Widow
Citation: Pfc. Wilson distinguished himself by conspicuous gallantry and intrepidity above and beyond the call of duty in action. As medical aidman attached to Company I, he accompanied the unit during a reconnaissance-in-force through the hilly country near Opari. The main body of the company was passing through a narrow valley flanked on three sides by high hills when the enemy laid down a barrage of mortar, automatic-weapons, and small-arms fire. The company suffered a large number of casualties from the intense hostile fire while fighting its way out of the ambush. Pfc. Wilson proceeded at once to move among the wounded and administered aid to them oblivious of the danger to himself, constantly exposing himself to hostile fire. The company commander ordered a withdrawal as the enemy threatened to encircle and isolate the company. As his unit withdrew Pvt. Wilson assisted wounded men to safety and assured himself that none were left behind. After the company had pulled back he learned that a comrade previously thought dead had been seen to be moving and attempting to crawl to safety. Despite the protests of his comrades, unarmed and facing a merciless enemy, Pfc. Wilson returned to the dangerous position in search of his comrade. Two days later a patrol found him lying beside the man he returned to aid. He had been shot several times while trying to shield and administer to the wounded man. Pfc. Wilson's superb personal bravery, consummate courage, and willing self-sacrifice for his comrades reflect untold glory upon himself and uphold the esteemed traditions of the military service.

3156 ◆ *WINDRICH, WILLIAM GORDON

Rank: Staff Sergeant
Service: U.S. Marine Corps
Birthday: 14 May 1921
Place of Birth: Chicago, Cook County, Illinois
Date of Death: 2 December 1950
Cemetery: Arlington National Cemetery (31-4856) (MH)—Arlington, Virginia
Entered Service at: Hammond, Lake County, Indiana
Unit: Company I, 3d Battalion, 5th Marines, 1st Marine Division (Rein)
Served as: Platoon Sergeant
Battle or Place of Action: vinicity of Yudam-ni, Korea
Date of Action: 1 December 1950
Date of Presentation: 8 February 1952
Place of Presentation: The Pentagon, presented by Under Sec. of the Navy Francis P. Whitehair to his Widow
Citation: For conspicuous gallantry and intrepidity at the risk of his life above and beyond the call of duty as a platoon sergeant of Company I, in action against enemy aggressor forces the night of 1 December 1950. Promptly organizing a squad of men when the enemy launched a sudden, vicious counterattack against the forward elements of his company's position, rendering it untenable, S/Sgt. Windrich, armed with a carbine, spearheaded the assault to the top of the knoll immediately confronting the overwhelming forces and, under shattering hostile automatic-weapons, mortar, and grenade fire, directed effective fire to hold back the attackers and cover the withdrawal of our troops to commanding ground. With seven of his men struck down during the furious action and himself wounded in the head by a bursting grenade, he made his way to his company's position and, organizing a

small group of volunteers, returned with them to evacuate the wounded and dying from the frozen hillside, staunchly refusing medical attention himself. Immediately redeploying the remainder of his troops, S/Sgt. Windrich placed them on the left flank of the defensive sector before the enemy again attacked in force. Wounded in the leg during the bitter fight that followed, he bravely fought on with his men, shouting words of encouragement and directing their fire until the attack was repelled. Refusing evacuation although unable to stand, he still continued to direct his platoon in setting up defensive positions until weakened by the bitter cold, excessive loss of blood, and severe pain, he lapsed into unconsciousness and died. His valiant leadership, fortitude, and courageous fighting spirit against tremendous odds served to inspire others to heroic endeavor in holding the objective and reflect the highest credit upon S/Sgt. Windrich and the U.S. Naval Service. He gallantly gave his life for his country.

3157 ◆ *WOMACK, BRYANT HOMER

Rank: Private
Service: U.S. Army
Birthday: 12 May 1931
Place of Birth: Mill Spring, Polk County, North Carolina
Date of Death: 12 March 1952
Place of Death: Sokso-ri, Korea
Cemetery: Lebanon Church Cemetery (MH)—Mill Spring, North Carolina
Entered Service at: Mill Spring, Polk County, North Carolina
Unit: Medical Company, 14th Infantry Regiment, 25th Infantry Division
Served as: Medical Aidman
Battle or Place of Action: near Sokso-ri, Korea
Date of Action: 12 March 1952
G.O. Number, Date: 5, 12 January 1953
Date of Presentation: 7 January 1953
Place of Presentation: The Pentagon, presented by Sec. of the Army Frank C. Pace to his family
Citation: Pfc. Womack distinguished himself by conspicuous gallantry above and beyond the call of duty in action against the enemy. Pfc. Womack was the only medical aidman attached to a night combat patrol when sudden contact with a numerically superior enemy produced numerous casualties. Pfc. Womack went immediately to their aid, although this necessitated exposing himself to a devastating hail of enemy fire, during which he was seriously wounded. Refusing medical aid for himself, he continued moving among his comrades to administer aid. While he was aiding one man, he was again struck by enemy mortar fire, this time suffering the loss of his right arm. Although he knew the consequences should immediate aid not be administered, he still refused aid and insisted that all efforts be made for the benefit of others that were wounded. Although unable to perform the task himself, he remained on the scene and directed others in first-aid techniques. The last man to withdraw, he walked until he collapsed from loss of blood, and died a few minutes later while being carried by his comrades. The extraordinary heroism, outstanding courage, and unswerving devotion to his duties displayed by Pfc. Womack reflect the utmost distinction upon himself and uphold the esteemed traditions of the U.S. Army.

3158 ◆ *YOUNG, ROBERT HARLEY

Rank: Private First Class (highest rank: Corporal)
Service: U.S. Army
Birthday: 4 March 1929
Place of Birth: Oroville, Butte County, California
Date of Death: 5 November 1950
Cemetery: Golden Gate National Cemetery (0-8) (MH)—San Bruno, California
Entered Service at: Vallejo, Solano County, California
Unit: Company E, 8th Cavalry Regiment, 1st Cavalry Division
Battle or Place of Action: north of Kaesong, Korea
Date of Action: 9 October 1950
G.O. Number, Date: 65, 2 August 1951
Date of Presentation: 21 June 1951
Place of Presentation: The Pentagon, presented by Gen. Omar N. Bradley to his Father
Citation: Pfc. Young distinguished himself by conspicuous gallantry and intrepidity above and beyond the call of duty in action. His company, spearheading a battalion drive deep in enemy territory, suddenly came under a devastating barrage of enemy mortar and automatic-weapons crossfire which inflicted heavy casualties among his comrades and wounded him in the face and shoulder. Refusing to be evacuated, Pfc. Young remained in position and continued to fire at the enemy until wounded a second time. As he awaited first aid near the company command post, the enemy attempted an enveloping movement. Disregarding medical treatment he took an exposed position and firing with deadly accuracy killed five of the enemy. During this action he was again hit by hostile fire which knocked him to the ground and destroyed his helmet. Later when supporting tanks moved forward, Pfc. Young, his wounds still unattended, directed tank fire which destroyed three enemy gun positions and enabled the company to advance. Wounded again by an enemy mortar burst, and while aiding several of his injured comrades, he demanded that all others be evacuated first. Throughout the course of this action the leadership and combative instinct displayed by Pfc. Young exerted a profound influence on the conduct of the company. His aggressive example affected the whole course of the action and was responsible for its success. Pfc. Young's dauntless courage and intrepidity reflect the highest credit upon himself and uphold the esteemed traditions of the U.S. Army.

VIETNAM WAR

3159 ◆ *ADAMS, WILLIAM EDWARD

Rank: Major
Service: U.S. Army
Birthday: 16 June 1939
Place of Birth: Casper, Natrona County, Wyoming
Date of Death: 25 May 1971
Place of Death: Republic of Vietnam
Cemetery: Fort Logan National Cemetery (P-3831) (MH)—Denver, Colorado
Entered Service at: Kansas City, Clay County, Missouri
Unit: A/227th Assault Helicopter Company, 52d Aviation Battalion, 17th Aviation Group, 1st Aviation Brigade
Served as: Helicopter Pilot
Battle or Place of Action: Kontum Province, Republic of Vietnam
Date of Action: 25 May 1971
G.O. Number, Date: 38, 6 September 1974
Date of Presentation: 8 August 1974
Place of Presentation: Blair House, presented by Vice Pres. Gerald R. Ford to his family
Citation: Maj. Adams distinguished himself on 25 May 1971 while serving as a helicopter pilot in Kontum province in the Republic of Vietnam. On that date, Maj. Adams volunteered to fly a lightly armed helicopter in an attempt to evacuate three seriously wounded soldiers from a small fire base which was under attack by a large enemy force. He made the decision with full knowledge that numerous antiaircraft weapons were positioned around the base and that the clear weather would afford the enemy gunners an unobstructed view of all routes into the base. As he approached the base, the enemy gunners opened fire with heavy machine guns, rocket-propelled grenades, and small arms. Undaunted by the fusillade, he continued his approach determined to accomplish the mission. Displaying tremendous courage under fire, he calmly directed the attacks of supporting gunships while maintaining absolute control of the helicopter he was flying. He landed the aircraft at the fire base despite the ever-increasing enemy fire and calmly waited until the wounded soldiers were placed on board. As his aircraft departed from the fire base, it was struck and seriously damaged by enemy antiaircraft fire and began descending. Flying with exceptional skill, he immediately regained control of the crippled aircraft and attempted a controlled landing. Despite his valiant efforts, the helicopter exploded, overturned, and plummeted to earth amid the hail of enemy fire. Maj. Adams' conspicuous gallantry, intrepidity, and humanitarian regard for his fellow man were in keeping with the most cherished traditions of the military service and reflected utmost credit on him and the U.S. Army.

3160 ◆ *ALBANESE, LEWIS

Rank: Private First Class
Service: U.S. Army
Birthday: 27 April 1946
Place of Birth: Venice, Italy
Date of Death: 1 December 1966
Place of Death: Republic of Vietnam
Cemetery: Evergreen-Washelli Memorial Park—Seattle, Washington
Entered Service at: Seattle, King County, Washington
Unit: Company B, 5th Battalion, 7th Cavalry, 1st Cavalry Division (Airmobile)
Battle or Place of Action: near Phu Muu II, Republic of Vietnam
Date of Action: 1 December 1966
G.O. Number, Date: 12, 3 April 1968
Date of Presentation: 16 February 1968
Place of Presentation: The Pentagon, presented by Sec. of the Army Stanley R. Resor to his family
Citation: For conspicuous gallantry and intrepidity in action at the risk of his life above and beyond the call of duty. Pfc. Albanese's platoon, while advancing through densely covered terrain to establish a blocking position, received intense automatic-weapons fire from close range. As other members maneuvered to assault the enemy position, Pfc. Albanese was ordered to provide security for the left flank of the platoon. Suddenly, the left flank received fire from enemy located in a well-concealed ditch. Realizing the imminent danger to his comrades from this fire, Pfc. Albanese fixed his bayonet and moved aggressively into the ditch. His action silenced the sniper fire, enabling the platoon to resume movement toward the main enemy position. As the platoon continued to advance, the sound of heavy firing emanated from the left flank from a pitched battle that ensued in the ditch which Pfc. Albanese had entered. The ditch was actually a well-organized complex of enemy defenses designed to bring devastating flanking fire on the forces attacking the main position. Pfc. Albanese, disregarding the danger to himself, advanced 100 meters along the trench and killed six of the snipers, who were armed with automatic weapons. Having exhausted his ammunition, Pfc. Albanese was mortally wounded when he engaged and killed two more enemy soldiers in fierce hand-to-hand combat. His unparalleled actions saved the lives of many members of his platoon who otherwise would have fallen to the sniper fire from the ditch, and enabled his platoon to successfully advance against an enemy force of overwhelming numerical superiority. Pfc. Albanese's extraordinary heroism and supreme dedication to his comrades were commensurate with the finest traditions of the military service and remain a tribute to himself, his unit, and the U.S. Army.

3161 ◆ *ANDERSON JR., JAMES

Rank: Private First Class
Service: U.S. Marine Corps
Birthday: 22 January 1947
Place of Birth: Los Angeles, Los Angeles County, California
Date of Death: 28 February 1967
Place of Death: Republic of Vietnam
Cemetery: Lincoln Memorial Park—Compton, California
Entered Service at: Los Angeles, Los Angeles County, California
Unit: 2d Platoon, Company F, 2d Battalion, 3d Marines, 3d Marine Division (Rein) FMF
Served as: Rifleman
Battle or Place of Action: northwest of Cam Lo, Republic of Vietnam
Date of Action: 28 February 1967
Date of Presentation: 21 August 1968
Place of Presentation: Marine Barracks, Washington, D.C., presented by Sec. of the Navy Paul R. Ignatius to his family
Citation: For conspicuous gallantry and intrepidity at the risk of his life above and beyond the call of duty. Company F was advancing in dense jungle northwest of Cam Lo in an effort to extract a heavily besieged reconnaissance patrol. Pfc. Anderson's platoon was the lead element and had advanced only about 200 meters when they were brought under extremely intense enemy small-arms and automatic-weapons fire. The platoon reacted swiftly, getting on line as best they could in the thick terrain, and began returning fire. Pfc. Anderson found himself tightly bunched together with the other members of the platoon only 20 meters from the enemy positions. As the firefight continued several of the men were wounded by the deadly enemy assault. Suddenly, an enemy grenade landed in the midst of the marines and rolled alongside Pfc. Anderson's head. Unhesitatingly and with complete disregard for his personal safety, he reached out, grasped the grenade, pulled it to his chest and curled around it as it went off. Although several marines received shrapnel from the grenade, his body absorbed the major force of the explosion. In this singularly heroic act, Pfc. Anderson saved his comrades from serious injury and possible death. His personal heroism, extraordinary valor, and inspirational supreme self-sacrifice reflected great credit upon himself and the Marine Corps and upheld the highest traditions of the U.S. Naval Service. He gallantly gave his life for his country.

3162 ◆ *ANDERSON, RICHARD ALLEN

Rank: Lance Corporal
Service: U.S. Marine Corps
Birthday: 16 April 1948
Place of Birth: Washington, D.C.
Date of Death: 24 August 1969
Place of Death: Republic of Vietnam
Cemetery: Forest Park Cemetery—Houston, Texas
Entered Service at: Houston, Harris County, Texas
Unit: Company E, 3d Reconnaissance Battalion, 3d Marine Division (Rein) FMF
Served as: Assistant Team Leader
Battle or Place of Action: Quang Tri Province, Republic of Vietnam
Date of Action: 24 August 1969
Date of Presentation: 15 September 1971
Place of Presentation: The White House, presented by Vice Pres. Spiro T. Agnew to his family
Citation: For conspicuous gallantry and intrepidity at the risk of his life above and beyond the call of duty while serving as an assistant team leader with Company E, in connection with combat operations against an armed enemy. While conducting a patrol during the early morning hours L/Cpl. Anderson's reconnaissance team came under a heavy volume of automatic-weapons and machine-gun fire from a numerically superior and well-concealed enemy force. Although painfully wounded in both legs and knocked to the ground during the initial moments of the fierce firefight, L/Cpl. Anderson assumed a prone position and continued to deliver intense suppressive fire in an attempt to repulse the attackers. Moments later he was wounded a second time by an enemy soldier who had approached to within eight feet of the team's position. Undaunted, he continued to pour a relentless stream of fire at the assaulting unit, even while a companion was treating his leg wounds. Observing an enemy grenade land between himself and the other marine, L/Cpl. Anderson immediately rolled over and covered the lethal weapon with his body, absorbing the full effects of the detonation. By his indomitable courage, inspiring initiative, and selfless devotion to duty, L/Cpl. Anderson was instrumental in saving several marines from serious injury or possible death. His actions were in keeping with the highest traditions of the Marine Corps and of the U.S. Naval Service. He gallantly gave his life in the service of his country.

3163 ◆ ANDERSON, WEBSTER

Rank: Sergeant First Class (rank at time of action: Staff Sergeant)
Service: U.S. Army
Birthday: 15 July 1933
Place of Birth: Winnsboro, Fairfield County, South Carolina
Entered Service at: Winnsboro, Fairfield County, South Carolina
Unit: Battery A, 2d Battalion, 320th Artillery, 101st Airborne Division (Airmobile)
Served as: Battery Section Chief
Battle or Place of Action: Tam Ky, Republic of Vietnam
Date of Action: 15 October 1967
G.O. Number, Date: 80, 4 December 1969
Date of Presentation: 24 November 1969
Place of Presentation: The White House, presented by Pres. Richard M. Nixon
Citation: Sfc. Anderson (then S/Sgt.) distinguished himself by conspicuous gallantry and intrepidity in action while serving as chief of section in Battery A, against a hostile force. During the early morning hours Battery A's defensive position was attacked by a determined North Vietnamese Army infantry unit supported by heavy mortar, recoilless-rifle, rocket-propelled-grenade and automatic-weapons fire. The initial enemy onslaught breached the battery defensive perimeter. Sfc. Anderson, with complete disregard for his personal safety,

mounted the exposed parapet of his howitzer position and became the mainstay of the defense of the battery position. Sfc. Anderson directed devastating direct howitzer fire on the assaulting enemy while providing rifle and grenade defensive fire against enemy soldiers attempting to overrun his gun section position. While protecting his crew and directing their fire against the enemy from his exposed position, two enemy grenades exploded at his feet knocking him down and severely wounding him in the legs. Despite the excruciating pain and though not able to stand, Sfc. Anderson valorously propped himself on the parapet and continued to direct howitzer fire upon the closing enemy and to encourage his men to fight on. Seeing an enemy grenade land within the gun pit near a wounded member of his gun crew, Sfc. Anderson heedless of his own safety, seized the grenade and attempted to throw it over the parapet to save his men. As the grenade was thrown from the position it exploded and Sfc. Anderson was again grievously wounded. Although only partially conscious and severely wounded, Sfc. Anderson refused medical evacuation and continued to encourage his men in the defense of the position. Sfc. Anderson, by his inspirational leadership, professionalism, devotion to duty, and complete disregard for his welfare, was able to maintain the defense of his section position and to defeat a determined attack. Sfc. Anderson's gallantry and extraordinary heroism at the risk of his life above and beyond the call of duty are in the highest traditions of the military service and reflect great credit upon himself, his unit, and the U.S. Army.

3164 ◆ *ASHLEY JR., EUGENE

Rank: Sergeant First Class
Service: U.S. Army
Birthday: 12 October 1931
Place of Birth: Wilmington, New Hanover County, North Carolina
Date of Death: 7 February 1968
Place of Death: Republic of Vietnam
Cemetery: Rochfish Memorial Cemetery (MH)—Fayetteville, North Carolina
Entered Service at: New York, New York
Unit: Detachment A-101, Company C, 5th Special Forces Group (Airborne), 1st Special Forces
Served as: Senior Advisor
Battle or Place of Action: near Lang Vei, Republic of Vietnam
Date of Action: 6-7 February 1968
G.O. Number, Date: 84, 12 December 1969
Date of Presentation: 2 December 1969
Place of Presentation: The White House, presented by Vice Pres. Spiro T. Agnew to his family
Citation: Sfc. Ashley distinguished himself by conspicuous gallantry and intrepidity while serving with Detachment A-101, Company C. Sfc. Ashley was the senior Special Forces Advisor of a hastily organized assault force whose mission was to rescue entrapped U.S. Special Forces advisers at Camp Lang Vei. During the initial attack on the Special Forces camp by North Vietnamese Army forces, Sfc. Ashley supported the camp with high-explosive and illumination mortar rounds. When communications were lost with the main camp, he assumed the additional responsibility of directing air strikes and artillery support. Sfc. Ashley organized and equipped a small assault force composed of local friendly personnel. During the ensuing battle, Sfc. Ashley led a total of five vigorous assaults against the enemy, continuously exposing himself to a voluminous hail of enemy grenades, machine gun and automatic-weapons fire. Throughout these assaults, he was plagued by numerous boobytrapped satchel charges in all bunkers on his avenue of approach. During his fifth and final assault, he adjusted air strikes nearly on top of his assault element, forcing the enemy to withdraw and resulting in friendly control of the summit of the hill. While exposing himself to intense enemy fire, he was seriously wounded by machine-gun fire but continued his mission without regard for his personal safety. After the fifth assault he lost consciousness and was carried from the summit by his comrades only to suffer a fatal wound when an enemy artillery round landed in the area. Sfc. Ashley displayed extraordinary heroism in risking his life in an attempt to save the lives of his entrapped comrades and commanding officer. His total disregard for his personal safety while exposed to enemy observation and automatic-weapons fire was an inspiration to all men committed to the assault. The resolute valor with which he led five gallant charges placed critical diversionary pressure on the attacking enemy and his valiant efforts carved a channel in the overpowering enemy forces and weapons positions through which the survivors of Camp Lang Vei eventually escaped to freedom. Sfc. Ashley's bravery at the cost of his life was in the highest traditions of the military service, and reflects great credit upon himself, his unit, and the U.S. Army.

3165 ◆ *AUSTIN, OSCAR PALMER

Rank: Private First Class
Service: U.S. Marine Corps
Birthday: 15 January 1948
Place of Birth: Nacogdoches, Nacogdoches County, Texas
Date of Death: 23 February 1969
Place of Death: Republic of Vietnam
Cemetery: Greenwood Memorial Park—Phoenix, Arizona
Entered Service at: Phoenix, Maricopa County, Arizona
Unit: Company E, 2d Battalion, 7th Marines, 1st Marine Division (Rein) FMF
Served as: Assistant Machine Gunner
Battle or Place of Action: west of Da Nang, Republic of Vietnam
Date of Action: 23 February 1969
Date of Presentation: 20 April 1970
Place of Presentation: The White House, presented by Vice Pres. Spiro T. Agnew to his family
Citation: For conspicuous gallantry and intrepidity at the risk of his life above and beyond the call of duty while serving as an assistant machine gunner with Company E, in connection with operations against enemy forces. During the early morning hours Pfc. Austin's observation post was subjected to a fierce ground attack by a large North Vietnamese Army force supported by a heavy volume of hand grenades, satchel charges, and small-arms fire. Observing that one of his

wounded companions had fallen unconscious in a position dangerously exposed to the hostile fire, Pfc. Austin unhesitatingly left the relative security of his fighting hole and, with complete disregard for his safety, raced across the fire-swept terrain to assist the marine to a covered location. As he neared the casualty, he observed an enemy grenade land nearby and reacting instantly, leaped between the injured marine and the lethal object, absorbing the effects of its detonation. As he ignored his painful injuries and turned to examine the wounded man, he saw a North Vietnamese Army soldier aiming a weapon at his unconscious companion. With full knowledge of the probable consequences and thinking only to protect the marine, Pfc. Austin resolutely threw himself between the casualty and the hostile soldier, and in so doing, was mortally wounded. Pfc. Austin's indomitable courage, inspiring initiative and selfless devotion to duty upheld the highest traditions of the Marine Corps and the U.S. Naval Service. He gallantly gave his life for his country.

3166 ◆ BACA, JOHN PHILIP

Rank: Specialist Fourth Class (highest rank: Sergeant)
Service: U.S. Army
Birthday: 10 January 1949
Place of Birth: Providence, Providence County, Rhode Island
Entered Service at: Fort Ord, Monterey County, California
Unit: 4th Platoon, Company D, 1st Battalion, 12th Cavalry, 1st Cavalry Division
Served as: Recoilless Rifle Team Member
Battle or Place of Action: near Quan Loi, Phuoc Long Province, Republic of Vietnam
Date of Action: 10 February 1970
G.O. Number, Date: 37, 16 July 1971
Date of Presentation: 15 June 1971
Place of Presentation: The White House (East Ballroom), presented by Pres. Richard M. Nixon
Citation: For conspicuous gallantry and intrepidity in action at the risk of his life above and beyond the call of duty. Sp4c. Baca, Company D, distinguished himself while serving on a recoilless-rifle team during a night ambush mission. A platoon from his company was sent to investigate the detonation of an automatic ambush device forward of his unit's main position and soon came under intense enemy fire from concealed positions along the trail. Hearing the heavy firing from the platoon position and realizing that his recoilless-rifle team could assist the members of the besieged patrol, Sp4c. Baca led his team through the hail of enemy fire to a firing position within the patrol's defensive perimeter. As they prepared to engage the enemy, a fragmentation grenade was thrown into the midst of the patrol. Fully aware of the danger to his comrades, Sp4c. Baca unhesitatingly and with complete disregard for his own safety, covered the grenade with his steel helmet and fell on it as the grenade exploded, thereby absorbing the lethal fragments and concussion with his body. His gallant action and total disregard for his personal well-being directly saved eight men from certain serious injury or death. The extraordinary courage and selflessness displayed by Sp4c. Baca, at the risk of his life, are in the highest traditions of the military service and reflect great credit on him, his unit, and the U.S. Army.

3167 ◆ BACON, NICKY DANIEL

Rank: Staff Sergeant (highest rank: First Sergeant)
Service: U.S. Army
Birthday: 25 November 1945
Place of Birth: Caraway, Craighead County, Arkansas
Entered Service at: Phoenix, Maricopa County, Arizona
Unit: Company B, 4th Battalion, 21st Infantry, 11th Infantry Brigade, Americal Division
Served as: Squad Leader
Battle or Place of Action: west of Tam Ky, Republic of Vietnam
Date of Action: 26 August 1968
G.O. Number, Date: 81, 4 December 1969
Date of Presentation: 24 November 1969
Place of Presentation: The White House, presented by Pres. Richard M. Nixon
Citation: For conspicuous gallantry and intrepidity in action at the risk of his life above and beyond the call of duty. S/Sgt. Bacon distinguished himself while serving as a squad leader with the 1st Platoon, Company B, during an operation west of Tam Ky. When Company B came under fire from an enemy bunker line to the front, S/Sgt. Bacon quickly organized his men and led them forward in an assault. He advanced on a hostile bunker and destroyed it with grenades. As he did so, several fellow soldiers, including the 1st Platoon leader, were struck by machine-gun fire and fell wounded in an exposed position forward of the rest of the platoon. S/Sgt. Bacon immediately assumed command of the platoon and assaulted the hostile gun position, finally killing the enemy gun crew in a singlehanded effort. When the 3d Platoon moved to S/Sgt. Bacon's location, its leader was also wounded. Without hesitation S/Sgt. Bacon took charge of the additional platoon and continued the fight. In the ensuing action he personally killed four more enemy soldiers and silenced an antitank weapon. Under his leadership and example, the members of both platoons accepted his authority without question. Continuing to ignore the intense hostile fire, he climbed up on the exposed deck of a tank and directed fire into the enemy position while several wounded men were evacuated. As a result of S/Sgt. Bacon's extraordinary efforts, his company was able to move forward, eliminate the enemy positions, and rescue the men trapped to the front. S/Sgt. Bacon's bravery at the risk of his life was in the highest traditions of the military service and reflects great credit upon himself, his unit, and the U.S. Army.

3168 ◆ BAKER JR., JOHN FRANKLIN

Rank: Sergeant (rank at time of action: Private First Class) (highest rank: Master Sergeant)
Service: U.S. Army
Birthday: 30 October 1945
Place of Birth: Davenport, Scott County, Iowa
Entered Service at: Moline, Rock Island County, Illinois

Unit: Company A, 2d Battalion, 27th Infantry, 25th Infantry Division
Served as: Machine Gunner
Battle or Place of Action: near Dau Tieng, Republic of Vietnam
Date of Action: 5 November 1966
G.O. Number, Date: 24, 13 June 1968
Date of Presentation: 1 May 1968
Place of Presentation: The White House (East Ballroom), presented by Pres. Lyndon B. Johnson
Citation: For conspicuous gallantry and intrepidity in action at the risk of his life above and beyond the call of duty. En route to assist another unit that was engaged with the enemy, Company A came under intense enemy fire and the lead man was killed instantly. Sgt. Baker immediately moved to the head of the column and together with another soldier knocked out two enemy bunkers. When his comrade was mortally wounded, Sgt. Baker, spotting four Viet Cong snipers, killed all of them, evacuated the fallen soldier, and returned to lead repeated assaults against the enemy positions, killing several more Viet Cong. Moving to attack two additional enemy bunkers, he and another soldier drew intense enemy fire and Sgt. Baker was blown from his feet by an enemy grenade. He quickly recovered and singlehandedly destroyed one bunker before the other soldier was wounded. Seizing his fallen comrade's machine gun, Sgt. Baker charged through the deadly fusillade to silence the other bunker. He evacuated his comrade, replenished his ammunition, and returned to the forefront to brave the enemy fire and continue the fight. When the forward element was ordered to withdraw, he carried one wounded man to the rear. As he returned to evacuate another soldier, he was taken under fire by snipers, but raced beyond the friendly troops to attack and kill the snipers. After evacuating the wounded man, he returned to cover the deployment of the unit. His ammunition now exhausted, he dragged two more of his fallen comrades to the rear. Sgt. Baker's selfless heroism, indomitable fighting spirit, and extraordinary gallantry were directly responsible for saving the lives of several of his comrades, and inflicting serious damage on the enemy. His acts were in keeping with the highest traditions of the U.S. Army and reflect great credit upon himself and the Armed Forces of his country.

3169 ♦ BALLARD, DONALD EVERETT

Rank: Hospital Corpsman Second Class (current rank: Lieutenant Colonel (ARNG))
Service: U.S. Navy
Birthday: 5 December 1945
Place of Birth: Kansas City, Clay County, Missouri
Entered Service at: Kansas City, Clay County, Missouri
Unit: Company M, 3d Battalion, 4th Marines, 3d Marine Division
Served as: Medical Corpsman
Battle or Place of Action: Quang Tri Province, Republic of Vietnam
Date of Action: 16 May 1968
Date of Presentation: 14 May 1970
Place of Presentation: The White House, presented by Pres. Richard M. Nixon
Citation: For conspicuous gallantry and intrepidity at the risk of his life above and beyond the call of duty while serving as a HC2c. with Company M, in connection with operations against enemy aggressor forces. During the afternoon hours, Company M was moving to join the remainder of the 3d Battalion in Quang Tri province. After treating and evacuating two heat casualies, HC2c. Ballard was returning to his platoon from the evacuation landing zone when the company was ambushed by a North Vietnamese Army unit employing automatic weapons and mortars, and sustained numerous casualies. Observing a wounded marine, HC2c. Ballard unhesitatingly moved across the fire-swept terrain to the injured man and swiftly rendered medical assistance to his comrade. HC2c. Ballard then directed four marines to carry the casualty to a position of relative safety. As the four men prepared to move the wounded marine, an enemy soldier suddenly left his concealed position and, after hurling a hand grenade which landed near the casualty, commenced firing upon the small group of men. Instantly shouting a warning to the marines, HC2c. Ballard fearlessly threw himself upon the lethal explosive device to protect his comrades from the deadly blast. When the grenade failed to detonate, he calmly arose from his dangerous position and resolutely continued his determined efforts in treating other marine casualties. HC2c. Ballard's heroic actions and selfless concern for the welfare of his companions served to inspire all who observed him and prevented possible injury or death to his fellow marines. His courage, daring initiative, and unwavering devotion to duty in the face of extreme personal danger, sustain and enhance the finest traditions of the U.S. Naval Service.

3170 ♦ *BARKER, JEDH COLBY

Rank: Lance Corporal
Service: U.S. Marine Corps
Birthday: 20 June 1945
ce of Birth: Franklin, Merrimack County, New Hampshire
Date of Death: 21 September 1967
Place of Death: Republic of Vietnam
Cemetery: George Washington Memorial Cemetery (MH)—Paramus, New Jersey
Entered Service at: Park Ridge, Bergen County, New Jersey
Unit: Company F, 2d Battalion, 4th Marines, 3d Marine Division (Rein) FMF
Served as: Machine Gunner
Battle or Place of Action: near Con Thein, Republic of Vietnam
Date of Action: 21 September 1967
Date of Presentation: 31 October 1969
Place of Presentation: The White House, presented by Vice Pres. Spiro T. Agnew to his family
Citation: For conspicuous gallantry and intrepidity at the risk of his life above and beyond the call of duty while serving as a machine gunner with Company F. During a reconnaissance operation L/Cpl. Barker's squad was suddenly hit by enemy sniper fire. The squad immediately deployed to a combat formation and advanced to a strongly fortified enemy

position, when it was again struck by small-arms and automatic-weapons fire, sustaining numerous casualties. Although wounded by the initial burst of fire, L/Cpl. Barker boldly remained in the open, delivering a devastating volume of accurate fire on the numerically superior force. The enemy was intent upon annihilating the small marine force and, realizing that L/Cpl. Barker was a threat to their position, directed the preponderance of their fire on his position. He was again wounded, this time in the right hand, which prevented him from operating his vitally needed machine gun. Suddenly and without warning, an enemy grenade landed in the midst of the few surviving marines. Unhesitatingly and with complete disregard for his personal safety, L/Cpl. Barker threw himself upon the deadly grenade, absorbing with his body the full and tremendous force of the explosion. In a final act of bravery, he crawled to the side of a wounded comrade and administered first aid before succumbing to his grievous wounds. His bold initiative, intrepid fighting spirit and unwavering devotion to duty in the face of almost certain death undoubtedly saved his comrades from further injury or possible death and reflect great credit upon himself, the Marine Corps, and the U.S. Naval Service. He gallantly gave his life for his country.

3171 ◆ *BARNES III, JOHN ANDREW

Rank: Private First Class
Service: U.S. Army
Birthday: 16 April 1945
Place of Birth: Boston, Suffolk County, Massachusetts
Date of Death: 12 November 1967
Place of Death: Republic of Vietnam
Cemetery: Brookdale Cemetery (MH)—Dedham, Massachusetts
Entered Service at: Boston, Suffolk County, Massachusetts
Unit: Company C, 1st Battalion, 503d Infantry, 173d Airborne Brigade
Served as: Grenadier
Battle or Place of Action: Dak To, Republic of Vietnam
Date of Action: 12 November 1967
G.O. Number, Date: 73, 20 November 1969
Date of Presentation: 4 November 1969
Place of Presentation: The White House, presented by Vice Pres. Spiro T. Agnew to his family
Citation: For conspicuous gallantry and intrepidity in action at the risk of his life above and beyond the call of duty. Pfc. Barnes distinguished himself by exceptional heroism while engaged in combat against hostile forces. Pfc. Barnes was serving as a grenadier when his unit was attacked by a North Vietnamese force, estimated to be a battalion. Upon seeing the crew of a machine-gun team killed, Pfc. Barnes, without hesitation, dashed through the bullet-swept area, manned the machinegun, and killed nine enemy soldiers as they assaulted his position. While pausing just long enough to retrieve more ammunition, Pfc. Barnes observed an enemy grenade thrown into the midst of some severely wounded personnel close to his position. Realizing that the grenade could further injure or kill the majority of the wounded presonnel, he sacrificed his life by throwing himself directly onto the hand grenade as it exploded. Through his indomitable courage, complete disregard for his own safety, and profound concern for his fellow soldiers, he averted a probable loss of life and injury to the wounded members of his unit. Pfc. Barnes' extraordinary heroism and intrepidity at the cost of his life, above and beyond the call of duty, are in the highest traditions of military service and reflect great credit upon himself, his unit, and the U.S. Army.

3172 ◆ BARNUM JR., HARVEY CURTISS "BARNEY"

Rank: Captain (rank at time of action: First Lieutenant) (highest rank: Colonel)
Service: U.S. Marine Corps
Birthday: 21 July 1940
Place of Birth: Cheshire, New Haven County, Connecticut
Entered Service at: Cheshire, New Haven County, Connecticut
Unit: Company H, 2d Battalion, 9th Marines, 3d Marine Division (Rein) FMF
Served as: Forward Observer
Battle or Place of Action: outside the village of Ky Phu, Quang Tin Province, Republic of Vietnam
Date of Action: 18 December 1965
Date of Presentation: 27 February 1967
Place of Presentation: Marine Barracks, Washington, D.C., presented by Sec. of the Navy Paul H. Nitze
Citation: For conspicuous gallantry and intrepidity at the risk of his life above and beyond the call of duty. When the company was suddenly pinned down by a hail of extremely accurate enemy fire and was quickly separated from the remainder of the battalion by over 500 meters of open and fire-swept ground and casualties mounted rapidly, Lt. Barnum quickly made a hazardous reconnaissance of the area, seeking targets for his artillery. Finding the rifle company commander mortally wounded and the radio operator killed, he, with complete disregard for his safety, gave aid to the dying commander, then removed the radio from the dead operator and strapped it to himself. He immediately assumed command of the rifle company, and moving at once into the midst of the heavy fire, rallying and giving encouragement to all units, reorganizing them to replace the loss of key personnel and lead their attack on enemy positions from which deadly fire continued to come. His sound and swift decisions and his obvious calm served to stabilize the badly decimated units and his gallant example as he stood exposed repeatedly to point out targets served as an inspiration to all. Provided with two armed helicopters, he moved fearlessly through enemy fire to control the air attacks against the firmly entrenched enemy while skillfully directing one platoon in a successful counterattack on the key enemy positions. Having thus cleared a small area, he requested and directed the landing of two transport helicopters for the evacuation of the dead and wounded. He then assisted in the mopping-up and final seizure of the battalion's objective. His gallant initiative and heroic conduct reflected great credit upon himself and were in keeping with the highest traditions of the Marine Corps and the U.S. Naval Service.

3173 ◆ BEIKIRCH, GARY BURNELL

Rank: Sergeant
Service: U.S. Army
Birthday: 29 August 1947
Place of Birth: Rochester, Monroe County, New York
Entered Service at: Buffalo, Erie County, New York
Unit: Detachment 8245, Company B, 5th Special Forces Group (Airborne), 1st Special Forces
Served as: Medical Aidman
Battle or Place of Action: Dak Seang Special Forces A Camp, Kontum Province, Republic of Vietnam
Date of Action: 1 April 1970
G.O. Number, Date: 37, 5 November 1973
Date of Presentation: 15 October 1973
Place of Presentation: The White House, presented by Pres. Richard M. Nixon
Citation: For conspicuous gallantry and intrepidity in action at the risk of his life above and beyond the call of duty. Sgt. Beikirch, medical aidman, Detachment B-24, Company B, distinguished himself during the defense of Camp Dak Seang. The allied defenders suffered a number of casualties as a result of an intense, devastating attack launched by the enemy from well-concealed positions surrounding the camp. Sgt. Beikirch, with complete disregard for his personal safety, moved unhesitatingly through the withering enemy fire to his fallen comrades, applied first aid to their wounds and assisted them to the medical-aid station. When informed that a seriously injured American officer was lying in an exposed position, Sgt. Beikirch ran immediately through the hail of fire. Although he was wounded seriously by fragments from an exploding enemy mortar shell, Sgt. Beikirch carried the officer to a medical aid station. Ignoring his own serious injuries, Sgt. Beikirch left the relative safety of the medical bunker to search for and evacuate other men who had been injured. He was again wounded as he dragged a critically injured Vietnamese soldier to the medical bunker while simultaneously applying mouth-to-mouth resuscitation to sustain his life. Sgt. Beikirch again refused treatment and continued his search for other casualties until he collapsed. Only then did he permit himself to be treated. Sgt. Beikirch's complete devotion to the welfare of his comrades, at the risk of his life, are in keeping with the highest traditions of the military service and reflect great credit on him, his unit, and the U.S. Army.

3174 ◆ *BELCHER, TED

Rank: Sergeant
Service: U.S. Army
Birthday: 21 July 1924
Place of Birth: Accoville, Logan County, West Virginia
Date of Death: 19 November 1966
Place of Death: Republic of Vietnam
Cemetery: Greenwood Cemetery—Zanesville, Ohio
Entered Service at: Huntington, Cabell County, West Virginia
Unit: Company C, 1st Battalion, 14th Infantry, 25th Infantry Division
Served as: Squad Leader
Battle or Place of Action: Plei Djerang, Republic of Vietnam
Date of Action: 19 November 1966
G.O. Number, Date: 82, 20 December 1968
Date of Presentation: 6 December 1968
Place of Presentation: The Pentagon, presented by Sec. of the Army Stanley R. Resor to his family
Citation: Distinguishing himself by conspicuous gallantry and intrepidity at the risk of his life. Sgt. Belcher's unit was engaged in a search-and-destroy mission with Company B, 1st Battalion, 14th Infantry, the Battalion Reconnaissance Platoon, and a Special Forces company of Civilian Irregular Defense Group personnel. As a squad leader of the 2d Platoon of Company C, Sgt. Belcher was leading his men when they encountered a bunker complex. The reconnaissance platoon, located a few hundred meters northwest of Company C, received a heavy volume of fire from well-camouflaged snipers. As the 2d Platoon moved forward to assist the unit under attack, Sgt. Belcher and his squad, advancing only a short distance through the dense jungle terrain, met heavy and accurate automatic-weapons and sniper fire. Sgt. Belcher and his squad were momentarily stopped by the deadly volume of enemy fire. He quickly gave the order to return fire and resume the advance toward the enemy. As he moved up with his men, a hand grenade landed in the midst of the sergeant's squad. Instantly realizing the immediate danger to his men, Sgt. Belcher, unhesitatingly and with complete disregard for his safety, lunged forward, covering the grenade with his body. Absorbing the grenade blast at the cost of his life, he saved his comrades from becoming casualties. Sgt. Belcher's profound concern for his fellow soldiers, at the risk of his life above and beyond the call of duty, are in keeping with the highest tradition of the U.S. Army and reflect credit upon himself and the Armed Forces of his country.

3175 ◆ *BELLRICHARD, LESLIE ALLEN

Rank: Private First Class
Service: U.S. Army
Birthday: 4 December 1941
Place of Birth: Janesville, Rock County, Wisconsin
Date of Death: 20 May 1967
Place of Death: Republic of Vietnam
Cemetery: Oakhill Cemetery (MH)—Janesville, Wisconsin
Entered Service at: Oakland, Alameda County, California
Unit: Company C, 1st Battalion, 8th Infantry, 4th Infantry Division
Served as: Fire Team Leader
Battle or Place of Action: Kontum Province, Republic of Vietnam
Date of Action: 20 May 1967
G.O. Number, Date: 53, 8 August 1969
Date of Presentation: 10 July 1969
Place of Presentation: The White House, presented by Pres. Richard M. Nixon to his family
Citation: For conspicuous gallantry and intrepidity in action at the risk of his life above and beyond the call of duty.

Acting as a fire-team leader with Company C during combat operations Pfc. Bellrichard was with four fellow soldiers in a foxhole on their unit's perimeter when the position came under a massive enemy attack. Following a 30-minute mortar barrage, the enemy launched a strong ground assault. Pfc. Bellrichard rose in face of a group of charging enemy soldiers and threw hand grenades into their midst, eliminating several of the foe and forcing the remainder to withdraw. Failing in their initial attack, the enemy repeated the mortar and rocket bombardment of the friendly perimeter, then once again charged against the defenders in a concerted effort to overrun the position. Pfc. Bellrichard resumed throwing hand grenades at the onrushing attackers. As he was about to hurl a grenade, a mortar round exploded just in front of his position, knocking him into the foxhole and causing him to lose his grip on the already armed grenade. Recovering instantly, Pfc. Bellrichard recognized the threat to the lives of his four comrades and threw himself upon the grenade, shielding his companions from the blast that followed. Although seriously wounded, Pfc. Bellrichard struggled into an upright position in the foxhole and fired his rifle at the enemy until he succumbed to his wounds. His selfless heroism contributed greatly to the successful defense of the position, and he was directly responsible for saving the lives of several of his comrades. His acts are in keeping with the highest traditions of the military service and reflect great credit upon himself and the U.S. Army.

3176 ◆ BENAVIDEZ, ROY PEREZ

Rank: Master Sergeant (rank at time of action: Staff Sergeant)
Service: U.S. Army
Birthday: 5 August 1935
Place of Birth: Cuero, DeWitt County, Texas
Entered Service at: Houston, Harris County, Texas
Unit: 5th Special Forces Group (Airborne), Detachment B-56, 1st Special Forces
Served as: Operation Intelligence Sergeant
Battle or Place of Action: west of Loc Ninh, Cambodia
Date of Action: 2 May 1968
G.O. Number, Date: 8, 16 March 1981
Date of Presentation: 24 February 1981
Place of Presentation: The Pentagon (courtyard), presented by Pres. Ronald Reagan
Citation: M/Sgt. (then S/Sgt.) Roy P. Benavidez, 455-02-5039, United States Army, who distinguished himself by a series of daring and extremely valorous actions on 2 May 1968 while assigned to Detachment B-56, 5th Special Forces Group (Airborne), 1st Special Forces, Republic of Vietnam. On the morning of 2 May 1968, a 12-man Special Forces Reconnaissance Team was inserted by helicopters in a dense jungle area west of Loc Ninh, Vietnam, to gather intelligence information about confirmed large-scale enemy activity. This area was controlled and routinely patrolled by the North Vietnamese Army. After a short period of time on the ground, the team met heavy enemy resistance, and requested emergency extraction. Three helicopters attempted extraction, but were unable to land due to intense enemy small-arms and anti-aircraft fire. Sgt. Benavidez was at the Forward Operating Base in Loc Ninh monitoring the operation by radio when these helicopters returned to off-load wounded crewmembers and to assess aircraft damage. Sgt. Benavidez voluntarily boarded a returning aircraft to assist in another extraction attempt. Realizing that all the team members were either dead or wounded and unable to move to the pickup zone, he directed the aircraft to a nearby clearing while he jumped from the hovering helicopter, and ran approximately 75 meters under withering small-arms fire to the crippled team. Prior to reaching the team's position he was wounded in his right leg, face, and head. Despite these painful injuries, he took charge, repositioning the team members and directing their fire to facilitate the landing of the extraction aircraft and the loading of the wounded and dead team members. He then threw smoke canisters to direct the aircraft to the team's position. Despite his severe wounds and under intense enemy fire, he carried and dragged half of the wounded team members to the awaiting aircraft. He then provided protective fire by running alongside the aircraft as it moved to pick up the remaining team members. As the enemy's fire intensified, he hurried to recover the body and classified documents on the dead team leader. When he reached the leader's body, Sgt. Benavidez was severely wounded by small-arms fire in the abdomen and grenade fragments in his back. At nearly the same moment, the aircraft pilot was mortally wounded, and his helicopter crashed. Although in extremely critical condition due to his multiple wounds, Sgt. Benavidez secured the classified documents and made his way back to the wreckage, where he aided the wounded out of the overturned aircraft, and gathered the stunned survivors into a defensive perimeter. Under increasing enemy automatic-weapons and grenade fire, he moved around the perimeter distributing water and ammunition to his weary men, reinstilling in them a will to live and fight. Facing a buildup of enemy opposition with a beleaguered team, Sgt. Benavidez mustered his strength, began calling in tactical air strikes and directed the fire from supporting gunships to suppress the enemy's fire and so permitted another extraction attempt. He was wounded again in his thigh by small-arms fire while administering first aid to a wounded team member just before another extraction helicopter was able to land. His indomitable spirit kept him going as he began to ferry his comrades to the craft. On his second trip with the wounded, he was clubbed from additional wounds to his head and arms before killing his adversary. He then continued under devastating fire to carry the wounded to the helicopter. Upon reaching the aircraft, he spotted and killed two enemy soldiers who were rushing the craft from an angle that prevented the aircraft door-gunner from firing upon them. With little strength remaining, he made one last trip to the perimeter to ensure that all classified material had been collected or destroyed and to bring in the remaining wounded. Only then, in extremely serious condition from numerous wounds and loss of blood, did he allow himself to be pulled into the extraction aircraft. Sgt. Benavidez' gallant choice to join voluntarily his comrades who were in critical straits, to expose himself constantly to withering enemy fire, and his refusal to be stopped despite numerous severe wounds, saved the lives of at least eight

men. His fearless personal leadership, tenacious devotion to duty, and extremely valorous actions in the face of overwhelming odds were in keeping with the highest traditions of the military service and reflect the utmost credit on him and the United States Army.

3177 ◆ *BENNETT, STEVEN LOGAN

Rank: Captain
Service: U.S. Air Force
Birthday: 22 April 1946
Place of Birth: Palestine, Anderson County, Texas
Date of Death: 29 June 1972
Place of Death: Gulf of Tonkin
Cemetery: Lafayette Memorial Park—Lafayette, Louisiana
Entered Service at: Lafayette, Lafayette County, Louisiana
Unit: 20th Tactical Air Support Squadron, Da Nang Air Base, Pacific Air Forces
Served as: Forward Air Controller; Pilot of a OV-10 Bronco
Battle or Place of Action: Quang Tri Province, Republic of Vietnam
Date of Action: 29 June 1972
G.O. Number, Date: GB-1007, 6 September 1974
Date of Presentation: 8 August 1974
Place of Presentation: Blair House, presented by Vice Pres. Gerald R. Ford to his family
Citation: Capt. Bennett was the pilot of a light aircraft flying an artillery adjustment mission along a heavily defended segment of route structure. A large concentration of enemy troops were massing for an attack on a friendly unit. Capt. Bennett requested tactical air support but was advised that none was available. He also requested artillery support, but this too was denied due to the close proximity of friendly troops to the target. Capt. Bennett was determined to aid the endangered unit and elected to strafe the hostile positions. After four such passes, the enemy forces began to retreat. Capt. Bennett continued the attack, but, as he completed his fifth strafing pass, his aircraft was struck by a surface-to-air missile which severely damaged the left engine and the left main landing gear. As fire spread in the left engine, Capt. Bennett realized that recovery at a friendly airfield was impossible. He instructed his observer to prepare for ejection, but was informed by the observer that his parachute had been shredded by the force of the impacting missile. Although Capt. Bennett had a good parachute, he knew that if he ejected, the observer would have no chance of survival. With complete disregard for his own life, Capt. Bennett elected to ditch the aircraft into the Gulf of Tonkin, even though he realized that a pilot of this type aircraft had never survived a ditching. The ensuing impact upon the water caused the aircraft to cartwheel and severely damage the front cockpit, making escape for Capt. Bennett impossible. The observer successfully made his way out of the aircraft and was rescued. Capt. Bennett's unparalleled concern for his companion, extraordinary heroism, and intrepidity above and beyond the call of duty, at the cost of his life, were in keeping with the highest traditions of the military service and reflect great credit upon himself and the U.S. Air Force.

3178 ◆ *BENNETT, THOMAS WILLIAM

Rank: Corporal
Service: U.S. Army
Birthday: 7 April 1947
Place of Birth: Morgantown, Monongalia County, West Virginia
Date of Death: 11 February 1969
Place of Death: Republic of Vietnam
Cemetery: East Oak Grove Cemetery—Morgantown, West Virginia
Entered Service at: Fairmont, Marion County, West Virginia
Unit: 2d Platoon, Company B, 1st Battalion, 14th Infantry, 4th Infantry Division
Served as: Medical Aidman
Battle or Place of Action: Chu Pa Region, Pleiku Province, Republic of Vietnam
Date of Action: 9-11 February 1969
G.O. Number, Date: 10, 23 April 1970
Date of Presentation: 7 April 1970
Place of Presentation: The White House (Oval Office), presented by Pres. Richard M. Nixon to his family
Citation: For conspicuous gallantry and intrepidity in action at the risk of his life above and beyond the call of duty. Cpl. Bennett distinguished himself while serving as a platoon medical aidman with the 2d Platoon, Company B, during a reconnaissance-in-force mission. On 9 February the platoon was moving to assist the 1st Platoon of Company D, which had run into a North Vietnamese ambush, when it became heavily engaged by the intense small-arms, automatic-weapons, mortar and rocket fire from a well-fortified and numerically superior enemy unit. In the initial barrage of fire, three of the point members of the platoon fell wounded. Cpl. Bennett, with complete disregard for his safety, ran through the heavy fire to his fallen comrades, administered life-saving first aid under fire, and then made repeated trips carrying the wounded men to positions of relative safety from which they would be medically evacuated from the battle position. Cpl. Bennett repeatedly braved the intense enemy fire, moving across open areas to give aid and comfort to his wounded comrades. He valiantly exposed himself to the heavy fire in order to retrieve the bodies of several fallen personnel. Throughout the night and following day, Cpl. Bennett moved from position to position treating and comforting several personnel who had suffered shrapnel and gunshot wounds. On 11 February, Company B again moved in an assault on the well-fortified enemy positions and became heavily engaged with the numerically superior enemy force. Five members of the company fell wounded in the initial assault. Cpl. Bennett ran to their aid without regard to the heavy fire. He treated one wounded comrade and began running toward another seriously wounded man. Although the wounded man was located forward of the company position covered by heavy enemy grazing fire and Cpl. Bennett was warned that it was impossible to reach the position, he leaped forward with complete disregard for his safety to save his comrade's life. In an attempt to save his fellow soldier, he was mortally wounded. Cpl. Bennett's undaunted concern for his comrades at the cost of his life

above and beyond the call of duty are in keeping with the highest traditions of the military service and reflect great credit upon himself, his unit, and the U.S. Army.

3179 ◆ *BLANCHFIELD, MICHAEL REINERT

Rank: Specialist Fourth Class
Service: U.S. Army
Birthday: 4 January 1950
Place of Birth: Minneapolis, Hennepin County, Minnesota
Date of Death: 3 July 1969
Place of Death: Republic of Vietnam
Cemetery: All Saints Cemetery (MH)—Des Plains, Illinois
Entered Service at: Chicago, Cook County, Illinois
Unit: Company A, 4th Battalion, 503d Infantry, 173d Airborne Brigade
Served as: Rifleman
Battle or Place of Action: Binh Dinh Province, Republic of Vietnam
Date of Action: 3 July 1969
G.O. Number, Date: 25, 21 May 1971
Date of Presentation: 22 April 1971
Place of Presentation: The White House, presented by Pres. Richard M. Nixon to his family
Citation: For conspicuous gallantry and intrepidity in action at the risk of his life above and beyond the call of duty. Sp4c. Blanchfield distinguished himself while serving as a rifleman in Company A on a combat patrol. The patrol surrounded a group of houses to search for suspects. During the search of one of the huts, a man suddenly ran out toward a nearby treeline. Sp4c. Blanchfield, who was on guard outside the hut, saw the man, shouted for him to halt, and began firing at him as the man ignored the warning and continued to run. The suspect suddenly threw a grenade toward the hut and its occupants. Although the exploding grenade severely wounded Sp4c. Blanchfield and several others, he regained his feet to continue the pursuit of the enemy. The fleeing enemy threw a second grenade which landed near Sp4c. Blanchfield and several members of his patrol. Instantly realizing the danger, he shouted a warning to his comrades. Sp4c. Blanchfield unhesitatingly and with complete disregard for his safety threw himself on the grenade, absorbing the full and fatal impact of the explosion. By his gallant action and self-sacrifice, he was able to save the lives and prevent injury to four members of the patrol and several Vietnamese civilians in the immediate area. Sp4c. Blanchfield's extraordinary courage and gallantry at the cost of his life above and beyond the call of duty are in keeping with the highest traditions of the military service and reflect great credit upon himself, his unit, and the U.S. Army.

3180 ◆ *BOBO, JOHN PAUL

Rank: Second Lieutenant
Service: U.S. Marine Corps Reserve
Birthday: 14 February 1943
Place of Birth: Niagara Falls, Niagara County, New York
Date of Death: 30 March 1967
Place of Death: Republic of Vietnam
Cemetery: Gate of Heaven Cemetery—Niagara Falls, New York
Entered Service at: Buffalo, Erie County, New York
Unit: Company I, 3d Battalion, 9th Marines, 3d Marine Division (Rein) FMF
Served as: Weapons Platoon Commander
Battle or Place of Action: Quang Tri Province, Republic of Vietnam
Date of Action: 30 March 1967
Date of Presentation: 27 August 1968
Place of Presentation: Marine Barracks, Washington, D.C., presented by Sec. of the Navy Paul R. Ignatius to his family
Citation: For conspicuous gallantry and intrepidity at the risk of his life above and beyond the call of duty. Company I was establishing night ambush sites when the command group was attacked by a reinforced North Vietnamese company supported by heavy automatic-weapons and mortar fire. 2d Lt. Bobo immediately organized a hasty defense and moved from position to position encouraging the outnumbered marines despite the murderous enemy fire. Recovering a rocket launcher from among the friendly casualties, he organized a new launcher team and directed its fire into the enemy machine-gun positions. When an exploding enemy mortar round severed 2d Lt. Bobo's right leg below the knee, he refused to be evacuated and insisted upon being placed in a firing position to cover the movement of the command group to a better location. With a web belt around his leg serving as a tourniquet and with his leg jammed into the dirt to contain the bleeding he remained in this position and delivered devastating fire into the ranks of the enemy attempting to overrun the marines. 2d Lt. Bobo was mortally wounded while firing his weapon into the mainpoint of the enemy attack but his valiant spirit inspired his men to heroic efforts, and his tenacious stand enabled the command group to gain a protective position where it repulsed the enemy onslaught. 2d Lt. Bobo's superb leadership, dauntless courage, and bold initiative reflected great credit upon himself and upheld the highest traditions of the Marine Corps and the U.S. Naval Service. He gallantly gave his life for his country.

3181 ◆ BONDSTEEL, JAMES LEROY

Rank: Staff Sergeant (highest rank: Master Sergeant)
Service: U.S. Army
Birthday: 18 July 1947
Place of Birth: Jackson, Jackson County, Michigan
Date of Death: 9 April 1987
Place of Death: Kinik River Bridge, Anchorage, Alaska
Cemetery: Fort Richardson National Cemetery (H-19) (MH)—Fort Richardson, Alaska
Entered Service at: Detroit, Wayne County, Michigan
Unit: Company A, 2d Battalion, 2d Infantry, 1st Infantry Division
Served as: Platoon Sergeant
Battle or Place of Action: near the village of Lang Sau, An Loc Province, Republic of Vietnam
Date of Action: 24 May 1969
G.O. Number, Date: 38, 5 November 1973
Date of Presentation: 15 October 1973

Place of Presentation: The White House, presented by Pres. Richard M. Nixon
Citation: For conspicuous gallantry and intrepidity in action at the risk of his life above and beyond the call of duty. S/Sgt. Bondsteel distinguished himself while serving as a platoon sergeant with Company A, near the village of Lang Sau. Company A was directed to assist a friendly unit which was endangered by intense fire from a North Vietnamese battalion located in a heavily fortified base camp. S/Sgt. Bondsteel quickly organized the men of his platoon into effective combat teams and spearheaded the attack by destroying four enemy-occupied bunkers. He then raced some 200 meters under heavy enemy fire to reach an adjoining platoon which had begun to falter. After rallying this unit and assisting their wounded, S/Sgt. Bondsteel returned to his own sector with critically needed munitions. Without pausing he moved to the forefront and destroyed four enemy-occupied bunkers and a machine gun which had threatened his advancing platoon. Although painfully wounded by an enemy grenade, S/Sgt. Bondsteel refused medical attention and continued his assault by neutralizing two more enemy bunkers nearby. While searching one of these emplacements, S/Sgt. Bondsteel narrowly escaped death when an enemy soldier detonated a grenade at close range. Shortly thereafter, he ran to the aid of a seriously wounded officer and struck down an enemy soldier who was threatening the officer's life. S/Sgt. Bondsteel then continued to rally his men and lead them through the entrenched enemy until his company was relieved. His exemplary leadership and great personal courage throughout the four-hour battle ensured the success of his own and nearby units, and resulted in the saving of numerous lives of his fellow soldiers. By individual acts of bravery he destroyed 10 enemy bunkers and accounted for a large toll of the enemy, including two key enemy commanders. His extraordinary heroism at the risk of his life was in the highest traditions of the military service and reflect great credit upon him, his unit, and the U.S. Army.

3182 ◆ *BOWEN JR., HAMMETT LEE

Rank: Staff Sergeant
Service: U.S. Army
Birthday: 30 November 1947
Place of Birth: LaGrange, Troup County, Georgia
Date of Death: 27 June 1969
Place of Death: Republic of Vietnam
Cemetery: Restlawn Memory Garden Cemetery (MH)—La Grange, Georgia
Entered Service at: Jacksonville, Duval County, Florida
Unit: Company C, 2d Battalion, 14th Infantry, 25th Infantry Division
Served as: Platoon Sergeant
Battle or Place of Action: Binh Duong Province, Republic of Vietnam
Date of Action: 27 June 1969
G.O. Number, Date: 43, 12 September 1974
Date of Presentation: 17 July 1974
Place of Presentation: Blair House (Courtyard), presented by Vice Pres. Gerald R. Ford to his family
Citation: S/Sgt. Bowen distinguished himself while serving as a platoon sergeant during combat operations in Binh Duong Province, Republic of Vietnam. S/Sgt. Bowen's platoon was advancing on a reconnaissance mission into enemy-controlled terrain when it came under the withering crossfire of small arms and grenades from an enemy ambush force. S/Sgt. Bowen placed heavy suppressive fire on the enemy positions and ordered his men to fall back. As the platoon was moving back, an enemy grenade was thrown amid S/Sgt. Bowen and three of his men. Sensing the danger to his comrades, S/Sgt. Bowen shouted a warning to his men and hurled himself on the grenade, absorbing the explosion with his body while saving the lives of his fellow soldiers. S/Sgt. Bowen's extraordinary courage and concern for his men at the cost of his life served as an inspiration to his comrades and are in the highest traditions of the military service and the U.S. Army.

3183 ◆ BRADY, PATRICK HENRY

Rank: Major (highest rank: Major General)
Service: U.S. Army
Birthday: 1 October 1936
Place of Birth: Philip, Haakon County, South Dakota
Entered Service at: Seattle, King County, Washington
Unit: Medical Service Corps, 54th Medical Detachment, 67th Medical Group, 44th Medical Brigade
Served as: Medivac Helicopter Pilot
Battle or Place of Action: near Chu Lai, Republic of Vietnam
Date of Action: 6 January 1968
G.O. Number, Date: 62, 27 October 1969
Date of Presentation: 9 October 1969
Place of Presentation: The White House, presented by Pres. Richard M. Nixon
Citation: For conspicuous gallantry and intrepidity in action at the risk of his life above and beyond the call of duty, Maj. Brady distinguished himself while serving in the Republic of Vietnam commanding a UH-1H ambulance helicopter, volunteered to rescue wounded men from a site in enemy-held territory which was reported to be heavily defended and to be blanketed by fog. To reach the site, he descended through heavy fog and smoke and hovered slowly along a valley trail, turning his ship sideward to blow away the fog with the backwash from his rotor blades. Despite the unchallenged, close-range enemy fire, he found the dangerously small site, where he successfully landed and evacuated two badly wounded South Vietnamese soldiers. He was then called to another area completely covered by dense fog where American casualties lay only 50 meters from the enemy. Two aircraft had previously been shot down and others had made unsuccessful attempts to reach this site earlier in the day. With unmatched skill and extraordinary courage, Maj. Brady made four flights to this embattled landing zone and successfully rescued all of the wounded. On his third mission of the day, Maj. Brady once again landed at a site surrounded by the enemy. The friendly ground force, pinned down by enemy fire, had been unable to reach and secure the landing zone. Although his aircraft had been badly damaged and his controls partially

shot away during his initial entry into this area, he returned minutes later and rescued the remaining injured. Shortly thereafter obtaining a replacement aircraft, Maj. Brady was requested to land in an enemy mine field where a platoon of American soldiers was trapped. A mine detonated near his helicopter, wounding two crewmembers and damaging his ship. In spite of this, he managed to fly six severely injured patients to medical aid. Throughout that day Maj. Brady utilized three helicopters to evacuate a total of 51 seriously wounded men, many of whom would have perished without prompt medical treatment. Maj. Brady's bravery was in the highest traditions of the military service and reflects great credit upon himself and the U.S. Army.

3184 ◆ *BRUCE, DANIEL DEAN

Rank: Private First Class
Service: U.S. Marine Corps
Birthday: 18 May 1950
Place of Birth: Michigan City, La Porte County, Indiana
Date of Death: 1 March 1969
Place of Death: Republic of Vietnam
Cemetery: Greenwood Cemetery—Michigan City, Indiana
Entered Service at: Chicago, Cook County, Illinois
Unit: Headquarters & Service Company, 3d Battalion, 5th Marines, 1st Marine Division (Rein) FMF
Served as: Mortar Man
Battle or Place of Action: Fire Support Base Tomahawk, Quang Nam Province, Republic of Vietnam
Date of Action: 1 March 1969
Date of Presentation: 16 February 1971
Place of Presentation: The White House (East Ballroom), presented by Pres. Richard M. Nixon to his family
Citation: For conspicuous gallantry and intrepidity at the risk of his life above and beyond the call of duty while serving as a mortar man with Headquarters and Service Company 3d Battalion, against the enemy. Early in the morning Pfc. Bruce was on watch in his night defensive position at Fire Support Base Tomahawk when he heard movements ahead of him. An enemy explosive charge was thrown toward his position and he reacted instantly, catching the device and shouting to alert his companions. Realizing the danger to the adjacent position with its two occupants, Pfc. Bruce held the device to his body and attempted to carry it from the vicinity of the entrenched marines. As he moved away, the charge detonated and he absorbed the full force of the explosion. Pfc. Bruce's indomitable courage, inspiring valor and selfless devotion to duty saved the lives of three of his fellow marines and upheld the highest traditions of the Marine Corps and the U.S. Naval Service. He gallantly gave his life for his country.

3185 ◆ *BRYANT, WILLIAM MAUD

Rank: Sergeant First Class
Service: U.S. Army
Birthday: 16 February 1933
Place of Birth: Cochran, Bleckley County, Georgia
Date of Death: 24 March 1969
Place of Death: Republic of Vietnam
Cemetery: Raleigh National Cemetery (15-1227) (MH)—Raleigh, North Carolina
Entered Service at: Detroit, Wayne County, Michigan
Unit: Company A, 5th Special Forces Group, 1st Special Forces
Served as: Commanding Officer of C.I.D.G.Co. 321
Battle or Place of Action: Long Khanh Province, Republic of Vietnam
Date of Action: 24 March 1969
G.O. Number, Date: 8, 9 March 1971
Date of Presentation: 16 February 1971
Place of Presentation: The White House (East Ballroom), presented by Pres. Richard M. Nixon to his family
Citation: For conspicuous gallantry and intrepidity in action at the risk of his life above and beyond the call of duty. Sfc. Bryant, assigned to Company A, distinguished himself while serving as commanding officer of Civilian Irregular Defense Group Company 321, 2d Battalion, 3d Mobile Strike Force Command, during combat operations. The battalion came under heavy fire and became surrounded by the elements of three enemy regiments. Sfc. Bryant displayed extraordinary heroism throughout the succeeding 34 hours of incessant attack as he moved throughout the company position heedless of the intense hostile fire while establishing and improving the defensive perimeter, directing fire during critical phases of the battle, distributing ammunition, assisting the wounded, and providing the leadership and inspirational example of courage to his men. When a helicopter drop of ammunition was made to resupply the beleaguered force, Sfc. Bryant with complete disregard for his safety ran through the heavy enemy fire to retrieve the scattered ammunition boxes and distributed needed ammunition to his men. During a lull in the intense fighting, Sfc. Bryant led a patrol outside the perimeter to obtain information of the enemy. The patrol came under intense automatic-weapons fire and was pinned down. Sfc. Bryant singlehandedly repulsed one enemy attack on his small force and by his heroic action inspired his men to fight off other assaults. Seeing a wounded enemy soldier some distance from the patrol location, Sfc. Bryant crawled forward alone under heavy fire to retrieve the soldier for intelligence purposes. Finding that the enemy soldier had expired, Sfc. Bryant crawled back to his patrol and led his men back to the company position where he again took command of the defense. As the siege continued, Sfc. Bryant organized and led a patrol in a daring attempt to break through the enemy encirclement. The patrol had advanced some 200 meters by heavy fighting when it was pinned down by the intense automatic-weapons fire from heavily fortified bunkers and Sfc. Bryant was severely wounded. Despite his wounds he rallied his men, called for helicopter gunship support, and directed heavy suppressive fire upon the enemy positions. Following the last gunship attack, Sfc. Bryant fearlessly charged an enemy automatic-weapons position, overrunning it and singlehandedly destroying its three defenders. Inspired by his heroic example, his men renewed their attack on the entrenched enemy. While regrouping his small force for the final assault against the enemy, Sfc. Bryant fell mortally wounded by an enemy rocket. Sfc. Bryant's selfless concern for his comrades, at the cost of his life above and beyond the

call of duty, are in keeping with the highest traditions of the military service and reflect great credit upon himself, his unit, and the U.S. Army.

3186 ◆ BUCHA, PAUL WILLIAM

Rank: Captain
Service: U.S. Army
Birthday: 1 August 1943
Place of Birth: Washington, D.C.
Entered Service at: USMA West Point, Orange County, New York
Unit: Company D, 3d Battalion, 187th Infantry, 3d Brigade, 101st Airborne Division
Served as: Company Commander
Battle or Place of Action: near Phuoc Vinh, Binh Duong Province, Republic of Vietnam
Date of Action: 16-19 March 1968
G.O. Number, Date: 30, 5 June 1970
Date of Presentation: 14 May 1970
Place of Presentation: The White House, presented by Pres. Richard M. Nixon
Citation: For conspicuous gallantry and intrepidity in action at the risk of his life above and beyond the call of duty. Capt. Bucha distinguished himself while serving as commanding officer, Company D, on a reconnaissance-in-force mission against enemy forces near Phuoc Vinh. The company was inserted by helicopter into the suspected enemy stronghold to locate and destroy the enemy. During this period Capt. Bucha aggressively and courageously led his men in the destruction of enemy fortifications and base areas and eliminated scattered resistance impeding the advance of the company. On 18 March while advancing to contact, the lead elements of the company became engaged by the heavy automatic-weapon, heavy machine-gun, rocket-propelled-grenade, claymore-mine and small-arms fire of an estimated battalion-size force. Capt. Bucha, with complete disregard for his safety, moved to the threatened area to direct the defense and ordered reinforcements to the aid of the lead element. Seeing that his men were pinned down by heavy machine-gun fire from a concealed bunker located some 40 meters to the front of the positions, Capt. Bucha crawled through the hail of fire to singlehandedly destroy the bunker with grenades. During this heroic action Capt. Bucha received a painful shrapnel wound. Returning to the perimeter, he observed that his unit could not hold its positions and repel the human wave assaults launched by the determined enemy. Capt. Bucha ordered the withdrawal of the unit elements and covered the withdrawal to positions of a company perimeter from which he could direct fire upon the charging enemy. When one friendly element retrieving casualties was ambushed and cut off from the perimeter, Capt. Bucha ordered them to feign death and he directed artillery fire around them. During the night Capt. Bucha moved throughout the position, distributing ammunition, providing encouragement, and insuring the integrity of the defense. He directed artillery, helicopter-gunship and Air Force-gunship fire on the enemy strong points and attacking forces, marking the positions with smoke grenades. Using flashlights in complete view of enemy snipers, he directed the medical evacuation of three air-ambulance loads of seriously wounded personnel and the helicopter supply of his company. At daybreak Capt. Bucha led a rescue party to recover the dead and wounded members of the ambushed element. During the period of intensive combat, Capt. Bucha, by his extraordinary heroism, inspirational example, outstanding leadership, and professional competence, led his company in the decimation of a superior enemy force which left 156 dead on the battlefield. His bravery and gallantry at the risk of his life are in the highest traditions of the military service. Capt. Bucha has reflected great credit on himself, his unit, and the U.S. Army.

3187 ◆ *BUKER, BRIAN LEROY

Rank: Sergeant
Service: U.S. Army
Birthday: 3 November 1949
Place of Birth: Benton, Maine
Date of Death: 5 April 1970
Place of Death: Republic of Vietnam
Cemetery: Brown Cemetery (MH)—Benton, Maine
Entered Service at: Bangor, Penobscot County, Maine
Unit: Detachment B-55, 5th Special Forces Group (Airborne), 1st Special Forces
Served as: Platoon Advisor
Battle or Place of Action: Chau Doc Province, Republic of Vietnam
Date of Action: 5 April 1970
G.O. Number, Date: 6, 25 January 1972
Date of Presentation: 16 December 1971
Place of Presentation: Old Executive Office Building, presented by Vice Pres. Spiro T. Agnew to his family
Citation: For conspicuous gallantry and intrepidity in action at the risk of his life above and beyond the call of duty. Sgt. Buker, Detachment B-55, distinguished himself while serving as a platoon adviser of a Vietnamese mobile strike force company during an offensive mission. Sgt. Buker personally led the platoon, cleared a strategically located well-guarded pass, and established the first foothold at the top of what had been an impenetrable mountain fortress. When the platoon came under intense fire from a determined enemy located in two heavily fortified bunkers, and realizing that withdrawal would result in heavy casualties, Sgt. Buker unhesitatingly, and with complete disregard for his personal safety, charged through the hail of enemy fire and destroyed the first bunker with hand grenades. While reorganizing his men for the attack on the second bunker, Sgt. Buker was seriously wounded. Despite his wounds and the deadly fire, he crawled forward and destroyed the second bunker. Sgt. Buker refused medical attention and was reorganizing his men to continue the attack when he was mortally wounded. As a direct result of his heroic actions, many casualties were averted, and the assault of the enemy position was successful. Sgt. Buker's extraordinary heroism at the cost of his life are in the highest traditions of the military service and reflect great credit on him, his unit, and the U.S. Army.

3188 ◆ *BURKE, ROBERT CHARLES

Rank: Private First Class
Service: U.S. Marine Corps

Birthday: 7 November 1949
Place of Birth: Monticello, Piatt County, Illinois
Date of Death: 17 May 1968
Place of Death: Republic of Vietnam
Cemetery: Monticello Cemetery (MH)—Monticello, Illinois
Entered Service at: Chicago, Cook County, Illinois
Unit: Company I, 3d Battalion, 27th Marines, 1st Marine Division (Rein) FMF
Served as: Machine Gunner
Battle or Place of Action: Le Nam 1, Go Nai Island, southern Quang Nam Province, Republic of Vietnam
Date of Action: 17 May 1968
Date of Presentation: 20 April 1970
Place of Presentation: The White House, presented by Vice Pres. Spiro T. Agnew to his family
Citation: For conspicuous gallantry and intrepidity at the risk of his life above and beyond the call of duty for service as a machine gunner with Company I. While on Operation Allen Brook, Company I was approaching a dry river bed with a heavily wooded treeline that borders the hamlet of Le Nam (1), when they suddenly came under intense mortar, rocket-propelled-grenade, automatic-weapons, and small-arms fire from a large, well-concealed enemy force which halted the company's advance and wounded several marines. Realizing that key points of resistance had to be eliminated to allow the units to advance and casualties to be evacuated, Pfc. Burke, without hesitation, seized his machine gun and launched a series of one-man assaults against the fortified emplacements. As he aggressively maneuvered to the edge of the steep river bank, he delivered accurate suppressive fire upon several enemy bunkers, which enabled his comrades to advance and move the wounded marines to positions of relative safety. As he continued his combative actions, he located an opposing automatic-weapons emplacement and poured intense fire into the position, killing three North Vietnamese soldiers as they attempted to flee. Pfc. Burke then fearlessly moved from one position to another, quelling the hostile fire until his weapon malfunctioned. Obtaining a casualty's rifle and hand grenades, he advanced further into the midst of the enemy fire in an assault against another pocket of resistance, killing two more of the enemy. Observing that a fellow marine had cleared his malfunctioning machine gun, he grasped his weapon and moved into a dangerously exposed area and saturated the hostile treeline until he fell mortally wounded. Pfc. Burke's gallant actions upheld the highest traditions of the Marine Corps and the U.S. Naval Service. He gallantly gave his life for his country.

3189 ◆ *CAPODANNO, VINCENT ROBERT

Rank: Lieutenant
Service: U.S. Navy
Birthday: 13 February 1929
Place of Birth: Staten Island, Richmond County, New York
Date of Death: 4 September 1967
Place of Death: Republic of Vietnam
Cemetery: Saint Peter's Cemetery—Staten Island, New York
Entered Service at: Staten Island, Richmond County, New York
Unit: Chaplain Corps, 3d Battalion, 5th Marines, 1st Marine Division (Rein) FMF
Served as: Chaplain
Battle or Place of Action: Quang Tin Province, Republic of Vietnam
Date of Action: 4 September 1967
Date of Presentation: 7 January 1969
Place of Presentation: The Washington Navy Yard, presented by Sec. of the Navy Paul R. Ignatius to his family
Citation: For conspicuous gallantry and intrepidity at the risk of his life above and beyond the call of duty as Chaplain of the 3d Battalion, in connection with operations against enemy forces. In response to reports that the 2d Platoon of M Company was in danger of being overrun by a massed enemy assaulting force, Lt. Capodanno left the relative safety of the company command post and ran through an open area raked with fire, directly to the beleaguered platoon. Disregarding the intense enemy small-arms, automatic-weapons, and mortar fire, he moved about the battlefield administering last rites to the dying and giving medical aid to the wounded. When an exploding mortar round inflicted painful multiple wounds to his arms and legs, and severed a portion of his right hand, he steadfastly refused all medical aid. Instead, he directed the corpsmen to help their wounded comrades and, with calm vigor, continued to move about the battlefield as he provided encouragement by voice and example to the valiant marines. Upon encountering a wounded corpsman in the direct line of fire of an enemy machine gunner positioned approximately 15 yards away, Lt. Capodanno rushed in a daring attempt to aid and assist the mortally wounded corpsman. At that instant, only inches from his goal, he was struck down by a burst of machine-gun fire. By his heroic conduct on the battlefield, and his inspiring example, Lt. Capodanno upheld the finest traditions of the U.S. Naval Service. He gallantly gave his life in the cause of freedom.

3190 ◆ *CARON, WAYNE MAURICE

Rank: Hospital Corpsman Third Class
Service: U.S. Navy
Birthday: 2 November 1946
Place of Birth: Middleboro, Plymouth County, Massachusetts
Date of Death: 28 July 1968
Place of Death: Republic of Vietnam
Cemetery: Arlington National Cemetery (51-2600) (MH)—Arlington, Virginia
Entered Service at: Boston, Suffolk County, Massachusetts
Unit: Headquarters & Service Company, 3d Battalion, 7th Marines, 1st Marine Division (Rein) FMF
Served as: Medical Corpsman
Battle or Place of Action: Quang Nam Province, Republic of Vietnam
Date of Action: 28 July 1968
Date of Presentation: 20 April 1970
Place of Presentation: The White House, presented by Vice Pres. Spiro T. Agnew to his family
Citation: For conspicuous gallantry and intrepidity at the risk of his life above and beyond the call of duty while serving as platoon corpsman with Company K, during combat opera-

tions against enemy forces. While on a sweep through an open rice field, HC3c. Caron's unit started receiving enemy small-arms fire. Upon seeing two marine casualties fall, he immediately ran forward to render first aid, but found that they were dead. At this time the platoon was taken under intense small-arms and automatic-weapons fire, sustaining additional casualties. As he moved to the aid of his wounded comrades, HC3c. Caron was hit in the arm by enemy fire. Although knocked to the ground, he regained his feet and continued to the injured marines. He rendered medical assistance to the first marine he reached, who was grievously wounded, and undoubtedly was instrumental in saving the man's life. HC3c. Caron then ran toward the second wounded marine, but was again hit by enemy fire, this time in the leg. Nonetheless, he crawled the remaining distance and provided medical aid for this severely wounded man. HC3c. Caron started to make his way to yet another injured comrade, when he was again struck by enemy small-arms fire. Courageously and with unbelievable determination, HC3c. Caron continued his attempt to reach the third marine until he was killed by an enemy rocket round. His inspiring valor, steadfast determination, and selfless dedication in the face of extreme danger, sustain and enhance the finest traditions of the U.S. Naval Service.

3191 ◆ *CARTER, BRUCE WAYNE

Rank: Private First Class
Service: U.S. Marine Corps
Birthday: 7 May 1950
Place of Birth: Schenectady, Schenectady County, New York
Date of Death: 7 August 1969
Place of Death: Republic of Vietnam
Cemetery: Vista Memorial Gardens (MH)—Hialeah, Florida
Entered Service at: Jacksonville, Duval County, Florida
Unit: Company H, 2d Battalion, 3d Marines, 3d Marine Division (Rein) FMF
Served as: Grenadier
Battle or Place of Action: Quang Tri Province, Republic of Vietnam
Date of Action: 7 August 1969
Date of Presentation: 9 September 1971
Place of Presentation: The White House, presented by Vice Pres. Spiro T. Agnew to his family
Citation: For conspicuous gallantry and intrepidity at the risk of his life above and beyond the call of duty while serving as grenadier with Company H in connection with combat operations against the enemy. Pfc. Carter's unit was maneuvering against the enemy during Operation Idaho Canyon and came under a heavy volume of fire from a numerically superior hostile force. The lead element soon became separated from the main body of the squad by a brush fire. Pfc. Carter and his fellow marines were pinned down by vicious crossfire when, with complete disregard for his safety, he stood in full view of the North Vietnamese Army soldiers to deliver a devastating volume of fire at their positions. The accuracy and aggressiveness of his attack caused several enemy casualties and forced the remainder of the soldiers to retreat from the immediate area. Shouting directions to the marines around him, Pfc. Carter then commenced leading them from the path of the rapidly approaching brush fire when he observed a hostile grenade land between him and his companions. Fully aware of the probable consequences of his action but determined to protect the men following him, he unhesitatingly threw himself over the grenade, absorbing the full effects of its detonation with his body. Pfc. Carter's indomitable courage, inspiring initiative, and selfless devotion to duty upheld the highest traditions of the Marine Corps and the U.S. Naval Service. He gallantly gave his life in the service of his country.

3192 ◆ CAVAIANI, JON ROBERT

Rank: Staff Sergeant (highest rank: Sergeant Major)
Service: U.S. Army
Birthday: 2 August 1943
Place of Birth: Royston, England
Entered Service at: Fresno, Fresno County, California
Unit: Vietnam Training Advisory Group, Republic of Vietnam
Served as: Platoon Leader
Battle or Place of Action: Hill 1050, overlooking Khesahn Airfield, Republic of Vietnam
Date of Action: 4-5 June 1971
G.O. Number, Date: 2, 3 January 1975
Date of Presentation: 12 December 1974
Place of Presentation: The White House, presented by Pres. Gerald R. Ford
Citation: S/Sgt. Cavaiani distinguished himself by conspicuous gallantry and intrepidity at the risk of his life above and beyond the call of duty in action in the Republic of Vietnam on 4 and 5 June 1971 while serving as a platoon leader to a security platoon providing security for an isolated radio relay site located within enemy-held territory. On the morning of 4 June 1971, the entire camp came under an intense barrage of enemy small-arms, automatic-weapons, rocket-propelled-grenade and mortar fire from a superior size enemy force. S/Sgt. Cavaiani acted with complete disregard for his personal safety as he repeatedly exposed himself to heavy enemy fire in order to move about the camp's perimeter directing the platoon's fire and rallying the platoon in a desperate fight for survival. S/Sgt. Cavaiani also returned heavy suppressive fire upon the assaulting enemy force during this period with a variety of weapons. When the entire platoon was to be evacuated, S/Sgt. Cavaiani unhesitatingly volunteered to remain on the ground and direct the helicopters into the landing zone. S/Sgt. Cavaiani was able to direct the first three helicopters in evacuating a major portion of the platoon. Due to intense increase in enemy fire, S/Sgt. Cavaiani was forced to remain at the camp overnight where he calmly directed the remaining platoon members in strengthening their defenses. On the morning of 5 June, a heavy ground fog restricted visibility. The superior size enemy force launched a major ground attack in an attempt to completely annihilate the remaining small force. The enemy force advanced in two ranks, first firing a heavy volume of small-arms, automatic-weapons, and rocket-propelled-grenade fire while the second rank continuously threw a steady barrage of hand grenades at the belea-

guered force. S/Sgt. Cavaiani returned a heavy barrage of small-arms and hand-grenade fire on the assaulting enemy force but was unable to slow them down. He ordered the remaining platoon members to attempt to escape while he provided them with cover fire. With one last courageous exertion, S/Sgt. Cavaiani recovered a machine gun, stood up, completely exposing himself to the heavy enemy fire directed at him, and began firing the machine gun in a sweeping motion along the two ranks of advancing enemy soldiers. Through S/Sgt. Cavaiani's valiant efforts with complete disregard for his safety, the majority of the remaining platoon members were able to escape. While inflicting severe losses on the advancing enemy force, S/Sgt. Cavaiani was wounded numerous times. S/Sgt. Cavaiani's conspicuous gallantry, extraordinary heroism, and intrepidity at the risk of his life, above and beyond the call of duty, were in keeping with the highest traditions of the military service and reflect great credit upon himself and the U.S. Army.

3193 ◆ CLAUSEN JR., RAYMOND MICHAEL "RED"

Rank: Private First Class
Service: U.S. Marine Corps
Birthday: 14 October 1947
Place of Birth: New Orleans, Orleans County, Louisiana
Entered Service at: New Orleans, Orleans County, Louisiana
Unit: Marine Medium Helicopter Squadron 263, Marine Aircraft Group 16, 1st Marine Aircraft Wing
Served as: Crew Chief of a HC-46 Helicopter
Battle or Place of Action: Republic of Vietnam
Date of Action: 31 January 1970
Date of Presentation: 15 June 1971
Place of Presentation: The White House (East Ballroom), presented by Pres. Richard M. Nixon
Citation: For conspicuous gallantry and intrepidity at the risk of his life above and beyond the call of duty while serving with Marine Medium Helicopter Squadron 263 during operations against enemy forces. Participating in a helicopter rescue mission to extract elements of a platoon which had inadvertently entered a minefield while attacking enemy positions, Pfc. Clausen skillfully guided the helicopter pilot to a landing in an area cleared by one of several mine explosions. With 11 marines wounded, and one dead, and the remaining eight marines holding their positions for fear of detonating other mines, Pfc. Clausen quickly leaped from the helicopter and, in the face of enemy fire, moved across the extremely hazardous mineladen area to assist in carrying casualties to the waiting helicopter and in placing them aboard. Despite the ever-present threat of further mine explosions, he continued his valiant efforts, leaving the comparatively safe area of the helicopter on six separate occasions to carry out his rescue efforts. On one occasion while he was carrying one of the wounded, another mine detonated, killing a corpsman and wounding three other men. Only when he was certain that all marines were safely aboard did he signal the pilot to lift the helicopter. By the courageous, determined, and inspiring efforts in the face of the utmost danger, Pfc. Clausen upheld the highest traditions of the Marine Corps and the U.S. Naval Service.

3194 ◆ *COKER, RONALD LEROY

Rank: Private First Class
Service: U.S. Marine Corps
Birthday: 9 August 1947
Place of Birth: Alliance, Box Butte County, Nebraska
Date of Death: 24 March 1969
Place of Death: Republic of Vietnam
Cemetery: Fairview Cemetery—Alliance, Nebraska
Entered Service at: Denver, Denver County, Colorado
Unit: 2d Platoon, Company M, 3d Battalion, 3d Marines, 3d Marine Division (Rein) FMF
Served as: Rifleman
Battle or Place of Action: northwest Quang Tri Province, Republic of Vietnam
Date of Action: 24 March 1969
Date of Presentation: 20 April 1970
Place of Presentation: The White House, presented by Vice Pres. Spiro T. Agnew to his family
Citation: For conspicuous gallantry and intrepidity at the risk of his life above and beyond the call of duty while serving as a rifleman with Company M in action against enemy forces. While serving as point man for the 2d Platoon, Pfc. Coker was leading his patrol when he encountered five enemy soldiers on a narrow jungle trail. Pfc. Coker's squad aggressively pursued them to a cave. As the squad neared the cave, it came under intense hostile fire, seriously wounding one marine and forcing the others to take cover. Observing the wounded man lying exposed to continuous enemy fire, Pfc. Coker disregarded his safety and moved across the fire-swept terrain toward his companion. Although wounded by enemy small-arms fire, he continued to crawl across the hazardous area and skillfully threw a hand grenade into the enemy positions, suppressing the hostile fire sufficiently to enable him to reach the wounded man. As he began to drag his injured comrade toward safety, a grenade landed on the wounded marine. Unhesitatingly, Pfc. Coker grasped it with both hands and turned away from his wounded companion, but before he could dispose of the grenade it exploded. Severely wounded, but undaunted, he refused to abandon his comrade. As he moved toward friendly lines, two more enemy grenades exploded near him, inflicting still further injuries. Concerned only for the safety of his comrade, Pfc. Coker, with supreme effort, continued to crawl and pull the wounded marine with him. His heroic deeds inspired his fellow marines to such aggressive action that the enemy fire was suppressed sufficiently to enable others to reach him and carry him to a relatively safe area where he succumbed to his extensive wounds. Pfc. Coker's indomitable courage, inspiring initiative, and selfless devotion to duty upheld the highest traditions of the Marine Corps and of the U.S. Naval Service. He gallantly gave his life for his country.

3195 ◆ *CONNOR, PETER SPENCER

Rank: Staff Sergeant
Service: U.S. Marine Corps
Birthday: 4 September 1932
Place of Birth: Orange, Essex County, New Jersey
Date of Death: 8 March 1966

Place of Death: on board Hospital Ship U.S.S. *Repose*
Cemetery: Fort Rosecrans National Cemetery (A-E-1005) (MH)—San Diego, California
Entered Service at: South Orange, Essex County, New Jersey
Unit: Company F, 2d Battalion, 3d Marines, 1st Marine Division (Rein) FMF
Served as: Platoon Sergeant
Battle or Place of Action: Quang Ngai Province, Republic of Vietnam
Date of Action: 25 February 1966
Date of Presentation: 2 May 1967
Place of Presentation: The White House (Rose Garden), presented by Pres. Lyndon B. Johnson to his family
Citation: For conspicuous gallantry and intrepidity in action against enemy Viet Cong forces at the risk of his life above and beyond the call of duty. Leading his platoon on a search-and-destroy operation in an area made particularly hazardous by extensive cave and tunnel complexes, S/Sgt. Connor maneuvered his unit aggressively forward under intermittent enemy small-arms fire. Exhibiting particular alertness and keen observation, he spotted an enemy spider hole emplacement approximately 15 meters to his front. He pulled the pin from a fragmentation grenade intending to charge the hole boldly and drop the missile into its depths. Upon pulling the pin he realized that the firing mechanism was faulty, and that even as he held the safety device firmly in place, the fuse charge was already activated. With only precious seconds to decide, he further realized that he could not cover the distance to the small opening of the spider hole in sufficient time, and that to hurl the deadly bomb in any direction would result in death or injury to some of his comrades tactically deployed near him. Manifesting extraordinary gallantry and with utter disregard for his personal safety, he chose to hold the grenade against his body in order to absorb the terrific explosion and spare his comrades. His act of extreme valor and selflessness in the face of virtually certain death, although leaving him mortally wounded, spared many of his fellow marines from death or injury. His gallant action in giving his life in the cause of freedom reflects the highest credit upon the Marine Corps and the Armed Forces of the United States.

3196 ◆ *COOK, DONALD GILBERT

Rank: Colonel (rank at time of action: Captain)
Service: U.S. Marine Corps
Birthday: 9 August 1934
Place of Birth: Brooklyn, Kings County, New York
Date of Death: 8 December 1967
Place of Death: Republic of Vietnam
Cemetery: Arlington National Cemetery ('In Memory' marker) (M1-110)—Arlington, Virginia
Entered Service at: Brooklyn, Kings County, New York
Unit: Naval Advisor Group, Military Assistance Command
Served as: Battalion Advisor
Battle or Place of Action: in the vicinity of Binh Gia, Phouc Tuy Province, Republic of Vietnam
Date of Action: 31 December 1964—8 December 1967
Date of Presentation: 16 May 1980
Place of Presentation: The Pentagon (Hall of Heroes), presented by Sec. of the Navy Edward Hidalgo to his family
Citation: For conspicuous gallantry and intrepidity at the risk of his life above and beyond the call of duty while interned as a Prisoner of War by the Viet Cong in the Republic of Vietnam during the period from 31 December 1964 to 8 December 1967. Despite the fact that by so doing he would bring about harsher treatment for himself, Col. (then Capt.) Cook established himself as the senior prisoner, even though in actuality he was not. Repeatedly assuming more than his share of the manual labor in order that the other Prisoners of War could improve the state of their health, Col. Cook willingly and unselfishly put the interests of his comrades before that of his own well-being and, eventually, his life. Giving more needy men his medicine and drug allowance while constantly nursing them, he risked infection from contagious diseases while in a rapidly deteriorating state of health. This unselfish and exemplary conduct, coupled with his refusal to stray even the slightest from the Code of Conduct, earned him the deepest respect from not only his fellow prisoners, but his captors as well. Rather than negotiate for his own release or better treatment, he steadfastly frustrated attempts by the Viet Cong to break his indomitable spirit, and passed this same resolve on to the men with whose well-being he so closely associated himself. Knowing his refusals would prevent his release prior to the end of the war, and also knowing his chances for prolonged survival would be small in the event of continued refusal, he chose nevertheless to adhere to a Code of Conduct far above that which could be expected. His personal valor and exceptional spirit of loyalty in the face of almost certain death reflected the highest credit upon Col. Cook, the Marine Corps, and the United States Naval Service.
Notes: POW from 31 December 1964—8 December 1967

3197 ◆ *CREEK, THOMAS ELBERT

Rank: Lance Corporal
Service: U.S. Marine Corps
Birthday: 7 April 1950
Place of Birth: Joplin, Jasper County, Missouri
Date of Death: 13 February 1969
Place of Death: Republic of Vietnam
Cemetery: Lland Cemetery (MH)—Amarillo, Texas
Entered Service at: Amarillo, Potter County, Texas
Unit: Company I, 3d Battalion, 9th Marines, 3d Marine Division (Rein) FMF
Served as: Rifleman
Battle or Place of Action: near Cam Lo, Republic of Vietnam
Date of Action: 13 February 1969
Date of Presentation: 20 April 1970
Place of Presentation: The White House, presented by Vice Pres. Spiro T. Agnew to his family
Citation: For conspicuous gallantry and intrepidity at the risk of his life above and beyond the call of duty while serving as a rifleman with Company I in action against enemy forces. L/Cpl. Creek's squad was providing security for a convoy moving to resupply the Vandergrift Command Base when an

enemy command-detonated mine destroyed one of the vehicles and halted the convoy near the Cam Lo Resettlement Village. Almost immediately, the marines came under a heavy volume of hostile mortar fire followed by intense small-arms fire from a well-concealed enemy force. As his squad deployed to engage the enemy, L/Cpl. Creek quickly moved to a fighting position and aggressively engaged in the firefight. Observing a position from which he could more effectively deliver fire against the hostile forces, he completely disregarded his own safety as he fearlessly dashed across the fire-swept terrain and was seriously wounded by enemy fire. At the same time, an enemy grenade was thrown into the gully where he had fallen, landing between him and several companions. Fully realizing the inevitable results of his action, L/Cpl. Creek rolled on the grenade and absorbed the full force of the explosion with his body, thereby saving the lives of five of his fellow marines. As a result of his heroic action, his men were inspired to such aggressive action that the enemy was defeated and the convoy was able to continue its vital mission. L/Cpl. Creek's indomitable courage inspired the Marine Corps and the U.S. Naval Service. He gallantly gave his life for his country.

3198 ◆ *CRESCENZ, MICHAEL JOSEPH

Rank: Corporal
Service: U.S. Army
Birthday: 14 January 1949
Place of Birth: Philadelphia, Philadelphia County, Pennsylvania
Date of Death: 20 November 1968
Place of Death: Republic of Vietnam
Cemetery: Holy Sepulchre Cemetery—Philadelphia, Pennsylvania
Entered Service at: Philadelphia, Philadelphia County, Pennsylvania
Unit: Company A, 4th Battalion, 31st Infantry, 196th Infantry Brigade, Americal Division
Served as: Rifleman
Battle or Place of Action: Hiep Duc Valley area, Republic of Vietnam
Date of Action: 20 November 1968
G.O. Number, Date: 11, 23 April 1970
Date of Presentation: 7 April 1970
Place of Presentation: The White House, presented by Pres. Richard M. Nixon to his family
Citation: Cpl. Crescenz distinguished himself by conspicuous gallantry and intrepidity in action while serving as a rifleman with Company A. In the morning his unit engaged a large, well-entrenched force of the North Vietnamese Army whose initial burst of fire pinned down the lead squad and killed the two point men, halting the advance of Company A. Immediately, Cpl. Crescenz left the relative safety of his own position, seized a nearby machine gun and, with complete disregard for his safety, charged 100 meters up a slope toward the enemy bunkers which he effectively silenced, killing the two occupants of each. Undaunted by the withering machine-gun fire around him, Cpl. Crescenz courageously moved forward toward a third bunker which he also succeeded in silencing, killing two more of the enemy and momentarily clearing the route of advance for his comrades. Suddenly, intense machine-gun fire erupted from an unseen, camouflaged bunker. Realizing the danger to his fellow soldiers, Cpl. Crescenz disregarded the barrage of hostile fire directed at him and daringly advanced toward the position. Assaulting with his machine gun, Cpl. Crescenz was within five meters of the bunker when he was mortally wounded by the fire from the enemy machine gun. As a direct result of his heroic actions, his company was able to maneuver freely with minimal danger and to complete its mission, defeating the enemy. Cpl. Crescenz's bravery and extraordinary heroism at the cost of his life are in the highest traditions of the military service and reflect great credit on himself, his unit, and the U.S. Army.

3199 ◆ *CUTINHA, NICHOLAS JOSEPH

Rank: Specialist Fourth Class
Service: U.S. Army
Birthday: 13 January 1945
Place of Birth: Fernandina Beach, Nassau County, Florida
Date of Death: 2 March 1968
Place of Death: Republic of Vietnam
Cemetery: Fort Denaud Cemetery—Fort Denaud, Florida
Entered Service at: Coral Gables, Dade County, Florida
Unit: Company C, 4th Battalion, 9th Infantry Regiment, 25th Infantry Division
Served as: Machine Gunner
Battle or Place of Action: near Gia Dinh, Republic of Vietnam
Date of Action: 2 March 1968
G.O. Number, Date: 26, 23 April 1970
Date of Presentation: 7 April 1970
Place of Presentation: The White House, presented by Pres. Richard M. Nixon to his family
Citation: For conspicuous gallantry and intrepidity in action at the risk of his life above and beyond the call of duty. While serving as a machine gunner with Company C, Sp4c. Cutinha accompanied his unit on a combat mission near Gia Dinh. Suddenly his company came under small-arms, automatic-weapons, mortar, and rocket-propelled grenade fire, from a battalion-size enemy unit. During the initial hostile attack, communications with the battalion was lost and the company commander and numerous members of the company became casualties. When Sp4c. Cutinha observed that his company was pinned down and disorganized, he moved to the front with complete disregard for his safety, firing his machine gun at the charging enemy. As he moved forward he drew fire on his own position and was seriously wounded in the leg. As the hostile fire intensified and half of the company was killed or wounded, Sp4c. Cutinha assumed command of all the survivors in his area and initiated a withdrawal while providing cover fire for the evacuation of the wounded. He killed several enemy soldiers but sustained another leg wound when his machine gun was destroyed by incoming rounds. Undaunted, he crawled through a hail of enemy fire to an operable machine gun in order to continue the defense of his injured comrades who were being administered medical treatment. Sp4c. Cutinha maintained this position, refused assistance,

and provided defensive fire for his comrades until he fell mortally wounded. He was solely responsible for killing 15 enemy soldiers while saving the lives of at least nine members of his own unit. Sp4c. Cutinha's gallantry and extraordinary heroism were in keeping with the highest traditions of the military service and reflect great credit upon himself, his unit, and the U.S. Army.

3200 ◆ *DAHL, LARRY GILBERT

Rank: Specialist Fourth Class
Service: U.S. Army
Birthday: 10 June 1949
Place of Birth: Oregon City, Clackamas County, Oregon
Date of Death: 23 February 1971
Place of Death: Republic of Vietnam
Cemetery: Willamette National Cemetery (S-3512) (MH)—Portland, Oregon
Entered Service at: Portland, Multnomah County, Oregon
Unit: 359th Transportation Company, 27th Transportation Battalion, U.S. Army Support Command
Served as: Machine Gunner
Battle or Place of Action: An Khe, Binh Dinh Province, Republic of Vietnam
Date of Action: 23 February 1971
G.O. Number, Date: 36, 6 September 1974
Date of Presentation: 8 August 1974
Place of Presentation: Blair House, presented by Vice Pres. Gerald R. Ford to his family
Citation: Sp4c. Dahl distinguished himself by conspicuous gallantry and intrepidity while serving as a machine gunner on a gun truck near An Khe, Binh Dinh Province. The gun truck in which Sp4c. Dahl was riding was sent with two other gun trucks to assist in the defense of a convoy that had been ambushed by an enemy force. The gun trucks entered the battle zone and engaged the attacking enemy troops with a heavy volume of machine-gun fire, causing a large number of casualties. After a brief period of intense fighting the attack subsided. As the gun trucks were preparing to return to their normal escort duties, an enemy hand grenade was thrown into the truck in which Sp4c. Dahl was riding. Instantly realizing the great danger, Sp4c. Dahl called a warning to his companions and threw himself directly onto the grenade. Through his indomitable courage, complete disregard for his safety, and profound concern for his fellow soldiers, Sp4c. Dahl saved the lives of the other members of the truck crew while sacrificing his own. Sp4c. Dahl's conspicuous gallantry, extraordinary heroism, and intrepidity at the cost of his life, above and beyond the call of duty, are in keeping with the highest traditions of the military service and reflect great credit on himself, his unit, and the U.S. Army.

3201 ◆ *DAVIS, RODNEY MAXWELL

Rank: Sergeant
Service: U.S. Marine Corps
Birthday: 7 April 1942
Place of Birth: Macon, Bibb County, Georgia
Date of Death: 6 September 1967
Place of Death: Republic of Vietnam
Cemetery: Linwood Cemetery—Macon, Georgia
Entered Service at: Macon, Bibb County, Georgia
Unit: 2d Platoon, Company B, 1st Battalion, 5th Marines, 1st Marine Division
Served as: Right Guide
Battle or Place of Action: Quang Nam Province, Republic of Vietnam
Date of Action: 6 September 1967
Date of Presentation: 26 March 1969
Place of Presentation: The Executive Office Building, presented by Vice Pres. Spiro T. Agnew to his family
Citation: For conspicuous gallantry and intrepidity at the risk of his life above and beyond the call of duty while serving as the right guide of the 2d Platoon, Company B, in action against enemy forces. Elements of the 2d Platoon were pinned down by a numerically superior force of attacking North Vietnamese Army regulars. Remnants of the platoon were located in a trench line where Sgt. Davis was directing the fire of his men in an attempt to repel the enemy attack. Disregarding the enemy hand grenades and high volume of small-arms and mortar fire, Sgt. Davis moved from man to man shouting words of encouragement to each of them while firing and throwing grenades at the onrushing enemy. When an enemy grenade landed in the trench in the midst of his men, Sgt. Davis realizing the gravity of the situation, and in a final valiant act of complete self-sacrifice, instantly threw himself upon the grenade, absorbing with his body the full and terrific force of the explosion. Through his extraordinary initiative and inspiring valor in the face of almost certain death, Sgt. Davis saved his comrades from injury and possible loss of life, enabled his platoon to hold its vital position, and upheld the highest traditions of the Marine Corps and the U.S. Naval Service. He gallantly gave his life for his country.

3202 ◆ DAVIS, SAMMY LEE

Rank: Sergeant (rank at time of action: Private First Class) (highest rank: Sergeant First Class)
Service: U.S. Army
Birthday: 1 November 1946
Place of Birth: Dayton, Montgomery County, Ohio
Entered Service at: Indianapolis, Marion County, Indiana
Unit: Battery C, 2d Battalion, 4th Artillery, 9th Infantry Division
Served as: Cannoneer
Battle or Place of Action: Firebase Cudgil, west of Cai Lay, Republic of Vietnam
Date of Action: 18 November 1967
G.O. Number, Date: 75, 10 December 1968
Date of Presentation: 19 November 1968
Place of Presentation: The White House, presented by Pres. Lyndon B. Johnson
Citation: For conspicuous gallantry and intrepidity in action at the risk of his life above and beyond the call of duty. Sgt. Davis (then Pfc.) distinguished himself during the early morning hours while serving as a cannoneer with Battery C, at a remote fire support base. At approximately 0200 hours the fire support base was under heavy enemy mortar attack.

Simultaneously, an estimated reinforced Viet Cong battalion launched a fierce ground assault upon the fire support base. The attacking enemy drove to within 25 meters of the friendly positions. Only a river separated the Viet Cong from the fire support base. Detecting a nearby enemy position, Sgt. Davis seized a machine gun and provided covering fire for his gun crew, as they attempted to bring direct artillery fire on the enemy. Despite his efforts, an enemy recoilless-rifle round scored a direct hit upon the artillery piece. The resultant blast hurled the gun crew from their weapon and blew Sgt. Davis into a foxhole. He struggled to his feet and returned to the howitzer, which was burning furiously. Ignoring repeated warnings to seek cover, Sgt. Davis rammed a shell into the gun. Disregarding a withering hail of enemy fire directed against his position, he aimed and fired the howitzer which rolled backward, knocking Sgt. Davis violently to the ground. Undaunted, he returned to the weapon to fire again when an enemy mortar round exploded within 20 meters of his position, injuring him painfully. Nevertheless, Sgt. Davis loaded the artillery piece, aimed, and fired. Again he was knocked down by the recoil. In complete disregard for his safety, Sgt. Davis loaded and fired three more shells into the enemy. Disregarding his extensive injuries and his inability to swim, Sgt. Davis picked up an air mattress and struck out across the deep river to rescue three wounded comrades on the far side. Upon reaching the three wounded men, he stood upright and fired into the dense vegetation to prevent the Viet Cong from advancing. While the most seriously wounded soldier was helped across the river, Sgt. Davis protected the two remaining casualties until he could pull them across the river to the fire support base. Though suffering from painful wounds, he refused medical attention, joining another howitzer crew which fired at the large Viet Cong force until it broke contact and fled. Sgt. Davis' extraordinary heroism, at the risk of his life, is in keeping with the highest traditions of the military service and reflect great credit upon himself and the U.S. Army.

3203 ◆ DAY, GEORGE EVERETTE "BUD"

Rank: Colonel (rank at time of action: Major)
Service: U.S. Air Force
Birthday: 24 February 1925
Place of Birth: Sioux City, Woodbury County, Iowa
Entered Service at: Sioux City, Woodbury County, Iowa
Unit: Misty Super FAC's F-100 Squadron, Phu Cat Air Base
Served as: Pilot of an F-100
Battle or Place of Action: over North Vietnam
Date of Action: 26 August 1967
G.O. Number, Date: GB-180, 22 March 1976
Date of Presentation: 6 March 1976
Place of Presentation: The White House, presented by Pres. Gerald R. Ford
Citation: On 26 August 1967, Col. Day was forced to eject from his aircraft over North Vietnam when it was hit by ground fire. His right arm was broken in three places, and his left knee was badly sprained. He was immediately captured by hostile forces and taken to a prison camp where he was interrogated and severely tortured. After causing the guards to relax their vigilance, Col. Day escaped into the jungle and began the trek toward South Vietnam. Despite injuries inflicted by fragments of a bomb or rocket, he continued southward surviving only on a few berries and uncooked frogs. He successfully evaded enemy patrols and reached the Ben Hai River, where he encountered U.S. artillery barrages. With the aid of a bamboo log float, Col. Day swam across the river and entered the demilitarized zone. Due to delirium, he lost his sense of direction and wandered aimlessly for several days. After several unsuccessful attempts to signal U.S. aircraft, he was ambushed and recaptured by the Viet Cong, sustaining gunshot wounds to his left hand and thigh. He was returned to the prison from which he had escaped and later was moved to Hanoi after giving his captors false information to questions put before him. Physically, Col. Day was totally debilitated and unable to perform even the simplest task for himself. Despite his many injuries, he continued to offer maximum resistance. His personal bravery in the face of deadly enemy pressure was significant in saving the lives of fellow aviators who were still flying against the enemy. Col. Day's conspicuous gallantry and intrepidity at the risk of his life above and beyond the call of duty are in keeping with the highest traditions of the U.S. Air Force and reflect great credit upon himself and the U.S. Armed Forces.
Notes: POW from 26 August 1967—February 1973 Shot down over North Vietnam on 26 August 1967, he spent 67 months as a prisoner of war. Col. Day was the only POW to escape from prison in North Vietnam and then be recaptured by the Viet Cong in the South.

3204 ◆ *DE LA GARZA JR., EMILIO ALBERT

Rank: Lance Corporal
Service: U.S. Marine Corps
Birthday: 23 June 1949
Place of Birth: East Chicago, Lake County, Indiana
Date of Death: 11 April 1970
Place of Death: Republic of Vietnam
Cemetery: Saint John's Cemetery (MH)—Hammond, Indiana
Entered Service at: Chicago, Cook County, Illinois
Unit: Company E, 2d Battalion, 1st Marines, 1st Marine Division (Rein) FMF
Served as: Machine Gunner
Battle or Place of Action: near Da Nang, Republic of Vietnam
Date of Action: 11 April 1970
Date of Presentation: 9 September 1971
Place of Presentation: The White House, presented by Vice Pres. Spiro T. Agnew to his family
Citation: For conspicuous gallantry and intrepidity at the risk of his life above and beyond the call of duty while serving as a machine gunner with Company E. Returning with his squad from a night ambush operation, L/Cpl. De La Garza joined his platoon commander and another marine in searching for two enemy soldiers who had been observed fleeing for cover toward a small pond. Moments later, he located one of the enemy soldiers hiding among the reeds and brush. As the three marines attempted to remove the resisting soldier from

the pond, L/Cpl. De La Garza observed him pull the pin on a grenade. Shouting a warning, L/Cpl. De La Garza placed himself between the other two marines and the ensuing blast from the grenade, thereby saving the lives of his comrades at the sacrifice of his life. By his prompt and decisive action and his great personal valor in the face of almost certain death, L/Cpl. De La Garza upheld and further enhanced the finest traditions of the Marine Corps and the U.S. Naval Service.

3205 ◆ DETHLEFSEN, MERLYN HANS

Rank: Major (rank at time of action: Captain) (highest rank: Colonel)
Service: U.S. Air Force
Birthday: 29 June 1934
Place of Birth: Greenville, Clay County, Iowa
Date of Death: 14 December 1987
Place of Death: Fort Worth, Texas
Cemetery: Arlington National Cemetery (65-1626) (MH)—Arlington, Virginia
Entered Service at: Royal, Clay County, Iowa
Unit: 354th Tactical Fighter Squadron, Takhli Royal Thai AFB, Thailand
Served as: Pilot of an F-105
Battle or Place of Action: Thai Nguyen, North Vietnam
Date of Action: 10 March 1967
G.O. Number, Date: GB-51, 8 February 1968
Date of Presentation: 1 February 1968
Place of Presentation: The White House, presented by Pres. Lyndon B. Johnson
Citation: Maj. Dethlefsen was one of a flight of F-105 aircraft engaged in a fire suppression mission designed to destroy a key antiaircraft defensive complex containing surface-to-air missiles (SAM), an exceptionally heavy concentration of antiaircraft artillery, and other automatic weapons. The defensive network was situated to dominate the approach and provide protection to an important North Vietnam industrial center that was scheduled to be attacked by fighter bombers immediately after the strike by Maj. Dethlefsen's flight. In the initial attack on the defensive complex the lead aircraft was crippled, and Maj. Dethlefsen's aircraft was extensively damaged by the intense enemy fire. Realizing that the success of the impending fighter bomber attack on the center now depended on his ability to effectively suppress the defensive fire, Maj. Dethlefsen ignored the enemy's overwhelming firepower and the damage to his aircraft and pressed his attack. Despite a continuing hail of antiaircraft fire, deadly surface-to-air missiles, and counterattacks by MIG interceptors, Maj. Dethlefsen flew repeated close-range strikes to silence the enemy defensive positions with bombs and cannon fire. His action in rendering ineffective the defensive SAM and antiaircraft artillery sites enabled the ensuing fighter bombers to strike successfully the important industrial target without loss or damage to their aircraft, thereby appreciably reducing the enemy's ability to provide essential war material. Maj. Dethlefsen's consummate skill and selfless dedication to this significant mission were in keeping with the highest traditions of the U.S. Air Force and reflect great credit upon himself and the Armed Forces of his country.

3206 ◆ *DEVORE JR., EDWARD ALLEN

Rank: Specialist Fourth Class
Service: U.S. Army
Birthday: 15 June 1947
Place of Birth: Torrance, Los Angeles County, California
Date of Death: 17 March 1968
Place of Death: Republic of Vietnam
Cemetery: Green Hills Memorial Park—San Pedro, California
Entered Service at: Harbor City, Los Angeles County, California
Unit: Company B, 4th Battalion, 39th Infantry, 9th Infantry Division
Served as: Machine Gunner
Battle or Place of Action: near Saigon, Republic of Vietnam
Date of Action: 17 March 1968
G.O. Number, Date: 16, 23 April 1970
Date of Presentation: 7 April 1970
Place of Presentation: The White House, presented by Pres. Richard M. Nixon to his family
Citation: For conspicuous gallantry and intrepidity in action at the risk of his life above and beyond the call of duty. Sp4c. Devore distinguished himself by exceptionally valorous actions on the afternoon of 17 March 1968, while serving as a machine gunner with Company B, on a reconnaissance-in-force mission approximately five kilometers south of Saigon. Sp4c. Devore's platoon, the company's lead element, abruptly came under intense fire from automatic weapons, claymore mines, rockets, and grenades from well-concealed bunkers in a nipa palm swamp. One man was killed and three wounded about 20 meters from the bunker complex. Sp4c. Devore raced through a hail of fire to provide a base of fire with his machine gun, enabling the point element to move the wounded back to friendly lines. After supporting artillery, gunships, and air strikes had been employed on the enemy positions, a squad was sent forward to retrieve their fallen comrades. Intense enemy frontal and enfilading automatic-weapons fire pinned down this element in the kill zone. With complete disregard for his personal safety, Sp4c. Devore assaulted the enemy positions. Hit in the shoulder and knocked down about 35 meters short of his objectives, Sp4c. Devore, ignoring his pain and the warnings of his fellow soldiers, jumped to his feet and continued his assault under intense hostile fire. Although mortally wounded during this advance, he continued to place highly accurate suppressive fire upon the entrenched insurgents. By drawing the enemy fire upon himself, Sp4c. Devore enabled the trapped squad to rejoin the platoon in safety. Sp4c. Devore's extraordinary heroism and devotion to duty in close combat were in keeping with the highest traditions of the military service and reflect great credit upon himself, the 39th Infantry, and the U.S. Army.

3207 ◆ *DIAS, RALPH ELLIS

Rank: Private First Class
Service: U.S. Marine Corps
Birthday: 15 July 1950

Place of Birth: Shelocta, Armstrong County, Pennsylvania
Date of Death: 12 November 1969
Place of Death: Republic of Vietnam
Cemetery: Oakdale Cemetery (MH)—Leetonia, Ohio
Entered Service at: Pittsburgh, Allegheny County, Pennsylvania
Unit: 3d Platoon, Company D, 1st Battalion, 7th Marines, 1st Marine Division (Rein) FMF
Served as: Rifleman
Battle or Place of Action: Que Son Mountains, Republic of Vietnam
Date of Action: 12 November 1969
Date of Presentation: 17 July 1974
Place of Presentation: Blair House, presented by Vice Pres. Gerald R. Ford to his family
Citation: As a member of a reaction force which was pinned down by enemy fire while assisting a platoon in the same circumstance, Pfc. Dias, observing that both units were sustaining casualties, initiated an aggressive assault against an enemy machine-gun bunker which was the principal source of hostile fire. Severely wounded by enemy snipers while charging across the open area, he pulled himself to the shelter of a nearby rock. Braving enemy fire for a second time, Pfc. Dias was again wounded. Unable to walk, he crawled 15 meters to the protection of a rock located near his objective and, repeatedly exposing himself to intense hostile fire, unsuccessfully threw several hand grenades at the machine-gun emplacement. Still determined to destroy the emplacement, Pfc. Dias again moved into the open and was wounded a third time by sniper fire. As he threw a last grenade, which destroyed the enemy position, he was mortally wounded by another enemy round. Pfc. Dias' indomitable courage, dynamic initiative, and selfless devotion to duty upheld the highest traditions of the Marine Corps and the U.S. Naval Service. He gallantly gave his life in the service of his country.

3208 ◆ *DICKEY, DOUGLAS EUGENE

Rank: Private First Class
Service: U.S. Marine Corps
Birthday: 24 December 1946
Place of Birth: Greenville, Darke County, Ohio
Date of Death: 26 March 1967
Place of Death: Republic of Vietnam
Cemetery: Brock Cemetery (MH)—Rossburg, Ohio
Entered Service at: Cincinnati, Hamilton County, Ohio
Unit: 2d Platoon, Company C, 1st Battalion, 4th Marines, 9th Marine Amphibious Brigade, 3d Marine Division (Rein) FMF
Served as: Rifleman
Battle or Place of Action: near Gio An, Quang Tri Province, Republic of Vietnam
Date of Action: 26 March 1967
Date of Presentation: 16 April 1968
Place of Presentation: Marine Barracks, Washington, D.C., presented by Sec. of the Navy Paul R. Ignatius to his family
Citation: For conspicuous gallantry and intrepidity at the risk of his life above and beyond the call of duty. While participating in Operation Beacon Hill 1, the 2d Platoon was engaged in a fierce battle with the Viet Cong at close-range in dense jungle foliage. Pfc. Dickey had come forward to replace a radio operator who had been wounded in this intense action and was being treated by a medical corpsman. Suddenly an enemy grenade landed in the midst of a group of marines, which included the wounded radio operator who was immobilized. Fully realizing the inevitable result of his actions, Pfc. Dickey, in a final valiant act, quickly and unhesitatingly threw himself upon the deadly grenade, absorbing with his body the full and complete force of the explosion. Pfc. Dickey's personal heroism, extraordinary valor and selfless courage saved a number of his comrades from certain injury and possible death at the cost of his life. His actions reflected great credit upon himself, the Marine Corps, and the U.S. Naval Service. He gallantly gave his life for his country.

3209 ◆ DIX, DREW DENNIS

Rank: Staff Sergeant (highest rank: Major)
Service: U.S. Army
Birthday: 14 December 1944
Place of Birth: West Point, Orange County, New York
Entered Service at: Denver, Denver County, Colorado
Unit: Senior Advisor Group, IV Corps, Military Assistance Command
Served as: Unit Advisor
Battle or Place of Action: Chau Doc Province, Republic of Vietnam
Date of Action: 31 January-1 February 1968
G.O. Number, Date: 10, 6 February 1969
Date of Presentation: 16 January 1969
Place of Presentation: The White House, presented by Pres. Lyndon B. Johnson
Citation: For conspicuous gallantry and intrepidity in action at the risk of his life above and beyond the call of duty. S/Sgt. Dix distinguished himself by exceptional heroism while serving as a unit adviser. Two heavily armed Viet Cong battalions attacked the province capital city of Chau Phu resulting in the complete breakdown and fragmentation of the defenses of the city. S/Sgt. Dix with a patrol of Vietnamese soldiers, was recalled to assist in defense of Chau Phu. Learning that a nurse was trapped in a house near the center of the city, S/Sgt. Dix organized a relief force, successfully rescued the nurse, and returned her to the safety of the Tactical Operations Center. Being informed of other trapped civilians within the city, S/Sgt. Dix voluntarily led another force to rescue eight civilian employees located in a building which was under heavy mortar and small-arms fire. S/Sgt. Dix then returned to the center of the city. Upon approaching a building, he was subjected to intense automatic rifle and machine-gun fire from an unknown number of Viet Cong. He personally assaulted the building, killing six Viet Cong, and rescuing two Filipinos. The following day S/Sgt. Dix, still on his own volition, assembled a 20-man force and though under intense enemy fire cleared the Viet Cong out of the hotel, theater, and other adjacent buildings within the city. During this portion of the attack, Army of the Republic of Vietnam soldiers inspired by the heroism and success of S/Sgt. Dix, rallied and commenced firing upon the Viet

Cong. S/Sgt. Dix captured 20 prisoners, including a high-ranking Viet Cong official. He then attacked enemy troops who had entered the residence of the Deputy Province Chief and was successful in rescuing the official's wife and children. S/Sgt. Dix's personal heroic actions resulted in 14 confirmed Viet Cong killed in action and possibly 25 more, the capture of 20 prisoners, 15 weapons, and the rescue of the 14 United States and free-world civilians. The heroism of S/Sgt. Dix was in the highest tradition and reflects great credit upon the U.S. Army.

3210 ◆ *DOANE, STEPHEN HOLDEN

Rank: First Lieutenant
Service: U.S. Army
Birthday: 13 October 1947
Place of Birth: Beverly, Essex County, Massachusetts
Date of Death: 25 March 1969
Place of Death: Republic of Vietnam
Cemetery: Arlington National Cemetery (59-1617) (MH)—Arlington, Virginia
Entered Service at: Albany, Albany County, New York
Unit: Company B, 1st Battalion, 5th Infantry, 25th Infantry Division
Served as: Platoon Leader
Battle or Place of Action: Hau Nghia Province, Republic of Vietnam
Date of Action: 25 March 1969
G.O. Number, Date: 7, 9 March 1971
Date of Presentation: 16 February 1971
Place of Presentation: The White House (East Ballroom), presented by Pres. Richard M. Nixon to his family
Citation: For conspicuous gallantry and intrepidity in action at the risk of his life above and beyond the call of duty. 1st Lt. Doane was serving as a platoon leader when his company, engaged in a tactical operation, abruptly contacted an enemy force concealed in protected bunkers and trenches. Three of the leading soldiers were pinned down by enemy crossfire. One was seriously wounded. After efforts of one platoon to rescue these men had failed, it became obvious that only a small group could successfully move close enough to destroy the enemy position and rescue or relieve the trapped soldiers. 1st Lt. Doane, although fully aware of the danger of such an action, crawled to the nearest enemy bunker and silenced it. He was wounded but continued to advance to a second enemy bunker. As he prepared to throw a grenade, he was again wounded. Undaunted, he deliberately pulled the pin on the grenade and lunged with it into the enemy bunker, destroying this final obstacle. 1st Lt. Doane's supreme act enabled his company to rescue the trapped men without further casualties. The extraordinary courage and selflessness displayed by this officer were an inspiration to his men and are in the highest traditions of the U.S. Army.

3211 ◆ DOLBY, DAVID CHARLES

Rank: Sergeant (rank at time of action: Specialist Fourth Class) (highest rank: Staff Sergeant)
Service: U.S. Army
Birthday: 14 May 1946
Place of Birth: Norristown, Montgomery County, Pennsylvania
Entered Service at: Philadelphia, Philadelphia County, Pennsylvania
Unit: Company B, 1st Battalion (Airborne), 8th Cavalry, 1st Cavalry Division
Served as: Machine Gunner
Battle or Place of Action: Republic of Vietnam
Date of Action: 21 May 1966
G.O. Number, Date: 45, 20 October 1967
Date of Presentation: 28 September 1967
Place of Presentation: The White House, presented by Pres. Lyndon B. Johnson
Citation: For conspicuous gallantry and intrepidity at the risk of his life above and beyond the call of duty, when his platoon, while advancing tactically, suddenly came under intense fire from the enemy located on a ridge immediately to the front. Six members of the platoon were killed instantly and a number were wounded, including the platoon leader. Sgt. Dolby's every move brought fire from the enemy. However, aware that the platoon leader was critically wounded, and that the platoon was in a precarious situation, Sgt. Dolby moved the wounded men to safety and deployed the remainder of the platoon to engage the enemy. Subsequently, his dying platoon leader ordered Sgt. Dolby to withdraw the forward elements to rejoin the platoon. Despite the continuing intense enemy fire and with utter disregard for his own safety, Sgt. Dolby positioned abled-bodied men to cover the withdrawal of the forward elements, assisted the wounded to the new position, and he, alone, attacked enemy positions until his ammunition was expended. Replenishing his ammunition, he returned to the area of most intense action, single-handedly killed three enemy machine gunners, and neutralized the enemy fire, thus enabling friendly elements on the flank to advance on the enemy redoubt. He defied the enemy fire to personally carry a seriously wounded soldier to safety where he could be treated and, returning to the forward area, he crawled through withering fire to within 50 meters of the enemy bunkers and threw smoke grenades to mark them for air strikes. Although repeatedly under fire at close range from enemy snipers and automatic weapons, Sgt. Dolby directed artillery fire on the enemy and succeeded in silencing several enemy weapons. He remained in his exposed location until his comrades had displaced to more secure positions. His actions of unsurpassed valor during four hours of intense combat were a source of inspiration to his entire company, contributed significantly to the success of the overall assault on the enemy position, and were directly responsible for saving the lives of a number of his fellow soldiers. Sgt. Dolby's heroism was in the highest traditions of the U.S. Army.

3212 ◆ DONLON, ROGER HUGH CHARLES

Rank: Captain (highest rank: Colonel)
Service: U.S. Army
Birthday: 30 January 1934
Place of Birth: Saugerties, Ulster County, New York
Entered Service at: Saugerties, Ulster County, New York

Unit: Detachment A-726, 7th Special Forces Group (Airborne), 1st Special Forces
Served as: Commanding Officer
Battle or Place of Action: near Nam Dong, Republic of Vietnam
Date of Action: 6 July 1964
G.O. Number, Date: 41, 17 December 1964
Date of Presentation: 5 December 1964
Place of Presentation: The White House (East Ballroom), presented by Pres. Lyndon B. Johnson
Citation: For conspicuous gallantry and intrepidity at the risk of his life above and beyond the call of duty while defending a U.S. military installation against a fierce attack by hostile forces. Capt. Donlon was serving as the commanding officer of the U.S. Army Special Forces Detachment A-726 at Camp Nam Dong when a reinforced Viet Cong battalion suddenly launched a full-scale, predawn attack on the camp. During the violent battle that ensued, lasting five hours and resulting in heavy casualties on both sides, Capt. Donlon directed the defense operations in the midst of an enemy barrage of mortar shells, falling grenades, and extremely heavy gunfire. Upon the initial onslaught, he swiftly marshaled his forces and ordered the removal of the needed ammunition from a blazing building. He then dashed through a hail of small arms and exploding hand grenades to abort a breach of the main gate. En route to this position he detected an enemy demolition team of three in the proximity of the main gate and quickly annihilated them. Although exposed to the intense grenade attack, he then succeeded in reaching a 60-mm mortar position despite sustaining a severe stomach wound as he was within five yards of the gun pit. When he discovered that most of the men in this gun pit were also wounded, he completely disregarded his own injury, directed their withdrawal to a location 30 meters away, and again risked his life by remaining behind and covering the movement with the utmost effectiveness. Noticing that his team sergeant was unable to evacuate the gun pit he crawled toward him and, while dragging the fallen soldier out of the gun pit, an enemy mortar exploded and inflicted a wound in Capt. Donlon's left shoulder. Although suffering from multiple wounds, he carried the abandoned 60-mm mortar weapon to a new location 30 meters away where he found three wounded defenders. After administering first aid and encouragement to these men, he left the weapon with them, headed toward another position, and retrieved a 57-mm recoilless rifle. Then with great courage and coolness under fire, he returned to the abandoned gun pit, evacuated ammunition for the two weapons, and while crawling and dragging the urgently needed ammunition, received a third wound in his leg by an enemy hand grenade. Despite his critical physical condition, he again crawled 175 meters to an 81-mm mortar position and directed firing operations which protected the seriously threatened east sector of the camp. He then moved to an eastern 60-mm mortar position and upon determining that the vicious enemy assault had weakened, crawled back to the gun pit with the 60-mm mortar, set it up for defensive operations, and turned it over to two defenders with minor wounds. Without hesitation, he left this sheltered position, and moved from position to position around the beleaguered perimeter while hurling hand grenades at the enemy and inspiring his men to superhuman effort. As he bravely continued to move around the perimeter, a mortar shell exploded, wounding him in the face and body. As the long awaited daylight brought defeat to the enemy forces and their retreat back to the jungle leaving behind 54 of their dead, many weapons, and grenades, Capt. Donlon immediately reorganized his defenses and administered first aid to the wounded. His dynamic leadership, fortitude, and valiant efforts inspired not only the American personnel but the friendly Vietnamese defenders as well and resulted in the successful defense of the camp. Capt. Donlon's extraordinary heroism, at the risk of his life above and beyond the call of duty, are in the highest traditions of the U.S. Army and reflect great credit upon himself and the Armed Forces of his country.

3213 ◆ DUNAGAN, KERN WAYNE

Rank: Major (rank at time of action: Captain) (highest rank: Colonel)
Service: U.S. Army
Birthday: 20 February 1934
Place of Birth: Superior, Pinal County, Arizona
Date of Death: 27 December 1991
Place of Death: Nevada City, California
Cemetery: Golden Gate National Cemetery (1-3-92) (WS-117-1) (MH)—San Francisco, California
Entered Service at: Los Angeles, Los Angeles County, California
Unit: Company A, 1st Battalion, 46th Infantry, Americal Division
Served as: Commanding Officer
Battle or Place of Action: Quang Tin Province, Republic of Vietnam
Date of Action: 13 May 1969
G.O. Number, Date: 39, 23 July 1971
Date of Presentation: 15 June 1971
Place of Presentation: The White House (East Ballroom), presented by Pres. Richard M. Nixon
Citation: For conspicuous gallantry and intrepidity in action at the risk of his life above and beyond the call of duty. Maj. (then Capt.) Dunagan distinguished himself during the period 13 and 14 May 1969, while serving as commanding officer, Company A. On 13 May 1969, Maj. Dunagan was leading an attack to relieve pressure on the battalion's forward support base when his company came under intense fire from a well-entrenched enemy battalion. Despite continuous hostile fire from a numerically superior force, Maj. Dunagan repeatedly and fearlessly exposed himself in order to locate enemy positions, direct friendly supporting artillery, and position the men of his company. In the early evening, while directing an element of his unit into perimeter guard, he was seriously wounded during an enemy mortar attack, but he refused to leave the battlefield and continued to supervise the evacuation of dead and wounded and to lead his command in the difficult task of disengaging from an aggressive enemy. In spite of painful wounds and extreme fatigue, Maj. Dunagan risked heavy fire on two occasions to rescue critically wounded men. He was again seriously wounded. Undaunted, he

continued to display outstanding courage, professional competence, and leadership and successfully extricated his command from its untenable position on the evening of 14 May. Having maneuvered his command into contact with an adjacent friendly unit, he learned that a six-man party from his company was under fire and had not reached the new perimeter. Maj. Dunagan unhesitatingly went back and searched for his men. Finding one soldier critically wounded, Maj. Dunagan, ignoring his wounds, lifted the man to his shoulders and carried him to the comparative safety of the friendly perimeter. Before permitting himself to be evacuated, he insured all of his wounded received emergency treatment and were removed from the area. Throughout the engagement, Maj. Dunagan's actions gave great inspiration to his men and were directly responsible for saving the lives of many of his fellow soldiers. Maj. Dunagan's extraordinary heroism, above and beyond the call of duty, are in the highest traditions of the U.S. Army and reflect great credit on him, his unit, and the U.S. Army.

3214 ◆ *DURHAM JR., HAROLD BASCOM

Rank: Second Lieutenant
Service: U.S. Army
Birthday: 12 October 1942
Place of Birth: Rocky Mount, Edgecombe County, North Carolina
Date of Death: 17 October 1967
Place of Death: Republic of Vietnam
Cemetery: Oakridge Cemetery—Tifton, Georgia
Entered Service at: Atlanta, Fulton County, Georgia
Unit: Battery C, 6th Battalion, 15th Artillery, 1st Infantry Division
Served as: Forward Observer
Battle or Place of Action: Republic of Vietnam
Date of Action: 17 October 1967
G.O. Number, Date: 74, 20 November 1969
Date of Presentation: 31 October 1969
Place of Presentation: The Executive Office Building, presented by Vice Pres. Spiro T. Agnew to his family
Citation: 2nd Lt. Durham, Artillery, distinguished himself by conspicuous gallantry and intrepidity at the cost of his life above and beyond the call of duty while assigned to Battery C. 2nd Lt. Durham was serving as a forward observer with Company D, 2d Battalion, 28th Infantry during a battalion reconnaissance-in-force mission. At approximately 1015 hours contact was made with an enemy force concealed in well-camouflaged positions and fortified bunkers. 2nd Lt. Durham immediately moved into an exposed position to adjust the supporting artillery fire onto the insurgents. During a brief lull in the battle he administered emergency first aid to the wounded in spite of heavy enemy sniper fire directed toward him. Moments later, as enemy units assaulted friendly positions, he learned that Company A, bearing the brunt of the attack, had lost its forward observer. While he was moving to replace the wounded observer, the enemy detonated a claymore mine, severely wounding him in the head and impairing his vision. In spite of the intense pain, he continued to direct the supporting artillery fire and to employ his individual weapon in support of the hard-pressed infantrymen. As the enemy pressed their attack, 2d Lt. Durham called for supporting fire to be placed almost directly on his position. Twice the insurgents were driven back, leaving many dead and wounded behind. 2nd Lt. Durham was then taken to a secondary defensive position. Even in his extremely weakened condition, he continued to call artillery fire onto the enemy. He refused to seek cover and instead positioned himself in a small clearing which offered a better vantage point from which to adjust the fire. Suddenly, he was severely wounded a second time by enemy machine-gun fire. As he lay on the ground near death, he saw two Viet Cong approaching, shooting the defenseless wounded men. With his last effort, 2d Lt. Durham shouted a warning to a nearby soldier who immediately killed the insurgents. 2nd Lt. Durham died moments later, still grasping the radio handset. 2nd Lt. Durham's gallant actions in close combat with an enemy force are in keeping with the highest traditions of the military service and reflect great credit upon himself, his unit, and the U.S. Army.

3215 ◆ *ENGLISH JR., GLENN HARRY

Rank: Staff Sergeant
Service: U.S. Army
Birthday: 23 April 1940
Place of Birth: Altoona, Blair County, Pennsylvania
Date of Death: 7 September 1970
Place of Death: Republic of Vietnam
Cemetery: Fort Bragg Post Cemetery (I-288-A) (MH)—Fort Bragg, North Carolina
Entered Service at: Philadelphia, Philadelphia County, Pennsylvania
Unit: Company E, 3d Battalion, 503d Infantry, 173d Airborne Brigade
Served as: Squad Leader
Battle or Place of Action: Phu My District, Republic of Vietnam
Date of Action: 7 September 1970
G.O. Number, Date: 39, 6 September 1974
Date of Presentation: 8 August 1974
Place of Presentation: Blair House, presented by Vice Pres. Gerald R. Ford to his family
Citation: S/Sgt. English was riding in the lead armored personnel carrier in a four-vehicle column when an enemy mine exploded in front of his vehicle. As the vehicle swerved from the road, a concealed enemy force waiting in ambush opened fire with automatic weapons and antitank grenades, striking the vehicle several times and setting it on fire. S/Sgt. English escaped from the disabled vehicle and, without pausing to extinguish the flames on his clothing, rallied his stunned unit. He then led it in a vigorous assault, in the face of heavy enemy automatic-weapons fire, on the entrenched enemy position. This prompt and courageous action routed the enemy and saved his unit from destruction. Following the assault, S/Sgt. English heard the cries of three men still trapped inside the vehicle. Paying no heed to warnings that the ammunition and fuel in the burning personnel carrier might explode at any moment, S/Sgt. English raced to the vehicle and climbed inside to rescue his wounded comrades. As he was lifting one of the men to safety, the vehicle exploded, mortally wounding him and the man he was attempting

to save. By his extraordinary devotion to duty, indomitable courage, and utter disregard for his own safety, S/Sgt. English saved his unit from destruction and selflessly sacrificed his life in a brave attempt to save three comrades. S/Sgt. English's conspicuous gallantry and intrepidity in action at the cost of his life were an inspiration to his comrades and are in the highest traditions of the U.S. Army.

3216 ◆ *ESTOCIN, MICHAEL JOHN

Rank: Captain (rank at time of action: Lieutenant Commander)
Service: U.S. Navy
Birthday: 27 April 1931
Place of Birth: Turtle Creek, Allegheny County, Pennsylvania
Date of Death: 26 April 1967
Place of Death: North Vietnam
Cemetery: Fort Rosecrans National Cemetery ('In Memory' marker) (MA-112)—San Diego, California
Entered Service at: Akron, Summit County, Ohio
Unit: Attack Squadron 192, U.S.S. *Ticonderoga* (CVA-14)
Served as: Pilot
Battle or Place of Action: Haiphong, North Vietnam
Date of Action: 20, 26 April 1967
Date of Presentation: 27 February 1978
Place of Presentation: The Pentagon (Hall of Heroes), presented by Sec. of the Navy W. Graham Claytor Jr. to his family
Citation: For conspicuous gallantry and intrepidity at the risk of his life above and beyond the call of duty on 20 and 26 April 1967 as a pilot in Attack Squadron 192, embarked in U.S.S. *Ticonderoga* (CVA-14). Leading a three-plane group of aircraft in support of a coordinated strike against two thermal powerplants in Haiphong, North Vietnam, on 20 April 1967, Capt. Estocin provided continuous warnings to the strike group leaders of the surface-to-air missile (SAM) threats, and personally neutralized three SAM sites. Although his aircraft was severely damaged by an exploding missile, he reentered the target area and relentlessly prosecuted a SHRIKE attack in the face of intense antiaircraft fire. With less than five minutes of fuel remaining he departed the target area and commenced in-flight refueling which continued for over 100 miles. Three miles aft of the *Ticonderoga*, and without enough fuel for a second approach, he disengaged from the tanker and executed a precise approach to a fiery arrested landing. On 26 April 1967, in support of a coordinated strike against the vital fuel facilities in Haiphong, he led an attack on a threatening SAM site, during which his aircraft was seriously damaged by an exploding SAM, nevertheless, he regained control of his burning aircraft and courageously launched his SHRIKE missiles before departing the area. By his inspiring courage and unswerving devotion to duty in the face of grave personal danger, Capt. Estocin upheld the highest traditions of the U.S. Naval Service.

3217 ◆ *EVANS JR., DONALD WARD

Rank: Specialist Fourth Class
Service: U.S. Army
Birthday: 23 July 1943
Place of Birth: Covina, Los Angeles County, California
Date of Death: 27 January 1967
Place of Death: Republic of Vietnam
Cemetery: Oakdale Memorial Park—Glendora, California
Entered Service at: Covina, Los Angeles County, California
Unit: Company A, 2d Battalion, 12th Infantry, 4th Infantry Division
Served as: Medical Aidman
Battle or Place of Action: Tri Tam, Republic of Vietnam
Date of Action: 27 January 1967
G.O. Number, Date: 34, 5 July 1968
Date of Presentation: 4 June 1968
Place of Presentation: The Pentagon, presented by Sec. of the Army Stanley R. Resor to his family
Citation: For conspicuous gallantry and intrepidity in action at the risk of his life above and beyond the call of duty. He left his position of relative safety with his platoon which had not yet been committed to the battle to answer the calls for medical aid from the wounded men of another platoon which was heavily engaged with the enemy force. Dashing across 100 meters of open area through a withering hail of enemy fire and exploding grenades, he administered lifesaving treatment to one individual and continued to expose himself to the deadly enemy fire as he moved to treat each of the other wounded men and to offer them encouragement. Realizing that the wounds of one man required immediate attention, Sp4c. Evans dragged the injured soldier back across the dangerous fire-swept area, to a secure position from which he could be further evacuated. Miraculously escaping the enemy fusillade, Sp4c. Evans returned to the forward location. As he continued the treatment of the wounded, he was struck by fragments from an enemy grenade. Despite his serious and painful injury he succeeded in evacuating another wounded comrade, rejoined his platoon as it was committed to battle and was soon treating other wounded soldiers. As he evacuated another wounded man across the fire-covered field, he was severely wounded. Continuing to refuse medical attention and ignoring advice to remain behind, he managed with his waning strength to move yet another wounded comrade across the dangerous open area to safety. Disregarding his painful wounds and seriously weakened from profuse bleeding, he continued his lifesaving medical aid and was killed while treating another wounded comrade. Sp4c. Evan's extraordinary valor, dedication, and indomitable spirit saved the lives of several of his fellow soldiers, served as an inspiration to the men of his company, were instrumental in the success of their mission, and reflect great credit upon himself and the Armed Forces of his country.

3218 ◆ *EVANS, RODNEY JOHN

Rank: Sergeant
Service: U.S. Army
Birthday: 17 July 1948
Place of Birth: Chelsea, Suffolk County, Massachusetts
Date of Death: 18 July 1969
Place of Death: Republic of Vietnam
Cemetery: Liberty Hill Cemetery—Florala, Alabama
Entered Service at: Montgomery, Montgomery County, Alabama

Unit: Company D, 1st Battalion, 12th Cavalry, 1st Cavalry Division
Served as: Squad Leader
Battle or Place of Action: Tay Ninh Province, Republic of Vietnam
Date of Action: 18 July 1969
G.O. Number, Date: 29, 5 July 1972
Date of Presentation: 22 April 1971
Place of Presentation: The White House, presented by Pres. Richard M. Nixon to his family
Citation: For conspicuous gallantry and intrepidity in action at the risk of his life above and beyond the call of duty. Sgt. Evans distinguished himself by extraordinary heroism while serving as a squad leader in a reconnaissance sweep through heavy vegetation to reconnoiter a strong enemy position. As the force approached a well-defined trail, the platoon scout warned that the trail was booby-trapped. Sgt. Evans led his squad on a route parallel to the trail. The force had started to move forward when a nearby squad was hit by the blast of a concealed mine. Looking to his right Sgt. Evans saw a second enemy device. With complete disregard for his safety he shouted a warning to his men, dived to the ground, and crawled toward the mine. Just as he reached it an enemy soldier detonated the explosive and Sgt. Evans absorbed the full impact with his body. His gallant and selfless action saved his comrades from probable death or injury and served as an inspiration to his entire unit. Sgt. Evans' gallantry in action at the cost of his life was in keeping with the highest traditions of the military service and reflect great credit upon himself, his unit, and the U.S. Army.

3219 ◆ FERGUSON, FREDERICK EDGAR

Rank: Chief Warrant Officer (highest rank: Major)
Service: U.S. Army
Birthday: 18 August 1939
Place of Birth: Pilot Point, Denton County, Texas
Entered Service at: Phoenix, Maricopa County, Arizona
Unit: Company C, 227th Aviation Battalion, 1st Cavalry Division (Airmobile)
Served as: Helicopter Commander
Battle or Place of Action: Hue, Republic of Vietnam
Date of Action: 31 January 1968
G.O. Number, Date: 38, 13 June 1969
Date of Presentation: 17 May 1969
Place of Presentation: The White House, presented by Pres. Richard M. Nixon
Citation: For conspicuous gallantry and intrepidity in action at the risk of his life above and beyond the call of duty. CWO Ferguson, commander of a resupply helicopter monitoring an emergency call from wounded passengers and crewmen of a downed helicopter under heavy attack within the enemy-controlled city of Hue, unhesitatingly volunteered to attempt evacuation. Despite warnings from all aircraft to stay clear of the area due to heavy antiaircraft fire, CWO Ferguson began a low-level flight at maximum airspeed along the Perfume River toward the tiny, isolated South Vietnamese Army compound in which the crash survivors had taken refuge. Coolly and skillfully maintaining his course in the face of intense, short-range fire from enemy-occupied buildings and boats, he displayed superior flying skill and tenacity of purpose by landing his aircraft in an extremely confined area in a blinding dust cloud under heavy mortar and small-arms fire. Although the helicopter was severely damaged by mortar fragments during the loading of the wounded, CWO Ferguson disregarded the damage and, taking off through the continuing hail of mortar fire, he flew his crippled aircraft on the return route through the rain of fire that he had experienced earlier and safely returned his wounded passengers to friendly control. CWO Ferguson's extraordinary determination saved the lives of five of his comrades. His actions are in the highest traditions of the military service and reflect great credit on himself and the U.S. Army.

3220 ◆ *FERNANDEZ, DANIEL

Rank: Specialist Fourth Class
ice: U.S. Army
Birthday: 30 June 1944
Place of Birth: Albuquerque, Bernalillo County, New Mexico
Date of Death: 18 February 1966
Place of Death: Republic of Vietnam
Cemetery: Santa Fe National Cemetery (S-249) (MH)—Santa Fe, New Mexico
Entered Service at: Albuquerque, Bernalillo County, New Mexico
Unit: Company C, 1st Battalion, 5th Infantry (Mechanized), 25th Infantry Division
Battle or Place of Action: Cu Chi, Hau Nghia Province, Republic of Vietnam
Date of Action: 18 February 1966
G.O. Number, Date: 21, 26 April 1967
Date of Presentation: 6 April 1967
Place of Presentation: The White House (Rose Garden), presented by Pres. Lyndon B. Johnson to his family
Citation: For conspicuous gallantry and intrepidity at the risk of his life above and beyond the call of duty. Sp4c. Fernandez demonstrated indomitable courage when the patrol was ambushed by a Viet Cong rifle company and driven back by the intense enemy automatic-weapons fire before it could evacuate an American soldier who had been wounded in the Viet Cong attack. Sp4c. Fernandez, a sergeant, and two other volunteers immediately fought their way through devastating fire and exploding grenades to reach the fallen soldier. Upon reaching their fallen comrade the sergeant was struck in the knee by machine-gun fire and immobilized. Sp4c. Fernandez took charge, rallied the left flank of his patrol, and began to assist in the recovery of the wounded sergeant. While first aid was being administered to the wounded man, a sudden increase in the accuracy and intensity of the enemy fire forced the volunteer group to take cover. As they did, an enemy grenade landed in the midst of the group, although some men did not see it. Realizing there was no time for the wounded sergeant or the other men to protect themselves from the grenade blast, Sp4c. Fernandez vaulted over the wounded sergeant and threw himself on the grenade as it exploded, saving the lives of his four comrades at the sacrifice of his life. Sp4c. Fernandez' profound concern for his fellow soldiers, at

the risk of his life above and beyond the call of duty, are in the highest traditions of the U.S. Army and reflect great credit upon himself and the Armed Forces of his country.

3221 ◆ FISHER, BERNARD FRANCIS

Rank: Major (highest rank: Colonel)
Service: U.S. Air Force
Birthday: 11 January 1927
Place of Birth: San Bernardino, San Bernardino County, California
Entered Service at: Kuna, Ada County, Idaho
Unit: 1st Air Commandos, United States Air Force
Served as: Pilot of a A-1E Skyraider
Battle or Place of Action: Bien Hoa and Pleiku, Republic of Vietnam
Date of Action: 10 March 1966
G.O. Number, Date: GB-41, 23 January 1967
Date of Presentation: 19 January 1967
Place of Presentation: The White House, presented by Pres. Lyndon B. Johnson
Citation: For conspicuous gallantry and intrepidity at the risk of his life above and beyond the call of duty. On that date, the Special Forces camp at A Shau was under attack by 2,000 North Vietnamese Army regulars. Hostile troops had positioned themselves between the airstrip and the camp. Other hostile troops had surrounded the camp and were continuously raking it with automatic-weapons fire from the surrounding hills. The tops of the 1,500-foot hills were obscured by an 800 foot ceiling, limiting aircraft maneuverability and forcing pilots to operate within range of hostile gun positions, which often were able to fire down on attacking aircraft. During the battle, Maj. Fisher observed a fellow airman crash land on the battle-torn airstrip. In the belief that the downed pilot was seriously injured and in imminent danger of capture, Maj. Fisher announced his intention to land on the airstrip to effect a rescue. Although aware of the extreme danger and likely failure of such an attempt, he elected to continue. Directing his own air cover, he landed his aircraft and taxied almost the full length of the runway, which was littered with battle debris and parts of an exploded aircraft. While effecting a successful rescue of the downed pilot, heavy ground fire was observed, with 19 bullets striking his aircraft. In the face of withering ground fire, he applied power and gained enough speed to lift-off at the overrun of the airstrip. Maj. Fisher's profound concern for his fellow airman, at the risk of his life above and beyond the call of duty, are in the highest traditions of the U.S. Air Force and reflect great credit upon himself and the Armed Forces of his country.

3222 ◆ FITZMAURICE, MICHAEL JOHN

Rank: Specialist Fourth Class
Service: U.S. Army
Birthday: 9 March 1950
Place of Birth: Jamestown, Stutsman County, North Dakota
Entered Service at: Cavour, Beadle County, South Dakota
Unit: 3d Squad, Troop D, 2d Squadron, 17th Cavalry, 101st Airborne Division (Airmobile)
Served as: Rifleman
Battle or Place of Action: Khesanh, Republic of Vietnam
Date of Action: 23 March 1971
G.O. Number, Date: 39, 5 November 1973
Date of Presentation: 15 October 1973
Place of Presentation: The White House, presented by Pres. Richard M. Nixon
Citation: For conspicuous gallantry and intrepidity in action at the risk of his life above and beyond the call of duty. Sp4c. Fitzmaurice, 3d Platoon, Troop D, distinguished himself at Khesanh. Sp4c. Fitzmaurice and three fellow soldiers were occupying a bunker when a company of North Vietnamese sappers infiltrated the area. At the onset of the attack Sp4c. Fitzmaurice observed three explosive charges which had been thrown into the bunker by the enemy. Realizing the imminent danger to his comrades, and with complete disregard for his personal safety, he hurled two of the charges out of the bunker. He then threw his flak vest and himself over the remaining charge. By this courageous act he absorbed the blast and shielded his fellow soldiers. Although suffering from serious multiple wounds and partial loss of sight, he charged out of the bunker and engaged the enemy until his rifle was damaged by the blast of an enemy hand grenade. While in search of another weapon, Sp4c. Fitzmaurice encountered and overcame an enemy sapper in hand-to-hand combat. Having obtained another weapon, he returned to his original fighting position and inflicted additional casualties on the attacking enemy. Although seriously wounded, Sp4c. Fitzmaurice refused to be medically evacuated, preferring to remain at his post. Sp4c. Fitzmaurice's extraordinary heroism in action at the risk of his life contributed significantly to the successful defense of the position and resulted in saving the lives of a number of his fellow soldiers. These acts of heroism go above and beyond the call of duty, are in keeping with the highest traditions of the military service, and reflect great credit on Sp4c. Fitzmaurice and the U.S. Army.

3223 ◆ *FLEEK, CHARLES CLINTON

Rank: Sergeant
Service: U.S. Army
Birthday: 28 August 1947
Place of Birth: Petersburg, Boone County, Kentucky
Date of Death: 27 May 1967
Place of Death: Republic of Vietnam
Cemetery: Petersburg Cemetery (MH)—Petersburg, Kentucky
Entered Service at: Cincinnati, Hamilton County, Ohio
Unit: Company C, 1st Battalion, 27th Infantry, 25th Infantry Division
Served as: Squad Leader
Battle or Place of Action: Binh Duong Province, Republic of Vietnam
Date of Action: 27 May 1967
G.O. Number, Date: 10, 9 March 1971
Date of Presentation: 16 February 1971
Place of Presentation: The White House (East Ballroom), presented by Pres. Richard M. Nixon to his family
Citation: For conspicuous gallantry and intrepidity in action

at the risk of his life above and beyond the call of duty. Sgt. Fleek distinguished himself while serving as a squad leader in Company C, during an ambush operation. Sgt. Fleek's unit was deployed in ambush locations when a large enemy force approached the position. Suddenly, the leading enemy element, sensing the ambush, halted and started to withdraw. Reacting instantly, Sgt. Fleek opened fire and directed the effective fire of his men upon the numerically superior enemy force. During the fierce battle that followed, an enemy soldier threw a grenade into the squad position. Realizing that his men had not seen the grenade, Sgt. Fleek, although in a position to seek cover, shouted a warning to his comrades and threw himself onto the grenade, absorbing its blast. His gallant action undoubtedly saved the lives or prevented the injury of at least eight of his fellow soldiers. Sgt. Fleek's gallantry and willing self-sacrifice were in keeping with the highest traditions of the military service and reflect great credit on himself, his unit, and the U.S. Army.

3224 ◆ FLEMING, JAMES PHILLIP

Rank: Captain (rank at time of action: First Lieutenant) (highest rank: Colonel)
Service: U.S. Air Force
Birthday: 12 March 1943
Place of Birth: Sedalia, Pettis County, Missouri
Entered Service at: Pullman, Whitman County, Washington
Unit: 20th Special Operations Squadron, United States Air Force
Served as: UF-1F Helicopter Commander
Battle or Place of Action: near Duc Co, Republic of Vietnam
Date of Action: 26 November 1968
G.O. Number, Date: GB-477, 23 June 1970
Date of Presentation: 14 May 1970
Place of Presentation: The White House, presented by Pres. Richard M. Nixon
Citation: For conspicuous gallantry and intrepidity in action at the risk of his life above and beyond the call of duty. Capt. Fleming (then 1st Lt.) distinguished himself as the aircraft commander of a UH-1F transport helicopter. Capt. Fleming went to the aid of a six-man Special Forces long-range reconnaissance patrol that was in danger of being overrun by a large, heavily armed hostile force. Despite the knowledge that one helicopter had been downed by intense hostile fire, Capt. Fleming descended, and balanced his helicopter on a river bank with the tail boom hanging over open water. The patrol could not penetrate to the landing site and he was forced to withdraw. Dangerously low on fuel, Capt. Fleming repeated his original landing maneuver. Disregarding his own safety, he remained in this exposed position. Hostile fire crashed through his windscreen as the patrol boarded his helicopter. Capt. Fleming made a successful takeoff through a barrage of hostile fire and recovered safely at a forward base. Capt. Fleming's profound concern for his fellow men, at the risk of his life above and beyond the call of duty, are in keeping with the highest traditions of the U.S. Air Force and reflect great credit upon himself and the Armed Forces of his country.

3225 ◆ FOLEY, ROBERT FRANKLIN

Rank: Captain (highest rank: Major General)
Service: U.S. Army
Birthday: 30 May 1941
Place of Birth: Newton, Middlesex County, Massachusetts
Entered Service at: Newton, Middlesex County, Massachusetts
Unit: Company A, 2d Battalion, 27th Infantry, 25th Infantry Division
Served as: Company Commander
Battle or Place of Action: near Quan Dau Tieng, Republic of Vietnam
Date of Action: 5 November 1966
G.O. Number, Date: 28, 21 June 1968
Date of Presentation: 1 May 1968
Place of Presentation: The White House, presented by Pres. Lyndon B. Johnson
Citation: For conspicuous gallantry and intrepidity in action at the risk of his life above and beyond the call of duty. Capt. Foley's company was ordered to extricate another company of the battalion. Moving through the dense jungle to aid the besieged unit, Company A encountered a strong enemy force occupying well-concealed, defensive positions, and the company's leading element quickly sustained several casualties. Capt. Foley immediately ran forward to the scene of the most intense action to direct the company's efforts. Deploying one platoon on the flank, he led the other two platoons in an attack on the enemy in the face of intense fire. During this action both radio operators accompanying him were wounded. At grave risk to himself, he defied the enemy's murderous fire and helped the wounded operators to a position where they could receive medical care. As he moved forward again one of his machine-gun crews was wounded. Seizing the weapon, he charged forward firing the machine gun, shouting orders, and rallying his men, thus maintaining the momentum of the attack. Under increasingly heavy enemy fire he ordered his assistant to take cover and, alone, Capt. Foley continued to advance firing the machine gun until the wounded had been evacuated and the attack in this area could be resumed. When movement on the other flank was halted by the enemy's fanatical defense, Capt. Foley moved to personally direct this critical phase of the battle. Leading the renewed effort he was blown off his feet and wounded by an enemy grenade. Despite his painful wounds he refused medical aid and persevered in the forefront of the attack on the enemy redoubt. He led the assault on several enemy gun emplacements and, singlehandedly, destroyed three such positions. His outstanding personal leadership under intense enemy fire during the fierce battle which lasted for several hours inspired his men to heroic efforts and was instrumental in the ultimate success of the operation. Capt. Foley's magnificent courage, selfless concern for his men, and professional skill reflect the utmost credit upon himself and the U.S. Army.

3226 ◆ *FOLLAND, MICHAEL FLEMING

Rank: Corporal
Service: U.S. Army

Birthday: 15 April 1949
Place of Birth: Richmond, Richmond County, Virginia
Date of Death: 3 July 1969
Place of Death: Republic of Vietnam
Cemetery: Glendale National Cemetery (H-846) (MH)—Richmond, Virginia
Entered Service at: Richmond, Richmond County, Virginia
Unit: Weapons Platoon, Company D, 2d Battalion, 3d Infantry, 199th Infantry Brigade
Served as: Ammunition Bearer
Battle or Place of Action: Long Khanh Province, Republic of Vietnam
Date of Action: 3 July 1969
G.O. Number, Date: 8, 25 January 1972
Date of Presentation: 16 December 1971
Place of Presentation: The Executive Office Building, presented by Vice Pres. Spiro T. Agnew to his family
Citation: For conspicuous gallantry and intrepidity in action at the risk of his life above and beyond the call of duty. Cpl. Folland distinguished himself while serving as an ammunition bearer with the weapons platoon of Company D, during a reconnaissance patrol mission. As the patrol was moving through a dense jungle area, it was caught in an intense crossfire from heavily fortified and concealed enemy ambush positions. As the patrol reacted to neutralize the ambush, it became evident that the heavy weapons could not be used in the cramped fighting area. Cpl. Folland dropped his recoilless-rifle ammunition and ran forward to join his commander in an assault on the enemy bunkers. The assaulting force moved forward until it was pinned down directly in front of the heavily fortified bunkers by machine-gun fire. Cpl. Folland stood up to draw enemy fire on himself and to place suppressive fire on the enemy positions while his commander attempted to destroy the machine-gun positions with grenades. Before the officer could throw a grenade, an enemy grenade landed in the position. Cpl. Folland alerted his comrades and his commander hurled the grenade from the position. When a second enemy grenade landed in the position, Cpl. Folland again shouted a warning to his fellow soldiers. Seeing that no one could reach the grenade and realizing that it was about to explode, Cpl. Folland, with complete disregard for his safety, threw himself on the grenade. By his dauntless courage, Cpl. Folland saved the lives of his comrades although he was mortally wounded by the explosion. Cpl. Folland's extraordinary heroism, at the cost of his life, was in keeping with the highest traditions of the military service and reflect great credit upon himself, his unit, and the U.S. Army.

3227 ◆ *FOSTER, PAUL HELLSTROM

Rank: Sergeant
Service: U.S. Marine Corps Reserve
Birthday: 17 April 1939
Place of Birth: San Mateo, San Mateo County, California
Date of Death: 14 October 1967
Place of Death: Republic of Vietnam
Cemetery: Golden Gate National Cemetery (V-4764) (MH)—San Bruno, California
Entered Service at: San Francisco, San Francisco County, California
Unit: 2d Battalion, 4th Marines, 3d Marine Division (Rein) FMF
Served as: Artillery Liaison Operations Chief
Battle or Place of Action: near Con Thien, Quang Tri Province, Republic of Vietnam
Date of Action: 14 October 1967
Date of Presentation: 20 June 1969
Place of Presentation: The White House, presented by Pres. Richard M. Nixon to his family
Citation: For conspicuous gallantry and intrepidity at the risk of his life above and beyond the call of duty while serving as an artillery liaison operations chief with the 2d Battalion. In the early morning hours the 2d Battalion was occupying a defensive position which protected a bridge on the road leading from Con Thien to Cam Lo. Suddenly, the marines' position came under a heavy volume of mortar and artillery fire, followed by an aggressive enemy ground assault. In the ensuing engagement, the hostile forces penetrated the perimeter and brought a heavy concentration of small-arms, automatic-weapons, and rocket fire to bear on the battalion command post. Although his position in the fire support coordination center was dangerously exposed to enemy fire and he was wounded when an enemy hand grenade exploded near his position, Sgt. Foster resolutely continued to direct accurate mortar and artillery fire on the advancing North Vietnamese troops. As the attack continued, a hand grenade landed in the midst of Sgt. Foster and his five companions. Realizing the danger, he shouted a warning, threw his armored vest over the grenade, and unhesitatingly placed his body over the armored vest. When the grenade exploded, Sgt. Foster absorbed the entire blast with his body and was mortally wounded. His heroic actions undoubtedly saved his comrades from further injury or possible death. Sgt. Foster's courage, extraordinary heroism, and unfaltering devotion to duty reflected great credit upon himself and the Marine Corps and upheld the highest traditions of the U.S. Naval Service. He gallantly gave his life for his country.

3228 ◆ *FOURNET, DOUGLAS BERNARD

Rank: First Lieutenant
Service: U.S. Army
Birthday: 7 May 1943
Place of Birth: Lake Charles, Calcasieu County, Louisiana
Date of Death: 4 May 1968
Place of Death: Republic of Vietnam
Cemetery: McGrill Cemetery—Kinder, Louisiana
Entered Service at: New Orleans, Orleans County, Louisiana
Unit: 2d Platoon, Company B, 1st Battalion, 7th Cavalry, 1st Cavalry Division (Airmobile)
Served as: Platoon Leader
Battle or Place of Action: A Shau Valley, Republic of Vietnam
Date of Action: 4 May 1968
G.O. Number, Date: 18, 23 April 1970
Date of Presentation: 7 April 1970

Place of Presentation: The White House, presented by Pres. Richard M. Nixon to his family
Citation: For conspicuous gallantry and intrepidity in action at the risk of his life above and beyond the call of duty. 1st Lt. Fournet, Infantry, distinguished himself in action while serving as rifle platoon leader of the 2d Platoon, Company B. While advancing uphill against fortified enemy positions in the A Shau Valley, the platoon encountered intense sniper fire, making movement very difficult. The right flank man suddenly discovered an enemy claymore mine covering the route of advance and shouted a warning to his comrades. Realizing that the enemy would also be alerted, 1st Lt. Fournet ordered his men to take cover and ran uphill toward the mine, drawing a sheath knife as he approached it. With complete disregard for his safety and realizing the imminent danger to members of his command, he used his body as a shield in front of the mine as he attempted to slash the control wires leading from the enemy positions to the mine. As he reached for the wire the mine was detonated, killing him instantly. Five men nearest the mine were slightly wounded, but 1st Lt. Fournet's heroic and unselfish act spared his men of serious injury or death. His gallantry and willing self-sacrifice are in keeping with the highest traditions of the military service and reflect great credit upon himself, his unit, and the U.S. Army.

3229 ◆ *FOUS, JAMES WILLIAM

Rank: Private First Class
Service: U.S. Army
Birthday: 14 October 1946
Place of Birth: Omaha, Douglas County, Nebraska
Date of Death: 14 May 1968
Place of Death: Republic of Vietnam
Cemetery: Fort McPherson National Cemetery (G-685) (MH)—Maxwell, Nebraska
Entered Service at: Omaha, Douglas County, Nebraska
Unit: Company E, 4th Battalion, 47th Infantry, 9th Infantry Division
Served as: Rifleman
Battle or Place of Action: Kien Hoa Province, Republic of Vietnam
Date of Action: 14 May 1968
G.O. Number, Date: 8, 23 April 1970
Date of Presentation: 7 April 1970
Place of Presentation: The White House, presented by Pres. Richard M. Nixon to his family
Citation: For conspicuous gallantry and intrepidity in action at the risk of his life above and beyond the call of duty. Pfc. Fous distinguished himself at the risk of his life while serving as a rifleman with Company E. Pfc. Fous was participating in a reconnaissance-in-force mission when his unit formed its perimeter defense for the night. Pfc. Fous, together with three other American soldiers, occupied a position in a thickly vegetated area facing a woodline. Pfc. Fous detected three Viet Cong maneuvering toward his position and, after alerting the other men, directed accurate fire upon the enemy soldiers, silencing two of them. The third Viet Cong soldier managed to escape in the thick vegetation after throwing a hand grenade into Pfc. Fous' position. Without hesitation, Pfc. Fous shouted a warning to his comrades and leaped upon the lethal explosive, absorbing the blast with his body to save the lives of the three men in the area at the sacrifice of his life. Pfc. Fous' extraordinary heroism at the cost of his life were in keeping with the highest traditions of the military service and reflect great credit upon himself, his unit, and the U.S. Army.

3230 ◆ FOX, WESLEY LEE

Rank: Captain (rank at time of action: First Lieutenant) (highest rank: Colonel)
Service: U.S. Marine Corps
Birthday: 30 September 1931
Place of Birth: Herndon, Fairfax County, Virginia
Entered Service at: Leesburg, Loudoun County, Virginia
Unit: Company A, 1st Battalion, 9th Marines, 3d Marine Division (Rein) FMF
Served as: Commanding Officer
Battle or Place of Action: A Shau Valley, Quang Tri Province, Republic of Vietnam
Date of Action: 22 February 1969
Date of Presentation: 2 March 1971
Place of Presentation: The White House (East Ballroom), presented by Pres. Richard M. Nixon
Citation: For conspicuous gallantry and intrepidity at the risk of his life above and beyond the call of duty while serving as commanding officer of Company A, in action against the enemy in the northern A Shau Valley. Capt. (then 1st Lt.) Fox's company came under intense fire from a large well-concealed enemy force. Capt. Fox maneuvered to a position from which he could assess the situation and confer with his platoon leaders. As they departed to execute the plan he had devised, the enemy attacked and Capt. Fox was wounded along with all of the other members of the command group, except the executive officer. Capt. Fox continued to direct the activity of his company. Advancing through heavy enemy fire, he personally neutralized one enemy position and calmly ordered an assault against the hostile emplacements. He then moved through the hazardous area coordinating aircraft support with the activities of his men. When his executive officer was mortally wounded, Capt. Fox reorganized the company and directed the fire of his men as they hurled grenades against the enemy and drove the hostile forces into retreat. Wounded again in the final assault, Capt. Fox refused medical attention, established a defensive posture, and supervised the preparation of casualties for medical evacuation. His indomitable courage, inspiring initiative, and unwavering devotion to duty in the face of grave personal danger inspired his marines to such aggressive action that they overcame all enemy resistance and destroyed a large bunker complex. Capt. Fox's heroic actions reflect great credit upon himself and the Marine Corps and uphold the highest traditions of the U.S. Naval Service.

3231 ◆ *FRATELLENICO, FRANK ROCCO

Rank: Corporal
Service: U.S. Army

Birthday: 14 July 1951
Place of Birth: Sharon, Litchfield County, Connecticut
Date of Death: 19 August 1970
Place of Death: Republic of Vietnam
Cemetery: Private Cemetery (MH)—Chatham, New York
Entered Service at: Albany, Albany County, New York
Unit: Company B, 2d Battalion, 502d Infantry, 1st Brigade, 101st Airborne Division
Served as: Rifleman
Battle or Place of Action: near Fire Base Barnett, Quang Tri Province, Republic of Vietnam
Date of Action: 19 August 1970
G.O. Number, Date: 37, 6 September 1974
Date of Presentation: 8 August 1974
Place of Presentation: Blair House, presented by Vice Pres. Gerald R. Ford to his family
Citation: Cpl. Fratellenico distinguished himself while serving as a rifleman with Company B. Cpl. Fratellenico's squad was pinned down by intensive fire from two well-fortified enemy bunkers. At great personal risk Cpl. Fratellenico maneuvered forward and, using hand grenades, neutralized the first bunker which was occupied by a number of enemy soldiers. While attacking the second bunker, enemy fire struck Cpl. Fratellenico, causing him to fall to the ground and drop a grenade which he was preparing to throw. Alert to the imminent danger to his comrades, Cpl. Fratellenico retrieved the grenade and fell upon it an instant before it exploded. His heroic actions prevented death or serious injury to four of his comrades nearby and inspired his unit, which subsequently overran the enemy position. Cpl. Fratellenico's conspicuous gallantry, extraordinary heroism, and intrepidity at the cost of his life, above and beyond the call of duty, are in keeping with the highest traditions of the military service and reflect great credit upon him, his unit, and the U.S. Army.

3232 ◆ FRITZ, HAROLD ARTHUR

Rank: Captain (rank at time of action: First Lieutenant) (highest rank: Lieutenant Colonel)
Service: U.S. Army
Birthday: 21 February 1944
Place of Birth: Chicago, Cook County, Illinois
Entered Service at: Milwaukee, Milwaukee County, Wisconsin
Unit: Troop A, 1st Squadron, 11th Armored Cavalry Regiment
Served as: Platoon Leader
Battle or Place of Action: near An Loc, Binh Long Province, Republic of Vietnam
Date of Action: 11 January 1969
G.O. Number, Date: 15, 24 March 1971
Date of Presentation: 2 March 1971
Place of Presentation: The White House (East Ballroom), presented by Pres. Richard M. Nixon
Citation: For conspicuous gallantry and intrepidity in action at the risk of his life above and beyond the call of duty. Capt. (then 1st Lt.) Fritz, Armor, U.S. Army, distinguished himself while serving as a platoon leader with Troop A, near Quan Loi. Capt. Fritz was leading his seven-vehicle armored column along Highway 13 to meet and escort a truck convoy when the column suddenly came under intense crossfire from a reinforced enemy company deployed in ambush positions. In the initial attack, Capt. Fritz' vehicle was hit and he was seriously wounded. Realizing that his platoon was completely surrounded, vastly outnumbered, and in danger of being overrun, Capt. Fritz leaped to the top of his burning vehicle and directed the positioning of his remaining vehicles and men. With complete disregard for his wounds and safety, he ran from vehicle to vehicle in complete view of the enemy gunners in order to reposition his men, to improve the defenses, to assist the wounded, to distribute ammunition, to direct fire, and to provide encouragement to his men. When a strong enemy force assaulted the position and attempted to overrun the platoon, Capt. Fritz manned a machine gun and through his exemplary action inspired his men to deliver intense and deadly fire which broke the assault and routed the attackers. Moments later a second enemy force advanced to within two meters of the position and threatened to overwhelm the defenders. Capt. Fritz, armed only with a pistol and bayonet, led a small group of his men in a fierce and daring charge which routed the attackers and inflicted heavy casualties. When a relief force arrived, Capt. Fritz saw that it was not deploying effectively against the enemy positions, and he moved through the heavy enemy fire to direct its deployment against the hostile positions. This deployment forced the enemy to abandon the ambush site and withdraw. Despite his wounds, Capt. Fritz returned to his position, assisted his men, and refused medical attention until all of his wounded comrades had been treated and evacuated. The extraordinary courage and selflessness displayed by Capt. Fritz, at the repeated risk of his own life above and beyond the call of duty, were in keeping with the highest traditions of the U.S. Army and reflect greatest credit upon himself, his unit, and the Armed Forces.

3233 ◆ *GARDNER, JAMES ALTON

Rank: First Lieutenant
Service: U.S. Army
Birthday: 7 February 1943
Place of Birth: Dyersburg, Dyer County, Tennessee
Date of Death: 7 February 1966
Place of Death: Republic of Vietnam
Cemetery: Fairview Cemetery—Dyersburg, Tennessee
Entered Service at: Memphis, Shelby County, Tennessee
Unit: Headquarters & Headquarters Company, 1st Battalion (Airborne), 327th Infantry, 1st Brigade, 101st Airborne Division
Served as: Platoon Leader
Battle or Place of Action: My Canh, Republic of Vietnam
Date of Action: 7 February 1966
G.O. Number, Date: 49, 30 November 1967
Date of Presentation: 19 October 1967
Place of Presentation: The Pentagon, presented by Sec. of the Army Stanley R. Resor to his family
Citation: For conspicuous gallantry and intrepidity in action at the risk of his life above and beyond the call of duty. 1st Lt. Gardner's platoon was advancing to relieve a company of

the 1st Battalion that had been pinned down for several hours by a numerically superior enemy force in the village of My Canh, Vietnam. The enemy occupied a series of strongly fortified bunker positions which were mutually supporting and expertly concealed. Approaches to the position were well-covered by an integrated pattern of fire including automatic weapons, machine guns, and mortars. Air strikes and artillery placed on the fortifications had little effect. 1st Lt. Gardner's platoon was to relieve the friendly company by encircling and destroying the enemy force. Even as it moved to begin the attack, the platoon was under heavy enemy fire. During the attack, the enemy fire intensified. Leading the assault and disregarding his own safety, 1st Lt. Gardner charged through a withering hail of fire across an open rice paddy. On reaching the first bunker he destroyed it with a grenade and without hesitation dashed to the second bunker and eliminated it by tossing a grenade inside. Then, crawling swiftly along the dike of a rice paddy, he reached the third bunker. Before he could arm a grenade, the enemy gunner leaped forth, firing at him. 1st Lt. Gardner instantly returned the fire and killed the enemy gunner at a distance of six feet. Following the seizure of the main enemy position, he reorganized the platoon to continue the attack. Advancing to the new assault position, the platoon was pinned down by an enemy machine gun emplaced in a fortified bunker. 1st Lt. Gardner immediately collected several grenades and charged the enemy position, firing his rifle as he advanced to neutralize the defenders. He dropped a grenade into the bunker and vaulted beyond. As the bunker blew up, he came under fire again. Rolling into a ditch to gain cover, he moved toward the new source of fire. Nearing the position, he leaped from the ditch and advanced with a grenade in one hand and firing his rifle with the other. He was gravely wounded just before he reached the bunker, but with a last valiant effort he staggered forward and destroyed the bunker, and its defenders, with a grenade. Although he fell dead on the rim of the bunker, his extraordinary actions so inspired the men of his platoon that they resumed the attack and completely routed the enemy. 1st Lt. Gardner's conspicuous gallantry were in the highest traditions of the U.S. Army.

3234 ◆ *GERTSCH, JOHN GERRY

Rank: Staff Sergeant
Service: U.S. Army
Birthday: 29 September 1944
Place of Birth: Jersey City, Hudson County, New Jersey
Date of Death: 19 July 1969
Place of Death: Republic of Vietnam
Cemetery: Northside Catholic Cemetery (MH)—Pittsburgh, Pennsylvania
Entered Service at: Buffalo, Erie County, New York
Unit: Company E, 1st Battalion, 327th Infantry, 101st Airborne Division
Served as: Platoon Sergeant/Platoon Leader
Battle or Place of Action: A Shau Valley, Republic of Vietnam
Date of Action: 15-19 July 1969
G.O. Number, Date: 34, 6 September 1974
Date of Presentation: 17 July 1974
Place of Presentation: Blair House (Courtyard), presented by Vice Pres. Gerald R. Ford to his family
Citation: S/Sgt. Gertsch distinguished himself while serving as a platoon sergeant and platoon leader during combat operations in the A Shau Valley. During the initial phase of an operation to seize a strongly defended enemy position, S/Sgt. Gertsch's platoon leader was seriously wounded and lay exposed to intense enemy fire. Forsaking his own safety, without hesitation S/Sgt. Gertsch rushed to aid his fallen leader and dragged him to a sheltered position. He then assumed command of the heavily engaged platoon and led his men in a fierce counterattack that forced the enemy to withdraw. Later, a small element of S/Sgt. Gertsch's unit was reconnoitering when attacked again by the enemy. S/Sgt. Gertsch moved forward to his besieged element and immediately charged, firing as he advanced. His determined assault forced the enemy troops to withdraw in confusion and made possible the recovery of two wounded men who had been exposed to heavy enemy fire. Sometime later his platoon came under attack by an enemy force employing automatic-weapons, grenade, and rocket fire. S/Sgt. Gertsch was severely wounded during the onslaught but continued to command his platoon despite his painful wound. While moving under fire and encouraging his men he sighted an aidman treating a wounded officer from an adjacent unit. Realizing that both men were in imminent danger of being killed, he rushed forward and positioned himself between them and the enemy nearby. While the wounded officer was being moved to safety S/Sgt. Gertsch was mortally wounded by enemy fire. Without S/Sgt. Gertsch's courage, ability to inspire others, and profound concern for the welfare of his men, the loss of life among his fellow soldiers would have been significantly greater. His conspicuous gallantry, extraordinary heroism, and intrepidity at the cost of his life, above and beyond the call of duty, are in the highest traditions of the U.S. Army and reflect great credit on him and the Armed Forces of his country.

3235 ◆ *GONZALEZ, ALFREDO (FREDDY)

Rank: Sergeant
Service: U.S. Marine Corps
Birthday: 23 May 1946
Place of Birth: Edinburg, Hidalgo County, Texas
Date of Death: 4 February 1968
Place of Death: Republic of Vietnam
Cemetery: Hillcrest Cemetery (MH)—Edenburg, Texas
Entered Service at: San Antonio, Bexar County, Texas
Unit: 3d Platoon, Company A, 1st Battalion, 1st Marines, 1st Marine Division (Rein) FMF
Served as: Platoon Commander
Battle or Place of Action: near Thua Thien, Republic of Vietnam
Date of Action: 4 February 1968
Date of Presentation: 31 October 1969
Place of Presentation: The White House, presented by Vice Pres. Spiro T. Agnew to his family
Citation: For conspicuous gallantry and intrepidity at the risk of his life above and beyond the call of duty while serving

as platoon commander, 3d Platoon, Company A. On 31 January 1968, during the initial phase of Operation Hue City, Sgt. Gonzalez' unit was formed as a reaction force and deployed to Hue to relieve the pressure on the beleaguered city. While moving by truck convoy along Route No. 1, near the village of Lang Van Lrong, the marines received a heavy volume of enemy fire. Sgt. Gonzalez aggressively maneuvered the marines in his platoon, and directed their fire until the area was cleared of snipers. Immediately after crossing a river south of Hue, the column was again hit by intense enemy fire. One of the marines on top of a tank was wounded and fell to the ground in an exposed position. With complete disregard for his safety, Sgt. Gonzalez ran through the fire-swept area to the assistance of his injured comrade. He lifted him up and though receiving fragmentation wounds during the rescue, he carried the wounded marine to a covered position for treatment. Due to the increased volume and accuracy of enemy fire from a fortified machine-gun bunker on the side of the road, the company was temporarily halted. Realizing the gravity of the situation, Sgt. Gonzalez exposed himself to the enemy fire and moved his platoon along the east side of a bordering rice paddy to a dike directly across from the bunker. Though fully aware of the danger involved, he moved to the fire-swept road and destroyed the hostile position with hand grenades. Although seriously wounded again on 3 February, he steadfastly refused medical treatment and continued to supervise his men and lead the attack. On 4 February, the enemy had again pinned the company down, inflicting heavy casualties with automatic-weapons and rocket fire. Sgt. Gonzalez, utilizing a number of light antitank assault weapons, fearlessly moved from position to position firing numerous rounds at the heavily fortified enemy emplacements. He successfully knocked out a rocket position and suppressed much of the enemy fire before falling mortally wounded. The heroism, courage, and dynamic leadership displayed by Sgt. Gonzalez reflected great credit upon himself and the Marine Corps and were in keeping with the highest traditions of the U.S. Naval Service. He gallantly gave his life for his country.

3236 ◆ *GRAHAM, JAMES ALBERT

Rank: Captain
Service: U.S. Marine Corps
Birthday: 25 August 1940
Place of Birth: Wilkinsburg, Allegheny County, Pennsylvania
Date of Death: 2 June 1967
Place of Death: Republic of Vietnam
Cemetery: Arlington National Cemetery (13-8576-F) (MH)—Arlington, Virginia
Entered Service at: Prince Georges, Prince Georges County, Maryland
Unit: Company F, 2d Battalion, 5th Marines, 1st Marine Division (Rein) FMF
Served as: Company Commander
Battle or Place of Action: Quang Tin Province, Republic of Vietnam
Date of Action: 2 June 1967

Date of Presentation: 29 October 1968
Place of Presentation: Marine Barracks, Washington D.C., presented by Sec. of the Navy Paul R. Ignatius to his family
Citation: For conspicuous gallantry and intrepidity at the risk of his life above and beyond the call of duty. During Operation Union II, the 1st Battalion, 5th Marines, consisting of Companies A and D, with Capt. Graham's company attached, launched an attack against an enemy-occupied position with two companies assaulting and one in reserve. Company F, a leading company, was proceeding across a clear paddy area 1,000 meters wide, attacking toward the assigned objective, when it came under fire from mortars and small arms which immediately inflicted a large number of casualties. Hardest hit by the enemy fire was the 2d platoon of Company F, which was pinned down in the open paddy area by intense fire from two concealed machine guns. Forming an assault unit from members of his small company headquarters, Capt. Graham boldly led a fierce assault through the second platoon's position, forcing the enemy to abandon the first machine-gun position, thereby relieving some of the pressure on his second platoon, and enabling evacuation of the wounded to a more secure area. Resolute to silence the second machine gun, which continued its devastating fire, Capt. Graham's small force stood steadfast in its hard-won enclave. Subsequently, during the afternoon's fierce fighting, he suffered two minor wounds while personally accounting for an estimated 15 enemy killed. With the enemy position remaining invincible upon each attempt to withdraw to friendly lines, and although knowing that he had no chance of survival, he chose to remain with one man who could not be moved due to the seriousness of his wounds. The last radio transmission from Capt. Graham reported that he was being assaulted by a force of 25 enemy soldiers; he died while protecting himself and the wounded man he chose not to abandon. Capt. Graham's actions throughout the day were a series of heroic achievements. His outstanding courage, superb leadership, and indomitable fighting spirit undoubtedly saved the second platoon from annihilation and reflected great credit upon himself, the Marine Corps, and the U.S. Naval Service. He gallantly gave his life for his country.

3237 ◆ *GRANDSTAFF, BRUCE ALAN

Rank: Platoon Sergeant
Service: U.S. Army
Birthday: 2 June 1934
Place of Birth: Spokane, Spokane County, Washington
Date of Death: 18 May 1967
Place of Death: Republic of Vietnam
Cemetery: Greenwood Riverside Memorial Park—Spokane, Washington
Entered Service at: Spokane, Spokane County, Washington
Unit: Weapons Platoon, Company B, 1st Battalion, 8th Infantry, 4th Infantry Division
Served as: Platoon Leader
Battle or Place of Action: Pleiku Province, Republic of Vietnam
Date of Action: 18 May 1967
G.O. Number, Date: 52, 8 August 1967

Date of Presentation: 10 July 1969
Place of Presentation: The White House, presented by Pres. Richard M. Nixon to his family
Citation: For conspicuous gallantry and intrepidity in action at the risk of his life above and beyond the call of duty. P/Sgt. Grandstaff distinguished himself while leading the Weapons Platoon, Company B, on a reconnaissance mission near the Cambodian border. His platoon was advancing through intermittent enemy contact when it was struck by heavy small-arms and automatic-weapons fire from three sides. As he established a defensive perimeter, P/Sgt. Grandstaff noted that several of his men had been struck down. He raced 30 meters through the intense fire to aid them but could only save one. Denied freedom to maneuver his unit by the intensity of the enemy onslaught, he adjusted artillery to within 45 meters of his position. When helicopter gunships arrived, he crawled outside the defensive position to mark the location with smoke grenades. Realizing his first marker was probably ineffective, he crawled to another location and threw his last smoke grenade but the smoke did not penetrate the jungle foliage. Seriously wounded in the leg during this effort he returned to his radio and, refusing medical aid, adjusted the artillery even closer as the enemy advanced on his position. Recognizing the need for additional firepower, he again braved the enemy fusillade, crawled to the edge of his position, and fired several magazines of tracer ammunition through the jungle canopy. He succeeded in designating the location to the gunships but this action again drew the enemy fire and he was wounded in the other leg. Now enduring intense pain and bleeding profusely, he crawled to within 10 meters of an enemy machine gun which had caused many casualties among his men. He destroyed the position with hand grenades but received additional wounds. Rallying his remaining men to withstand the enemy assaults, he realized his position was being overrun and asked for artillery directly on his location. He fought until mortally wounded by an enemy rocket. Although every man in the platoon was a casualty, survivors attest to the indomitable spirit and exceptional courage of this outstanding combat leader who inspired his men to fight courageously against overwhelming odds and cost the enemy heavy casualties. P/Sgt. Grandstaff's selfless gallantry, above and beyond the call of duty, are in the highest traditions of the U.S. Army and reflect great credit upon himself and the Armed Forces of his country.

3238 ◆ *GRANT, JOSEPH XAVIER

Rank: Captain (rank at time of action: First Lieutenant)
Service: U.S. Army
Birthday: 28 March 1940
Place of Birth: Cambridge, Middlesex County, Massachusetts
Date of Death: 13 November 1966
Place of Death: Republic of Vietnam
Cemetery: Arlington National Cemetery (30-1648-2) (MH)—Arlington, Virginia
Entered Service at: Boston, Suffolk County, Massachusetts
Unit: Company A, 1st Battalion, 14th Infantry, 25th Infantry Division
Served as: Platoon Leader
Battle or Place of Action: near Plei Djereng, Republic of Vietnam
Date of Action: 13 November 1966
G.O. Number, Date: 4, 29 January 1968
Date of Presentation: 30 November 1967
Place of Presentation: The Pentagon, presented by Sec. of the Army Stanley R. Resor to his family
Citation: For conspicuous gallantry and intrepidity in action at the risk of his life above and beyond the call of duty. Company A was participating in a search-and-destroy operation when the leading platoon made contact with the enemy and a fierce fire-fight ensued. Capt. Grant was ordered to disengage the two remaining platoons and to maneuver them to envelop and destroy the enemy. After beginning their movement, the platoon encountered intense automatic-weapons and mortar fire from the front and flank. Capt. Grant was ordered to deploy the platoons in a defensive position. As this action was underway, the enemy attacked, using "human wave" assaults, in an attempt to literally overwhelm Capt. Grant's force. In a magnificent display of courage and leadership, Capt. Grant moved under intense fire along the hastily formed defensive line repositioning soldiers to fill gaps created by the mounting casualties and inspiring and directing the efforts of his men to successfully repel the determined enemy onslaught. Seeing a platoon leader wounded, Capt. Grant hastened to his aid, in the face of the mass of fire of the entire enemy force, and moved him to a more secure position. During this action, Capt. Grant was wounded in the shoulder. Refusing medical treatment, he returned to the forward part of the perimeter, where he continued to lead and to inspire his men by his own indomitable example. While attempting to evacuate a wounded soldier, he was pinned down by fire from an enemy machine gun. With a supply of hand grenades, he crawled forward under a withering hail of fire and knocked out the machine gun, killing the crew, after which he moved the wounded man to safety. Learning that several other wounded men were pinned down by enemy fire forward of his position, Capt. Grant disregarded his painful wound and led five men across the fire-swept open ground to effect a rescue. Following the return of the wounded men to the perimeter, a concentration of mortar fire landed in their midst and Capt. Grant was killed instantly. His heroic actions saved the lives of a number of his comrades and enabled the task force to repulse the vicious assaults and defeat the enemy. Capt. Grant's actions reflect great credit upon himself and were in keeping with the finest traditions of the U.S. Army.

3239 ◆ *GRAVES, TERRENCE COLLINSON

Rank: Second Lieutenant
Service: U.S. Marine Corps
Birthday: 6 July 1945
Place of Birth: Corpus Christi, Nueces County, Texas
Date of Death: 17 February 1968
Place of Death: Republic of Vietnam
Cemetery: Woodlawn Cemetery (MH)—Hamilton, New York
Entered Service at: New York

Unit: 3d Force Reconnaissance Company, 3d Reconnaissance Battalion, 3d Marine Division (Rein) FMF
Served as: Platoon Commander
Battle or Place of Action: Quang Tri Province, Republic of Vietnam
Date of Action: 16 February 1968
Date of Presentation: 2 December 1969
Place of Presentation: The White House, presented by Vice Pres. Spiro T. Agnew to his family
Citation: For conspicuous gallantry and intrepidity at the risk of his life above and beyond the call of duty as a platoon commander with the 3d Force Reconnaissance Company. While on a long-range reconnaissance mission, 2d Lt. Graves' eight-man patrol observed seven enemy soldiers approaching their position. Reacting instantly, he deployed his men and directed their fire on the approaching enemy. After the fire had ceased, he and two patrol members commenced a search on the area, and suddenly came under a heavy volume of hostile small-arms and automatic-weapons fire from a numerically superior enemy force. When one of his men was hit by the enemy fire, 2d Lt. Graves moved through the fire-swept area to his radio and, while directing suppressive fire from his men, requested air support and adjusted a heavy volume of artillery and helicopter gunship fire upon the enemy. After attending the wounded, 2d Lt. Graves, accompanied by another marine, moved from his relatively safe position to confirm the results of the earlier engagement. Observing that several of the enemy were still alive, he launched a determined assault, eliminating the remaining enemy troops. He then began moving the patrol to a landing zone for extraction, when the unit again came under intense fire which wounded two more marines and 2d Lt. Graves. Refusing medical attention, he once more adjusted air strikes and artillery fire upon the enemy while directing the fire of his men. He led his men to a new landing site into which he skillfully guided the incoming aircraft and boarded his men while remaining exposed to the hostile fire. Realizing that one of the wounded had not embarked, he directed the aircraft to depart and, along with another marine, moved to the side of the casualty. Confronted with a shortage of ammunition, 2d Lt. Graves utilized supporting arms and directed fire until a second helicopter arrived. At this point, the volume of enemy fire intensified, hitting the helicopter and causing it to crash shortly after liftoff. All aboard were killed. Second Lt. Graves' outstanding courage, superb leadership, and indomitable fighting spirit throughout the day were in keeping with the highest traditions of the Marine Corps and the U.S. Naval Service. He gallantly gave his life for his country.

3240 ◆ *GUENETTE, PETER MATHEW

Rank: Specialist Fourth Class
Service: U.S. Army
Birthday: 4 January 1948
Place of Birth: Troy, Rensselaer County, New York
Date of Death: 18 May 1968
Place of Death: Republic of Vietnam
Cemetery: Saint John's Cemetery—North Troy, New York
Entered Service at: Albany, Albany County, New York
Unit: Company D, 2d Battalion (Airborne), 506th Infantry, 101st Airborne Division
Served as: Machine Gunner
Battle or Place of Action: Quan Tan Uyen Province, Republic of Vietnam
Date of Action: 18 May 1968
G.O. Number, Date: 9, 23 April 1970
Date of Presentation: 7 April 1970
Place of Presentation: The White House, presented by Pres. Richard M. Nixon to his family
Citation: For conspicuous gallantry and intrepidity in action at the risk of his life above and beyond the call of duty. Sp4c. Guenette distinguished himself serving as a machine gunner with Company D, during combat operations. While Sp4c. Guenette's platoon was sweeping a suspected enemy base camp, it came under light harassing fire from a well-equipped and firmly entrenched squad of North Vietnamese Army regulars which was serving as a delaying force at the entrance to their base camp. As the platoon moved within 10 meters of the fortified positions, the enemy fire became intense. Sp4c. Guenette and his assistant gunner immediately began to provide a base of suppressive fire, ceasing momentarily to allow the assistant gunner time to throw a grenade into the bunker. Seconds later, an enemy grenade was thrown to Sp4c. Guenette's right flank. Realizing that the grenade would kill or wound at least four men and destroy the machine gun, he shouted a warning and smothered the grenade with his body, absorbing its blast. Through his actions, he prevented loss of life or injury to at least three men and enabled his comrades to maintain their fire superiority. By his gallantry at the cost of his life in keeping with the highest traditions of the military service, Sp4c. Guenette has reflected great credit upon himself, his unit, and the U.S. Army.

3241 ◆ HAGEMEISTER, CHARLES CRIS

Rank: Specialist Fifth Class (rank at time of action: Specialist Fourth Class) (highest rank: Lieutenant Colonel)
Service: U.S. Army
Birthday: 21 August 1946
Place of Birth: Lincoln, Lancaster County, Nebraska
Entered Service at: Lincoln, Lancaster County, Nebraska
Unit: Headquarters & Headquarters Company, 1st Battalion, 5th Cavalry, 1st Cavalry Division (Airmobile)
Served as: Medical Aidman
Battle or Place of Action: Binh Dinh Province, Republic of Vietnam
Date of Action: 20 March 1967
G.O. Number, Date: 29, 24 June 1968
Date of Presentation: 14 May 1968
Place of Presentation: Pentagon (Inner Courtyard), Hall of Heroes, presented by Pres. Lyndon B. Johnson
Citation: For conspicuous gallantry and intrepidity in action at the risk of his life above and beyond the call of duty. While conducting combat operations against a hostile force, Sp5c. Hagemeister's platoon suddenly came under heavy attack from three sides by an enemy force occupying well-concealed, fortified positions and supported by machine guns and mortars. Seeing two of his comrades seriously wounded in the ini-

tial action, Sp5c. Hagemeister, unhesitatingly and with total disregard for his safety, raced through the deadly hail of enemy fire to provide them medical aid. Upon learning that the platoon leader and several other soldiers had been wounded, Sp5c. Hagemeister continued to brave the withering enemy fire and crawled forward to render lifesaving treatment and to offer words of encouragement. Attempting to evacuate the seriously wounded soldiers, Sp5c. Hagemeister was taken under fire at close range by an enemy sniper. Realizing that the lives of his fellow soldiers depended on his actions, Sp5c. Hagemeister seized a rifle from a fallen comrade, killed the sniper, three other enemy soldiers who were attempting to encircle his position, and silenced an enemy machine gun that covered the area with deadly fire. Unable to remove the wounded to a less exposed location and aware of the enemy efforts to isolate his unit, he dashed through the fusillade of fire to secure help from a nearby platoon. Returning with help, he placed men in positions to cover his advance as he moved to evacuate the wounded forward of his location. These efforts successfully completed, he then moved to the other flank and evacuated additional wounded men despite the fact that his every move drew fire from the enemy. Sp5c. Hagemeister's repeated heroic and selfless actions at the risk of his life saved the lives of many of his comrades and inspired their actions in repelling the enemy assault. Sp5c. Hagemeister's indomitable courage was in the highest traditions of the Armed Forces and reflect great credit upon himself.

3242 ◆ *HAGEN, LOREN DOUGLAS

Rank: First Lieutenant
Service: U.S. Army
Birthday: 25 February 1946
Place of Birth: Fargo, Cass County, North Dakota
Date of Death: 7 August 1971
Place of Death: Republic of Vietnam
Cemetery: Arlington National Cemetery (28-1204) (MH)—Arlington, Virginia
Entered Service at: Fargo, Cass County, North Dakota
Unit: U.S. Army Training Advisory Group
Served as: Team Leader
Battle or Place of Action: Republic of Vietnam
Date of Action: 7 August 1971
G.O. Number, Date: 40, 6 September 1974
Date of Presentation: 8 August 1974
Place of Presentation: Blair House, presented by Vice Pres. Gerald R. Ford to his family
Citation: 1st Lt. Hagen distinguished himself in action while serving as the team leader of a small reconnaissance team operating deep within enemy-held territory. At approximately 0600 hours on the morning of 7 August 1971 the small team came under a fierce assault by a superior-sized enemy force using heavy small-arms, automatic-weapons, mortar, and rocket fire. 1st Lt. Hagen immediately began returning small-arms fire upon the attackers and successfully led his team in repelling the first enemy onslaught. He then quickly deployed his men into more strategic defense locations before the enemy struck again in an attempt to overrun and annihilate the beleaguered team's members. 1st Lt. Hagen repeatedly exposed himself to the enemy fire directed at him as he constantly moved about the team's perimeter, directing fire, rallying the members, and resupplying the team with ammunition, while courageously returning small-arms and hand-grenade fire in a valorous attempt to repel the advancing enemy force. The courageous actions and expert leadership abilities of 1st Lt. Hagen were a great source of inspiration and instilled confidence in the team members. After observing an enemy rocket make a direct hit on and destroy one of the team's bunkers, 1st Lt. Hagen moved toward the wrecked bunker in search for team members despite the fact that the enemy force now controlled the bunker area. With total disregard for his own personal safety, he crawled through the enemy fire while returning small-arms fire upon the enemy force. Undaunted by the enemy rockets and grenades impacting all around him, 1st Lt. Hagen desperately advanced upon the destroyed bunker until he was fatally wounded by enemy small-arms and automatic-weapons fire. With complete disregard for his personal safety, 1st Lt. Hagen's courageous gallantry, extraordinary heroism, and intrepidity above and beyond the call of duty, at the cost of his own life, were in keeping with the highest traditions of the military service and reflect great credit upon him and the U.S. Army.

3243 ◆ *HARTSOCK, ROBERT WILLARD

Rank: Staff Sergeant
Service: U.S. Army
Birthday: 24 January 1945
Place of Birth: Cumberland, Allegany County, Maryland
Date of Death: 23 February 1969
Place of Death: Republic of Vietnam
Cemetery: Rocky Gap Veterans Cemetery (MH)—Flintstone, Maryland
Entered Service at: Fairmont, Marion County, West Virginia
Unit: 44th Infantry Platoon (Scout Dog), 3d Brigade, 25th Infantry Division
Served as: Section Leader
Battle or Place of Action: Dau Tieng Base Camp, Hau Nghia Province, Republic of Vietnam
Date of Action: 23 February 1969
G.O. Number, Date: 47, 8 September 1970
Date of Presentation: 6 August 1970
Place of Presentation: The White House, presented by Pres. Richard M. Nixon to his family
Citation: For conspicuous gallantry and intrepidity in action at the risk of his life above and beyond the call of duty. S/Sgt. Hartsock distinguished himself in action while serving as section leader with the 44th Infantry Platoon. When the Dau Tieng Base Camp came under a heavy enemy rocket and mortar attack, S/Sgt. Hartsock and his platoon commander spotted an enemy sapper squad which had infiltrated the camp undetected. Realizing the enemy squad was heading for the brigade tactical operations center and nearby prisoner compound, they concealed themselves and, although heavily outnumbered, awaited the approach of the enemy soldiers.

When the enemy was almost upon them, S/Sgt. Hartsock and his platoon commander opened fire on the squad. As a wounded enemy soldier fell, he managed to detonate a satchel charge he was carrying. S/Sgt. Hartsock, with complete disregard for his life, threw himself on the charge and was gravely wounded. In spite of his wounds, S/Sgt. Hartsock crawled about five meters to a ditch and provided heavy suppressive fire, completely pinning down the enemy and allowing his commander to seek shelter. S/Sgt. Hartsock continued his deadly stream of fire until he succumbed to his wounds. S/Sgt. Hartsock's extraordinary heroism and profound concern for the lives of his fellow soldiers were in keeping with the highest traditions of the military service and reflect great credit upon him, his unit, and the U.S. Army.

3244 ◆ *HARVEY JR., CARMEL BERNON

Rank: Specialist Fourth Class
Service: U.S. Army
Birthday: 6 October 1946
Place of Birth: Montgomery, Fayette County, West Virginia
Date of Death: 21 June 1967
Place of Death: Republic of Vietnam
Cemetery: Cedar Park Cemetery—Chicago, Illinois
Entered Service at: Chicago, Cook County, Illinois
Unit: Company B, 1st Battalion, 5th Cavalry, 1st Cavalry Division (Airmobile)
Served as: Fire Team Leader
Battle or Place of Action: Binh Dinh Province, Republic of Vietnam
Date of Action: 21 June 1967
G.O. Number, Date: 67, 27 October 1969
Date of Presentation: 16 October 1969
Place of Presentation: The White House, presented by Pres. Richard M. Nixon to his family
Citation: For conspicuous gallantry and intrepidity in action at the risk of his life above and beyond the call of duty. Sp4c. Harvey distinguished himself as a fire team leader with Company B, during combat operations. Ordered to secure a downed helicopter, his platoon established a defensive perimeter around the aircraft, but shortly thereafter a large enemy force attacked the position from three sides. Sp4c. Harvey and two members of his squad were in a position directly in the path of the enemy onslaught, and their location received the brunt of the fire from an enemy machine gun. In short order, both of his companions were wounded, but Sp4c. Harvey covered this loss by increasing his deliberate rifle fire at the foe. The enemy machine gun seemed to concentrate on him and the bullets struck the ground all around his position. One round hit and armed a grenade attached to his belt. Quickly, he tried to remove the grenade but was unsuccessful. Realizing the danger to his comrades if he remained and despite the hail of enemy fire, he jumped to his feet, shouted a challenge at the enemy, and raced toward the deadly machine gun. He nearly reached the enemy position when the grenade on his belt exploded, mortally wounding Sp4c. Harvey, and stunning the enemy machine-gun crew. His final act caused a pause in the enemy fire, and the wounded men were moved from the danger area. Sp4c. Harvey's dedication to duty, high sense of responsibility, and heroic actions inspired the others in his platoon to decisively beat back the enemy attack. His acts are in keeping with the highest traditions of the military service and reflect great credit upon himself and the U.S. Army.

3245 ◆ HERDA, FRANK ALOYSIOUS

Rank: Specialist Fourth Class (rank at time of action: Private First Class)
Service: U.S. Army
Birthday: 13 September 1947
Place of Birth: Cleveland, Cuyahoga County, Ohio
Entered Service at: Cleveland, Cuyahoga County, Ohio
Unit: Company A, 1st Battalion (Airborne), 506th Infantry, 101st Airborne Division (Airmobile)
Served as: Grenadier
Battle or Place of Action: near Dak To, Quang Trang Province, Republic of Vietnam
Date of Action: 29 June 1968
G.O. Number, Date: 32, 5 June 1970
Date of Presentation: 14 May 1970
Place of Presentation: The White House, presented by Pres. Richard M. Nixon
Citation: For conspicuous gallantry and intrepidity in action at the risk of his life above and beyond the call of duty. Sp4c. Herda (then Pfc.) distinguished himself while serving as a grenadier with Company A. Company A was part of a battalion-size night defensive perimeter when a large enemy force initiated an attack on the friendly units. While other enemy elements provided diversionary fire and indirect weapons fire to the west, a sapper force of approximately 30 men armed with hand grenades and small charges attacked Company A's perimeter from the east. As the sappers were making a last, violent assault, five of them charged the position defended by Sp4c. Herda and two comrades, one of whom was wounded and lay helpless in the bottom of the foxhole. Sp4c. Herda fired at the aggressors until they were within 10 feet of his position and one of their grenades landed in the foxhole. He fired one last round from his grenade launcher, hitting one of the enemy soldiers in the head, and then, with no concern for his safety, Sp4c. Herda immediately covered the blast of the grenade with his body. The explosion wounded him grievously, but his selfless action prevented his two comrades from being seriously injured or killed and enabled the remaining defender to kill the other sappers. By his gallantry at the risk of his life in the highest traditions of the military service, Sp4c. Herda has reflected great credit on himself, his unit, and the U.S. Army.

3246 ◆ *HIBBS, ROBERT JOHN

Rank: Second Lieutenant
Service: U.S. Army
Birthday: 21 April 1943
Place of Birth: Omaha, Douglas County, Nebraska
Date of Death: 5 March 1966
Place of Death: Republic of Vietnam
Cemetery: Greenwood Cemetery (MH)—Cedar Falls, Iowa

Entered Service at: Des Moines, Polk County, Iowa
Unit: Company B, 2d Battalion, 28th Infantry, 1st Infantry Division
Served as: Patrol Commander
Battle or Place of Action: Don Dien Lo Ke, Republic of Vietnam
Date of Action: 5 March 1966
G.O. Number, Date: 8, 24 February 1967
Date of Presentation: 26 January 1967
Place of Presentation: Fort Myers, Virginia, presented by Sec. of the Army Stanley R. Resor to his family
Citation: For conspicuous gallantry and intrepidity at the risk of his life above and beyond the call of duty. 2d Lt. Hibbs was in command of a 15-man ambush patrol of the 2d Battalion, when his unit observed a company of Viet Cong advancing along the road toward the 2d Battalion's position. Informing his command post by radio of the impending attack, he prepared his men for the oncoming Viet Cong, emplaced two mines in their path, and, when the insurgents were within 20 feet of the patrol's position, he fired the two antipersonnel mines, wounding or killing half of the enemy company. Then, to cover the withdrawl of his patrol, he threw hand grenades, stepped onto the open road, and opened fire on the remainder of the Viet Cong force of approximately 50 men. Having rejoined his men, he was leading them toward the battalion perimeter when the patrol encountered the rear elements of another Viet Cong company deployed to attack the battalion. With the advantage of surprise, he directed a charge against the Viet Cong, which carried the patrol through the insurgent force, completely disrupting its attack. Learning that a wounded patrol member was wandering in the area between the two opposing forces and although moments from safety and wounded in the leg himself, he and a sergeant went back to the battlefield to recover the stricken man. After they maneuvered through the withering fire of two Viet Cong machine guns, the sergeant grabbed the dazed soldier and dragged him back toward the friendly lines while 2d Lt. Hibbs remained behind to provide covering fire. Armed only with a M-16 rifle and a pistol, but determined to destroy the enemy positions, he then charged the two machine-gun emplacements and was struck down. Before succumbing to his mortal wounds, he destroyed the starlight telescopic sight attached to his rifle to prevent its capture and use by the Viet Cong. 2d Lt. Hibbs' profound concern for his fellow soldiers and his intrepidity at the risk of his life above and beyond the call of duty are in the highest traditions of the U.S. Army and reflect great credit upon himself and the Armed Forces of his country.

3247 ◆ *HOLCOMB, JOHN NOBLE

Rank: Sergeant
Service: U.S. Army
Birthday: 11 June 1946
Place of Birth: Baker, Baker County, Oregon
Date of Death: 3 December 1968
Place of Death: Republic of Vietnam
Cemetery: Eagle Valley Cemetery (MH)—Richland, Oregon

Entered Service at: Corvallis, Benton County, Oregon
Unit: Company D, 2d Battalion, 7th Cavalry, 1st Cavalry Division
Served as: Squad Leader
Battle or Place of Action: near Quan Loi, Republic of Vietnam
Date of Action: 3 December 1968
G.O. Number, Date: 9, 9 March 1971
Date of Presentation: 16 February 1971
Place of Presentation: The White House (East Ballroom), presented by Pres. Richard M. Nixon to his family
Citation: For conspicuous gallantry and intrepidity in action at the risk of his life above and beyond the call of duty. Sgt. Holcomb distinguished himself while serving as a squad leader in Company D during a combat assault mission. Sgt. Holcomb's company assault had landed by helicopter and deployed into a hasty defensive position to organize for a reconnaissance-in-force mission when it was attacked from three sides by an estimated battalion-size enemy force. Sgt. Holcomb's squad was directly in the path of the main enemy attack. With complete disregard for the heavy fire, Sgt. Holcomb moved among his men giving encouragement and directing fire on the assaulting enemy. When his machine gunner was knocked out, Sgt. Holcomb seized the weapon, ran to a forward edge of the position, and placed withering fire on the enemy. His gallant actions caused the enemy to withdraw. Sgt. Holcomb treated and carried his wounded to a position of safety and reorganized his defensive sector despite a raging grass fire ignited by the incoming enemy mortar and rocket rounds. When the enemy assaulted the position a second time, Sgt. Holcomb again manned the forward machine gun, devastating the enemy attack and forcing the enemy to again break contact and withdraw. During the enemy withdrawal an enemy rocket hit Sgt. Holcomb's position, destroying his machine gun and severely wounding him. Despite his painful wounds, Sgt. Holcomb crawled through the grass fire and exploding mortar and rocket rounds to move the members of his squad, every one of whom had been wounded, to more secure positions. Although grievously wounded and sustained solely by his indomitable will and courage, Sgt. Holcomb as the last surviving leader of his platoon organized his men to repel the enemy, crawled to the platoon radio, and reported the third enemy assault on his position. His report brought friendly supporting fires on the charging enemy and broke the enemy attack. Sgt. Holcomb's inspiring leadership, fighting spirit, in action at the cost of his life, were in keeping with the highest traditions of the military service and reflect great credit on himself, his unit, and the U.S. Army.

3248 ◆ HOOPER, JOE RONNIE

Rank: Staff Sergeant (rank at time of action: Sergeant) (highest rank: Captain)
Service: U.S. Army
Birthday: 8 August 1938
Place of Birth: Piedmont, Greenville County, South Carolina
Date of Death: 6 May 1979
Place of Death: Louisville, Kentucky

Cemetery: Arlington National Cemetery (46-656-17) (MH)—Arlington, Virginia
Entered Service at: Los Angeles, Los Angeles County, California
Unit: Company A, 1st Battalion (Airborne), 506th Infantry, 101st Airborne Division (Airmobile)
Served as: Squad Leader
Battle or Place of Action: near Hue, Republic of Vietnam
Date of Action: 21 February 1968
G.O. Number, Date: 24, 17 April 1969
Date of Presentation: 7 March 1969
Place of Presentation: The White House, presented by Pres. Richard M. Nixon
Citation: For conspicuous gallantry and intrepidity in action at the risk of his life above and beyond the call of duty. S/Sgt. (then Sgt.) Hooper, U.S. Army, distinguished himself while serving as squad leader with Company D. Company D was assaulting a heavily defended enemy position along a river bank when it encountered a withering hail of fire from rockets, machine guns, and automatic weapons. S/Sgt. Hooper rallied several men and stormed across the river, overrunning several bunkers on the opposite shore. Thus inspired, the rest of the company moved to the attack. With utter disregard for his own safety, he moved out under the intense fire again and pulled back the wounded, moving them to safety. During this act S/Sgt. Hooper was seriously wounded, but he refused medical aid and returned to his men. With the relentless enemy fire disrupting the attack, he singlehandedly stormed three enemy bunkers, destroying them with hand grenades and rifle fire, and shot two enemy soldiers who had attacked and wounded the chaplain. Leading his men forward in a sweep of the area, S/Sgt. Hooper destroyed three buildings housing enemy riflemen. At this point he was attacked by a North Vietnamese officer whom he fatally wounded with his bayonet. Finding his men under heavy fire from a house to the front, he proceeded alone to the building, killing its occupants with rifle fire and grenades. By now his initial body wound had been compounded by grenade fragments, yet despite the multiple wounds and loss of blood, he continued to lead his men against the intense enemy fire. As his squad reached the final line of enemy resistance, it received devastating fire from four bunkers in line on its left flank. S/Sgt. Hooper gathered several hand grenades and raced down a small trench which ran the length of the bunker line, tossing grenades into each bunker as he passed by, killing all but two of the occupants. With these positions destroyed, he concentrated on the last bunkers facing his men, destroying the first with an incendiary grenade and neutralizing two more by rifle fire. He then raced across an open field, still under enemy fire, to rescue a wounded man who was trapped in a trench. Upon reaching the man, he was faced by an armed enemy soldier whom he killed with a pistol. Moving his comrade to safety and returning to his men, he neutralized the final pocket of enemy resistance by fatally wounding three North Vietnamese officers with rifle fire. S/Sgt. Hooper then established a final line and reorganized his men, not accepting treatment until this was accomplished and not consenting to evacuation until the following morning. His supreme valor, inspiring leadership, and heroic self-sacrifice were directly responsible for the company's success and provided a lasting example in personal courage for every man on the field. S/Sgt. Hooper's actions were in keeping with the highest traditions of the military service and reflect great credit upon himself and the U.S. Army.

3249 ◆ *HOSKING JR., CHARLES ERNEST

Rank: Master Sergeant (rank at time of action: Staff Sergeant)
Service: U.S. Army
Birthday: 12 May 1924
Place of Birth: Ramsey, Bergen County, New Jersey
Date of Death: 21 March 1967
Place of Death: Republic of Vietnam
Cemetery: Valleau Cemetery—Ridgewood, New Jersey
Entered Service at: Fort Dix, Mercer County, New Jersey
Unit: Detachment A-302, Company A, 5th Special Forces Group (Airborne), 1st Special Forces
Served as: Company Advisor
Battle or Place of Action: Don Luan District, Phuoc Long Province, Republic of Vietnam
Date of Action: 21 March 1967
G.O. Number, Date: 39, 13 June 1969
Date of Presentation: 23 May 1969
Place of Presentation: The White House, presented by Pres. Richard M. Nixon to his Widow
Citation: For conspicuous gallantry and intrepidity in action at the risk of his life above and beyond the call of duty. M/Sgt. Hosking (then Sfc.), Detachment A-302, Company A, greatly distinguished himself while serving as company adviser in the III Corps Civilian Irregular Defense Group Reaction Battalion during combat operations in Don Luan District. A Viet Cong suspect was apprehended and subsequently identified as a Viet Cong sniper. While M/Sgt. Hosking was preparing the enemy for movement back to the base camp, the prisoner suddenly grabbed a hand grenade from M/Sgt. Hosking's belt, armed the grenade, and started running towards the company command group which consisted of two Americans and two Vietnamese who were standing a few feet away. Instantly realizing that the enemy intended to kill the other men, M/Sgt. Hosking immediately leaped upon the Viet Cong's back. With utter disregard for his personal safety, he grasped the Viet Cong in a "Bear Hug" forcing the grenade against the enemy soldier's chest. He then wrestled the Viet Cong to the ground and covered the enemy's body with his body until the grenade detonated. The blast instantly killed both M/Sgt. Hosking and the Viet Cong. By absorbing the full force of the exploding grenade with his body and that of the enemy, he saved the other members of his command group from death or serious injury. M/Sgt. Hosking's risk of his life above and beyond the call of duty are in the highest traditions of the U.S. Army and reflect great credit upon himself and the Armed Forces of his country.

3250 ◆ HOWARD, JIMMIE EARL

Rank: Gunnery Sergeant (rank at time of action: Staff Sergeant) (highest rank: First Sergeant)
Service: U.S. Marine Corps

Birthday: 27 July 1929
Place of Birth: Burlington, Des Moines County, Iowa
Date of Death: 12 November 1993
Place of Death: San Diego, California
Cemetery: Fort Rosecrans National Cemetery (O-3759)—San Diego, California
Entered Service at: Burlington, Des Moines County, Iowa
Unit: Company C, 1st Reconnaissance Battalion, 1st Marine Division (Rein) FMF
Served as: Platoon Sergeant
Battle or Place of Action: near Chu Lai, Republic of Vietnam
Date of Action: 16 June 1966
Date of Presentation: 21 August 1967
Place of Presentation: The White House, presented by Pres. Lyndon B. Johnson
Citation: For conspicuous gallantry and intrepidity at the risk of his life above and beyond the call of duty. G/Sgt. Howard and his 18-man platoon were occupying an observation post deep within enemy-controlled territory. Shortly after midnight a Viet Cong force of estimated battalion size approached the marines' position and launched a vicious attack with small-arms, automatic-weapons, and mortar fire. Reacting swiftly and fearlessly in the face of the overwhelming odds, G/Sgt. Howard skillfully organized his small but determined force into a tight perimeter defense and calmly moved from position to position to direct his men's fire. Throughout the night, during assault after assault, his courageous example and firm leadership inspired and motivated his men to withstand the unrelenting fury of the hostile fire in the seemingly hopeless situation. He constantly shouted encouragement to his men and exhibited imagination and resourcefulness in directing their return fire. When fragments of an exploding enemy grenade wounded him severely and prevented him from moving his legs, he distributed his ammunition to the remaining members of his platoon and proceeded to maintain radio communications and direct air strikes on the enemy with uncanny accuracy. At dawn, despite the fact that five men were killed and all but one wounded, his beleaguered platoon was still in command of its position. When evacuation helicopters approached his position, G/Sgt. Howard warned them away and called for additional air strikes and directed devastating small-arms fire and air strikes against enemy automatic-weapons positions in order to make the landing zone as secure as possible. Through his extraordinary courage and resolute fighting spirit, G/Sgt. Howard was largely responsible for preventing the loss of his entire platoon. His valiant leadership and courageous fighting spirit served to inspire the men of his platoon to heroic endeavor in the face of overwhelming odds, and reflect the highest credit upon G/Sgt. Howard, the Marine Corps, and the U.S. Naval Service.

3251 ◆ HOWARD, ROBERT LEWIS

Rank: First Lieutenant (rank at time of action: Sergeant First Class) (highest rank: Colonel)
Service: U.S. Army
Birthday: 11 July 1939
Place of Birth: Opelika, Lee County, Alabama
Entered Service at: Montgomery, Montgomery County, Alabama
Unit: 5th Special Forces Group (Airborne), 1st Special Forces
Served as: Platoon Sergeant
Battle or Place of Action: Republic of Vietnam
Date of Action: 30 December 1968
G.O. Number, Date: 16, 24 March 1971
Date of Presentation: 2 March 1971
Place of Presentation: The White House (East Ballroom), presented by Pres. Richard M. Nixon
Citation: For conspicuous gallantry and intrepidity in action at the risk of his life above and beyond the call of duty. 1st Lt. Howard (then Sfc.) distinguished himself while serving as platoon sergeant of an American-Vietnamese platoon which was on a mission to rescue a missing American soldier in enemy-controlled territory in the Republic of Vietnam. The platoon had left its helicopter landing zone and was moving out on its mission when it was attacked by an estimated two-company force. During the initial engagement, 1st Lt. Howard was wounded and his weapon destroyed by a grenade explosion. 1st Lt. Howard saw his platoon leader had been wounded seriously and was exposed to fire. Although unable to walk, and weaponless, 1st Lt. Howard unhesitatingly crawled through a hail of fire to retrieve his wounded leader. As 1st Lt. Howard was administering first aid and removing the officer's equipment, an enemy bullet struck one of the ammunition pouches on the lieutenant's belt, detonating several magazines of ammunition. 1st Lt. Howard momentarily sought cover and then realizing that he must rejoin the platoon, which had been disorganized by the enemy attack, he again began dragging the seriously wounded officer toward the platoon area. Through his outstanding example of indomitable courage and bravery, 1st Lt. Howard was able to rally the platoon into an organized defense force. With complete disregard for his safely, 1st Lt. Howard crawled from position to position, administering first aid to the wounded, giving encouragement to the defenders and directing their fire on the encircling enemy. For 3 1/2 hours 1st Lt. Howard's small force and supporting aircraft successfully repulsed enemy attacks and finally were in sufficient control to permit the landing of rescue helicopters. 1st Lt. Howard personally supervised the loading of his men and did not leave the bullet-swept landing zone until all were aboard safety. 1st Lt. Howard's gallantry in action, his complete devotion to the welfare of his men at the risk of his life were in keeping with the highest traditions of the military service and reflect great credit on himself, his unit, and the U.S. Army.

3252 ◆ *HOWE, JAMES DONNIE

Rank: Lance Corporal
Service: U.S. Marine Corps
Birthday: 17 December 1948
Place of Birth: Six Mile, Pickens County, South Carolina
Date of Death: 6 May 1970
Place of Death: Republic of Vietnam
Cemetery: Liberty Memorial Gardens Cemetery (MH)—Liberty, South Carolina

Entered Service at: Fort Jackson, Richland County, South Carolina
Unit: Company I, 3d Battalion, 7th Marines, 1st Marine Division (Rein) FMF
Served as: Rifleman
Battle or Place of Action: Republic of Vietnam
Date of Action: 6 May 1970
Date of Presentation: 15 September 1971
Place of Presentation: The White House, presented by Vice Pres. Spiro T. Agnew to his family
Citation: For conspicuous gallantry and intrepidity at the risk of his life above and beyond the call of duty while serving as a rifleman with Company I, during operations against enemy forces. In the early morning hours L/Cpl. Howe and two other marines were occupying a defensive position in a sandy beach area fronted by bamboo thickets. Enemy sappers suddenly launched a grenade attack against the position, utilizing the cover of darkness to carry out their assault. Following the initial explosions of the grenades, L/Cpl. Howe and his two comrades moved to a more advantageous position in order to return suppressive fire. When an enemy grenade landed in their midst, L/Cpl. Howe immediately shouted a warning and then threw himself upon the deadly missile, thereby protecting the lives of the fellow marines. His heroic and selfless action was in keeping with the finest traditions of the Marine Corps and of the U.S. Naval Service. He valiantly gave his life in the service of his country.

3253 ◆ *INGALLS, GEORGE ALAN

Rank: Specialist Fourth Class
Service: U.S. Army
Birthday: 9 March 1946
Place of Birth: Hanford, Kings County, California
Date of Death: 16 April 1967
Place of Death: Republic of Vietnam
Cemetery: Crestlawn Memorial Park (MH)—Riverside, California
Entered Service at: Los Angeles, Los Angeles County, California
Unit: Company A, 2d Battalion, 5th Cavalry, 1st Cavalry Division (Airmobile)
Served as: Rifleman
Battle or Place of Action: near Duc Pho, Republic of Vietnam
Date of Action: 16 April 1967
G.O. Number, Date: 11, 6 February 1969
Date of Presentation: 30 January 1969
Place of Presentation: The Pentagon, presented by Sec. of the Army Stanley R. Resor to his family
Citation: For conspicuous gallantry and intrepidity in action at the risk of his life above and beyond the call of duty. Sp4c. Ingalls, a member of Company A, accompanied his squad on a night ambush mission. Shortly after the ambush was established, an enemy soldier entered the killing zone and was shot when he tried to evade capture. Other enemy soldiers were expected to enter the area, and the ambush was maintained in the same location. Two quiet hours passed without incident, then suddenly a hand grenade was thrown from the nearby dense undergrowth into the center of the squad's position. The grenade did not explode, but shortly thereafter a second grenade landed directly between Sp4c. Ingalls and a nearby comrade. Although he could have jumped to a safe position, Sp4c. Ingalls, in a spontaneous act of great courage, threw himself on the grenade and absorbed its full blast. The explosion mortally wounded Sp4c. Ingalls, but his heroic action saved the lives of the remaining members of his squad. His gallantry and selfless devotion to his comrades are in keeping with the highest traditions of the military service and reflects great credit upon Sp4c. Ingalls, his unit, and the U.S. Army.

3254 ◆ JACKSON, JOE MADISON

Rank: Lieutenant Colonel (highest rank: Colonel)
Service: U.S. Air Force
Birthday: 14 March 1923
Place of Birth: Newnan, Coweta County, Georgia
Entered Service at: Newnan, Coweta County, Georgia
Unit: 311th Air Commando Squadron, Da Nang, Republic of Vietnam
Served as: Pilot of an C-123
Battle or Place of Action: Kham Duc, Republic of Vietnam
Date of Action: 12 May 1968
G.O. Number, Date: GB-40, 27 January 1969
Date of Presentation: 16 January 1969
Place of Presentation: The White house, presented by Pres. Lyndon B. Johnson
Citation: For conspicuous gallantry and intrepidity in action at the risk of his life above and beyond the call of duty. Lt. Col. Jackson distinguished himself as a pilot of a C-123 aircraft. Lt. Col. Jackson volunteered to attempt the rescue of a three-man USAF Combat Control Team from the Special Forces camp at Kham Duc. Hostile forces had overrun the forward outpost and established gun positions on the airstrip. They were raking the camp with small-arms, mortars, light and heavy automatic-weapons, and recoilless-rifle fire. The camp was engulfed in flames and ammunition dumps were continuously exploding and littering the runway with debris. In addition, eight aircraft had been destroyed by the intense enemy fire and one aircraft remained on the runway reducing its usable length to only 2,200 feet. To further complicate the landing, the weather was deteriorating rapidly, thereby permitting only one air strike prior to his landing. Although fully aware of the extreme danger and likely failure of such an attempt, Lt. Col. Jackson elected to land his aircraft and attempt to rescue. Displaying superb airmanship and extraordinary heroism, he landed his aircraft near the point where the combat control team was reported to be hiding. While on the ground, his aircraft was the target of intense hostile fire. A rocket landed in front of the nose of the aircraft but failed to explode. Once the combat control team was aboard, Lt. Col. Jackson succeeded in getting airborne despite the hostile fire directed across the runway in front of his aircraft. Lt. Col. Jackson's profound concern for his fellow men, at the risk of his life above and beyond the call of duty, are in keeping with the highest traditions of the U.S. Air Force and reflect great credit upon himself and the Armed Forces of his country.

3255 ◆ JACOBS, JACK HOWARD

Rank: Captain (rank at time of action: First Lieutenant) (highest rank: Colonel)
Service: U.S. Army
Birthday: 2 August 1945
Place of Birth: Brooklyn, Kings County, New York
Entered Service at: Trenton, Mercer County, New Jersey
Unit: U.S. Military Assistance Command, Army Element
Served as: Assistant Battalion Advisor
Battle or Place of Action: Kien Phong Province, Republic of Vietnam
Date of Action: 9 March 1968
G.O. Number, Date: 63, 27 October 1969
Date of Presentation: 9 October 1969
Place of Presentation: The White House, presented by Pres. Richard M. Nixon
Citation: For conspicuous gallantry and intrepidity in action at the risk of his life above and beyond the call of duty. Capt. Jacobs (then 1st Lt.), Infantry, distinguished himself while serving as assistant battalion adviser, 2d Battalion, 16th Infantry, 9th Infantry Division, Army of the Republic of Vietnam. The 2d Battalion was advancing to contact when it came under intense heavy machine-gun and mortar fire from a Viet Cong battalion positioned in well-fortified bunkers. As the 2d Battalion deployed into attack formation, its advance was halted by devastating fire. Capt. Jacobs, with the command element of the lead company, called for and directed air strikes on the enemy positions to facilitate a renewed attack. Due to the intensity of the enemy fire and heavy casualties to the command group, including the company commander, the attack stopped and the friendly troops became disorganized. Although wounded by mortar fragments, Capt. Jacobs assumed command of the allied company, ordered a withdrawal from the exposed position, and established a defensive perimeter. Despite profuse bleeding from head wounds which impaired his vision, Capt. Jacobs, with complete disregard for his safety, returned under intense fire to evacuate a seriously wounded adviser to the safety of a wooded area where he administered lifesaving first aid. He then returned through heavy automatic-weapons fire to evacuate the wounded company commander. Capt. Jacobs made repeated trips across the fire-swept, open rice paddies, evacuating wounded and their weapons. On three separate occasions, Capt. Jacobs contacted and drove off Viet Cong squads who were searching for allied wounded and weapons, singlehandedly killing three and wounding several others. His gallant actions and extraordinary heroism saved the lives of one U.S. adviser and 13 allied soldiers. Through his effort the allied company was restored to an effective fighting unit and prevented defeat of the friendly forces by a strong and determined enemy. Capt. Jacobs, by his gallantry and bravery in action in the highest traditions of the military service, has reflected great credit upon himself, his unit, and the U.S. Army.

3256 ◆ JENKINS, DON

Rank: Staff Sergeant (rank at time of action: Private First Class)
Service: U.S. Army
Birthday: 18 April 1948
Place of Birth: Quality, Butler County, Kentucky
Entered Service at: Nashville, Davidson County, Tennessee
Unit: Company A, 2d Battalion, 39th Infantry, 9th Infantry Division
Served as: Machine Gunner
Battle or Place of Action: Kien Phong Province, Republic of Vietnam
Date of Action: 6 January 1969
G.O. Number, Date: 17, 24 March 1971
Date of Presentation: 2 March 1971
Place of Presentation: The White House (East Ballroom), presented by Pres. Richard M. Nixon
Citation: For conspicuous gallantry and intrepidity in action at the risk of his life above and beyond the call of duty. S/Sgt. Jenkins (then Pfc.), Company A, distinguished himself while serving as a machine gunner on a reconnaissance mission. When his company came under heavy crossfire from an enemy complex, S/Sgt. Jenkins unhesitatingly maneuvered forward to a perilously exposed position and began placing suppressive fire on the enemy. When his own machine gun jammed, he immediately obtained a rifle and continued to fire into the enemy bunkers until his machine gun was made operative by his assistant. He exposed himself to extremely heavy fire when he repeatedly both ran and crawled across open terrain to obtain resupplies of ammunition until he had exhausted all that was available for his machine gun. Displaying tremendous presence of mind, he then armed himself with two antitank weapons and, by himself, maneuvered through the hostile fusillade to within 20 meters of an enemy bunker to destroy that position. After moving back to the friendly defensive perimeter long enough to secure yet another weapon, a grenade launcher, S/Sgt. Jenkins moved forward to a position providing no protection and resumed placing accurate fire on the enemy until his ammunition was again exhausted. During this time he was seriously wounded by shrapnel. Undaunted and displaying great courage, he moved forward 100 meters to aid a friendly element that was pinned down only a few meters from the enemy. This he did with complete disregard for his own wound and despite having been advised that several previous rescue attempts had failed at the cost of the life of one and wounding of others. Ignoring the continuing intense fire and his painful wounds, and hindered by darkness, he made three trips to the beleaguered unit, each time pulling a wounded comrade back to safety. S/Sgt. Jenkins' extraordinary valor, dedication, and indomitable spirit inspired his fellow soldiers to repulse the determined enemy attack and ultimately to defeat the larger force. S/Sgt. Jenkins' risk of his life reflect great credit upon himself, his unit, and the U.S. Army.

3257 ◆ *JENKINS JR., ROBERT HENRY

Rank: Private First Class
Service: U.S. Marine Corps
Birthday: 1 June 1948
Place of Birth: Interlachen, Putnam County, Florida
Date of Death: 5 March 1969
Place of Death: Republic of Vietnam

Cemetery: Sister Spring Baptist Cemetery (MH)—Interlachen, Florida
Entered Service at: Jacksonville, Duval County, Florida
Unit: 3d Reconnaissance Battalion, 3d Marine Division (Rein) FMF
Served as: Machine Gunner
Battle or Place of Action: Fire Support Base Argonne, DMZ
Date of Action: 5 March 1969
Date of Presentation: 20 April 1970
Place of Presentation: The White House, presented by Vice Pres. Spiro T. Agnew to his family
Citation: For conspicuous gallantry and intrepidity at the risk of his life above and beyond the call of duty while serving as a machine gunner with Company C, 3d Reconnaissance Battalion, in connection with operations against enemy forces. Early in the morning Pfc. Jenkins' 12-man reconnaissance team was occupying a defensive position at Fire Support Base Argonne south of the Demilitarized Zone. Suddenly, the marines were assaulted by a North Vietnamese Army platoon employing mortars, automatic weapons, and hand grenades. Reacting instantly, Pfc. Jenkins and another marine quickly moved into a two-man fighting emplacement, and as they boldly delivered accurate machine-gun fire against the enemy, a North Vietnamese soldier threw a hand grenade into the friendly emplacement. Fully realizing the inevitable results of his actions, Pfc. Jenkins quickly seized his comrade, and pushing the man to the ground, he leaped on top of the marine to shield him from the explosion. Absorbing the full impact of the detonation, Pfc. Jenkins was seriously injured and subsequently succumbed to his wounds. His courage, inspiring valor, and selfless devotion to duty saved a fellow marine from serious injury or possible death and upheld the highest traditions of the Marine Corps and the U.S. Naval Service. He gallantly gave his life for his country.

3258 ◆ JENNINGS, DELBERT OWEN

Rank: Staff Sergeant (highest rank: Command Sergeant Major)
Service: U.S. Army
Birthday: 23 July 1936
Place of Birth: Silver City, Grant County, New Mexico
Entered Service at: San Francisco, San Francisco County, California
Unit: 3d Squad, 4th Platoon, Company C, 1st Battalion (Airborne), 12th Cavalry, 1st Air Cavalry Division
Served as: Squad Leader
Battle or Place of Action: Kim Song Valley, Republic of Vietnam
Date of Action: 27 December 1966
G.O. Number, Date: 60, 22 October 1968
Date of Presentation: 19 September 1968
Place of Presentation: The White House, presented by Pres. Lyndon B. Johnson
Citation: For conspicuous gallantry and intrepidity at the risk of his life above and beyond the call of duty. Part of Company C was defending an artillery position when attacked by a North Vietnamese Army regiment supported by mortar, recoilless-rifle, and machine-gun fire. At the outset, Sgt. Jennings sprang to his bunker, astride the main attack route, and slowed the on-coming enemy wave with highly effective machine-gun fire. Despite a tenacious defense in which he killed at least 12 of the enemy, his squad was forced to the rear. After covering the withdrawal of the squad, he rejoined his men, destroyed an enemy demolition crew about to blow up a nearby howitzer, and killed three enemy soldiers at his initial bunker position. Ordering his men back into a secondary position, he again covered their withdrawal, killing one enemy with the butt of his weapon. Observing that some of the defenders were unaware of a enemy force in their rear, he raced through a fire-swept area to warn the men, turn their fire on the enemy, and lead them into a secondary perimeter. Assisting in the defense of the new position, he aided the air-landing of reinforcements by throwing white phosphorous grenades on the landing zone despite dangerously silhouetting himself with the light. After helping to repulse the final enemy assaults, he led a group of volunteers well beyond friendly lines to an area where eight seriously wounded men lay. Braving enemy sniper fire and ignoring the presence of booby traps in the area, they recovered the eight men who would have probably perished without early medical treatment. Sgt. Jenning's extraordinary heroism and inspirational leadership saved the lives of many of his comrades and contributed greatly to the defeat of a superior enemy force. His actions stand with the highest traditions of the military profession and reflect great credit upon himself, his unit, and the U.S. Army.

3259 ◆ *JIMENEZ, JOSE FRANCISCO

Rank: Lance Corporal
Service: U.S. Marine Corps
Birthday: 20 March 1946
Place of Birth: Mexico City, Mexico
Date of Death: 28 August 1969
Place of Death: Republic of Vietnam
Cemetery: Panteon Municipal Cemetery (MH)—Morelia, Mexico
Entered Service at: Phoenix, Maricopa County, Arizona
Unit: Company K, 3d Battalion, 7th Marines, 1st Marine Division (Rein) FMF
Served as: Fire Team Leader
Battle or Place of Action: south of Da Nang, Quang Nam Province, Republic of Vietnam
Date of Action: 28 August 1969
Date of Presentation: 6 August 1970
Place of Presentation: The White House, presented by Pres. Richard M. Nixon to his family
Citation: For conspicuous gallantry and intrepidity at the risk of his life above and beyond the call of duty while serving as a fire team leader with Company K, in operations against the enemy. L/Cpl. Jimenez' unit came under heavy attack by North Vietnamese soldiers concealed in well-camouflaged emplacements. L/Cpl. Jimenez reacted by seizing the initiative and plunging forward toward the enemy positions. He personally destroyed several enemy personnel and silenced an antiaircraft weapon. Shouting encouragement to his companions, L/Cpl. Jimenez continued his aggressive forward movement. He slowly maneuvered to within 10 feet of hostile sol-

diers who were firing automatic weapons from a trench and, in the face of vicious enemy fire, destroyed the position. Although he was by now the target of concentrated fire from hostile gunners intent upon halting his assault, L/Cpl. Jimenez continued to press forward. As he moved to attack another enemy soldier, he was mortally wounded. L/Cpl. Jimenez' indomitable courage, aggressive fighting spirit, and unfaltering devotion to duty upheld the highest traditions of the Marine Corps and of the U.S. Naval Service.

3260 ◆ JOEL, LAWRENCE

Rank: Specialist Sixth Class (rank at time of action: Specialist Fifth Class) (highest rank: Sergeant First Class)
Service: U.S. Army
Birthday: 22 February 1928
Place of Birth: Winston-Salem, Forsyth County, North Carolina
Date of Death: 4 February 1984
Place of Death: Winston-Salem, North Carolina
Cemetery: Arlington National Cemetery (46-15-1) (MH)—Arlington, Virginia
Entered Service at: New York, New York
Unit: Headquarters & Headquarters Company, 1st Battalion (Airborne), 503d Infantry, 173d Airborne Brigade
Served as: Medical Aidman
Battle or Place of Action: Republic of Vietnam
Date of Action: 8 November 1965
G.O. Number, Date: 15, 5 April 1967
Date of Presentation: 9 March 1967
Place of Presentation: The White House (Lawn), presented by Pres. Lyndon b. Johnson
Citation: For conspicuous gallantry and intrepidity at the risk of his life above and beyond the call of duty. Sp6c. Joel demonstrated indomitable courage, determination, and professional skill when a numerically superior and well-concealed Viet Cong element launched a vicious attack which wounded or killed nearly every man in the lead squad of the company. After treating the men wounded by the initial burst of gunfire, he bravely moved forward to assist others who were wounded while proceeding to their objective. While moving from man to man, he was struck in the right leg by machinegun fire. Although painfully wounded his desire to aid his fellow soldiers transcended all personal feeling. He bandaged his own wound and self-administered morphine to deaden the pain enabling him to continue his dangerous undertaking. Through this period of time, he constantly shouted words of encouragement to all around him. Then, completely ignoring the warnings of others and his pain, he continued his search for wounded, exposing himself to hostile fire; and, as the bullets dug up the dirt around him, he held plasma bottles high while kneeling completely engrossed in his lifesaving mission. Then, after being struck a second time and with a bullet lodged in his thigh, he dragged himself over the battlefield and succeeded in treating 13 more men before his medical supplies ran out. Displaying resourcefulness, he saved the life of one man by placing a plastic bag over a severe chest wound to congeal the blood. As one of the platoons pursued the Viet Cong, an insurgent force in concealed positions opened fire on the platoon and wounded many more soldiers. With a new stock of medical supplies, Sp6c. Joel again shouted words of encouragement as he crawled through an intense hail of gunfire to the wounded men. After the 24-hour battle subsided and the Viet Cong dead numbered 410, snipers continued to harass the company. Throughout the long battle, Sp6c. Joel never lost sight of his mission as a medical aidman and continued to comfort and treat the wounded until his own evacuation was ordered. His meticulous attention to duty saved a large number of lives and his unselfish, daring example under most adverse conditions was an inspiration to all. Sp6c. Joel's profound concern for his fellow soldiers, at the risk of his life above and beyond the call of duty, are in the highest traditions of the U.S. Army and reflect great credit upon himself and the Armed Forces of his country.

3261 ◆ JOHNSON, DWIGHT HAL

Rank: Specialist Fifth Class
Service: U.S. Army
Birthday: 7 May 1947
Place of Birth: Detroit, Wayne County, Michigan
Date of Death: 30 April 1971
Place of Death: Detroit, Michigan
Cemetery: Arlington National Cemetery (31-471) (MH)—Arlington, Virginia
Entered Service at: Detroit, Wayne County, Michigan
Unit: Company B, 1st Battalion, 69th Armor, 4th Infantry Division
Served as: Tank Driver
Battle or Place of Action: near Dak To, Kontum Province, Republic of Vietnam
Date of Action: 15 January 1968
G.O. Number, Date: 76, 10 December 1968
Date of Presentation: 19 November 1968
Place of Presentation: The White House, presented by Pres. Lyndon B. Johnson
Citation: For conspicuous gallantry and intrepidity at the risk of his life above and beyond the call of duty. Sp5c. Johnson, a tank driver with Company B, was a member of a reaction force moving to aid other elements of his platoon, which was in heavy contact with a battalion-size North Vietnamese force. Sp5c. Johnson's tank, upon reaching the point of contact, threw a track and became immobilized. Realizing that he could do no more as a driver, he climbed out of the vehicle, armed only with a .45 caliber pistol. Despite intense hostile fire, Sp5c. Johnson killed several enemy soldiers before he had expended his ammunition. Returning to his tank through a heavy volume of antitank-rocket, small-arms and automatic weapon fire, he obtained a submachine gun with which to continue his fight against the advancing enemy. Armed with this weapon, Sp5c. Johnson again braved deadly enemy fire to return to the center of the ambush site where he courageously eliminated more of the determined foe. Engaged in extremely close combat when the last of his ammunition was expended, he killed an enemy soldier with the stock end of his submachine gun. Now weaponless, Sp5c. Johnson ignored the enemy fire around him, climbed into his platoon sergeant's tank, extricated a wound-

ed crewmember and carried him to an armored personnel carrier. He then returned to the same tank and assisted in firing the main gun until it jammed. In a magnificent display of courage, Sp5c. Johnson exited the tank and again armed only with a .45 caliber pistol, engaged several North Vietnamese troops in close proximity to the vehicle. Fighting his way through devastating fire and remounting his own immobilized tank, he remained fully exposed to the enemy as he bravely and skillfully engaged them with the tank's externally mounted .50 caliber machine gun, where he remained until the situation was brought under control. Sp5c. Johnson's profound concern for his fellow soldiers, at the risk of his life above and beyond the call of duty, are in keeping with the highest traditions of the military service and reflect great credit upon himself and the U.S. Army.

3262 ◆ *JOHNSON, RALPH HENRY

Rank: Private First Class
Service: U.S. Marine Corps
Birthday: 11 January 1949
Place of Birth: Charleston, Charleston County, South Carolina
Date of Death: 5 March 1968
Place of Death: Republic of Vietnam
Cemetery: Beaufort National Cemetery (3-21) (MH)—Beaufort, South Carolina
Entered Service at: Oakland, Alameda County, California
Unit: Company A, 1st Reconnaissance Battalion, 1st Marine Division (Rein) FMF
Served as: Reconnaissance Scout
Battle or Place of Action: Hill-146, near Quan Duc Valley, Republic of Vietnam
Date of Action: 5 March 1968
Date of Presentation: 20 April 1970
Place of Presentation: The White House, presented by Vice Pres. Spiro T. Agnew to his family
Citation: For conspicuous gallantry and intrepidity at the risk of his life above and beyond the call of duty while serving as a reconnaissance scout with Company A, in action against the North Vietnamese Army and Viet Cong forces. In the early morning hours during Operation Rock, Pfc. Johnson was a member of a 15-man reconnaissance patrol manning an observation post on Hill 146 overlooking the Quan Duc Valley deep in enemy-controlled territory. They were attacked by a platoon-size hostile force employing automatic weapons, satchel charges, and hand grenades. Suddenly, a hand grenade landed in the three-man fighting hole occupied by Pfc. Johnson and two fellow marines. Realizing the inherent danger to his two comrades, he shouted a warning and unhesitatingly hurled himself on the explosive device. When the grenade exploded, Pfc. Johnson absorbed the tremendous impact of the blast and was killed instantly. His prompt and heroic act saved the life of one marine at the cost of his life and undoubtedly prevented the enemy from penetrating his sector of the patrol's perimeter. Pfc. Johnson's courage, inspiring valor, and selfless devotion to duty were in keeping with the highest traditions of the Marine Corps and the U.S. Naval Service. He gallantly gave his life for his country.

3263 ◆ *JOHNSTON, DONALD RAY

Rank: Specialist Fourth Class
Service: U.S. Army
Birthday: 19 November 1947
Place of Birth: Columbus, Muscogee County, Georgia
Date of Death: 21 March 1969
Place of Death: Republic of Vietnam
Cemetery: Fort Benning Post Cemetery (E-43-A) (MH)—Fort Benning, Georgia
Entered Service at: Columbus, Muscogee County, Georgia
Unit: Company D, 1st Battalion, 8th Cavalry, 1st Cavalry Division
Served as: Mortarman
Battle or Place of Action: Tay Ninh Province, Republic of Vietnam
Date of Action: 21 March 1969
G.O. Number, Date: 11, 9 March 1971
Date of Presentation: 16 February 1971
Place of Presentation: The White House (East Ballroom), presented by Pres. Richard M. Nixon to his family
Citation: For conspicuous gallantry and intrepidity in action at the risk of his life above and beyond the call of duty. Sp4c. Johnston distinguished himself while serving as a mortarman with Company D, at a fire support base in Tay Ninh Province. Sp4c. Johnston's company was in defense positions when it came under a devastating rocket and mortar attack. Under cover of the bombardment, enemy sappers broke through the defensive perimeter and began hurling explosive charges into the main defensive bunkers. Sp4c. Johnston and six of his comrades had moved from their exposed position to one of the bunkers to continue their fight against the enemy attackers. As they were firing from the bunker, an enemy soldier threw three explosive charges into their position. Sensing the danger to his comrades, Sp4c. Johnston, with complete disregard for his safety, hurled himself onto the explosive charges, smothering the detonations with his body and shielding his fellow soldiers from the blast. His heroic action saved the lives of six of his comrades. Sp4c. Johnston's concern for his fellow men at the cost of his life were in the highest traditions of the military service and reflect great credit upon himself, his unit, and the U.S. Army.

3264 ◆ *JONES III, WILLIAM ATKINSON

Rank: Colonel
Service: U.S. Air Force
Birthday: 31 May 1922
Place of Birth: Norfolk, Norfolk County, Virginia
Date of Death: 15 November 1969
Place of Death: near Woodbridge, Virginia
Cemetery: Saint John's Church Cemetery—Warsaw, Virginia
Entered Service at: Charlottesville, Charlottesville County, Virginia
Unit: 602d Special Operations Squadron, Nakon Phanom Royal Thai AFB Thailand
Served as: Pilot of an A-1H Skyraider
Battle or Place of Action: near Dong Hoi, North Vietnam

Date of Action: 1 September 1968
G.O. Number, Date: GB-826, 23 June 1970
Date of Presentation: 6 August 1970
Place of Presentation: The White House, presented by Pres. Richard M. Nixon to his family
Citation: For conspicuous gallantry and intrepidity in action at the risk of his life above and beyond the call of duty. Col. Jones distinguished himself as the pilot of an A-1H Skyraider aircraft near Dong Hoi, North Vietnam. On that day, as the on-scene commander in the attempted rescue of a downed U.S. pilot, Col. Jones' aircraft was repeatedly hit by heavy and accurate antiaircraft fire. On one of his low passes, Col. Jones felt an explosion beneath his aircraft and his cockpit rapidly filled with smoke. With complete disregard of the possibility that his aircraft might still be burning, he unhesitatingly continued his search for the downed pilot. On this pass, he sighted the survivor and a multiple-barrel gun position firing at him from near the top of a karst formation. He could not attack the gun position on that pass for fear he would endanger the downed pilot. Leaving himself exposed to the gun position, Col. Jones attacked the position with cannon and rocket fire on two successive passes. On his second pass, the aircraft was hit with multiple rounds of automatic-weapons fire. One round impacted the Yankee Extraction System rocket mounted directly behind the headrest, igniting the rocket. His aircraft was observed to burst into flames in the center fuselage section, with flames engulfing the cockpit area. He pulled the extraction handle, jettisoning the canopy. The influx of fresh air made the fire burn with greater intensity for a few moments, but since the rocket motor had already burned, the extraction system did not pull Col. Jones from the aircraft. Despite searing pains from severe burns sustained on his arms, hands, neck, shoulders, and face, Col. Jones pulled his aircraft into a climb and attempted to transmit the location of the downed pilot and the enemy gun position to the other aircraft in the area. His calls were blocked by other aircraft transmissions repeatedly directing him to bail out and within seconds his transmitters were disabled and he could receive only on one channel. Completely disregarding his injuries, he elected to fly his crippled aircraft back to his base and pass on essential information for the rescue rather than bail out. Col. Jones successfully landed his heavily damaged aircraft and passed the information to a debriefing officer while on the operating table. As a result of his heroic actions and complete disregard for his personal safety, the downed pilot was rescued later in the day. Col. Jones' profound concern for his fellow man at the risk of his life, above and beyond the call of duty, are in keeping with the highest traditions of the U.S. Air Force and reflect great credit upon himself and the Armed Forces of his country.

3265 ◆ *KAROPCZYC, STEPHEN EDWARD

Rank: First Lieutenant
Service: U.S. Army
Birthday: 5 March 1944
Place of Birth: New York, New York
Date of Death: 12 March 1967
Place of Death: Republic of Vietnam
Cemetery: Long Island National Cemetery (DSS-5-A) (MH)—Farmingdale, New York
Entered Service at: Bethpage, Nassau County, New York
Unit: 3d Platoon, Company A, 2d Battalion, 35th Infantry, 25th Infantry Division
Served as: Platoon Leader
Battle or Place of Action: Kontum Province, Republic of Vietnam
Date of Action: 12 March 1967
G.O. Number, Date: 4, 24 January 1969
Date of Presentation: 9 January 1969
Place of Presentation: The Pentagon, presented by Sec. of the Army Stanley R. Resor to his family
Citation: For conspicuous gallantry and intrepidity in action at the risk of his life above and beyond the call of duty. While leading the 3d Platoon, Company A, on a flanking maneuver against a superior enemy force, 1st Lt. Karopczyc observed that his lead element was engaged with a small enemy unit along his route. Aware of the importance of quickly pushing through to the main enemy force in order to provide relief for a hard-pressed friendly platoon, he dashed through the intense enemy fire into the open and hurled colored smoke grenades to designate the foe for attack by helicopter gunships. He moved among his men to embolden their advance, and he guided their attack by marking enemy locations with bursts of fire from his own weapon. His forceful leadership quickened the advance, forced the enemy to retreat, and allowed his unit to close with the main hostile force. Continuing the deployment of his platoon, he constantly exposed himself as he ran from man to man to give encouragement and to direct their efforts. A shot from an enemy sniper struck him above the heart but he refused aid for this serious injury, plugging the bleeding wound with his finger until it could be properly dressed. As the enemy strength mounted, he ordered his men to organize a defensive position in and around some abandoned bunkers where he conducted a defense against the increasingly strong enemy attacks. After several hours, a North Vietnamese soldier hurled a hand grenade to within a few feet of 1st Lt. Karopczyc and two other wounded men. Although his position protected him, he leaped up to cover the deadly grenade with a steel helmet. It exploded to drive fragments into 1st Lt. Karopczyc's legs, but his action prevented further injury to the two wounded men. Severely weakened by his multiple wounds, he continued to direct the actions of his men until he succumbed two hours later. 1st Lt. Karopczyc's heroic leadership, unyielding perseverance, and selfless devotion to his men were directly responsible for the successful and spirited action of his platoon throughout the battle and are in keeping with the highest traditions of the U.S. Army.

3266 ◆ *KAWAMURA, TERRY TERUO

Rank: Corporal
Service: U.S. Army
Birthday: 10 December 1949
Place of Birth: Wahiawa, Honolulu County, Oahu, Hawaii
Date of Death: 20 March 1969
Place of Death: Republic of Vietnam

Cemetery: Mililani Memorial Park—Pearl City, Hawaii
Entered Service at: Oahu, Hawaii
Unit: 173d Engineer Company, 173d Airborne Brigade
Battle or Place of Action: Camp Radcliff, Republic of Vietnam
Date of Action: 20 March 1969
G.O. Number, Date: 12, 9 March 1971
Date of Presentation: 16 February 1971
Place of Presentation: The White House (East Ballroom), presented by Pres. Richard M. Nixon to his family
Citation: For conspicuous gallantry and intrepidity in action at the risk of his life above and beyond the call of duty. Cpl. Kawamura distinguished himself by heroic action while serving as a member of the 173d Engineer Company. An enemy demolition team infiltrated the unit quarters area and opened fire with automatic weapons. Disregarding the intense fire, Cpl. Kawamura ran for his weapon. At that moment, a violent explosion tore a hole in the roof and stunned the occupants of the room. Cpl. Kawamura jumped to his feet, secured his weapon and, as he ran toward the door to return the enemy fire, he observed that another explosive charge had been thrown through the hole in the roof to the floor. He immediately realized that two stunned fellow soldiers were in great peril and shouted a warning. Although in a position to escape, Cpl. Kawamura unhesitatingly wheeled around and threw himself on the charge. In completely disregarding his safety, Cpl. Kawamura prevented serious injury or death to several members of his unit. The extraordinary courage and selflessness displayed by Cpl. Kawamura are in the highest traditions of the military service and reflect great credit upon himself, his unit, and the U.S. Army.

3267 ◆ KAYS, KENNETH MICHAEL

Rank: Private First Class (rank at time of action: Private)
Service: U.S. Army
Birthday: 22 September 1949
Place of Birth: Mount Vernon, Jefferson County, Illinois
Date of Death: 25 November 1991
Place of Death: Fairfield, Illinois
Cemetery: Maple Hill Cemetery Veterans Section (MH)—Fairfield, Illinois
Entered Service at: Fairfield, Wayne County, Illinois
Unit: Headquarters & Headquarters Company, 1st Battalion, 506th Infantry, 101st Airborne Division
Served as: Medical Aidman
Battle or Place of Action: Thua Thien Province, Republic of Vietnam
Date of Action: 7 May 1970
G.O. Number, Date: 40, 5 November 1973
Date of Presentation: 15 October 1973
Place of Presentation: The White House, presented by Pres. Richard M. Nixon
Citation: For conspicuous gallantry and intrepidity in action at the risk of his life above and beyond the call of duty. Pfc. (then Pvt.) Kays distinguished himself while serving as a medical aidman with Company D, 1st Battalion, 101st Airborne Division near Fire Support Base Maureen. A heavily armed force of enemy sappers and infantrymen assaulted Company D's night defensive position, wounding and killing a number of its members. Disregarding the intense enemy fire and ground assault, Pfc. Kays began moving toward the perimeter to assist his fallen comrades. In doing so he became the target of concentrated enemy fire and explosive charges, one of which severed the lower portion of his left leg. After applying a tourniquet to his leg, Pfc. Kays moved to the fire-swept perimeter, administered medical aid to one of the wounded, and helped move him to an area of relative safety. Despite his severe wound and excruciating pain, Pfc. Kays returned to the perimeter in search of other wounded men. He treated another wounded comrade, and, using his own body as a shield against enemy bullets and fragments, moved him to safety. Although weakened from a great loss of blood, Pfc. Kays resumed his heroic lifesaving efforts by moving beyond the company's perimeter into the enemy-held territory to treat a wounded American lying there. Only after his fellow wounded soldiers had been treated and evacuated did Pfc. Kays allow his own wounds to be treated. These courageous acts by Pfc. Kays resulted in the saving of numerous lives and inspired others in his company to repel the enemy. Pfc. Kays' heroism at the risk of his life are in keeping with the highest traditions of the service and reflect great credit upon him, his unit, and the U.S. Army.

3268 ◆ *KEDENBURG, JOHN JAMES

Rank: Specialist Fifth Class
Service: U.S. Army
Birthday: 31 July 1946
Place of Birth: Brooklyn, Kings County, New York
Date of Death: 14 June 1968
Place of Death: Republic of Vietnam
Cemetery: Long Island National Cemetery (2H-3684) (MH)—Farmingdale, New York
Entered Service at: Brooklyn, Kings County, New York
Unit: Command and Control Detachment North, Forward Operating Base 2, 5th Special Forces Group (Airborne), 1st Special Forces
Served as: Advisor
Battle or Place of Action: Republic of Vietnam
Date of Action: 13 June 1968
G.O. Number, Date: 17, 23 April 1970
Date of Presentation: 7 April 1970
Place of Presentation: The White House, presented by Pres. Richard M. Nixon to his family
Citation: For conspicuous gallantry and intrepidity in action at the risk of his life above and beyond the call of duty. Sp5c. Kedenburg, U.S. Army, Command and Control Detachment North, Forward Operating Base 2, 5th Special Forces Group (Airborne), distinguished himself while serving as adviser to a long-range reconnaissance team of South Vietnamese irregular troops. The team's mission was to conduct counterguerrilla operations deep within enemy-held territory. Prior to reaching the day's objective, the team was attacked and encircled by a battalion-size North Vietnamese Army force. Sp5c. Kedenburg assumed immediate command of the team which succeeded, after a fierce fight, in breaking out of the encirclement. As the team moved through thick jungle to a posi-

tion from which it could be extracted by helicopter, Sp5c. Kedenburg conducted a gallant rear guard fight against the pursuing enemy and called for tactical air support and rescue helicopters. His withering fire against the enemy permitted the team to reach a preselected landing zone with the loss of only one man, who was unaccounted for. Once in the landing zone, Sp5c. Kedenburg deployed the team into a perimeter defense against the numerically superior enemy force. When tactical air support arrived, he skillfully directed air strikes against the enemy, suppressing their fire so that helicopters could hover over the area and drop slings to be used in the extraction of the team. After half of the team was extracted by helicopter, Sp5c. Kedenburg and the remaining three members of the team harnessed themselves to the sling on a second hovering helicopter. Just as the helicopter was to lift them out of the area, the South Vietnamese team member who had been unaccounted for after the initial encounter with the enemy appeared in the landing zone. Sp5c. Kedenburg unhesitatingly gave up his place in the sling to the man and directed the helicopter pilot to leave the area. He then continued to engage the enemy who were swarming into the landing zone, killing six enemy soldiers before he was overpowered. Sp5c. Kedenburg's inspiring leadership, consummate courage, and willing self-sacrifice permitted his small team to inflict heavy casualties on the enemy and escape almost certain annihilation. His actions reflect great credit upon himself and the U.S. Army.

3269 ◆ *KEITH, MIGUEL

R Lance Corporal
Service: U.S. Marine Corps
Birthday: 2 June 1951
Place of Birth: San Antonio, Bexar County, Texas
Date of Death: 8 May 1970
Place of Death: Republic of Vietnam
Cemetery: Forest Lawn Cemetery (MH)—Omaha, Nebraska
Entered Service at: Omaha, Douglas County, Nebraska
Unit: Combined Action Platoon 1-3-2, III Marine Amphibious Force
Served as: Machine Gunner
Battle or Place of Action: Quang Ngai Province, Republic of Vietnam
Date of Action: 8 May 1970
Date of Presentation: 15 September 1971
Place of Presentation: The White House, presented by Vice Pres. Spiro T. Agnew to his family
Citation: For conspicuous gallantry and intrepidity at the risk of his life above and beyond the call of duty while serving as a machine gunner with Combined Action Platoon 1-3-2. During the early morning L/Cpl. Keith was seriously wounded when his platoon was subjected to a heavy ground attack by a greatly outnumbering enemy force. Despite his painful wounds, he ran across the fire-swept terrain to check the security of vital defensive positions and then, while completely exposed to view, proceeded to deliver a hail of devastating machine-gun fire against the enemy. Determined to stop five of the enemy soldiers approaching the command post, he rushed forward, firing as he advanced. He succeeded in disposing of three of the attackers and in dispersing the remaining two. At this point, a grenade detonated near L/Cpl. Keith, knocking him to the ground and inflicting further severe wounds. Fighting pain and weakness from loss of blood, he again braved the concentrated hostile fire to charge an estimated 25 enemy soldiers who were massing to attack. The vigor of his assault and his well-placed fire eliminated four of the enemy soldiers while the remainder fled for cover. During this valiant effort, he was mortally wounded by an enemy soldier. By his courageous and inspiring performance in the face of almost overwhelming odds, L/Cpl. Keith contributed in large measure to the success of his platoon in routing a numerically superior enemy force, and upheld the finest traditions of the Marine Corps and of the U.S. Naval Service.

3270 ◆ KELLER, LEONARD BERT

Rank: Sergeant
Service: U.S. Army
Birthday: 25 February 1947
Place of Birth: Rockford, Winnebago County, Illinois
Entered Service at: Chicago, Cook County, Illinois
Unit: Company A, 3d Battalion, 60th Infantry, 9th Infantry Division
Served as: Machine Gunner
Battle or Place of Action: Ap Bac Zone, Republic of Vietnam
Date of Action: 2 May 1967
G.O. Number, Date: 61, 22 October 1968
Date of Presentation: 19 September 1968
Place of Presentation: The White House, presented by Pres. Lyndon B. Johnson
Citation: For conspicuous gallantry and intrepidity in action at the risk of his life above and beyond the call of duty. Sweeping through an area where an enemy ambush had occurred earlier, Sgt. Keller's unit suddenly came under intense automatic-weapons and small-arms fire from a number of enemy bunkers and numerous snipers in nearby trees. Sgt. Keller quickly moved to a position where he could fire at a bunker from which automatic fire was received, killing one Viet Cong who attempted to escape. Leaping to the top of a dike, he and a comrade charged the enemy bunkers, dangerously exposing themselves to the enemy fire. Armed with a light machine gun, Sgt. Keller and his comrade began a systematic assault on the enemy bunkers. While Sgt. Keller neutralized the fire from the first bunker with his machine gun, the other soldier threw in a hand grenade killing its occupant. Then he and the other soldier charged a second bunker, killing its occupant. A third bunker contained a automatic rifleman who had pinned down much of the friendly platoon. Again, with utter disregard for the fire directed to them, the two-men charged, killing the enemy within. Continuing their attack, Sgt. Keller and his comrade assaulted four more bunkers, killing the enemy within. During their furious assault, Sgt. Keller and his comrade had been almost continuously exposed to intense sniper fire as the enemy desperately sought to stop their attack. The ferocity of their assault had

carried the soldiers beyond the line of bunkers into the treeline, forcing the snipers to flee. The two men gave immediate chase, driving the enemy away from the friendly unit. When his ammunition was exhausted, Sgt. Keller returned to the platoon to assist in the evacuation of the wounded. The two man assault had driven an enemy platoon from a well-prepared position, accounted for numerous enemy dead, and prevented further friendly casualties. Sgt. Keller's selfless heroism and indomitable fighting spirit saved the lives of many of his comrades and inflicted serious damage on the enemy. His acts were in keeping with the highest traditions of the military service and reflect great credit upon himself and the U.S. Army.

3271 ◆ KELLEY, THOMAS GUNNING

Rank: Lieutenant Commander (rank at time of action: Lieutenant) (highest rank: Captain)
Service: U.S. Navy
Birthday: 13 May 1939
Place of Birth: Boston, Suffolk County, Massachusetts
Entered Service at: Boston, Suffolk County, Massachusetts
Unit: River Assault Division 152
Served as: Division Commander
Battle or Place of Action: Ong Muong Canal, Kien Hoa Province, Republic of Vietnam
Date of Action: 15 June 1969
Date of Presentation: 14 May 1970
Place of Presentation: The White House, presented by Pres. Richard M. Nixon
Citation: For conspicuous gallantry and intrepidity at the risk of his life above and beyond the call of duty in the afternoon while serving as commander of River Assault Division 152 during combat operations against enemy aggressor forces. Lt. Comdr. (then Lt.) Kelley was in charge of a column of eight river assault craft which were extracting one company of U.S. Army infantry troops on the east bank of the Ong Muong Canal in Kien Hoa Province, when one of the armored troop carriers reported a mechanical failure of a loading ramp. At approximately the same time, Viet Cong forces opened fire from the opposite bank of the canal. After issuing orders for the crippled troop carrier to raise its ramp manually, and for the remaining boats to form a protective cordon around the disabled craft, Lt. Comdr. Kelley, realizing the extreme danger to his column and its inability to clear the ambush site until the crippled unit was repaired, boldly maneuvered the monitor in which he was embarked to the exposed side of the protective cordon in direct line with the enemy's fire, and ordered the monitor to commence firing. Suddenly, an enemy rocket scored a direct hit on the coxswain's flat, the shell penetrating the thick armor plate, and the explosion spraying shrapnel in all directions. Sustaining serious head wounds from the blast, which hurled him to the deck of the monitor, Lt. Comdr. Kelley disregarded his severe injuries and attempted to continue directing the other boats. Although unable to move from the deck or to speak clearly into the radio, he succeeded in relaying his commands through one of his men until the enemy attack was silenced and the boats were able to move to an area of safety. Lt. Comdr. Kelley's brilliant leadership, bold initiative, and resolute determination served to inspire his men and provide the impetus needed to carry out the mission after he was medically evacuated by helicopter. His extraordinary courage under fire and his selfless devotion to duty sustain and enhance the finest traditions of the U.S. Naval Service.

3272 ◆ KELLOGG JR., ALLAN JAY

Rank: Gunnery Sergeant (rank at time of action: Staff Sergeant) (highest rank: Sergeant Major)
Service: U.S. Marine Corps
Birthday: 1 October 1943
Place of Birth: Bethel, Fairfield County, Connecticut
Entered Service at: Bridgeport, Fairfield County, Connecticut
Unit: Company G, 2d Battalion, 5th Marines, 1st Marine Division
Served as: Platoon Sergeant
Battle or Place of Action: Quang Nam Province, Republic of Vietnam
Date of Action: 11 March 1970
Date of Presentation: 15 October 1973
Place of Presentation: The White House, presented by Pres. Richard M. Nixon
Citation: For conspicuous gallantry and intrepidity at the risk of his life above and beyond the call of duty while serving as a platoon sergeant with Company G, in connection with combat operations against the enemy on the night of 11 March 1970. Under the leadership of G/Sgt. Kellogg, a small unit from Company G was evacuating a fallen comrade when the unit came under a heavy volume of small-arms and automatic-weapons fire from a numerically superior enemy force occupying well-concealed emplacements in the surrounding jungle. During the ensuing fierce engagement, an enemy soldier managed to maneuver through the dense foliage to a position near the marines, and hurled a hand grenade into their midst which glanced off the chest of G/Sgt. Kellogg. Quick to act, he forced the grenade into the mud in which he was standing, threw himself over the lethal weapon and absorbed the full effects of its detonation with his body, thereby preventing serious injury or possible death to several of his fellow marines. Although suffering multiple injuries to his chest and his right shoulder and arm, G/Sgt. Kellogg resolutely continued to direct the efforts of his men until all were able to maneuver to the relative safety of the company perimeter. By his heroic and decisive action in risking his life to save the lives of his comrades, G/Sgt. Kellogg reflected the highest credit upon himself and upheld the finest traditions of the Marine Corps and the U.S. Naval Service.

3273 ◆ KERREY, JOSEPH ROBERT

Rank: Lieutenant (j.g.)
Service: U.S. Naval Reserve
Birthday: 27 August 1943
Place of Birth: Lincoln, Lancaster County, Nebraska
Entered Service at: Omaha, Douglas County, Nebraska

Unit: Sea, Air, and Land Team 1 (SEAL)
Served as: SEAL Team Leader
Battle or Place of Action: near Nha Trang Bay, Republic of Vietnam
Date of Action: 14 March 1969
Date of Presentation: 14 May 1970
Place of Presentation: The White House, presented by Pres. Richard M. Nixon
Citation: For conspicuous gallantry and intrepidity at the risk of his life above and beyond the call of duty while serving as a SEAL team leader during action against enemy aggressor (Viet Cong) forces. Acting in response to reliable intelligence, Lt. (j.g.) Kerrey led his SEAL team on a mission to capture important members of the enemy's area political cadre known to be located on an island in the bay of Nha Trang. In order to surprise the enemy, he and his team scaled a 350-foot sheer cliff to place themselves above the ledge on which the enemy was located. Splitting his team in two elements and coordinating both, Lt. (j.g.) Kerrey led his men in the treacherous downward descent to the enemy's camp. Just as they neared the end of their descent, intense enemy fire was directed at them, and Lt. (j.g.) Kerrey received massive injuries from a grenade which exploded at his feet and threw him backward on the jagged rocks. Although bleeding profusely and suffering great pain, he displayed outstanding courage and presence of mind in immediately directing his element's fire into the heart of the enemy camp. Utilizing his radioman, Lt. (j.g.) Kerrey called in a second element's fire support which caught the confused Viet Cong in a devastating crossfire. After successfully suppressing the enemy's fire, and although immobilized by his multiple wounds, he continued to maintain calm, superlative control as he ordered his team to secure and defend an extraction site. Lt. (j.g.) Kerrey resolutely directed his men, despite his near-unconscious state, until he was eventually evacuated by helicopter. The havoc brought to the enemy by this very successful mission cannot be over-estimated. The enemy soldiers who were captured provided critical intelligence to the allied effort. Lt. (j.g.) Kerrey's courageous and inspiring leadership, valiant fighting spirit, and tenacious devotion to duty in the face of almost overwhelming opposition sustain and enhance the finest traditions of the U.S. Naval Service.

3274 ◆ KINSMAN, THOMAS JAMES

Rank: Specialist Fourth Class (rank at time of action: Private First Class)
Service: U.S. Army
Birthday: 4 March 1945
Place of Birth: Renton, King County, Washington
Entered Service at: Seattle, King County, Washington
Unit: Company B, 3d Battalion, 60th Infantry, 9th Infantry Division
Served as: Rifleman
Battle or Place of Action: near Vinh Long, Republic of Vietnam
Date of Action: 6 February 1968
G.O. Number, Date: 40, 13 June 1969
Date of Presentation: 17 May 1969
Place of Presentation: The White House (Lawn), presented by Pres. Richard M. Nixon
Citation: For conspicuous gallantry and intrepidity in action at the risk of his life above and beyond the call of duty Sp4c. Kinsman (then Pfc.) distinguished himself in action in the afternoon while serving as a rifleman with Company B, on a reconnaissance-in-force mission. As his company was proceeding up a narrow canal in armored troop carriers, it came under sudden and intense rocket, automatic-weapons and small-arms fire from a well-entrenched Viet Cong force. The company immediately beached and began assaulting the enemy bunker complex. Hampered by exceedingly dense undergrowth which limited visibility to 10 meters, a group of eight men became cut off from the main body of the company. As they were moving through heavy enemy fire to effect a link-up, an enemy soldier in a concealed position hurled a grenade into their midst. Sp4c. Kinsman immediately alerted his comrades of the danger, then unhesitatingly threw himself on the grenade and blocked the explosion with his body. As a result of his courageous action, he received severe head and chest wounds. Through his indomitable courage, complete disregard for his personal safety and profound concern for his fellow soldiers, Sp4c. Kinsman averted loss of life and injury to the other seven men in his element. Sp4c. Kinsman's extraordinary heroism at the risk of his life, above and beyond the call of duty, are in keeping with the highest traditions of the military service and reflect great credit upon himself, his unit, and the U.S. Army.

3275 ◆ LAMBERS, PAUL RONALD

Rank: Staff Sergeant
Service: U.S. Army
Birthday: 25 June 1942
Place of Birth: Holland, Ottawa County, Michigan
Date of Death: 1 December 1970
Place of Death: Holland, Michigan
Cemetery: Drowned in Lake Michigan, body not recovered.
Entered Service at: Holland, Ottawa County, Michigan
Unit: 3d Platoon, Company A, 2d Battalion, 27th Infantry, 25th Infantry Division
Battle or Place of Action: Tay Ninh Province, Republic of Vietnam
Date of Action: 20 August 1968
G.O. Number, Date: 79, 4 December 1969
Date of Presentation: 24 November 1969
Place of Presentation: The White House, presented by Pres. Richard M. Nixon
Citation: For conspicuous gallantry and intrepidity in action at the risk of his life above and beyond the call of duty. S/Sgt. (then Sgt.) Lambers distinguished himself in action while serving with the 3d Platoon, Company A. The unit had established a night defensive position astride a suspected enemy infiltration route, when it was attacked by an estimated Viet Cong battalion. During the initial enemy onslaught, the platoon leader fell seriously wounded and S/Sgt. Lambers assumed command of the platoon. Disregarding the intense enemy fire, S/Sgt. Lambers left his covered position, secured the platoon radio, and moved to the command post to direct

the defense. When his radio became inoperative due to enemy action, S/Sgt. Lambers crossed the fire-swept position to secure the 90-mm recoilless-rifle crew's radio in order to reestablish communications. Upon discovering that the 90-mm recoilless rifle was not functioning, S/Sgt. Lambers assisted in the repair of the weapon and directed cannister fire at point-blank range against the attacking enemy who had breached the defensive wire of the position. When the weapon was knocked out by enemy fire, he singlehandedly repulsed a penetration of the position by detonating claymore mines and throwing grenades into the midst of the attackers, killing four more of the Viet Cong with well-aimed hand grenades. S/Sgt. Lambers maintained command of the platoon elements by moving from position to position under the hail of enemy fire, providing assistance where the assault was the heaviest and by his outstanding example inspiring his men to the utmost efforts of courage. He displayed great skill and valor throughout the five-hour battle by personally directing artillery and helicopter fire, placing them at times within five meters of the defensive position. He repeatedly exposed himself to hostile fire at great risk to his own life in order to redistribute ammunition and to care for seriously wounded comrades and to move them to sheltered positions. S/Sgt. Lambers' superb leadership, professional skill, and magnificent courage saved the lives of his comrades, resulted in the virtual annihilation of a vastly superior enemy force, and were largely instrumental in thwarting an enemy offensive against Tay Ninh City. His gallantry at the risk of his life is in keeping with the highest traditions of the military service and reflects great credit upon himself, his unit, and the U.S. Army.

3276 ◆ LANG, GEORGE CHARLES

Rank: Specialist Fourth Class
Service: U.S. Army
Birthday: 20 April 1947
Place of Birth: Flushing, Queens County, New York
Entered Service at: Brooklyn, Kings County, New York
Unit: 3d Squad, 3d Platoon, Company A, 4th Battalion, 47th Infantry, 9th Infantry Division
Served as: Squad Leader
Battle or Place of Action: near Ben Tre City, Kien Hoa Province, Republic of Vietnam
Date of Action: 22 February 1969
G.O. Number, Date: 18, 24 March 1971
Date of Presentation: 2 March 1971
Place of Presentation: The White House (East Ballroom), presented by Pres. Richard M. Nixon
Citation: For conspicuous gallantry and intrepidity in action at the risk of his life above and beyond the call of duty. Sp4c. Lang, Company A, was serving as a squad leader when his unit, on a reconnaissance-in-force mission, encountered intense fire from a well-fortifed enemy bunker complex. Sp4c. Lang observed an emplacement from which heavy fire was coming. Unhesitatingly, he assaulted the position and destroyed it with hand grenades and rifle fire. Observing another emplacement approximately 15 meters to his front, Sp4c. Lang jumped across a canal, moved through heavy enemy fire to within a few feet of the position, and eliminated it, again using hand grenades and rifle fire. Nearby, he discovered a large cache of enemy ammunition. As he maneuvered his squad forward to secure the cache, they came under fire from yet a third bunker. Sp4c. Lang immediately reacted, assaulted this position, and destroyed it with the remainder of his grenades. After returning to the area of the arms cache, his squad again came under heavy enemy rocket and automatic-weapons fire from three sides and suffered six casualties. Sp4c. Lang was one of those seriously wounded. Although immobilized and in great pain, he continued to direct his men until his evacuation was ordered over his protests. The sustained extraordinary courage and selflessness exhibited by this soldier over an extended period of time were an inspiration to his comrades and are in keeping with the highest traditions of the U.S. Army.

3277 ◆ *LANGHORN, GARFIELD McCONNELL

Rank: Private First Class
Service: U.S. Army
Birthday: 10 September 1948
Place of Birth: Cumberland, Cumberland County, Virginia
Date of Death: 15 January 1969
Place of Death: Republic of Vietnam
Cemetery: Riverhead Cemetery (MH)—Riverhead, New York
Entered Service at: Brooklyn, Kings County, New York
Unit: Troop C, 7th Squadron (Airmobile), 17th Cavalry, 1st Aviation Brigade
Served as: Radio Operator
Battle or Place of Action: near Plei Djereng, Pleiku Province, Republic of Vietnam
Date of Action: 15 January 1969
G.O. Number, Date: 19, 23 April 1970
Date of Presentation: 7 April 1970
Place of Presentation: The White House, presented by Pres. Richard M. Nixon to his family
Citation: For conspicuous gallantry and intrepidity in action at the risk of his life above and beyond the call of duty. Pfc. Langhorn distinguished himself while serving as a radio operator with Troop C, near Plei Djereng in Pleiku Province. Pfc. Langhorn's platoon was inserted into a landing zone to rescue two pilots of a Cobra helicopter shot down by enemy fire on a heavily timbered slope. He provided radio coordination with the command-and-control aircraft overhead while the troops hacked their way through dense undergrowth to the wreckage, where both aviators were found dead. As the men were taking the bodies to a pickup site, they suddenly came under intense fire from North Vietnamese soldiers in camouflaged bunkers to the front and right flank, and within minutes they were surrounded. Pfc. Langhorn immediately radioed for help from the orbiting gunships, which began to place minigun and rocket fire on the aggressors. He then lay between the platoon leader and another man, operating the radio and providing covering fire for the wounded who had been moved to the center of the small perimeter. Darkness

soon fell, making it impossible for the gunships to give accurate support, and the aggressors began to probe the perimeter. An enemy hand grenade landed in front of Pfc. Langhorn and a few feet from personnel who had become casualties. Choosing to protect these wounded, he unhesitatingly threw himself on the grenade, scooped it beneath his body, and absorbed the blast. By sacrificing himself, he saved the lives of his comrades. Pfc. Langhorn's extraordinary heroism at the cost of his life was in keeping with the highest traditions of the military service and reflect great credit on himself, his unit, and the U.S. Army.

3278 ◆ *LAPOINTE JR., JOSEPH GUY

Rank: Specialist Fourth Class
Service: U.S. Army
Birthday: 2 July 1948
Place of Birth: Dayton, Montgomery County, Ohio
Date of Death: 2 June 1969
Place of Death: Republic of Vietnam
Cemetery: Riverside Cemetery—West Milton, Ohio
Entered Service at: Cincinnati, Hamilton County, Ohio
Unit: Headquarters & Headquarters Troop, 2d Squadron, 17th Cavalry, 101st Airborne Division
Served as: Medical Aidman
Battle or Place of Action: Quang Tin Province, Republic of Vietnam
Date of Action: 2 June 1969
G.O. Number, Date: 7, 25 January 1972
Date of Presentation: 16 December 1971
Place of Presentation: Old Executive Office Building, presented by Vice Pres. Spiro T. Agnew to his family
Citation: For conspicuous gallantry and intrepidity in action at the risk of his life above and beyond the call of duty. Sp4c. LaPointe, Headquarters and Headquarters Troop, 2d Squadron, distinguished himself while serving as a medical aidman during a combat helicopter assault mission. Sp4c. LaPointe's patrol was advancing from the landing zone through an adjoining valley when it suddenly encountered heavy automatic-weapons fire from a large enemy force entrenched in well-fortified bunker positions. In the initial hail of fire, two soldiers in the formation vanguard were seriously wounded. Hearing a call for aid from one of the wounded, Sp4c. LaPointe ran forward through heavy fire to assist his fallen comrades. To reach the wounded men, he was forced to crawl directly in view of an enemy bunker. As members of his unit attempted to provide covering fire, he administered first aid to one man, shielding the other with his body. He was hit by a burst of fire from the bunker while attending the wounded soldier. In spite of his painful wounds, Sp4c. LaPointe continued his lifesaving duties until he was again wounded and knocked to the ground. Making strenuous efforts, he moved back again into a shielding position to continue administering first aid. An exploding enemy grenade mortally wounded all three men. Sp4c. LaPointe's courageous actions at the cost of his life were an inspiration to his comrades. His gallantry and selflessness are in the highest traditions of the military service and reflect great credit on him, his unit, and the U.S. Army.

3279 ◆ LASSEN, CLYDE EVERETT

Rank: Lieutenant (highest rank: Commander)
Service: U.S. Navy
Birthday: 14 March 1942
Place of Birth: Fort Myers, Lee County, Florida
Date of Death: 1 April 1994
Place of Death: Pensacola, Florida
Cemetery: Barrancas National Cemetery (MH)(38-113)—Pensacola, Florida
Entered Service at: Jacksonville, Duval County, Florida
Unit: U.S.S. *Preble* (DLG-15), Detachment 104, Helicopter Support Squadron 7
Served as: Search & Rescue Helicopter Pilot
Battle or Place of Action: Republic of Vietnam
Date of Action: 19 June 1968
Date of Presentation: 16 January 1969
Place of Presentation: The White House, presented by Pres. Lyndon B. Johnson
Citation: For conspicuous gallantry and intrepidity at the risk of his life above and beyond the call of duty as pilot and aircraft commander of a search-and-rescue helicopter, attached to Helicopter Support Squadron 7, during operations against enemy forces in North Vietnam. Launched shortly after midnight to attempt the rescue of two downed aviators, Lt. (then Lt. (j.g.) Lassen skillfully piloted his aircraft over unknown and hostile terrain to a steep, tree-covered hill on which the survivors had been located. Although enemy fire was being directed at the helicopter, he initially landed in a clear area near the base of the hill, but, due to the dense undergrowth, the survivors could not reach the helicopter. With the aid of flare illumination, Lt. Lassen successfully accomplished a hover between two trees at the survivors' position. Illumination was abruptly lost as the last of the flares were expended, and the helicopter collided with a tree, commencing a sharp descent. Expertly righting his aircraft and maneuvering clear, Lt. Lassen remained in the area, determined to make another rescue attempt, and encouraged the downed aviators while awaiting resumption of flare illumination. After another unsuccessful, illuminated rescue attempt, and with his fuel dangerously low and his aircraft significantly damaged, he launched again and commenced another approach in the face of the continuing enemy opposition. When flare illumination was again lost, Lt. Lassen, fully aware of the dangers in clearly revealing his position to the enemy, turned on his landing lights and completed the landing. On this attempt, the survivors were able to make their way to the helicopter. En route to the coast he encountered and successfully evaded additional hostile antiaircraft fire and, with fuel for only five minutes of flight remaining, landed safely aboard U.S.S. *Jouett* (DLG-29).

3280 ◆ *LAUFFER, BILLY LANE

Rank: Private First Class
Service: U.S. Army
Birthday: 20 October 1945
Place of Birth: Murray, Calloway County, Kentucky
Date of Death: 21 September 1966

Place of Death: Republic of Vietnam
Cemetery: Murray Memorial Gardens—Murray, Kentucky
Entered Service at: Phoenix, Maricopa County, Arizona
Unit: Company C, 2d Battalion, 5th Cavalry, 1st Air Cavalry Division
Served as: Rifleman
Battle or Place of Action: near Bon Son, Binh Dinh Province, Republic of Vietnam
Date of Action: 21 September 1966
G.O. Number, Date: 49, 14 September 1968
Date of Presentation: 15 August 1968
Place of Presentation: The Pentagon, presented by Sec. of the Army Stanley R. Resor to his family
Citation: For conspicuous gallantry and intrepidity in action at the risk of his life above and beyond the call of duty. Pfc. Lauffer's squad, a part of Company C, was suddenly struck at close range by an intense machine-gun crossfire from two concealed bunkers astride the squad's route. Pfc. Lauffer, the second man in the column, saw the leadman fall and noted that the remainder of the squad was unable to move. Two comrades, previously wounded and being carried on litters, were lying helpless in the beaten zone of the enemy fire. Reacting instinctively, Pfc. Lauffer quickly engaged both bunkers with fire from his rifle, but when the other squad members attempted to maneuver under his cover fire, the enemy fusillade increased in volume and thwarted every attempt to move. Seeing this and his wounded comrades helpless in the open, Pfc. Lauffer rose to his feet and charged the enemy machine-gun positions, firing his weapon and drawing the enemy's attention. Keeping the enemy confused and off balance, his one-man assault provided the crucial moments for the wounded point man to crawl to a covered position, the squad to move the exposed litter patients to safety, and his comrades to gain more advantageous positions. Pfc. Lauffer was fatally wounded during his selfless act of courage and devotion to his fellow soldiers. His gallantry at the cost of his life served as an inspiration to his comrades and saved the lives of an untold number of his companions. His actions are in keeping with the highest traditions of military service and reflect great credit upon himself, his unit, and the U.S. Army.

3281 ◆ *LAW, ROBERT DAVID

Rank: Specialist Fourth Class
Service: U.S. Army
Birthday: 15 September 1944
Place of Birth: Fort Worth, Tarrant County, Texas
Date of Death: 22 February 1969
Place of Death: Republic of Vietnam
Cemetery: Mount Olivet Cemetery—Fort Worth, Texas
Entered Service at: Dallas, Collin County, Texas
Unit: Company I (Ranger), 75th Infantry, 1st Infantry Division
Battle or Place of Action: Tinh Phuoc Thanh Province, Republic of Vietnam
Date of Action: 22 February 1969
G.O. Number, Date: 45, 28 August 1970
Date of Presentation: 6 August 1970
Place of Presentation: The White House, presented by Pres. Richard M. Nixon to his family
Citation: For conspicuous gallantry and intrepidity in action at the risk of his life above and beyond the call of duty. Sp4c. Law distinguished himself while serving with Company I. While on a long-range reconnaissance patrol in Tinh Phuoc Thanh Province, Sp4c. Law and five comrades made contact with a small enemy patrol. As the opposing elements exchanged intense fire, he maneuvered to a perilously exposed position flanking his comrades and began placing suppressive fire on the hostile troops. Although his team was hindered by a low supply of ammunition and suffered from an unidentified irritating gas in the air, Sp4c. Law's spirited defense and challenging counterassault rallied his fellow soldiers against the well-equipped hostile troops. When an enemy grenade landed in his team's position, Sp4c. Law, instead of diving into the safety of a stream behind him, threw himself on the grenade to save the lives of his comrades. Sp4c. Law's extraordinary courage and profound concern for his fellow soldiers were in keeping with the highest traditions of the military service and reflect great credit on himself, his unit, and the U.S. Army.

3282 ◆ LEE, HOWARD VINCENT

Rank: Major (rank at time of action: Captain) (highest rank: Colonel)
Service: U.S. Marine Corps
Birthday: 1 August 1933
Place of Birth: New York, New York
Entered Service at: Dumfries, Prince William County, Virginia
Unit: Company E, 2d Battalion, 4th Marines, 3d Marine Division (Rein) FMF
Served as: Company Commander
Battle or Place of Action: near Cam Lo, Republic of Vietnam
Date of Action: 8-9 August 1966
Date of Presentation: 25 October 1967
Place of Presentation: The White House, presented by Pres. Lyndon B. Johnson
Citation: For conspicuous gallantry and intrepidity at the risk of his life above and beyond the call of duty. A platoon of Maj. (then Capt.) Lee's company, while on an operation deep in enemy territory, was attacked and surrounded by a large Vietnamese force. Realizing that the unit had suffered numerous casualties, depriving it of effective leadership, and fully aware that the platoon was even then under heavy attack by the enemy, Maj. Lee took seven men and proceeded by helicopter to reinforce the beleaguered platoon. Maj. Lee disembarked from the helicopter with two of his men and, braving withering enemy fire, led them into the perimeter, where he fearlessly moved from position to position, directing and encouraging the overtaxed troops. The enemy then launched a massive attack with the full might of their forces. Although painfully wounded by fragments from an enemy grenade in several areas of his body, including his eye, Maj. Lee continued undauntedly throughout the night to direct the valiant defense, coordinate supporting fire, and apprise higher headquarters of the plight of the platoon. The next morning he

collapsed from his wounds and was forced to relinquish command. However the small band of marines had held their position and repeatedly fought off many vicious enemy attacks for a grueling six hours until their evacuation was effected the following morning. Maj. Lee's actions saved his men from capture, minimized the loss of lives, and dealt the enemy a severe defeat. His indomitable fighting spirit, superb leadership, and great personal valor in the face of tremendous odds, reflect great credit upon himself and are in keeping with the highest traditions of the Marine Corps and the U.S. Naval Service.

3283 ◆ *LEE, MILTON ARTHUR

Rank: Private First Class
Service: U.S. Army
Birthday: 28 February 1949
Place of Birth: Shreveport, Caddo County, Louisiana
Date of Death: 26 April 1968
Place of Death: Republic of Vietnam
Cemetery: Fort Sam Houston National Cemetery (X-2475) (MH)—San Antonio, Texas
Entered Service at: San Antonio, Bexar County, Texas
Unit: 3d Platoon, Company B, 2d Battalion, 502d Infantry, 1st Brigade, 101st Airborne Division (Airmobile)
Served as: Radio Operator
Battle or Place of Action: near Phu Bai, Thua Thien Province, Republic of Vietnam
Date of Action: 26 April 1968
G.O. Number, Date: 13, 23 April 1970
Date of Presentation: 7 April 1970
Place of Presentation: The White House, presented by Pres. Richard M. Nixon to his family
Citation: For conspicuous gallantry and intrepidity in action at the risk of his life above and beyond the call of duty. Pfc. Lee distinguished himself near the city of Phu Bai in the province of Thua Thien. Pfc. Lee was serving as the radio telephone operator with the 3d Platoon, Company B. As lead element for the company, the 3d Platoon received intense surprise hostile fire from a force of North Vietnamese Army regulars in well-concealed bunkers. With 50 percent casualties, the platoon maneuvered to a position of cover to treat their wounded and reorganize, while Pfc. Lee moved through the heavy enemy fire giving lifesaving first aid to his wounded comrades. During the subsequent assault on the enemy defensive positions, Pfc. Lee continuously kept close radio contact with the company commander, relaying precise and understandable orders to his platoon leader. While advancing with the front rank toward the objective, Pfc. Lee observed four North Vietnamese soldiers with automatic weapons and a rocket launcher lying in wait for the lead element of the platoon. As the element moved forward, unaware of the concealed danger, Pfc. Lee immediately and with utter disregard for his own personal safety, passed his radio to another soldier and charged through the murderous fire. Without hesitation he continued his assault, overrunning the enemy position, killing all occupants, and capturing four automatic weapons and a rocket launcher. Pfc. Lee continued his one-man assault on the second position through a heavy barrage of enemy automatic-weapons fire. Grievously wounded, he continued to press the attack, crawling forward into a firing position and delivering accurate covering fire to enable his platoon to maneuver and destroy the position. Not until the position was overrun did Pfc. Lee falter in his steady volume of fire and succumb to his wounds. Pfc. Lee's heroic actions saved the lives of the lead element and were instrumental in the destruction of the key position of the enemy defense. Pfc. Lee's gallantry at the risk of life above and beyond the call of duty are in keeping with the highest traditions of the military service and reflect great credit on himself, the 502d Infantry, and the U.S. Army.

3284 ◆ *LEISY, ROBERT RONALD

Rank: Second Lieutenant
Service: U.S. Army
Birthday: 1 March 1945
Place of Birth: Stockton, San Joaquin County, California
Date of Death: 2 December 1969
Place of Death: Republic of Vietnam
Cemetery: Evergreen-Washelli Memorial Park—Seattle, Washington
Entered Service at: Seattle, King County, Washington
Unit: Company B, 1st Battalion, 8th Cavalry, 1st Cavalry Division
Served as: Platoon Leader
Battle or Place of Action: Phuoc Long Province, Republic of Vietnam
Date of Action: 2 December 1969
G.O. Number, Date: 4, 25 January 1972
Date of Presentation: 16 December 1971
Place of Presentation: Old Executive Office Building, presented by Vice Pres. Sprio T. Agnew to his family
Citation: For conspicuous gallantry and intrepidity in action at the risk of his life above and beyond the call of duty. 2d Lt. Leisy, Infantry, Company B, distinguished himself while serving as platoon leader during a reconnaissance mission. One of his patrols became heavily engaged by the fire from a numerically superior enemy force located in a well-entrenched bunker complex. As 2d Lt. Leisy deployed the remainder of his platoon to rescue the beleaguered patrol, the platoon also came under intense enemy fire from the front and both flanks. In complete disregard for his safety, 2d Lt. Leisy moved from position to position deploying his men to effectively engage the enemy. Accompanied by his radio operator he moved to the front and spotted an enemy sniper in a tree in the act of firing a rocket-propelled grenade at them. Realizing there was neither time to escape the grenade nor shout a warning, 2d Lt. Leisy unhesitatingly, and with full knowledge of the consequences, shielded the radio operator with his body and absorbed the full impact of the explosion. This valorous act saved the life of the radio operator and protected other men of his platoon who were nearby from serious injury. Despite his mortal wounds, 2d Lt. Leisy calmly and confidently continued to direct the platoon's fire. When medical aid arrived 2d Lt. Leisy valiantly refused attention until the other seriously wounded were treated. His display of extraordinary courage and exemplary devotion to duty provided the inspiration and leadership that enabled his platoon to successfully withdraw without further casualties. 2d Lt.

Leisy's gallantry at the cost of his life are in keeping with the highest traditions of the military service and reflect great credit on him, his unit, and the U.S. Army

3285 ◆ LEMON, PETER CHARLES

Rank: Sergeant (rank at time of action: Specialist Fourth Class)
Service: U.S. Army
Birthday: 5 June 1950
Place of Birth: Toronto, Canada
Entered Service at: Tawas City, Iosco County, Michigan
Unit: Company E (Recon), 2d Battalion, 8th Cavalry, 1st Cavalry Division
Served as: Assistant Machine Gunner
Battle or Place of Action: Fire Support Base Illingworth, Tay Ninh Province, Republic of Vietnam
Date of Action: 1 April 1970
G.O. Number, Date: 36, 16 July 1971
Date of Presentation: 15 June 1971
Place of Presentation: The White House, presented by Pres. Richard M. Nixon
Citation: For conspicuous gallantry and intrepidity in action at the risk of his life above and beyond the call of duty. Sgt. Lemon (then Sp4c.), Company E, distinguished himself while serving as an assistant machine gunner during the defense of Fire Support Base Illingworth. When the base came under heavy enemy attack, Sgt. Lemon engaged a numerically superior enemy with machine-gun and rifle fire from his defensive position until both weapons malfunctioned. He then used hand grenades to fend off the intensified enemy attack launched in his direction. After eliminating all but one of the enemy soldiers in the immediate vicinity, he pursued and disposed of the remaining soldier in hand-to-hand combat. Despite fragment wounds from an exploding grenade, Sgt. Lemon regained his position, carried a more seriously wounded comrade to an aid station, and, as he returned, was wounded a second time by enemy fire. Disregarding his personal injuries, he moved to his position through a hail of small-arms and grenade fire. Sgt. Lemon immediately realized that the defensive sector was in danger of being overrun by the enemy and unhesitatingly assaulted the enemy soldiers by throwing hand grenades and engaging in hand-to-hand combat. He was wounded yet a third time, but his determined efforts successfully drove the enemy from the position. Securing an operable machine gun, Sgt. Lemon stood atop an embankment fully exposed to enemy fire, and placed effective fire upon the enemy until he collapsed from his multiple wounds and exhaustion. After regaining consciousness at the aid station, he refused medical evacuation until his more seriously wounded comrades had been evacuated. Sgt. Lemon's gallantry and extraordinary heroism are in keeping with the highest traditions of the military service and reflect great credit on him, his unit, and the U.S. Army.

3286 ◆ *LEONARD, MATTHEW

Rank: Sergeant First Class
Service: U.S. Army
Birthday: 26 November 1929
Place of Birth: Eutaw, Greene County, Alabama
Date of Death: 28 February 1967
Place of Death: Republic of Vietnam
Cemetery: Shadow Lawn Cemetery (MH)—Birmingham, Alabama
Entered Service at: Birmingham, Jefferson County, Alabama
Unit: Company B, 1st Battalion, 16th Infantry, 1st Infantry Division
Served as: Platoon Sergeant
Battle or Place of Action: near Suoi Da, Republic of Vietnam
Date of Action: 28 February 1967
G.O. Number, Date: 2, 9 January 1969
Date of Presentation: 19 December 1968
Place of Presentation: The Pentagon, presented by Sec. of the Army Stanley R. Resor to his family
Citation: For conspicuous gallantry and intrepidity in action at the risk of his life above and beyond the call of duty. His platoon was suddenly attacked by a large enemy force employing small-arms, automatic weapons, and hand grenades. Although the platoon leader and several other key leaders were among the first wounded, P/Sgt. Leonard quickly rallied his men to throw back the initial enemy assaults. During the short pause that followed, he organized a defensive perimeter, redistributed ammunition, and inspired his comrades through his forceful leadership and words of encouragement. Noticing a wounded companion outside the perimeter, he dragged the man to safety but was struck by a sniper's bullet which shattered his left hand. Refusing medical attention and continuously exposing himself to the increasing fire as the enemy again assaulted the perimeter, P/Sgt. Leonard moved from position to position to direct the fire of his men against the well-camouflaged foe. Under the cover of the main attack, the enemy moved a machine gun into a location where it could sweep the entire perimeter. This threat was magnified when the platoon machine gun in this area malfunctioned. P/Sgt. Leonard quickly crawled to the gun position and was helping to clear the malfunction when the gunner and other men in the vicinity were wounded by fire from the enemy machine gun. P/Sgt. Leonard rose to his feet, charged the enemy gun, and destroyed the hostile crew despite being hit several times by enemy fire. He moved to a tree, propped himself against it, and continued to engage the enemy until he succumbed to his many wounds. His fighting spirit, heroic leadership, and valiant acts inspired the remaining members of his platoon to hold back the enemy until assistance arrived. P/Sgt. Leonard's profound courage and devotion to his men are in keeping with the highest traditions of the military service, and his gallant actions reflect great credit upon himself and the U.S. Army.

3287 ◆ LEVITOW, JOHN LEE

Rank: Sergeant (rank at time of action: Airman First Class)
Service: U.S. Air Force
Birthday: 1 November 1945
Place of Birth: Hartford, Hartford County, Connecticut
Entered Service at: New Haven, New Haven County, Connecticut
Unit: 3d Special Operations Squadron

Served as: Loadmaster
Battle or Place of Action: over Long Binh Army Post, Republic of Vietnam
Date of Action: 24 February 1969
G.O. Number, Date: GB-476, 23 June 1970
Date of Presentation: 14 May 1970
Place of Presentation: The White House, presented by Pres. Richard M. Nixon
Citation: For conspicuous gallantry and intrepidity in action at the risk of his life above and beyond the call of duty. Sgt. Levitow (then A1c.), U.S. Air Force, distinguished himself by exceptional heroism while assigned as a loadmaster aboard an AC-47 aircraft flying a night mission in support of Long Binh Army Post. Sgt. Levitow's aircraft was struck by a hostile mortar round. The resulting explosion ripped a hole two feet in diameter through the wing and fragments made over 3,500 holes in the fuselage. All occupants of the cargo compartment were wounded and helplessly slammed against the floor and fuselage. The explosion tore an activated flare from the grasp of a crewmember who had been launching flares to provide illumination for Army ground troops engaged in combat. Sgt. Levitow, though stunned by the concussion of the blast and suffering from over 40 fragment wounds in the back and legs, staggered to his feet and turned to assist the man nearest to him who had been knocked down and was bleeding heavily. As he was moving his wounded comrade forward and away from the opened cargo compartment door, he saw the smoking flare ahead of him in the aisle. Realizing the danger involved and completely disregarding his own wounds, Sgt. Levitow started toward the burning flare. The aircraft was partially out of control and the flare was rolling wildly from side to side. Sgt. Levitow struggled forward despite the loss of blood from his many wounds and the partial loss of feeling in his right leg. Unable to grasp the rolling flare with his hands, he threw himself bodily upon the burning flare. Hugging the deadly device to his body, he dragged himself back to the rear of the aircraft and hurled the flare through the open cargo door. At that instant the flare separated and ignited in the air, but clear of the aircraft. Sgt. Levitow, by his selfless and heroic actions, saved the aircraft and its entire crew from certain death and destruction. Sgt. Levitow's gallantry, his profound concern for his fellow men, at the risk of his life above and beyond the call of duty, are in keeping with the highest traditions of the U.S. Air Force and reflect great credit upon himself and the Armed Forces of his country.

3288 ◆ LITEKY, CHARLES JAMES (ANGELO)

Rank: Captain
Service: U.S. Army
Birthday: 14 February 1931
Place of Birth: Washington, D.C.
Entered Service at: Fort Hamilton, Kings County, New York
Unit: Headquarters & Headquarters Company, 199th Infantry Brigade (Separate) (Light)
Served as: Chaplain
Battle or Place of Action: near Phuoc-Lac, Bien Hoa Province, Republic of Vietnam
Date of Action: 6 December 1967
G.O. Number, Date: 77, 10 December 1968
Date of Presentation: 19 November 1968
Place of Presentation: The White House, presented by Pres. Lyndon B. Johnson
Citation: Chaplain Liteky distinguished himself by exceptional heroism while serving with Company A, 4th Battalion, 12th Infantry, 199th Light Infantry Brigade. He was participating in a search-and-destroy operation when Company A came under intense fire from a battalion-size enemy force. Momentarily stunned from the immediate encounter that ensued, the men hugged the ground for cover. Observing two wounded men, Chaplain Liteky moved to within 15 meters of an enemy machine-gun position to reach them, placing himself between the enemy and the wounded men. When there was a brief respite in the fighting, he managed to drag them to the relative safety of the landing zone. Inspired by his courageous actions, the company rallied and began placing a heavy volume of fire upon the enemy positions. In a magnificent display of courage and leadership, Chaplain Liteky began moving upright through the enemy fire, administering last rites to the dying and evacuating the wounded. Noticing another trapped and seriously wounded man, Chaplain Liteky crawled to his aid. Realizing that the wounded man was too heavy to carry, he rolled on his back, placed the man on his chest and through sheer determination and fortitude crawled back to the landing zone using his elbows and heels to push himself along. Pausing for breath momentarily, he returned to the action and came upon a man entangled in the dense, thorny underbrush. Once more intense enemy fire was directed at him, but Chaplain Liteky stood his ground and calmly broke the vines and carried the man to the landing zone for evacuation. On several occasions when the landing zone was under small-arms and rocket fire, Chaplain Liteky stood up in the face of hostile fire and personally directed the medivac helicopters into and out of the area. With the wounded safely evacuated, Chaplain Liteky returned to the perimeter, constantly encouraging and inspiring the men. Upon the unit's relief on the morning of 7 December 1967, it was discovered that despite painful wounds in the neck and foot, Chaplain Liteky had personally carried over 20 men to the landing zone for evacuation during the savage fighting. Through his indomitable inspiration and heroic actions, Chaplain Liteky saved the lives of a number of his comrades and enabled the company to repulse the enemy. Chaplain Liteky's actions reflect great credit upon himself and were in keeping with the highest traditions of the U.S. Army.

3289 ◆ LITTRELL, GARY LEE

Rank: Sergeant First Class (highest rank: Command Sergeant Major)
Service: U.S. Army
Birthday: 26 October 1944
Place of Birth: Henderson, Henderson County, Kentucky
Entered Service at: Los Angeles, Los Angeles County, California
Unit: U.S. Military Assistance Command, II Corps Advisory Group, Advisory Team 21

Served as: Light Weapons Infantry Advisor
Battle or Place of Action: Kontum Province, Republic of Vietnam
Date of Action: 4-8 April 1970
G.O. Number, Date: 41, 5 November 1973
Date of Presentation: 15 October 1973
Place of Presentation: The White House, presented by Pres. Richard M. Nixon
Citation: For conspicuous gallantry and intrepidity in action at the risk of his life above and beyond the call of duty. Sfc. Littrell, U.S. Military Assistance Command, Vietnam, Advisory Team 21, distinguished himself while serving as a Light Weapons Infantry adviser with the 23d Battalion, 2d Ranger Group, Republic of Vietnam Army, near Dak Seang. After establishing a defensive perimeter on a hill on 4 April, the battalion was subjected to an intense enemy mortar attack which killed the Vietnamese commander, one adviser, and seriously wounded all the advisers except Sfc. Littrell. During the ensuing four days, Sfc. Littrell exhibited near superhuman endurance as he singlehandedly bolstered the besieged battalion. Repeatedly abandoning positions of relative safety, he directed artillery and air support by day and marked the unit's location by night, despite the heavy, concentrated enemy fire. His dauntless will instilled in the men of the 23d Battalion a deep desire to resist. Assault after assault was repulsed as the battalion responded to the extraordinary leadership and personal example exhibited by Sfc. Littrell as he continuously moved to those points most seriously threatened by the enemy, redistributed ammunition, strengthened faltering defenses, cared for the wounded, and shouted encouragement to the Vietnamese in their own language. When the beleaguered battalion was finally ordered to withdraw, numerous ambushes were encountered. Sfc. Littrell repeatedly prevented widespread disorder by directing air strikes to within 50 meters of their position. Through his indomitable courage and complete disregard for his safety, he averted excessive loss of life and injury to the members of the battalion. The sustained extraordinary courage and selflessness displayed by Sfc. Littrell over an extended period of time were in keeping with the highest traditions of the military service and reflect great credit on him and the U.S. Army.

3290 ◆ LIVINGSTON, JAMES EVERTTE

Rank: Captain (current rank: Major General)
Service: U.S. Marine Corps
Birthday: 12 January 1940
Place of Birth: Towns, Telfair County, Georgia
Entered Service at: McRae, Telfair County, Georgia
Unit: Company E, 2d Battalion, 4th Marines, 9th Marine Amphibious Brigade
Served as: Commanding Officer
Battle or Place of Action: Dai Do, Quang Tri Province, Republic of Vietnam
Date of Action: 2 May 1968
Date of Presentation: 14 May 1970
Place of Presentation: The White House, presented by Pres. Richard M. Nixon
Citation: For conspicuous gallantry and intrepidity at the risk of his life above and beyond the call of duty while serving as Commanding Officer, Company E, in action against enemy forces. Company E launched a determined assault on the heavily fortified village of Dai Do, which had been seized by the enemy on the preceding evening isolating a marine company from the remainder of the battalion. Skillfully employing screening agents, Capt. Livingston maneuvered his men to assault positions across 500 meters of dangerous open rice paddy while under intense enemy fire. Ignoring hostile rounds impacting near him, he fearlessly led his men in a savage assault against enemy emplacements within the village. While adjusting supporting arms fire, Capt. Livingston moved to the points of heaviest resistance, shouting words of encouragement to his marines, directing their fire, and spurring the dwindling momentum of the attack on repeated occasions. Although twice painfully wounded by grenade fragments, he refused medical treatment and courageously led his men in the destruction of over 100 mutually supporting bunkers, driving the remaining enemy from their positions and relieving the pressure on the stranded marine company. As the two companies consolidated positions and evacuated casualties, a third company passed through the friendly lines launching an assault on the adjacent village of Dinh To, only to be halted by a furious counterattack of an enemy battalion. Swiftly assessing the situation and disregarding the heavy volume of enemy fire, Capt. Livingston boldly maneuvered the remaining effective men of his company forward, joined forces with the heavily engaged marines, and halted the enemy's counterattack. Wounded a third time and unable to walk, he steadfastly remained in the dangerously exposed area, deploying his men to more tenable positions and supervising the evacuation of casualties. Only when assured of the safety of his men did he allow himself to be evacuated. Capt. Livingston's gallant actions uphold the highest traditions of the Marine Corps and the U.S. Naval Service.

3291 ◆ *LONG, DONALD RUSSELL

Rank: Sergeant
Service: U.S. Army
Birthday: 27 August 1939
Place of Birth: Blackfork, Ohio
Date of Death: 30 June 1966
Place of Death: Republic of Vietnam
Cemetery: Union Baptist Church Cemetery—Blackfork, Ohio
Entered Service at: Ashland, Boyd County, Kentucky
Unit: Troop C, 1st Squadron, 4th Cavalry, 1st Infantry Division
Served as: Assistant Platoon Leader
Battle or Place of Action: Republic of Vietnam
Date of Action: 30 June 1966
G.O. Number, Date: 13, 4 April 1968
Date of Presentation: 8 February 1968
Place of Presentation: The Pentagon, presented by Sec. of the Army Stanley R. Resor to his family
Citation: For conspicuous gallantry and intrepidity in action at the risk of his life above and beyond the call of duty. Troops B and C, while conducting a reconnaissance mission

along a road were suddenly attacked by a Viet Cong regiment, supported by mortars, recoilless rifles, and machine guns from concealed positions astride the road. Sgt. Long abandoned the relative safety of his armored personnel carrier and braved a withering hail of enemy fire to carry wounded men to evacuation helicopters. As the platoon fought its way forward to resupply advanced elements, Sgt. Long repeatedly exposed himself to enemy fire at point-blank range to provide the needed supplies. While assaulting the Viet Cong position, Sgt. Long inspired his comrades by fearlessly standing unprotected to repel the enemy with rifle fire and grenades as they attempted to mount his carrier. When the enemy threatened to overrun a disabled carrier nearby, Sgt. Long again disregarded his own safety to help the severely wounded crew to safety. As he was handing arms to the less seriously wounded and reorganizing them to press the attack, an enemy grenade was hurled onto the carrier deck. Immediately recognizing the imminent danger, he instinctively shouted a warning to the crew and pushed to safety one man who had not heard his warning over the roar of battle. Realizing that these actions would not fully protect the exposed crewmen from the deadly explosion, he threw himself over the grenade to absorb the blast and thereby saved the lives of eight of his comrades at the expense of his life. Throughout the battle, Sgt. Long's extraordinary heroism, courage and supreme devotion to his men were in the finest tradition of the military service, and reflect great credit upon himself and the U.S. Army.

3292 ◆ *LOZADA, CARLOS JAMES

Rank: Private First Class
Service: U.S. Army
Birthday: 6 September 1946
Place of Birth: Caguas, Caguas County, Puerto Rico
Date of Death: 20 November 1967
Place of Death: Republic of Vietnam
Cemetery: Long Island National Cemetery (T-2295) (MH)—Farmingdale, New York
Entered Service at: New York, New York
Unit: 1st Platoon, Company A, 2d Battalion, 503d Infantry, 173d Airborne Brigade
Served as: Machine Gunner
Battle or Place of Action: Hill 875, near Dak To, Kontum Province, Republic of Vietnam
Date of Action: 20 November 1967
G.O. Number, Date: 77, 4 December 1969
Date of Presentation: 18 November 1969
Place of Presentation: The White House, presented by Vice Pres. Spiro T. Agnew to his family
Citation: For conspicuous gallantry and intrepidity in action at the risk of his life above and beyond the call of duty. Pfc. Lozada, U.S. Army, distinguished himself at the risk of his life above and beyond the call of duty in the battle of Dak To. While serving as a machine gunner with 1st Platoon, Company A, Pfc. Lozada was part of a four-man early warning outpost, located 35 meters from his company's lines. At 1400 hours a North Vietnamese Army company rapidly approached the outpost along a well-defended trail. Pfc. Lozada alerted his comrades and commenced firing at the enemy who were within 10 meters of the outpost. His heavy and accurate machine-gun fire killed at least 20 North Vietnamese soldiers and completely disrupted their initial attack. Pfc. Lozada remained in an exposed position and continued to pour deadly fire upon the enemy despite the urgent pleas of his comrades to withdraw. The enemy continued their assault, attempting to envelop the outpost. At the same time enemy forces launched a heavy attack on the forward west flank of Company A with the intent to cut them off from their battalion. Company A was given the order to withdraw. Pfc. Lozada apparently realized that if he abandoned his position there would be nothing to hold back the surging North Vietnamese soldiers and that the entire company withdrawal would be jeopardized. He called for his comrades to move back and that he would stay and provide cover for them. He made this decision realizing that the enemy was converging on three sides of his position and only meters away, and a delay in withdrawal meant almost certain death. Pfc. Lozada continued to deliver a heavy, accurate volume of suppressive fire against the enemy until he was mortally wounded and had to be carried during the withdrawal. His heroic deed served as an example and an inspiration to his comrades throughout the ensuing four-day battle. Pfc. Lozada's actions are in the highest traditions of the U.S. Army and reflect great credit upon himself, his unit, and the U.S. Army.

3293 ◆ *LUCAS, ANDRE CAVARO

Rank: Lieutenant Colonel
Service: U.S. Army
Birthday: 2 October 1930
Place of Birth: Washington, D.C.
Date of Death: 23 July 1970
Place of Death: Republic of Vietnam
Cemetery: U.S Military Academy Cemetery (7-C-160)—West Point, New York
Entered Service at: West Point, Orange County, New York
Unit: 2d Battalion, 506th Infantry, 101st Airborne Division
Served as: Battalion Commander
Battle or Place of Action: Fire Support Base Ripcord, Republic of Vietnam
Date of Action: 1-23 July 1970
G.O. Number, Date: 33, 6 September 1974
Date of Presentation: 17 July 1974
Place of Presentation: Blair House (Courtyard), presented by Vice Pres. Gerald R. Ford to his family
Citation: Lt. Col. Lucas distinguished himself by extraordinary heroism while serving as the commanding officer of the 2d Battalion. Although the fire base was constantly subjected to heavy attacks by a numerically superior enemy force throughout this period, Lt. Col. Lucas, forsaking his own safety, performed numerous acts of extraordinary valor in directing the defense of the allied position. On one occasion, he flew in a helicopter at treetop level above an entrenched enemy directing the fire of one of his companies for over three hours. Even though his helicopter was heavily damaged by enemy fire, he remained in an exposed position until the

company expended its supply of grenades. He then transferred to another helicopter, dropped critically needed grenades to the troops, and resumed his perilous mission of directing fire on the enemy. These courageous actions by Lt. Col. Lucas prevented the company from being encircled and destroyed by a larger enemy force. On another occasion, Lt. Col. Lucas attempted to rescue a crewman trapped in a burning helicopter. As the flames in the aircraft spread, and enemy fire became intense, Lt. Col. Lucas ordered all members of the rescue party to safety. Then, at great personal risk, he continued the rescue effort amid concentrated enemy mortar fire, intense heat, and exploding ammunition until the aircraft was completely engulfed in flames. Lt. Col. Lucas was mortally wounded while directing the successful withdrawal of his battalion from the fire base. His actions throughout this extended period inspired his men to heroic efforts, and were instrumental in saving the lives of many of his fellow soldiers while inflicting heavy casualties on the enemy. Lt. Col. Lucas' conspicuous gallantry and intrepidity in action, at the cost of his own life, were in keeping with the highest traditions of the military service and reflect great credit on him, his unit, and the U.S. Army.

3294 ◆ LYNCH, ALLAN JAMES

Rank: Sergeant (rank at time of action: Specialist Fourth Class)
Service: U.S. Army
Birthday: 28 October 1945
Place of Birth: Chicago, Cook County, Illinois
Entered Service at: Chicago, Cook County, Illinois
Unit: Company D, 1st Battalion (Airmobile), 12th Cavalry, 1st Cavalry Division
Served as: Radio Operator
Battle or Place of Action: near My An (2), Binh Dinh Province, Republic of Vietnam
Date of Action: 15 December 1967
G.O. Number, Date: 33, 5 June 1970
Date of Presentation: 14 May 1970
Place of Presentation: The White House, presented by Pres. Richard M. Nixon
Citation: For conspicuous gallantry and intrepidity in action at the risk of his life above and beyond the call of duty. Sgt. Lynch (then Sp4c.) distinguished himself while serving as a radio telephone operator with Company D. While serving in the forward element on an operation near the village of My An, his unit became heavily engaged with a numerically superior enemy force. Quickly and accurately assessing the situation, Sgt. Lynch provided his commander with information which subsequently proved essential to the unit's successful actions. Observing three wounded comrades lying exposed to enemy fire, Sgt. Lynch dashed across 50 meters of open ground through a withering hail of enemy fire to administer aid. Reconnoitering a nearby trench for a covered position to protect the wounded from intense hostile fire, he killed two enemy soldiers at point-blank range. With the trench cleared, he unhesitatingly returned to the fire-swept area three times to carry the wounded men to safety. When his company was forced to withdraw by the superior firepower of the enemy, Sgt. Lynch remained to aid his comrades at the risk of his life rather than abandon them. Alone, he defended his isolated position for two hours against the advancing enemy. Using only his rifle and a grenade, he stopped them just short of his trench, killing five. Again, disregarding his safety in the face of withering hostile fire, he crossed 70 meters of exposed terrain five times to carry his wounded comrades to a more secure area. Once he had assured their comfort and safety, Sgt. Lynch located the counterattacking friendly company to assist in directing the attack and evacuating the three casualties. His gallantry at the risk of his life is in the highest traditions of the military service. Sgt. Lynch has reflected great credit on himself, the 12th Cavalry, and the U.S. Army.

3295 ◆ MARM JR., WALTER JOSEPH

Rank: First Lieutenant (rank at time of action: Second Lieutenant) (current rank: Colonel)
Service: U.S. Army
Birthday: 20 November 1941
Place of Birth: Washington, Washington County, Pennsylvania
Entered Service at: Pittsburgh, Allegheny County, Pennsylvania
Unit: Company A, 1st Battalion, 7th Cavalry, 1st Cavalry Division (Airmobile)
Served as: Platoon Leader
Battle or Place of Action: vicinity of Ia Drang Valley, Republic of Vietnam
Date of Action: 14 November 1965
G.O. Number, Date: 7, 15 February 1967
Date of Presentation: 19 December 1966
Place of Presentation: The Pentagon, presented by Sec. of the Army Stanley R. Resor
Citation: For conspicuous gallantry and intrepidity at the risk of his life above and beyond the call of duty. As a platoon leader in the 1st Cavalry Division (Airmobile), 1st Lt. Marm demonstrated indomitable courage during a combat operation. His company was moving through the valley to relieve a friendly unit surrounded by an enemy force of estimated regimental size. 1st Lt. Marm led his platoon through withering fire until they were finally forced to take cover. Realizing that his platoon could not hold very long, and seeing four enemy soldiers moving into his position, he moved quickly under heavy fire and annihilated all four. Then, seeing that his platoon was receiving intense fire from a concealed machine gun, he deliberately exposed himself to draw its fire. Thus locating its position, he attempted to destroy it with an antitank weapon. Although he inflicted casualties, the weapon did not silence the enemy fire. Quickly, disregarding the intense fire directed on him and his platoon, he charged 30 meters across open ground and hurled grenades into the enemy position, killing some of the eight insurgents manning it. Although severely wounded, when his grenades were expended, armed with only a rifle, he continued the momentum of his assault on the position and killed the remainder of the enemy. 1st Lt. Marm's selfless actions reduced the fire on his platoon, broke the enemy assault, and rallied his unit to continue toward the accomplishment of this mission. 1st Lt. Marm's gallantry on

the battlefield and his extraordinary intrepidity at the risk of his life are in the highest traditions of the U.S. Army and reflect great credit upon himself and the Armed Forces of his country.

3296 ◆ *MARTINI, GARY WAYNE

Rank: Private First Class
Service: U.S. Marine Corps
Birthday: 21 September 1948
Place of Birth: Lexington, Lexington County, Virginia
Date of Death: 21 April 1967
Place of Death: Republic of Vietnam
Cemetery: Rosewood Cemetery—Lewisburg, West Virginia
Entered Service at: Portland, Multnomah County, Oregon
Unit: Company F, 2d Battalion, 1st Marines, 1st Marine Division (Rein) FMF
Served as: Rifleman
Battle or Place of Action: Binh Son, Republic of Vietnam
Date of Action: 21 April 1967
Date of Presentation: 22 October 1968
Place of Presentation: Marine Barracks, Washington D.C., presented by Secretary of the Navy Paul R. Ignatius to his family
Citation: For conspicuous gallantry and intrepidity at the risk of his life above and beyond the call of duty. On 21 April 1967, during Operation Union, elements of Company F, conducting offensive operations at Binh Son, encountered a firmly entrenched enemy force and immediately deployed to engage them. The marines in Pfc. Martini's platoon assaulted across an open rice paddy to within 20 meters of the enemy trench line where they were suddenly struck by hand grenades, intense small-arms, automatic-weapons, and mortar fire. The enemy onslaught killed 14 and wounded 18 marines, pinning the remainder of the platoon down behind a low paddy dike. In the face of imminent danger, Pfc. Martini immediately crawled over the dike to a forward open area within 15 meters of the enemy position where, continuously exposed to the hostile fire, he hurled hand grenades, killing several of the enemy. Crawling back through the intense fire, he rejoined his platoon which had moved to the relative safety of a trench line. From this position he observed several of his wounded comrades lying helpless in the fire-swept paddy. Although he knew that one man had been killed attempting to assist the wounded, Pfc. Martini raced through the open area and dragged a comrade back to a friendly position. In spite of a serious wound received during this first daring rescue, he again braved the unrelenting fury of the enemy fire to aid another companion lying wounded only 20 meters in front of the enemy trench line. As he reached the fallen marine, he received a mortal wound, but disregarding his own condition, he began to drag the marine toward his platoon's position. Observing men from his unit attempting to leave the security of their position to aid him, concerned only for their safety, he called to them to remain under cover, and through a final supreme effort, moved his injured comrade to where he could be pulled to safety, before he fell, succumbing to his wounds. Stouthearted and indomitable, Pfc. Martini unhesitatingly yielded his life to save two of his comrades and insure the safety of the remainder of his platoon. His outstanding courage, valiant fighting spirit and selfless devotion to duty reflected the highest credit upon himself, the Marine Corps, and the U.S. Naval Service. He gallantly gave his life for his country.

3297 ◆ *MAXAM, LARRY LEONARD

Rank: Corporal
Service: U.S. Marine Corps
Birthday: 9 January 1948
Place of Birth: Glendale, Los Angeles County, California
Date of Death: 2 February 1968
Place of Death: Republic of Vietnam
Cemetery: National Memorial Cemetery of the Pacific (J-388) (MH)—Honolulu, Hawaii
Entered Service at: Los Angeles, Los Angeles County, California
Unit: Company D, 1st Battalion, 4th Marines, 3d Marine Division (Rein) FMF
Served as: Fire Team Leader
Battle or Place of Action: Cam Lo District, Quang Tri Province, Republic of Vietnam
Date of Action: 2 February 1968
Date of Presentation: 20 April 1970
Place of Presentation: The White House, presented by Pres. Richard M. Nixon to his family
Citation: For conspicuous gallantry and intrepidity at the risk of his life above and beyond the call of duty while serving as a fire team leader with Company D. The Cam Lo District Headquarters came under extremely heavy rocket, artillery, mortar, and recoilless-rifle fire from a numerically superior enemy force destroying a portion of the defense perimeter. Cpl. Maxam observing the enemy massing for an assault into the compound across the remaining defensive wire, instructed his assistant fire team leader to take charge of the fire team, and unhesitatingly proceeded to the weakened section of the perimeter. Completely exposed to the concentrated enemy fire, he sustained multiple fragmentation wounds from exploding grenades as he ran to an abandoned machine-gun position. Reaching the emplacement, he grasped the machine gun and commenced to deliver effective fire on the advancing enemy. As the enemy directed maximum firepower against the determined marine, Cpl. Maxam's position received a direct hit from a rocket-propelled grenade, knocking him backwards and inflicting severe fragmentation wounds to his face and right eye. Although momentarily stunned and in intense pain, Cpl. Maxam courageously assumed his firing position and subsequently was struck again by small-arms fire. With resolute determination, he gallantly continued to deliver intense machine-gun fire, causing the enemy to retreat through the defensive wire to positions of cover. In a desperate attempt to silence his weapon, the North Vietnamese threw hand grenades and directed recoilless-rifle fire against him inflicting two additional wounds. Too weak to reload his machine gun, Cpl. Maxam fell to a prone position and valiantly continued to deliver effective fire with his rifle. After 1 1/2 hours, during which he was hit repeatedly by fragments from exploding grenades and concentrated small-arms

fire, he succumbed to his wounds, having successfully defended nearly half of the perimeter singlehandedly. Cpl. Maxam's aggressive fighting spirit, inspiring valor and selfless devotion to duty, reflected great credit upon himself and the Marine Corps and upheld the highest traditions of the U.S. Naval Service. He gallantly gave his life for his country.

3298 ◆ McCLEERY, FINNIS DAWSON

Rank: Sergeant First Class
Service: U.S. Army
Birthday: 25 December 1927
Place of Birth: Stephenville, Erath County, Texas
Entered Service at: San Angelo, Tom Green County, Texas
Unit: 1st Platoon, Company A, 1st Battalion, 6th U.S. Infantry, Americal Division
Served as: Platoon Leader
Battle or Place of Action: Quang Tin Province, Republic of Vietnam
Date of Action: 14 May 1968
G.O. Number, Date: 19, 24 March 1971
Date of Presentation: 2 March 1971
Place of Presentation: The White House (East Ballroom), presented by Pres. Richard M. Nixon
Citation: For conspicuous gallantry and intrepidity in action at the risk of his life above and beyond the call of duty. P/Sgt. McCleery, U.S. Army, distinguished himself while serving as platoon leader of the 1st Platoon of Company A. A combined force was assigned the mission of assaulting a reinforced company of North Vietnamese Army regulars, well-entrenched on Hill 352, 17 miles west of Tam Ky. As P/Sgt. McCleery led his men up the hill and across an open area to close with the enemy, his platoon and other friendly elements were pinned down by tremendously heavy fire coming from the fortified enemy positions. Realizing the severe damage that the enemy could inflict on the combined force in the event that their attack was completely halted, P/Sgt. McCleery rose from his sheltered position and began a one-man assault on the bunker complex. With extraordinary courage, he moved across 60 meters of open ground as bullets struck all around him and rockets and grenades literally exploded at his feet. As he came within 30 meters of the key enemy bunker, P/Sgt. McCleery began firing furiously from the hip and throwing hand grenades. At this point in his assault, he was painfully wounded by shrapnel, but, with complete disregard for his wound, he continued his advance on the key bunker and killed all of its occupants. Having successfully and singlehandedly reached the enemy perimeter, he climbed to the top of the bunker he had just captured and, in full view of the enemy, shouted encouragement to his men to follow his assault. As the friendly forces moved forward, P/Sgt. McCleery began a lateral assault on the enemy bunker line. He continued to expose himself to the intense enemy fire as he moved from bunker to bunker, destroying each in turn. He was wounded a second time by shrapnel as he destroyed and routed the enemy from the hill. P/Sgt. McCleery is personally credited with eliminating several key enemy positions and inspiring the assault that resulted in gaining control of Hill 352. His extraordinary heroism at the risk of his life above and beyond the call of duty was in keeping with the highest standards of the military service, and reflects great credit on him, the Americal Division, and the U.S. Army.

3299 ◆ *McDONALD, PHILL GENE

Rank: Private First Class
Service: U.S. Army
Birthday: 13 September 1941
Place of Birth: Avondale, McDowell County, West Virginia
Date of Death: 7 June 1968
Place of Death: Republic of Vietnam
Cemetery: Guilford Memorial Park (MH)—Greensboro, North Carolina
Entered Service at: Beckley, Raleigh County, West Virginia
Unit: 1st Platoon, Company A, 1st Battalion, 14th Infantry, 4th Infantry Division
Served as: Team Leader
Battle or Place of Action: near Kontum City, Republic of Vietnam
Date of Action: 7 June 1968
G.O. Number, Date: 20, 23 April 1970
Date of Presentation: 7 April 1970
Place of Presentation: The White House, presented by Pres. Richard M. Nixon to his family
Citation: For conspicuous gallantry and intrepidity in action at the risk of his life above and beyond the call of duty. Pfc. McDonald distinguished himself while serving as a team leader with the 1st Platoon of Company A. While on a combat mission his platoon came under heavy barrage of automatic-weapons fire from a well-concealed company-size enemy force. Volunteering to escort two wounded comrades to an evacuation point, Pfc. McDonald crawled through intense fire to destroy with a grenade an enemy automatic weapon threatening the safety of the evacuation. Returning to his platoon, he again volunteered to provide covering fire for the maneuver of the platoon from its exposed position. Realizing the threat he posed, enemy gunners concentrated their fire on Pfc. McDonald's position, seriously wounding him. Despite his painful wounds, Pfc. McDonald recovered the weapon of a wounded machine gunner to provide accurate covering fire for the gunner's evacuation. When other soldiers were pinned down by a heavy volume of fire from a hostile machine gun to his front, Pfc. McDonald crawled toward the enemy position to destroy it with grenades. He was mortally wounded in this intrepid action. Pfc. McDonald's gallantry at the risk of his life, which resulted in the saving of the lives of his comrades, is in keeping with the highest traditions of the military service and reflect great credit upon himself, his unit, and the U.S. Army.

3300 ◆ McGINTY III, JOHN JAMES

Rank: Second Lieutenant (rank at time of action: Staff Sergeant) (highest rank: Captain)
Service: U.S. Marine Corps
Birthday: 21 January 1940
Place of Birth: Boston, Suffolk County, Massachusetts

Entered Service at: Laurel Bay, South Carolina
Unit: Company K, 3d Battalion, 4th Marines, 3d Marine Division (Rein) FMF
Served as: Acting Platoon Leader
Battle or Place of Action: Quang Tri Province, Republic of Vietnam
Date of Action: 18 July 1966
Date of Presentation: 12 March 1968
Place of Presentation: The White House, presented by Pres. Lyndon B. Johnson
Citation: For conspicuous gallantry and intrepidity at the risk of his life above and beyond the call of duty. 2d Lt. McGinty's platoon, which was providing rear security to protect the withdrawal of the battalion from a position which had been under attack for three days, came under heavy small-arms, automatic-weapons, and mortar fire from an estimated enemy regiment. With each successive human wave which assaulted his 32-man platoon during the four-hour battle, 2d Lt. McGinty rallied his men to beat off the enemy. In one bitter assault, two of the squads became separated from the remainder of the platoon. With complete disregard for his safety, 2d Lt. McGinty charged through intense automatic-weapons and mortar fire to their position. Finding 20 men wounded and the medical corpsman killed, he quickly reloaded ammunition magazines and weapons for the wounded men and directed their fire upon the enemy. Although he was painfully wounded as he moved to care for the disabled men, he continued to shout encouragement to his troops and to direct their fire so effectively that the attacking hordes were beaten off. When the enemy tried to out-flank his position, he killed five of them at point-blank range with his pistol. When they again seemed on the verge of overrunning the small force, he skillfully adjusted artillery and air strikes within 50 yards of his position. This destructive firepower routed the enemy, who left an estimated 500 bodies on the battlefield. 2d Lt. McGinty's personal heroism, indomitable leadership, selfless devotion to duty, and bold fighting spirit inspired his men to resist the repeated attacks by a fanatical enemy, reflected great credit upon himself, and upheld the highest traditions of the Marine Corps and the U.S. Naval Service.

3301 ◆ McGONAGLE, WILLIAM LOREN

Rank: Captain (rank at time of action: Commander)
Service: U.S. Navy
Birthday: 19 November 1925
Place of Birth: Wichita, Sedgwick County, Kansas
Entered Service at: Thermal, Riverside County, California
Unit: U.S.S. *Liberty* (AGTR-5)
Served as: Captain
Battle or Place of Action: International waters, Eastern Mediterranean
Date of Action: 8-9 June 1967
Date of Presentation: 6 June 1968
Place of Presentation: Admiral Leutze Park, Washington Navy Yard, presented by Sec. of the Navy Paul R. Ignatius
Citation: For conspicuous gallantry and intrepidity at the risk of his life above and beyond the call of duty. Sailing in international waters, the *Liberty* was attacked without warning by a jet fighter aircraft and motor torpedo boats which inflicted many casualties among the crew and caused extreme damage to the ship. Although severely wounded during the first air attack, Capt. McGonagle remained at his battle station on the badly damaged bridge and, with full knowledge of the seriousness of his wounds, subordinated his own welfare to the safety and survival of his command. Steadfastly refusing any treatment which would take him away from his post, he calmly continued to exercise firm command of his ship. Despite continuous exposure to fire, he maneuvered his ship, directed its defense, supervised the control of flooding and fire, and saw to the care of the casualties. Capt. McGonagle's extraordinary valor under these conditions inspired the surviving members of the *Liberty*'s crew, many of them seriously wounded, to heroic efforts to overcome the battle damage and keep the ship afloat. Subsequent to the attack, although in great pain and weak from loss of blood, Capt. McGonagle remained at his battle station and continued to command his ship for more than 17 hours. It was only after rendezvous with a U.S. destroyer that he relinquished personal control of the *Liberty* and permitted himself to be removed from the bridge. Even then, he refused much needed medical attention until convinced that the seriously wounded among his crew had been treated. Capt. McGonagle's superb professionalism, courageous fighting spirit, and valiant leadership saved his ship and many lives. His actions sustain and enhance the finest traditions of the U.S. Naval Service.

3302 ◆ *McKIBBEN, RAY

Rank: Sergeant
Service: U.S. Army
Birthday: 27 October 1946
Place of Birth: Felton, Haralson County, Georgia
Date of Death: 8 December 1968
Place of Death: Republic of Vietnam
Cemetery: Center Baptist Cemetery (MH)—Felton, Georgia
Entered Service at: Atlanta, Fulton County, Georgia
Unit: Troop B, 7th Squadron (Airmobile), 17th Cavalry, 1st Aviation Brigade
Served as: Team Leader
Battle or Place of Action: near Song Mao, Republic of Vietnam
Date of Action: 8 December 1968
G.O. Number, Date: 21, 23 April 1970
Date of Presentation: 7 April 1970
Place of Presentation: The White House, presented by Pres. Richard M. Nixon to his family
Citation: For conspicuous gallantry and intrepidity in action at the risk of his life above and beyond the call of duty. Sgt. McKibben distinguished himself in action while serving as team leader of the point element of a reconnaissance patrol of Troop B, operating in enemy territory. Sgt. McKibben was leading his point element in a movement to contact along a well-traveled trail when the lead element came under heavy automatic-weapons fire from a fortified bunker position, forcing the patrol to take cover. Sgt. McKibben, appraising the situation and without regard for his own safety, charged

through bamboo and heavy brush to the fortified position, killed the enemy gunner, secured the weapon and directed his patrol element forward. As the patrol moved out, Sgt. McKibben observed enemy movement to the flank of the patrol. Fire support from helicopter gunships was requested and the area was effectively neutralized. The patrol again continued its mission and as the lead element rounded the bend of a river it came under heavy automatic-weapons fire from camouflaged bunkers. As Sgt. McKibben was deploying his men to covered positions, he observed one of his men fall wounded. Although bullets were hitting all around the wounded man, Sgt. McKibben, with complete disregard for his safety, sprang to his comrade's side and under heavy enemy fire pulled him to safety behind the cover of a rock emplacement where he administered hasty first aid. Sgt. McKibben, seeing that his comrades were pinned down and were unable to deliver effective fire against the enemy bunkers, again undertook a singlehanded assault of the enemy defenses. He charged through the brush and hail of automatic-weapons fire closing on the first bunker, killing the enemy with accurate rifle fire and securing the enemy's weapon. He continued his assault against the next bunker, firing his rifle as he charged. As he approached the second bunker his rifle ran out of ammunition, however; he used the captured enemy weapon until it too was empty, at that time he silenced the bunker with well-placed hand grenades. He reloaded his weapon and covered the advance of his men as they moved forward. Observing the fire of another bunker impeding the patrol's advance, Sgt. McKibben again singlehandedly assaulted the new position. As he neared the bunker he was mortally wounded but was able to fire a final burst from his weapon killing the enemy and enabling the patrol to continue the assault. Sgt. McKibben's indomitable courage, extraordinary heroism, profound concern for the welfare of his fellow soldiers, and disregard for his personal safety saved the lives of his comrades and enabled the patrol to accomplish its mission. Sgt. McKibben's gallantry in action at the cost of his life above and beyond the call of duty are in the highest traditions of the military service and reflect great credit upon himself, his unit, and the U.S. Army.

3303 ◆ *McMAHON, THOMAS JOSEPH

Rank: Specialist Fourth Class
Service: U.S. Army
Birthday: 24 June 1948
Place of Birth: Washington, D.C.
Date of Death: 19 March 1969
Place of Death: Republic of Vietnam
Cemetery: Mount Hope Cemetery (MH)—Lewiston, Maine
Entered Service at: Portland, Cumberland County, Maine
Unit: Company A, 2d Battalion, 1st Infantry, 196th Infantry Brigade, Americal Division
Served as: Medical Aidman
Battle or Place of Action: Quang Tin Province, Republic of Vietnam
Date of Action: 19 March 1969
G.O. Number, Date: 46, 28 August 1970
Date of Presentation: 6 August 1970
Place of Presentation: The White House, presented by Pres. Richard M. Nixon to his family
Citation: For conspicuous gallantry and intrepidity in action at the risk of his life above and beyond the call of duty. Sp4c. McMahon distinguished himself while serving as medical aidman with Company A. When the lead elements of his company came under heavy fire from well-fortified enemy positions, three soldiers fell seriously wounded. Sp4c. McMahon, with complete disregard for his safety, left his covered position and ran through intense enemy fire to the side of one of the wounded, administered first aid, and then carried him to safety. He returned through the hail of fire to the side of a second wounded man. Although painfully wounded by an exploding mortar round while returning the wounded man to a secure position, Sp4c. McMahon refused medical attention and heroically ran back through the heavy enemy fire toward his remaining wounded comrade. He fell mortally wounded before he could rescue the last man. Sp4c. McMahon's undaunted concern for the welfare of his comrades at the cost of his life are in keeping with the highest traditions of the military service and reflect great credit on himself, his unit, and the U.S. Army.

3304 ◆ McNERNEY, DAVID HERBERT

Rank: First Sergeant
Service: U.S. Army
Birthday: 2 June 1931
Place of Birth: Lowell, Middlesex County, Massachusetts
Entered Service at: Fort Bliss, El Paso County, Texas
Unit: Company A, 1st Battalion, 8th Infantry, 4th Infantry Division
Served as: Company First Sergeant
Battle or Place of Action: Polei Doc, Republic of Vietnam
Date of Action: 22 March 1967
G.O. Number, Date: 62, 22 October 1968
Date of Presentation: 19 September 1968
Place of Presentation: The White House, presented by Pres. Lyndon B. Johnson
Citation: 1st Sgt. McNerney distinguished himself when his unit was attacked by a North Vietnamese battalion near Polei Doc. Running through the hail of enemy fire to the area of heaviest contact, he was assisting in the development of a defensive perimeter when he encountered several enemy at close range. He killed the enemy but was painfully injured when blown from his feet by a grenade. In spite of this injury, he assaulted and destroyed an enemy machine-gun position that had pinned down five of his comrades beyond the defensive line. Upon learning his commander and artillery forward observer had been killed, he assumed command of the company. He adjusted artillery fire to within 20 meters of the position in a daring measure to repulse enemy assaults. When the smoke grenades used to mark the position were gone, he moved into a nearby clearing to designate the location to friendly aircraft. In spite of enemy fire he remained exposed until he was certain the position was spotted and then climbed into a tree and tied the identification panel to its highest branches. Then he moved among his men readjusting

their position, encouraging the defenders and checking the wounded. As the hostile assaults slackened, he began clearing a helicopter landing site to evacuate the wounded. When explosives were needed to remove large trees, he crawled outside the relative safety of his perimeter to collect demolition material from abandoned rucksacks. Moving through a fusillade of fire he returned with the explosives that were vital to the clearing of the landing zone. Disregarding the pain of his injury and refusing medical evacuation, 1st Sgt. McNerney remained with his unit until the next day when the new commander arrived. 1st Sgt. McNerney's outstanding heroism and leadership were inspirational to his comrades. His actions were in keeping with the highest traditions of the U.S. Army and reflect great credit upon himself and the Armed Forces of his country.

3305 ◆ *McWETHY JR., EDGAR LEE

Rank: Specialist Fifth Class
Service: U.S. Army
Birthday: 22 November 1944
Place of Birth: Leadville, Lake County, Colorado
Date of Death: 21 June 1967
Place of Death: Republic of Vietnam
Cemetery: Pence Cemetery—Baxter Springs, Kansas
Entered Service at: Denver, Denver County, Colorado
Unit: Company B, 1st Battalion, 5th Cavalry, 1st Cavalry Division (Airmobile)
Served as: Medical Aidman
Battle or Place of Action: Binh Dinh Province, Republic of Vietnam
Date of Action: 21 June 1967
G.O. Number, Date: 68, 27 October 1969
Date of Presentation: 16 October 1969
Place of Presentation: The White House, presented by Pres. Richard M. Nixon to his family
Citation: For conspicuous gallantry and intrepidity in action at the risk of his life above and beyond the call of duty. Serving as a medical aidman with Company B, Sp5c. McWethy accompanied his platoon to the site of a downed helicopter. Shortly after the platoon established a defensive perimeter around the aircraft, a large enemy force attacked the position from three sides with a heavy volume of automatic-weapons fire and grenades. The platoon leader and his radio operator were wounded almost immediately, and Sp5c. McWethy rushed across the fire-swept area to their assistance. Although he could not help the mortally wounded radio operator, Sp5c. McWethy's timely first aid enabled the platoon leader to retain command during this critical period. Hearing a call for aid, Sp5c. McWethy started across the open toward the injured men, but was wounded in the head and was knocked to the ground. He regained his feet and continued on but was hit again, this time in the leg. Struggling onward despite his wounds, he gained the side of his comrades and treated their injuries. Observing another fallen rifleman lying in an exposed position raked by enemy fire, Sp5c. McWethy moved toward him without hesitation. Although the enemy fire wounded him a third time, Sp5c. McWethy reached his fallen companion. Though weakened and in extreme pain, Sp5c. McWethy gave the wounded man artificial respiration but suffered a fourth and fatal wound. Through his indomitable courage, complete disregard for his safety, and demonstrated concern for his fellow soldiers, Sp5c. McWethy inspired the members of his platoon and contributed in great measure to their successful defense of the position and the ultimate rout of the enemy force. Sp5c. McWethy's profound sense of duty, bravery, and his willingness to accept extraordinary risks in order to help the men of his unit are characteristic of the highest traditions of the military service and reflect great credit upon himself and the U.S. Army.

3306 ◆ *MICHAEL, DON LESLIE

Rank: Specialist Fourth Class
Service: U.S. Army
Birthday: 31 July 1947
Place of Birth: Florence, Lauderdale County, Alabama
Date of Death: 8 April 1967
Place of Death: Republic of Vietnam
Cemetery: Mount Pleasant Cemetery (MH)—Lexington, Alabama
Entered Service at: Montgomery, Montgonery County, Alabama
Unit: Company C, 4th Battalion, 503d Infantry, 173d Airborne Brigade
Served as: Rifleman
Battle or Place of Action: Republic of Vietnam
Date of Action: 8 April 1967
G.O. Number, Date: 41, 13 June 1969
Date of Presentation: 23 May 1969
Place of Presentation: The White House, presented by Pres. Richard M. Nixon to his family
Citation: For conspicuous gallantry and intrepidity at the risk of his life above and beyond the call of duty. Sp4c. Michael, U.S. Army, distinguished himself while serving with Company C. Sp4c. Michael was part of a platoon which was moving through an area of suspected enemy activity. While the rest of the platoon stopped to provide security, the squad to which Sp4c. Michael was assigned moved forward to investigate signs of recent enemy activity. After moving approximately 125 meters, the squad encountered a single Viet Cong soldier. When he was fired upon by the squad's machine gunner, other Viet Cong opened fire with automatic weapons from a well-concealed bunker to the squad's right front. The volume of enemy fire was so withering as to pin down the entire squad and halt all forward movement. Realizing the gravity of the situation, Sp4c. Michael exposed himself to throw two grenades, but failed to eliminate the enemy position. From his position on the left flank, Sp4c. Michael maneuvered forward with two more grenades until he was within 20 meters of the enemy bunkers, when he again exposed himself to throw two grenades, which failed to detonate. Undaunted, Sp4c. Michael made his way back to the friendly positions to obtain more grenades. With two grenades in hand, he again started his perilous move towards the enemy bunker, which by this time was under intense artillery fire from friendly positions. As he neared the bunker,

an enemy soldier attacked him from a concealed position. Sp4c. Michael killed him with his rifle and, in spite of the enemy fire and the exploding artillery rounds, was successful in destroying the enemy positions. Sp4c. Michael took up pursuit of the remnants of the retreating enemy. When his comrades reached Sp4c. Michael, he had been mortally wounded. His inspiring display of determination and courage saved the lives of many of his comrades and successfully eliminated a destructive enemy force. Sp4c. Michael's actions were in keeping with the highest traditions of the military service and reflect the utmost credit upon himself and the U.S. Army.

3307 ◆ MILLER, FRANKLIN DOUGLAS

Rank: Staff Sergeant (highest rank: Command Sergeant Major)
Service: U.S. Army
Birthday: 27 January 1945
Place of Birth: Elizabeth City, Pasquotank County, North Carolina
Entered Service at: Albuquerque, Bernalillo County, New Mexico
Unit: 5th Special Forces Group, 1st Special Forces
Served as: Team Leader
Battle or Place of Action: Kontum Province, Republic of Vietnam
Date of Action: 5 January 1970
G.O. Number, Date: 35, 16 July 1971
Date of Presentation: 15 June 1971
Place of Presentation: The White House, presented by Pres. Richard M. Nixon
Citation: For conspicuous gallantry and intrepidity in action at the risk of his life above and beyond the call of duty. S/Sgt. Miller, 5th Special Forces Group, distinguished himself while serving as team leader of an American-Vietnamese long-range reconnaissance patrol operating deep within enemy-controlled territory. Leaving the helicopter insertion point, the patrol moved forward on its mission. Suddenly, one of the team members tripped a hostile booby trap which wounded four soldiers. S/Sgt. Miller, knowing that the explosion would alert the enemy, quickly administered first aid to the wounded and directed the team into positions across a small stream bed at the base of a steep hill. Within a few minutes, S/Sgt. Miller saw the lead element of what he estimated to be a platoon-size enemy force moving toward his location. Concerned for the safety of his men, he directed the small team to move up the hill to a more secure position. He remained alone, separated from the patrol, to meet the attack. S/Sgt. Miller singlehandedly repulsed two determined attacks by the numerically superior enemy force and caused them to withdraw in disorder. He rejoined his team, established contact with a forward air controller, and arranged the evacuation of his patrol. However, the only suitable extraction location in the heavy jungle was a bomb crater some 150 meters from the team location. S/Sgt. Miller reconnoitered the route to the crater and led his men through the enemy-controlled jungle to the extraction site. As the evacuation helicopter hovered over the crater to pick up the patrol, the enemy launched a savage automatic-weapons and rocket-propelled-grenade attack against the beleaguered team, driving off the rescue helicopter. S/Sgt. Miller led the team in a valiant defense which drove back the enemy in its attempt to overrun the small patrol. Although seriously wounded and with every man in his patrol a casualty, S/Sgt. Miller moved forward to again singlehandedly meet the hostile attackers. From his forward exposed position, S/Sgt. Miller gallantly repelled two attacks by the enemy before a friendly relief force reached the patrol location. S/Sgt. Miller's gallantry, intrepidity in action, and selfless devotion to the welfare of his comrades are in keeping with the highest traditions of the military service and reflect great credit on him, his unit, and the U.S. Army.

3308 ◆ *MILLER, GARY LEE

Rank: First Lieutenant
Service: U.S. Army
Birthday: 19 March 1947
Place of Birth: Covington, Covington County, Virginia
Date of Death: 16 February 1969
Place of Death: Republic of Vietnam
Cemetery: Allegheny Memorial Park—Covington, Virginia
Entered Service at: Roanoke, Roanoke County, Virginia
Unit: Company A, 1st Battalion, 28th Infantry, 1st Infantry Division
Served as: Platoon Leader
Battle or Place of Action: Binh Duong Province, Republic of Vietnam
Date of Action: 16 February 1969
G.O. Number, Date: 44, 28 August 1970
Date of Presentation: 6 August 1970
Place of Presentation: The White House, presented by Pres. Richard M. Nixon to his family
Citation: For conspicuous gallantry and intrepidity in action at the risk of his life above and beyond the call of duty. 1st Lt. Miller, Infantry, Company A, was serving as a platoon leader at night when his company ambushed a hostile force infiltrating from Cambodian sanctuaries. After contact with the enemy was broken, 1st Lt. Miller led a reconnaissance patrol from their prepared positions through the early evening darkness and dense tropical growth to search the area for enemy casualties. As the group advanced they were suddenly attacked. 1st Lt. Miller was seriously wounded. However, the group fought back with telling effect on the hostile force. An enemy grenade was thrown into the midst of the friendly patrol group and all took cover except 1st Lt. Miller, who in the dim light located the grenade and threw himself on it, absorbing the force of the explosion with his body. His action saved nearby members of his patrol from almost certain serious injury. The extraordinary courage and selflessness displayed by this officer were an inspiration to his comrades and are in the highest traditions of the U.S. Army.

3309 ◆ MODRZEJEWSKI, ROBERT JOSEPH

Rank: Major (rank at time of action: Captain) (highest rank: Colonel)
Service: U.S. Marine Corps

Birthday: 3 July 1934
Place of Birth: Milwaukee, Milwaukee County, Wisconsin
Entered Service at: Milwaukee, Milwaukee County, Wisconsin
Unit: Company K, 3d Battalion, 4th Marines, 3d Marine Division (Rein) FMF
Served as: Company Commander
Battle or Place of Action: Republic of Vietnam
Date of Action: 15-18 July 1966
Date of Presentation: 12 March 1968
Place of Presentation: The White House, presented by Pres. Lyndon B. Johnson
Citation: For conspicuous gallantry and intrepidity at the risk of his life above and beyond the call of duty. On 15 July, during Operation Hastings, Company K was landed in an enemy-infested jungle area to establish a blocking position at a major enemy trail network. Shortly after landing, the company encountered a reinforced enemy platoon in a well-organized, defensive position. Maj. Modrzejewski led his men in the successful seizure of the enemy redoubt, which contained large quantities of ammunition and supplies. That evening, a numerically superior enemy force counterattacked in an effort to retake the vital supply area, thus setting the pattern of activity for the next 2 1/2 days. In the first series of attacks, the enemy assaulted repeatedly in overwhelming numbers but each time was repulsed by the gallant marines. The second night, the enemy struck in battalion strength, and Maj. Modrzejewski was wounded in this intensive action which was fought at close quarters. Although exposed to enemy fire, and despite his painful wounds, he crawled 200 meters to provide critically needed ammunition to an exposed element of his command and was constantly present wherever the fighting was the heaviest; despite numerous casualties, a dwindling supply of ammunition, and the knowledge that they were surrounded, he skillfully directed artillery fire to within a few meters of his position and courageously inspired the efforts of his company in repelling the aggressive enemy attack. On 18 July, Company K was attacked by a regimental-size enemy force. Although his unit was vastly outnumbered and weakened by the previous fighting, Maj. Modrzejewski reorganized his men and calmly moved among them to encourage and direct their efforts to heroic limits as they fought to overcome the vicious enemy onslaught. Again he called in air and artillery strikes at close-range with devastating effect on the enemy, which together with the bold and determined fighting of the men of Company K, repulsed the fanatical attack of the larger North Vietnamese force. His unparalleled personal heroism and indomitable leadership inspired his men to a significant victory over the enemy force and reflected great credit upon himself, the Marine Corps, and the U.S. Naval Service.

3310 ◆ *MOLNAR, FRANKIE ZOLY

Rank: Staff Sergeant
Service: U.S. Army
Birthday: 14 February 1943
Place of Birth: Logan, Logan County, West Virginia
Date of Death: 20 May 1967
Place of Death: Republic of Vietnam
Cemetery: Highland Memorial Gardens Cemetery—Logan, West Virginia
Entered Service at: Fresno, Fresno County, California
Unit: Company B, 1st Battalion, 8th Infantry, 4th Infantry Division
Served as: Squad Leader
Battle or Place of Action: Kontum Province, Republic of Vietnam
Date of Action: 20 May 1967
G.O. Number, Date: 51, 8 August 1969
Date of Presentation: 10 July 1969
Place of Presentation: The White House, presented by Pres. Richard M. Nixon to his family
Citation: For conspicuous gallantry and intrepidity in action at the risk of his life above and beyond the call of duty. S/Sgt. Molnar distinguished himself while serving as a squad leader with Company B, during combat operations. Shortly after the battalion's defensive perimeter was established, it was hit by intense mortar fire as the prelude to a massive enemy night attack. S/Sgt. Molnar immediately left his sheltered location to insure the readiness of his squad to meet the attack. As he crawled through the position, he discovered a group of enemy soldiers closing in on his squad area. His accurate rifle fire killed five of the enemy and forced the remainder to flee. When the mortar fire stopped, the enemy attacked in a human wave supported by grenades, rockets, automatic-weapons, and small-arms fire. After assisting to repel the first enemy assault, S/Sgt. Molnar found that his squad's ammunition and grenade supply were nearly expended. Again leaving the relative safety of his position, he crawled through intense enemy fire to secure additional ammunition and distribute it to his squad. He rejoined his men to beat back the renewed enemy onslaught, and he moved about his area providing medical aid and assisting in the evacuation of the wounded. With the help of several men, he was preparing to move a severely wounded soldier when an enemy hand grenade was thrown into the group. The first to see the grenade, S/Sgt. Molnar threw himself on it and absorbed the deadly blast to save his comrades. His demonstrated selflessness and inspirational leadership on the battlefield were a major factor in the successful defense of the American position and are in keeping with the finest traditions of the U.S. Army. S/Sgt. Molnar's actions reflect great credit upon himself, his unit, and the U.S. Army.

3311 ◆ *MONROE, JAMES HOWARD

Rank: Private First Class
Service: U.S. Army
Birthday: 17 October 1944
Place of Birth: Aurora, Du Page County, Illinois
Date of Death: 16 February 1967
Place of Death: Republic of Vietnam
Cemetery: Wheaton Cemetery—Wheaton, Illinois
Entered Service at: Chicago, Cook County, Illinois
Unit: Headquarters & Headquarters Company, 1st Battalion, 8th Cavalry, 1st Cavalry Division (Airmobile)
Served as: Medical Aidman

Battle or Place of Action: Bong Son, Hoai Nhon Province, Republic of Vietnam
Date of Action: 16 February 1967
G.O. Number, Date: 68, 5 November 1968
Date of Presentation: 17 October 1968
Place of Presentation: The Pentagon, presented by Sec. of the Army Stanley R. Resor to his family
Citation: For conspicuous gallantry and intrepidity in action at the risk of his life above and beyond the call of duty. His platoon was deployed in a night ambush when the position was suddenly subjected to an intense and accurate grenade attack, and one foxhole was hit immediately. Responding without hesitation to the calls for help from the wounded men, Pfc. Monroe moved forward through heavy small-arms fire to the foxhole but found that all of the men had expired. He turned immediately and crawled back through the deadly hail of fire toward other calls for aid. He moved to the platoon sergeant's position where he found the radio operator bleeding profusely from fragmentation and bullet wounds. Ignoring the continuing enemy attack, Pfc. Monroe began treating the wounded man when he saw a live grenade fall directly in front of the position. He shouted a warning to all those nearby, pushed the wounded radio operator and the platoon sergeant to one side, and lunged forward to smother the grenade's blast with his body. Through his valorous actions, performed in a flash of inspired selflessness, Pfc. Monroe saved the lives of two of his comrades and prevented the probable injury of several others. His gallantry and intrepidity were in the highest traditions of the U.S. Army, and reflect great credit upon himself and the Armed Forces of his country.

3312 ◆ *MORGAN, WILLIAM DAVID

Rank: Corporal
Service: U.S. Marine Corps
Birthday: 17 September 1947
Place of Birth: Pittsburgh, Allegheny County, Pennsylvania
Date of Death: 25 February 1969
Place of Death: Republic of Vietnam
Cemetery: Mount Lebanon Cemetery (MH)—Pittsburgh, Pennsylvania
Entered Service at: Pittsburgh, Allegheny County, Pennsylvania
Unit: Company H, 2d Battalion, 9th Marines, 3d Marine Division (Rein) FMF
Served as: Squad Leader
Battle or Place of Action: southeast of Vandegrift Combat Base, Quang Tri Province, Republic of Vietnam
Date of Action: 25 February 1969
Date of Presentation: 6 August 1970
Place of Presentation: The White House, presented by Pres. Richard M. Nixon to his family
Citation: For conspicuous gallantry and intrepidity at the risk of his life above and beyond the call of duty while serving as a squad leader with Company H, in operations against the enemy. While participating in Operation Dewey Canyon southeast of Vandegrift Combat Base, one of the squads of Cpl. Morgan's platoon was temporarily pinned down and sustained several casualties while attacking a North Vietnamese Army force occupying a heavily fortified bunker complex. Observing that two of the wounded marines had fallen in a position dangerously exposed to the enemy fire and that all attempts to evacuate them were halted by a heavy volume of automatic-weapons fire and rocket-propelled grenades. Cpl. Morgan unhesitatingly maneuvered through the dense jungle undergrowth to a road that passed in front of a hostile emplacement which was the principal source of enemy fire. Fully aware of the possible consequences of his valiant action, but thinking only of the welfare of his injured companions, Cpl. Morgan shouted words of encouragement to them as he initiated an aggressive assault against the hostile bunker. While charging across the open road, he was clearly visible to the hostile soldiers who turned their fire in his direction and mortally wounded him, but his diversionary tactic enabled the remainder of his squad to retrieve their casualties and overrun the North Vietnamese Army position. His heroic and determined actions saved the lives of two fellow marines and were instrumental in the subsequent defeat of the enemy. Cpl. Morgan's indomitable courage, inspiring initiative, and selfless devotion to duty upheld the highest traditions of the Marine Corps and of the U.S. Naval Service. He gallantly gave his life for his country.

3313 ◆ MORRIS, CHARLES BEDFORD

Rank: Staff Sergeant (rank at time of action: Sergeant) (highest rank: Sergeant Major)
Service: U.S. Army
Birthday: 29 December 1931
Place of Birth: Carroll County, Virginia
Entered Service at: Roanoke, Roanoke County, Virginia
Unit: Company A, 2d Battalion (Airborne), 503d Infantry, 173d Airborne Brigade (Separate)
Served as: Platoon Sergeant
Battle or Place of Action: near Xuan Loc, Republic of Vietnam
Date of Action: 29 June 1966
G.O. Number, Date: 51, 14 December 1967
Date of Presentation: 16 November 1967
Place of Presentation: The White House, presented by Pres. Lyndon B. Johnson
Citation: For conspicuous gallantry and intrepidity at the risk of his life above and beyond the call of duty. Seeing indications of the enemy's presence in the area, S/Sgt. Morris deployed his squad and continued forward alone to make a reconnaissance. He unknowingly crawled within 20 meters of an enemy machine gun, whereupon the gunner fired, wounding him in the chest. S/Sgt. Morris instantly returned the fire and killed the gunner. Continuing to crawl within a few feet of the gun, he hurled a grenade and killed the remainder of the enemy crew. Although in pain and bleeding profusely, S/Sgt. Morris continued his reconnaissance. Returning to the platoon area, he reported the results of his reconnaissance to the platoon leader. As he spoke, the platoon came under heavy fire. Refusing medical attention for himself, he deployed his men in better firing positions confronting the entrenched enemy to his front. Then for eight hours the pla-

toon engaged the numerically superior enemy force. Withdrawal was impossible without abandoning many wounded and dead. Finding the platoon medic dead, S/Sgt. Morris administered first aid to himself and was returning to treat the wounded members of his squad with the medic's first-aid kit when he was again wounded. Knocked down and stunned, he regained consciousness and continued to treat the wounded, reposition his men, and inspire and encourage their efforts. Wounded again when an enemy grenade shattered his left hand, nonetheless he personally took up the fight and armed and threw several grenades which killed a number of enemy soldiers. Seeing that an enemy machine gun had maneuvered behind his platoon and was delivering the fire upon his men, S/Sgt. Morris and another man crawled toward the gun to knock it out. His comrade was killed and S/Sgt. Morris sustained another wound, but, firing his rifle with one hand, he silenced the enemy machine gun. Returning to the platoon, he courageously exposed himself to the devastating enemy fire to drag the wounded to a protected area, and with utter disregard for his personal safety and the pain he suffered, he continued to lead and direct the efforts of his men until relief arrived. Upon termination of the battle, important documents were found among the enemy dead revealing a planned ambush of a Republic of Vietnam battalion. Use of this information prevented the ambush and saved many lives. S/Sgt. Morris' gallantry was instrumental in the successful defeat of the enemy, saved many lives, and was in the highest traditions of the U.S. Army.

3314 ◆ *MURRAY, ROBERT CHARLES

Rank: Staff Sergeant
Service: U.S. Army
Birthday: 10 December 1946
Place of Birth: Bronx County, New York
Date of Death: 7 June 1970
Place of Death: Republic of Vietnam
Cemetery: Gate of Heaven Cemetery—Hawthorne, New York
Entered Service at: New York, New York
Unit: Company B, 4th Battalion, 31st Infantry, 196th Infantry Brigade, Americal Division
Served as: Squad Leader
Battle or Place of Action: near the village of Hiep Duc, Republic of Vietnam
Date of Action: 7 June 1970
G.O. Number, Date: 41, 6 September 1974
Date of Presentation: 8 August 1974
Place of Presentation: Blair House, presented by Vice Pres. Gerald R. Ford to his family
Citation: S/Sgt. Murray distinguished himself while serving as a squad leader with Company B. S/Sgt. Murray's squad was searching for an enemy mortar that had been threatening friendly positions when a member of the squad tripped an enemy grenade rigged as a booby trap. Realizing that he had activated the enemy booby trap, the soldier shouted for everybody to take cover. Instantly assessing the danger to the men of his squad, S/Sgt. Murray unhesitatingly and with complete disregard for his own safety threw himself on the grenade absorbing the full and fatal impact of the explosion. By his gallant action and self sacrifice, he prevented the death or injury of the other members of his squad. S/Sgt. Murray's extraordinary courage and gallantry, at the cost of his life above and beyond the call to duty, are in keeping with the highest traditions of the military service and reflect great credit on him, his unit, and the U.S. Army.

3315 ◆ *NASH, DAVID PAUL

Rank: Private First Class
Service: U.S. Army
Birthday: 3 November 1947
Place of Birth: Whitesville, Daviess County, Kentucky
Date of Death: 29 December 1968
Place of Death: Republic of Vietnam
Cemetery: Saint Mary's of the Woods Cemetery (MH)—Whitesville, Kentucky
Entered Service at: Louisville, Jefferson County, Kentucky
Unit: Company B, 2d Battalion, 39th Infantry, 9th Infantry Division
Served as: Grenadier
Battle or Place of Action: Giao Duc District, Dinh Tuong Province, Republic of Vietnam
Date of Action: 29 December 1968
G.O. Number, Date: 23, 23 April 1970
Date of Presentation: 7 April 1970
Place of Presentation: The White House, presented by Pres. Richard M. Nixon to his family
Citation: For conspicuous gallantry and intrepidity in action at the risk of his life above and beyond the call of duty. Pfc. Nash distinguished himself while serving as a grenadier with Company B, in Giao Duc district. When an ambush patrol of which he was a member suddenly came under intense attack before reaching its destination, he was the first to return the enemy fire. Taking an exposed location, Pfc. Nash suppressed the hostile fusillade with a rapid series of rounds from his grenade launcher, enabling artillery fire to be adjusted on the enemy. After the foe had been routed, his small element continued to the ambush site where he established a position with three fellow soldiers on a narrow dike. Shortly past midnight, while Pfc. Nash and a comrade kept watch and the two other men took their turn sleeping, an enemy grenade wounded two soldiers in the adjacent position. Seconds later, Pfc. Nash saw another grenade land only a few feet from his own position. Although he could have escaped harm by rolling down the other side of the dike, he shouted a warning to his comrades and leaped upon the lethal explosive. Absorbing the blast with his body, he saved the lives of the three men in the area at the sacrifice of his own life. By his gallantry at the cost of his life and in the highest traditions of the military service, Pfc. Nash has reflected great credit on himself, his unit, and the U.S. Army.

3316 ◆ *NEWLIN, MELVIN EARL

Rank: Private First Class
Service: U.S. Marine Corps
Birthday: 27 September 1948

Place of Birth: Wellsville, Columbiana County, Ohio
Date of Death: 4 July 1967
Place of Death: Republic of Vietnam
Cemetery: Spring Hill Cemetery (MH)—Wellsville, Ohio
Entered Service at: Cleveland, Cuyahoga County, Ohio
Unit: Company F, 2d Battalion, 5th Marines, 1st Marine Division (Rein) FMF
Served as: Machine Gunner
Battle or Place of Action: Quang Nam Province, Republic of Vietnam
Date of Action: 3-4 July 1967
Date of Presentation: 18 March 1969
Place of Presentation: The White House, presented by Pres. Richard M. Nixon to his family
Citation: For conspicuous gallantry and intrepidity at the risk of his life above and beyond the call of duty while serving as a machine gunner attached to the 1st Platoon, Company F, 2d Battalion, on 3 and 4 July 1967. Pfc. Newlin, with four other marines, was manning a key position on the perimeter of the Nong Son outpost when the enemy launched a savage and well-coordinated mortar and infantry assault, seriously wounding him and killing his four comrades. Propping himself against his machine gun, he poured a deadly accurate stream of fire into the charging ranks of the Viet Cong. Though repeatedly hit by small-arms fire, he twice repelled enemy attempts to overrun his position. During the third attempt, a grenade explosion wounded him again and knocked him to the ground, unconscious. The Viet Cong guerrillas, believing him dead, bypassed him and continued their assault on the main force. Meanwhile, Pfc. Newlin regained consciousness, crawled back to his weapon, and brought it to bear on the rear of the enemy causing havoc and confusion among them. Spotting the enemy attempting to bring a captured 106 recoilless weapon to bear on other marine positions, he shifted his fire, inflicting heavy casualties on the enemy and preventing them from firing the captured weapon. He then shifted his fire back to the primary enemy force, causing the enemy to stop their assault on the marine bunkers and to once again attack his machine-gun position. Valiantly fighting off two more enemy assaults, he firmly held his ground until mortally wounded. Pfc. Newlin had single-handedly broken up and disorganized the entire enemy assault force, causing them to lose momentum and delaying them long enough for his fellow marines to organize a defense and beat off their secondary attack. His indomitable courage, fortitude, and unwavering devotion to duty in the face of almost certain death reflected great credit upon himself and the Marine Corps and upheld the highest traditions of the U.S. Naval Service.

3317 ◆ *NOONAN JR., THOMAS PATRICK

Rank: Lance Corporal
Service: U.S. Marine Corps
Birthday: 18 November 1943
Place of Birth: Brooklyn, Kings County, New York
Date of Death: 5 February 1969
Place of Death: Republic of Vietnam
Cemetery: First Calvary Cemetery—Woodside, New York
Entered Service at: Brooklyn, Kings County, New York
Unit: Company G, 2d Battalion, 9th Marines, 3d Marine Division (Rein) FMF
Served as: Fire Team Leader
Battle or Place of Action: near Vandergrift Combat Base, A Shau Valley, Republic of Vietnam
Date of Action: 5 February 1969
Date of Presentation: 16 February 1971
Place of Presentation: The White House (East Ballroom), presented by Pres. Richard M. Nixon to his family
Citation: For conspicuous gallantry and intrepidity at the risk of his life above and beyond the call of duty while serving as a fire team leader with Company G, in operations against the enemy in Quang Tri province. Company G was directed to move from a position which they had been holding southeast of the Vandergrift Combat Base to an alternate location. As the marines commenced a slow and difficult descent down the side of the hill made extremely slippery by the heavy rains, the leading element came under a heavy fire from a North Vietnamese Army unit occupying well-concealed positions in the rocky terrain. Four men were wounded, and repeated attempts to recover them failed because of the intense hostile fire. L/Cpl. Noonan moved from his position of relative security and, maneuvering down the treacherous slope to a location near the injured men, took cover behind some rocks. Shouting words of encouragement to the wounded men to restore their confidence, he dashed across the hazardous terrain and commenced dragging the most seriously wounded man away from the fire-swept area. Although wounded and knocked to the ground by an enemy round, L/Cpl. Noonan recovered rapidly and resumed dragging the man toward the marginal security of a rock. He was, however, mortally wounded before he could reach his destination. His heroic actions inspired his fellow marines to such aggressiveness that they initiated a spirited assault which forced the enemy soldiers to withdraw. L/Cpl. Noonan's indomitable courage, inspiring initiative, and selfless devotion to duty upheld the highest traditions of the Marine Corps and the U.S. Naval Service. He gallantly gave his life for his country.

3318 ◆ NORRIS, THOMAS ROLLAND

Rank: Lieutenant
Service: U.S. Navy
Birthday: 14 January 1944
Place of Birth: Jacksonville, Duval County, Florida
Entered Service at: Silver Spring, Montgomery County, Maryland
Unit: United States Military Assistance Command, Headquarters, SEAL Advisor, Strategic Technical Directorate Assistance Team
Served as: SEAL Advisor
Battle or Place of Action: Quang Tri Province, Republic of Vietnam
Date of Action: 10-13 April 1972
Date of Presentation: 6 March 1976
Place of Presentation: The White House, presented by Pres. Gerald R. Ford
Citation: Lt. Norris completed an unprecedented ground

rescue of two downed pilots deep within heavily controlled enemy territory in Quang Tri Province. Lt. Norris, on the night of 10 April, led a five-man patrol through 2,000 meters of heavily controlled territory, located one of the downed pilots at daybreak, and returned to the Forward Operating Base (FOB). On 11 April, after a devastating mortar and rocket attack on the small FOB, Lt. Norris led a three-man team on two unsuccessful rescue attempts for the second pilot. On the afternoon of the 12th, a forward air controller located the pilot and notified Lt. Norris. Dressed in fishermen disguises and using a sampan, Lt. Norris and one Vietnamese traveled throughout the night and found the injured pilot at dawn. Covering the pilot with bamboo and vegetation, they began the return journey, successfully evading a North Vietnamese patrol. Approaching the FOB, they came under heavy machine-gun fire. Lt. Norris called in an air strike which provided suppression fire and a smoke screen, allowing the rescue party to reach the FOB. By his outstanding display of decisive leadership, undaunted courage, and selfless dedication in the face of extreme danger, Lt. Norris enhanced the finest traditions of the U.S. Naval service.

3319 ◆ NOVOSEL, MICHAEL JOSEPH

Rank: Chief Warrant Officer (highest rank: Chief Warrant Officer 4)
Service: U.S. Army
Birthday: 3 September 1922
Place of Birth: Etna, Allegheny County, Pennsylvania
Entered Service at: Kenner, Jefferson County, Louisiana
Unit: 82d Medical Detachment, 45th Medical Company, 68th Medical Group
Served as: Commander of a Medivac Helicopter
Battle or Place of Action: Kien Tuong Province, Republic of Vietnam
Date of Action: 2 October 1969
G.O. Number, Date: 34, 16 July 1971
Date of Presentation: 15 June 1971
Place of Presentation: The White House, presented by Pres. Richard M. Nixon
Citation: For conspicuous gallantry and intrepidity in action at the risk of his life above and beyond the call of duty. CWO Novosel, 82d Medical Detachment, distinguished himself while serving as commander of a medical evacuation helicopter. He unhesitatingly maneuvered his helicopter into a heavily fortified and defended enemy training area where a group of wounded Vietnamese soldiers were pinned down by a large enemy force. Flying without gunship or other cover and exposed to intense machine-gun fire, CWO Novosel was able to locate and rescue a wounded soldier. Since all communications with the beleaguered troops had been lost, he repeatedly circled the battle area, flying at low level under continuous heavy fire, to attract the attention of the scattered friendly troops. This display of courage visibly raised their morale, as they recognized this as a signal to assemble for evacuation. On six occasions he and his crew were forced out of the battle area by the intense enemy fire, only to circle and return from another direction to land and extract additional troops. Near the end of the mission, a wounded soldier was spotted close to an enemy bunker. Fully realizing that he would attract a hail of enemy fire, CWO Novosel nevertheless attempted the extraction by hovering the helicopter backward. As the man was pulled on board, enemy automatic weapons opened fire at close-range, damaged the aircraft and wounded CWO Novosel. He momentarily lost control of the aircraft, but quickly recovered and departed under the withering enemy fire. In all 15 extremely hazardous extractions were performed in order to remove wounded personnel. As a direct result of his selfless conduct, the lives of 29 soldiers were saved. The extraordinary heroism displayed by CWO Novosel was an inspiration to his comrades in arms and reflect great credit on him, his unit, and the U.S. Army.

3320 ◆ *OLIVE III, MILTON LEE

Rank: Private First Class
Service: U.S. Army
Birthday: 7 November 1946
Place of Birth: Chicago, Cook County, Illinois
Date of Death: 22 October 1965
Place of Death: Republic of Vietnam
Cemetery: West Grove Cemetery—Lexington, Mississippi
Entered Service at: Chicago, Cook County, Illinois
Unit: 3d Platoon, Company B, 2d Battalion [Airborne], 503d Infantry, 173d Airborne Brigade
Battle or Place of Action: Phu Cuong, Republic of Vietnam
Date of Action: 22 October 1965
G.O. Number, Date: 18, 26 April 1966
Date of Presentation: 21 April 1966
Place of Presentation: The White house, presented by Pres. Lyndon B. Johnson to his family
Citation: For conspicuous gallantry and intrepidity at the risk of his life above and beyond the call of duty. Pfc. Olive was a member of the 3d Platoon of Company B, as it moved through the jungle to find the Viet Cong operating in the area. Although the platoon was subjected to a heavy volume of enemy gunfire and pinned down temporarily, it retaliated by assaulting the Viet Cong positions, causing the enemy to flee. As the platoon pursued the insurgents, Pfc. Olive and four other soldiers were moving through the jungle together when a grenade was thrown into their midst. Pfc. Olive saw the grenade, and then saved the lives of his fellow soldiers at the sacrifice of his by grabbing the grenade in his hand and falling on it to absorb the blast with his body. Through his bravery, unhesitating actions, and complete disregard for his safety, he prevented additional loss of life or injury to the members of his platoon. Pfc. Olive's extraordinary heroism, at the risk of his life above and beyond the call of duty, are in the highest traditions of the U.S. Army and reflect great credit upon himself and the Armed Forces of his country.

3321 ◆ *OLSON, KENNETH LEE

Rank: Specialist Fourth Class
Service: U.S. Army
Birthday: 26 May 1945
Place of Birth: Willmar, Kandiyohi County, Minnesota
Date of Death: 13 May 1968

Place of Death: Republic of Vietnam
Cemetery: Paynesville Cemetery (MH)—Paynesville, Minnesota
Entered Service at: Minneapolis, Hennepin County, Minnesota
Unit: Company A, 5th Battalion, 12th Infantry, 199th Infantry Brigade (Separate)
Served as: Team Leader
Battle or Place of Action: Republic of Vietnam
Date of Action: 13 May 1968
G.O. Number, Date: 22, 23 April 1970
Date of Presentation: 7 April 1970
Place of Presentation: The White House, presented by Pres. Richard M. Nixon to his family
Citation: For conspicuous gallantry and intrepidity in action at the risk of his life above and beyond the call of duty. Sp4c. Olson distinguished himself at the cost of his life while serving as a team leader with Company A. Sp4c. Olson was participating in a mission to reinforce a reconnaissance platoon which was heavily engaged with a well-entrenched Viet Cong force. When his platoon moved into the area of contact and had overrun the first line of enemy bunkers, Sp4c. Olson and a fellow soldier moved forward of the platoon to investigate another suspected line of bunkers. As the two men advanced they were pinned down by intense automatic-weapons fire from an enemy position 10 meters to their front. With complete disregard for his safety, Sp4c. Olson exposed himself and hurled a hand grenade into the Viet Cong position. Failing to silence the hostile fire, he again exposed himself to the intense fire in preparation to assault the enemy position. As he prepared to hurl the grenade, he was wounded, causing him to drop the activated device within his own position. Realizing that it would explode immediately, Sp4c. Olson threw himself upon the grenade and pulled it in to his body to take the full force of the explosion. By this unselfish action Sp4c. Olson sacrificed his own life to save the lives of his fellow comrades-in-arms. His extraordinary heroism inspired his fellow soldiers to renew their efforts and totally defeat the enemy force. Sp4c. Olson's profound courage and intrepidity were in keeping with the highest traditions of the military service and reflect great credit upon himself, his unit, and the U.S. Army.

3322 ◆ O'MALLEY, ROBERT EMMETT

Rank: Sergeant (rank at time of action: Corporal)
Service: U.S. Marine Corps
Birthday: 3 June 1943
Place of Birth: Woodside, Queens County, New York
Entered Service at: New York, New York
Unit: Company I, 3d Battalion, 3d Marine Regiment, 3d Marine Division (Rein) FMF
Served as: Squad Leader
Battle or Place of Action: near An Cu'ong 2, Republic of Vietnam
Date of Action: 18 August 1965
Date of Presentation: 6 December 1966
Place of Presentation: The Federal Building, Austin, Texas, presented by Pres. Lyndon B. Johnson
Citation: For conspicuous gallantry and intrepidity in action against the communist (Viet Cong) forces at the risk of his life above and beyond the call of duty. While leading his squad in the assault against a strongly entrenched enemy force, his unit came under intense small-arms fire. With complete disregard for his personal safety, Sgt. O'Malley raced across an open rice paddy to a trench line where the enemy forces were located. Jumping into the trench, he attacked the Viet Cong with his rifle and grenades, singlehandedly killed eight of the enemy. He then led his squad to the assistance of an adjacent marine unit which was suffering heavy casualties. Continuing to press forward, he reloaded his weapon and fired with telling effect into the enemy emplacement. He personally assisted in the evacuation of several wounded marines, and again regrouping the remnants of his squad, he returned to the point of the heaviest fighting. Ordered to an evacuation point by an officer, Sgt. O'Malley gathered his besieged and badly wounded squad, and boldly led them under fire to a helicopter for withdrawal. Although three times wounded in this encounter, and facing imminent death from a fanatic and determined enemy, he steadfastly refused evacuation and continued to cover his squad's boarding of the helicopters while, from an exposed position, he delivered fire against the enemy until his wounded men were evacuated. Only then, with his last mission accomplished, did he permit himself to be removed from the battlefield. By his valor, leadership, and courageous efforts in behalf of his comrades, he served as an inspiration to all who observed him, and reflected the highest credit upon the Marine Corps and the U.S. Naval Service.

3323 ◆ *OUELLET, DAVID GEORGE

Rank: Seaman
Service: U.S. Navy
Birthday: 13 June 1944
Place of Birth: Newton, Middlesex County, Massachusetts
Date of Death: 6 March 1967
Place of Death: Republic of Vietnam
Cemetery: Woodlawn Cemetery (MH)—Wellesley, Massachusetts
Entered Service at: Boston, Suffolk County, Massachusetts
Unit: River Patrol Boat (PBR-124), My Tho Detachment 532, River Squadron 5
Served as: Forward Machine Gunner
Battle or Place of Action: Mekong River, Republic of Vietnam
Date of Action: 6 March 1967
Date of Presentation: 30 January 1968
Place of Presentation: The Pentagon, presented by Sec. of the Navy Paul R. Ignatius to his family
Citation: For conspicuous gallantry and intrepidity at the risk of his life above and beyond the call of duty. As the forward machine gunner on River Patrol Boat (PBR) 124, which was on patrol during the early evening hours, Seaman Ouellet observed suspicious activity near the river bank, alerted his boat captain, and recommended movement of the boat to the area to investigate. While the PBR was making a high-speed

run along the river bank, Seaman Ouellet spotted an incoming enemy grenade falling toward the boat. He immediately left the protected position of his gun mount and ran aft for the full length of the speeding boat, shouting to his fellow crewmembers to take cover. Observing the boat captain standing unprotected on the boat, Seaman Ouellet bounded on to the engine compartment cover, and pushed the boat captain down to safety. In the split second that followed the grenade's landing, and in the face of certain death, Seaman Ouellet fearlessly placed himself between the deadly missile and his shipmates, courageously absorbing most of the blast fragments with his body in order to protect his shipmates from injury and death. His extraordinary heroism and his selfless and courageous actions on behalf of his comrades at the expense of his life were in the finest traditions of the U.S. Naval Service.

3324 ◆ PATTERSON, ROBERT MARTIN

Rank: Sergeant (rank at time of action: Specialist Fourth Class) (highest rank: Command Sergeant Major)
Service: U.S. Army
Birthday: 16 April 1948
Place of Birth: Durham, Durham County, North Carolina
Entered Service at: Raleigh, Wake County, North Carolina
Unit: 3d Platoon, Troop B, 2d Squadron, 17th Cavalry, 101st Airborne Division
Served as: Fire Team Leader
Battle or Place of Action: near La Chu, Republic of Vietnam
Date of Action: 6 May 1968
G.O. Number, Date: 65, 25 October 1969
Date of Presentation: 9 October 1969
Place of Presentation: The White House, presented by Pres. Richard M. Nixon
Citation: For conspicuous gallantry and intrepidity in action at the risk of his life above and beyond the call of duty. Sgt. Patterson (then Sp4c.) distinguished himself while serving as a fire team leader of the 3d Platoon, Troop B, during an assault against a North Vietnamese Army battalion which was entrenched in a heavily fortified position. When the leading squad of the 3d Platoon was pinned down by heavy interlocking automatic-weapons and rocket-propelled-grenade fire from two enemy bunkers, Sgt. Patterson and the two other members of his assault team moved forward under a hail of enemy fire to destroy the bunkers with grenade and machine-gun fire. Observing that his comrades were being fired on from a third enemy bunker covered by enemy gunners in one-man spider holes, Sgt. Patterson, with complete disregard for his safety and ignoring the warnings of his comrades that he was moving into a bunker complex, assaulted and destroyed the position. Although exposed to intensive small-arms and grenade fire from the bunkers and their mutually supporting emplacements, Sgt. Patterson continued his assault upon the bunkers which were impeding the advance of his unit. Sgt. Patterson singlehandedly destroyed by rifle and grenade fire five enemy bunkers, killed eight enemy soldiers, and captured seven weapons. His dauntless courage and heroism inspired his platoon to resume the attack and to penetrate the enemy defensive position. Sgt. Patterson's action at the risk of his life has reflected great credit upon himself, his unit, and the U.S. Army.

3325 ◆ *PAUL, JOE CALVIN

Rank: Lance Corporal
Service: U.S. Marine Corps
Birthday: 23 April 1946
Place of Birth: Williamsburg, Whitley County, Kentucky
Date of Death: 19 August 1965
Place of Death: Republic of Vietnam
Cemetery: Memorial Park—Dayton, Ohio
Entered Service at: Dayton, Montgomery County, Ohio
Unit: Company H, 2d Battalion, 4th Marines, 3d Marine Division (Rein) FMF
Served as: Fire Team Leader
Battle or Place of Action: near Chu Lai, Republic of Vietnam
Date of Action: 18 August 1965
Date of Presentation: 7 February 1967
Place of Presentation: Marine Barracks, Washington D.C., presented by Under Sec. of the Navy to his family
Citation: For conspicuous gallantry and intrepidity at the risk of his life above and beyond the call of duty. In violent battle, L/Cpl. Paul's platoon sustained five casualties as it was temporarily pinned down, by devastating mortar, recoilless-rifle, automatic-weapons, and rifle fire delivered by insurgent communist (Viet Cong) forces in well-entrenched positions. The wounded marines were unable to move from their perilously exposed positions forward of the remainder of their platoon, and were suddenly subjected to a barrage of white phosphorous rifle grenades. L/Cpl. Paul, fully aware that his tactics would almost certainly result in serious injury or death to himself, chose to disregard his safety and boldly dashed across the fire-swept rice paddies, placed himself between his wounded comrades and the enemy, and delivered effective suppressive fire with his automatic weapon in order to divert the attack long enough to allow the casualties to be evacuated. Although critically wounded during the course of the battle, he resolutely remained in his exposed position and continued to fire his rifle until he collapsed and was evacuated. By his fortitude and gallant spirit of self-sacrifice in the face of almost certain death, he saved the lives of several of his fellow marines. His heroic action served to inspire all who observed him and reflect the highest credit upon himself, the Marine Corps, and the U.S. Naval Service. He gallantly gave his life in the cause of freedom.

3326 ◆ PENRY, RICHARD ALLEN

Rank: Sergeant
Service: U.S. Army
Birthday: 18 November 1948
Place of Birth: Petaluma, Sonoma County, California
Date of Death: 9 May 1994
Place of Death: Petaluma, California

Cemetery: Cypress Hills Memorial Park (MH)—Petaluma, California
Entered Service at: Oakland, Alameda County, California
Unit: Company C, 4th Battalion, 12th Infantry, 199th Infantry Brigade
Served as: Rifleman
Battle or Place of Action: Binh Tuy Province, Republic of Vietnam
Date of Action: 31 January 1970
G.O. Number, Date: 40, 23 July 1971
Date of Presentation: 15 June 1971
Place of Presentation: The White House, presented by Pres. Richard M. Nixon
Citation: For conspicuous gallantry and intrepidity in action at the risk of his life above and beyond the call of duty. Sgt. Penry, Company C, distinguished himself while serving as a rifleman during a night ambush mission. As the platoon was preparing the ambush position, it suddenly came under an intense enemy attack from mortar, rocket, and automatic-weapons fire which seriously wounded the company commander and most of the platoon members, leaving small isolated groups of wounded men throughout the area. Sgt. Penry, seeing the extreme seriousness of the situation, worked his way through the deadly enemy fire to the company command post where he administered first aid to the wounded company commander and other personnel. He then moved the command post to a position which provided greater protection and visual communication and control of other platoon elements. Realizing the company radio was damaged and recognizing the urgent necessity to reestablish communications with the battalion headquarters, he ran outside the defensive perimeter through a fusillade of hostile fire to retrieve a radio. Finding it inoperable, Sgt. Penry returned through heavy fire to retrieve two more radios. Turning his attention to the defense of the area, he crawled to the edge of the perimeter, retrieved needed ammunition and weapons, and resupplied the wounded men. During a determined assault by over 30 enemy soldiers, Sgt. Penry occupied the most vulnerable forward position, placing heavy, accurate fire on the attacking enemy and exposing himself several times to throw hand grenades into the advancing enemy troops. He succeeded virtually singlehandedly in stopping the attack. Learning that none of the radios were operable, Sgt. Penry again crawled outside the defensive perimeter, retrieved a fourth radio, and established communications with higher headquarters. Sgt. Penry then continued to administer first aid to the wounded and repositioned them to better repel further enemy attacks. Despite continuous and deadly sniper fire, he again left the defensive perimeter, moved to within a few feet of enemy positions, located five isolated wounded soldiers, and led them to safety. When evacuation helicopters approached, Sgt. Penry voluntarily left the perimeter, set up a guiding beacon, established the priorities for evacuation, and successively carried 18 wounded men to the extraction site. After all wounded personnel had been evacuated, Sgt. Penry joined another platoon and assisted in the pursuit of the enemy. Sgt. Penry's extraordinary heroism at the risk of his own life are in keeping with the highest traditions of the military service and reflect great credit on him, his unit, and the U.S. Army.

3327 ◆ *PERKINS JR., WILLIAM THOMAS

Rank: Corporal
Service: U.S. Marine Corps
Birthday: 10 August 1947
Place of Birth: Rochester, Monroe County, New York
Date of Death: 12 October 1967
Place of Death: Republic of Vietnam
Cemetery: San Fernando Mission Cemetery—San Fernando, California
Entered Service at: San Francisco, San Francisco County, California
Unit: Company C, 1st Battalion, 1st Marines, 1st Marine Division (Rein) FMF
Served as: Combat Photographer
Battle or Place of Action: Quang Tri Province, Republic of Vietnam
Date of Action: 12 October 1967
Date of Presentation: 20 June 1969
Place of Presentation: The White House, presented by Pres. Richard M. Nixon to his family
Citation: For conspicuous gallantry and intrepidity at the risk of his life above and beyond the call of duty while serving as a combat photographer attached to Company C. During Operation Medina, a major reconnaissance-in-force southwest of Quang Tri, Company C made heavy combat contact with a numerically superior North Vietnamese Army force estimated at from two to three companies. The focal point of the intense fighting was a helicopter landing zone which was also serving as the Command Post of Company C. In the course of a strong hostile attack, an enemy grenade landed in the immediate area occupied by Cpl. Perkins and three other marines. Realizing the inherent danger, he shouted the warning, "Incoming Grenade" to his fellow marines, and in a valiant act of heroism, hurled himself upon the grenade absorbing the impact of the explosion with his body, thereby saving the lives of his comrades at the cost of his life. Through his exceptional courage and inspiring valor in the face of certain death, Cpl. Perkins reflected great credit upon himself and the Marine Corps and upheld the highest traditions of the U.S. Naval Service. He gallantly gave his life for his country.

3328 ◆ *PETERS, LAWRENCE DAVID

Rank: Sergeant
Service: U.S. Marine Corps
Birthday: 16 September 1946
Place of Birth: Johnson City, Broome County, New York
Date of Death: 4 September 1967
Place of Death: Republic of Vietnam
Cemetery: Chenango Valley Cemetery (MH)—Binghamton, New York
Entered Service at: Binghamton, Broome County, New York
Unit: Company M, 3d Battalion, 5th Marines, 1st Marine Division (Rein) FMF
Served as: Squad Leader
Battle or Place of Action: Quang Tin Province, Republic of Vietnam

Date of Action: 4 September 1967
Date of Presentation: 20 April 1970
Place of Presentation: The White House, presented by Vice Pres. Spiro T. Agnew to his family
Citation: For conspicuous gallantry and intrepidity at the risk of his life above and beyond the call of duty while serving as a squad leader with Company M. During Operation Swift, the marines of the 2d Platoon of Company M were struck by intense mortar, machine-gun, and small-arms fire from an entrenched enemy force. As the company rallied its forces, Sgt. Peters maneuvered his squad in an assault on an enemy-defended knoll. Disregarding his safety, as enemy rounds hit all about him, he stood in the open, pointing out enemy positions until he was painfully wounded in the leg. Disregarding his wound, he moved forward and continued to lead his men. As the enemy fire increased in accuracy and volume, his squad lost its momentum and was temporarily pinned down. Exposing himself to devastating enemy fire, he consolidated his position to render more effective fire. While directing the base of fire, he was wounded a second time in the face and neck from an exploding mortar round. As the enemy attempted to infiltrate the position of an adjacent platoon, Sgt. Peters stood erect in the full view of the enemy firing burst after burst forcing them to disclose their camouflaged positions. Sgt. Peters steadfastly continued to direct his squad in spite of two additional wounds and persisted in his efforts to encourage and supervise his men until he lost consciousness and succumbed. Inspired by his selfless actions, the squad regained fire superiority and once again carried the assault to the enemy. By his outstanding valor, indomitable fighting spirit and tenacious determination in the face of overwhelming odds, Sgt. Peters upheld the highest traditions of the Marine Corps and the U.S. Naval Service. He gallantly gave his life for his country.

3329 ◆ *PETERSEN, DANNY JOHN

Rank: Specialist Fourth Class
Service: U.S. Army
Birthday: 11 March 1949
Place of Birth: Horton, Brown County, Kansas
Date of Death: 9 January 1970
Place of Death: Republic of Vietnam
Cemetery: Netawaka Cemetery (MH)—Netawaka, Kansas
Entered Service at: Kansas City, Clay County, Missouri
Unit: Company B, 4th Battalion, 23d Infantry, 25th Infantry Division
Served as: A.P.C. Commander
Battle or Place of Action: Tay Ninh Province, Republic of Vietnam
Date of Action: 9 January 1970
G.O. Number, Date: 44, 12 September 1974
Date of Presentation: 17 July 1974
Place of Presentation: Blair House, presented by Vice Pres. Gerald R. Ford to his family
Citation: Sp4c. Petersen distinguished himself while serving as an armored personnel carrier commander with Company B during a combat operation against a North Vietnamese Army force estimated to be of battalion size. During the initial contact with the enemy, an armored personnel carrier was disabled and the crewmen were pinned down by the heavy onslaught of enemy small-arms, automatic-weapons, and rocket-propelled-grenade fire. Sp4c. Petersen immediately maneuvered his armored personnel carrier to a position between the disabled vehicle and the enemy. He placed suppressive fire on the enemy's well-fortified position, thereby enabling the crewmembers of the disabled personnel carrier to repair their vehicle. He then maneuvered his vehicle, while still under heavy hostile fire, to within 10 feet of the enemy's defensive emplacement. After a period of intense fighting, his vehicle received a direct hit and the driver was wounded. With extraordinary courage and selfless disregard for his own safety, Sp4c. Petersen carried his wounded comrade 45 meters across the bullet-swept field to a secure area. He then voluntarily returned to his disabled armored personnel carrier to provide covering fire for both the other vehicles and the dismounted personnel of his platoon as they withdrew. Despite heavy fire from three sides, he remained with his disabled vehicle, alone and completely exposed. Sp4c. Petersen was standing on top of his vehicle, firing his weapon, when he was mortally wounded. His heroic and selfless actions prevented further loss of life in his platoon. Sp4c. Petersen's conspicuous gallantry and extraordinary heroism are in the highest traditions of the military service and reflect great credit upon him, his unit, and the U.S. Army.

3330 ◆ *PHIPPS, JIMMY WAYNE

Rank: Private First Class
Service: U.S. Marine Corps
Birthday: 1 November 1950
Place of Birth: Santa Monica, Los Angeles County, California
Date of Death: 27 May 1969
Place of Death: Republic of Vietnam
Cemetery: Woodlawn Cemetery—Santa Monica, California
Entered Service at: Culver City, Los Angeles County, California
Unit: Company B, 1st Engineer Battalion, 1st Marine Division (Rein) FMF
Served as: Combat Engineer
Battle or Place of Action: near An Hoa, Republic of Vietnam
Date of Action: 27 May 1969
Date of Presentation: 20 April 1970
Place of Presentation: The White House, presented by Vice Pres. Spiro T. Agnew to his family
Citation: For conspicuous gallantry and intrepidity at the risk of his life above and beyond the call of duty while serving as a combat engineer with Company B in connection with combat operations against the enemy. Pfc. Phipps was a member of a two-man combat engineer demolition team assigned to locate and destroy enemy artillery ordnance and concealed firing devices. After he had expended all of his explosives and blasting caps, Pfc. Phipps discovered a 175-mm high-explosive artillery round in a rice paddy. Suspecting that the enemy had attached the artillery round to a secondary explosive device, he warned other marines in the area to move to covered positions and perpared to destroy the

round with a hand grenade. As he was attaching the hand grenade to a stake beside the artillery round, the fuse of the enemy's secondary explosive device ignited. Realizing that his assistant and the platoon commander were both within a few meters of him and that the imminent explosion could kill all three men, Pfc. Phipps grasped the hand grenade to his chest and dived forward to cover the enemy's explosive and the artillery round with his body, thereby shielding his companions from the detonation while absorbing the full and tremendous impact with his body. Pfc. Phipps' indomitable courage, inspiring initiative, and selfless devotion to duty saved the lives of two marines and upheld the highest traditions of the Marine Corps and the U.S. Naval Service. He gallantly gave his life for his country.

3331 ◆ *PIERCE, LARRY STANLEY

Rank: Sergeant
Service: U.S. Army
Birthday: 6 July 1941
Place of Birth: Wewoka, Seminole County, Oklahoma
Date of Death: 20 September 1965
Place of Death: Republic of Vietnam
Cemetery: Wasco Cemetery—Wasco, California
Entered Service at: Fresno, Fresno County, California
Unit: Headquarters & Headquarters Company, 1st Battalion (Airborne), 503d Infantry, 173d Airborne Brigade
Served as: Squad Leader
Battle or Place of Action: near Ben Cat, Republic of Vietnam
Date of Action: 20 September 1965
G.O. Number, Date: 7, 24 February 1966
Date of Presentation: 24 February 1966
Place of Presentation: The White House, presented by Pres. Lyndon B. Johnson to his family
Citation: For conspicuous gallantry and intrepidity at the risk of his life above and beyond the call of duty. Sgt. Pierce was serving as squad leader in a reconnaissance platoon when his patrol was ambushed by hostile forces. Through his inspiring leadership and personal courage, the squad succeeded in eliminating an enemy machine gun and routing the opposing force. While pursuing the fleeing enemy, the squad came upon a dirt road and, as the main body of his men entered the road, Sgt. Pierce discovered an antipersonnel mine emplaced in the road bed. Realizing that the mine could destroy the majority of his squad, Sgt. Pierce saved the lives of his men at the sacrifice of his life by throwing himself directly onto the mine as it exploded. Through his indomitable courage, complete disregard for his safety, and profound concern for his fellow soldiers, he averted loss of life and injury to the members of his squad. Sgt. Pierce's extraordinary heroism, at the cost of his life, are in the highest traditions of the U.S. Army and reflect great credit upon himself and the Armed Forces of his country.

3332 ◆ PITTMAN, RICHARD ALLAN

Rank: Sergeant (rank at time of action: Lance Corporal) (highest rank: Master Sergeant)
Service: U.S. Marine Corps
Birthday: 26 May 1945
Place of Birth: French Camp, San Joaquin County, California
Entered Service at: Stockton, San Joaquin County, California
Unit: Company I, 3d Battalion, 5th Marines, 1st Marine Division (Rein) FMF
Served as: Rifleman/Squad Leader
Battle or Place of Action: near the Demilitarized Zone, Republic of Vietnam
Date of Action: 24 July 1966
Date of Presentation: 14 May 1968
Place of Presentation: The Pentagon (Inner Courtyard), Hall of Heroes, presented by Pres. Lyndon B. Johnson
Citation: For conspicuous gallantry and intrepidity at the risk of his life above and beyond the call of duty. While Company I was conducting an operation along the axis of a narrow jungle trail, the leading company elements suffered numerous casualties when they suddenly came under heavy fire from a well-concealed and numerically superior force. Hearing the engaged marines' calls for more firepower, Sgt. Pittman quickly exchanged his rifle for a machine gun and several belts of ammunition, left the relative safety of his platoon, and unhesitatingly rushed forward to aid his comrades. Taken under intense enemy small-arms fire at point-blank range during his advance, he returned the fire, silencing the enemy position. As Sgt. Pittman continued to forge forward to aid members of the leading platoon, he again came under heavy fire from two automatic weapons which he promptly destroyed. Learning that there were additional wounded marines 50 yards further along the trail, he braved a withering hail of enemy mortar and small-arms fire to continue onward. As he reached the position where the leading marines had fallen, he was suddenly confronted with a bold frontal attack by 30 to 40 enemy. Totally disregarding his safety, he calmly established a position in the middle of the trail and raked the advancing enemy with devastating machine-gun fire. His weapon rendered ineffective, he picked up an enemy submachine gun and, together with a pistol seized from a fallen comrade, continued his lethal fire until the enemy force had withdrawn. Having exhausted his ammunition except for a grenade which he hurled at the enemy, he then rejoined his platoon. Sgt. Pittman's daring initiative, bold fighting spirit, and selfless devotion to duty inflicted many enemy casualties, disrupted the enemy attack, and saved the lives of many of his wounded comrades. His personal valor at grave risk to himself reflects the highest credit upon himself, the Marine Corps, and the U.S. Naval Service.

3333 ◆ *PITTS, RILEY LEROY

Rank: Captain
Service: U.S. Army
Birthday: 15 October 1937
Place of Birth: Fallis, Oklahoma
Date of Death: 31 October 1967
Place of Death: Republic of Vietnam
Cemetery: Hillcrest Memorial Gardens Cemetery (MH)—Spencer, Oklahoma
Entered Service at: Wichita, Sedgwick County, Kansas

Unit: Company C, 2d Battalion, 27th Infantry, 25th Infantry Division
Served as: Company Commander
Battle or Place of Action: Ap Dong, Republic of Vietnam
Date of Action: 31 October 1967
G.O. Number, Date: 84, 31 December 1968
Date of Presentation: 10 December 1968
Place of Presentation: The White House, presented by Pres. Lyndon B. Johnson to his family
Citation: Distinguishing himself by exceptional heroism while serving as company commander during an airmobile assault. Immediately after his company landed in the area, several Viet Cong opened fire with automatic weapons. Despite the enemy fire, Capt. Pitts forcefully led an assault which overran the enemy positions. Shortly thereafter, Capt. Pitts was ordered to move his unit to the north to reinforce another company heavily engaged against a strong enemy force. As Capt. Pitts' company moved forward to engage the enemy, intense fire was received from three directions, including fire from four enemy bunkers, two of which were within 15 meters of Capt. Pitts' position. The severity of the incoming fire prevented Capt. Pitts from maneuvering his company. His rifle fire proving ineffective against the enemy due to the dense jungle foliage, he picked up an M-79 grenade launcher and began pinpointing the targets. Seizing a Chinese Communist grenade which had been taken from a captured Viet Cong's web gear, Capt. Pitts lobbed the grenade at a bunker to his front, but it hit the dense jungle foliage and rebounded. Without hesitation, Capt. Pitts threw himself on top of the grenade which, fortunately, failed to explode. Capt. Pitts then directed the repositioning of the company to permit friendly artillery to be fired. Upon completion of the artillery fire mission, Capt. Pitts again led his men toward the enemy positions, personally killing at least one more Viet Cong. The jungle growth still prevented effective fire to be placed on the enemy bunkers. Capt. Pitts, displaying complete disregard for his life and personal safety, quickly moved to a position which permitted him to place effective fire on the enemy. He maintained a continuous fire, pinpointing the enemy's fortified positions, while at the same time directing and urging his men forward, until he was mortally wounded. Capt. Pitts' conspicuous gallantry, extraordinary heroism, and intrepidity at the cost of his life, above and beyond the call of duty, are in the highest traditions of the U.S. Army and reflect great credit upon himself, his unit, and the Armed Forces of his country.

3334 ◆ PLESS, STEPHEN WESLEY

Rank: Major (rank at time of action: Captain)
Service: U.S. Marine Corps
Birthday: 6 September 1939
Place of Birth: Newnan, Coweta County, Georgia
Date of Death: 20 July 1969
Place of Death: Pensacola, Florida
Cemetery: Barrancas National Cemetery (21-929A) (MH)—Pensacola, Florida
Entered Service at: Atlanta, Fulton County, Georgia
Unit: Marine Observation Squadron 6, Marine Aircraft Group 36, 1st Marine Aircraft Wing
Served as: Helicopter Gunship Pilot
Battle or Place of Action: near Quang Nai, Republic of Vietnam
Date of Action: 19 August 1967
Date of Presentation: 16 January 1969
Place of Presentation: The White House, presented by Pres. Lyndon B. Johnson
Citation: For conspicuous gallantry and intrepidity at the risk of his life above and beyond the call of duty while serving as a helicopter gunship pilot attached to Marine Observation Squadron 6 in action against enemy forces. During an escort mission Maj. Pless monitored an emergency call that four American soldiers stranded on a nearby beach were being overwhelmed by a large Viet Cong force. Maj. Pless flew to the scene and found 30 to 50 enemy soldiers in the open. Some of the enemy were bayoneting and beating the downed Americans. Maj. Pless displayed exceptional airmanship as he launched a devastating attack against the enemy force, killing or wounding many of the enemy and driving the remainder back into a treeline. His rockets and machine-gun attacks were made at such low levels that the aircraft flew through debris created by explosions from its rockets. Seeing one of the wounded soldiers gesture for assistance, he maneuvered his helicopter into a position between the wounded man and the enemy, providing a shield which permitted his crew to retrieve the wounded. During the rescue the enemy directed intense fire at the helicopter and rushed the aircraft again and again, closing to within a few feet before being beaten back. When the wounded men were aboard, Maj. Pless maneuvered the helicopter out to sea. Before it became safely airborne, the overloaded aircraft settled four times into the water. Displaying superb airmanship, he finally got the helicopter aloft. Maj. Pless' extraordinary heroism coupled with his outstanding flying skill prevented the annihilation of the tiny force. His courageous actions reflect great credit upon himself and uphold the highest traditions of the Marine Corps and the U.S. Naval Service.

3335 ◆ *PORT, WILLIAM DAVID

Rank: Sergeant (rank at time of action: Private First Class)
Service: U.S. Army
Birthday: 31 October 1941
Place of Birth: Petersburg, Huntingdon County, Pennsylvania
Date of Death: 27 November 1968
Place of Death: Republic of Vietnam
Cemetery: Arlington National Cemetery (7-8120-B) (MH)—Arlington, Virginia
Entered Service at: Harrisburg, Dauphin County, Pennsylvania
Unit: Company C, 5th Battalion, 7th Cavalry, 1st Air Cavalry Division
Served as: Rifleman
Battle or Place of Action: Que Son Valley, Heip Duc Province
Date of Action: 12 January 1968

G.O. Number, Date: 48, 8 September 1970
Date of Presentation: 6 August 1970
Place of Presentation: The White House, presented by Pres. Richard M. Nixon to his family
Citation: For conspicuous gallantry and intrepidity at the risk of his life above and beyond the call of duty. Sgt. Port distinguished himself while serving as a rifleman with Company C, which was conducting combat operations against an enemy force in the Que Son Valley. As Sgt. Port's platoon was moving to cut off a reported movement of enemy soldiers, the platoon came under heavy fire from an entrenched enemy force. The platoon was forced to withdraw due to the intensity and ferocity of the fire. Although wounded in the hand as the withdrawal began, Sgt. Port, with complete disregard for his safety, ran through the heavy fire to assist a wounded comrade back to the safety of the platoon perimeter. As the enemy forces assaulted in the perimeter, Sgt. Port and three comrades were in position behind an embankment when an enemy grenade landed in their midst. Sgt. Port, realizing the danger to his fellow soldiers, shouted the warning, "Grenade," and unhesitatingly hurled himself towards the grenade to shield his comrades from the explosion. Through his exemplary courage and devotion he saved the lives of his fellow soldiers and gave the members of his platoon the inspiration needed to hold their position. Sgt. Port's selfless concern for his comrades, at the risk of his life above and beyond the call of duty, are in keeping with the highest traditions of the military service and reflect great credit on himself, his unit, and the U.S. Army.
Notes: POW from 12 January 1968—27 November 1968

3336 ◆ *POXON, ROBERT LESLIE

Rank: First Lieutenant
Service: U.S. Army
Birthday: 3 January 1947
Place of Birth: Detroit, Wayne County, Michigan
Date of Death: 2 June 1969
Place of Death: Republic of Vietnam
Cemetery: Forest Lawn Cemetery—Detroit, Michigan
Entered Service at: Detroit, Wayne County, Michigan
Unit: Troop B, 1st Squadron, 9th Cavalry, 1st Cavalry Division
Served as: Platoon Leader
Battle or Place of Action: Tay Ninh Province, Republic of Vietnam
Date of Action: 2 June 1969
G.O. Number, Date: 6, 9 March 1971
Date of Presentation: 16 February 1971
Place of Presentation: The White House (East Ballroom), presented by Pres. Richard M. Nixon to his family
Citation: For conspicuous gallantry and intrepidity in action at the risk of his life above and beyond the call of duty. 1st Lt. Poxon, Armor, Troop B, distinguished himself while serving as a platoon leader on a reconnaissance mission. Landing by helicopter in a area suspected of being occupied by the enemy, the platoon came under intense fire from enemy soldiers in concealed positions and fortifications around the landing zone. A soldier fell, hit by the first burst of fire. 1st Lt. Poxon dashed to his aid, drawing the majority of the enemy fire as he crossed 20 meters of open ground. The fallen soldier was beyond help and 1st Lt. Poxon was seriously and painfully wounded. 1st Lt. Poxon, with indomitable courage, refused medical aid and evacuation and turned his attention to seizing the initiative from the enemy. With sure instinct he marked a central enemy bunker as the key to success. Quickly instructing his men to concentrate their fire on the bunker, and in spite of his wound, 1st Lt. Poxon crawled toward the bunker, readied a hand grenade, and charged. He was hit again but continued his assault. After succeeding in silencing the enemy guns in the bunker he was struck once again by enemy fire and fell, mortally wounded. 1st Lt. Poxon's comrades followed their leader, pressed the attack, and drove the enemy from their positions. 1st Lt. Poxon's gallantry, indomitable will, and courage are in keeping with the highest traditions of the military service and reflect great credit on himself, his unit, and the U.S. Army.

3337 ◆ *PROM, WILLIAM RAYMOND

Rank: Lance Corporal
Service: U.S. Marine Corps
Birthday: 17 November 1948
Place of Birth: Pittsburgh, Allegheny County, Pennsylvania
Date of Death: 9 February 1969
Place of Death: Republic of Vietnam
Cemetery: Allegheny County Memorial Park (MH)—Pittsburgh, Pennsylvania
Entered Service at: Pittsburgh, Allegheny County, Pennsylvania
Unit: Company I, 3d Battalion, 3d Marines, 3d Marine Division (Rein) FMF
Served as: Squad Leader/Machine Gunner
Battle or Place of Action: near An Hoa, Republic of Vietnam
Date of Action: 9 February 1969
Date of Presentation: 20 April 1970
Place of Presentation: The White House, presented by Vice Pres. Spiro T. Agnew to his family
Citation: For conspicuous gallantry and intrepidity at the risk of his life above and beyond the call of duty while serving as a machine-gun squad leader with Company I, in action against the enemy. While returning from a reconnaissance operation during Operation Taylor Common, two platoons of Company I came under an intense automatic-weapons fire and grenade attack from a well-concealed North Vietnamese Army force in fortified positions. The leading element of the platoon was isolated and several marines were wounded. L/Cpl. Prom immediately assumed control of one of his machine guns and began to deliver return fire. Disregarding his safety he advanced to a position from which he could more effectively deliver covering fire while first aid was administered to the wounded men. Realizing that the enemy would have to be destroyed before the injured marines could be evacuated, L/Cpl. Prom again moved forward and delivered a heavy volume of fire with such accuracy that he was instrumental in routing the enemy, thus permitting his men to regroup and resume their march. Shortly thereafter, the

platoon again came under heavy fire in which one man was critically wounded. Reacting instantly, L/Cpl. Prom moved forward to protect his injured comrade. Unable to continue his fire because of severe wounds, he continued to advance to within a few yards to the enemy positions. There, standing in full view of the enemy, he accurately directed the fire of his support elements until he was mortally wounded. Inspired by his heroic actions, the marines launched an assault that destroyed the enemy. L/Cpl. Prom's indomitable courage, inspiring initiative and selfless devotion to duty upheld the highest traditions of the Marine Corps and the U.S. Naval Service. He gallantly gave his life for his country.

3338 ◆ *PRUDEN, ROBERT JOSEPH

Rank: Staff Sergeant
Service: U.S. Army
Birthday: 9 September 1949
Place of Birth: St.Paul, Ramsey County, Minnesota
Date of Death: 29 November 1969
Place of Death: Republic of Vietnam
Cemetery: Fort Snelling National Cemetery (M-5710) (MH)—Minneapolis, Minnesota
Entered Service at: Minneapolis, Hennepin County, Minnesota
Unit: Company G, 75th Infantry, Americal Division
Served as: Reconnaissance Team Leader
Battle or Place of Action: Quang Ngai Province, Republic of Vietnam
Date of Action: 29 November 1969
G.O. Number, Date: 26, 26 May 1971
Date of Presentation: 22 April 1971
Place of Presentation: The White House, presented by Pres. Richard M. Nixon to his family
Citation: For conspicuous gallantry and intrepidity in action at the risk of his life above and beyond the call of duty. S/Sgt. Pruden, Company G, distinguished himself while serving as a reconnaissance team leader during an ambush mission. The six-man team was inserted by helicopter into enemy-controlled territory to establish an ambush position and to obtain information concerning enemy movements. As the team moved into the preplanned area, S/Sgt. Pruden deployed his men into two groups on the opposite sides of a well-used trail. As the groups were establishing their defensive positions, one member of the team was trapped in the open by the heavy fire from an enemy squad. Realizing that the ambush position had been compromised, S/Sgt. Pruden directed his team to open fire on the enemy force. Immediately, the team came under heavy fire from a second enemy element. S/Sgt. Pruden, with full knowledge of the extreme danger involved, left his concealed position and, firing as he ran, advanced toward the enemy to draw the hostile fire. He was seriously wounded twice but continued his attack until he fell for a third time, in front of the enemy positions. S/Sgt. Pruden's actions resulted in several enemy casualties and withdrawal of the remaining enemy force. Although grievously wounded, he directed his men into defensive positions and called for evacuation helicopters, which safely withdrew the members of the team. S/Sgt. Pruden's outstanding courage, selfless concern for the welfare of his men, and intrepidity in action at the cost of his life were in keeping with the highest traditions of the military service and reflect great credit upon himself, his unit, and the U.S. Army.

3339 ◆ *RABEL, LASZLO

Rank: Staff Sergeant
Service: U.S. Army
Birthday: 21 September 1937
Place of Birth: Budapest, Hungary
Date of Death: 13 November 1968
Place of Death: Republic of Vietnam
Cemetery: Arlington National Cemetery (52-1326) (MH)—Arlington, Virginia
Entered Service at: Minneapolis, Hennepin County, Minnesota
Unit: Team Delta, 74th Infantry Detachment (Long Range Patrol), 173d Airborne Brigade
Served as: Team Leader
Battle or Place of Action: Binh Dinh Province, Republic of Vietnam
Date of Action: 13 November 1968
G.O. Number, Date: 6, 23 April 1970
Date of Presentation: 7 April 1970
Place of Presentation: The White House, presented by Pres. Richard M. Nixon to his family
Citation: For conspicuous gallantry and intrepidity in action at the risk of his life above and beyond the call of duty. S/Sgt. Rabel distinguished himself while serving as leader of Team Delta, 74th Infantry Detachment. At 1000 hours on this date, Team Delta was in a defensive perimeter conducting reconnaissance of enemy trail networks when a member of the team detected enemy movement to the front. As S/Sgt. Rabel and a comrade prepared to clear the area, he heard an incoming grenade as it landed in the midst of the team's perimeter. With complete disregard for his life, S/Sgt. Rabel threw himself on the grenade and, covering it with his body, received the complete impact of the immediate explosion. Through his indomitable courage, complete disregard for his safety, and profound concern for his fellow soldiers, S/Sgt. Rabel averted the loss of life and injury to the other members of Team Delta. By his gallantry at the cost of his life in the highest traditions of the military service, S/Sgt. Rabel has reflected great credit upon himself, his unit, and the U.S. Army.

3340 ◆ *RAY, DAVID ROBERT

Rank: Hospital Corpsman Second Class
Service: U.S. Navy
Birthday: 14 February 1945
Place of Birth: McMinnville, Warren County, Tennessee
Date of Death: 19 March 1969
Place of Death: Republic of Vietnam
Cemetery: Mountain View Cemetery—McMinnville, Tennessee
Entered Service at: Nashville, Davidson County, Tennessee
Unit: Battery D, 2d Battalion, 11th Marines, 1st Marine Division

Served as: Medical Corpsman
Battle or Place of Action: Phu Loc 6, near An Hoa, Quang Nam Province, Republic of Vietnam
Date of Action: 19 March 1969
Date of Presentation: 20 April 1970
Place of Presentation: The White House, presented by Vice Pres. Spiro T. Agnew to his family
Citation: For conspicuous gallantry and intrepidity at the risk of his life above and beyond the call of duty while serving as a HC2c. with Battery D, 2d Battalion, at Phu Loc 6, near An Hoa. During the early morning hours, an estimated battalion-size enemy force launched a determined assault against the battery's position, and succeeded in effecting a penetration of the barbed-wire perimeter. The initial burst of enemy fire caused numerous casualties among the marines who had immediately manned their howitzers during the rocket and mortar attack. Undaunted by the intense hostile fire, HC2c. Ray moved from parapet to parapet, rendering emergency medical treatment to the wounded. Although seriously wounded himself while administering first aid to a marine casualty, he refused medical aid and continued his lifesaving efforts. While he was bandaging and attempting to comfort another wounded marine, HC2c. Ray was forced to battle two enemy soldiers who attacked his position, personally killing one and wounding the other. Rapidly losing his strength as a result of his severe wounds, he nonetheless managed to move through the hail of enemy fire to other casualties. Once again, he was faced with the intense fire of oncoming enemy troops and, despite the grave personal danger and insurmountable odds, succeeded in treating the wounded and holding off the enemy until he ran out of ammunition, at which time he sustained fatal wounds. HC2c. Ray's final act of heroism was to protect the patient he was treating. He threw himself upon the wounded marine, thus saving the man's life when an enemy grenade exploded nearby. By his determined and persevering actions, courageous spirit, and selfless devotion to the welfare of his marine comrades, HC2c. Ray served to inspire the men of Battery D to heroic efforts in defeating the enemy. His conduct throughout was in keeping with the finest traditions of the U.S. Naval Service.

3341 ◆ RAY, RONALD ERIC

Rank: Captain (rank at time of action: First Lieutenant) (highest rank: Lieutenant Colonel)
Service: U.S. Army
Birthday: 7 December 1941
Place of Birth: Cordele, Crisp County, Georgia
Entered Service at: Atlanta, Fulton County, Georgia
Unit: Company A, 2d Battalion, 35th Infantry, 25th Infantry Division
Served as: Platoon Leader
Battle or Place of Action: Ia Drang Valley, Republic of Vietnam
Date of Action: 19 June 1966
G.O. Number, Date: 31, 5 June 1970
Date of Presentation: 14 May 1970
Place of Presentation: The White House, presented by Pres. Richard M. Nixon
Citation: For conspicuous gallantry and intrepidity in action at the risk of his life above and beyond the call of duty. Capt. Ray distinguished himself while serving as a platoon leader with Company A. When one of his ambush patrols was attacked by an estimated reinforced Viet Cong company, Capt. Ray organized a reaction force and quickly moved through two kilometers of mountainous jungle terrain to the contact area. After breaking through the hostile lines to reach the beleaguered patrol, Capt. Ray began directing the reinforcement of the site. When an enemy position pinned down three of his men with a heavy volume of automatic-weapons fire, he silenced the emplacement with a grenade and killed four Viet Cong with his rifle fire. As medics were moving a casualty toward a sheltered position, they began receiving intense hostile fire. While directing suppressive fire on the enemy position, Capt. Ray moved close enough to silence the enemy with a grenade. A few moments later Capt. Ray saw an enemy grenade land, unnoticed, near two of his men. Without hesitation or regard for his safety he dove between the grenade and the men, thus shielding them from the explosion while receiving wounds in his exposed feet and legs. He immediately sustained additional wounds in his legs from an enemy machine gun, but nevertheless he silenced the emplacement with another grenade. Although suffering great pain from his wounds, Capt. Ray continued to direct his men, providing the outstanding courage and leadership they vitally needed, and prevented their annihilation by successfully leading them from their surrounded position. Only after assuring that his platoon was no longer in immediate danger did he allow himself to be evacuated for medical treatment. By his gallantry at the risk of his life in the highest traditions of the military service, Capt. Ray has reflected great credit upon himself, his unit, and the U.S. Army.

3342 ◆ *REASONER, FRANK STANLEY

Rank: First Lieutenant
Service: U.S. Marine Corps
Birthday: 16 September 1937
Place of Birth: Spokane, Spokane County, Washington
Date of Death: 12 July 1965
Place of Death: Republic of Vietnam
Cemetery: Greenwood Cemetery (MH)—Kellogg, Idaho
Entered Service at: Kellogg, Shoshone County, Idaho
Unit: Company A, 3d Reconnaissance Battalion, 3d Marine Division (Rein) FMF
Served as: Commanding Officer
Battle or Place of Action: near Da Nang, Republic of Vietnam
Date of Action: 12 July 1965
Date of Presentation: 31 January 1967
Place of Presentation: The Pentagon, presented by the Sec. of the Navy Paul H. Nitze to his family
Citation: For conspicuous gallantry and intrepidity at the risk of his life above and beyond the call of duty. The reconnaissance patrol led by 1st Lt. Reasoner had deeply penetrated heavily controlled enemy territory when it came under extremely heavy fire from an estimated 50 to 100 Viet Cong insurgents. Accompanying the advance party and the point

that consisted of five men, he immediately deployed his men for an assault after the Viet Cong had opened fire from numerous concealed positions. Boldly shouting encouragement, and virtually isolated from the main body, he organized a base of fire for an assault on the enemy positions. The slashing fury of the Viet Cong machine-gun and automatic-weapons fire made it impossible for the main body to move forward. Repeatedly exposing himself to the devastating attack he skillfully provided covering fire, killing at least two Viet Cong and effectively silencing an automatic-weapons position in a valiant attempt to effect evacuation of a wounded man. As casualties began to mount his radio operator was wounded and 1st Lt. Reasoner immediately moved to his side and tended his wounds. When the radio operator was hit a second time while attempting to reach a covered position, 1st Lt. Reasoner courageously running to his aid through the grazing machine-gun fire fell mortally wounded. His indomitable fighting spirit, valiant leadership, and unflinching devotion to duty provided the inspiration that was to enable the patrol to complete its mission without further casualties. In the face of almost certain death he gallantly gave his life in the service of his country. His actions upheld the highest traditions of the Marine Corps and the U.S. Naval Service.

3343 ◆ *ROARK, ANUND CHARLES

Rank: Sergeant
Service: U.S. Army
Birthday: 17 February 1948
Place of Birth: Vallejo, Solano County, California
Date of Death: 16 May 1968
Place of Death: Republic of Vietnam
Cemetery: Fort Rosecrans National Cemetery (0-1855) (MH)—San Diego, California
Entered Service at: Los Angeles, Los Angeles County, California
Unit: Company C, 1st Battalion, 12th Infantry, 4th Infantry Division
Served as: Squad Leader
Battle or Place of Action: Kontum Province, Republic of Vietnam
Date of Action: 16 May 1968
G.O. Number, Date: 25, 23 April 1970
Date of Presentation: 7 April 1970
Place of Presentation: The White House, presented by Pres. Richard M. Nixon to his family
Citation: For conspicuous gallantry and intrepidity in action at the risk of his life above and beyond the call of duty. Sgt. Roark distinguished himself by extraordinary gallantry while serving with Company C. Sgt. Roark was the point squad leader of a small force which had the mission of rescuing 11 men in a hilltop observation post under heavy attack by a company-size force, approximately 1,000 meters from the battalion perimeter. As lead elements of the relief force reached the besieged observation post, intense automatic-weapons fire from enemy-occupied bunkers halted their movement. Without hesitation, Sgt. Roark maneuvered his squad, repeatedly exposing himself to withering enemy fire to hurl grenades and direct the fire of his squad to gain fire superiority and cover the withdrawal of the outpost and evacuation of its casualties. Frustrated in their effort to overrun the position, the enemy swept the hilltop with small arms and volleys of grenades. Seeing a grenade land in the midst of his men, Sgt. Roark, with complete disregard for his safety, hurled himself upon the grenade, absorbing its blast with his body. Sgt. Roark's magnificent leadership and dauntless courage saved the lives of many of his comrades and were the inspiration for the successful relief of the outpost. His actions which culminated in the supreme sacrifice of his life were in keeping with the highest traditions of the military service, and reflect great credit on himself and the U.S. Army.

3344 ◆ ROBERTS, GORDON RAY

Rank: Sergeant (rank at time of action: Specialist Fourth Class) (highest rank: Master Sergeant)
Service: U.S. Army
Birthday: 14 June 1950
Place of Birth: Middletown, Butler County, Ohio
Entered Service at: Cincinnati, Hamilton County, Ohio
Unit: Company B, 1st Battalion, 506th Infantry, 101st Airborne Division (Airmobile)
Served as: Rifleman
Battle or Place of Action: Thua Thien Province, Republic of Vietnam
Date of Action: 11 July 1969
G.O. Number, Date: 20, 24 March 1971
Date of Presentation: 2 March 1971
Place of Presentation: The White House (East Ballroom), presented by Pres. Richard M. Nixon
Citation: For conspicuous gallantry and intrepidity in action at the risk of his life above and beyond the call of duty. Sgt. Roberts distinguished himself while serving as a rifleman with Company B, during combat operations. Sgt. Roberts' platoon was maneuvering along a ridge to attack heavily fortified enemy bunker positions which had pinned down an adjoining friendly company. As the platoon approached the enemy positions, it was suddenly pinned down by heavy automatic-weapons and grenade fire from camouflaged enemy fortifications atop the overlooking hill. Seeing his platoon immobilized and in danger of failing in its mission, Sgt. Roberts crawled rapidly toward the closest enemy bunker. With complete disregard for his safety, he leaped to his feet and charged the bunker, firing as he ran. Despite the intense enemy fire directed at him, Sgt. Roberts silenced the two-man bunker. Without hesitation, Sgt. Roberts continued his one-man assault on a second bunker. As he neared the second bunker, a burst of enemy fire knocked his rifle from his hands. Sgt. Roberts picked up a rifle dropped by a comrade and continued his assault, silencing the bunker. He continued his charge against a third bunker and destroyed it with well-thrown hand grenades. Although Sgt. Roberts was now cut off from his platoon, he continued his assault against a fourth enemy emplacement. He fought through a heavy hail of fire to join elements of an adjoining company which had been pinned down by the enemy fire. Although continually exposed to hostile fire, he assisted in moving wounded personnel from exposed positions on the hilltop to an evacuation

area before returning to his unit. By his gallant and selfless actions, Sgt. Roberts contributed directly in saving the lives of his comrades and served as an inspiration to his fellow soldiers in the defeat of the enemy force. Sgt. Roberts' extraordinary heroism in action at the risk of his life were in keeping with the highest traditions of the military service and reflect great credit upon himself, his unit, and the U.S. Army.

3345 ◆ *ROBINSON JR., JAMES WILLIAM

Rank: Sergeant
Service: U.S. Army
Birthday: 30 August 1940
Place of Birth: Hinsdale, Du Page County, Illinois
Date of Death: 11 April 1966
Place of Death: Republic of Vietnam
Cemetery: Clarendon Hills Cemetery (MH)—Westmont, Illinois
Entered Service at: Chicago, Cook County, Illinois
Unit: Company D, 2d Battalion, 16th Infantry, 1st Infantry Division
Served as: Fire Team Leader
Battle or Place of Action: Republic of Vietnam
Date of Action: 11 April 1966
G.O. Number, Date: 35, 13 September 1967
Date of Presentation: 16 July 1967
Place of Presentation: The Pentagon, presented by Sec. of the Army Stanley R. Resor to his family
Citation: For conspicuous gallantry and intrepidity in action at the risk of his life above and beyond the call of duty. Company C was engaged in fierce combat with a Viet Cong battalion. Despite the heavy fire, Sgt. Robinson moved among the men of his fire team, instructing and inspiring them, and placing them in advantageous positions. Enemy snipers located in nearby trees were inflicting heavy casualties on forward elements of Sgt. Robinson's unit. Upon locating the enemy sniper whose fire was taking the heaviest toll, he took a grenade launcher and eliminated the sniper. Seeing a medic hit while administering aid to a wounded sergeant in front of his position and aware that now the two wounded men were at the mercy of the enemy, he charged through a withering hail of fire and dragged his comrades to safety, where he rendered first aid and saved their lives. As the battle continued and casualties mounted, Sgt. Robinson moved about under intense fire to collect from the wounded their weapons and ammunition and redistribute them to able-bodied soldiers. Adding his fire to that of his men, he assisted in eliminating a major enemy threat. Seeing another wounded comrade in front of his position, Sgt. Robinson again defied the enemy's fire to effect a rescue. In so doing he was himself wounded in the shoulder and leg. Despite his painful wounds, he dragged the soldier to shelter and saved his life by administering first aid. While patching his own wounds, he spotted an enemy machine gun which had inflicted a number of casualties on the American force. His rifle ammunition expended, he seized two grenades and, in an act of unsurpassed heroism, charged toward the entrenched enemy weapon. Hit again in the leg, this time with a tracer round which set fire to his clothing, Sgt. Robinson ripped the burning clothing from his body and staggered indomitably through the enemy fire, now concentrated solely on him, to within grenade range of the enemy machine-gun position. Sustaining two additional chest wounds, he marshalled his fleeting physical strength and hurled the two grenades, thus destroying the enemy gun position, as he fell dead upon the battlefield. His magnificent display of leadership and bravery saved several lives and inspired his soldiers to defeat the numerically superior enemy force. Sgt. Robinson's conspicuous gallantry and intrepidity, at the cost of his life, are in keeping with the finest traditions of the U.S. Army and reflect great credit upon the 1st Infantry Division and the U.S. Armed Forces.

3346 ◆ ROCCO, LOUIS RICHARD

Rank: Warrant Officer (rank at time of action: Sergeant First Class) (highest rank: Chief Warrant Officer 2)
Service: U.S. Army
Birthday: 19 November 1938
Place of Birth: Albuquerque, Bernalillo County, New Mexico
Entered Service at: Los Angeles, Los Angeles County, California
Unit: U.S. Military Assistance Command, Advisory Team 162
Served as: Medical Advisor
Battle or Place of Action: Northeast of Katum, Republic of Vietnam
Date of Action: 24 May 1970
G.O. Number, Date: 1, 3 January 1975
Date of Presentation: 12 December 1974
Place of Presentation: The White House, presented by Pres. Gerald R. Ford
Citation: WO Rocco distinguished himself when he volunteered to accompany a medical evacuation team on an urgent mission to evacuate eight critically wounded Army of the Republic of Vietnam personnel. As the helicopter approached the landing zone, it became the target for intense enemy automatic-weapons fire. Disregarding his own safety, WO Rocco identified and placed accurate suppressive fire on the enemy positions as the aircraft descended toward the landing zone. Sustaining major damage from the enemy fire, the aircraft was forced to crash land, causing WO Rocco to sustain a fractured wrist and hip and severely bruised back. Ignoring his injuries, he extracted the survivors from the burning wreckage, sustaining burns to his own body. Despite intense enemy fire, WO Rocco carried each unconscious man across approximately 20 meters of exposed terrain to the Army of the Republic of Vietnam perimeter. On each trip, his severely burned hands and broken wrist caused excruciating pain, but the lives of the unconscious crash survivors were more important than his personal discomfort, and he continued his rescue efforts. Once inside the friendly position, WO Rocco helped administer first aid to his wounded comrades until his wounds and burns caused him to collapse and lose consciousness. His bravery under fire and intense devotion to duty were directly responsible for saving three of his fellow soldiers from certain death. His unparalleled bravery in the face of enemy fire, his complete disregard for his own pain and injuries, and his per-

formance were far above and beyond the call of duty and were in keeping with the highest traditions of self-sacrifice and courage of the military service.

3347 ◆ ROGERS, CHARLES CALVIN

Rank: Lieutenant Colonel (highest rank: Major General)
Service: U.S. Army
Birthday: 6 September 1929
Place of Birth: Claremont, West Virginia
Date of Death: 21 September 1990
Place of Death: Munich, Germany
Cemetery: Arlington National Cemetery (7-A-99) (MH)—Arlington, Virginia
Entered Service at: Institute, Kanawha County, West Virginia
Unit: 1st Battalion, 5th Artillery, 1st Infantry Division
Served as: Battalion Commander
Battle or Place of Action: Fishhook near Cambodian border, Republic of Vietnam
Date of Action: 1 November 1968
G.O. Number, Date: 29, 5 June 1970
Date of Presentation: 14 May 1970
Place of Presentation: The White House, presented by Pres. Richard M. Nixon
Citation: For conspicuous gallantry and intrepidity in action at the risk of his life above and beyond the call of duty. Lt. Col. Rogers, Field Artillery, distinguished himself in action while serving as commanding officer, 1st Battalion, during the defense of a forward fire support base. In the early morning hours, the fire support base was subjected to a concentrated bombardment of heavy mortar, rocket, and rocket-propelled grenade fire. Simultaneously the position was struck by a human wave ground assault, led by sappers who breached the defensive barriers with bangalore torpedoes and penetrated the defensive perimeter. Lt. Col. Rogers with complete disregard for his safety moved through the hail of fragments from bursting enemy rounds to the embattled area. He aggressively rallied the dazed artillery crewmen to man their howitzers and he directed their fire on the assaulting enemy. Although knocked to the ground and wounded by an exploding round, Lt. Col. Rogers sprang to his feet and led a small counterattack force against an enemy element that had penetrated the howitzer position. Although painfully wounded a second time during the assault, Lt. Col. Rogers pressed the attack killing several of the enemy and driving the remainder from their positions. Refusing medical treatment, Lt. Col. Rogers reestablished and reinforced the defensive positions. As a second human wave attack was launched against another sector of the perimeter, Lt. Col. Rogers directed artillery fire on the assaulting enemy and led a second counterattack against the charging forces. His valorous example rallied the beleaguered defenders to repulse and defeat the enemy onslaught. Lt. Col. Rogers moved from position to position through the heavy enemy fire, giving encouragement and direction to his men. At dawn the determined enemy launched a third assault against the fire base in an attempt to overrun the position. Lt. Col. Rogers moved to the threatened area and directed lethal fire on the enemy f orces. Seeing a howitzer inoperative due to casualties, Lt. Col. Rogers joined the surviving members of the crew to return the howitzer to action. While directing the position defense, Lt. Col. Rogers was seriously wounded by fragments from a heavy mortar round which exploded on the parapet of the gun position. Although too severely wounded to physically lead the defenders, Lt. Col. Rogers continued to give encouragement and direction to his men in the defeating and repelling of the enemy attack. Lt. Col. Rogers' dauntless courage and heroism inspired the defenders of the fire support base to the heights of valor to defeat a determined and numerically superior enemy force. His relentless spirit of aggressiveness in action are in the highest traditions of the military service and reflect great credit upon himself, his unit, and the U.S. Army.

3348 ◆ *RUBIO, EURIPIDES

Rank: Captain
Service: U.S. Army
Birthday: 1 March 1938
Place of Birth: Ponce, Ponce County, Puerto Rico
Date of Death: 8 November 1966
Place of Death: Republic of Vietnam
Cemetery: Puerto Rico National Cemetery (HSA-5) (MH)—Bayamon, Puerto Rico
Entered Service at: Fort Buchanan, San Juan County, Puerto Rico
Unit: Headquarters & Headquarters Company, 1st Battalion, 28th Infantry, 1st Infantry Division
Served as: Communications Officer
Battle or Place of Action: Tay Ninh Province, Republic of Vietnam
Date of Action: 8 November 1966
G.O. Number, Date: 39, 2 August 1968
Date of Presentation: 11 July 1968
Place of Presentation: The Pentagon, presented by Sec. of the Army Stanley R. Resor to his family
Citation: For conspicuous gallantry and intrepidity in action at the risk of his life above and beyond the call of duty. Capt. Rubio, Infantry, was serving as communications officer, 1st Battalion, when a numerically superior enemy force launched a massive attack against the battalion defense position. Intense enemy machine-gun fire raked the area while mortar rounds and rifle grenades exploded within the perimeter. Leaving the relative safety of his post, Capt. Rubio received two serious wounds as he braved the withering fire to go to the area of most intense action where he distributed ammunition, reestablished positions, and rendered aid to the wounded. Disregarding the painful wounds, he unhesitatingly assumed command when a rifle company commander was medically evacuated. Capt. Rubio was wounded a third time as he selflessly exposed himself to the devastating enemy fire to move among his men to encourage them to fight with renewed effort. While aiding the evacuation of wounded personnel, he noted that a smoke grenade which was intended to mark the Viet Cong position for air strikes had fallen dangerously close to the friendly lines. Capt. Rubio ran to reposition the grenade but was immediately struck to his knees by enemy

fire. Despite his several wounds, Capt. Rubio scooped up the grenade, ran through the deadly hail of fire to within 20 meters of the enemy position and hurled the already smoking grenade into the midst of the enemy before he fell for the final time. Using the reposition grenade as a marker, friendly air strikes were directed to destroy the hostile positions. Capt. Rubio's singularly heroic act turned the tide of battle, and his extraordinary leadership and valor were a magnificent inspiration to his men. His remarkable bravery and selfless concern for his men are in keeping with the highest traditions of the military service and reflect great credit on Capt. Rubio and the U.S. Army.

3349 ◆ *SANTIAGO-COLON, HECTOR

Rank: Specialist Fourth Class
Service: U.S. Army
Birthday: 20 December 1942
Place of Birth: Salinas, Salinas County, Puerto Rico
Date of Death: 28 June 1968
Place of Death: Republic of Vietnam
Cemetery: Salinas Municipal Cemetery (MH)—Salinas, Puerto Rico
Entered Service at: New York, New York
Unit: Company B, 5th Battalion, 7th Cavalry, 1st Cavalry Division (Airmobile)
Served as: Gunner in Mortar Platoon
Battle or Place of Action: Quang Tri Province, Republic of Vietnam
Date of Action: 28 June 1968
G.O. Number, Date: 24, 23 April 1970
Date of Presentation: 7 April 1970
Place of Presentation: The White House, presented by Pres. Richard M. Nixon to his family
Citation: For conspicuous gallantry and intrepidity in action at the risk of his life above and beyond the call of duty. Sp4c. Santiago-Colon distinguished himself at the cost of his life while serving as a gunner in the mortar platoon of Company B. While serving as a perimeter sentry, Sp4c. Santiago-Colon heard distinct movement in the heavily wooded area to his front and flanks. Immediately he alerted his fellow sentries in the area to move to their foxholes and remain alert for any enemy probing forces. From the wooded area around his position heavy enemy automatic-weapons and small-arms fire suddenly broke out, but extreme darkness rendered difficult the precise location and identification of the hostile force. Only the muzzle flashes from the enemy weapons indicated their positions. Sp4c. Santiago-Colon and the other members of his platoon immediately began to repel the attackers, utilizing hand grenades, antipersonnel mines and small-arms fire. Due to the heavy volume of enemy fire and exploding grenades around them, a North Vietnamese soldier was able to crawl, undetected, to their position. Suddenly, the enemy soldier lobbed a hand grenade into Sp4c. Santiago-Colon's foxhole. Realizing that there was no time to throw the grenade out of his position, Sp4c. Santiago-Colon retrieved the grenade, tucked it into his stomach and, turning away from his comrades, absorbed the full impact of the blast. His heroic self-sacrifice saved the lives of those who occupied the foxhole with him, and provided them with the inspiration to continue fighting until they had forced the enemy to retreat from the perimeter. By his gallantry at the cost of his life and in the highest traditions of the military service, Sp4c. Santiago-Colon has reflected great credit upon himself, his unit, and the U.S. Army.

3350 ◆ *SARGENT, RUPPERT LEON

Rank: First Lieutenant
Service: U.S. Army
Birthday: 6 January 1938
Place of Birth: Hampton, Hampton County, Virginia
Date of Death: 15 March 1967
Place of Death: Republic of Vietnam
Cemetery: Hampton National Cemetery (F-17596) (MH)—Hampton Virginia,
Entered Service at: Richmond, Richmond County, Virginia
Unit: Company B, 4th Battalion, 9th Infantry, 25th Infantry Division
Served as: Platoon Leader
Battle or Place of Action: Hau Nghia Province, Republic of Vietnam
Date of Action: 15 March 1967
G.O. Number, Date: 25, 17 April 1969
Date of Presentation: 10 March 1969
Place of Presentation: At Widow's home, Hampton, Va., presented by Gen. Donley P. Bolton
Citation: For conspicuous gallantry and intrepidity in action at the risk of his life above and beyond the call of duty. While leading a platoon of Company B, 1st Lt. Sargent was investigating a reported Viet Cong meetinghouse and weapons cache. A tunnel entrance which 1st Lt. Sargent observed was booby-trapped. He tried to destroy the booby trap and blow the cover from the tunnel using hand grenades, but this attempt was not successful. He and his demolition man moved in to destroy the booby trap and cover which flushed a Viet Cong soldier from the tunnel, who was immediately killed by the nearby platoon sergeant. First Lt. Sargent, the platoon sergeant, and a forward observer moved toward the tunnel entrance. As they approached, another Viet Cong emerged and threw two hand grenades that landed in the midst of the group. First Lt. Sargent fired three shots at the enemy then turned and unhesitatingly threw himself over the two grenades. He was mortally wounded, and his two companions were lightly wounded when the grenades exploded. By his courageous and selfless act of exceptional heroism, he saved the lives of the platoon sergeant and forward observer and prevented the injury or death of several other nearby comrades. First Lt. Sargent's actions were in keeping with the highest traditions of the military service and reflect great credit upon himself and the U.S. Army.

3351 ◆ SASSER, CLARENCE EUGENE

Rank: Specialist Fifth Class (rank at time of action: Private First Class)
Service: U.S. Army
Birthday: 12 September 1947

Place of Birth: Chenango, Texas
Entered Service at: Houston, Harris County, Texas
Unit: Headquarters & Headquarters Company, 3d Battalion, 60th Infantry, 9th Infantry Division
Served as: Medical Aidman
Battle or Place of Action: Ding Tuong Province, Republic of Vietnam
Date of Action: 10 January 1968
G.O. Number, Date: 26, 17 April 1969
Date of Presentation: 7 March 1969
Place of Presentation: The White House, presented by Pres. Richard M. Nixon
Citation: For conspicuous gallantry and intrepidity in action at the risk of his life above and beyond the call of duty. Sp5c. Sasser distinguished himself while assigned to Headquarters and Headquarters Company, 3d Battalion. He was serving as a medical aidman with Company A, 3d Battalion, on a reconnaissance-in-force operation. His company was making an air assault when suddenly it was taken under heavy small-arms, recoilless-rifle, machine-gun, and rocket fire from well-fortified enemy positions on three sides of the landing zone. During the first few minutes, over 30 casualties were sustained. Without hesitation, Sp5c. Sasser ran across an open rice paddy through a hail of fire to assist the wounded. After helping one man to safety, he was painfully wounded in the left shoulder by fragments of an exploding rocket. Refusing medical attention, he ran through a barrage of rocket and automatic-weapons fire to aid casualties of the initial attack and, after giving them urgently needed treatment, continued to search for other wounded. Despite two additional wounds immobilizing his legs, he dragged himself through the mud toward another soldier 100 meters away. Although in agonizing pain and faint from loss of blood, Sp5c. Sasser reached the man, treated him, and proceeded on to encourage another group of soldiers to crawl 200 meters to relative safety. There he attended their wounds for five hours until they were evacuated. Sp5c. Sasser's extraordinary heroism is in keeping with the highest traditions of the military service and reflect great credit upon himself, his unit, and the U.S. Army.

3352 ◆ *SEAY, WILLIAM WAYNE

Rank: Sergeant
Service: U.S. Army
Birthday: 24 October 1948
Place of Birth: Brewton, Escambia County, Alabama
Date of Death: 25 August 1968
Place of Death: Republic of Vietnam
Cemetery: Weaver Cemetery—Brewton, Alabama
Entered Service at: Montgomery, Montgomery County, Alabama
Unit: 62d Transportation Company (Medium Truck), 7th Transportation Battalion, 48th Transportation Group
Served as: Driver
Battle or Place of Action: near Ap Nhi, Republic of Vietnam
Date of Action: 25 August 1968
G.O. Number, Date: 12, 23 April 1970
Date of Presentation: 7 April 1970
Place of Presentation: The White House, presented by Pres. Richard M. Nixon to his family
Citation: For conspicuous gallantry and intrepidity in action at the risk of his life above and beyond the call of duty. Sgt. Seay distinguished himself while serving as a driver with the 62d Transportation Company, on a resupply mission. The convoy with which he was traveling, carrying critically needed ammunition and supplies from Long Binh to Tay Ninh, was ambushed by a reinforced battalion of the North Vietnamese Army. As the main elements of the convoy entered the ambush killing zone, they were struck by intense rocket, machine-gun, and automatic-weapons fire from the well-concealed and entrenched enemy force. When his convoy was forced to stop, Sgt. Seay immediately dismounted and took a defensive position behind the wheels of a vehicle loaded with high-explosive ammunition. As the violent North Vietnamese assault approached to within 10 meters of the road, Sgt. Seay opened fire, killing two of the enemy. He then spotted a sniper in a tree approximately 75 meters to his front and killed him. When an enemy grenade was thrown under an ammunition trailer near his position, without regard for his own safety he left his protective cover, exposing himself to intense enemy fire, picked up the grenade, and threw it back to the North Vietnamese position, killing four more of the enemy and saving the lives of the men around him. Another enemy grenade landed approximately three meters from Sgt. Seay's position. Again Sgt. Seay left his covered position and threw the armed grenade back upon the assaulting enemy. After returning to his position he was painfully wounded in the right wrist, however, Sgt. Seay continued to give encouragement and direction to his fellow soldiers. After moving to the relative cover of a shallow ditch, he detected three enemy soldiers who had penetrated the position and were preparing to fire on his comrades. Although weak from loss of blood and with his right hand immobilized, Sgt. Seay stood up and fired his rifle with his left hand, killing all th
ree and saving the lives of the other men in his location. As a result of his heroic action, Sgt. Seay was mortally wounded by a sniper's bullet. Sgt. Seay, by his gallantry in action at the cost of his life, has reflected great credit upon himself, his unit, and the U.S. Army.

3353 ◆ *SHEA, DANIEL JOHN

Rank: Private First Class
Service: U.S. Army
Birthday: 29 January 1947
Place of Birth: Norwalk, Fairfield County, Connecticut
Date of Death: 14 May 1969
Place of Death: Republic of Vietnam
Cemetery: Saint John's Cemetery (MH)—Norwalk, Connecticut
Entered Service at: New Haven, New Haven County, Connecticut
Unit: Headquarters Company, 3d Battalion, 21st Infantry, 196th Infantry Brigade, Americal Division
Served as: Medical Aidman
Battle or Place of Action: Quang Tri Province, Republic of Vietnam

Date of Action: 14 May 1969
G.O. Number, Date: 13, 9 March 1971
Date of Presentation: 16 February 1971
Place of Presentation: The White House, presented by Pres. Richard M. Nixon presented to his family
Citation: For conspicuous gallantry and intrepidity in action at the risk of his life above and beyond the call of duty. Pfc. Shea, Headquarters and Headquarters Company, 3d Battalion, distinguished himself while serving as a medical aidman with Company C, 3d Battalion, during a combat patrol mission. As the lead platoon of the company was crossing a rice paddy, a large enemy force in ambush positions opened fire with mortars, grenades, and automatic weapons. Under heavy crossfire from three sides, the platoon withdrew to a small island in the paddy to establish a defensive perimeter. Pfc. Shea, seeing that a number of his comrades had fallen in the initial hail of fire, dashed from the defensive position to assist the wounded. With complete disregard for his safety and braving the intense hostile fire sweeping the open rice paddy, Pfc. Shea made four trips to tend wounded soldiers and to carry them to the safety of the platoon position. Seeing a fifth wounded comrade directly in front of one of the enemy strong points, Pfc. Shea ran to his assistance. As he reached the wounded man, Pfc. Shea was grievously wounded. Disregarding his welfare, Pfc. Shea tended his wounded comrade and began to move him back to the safety of the defensive perimeter. As he neared the platoon position, Pfc. Shea was mortally wounded by a burst of enemy fire. By his heroic actions Pfc. Shea saved the lives of several of his fellow soldiers. Pfc. Shea's gallantry in action at the cost of his life were in keeping with the highest traditions of the military service and reflect great credit upon himself, his unit, and the U.S. Army.

3354 ◆ *SHIELDS, MARVIN GLEN

Rank: Construction Mechanic Third Class
Service: U.S. Navy
Birthday: 30 December 1939
Place of Birth: Port Townsend, Jefferson County, Washington
Date of Death: 10 June 1965
Place of Death: Republic of Vietnam
Cemetery: Gardiner Cemetery (MH)—Gardiner, Washington
Entered Service at: Seattle, King County, Washington
Unit: Seabee Team 1104, Mobile Construction Battalion 11
Served as: Seabee
Battle or Place of Action: Dong Xoai, Republic of Vietnam
Date of Action: 10 June 1965
Date of Presentation: 13 September 1966
Place of Presentation: The White House, presented by Pres. Lyndon B. Johnson to his family
Citation: For conspicuous gallantry and intrepidity at the risk of his life above and beyond the call of duty. Although wounded when the compound of Detachment A-342, 5th Special Forces Group (Airborne), 1st Special Forces, came under intense fire from an estimated reinforced Viet Cong regiment employing machine guns, heavy weapons, and small arms, Shields continued to resupply his fellow Americans who needed ammunition and to return the enemy fire for a period of approximately three hours, at which time the Viet Cong launched a massive attack at close-range with flamethrowers, hand grenades and small-arms fire. Wounded a second time during this attack, Shields nevertheless assisted in carrying a more critically wounded man to safety, and then resumed firing at the enemy for four more hours. When the commander asked for a volunteer to accompany him in an attempt to knock out an enemy machine-gun emplacement which was endangering the lives of all personnel in the compound because of the accuracy of its fire, Shields unhesitatingly volunteered for this extremely hazardous mission. Proceeding toward their objective with a 3.5-inch rocket launcher, they succeeded in destroying the enemy machine-gun emplacement, thus undoubtedly saving the lives of many of their fellow servicemen in the compound. Shields was mortally wounded by hostile fire while returning to his defensive position. His heroic initiative and great personal valor in the face of intense enemy fire sustain and enhance the finest traditions of the U.S. Naval Service.

3355 ◆ *SIJAN, LANCE PETER

Rank: Captain
Service: U.S. Air Force
Birthday: 13 April 1942
Place of Birth: Milwaukee, Milwaukee County, Wisconsin
Date of Death: 22 January 1968
Place of Death: Hoa Lo Prison, Hanoi, North Vietnam
Cemetery: Arlington Park Cemetery (MH)—Milwaukee, Wisconsin
Entered Service at: Milwaukee, Milwaukee County, Wisconsin
Unit: 480th Tactical Fighter Squadron, Da Nang AFB, Republic of Vietnam
Served as: Pilot of an F-4C Aircraft
Battle or Place of Action: Ban Loboy Ford, Laos and Ban Kari Pass & Hoa Lo Prison, North Vietnam
Date of Action: 9 November 1967
G.O. Number, Date: GB-181, 23 March 1976
Date of Presentation: 6 March 1976
Place of Presentation: The White House, presented by Pres. Gerald R. Ford to his family
Citation: While on a flight over North Vietnam, Capt. Sijan ejected from his disabled aircraft and successfully evaded capture for more than six weeks. During this time, he was seriously injured and suffered from shock and extreme weight loss due to lack of food. After being captured by North Vietnamese soldiers, Capt. Sijan was taken to a holding point for subsequent transfer to a prisoner-of-war camp. In his emaciated and crippled condition, he overpowered one of his guards and crawled into the jungle, only to be recaptured after several hours. He was then transferred to another prison camp where he was kept in solitary confinement and interrogated at length. During interrogation, he was severely tortured; however, he did not divulge any information to his captors. Capt. Sijan lapsed into delirium and was placed in the care of another prisoner. During his intermittent periods of

consciousness until his death, he never complained of his physical condition and, on several occasions, spoke of future escape attempts. Capt. Sijan's extraordinary heroism and intrepidity above and beyond the call of duty at the cost of his life are in keeping with the highest traditions of the U.S. Air Force and reflect great credit upon himself and the U.S. Armed Forces.
Notes: POW from 9 November 1967—22 January 1968

3356 ◆ *SIMS, CLIFFORD CHESTER

Rank: Staff Sergeant
Service: U.S. Army
Birthday: 18 June 1942
Place of Birth: Port St. Joe, Gulf County, Florida
Date of Death: 21 February 1968
Place of Death: Republic of Vietnam
Cemetery: Barrancas National Cemetery (29-546) (MH)—Pensacola, Florida
Entered Service at: Jacksonville, Duval County, Florida
Unit: Company D, 2d Battalion (Airborne), 501st Infantry, 101st Airborne Division
Served as: Squad Leader
Battle or Place of Action: near Hue, Republic of Vietnam
Date of Action: 21 February 1968
G.O. Number, Date: 83, 12 December 1969
Date of Presentation: 2 December 1969
Place of Presentation: The White House, presented by Vice Pres. Spiro T. Agnew to his family
Citation: For conspicuous gallantry and intrepidity in action at the risk of his life above and beyond the call of duty. S/Sgt. Sims distinguished himself while serving as a squad leader with Company D. Company D was assaulting a heavily fortified enemy position concealed within a dense wooded area when it encountered strong enemy defensive fire. Once within the woodline, S/Sgt. Sims led his squad in a furious attack against an enemy force which had pinned down the 1st Platoon and threatened to overrun it. His skillful leadership provided the platoon with freedom of movement and enabled it to regain the initiative. S/Sgt. Sims was then ordered to move his squad to a position where he could provide covering fire for the company command group and to link up with the 3d Platoon which was under heavy enemy pressure. After moving no more than 30 meters S/Sgt. Sims noticed that a brick structure in which ammunition was stocked was on fire. Realizing the danger, S/Sgt. Sims took immediate action to move his squad from this position. Though in the process of leaving the area two members of his squad were injured by the subsequent explosion of the ammunition, S/Sgt. Sims' prompt actions undoubtedly prevented more serious casualties from occurring. While continuing through the dense woods amidst heavy enemy fire, S/Sgt. Sims and his squad were approaching a bunker when they heard an unmistakable noise of a concealed booby trap being triggered immediately to their front. S/Sgt. Sims warned his comrades of the danger and unhesitatingly hurled himself upon the device as it exploded, taking the full impact of the blast. In so protecting his fellow soldiers, he willingly sacrificed his life. S/Sgt. Sims' extraordinary heroism at the cost of his life is in keeping with the highest traditions of the military service and reflect great credit upon himself and the U.S. Army.

3357 ◆ *SINGLETON, WALTER KEITH

Rank: Sergeant
Service: U.S. Marine Corps
Birthday: 7 December 1944
Place of Birth: Memphis, Shelby County, Tennessee
Date of Death: 24 March 1967
Place of Death: Republic of Vietnam
Cemetery: Memory Hill Gardens Cemetery—Memphis, Tennessee
Entered Service at: Memphis, Shelby County, Tennessee
Unit: Company A, 1st Battalion, 9th Marines, 3d Marine Division (Rein) FMF
Served as: Supply Sergeant
Battle or Place of Action: Gio Linh District, Quang Tri Province, Republic of Vietnam
Date of Action: 24 March 1967
Date of Presentation: 4 September 1968
Place of Presentation: Marine Barracks, Washington, D.C., presented by Secretary of the Navy Paul R. Ignatius to his family
Citation: For conspicuous gallantry and intrepidity at the risk of his life above and beyond the call of duty. Sgt. Singleton's company was conducting combat operations when the lead platoon received intense small-arms, automatic-weapons, rocket, and mortar fire from a well-entrenched enemy force. As the company fought its way forward, the extremely heavy enemy fire caused numerous friendly casualties. Sensing the need for early treatment of the wounded, Sgt. Singleton quickly moved from his relatively safe position in the rear of the foremost point of the advance and made numerous trips through the enemy killing zone to move the injured men out of the danger area. Noting that a large part of the enemy fire was coming from a hedgerow, he seized a machine gun and assaulted the key enemy location, delivering devastating fire as he advanced. He forced his way through the hedgerow directly into the enemy strong point. Although he was mortally wounded, his fearless attack killed eight of the enemy and drove the remainder from the hedgerow. Sgt. Singleton's bold actions completely disorganized the enemy defense and saved the lives of many of his comrades. His daring initiative, selfless devotion to duty and indomitable fighting spirit reflected great credit upon himself and the Marine Corps, and his performance upheld the highest traditions of the U.S. Naval Service.

3358 ◆ *SISLER, GEORGE KENTON

Rank: First Lieutenant
Service: U.S. Army
Birthday: 19 September 1937
Place of Birth: Dexter, Stoddard County, Missouri
Date of Death: 7 February 1967
Place of Death: Republic of Vietnam
Cemetery: Dexter Cemetery—Dexter, Missouri
Entered Service at: Dexter, Stoddard County, Missouri

Unit: Headquarters & Headquarters Company, 5th Special Forces Group (Airborne), 1st Special Forces
Served as: Platoon Leader/Advisor
Battle or Place of Action: Republic of Vietnam
Date of Action: 7 February 1967
G.O. Number, Date: 35, 16 July 1968
Date of Presentation: 27 June 1968
Place of Presentation: The Pentagon, presented by Sec. of the Army Stanley R. Resor to his family
Citation: For conspicuous gallantry and intrepidity at the risk of his life above and beyond the call of duty. 1st Lt. Sisler was the platoon leader/adviser to a Special United States/Vietnam exploitation force. While on patrol deep within enemy-dominated territory, 1st Lt. Sisler's platoon was attacked from three sides by a company-sized enemy force. 1st Lt. Sisler quickly rallied his men, deployed them to a better defensive position, called for air strikes, and moved among his men to encourage and direct their efforts. Learning that two men had been wounded and were unable to pull back to the perimeter, 1st Lt. Sisler charged from the position through intense enemy fire to assist them. He reached the men and began carrying one of them back to the perimeter, when he was taken under more intensive weapons fire by the enemy. Laying down his wounded comrade, he killed three onrushing enemy soldiers by firing his rifle and silenced the enemy machine gun with a grenade. As he returned the wounded man to the perimeter, the left flank of the position came under extremely heavy attack by the superior enemy force and several additional men of his platoon were quickly wounded. Realizing the need for instant action to prevent his position from being overrun, 1st Lt. Sisler picked up some grenades and charged singlehandedly into the enemy onslaught, firing his weapon and throwing grenades. This singularly heroic action broke up the vicious assault and forced the enemy to begin withdrawing. Despite the continuing enemy fire, 1st Lt. Sisler was moving about the battlefield directing force and several men of his platoon were quickly wounded. His extraordinary leadership, infinite courage, and selfless concern for his men saved the lives of a number of his comrades. His actions reflect great credit upon himself and uphold the highest traditions of the military service.

3359 ◆ *SKIDGEL, DONALD SIDNEY

Rank: Sergeant
Service: U.S. Army
Birthday: 13 October 1948
Place of Birth: Caribou, Aroostook County, Maine
Date of Death: 14 September 1969
Place of Death: Republic of Vietnam
Cemetery: Sawyer Cemetery (MH)—Plymouth, Maine
Entered Service at: Bangor, Penobscot County, Maine
Unit: Troop D, 1st Squadron, 9th Cavalry, 1st Cavalry Division
Served as: Reconnaissance Section Leader
Battle or Place of Action: near Song Be, Republic of Vietnam
Date of Action: 14 September 1969
G.O. Number, Date: 5, 25 January 1972
Date of Presentation: 16 December 1971
Place of Presentation: Old Executive Office Building, presented by Vice Pres. Spiro T. Agnew to his family
Citation: For conspicuous gallantry and intrepidity in action at the risk of his life above and beyond the call of duty. Sgt. Skidgel distinguished himself while serving as a reconnaissance section leader in Troop D. On a road near Song Be in Binh Long Province, Sgt. Skidgel and his section with other elements of his troop were acting as a convoy security-and-screening force when contact occurred with an estimated enemy battalion concealed in tall grass and in bunkers bordering the road. Sgt. Skidgel maneuvered off the road and began placing effective machine-gun fire on the enemy automatic-weapons and rocket-propelled-grenade positions. After silencing at least one position, he ran with his machine gun across 60 meters of bullet-swept ground to another location from which he continued to rake the enemy positions. Running low on ammunition, he returned to his vehicle over the same terrain. Moments later he was alerted that the command element was receiving intense automatic-weapons, rocket-propelled-grenade and mortar fire. Although he knew the road was saturated with enemy fire, Sgt. Skidgel calmly mounted his vehicle and with his driver advanced toward the command group in an effort to draw the enemy fire onto himself. Despite the hostile fire concentrated on him, he succeeded in silencing several enemy positions with his machine gun. Moments later Sgt. Skidgel was knocked down onto the rear fender by the explosion of an enemy rocket-propelled grenade. Ignoring his extremely painful wounds, he staggered back to his feet and placed effective fire on several other enemy positions until he was mortally wounded by hostile small-arms fire. His selfless actions enabled the command group to withdraw to a better position without casualties and inspired the rest of his fellow soldiers to gain fire superiority and defeat the enemy. Sgt. Skidgel's gallantry at the cost of his life were in keeping with the highest traditions of the military service and reflect great credit upon himself, his unit, and the U.S. Army.

3360 ◆ *SMEDLEY, LARRY EUGENE

Rank: Corporal
Service: U.S. Marine Corps
Birthday: 4 March 1949
Place of Birth: Front Royal, Warren County, Virginia
Date of Death: 21 December 1967
Place of Death: Republic of Vietnam
Cemetery: Arlington National Cemetery (31-6486) (MH)—Arlington, Virginia
Entered Service at: Orlando, Orange County, Florida
Unit: Company D, 1st Battalion, 7th Marines, 1st Marine Division (Rein) FMF
Served as: Squad Leader
Battle or Place of Action: at the mouth of Happy Valley, near Phouc Ninh (2), Quang Nam Province, Republic of Vietnam
Date of Action: 20-21 December 1967
Date of Presentation: 20 June 1969
Place of Presentation: The White House, presented by Pres. Richard M. Nixon to his family

Citation: For conspicuous gallantry and intrepidity at the risk of his life above and beyond the call of duty while serving as a squad leader with Company D, in connection with operations against the enemy. On the evenings of 20 and 21 December 1967, Cpl. Smedley led his six-man squad to an ambush site at the mouth of Happy Valley, near Phouc Ninh (2) in Quang Nam Province. Later that night an estimated 100 Viet Cong and North Vietnamese Army regulars, carrying 122-mm rocket launchers and mortars, were observed moving toward Hill 41. Realizing this was a significant enemy move to launch an attack on the vital Da Nang complex, Cpl. Smedley immediately took sound and courageous action to stop the enemy threat. After he radioed for a reaction force, he skillfully maneuvered his men to a more advantageous position and led an attack on the numerically superior enemy force. A heavy volume of fire from an enemy machine-gun positioned on the left flank of the squad inflicted several casualties on Cpl. Smedley's unit. Simultaneously, an enemy rifle grenade exploded nearby, wounding him in the right foot and knocking him to the ground. Cpl. Smedley disregarded this serious injury and valiantly struggled to his feet, shouting words of encouragement to his men. He fearlessly led a charge against the enemy machine-gun emplacement, firing his rifle and throwing grenades, until he was again struck by enemy fire and knocked to the ground. Gravely wounded and weak from loss of blood, he rose and commenced a one-man assault against the enemy position. Although his aggressive and singlehanded attack resulted in the destruction of the machine gun, he was struck in the chest by enemy fire and fell mortally wounded. Cpl. Smedley's inspiring and courageous actions, bold initiative, and selfless devotion to duty in the face of certain death were in keeping with the highest traditions of the Marine Corps and the U.S. Naval Service. He gallantly gave his life for his country.

3361 ◆ *SMITH, ELMELINDO RODRIQUES

Rank: Sergeant First Class (rank at time of action: Staff Sergeant)
Service: U.S. Army
Birthday: 27 July 1935
Place of Birth: Honolulu, Honolulu County, Hawaii
Date of Death: 16 February 1967
Place of Death: Republic of Vietnam
Cemetery: National Memorial Cemetery of the Pacific (W-131) (MH)—Honolulu, Hawaii
Entered Service at: Honolulu, Honolulu County, Hawaii
Unit: 1st Platoon, Company C, 2d Battalion, 8th Infantry, 4th Infantry Division
Served as: Platoon Sergeant
Battle or Place of Action: Republic of Vietnam
Date of Action: 16 February 1967
G.O. Number, Date: 63, 22 October 1968
Date of Presentation: 3 October 1968
Place of Presentation: The Pentagon, presented by Sec. of the Army Stanley R. Resor to his family
Citation: For conspicuous gallantry and intrepidity at the risk of his life above and beyond the call of duty. During a reconnaissance patrol, his platoon was suddenly engaged by intense machine-gun fire hemming in the platoon on three sides. A defensive perimeter was hastily established, but the enemy added mortar and rocket fire to the deadly fusillade and assaulted the position from several directions. With complete disregard for his safety, P/Sgt. Smith moved through the deadly fire along the defensive line, positioning soldiers, distributing ammunition, and encouraging his men to repel the enemy attack. Struck to the ground by enemy fire which caused a severe shoulder wound, he regained his feet, killed the enemy soldier, and continued to move about the perimeter. He was again wounded in the shoulder and stomach but continued moving on his knees to assist in the defense. Noting the enemy massing at a weakened point on the perimeter, he crawled into the open and poured deadly fire into the enemy ranks. As he crawled on, he was struck by a rocket. Moments later, he regained consciousness, and drawing on his fast dwindling strength, continued to crawl from man to man. When he could move no farther, he chose to remain in the open where he could alert the perimeter to the approaching enemy. P/Sgt. Smith perished, never relenting in his determined effort against the enemy. The valorous acts and heroic leadership of this outstanding soldier inspired those remaining members of his platoon to beat back the enemy assaults. P/Sgt. Smith's gallant actions were in keeping with the highest traditions of the U.S. Army and they reflect great credit upon him and the Armed Forces of his country.

3362 ◆ SPRAYBERRY, JAMES MICHAEL

Rank: Captain (rank at time of action: First Lieutenant) (highest rank: Lieutenant Colonel)
Service: U.S. Army
Birthday: 24 April 1947
Place of Birth: LaGrange, Troup County, Georgia
Entered Service at: Montgomery, Montgomery County, Alabama
Unit: Company D, 5th Battalion, 7th Cavalry, 1st Cavalry Division (Airmobile)
Served as: Executive Officer
Battle or Place of Action: Republic of Vietnam
Date of Action: 25 April 1968
G.O. Number, Date: 64, 27 October 1969
Date of Presentation: 9 October 1969
Place of Presentation: The White House (South Lawn), presented by Pres. Richard M. Nixon
Citation: For conspicuous gallantry and intrepidity in action at the risk of his life above and beyond the call of duty. Capt. Sprayberry, Armor, U.S. Army, distinguished himself by exceptional bravery while serving as executive officer of Company D. His company commander and a great number of the men were wounded and separated from the main body of the company. A daylight attempt to rescue them was driven back by the well-entrenched enemy's heavy fire. Capt. Sprayberry then organized and led a volunteer night patrol to eliminate the intervening enemy bunkers and to relieve the surrounded element. The patrol soon began receiving enemy machine-gun fire. Capt. Sprayberry quickly moved the men to protective cover and without regard for his own safety, crawled within close range of the bunker from which the fire

was coming. He silenced the machine gun with a hand grenade. Identifying several one-man enemy positions nearby, Capt. Sprayberry immediately attacked them with the rest of his grenades. He crawled back for more grenades and when two grenades were thrown at his men from a position to the front, Capt. Sprayberry, without hesitation, again exposed himself and charged the enemy-held bunker, killing its occupants with a grenade. Placing two men to cover his advance, he crawled forward and neutralized three more bunkers with grenades. Immediately thereafter, Capt. Sprayberry was surprised by an enemy soldier who charged from a concealed position. He killed the soldier with his pistol and with continuing disregard for the danger neutralized another enemy emplacement. Capt. Sprayberry then established radio contact with the isolated men, directing them toward his position. When the two elements made contact he organized his men into litter parties to evacuate the wounded. As the evacuation was nearing completion, he observed an enemy machine-gun position which he silenced with a grenade. Capt. Sprayberry returned to the rescue party, established security, and moved to friendly lines with the wounded. This rescue operation, which lasted approximately 7 1/2 hours, saved the lives of many of his fellow soldiers. Capt. Sprayberry personally killed 12 enemy soldiers, eliminated two machine guns, and destroyed numerous enemy bunkers. Capt. Sprayberry's indomitable spirit and gallant action at great personal risk to his life are in keeping with the highest traditions of the military service and reflect great credit upon himself, his unit, and the U.S. Army.

3363 ◆ *STEINDAM, RUSSELL ALBERT

Rank: First Lieutenant
Service: U.S. Army
Birthday: 27 August 1946
Place of Birth: Austin, Travis County, Texas
Date of Death: 1 February 1970
Place of Death: Republic of Vietnam
Cemetery: Restland Memorial Park (MH)—Dallas, Texas
Entered Service at: Austin, Travis County, Texas
Unit: Troop B, 3d Squadron, 4th Cavalry, 25th Infantry Division
Served as: Platoon Leader
Battle or Place of Action: Tay Ninh Province, Republic of Vietnam
Date of Action: 1 February 1970
G.O. Number, Date: 3, 25 January 1972
Date of Presentation: 16 December 1971
Place of Presentation: Old Executive Office Building, presented by Vice Pres. Spiro T. Agnew to his family
Citation: For conspicuous gallantry and intrepidity in action at the risk of his life above and beyond the call of duty. First Lt. Steindam, Troop B, while serving as a platoon leader, led members of his platoon on a night ambush operation. On the way to the ambush site, suspected enemy movement was detected on one flank and the platoon's temporary position was subjected to intense small-arms and automatic-weapons fire as well as a fusillade of hand and rocket-propelled grenades. After the initial barrage, 1st Lt. Steindam ordered fire placed on the enemy position and the wounded men to be moved to a shallow bomb crater. As he directed the return fire against the enemy from his exposed position, a fragmentation grenade was thrown into the site occupied by his command group. Instantly realizing the extreme gravity of the situation, 1st Lt. Steindam shouted a warning to alert his fellow soldiers in the immediate vicinity. Then, unhesitatingly and with complete disregard for his safety, 1st Lt. Steindam deliberately threw himself on the grenade, absorbing the full and fatal force of the explosion as it detonated. By his gallant action and self-sacrifice, he was able to save the lives of the nearby members of his command group. The extraordinary courage and selflessness displayed by 1st Lt. Steindam were an inspiration to his comrades and are in the highest traditions of the U.S. Army.

3364 ◆ *STEWART, JIMMY GOETHEL

Rank: Staff Sergeant
Service: U.S. Army
Birthday: 25 December 1942
Place of Birth: West Columbia, Mason County, West Virginia
Date of Death: 18 May 1966
Place of Death: Republic of Vietnam
Cemetery: Riverview Cemetery—Middleport, Oklahoma
Entered Service at: Ashland, Boyd County, Kentucky
Unit: Company B, 2d Battalion, 12th Cavalry, 1st Cavalry Division (Airmobile)
Battle or Place of Action: Republic of Vietnam
Date of Action: 18 May 1966
G.O. Number, Date: 41, 22 September 1967
Date of Presentation: 24 August 1967
Place of Presentation: The Pentagon, presented by Sec. of the Army Stanley R. Resor to his family
Citation: For conspicuous gallantry and intrepidity in action at the risk of his life above and beyond the call of duty. Early in the morning a reinforced North Vietnamese company attacked Company B, which was manning a defensive perimeter in Vietnam. The surprise onslaught wounded five members of a six-man squad caught in the direct path of the enemy's thrust. S/Sgt. Stewart became a lone defender of vital terrain—virtually one man against a hostile platoon. Refusing to take advantage of a lull in the firing which would have permitted him to withdraw, S/Sgt. Stewart elected to hold his ground to protect his fallen comrades and prevent an enemy penetration of the company perimeter. As the full force of the platoon-sized attack struck his lone position, he fought like a man possessed; emptying magazine after magazine at the determined, oncharging enemy. The enemy drove almost to his position and hurled grenades, but S/Sgt. Stewart decimated them by retrieving and throwing the grenades back. Exhausting his ammunition, he crawled, under intense fire, to his wounded team members and collected ammunition that they were unable to use. Far past the normal point of exhaustion, he held his position for four harrowing hours and through three assaults, annihilating the enemy as they approached and before they could get a foothold. As a result of his defense, the company position held until the

arrival of a reinforcing platoon which counterattacked the enemy, now occupying foxholes to the left of S/Sgt. Stewart's position. After the counterattack, his body was found in a shallow enemy hole where he had advanced in order to add his fire to that of the counterattacking platoon. Eight enemy dead were found around his immediate position, with evidence that 15 others had been dragged away. The wounded whom he gave his life to protect were recovered and evacuated. S/Sgt. Stewart's indomitable courage, in the face of overwhelming odds, stands as a tribute to himself and an inspiration to all men of his unit. His actions were in the highest traditions of the U.S. Army and the Armed Forces of his country.

3365 ◆ STOCKDALE, JAMES BOND

Rank: Rear Admiral (rank at time of action: Captain) (highest rank: Vice Admiral)
Service: U.S. Navy
Birthday: 23 December 1923
Place of Birth: Abingdon, Knox County, Illinois
Entered Service at: Abingdon, Knox County, Illinois
Unit: Attack Carrier Air Wing 16, U.S.S. *Oriskany*
Served as: Pilot, Senior Naval Officer
Battle or Place of Action: Hoa Lo Prison, Hanoi
Date of Action: 4 September 1969
Date of Presentation: 6 March 1976
Place of Presentation: The White House, presented by Pres. Gerald R. Ford
Citation: For conspicuous gallantry and intrepidity at the risk of his life above and beyond the call of duty while senior naval officer in the prisoner-of-war camps of North Vietnam. Recognized by his captors as the leader in the prisoners' of war resistance to interrogation and in their refusal to participate in propaganda exploitation, Rear Adm. Stockdale was singled out for interrogation and attendant torture after he was detected in a covert communications attempt. Sensing the start of another purge, and aware that his earlier efforts at self-disfiguration to dissuade his captors from exploiting him for propaganda purposes had resulted in cruel and agonizing punishment, Rear Adm. Stockdale resolved to make himself a symbol of resistance regardless of personal sacrifice. He deliberately inflicted a near-mortal wound to his person in order to convince his captors of his willingness to give up his life rather than capitulate. He was subsequently discovered and revived by the North Vietnamese who, convinced of his indomitable spirit, abated in their employment of excessive harassment and torture toward all the prisoners of war. By his heroic actions, at great peril to himself, he earned the everlasting gratitude of his fellow prisoners and of his country. Rear Adm. Stockdale's valiant leadership and extraordinary courage in a hostile environment sustain and enhance the finest traditions of the U.S. Naval Service.
Notes: POW from 9 September 1965—February 1973

3366 ◆ *STONE JR., LESTER RAYMOND

Rank: Sergeant
Service: U.S. Army
Birthday: 4 June 1947
Place of Birth: Binghamton, Broome County, New York
Date of Death: 3 March 1969
Place of Death: Republic of Vietnam
Cemetery: Chenango Valley Cemetery (MH)—Binghamton, New York
Entered Service at: Syracuse, Onondaga County, New York
Unit: 1st Platoon, Company B, 1st Battalion, 20th Infantry, 11th Infantry Brigade, 23d Infantry Division (Americal)
Served as: Squad Leader
Battle or Place of Action: west of Landing Zone Liz, Republic of Vietnam
Date of Action: 3 March 1969
G.O. Number, Date: 14, 23 April 1970
Date of Presentation: 7 April 1970
Place of Presentation: The White House, presented by Pres. Richard M. Nixon to his family
Citation: For conspicuous gallantry and intrepidity in action at the risk of his life above and beyond the call of duty. Sgt. Stone distinguished himself while serving as squad leader of the 1st Platoon. The 1st Platoon was on a combat patrol mission just west of Landing Zone Liz when it came under intense automatic-weapons and grenade fire from a well-concealed company-size force of North Vietnamese regulars. Observing the platoon machine gunner fall critically wounded, Sgt. Stone remained in the exposed area to provide cover fire for the wounded soldier who was being pulled to safety by another member of the platoon. With enemy fire impacting all around him, Sgt. Stone had a malfunction in the machine gun, preventing him from firing the weapon automatically. Displaying extraordinary courage under the most adverse conditions, Sgt. Stone repaired the weapon and continued to place on the enemy positions effective suppressive fire which enabled the rescue to be completed. In a desperate attempt to overrun his position, an enemy force left its cover and charged Sgt. Stone. Disregarding the danger involved, Sgt. Stone rose to his knees and began placing intense fire on the enemy at point-blank range, killing six of the enemy before falling mortally wounded. His actions of unsurpassed valor were a source of inspiration to his entire unit, and he was responsible for saving the lives of a number of his fellow soldiers. His actions were in keeping with the highest traditions of the military profession and reflect great credit on him, his unit, and the U.S. Army.

3367 ◆ *STOUT, MITCHELL WILLIAM

Rank: Sergeant
Service: U.S. Army
Birthday: 24 February 1950
Place of Birth: Knoxville, Knox County, Tennessee
Date of Death: 12 March 1970
Place of Death: Republic of Vietnam
Cemetery: Virture Cemetery (MH)—Concord, Tennessee
Entered Service at: Raleigh, Wake County, North Carolina
Unit: Battery C, 1st Battalion, 44th Artillery
Battle or Place of Action: Khe Gio Bridge, Republic of Vietnam
Date of Action: 12 March 1970
G.O. Number, Date: 42, 12 September 1974
Date of Presentation: 17 July 1974

Place of Presentation: Blair House (Courtyard), presented by Vice Pres. Gerald R. Ford to his family
Citation: Sgt. Stout distinguished himself during an attack by a North Vietnamese Army Sapper company on his unit's firing position at Khe Gio Bridge. Sgt. Stout was in a bunker with members of a searchlight crew when the position came under heavy enemy mortar fire and ground attack. When the intensity of the mortar attack subsided, an enemy grenade was thrown into the bunker. Displaying great courage, Sgt. Stout ran to the grenade, picked it up, and started out of the bunker. As he reached the door, the grenade exploded. By holding the grenade close to his body and shielding its blast, he protected his fellow soldiers in the bunker from further injury or death. Sgt. Stout's conspicuous gallantry and intrepidity in action, at the cost of his own life, are in keeping with the highest traditions of the military service and reflect great credit upon him, his unit, and the U.S. Army.

3368 ◆ *STRYKER, ROBERT FRANCIS

Rank: Specialist Fourth Class
Service: U.S. Army
Birthday: 9 November 1944
Place of Birth: Auburn, Cayuga County, New York
Date of Death: 7 November 1967
Place of Death: Republic of Vietnam
Cemetery: Pine Hill Cemetery—Throopsville, New York
Entered Service at: Throop, Cayuga County, New York
Unit: Company C, 1st Battalion, 26th Infantry, 1st Infantry Division
Served as: Grenadier
Battle or Place of Action: near Loc Ninh, Republic of Vietnam
Date of Action: 7 November 1967
G.O. Number, Date: 72, 20 November 1969
Date of Presentation: 4 November 1969
Place of Presentation: The White House, presented by Vice Pres. Spiro T. Agnew to his family
Citation: For conspicuous gallantry and intrepidity at the risk of his life above and beyond the call of duty. Sp4c. Stryker, U.S. Army, distinguished himself while serving with Company C. Sp4c. Stryker was serving as a grenadier in a multicompany reconnaissance-in-force near Loc Ninh. As his unit moved through the dense underbrush, it was suddenly met with a hail of rocket, automatic-weapons, and small-arms fire from enemy forces concealed in fortified bunkers and in the surrounding trees. Reacting quickly, Sp4c. Stryker fired into the enemy positions with his grenade launcher. During the devastating exchange of fire, Sp4c. Stryker detected enemy elements attempting to encircle his company and isolate it from the main body of the friendly force. Undaunted by the enemy machine-gun and small-arms fire, Sp4c. Stryker repeatedly fired grenades into the trees, killing enemy snipers and enabling his comrades to sever the attempted encirclement. As the battle continued, Sp4c. Stryker observed several wounded members of his squad in the killing zone of an enemy claymore mine. With complete disregard for his safety, he threw himself upon the mine as it was detonated. He was mortally wounded as his body absorbed the blast and shielded his comrades from the explosion. His unselfish actions were responsible for saving the lives of at least six of his fellow soldiers. Sp4c. Stryker's great personal bravery was in keeping with the highest traditions of the military service and reflects great credit upon himself, his unit, and the U.S. Army.

3369 ◆ STUMPF, KENNETH EDWARD

Rank: Sergeant (rank at time of action: Specialist Fourth Class) (highest rank: Sergeant Major)
Service: U.S. Army
Birthday: 28 September 1944
Place of Birth: Neenah, Winnebago County, Wisconsin
Entered Service at: Milwaukee, Milwaukee County, Wisconsin
Unit: 3d Platoon, Company C, 1st Battalion, 35th Infantry, 25th Infantry Division
Served as: Squad Leader
Battle or Place of Action: near Duc Pho, Republic of Vietnam
Date of Action: 25 April 1967
G.O. Number, Date: 64, 22 October 1968
Date of Presentation: 19 September 1968
Place of Presentation: The White House, presented by Pres. Lyndon B. Johnson
Citation: For conspicuous gallantry and intrepidity in action at the risk of his life above and beyond the call of duty. S/Sgt. Stumpf distinguished himself while serving as a squad leader of the 3d Platoon, Company C, on a search-and-destroy mission. As S/Sgt. Stumpf's company approached a village, it encountered a North Vietnamese rifle company occupying a well-fortified bunker complex. During the initial contact, three men from his squad fell wounded in front of a hostile machine-gun emplacement. The enemy's heavy volume of fire prevented the unit from moving to the aid of the injured men, but S/Sgt. Stumpf left his secure position in a deep trench and ran through the barrage of incoming rounds to reach his wounded comrades. He picked up one of the men and carried him back to the safety of the trench. Twice more S/Sgt. Stumpf dashed forward while the enemy turned automatic weapons and machine guns upon him, yet he managed to rescue the remaining two wounded squad members. He then organized his squad and led an assault against several enemy bunkers from which continuously heavy fire was being received. He and his squad successfully eliminated two of the bunker positions, but one to the front of the advancing platoon remained a serious threat. Arming himself with extra hand grenades, S/Sgt. Stumpf ran over open ground, through a volley of fire directed at him by a determined enemy, toward the machine-gun position. As he reached the bunker, he threw a hand grenade through the aperture. It was immediately returned by the occupants, forcing S/Sgt. Stumpf to take cover. Undaunted, he pulled the pins on two more grenades, held them for a few seconds after activation, then hurled them into the position, this time successfully destroying the emplacement. With the elimination of this key position, his unit was able to assault and overrun the enemy. S/Sgt. Stumpf's relentless spirit of aggressiveness, intrepidity, and ultimate concern for the lives of his men, are in the highest traditions of the military service and reflect great credit upon himself and the U.S. Army.

3370 ◆ TAYLOR, JAMES ALLEN

Rank: Captain (rank at time of action: First Lieutenant) (highest rank: Major)
Service: U.S. Army
Birthday: 31 December 1937
Place of Birth: Arcata, Humboldt County, California
Entered Service at: San Francisco, San Francisco County, California
Unit: Troop B, 1st Squadron, 1st Cavalry, Americal Division
Served as: Executive Officer
Battle or Place of Action: west of Que Son, Republic of Vietnam
Date of Action: 9 November 1967
G.O. Number, Date: 78, 10 December 1968
Date of Presentation: 19 November 1968
Place of Presentation: The White House, presented by Pres. Lyndon B. Johnson
Citation: Capt. Taylor, Armor, was serving as executive officer of Troop B, 1st Squadron. His troop was engaged in an attack on a fortified position west of Que Son when it came under intense enemy recoilless-rifle, mortar, and automatic-weapons fire from an enemy strong point located immediately to its front. One armored cavalry assault vehicle was hit immediately by recoilless-rifle fire and all five crewmembers were wounded. Aware that the stricken vehicle was in grave danger of exploding, Capt. Taylor rushed forward and personally extracted the wounded to safety despite the hail of enemy fire and exploding ammunition. Within minutes a second armored cavalry assault vehicle was hit by multiple recoilless-rifle rounds. Despite the continuing intense enemy fire, Capt. Taylor moved forward on foot to rescue the wounded men from the burning vehicle and personally removed all the crewmen to the safety of a nearby dike. Moments later the vehicle exploded. As he was returning to his vehicle, a bursting mortar round painfully wounded Capt. Taylor yet he valiantly returned to his vehicle to relocate the medical evacuation zone to an area closer to the front lines. As he was moving his vehicle, it came under machine-gun fire from an enemy position not 50 yards away. Capt. Taylor engaged the position with his machine gun, killing the three-man crew. Upon arrival at the new evacuation site, still another vehicle was struck. Once again Capt. Taylor rushed forward and pulled the wounded from the vehicle, loaded them aboard his vehicle, and returned them safely to the evacuation site. His actions of unsurpassed valor were a source of inspiration to his entire troop, contributed significantly to the success of the overall assault on the enemy position, and were directly responsible for saving the lives of a number of his fellow soldiers. His actions were in keeping with the highest traditions of the military profession and reflect great credit upon himself, his unit, and the U.S. Army.

3371 ◆ *TAYLOR SR., KARL GORMAN

Rank: Staff Sergeant
Service: U.S. Marine Corps
Birthday: 14 July 1939
Place of Birth: Laurel, Prince George's County, Maryland
Date of Death: 8 December 1968
Place of Death: Republic of Vietnam
Cemetery: Independence Cemetery—Independence, Pennsylvania
Entered Service at: Baltimore, Baltimore County, Maryland
Unit: Company I, 3d Battalion, 26th Marines Regiment, 3d Marine Division (Rein) FMF
Served as: Gunnery Sergeant
Battle or Place of Action: Republic of Vietnam
Date of Action: 8 December 1968
Date of Presentation: 16 February 1971
Place of Presentation: The White House, presented by Pres. Richard M. Nixon to his family
Citation: For conspicuous gallantry and intrepidity at the risk of his life above and beyond the call of duty while serving at night as a company gunnery sergeant during Operation Meade River. Informed that the commander of the lead platoon had been mortally wounded when his unit was pinned down by a heavy volume of enemy fire, S/Sgt. Taylor, along with another marine, crawled forward to the beleaguered unit through a hail of hostile fire, shouted encouragement and instructions to the men, and deployed them to covered positions. With his companion, he then repeatedly maneuvered across an open area to rescue those marines who were too seriously wounded to move by themselves. Upon learning that there were still other wounded men lying in another open area, in proximity to an enemy machine-gun position, S/Sgt. Taylor, accompanied by four comrades, led his men forward across the fire-swept terrain in an attempt to rescue the marines. When his group was halted by devastating fire, he directed his companions to return to the company command post; whereupon he took his grenade launcher and, in full view of the enemy, charged across the open rice paddy toward the machine-gun position, firing his weapon as he ran. Although wounded several times, he succeeded in reaching the machine-gun bunker and silencing the fire from that sector, moments before he was mortally wounded. Directly instrumental in saving the lives of several of his fellow marines, S/Sgt. Taylor, by his indomitable courage, inspiring leadership, and selfless dedication, upheld the highest traditions of the Marine Corps and of the U.S. Naval Service.

3372 ◆ THACKER, BRIAN MILES

Rank: First Lieutenant
Service: U.S. Army
Birthday: 25 April 1945
Place of Birth: Columbus, Franklin County, Ohio
Entered Service at: Salt Lake City, Salt Lake County, Utah
Unit: Battery A, 1st Battalion, 92d Artillery
Served as: Team Leader
Battle or Place of Action: Fire Base 6, Kontum Province, Republic of Vietnam
Date of Action: 31 March 1971
G.O. Number, Date: 42, 5 November 1973
Date of Presentation: 15 October 1973
Place of Presentation: The White House, presented by Pres. Richard M. Nixon
Citation: For conspicuous gallantry and intrepidity in action at the risk of his life above and beyond the call of duty. 1st

Lt. Thacker, Field Artillery, Battery A, distinguished himself while serving as the team leader of an Integrated Observation System collocated with elements of two Army of the Republic of Vietnam units at Fire Base 6. A numerically superior North Vietnamese Army force launched a well-planned dawn attack on the small, isolated, hilltop fire base. Employing rockets, grenades, flamethrowers, and automatic weapons, the enemy forces penetrated the perimeter defenses and engaged the defenders in hand-to-hand combat. Throughout the morning and early afternoon, 1st Lt. Thacker rallied and encouraged the U.S. and Republic of Vietnam soldiers in heroic efforts to repulse the enemy. He occupied a dangerously exposed observation position for a period of four hours while directing friendly air strikes and artillery fire against the assaulting enemy forces. His personal bravery and inspired leadership enabled the outnumbered friendly forces to inflict a maximum of casualties on the attacking enemy forces and prevented the base from being overrun. By late afternoon, the situation had become untenable. 1st Lt. Thacker organized and directed the withdrawal of the remaining friendly forces. With complete disregard for his personal safety, he remained inside the perimeter alone to provide covering fire with his M-16 rifle until all other friendly forces had escaped from the besieged fire base. Then, in an act of supreme courage, he called for friendly artillery fire on his own position to allow his comrades more time to withdraw safely from the area and, at the same time, inflict even greater casualties on the enemy forces. Although wounded and unable to escape from the area himself, he successfully eluded the enemy forces for eight days until friendly forces regained control of the fire base. The extraordinary courage and selflessness displayed by 1st Lt. Thacker were an inspiration to his comrades and are in the highest traditions of the military service.

3373 ◆ THORNTON, MICHAEL EDWIN

Rank: Engineman First Class (highest rank: Lieutenant)
Service: U.S. Navy
Birthday: 23 March 1949
Place of Birth: Greenville, Greenville County, South Carolina
Entered Service at: Spartanburg, Spartanburg County, South Carolina
Unit: Naval Advisory Group
Served as: Assistant U.S. Navy Advisor
Battle or Place of Action: Republic of Vietnam
Date of Action: 31 October 1972
Date of Presentation: 15 October 1973
Place of Presentation: The White House, presented by Pres. Richard M. Nixon
Citation: For conspicuous gallantry and intrepidity at the risk of his life above and beyond the call of duty while participating in a daring operation against enemy forces. PO Thornton, as assistant U.S. Navy adviser, along with a U.S. Navy lieutenant serving as senior adviser, accompanied a three-man Vietnamese Navy SEAL patrol on an intelligence-gathering and prisoner capture operation against an enemy-occupied naval river base. Launched from a Vietnamese Navy junk in a rubber boat, the patrol reached land and was continuing on foot toward its objective when it suddenly came under heavy fire from a numerically superior force. The patrol called in naval gunfire support and then engaged the enemy in a fierce firefight, accounting for many enemy casualties before moving back to the waterline to prevent encirclement. Upon learning that the senior adviser had been hit by enemy fire and was believed to be dead, PO Thornton returned through a hail of fire to the lieutenant's last position, quickly disposed of two enemy soldiers about to overrun the position, and succeeded in removing the seriously wounded and unconscious Senior Naval Advisor to the water's edge. He then inflated the lieutenant's lifejacket and towed him seaward for approximately two hours until picked up by support craft. By his extraordinary courage and perseverance, PO Thornton was directly responsible for saving the life of his superior officer and enabling the safe extraction of all patrol members, thereby upholding the highest traditions of the U.S. Naval Service.

3374 ◆ THORSNESS, LEO KEITH

Rank: Lieutenant Colonel (rank at time of action: Major) (highest rank: Colonel)
Service: U.S. Air Force
Birthday: 14 February 1932
Place of Birth: Walnut Grove, Redwood County, Minnesota
Entered Service at: Walnut Grove, Redwood County, Minnesota
Unit: 357th Tactical Fighter Squadron, 355th Tactical Fighter Wing
Served as: Pilot of a F-105
Battle or Place of Action: over North Vietnam
Date of Action: 19 April 1967
G.O. Number, Date: GB-796, 6 November 1973
Date of Presentation: 15 October 1973
Place of Presentation: The White House, presented by Pres. Richard M. Nixon
Citation: For conspicuous gallantry and intrepidity in action at the risk of his life above and beyond the call of duty. As pilot of an F-105 aircraft, Lt. Col. Thorsness was on a surface-to-air missile suppression mission over North Vietnam. Lt. Col. Thorsness and his wingman attacked and silenced a surface-to-air missile site with air-to-ground missiles, and then destroyed a second surface-to-air missile site with bombs. In the attack on the second missile site, Lt. Col. Thorsness' wingman was shot down by intensive antiaircraft fire, and the two crewmembers abandoned their aircraft. Lt. Col. Thorsness circled the descending parachutes to keep the crewmembers in sight and relay their position to the Search and Rescue Center. During this maneuver, a MIG-17 was sighted in the area. Lt. Col. Thorsness immediately initiated an attack and destroyed the MIG. Because his aircraft was low on fuel, he was forced to depart the area in search of a tanker. Upon being advised that two helicopters were orbiting over the downed crew's position and that there were hostile MIGs in the area posing a serious threat to the helicopters, Lt. Col. Thorsness, despite his low fuel condition, decided to return alone through a hostile environment of surface-to-air missile and antiaircraft defenses to the downed crew's position. As he approached the area, he spotted four MIG-17 aircraft and

immediately initiated an attack on the MIGs, damaging one and driving the others away from the rescue scene. When it became apparent that an aircraft in the area was critically low on fuel and the crew would have to abandon the aircraft unless they could reach a tanker, Lt. Col. Thorsness, although critically short on fuel himself, helped to avert further possible loss of life and a friendly aircraft by recovering at a forward operating base, thus allowing the aircraft in emergency fuel condition to refuel safely. Lt. Col. Thorsness' extraordinary heroism, self-sacrifice, and personal bravery involving conspicuous risk of life were in the highest traditions of the military service, and have reflected great credit upon himself and the U.S. Air Force.
Notes: POW from April 1967—March 1973

3375 ◆ VARGAS, JAY R.

Rank: Major (rank at time of action: Captain) (highest rank: Colonel
Service: U.S. Marine Corps
Birthday: 29 July 1937
Place of Birth: Winslow, Navajo County, Arizona
Entered Service at: Winslow, Navajo County, Arizona
Unit: Company G, 2d Battalion, 4th Marines, 9th Marine Amphibious Brigade
Served as: Commanding Officer
Battle or Place of Action: Dai Do, Quang Tri Province, Republic of Vietnam
Date of Action: 30 April-2 May 1968
Date of Presentation: 14 May 1970
Place of Presentation: The White House, presented by Pres. Richard M. Nixon
Citation: For conspicuous gallantry and intrepidity at the risk of his life above and beyond the call of duty while serving as commanding officer, Company G, in action against enemy forces from 30 April to 2 May 1968. On 1 May 1968, though suffering from wounds he had incurred while relocating his unit under heavy enemy fire the preceding day, Maj. Vargas combined Company G with two other companies and led his men in an attack on the fortified village of Dai Do. Exercising expert leadership, he maneuvered his marines across 700 meters of open rice paddy while under intense enemy mortar, rocket, and artillery fire and obtained a foothold in two hedgerows on the enemy perimeter, only to have elements of his company become pinned down by the intense enemy fire. Leading his reserve platoon to the aid of his beleaguered men, Maj. Vargas inspired his men to renew their relentless advance, while destroying a number of enemy bunkers. Again wounded by grenade fragments, he refused aid as he moved about the hazardous area reorganizing his unit into a strong defensive perimeter at the edge of the village. Shortly after the objective was secured the enemy commenced a series of counterattacks and probes which lasted throughout the night but were unsuccessful as the gallant defenders of Company G stood firm in their hard-won enclave. Reinforced the following morning, the marines launched a renewed assault through Dai Do on the village of Dinh To, to which the enemy retaliated with a massive counterattack resulting in hand-to-hand combat. Maj. Vargas remained in the open, encouraging and rendering assistance to his marines when he was hit for a third time in the three-day battle. Observing his battalion commander sustain a serious wound, he disregarded his excruciating pain, crossed the fire-swept area, and carried his commander to a covered position, then resumed supervising and encouraging his men while simultaneously assisting in organizing the battalion's perimeter defense. His gallant actions uphold the highest traditions of the Marine Corps and the U.S. Naval Service.

3376 ◆ *WARREN JR., JOHN EARL

Rank: First Lieutenant
Service: U.S. Army
Birthday: 16 November 1946
Place of Birth: Brooklyn, Kings County, New York
Date of Death: 14 January 1969
Place of Death: Republic of Vietnam
Cemetery: Long Island National Cemetery (0-33144) (MH)—Farmingdale, New York
Entered Service at: New York, New York
Unit: Company C, 2d Battalion (Mechanized), 22d Infantry, 25th Infantry Division
Served as: Platoon Leader
Battle or Place of Action: Tay Ninh Province, Republic of Vietnam
Date of Action: 14 January 1969
G.O. Number, Date: 49, 8 September 1970
Date of Presentation: 6 August 1970
Place of Presentation: The White House, presented by Pres. Richard M. Nixon to his family
Citation: For conspicuous gallantry and intrepidity in action at the risk of his life above and beyond the call of duty. 1st Lt. Warren distinguished himself at the cost of his life while serving as a platoon leader with Company C. While moving through a rubber plantation to reinforce another friendly unit, Company C came under intense fire from a well-fortified enemy force. Disregarding his safety, 1st Lt. Warren with several of his men began maneuvering through the hail of enemy fire toward the hostile positions. When he had come to within six feet of one of the enemy bunkers and was preparing to toss a hand grenade into it, an enemy grenade was suddenly thrown into the middle of his small group. Thinking only of his men, 1st Lt. Warren fell in the direction of the grenade, thus shielding those around him from the blast. His action, performed at the cost of his life, saved three men from serious or mortal injury. 1st Lt. Warren's ultimate action of sacrifice to save the lives of his men was in keeping with the highest traditions of the military service and reflects great credit on him, his unit, and the U.S. Army.

3377 ◆ *WATTERS, CHARLES JOSEPH

Rank: Major
Service: U.S. Army
Birthday: 17 January 1927
Place of Birth: Jersey City, Hudson County, New Jersey
Date of Death: 19 November 1967
Place of Death: Republic of Vietnam

Cemetery: Arlington National Cemetery (2-E-186-A) (MH)—Arlington, Virginia
Entered Service at: Fort Dix, Mercer County, New Jersey
Unit: Company A, 173d Support Battalion, 173d Airborne Brigade
Served as: Chaplain
Battle or Place of Action: Hill 875, near Dak To, Kontum Province, Republic of Vietnam
Date of Action: 19 November 1967
G.O. Number, Date: 71, 20 November 1969
Date of Presentation: 4 November 1969
Place of Presentation: The White House, presented by Vice Pres. Spiro T. Agnew to his family
Citation: For conspicuous gallantry and intrepidity in action at the risk of his life above and beyond the call of duty. Chaplain Watters distinguished himself during an assault in the vicinity of Dak To. Chaplain Watters was moving with one of the companies when it engaged a heavily armed enemy battalion. As the battle raged and the casualties mounted, Chaplain Watters, with complete disregard for his safety, rushed forward to the line of contact. Unarmed and completely exposed, he moved among, as well as in front of, the advancing troops, giving aid to the wounded, assisting in their evacuation, giving words of encouragement, and administering the last rites to the dying. When a wounded paratrooper was standing in shock in front of the assaulting forces, Chaplain Watters ran forward, picked the man up on his shoulders, and carried him to safety. As the troopers battled to the first enemy entrenchment, Chaplain Watters ran through the intense enemy fire to the front of the entrenchment to aid a fallen comrade. A short time later, the paratroopers pulled back in preparation for a second assault, Chaplain Watters exposed himself to both friendly and enemy fire between the two forces in order to recover two wounded soldiers. Later, when the battalion was forced to pull back into a perimeter, Chaplain Watters noticed that several wounded soldiers were lying outside the newly formed perimeter. Without hesitation and ignoring attempts to restrain him, Chaplain Watters left the perimeter three times in the face of small-arms, automatic-weapons, and mortar fire to carry and to assist the injured troopers to safety. Satisfied that all of the wounded were inside the perimeter, he began aiding the medics—applying field bandages to open wounds, obtaining and serving food and water, giving spiritual and mental strength and comfort. During his ministering, he moved out to the perimeter from position to position redistributing food and water and tending to the needs of his men. Chaplain Watters was giving aid to the wounded when he himself was mortally wounded. Chaplain Watters' unyielding perseverance and selfless devotion to his comrades was in keeping with the highest traditions of the U.S. Army.

3378 ◆ *WAYRYNEN, DALE EUGENE

Rank: Specialist Fourth Class
Service: U.S. Army
Birthday: 18 January 1947
Place of Birth: Moose Lake, Carlton County, Minnesota
Date of Death: 18 May 1967
Place of Death: Republic of Vietnam
Cemetery: Rice River Lutheran Cemetery (MH)—McGregor, Minnesota
Entered Service at: Minneapolis, Hennepin County, Minnesota
Unit: Company B, 2d Battalion, 502d Infantry, 1st Brigade, 101st Airborne Division
Battle or Place of Action: near Duc Pho, Quang Ngai Province, Republic of Vietnam
Date of Action: 18 May 1967
G.O. Number, Date: 66, 27 October 1969
Date of Presentation: 16 October 1969
Place of Presentation: The White House, presented by Pres. Richard M. Nixon to his family
Citation: For conspicuous gallantry and intrepidity in action at the risk of his life above and beyond the call of duty. Sp4c. Wayrynen distinguished himself with Company B, during combat operations near Duc Pho. His platoon was assisting in the night evacuation of the wounded from an early enemy contact when the leadman of the unit met face to face with a Viet Cong soldier. The American's shouted warning also alerted the enemy who immediately swept the area with automatic-weapons fire from a strongly built bunker close to the trail and threw hand grenades from another nearby fortified position. Almost immediately, the leadman was wounded and knocked from his feet. Sp4c. Wayrynen, the second man in the formation, leaped beyond his fallen comrade to kill another enemy soldier who appeared on the trail, and he dragged his injured companion back to where the point squad had taken cover. Suddenly, a live enemy grenade landed in the center of the tightly grouped men. Sp4c. Wayrynen, quickly assessing the danger to the entire squad as well as to his platoon leader who was nearby, shouted a warning, pushed one soldier out of the way, and threw himself on the grenade at the moment it exploded. He was mortally wounded. His deep and abiding concern for his fellow soldiers was significantly reflected in his supreme and courageous act that preserved the lives of his comrades. Sp4c. Wayrynen's heroic actions are in keeping with the highest traditions of the service, and they reflect great credit upon himself and the U.S. Army.

3379 ◆ *WEBER, LESTER WILLIAM

Rank: Lance Corporal
Service: U.S. Marine Corps
Birthday: 30 July 1948
Place of Birth: Aurora, Du Page County, Illinois
Date of Death: 23 February 1969
Place of Death: Republic of Vietnam
Cemetery: Clarendon Hills Cemetery (MH)—Westmont, Illinois
Entered Service at: Chicago, Cook County, Illinois
Unit: 2d Platoon, Company M, 3d Battalion, 7th Marines, 1st Marine Division (Rein) FMF
Served as: Squad Leader/Machine Gunner
Battle or Place of Action: Bo Ban area, Hieu Duc District, Quang Nam Province, Republic of Vietnam
Date of Action: 23 February 1969
Date of Presentation: 16 February 1971

Place of Presentation: The White House, presented by Pres. Richard M. Nixon to his family
Citation: For conspicuous gallantry and intrepidity at the risk of his life above and beyond the call of duty while serving as a machine-gun squad leader with Company M, in action against the enemy. The 2d Platoon of Company M was dispatched to the Bo Ban area of Hieu Duc district to assist a squad from another platoon which had become heavily engaged with a well-entrenched enemy battalion. While moving through a rice paddy covered with tall grass L/Cpl. Weber's platoon came under heavy attack from concealed hostile soldiers. He reacted by plunging into the tall grass, successfully attacking one enemy, and forcing 11 others to break contact. Upon encountering a second North Vietnamese Army soldier he overwhelmed him in fierce hand-to-hand combat. Observing two other soldiers firing upon his comrades from behind a dike, L/Cpl. Weber ignored the frenzied firing of the enemy and, racing across the hazardous area, dived into their position. He neutralized the position by wrestling weapons from the hands of the two soldiers and overcoming them. Although by now the target for concentrated fire from hostile riflemen, L/Cpl. Weber remained in a dangerously exposed position to shout words of encouragement to his emboldened companions. As he moved forward to attack a fifth enemy soldier, he was mortally wounded. L/Cpl. Weber's indomitable courage, aggressive fighting spirit, and unwavering devotion to duty upheld the highest traditions of the Marine Corps and of the U.S. Naval Service. He gallantly gave his life for his country.

3380 ◆ WETZEL, GARY GEORGE

Rank: Specialist Fourth Class [rank at time of action: Private First Class]
Service: U.S. Army
Birthday: 29 September 1947
Place of Birth: South Milwaukee, Milwaukee County, Wisconsin
Entered Service at: Milwaukee, Milwaukee County, Wisconsin
Unit: 173d Assault Helicopter Company, 11th Combat Aviation Battalion, 1st Aviation Brigade
Served as: Door Gunner
Battle or Place of Action: near Ap Dong An, Republic of Vietnam
Date of Action: 8 January 1968
G.O. Number, Date: 79, 10 December 1968
Date of Presentation: 19 November 1968
Place of Presentation: The White House, presented by Pres. Lyndon B. Johnson
Citation: Sp4c. Wetzel, 173d Assault Helicopter Company, distinguished himself by conspicuous gallantry and intrepidity at the risk of his life above and beyond the call of duty. Sp4c. Wetzel was serving as door gunner aboard a helicopter which was part of an insertion force trapped in a landing zone by intense and deadly hostile fire. Sp4c. Wetzel was going to the aid of his aircraft commander when he was blown into a rice paddy and critically wounded by two enemy rockets that exploded just inches from his location. Although bleeding profusely due to the loss of his left arm and severe wounds in his right arm, chest, and left leg, Sp4c. Wetzel staggered back to his original position in his gun-well and took the enemy forces under fire. His machine gun was the only weapon placing effective fire on the enemy at that time. Through a resolve that overcame the shock and intolerable pain of his injuries, Sp4c. Wetzel remained at his position until he had eliminated the automatic-weapons emplacement that had been inflicting heavy casualties on the American troops and preventing them from moving against this strong enemy force. Refusing to attend his own extensive wounds, he attempted to return to the aid of his aircraft commander but passed out from loss of blood. Regaining consciousness, he persisted in his efforts to drag himself to the aid of his fellow crewman. After an agonizing effort, he came to the side of the crew chief who was attempting to drag the wounded aircraft commander to the safety of a nearby dike. Unswerving in his devotion to his fellow man, Sp4c. Wetzel assisted his crew chief even though he lost consciousness once again during this action. Sp4c. Wetzel displayed extraordinary heroism in his efforts to aid his fellow crewmen. His gallant actions were in keeping with the highest traditions of the U.S. Army and reflect great credit upon himself and the Armed Forces of his country.

3381 ◆ *WHEAT, ROY MITCHELL

Rank: Lance Corporal
Service: U.S. Marine Corps
Birthday: 24 July 1947
Place of Birth: Moselle, Jones County, Mississippi
Date of Death: 11 August 1967
Place of Death: Republic of Vietnam
Cemetery: Eastabuchie Cemetery (MH)—Eastabuchie, Mississippi
Entered Service at: Jackson, Hinds County, Mississippi
Unit: Company K, 3d Battalion, 7th Marines, 1st Marine Division
Served as: Fire Team Leader
Battle or Place of Action: along Liberty Road, Dien Ban District, Quang Nam Province, Republic of Vietnam
Date of Action: 11 August 1967
Date of Presentation: 23 September 1968
Place of Presentation: Marine Barracks, Washington, D.C., presented by Sec. of the Navy Paul R. Ignatius to his family
Citation: For conspicuous gallantry and intrepidity at the risk of his life above and beyond the call of duty. L/Cpl. Wheat and two other marines were assigned the mission of providing security for a Navy construction battalion crane and crew operating along Liberty Road in the vicinity of the Dien Ban district, Quang Nam Province. After the marines had set up security positions in a treeline adjacent to the work site, L/Cpl. Wheat reconnoitered the area to the rear of their location for the possible presence of guerrillas. He then returned to within 10 feet of the friendly position and here unintentionally triggered a well-concealed, bounding type antipersonnel mine. Immediately, a hissing sound was heard which was identified by the three marines as that of a burning time fuse. Shouting a warning to his comrades, L/Cpl. Wheat in a valiant act of heroism hurled himself upon the mine, absorbing the tremendous impact of the explosion with his body. The inspirational personal heroism and extraordinary valor of his unselfish action saved his fellow marines from cer-

tain injury and possible death, reflected great credit upon himself, and upheld the highest traditions of the Marine Corps and the U.S. Naval Service. He gallantly gave his life for his country.

3382 ◆ *WICKAM, JERRY WAYNE

Rank: Corporal
Service: U.S. Army
Birthday: 19 January 1942
Place of Birth: Rockford, Winnebago County, Illinois
Date of Death: 6 January 1968
Place of Death: Republic of Vietnam
Cemetery: Lightsville Cemetery—Leaf River, Illinois
Entered Service at: Chicago, Cook County, Illinois
Unit: Troop F, 2d Squadron, 11th Armored Cavalry Regiment
Battle or Place of Action: near Loc Ninh, Republic of Vietnam
Date of Action: 6 January 1968
G.O. Number, Date: 78, 4 December 1969
Date of Presentation: 18 November 1969
Place of Presentation: The White House, presented by Vice Pres. Spiro T. Agnew to his family
Citation: For conspicuous gallantry and intrepidity in action at the risk of his life above and beyond the call of duty. Cpl. Wickam distinguished himself while serving with Troop F. Troop F was conducting a reconnaissance-in-force mission southwest of Loc Ninh when the lead element of the friendly force was subjected to a heavy barrage of rocket, automatic-weapons, and small-arms fire from a well-concealed enemy bunker complex. Disregarding the intense fire, Cpl. Wickam leaped from his armored vehicle and assaulted one of the enemy bunkers and threw a grenade into it, killing two enemy soldiers. He moved into the bunker and, with the aid of another soldier, began to remove the body of one Viet Cong when he detected the sound of an enemy grenade being charged. Cpl. Wickam warned his comrade and physically pushed him away from the grenade thus protecting him from the force of the blast. When a second Viet Cong bunker was discovered, he ran through a hail of enemy fire to deliver deadly fire into the bunker, killing one enemy soldier. He also captured one Viet Cong who later provided valuable information on enemy activity in the Loc Ninh area. After the patrol withdrew and an air strike was conducted, Cpl. Wickam led his men back to evaluate the success of the strike. They were immediately attacked again by enemy fire. Without hesitation, he charged the bunker from which the fire was being directed, enabling the remainder of his men to seek cover. He threw a grenade inside of the enemy's position killing two Viet Cong and destroying the bunker. Moments later he was mortally wounded by enemy fire. Cpl. Wickam's extraordinary heroism at the cost of his life were in keeping with the highest traditions of the military service and reflect great credit upon himself and the U.S. Army.

3383 ◆ *WILBANKS, HILLIARD ALMOND

Rank: Captain
Service: U.S. Air Force
Birthday: 26 July 1933
Place of Birth: Cornelia, Habersham County, Georgia
Date of Death: 24 February 1967
Place of Death: Republic of Vietnam
Cemetery: Fayette Methodist Cemetery—Fayette, Mississippi
Entered Service at: Atlanta, Fulton County, Georgia
Unit: 21st Tactical Air Support Squadron, Nha Trang Air Force Base, Republic of Vietnam
Served as: Pilot of a O-E1 Bird Dog
Battle or Place of Action: near Dalat, Republic of Vietnam
Date of Action: 24 February 1967
G.O. Number, Date: GB-50, 8 February 1968
Date of Presentation: 24 January 1968
Place of Presentation: The Pentagon, presented by Sec. of the Air Force Harold Brown to his family
Citation: For conspicuous gallantry and intrepidity in action at the risk of his life above and beyond the call of duty. As a forward air controller Capt. Wilbanks was pilot of an unarmed, light aircraft flying visual reconnaissance ahead of a South Vietnam Army Ranger Battalion. His intensive search revealed a well-concealed and numerically superior hostile force poised to ambush the advancing Rangers. The Viet Cong, realizing that Capt. Wilbanks' discovery had compromised their position and ability to launch a surprise attack, immediately fired on the small aircraft with all available firepower. The enemy then began advancing against the exposed forward elements of the ranger force which were pinned down by devastating fire. Capt. Wilbanks recognized that close support aircraft could not arrive in time to enable the rangers to withstand the advancing enemy onslaught. With full knowledge of the limitations of his unarmed, unarmored light reconnaissance aircraft, and the great danger imposed by the enemy's vast firepower, he unhesitatimgly assumed a covering, close support role. Flying through a hail of withering fire at treetop level, Capt. Wilbanks passed directly over the advancing enemy and inflicted many casualties by firing his rifle out of the side window of his aircraft. Despite increasingly intense antiaircraft fire, Capt. Wilbanks continued to completely disregard his own safety and made repeated low passes over the enemy to divert their fire away from the rangers. His daring tactics successfully interrupted the enemy advance, allowing the rangers to withdraw to safety from their perilous position. During his final courageous attack to protect the withdrawing forces, Capt. Wilbanks was mortally wounded and his bullet-riddled aircraft crashed between the opposing forces. Capt. Wilbanks' magnificent action saved numerous friendly personnel from certain injury or death. His unparalleled concern for his fellow man and his extraordinary heroism were in the highest traditions of the military service, and have reflected great credit upon himself and the U.S. Air Force.

3384 ◆ *WILLETT, LOUIS EDWARD

Rank: Private First Class
Service: U.S. Army
Birthday: 19 June 1945
Place of Birth: Brooklyn, Kings County, New York
Date of Death: 15 February 1967

Place of Death: Republic of Vietnam
Cemetery: Saint John's Cemetery (MH)—Middle Village, New York
Entered Service at: Brooklyn, Kings County, New York
Unit: Company C, 1st Battalion, 12th Infantry, 4th Infantry Division
Served as: Rifleman
Battle or Place of Action: Kontum Province, Republic of Vietnam
Date of Action: 15 February 1967
G.O. Number, Date: 52, 30 September 1968
Date of Presentation: 5 September 1968
Place of Presentation: The Pentagon, presented by Sec. of the Army Stanley R. Resor to his family
Citation: For conspicuous gallantry and intrepidity at the risk of his life above and beyond the call of duty. Pfc. Willett distinguished himself while serving as a rifleman in Company C, during combat operations. His squad was conducting a security sweep when it made contact with a large enemy force. The squad was immediately engaged with a heavy volume of automatic-weapons fire and pinned to the ground. Despite the deadly fusillade, Pfc. Willett rose to his feet firing rapid bursts from his weapon and moved to a position from which he placed highly effective fire on the enemy. His action allowed the remainder of his squad to begin to withdraw from the superior enemy force toward the company perimeter. Pfc. Willett covered the squad's withdrawal, but his position drew heavy enemy machine-gun fire, and he received multiple wounds enabling the enemy again to pin down the remainder of the squad. Pfc. Willett struggled to an upright position, and, disregarding his painful wounds, he again engaged the enemy with his rifle to allow his squad to continue its movement and to evacuate several of his comrades who were by now wounded. Moving from position to position, he engaged the enemy at close-range until he was mortally wounded. By his unselfish acts of bravery, Pfc. Willett insured the withdrawal of his comrades to the company position, saving their lives at the cost of his life. Pfc. Willett's valorous actions were in keeping with the highest traditions of the U.S. Army and reflect great credit upon himself and the Armed Forces of his country.

3385 ◆ WILLIAMS, CHARLES QUINCY

Rank: First Lieutenant (rank at time of action: Second Lieutenant) (highest rank: Major)
Service: U.S. Army
Birthday: 17 September 1933
Place of Birth: Charleston, Charleston County, South Carolina
Date of Death: 15 October 1982
Place of Death: Columbia, South Carolina
Cemetery: Arlington National Cemetery (65-1491) (MH)—Arlington, Virginia
Entered Service at: Fort Jackson, South Carolina
Unit: Detachment A, 5th Special Forces Group, 1st Special Forces
Served as: Executive Officer
Battle or Place of Action: Dong Xoai, Republic of Vietnam
Date of Action: 9-10 June 1965
G.O. Number, Date: 30, 5 July 1966
Date of Presentation: 23 June 1966
Place of Presentation: The White House, presented by Pres. Lyndon B. Johnson
Citation: 1st Lt. Williams distinguished himself by conspicuous gallantry and intrepidity at the risk of his life above and beyond the call of duty while defending the Special Forces camp against a violent attack by hostile forces that lasted for 14 hours. 1st Lt. Williams was serving as executive officer of a Special Forces detachment when an estimated Viet Cong reinforced regiment struck the camp and threatened to overrun it and the adjacent district headquarters. He awoke personnel, organized them, determined the source of the insurgents' main effort, and led the troops to their defensive positions on the south and west walls. Then, after running to the district headquarters to establish communications, he found that there was no radio operational with which to communicate with his commanding officer in another compound. To reach the other compound, he traveled through darkness but was halted in this effort by a combination of shrapnel in his right leg and the increase of Viet Cong gunfire. Ignoring his wound, he returned to the district headquarters and directed the defense against the first assault. As the insurgents attempted to scale the walls and as some of the Vietnamese defenders began to retreat, he dashed through a barrage of gunfire, succeeded in rallying these defenders, and led them back to their positions. Although wounded in the thigh and left leg during this gallant action, he returned to his position and, upon being told that communications were reestablished and that his commanding officer was seriously wounded, 1st Lt. Williams took charge of actions in both compounds. Then, in an attempt to reach the communications bunker, he sustained wounds in the stomach and right arm from grenade fragments. As the defensive position on the walls had been held for hours and casualties were mounting, he ordered the consolidation of the American personnel from both compounds to establish a defense in the district building. After radio contact was made with a friendly air controller, he disregarded his wounds and directed the defense from the district building, using descending flares as reference points to adjust air strikes. By his courage, he inspired his team to hold out against the insurgent force that was closing in on them and throwing grenades into the windows of the building. As daylight arrived and the Viet Cong continued to besiege the stronghold, firing a machine gun directly south of the district building, he was determined to eliminate this menace that threatened the lives of his men. Taking a 3.5 rocket launcher and a volunteer to load it, he worked his way across open terrain, reached the berm south of the district headquarters, and took aim at the Viet Cong machine gun 150 meters away. Although the sight was faulty, he succeeded in hitting the machine gun. While he and the loader were trying to return to the district headquarters, they were both wounded. With a fourth wound, this time in the right arm and leg, and realizing he was unable to carry his wounded comrade back to the district building, 1st Lt. Williams pulled him to a covered position and then made his way back to the district building where he sought the help of others who went out and evacu-

ated the injured soldier. Although seriously wounded and tired, he continued to direct the air strikes closer to the defensive position. As morning turned to afternoon and the Viet Cong pressed their effort with direct recoilless-rifle fire into the building, he ordered the evacuation of the seriously wounded to the safety of the communications bunker. When informed that helicopters would attempt to land as the hostile gunfire had abated, he led his team from the building to the artillery position, making certain of the timely evacuation of the wounded from the communications area, and then on to the pickup point. Despite resurgent Viet Cong gunfire, he directed the rapid evacuation of all personnel. Throughout the long battle, he was undaunted by the vicious Viet Cong assault and inspired the defenders in decimating the determined insurgents. 1st Lt. Williams' extraordinary heroism is in the highest traditions of the U.S. Army and reflect great credit upon himself and the Armed Forces of his country.

3386 ◆ *WILLIAMS, DEWAYNE THOMAS

Rank: Private First Class
Service: U.S. Marine Corps
Birthday: 18 September 1949
Place of Birth: Brown City, Sanilac County, Michigan
Date of Death: 18 September 1968
Place of Death: Republic of Vietnam
Cemetery: St. Mary's Cemetery (MH)—St. Clair, Michigan
Entered Service at: Saint Clair, Saint Clair County, Michigan
Unit: 1st Platoon, Company H, 2d Battalion, 1st Marines, 1st Marine Division
Served as: Rifleman
Battle or Place of Action: Quang Nam Province, Republic of Vietnam
Date of Action: 18 September 1968
Date of Presentation: 20 April 1970
Place of Presentation: The White House, presented by Vice Pres. Spiro T. Agnew to his family
Citation: For conspicuous gallantry and intrepidity at the risk of his life above and beyond the call of duty while serving as a rifleman with the 1st Platoon, Company H, in action against communist insurgent forces. Pfc. Williams was a member of a combat patrol sent out from the platoon with the mission of establishing positions in the company's area of operations from which it could intercept and destroy enemy sniper teams operating in the area. In the night as the patrol was preparing to move from its daylight position to a preselected night position, it was attacked from ambush by a squad of enemy using small arms and hand grenades. Although severely wounded in the back by the close intense fire, Pfc. Williams, recognizing the danger to the patrol, immediately began to crawl forward toward a good firing position. While he was moving under the continuing intense fire, he heard one of the members of the patrol sound the alert that an enemy grenade had landed in their position. Reacting instantly to the alert, he saw that the grenade had landed close to where he was lying and without hesitation, in a valiant act of heroism, rolled on top of the grenade as it exploded, absorbing the full and tremendous impact of the explosion with his body. Through his extraordinary initiative and inspiring valor in the face of certain death, he saved the other members of his patrol from serious injury and possible loss of life, and enabled them to successfully defeat the attackers and hold their position until assistance arrived. His personal heroism and devotion to duty upheld the highest traditions of the Marine Corps and the U.S. Naval Service. He gallantly gave his life for his country.

3387 ◆ WILLIAMS, JAMES ELLIOTT

Rank: Boatswain's Mate First Class
Service: U.S. Navy
Birthday: 13 June 1930
Place of Birth: Rock Hill, York County, South Carolina
Entered Service at: Columbia, Richland County, South Carolina
Unit: River Patrol Boat 105, River Section 531, My Tho, Republic of Vietnam
Served as: Boat Captain/Patrol Officer
Battle or Place of Action: Mekong River, Republic of Vietnam
Date of Action: 31 October 1966
Date of Presentation: 14 May 1968
Place of Presentation: The Pentagon (Inner Courtyard), Hall of Heroes, presented by Pres. Lyndon B. Johnson
Citation: For conspicuous gallantry and intrepidity at the risk of his life above and beyond the call of duty. PO1c. Williams was serving as boat captain and patrol officer aboard River Patrol Boat (PBR) 105 accompanied by another patrol boat when the patrol was suddenly taken under fire by two enemy sampans. PO1c. Williams immediately ordered the fire returned, killing the crew of one enemy boat and causing the other sampan to take refuge in a nearby river inlet. Pursuing the fleeing sampan, the U.S. patrol encountered a heavy volume of small-arms fire from enemy forces, at close-range, occupying well-concealed positions along the river bank. Maneuvering through this fire, the patrol confronted a numerically superior enemy force aboard two enemy junks and eight sampans augmented by heavy automatic-weapons fire from ashore. In the savage battle that ensued, PO1c. Williams, with utter disregard for his safety, exposed himself to the withering hail of enemy fire to direct counterfire and inspire the actions of his patrol. Recognizing the overwhelming strength of the enemy force, PO1c. Williams deployed his patrol to await the arrival of armed helicopters. In the course of his movement he discovered an even larger concentration of enemy boats. Not waiting for the arrival of the armed helicopters, he displayed great initiative and boldly led the patrol through the intense enemy fire and damaged or destroyed 50 enemy sampans and seven junks. This phase of the action completed, and with the arrival of the armed helicopters, PO1c. Williams directed the attack on the remaining enemy force. Now virtually dark, and although PO1c. Williams was aware that his boats would become even better targets, he ordered the patrol boats' search lights turned on to better illuminate the area and moved the patrol perilously close to shore to press the attack. Despite a waning supply of ammunition, the patrol successfully engaged the enemy ashore and

completed the rout of the enemy force. Under the leadership of PO1c. Williams who demonstrated unusual professional skill and indomitable courage throughout the three-hour battle, the patrol accounted for the destruction or loss of 65 enemy boats and inflicted numerous casualties on the enemy personnel. His extraordinary heroism and exemplary fighting spirit in the face of grave risks inspired the efforts of his men to defeat a larger enemy force and are in keeping with the finest traditions of the U.S. Naval Service.

3388 ◆ *WILSON, ALFRED MAC

Rank: Private First Class
Service: U.S. Marine Corps
Birthday: 13 January 1948
Place of Birth: Olney, Richland County, Illinois
Date of Death: 3 March 1969
Place of Death: Republic of Vietnam
Cemetery: Sunset Memorial Cemetery (MH)—Odessa, Texas
Entered Service at: Abilene, Taylor County, Texas
Unit: 1st Platoon, Company M, 3d Battalion, 9th Marines, 3d Marine Division
Served as: Rifleman
Battle or Place of Action: Fire Support Base Cunningham, Quang Tri Province, Republic of Vietnam
Date of Action: 3 March 1969
Date of Presentation: 20 April 1970
Place of Presentation: The White House, presented by Vice Pres. Spiro T. Agnew to his family
Citation: For conspicuous gallantry and intrepidity at the risk of his life above and beyond the call of duty while serving as a rifleman with Company M in action against hostile forces. While returning from a reconnaissance-in-force mission in the vicinity of Fire Support Base Cunningham, the 1st Platoon of Company M came under intense automatic-weapons fire and a grenade attack from a well-concealed enemy force. As the center of the column was pinned down, the leading squad moved to outflank the enemy. Pfc. Wilson, acting as squad leader of the rear squad, skillfully maneuvered his men to form a base of fire and act as a blocking force. In the ensuing firefight, both his machine gunner and assistant machine gunner were seriously wounded and unable to operate their weapons. Realizing the urgent need to bring the weapon into operation again, Pfc. Wilson, followed by another marine and with complete disregard for his safety, fearlessly dashed across the fire-swept terrain to recover the weapon. As they reached the machine gun, an enemy soldier stepped from behind a tree and threw a grenade toward the two marines. Observing the grenade fall between himself and the other marine, Pfc. Wilson, fully realizing the inevitable result of his action, shouted to his companion and unhesitatingly threw himself on the grenade, absorbing the full force of the explosion with his own body. His heroic actions inspired his platoon members to maximum effort as they aggressively attacked and defeated the enemy. Pfc. Wilson's indomitable courage, inspiring valor, and selfless devotion to duty upheld the highest traditions of the Marine Corps and the U.S. Naval Service. He gallantly gave his life for his country.

3389 ◆ *WINDER, DAVID FRANCIS

Rank: Private First Class
Service: U.S. Army
Birthday: 10 August 1946
Place of Birth: Edinboro, Erie County, Pennsylvania
Date of Death: 13 May 1970
Place of Death: Republic of Vietnam
Cemetery: Mansfield Memorial Park—Mansfield, Ohio
Entered Service at: Columbus, Franklin County, Ohio
Unit: Headquarters & Headquarters Company, 3d Battalion, 1st Infantry, 11th Infantry Brigade, Americal Division
Served as: Senior Medical Aidman
Battle or Place of Action: Republic of Vietnam
Date of Action: 13 May 1970
G.O. Number, Date: 35, 6 September 1974
Date of Presentation: 17 July 1974
Place of Presentation: Blair House (Courtyard), presented by Vice Pres. Gerald R. Ford to his family
Citation: Pfc. Winder distinguished himself while serving in the Republic of Vietnam as a senior medical aidman with Company A. After moving through freshly cut rice paddies in search of a suspected company-size enemy force, the unit started a thorough search of the area. Suddenly they were engaged with intense automatic-weapons and rocket-propelled-grenade fire by a well-entrenched enemy force. Several friendly soldiers fell wounded in the initial contact and the unit was pinned down. Responding instantly to the cries of his wounded comrades, Pfc. Winder began maneuvering across approximately 100 meters of open, bullet-swept terrain toward the nearest casualty. Unarmed and crawling most of the distance, he was wounded by enemy fire before reaching his comrades. Despite his wounds and with great effort, Pfc. Winder reached the first casualty and administered medical aid. As he continued to crawl across the open terrain toward a second wounded soldier he was forced to stop when wounded a second time. Aroused by the cries of an injured comrade for aid, Pfc. Winder's great determination and sense of duty impelled him to move forward once again, despite his wounds, in a courageous attempt to reach and assist the injured man. After struggling to within 10 meters of the man, Pfc. Winder was mortally wounded. His dedication and sacrifice inspired his unit to initiate an aggressive counterassault which led to the defeat of the enemy. Pfc. Winder's conspicuous gallantry and intrepidity in action at the cost of his life were in keeping with the highest traditions of the military service and reflect great credit on him, his unit, and the U.S. Army.

3390 ◆ *WORLEY, KENNETH LEE

Rank: Lance Corporal
Service: U.S. Marine Corps
Birthday: 27 April 1948
Place of Birth: Farmington, San Juan County, New Mexico
Date of Death: 12 August 1968
Place of Death: Republic of Vietnam
Cemetery: Westminster Memorial Park—Westminster, California

Entered Service at: Fresno, Fresno County, California
Unit: Company L, 3d Battalion, 7th Marines, 1st Marine Division (Rein) FMF
Served as: Machine Gunner
Battle or Place of Action: Bo Ban, Quang Nam Province, Republic of Vietnam
Date of Action: 12 August 1968
Date of Presentation: 20 April 1970
Place of Presentation: The White House, presented by Vice Pres. Spiro T. Agnew to his family
Citation: For conspicuous gallantry and intrepidity at the risk of his life above and beyond the call of duty while serving as a machine gunner with Company L, 3d Battalion, in action against enemy forces. After establishing a night ambush position in a house in Bo Ban, a hamlet of Quang Nam Province, security was set up and the remainder of the patrol members retired until their respective watch. During the early morning hours the marines were abruptly awakened by the platoon leader's warning that "grenades" had landed in the house. Fully realizing the inevitable result of his actions, L/Cpl. Worley, in a valiant act of heroism, instantly threw himself upon the grenade nearest him and his comrades, absorbing with his body, the full and tremendous force of the explosion. Through his extraordinary initiative and inspiring valor in the face of almost certain death, he saved his comrades from serious injury and possible loss of life although five of his fellow marines incurred minor wounds as the other grenades exploded. L/Cpl. Worley's gallant actions upheld the highest traditions of the Marine Corps and the U.S. Naval Service. He gallantly gave his life for his country.

3391 ◆ WRIGHT, RAYMOND RICHARD "BUZZER"

Rank: Specialist Fourth Class
Service: U.S. Army
Birthday: 5 December 1945
Place of Birth: Moriah, Essex County, New York
Entered Service at: Moriah, Essex County, New York
Unit: Company A, 3d Battalion, 60th Infantry, 9th Infantry Division
Served as: Rifleman
Battle or Place of Action: Ap Bac Zone, Republic of Vietnam
Date of Action: 2 May 1967
G.O. Number, Date: 65, 22 October 1968
Date of Presentation: 19 September 1968
Place of Presentation: The White House, presented by Pres. Lyndon B. Johnson
Citation: For conspicuous gallantry and intrepidity at the risk of his life above and beyond the call of duty. While serving as a rifleman with Company A, Sp4c. Wright distinguished himself during a combat patrol in an area where an enemy ambush had occurred earlier. Sp4c. Wright's unit suddenly came under intense automatic-weapons and small-arms fire from an enemy bunker system protected by numerous snipers in nearby trees. Despite the heavy enemy fire, Sp4c. Wright and another soldier leaped to the top of a dike to assault the position. Armed with a rifle and several grenades, he and his comrade exposed themselves to intense fire from the bunkers as they charged the nearest one. Sp4c. Wright raced to the bunker, threw in a grenade, killing its occupant. The two soldiers then ran through a hail of fire to a second bunker. While his comrade covered him with his machine gun, Sp4c. Wright charged the bunker and succeeded in killing its occupant with a grenade. A third bunker contained an automatic rifleman who had pinned down much of the friendly platoon. While his comrade again covered him with machine-gun fire, Sp4c. Wright charged in and killed the enemy rifleman with a grenade. The two soldiers worked their way through the remaining bunkers, knocking out four of them. Throughout their furious assault, Sp4c. Wright and his comrade had been almost continuously exposed to intense sniper fire from the treeline as the enemy desperately sought to stop their attack. Overcoming stubborn resistance from the bunker system, the men advanced into the treeline, forcing the snipers to retreat, giving immediate chase, and driving the enemy away from the friendly unit so that it advanced across the open area without further casualty. When his ammunition was exhausted, Sp4c. Wright returned to his unit to assist in the evacuation of the wounded. This two-man assault had driven an enemy platoon from a well-prepared position, accounted for numerous enemy casualties, and adverted further friendly casualties. Sp4c. Wright's extraordinary heroism, courage, and indomitable fighting spirit saved the lives of many of his comrades and inflicted serious damage on the enemy. His acts were in keeping with the highest traditions of the military service and reflect great credit upon himself and the U.S. Army.

3392 ◆ *YABES, MAXIMO

Rank: First Sergeant
Service: U.S. Army
Birthday: 29 January 1932
Place of Birth: Lodi, San Joaquin County, California
Date of Death: 26 February 1967
Place of Death: Republic of Vietnam
Cemetery: Fort Logan National Cemetery (R-369) (MH)—Denver, Colorado
Entered Service at: Eugene, Lane County, Oregon
Unit: Company A, 4th Battalion, 9th Infantry, 25th Infantry Division
Served as: Company First Sergeant
Battle or Place of Action: near Phu Hoa Dong, Republic of Vietnam
Date of Action: 26 February 1967
G.O. Number, Date: 71, 15 November 1968
Date of Presentation: 31 October 1968
Place of Presentation: The Pentagon, presented by Sec. of the Army Stanley R. Resor to his family
Citation: For conspicuous gallantry and intrepidity at the risk of his life above and beyond the call of duty. First Sgt. Yabes distinguished himself with Company A, which was providing security for a land-clearing operation. Early in the morning the company suddenly came under intense automatic-weapons and mortar fire followed by a ybattalion-battalion-sized assault from three sides. Penetrating the defensive

perimeter, the enemy advanced on the company command post bunker. The command post received increasingly heavy fire and was in danger of being overwhelmed. When several enemy grenades landed within the command post, 1st Sgt. Yabes shouted a warning and used his body as a shield to protect others in the bunker. Although painfully wounded by numerous grenade fragments, and despite the vicious enemy fire on the bunker, he remained there to provide covering fire and enable the others in the command group to relocate. When the command group had reached a new position, 1st Sgt. Yabes moved through a withering hail of enemy fire to another bunker 50 meters away. There he secured a grenade launcher from a fallen comrade and fired point-blank into the attacking Viet Cong, stopping further penetration of the perimeter. Noting two wounded men helpless in the fire-swept area, he moved them to a safer position where they could be given medical treatment. He resumed his accurate and effective fire, killing several enemy soldiers and forcing others to withdraw from the vicinity of the command post. As the battle continued, he observed an enemy machine gun within the perimeter which threatened the whole position. On his own, he dashed across the exposed area, assaulted the machine gun, killed the crew, destroyed the weapon, and fell mortally wounded. First Sgt. Yabes' valiant and selfless actions saved the lives of many of his fellow soldiers and inspired his comrades to effectively repel the enemy assault. His indomitable fighting spirit, extraordinary courage, and intrepidity at the cost of his life are in the highest military traditions and reflect great credit upon himself and the Armed Forces of his country.

3393 ◆ *YANO, RODNEY JAMES TADASHI

Rank: First Sergeant
Service: U.S. Army
Birthday: 13 December 1943
Place of Birth: Kealakekua Kona, Hawaii County, Hawaii
Date of Death: 1 January 1969
Place of Death: Republic of Vietnam
Cemetery: National Memorial Cemetery of the Pacific (W-614) (MH)—Honolulu, Hawaii
Entered Service at: Honolulu, Honolulu County, Hawaii
Unit: Air Cavalry Troop, 11th Armored Cavalry Regiment
Served as: Crew Chief
Battle or Place of Action: near Bien Hao, Republic of Vietnam
Date of Action: 1 January 1969
G.O. Number, Date: 15, 23 April 1970
Date of Presentation: 7 April 1970
Place of Presentation: The White House, presented by Pres. Richard M. Nixon to his family
Citation: Sfc. Yano distinguished himself while serving with the Air Cavalry Troop. Sfc. Yano was performing the duties of crew chief aboard the troop's command-and-control helicopter during action against enemy forces entrenched in dense jungle. From an exposed position in the face of small-arms and antiaircraft fire he delivered suppressive fire upon the enemy forces and marked their positions with smoke and white phosphorous grenades, thus enabling his troop commander to direct accurate and effective artillery fire against the hostile emplacements. A grenade, exploding prematurely, covered him with burning phosphorous, and left him severely wounded. Flaming fragments within the helicopter caused supplies and ammunition to detonate. Dense white smoke filled the aircraft, obscuring the pilot's vision and causing him to lose control. Although having the use of only one arm and being partially blinded by the initial explosion, Sfc. Yano completely disregarded his welfare and began hurling blazing ammunition from the helicopter. In so doing he inflicted additional wounds upon himself, yet he persisted until the danger was past. Sfc. Yano's indomitable courage and profound concern for his comrades averted loss of life and additional injury to the rest of the crew. By his conspicuous gallantry at the cost of his life, in the highest traditions of the military service, Sfc. Yano has reflected great credit on himself, his unit, and the U.S. Army.

3394 ◆ *YNTEMA, GORDON DOUGLAS

Rank: Sergeant
Service: U.S. Army
Birthday: 26 June 1945
Place of Birth: Bethesda, Montgomery County, Maryland
Date of Death: 18 January 1968
Place of Death: Republic of Vietnam
Cemetery: Pilgrim Home Cemetery—Holland, Michigan
Entered Service at: Detroit, Wayne County, Michigan
Unit: Detachment A-431, Company D, 5th Special Forces Group (Airborne), 1st Special Forces
Served as: Advisor
Battle or Place of Action: near Thong Binh, Republic of Vietnam
Date of Action: 16-18 January 1968
G.O. Number, Date: 76, 3 December 1969
Date of Presentation: 18 November 1969
Place of Presentation: The White House, presented by Vice Pres. Spiro T. Agnew to his family
Citation: For conspicuous gallantry and intrepidity in action at the risk of his life above and beyond the call of duty. Sgt. Yntema, U.S. Army, distinguished himself while assigned to Detachment A-431, Company D. As part of a larger force of civilian irregulars from Camp Cai Cai, he accompanied two platoons to a blocking position east of the village of Thong Binh, where they became heavily engaged in a small-arms firefight with the Viet Cong. Assuming control of the force when the Vietnamese commander was seriously wounded, he advanced his troops to within 50 meters of the enemy bunkers. After a fierce 30-minute firefight, the enemy forced Sgt. Yntema to withdraw his men to a trench in order to afford them protection and still perform their assigned blocking mission. Under cover of machine-gun fire, approximately one company of Viet Cong maneuvered into a position which pinned down the friendly platoons from three sides. A dwindling ammunition supply, coupled with a Viet Cong mortar barrage which inflicted heavy losses on the exposed friendly troops, caused many of the irregulars to withdraw. Seriously wounded and ordered to withdraw himself, Sgt. Yntema refused to leave his fallen comrades. Under withering small-

arms and machine-gun fire, he carried the wounded Vietnamese commander and a mortally wounded American Special Forces adviser to a small gully 50 meters away in order to shield them from the enemy fire. Sgt. Yntema then continued to repulse the attacking Viet Cong attempting to overrun his position until, out of ammunition and surrounded, he was offered the opportunity to surrender. Refusing, Sgt. Yntema stood his ground, using his rifle as a club to fight the approximately 15 Viet Cong attempting his capture. His resistance was so fierce that the Viet Cong were forced to shoot in order to overcome him. Sgt. Yntema's personal bravery in the face of insurmountable odds and supreme self-sacrifice were in keeping with the highest traditions of the military service and reflect the utmost credit upon himself, the 1st Special Forces, and the U.S. Army.

3395 ◆ YOUNG, GERALD ORREN

Rank: Captain (highest rank: Lieutenant Colonel)
Service: U.S. Air Force
Birthday: 19 May 1930
Place of Birth: Chicago, Cook County, Illinois
Date of Death: 6 June 1990
Place of Death: Anacortes, Washington
Cemetery: Arlington National Cemetery (7-A-87) (MH)—Arlington, Virginia
Entered Service at: Colorado Springs, El Paso County, Colorado
Unit: 37th Air Rescue Service, Da Nang Air Force Base, Republic of Vietnam
Served as: Rescue Helicopter Crew Commander/Pilot—HH-3E
Battle or Place of Action: Khesanh, Republic of Vietnam
Date of Action: 9 November 1967
G.O. Number, Date: GB-208, 20 May 1968
Date of Presentation: 14 May 1968
Place of Presentation: The Pentagon (Inner Courtyard), Hall of Heroes, presented by Pres. Lyndon B. Johnson
Citation: For conspicuous gallantry and intrepidity at the risk of his life above and beyond the call of duty. Capt. Young distinguished himself while serving as a helicopter rescue crew commander. Capt. Young was flying escort for another helicopter attempting the night rescue of an Army ground reconnaissance team in imminent danger of death or capture. Previous attempts had resulted in the loss of two helicopters to hostile ground fire. The endangered team was positioned on the side of a steep slope which required unusual airmanship on the part of Capt. Young to effect pickup. Heavy automatic weapons fire from the surrounding enemy severely damaged one rescue helicopter, but it was able to extract three of the team. The commander of this aircraft recommended to Capt. Young that further rescue attempts be abandoned because it was not possible to suppress the concentrated fire from enemy automatic weapons. With full knowledge of the danger involved, and the fact that supporting helicopter gunships were low on fuel and ordnance, Capt. Young hovered under intense fire until the remaining survivors were aboard. As he maneuvered the aircraft for takeoff, the enemy appeared at point-blank range and raked the aircraft with automatic-weapons fire. The aircraft crashed, inverted, and burst into flames. Capt. Young escaped through a window of the burning aircraft. Disregarding serious burns, Capt. Young aided one of the wounded men and attempted to lead the hostile forces away from his position. Later, despite intense pain from his burns, he declined to accept rescue because he had observed hostile forces setting up automatic-weapons positions to entrap any rescue aircraft. For more than 17 hours he evaded the enemy until rescue aircraft could be brought into the area. Through his extraordinary heroism, aggressiveness, and concern for his fellow man, Capt. Young reflected the highest credit upon himself, the U.S. Air Force, and the Armed Forces of his country.

3396 ◆ *YOUNG, MARVIN REX

Rank: Staff Sergeant
Service: U.S. Army
Birthday: 11 May 1947
Place of Birth: Alpine, Brewster County, Texas
Date of Death: 21 August 1968
Place of Death: Republic of Vietnam
Cemetery: Sunset Memorial Cemetery (MH)—Odessa, Texas
Entered Service at: Odessa, Ector County, Texas
Unit: Company C, 1st Battalion (Mechanized), 5th Infantry, 25th Infantry Division
Served as: Squad Leader
Battle or Place of Action: near Ben Cui, Republic of Vietnam
Date of Action: 21 August 1968
G.O. Number, Date: 27, 23 April 1970
Date of Presentation: 7 April 1970
Place of Presentation: The White House, presented by Pres. Richard M. Nixon to his family
Citation: For conspicuous gallantry and intrepidity in action at the risk of his life above and beyond the call of duty. S/Sgt. Young distinguished himself at the cost of his life while serving as a squad leader with Company C. While conducting a reconnaissance mission in the vicinity of Ben Cui, Company C was suddenly engaged by an estimated regimental-size force of the North Vietnamese Army. During the initial volley of fire the point element of the 1st Platoon was pinned down, sustaining several casualties, and the acting platoon leader was killed. S/Sgt. Young unhesitatingly assumed command of the platoon and immediately began to organize and deploy his men into a defensive position in order to repel the attacking force. As a human wave attack advanced on S/Sgt. Young's platoon, he moved from position to position, encouraging and directing fire on the hostile insurgents while exposing himself to the hail of enemy bullets. After receiving orders to withdraw to a better defensive position, he remained behind to provide covering fire for the withdrawal. Observing that a small element of the point squad was unable to extract itself from its position, and completely disregarding his personal safety, S/Sgt. Young began moving toward their position, firing as he maneuvered. When halfway to their position he sustained a critical head injury, yet he continued his mission and ordered the element to withdraw. Remaining

with the squad as it fought its way to the rear, he was twice seriously wounded in the arm and leg. Although his leg was badly shattered, S/Sgt. Young refused assistance that would have slowed the retreat of his comrades, and he ordered them to continue their withdrawal while he provided protective covering fire. With indomitable courage and heroic self-sacrifice he continued his self-assigned mission until the enemy force engulfed his position. By his gallantry at the cost of his life and in the highest traditions of the military service, S/Sgt. Young has reflected great credit upon himself, his unit and the U.S. Army.

3397 ◆ ZABITOSKY, FRED WILLIAM

Rank: Sergeant First Class (rank at time of action: Staff Sergeant) (highest rank: Master Sergeant)
Service: U.S. Army
Birthday: 27 October 1942
Place of Birth: Trenton, Mercer County, New Jersey
Entered Service at: Trenton, Mercer County, New Jersey
Unit: 5th Special Forces Group (Airborne), 1st Special Forces
Served as: Assistant Team Leader
Battle or Place of Action: Laos
Date of Action: 19 February 1968
G.O. Number, Date: 27, 17 April 1969
Date of Presentation: 7 March 1969
Place of Presentation: The White House (East Ballroom), presented by Pres. Richard M. Nixon
Citation: For conspicuous gallantry and intrepidity in action at the risk of his life above and beyond the call of duty. Sfc. Zabitosky, U.S. Army, distinguished himself while serving as an assistant team leader of a nine-man Special Forces long-range reconnaissance patrol. Sfc. Zabitosky's patrol was operating deep within enemy controlled territory when they were attacked by a numerically superior North Vietnamese Army unit. Sfc. Zabitosky rallied his team members, deployed them into defensive positions, and, exposing himself to concentrated enemy automatic weapons fire, directed their return fire. Realizing the gravity of the situation, Sfc. Zabitosky ordered his patrol to move to a landing zone for helicopter extraction while he covered their withdrawal with rifle fire and grenades. Rejoining the patrol under increasing enemy pressure, he positioned each man in a tight perimeter defense and continually moved from man to man, encouraging them and controlling their defensive fire. Mainly due to his example, the outnumbered patrol maintained its precarious position until the arrival of tactical air support and a helicopter extraction team. As the rescue helicopters arrived, the determined North Vietnamese pressed their attack. Sfc. Zabitosky repeatedly exposed himself to their fire to adjust suppressive helicopter-gunship fire around the landing zone. After boarding one of the rescue helicopters, he positioned himself in the door delivering fire on the enemy as the ship took off. The helicopter was engulfed in a hail of bullets and Sfc. Zabitosky was thrown from the craft as it spun out of control and crashed. Recovering consciousness, he ignored his extremely painful injuries and moved to the flaming wreckage. Heedless of the danger of exploding ordnance and fuel, he pulled the severely wounded pilot from the searing blaze and made repeated attempts to rescue his patrol members but was driven back by the intense heat. Despite his serious burns and crushed ribs, he carried and dragged the unconscious pilot through a curtain of enemy fire to within 10 feet of a hovering rescue helicopter before collapsing. Sfc. Zabitosky's extraordinary heroism and devotion to duty were in keeping with the highest traditons of the miltary serrvice and reflect great credit upon himself, his unit, and the U.S. Army.

SOMALIA
(OPERATION RESTORE HOPE)

3398 ♦ *GORDON, GARY IVAN

Rank: Master Sergeant
Service: U.S. Army
Birthday: 30 August 1960
Place of Birth: Lincoln, Penobscot County, Maine
Date of Death: 3 October 1993
Place of Death: Mogadishu, Somalia
Cemetery: Lincoln Cemetery—Lincoln, Maine
Entered Service at: Lincoln, Penobscot County, Maine
Unit: Task Force Ranger, Special Operations Command
Served as: Sniper Team Leader
Battle or Place of Action: Mogadishu, Somalia
Date of Action: 3 October 1993
Date of Presentation: 23 May 1994
Place of Presentation: The White House, presented by Pres. William J. Clinton to his Widow
Citation: M/Sgt. Gary I. Gordon, United States Army, distinguished himself by action above and beyond the call of duty on 3 October 1993, while serving as a Sniper Team Leader, United States Army Special Operations Command with Task Force Ranger in Mogadishu, Somalai. M/Sgt. Gordon's sniper team provided precision fires from the lead helicopter during an assault, and at two helicopter crash sites, while subjected to intense automatic weapons and rocket propelled grenade fires. When M/Sgt. Gordon learned that ground forces were not immediately available to secure the crash site, he and another sniper unhesitatingly volunteered to be inserted to protect the four critcally wounded personnel, despite being well aware of the growing number of enemy personnel closing in on the site. After his third request to be inserted, M/Sgt. Gordon received permission to perform his volunteer mission. When debris and enemy ground fires at the site caused him to abort the first attempt, M/Sgt. Gordon was inserted one hundred meters south of the crash site. Equipped with only his sniper rifle and pistol, M/Sgt. Gordon and his fellow sniper, while under intense small arms fire from the enemy, fought their way through a dense maze of shanties and shacks to reach the critically injured crew members. M/Sgt. Gordon immediately pulled the pilot and other crew members from the aircraft, establishing a perimeter which placed him and his fellow sniper in the most vulnerable position. M/Sgt. Gordon used his long range rifle and side arm to kill an undetermined number of attackers until he depleted his ammunition. M/Sgt. Gordon then went back to the wreckage, recovering some of the crew's weapons and ammunition. Despite the fact that he was critically low on ammunition he provided some of it to the dazed pilot and then radioed for help. M/Sgt. Gordon continued to travel the perimeter, protecting the downed crew. After his team member was fatally wounded, and his own rifle ammunition exhausted, M/Sgt. Gordon returned to the wreckage, recovering a rifle with the last five rounds of ammunition and gave it to the pilot with the words "Good Luck." Then, armed only with his pistol, M/Sgt. Gordon continued to fight until he was fatally wounded. His actions saved the pilot's life. M/Sgt. Gordon's extraordinary heroism and devotion to duty were in keeping with the highest standards of military service and reflect great credit on him, his unit, and the United States Army.

3399 ♦ *SHUGHART, RANDALL DAVID

Rank: Sergeant First Class
Service: U.S. Army
Birthday: 13 August 1958
Place of Birth: Lincoln, Lancaster County, Nebraska
Date of Death: 3 October 1993
Place of Death: Mogadishu, Somalia
Cemetery: Westminster Cemetery, Garden of Benediction (230-3-2)—North Middleton Township, Pennsylvania
Entered Service at: Newville, Cumberland County, Pennsylvania
Unit: Task Force Ranger, Special Operations Command
Served as: Sniper Team Member
Battle or Place of Action: Mogadishu, Somalia
Date of Action: 3 October 1993
Date of Presentation: 23 May 1994
Place of Presentation: The White House, presented by Pres. William J. Clinton to his Widow
Citation: Sfc. Randall D. Shughart, United States Army, distinguished himself by actions above and beyond the call of duty on 3 October 1993, while serving as a Sniper Team Member, United States Army Special Operations Command with Task Force Ranger in Mogadishu, Somalia. Sfc. Stughart provided precision sniper fires from the lead helicopter during an assault on a building and at two helicopter crash sites, while subjected to intense automatic weapons and rocket propelled grenade fires. While providing critical suppressive fires at the second crash site, Sfc. Stughart and his team leader learned that ground forces were not immediately available to secure the site. Sfc. Shughart and his team leader unhesitatingly volunteered to be inserted to protect the four critically wounded personnel, despite being well aware of the growing number of enemy personnel closing in on the site. After their third request to be inserted, Sfc. Shughart and his team leader received permission to perform this volunteer mission. When debris and enemy ground fires at the site caused them to

abort the first attempt, Sfc. Shughart and his team leader were inserted one hundred meters south of the crash site. Equipped with only his sniper rifle and a pistol, Sergeant First Class Shughart and his team leader, while under intense small arms fire from the enemy, fought their way through a dense maze of shanties and shacks to reach the critically injured crew members. Sfc. Shughart pulled the pilot and the other crew members from the aircraft, establishing a perimeter which placed him and his fellow sniper in the most vulnerable position. Sfc. Shughart used his long range rifle and side arm to kill an undetermined number of attackers while travelling the perimeter, protecting the downed crew. Sfc. Shughart continued his protective fire until he depleted his ammunition and was fatally wounded. His actions saved the pilot's life. Sfc. Shughart's extraordinary heroism and devotion to duty were in keeping with the highest standards of military service and reflect great credit on him, his unit, and the United States Army.

MEDALS OF HONOR AWARDED TO UNKNOWNS

On Armistice Day, 1921, the Medal of Honor was pinned to the flag-draped coffin of the American Unknown Soldier by President Harding during services at the Arlington National Cemetery. A special bill was passed by Congress permitting the award to an unknown as "typifying the gallantry and intrepidity, at the risk of life above and beyond the call of duty, or our beloved heroes who made the supreme sacrifice in the World War." Medals of Honor were also awarded by special legislation to the unknown soldiers of Belgium, Great Britain, France, Italy, and Rumania.

BELGIUM

* * *By virtue of the authority vested in the President of the United States, The Congressional Medal of Honor, emblem of the highest military ideals and virtues, is bestowed in the name of the Congress of the United States upon the unknown, unidentified Belgian soldier in a desire to add all that is possible to the imperishable glory won by the soldiers of Belgium who fought as comrades of the American soldiers during the World War, and to commemorate with them the deeds of the nations associated with the United States of America, by paying this tribute to their unknown dead (A.G. 220.523) (War Department General Orders, No.52, 1 December 1922, Sec. I).

GREAT BRITAIN AND FRANCE

* * * By virtue of an act of Congress approved 4 March 1921, the Medal of Honor, emblem of highest ideals and virtues, is bestowed in the name of the Congress of the United States upon the unknown, unidentified British soldier and French soldier buried, respectively, in Westminster Abbey and Arc de Triomphe.

Whereas Great Britain and France, two of the Allies of the United States in the World War, have done honor to the unknown dead of their armies by placing with fitting ceremony the body of an unidentified soldier, respectively, in Westminster Abbey and in the Arc de Triomphe; and

Whereas animated by the same spirit of comradeship in which we of the American Forces fought alongside these allies, we desire to add whatever we can to the imperishable glory won by the deeds of our Allies and commemorated in part by this tribute to their unknown dead:

Now therefore,

Be it enacted by the Senate and House of Representatives of the United States of America assembled, That the President of the United States of America be, and he hereby is, authorized to bestow with appropriate ceremonies, military and civil, the Congressional Medal of Honor upon the unknown, unidentified British soldier buried in Westminster Abbey, London, England, and upon the unknown, unidentified French soldier buried in the Arc de Triomphe, Paris, France (A.G. 220.523) (War Department General Orders, No. 52, 1 December 1922, Sec. II).

ITALY

* * * By virtue of a joint resolution of Congress, approved 12 October 1921, the Medal of Honor, emblem of highest ideals and virtues, is bestowed in the name of Congress of the United States of America upon the unknown, unidentified Italian soldier to be buried in the National Monument to Victor Emanuel II, in Rome.

Whereas the Congress has authorized the bestowal of the Congressional Medal of Honor upon the unknown, unidentified British and French soldiers buried in Westminster Abbey, London, England, and the Arc de Triomphe, Paris, France, respectfully, who fought beside our soldiers in the recent war; and

Whereas, animated by the same spirit of friendship toward the soldiers of Italy who also fought as comrades of the American soldiers during the World War, we desire to add whatever we can to the imperishable glory won by their deeds and to participate in paying tribute to their unknown dead: Now, therefore, be it

Resolved by the Senate and House of Representatives of the United States of America in Congress assembled, That the President of the United States be, and he is hereby, authorized to bestow, with appropriate ceremonies, military and civil, the Congressional Medal of Honor upon the unknown, unidentified Italian soldier to be buried in the National Monument to Victor Emanuel II, in Rome, Italy (A.G. 220.523) (War Department General Orders, No. 52, 1 December 1922, Sec. III).

RUMANIA

* * * By virtue of the authority vested by law in the President of the United States, The Congressional Medal of Honor, emblem of the highest military ideals and virtues, is bestowed in the name of the Congress of the United States upon the unknown, unidentified Rumanian soldier in a desire to add all that is possible to the imperishable glory won by the soldiers of Rumania who fought as comrades of the American soldiers during the World War, and to commemorate with them the deeds of the nations associated with the United States of America, by paying tribute to their unknown dead. The medal is on display at the National Minority Museum in Bucharest, Rumania (A.G. 220.52, 17 May 1923) (War Department General Orders, No. 22, 6 June 1923).

UNITED STATES

* * * By virtue of an Act of Congress approved 24 August 1921, the Medal of Honor, emblem of highest ideals and virtues is bestowed in the name of Congress of the United States upon the unknown American, typifying the gallantry and intrepidity, at the risk of life above and beyond the call of duty, of our beloved heroes who made the supreme sacrifice in the World War. They died in order that others might live (293.8, A.G.O.) (War Department General Orders, No. 59, 13 December 1921, Sec. I).

AN ACT To authorize the President to award the Medal of Honor to the unknown Americans who lost his life while serving overseas in the armed forces of the United States during the Second World War.

Be it enacted by the Senate and House of Representatives of the United States of America assembled, That the President is hereby authorized and directed to award, in the name of Congress, a Medal of Honor to the unknown American who lost his life while serving overseas in the armed forces of the United States during the Second World War, and who will lie buried in the Memorial Amphitheater of the National Cemetery at Arlington, Virginia, as authorized by the Act of June 24, 1946, Public Law 438, Seventy-ninth Congress.

Approved March 9, 1948, Public Law 438, Eightieth Congress.

AN ACT TO authorize the President to award the Medal of Honor to the unknown American who lost his life while serving overseas in the Armed Forces of the United States during the Korean War.

Be it enacted by the Senate and the House of Representatives of the United States of America assembled, That the President is hereby authorized and directed to award, in the name of Congress, a Medal of Honor to the unknown American who lost his life while serving overseas in the Armed Forces of the United States during the Korean War, and who will lie buried in the Memorial Amphitheater of the National Cemetery at Arlington, Virginia, as authorized by the Act of August 3, 1956, Public Law 975, Eighty-fourth Congress.

Approved August 31, 1957, Public Law 85-251, Eighty-fifth Congress.

AN ACT TO authorize the President to award the Medal of Honor to the unknown American who lost his life while serving in the Armed Forces of the United States in Southeast Asia during the Vietnam Era and who has been selected to be buried in the Memorial Amphitheater at Arlington National Cemetery.

Be it enacted by the Senate and the House of Representatives of the United States of America assembled, That the President may award, and present in the name of Congress, the Medal of Honor to the unknown American who lost his life while serving in Southeast Asia during the Vietnam Era as a member of the Armed Forces of the United States of America and who has been selected to lie buried in the Memorial Amphitheater of the National Cemetery at Arlington, Virginia, as authorized by Section 9 of the National Cemeteries Act of 1973 (Pubic Law 93-43), Ninety-third Congress.

Approved May 25, 1984. Public Law 98-301, Ninety-eighth Congress.

APPENDIXES

ABBREVIATIONS

A1c.	airman first class	LCS	landing craft, support
A.A.C.	army air corp	LST	landing ship tank
A.G.	adjutant general	Lt.	lieutenant
Adm.	admiral	M/Sgt.	master sergeant
AFB	air force base	Maj.	major
AGTR	technical research ship	MH	Medal of Honor
ARNG	Army National Guard	PBR	patrol boat, river
Brig.	brigadier	Pfc.	private first class
C.B.	cabin boy	PmS.	paymaster's steward
C.G.	chief gunner	Pvt.	private
C.H.	coal heaver	Q.G.	quarter gunner
C.S.A.	Confederate States of America	Q.M.	quartermaster
C.S.S.	Confederate steamship	Recon.	reconnaissance
Capt.	captain	Rein	Reinforced (unit composed of men from other units to bring the unit up to full strength)
Col.	colonel		
Comdr.	commander	Ret.	retired
Cpl.	corporal	S/man	seaman
CWO	chief warrant officer	S/Q.M.	signal quartermaster
DE	destroyer escort	S/Sgt.	staff sergeant
Ens.	ensign	SCARNG	South Carolina Army National Guard
FAC	forward air controller	SEAL	sea, air and land
FMF	fleet marine force	Sec.	secretary
G.O.#	general order number	Sfc.	sergeant first class
G/Sgt.	gunnery sergeant	Sgt.	sergeant
Gen.	general	Sp4c.	specialist fourth class
Gp.	group	Sp5c.	specialist fifth class
HC2c.	hospital corpsman second class	Surg.	surgeon
HC3c.	hospital corpsman third class	T/Sgt.	technical sergeant
HC	hospital corpsman	Tech.	technician
j.g.	junior grade	U.S.A.	U.S. Army
L/Cpl.	lance corporal	U.S.S.	United States ship
LCI(G)	landing craft infantry gunboat	WO	warrant officer

RECIPIENTS BY STATE OF ENLISTMENT & BIRTH

ALABAMA

U.S. Army

BOLDEN, Paul Luther — ES: Madison, Madison Co., AL
B: Hobbes Island, AL

BOLTON, Cecil Hamilton — ES: Huntsville, Madison Co., AL
B: Crawfordville, Wakulla Co., FL

DAVIS, Charles Willis — ES: Montgomery, Montgomery Co., AL
B: Gordo, Pickens Co., AL

*EVANS, Rodney John — ES: Montgomery, Montgomery Co., AL
B: Chelsea, Suffolk Co., MA

HOWARD, Robert Lewis — ES: Montgomery, Montgomery Co., AL
B: Opelika, Lee Co., AL

JOHNSTON, Gordon — ES: Birmingham, Jefferson Co., AL
B: Charlotte, Mecklenburg Co., NC

*LEONARD, Matthew — ES: Birmingham, Jefferson Co., AL
B: Eutaw, Greene Co., AL

LINDSEY Sr., Jake William — ES: Lucedale, George Co., MS
B: Isney, AL

MANNING, Sidney E. — ES: Flomaton, Escambia Co., AL
B: Butler Co., AL

*MICHAEL, Don Leslie — ES: Montgomery, Montgonery Co., AL
B: Florence, Lauderdale Co., AL

MIZE, Ola Lee — ES: Gadsden, Etowah Co., AL
B: Albertville, Marshall Co., AL

*SEAY, William Wayne — ES: Montgomery, Montgomery Co., AL
B: Brewton, Escambia Co., AL

SPRAYBERRY, James Michael — ES: Montgomery, Montgomery Co., AL
B: LaGrange, Troup Co., GA

TAYLOR, Richard — ES: Indianapolis, Marion Co., IN
B: Madison Co., AL

TREADWELL, Jack Lemaster — ES: Snyder, Kiowa Co., OK
B: Ashland, Clay Co., AL

U.S. Army Air Corps/U.S. Air Force

ERWIN, Henry Eugene "Red" — ES: Bessemer, Jefferson Co., AL
B: Adamsville, Jefferson Co., AL

LAWLEY Jr., William Robert — ES: Birmingham, Jefferson Co., AL
B: Leeds, Jefferson Co., AL

U.S. Navy

*GILMORE, Howard Walter — ES: LA
B: Selma, Dallas Co., AL

HOBSON, Richmond Pearson — ES: NY
B: Greensboro, Hale Co., AL

HOUGHTON, Edward J. — ES: AL
B: Mobile, Mobile Co., AL

*INGRAM, Osmond Kelly — ES: AL
B: Platt City, AL

McCAMPBELL, David — ES: West Palm Beach, Palm Beach Co., FL
B: Bessemer, Jefferson Co., AL

U.S. Marine Corps

*GRAY, Ross Franklin — ES: AL
B: Marvel Valley, AL

McLAUGHLIN, Alford Lee — ES: Leeds, Jefferson Co., AL
B: Leeds, Jefferson Co., AL

*NEW, John Dury — ES: AL
B: Mobile, Mobile Co., AL

WATSON, Wilson Douglas — ES: Earle, Crittenden Co., AR
B: Tuscumbia, Colbert Co., AL

WILSON, Harold Edward "Speedy" — ES: Birmingham, Jefferson Co., AL
B: Birmingham, Jefferson Co., AL

ALASKA

U.S. Marine Corps

VAN WINKLE, Archie — ES: Arlington, Snohomish Co., WA
B: Juneau, Juneau Co., AK

ARIZONA

U.S. Army

ALCHESAY, William — ES: Camp Verde, Yavapai Co., Arizona Territory
B: AZ

BACON, Nicky Daniel — ES: Phoenix, Maricopa Co., AZ
B: Caraway, Craighead Co., AR

BLANQUET — B: AZ

CHIQUITO	ES: San Carlos, Gila Co., AZ B: AZ	HENDRIX, James Richard	ES: Lepanto, Poinsett Co., AR B: Lepanto, Poinsett Co., AR
DUNAGAN, Kern Wayne	ES: Los Angeles, Los Angeles Co., CA B: Superior, Pinal Co., AZ	*LLOYD, Edgar Harold	ES: Blytheville, Mississippi Co., AR B: Blytheville, Mississippi Co., AR
ELSATSOOSH	B: Arizona Territory	MacARTHUR, Douglas	ES: Ashland, Ashland Co., WI B: Little Rock, Pulaski Co., AR
FERGUSON, Frederick Edgar	ES: Phoenix, Maricopa Co., AZ B: Pilot Point, Denton Co., TX	*MILLER, Oscar F.	ES: Los Angeles, Los Angeles Co., CA B: Franklin Co., AR
HERRERA, Silvestre Santana	ES: Phoenix, Maricopa Co., AZ B: El Paso, El Paso Co., TX	STONE, James Lamar	ES: Houston, Harris Co., TX B: Pine Bluff, Jefferson Co., AR
JIM	ES: Camp Verde, Yavapia Co., Arizona Territory B: Arizona Territory	*TERRY, Seymour W.	ES: Little Rock, Pulaski Co., AR B: Little Rock, Pulaski Co., AR
KELSAY	ES: Arizona Territory B: Arizona Territory	*THOMAS, William H.	ES: Ypsilanti, Washtenaw Co., MI B: Wynne, Cross Co., AR
KOSOHA	B: Arizona Territory	WARD, John	ES: Fort Duncan, TX B: AR
*LAUFFER, Billy Lane	ES: Phoenix, Maricopa Co., AZ B: Murray, Calloway Co., KY	*WATKINS, Travis E.	ES: TX B: Waldo, Columbia Co., AR
MACHOL	B: Arizona Territory	WHEELER, Henry W.	ES: Bangor, Penobscot Co., ME B: Fort Smith, Sebastian Co., AR

U.S. Navy

NANNASADDIE	B: Arizona Territory
NANTAJE (NANTAHE)	B: Arizona Territory
ROWDY	ES: San Carlos, Gila Co., AZ B: Arizona Territory
SMITH, Cornelius Cole	ES: Helena, Lewis & Clark Co., MT B: Tucson, Pima Co., AZ

FRANKS, William J.	ES: De Valls Bluff, Prairie Co., AR B: Chatham Co., NC
GORDON, Nathan Green	ES: Morrilton, Conway Co., AR B: Morrilton, Conway Co., AR
*WILLIAMS, Jack	ES: AR B: Harrison, Boone Co., AR

U.S. Marine Corps

U.S. Army Air Service

*LUKE Jr., Frank	ES: Phoenix, Maricopa Co., AZ B: Phoenix, Maricopa Co., AZ

*LITTLETON, Herbert A.	ES: Black Hawk, Meade Co., SD B: Mena, Polk Co., AR
*PRUITT, John Henry	ES: Phoenix, Maricopa Co., AZ B: Fayetteville, Washington Co., AR
WATSON, Wilson Douglas	ES: Earle, Crittenden Co., AR B: Tuscumbia, Colbert Co., AL

U.S. Marine Corps

*AUSTIN, Oscar Palmer	ES: Phoenix, Maricopa Co., AZ B: Nacogdoches, Nacogdoches Co., TX
*JIMENEZ, Jose Francisco	ES: Phoenix, Maricopa Co., AZ B: Mexico City, Mexico
*PRUITT, John Henry	ES: Phoenix, Maricopa Co., AZ B: Fayetteville, Washington Co., AR
VARGAS, Jay R.	ES: Winslow, Navajo Co., AZ B: Winslow, Navajo Co., AZ

CALIFORNIA

U.S. Army

BACA, John Philip	ES: Fort Ord, Monterey Co., CA B: Providence, Providence Co., RI
BARNES, Will Croft	ES: Washington, D.C. B: San Francisco, San Francisco Co., CA
*BELLRICHARD, Leslie Allen	ES: Oakland, Alameda Co., CA B: Janesville, Rock Co., WI
BROPHY, James	ES: Stockton, San Joaquin Co., CA B: Kilkenny, Ireland
BURKE, Patrick J.	ES: Vallejo, Solano Co., CA B: Kilkenny, Ireland
CARR, John	ES: San Jose, Santa Clara Co., CA B: Columbus, Franklin Co., OH
CARTER, George	ES: Vallejo, Solano Co., CA B: Dublin, Ireland
CAVAIANI, Jon Robert	ES: Fresno, Fresno Co., CA B: Royston, England
CRAFT, Clarence Byrle	ES: Santa Ana, Orange Co., CA B: San Bernardino, San Bernardino Co., CA
CROCKER, Henry H.	ES: San Francisco, San Francisco Co., CA B: Colchester, New London Co., CT

ARKANSAS

U.S. Army

BACON, Nicky Daniel	ES: Phoenix, Maricopa Co., AZ B: Caraway, Craighead Co., AR
BRITT, Maurice Lee "Footsie"	ES: Lonoke, Lonoke Co., AR B: Carlisle, Lonoke Co., AR
BURKE, Lloyd Leslie "Scooter"	ES: Stuttgart, Arkansas Co., AR B: Tichnor, Arkansas Co., AR
*CHILES, Marcellus Holmes	ES: Denver, Denver Co., CO B: Eureka Springs, Carroll Co., AR
*COLLIER, Gilbert G.	S: Tichnor, Arkansas Co., AR B: Hunter, Woodruff Co., AR
FACTOR, Pompey	ES: Fort Duncan, TX B: AR
*GILLILAND, Charles L.	ES: Yellville, Marion Co., AR B: Mountain Home, Baxter Co., AR

DEAN Sr., William Frishe	ES: CA B: Carlyle, Clinton Co., IL	LAWRENCE, James	ES: Sacramento, Sacramento Co., CA B: Aberdeen, Scotland
*DESIDERIO, Reginald Benjamin	ES: Gilroy, Santa Clara Co., CA B: Clairton, Allegheny Co., PA	*LEAHY, Cornelius J.	ES: San Francisco, San Francisco Co., CA B: Limerick, Ireland
*DEVORE Jr., Edward Allen	ES: Harbor City, Los Angeles Co., CA B: Torrance, Los Angeles Co., CA	*LEISY, Robert Ronald	ES: Seattle, King Co., WA B: Stockton, San Joaquin Co., CA
DICKENS, Charles H.	ES: San Francisco, San Francisco Co., CA B: Dublin, Ireland	LITTRELL, Gary Lee	ES: Los Angeles, Los Angeles Co., CA B: Henderson, Henderson Co., KY
DUNAGAN, Kern Wayne	ES: Los Angeles, Los Angeles Co., CA B: Superior, Pinal Co., AZ	LYTTON, Jeptha L.	ES: San Francisco, San Francisco Co., CA B: Lawrence Co., IN
ELWOOD, Edwin L.	ES: San Jose, Santa Clara Co., CA B: St. Louis, St Louis Co., MO	MAHERS, Herbert	ES: Wilmington, Los Angeles Co., CA B: Canada
*EVANS Jr., Donald Ward	ES: Covina, Los Angeles Co., CA B: Covina, Los Angeles Co., CA	McKINLEY, Daniel	ES: San Francisco, San Francisco Co., CA B: Boston, Suffolk Co., MA
FALCOTT, Henry	ES: San Francisco, San Francisco Co., CA B: Champagne, France	McMAHON, Martin Thomas	ES: CA B: LaPrairie, Quebec, Canada
GARDNER, Charles	ES: San Francisco, San Francisco Co., CA B: Bavaria, Germany	McVEAGH, Charles H.	ES: San Francisco, San Francisco Co., CA B: New York, NY
GOLDEN, Patrick	ES: San Francisco, San Francisco Co., CA B: County Sligo, Ireland	*MILLER, Oscar F.	ES: Los Angeles, Los Angeles Co., CA B: Franklin Co., AR
*GONZALES, David M.	ES: Pacoima, Los Angeles Co., CA B: Pacoima, Los Angeles Co., CA	*MOLNAR, Frankie Zoly	ES: Fresno, Fresno Co., CA B: Logan, Logan Co., WV
GREEN, Francis C.	ES: Sacramento, Sacramento Co., CA B: Mount Vernon, Posey Co., IN	*MOON Jr., Harold Herman	ES: Gardena, Los Angeles Co., CA B: Albuquerque, Bernalillo Co., NM
GUMPERTZ, Sydney G.	ES: Chicago, Cook Co., IL B: San Raphael, Marin Co., CA	MORAN, John	ES: Marysville, Yuba Co., CA B: Lyon, France
HALL, John	ES: Sacramento, Sacramento Co., CA B: Logan Co., IL	*MUNEMORI, Sadao S.	ES: Los Angeles, Los Angeles Co., CA B: Los Angeles, Los Angeles Co., CA
HAMILTON, Frank	ES: Sacramento, Sacramento Co., CA B: County Tyrone, Ireland	MURPHY, Thomas	ES: San Francisco, San Francisco Co., CA B: County Kerry, Ireland
*HARMON, Roy W.	ES: Pixley, Tulare Co., CA B: Talala, Rogers Co., OK	O'CALLAGHAN, John	ES: San Francisco, San Francisco Co., CA B: New York, NY
HARVEY, Raymond	ES: Pasadena, Los Angeles Co., CA B: Ford City, Armstrong Co., PA	PENRY, Richard Allen	ES: Oakland, Alameda Co., CA B: Petaluma, Sonoma Co., CA
HAWK, John Druse "Bud"	ES: Bremerton, Kitsap Co., WA B: San Francisco, San Francisco Co., CA	*PIERCE, Larry Stanley	ES: Fresno, Fresno Co., CA B: Wewoka, Seminole Co., OK
HEARTERY, Richard	ES: San Francisco, San Francisco Co., CA B: Ireland	QUINN, Peter H.	ES: San Francisco, San Francisco Co., CA B: San Francisco, San Francisco Co., CA
HERNANDEZ, Rodolfo Perez	ES: Fowler, Fresno Co., CA B: Colton, San Bernardino Co., CA	REED, James C.	ES: San Francisco, San Francisco Co., CA B: Kilkenny, Ireland
HIGGINS, Thomas P.	ES: Napa, Napa Co., CA B: Longford, Ireland	REGAN, Patrick J.	ES: Los Angeles, Los Angeles Co., CA B: Middleboro, Plymouth Co., MA
HIGH, Frank Charles	ES: Ashland, Jackson Co., OR B: Dunningham, Yolo Co., CA	*ROARK, Anund Charles	ES: Los Angeles, Los Angeles Co., CA B: Vallejo, Solano Co., CA
HOLDERMAN, Nelson Miles	ES: Santa Ana, Orange Co., CA B: Trumbull, Clay Co., NE	*ROBERTS, Harold W.	ES: San Francisco, San Francisco Co., CA B: San Francisco, San Francisco Co., CA
HOOPER, Joe Ronnie	ES: Los Angeles, Los Angeles Co., CA B: Piedmont, Greenville Co., SC	ROCCO, Louis Richard	ES: Los Angeles, Los Angeles Co., CA B: Albuquerque, Bernalillo Co., NM
*INGALLS, George Alan	ES: Los Angeles, Los Angeles Co., CA B: Hanford, Kings Co., CA	RODRIGUEZ, Joseph Charles	ES: San Bernardino, San Bernardino Co., CA B: San Bernardino, San Bernardino Co., CA
JENNINGS, Delbert Owen	ES: San Francisco, San Francisco Co., CA B: Silver City, Grant Co., NM	SEIBERT, Lloyd Martin	ES: Salinas, Monterey Co., CA B: Caledonia, Kent Co., MI
*KANDLE, Victor Leonard	ES: Redwood City, San Mateo Co., CA B: Roy, Pierce Co., WA	SHIELS, George Franklin	ES: CA B: CA
KATZ, Phillip Carl	ES: San Francisco, San Francisco Co., CA B: San Francisco, San Francisco Co., CA	*SHOCKLEY, William Ralph	ES: Selma, Fresno Co., CA B: Bokoshe, LeFlore Co., OK
KEENAN, John	ES: San Francisco, San Francisco Co., CA B: Tubbercurry, County Sligo, Ireland	SMITH, Otto	ES: Sacramento, Sacramento Co., CA B: Baltimore, Baltimore Co., MD
		SMITH, William	ES: San Francisco, San Francisco Co., CA B: Bath, Sagadahoc Co., ME

STANLEY, Edward	ES: San Francisco, San Francisco Co., CA B: New York, NY	*JONES, Herbert Charpoit	ES: CA B: Los Angeles, Los Angeles Co., CA
STRIVSON, Benoni	ES: Sacramento, Sacramento Co., CA B: Overton, TN	*KOELSCH, John Kelvin	ES: Los Angeles, Los Angeles Co., CA B: London, England U.S. Marine Corps
TAYLOR, James Allen	ES: San Francisco, San Francisco Co., CA B: Arcata, Humboldt Co., CA	LAVERTY, John	ES: CA B: County Tyrone, Ireland
TURNER, George Benton	ES: Los Angeles, Los Angeles Co., CA B: Longview, Gregg Co., TX	McALLISTER, Samuel	ES: CA B: Belfast, County Antrim, Ireland
*VIALE, Robert M.	ES: Ukiah, Mendocino Co., CA B: Bayside, Humboldt Co., CA	McGONAGLE, William Loren	ES: Thermal, Riverside Co., CA B: Wichita, Sedgwick Co., KS
*VILLEGAS, Ysmael R.	ES: Casa Blanca, CA B: Casa Blanca, CA	PHARRIS, Jackson Charles	ES: CA B: Columbus, Muscogee Co., GA
VON SCHLICK, Robert H.	ES: San Francisco, San Francisco Co., CA B: Germany	SMITH, Eugene P.	ES: CA B: Illinois
WARE, Keith Lincoln	ES: Glendale, Los Angeles Co., CA B: Denver, Denver Co., CO	STOLTENBERG, Andrew Vincent	ES: CA B: Bodo, Norway
WAYBUR, David Crowder	ES: Piedmont, Alameda Co., CA B: Oakland, Alameda Co., CA	VOLZ, Robert	ES: VA B: San Francisco, San Francisco Co., CA
WEAVER, Amos	ES: San Francisco, San Francisco Co., CA B: Niles Township, Delaware Co., IN	WESTERMARK, Axel	ES: CA B: Bergo, Finland
WEST, Chester Howard	ES: Los Banos, Merced Co., CA B: Fort Collins, Larimer Co., CO	WILLIAMS, Louis	ES: CA B: Christiana (now Oslo), Norway
WILLISTON, Edward Bancroft	ES: San Francisco, San Francisco Co., CA B: Norwich, Windsor Co., VT	WOODS, Samuel	ES: CA B: San Francisco, San Francisco Co., CA
*YABES, Maximo	ES: Eugene, Lane Co., OR B: Lodi, San Joaquin Co., CA		
*YOUNG, Robert Harley	ES: Vallejo, Solano Co., CA B: Oroville, Butte Co., CA		
YOUNT, John P.	ES: Sacramento, Sacramento Co., CA B: Putnam Co., IN		

U.S. Army Air Corps/U.S. Air Force

*CHELI, Ralph	ES: Brooklyn, Kings Co., NY B: San Francisco, San Francisco Co., CA
DOOLITTLE, James Harold	ES: Berkeley, Alameda Co., CA B: Alameda, Alameda Co., CA

U.S. Air Force

FISHER, Bernard Francis	ES: Kuna, Ada Co., ID B: San Bernardino, San Bernardino Co., CA

U.S. Navy

BROCK, George F.	ES: CA B: Cleveland, Montgomery Co., OH
*CALLAGHAN, Daniel Judson	ES: Oakland, Alameda Co., CA B: San Francisco, San Francisco Co., CA
CLAUSEY, John Joseph	ES: CA B: San Francisco, San Francisco Co., CA
COVINGTON, Jesse Whitfield	ES: CA B: Haywood, TN
FINN, John William	ES: Belle Vernon Acres, CA B: Los Angeles, Los Angeles Co., CA
FISHER, Frederick Thomas	ES: CA B: England
HALFORD, William	ES: San Francisco, San Francisco Co., CA B: Gloucester, Gloucestershire, England
HANSEN, Hans Anton	ES: CA B: Germany
HENRECHON, George Francis	ES: CA B: Hartford, Hartford Co., CT
ITRICH, Franz Anton	ES: CA B: Gross Katz, Germany

U.S. Marine Corps

*ANDERSON Jr., James	ES: Los Angeles, Los Angeles Co., CA B: Los Angeles, Los Angeles Co., CA
BOYDSTON, Erwin Jay	ES: CA B: Deer Creek, CO
BURNES, James	ES: CA B: Worcester, Worcester Co., MA
COLEMAN, John	ES: CA B: County Cork, Ireland
DAHLGREN, John Olof	ES: CA B: Kahliwar, Sweden
*FOSTER, Paul Hellstrom	ES: San Francisco, San Francisco Co., CA B: San Mateo, San Mateo Co., CA
*GONSALVES, Harold	ES: CA B: Alameda, Alameda Co., CA
HEISCH, Henry William	ES: CA B: Latendorf, Germany
HULBERT, Henry Lewis	ES: CA B: Kingston upon Hull, Humberside Co., England
*JOHNSON, Ralph Henry	ES: Oakland, Alameda Co., CA B: Charleston, Charleston Co., SC
*KELSO, Jack William	ES: Caruthers, Fresno Co., CA B: Madera, Madera Co., CA
*MATTHEWS, Daniel Paul	ES: Van Nuys, Los Angeles Co., CA B: Van Nuys, Los Angeles Co., CA
*MAXAM, Larry Leonard	ES: Los Angeles, Los Angeles Co., CA B: Glendale, Los Angeles Co., CA
McNALLY, Michael Joseph	ES: CA B: New York, NY
MOORE, Albert	ES: CA B: Merced, Merced Co., CA
*OBREGON, Eugene Arnold	ES: Los Angeles, Los Angeles Co., CA B: Los Angeles, Los Angeles Co., CA
ORNDOFF, Harry Westley	ES: CA B: Sandusky, Erie Co., OH

*PERKINS Jr., William Thomas   ES: San Francisco, San Francisco Co., CA
B: Rochester, Monroe Co., NY

PHILLIPS, Reuben Jasper   ES: CA
B: Cambria, San Luis Obispo Co., CA

*PHIPPS, Jimmy Wayne   ES: Culver City, Los Angeles Co., CA
B: Santa Monica, Los Angeles Co., CA

PITTMAN, Richard Allan   ES: Stockton, San Joaquin Co., CA
B: French Camp, San Joaquin Co., CA

*POYNTER, James Irsley   ES: Downey, Los Angeles Co., CA
B: Bloomington, McLean Co., IL

SILVA, France   ES: San Francisco, San Francisco Co., CA
B: Hayward, Alameda Co., CA

SWETT, James Elms   ES: San Mateo, San Mateo Co., CA
B: Seattle, King Co., WA

*WORLEY, Kenneth Lee   ES: Fresno, Fresno Co., CA
B: Farmington, San Juan Co., NM

ZION, William F.   ES: CA
B: Knightstown, Henry Co., IN

COLORADO

U.S. Army

*CHILES, Marcellus Holmes   ES: Denver, Denver Co., CO
B: Eureka Springs, Carroll Co., AR

CRAWFORD, William John   ES: Pueblo, Pueblo Co., CO
B: Pueblo, Pueblo Co., CO

DIX, Drew Dennis   ES: Denver, Denver Co., CO
B: West Point, Orange Co., NY

*FRYAR, Elmer E.   ES: Denver, Denver Co., CO
B: Denver, Denver Co., CO

FUNK, Jesse N.   ES: Calhan, El Paso Co., CO
B: New Hampton, Harrison Co., MO

GROVE, William Remsburg   ES: Denver, Denver Co., CO
B: Montezuma, Poweshiek Co., IA

KNIGHT, Joseph F.   ES: Denver, Denver Co., CO
B: Danville, Vermilion Co., IL

*LINDSTROM, Floyd K.   ES: Colorado Springs, El Paso Co., CO
B: Holdrege, Phelps Co., NE

*MARTINEZ, Joe P.   ES: Ault, Weld Co., CO
B:aos, Taos Co., NM

MAXWELL, Robert Dale   ES: Creswell, Larimer Co., CO
B: Boise, Ada Co., ID

*McWETHY Jr., Edgar Lee   ES: Denver, Denver Co., CO
B: Leadville, Lake Co., CO

WALLACE, George Weed   ES: Denver, Denver Co., CO
B: Fort Riley, Geary Co., KS

WARE, Keith Lincoln   ES: Glendale, Los Angeles Co., CA
B: Denver, Denver Co., CO

WEST, Chester Howard   ES: Los Banos, Merced Co., CA
B: Fort Collins, Larimer Co., CO

*WICKERSHAM, J. Hunter   ES: Denver, Denver Co., CO
B: New York, NY

U.S. Army Air Corps/U.S. Air Force

*PUCKET, Donald Dale   ES: Boulder, Boulder Co., CO
B: Longmont, Boulder Co., CO

*WALKER, Kenneth Newton   ES: Denver, Denver Co., CO
B: Cerrillos, Santa Fe Co., NM

YOUNG, Gerald Orren   ES: Colorado Springs, El Paso Co., CO
B: Chicago, Cook Co., IL

U.S. Navy

GRAVES, Ora   ES: NE
B: Las Animas, Bent Co., CO

McCANDLESS, Bruce   ES: CO
B: Washington, D.C.

ROSS, Donald Kirby   ES: Denver, Denver Co., CO
B: Beverly, Lincoln Co., KS

UPTON, Frank Monroe   ES: CO
B: Loveland, Larimer Co., CO

U.S. Marine Corps

BOYDSTON, Erwin Jay   ES: CA
B: Deer Creek, CO

*COKER, Ronald Leroy   ES: Denver, Denver Co., CO
B: Alliance, Box Butte Co., NE

*GUILLEN, Ambrosio   ES: El Paso, El Paso Co., TX
B: La Junta, Otero Co., CO

MURPHY, Raymond Gerald   ES: Pueblo, Pueblo Co., CO
B: Pueblo, Pueblo Co., CO

SITTER, Carl Leonard   ES: Pueblo, Pueblo Co., CO
B: Syracuse, Morgan Co., MO

CONNECTICUT

U.S. Army

BABCOCK, John   ES: Stonington, New London Co., CT
B: New Orleans, Orleans Co., LA

BABOCK, William J.   ES: South Kingston, Washington Co., RI
B: Griswold, CT

*BACON, Elijah William   ES: New Britain, Hartford Co., CT
B: Burlington, Hartford Co., CT

BAIRD, George William   ES: Milford, New Haven Co., CT
B: Milford, New Haven Co., CT

BECKWITH, Wallace A.   ES: New London, New London Co., CT
B: New London, New London Co., CT

BRIGGS, Elijah A.   ES: Salisbury, Litchfield Co., CT
B: Salisbury, Litchfield Co., CT

BUCK, Frederick Clarence   ES: Windsor, Hartford Co., CT
B: Hartford, Hartford Co., CT

BURKE, Daniel Webster   ES: New Haven, New Haven Co., CT
B: New Haven, New Haven Co., CT

CANFIELD, Heth   ES: Carlisle, Cumberland Co., PA
B: New Milford, Litchfield Co., CT

CORLISS, George W.   ES: Hartford, Hartford Co., CT
B: CT

CROCKER, Henry H.   ES: San Francisco, San Francisco Co., CA
B: Colchester, New London Co., CT

CURTIS, John Calvin   ES: Bridgeport, Fairfield Co., CT
B: Bridgeport, Fairfield Co., CT

DALY, Michael Joseph   ES: Southport, Fairfield Co., CT
B: New York, NY

DOWNS, Willis H.   ES: Jamestown, Stutsman Co., ND
B: Mount Carmel, CT

ENNIS, Charles D.   ES: Charleston, Washington Co., RI
B: Stonington, New London Co., CT

FLYNN, Christopher   ES: Hartford, Hartford Co., CT
B: Ireland

FORSYTH, Thomas Hall   ES: St. Louis, St. Louis Co., MO
B: Hartford, Hartford Co., CT

*FOURNIER, William Grant   ES: Winterport, Waldo Co., ME
B: Norwich, New London Co., CT

FOX, Nicholas   ES: Greenwich, Fairfield Co., CT

*FRATELLENICO, Frank Rocco	ES: Albany, Albany Co., NY B: Sharon, Litchfield Co., CT	TRACY, Charles H.	ES: Springfield, Hampden Co., MA B: Jewett City, New London Co., CT
GIBBS, Wesley	ES: Salisbury, Litchfield Co., CT B: Sharon, Litchfield Co., CT	TUCKER, Allen	ES: Sprague, CT B: Lyme, CT
GRAY, Robert A.	ES: Groton, New London Co., CT B: Philadelphia, Philadelphia Co., PA	WEEKS, John Henry	ES: Hartwick Seminary, Oswego Co., NY B: Hampton, Windham Co., CT
*HARTELL, Lee Ross	ES: Danbury, Fairfield Co., CT B: Philadelphia, Philadelphia Co., PA	WHITAKER, Edward Washburn	ES: Hartford, Hartford Co., CT B: Killingly, CT
HICKOK, Nathan E.	ES: Danbury, Fairfield Co., CT B: Danbury, Fairfield Co., CT	WILLIAMS, George C.	ES: New London, New London Co., CT B: England
HINCKS, William B.	ES: Bridgeport, Fairfield Co., CT B: Bucksport, Hancock Co., ME	WILSON, Christopher W.	ES: West Meriden, New Haven Co., CT B: Ireland
HOOPER, William B.	ES: Jersey City, Hudson Co., NJ B: Willimantic, Windham Co., CT	WRIGHT, Robert	ES: Woodstock, Windham Co., CT B: Ireland
HORNE, Samuel Belton	ES: Winsted, Litchfield Co., CT B: Belleek, County Fermanagh, Ireland		

U.S. Air Force

LEVITOW, John Lee	ES: New Haven, New Haven Co., CT B: Hartford, Hartford Co., CT

U.S. Navy

HUBBELL, William Stone	ES: North Stonington, New London Co., CT B: Wolcottville, New Haven Co., CT	BREAULT, Henry	ES: VT B: Putnam, Windham Co., CT
JACKSON, Frederick Randolph	ES: New Haven, New Haven Co., CT B: New Haven, New Haven Co., CT	CANN, Tedford Harris	ES: NY B: Bridgeport, Fairfield Co., CT
JOHNSTON Sr., William James	ES: Colchester, New London Co., CT B: Trenton, Mercer Co., NJ	CRANDALL, Orson Leon	ES: CT B: St. Joseph, Buchanan Co., MO
LANFARE, Aaron Steven	ES: Branford, New Haven Co., CT B: Branford, New Haven Co., CT	*DENNING, Lorenzo	ES: New Britain, Hartford Co., CT B: Granby, Hartford Co., CT
*LIBBY, George Dalton	ES: Waterbury, New Haven Co., CT B: Bridgton, Cumberland Co., ME	GARVIN, William	ES: Plymouth, Litchfield Co., CT B: west Canada
*MAGRATH, John D.	ES: East Norwalk, Fairfield Co., CT B: East Norwalk, Fairfield Co., CT	HARDING, Thomas	ES: CT B: Middletown, Middlesex Co., CT
MARSH, Charles H.	ES: New Milford, Litchfield Co., CT B: Milford, New Haven Co., CT	HENRECHON, George Francis	ES: CA B: Hartford, Hartford Co., CT
MURPHY, James T.	ES: New Haven, New Haven Co., CT B: Canada	JONES, John	ES: Acton, Middlesex Co., MA B: Bridgeport, Fairfield Co., CT
NETT, Robert Burton	ES: New Haven, New Haven Co., CT B: New Haven, New Haven Co., CT	MacKENZIE, John	ES: MA B: Bridgeport, Fairfield Co., CT
NEVILLE, Edwin Michael	ES: Waterbury, New Haven Co., CT B: Waterbury, New Haven Co., CT	MANNING, Henry J.	ES: CT B: New Haven, New Haven Co., CT
NORTON, Elliott Malloy	ES: Cooper, MI B: CT	MONTGOMERY, Robert William	ES: Norwich, New London Co., CT B: Ireland
O'NEILL, William	ES: New York, NY B: Tariffville, Hartford Co., CT	NEIL, John	ES: Norwich, New London Co., CT B: Newfoundland, Canada
PALMER, John Gideon	ES: Montville, New London Co., CT B: Montville, New London Co., CT	PECK, Oscar E.	ES: CT B: Bridgeport, Fairfield Co., CT
SCOFIELD, David H.	ES: Stamford, Fairfield Co., CT B: Mamaroneck, Westchester Co., NY	*REEVES, Thomas James	ES: CT B: Thomaston, Litchfield Co., CT
SHALER, Alexander	ES: New York, NY B: Haddam, Middlesex Co., CT	ROBERTS, James	ES: Hartford, Hartford Co., CT B: England
*SHEA, Daniel John	ES: New Haven, New Haven Co., CT B: Norwalk, Fairfield Co., CT	ROSE, George Harry	ES: CT B: Stamford, Fairfield Co., CT
SHEPPARD, Charles	ES: St. Louis, St. Louis Co., MO B: Rocky Hill, Hartford Co., CT	RYAN, Richard	ES: CT B: CT
SIMONDS, William Edgar	ES: Canton, Hartford Co., CT B: Collinsville, Hartford Co., CT	SULLIVAN, James	ES: Danbury, Fairfield Co., CT B: New York, NY
SODERMAN, William Adolph	ES: West Haven, New Haven Co., CT B: West Haven, New Haven Co., CT		

U.S. Marine Corps

SWIFT, Frederic William	ES: Detroit, Wayne Co., MI B: Mansfield Center, Tolland Co., CT	BARNUM Jr., Harvey Curtiss "Barney"	ES: Cheshire, New Haven Co., CT B: Cheshire, New Haven Co., CT
TINKHAM, Eugene M.	ES: Waterloo, Seneca Co., NY B: Sprague, CT		

HILL, Frank	ES: CT B: Hartford, Hartford Co., CT		CONDON, Clarence Milville	ES: St. Augustine, St. Johns Co., FL B: South Brooksville, Hancock Co., ME
KELLOGG Jr., Allan Jay	ES: Bridgeport, Fairfield Co., CT B: Bethel, Fairfield Co., CT		*CUTINHA, Nicholas Joseph	ES: Coral Gables, Dade Co., FL B: Fernandina Beach, Nassau Co., FL
*SKINNER Jr., Sherrod Emerson	ES: East Lansing, Ingham Co., MI B: Hartford, Hartford Co., CT		MILLS, James Henry	ES: Fort Meade, Polk Co., FL B: Fort Meade, Polk Co., FL
*TALBOT, Ralph	ES: CT B: South Weymouth, Norfolk Co., MA		*NININGER Jr., Alexander Ramsey	ES: Fort Lauderdale, Broward Co., FL B: Gainesville, Hall Co., GA
*WITEK, Frank Peter	ES: Illinois B: Derby, New Haven Co., CT		PAINE, Adam	ES: Fort Duncan, TX B: FL

DELAWARE

U.S. Army

BUCKINGHAM, David E.	ES: Wilmington, New Castle Co., DE B: Pleasant Hill, DE
CONNOR, James Phillip	ES: Wilmington, New Castle Co., DE B: Wilmington, New Castle Co., DE
Du PONT, Henry Algernon	ES: Wilmington, New Castle Co., DE B: Eleutherean Mills, New Castle Co., DE
MAYBERRY, John B.	ES: Dover, Kent Co., DE B: Smyrna, Kent Co., DE
McCARREN, Bernard	ES: Wilmimgton, New Castle Co., DE B: Ireland
*NELSON, William Lancaster	ES: Middletown, New Castle Co., DE B: Dover, Kent Co., DE
PALMER, William Jackson	ES: Philadelphia, Philadelphia Co., PA B: Leipsic, Kent Co., DE
PIERCE, Charles H.	ES: Delaware City, New Castle Co., DE B: Cecil Co., MD
POSTLES, James Parke	ES: Wilmimgton, New Castle Co., DE B: Camden, Kent Co., DE
SACRISTE, Louis Jeanottelle	ES: Philadelphia, Philadelphia Co., PA B: New Castle Co., DE
SEWARD, Griffin	ES: Philadelphia, Philadelphia Co., PA B: Dover, Kent Co., DE
SHILLING, John	ES: Felton, Kent Co., DE B: England
SMITH, Samuel Rodmond	ES: Wilmington, New Castle Co., DE B: Wilmington, New Castle Co., DE
TANNER, Charles B.	ES: Wilmimgton, New Castle Co., DE B: Philadelphia, Philadelphia Co., PA

U.S. Navy

BALDWIN, Charles H.	ES: Philadelphia, Philadelphia Co., PA B: Wilmington, New Castle Co., DE
CHADWICK, Leonard B.	ES: DE B: Middletown, New Castle Co., DE
HAND, Allexander	ES: DE B: DE

FLORIDA

U.S. Army

*BENNETT, Emory L.	ES: Cocoa, Brevard Co., FL B: New Smyrna Beach, Volusia Co., FL
BOLTON, Cecil Hamilton	ES: Huntsville, Madison Co., AL B: Crawfordville, Wakulla Co., FL
*BOWEN Jr., Hammett Lee	ES: Jacksonville, Duval Co., FL B: LaGrange, Troup Co., GA

*SIMS, Clifford Chester	ES: Jacksonville, Duval Co., FL B: Port St. Joe, Gulf Co., FL
VARNUM, Charles Albert	ES: Pensacola, Escambia Co., FL B: Troy, Rensselaer Co., NY

U.S. Army Air Corps

*FEMOYER, Robert Edward	ES: Jacksonville, Duval Co., FL B: Huntington, Cabell Co., WV
*McGUIRE Jr., Thomas Buchanan	ES: Sebring, Highlands Co., FL B: Ridgewood, Bergen Co., NJ

U.S. Navy

*CORRY Jr., William Merrill	ES: FL B: Quincy, Gadsden Co., FL
LASSEN, Clyde Everett	ES: Jacksonville, Duval Co., FL B: Fort Myers, Lee Co., FL
McCAMPBELL, David	ES: West Palm Beach, Palm Beach Co., FL B: Bessemer, Jefferson Co., AL
NORRIS, Thomas Rolland	ES: Silver Spring, Montgomery Co., MD B: Jacksonville, Duval Co., FL
ORMSBEE Jr., Francis Edward	ES: FL B: Providence, Providence Co., RI

U.S. Marine Corps

*CARTER, Bruce Wayne	ES: Jacksonville, Duval Co., FL B: Schenectady, Schenectady Co., NY
*JENKINS Jr., Robert Henry	ES: Jacksonville, Duval Co., FL B: Interlachen, Putnam Co., FL
*LOPEZ, Baldomero	ES: Tampa, Hillsborough Co., FL B: Tampa, Hillsborough Co., FL
*McTUREOUS Jr., Robert Miller	ES: FL B: Altoona, Lake Co., FL
*SMEDLEY, Larry Eugene	ES: Orlando, Orange Co., FL B: Front Royal, Warren Co., VA

GEORGIA

U.S. Army

*BOWEN Jr., Hammett Lee	ES: Jacksonville, Duval Co., FL B: LaGrange, Troup Co., GA
BROWN Jr., Bobbie Evan	ES: Atlanta, Fulton Co., GA B: Dublin, Laurens Co., GA
*BRYANT, William Maud	ES: Detroit, Wayne Co., MI B: Cochran, Bleckley Co., GA
CARTER, Mason	ES: Augusta, Richmond Co., GA B: Augusta, Richmond Co., GA
*DURHAM Jr., Harold Bascom	ES: Atlanta, Fulton Co., GA B: Rocky Mount, Edgecombe Co., NC

GARLINGTON, Ernest Albert — ES: Athens, Clarke Co., GA
B: Newberry Hill, Newberry Co., SC

*JOHNSTON, Donald Ray — ES: Columbus, Muscogee Co., GA
B: Columbus, Muscogee Co., GA

LEE Sr., Daniel Warnel — ES: Alma, Bacon Co., GA
B: Alma, Bacon Co., GA

*McKIBBEN, Ray — ES: Atlanta, Fulton Co., GA
B: Felton, Haralson Co., GA

McKINNEY, John R. — ES: Woodcliff, GA
B: Woodcliff, GA

*NININGER Jr., Alexander Ramsey — ES: Fort Lauderdale, Broward Co., FL
B: Gainesville, Hall Co., GA

RAY, Ronald Eric — ES: Atlanta, Fulton Co., GA
B: Cordele, Crisp Co., GA

SPRAYBERRY, James Michael — ES: Montgomery, Montgomery Co., AL
B: LaGrange, Troup Co., GA

*STORY, Luther H. — ES: GA
B: Buena Vista, Marion Co., GA

U.S. Air Force

JACKSON, Joe Madison — ES: Newnan, Coweta Co., GA
B: Newnan, Coweta Co., GA

WILBANKS, Hilliard Almond — ES: Atlanta, Fulton Co., GA
B: Cornelia, Habersham Co., GA

U.S. Navy

LELAND, George W. — ES: GA
B: Savannah, Chatham Co., GA

PHARRIS, Jackson Charles — ES: CA
B: Columbus, Muscogee Co., GA

U.S. Marine Corps

*BONNYMAN Jr., Alexander "Sandy" — ES: NM
B: Atlanta, Fulton Co., GA

DAVIS, Raymond Gilbert — ES: Atlanta, Fulton Co., GA
B: Fitzgerald, Ben Hill Co., GA

*DAVIS, Rodney Maxwell — ES: Macon, Bibb Co., GA
B: Macon, Bibb Co., GA

*DYESS, Aquilla James — ES: GA
B: Augusta, Richmond Co., GA

*ELROD, Henry Talmage — ES: Ashburn, Turner Co., GA
B: Rebecca, Turner Co., GA

LIVINGSTON, James Evertte — ES: McRae, Telfair Co., GA
B: Towns, Telfair Co., GA

*PHILLIPS, Lee Hugh — ES: Ben Hill, Fulton Co., GA
B: Stockbridge, Henry Co., GA

PLESS, Stephen Wesley — ES: Atlanta, Fulton Co., GA
B: Newnan, Coweta Co., GA

*THOMASON, Clyde A. — ES: GA
B: Atlanta, Fulton Co., GA

HAWAII

U.S. Army

*KAWAMURA, Terry Teruo — ES: Oahu, HI
B: Wahiawa, Honolulu Co., Oahu, HI

*MENDONCA, Leroy A. — ES: Honolulu, Honolulu Co., Territory of Hawaii
B: Honolulu, Honolulu Co., Territory of Hawaii

*PILILAAU, Herbert K. — ES: Oahu, Territory of Hawaii
B: Waianae, Oahu, Territory of Hawaii

*SMITH, Elmelindo Rodriques — ES: Honolulu, Honolulu Co., HI
B: Honolulu, Honolulu Co., HI

*YANO, Rodney James Tadashi — ES: Honolulu, Honolulu Co., HI
B: Kealakekua Kona, Hawaii Co., HI

U.S. Navy

SMITH, James — ES: New York
B: Hawaiian Islands

IDAHO

U.S. Army

BLEAK, David Bruce — ES: Shelley, Bingham Co., ID
B: Idaho Falls, Bonneville Co., ID

*BROSTROM, Leonard C. — ES: Preston, Franklin Co., ID
B: Preston, Franklin Co., ID

MAXWELL, Robert Dale — ES: Creswell, Larimer Co., CO
B: Boise, Ada Co., ID

McCARTER, Lloyd G. — ES: Tacoma, Pierce Co., WA
B: St. Maries, Benewah Co., ID

NEIBAUR, Thomas Croft — ES: Sugar City, Madison Co., ID
B: Sharon, ID

*SCHOONOVER, Dan D. — ES: Boise, Ada Co., ID
B: Boise, Ada Co., ID

*VAN NOY Jr., Nathan — ES: Preston, Franklin Co., ID
B: Grace, Caribou Co., ID

U.S. Air Force

FISHER, Bernard Francis — ES: Kuna, Ada Co., ID
B: San Bernardino, San Bernardino Co., CA

U.S. Marine Corps

BOYINGTON, Gregory "Pappy" — ES: WA
B: Coeur D'Alene, Kootenai Co., ID

*JOHNSON, James Edmund — ES: Washington, D.C.
B: Pocatello, Bannock Co., ID

MYERS, Reginald Rodney — ES: Boise, Ada Co., ID
B: Boise, Ada Co., ID

*REASONER, Frank Stanley — ES: Kellogg, Shoshone Co., ID
B: Spokane, Spokane Co., WA

ILLINOIS

U.S. Army

ALLEN, Abner Peeler — ES: Bloomington, McLean Co., IL
B: Woodford Co., IL

ALLEX, Jake — ES: Chicago, Cook Co., IL
B: Streska, near Prizren, Serbia

ANDERSON, Johannes Seigfried — ES: Chicago, Cook Co., IL
B: Bjoroky, Finland

ARCHER, James W. — ES: Spencer, Owen Co., IN
B: Edgar Co., IL

AYERS, John G. K. — ES: Pekin, Tazwell Co., IL
B: Washtenaw Co., MI

BAKER Jr., John Franklin — ES: Moline, Rock Island Co., IL
B: Davenport, Scott Co., IA

BANCROFT, Neil	ES: Chicago, Cook Co., IL B: Oswego, Oswego Co., NY	DEAN Sr., William Frishe	ES: California B: Carlyle, Clinton Co., IL
BATSON, Matthew Arlington	ES: Carbondale, Jackson Co., IL B: Anna, Union Co., IL	DICKIE, David	ES: Gillespie, Macoupin Co., IL B: Scotland
BENDER, Stanley	ES: Chicago, Cook Co., IL B: Carlisle, WV	DUNHAM, Russell	ES: Brighton, Jersey Co., IL B: East Carondelet, St. Clair Co., IL
BERG, George Francis	ES: Fort Omaha, Douglas Co., NE B: Mount Erie, Wayne Co., IL	DUNNE, James	ES: Chicago, Cook Co., IL B: Detroit, Wayne Co., MI
BERTOLDO, Vito R.	ES: Decatur, Macon Co., IL B: Decatur, Macon Co., IL	ELLIS, Michael B.	ES: East St. Louis, St. Clair Co., IL B: St. Louis, St. Louis Co., MO
BICKFORD, Matthew	ES: Trivolia, Peoria Co., IL B: Peoria Co., IL	FARQUHAR, John Mcgreath	ES: Chicago, Cook Co., IL B: near Ayr, Scotland
BLACK, John Charles	ES: Danville, Vermillion Co., IL B: Lexington, Holmes Co., MS	FISHER, John H.	ES: Chicago, Cook Co., IL B: Monmouth, PA
BLACK, William Perkins	ES: Danville, Vermillion Co., IL B: Woodford, KY	FLYNN, James Edward	ES: St. Louis, St. Louis Co., MO B: Pittsfield, Pike Co., IL
*BLANCHFIELD, Michael Reinert	ES: Chicago, Cook Co., IL B: Minneapolis, Hennepin Co., MN	FOX, Henry	ES: Lincoln, Logan Co., IL B: Reuthingen, Wurtemberg, Germany
BLODGETT, Wells H.	ES: Chicago, Cook Co., IL B: Downer's Grove, Du Page Co., IL	FRASER, William W.	ES: Alton, Madison Co., IL B: Burn Brac, Scotland
BOURKE, John Gregory	ES: Chicago, Cook Co., IL B: Philadelphia, Philadelphia Co., PA	FRITZ, Harold Arthur	ES: Milwaukee, Milwaukee Co., WI B: Chicago, Cook Co., IL
BOWEN, Emmer	ES: Hampshire, Kane Co., IL B: Erie Co., NY	GAGE, Richard J.	ES: Ottawa, La Salle Co., IL B: Grafton Co., NH
BURRITT, William Wallace	ES: Chicago, Cook Co., IL B: Campbell, Steuben Co., NY	GARMAN, Harold Alva	ES: Albion, Edwards Co., IL B: Fairfield, Wayne Co., IL
CALLAHAN, John H.	ES: Scottville, Macoupin Co., IL B: Shelby Co., KY	GERSTUNG, Robert E.	ES: Chicago, Cook Co., IL B: Chicago, Cook Co., IL
CALVERT, James Spencer	ES: Springfield, Sangamon Co., IL B: Athens Co., OH	GESCHWIND, Nicholas	ES: Pleasant Hill, Pike Co., IL B: France
*CAPRON Jr., Horace	ES: Peoria, Peoria Co., IL B: Laurel, Prince George's Co., MD	*GIBSON, Eric Gunnar	ES: Chicago, Cook Co., IL B: Nysund, Sweden
CARROLL, Thomas	ES: Chicago, Cook Co., IL B: Kilkenny, Ireland	GOLDIN, Theodore W. B.	ES: Chicago, Cook Co., IL B: Avon, Rock Co., WI
CHOATE, Clyde Lee	ES: Anna, Union Co., IL B: West Frankfort, Franklin Co., IL	GOLDSBERY, Andrew E.	ES: St. Charles, Kane Co., IL B: St. Charles, Kane Co., IL
CHURCH, James Robb	ES: Washington, D.C. B: Chicago, Cook Co., IL	GOULD, Newton Thomas	ES: Elk Grove, Cook Co., IL B: Elk Grove, Cook Co., IL
CHURCHILL, Samuel Joseph	ES: DeKalb, DeKalb Co., IL B: Rutland, Rutland Co., VT	GUMPERTZ, Sydney G.	ES: Chicago, Cook Co., IL B: San Raphael, Marin Co., CA
COLBY, Carlos W.	ES: Madison Co., IL B: Merrimack, Hillsborough Co., NH	HALL, John	ES: Sacramento, Sacramento Co., CA B: Logan Co., IL
COOK, John Henry	ES: Quincy, Adams Co., IL B: London, England	*HAMMOND Jr., Lester	ES: Quincy, Adams Co., IL B: Wayland, Clark Co., MO
COX, Robert Mitchell	ES: Prairie City, McDonough Co., IL B: Guernsey Co., OH	HANEY, Milton Lorenzi	ES: Bushnell, McDonough Co., IL B: Savannah, Ashland Co., OH
CRAIG, Samuel Henry	ES: Chicago, Cook Co., IL B: New Market, Rockingham Co., NH	HAPEMAN, Douglas	ES: Ottawa, La Salle Co., IL B: Ephrata, Fulton Co., NY
CREED, John	ES: Chicago, Cook Co., IL B: Tipperary, County Tipperary, Ireland	*HARDENBERGH, Henry M.	ES: Bremen, IL B: Noble Co., IN
CUNNINGHAM, James Smith	ES: Bloomington, McLean Co., IL B: Washington Co., PA	*HARVEY Jr., Carmel Bernon	ES: Chicago, Cook Co., IL B: Montgomery, Fayette Co., WV
DANIELS, James Thomas	ES: Fort Leavenworth, Leavenworth Co., KS B: Richland Co., IL	HENRY, James	ES: Kankakee, Kankakee Co., IL B: Sunfish, OH
		HIGGINS, Thomas J.	ES: Barry, Pike Co., IL B: Riverlequerre, Quebec, Canada
DARROUGH, John S.	ES: Concord, Morgan Co., IL B: Maysville, Mason Co., KY	HIGHLAND, Patrick	ES: Chicago, Cook Co., IL B: Tipperary, Ireland
		HILL, Ralyn M.	ES: Oregon, Ogle Co., IL B: Lindenwood, Ogle Co., IL
DAVIS, Martin K.	ES: Stonington, Christian Co., IL B: Marion, Williamson Co., IL	HOBDAY, George	ES: Memphis, Shelby Co., TN B: Pulaski Co., IL

HOLLAND, Lemuel F.	ES: Tiskilwa, Bureau Co., IL B: Burlington, OH	LUCAS, George Washington	ES: Mount Sterling, Brown Co., IL B: Adams Co., IL
HOLMES, William T.	ES: Indianapolis, Marion Co., IN B: Vermilion Co., IL	LUCE, Moses Augustine	ES: Adrian, Lenawee Co., MI B: Payson, Adams Co., IL
HOUGHTON, George L.	ES: Brookfield, Cook Co., IL B: Yarmouth, West Canada	LYNCH, Allan James	ES: Chicago, Cook Co., IL B: Chicago, Cook Co., IL
HOWE, Orion P.	ES: Waukegan, Lake Co., IL B: Hiram, Portage Co., OH	MARSH, George	ES: Brookfield, Cook Co., IL B: Brookfield, Cook Co., IL
HUGGINS, Eli Lundy	ES: MN B: Schuyler Co., IL	McCLERNAND, Edward John	ES: Springfield, Sangamon Co., IL B: Jacksonville, Morgan Co., IL
HUGHEY, John P.	ES: Anna, Union Co., IL B: Louisville, Jefferson Co., KY	McCONNELL, Samuel	ES: Bushnell, McDonough Co., IL B: Belmont Co., OH
HYATT, Theodore	ES: Gardner, Grundy Co., IL B: PA	McCORNACK, Andrew	ES: Rutland, La Salle Co., IL B: Kane, Greene Co., IL
HYMER, Samuel	ES: Rushville, Schuyler Co., IL B: Harrison Co., IN	McDONALD, James	ES: Chicago, Cook Co., IL B: Edinburgh, Scotland
JOHNS, Elisha	ES: Martinton, Iroquois Co., IL B: Clinton, Summit Co., OH	McDONALD, John Wade	ES: Waynesville, DeWitt Co., IL B: Lancaster, Fairfield Co., OH
JOHNSON, Andrew	ES: Assumption, Christian Co., IL B: Delaware Co., OH	McGRAW, Thomas	ES: Chicago, Cook Co., IL B: Ireland
JOHNSTON, David H.	ES: Warsaw, Hancock Co., IL B: Indiana Co., PA	McGUIRE, Patrick	ES: Chicago, Cook Co., IL B: Ireland
JOHNSTON, Edward	ES: Chicago, Cook Co., IL B: Pen Yan, Yates Co., NY	McKEEN, Nineveh S.	ES: Marshall, Clark Co., IL B: Marshall, Clark Co., IL
JOHNSTON, Harold Irving	ES: Chicago, Cook Co., IL B: Kendall, Hamilton Co., KS	MERRIFIELD, James K.	ES: Manlius, Bureau Co., IL B: Hyde Park, Westmoreland Co., PA
JOSSELYN, Simeon T.	ES: Amboy, Lee Co., IL B: Buffalo, Erie Co., NY	MILLER, Archie	ES: St. Louis, St. Louis Co., MO B: Fort Sheridan, Lake Co., IL
KAYS, Kenneth Michael	ES: Fairfield, Wayne Co., IL B: Mount Vernon, Jefferson Co., IL	MILLER, Henry August	ES: Decatur, Macon Co., IL B: Germany
KELLER, Leonard Bert	ES: Chicago, Cook Co., IL B: Rockford, Winnebago Co., IL	MILLER, Jacob C.	ES: Elgin, Kane Co., IL B: Bellevue, Huron Co., OH
KELLEY, Leverett Mansfield	ES: Rutland, La Salle Co., IL B: Schenectady, Schenectady Co., NY	MITCHELL, John	ES: Peoria, Peoria Co., IL B: Dublin, Ireland
KELLY, John J. H.	ES: Springfield, Sangamon Co., IL B: Schuyler Co., IL	*MONROE, James Howard	ES: Chicago, Cook Co., IL B: Aurora, Du Page Co., IL
*KENNEDY, Philip	ES: Evansville, Randolph Co., IL B: County Galway, Ireland	MOORE, Wilbur F.	ES: Lebanon, St. Clair Co., IL B: Lebanon, St. Clair Co., IL
KLOTH, Charles H.	ES: Chicago, Cook Co., IL B: Europe	MORELOCK, Sterling Lewis	ES: Oquawka, Henderson Co., IL B: Silver Run, MD
KNIGHT, Joseph F.	ES: Denver, Denver Co., CO B: Danville, Vermilion Co., IL	MORFORD, Jerome	ES: Bridgers Co., IL B: Mercer Co., PA
KRETSINGER, George	ES: Chicago, Cook Co., IL B: Fairfield, Herkimer Co., NY	*MOSKALA, Edward J.	ES: Chicago, Cook Co., IL B: Chicago, Cook Co., IL
*KROTIAK, Anton L.	ES: Chicago, Cook Co., IL B: Chicago, Cook Co., IL	MURPHY, Philip	ES: Chicago, Cook Co., IL B: County Killkenny, Ireland
*KRZYZOWSKI, Edward C.	ES: Cicero, Cook Co., IL B: Chicago, Cook Co., IL	MURPHY, Robinson Barr	ES: Oswego, Kendall Co., IL B: Oswego, Kendall Co., IL
LABILL, Joseph S.	ES: Vandalia, Fayette Co., IL B: Belgium	MURPHY, Thomas C.	ES: Pekin, Tazewell Co., IL B: Ireland
LARRABEE, James W.	ES: Mendota, La Salle Co., IL B: Rensselaer Co., NY	NEWMAN, Marcellus J.	ES: Richview, Washington Co., IL B: Richview, Washington Co., IL
*LOGAN Jr., John Alexander	ES: Youngstown, Mahoning Co., OH B: Carbondale, Jackson Co., IL	O'DEA, John	ES: Bloomington, McLean Co., IL B: Limerick, County Limerick, Ireland
LOMAN, Berger Holton	ES: Chicago, Cook Co., IL B: Bergen, Norway	O'DONNELL, Menomen	ES: Sumner, Lawrence Co., IL B: Drumbarty, Ireland
LONGFELLOW, Richard Moses	ES: Mandan, Morton Co., ND B: Logan Co., IL	OGDEN Sr., Carlos Carnes	ES: Fairmount, Vermillion Co., IL B: Borton, Edgar Co., IL
		*OLIVE III, Milton Lee	ES: Chicago, Cook Co., IL B: Chicago, Cook Co., IL
LOWER, Robert A.	ES: Elmwood, Peoria Co., IL B: IL	PALMER, George Henry	ES: Monmouth, Warren Co., IL B: NY

PARKS, James W.	ES: Xenia, Clay Co., IL B: Lawrence Co., OH	STOKES, George	ES: Jerseyville, Jersey Co., IL B: England
PAYNE, Thomas H. L.	ES: Mendota, La Salle Co., IL B: Boston Suffolk Co., MA	SUMNER, James	ES: Chicago, Cook Co., IL B: London, England
PENTZER, Patrick Henry	ES: Gillespie, Macoupin Co., IL B: Marion Co., MO	TAYLOR, Henry H.	ES: Galena, Jo Daviess Co., IL B: Near Galena, Jo Daviess Co., IL
*PEREZ Jr., Manuel	ES: Chicago, Cook Co., IL B: Oklahoma City, Oklahoma Co., OK	THOMPSON, John	ES: Chicago, Cook Co., IL B: Glasgow, Scotland
PIKE, Edward M.	ES: Bloomington, McLean Co., IL B: Casco, Cumberland Co., ME	TOOMER, William	ES: Chicago, Cook Co., IL B: Dublin, Ireland
POND, George F.	ES: Fairwater, Fond du Lac Co., WI B: Libertyville, Lake Co., IL	TOY, Frederick Ernest	ES: Chicago, Cook Co., IL B: Buffalo, Erie Co., NY
POPE, Thomas A.	ES: Chicago, Cook Co., IL B: Chicago, Cook Co., IL	TRACY, John	ES: Chicago, Cook Co., IL B: Dublin, Ireland
POST, Philip Sidney	ES: Galesburg, Knox Co., IL B: Florida, Orange Co., NY	VERNAY, James David	ES: Lacon, Marshall Co., IL B: Lacon, Marshall Co., IL
POWERS, Wesley James	ES: Virgil, Kane Co., IL B: Orono, Ontario, Canada	VOKES, Leroy H.	ES: St. Louis, St. Louis Co., MO B: Lake Co., IL
PUTNAM, Winthrop D.	ES: Peoria, Peoria Co., IL B: Southbridge, Worcester Co., MA	WARD, Thomas J.	ES: Decatur, Macon Co., IL B: Romney, Hampshire Co., WV
REBMANN, George F.	ES: Rushville, Schuyler Co., IL B: Schuyler Co., IL	WARDEN, John	ES: Lemont, Du Page Co., IL B: Cook Co., IL
REED, William	ES: Pekin, Tazewell Co., IL B: Union Co., PA	WATSON, Joseph	ES: Chicago, Cook Co., IL B: Union City, Branch Co., MI
*ROBINSON Jr., James William	ES: Chicago, Cook Co., IL B: Hinsdale, Du Page Co., IL	WHEATON, Loyd	ES: Peoria, Peoria Co., IL B: Penfield, MI
ROSS, Frank Fulton	ES: Langdon, Cavalier Co., ND B: Avon, Fulton Co., IL	WHITE, Patrick H.	ES: Chicago, Cook Co., IL B: County Sligo, Ireland
RUNDLE, Charles Wesley	ES: Oakley, Macon Co., IL B: Covington, Campbell Co., KY	WHITMORE, John W.	ES: Camden, Schuyler Co., IL B: Brown Co., IL
SANFORD, Jacob	ES: Prairie City, McDonough Co., IL B: Fulton Co., IL	*WICKAM, Jerry Wayne	ES: Chicago, Cook Co., IL B: Rockford, Winnebago Co., IL
SCHENCK, Benjamin W.	ES: Maroa, Macon Co., IL B: Butler Co., OH	WIDICK, Andrew J.	ES: Decatur, Macon Co., IL B: Macon Co., IL
SCHOFIELD, John McAllister	ES: Freeport, Stephenson Co., IL B: Gerry, Chautauga Co., NY	WILLIAMS, Elwood N.	ES: Havana, Mason Co., IL B: Philadelphia, Philadelphia Co., PA
SCHROEDER, Henry Frank	ES: Chicago, Cook Co., IL B: Chicago, Cook Co., IL	WILSON, Arthur Harrison	ES: Springfield, Sangamon Co., IL B: Springfield, Sangamon Co., IL
SHAPLAND, John	ES: Ottawa, La Salle Co., IL B: Barnstable, Devonshire, England	WILSON, Charles	ES: Springfield, Sangamon Co., IL B: Petersburg, Menard Co., IL
SIMMONS, William Thomas	ES: Springfield, Sangamon Co., IL B: Greene Co., IL	*WILSON, Richard G.	ES: Cape Girardeau, Cape Girardeau Co., MO B: Marion, Williamson Co., IL
SLAGLE, Oscar	ES: Manlius, Bureau Co., IL B: Fulton Co., OH	WOOD, Richard H.	ES: Woodburn, Macoupin Co., IL B: Canton, NJ
SMALLEY, Reuben S.	ES: Brookfield, Cook Co., IL B: Washington Co., PA		

U.S. Army Air Corps/U.S. Air Force

*SMITH, Fred E.	ES: Bartlett, ND B: Rockford, Winnebago Co., IL	*BAKER, Addison Earl	ES: Akron, Summit Co., OH B: Chicago, Cook Co., IL
SNOW, Elmer A.	ES: Chicago, Cook Co., IL B: Hardwick, Worcester Co., MA	*GOETTLER, Harold Ernest	ES: Chicago, Cook Co., IL B: Chicago, Cook Co., IL
SPALDING, Edward Burson	ES: Rockford, Winnebago Co., IL B: Byron, Ogle Co., IL	MICHAEL, Edward Stanley	ES: Chicago, Cook Co., IL B: Chicago, Cook Co., IL
SPRAGUE, Benona	ES: Cheney Grove, IL B: Satina Onondaga Co., NY	*SEBILLE, Louis Joseph	ES: Chicago, Cook Co., IL B: Harbor Beach, Huron Co., MI
STEPHENS, William G.	ES: Chicago, Cook Co., IL B: New York, NY	*TRUEMPER, Walter Edward	ES: Aurora, Du Page Co., IL B: Aurora, Du Page Co., IL
STERLING, John T.	ES: Indianapolis, Marion Co., IN B: Edgar Co., IL	YOUNG, Gerald Orren	ES: Colorado Springs, El Paso Co., CO B: Chicago, Cook Co., IL

U.S. Navy

STOCKMAN, George Henry	ES: Chicago, Cook Co., IL B: Muenden, Germany
ASTEN, Charles	ES: Chicago, Cook Co., IL B: Halifax, Nova Scotia, Canada

BADDERS, William — ES: Indianapolis, Marion Co., IN
B: Harrisburg, Saline Co., IL

*BIGELOW, Elmer Charles — ES: IL
B: Hebron, McHenry Co., IL

CATHERWOOD, John Hugh — ES: IL
B: Springfield, Sangamon Co., IL

COURTNEY, Henry C. — ES: IL
B: Springfield, Sangamon Co., IL

*CROMWELL, John Philip — ES: IL
B: Henry, Marshall Co., IL

CRONAN, William (Willie) — ES: IL
B: Chicago, Cook Co., IL

DOW, Henry — ES: IL
B: Scotland

FERRELL, John H. — ES: IL
B: Bedford Co., TN

FLUCKEY, Eugene Bennett — ES: Neoga, Cumberland Co., IL
B: Washington, D.C.

GRBITCH, Rade — ES: IL
B: Austria

HOLYOKE, William Edward — ES: IL
B: Groveton, Coos Co., NH

HULL, James Lott — ES: IL
B: Patoka, Marion Co., IL

HYLAND, John — ES: IL
B: Ireland

IZAC, Edouard Victor Michel — ES: IL
B: Cresco, Howard Co., IA

JOHNSTON, William P. — ES: Chicago, Cook Co., IL
B: Chicago, Cook Co., IL

*KILMER, John Edward — ES: Houston, Harris Co., TX
B: Highland Park, Lake Co., IL

*LESTER, Fred Faulkner — ES: IL
B: Downers Grove, Du Page Co., IL

MARTIN, William — ES: Cairo, Alexander Co., IL
B: New York, NY

McCORMICK, Michael — ES: Chicago, Cook Co., IL
B: Ireland

MEYER, William — ES: IL
B: Germany

MOLLOY, Hugh — ES: Joliet, Will Co., IL
B: County Wexford, Ireland

MULLIN, Hugh Patrick — ES: Chicago, Cook Co., IL
B: Richmond, McHenry Co., IL

NOBLE, Daniel — ES: Chicago, Cook Co., IL
B: Bath Co., KY

*OSBORNE, Weedon E. — ES: IL
B: Chicago, Cook Co., IL

ROBERTS, Charles Church — ES: IL
B: Newton, Middlesex Co., MA

SMITH, Eugene P. — ES: CA
B: IL

STOCKDALE, James Bond — ES: Abingdon, Knox Co., IL
B: Abingdon, Knox Co., IL

U.S. Marine Corps

*BAILEY, Kenneth Dillon — ES: Illinois
B: Pawnee, Pawnee Co., OK

*BRUCE, Daniel Dean — ES: Chicago, Cook Co., IL
B: Michigan City, La Porte Co., IN

*BURKE, Robert Charles — ES: Chicago, Cook Co., IL
B: Monticello, Piatt Co., IL

*De La GARZA Jr., Emilio Albert — ES: Chicago, Cook Co., IL
B: East Chicago, Lake Co., IN

DUNLAP, Robert Hugo — ES: Monmouth, Warren Co., IL
B: Abingdon, Knox Co., IL

*FARDY, John Peter — ES: Illinois
B: Chicago, Cook Co., IL

HELMS, John Henry — ES: Illinois
B: Chicago, Cook Co., IL

HORTON, William M. Charlie — ES: Philadelphia, Philadelphia Co., PA
B: Chicago, Cook Co., IL

KELLY, John Joseph — ES: Chicago, Cook Co., IL
B: Chicago, Cook Co., IL

*KRAUS, Richard Edward — ES: MN
B: Chicago, Cook Co., IL

LEIMS, John Harold — ES: Chicago, Cook Co., IL
B: Chicago, Cook Co., IL

McCARTHY, Joseph Jeremiah — ES: Chicago, Cook Co., IL
B: Chicago, Cook Co., IL

*OZBOURN, Joseph William — ES: IL
B: Herrin, Williamson Co., IL

*POYNTER, James Irsley — ES: Downey, Los Angeles Co., CA
B: Bloomington, McLean Co., IL

ROBINSON, Robert Guy — ES: Chicago, Cook Co., IL
B: New York, NY

SCHILT, Christian Franklin — ES: IL
B: Richland Co., IL

UPHAM, Oscar Jefferson — ES: IL
B: Toledo, Lucas Co., OH

*WEBER, Lester William — ES: Chicago, Cook Co., IL
B: Aurora, Du Page Co., IL

WILLIAMS, Ernest Calvin — ES: IL
B: Broadwell, Elkhart Co., IL

*WILSON, Alfred Mac — ES: Abilene, Taylor Co., TX
B: Olney, Richland Co., IL

*WILSON, Robert Lee — ES: IL
B: Centralia, Marion Co., IL

*WINDRICH, William Gordon — ES: Hammond, Lake Co., IN
B: Chicago, Cook Co., IL

*WITEK, Frank Peter — ES: IL
B: Derby, New Haven Co., CT

INDIANA

U.S. Army

ANDERSON, Marion T. — ES: Kokomo, Howard Co., IN
B: Decatur Co., IN

ARCHER, James W. — ES: Spencer, Owen Co., IN
B: Edgar Co., IL

ARMSTRONG, Clinton Lycurgus — ES: Indianapolis, Marion Co., IN
B: Franklin, Johnson Co., IN

BANKS, George Lovell — ES: Lafayette, Tippecanoe Co., IN
B: Lake Co., OH

BIDDLE, Melvin Earl — ES: Anderson, Madison Co., IN
B: Daleville, Delaware Co., IN

BIEGLER, George Wesley — ES: Terre Haute, Vigo Co., IN
B: Terre Haute, Vigo Co., IN

BLASDEL, Thomas A. — ES: Guilford, Dearborn Co., IN
B: Dearborn Co., IN

BOX, Thomas J.	ES: Bedford, Lawrence Co., IN B: IN
BROUSE, Charles W.	ES: Indianapolis, Marion Co., IN
BROWN, Lorenzo Dow	ES: Indianapolis, Marion Co., IN B: Davidson Co., NC
BRUNER, Louis J.	ES: Clifty Brumer, IN B: Monroe Co., IN
BUCKLES, Abram J.	ES: Muncie, Delaware Co., IN B: Delaware Co., IN
CHAMBERLAIN, Orville Tyron	ES: Elkhart, Elkhart Co., IN B: Leesburgh, Kosciusko Co., IN
CHISMAN, William W.	ES: Wilmington, IN B: Dearborn Co., IN
CONAWAY, John Wesley	ES: Hartford, Blackford Co., IN B: Dearborn Co., IN
CUMMINS, Andrew Johnson	ES: Alexandria, Madison Co., IN B: Alexandria, Madison Co., IN
DAVIS, John	ES: Indanapolis, Marion Co., IN B: Carroll, KY
DAVIS, Sammy Lee	ES: Indianapolis, Marion Co., IN B: Dayton, Montgomery Co., OH
DOUGALL, Allan Houston	ES: New Haven, Allen Co., IN B: Scotland
DUNLAVY, James	ES: Bloomfield, Davis Co., IA B: Decatur Co., IN
EVANS, Coron D.	ES: Madison, Jefferson Co., IN B: Jefferson Co., IN
*FAITH Jr., Don Carlos	ES: Washington, Daviess Co., IN B: Washington, Daviess Co., IN
FALL, Charles S.	ES: Hamburg, Livingston Co., MI B: Noble Co., IN
FANNING, Nicholas	ES: Independence, Buchanan Co., IA B: Carroll Co., IN
FERRIER, Daniel Tweed	ES: Delphi, Carroll Co., IN B: IN
FOUT, Frederick W.	ES: Indianapolis, Marion Co., IN B: Germany
FRANTZ, Joseph	ES: Osgood, Ripley Co., IN B: Eurapae, France
GARLAND, Harry	ES: Indianapolis, Marion Co., IN B: Boston, Suffolk Co., MA
GRAHAM, Thomas N.	ES: Westville, La Porte Co., IN
GRANT, George	ES: Indianapolis, Marion Co., IN B: Raleigh, Shelby Co., TN
GRAVES, Thomas J.	ES: Millville, IN B: Milton, Wayne Co., IN
GREEN, Francis C.	ES: Sacramento, Sacramento Co., CA B: Mount Vernon, Posey Co., IN
*HARDENBERGH, Henry M.	ES: Bremen, IL B: Noble Co., IN
HARRIS, David W.	ES: Cincinnati, Hamilton Co., OH B: Indianapolis, Marion Co., IN
HELMS, David H.	ES: Farmers Retreat, IN B: Dearborn Co., IN
HOLMES, William T.	ES: Indianapolis, Marion Co., IN B: Vermilion Co., IL
HORNADAY, Elisha Simpson	ES: Des Moines, Polk Co., IA B: Hendricks Co., IN
HOUGH, Ira	ES: Middletown, Henry Co., IN B: Henry Co., IN
HUDSON, Aaron R.	ES: Indianapolis, Marion Co., IN B: Madison Co., KY
HUNT, Louis T.	ES: Jefferson Co., MO B: Montgomery Co., IN
HYMER, Samuel	ES: Rushville, Schuyler Co., IL B: Harrison Co., IN
JOHNSON, Ruel M.	ES: Goshen, Elkhart Co., IN B: Harbor Creek Township, Erie Co., PA
JORDAN, Absalom	ES: North Madison, Jefferson Co., IN B: Brown Co., OH
KELLEY, Andrew John	ES: Ypsilanti, Washtenaw Co., MI B: La Grange Co., IN
KENDALL, William Wesley	ES: Jeffersonville, Clark Co., IN B: Hall Township, Dubois Co., IN
KISTERS, Gerry Herman	ES: Bloomington, Monroe Co., IN B: Salt Lake City, Salt Lake Co., UT
KUDER, Jeremiah	ES: Warsaw, Kosciusko Co., IN B: Tiffin, Seneca Co., OH
LAWTON, Henry Ware	ES: Fort Wayne, Allen Co., IN B: Manhattan, Lucas Co., OH
LYTTON, Jeptha L.	ES: San Francisco, San Francisco Co., CA B: Lawrence Co., IN
MASON, Elihu H.	ES: Pemberville, Wood Co., OH B: Wayne Co., IN
McCALL, Thomas Edward	ES: Veedersburg, Fountain Co., IN B: Burrton, Harvey Co., KS
*McGEE, William D.	ES: Indianapolis, Marion Co., IN B: Indianapolis, Marion Co., IN
*MICHAEL, Harry J.	ES: Milford, Kosciusko Co., IN B: Benton, IN
MORGAN, Richard H.	ES: Taylor, Freemont Co., IA B: Dubois Co., IN
NOLAN, Joseph A.	ES: South Bend, St. Joseph Co., IN B: Elkhart, Elkhart Co., IN
OPEL, John N.	ES: Rossburg, Decatur Co., IN B: Hoflas, Bavaria, Germany
OVERTURF, Jacob H.	ES: Holton, Ripley Co., IN B: Jefferson Co., IN
PRENTICE, Joseph Rollin	ES: Fort Wayne, Allen Co., IN B: Lancaster, Fairfield Co., OH
ROOD, Oliver P.	ES: Terre Haute, Vigo Co., IN B: Frankfort Co., KY
RUSSELL, Milton F.	ES: North Salem, Hendricks Co., IN B: Hendricks Co., IN
RYAN, Peter J.	ES: Terre Haute, Vigo Co., IN B: Tiperrary, County Tiperrary, Ireland
*SESTON, Charles H.	ES: New Albany, Floyd Co., IN B: New Albany, Floyd Co., IN
SHEPHERD, William	ES: Washington, D.C. B: Dillsboro, Ohio Co., IN
SMALLEY, Reuben	ES: Holton, Ripley Co., IN B: Reading, Schuyler Co., NY
STEINMETZ, William	ES: Sunman, Ripley Co., IN B: Newport, Campbell Co., KY
STERLING, John T.	ES: Indianapolis, Marion Co., IN B: Edgar Co., IL
STOLZ, Frank	ES: Sunman, Ripley Co., IN B: Dearborn Co., IN
SUTHERLAND, John Alexander	ES: Indianapolis, Marion Co., IN B: Harrodsburg, Monroe Co., IN

TAYLOR, Richard	ES: Indianapolis, Marion Co., IN B: Madison Co., AL
*THOMPSON, William P.	ES: Lafayette, Tippecanoe Co., IN B: Brooklyn, Kings Co., NY
TIBBETS, Andrew W.	ES: Centerville, Appanoose Co., IA B: Clark Co., IN
WALKER, Allen	ES: Cincinnati, Hamilton Co., OH B: Patriot, Switzerland Co., IN
WEAVER, Amos	ES: San Francisco, San Francisco Co., CA B: Niles Township, Delaware Co., IN
WEISS, Enoch R.	ES: St. Louis, St. Louis Co., MO B: Kosciusko Co., IN
*WETHERBY, John C.	ES: Martinsville, Morgan Co., IN B: Morgan Co., IN
WHITEHEAD, John Milton	ES: Westville, La Porte Co., IN B: Wayne Co., IN
*WIGLE, Thomas W.	ES: Detroit, Wayne Co., MI B: Indianapolis, Marion Co., IN
WINDUS, Claron	ES: Indianapolis, Marion Co., IN B: Janesville, Rock Co., WI
WOODFILL, Samuel	ES: Bryantsburg, IN B: Jefferson Co., IN
WRIGHT, Samuel	ES: Mankato, Blue Earth Co., MN B: IN
YOUNT, John P.	ES: Sacramento, Sacramento Co., CA B: Putnam Co., IN

U.S. Navy

ANTRIM, Richard Nott	ES: IN B: Peru, Miami Co., IN
BADDERS, William	ES: INpolis, Marion Co., IN B: Harrisburg, Saline Co., IL
BUCHANAN, Allen	ES: IN B: Evansville, Vanderburgh Co., IN
CAMPBELL, William	ES: IN B: IN
DITZENBACK, John	ES: IN B: New York, NY
HILL, Frank Ebenezer	ES: IN B: La Grange, La Grange Co., IN
INGRAM, Jonas Howard	ES: IN B: Jeffersonville, Clark Co., IN
*SCOTT, Norman	ES: IN B: INpolis, Marion Co., IN
WILKES, Perry	ES: Jeffersonville, Clark Co., IN B: IN
WILLIAMS, Jay P.	ES: OH B: Orland, Steuben Co., IN

U.S. Marine Corps

*ABRELL, Charles Gene	ES: Terre Haute, Vigo Co., IN B: Terre Haute, Vigo Co., IN
BEARSS, Hiram Iddings	ES: IN B: Peru, Miami Co., IN
*BRUCE, Daniel Dean	ES: Chicago, Cook Co., IL B: Michigan City, La Porte Co., IN
*De La GARZA Jr., Emilio Albert	ES: Chicago, Cook Co., IL B: East Chicago, Lake Co., IN
SHOUP, David Monroe	ES: IN B: Battle Ground, Tippecanoe Co., IN
WINANS, Roswell	ES: WA B: Brookville, Franklin Co., IN
*WINDRICH, William Gordon	ES: Hammond, Lake Co., IN B: Chicago, Cook Co., IL
ZION, William F.	ES: CA B: Knightstown, Henry Co., IN

IOWA

U.S. Army

BAKER Jr., John Franklin	ES: Moline, Rock Island Co., IL B: Davenport, Scott Co., IA
BATES, Norman Francis	ES: Grinnell, Poweshiek Co., IA B: Derry, VT
BEBB, Edward James	ES: Mount Pleasant, Henry Co., IA B: Butler Co., OH
BENNETT, Orson W.	ES: Dubuque, Dubuque Co., IA B: Union City, Branch Co., MI
BEYER, Arthur O.	ES: St. Ansgar, Mitchell Co., IA B: Rock Township, Mitchell Co., IA
BIRDSALL, Horatio L.	ES: Keokuk, Lee Co., IA B: Monroe Co., NY
BIRKHIMER, William Edward	ES: IA B: Somerset, Perry Co., OH
BOUQUET, Nicholas S.	ES: Burlington, Des Moines Co., IA B: Landau, Bavaria, Germany
BRAS, Edgar A.	ES: Wapello, Louisa Co., IA B: Jefferson Co., IA
BRILES, Herschel Floyd "Pete"	ES: Fort Des Moines, Polk Co., IA B: Colfax, Jasper Co., IA
*CHRISTENSEN, Dale Eldon	ES: Gray, Audubon Co., IA B: Cameron Township, Audubon Co., IA
CODY, William Frederick "Buffalo Bill"	ES: Fort McPherson, NE B: Scott Co., IA
COSGRIFF, Richard H.	ES: Wapello, Louisa Co., IA B: Dunkirk Co., NY
DUNLAVY, James	ES: Bloomfield, Davis Co., IA B: Decatur Co., IN
*EDWARDS, Junior Dean	ES: Indianola, Warren Co., IA B: Indianola, Warren Co., IA
ELSON, James M.	ES: Shellsburg, Benton Co., IA B: Coshocton, Coshocton Co., OH
FANNING, Nicholas	ES: Independence, Buchanan Co., IA B: Carroll Co., IN
GATES, George	ES: Dubuque, Dubuque Co., IA B: Delaware Co., OH
GODLEY, Leonidas Mahlon	ES: Ashland, IA B: Mason Co., WV
GROVE, William Remsburg	ES: Denver, Denver Co., CO B: Montezuma, Poweshiek Co., IA
HAYS, John H.	ES: Oskaloosa, Mahaska Co., IA B: Jefferson Co., OH
HEALEY, George Washington	ES: Dubuque, Dubuque Co., IA B: Dubuque, Dubuque Co., IA
HERINGTON, Pitt B.	ES: Tipton, Cedar Co., IA B: MI
*HIBBS, Robert John	ES: Des Moines, Polk Co., IA B: Omaha, Douglas Co., NE

HILL, James	ES: Cascade, Dubuque Co., IA
	B: Bristol, Avon Co., England
HORNADAY, Elisha Simpson	ES: Des Moines, Polk Co., IA
	B: Hendricks Co., IN
HUNTSMAN, John A.	ES: Lawrence, Douglas Co., KS
	B: Oskaloosa, Mahaska Co., IA
KALTENBACH, Luther	ES: Honey Creek, Pottawattamie Co., IA
	B: Germany
KEPHART, James	ES: Dubuque, Dubuque Co., IA
	B: Venango Co., PA
KNOX, John W.	ES: Fort Leavenworth, Leavenworth Co., KS
	B: Burlington, Des Moines Co., IA
LAWTON, Louis Bowem	ES: Auburn, Cayuga Co., NY
	B: Independence, Buchanan Co., IA
*LEMERT, Milo	ES: Crossville, Cumberland Co., TN
	B: Marshalltown, Marshall Co., IA
MAY, William C.	ES: Maysville, Franklin Co., IA
	B: PA
MAYES, William B.	ES: DeWitt, Clinton Co., IA
	B: Marion Co., OH
MILLER, James P.	ES: Henry Co., IA
	B: Franklin, Warren Co., OH
MORGAN, Richard H.	ES: Taylor, Freemont Co., IA
	B: Dubois Co., IN
NEPPEL, Ralph George	ES: Glidden, Carroll Co., IA
	B: Willey, Carroll Co., IA
*OLSON, Arlo L.	ES: Toronto, Deuel Co., SD
	B: Greenville, Clay Co., IA
PHIFE, Lewis	ES: Marion, Marion Co., OR
	B: Des Moines Co., IA
*PIKE, Emory Jenison	ES: Sigourney, Keokuk Co., IA
	B: Columbus City, Louisa Co., IA
POWER, Albert	ES: Bloomfield, Davis Co., IA
	B: Liberty, Guernsey Co., OH
*RIORDAN, Paul F.	ES: Kansas City, Clay Co., MO
	B: Charles City, Floyd Co., IA
SALE, Albert	ES: Dubuque, Dubuque Co., IA
	B: Broome Co., NY
SLOAN, Andrew Jackson	ES: Colesburg, Delaware Co., IA
	B: Bedford Co., PA
SMITH, Henry I.	ES: Shell Rock Fall, Butler Co., IA
	B: Nottingham, Nottinghamshire, England
STANLEY, Eben	ES: Santa Fe, Santa Fe Co., NM
	B: Decatur Co., IA
STRAUB, Paul Frederick	ES: Mount Pleasant, Henry Co., IA
	B: Baden, Germany
SWAN, Charles Alexander	ES: Mount Pleasant, Henry Co., IA
	B: Greene Co., PA
*THORSON, John F.	ES: Armstrong, Emmet Co., IA
	B: Armstrong, Emmet Co., IA
TIBBETS, Andrew W.	ES: Centerville, Appanoose Co., IA
	B: Clark Co., IN
TITUS, Calvin Pearl	ES: IA
	B: Vinton, Benton Co., IA
TWOMBLY, Voltare Paine	ES: Keosauqua, Van Buren Co., IA
	B: Farmington, Van Buren Co., IA
WELCH, George W.	ES: Keokuk, Lee Co., IA
	B: Brown Co., IA
WILLIAMSON, James Alexander	ES: Des Moines, Polk Co., IA
	B: Columbia, Adair Co., KY
YOUNG, Calvary Morris	ES: Hopeville, Clark Co., IA
	B: Washington Co., OH

U.S. Army Air Corps/U.S. Air Force

DAY, George Everette "Bud"	ES: Sioux City, Woodbury Co., IA
	B: Sioux City, Woodbury Co., IA
DETHLEFSEN, Merlyn Hans	ES: Royal, Clay Co., IA
	B: Greenville, Clay Co., IA
*LINDSEY, Darrell Robins	ES: Storm Lake, Buena Vista Co., IA
	B: Jefferson, Greene Co., IA

U.S. Navy

DEIGNAN, Osborn Warren	ES: IA
	B: Stuart, Guthrie Co., IA
FITZ, Joseph	ES: Des Moines, Polk Co., IA
	B: Austria
FLETCHER, Frank Friday	ES: IA
	B: Oskaloosa, Mahaska Co., IA
FLETCHER, Frank Jack	ES: IA
	B: Marshalltown, Marshall Co., IA
IZAC, Edouard Victor Michel	ES: IL
	B: Cresco, Howard Co., IA
PIERCE, Francis Junior	ES: IA
	B: Earlville, Delaware Co., IA

U.S. Marine Corps

HOWARD, Jimmie Earl	ES: Burlington, Des Moines Co., IA
	B: Burlington, Des Moines Co., IA

KANSAS

U.S. Army

ADAMS, Stanley Taylor	ES: Olathe, Johnson Co., KS
	B: DeSoto, Johnson Co., KS
*COWAN, Richard Eller	ES: Wichita, Sedgwick Co., KS
	B: Lincoln, Lancaster Co., NE
DANIELS, James Thomas	ES: Fort Leavenworth, Leavenworth Co., KS
	B: Richland Co., IL
EHLERS, Walter David	ES: Manhattan, Riley Co., KS
	B: Junction City, Geary Co., KS
FERGUSON, Arthur Medworth	ES: Burlington, Coffey Co., KS
	B: Coffey Co., KS
FUNSTON Sr., Frederick	ES: Iola, Allen Co., KS
	B: New Carlisle, Clark Co., OH
*HADDOO Jr., John	ES: Columbus, Cherokee Co., KS
	B: Hooksett, Merrimack Co., NH
HAY, Fred Stewart	ES: Fort Leavenworth, Leavenworth Co., KS
	B: Stirlingshire, Scotland
HENDERSON, Joseph	ES: Leavenworth, Leavenworth Co., KS
	B: Leavenworth, Leavenworth Co., KS
HOLLAND, David	ES: Fort Leavenworth, Leavenworth Co., KS
	B: Dearborn, Wayne Co., MI
HUNT, Frederick O.	ES: Fort Leavenworth, Leavenworth Co., KS
	B: London, England
HUNTSMAN, John A.	ES: Lawrence, Douglas Co., KS
	B: Oskaloosa, Mahaska Co., IA

IMMELL, Lorenzo Dow	ES: Fort Leavenworth, Leavenworth Co., KS B: Ross, Butler Co., OH	*TIMMERMAN, Grant Frederick	ES: KS B: Americus, Lyon Co., KS
JOHNSTON, Harold Irving	ES: Chicago, Cook Co., IL B: Kendall, Hamilton Co., KS		

KENTUCKY

U.S. Army

KNOX, John W.	ES: Fort Leavenworth, Leavenworth Co., KS B: Burlington, Des Moines Co., IA
MALLON, George H.	ES: Minneapolis, Hennepin Co., MN B: Ogden, Riley Co., KS
McCALL, Thomas Edward	ES: Veedersburg, Fountain Co., IN B: Burrton, Harvey Co., KS
*PEDEN, Forrest E.	ES: Wathena, Doniphan Co., KS B: St. Joseph, Buchanan Co., MO
*PETERSEN, Danny John	ES: Kansas City, Clay Co., MO B: Horton, Brown Co., KS
*PITTS, Riley Leroy	ES: Wichita, Sedgwick Co., KS B: Fallis, OK
POPPE, John A.	ES: Fort Dodge, Ford Co., KS B: Cincinnati, Hamilton Co., OH
ROACH, Hampton Mitchell	ES: Fort Dodge, Ford Co., KS B: Concord, LA
ROBB, George Seanor	ES: Salina, Saline Co., KS B: Assaria, Saline Co., KS
RODENBURG, Henry	ES: Fort Leavenworth, Leavenworth Co., KS B: Germany
SCHMIDT, Conrad	ES: Fort Leavenworth, Leavenworth Co., KS B: Wurttemberg, Germany
TREMBLEY, William Beattie	ES: Kansas City, Wyandotte Co., KS B: Johnson, Stanton Co., KS
WALLACE, George Weed	ES: Denver, Denver Co., CO B: Fort Riley, Geary Co., KS
WHITE, Edward	ES: Kansas City, Wyandotte Co., KS B: Seneca, Nemaha Co., KS

U.S. Army Air Corps/U.S. Air Force

*BLECKLEY, Erwin Russell	ES: Wichita, Sedgwick Co., KS B: Wichita, Sedgwick Co., KS
JOHNSON, Leon William	ES: Moline, Elk Co., KS B: Columbia, Boone Co., MO

U.S. Navy

BALCH, John Henry	ES: Kansas City, Clay Co., MO B: Edgerton, Johnson Co., KS
FOSTER, Paul Frederick	ES: KS B: Wichita, Sedgwick Co., KS
McGONAGLE, William Loren	ES: Thermal, Riverside Co., CA B: Wichita, Sedgwick Co., KS
ROSS, Donald Kirby	ES: Denver, Denver Co., CO B: Beverly, Lincoln Co., KS
TRIPLETT, Samuel S.	ES: NY B: Cherokee, Crawford Co., KS

U.S. Marine Corps

*BAUER, Harold William "Indian Joe"	ES: NE B: Woodruff, KS
*DAVENPORT, Jack Arden	ES: Mission, Johnson Co., KS B: Kansas City, Clay Co., MO
*HAWKINS, William Deane	ES: El Paso, El Paso Co., TX B: Fort Scott, Bourbon Co., KS

U.S. Army

BELL, James Franklin	ES: Shelbyville, Shelby Co., KY B: Shelbyville, Shelby Co., KY
BLACK, William Perkins	ES: Danville, Vermillion Co., IL B: Woodford, KY
*BRATLING, Frank	ES: Louisville, Jefferson Co., KY B: Bavaria, Germany
CALLAHAN, John H.	ES: Scottville, Macoupin Co., IL B: Shelby Co., KY
*COLLIER, John Walton	ES: Worthington, Greenup Co., KY B: Worthington, Greenup Co., KY
*CRAIN, Morris E.	ES: Paducah, McCracken Co., KY B: Bandana, Ballard Co., KY
CRUSE, Thomas	ES: Owensboro, Daviess Co., KY B: Owensboro, Daviess Co., KY
DARROUGH, John S.	ES: Concord, Morgan Co., IL B: Maysville, Mason Co., KY
DAVIS, John	ES: Indianapolis, Marion Co., IN B: Carroll, KY
DAY, William L.	ES: Louisville, Jefferson Co., KY B: Barron Co., KY
DODD, Carl Henry	ES: Kenvir, Harlan Co., KY B: Coats, Harlan Co., KY
*FLEEK, Charles Clinton	ES: Cincinnati, Hamilton Co., OH B: Petersburg, Boone Co., KY
*GIVEN, John J.	ES: Cincinnati, Hamilton Co., OH B: Daviess Co., KY
HARDAWAY, Benjamin Franklin	ES: Fort Totten, Benson Co., Dakota Territory B: Benleyville, KY
HARRIS, William M.	ES: Mount Vernon, Rockcastle Co., KY B: Madison Co., KY
HAWTHORNE, Harry Leroy	ES: KY B: MN
HORSFALL, William H.	ES: Fort Cox, Charleston, WV B: Campbell Co., KY
HUDSON, Aaron R.	ES: Indianapolis, Marion Co., IN B: Madison Co., KY
HUGHES, Oliver	ES: Albany, Clinton Co., KY B: Fentress Co., TN
HUGHEY, John P.	ES: Anna, Union Co., IL B: Louisville, Jefferson Co., KY
JENKINS, Don	ES: Nashville, Davidson Co., TN B: Quality, Butler Co., KY
JONES, William H.	ES: Louisville, Jefferson Co., KY B: Davidson Co., NC
KERR, John Brown	ES: Hutchison Station, Bourbon Co., KY B: Lexington, Fayette Co., KY
*KYLE, Darwin K.	ES: Racine, Boone Co., WV B: Jenkins, Letcher Co., KY
*LAUFFER, Billy Lane	ES: Phoenix, Maricopa Co., AZ B: Murray, Calloway Co., KY
LITTRELL, Gary Lee	ES: Los Angeles, Los Angeles Co., CA B: Henderson, Henderson Co., KY

*LONG, Donald Russell	ES: Ashland, Boyd Co., KY B: Blackfork, OH	WOODS, Brent	ES: Louisville, Jefferson Co., KY B: Pulaski Co., KY
MATTINGLY, Henry B.	ES: Lebanon, Marion Co., KY B: Marion Co., KY		

U.S. Navy

BOERS, Edward William	ES: KY B: Cincinnati, Hamilton Co., OH
CLARY, Edward Alvin	ES: KY B: Foxport, KY
HOLT, George	ES: KY B: KY
NOBLE, Daniel	ES: Chicago, Cook Co., IL B: Bath Co., KY

McDONALD, Franklin M.	ES: Fort Griffin, TX B: Bowling Green, Warren Co., KY
McDONALD, Robert	ES: Newport, Campbell Co., KY B: Erie Co., NY
McLOUGHLIN, Michael	ES: Louisville, Jefferson Co., KY B: County Sligo, Ireland
McMILLEN, Francis M.	ES: Piqua, Miami Co., OH B: Bracken Co., KY
MORRIS, William W.	ES: Louisville, Jefferson Co., KY B: Stewart Co., TN

U.S. Marine Corps

BARBER, William Earl	ES: West Liberty, Morgan Co., KY B: Dehart, Morgan Co., KY
*BAUGH, William Bernard	ES: Harrison, Hamilton Co., OH B: McKinney, Lincoln Co., KY
BUSH, Richard Earl	ES: KY B: Glasgow, Barren Co., KY
*MASON, Leonard Foster	ES: OH B: Middlesboro, Bell Co., KY
*PAUL, Joe Calvin	ES: Dayton, Montgomery Co., OH B: Williamsburg, Whitley Co., KY
*PHELPS, Wesley	ES: KY B: Neafus, Grayson Co., KY
SKAGGS Jr., Luther	ES: KY B: Henderson, Henderson Co., KY

*NASH, David Paul	ES: Louisville, Jefferson Co., KY B: Whitesville, Daviess Co., KY
NASH, James J.	ES: Louisville, Jefferson Co., KY B: Louisville, Jefferson Co., KY
ROOD, Oliver P.	ES: Terre Haute, Vigo Co., IN B: Frankfort Co., KY
ROSS, Wilburn Kirby	ES: Strunk, McCreary Co., KY B: Strunk, McCreary Co., KY
RUNDLE, Charles Wesley	ES: Oakley, Macon Co., IL B: Covington, Campbell Co., KY
SANDLIN, Willie	ES: Hyden, Leslie Co., KY B: Jackson, Breathitt Co., KY
SCOTT, George D.	ES: Mount Vernon, Rockcastle Co., KY B: Lancaster, Garrard Co., KY
SHAW, Thomas	ES: Baton Rouge, Baton Rouge Co., LA B: Covington, Kenton Co., KY

LOUISIANA

U.S. Army

BABCOCK, John	ES: Stonington, New London Co., CT B: New Orleans, Orleans Co., LA
BEAUFORT, Jean J.	ES: New Orleans, Orleans Co., LA B: France
CLARKE, Powhatan Henry	ES: Baltimore, Baltimore Co., MD B: Alexandria, Rapides Co., LA
*DIAMOND, James H.	ES: Gulfport, Harrison Co., MS B: New Orleans, Orleans Co., LA
*FOURNET, Douglas Bernard	ES: New Orleans, Orleans Co., LA B: Lake Charles, Calcasieu Co., LA
GREELY, Adolphus Washington	ES: LA B: Newburyport, Essex Co., MA
*JOHNSON, Leroy	ES: Oakdale, Allen Co., LA B: Caney Creek, LA
*LEE, Milton Arthur	ES: San Antonio, Bexar Co., TX B: Shreveport, Caddo Co., LA
NOVOSEL, Michael Joseph	ES: Kenner, Jefferson Co., LA B: Etna, Allegheny Co., PA
RILEY, Thomas	ES: New Orleans, Orleans Co., LA B: Ireland
ROACH, Hampton Mitchell	ES: Fort Dodge, Ford Co., KS B: Concord, LA
SCHOWALTER Jr., Edward Rightor	ES: Metairie, Jefferson Co., LA B: New Orleans, Orleans Co., LA
SHAW, Thomas	ES: Baton Rouge, Baton Rouge Co., LA B: Covington, Kenton Co., KY
STANCE, Emanuel	ES: East Carroll Parish, LA B: Carroll Parish, LA

*SMITH, David Monroe	ES: Livingston, Rockcastle Co., KY B: Livingston, Rockcastle Co., KY
SPURRIER, Junior James	ES: Riggs, KY B: Russell Co., KY
*SQUIRES, John C.	ES: Louisville, Jefferson Co., KY B: Louisville, Jefferson Co., KY
STEINMETZ, William	ES: Sunman, Ripley Co., IN B: Newport, Campbell Co., KY
STEVERS, Thomas W.	ES: Mount Vernon, Rockcastle Co., KY B: Madison Co., KY
*STEWART, Jimmy Goethel	ES: Ashland, Boyd Co., KY B: West Columbia, Mason Co., WV
SULLIVAN, Thomas	ES: Cincinnati, Hamilton Co., OH B: Covington, Kenton Co., KY
SWEGHEIMER, Jacob	ES: Paducah, McCracken Co., KY B: Oldtown, Baden, Germany
THORN, Walter	ES: Camp Nelson, KY B: Brooklyn, Kings Co., NY
VOIT, Otto Emil	ES: Louisville, Jefferson Co., KY B: Baden, Germany
WALKER, Mary Edwards	ES: Louisville, Jefferson Co., KY B: Oswego Co., NY
WEST, Ernest Edison	ES: Wurtland, Greenup Co., KY B: Russell, Greenup Co., KY
WESTON, John Francis	ES: Camp Anderson, KY B: Louisville, Jefferson Co., KY
WHITEHEAD, Patton G.	ES: Louisville, Jefferson Co., KY B: Russell Co., VA
WILLIAMSON, James Alexander	ES: Des Moines, Polk Co., IA B: Columbia, Adair Co., KY

WHITTINGTON, Hulon Brooke ES: Bastrop, Morehouse Co., LA
B: Bogalusa, Washington Co., LA

WILLIAMS, Moses ES: East Carroll Parish, LA
B: Carrollton, Orleans Parish, LA

WISE, Homer L. ES: Baton Rouge, East Baton Rouge Co., LA
B: Baton Rouge, East Baton Rouge Co., LA

U.S. Army Air Corps/U.S. Air Force

*BENNETT, Steven Logan ES: Lafayette, Lafayette Co., LA
B: Palestine, Anderson Co., TX

*HUGHES, Lloyd Herbert ES: San Antonio, Bexar Co., TX
B: Alexandria, Rapides Co., LA

KANE, John Riley ES: Shreveport, Caddo Co., LA
B: McGregor, McLennan Co., TX

U.S. Navy

*GILMORE, Howard Walter ES: LA
B: Selma, Dallas Co., AL

OSBORNE, John ES: LA
B: New Orleans, Orleans Co., LA

RYAN Jr., Thomas John ES: LA
B: New Orleans, Orleans Co., LA

WEISBOGEL, Albert ES: LA
B: New Orleans, Orleans Co., LA

WILKINSON Jr., Theodore Stark ES: LA
B: Annapolis, Anne Arundel Co., MD

WILLIAMS, John ES: LA
B: New Orleans, Orleans Co., LA

U.S. Marine Corps

CLAUSEN Jr., Raymond Michael "Red" ES: New Orleans, Orleans Co., LA
B: New Orleans, Orleans Co., LA

DeBLANC, Jefferson Joseph ES: Lockport, Lafourche Co., LA
B: Lockport, Lafourche Co., LA

MAINE

U.S. Army

AMES, Adelbert ES: Rockland, Knox Co., ME
B: Rockland, Knox Co., ME

BAILEY, James E. ES: Boston, Suffolk Co., MA
B: Dexter, Penobscot Co., ME

BELCHER, Thomas ES: Bangor, Penobscot Co., ME
B: Bangor, Penobscot Co., ME

BOODY, Robert M. ES: Amesbury, Essex Co., MA
B: Lemington, ME

BOWMAN, Alonzo ES: Boston, Suffolk Co., MA
B: Washington Township, Knox Co., ME

BRETT, Lloyd Milton ES: Malden, Middlesex Co., MA
B: Dead River, ME

*BUKER, Brian Leroy ES: Bangor, Penobscot Co., ME
B: Benton, ME

CARTER, Robert Goldthwaite ES: Bradford, Essex Co., MA
B: Bridgton, Cumberland Co., ME

CHAMBERLAIN, Joshua Lawrence ES: Brunswick, Cumberland Co., ME
B: Brewer, Penobscot Co., ME

CHAPMAN, John ES: Limerick, York Co., ME
B: Strasburg, France

CHASE, John F. ES: Augusta, Kennebec Co., ME
B: Chelsea, ME

CLARK, Charles Amory ES: Forcroft, ME
B: Sangerville, Piscataquis Co., ME

CONDON, Clarence Milville ES: St. Augustine, St. Johns Co., FL
B: South Brooksville, Hancock Co., ME

DAHLGREN, Edward Carl ES: Caribou, Aroostook Co., ME
B: Perham, Aroostook Co., ME

DOHERTY, Thomas M. ES: Newcastle, Lincoln Co., ME
B: Mitchelstown, County Cork, Ireland

ESTES, Lewellyn Garrish ES: Oldtown, Penobscot Co., ME
B: Oldtown, Penobscot Co., ME

FERNALD, Albert E. ES: Winterport, Waldo Co., ME
B: Winterport, Waldo Co., ME

*FOURNIER, William Grant ES: Winterport, Waldo Co., ME
B: Norwich, New London Co., CT

*GOODBLOOD, Clair ES: Burnham, Waldo Co., ME
B: Fort Kent, Aroostook Co., ME

*GORDON, Gary Ivan ES: Lincoln, Penobscot Co., ME
B: Lincoln, Penobscot Co., ME

HANNA, Marcus A. ES: Rockport, Essex Co., MA
B: Bristol, Lincoln Co., ME

HANSCOM, Moses C. ES: Bowdoinham, Sagadahoc Co., ME
B: Danville, Androscoggin Co., ME

HARRINGTON, Ephraim W. ES: Kirby, VT
B: Waterford, Oxford Co., ME

HASKELL, Frank W. ES: Waterville, Kennebec Co., ME
B: Benton, ME

HAYNES, Asbury F. ES: Passadumkeag, Penobscot Co., ME
B: Edinburgh, ME

HESSELTINE, Francis Snow ES: Waterville, Kennebec Co., ME
B: Bangor, Penobscot Co., ME

HINCKS, William B. ES: Bridgeport, Fairfield Co., CT
B: Bucksport, Hancock Co., ME

HOWARD, Oliver Otis ES: Leeds, Androscoggin Co., ME
B: Leeds, Androscoggin Co., ME

HYDE, Henry J. ES: New York, NY
B: Bangor, Penobscot Co., ME

HYDE, Thomas Worcester ES: Bath, Sagadahoc Co., ME
B: Florence, Italy

KING, Horatio Collins ES: Brooklyn, Kings Co., NY
B: Portland, Cumberland Co., ME

KNOWLES, Abiather J. ES: Willets Point, Queens Co., NY
B: La Grange, Penobscot Co., ME

*LIBBY, George Dalton ES: Waterbury, New Haven Co., CT
B: Bridgton, Cumberland Co., ME

LITTLEFIELD, George H. ES: Skowhegan, Somerset Co., ME
B: Skowhegan, Somerset Co., ME

LUNT, Alphonso M. ES: Cambridge, Middlesex Co., MA
B: Berwick, York Co., ME

MATTOCKS, Charles Porter ES: Portland, Cumberland Co., ME
B: Danville, Caledonia Co., VT

*McMAHON, Thomas Joseph ES: Portland, Cumberland Co., ME
B: Washington, D.C.

*McMASTERS, Henry A. ES: Augusta, Kennebec Co., ME
B: Augusta, Kennebec Co., ME

MERRIAM, Henry Clay ES: Houlton, Aroostook Co., ME
B: Houlton, Aroostook Co., ME

MERRILL, Augustus ES: Lyndon, ME
B: Byron, ME

MILLETT, Lewis Lee "Red"	ES: Mechanic Falls, Androscoggin Co., ME B: Mechanic Falls, Androscoggin Co., ME	BLAIR, Robert M.	ES: Portland, Cumberland Co., ME B: Peacham, Caledonia Co., VT
MORRILL, Walter Goodale	ES: Brownville, Piscataquis Co., ME B: Williamsburg, ME	BOWMAN, Edward R.	ES: ME B: Eastport, Washington Co., ME
O'BRIEN, Henry D.	ES: St. Anthony Falls, MN B: Colois, ME	DAVIS, Samuel W.	ES: ME B: Brewer, Penobscot Co., ME
PIKE, Edward M.	ES: Bloomington, McLean Co., IL B: Casco, Cumberland Co., ME	DUNCAN, Adam	ES: Boston, Suffolk Co., MA B: ME
REED, Axel Hayford	ES: Glencoe, McLeod Co., MN B: Hartford, Oxford Co., ME	DUNN, William	ES: ME B: Lisbon, Androscoggin Co., ME
*RICHMOND, James	ES: Fremont, Sandusky Co., OH B: ME	FARLEY, William	ES: ME B: Whitefield, Lincoln Co., ME
ROBERTS, Otis O.	ES: Dexter, Penobscot Co., ME B: Sangerville, Piscataquis Co., ME	FOSS, Herbert Louis	ES: ME B: Belfast, Waldo Co., ME
*SKIDGEL, Donald Sidney	ES: Bangor, Penobscot Co., ME B: Caribou, Aroostook Co., ME	FRISBEE, John B.	ES: Brookline, Norfolk Co., MA B: Phippsburg, Sagadahoc Co., ME
SMITH, Charles Henry	ES: Eastport, Washington Co., ME B: Hollis, York Co., ME	GIDDING, Charles	ES: ME B: Bangor, Penobscot Co., ME
SMITH, Joseph Sewall	ES: Wiscasset, Lincoln Co., ME B: Wiscasset, Lincoln Co., ME	HAYDEN, Cyrus	ES: ME B: York, York Co., ME
SMITH, William	ES: San Francisco, San Francisco Co., CA B: Bath, Sagadahoc Co., ME	KENDRICK, Thomas	ES: ME B: Bath, Sagadahoc Co., ME
SPURLING, Andrew Barclay	ES: Augusta, Kennebec Co., ME B: Cranberry Isles, Hancock Co., ME	MACK, John	ES: ME B: Brooksville, Hancock Co., ME
TAYLOR, Wilbur Nelson	ES: Boston, Suffolk Co., MA B: Hampden, Penobscot Co., ME	McCULLOCK, Adam	ES: Augusta, Kennebec Co., ME B: ME
TERRY, John Darling	ES: Boston, Suffolk Co., MA B: Montville, ME	McLEOD, James	ES: ME B: Scotland
THAXTER, Sidney Warren	ES: Bangor, Penobscot Co., ME B: Bangor, Penobscot Co., ME	MILLIKEN, Daniel	ES: New York, NY B: Saco, York Co., ME
TOBIE Jr., Edward Parsons	ES: Lewiston, Androscoggin Co., ME B: Lewiston, Androscoggin Co., ME	POOLE, William B.	ES: ME B: Cape Elizabeth, Cumberland Co., ME
TOZIER, Andrew Jackson	ES: Bangor, Penobscot Co., ME B: Monmouth, Kennebec Co., ME	RICE, Charles	ES: Portland, Cumberland Co., ME B: Russia
TRACY, Amasa Sawyer	ES: Middlebury, Addison Co., VT B: Dover, Piscataquis Co., ME	ROBINSON, John	ES: ME B: Cuba
*WAUGH, Robert T.	ES: Augusta, Kennebec Co., ME B: Ashton, RI	SAVAGE, Auzella	ES: Boston, Suffolk Co., MA B: Anson, Somerset Co., ME
WHEELER, Henry W.	ES: Bangor, Penobscot Co., ME B: Fort Smith, Sebastian Co., AR	SCHONLAND, Herbert Emery	ES: Portland, Cumberland Co., ME B: Portland, Cumberland Co., ME
WHITMAN, Frank M.	ES: Ayersville, MA B: Woodstock, ME	SEWARD, Richard Henry	ES: Kittery, York Co., ME B: Kittery, York Co., ME
WHITTIER, Edward Newton	ES: Gorham, Cumberland Co., ME B: Portland, Cumberland Co., ME	SMITH, Charles H.	ES: ME B: Standish, Cumberland Co., ME
WOOD, Henry Clay	ES: Winthrop, Kennebec Co., ME B: Winthrop, Kennebec Co., ME	TAYLOR, Thomas	ES: ME B: Bangor, Penobscot Co., ME

U.S. Army Air Corps/U.S. Air Force

*LORING Jr., Charles Joseph	ES: Portland, Cumberland Co., ME B: Portland, Cumberland Co., ME
ZEAMER Jr., Jay	ES: Machias, Washington Co., ME B: Carlisle, Cumberland Co., PA

U.S. Navy

ANGLING, John	ES: Portland, Cumberland Co., ME B: Portland, Cumberland Co., ME
BIBBER, Charles James	ES: Portland, Cumberland Co., ME B: Portland, Cumberland Co., ME
BICKFORD, John F.	ES: Boston, Suffolk Co., MA B: Tremont, ME

TRIPP, Othniel	ES: ME B: ME
VERNEY, James W.	ES: Portland, Cumberland Co., ME B: Bath, Sagadahoc Co., ME
WILLIAMS, Anthony	ES: Portsmouth, ME B: Plymouth, Plymouth Co., MA
YOUNG, Horatio Nelson	ES: Boston, Suffolk Co., MA B: Calais, Washington Co., ME

U.S. Marine Corps

*CHAMPAGNE, David Bernard	ES: Wakefield, Washington Co., RI B: Waterville, Kennebec Co., ME

MARYLAND

U.S. Army

ANDERSON, Charles W.	ES: near Winchester, Frederick Co., VA	
	B: Baltimore, Baltimore Co., MD	
BARNES, William Henry	ES: Norfolk, Norfolk Co., VA	
	B: St. Marys Co., MD	
BEAUFORD, Clay	ES: Nashville, Davidson Co., TN	
	B: Washington Co., MD	
BOYNE, Thomas	ES: Norfolk, Norfolk Co., VA	
	B: Prince Georges Co., MD	
BUFFINGTON, John C.	ES: Westminster, Carroll Co., MD	
	B: Carroll Co., MD	
CADWALLADER, Abel G.	ES: Frederick, Frederick Co., MD	
	B: Baltimore, Baltimore Co., MD	
*CAPRON Jr., Horace	ES: Peoria, Peoria Co., IL	
	B: Laurel, Prince George's Co., MD	
CARTER, Joseph Franklin	ES: Baltimore, Baltimore Co., MD	
	B: Baltimore, Baltimore Co., MD	
CLARKE, Powhatan Henry	ES: Baltimore, Baltimore Co., MD	
	B: Alexandria, Rapides Co., LA	
*COSTIN, Henry G.	ES: Baltimore, Baltimore Co., MD	
	B: Baltimore, Baltimore Co., MD	
CRIST, John	ES: Baltimore, Baltimore Co., MD	
	B: Baltimore, Baltimore Co., MD	
DEETLINE, Frederick	ES: Baltimore, Baltimore Co., MD	
	B: Offenheim, Germany	
DONAHUE, John L.	ES: Baltimore, Baltimore Co., MD	
	B: Baltimore Co., MD	
DORSEY, Decatur	ES: Baltimore, Baltimore Co., MD	
	B: Howard Co., MD	
FLEETWOOD, Christian A.	ES: Baltimore, Baltimore Co., MD	
	B: Baltimore, Baltimore Co., MD	
FOSTER, William	ES: Bakersville, MD	
	B: Somerset Co., England	
GALT, Sterling Archibald	ES: Taneytown, Carroll Co., MD	
	B: Taneytown, Carroll Co., MD	
GREAVES, Clinton	ES: Baltimore, Baltimore Co., MD	
	B: Madison Co., VA	
HARRIS, James H.	ES: Great Mills, St. Mary's Co., MD	
	B: St. Mary's Co., MD	
HART, John William	ES: Cumberland, Allegany Co., MD	
	B: Germany	
*HARTSOCK, Robert Willard	ES: Fairmont, Marion Co., WV	
	B: Cumberland, Allegany Co., MD	
HAUPT, Paul	ES: Baltimore, Baltimore Co., MD	
	B: Germany (Prussia)	
*HILTON, Alfred B.	ES: Baltimore, Baltimore Co., MD	
	B: Harford Co., MD	
HINEMANN, Lehmann	ES: Baltimore, Baltimore Co., MD	
	B: Lanback, Germany	
*HOOKER, George	ES: Washington, D.C.	
	B: Frederick, Frederick Co., MD	
*JACHMAN, Isadore Seigfried	ES: Baltimore, Baltimore Co., MD	
	B: Berlin, Germany	
*JECELIN, William R.	ES: Baltimore, Baltimore Co., MD	
	B: Baltimore, Baltimore Co., MD	
KEOUGH, John	ES: Annapolis, Anne Arundel Co., MD	
	B: County Tipperary, Ireland	
KOOGLE, Jacob	ES: Middletown, Frederick Co., MD	
	B: Frederick, Frederick Co., MD	
MATHEWS, William Henry	ES: Baltimore, Baltimore Co., MD	
	B: Devizes, Wiltshire, England	
MAUS, Marion Perry	ES: Tennallytown, Montgomery Co., MD	
	B: Burnt Mills, Montgomery Co., MD	
McALWEE, Benjamin Franklin	ES: Baltimore, Baltimore Co., MD	
	B: Washington, D.C.	
McGONNIGLE, Andrew Jackson	ES: Cumberland, Allegany Co., MD	
	B: New York, NY	
McNAMARA, William	ES: Baltimore, Baltimore Co., MD	
	B: County Cork, Ireland	
MILES, Louis Wardlaw	ES: Princeton, Mercer Co., NJ	
	B: Baltimore, Baltimore Co., MD	
MORELOCK, Sterling Lewis	ES: Oquawka, Henderson Co., IL	
	B: Silver Run, MD	
MOTT, John	ES: Baltimore, Baltimore Co., MD	
	B: Fifeshire, Scotland	
MURRAY Jr., Charles Patrick "Chuck"	ES: Wilmington, New Hanover Co., NC	
	B: Baltimore, Baltimore Co., MD	
MYERS, William H.	ES: Baltimore, Baltimore Co., MD	
	B: Philadelphia, Philadelphia Co., PA	
OLIVER, Francis	ES: Fort Filmore, NM	
	B: Baltimore, Baltimore Co., MD	
PENNSYL, Josiah	ES: Carlisle, Cumberland Co., PA	
	B: Frederick Co., MD	
PHELPS, Charles Edwards	ES: Baltimore, Baltimore Co., MD	
	B: Guilford, VT	
PHILIPSEN, Wilhelm O.	ES: Baltimore, Baltimore Co., MD	
	B: Schleswig, Germany	
PIERCE, Charles H.	ES: Delaware City, New Castle Co., DE	
	B: Cecil Co., MD	
PORTER, Ambrose	ES: Rockport, Atchison Co., MO	
	B: Allegany Co., MD	
*PORTER, Donn F.	ES: Baltimore, Baltimore Co., MD	
	B: Sewickley, Allegheny Co., PA	
PORTER, Samuel	ES: Washington, D.C.	
	B: Montgomery Co., MD	
*PRUSSMAN, Ernest W.	ES: Brighton, Suffolk Co., MA	
	B: Baltimore, Baltimore Co., MD	
SCHNEIDER, George	ES: Baltimore, Baltimore Co., MD	
	B: Baltimore, Baltimore Co., MD	
SHEA, Joseph Henry	ES: New Bern, Craven Co., NC	
	B: Baltimore, Baltimore Co., MD	
SHEERIN, John	ES: Baltimore, Baltimore Co., MD	
	B: Camden Co., NJ	
*SHERIDAN, Carl Vernon	ES: Baltimore, Baltimore Co., MD	
	B: Baltimore, Baltimore Co., MD	
SKINNER, John Oscar	ES: MD	
	B: Baltimore, Baltimore Co., MD	
SMITH, Andrew J.	ES: Baltimore, Baltimore Co., MD	
	B: Baltimore, Baltimore Co., MD	
SMITH, Francis M.	ES: Frederick, Frederick Co., MD	
	B: Baltimore, Baltimore Co., MD	
SMITH, Otto	ES: Sacramento, Sacramento Co., CA	
	B: Baltimore, Baltimore Co., MD	
STEWART, Joseph	ES: Baltimore, Baltimore Co., MD	
	B: Ireland	
TAYLOR, Charles	ES: St. Louis, St. Louis Co., MO	
	B: Baltimore, Baltimore Co., MD	

TAYLOR, William	ES: Frederick, Frederick Co., MD B: Washington, D.C.	JONES, Thomas	ES: Baltimore, Baltimore Co., MD B: Baltimore, Baltimore Co., MD
THOMPSON, John J.	ES: Baltimore, Baltimore Co., MD B: Holstein, Germany	JORDAN, Thomas H.	ES: Baltimore, Baltimore Co., MD B: Portsmouth, Portsmouth Co., VA
TUCKER, Jacob R.	ES: Baltimore, Baltimore Co., MD B: Chester Co., PA	LAKIN, Daniel	ES: MD B: Baltimore, Baltimore Co., MD
VEAL, Charles	ES: Baltimore, Baltimore Co., MD B: Portsmouth, Portsmouth Co., VA	MAGEE, John W.	ES: MD B: MD
WAGNER, John W.	ES: St. Louis, St. Louis Co., MO B: Clear Spring, Washington Co., MD	McDONNELL, Edward Orrick	ES: MD B: Baltimore, Baltimore Co., MD
WALLEY, Augustus	ES: Baltimore, Baltimore Co., MD B: Reistertown, Baltimore Co., MD	McNAIR Jr., Frederick Vallette	ES: Appointed at large B: Maryland
WARFEL, Henry Clay	ES: Monocacy Junction, MD B: Mill Creek, Huntingdon Co., PA	MORTON, Charles W.	ES: MD B: Ireland
WEINERT, Paul H.	ES: Baltimore, Baltimore Co., MD B: Frankfort, Germany	MULLEN, Patrick	ES: Baltimore, Baltimore Co., MD B: Ireland
WELD, Seth Lathrop	ES: Altamont, Grundy Co., TN B: Sandy Hook, MD	NORRIS, Thomas Rolland	ES: Silver Spring, Montgomery Co., MD B: Jacksonville, Duval Co., FL
WIEDORFER, Paul Joseph	ES: Baltimore, Baltimore Co., MD B: Baltimore, Baltimore Co., MD	PRESTON, Arthur Murray	ES: MD B: Washington, D.C.
WILSON, William O.	ES: St. Paul, Ramsey Co., MN B: Hagerstown, Washington Co., MD	*RICKETTS, Milton Ernest	ES: MD B: Baltimore, Baltimore Co., MD
WOODWARD, Evan M.	ES: Sandy Hook, MD B: Philadelphia, Philadelphia Co., PA	RINGOLD, Edward	ES: MD B: Baltimore, Baltimore Co., MD
*YNTEMA, Gordon Douglas	ES: Detroit, Wayne Co., MI B: Bethesda, Montgomery Co., MD	SHUTES, Henry	ES: MD B: Baltimore, Baltimore Co., MD
ZIEGNER, Herman	ES: Baltimore, Baltimore Co., MD B: Aploda, Germany	STERLING, James E.	ES: MD B: Baltimore, Baltimore Co., MD

U.S. Air Force

*WALMSLEY Jr., John Springer	ES: Baltimore, Baltimore Co., MD B: Baltimore, Baltimore Co., MD	SWEARER, Benjamin	ES: MD B: Baltimore, Baltimore Co., MD
		*TALLENTINE, James	ES: Baltimore, Baltimore Co., MD B: England
		TRUETT, Alexander H.	ES: MD B: Baltimore, Baltimore Co., MD

U.S. Navy

ANDREWS, John	ES: MD B: York Co., PA	WILKINSON Jr., Theodore Stark	ES: LA B: Annapolis, Anne Arundel Co., MD
BROWN, John	ES: MD B: Denmark	WRIGHT, William	ES: Baltimore, Baltimore Co., MD B: London, England
BROWN, William H.	ES: MD B: Baltimore, Baltimore Co., MD		

U.S. Marine Corps

BUCK, James	B: Baltimore, Baltimore Co., MD	*GRAHAM, James Albert	ES: Prince Georges, Prince Georges Co., MD B: Wilkinsburg, Allegheny Co., PA
CARR, William M.	ES: Baltimore, Baltimore Co., MD B: Baltimore, Baltimore Co., MD	*SHUCK Jr., William Edward	ES: Cumberland, Allegany Co., MD B: Cumberland, Allegany Co., MD
CHATHAM, John Purness	ES: MD B: Warchester, MD	*TAYLOR Sr., Karl Gorman	ES: Baltimore, Baltimore Co., MD B: Laurel, Prince George's Co., MD
CONNOR, Thomas	ES: Baltimore, Baltimore Co., MD B: Ireland		

MASSACHUSETTS

U.S. Army

DIGGINS, Bartholomew	ES: MD B: Baltimore, Baltimore Co., MD		
DURNEY, Austin Joseph	ES: Woodland, MD B: Philadelphia, Philadelphia Co., PA	ADAMS, John Gregory Bishop	ES: West Newbury, Essex Co., MA B: Groveland, Essex Co., MA
HAMMANN, Charles Hazeltine	ES: MD B: Baltimore, Baltimore Co., MD	ALLEN, Nathaniel M.	ES: Boston, Suffolk Co., MA B: Boston, Suffolk Co., MA
HAYDEN, Joseph B.	ES: MD B: St. Mary's City, St. Mary's Co., MD	ANDERSON, Frederick Charles	ES: Dedham, Norfolk Co., MA B: Boston, Suffolk Co., MA
JARRETT, Berrie Henry	ES: MD B: Baltimore, Baltimore Co., MD	BAILEY, James E.	ES: Boston, Suffolk Co., MA B: Dexter, Penobscot Co., ME
JOHANSON, John Peter	ES: MD B: Oskarshamn, Sweden		

*BARNES III, John Andrew	ES: Boston, Suffolk Co., MA B: Boston, Suffolk Co., MA	*DeFRANZO, Arthur Frederick	ES: Saugus, Essex Co., MA B: Saugus, Essex Co., MA
BAYBUTT, Philip	ES: Fall River, Bristol Co., MA B: Manchester, Greater Manchester Co., England	DELAND, Frederick Nelson	ES: Great Barrington, Berkshire Co., MA B: Sheffield, Berkshire Co., MA
*BEAUDOIN, Raymond Ovila	ES: Holyoke, Hampden Co., MA B: Holyoke, Hampden Co., MA	DILLON, Michael A.	ES: Wilton, Hillsborough Co., NH B: Chelmsford, Middlesex Co., MA
BERGENDAHL, Frederick	ES: Boston, Suffolk Co., MA B: Gothenburg, Sweden	*DOANE, Stephen Holden	ES: Albany, Albany Co., NY B: Beverly, Essex Co., MA
BESSEY, Charles Albert	ES: Boston, Suffolk Co., MA B: Reading, Middlesex Co., MA	DODGE, Francis Safford	ES: Danvers, Essex Co., MA B: Danvers, Essex Co., MA
BOODY, Robert M.	ES: Amesbury, Essex Co., MA B: Lemington, ME	DOWNEY, William	ES: Fall River, Bristol Co., MA B: Ireland
BOSS, Orlando Phidelio	ES: Fitchburg, Worcester Co., MA B: Fitchburg, Worcester Co., MA	DUFFEY, John	ES: New Bedford, Bristol Co., MA B: New Bedford, Bristol Co., MA
BOWDEN, Samuel	ES: Boston, Suffolk Co., MA B: Salem, Essex Co., MA	EDDY, Samuel E.	ES: Chesterfield, Hampshire Co., MA B: Whitingham, Windham Co., VT
BOWMAN, Alonzo	ES: Boston, Suffolk Co., MA B: Washington Township, Knox Co., ME	ELLIOTT, Russell C.	ES: Boston, Suffolk Co., MA B: Concord, Merrimack Co., NH
BOYNTON, Henry Van Ness	ES: Hamilton, Butler Co., OH B: West Stockbridge, Berkshire Co., MA	ELLSWORTH, Thomas Foulds	ES: Boston, Suffolk Co., MA B: Ipswich, Essex Co., MA
BRADY, James	ES: Kingston, Rockingham Co., NH B: Boston, Suffolk Co., MA	*EVANS, Rodney John	ES: Montgomery, Montgomery Co., AL B: Chelsea, Suffolk Co., MA
BRETT, Lloyd Milton	ES: Malden, Middlesex Co., MA B: Dead River, ME	*FALLS, Benjamin Frank	ES: Lynn, Essex Co., MA B: Portsmouth, Rockingham Co., NH
BROWN, John	ES: Cincinnati, Hamilton Co., OH B: Boston, Suffolk Co., MA	FERRIS, Eugene W.	ES: Lowell, Middlesex Co., MA B: Springfield, Windsor Co., VT
BROWN, John Harties	ES: Charlestown, Suffolk Co., MA B: New Brunswick, Canada	FOLEY, John H.	ES: Boston, Suffolk Co., MA B: Cork, Ireland
BRYANT, Andrew Symmes	ES: Springfield, Hampden Co., MA B: Springfield, Hampden Co., MA	FOLEY, Robert Franklin	ES: Newton, Middlesex Co., MA B: Newton, Middlesex Co., MA
BUFFUM, Robert	ES: Gilead, Wood Co., OH B: Salem, Essex Co., MA	FUNK, West	ES: Philadelphia, Philadelphia Co., PA B: Boston, Suffolk Co., MA
BURT, James Montross	ES: Lee, Berkshire Co., MA B: Hinsdale, Berkshire Co., MA	GARDNER, Charles N.	ES: Scituate, Plymouth Co., MA B: South Scituate, Plymouth Co., MA
CALLEN, Thomas Joseph	ES: Boston, Suffolk Co., MA B: County Louth, Ireland	GARDNER, Robert J.	ES: Egremont, Berkshire Co., MA B: Livingston, Columbia Co., NY
CARNEY, William Harvey	ES: New Bedford, Bristol Co., MA B: Norfolk, Norfolk Co., VA	GARLAND, Harry	ES: Indianapolis, Marion Co., IN B: Boston, Suffolk Co., MA
CARSON, Anthony J.	ES: Malden, Middlesex Co., MA B: Boston, Suffolk Co., MA	GAY, Thomas H.	ES: Boston, Suffolk Co., MA B: Prince Edward Island, Canada
CARTER, Robert Goldthwaite	ES: Bradford, Essex Co., MA B: Bridgton, Cumberland Co., ME	GAYLORD, Levi B.	ES: Boston, Suffolk Co., MA B: Boston, Suffolk Co., MA
CASEY, David P.	ES: Northbridge, Worcester Co., MA B: Ireland	GIBSON, Edward Herrick	ES: Boston, Suffolk Co., MA B: Boston, Suffolk Co., MA
CHANDLER, Henry Flint	ES: Andover, Essex Co., MA B: Andover, Essex Co., MA	GIFFORD, David L.	ES: New Bedford, Bristol Co., MA B: Dartmouth, Bristol Co., MA
COSGROVE, Thomas	ES: East Stoughton, Norfolk Co., MA B: County Galway, Ireland	GOODMAN, David	ES: Boston, Suffolk Co., MA B: Paxton, Worcester Co., MA
*CRAIG, Gordon Maynard	ES: Brockton, Plymouth Co., MA B: Brockton, Plymouth Co., MA	GRACE, Peter	ES: Berkshire, Berkshire Co., MA B: Berkshire, Berkshire Co., MA
CRANDALL, Charles	ES: Philadelphia, Philadelphia Co., PA B: Worcester, Worcester Co., MA	*GRANT, Joseph Xavier	ES: Boston, Suffolk Co., MA B: Cambridge, Middlesex Co., MA
DAVIS, George Evans	ES: Burlington, Chittenden Co., VT B: Dunstable, Middlesex Co., MA	GREELY, Adolphus Washington	ES: LA B: Newburyport, Essex Co., MA
DAWSON, Michael	ES: New York, NY B: Boston, Suffolk Co., MA	GRIMES, Edward P.	ES: Boston, Suffolk Co., MA B: Dover, Strafford Co., NH
DEANE, John Milton	ES: Freetown, Bristol Co., MA B: Assonet Village, Bristol Co., MA	HALL, George John	ES: Boston, Suffolk Co., MA B: Stoneham, Middlesex Co., MA
DeCASTRO, Joseph H.	ES: Boston, Suffolk Co., MA B: Boston, Suffolk Co., MA		

HANLEY, Richard P.	ES: Cincinnati, Hamilton Co., OH B: Boston, Suffolk Co., MA	MAHONEY, Gregory	ES: Boston, Suffolk Co., MA B: Pettypool, South Wales
HANNA, Marcus A.	ES: Rockport, Essex Co., MA B: Bristol, Lincoln Co., ME	MAHONEY, Jeremiah	ES: Fall River, Bristol Co., MA
HARBOURNE, John H.	ES: Readville, Suffolk Co., MA B: England	MANNING, Joseph S.	ES: Boston, Suffolk Co., MA B: Ipswich, Essex Co., MA
HARRIS, Moses	ES: Boston, Suffolk Co., MA B: Andover, Merrimack Co., NH	MARLAND, William	ES: Andover, Essex Co., MA B: Andover, Essex Co., MA
HASKELL, Marcus M.	ES: Chelsea, Suffolk Co., MA B: Chelsea, Suffolk Co., MA	MATHEWS, George William	ES: Worcester, Worcester Co., MA B: Worcester, Worcester Co., MA
HOLDEN, Henry	ES: Boston, Suffolk Co., MA B: Brighton, Sussex Co., England	MATTHEWS, David A.	ES: Boston, Suffolk Co., MA B: Boston, Suffolk Co., MA
HOLEHOUSE, James	ES: Fall River, Bristol Co., MA B: Stockport, Greater Manchester Co., England	MAXHAM, Lowell Mason	ES: Taunton, Bristol Co., MA B: Carver, Plymouth Co., MA
HOMAN, Conrad	ES: Boston, Suffolk Co., MA B: Roxbury, Suffolk Co., MA	MAYNARD, George Henry	ES: Boston, Suffolk Co., MA B: Waltham, Middlesex Co., MA
HOOKER, George White	ES: Boston, Suffolk Co., MA B: Salem, Washington Co., NY	McGAR, Owen	ES: Providence, Providence Co., RI B: North Attleboro, Bristol Co., MA
HOWE, William H.	ES: Boston, Suffolk Co., MA B: Haverhill, Essex Co., MA	McKINLEY, Daniel	ES: San Francisco, San Francisco Co., CA B: Boston, Suffolk Co., MA
HUNTER, Charles Adams	ES: Spencer, Worcester Co., MA B: Spencer, Worcester Co., MA	McNERNEY, David Herbert	ES: Fort Bliss, El Paso Co., TX B: Lowell, Middlesex Co., MA
INGALLS, Lewis J.	ES: Belvidere, Lamoille Co., VT B: Boston, Suffolk Co., MA	MILES, Nelson Appleton	ES: Roxbury, Suffolk Co., MA B: Westminster, Worcester Co., MA
JELLISON, Benjamin H.	ES: Newburyport, Essex Co., MA B: Newburyport, Essex Co., MA	MILLER, George	ES: Boston, Suffolk Co., MA B: Brooklyn, Kings Co., NY
JOHNS, Henry T.	ES: Hinsdale, Berkshire Co., MA B: Philadelphia, Philadelphia Co., PA	MORIARITY, John	ES: Boston, Suffolk Co., MA B: Huddersfield, Yorkshire, England
*JOHNSON, Elden Harvey	ES: East Weymouth, Norfolk Co., MA B: Bivale, Cumberland Co., NJ	MOSHER, Louis C.	ES: Brockton, Plymouth Co., MA B: Westport, Bristol Co., MA
KARPELES, Leopold	ES: Springfield, Hampden Co., MA B: Prague, Austria-Hungary	MOYLAN, Myles	ES: Essex, Essex Co., MA B: Amesbury, Essex Co., MA
KEATING, Daniel	ES: Boston, Suffolk Co., MA B: County Cork, Ireland	*MULLER, Joseph E.	ES: New York, NY B: Holyoke, Hampden Co., MA
LARKIN, David	ES: Boston, Suffolk Co., MA B: Cork, Ireland	MURPHY, Daniel J.	ES: Lowell, Middlesex Co., MA B: Philadelphia, Philadelphia Co., PA
LAWTON, John Sterling	ES: Boston, Suffolk Co., MA B: Bristol, Bristol Co., RI	MURPHY, Dennis J. F.	ES: Lowell, Middlesex Co., MA B: County Cork, Ireland
LEONARD, Edwin	ES: Agawam, Hampden Co., MA B: Agawam, Hampden Co., MA	*MURPHY, Frederick C.	ES: Weymouth, Norfolk Co., MA B: Boston, Suffolk Co., MA
LEWIS, William B.	ES: Boston, Suffolk Co., MA B: Boston, Suffolk Co., MA	MURPHY, Jeremiah J.	ES: Boston, Suffolk Co., MA B: County Cork, Ireland
LORD, William	ES: Lawrence, Essex Co., MA B: Bradford, England	NEAL, Solon D.	ES: Boston, Suffolk Co., MA B: Hanover, Grafton Co., NH
LOVERING, George Mason	ES: East Randolph, Norfolk Co., MA B: Springfield, NH	NEE, George Henry	ES: Boston, Suffolk Co., MA B: Boston, Suffolk Co., MA
LOWTHERS, James	ES: Boston, Suffolk Co., MA B: Boston, Suffolk Co., MA	NEILON, Frederick S.	ES: Watertown, Middlesex Co., MA B: Boston, Suffolk Co., MA
LUNT, Alphonso M.	ES: Cambridge, Middlesex Co., MA B: Berwick, York Co., ME	O'REGAN, Michael	ES: Boston, Suffolk Co., MA B: Fall River, Bristol Co., MA
LUTHER, James Hezikiah	ES: Taunton, Bristol Co., MA B: Dighton, Bristol Co., MA	OSBORNE, William	ES: Boston, Suffolk Co., MA B: Boston, Suffolk Co., MA
LYON, Frederick A.	ES: Burlington, Chittenden Co., VT B: Williamsburg, Hampshire Co., MA	OSBORNE, William Henry	ES: East Bridgewater, Plymouth Co., MA B: Scituate, Plymouth Co., MA
MacARTHUR Jr., Arthur	ES: Milwaukee, Milwaukee Co., WI B: Springfield, Hampden Co., MA	*OUELLETTE, Joseph R.	ES: Lowell, Middlesex Co., MA B: Lowell, Middlesex Co., MA
MacGILLIVARY, Charles Andrew	ES: Boston, Suffolk Co., MA B: Charlottetown, Prince Edward Island, Canada	PAYNE, Thomas H. L.	ES: Mendota, La Salle Co., IL B: Boston Suffolk Co., MA
		*PERKINS, Michael J.	ES: Boston, Suffolk Co., MA B: Boston, Suffolk Co., MA
		PINKHAM, Charles H.	ES: Worcester, Worcester Co., MA B: Grafton, Worcester Co., MA

PLUNKETT, Thomas	ES: West Boylston, Worcester Co., MA B: Ireland	TURPIN, James H.	ES: Boston, Suffolk Co., MA B: Easton, Bristol Co., MA
*PRUSSMAN, Ernest W.	ES: Brighton, Suffolk Co., MA B: Baltimore, Baltimore Co., MD	WALKER, Frank T. O.	ES: Burlington, Middlesex Co., MA B: South Boston, Suffolk Co., MA
PUTNAM, Winthrop D.	ES: Peoria, Peoria Co., IL B: Southbridge, Worcester Co., MA	WALSH, John	ES: Springfield, Hampden Co., MA B: Tipperary, Ireland
PYM, James	ES: Boston, Suffolk Co., MA B: Oxfordshire, England	WARD, James	ES: Boston, Suffolk Co., MA B: Quincy, Norfolk Co., MA
REED, Charles Wellington	ES: Malden, Middlesex Co., MA B: Charlestown, Suffolk Co., MA	WARREN, Francis Emroy	ES: Hinsdale, Berkshire Co., MA B: Hinsdale, Berkshire Co., MA
REGAN, Patrick J.	ES: Los Angeles, Los Angeles Co., CA B: Middleboro, Plymouth Co., MA	WELCH, Richard	ES: Williamstown, Berkshire Co., MA B: Ireland
RICE, Edmund	ES: Cambridge, Middlesex Ccounty, MA B: Brighton, Suffolk Co., MA	WHITMAN, Frank M.	ES: Ayersville, MA B: Woodstock, ME
RICH, Carlos H.	ES: Northfield, Franklin Co., MA B: Canada	WHITTLESEY, Charles White	ES: Pittsfield, Berkshire Co., MA B: Florence, Florence Co., WI
ROBBINS, Marcus M.	ES: Boston, Suffolk Co., MA B: Elba, Dodge Co., WI	WILBUR, William Hale	ES: Palmer, Hampden Co., MA B: Palmer, Hampden Co., MA
ROBINSON, John H.	ES: Roxbury, Suffolk Co., MA B: Ireland	*WILKIN, Edward G.	ES: Longmeadow, Hampden Co., MA B: Burlington, Chittenden Co., VT
ROBINSON, Joseph	ES: Boston, Suffolk Co., MA B: Montreal, Canada	WINTERBOTTOM, William	ES: Boston, Suffolk Co., MA B: Manchester, Greater Manchester Co., England
SAXTON Jr., Rufus	ES: Deerfield, Franklin Co., MA B: Greenfield, Franklin Co., MA	WITHINGTON, William Herbert	ES: Jackson, Jackson Co., MI B: Dorchester, Suffolk Co., MA
SCANLAN, Patrick	ES: Spencer, Worcester Co., MA B: Ireland	WOOD, Leonard	ES: Boston, Suffolk Co., MA B: Winchester, Cheshire Co., NH
SCHWENK, Martin	ES: Boston, Suffolk Co., MA B: Baden, Germany	WORTMAN, George G.	ES: Boston, Suffolk Co., MA B: Monckton, New Brunswick, Canada
SLADEN, Joseph Alton	ES: Lowell, Middlesex Co., MA B: Rockdale, England	WRIGHT, Samuel Cole	ES: Plympton, Plymouth Co., MA B: Plympton, Plymouth Co., MA
SMITH, Thomas	ES: Fort Adams, RI B: Boston, Suffolk Co., MA		
SNOW, Elmer A.	ES: Chicago, Cook Co., IL B: Hardwick, Worcester Co., MA		

U.S. Army Air Corps

*PEASE Jr., Harl	ES: Boston, Suffolk Co., MA B: Plymouth, Grafton Co., NH

U.S. Navy

STEWART, Benjamin F.	ES: Boston, Suffolk Co., MA B: Norfolk, Norfolk Co., VA	ARTHER, Matthew	ES: Boston, Suffolk Co., MA B: Scotland
STRONG, James N.	ES: Pittsfield, Berkshire Co., MA B: Pittsfield, Berkshire Co., MA	ATKINSON, Thomas E.	ES: MA B: Salem, Essex Co., MA
SWEATT, Joseph Sewell Gerrish	ES: Lowell, Middlesex Co., MA B: Boscawen, Merrimack Co., NH	BAKER, Benjamin F.	B: Dennis Port, Barnstable Co., MA
TABOR, William L. S.	ES: Concord, Merrimack Co., NH B: Metheun, Essex Co., MA	BARNUM, James	ES: MA B: MA
TAGGART, Charles A.	ES: Otis, Berkshire Co., MA B: Blandford, Hampden Co., MA	BAZAAR, Philip	ES: New Bedford, Bristol Co., MA B: Chile
TAYLOR, Wilbur Nelson	ES: Boston, Suffolk Co., MA B: Hampden, Penobscot Co., ME	BEYER, Albert	ES: Boston, Suffolk Co., MA B: Hanover, Germany
TERRY, John Darling	ES: Boston, Suffolk Co., MA B: Montville, ME	BICKFORD, John F.	ES: Boston, Suffolk Co., MA B: Tremont, ME
TOBIN, John Michael	ES: Boston, Suffolk Co., MA B: Waterford, Ireland	BOIS, Frank	ES: Northampton, Hampshire Co., MA B: Quebec, Canada
TOLAN, Frank	ES: Boston, Suffolk Co., MA B: Malone, Franklin Co., NY	BOND, William S.	ES: Boston, Suffolk Co., MA B: Boston, Suffolk Co., MA
TRACY, Charles H.	ES: Springfield, Hampden Co., MA B: Jewett City, New London Co., CT	BRADLEY, Alexander	ES: MA B: Boston, Suffolk Co., MA
TRUELL, Edwin M.	ES: Mantson, WI B: Lowell, Middlesex Co., MA	BRENNAN, Christopher	ES: Boston, Suffolk Co., MA B: Ireland
*TURNER, Charles William	ES: MA B: Boston, Suffolk Co., MA	BRESNAHAN, Patrick Francis	ES: VT B: Peabody, Essex Co., MA
*TURNER, William Bradford	ES: Garden City, Nassau Co., NY B: Dorchester, Suffolk Co., MA		

*CARON, Wayne Maurice	ES: Boston, Suffolk Co., MA B: Middleboro, Plymouth Co., MA	HORTON, Lewis Augustine	ES: Taunton, Bristol Co., MA B: Bristol Co., MA
CHANDLER, James B.	ES: Boston, Suffolk Co., MA B: Plymouth, Plymouth Co., MA	HOWARD, Peter	ES: Boston, Suffolk Co., MA B: France
CHARETTE, George	ES: Lowell, Middlesex Co., MA B: Lowell, Middlesex Co., MA	HUDNER Jr., Thomas Jerome	ES: Fall River, Bristol Co., MA B: Fall River, Bristol Co., MA
CONNOLLY, Michael	ES: MA B: Boston, Suffolk Co., MA	JAMES, John H.	ES: MA B: Boston, Suffolk Co., MA
CRAMEN, Thomas	ES: MA B: Ireland	JONES, John	ES: Acton, Middlesex Co., MA B: Bridgeport, Fairfield Co., CT
DEMPSEY, John	ES: Boston, Suffolk Co., MA B: Ireland	KELLEY, Thomas Gunning	ES: Boston, Suffolk Co., MA B: Boston, Suffolk Co., MA
DENEEF, Michael	ES: MA B: MA	KELLY, Francis	ES: MA B: Boston, Suffolk Co., MA
DENNIS, Richard	ES: Boston, Suffolk Co., MA B: Charlestown, Suffolk Co., MA	KENNA, Barnett	ES: Newburyport, Essex Co., MA B: Canterbury, Kent Co., England
*DEWERT, Richard David	ES: Taunton, Bristol Co., MA B: Taunton, Bristol Co., MA	KERSEY, Thomas Joseph	ES: MA B: St. Johns, Newfoundland, Canada
DORAN, John James	ES: MA B: Boston, Suffolk Co., MA	KRAMER, Franz	ES: MA B: Nierstein, Germany
DUNCAN, Adam	ES: Boston, Suffolk Co., MA B: ME	KYLE, Patrick J.	ES: MA B: Ireland
ENRIGHT, John	ES: MA B: Lynn, Essex Co., MA	LAFFEY, Bartlett	ES: Boston, Suffolk Co., MA B: Galway, County Galway, Ireland
FITZPATRICK, Thomas	ES: Taunton, Bristol Co., MA B: Canada	LOGAN, Hugh	ES: Boston, Suffolk Co., MA B: Ireland
FOY, Charles H.	ES: Springfield, Hampden Co., MA B: Portsmouth, Rockingham Co., NH	LYLE, Alexander Gordon	ES: MA B: Gloucester, Essex Co., MA
FRISBEE, John B.	ES: Brookline, Norfolk Co., MA B: Phippsburg, Sagadahoc Co., ME	LYONS, Thomas G.	ES: MA B: Salem, Essex Co., MA
GILE, Frank S.	ES: MA B: MA	MacKENZIE, John	ES: MA B: Bridgeport, Fairfield Co., CT
GILL, Freeman	ES: MA B: Boston, Suffolk Co., MA	MADDIN, Edward	ES: MA B: Newfoundland, Canada
GISBURNE, Edward Allen	ES: MA B: Providence, Providence Co., RI	MAHONEY, George	ES: Pennsylvania B: Worcester, Worcester Co., MA
GRADY, John	ES: MA B: New Brunswick, Canada	McDONALD, John	ES: Boston, Suffolk Co., MA B: Perth, Scotland
GRIFFITHS, John	ES: MA B: Wales	McFARLAND, John C.	ES: Boston, Suffolk Co., MA B: Boston, Suffolk Co., MA
GRISWOLD, Luke M.	ES: Springfield, Hampden Co., MA B: MA	MIHALOWSKI, John	ES: MA B: Worcester, Worcester Co., MA
HAMILTON, Thomas W.	ES: Weymouth, Norfolk Co., MA B: Scotland	MILLER, Harry Herbert	ES: MA B: Noel Shore, Hants Co., Nova Scotia, Canada
HANDRAN, John	ES: MA B: MA	MILLER, James	ES: Boston, Suffolk Co., MA B: Denmark
HARCOURT, Thomas	ES: MA B: Boston, Suffolk Co., MA	MILLER, Willard D.	ES: MA B: Noel Shore, Hants Co., Nova Scotia, Canada
HARRINGTON, Daniel C.	ES: MA B: Ireland	MOORE, George	ES: Boston, Suffolk Co., MA B: Philadelphia, Philadelphia Co., PA
HARRISON, George H.	ES: Somerset, Bristol Co., MA B: Middleton, Essex Co., MA	MOORE, William	ES: MA B: Boston, Suffolk Co., MA
HART, William	ES: MA B: MA	MULLER, Frederick	ES: MA B: Copenhagen, Denmark
HATHAWAY, Edward W.	ES: Plymouth, Plymouth Co., MA B: Plymouth, Plymouth Co., MA	NEWLAND, William D.	ES: MA B: Medway, Norfolk Co., MA
HAYES, John	ES: New Bedford, Bristol Co., MA B: Brogus, Newfoundland, Canada	O'BRIEN, Oliver Albert	ES: Boston, Suffolk Co., MA B: Boston, Suffolk Co., MA
HORTON, James	ES: MA B: England	O'CALLAHAN, Joseph Timothy	ES: MA B: Boston, Suffolk Co., MA
HORTON, James	ES: MA B: Boston, Suffolk Co., MA		

OLSEN, Anton	ES: MA B: Christiana (now Oslo), Norway
*OUELLET, David George	ES: Boston, Suffolk Co., MA B: Newton, Middlesex Co., MA
PARKER, William	ES: MA B: Boston, Suffolk Co., MA
PILE, Richard	ES: MA B: West Indies
PRANCE, George	ES: Boston, Suffolk Co., MA B: France
PRESTON, John	ES: Boston, Suffolk Co., MA B: Ireland
PROVINCE, George	ES: Boston, Suffolk Co., MA B: Newport, Newport Co., RI
RAMAGE, Lawson Paterson "Red"	ES: VT B: Monroe Bridge, Franklin Co., MA
REGAN, Jeremiah	ES: Boston, Suffolk Co., MA B: Boston, Suffolk Co., MA
RILLEY, John Phillip	ES: MA B: Allentown, Lehigh Co., PA
ROBERTS, Charles Church	ES: IL B: Newton, Middlesex Co., MA
ROUNTRY, John	ES: Boston, Suffolk Co., MA B: MA
RYAN, Francis Thomas	ES: MA B: MA
SADLER, William	ES: MA B: Boston, Suffolk Co., MA
SAUNDERS, James	ES: Boston, Suffolk Co., MA B: MA
SAVAGE, Auzella	ES: Boston, Suffolk Co., MA B: Anson, Somerset Co., ME
SEACH, William	ES: MA B: London, England
SEANOR, James	ES: New York, NY B: Boston, Suffolk Co., MA
SMITH, Frank Elmer	ES: VA B: Boston, Suffolk Co., MA
SMITH, John	ES: MA B: Boston, Suffolk Co., MA
STACY, William Bradford	ES: New Bedford, Bristol Co., MA B: Fall River, Bristol Co., MA
STANLEY, William A.	ES: MA B: MA
STEVENS, Daniel Dickerson	ES: MA B: La Grange, Fayette Co., TN
STICKNEY, Herman Osman	ES: MA B: Pepperell, Middlesex Co., MA
SULLIVAN, James F.	ES: MA B: Lowell, Middlesex Co., MA
SWANSON, John	ES: MA B: Gothenburg, Sweden
SWATTON, Edward	ES: Boston, Suffolk Co., MA B: New York, NY
SWEENEY, William	ES: MA B: Boston, Suffolk Co., MA
TALBOTT, William	ES: Boston, Suffolk Co., MA B: England
THIELBERG, Henry	ES: Dudley, Webster Co., MA B: Germany
THOMPSON, William	ES: Boston, Suffolk Co., MA B: Cape May Co., NJ
TROY, William	ES: MA B: Boston, Suffolk Co., MA
WILLEY, Charles H.	ES: MA B: East Boston, Suffolk Co., MA
WILLIAMS, Anthony	ES: Portsmouth, ME B: Plymouth, Plymouth Co., MA
WILLIAMS, Augustus	ES: MA B: Kristiansand, Norway
WILLIS, George	ES: MA B: Boston, Suffolk Co., MA
YOUNG, Horatio Nelson	ES: Boston, Suffolk Co., MA B: Calais, Washington Co., ME

U.S. Marine Corps

ADAMS, John Mapes	ES: MA B: Haverhill, Essex Co., MA
ADRIANCE, Harry Chapman	ES: MA B: Oswego, Oswego Co., NY
BURNES, James	ES: CA B: Worcester, Worcester Co., MA
*CADDY, William Robert	ES: MA B: Quincy, Norfolk Co., MA
CAMPBELL, Daniel J.	ES: Boston, Suffolk Co., MA B: Prince Edward Island, Canada
CARR, William Louis	ES: Boston, Suffolk Co., MA B: Peabody, Essex Co., MA
COONEY, James	ES: MA B: Limerick, Ireland
FORSTERER, Bruno Albert	ES: MA B: Koenigsberg, Germany
*HANSON, Robert Murray	ES: MA B: Lucknow, India
HILL, Walter Newell	ES: MA B: Haverhill, Essex Co., MA
HUNT, Martin	ES: Boston, Suffolk Co., MA B: County Mayo, Ireland
*JULIAN, Joseph Rodolph	ES: MA B: Sturbridge, Worcester Co., MA
KEARNEY, Michael	ES: MA B: Newmarket, County Cork, Ireland
McGINTY III, John James	ES: Laurel Bay, SC B: Boston, Suffolk Co., MA
MEREDITH, James	ES: Boston, Suffolk Co., MA B: Omaha, Douglas Co., NE
*MONEGAN Jr., Walter Carleton	ES: Seattle, King Co., WA B: Melrose, Middlesex Co., MA
NUGENT, Christopher	ES: MA B: County Cavan, Ireland
POPE, Everett Parker	ES: Quincy, Norfolk Co., MA B: Milton, Norfolk Co., MA
*POWER, John Vincent	ES: MA B: Worcester, Worcester Co., MA
PRENDERGAST, Thomas Francis	ES: MA B: Waterford, Ireland
SCANNELL, David John	ES: Boston, Suffolk Co., MA B: Boston, Suffolk Co., MA
SCOTT, Joseph Francis	ES: Cambridge, Middlesex Co., MA B: Boston, Suffolk Co., MA

SULLIVAN, Edward	ES: MA B: Cork, Ireland	*ESSEBAGGER Jr., John	ES: Holland, Ottawa Co., MI B: Holland, Ottawa Co., MI
*TALBOT, Ralph	ES: CT B: South Weymouth, Norfolk Co., MA	FALCONER, John A.	ES: Manchester, Washtenaw Co., MI B: Washtenaw, MI
*VITTORI, Joseph	ES: Beverly, Essex Co., MA B: Beverly, Essex Co., MA	FALL, Charles S.	ES: Hamburg, Livingston Co., MI B: Noble Co., IN
*WALSH, William Gary	ES: MA B: Roxbury, Suffolk Co., MA	FORMAN, Alexander A.	ES: Jonesville, Hillsdale Co., MI B: Scipio Township, Hillsdale Co., MI

MICHIGAN

U.S. Army

ALBER, Frederick	ES: Manchester, Washtenaw Co., MI B: Germany	FOX, Henry M.	ES: Coldwater, Branch Co., MI B: Trumbull, OH
AYERS, John G. K.	ES: Pekin, Tazwell Co., IL B: Washtenaw Co., MI	FRENCH, Samuel S.	ES: Gifford, Tuscola Co., MI B: Erie Co., NY
BALDWIN, Frank Dwight	ES: Constantine, St. Joseph Co., MI B: Manchester, Washtenaw Co., MI	FURLONG, Harold Arthur	ES: Detroit, Wayne Co., MI B: Pontiac, Oakland Co., MI
BALLEN, Frederick A.	ES: Adrian, Lenawee Co., MI B: Germany	GAUJOT, Antoine August	ES: Williamson, Mingo Co., WV B: Keweenaw, Baraga Co., MI
BARRELL, Charles L.	ES: Leighton, Allegan Co., MI B: Conquest, NY	GAUJOT, Julien Edmund	ES: Williamson, Mingo Co., WV B: Keweenaw, Baraga Co., MI
BENNETT, Orson W.	ES: Dubuque, Dubuque Co., IA B: Union City, Branch Co., MI	HACK, John	ES: Adrian, Lenawee Co., MI B: Germany
BICKFORD, Henry H.	ES: Middleport, Niagara Co., NY B: Ypsilanti, Washtenaw Co., MI	HADLEY, Cornelius Minor	ES: Adrian, Lenawee Co., MI B: Sandy Creek, Oswego Co., NY
BONDSTEEL, James Leroy	ES: Detroit, Wayne Co., MI B: Jackson, Jackson Co., MI	HAIGHT, Sidney	ES: Goodland, MI B: Reading, Hillsdale Co., MI
BRANDLE, Joseph E.	ES: Colon, St. Joseph Co., MI B: Seneca Co., OH	HARRINGTON, John	ES: Cleveland, Cuyahoga Co., OH B: Detroit, Wayne Co., MI
*BRYANT, William Maud	ES: Detroit, Wayne Co., MI B: Cochran, Bleckley Co., GA	HARTZOG, Joshua B.	ES: Detroit, Wayne Co., MI B: Paulding Co., OH
CAWETZKA, Charles	ES: Wayne, Wayne Co., MI B: Detroit, Wayne Co., MI	HASTINGS, Smith H.	ES: Coldwater, Branch Co., MI B: Quincy, Branch Co., MI
CHANDLER, Stephen Edwin	ES: Grandby, Oswego Co., NY B: Convis, MI	HERINGTON, Pitt B.	ES: Tipton, Cedar Co., IA B: MI
CHAPMAN, Amos	ES: Fort Supply, Indian Territory (Oklahoma) B: Kalamazoo, Kalamazoo Co., MI	HILL, Edward	ES: Detroit, Wayne Co., MI B: Liberty, Sullivan Co., NY
CHRISTIANCY, James Isaac	ES: Monroe Co., MI B: Monroe Co., MI	HILLOCK, Marvin C.	ES: Detroit, Wayne Co., MI B: Port Huron, St. Clair Co., MI
CLUTE, George Washington	ES: Marathon, MI B: Marathon, MI	HODGES, Addison J.	ES: Adrian, Lenawee Co., MI B: Hillsdale, Hillsdale Co., MI
COLE, Gabriel	ES: New Salem, Washtenaw Co., MI B: Chenango Co., NY	HOLLAND, David	ES: Fort Leavenworth, Leavenworth Co., KS B: Dearborn, Wayne Co., MI
CUSTER, Thomas Ward	ES: Monroe, Monroe Co., MI B: New Rumley, Harrison Co., OH	HOLTON, Charles Maynard	ES: Battle Creek, Calhoun Co., MI B: Potter, Yates Co., NY
CUTCHEON, Byron M.	ES: Ypsilanti, Washtenaw Co., MI B: Pembroke, Suncook Co., NH	IRWIN, Patrick	ES: Ann Arbor, Washtenaw Co., MI B: Ireland
DePUY, Charles H.	ES: St. Louis, St. Louis Co., MO B: Sherman, MI	JARVIS, Frederick	ES: Hudson, Lenawee Co., MI B: Essex Co., NY
DODD, Robert Fulton	ES: Detroit, Wayne Co., MI B: Canada	JOHNSON, Dwight Hal	ES: Detroit, Wayne Co., MI B: Detroit, Wayne Co., MI
DOUGHERTY, William	ES: Philadelphia, Philadelphia Co., PA B: Detroit, Wayne Co., MI	JOHNSON, Henry	ES: Detroit, Wayne Co., MI B: Boydton, Mecklenburg Co., VA
DROWLEY, Jesse Ray	ES: Wayne Co., MI B: St. Charles, Saginaw Co., MI	JOHNSON Jr., Oscar Godfrey	ES: Foster City, Dickinson Co., MI B: Foster City, Dickinson Co., MI
DUNNE, James	ES: Chicago, Cook Co., IL B: Detroit, Wayne Co., MI	KEEN, Joseph S.	ES: Detroit, Wayne Co., MI B: Vale, Guernsey, England
ELDRIDGE, George H.	ES: Detroit, Wayne Co., MI B: Sackets Harbor, Jefferson Co., NY	KELLEY, Andrew John	ES: Ypsilanti, Washtenaw Co., MI B: La Grange Co., IN
		KEMP, Joseph Bell	ES: Sault Ste. Marie, Chippewa Co., MI B: Lima, Allen Co., OH
		LAMBERS, Paul Ronald	ES: Holland, Ottawa Co., MI B: Holland, Ottawa Co., MI

LANE, Morgan D.	ES: Allegan, Allegan Co., MI B: Monroe, Orange Co., NY	SHEPARD, Irwin	ES: Chelsea, Washtenaw Co., MI B: Skaneateles, Onondaga Co., NY
LEMON, Peter Charles	ES: Tawas City, Iosco Co., MI B: Toronto, Canada	SIDMAN, George Dallas	ES: Owosso, Shiawassee Co., MI B: Rochester, Monroe Co., NY
LEONARD, William	ES: Detroit, Wayne Co., MI B: Ypsilanti, Washtenaw Co., MI	SJOGREN, John Carleton	ES: Rockford, Kent Co., MI B: Rockford, Kent Co., MI
LEWIS, Henry	ES: Adrian, Lenawee Co., MI B: Belleville, Wayne Co., MI	SMITH, Alonzo	ES: Jonesville, Hillsdale Co., MI B: Niagara Co., NY
LUCE, Moses Augustine	ES: Adrian, Lenawee Co., MI B: Payson, Adams Co., IL	SMITH, William H.	ES: Cincinnati, Hamilton Co., OH B: Lapeer, Lapeer Co., MI
McCONNELL, James	ES: Detroit, Wayne Co., MI B: Syracuse, Onondaga Co., NY	SWIFT, Frederic William	ES: Detroit, Wayne Co., MI B: Mansfield Center, Tolland Co., CT
McFALL, Daniel Robert	ES: Ypsilanti, Washtenaw Co., MI B: Niagara Co., NY	SYPE, Peter	ES: Adrian, Lenawee Co., MI B: Monroe Co., MI
McHALE, Alexander U.	ES: Muskegon, Muskegon Co., MI B: Ireland	THATCHER, Charles M.	ES: Grand Haven, Ottawa Co., MI B: Coldwater, Branch Co., MI
MENTER, John William	ES: Detroit, Wayne Co., MI B: Palmer, NY	*THOMAS, William H.	ES: Ypsilanti, Washtenaw Co., MI B: Wynne, Cross Co., AR
MORSE, Benjamin	ES: Grand Rapids, Kent Co., MI B: Livingston, Columbia Co., NY	THOMPSON, Charles Augustus	ES: Kalamazoo, Kalamazoo Co., MI B: Perrysburg, Wood Co., OH
*MOYER, Donald Raymond	ES: Keego Harbor, Oakland Co., MI B: Pontiac, Oakland Co., MI	TOBAN, James W.	ES: Northfield, MI B: Northfield, MI
MUNDELL, Walter L.	ES: Dallas, MI B: MI	VLUG, Dirk John	ES: Grand Rapids, Kent Co., MI B: Maple Lake, Wright Co., MN
NASH, Henry H.	ES: Adrian, Lenawee Co., MI B: Lenawee Co., MI	WALKER, John	ES: Detroit, Wayne Co., MI B: Leon, France
NOLL, Conrad	ES: Ann Arbor, Washtenaw Co., MI B: Germany	WARD, William Henry	ES: Adrian, Lenawee Co., MI B: Adrian, Lenawee Co., MI
NORTON, Elliott Malloy	ES: Cooper, MI B: CT	WATSON, Joseph	ES: Chicago, Cook Co., IL B: Union City, Branch Co., MI
NORTON, John R.	ES: Grand Rapids, Kent Co., MI B: St. John's Parish, Roscommon, County Ballaugh, Ireland	*WETZEL, Walter C.	ES: Roseville, Macomb Co., MI B: Huntington, Cabell Co., WV
PETERS, Henry Carlton	ES: Adrian, Lenawee Co., MI B: Monroe Co., MI	WHEATON, Loyd	ES: Peoria, Peoria Co., IL B: Penfield, MI
PLANT, Henry E.	ES: Cockery, MI B: Oswego Co., NY	WHITNEY, William G.	ES: Quincy, Branch Co., MI B: Allen, Hillsdale Co., MI
POLOND, Alfred	ES: Lapeer, Lapeer Co., MI B: Lapeer, Lapeer Co., MI	*WIGLE, Thomas W.	ES: Detroit, Wayne Co., MI B: INpolis, Marion Co., IN
POWERS, Thomas	ES: Detroit, Wayne Co., MI B: New York, NY	WILDER, Wilber Elliott	ES: Detroit, Wayne Co., MI B: Atlas, Genesee Co., MI
*POXON, Robert Leslie	ES: Detroit, Wayne Co., MI B: Detroit, Wayne Co., MI	WILLCOX, Orlando Bolivar	ES: Detroit, Wayne Co., MI B: Detroit, Wayne Co., MI
RANNEY, George E.	ES: Grand Rapids, Kent Co., MI B: Batavia, Genesee Co., NY	WITHINGTON, William Herbert	ES: Jackson, Jackson Co., MI B: Dorchester, Suffolk Co., MA
RHODES, Julius Dexter	ES: Springville, Erie Co., NY B: Monroe Co., MI	WOODRUFF, Alonzo	ES: Ionia, Ionia Co., MI B: Ionia, Ionia Co., MI
*ROBINSON, James H.	ES: Victor, MI B: Oakland Co., MI	*YNTEMA, Gordon Douglas	ES: Detroit, Wayne Co., MI B: Bethesda, Montgomery Co., MD
ROMEYN, Henry	ES: MI B: Galen, Wayne Co., NY	YOUNG, Benjamin F.	ES: Detroit, Wayne Co., MI B: Canada
SANCRAINTE, Charles Francis	ES: Monroe, Monroe Co., MI B: Monroe, Monroe Co., MI	*ZUSSMAN, Raymond	ES: Detroit, Wayne Co., MI B: Hamtramck, Wayne Co., MI
SAVACOOL, Edwin F.	ES: Marshall, Calhoun Co., MI B: Jackson, Jackson Co., MI		
SEIBERT, Lloyd Martin	ES: Salinas, Monterey Co., CA B: Caledonia, Kent Co., MI		
SHAFTER, William Rufus	ES: Galesburg, Kalamazoo Co., MI B: Kalamazoo, Kalamazoo Co., MI		
SHAW, George Clymer	ES: Washington, D.C. B: Pontiac, Oakland Co., MI		

U.S. Army Air Corps/U.S. Air Force

*CRAW, Demas Thurlow	ES: MI B: Traverse City, Grand Traverse Co., MI
LINDBERGH Jr., Charles Augustus	ES: Little Falls, Morrison Co., MN B: Detroit, Wayne Co., MI
*SEBILLE, Louis Joseph	ES: Chicago, Cook Co., IL B: Harbor Beach, Huron Co., MI

SMITH Sr., Maynard Harrison ES: Cairo, MI
B: Cairo, MI

U.S. Navy

CHARETTE, William Richard ES: Ludington, Mason Co., MI
B: Ludington, Mason Co., MI

CRONIN, Cornelius ES: MI
B: Ireland

*FLAHERTY, Francis Charles ES: MI
B: Charlotte, Eaton Co., MI

*HAMMERBERG, Owen Francis Patrick ES: MI
B: Daggett, Menominee Co., MI

STODDARD, James ES: Detroit, Wayne Co., MI
B: Port Robinson, Canada (West)

ZUIDERVELD, William ES: MI
B: MI

U.S. Marine Corps

*CANNON, George Ham ES: MI
B: Webster Groves, St. Louis Co., MO

DEWEY, Duane Edgar ES: Muskegon, Muskegon Co., MI
B: Grand Rapids, Kent Co., MI

GLOWIN, Joseph Anthony ES: MI
B: Detroit, Wayne Co., MI

SIMANEK, Robert Ernest ES: Detroit, Wayne Co., MI
B: Detroit, Wayne Co., MI

*SKINNER Jr., Sherrod Emerson ES: East Lansing, Ingham Co., MI
B: Hartford, Hartford Co., CT

SMITH, Albert Joseph ES: MI
B: Calumet, Houghton Co., MI

*STOCKHAM, Fred William ES: New York, NY
B: Detroit, Wayne Co., MI

*WILLIAMS, Dewayne Thomas ES: Saint Clair, Saint Clair Co., MI
B: Brown City, Sanilac Co., MI

MINNESOTA

U.S. Army

ALBEE, George Emerson ES: Owatonna, Steele Co., MN
B: Lisbon, Grafton Co., NH

BARRICK, Jesse ES: Fort Snelling, St. Paul Co., MN
B: Columbiana Co., OH

BELL, Harry ES: Minneapolis, Hennepin Co., MN
B: Milwaukee, Milwaukee Co., WI

*BIANCHI, Willibald Charles ES: New Ulm, Brown Co., MN
B: New Ulm, Brown Co., MN

*BLANCHFIELD, Michael Reinert ES: Chicago, Cook Co., IL
B: Minneapolis, Hennepin Co., MN

BURGER, Joseph ES: Crystal Lake, Hennepin Co., MN
B: Austria or Swiss Tyrol

BURKARD, Oscar R. ES: Fort Snelling, St. Paul Co., MN
B: Baden Achern, Germany

CILLEY, Clinton Albert ES: Sasioja, MN
B: Rockingham Co., NH

CLARK, William A. ES: Shelbyville, MN
B: PA

COLALILLO, Michael "Mike" ES: Duluth, St. Louis Co., MN
B: Hibbing, St. Louis Co., MN

DAVIS, Charles P. ES: Valley City, Barnes Co., ND
B: Long Prairie, Todd Co., MN

FLANNIGAN, James ES: Fort Snelling, St. Paul Co., MN
B: Canada

GERE, Thomas Parke ES: Fort Snelling, St. Paul Co., MN
B: Wellsburg, Chemung Co., NY

HANNA, Milton ES: Henderson, Sibley Co., MN
B: Licking Co., OH

HAWKS, Lloyd C. ES: Park Rapids, Hubbard Co., MN
B: Becker, Sherburne Co., MN

HAWTHORNE, Harry Leroy ES: KY
B: MN

HOLMES, Lovilo N. ES: Mankato, Blue Earth Co., MN
B: Farmersville, Cattaraugus Co., NY

HUGGINS, Eli Lundy ES: MN
B: Schuyler Co., IL

MALLON, George H. ES: Minneapolis, Hennepin Co., MN
B: Ogden, Riley Co., KS

McMILLIAN, Albert Walter ES: Jefferson Barracks, MO
B: Stillwater, Washington Co., MN

MERRITT, John G. ES: Fort Snelling, St. Paul Co., MN
B: New York, NY

MONTROSE, Charles H. ES: New York, NY
B: St. Paul, Ramsey Co., MN

MORGAN, George Horace ES: Minneapolis, Hennepin Co., MN
B: St. Catherines, Canada

O'BRIEN, Henry D. ES: St. Anthony Falls, MN
B: Colois, ME

*OLSON, Kenneth Lee ES: Minneapolis, Hennepin Co., MN
B: Willmar, Kandiyohi Co., MN

*PAGE, John Upshur Dennis ES: St. Paul, Ramsey Co., MN
B: Malahi Island, Luzon, Philippine Islands

PAY, Byron E. ES: Mankato, Blue Earth Co., MN
B: LeRoy Township, Jefferson Co., NY

PICKLE, Alonzo H. ES: Dover, Olmsted Co., MN
B: Canada

*PRUDEN, Robert Joseph ES: Minneapolis, Hennepin Co., MN
B: St.Paul, Ramsey Co., MN

*RABEL, Laszlo ES: Minneapolis, Hennepin Co., MN
B: Budapest, Hungary

REED, Axel Hayford ES: Glencoe, McLeod Co., MN
B: Hartford, Oxford Co., ME

RUDOLPH, Donald Eugene ES: Minneapolis, Hennepin Co., MN
B: South Haven, Wright Co., MN

SHERMAN, Marshall ES: St. Paul, Ramsey Co., MN
B: Burlington, Chittenden Co., VT

VALE, John ES: Rochester, Olmsted Co., MN
B: London, England

VLUG, Dirk John ES: Grand Rapids, Kent Co., MI
B: Maple Lake, Wright Co., MN

*WAYRYNEN, Dale Eugene ES: Minneapolis, Hennepin Co., MN
B: Moose Lake, Carlton Co., MN

WELCH, Charles H. ES: Fort Snelling, St. Paul Co., MN
B: New York, NY

WILSON, William O. ES: St. Paul, Ramsey Co., MN
B: Hagerstown, Washington Co., MD

*WOLD, Nels T. ES: Minnewaukan, Benson Co., ND
B: Winger, Polk Co., MN

WRIGHT, Samuel ES: Mankato, Blue Earth Co., MN
B: IN

U.S. Army Air Corps/U.S. Air Force

LINDBERGH Jr., Charles Augustus	ES: Little Falls, Morrison Co., MN B: Detroit, Wayne Co., MI
THORSNESS, Leo Keith	ES: Walnut Grove, Redwood Co., MN B: Walnut Grove, Redwood Co., MN

U.S. Navy

DAVIS, Raymond Erwin	ES: Puget Sound, WA B: Mankato, Blue Earth Co., MN
NELSON, Oscar Frederick	ES: MN B: Minneapolis, Hennepin Co., MN
*RUD, George William	ES: MN B: Minneapolis, Hennepin Co., MN
*VAN VALKENBURGH, Franklin	ES: WI B: Minneapolis, Hennepin Co., MN

U.S. Marine Corps

CATLIN, Albertus Wright	ES: MN B: Gowanda, Cattaraugus Co., NY
*COURTNEY Jr., Henry Alexius	ES: MN B: Duluth, St. Louis Co., MN
CUKELA, Louis	ES: Minneapolis, Hennepin Co., MN B: Spalato, Yugoslavia
DYER, Jesse Farley	ES: MN B: St. Paul, Ramsey Co., MN
*FLEMING, Richard Eugene	ES: MN B: St. Paul, Ramsey Co., MN
*HAUGE Jr., Louis James	ES: MN B: Ada, Norman Co., MN
*KRAUS, Richard Edward	ES: MN B: Chicago, Cook Co., IL
*La BELLE, James Dennis	ES: MN B: Columbia Heights, Hennepin Co., MN
SORENSON, Richard Keith	ES: Anoka, Anoka Co., MN B: Anoka, Anoka Co., MN

MISSISSIPPI

U.S. Army

BARFOOT, Van Thomas	ES: Carthage, Leake Co., MS B: Edinburg, Leake Co., MS
BLACK, John Charles	ES: Danville, Vermillion Co., IL B: Lexington, Holmes Co., MS
*DIAMOND, James H.	ES: Gulfport, Harrison Co., MS B: New Orleans, Orleans Co., LA
DORLEY, August	ES: Natchez, Adams Co., MS B: Germany
*HANSON, Jack G.	ES: Galveston, Galveston Co., TX B: Escatawpa, Jackson Co., MS
HEARD, John William	ES: MS B: Woodstock, MS
*HENRY, Robert T.	ES: Greenville, Washington Co., MS B: Greenville, Washington Co., MS
*JORDON, Mack A.	ES: Collins, Covington Co., MS B: Collins, Covington Co., MS
LEE, Hubert Louis	ES: Leland, Washington Co., MS B: Arburg, MO
LINDSEY Sr., Jake William	ES: Lucedale, George Co., MS B: Isney, AL
PITTMAN, John Albert	ES: Carrollton, Carroll Co., MS B: Carrollton, Carroll Co., MS
SLATON, James Daniel	ES: Gulfport, Harrison Co., MS B: Laurel, Jones Co., MS
WELBORN, Ira Clinton	ES: Mico, MS B: Mico, MS

U.S. Navy

BROWN, Wilson	ES: MS River, MS B: Natchez, Adams Co., MS
FREEMAN, Martin	ES: Ship's Island, Jackson Co., MS B: Germany
MADISON, James Jonas	ES: MS B: Jersey City, Hudson Co., NJ

U.S. Marine Corps

COMMISKEY Sr., Henry Alfred	ES: Hattiesburg, Forrest Co., MS B: Hattiesburg, Forrest Co., MS
*WHEAT, Roy Mitchell	ES: Jackson, Hinds Co., MS B: Moselle, Jones Co., MS
WILSON Jr., Louis Hugh	ES: MS B: Brandon, Rankin Co., MS

MISSOURI

U.S. Army

*ADAMS, William Edward	ES: Kansas City, Clay Co., MO B: Casper, Natrona Co., WY
ANDERSON, James	ES: St. Louis, St. Louis Co., MO B: East Canada
BARGER, Charles Denver	ES: Stotts City, Lawrence Co., MO B: Mount Vernon, Lawrence Co., MO
BARKLEY, John Lewis	ES: Blairstown, Henry Co., MO B: Blairstown, Henry Co., MO
BIEGER, Charles	ES: St. Louis, St. Louis Co., MO B: Wiesbaden, Germany
*BRANT, Abram B.	ES: St. Louis, St. Louis Co., MO B: New York, NY
BRYAN, William C.	ES: St. Louis, St. Louis Co., MO B: Zanesville, Muskingum Co., OH
BURR, Herbert Hoover	ES: Kansas City, Clay Co., MO B: St. Joseph, Buchanan Co., MO
CABLE, Joseph A.	ES: Madison, Dane Co., WI B: Cape Girardeau, Cape Girardeau Co., MO
DePUY, Charles H.	ES: St. Louis, St. Louis Co., MO B: Sherman, MI
ELLIS, Michael B.	ES: East St. Louis, St. Clair Co., IL B: St. Louis, St. Louis Co., MO
ELWOOD, Edwin L.	ES: San Jose, Santa Clara Co., CA B: St. Louis, St Louis Co., MO
EPPS, Joseph L.	ES: Oklahoma Indian Territory B: Jamestown, Moniteau Co., MO
EVANS, William	ES: St. Louis, St. Louis Co., MO B: Annagh, Ireland
FLYNN, James Edward	ES: St. Louis, St. Louis Co., MO B: Pittsfield, Pike Co., IL
FOLLETT, Joseph Leonard	ES: St. Louis, St. Louis Co., MO B: Newark, Essex Co., NJ
FORAN, Nicholas	ES: St. Louis, St. Louis Co., MO B: County Waterford, Ireland

FORREST, Arthur J.	ES: Hannibal, Marion Co., MO B: St. Louis, St. Louis Co., MO	PHILLIPS, Samuel D.	ES: St. Louis, St. Louis Co., MO B: Butler Co., OH
FORSYTH, Thomas Hall	ES: St. Louis, St. Louis Co., MO B: Hartford, Hartford Co., CT	PHOENIX, Edwin	ES: St. Louis, St. Louis Co., MO B: St. Louis, St. Louis Co., MO
FRIZZELL, Henry F.	ES: Pilot Knob, Iron Co., MO B: Madison Co., MO	PORTER, Ambrose	ES: Rockport, Atchison Co., MO B: Allegany Co., MD
FUNK, Jesse N.	ES: Calhan, El Paso Co., CO B: New Hampton, Harrison Co., MO	RAY, Charles W.	ES: St. Louis, St. Louis Co., MO B: Pensacola, Yancey Co., NC
GEIGER, George	ES: St. Louis, St. Louis Co., MO B: Cincinnati, Hamilton Co., OH	*RIORDAN, Paul F.	ES: Kansas City, Clay Co., MO B: Charles City, Floyd Co., IA
GREBE, M. R. William	ES: St. Louis, St. Louis Co., MO B: Hildesheim, Germany	SCHROETER, Charles	ES: St. Louis, St. Louis Co., MO B: Lindberg, Hanover, Germany
GUERIN, Fitz W.	ES: St. Louis, St. Louis Co., MO B: New York, NY	SCOTT, Robert B.	ES: St. Louis, St. Louis Co., MO B: Washington Co., NY
GWYNNE, Nathaniel McClean	ES: Fairmount, MO B: Urbana, Champaign Co., OH	SHEPPARD, Charles	ES: St. Louis, St. Louis Co., MO B: Rocky Hill, Hartford Co., CT
HALL, William Preble	ES: Huntsville, Randolph Co., MO B: Randolph Co., MO	SHINGLE, John Henry	ES: St. Louis, St. Louis Co., MO B: Philadelphia, Philadelphia Co., PA
HAMMEL, Henry A.	ES: St. Louis, St. Louis Co., MO B: Germany	*SISLER, George Kenton	ES: Dexter, Stoddard Co., MO B: Dexter, Stoddard Co., MO
*HAMMOND Jr., Lester	ES: Quincy, Adams Co., IL B: Wayland, Clark Co., MO	*SKINKER, Alexander Rives	ES: St. Louis, St. Louis Co., MO B: St. Louis, St. Louis Co., MO
HARDING, Mosher A.	ES: St. Louis, St. Louis Co., MO B: West Canada	SMITH, Charles E.	ES: St. Louis, St. Louis Co., MO B: Auburn, Cayuga Co., NY
HATLER, M. Waldo	ES: Neosho, Newton Co., MO B: Bolivar, Polk Co., MO	*SPECKER, Joe C.	ES: Odessa, Lafayette Co., MO B: Odessa, Lafayette Co., MO
HILL, Frank E.	ES: St. Louis, St. Louis Co., MO B: Mayfield, WI	STEINER, Christian	ES: St. Louis, St. Louis Co., MO B: Wurttemberg, Germany
HUNT, Louis T.	ES: Jefferson Co., MO B: Montgomery Co., IN	*TAYLOR, Bernard	ES: Washington, D.C. B: St. Louis, St. Louis Co., MO
*KANELL, Billie Gene	ES: Poplar Bluff, Butler Co., MO B: Poplar Bluff, Butler Co., MO	TAYLOR, Charles	ES: St. Louis, St. Louis Co., MO B: Baltimore, Baltimore Co., MD
*KELLEY, Ova Art	ES: Norwood, Wright Co., MO B: Norwood, Wright Co., MO	TROGDEN, Howell G.	ES: St. Louis, St. Louis Co., MO B: Cedar Falls, Randolph Co., NC
KIRBY, Dennis Thomas	ES: St. Louis, St. Louis Co., MO B: Niagara Falls, Niagara Co., NY	TURNER, Harold Leo	ES: Seminole, Seminole Co., OK B: Aurora, Lawrence Co., MO
LEE, Hubert Louis	ES: Leland, Washington Co., MS B: Arburg, MO	VOKES, Leroy H.	ES: St. Louis, St. Louis Co., MO B: Lake Co., IL
*LONG, Charles Richard	ES: Kansas City, Clay Co., MO B: Kansas City, Clay Co., MO	WAGNER, John W.	ES: St. Louis, St. Louis Co., MO B: Clear Spring, Washington Co., MD
McCAMMON, William Wallace	ES: Montgomery City, Montgomery Co., MO B: Shippensburg, Cumberland Co., PA	WEISS, Enoch R.	ES: St. Louis, St. Louis Co., MO B: Kosciusko Co., IN
McGANN, Michael A.	ES: St. Louis, St. Louis Co., MO B: County Roscommon, Ireland	WHERRY, William Macky	ES: St. Louis, St. Louis Co., MO B: St. Louis, St. Louis Co., MO
McMILLIAN, Albert Walter	ES: Jefferson Barracks, MO B: Stillwater, Washington Co., MN	WILLS, Henry	ES: St. Louis, St. Louis Co., MO B: Gracon, VA
MILLER, Archie	ES: St. Louis, St. Louis Co., MO B: Fort Sheridan, Lake Co., IL	*WILSON, Richard G.	ES: Cape Girardeau, Cape Girardeau Co., MO B: Marion, Williamson Co., IL
MYERS, Fred	ES: St. Louis, St. Louis Co., MO B: Brunswick, Germany	WORTICK, Joseph	ES: Hannibal, Marion Co., MO B: Fayette Co., PA
NEDER, Adam	ES: St. Louis, St. Louis Co., MO B: Bavaria, Germany		
*PEDEN, Forrest E.	ES: Wathena, Doniphan Co., KS B: St. Joseph, Buchanan Co., MO		
PENTZER, Patrick Henry	ES: Gillespie, Macoupin Co., IL B: Marion Co., MO		
PESCH, Joseph M.	ES: St. Louis, St. Louis Co., MO B: Grossleiton, Prussia		
*PETERSEN, Danny John	ES: Kansas City, Clay Co., MO B: Horton, Brown Co., KS		

U.S. Army Air Corps/U.S. Air Force

FLEMING, James Phillip	ES: Pullman, Whitman Co., WA B: Sedalia, Pettis Co., MO
HOWARD, James Howell	ES: St. Louis, St. Louis Co., MO B: Canton, China
JOHNSON, Leon William	ES: Moline, Elk Co., KS B: Columbia, Boone Co., MO

U.S. Navy

BALCH, John Henry	ES: Kansas City, Clay Co., MO B: Edgerton, Johnson Co., KS

BALLARD, Donald Everett	ES: Kansas City, Clay Co., MO B: Kansas City, Clay Co., MO	
CARY, Robert Webster	ES:ton, Cooper Co., MO B: Kansas City, Clay Co., MO	
CRANDALL, Orson Leon	ES: CT B: St. Joseph, Buchanan Co., MO	
*DAVID, Albert Leroy	ES: MO B: Maryville, Nodaway Co., MO	
FUQUA, Samuel Glenn	ES: Laddonia, Audrain Co., MO B: Laddonia, Audrain Co., MO	
HOLTZ, August	ES: St. Louis, St. Louis Co., MO B: St. Louis, St. Louis Co., MO	
McGUIRE, Fred Henry	ES: Gordonville, Cape Girardeau Co., MO B: Gordonville, Cape Girardeau Co., MO	
O'HARE, Edward Henry "Butch"	ES: St. Louis, St. Louis Co., MO B: St. Louis, St. Louis Co., MO	
TOWNSEND, Julius Curtis	ES: Athens, MO B: Athens, MO	

U.S. Marine Corps

BUTTON, William Robert	ES: St. Louis, St. Louis Co., MO B: St. Louis, St. Louis Co., MO
*CANNON, George Ham	ES: MI B: Webster Groves, St. Louis Co., MO
*COLE, Daril Samuel	ES: Esther, San Francois Co., MO B: Flat River, San Francois Co., MO
*CREEK, Thomas Elbert	ES: Amarillo, Potter Co., TX B: Joplin, Jasper Co., MO
*DAVENPORT, Jack Arden	ES: Mission, Johnson Co., KS B: Kansas City, Clay Co., MO
GAIENNIE, Louis Rene	ES: St. Louis, St. Louis Co., MO B: St. Louis, St. Louis Co., MO
HANNEKEN, Herman Henry	ES: St. Louis, St. Louis Co., MO B: St. Louis, St. Louis Co., MO
*PHILLIPS, George	ES: Labadie, Franklin Co., MO B: Rich Hill, Vernon Co., MO
SITTER, Carl Leonard	ES: Pueblo, Pueblo Co., CO B: Syracuse, Morgan Co., MO

MONTANA

U.S. Army

*GALT, William Wylie	ES: Stanford, Judith Basin Co., MT B: Geyser, Judith Basin Co., MT
McLENNON, John	ES: Fort Ellis, MT B: Fort Belknap, TX
MORAN, John E.	ES: Cascade Co., MT B: Vernon, Windham Co., VT
*PARRISH, Laverne	ES: Ronan, Lake Co., MT B: Knox City, MT
POWERS, Leo J.	ES: Alder Gulch, Madison Co., MT B: Anselmo, Custer Co., NE
SCHAUER, Henry	ES: Scobey, Daniels Co., MT B: Clinton, Custer Co., OK
SMITH, Cornelius Cole	ES: Helena, Lewis & Clark Co., MT B: Tucson, Pima Co., AZ

U.S. Marine Corps

*RUHL, Donald Jack	ES: MT B: Columbus, Stillwater Co., MT

NEBRASKA

U.S. Army

BERG, George Francis	ES: Fort Omaha, Douglas Co., NE B: Mount Erie, Wayne Co., IL
*BOOKER, Robert D.	ES: Callaway, Custer Co., NE B: Callaway, Custer Co., NE
CO-RUX-TE-CHOD-ISH (MAD BEAR)	ES: Columbus, Platte Co., NE B: NE
CODY, William Frederick "Buffalo Bill"	ES: Fort McPherson, NE B: Scott Co., IA
*COWAN, Richard Eller	ES: Wichita, Sedgwick Co., KS B: Lincoln, Lancaster Co., NE
*FOUS, James William	ES: Omaha, Douglas Co., NE B: Omaha, Douglas Co., NE
HAGEMEISTER, Charles Cris	ES: Lincoln, Lancaster Co., NE B: Lincoln, Lancaster Co., NE
*HIBBS, Robert John	ES: Des Moines, Polk Co., IA B: Omaha, Douglas Co., NE
HOLDERMAN, Nelson Miles	ES: Santa Ana, Orange Co., CA B: Trumbull, Clay Co., NE
KIRKWOOD, John A.	ES: North Platte Barracks, Lincoln Co., NE B: Allegheny City, Allegheny Co., PA
KOUMA, Ernest Richard	ES: Dwight, Butler Co., NE B: Dwight, Butler Co., NE
*LINDSTROM, Floyd K.	ES: Colorado Springs, El Paso Co., CO B: Holdrege, Phelps Co., NE
LOHNES, Frank W.	ES: Omaha, Douglas Co., NE B: Oneida Co., NY
POWERS, Leo J.	ES: Alder Gulch, Madison Co., MT B: Anselmo, Custer Co., NE
*SHUGHART, Randall David	ES: Newville, Cumberland Co., PA B: Lincoln, Lancaster Co., NE
VIFQUAIN, Victor	ES: Salene Co., NE B: Brussels, Belgium

U.S. Navy

EHLE, John Walter	ES: NE B: Kearney, Buffalo Co., NE
GRAVES, Ora	ES: NE B: Las Animas, Bent Co., CO
KERREY, Joseph Robert	ES: Omaha, Douglas Co., NE B: Lincoln, Lancaster Co., NE
*PARLE, John Joseph	ES: NE B: Omaha, Douglas Co., NE
SCHMIDT, Otto Diller	ES: NE B: Blair, Washington Co., NE
VOLZ, Jacob	ES: NE B: Sutton, Clay Co., NE

U.S. Marine Corps

*BAUER, Harold William "Indian Joe"	ES: NE B: Woodruff, KS
*COKER, Ronald Leroy	ES: Denver, Denver Co., CO B: Alliance, Box Butte Co., NE
*GOMEZ, Edward	ES: Omaha, Douglas Co., NE B: Omaha, Douglas Co., NE
*HANSEN, Dale Merlin	ES: NE B: Wisner, Cuming Co., NE

*KEITH, Miguel	ES: Omaha, Douglas Co., NE B: San Antonio, Bexar Co., TX
MEREDITH, James	ES: Boston, Suffolk Co., MA B: Omaha, Douglas Co., NE

NEVADA

U.S. Army

BLAIR, James	ES: Camp Winfield Scott, Humbolt Co., NV B: Schuyler Co., PA

U.S. Navy

*VAN VOORHIS, Bruce Avery	ES: NV B: Aberdeen, Grays Harbor Co., WA

NEW HAMPSHIRE

U.S. Army

ALBEE, George Emerson	ES: Owatonna, Steele Co., MN B: Lisbon, Grafton Co., NH
APPLETON, William H.	ES: Portsmouth, Rockingham Co., NH B: Chichester, NH
BARKER, Nathaniel C.	ES: Manchester, Hillsborough Co., NH B: Piermont, Grafton Co., NH
BATCHELDER, Richard Napoleon	ES: Manchester, Hillsborough Co., NH B: Lake Village (Now Lakeport), Belknap Co., NH
BOUTWELL, John W.	ES: West Lebanon, Grafton Co., NH B: Hanover, Grafton Co., NH
BRADY, James	ES: Kingston, Rockingham Co., NH B: Boston, Suffolk Co., MA
CAMP, Carlton N.	ES: Hanover, Grafton Co., NH B: Hanover, Grafton Co., NH
CARR, Chris	ES: Manchester, Hillsborough Co., NH B: Manchester, Hillsborough Co., NH
CILLEY, Clinton Albert	ES: Sasioja, MN B: Rockingham Co., NH
COHN, Abraham	ES: Campton, Grafton Co., NH B: Guttentag, Silesia, Prussia
COLBY, Carlos W.	ES: Madison Co., IL B: Merrimack, Hillsborough Co., NH
COPP, Charles Dearborn	ES: Nashua, Hillsborough Co., NH B: Warren Co., NH
COUGHLIN, John	ES: Manchester, Hillsborough Co., NH B: VT
CRAIG, Samuel Henry	ES: Chicago, Cook Co., IL B: New Market, Rockingham Co., NH
CUTCHEON, Byron M.	ES: Ypsilanti, Washtenaw Co., MI B: Pembroke, Suncook Co., NH
*DILBOY, George	ES: Keene, Cheshire Co., NH B: Greece
DILLON, Michael A.	ES: Wilton, Hillsborough Co., NH B: Chelmsford, Middlesex Co., MA
DOW, George P.	ES: Manchester, Hillsborough Co., NH B: Atkinson, Rockingham Co., NH
ELLIOTT, Russell C.	ES: Boston, Suffolk Co., MA B: Concord, Merrimack Co., NH
EVANS, Ira Hobart	ES: Barre, Washington Co., VT B: Piermont, Grafton Co., NH
*FALLS, Benjamin Frank	ES: Lynn, Essex Co., MA B: Portsmouth, Rockingham Co., NH
GAGE, Richard J.	ES: Ottawa, La Salle Co., IL B: Grafton Co., NH
GOODALL, Francis Henry	ES: Bath, Grafton Co., NH B: Bath, Grafton Co., NH
GRIMES, Edward P.	ES: Boston, Suffolk Co., MA B: Dover, Strafford Co., NH
*HADDOO Jr., John	ES: Columbus, Cherokee Co., KS B: Hooksett, Merrimack Co., NH
HADLEY, Osgood Towns	ES: Peterborough, Hillsborough Co., NH B: Nashua, Hillsborough Co., NH
HARRIS, Moses	ES: Boston, Suffolk Co., MA B: Andover, Merrimack Co., NH
KIMBALL, Joseph	ES: Ironton, Lawrence Co., OH B: Littleton, Grafton Co., NH
KNIGHT, Charles H.	ES: Keene, Cheshire Co., NH B: Keene, Cheshire Co., NH
LITTLE, Henry F. W.	ES: Manchester, Hillsborough Co., NH B: Manchester, Hillsborough Co., NH
LOVERING, George Mason	ES: East Randolph, Norfolk Co., MA B: Springfield, NH
NEAL, Solon D.	ES: Boston, Suffolk Co., MA B: Hanover, Grafton Co., NH
NOLAN, John J.	ES: Nashua, Hillsborough Co., NH B: Thurles, County Tipperary, Ireland
PINGREE, Samuel E.	ES: Hartford, Windsor Co., VT B: Salisbury, Merrimack Co., NH
ROBIE, George Frank	ES: Manchester, Hillsborough Co., NH B: Candia, Rockingham Co., NH
ROWE, Henry Walker	ES: Candia, Rockingham Co., NH B: Candia, Rockingham Co., NH
SIMONS, Charles Jenks	ES: Exeter, Rockingham Co., NH B: Bombay, India
SWEATT, Joseph Sewell Gerrish	ES: Lowell, Middlesex Co., MA B: Boscawen, Merrimack Co., NH
TABOR, William L. S.	ES: Concord, Merrimack Co., NH B: Metheun, Essex Co., MA
TILTON, William	ES: Hanover, Grafton Co., NH B: St. Albans, Franklin Co., VT
VEAZEY, Wheelock Graves	ES: Springfield, Windsor Co., VT B: Brentwood, Coos Co., NH
WILCOX, William H.	ES: Lempster, Sullivan Co., NH B: Lempster, Sullivan Co., NH
WILKINS, Leander A.	ES: Northumberland, NH B: Lancaster, Coos Co., NH
WOOD, Leonard	ES: Boston, Suffolk Co., MA B: Winchester, Cheshire Co., NH
WOODBURY, Eri Davidson	ES: St. Johnsbury, Caledonia Co., VT B: Francistown, Hillsborough Co., NH

U.S. Army Air Corps

*PEASE Jr., Harl	ES: Boston, Suffolk Co., MA B: Plymouth, Grafton Co., NH

U.S. Navy

ANDERSON, Robert N.	ES: NH B: Ireland
FOY, Charles H.	ES: Springfield, Hampden Co., MA B: Portsmouth, Rockingham Co., NH

FRANKLIN, Frederick H.	ES: NH B: Portsmouth, Rockingham Co., NH	DRAKE, James Madison	ES: Elizabeth, Union Co., NJ B: Washington Valley, Somerset Co., NJ
GEORGE, Daniel Griffin	ES: NH B: Plaistow, Rockingham Co., NH	*DUTKO, John W.	ES: Riverside, Burlington Co., NJ B: Dilltown, Indiana Co., PA
HAM, Mark G.	ES: Portsmouth, Rockingham Co., NH B: Portsmouth, Rockingham Co., NH	EGGERS, Alan Louis	ES: Summit, Union Co., NJ B: Saranac Lake, Franklin Co., NY
HAWKINS, Charles	ES: Portsmouth, Rockingham Co., NH B: Scotland	ENGLISH, Edmund	ES: Newark, Essex Co., NJ B: New York, NY
HOLYOKE, William Edward	ES: IL B: Groveton, Coos Co., NH	FALLON, Thomas Timothy	ES: Freehold, Monmouth Co., NJ B: County Galway, Ireland
MELVILLE, Charles	ES: NH B: Dover, Strafford Co., NH	FESQ, Frank E.	ES: Newark, Essex Co., NJ B: Germany
MERTON, James F.	ES: Portsmouth, Rockingham Co., NH B: Cheshire, England	FOLLETT, Joseph Leonard	ES: St. Louis, St. Louis Co., MO B: Newark, Essex Co., NJ
O'KANE, Richard Hetherington	ES: Durham, Strafford Co., NH B: Dover, Strafford Co., NH	FOLLY, William H.	ES: New York, NY B: Bergen Co., NJ
SMITH, William	ES: Concord, Merrimack Co., NH B: Ireland	*GERTSCH, John Gerry	ES: Buffalo, Erie Co., NY B: Jersey City, Hudson Co., NJ
TODD, Samuel	ES: NH B: Portsmouth, Rockingham Co., NH	GRANT, Gabriel	ES: Trenton, Mercer Co., NJ B: Newark, Essex Co., NJ

U.S. Marine Corps

*BARKER, Jedh Colby	ES: Park Ridge, Bergen Co., NJ B: Franklin, Merrimack Co., NH	GREGG, Stephen Raymond	ES: Bayonne, Hudson Co., NJ B: New York, NY
WEST, Walter Scott	ES: NH B: Bradford, Merrimack Co., NH	HEYL, Charles Pettit heath	ES: Camden, Camden Co., NJ B: Philadelphia, Philadelphia Co., PA

NEW JERSEY

U.S. Army

BART, Frank J.	ES: Newark, Essex Co., NJ B: New York, NY	HOOPER, William B.	ES: Jersey City, Hudson Co., NJ B: Willimantic, Windham Co., CT
BEECH, John P.	ES: Trenton, Mercer Co., NJ B: Stratfordshire Co., England	HOPKINS, Charles F.	ES: Trenton, Mercer Co., NJ B: Hope, Warren Co., NJ
*BENJAMIN Jr., George	ES: Carney's Point, Salem Co., NJ B: Philadelphia, Philadelphia Co., PA	*HOSKING Jr., Charles Ernest	ES: Fort Dix, Mercer Co., NJ B: Ramsey, Bergen Co., NJ
BRADBURY, Sanford	ES: Washington, D.C. B: Newton, Sussex Co., NJ	HOWARD, James	ES: Brooklyn, Kings Co., NY B: Newton, Sussex Co., NJ
BRANT Jr., William	ES: Trenton, Mercer Co., NJ B: Elizabeth, Union Co., NJ	JACKSON, James	ES: NJ B: NJ
BREWSTER, Andre Walker	ES: Philadelphia, Philadelphia Co., PA B: Hoboken, Hudson Co., NJ	JACOBS, Jack Howard	ES: Trenton, Mercer Co., NJ B: Brooklyn, Kings Co., NY
*BRITTIN, Nelson Vogel	ES: Audubon, Camden Co., NJ B: Audubon, Camden Co., NJ	*JOHNSON, Elden Harvey	ES: East Weymouth, Norfolk Co., MA B: Bivale, Cumberland Co., NJ
BURKE, Francis Xavier	ES: Jersey City, Hudson Co., NJ B: New York, NY	JOHNSTON Sr., William James	ES: Colchester, New London Co., CT B: Trenton, Mercer Co., NJ
CARMIN, Isaac Harrison	ES: New Lexington, Perry Co., OH B: Monmouth Co., NJ	LATHAM, John Cridland	ES: Rutherford, Bergen Co., NJ B: Windemere, Cumbria Co., England
CARPENTER, Louis Henry	ES: Philadelphia, Philadelphia Co., PA B: Glassboro, Gloucester Co., NJ	LOCKE, Lewis	ES: Jersey City, Hudson Co., NJ B: Clintonville, Essex Co., NY
CLANCY, James T.	ES: Camden, Camden Co., NJ B: Albany, Albany Co., NY	MAGEE, William	ES: Newark, Essex Co., NJ B: Newark, Essex Co., NJ
CONNER, Richard	ES: Burlington, Burlington Co., NJ B: Philadelphia, Philadelphia Co., PA	*MAY, Martin O.	ES: Phillipsburg, Warren Co., NJ B: Phillipsburg, Warren Co., NJ
*COURSEN, Samuel Streit	ES: Madison, Morris Co., NJ B: Madison, Morris Co., NJ	*McGRAW, Francis Xavier	ES: Camden, Camden Co., NJ B: Philadelphia, Philadelphia Co., PA
CUMMINGS, Amos Jay	ES: Irvington, Essex Co., NJ B: Conklin, Broome Co., NY	MEAGHER, John William	ES: Jersey City, Hudson Co., NJ B: Jersey City, Hudson Co., NJ
DONELLY, John S.	ES: Jersey City, Hudson Co., NJ B: County Kerry, Ireland	MILES, Louis Wardlaw	ES: Princeton, Mercer Co., NJ B: Baltimore, Baltimore Co., MD
		*MINUE, Nicholas	ES: Carteret, Middlesex Co., NJ B: Sedden, Poland
		*O'SHEA, Thomas E.	ES: Summit, Union Co., NJ B: New York, NY
		ORESKO, Nicholas	ES: Bayonne, Hudson Co., NJ B: Bayonne, Hudson Co., NJ

OSS, Albert	ES: Newark, Essex Co., NJ B: Belgium	WOOD, Richard H.	ES: Woodburn, Macoupin Co., IL B: Canton, NJ
PARKER, James	ES: Newark, Essex Co., NJ B: Newark, Essex Co., NJ	ZABITOSKY, Fred William	ES: Trenton, Mercer Co., NJ B: Trenton, Mercer Co., NJ
PITMAN, George J.	ES: Philadelphia, Philadelphia Co., PA B: Recklestown, NJ	*U.S. Army Air Corps*	
PORTER, William	ES: Trenton, Mercer Co., NJ B: New York, NY	*CASTLE, Frederick Walker	ES: Mountain Lakes, Morris Co., NJ B: Manila, Philippine Island
QUINN, Alexander M.	ES: Philadelphia, Philadelphia Co., PA B: Passaic, Passaic Co., NJ	*McGUIRE Jr., Thomas Buchanan	ES: Sebring, Highlands Co., FL B: Ridgewood, Bergen Co., NJ
*SADOWSKI, Joseph John	ES: Perth Amboy, Middlesex Co., NJ B: Perth Amboy, Middlesex Co., NJ	*U.S. Navy*	
SAGELHURST, John Christopher	ES: Jersey City, Hudson Co., NJ B: Buffalo, Erie Co., NY	BEHNE, Frederick	ES: NJ B: Lodi, Bergen Co., NJ
*SAWELSON, William	ES: Harrison, Hudson Co., NJ B: Newark, Essex Co., NJ	BLUME, Robert	ES: NJ B: Pittsburgh, Allegheny Co., PA
SEWELL, William Joyce	ES: Camden, Camden Co., NJ B: Castlebar, County Mayo, Ireland	BREEMAN, George	ES: NJ B: Passaic, Passaic Co., NJ
SHEERIN, John	ES: Baltimore, Baltimore Co., MD B: Camden Co., NJ	*CHOLISTER, George Robert	ES: NJ B: Camden, Camden Co., NJ
SMITH, Theodore F.	ES: Harrisburg, Dauphin Co., PA B: Rahway, Union Co., NJ	COONEY, Thomas C.	ES: NJ B: Westport, Nova Scotia, Canada
SOUTHARD, David	ES: Florence, Burlington Co., NJ B: Ocean Co., NJ	CRILLEY, Frank William	ES: PA B: Trenton, Mercer Co., NJ
STEWART, George W.	ES: Salem, Salem Co., NJ B: Salem, Salem Co., NJ	DAVIS, John	ES: NJ B: Cedarville, Cumberland Co., NJ
STREILE, Christian	ES: Jersey City, Hudson Co., NJ B: Germany	EILERS, Henry A.	ES: NJ B: Newark, Essex Co., NJ
SULLIVAN, Thomas	ES: Newark, Essex Co., NJ B: County Meath, Ireland	HAMBERGER, William Francis	ES: NJ B: Newark, Essex Co., NJ
TAYLOR, Anthony	ES: Philadelphia, Philadelphia Co., PA B: Burlington, Burlington Co., NJ	KANE, Thomas	ES: NJ B: Jersey City, Hudson Co., NJ
TAYLOR, Forrester L.	ES: Beverly, Burlington Co., NJ B: Philadelphia, Philadelphia Co., PA	MADISON, James Jonas	ES: MS B: Jersey City, Hudson Co., NJ
THOMPKINS, William H.	ES: Paterson, Passaic Co., NJ B: Paterson, Passaic Co., NJ	MAGER, George Frederick	ES: NJ B: Phillipsburg, Warren Co., NJ
*THORNE, Horace Marvin	ES: Keyport, Monmouth Co., NJ B: Keansburg, Monmouth Co., NJ	PARKER, Alexander	ES: NJ B: Kensington, NJ
TILTON, Henry Remsen	ES: Jersey City, Hudson Co., NJ B: Barnegat, Ocean Co., NJ	PETERSEN, Carl Emil	ES: NJ B: Hamburg, Germany
TITUS, Charles	ES: New Brunswick, Middlesex Co., NJ B: Millstone, NJ	SHERIDAN, James	ES: New York, NY B: Newark, Essex Co., NJ
TOFFEY, John James	ES: Hudson, Hudson Co., NJ B: Quaker Hill, Dutchess Co., NY	SIEGEL, John Otto	ES: NJ B: Milwaukee, Milwaukee Co., WI
TOMPKINS, Aaron B.	ES: Jersey City, Hudson Co., NJ B: Orange, Essex Co., NJ	STRAHAN, Robert	ES: NJ B: NJ
TRAYNOR, Andrew	ES: Rome, Oneida Co., NY B: Newark, Essex Co., NJ	SWEENEY, Robert Augustus	ES: NJ B: Montserrat, West Indies
VAN IERSEL, Ludovicus M. M.	ES: Glen Rock, Bergen Co., NJ B: Dussen, Holland	TEYTAND, August P.	ES: NJ B: Santa Cruz, West Indies
VEALE, Moses	ES: Philadelphia, Philadelphia Co., PA B: Bridgeton, Cumberland Co., NJ	THOMPSON, William	ES: Boston, Suffolk Co., MA B: Cape May Co., NJ
WANTON, George Henry	ES: Paterson, Passaic Co., NJ B: Paterson, Passaic Co., NJ	*TOMICH, Peter	ES: NJ B: Prolog, Austria
*WATTERS, Charles Joseph	ES: Fort Dix, Mercer Co., NJ B: Jersey City, Hudson Co., NJ	VAN ETTEN, Hudson	ES: NJ B: Port Jervis, Orange Co., NY
WILSON, Charles E.	ES: Hatborough, Montgomery Co., NJ B: Bucks Co., PA	WEEKS, Charles H.	ES: NJ B: NJ
WILSON, John	ES: Jersey City, Hudson Co., NJ B: England	WHITFIELD, Daniel	ES: NJ B: Newark, Essex Co., NJ

WILLIAMS II, John	ES: NY B: Elizabethtown, NJ		
YOUNG, Edward B.	ES: NJ B: Bergen, Hudson Co., NJ		

U.S. Marine Corps

*BARKER, Jedh Colby	ES: Park Ridge, Bergen Co., NJ B: Franklin, Merrimack Co., NH
BASILONE, John "Manila Jonn"	ES: NJ B: Buffalo, Erie Co., NY
CAFFERATA Jr., Hector Albert	ES: Dover, Morris Co., NJ B: New York, NY
*CONNOR, Peter Spencer	ES: South Orange, Essex Co., NJ B: Orange, Essex Co., NJ
FIELD, Oscar Wadsworth	ES: NY B: Jersey City, Hudson Co., NJ
FRYER, Eli Thompson	ES: NJ B: Hightstown, Mercer Co., NJ
HARVEY, Harry	ES: NJ B: New York, NY
PFEIFER, Louis Fred	ES: NJ B: Philadelphia, Philadelphia Co., PA
PRESTON, Herbert Irving	ES: NJ B: Berkeley, Union Co., NJ
ROUH, Carlton Robert	ES: NJ B: Lindenwold, Camden Co., NJ
SHIVERS, John	ES: NJ B: Canada
SIGLER, Franklin Earl	ES: Little Falls, Passaic Co., NJ B: Glen Ridge, Essex Co., NJ
TOMLIN, Andrew J.	ES: NJ B: Goshen, Cape May Co., NJ

NEW MEXICO

U.S. Army

*FERNANDEZ, Daniel	ES: Albuquerque, Bernalillo Co., NM B: Albuquerque, Bernalillo Co., NM
JENNINGS, Delbert Owen	ES: San Francisco, San Francisco Co., CA B: Silver City, Grant Co., NM
*MARTINEZ, Joe P.	ES: Ault, Weld Co., CO B: Taos, Taos Co., NM
MILLER, Franklin Douglas	ES: Albuquerque, Bernalillo Co., NM B: Elizabeth City, Pasquotank Co., NC
MIYAMURA, Hiroshi	ES: Gallup, McKinley Co., NM B: Gallup, McKinley Co., NM
*MOON Jr., Harold Herman	ES: Gardena, Los Angeles Co., CA B: Albuquerque, Bernalillo Co., NM
OLIVER, Francis	ES: Fort Filmore, NM B: Baltimore, Baltimore Co., MD
ROCCO, Louis Richard	ES: Los Angeles, Los Angeles Co., CA B: Albuquerque, Bernalillo Co., NM
RUIZ, Alejandro Renteria	ES: Carlsbad, Eddy Co., NM B: Loving, Eddy Co., NM
SCOTT, Robert Sheldon	ES: Santa Fe, Santa Fe Co., NM B: Washington, D.C.
STANLEY, Eben	ES: Santa Fe, Santa Fe Co., NM B: Decatur Co., IA
*VALDEZ, Jose F.	ES: Pleasant Grove, Utah Co., UT B: Governador, NM

U.S. Army Air Corps

*WALKER, Kenneth Newton	ES: Denver, Denver Co., CO B: Cerrillos, Santa Fe Co., NM

U.S. Marine Corps

*BONNYMAN Jr., Alexander "Sandy"	ES: NM B: Atlanta, Fulton Co., GA
*WORLEY, Kenneth Lee	ES: Fresno, Fresno Co., CA B: Farmington, San Juan Co., NM

NEW YORK

U.S. Army

ALLEN, James	ES: Potsdam, St. Lawrence Co., NY B: Ireland
ANDERSON, Bruce	ES: Albany, Albany Co., NY B: Mexico City, Mexico
*ARCHER, Lester	ES: Plattsburgh, Clinton Co., NY B: Fort Ann, Washington Co., NY
*ASHLEY Jr., Eugene	ES: New York, NY B: Wilmington, New Hanover Co., NC
AUSTIN, William Grafton	ES: New York, NY B: Galveston, Galveston Co., TX
BAKER, John	ES: Brooklyn, Kings Co., NY B: Hessen, Germany
*BAKER Jr., Thomas Alexander	ES: Troy, Rensselaer Co., NY B: Troy, Rensselaer Co., NY
BANCROFT, Neil	ES: Chicago, Cook Co., IL B: Oswego, Oswego Co., NY
BARNUM, Henry Alanson	ES: Syracuse, Onondaga Co., NY B: Jamesville, Onondaga Co., NY
BARRELL, Charles L.	ES: Leighton, Allegan Co., MI B: Conquest, NY
BARRETT, Carlton William	ES: Albany, Albany Co., NY B: Fulton, Oswego Co., NY
BARRETT, Richard	ES: Buffalo, Erie Co., NY B: County Mayo, Ireland
BARRY, Augustus	ES: New York, NY B: Ireland
BART, Frank J.	ES: Newark, Essex Co., NJ B: New York, NY
BATES, Delavan	ES: Mohawk, Herkimer Co., NY B: Schoharie Co., NY
BEDDOWS, Richard	ES: Flushing, Queens Co., NY B: Liverpool, Merseyside Co., England
BEEBE, William Sully	ES: Philadelphia, Philadelphia Co., PA B: Ithaca, Tompkins Co., NY
*BEGLEY, Terrence	ES: Albany, Albany Co., NY B: Ireland
BEIKIRCH, Gary Burnell	ES: Buffalo, Erie Co., NY B: Rochester, Monroe Co., NY
BELL, Bernard Pious	ES: New York, NY B: Grantsville, Calhoun Co., WV
BELL, James	ES: Troy, Rensselaer Co., NY B: County Antrim, Ireland
BENJAMIN, John Francis	ES: Newburgh, Orange Co., NY B: Orange Co., NY
BENJAMIN, Samuel Nicholl	ES: New York, NY B: New York, NY

BICKFORD, Henry H.	ES: Middleport, Niagara Co., NY B: Ypsilanti, Washtenaw Co., MI	BUTLER, Edmond Thomas	ES: Brooklyn, Kings Co., NY B: Clonmel, County Tipperary, Ireland
BIRDSALL, Horatio L.	ES: Keokuk, Lee Co., IA B: Monroe Co., NY	BUTTERFIELD, Daniel Adams	ES: Washington, D.C. B: Utica, Oneida Co., NY
BLUNT, John W.	ES: Four Corners, Chatham, Columbia Co., NY B: Columbia Co., NY	*BUTTS, John Edward	ES: Buffalo, Erie Co., NY B: Medina, Orleans Co., NY
BOEHM, Peter Martin	ES: Brooklyn, Kings Co., NY B: Albany, Albany Co., NY	BYRNE, Denis	ES: New York, NY B: Wexford, Ireland
BOWEN, Chester Bennett	ES: Nunda, Livingston Co., NY B: Nunda, Livingston Co., NY	CADWELL, Luman Lewis	ES: Troy, Rensselaer Co., NY B: Nanticoke Springs, Broome Co., NY
BOWEN, Emmer	ES: Hampshire, Kane Co., IL B: Erie Co., NY	CALKIN, Ivers S.	ES: Willsboro, Essex Co., NY B: Elizabethtown, Essex Co., NY
*BOYCE Jr., George W. G.	ES: Cornwall, Orange Co., NY B: New York, NY	CALL, Donald Marshall	ES: France B: New York, NY
BRADLEY, Thomas Wilson	ES: Walden, Orange Co., NY B: Sheffield, Yorkshire Co., England	CAMPBELL, James A.	ES: New York, NY B: Brooklyn, Kings Co., NY
BRANAGAN, Edward	ES: New York, NY B: County Louth, Ireland	*CAREY, Hugh	ES: New York, NY B: Ireland
*BRANT, Abram B.	ES: St. Louis, St. Louis Co., MO B: New York, NY	CAREY, James Lemuel	ES: Syracuse, Onondaga Co., NY B: Jamesville, Onondaga Co., NY
BREWER, William John	ES: Newburgh, Orange Co., NY B: Putnam Co., NY	CARMAN, Warren	ES: Victor, Ontario Co., NY B: England
BRINGLE, Andrew	ES: Buffalo, Erie Co., NY B: Buffalo, Erie Co., NY	CARR, Eugene Asa	ES: Hamburg, Erie Co., NY B: Boston Corner, Erie Co., NY
BRONNER, August Frederick	ES: New York, NY B: Germany	CARTER, John Joice	ES: Nunda, Livingston Co., NY B: Troy, Rensselaer Co., NY
BROSNAN, John	ES: New York, NY B: Ireland	CARTER, William Harding	ES: New York, NY B: Nashville, Davidson Co., TN
BROWN, Henri Le Fevre	ES: Ellicott, Erie Co., NY B: Jamestown, Chautauqua Co., NY	CARUANA, Orlando Emanuel	ES: New York, NY B: Ca Valletta, Malta
BROWN, James	ES: New York, NY B: Wexford, Ireland	CASEY, James Seaman	ES: New York, NY B: Philadelphia, Philadelphia Co., PA
BROWN Jr., Edward	ES: New York, NY B: Ireland	CATLIN, Isaac Swartwood	ES: Owego, Tioga Co., NY B: Near Owego, Tioga Co., NY
*BROWN Jr., Morris	ES: Geneva, Ontario Co., NY B: Hammondsport, Steuben Co., NY	CAYER, Ovila	ES: Malone, Franklin Co., NY B: St. Remi, Canada
BROWNELL, Francis Edwin	ES: Troy, Rensselaer Co., NY B: Troy, Rensselaer Co., NY	CHANDLER, Stephen Edwin	ES: Grandby, Oswego Co., NY B: Convis, MI
BRUSH, George Washington	ES: Huntington, Suffolk Co., NY B: West Hills, Suffolk Co., NY	CHAPIN, Alaric B.	ES: Pamelia, Jefferson Co., NY B: Ogdensburg, St. Lawrence Co., NY
BRUTON, Christopher C.	ES: Riga, Monroe Co., NY B: Ireland	*CHARLTON, Cornelius H.	ES: Bronx Co., NY B: East Gulf, Raleigh Co., WV
BUCHA, Paul William	ES: USMA West Point, Orange Co., NY B: Washington, D.C.	CLANCY, James T.	ES: Camden, Camden Co., NJ B: Albany, Albany Co., NY
*BUCHANAN, George A.	ES: Canaoaigua, Ontario Co., NY B: Victor, Ontario Co., NY	CLANCY, John E.	ES: Vancouver Barracks, Clark Co., WA B: New York, NY
*BUCKLEY, Denis	ES: Avon, Livingston Co., NY B: Canada	CLAPP, Albert Adams	ES: Painesville, Lake Co., OH B: Pompey, Onondaga Co., NY
BURK, E. Michael	ES: Troy, Rensselaer Co., NY B: Ireland	CLARK, Francis J.	ES: Salem, NY B: Whitehall, Washington Co., NY
BURK, Thomas	ES: Harrisburgh, Lewis Co., NY B: Lewis Co., NY	CLARK, Harrison	ES: Chatham, Columbia Co., NY B: Chatham, Columbia Co., NY
BURKE, Francis Xavier	ES: Jersey City, Hudson Co., NJ B: New York, NY	CLARKE, Dayton P.	ES: Hermon, St. Lawrence Co., NY B: DeKalb, St. Lawrence Co., NY
BURKE, Richard	ES: New York, NY B: Tipperary, Ireland	CLEVELAND, Charles Franklin	ES: Elmira, Chemung Co., NY B: Hartford, Washington Co., NY
BURKE, Thomas	ES: New York, NY B: Ireland	COEY, James	ES: Oswego, Oswego Co., NY B: New York, NY
BURRITT, William Wallace	ES: Chicago, Cook Co., IL B: Campbell, Steuben Co., NY		

COLE, Gabriel	ES: New Salem, Washtenaw Co., MI B: Chenango Co., NY	*DIETZ, Robert H.	ES: Kingston, Ulster Co., NY B: Kingston, Ulster Co., NY
COLLINS Sr., Thomas D.	ES: Liberty, Sullivan Co., NY B: Neversink Flats, Sullivan Co., NY	DILGER, Hubert	ES: New York, NY B: Germany
*COLYER, Wilbur E.	ES: South Ozone, Queens Co., NY B: Brooklyn, Kings Co., NY	DIX, Drew Dennis	ES: Denver, Denver Co., CO B: West Point, Orange Co., NY
COMPSON, Hartwell B.	ES: Seneca Falls, Seneca Co., NY B: Seneca Falls, Seneca Co., NY	*DOANE, Stephen Holden	ES: Albany, Albany Co., NY B: Beverly, Essex Co., MA
CONBOY, Martin	ES: New York, NY B: Roscommon, Ballagh Co., Ireland	DOCKUM, Warren C.	ES: Plattsburgh, Clinton Co., NY B: Clintonville, Clinton Co., NY
CONNORS, James	ES: Canajoharie, Montgomery Co., NY B: Kildare, Ireland	DODDS, Edward Edwin	ES: Rochester, Monroe Co., NY B: Canada
CORLISS, Stephen Potter	ES: Albany, Albany Co., NY B: Albany, Albany Co., NY	DOLLOFF, Charles W.	ES: St. Johnsbury, Caledonia Co., VT B: Parishville, St. Lawrence Co., NY
COSGRIFF, Richard H.	ES: Wapello, Louisa Co., IA B: Dunkirk Co., NY	DONALDSON, Michael Aloyisius	ES: Haverstraw, Rockland Co., NY B: Haverstraw, Rockland Co., NY
COYNE, John Nicholas	ES: New York, NY B: New York, NY	DONAVAN, Cornelius	ES: New York, NY B: County Cork, Ireland
CROSIER, William Henry Harrison	ES: Skaneateles, Onondaga Co., NY B: Skaneateles, Onondaga Co., NY	DONLON, Roger Hugh Charles	ES: Saugerties, Ulster Co., NY B: Saugerties, Ulster Co., NY
CROSS, James Edwin	ES: Batavia, Genesee Co., NY B: Darien, Genesee Co., NY	DONOGHUE, Timothy	ES: New York, NY B: Ireland
CROWLEY, Michael	ES: Rochester, Monroe Co., NY B: Rochester, Monroe Co., NY	DONOVAN, William Joseph "Wild Bill"	ES: Buffalo, Erie Co., NY B: Buffalo, Erie Co., NY
CULLEN, Thomas	ES: New York, NY B: Ireland	DOODY, Patrick H.	ES: New York, NY B: Ireland
CUMMINGS, Amos Jay	ES: Irvington, Essex Co., NJ B: Conklin, Broome Co., NY	DORE, George H.	ES: West Bloomfield, Ontario Co., NY B: England
CUNNINGHAM, Charles	ES: New York, NY B: Hudson, Columbia Co., NY	*DUNN, Parker F.	ES: Albany, Albany Co., NY B: Albany, Albany Co., NY
CURRAN, Richard J.	ES: Seneca Falls, Seneca Co., NY B: Ennis, County Clare, Ireland	DURHAM, John S.	ES: Malone, Fond Du Lac Co., WI B: New York, NY
CURREY, Francis Sherman "Frank"	ES: Hurleyville, Sullivan Co., NY B: Loch Sheldrake, Sullivan Co., NY	EDWARDS, David	ES: Sangerfield, Oneida Co., NY B: Wales
CURTIS, Newton Martin	ES: De Peyster, St. Lawrence Co., NY B: De Peyster, St. Lawrence Co., NY	EDWARDS, William D.	ES: Brooklyn, Kings Co., NY B: Brooklyn, Kings Co., NY
DALESSONDRO, Peter Joseph	ES: Watervliet, Albany Co., NY B: Watervliet, Albany Co., NY	EGGERS, Alan Louis	ES: Summit, Union Co., NJ B: Saranac Lake, Franklin Co., NY
DALY, Michael Joseph	ES: Southport, Fairfield Co., CT B: New York, NY	ELDRIDGE, George H.	ES: Detroit, Wayne Co., MI B: Sackets Harbor, Jefferson Co., NY
DAVIDSON, Andrew	ES: Middlefield, Otsego Co., NY B: Morebattle, Roxburgshire, Scotland	EMBLER, Andrew Henry	ES: NY B: New York, NY
DAVIS, Thomas	ES: New York, NY B: Haverford, West Wales	EMMET, Robert Temple	ES: New York, NY B: New York, NY
DAWSON, Michael	ES: New York, NY B: Boston, Suffolk Co., MA	ENGLISH, Edmund	ES: Newark, Essex Co., NJ B: New York, NY
DAY, Charles	ES: Richmond, Philadelphia Co., PA B: West Laurens, Otsego Co., NY	EVANS, James Robert	ES: New York, NY B: New York, NY
*De ARMOND, William	ES: New York, NY B: Butler Co., OH	EVERSON, Adelbert	ES: Salina, Onondaga Co., NY B: Cicero, Onondaga Co., NY
*DeGLOPPER, Charles N.	ES: Grand Island, Erie Co., NY B: Grand Island, Erie Co., NY	FARNSWORTH, Herbert E.	ES: Gowanda, Cattaraugus Co., NY B: Perrysburg, Cattaraugus Co., NY
DENNY, John	ES: Elmira, Chemung Co., NY B: Big Flats, Chemung Co., NY	FEGAN, James	ES: New York, NY B: Athlone, County Westmeath, Ireland
Di CESNOLA, Louis Palma	ES: New York, NY B: Rivarola, Piedmont, Italy	FERRARI, George	ES: Cleveland, Cuyahoga Co., OH B: New York, NY
DICKEY, William Donaldson	ES: Newburgh, Orange Co., NY B: Newburgh, Orange Co., NY	FICHTER, Hermann Emil	ES: New York, NY B: Baden, Germany

FISHER, Almond Edward	ES: Brooklyn, Kings Co., NY B: Hume, Allegany Co., NY	GREIG, Theodore W.	ES: Staten Island, Richmond Co., NY B: NY
FOLLY, William H.	ES: New York, NY B: Bergen Co., NJ	GRIBBEN, James H.	ES: New York, NY B: Ireland
FORD, George W.	ES: New York, NY B: Ireland	GRINDLAY, James G.	ES: Utica, Oneida Co., NY B: Odinburgh, Scotland
FOURNIA, Frank Ottis	ES: Plattsburgh, Clinton Co., NY B: Rome, Oneida Co., NY	GRUEB, George M.	ES: Brooklyn, Kings Co., NY B: Wurttemberg, Germany
*FRATELLENICO, Frank Rocco	ES: Albany, Albany Co., NY B: Sharon, Litchfield Co., CT	*GUENETTE, Peter Mathew	ES: Albany, Albany Co., NY B: Troy, Rensselaer Co., NY
FREEMAN, Archibald	ES: Newburgh, Orange Co., NY B: Newburgh, Orange Co., NY	GUERIN, Fitz W.	ES: St. Louis, St. Louis Co., MO B: New York, NY
FREEMAN, William Henry	ES: Troy, Rensselaer Co., NY B: Troy, Rensselaer Co., NY	HACK, Lester Goodel	ES: Salisbury, Addison Co., VT B: Cadwell, Warren Co., NY
FREEMEYER, Christopher	ES: New York, NY B: Bavaria, Germany	HADLEY, Cornelius Minor	ES: Adrian, Lenawee Co., MI B: Sandy Creek, Oswego Co., NY
FRENCH, Samuel S.	ES: Gifford, Tuscola Co., MI B: Erie Co., NY	HAGERTY, Asel	ES: New York, NY B: Canada
FUGER, Frederick W.	ES: New York, NY B: Wurttemberg, Germany	HAIGHT, John H.	ES: Westfield, Chautauqua Co., NY B: Westfield, Chautauqua Co., NY
GAFFNEY, Frank J.	ES: Niagara Falls, Niagara Co., NY B: Buffalo, Erie Co., NY	HALL, Francis Bloodgood	ES: Plattsburgh, Clinton Co., NY B: New York, NY
GARDINER, Peter W.	ES: New York, NY B: Carlisle, Schoharie Co., NY	HALL, Henry Seymour	ES: Elmira, Chemung Co., NY B: Barkersville, Saratoga Co., NY
GARDNER, Robert J.	ES: Egremont, Berkshire Co., MA B: Livingston, Columbia Co., NY	HALLOCK, Nathan Mullock	ES: Middletown, Orange Co., NY B: Mount Hope, Orange Co., NY
*GASSON, Richard	ES: New York, NY B: Ireland	HAMILTON, Mathew H.	ES: New York, NY B: Hobart, Australia
GEORGIAN, John	ES: Buffalo, Erie Co., NY B: Germany	HANFORD, Edward R.	ES: Cortland, Cortland Co., NY B: Allegany Co., NY
GERBER, Frederick William	ES: Brooklyn, Kings Co., NY B: Dresden, Germany	HAPEMAN, Douglas	ES: Ottawa, La Salle Co., IL B: Ephrata, Fulton Co., NY
GERE, Thomas Parke	ES: Fort Snelling, St. Paul Co., MN B: Wellsburg, Chemung Co., NY	HARING, Abram Pye	ES: New York, NY B: New York, NY
*GERTSCH, John Gerry	ES: Buffalo, Erie Co., NY B: Jersey City, Hudson Co., NJ	HARRIS, Charles D.	ES: Rochester, Monroe Co., NY B: Albion, Orleans Co., NY
GIFFORD, Benjamin	ES: German Flats, Herkimer Co., NY B: German Flats, Herkimer Co., NY	HART, William E.	ES: Rushville, Yates Co., NY B: Rushville, Yates Co., NY
GILMORE, John Curtis	ES: Potsdam, St. Lawrence Co., NY B: Canada	HARVEY, Harry	ES: Rochester, Monroe Co., NY B: England
GINLEY, Patrick	ES: New York, NY B: Ireland	HATCH, John Porter	ES: Oswego, Oswego Co., NY B: Oswego, Oswego Co., NY
GLOVER, Thaddeus Brown	ES: New York, NY B: New York, NY	HAWTHORNE, Harris Smith	ES: Otsego Co., NY B: Salem, Washington Co., NY
GLYNN, Michael	ES: New York, NY B: Galway, Ireland	HEERMANCE, William Laing	ES: Kinderhook, Columbia Co., NY B: Kinderhook, Columbia Co., NY
GOETTEL, Philip	ES: Syracuse, Onondaga Co., NY B: Salina, Onondaga Co., NY	HEISE, Clamor	ES: New York, NY B: Germany
GOHEEN, Charles Arthur	ES: Rochester, Monroe Co., NY B: Groveland, Livingston Co., NY	HIBSON, Joseph C.	ES: New York, NY B: London, England
GOODRICH, Edwin	ES: Westfield, Chautauqua Co., NY B: New York, NY	HICKEY, Dennis William	ES: Plattsburgh, Clinton Co., NY B: Troy, Rensselaer Co., NY
GOURAUD, George Edward	ES: New York, NY B: New York, NY	HILL, Edward	ES: Detroit, Wayne Co., MI B: Liberty, Sullivan Co., NY
*GRABIARZ, William J.	ES: Buffalo, Erie Co., NY B: Buffalo, Erie Co., NY	HILL, James Samuel	ES: Lyons, Wayne Co., NY B: Lyons, Wayne Co., NY
GREENE, Oliver Duff	ES: Scott, Cortland Co., NY B: Scott, Cortland Co., NY	HILLIKER, Benjamin F.	ES: Waupaca Township, Waupaca Co., WI B: Golden, Erie Co., NY
GREGG, Stephen Raymond	ES: Bayonne, Hudson Co., NJ B: New York, NY	HILLS, William Giles	ES: East Randolph, Cattaraugus Co., NY B: Conewango, Cattaraugus Co., NY
		HOGAN, Henry	ES: New York, NY B: County Clare, Ireland

HOGARTY, William P.	ES: Elmira, Chemung Co., NY B: New York, NY	*KAROPCZYC, Stephen Edward	ES: Bethpage, Nassau Co., NY B: New York, NY
HOLMES, Lovilo N.	ES: Mankato, Blue Earth Co., MN B: Farmersville, Cattaraugus Co., NY	KAUFMAN, Benjamin	ES: Brooklyn, Kings Co., NY B: Buffalo, Erie Co., NY
HOLTON, Charles Maynard	ES: Battle Creek, Calhoun Co., MI B: Potter, Yates Co., NY	KAUSS, August	ES: New York, NY B: Germany
HOOKER, George White	ES: Boston, Suffolk Co., MA B: Salem, Washington Co., NY	*KEDENBURG, John James	ES: Brooklyn, Kings Co., NY B: Brooklyn, Kings Co., NY
HORAN, Thomas	ES: Dunkirk, Chautauqua Co., NY	KEELE, Joseph	ES: Staten Island, Richmond Co., NY B: Ireland
HOUGHTON, Charles H.	ES: Ogdensburg, St. Lawrence Co., NY B: Macomb, St. Lawrence Co., NY	KEENAN, Bartholomew T.	ES: Cincinnati, Hamilton Co., OH B: Brooklyn, Kings Co., NY
HOULTON, William M.	ES: Athens, Athens Co., OH B: Clymer, Chautauqua Co., NY	KEENE, Joseph	ES: Utica, Oneida Co., NY B: England
HOWARD, James	ES: Brooklyn, Kings Co., NY B: Newton, Sussex Co., NJ	KELLER, William G.	ES: Buffalo, Erie Co., NY B: Buffalo, Erie Co., NY
HUMPHREY, Charles Frederic	ES: Buffalo, Erie Co., NY B: Cortland, Cortland Co., NY	KELLEY, Charles	ES: New York, NY B: County Clare, Ireland
HYDE, Henry J.	ES: New York, NY B: Bangor, Penobscot Co., ME	KELLEY, Leverett Mansfield	ES: Rutland, La Salle Co., IL B: Schenectady, Schenectady Co., NY
IRSCH, Francis	ES: New York, NY B: Saarburg, Germany	KELLY, Daniel	ES: Groveland, Livingston Co., NY B: Groveland, Livingston Co., NY
IRWIN, Bernard John Dowling	ES: New York, NY B: Ireland	KELLY, Thomas	ES: New York, NY B: Ireland
JACOBS, Jack Howard	ES: Trenton, Mercer Co., NJ B: Brooklyn, Kings Co., NY	KELLY, Thomas	ES: New York, NY B: County Mayo, Ireland
JACOBSON, Eugene Philip	ES: New York, NY B: Prussia	KELLY, Thomas	ES: NY B: Ireland
JAMES, John	ES: Albany, Albany Co., NY B: Manchester, Greater Manchester Co., England	KELLY, Thomas Joseph	ES: Brooklyn, Kings Co., NY B: Brooklyn, Kings Co., NY
JAMIESON, Walter	ES: New York, NY B: Boulogne, France	KENNEDY, John	ES: New York, NY B: Cavan, County Cavan, Ireland
JARVIS, Frederick	ES: Hudson, Lenawee Co., MI B: Essex Co., NY	KENYON, John Snyders	ES: Schenevus, Otsego Co., NY B: Grosvenors Corners, Schoharie Co., NY
JETTER, Bernhard	ES: New York, NY B: Wurttemberg, Germany	KENYON, Samuel P.	ES: Augusta, NY B: Ira, Cayuga Co., NY
JOEL, Lawrence	ES: New York, NY B: Winston-Salem, Forsyth Co., NC	KERRIGAN, Thomas	ES: New York, NY B: County Tipperary, Ireland
JOHNDRO, Franklin	ES: Queensbury, Warren Co., NY B: Highgate Falls, Franklin Co., VT	KIGGINS, John	ES: Syracuse, Onondaga Co., NY B: Syracuse, Onondaga Co., NY
JOHNSON, Follett	ES: Ogdensburg, St. Lawrence Co., NY B: Brasher, St. Lawrence Co., NY	KING, Horatio Collins	ES: Brooklyn, Kings Co., NY B: Portland, Cumberland Co., ME
JOHNSON, Wallace W.	ES: Waverly, Tioga Co., NY B: Newfield, Thompkins Co., NY	KING Jr., Rufus	ES: NY B: NY
JOHNSTON, Edward	ES: Chicago, Cook Co., IL B: Pen Yan, Yates Co., NY	KIRBY, Dennis Thomas	ES: St. Louis, St. Louis Co., MO B: Niagara Falls, Niagara Co., NY
JOHNSTON, William "Willie"	ES: St. Johnsbury, Caledonia Co., VT B: Morristown, Morristown Co., NY	KLINE, Harry	ES: Syracuse, Onondaga Co., NY B: Germany
*JONES, William	ES: New York, NY B: Wicklow, County Wicklow, Ireland	KNOWLES, Abiather J.	ES: Willets Point, Queens Co., NY B: La Grange, Penobscot Co., ME
JOSSELYN, Simeon T.	ES: Amboy, Lee Co., IL B: Buffalo, Erie Co., NY	KNOX, Edward M.	ES: New York, NY B: New York, NY
JUDGE, Francis W.	ES: New York, NY B: England	KOELPIN, William	ES: Brooklyn, Kings Co., NY B: Stetten, Prussia
KAISER, John	ES: New York, NY B: Nerzogenaurach, Germany	KRETSINGER, George	ES: Chicago, Cook Co., IL B: Fairfield, Herkimer Co., NY
KANE, John	ES: Marilla, Erie Co., NY B: Ireland	KUDER, Andrew	ES: Rochester, Monroe Co., NY B: Groveland, Livingston Co., NY
KAPPESSER, Peter	ES: Syracuse, Onondaga Co., NY B: Germany	LADD, George	ES: Camillus, Onondaga Co., NY B: Camillus, Onondaga Co., NY

*LAING, William	ES: Brooklyn, Kings Co., NY B: Hempstead, Nassau Co., NY	MARSH, Albert	ES: Randolph, Cattaraugus Co., NY B: Randolph, Cattaraugus Co., NY
LANE, Morgan D.	ES: Allegan, Allegan Co., MI B: Monroe, Orange Co., NY	MARTIN, Patrick	ES: New York, NY B: County Offaly, Ireland
LANG, George Charles	ES: Brooklyn, Kings Co., NY B: Flushing, Queens Co., NY	McBRIDE, Bernard	ES: Washington, D.C. B: Brooklyn, Kings Co., NY
LANGBEIN, Johann Christoph Julius	ES: New York, NY B: Germany	McBRYAR, William	ES: New York, NY B: Elizabethtown, Bladen Co., NC
*LANGHORN, Garfield McConnell	ES: Brooklyn, Kings Co., NY B: Cumberland, Cumberland Co., VA	McCANN, Bernard	ES: New York, NY B: County Roscommon, Ireland
LARRABEE, James W.	ES: Mendota, La Salle Co., IL B: Rensselaer Co., NY	McCARTHY, Michael	ES: New York, NY B: St. John's, Newfoundland, Canada
LAWTON, Louis Bowem	ES: Auburn, Cayuga Co., NY B: Independence, Buchanan Co., IA	McCONNELL, James	ES: Detroit, Wayne Co., MI B: Syracuse, Onondaga Co., NY
LEONARD, Patrick Thomas	ES: New York, NY B: County Clare, Ireland	McDONALD, Robert	ES: Newport, Campbell Co., KY B: Erie Co., NY
LESLIE, Frank	ES: New York, NY B: London, England	McENROE, Patrick H.	ES: Schodack, Rensselaer Co., NY B: Ireland
LEVY, Benjamin Bennett	ES: Newport News, Newport News Co., VA B: New York, NY	McFALL, Daniel Robert	ES: Ypsilanti, Washtenaw Co., MI B: Niagara Co., NY
LIBAIRE, Adolph	ES: New York, NY B: Baccarat, France	McGINN, Edward	ES: Cincinnati, Hamilton Co., OH B: New York, NY
LITEKY, Charles James (Angelo)	ES: Fort Hamilton, Kings Co., NY B: Washington, D.C.	McGONNIGLE, Andrew Jackson	ES: Cumberland, Allegany Co., MD B: New York, NY
LITTLE, Thomas	ES: New York, NY B: Barbados, West Indians	McGOUGH, Owen	ES: Cornwall, Orange Co., NY B: Monaghan, Ireland
LOCKE, Lewis	ES: Jersey City, Hudson Co., NJ B: Clintonville, Essex Co., NY	McHUGH, John	ES: New York, NY B: Syracuse, Onondaga Co., NY
LOHNES, Frank W.	ES: Omaha, Douglas Co., NE B: Oneida Co., NY	McKAY, Charles W.	ES: Allegany, Cattaraugus Co., NY B: Mansfield, Cattaraugus Co., NY
LONG, Oscar Fitzalan	ES: Utica, Oneida Co., NY B: Utica, Oneida Co., NY	McKEE, George	ES: Rochester, Monroe Co., NY B: County Tyrone, Ireland
LONSWAY, Joseph	ES: Sackets Harbor, Jefferson Co., NY B: Clayton, Jefferson Co., NY	McMURTRY, George G.	ES: New York, NY B: Pittsburgh, Allegheny Co., PA
LORISH, Andrew J.	ES: Attica, Wyoming Co., NY B: Dansville, Livingston Co., NY	McNALLY, James	ES: Albany, Albany Co., NY B: County Monaghan, Ireland
LOVE, George Maltby	ES: Elmira, Chemung Co., NY B: Buffalo, Erie Co., NY	McPHELAN, Robert	ES: New York, NY B: County Laois, Ireland
*LOZADA, Carlos James	ES: New York, NY B: Caguas, Caguas Co., Puerto Rico	McVEAGH, Charles H.	ES: San Francisco, San Francisco Co., CA B: New York, NY
*LUCAS, Andre Cavaro	ES: West Point, Orange Co., NY B: Washington, D.C.	*McVEANE, John P.	ES: Buffalo, Erie Co., NY B: Toronto, Canada
LUDGATE, William	ES: New York, NY B: London, England	MEACH, George E.	ES: New York, NY B: NY
LUDWIG, Carl	ES: Flushing, Queens Co., NY B: France	MEAGHER, Thomas	ES: Brooklyn, Kings Co., NY B: Scotland
LUTES, Franklin W.	ES: Geddes, NY B: Dundee, Yates Co., NY	MENTER, John William	ES: Detroit, Wayne Co., MI B: Palmer, NY
LYMAN, Joel H.	ES: Randolph, Cattaraugus Co., NY B: East Randolph, Cattaraugus Co., NY	*MERRELL, Joseph Frederick	ES: Staten Island, Richmond Co., NY B: Staten Island, Richmond Co., NY
MADDEN, Michael	ES: New York, NY B: County Limerick, Ireland	MERRILL, George	ES: Moreau, NY B: Queensberry, Warren Co., NY
MADISON, James	ES: Fairport, Monroe Co., NY B: Niagara, Niagara Co., NY	MERRILL, John Mitchell	ES: New York, NY B: New York, NY
MANDY, Harry J.	ES: New York, NY B: England	MERRITT, John G.	ES: Fort Snelling, St. Paul Co., MN B: New York, NY
MANGAM, Richard Christopher	ES: Auburn, Cayuga Co., NY B: Ireland	MEYER, Henry Coddington	ES: Dobbs Ferry, Westchester Co., NY B: Hamburg, Erie Co., NY
		MILLER, Frank	ES: Jamaica, Queens Co., NY B: NY

MILLER, George	ES: Boston, Suffolk Co., MA B: Brooklyn, Kings Co., NY	O'NEILL, William	ES: New York, NY B: Tariffville, Hartford Co., CT
MILLER, John	ES: Rochester, Monroe Co., NY B: Kurhessen, Germany	*O'SHEA, Thomas E.	ES: Summit, Union Co., NJ B: New York, NY
MILLS, Albert Leopold	ES: New York, NY B: New York City (Washington Heights), NY	O'SULLIVAN, John Francis	ES: New York, NY B: County Kerry, Ireland
MILLS, Frank W.	ES: Middletown, Orange Co., NY B: Middletown, Orange Co., NY	OLIVER, Paul Ambrose	ES: New York, NY B: At sea in the English Channel aboard American flagship Louisiana.
MOFFITT, John Henry	ES: Plattsburgh, Clinton Co., NY B: Chazy, Clinton Co., NY	ORR, Charles Alvin	ES: Bennington, Wyoming Co., NY B: Holland, Erie Co., NY
MONTROSE, Charles H.	ES: New York, NY B: St. Paul, Ramsey Co., MN	PACKARD, Loron F.	ES: Cuba, Allegany Co., NY B: Cattaraugus Co., NY
MOQUIN, George	ES: Brooklyn, Kings Co., NY B: New York, NY	PALMER, George Henry	ES: Monmouth, Warren Co., IL B: NY
MORSE, Benjamin	ES: Grand Rapids, Kent Co., MI B: Livingston, Columbia Co., NY	PARKS, Henry Jeremiah	ES: Orangeville, Wyoming Co., NY B: Orangeville, Wyoming Co., NY
MORSE, Charles E.	ES: NY B: France	PARNELL, William Russell	ES: Brooklyn, Kings Co., NY B: Dublin, Ireland
*MULLER, Joseph E.	ES: New York, NY B: Holyoke, Hampden Co., MA	PATTERSON, John Henry	ES: NY B: NY
MUNSELL, Harvey May	ES: Philadelphia, Philadelphia Co., PA B: Painted Post, Steuben Co., NY	PAY, Byron E.	ES: Mankato, Blue Earth Co., MN B: LeRoy Township, Jefferson Co., NY
MURPHY, Charles Joseph	ES: New York, NY B: Stockport, Greater Manchester Co., England	PAYNE, Irvin C.	ES: New York, NY B: Wayne Co., PA
MURPHY, Edward	ES: New York, NY B: County Cork, Ireland	PECK, Archie A.	ES: Hornell, Steuben Co., NY B: Tyrone, Schuyler Co., NY
MURPHY, Michael C.	ES: New York, NY B: Limerick, County Limerick, Ireland	PENGALLY, Edward	ES: Albany, Albany Co., NY B: Devonshire, England
MURPHY, Thomas	ES: Brooklyn, Kings Co., NY B: New York, NY	*PETERSON, George	ES: Brooklyn, Kings Co., NY B: Brooklyn, Kings Co., NY
MURPHY, Thomas J.	ES: New York, NY B: Ireland	PFISTERER, Herman	ES: New York, NY B: Brooklyn, Kings Co., NY
*MURRAY, Robert Charles	ES: New York, NY B: Bronx Co., NY	PHILLIPS, Josiah	ES: Ulysses, Potter Co., PA B: Wyoming Co., NY
MURRAY, Thomas	ES: New York, NY B: County Monaghan, Ireland	PLANT, Henry E.	ES: Cockery, MI B: Oswego Co., NY
NEAHR, Zachariah C.	ES: Canajoharie, Montgomery Co., NY B: Palatine, Montgomery Co., NY	PLATTEN, Frederick	ES: New York, NY B: Torbeck, Ireland
NEWMAN, William Henry	ES: Port Jervis, Orange Co., NY B: Highland Mills, Orange Co., NY	PLIMLEY, William	ES: Catskill, Greene Co., NY B: Catskill, Greene Co., NY
NIHILL, John	ES: Brooklyn, Kings Co., NY B: Nenagh, County Tipperary, Ireland	POND, James Burton	ES: Janesville, Rock Co., WI B: Allegany, Cattaraugus Co., NY
NIVEN, Robert	ES: Rochester, Monroe Co., NY B: Harlem, NY	PORTER, William	ES: Trenton, Mercer Co., NJ B: New York, NY
NORTON, Llewellyn Powell	ES: Scott, Cortland Co., NY B: Scott, Cortland Co., NY	POST, Philip Sidney	ES: Galesburg, Knox Co., IL B: Florida, Orange Co., NY
NUTTING, Lee	ES: New York, NY B: New York, NY	POTTER, Norman F.	ES: Pompey, Onondaga Co., NY B: Pompey, Onondaga Co., NY
O'BEIRNE, James Rowan	ES: New York, NY B: Roscommon, County Ballagh, Ireland	POWERS, Thomas	ES: Detroit, Wayne Co., MI B: New York, NY
O'BRIEN, Peter	ES: New York, NY B: Dublin, County Dublin, Ireland	PRESTON, Noble Delance	ES: Fulton, Oswego Co., NY B: Madison, Madison Co., NY
O'BRIEN, William Joseph	ES: Troy, Rensselaer Co., NY B: Troy, Rensselaer Co., NY	PUTNAM, Edgar Pierpont	ES: Stockton, Chautauqua Co., NY B: Stockton, Chautauqua Co., NY
O'CALLAGHAN, John	ES: San Francisco, San Francisco Co., CA B: New York, NY	QUINLAN, James	ES: New York, NY B: Clomwell, County Tipperary, Ireland
O'NEILL, Richard William	ES: New York, NY B: New York, NY	RAFFERTY, Peter F.	ES: New York, NY B: County Tyrone, Ireland
O'NEILL, Stephen	ES: New York, NY B: St. Johns, New Brunswick, Canada	RAGNAR, Theodore	ES: New York, NY B: Linkoping, Sweden

RAND, Charles Franklin	ES: Batavia, Genesee Co., NY B: Batavia, Genesee Co., NY	SCHILLER, John	ES: New York, NY B: Hessen, Germany
RANNEY, George E.	ES: Grand Rapids, Kent Co., MI B: Batavia, Genesee Co., NY	SCHLACHTER, Philipp	ES: New York, NY B: Germany
RANNEY, Myron H.	ES: Dansville, Livingston Co., NY B: Franklinville, Cattaraugus Co., NY	SCHMAL, George William	ES: Buffalo, Erie Co., NY B: Germany
*RAY, Bernard James	ES: Baldwin, Nassau Co., NY B: Brooklyn, Kings Co., NY	SCHNITZER, John	ES: New York, NY B: Kempten, Bavaria, Germany
RAYMOND, William H.	ES: Penfield, Monroe Co., NY B: Penfield, Monroe Co., NY	SCHOFIELD, John McAllister	ES: Freeport, Stephenson Co., IL B: Gerry, Chautauga Co., NY
READ, Morton A.	ES: Brockport, Monroe Co., NY B: Brockport, Monroe Co., NY	SCHOU, Julius Alexis	ES: Brooklyn, Kings Co., NY B: Copenhagen, Denmark
REYNOLDS, George	ES: New York, NY B: Ireland	SCHUBERT, Martin	ES: Elmira, Chemung Co., NY B: Germany
RHODES, Julius Dexter	ES: Springville, Erie Co., NY B: Monroe Co., MI	SCHWAN, Theodore	ES: NY B: Hanover, Germany
RIDDELL, Rudolph R.	ES: Hamilton, Madison Co., NY B: Hamilton, Madison Co., NY	SCOFIELD, David H.	ES: Stamford, Fairfield Co., CT B: Mamaroneck, Westchester Co., NY
ROBERTSON, Robert Stoddart	ES: Argyle, Washington Co., NY B: Argyle, Washington Co., NY	SCOTT, Robert B.	ES: St. Louis, St. Louis Co., MO B: Washington Co., NY
ROBINSON, John Cleveland	ES: Binghamton, Broome Co., NY B: Binghamton, Broome Co., NY	SEARS, Cyrus	ES: Bucyrus, Crawford Co., OH B: Meredith Township, Delaware Co., NY
ROCHE, David	ES: New York, NY B: County Kerry, Ireland	SHALER, Alexander	ES: New York, NY B: Haddam, Middlesex Co., CT
ROCKEFELLER, Charles Mortimer	ES: New York, NY B: Gallatin Columbia Co., NY	SHEA, Charles William	ES: New York, NY B: Bronx Co., NY
ROMEYN, Henry	ES: MI B: Galen, Wayne Co., NY	SHEPARD, Irwin	ES: Chelsea, Washtenaw Co., MI B: Skaneateles, Onondaga Co., NY
ROONEY, Edward	ES: Poughkeepsie, Dutchess Co., NY B: Poughkeepsie, Dutchess Co., NY	SHIPLEY, Robert F.	ES: Penn Yan, Yates Co., NY B: Wayne, Schuyler Co., NY
*ROOSEVELT Jr., Theodore	ES: Oyster Bay, Nassau Co., NY B: Oyster Bay, Nassau Co., NY	*SHOUP, Curtis F.	ES: Buffalo, Erie Co., NY B: Napanoch, Ulster Co., NY
ROSSBACH, Valentine	ES: Flushing, Queens Co., NY B: Germany	SHUBERT, Frank	ES: Canojaharie, Montgomery Co., NY B: Hesse, Germany
ROTH, Peter Paul	ES: Brooklyn, Kings Co., NY B: Wurttemberg, Germany	SICKLES, Daniel Edgar	ES: New York, NY B: New York, NY
ROUNDS, Lewis A.	ES: Norwalk, Huron Co., OH B: Cattaraugus Co., NY	SICKLES, William H.	ES: Fall River, Columbia Co., WI B: Danube, Herkimer Co., NY
RUSSELL, Charles L.	ES: Malone, Franklin Co., NY B: Malone, Franklin Co., NY	SIDMAN, George Dallas	ES: Owosso, Shiawassee Co., MI B: Rochester, Monroe Co., NY
RUSSELL, James	ES: New York, NY B: New York, NY	SIMMONS, John	ES: Liberty, Sullivan Co., NY B: Bethel, Sullivan Co., NY
RUTHERFORD, John T.	ES: Canton, St. Lawrence Co., NY B: Russell, St. Lawrence Co., NY	SKELLIE, Ebenezer	ES: Mina, Chautauqua Co., NY B: Mina, Chautauqua Co., NY
RYAN, Denis	ES: New York, NY B: Cork, Ireland	SMALLEY, Reuben	ES: Holton, Ripley Co., IN B: Reading, Schuyler Co., NY
SAGE, William Hampden	ES: Binghamton, Broome Co., NY B: Centerville, Allegany Co., NY	SMITH, Alonzo	ES: Jonesville, Hillsdale Co., MI B: Niagara Co., NY
SAGELHURST, John Christopher	ES: Jersey City, Hudson Co., NJ B: Buffalo, Erie Co., NY	SMITH, Charles E.	ES: St. Louis, St. Louis Co., MO B: Auburn, Cayuga Co., NY
SALE, Albert	ES: Dubuque, Dubuque Co., IA B: Broome Co., NY	SMITH, David Lafayette	ES: Bath, Steuben Co., NY B: Cameron, Steuben Co., NY
*SANTIAGO-COLON, Hector	ES: New York, NY B: Salinas, Salinas Co., Puerto Rico	*SMITH, George W.	ES: New York, NY B: Greenfield, Saratoga Co., NY
SARTWELL, Henry	ES: Fort Ann, Washington Co., NY B: Ticonderoga, Essex Co., NY	SMITH, Richard	ES: Haverstraw, Rockland Co., NY B: Haverstraw, Rockland Co., NY
SCHAEFER, Joseph E.	ES: Long Island, NY B: New York, NY	SMITH, Thomas J.	ES: New York, NY B: Liverpool, Merseyside Co., England
		SMITH, Wilson	ES: Madison, Madison Co., NY B: Madison, Madison Co., NY

SOVA, Joseph E.	ES: Rochester, Monroe Co., NY B: Chili, Monroe, NY	TRACY, William Gardner	ES: Albany, Albany Co., NY B: Syracuse, Onondaga Co., NY
SPILLANE, Timothy	ES: Waterford, Saratoga Co., NY B: County Kerry, Ireland	TRAYNOR, Andrew	ES: Rome, Oneida Co., NY B: Newark, Essex Co., NJ
SPRAGUE, Benona	ES: Cheney Grove, IL B: Satina Onondaga Co., NY	TREMAIN, Henry Edwin	ES: New York, NY B: New York, NY
*SPRAGUE, John Wilson	ES: Sandusky, Erie Co., OH B: White Creek, Washington Co., NY	TRIBE, John	ES: Oswego, Oswego Co., NY B: Tioga Co., NY
STAHEL, Julius H.	ES: New York, NY B: Szegedin, Hungary	*TURNER, William Bradford	ES: Garden City, Nassau Co., NY B: Dorchester, Suffolk Co., MA
STANLEY, Edward	ES: San Francisco, San Francisco Co., CA B: New York, NY	UHRL, George	ES: New York, NY B: Baden, Germany
STARKINS, John H.	ES: Flushing, Queens Co., NY B: Great Neck, Nassau Co., NY	URBAN, Matt Louis	ES: Fort Bragg, Cumberland Co., NC B: Buffalo, Erie Co., NY
STEPHENS, William G.	ES: Chicago, Cook Co., IL B: New York, NY	URELL, Michael Emmet	ES: New York, NY B: County Cork, Ireland
STEWART, George Evans	ES: New York, NY B: New South Wales (Australia)	VALENTE, Michael	ES: Ogdensburg, St. Lawrence Co., NY B: Cassino, Italy
*STONE Jr., Lester Raymond	ES: Syracuse, Onondaga Co., NY B: Binghamton, Broome Co., NY	VAN SCHAICK, Louis Joseph	ES: Cobleskill, Schoharie Co., NY B: Cobleskill, Schoharie Co., NY
*STRYKER, Robert Francis	ES: Throop, Cayuga Co., NY B: Auburn, Cayuga Co., NY	VAN WINKLE, Edward (Edwin)	ES: Phelps, Ontario Co., NY B: Phelps, Ontario Co., NY
SWAP, Jacob E.	ES: Springs, Somerset Co., PA B: Coeymans, Albany Co., NY	VARNUM, Charles Albert	ES: Pensacola, Escambia Co., FL B: Troy, Rensselaer Co., NY
SWIFT, Harlan J.	ES: Buffalo, Erie Co., NY B: New Hudson, Columbia Co., NY	VON MEDEM, Rudolph	ES: New York, NY B: Germany (Prussia)
THACKRAH, Benjamin	ES: Johnsonville, Rensselaer Co., NY B: Scotland	VON VEGESACK, Ernest	ES: New York, NY B: Gotland, Sweden
THOMPKINS, George W.	ES: Port Jervis, Orange Co., NY B: Orange Co., NY	WAALER, Reidar	ES: New York, NY B: Christiana, now Oslo, Norway
THOMPSON, Allen	ES: Sandy Creek, Oswego Co., NY B: New York, NY	WAINWRIGHT IV, Jonathan Mayhew	ES: Skaneateles, Onondaga Co., NY B: Fort Walla Walla, Walla Walla Co., WA
THOMPSON, George Washington	ES: Syracuse, Onondaga Co., NY B: Victory, Cayuga Co., NY	WAINWRIGHT, John	ES: West Chester, Chester Co., PA B: Syracuse, Onondaga Co., NY
THOMPSON, James Granville	ES: Sandy Creek, Oswego Co., NY B: Sandy Creek, Oswego Co., NY	WALKER, Mary Edwards	ES: Louisville, Jefferson Co., KY B: Oswego Co., NY
THOMPSON, James Harry	ES: New York, NY B: England	WALL, Jerry C.	ES: Milo, NY B: Geneva Ontario Co., NY
*THOMPSON, William Henry	ES: Bronx Co., NY B: New York, NY	WALLACE, William	ES: New York, NY B: County Donegal, Ireland
*THOMPSON, William P.	ES: Lafayette, Tippecanoe Co., IN B: Brooklyn, Kings Co., NY	WALLING, William Henry	ES: Folly Island, Charleston Co., SC B: Hartford, Washington Co., NY
THOMSON, Clifford	ES: New York, NY B: Fulton, Oswego Co., NY	WAMBSGAN, Martin	ES: Clyde, Wayne Co., NY B: Nusdorof, Bavaria, Germany
THORN, Walter	ES: Camp Nelson, KY B: Brooklyn, Kings Co., NY	*WARREN Jr., John Earl	ES: New York, NY B: Brooklyn, Kings Co., NY
TINKHAM, Eugene M.	ES: Waterloo, Seneca Co., NY B: Sprague, CT	WATSON, James C.	ES: Philadelphia, Philadelphia Co., PA B: Cochecton, Sullivan Co., NY
TOFFEY, John James	ES: Hudson, Hudson Co., NJ B: Quaker Hill, Dutchess Co., NY	WEBB, Alexander Stewart	ES: New York, NY B: New York, NY
TOLAN, Frank	ES: Boston, Suffolk Co., MA B: Malone, Franklin Co., NY	WEBB, James W.	ES: New York, NY B: Brooklyn, Kings Co., NY
TOMPKINS, Charles Henry	ES: Brooklyn, Kings Co., NY B: Fort Monroe, Hampton Co., VA	WEBBER, Alason P.	ES: Chillicothe, Ross Co., OH B: Greene Co., NY
TOOHEY, Thomas	ES: Milwaukee, Milwaukee Co., WI B: New York, NY	WEEKS, John Henry	ES: Hartwick Seminary, Oswego Co., NY B: Hampton, Windham Co., CT
TOY, Frederick Ernest	ES: Chicago, Cook Co., IL B: Buffalo, Erie Co., NY	WEIR, Henry Cary	ES: Bolivar, WV B: West Point, Orange Co., NY
TRACY, Benjamin Franklin	ES: Owego, Tioga Co., NY B: Owego, Tioga Co., NY	WELCH, Charles H.	ES: Fort Snelling, St. Paul Co., MN B: New York, NY

WELCH, Michael	ES: New York, NY B: Poughkeepsie, Dutchess Co., NY	BATES, Richard	ES: NY B: Wales
WELCH, Stephen	ES: Allegany, Cattaraugus Co., NY B: Groton, Tompkins Co., NY	BELL, George	ES: New York, NY B: Sunderland, England
*WELLS, Henry S.	ES: Phelps, Ontario Co., NY	*BENFOLD, Edward Clyde "Ted"	ES: Philadelphia, Philadelphia Co., PA B: Staten Island, Richmond Co., NY
WELLS, Thomas McCoy	ES: DeKalb, St. Lawrence Co., NY B: Ather, Ireland	BENNETT, Floyd	ES: NY B: Warrensburg, Warren Co., NY
WEST, Frank	ES: Mohawk, Herkimer Co., NY B: Mohawk, Herkimer Co., NY	BENNETT, James Harvey	ES: NY B: Haverstraw, Rockland Co., NY
WESTERHOLD, William	ES: New York, NY B: Binde, Prussia	BETHAM, Asa	ES: New York, NY B: New York, NY
*WICKERSHAM, J. Hunter	ES: Denver, Denver Co., CO B: New York, NY	BJORKMAN, Ernest H.	ES: NY B: Malmo, Sweden
*WILL, Walter J.	ES: West Winfield, Herkimer Co., NY B: Pittsburgh, Allegheny Co., PA	BLAGHEEN, William	ES: New York, NY B: Devonshire Co., England
*WILLETT, Louis Edward	ES: Brooklyn, Kings Co., NY B: Brooklyn, Kings Co., NY	BOURNE, Thomas	ES: New York, NY B: England
WILLIAMS, Leroy	ES: Batavia, Genesee Co., NY B: Oswego, Oswego Co., NY	BRADLEY, Amos	ES: NY B: Dansville, Livingston Co., NY
WINDOLPH, Charles	ES: Brooklyn, Kings Co., NY B: Bergen, Germany	BRADLEY, Charles	ES: New York, NY B: Ireland
WINEGAR, William W.	ES: Mount Morris, Livingston Co., NY B: Springport, NY	BRADLEY, George	ES: Rhode Island B: New York, NY
WISNER, Lewis S.	ES: Wallkill, Ulster Co., NY B: Wallkill, Ulster Co., NY	BRADLEY Jr., Willis Winter	ES: North Dakota B: Ransomville, Niagara Co., NY
WOODRUFF, Carle Augustus	ES: Washington, D.C. B: Buffalo, Erie Co., NY	BRADY, George F.	ES: NY B: Ireland
WRIGHT, Raymond Richard "Buzzer"	ES: Moriah, Essex Co., NY B: Moriah, Essex Co., NY	BREEN, John	ES: New York, NY B: New York, NY
YOUNG, James Marvin	ES: Chautauqua Co., NY B: Ellicott, Erie Co., NY	BRINN, Andrew	ES: New York, NY B: Scotland

U.S. Army Air Corps

		BROWN, James	ES: NY B: Rochester, Monroe Co., NY
*CHELI, Ralph	ES: Brooklyn, Kings Co., NY B: San Francisco, San Francisco Co., CA	BROWN, John	ES: New York, NY B: Glasgow, Scotland
HAMILTON, Pierpont Morgan	ES: New York, NY B: Tuxedo Park, Orange Co., NY	BROWN, Robert	ES: NY B: Norway
*VANCE Jr., Leon Robert	ES: Garden City, Nassau Co., NY B: Enid, Garfield Co., OK	BROWNELL, William P.	ES: NY B: NY
VOSLER, Forrest Lee "Woody"	ES: Rochester, Monroe Co., NY B: Lyndonville, Orleans Co., NY	BURKE, Thomas	ES: NY B: Ireland

U.S. Navy

		BURNS, John M.	ES: NY B: Hudson, Columbia Co., NY
AHERN, William	ES: NY B: Ireland	BURTON, Albert	ES: NY B: England
ALLEN, Edward G.	ES: NY B: Amsterdam, Holland	BUTTS, George	ES: Cleveland, Cuyahoga Co., OH B: Rome, Oneida Co., NY
ANDERSON, William	ES: NY B: Sweden	BYRNES, James	ES: NY B: Ireland
AUER, John F.	ES: NY B: NY	CAHEY, Thomas	ES: NY B: Belfast, County Antrim, Ireland
AVERY, James	ES: NY B: Scotland	CANN, Tedford Harris	ES: NY B: Bridgeport, Fairfield Co., CT
BAKER, Charles	ES: New York, NY B: Georgetown, D.C.	*CAPODANNO, Vincent Robert	ES: Staten Island, Richmond Co., NY B: Staten Island, Richmond Co., NY
BARTER, Gurdon H.	ES: New York, NY B: Williamsburg, Kings Co., NY	CAREY, James	ES: NY B: Ireland
BASS, David L.	ES: New York, NY B: Ireland	CASSIDY, Michael	ES: New York, NY B: Ireland

CAVANAUGH, Thomas	ES: NY B: Ireland	FLOOD, Thomas S.	ES: NY B: Ireland
CHANDRON, August	ES: NY B: France	FORBECK, Andrew Peter	ES: NY B: NY
CHAPUT, Louis G.	ES: New York, NY B: Canada	FOWLER, Christopher	ES: NY B: NY
CLANCY, Joseph	B: New York, NY	GALBRAITH, Robert	ES: NY B: Brooklyn, Kings Co., NY
CLAUSEN, Claus Kristian Randolph	ES: NY B: Denmark	GARDNER, William	ES: New York, NY B: Ireland
COLBERT, Patrick	ES: NY B: Ireland	GARRISON, James R.	ES: New York, NY B: Poughkeepsie, Dutchess Co., NY
CONLAN, Dennis	ES: New York, NY B: New York, NY	GIBBONS, Michael	ES: NY B: Ireland
COOPER, John	ES: New York, NY B: Dublin, County Dublin, Ireland	GOWAN, William Henry	ES: NY B: Rye, Westchester Co., NY
CORAHORGI, Demetri	ES: NY B: Trieste, Austria	GRAHAM, Robert	ES: NY B: England
CORCORAN, Thomas E.	ES: New York, NY B: Dublin, County Dublin, Ireland	GREENE, John	ES: NY
COREY, William	ES: NY B: New York, NY	HALLING, Luovi	ES: NY B: Stockholm, Sweden
COSTELLO, John	ES: NY B: Rouses Point, Clinton Co., NY	HALSTEAD, William W.	ES: NY B: Alplaus, Schenectady Co., NY
COTTON, Peter	ES: NY B: New York, NY	HAMILTON, Hugh	ES: New York, NY B: New York, NY
CREELMAN, William James	ES: NY B: Brooklyn, Kings Co., NY	HARLEY, Bernard	ES: New York, NY B: Brooklyn, Kings Co., NY
CREGAN, George	ES: NY B: New York, NY	HARRIS, John	ES: New York, NY B: Norway
DAVIS, John	ES: New York, NY B: Germany	HARTIGAN, Charles Conway	ES: Norwich, Chenango Co., NY B: Middletown, Orange Co., NY
DEAKIN, Charles	ES: Philadelphia, Philadelphia Co., PA B: New York, NY	HILL, George	ES: New York, NY B: England
DECKER, Percy A.	ES: NY B: New York, NY	HILL, William Lowell	ES: NY B: Brooklyn, Kings Co., NY
DENHAM, Austin	ES: NY B: England	HINNEGAN, William	ES: NY B: Ireland
DENSMORE, William	ES: NY B: NY	HOBAN, Thomas	ES: NY B: New York, NY
DITZENBACK, John	ES: IN B: New York, NY	HOBSON, Richmond Pearson	ES: NY B: Greensboro, Hale Co., AL
DONNELLY, John C.	ES: New York, NY B: England	HOLLAT, George	ES: NY
DOUGHERTY, Patrick	ES: New York, NY B: Ireland	HOWARD, Martin	ES: New York, NY B: Ireland
DUNPHY, Richard D.	ES: New York, NY B: Ireland	HUSE, Henry McLaren Pinckney	ES: NY B: USMA, West Point, Orange Co., NY
EGLIT, John	ES: NY B: Finland	HUSKEY, Michael	ES: NY B: Niagara Co., NY
ENGLISH, Thomas	ES: New York, NY B: New York, NY	*HUTCHINS, Carlton Barmore	ES: NY B: Albany, Albany Co., NY
ERICKSON, John P.	ES: Brooklyn, Kings Co., NY B: London, England	IRLAM, Joseph	ES: New York, NY B: Liverpool, Merseyside Co., England
ERICKSON, Nicholas	ES: NY B: Finland	IRVING, John	ES: New York, NY B: East Brooklyn, Kings Co., NY
EVERETTS, John	ES: NY B: Thorold, Canada	IRVING, Thomas	ES: New York, NY B: England
FARRELL, Edward	ES: New York, NY B: Saratoga, Saratoga Co., NY	IRWIN, Nicholas	ES: New York, NY B: Denmark
FLANNAGAN, John	ES: NY B: Ireland	JOHANSSON, Johan J.	ES: NY B: Sweden

JOHNSON, Henry	ES: New York, NY B: Norway	McKNIGHT, William	ES: New York, NY B: Ulster Co., NY
JOHNSON, William	ES: NY B: St. Vincent, West Indies	MILLIKEN, Daniel	ES: New York, NY B: Saco, York Co., ME
JONES, Andrew	ES: New York, NY B: Limerick, County Limerick, Ireland	MILLMORE, John	ES: NY B: New York, NY
JONES, John E.	ES: NY B: New York, NY	MILLS, Charles	ES: Brooklyn, Kings Co., NY B: Ulster, Ulster Co., NY
JORDAN, Robert	ES: NY B: New York, NY	MITCHELL, Thomas	ES: NY B: New York, NY
KENYON, Charles W.	ES: New York, NY B: Oneida, Madison Co., NY	MOORE, Charles	ES: New York, NY B: Ireland
KING, Hugh	ES: NY B: Ireland	MOORE, Francis	ES: NY B: NY
KING, John	ES: NY B: County Mayo, Ireland	MORGAN, James H.	ES: New York, NY B: NY
KING, Robert Henry	ES: NY B: NY	MORIN, William Henry	ES: NY B: Birmingham, West Midlands Co., England
KINNAIRD, Samuel W.	ES: New York, NY B: New York, NY	MORRISON, John G.	ES: Lansingburg, Tompkins Co., NY B: Ireland
KRAUSE, Ernest	ES: NY B: Lubeck, Germany	MORSE, William	ES: NY B: Germany
LAFFERTY, John	ES: PA B: New York, NY	MURPHY, John Edward	ES: NY B: Ireland
LAKIN, Thomas	ES: NY B: NY	MURPHY, Patrick	ES: New York, NY B: Ireland
LANN, John S.	ES: New York, NY B: Rochester, Monroe Co., NY	NAYLOR, David Johnson	ES: New York, NY B: Thompsonville, Sullivan Co., NY
LEE, James H.	ES: New York, NY B: NY	NIBBE, John H.	ES: NY B: Germany
LEJEUNE, Emile	ES: NY B: France	NICHOLS, William	ES: NY B: New York, NY
LLOYD, John W.	ES: NY B: New York, NY	NOIL, Joseph B.	ES: NY B: Nova Scotia, Canada
LOW, George	ES: NY B: Canada	NORDSIEK, Charles Luers	ES: NY B: New York, NY
LUCY, John	ES: NY B: New York, NY	NORDSTROM, Isador A.	ES: NY B: Goteborg, Sweden
MACHON, James	ES: New York, NY B: Derby, Derbyshire, England	NORRIS, J. W.	ES: NY B: England
MACK, Alexander	ES: New York, NY B: Rotterdam, Holland	O'CONNELL, Thomas	ES: New York, NY B: Ireland
MADDEN, William	ES: New York, NY B: Devonshire, England	O'DONOGHUE, Timothy	ES: NY B: Rochester, Monroe Co., NY
MARTIN, William	ES: NY B: Ireland	OAKLEY, William	ES: NY B: Colchester, Essex Co., England
MARTIN, William	ES: Cairo, Alexander Co., IL B: New York, NY	OHMSEN, August	ES: NY B: Lubeck, Germany
MAXWELL, John	ES: NY B: Brooklyn, Kings Co., NY	OSEPINS, Christian	ES: NY B: Holland
McCARTON, John	ES: NY B: Brooklyn, Kings Co., NY	PARKS, George	ES: New York, NY B: Schenectady, Schenectady Co., NY
McCLELLAND, Matthew	ES: Brooklyn, Kings Co., NY B: Brooklyn, Kings Co., NY	PEASE, Joachim	ES: New York, NY B: Long Island, NY
McCLOY, John	ES: NY B: Brewster, Putnam Co., NY	PELHAM, William	ES: New York, NY B: Halifax, Nova Scotia, Canada
McGOWAN, John	ES: New York, NY B: Ireland	PERRY, Thomas	ES: NY B: NY
McINTOSH, James	ES: New York, NY B: Canada	PETERSON, Alfred	ES: New York, NY B: Sweden
McKENZIE, Alexander	ES: NY B: Glasgow, Scotland		

PHINNEY, William	ES: New York, NY B: Norway	SMITH, Oloff	ES: New York, NY B: Sweden
*POWERS, John James	ES: NY B: New York, NY	SMITH, Thomas	ES: New York, NY B: England
PRICE, Edward	ES: New York, NY B: New York, NY	SMITH, Walter B.	ES: New York, NY B: NY
PYNE, George	ES: New York, NY B: England	SMITH, Wilhelm	ES: NY B: Germany
QUICK, Joseph	ES: NY B: NY	SPICER, William	ES: NY B: Liverpool, Merseyside Co., England
READ, Charles	ES: New York, NY B: Cambridge, Washington Co., NY	STANLEY, Robert Henry	ES: aboard U.S.S. *Vermont* B: Brooklyn, Kings Co., NY
REGAN, Patrick	ES: NY B: Queenstown, County Cork, Ireland	STANTON, Thomas	ES: NY B: Ireland
REID, Patrick	ES: NY B: Dublin, Ireland	STOKES, John S.	ES: NY B: New York, NY
RICHARDS, Louis	ES: New York, NY B: New York, NY	STOUT, Richard	ES: NY B: Owego, Tioga Co., NY
ROBINSON, Alexander	ES: New York, NY B: England	SULLIVAN, James	ES: Danbury, Fairfield Co., CT B: New York, NY
ROBINSON, Charles	ES: New York, NY B: Dundee, Scotland	SULLIVAN, John	ES: NY B: New York, NY
ROBINSON, Thomas	ES: NY B: Norway	SULLIVAN, Timothy	ES: New York, NY B: Ireland
ROGERS, Samuel F.	ES: NY B: Buffalo, Erie Co., NY	SUMMERS, Robert	ES: New York, NY B: Prussia
RUSSELL, Henry Peter	ES: NY B: Quebec, Canada	SUNDQUIST, Gustav Adolf	ES: NY B: Sweden
RUSSELL, John	ES: NY B: New York, NY	SWATTON, Edward	ES: Boston, Suffolk Co., MA B: New York, NY
SCHEPKE, Charles Stephen	ES: NY B: New York, NY	TAYLOR, George	ES: New York, NY B: Reddich, Hereford & Worcester Co., England
SCHNEPEL, Fred Jurgen	ES: NY B: New York, NY	THOMAS, Karl	ES: NY B: Germany
SCHUTT, George	ES: New York, NY B: Ireland	THORDSEN, William George	ES: NY B: Frederikstadt, Germany
SEANOR, James	ES: New York, NY B: Boston, Suffolk Co., MA	TRIPLETT, Samuel S.	ES: NY B: Cherokee, Crawford Co., KS
SHANAHAN, Patrick	ES: NY B: Shanat Castle, County Limerick, Ireland	TROY, Jeremiah	ES: NY B: New York, NY
SHARP, Hendrick	ES: New York, NY B: Spain	VADAS, Albert	ES: NY B: Austria-Hungary
SHERIDAN, James	ES: New York, NY B: Newark, Essex Co., NJ	VAN ETTEN, Hudson	ES: NJ B: Port Jervis, Orange Co., NY
SHIPMAN, William	ES: New York, NY B: New York, NY	WAGG, Maurice	ES: New York, NY B: Hampshire, England
SIMKINS, Lebbeus	ES: NY B: Utica, Oneida Co., NY	WALSH, James Aloysius	ES: New York, NY B: New York, NY
SIMPSON, D. Henry Lakin	ES: NY B: London, England	WARD, James	ES: New York, NY B: New York, NY
SMITH, Edwin	ES: NY B: New York, NY	WARREN, David	ES: New York, NY B: Glasgow, Scotland
SMITH, James	ES: New York, NY B: Belfast, County Antrim, Ireland	WEBSTER, Henry S.	ES: Brooklyn, Kings Co., NY B: Stockholm, NY
SMITH, James	ES: NY B: Hawaiian Islands	WEISSEL, Adam	ES: NY B: Germany
SMITH, James A.	ES: NY B: NY	WELLS, William	ES: New York, NY B: Germany
SMITH, John	ES: New York, NY B: Albany, Albany Co., NY	WESTA, Karl	ES: NY B: Norway
SMITH, John	ES: NY B: Bermuda		

WILCOX, Franklin L.	ES: NY B: Paris, Oneida Co., NY	HUDSON, Michael	ES: NY B: County Sligo, Ireland
WILKE, Julius August Robert	ES: NY B: Germany	HUGHES, John Arthur	ES: NY B: New York, NY
WILKES, Henry	ES: New York, NY B: New York, NY	JACOBSON, Douglas Thomas	ES: NY B: Rochester, Monroe Co., NY
WILLIAMS, Frank	ES: NY B: Danzig, Germany	KATES, Thomas Wilbur	ES: NY B: Shelby Center, NY
WILLIAMS, Robert	ES: NY B: New York, NY	*KOCAK, Matej	ES: New York, NY B: Gbely (Slovakia), Austria
WILLIAMS II, John	ES: NY B: Elizabethtown, NJ	KUCHNEISTER, Hermann Wilhelm	ES: NY B: Hamburg, Germany
WILSON, August	ES: NY B: Danzig, Germany	LEE, Howard Vincent	ES: Dumfries, Prince William Co., VA B: New York, NY
WOON, John	ES: New York, NY B: England	LEONARD, Joseph H.	ES: New York, NY B: Cohoes, Albany Co., NY
WORAM, Charles B.	ES: New York, NY B: New York, NY	MACKIE, John Freeman	ES: New York, NY B: New York, NY
WRIGHT, Edward	ES: New York, NY B: New York, NY	*MAUSERT III, Frederick William	ES: Dresher, Montgomery Co., PA B: Cambridge, Washington Co., NY
YOUNG, William	ES: New York, NY B: NY	*McCARD, Robert Howard	ES: NY B: Syracuse, Onondaga Co., NY

U.S. Marine Corps

ADRIANCE, Harry Chapman	ES: Massachusetts B: Oswego, Oswego Co., NY	McNALLY, Michael Joseph	ES: CA B: New York, NY
APPLETON, Edwin Nelson	ES: NY B: Brooklyn, Kings Co., NY	McNAMARA, Michael	ES: NY B: Clure, Ireland
BASILONE, John "Manila John"	ES: NJ B: Buffalo, Erie Co., NY	MORRIS, John	ES: NY B: NY
*BOBO, John Paul	ES: Buffalo, Erie Co., NY B: Niagara Falls, Niagara Co., NY	MURPHY, John Alphonsus	ES: Washington, D.C. B: New York, NY
BROWN, Charles	ES: Hong Kong B: New York, NY	MURRAY, William Henry	ES: Brooklyn, Kings Co., NY B: Brooklyn, Kings Co., NY
BUCKLEY, Howard Major	ES: NY B: Croton Falls, Westchester Co., NY	*NOONAN Jr., Thomas Patrick	ES: Brooklyn, Kings Co., NY B: Brooklyn, Kings Co., NY
CAFFERATA Jr., Hector Albert	ES: Dover, Morris Co., NJ B: New York, NY	O'MALLEY, Robert Emmett	ES: New York, NY B: Woodside, Queens Co., NY
*CARTER, Bruce Wayne	ES: Jacksonville, Duval Co., FL B: Schenectady, Schenectady Co., NY	OVIATT, Miles M.	ES: NY B: Cattaraugus Co., NY
CASAMENTO, Anthony	ES: New York, NY B: New York, NY	OWENS, Michael	ES: NY B: New York, NY
CATLIN, Albertus Wright	ES: MN B: Gowanda, Cattaraugus Co., NY	*PERKINS Jr., William Thomas	ES: San Francisco, San Francisco Co., CA B: Rochester, Monroe Co., NY
*COOK, Donald Gilbert	ES: Brooklyn, Kings Co., NY B: Brooklyn, Kings Co., NY	*PETERS, Lawrence David	ES: Binghamton, Broome Co., NY B: Johnson City, Broome Co., NY
DALY, Daniel Joseph	ES: NY B: Glen Cove, Nassau Co., NY	ROANTREE, James S.	ES: NY B: Dublin, County Dublin, Ireland
FIELD, Oscar Wadsworth	ES: NY B: Jersey City, Hudson Co., NJ	ROBINSON, Robert Guy	ES: Chicago, Cook Co., IL B: New York, NY
FITZGERALD, John	ES: NY B: Limerick, Ireland	SMITH, Willard M.	ES: NY B: Allegany, Cattaraugus Co., NY
FRANKLIN, Joseph John	ES: NY B: Buffalo, Erie Co., NY	SPROWLE, David	ES: NY B: Lisbon, St. Lawrence Co., NY
*GRAVES, Terrence Collinson	ES: NY B: Corpus Christi, Nueces Co., TX	*STOCKHAM, Fred William	ES: New York, NY B: Detroit, Wayne Co., MI
HARVEY, Harry	ES: NJ B: New York, NY	WALKER, Edward Alexander	ES: Brooklyn, Kings Co., NY B: Huntley, Scotland
HOFFMAN, Charles F.	ES: Brooklyn, Kings Co., NY B: New York, NY	WALSH, Kenneth Ambrose	ES: Brooklyn, Kings Co., NY B: Brooklyn, Kings Co., NY

NORTH CAROLINA

U.S. Army

*ASHLEY Jr., Eugene	ES: New York, NY B: Wilmington, New Hanover Co., NC
*BLACKWELL, Robert Lester	ES: Hurdle Mills, Person Co., NC B: Person Co., NC
BROWN, Lorenzo Dow	ES: Indianapolis, Marion Co., IN B: Davidson Co., NC
CRUMP, Jerry Kirt	ES: Forest City, Rutherford Co., NC B: Charlotte, Mecklenburg Co., NC
*DURHAM Jr., Harold Bascom	ES: Atlanta, Fulton Co., GA B: Rocky Mount, Edgecombe Co., NC
*EUBANKS, Ray E.	ES: LaGrange, Lenoir Co., NC B: Snow Hill, Greene Co., NC
*GEORGE, Charles	ES: Whittier, Jackson Co., NC B: Cherokee, Swain Co., NC
JOEL, Lawrence	ES: New York, NY B: Winston-Salem, Forsyth Co., NC
JOHNSTON, Gordon	ES: Birmingham, Jefferson Co., AL B: Charlotte, Mecklenburg Co., NC
JONES, William H.	ES: Louisville, Jefferson Co., KY B: Davidson Co., NC
McBRYAR, William	ES: New York, NY B: Elizabethtown, Bladen Co., NC
MILLER, Franklin Douglas	ES: Albuquerque, Bernalillo Co., NM B: Elizabeth City, Pasquotank Co., NC
MURRAY Jr., Charles Patrick "Chuck"	ES: Wilmington, New Hanover Co., NC B: Baltimore, Baltimore Co., MD
PARKER, Samuel Iredell	ES: Monroe, Union Co., NC B: Monroe, Union Co., NC
PATTERSON, Robert Martin	ES: Raleigh, Wake Co., NC B: Durham, Durham Co., NC
RAY, Charles W.	ES: St. Louis, St. Louis Co., MO B: Pensacola, Yancey Co., NC
SHEA, Joseph Henry	ES: New Bern, Craven Co., NC B: Baltimore, Baltimore Co., MD
*STOUT, Mitchell William	ES: Raleigh, Wake Co., NC B: Knoxville, Knox Co., TN
THOMPSON, Max	ES: Canton, Haywood Co., NC B: Bethel, Pitt Co., NC
TROGDEN, Howell G.	ES: St. Louis, St. Louis Co., MO B: Cedar Falls, Randolph Co., NC
URBAN, Matt Louis	ES: Fort Bragg, Cumberland Co., NC B: Buffalo, Erie Co., NY
*WARNER, Henry F.	ES: Troy, Montgomery Co., NC B: Troy, Montgomery Co., NC
*WOMACK, Bryant Homer	ES: Mill Spring, Polk Co., NC B: Mill Spring, Polk Co., NC

U.S. Navy

ANDERSON, Edwin Alexander	ES: Wilmington, New Hanover Co., NC B: Wilmington, New Hanover Co., NC
BARROW, David Duffy	ES: Norfolk, Norfolk Co., VA B: Reelsboro, NC
FRANKS, William J.	ES: De Valls Bluff, Prairie Co., AR B: Chatham Co., NC
*HALYBURTON Jr., William David	ES: NC B: Canton, Haywood Co., NC
HERRING, Rufus Geddie	ES: Roseboro, Sampson Co., NC B: Roseboro, Sampson Co., NC
JOHNSTON Jr., Rufus Zenas	ES: NC B: Lincolnton, Lincoln Co., NC
SANDERSON, Aaron	ES: Philadelphia, Philadelphia Co., PA B: North Carolina
STATON, Adolphus	ES: NC B: Tarboro, Edgecombe Co., NC

U.S. Marine Corps

LUCAS, Jacklyn Harold	ES: Norfolk, Norfolk Co., VA B: Plymouth, Washington Co., NC
PARKER, Pomeroy	ES: NC B: Gates Co., NC

NORTH DAKOTA

U.S. Army

ANDERS, Frank Lafayette	ES: Fargo, Cass Co., ND B: Fort Lincoln, Dakota Territory
BLOCH, Orville Emil	ES: Streeter, Stutsman Co., ND B: Big Falls, Waupaca Co., WI
BOEHLER, Otto A.	ES: Wahpeton, Richland Co., ND B: Germany
DAVIS, Charles P.	ES: Valley City, Barnes Co., ND B: Long Prairie, Todd Co., MN
DOWNS, Willis H.	ES: Jamestown, Stutsman Co., ND B: Mount Carmel, CT
FITZMAURICE, Michael John	ES: Cavour, Beadle Co., SD B: Jamestown, Stutsman Co., ND
*HAGEN, Loren Douglas	ES: Fargo, Cass Co., ND B: Fargo, Cass Co., ND
HARDAWAY, Benjamin Franklin	ES: Fort Totten, Benson Co., Dakota Territory B: Benleyville, KY
JENSEN, Gotfred	ES: Devils Lake, Ramsey Co., ND B: Denmark
KINNE, John Baxter	ES: Fargo, Cass Co., ND B: Beloit, Rock Co., WI
LONGFELLOW, Richard Moses	ES: Mandan, Morton Co., ND B: Logan Co., IL
*PENDLETON, Jack James	ES: Yakima, Yakima Co., WA B: Sentinel Butte, Golden Valley Co., ND
ROSS, Frank Fulton	ES: Langdon, Cavalier Co., ND B: Avon, Fulton Co., IL
SLETTELAND, Thomas	ES: Grafton, Walsh Co., ND B: Bergen, Norway
*SMITH, Fred E.	ES: Bartlett, ND B: Rockford, Winnebago Co., IL
*WOLD, Nels T.	ES: Minnewaukan, Benson Co., ND B: Winger, Polk Co., MN

U.S. Navy

BRADLEY Jr., Willis Winter	ES: ND B: Ransomville, Niagara Co., NY
CARTER, Joseph Edward	ES: ND B: Manchester, Greater Manchester Co., England

U.S. Marine Corps

*GURKE, Henry   ES: ND
  B: Neche, Pembina Co., ND

OHIO

U.S. Army

ALBERT, Christian	ES: Cincinnati, Hamilton Co., OH B: Cincinnati, Hamilton Co., OH	BROWN, Uriah H.	ES: Steubenville, Jefferson Co., OH B: Covington, Miami Co., OH
*ANTOLAK, Sylvester	ES: Clairsville, OH B: Clairsville, OH	BROWN, Wilson W.	ES: Findlay, Hancock Co., OH B: Logan Co., OH
ARCHINAL, William J.	ES: Canaldover, OH B: Felsburg, Hesse, Germany	BRYAN, William C.	ES: St. Louis, St. Louis Co., MO B: Zanesville, Muskingum Co., OH
ASTON, Edgar R.	ES: Cincinnati, Hamilton Co., OH B: Clermont Co., OH	BUFFUM, Robert	ES: Gilead, Wood Co., OH B: Salem, Essex Co., MA
AYERS, David	ES: Upper Sandusky, Wyandot Co., OH B: Kalida, Putnam Co., OH	BUHRMAN, Henry G.	ES: Cincinnati, Hamilton Co., OH B: Cincinnati, Hamilton Co., OH
*BAESEL, Albert E.	ES: Berea, Cuyahoga Co., OH B: Berea, Cuyahoga Co., OH	BURNS, James Madison	ES: Wellsburg, Brooke Co., WV B: Wells Township, Jefferson Co., OH
BAKER Jr., Edward Lee	ES: Cincinnati, Hamilton Co., OH B: Platte River, Laramie Co., WY	CALVERT, James Spencer	ES: Springfield, Sangamon Co., IL B: Athens Co., OH
BANKS, George Lovell	ES: Lafayette, Tippecanoe Co., IN B: Lake Co., OH	CAMPBELL, William	ES: New Philadelphia, Tuscarawas Co., OH B: County Down, Ireland
BARRICK, Jesse T.	ES: Fort Snelling, St. Paul Co., MN B: Columbiana Co., OH	CAPEHART, Henry	ES: Bridgeport, Belmont Co., OH B: Johnstown, Cambria Co., PA
BARRINGER, William H.	ES: Mason City, Mason Co., WV B: Long Bottom, Meigs Co., OH	CARMIN, Isaac Harrison	ES: New Lexington, Perry Co., OH B: Monmouth Co., NJ
BEATY, Powhatan	ES: Cincinnati, Hamilton Co., OH B: Richmond, Richmond Co., VA	CARR, Franklin	ES: Toledo, Lucas Co., OH B: Stark Co., OH
BEBB, Edward James	ES: Mount Pleasant, Henry Co., IA B: Butler Co., OH	CARR, John	ES: San Jose, Santa Clara Co., CA B: Columbus, Franklin Co., OH
BELL, James Bennett	ES: Troy, Miami Co., OH B: Branot, OH	CARSON, William J.	ES: North Greenfield, Highland Co., OH B: Washington Co., PA
BENNETT, Edward Andrew	ES: Middleport, Meigs Co., OH B: Middleport, Meigs Co., OH	CASEY, Henry	ES: Bloomingburg, Fayette Co., OH B: New Geneva, Fayette Co., PA
BENSINGER, William	ES: McComb, Hancock Co., OH B: Waynesburg, Stark Co., OH	*CHRISTIAN, Herbert F.	ES: Steubenville, Jefferson Co., OH B: Byesville, Guernsey Co., OH
BERTRAM, Heinrich	ES: Cincinnati, Hamilton Co., OH B: Brunswick, Germany	*CICCHETTI, Joseph J.	ES: Waynesburg, Stark Co., OH B: Waynesburg, Stark Co., OH
BICKHAM, Charles Goodwin	ES: Dayton, Montgomery Co., OH B: Dayton, Montgomery Co., OH	CLAPP, Albert Adams	ES: Painesville, Lake Co., OH B: Pompey, Onondaga Co., NY
BIRKHIMER, William Edward	ES: IA B: Somerset, Perry Co., OH	COCKLEY, David L.	ES: Columbus, Franklin Co., OH B: Lexington, Richland Co., OH
BISHOP, Daniel	ES: Wheeling, Ohio Co., WV B: Monroe Co., OH	COLWELL, Oliver	ES: Columbus, Franklin Co., OH B: Champaign Co., OH
BLICKENSDERGER, Milton	ES: Shanesville, OH B: Lancaster, Lancaster Co., PA	COOK, John	ES: Cincinnati, Hamilton Co., OH B: Cincinnati, Hamilton Co., OH
BOURY, Richard	ES: Wirt Courthouse, WV B: Monroe Co., OH	COONROD, Aquilla	ES: Bryan, Williams Co., OH B: Williams Co., OH
BOYNTON, Henry Van Ness	ES: Hamilton, Butler Co., OH B: West Stockbridge, Berkshire Co., MA	COX, Robert Mitchell	ES: Prairie City, McDonough Co., IL B: Guernsey Co., OH
BRANDLE, Joseph E.	ES: Colon, St. Joseph Co., MI B: Seneca Co., OH	*CRAIG, Robert	ES: Toledo, Lucas Co., OH B: Scotland
BRONSON, James H.	ES: Trumbell Co., OH B: Indiana Co., PA	CRANSTON, William Wallace	ES: Urbana, Champaign Co., OH B: near Woodstock, Champaign Co., OH
BROOKIN, Oscar	ES: Green Co., OH B: Byron, Fond Du Lac Co., WI	CRISWELL, Benjamin C.	ES: Cincinnati, Hamilton Co., OH B: Moundsville, Marshall Co., WV
BROWN, John	ES: Cincinnati, Hamilton Co., OH B: Boston, Suffolk Co., MA	CROCKER, Ulric Lyona	ES: Vergennes, OH B: OH
BROWN, Robert Burns	ES: Zanesville, Muskingum Co., OH B: New Concord, Muskingum Co., OH	CUBBERLY, William G.	ES: Cincinnati, Hamilton Co., OH B: Butler Co., OH
		CUMPSTON, James M.	ES: Portsmouth, Scioto Co., OH B: Gallia Co., OH
		CUSTER, Thomas Ward	ES: Monroe, Monroe Co., MI B: New Rumley, Harrison Co., OH
		DAVIDSON, Andrew	ES: Cincinnati, Hamilton Co., OH B: Middlebury, Addison Co., VT
		DAVIS, Freeman	ES: Newcomerstown, Tuscarawas Co., OH B: Newcomerstown, Tuscarawas Co., OH

DAVIS, Harry Clay	ES: Columbus, Franklin Co., OH B: Franklin Co., OH	GODFREY, Edward Settle	ES: Ottawa, Putnam Co., OH B: Kalida, Putnam Co., OH
DAVIS, Joseph	ES: East Palestine, Columbiana Co., OH B: Monmouth Co., Wales	GRAY, John	ES: Cincinnati, Hamilton Co., OH B: Dundee, Scotland
DAVIS, Sammy Lee	ES: Indianapolis, Marion Co., IN B: Dayton, Montgomery Co., OH	GREEN, George	ES: Columbus, Franklin Co., OH B: Elsham, Lincolnshire Co., England
DAY, David Frakes	ES: Cincinnati, Hamilton Co., OH B: Dallasburg, OH	GREEN, John	ES: Columbus, Franklin Co., OH B: Wurttemberg, Germany
DAY, Matthias Walter	ES: Oberlin, Lorain Co., OH B: Mansfield, Richland Co., OH	GREENAWALT, Abraham	ES: Salem, Columbiana Co., OH B: Montgomery Co., PA
*De ARMOND, William	ES: New York, NY B: Butler Co., OH	GREGG, Joseph Olds	ES: Columbus, Franklin Co., OH B: Lithopolis, Fairfield Co., OH
DeLAVIE, Hiram H.	ES: Allegheny Co., PA B: Stark Co., OH	GRIMSHAW, Samuel	ES: Smithfield, Jefferson Co., OH B: Jefferson Co., OH
*DELEAU Jr., Emile	ES: Blaine, Belmont Co., OH B: Lansing, Belmont Co., OH	GUINN, Thomas	ES: Oxford, Butler Co., OH B: Clinton Co., OH
DeWITT, Richard Willis	ES: Oxford, Butler Co., OH B: Butler Co., OH	GWYNNE, Nathaniel McClean	ES: Fairmount, MO B: Urbana, Champaign Co., OH
DORSEY, Daniel Allen	ES: Chillicothe, Ross Co., OH B: Lancaster, Fairfield Co., OH	*HALL, Lewis R.	ES: Columbus, Franklin Co., OH B: Bloom, OH
DOWLING, James	ES: Cleveland, Cuyahoga Co., OH B: County Meath, Ireland	HALL, Newton H.	ES: Brimfield, Portage Co., OH B: Brimfield, Portage Co., OH
EDGERTON, Nathan Huntley	ES: Philadelphia, Philadelphia Co., PA B: Barnesville, Belmont Co., OH	HANEY, Milton Lorenzi	ES: Bushnell, McDonough Co., IL B: Savannah, Ashland Co., OH
ELSON, James M.	ES: Shellsburg, Benton Co., IA B: Coshocton, Coshocton Co., OH	HANKS, Joseph	ES: Chillicothe, Ross Co., OH B: Chillicothe, Ross Co., OH
ENDERLIN, Richard	ES: Chillicothe, Ross Co., OH B: Germany	HANLEY, Richard P.	ES: Cincinnati, Hamilton Co., OH B: Boston, Suffolk Co., MA
EVERHART Sr., Forrest Eugene	ES: Texas City, Galveston Co., TX B: Bainbridge, Ross Co., OH	HANNA, Milton	ES: Henderson, Sibley Co., MN B: Licking Co., OH
FEASTER, Mosheim	ES: Cleveland, Cuyahoga Co., OH B: Schellsburg, Bedford Co., PA	HARRINGTON, John	ES: Cleveland, Cuyahoga Co., OH B: Detroit, Wayne Co., MI
FERRARI, George	ES: Cleveland, Cuyahoga Co., OH B: New York, NY	HARRIS, David W.	ES: Cincinnati, Hamilton Co., OH B: Indianapolis, Marion Co., IN
FINKENBINER, Henry S.	ES: Pike Township, OH B: North Industry, Stark Co., OH	HARRIS, Sampson	ES: Olive, OH B: Noble Co., OH
*FLEEK, Charles Clinton	ES: Cincinnati, Hamilton Co., OH B: Petersburg, Boone Co., KY	HARTZOG, Joshua B.	ES: Detroit, Wayne Co., MI B: Paulding Co., OH
FORCE, Manning Ferguson	ES: Cincinnati, Hamilton Co., OH B: Washington, D.C.	*HASTINGS, Joe R.	ES: Magnolia, Stark Co., OH B: Malvern, Carroll Co., OH
FOX, Henry M.	ES: Coldwater, Branch Co., MI B: Trumbull, OH	HAWKINS, Martin Jones	ES: Portsmouth, Scioto Co., OH B: Mercer Co., PA
FREEMAN, Henry Blanchard	ES: Mount Vernon, Knox Co., OH B: Mount Vernon, Knox Co., OH	HAWKINS, Thomas R.	ES: Philadelphia, Philadelphia Co., PA B: Cincinnati, Hamilton Co., OH
FREY, Franz	ES: Cleveland, Cuyahoga Co., OH B: Switzerland	HAYES, Webb Cook	ES: Fremont, Sandusky Co., OH B: Cincinnati, Hamilton Co., OH
FUNSTON Sr., Frederick	ES: Iola, Allen Co., KS B: New Carlisle, Clark Co., OH	HAYS, John H.	ES: Oskaloosa, Mahaska Co., IA B: Jefferson Co., OH
GARRETT, William	ES: Chardon, Geauga Co., OH B: Isle of Man, England	HEDGES, Joseph S.	ES: Mansfield, Richland Co., OH B: Mansfield, Richland Co., OH
GATES, George	ES: Dubuque, Dubuque Co., IA B: Delaware Co., OH	HELLER, Henry	ES: Urbana, Champaign Co., OH
GAUNT, John C.	ES: Damascoville, OH B: Columbiana Co., OH	HENRY, James	ES: Kankakee, Kankakee Co., IL B: Sunfish, OH
GAUSE, Isaac	ES: Canfield, Mahoning Co., OH B: Trumbull Co., OH	HERDA, Frank Aloysious	ES: Cleveland, Cuyahoga Co., OH B: Cleveland, Cuyahoga Co., OH
GEIGER, George	ES: St. Louis, St. Louis Co., MO B: Cincinnati, Hamilton Co., OH	HILL, James Madison	ES: Cincinnati, Hamilton Co., OH B: Washington Co., PA
*GIVEN, John J.	ES: Cincinnati, Hamilton Co., OH B: Daviess Co., KY	HOFFMAN, Henry	ES: Cincinnati, Hamilton Co., OH B: Wurttemberg, Germany
		HOLCOMB, Daniel Irving	ES: Hartford, Trumbull Co., OH B: Hartford, Trumbull Co., OH

HOLLAND, Lemuel F.	ES: Tiskilwa, Bureau Co., IL B: Burlington, OH	LEONARD, Patrick James	ES: Cincinnati, Hamilton Co., OH B: County Meath, Ireland
HOLLAND, Milton Murray	ES: Albany, Athens Co., OH B: Austin, Travis Co., TX	*LOGAN Jr., John Alexander	ES: Youngstown, Mahoning Co., OH B: Carbondale, Jackson Co., IL
HOULTON, William M.	ES: Athens, Athens Co., OH B: Clymer, Chautauqua Co., NY	*LONG, Donald Russell	ES: Ashland, Boyd Co., KY B: Blackfork, OH
HOWARD, Hiram Reese	ES: Cincinnati, Hamilton Co., OH B: Urbana, Champaign Co., OH	LONGSHORE, William Henry	ES: Columbus, Franklin Co., OH B: Zanesville, Muskingum Co., OH
HOWE, Orion P.	ES: Waukegan, Lake Co., IL B: Hiram, Portage Co., OH	LOYD, George A.	ES: Zanesville, Muskingum Co., OH B: Muskingum Co., OH
HUTCHINSON, Rufus D.	ES: Cincinnati, Hamilton Co., OH B: Butlerville, OH	LYTLE, Leonidas S.	ES: Cleveland, Cuyahoga Co., OH B: Warren Co., PA
IMMELL, Lorenzo Dow	ES: Fort Leavenworth, Leavenworth Co., KS B: Ross, Butler Co., OH	MASON, Elihu H.	ES: Pemberville, Wood Co., OH B: Wayne Co., IN
INSCHO, Leonidas H.	ES: Newark, Licking Co., OH B: Chatham, Licking Co., OH	MAYES, William B.	ES: DeWitt, Clinton Co., IA B: Marion Co., OH
JAMES, Isaac	ES: Mississinawa Township, OH B: Jefferson Township, Ashtabula Co., OH	MAYFIELD, Melvin	ES: Nashport, Muskingum Co., OH B: Salem, Harrison Co., WV
JARDINE, James	ES: Hamilton Co., OH B: Helensburgh, Dunbartonshire, Scotland	MAYS, Isaiah	ES: Columbus Barracks, Franklin Co., OH B: Carters Bridge, VA
JOHN, William F.	ES: Chillicothe, Ross Co., OH B: Germany	McCLEARY, Charles H.	ES: Clyde, Sandusky Co., OH B: Sandusky Co., OH
JOHNS, Elisha	ES: Martinton, Iroquois Co., IL B: Clinton, Summit Co., OH	McCLELLAND, James M.	ES: Ohio B: Harrison Co., OH
JOHNSON, Andrew	ES: Assumption, Christian Co., IL B: Delaware Co., OH	McCONNELL, Samuel	ES: Bushnell, McDonough Co., IL B: Belmont Co., OH
JONES, David	ES: Washington Courthouse, Fayette Co., OH B: Fayette Co., OH	McDONALD, John Wade	ES: Waynesville, DeWitt Co., IL B: Lancaster, Fairfield Co., OH
JORDAN, Absalom	ES: North Madison, Jefferson Co., IN B: Brown Co., OH	McELHINNY, Samuel O.	ES: Point Pleasant, Mason Co., WV B: Meigs Co., OH
KEENAN, Bartholomew T.	ES: Cincinnati, Hamilton Co., OH B: Brooklyn, Kings Co., NY	McGINN, Edward	ES: Cincinnati, Hamilton Co., OH B: New York, NY
*KEFURT, Gus	ES: Youngstown, Mahoning Co., OH B: Greenville, Mercer Co., PA	McGONAGLE, Wilson	ES: Cadiz, Harrison Co., OH B: Jefferson Co., OH
KELLEY, George V.	ES: Massillon, Stark Co., OH B: Massillon, Stark Co., OH	McMILLEN, Francis M.	ES: Piqua, Miami Co., OH B: Bracken Co., KY
KEMP, Joseph Bell	ES: Sault Ste. Marie, Chippewa Co., MI B: Lima, Allen Co., OH	MEAHER, Nicholas	ES: Cincinnati, Hamilton Co., OH B: Perry Co., OH
*KESSLER, Patrick L.	ES: Middletown, Butler Co., OH B: Middletown, Butler Co., OH	MILLER, Daniel H.	ES: Columbus, Franklin Co., OH B: Fairfield Co., OH
KIMBALL, Joseph	ES: Ironton, Lawrence Co., OH B: Littleton, Grafton Co., NH	MILLER, Jacob C.	ES: Elgin, Kane Co., IL B: Bellevue, Huron Co., OH
KIRK, Jonathan C.	ES: Wilmington, Clinton Co., OH B: Clinton Co., OH	MILLER, James P.	ES: Henry Co., IA B: Franklin, Warren Co., OH
KNAAK, Albert	ES: Cincinnati, Hamilton Co., OH B: Luxenburg, Switzerland	MILLER, John G.	ES: Camp Dennison, Hamilton Co., OH B: Germany
KNIGHT, William J.	ES: Farmers Center, Defiance Co., OH B: Apple Creek, Wayne Co., OH	MOREY, Delano	ES: Kenton, Hardin Co., OH B: Licking Co., OH
KOUNTZ, John S.	ES: Maumee, Lucas Co., OH B: Maumee, Lucas Co., OH	*MORGAN, Lewis	ES: Delaware Co., OH B: Delaware Co., OH
KUDER, Jeremiah	ES: Warsaw, Kosciusko Co., IN B: Tiffin, Seneca Co., OH	MURPHY, John P.	ES: Cincinnati, Hamilton Co., OH B: Killarney, County Kerry, Ireland
KYLE, John	ES: Nashville, Davidson Co., TN B: Cincinnati, Hamilton Co., OH	MYERS, George S.	ES: Tiffin, Seneca Co., OH B: Fairfield, Butler Co., OH
*LAPOINTE Jr., Joseph Guy	ES: Cincinnati, Hamilton Co., OH B: Dayton, Montgomery Co., OH	NEWMAN, Henry	ES: Cincinnati, Hamilton Co., OH B: Hanover, Germany
LARIMER, Smith	ES: Columbus, Franklin Co., OH B: Richland Co., OH	NORTH, Jasper N.	ES: Amesville, Athens Co., OH B: OH
LAWTON, Henry Ware	ES: Fort Wayne, Allen Co., IN B: Manhattan, Lucas Co., OH	ORBANSKY, David	ES: Columbus, Franklin Co., OH B: Lautenburg, Prussia

PARKS, James W.	ES: Xenia, Clay Co., IL B: Lawrence Co., OH	*ROSS, Marion A.	ES: Christianburg, Champaign Co., OH B: Christianburg, Champaign Co., OH
PARROTT, Jacob	ES: Kenton, Hardin Co., OH B: Fairfield Co., OH	ROSSER, Ronald Eugene	ES: Crooksville, Perry Co., OH B: Columbus, Franklin Co., OH
PATTERSON, John T.	ES: McConnelsville, Morgan Co., OH B: Morgan Co., OH	ROUNDS, Lewis A.	ES: Norwalk, Huron Co., OH B: Cattaraugus Co., NY
PEARSALL, Platt	ES: Downington, OH B: Meigs Co., OH	ROWALT, John F.	ES: Cincinnati, Hamilton Co., OH B: Belleville, Richland Co., OH
PEIRSOL, James Kastor	ES: Waynesboro, OH B: Beaver Co., PA	ROY, Stanislaus	ES: Cincinnati, Hamilton Co., OH B: France
*PETRARCA, Frank Joseph	ES: Cleveland, Cuyahoga Co., OH B: Cleveland, Cuyahoga Co., OH	SCHENCK, Benjamin W.	ES: Maroa, Macon Co., IL B: Butler Co., OH
PHILLIPS, Samuel D.	ES: St. Louis, St. Louis Co., MO B: Butler Co., OH	SCHMAUCH, Andrew	ES: Portsmouth, Scioto Co., OH B: Germany
PHISTERER, Frederick	ES: Medina Co., OH B: Germany	SCHMIDT, William	ES: Maumee, Lucas Co., OH B: Tiffin, Seneca Co., OH
PINN, Robert A.	ES: Massillon, Stark Co., OH B: Stark Co., OH	SCHNELL, Christian	ES: Wapakoneta, Auglaize Co., OH B: VA
PITTINGER, William	ES: Steubenville, Jefferson Co., OH B: Knoxville, Jefferson Co., OH	*SCOTT, John Morehead	ES: Findley, Hancock Co., OH B: Stark Co., OH
POPPE, John A.	ES: Fort Dodge, Ford Co., KS B: Cincinnati, Hamilton Co., OH	SEAMAN, Elisha B.	ES: Logan Co., OH B: Logan Co., OH
PORTER, John Reed	ES: McComb, Hancock Co., OH B: Delaware Co., OH	SEARS, Cyrus	ES: Bucyrus, Crawford Co., OH B: Meredith Township, Delaware Co., NY
POWELL, William Henry	ES: Ironton, Lawrence Co., OH B: Pontypool, Monmouthshire, South Wales	SHAFFER, William	ES: Cincinnati, Hamilton Co., OH B: Bavaria, Germany
POWER, Albert	ES: Bloomfield, Davis Co., IA B: Liberty, Guernsey Co., OH	SHARPLESS, Edward Clay	ES: Columbus, Franklin Co., OH B: Marion Co., OH
PRATT, James N.	ES: Bellefontaine, Logan Co., OH B: Bellefontaine, Logan Co., OH	SHIELDS, Bernard	ES: Ironton, Lawrence Co., OH B: Ireland
PRENTICE, Joseph Rollin	ES: Fort Wayne, Allen Co., IN B: Lancaster, Fairfield Co., OH	SLAGLE, Oscar	ES: Manlius, Bureau Co., IL B: Fulton Co., OH
RAERICK, John	ES: Cincinnati, Hamilton Co., OH B: Baden, Germany	*SLAVENS, Samuel	ES: Wakefield, Pike Co., OH B: Pike Co., OH
RANSBOTTOM, Alfred	ES: Nashport, Muskingum Co., OH B: South Zanesville, Delaware Co., OH	SMITH, James (Ovid)	ES: Circleville, Pickaway Co., OH B: Fredericksburg, Fredericksburg Co., VA
REDDICK, William Henry Harrison	ES: Portsmouth, Scioto Co., OH B: Locust Grove, Adams Co., OH	SMITH, Otis W.	ES: Champaign, OH B: Logan Co., OH
RENNINGER, Louis	ES: Liverpool, OH B: Liverpool, OH	SMITH, William H.	ES: Cincinnati, Hamilton Co., OH B: Lapeer, Lapeer Co., MI
RICHARDSON, William R.	ES: Washington, OH B: Cleveland, Cuyahoga Co., OH	SPENCE, Orizoba	ES: Cincinnati, Hamilton Co., OH B: Forest Co., PA
RICHEY, William E.	ES: New Concord, Muskingum Co., OH B: Athens Co., OH	*SPRAGUE, John Wilson	ES: Sandusky, Erie Co., OH B: White Creek, Washington Co., NY
RICHMAN, Samuel	ES: Cleveland, Cuyahoga Co., OH B: Cleveland, Cuyahoga Co., OH	STACEY, Charles	ES: Norwalk, Huron Co., OH B: England
*RICHMOND, James	ES: Fremont, Sandusky Co., OH B: ME	STANLEY, David Sloane	ES: Congress, Wayne Co., OH B: Cedar Valley, OH
RICKSECKER, John Henry	ES: Aurora, Portage Co., OH B: Mansfield, Richland Co., OH	STAUFFER, Rudolph	ES: Cincinnati, Hamilton Co., OH B: Berne, Switzerland
ROBERTS, Gordon Ray	ES: Cincinnati, Hamilton Co., OH B: Middletown, Butler Co., OH	STEELE, John Whedon	ES: Oberlin, Lorain Co., OH B: Middleburg, Logan Co., OH
*ROBERTSON, Samuel	ES: Boarneville, Ross Co., OH B: Muskingum Co., OH	STICKELS, Joseph	ES: Bethany, OH B: Butler Co., OH
ROBINSON, Elbridge	ES: McConnelsville, Morgan Co., OH B: Morgan Co., OH	STICKOFFER, Julius Henry	ES: Cincinnati, Hamilton Co., OH B: Switzerland
*ROBINSON Jr., James E.	ES: Waco, McLennan Co., TX B: Toledo, Lucas Co., OH	STOKES, Alonzo	ES: Cincinnati, Hamilton Co., OH B: Logan Co., OH
ROCK, Frederick	ES: Cleveland, Cuyahoga Co., OH B: Darmstadt, Germany	STURGEON, James K.	ES: Lancaster, Fairfield Co., OH B: Perry Co., OH
		SULLIVAN, Thomas	ES: Cincinnati, Hamilton Co., OH B: Covington, Kenton Co., KY

SURLES, William H.	ES: Steubenville, Jefferson Co., OH B: Steubenville, Jefferson Co., OH	*WOODFORD, Howard E.	ES: Barberton, Summit Co., OH B: Barberton, Summit Co., OH
SWAYNE, Wager	ES: Columbus, Franklin Co., OH B: Columbus, Franklin Co., OH	WOODS, Daniel A. (Wood)	ES: Wheeling, Ohio Co., WV B: OH Co., WV
THACKER, Brian Miles	ES: Salt Lake City, Salt Lake Co., UT B: Columbus, Franklin Co., OH	YEAGER, Jacob F.	ES: Tiffin, Seneca Co., OH B: New Texas, Lehigh Co., PA
*THOMAS, Charles L.	ES: Cincinnati, Hamilton Co., OH B: Philadelphia, Philadelphia Co., PA	YOUNG, Calvary Morris	ES: Hopeville, Clark Co., IA B: Washington Co., OH
THOMPSON, Charles Augustus	ES: Kalamazoo, Kalamazoo Co., MI B: Perrysburg, Wood Co., OH	*YOUNG, Rodger W.	ES: Clyde, Sandusky Co., OH B: Tiffin, Seneca Co., OH
THOMPSON, Freeman C.	ES: Marietta, Washington Co., OH B: Monroe Co., OH	YOUNKER, John L.	ES: Lancaster, Fairfield Co., OH B: Wurttemberg, Germany
THOMPSON, Thomas W.	ES: Urbana, Champaign Co., OH B: Champaign Co., OH	*U.S. Army Air Corps*	
TORGLER, Ernest R.	ES: Toledo, Lucas Co., OH B: Mecklenburg, Germany	*BAKER, Addison Earl	ES: Akron, Summit Co., OH B: Chicago, Cook Co., IL
*TOWLE, John Roderick	ES: Cleveland, Cuyahoga Co., OH B: Cleveland, Cuyahoga Co., OH	*METZGER Jr., William Edward	ES: Lima, Allen Co., OH B: Lima, Allen Co., OH
TREAT, Howell B.	ES: Painesville, Lake Co., OH B: Painesville, Lake Co., OH	RICKENBACKER, Edward Vernon	ES: Columbus, Franklin Co., OH B: Columbus, Franklin Co., OH
TYRRELL, George William	ES: Cincinnati, Hamilton Co., OH B: Ireland	*U.S. Navy*	
VAN MATRE, Joseph	ES: Middleport, Meigs Co., OH B: Mason Co., WV	BARTON, Thomas	ES: OH B: Cleveland, Cuyahoga Co., OH
VANCE, Wilson J.	ES: Findlay, Hancock Co., OH B: Findlay, Hancock Co., OH	BEASLEY, Harry C.	ES: OH B: OH
WAGEMAN, John H.	ES: Amelia, Clermont Co., OH B: Amelia, Clermont Co., OH	BOERS, Edward William	ES: KY B: Cincinnati, Hamilton Co., OH
WALKER, Allen	ES: Cincinnati, Hamilton Co., OH B: Patriot, Switzerland Co., IN	BROCK, George F.	ES: CA B: Cleveland, Montgomery Co., OH
WALKER, James C.	ES: Springfield, Clark Co., OH B: Harmony, Clark Co., OH	BUTTS, George	ES: Cleveland, Cuyahoga Co., OH B: Rome, Oneida Co., NY
WALLER, Francis A.	ES: DeSoto, Vernon Co., WI B: Gurney, OH	DORMAN, John Henry	ES: Cincinnati, Hamilton Co., OH B: Cincinnati, Hamilton Co., OH
WARD, Nelson W.	ES: Rutland, Meigs Co., OH B: Madison Township, Columbiana Co., OH	*ESTOCIN, Michael John	ES: Akron, Summit Co., OH B: Turtle Creek, Allegheny Co., PA
WEBBER, Alason P.	ES: Chillicothe, Ross Co., OH B: Greene Co., NY	GARY, Donald Arthur	ES: OH B: Findlay, Hancock Co., OH
WELSH, Edward	ES: Cincinnati, Hamilton Co., OH B: Ireland	HALEY, James	ES: OH B: Ireland
WENDE, Bruno	ES: Canton, Stark Co., OH B: Germany	HANFORD, Burke	ES: OH B: Toledo, Lucas Co., OH
*WILEY, James	ES: Bellville, Richland Co., OH B: OH	HARNER, Joseph Gabriel	ES: OH B: Louisville, Stark Co., OH
WILHELM, George	ES: Lancaster, Fairfield Co., OH B: Scioto Co., OH	JARDINE, Alexander	ES: OH B: Inverness, Scotland
WILLIAMS, William Haliday	ES: Lima, Allen Co., OH B: Williamstown, Hancock Co., OH	*KIDD, Isaac Campbell	ES: OH B: Cleveland, Cuyahoga Co., OH
WILSON, Benjamin	ES: Cincinnati, Hamilton Co., OH B: Pittsburgh, Allegheny Co., PA	McGUNIGAL, Patrick	ES: OH B: Hubbard, Trumbull Co., OH
WILSON, John Alfred	ES: Perrysburg, Wood Co., OH B: Columbus, Franklin Co., OH	McHUGH, Martin	ES: OH B: Cincinnati, Hamilton Co., OH
WILSON, Milden H.	ES: Newark, Licking Co., OH B: Huron Co., OH	PETTY, Orlando Henderson	ES: PA B: Harrison, Hamilton Co., OH
*WINDER, David Francis	ES: Columbus, Franklin Co., OH B: Edinboro, Erie Co., PA	READ, Charles A.	ES: OH B: Sweden
WOLLAM, John	ES: Jackson, Jackson Co., OH B: Hamilton, Butler Co., OH	*SCOTT, Robert Raymond	ES: OH B: Massillon, Stark Co., OH
WOOD, Mark	ES: Portage, Wood Co., OH B: England	SHEPARD, Louis Capet	ES: OH B: Ashtabula, Ashtabula Co., OH

STUPKA, Laddie	ES: OH B: Cleveland, Cuyahoga Co., OH	*HARMON, Roy W.	ES: Pixley, Tulare Co., CA B: Talala, Rogers Co., OK
*WARD, James Richard	ES: Springfield, Clark Co., OH B: Springfield, Clark Co., OH	HAYS, George Price	ES: Okarche, Kingfisher Co., OK B: Chee Foo, China
WILLIAMS, Jay P.	ES: OH B: Orland, Steuben Co., IN	*HENRY, Frederick F.	ES: Clinton, Custer Co., OK B: Vian, Sequoyah Co., OK
WOOD, Robert B.	ES: OH B: New Garden, OH	*KINER, Harold G.	ES: Enid, Garfield Co., OK B: Aline, Alfalfa Co., OK

U.S. Marine Corps

*BAUGH, William Bernard	ES: Harrison, Hamilton Co., OH B: McKinney, Lincoln Co., KY	*McGILL, Troy A.	ES: Ada, Pontotoc Co., OK B: Knoxville, Knox Co., TN
*BERRY, Charles Joseph	ES: Ohio B: Lorain, Lorain Co., OH	MONTGOMERY, Jack Cleveland	ES: Sallisaw, Sequoyah Co., OK B: Long, OK
*DICKEY, Douglas Eugene	ES: Cincinnati, Hamilton Co., OH B: Greenville, Darke Co., OH	*PEREZ Jr., Manuel	ES: Chicago, Cook Co., IL B: Oklahoma City, Oklahoma Co., OK
*EPPERSON, Harold Glenn	ES: OH B: Akron, Summit Co., OH	*PIERCE, Larry Stanley	ES: Fresno, Fresno Co., CA B: Wewoka, Seminole Co., OK
*FOSTER, William Adelbert	ES: OH B: Cleveland, Cuyahoga Co., OH	*PITTS, Riley Leroy	ES: Wichita, Sedgwick Co., KS B: Fallis, OK
JACKSON, Arthur Junior	ES: Portland, Multnomah Co., OR B: Cleveland, Cuyahoga Co., OH	*REESE Jr., John N.	ES: Pryor, Mayes Co., OK B: Muskogee, Muskogee Co., OK
*KELLY, John Doran	ES: Homestead, Allegheny Co., PA B: Youngstown, Mahoning Co., OH	SAMPLER, Samuel M.	ES: Altus, Jackson Co., OK B: Decatur, Wise Co., TX
*MARTIN, Harry Linn	ES: OH B: Bucyrus, Crawford Co., OH	SCHAUER, Henry	ES: Scobey, Daniels Co., MT B: Clinton, Custer Co., OK
*MASON, Leonard Foster	ES: OH B: Middlesboro, Bell Co., KY	*SHOCKLEY, William Ralph	ES: Selma, Fresno Co., CA B: Bokoshe, LeFlore Co., OK
*NEWLIN, Melvin Earl	ES: Cleveland, Cuyahoga Co., OH B: Wellsville, Columbiana Co., OH	TREADWELL, Jack Lemaster	ES: Snyder, Kiowa Co., OK B: Ashland, Clay Co., AL
ORNDOFF, Harry Westley	ES: CA B: Sandusky, Erie Co., OH	TURNER, Harold Leo	ES: Seminole, Seminole Co., OK B: Aurora, Lawrence Co., MO
OSTERMANN, Edward Albert	ES: OH B: Columbus, Franklin Co., OH	*WALLACE, Herman C.	ES: Lubbock, Lubbock Co., TX B: Marlow, Stephens Co., OK

U.S. Army Air Corps

*GOTT, Donald Joseph	ES: Arnett, Ellis Co., OK B: Arnett, Ellis Co., OK
*VANCE Jr., Leon Robert	ES: Garden City, Nassau Co., NY B: Enid, Garfield Co., OK

*PAUL, Joe Calvin	ES: Dayton, Montgomery Co., OH B: Williamsburg, Whitley Co., KY		
REID, George Croghan	ES: OH B: Lorain, Lorain Co., OH		
*STEIN, Tony	ES: OH B: Dayton, Montgomery Co., OH		
*THOMAS, Herbert Joseph	ES: WV B: Columbus, Franklin Co., OH		
UPHAM, Oscar Jefferson	ES: IL B: Toledo, Lucas Co., OH		

U.S. Navy

*EVANS, Ernest Edwin "Chief"	ES: OK B: Pawnee, Pawnee Co., OK
McCOOL Jr., Richard Miles	ES: OK B: Tishomingo, Johnston Co., OK

U.S. Marine Corps

*BAILEY, Kenneth Dillon	ES: IL B: Pawnee, Pawnee Co., OK
*SCHWAB, Albert Ernest	ES: Tulsa, Tulsa Co., OK B: Washington, D.C.
SMITH, John Lucian	ES: OK B: Lexington, Cleveland Co., OK

OKLAHOMA

U.S. Army

*BURRIS, Tony K.	ES: Blanchard, McClain Co., OK B: Blanchard, McClain Co., OK
*CAREY Jr., Charles F.	ES: Cheyenne, Laramie Co., WY B: Canadian, Pittsburg Co., OK
CHAPMAN, Amos	ES: Fort Supply, Indian Territory (Oklahoma) B: Kalamazoo, Kalamazoo Co., MI
CHILDERS, Ernest "Chief"	ES: Tulsa, Tulsa Co., OK B: Broken Arrow, Tulsa Co., OK
CREWS, John R.	ES: Bowlegs, Seminole Co., OK B: Golden, McCurtain Co., OK
EPPS, Joseph L.	ES: Indian Territory (Oklahoma) B: Jamestown, Moniteau Co., MO

OREGON

U.S. Army

ALLWORTH, Edward C.	ES: Corvallis, Benton Co., OR B: Crawford, WA
*DAHL, Larry Gilbert	ES: Portland, Multnomah Co., OR B: Oregon City, Clackamas Co., OR

HIGH, Frank Charles	ES: Ashland, Jackson Co., OR B: Dunningham, Yolo Co., CA	BETTS, Charles Malone	ES: Philadelphia, Philadelphia Co., PA B: Bucks Co., PA
*HOLCOMB, John Noble	ES: Corvallis, Benton Co., OR B: Baker, Baker Co., OR	BEYER, Hillary	ES: Philadelphia, Philadelphia Co., PA B: Montgomery Co., PA
*KAUFMAN, Loren R.	ES: The Dalles, Wasco Co., OR B: The Dalles, Wasco Co., OR	BINGHAM, Henry Harrison Pensylvania	ES: Canonsburg, Washington Co., B: Philadelphia, Philadelphia Co., PA
KILBOURNE Jr., Charles Evans	ES: Portland, Multnomah Co., OR B: Fort Myer, Arlington Co., VA	BISHOP, Francis A.	ES: Harrisburg, Dauphin Co., PA B: Bradford Co., PA
PHIFE, Lewis	ES: Marion, Marion Co., OR B: Des Moines Co., IA	BLACKMAR, Wilmon Whilldin	ES: Philadelphia, Philadelphia Co., PA B: Bristol, Bucks Co., PA
ROBERTSON, Marcus William	ES: Hood River, Hood River Co., OR B: Flintville, WI	BLACKWOOD, William Robert Douglas	ES: Philadelphia, Philadelphia Co., PA B: Hollywood, County Wicklow, Ireland
*STRYKER, Stuart S.	ES: Portland, Multnomah Co., OR B: Portland, Multnomah Co., OR	BLAIR, James	ES: Camp Winfield Scott, Humbolt Co., NV B: Schuyler Co., PA
*YABES, Maximo	ES: Eugene, Lane Co., OR B: Lodi, San Joaquin Co., CA	BLICKENSDERGER, Milton	ES: Shanesville, OH B: Lancaster, Lancaster Co., PA

U.S. Army Air Corps

*KINGSLEY, David Richard	ES: Portland, Multnomah Co., OR B: Portland, Multnomah Co., OR	BLUCHER, Charles	ES: Philadelphia, Philadelphia Co., PA B: Germany
		BONEBRAKE, Henry G.	ES: Franklin Co., PA B: Waynesboro, Franklin Co., PA

U.S. Navy

FADDEN, Harry Delmar	ES: WA B: The Dalles, Wasco Co., OR	BONNAFFON Jr., Sylvester	ES: Philadelphia, Philadelphia Co., PA B: Philadelphia, Philadelphia Co., PA
		BOON, Hugh Patterson	ES: Washington, Washington Co., PA B: Washington, Washington Co., PA

U.S. Marine Corps

JACKSON, Arthur Junior	ES: Portland, Multnomah Co., OR B: Cleveland, Cuyahoga Co., OH	BOURKE, John Gregory	ES: Chicago, Cook Co., IL B: Philadelphia, Philadelphia Co., PA
*MARTINI, Gary Wayne	ES: Portland, Multnomah Co., OR B: Lexington, Lexington Co., VA	BRANNIGAN, Felix	ES: Pittsburgh, Allegheny Co., PA B: Ireland

PENNSYLVANIA

U.S. Army

ALLEN, William	ES: Philadelphia, Philadelphia Co., PA B: Philadelphia, Philadelphia Co., PA	BREST, Lewis Francis	ES: Pittsburgh, Allegheny Co., PA B: Mercer, Mercer Co., PA
AMMERMAN, Robert Wesley	ES: Milesburg, Centre Co., PA B: Centre Co., PA	BREWSTER, Andre Walker	ES: Philadelphia, Philadelphia Co., PA B: Hoboken, Hudson Co., NJ
ANDERSON, Everett W.	ES: Philadelphia, Philadelphia Co., PA B: near Phoenixville, Chester Co., PA	BREYER, Charles	ES: Philadelphia, Philadelphia Co., PA B: England
ANDERSON, Thomas	ES: Wheeling, Ohio Co., WV B: Scenery Hill, Washington Co., PA	BROGAN, James	ES: Harrisburg, Dauphin Co., PA B: County Donegal, Ireland
APPLE, Andrew O.	ES: New Manchester, Hancock Co., WV B: Northampton, Northampton Co., PA	BRONSON, James H.	ES: Trumbell Co., OH B: Indiana Co., PA
ARNOLD, Abraham Kerns	ES: Bedford, Bedford Co., PA B: Bedford, Bedford Co., PA	BROWN, Benjamin	ES: Harrisburg, Dauphin Co., PA B: Spotsylvania Co., VA
BAIRD, Absalom	ES: Washington, Washington Co., PA B: Washington, Washington Co., PA	BROWN, Charles E.	ES: Schuylkill Haven, Schuylkill Co., PA B: Schuylkill Co., PA
BEAUMONT, Eugene Beauharnais	ES: Wilks-Barre, Luzerne Co., PA B: Wilks-Barre, Luzerne Co., PA	BROWN, Jeremiah Z.	ES: Curllsville, Clarion Co., PA B: near Rural Valley, Armstrong Co., PA
BEEBE, William Sully	ES: Philadelphia, Philadelphia Co., PA B: Ithaca, Tompkins Co., NY	*BROWN, Melvin L.	ES: Erie, Erie Co., PA B: Mahaffey, Clearfield Co., PA
*BENJAMIN Jr., George	ES: Carney's Point, Salem Co., NJ B: Philadelphia, Philadelphia Co., PA	BURNETT, George Ritter	ES: Spring Mills, Centre Co., PA B: Lower Providence Township, PA
BENNETT, Orrin	ES: Towanda, Bradford Co., PA B: Bradford Co., PA	BUZZARD, Ulysses G.	ES: Pittsburgh, Allegheny Co., PA B: Armstrong, PA
BENYAURD, William Henry Harrison	ES: Philadelphia, Philadelphia Co., PA B: Philadelphia, Philadelphia Co., PA	CALDWELL, Daniel G.	ES: Philadelphia, Philadelphia Co., PA B: Marble Hill, Montgomery Co., PA
		CANFIELD, Heth	ES: Carlisle, Cumberland Co., PA B: New Milford, Litchfield Co., CT
		CAPEHART, Charles E.	ES: Washington, D.C. B: Conemaugh Township, PA
		CAPEHART, Henry	ES: Bridgeport, Belmont Co., OH B: Johnstown, Cambria Co., PA

*CAREY, Alvin P.	ES: Laughlintown, Westmoreland Co., PA B: Lycippus, PA	DEARY, George	ES: Philadelphia, Philadelphia Co., PA B: Philadelphia, Philadelphia Co., PA
CARLISLE, Casper R.	ES: Pittsburgh, Allegheny Co., PA B: Allegheny Co., PA	DeLACEY, Patrick	ES: Scranton, Lackawanna Co., PA B: Carbondale, Lackawanna Co., PA
CARPENTER, Louis Henry	ES: Philadelphia, Philadelphia Co., PA B: Glassboro, Gloucester Co., NJ	DELANEY, John Carroll	ES: Honesdale, Wayne Co., PA B: Ireland
CARSON, William J.	ES: North Greenfield, Highland Co., OH B: Washington Co., PA	DeLAVIE, Hiram H.	ES: Allegheny Co., PA B: Stark Co., OH
CART, Jacob	ES: Carlisle, Cumberland Co., PA B: Carlisle, Cumberland Co., PA	*DESIDERIO, Reginald Benjamin	ES: Gilroy, Santa Clara Co., CA B: Clairton, Allegheny Co., PA
CASEY, Henry	ES: Bloomingbug, Fayette Co., OH B: New Geneva, Fayette Co., PA	DeSWAN, John Francis	ES: Philadelphia, Philadelphia Co., PA B: Philadelphia, Philadelphia Co., PA
CASEY, James Seaman	ES: New York, NY B: Philadelphia, Philadelphia Co., PA	DOLBY, David Charles	ES: Philadelphia, Philadelphia Co., PA B: Norristown, Montgomery Co., PA
CHAMBERS, Joseph B.	ES: East Brook, PA B: Beaver Co., PA	DONALDSON, John P.	ES: Butler, Butler Co., PA B: Butler Co., PA
CLARK, James G.	ES: Philadelphia, Philadelphia Co., PA B: Germantown, Philadelphia Co., PA	DOUGHERTY, Michael	ES: Philadelphia, Philadelphia Co., PA B: Falcarragh, County Donegal, Ireland
CLARK, Wilfred	ES: Philadelphia, Philadelphia Co., PA B: Philadelphia, Philadelphia Co., PA	DOUGHERTY, William	ES: Philadelphia, Philadelphia Co., PA B: Detroit, Wayne Co., MI
CLARK, William A.	ES: Shelbyville, MN B: PA	*DUTKO, John W.	ES: Riverside, Burlington Co., NJ B: Dilltown, Indiana Co., PA
CLAUSEN, Charles H.	ES: Philadelphia, Philadelphia Co., PA B: Philadelphia, Philadelphia Co., PA	EDGERTON, Nathan Huntley	ES: Philadelphia, Philadelphia Co., PA B: Barnesville, Belmont Co., OH
CLAY, Cecil	ES: Philadelphia, Philadelphia Co., PA B: Philadelphia, Philadelphia Co., PA	ELLIOTT, Alexander	ES: North Sewickley, Allegheny Co., PA B: Beaver Co., PA
CLOPP, John E.	ES: Philadelphia, Philadelphia Co., PA B: Philadelphia, Philadelphia Co., PA	ELLIS, Horace	ES: Chippewa Falls, Chippewa Co., WI B: Mercer Co., PA
COLLIS, Charles Henry Tucky	ES: Philadelphia, Philadelphia Co., PA B: Cork, County Cork, Ireland	ENGLE, James Edgar	ES: Chester, Delaware Co., PA B: Chester, Delaware Co., PA
COMFORT, John W.	ES: Philadelphia, Philadelphia Co., PA B: Philadelphia, Philadelphia Co., PA	*ENGLISH Jr., Glenn Harry	ES: Philadelphia, Philadelphia Co., PA B: Altoona, Blair Co., PA
CONNELL, Trustrim	ES: Port Kennedy, PA B: Lancaster, Lancaster Co., PA	EVANS, Thomas	ES: Johnstown, Cambria Co., PA B: Wales
CONNER, Richard	ES: Burlington, Burlington Co., NJ B: Philadelphia, Philadelphia Co., PA	EWING, John C.	ES: Greensburg, Westmoreland Co., PA B: Ligonier Valley, Westmoreland Co., PA
COOKE, Walter Howard	ES: Norristown, Montgomery Co., PA B: Norristown, Montgomery Co., PA	FARREN, Daniel	ES: Philadelphia, Philadelphia Co., PA B: County Derry, Ireland
CORCORAN, Michael	ES: Wheeling, Ohio Co., WV B: Philadelphia, Philadelphia Co., PA	FASNACHT, Charles H.	ES: Philadelphia, Philadelphia Co., PA B: Lancaster Co., PA
CORSON, Joseph Kirby	ES: Philadelphia, Philadelphia Co., PA B: Plymouth Meeting, Montgomery Co., PA	FASSETT, John Barclay	ES: Philadelphia, Philadelphia Co., PA B: Philadelphia, Philadelphia Co., PA
CRANDALL, Charles	ES: Philadelphia, Philadelphia Co., PA B: Worcester, Worcester Co., MA	FEASTER, Mosheim	ES: Cleveland, Cuyahoga Co., OH B: Schellsburg, Bedford Co., PA
*CRESCENZ, Michael Joseph	ES: Philadelphia, Philadelphia Co., PA B: Philadelphia, Philadelphia Co., PA	FISHER, John H.	ES: Chicago, Cook Co., IL B: Monmouth, PA
CUNNINGHAM, Francis Marion	ES: Springfield, Delaware Co., PA B: Somerset, Somerset Co., PA	FISHER, Joseph	ES: Philadelphia, Philadelphia Co., PA B: Philadelphia, Philadelphia Co., PA
CUNNINGHAM, James Smith	ES: Bloomington, McLean Co., IL B: Washington Co., PA	FLANAGAN, Augustin D.	ES: Chester Springs, Chester Co., PA B: Loretto, Cambria Co., PA
DAILY, Charles	ES: Philadelphia, Philadelphia Co., PA B: Mallow, County Cork, Ireland	FOX, William R.	ES: Philadelphia, Philadelphia Co., PA B: Philadelphia, Philadelphia Co., PA
DAVIDSIZER, John A.	ES: Lewistown, Mifflin Co., PA B: Milford, Pike Co., PA	FRICK, Jacob G.	ES: Pottsville, Schuylkill Co., PA B: Northumberland, Northumberland Co., PA
DAVIS, Charles C.	ES: Harrisburg, Dauphin Co., PA B: Harrisburg, Dauphin Co., PA	FUNK, West	ES: Philadelphia, Philadelphia Co., PA B: Boston, Suffolk Co., MA
DAY, Charles	ES: Richmond, Philadelphia Co., PA B: West Laurens, Otsego Co., NY	FUNK Jr., Leonard Alfred	ES: Wilkinsburg, Allegheny Co., PA B: Braddock Township, Allegheny Co., PA

FURMAN, Chester S.	ES: Bloomsburg, Columbia Co., PA B: Columbia, Lancaster Co., PA	HIMMELSBACK, Michael	ES: Harrisburg, Dauphin Co., PA B: Allegheny Co., PA
FURNESS, Frank	ES: Philadelphia, Philadelphia Co., PA B: Philadelphia, Philadelphia Co., PA	HOFFMAN, Thomas W.	ES: Harrisburg, Dauphin Co., PA B: Perrysburg, Allegheny Co., PA
GALLOWAY, George Norton	ES: Philadelphia, Philadelphia Co., PA B: Philadelphia, Philadelphia Co., PA	HOGAN, Franklin	ES: Howard, Centre Co., PA B: Centre Co., PA
GALLOWAY, John	ES: Philadelphia, Philadelphia Co., PA B: Philadelphia, Philadelphia Co., PA	HOOVER, Samuel	ES: Harrisburg, Dauphin Co., PA B: Dauphin Co., PA
GEDEON, Louis	ES: Pittsburgh, Allegheny Co., PA B: Pittsburgh, Allegheny Co., PA	HORNER, Freeman Victor	ES: Shamokin, Northumberland Co., PA B: Mount Carmel, Northumberland Co., PA
GILLIGAN, Edward Lyons	ES: Philadelphia, Philadelphia Co., PA B: Philadelphia, Philadelphia Co., PA	HOTTENSTINE, Solomon J.	ES: Philadelphia, Philadelphia Co., PA B: Lehigh Co., PA
GION, Joseph	ES: Allegheny Co., PA B: Alsace-Lorraine area, Germany	HOWARD, Henderson Calvin	ES: Indiana, Indiana Co., PA B: Indiana Co., PA
GLAVINSKI, Albert	ES: Pittsburgh, Allegheny Co., PA B: Germany (Prussia)	HUBBARD, Thomas H.	ES: Philadelphia, Philadelphia Co., PA B: Philadelphia, Philadelphia Co., PA
GOODMAN, William Ernest	ES: Philadelphia, Philadelphia Co., PA B: Philadelphia, Philadelphia Co., PA	HUFF, James W.	ES: Vanburan, PA B: Washington, Washington Co., PA
GRAUL, William L.	ES: Reading, Berks Co., PA B: Reading, Berks Co., PA	HUIDEKOPER, Henry Shippen	ES: Philadelphia, Philadelphia Co., PA B: Meadville, Crawford Co., PA
GRAY, Robert A.	ES: Groton, New London Co., CT B: Philadelphia, Philadelphia Co., PA	HUNTERSON, John C.	ES: Philadelphia, Philadelphia Co., PA B: Philadelphia, Philadelphia Co., PA
GREENAWALT, Abraham	ES: Salem, Columbiana Co., OH B: Montgomery Co., PA	HYATT, Theodore	ES: Gardner, Grundy Co., IL B: PA
GRESSER, Ignatz	ES: Allentown, Lehigh Co., PA B: Malach, Germany	ILGENFRITZ, Charles Henry	ES: Harrisburg, Dauphin Co., PA B: York Co., PA
GUNTHER, Jacob	ES: Philadelphia, Philadelphia Co., PA B: Schuylkill Co., PA	JENNINGS, James T.	ES: Luzerne, Luzerne Co., PA B: Devonshire, England
*HALLMAN, Sherwood H.	ES: Spring City, Chester Co., PA B: Spring City, Chester Co., PA	JOHNS, Henry T.	ES: Hinsdale, Berkshire Co., MA B: Philadelphia, Philadelphia Co., PA
HARMON, Amzi Davis	ES: Greensburg, Westmoreland Co., PA B: Wilkinsburg, Allegheny Co., PA	JOHNSON, Joseph Esrey	ES: Philadelphia, Philadelphia Co., PA B: Lower Merion, Montgomery Co., PA
*HARR, Harry R.	ES: East Freedom, Blair Co., PA B: Pine Croft, PA	JOHNSON, Ruel M.	ES: Goshen, Elkhart Co., IN B: Harbor Creek Township, Erie Co., PA
HARRIS, George W.	ES: Bellefonte, Centre Co., PA B: Schuylkill, Philadelphia Co., PA	JOHNSON, Samuel	ES: Connellsville, Fayette Co., PA B: Springfield Township, Delaware Co., PA
*HARTELL, Lee Ross	ES: Danbury, Fairfield Co., CT B: Philadelphia, Philadelphia Co., PA	JOHNSTON, David H.	ES: Warsaw, Hancock Co., IL B: Indiana Co., PA
HARTRANFT, John Frederic	ES: Norristown, Montgomery Co., PA B: New Hanover Township, Montgomery Co., PA	KAY, John	ES: Philadelphia, Philadelphia Co., PA B: Lancashire, England
HARVEY, Raymond	ES: Pasadena, Los Angeles Co., CA B: Ford City, Armstrong Co., PA	*KEFURT, Gus	ES: Youngstown, Mahoning Co., OH B: Greenville, Mercer Co., PA
HAWKINS, Martin Jones	ES: Portsmouth, Scioto Co., OH B: Mercer Co., PA	KELLY, Alexander	ES: Allegheny, Allegheny Co., PA B: Saltsburg, Indiana Co., PA
HAWKINS, Thomas R.	ES: Philadelphia, Philadelphia Co., PA B: Cincinnati, Hamilton Co., OH	KELLY, Charles E.	ES: Pittsburgh, Allegheny Co., PA B: Pittsburgh, Allegheny Co., PA
HENRY, Guy Vernor	ES: Reading, Berks Co., PA B: Fort Smith, Indian Territory	*KELLY, John D.	ES: Cambridge Springs, Crawford Co., PA B: Venango Township, Crawford Co., PA
HERRON, Francis Jay	ES: Pittsburgh, Allegheny Co., PA B: Pittsburgh, Allegheny Co., PA	KEPHART, James	ES: Dubuque, Dubuque Co., IA B: Venango Co., PA
HERRON, Leander	ES: Pittsburgh, Allegheny Co., PA B: Bucks Co., PA	KERR, Thomas R.	ES: Pittsburgh, Allegheny Co., PA B: near Colleraine, County Derry, Ireland
HEYL, Charles Pettit Heath	ES: Camden, Camden Co., NJ B: Philadelphia, Philadelphia Co., PA	KILMARTIN, John	ES: Philadelphia, Philadelphia Co., PA B: Montreal, Canada
HIGBY, Charles	ES: New Brighton, Beaver Co., PA B: Pittsburgh, Allegheny Co., PA	KINDIG, John M.	ES: Wilkins, Allegheny Co., PA B: East Liberty, Allegheny Co., PA
HILL, Henry	ES: Harrisburg, Dauphin Co., PA B: Schuylkill Co., PA	KINSEY, John	ES: Maytown, Lancaster Co., PA B: Lancaster Co., PA
HILL, James Madison	ES: Cincinnati, Hamilton Co., OH B: Washington Co., PA	KIRK, John	ES: Harrisburg, Dauphin Co., PA B: York, York Co., PA

KIRKWOOD, John A.	ES: North Platte Barracks, Lincoln Co., NE B: Allegheny City, Allegheny Co., PA	McMURTRY, George G.	ES: New York, NY B: Pittsburgh, Allegheny Co., PA
KITCHEN, George Krause	ES: Harrisburg, Dauphin Co., PA B: Lebanon Co., PA	*McVEIGH, John J.	ES: Philadelphia, Philadelphia Co., PA B: Philadelphia, Philadelphia Co., PA
KNAPPENBERGER, Alton W.	ES: Almount, Bucks Co., PA B: Coopersburg, Lehigh Co., PA	MEARS, George W.	ES: Bloomsburg, Columbia Co., PA B: Bloomsburg, Columbia Co., PA
KRAMER, Theodore L.	ES: Danville, Montour Co., PA B: Luzerne Co., PA	MECHLIN, Henry W.B.	ES: Pittsburgh, Allegheny Co., PA B: Mount Pleasant, Westmoreland Co., PA
*KREHER, Wendelin	ES: Philadelphia, Philadelphia Co., PA B: Stetten, Prussia	MERLI, Gino Joseph	ES: Peckville, Lackawanna Co., PA B: Scranton, Lackawanna Co., PA
LANDIS, James Parker	ES: Reedsville, Mifflin Co., PA B: Mifflin Co., PA	MERRIFIELD, James K.	ES: Manlius, Bureau Co., IL B: Hyde Park, Westmoreland Co., PA
LAWS, Robert Earl	ES: Altoona, Blair Co., PA B: Altoona, Blair Co., PA	*MESSERSCHMIDT, Harold O.	ES: Chester, Delaware Co., PA B: Grier City, PA
LEE, Fitz	ES: Philadelphia, Philadelphia Co., PA B: Dinwiddie Co., VA	*MESTROVITCH, James I.	ES: Pittsburgh, Allegheny Co., PA B: Crna Cora, Yugoslavia
LEONARD, William Edman	ES: Jacksonville, PA B: Greene Co., PA	MILLER, George W.	ES: Philadelphia, Philadelphia Co., PA B: Philadelphia, Philadelphia Co., PA
LEWIS, Dewitt Clinton	ES: West Chester, Chester Co., PA B: West Chester, Chester Co., PA	MILLER, William Edward	ES: Newville, Cumberland Co., PA B: West Hill, Cumberland Co., PA
LILLEY, John	ES: Lewistown, Mifflin Co., PA B: Mifflin Co., PA	MINDIL, George Washington	ES: Philadelphia, Philadelphia Co., PA B: near Frankfort, Germany
*LOBAUGH, Donald Ronald	ES: Freeport, Armstrong Co., PA B: Freeport, Armstrong Co., PA	*MINICK, John W.	ES: Carlisle, Cumberland Co., PA B: Wall, Allegheny Co., PA
LOWER, Cyrus B.	ES: New Castle, Lawrence Co., PA B: Lawrence, PA	MITCHELL, Alexander H.	ES: Hamilton, Jefferson Co., PA B: Perrysville, Allegheny Co., PA
LUTY, Gotlieb	ES: West Manchester, York Co., PA B: Allegheny Co., PA	MITCHELL, John James	ES: Philadelphia, Philadelphia Co., PA B: County Tyrone, Ireland
LYTLE, Leonidas S.	ES: Cleveland, Cuyahoga Co., OH B: Warren Co., PA	MITCHELL, Theodore	ES: Pittsburgh, Allegheny Co., PA B: Tarentum, Allegheny Co., PA
MACLAY, William Palmer	ES: Altoona, Blair Co., PA B: Spruce Creek, Huntingdon Co., PA	MONAGHAN, Patrick H.	ES: Minersville, Schuylkill Co., PA B: Ireland
MARM Jr., Walter Joseph	ES: Pittsburgh, Allegheny Co., PA B: Washington, Washington Co., PA	MORFORD, Jerome	ES: Bridgers Co., IL B: Mercer Co., PA
MARQUETTE, Charles D.	ES: Campbelltown, Lebanon Co., PA B: Lebanon Co., PA	MORRIS, James L.	ES: Philadelphia, Philadelphia Co., PA B: County Kerry, Ireland
MARTIN, Sylvester Hopkins	ES: Philadelphia, Philadelphia Co., PA B: Chester Co., PA	MORRIS, William Powers	ES: Philadelphia, Philadelphia Co., PA B: Philadelphia, Philadelphia Co., PA
MATTHEWS, John C.	ES: Greensburg, Westmoreland Co., PA B: Westmoreland Co., PA	MORRISON, Francis	ES: Drakestown, PA B: Ohiopyle, Fayette Co., PA
MATTHEWS, Milton	ES: Pittsburgh, Allegheny Co., PA B: Pittsburgh, Allegheny Co., PA	MOSTOLLER, John William	ES: Stoystown, Somerset Co., PA B: Stoystown, Somerset Co., PA
MAY, John	ES: Philadelphia, Philadelphia Co., PA B: Wurttemberg, Germany	MULHOLLAND, St. Clair Agustin	ES: Philadelphia, Philadelphia Co., PA B: Lisburn, County Antrim, Ireland
MAY, William C.	ES: Maysville, Franklin Co., IA B: PA	MUNSELL, Harvey May	ES: Philadelphia, Philadelphia Co., PA B: Painted Post, Steuben Co., NY
McADAMS, Peter	ES: Philadelphia, Philadelphia Co., PA B: Armagh, County Armagh, Ireland	MURPHY, Daniel J.	ES: Lowell, Middlesex Co., MA B: Philadelphia, Philadelphia Co., PA
McANALLY, Charles	ES: Philadelphia, Philadelphia Co., PA B: Ireland	MURPHY, Edward F.	ES: Philadelphia, Philadelphia Co., PA B: Wayne Co., PA
McCAMMON, William Wallace	ES: Montgomery City, Montgomery Co., MO B: Shippensburg, Cumberland Co., PA	MYERS, William H.	ES: Baltimore, Baltimore Co., MD B: Philadelphia, Philadelphia Co., PA
McCORMICK, Michael P.	ES: Harrisburg, Dauphin Co., PA B: Rutland, Rutland Co., VT	NOVOSEL, Michael Joseph	ES: Kenner, Jefferson Co., LA B: Etna, Allegheny Co., PA
*McGRAW, Francis Xavier	ES: Camden, Camden Co., NJ B: Philadelphia, Philadelphia Co., PA	OLIVER, Charles	ES: Webster, Westmoreland Co., PA B: Allegheny Co., PA
McKEEVER, Michael	ES: Philadelphia, Philadelphia Co., PA B: Ireland	ORR, Moses	ES: Philadelphia, Philadelphia Co., PA B: County Tyrone, Ireland
McKOWN, Nathaniel A.	ES: Philadelphia, Philadelphia Co., PA B: Susquehanna Co., PA	ORR, Robert Levan	ES: Philadelphia, Philadelphia Co., PA B: Philadelphia, Philadelphia Co., PA

ORTH, Jacob George	ES: Philadelphia, Philadelphia Co., PA B: Philadelphia, Philadelphia Co., PA	ROBINSON, Thomas	ES: Tamaqua, Schuylkill Co., PA B: Ireland
PALMER, William Jackson	ES: Philadelphia, Philadelphia Co., PA B: Leipsic, Kent Co., DE	RODENBOUGH, Theophilus Francis	ES: PA B: Easton, Northampton Co., PA
PAUL, William H.	ES: Philadelphia, Philadelphia Co., PA B: Philadelphia, Philadelphia Co., PA	*ROEDER, Robert E.	ES: Summit Station, Schuylkill Co., PA B: Summit Station, Schuylkill Co., PA
PAYNE, Irvin C.	ES: New York, NY B: Wayne Co., PA	ROGAN, Patrick	ES: Reading, Berks Co., PA B: County Leitrim, Ireland
PEARSON, Alfred L.	ES: Pittsburgh, Allegheny Co., PA B: Pittsburgh, Allegheny Co., PA	ROHM, Ferdinand Frederick	ES: Juniata Co., PA B: Patterson, Juniata Co., PA
PEIRSOL, James Kastor	ES: Waynesboro, OH B: Beaver Co., PA	ROOSEVELT, George Washington	ES: Chester Co., PA B: Chester Co., PA
PENNSYL, Josiah	ES: Carlisle, Cumberland Co., PA B: Frederick Co., MD	ROUGHT, Stephen	ES: Crampton, PA B: Bradford Co., PA
PENNYPACKER, Galusha	ES: West Chester, Chester Co., PA B: Near Valley Forge, Chester Co., PA	ROUSH, James Levi	ES: Chambersburg, Franklin Co., PA B: Bedford Co., PA
PETTY, Philip	ES: Troy, Bradford Co., PA B: Tingswich, Buckinghamshire, England	ROWAND Jr., Archibald Hamilton	ES: Pittsburgh, Allegheny Co., PA B: Philadelphia, Philadelphia Co., PA
PHILLIPS, Josiah	ES: Ulysses, Potter Co., PA B: Wyoming Co., NY	RUTTER, James May	ES: Wilkes-Barre, Luzerne Co., PA B: Wilkes-Barre, Luzerne Co., PA
*PINDER Jr., John J.	ES: Burgettstown, Washington Co., PA B: McKees Rocks, Allegheny Co., PA	RYAN, David	ES: Philadelphia, Philadelphia Co., PA B: County Kilkenny, Ireland
PIPES, James Milton	ES: Waynesburg, Greene Co., PA B: Morrisville, Bucks Co., PA	SACRISTE, Louis Jeanottelle	ES: Philadelphia, Philadelphia Co., PA B: New Castle Co., DE
PITMAN, George J.	ES: Philadelphia, Philadelphia Co., PA B: Recklestown, NJ	SANDS, William	ES: Reading, Berks Co., PA B: Reading, Berks Co., PA
PLATT, George Crawford	ES: Philadelphia, Philadelphia Co., PA B: Ireland	*SAYERS, Foster Joseph	ES: Howard, Centre Co., PA B: Marshalls Creek, Monroe Co., PA
*PORT, William David	ES: Harrisburg, Dauphin Co., PA B: Petersburg, Huntingdon Co., PA	SCHAFFNER, Dwite H.	ES: Falls Creek, Jefferson Co., PA B: Arroya, PA
*PORTER, Donn F.	ES: Baltimore, Baltimore Co., MD B: Sewickley, Allegheny Co., PA	SCHEIBNER, Martin E.	ES: Philadelphia, Philadelphia Co., PA B: Valdai, Russia
PORTER, Horace	ES: Harrisburg, Dauphin Co., PA B: Huntingdon, Huntingdon Co., PA	SCHOONMAKER, James Martinus	ES: Pittsburgh, Allegheny Co., PA B: Pittsburgh, Allegheny Co., PA
PURCELL, Hiram W.	ES: Doylestown, Bucks Co., PA B: Upper Black Eddy, Bucks Co., PA	SCOTT, John Wallace	ES: Philadelphia, Philadelphia Co., PA B: Chester Co., PA
PURMAN, James Jackson	ES: Waynesburg, Greene Co., PA B: Greene Co., PA	SEITZINGER, James M.	ES: Worcester, Montgomery Co., PA B: Germany
QUAY, Matthew Stanley	ES: Harrisburg, Dauphin Co., PA B: Dillsburg, York Co., PA	SELLERS, Alfred Jacob	ES: Philadelphia, Philadelphia Co., PA B: Plumsteadville, Bucks Co., PA
QUINN, Alexander M.	ES: Philadelphia, Philadelphia Co., PA B: Passaic, Passaic Co., NJ	SEWARD, Griffin	ES: Philadelphia, Philadelphia Co., PA B: Dover, Kent Co., DE
RANKIN, William	ES: Harrisburg, Dauphin Co., PA B: Lewistown, Mifflin Co., PA	SHAMBAUGH, Charles	ES: Indian Town, Lebanon Co., PA B: Prussia, Germany
RAUB, Jacob F.	ES: Weaversville, PA B: Raubsville, Northampton Co., PA	SHELLENBERGER, John	ES: Perryopolis, Fayette Co., PA B: Fayette Co., PA
REED, George W.	ES: Johnstown, Cambria Co., PA B: Cambria Co., PA	SHEPHERD, Warren Julius	ES: Westover, Clearfield Co., PA B: Cherry Tree, Indiana Co., PA
REED, William	ES: Pekin, Tazewell Co., IL B: Union Co., PA	SHIEL, John	ES: Philadelphia, Philadelphia Co., PA B: Scotland
*REESE, James W.	ES: Chester, Delaware Co., PA B: Chester, Delaware Co., PA	SHINGLE, John Henry	ES: St. Louis, St. Louis Co., MO B: Philadelphia, Philadelphia Co., PA
REID, Robert Alexander	ES: Pottsville, Schuylkill Co., PA B: Raploch, Scotland	SHOPP, George J.	ES: Reading, Berks Co., PA B: Equinunk, Wayne Co., PA
REIGLE, Daniel P.	ES: Gettysburg, Adams Co., PA B: Adams Co., PA	*SHUGHART, Randall David	ES: Newville, Cumberland Co., PA B: Lincoln, Lancaster Co., NE
REISINGER, James Monroe	ES: Meadville, Crawford Co., PA B: Beaver Co., PA	SILK, Edward A.	ES: Johnstown, Cambria Co., PA B: Johnstown, Cambria Co., PA
RESSLER, Norman W.	ES: Dalmatia, Northumberland Co., PA B: Dalmatia, Northumberland Co., PA		
RHODES, Sylvester D.	ES: Wilkes-Barre, Luzerne Co., PA B: Plains, PA		

*SITMAN, William S.	ES: Bellwood, Blair Co., PA B: Bellwood, Blair Co., PA	TWEEDALE, John	ES: Philadelphia, Philadelphia Co., PA B: Frankford, Philadelphia Co., PA
SLOAN, Andrew Jackson	ES: Colesburg, Delaware Co., IA B: Bedford Co., PA	VANDERSLICE, John Mitchell	ES: Philadelphia, Philadelphia Co., PA B: near Valley Forge, Chester Co., PA
SLUSHER, Henry C.	ES: Washington, Washington Co., PA B: Washington Co., PA	VEALE, Moses	ES: Philadelphia, Philadelphia Co., PA B: Bridgeton, Cumberland Co., NJ
SMALLEY, Reuben S.	ES: Brookfield, Cook Co., IL B: Washington Co., PA	WAINWRIGHT, John	ES: West Chester, Chester Co., PA B: Syracuse, Onondaga Co., NY
SMITH, Robert	ES: Philadelphia, Philadelphia Co., PA B: Philadelphia, Philadelphia Co., PA	WALTON, George Washington	ES: Upper Oxford Township, Chester Co., PA B: Upper Oxford Township, Chester Co., PA
SMITH, Thaddeus S.	ES: Harrisburg, Dauphin Co., PA B: Cumberland, Franklin Co., PA	WARD, Charles H.	ES: Philadelphia, Philadelphia Co., PA B: Bradford, England
SMITH, Theodore F.	ES: Harrisburg, Dauphin Co., PA B: Rahway, Union Co., NJ	WARFEL, Henry Clay	ES: Monocacy Junction, MD B: Mill Creek, Huntingdon Co., PA
SNEDDEN, James	ES: Johnstown, Cambria Co., PA B: Edinburgh, Scotland	WATSON, James C.	ES: Philadelphia, Philadelphia Co., PA B: Cochecton, Sullivan Co., NY
SOWERS, Michael	ES: Pittsburgh, Allegheny Co., PA B: Pittsburgh, Allegheny Co., PA	WEAHER, Andrew J.	ES: Philadelphia, Philadelphia Co., PA B: Philadelphia, Philadelphia Co., PA
*SPEICHER, Clifton T.	ES: Gray, Somerset Co., PA B: Gray, Somerset Co., PA	*WEICHT, Ellis R.	ES: Bedford, Bedford Co., PA B: Clearville, Bedford Co., PA
SPENCE, Orizoba	ES: Cincinnati, Hamilton Co., OH B: Forest Co., PA	WHITE, John Henry	ES: Philadelphia, Philadelphia Co., PA B: Philadelphia, Philadelphia Co., PA
SPRINGER, George	ES: Harrisburg, Dauphin Co., PA B: York Co., PA	WIDMER, Jacob	ES: Philadelphia, Philadelphia Co., PA B: Wurttemberg, Germany
STOREY, John Hamilton Reid	ES: Philadelphia, Philadelphia Co., PA B: Philadelphia, Philadelphia Co., PA	WILKENS, Henry	ES: Pittsburgh, Allegheny Co., PA B: Germany
*STRAUSBURGH, Bernard A.	ES: Warfordsburg, Fulton Co., PA B: Adams Co., PA	*WILL, Walter J.	ES: West Winfield, Herkimer Co., NY B: Pittsburgh, Allegheny Co., PA
STRAYER, William H.	ES: Carlisle, Cumberland Co., PA B: Maytown, Lancaster Co., PA	WILLIAMS, Elwood N.	ES: Havana, Mason Co., IL B: Philadelphia, Philadelphia Co., PA
SWAN, Charles Alexander	ES: Mount Pleasant, Henry Co., IA B: Greene Co., PA	*WILSON, Alfred Leonard	ES: Fairchance, Fayette Co., PA B: Fairchance, Fayette Co., PA
SWAP, Jacob E.	ES: Springs, Somerset Co., PA B: Coeymans, Albany Co., NY	WILSON, Benjamin	ES: Cincinnati, Hamilton Co., OH B: Pittsburgh, Allegheny Co., PA
TANNER, Charles B.	ES: Wilmimgton, New Castle Co., DE B: Philadelphia, Philadelphia Co., PA	WILSON, Charles E.	ES: Hatborough, Montgomery Co., NJ B: Bucks Co., PA
TAYLOR, Anthony	ES: Philadelphia, Philadelphia Co., PA B: Burlington, Burlington Co., NJ	WILSON, Francis A.	ES: Philadelphia, Philadelphia Co., PA B: Philadelphia, Philadelphia Co., PA
TAYLOR, Forrester L.	ES: Beverly, Burlington Co., NJ B: Philadelphia, Philadelphia Co., PA	WILSON, William	ES: Philadelphia, Philadelphia Co., PA B: Philadelphia, Philadelphia Co., PA
TEA, Richard Longstreet	ES: Philadelphia, Philadelphia Co., PA B: Philadelphia, Philadelphia Co., PA	*WINDER, David Francis	ES: Columbus, Franklin Co., OH B: Edinboro, Erie Co., PA
*THOMAS, Charles L.	ES: Cincinnati, Hamilton Co., OH B: Philadelphia, Philadelphia Co., PA	WITCOME, Joseph	ES: Carlisle, Cumberland Co., PA B: Mechanicsburg, Cumberland Co., PA
THOMAS, Hampton Sidney	ES: Harrisburg, Dauphin Co., PA B: Quakertown, Bucks Co., PA	WOODALL, Zachariah	ES: Carlisle, Cumberland Co., PA B: Alexandria, Alexandria Co., VA
THOMPSON, James B.	ES: Perrysville, Allegheny Co., PA B: Juniata Co., PA	WOODWARD, Evan M.	ES: Sandy Hook, MD B: Philadelphia Philadelphia Co., PA
THOMPSON, Joseph Henry	ES: Beaver Falls, Beaver Co., PA B: Kilkeel, County Down, Ireland	WORTICK, Joseph	ES: Hannibal, Marion Co., MO B: Fayette Co., PA
THOMPSON, Peter	ES: Pittsburgh, Allegheny Co., PA B: Scotland	WRAY, William J.	ES: Philadelphia, Philadelphia Co., PA B: Philadelphia, Philadelphia Co., PA
TOMINAC, John Joseph	ES: Conemaugh, Cambria Co., PA B: Conemaugh, Cambria Co., PA	WRIGHT, Albert D.	ES: Wellsboro, Tioga Co., PA B: Elkland, Tioga Co., PA
TRAUTMAN, Jacob	ES: Pittsburgh, Allegheny Co., PA B: Hamburg, Germany	YEAGER, Jacob F.	ES: Tiffin, Seneca Co., OH B: New Texas, Lehigh Co., PA
TUCKER, Jacob R.	ES: Baltimore, Baltimore Co., MD B: Chester Co., PA	YOUNG, Andrew J.	ES: Carmichaels, Greene Co., PA B: Greene Co., PA
*TURNER, Day G.	ES: Nescopeck, Luzerne Co., PA B: Berwick, Columbia Co., PA		

U.S. Army Air Corps/U.S. Air Force

*MATHIES, Archibald — ES: Pittsburgh, Allegheny Co., PA / B: Scotland

*SARNOSKI, Joseph Raymond — ES: Simpson, Lackawanna Co., PA / B: Simpson, Lackawanna Co., PA

SHOMO, William Arthur — ES: Westmoreland Co., PA / B: Jeannette, Westmoreland Co., PA

ZEAMER Jr., Jay — ES: Machias, Washington Co., ME / B: Carlisle, Cumberland Co., PA

U.S. Navy

ANDREWS, John — ES: Maryland / B: York Co., PA

BALDWIN, Charles H. — ES: Philadelphia, Philadelphia Co., PA / B: Wilmington, New Castle Co., DE

BARRETT, Edward — ES: PA / B: Philadelphia, Philadelphia Co., PA

*BENFOLD, Edward Clyde "Ted" — ES: Philadelphia, Philadelphia Co., PA / B: Staten Island, Richmond Co., NY

BISHOP, Charles Francis — ES: PA / B: Pittsburgh, Allegheny Co., PA

BLUME, Robert — ES: NJ / B: Pittsburgh, Allegheny Co., PA

BOONE, Joel Thompson — ES: St. Clair, Schuylkill Co., PA / B: St. Clair, Schuylkill Co., PA

BRAZELL, John — ES: PA / B: Philadelphia, Philadelphia Co., PA

BRUTSCHE, Henry — ES: PA / B: Philadelphia, Philadelphia Co., PA

BUCHANAN, David M. — ES: PA / B: Philadelphia, Philadelphia Co., PA

CLIFFORD, Robert Teleford — ES: PA / B: PA

CONNOR, William C. — ES: PA / B: Cork, County Coke, Ireland

CRAWFORD, Alexander — ES: Philadelphia, Philadelphia Co., PA / B: Philadelphia, Philadelphia Co., PA

CRILLEY, Frank William — ES: PA / B: Trenton, Mercer Co., NJ

CRIPPS, Thomas H. — ES: PA / B: Philadelphia, Philadelphia Co., PA

CROUSE, William Adolphus — ES: PA / B: Tannettsburg, Franklin Co., PA

CUTTER, George W. — ES: PA / B: Philadelphia, Philadelphia Co., PA

DAVIS, Joseph H. — ES: Philadelphia, Philadelphia Co., PA / B: Philadelphia, Philadelphia Co., PA

DEAKIN, Charles — ES: Philadelphia, Philadelphia Co., PA / B: New York, NY

DEMPSTER, John — ES: Philadelphia, Philadelphia Co., PA / B: Scotland

DOOLEN, William — ES: Philadelphia, Philadelphia Co., PA / B: Ireland

*DREXLER, Henry Clay — ES: PA / B: Braddock, Allegheny Co., PA

DRUSTRUP, Niels — ES: PA / B: Denmark

Du MOULIN, Frank — ES: PA / B: Philadelphia, Philadelphia Co., PA

DUNCAN, James K. L. — ES: PA / B: Frankfort Mineral Springs, Washington Co., PA

DURNEY, Austin Joseph — ES: Woodland, MD / B: Philadelphia, Philadelphia Co., PA

EDWARDS, Walter Atlee — ES: PA / B: Philadelphia, Philadelphia Co., PA

*ESTOCIN, Michael John — ES: Akron, Summit Co., OH / B: Turtle Creek, Allegheny Co., PA

GIRANDY, Alphonse — ES: PA / B: Guadaloupe, West Indies

GRACE, Patrick Henry — ES: PA / B: Ireland

HAFFEE, Edmund — ES: Philadelphia, Philadelphia Co., PA / B: Philadelphia, Philadelphia Co., PA

HAMILTON, Richard — ES: PA / B: Philadelphia, Philadelphia Co., PA

HICKMAN, John S. — ES: PA / B: Blair Co., PA

*HILL, Edwin Joseph — ES: PA / B: Philadelphia, Philadelphia Co., PA

HUBER, William Russell — ES: PA / B: Harrisburg, Dauphin Co., PA

JOHNSEN, Hans — ES: PA / B: Sandnes, Norway

JOHNSON, John — ES: PA / B: Philadelphia, Philadelphia Co., PA

JOHNSON, Peter — ES: PA / B: Sumerland, England

JONES, William — ES: PA / B: Philadelphia, Philadelphia Co., PA

KILLACKEY, Joseph — ES: PA / B: County Cork, Ireland

LAFFERTY, John — ES: PA / B: New York, NY

LAWSON, John — ES: PA / B: Philadelphia, Philadelphia Co., PA

LEAR, Nicholas — ES: Philadelphia, Philadelphia Co., PA / B: Rhode Island

LEON, Pierre — ES: Philadelphia, Philadelphia Co., PA / B: France

LEVERY, William — ES: PA / B: Philadelphia, Philadelphia Co., PA

LLOYD, Benjamin — ES: Philadelphia, Philadelphia Co., PA / B: Liverpool, Merseyside Co., England

LOWRY, George Maus — ES: PA / B: Erie, Erie Co., PA

MAHONEY, George — ES: PA / B: Worcester, Worcester Co., MA

MARTIN, Edward S. — ES: Philadelphia, Philadelphia Co., PA / B: Ireland

MATTHEWS, Joseph — ES: PA / B: Malta

McWILLIAMS, George Washington — ES: PA / B: Waterford, Erie Co., PA

MILLER, Hugh — ES: PA / B: Philadelphia, Philadelphia Co., PA

MITCHELL, Joseph Andrew — ES: PA / B: Philadelphia, Philadelphia Co., PA

MOORE, George — ES: Boston, Suffolk Co., MA / B: Philadelphia, Philadelphia Co., PA

O'NEAL, John	ES: PA B: Ireland	DOUGHERTY, James	ES: PA B: Langhash, Ireland
ORTEGA, John	ES: PA B: Spain	*FISHER, Harry	ES: PA B: McKeesport, Allegheny Co., PA
PETERS, Alexander	ES: PA B: Russia	FOLEY, Alexander Joseph	ES: PA B: Heckersville, PA
PETTY, Orlando Henderson	ES: PA B: Harrison, Hamilton Co., OH	FRANCIS, Charles Robert	ES: Philadelphia, Philadelphia Co., PA B: Doylestown, Bucks Co., PA
RILLEY, John Phillip	ES: Massachusetts B: Allentown, Lehigh Co., PA	FRY, Isaac N.	ES: Philadelphia, Philadelphia Co., PA B: Lancaster, Lancaster Co., PA
RUSH, William Rees	ES: PA B: Philadelphia, Philadelphia Co., PA	GAUGHAN, Philip	ES: PA B: Belmullet, County Mayo, Ireland
SANDERSON, Aaron	ES: Philadelphia, Philadelphia Co., PA B: NC	*GRAHAM, James Albert	ES: Prince Georges, Prince Georges Co., MD B: Wilkinsburg, Allegheny Co., PA
SAPP, Isaac	ES: PA B: Philadelphia, Philadelphia Co., PA	GROSS, Samuel	ES: PA B: Philadelphia, Philadelphia Co., PA
SCHMIDT Jr., Oscar	ES: PA B: Philadelphia, Philadelphia Co., PA	HORTON, William M. Charlie	ES: Philadelphia, Philadelphia Co., PA B: Chicago, Cook Co., IL
SEMPLE, Robert	ES: PA B: Pittsburgh, Allegheny Co., PA	IAMS, Ross Lindsey	ES: PA B: Graysville, Greene Co., PA
SINNETT, Lawrence Clinton	ES: PA B: Burnt House, WV	*KELLY, John Doran	ES: Homestead, Allegheny Co., PA B: Youngstown, Mahoning Co., OH
SNYDER, William Ellsworth	ES: PA B: South Bethlehem, Northampton Co., PA	MacNEAL, Harry Lewis	ES: PA B: Philadelphia, Philadelphia Co., PA
SUNDQUIST, Axel Leonard	ES: PA B: Finland	MARTIN, James	ES: PA B: Derry, Ireland
TAYLOR, William G.	ES: Philadelphia, Philadelphia Co., PA B: Philadelphia, Philadelphia Co., PA	MATHIAS, Clarence Edward	ES: PA B: Royalton, Dauphin Co., PA
THAYER, James	ES: PA B: Ireland	*MAUSERT III, Frederick William	ES: Dresher, Montgomery Co., PA B: Cambridge, Washington Co., NY
THORNTON, Michael	ES: PA B: Ireland	*MORGAN, William David	ES: Pittsburgh, Allegheny Co., PA B: Pittsburgh, Allegheny Co., PA
TROUT, James M.	ES: PA B: Philadelphia, Philadelphia Co., PA	PAIGE, Mitchell	ES: PA B: Charleroi, Washington Co., PA
VANTINE, Joseph E.	ES: Pennslyvania B: Philadelphia, Philadelphia Co., PA	PFEIFER, Louis Fred	ES: NJ B: Philadelphia, Philadelphia Co., PA
WHITE, Joseph	ES: Philadelphia, Philadelphia Co., PA B: Washington, D.C.	*PROM, William Raymond	ES: Pittsburgh, Allegheny Co., PA B: Pittsburgh, Allegheny Co., PA
WILLIAMS, Henry	ES: PA B: Canada	PURVIS, Hugh	ES: PA B: Philadelphia, Philadelphia Co., PA
WILLIAMS, John	ES: PA B: Blair Co., PA	QUICK, John Henry	ES: PA B: Charleston, Kanawha Co., WV
WILLIAMS, Peter	ES: PA B: Norway	*RAMER, George Henry	ES: Lewisburg, Union Co., PA B: Meyersdale, Somerset Co., PA
WILLIAMS, William	ES: PA B: Ireland	RANNAHAN, John	ES: PA B: County Monaghan, Ireland
WILLIS, Richard	ES: Philadelphia, Philadelphia Co., PA B: England	*REEM, Robert Dale	ES: Elizabethtown, Lancaster Co., PA B: Lancaster, Lancaster Co., PA

U.S. Marine Corps

BINDER, Richard	ES: PA B: Germany	STEWART, James A.	ES: PA B: Philadelphia, Philadelphia Co., PA
BUTLER, Smedley Darlington	ES: PA B: West Chester, Chester Co., PA	THOMPSON, Henry A.	ES: PA B: England
CAMPBELL, Albert Ralph	ES: PA B: Williamsport, Lycoming Co., PA	VAUGHN, Pinkerton Ross	ES: PA B: Downingtown, Chester Co., PA
*DAMATO, Anthony Peter	ES: PA B: Shenandoah, Schuylkill Co., PA		

RHODE ISLAND

U.S. Army

DENIG, J. Henry	ES: PA B: York, York Co., PA	AVERY, William B.	ES: Providence, Providence Co., RI B: Providence, Providence Co., RI
*DIAS, Ralph Ellis	ES: Pittsburgh, Allegheny Co., PA B: Shelocta, Armstrong Co., PA		

BABOCK, William J. — ES: South Kingston, Washington Co., RI; B: Griswold, CT

BACA, John Philip — ES: Fort Ord, Monterey Co., CA; B: Providence, Providence Co., RI

BARBER, James Albert — ES: Westerly, Washington Co., RI; B: Westerly, Washington Co., RI

BLISS, George Newman — ES: Pawtucket, Providence Co., RI; B: Tiverton, Newport Co., RI

BLISS, Zenas Randall — ES: Johnston, Providence Co., RI; B: Johnston, Providence Co., RI

BUCKLYN, John Knight — ES: Providence, Providence Co., RI; B: Foster Creek, Providence Co., RI

BURBANK, James H. — ES: Providence, Providence Co., RI; B: Stavorey, Holland

CHILD, Benjamin Ham — ES: Providence, Providence Co., RI; B: Providence, Providence Co., RI

CORCORAN, John — ES: Pawtucket, Providence Co., RI; B: Pawtucket, Providence Co., RI

CUTTS, James Madison — ES: Providence, Providence Co., RI; B: Washington, D.C.

ENNIS, Charles D. — ES: Charleston, Washington Co., RI; B: Stonington, New London Co., CT

HAVRON, John H. — ES: Providence, Providence Co., RI; B: Ireland

LAWTON, John Sterling — ES: Boston, Suffolk Co., MA; B: Bristol, Bristol Co., RI

LEWIS, Samuel E. — ES: Coventry, Kent Co., RI; B: Coventry, Kent Co., RI

McDONALD, George E. — ES: Warwick, Kent Co., RI; B: Warwick, Kent Co., RI

McGAR, Owen — ES: Providence, Providence Co., RI; B: North Attleboro, Bristol Co., MA

MOLBONE, Archibald — ES: Johnston, Providence Co., RI; B: West Greenwich, RI

PARKER, Thomas — ES: Providence, Providence Co., RI; B: England

*PETERS, George J. — ES: Cranston, Providence Co., RI; B: Cranston, Providence Co., RI

POTTER, George W. — ES: Coventry, Kent Co., RI; B: Coventry, Kent Co., RI

SMITH, Thomas — ES: Fort Adams, RI; B: Boston, Suffolk Co., MA

STEVENS, Hazard — ES: Olympia, Thurston Co., Washington Territory; B: Newport, Newport Co., RI

TAYLOR, Joseph — ES: Burrillville, RI; B: England

WAINWRIGHT, Jonathan Mayhew — ES: Skaneateles, Onondaga Co., NY; B: Fort Walla Walla, Walla Walla Co., WA

*WAUGH, Robert T. — ES: Augusta, Kennebec Co., ME; B: Ashton, RI

WELSH, James — ES: Slatersville, Providence Co., RI; B: Ireland

U.S. Navy

BRADLEY, George — ES: Rhode Island; B: New York, NY

EADIE, Thomas — ES: Newport, Newport Co., RI; B: Scotland

EDWARDS, John — ES: Rhode Island; B: Providence, Providence Co., RI

GILLICK, Matthew — ES: Rhode Island; B: Providence, Providence Co., RI

GISBURNE, Edward Allen — ES: Massachusetts; B: Providence, Providence Co., RI

HAYES, Thomas — ES: Rhode Island; B: Rhode Island

LEAR, Nicholas — ES: Philadelphia, Philadelphia Co., PA; B: Rhode Island

MOORE, Philip — ES: Rhode Island; B: Newfoundland, Canada

ORMSBEE Jr., Francis Edward — ES: Florida; B: Providence, Providence Co., RI

PROVINCE, George — ES: Boston, Suffolk Co., MA; B: Newport, Newport Co., RI

READ, George E. — ES: RI; B: RI

WALSH, Michael — ES: RI; B: Newport, Newport Co., RI

U.S. Marine Corps

*CHAMPAGNE, David Bernard — ES: Wakefield, Washington Co., RI; B: Waterville, Kennebec Co., ME

SOUTH CAROLINA

U.S. Army

ANDERSON, Webster — ES: Winnsboro, Fairfield Co., SC; B: Winnsboro, Fairfield Co., SC

ATKINS, Thomas E. — ES: Campobello, Spartanburg Co., SC; B: Campobello, Spartanburg Co., SC

*BARKER, Charles H. — ES: Pickens Co., SC; B: Pickens Co., SC

DOZIER, James C. — ES: Rock Hill, York Co., SC; B: Galivants Ferry, Horry Co., SC

FOSTER, Gary Evans — ES: Inman, Spartanburg Co., SC; B: Spartanburg, Spartanburg Co., SC

GARLINGTON, Ernest Albert — ES: Athens, Clarke Co., GA; B: Newberry Hill, Newberry Co., SC

*HALL, Thomas Lee — ES: Fort Mill, York Co., SC; B: Fort Mill, York Co., SC

*HERIOT, James Davidson — ES: Providence, SC; B: Providence, SC

HILTON, Richmond Hobson — ES: Westville, Kershaw Co., SC; B: Westville, Kershaw Co., SC

HOOPER, Joe Ronnie — ES: Los Angeles, Los Angeles Co., CA; B: Piedmont, Greenville Co., SC

KENNEDY, John Thomas — ES: Orangeburg, Orangeburg Co., SC; B: Hendersonville, SC

*KNIGHT, Noah Odell — ES: Jefferson, Chesterfield Co., SC; B: Chesterfield Co., SC

MABRY Jr., George Lafayette — ES: Sumter, Sumter Co., SC; B: Sumter, Sumter Co., SC

*McWHORTER, William A. — ES: Liberty, Pickens Co., SC; B: Liberty, Pickens Co., SC

*SMITH, Furman L. — ES: Central, Pickens Co., SC; B: Six Mile, Pickens Co., SC

*STOWERS, Freddie — ES: Anderson Co., SC; B: Sandy Springs, Anderson Co., SC

VILLEPIGUE, John Cantey — ES: Camden, Kershaw Co., SC; B: Camden, Kershaw Co., SC

WALLING, William Henry   ES: Folly Island, Charleston Co., SC
B: Hartford, Washington Co., NY

WILLIAMS, Charles Quincy   ES: Fort Jackson, SC
B: Charleston, Charleston Co., SC

U.S. Navy

ELLIOTT, Middleton Stuart   ES: SC
B: Beauford, Beauford Co., SC

FLOYD, Edward   ES: SC
B: Ireland

MOFFETT, William Adger   ES: Charleston, Charleston Co., SC
B: Charleston, Charleston Co., SC

SULLIVAN, Daniel Augustus Joseph   ES: SC
B: Charleston, Charleston Co., SC

THORNTON, Michael Edwin   ES: Spartanburg, Spartanburg Co., SC
B: Greenville, Greenville Co., SC

WHEELER, George Huber   ES: Washington, D.C.
B: Charleston, Charleston Co., SC

WILLIAMS, James Elliott   ES: Columbia, Richland Co., SC
B: Rock Hill, York Co., SC

U.S. Marine Corps

*HOWE, James Donnie   ES: Fort Jackson, Richland Co., SC
B: Six Mile, Pickens Co., SC

*JOHNSON, Ralph Henry   ES: Oakland, Alameda Co., CA
B: Charleston, Charleston Co., SC

KENNEMORE, Robert Sidney   ES: Greenville, Greenville Co., SC
B: Greenville, Greenville Co., SC

McGINTY III, John James   ES: Laurel Bay, SC
B: Boston, Suffolk Co., MA

*OWENS, Robert Allen   ES: SC
B: Greenville, Greenville Co., SC

TRUESDELL, Donald Leroy   ES: SC
B: Lugoff, Kershaw Co., SC

*WATKINS, Lewis George   ES: Seneca, Oconee Co., SC
B: Seneca, Oconee Co., SC

SOUTH DAKOTA

U.S. Army

ANDERS, Frank Lafayette   ES: Fargo, Cass Co., ND
B: Fort Lincoln, Dakota Territory

BRADY, Patrick Henry   ES: Seattle, King Co., WA
B: Philip, Haakon Co., SD

FITZMAURICE, Michael John   ES: Cavour, Beadle Co., SD
B: Jamestown, Stutsman Co., ND

HARDAWAY, Benjamin Franklin   ES: Fort Totten, Benson Co., Dakota Territory
B: Benleyville, KY

*OLSON, Arlo L.   ES: Toronto, Deuel Co., SD
B: Greenville, Clay Co., IA

ROBERTS, Charles Duval   ES: Fort D.A. Russell, WY
B: Cheyenne Agency, Dakota

U.S. Marine Corps

FOSS, Joseph Jacob   ES: Sioux Falls, Minnehaha Co., SD
B: Sioux Falls, Minnehaha Co., SD

*LITTLETON, Herbert A.   ES: Black Hawk, Meade Co., SD
B: Mena, Polk Co., AR

TENNESSEE

U.S. Army

ADKINSON, Joseph B.   ES: Memphis, Shelby Co., TN
B: Egypt, TN

BEAUFORD, Clay   ES: Nashville, Davidson Co., TN
B: Washington Co., MD

CANTRELL, Charles P.   ES: Nashville, Davidson Co., TN
B: Smithville, Dekalb Co., TN

CARTER, William Harding   ES: New York, NY
B: Nashville, Davidson Co., TN

CECIL, Joseph Samuel   ES: New River, TN
B: New River, TN

COLLINS, Harrison   ES: Cumberland Gap, Claiborne Co., TN
B: Hawkins Co., TN

COOLEY, Raymond Henry   ES: Richard City, TN
B: Dunlap, Sequatchie Co., TN

COOLIDGE, Charles Henry   ES: Signal Mountain, Hamilton Co., TN
B: Signal Mountain, Hamilton Co., TN

DOZIER, James B.   ES: Fort Richardson, TX
B: Warren Co., TN

*DUKE, Ray E.   ES: Whitwell, Marion Co., TN
B: Whitwell, Marion Co., TN

*GARDNER, James Alton   ES: Memphis, Shelby Co., TN
B: Dyersburg, Dyer Co., TN

GILLESPIE Jr., George Lewis   ES: Chattanooga, Hamilton Co., TN
B: Kingston, Roane Co., TN

GRANT, George   ES: Indianapolis, Marion Co., IN
B: Raleigh, Shelby Co., TN

GREER, Allen James   ES: Memphis, Shelby Co., TN
B: Memphis, Shelby Co., TN

HOBDAY, George   ES: Memphis, Shelby Co., TN
B: Pulaski Co., IL

HUFF, Paul Bert   ES: Cleveland, Bradley Co., TN
B: Cleveland, Bradley Co., TN

HUGHES, Oliver   ES: Albany, Clinton Co., KY
B: Fentress Co., TN

JENKINS, Don   ES: Nashville, Davidson Co., TN
B: Quality, Butler Co., KY

JORDAN, George   ES: Nashville, Davidson Co., TN
B: Williamson Co., TN

KARNES, James Ernest   ES: Knoxville, Knox Co., TN
B: Arlington, Shelby Co., TN

KYLE, John   ES: Nashville, Davidson Co., TN
B: Cincinnati, Hamilton Co., OH

LAWSON, Gaines   ES: Rogersville, Hawkins Co., TN
B: Hawkins Co., TN

*LEMERT, Milo   ES: Crossville, Cumberland Co., TN
B: Marshalltown, Marshall Co., IA

*LYELL, William Franklin   ES: Old Hickory, Davidson Co., TN
B: Hickman Co., TN

McGAHA, Charles L.   ES: Crosby, TN
B: Crosby, TN

McGARITY, Vernon   ES: Model, TN
B: Right, TN

*McGILL, Troy A.   ES: Ada, Pontotoc Co., OK
B: Knoxville, Knox Co., TN

MORRIS, William W.   ES: Louisville, Jefferson Co., KY
B: Stewart Co., TN

*PENDLETON, Charles F.   ES: Fort Worth, TX
B: Camden, Benton Co., TN

*STOUT, Mitchell William	ES: Raleigh, Wake Co., NC B: Knoxville, Knox Co., TN	FIELDS, James H.	ES: Houston, Harris Co., TX B: Caddo, Stephens Co., TX
STRIVSON, Benoni	ES: Sacramento, Sacramento Co., CA B: Overton, TN	*FOWLER, Thomas Weldon	ES: Wichita Falls, Wichita Co., TX B: Wichita Falls, Wichita Co., TX
TALLEY, Edward R.	ES: Russellville, Hamblen Co., TN B: Russellville, Hamblen Co., TN	GARCIA, Marcario	ES: Sugar Land, Fort Bend Co., TX B: Villa de Castano, Mexico
WARD, Calvin John	ES: Morristown, Hamblen Co., TN B: Green Co., TN	*HANSON, Jack G.	ES: Galveston, Galveston Co., TX B: Escatawpa, Jackson Co., MS
WELD, Seth Lathrop	ES: Altamont, Grundy Co., TN B: Sandy Hook, MD	*HARRIS, James Lindell	ES: Hillsboro, Hill Co., TX B: Hillsboro, Hill Co., TX
YORK, Alvin Cullium	ES: Pall Mall, Fentress Co., TN B: Fentress Co., TN	HERRERA, Silvestre Santana	ES: Phoenix, Maricopa Co., AZ B: El Paso, El Paso Co., TX

U.S. Navy

BONNEY, Robert Earl	ES: Nashville, Davidson Co., TN B: Maryville, Blount Co., TN	HOLLAND, Milton Murray	ES: Albany, Athens Co., OH B: Austin, Travis Co., TX
COVINGTON, Jesse Whitfield	ES: CA B: Haywood, TN	HOWZE, Robert Lee	ES: Overton, Rusk Co., TX B: Overton, Rusk Co., TX
FERRELL, John H.	ES: IL B: Bedford Co., TN	*KEATHLEY, George D.	ES: Lamesa, Dawson Co., TX B: Olney, Young Co., TX
HARRISON, Bolden Reush	ES: TN B: Savannah, Hardin Co., TN	*KIMBRO, Truman	ES: Houston, Harris Co., TX B: Madisonville, Madison Co., TX
*RAY, David Robert	ES: Nashville, Davidson Co., TN B: McMinnville, Warren Co., TN	*KNIGHT, Jack Llewellyn	ES: Weatherford, Parker Co., TX B: Garner, TX
STEVENS, Daniel Dickerson	ES: MA B: La Grange, Fayette Co., TN	*LAW, Robert David	ES: Dallas, Collin Co., TX B: Fort Worth, Tarrant Co., TX
*WILLIS, John Harlan	ES: Tennessee B: Columbia, Maury Co., TN	*LEE, Milton Arthur	ES: San Antonio, Bexar Co., TX B: Shreveport, Caddo Co., LA

U.S. Marine Corps

*KINSER, Elbert Luther	ES: Tennessee B: Greeneville, Greene Co., TN	*LEONARD, Turney White	ES: Dallas, Collin Co., TX B: Dallas, Collin Co., TX
*SINGLETON, Walter Keith	ES: Memphis, Shelby Co., TN B: Memphis, Shelby Co., TN	LLOYD, George	ES: Canton, Van Zandt Co., TX B: County Tyrone, Ireland

TEXAS

U.S. Army

ADAMS, Lucian	ES: Port Arthur, Jefferson Co., TX B: Port Arthur, Jefferson Co., TX	LOGAN, James Marion	ES: Luling, Caldwell Co., TX B: McNeil, Travis Co., TX
AUSTIN, William Grafton	ES: New York, NY B: Galveston, Galveston Co., TX	LOPEZ, Jose Mendoza	ES: Brownsville, Cameron Co., TX B: Mission, Hidalgo Co., TX
*BARKELEY, David B.	ES: San Antonio, Bexar Co., TX B: Laredo, Webb Co., TX	*MARTINEZ, Benito	ES: Fort Hancock, Hudspeth Co., TX B: Fort Hancock, Hudspeth Co., TX
BENAVIDEZ, Roy Perez	ES: Houston, Harris Co., TX B: Cuero, DeWitt Co., TX	McCABE, William	ES: Fort Duncan, TX B: Belfast, County Antrim, Ireland
*COLE, Robert George	ES: San Antonio, Bexar Co., TX B: Fort Sam Houston, Bexar Co., TX	McCLEERY, Finnis Dawson	ES: San Angelo, Tom Green Co., TX B: Stephenville, Erath Co., TX
CONNOR, John	ES: Jefferson, Marion Co., TX B: Galway, Ireland	McDONALD, Franklin M.	ES: Fort Griffin, TX B: Bowling Green, Warren Co., KY
DOZIER, James B.	ES: Fort Richardson, TX B: Warren Co., TN	McLENNON, John	ES: Fort Ellis, MT B: Fort Belknap, TX
EDWARDS, Daniel Richmond	ES: Bruceville, McLennan Co., TX B: Mooreville, TX	McNERNEY, David Herbert	ES: Fort Bliss, El Paso Co., TX B: Lowell, Middlesex Co., MA
EVERHART Sr., Forrest Eugene	ES: Texas City, Galveston Co., TX B: Bainbridge, Ross Co., OH	MURPHY, Audie Leon	ES: Dallas, Collin Co., TX B: near Kingston, Hunt Co., TX
FACTOR, Pompey	ES: Fort Duncan, TX B: AR	PAINE, Adam	ES: Fort Duncan, TX B: FL
FERGUSON, Frederick Edgar	ES: Phoenix, Maricopa Co., AZ B: Pilot Point, Denton Co., TX	PAYNE, Isaac	ES: Fort Duncan, TX B: Mexico
		*PENDLETON, Charles F.	ES: Fort Worth, TX B: Camden, Benton Co., TN
		*ROBINSON Jr., James E.	ES: Waco, McLennan Co., TX B: Toledo, Lucas Co., OH
		RODRIGUEZ, Cleto L.	ES: San Antonio, Bexar Co., TX B: San Marcos, Hays Co., TX
		SAMPLER, Samuel M.	ES: Altus, Jackson Co., OK B: Decatur, Wise Co., TX
		SASSER, Clarence Eugene	ES: Houston, Harris Co., TX B: Chenango, TX

SHELTON, George Mathews	ES: Bellington, TX B: Brownwood, Brown Co., TX	*CREEK, Thomas Elbert	ES: Amarillo, Potter Co., TX B: Joplin, Jasper Co., MO
*STEINDAM, Russell Albert	ES: Austin, Travis Co., TX B: Austin, Travis Co., TX	*GONZALEZ, Alfredo (Freddy)	ES: San Antonio, Bexar Co., TX B: Edinburg, Hidalgo Co., TX
STONE, James Lamar	ES: Houston, Harris Co., TX B: Pine Bluff, Jefferson Co., AR	*GRAVES, Terrence Collinson	ES: NY B: Corpus Christi, Nueces Co., TX
TURNER, George Benton	ES: Los Angeles, Los Angeles Co., CA B: Longview, Gregg Co., TX	*GUILLEN, Ambrosio	ES: El Paso, El Paso Co., TX B: La Junta, Otero Co., CO
*WALLACE, Herman C.	ES: Lubbock, Lubbock Co., TX B: Marlow, Stephens Co., OK	HARRELL, William George	ES: Mercedes, Hidalgo Co., TX B: Rio Grande City, Starr Co., TX
WARD, John	ES: Fort Duncan, TX B: AR	*HAWKINS, William Deane	ES: El Paso, El Paso Co., TX B: Fort Scott, Bourbon Co., KS
*WATKINS, Travis E.	ES: Texas B: Waldo, Columbia Co., AR	*KEITH, Miguel	ES: Omaha, Douglas Co., NE B: San Antonio, Bexar Co., TX

U.S. Army Air Corps/U.S. Air Force

(Texas continued)

*LUMMUS, Jack	ES: TX B: Ennis, Ellis Co., TX
*MITCHELL, Frank Nicias	ES: Roaring Springs, Motley Co., TX B: Indian Gap, Hamilton Co., TX
*MORELAND, Whitt Lloyd	ES: Austin, Travis Co., TX B: Waco, McLennan Co., TX
O'BRIEN Jr., George Herman	ES: Big Spring, Howard Co., TX B: Fort Worth, Tarrant Co., TX
*ROAN, Charles Howard	ES: TX B: Claude, Armstrong Co., TX
*WILSON, Alfred Mac	ES: Abilene, Taylor Co., TX B: Olney, Richland Co., IL

(Texas continued, left column)

*BENNETT, Steven Logan	ES: Lafayette, Lafayette Co., LA B: Palestine, Anderson Co., TX
*CARSWELL Jr., Horace Seaver	ES: San Angelo, Tom Green Co., TX B: Fort Worth, Tarrant Co., TX
*DAVIS Jr., George Andrew	ES: Lubbock, Lubbock Co., TX B: Dublin, Erath Co., TX
*HUGHES, Lloyd Herbert	ES: San Antonio, Bexar Co., TX B: Alexandria, Rapides Co., LA
KANE, John Riley	ES: Shreveport, Caddo Co., LA B: McGregor, McLennan Co., TX
KEARBY, Neel Ernest	ES: Dallas, Collin Co., TX B: Wichita Falls, Wichita Co., TX
*KNIGHT, Raymond Larry	ES: Houston, Harris Co., TX B: Houston, Harris Co., TX
*MATHIS, Jack Warren	ES: San Angelo, Tom Green Co., TX B: San Angelo, Tom Green Co., TX
MORGAN, John Cary "Red"	ES: London, England B: Vernon, Wilbarger Co., TX

U.S. Navy

BULKELEY, John Duncan	ES: TX B: San Antonio, Bexar Co., TX
*DEALEY, Samuel David	ES: TX B: Dallas, Collin Co., TX
HARRISON, William Kelly	ES: TX B: Waco, McLennan Co., TX
HAYDEN, David Ephraim	ES: TX B: Florence, Williamson Co., TX
*HUTCHINS, Johnnie David	ES: TX B: Weimer, Colorado Co., TX
*KILMER, John Edward	ES: Houston, Harris Co., TX B: Highland Park, Lake Co., IL
PHILLIPS, George Frederick	ES: Galveston, Galveston Co., TX B: St. John, New Brunswick, Canada

U.S. Marine Corps

*ANDERSON, Richard Allen	ES: Houston, Harris Co., TX B: Washington, D.C.
*AUSTIN, Oscar Palmer	ES: Phoenix, Maricopa Co., AZ B: Nacogdoches, Nacogdoches Co., TX
*BORDELON, William James	ES: TX B: San Antonio, Bexar Co., TX

UTAH

U.S. Army

KISTERS, Gerry Herman	ES: Bloomington, Monroe Co., IN B: Salt Lake City, Salt Lake Co., UT
THACKER, Brian Miles	ES: Salt Lake City, Salt Lake Co., UT B: Columbus, Franklin Co., OH
*VALDEZ, Jose F.	ES: Pleasant Grove, Utah Co., UT B: Governador, NM

U.S. Navy

*BENNION, Mervyn Sharp	ES: Utah B: Vernon, Tooele Co., UT
HALL, William Edward	ES: Mohrland, Emery Co., UT B: Storrs, Carbon Co., UT
WAHLEN, George Edward	ES: Ogden, Weber Co., UT B: Ogden, Weber Co., UT

VERMONT

U.S. Army

BATES, Norman Francis	ES: Grinnell, Poweshiek Co., IA B: Derry, VT
BEATTY, Alexander Mitchell	ES: Guildhall, Essex Co., VT B: Ryegate, Caledonia Co., VT
BENEDICT, George Greenville	ES: Burlington, Chittenden Co., VT B: Burlington, Chittenden Co., VT
BUTTERFIELD, Franklin George	ES: Rockingham, Windham Co., VT B: Rockingham, Windham Co., VT
CHURCHILL, Samuel Joseph	ES: DeKalb, DeKalb Co., IL B: Rutland, Rutland Co., VT
CLARK, John Wesley	ES: VT B: Montpelier, Washington Co., VT

COFFEY, Robert John	ES: Montpelier, Washington Co., VT B: St. John, New Brunswick, Canada	PECK, Cassius	ES: West Randolph, Orange Co., VT B: Brookfield, Orange Co., VT
COUGHLIN, John	ES: Manchester, Hillsborough Co., NH B: VT	PECK, Theodore Safford	ES: Burlington, Chittenden Co., VT B: Burlington, Chittenden Co., VT
DAVIDSON, Andrew	ES: Cincinnati, Hamilton Co., OH B: Middlebury, Addison Co., VT	PHELPS, Charles Edwards	ES: Baltimore, Baltimore Co., MD B: Guilford, VT
DAVIS, George Evans	ES: Burlington, Chittenden Co., VT B: Dunstable, Middlesex Co., MA	PINGREE, Samuel E.	ES: Hartford, Windsor Co., VT B: Salisbury, Merrimack Co., NH
DOLLOFF, Charles W.	ES: St. Johnsbury, Caledonia Co., VT B: Parishville, St. Lawrence Co., NY	RIPLEY, William Young Warren	ES: Rutland, Rutland Co., VT B: Middlebury, Addison Co., VT
DOWNS, Henry W.	ES: Newfane, Windham Co., VT B: Jamaica, Windham Co., VT	ROBBINS, Augustus J.	ES: Grafton, Windham Co., VT B: Grafton, Windham Co., VT
DRURY, James	ES: Chester, Windsor Co., VT B: Limerick, County Limerick, Ireland	SARGENT, Jackson	ES: Stowe, Lamoille Co., VT B: Stowe, Lamoille Co., VT
EDDY, Samuel E.	ES: Chesterfield, Hampshire Co., MA B: Whitingham, Windham Co., VT	SCOTT, Alexander	ES: Winooski, Chittenden Co., VT B: Montreal, Canada
EVANS, Ira Hobart	ES: Barre, Washington Co., VT B: Piermont, Grafton Co., NH	SCOTT, Julian A.	ES: Johnson, Lamoille Co., VT B: Johnson, Lamoille Co., VT
FERRIS, Eugene W.	ES: Lowell, Middlesex Co., MA B: Springfield, Windsor Co., VT	SEAVER, Thomas Orville	ES: Pomfret, VT B: Cavendish, Windsor Co., VT
GOULD, Charles Gilbert	ES: Windham Co., VT B: Windham Co., VT	SHERMAN, Marshall	ES: St. Paul, Ramsey Co., MN B: Burlington, Chittenden Co., VT
GRANT, Lewis Addison	ES: Bellows Falls, Windham Co., VT B: Winhall, VT	SPERRY, William Joseph	ES: Cavendish, Windsor Co., VT B: Cavendish, Windsor Co., VT
HACK, Lester Goodel	ES: Salisbury, Addison Co., VT B: Cadwell, Warren Co., NY	SWEENEY, James	ES: Essex, Chittenden Co., VT B: Manchester, Greater Manchester Co., England
HARRINGTON, Ephraim W.	ES: Kirby, VT B: Waterford, Oxford Co., ME	THOMAS, Stephen	ES: West Fairlee, Orange Co., VT B: Bethel, Windsor Co., VT
HAWKINS, Gardner C.	ES: Woodstock, Windsor Co., VT B: Pomfret, VT	TILTON, William	ES: Hanover, Grafton Co., NH B: St. Albans, Franklin Co., VT
HENRY, William Wirt	ES: Waterbury, Washington Co., VT B: Waterbury, Washington Co., VT	TRACY, Amasa Sawyer	ES: Middlebury, Addison Co., VT B: Dover, Piscataquis Co., ME
HOLTON, Edward A.	ES: Williston, Chittenden Co., VT B: Westminster, Windham Co., VT	VEAZEY, Wheelock Graves	ES: Springfield, Windsor Co., VT B: Brentwood, Coos Co., NH
HOWARD, Squire Edward	ES: Townshend, Windham Co., VT B: Jamaica, Windham Co., VT	WELLS, William	ES: Waterbury, Washington Co., VT B: Waterbury, Washington Co., VT
INGALLS, Lewis J.	ES: Belvidere, Lamoille Co., VT B: Boston, Suffolk Co., MA	WHEELER, Daniel Davis	ES: Cavendish, Windsor Co., VT B: Cavendish, Windsor Co., VT
JEWETT, Erastus W.	ES: St. Albans, Franklin Co., VT B: St. Albans, Franklin Co., VT	*WILKIN, Edward G.	ES: Longmeadow, Hampden Co., MA B: Burlington, Chittenden Co., VT
JOHNDRO, Franklin	ES: Queensbury, Warren Co., NY B: Highgate Falls, Franklin Co., VT	WILLISTON, Edward Bancroft	ES: San Francisco, San Francisco Co., CA B: Norwich, Windsor Co., VT
JOHNSTON, William (Willie)	ES: St. Johnsbury, Caledonia Co., VT B: Morristown, Morristown Co., NY	WOODBURY, Eri Davidson	ES: St. Johnsbury, Caledonia Co., VT B: Francistown, Hillsborough Co., NH
LIVINGSTON, Josiah O.	ES: Marshfield, Washington Co., VT B: Walden, VT	*U.S. Navy*	
LONERGAN, John	ES: Burlington, Chittenden Co., VT B: Carrick, County Donegal, Ireland	BLAIR, Robert M.	ES: Portland, Cumberland Co., ME B: Peacham, Caledonia Co., VT
LYON, Frederick A.	ES: Burlington, Chittenden Co., VT B: Williamsburg, Hampshire Co., MA	BREAULT, Henry	ES: VT B: Putnam, Windham Co., CT
MATTOCKS, Charles Porter	ES: Portland, Cumberland Co., ME B: Danville, Caledonia Co., VT	BRESNAHAN, Patrick Francis	ES: VT B: Peabody, Essex Co., MA
McCORMICK, Michael P.	ES: Harrisburg, Dauphin Co., PA B: Rutland, Rutland Co., VT	RAMAGE, Lawson Paterson "Red"	ES: VT B: Monroe Bridge, Franklin Co., MA
MORAN, John E.	ES: Cascade Co., MT B: Vernon, Windham Co., VT	*U.S. Marine Corps*	
NICHOLS, Henry Clay	ES: St. Albans, Franklin Co., VT B: Brandon, Rutland Co., VT	EDSON, Merritt Austin	ES: VT B: Rutland, Rutland Co., VT
NOYES, William W.	ES: Montpelier, Washington Co., VT B: Montpelier, Washington Co., VT		

VIRGINIA

U.S. Army

ANDERSON, Charles W.	ES: near Winchester, Frederick Co., VA B: Baltimore, Baltimore Co., MD	
AYERS, James F.	ES: Richmond, Richmond Co., VA B: Collinstown, Henry Co., VA	
BARNES, William H.	ES: Norfolk, Norfolk Co., VA B: St. Marys Co., MD	
BEATY, Powhatan	ES: Cincinnati, Hamilton Co., OH B: Richmond, Richmond Co., VA	
BOYNE, Thomas	ES: Norfolk, Norfolk Co., VA B: Prince Georges Co., MD	
BROWN, Benjamin	ES: Harrisburg, Dauphin Co., PA B: Spotsylvania Co., VA	
BYRNE, Bernard Albert	ES: Washington, D.C. B: Newport Barracks, Giles Co., VA	
CARNEY, William Harvey	ES: New Bedford, Bristol Co., MA B: Norfolk, Norfolk Co., VA	
DERVISHIAN, Ernest Herbert	ES: Richmond, Richmond Co., VA B: Richmond, Richmond Co., VA	
DOSS, Desmond Thomas	ES: Lynchburg, Lynchburg Co., VA B: Lynchburg, Lynchburg Co., VA	
DURHAM, James R.	ES: Clarksburg, Harrison Co., NV B: Richmond, Richmond Co., VA	
FOLLAND, Michael F.	ES: Richmond, Richmond Co., VA B: Richmond, Richmond Co., VA	
*GAMMON, Archer T.	ES: Roanoke, Roanoke Co., VA B: Chatham, Pittsylvania Co., VA	
GARDINER, James	ES: Yorktown, York Co., VA B: Gloucester, Gloucester Co., VA	
GILLENWATER, James Robert Lee	ES: Rye Cove, VA B: Rye Cove, VA	
GREAVES, Clinton	ES: Baltimore, Baltimore Co., MD B: Madison Co., VA	
GREGORY, Earl D.	ES: Chase City, Mecklenburg Co., VA B: Chase City, Mecklenburg Co., VA	
GRESHAM, John Chowning	ES: Lancaster Courthouse, Lancaster Co., VA B: VA	
JAMES, Miles	ES: Portsmouth, Portsmouth Co., VA B: Princess Anne Co., VA	
JOHNSON, Henry	ES: Detroit, Wayne Co., MI B: Boydton, Mecklenburg Co., VA	
KILBOURNE Jr., Charles Evans	ES: Portland, Multnomah Co., OR B: Fort Myer, Arlington Co., VA	
*LANGHORN, Garfield McConnell	ES: Brooklyn, Kings Co., NY B: Cumberland, Cumberland Co., PA	
LEE, Fitz	ES: Philadelphia, Philadelphia Co., PA B: Dinwiddie Co., VA	
LEVY, Benjamin Bennett	ES: Newport News, Newport News Co., VA B: New York, NY	
MAYS, Isaiah	ES: Columbus Barracks, Franklin Co., OH B: Carters Bridge, VA	
*MILLER, Gary Lee	ES: Roanoke, Roanoke Co., VA B: Covington, Covington Co., VA	
*MONTEITH Jr., Jimmie W.	ES: Richmond, Richmond Co., VA B: Low Moor, Alleghany Co., VA	
MORRIS, Charles Bedford	ES: Roanoke, Roanoke Co., VA B: Carroll Co., VA	
O'CONNOR, Timothy	ES: New Creek, VA B: Ireland	
*PEREGORY, Frank D.	ES: Charlottesville, Charlottesville Co., VA B: Esmont, Albemarle Co., VA	
RATCLIFF, Edward	ES: Yorktown, York Co., VA B: James Co., VA	
*SARGENT, Ruppert Leon	ES: Richmond, Richmond Co., VA B: Hampton, Hampton Co., VA	
SCHNELL, Christian	ES: Wapakoneta, Auglaize Co., OH B: VA	
*SHEA Jr., Richard Thomas	ES: Portsmouth, Portsmouth Co., VA B: Portsmouth, Portsmouth Co., VA	
SMITH, James (Ovid)	ES: Circleville, Pickaway Co., OH B: Fredericksburg, Fredericksburg Co., VA	
STEWART, Benjamin F.	ES: Boston, Suffolk Co., MA B: Norfolk, Norfolk Co., VA	
TOMPKINS, Charles Henry	ES: Brooklyn, Kings Co., NY B: Fort Monroe, Hampton Co., VA	
VEAL, Charles	ES: Baltimore, Baltimore Co., MD B: Portsmouth, Portsmouth Co., VA	
WHITEHEAD, Patton G.	ES: Louisville, Jefferson Co., KY B: Russell Co., VA	
WILLS, Henry	ES: St. Louis, St. Louis Co., MO B: Gracon, VA	
WOODALL, William H.	ES: Winchester, Frederic Co., VA B: Lynchburg, Lynchburg Co., VA	
WOODALL, Zachariah	ES: Carlisle, Cumberland Co., PA B: Alexandria, Alexandria Co., VA	

U.S. Army Air Corps/U.S. Air Force

*JONES III, William Atkinson	ES: Charlottesville, Charlottesville Co., VA B: Norfolk, Norfolk Co., VA
*WILKINS, Raymond Harrell	ES: Portsmouth, Portsmouth Co., VA B: Portsmouth, Portsmouth Co., VA

U.S. Navy

ATKINS, Daniel	ES: VA B: Brunswick, VA
BARROW, David Duffy	ES: Norfolk, Norfolk Co., VA B: Reelsboro, NC
BLAKE, Robert	ES: Port Royal, Caroline Co., VA B: VA
BRIGHT, George Washington	ES: VA B: Norfolk, Norfolk Co., VA
BYRD Jr., Richard Evelyn	ES: VA B: Winchester, Frederick Co., VA
*HAMMOND, Francis Colton	ES: Alexandria, Alexandria Co., VA B: Alexandria, Alexandria Co., VA
JORDAN, Thomas H.	ES: Baltimore, Baltimore Co., MD B: Portsmouth, Portsmouth Co., VA
LANGHORNE, Cary DeVall	ES: VA B: Lynchburg, Lynchburg Co., VA
LANNON, James Patrick	ES: VA B: Alexandria, Alexandria Co., VA
MIFFLIN, James	ES: VA B: Richmond, Richmond Co., VA
O'CONNER, James Francis	ES: VA B: Portsmouth, Portsmouth Co., VA

PENN, Robert	ES: VA B: City Point, VA		HAWK, John Druse "Bud"	ES: Bremerton, Kitsap Co., WA B: San Francisco, San Francisco Co., CA
SHACKLETTE, William Sidney	ES: VA B: Delaplane, Fauquier Co., VA		*KANDLE, Victor Leonard	ES: Redwood City, San Mateo Co., CA B: Roy, Pierce Co., WA
SMITH, Frank Elmer	ES: VA B: Boston, Suffolk Co., MA		KERSTETTER, Dexter James	ES: Centralia, Lewis Co., WA B: Centralia, Lewis Co., WA
SMITH, Thomas	ES: VA B: Ireland		KINSMAN, Thomas James	ES: Seattle, King Co., WA B: Renton, King Co., WA
STREET III, George Levick	ES: Richmond, Richmond Co., VA B: Richmond, Richmond Co., VA		*LEISY, Robert Ronald	ES: Seattle, King Co., WA B: Stockton, San Joaquin Co., CA
TAYLOR, Richard Hamilton	ES: VA B: Staunton, Staunton Co., VA		LYON, Edward Eugene	ES: Amboy, Clark Co., WA B: Hixton, Jackson Co., WI
TORGERSON, Martin Torinus	ES: VA B: Oleesen, Norway		*MANN, Joe Eugene	ES: Seattle, King Co., WA B: Reardan, Lincoln Co., WA
VOLZ, Robert	ES: VA B: San Francisco, San Francisco Co., CA		McCARTER, Lloyd G.	ES: Tacoma, Pierce Co., WA B: St. Maries, Benewah Co., ID
			*PENDLETON, Jack James	ES: Yakima, Yakima Co., WA B: Sentinel Butte, Golden Valley Co., ND
			STEVENS, Hazard	ES: Olympia, Thurston Co., Washington Territory B: Newport, Newport Co., RI

U.S. Marine Corps

*BAUSELL, Lewis Kenneth	ES: Washington, D.C. B: Pulaski, Montgomery Co., VA		WILSON, Benjamin F.	ES: Vashon, King Co., WA B: Vashon, King Co., WA
BERKELEY, Randolph Carter	ES: Appointed from: Washington, D.C B: Staunton, Staunton Co., VA		WILSON, John Moulder	ES: Olympia, Thurston Co., Washington Territory B: Washington, D.C.
FOX, Wesley Lee	ES: Leesburg, Loudoun Co., VA B: Herndon, Fairfax Co., VA			

U.S. Air Force

FLEMING, James Phillip	ES: Pullman, Whitman Co., WA B: Sedalia, Pettis Co., MO

LEE, Howard Vincent	ES: Dumfries, Prince William Co., VA B: New York, NY			
LUCAS, Jacklyn Harold	ES: Norfolk, Norfolk Co., VA B: Plymouth, Washington Co., NC			

U.S. Navy

BUSH, Robert Eugene	ES: WA B: Tacoma, Pierce Co., WA
DAVIS, Raymond Erwin	ES: Puget Sound, WA B: Mankato, Blue Earth Co., MN
FADDEN, Harry Delmar	ES: WA B: The Dalles, Wasco Co., OR
*KEPPLER, Reinhardt John	ES: WA B: Ralston, WA
*ROOKS, Albert Harold	ES: WA B: Colton, Whitman Co., WA
*SHIELDS, Marvin Glen	ES: Seattle, King Co., WA B: Port Townsend, Jefferson Co., WA
*VAN VOORHIS, Bruce Avery	ES: Nevada B: Aberdeen, Grays Harbor Co., WA

*MARTINI, Gary Wayne	ES: Portland, Multnomah Co., OR B: Lexington, Lexington Co., VA	
NEVILLE, Wendell Cushing	ES: VA B: Portsmouth, Portsmouth Co., VA	
*SMEDLEY, Larry Eugene	ES: Orlando, Orange Co., FL B: Front Royal, Warren Co., VA	
SUTTON, Clarence Edwin	ES: Washington, D.C. B: Urbanna, Middlesex Co., VA	
UPSHUR, William Peterkin	ES: VA B: Richmond, Richmond Co., VA	
VANDEGRIFT, Alexander Archer	ES: VA B: Charlottesville, Charlottesville Co., VA	

WASHINGTON

U.S. Army

*ALBANESE, Lewis	ES: Seattle, King Co., WA B: Venice, Italy
ALLWORTH, Edward C.	ES: Corvallis, Benton Co., OR B: Crawford, WA
BJORKLUND, Arnold L.	ES: Seattle, King Co., WA B: Clinton, Island Co., WA
BRADY, Patrick Henry	ES: Seattle, King Co., WA B: Philip, Haakon Co., SD
BRONSON, Deming	ES: Seattle, King Co., WA B: Rhinelander, Oneida Co., WI
CLANCY, John E.	ES: Vancouver Barracks, Clark Co., WA B: New York, NY
*GRANDSTAFF, Bruce Alan	ES: Spokane, Spokane Co., WA B: Spokane, Spokane Co., WA

U.S. Coast Guard

*MUNRO, Douglas Albert	ES: WA B: Vancouver, British Columbia, Canada

U.S. Marine Corps

*ANDERSON, Richard Beatty	ES: WA B: Tacoma, Pierce Co., WA
BOYINGTON, Gregory "Pappy"	ES: WA B: Coeur D'Alene, Kootenai Co., ID
GALER, Robert Edward	ES: Seattle, King Co., WA B: Seattle, King Co., WA
*MONEGAN Jr., Walter Carleton	ES: Seattle, King Co., WA B: Melrose, Middlesex Co., MA

*REASONER, Frank Stanley   ES: Kellogg, Shoshone Co., ID
B: Spokane, Spokane Co., WA

SWETT, James Elms   ES: San Mateo, San Mateo Co., CA
B: Seattle, King Co., WA

VAN WINKLE, Archie   ES: Arlington, Snohomish Co., WA
B: Juneau, Juneau Co., AK

WINANS, Roswell   ES: WA
B: Brookville, Franklin Co., IN

WEST VIRGINIA

U.S. Army

ADAMS, James F.   ES: Ceredo, Wayne Co., WV
B: Cabell Co., WV

ANDERSON, Thomas   ES: Wheeling, Ohio Co., WV
B: Scenery Hill, Washington Co., PA

APPLE, Andrew O.   ES: New Manchester, Hancock Co., WV
B: Northampton, Northampton Co., PA

BARRINGER, William H.   ES: Mason City, Mason Co., WV
B: Long Bottom, Meigs Co., OH

*BELCHER, Ted   ES: Huntington, Cabell Co., WV
B: Accoville, Logan Co., WV

BELL, Bernard Pious   ES: New York, NY
B: Grantsville, Calhoun Co., WV

BENDER, Stanley   ES: Chicago, Cook Co., IL
B: Carlisle, WV

*BENNETT, Thomas William   ES: Fairmont, Marion Co., WV
B: Morgantown, Monongalia Co., WV

BISHOP, Daniel   ES: Wheeling, Ohio Co., WV
B: Monroe Co., OH

BOURY, Richard   ES: Wirt Courthouse, WV
B: Monroe Co., OH

BUCKLEY, John C.   ES: Mount Pleasant, WV
B: Fayette Co., WV

BUMGARNER, William   ES: Mason City, Mason Co., WV
B: Mason Co., WV

BURNS, James Madison   ES: Wellsburg, Brooke Co., WV
B: Wells Township, Jefferson Co., OH

*CHARLTON, Cornelius H.   ES: Bronx Co., NY
B: East Gulf, Raleigh Co., WV

CORCORAN, Michael   ES: Wheeling, Ohio Co., WV
B: Philadelphia, Philadelphia Co., PA

CRISWELL, Benjamin C.   ES: Cincinnati, Hamilton Co., OH
B: Moundsville, Marshall Co., WV

CURTIS, Josiah M.   ES: West Liberty, Ohio Co., WV
B: Ohio Co., WV

DIXON, William "Billy"   ES: Indian Territory
B: Ohio Co., WV

DURHAM, James R.   ES: Clarksburg, Harrison Co., WV
B: Richmond, Richmond Co., VA

ECKES, John N.   ES: Weston, Lewis Co., WV
B: Lewis Co., WV

GAUJOT, Antoine August   ES: Williamson, Mingo Co., WV
B: Keweenaw, Baraga Co., MI

GAUJOT, Julien Edmund   ES: Williamson, Mingo Co., WV
B: Keweenaw, Baraga Co., MI

GODLEY, Leonidas Mahlon   ES: Ashland, IA
B: Mason Co., WV

*HARTSOCK, Robert Willard   ES: Fairmont, Marion Co., WV
B: Cumberland, Allegany Co., MD

*HARVEY Jr., Carmel Bernon   ES: Chicago, Cook Co., IL
B: Montgomery, Fayette Co., WV

*HEDRICK, Clinton M.   ES: Riverton, Pendleton Co., WV
B: Cherry Grove, WV

HORSFALL, William H.   ES: Fort Cox, Charleston, WV
B: Campbell Co., KY

*KELLEY, Jonah Edward High   ES: Keyser, Mineral Co., WV
B: Roda, WV

*KYLE, Darwin K.   ES: Racine, Boone Co., WV
B: Jenkins, Letcher Co., KY

MAYFIELD, Melvin   ES: Nashport, Muskingum Co., OH
B: Salem, Harrison Co., WV

McCAUSLIN, Joseph   ES: West Liberty, Ohio Co., WV
B: Ohio Co., WV

*McDONALD, Phill Gene   ES: Beckley, Raleigh Co., WV
B: Avondale, McDowell Co., WV

McELHINNY, Samuel O.   ES: Point Pleasant, Mason Co., WV
B: Meigs Co., OH

McWHORTER, Walter F.   ES: Clarksburg, Harrison Co., WV
B: Lewis Co., WV

*MOLNAR, Frankie Zoly   ES: Fresno, Fresno Co., CA
B: Logan, Logan Co., WV

MOORE, George G.   ES: Parkersburg, Wood Co., WV
B: Tyler Co., WV

PARSONS, Joel   ES: Mason City, Mason Co., WV
B: Jackson Co., WV

*POMEROY, Ralph Eugene   ES: Quinwood, Greenbrier Co., WV
B: Quinwood, Greenbrier Co., WV

REEDER, Charles A.   ES: Shinnston, Harrison Co., WV
B: Harrison, Clay Co., WV

ROGERS, Charles Calvin   ES: Institute, Kanawha Co., WV
B: Claremont, WV

SCHORN, Charles   ES: Mason City, Mason Co., WV
B: Germany

SHAHAN, Emisire   ES: Clarksburg, Harrison Co., WV
B: Preston Co., WV

SHANES, John   ES: Warren, WV
B: Monongalia Co., WV

SHOEMAKER, Levi   ES: Clarksburg, Harrison Co., WV
B: Monongalia Co., WV

*STEWART, Jimmy Goethel   ES: Ashland, Boyd Co., KY
B: West Columbia, Mason Co., WV

SUMMERS, James Calvin   ES: Point Pleasant, Mason Co., WV
B: on Elk River six miles above Charleston, Kanawha Co., WV

VAN MATRE, Joseph   ES: Middleport, Meigs Co., OH
B: Mason Co., WV

WARD, Thomas J.   ES: Decatur, Macon Co., IL
B: Romney, Hampshire Co., WV

WEIR, Henry Cary   ES: Bolivar, WV
B: West Point, Orange Co., NY

*WETZEL, Walter C.   ES: Roseville, Macomb Co., MI
B: Huntington, Cabell Co., WV

WHITE, Adam   ES: Parkersburg, Wood Co., WV
B: Switzerland

WOODS, Daniel A. (Wood)   ES: Wheeling, Ohio Co., WV
B: Ohio Co., WV

U.S. Army Air Corps

*FEMOYER, Robert Edward   ES: Jacksonville, Duval Co., FL
B: Huntington, Cabell Co., WV

U.S. Navy

COX, Robert Edward   ES: WV
B: St. Albans, Kanawha Co., WV

FRAZER, Hugh Carroll	ES: WV B: Martinsburg, Berkeley Co., WV		*HANDRICH, Melvin O.	ES: Manawa, Waupaca Co., WI B: Manawa, Waupaca Co., WI
JONES, Claud Ashton	ES: WV B: Fire Creek, WV		HILL, Frank E.	ES: St. Louis, St. Louis Co., MO B: Mayfield, WI
NICKERSON, Henry Nehemiah	ES: WV B: Edgewood, WV		HILLIKER, Benjamin F.	ES: Waupaca Township, Waupaca Co., WI B: Golden, Erie Co., NY
SINNETT, Lawrence Clinton	ES: PA B: Burnt House, WV		INGMAN Jr., Einar Harold	ES: West Bend, Washington Co., WI B: Milwaukee, Milwaukee Co., WI

U.S. Marine Corps

CHAMBERS, Justice Marion	ES: Washington, D.C. B: Huntington, Cabell Co., WV
QUICK, John Henry	ES: PA B: Charleston, Kanawha Co., WV
*THOMAS, Herbert Joseph	ES: WV B: Columbus, Franklin Co., OH
WILLIAMS, Hershel Woodrow "Woody"	ES: Fairmont, Marion Co., WV B: Quiet Dell, Marion Co., WV

WISCONSIN

U.S. Army

ANDERSON, Beauford Theodore	ES: Soldiers Grove, Crawford Co., WI B: Eagle, Waukesha Co., WI
ANDERSON, Peter T.	ES: Wiota, WI B: Darlington, Lafayette Co., WI
BELL, Harry	ES: Minneapolis, Hennepin Co., MN B: Milwaukee, Milwaukee Co., WI
*BELLRICHARD, Leslie Allen	ES: Oakland, Alameda Co., CA B: Janesville, Rock Co., WI
BLOCH, Orville Emil	ES: Streeter, Stutsman Co., ND B: Big Falls, Waupaca Co., WI
BRONSON, Deming	ES: Seattle, King Co., WA B: Rhinelander, Oneida Co., WI
BROOKIN, Oscar	ES: Green Co., OH B: Byron, Fond Du Lac Co., WI
*BURR, Elmer J.	ES: Menasha, Winnebago Co., WI B: Neenah, Winnebago Co., WI
CABLE, Joseph A.	ES: Madison, Dane Co., WI B: Cape Girardeau, Cape Girardeau Co., MO
COATES, Jefferson	ES: Boscobel, Grant Co., WI B: Grant Co., WI
CROFT, James E.	ES: Janesville, Rock Co., WI B: Yorkshire, England
DURHAM, John S.	ES: Malone, Fond Du Lac Co., WI B: New York, NY
ELLIS, Horace	ES: Chippewa Falls, Chippewa Co., WI B: Mercer Co., PA
ELLIS, William	ES: Watertown, Jefferson Co., WI B: England
*ENDL, Gerald Leon	ES: Janesville, Rock Co., WI B: Fort Atkinson, Jefferson Co., WI
FRITZ, Harold Arthur	ES: Milwaukee, Milwaukee Co., WI B: Chicago, Cook Co., IL
GOLDIN, Theodore W. B.	ES: Chicago, Cook Co., IL B: Avon, Rock Co., WI
*GRUENNERT, Kenneth E.	ES: Helenville, Jefferson Co., WI B: Helenville, Jefferson Co., WI
JOHNSON, John	ES: Janesville, Rock Co., WI B: Toten Christiana (now Olso), Norway
KINNE, John Baxter	ES: Fargo, Cass Co., ND B: Beloit, Rock Co., WI
LYON, Edward Eugene	ES: Amboy, Clark Co., WA B: Hixton, Jackson Co., WI
MacARTHUR, Douglas	ES: Ashland, Ashland Co., WI B: Little Rock, Pulaski Co., AR
MacARTHUR Jr., Arthur	ES: Milwaukee, Milwaukee Co., WI B: Springfield, Hampden Co., MA
*McGRATH, Hugh Jocelyn	ES: Eau Claire, Eau Claire Co., WI B: Fond Du Lac, Fond Du Lac Co., WI
*MILLER, Andrew	ES: Two Rivers, Manitowoc Co., WI B: Manitowoc, Manitowoc Co., WI
MOORE, Daniel B.	ES: Mifflin, Iowa Co., WI B: Mifflin, Iowa Co., WI
*MOWER, Charles E.	ES: Chippewa Falls, Chippewa Co., WI B: Chippewa Falls, Chippewa Co., WI
NEWMAN, Beryl Richard	ES: Baraboo, Sauk Co., WI B: Baraboo, Sauk Co., WI
NOLAN, Richard J.	ES: Milwaukee, Milwaukee Co., WI B: Ireland
O'CONNOR, Albert	ES: Lodi, Columbia Co., WI B: Herford, Canada
*OLSON, Truman O.	ES: Cambridge, Dane Co., WI B: Christiana, WI
POND, George F.	ES: Fairwater, Fond du Lac Co., WI B: Libertyville, Lake Co., IL
POND, James Burton	ES: Janesville, Rock Co., WI B: Allegany, Cattaraugus Co., NY
*RED CLOUD Jr., Mitchell	ES: Merrillan, Jackson Co., WI B: Hatfield, WI
ROBBINS, Marcus M.	ES: Boston, Suffolk Co., MA B: Elba, Dodge Co., WI
ROBERTSON, Marcus William	ES: Hood River, Hood River Co., OR B: Flintville, WI
SICKLES, William H.	ES: Fall River, Columbia Co., WI B: Danube, Herkimer Co., NY
SLACK, Clayton Kirk	ES: Madison, Dane Co., WI B: Plover, Portage Co., WI
STUMPF, Kenneth Edward	ES: Milwaukee, Milwaukee Co., WI B: Neenah, Winnebago Co., WI
*SUDUT, Jerome A.	ES: WI B: Wausau, Marathon Co., WI
TOOHEY, Thomas	ES: Milwaukee, Milwaukee Co., WI B: New York, NY
TRUELL, Edwin M.	ES: Mantson, WI B: Lowell, Middlesex Co., MA
WALLER, Francis A.	ES: DeSoto, Vernon Co., WI B: Gurney, OH
WETZEL, Gary George	ES: Milwaukee, Milwaukee Co., WI B: South Milwaukee, Milwaukee Co., WI

WHITTLESEY, Charles White   ES: Pittsfield, Berkshire Co., MA
B: Florence, Florence Co., WI

WINDUS, Claron   ES: Indianapolis, Marion Co., IN
B: Janesville, Rock Co., WI

U.S. Army Air Corps/U.S. Air Force

BONG, Richard Ira   ES: Poplar, Douglas Co., WI
B: Superior, Douglas Co., WI

*JERSTAD, John Louis   ES: Racine, Racine Co., WI
B: Racine, Racine Co., WI

*SIJAN, Lance Peter   ES: Milwaukee, Milwaukee Co., WI
B: Milwaukee, Milwaukee Co., WI

U.S. Navy

CASTLE, Guy Wilkinson Stuart   ES: WI

De SOMER, Abraham   ES: WI
B: Milwaukee, Milwaukee Co., WI

*PETERSON, Oscar Verner   ES: WI
B: Prentice, Price Co., WI

SIEGEL, John Otto   ES: NJ
B: Milwaukee, Milwaukee Co., WI

*VAN VALKENBURGH, Franklin   ES: WI
B: Minneapolis, Hennepin Co., MN

YOUNG, Cassin   ES: WI
B: Washington, D.C.

U.S. Marine Corps

*AGERHOLM, Harold Christ   S: Wisconsin
B: Racine, WI

*CHRISTIANSON, Stanley Reuben   ES: Mindoro, La Crosse Co., WI
B: Mindoro, La Crosse Co., WI

MODRZEJEWSKI, Robert Joseph   ES: Milwaukee, Milwaukee Co., WI
B: Milwaukee, Milwaukee Co., WI

YOUNG, Frank Albert   ES: Wisconsin
B: Milwaukee, Milwaukee Co., WI

WYOMING

U.S. Army

*ADAMS, William Edward   ES: Kansas City, Clay Co., MO
B: Casper, Natrona Co., WY

BAKER Jr., Edward Lee   ES: Cincinnati, Hamilton Co., OH
B: Platte River, Laramie Co., WY

*CAREY Jr., Charles F.   ES: Cheyenne, Laramie Co., WY
B: Canadian, Pittsburg Co., OK

ROBERTS, Charles Duval   ES: Fort D.A. Russell, WY
B: Cheyenne Agency, Dakota

WASHINGTON, D.C.

U.S. Army

BARNES, Will Croft   ES: Washington, D.C.
B: San Francisco, San Francisco Co., CA

BELL, Dennis   ES: Washington, D.C.
B: Washington, D.C.

BERKELEY, Randolph Carter   ES: Washington, D.C.
B: Stauton, Stauton Co., VA

BRADBURY, Sanford   ES: Washington, D.C.
B: Newton, Sussex County, New Jersey

BUCHA, Paul William   ES: USMA West Point, Orange County, New York
B: Washington, D.C.

BUTTERFIELD, Daniel Adams   ES: Washington, D.C.
B: Utica, Oneida County, New York

BYRNE, Bernard Albert   ES: Washington, D.C.
B: Newport Barracks, Giles County, Virginia

CAPEHART, Charles E.   ES: Washington, D.C.
B: Conemaugh Township, Pennsylvania

CHEEVER Jr., Benjamin Harrison   ES: Washington, D.C.
B: Washington, D.C.

CHURCH, James Robb   ES: Washington, D.C.
B: Chicago, Cook County, Illinois

CUTTS, James Madison   ES: Providence, Providence County, Rhode Island
B: Washington, D.C.

FORCE, Manning Ferguson   ES: Cincinnati, Hamilton County, Ohio
B: Washington, D.C.

*HOOKER, George   ES: Washington, D.C.
B: Frederick, Frederick County, Maryland

LENIHAN, James   ES: Washington, D.C.
B: County Kerry, Ireland

LITEKY, Charles James (Angelo)   ES: Fort Hamilton, Kings County, New York
B: Washington, D.C.

*LUCAS, Andre Cavaro   ES: West Point, Orange County, New York
B: Washington, D.C.

McALWEE, Benjamin Franklin   ES: Baltimore, Baltimore County, Maryland
B: Washington, D.C.

McBRIDE, Bernard   ES: Washington, D.C.
B: Brooklyn, Kings County, New York

*McGOVERN, Robert Milton   ES: Washington, D.C.
B: Washington, D.C.

*McMAHON, Thomas Joseph   ES: Portland, Cumberland County, Maine
B: Washington, D.C.

PLOWMAN, George H.   ES: Washington, D.C.
B: Oxford, Oxfordshire, England

PORTER, Samuel   ES: Washington, D.C.
B: Montgomery County, Maryland

SCOTT, Robert Sheldon   ES: Santa Fe, Santa Fe County, New Mexico
B: Washington, D.C.

SHAW, George Clymer   ES: Washington, D.C.
B: Pontiac, Oakland County, Michigan

SHEPHERD, William   ES: Washington, D.C.
B: Dillsboro, Ohio County, Indiana

*TAYLOR, Bernard   ES: Washington, D.C.
B: St. Louis, St. Louis County, Missouri

TAYLOR, William   ES: Frederick, Frederick County, Maryland
B: Washington, D.C.

WARRINGTON, Lewis   ES: Washington, D.C.
B: Washington, D.C.

WILSON, John Moulder   ES: Olympia, Thurston County, Washington Territory
B: Washington, D.C.

WOODRUFF, Carle Augustus   ES: Washington, D.C.
B: Buffalo, Erie County, New York

U.S. Navy

BADGER, Oscar Charles	ES: Washington, D.C. B: Washington, D.C.
BAKER, Charles	ES: New York, NY B: Washington, D.C.
BEHNKE, Heinrich	ES: Washington, D.C. B: Germany
COURTS, George McCall	ES: Washington, D.C. B: Washington, D.C.
FLUCKEY, Eugene Bennett	ES: Neoga, Cumberland County, Illinois B: Washington, D.C.
HARRINGTON, David	ES: Washington, D.C. B: Washington, D.C.
HAYDEN, John	ES: Washington, D.C. B: Washington, D.C.
KEEFER, Philip Bogan	ES: Washington, D.C. B: Washington, D.C.
LIPSCOMB, Harry	ES: Washington, D.C. B: Washington, D.C.
McCANDLESS, Bruce	ES: Colorado B: Washington, D.C.
McDONALD, James Harper	ES: Washington, D.C. B: Newmaud, Scotland
PRESTON, Arthur Murray	ES: Maryland B: Washington, D.C.
RUSH, John	ES: Washington, D.C. B: Washington, D.C.
WAINWRIGHT Jr., Richard	ES: Washington, D.C. B: Washington, D.C.
WHEELER, George Huber	ES: Washington, D.C. B: Charleston Co., S.C.
WHITE, Joseph	ES: Philadelphia, Philadelphia County, Pennsylvania B: Washington, D.C.
YOUNG, Cassin	ES: Wisconsin B: Washington, D.C.

U.S. Marine Corps

*ANDERSON, Richard Allen	ES: Houston, Harris County, Texas B: Washington, D.C.
*BAUSELL, Lewis Kenneth	ES: Washington, D.C. B: Pulaski, Montgomery County, Virginia
CHAMBERS, Justice Marion	ES: Washington, D.C. B: Huntington, Cabell County, West Virginia
*JOHNSON, James Edmund	ES: Washington, D.C. B: Pocatello, Bannock County, Idaho
MILLER, Andrew	ES: Washington, D.C. B: Germany
MURPHY, John Alphonsus	ES: Washington, D.C. B: New York, New York
PORTER, David Dixon	ES: Washington, D.C. B: Washington, D.C.
*SCHWAB, Albert Ernest	ES: Tulsa, Tulsa County, Oklahoma B: Washington, D.C.
STEWART, Peter	ES: Washington, D.C. B: Airdrie, Scotland
SUTTON, Clarence Edwin	ES: Washington, D.C. B: Urbanna, Middlesex County, Virginia

FOREIGN-BORN RECIPIENTS

AUSTRALIA
BELPITT, William Henry, USN	B: Sydney, Australia
HAMILTON, Mathew H., USA	B: Hobert, Australia
STEWART, George Evans, USA	B: New South Wales (Australia)

AUSTRIA
BURGER, Joseph, USA	B: Swiss Tyrol, Austria
CORAHORGI, Demetri, USN	B: Triste, Austria
CUKELA, Louis, USMC	B: Sebenes, Austria
FITZ, Joseph, USN	B: Austria
GRBITCH, Rade, USN	B: Austria
KARPELES, Leopold, USA	B: Prague, Austria - Hungary
*KOCAK, Matej, USMC	B: Gbely, Austria
*TOMICH, Peter, USN	B: Prolog, Austria
VADAS, Albert (WADAS), USN	B: Austria - Hungary

BELGIUM
LABILL, Joseph S., USA	B: Belgium
OSS, Albert, USA	B: Belgium
VIFQUAIN, Victor, USA	B: Brussels, Belgium

BERMUDA
SMITH, John, USN	B: Bermuda

CANADA
ANDERSON, James (SMYTH), USA	B: Canada (east)
ASTEN, Charles (Michael), USN	B: Halifax, Nova Scotia, Canada
BOIS, Frank, USN	B: Canada
BROWN, John Harties, USA	B: New Brunswick, Canada
*BUCKLEY, Denis, USA	B: Canada
CAMPBELL, Daniel J., USMC	B: Prince Edward Island, Canada
CAYER, Ovila, USA	B: St. Remi, Canada
CHAPUT, Louis G., USN	B: Canada
COFFEY, Robert John, USA	B: St. John, New Brunswick, Canada
COONEY, Thomas C., USN	B: Westport, Nova Scotia, Canada
DODD, Robert Fulton, USA	B: Canada
DODDS, Edward Edwin, USA	B: Canada
EVERETTS, John, USN	B: Therold, Canada
FITZPATRICK, Thomas, USN	B: Canada
FLANNIGAN, James (FLANAGAN), USA	B: Canada
GARVIN, William, USN	B: Canada (west)
GAY, Thomas H., USA	B: Prince Edward Island, Canada
GILMORE, John Curtis, USA	B: Canada
GRADY, John, USN	B: New Brunswick, Canada
HAGERTY, Asel (HAGERT, Asa), USA	B: Canada
HARDING, Mosher A., USA	B: Canada (west)
HAYES, John, USN	B: Brogus, Newfoundland, Canada
HIGGINS, Thomas J., USA	B: Riverlequerre, Quebec, Canada
HOUGHTON, George L., USA	B: Yarmouth, Canada (west)
KERSEY, Thomas Joseph, USN	B: St. Johns, Newfoundland, Canada
KILMARTIN, John (GILMARTIN), USA	B: Montreal, Canada
LEMON, Peter Charles, USA	B: Toronto, Canada
LOW, George (EVATT), USN	B: Canada
MacGILLIVARY, Charles Andrew, USA	B: Prince Edward Island, Canada
MADDIN, Edward (MADDEN), USN	B: Newfoundland, Canada
McCARTHY, Michael, USA	B: St. Johns, Newfoundland, Canada
McINTOSH, James, USN	B: Canada
McMAHON, Martin Thomas, USA	B: LaPraire, Quebec, Canada
*McVEANE, John P. (McVEAN), USA	B: Toronto, Canada
MILLER, Harry Herbert, USN	B: Nova Scotia, Canada
MILLER, Willard D., USN	B: Nova Scotia, Canada
MOORE, Philip, USN	B: Newfoundland, Canada
MORGAN, George Horace, USA	B: Canada
*MUNRO, Douglas Albert, USCG	B: Vancouver, British Columbia, Canada
MURPHY, James T., USA	B: Canada
NEIL, John, USN	B: Newfoundland, Canada
NOIL, Joseph B., USN	B: Nova Scotia, Canada
O'CONNOR, Albert, USA	B: Herford, Canada
O'NEILL, Stephen, USA	B: St. John, New Brunswick, Canada
PELHAM, William, USN	B: Halifax, Nova Scotia, Canada
PHILLIPS, George Frederick, USN	B: St. John, New Brunswick, Canada
PICKLE, Alonzo H., USA	B: Canada

POWERS, Wesley James, USA	B: Orono, Ontario, Canada	ELMORE, Walter, USN	B: England
RICH, Carlos H., USA	B: Canada	ERICKSON, John P., USN	B: London, England
ROBINSON, Joseph, USA	B: Montreal, Canada	FISHER, Frederick Thomas, USN	B: England
RUSSELL, Henry Peter, USN	B: Quebec, Canada	FOSTER, William, USA	B: Somerset Co., England
SCOTT, Alexander, USA	B: Canada	GARRETT, William, USA	B: Isle of Man, England
SHIVERS, John, USMC	B: Canada	GRAHAM, Robert (HALL, Fred), USN	B: England
STODDARD, James, USN	B: Port Robinson, Canada (west)	GREEN, George, USA	B: Elsham, Lincolnshire
WILLIAMS, Henry, USN	B: Canada	HALFORD, William, USN	B: Gloucester, Gloucestershire
WORTMAN, George G., USA	B: Monckton, New Brunswick, Canada	HARBOURNE, John H., USA	B: England
		HARVEY, Harry (HUCKMAN), USA	B: England
YOUNG, Benjamin F., USA	B: Canada	HIBSON, Joseph C., USA	B: London, England
		HILL, George, USN	B: England

CHILE

BAZAAR, Philip, USN — B: Chile

CHINA

HAYS, George Price, USA — B: China
HOWARD, James Howell, USAAC/USAF — B: Canton, China

CUBA

ROBINSON, John, USN — B: Cuba

DENMARK

BENSON, James, USN	B: Denmark
BROWN, John, USN	B: Denmark
CLAUSEN, Claus Kristian Randolph, USN	B: Denmark
DRUSTRUP, Niels, USN	B: Denmark
IRWIN, Nicholas, USN	B: Denmark
JENSEN, Gotfred, USA	B: Denamrk
MILLER, James, USN	B: Denmark
MULLER, Frederick, USN	B: Copenhagen, Denmark
SCHOU, Julius Alexis, USA	B: Copenhagen, Denamrk

ENGLAND

BAYBUTT, Philip, USA	B: Manchester, Greater Manchester Co.
BEDDOWS, Richard, USA	B: Liverpool, Merseyside Co.
BEECH, John P., USA	B: Stratfordshire, England
BELL, George H., USN	B: Sunderland, England
BLAGHEEN, William (BLAGDEN), USN	B: Devonshire, England
BOURNE, Thomas, USN	B: England
BRADLEY, Thomas Wilson, USA	B: Sheffield, Yorkshire, England
BREYER, Charles, USA	B: England
BURTON, Albert, USN	B: England
CARMAN, Warren, USA	B: England
CARTER, Joseph Edward, USN	B: Manchester, Greater Manchester Co.
CAVAIANI, Jon Robert, USA	B: Royston, England
COOK, John Henry, USA	B: London, England
CROFT, James E., USA	B: Yorkshire, England
DENHAM, Austin, USN	B: England
DONNELLY, John C., USN	B: England
DORE, George H., USA	B: England
ELLIS, William, USA	B: England
HILL, James, USA	B: Bristol, Avon Co., England
HOLDEN, Henry, USA	B: Brighton, Sussex Co.,
HOLEHOUSE, James, USA	B: Stockport, Greater Manchester Co.
HORTON, James (Joseph), USN	B: England
HULBERT, Henry Lewis, USMC	B: Kingston-upon-Hull, Humberside Co.
HUNT, Frederick O., USA	B: London, England
IRLAM, Joseph, USN	B: Liverpool, Merseyside Co.
IRVING, Thomas, USN	B: England
JAMES, John, USA	B: Manchester, Greater Manchester Co.
JENNINGS, James T., USA	B: Devonshire, England
JOHNSON, Peter, USN	B: Sumerland, England
JUDGE, Francis W., USA	B: England
KAY, John, USA	B: Lancashire Co., England
KEEN, Joseph S., USA	B: Vale, Guernsey, England
KEENE, Joseph, USA	B: England
KENNA, Barnett, USN	B: Canterbury, Kent Co., England
*KOELSCH, John Kelvin, USN	B: London, England
LATHAM, John Cridland, USA	B: Windemere, Cumbria Co., England
LESLIE, Frank, USA	B: London, England
LLOYD, Benjamin, USN	B: Liverpool, Merseyside Co.
LORD, William, USA	B: Bradford, England
LUDGATE, William, USA	B: London, England
MACHON, James, USN	B: Derby, Derbyshire, England
MADDEN, William, USN	B: Devonshire, England
MANDY, Harry J., USA	B: England
MATHEWS, William Henry	B: Devizes, Wiltshire, England
MERTON, James F., USN	B: Cheshire, England
MORIARITY, John, USA	B: Huddersfield, Yorkshire
MORIN, William Henry, USN	B: Birmingham, West Midlands Co.
MURPHY, Charles Joseph, USA	B: Stockport, Greater Manchester Co.
NORRIS, J. W., USN	B: England
OAKLEY, William, USN	B: Colchester, Essex Co., England
PARKER, Thomas, USA	B: England
PENGALLY, Edward, USA	B: Devonshire, England
PETTY, Philip, USA	B: Tingswich, Buckinghamshire
PLOWMAN, George H., USA	B: Oxford, Oxfordshire
PYM, James, USA	B: Oxfordshire, England
PYNE, George, USN	B: England

ROBERTS, James, USN	B: England
ROBINSON, Alexander, USN	B: England
SEACH, William, USN	B: London, England
SHAPLAND, John, USA	B: Barnstable, Devonshire
SHILLING, John, USA	B: England
SIMPSON, D. Henry Lakin, USN	B: London, England
SLADEN, Joseph Alton, USA	B: Rockdale, England
SMITH, Henry I., USA	B: Nottingham, Nottinghamshire
SMITH, Thomas, USN	B: England
SMITH, Thomas J., USA	B: Liverpool, Merseyside Co.
SPICER, William, USN	B: Liverpool, Merseyside Co.
STACEY, Charles, USA	B: England
STOKES, George, USA	B: England
SUMNER, James, USA	B: London, England
SWEENEY, James (2nd), USA	B: Manchester, Greater Manchester Co.
TALBOTT, William, USN	B: England
*TALLENTINE, James, USN	B: England
TAYLOR, George (JOHNSON), USN	B: Reddich, Hereford & Worcester Co.
TAYLOR, Joseph, USA	B: England
THOMPSON, Henry A. (CONNELLY, Roderick P.), USMC	B: England
THOMPSON, James Harry, USA	B: England
VALE, John, USA	B: London, England
WAGG, Maurice, USN	B: Hampshire Co. England
WARD, Charles H., USA	B: Bradford, England
WILLIAMS, George C., USA	B: England
WILLIS, Richard, USN	B: England
WILSON, John, USA	B: England
WINTERBOTTOM, William, USA	B: Manchester, Greater Manchester Co.
WOOD, Mark, USA	B: England
WOON, John, USN	B: England
WRIGHT, William, USN	B: London, England

FINLAND

ANDERSON, Johannes Seigfried, USA	B: Bjoroky, Finland
EGLIT, John, USN	B: Finland
ERICKSON, Nicholas, USN	B: Finland
WESTERMARK, Axel, USN	B: Bergo, Finland

FRANCE

BEAUFORT, Jean J., USA	B: France
CHANDRON, August, USN	B: France
CHAPMAN, John (KAUFMAN, Charles F.), USA	B: Strasburg, France
FALCOTT, Henry, USA	B: Champagne, France
FRANTZ, Joseph, USA	B: Eurapae, France
GESCHWIND, Nicholas, USA	B: France
HOWARD, Peter, USN	B: France
JAMIESON, Walter, USA	B: Boulogne, France
LEJEUNE, Emile, USN	B: France
LEON, Pierre, USN	B: France
LIBAIRE, Adolph, USA	B: Bacarrt, France
LUDWIG, Carl, USA	B: France
MORAN, John, USA	B: Lyon, France
MORSE, Charles F., USA	B: France
PRANCE, George, USN	B: France
ROY, Stanislaus (Stanilas), USA	B: France
TOBIN, Paul, USN	B: Plybin, France
WALKER, John, USA	B: Leon, France

GERMANY & PRUSSIA

ALBER, Frederick, USA	B: Germany
ARCHINAL, William J., USA	B: Felsburg, Hesse, Germany
BAKER, John, USA	B: Hesse, Germany
BALLEN, Frederick A., USA	B: Germany
BEHNKE, Heinrich, USN	B: Germany
BERTRAM, Heinrich, USA	B: Brunswick, Germany
BEYER, Albert, USN	B: Hanover, Germany
BIEGER, Charles, USA	B: Wiesbaden, Germany
BINDER, Richard, USMC	B: Germany
BLUCHER, Charles, USA	B: Germany
BOEHLER, Otto A., USA	B: Germany
BOUQUET, Nicholas S., USA	B: Landau, Bavaria, Germany
*BRATLING, Frank, USA	B: Bavaria, Germany
BRONNER, August Frederick, USA	B: Germany
BURKARD, Oscar R., USA	B: Achern, Baden, Germany
COHN, Abraham, USA	B: Guttentag, Silesia, Prussia
DAVIS, John, USN	B: Germany
DEETLINE, Frederick, USA	B: Offenheim, Germany
DILGER, Hubert, USA	B: Germany
DORLEY, August (DOERLE), USA	B: Germany
ENDERLIN, Richard, USA	B: Germany
FESQ, Frank E., USA	B: Germany (Purssia)
FICHTER, Hermann Emil, USA	B: Baden, Germany
FORSTERER, Bruno Albert, USMC	B: Koenigsberg, Germany
FOUT, Frederick W., USA	B: Germany
FOX, Henry, USA	B: Reuthingen, Wurttemberg, Germany
FREEMAN, Martin, USN	B: Germany
FREEMEYER, Christopher, USA	B: Bavaria, Germany
FUGER, Frederick W., USA	B: Wurttemberg, Germany
GARDNER, Charles (SCHLER, Simon), USA	B: Bavaria, Germany
GEORGIAN, John, USA	B: Germany
GERBER, Frederick William, USA	B: Dresden, Germany
GION, Joseph, USA	B: Alsace-Lorraine area, Germany
GLAVINSKI, Albert (GLAWINSKI), USA	B: Germany
GREBE, M. R. William, USA	B: Hildesheim, Germany
GREEN, John, USA	B: Wurttemberg, Germany
GRESSER, Ignatz, USA	B: Malach, Germany
GRUEB, George M., USA	B: Wurttemberg, Germany
HACK, John, USA	B: Germany
HAMMEL, Henry A., USA	B: Germany
HANSEN, Hans Anton, USN	B: Germany
HART, John William, USA	B: Germany
HAUPT, Paul, USA	B: Prussia (Germany)
HEISCH, Henry William, USMC	B: Latendorf, Germany

HEISE, Clamor, USA	B: Germany	SCHMAUCH, Andrew, USA	B: Germany
HENDRICKSON, Henry, USN	B: Germany	SCHMIDT, Conrad, USA	B: Wurttemberg, Germany
HINEMANN, Lehmann, USA	B: Lanback, Germany	SCHNITZER, John, USA	B: Kempten, Bavaria, Germany
HOFFMAN, Henry, USA	B: Wurttemberg, Germany	SCHORN, Charles, USA	B: Germany
IRSCH, Francis, USA	B: Saarburg, Germany	SCHROETER, Charles, USA	B: Lindberg, Hanover, Germany
ITRICH, Franz Anton, USN	B: Gross Katz, Germany	SCHUBERT, Martin, USA	B: Germany
*JACHMAN, Isadore Seigfried, USA	B: Berlin, Germany	SCHWAN, Theodore, USA	B: Hanover, Germany
JACOBSON, Eugene Philip, USA	B: Prussia	SCHWENK, Martin (MARTIN, George), USA	B: Baden, Germany
JETTER, Bernard, USA	B: Wurttemberg, Germany	SEITZINGER, James M., USA	B: Germany
JOHN, William F., USA	B: Germany	SHAFFER, William (SCHAFFER), USA	B: Bavaria, Germany
KAISER, John, USA	B: Nerzogenaurach, Germany	SHAMBAUGH, Charles, USA	B: Prussia, Germany
KALTENBACH, Luther, USA	B: Germany	SHUBERT, Frank, USA	B: Hesse, Germany
KAPPESSER, Peter, USA	B: Germany	SMITH, Wilhelm, USN	B: Germany
KAUSS, August, USA	B: Germany	STEINER, Christian, USA	B: Wurttemberg, Germany
KLEIN, Robert, USN	B: Gerdonen, Germany	STOCKMAN, George Henry, USA	B: Muenden, Germany
KLINE, Harry (KLIEN, Henry), USA	B: Germany	STRAUB, Paul Frederick, USA	B: Baden, Germany
KOELPIN, William, USA	B: Stetten, Prussia	STREILE, Christian, USA	B: Germany
KRAMER, Franz, USN	B: Nierstein, Germany	SUMMERS, Robert (SOMMERS), USN	B: Prussia
KRAUSE, Ernest, USN	B: Lubeck, Germany	SWEGHEIMER, Jacob (John Jacob), USA	B: Oldtown, Baden, Germany
*KREHER, Wendelin,	B: Stetten, Prussia	THIELBERG, Henry, USN	B: Germany
KUCHMEISTER, Hermann W., USMC	B: Hamburg, Germany	THOMAS, Karl, USN	B: Germany
LANGBEIN, Johann Christian Julius, USA	B: Germany	THOMPSON, John J., USA	B: Holstein, Germany
LUKES, William F., USN	B: Niderbergdorf, Bohemia	THORDSEN, William George, USN	B: Fredericstadt, Germany
MAY, John, USA	B: Wurttemberg, Germany	TORGLER, Ernest R., USA	B: Mecklenburg, Germany
MEYER, William, USN	B: Germany	TRAUTMAN, Jacob, USA	B: Hamburg, Germany
MILLER, Andrew, USMC	B: Germany	UHRL, George (Uhri), USA	B: Baden, Germany
MILLER, Henry August, USA	B: Germany	VOIT, Otto Emil, USA	B: Baden, Germany
MILLER, John (FEY, Henry), USA	B: Kurhessen, Germany	VON MEDEM, Rudolph, USA	B: Germany (Prussia)
MILLER, John G., USA	B: Germany	VON SCHLICK, Robert H., USA	B: Germany
MINDIL, George Washington, USA	B: near Frankfort, Germany	WAMBSGAN, Martin, USA	B: Nusdorof, Bavaria, Germany
MORSE, William, USN	B: Germany	WEINERT, Paul H., USA	B: Frankfort, Germany
MYERS, Fred, USA	B: Brunswick, Germany	WEISSEL, Adam, USN	B: Germany
NEDER, Adam, USA	B: Bavaria, Germany	WELLS, William, USN	B: Germany
NEWMAN, Henry, USA	B: Hanover, Germany	WENDE, Bruno, USA	B: Germany
NIBBE, John H., USN	B: Germany	WESTERHOLD, William, USA	B: Binde, Prussia
NOIL, Joseph B., USA	B: Germany	WIDMER, Jacob, USA	B: Wurttemberg, Germany
OHMSEN, August, USN	B: Lubeck, Germany	WILKE, Julius August Robert, USN	B: Germany
OPEL, John N., USA	B: Hoflas, Bavaria, Germany	WILKENS, Henry, USA	B: Germany
ORBANSKY, David (URBANSKY), USA	B: Lautenburg, Prussia	WILLIAMS, Frank, USN	B: Danzig, Germany
PESCH, Joseph M., USA	B: Grossleiton, Prussia	WILSON, August, USN	B: Danzig, Germany
PETERSEN, Carl Emil, USN	B: Hamburg, Germany	WINDOLPH, Charles, USA	B: Bergen, Germany
PHILIPSEN, Wilhelm O., USA	B: Schleswig, Germany	YOUNKER, John L., USA	B: Wurttemberg, Germany
PHISTERER, Frederick, USA	B: Germany	ZIEGNER, Herman, USA	B: Aploda, Germany
RAERICK, John, USA	B: Baden, Germany		
ROCK, Frederick, USA	B: Darmstadt, Germany		

GREECE

*DILBOY, George, USA	B: Greece

HOLLAND

ALLEN, Edward G., USN	B: Amsterdam, Holland
BURBANK, James H., USA	B: Stavorey, Holland
FASSEUR, Isaac L., USN	B: Fushing, Holland
MACK, Alexander, USN	B: Rotterdam, Holland

RODENBURG, Henry, USA	B: Germany
ROSSBACH, Valentine, USA	B: Germany
ROTH, Peter Paul, USA	B: Wurttemberg, Germany
SCHILLER, John (SCHILLING), USA	B: Hesse, Germany
SCHLACHTER, Philipp, USA	B: Germany
SCHMAL, George William, USA	B: Germany

FOREIGN-BORN RECIPIENTS

MOORE, Charles, USN — B: Holland
OSEPINS, Christian, USN — B: Holland
VAN IERSEL, Ludovicus M. M., USA — B: Dussen, Holland

HUNGARY

*RABEL, Laszlo, USA — B: Budapest, Hungary
STAHEL, Julius H., USA — B: Szegedin, Hungary

INDIA

*HANSON, Robert Murray, USMC — B: Lucknow, India
SIMONS, Charles Jenks, USA — B: India

IRELAND

AHERN, William, USN — B: Ireland
ALLEN, James, USA — B: Ireland
ANDERSON, Robert N., USN — B: Ireland
BARRETT, Richard, USA — B: County Mayo, Ireland
BARRY, Augustus, USA — B: Ireland
BASS, David L., USN — B: Ireland
*BEGLEY, Terrence, USA — B: Ireland
BELL, James, USA — B: County Antrim, Ireland
BLACKWOOD, William Robert Douglas, USA — B: Hollywood, County Wicklow, Ireland
BRADLEY, Charles, USN — B: Ireland
BRADY, George F., USN — B: Ireland
BRANAGAN, Edward, USA — B: County Louth, Ireland
BRANNIGAN, Felix, USA — B: Ireland
BRENNAN, Christopher, USN — B: Ireland
BROGAN, James (Edward James), USA — B: County Donegal, Ireland
BROPHY, James, USA — B: Kilkenny, Ireland
BROSNAN, John, USA — B: Ireland
BROWN, Edward Jr. (BROWNE), USA — B: Ireland
BROWN, James, USA — B: Wexford, Ireland
BRUTON, Christopher C. — B: Ireland
BURK, E. Michael (BURKE, Michael), USA — B: Ireland
BURKE, Patrick J., USA — B: Kilkenny, Ireland
BURKE, Richard, USA — B: Tipperary, Ireland
BURKE, Thomas, USN — B: Ireland
BURKE, Thomas, USA — B: Ireland
BUTLER, Edmond Thomas, USA — B: Clonmel, County Tipperary, Ireland
BYRNE, Denis, USA — B: Wexford, Ireland
BYRNES, James, USN — B: Ireland
CAHEY, Thomas, USN — B: Belfast, County Antrim, Ireland
CALLEN, Thomas Joseph (CALLAN), USA — B: County Louth, Ireland
CAMPBELL, William, USA — B: County Down, Ireland
CAREY, Hugh, USA — B: Ireland
CAREY, James, USN — B: Ireland
CARROLL, Thomas, USA — B: Kilkenny, Ireland
CARTER, George, USA — B: Dublin, Ireland
CASEY, David P., USA — B: Ireland
CASSIDY, Michael, USN — B: Ireland
CAVANAUGH, Thomas, USN — B: Ireland
COLBERT, Patrick, USN — B: Ireland
COLEMAN, John, USMC — B: County Cork, Ireland
COLLIS, Charles Henry Tucky, USA — B: County Cork, Ireland
CONBOY, Martin, USA — B: Roscommon, County Ballagh, Ireland
CONNOR, John, USA — B: Galway, Ireland
CONNOR, Thomas, USN — B: Ireland
CONNOR, William C., USN — B: County Cork, Ireland
CONNORS, James, USA — B: Kildare, Ireland
COONEY, James, USMC — B: Limerick, Ireland
COOPER, John (MATHER, John Laver), USN — B: County Dublin, Ireland
CORCORAN, Thomas E., USN — B: Dublin, County Dublin, Ireland
COSGROVE, Thomas, USA — B: County Galway, Ireland
CRAMEN, Thomas, USN — B: Ireland
CREED, John, USA — B: Tipperary, County Tipperary, Ireland
CRONIN, Cornelius, USN — B: Ireland
CULLEN, Thomas, USA — B: Ireland
CURRAN, Richard J., USA — B: Ennis, County Clare, Ireland
DAILY, Charles, USA — B: Mallow, County Cork, Ireland
DELANEY, John Carroll, USA — B: Ireland
DEMPSEY, John, USN — B: Ireland
DICKENS, Charles H., USA — B: Dublin, Ireland
DOHERTY, Thomas M., USA — B: Mitchelstown, County Cork, Ireland
DONAVAN, Cornelius (DONOVAN), USA — B: County Cork, Ireland
DONELLY, John S. (DONNELLY), USA — B: County Kerry, Ireland
DONOGHUE, Timothy (DONAHUE), USA — B: Ireland
DOODY, Patrick H., USA — B: Ireland
DOOLEN, William, USN — B: Ireland
DOUGHERTY, James, USMC — B: Langhash, Ireland
DOUGHERTY, Michael, USA — B: Falcarragh, County Donegal, Ireland
DOUGHERTY, Patrick, USN — B: Ireland
DOWLING, James, USA — B: County Meath, Ireland
DOWNEY, William, USA — B: Ireland
DRURY, James, USA — B: Limerick, County Limerick, Ireland
DUNPHY, Richard D., USN — B: Ireland
EVANS, William, USA — B: Annagh, Ireland
FALLON, Thomas Timothy, USA — B: County Galway, Ireland
FARREN, Daniel, USA — B: County Derry, Ireland
FEGAN, James, USA — B: Athlone, County Westmeath, Ireland
FITZGERALD, John, USMC — B: Limerick, Ireland
FLANNAGAN, John, USN — B: Ireland
FLOOD, Thomas S., USN — B: Ireland
FLOYD, Edward, USN — B: Ireland
FLYNN, Christopher, USA — B: Ireland
FOLEY, John H., USA — B: Cork, Ireland

FORAN, Nicholas, USA	B: County Waterford, Ireland	LAFFEY, Bartlett, USN	B: Galway, County Galway, Ireland
FORD, George W., USA	B: Ireland	LARKIN, David, USA	B: Cork, Ireland
GARDNER, William, USN	B: Ireland	LAVERTY, John, USN	B: County Tyrone, Ireland
*GASSON, Richard, USA	B: Ireland	*LEAHY, Cornelius J., USA	B: Limerick, Ireland
GAUGHAN, Philip, USMC	B: Belmullet, County Mayo, Ireland	LENIHAN, James, USA	B: County Kerry, Ireland
GIBBONS, Michael, USN	B: Ireland	LEONARD, Patrick James, USA	B: County Meath, Ireland
GINLEY, Patrick, USA	B: Ireland	LEONARD, Patrick Thomas, USA	B: County Clare, Ireland
GLYNN, Michael, USA	B: Galway, Ireland	LLOYD, George (LOYD), USA	B: County Tyrone, Ireland
GOLDEN, Patrick, USA	B: County Sligo, Ireland	LOGAN, Hugh, USN	B: Ireland
GRACE, Patrick Henry (Henry Patrick), USN	B: Ireland	LONERGAN, John, USA	B: Carrick, County Donegal, Ireland
GRIBBEN, James H., USA	B: Ireland	MADDEN, Michael, USA	B: County Limerick, Ireland
HALEY, James, USN	B: Ireland	MANGAM, Richard Christopher, USA	B: Ireland
HAMILTON, Frank, USA	B: County Tyrone, Ireland	MARTIN, Edward S., USN	B: Ireland
HARRINGTON, Daniel C., USN	B: Ireland	MARTIN, James, USMC	B: Derry, Ireland
HAVRON, John H., USA	B: Ireland	MARTIN, Patrick, USA	B: County Offaly, Ireland
HEARTERY, Richard, USA	B: Ireland	MARTIN, William, USN	B: Ireland
HIGGINS, Thomas P., USA	B: Longford, Ireland	McADAMS, Peter, USA	B: Armagh, County Armagh, Ireland
HIGHLAND, Patrick, USA	B: Tipperary, Ireland	McALLISTER, Samuel, USN	B: Belfast, County Antrim, Ireland
HINNEGAN, William, USN	B: Ireland	McANALLY, Charles, USA	B: Ireland
HOGAN, Henry, USA	B: County Clare, Ireland	McCABE, William, USA	B: Belfast, County Antrim, Ireland
HORNE, Samuel Belton, USA	B: Belleek, County Fermanagh, Ireland	McCANN, Bernard, USA	B: County Roscommon, Ireland
HOWARD, Martin (HORGAN, Michael C.), USN	B: Ireland	McCARREN, Bernard, USA	B: Ireland
HUDSON, Michael, USMC	B: County Sligo, Ireland	McCORMICK, Michael, USN	B: Ireland
HUNT, Martin, USMC	B: County Mayo, Ireland	McENROE, Patrick H., USA	B: Ireland
HYLAND, John, USN	B: Ireland	McGANN, Michael A., USA	B: County Roscommon, Ireland
IRWIN, Bernard John Dowling, USA	B: Ireland	McGOUGH, Owen, USA	B: Monaghan, Ireland
IRWIN, Patrick, USA	B: Ireland	McGOWAN, John, USN	B: Ireland
JONES, Andrew, USN	B: Limerick, County Limerick, Ireland	McGRAW, Thomas, USA	B: Ireland
JONES, William, USA	B: Wicklow, County Wicklow, Ireland	McGUIRE, Patrick, USA	B: Ireland
KANE, John, USA	B: Ireland	McHALE, Alexander U., USA	B: Ireland
KEARNEY, Michael, USMC	B: Newmarket, County Cork, Ireland	McKEE, George, USA	B: County Tyrone, Ireland
KEATING, Daniel, USA	B: County Cork, Ireland	McKEEVER, Michael, USA	B: Ireland
KEELE, Joseph, USA	B: Ireland	McLOUGHLIN, Michael, USA	B: County Sligo, Ireland
KEENAN, John, USA	B: Tubbercurry, County Sligo, Ireland	McNALLY, James, USA	B: County Monaghan, Ireland
KELLEY, Charles, USA	B: County Clare, Ireland	McNAMARA, Michael, USMC	B: Clure, Ireland
KELLEY, John, USN	B: Ireland	McNAMARA, William, USA	B: County Cork, Ireland
KELLY, Thomas, USA	B: County Mayo, Ireland	McPHELAN, Robert, USA	B: County Laois, Ireland
KELLY, Thomas Gunning, USA	B: Ireland	MITCHELL, John, USA	B: Dublin, Ireland
KENNEDY, John, USA	B: Cavan, County Cavan, Ireland	MITCHELL, John James, USA	B: County Tyrone, Ireland
KENNEDY, Philip, USA	B: County Galway, Ireland	MOLLOY, Hugh, USN	B: County Wexford, Ireland
KEOUGH, John, USA	B: County Tipperary, Ireland	MONAGHAN, Patrick H., USA	B: Ireland
KERR, Thomas R., USA	B: Near Colleraine, County Derry, Ireland	MONTAGUE, Daniel, USN	B: Wicklow, Ireland
KERRIGAN, Thomas, USA	B: County Tipperary, Ireland	MONTGOMERY, Robert William, USN	B: Ireland
KILLACKEY, Joseph, USN	B: County Cork, Ireland	MOORE, Charles, USN	B: Ireland
KING, Hugh, USN	B: Ireland	MORRIS, James L., USA	B: County Kerry, Ireland
KING, John, USN	B: County Mayo, Ireland	MORRISON, John G., USN	B: Ireland
KYLE, Patrick J., USN	B: Ireland	MORTON, Charles W., USN	B: Ireland
		MULHOLLAND, St. Clair Agustin, USA	B: Lisburn, County Antrim, Ireland
		MULLEN, Patrick, USN	B: Ireland
		MURPHY, Dennis J. F., USA	B: County Cork, Ireland
		MURPHY, Edward, USA	B: County Cork, Ireland

MURPHY, Jeremiah J., USA	B: County Cork, Ireland
MURPHY, John Edward, USN	B: Ireland
MURPHY, John P., USA	B: Killarney, County Kerry, Ireland
MURPHY, Michael C., USA	B: Limerick, County Limerick, Ireland
MURPHY, Patrick, USN	B: Ireland
MURPHY, Philip, USA	B: County Killkenny, Ireland
MURPHY, Thomas, USA	B: County Kerry, Ireland
MURPHY, Thomas C., USA	B: Ireland
MURPHY, Thomas J., USA	B: Ireland
MURRAY, Thomas, USA	B: County Monaghan, Ireland
NIHILL, John, USA	B: Nenagh, County Tipperary, Ireland
NOLAN, John J., USA	B: Thurles, County Tipperary, Ireland
NOLAN, Richard J., USA	B: Ireland
NORTON, John R., USA	B: St. John's Parish, County Roscommon, Ireland
NUGENT, Christopher, USMC	B: County Cavan, Ireland
O'BEIRNE, James Rowan, USA	B: Roscommon, County Ballagh, Ireland
O'BRIEN, Peter, USA	B: Dublin, County Dublin, Ireland
O'CONNELL, Thomas, USN	B: Ireland
O'CONNOR, Timothy, USA	B: Ireland
O'DEA, John, USA	B: Limerick, County Limerick, Ireland
O'DONNELL, Menomen, USA	B: Drumbarty, Ireland
O'NEAL, John, USN	B: Ireland
O'SULLIVAN, John Francis, USA	B: County Kerry, Ireland
ORR, Moses, USA	B: County Tyrone, Ireland
PARNELL, William Russell, USA	B: Dublin, Ireland
PLATT, George Crawford, USA	B: Ireland
PLATTEN, Frederick, USA	B: Torbeck, Ireland
PLUNKETT, Thomas, USA	B: Ireland
PRENDERGAST, Thomas Francis, USMC	B: Waterford, Ireland
PRESTON, John, USN	B: Ireland
QUINLAN, James, USA	B: Clomwell, County Tipperary, Ireland
RAFFERTY, Peter F., USA	B: County Tyrone, Ireland
RANNAHAN, John, USMC	B: County Monaghan, Ireland
REED, James C., USA	B: Kilkenny, Ireland
REGAN, Patrick, USN	B: Queenstown, County Cork, Ireland
REID, Patrick, USN	B: Dublin, Ireland
REYNOLDS, George, USA	B: Ireland
RILEY, Thomas, USA	B: Ireland
ROANTREE, James S., USMC	B: Dublin, County Dublin, Ireland
ROBINSON, John H., USA	B: Ireland
ROBINSON, Thomas, USA	B: Ireland
ROCHE, David, USA	B: County Kerry, Ireland
ROGAN, Patrick, USA	B: County Lietrim, Ireland
RYAN, David, USA	B: County Kilkenny, Ireland
RYAN, Denis, USA	B: Cork, Ireland
RYAN, Peter J., USA	B: Tipperary, Ireland
SCANLAN, Patrick (SCANLON), USA	B: Ireland
SCHUTT, George, USN	B: Ireland
SEWELL, William Joyce, USA	B: Castlebar, County Mayo, Ireland
SHANAHAN, Patrick, USN	B: Shanat Castle, County Limerick, Ireland
SHIELDS, Bernard, USA	B: Ireland
SMITH, James, USN	B: Belfast, County Antrim, Ireland
SMITH, Thomas, USN	B: Ireland
SMITH, William, USN	B: Ireland
SPILLANE, Timothy, USA	B: County Kerry, Ireland
STANTON, Thomas, USN	B: Ireland
STEWART, Joseph, USA	B: Ireland
SULLIVAN, Edward, USMC	B: Cork, Ireland
SULLIVAN, Thomas, USA	B: County Meath, Ireland
SULLIVAN, Timothy, USN	B: Ireland
THAYER, James, USN	B: Ireland
THOMPSON, Joseph Henry, USA	B: Kilkeel, County Down, Ireland
THORNTON, Michael, USN	B: Ireland
TOBIN, John Michael, USA	B: Waterford, Ireland
TOOMER, William, USA	B: Dublin, Ireland
TRACY, John (NABERS, Henry G.), USA	B: Dublin, Ireland
TYRRELL, George William, USA	B: Ireland
URELL, Michael Emmet, USA	B: County Cork, Ireland
WALLACE, William, USA	B: County Donegal, Ireland
WALSH, John, USA	B: Tipperary, Ireland
WELCH, Richard, USA	B: Ireland
WELLS, Thomas McCoy, USA	B: Ather, Ireland
WELSH, Edward, USA	B: Ireland
WELSH, James, USA	B: Ireland
WHITE, Patrick H., USA	B: County Sligo, Ireland
WILLIAMS, William, USN	B: Ireland
WILSON, Christopher W., USA	B: Ireland
WRIGHT, Robert, USA	B: Ireland

ITALY

*ALBANESE, Lewis, USA	B: Venice, Italy
Di CESNOLA, Louis Palma, USA	B: Rivarola, Piedmont, Italy
HYDE, Thomas Worcester, USA	B: Florence, Italy
VALENTE, Michael, USA	B: Cassino, Italy

MALTA

CARUANA, Orlando Emanuel, USA	B: Ca Valletta, Malta
MATTHEWS, Joseph, USN	B: Malta
WILLIAMS, Antonio, USN	B: Malta

MEXICO

ANDERSON, Bruce, USA	B: Mexico City, Mexico
GARCIA, Marcario, USA	B: Villa de Castano, Mexico
*JIMENEZ, Jose Francisco, USMC	B: Mexico City, Mexico
PAYNE, Isaac, USA	B: Mexico

NORWAY

BROWN, Robert, USN	B: Norway
HARRIS, John, USN	B: Norway

JOHANNESSEN, Johannes J., USN	B: Bodo, Norway
JOHNSEN, Hans, USN	B: Sandnes, Norway
JOHNSON, Henry, USN	B: Norway
JOHNSON, John, USA	B: Toten Christiania, (now Oslo), Norway
LOMAN, Berger Holton, USA	B: Bergen, Norway
MONSSEN, Mons, USN	B: Bergen, Norway
NELSON, Lauritz, USN	B: Norway
OLSEN, Anton, USN	B: Christiana, (now Oslo), Norway
PHINNEY, William, USN	B: Norway
ROBINSON, Thomas, USN	B: Norway
SLETTELAND, Thomas, USA	B: Bergen, Norway
STOLTENBERG, Andrew Vincent, USN	B: Boto, Norway
TORGERSON, Martin Torinus, USN	B: Oleesen, Norway
WAALER, Reidar, USA	B: Christiana, (now Oslo), Norway
WESTA, Karl, USN	B: Norway
WILLIAMS, Augustus, USN	B: Kristiansand, Norway
WILLIAMS, Louis, USN	B: Christiana, (now Oslo), Norway
WILLIAMS, Peter, USN	B: Norway

PHILIPPINE ISLANDS

CALUGAS, Jose, USA	B: Iliolo, Leon, Barrio Tagsing, PI
*CASTLE, Frederick Walker, USAAC	B: Manila, PI
*DAVIS, George Fleming, USN	B: Manila, PI
NISPEROS, Jose B., USA	B: San Fernandos Union, PI
*PAGE, John Upshur Dennis, USA	B: Luzon, Malahi Island, PI
TRINIDAD, Telesforo Delacruz, USN	B: New Washington Capig, PI

POLAND

MINUE, Nicholas, USA	B: Sedden, Poland

PUERTO RICO

*GARCIA, Fernando Luis, USMC	B: Utuado, Utusdo Co. PR
*LOZADA, Carlos James, USA	B: Caguas, Caguas Co. PR
*RUBIO, Euripides, USA	B: Ponce, Ponce Co. PR
*SANTIAGO-COLON, Hector, USA	B: Salinas, Salinas Co. PR

RUSSIA

PETERS, Alexander, USN	B: Russia
RICE, Charles, USN	B: Russia
SCHEIBNER, Martin E., USA	B: Valdia, Russia
SUNDQUIST, Axel Leohard, USN	B: Finland, Russia
TURVELIN, Alexander Haure, USN	B: Russia

SCOTLAND

ARTHER, Matthew, USN	B: Scotland
AVERY, James, USN	B: Scotland
BRINN, Andrew, USN	B: Scotland
BROWN, John (HAYES, Thomas), USN	B: Glasgow, Scotland
*CRAIG, Robert, USA	B: Scotland
DAVIDSON, Andrew, USA	B: Morebattle, Scotland
DEMPSTER, John, USN	B: Scotland
DICKIE, David, USA	B: Scotland
DOUGALL, Allan Houston, USA	B: Scotland
DOW, Henry, USN	B: Scotland
EADIE, Thomas, USN	B: Scotland
FARQUHAR, John McGreath, USA	B: Near Ayr, Scotland
FRASER, William W., USA	B: Burn Brac, Scotland
GRAY, John, USA	B: Dunde, Scotland
GRINDLAY, James G., USA	B: Odinburgh, Scotland
HAMILTON, Thomas W., USN	B: Scotland
HAWKINS, Charles, USN	B: Scotland
HAY, Fred Stewart (SCHWABE, Frederick H.), USA	B: Stirlingshire, Scotland
JARDINE, Alexander, USN	B: Inverness, Scotland
JARDINE, James, USA	B: Helensburg, Dumbartonshire, Scotland
LAWRENCE, James, USA	B: Aberdeen, Scotland
*MATHIES, Archibald, USAAC	B: Scotland
McDONALD, James, USA	B: Edinburgh, Scotland
McDONALD, James Harper, USN	B: Newmaud, Scotland
McDONALD, John, USN	B: Perth, Scotland
McKENZIE, Alexander, USN	B: Glasgow, Scotland
McLEOD, James, USN	B: Scotland
MEAGHER, Thomas (MARR, Thomas W.), USA	B: Scotland
MOTT, John (McMAHAN, John Mott), USA	B: Fifeshire County, Scotland
REID, Robert Alexander, USA	B: Raplock, Scotland
ROBINSON, Charles, USN	B: Dundee, Scotland
SHIEL, John, USA	B: Scotland
SNEDDEN, James, USA	B: Edinburgh, Scotland
STEWART, Peter, USMC	B: Airdrie, Scotland
THACKRAH, Benjamin, USA	B: Scotland
THOMPSON, John, USA	B: Glasgow, Scotland
THOMPSON, Peter, USA	B: Scotland
WALKER, Edward Alexander, USMC	B: Huntley, Scotland
WARREN, David, USN	B: Glasgow, Scotland

SPAIN

ORTEGA, John, USN	B: Spain
SHARP, Hendrick, USN	B: Spain

SWEDEN

ANDERSON, William, USN	B: Sweden
BERGENDAHL, Frederick, USA	B: Gothenburg, Sweden
BJORKMAN, Ernest H., USN	B: Malmo, Sweden
DAHLGREN, John Olof, USMC	B: Kahliwar, Sewden
*GIBSON, Eric Gunnar, USA	B: Nysund, Sweden
HALLING, Luovi, USN	B: Stockholm, Sweden
JOHANSON, John Peter, USN	B: Oskarshamn, Sweden
JOHANSSON, Johan J., USN	B: Sweden
NORDSTROM, Isador A., USN	B: Gotegorg, Sweden
PETERSON, Alfred, USN	B: Sweden
RAGNAR, Theodore, USA	B: Linkoping, Sweden
READ, Charles A., USN	B: Sweden
SMITH, Oloff, USN	B: Sweden

FOREIGN-BORN RECIPIENTS

SUNDQUIST, Gustav Adolf, USN	B: Sweden	GRIFFITHS, John, USN	B: Wales
SWANSON, John, USN	B: Gothenburg, Sweden	MAHONEY, Gregory, USA	B: Pettypool, South Wales
VON VEGESACK, Ernest, USA	B: Gotland, Sweden	POWELL, William Henry, USA	B: Pontypool, Monmouthshire, South Wales

SWITZERLAND

FREY, Franz (Frank Xaiver), USA	B: Switzerland
KNAAK, Albert, USA	B: Luxenburg, Switzerland
STAUFFER, Rudolph, USA	B: Berne, Switzerland
STICKOFFER, Julius Henry, USA	B: Switzerland
VEUVE, Ernest, USA	B: New Castle, Switzerland
WHITE, Adam, USA	B: Switzerland

WEST INDIES

DAVIS, John, USN	B: Kingslow, Jamaica, West Indies
GIRANDY, Alphonse, USN	B: Guadaloupe, West Indies
JOHNSON, William, USN	B: St. Vincent, West Indies
LITTLE, Thomas, USA	B: Barbados, West Indies
PILE, Richard, USN	B: West Indies
SWEENEY, Robert Augustus, USN	B: Montserrat, West Indies
TEYTAND, August P. (TEYTARD), USN	B: Santa Cruz, West Indies

WALES

BATES, Richard, USN	B: Wales
DAVIS, Joseph, USA	B: Monmouth County, Wales
DAVIS, Thomas, USA	B: Haverford, West Wales
EDWARDS, David, USA	B: Wales
EVANS, Thomas, USA	B: Wales

YUGOSLAVIA

ALLEX, Jake (MANDUSHICH, Jake Allex), USA	B: near Prizren, Streska, Serbia
*MESTROVITCH, James I., USA	B: Crna Cora, Yugoslavia

TABLE OF MEDAL RECIPIENTS 1863–1994

ACTION	ARMY	NAVY	MARINE CORPS	AIR FORCE	COAST GUARD	TOTAL
CIVIL WAR	1195	308	17	0	0	1520
INTERIM 1865-1870	0	13	0	0	0	13
INDIAN CAMPAIGNS	424	0	0	0	0	424
KOREAN CAMPAIGN 1871	0	8	7	0	0	15
INTERIM 1871-1898	0	98	2	0	0	100
SPANISH-AMERICAN WAR	30	64	15	0	0	109
SAMOA CAMPAIGN	0	1	3	0	0	4
PHILILIPPINE INSURRECT.	69	5	6	0	0	80
CHINA RELIEF EXPEDITION	4	22	33	0	0	59
INTERIM 1899-1910	0	48	2	0	0	50
PHILIPPINES 1911	1	5	0	0	0	6
MEXICAN CAMPAIGN	1	46	9	0	0	56
HAITIAN CAMPAIGN 1915	0	0	6	0	0	6
INTERIM 1915-1916	0	8	0	0	0	8
DOMINICAN CAMPAIGN	0	0	3	0	0	3
WORLD WAR I	90	21	8	0	0	119
HAITIAN CAMPAIGN 1919-1920	0	0	2	0	0	2
2ND NICARAGUAN CAMPAIGN	0	0	2	0	0	2
INTERIM 1919-1940	2	15	1	0	0	18
WORLD WAR II	294	57	81	0	1	433
KOREAN WAR	78	7	42	4	0	131
VIETNAM WAR & ERA	155	15	57	12	0	239
SOMALIA	2	0	0	0	0	2
UNKNOWNS	9	0	0	0	0	9
TOTALS	2354	741	296	16	1	3408*

*Seven double awardees won medals in two different actions

A SELECT MEDAL OF HONOR BIBLIOGRAPHY

This Medal of Honor bibliography is somewhat selective. To include all sources would involve an endless compilation of materials, the good with the bad, the scholarly with the unscholarly. The exclusion and/or inclusion of entries was solely my decision. So, too, was the method of presentation and the division of titles.

I've attempted to shorten the list in various ways. For example, hundreds of military units have written their own histories, detailed accounts of their combat action in the campaigns of the various wars. Many contain accounts where Medals were won; to include all of these would mean nearly 600 more entries.

There is much information about actions where Medals were awarded in the excellent official histories published by the services. Here I've listed the series name rather than individual titles, in order to call the reader's attention to them.

Not all Medal of Honor biographies are listed. Some Medal winners have had many volumes written about them, for instance Douglas MacArthur, O. O. Howard and Leonard Wood, all of whom were controversial figures. Nearly 20 books cover the various aspects of Howard's career, much of this material being redundant, poorly written or just boring. Those works included here are well written and very much to the point. This basis for selection has been applied to other material throughout.

Similarly the section "Books with Anecdotes about the Medals and Their Recipients" has been edited to present only the relevant material. For example, Edward Beach's *The Wreck of the Memphis* focuses on the *Memphis* disaster, but within the main story lies the story of how three of her crew won Medals of Honor. And then again, just two brief paragraphs in Ross Carter's *Those Devils in Baggy Pants* relate how Pvt. John R. Towle announced to his comrades that he was going to win a Medal of Honor, as he took on two German tanks and their infantry, stopping them cold, winning a Medal posthumously.

GENERAL BIBLIOGRAPHY

Anders, Curt. *Fighting Generals.* New York: Putnam, 1965.

Army Times (eds.). *American Heroes of Asian Wars.* New York: Dodd, Mead, 1968.

Barrows, N. *Blow All Ballast: The Story of the Squalus.* New York: Dodd, Mead, 1940.

Belden, Bauman. *United States War Medals.* Greenwich, Conn.: F. Flayderman, 1962.

Benavidez, Roy B. *The Last Medal of Honor Winner.* McLean, Va.: Brasseys U.S., 1995.

Beyer, W. F., and O.F. Keyel (eds.). *Deeds of Valor from Records in the Archives of the United States Government: How American Heroes Won the Medal of Honor.* 2 vols. Detroit: Perrien-Keydel, 1906-07.

Bigler, Philip. *In Honored Glory: the Story of Arlington Cemetery.* New York: Vandamere, 1966.

Blakeney, Jane. *Heroes, U.S. Marine Corps, 1861-1955.* Washington, D.C.: Blakeney Pub., 1957.

Blassingame, Wyatt. *Medical Corps Heroes of World War II.* New York: Garrard, 1969.

Boswell, Rolfe. *Medals for Marines.* New York: Thomas Y. Crowell, 1945.

Bozich, Stanley J. *Detroit's Own.* Frankenmuth, Mich.: Polar Bear Pub., 1985.

Braun, Saul M. *Seven Heroes . . . Medal of Honor Stories of the War in the Pacific.* New York: Putnam, 1965.

Chase, Joseph C. *Soldiers All: Portraits and Sketches of the Men of the A.E.F.* New York: George H. Doran, 1920.

Cook, John L. *Dust Off.* Toronto: Bantam Books, 1988.

Cooke, Donald E. *For Conspicuous Gallantry: Winners of the Medal of Honor.* Maplewood, N.J.: Hammond, 1966.

Curtis, Arthur S. *The Congressional Medal of Honor.* Annapolis, Md.: The American Serviceman's Library, 1945.

Dell Publishing (ed.). *The Congressional Medal of Honor Library: the Names, the Deeds, Korea.* New York: Dell Publishing, 1987.

———. *Congressional Medal of Honor Library: The Names, the Deeds, World War II.* New York: Dell Publishing, 1986.

Delong, Kent. *War Heroes: True Stories of Congressional Medal of Honor Recipients.* Westport, Conn.: Praeger, 1993.

Donovan, Frank. *The Medal: The Story of the Medal of Honor.* New York: Dodd, Mead, 1962.

Dorling, H. Taprell. *Ribbons and Medals.* London: Philip, 1963.

DuPre, Flint O. *U.S. Air Force Biographical Dictionary.* New York: Watts, 1965.

Engle, Eloise K. *Medic: America's Medical Soldiers, Sailors and Airmen from the Revolutionary War to Vietnam.* New York: Day, 1967.

Faber, Harold and Doris. *American Heroes of the 20th Century.* New York: Random House, 1967.

Feeny, William D. *In Their Honor.* New York: Duell, 1963.

Ferrel, P. V. *The Heroes of the War for the Union and Their Achievements.* Cincinatti, 1865.

Floherty, John J. *The Courage and the Glory.* New York: J. B. Lippincott, 1942.

Fredman, J. George, and Louis A. Falk. *Jews in American Wars.* New York: Jewish War Veterans of the United States, 1943.

Friederich, Rudolf J. *Medal of Honor Citation Supplements.* Chicago: Orders & Medals Society of America, 1968.

Gallery, Daniel V. *Twenty Million Tons Under the Sea (U-505).* Chicago: H. Regnery, 1956.

Garland, Albert N. (ed.). *Infantry in Vietnam.* New York: Jove Pubns., 1985.

Gibbons, Cromwell. *Military Decorations and Campaign Service Bars of the United States.* New York: U.S. Insignia, 1943.

Greene, J. I. (ed.). *The Infantry Journal Reader.* Garden City, N.Y.: Doubleday, Doran, 1943.

Gurney, Gene. *Arlington National Cemetery: a Picture Story.* New York: Crown Publishers, 1965.

———. *Five Down and Glory.* New York: Putnam, 1958.

Harr, B. *Combat Boots.* New York: Exposition Press, 1952.

Heaps, Willard A. *The Bravest Teenage Yanks.* New York: Duell, 1963.

Hero Tales of the American Soldier and Sailor as Told by the Heroes Themselves and Their Comrades. Philadelphia: merchants Library Association, 1899.

Hicken, Victor. *The American Fighting Man.* New York: Macmillan, 1969.

Hinkel, John V. *Arlington: Monument to Heroes.* Englewood Cliffs, N.J.: Prentice Hall, 1965.

Hirsch, Phil (ed.). *Great Combat Stories of the Korean War.* New York: Pyramid, 1968.

Holbrook, Stewart. *None More Courageous: American War Heroes of Today.* New York: Macmillan, 1942.

Howell, Glenn. *Medals of Honor.* New York: L. MacVeagh, Dial Press, 1931.

Hume, Edgar E. *The Medical Book of Merit.* Washington, D.C.: The Association of Medical Surgeons, 1925.

Jacobs, Bruce. *Heroes of the Army: The Medal of Honor and Its Winners.* New York: Norton, 1956.

———. *Korea's Heroes: The Medal of Honor Story.* New York, Berkley Pub., 1961.

Kayser, Hugh F. *The Spirit of America.* Palm Springs, Calif: ETC Publs., 1982.

Kerrigan, Evans E. *American War Medals and Decorations.* New York: Macmillan, 1964.

———. *American Medals and Decorations.* Westport, Conn.: Medallic Pub., 1990.

———. *Current American War Medals and Decorations, 1963-1969.* Noroton Heights, Conn.: Medallic Pub., 1969.

Lavender, David. *Mike Maroney, Raider.* Philadelphia: Westminster Press, 1945.

———. *Medal of Honor in Vietnam.* Westport, Conn.: Medallic Pub., 1976.

Lee, Irvin H. *Negro Medal of Honor Men.* New York: Dodd, Mead, 1967.

———. *Medal of Honor.* New York: Dodd, Mead, 1967.

Lockwood, C., and H. C. Adamson. *Hellcats of the Sea.* New York: Greenberg, 1955.

Lockwood, Charles. *Sink 'Em All.* New York: Dutton, 1951.

Look Magazine (eds.). *Our American Heroes.* New York: Look, 1943.

Loubat, Joseph F. *The Medallic History of the United States of America, 1776-1876.* New York: the author, 1880.

Merrill, James M. (ed.). *Uncommon Valor: The Exciting Story of the Army.* New York, 1964.

Meyer, N. S. *Military Insignia and Equipment.* New York: N. S. Meyer, 1930.

Millbook, Minnie. *A Study in Valor: Michigan Medal of Honor Winners in the Civil War.* Lansing, Mich., 1966.

Miller, Warren H. *Boys of 1917: Famous American Heroes of the World War.* Boston: L. C. Page, 1939.

Mingos, Howard. *American Heroes of the War in the Air.* 2 vols. New York: Lanciar Publishers, 1943.

Mitchell, Joseph B. *The Badge of Gallantry: Recollections of the Civil War Congressional Medal of Honor Winners.* New York: Macmillan, 1968

Morgan, Joseph M. *Military Medals and Insignia of the United States.* Glendale, Calif.: Griffin-Patterson Publishing, 1941.

Mulholland, St. Clair A. *Medal of Honor Legion of the United States.* Philadelphia: Town Printing, 1905.

Murphy, Edward F. *World War II Heroes.* Novato, Calif., Presidio Press, 1990.

———. *Korean War Heroes.* Novato, Calif.: Presidio Press, 1992.

———. *Vietnam Medal of Honor Heroes.* New York: Ballantine Books, 1987.

Musciano, Walter A. *Corsair Aces: The Bent-Wing Birds over the Pacific.* New York: Prentice Hall, 1979.

Nagle, John T. *The Status of Acting Assistant Surgeons of the United States Army.* New York: M. B. Brown, printer, 1893.

National Geographic Society. *Insignias and Decorations of the U.S. Armed Forces.* Washington, D.C.: National Geographic Society, 1944.

Navy Times (eds.). *They Fought Under the Sea.* Washington, D.C.: Navy Times Books, 1968.

Official Records of the Union and Confederate Navies in the War of Rebellion. 31 vols. Washington, D.C.: U.S. Naval War Records Office, 1894-1927.

O'Neill, Charles K. *Wild Train: The Story of the Andrews Raiders.* New York: Random House, 1956.

Parker, William R. (ed.). *Above and Beyond the Call of Duty; Commemorating the One Hundredth Anniversary of the Medal of Honor.* New York: McFadden Books, 1963.

Petersen, Gordon A. *A Guide to U.S. Army Insignia and Decorations.* Racine, Wis.: Whitman, 1942.

Pullen, John J. *A Shower of Stars: The Medal of Honor and the 27th Maine.* Philadelphia: Lippincott, 1966.

Reck, Franklin M. *Beyond the Call of Duty.* New York: Thomas Y. Crowell, 1944.

Reeder, Russell P. (Red). *Medal of Honor Heroes.* New York: Random House, 1965.

Reynolds, Quentin J. *Known But to God.* New York: John Day, 1962.

Roberts, MacLennan. *The Great Locomotive Chase.* New York: Dell Publishing, 1956.

Rodenbough, Theo. F.(ed. and comp.). *The Bravest Five Hundred of '61.* New York: G. W. Dillingham, 1891.

Rovere, Richard H., and Athur A. Schlesinger. *The MacArthur Controversy and American Foreign Policy.* New York: Farrar, Straus, & Giroux, 1965.

Schott, Joseph L. *Above and Beyond: The Story of the Congressional Medal of Honor.* New York: Putnam, 1963.

Schuon, Karl. *U.S. Marine Corps Biographical Dictionary.* New York: Franklin Watts, 1963.

Scott, J. (pseud.). *Marine War Heroes: Daring Exploits of Marine Winners of the ... Medal of Honor.* Derby, Conn.: Monarch Books, 1963.

Scott, Jay. *America's War Heroes: Dramatic True Tales of ... Men Whose Exploits Won Them the ... Medal of Honor.* Derby, CT, 1963.

Shane, Ted. *Heroes of the Pacific.* New York: J. Messner, 1944.

Sims, Edward H. *Greatest Fighter Missions of the Top Navy and Marine Air Aces of World War II.* New York: Harper, 1962.

———. *The Greatest Aces.* New York: Harper, 1968.

Snowden, James R. *A Description of the Medals of Washington.* Philadelphia: J. B. Lippincott, 1861.

South Carolina Adjutant-General's Office. *The Medal of Honor, Army and Navy.* Columbia, S.C.: South Carolina State Adjutant General's Office, 1956.

Stillman, Richard J. *The U.S. Infantry: Queen of Battle.* New York: Franklin Watts, 1965.

Stringer, Harry. *Heroes All!* Washington, D.C.: Fassett, 1919.

Studley, George W. *Regulation War Medals.* Avon, N.Y.: Studley, G.W., 1939.

Talley, Naomi. *Medals for Brave Men.* New York: Dial Press, 1963.

Tassin, R. *Double Winners of the Medal of Honor.* Canton, Ohio: Daring Books, 1987.

Tibbets, Albert B. *American Heroes All.* Boston: Little, Brown, 1966.

Thomas, Lowell J. *These Men Shall Never Die.* Philadelphia: The John C. Winston, 1943.

Tolliver, Raymond F. *Fighter Aces.* New York: Macmillan, 1965.

Townsend, Edward D. *Anecdotes of the Civil War in the United States.* New York: D. Appleton, 1884.

U.S. Army Artillery and Missile School. *The Medal of Honor Among Artillerymen.* Ft. Sill, Okla.: 1961.

U.S. Army Corps of Engineers. *Medal of Honor Winners.* Washington, D.C.: 1964.

U.S. Infantry Association. *Army Regulations Applicable to Individual Soldiers and the Administration of Units of the Army.* Washington, D.C.: 1923.

U.S. Military Academy. *Memorial Booklet West Point Graduate ... Medal of Honor.* West Point, N.Y.: U.S. Military Academy, 1963.

U.S. National Historic Publishers Association. *The World War and Historic Deeds of Valor from Official Records and Illustrations of the Untied States and Allied Governments. Vol. VI.* Chicago: U.S. Hist. Publ. Assn., 1919.

Wells, Linton. *Salute to Valor.* New York: Random House, 1942.

Werlich, Robert. *Orders and Decorations of All Nations.* Washington, D.C.: Quaker Press, 1966.

Whitehouse, Arthur G. J. *Epics and Legends of the First War.* London: F. Muller, 1964.

Wyllie, Robert E. *Orders, Decorations and Insignia: Military and Civil.* New York: G. P. Putnam's Sons, 1921.

Yolen, Will, and Kenneth Seeman. *Heroes for Our Times.* Harrisburg, Pa.: Stackpole Books, 1968.

AUTOBIOGRAPHIES AND BIOGRAPHIES OF MEDAL OF HONOR WINNERS

Army Times (eds.). *The Banner and the Glory: The Story of Gen. Douglas MacArthur.* New York: Dodd, Mead, 1966.

Baldwin, Alice B. *Memoirs of the Late Major-General Frank D. Baldwin.* Los Angeles: Wetzel Publishing, 1929.

Beamish, Richard J. *The Boy's Story of Lindbergh, The Lone Eagle.* Chicago: John C. Winston, 1928.

Benavidez, Roy, and Oscar Griffin. *The Three Wars of Roy Benavidez.* San Antonio, Tex., 1988.

Billac, Pete (ed.). *The Last Medal of Honor.* New York: Swan Publications, 1990.

Bourke, John G. *Apache Campaign.* New York: Scribner, 1958.

———. *On the Border with Crook.* Lincoln, Neb.: University of Nebraska Press, 1971.

Boyington, Gregory. *Baa Baa Black Sheep.* New York: Putnam, 1958.

Boynton, Henry V. (ed.). *U.S. Congress, Joint Committee on Dedication of Chickamauga and Chattanooga National Military Park Sept. 18-20, 1895.* Washington, D.C.: U.S. Government Printing Office, 1896.

Bradley, James H. *The March of the Montana Column: Godfrey's Diary.* Norman, Okla.: University of Oklahoma Press, 1963.

Brent, Rafer (pseud.). *Great War Stories.* New York: Bartholemew House, 1957.

Breuer, William B. *Sea Wolf.* Novato, Calif.: Presidio Press, 1987.

Butler, Smedley D. *War Is a Racket.* New York: Round Table Press, 1935.

Butterfield, Julia L. (ed.). *A Biographical Memorial of General Daniel Butterfield.* New York: Grafton Press, 1904.

Byrd, Richard E. *Alone.* New York: G. P. Putnam's Sons, 1938.

———. *Little America.* New York: Putnam, 1930.

Carpenter, John A. *Sword and Olive Branch: Oliver Otis Howard.* Pittsburgh: University of Pittsburgh Press, 1964.

Carr, William H. A. *The DuPonts of Delaware.* Toronto: Dodd, 1964.

Carter, R. G. *The Old Sergeant's Story.* New York: Hitchcock, 1926.

Cavanagh, Michael. *Memoirs of Gen. Thomas Francis Meagher.* Worcester, Mass.: Messenger Press, 1892.

Chamberlain, Joshua L. *The Passing of the Armies.* New York: G. P. Putnam's Sons, 1915.

Cleveland, E. J. *The Genealogy of the Cleveland and Cleaveland Families.* Hartford, Conn.: Case, Lockwood & Brainard, 1899.

Cody, William F. *The Adventures of Buffalo Bill.* New York: Harper & Row, 1904.

Considine, Robert B. *General Douglas MacArthur.* New York, 1964.

Cowan, Sam K. *Sergeant York and His People.* New York: Funk & Wagnalls, 1922.

Cruse, Thomas. *Apache Days and After.* Caldwell, Idaho: Caxton Printers, 1941.

Cummings, Damon E. *Admiral Richard Wainwright and the United States Fleet.* Washington, D.C.: U.S. Government Printing Office, 1962.

Cutler, Thomas J. *Brown Water, Black Berets.* Annapolis, Md.: Naval Institute Press, 1988.

Davis, Kenneth S. *Hero: Charles A. Lindbergh and the American Dream.* New York: Doubleday, 1959.

Day, George E. *Return with Honor.* Mesa, AZ: 1989

Dean, William F. *General Dean's Story.* New York: Viking Press, 1954.

Donlon, Roger. *Outpost of Freedom.* New York: McGraw-Hill, 1965.

Dougherty, Michael. *Prison Diary of Michael Dougherty.* Bristol, Pa.: C. A. Dougherty, 1908.

DuPont, Henry A. *Campaign of 1864 in the Valley of Virginia.* New York: National Americana Society, 1925.

Eadie, Tom. *I Like Diving: A Professional's Story.* Boston: Houghton Mifflin, 1929.

Edwards, D. K. *This Side of Hell.* New York: Doubleday, 1932.

Ellsberg, Edward. *Men Under the Sea.* New York: Dodd, Mead, 1940.

———. *On the Bottom.* Rahway, N.J.: 1939.

Fluckey, Eugene B. *Thunder Below!* Chicago: University of Illinois Press, 1992.

Force, Manning F. . . . *General Sherman.* New York: D. Appleton and Company, 1899.

Foss, Joe. *Joe Foss, Flying Marine.* New York: Books, Inc., 1943; distributed by E. P. Dutton.

Foss, Joe, and Donna W. Foss. *Proud American.* New York: Pocket Books, 1992.

Foster, C. *Rear Admiral Byrd and the Polar Expeditions.* New York: Burt, 1930.

Foster, John. *Guadalcanal General: The Story of A. A. Vandergrift, USMC.* New York: Morrow, 1966.

Fredericks, Edgar J. *MacArthur: His Mission and Meaning.* Philadelphia: J. Whitmore, 1969.

Funston, Frederick. *Memories of Two Wars.* New York: Scribner, 1914.

Ganoe, William A. *MacArthur Close-Up: Much Then and Some Now.* New York: Vantage, 1962.

Gladych, Michael. *Admiral Byrd of Antarctica.* New York: Messner, 1960.

Glines, Carroll V. *Doolittle's Tokyo Raiders.* New York: Van Nostrand, 1964.

Godfrey, Edward S. *Some Reminiscences, Including the Washita Battle November 27, 1868.* Reprinted from the Cavalry Journal 37 No. 153; (1928).

Graham, Don. *No Name on the Bullet.* New York: Viking Press, 1989.

Greely, Maj. Gen. A. W. *Reminiscences of Adventure and Service.* New York: C. Scribner's Sons, 1927.

Greely, Lt. A. W. *Three Years of Arctic Service.* New York: C. Scribner's Sons, 1886.

Gumpertz, Sydney G. *The Jewish Legion of Valor.* New York: S. G. Gumpertz, 1946.

Hagedorn, Hermann. *Leonard Wood: A Biography.* 2 vols. New York: Harper & Brothers, 1931.

Hall, Norman S. *The Balloon Buster.* New York: Bantam Books, 1928, 1966.

Herndon, B. *The Unlikeliest Hero: The Story of PFC Desmond Doss, Conscientious Objector Who Won His Nation's Highest Military Honor.* Mountain View, Calif.: Pacific, 1967.

Hobson, Richmond P. *The Sinking of the Merrimac: A Personal Narrative.* New York: Century, 1899.

Howard, James H., Paul McCarthy (ed.). *Roar of the Tiger.* New York: Crown Publishing Group, 1991.

Howard, Oliver O. *Autobiography of Oliver Otis Howard.* 2 vols. New York: Baker & Taylor, 1907.

Hoyt, Edwin P. *The Last Explorer: The Adventures of Admiral Byrd.* New York: John Day, 1968.

Huff, Sidney. *My Fifteen Years with General MacArthur.* New York: Paperback Library, 1964.

Huie, William B. *The Hero of Iwo Jima.* New York: New American Library, 1962.

Hunt, Frazier. *MacArthur and the War Against Japan.* New York: C. Scribner's Sons, 1944.

———. *Untold Story of Douglas MacArthur.* New York: Devin-Adair, 1954.

Izac, Edouard. *Prisoner of the U-90.* Boston: Houghton, Mifflin, 1919.

Jablonski, Edward. *Flying Fortress: Illustrated Biography of the B-17s and the Men Who Flew Them.* New York: Doubleday, 1965.

Johnson, Virginia W. *The Unregimented General; a Biography of Nelson A. Miles.* Cambridge, Mass.: Houghton Mifflin, 1962.

Kelly, Charles. *One Man's War.* New York: A. A. Knopf, 1944.

Kenney, George C. *Dick Bong; Ace of Aces.* New York: Duell, 1960.

Keyhoe, Donald E. *Flying with Lindbergh.* New York: Putnam, 1928.

King, James T. *War Eagle: A Life of General Eugene A. Carr.* Lincoln, Neb.: University of Nebraska Press, 1963.

Klemme, Otto. *General Lawton's Day.* Leipzig: Verlag fur Literatur, Kunst und Musik, 1907.

Langford, Laura C. Holloway. *Howard: The Christian Hero.* New York: Funk & Wagnalls, 1885.

Lawrence, J. S. *The Descendants of Moses and Sarah Kilham Porter.* Grand Rapids, Mich.: F. A. Onderdonk, printer, 1910.

Lawson, Ted. *Thirty Seconds Over Tokyo.* New York: Random House, 1953.

Lindbergh, Charles A. *Of Flight and Life.* New York: Scribner's Sons, 1948.

———. *The Spirit of St. Louis.* New York: Scribner, 1953.

———. *We.* New York: Putnam, 1927.

Lockwood, Charles A., and Hans C. Adamson. *Through Hell and Deep Water: The Story of the Submarine U.S.S. Harder.* New York: Greenberg, 1956.

Lowry, Timothy S. *And Brave Men, Too.* New York: Crown Pub., 1985.

MacArthur, Douglas. *Reminiscences.* New York: McGraw-Hill, 1964.

Mende, Elsie P. *An American Soldier and Diplomat: Horace Porter.* New York: Frederick A. Stokes, 1927.

Merrill, James M. *Target Tokyo: The Halsey-Doolittle Raid.* New York: Rand-McNally, 1964.

Miles, Nelson A. *Personal Recollections and Observations of General Nelson A. Miles.* New York: Werner, 1896.

———. *Serving the Republic.* New York: Harper, 1911.

Miley, John D. *In Cuba with Shafter.* New York: C. Scribner's Sons, 1899.

Miller, Franklin D. with Elwood J. C. Kureth. *Reflections of a Warrior.* Novato, Calif.: Presidio Press, 1991.

Miller, Francis T. *General Douglas MacArthur.* Philadelphia: John C. Winston, 1944.

Mullholland, St. Clair A. *The Story of the 116th Regiment, Pennsylvania Infantry.* Philadelphia: F. McManus, Jr., printer, 1899.

Murphy, Audie. *To Hell and Back.* New York: H. Holt, 1949.

Murphy, Francis X. *Fight Admiral.* New York: Vantage Press, 1952.

New York Monuments Commission. *In Memoriam, Alexander Steward Webb.* Albany, N.Y.: New York Monuments Commission, 1916.

Nicolay, Helen. *MacArthur of Bataan.* New York: D. Appleton-Century, 1942.

O'Callahan, Joseph, S. J. *I Was a Chaplain on the Franklin.* New York: Macmillan, 1956.

O'Kane, Richard H. *Clear the Bridge.* Chicago: Rand McNally, 1977.

———. *Wahoo.* Novato, Calif: Presidio Press, 1987.

Parker, James. *The Mounted Rifleman.* Menasha, Wis.: Banta, 1916.

Pearl, Jack. *General Douglas MacArthur.* Derby, Conn.: Monarch Books, 1961.

Pinchon, Edgcumb. *Dan Sickles: Hero of Gettysburg and "Yankee King of Spain."* Garden City, N.Y.: Doubleday, Doran, 1945.

Pittenger, William. *Daring and Suffering: a History of the Great Railroad Adventure.* Philadelphia: J. W. Daughaday, 1863.

———. *In Pursuit of the General.* reprint, San Marino, Calif.: Golden West Books, 1966.

Place, Marion. *The Frontiersman:.* New York: Holt, 1967.

Pond, George. *The Shenandoah Valley in 1864.* New York: C. Scribner's Sons, 1883.

Porter, Horace. *Campaigning with Grant.* New York: Century, 1897.

Reynolds, Quentin. *The Amazing Mr. Doolittle.* New York: Appleton-Century Crofts, 1953.

Rickenbacker, Edward V. *Fighting the Flying Circus.* Garden City, N.Y.: Doubleday, 1965.

———. *Rickenbacker.* Englewood Cliffs, N.J.: Prentice Hall, 1967.

———. *Seven Came Through.* New York: Doubleday, 1943.

Roosevelt, E. B. A. *Day Before Yesterday; Reminiscences.* New York: Doubleday, 1959.

Roske, Ralph, and C. Van Doren. *Lincoln's Commando.* New York: Harper, 1957.

Ross, Helen L. *Touch of Smile.* Burley, Wash.: Coffee Break Press, 1978.

Ross, Walter S. *The Last Hero: Charles A. Lindbergh.* New York: Harper, 1968.

Rovere, Richard H., and Arthur M. Schlesinger, Jr. *The General and the President.* New York: Farrar, Straus and Young, 1951.

Schofield, John M. *Forty-six Years in the Army.* New York: Century, 1897.

Stanley, David S. *Personal Memoirs of Major-General D. S. Stanley.* Cambridge, Mass.: Harvard University Press, 1917.

Strandberg, John E., and Roger James Bender. *Call of Duty: Military Awards & Decorations of the United States of America.* San Jose, Calif.: Bender, 1994.

Swanberg, W. A. *Sickles the Incredible.* New York: Scribner, 1956.

Thomas, Lowell J. *Old Gimlet Eye.* New York: Farrar & Rinehart, 1933.

Todd, Alden L. *Abandoned: The Story of the Greely Arctic Expedition, 1881-1884.* New York: McGraw-Hill, 1961.

Tolman, Newton F. *The Search for General Miles.* New York: Putnam, 1968.

Tremain, Henry E. *Sailor's Creek to Appomattox Court House.* New York: C. H. Ludwig, printer, 1885.

———. *Two Days of War: A Gettysburg Narrative.* New York: Bonnell, 1905.

Urban, Matt, and Charles F. Conrad. *Matt Urban Story: Life and World War Two Experiences.* Holland, Mich.: Matt Urban Story, 1989.

Vandegrift, Alexander A. *Once a Marine: The Memoirs of General A. A. Vandegrift, U.S.M.C.* New York: Norton, 1964.

Vanderslice, John M. *Gettysburg.* Philadelphia: J. B. Lippincott, 1897.

Wainwright, Jonathan, Robert Considine (ed.). *General Wainwright's Story.* Garden City, N.Y.: Doubleday & Co., 1946.

Wallace, Willard M. *Soul of the Lion: A Biography of General Joshua L. Chamberlain.* New York: Nelson, 1960.

Webb, Alexander S. *The Peninsula: McClellan's Campaign of 1862.* New York: C. Scribner's Sons, 1881.

Wetzel, Gary G. *Jake: The Forgotten Warrior.* Oak Creek, WI: 1984.

Wheeler, Richard. *The Bloody Battle for Suribachi*. New York: Crowell, 1965.

White, W. L. *They Were Expendable*. New York: Harcourt, 1942.

Whiting, Charles. *Hero: The Life and Death of Audie Murphy*. Chelsea, Mich.: Madison Books, 1990.

Whitney, Courtney. *MacArthur, His Rendezvous with History*. New York: Knopf, 1956.

Whorf, Mike. *Old Soldiers Never Die*. Birmingham, Mich.: Mike Whorf, 1970, 1964.

Wilhelm, Maria. *The Fighting Irishman: The Story of "Wild Bill" Donovan*. New York: Hawthorn Books, 1964.

Willcox, Orlando B. (Majro March, Pseud.). *Faca, An Army Memoir*. Boston, E. O. Libby, 1858.

Wilson, D Ray. *Episode on Hill 616*. Alton, IL., 1981.

Wilson, John A. *Adventures of Alf Wilson*. Toledo, Ohio: Blade Printing & Paper, 1880.

Windolph, Charles A. *I Fought with Custer*. New York: C. Scribner's Sons, 1947.

Woodfill, Samuel. *Woodfill of the Regulars*. New York: Doubleday, Doran, 1929.

York, Alvin, and Tom Skeyhill (ed.). *Sergeant York: His Own Life Story and War Diary*. Garden City, N.Y.: Doubleday, Doran, 1931.

GOVERNMENT DOCUMENTS
(Washington, D.C., U.S. Government Printing Office, unless otherwise noted.)

Annual Report of the Chief of the Record and Pension Office, 1901-1906

Annual Report of the Secretary of Defense, 1948-1969.

Annual Report of the Secretary of the Navy, 1863-1947.

Annual Report of the Secretary of War, 1863-1865, 1890-1947.

Congressional Document. *Medal of Honor, 1863-1968*. (Revision of 1964 ed.) 90th Cong., 2nd Sess., Washington, D.C., 1968.

———. *General Staff Corps and Medals of Honor*. S. Doc. 58, 66th Cong., 1st Sess., 1919.

U.S. Army and Navy Regulations, 1895-1969; Air Force Regulations, 1948-1969. (Pertinent to wearing the Medals, display and Medal design.)

U.S. Army War College. *Rewards and Commendations*. Fort Carlysle, 1928.

U.S. Congress. House Committee on Military Affairs. *Presenting A Medal of Honor to General (A.L.) Greely, Feb. 22, 1935*. House Rpt. No. 210, 74th Cong., 1st Sess., 1935.

U.S. Commission of Fine Arts. *Critical Appraisal of the Present Medal of Honor*. 1920.

U.S. Department of the Army. *The Medal of Honor of the United States Army*. 1948.

U.S. Department of Defense. *The Unknowns of World War II and Korea*. 1960.

U.S. Department of the Navy. *Roll of Honor: a Record of the Medals of Honor Issued to the Enlisted Men and Marines of the Navy*. 1888.

U.S. Department of the Navy. Bureau of Naval Personnel. *Records of Medals of Honor Issued to Bluejackets and marines of the United States Navy, 1862-1910*. 1910.

U.S. Department of the Navy. Bureau of Naval Personnel. *Record of Medals of Honor Issued to the Bluejackets and Marines of the United States Navy, 1862-1920*. 1921.

U.S. Department of the Navy. *Medal of Honor, 1861-1949*. 1950.

U.S. Navy. Division of Naval Intelligence. *Decorations, Medals and Campaign Ribbons of the U.S. Armed Forces*. 1943.

U.S. Senate, Committee on Pensions. *Petition of Wilson W. Brown and Other Members of the "Mitchell Raiders"*. Rpt. No. 361, 48th Cong., 1st Sess., 1884.

U.S. Senate, Committee on Rules and Administration. *Representative Speeches of General of the Army Douglas MacArthur*. S. Doc. 95, 88th Cong., 2nd Sess., 1964.

U.S. Senate, Subcommittee on Veterans' Affairs of the Committee on Labor and Public Welfare. *Medal of Honor, 1863-1964*. 88th Cong., 2nd Sess., Washington, 1964.

U.S. War Department. *Regulations for the Army of the United States*. Washington, D.C., 1889.

———. *Medals of Honor and Certificates of Merit*. 1904.

———. *Medals of Honor Issued by the War Department from January 1, 1907 to December 31, 1909*. 1910.

———. *Medals of Honor Issued by the War Department from September 1, 1904 to June 30, 1915, together with the List of Corrections Made in the Medal of Honor Circular of September 1, 1904*.

War Department Document. *Medals of Honor Issued by the War Department Up to and Including October 31, 1897*. Washington, D.C., 1897.

———. Adjutant-General's Office. *Congressional Medal of Honor, the Distinguished Service Cross and the Distinguished Service Medal Issued by the War Department Since April 6, 1917, Up To and Including General Orders, No. 126, War Department, November 11, 1919*.

———. *American Decorations: A List of the Awards of the Congressional Medal of Honor... 1862-1926*. 1927.

———. *Decorations, United States Army, Supplements to 1927 Report, Nos. I, II, III, IV and V*. 1937-1940.

MEDAL OF HONOR FICTION

Condon, Richard. *The Manchurian Candidate.* New York: McGraw, 1959.

Hoffenberg, John. *A Hero for Regis.* New York: Dutton, 1963.

Huie, William B. *The Klansman.* New York: Dial Press, 1968.

King, Charles. *The Medal of Honor.* New York: H. B. Claflin, 1905.

Little, Charles. *The Bold and the Lonely.* New York: McKay, 1966.

Myrer, Anton. *Once an Eagle.* New York: Holt, 1968.

Swarthout, Glendon. *They Came to Cordura.* New York: Random House, 1958.

Taggart, Donald G. *Reunion of the 108th.* New York: Doubleday, 1968.

BOOKS BY MEDAL WINNERS

Birkhimer, William E. *Historical Sketch of the Organization, Administration, Material, and Tactics of the Artillery, United States Army.* Washington, D.C.: J. J. Chapman, agent, 1884.

Carter, Robert G. *The Art and Science of War Versus the Art of Fighting.* Washington, D.C.: National Publishing, 1922.

Wood, Leonard. *America's Duty as Shown by Our Military History: Its Facts and Fallacies.* Chicago: Reilly & Lee, 1921.

BOOKS WITH ANECDOTES ABOUT THE MEDALS AND THEIR RECIPIENTS

American Council of Learned Societies. Schuyler, R. L. (ed.). *Dictionary of American Biography.* 22 vols. New York: Schribner, 1958.

Anders, Curtis. *Fighting Airmen.* New York: Putnam, 1966.

Anderson, Bern. *By Sea and By River: The Naval History of the Civil War.* New York: A. Knopf, 1962.

Appleman, Roy E. *The U.S. Army in Korea. vol. 1: South to the Naktong, North to the Yalu.* Rutland, Vt.: C. E. Tuttle, 1961.

Army Times (eds.). *The Daring Regiments: Adventures of the A.E.F. in World War I.* New York: Dodd, Mead, 1967.

———. *The Yanks Are Coming, Story of General John J. Pershing.* New York: Putnam, 1960.

Asprey, Robert B. *At Belleau Wood.* New York: Putnam, 1965.

Bailey, Tom. *Tarawa.* Derby, CT, 1962.

Bartley, Whitman S. *Iwo Jima: Amphibious Epic.* Nashville, Tenn.: Battery Press, 1954.

Bayler, Walter Louis John as told to Cecil Carnes. *Last Man Off Wake Island.* New York: Bobbs Merrill, 1943.

Beach, Edward I. *The Wreck of the Memphis.* New York: Holt Rinehart, 1966.

Belote, James H., and William M. *Corregidor: the Saga of a Fortress.* New York: Harper, 1968.

Boatner, Mark M. *The Civil War Dictionary.* New York: David McKay 1959.

Boswell, Rolfe. *Leathernecks: Our Marines in Fact & Picture.* New York: Thomas Y. Crowell, 1943.

Bourke, John G. *An Apache Campaign.* New York, 1958.

Brininstool, E. A. *Troopers with Custer: historic incidents of the battle of the Little Big Horn.* Harrisburg: Pa.: Stackpole, 1952.

Brown, Ashley. *U.S. Marines in Action.* New York: Villard Books, 1986.

Brown, Ashley, and Jonathan Reed. *Marines.* Harrisburg, Penna.: Nat'l Hist. Soc., 1983.

Bryan, J. *Aircraft Carrier.* New York: Ballantine Books, 1954.

Bulkley, Robert J. *At Close Quarters: PT Boats in the United States Navy.* Washington, D.C.: The Naval History Division, 1962.

Burchard, Peter. *One Gallant Rush: Robert Gould Shaw and His Brave Black Regiment.* New York: St. Martin's Press, 1965.

Cagle, Malcolm W., and F. A. Manson. *The Sea War in Korea.* Annapolis, Md.: U.S. Naval Institute, 1957.

Caldin, Martin. *Air Force: A Pictorial History of American Airpower.* New York: Bramhall House, 1957.

———. *Black Thursday.* New York: Dutton, 1960.

———. *The Ragged, Rugged Warriors: The Heroic Story of American Pilots in the Early Air War Against Japan.* New York: Dutton, 1966.

Carter, Ross S. *Those Devils in Baggy Pants.* New York: Appleton-Century Crofts, 1951.

Cass, Bevan G. (ed.). *History of the Sixth Marine Division, Melanesia, Micronesia, Orient.* Washington, D.C.: Infantry Journal Press, 1948.

Catlin, Albertus Wright. *With the Help of God and a Few Marines.* Garden City, N.Y.: Doubleday, Page, 1919.

Chadwick, Joseph. *The Apache Wars.* Derby, Conn.: Monarch Books, 1961.

———. *The Sioux Indian Wars.* Derby, Conn.: Monarch Books, 1962.

Chambliss, Wiliam. *The Silent Service.* New York: New American Library, 1959.

Cohlmia, Robert A., Arthur and Kenneth. *The Third Marine Division.* Washington, D.C.: Infantry Press Journal, 1948.

Congdon, Don (ed.). *Combat: the Civil War.* New York: Dial Press, 1968.

Conner, Howard. *The Spearhead: The World War II History of the Fifth Marine Division.* Washington, D.C.: Infantry Journal Press, 1950.

Crane, Stephen. *Red Badge of Courage and Other Stories.* New York: Collier, 1962.

Cunningham, W. Scott. *Wake Island Command.* New York: Little, 1962.

Custer, Elizabeth. *Boots and Saddles.* New York: Harper & Brothers, 1885.

———. *Following the Guidon.* New York: Harper, 1890.

Devereux, James. *The Story of Wake Island.* New York: J. B. Lippincott, 1947.

Dornbusch, Charles E. (comp.). *Histories of American Army Units, World Wars I and II and Korean Conflict.* Washington, D.C.: Adjuctant General's Office, 1956.

Downey, Fairfax D. *General Crook, Indian Fighter.* Philadelphia: Westminster Press, 1957.

Dugan, James, and Stewart Carroll. *Ploesti: the Great Ground-Air Battle of 1 August 1943.* New York: Random House, 1963.

Dupuy, Richard E. *Brave Men and Great Captains.* New York: Harper, 1959.

———. *The Compact History of the United States Army.* Englewood Cliffs, N.J.: Hawthorn Books, 1961.

———. *Men of West Point.* New York: McLeod, 1952.

Dupuy, R. Ernest. *Where They Have Trod.* New York: Stokes, 1940.

Dupuy, R. Ernest, and William H. Baumer. *The Little Wars of the United States.* New York: Hawthorn Books, 1968.

Dupuy, R. Ernest, and N. Trevon. *Military Heritage of America.* New York: McGraw, 1956.

Edmonds, James E. *Fighting Fools.* New York: D. Appleton-Century, 1938.

Elsinger, Larry (ed.). *Sky Fighters of World War I.* Greenwich, Conn.: Fawcett, 1961.

Faulk, Odie B. *The Geronimo Campaign.* New York: Oxford, 1969.

Fehrenbach, T. R. *This Kind of War: A Study in Unpreparedness.* New York: Macmillan, 1963.

Field, James A. Jr. *History of U.S. Naval Operations: Korea.* Washington, D.C., 1962.

Forsberg, Franklin (ed.). *Highlights from "Yank," The Army Weekly.* New York: Royal Books, 1953.

Foster, John. *Hell in the Heavens.* New York: Putnam, 1961.

Freidel, Frank. *Over There: The Story of America's First Great Overseas Crusade.* New York: McGraw Hill, 1990.

Futrell, Robert F. *The United States Air Force in Korea, 1950-1953.* New York: Duell, 1961.

Gallant, Thomas G. *On Valor's Side.* New York: Doubleday, 1963.

———. *The Friendly Dead.* New York: Doubleday, 1964.

Garroe, William A. *The History of the United States Army.* New York, 1924.

Gibbons, Floyd. *And They Thought We Wouldn't Fight.* New York: George H. Doran, 1918.

Glass, E. L. N. *The History of the Tenth Cavalry.* Tucson, Ariz.: Acme Printing, 1921.

Glazier, Willard. *The Capture, Prison Pen and the Escape.* New York, United States Publishing, 1868.

Greer, Andrew C. *The New Breed: The Story of the U. S. Marines in Korea.* New York: Harper, 1952.

Grider, George W. *War Fish.* Boston: Little, Brown & Co., 1958.

Grolier's History of the First World War. 4 vols. New York: Grolier, 1966.

Gugeler, Russell A. *Combat Actions in Korea.* Washington, D.C.: Combat Forces Press, 1954.

Gurney, Gene. *Flying Aces of World War I.* New York: Random House, 1965.

———. *Journey of the Giants (Story of the B-29).* New York: Cowar-McCann, 1961.

———. *The War in the Air: A Pictorial History of World War II Air Forces in Combat.* New York: Crown, 1962.

Hammer, Kenneth. *Little Big Horn Biographies.* Brookings, S. Dak.: Custer Battlefield Historical & Museum Association, 1965.

Handleman, Howard. *Bridge to Victory.* New York: Random House, 1943.

Harbord, James G. *The American Army in France, 1917-19.* Boston: Little, Brown, 1936.

Harper, Robert S. *Ohio Handbook of the Civil War.* Columbus, Ohio: LBS Archival Products, 1961.

Heavey, William F. *Down Ramp!.* Washington, D.C.: Infantry Journal Press, 1947.

Heinl, Robert D. Jr. *Victory at High Tide: The Inchon-Seoul Campaign.* New York: Lippincott, 1968.

Heitman, Francis B. *Historical Register and Dictionary of the United States Army.* Washington, D.C.: U.S. Government Printing Office, 1903. Revised, 1965.

Hilliard, Jack B. *An Annotated Reading List of United States marine Corps History.* Washington, D.C.: U.S. Marine Corp, Historical Branch, G3 Div., 1966.

Hirsh, Phil. *Fighting Eagles.* New York: Pyramid Books, 1961.

Hoehling, Adolph A. *The Fierce Lambs.* Boston: Little, Brown, 1960.

Honeywell, Roy J. *Chaplains of the United States Army.* Washington, D.C.: Office of Chief of Chaplains, 1958.

Hough, Frank O. *The Island War: The United States Marine Corps in the Pacific.* Philadelphia: J. B. Lippincott, 1947.

Hoyt, Edwin P. *The Battle of Leyte Gulf.* New York: Jove Publications, 1988.

Hubler, Richard G., and John A. DeChant. *Flying Leathernecks.* Garden City, N.Y.: Doubleday, Doran, 1944.

Hunt, George P. *Coral Comes High.* New York: Harper & Brothers, 1946.

———. *The Story of the United States Marines.* New York: Random House, 1951.

Jablonski, Edward. *Pictorial History of World War I Years.* New York: Doubleday, 1985.

Jacobs, Bruce. *Soldiers: The Fighting Divisions of the Regular Army.* New York: Norton, 1958.

Johnston, R. W. *Follow Me!* New York: Random House, 1948.

Karig, Walter. *Battle Report.* vol. 6. New York: Farrar & Rinehart, 1944-52.

Kenney, George C. *General Kenney Reports: A Personal History of the Pacific War.* New York: Duell, Sloan & Pearce, 1949.

King, Charles. *Campaigning with Crook.* Norman, Okla: University of Oklahoma Press, 1964.

Knox, Dudley W. *A History of the United States Navy.* New York, 1963.

Leckie, Robert. *Challenge for the Pacific.* New York: Doubleday, 1965.

———. *Conflict: The History of the Korean War.* New York: Putnam, 1962.

———. *March to Glory.* New York: Bantam, 1990.

———. *Strong Men Armed: The United States Marines Against Japan.* New York: Random House, 1962.

Leckie, William H. *The Buffalo Soldiers: A Narrative of the Negro Cavalry in the West.* Norman, Okla.: University of Oklahoma Press, 1967.

———. *The Military Conquest of the Southern Plains.* Norman, Okla.: University of Oklahoma Press, 1963.

Lejeune, John A. *Reminiscences of a Marine.* Philadelphia: Dorrance, 1930.

Lewis, Winston B. *The Battle of Savo Island.* Washington, D.C.: Naval Historical Center, 1993.

Life Magazine (eds.). *The First World War.* New York: Life, 1965.

Livesay, Anthony. *Great Battles of World War I.* New York: Macmillan, 1989.

Lockwood, Charles. *Sink 'Em All.* New York: Dutton, 1951.

Lockwood, Charles A., and H. C. Adamson. *Hell at 50 Fathoms.* Philadelphia: Chilton, 1962.

Loomis, Robert. *Great American Fighter Pilots of World War II.* New York: Random House, 1961.

Lord, Walter. *Day of Infamy.* New York: Holt, 1957.

———. *Incredible Victory.* New York: Harper & Row, 1967.

Love, Edmund G. *War Is a Private Affair.* New York: Harcourt, 1959.

Mandel, Paul, and Life Magazine (eds.). *Great Battles of the Civil War.* New York: Life, 1961.

Mann, Carl. *Air Heraldry.* New York: R. M. McBride, 1944.

Marshall, S. L. A. *The American Heritage History of World War I.* New York: Dell, 1966.

———. *Battle at Best.* New York: Morrow, 1963.

———. *Battles in the Monsoon: Campaigning in the Central Vietnam, Summer 1966.* New York: Morrow, 1967.

———. *Men Against Fire.* New York: Morrow, 1947.

———. *Night Drop.* New York: Macmillan, 1963.

———. *The Officer as a Leader.* Harrisburg, Pa.: Stackpole Co., 1966.

———. *Pork Chop Hill: the American Fighting Man in Action, Korea, Spring, 1952.* Nashville, Battery Press, 1986.

———. *West to Cambodia.* New York: Cowles, 1968.

Macaulay, Neill W. *The Sandino Affair.* Chicago: Quadrangle Books, 1967.

MacDonald, Charles B. *The Battle of the Huertgen Forest.* New York: Lippincott, 1963.

McCahill, William. *First to Fight.* Philadelphia: David McKay, 1943.

McCollum, Lee Charles. *History and Rhymes of the Lost Battalion.* Chicago: Foley, printers, 1922.

McMillan, George. *The Old Breed.* Washington, D.C.: Infantry Journal Press, 1949.

———. *Uncommon Valor: Marine Divisions in Action.* Washington, D.C.: Infantry Journal Press, 1946.

Mercey, A. A. *Sea, Surf and Hell.* New York: Prentice Hall, 1945.

Merrill, James M. (ed.). *Uncommon Valor: The Exciting Story of the Army.* New York: Rand-McNally, 1964.

Metcalfe, Clyde H. *A History of the United States Marine Corps.* New York: G. Putnam's Sons, 1939.

———. *Marine Corps Reader.* New York: Putnam, 1944.

Miller, F. T. *World in the Air: The Story of Flying in Pictures.* 2 vols. New York: Putnam, 1930.

Miller, Harold B. *Navy Wings.* New York: Dodd, Mead, 1937, 1942.

Monks, John, Jr. *Ribbon and Star: The Third Marines at Bougainville.* Washington, D.C.: Zenger, 1979.

Montross, Lynn. *The United States Marines: A Pictorial History.* New York: Holt, Rinehart & Winston, 1959.

Moore, Robin. *The Green Berets.* New York: Crown, 1965.

Morison, Samuel Eliot. *History of United States Naval Operations in World War II.* 15 vols. Boston: Little, Brown, 1947-1962.

Mulvey, Timothy J. *These Are Your Sons.* New York: McGraw-Hill, 1952.

Muphy, Jack. *History of United States Marine Corps Operations in World War II.* 3 vols. Washington, D.C.:, 1961-1968.

———. *A History of the United States.* Stamford, Conn.: Longmeadow Press, 1993.

Murphy, Robert. *Diplomat Among Warriors* New York: Doubleday, 1964.

Murphy, Thomas D. *Ambassadors in Arms.* Honolulu: University of Hawaii Press, 1954.

Nason, Elias. *The Life and Public Services of Henry Wilson.* Boston: D. Lothrup, c. 1881.

Navy Times (eds.). *They Fought Under the Sea.* Springfield, Va: Navy Times Publishing, 1963.

Newcomb, Richard F. *Battle of Iwo Jima.* New York: Crowell, 1966.

———. *Savo: the Incredible Naval Debacle Off Guadalcanal.* New York: Holt, Rinehart & Winston, 1961.

Nolan, Alan T. *The Iron Brigade.* New York: Macmillan, 1961.

Office of the Chief of Military History. *The United States Army in World War II.* 84 vols. Washington, D.C.: U.S. Government Printing Office, 1947-1968.

Official Records of the Union and Confederate Navies in the War of Rebellion. 31 vols. Washington, D.C.: U.S. Naval War Records Office, 1894-1927.

Parrott, Marc. *Hazard: Marines on Mission.* Garden City, N.Y.: Doubleday, 1962.

Pearl, Jack. *Aerial Dogfights of World War II.* Derby, Conn.: Monarch Books, 1962.

Pershing, John J. *My Experiences in the World War.* New York: Frederick A. Stokes, 1931.

Phisterer, Frederick (comp.). *New York in the War of the Rebellion, 1861 to 1865, vol. 5,* Albany, N.Y.: J. B. Lyon, State Printers, 1912.

Pierce, Philip N., and Frank D. Hough. *The Compact History of the United States Marine Corps.* New York: Hawthorn Books, 1960.

Plank, Will. *Banners and Bugles.* Marlborough, N.Y.: Centennial Press, 1963.

Platt, Frank C. (ed.). *Great Battles of World War I: In the Air.* New York: New American Library, 1966.

———. *Great Battles of World War I; On the Land.* New York, 1966.

Powell, William H. *Officers of the Army and Navy: Volunteers Who Served in the Civil War.* Philadelphia: L. R. Hamersly, 1893.

Pratt, Fletcher. *The Compact History of the U.S. Navy.* New York: Hawthorn Books, 1962.

Proehl, Carl W. (ed.). *The Fourth Marine Division in World War II.* Nashville: Battery Press, 1988.

Public Papers of the Presidents of the United States. Harry S. Truman, 1945-1953. 8 vols. *Dwight D. Eisenhower, 1953-1961. John F. Kennedy, 1961-1963.* 3 vols. *Lyndon B. Johnson, 1963-1967.* 5 vols. Millwood, N.Y.: KTO Press, 1978.

Pullen, John. *The 20th Maine: a Volunteer Regiment in the Civil War.* Philadelphia: Lippincott, 1962.

Quarles, Benjamin. *The Negro in the Civil War.* Boston: Little, Brown, 1953.

Randall, Ruth. *Colonel Elmer Ellsworth.* Boston: Little, Brown, 1960.

Reeder, Russell P. (Red), and N. R. Campion. *The West Point Story.* New York: Random House, 1956.

Reynolds, Quentin J. *They Fought for the Sky [The Dramatic Story of the First War in the Air].* New York: Rinehart, 1957.

Rickey, Don Jr. *Forty Miles a Day on Beans and Hay.* Norman, Okla.: University of Oklahoma Press, 1963.

Ridgway, Matthew B. *The Korean War.* New York: Doubleday, 1967.

Riesnberg, Felix. *The Story of the Naval Academy.* New York: Random House, 1958.

Robinson, D. B. (ed.). *The Dirty Wars.* New York, Dial Press, 1967.

Robinson, Donald (ed.). *The Day I Was Proudest To Be An American.* Garden City, N.Y.: Doubleday, 1958.

Roosevelt, Theodore. *The Rough Riders.* New York: New American Library, 1961.

Roscoe, Theodore. *Pig Boats: The True Story of the Fighting Submarines of World War II.* New York: Bantam Books, 1958.

Ryan, Cornelius. *The Longest Day: June 6, 1944.* New York: Simon & Schuster, 1959.

Saturday Evening Post (eds.). *Battle: Great True Stories of Combat in World War II.* New York: Saturday Evening Post, 1968.

Schott, Joseph L. *The Ordeal of Samar*. Indianapolis: Bobbs-Merrill, 1965.

Schuon, Karl (ed.). *The Leathernecks: an Informal History of the U.S. Marine Corps*. New York: Franklin Watts, 1963.

Shaw, Henry T. Jr. *Tarawa: A Legend Is Born*. New York: Ballantine Books, 1968.

Shelford, W. *Subsunk*. Garden City, N.Y.: Doubleday, 1960.

Sherrod, Robert. *History of Marine Corps Aviation in World War II*. Washington, D.C.: Combat Forces Press, 1952.

———. *On To Westward*. New York: Duell, 1945.

Sims, William S., and Burton Jesse Hendrick. *Victory at Sea*. New York: Doubleday, 1920.

Smith, Holland. *Coral and Brass*. New York: C. Scribner's Sons, 1949.

Smith, Stanley E. *The U.S. in Navy World War II*. New York: Morrow, 1966.

Smith, William W. *Midway, Turning Point of the Pacific*. New York: Crowell, 1966.

Stackpole Co. (eds.). *The Army Almanac*. Harrisburg, Pa.: Stackpole Co., 1959.

Stallings, Laurence. *The Doughboys: The Story of the AEF, 1917-1918*. New York: Harper & Row, 1963.

Sterling, Forest J. *Wake of the Wahoo*. Philadelphia: Chilton Co., 1960.

Stewart, Edgar I. *Custer's Luck*. Norman, Okla.: University of Oklahoma Press, 1955.

Sweetman, Jack. *The Landing at Veracruz: 1914*. Annapolis, Md.: U.S. Naval Institute, 1968.

Thomason, John W. *And a Few Marines*. New York: Scribner, 1943.

———. *Fix Bayonets*. New York: Scribner, 1926.

Todd, Frederick P., and Fritz Kredel. *Soldiers of the American Army, 1775-1954*. Chicago: H. Regnery, 1954.

Toand, John. *Battle: The Story of the Bulge*. New York: Random House, 1959.

———. *But Not in Shame: The Six Months After Pearl Harbor*. New York: Random House, 1961.

———. *The Last 100 Days*. New York: Random House, 1966.

Townsend, Thomas S. *The Honors of the Empire State in the War of the Rebellion*. New York: A. Lovell, 1889.

Tregaskis, Richard. *Guadalcanal Diary*. New York: Random House, 1955.

True, The Man's Magazine. *True Civil War Stories. Edited by Joseph Millard*. Greenwich, Conn., Fawcett, 1961.

Ulanoff, Stanley. *Fighter Pilot*. Garden City, N.Y.: Doubleday, 1962.

U.S. Marine Corps and Nicholas Canzona. *United States Marine Operations in Korea, 1950-1953*. 4 vols. Grosse Point, Mich.: Scholarly Press, 1969.

U.S. Naval History Division. *Aviation in the United States Navy*. Washington, D.C.: U.S. Government Printing Office, 1961.

———. *The Submarine in the United States Navy*. Washington, D.C.: U.S. Government Printing Office, 1969.

Warner, Ezra J. *Generals in Blue*. Baton Rouge, La.: Louisiana State University Press, 1964.

Weigley, Russell F. *History of the United States Army*. New York: Macmillan, 1967.

Wellman, Paul I. *The Indian Wars of the West*. New York: Doubleday, 1954.

Westermier, Clifford P. *Who Rush to Glory: the Cowboy Volunteers of 1898*. Caldwell, Idaho: Caxton Printers, 1958.

White, W. L. *They Were Expendable*. New York: 1942.

Whitehouse, A. G. L. (Arch). *The Years of the War Birds*. Garden City, N.Y.: Doubleday, 1960.

———. *The Years of the Sky Kings*. Garden City, N.Y.: Doubleday, 1959.

Whitman, Sidney E. *The Troopers: An Informal History of the Plains Cavalry, 1865-1890*. New York: Hastings House Publishers, 1962.

Wiley, Bell I. *The Common Soldier of the Union*. Indianapolis: Bobbs-Merrill, 1952.

Willson, Arobella M. *Disaster, Struggle, Triumph*. Albany, N.Y.: Argus, 1870.

Wise, Frederick M. *A Marine Tells It to You*. New York: J. H. Sears Co., 1929.

Wise, Wm. H. and Company Inc.(ed.). *The 100 Best True Stories of World War II*. New York: W. H. Wise, 1945.

Wolff, Leon. *Little Brown Brother*. New York: Doubleday, 1961.

———. *Low Level Mission*. New York: Doubleday, 1957.

Wormser, Richard. *The Yellowlegs: the Story of the United States Cavalry*. Garden City, N.Y.: Doubleday, 1966.

Wright, Elsie N. (Grayson, J. J. Pseud.). *Famous Flyers*. Cleveland, Ohio: World Syndicate Pub., 1932.

— Eugene V. McAndrews

INDEX

NAME	CITATION NUMBER
ABRELL, Charles Gene, *U.S. Marine Corps*	3028
ADAMS, James F., *U.S. Army*	1
ADAMS, John Gregory Bishop, *U.S. Army*	2
ADAMS, John Mapes, *U.S. Marine Corps*	2266
ADAMS, Lucian, *U.S. Army*	2595
ADAMS, Stanley Taylor, *U.S. Army*	3029
ADAMS, William Edward, *U.S. Army*	3159
ADKINSON, Joseph B., *U.S. Army*	2454
ADRIANCE, Harry Chapman, *U.S. Marine Corps*	2267
AGERHOLM, Harold Christ, *U.S. Marine Corps Reserve*	2596
AHEAM, Michael, *U.S. Navy*	3
AHERN, William, *U.S. Navy*	1973
ALBANESE, Lewis, *U.S. Army*	3160
ALBEE, George Emerson, *U.S. Army*	1534
ALBER, Frederick, *U.S. Army*	4
ALBERT, Christian, *U.S. Army*	5
ALCHESAY, William, *U.S. Army*	1535
ALLEN, Abner Peeler, *U.S. Army*	6
ALLEN, Edward G., *U.S. Navy*	2268
ALLEN, James, *U.S. Army*	7
ALLEN, Nathaniel M., *U.S. Army*	8
ALLEN, William, *U.S. Army*	1536
ALLEX, Jake, *U.S. Army*	2455
ALLWORTH, Edward C., *U.S. Army*	2456
AMES, Adelbert, *U.S. Army*	9
AMMERMAN, Robert Wesley, *U.S. Army*	10
ANDERS, Frank Lafayette, *U.S. Army*	2186
ANDERSON, Beauford Theodore, *U.S. Army*	2597
ANDERSON, Bruce, *U.S. Army*	11
ANDERSON, Charles W., *U.S. Army*	12
ANDERSON, Edwin Alexander, *U.S. Navy*	2381
ANDERSON, Everett W., *U.S. Army*	13
ANDERSON, Frederick Charles, *U.S. Army*	14
ANDERSON, James, *U.S. Army*	1537
ANDERSON Jr., James, *U.S. Marine Corps*	3161
ANDERSON, Johannes Seigfried, *U.S. Army*	2457
ANDERSON, Marion T., *U.S. Army*	15
ANDERSON, Peter T., *U.S. Army*	16
ANDERSON, Richard Allen, *U.S. Marine Corps*	3162
ANDERSON, Richard Beatty, *U.S. Marine Corps*	2598
ANDERSON, Robert N., *U.S. Navy*	17
ANDERSON, Thomas, *U.S. Army*	18
ANDERSON, Webster, *U.S. Army*	3163
ANDERSON, William, *U.S. Navy*	1974
ANDREWS, John, *U.S. Navy*	1958
ANGLING, John, *U.S. Navy*	19
ANTOLAK, Sylvester, *U.S. Army*	2599
ANTRIM, Richard Nott, *U.S. Navy*	2600
APPLE, Andrew O., *U.S. Army*	20
APPLETON, Edwin Nelson, *U.S. Marine Corps*	2269
APPLETON, William H., *U.S. Army*	21
ARCHER, James W., *U.S. Army*	22
ARCHER, Lester, *U.S. Army*	23
ARCHINAL, William J., *U.S. Army*	24
ARMSTRONG, Clinton Lycurgus, *U.S. Army*	25
ARNOLD, Abraham Kerns, *U.S. Army*	26
ARTHER, Matthew, *U.S. Navy*	27
ASHLEY Jr., Eugene, *U.S. Army*	3164
ASTEN, Charles, *U.S. Navy*	28
ASTON, Edgar R., *U.S. Army*	1538
ATKINS, Daniel, *U.S. Navy*	1975
ATKINS, Thomas E., *U.S. Army*	2601
ATKINSON, Thomas E., *U.S. Navy*	29
AUER, John F., *U.S. Navy*	1976
AUSTIN, Oscar Palmer, *U.S. Marine Corps*	3165
AUSTIN, William Grafton, *U.S. Army*	1539
AVERY, James, *U.S. Navy*	30
AVERY, William B., *U.S. Army*	31
AYERS, David, *U.S. Army*	32
AYERS, James F., *U.S. Army*	1540
AYERS, John G. K., *U.S. Army*	33
BABCOCK, John, *U.S. Army*	1541
BABOCK, William J., *U.S. Army*	34
BACA, John Philip, *U.S. Army*	3166
BACON, Elijah William, *U.S. Army*	35
BACON, Nicky Daniel, *U.S. Army*	3167
BADDERS, William, *U.S. Navy*	2577
BADGER, Oscar Charles, *U.S. Navy*	2382
BAESEL, Albert E., *U.S. Army*	2458
BAILEY, James E., *U.S. Army*	1542
BAILEY, Kenneth Dillon, *U.S. Marine Corps*	2602
BAIRD, Absalom, *U.S. Army*	36
BAIRD, George William, *U.S. Army*	1543

Name	Page
BAKER, Addison Earl, *U.S. Army Air Corps*	2603
BAKER, Benjamin F., *U.S. Navy*	2073
BAKER, Charles, *U.S. Navy*	37
BAKER Jr., Edward Lee, *U.S. Army*	2074
BAKER, John, *U.S. Army*	1544
BAKER Jr., John Franklin, *U.S. Army*	3168
BAKER Jr., Thomas Alexander, *U.S. Army*	2604
BALCH, John Henry, *U.S. Navy*	2459
BALDWIN, Charles H., *U.S. Navy*	38
BALDWIN, Frank Dwight, *U.S. Army*	39, 1545
BALLARD, Donald Everett, *U.S. Navy*	3169
BALLEN, Frederick A., *U.S. Army*	40
BANCROFT, Neil, *U.S. Army*	1546
BANKS, George Lovell, *U.S. Army*	41
BARBER, James Albert, *U.S. Army*	42
BARBER, William Earl, *U.S. Marine Corps*	3030
BARFOOT, Van Thomas, *U.S. Army*	2605
BARGER, Charles Denver, *U.S. Army*	2460
BARKELEY, David B., *U.S. Army*	2461
BARKER, Chalres H., *U.S. Army*	3031
BARKER, Jedh Colby, *U.S. Marine Corps*	3170
BARKER, Nathaniel C., *U.S. Army*	43
BARKLEY, John Lewis, *U.S. Army*	2462
BARNES, Will Croft, *U.S. Army*	1547
BARNES, William H., *U.S. Army*	44
BARNES III, John Andrew, *U.S. Army*	3171
BARNUM Jr., Harvey Curtiss "Barney", *U.S. Marine Corps*	3172
BARNUM, Henry Alanson, *U.S. Army*	45
BARNUM, James, *U.S. Navy*	46
BARRELL, Charles L., *U.S. Army*	47
BARRETT, Carlton William, *U.S. Army*	2606
BARRETT, Edward, *U.S. Navy*	1977
BARRETT, Richard, *U.S. Army*	1548
BARRICK, Jesse, *U.S. Army*	48
BARRINGER, William H., *U.S. Army*	49
BARROW, David Duffy, *U.S. Navy*	2075
BARRY, Augustus, *U.S. Army*	50
BART, Frank J., *U.S. Army*	2463
BARTER, Gurdon H., *U.S. Navy*	51
BARTON, Thomas, *U.S. Navy*	52
BASILONE, John "Manila Jonn", *U.S. Marine Corps*	2607
BASS, David L., *U.S. Navy*	53
BATCHELDER, Richard Napoleon, *U.S. Army*	54
BATES, Delavan, *U.S. Army*	55
BATES, Norman Francis, *U.S. Army*	56
BATES, Richard, *U.S. Navy*	1521
BATSON, Matthew Arlington, *U.S. Army*	2187
BAUER, Harold William "Indian Joe", *U.S. Marine Corps*	2608
BAUGH, William Bernard, *U.S. Marine Corps*	3032
BAUSELL, Lewis Kenneth, *U.S. Marine Corps*	2609
BAYBUTT, Philip, *U.S. Army*	57
BAZAAR, Philip, *U.S. Army*	58
BEARSS, Hiram Iddings, *U.S. Marine Corps*	2188
BEASLEY, Harry C., *U.S. Navy*	2383
BEATTY, Alexander Mitchell, *U.S. Army*	59
BEATY, Powhatan, *U.S. Army*	60
BEAUDOIN, Raymond Ovila, *U.S. Army*	2610
BEAUFORD, Clay, *U.S. Army*	1549
BEAUFORT, Jean J., *U.S. Army*	61
BEAUMONT, Eugene Beauharnais, *U.S. Army*	62
BEBB, Edward James, *U.S. Army*	63
BECKWITH, Wallace A., *U.S. Army*	64
BEDDOWS, Richard, *U.S. Army*	65
BEEBE, William Sully, *U.S. Army*	66
BEECH, John P., *U.S. Army*	67
BEGLEY, Terrence, *U.S. Army*	68
BEHNE, Frederick, *U.S. Navy*	2325
BEHNKE, Heinrich, *U.S. Navy*	2326
BEIKIRCH, Gary Burnell, *U.S. Army*	3173
BELCHER, Ted, *U.S. Army*	3174
BELCHER, Thomas, *U.S. Army*	69
BELL, Bernard Pious, *U.S. Army*	2611
BELL, Dennis, *U.S. Army*	2076
BELL, George, *U.S. Navy*	70
BELL, Harry, *U.S. Army*	2189
BELL, James, *U.S. Army*	1550
BELL, James Bennett, *U.S. Army*	71
BELL, James Franklin, *U.S. Army*	2190
BELLRICHARD, Leslie Allen, *U.S. Army*	3175
BELPITT, William Henry, *U.S. Navy*	1978
BENAVIDEZ, Roy Perez, *U.S. Army*	3176
BENDER, Stanley, *U.S. Army*	2612
BENEDICT, George Greenville, *U.S. Army*	72
BENFOLD, Edward Clyde "Ted", *U.S. Navy*	3033
BENJAMIN Jr., George, *U.S. Army*	2613
BENJAMIN, John Francis, *U.S. Army*	73
BENJAMIN, Samuel Nicholl, *U.S. Army*	74
BENNETT, Edward Andrew, *U.S. Army*	2614
BENNETT, Emory L., *U.S. Army*	3034
BENNETT, Floyd, *U.S. Navy*	2578
BENNETT, James Harvey, *U.S. Navy*	2077
BENNETT, Orrin, *U.S. Army*	75
BENNETT, Orson W., *U.S. Army*	76
BENNETT, Steven Logan, *U.S. Air Force*	3177
BENNETT, Thomas William, *U.S. Army*	3178
BENNION, Mervyn Sharp, *U.S. Navy*	2615
BENSINGER, William, *U.S. Army*	77
BENSON, James, *U.S. Navy*	1979
BENYAURD, William Henry Harrison, *U.S. Army*	78
BERG, George Francis, *U.S. Army*	2078
BERGENDAHL, Frederick, *U.S. Army*	1551
BERKELEY, Randolph Carter, *U.S. Marine Corps*	2384
BERRY, Charles Joseph, *U.S. Marine Corps*	2616
BERTOLDO, Vito R., *U.S. Army*	2617
BERTRAM, Heinrich, *U.S. Army*	1552
BESSEY, Charles Albert, *U.S. Army*	1553
BETHAM, Asa, *U.S. Navy*	79
BETTS, Charles Malone, *U.S. Army*	80
BEYER, Albert, *U.S. Navy*	2079
BEYER, Arthur O., *U.S. Army*	2618
BEYER, Hillary, *U.S. Army*	81
BIANCHI, Willibald Charles, *U.S. Army*	2619
BIBBER, Charles James, *U.S. Navy*	82
BICKFORD, Henry H., *U.S. Army*	83
BICKFORD, John F., *U.S. Navy*	84
BICKFORD, Matthew, *U.S. Army*	85
BICKHAM, Charles Goodwin, *U.S. Army*	2191
BIDDLE, Melvin Earl, *U.S. Army*	2620

Name	Page
BIEGER, Charles, *U.S. Army*	86
BIEGLER, George Wesley, *U.S. Army*	2192
BIGELOW, Elmer Charles, *U.S. Naval Reserve*	2621
BINDER, Richard, *U.S. Marine Corps*	87
BINGHAM, Henry Harrison, *U.S. Army*	88
BIRDSALL, Horatio L., *U.S. Army*	89
BIRKHIMER, William Edward, *U.S. Army*	2193
BISHOP, Charles Francis, *U.S. Navy*	2385
BISHOP, Daniel, *U.S. Army*	1554
BISHOP, Francis A., *U.S. Army*	90
BJORKLUND, Arnold L., *U.S. Army*	2622
BJORKMAN, Ernest H., *U.S. Navy*	2327
BLACK, John Charles, *U.S. Army*	91
BLACK, William Perkins, *U.S. Army*	92
BLACKMAR, Wilmon Whilldin, *U.S. Army*	93
BLACKWELL, Robert Lester, *U.S. Army*	2464
BLACKWOOD, William Robert Douglas, *U.S. Army*	94
BLAGHEEN, William, *U.S. Navy*	95
BLAIR, James, *U.S. Army*	1555
BLAIR, Robert M., *U.S. Navy*	96
BLAKE, Robert, *U.S. Navy*	97
BLANCHFIELD, Michael Reinert, *U.S. Army*	3179
BLANQUET, *U.S. Army*	1556
BLASDEL, Thomas A., *U.S. Army*	98
BLEAK, David Bruce, *U.S. Army*	3035
BLECKLEY, Erwin Russell, *U.S. Army Air Service*	2465
BLICKENSDERGER, Milton, *U.S. Army*	99
BLISS, George Newman, *U.S. Army*	100
BLISS, Zenas Randall, *U.S. Army*	101
BLOCH, Orville Emil, *U.S. Army*	2623
BLODGETT, Wells H., *U.S. Army*	102
BLUCHER, Charles, *U.S. Army*	103
BLUME, Robert, *U.S. Navy*	2080
BLUNT, John W., *U.S. Army*	104
BOBO, John Paul, *U.S. Marine Corps Reserve*	3180
BOEHLER, Otto A., *U.S. Army*	2194
BOEHM, Peter Martin, *U.S. Army*	105
BOERS, Edward William, *U.S. Navy*	2328
BOIS, Frank, *U.S. Navy*	106
BOLDEN, Paul Luther, *U.S. Army*	2624
BOLTON, Cecil Hamilton, *U.S. Army*	2625
BOND, William S., *U.S. Navy*	107
BONDSTEEL, James Leroy, *U.S. Army*	3181
BONEBRAKE, Henry G., *U.S. Army*	108
BONG, Richard Ira, *U.S. Army Air Corps*	2626
BONNAFFON Jr., Sylvester, *U.S. Army*	109
BONNEY, Robert Earl, *U.S. Navy*	2329
BONNYMAN Jr., Alexander "Sandy", *U.S. Marine Corps Reserve*	2627
BOODY, Robert M., *U.S. Army*	110
BOOKER, Robert D., *U.S. Army*	2628
BOON, Hugh Patterson, *U.S. Army*	111
BOONE, Joel Thompson, *U.S. Navy*	2466
BORDELON, William James, *U.S. Marine Corps*	2629
BOSS, Orlando Phidelio, *U.S. Army*	112
BOUQUET, Nicholas S., *U.S. Army*	113
BOURKE, John Gregory, *U.S. Army*	114
BOURNE, Thomas, *U.S. Navy*	115
BOURY, Richard, *U.S. Army*	116
BOUTWELL, John W., *U.S. Army*	117
BOWDEN, Samuel, *U.S. Army*	1557
BOWEN, Chester Bennett, *U.S. Army*	118
BOWEN, Emmer, *U.S. Army*	119
BOWEN Jr., Hammett Lee, *U.S. Army*	3182
BOWMAN, Alonzo, *U.S. Army*	1558
BOWMAN, Edward R., *U.S. Navy*	120
BOX, Thomas J., *U.S. Army*	121
BOYCE Jr., George W. G., *U.S. Army*	2630
BOYDSTON, Erwin Jay, *U.S. Marine Corps*	2270
BOYINGTON, Gregory "Pappy", *U.S. Marine Corps Reserve*	2631
BOYNE, Thomas, *U.S. Army*	1559
BOYNTON, Henry Van Ness, *U.S. Army*	122
BRADBURY, Sanford, *U.S. Army*	1560
BRADLEY, Alexander, *U.S. Navy*	1980
BRADLEY, Amos, *U.S. Navy*	123
BRADLEY, Charles, *U.S. Navy*	124
BRADLEY, George, *U.S. Navy*	2386
BRADLEY, Thomas Wilson, *U.S. Army*	125
BRADLEY Jr., Willis Winter, *U.S. Navy*	2467
BRADY, George F., *U.S. Navy*	2081
BRADY, James, *U.S. Army*	126
BRADY, Patrick Henry, *U.S. Army*	3183
BRANAGAN, Edward, *U.S. Army*	1561
BRANDLE, Joseph E., *U.S. Army*	127
BRANNIGAN, Felix, *U.S. Army*	128
BRANT, Abram B., *U.S. Army*	1562
BRANT Jr., William, *U.S. Army*	129
BRAS, Edgar A., *U.S. Army*	130
BRATLING, Frank, *U.S. Army*	1563
BRAZELL, John, *U.S. Navy*	131
BREAULT, Henry, *U.S. Navy*	2579
BREEMAN, George, *U.S. Navy*	2330
BREEN, John, *U.S. Navy*	132
BRENNAN, Christopher, *U.S. Navy*	133
BRESNAHAN, Patrick Francis, *U.S. Navy*	2331
BREST, Lewis Francis, *U.S. Army*	134
BRETT, Lloyd Milton, *U.S. Army*	1564
BREWER, William John, *U.S. Army*	135
BREWSTER, Andre Walker, *U.S. Army*	2271
BREYER, Charles, *U.S. Army*	136
BRIGGS, Elijah A., *U.S. Army*	137
BRIGHT, George Washington, *U.S. Navy*	2082
BRILES, Herschel Floyd "Pete", *U.S. Army*	2632
BRINGLE, Andrew, *U.S. Army*	138
BRINN, Andrew, *U.S. Navy*	139
BRITT, Maurice Lee (Footsie), *U.S. Army*	2633
BRITTIN, Nelson Vogel, *U.S. Army*	3036
BROCK, George F., *U.S. Navy*	2332
BROGAN, James, *U.S. Army*	1565
BRONNER, August Frederick, *U.S. Army*	140
BRONSON, Deming, *U.S. Army*	2468
BRONSON, James H., *U.S. Army*	141
BROOKIN, Oscar, *U.S. Army*	2083
BROPHY, James, *U.S. Army*	1566
BROSNAN, John, *U.S. Army*	142
BROSTROM, Leonard C., *U.S. Army*	2634
BROUSE, Charles W., *U.S. Army*	143
BROWN, Benjamin, *U.S. Army*	1567
BROWN Jr., Bobbie Evan, *U.S. Army*	2635

Name	Page
BROWN, Charles, *U.S. Marine Corps*	1959
BROWN, Charles E., *U.S. Army*	144
BROWN Jr., Edward, *U.S. Army*	145
BROWN, Henri Le Fevre, *U.S. Army*	146
BROWN, James, *U.S. Army*	1568
BROWN, James, *U.S. Navy*	147
BROWN, Jeremiah Z., *U.S. Army*	148
BROWN, John, *U.S. Army*	150
BROWN, John, *U.S. Navy*	149
BROWN, John, *U.S. Navy*	1522
BROWN, John Harties, *U.S. Army*	151
BROWN, Lorenzo Dow, *U.S. Army*	1569
BROWN, Melvin L., *U.S. Army*	3037
BROWN Jr., Morris, *U.S. Army*	152
BROWN, Robert, *U.S. Navy*	153
BROWN, Robert Burns, *U.S. Army*	154
BROWN, Uriah H., *U.S. Army*	155
BROWN, William H., *U.S. Navy*	156
BROWN, Wilson, *U.S. Navy*	157
BROWN, Wilson W., *U.S. Army*	158
BROWNELL, Francis Edwin, *U.S. Army*	159
BROWNELL, William P., *U.S. Navy*	160
BRUCE, Daniel Dean, *U.S. Marine Corps*	3184
BRUNER, Louis J., *U.S. Army*	161
BRUSH, George Washington, *U.S. Army*	162
BRUTON, Christopher C., *U.S. Army*	163
BRUTSCHE, Henry, *U.S. Navy*	164
BRYAN, William C., *U.S. Army*	1570
BRYANT, Andrew Symmes, *U.S. Army*	165
BRYANT, William Maud, *U.S. Army*	3185
BUCHA, Paul William, *U.S. Army*	3186
BUCHANAN, Allen, *U.S. Navy*	2387
BUCHANAN, David M., *U.S. Navy*	1981
BUCHANAN, George A., *U.S. Army*	166
BUCK, Frederick Clarence, *U.S. Army*	167
BUCK, James, *U.S. Navy*	168
BUCKINGHAM, David E., *U.S. Army*	169
BUCKLES, Abram J., *U.S. Army*	170
BUCKLEY, Denis, *U.S. Army*	171
BUCKLEY, Howard Major, *U.S. Marine Corps*	2195
BUCKLEY, John C., *U.S. Army*	172
BUCKLYN, John Knight, *U.S. Army*	173
BUFFINGTON, John C., *U.S. Army*	174
BUFFUM, Robert, *U.S. Army*	175
BUHRMAN, Henry G., *U.S. Army*	176
BUKER, Brian Leroy, *U.S. Army*	3187
BULKELEY, John Duncan, *U.S. Navy*	2636
BUMGARNER, William, *U.S. Army*	177
BURBANK, James H., *U.S. Army*	178
BURGER, Joseph, *U.S. Army*	179
BURK, E. Michael, *U.S. Army*	180
BURK, Thomas, *U.S. Army*	181
BURKARD, Oscar R., *U.S. Army*	1571
BURKE, Daniel Webster, *U.S. Army*	182
BURKE, Francis Xavier, *U.S. Army*	2637
BURKE, Lloyd Leslie "Scooter", *U.S. Army*	3038
BURKE, Patrick J., *U.S. Army*	1572
BURKE, Richard, *U.S. Army*	1573
BURKE, Robert Charles, *U.S. Marine Corps*	3188
BURKE, Thomas, *U.S. Army*	183
BURKE, Thomas, *U.S. Navy*	1523
BURNES, James, *U.S. Marine Corps*	2272
BURNETT, George Ritter, *U.S. Army*	1574
BURNS, James Madison, *U.S. Army*	184
BURNS, John M., *U.S. Navy*	185
BURR, Elmer J., *U.S. Army*	2638
BURR, Herbert Hoover, *U.S. Army*	2639
BURRIS, Tony K., *U.S. Army*	3039
BURRITT, William Wallace, *U.S. Army*	186
BURT, James Montross, *U.S. Army*	2640
BURTON, Albert, *U.S. Navy*	187
BUSH, Richard Earl, *U.S. Marine Corps Reserve*	2641
BUSH, Robert Eugene, *U.S. Navy Reserve*	2642
BUTLER, Edmond Thomas, *U.S. Army*	1575
BUTLER, Smedley Darlington, *U.S. Marine Corps*	2388, 2437
BUTTERFIELD, Daniel Adams, *U.S. Army*	188
BUTTERFIELD, Franklin George, *U.S. Army*	189
BUTTON, William Robert, *U.S. Marine Corps*	2573
BUTTS, George, *U.S. Navy*	190
BUTTS, John Edward, *U.S. Army*	2643
BUZZARD, Ulysses G., *U.S. Army*	2084
BYRD Jr., Richard Evelyn, *U.S. Navy*	2580
BYRNE, Bernard Albert, *U.S. Army*	2196
BYRNE, Denis, *U.S. Army*	1576
BYRNES, James, *U.S. Navy*	191
CABLE, Joseph A., *U.S. Army*	1577
CADDY, William Robert, *U.S. Marine Corps Reserve*	2644
CADWALLADER, Abel G., *U.S. Army*	192
CADWELL, Luman Lewis, *U.S. Army*	193
CAFFERATA Jr., Hector Albert, *U.S. Marine Corps Reserve*	3040
CAHEY, Thomas, *U.S. Navy*	2333
CALDWELL, Daniel G., *U.S. Army*	194
CALKIN, Ivers S., *U.S. Army*	195
CALL, Donald Marshall, *U.S. Army*	2469
CALLAGHAN, Daniel Judson, *U.S. Navy*	2645
CALLAHAN, John H., *U.S. Army*	196
CALLEN, Thomas Joseph, *U.S. Army*	1578
CALUGAS, Jose, *U.S. Army*	2646
CALVERT, James Spencer, *U.S. Army*	1579
CAMP, Carlton N., *U.S. Army*	197
CAMPBELL, Albert Ralph, *U.S. Marine Corps*	2273
CAMPBELL, Daniel J., *U.S. Marine Corps*	2085
CAMPBELL, James A., *U.S. Army*	198
CAMPBELL, William, *U.S. Army*	199
CAMPBELL, William, *U.S. Navy*	200
CANFIELD, Heth, *U.S. Army*	1580
CANN, Tedford Harris, *U.S. Navy*	2470
CANNON, George Ham, *U.S. Marine Corps*	2647
CANTRELL, Charles P., *U.S. Army*	2086
CAPEHART, Charles E., *U.S. Army*	201
CAPEHART, Henry, *U.S. Army*	202
CAPODANNO, Vincent Robert, *U.S. Navy*	3189
CAPRON Jr., Horace, *U.S. Army*	203
CAREY, Alvin P., *U.S. Army*	2648
CAREY Jr., Charles F., *U.S. Army*	2649
CAREY, Hugh, *U.S. Army*	204
CAREY, James, *U.S. Navy*	1524
CAREY, James Lemuel, *U.S. Army*	205

Name	Page
CARLISLE, Casper R., *U.S. Army*	206
CARMAN, Warren, *U.S. Army*	207
CARMIN, Isaac Harrison, *U.S. Army*	208
CARNEY, William Harvey, *U.S. Army*	209
CARON, Wayne Maurice, *U.S. Navy*	3190
CARPENTER, Louis Henry, *U.S. Army*	1581
CARR, Chris, *U.S. Army*	2650
CARR, Eugene Asa, *U.S. Army*	210
CARR, Franklin, *U.S. Army*	211
CARR, John, *U.S. Army*	1582
CARR, William Louis, *U.S. Marine Corps*	2274
CARR, William M., *U.S. Navy*	212
CARROLL, Thomas, *U.S. Army*	1583
CARSON, Anthony J., *U.S. Army*	2197
CARSON, William J., *U.S. Army*	213
CARSWELL Jr., Horace Seaver, *U.S. Army Air Corps*	2651
CART, Jacob, *U.S. Army*	214
CARTER, Bruce Wayne, *U.S. Marine Corps*	3191
CARTER, George, *U.S. Army*	1584
CARTER, John Joice, *U.S. Army*	215
CARTER, Joseph Edward, *U.S. Navy*	2087
CARTER, Joseph Franklin, *U.S. Army*	216
CARTER, Mason, *U.S. Army*	1585
CARTER, Robert Goldthwaite, *U.S. Army*	1586
CARTER, William Harding, *U.S. Army*	1587
CARUANA, Orlando Emanuel, *U.S. Army*	217
CARY, Robert Webster, *U.S. Navy*	2443
CASAMENTO, Anthony, *U.S. Marine Corps*	2652
CASEY, David P., *U.S. Army*	218
CASEY, Henry, *U.S. Army*	219
CASEY, James Seaman, *U.S. Army*	1588
CASSIDY, Michael, *U.S. Navy*	220
CASTLE, Frederick Walker, *U.S. Army Air Corps*	2653
CASTLE, Guy Wilkinson Stuart, *U.S. Navy*	2389
CATHERWOOD, John Hugh, *U.S. Navy*	2375
CATLIN, Albertus Wright, *U.S. Marine Corps*	2390
CATLIN, Isaac Swartwood, *U.S. Army*	221
CAVAIANI, Jon Robert, *U.S. Army*	3192
CAVANAUGH, Thomas, *U.S. Navy*	1982
CAWETZKA, Charles, *U.S. Army*	2198
CAYER, Ovila, *U.S. Army*	222
CECIL, Joseph Samuel, *U.S. Army*	2199
CHADWICK, Leonard B., *U.S. Navy*	2088
CHAMBERLAIN, Joshua Lawrence, *U.S. Army*	223
CHAMBERLAIN, Orville Tyron, *U.S. Army*	224
CHAMBERS, Joseph B., *U.S. Army*	225
CHAMBERS, Justice Marion, *U.S. Marine Corps Reserve*	2654
CHAMPAGNE, David Bernard, *U.S. Marine Corps*	3041
CHANDLER, Henry Flint, *U.S. Army*	226
CHANDLER, James B., *U.S. Navy*	227
CHANDLER, Stephen Edwin, *U.S. Army*	228
CHANDRON, August, *U.S. Navy*	1983
CHAPIN, Alaric B., *U.S. Army*	229
CHAPMAN, Amos, *U.S. Army*	1589
CHAPMAN, John, *U.S. Army*	230
CHAPUT, Louis G., *U.S. Navy*	231
CHARETTE, George, *U.S. Navy*	2089
CHARETTE, William Richard, *U.S. Navy*	3042
CHARLTON, Cornelius H., *U.S. Army*	3043
CHASE, John F., *U.S. Army*	232
CHATHAM, John Purness, *U.S. Navy*	2275
CHEEVER Jr., Benjamin Harrison, *U.S. Army*	1590
CHELI, Ralph, *U.S. Army Air Corps*	2655
CHILD, Benjamin Ham, *U.S. Army*	233
CHILDERS, Ernest "Chief", *U.S. Army*	2656
CHILES, Marcellus Holmes, *U.S. Army*	2471
CHIQUITO, *U.S. Army*	1591
CHISMAN, William W., *U.S. Army*	234
CHOATE, Clyde Lee, *U.S. Army*	2657
CHOLISTER, George Robert, *U.S. Navy*	2581
CHRISTENSEN, Dale Eldon, *U.S. Army*	2658
CHRISTIAN, Herbert F., *U.S. Army*	2659
CHRISTIANCY, James Isaac, *U.S. Army*	235
CHRISTIANSON, Stanley Reuben, *U.S. Marine Corps*	3044
CHURCH, James Robb, *U.S. Army*	2090
CHURCHILL, Samuel Joseph, *U.S. Army*	236
CICCHETTI, Joseph J., *U.S. Army*	2660
CILLEY, Clinton Albert, *U.S. Army*	237
CLANCY, James T., *U.S. Army*	238
CLANCY, John E., *U.S. Army*	1592
CLANCY, Joseph, *U.S. Navy*	2276
CLAPP, Albert Adams, *U.S. Army*	239
CLARK, Charles Amory, *U.S. Army*	240
CLARK, Francis J., *U.S. Army*	2661
CLARK, Harrison, *U.S. Army*	241
CLARK, James G., *U.S. Army*	242
CLARK, John Wesley, *U.S. Army*	243
CLARK, Wilfred, *U.S. Army*	1593
CLARK, William A., *U.S. Army*	244
CLARKE, Dayton P., *U.S. Army*	245
CLARKE, Powhatan Henry, *U.S. Army*	1594
CLARY, Edward Alvin, *U.S. Navy*	2334
CLAUSEN, Charles H., *U.S. Army*	246
CLAUSEN, Claus Kristian Randolph, *U.S. Navy*	2091
CLAUSEN Jr., Raymond Michael "Red", *U.S. Marine Corps*	3193
CLAUSEY, John Joseph, *U.S. Navy*	2335
CLAY, Cecil, *U.S. Army*	247
CLEVELAND, Charles Franklin, *U.S. Army*	248
CLIFFORD, Robert Teleford, *U.S. Navy*	249
CLOPP, John E., *U.S. Army*	250
CLUTE, George Washington, *U.S. Army*	251
CO-RUX-TE-CHOD-ISH (MAD BEAR), *U.S. Army*	1600
COATES, Jefferson, *U.S. Army*	252
COCKLEY, David L., *U.S. Army*	253
CODY, William Frederick "Buffalo Bill", *U.S. Army*	1595
COEY, James, *U.S. Army*	254
COFFEY, Robert John, *U.S. Army*	255
COHN, Abraham, *U.S. Army*	256
COKER, Ronald Leroy, *U.S. Marine Corps*	3194
COLALILLO, Michael "Mike", *U.S. Army*	2662
COLBERT, Patrick, *U.S. Navy*	257
COLBY, Carlos W., *U.S. Army*	258
COLE, Daril Samuel, *U.S. Marine Corps Reserve*	2663
COLE, Gabriel, *U.S. Army*	259
COLE, Robert George, *U.S. Army*	2664
COLEMAN, John, *U.S. Marine Corps*	1960
COLLIER, Gilbert G., *U.S. Army*	3045
COLLIER, John Walton, *U.S. Army*	3046

Name	Page
COLLINS, Harrison, *U.S. Army*	260
COLLINS Sr., Thomas D., *U.S. Army*	261
COLLIS, Charles Henry Tucky, *U.S. Army*	262
COLWELL, Oliver, *U.S. Army*	263
COLYER, Wilbur E., *U.S. Army*	2472
COMFORT, John W., *U.S. Army*	1596
COMMISKEY SR., Henry Alfred, *U.S. Marine Corps*	3047
COMPSON, Hartwell B., *U.S. Army*	264
CONAWAY, John Wesley, *U.S. Army*	265
CONBOY, Martin, *U.S. Army*	266
CONDON, Clarence Milville, *U.S. Army*	2200
CONLAN, Dennis, *U.S. Navy*	267
CONNELL, Trustrim, *U.S. Army*	268
CONNER, Richard, *U.S. Army*	269
CONNOLLY, Michael, *U.S. Navy*	1984
CONNOR, James Phillip, *U.S. Army*	2665
CONNOR, John, *U.S. Army*	1597
CONNOR, Peter Spencer, *U.S. Marine Corps*	3195
CONNOR, Thomas, *U.S. Navy*	270
CONNOR, William C., *U.S. Navy*	271
CONNORS, James, *U.S. Army*	272
COOK, Donald Gilbert, *U.S. Marine Corps*	3196
COOK, John, *U.S. Army*	273
COOK, John Henry, *U.S. Army*	274
COOKE, Walter Howard, *U.S. Army*	275
COOLEY, Raymond Henry, *U.S. Army*	2666
COOLIDGE, Charles Henry, *U.S. Army*	2667
COONEY, James, *U.S. Marine Corps*	2277
COONEY, Thomas C., *U.S. Navy*	2092
COONROD, Aquilla, *U.S. Army*	1598
COOPER, John, *U.S. Navy*	276, 1525
COPP, Charles Dearborn, *U.S. Army*	277
CORAHORGI, Demetri, *U.S. Navy*	2336
CORCORAN, John, *U.S. Army*	278
CORCORAN, Michael, *U.S. Army*	1599
CORCORAN, Thomas E., *U.S. Navy*	279
COREY, William, *U.S. Navy*	1985
CORLISS, George W., *U.S. Army*	280
CORLISS, Stephen Potter, *U.S. Army*	281
CORRY Jr., William Merrill, *U.S. Navy*	2582
CORSON, Joseph Kirby, *U.S. Army*	282
COSGRIFF, Richard H., *U.S. Army*	283
COSGROVE, Thomas, *U.S. Army*	284
COSTELLO, John, *U.S. Navy*	1986
COSTIN, Henry G., *U.S. Army*	2473
COTTON, Peter, *U.S. Navy*	285
COUGHLIN, John, *U.S. Army*	286
COURSEN, Samuel Streit, *U.S. Army*	3048
COURTNEY Jr., Henry Alexius, *U.S. Marine Corps Reserve*	2668
COURTNEY, Henry C., *U.S. Navy*	1987
COURTS, George McCall, *U.S. Navy*	2391
COVINGTON, Jesse Whitfield, *U.S. Navy*	2474
COWAN, Richard Eller, *U.S. Army*	2669
COX, Robert Edward, *U.S. Navy*	2337
COX, Robert Mitchell, *U.S. Army*	287
COYNE, John Nicholas, *U.S. Army*	288
CRAFT, Clarence Byrle, *U.S. Army*	2670
CRAIG, Gordon Maynard, *U.S. Army*	3049
CRAIG, Robert, *U.S. Army*	2671
CRAIG, Samuel Henry, *U.S. Army*	1601
CRAIN, Morris E., *U.S. Army*	2672
CRAMEN, Thomas, *U.S. Navy*	1988
CRANDALL, Charles, *U.S. Army*	1602
CRANDALL, Orson Leon, *U.S. Navy*	2583
CRANSTON, William Wallace, *U.S. Army*	289
CRAW, Demas Thurlow, *U.S. Army Air Corps*	2673
CRAWFORD, Alexander, *U.S. Navy*	290
CRAWFORD, William John, *U.S. Army*	2674
CREED, John, *U.S. Army*	291
CREEK, Thomas Elbert, *U.S. Marine Corps*	3197
CREELMAN, William James, *U.S. Navy*	1989
CREGAN, George, *U.S. Navy*	2392
CRESCENZ, Michael Joseph, *U.S. Army*	3198
CREWS, John R., *U.S. Army*	2675
CRILLEY, Frank William, *U.S. Navy*	2444
CRIPPS, Thomas H., *U.S. Navy*	292
CRIST, John, *U.S. Army*	1603
CRISWELL, Benjamin C., *U.S. Army*	1604
CROCKER, Henry H., *U.S. Army*	293
CROCKER, Ulric Lyona, *U.S. Army*	294
CROFT, James E., *U.S. Army*	295
CROMWELL, John Philip, *U.S. Navy*	2676
CRONAN, William (Willie), *U.S. Navy*	2338
CRONIN, Cornelius, *U.S. Navy*	296
CROSIER, William Henry Harrison, *U.S. Army*	297
CROSS, James Edwin, *U.S. Army*	298
CROUSE, William Adolphus, *U.S. Navy*	2093
CROWLEY, Michael, *U.S. Army*	299
CRUMP, Jerry Kirt, *U.S. Army*	3050
CRUSE, Thomas, *U.S. Army*	1605
CUBBERLY, William G., *U.S. Army*	1606
CUKELA, Louis, *U.S. Marine Corps*	2475
CULLEN, Thomas, *U.S. Army*	300
CUMMINGS, Amos Jay, *U.S. Army*	301
CUMMINS, Andrew Johnson, *U.S. Army*	2094
CUMPSTON, James M., *U.S. Army*	302
CUNNINGHAM, Charles, *U.S. Army*	1607
CUNNINGHAM, Francis Marion, *U.S. Army*	303
CUNNINGHAM, James Smith, *U.S. Army*	304
CURRAN, Richard J., *U.S. Army*	305
CURREY, Francis Sherman "Frank", *U.S. Army*	2677
CURTIS, John Calvin, *U.S. Army*	306
CURTIS, Josiah M., *U.S. Army*	307
CURTIS, Newton Martin, *U.S. Army*	308
CUSTER, Thomas Ward, *U.S. Army*	309
CUTCHEON, Byron M., *U.S. Army*	310
CUTINHA, Nicholas Joseph, *U.S. Army*	3199
CUTTER, George W., *U.S. Navy*	1990
CUTTS, James Madison, *U.S. Army*	311
DAHL, Larry Gilbert, *U.S. Army*	3200
DAHLGREN, Edward Carl, *U.S. Army*	2678
DAHLGREN, John Olof, *U.S. Marine Corps*	2278
DAILY, Charles, *U.S. Army*	1608
DALESSONDRO, Peter Joseph, *U.S. Army*	2679
DALY, Daniel Joseph, *U.S. Marine Corps*	2279, 2438
DALY, Michael Joseph, *U.S. Army*	2680
DAMATO, Anthony Peter, *U.S. Marine Corps*	2681
DANIELS, James Thomas, *U.S. Army*	1609

Name	Page
DARROUGH, John S., *U.S. Army*	312
DAVENPORT, Jack Arden, *U.S. Marine Corps*	3051
DAVID, Albert Leroy, *U.S. Navy*	2682
DAVIDSIZER, John A., *U.S. Army*	313
DAVIDSON, Andrew, *U.S. Army*	314
DAVIDSON, Andrew, *U.S. Army*	315
DAVIS, Charles C., *U.S. Army*	316
DAVIS, Charles P., *U.S. Army*	2201
DAVIS, Charles Willis, *U.S. Army*	2683
DAVIS, Freeman, *U.S. Army*	317
DAVIS Jr., George Andrew, *U.S. Air Force*	3052
DAVIS, George Evans, *U.S. Army*	318
DAVIS, George Fleming, *U.S. Navy*	2684
DAVIS, Harry Clay, *U.S. Army*	319
DAVIS, John, *U.S. Army*	321
DAVIS, John, *U.S. Navy*	320
DAVIS, John, *U.S. Navy*	1991
DAVIS, John, *U.S. Navy*	2095
DAVIS, Joseph, *U.S. Army*	322
DAVIS, Joseph H., *U.S. Navy*	1992
DAVIS, Martin K., *U.S. Army*	323
DAVIS, Raymond Erwin, *U.S. Navy*	2339
DAVIS, Raymond Gilbert, *U.S. Marine Corps*	3053
DAVIS, Rodney Maxwell, *U.S. Marine Corps*	3201
DAVIS, Sammy Lee, *U.S. Army*	3202
DAVIS, Samuel W., *U.S. Navy*	324
DAVIS, Thomas, *U.S. Army*	325
DAWSON, Michael, *U.S. Army*	1610
DAY, Charles, *U.S. Army*	326
DAY, David Frakes, *U.S. Army*	327
DAY, George Everette "Bud", *U.S. Air Force*	3203
DAY, Matthias Walter, *U.S. Army*	1611
DAY, William L., *U.S. Army*	1612
De ARMOND, William, *U.S. Army*	1613
De La GARZA Jr., Emilio Albert, *U.S. Marine Corps*	3204
DEAKIN, Charles, *U.S. Navy*	328
DEALEY, Samuel David, *U.S. Navy*	2685
DEAN Sr., William Frishe, *U.S. Army*	3054
DEANE, John Milton, *U.S. Army*	329
DEARY, George, *U.S. Army*	1614
DEBLANC, Jefferson Joseph, *U.S. Marine Corps Reserve*	2686
DeCASTRO, Joseph H., *U.S. Army*	330
DECKER, Percy A., *U.S. Navy*	2393
DEETLINE, Frederick, *U.S. Army*	1615
DEFRANZO, Arthur Frederick, *U.S. Army*	2687
DEGLOPPER, Charles N., *U.S. Army*	2688
DEIGNAN, Osborn Warren, *U.S. Navy*	2096
DeLACEY, Patrick, *U.S. Army*	331
DeLAND, Frederick Nelson, *U.S. Army*	332
DELANEY, John Carroll, *U.S. Army*	333
DeLAVIE, Hiram H., *U.S. Army*	334
DELEAU Jr., Emile, *U.S. Army*	2689
DEMPSEY, John, *U.S. Navy*	1993
DEMPSTER, John, *U.S. Navy*	335
DENEEF, Michael, *U.S. Navy*	1994
DENHAM, Austin, *U.S. Navy*	1995
DENIG, J. Henry, *U.S. Marine Corps*	336
DENNING, Lorenzo, *U.S. Navy*	337
DENNIS, Richard, *U.S. Navy*	338
DENNY, John, *U.S. Army*	1616
DENSMORE, William, *U.S. Navy*	339
DePUY, Charles H., *U.S. Army*	340
DERVISHIAN, Ernest Herbert, *U.S. Army*	2690
DESIDERIO, Reginald Benjamin, *U.S. Army*	3055
DeSOMER, Abraham, *U.S. Navy*	2394
DeSWAN, John Francis, *U.S. Army*	2097
DETHLEFSEN, Merlyn Hans, *U.S. Air Force*	3205
DEVORE Jr., Edward Allen, *U.S. Army*	3206
DEWERT, Richard David, *U.S. Navy*	3056
DEWEY, Duane Edgar, *U.S. Marine Corps Reserve*	3057
DEWITT, Richard Willis, *U.S. Army*	341
Di CESNOLA, Louis Palma, *U.S. Army*	342
DIAMOND, James H., *U.S. Army*	2691
DIAS, Ralph Ellis, *U.S. Marine Corps*	3207
DICKENS, Charles H., *U.S. Army*	1617
DICKEY, Douglas Eugene, *U.S. Marine Corps*	3208
DICKEY, William Donaldson, *U.S. Army*	343
DICKIE, David, *U.S. Army*	344
DIETZ, Robert H., *U.S. Army*	2692
DIGGINS, Bartholomew, *U.S. Navy*	345
DILBOY, George, *U.S. Army*	2476
DILGER, Hubert, *U.S. Army*	346
DILLON, Michael A., *U.S. Army*	347
DITZENBACK, John, *U.S. Navy*	348
DIX, Drew Dennis, *U.S. Army*	3209
DIXON, William "Billy", *U.S. Army*	1618
DOANE, Stephen Holden, *U.S. Army*	3210
DOCKUM, Warren C., *U.S. Army*	349
DODD, Carl Henry, *U.S. Army*	3058
DODD, Robert Fulton, *U.S. Army*	350
DODDS, Edward Edwin, *U.S. Army*	351
DODGE, Francis Safford, *U.S. Army*	1619
DOHERTY, Thomas M., *U.S. Army*	2098
DOLBY, David Charles, *U.S. Army*	3211
DOLLOFF, Charles W., *U.S. Army*	352
DONAHUE, John L., *U.S. Army*	1620
DONALDSON, John P., *U.S. Army*	353
DONALDSON, Michael Aloyisius, *U.S. Army*	2477
DONAVAN, Cornelius, *U.S. Army*	1621
DONELLY, John S., *U.S. Army*	1622
DONLON, Roger Hugh Charles, *U.S. Army*	3212
DONNELLY, John C., *U.S. Navy*	354
DONOGHUE, Timothy, *U.S. Army*	355
DONOVAN, William Joseph "Wild Bill", *U.S. Army*	2478
DOODY, Patrick H., *U.S. Army*	356
DOOLEN, William, *U.S. Navy*	357
DOOLITTLE, James Harold, *U.S. Army Air Corps/U.S. Air Force*	2693
DORAN, John James, *U.S. Navy*	2099
DORE, George H., *U.S. Army*	358
DORLEY, August, *U.S. Army*	359
DORMAN, John Henry, *U.S. Navy*	360
DORSEY, Daniel Allen, *U.S. Army*	361
DORSEY, Decatur, *U.S. Army*	362
DOSS, Desmond Thomas, *U.S. Army*	2694
DOUGALL, Allan Houston, *U.S. Army*	363
DOUGHERTY, James, *U.S. Marine Corps*	1961
DOUGHERTY, Michael, *U.S. Army*	364
DOUGHERTY, Patrick, *U.S. Navy*	365

Name	Page
DOUGHERTY, William, *U.S. Army*	1623
DOW, George P., *U.S. Army*	366
DOW, Henry, *U.S. Navy*	367
DOWLING, James, *U.S. Army*	1624
DOWNEY, William, *U.S. Army*	368
DOWNS, Henry W., *U.S. Army*	369
DOWNS, Willis H., *U.S. Army*	2202
DOZIER, James B., *U.S. Army*	1625
DOZIER, James C., *U.S. Army*	2479
DRAKE, James Madison, *U.S. Army*	370
DREXLER, Henry Clay, *U.S. Navy*	2584
DROWLEY, Jesse Ray, *U.S. Army*	2695
DRURY, James, *U.S. Army*	371
DRUSTRUP, Niels, *U.S. Navy*	2395
Du MOULIN, Frank, *U.S. Navy*	1526
Du PONT, Henry Algernon, *U.S. Army*	379
DUFFEY, John, *U.S. Army*	372
DUKE, Ray E., *U.S. Army*	3059
DUNAGAN, Kern Wayne, *U.S. Army*	3213
DUNCAN, Adam, *U.S. Navy*	373
DUNCAN, James K. L., *U.S. Navy*	374
DUNHAM, Russell, *U.S. Army*	2696
DUNLAP, Robert Hugo, *U.S. Marine Corps Reserve*	2697
DUNLAVY, James, *U.S. Army*	375
DUNN, Parker F., *U.S. Army*	2480
DUNN, William, *U.S. Navy*	376
DUNNE, James, *U.S. Army*	377
DUNPHY, Richard D., *U.S. Navy*	378
DURHAM Jr., Harold Bascom, *U.S. Army*	3214
DURHAM, James R., *U.S. Army*	380
DURHAM, John S., *U.S. Army*	381
DURNEY, Austin Joseph, *U.S. Navy*	2100
DUTKO, John W., *U.S. Army*	2698
DYER, Jesse Farley, *U.S. Marine Corps*	2396
DYESS, Aquilla James, *U.S. Marine Corps Reserve*	2699
EADIE, Thomas, *U.S. Navy*	2585
ECKES, John N., *U.S. Army*	382
EDDY, Samuel E., *U.S. Army*	383
EDGERTON, Nathan Huntley, *U.s. Army*	384
EDSON, Merritt Austin, *U.S. Marine Corps*	2700
EDWARDS, Daniel Richmond, *U.S. Army*	2481
EDWARDS, David, *U.S. Army*	385
EDWARDS, John, *U.S. Navy*	386
EDWARDS, Junior Dean, *U.S. Army*	3060
EDWARDS, Walter Atlee, *U.S. Navy*	2586
EDWARDS, William D., *U.S. Army*	1626
EGGERS, Alan Louis, *U.S. Army*	2482
EGLIT, John, *U.S. Navy*	2101
EHLE, John Walter, *U.S. Navy*	2102
EHLERS, Walter David, *U.S. Army*	2701
EILERS, Henry A., *U.S. Navy*	1996
ELDRIDGE, George H., *U.S. Army*	1627
ELLIOTT, Alexander, *U.S. Army*	387
ELLIOTT, Middleton Stuart, *U.S. Navy*	2397
ELLIOTT, Russell C., *U.S. Army*	388
ELLIS, Horace, *U.S. Army*	389
ELLIS, Michael B., *U.S. Army*	2483
ELLIS, William, *U.S. Army*	390
ELLSWORTH, Thomas Foulds, *U.S. Army*	391
ELMORE, Walter, *U.S. Navy*	1997
ELROD, Henry Talmage, *U.S. Marine Corps*	2702
ELSATSOOSH, *U.S. Army*	1628
ELSON, James M., *U.S. Army*	392
ELWOOD, Edwin L., *U.S. Army*	1629
EMBLER, Andrew Henry, *U.S. Army*	393
EMMET, Robert Temple, *U.S. Army*	1630
ENDERLIN, Richard, *U.S. Army*	394
ENDL, Gerald Leon, *U.S. Army*	2703
ENGLE, James Edgar, *U.S. Army*	395
ENGLISH, Edmund, *U.S. Army*	396
ENGLISH Jr., Glenn Harry, *U.S. Army*	3215
ENGLISH, Thomas, *U.S. Navy*	397
ENNIS, Charles D., *U.S. Army*	398
ENRIGHT, John, *U.S. Navy*	1998
EPPERSON, Harold Glenn, *U.S. Marine Corps Reserve*	2704
EPPS, Joseph L., *U.S. Army*	2203
ERICKSON, John P., *U.S. Navy*	399
ERICKSON, Nicholas, *U.S. Navy*	2103
ERWIN, Henry Eugene "Red", *U.S. Army Air Corps*	2705
ESSEBAGGER Jr., John, *U.S. Army*	3061
ESTES, Lewellyn Garrish, *U.S. Army*	400
ESTOCIN, Michael John, *U.S. Navy*	3216
EUBANKS, Ray E., *U.S. Army*	2706
EVANS, Coron D., *U.S. Army*	401
EVANS Jr., Donald Ward, *U.S. Army*	3217
EVANS, Ernest Edwin "Chief", *U.S. Navy*	2707
EVANS, Ira Hobart, *U.S. Army*	402
EVANS, James Robert, *U.S. Army*	403
EVANS, Rodney John, *U.S. Army*	3218
EVANS, Thomas, *U.S. Army*	404
EVANS, William, *U.S. Army*	1631
EVERETTS, John, *U.S. Navy*	1999
EVERHART Sr., Forrest Eugene, *U.S. Army*	2708
EVERSON, Adelbert, *U.S. Army*	405
EWING, John C., *U.S. Army*	406
FACTOR, Pompey, *U.S. Army*	1632
FADDEN, Harry Delmar, *U.S. Navy*	2340
FAITH Jr., Don Carlos, *U.S. Army*	3062
FALCONER, John A., *U.S. Army*	407
FALCOTT, Henry, *U.S. Army*	1633
FALL, Charles S., *U.S. Army*	408
FALLON, Thomas Timothy, *U.S. Army*	409
FALLS, Benjamin Frank, *U.S. Army*	410
FANNING, Nicholas, *U.S. Army*	411
FARDY, John Peter, *U.S. Marine Corps*	2709
FARLEY, William, *U.S. Navy*	412
FARNSWORTH, Herbert E., *U.S. Army*	413
FARQUHAR, John Mcgreath, *U.S. Army*	414
FARRELL, Edward, *U.S. Navy*	415
FARREN, Daniel, *U.S. Army*	1634
FASNACHT, Charles H., *U.S. Army*	416
FASSETT, John Barclay, *U.S. Army*	417
FASSEUR, Isaac L., *U.S. Navy*	2000
FEASTER, Mosheim, *U.S. Army*	1635
FEGAN, James, *U.S. Army*	1636
FEMOYER, Robert Edward, *U.S. Army Air Corps*	2710
FERGUSON, Arthur Medworth, *U.S. Army*	2204
FERGUSON, Frederick Edgar, *U.S. Army*	3219

FERNALD, Albert E., *U.S. Army*	418	FOURNIA, Frank Ottis, *U.S. Army*	2107
FERNANDEZ, Daniel, *U.S. Army*	3220	FOURNIER, William Grant, *U.S. Army*	2719
FERRARI, George, *U.S. Army*	1637	FOUS, James William, *U.S. Army*	3229
FERRELL, John H., *U.S. Navy*	419	FOUT, Frederick W., *U.S. Army*	437
FERRIER, Daniel Tweed, *U.S. Army*	420	FOWLER, Christopher, *U.S. Navy*	2002
FERRIS, Eugene W., *U.S. Army*	421	FOWLER, Thomas Weldon, *U.S. Army*	2720
FESQ, Frank E., *U.S. Army*	422	FOX, Henry, *U.S. Army*	438
FICHTER, Hermann Emil, *U.S. Army*	1638	FOX, Henry M., *U.S. Army*	439
FIELD, Oscar Wadsworth, *U.S. Marine Corps*	2104	FOX, Nicholas, *U.S. Army*	440
FIELDS, James H., *U.S. Army*	2711	FOX, Wesley Lee, *U.S. Marine Corps*	3230
FINKENBINER, Henry S., *U.S. Army*	423	FOX, William R., *U.S. Army*	441
FINN, John William, *U.S. Navy*	2712	FOY, Charles H., *U.S. Navy*	442
FISHER, Almond Edward, *U.S. Army*	2713	FRANCIS, Charles Robert, *U.S. Marine Corps*	2282
FISHER, Bernard Francis, *U.S. Air Force*	3221	FRANKLIN, Frederick H., *U.S. Navy*	1962
FISHER, Frederick Thomas, *U.S. Navy*	2182	FRANKLIN, Joseph John, *U.S. Marine Corps*	2108
FISHER, Harry, *U.S. Marine Corps*	2280	FRANKS, William J., *U.S. Navy*	443
FISHER, John H., *U.S. Army*	424	FRANTZ, Joseph, *U.S. Army*	444
FISHER, Joseph, *U.S. Army*	425	FRASER, William W., *U.S. Army*	445
FITZ, Joseph, *U.S. Navy*	2205	FRATELLENICO, Frank Rocco, *U.S. Army*	3231
FITZGERALD, John, *U.S. Marine Corps*	2105	FRAZER, Hugh Carroll, *U.S. Navy*	2401
FITZMAURICE, Michael John, *U.S. Army*	3222	FREDERICKSEN, Emil, *U.S. Navy*	2342
FITZPATRICK, Thomas, *U.S. Navy*	426	FREEMAN, Archibald, *U.S. Army*	446
FLAHERTY, Francis Charles, *U.S. Naval Reserve*	2714	FREEMAN, Henry Blanchard, *U.S. Army*	447
FLANAGAN, Augustin D., *U.S. Army*	427	FREEMAN, Martin, *U.S. Navy*	448
FLANNAGAN, John, *U.S. Navy*	2001	FREEMAN, William Henry, *U.S. Army*	449
FLANNIGAN, James, *U.S. Army*	428	FREEMEYER, Christopher, *U.S. Army*	1644
FLEEK, Charles Clinton, *U.S. Army*	3223	FRENCH, Samuel S., *U.S. Army*	450
FLEETWOOD, Christian A., *U.S. Army*	429	FREY, Franz, *U.S. Army*	451
FLEMING, James Phillip, *U.S. Air Force*	3224	FRICK, Jacob G., *U.S. Army*	452
FLEMING, Richard Eugene, *U.S. Marine Corps Reserve*	2715	FRISBEE, John B., *U.S. Navy*	453
FLETCHER, Frank Friday, *U.S. Navy*	2398	FRITZ, Harold Arthur, *U.S. Army*	3232
FLETCHER, Frank Jack, *U.S. Navy*	2399	FRIZZELL, Henry F., *U.S. Army*	454
FLOOD, Thomas S., *U.S. Navy*	430	FRY, Isaac N., *U.S. Marine Corps*	455
FLOYD, Edward, *U.S. Navy*	2341	FRYAR, Elmer E., *U.S. Army*	2721
FLUCKEY, Eugene Bennett, *U.S. Navy*	2716	FRYER, Eli Thompson, *U.S. Marine Corps*	2402
FLYNN, Christopher, *U.S. Army*	431	FUGER, Frederick W., *U.S. Army*	456
FLYNN, James Edward, *U.S. Army*	432	FUNK, Jesse N., *U.S. Army*	2486
FOLEY, Alexander Joseph, *U.S. Marine Corps*	2281	FUNK Jr., Leonard Alfred, *U.S. Army*	2722
FOLEY, John H., *U.S. Army*	1639	FUNK, West, *U.S. Army*	457
FOLEY, Robert Franklin, *U.S. Army*	3225	FUNSTON Sr., Frederick, *U.S. Army*	2207
FOLLAND, Michael Fleming, *U.S. Army*	3226	FUQUA, Samuel Glenn, *U.S. Navy*	2723
FOLLETT, Joseph Leonard, *U.S. Army*	433	FURLONG, Harold Arthur, *U.S. Army*	2487
FOLLY, William H., *U.S. Army*	1640	FURMAN, Chester S., *U.S. Army*	458
FORAN, Nicholas, *U.S. Army*	1641	FURNESS, Frank, *U.S. Army*	459
FORBECK, Andrew Peter, *U.S. Navy*	2206	GAFFNEY, Frank J., *U.S. Army*	2488
FORCE, Manning Ferguson, *U.S. Army*	434	GAGE, Richard J., *U.S. Army*	460
FORD, George W., *U.S. Army*	435	GAIENNIE, Louis Rene, *U.S. Marine Corps*	2283
FORMAN, Alexander A., *U.S. Army*	436	GALBRAITH, Robert, *U.S. Navy*	2208
FORREST, Arthur J., *U.S. Army*	2484	GALER, Robert Edward, *U.S. Marine Corps*	2724
FORSTERER, Bruno Albert, *U.S. Marine Corps*	2183	GALLOWAY, George Norton, *U.S. Army*	461
FORSYTH, Thomas Hall, *U.S. Army*	1642	GALLOWAY, John, *U.S. Army*	462
FOSS, Herbert Louis, *U.S. Navy*	2106	GALT, Sterling Archibald, *U.S. Army*	2209
FOSS, Joseph Jacob, *U.S. Marine Corps Reserve*	2717	GALT, William Wylie, *U.S. Army*	2725
FOSTER, Gary Evans, *U.S. Army*	2485	GAMMON, Archer T., *U.S. Army*	2726
FOSTER, Paul Frederick, *U.S. Navy*	2400	GARCIA, Fernando Luis, *U.S. Marine Corps*	3063
FOSTER, Paul Hellstrom, *U.S. Marine Corps Reserve*	3227	GARCIA, Marcario, *U.S. Army*	2727
FOSTER, William, *U.S. Army*	1643	GARDINER, James, *U.S. Army*	463
FOSTER, William Adelbert, *U.S. Marine Corps Reserve*	2718	GARDINER, Peter W., *U.S. Army*	1645
FOURNET, Douglas Bernard, *U.S. Army*	3228	GARDNER, Charles, *U.S. Army*	1646

GARDNER, Charles N., *U.S. Army*	464		GOHEEN, Charles Arthur, *U.S. Army*	488
GARDNER, James Alton, *U.S. Army*	3233		GOLDEN, Patrick, *U.S. Army*	1658
GARDNER, Robert J., *U.S. Army*	465		GOLDIN, Theodore W. B., *U.S. Army*	1659
GARDNER, William, *U.S. Navy*	466		GOLDSBERY, Andrew E., *U.S. Army*	489
GARLAND, Harry, *U.S. Army*	1647		GOMEZ, Edward, *U.S. Marine Corps*	3066
GARLINGTON, Ernest Albert, *U.S. Army*	1648		GONSALVES, Harold, *U.S. Marine Corps Reserve*	2733
GARMAN, Harold Alva, *U.S. Army*	2728		GONZALES, David M., *U.S. Army*	2734
GARRETT, William, *U.S. Army*	467		GONZALEZ, Alfredo (Freddy), *U.S. Marine Corps*	3235
GARRISON, James R., *U.S. Navy*	468		GOODALL, Francis Henry, *U.S. Army*	490
GARVIN, William, *U.S. Navy*	469		GOODBLOOD, Clair, *U.S. Army*	3067
GARY, Donald Arthur, *U.S. Navy*	2729		GOODMAN, David, *U.S. Army*	1660
GASSON, Richard, *U.S. Army*	470		GOODMAN, Willaim Ernest, *U.S. Army*	491
GATES, George, *U.S. Army*	1649		GOODRICH, Edwin, *U.S. Army*	492
GAUGHAN, Philip, *U.S. Marine Corps*	2109		GORDON, Gary Ivan, *U.S. Army*	3398
GAUJOT, Antoine August, *U.S. Army*	2210		GORDON, Nathan Green, *U.S. Navy*	2735
GAUJOT, Julien Edmund, *U.S. Army*	2403		GOTT, Donald Joseph, *U.S. Army Air Corps*	2736
GAUNT, John C., *U.S. Army*	471		GOULD, Charles Gilbert, *U.S. Army*	493
GAUSE, Isaac, *U.S. Army*	472		GOULD, Newton Thomas, *U.S. Army*	494
GAY, Thomas H., *U.S. Army*	1650		GOURAUD, George Edward, *U.S. Army*	495
GAYLORD, Levi B., *U.S. Army*	473		GOWAN, William Henry, *U.S. Navy*	2344
GEDEON, Louis, *U.S. Army*	2211		GRABIARZ, William J., *U.S. Army*	2737
GEIGER, George, *U.S. Army*	1651		GRACE, Patrick Henry, *U.S. Navy*	1963
GEORGE, Charles, *U.S. Army*	3064		GRACE, Peter, *U.S. Army*	496
GEORGE, Daniel Griffin, *U.S. Navy*	474		GRADY, John, *U.S. Navy*	2405
GEORGIAN, John, *U.S. Army*	1652		GRAHAM, James Albert, *U.S. Marine Corps*	3236
GERBER, Frederick William, *U.S. Army*	1527		GRAHAM, Robert, *U.S. Navy*	497
GERE, Thomas Parke, *U.S. Army*	475		GRAHAM, Thomas N., *U.S. Army*	498
GERSTUNG, Robert E., *U.S. Army*	2730		GRANDSTAFF, Bruce Alan, *U.S. Army*	3237
GERTSCH, John Gerry, *U.S. Army*	3234		GRANT, Gabriel, *U.S. Army*	499
GESCHWIND, Nicholas, *U.S. Army*	476		GRANT, George, *U.S. Army*	1661
GIBBONS, Michael, *U.S. Navy*	2110		GRANT, Joseph Xavier, *U.S. Army*	3238
GIBBS, Wesley, *U.S. Army*	477		GRANT, Lewis Addison, *U.S. Army*	500
GIBSON, Edward Herrick, *U.S. Army*	2212		GRAUL, William L., *U.S. Army*	501
GIBSON, Eric Gunnar, *U.S. Army*	2731		GRAVES, Ora, *U.S. Navy*	2490
GIDDING, Charles, *U.S. Navy*	2003		GRAVES, Terrence Collinson, *U.S. Marine Corps*	3239
GIFFORD, Benjamin, *U.S. Army*	478		GRAVES, Thomas J., *U.S. Army*	2112
GIFFORD, David L., *U.S. Army*	479		GRAY, John, *U.S. Army*	502
GILE, Frank S., *U.S. Navy*	480		GRAY, Robert A., *U.S. Army*	503
GILL, Freeman, *U.S. Navy*	2111		GRAY, Ross Franklin, *U.S. Marine Corps Reserve*	2738
GILLENWATER, James Robert Lee, *U.S. Army*	2213		GRBITCH, Rade, *U.S. Navy*	2345
GILLESPIE Jr., George Lewis, *U.S. Army*	481		GREAVES, Clinton, *U.S. Army*	1662
GILLICK, Matthew, *U.S. Navy*	2004		GREBE, M. R. William, *U.S. Army*	504
GILLIGAN, Edward Lyons, *U.S. Army*	482		GREELY, Adolphus Washington, *U.S. Army Ret.*	2587
GILLILAND, Charles L., *U.S. Army*	3065		GREEN, Francis C., *U.S. Army*	1663
GILMORE, Howard Walter, *U.S. Navy*	2732		GREEN, George, *U.S. Army*	505
GILMORE, John Curtis, *U.S. Army*	483		GREEN, John, *U.S. Army*	1664
GINLEY, Patrick, *U.S. Army*	484		GREENAWALT, Abraham, *U.S. Army*	506
GION, Joseph, *U.S. Army*	485		GREENE, John, *U.S. Navy*	507
GIRANDY, Alphonse, *U.S. Navy*	2343		GREENE, Oliver Duff, *U.S. Army*	508
GISBURNE, Edward Allen, *U.S. Navy*	2404		GREER, Allen James, *U.S. Army*	2214
GIVEN, John J., *U.S. Army*	1653		GREGG, Joseph Olds, *U.S. Army*	509
GLAVINSKI, Albert, *U.S. Army*	1654		GREGG, Stephen Raymond, *U.S. Army*	2739
GLOVER, Thaddeus Brown, *U.S. Army*	1655		GREGORY, Earl D., *U.S. Army*	2491
GLOWIN, Joseph Anthony, *U.S. Marine Corps*	2451		GREIG, Theodore W., *U.S. Army*	510
GLYNN, Michael, *U.S. Army*	1656		GRESHAM, John Chowning, *U.S. Army*	1665
GODFREY, Edward Settle, *U.S. Army*	1657		GRESSER, Ignatz, *U.S. Army*	511
GODLEY, Leonidas Mahlon, *U.S. Army*	486		GRIBBEN, James H., *U.S. Army*	512
GOETTEL, Philip, *U.S. Army*	487		GRIFFITHS, John, *U.S. Navy*	513
GOETTLER, Harold Ernest, *U.S. Army Air Service*	2489		GRIMES, Edward P., *U.S. Army*	1666

GRIMSHAW, Samuel, *U.S. Army*	514
GRINDLAY, James G., *U.S. Army*	515
GRISWOLD, Luke M., *U.S. Navy*	516
GROSS, Samuel, *U.S. Marine Corps*	2439
GROVE, William Remsburg, *U.S. Army*	2215
GRUEB, George M., *U.S. Army*	517
GRUENNERT, Kenneth E., *U.S. Army*	2740
GUENETTE, Peter Mathew, *U.S. Army*	3240
GUERIN, Fitz W., *U.S. Army*	518
GUILLEN, Ambrosio, *U.S. Marine Corps*	3068
GUINN, Thomas, *U.S. Army*	519
GUMPERTZ, Sydney G., *U.S. Army*	2492
GUNTHER, Jacob, *U.S. Army*	1667
GURKE, Henry, *U.S. Marine Corps*	2741
GWYNNE, Nathaniel McClean, *U.S. Army*	520
HACK, John, *U.S. Army*	521
HACK, Lester Goodel, *U.S. Army*	522
HADDOO Jr., John, *U.S. Army*	1668
HADLEY, Cornelius Minor, *U.S. Army*	523
HADLEY, Osgood Towns, *U.S. Army*	524
HAFFEE, Edmund, *U.S. Navy*	525
HAGEMEISTER, Charles Cris, *U.S. Army*	3241
HAGEN, Loren Douglas, *U.S. Army*	3242
HAGERTY, Asel, *U.S. Army*	526
HAIGHT, John H., *U.S. Army*	527
HAIGHT, Sidney, *U.S. Army*	528
HALEY, James, *U.S. Navy*	529
HALFORD, William, *U.S. Navy*	1528
HALL, Francis Bloodgood, *U.S. Army*	530
HALL, George John, *U.S. Army*	2742
HALL, Henry Seymour, *U.S. Army*	531
HALL, John, *U.S. Army*	1669
HALL, Lewis R., *U.S. Army*	2743
HALL, Newton H., *U.S. Army*	532
HALL, Thomas Lee, *U.S. Army*	2493
HALL, William Edward, *U.S. Navy*	2744
HALL, William Preble, *U.S. Army*	1670
HALLING, Luovi, *U.S. Navy*	2346
HALLMAN, Sherwood H., *U.S. Army*	2745
HALLOCK, Nathan Mullock, *U.S. Army*	533
HALSTEAD, William W., *U.S. Navy*	534
HALYBURTON Jr., William David, *U.S. Naval Reserve*	2746
HAM, Mark G., *U.S. Navy*	535
HAMBERGER, William Francis, *U.S. Navy*	2284
HAMILTON, Frank, *U.S. Army*	1671
HAMILTON, Hugh, *U.S. Navy*	536
HAMILTON, Mathew H., *U.S. Army*	1672
HAMILTON, Pierpont Morgan, *U.S. Army Air Corps*	2747
HAMILTON, Richard, *U.S. Navy*	537
HAMILTON, Thomas W., *U.S. Navy*	538
HAMMANN, Charles Hazeltine, *U.S. Naval Reserve Fleet*	2494
HAMMEL, Henry A., *U.S. Army*	539
HAMMERBERG, Owen Francis Patrick, *U.S. Navy*	2748
HAMMOND, Francis Colton, *U.S. Navy*	3069
HAMMOND Jr., Lester, *U.S. Army*	3070
HAND, Allexander, *U.S. Navy*	540
HANDRAN, John, *U.S. Navy*	2005
HANDRICH, Melvin O., *U.S. Army*	3071
HANEY, Milton Lorenzi, *U.S. Army*	541
HANFORD, Burke, *U.S. Navy*	2285
HANFORD, Edward R., *U.S. Army*	542
HANKS, Joseph, *U.S. Army*	543
HANLEY, Richard P., *U.S. Army*	1673
HANNA, Marcus A., *U.S. Army*	544
HANNA, Milton, *U.S. Army*	545
HANNEKEN, Herman Henry, *U.S. Marine Corps*	2574
HANSCOM, Moses C., *U.S. Army*	546
HANSEN, Dale Merlin, *U.S. Marine Corps*	2749
HANSEN, Hans Anton, *U.S. Navy*	2286
HANSON, Jack G., *U.S. Army*	3072
HANSON, Robert Murray, *U.S. Marine Corps Reserve*	2750
HAPEMAN, Douglas, *U.S. Army*	547
HARBOURNE, John H., *U.S. Army*	548
HARCOURT, Thomas, *U.S. Navy*	549
HARDAWAY, Benjamin Franklin, *U.S. Army*	2113
HARDENBERGH, Henry M., *U.S. Army*	550
HARDING, Mosher A., *U.S. Army*	1674
HARDING, Thomas, *U.S. Navy*	551
HARING, Abram Pye, *U.S. Army*	552
HARLEY, Bernard, *U.S. Navy*	553
HARMON, Amzi Davis, *U.S. Army*	554
HARMON, Roy W., *U.S. Army*	2751
HARNER, Joseph Gabriel, *U.S. Navy*	2406
HARR, Harry R., *U.S. Army*	2752
HARRELL, William George, *U.S. Marine Corps*	2753
HARRINGTON, Daniel C., *U.S. Navy*	555
HARRINGTON, David, *U.S. Navy*	2006
HARRINGTON, Ephraim W., *U.S. Army*	556
HARRINGTON, John, *U.S. Army*	1675
HARRIS, Charles D., *U.S. Army*	1676
HARRIS, David W., *U.S. Army*	1677
HARRIS, George W., *U.S. Army*	557
HARRIS, James H., *U.S. Army*	558
HARRIS, James Lindell, *U.S. Army*	2754
HARRIS, John, *U.S. Navy*	559
HARRIS, Moses, *U.S. Army*	560
HARRIS, Sampson, *U.S. Army*	561
HARRIS, William M., *U.S. Army*	1678
HARRISON, Bolden Reush, *U.S. Navy*	2376
HARRISON, George H., *U.S. Navy*	562
HARRISON, William Kelly, *U.S. Navy*	2407
HART, John William, *U.S. Army*	563
HART, William, *U.S. Navy*	2114
HART, William E., *U.S. Army*	564
HARTELL, Lee Ross, *U.S. Army*	3073
HARTIGAN, Charles Conway, *U.S. Navy*	2408
HARTRANFT, John Frederic, *U.S. Army*	565
HARTSOCK, Robert Willard, *U.S. Army*	3243
HARTZOG, Joshua B., *U.S. Army*	1679
HARVEY Jr., Carmel Bernon, *U.S. Army*	3244
HARVEY, Harry, *U.S. Army*	566
HARVEY, Harry, *U.S. Marine Corps*	2216
HARVEY, Raymond, *U.S. Army*	3074
HASKELL, Frank W., *U.S. Army*	567
HASKELL, Marcus M., *U.S. Army*	568
HASTINGS, Joe R., *U.S. Army*	2755
HASTINGS, Smith H., *U.S. Army*	569
HATCH, John Porter, *U.S. Army*	570

Name	Page
HATHAWAY, Edward W., *U.S. Navy*	571
HATLER, M. Waldo, *U.S. Army*	2495
HAUGE Jr., Louis James, *U.S. Marine Corps Reserve*	2756
HAUPT, Paul, *U.S. Army*	1680
HAVRON, John H., *U.S. Army*	572
HAWK, John Druse "Bud", *U.S. Army*	2757
HAWKINS, Charles, *U.S. Navy*	573
HAWKINS, Gardner C., *U.S. Army*	574
HAWKINS, Martin Jones, *U.S. Army*	575
HAWKINS, Thomas R., *U.S. Army*	576
HAWKINS, William Deane, *U.S. Marine Corps*	2758
HAWKS, Lloyd C., *U.S. Army*	2759
HAWTHORNE, Harris Smith, *U.S. Army*	577
HAWTHORNE, Harry Leroy, *U.S. Army*	1681
HAY, Fred Stewart, *U.S. Army*	1682
HAYDEN, Cyrus, *U.S. Navy*	1964
HAYDEN, David Ephraim, *U.S. Navy*	2496
HAYDEN, John, *U.S. Navy*	2007
HAYDEN, Joseph B., *U.S. Navy*	578
HAYES, John, *U.S. Navy*	579
HAYES, Thomas, *U.S. Navy*	580
HAYES, Webb Cook, *U.S. Army*	2217
HAYNES, Asbury F., *U.S. Army*	581
HAYS, George Price, *U.S. Army*	2497
HAYS, John H., *U.S. Army*	582
HEALEY, George Washington, *U.S. Army*	583
HEARD, John William, *U.S. Army*	2115
HEARTERY, Richard, *U.S. Army*	1683
HEDGES, Joseph S., *U.S. Army*	584
HEDRICK, Clinton M., *U.S. Army*	2760
HEERMANCE, William Laing, *U.S. Army*	585
HEISCH, Henry William, *U.S. Marine Corps*	2287
HEISE, Clamor, *U.S. Army*	1684
HELLER, Henry, *U.S. Army*	586
HELMS, David H., *U.S. Army*	587
HELMS, John Henry, *U.S. Marine Corps*	2347
HENDERSON, Joseph, *U.S. Army*	2218
HENDRICKSON, Henry, *U.S. Navy*	2116
HENDRIX, James Richard, *U.S. Army*	2761
HENRECHON, George Francis, *U.S. Navy*	2377
HENRY, Frederick F., *U.S. Army*	3075
HENRY, Guy Vernor, *U.S. Army*	588
HENRY, James, *U.S. Army*	589
HENRY, Robert T., *U.S. Army*	2762
HENRY, William Wirt, *U.S. Army*	590
HERDA, Frank Aloysious, *U.S. Army*	3245
HERINGTON, Pitt B., *U.S. Army*	591
HERIOT, James Davidson, *U.S. Army*	2498
HERNANDEZ, Rodolfo Perez, *U.S. Army*	3076
HERRERA, Silvestre Santana, *U.S. Army*	2763
HERRING, Rufus Geddie, *U.S. Navy*	2764
HERRON, Francis Jay, *U.S. Army*	592
HERRON, Leander, *U.S. Army*	1685
HESSELTINE, Francis Snow, *U.S. Army*	593
HEYL, Charles Pettit heath, *U.S. Army*	1686
HIBBS, Robert John, *U.S. Army*	3246
HIBSON, Joseph C., *U.S. Army*	594
HICKEY, Dennis William, *U.S. Army*	595
HICKMAN, John S., *U.S. Navy*	596
HICKOK, Nathan E., *U.S. Army*	597
HIGBY, Charles, *U.S. Army*	598
HIGGINS, Thomas J., *U.S. Army*	599
HIGGINS, Thomas P., *U.S. Army*	1687
HIGH, Frank Charles, *U.S. Army*	2219
HIGHLAND, Patrick, *U.S. Army*	600
HILL, Edward, *U.S. Army*	601
HILL, Edwin Joseph, *U.S. Navy*	2765
HILL, Frank, *U.S. Marine Corps*	2117
HILL, Frank E., *U.S. Army*	1688
HILL, Frank Ebenezer, *U.S. Navy*	2348
HILL, George, *U.S. Navy*	2008
HILL, Henry, *U.S. Army*	602
HILL, James, *U.S. Army*	603
HILL, James Madison, *U.S. Army*	1689
HILL, James Samuel, *U.S. Army*	604
HILL, Ralyn M., *U.S. Army*	2499
HILL, Walter Newell, *U.S. Marine Corps*	2409
HILL, William Lowell, *U.S. Navy*	2009
HILLIKER, Benjamin F., *U.S. Army*	605
HILLOCK, Marvin C., *U.S. Army*	1690
HILLS, William Giles, *U.S. Army*	606
HILTON, Alfred B., *U.S. Army*	607
HILTON, Richmond Hobson, *U.S. Army*	2500
HIMMELSBACK, Michael, *U.S. Army*	1691
HINCKS, William B., *U.S. Army*	608
HINEMANN, Lehmann, *U.S. Army*	1692
HINNEGAN, William, *U.S. Navy*	609
HOBAN, Thomas, *U.S. Navy*	2118
HOBDAY, George, *U.S. Army*	1693
HOBSON, Richmond Pearson, *U.S. Navy*	2119
HODGES, Addison J., *U.S. Army*	610
HOFFMAN, Charles F., *U.S. Marine Corps*	2501
HOFFMAN, Henry, *U.S. Army*	611
HOFFMAN, Thomas W., *U.S. Army*	612
HOGAN, Franklin, *U.S. Army*	613
HOGAN, Henry, *U.S. Army*	1694
HOGARTY, William P., *U.S. Army*	614
HOLCOMB, Daniel Irving, *U.S. Army*	615
HOLCOMB, John Noble, *U.S. Army*	3247
HOLDEN, Henry, *U.S. Army*	1695
HOLDERMAN, Nelson Miles, *U.S. Army*	2502
HOLEHOUSE, James, *U.S. Army*	616
HOLLAND, David, *U.S. Army*	1696
HOLLAND, Lemuel F., *U.S. Army*	617
HOLLAND, Milton Murray, *U.S. Army*	618
HOLLAT, George, *U.S. Navy*	619
HOLMES, Lovilo N., *U.S. Army*	620
HOLMES, William T., *U.S. Army*	621
HOLT, George, *U.S. Navy*	2010
HOLTON, Charles Maynard, *U.S. Army*	622
HOLTON, Edward A., *U.S. Army*	623
HOLTZ, August, *U.S. Navy*	2349
HOLYOKE, William Edward, *U.S. Navy*	2288
HOMAN, Conrad, *U.S. Army*	624
HOOKER, George, *U.S. Army*	1697
HOOKER, George White, *U.S. Army*	625
HOOPER, Joe Ronnie, *U.S. Army*	3248
HOOPER, William B., *U.S. Army*	626

Name	Page
HOOVER, Samuel, *U.S. Army*	1698
HOPKINS, Charles F., *U.S. Army*	627
HORAN, Thomas, *U.S. Army*	628
HORNADAY, Elisha Simpson, *U.S. Army*	1699
HORNE, Samuel Belton, *U.S. Army*	629
HORNER, Freeman Victor, *U.S. Army*	2766
HORSFALL, William H., *U.S. Army*	630
HORTON, James, *U.S. Navy*	631
HORTON, James, *U.S. Navy*	2011
HORTON, Lewis Augustine, *U.S. Navy*	632
HORTON, William M. Charlie, *U.S. Marine Corps*	2289
HOSKING Jr., Charles Ernest, *U.S. Army*	3249
HOTTENSTINE, Solomon J., *U.S. Army*	633
HOUGH, Ira, *U.S. Army*	634
HOUGHTON, Charles H., *U.S. Army*	635
HOUGHTON, Edward J., *U.S. Navy*	636
HOUGHTON, George L., *U.S. Army*	637
HOULTON, William M., *U.S. Army*	638
HOWARD, Henderson Calvin, *U.S. Army*	639
HOWARD, Hiram Reese, *U.S. Army*	640
HOWARD, James, *U.S. Army*	641
HOWARD, James Howell, *U.S. Army Air Corps/U.S. Air Force*	2767
HOWARD, Jimmie Earl, *U.S. Marine Corps*	3250
HOWARD, Martin, *U.S. Navy*	642
HOWARD, Oliver Otis, *U.S. Army*	643
HOWARD, Peter, *U.S. Navy*	644
HOWARD, Robert Lewis, *U.S. Army*	3251
HOWARD, Squire Edward, *U.S. Army*	645
HOWE, James Donnie, *U.S. Marine Corps*	3252
HOWE, Orion P., *U.S. Army*	646
HOWE, William H., *U.S. Army*	647
HOWZE, Robert Lee, *U.S. Army*	1700
HUBBARD, Thomas H., *U.S. Army*	1701
HUBBELL, William Stone, *U.S. Army*	648
HUBER, William Russell, *U.S. Navy*	2588
HUDNER Jr., Thomas Jerome, *U.S. Navy*	3077
HUDSON, Aaron R., *U.S. Army*	649
HUDSON, Michael, *U.S. Marine Corps*	650
HUFF, James W., *U.S. Army*	1702
HUFF, Paul Bert, *U.S. Army*	2768
HUGGINS, Eli Lundy, *U.S. Army*	1703
HUGHES, John Arthur, *U.S. Marine Corps*	2410
HUGHES, Lloyd Herbert, *U.S. Army Air Corps*	2769
HUGHES, Oliver, *U.S. Army*	651
HUGHEY, John P., *U.S. Army*	652
HUIDEKOPER, Henry Shippen, *U.S. Army*	653
HULBERT, Henry Lewis, *U.S. Marine Corps*	2184
HULL, James Lott, *U.S. Navy*	2120
HUMPHREY, Charles Frederic, *U.S. Army*	1704
HUNT, Frederick O., *U.S. Army*	1705
HUNT, Louis T., *U.S. Army*	654
HUNT, Martin, *U.S. Marine Corps*	2290
HUNTER, Charles Adams, *U.S. Army*	655
HUNTERSON, John C., *U.S. Army*	656
HUNTSMAN, John A., *U.S. Army*	2220
HUSE, Henry McLaren Pinckney, *U.S. Navy*	2411
HUSKEY, Michael, *U.S. Navy*	657
HUTCHINS, Carlton Barmore, *U.S. Navy*	2589
HUTCHINS, Johnnie David, *U.S. Naval Reserve*	2770
HUTCHINSON, Rufus D., *U.S. Army*	1706
HYATT, Theodore, *U.S. Army*	658
HYDE, Henry J., *U.S. Army*	1707
HYDE, Thomas Worcester, *U.S. Army*	659
HYLAND, John, *U.S. Navy*	660
HYMER, Samuel, *U.S. Army*	661
IAMS, Ross Lindsey, *U.S. Marine Corps*	2440
ILGENFRITZ, Charles Henry, *U.S. Army*	662
IMMELL, Lorenzo Dow, *U.S. Army*	663
INGALLS, George Alan, *U.S. Army*	3253
INGALLS, Lewis J., *U.S. Army*	664
INGMAN Jr., Einar Harold, *U.S. Army*	3078
INGRAM, Jonas Howard, *U.S. Navy*	2412
INGRAM, Osmond Kelly, *U.S. Navy*	2503
INSCHO, Leonidas H., *U.S. Army*	665
IRLAM, Joseph, *U.S. Navy*	666
IRSCH, Francis, *U.S. Army*	667
IRVING, John, *U.S. Navy*	668
IRVING, Thomas, *U.S. Navy*	669
IRWIN, Bernard John Dowling, *U.S. Army*	1708
IRWIN, Nicholas, *U.S. Navy*	670
IRWIN, Patrick, *U.S. Army*	671
ITRICH, Franz Anton, *U.S. Navy*	2121
IZAC, Edouard Victor Michel, *U.S. Navy*	2504
JACHMAN, Isadore Seigfreid, *U.S. Army*	2771
JACKSON, Arthur Junior, *U.S. Marine Corps*	2772
JACKSON, Frederick Randolph, *U.S. Army*	672
JACKSON, James, *U.S. Army*	1709
JACKSON, Joe Madison, *U.S. Air Force*	3254
JACOBS, Jack Howard, *U.S. Army*	3255
JACOBSON, Douglas Thomas, *U.S. Marine Corps Reserve*	2773
JACOBSON, Eugene Philip, *U.S. Army*	673
JAMES, Isaac, *U.S. Army*	674
JAMES, John, *U.S. Army*	1710
JAMES, John H., *U.S. Navy*	675
JAMES, Miles, *U.S. Army*	676
JAMIESON, Walter, *U.S. Army*	677
JARDINE, Alexander, *U.S. Navy*	2012
JARDINE, James, *U.S. Army*	678
JARRETT, Berrie Henry, *U.S. Navy*	2413
JARVIS, Frederick, *U.S. Army*	1711
JECELIN, William R., *U.S. Army*	3079
JELLISON, Benjamin H., *U.S. Army*	679
JENKINS, Don, *U.S. Army*	3256
JENKINS Jr., Robert Henry, *U.S. Marine Corps*	3257
JENKINS, Thomas, *U.S. Navy*	680
JENNINGS, Delbert Owen, *U.S. Army*	3258
JENNINGS, James T., *U.S. Army*	681
JENSEN, Gotfred, *U.S. Army*	2221
JERSTAD, John Louis, *U.S. Army Air Corps*	2774
JETTER, Bernhard, *U.S. Army*	1712
JEWETT, Erastus W., *U.S. Army*	682
JIM, *U.S. Army*	1713
JIMENEZ, Jose Francisco, *U.S. Marine Corps*	3259
JOEL, Lawrence, *U.S. Army*	3260
JOHANNESSEN, Johannes J., *U.S. Navy*	2350
JOHANSON, John Peter, *U.S. Navy*	2122
JOHANSSON, Johan J., *U.S. Navy*	2123
JOHN, William F., *U.S. Army*	683

JOHNDRO, Franklin, *U.S. Army*	684	KARNES, James Ernest, *U.S. Army*	2506
JOHNS, Elisha, *U.S. Army*	685	KAROPCZYC, Stephen Edward, *U.S. Army*	3265
JOHNS, Henry T., *U.S. Army*	686	KARPELES, Leopold, *U.S. Army*	715
JOHNSEN, Hans, *U.S. Navy*	2124	KATES, Thomas Wilbur, *U.S. Marine Corps*	2291
JOHNSON, Andrew, *U.S. Army*	687	KATZ, Phillip Carl, *U.S. Army*	2507
JOHNSON, Dwight Hal, *U.S. Army*	3261	KAUFMAN, Benjamin, *U.S. Army*	2508
JOHNSON, Elden Harvey, *U.S. Army*	2775	KAUFMAN, Loren R., *U.S. Army*	3083
JOHNSON, Follett, *U.S. Army*	688	KAUSS, August, *U.S. Army*	716
JOHNSON, Henry, *U.S. Army*	1714	KAWAMURA, Terry Teruo, *U.S. Army*	3266
JOHNSON, Henry, *U.S. Navy*	689	KAY, John, *U.S. Army*	1718
JOHNSON, James Edmund, *U.S. Marine Corps*	3080	KAYS, Kenneth Michael, *U.S. Army*	3267
JOHNSON, John, *U.S. Army*	690	KEARBY, Neel Ernest, *U.S. Army Air Corps*	2784
JOHNSON, John, *U.S. Navy*	2013	KEARNEY, Michael, *U.S. Marine Corps*	2126
JOHNSON, Joseph Esrey, *U.S. Army*	691	KEATHLEY, George D., *U.S. Army*	2785
JOHNSON, Leon William, *U.S. Army Air Corps/U.S. Air Force*	2776	KEATING, Daniel, *U.S. Army*	1719
JOHNSON, Leroy, *U.S. Army*	2777	KEDENBURG, John James, *U.S. Army*	3268
JOHNSON Jr., Oscar Godfrey, *U.S. Army*	2778	KEEFER, Philip Bogan, *U.S. Navy*	2127
JOHNSON, Peter, *U.S. Navy*	2125	KEELE, Joseph, *U.S. Army*	717
JOHNSON, Ralph Henry, *U.S. Marine Corps*	3262	KEEN, Joseph S., *U.S. Army*	718
JOHNSON, Ruel M., *U.S. Army*	692	KEENAN, Bartholomew T., *U.S. Army*	1720
JOHNSON, Samuel, *U.S. Army*	693	KEENAN, John, *U.S. Army*	1721
JOHNSON, Wallace W., *U.S. Army*	694	KEENE, Joseph, *U.S. Army*	719
JOHNSON, William, *U.S. Navy*	2014	KEFURT, Gus, *U.S. Army*	2786
JOHNSTON, David H., *U.S. Army*	695	KEITH, Miguel, *U.S. Marine Corps*	3269
JOHNSTON, Donald Ray, *U.S. Army*	3263	KELLER, Leonard Bert, *U.S. Army*	3270
JOHNSTON, Edward, *U.S. Army*	1715	KELLER, William G., *U.S. Army*	2128
JOHNSTON, Gordon, *U.S. Army*	2222	KELLEY, Andrew John, *U.S. Army*	720
JOHNSTON, Harold Irving, *U.S. Army*	2505	KELLEY, Charles, *U.S. Army*	1722
JOHNSTON Jr., Rufus Zenas, *U.S. Navy*	2414	KELLEY, George V., *U.S. Army*	721
JOHNSTON, William (Willie), *U.S. Army*	697	KELLEY, John, *U.S. Navy*	722
JOHNSTON, William P., *U.S. Navy*	696	KELLEY, Jonah Edward High, *U.S. Army*	2787
JOHNSTON Sr., William James, *U.S. Army*	2779	KELLEY, Leverett Mansfield, *U.S. Army*	723
JONES, Andrew, *U.S. Navy*	698	KELLEY, Ova Art, *U.S. Army*	2788
JONES, Claud Ashton, *U.S. Navy*	2445	KELLEY, Thomas Gunning, *U.S. Navy*	3271
JONES, David, *U.S. Army*	699	KELLOGG Jr., Allan Jay, *U.S. Marine Corps*	3272
JONES, Herbert Charpoit, *U.S. Naval Reserve*	2780	KELLY, Alexander, *U.S. Army*	724
JONES, John, *U.S. Navy*	700	KELLY, Charles E., *U.S. Army*	2789
JONES, John E., *U.S. Navy*	701	KELLY, Daniel, *U.S. Army*	725
JONES, Thomas, *U.S. Navy*	702	KELLY, Francis, *U.S. Navy*	2129
JONES, William, *U.S. Army*	704	KELLY, John D., *U.S. Army*	2790
JONES, William, *U.S. Navy*	703	KELLY, John Doran, *U.S. Marine Corps*	3084
JONES, William H., *U.S. Army*	1716	KELLY, John J. H., *U.S. Army*	1723
JONES III, William Atkinson, *U.S. Air Force*	3264	KELLY, John Joseph, *U.S. Marine Corps*	2509
JORDAN, Absalom, *U.S. Army*	705	KELLY, Thomas, *U.S. Army (Civil War)*	726
JORDAN, George, *U.S. Army*	1717	KELLY, Thomas, *U.S. Army (Indian Campaigns)*	1724
JORDAN, Robert, *U.S. Navy*	706	KELLY, Thomas, *U.S. Army (Sp.-Am. War)*	2130
JORDAN, Thomas H., *U.S. Navy*	707	KELLY, Thomas Joseph, *U.S. Army*	2791
JORDON, Mack A., *U.S. Army*	3081	KELSAY, *U.S. Army*	1725
JOSSELYN, Simeon T., *U.S. Army*	708	KELSO, Jack William, *U.S. Marine Corps*	3085
JUDGE, Francis W., *U.S. Army*	709	KEMP, Joseph Bell, *U.S. Army*	727
JULIAN, Joseph Rodolph, *U.S. Marine Corps Reserve*	2781	KENDALL, William Wesley, *U.S. Army*	728
KAISER, John, *U.S. Army*	710	KENDRICK, Thomas, *U.S. Navy*	729
KALTENBACH, Luther, *U.S. Army*	711	KENNA, Barnett, *U.S. Navy*	730
KANDLE, Victor Leonard, *U.S. Army*	2782	KENNEDY, John, *U.S. Army*	731
KANE, John, *U.S. Army*	712	KENNEDY, John Thomas, *U.S. Army*	2223
KANE, John Riley, *U.S. Army Air Corps/U.S. Air Force*	2783	KENNEDY, Philip, *U.S. Army*	1726
KANE, Thomas, *U.S. Navy*	713	KENNEMORE, Robert Sidney, *U.S. Marine Corps*	3086
KANELL, Billie Gene, *U.S. Army*	3082	KENYON, Charles W., *U.S. Navy*	732
KAPPESSER, Peter, *U.S. Army*	714	KENYON, John Snyders, *U.S. Army*	733

Name	Page
KENYON, Samuel P., *U.S. Army*	734
KEOUGH, John, *U.S. Army*	735
KEPHART, James, *U.S. Army*	736
KEPPLER, Reinhardt John, *U.S. Navy*	2792
KERR, John Brown, *U.S. Army*	1727
KERR, Thomas R., *U.S. Army*	737
KERREY, Joseph Robert, *U.S. Naval Reserve*	3273
KERRIGAN, Thomas, *U.S. Army*	1728
KERSEY, Thomas Joseph, *U.S. Navy*	2015
KERSTETTER, Dexter James, *U.S. Army*	2793
KESSLER, Patrick L., *U.S. Army*	2794
KIDD, Isaac Campbell, *U.S. Navy*	2795
KIGGINS, John, *U.S. Army*	738
KILBOURNE Jr., Charles Evans, *U.S. Army*	2224
KILLACKEY, Joseph, *U.S. Navy*	2292
KILMARTIN, John, *U.S. Army*	1729
KILMER, John Edward, *U.S. Navy*	3087
KIMBALL, Joseph, *U.S. Army*	739
KIMBRO, Truman, *U.S. Army*	2796
KINDIG, John M., *U.S. Army*	740
KINER, Harold G., *U.S. Army*	2797
KING, Horatio Collins, *U.S. Army*	741
KING, Hugh, *U.S. Navy*	2016
KING, John, *U.S. Navy*	2351
KING, Robert Henry, *U.S. Navy*	742
KING Jr., Rufus, *U.S. Army*	743
KINGSLEY, David Richard, *U.S. Army Air Corps*	2798
KINNAIRD, Samuel W., *U.S. Navy*	744
KINNE, John Baxter, *U.S. Army*	2225
KINSER, Elbert Luther, *U.S. Marine Corps Reserve*	2799
KINSEY, John, *U.S. Army*	745
KINSMAN, Thomas James, *U.S. Army*	3274
KIRBY, Dennis Thomas, *U.S. Army*	746
KIRK, John, *U.S. Army*	1730
KIRK, Jonathan C., *U.S. Army*	747
KIRKWOOD, John A., *U.S. Army*	1731
KISTERS, Gerry Herman, *U.S. Army*	2800
KITCHEN, George Krause, *U.S. Army*	1732
KLEIN, Robert, *U.S. Navy*	2352
KLINE, Harry, *U.S. Army*	748
KLOTH, Charles H., *U.S. Army*	749
KNAAK, Albert, *U.S. Army*	1733
KNAPPENBERGER, Alton W., *U.S. Army*	2801
KNIGHT, Charles H., *U.S. Army*	750
KNIGHT, Jack Llewellyn, *U.S. Army*	2802
KNIGHT, Joseph F., *U.S. Army*	1734
KNIGHT, Noah Odell, *U.S. Army*	3088
KNIGHT, Raymond Larry, *U.S. Army Air Corps*	2803
KNIGHT, William J., *U.S. Army*	751
KNOWLES, Abiather J., *U.S. Army*	752
KNOX, Edward M., *U.S. Army*	753
KNOX, John W., *U.S. Army*	1735
KOCAK, Matej, *U.S. Marine Corps*	2510
KOELPIN, William, *U.S. Army*	1736
KOELSCH, John Kelvin, *U.S. Navy*	3089
KOOGLE, Jacob, *U.S. Army*	754
KOSOHA, *U.S. Army*	1737
KOUMA, Ernest Richard, *U.S. Army*	3090
KOUNTZ, John S., *U.S. Army*	755
KRAMER, Franz, *U.S. Navy*	2131
KRAMER, Theodore L., *U.S. Army*	756
KRAUS, Richard Edward, *U.S. Marine Corps Reserve*	2804
KRAUSE, Ernest, *U.S. Navy*	2132
KREHER, Wendelin, *U.S. Army*	1738
KRETSINGER, George, *U.S. Army*	757
KROTIAK, Anton L., *U.S. Army*	2805
KRZYZOWSKI, Edward C., *U.S. Army*	3091
KUCHNEISTER, Hermann Wilhelm, *U.S. Marine Corps*	2133
KUDER, Andrew, *U.S. Army*	758
KUDER, Jeremiah, *U.S. Army*	759
KYLE, Darwin K., *U.S. Army*	3092
KYLE, John, *U.S. Army*	1739
KYLE, Patrick J., *U.S. Navy*	2017
LA BELLE, James Dennis, *U.S. Marine Corps Reserve*	2806
LABILL, Joseph S., *U.S. Army*	760
LADD, George, *U.S. Army*	761
LAFFERTY, John, *U.S. Navy*	762
LAFFEY, Bartlett, *U.S. Navy*	763
LAING, William, *U.S. Army*	764
LAKIN, Daniel, *U.S. Navy*	765
LAKIN, Thomas, *U.S. Navy*	2018
LAMBERS, Paul Ronald, *U.S. Army*	3275
LANDIS, James Parker, *U.S. Army*	766
LANE, Morgan D., *U.S. Army*	767
LANFARE, Aaron Steven, *U.S. Army*	768
LANG, George Charles, *U.S. Army*	3276
LANGBEIN, Johann Christoph Julius, *U.S. Army*	769
LANGHORN, Garfield McConnell, *U.S. Army*	3277
LANGHORNE, Cary DeVall, *U.S. Navy*	2415
LANN, John S., *U.S. Navy*	770
LANNON, James Patrick, *U.S. Navy*	2416
LAPOINTE Jr., Joseph Guy, *U.S. Army*	3278
LARIMER, Smith, *U.S. Army*	771
LARKIN, David, *U.S. Army*	1740
LARRABEE, James W., *U.S. Army*	772
LASSEN, Clyde Everett, *U.S. Navy*	3279
LATHAM, John Cridland, *U.S. Army*	2511
LAUFFER, Billy Lane, *U.S. Army*	3280
LAVERTY, John, *U.S. Navy*	2019
LAW, Robert David, *U.S. Army*	3281
LAWLEY Jr., William Robert, *U.S. Army Air Corp/U.S. Air Force*	2807
LAWRENCE, James, *U.S. Army*	1741
LAWS, Robert Earl, *U.S. Army*	2808
LAWSON, Gaines, *U.S. Army*	773
LAWSON, John, *U.S. Navy*	774
LAWTON, Henry Ware, *U.S. Army*	775
LAWTON, John Sterling, *U.S. Army*	1742
LAWTON, Louis Bowem, *U.S. Army*	2293
LEAHY, Cornelius J., *U.S. Army*	2226
LEAR, Nicholas, *U.S. Navy*	776
LEE, Fitz, *U.S. Army*	2134
LEE, Howard Vincent, *U.S. Marine Corps*	3282
LEE, Hubert Louis, *U.S. Army*	3093
LEE, James H., *U.S. Navy*	777
LEE, Milton Arthur, *U.S. Army*	3283
LEE Sr., Daniel Warnel, *U.S. Army*	2809
LEIMS, John Harold, *U.S. Marine Corps Reserve*	2810
LEISY, Robert Ronald, *U.S. Army*	3284

Name	Page
LEJEUNE, Emile, *U.S. Navy*	2020
LELAND, George W., *U.S. Navy*	778
LEMERT, Milo, *U.S. Army*	2512
LEMON, Peter Charles, *U.S. Army*	3285
LENIHAN, James, *U.S. Army*	1743
LEON, Pierre, *U.S. Navy*	779
LEONARD, Edwin, *U.S. Army*	780
LEONARD, Joseph H., *U.S. Marine Corps*	2227
LEONARD, Matthew, *U.S. Army*	3286
LEONARD, Patrick James, *U.S. Army*	1744
LEONARD, Patrick Thomas, *U.S. Army*	1745
LEONARD, Turney White, *U.S. Army*	2811
LEONARD, William, *U.S. Army*	1746
LEONARD, William Edman, *U.S. Army*	781
LESLIE, Frank, *U.S. Army*	782
LESTER, Fred Faulkner, *U.S. Navy*	2812
LEVERY, William, *U.S. Navy*	2135
LEVITOW, John Lee, *U.S. Air Force*	3287
LEVY, Benjamin Bennett, *U.S. Army*	783
LEWIS, Dewitt Clinton, *U.S. Army*	784
LEWIS, Henry, *U.S. Army*	785
LEWIS, Samuel E., *U.S. Army*	786
LEWIS, William B., *U.S. Army*	1747
LIBAIRE, Adolph, *U.S. Army*	787
LIBBY, George Dalton, *U.S. Army*	3094
LILLEY, John, *U.S. Army*	788
LINDBERGH Jr., Charles Augustus, *U.S. Army Air Corp Reserve*	2590
LINDSEY, Darrell Robins, *U.S. Army Air Corps*	2813
LINDSEY Sr., Jake William, *U.S. Army*	2814
LINDSTROM, Floyd K., *U.S. Army*	2815
LIPSCOMB, Harry, *U.S. Navy*	2353
LITEKY, Charles James (Angelo), *U.S. Army*	3288
LITTLE, Henry F. W., *U.S. Army*	789
LITTLE, Thomas, *U.S. Army*	1748
LITTLEFIELD, George H., *U.S. Army*	790
LITTLETON, Herbert A., *U.S. Marine Corps Reserve*	3095
LITTRELL, Gary Lee, *U.S. Army*	3289
LIVINGSTON, James Evertte, *U.S. Marine Corps*	3290
LIVINGSTON, Josiah O., *U.S. Army*	791
LLOYD, Benjamin, *U.S. Navy*	792
LLOYD, Edgar Harold, *U.S. Army*	2816
LLOYD, George, *U.S. Army*	1749
LLOYD, John W., *U.S. Navy*	793
LOBAUGH, Donald Ronald, *U.S. Army*	2817
LOCKE, Lewis, *U.S. Army*	794
LOGAN, Hugh, *U.S. Navy*	795
LOGAN, James Marion, *U.S. Army*	2818
LOGAN Jr., John Alexander, *U.S. Army*	2228
LOHNES, Frank W., *U.S. Army*	1750
LOMAN, Berger Holton, *U.S. Army*	2513
LONERGAN, John, *U.S. Army*	796
LONG, Charles Richard, *U.S. Army*	3096
LONG, Donald Russell, *U.S. Army*	3291
LONG, Oscar Fitzalan, *U.S. Army*	1751
LONGFELLOW, Richard Moses, *U.S. Army*	2229
LONGSHORE, William H., *U.S. Army*	797
LONSWAY, Joseph, *U.S. Army*	798
LOPEZ, Baldomero, *U.S. Marine Corps*	3097
LOPEZ, Jose Mendoza, *U.S. Army*	2819
LORD, William, *U.S. Army*	799
LORING Jr., Charles Joseph, *U.S. Air Force*	3098
LORISH, Andrew J., *U.S. Army*	800
LOVE, George Maltby, *U.S. Army*	801
LOVERING, George Mason, *U.S. Army*	802
LOW, George, *U.S. Navy*	2021
LOWER, Cyrus B., *U.S. Army*	803
LOWER, Robert A., *U.S. Army*	804
LOWRY, George Maus, *U.S. Navy*	2417
LOWTHERS, James, *U.S. Army*	1752
LOYD, George A., *U.S. Army*	805
LOZADA, Carlos James, *U.S. Army*	3292
LUCAS, Andre Cavaro, *U.S. Army*	3293
LUCAS, George Washington, *U.S. Army*	806
LUCAS, Jacklyn Harold, *U.S. Marine Corps Reserve*	2820
LUCE, Moses Augustine, *U.S. Army*	807
LUCY, John, *U.S. Navy*	2022
LUDGATE, William, *U.S. Army*	808
LUDWIG, Carl, *U.S. Army*	809
LUKE Jr., Frank, *U.S. Army Air Service*	2514
LUKES, William F., *U.S. Navy*	1965
LUMMUS, Jack, *U.S. Marine Corps Reserve*	2821
LUNT, Alphonso M., *U.S. Army*	810
LUTES, Franklin W., *U.S. Army*	811
LUTHER, James Hezikiah, *U.S. Army*	812
LUTY, Gotlieb, *U.S. Army*	813
LYELL, William Franklin, *U.S. Army*	3099
LYLE, Alexander Gordon, *U.S. Navy*	2515
LYMAN, Joel H., *U.S. Army*	814
LYNCH, Allan James, *U.S. Army*	3294
LYON, Edward Eugene, *U.S. Army*	2230
LYON, Frederick A., *U.S. Army*	815
LYONS, Thomas G., *U.S. Navy*	816
LYTLE, Leonidas S., *U.S. Army*	1753
LYTTON, Jeptha L., *U.S. Army*	1754
MABRY Jr., George Lafayette, *U.S. Army*	2822
MacARTHUR Jr., Arthur, *U.S. Army*	817
MacARTHUR, Douglas, *U.S. Army*	2823
MacGILLIVARY, Charles Andrew, *U.S. Army*	2824
MACHOL, *U.S. Army*	1755
MACHON, James, *U.S. Navy*	818
MACK, Alexander, *U.S. Navy*	819
MACK, John, *U.S. Navy*	820
MacKENZIE, John, *U.S. Navy*	2516
MACKIE, John Freeman, *U.S. Marine Corps*	821
MACLAY, William Palmer, *U.S. Army*	2231
MacNEAL, Harry Lewis, *U.S. Marine Corps*	2136
MADDEN, Michael, *U.S. Army*	822
MADDEN, William, *U.S. Navy*	823
MADDIN, Edward, *U.S. Navy*	2023
MADISON, James, *U.S. Army*	824
MADISON, James Jonas, *U.S. Naval Reserve Force*	2517
MAGEE, John W., *U.S. Navy*	2024
MAGEE, William, *U.S. Army*	825
MAGER, George Frederick, *U.S. Navy*	2137
MAGRATH, John D., *U.S. Army*	2825
MAHERS, Herbert, *U.S. Army*	1756
MAHONEY, George, *U.S. Navy*	2138
MAHONEY, Gregory, *U.S. Army*	1757

MAHONEY, Jeremiah, *U.S. Army*	826	McCALL, Thomas Edward, *U.S. Army*	2835
MALLON, George H., *U.S. Army*	2518	McCAMMON, William Wallace, *U.S. Army*	854
MANDY, Harry J., *U.S. Army*	827	McCAMPBELL, David, *U.S. Navy*	2836
MANGAM, Richard Christopher, *U.S. Army*	828	McCANDLESS, Bruce, *U.S. Navy*	2837
MANN, Joe Eugene, *U.S. Army*	2826	McCANN, Bernard, *U.S. Army*	1766
MANNING, Henry J., *U.S. Navy*	2025	McCARD, Robert Howard, *U.S. Marine Corps*	2838
MANNING, Joseph S., *U.S. Army*	829	McCARREN, Bernard, *U.S. Army*	855
MANNING, Sidney E., *U.S. Army*	2519	McCARTER, Lloyd G., *U.S. Army*	2839
MARLAND, William, *U.S. Army*	830	McCARTHY, Joseph Jeremiah, *U.S. Marine Corps Reserve*	2840
MARM Jr., Walter Joseph, *U.S. Army*	3295	McCARTHY, Michael, *U.S. Army*	1767
MARQUETTE, Charles D., *U.S. Army*	831	McCARTON, John, *U.S. Navy*	2027
MARSH, Albert, *U.S. Army*	832	McCAUSLIN, Joseph, *U.S. Army*	856
MARSH, Charles H., *U.S. Army*	833	McCLEARY, Charles H., *U.S. Army*	857
MARSH, George, *U.S. Army*	834	McCLEERY, Finnis Dawson, *U.S. Army*	3298
MARTIN, Edward S., *U.S. Navy*	835	McCLELLAND, James M., *U.S. Army*	858
MARTIN, Harry Linn, *U.S. Marine Corps Reserve*	2827	McCLELLAND, Matthew, *U.S. Navy*	859
MARTIN, James, *U.S. Marine Corps*	836	McCLERNAND, Edward John, *U.S. Army*	1768
MARTIN, Patrick, *U.S. Army*	1758	McCLOY, John, *U.S. Navy*	2296, 2418
MARTIN, Sylvester Hopkins, *U.S. Army*	837	McCONNELL, James, *U.S. Army*	2233
MARTIN, William, *U.S. Navy*	838	McCONNELL, Samuel, *U.S. Army*	860
MARTIN, William, *U.S. Navy*	839	McCOOL Jr., Richard Miles, *U.S. Navy*	2841
MARTINEZ, Benito, *U.S. Army*	3100	McCORMICK, Michael, *U.S. Navy*	861
MARTINEZ, Joe P., *U.S. Army*	2828	McCORMICK, Michael P., *U.S. Army*	1769
MARTINI, Gary Wayne, *U.S. Marine Corps*	3296	McCORNACK, Andrew, *U.S. Army*	862
MASON, Elihu H., *U.S. Army*	840	McCULLOCK, Adam, *U.S. Navy*	863
MASON, Leonard Foster, *U.S. Marine Corps*	2829	McDONALD, Franklin M., *U.S. Army*	1770
MATHEWS, George William, *U.S. Army*	2232	McDONALD, George E., *U.S. Army*	864
MATHEWS, William Henry, *U.S. Army*	841	McDONALD, James, *U.S. Army*	1771
MATHIAS, Clarence Edward, *U.S. Marine Corps*	2294	McDONALD, James Harper, *U.S. Navy*	2591
MATHIES, Archibald, *U.S. Army Air Corps*	2830	McDONALD, John, *U.S. Navy*	865
MATHIS, Jack Warren, *U.S. Army Air Corps*	2831	McDONALD, John Wade, *U.S. Army*	866
MATTHEWS, Daniel Paul, *U.S. Marine Corps*	3101	McDONALD, Phill Gene, *U.S. Army*	3299
MATTHEWS, David A., *U.S. Army*	1759	McDONALD, Robert, *U.S. Army*	1772
MATTHEWS, John C., *U.S. Army*	842	McDONNELL, Edward Orrick, *U.S. Navy*	2419
MATTHEWS, Joseph, *U.S. Navy*	2026	McELHINNY, Samuel O., *U.S. Army*	867
MATTHEWS, Milton, *U.S. Army*	843	McENROE, Patrick H., *U.S. Army*	868
MATTINGLY, Henry B., *U.S. Army*	844	McFALL, Daniel Robert, *U.S. Army*	869
MATTOCKS, Charles Porter, *U.S. Army*	845	McFARLAND, John C., *U.S. Navy*	870
MAUS, Marion Perry, *U.S. Army*	1760	McGAHA, Charles L., *U.S. Army*	2842
MAUSERT III, Frederick William, *U.S. Marine Corps*	3102	McGANN, Michael A., *U.S. Army*	1773
MAXAM, Larry Leonard, *U.S. Marine Corps*	3297	McGAR, Owen, *U.S. Army*	1774
MAXHAM, Lowell Mason, *U.S. Army*	846	McGARITY, Vernon, *U.S. Army*	2843
MAXWELL, John, *U.S. Navy*	2139	McGEE, William D., *U.S. Army*	2844
MAXWELL, Robert Dale, *U.S. Army*	2832	McGILL, Troy A., *U.S. Army*	2845
MAY, John, *U.S. Army*	1761	McGINN, Edward, *U.S. Army*	871
MAY, Martin O., *U.S. Army*	2833	McGINTY III, John James, *U.S. Marine Corps*	3300
MAY, William C., *U.S. Army*	847	McGONAGLE, William Loren, *U.S. Navy*	3301
MAYBERRY, John B., *U.S. Army*	848	McGONAGLE, Wilson, *U.S. Army*	872
MAYES, William B., *U.S. Army*	849	McGONNIGLE, Andrew Jackson, *U.S. Army*	873
MAYFIELD, Melvin, *U.S. Army*	2834	McGOUGH, Owen, *U.S. Army*	874
MAYNARD, George Henry, *U.S. Army*	850	McGOVERN, Robert Milton, *U.S. Army*	3103
MAYS, Isaiah, *U.S. Army*	1762	McGOWAN, John, *U.S. Navy*	875
McADAMS, Peter, *U.S. Army*	851	McGRATH, Hugh Jocelyn, *U.S. Army*	2234
McALLISTER, Samuel, *U.S. Navy*	2295	McGRAW, Francis Xavier, *U.S. Army*	2846
McALWEE, Benjamin Franklin, *U.S. Army*	852	McGRAW, Thomas, *U.S. Army*	876
McANALLY, Charles, *U.S. Army*	853	McGUIRE, Fred Henry, *U.S. Navy*	2378
McBRIDE, Bernard, *U.S. Army*	1763	McGUIRE, Patrick, *U.S. Army*	877
McBRYAR, William, *U.S. Army*	1764	McGUIRE Jr., Thomas Buchanan, *U.S. Army Air Corps*	2847
McCABE, William, *U.S. Army*	1765	McGUNIGAL, Patrick, *U.S. Navy*	2520

Name	Page
McHALE, Alexander U., *U.S. Army*	878
McHUGH, John, *U.S. Army*	1775
McHUGH, Martin, *U.S. Navy*	879
McINTOSH, James, *U.S. Navy*	880
McKAY, Charles W., *U.S. Army*	881
McKEE, George, *U.S. Army*	882
McKEEN, Nineveh S., *U.S. Army*	883
McKEEVER, Michael, *U.S. Army*	884
McKENZIE, Alexander, *U.S. Navy*	1966
McKIBBEN, Ray, *U.S. Army*	3302
McKINLEY, Daniel, *U.S. Army*	1776
McKINNEY, John R., *U.S. Army*	2848
McKNIGHT, William, *U.S. Navy*	885
McKOWN, Nathaniel A., *U.S. Army*	886
McLAUGHLIN, Alford Lee, *U.S. Marine Corps*	3104
McLENNON, John, *U.S. Army*	1777
McLEOD, James, *U.S. Navy*	887
McLOUGHLIN, Michael, *U.S. Army*	1778
McMAHON, Martin Thomas, *U.S. Army*	888
McMAHON, Thomas Joseph, *U.S. Army*	3303
McMASTERS, Henry A., *U.S. Army*	1779
McMILLEN, Francis M., *U.S. Army*	889
McMILLIAN, Albert Walter, *U.S. Army*	1780
McMURTRY, George G., *U.S. Army*	2521
McNAIR Jr., Frederick Vallette, *U.S. Navy*	2420
McNALLY, James, *U.S. Army*	1781
McNALLY, Michael Joseph, *U.S. Marine Corps*	2185
McNAMARA, Michael, *U.S. Marine Corps*	1967
McNAMARA, William, *U.S. Army*	1782
McNERNEY, David Herbert, *U.S. Army*	3304
McPHELAN, Robert, *U.S. Army*	1783
McTUREOUS Jr., Robert Miller, *U.S. Marine Corps*	2849
McVEAGH, Charles H., *U.S. Army*	1784
McVEANE, John P., *U.S. Army*	890
McVEIGH, John J., *U.S. Army*	2850
McWETHY Jr., Edgar Lee, *U.S. Army*	3305
McWHORTER, Walter F., *U.S. Army*	891
McWHORTER, William A., *U.S. Army*	2851
McWILLIAMS, George Washington, *U.S. Navy*	892
MEACH, George E., *U.S. Army*	893
MEAGHER, John William, *U.S. Army*	2852
MEAGHER, Thomas, *U.S. Army*	894
MEAHER, Nicholas, *U.S. Army*	1785
MEARS, George W., *U.S. Army*	895
MECHLIN, Henry W.B., *U.S. Army*	1786
MELVILLE, Charles, *U.S. Navy*	896
MENDONCA, Leroy A., *U.S. Army*	3105
MENTER, John William, *U.S. Army*	897
MEREDITH, James, *U.S. Marine Corps*	2140
MERLI, Gino Joseph, *U.S. Army*	2853
MERRELL, Joseph Frederick, *U.S. Army*	2854
MERRIAM, Henry Clay, *U.S. Army*	898
MERRIFIELD, James K., *U.S. Army*	899
MERRILL, Augustus, *U.S. Army*	900
MERRILL, George, *U.S. Army*	901
MERRILL, John Mitchell, *U.S. Army*	1787
MERRITT, John G., *U.S. Army*	902
MERTON, James F., *U.S. Navy*	1968
MESSERSCHMIDT, Harold O., *U.S. Army*	2855
MESTROVITCH, James I., *U.S. Army*	2522
METZGER Jr., William Edward, *U.S. Army Air Corps*	2856
MEYER, Henry Coddington, *U.S. Army*	903
MEYER, William, *U.S. Navy*	2141
MICHAEL, Don Leslie, *U.S. Army*	3306
MICHAEL, Edward Stanley, *U.S. Army Air Corps/U.S. Air Force*	2857
MICHAEL, Harry J., *U.S. Army*	2858
MIFFLIN, James, *U.S. Navy*	904
MIHALOWSKI, John, *U.S. Navy*	2592
MILES, Louis Wardlaw, *U.S. Army*	2523
MILES, Nelson Appleton, *U.S. Army*	905
MILLER, Andrew, *U.S. Army*	2859
MILLER, Andrew, *U.S. Marine Corps*	906
MILLER, Archie, *U.S. Army*	2235
MILLER, Daniel H., *U.S. Army*	1788
MILLER, Frank, *U.S. Army*	907
MILLER, Franklin Douglas, *U.S. Army*	3307
MILLER, Gary Lee, *U.S. Army*	3308
MILLER, George, *U.S. Army*	1789
MILLER, George W., *U.S. Army*	1790
MILLER, Harry Herbert, *U.S. Navy*	2142
MILLER, Henry August, *U.S. Army*	908
MILLER, Hugh, *U.S. Navy*	2028
MILLER, Jacob C., *U.S. Army*	909
MILLER, James, *U.S. Navy*	910
MILLER, James P., *U.S. Army*	911
MILLER, John, *U.S. Army*	912
MILLER, John G., *U.S. Army*	913
MILLER, Oscar F., *U.S. Army*	2524
MILLER, Willard D., *U.S. Navy*	2143
MILLER, William Edward, *U.S. Army*	914
MILLETT, Lewis Lee "Red", *U.S. Army*	3106
MILLIKEN, Daniel, *U.S. Navy*	915
MILLMORE, John, *U.S. Navy*	2029
MILLS, Albert Leopold, *U.S. Army*	2144
MILLS, Charles, *U.S. Navy*	916
MILLS, Frank W., *U.S. Army*	917
MILLS, James Henry, *U.S. Army*	2860
MINDIL, George Washington, *U.S. Army*	918
MINICK, John W., *U.S. Army*	2861
MINUE, Nicholas, *U.S. Army*	2862
MITCHELL, Alexander H., *U.S. Army*	919
MITCHELL, Frank Nicias, *U.S. Marine Corps*	3107
MITCHELL, John, *U.S. Army*	1791
MITCHELL, John James, *U.S. Army*	1792
MITCHELL, Joseph Andrew, *U.S. Navy*	2297
MITCHELL, Theodore, *U.S. Army*	920
MITCHELL, Thomas, *U.S. Navy*	2030
MIYAMURA, Hiroshi, *U.S. Army*	3108
MIZE, Ola Lee, *U.S. Army*	3109
MODRZEJEWSKI, Robert Joseph, *U.S. Marine Corps*	3309
MOFFETT, William Adger, *U.S. Navy*	2421
MOFFITT, John Henry, *U.S. Army*	921
MOLBONE, Archibald, *U.S. Army*	922
MOLLOY, Hugh, *U.S. Navy*	923
MOLNAR, Frankie Zoly, *U.S. Army*	3310
MONAGHAN, Patrick H., *U.S. Army*	924
MONEGAN Jr., Walter Carleton, *U.S. Marine Corps*	3110
MONROE, James Howard, *U.S. Army*	3311

MONSSEN, Mons, *U.S. Navy*	2354	MUNSELL, Harvey May, *U.S. Army*	949
MONTAGUE, Daniel, *U.S. Navy*	2145	MURPHY, Audie Leon, *U.S. Army*	2872
MONTEITH Jr., Jimmie W., *U.S. Army*	2863	MURPHY, Charles Joseph, *U.S. Army*	950
MONTGOMERY, Jack Cleveland, *U.S. Army*	2864	MURPHY, Daniel J., *U.S. Army*	951
MONTGOMERY, Robert William, *U.S. Navy*	925	MURPHY, Dennis J. F., *U.S. Army*	952
MONTROSE, Charles H., *U.S. Army*	1793	MURPHY, Edward, *U.S. Army*	1802
MOON Jr., Harold Herman, *U.S. Army*	2865	MURPHY, Edward F., *U.S. Army*	1803
MOORE, Albert, *U.S. Marine Corps*	2298	MURPHY, Frederick C., *U.S. Army*	2873
MOORE, Charles, *U.S. Navy*	926	MURPHY, James T., *U.S. Army*	953
MOORE, Charles, *U.S. Navy*	927	MURPHY, Jeremiah J., *U.S. Army*	1804
MOORE, Daniel B., *U.S. Army*	928	MURPHY, John Alphonsus, *U.S. Marine Corps*	2299
MOORE, Francis, *U.S. Navy*	2031	MURPHY, John Edward, *U.S. Navy*	2148
MOORE, George, *U.S. Navy*	929	MURPHY, John P., *U.S. Army*	954
MOORE, George G., *U.S. Army*	930	MURPHY, Michael C., *U.S. Army*	955
MOORE, Philip, *U.S. Navy*	2032	MURPHY, Patrick, *U.S. Navy*	956
MOORE, Wilbur F., *U.S. Army*	931	MURPHY, Philip, *U.S. Army*	1805
MOORE, William, *U.S. Navy*	932	MURPHY, Raymond Gerald, *U.S. Marine Corps*	3113
MOQUIN, George, *U.S. Army*	1794	MURPHY, Robinson Barr, *U.S. Army*	957
MORAN, John, *U.S. Army*	1795	MURPHY, Thomas, *U.S. Army*	958
MORAN, John E., *U.S. Army*	2236	MURPHY, Thomas, *U.S. Army*	1806
MORELAND, Whitt Lloyd, *U.S. Marine Corps*	3111	MURPHY, Thomas C., *U.S. Army*	959
MORELOCK, Sterling Lewis, *U.S. Army*	2525	MURPHY, Thomas J., *U.S. Army*	960
MOREY, Delano, *U.S. Army*	933	MURRAY Jr., Charles Patrick "Chuck", *U.S. Army*	2874
MORFORD, Jerome, *U.S. Army*	934	MURRAY, Robert Charles, *U.S. Army*	3314
MORGAN, George Horace, *U.S. Army*	1796	MURRAY, Thomas, *U.S. Army*	1807
MORGAN, James H., *U.S. Navy*	935	MURRAY, William Henry, *U.S. Marine Corps*	2300
MORGAN, John Cary "Red", *U.S. Army Air Corps/U.S. Air Force*	2866	MYERS, Fred, *U.S. Army*	1808
MORGAN, Lewis, *U.S. Army*	936	MYERS, George S., *U.S. Army*	961
MORGAN, Richard H., *U.S. Army*	937	MYERS, Reginald Rodney, *U.S. Marine Corps*	3114
MORGAN, William David, *U.S. Marine Corps*	3312	MYERS, William H., *U.S. Army*	962
MORIARITY, John, *U.S. Army*	1797	NANNASADDIE, *U.S. Army*	1809
MORIN, William Henry, *U.S. Navy*	2146	NANTAJE (NANTAHE), *U.S. Army*	1810
MORRILL, Walter Goodale, *U.S. Army*	938	NASH, David Paul, *U.S. Army*	3315
MORRIS, Charles Bedford, *U.S. Army*	3313	NASH, Henry H., *U.S. Army*	963
MORRIS, James L., *U.S. Army*	1798	NASH, James J., *U.S. Army*	2149
MORRIS, John, *U.S. Marine Corps*	2033	NAYLOR, David Johnson, *U.S. Navy*	964
MORRIS, William Powers, *U.S. Army*	939	NEAHR, Zachariah C., *U.S. Army*	965
MORRIS, William W., *U.S. Army*	1799	NEAL, Solon D., *U.S. Army*	1811
MORRISON, Francis, *U.S. Army*	940	NEDER, Adam, *U.S. Army*	1812
MORRISON, John G., *U.S. Navy*	941	NEE, George Henry, *U.S. Army*	2150
MORSE, Benjamin, *U.S. Army*	942	NEIBAUR, Thomas Croft, *U.S. Army*	2526
MORSE, Charles E., *U.S. Army*	943	NEIL, John, *U.S. Navy*	966
MORSE, William, *U.S. Navy*	2034	NEILON, Frederick S., *U.S. Army*	1813
MORTON, Charles W., *U.S. Navy*	944	NELSON, Lauritz, *U.S. Navy*	2151
MOSHER, Louis C., *U.S. Army*	2237	NELSON, Oscar Frederick, *U.S. Navy*	2356
MOSKALA, Edward J., *U.S. Army*	2867	NELSON, William Lancaster, *U.S. Army*	2875
MOSTOLLER, John William, *U.S. Army*	945	NEPPEL, Ralph George, *U.S. Army*	2876
MOTT, John, *U.S. Army*	1800	NETT, Robert Burton, *U.S. Army*	2877
MOWER, Charles E., *U.S. Army*	2868	NEVILLE, Edwin Michael, *U.S. Army*	967
MOYER, Donald Raymond, *U.S. Army*	3112	NEVILLE, Wendell Cushing, *U.S. Marine Corps*	2422
MOYLAN, Myles, *U.S. Army*	1801	NEW, John Dury, *U.S. Marine Corps*	2878
MULHOLLAND, St. Clair Agustin, *U.S. Army*	946	NEWLAND, William D., *U.S. Navy*	968
MULLEN, Patrick, *U.S. Navy*	947, 1529	NEWLIN, Melvin Earl, *U.S. Marine Corps*	3316
MULLER, Frederick, *U.S. Navy*	2147	NEWMAN, Beryl Richard, *U.S. Army*	2879
MULLER, Joseph E., *U.S. Army*	2869	NEWMAN, Henry, *U.S. Army*	1814
MULLIN, Hugh Patrick, *U.S. Navy*	2355	NEWMAN, Marcellus J., *U.S. Army*	969
MUNDELL, Walter L., *U.S. Army*	948	NEWMAN, William Henry, *U.S. Army*	970
MUNEMORI, Sadao S., *U.S. Army*	2870	NIBBE, John H., *U.S. Navy*	971
MUNRO, Douglas Albert, *U.S. Coast Guard*	2871	NICHOLS, Henry Clay, *U.S. Army*	972

Name	Page
NICHOLS, William, *U.S. Navy*	973
NICKERSON, Henry Nehemiah, *U.S. Navy*	2423
NIHILL, John, *U.S. Army*	1815
NININGER Jr., Alexander Ramsey, *U.S. Army*	2880
NISPEROS, Jose B., *U.S. Army*	2379
NIVEN, Robert, *U.S. Army*	974
NOBLE, Daniel, *U.S. Navy*	975
NOIL, Joseph B., *U.S. Navy*	2035
NOLAN, John J., *U.S. Army*	976
NOLAN, Joseph A., *U.S. Army*	2238
NOLAN, Richard J., *U.S. Army*	1816
NOLL, Conrad, *U.S. Army*	977
NOONAN Jr., Thomas Patrick, *U.S. Marine Corps*	3317
NORDSIEK, Charles Luers, *U.S. Navy*	2424
NORDSTROM, Isador A., *U.S. Navy*	2357
NORRIS, J. W., *U.S. Navy*	2036
NORRIS, Thomas Rolland, *U.S. Navy*	3318
NORTH, Jasper N., *U.S. Army*	978
NORTON, Elliott Malloy, *U.S. Army*	979
NORTON, John R., *U.S. Army*	980
NORTON, Llewellyn Powell, *U.S. Army*	981
NOVOSEL, Michael Joseph, *U.S. Army*	3319
NOYES, William W., *U.S. Army*	982
NUGENT, Christopher, *U.S. Marine Corps*	983
NUTTING, Lee, *U.S. Army*	984
O'BEIRNE, James Rowan, *U.S. Army*	985
O'BRIEN Jr., George Herman, *U.S. Marine Corps Reserve*	3116
O'BRIEN, Henry D., *U.S. Army*	986
O'BRIEN, Oliver Albert, *U.S. Navy*	987
O'BRIEN, Peter, *U.S. Army*	988
O'BRIEN, William Joseph, *U.S. Army*	2881
O'CALLAGHAN, John, *U.S. Army*	1817
O'CALLAHAN, Joseph Timothy, *U.S. Naval Reserve*	2882
O'CONNELL, Thomas, *U.S. Navy*	989
O'CONNER, James Francis, *U.S. Navy*	2037
O'CONNOR, Albert, *U.S. Army*	990
O'CONNOR, Timothy, *U.S. Army*	991
O'DEA, John, *U.S. Army*	992
O'DONNELL, Menomen, *U.S. Army*	993
O'DONOGHUE, Timothy, *U.S. Navy*	994
O'HARE, Edward Henry "Butch", *U.S. Navy*	2884
O'KANE, Richard Hetherington, *U.S. Navy*	2885
O'MALLEY, Robert Emmett, *U.S. Marine Corps*	3322
O'NEAL, John, *U.S. Navy*	2039
O'NEILL, Richard William, *U.S. Army*	2527
O'NEILL, Stephen, *U.S. Army*	997
O'NEILL, William, *U.S. Army*	1819
O'REGAN, Michael, *U.S. Army*	1820
O'SHEA, Thomas E., *U.S. Army*	2530
O'SULLIVAN, John Francis, *U.S. Army*	1823
OAKLEY, William, *U.S. Navy*	2152
OBREGON, Eugene Arnold, *U.S. Marine Corps*	3115
OGDEN Sr., Carlos Carnes, *U.S. Army*	2883
OHMSEN, August, *U.S. Navy*	2038
OLIVE III, Milton Lee, *U.S. Army*	3320
OLIVER, Charles, *U.S. Army*	995
OLIVER, Francis, *U.S. Army*	1818
OLIVER, Paul Ambrose, *U.S. Army*	996
OLSEN, Anton, *U.S. Navy*	2153
OLSON, Arlo L., *U.S. Army*	2886
OLSON, Kenneth Lee, *U.S. Army*	3321
OLSON, Truman O., *U.S. Army*	2887
OPEL, John N., *U.S. Army*	998
ORBANSKY, David, *U.S. Army*	999
ORESKO, Nicholas, *U.S. Army*	2888
ORMSBEE Jr., Francis Edward, *U.S. Navy*	2528
ORNDOFF, Harry Westley, *U.S. Marine Corps*	2301
ORR, Charles Alvin, *U.S. Army*	1000
ORR, Moses, *U.S. Army*	1821
ORR, Robert Levan, *U.S. Army*	1001
ORTEGA, John, *U.S. Navy*	1002
ORTH, Jacob George, *U.S. Army*	1003
OSBORNE, John, *U.S. Navy*	2040
OSBORNE, Weedon E., *U.S. Navy*	2529
OSBORNE, William, *U.S. Army*	1822
OSBORNE, William Henry, *U.S. Army*	1004
OSEPINS, Christian, *U.S. Navy*	2041
OSS, Albert, *U.S. Army*	1005
OSTERMANN, Edward Albert, *U.S. Marine Corps*	2441
OUELLET, David George, *U.S. Navy*	3323
OUELLETTE, Joseph R., *U.S. Army*	3117
OVERTURF, Jacob H., *U.S. Army*	1006
OVIATT, Miles M., *U.S. Marine Corps*	1007
OWENS, Michael, *U.S. Marine Corps*	1969
OWENS, Robert Allen, *U.S. Marine Corps*	2889
OZBOURN, Joseph William, *U.S. Marine Corps*	2890
PACKARD, Loron F., *U.S. Army*	1008
PAGE, John Upshur Dennis, *U.S. Army*	3118
PAIGE, Mitchell, *U.S. Marine Corps*	2891
PAINE, Adam, *U.S. Army*	1824
PALMER, George Henry, *U.S. Army*	1009
PALMER, John Gideon, *U.S. Army*	1010
PALMER, William Jackson, *U.S. Army*	1011
PARKER, Alexander, *U.S. Navy*	2042
PARKER, James, *U.S. Army*	2239
PARKER, Pomeroy, *U.S. Marine Corps*	2154
PARKER, Samuel Iredell, *U.S. Army*	2531
PARKER, Thomas, *U.S. Army*	1012
PARKER, William, *U.S. Navy*	1013
PARKS, George, *U.S. Navy*	1014
PARKS, Henry Jeremiah, *U.S. Army*	1015
PARKS, James W., *U.S. Army*	1016
PARLE, John Joseph, *U.S. Naval Reserve*	2892
PARNELL, William Russell, *U.S. Army*	1825
PARRISH, Laverne, *U.S. Army*	2893
PARROTT, Jacob, *U.S. Army*	1017
PARSONS, Joel, *U.S. Army*	1018
PATTERSON, John Henry, *U.S. Army*	1019
PATTERSON, John T., *U.S. Army*	1020
PATTERSON, Robert Martin, *U.S. Army*	3324
PAUL, Joe Calvin, *U.S. Marine Corps*	3325
PAUL, William H., *U.S. Army*	1021
PAY, Byron E., *U.S. Army*	1022
PAYNE, Irvin C., *U.S. Army*	1023
PAYNE, Isaac, *U.S. Army*	1826
PAYNE, Thomas H. L., *U.S. Army*	1024
PEARSALL, Platt, *U.S. Army*	1025
PEARSON, Alfred L., *U.S. Army*	1026

Name	Page
PEASE Jr., Harl, *U.S. Army Air Corps*	2894
PEASE, Joachim, *U.S. Navy*	1027
PECK, Archie A., *U.S. Army*	2532
PECK, Cassius, *U.S. Army*	1028
PECK, Oscar E., *U.S. Navy*	1029
PECK, Theodore Safford, *U.S. Army*	1030
PEDEN, Forrest E., *U.S. Army*	2895
PEIRSOL, James Kastor, *U.S. Army*	1031
PELHAM, William, *U.S. Navy*	1032
PENDLETON, Charles F., *U.S. Army*	3119
PENDLETON, Jack James, *U.S. Army*	2896
PENGALLY, Edward, *U.S. Army*	1827
PENN, Robert, *U.S. Navy*	2155
PENNSYL, Josiah, *U.S. Army*	1828
PENNYPACKER, Galusha, *U.S. Army*	1033
PENRY, Richard Allen, *U.S. Army*	3326
PENTZER, Patrick Henry, *U.S. Army*	1034
PEREGORY, Frank D., *U.S. Army*	2897
PEREZ Jr., Manuel, *U.S. Army*	2898
PERKINS, Michael J., *U.S. Army*	2533
PERKINS Jr., William Thomas, *U.S. Marine Corps*	3327
PERRY, Thomas, *U.S. Navy*	1035
PESCH, Joseph M., *U.S. Army*	1036
PETERS, Alexander, *U.S. Navy*	2358
PETERS, George J., *U.S. Army*	2899
PETERS, Henry Carlton, *U.S. Army*	1037
PETERS, Lawrence David, *U.S. Marine Corps*	3328
PETERSEN, Carl Emil, *U.S. Navy*	2302
PETERSEN, Danny John, *U.S. Army*	3329
PETERSON, Alfred, *U.S. Navy*	1038
PETERSON, George, *U.S. Army*	2900
PETERSON, Oscar Verner, *U.S. Navy*	2901
PETRARCA, Frank Joseph, *U.S. Army*	2902
PETTY, Orlando Henderson, *U.S. Naval Reserve Forces*	2534
PETTY, Philip, *U.S. Army*	1039
PFEIFER, Louis Fred, *U.S. Marine Corps*	2359
PFISTERER, Herman, *U.S. Army*	2156
PHARRIS, Jackson Charles, *U.S. Navy*	2903
PHELPS, Charles Edwards, *U.S. Army*	1040
PHELPS, Wesley, *U.S. Marine Corps Reserve*	2904
PHIFE, Lewis, *U.S. Army*	1829
PHILIPSEN, Wilhelm O., *U.S. Army*	1830
PHILLIPS, George, *U.S. Marine Corps Reserve*	2905
PHILLIPS, George Frederick, *U.S. Navy*	2157
PHILLIPS, Josiah, *U.S. Army*	1041
PHILLIPS, Lee Hugh, *U.S. Marine Corps*	3120
PHILLIPS, Reuben Jasper, *U.S. Marine Corps*	2303
PHILLIPS, Samuel D., *U.S. Army*	1831
PHINNEY, William, *U.S. Navy*	1042
PHIPPS, Jimmy Wayne, *U.S. Marine Corps*	3330
PHISTERER, Frederick, *U.S. Army*	1043
PHOENIX, Edwin, *U.S. Army*	1832
PICKLE, Alonzo H., *U.S. Army*	1044
PIERCE, Charles H., *U.S. Army*	2240
PIERCE, Francis Junior, *U.S. Navy*	2906
PIERCE, Larry Stanley, *U.S. Army*	3331
PIKE, Edward M., *U.S. Army*	1045
PIKE, Emory Jenison, *U.S. Army*	2535
PILE, Richard, *U.S. Navy*	2043
PILILAAU, Herbert K., *U.S. Army*	3121
PINDER Jr., John J., *U.S. Army*	2907
PINGREE, Samuel E., *U.S. Army*	1046
PINKHAM, Charles H., *U.S. Army*	1047
PINN, Robert A., *U.S. Army*	1048
PIPES, James Milton, *U.S. Army*	1049
PITMAN, George J., *U.S. Army*	1050
PITTINGER, William, *U.S. Army*	1051
PITTMAN, John Albert, *U.S. Army*	3122
PITTMAN, Richard Allan, *U.S. Marine Corps*	3332
PITTS, Riley Leroy, *U.S. Army*	3333
PLANT, Henry E., *U.S. Army*	1052
PLATT, George Crawford, *U.S. Army*	1053
PLATTEN, Frederick, *U.S. Army*	1833
PLESS, Stephen Wesley, *U.S. Marine Corps*	3334
PLIMLEY, William, *U.S. Army*	1054
PLOWMAN, George H., *U.S. Army*	1055
PLUNKETT, Thomas, *U.S. Army*	1056
POLOND, Alfred, *U.S. Army*	2158
POMEROY, Ralph Eugene, *U.S. Army*	3123
POND, George F., *U.S. Army*	1057
POND, James Burton, *U.S. Army*	1058
POOLE, William B., *U.S. Navy*	1059
POPE, Everett Parker, *U.S. Marine Corps*	2908
POPE, Thomas A., *U.S. Army*	2536
POPPE, John A., *U.S. Army*	1834
PORT, William David, *U.S. Army*	3335
PORTER, Ambrose, *U.S. Army*	1060
PORTER, David Dixon, *U.S. Marine Corps*	2241
PORTER, Donn F., *U.S. Army*	3124
PORTER, Horace, *U.S. Army*	1061
PORTER, John Reed, *U.S. Army*	1062
PORTER, Samuel, *U.S. Army*	1835
PORTER, William, *U.S. Army*	1063
POST, Philip Sidney, *U.S. Army*	1064
POSTLES, James Parke, *U.S. Army*	1065
POTTER, George W., *U.S. Army*	1066
POTTER, Norman F., *U.S. Army*	1067
POWELL, William Henry, *U.S. Army*	1068
POWER, Albert, *U.S. Army*	1069
POWER, John Vincent, *U.S. Marine Corps*	2909
POWERS, John James, *U.S. Navy*	2910
POWERS, Leo J., *U.S. Army*	2911
POWERS, Thomas, *U.S. Army*	1836
POWERS, Wesley James, *U.S. Army*	1070
POXON, Robert Leslie, *U.S. Army*	3336
POYNTER, James Irsley, *U.S. Marine Corps Reserve*	3125
PRANCE, George, *U.S. Navy*	1071
PRATT, James N., *U.S. Army*	1837
PRENDERGAST, Thomas Francis, *U.S. Marine Corps*	2242
PRENTICE, Joseph Rollin, *U.S. Army*	1072
PRESTON, Arthur Murray, *U.S. Naval Reserve*	2912
PRESTON, Herbert Irving, *U.S. Marine Corps*	2304
PRESTON, John, *U.S. Navy*	1073
PRESTON, Noble Delance, *U.S. Army*	1074
PRICE, Edward, *U.S. Navy*	1075
PROM, William Raymond, *U.S. Marine Corps*	3337
PROVINCE, George, *U.S. Navy*	1076
PRUDEN, Robert Joseph, *U.S. Army*	3338

Name	Number
PRUITT, John Henry, *U.S. Marine Corps*	2537
PRUSSMAN, Ernest W., *U.S. Army*	2913
PUCKET, Donald Dale, *U.S. Army Air Corps*	2914
PURCELL, Hiram W., *U.S. Army*	1077
PURMAN, James Jackson, *U.S. Army*	1078
PURVIS, Hugh, *U.S. Marine Corps*	1970
PUTNAM, Edgar Pierpont, *U.S. Army*	1079
PUTNAM, Winthrop D., *U.S. Army*	1080
PYM, James, *U.S. Army*	1838
PYNE, George, *U.S. Navy*	1081
QUAY, Matthew Stanley, *U.S. Army*	1082
QUICK, John Henry, *U.S. Marine Corps*	2159
QUICK, Joseph, *U.S. Navy*	2360
QUINLAN, James, *U.S. Army*	1083
QUINN, Alexander M., *U.S. Army*	2160
QUINN, Peter H., *U.S. Army*	2243
RABEL, Laszlo, *U.S. Army*	3339
RAERICK, John, *U.S. Army*	1839
RAFFERTY, Peter F., *U.S. Army*	1084
RAGNAR, Theodore, *U.S. Army*	1840
RAMAGE, Lawson Paterson "Red", *U.S. Navy*	2915
RAMER, George Henry, *U.S. Marine Corps Reserve*	3126
RAND, Charles Franklin, *U.S. Army*	1085
RANKIN, William, *U.S. Army*	1841
RANNAHAN, John, *U.S. Marine Corps*	1086
RANNEY, George E., *U.S. Army*	1087
RANNEY, Myron H., *U.S. Army*	1088
RANSBOTTOM, Alfred, *U.S. Army*	1089
RATCLIFF, Edward, *U.S. Army*	1090
RAUB, Jacob F., *U.S. Army*	1091
RAY, Bernard James, *U.S. Army*	2916
RAY, Charles W., *U.S. Army*	2244
RAY, David Robert, *U.S. Navy*	3340
RAY, Ronald Eric, *U.S. Army*	3341
RAYMOND, William H., *U.S. Army*	1092
READ, Charles, *U.S. Navy*	1093
READ, Charles A., *U.S. Navy*	1094
READ, George E., *U.S. Navy*	1095
READ, Morton A., *U.S. Army*	1096
REASONER, Frank Stanley, *U.S. Marine Corps*	3342
REBMANN, George F., *U.S. Army*	1097
RED CLOUD Jr., Mitchell, *U.S. Army*	3127
REDDICK, William Henry Harrison, *U.S. Army*	1098
REED, Axel Hayford, *U.S. Army*	1099
REED, Charles Wellington, *U.S. Army*	1100
REED, George W., *U.S. Army*	1101
REED, James C., *U.S. Army*	1842
REED, William, *U.S. Army*	1102
REEDER, Charles A., *U.S. Army*	1103
REEM, Robert Dale, *U.S. Marine Corps*	3128
REESE, James W., *U.S. Army*	2917
REESE Jr., John N., *U.S. Army*	2918
REEVES, Thomas James, *U.S. Navy*	2919
REGAN, Jeremiah, *U.S. Navy*	1104
REGAN, Patrick, *U.S. Navy*	2044
REGAN, Patrick J., *U.S. Army*	2538
REID, George Croghan, *U.S. Marine Corps*	2425
REID, Patrick, *U.S. Navy*	2361
REID, Robert Alexander, *U.S. Army*	1105
REIGLE, Daniel P., *U.S. Army*	1106
REISINGER, James Monroe, *U.S. Army*	1107
RENNINGER, Louis, *U.S. Army*	1108
RESSLER, Norman W., *U.S. Army*	2161
REYNOLDS, George, *U.S. Army*	1109
RHODES, Julius Dexter, *U.S. Army*	1110
RHODES, Sylvester D., *U.S. Army*	1111
RICE, Charles, *U.S. Navy*	1112
RICE, Edmund, *U.S. Army*	1113
RICH, Carlos H., *U.S. Army*	1114
RICHARDS, Louis, *U.S. Navy*	1115
RICHARDSON, William R., *U.S. Army*	1116
RICHEY, William E., *U.S. Army*	1117
RICHMAN, Samuel, *U.S. Army*	1843
RICHMOND, James, *U.S. Army*	1118
RICKENBACKER, Edward Vernon, *U.S. Army Air Service*	2539
RICKETTS, Milton Ernest, *U.S. Navy*	2920
RICKSECKER, John Henry, *U.S. Army*	1119
RIDDELL, Rudolph R., *U.S. Army*	1120
RILEY, Thomas, *U.S. Army*	1121
RILLEY, John Phillip, *U.S. Navy*	2162
RINGOLD, Edward, *U.S. Navy*	1122
RIORDAN, Paul F., *U.S. Army*	2921
RIPLEY, William Young Warren, *U.S. Army*	1123
ROACH, Hampton Mitchell, *U.S. Army*	1844
ROAN, Charles Howard, *U.S. Marine Corps Reserve*	2922
ROANTREE, James S., *U.S. Marine Corps*	1124
ROARK, Anund Charles, *U.S. Army*	3343
ROBB, George Seanor, *U.S. Army*	2540
ROBBINS, Augustus J., *U.S. Army*	1125
ROBBINS, Marcus M., *U.S. Army*	1845
ROBERTS, Charles Church, *U.S. Navy*	2362
ROBERTS, Charles Duval, *U.S. Army*	2163
ROBERTS, Gordon Ray, *U.S. Army*	3344
ROBERTS, Harold W., *U.S. Army*	2541
ROBERTS, James, *U.S. Navy*	1126
ROBERTS, Otis O., *U.S. Army*	1127
ROBERTSON, Marcus William, *U.S. Army*	2245
ROBERTSON, Robert Stoddart, *U.S. Army*	1128
ROBERTSON, Samuel, *U.S. Army*	1129
ROBIE, George Frank, *U.S. Army*	1130
ROBINSON, Alexander, *U.S. Navy*	1131
ROBINSON, Charles, *U.S. Navy*	1132
ROBINSON, Elbridge, *U.S. Army*	1133
ROBINSON Jr., James E., *U.S. Army*	2923
ROBINSON, James H., *U.S. Army*	1134
ROBINSON Jr., James William, *U.S. Army*	3345
ROBINSON, John, *U.S. Navy*	1530
ROBINSON, John Cleveland, *U.S. Army*	1135
ROBINSON, John H., *U.S. Army*	1136
ROBINSON, Joseph, *U.S. Army*	1846
ROBINSON, Robert Guy, *U.S. Marine Corps*	2542
ROBINSON, Thomas, *U.S. Army*	1137
ROBINSON, Thomas, *U.S. Navy*	1531
ROCCO, Louis Richard, *U.S. Army*	3346
ROCHE, David, *U.S. Army*	1847
ROCK, Frederick, *U.S. Army*	1138
ROCKEFELLER, Charles Mortimer, *U.S. Army*	1139
RODENBOUGH, Theophilus Francis, *U.S. Army*	1140

RODENBURG, Henry, *U.S. Army*	1848	SALE, Albert, *U.S. Army*	1859
RODRIGUEZ, Cleto L., *U.S. Army*	2924	SAMPLER, Samuel M., *U.S. Army*	2543
RODRIGUEZ, Joseph Charles, *U.S. Army*	3129	SANCRAINTE, Charles Francis, *U.S. Army*	1161
ROEDER, Robert E., *U.S. Army*	2925	SANDERSON, Aaron, *U.S. Navy*	1162
ROGAN, Patrick, *U.S. Army*	1849	SANDLIN, Willie, *U.S. Army*	2544
ROGERS, Charles Calvin, *U.S. Army*	3347	SANDS, William, *U.S. Army*	1163
ROGERS, Samuel F., *U.S. Navy*	1971	SANFORD, Jacob, *U.S. Army*	1164
ROHM, Ferdinand Frederick, *U.S. Army*	1141	SANTIAGO-COLON, Hector, *U.S. Army*	3349
ROMEYN, Henry, *U.S. Army*	1850	SAPP, Isaac, *U.S. Navy*	2049
ROOD, Oliver P., *U.S. Army*	1142	SARGENT, Jackson, *U.S. Army*	1165
ROOKS, Albert Harold, *U.S. Navy*	2926	SARGENT, Ruppert Leon, *U.S. Army*	3350
ROONEY, Edward, *U.S. Army*	1851	SARNOSKI, Joseph Raymond, *U.S. Army Air Corps*	2935
ROOSEVELT, George Washington, *U.S. Army*	1143	SARTWELL, Henry, *U.S. Army*	1166
ROOSEVELT Jr., Theodore, *U.S. Army*	2927	SASSER, Clarence Eugene, *U.S. Army*	3351
ROSE, George Harry, *U.S. Navy*	2305	SAUNDERS, James, *U.S. Navy*	1167
ROSS, Donald Kirby, *U.S. Navy*	2928	SAVACOOL, Edwin F., *U.S. Army*	1168
ROSS, Frank Fulton, *U.S. Army*	2246	SAVAGE, Auzella, *U.S. Navy*	1169
ROSS, Marion A., *U.S. Army*	1144	SAWELSON, William, *U.S. Army*	2545
ROSS, Wilburn Kirby, *U.S. Army*	2929	SAXTON Jr., Rufus, *U.S. Army*	1170
ROSSBACH, Valentine, *U.S. Army*	1145	SAYERS, Foster Joseph, *U.S. Army*	2936
ROSSER, Ronald Eugene, *U.S. Army*	3130	SCANLAN, Patrick, *U.S. Army*	1171
ROTH, Peter Paul, *U.S. Army*	1852	SCANNELL, David John, *U.S. Marine Corps*	2307
ROUGHT, Stephen, *U.S. Army*	1146	SCHAEFER, Joseph E., *U.S. Army*	2937
ROUH, Carlton Robert, *U.S. Marine Corps Reserve*	2930	SCHAFFNER, Dwite H., *U.S. Army*	2546
ROUNDS, Lewis A., *U.S. Army*	1147	SCHAUER, Henry, *U.S. Army*	2938
ROUNING, Johannes, *U.S. Navy*	2045	SCHEIBNER, Martin E., *U.S. Army*	1172
ROUNTRY, John, *U.S. Navy*	1148	SCHENCK, Benjamin W., *U.S. Army*	1173
ROUSH, James Levi, *U.S. Army*	1149	SCHEPKE, Charles Stephen, *U.S. Navy*	2363
ROWALT, John F., *U.S. Army*	1853	SCHILLER, John, *U.S. Army*	1174
ROWAND Jr., Archibald Hamilton, *U.S. Army*	1150	SCHILT, Christian Franklin, *U.S. Marine Corps*	2575
ROWDY, *U.S. Army*	1854	SCHLACHTER, Philipp, *U.S. Army*	1175
ROWE, Henry Walker, *U.S. Army*	1151	SCHMAL, George William, *U.S. Army*	1176
ROY, Stanislaus, *U.S. Army*	1855	SCHMAUCH, Andrew, *U.S. Army*	1177
RUBIO, Euripides, *U.S. Army*	3348	SCHMIDT, Conrad, *U.S. Army*	1178
RUD, George William, *U.S. Navy*	2446	SCHMIDT Jr., Oscar, *U.S. Navy*	2547
RUDOLPH, Donald Eugene, *U.S. Army*	2931	SCHMIDT, Otto Diller, *U.S. Navy*	2364
RUHL, Donald Jack, *U.S. Marine Corps Reserve*	2932	SCHMIDT, William, *U.S. Army*	1179
RUIZ, Alejandro Renteria, *U.S. Army*	2933	SCHNEIDER, George, *U.S. Army*	1180
RUNDLE, Charles Wesley, *U.S. Army*	1152	SCHNELL, Christian, *U.S. Army*	1181
RUSH, John, *U.S. Navy*	1153	SCHNEPEL, Fred Jurgen, *U.S. Navy*	2427
RUSH, William Rees, *U.S. Navy*	2426	SCHNITZER, John, *U.S. Army*	1860
RUSSELL, Charles L., *U.S. Army*	1154	SCHOFIELD, John McAllister, *U.S. Army*	1182
RUSSELL, Henry Peter, *U.S. Navy*	2164	SCHONLAND, Herbert Emery, *U.S. Navy*	2939
RUSSELL, James, *U.S. Army*	1856	SCHOONMAKER, James Martinus, *U.S. Army*	1183
RUSSELL, John, *U.S. Navy*	2046	SCHOONOVER, Dan D., *U.S. Army*	3131
RUSSELL, Milton F., *U.S. Army*	1155	SCHORN, Charles, *U.S. Army*	1184
RUTHERFORD, John T., *U.S. Army*	1156	SCHOU, Julius Alexis, *U.S. Army*	1861
RUTTER, James May, *U.S. Army*	1157	SCHOWALTER Jr., Edward Rightor, *U.S. Army*	3132
RYAN, David, *U.S. Army*	1857	SCHROEDER, Henry Frank, *U.S. Army*	2248
RYAN, Denis, *U.S. Army*	1858	SCHROETER, Charles, *U.S. Army*	1862
RYAN, Francis Thomas, *U.S. Navy*	2306	SCHUBERT, Martin, *U.S. Army*	1185
RYAN, Peter J., *U.S. Army*	1158	SCHUTT, George, *U.S. Navy*	1186
RYAN, Richard, *U.S. Navy*	2047	SCHWAB, Albert Ernest, *U.S. Marine Corps Reserve*	2940
RYAN Jr., Thomas John, *U.S. Navy*	2593	SCHWAN, Theodore, *U.S. Army*	1187
SACRISTE, Louis Jeanottelle, *U.S. Army*	1159	SCHWENK, Martin, *U.S. Army*	1188
SADLER, William, *U.S. Navy*	2048	SCOFIELD, David H., *U.S. Army*	1189
SADOWSKI, Joseph John, *U.S. Army*	2934	SCOTT, Alexander, *U.S. Army*	1190
SAGE, William Hampden, *U.S. Army*	2247	SCOTT, George D., *U.S. Army*	1863
SAGELHURST, John Christopher, *U.S. Army*	1160	SCOTT, John Morehead, *U.S. Army*	1191

Name	Page
SCOTT, John Wallace, *U.S. Army*	1192
SCOTT, Joseph Francis, *U.S. Marine Corps*	2165
SCOTT, Julian A., *U.S. Army*	1193
SCOTT, Norman, *U.S. Navy*	2941
SCOTT, Robert B., *U.S. Army*	1864
SCOTT, Robert Raymond, *U.S. Navy*	2942
SCOTT, Robert Sheldon, *U.S. Army*	2943
SEACH, William, *U.S. Navy*	2308
SEAMAN, Elisha B., *U.S. Army*	1194
SEANOR, James, *U.S. Navy*	1195
SEARS, Cyrus, *U.S. Army*	1196
SEAVER, Thomas Orville, *U.S. Army*	1197
SEAY, William Wayne, *U.S. Army*	3352
SEBILLE, Louis Joseph, *U.S. Air Force*	3133
SEIBERT, Lloyd Martin, *U.S. Army*	2548
SEITZINGER, James M., *U.S. Army*	1198
SELLERS, Alfred Jacob, *U.S. Army*	1199
SEMPLE, Robert, *U.S. Navy*	2428
SESTON, Charles H., *U.S. Army*	1200
SEWARD, Griffin, *U.S. Army*	1865
SEWARD, Richard Henry, *U.S. Navy*	1201
SEWELL, William Joyce, *U.S. Army*	1202
SHACKLETTE, William Sidney, *U.S. Navy*	2365
SHAFFER, William, *U.S. Army*	1866
SHAFTER, William Rufus, *U.S. Army*	1203
SHAHAN, Emisire, *U.S. Army*	1204
SHALER, Alexander, *U.S. Army*	1205
SHAMBAUGH, Charles, *U.S. Army*	1206
SHANAHAN, Patrick, *U.S. Navy*	2366
SHANES, John, *U.S. Army*	1207
SHAPLAND, John, *U.S. Army*	1208
SHARP, Hendrick, *U.S. Navy*	1209
SHARPLESS, Edward Clay, *U.S. Army*	1867
SHAW, George Clymer, *U.S. Army*	2249
SHAW, Thomas, *U.S. Army*	1868
SHEA, Charles William, *U.S. Army*	2944
SHEA, Daniel John, *U.S. Army*	3353
SHEA, Joseph Henry, *U.S. Army*	1210
SHEA Jr., Richard Thomas, *U.S. Army*	3134
SHEERIN, John, *U.S. Army*	1869
SHELLENBERGER, John, *U.S. Army*	1211
SHELTON, George Mathews, *U.S. Army*	2250
SHEPARD, Irwin, *U.S. Army*	1212
SHEPARD, Louis Capet, *U.S. Navy*	1213
SHEPHERD, Warren Julius, *U.S. Army*	2166
SHEPHERD, William, *U.S. Army*	1214
SHEPPARD, Charles, *U.S. Army*	1870
SHERIDAN, Carl Vernon, *U.S. Army*	2945
SHERIDAN, James, *U.S. Navy*	1215
SHERMAN, Marshall, *U.S. Army*	1216
SHIEL, John, *U.S. Army*	1218
SHIELDS, Bernard, *U.S. Army*	1217
SHIELDS, Marvin Glen, *U.S. Navy*	3354
SHIELS, George Franklin, *U.S. Army*	2251
SHILLING, John, *U.S. Army*	1219
SHINGLE, John Henry, *U.S. Army*	1871
SHIPLEY, Robert F., *U.S. Army*	1220
SHIPMAN, William, *U.S. Navy*	1221
SHIVERS, John, *U.S. Marine Corps*	1222
SHOCKLEY, William Ralph, *U.S. Army*	2946
SHOEMAKER, Levi, *U.S. Army*	1223
SHOMO, William Arthur, *U.S. Army Air Corps/U.S. Air Force*	2947
SHOPP, George J., *U.S. Army*	1224
SHOUP, Curtis F., *U.S. Army*	2948
SHOUP, David Monroe, *U.S. Marine Corps*	2949
SHUBERT, Frank, *U.S. Army*	1225
SHUCK Jr., William Edward, *U.S. Marine Corps*	3135
SHUGHART, Randall David, *U.S. Army*	3399
SHUTES, Henry, *U.S. Navy*	1226
SICKLES, Daniel Edgar, *U.S. Army*	1227
SICKLES, William H., *U.S. Army*	1228
SIDMAN, George Dallas, *U.S. Army*	1229
SIEGEL, John Otto, *U.S. Navy*	2549
SIGLER, Franklin Earl, *U.S. Marine Corps Reserve*	2950
SIJAN, Lance Peter, *U.S. Air Force*	3355
SILK, Edward A., *U.S. Army*	2951
SILVA, France, *U.S. Marine Corps*	2309
SIMANEK, Robert Ernest, *U.S. Marine Corps*	3136
SIMKINS, Lebbeus, *U.S. Navy*	1230
SIMMONS, John, *U.S. Army*	1231
SIMMONS, William Thomas, *U.S. Army*	1232
SIMONDS, William Edgar, *U.S. Army*	1233
SIMONS, Charles Jenks, *U.S. Army*	1234
SIMPSON, D. Henry Lakin, *U.S. Navy*	2050
SIMS, Clifford Chester, *U.S. Army*	3356
SINGLETON, Walter Keith, *U.S. Marine Corps*	3357
SINNETT, Lawrence Clinton, *U.S. Navy*	2429
SISLER, George Kenton, *U.S. Army*	3358
SITMAN, William S., *U.S. Army*	3137
SITTER, Carl Leonard, *U.S. Marine Corps*	3138
SJOGREN, John Carleton, *U.S. Army*	2952
SKAGGS Jr., Luther, *U.S. Marine Corps Reserve*	2953
SKELLIE, Ebenezer, *U.S. Army*	1235
SKIDGEL, Donald Sidney, *U.S. Army*	3359
SKINKER, Alexander Rives, *U.S. Army*	2550
SKINNER, John Oscar, *U.S. Army*	1872
SKINNER Jr., Sherrod Emerson, *U.S. Marine Corps Reserve*	3139
SLACK, Clayton Kirk, *U.S. Army*	2551
SLADEN, Joseph Alton, *U.S. Army*	1236
SLAGLE, Oscar, *U.S. Army*	1237
SLATON, James Daniel, *U.S. Army*	2954
SLAVENS, Samuel, *U.S. Army*	1238
SLETTELAND, Thomas, *U.S. Army*	2252
SLOAN, Andrew Jackson, *U.S. Army*	1239
SLUSHER, Henry C., *U.S. Army*	1240
SMALLEY, Reuben, *U.S. Army*	1241
SMALLEY, Reuben S., *U.S. Army*	1242
SMEDLEY, Larry Eugene, *U.S. Marine Corps*	3360
SMITH, Albert Joseph, *U.S. Marine Corps*	2594
SMITH, Alonzo, *U.S. Army*	1243
SMITH, Andrew J., *U.S. Army*	1873
SMITH, Charles E., *U.S. Army*	1874
SMITH, Charles H., *U.S. Navy*	1244
SMITH, Charles Henry, *U.S. Army*	1245
SMITH, Cornelius Cole, *U.S. Army*	1875
SMITH, David Lafayette, *U.S. Army*	1246
SMITH, David Monroe, *U.S. Army*	3140
SMITH, Edwin, *U.S. Navy*	1247

SMITH, Elmelindo Rodriques, *U.S. Army*	3361	SQUIRES, John C., *U.S. Army*	2962
SMITH, Eugene P., *U.S. Navy*	2447	STACEY, Charles, *U.S. Army*	1276
SMITH, Francis M., *U.S. Army*	1248	STACY, William Bradford, *U.S. Navy*	1532
SMITH, Frank Elmer, *U.S. Navy*	2310	STAHEL, Julius H., *U.S. Army*	1277
SMITH, Fred E., *U.S. Army*	2552	STANCE, Emanuel, *U.S. Army*	1887
SMITH, Furman L., *U.S. Army*	2955	STANLEY, David Sloane, *U.S. Army*	1278
SMITH, George W., *U.S. Army*	1876	STANLEY, Eben, *U.S. Army*	1888
SMITH, Henry I., *U.S. Army*	1249	STANLEY, Edward, *U.S. Army*	1889
SMITH, James, *U.S. Navy*	1250	STANLEY, Robert Henry, *U.S. Navy*	2312
SMITH, James, *U.S. Navy*	2051	STANLEY, William A., *U.S. Navy*	1279
SMITH, James (Ovid), *U.S. Army*	1251	STANTON, Thomas, *U.S. Navy*	2368
SMITH, James A., *U.S. Navy*	2311	STARKINS, John H., *U.S. Army*	1280
SMITH, John, *U.S. Navy*	1252	STATON, Adolphus, *U.S. Navy*	2430
SMITH, John, *U.S. Navy*	1253	STAUFFER, Rudolph, *U.S. Army*	1890
SMITH, John, *U.S. Navy*	2052	STEELE, John Whedon, *U.S. Army*	1281
SMITH, John Lucian, *U.S. Marine Corps*	2956	STEIN, Tony, *U.S. Marine Corps Reserve*	2963
SMITH, Joseph Sewall, *U.S. Army*	1254	STEINDAM, Russell Albert, *U.S. Army*	3363
SMITH, Oloff, *U.S. Navy*	1255	STEINER, Christian, *U.S. Army*	1891
SMITH, Otis W., *U.S. Army*	1256	STEINMETZ, William, *U.S. Army*	1282
SMITH, Otto, *U.S. Army*	1877	STEPHENS, William G., *U.S. Army*	1283
SMITH, Richard, *U.S. Army*	1257	STERLING, James E., *U.S. Navy*	1284
SMITH, Robert, *U.S. Army*	1878	STERLING, John T., *U.S. Army*	1285
SMITH, Samuel Rodmond, *U.S. Army*	1258	STEVENS, Daniel Dickerson, *U.S. Navy*	1286
SMITH, Thaddeus S., *U.S. Army*	1259	STEVENS, Hazard, *U.S. Army*	1287
SMITH, Theodore F., *U.S. Army*	1879	STEVERS, Thomas W., *U.S. Army*	1892
SMITH, Thomas, *U.S. Army*	1880	STEWART, Benjamin F., *U.S. Army*	1893
SMITH, Thomas, *U.S. Navy*	1260	STEWART, George Evans, *U.S. Army*	2253
SMITH, Thomas, *U.S. Navy*	2053	STEWART, George W., *U.S. Army*	1288
SMITH, Thomas J., *U.S. Army*	1881	STEWART, James A., *U.S. Marine Corps*	2054
SMITH, Walter B., *U.S. Navy*	1261	STEWART, Jimmy Goethel, *U.S. Army*	3364
SMITH, Wilhelm, *U.S. Navy*	2448	STEWART, Joseph, *U.S. Army*	1289
SMITH, Willard M., *U.S. Marine Corps*	1262	STEWART, Peter, *U.S. Marine Corps*	2313
SMITH, William, *U.S. Army*	1882	STICKELS, Joseph, *U.S. Army*	1290
SMITH, William, *U.S. Navy*	1263	STICKNEY, Herman Osman, *U.S. Navy*	2431
SMITH, William H., *U.S. Army*	1883	STICKOFFER, Julius Henry, *U.S. Army*	1894
SMITH, Wilson, *U.S. Army*	1264	STOCKDALE, James Bond, *U.S. Navy*	3365
SMITH Sr., Maynard Harrison, *U.S. Army Air Corps*	2957	STOCKHAM, Fred William, *U.S. Marine Corps*	2553
SNEDDEN, James, *U.S. Army*	1265	STOCKMAN, George Henry, *U.S. Army*	1291
SNOW, Elmer A., *U.S. Army*	1884	STODDARD, James, *U.S. Navy*	1292
SNYDER, William Ellsworth, *U.S. Navy*	2367	STOKES, Alonzo, *U.S. Army*	1895
SODERMAN, William Adolph, *U.S. Army*	2958	STOKES, George, *U.S. Army*	1293
SORENSON, Richard Keith, *U.S. Marine Corps Reserve*	2959	STOKES, John S., *U.S. Navy*	2369
SOUTHARD, David, *U.S. Army*	1266	STOLTENBERG, Andrew Vincent, *U.S. Navy*	2254
SOVA, Joseph E., *U.S. Army*	1267	STOLZ, Frank, *U.S. Army*	1294
SOWERS, Michael, *U.S. Army*	1268	STONE, James Lamar, *U.S. Army*	3142
SPALDING, Edward Burson, *U.S. Army*	1269	STONE Jr., Lester Raymond, *U.S. Army*	3366
SPECKER, Joe C., *U.S. Army*	2960	STOREY, John Hamilton Reid, *U.S. Army*	1295
SPEICHER, Clifton T., *U.S. Army*	3141	STORY, Luther H., *U.S. Army*	3143
SPENCE, Orizoba, *U.S. Army*	1885	STOUT, Mitchell William, *U.S. Army*	3367
SPERRY, William Joseph, *U.S. Army*	1270	STOUT, Richard, *U.S. Navy*	1296
SPICER, William, *U.S. Navy*	2167	STOWERS, Freddie, *U.S. Army*	2554
SPILLANE, Timothy, *U.S. Army*	1271	STRAHAN, Robert, *U.S. Navy*	1297
SPRAGUE, Benona, *U.S. Army*	1272	STRAUB, Paul Frederick, *U.S. Army*	2255
SPRAGUE, John Wilson, *U.S. Army*	1273	STRAUSBURGH, Bernard A., *U.S. Army*	1298
SPRAYBERRY, James Michael, *U.S. Army*	3362	STRAYER, William H., *U.S. Army*	1896
SPRINGER, George, *U.S. Army*	1886	STREET III, George Levick, *U.S. Navy*	2964
SPROWLE, David, *U.S. Marine Corps*	1274	STREILE, Christian, *U.S. Army*	1299
SPURLING, Andrew Barclay, *U.S. Army*	1275	STRIVSON, Benoni, *U.S. Army*	1897
SPURRIER, Junior James, *U.S. Army*	2961	STRONG, James N., *U.S. Army*	1300

Name	Number
STRYKER, Robert Francis, *U.S. Army*	3368
STRYKER, Stuart S., *U.S. Army*	2965
STUMPF, Kenneth Edward, *U.S. Army*	3369
STUPKA, Laddie, *U.S. Navy*	2370
STURGEON, James K., *U.S. Army*	1301
SUDUT, Jerome A., *U.S. Army*	3144
SULLIVAN, Daniel Augustus Joseph, *U.S. Naval Reserve Force*	2555
SULLIVAN, Edward, *U.S. Marine Corps*	2168
SULLIVAN, James, *U.S. Navy*	1302
SULLIVAN, James F., *U.S. Navy*	2055
SULLIVAN, John, *U.S. Navy*	1303
SULLIVAN, Thomas, *U.S. Army*	1898
SULLIVAN, Thomas, *U.S. Army*	1899
SULLIVAN, Timothy, *U.S. Navy*	1304
SUMMERS, James Calvin, *U.S. Army*	1305
SUMMERS, Robert, *U.S. Navy*	1306
SUMNER, James, *U.S. Army*	1900
SUNDQUIST, Axel Leohard, *U.S. Navy*	2169
SUNDQUIST, Gustav Adolf, *U.S. Navy*	2170
SURLES, William H., *U.S. Army*	1307
SUTHERLAND, John Alexander, *U.S. Army*	1901
SUTTON, Clarence Edwin, *U.S. Marine Corps*	2314
SWAN, Charles Alexander, *U.S. Army*	1308
SWANSON, John, *U.S. Navy*	1309
SWAP, Jacob E., *U.S. Army*	1310
SWATTON, Edward, *U.S. Navy*	1311
SWAYNE, Wager, *U.S. Army*	1312
SWEARER, Benjamin, *U.S. Navy*	1313
SWEATT, Joseph Sewell Gerrish, *U.S. Army*	1314
SWEENEY, James, *U.S. Army*	1315
SWEENEY, Robert Augustus, *U.S. Navy*	2056
SWEENEY, William, *U.S. Navy*	2057
SWEGHEIMER, Jacob, *U.S. Army*	1316
SWETT, James Elms, *U.S. Marine Corps Reserve*	2966
SWIFT, Frederic William, *U.S. Army*	1317
SWIFT, Harlan J., *U.S. Army*	1318
SYPE, Peter, *U.S. Army*	1319
TABOR, William L. S., *U.S. Army*	1320
TAGGART, Charles A., *U.S. Army*	1321
TALBOT, Ralph, *U.S. Marine Corps*	2556
TALBOTT, William, *U.S. Navy*	1322
TALLENTINE, James, *U.S. Navy*	1323
TALLEY, Edward R., *U.S. Army*	2557
TANNER, Charles B., *U.S. Army*	1324
TAYLOR, Anthony, *U.S. Army*	1325
TAYLOR, Bernard, *U.S. Army*	1902
TAYLOR, Charles, *U.S. Army*	1903
TAYLOR, Forrester L., *U.S. Army*	1326
TAYLOR, George, *U.S. Navy*	1327
TAYLOR, Henry H., *U.S. Army*	1328
TAYLOR, James Allen, *U.S. Army*	3370
TAYLOR, John, *U.S. Navy*	1533
TAYLOR, Joseph, *U.S. Army*	1329
TAYLOR, Richard, *U.S. Army*	1330
TAYLOR, Richard Hamilton, *U.S. Navy*	2058
TAYLOR, Thomas, *U.S. Navy*	1331
TAYLOR, Wilbur Nelson, *U.S. Army*	1904
TAYLOR, William, *U.S. Army*	1332
TAYLOR, William G., *U.S. Navy*	1333
TAYLOR Sr., Karl Gorman, *U.S. Marine Corps*	3371
TEA, Richard Longstreet, *U.S. Army*	1905
TERRY, John Darling, *U.S. Army*	1334
TERRY, Seymour W., *U.S. Army*	2967
TEYTAND, August P., *U.S. Navy*	2371
THACKER, Brian Miles, *U.S. Army*	3372
THACKRAH, Benjamin, *U.S. Army*	1335
THATCHER, Charles M., *U.S. Army*	1336
THAXTER, Sidney Warren, *U.S. Army*	1337
THAYER, James, *U.S. Navy*	2059
THIELBERG, Henry, *U.S. Navy*	1338
THOMAS, Charles L., *U.S. Army*	1906
THOMAS, Hampton Sidney, *U.S. Army*	1339
THOMAS, Herbert Joseph, *U.S. Marine Corps Reserve*	2968
THOMAS, Karl, *U.S. Navy*	2315
THOMAS, Stephen, *U.S. Army*	1340
THOMAS, William H., *U.S. Army*	2969
THOMASON, Clyde A., *U.S. Marine Corps Reserve*	2970
THOMPKINS, George W., *U.S. Army*	1341
THOMPKINS, William H., *U.S. Army*	2171
THOMPSON, Allen, *U.S. Army*	1342
THOMPSON, Charles Augustus, *U.S. Army*	1343
THOMPSON, Freeman C., *U.S. Army*	1344
THOMPSON, George Washington, *U.S. Army*	1907
THOMPSON, Henry, *U.S. Navy*	2060
THOMPSON, Henry A., *U.S. Marine Corps*	1345
THOMPSON, James B., *U.S. Army*	1346
THOMPSON, James Granville, *U.S. Army*	1347
THOMPSON, James Harry, *U.S. Army*	1348
THOMPSON, John, *U.S. Army*	1908
THOMPSON, John J., *U.S. Army*	1349
THOMPSON, Joseph Henry, *U.S. Army*	2558
THOMPSON, Max, *U.S. Army*	2971
THOMPSON, Peter, *U.S. Army*	1909
THOMPSON, Thomas W., *U.S. Army*	1350
THOMPSON, William, *U.S. Navy*	1351
THOMPSON, William Henry, *U.S. Army*	3145
THOMPSON, William P., *U.S. Army*	1352
THOMSON, Clifford, *U.S. Army*	1353
THORDSEN, William George, *U.S. Navy*	2256
THORN, Walter, *U.S. Army*	1354
THORNE, Horace Marvin, *U.S. Army*	2972
THORNTON, Michael, *U.S. Navy*	2061
THORNTON, Michael Edwin, *U.S. Navy*	3373
THORSNESS, Leo Keith, *U.S. Air Force*	3374
THORSON, John F., *U.S. Army*	2973
TIBBETS, Andrew W., *U.S. Army*	1355
TILTON, Henry Remsen, *U.S. Army*	1910
TILTON, William, *U.S. Army*	1356
TIMMERMAN, Grant Frederick, *U.S. Marine Corps*	2974
TINKHAM, Eugene M., *U.S. Army*	1357
TITUS, Calvin Pearl, *U.S. Army*	2316
TITUS, Charles, *U.S. Army*	1358
TOBAN, James W., *U.S. Army*	1359
TOBIE Jr., Edward Parsons, *U.S. Army*	1360
TOBIN, John Michael, *U.S. Army*	1361
TOBIN, Paul, *U.S. Navy*	2062
TODD, Samuel, *U.S. Navy*	1362
TOFFEY, John James, *U.S. Army*	1363

Name	Page
TOLAN, Frank, *U.S. Army*	1911
TOMICH, Peter, *U.S. Navy*	2975
TOMINAC, John Joseph, *U.S. Army*	2976
TOMLIN, Andrew J., *U.S. Marine Corps*	1364
TOMPKINS, Aaron B., *U.S. Army*	1365
TOMPKINS, Charles Henry, *U.S. Army*	1366
TOOHEY, Thomas, *U.S. Army*	1367
TOOMER, William, *U.S. Army*	1368
TORGERSON, Martin Torinus, *U.S. Navy*	2317
TORGLER, Ernest R., *U.S. Army*	1369
TOWLE, John Roderick, *U.S. Army*	2977
TOWNSEND, Julius Curtis, *U.S. Navy*	2432
TOY, Frederick Ernest, *U.S. Army*	1912
TOZIER, Andrew Jackson, *U.S. Army*	1370
TRACY, Amasa Sawyer, *U.S. Army*	1371
TRACY, Benjamin Franklin, *U.S. Army*	1372
TRACY, Charles H., *U.S. Army*	1373
TRACY, John, *U.S. Army*	1913
TRACY, William Gardner, *U.S. Army*	1374
TRAUTMAN, Jacob, *U.S. Army*	1914
TRAYNOR, Andrew, *U.S. Army*	1375
TREADWELL, Jack Lemaster, *U.S. Army*	2978
TREAT, Howell B., *U.S. Army*	1376
TREMAIN, Henry Edwin, *U.S. Army*	1377
TREMBLEY, William Beattie, *U.S. Army*	2257
TRIBE, John, *U.S. Army*	1378
TRINIDAD, Telesforo De La Cruz, *U.S. Navy*	2449
TRIPLETT, Samuel S., *U.S. Navy*	2172
TRIPP, Othniel, *U.S. Navy*	1379
TROGDEN, Howell G., *U.S. Army*	1380
TROUT, James M., *U.S. Navy*	2063
TROY, Jeremiah, *U.S. Navy*	2064
TROY, William, *U.S. Navy*	1972
TRUELL, Edwin M., *U.S. Army*	1381
TRUEMPER, Walter Edward, *U.S. Army Air Corps*	2979
TRUESDELL, Donald Leroy, *U.S. Marine Corps*	2576
TRUETT, Alexander H., *U.S. Navy*	1382
TUCKER, Allen, *U.S. Army*	1383
TUCKER, Jacob R., *U.S. Army*	1384
TURNER, Charles William, *U.S. Army*	3146
TURNER, Day G., *U.S. Army*	2980
TURNER, George Benton, *U.S. Army*	2981
TURNER, Harold Leo, *U.S. Army*	2559
TURNER, William Bradford, *U.S. Army*	2560
TURPIN, James H., *U.S. Army*	1915
TURVELIN, Alexander Haure, *U.S. Navy*	2065
TWEEDALE, John, *U.S. Army*	1385
TWOMBLY, Voltare Paine, *U.S. Army*	1386
TYRRELL, George William, *U.S. Army*	1387
UHRL, George, *U.S. Army*	1388
UPHAM, Oscar Jefferson, *U.S. Marine Corps*	2318
UPSHUR, William Peterkin, *U.S. Marine Corps*	2442
UPTON, Frank Monroe, *U.S. Navy*	2561
URBAN, Matt Louis, *U.S. Army*	2982
URELL, Michael Emmet, *U.S. Army*	1389
VADAS, Albert, *U.S. Navy*	2173
VALDEZ, Jose F., *U.S. Army*	2983
VALE, John, *U.S. Army*	1390
VALENTE, Michael, *U.S. Army*	2562
VAN ETTEN, Hudson, *U.S. Navy*	2174
VAN IERSEL, Ludovicus M.M., *U.S. Army*	2563
VAN MATRE, Joseph, *U.S. Army*	1393
VAN NOY Jr., Nathan, *U.S. Army*	2986
VAN SCHAICK, Louis Joseph, *U.S. Army*	2258
VAN VALKENBURGH, Franklin, *U.S. Navy*	2987
VAN VOORHIS, Bruce Avery, *U.S. Navy*	2988
VAN WINKLE, Archie, *U.S. Marine Corps Reserve*	3147
VAN WINKLE, Edward (Edwin), *U.S. Army*	1395
VANCE Jr., Leon Robert, *U.S. Army Air Corps*	2984
VANCE, Wilson J., *U.S. Army*	1391
VANDEGRIFT, Alexander Archer, *U.S. Marine Corps*	2985
VANDERSLICE, John Mitchell, *U.S. Army*	1392
VANTINE, Joseph E., *U.S. Navy*	1394
VARGAS, Jay R., *U.S. Marine Corps*	3375
VARNUM, Charles Albert, *U.S. Army*	1916
VAUGHN, Pinkerton Ross, *U.S. Marine Corps*	1396
VEAL, Charles, *U.S. Army*	1397
VEALE, Moses, *U.S. Army*	1398
VEAZEY, Wheelock Graves, *U.S. Army*	1399
VERNAY, James David, *U.S. Army*	1400
VERNEY, James W., *U.S. Navy*	1401
VEUVE, Ernest, *U.S. Army*	1917
VIALE, Robert M., *U.S. Army*	2989
VIFQUAIN, Victor, *U.S. Army*	1402
VILLEGAS, Ysmael R., *U.S. Army*	2990
VILLEPIGUE, John Cantey, *U.S. Army*	2564
VITTORI, Joseph, *U.S. Marine Corps Reserve*	3148
VLUG, Dirk John, *U.S. Army*	2991
VOIT, Otto Emil, *U.S. Army*	1918
VOKES, Leroy H., *U.S. Army*	1919
VOLZ, Jacob, *U.S. Navy*	2380
VOLZ, Robert, *U.S. Navy*	2175
VON MEDEM, Rudolph, *U.S. Army*	1920
VON SCHLICK, Robert H., *U.S. Army*	2319
VON VEGESACK, Ernest, *U.S. Army*	1403
VOSLER, Forrest Lee "Woody", *U.S. Army Air Corps*	2992
WAALER, Reidar, *U.S. Army*	2565
WAGEMAN, John H., *U.S. Army*	1404
WAGG, Maurice, *U.S. Navy*	1405
WAGNER, John W., *U.S. Army*	1406
WAHLEN, George Edward, *U.S. Navy*	2993
WAINWRIGHT, John, *U.S. Army*	1407
WAINWRIGHT Jr., Richard, *U.S. Navy*	2433
WAINWRIGHT IV, Jonathan Mayhew, *U.S. Army*	2994
WALKER, Allen, *U.S. Army*	1921
WALKER, Edward Alexander, *U.S. Marine Corps*	2320
WALKER, Frank T. O., *U.S. Army*	2259
WALKER, James C., *U.S. Army*	1408
WALKER, John, *U.S. Army*	1922
WALKER, Kenneth Newton, *U.S. Army Air Corps*	2995
WALKER, Mary Edwards, *U.S. Army*	1409
WALL, Jerry C., *U.S. Army*	1410
WALLACE, George Weed, *U.S. Army*	2260
WALLACE, Herman C., *U.S. Army*	2996
WALLACE, William, *U.S. Army*	1923
WALLER, Francis A., *U.S. Army*	1411
WALLEY, Augustus, *U.S. Army*	1924
WALLING, William Henry, *U.S. Army*	1412

Name	Page
WALMSLEY Jr., John Springer, *U.S. Air Force*	3149
WALSH, James Aloysius, *U.S. Navy*	2434
WALSH, John, *U.S. Army*	1413
WALSH, Kenneth Ambrose, *U.S. Marine Corps*	2997
WALSH, Michael, *U.S. Navy*	2372
WALSH, William Gary, *U.S. Marine Corps Reserve*	2998
WALTON, George Washington, *U.S. Army*	1414
WAMBSGAN, Martin, *U.S. Army*	1415
WANTON, George Henry, *U.S. Army*	2176
WARD, Calvin John, *U.S. Army*	2566
WARD, Charles H., *U.S. Army*	1925
WARD, James, *U.S. Army*	1926
WARD, James, *U.S. Navy*	1416
WARD, James Richard, *U.S. Navy*	2999
WARD, John, *U.S. Army*	1927
WARD, Nelson W., *U.S. Army*	1417
WARD, Thomas J., *U.S. Army*	1418
WARD, William Henry, *U.S. Army*	1419
WARDEN, John, *U.S. Army*	1420
WARE, Keith Lincoln, *U.S. Army*	3000
WARFEL, Henry Clay, *U.S. Army*	1421
WARNER, Henry F., *U.S. Army*	3001
WARREN, David, *U.S. Navy*	1422
WARREN, Francis Emroy, *U.S. Army*	1423
WARREN Jr., John Earl, *U.S. Army*	3376
WARRINGTON, Lewis, *U.S. Army*	1928
WATKINS, Lewis George, *U.S. Marine Corps*	3150
WATKINS, Travis E., *U.S. Army*	3151
WATSON, James C., *U.S. Army*	1929
WATSON, Joseph, *U.S. Army*	1930
WATSON, Wilson Douglas, *U.S. Marine Corps Reserve*	3002
WATTERS, Charles Joseph, *U.S. Army*	3377
WAUGH, Robert T., *U.S. Army*	3003
WAYBUR, David Crowder, *U.S. Army*	3004
WAYRYNEN, Dale Eugene, *U.S. Army*	3378
WEAHER, Andrew J., *U.S. Army*	1931
WEAVER, Amos, *U.S. Army*	2261
WEBB, Alexander Stewart, *U.S. Army*	1424
WEBB, James W., *U.S. Army*	1425
WEBBER, Alason P., *U.S. Army*	1426
WEBER, Lester William, *U.S. Marine Corps*	3379
WEBSTER, Henry S., *U.S. Navy*	1427
WEEKS, Charles H., *U.S. Navy*	1428
WEEKS, John Henry, *U.S. Army*	1429
WEICHT, Ellis R., *U.S. Army*	3005
WEINERT, Paul H., *U.S. Army*	1932
WEIR, Henry Cary, *U.S. Army*	1430
WEISBOGEL, Albert, *U.S. Navy*	2066
WEISS, Enoch R., *U.S. Army*	1933
WEISSEL, Adam, *U.S. Navy*	2067
WELBORN, Ira Clinton, *U.S. Army*	2177
WELCH, Charles H., *U.S. Army*	1934
WELCH, George W., *U.S. Army*	1431
WELCH, Michael, *U.S. Army*	1935
WELCH, Richard, *U.S. Army*	1432
WELCH, Stephen, *U.S. Army*	1433
WELD, Seth Lathrop, *U.S. Army*	2262
WELLS, Henry S., *U.S. Army*	1434
WELLS, Thomas McCoy, *U.S. Army*	1435
WELLS, William, *U.S. Army*	1437
WELLS, William, *U.S. Navy*	1436
WELSH, Edward, *U.S. Army*	1438
WELSH, James, *U.S. Army*	1439
WENDE, Bruno, *U.S. Army*	2178
WEST, Chester Howard, *U.S. Army*	2567
WEST, Ernest Edison, *U.S. Army*	3152
WEST, Frank, *U.S. Army*	1936
WEST, Walter Scott, *U.S. Marine Corps*	2179
WESTA, Karl, *U.S. Navy*	2373
WESTERHOLD, William, *U.S. Army*	1440
WESTERMARK, Axel, *U.S. Navy*	2321
WESTON, John Francis, *U.S. Army*	1441
WETHERBY, John C., *U.S. Army*	2263
WETZEL, Gary George, *U.S. Army*	3380
WETZEL, Walter C., *U.S. Army*	3006
WHEAT, Roy Mitchell, *U.S. Marine Corps*	3381
WHEATON, Loyd, *U.S. Army*	1442
WHEELER, Daniel Davis, *U.S. Army*	1443
WHEELER, George Huber, *U.S. Navy*	2374
WHEELER, Henry W., *U.S. Army*	1444
WHERRY, William Macky, *U.S. Army*	1445
WHITAKER, Edward Washburn, *U.S. Army*	1446
WHITE, Adam, *U.S. Army*	1447
WHITE, Edward, *U.S. Army*	2264
WHITE, John Henry, *U.S. Army*	1448
WHITE, Joseph, *U.S. Navy*	1449
WHITE, Patrick H., *U.S. Army*	1450
WHITEHEAD, John Milton, *U.S. Army*	1451
WHITEHEAD, Patton G., *U.S. Army*	1937
WHITELEY, Eli Lamar, *U.S. Army*	3007
WHITFIELD, Daniel, *U.S. Navy*	1452
WHITMAN, Frank M., *U.S. Army*	1453
WHITMORE, John W., *U.S. Army*	1454
WHITNEY, William G., *U.S. Army*	1455
WHITTIER, Edward Newton, *U.S. Army*	1456
WHITTINGTON, Hulon Brooke, *U.S. Army*	3008
WHITTLESEY, Charles White, *U.S. Army*	2568
WICKAM, Jerry Wayne, *U.S. Army*	3382
WICKERSHAM, J. Hunter, *U.S. Army*	2569
WIDICK, Andrew J., *U.S. Army*	1457
WIDMER, Jacob, *U.S. Army*	1938
WIEDORFER, Paul Joseph, *U.S. Army*	3009
WIGLE, Thomas W., *U.S. Army*	3010
WILBANKS, Hilliard Almond, *U.S. Air Force*	3383
WILBUR, William Hale, *U.S. Army*	3011
WILCOX, Franklin L., *U.S. Navy*	1458
WILCOX, William H., *U.S. Army*	1459
WILDER, Wilber Elliott, *U.S. Army*	1939
WILEY, James, *U.S. Army*	1460
WILHELM, George, *U.S. Army*	1461
WILKE, Julius August Robert, *U.S. Navy*	2180
WILKENS, Henry, *U.S. Army*	1940
WILKES, Henry, *U.S. Navy*	1462
WILKES, Perry, *U.S. Navy*	1463
WILKIN, Edward G., *U.S. Army*	3012
WILKINS, Leander A., *U.S. Army*	1464
WILKINS, Raymond Harrell, *U.S. Army Air Corps*	3013
WILKINSON Jr., Theodore Stark, *U.S. Navy*	2435

Name	Page
WILL, Walter J., *U.S. Army*	3014
WILLCOX, Orlando Bolivar, *U.S. Army*	1465
WILLETT, Louis Edward, *U.S. Army*	3384
WILLEY, Charles H., *U.S. Navy*	2450
WILLIAMS, Anthony, *U.S. Navy*	1466
WILLIAMS, Antonio, *U.S. Navy*	2068
WILLIAMS, Augustus, *U.S. Navy*	1467
WILLIAMS, Charles Quincy, *U.S. Army*	3385
WILLIAMS, Dewayne Thomas, *U.S. Marine Corps*	3386
WILLIAMS, Elwood N., *U.S. Army*	1468
WILLIAMS, Ernest Calvin, *U.S. Marine Corps*	2452
WILLIAMS, Frank, *U.S. Navy*	2181
WILLIAMS, George C., *U.S. Army*	1469
WILLIAMS, Henry, *U.S. Navy*	2069
WILLIAMS, Hershel Woodrow "Woody", *U.S. Marine Corps Reserve*	3015
WILLIAMS, Jack, *U.S. Naval Reserve*	3016
WILLIAMS, James Elliott, *U.S. Navy*	3387
WILLIAMS, Jay P., *U.S. Navy*	2322
WILLIAMS, John, *U.S. Navy (Civil War) (Capt. Maintop)*	1470
WILLIAMS, John, *U.S. Navy (Civil War) (Seaman)*	1471
WILLIAMS II, John, *U.S. Navy*	1472
WILLIAMS, Leroy, *U.S. Army*	1473
WILLIAMS, Louis, *U.S. Navy*	2070
WILLIAMS, Moses, *U.S. Army*	1941
WILLIAMS, Peter, *U.S. Navy*	1474
WILLIAMS, Robert, *U.S. Navy*	1475
WILLIAMS, William, *U.S. Navy*	1476
WILLIAMS, William Haliday, *U.S. Army*	1477
WILLIAMSON, James Alexander, *U.S. Army*	1478
WILLIS, George, *U.S. Navy*	2071
WILLIS, John Harlan, *U.S. Navy*	3017
WILLIS, Richard, *U.S. Navy*	1479
WILLISTON, Edward Bancroft, *U.S. Army*	1480
WILLS, Henry, *U.S. Army*	1942
WILSON, Alfred Leonard, *U.S. Army*	3018
WILSON, Alfred Mac, *U.S. Marine Corps*	3388
WILSON, Arthur Harrison, *U.S. Army*	2265
WILSON, August, *U.S. Navy*	2072
WILSON, Benjamin, *U.S. Army*	1943
WILSON, Benjamin F., *U.S. Army*	3153
WILSON, Charles, *U.S. Army*	1944
WILSON, Charles E., *U.S. Army*	1481
WILSON, Christopher W., *U.S. Army*	1482
WILSON, Francis A., *U.S. Army*	1483
WILSON, Harold Edward "Speedy", *U.S. Marine Corps Reserve*	3154
WILSON, John, *U.S. Army*	1484
WILSON, John Alfred, *U.S. Army*	1485
WILSON, John Moulder, *U.S. Army*	1486
WILSON Jr., Louis Hugh, *U.S. Marine Corps*	3019
WILSON, Milden H., *U.S. Army*	1945
WILSON, Richard G., *U.S. Army*	3155
WILSON, Robert Lee, *U.S. Marine Corps*	3020
WILSON, William O., *U.S. Army*	1947
WILSON, William, *U.S. Army*	1946
WINANS, Roswell, *U.S. Marine Corps*	2453
WINDER, David Francis, *U.S. Army*	3389
WINDOLPH, Charles, *U.S. Army*	1948
WINDRICH, William Gordon, *U.S. Marine Corps*	3156
WINDUS, Claron, *U.S. Army*	1949
WINEGAR, William W., *U.S. Army*	1487
WINTERBOTTOM, William, *U.S. Army*	1950
WISE, Homer L., *U.S. Army*	3021
WISNER, Lewis S., *U.S. Army*	1488
WITCOME, Joseph, *U.S. Army*	1951
WITEK, Frank Peter, *U.S. Marine Corps Reserve*	3022
WITHINGTON, William Herbert, *U.S. Army*	1489
WOLD, Nels T., *U.S. Army*	2570
WOLLAM, John, *U.S. Army*	1490
WOMACK, Bryant Homer, *U.S. Army*	3157
WOOD, Henry Clay, *U.S. Army*	1491
WOOD, Leonard, *U.S. Army*	1952
WOOD, Mark, *U.S. Army*	1492
WOOD, Richard H., *U.S. Army*	1493
WOOD, Robert B., *U.S. Navy*	1494
WOODALL, William H., *U.S. Army*	1495
WOODALL, Zachariah, *U.S. Army*	1953
WOODBURY, Eri Davidson, *U.S. Army*	1496
WOODFILL, Samuel, *U.S. Army*	2571
WOODFORD, Howard E., *U.S. Army*	3023
WOODRUFF, Alonzo, *U.S. Army*	1497
WOODRUFF, Carle Augustus, *U.S. Army*	1498
WOODS, Brent, *U.S. Army*	1954
WOODS, Daniel A. (Wood), *U.S. Army*	1499
WOODS, Samuel, *U.S. Navy*	1500
WOODWARD, Evan M., *U.S. Army*	1501
WOON, John, *U.S. Navy*	1502
WORAM, Charles B., *U.S. Navy*	1503
WORLEY, Kenneth Lee, *U.S. Marine Corps*	3390
WORTICK, Joseph, *U.S. Army*	1504
WORTMAN, George G., *U.S. Army*	1955
WRAY, William J., *U.S. Army*	1505
WRIGHT, Albert D., *U.S. Army*	1506
WRIGHT, Edward, *U.S. Navy*	1507
WRIGHT, Raymond Richard "Buzzer", *U.S. Army*	3391
WRIGHT, Robert, *U.S. Army*	1508
WRIGHT, Samuel, *U.S. Army*	1509
WRIGHT, Samuel Cole, *U.S. Army*	1510
WRIGHT, William, *U.S. Navy*	1511
YABES, Maximo, *U.S. Army*	3392
YANO, Rodney James Tadashi, *U.S. Army*	3393
YEAGER, Jacob F., *U.S. Army*	1512
YNTEMA, Gordon Douglas, *U.S. Army*	3394
YORK, Alvin Cullium, *U.S. Army*	2572
YOUNG, Andrew J., *U.S. Army*	1513
YOUNG, Benjamin F., *U.S. Army*	1514
YOUNG, Calvary Morris, *U.S. Army*	1515
YOUNG, Cassin, *U.S. Navy*	3024
YOUNG, Edward B., *U.S. Navy*	1516
YOUNG, Frank Albert, *U.S. Marine Corps*	2323
YOUNG, Gerald Orren, *U.S. Air Force*	3395
YOUNG, Horatio Nelson, *U.S. Navy*	1517
YOUNG, James Marvin, *U.S. Army*	1518
YOUNG, Marvin Rex, *U.S. Army*	3396
YOUNG, Robert Harley, *U.S. Army*	3158
YOUNG, Rodger W., *U.S. Army*	3025
YOUNG, William, *U.S. Navy*	1519
YOUNKER, John L., *U.S. Army*	1520
YOUNT, John P., *U.S. Army*	1956

ZABITOSKY, Fred William, *U.S. Army*	3397	ZION, William F., *U.S. Marine Corps*	2324
ZEAMER Jr., Jay, *U.S. Army Air Corps*	3026	ZUIDERVELD, William, *U.S. Navy*	2436
ZIEGNER, Herman, *U.S. Army*	1957	ZUSSMAN, Raymond, *U.S. Army*	3027